The Bill James Handbook 2007

Baseball Info Solutions

www.baseballinfosolutions.com

Published by ACTA Sports

A Division of ACTA Publications

Cover by Tom A. Wright

Cover Photos by Scott Jordan Levy

© Copyright 2006 by Baseball Info Solutions and Bill James

First Edition: November 2006

Published by:
ACTA Sports, a division of ACTA Publications
5559 W. Howard Street, Skokie, IL 60077
(800) 397-2282
www.actasports.com www.actapublications.com

ISBN-10: 0-87946-311-2
ISBN-13: 978-0-87946-311-3

Printed in the United States of America

Table of Contents

Dedication

This book is dedicated to my father Stan and my mother Ruth, who passed away this year. I miss you so much and look forward to seeing you again someday. Thank you both for everything you've done.

To my devoted wife Samphan who endures the countless hours I spend each season watching baseball.

God Bless you all,
Todd Radcliffe

Acknowledgements

This book was conceived by Bill James, who participates in the design and production of the book and who also wrote several articles which appear in these pages.

BIS is the best in the business, and a big reason for that is the hard work done by our owner, John Dewan, and president, Steve Moyer. Your experience and expertise has been vital to us having a successful season.

Damon Lichtenwalner has been with BIS since the very beginning in 2002. Damon is indispensable to the company; his computer programming ability coupled with the amount of dedication he shows is immeasurable. Thank you for everything you have done to enable BIS to flourish.

Nate Birtwell has been instrumental in recruiting our staff of interns, making sure everything runs smoothly on the operational end, and also in dealing with several of our clients. Thanks for all the energy and commitment you have shown and know that it has been appreciated.

Todd Radcliffe has been important in making sure the data you see in this book is as accurate as possible. Todd has spent numerous hours performing quality control on our data, and it is because of this that our data is second to none. Thank you for all that you have done.

Matt Lorenzo has been vital to BIS on both the programming and operational side. He always can be counted on to go the extra mile when working on important projects for various clients. Because of this, you deserve big thanks.

Jim Swavely is in his second season with us, and he has always been a big help with programming issues. However, in addition to that, this season Jim took on some added responsibilities on the operational side, and this has been a huge help. Thanks for your efforts.

Jon Vrecsics joined the full time staff shortly after the *Handbook* was published last season. During that time he has been involved in several projects and is willing to do what it takes to get the job done. Thank you for your dedication.

Andy Bausher was a huge help for BIS, especially in matters related to pitch analysis. Thank you for your efforts during your time at BIS.

A special thanks also needs to go out to Pat Quinn. Pat is extremely helpful in making this book possible, and he played a huge role with *The Fielding Bible* as well. Please know that your efforts have been appreciated.

Once again our crew of Video Scouts did an excellent job. Thank you to Jake Abry, Dedan Brozino, Francis Connolly, Adam Cromie, Kevin Davidson, Andrew Grim, Durward Hamil, Wes Koser, Neil Moyer, Erik Neander, Jay Paradise, Gino Pavan, Gary

Read, Steve Readey, Mark Shive, Mike Silverman, Charlie Stivali, Mike Thompson, and Tom Yost. A special thank you and congratulations is extended to Joel Kammeyer, as he began the season as an intern and is now the latest addition to our full-time staff.

Greg Pierce, Andrew Yankech, Charles Fiore, and the entire ACTA Sports staff are a tremendous help each year. Thanks to all of you.

Thanks to our friends in the baseball industry: Greg Ambrosius, Jeff Barton, Matthew Berry, Jim Callis, Mike Canter, Frank Cooney, Doug Dennis, Sue Dewan, Jeff Erickson, Steve Goldstein, Steve Greenberg, Jason Grey, John Hunt, Peter Kreutzer, Gene McCaffrey, Sig Mejdal, Bob Meyerhoff, Rob Neyer, Mat Olkin, Scott Pianowski, David Pinto, Mike Phillips, Hal Richman, Mike Salfino, Peter Schoenke, Ron Shandler, John Sickels, Sam Walker, Mark Watson, Rick Wilton, Rick Wolf, Trace Wood, and Todd Zola.

Many thanks to our remote video crew: Ted Ball, Jay Cramer, James Davis Jr., Jay De Leon, Brian Dewberry-Jones, David Dick, Joe Dimino, Mariusz Robert Dudek, Don Masi, Al Melchior, John Menna, Gus Papadopoulos, Theo Papadopoulos, Steve Paprocki, Daryl Ravani, Harold Richter, Bob Routier, Kyle Schmidt, Matthew Schultz, Wayne Sit, and John Wagner.

Introduction

It seems like just yesterday that the White Sox and Indians were sitting through a three-hour delay on a rainy Sunday night in Chicago to open the 2006 season. Now, the publication of the *Bill James Handbook* marks the end of an incredibly busy and fulfilling season here at Baseball Info Solutions.

As is always the case in baseball, remarkable things transpired throughout the season. On a team level, the Tigers seemingly came out of nowhere and were a major story all season as they pursued a division title just three seasons after the lowest of all lows—a 43-119 season. On the morning of June 11th, the Twins woke up with a 27-34 record, but they came roaring back to win the division title. On an individual level, Francisco Liriano made a remarkable debut until he was bit by the injury bug. After a disappointing initial season in New York, Carlos Beltran showed why the Mets signed him by posting an MVP caliber season. Ryan Howard more than fulfilled his power potential this season and was a huge reason why the Phillies made their playoff push. Barry Bonds was filled with controversy all season, but he had a solid year and has set himself up to challenge Hank Aaron's homerun record next season.

The 2007 *Bill James Handbook* contains all of the features that you have come to enjoy each November, as well as some changes and additions. The Fielding Bible Awards make their debut in this year's book. We've added a new section for Manufactured Runs, plus we have new charts in the Career Assessments section this year, as well as new leader boards for Park Indices. Just flip through the book randomly and you'll find a lot of nice surprises. I am sure you will enjoy this years *Handbook* more than ever!

Jon Vrecsics
Project Manager
Baseball Info Solutions

2006 Team Statistics

On the following pages you will find the most complete compilation of team statistics from the 2006 regular season that you can find. Do you want to know how many days the Rangers spent in first place? What about the last date they had at least a share of first? How about the breakdown of the season series between the Yankees and Red Sox? All of that info and more can be found here. So, go digging through the next few pages and see what you find.

2006 American League Standings

Overall

EAST

Team	W-L	Pct	GB	D1	LD1	LLd
New York Yankees	97-65	.599	0.0	87	10/1	12.0
Toronto Blue Jays	87-75	.537	10.0	3	4/28	0.0
Boston Red Sox	86-76	.531	11.0	99	7/31	4.0
Baltimore Orioles	70-92	.432	27.0	4	4/6	0.5
Tampa Bay Devil Rays	61-101	.377	36.0	0	-	0.0

CENTRAL

Team	W-L	Pct	GB	D1	LD1	LLd
Minnesota Twins	96-66	.593	0.0	4	10/1	1.0
Detroit Tigers*	95-67	.586	1.0	147	9/30	10.0
Chicago White Sox	90-72	.556	6.0	36	5/20	3.5
Cleveland Indians	78-84	.481	18.0	10	4/18	1.0
Kansas City Royals	62-100	.383	34.0	0	-	0.0

WEST

Team	W-L	Pct	GB	D1	LD1	LLd
Oakland Athletics	93-69	.574	0.0	128	10/1	8.5
Los Angeles Angels	89-73	.549	4.0	24	7/28	1.0
Texas Rangers	80-82	.494	13.0	58	7/15	5.0
Seattle Mariners	78-84	.481	15.0	5	4/15	1.0

* Clinched Wild Card Birth on 9/24. Division Clinch Dates: New York 9/20, Oakland 9/26, Minnesota 10/1.
D1 = Number of days a team had at least a share of first place of their division; LD1 = Last date the team had at least a share of first place; LLd = The largest number of games that a team led their division

East Division

Tm	Home	Road	East	Cent	West	NL	LHS	RHS	Day	Night	Grass	Turf	1-Rn	5+Rn	XInn	April	May	June	July	Aug	S/O	Pre	Post
NYY	50-31	47-34	46-28	23-12	18-17	10-8	31-17	66-48	35-23	62-42	86-55	11-10	24-22	38-21	7-3	13-10	18-10	14-12	16-9	18-12	18-12	50-36	47-29
Tor	50-31	37-44	43-31	18-17	17-18	9-9	28-19	59-56	30-26	57-49	28-40	59-35	20-10	29-24	7-1	12-11	17-12	16-11	12-14	12-17	18-10	49-39	38-36
Bos	48-33	38-43	40-35	15-19	15-20	16-2	25-31	61-45	25-21	61-55	80-59	6-17	29-20	24-25	5-7	14-11	17-9	17-9	15-12	9-21	14-14	53-33	33-43
Bal	40-41	30-51	31-44	17-17	13-22	9-9	16-33	54-59	23-33	47-59	60-79	10-13	22-20	16-31	3-6	13-13	12-15	12-16	11-15	12-14	10-19	41-49	29-43
TB	41-40	20-61	26-48	13-21	11-25	11-7	17-29	44-72	18-27	43-74	17-51	44-50	17-22	12-26	5-7	11-14	10-18	14-13	9-17	9-19	8-20	39-50	22-51

Central Division

Tm	Home	Road	East	Cent	West	NL	LHS	RHS	Day	Night	Grass	Turf	1-Rn	5+Rn	XInn	April	May	June	July	Aug	S/O	Pre	Post
Min	54-27	42-39	22-13	41-35	17-16	16-2	34-26	62-40	27-20	69-46	39-36	57-30	20-11	34-23	10-4	9-15	15-13	19-7	18-8	16-12	19-11	49-38	47-28
Det	46-35	49-32	16-17	45-30	19-17	15-3	33-20	62-47	28-30	67-37	87-58	8-9	24-20	30-18	4-8	16-9	19-9	20-7	15-10	13-16	12-16	59-29	36-38
CWS	49-32	41-40	17-17	40-36	19-15	14-4	31-34	59-38	35-23	55-49	81-62	9-10	24-21	29-21	7-8	17-7	16-12	19-8	10-15	16-13	12-17	57-31	33-41
Cle	44-37	34-47	19-14	35-40	16-20	8-10	25-32	53-52	24-22	54-62	72-75	6-9	18-26	33-20	5-3	13-12	13-14	9-17	10-16	18-10	15-15	40-47	38-37
KC	34-47	28-53	12-25	27-47	13-20	10-8	13-36	49-64	11-35	51-65	57-90	5-10	14-24	14-36	6-6	5-17	8-21	13-14	11-16	12-18	13-14	31-56	31-44

West Division

Tm	Home	Road	East	Cent	West	NL	LHS	RHS	Day	Night	Grass	Turf	1-Rn	5+Rn	XInn	April	May	June	July	Aug	S/O	Pre	Post
Oak	49-32	44-37	29-15	22-21	34-23	8-10	23-18	70-51	40-21	53-48	87-60	6-9	32-22	21-22	9-4	12-12	12-17	18-8	14-13	21-6	16-13	45-43	48-26
LAA	45-36	44-37	26-19	24-18	32-25	7-11	30-21	59-52	28-22	61-51	82-67	7-6	25-22	26-22	8-7	12-13	11-17	12-14	19-7	16-13	19-9	43-45	46-28
Tex	39-42	41-40	22-21	22-22	29-28	7-11	22-23	58-59	16-22	64-60	73-77	7-5	17-26	29-21	2-5	13-12	15-13	13-14	11-15	17-12	11-16	45-43	35-39
Sea	44-37	34-47	25-19	20-23	19-38	14-4	19-24	59-60	23-27	55-57	75-76	3-8	20-24	16-22	8-8	11-15	12-17	18-8	11-13	11-17	15-14	43-46	35-38

Team vs. Team Breakdown

	NYY	Tor	Bos	Bal	TB	Min	Det	CWS	Cle	KC	Oak	LAA	Tex	Sea
New York Yankees	-	10	11	12	13	3	5	4	4	7	3	4	8	3
Toronto Blue Jays	8	-	12	11	12	5	3	4	2	4	4	6	2	5
Boston Red Sox	8	7	-	15	10	1	3	4	3	4	3	3	5	4
Baltimore Orioles	7	8	3	-	13	3	3	2	4	5	2	4	3	4
Tampa Bay Devil Rays	5	6	9	6	-	1	3	3	1	5	3	2	3	3
Minnesota Twins	3	2	5	6	6	-	8	10	11	12	6	2	4	5
Detroit Tigers	2	3	3	3	5	11	-	7	13	14	5	3	5	6
Chicago White Sox	2	5	2	5	3	9	12	-	8	11	3	6	5	5
Cleveland Indians	3	4	4	2	6	8	6	11	-	10	3	4	5	4
Kansas City Royals	2	3	5	1	1	7	4	8	8	-	4	3	3	5
Oakland Athletics	6	6	7	4	6	4	4	3	6	5	-	8	9	17
Los Angeles Angels	6	4	3	6	7	4	5	3	5	7	11	-	11	10
Texas Rangers	2	4	4	6	6	5	5	5	4	3	10	8	-	11
Seattle Mariners	3	4	6	6	6	3	3	4	5	5	2	9	8	-

2006 National League Standings

Overall

EAST	W-L	Pct	GB	D1	LD1	LLd	CENTRAL	W-L	Pct	GB	D1	LD1	LLd	WEST	W-L	Pct	GB	D1	LD1	LLd
Team							Team							Team						
New York Mets	97-65	.599	0.0	181	10/1	16.5	St Louis Cardinals	83-78	.516	0.0	145	10/1	7.0	San Diego Padres	88-74	.543	0.0	73	10/1	3.5
Philadelphia Phillies	85-77	.525	12.0	0	-	0.0	Houston Astros	82-80	.506	1.5	17	4/27	1.5	Los Angeles Dodgers*	88-74	.543	0.0	59	10/1	4.0
Atlanta Braves	79-83	.488	18.0	2	4/5	0.5	Cincinnati Reds	80-82	.494	3.5	21	6/8	1.5	San Francisco Giants	76-85	.472	11.5	20	7/22	1.5
Florida Marlins	78-84	.481	19.0	0	-	0.0	Milwaukee Brewers	75-87	.463	8.5	10	4/15	1.0	Colorado Rockies	76-86	.469	12.0	34	7/5	1.5
Washington Nationals	71-91	.438	26.0	0	-	0.0	Pittsburgh Pirates	67-95	.414	16.5	0	-	0.0	Arizona Diamondbacks	76-86	.469	12.0	31	6/14	2.5
							Chicago Cubs	66-96	.407	17.5	3	4/12	0.0							

* Clinched Wild Card Birth on 9/30. Division Clinch Dates: New York 9/18, San Diego 10/1, St Louis 10/1.
D1 = Number of days a team had at least a share of first place of their division; LD1 = Last date the team had at least a share of first place; LLd = The largest number of games that a team led their division

East Division

	AT		VERSUS					CONDITIONS				GAME			MONTHLY						ALL-STAR	
Tm	Home	Road	East	Cent	West	AL	LHS	RHS	Day	Night	Grass	Turf	1-Rn	5+Rn	XInn	April	May	June	July	Aug	S/O	Pre	Post
NYM	50-31	47-34	45-29	23-17	23-10	6-9	25-22	72-43	36-19	61-46	95-64	2-1	31-16	34-17	9-5	16-8	16-12	15-12	16-9	19-9	15-15	53-36	44-29
Phi	41-40	44-37	41-34	20-17	19-13	5-13	23-22	62-55	29-23	56-54	84-75	1-2	22-23	21-21	5-11	10-14	17-11	9-18	13-12	18-11	18-11	40-47	45-30
Atl	40-41	39-42	35-38	22-17	17-18	5-10	18-23	61-60	24-24	55-59	77-82	2-1	19-33	24-20	8-3	10-14	18-11	6-21	14-10	15-13	16-14	40-49	39-34
Fla	42-39	36-45	33-42	22-17	14-16	9-9	20-28	58-56	22-24	56-60	78-81	0-3	20-26	23-23	5-7	6-16	11-18	18-7	14-15	16-12	13-16	38-48	40-36
Was	41-40	30-51	31-42	20-19	13-19	7-11	24-23	47-68	26-27	45-64	71-88	0-3	23-20	16-29	7-6	8-17	14-15	11-16	14-11	9-18	15-14	38-52	33-39

Central Division

	AT		VERSUS					CONDITIONS				GAME			MONTHLY						ALL-STAR	
Tm	Home	Road	East	Cent	West	AL	LHS	RHS	Day	Night	Grass	Turf	1-Rn	5+Rn	XInn	April	May	June	July	Aug	S/O	Pre	Post
StL	49-31	34-47	16-15	39-42	23-11	5-10	23-34	60-44	37-19	46-59	83-78	0-0	22-27	30-23	5-6	17-8	17-11	9-16	15-11	13-15	12-17	48-39	35-39
Hou	44-37	38-43	16-18	45-32	14-19	7-11	22-16	60-64	22-25	60-55	82-80	0-0	25-21	22-21	5-10	16-8	11-19	11-15	11-14	17-12	16-12	43-46	39-34
Cin	42-39	38-43	17-15	46-38	11-20	6-9	24-24	56-58	23-34	57-48	80-82	0-0	27-20	19-28	5-8	17-8	12-16	15-12	11-14	12-17	13-15	45-44	35-38
Mil	48-33	27-54	13-18	37-45	19-15	6-9	19-20	56-67	29-26	46-61	75-84	0-3	27-27	14-30	7-2	14-11	12-16	14-14	10-15	12-16	13-15	44-46	31-41
Pit	43-38	24-57	15-19	34-44	15-20	3-12	13-36	54-59	18-37	49-58	67-95	0-0	24-31	15-24	5-7	7-19	12-15	8-20	13-12	13-15	14-14	30-60	37-35
ChC	36-45	30-51	10-22	42-42	10-21	4-11	22-30	44-66	31-52	35-44	66-93	0-3	15-26	20-34	4-7	13-10	7-22	9-18	14-12	11-17	12-17	34-54	32-42

West Division

	AT		VERSUS					CONDITIONS				GAME			MONTHLY						ALL-STAR	
Tm	Home	Road	East	Cent	West	AL	LHS	RHS	Day	Night	Grass	Turf	1-Rn	5+Rn	XInn	April	May	June	July	Aug	S/O	Pre	Post
SD	43-38	45-36	16-18	26-12	39-36	7-8	17-17	71-57	32-22	56-52	88-74	0-0	30-22	23-16	10-12	9-15	19-10	14-12	13-13	13-15	20-9	48-40	40-34
LAD	49-32	39-42	19-13	21-20	43-31	5-10	19-16	69-58	27-22	61-52	88-71	0-3	20-20	30-23	3-8	12-13	18-10	11-15	9-17	21-7	17-12	46-42	42-32
SF	43-38	33-47	12-19	19-21	37-38	8-7	15-22	61-63	29-32	47-53	76-85	0-0	23-22	19-25	6-7	13-11	14-15	13-13	11-16	15-13	10-17	45-44	31-41
Col	44-37	32-49	18-15	16-23	31-44	11-4	17-12	59-74	22-21	54-65	76-86	0-0	19-25	25-20	8-4	15-10	12-16	14-12	10-16	11-17	14-15	44-43	32-43
Ari	39-42	37-44	11-21	24-16	37-38	4-11	21-19	55-67	19-30	57-56	76-83	0-3	22-26	21-21	7-5	12-13	18-9	8-20	16-9	10-18	12-17	43-45	33-41

Team vs. Team Breakdown

	EAST					CENTRAL						WEST				
	NYM	Phi	Atl	Fla	Was	StL	Hou	Cin	Mil	Pit	ChC	SD	LAD	SF	Ari	Col
New York Mets	-	11	11	11	12	4	4	4	3	5	3	5	4	3	6	5
Philadelphia Phillies	8	-	11	13	9	3	4	4	1	3	5	2	3	5	5	4
Atlanta Braves	7	7	-	11	10	4	3	4	2	3	6	7	3	3	1	3
Florida Marlins	8	6	8	-	11	1	3	2	7	5	4	3	1	3	4	3
Washington Nationals	6	10	8	7	-	3	4	1	5	3	4	1	2	5	5	0
St Louis Cardinals	2	3	2	5	4	-	7	6	9	9	8	2	7	4	3	7
Houston Astros	2	2	4	4	4	9	-	5	10	13	8	3	3	1	5	2
Cincinnati Reds	3	2	3	4	5	9	10	-	9	9	9	2	0	2	2	5
Milwaukee Brewers	3	5	4	0	1	7	5	10	-	7	8	4	2	6	3	4
Pittsburgh Pirates	4	3	3	2	3	6	3	7	9	-	9	1	4	6	1	3
Chicago Cubs	3	2	1	2	2	11	7	10	8	6	-	0	4	2	2	2
San Diego Padres	2	4	2	3	5	4	3	4	3	5	7	-	13	7	10	9
Los Angeles Dodgers	3	4	3	5	4	0	3	6	4	6	2	5	-	13	10	15
San Francisco Giants	3	1	4	3	1	1	5	5	3	1	4	12	6	-	11	8
Arizona Diamondbacks	1	1	6	2	1	4	4	4	3	5	4	9	8	8	-	12
Colorado Rockies	1	3	3	3	8	2	4	1	2	3	4	10	4	10	7	-

American League Batting

							BATTING													BASERUNNING					PERCENTAGES		
Tm	G	AB	H	2B	3B	HR	(Hm	Rd)	TB	R	RBI	TBB	IBB	SO	HBP	SH	SF	ShO	SB	CS	SB%	GDP	LOB	Avg	OBP	Slg
NYY	162	5651	1608	327	21	210	(111	99)	2607	930	902	649	43	1053	72	34	49	4	139	35	.80	139	1253	.285	.363	.461
Cle	162	5619	1576	351	27	196	(94	102)	2569	870	839	556	42	1204	54	30	43	6	55	23	.71	127	1162	.280	.349	.457
CWS	162	5657	1586	291	20	236	(136	100)	2625	868	839	502	33	1056	58	44	57	6	93	48	.66	118	1125	.280	.342	.464
Tex	162	5659	1571	357	23	183	(93	90)	2523	835	799	505	35	1061	40	18	50	7	53	24	.69	148	1139	.278	.338	.446
Det	162	5642	1548	294	40	203	(81	122)	2531	822	785	430	27	1133	45	45	36	8	60	40	.60	120	1068	.274	.329	.449
Bos	162	5619	1510	327	16	192	(83	109)	2445	820	777	672	56	1056	66	22	56	8	51	23	.69	136	1301	.269	.351	.435
Tor	162	5596	1591	348	27	199	(121	78)	2590	809	778	514	31	906	63	16	52	6	65	33	.66	166	1162	.284	.348	.463
Min	162	5602	1608	275	34	143	(69	74)	2380	801	754	490	46	872	50	31	55	14	101	42	.71	163	1143	.287	.347	.425
Oak	162	5500	1429	266	22	175	(84	91)	2264	771	735	650	28	976	50	25	56	11	61	20	.75	170	1187	.260	.340	.412
Bal	162	5610	1556	288	20	164	(100	64)	2376	768	727	474	35	878	73	40	41	8	121	32	.79	145	1177	.277	.339	.424
LAA	162	5609	1539	309	29	159	(69	90)	2383	766	737	486	49	914	42	31	53	8	148	57	.72	126	1121	.274	.334	.425
KC	162	5589	1515	335	37	124	(65	59)	2296	757	718	474	32	1040	64	52	48	11	65	34	.66	131	1144	.271	.332	.411
Sea	162	5670	1540	266	42	172	(81	91)	2406	756	703	404	49	974	63	38	38	15	106	37	.74	118	1110	.272	.325	.424
TB	162	5474	1395	267	33	190	(100	90)	2298	689	650	441	23	1106	47	35	43	7	134	52	.72	101	1038	.255	.314	.420
AL	1134	78497	21572	4301	391	2546	(1287	1259)	34293	11262	10743	7247	529	14229	787	461	677	119	1252	500	.71	1908	16130	.275	.339	.437

American League Pitching

HOW MUCH THEY PITCHED					WHAT THEY GAVE UP												THE RESULTS									
Tm	G	CG	Rel	IP	BFP	H	R	ER	HR	SH	SF	HB	TBB	IBB	SO	WP	Bk	W	L	Pct.	ShO	Sv-Op	Hld	OAvg	OOBP	OSlg	ERA
Det	162	3	390	1448.0	6145	1420	675	618	160	26	41	53	489	35	1003	44	2	95	67	.586	16	46-62	75	.257	.321	.405	3.84
Min	162	1	421	1439.1	6066	1490	683	632	182	40	48	36	356	25	1164	40	3	96	66	.593	6	40-50	68	.267	.312	.423	3.95
Oak	162	5	444	1451.2	6279	1525	727	679	162	32	49	55	529	47	1003	43	4	93	69	.574	11	54-74	83	.272	.338	.422	4.21
LAA	162	5	380	1452.2	6149	1410	732	652	158	40	43	50	471	27	1164	85	3	89	73	.549	12	50-63	50	.254	.316	.402	4.04
Tor	162	6	482	1428.1	6151	1447	754	694	185	25	31	59	504	56	1076	53	13	87	75	.537	6	42-62	87	.262	.328	.422	4.37
NYY	162	5	489	1443.2	6215	1463	767	708	170	31	39	59	496	41	1019	46	7	97	65	.599	8	43-60	83	.262	.326	.413	4.41
Cle	162	13	377	1423.1	6190	1583	782	698	166	35	55	51	429	35	948	46	2	78	84	.481	13	24-47	40	.282	.335	.431	4.41
Tex	162	3	489	1431.1	6237	1558	784	731	162	26	48	66	496	18	972	34	4	80	82	.494	8	42-65	79	.278	.341	.424	4.60
Sea	162	6	429	1446.2	6294	1500	792	739	183	31	39	53	560	50	1067	47	6	78	84	.481	6	47-67	72	.267	.337	.432	4.60
CWS	162	5	398	1449.0	6232	1534	794	743	200	29	48	58	433	59	1012	51	1	90	72	.556	11	46-63	64	.271	.326	.440	4.61
Bos	162	3	454	1441.1	6292	1570	825	773	181	31	47	68	509	25	1070	52	3	86	76	.531	4	46-58	80	.279	.343	.447	4.83
TB	162	3	444	1420.1	6374	1600	856	782	180	34	73	63	606	39	979	70	8	61	101	.377	7	33-54	47	.286	.358	.452	4.96
Bal	162	5	472	1419.0	6327	1579	899	843	216	45	61	48	613	26	1016	59	4	70	92	.432	9	35-56	58	.284	.357	.462	5.35
KC	162	3	473	1426.1	6434	1648	971	896	213	44	57	60	637	45	904	85	9	62	100	.383	5	35-66	66	.292	.367	.476	5.65
AL	1134	66	6142	20121.0	87385	21327	11041	10188	2518	469	678	779	7128	528	14397	755	69	1162	1106	.512	124	583-858	952	.272	.336	.432	4.56

American League Fielding

					Fielding															
Team	G	Inn	PO	Ast	OFAst	E	(Throw	Field)	TC	DP	GDP	SB	CS	SB%	CPkof	PPkof	PB	UER	UERA	FPct
Boston	162	1441.1	4324	1658	31	66	27	38	6048	174	148	108	23	.82	1	8	24	52	0.32	.989
Oakland	162	1451.2	4355	1622	23	84	39	45	6061	173	150	88	41	.68	1	3	10	47	0.29	.986
Minnesota	162	1439.1	4318	1646	31	84	43	41	6048	134	110	54	31	.64	0	3	5	51	0.32	.986
Seattle	162	1446.2	4340	1628	35	88	37	51	6056	150	130	72	38	.65	1	2	16	53	0.33	.985
Chicago	162	1449.0	4347	1649	16	90	38	51	6086	145	128	116	34	.77	0	6	13	51	0.32	.985
Texas	162	1431.1	4294	1750	41	98	41	57	6142	174	145	67	40	.63	2	1	11	51	0.32	.984
Toronto	162	1428.1	4285	1710	35	99	56	43	6094	157	127	130	32	.80	1	4	15	60	0.38	.984
Kansas City	162	1426.1	4279	1655	33	98	39	59	6032	189	161	58	30	.66	2	4	10	72	0.45	.984
Detroit	162	1448.0	4344	1768	30	106	45	61	6218	162	140	49	35	.58	1	8	6	55	0.34	.983
Baltimore	162	1419.0	4257	1607	30	102	47	55	5966	156	129	80	50	.62	4	0	15	55	0.35	.983
New York	162	1443.2	4331	1589	27	104	50	54	6024	145	126	92	47	.66	2	2	17	57	0.36	.983
Tampa Bay	162	1420.1	4261	1588	35	116	45	70	5965	156	128	108	46	.70	0	7	8	72	0.46	.981
Cleveland	162	1423.1	4270	1667	28	118	44	73	6055	165	143	128	34	.79	2	3	7	81	0.51	.981
Los Angeles	162	1452.2	4358	1538	33	124	43	80	6020	154	129	77	40	.66	4	4	8	80	0.50	.979
American League	1134	20121.0	60363	23075	428	1377	594	778	84815	2234	1894	1227	521	.70	21	55	165	837	0.37	.984

National League Batting

Tm	G	AB	H	2B	3B	HR	(Hm	Rd)	TB	R	RBI	TBB	IBB	SO	HBP	SH	SF	ShO	SB	CS	SB%	GDP	LOB	Avg	OBP	Slg
Phi	162	5687	1518	294	41	216	(112	104)	2542	865	823	626	67	1203	95	57	44	3	92	25	.79	115	1275	.267	.347	.447
Atl	162	5583	1510	312	26	222	(100	122)	2540	849	818	526	48	1169	52	78	44	4	52	35	.60	132	1105	.270	.337	.455
NYM	162	5558	1469	323	41	200	(96	104)	2474	834	800	547	63	1071	62	77	47	9	146	35	.81	114	1115	.264	.334	.445
LAD	162	5628	1552	307	58	153	(88	65)	2434	820	787	601	61	959	51	66	48	9	128	49	.72	140	1223	.276	.348	.432
Col	162	5562	1504	325	54	157	(75	82)	2408	813	761	561	64	1108	60	119	45	12	85	50	.63	119	1174	.270	.341	.433
StL	161	5522	1484	292	27	184	(85	99)	2382	781	745	531	70	922	61	71	40	8	59	32	.65	129	1158	.269	.337	.431
Ari	162	5645	1506	331	38	160	(86	74)	2393	773	743	504	47	965	67	61	53	7	76	30	.72	136	1166	.267	.331	.424
Fla	162	5502	1454	309	42	182	(84	98)	2393	758	713	497	55	1249	74	76	42	7	110	58	.65	109	1126	.264	.331	.435
Cin	162	5515	1419	291	12	217	(124	93)	2385	749	718	614	52	1192	59	66	38	14	124	33	.79	122	1196	.257	.336	.432
Was	162	5495	1437	322	22	164	(74	90)	2295	746	695	594	66	1156	69	76	49	8	123	62	.66	119	1194	.262	.338	.418
SF	161	5472	1418	297	52	163	(61	102)	2308	746	711	494	76	891	53	80	37	6	58	25	.70	137	1092	.259	.324	.422
Hou	162	5521	1407	275	27	174	(98	76)	2258	735	708	585	54	1076	73	100	46	13	79	36	.69	123	1191	.255	.332	.409
SD	162	5576	1465	298	38	161	(75	86)	2322	731	698	564	37	1104	40	59	47	7	123	31	.80	128	1188	.263	.332	.416
Mil	162	5433	1400	301	20	180	(96	84)	2281	730	695	502	48	1233	82	58	53	8	71	37	.66	134	1108	.258	.327	.420
ChC	162	5587	1496	271	46	166	(81	85)	2357	716	677	395	24	928	43	84	37	15	121	49	.71	135	1082	.268	.319	.422
Pit	162	5558	1462	286	17	141	(70	71)	2205	691	656	459	49	1200	89	62	49	11	68	23	.75	153	1175	.263	.327	.397
NL	1295	88844	23501	4834	561	2840	(1405	1435)	37977	12337	11748	8600	881	17426	1030	1190	719	141	1515	610	.71	2045	18568	.265	.334	.427

National League Pitching

Tm	G	CG	Rel	IP	BFP	H	R	ER	HR	SH	SF	HB	TBB	IBB	SO	WP	Bk	W	L	Pct.	ShO	Sv-Op	Hld	OAvg	OOBP	OSlg	ERA
SD	162	4	475	1463.2	6175	1385	679	629	176	68	32	50	468	63	1097	34	4	88	74	.543	11	50-71	81	.249	.312	.404	3.87
Hou	162	5	497	1468.2	6219	1425	719	666	182	72	41	54	480	65	1160	44	2	82	80	.506	12	42-60	75	.256	.319	.421	4.08
NYM	162	5	474	1461.1	6240	1402	731	673	180	67	53	62	527	39	1161	37	5	97	65	.599	12	43-58	73	.253	.323	.407	4.14
LAD	162	1	454	1460.1	6289	1524	751	686	152	63	38	41	492	40	1068	54	8	88	74	.543	10	40-61	56	.269	.330	.418	4.23
StL	161	6	469	1429.2	6196	1475	762	721	193	83	32	80	504	35	970	35	3	83	78	.516	9	38-57	73	.268	.337	.443	4.54
Fla	162	6	438	1433.1	6294	1465	772	696	166	71	35	74	622	58	1088	47	4	78	84	.481	6	41-68	69	.267	.347	.423	4.37
Ari	162	8	461	1459.2	6341	1503	788	727	168	76	34	61	536	44	1115	53	4	76	86	.469	9	34-54	75	.267	.335	.431	4.48
SF	161	7	438	1429.2	6225	1422	790	735	153	66	55	70	584	37	992	50	7	76	85	.472	9	37-59	68	.261	.337	.415	4.63
Pit	162	2	505	1435.0	6354	1545	797	720	156	102	55	70	620	62	1060	61	6	67	95	.414	10	39-60	72	.281	.357	.431	4.52
Cin	162	9	476	1445.2	6319	1576	801	725	213	84	40	60	464	55	1053	40	9	80	82	.494	10	36-60	49	.278	.337	.457	4.51
Atl	162	6	522	1441.1	6350	1529	805	736	183	68	54	55	572	69	1049	39	2	79	83	.488	6	38-67	56	.273	.343	.438	4.60
Phi	162	4	500	1460.1	6366	1561	812	747	211	63	49	62	512	63	1138	58	4	85	77	.525	6	42-64	85	.275	.339	.460	4.60
Col	162	5	499	1447.1	6318	1549	812	749	155	53	44	66	553	81	952	43	2	76	86	.469	8	34-59	76	.277	.346	.438	4.66
Mil	162	7	427	1425.2	6210	1454	833	763	177	77	51	74	514	34	1145	57	2	75	87	.463	8	43-67	59	.265	.333	.438	4.82
ChC	162	2	542	1439.0	6366	1396	834	758	210	82	46	67	687	44	1250	68	4	66	96	.407	7	29-46	68	.255	.342	.431	4.74
Was	162	1	517	1436.1	6424	1535	872	803	193	87	59	92	584	93	960	47	10	71	91	.438	3	32-55	62	.274	.349	.447	5.03
NL	1295	78	7694	23137.0	100686	23746	12558	11534	2868	1182	718	1038	8719	882	17258	767	76	1267	1323	.489	136	618-966	1097	.267	.337	.432	4.49

National League Fielding

Team	G	Inn	PO	Ast	OFAst	E	(Throw	Field)	TC	DP	GDP	SB	CS	SB%	CPkof	PPkof	PB	UER	UERA	FPct
Houston	162	1468.2	4406	1748	21	80	(26	53)	6234	163	144	78	28	.74	2	2	7	51	0.31	.987
Colorado	162	1447.1	4342	1814	34	91	(35	56)	6247	190	166	99	42	.70	1	3	8	63	0.39	.985
San Diego	162	1463.2	4391	1591	16	92	(41	50)	6074	139	120	150	26	.85	2	3	11	48	0.30	.985
San Francisco	161	1429.2	4289	1577	23	91	(43	48)	5957	132	108	98	40	.71	0	7	5	53	0.33	.985
St Louis	161	1429.2	4289	1777	15	98	(29	69)	6164	170	155	63	32	.66	7	1	8	41	0.26	.984
Atlanta	162	1441.1	4324	1605	24	99	(44	55)	6028	146	132	101	30	.77	0	3	8	60	0.43	.984
Arizona	162	1459.2	4379	1773	13	104	(48	56)	6256	171	141	90	45	.67	2	2	11	60	0.37	.983
Pittsburgh	162	1435.0	4305	1782	25	104	(43	61)	6191	168	144	102	52	.66	3	5	16	72	0.45	.983
Philadelphia	162	1460.1	4381	1683	32	104	(52	52)	6168	153	136	94	35	.73	1	2	11	64	0.39	.983
New York	162	1461.1	4384	1638	38	104	(54	50)	6126	131	105	111	40	.74	1	3	10	56	0.34	.983
Chicago	162	1439.0	4317	1475	15	106	(53	53)	5898	122	95	118	39	.75	0	2	12	76	0.48	.982
Los Angeles	162	1460.1	4381	1792	22	115	(52	63)	6288	174	154	110	38	.74	0	5	7	65	0.40	.982
Milwaukee	162	1425.2	4277	1576	24	117	(59	58)	5970	127	111	97	31	.76	0	7	3	68	0.43	.980
Florida	162	1433.1	4300	1585	24	126	(64	62)	6011	146	146	69	46	.60	2	5	14	76	0.48	.979
Cincinnati	162	1445.2	4337	1592	36	128	(66	62)	6057	139	112	50	35	.59	1	0	9	73	0.45	.979
Washington	162	1436.1	4309	1494	36	131	(61	69)	5934	123	90	110	30	.79	0	2	11	69	0.43	.978
National League	1295	23137.0	69411	26502	398	1690	(770	916)	97603	2414	2059	1540	589	.72	22	52	151	1004	0.39	.983

Team Efficiency Summary

Bill James

Baseball has individual statistics and team accomplishments. The foundation of sabermetrics is the realization that these two are related—that the number of wins by the team is a largely predictable outcome of things that are measured by individual statistics. This probably seems obvious to you, but I grew up in a world in which it was common to deny that there was any such relationship. The first ten years of my career as a writer were more or less devoted simply to convincing people that these relationships did exist—that the number of games a team won was an essentially predictable outcome of the number of runs they scored, that the number of runs scored was an essentially predictable outcome of individual batting statistics.

Essentially predictable; not perfectly predictable. This chart focuses on the exceptions, on the teams that win more games than they ought to, based on their individual stats, or fewer games than they ought to. "Hitting Efficiency" (Hit Eff) asks the question "Did this team score more runs or fewer runs than they should have, given their individual hitting stats?" "Pitching Efficiency" (Pit Eff) asks the question "Did this team allow more runs or fewer runs than they should have, given their individual pitching statistics?" "Run Efficiency" (Run Eff) asks the question "Did this team win more games or fewer games than they should have, given their runs scored and runs allowed?"

2006 American League Team Efficiency Summary

	RC	Runs	Hit Eff	Exp RA	RA	Pit Eff	Exp Wins	Wins	Runs Eff	Eff Wins	Wins	Overall Eff
Oakland Athletics	644	649	101	625	601	104	87	80	92	83	80	96
Tampa Bay Devil Rays	601	596	99	760	731	104	65	56	87	62	56	90
Detroit Tigers	676	690	102	561	551	102	99	85	86	96	85	89
Minnesota Twins	680	677	100	602	601	100	91	80	88	91	80	88
Baltimore Orioles	677	665	98	778	767	101	70	61	88	70	61	87
Los Angeles Angels	678	674	99	625	649	96	84	75	89	88	75	86
Boston Red Sox	754	718	95	690	713	97	82	75	92	88	75	85
Chicago White Sox	776	769	99	659	664	99	93	80	86	94	80	85
Seattle Mariners	633	625	99	656	652	101	78	66	85	78	66	84
Kansas City Royals	637	642	101	810	832	97	60	52	86	62	52	84
Texas Rangers	725	731	101	674	691	98	86	72	84	87	72	83
New York Yankees	814	784	96	615	649	95	96	83	86	103	83	80
Toronto Blue Jays	750	700	93	652	671	97	84	73	86	92	73	79
Cleveland Indians	761	748	98	664	675	98	89	66	74	92	66	72

2006 National League Team Efficiency Summary

	RC	Runs	Hit Eff	Exp RA	RA	Pit Eff	Exp Wins	Wins	Runs Eff	Eff Wins	Wins	Overall Eff
New York Mets	723	739	102	598	612	98	96	86	89	96	86	89
Cincinnati Reds	721	675	94	741	706	105	77	69	89	79	69	88
Florida Marlins	656	656	100	664	653	102	81	70	86	80	70	87
St Louis Cardinals	683	667	98	652	651	100	83	74	89	85	74	87
Philadelphia Phillies	740	739	100	723	719	101	83	70	84	83	70	84
Washington Nationals	661	636	96	734	736	100	69	61	88	73	61	84
San Francisco Giants	632	645	102	614	641	96	82	70	86	83	70	84
Milwaukee Brewers	624	627	100	661	713	93	71	64	91	76	64	84
Pittsburgh Pirates	624	614	98	735	715	103	69	56	81	68	56	83
Los Angeles Dodgers	718	695	97	639	646	99	87	74	85	90	74	82
Arizona Diamondbacks	671	669	100	678	696	97	78	65	84	80	65	81
Atlanta Braves	703	722	103	697	705	99	83	66	80	82	66	81
San Diego Padres	656	617	94	580	601	96	83	73	88	91	73	80
Chicago Cubs	618	596	97	708	720	98	66	56	85	70	56	80
Houston Astros	636	631	99	594	625	95	82	68	83	86	68	79
Colorado Rockies	658	638	97	628	648	97	80	63	79	85	63	74

The Fielding Bible Awards

John Dewan

As a follow-up to my book, *The Fielding Bible*, Bill James gave me a great suggestion. He suggested that I assemble a "panel of experts" to vote on the best defensive players at each position. That's what we've done here.

We asked our panel of ten experts to rank 10 players at each position from one to ten. We then use the same voting technique as the Major League Baseball MVP voting. A first place vote gets 10 points, second place 9 points, third place 8 points, etc. Total up the points for each player and the player with the most points wins the award. A perfect score is 100.

One important distinction that differentiates our award from most other baseball awards, such as the Gold Gloves, is that we only have one winner instead of separate winners for each league. Our intention is to stand up and say "This is the best fielder at this position in Major League Baseball last season."

Here are the results of the very first Fielding Bible Awards.

The Awards

First Base – Albert Pujols, St. Louis

It's amazing to think that the best hitter of this generation is also the best fielding player at his position. Pujols (87 points) wins in a close battle with two former Gold Glovers, Mark Teixeira (80 points) and Doug Mientkiewicz (77).

Second Base – Orlando Hudson, Arizona

Hudson (90 points) was finally recognized with a Gold Glove in 2005 after years of excellence and now wins the first Fielding Bible Award at second base. He was well ahead of the second place finisher, Oakland's Mark Ellis (67 points).

Third Base – Adrian Beltre, Seattle

What a battle this was! Joe Crede finished third with 74 points, just four points behind the tie for first place between Beltre and Scott Rolen (78 points each). The first tie-breaker for the voting is number of first-place votes, and we had another tie with Beltre and Rolen each being named to the top spot on three of the ten ballots. The next tie-breaker is to use our three tie-breaker ballots. These are ballots from three additional experts designed for this very purpose. Our three additional voters listed Beltre and Rolen as follows:

Voter	Beltre	Rolen
Steve Moyer	1st	8th
Todd Radcliffe	2nd	5th
Dave Studenmund	4th	5th

All three listed Beltre ahead of Rolen, giving Beltre the award.

Shortstop – Adam Everett, Houston

It was a landslide for Everett as he garnered all but two first-place votes from our panel. He received second place votes on the other two ballots, for a near-perfect point total of 98 points. Omar Vizquel was a distant second (61 points).

Left Field – Carl Crawford, Tampa Bay

Crawford was no surprise. Although he has never won a Gold Glove, his excellent defense is well known. Gold Gloves are usually given to center fielders. Our award system recognizes each outfield position separately, and Crawford finally gets his just reward. Crawford earned 87 points placing him ahead of the runner-up, Toronto's Reed Johnson (71 points).

Center Field – Carlos Beltran, New York Mets

I thought Andruw Jones would win this, and he did come in second with 78 points. But Beltran was the clear-cut winner with 90 points.

Right Field – Ichiro Suzuki, Seattle

As expected, Ichiro (95 points) easily won the first Fielding Bible Award in right field. It may be his last as a right fielder if he continues to play center field as he did for the last six weeks of the 2006 season. The competition will be much tougher in center. Suzuki is the second defender from Seattle to win a Fielding Bible award, while Toronto places another outfielder in second place with the 69 points earned by right-fielder Alexis Rios.

Cather – Ivan Rodriguez, Detroit

Rodriguez (96 points) and Yadier Molina (90) were named first and second on 11 of our 13 ballots. Rodriguez has always been known for his great arm, and 2006 was no exception as he threw out 46% of the runners who tried to steal on him, the highest percentage among all regulars. Miguel Oliva (53 points) was a distant third.

Pitcher – Greg Maddux, Chicago Cubs and Los Angeles Dodgers

Maddux (78 points) has won 15 of the last 16 National League Gold Gloves and now wins the first Fielding Bible Award at pitcher. Kenny Rogers has won four of the last six AL Gold Gloves and was a close second for the Fielding Bible Award with 72 points. Over the last three years, Rogers and Maddux also rank as the two best fielders at pitcher in the *Fielding Bible* plus/minus system, with scores of +22 and +21 respectively.

Interestingly, among the eight fielding positions with everyday players, four winners were from the American League and four were National Leaguers. The National League gets the overall nod with the winner at the ninth position, pitcher.

Background of the Fielding Bible Awards

While *The Fielding Bible* puts a lot of emphasis on the numbers, I feel that visual observation and subjective judgment are very important parts of determining the best defensive players. But there is now, and has been since 1957, one and only one source for organized subjective judgment about fielding: the Gold Glove Awards. That source doesn't work as well as it might, because

> a) the voting system is badly designed, and
> b) all it really offers us is one look at one player.

If you look at, say, Dave Cash, or Ted Sizemore, or Jim Gantner, or Julian Javier, or Johnny Ray or Steve Sax, and you ask "was he generally regarded, while active, as a good defensive second baseman?" you really have almost nothing to go on. The only thing you really know about any of these guys was that he never won a Gold Glove award. Javier was regarded as a brilliant second baseman, Sax as a not-very-good second baseman, but in the eyes of the Gold Glove voters, they're the same. That happens because only the winner of the Gold Glove voting is shown. You don't know who came in second or third.

We're taking a second look at the same issue, and trying to do this in a way that avoids the pitfalls and oversights of the Gold Glove vote. Here's how it works:

1. *I appointed a panel of experts to vote.* We have a panel of ten experts, plus three "tie-breaker" ballots.

2. *We rate everybody in one group*. The Gold Glove vote is divided into National League and American League. We make ours different by putting everybody together. Is playing shortstop in the American League one thing, and playing shortstop in the National League a different thing, or is it really very much the same? It's very much the same—thus, it's better to treat it as if it *were* the same.

3. *We use a ten-man ballot*. We use a ten-man ballot (I'm referring to the players listed, not the panel of experts). Ten points for first place, nine points for second place, etc, down to one point for tenth place. We feel strongly that a ten-man ballot with weighted positions leads to more accurate outcomes.

4. *We defined the list of candidates.* Only players who actually were regulars at the position are candidates. This eliminates the possibility of a vote going to somebody who wasn't really playing the position.

5. *We are publishing the balloting.* We summarize the voting at each position, clearly identifying who everybody voted for. Publishing the actual vote totals encourages the voters to take their votes more seriously. They understand that their ballots are going to

be published. Also, we felt the public would have more respect for the voting if they have more insight into the process.

There is something cool about having 10 experts and a 10-man ballot, because that gives you 100 points possible. . .if all 10 voters place Ivan Rodriguez first at catcher, he scores at 100.

Here are the tie-breaker rules we are using:
1. Most first-place votes wins.
2. If still tied, count the tie-breaker ballots.
3. If still tied, award goes to player with the higher plus/minus rating.

Ballots were due on the Tuesday after the end of the regular season.

At some point in the future we may use one panel of experts for outfielders, a second one for infielders, a third one for catchers.   That would allow more experts to climb on board the system, and it would also sharpen one's focus a little. If you knew in advance, for example, that you would only be voting on outfielders, then, in watching games during the season, you would focus more on the defense of the individual outfielders.   By the time the ballot was due, you would know more about them.

Of course, we can't make this award equal in prestige to the Gold Glove voting; the Gold Glove voting has a 50-year head start.   But we can provide an alternative.

The Panel

This is our ten-man panel of experts for The Fielding Bible Awards:

Since you have this book, you probably know **Bill James**, a baseball writer and analyst published for more than thirty years. Bill is the Senior Baseball Operations Advisor for the Boston Red Sox.

The **BIS Video Scouts** at Baseball Info Solutions (BIS) study every game of the season, sometimes multiple times, with the task to examine a huge list of valuable game details.

The man who created Strat-O-Matic Baseball, **Hal Richman**, continues to lead his company's annual in-depth analysis of each player's season. Hal cautions SOM players that his voting on this ballot may or may not reflect the eventual 2006 fielding ratings for players in his game. Ballots were due prior to the completion of his annual research effort to evaluate player defense.

Named the best sports columnist in America by the Associated Press Sports Editors in 2003 and 2005, **Joe Posnanski** writes for the Kansas City Star.

For over twenty years, BIS owner **John Dewan** has collected, published, and analyzed in-depth baseball statistics. He wrote *The Fielding Bible* in February 2006.

Now Player Acquisition Consultant to Seattle Mariners GM Bill Bavasi, **Mat Olkin** studied, analyzed, and wrote about baseball players for almost fifteen years.

On Chicago sports radio for more than twenty years, **Mike Murphy's** many strengths include keen baseball observations. He currently hosts a daily show on WSCR 670 AM *The Score*.

Nate Birtwell oversees the BIS data collection operation. When he was back in college, Nate played catcher for the Penn State Baseball Club.

Rob Neyer writes baseball for ESPN.com and appears regularly on ESPN radio and ESPNews.

The **Tom Tango Fan Poll** represents the results of a poll taken at the website, Tango on Baseball (www.tangotiger.net). Besides hosting the website, Tom writes research articles devoted to sabermetrics.

Our three tie-breakers are **Steve Moyer**, president of BIS, **Todd Radcliffe**, lead Video Scout at BIS, and **Dave Studenmund**, one of the owners of www.hardballtimes.com and the editor of *The Hardball Times Baseball Annual*.

The Fielding Bible Awards

Below we show the final point tally for The Fielding Bible Awards in the 2006 season. We asked a panel of experts to complete a ten-man ballot ranking the defensive ability of players from 1 to 10. We show the ranks in the tables below. We then awarded points in the same way as Major League Baseball's MVP voting: ten points for a first place vote, nine for second, etc., down to one point for tenth place. We cover all nine positions, looking at only their fielding work for the 2006 season. Non-pitchers are only eligible if they played at least 500 innings at the position. Pitchers require a minimum of 100 innings pitched.

First Basemen

First Basemen	Bill James	BIS Video Scouts	Hal Richman	Joe Posnanski	John Dewan	Mat Olkin	Mike Murphy	Nate Birtwell	Rob Neyer	Tom Tango Fan Poll	Total Points
Albert Pujols	2	1	6	1	1	2	2	3	2	3	87
Mark Teixeira	4	3	1	6	3	6	1	1	4	1	80
Doug Mientkiewicz	6	4	2	2	2	1		2	1	2	77
Kevin Youkilis	8	2	9	4	4	4		4	3	10	51
Nomar Garciaparra	3	6		3	5	7	3	7	9	7	49
Travis Lee		5	4	5	7	5		5	10	6	41
Todd Helton	1	10	5	10	9	10	4	10		5	35
Adrian Gonzalez	7	7	3				9		8	4	28
Lance Berkman	9	8		8	8	3		9	8		24
Lyle Overbay	10			7	10		8	6		8	17

Others receiving points: Justin Morneau 14, Nick Swisher 12, Richie Sexson 8, Sean Casey 7, Ryan Howard 6, Shea Hillenbrand 4, Adam LaRoche 4, Nick Johnson 3, Chris Shelton 2, Ben Broussard 1

Second Basemen

Second Basemen	Bill James	BIS Video Scouts	Hal Richman	Joe Posnanski	John Dewan	Mat Olkin	Mike Murphy	Nate Birtwell	Rob Neyer	Tom Tango Fan Poll	Total Points
Orlando Hudson	5	1	1	1	1	4	1	1	2	3	90
Mark Ellis	4	4	6	7	2	5	3	5	5	2	67
Chase Utley	3	6		2	4	8	7	6	1	6	56
Aaron Hill	1	5		4	8	1		2	3		53
Brian Roberts	9	8	5	5	3	7		4	6	1	51
Jamey Carroll	6	2	9		7	2	2	3	9	9	50
Mark Grudzielanek	2	3	10	3	9	10	4	8	8	8	45
Placido Polanco	8			8	6	3		9	7	5	31
Luis Castillo		7	2	6	5		10			7	29
Jose Valentin	7			9	10	6			4		19

Others receiving points: Brandon Phillips 15, Mark Loretta 9, Tadahito Iguchi 8, Daniel Uggla 6, Ronnie Belliard 6, Adam Kennedy 5, Jose Castillo 5, Jose Lopez 3, Craig Biggio 2

Third Basemen

Third Basemen	Bill James	BIS Video Scouts	Hal Richman	Joe Posnanski	John Dewan	Mat Olkin	Mike Murphy	Nate Birtwell	Rob Neyer	Tom Tango Fan Poll	Total Points
Adrian Beltre	3	1	5	4	2	3	7	1	1	5	78
Scott Rolen	6	4	1	3	1	4	4	5	3	1	78
Joe Crede	4	3	6	2	4	2	1	3	5	6	74
Eric Chavez	5	7	2	5	5	6	2	8	6	2	62
Mike Lowell	1	2	3	6	7	8	3	2	10	8	60
Brandon Inge	9	5	7	1	8	1	8	4	7	4	56
Pedro Feliz	2	8		8	3	5		7	2	9	44
Freddy Sanchez	7	6	10			7	5	9	4		29
Ryan Zimmerman		9	4	10		9		6		3	25
David Bell				8	6				8		11

Others receiving points: Troy Glaus 10, Nick Punto 9, David Wright 4. Morgan Ensberg 4, Miguel Cabrera 3, Aaron Boone 2, Alex Rodriguez 1

Shortstops

Shortstops	Bill James	BIS Video Scouts	Hal Richman	Joe Posnanski	John Dewan	Mat Olkin	Mike Murphy	Nate Birtwell	Rob Neyer	Tom Tango Fan Poll	Total Points
Adam Everett	1	1	1	1	1	1	2	2	1	1	98
Omar Vizquel	9	2	6	9	7	2	3	1	8	2	61
Jimmy Rollins	3	4	9	5	2	4	9	10	3	6	55
Alex Gonzalez	2	3	2					3		5	40
Rafael Furcal	8	10		3	3		1	8	4		40
Y. Betancourt		8	3	7	8	6		7		3	35
Clint Barmes	4			4	4	8	10		2		34
Craig Counsell		9		2	5	5		9	5		31
Jack Wilson		5	5	8	10	7		4	9	9	31
Khalil Greene	7	7	10		6	3		6		8	30

Others receiving points: Orlando Cabrera 16, Jose Reyes 11, Michael Young 10, John McDonald 7, Edgar Renteria 7, David Eckstein 7, Juan Uribe 7, Derek Jeter 7, Hanley Ramirez 6, Bill Hall 5, Jhonny Peralta 5, Jason Bartlett 4, Miguel Tejada 3

Left Fielders

Left Fielders	Bill James	BIS Video Scouts	Hal Richman	Joe Posnanski	John Dewan	Mat Olkin	Mike Murphy	Nate Birtwell	Rob Neyer	Tom Tango Fan Poll	Total Points
Carl Crawford	1	3	1	1	1	4	1	9	1	1	87
Reed Johnson	3	1	2	9	3	2		1	4	3	71
Dave Roberts	6	2	3	2	4	7		3	6	4	62
Melky Cabrera	4	8	9		6	1	2	7	3	6	53
Jason Bay	2	4	8	4	9	6	8	5	5	7	52
Alfonso Soriano	7			3	2	10	4		7	5	39
Ryan Langerhans		10	4		7	9		4	9	2	32
Raul Ibanez	10	6		10	8	3	3		8		29
Scott Podsednik	5			5	5				2		27
Frank Catalanotte		7		8		5		2			22

Others receiving points: Jason Michaels 21, Matt Diaz 11, Nick Swisher 11, Matt Murton 8, Andre Ethier 6, Emil Brown 6, Brad Wilkerson 5, Matt Holliday 4, Craig Monroe 3, Garret Anderson 1

Center Fielders

Center Fielders	Bill James	BIS Video Scouts	Hal Richman	Joe Posnanski	John Dewan	Mat Olkin	Mike Murphy	Nate Birtwell	Rob Neyer	Tom Tango Fan Poll	Total Points
Carlos Beltran	2	1	6	2	2	1	1	1	3	1	90
Andruw Jones	1	3	2	1	1	5	2	4	2		78
Corey Patterson	5	5		8	5	2		8	1	8	46
Gary Matthews Jr.	9	8		4	6	8	6	2	8	2	46
Curtis Granderson	8	6		6	9	3	9	7	5		35
Juan Pierre		4		3	8	6		6	4		35
Torii Hunter	4	9	1	9	7	10	3		10		35
Vernon Wells			3	7	4			3		4	34
Grady Sizemore	10	2	8	5			5	5	9		33
Willy Taveras	7	7	10	10	3	4			6	10	31

Others receiving points: Joey Gathright 18, Mike Cameron 13, Jim Edmonds 10, Mark Kotsay 10, Aaron Rowand 10, Chris Duffy 9, Chone Figgins 7, Jeremy Reed 5, Brian Anderson 4, Steve Finley 1

Right Fielders

Right Fielders	Bill James	BIS Video Scouts	Hal Richman	Joe Posnanski	John Dewan	Mat Olkin	Mike Murphy	Nate Birtwell	Rob Neyer	Tom Tango Fan Poll	Total Points
Ichiro Suzuki	4	1	1	1	1	2	2	1	1	1	95
Alexis Rios	2	3		2	2	1		2	3	4	69
J.D. Drew	1	5	2	4	3	3		4	2		64
Randy Winn	3	4		3	5	4	10	8	4		47
Austin Kearns	6		7	7	4	6	5	6	6	10	42
Jermaine Dye	8	7		6		10	4	5			26
Jeff Francoeur		6	5				3			5	25
Nicholas Markakis		2				9				2	20
Juan Encarnacion	5		6	5		8					20
Brian Giles	9				10	7		3		7	19

Others receiving points: Milton Bradley 19, Jose Guillen 18, Brad Hawpe 16, Trot Nixon 14, Mark DeRosa13, Geoff Jenkins 9, Mike Cuddyer 9, Casey Blake 7, Vladimir Guerrero 6, Reggie Sanders 3, Jason Lane 3, Bobby Abreu 3, Magglio Ordonez 2, Jacque Jones 1

Catchers

First Basemen	Bill James	BIS Video Scouts	Hal Richman	Joe Posnanski	John Dewan	Mat Olkin	Mike Murphy	Nate Birtwell	Rob Neyer	Tom Tango Fan Poll	Total Points
Ivan Rodriguez	1	2	2	2	1	2	1	1	1	1	96
Yadier Molina	2	1	1	4	2	1	2	2	2	3	90
Miguel Olivo	3	4		9	10	5	4	3	4	4	53
Joe Mauer		3	3	3	3	3	9	10		2	52
Brad Ausmus		6	5	1	4	6			8	9	38
Ramon Hernandez	6						3		3	5	27
Jorge Posada	7			6	7		5		5		25
Jason Kendall		8		5	5	10	8		6		24
Kenji Johjima		5				7	7		7		18
Gerald Laird	10			10	6			4		8	17

Others receiving points: Brian Schneider 16, Damian Miller 14, Jason Varitek 11, Russell Martin 10, Johnny Estrada 10, John Buck 9, Jose Molina 8, Yorvit Torrealba 7, Ronny Paulino 6, Dave Ross 6, Brian McCann 5, A.J. Pierzynski 4, Bengie Molina 3, Eliezer Alfonzo 1

Pitchers

First Basemen	Bill James	BIS Video Scouts	Hal Richman	Joe Posnanski	John Dewan	Mat Olkin	Mike Murphy	Nate Birtwell	Rob Neyer	Tom Tango Fan Poll	Total Points
Greg Maddux	2	1	1	1	1	6	1	8	10	1	78
Kenny Rogers	1	2	2	2	2	7	9	1	1		72
Mark Buehrle			7	5	3	1		2	5		43
Johan Santana		3	6	3	4	4			4		42
Zach Duke	4	10		9	8	3	6	4	9		35
Tom Glavine			4	8	6		8	7	2	8	34
Dontrelle Willis	8	6	8	6	10		2		6		31
Jake Westbrook		9		4	7		3	9		4	30
Aaron Cook		5		9			10	6	3	6	27
Mike Mussina		7	3		5				7		22

Others receiving points: Chris Capuano 19, Paul Maholm 19, Livan Hernandez 17, Bronson Arroyo 13, Jon Garland 11, Felix Hernandez 10, Orlando Hernandez 8, John Smoltz 7, Brad Radke 6, Cliff Lee 6, Kelvim Escobar 5, Andy Pettitte 4, Mark Redman 4, James Shields 2, Tim Wakefield 2, Cory Lidle 1, Jason Marquis 1, Kevin Millwood 1

Plus/Minus Leaders

John Dewan

My book, *The Fielding Bible*, goes into great length (*ad nauseum* to some) describing the new fielding system we developed at Baseball Info Solutions, the Plus/Minus System. Video Scouts at BIS review video of every play of every major league game and record detailed information on each play, such as the location of each batted ball, the speed, the type of hit, etc. Using this in-depth data, we're able to figure out how each player compares to his peers at his position. How often does Derek Jeter field that softly batted ball located 20 feet to the right of the normal shortstop position, for example, compared to all other major league shortstops?

A player gets credit (a "plus" number) if he makes a play that at least one other player at his position missed during the season, and he loses credit (a "minus" number) if he misses a play that at least one player made. The size of the credit is directly related to how often players make the play. Each play is looked at individually, and a score is given for each play. Sum up all the plays for each player at his position and you get his total plus/minus for the season. A total plus/minus score near zero means the player is average. A score above zero is above average and a negative score is below average. Adam Everett turned in the highest score we've had in four years of using the system with a +43 at shortstop in 2006. That means he made 43 more plays than the average MLB shortstop would make.

The charts on the next page summarize the leaders in plus/minus by position for the last three years and for 2006 by itself.

Enhancements

There were several enhancements made to the system since the publication of *The Fielding Bible* in February, 2006. Here's a summary:

- The system for outfielders was modified to count all batted balls hit within about five feet as the same location. This generally resulted in more extreme (higher and lower) plus/minus figures for outfielders. All years were restated.
- Also for outfielders: we added a new category called a "fliner." Prior to last year we categorized balls hit in the air as a fly or a liner. But, as baseball fans know, there are a lot of balls hit in the air that are in between. We call them fliners, and using this new category we are able to get better precision. This was implemented for 2006.
- For balls hit in the air in the infield (pop-ups and line drives), all batted balls within about three feet count as the same location. Again, all years were restated for the "air" component of infielders' plus/minus.
- We reviewed several other possible enhancements, such as using multi-year data as a basis to calculate an individual year. Other than the three mentioned above, however, none of them provided any improvement in the system and were discarded.

We plan to review, and hope to improve, the system as we go forward. And we anticipate publishing an updated *Fielding Bible* in the next year or two.

Plus/Minus Leaders

2004 - 2006

First Basemen		Second Basemen		Third Basemen		Shortstops	
Albert Pujols	+37	Orlando Hudson	+66	Adrian Beltre	+64	Adam Everett	+98
Doug Mientkiewicz	+31	Chase Utley	+52	Scott Rolen	+61	Clint Barmes	+46
Mark Teixeira	+26	Mark Grudzielanek	+30	Pedro Feliz	+54	Jack Wilson	+43
Darin Erstad	+22	Mark Ellis	+24	David Bell	+54	Jimmy Rollins	+40
Tino Martinez	+15	Brian Roberts	+24	Eric Chavez	+33	Rafael Furcal	+35
Justin Morneau	+12	Adam Kennedy	+22	Brandon Inge	+31	Neifi Perez	+28
Ryan Howard	+10	Ronnie Belliard	+18	Sean Burroughs	+26	Bill Hall	+28
Jeff Bagwell	+10	D'Angelo Jimenez	+16	Corey Koskie	+14	Craig Counsell	+23
Nick Johnson	+8	Luis Castillo	+13	Joe Crede	+13	Cesar Izturis	+21
Kevin Millar	+7	Placido Polanco	+13	Morgan Ensberg	+13	Juan Uribe	+20
				Chad Tracy	+13		

Left Fielders		Center Fielders		Right Fielders		Pitchers	
Carl Crawford	+56	Andruw Jones	+48	Ichiro Suzuki	+59	Kenny Rogers	+22
Reed Johnson	+39	Corey Patterson	+45	J.D. Drew	+46	Greg Maddux	+21
Scott Podsednik	+28	Vernon Wells	+34	Alexis Rios	+33	Jake Westbrook	+16
Raul Ibanez	+20	Jeremy Reed	+32	Austin Kearns	+21	Tom Glavine	+14
Jason Bay	+16	Aaron Rowand	+31	Brian Giles	+18	Livan Hernandez	+13
Luis Gonzalez	+13	Joey Gathright	+31	Trot Nixon	+18	Johan Santana	+13
Eric Byrnes	+7	Carlos Beltran	+30	Jose Guillen	+18	Mark Buehrle	+12
Matt Holliday	+6	Torii Hunter	+29	Richard Hidalgo	+15	Mark Mulder	+12
Moises Alou	+4	Willy Taveras	+28	Jeff Francoeur	+13	Dontrelle Willis	+11
Frank Catalanotto	+3	Curtis Granderson	+28	Casey Blake	+10	Mike Mussina	+10
				Geoff Jenkins	+10		

2006

First Basemen		Second Basemen		Third Basemen		Shortstops	
Albert Pujols	+19	Jose Valentin	+22	Brandon Inge	+27	Adam Everett	+43
Doug Mientkiewicz	+16	Aaron Hill	+22	Pedro Feliz	+25	Clint Barmes	+27
Kevin Youkilis	+10	Chase Utley	+19	Adrian Beltre	+23	Bill Hall	+18
Nomar Garciaparra	+7	Mark Ellis	+13	Joe Crede	+22	Craig Counsell	+17
Scott Hatteberg	+7	Tony Graffanino	+13	Nick Punto	+15	Jose Reyes	+13
Travis Lee	+7	Orlando Hudson	+11	Freddy Sanchez	+12	Jason Bartlett	+13
Chris Shelton	+6	Jamey Carroll	+11	Troy Glaus	+10	Jimmy Rollins	+12
Lance Berkman	+6	Mark Grudzielanek	+10	Scott Rolen	+8	Khalil Greene	+12
Richie Sexson	+6	Josh Barfield	+8	Mike Lowell	+8	Rafael Furcal	+7
Shea Hillenbrand	+5	Brian Roberts	+8	David Bell	+8	David Eckstein	+7

Left Fielders		Center Fielders		Right Fielders		Pitchers	
Dave Roberts	+16	Corey Patterson	+34	Randy Winn	+22	Johan Santana	+8
Carl Crawford	+15	Andruw Jones	+30	Alexis Rios	+20	Greg Maddux	+7
Alfonso Soriano	+15	Juan Pierre	+25	J.D. Drew	+19	Zach Duke	+7
Ryan Lanerhans	+15	Curtis Granderson	+18	Brian Giles	+18	Kenny Rogers	+6
Jason Bay	+14	Willy Taveras	+17	Ichiro Suzuki	+17	Felix Hernandez	+4
Reed Johnson	+12	Carlos Beltran	+16	Mark DeRosa	+12	Steve Trachsel	+4
Jason Michaels	+12	Mike Cameron	+15	Juan Encarnacion	+10	10 tied with	+3
Matt Diaz	+12	Vernon Wells	+15	Austin Kearns	+9		
Scott Podsednik	+11	Grady Sizemore	+10	Reggie Sanders	+8		
Matt Murton	+11	Brady Clark	+9	Jose Guillen	+5		
		Alfredo Amezaga	+9				

20

Career Register

The Career Register includes complete career statistics through the 2006 season for every major league player who played in 2006, plus a number of bonus players. Some of the bonus players are guys who missed the entire 2006 season with an injury but are expected to be back in 2007 (such as Brian Lawrence) as well as potential foreign imports. Overall, there are 21 bonus players included in the handbook this year, including nine Japanese players who might play major league baseball in 2007. Among these potential Japanese imports is the highly touted pitcher Daisuke Matsuzaka, who was the MVP of the World Baseball Classic and many feel is one of the top five pitchers in the world.

Players who have appeared in fewer than three major league seasons have their full minor league statistics included. Major leaguers with three or more years in the majors who spent time in the minor leagues in 2006 (for example, if they had a rehab assignment) only have their 2006 minor league statistics displayed; this is indicated by an asterisk. Of course, players who split time between the majors and minors in 2006 but have fewer than three years of major league experience will still have their full minor league stats included.

Players who led the league in a particular category will have that register total in boldface.

The Register also features Runs Created (RC) for hitters and Component ERA (ERC) for pitchers, in addition to the traditional statistics. Developed by Bill James, Runs Created is a method of measuring every facet of a hitter's strengths and weaknesses, and combining those factors into one production number. Component ERC estimates what a pitcher's ERA should have been based upon his raw pitching statistics and gives us a good indication of whether or not a pitcher actually deserved his ERA. An explanation of Bill's most current formulas for both RC and ERC can be found in the Baseball Glossary at the end of the *Handbook*.

Just as a refresher:

Age is seasonal as of June 30, 2007

For pitchers, **BFP** is batters facing pitcher; **TBB** is total walks (intentional and unintentional); **Op** is Save opportunities; **Hld** is holds.

For varying levels of Class-A ball we have used "A+" to denote High A and "A-" for Low A.

Finally, Bill James decided that we should start referring to all incarnations of the Los Angeles Angels of Anaheim as LAA. He cited the Philadelphia Blue Jays of 1943 and 1944 as a historical example of a very temporary team name being forgotten and eventually assimilated into the name they were called going forward—the Phillies.

David Aardsma

Pitches: R **Bats:** R **Pos:** RP-45   **Ht:** 6'4" **Wt:** 205 **Born:** 12/27/1981 **Age:** 25

Year	Team	Lg	G	GS	CG	GF	IP	BFP	H	R	ER	HR	SH	SF	HB	TBB	IBB	SO	WP	Bk	W	L	Pct	ShO	Sv-Op	Hld	ERC	ERA
2003	SnJos	A+	18	0	0	12	18.1	74	14	4	4	2	1	0	0	7	0	28	0	0	1	1	.500	0	8--	-	2.85	1.96
2004	Fresno	AAA	44	0	0	29	55.1	245	46	21	19	2	0	0	4	29	3	53	1	0	6	4	.600	0	11--	-	3.27	3.09
2005	Nrwich	AA	9	8	0	0	46.0	195	44	17	15	2	3	0	0	13	0	30	1	0	6	2	.750	0	0--	-	2.95	2.93
2005	WTenn	AA	33	3	0	8	50.2	232	48	22	22	3	2	2	4	32	3	43	1	0	4	1	.800	0	2--	-	4.55	3.91
2006	Iowa	AAA	29	0	0	20	36.1	150	31	15	13	1	4	2	0	15	2	36	3	0	2	3	.400	0	8--	-	2.81	3.22
2004	SF	NL	11	0	0	5	10.2	61	20	8	8	1	0	1	2	10	0	5	0	0	1	0	1.000	0	0-1	1	13.38	6.75
2006	ChC	NL	45	0	0	9	53.0	225	41	25	24	9	1	3	1	28	0	49	1	0	3	0	1.000	0	0-0	5	3.88	4.08
	2 ML YEARS		56	0	0	14	63.2	286	61	33	32	10	1	4	3	38	0	54	1	0	4	0	1.000	0	0-1	6	5.26	4.52

Andy Abad

Bats: L **Throws:** L **Pos:** PH-5   **Ht:** 6'0" **Wt:** 210 **Born:** 8/25/1972 **Age:** 34

Year	Team	Lg	G	AB	H	2B	3B	HR	(Hm	Rd)	TB	R	RBI	RC	TBB	IBB	SO	HBP	SH	SF	SB	CS	SB%	GDP	Avg	OBP	Slg
2006	Lsvlle*	AAA	82	266	71	12	0	9	(-	-)	110	36	32	39	26	1	31	6	5	1	0	1	.00	6	.267	.344	.414
2001	Oak	AL	1	1	0	0	0	0	(0	0)	0	0	0	0	0	0	0	0	0	0	0	0	-	0	.000	.000	.000
2003	Bos	AL	9	17	2	0	0	0	(0	0)	2	1	0	0	2	0	5	0	0	0	0	1	.00	1	.118	.211	.118
2006	Cin	NL	5	3	0	0	0	0	(0	0)	0	0	0	0	2	0	0	0	0	0	0	0	-	0	.000	.400	.000
	3 ML YEARS		15	21	2	0	0	0	(0	0)	2	1	0	0	4	0	5	0	0	0	0	1	.00	1	.095	.240	.095

Reggie Abercrombie

Bats: R **Throws:** R **Pos:** CF-87; RF-13; PR-13; PH-11; LF-3   **Ht:** 6'3" **Wt:** 220 **Born:** 7/15/1980 **Age:** 26

Year	Team	Lg	G	AB	H	2B	3B	HR	(Hm	Rd)	TB	R	RBI	RC	TBB	IBB	SO	HBP	SH	SF	SB	CS	SB%	GDP	Avg	OBP	Slg
2000	Gr Falls	R+	54	220	60	7	1	2	(-	-)	75	40	29	32	22	0	66	8	3	0	32	8	.80	1	.273	.360	.341
2001	Wilmg	A	125	486	110	17	3	10	(-	-)	163	63	41	49	19	1	154	12	12	2	44	11	.80	3	.226	.272	.335
2002	VeroB	A	132	526	145	23	13	10	(-	-)	224	80	56	74	27	0	158	9	6	1	41	17	.71	3	.276	.321	.426
2002	Jaxnvl	AA	1	4	1	0	0	0	(-	-)	1	1	0	0	0	0	1	0	0	0	1	0	1.00	0	.250	.250	.250
2003	Jaxnvl	AA	116	448	117	25	7	15	(-	-)	201	59	54	62	16	2	164	9	3	3	28	9	.76	3	.261	.298	.449
2004	VeroB	A	34	133	36	4	5	5	(-	-)	65	18	12	21	6	0	33	1	2	1	16	5	.76	1	.271	.305	.489
2004	Lancst	A+	29	120	41	10	2	3	(-	-)	64	24	19	23	2	0	24	1	0	0	8	1	.89	1	.342	.358	.533
2004	Jaxnvl	AA	41	168	29	6	4	4	(-	-)	55	17	20	9	4	0	66	1	1	3	3	3	.50	2	.173	.193	.327
2005	Jupiter	A+	76	299	82	12	3	15	(-	-)	145	51	45	47	14	2	87	5	2	1	19	6	.76	5	.274	.317	.485
2005	Carlina	AA	49	178	45	7	2	10	(-	-)	86	28	23	27	11	0	40	6	0	2	7	5	.58	1	.253	.315	.483
2006	Fla	NL	111	255	54	12	2	5	(1	4)	85	39	24	24	18	2	78	3	4	1	6	5	.55	2	.212	.271	.333

Bobby Abreu

Bats: L **Throws:** R **Pos:** RF-154; CF-2; DH-2; PH-2   **Ht:** 6'0" **Wt:** 210 **Born:** 3/11/1974 **Age:** 33

Year	Team	Lg	G	AB	H	2B	3B	HR	(Hm	Rd)	TB	R	RBI	RC	TBB	IBB	SO	HBP	SH	SF	SB	CS	SB%	GDP	Avg	OBP	Slg
1996	Hou	NL	15	22	5	1	0	0	(0	0)	6	1	1	1	2	0	3	0	0	0	0	0	-	1	.227	.292	.273
1997	Hou	NL	59	188	47	10	2	3	(3	0)	70	22	26	25	21	0	48	1	0	0	7	2	.78	6	.250	.329	.372
1998	Phi	NL	151	497	155	29	6	17	(10	7)	247	68	74	101	84	14	133	0	4	4	19	10	.66	6	.312	.409	.497
1999	Phi	NL	152	546	183	35	11	20	(13	7)	300	118	93	131	109	8	113	3	0	4	27	9	.75	13	.335	.446	.549
2000	Phi	NL	154	576	182	42	10	25	(14	11)	319	103	79	130	100	9	116	1	0	3	28	8	.78	12	.316	.416	.554
2001	Phi	NL	162	588	170	48	4	31	(13	18)	319	118	110	125	106	11	137	1	0	9	36	14	.72	13	.289	.393	.543
2002	Phi	NL	157	572	176	50	6	20	(8	12)	298	102	85	112	104	9	117	3	0	6	31	12	.72	11	.308	.413	.521
2003	Phi	NL	158	577	173	35	1	20	(11	9)	270	99	101	120	109	13	126	2	0	7	22	9	.71	13	.300	.409	.468
2004	Phi	NL	159	574	173	47	1	30	(13	17)	312	118	105	139	127	10	116	5	0	7	40	5	.89	5	.301	.428	.544
2005	Phi	NL	162	588	168	37	1	24	(15	9)	279	104	102	116	117	15	134	6	0	8	31	9	.78	13	.286	.405	.474
2006	2 Tms		156	548	163	41	2	15	(8	7)	253	98	107	123	124	6	138	3	2	9	30	6	.83	13	.297	.424	.462
06	Phi	NL	98	339	94	25	2	8	(5	3)	147	61	65	76	91	5	86	2	0	6	20	4	.83	8	.277	.427	.434
06	NYY	AL	58	209	69	16	0	7	(3	4)	106	37	42	47	33	1	52	1	2	3	10	2	.83	5	.330	.419	.507
	11 ML YEARS		1485	5276	1595	375	44	205	(108	97)	2673	951	883	1123	1003	95	1181	25	6	57	271	84	.76	94	.302	.412	.507

Winston Abreu

Pitches: R **Bats:** R **Pos:** RP-7   **Ht:** 6'2" **Wt:** 170 **Born:** 4/5/1977 **Age:** 30

Year	Team	Lg	G	GS	CG	GF	IP	BFP	H	R	ER	HR	SH	SF	HB	TBB	IBB	SO	WP	Bk	W	L	Pct	ShO	Sv-Op	Hld	ERC	ERA
1994	Braves	R	13	11	0	1	57.1	257	57	35	26	2	0	5	4	24	0	53	3	4	0	8	.000	0	0--	-	3.81	4.08
1995	Danvle	R+	13	13	1	0	74.0	277	54	29	19	5	4	1	1	13	0	90	2	0	6	3	.667	0	0--	-	1.84	2.31
1996	Macon	A	12	12	0	0	60.0	247	51	29	20	4	1	0	1	25	1	60	3	1	4	3	.571	0	0--	-	3.22	3.00
1998	Eugene	A-	17	10	0	3	45.1	206	39	36	32	6	0	2	5	31	0	52	6	0	0	4	.000	0	0--	-	5.11	6.35
1999	Macon	A	14	14	0	0	69.1	272	41	17	13	3	0	2	4	26	0	95	7	1	7	2	.778	0	0--	-	1.81	1.69
1999	MrtlBh	A+	13	12	0	0	68.2	290	53	26	25	7	2	4	0	41	0	76	3	1	3	2	.600	0	0--	-	3.66	3.28
2000	Braves	R	2	2	0	0	3.0	14	2	1	1	1	0	0	1	2	0	2	0	0	0	0	-	0	0--	-	6.25	3.00
2000	Macon	A	11	1	0	8	28.2	103	11	6	6	2	0	0	0	6	0	48	1	0	2	1	.667	0	3--	-	0.80	1.88
2000	Grnvlle	AA	1	1	0	0	4.0	17	4	1	1	0	0	0	0	3	0	5	0	0	0	1	.000	0	0--	-	5.14	2.25
2000	Rchmd	AAA	3	0	0	0	9.0	42	7	8	7	2	1	1	1	10	0	5	0	0	0	1	.000	0	0--	-	7.52	7.00
2001	Grnvlle	AA	34	7	0	4	73.2	319	56	40	38	9	5	2	5	45	2	93	2	1	3	5	.375	0	0--	-	3.96	4.64
2002	Wichta	AA	23	1	0	9	40.2	169	29	16	15	1	1	1	0	21	3	52	3	0	3	0	1.000	0	0--	-	2.38	3.32
2002	WTenn	AA	11	0	0	3	15.0	75	9	12	12	2	2	0	0	20	0	20	2	1	1	0	1.000	0	0--	-	5.50	7.20
2004	Jaxnvl	AA	3	2	0	0	9.2	46	10	7	6	4	0	0	1	7	0	12	0	0	1	1	.500	0	0--	-	8.70	5.59
2004	LsVgs	AAA	14	1	0	2	23.0	109	20	20	20	5	0	2	2	20	0	23	0	1	1	2	.333	0	0--	-	6.51	7.83
2004	Tucsn	AAA	28	0	0	9	44.1	205	44	28	28	10	0	1	2	25	1	41	6	0	1	0	1.000	0	3--	-	5.64	5.68

23

Year	Team	Lg	HOW MUCH HE PITCHED						WHAT HE GAVE UP											THE RESULTS							
			G	GS	CG	GF	IP	BFP	H	R	ER	HR	SH	SF	HB	TBB	IBB	SO	WP	Bk	W	L	Pct	ShO	Sv-Op	Hld	ERC	ERA
2005	Tucsn	AAA	27	0	0	10	33.1	150	37	24	24	6	0	0	0	15	0	42	2	0	2	3	.400	0	2--	-	5.47	6.48
2006	Ottawa	AAA	46	0	0	11	65.1	274	54	22	18	4	4	2	3	20	6	78	8	0	9	4	.692	0	1--	-	2.52	2.48
2006	Bal	AL	7	0	0	2	8.0	42	10	10	9	1	0	1	1	6	1	6	0	0	0	0	-	0	0-0	0	7.17	10.13

Jeremy Accardo

Pitches: R **Bats:** R **Pos:** RP-65   **Ht:** 6'2" **Wt:** 190 **Born:** 12/8/1981 **Age:** 25

Year	Team	Lg	HOW MUCH HE PITCHED						WHAT HE GAVE UP											THE RESULTS							
			G	GS	CG	GF	IP	BFP	H	R	ER	HR	SH	SF	HB	TBB	IBB	SO	WP	Bk	W	L	Pct	ShO	Sv-Op	Hld	ERC	ERA
2004	SnJos	A+	50	0	0	44	55.0	239	57	28	26	3	0	0	1	15	1	43	4	0	1	2	.333	0	27--	-	3.41	4.25
2004	Nrwich	AA	7	0	0	4	8.1	36	9	5	5	1	0	0	0	2	1	5	1	0	2	1	.667	0	1--	-	3.75	5.40
2005	SnJos	A+	2	0	0	2	2.0	8	1	0	0	0	0	0	1	1	0	3	0	0	0	0	-	0	1--	-	3.21	0.00
2005	Nrwich	AA	8	0	0	6	9.2	38	8	3	1	0	0	0	1	1	0	15	0	0	1	0	1.000	0	4--	-	1.57	0.93
2005	Fresno	AAA	25	0	0	11	32.1	132	25	7	7	0	1	0	0	10	1	30	2	0	2	0	1.000	0	3--	-	1.87	1.95
2006	Fresno	AAA	3	0	0	0	5.0	20	5	1	1	0	1	0	0	1	0	8	0	0	0	0	-	0	0--	-	2.76	1.80
2005	SF	NL	28	0	0	7	29.2	124	26	13	13	2	1	1	1	9	1	16	1	0	1	5	.167	0	0-1	4	2.87	3.94
2006	2 Tms		65	0	0	27	69.0	297	76	42	41	7	1	4	1	20	5	54	4	1	2	4	.333	0	3-8	10	4.17	5.35
06	SF	NL	38	0	0	16	40.1	170	38	23	22	2	0	4	1	11	3	40	2	0	1	3	.250	0	3-6	8	2.88	4.91
06	Tor	AL	27	0	0	11	28.2	127	38	19	19	5	1	0	0	9	2	14	2	1	1	1	.500	0	0-2	2	6.25	5.97
2 ML YEARS			93	0	0	34	98.2	421	102	55	54	9	2	5	2	29	6	70	5	1	3	9	.250	0	3-9	14	3.76	4.93

Mike Adams

Pitches: R **Bats:** R **Pos:** RP-2   **Ht:** 6'5" **Wt:** 190 **Born:** 7/29/1978 **Age:** 28

Year	Team	Lg	HOW MUCH HE PITCHED						WHAT HE GAVE UP											THE RESULTS							
			G	GS	CG	GF	IP	BFP	H	R	ER	HR	SH	SF	HB	TBB	IBB	SO	WP	Bk	W	L	Pct	ShO	Sv-Op	Hld	ERC	ERA
2006	Nashv*	AAA	15	0	0	9	16.1	72	17	8	6	2	2	0	0	8	0	18	2	0	1	1	.500	0	2--	-	4.86	3.31
2006	Norfolk*	AAA	13	0	0	7	14.2	61	13	8	8	0	1	0	0	7	0	12	1	0	0	0	-	0	0--	-	3.15	4.91
2006	Buffalo*	AAA	3	0	0	1	4.2	17	4	1	1	0	0	1	0	0	0	3	0	0	0	0	-	0	0--	-	1.52	1.93
2006	Portlnd*	AAA	17	0	0	10	23.2	106	29	16	11	1	1	1	0	7	0	15	0	0	0	2	.000	0	0--	-	4.45	4.18
2004	Mil	NL	46	0	0	13	53.0	225	50	21	20	5	5	2	2	14	2	39	2	0	2	3	.400	0	0-5	12	3.22	3.40
2005	Mil	NL	13	0	0	7	13.1	61	12	4	4	2	0	0	0	10	1	14	1	0	0	1	.000	0	1-2	2	5.12	2.70
2006	Mil	NL	2	0	0	0	2.1	13	4	3	3	1	0	0	0	2	0	1	0	0	0	0	-	0	0-0	0	13.74	11.57
3 ML YEARS			61	0	0	20	68.2	299	66	28	27	8	5	2	2	26	3	54	3	0	2	4	.333	0	1-7	14	3.86	3.54

Russ Adams

Bats: L **Throws:** R **Pos:** 2B-50; SS-36; PH-10; PR-5; DH-1   **Ht:** 6'0" **Wt:** 195 **Born:** 8/30/1980 **Age:** 26

Year	Team	Lg	BATTING																BASERUNNING				AVERAGES		
			G	AB	H	2B	3B	HR	(Hm | Rd)	TB	R	RBI	RC	TBB	IBB	SO	HBP	SH	SF	SB	CS	SB%	GDP	Avg	OBP	Slg
2006	Syrcse*	AAA	42	161	50	9	3	0	(- | -)	65	21	15	25	17	1	23	0	0	1	3	2	.60	3	.311	.374	.404
2004	Tor	AL	22	72	22	2	1	4	(1 | 3)	38	10	10	11	5	0	5	1	0	0	1	0	1.00	3	.306	.359	.528
2005	Tor	AL	139	481	123	27	5	8	(5 | 3)	184	68	63	66	50	1	57	3	3	8	11	2	.85	5	.256	.325	.383
2006	Tor	AL	90	251	55	14	1	3	(2 | 1)	80	31	28	23	22	0	41	1	3	3	1	2	.33	5	.219	.282	.319
3 ML YEARS			251	804	200	43	7	15	(8 | 7)	302	109	101	100	77	1	103	5	6	11	13	4	.76	13	.249	.314	.376

Jon Adkins

Pitches: R **Bats:** L **Pos:** RP-55   **Ht:** 6'0" **Wt:** 200 **Born:** 8/30/1977 **Age:** 29

Year	Team	Lg	HOW MUCH HE PITCHED						WHAT HE GAVE UP											THE RESULTS							
			G	GS	CG	GF	IP	BFP	H	R	ER	HR	SH	SF	HB	TBB	IBB	SO	WP	Bk	W	L	Pct	ShO	Sv-Op	Hld	ERC	ERA
2006	Portlnd*	AAA	13	0	0	12	13.0	54	12	2	2	0	0	0	0	3	0	11	0	0	1	0	1.000	0	7--	-	2.34	1.38
2003	CWS	AL	4	0	0	2	9.1	42	8	5	5	1	1	1	1	7	0	3	0	0	0	0	-	0	0-0	0	5.27	4.82
2004	CWS	AL	50	0	0	19	62.0	271	75	35	32	13	3	1	1	20	3	44	1	0	2	3	.400	0	0-0	5	5.90	4.65
2005	CWS	AL	5	0	0	4	8.1	42	13	8	8	0	0	0	1	4	2	1	0	0	1	0	1.000	0	0-0	0	6.94	8.64
2006	SD	NL	55	0	0	15	54.1	232	55	26	24	3	5	2	2	20	4	30	0	0	2	1	.667	0	0-0	8	3.77	3.98
4 ML YEARS			114	0	0	40	134.0	587	151	74	69	17	9	4	5	51	9	78	1	0	4	5	.444	0	0-0	13	5.04	4.63

Jeremy Affeldt

Pitches: L **Bats:** L **Pos:** RP-45; SP-9   **Ht:** 6'4" **Wt:** 225 **Born:** 6/6/1979 **Age:** 28

Year	Team	Lg	HOW MUCH HE PITCHED						WHAT HE GAVE UP											THE RESULTS							
			G	GS	CG	GF	IP	BFP	H	R	ER	HR	SH	SF	HB	TBB	IBB	SO	WP	Bk	W	L	Pct	ShO	Sv-Op	Hld	ERC	ERA
2002	KC	AL	34	7	0	4	77.2	353	85	41	40	8	2	1	3	37	4	67	5	2	3	4	.429	0	0-1	1	4.97	4.64
2003	KC	AL	36	18	0	5	126.0	533	126	58	55	12	2	5	5	38	1	98	2	1	7	6	.538	0	4-4	3	3.82	3.93
2004	KC	AL	38	8	0	26	76.1	344	91	49	42	6	4	4	3	32	2	49	4	3	3	4	.429	0	13-17	0	5.26	4.95
2005	KC	AL	49	0	0	13	49.2	232	56	35	29	3	0	1	0	29	2	39	5	0	0	2	.000	0	0-0	12	5.08	5.26
2006	2 Tms		54	9	0	12	97.1	448	102	74	67	13	4	4	2	55	3	48	2	0	8	8	.500	0	1-3	5	5.21	6.20
06	KC	AL	27	9	0	3	70.0	320	71	51	46	9	3	3	1	42	0	28	2	0	4	6	.400	0	0-0	2	5.18	5.91
06	Col	NL	27	0	0	9	27.1	128	31	23	21	4	1	1	1	13	3	20	0	0	4	2	.667	0	1-3	3	5.29	6.91
5 ML YEARS			211	42	0	60	427.0	1910	460	257	233	42	12	15	13	191	12	301	18	6	21	24	.467	0	18-25	21	4.74	4.91

Chris Aguila

Bats: R **Throws:** R **Pos:** RF-24; PH-17; LF-15; PR-2; CF-1; DH-1 **Ht:** 5'11" **Wt:** 180 **Born:** 2/23/1979 **Age:** 28

								BATTING														BASERUNNING				AVERAGES		
Year	Team	Lg	G	AB	H	2B	3B	HR	(Hm	Rd)	TB	R	RBI	RC	TBB	IBB	SO	HBP	SH	SF		SB	CS	SB%	GDP	Avg	OBP	Slg
2006	Albq*	AAA	78	302	96	15	3	11	(-	-)	150	53	61	56	26	1	54	1	0	4		7	3	.70	4	.318	.369	.497
2004	Fla	NL	29	45	10	2	1	3	(1	2)	23	10	5	3	2	0	12	0	1	0		0	0	-	0	.222	.255	.511
2005	Fla	NL	65	78	19	3	0	0	(0	0)	22	11	4	4	3	0	19	0	0	0		0	1	.00	0	.244	.272	.282
2006	Fla	NL	47	95	22	8	1	0	(0	0)	32	5	7	7	9	1	26	0	0	0		2	1	.67	2	.232	.298	.337
	3 ML YEARS		141	218	51	13	2	3	(1	2)	77	26	16	14	14	1	57	0	1	0		2	2	.50	2	.234	.280	.353

Matt Albers

Pitches: R **Bats:** L **Pos:** SP-2; RP-2 **Ht:** 6'0" **Wt:** 205 **Born:** 1/20/1983 **Age:** 24

			HOW MUCH HE PITCHED						WHAT HE GAVE UP											THE RESULTS						
Year	Team	Lg	G	GS	CG	GF	IP	BFP	H	R	ER	HR	SH	SF	HB	TBB	IBB	SO	WP	Bk	W	L	Pct	ShO	Sv-Op	Hld	ERC	ERA
2002	Mrtnsvl	R+	13	13	0	0	59.2	273	61	38	34	2	3	2	7	38	0	72	5	1	2	3	.400	0	0- -	-	5.19	5.13
2003	Tri-Cit	A	15	14	0	0	86.1	355	69	37	28	1	3	0	5	25	0	94	4	1	5	4	.556	0	0- -	-	2.24	2.92
2004	Lxngtn	A	22	21	0	0	111.1	474	95	51	41	3	4	6	6	57	0	140	11	0	8	3	.727	0	0- -	-	3.45	3.31
2005	Salem	A+	28	27	0	0	148.2	669	161	86	77	15	2	4	8	62	0	146	7	0	8	12	.400	0	0- -	-	4.78	4.66
2006	CpChr	AA	19	19	0	0	116.0	496	96	40	28	4	4	2	12	47	2	95	9	0	10	2	.833	0	0- -	-	3.05	2.17
2006	RdRck	AAA	4	4	0	0	25.0	107	24	11	11	2	0	0	2	10	0	26	0	0	2	1	.667	0	0- -	-	4.09	3.96
2006	Hou	NL	4	2	0	0	15.0	66	17	10	10	1	2	0	0	11	0	0	0	0	0	2	.000	0	0-0	-	4.97	6.00

Manny Alexander

Bats: R **Throws:** R **Pos:** 3B-13; SS-9; PR-2 **Ht:** 5'10" **Wt:** 180 **Born:** 3/20/1971 **Age:** 36

								BATTING														BASERUNNING				AVERAGES		
Year	Team	Lg	G	AB	H	2B	3B	HR	(Hm	Rd)	TB	R	RBI	RC	TBB	IBB	SO	HBP	SH	SF		SB	CS	SB%	GDP	Avg	OBP	Slg
2006	Portlnd*	AAA	102	430	114	21	0	7	(-	-)	156	78	37	54	35	1	58	3	1	3		14	4	.78	13	.265	.323	.363
1992	Bal	AL	4	5	1	0	0	0	(0	0)	1	1	0	0	0	0	3	0	0	0		0	0	-	0	.200	.200	.200
1993	Bal	AL	3	0	0	0	0	0	(0	0)	0	1	0	0	0	0	0	0	0	0		0	0	-	0	-	-	-
1995	Bal	AL	94	242	57	9	1	3	(2	1)	77	35	23	24	20	0	30	2	4	0		11	4	.73	2	.236	.299	.318
1996	Bal	AL	54	68	7	0	0	0	(0	0)	7	6	4	0	3	0	27	0	2	0		3	3	.50	2	.103	.141	.103
1997	2 Tms	NL	87	248	66	12	4	3	(0	3)	95	37	22	30	17	3	54	3	3	1		13	1	.93	6	.266	.320	.383
1998	ChC	NL	108	264	60	10	1	5	(1	4)	87	34	25	23	18	1	66	1	5	1		4	1	.80	6	.227	.278	.330
1999	ChC	NL	90	177	48	11	2	0	(0	0)	63	17	15	20	10	0	38	0	1	1		4	0	1.00	1	.271	.309	.356
2000	Bos	AL	101	194	41	4	3	4	(1	3)	63	30	19	16	13	0	41	0	2	0		2	0	1.00	0	.211	.261	.325
2004	Tex	AL	21	21	5	2	0	0	(0	0)	7	3	3	3	1	0	7	0	0	0		0	0	-	0	.238	.273	.333
2005	SD	NL	10	18	2	1	0	0	(0	0)	3	0	0	1	2	1	5	1	0	0		0	0	-	0	.111	.238	.167
2006	SD	NL	22	34	6	1	1	0	(0	0)	9	2	4	1	2	2	5	0	2	1		1	0	1.00	0	.176	.216	.265
97	ChC	NL	33	99	29	3	1	1	(0	1)	37	11	7	12	8	2	16	2	2	0		2	1	.67	3	.293	.358	.374
97	NYM	NL	54	149	37	9	3	2	(0	2)	58	26	15	18	9	1	38	1	1	1		11	0	1.00	3	.248	.294	.389
	11 ML YEARS		594	1271	293	50	12	15	(4	11)	412	166	115	118	86	7	276	7	19	4		37	10	.79	17	.231	.282	.324

Antonio Alfonseca

Pitches: R **Bats:** R **Pos:** RP-19 **Ht:** 6'5" **Wt:** 250 **Born:** 4/16/1972 **Age:** 35

			HOW MUCH HE PITCHED						WHAT HE GAVE UP											THE RESULTS						
Year	Team	Lg	G	GS	CG	GF	IP	BFP	H	R	ER	HR	SH	SF	HB	TBB	IBB	SO	WP	Bk	W	L	Pct	ShO	Sv-Op	Hld	ERC	ERA
2006	Frisco*	AA	1	0	0	0	1.0	3	0	0	0	0	0	0	0	0	0	0	0	0	0	0	-	0	0- -	-	0.00	0.00
2006	Okla*	AAA	3	0	0	1	3.0	11	4	2	2	0	0	0	1	0	1	0	0	0	1	.000	0	0- -	-	6.30	6.00
1997	Fla	NL	17	0	0	2	25.2	123	36	16	14	3	1	0	1	10	3	19	1	0	1	3	.250	0	0-2	0	6.41	4.91
1998	Fla	NL	58	0	0	27	70.2	316	75	32	32	10	7	6	3	33	9	46	1	0	4	6	.400	0	8-14	9	4.96	4.08
1999	Fla	NL	73	0	0	49	77.2	325	79	28	28	4	3	1	4	29	6	46	1	0	5	4	.444	0	21-25	5	3.96	3.24
2000	Fla	NL	68	0	0	62	70.0	311	82	35	33	7	3	1	1	24	3	47	0	2	5	6	.455	0	45-49	0	4.79	4.24
2001	Fla	NL	58	0	0	52	61.2	268	68	24	21	6	5	1	5	15	3	40	2	0	4	4	.500	0	28-34	0	4.24	3.06
2002	ChC	NL	66	0	0	55	74.1	330	73	34	33	5	4	3	3	36	3	61	0	0	2	5	.286	0	19-28	0	4.12	4.00
2003	ChC	NL	60	0	0	17	66.1	296	76	43	43	7	4	1	2	27	3	51	0	0	3	1	.750	0	0-4	9	5.05	5.83
2004	Atl	NL	79	0	0	11	73.2	313	71	24	21	5	6	1	0	28	5	45	5	0	6	4	.600	0	0-1	13	3.47	2.57
2005	Fla	NL	33	0	0	1	27.1	118	29	15	15	3	2	2	1	14	4	16	1	0	1	1	.500	0	0-2	8	4.96	4.94
2006	Tex	AL	19	0	0	3	16.0	74	23	10	10	3	0	1	0	7	0	5	0	0	0	0	-	0	0-0	8	7.86	5.63
	10 ML YEARS		531	0	0	279	563.1	2474	612	261	250	52	36	17	21	223	39	376	12	2	30	35	.462	0	121-159	52	4.56	3.99

Edgardo Alfonzo

Bats: R **Throws:** R **Pos:** 3B-15; 2B-12; 1B-2; DH-1; PH-1 **Ht:** 5'11" **Wt:** 210 **Born:** 11/8/1973 **Age:** 33

								BATTING														BASERUNNING				AVERAGES		
Year	Team	Lg	G	AB	H	2B	3B	HR	(Hm	Rd)	TB	R	RBI	RC	TBB	IBB	SO	HBP	SH	SF		SB	CS	SB%	GDP	Avg	OBP	Slg
2006	NHam*	AA	3	8	0	0	0	0	(-	-)	0	1	0	0	2	0	1	0	0	0		0	0	-	0	.000	.200	.000
2006	Norfolk*	AAA	42	141	34	6	0	3	(-	-)	49	10	19	17	16	0	15	2	0	2		1	0	1.00	4	.241	.323	.348
1995	NYM	NL	101	335	93	13	5	4	(0	4)	128	26	41	37	12	1	37	1	4	4		1	1	.50	7	.278	.301	.382
1996	NYM	NL	123	368	96	15	2	4	(2	2)	127	36	40	38	25	2	56	0	9	5		2	0	1.00	8	.261	.304	.345
1997	NYM	NL	151	518	163	27	2	10	(4	6)	224	84	72	91	63	0	56	5	8	5		11	6	.65	4	.315	.391	.432
1998	NYM	NL	144	557	155	28	2	17	(8	9)	238	94	78	85	65	1	77	3	2	3		8	3	.73	11	.278	.355	.427
1999	NYM	NL	158	628	191	41	1	27	(11	16)	315	123	108	121	85	2	85	3	1	9		9	2	.82	14	.304	.385	.502
2000	NYM	NL	150	544	176	40	2	25	(13	12)	295	109	94	122	95	1	70	5	0	6		3	2	.60	12	.324	.425	.542
2001	NYM	NL	124	457	111	22	0	17	(6	11)	184	64	49	62	51	0	62	5	1	5		5	0	1.00	5	.243	.322	.403
2002	NYM	NL	135	490	151	26	2	16	(8	8)	225	78	56	90	56	8	55	7	1	6		6	0	1.00	4	.308	.391	.459
2003	SF	NL	142	514	133	25	2	13	(6	7)	201	56	81	76	58	4	41	4	3	7		5	2	.71	14	.259	.334	.391
2004	SF	NL	139	519	150	26	1	11	(8	3)	211	66	77	75	46	2	40	5	2	4		1	1	.50	16	.289	.350	.407
2005	SF	NL	109	368	102	17	1	2	(2	0)	127	36	43	45	27	1	34	2	1	4		2	0	1.00	11	.277	.327	.345
2006	2 Tms	AL	30	87	11	2	0	0	(0	0)	13	5	5	1	4	0	4	1	0	0		0	0	-	2	.126	.200	.149

Year	Team	Lg	G	AB	H	2B	3B	HR	(Hm	Rd)	TB	R	RBI	RC	TBB	IBB	SO	HBP	SH	SF	SB	CS	SB%	GDP	Avg	OBP	Slg
06	LAA	AL	18	50	5	1	0	0	(0	0)	6	1	1	0	2	0	3	0	0	0	0	0	-	1	.100	.135	.120
06	Tor	AL	12	37	6	1	0	0	(0	0)	7	4	4	1	5	0	1	1	0	0	0	0	-	1	.162	.279	.189
	12 ML YEARS		1506	5385	1532	282	18	146	(68	78)	2288	777	744	843	596	22	617	41	31	55	53	17	.76	111	.284	.357	.425

Eliezer Alfonzo

Bats: R **Throws:** R **Pos:** C-84; PH-3   **Ht:** 6'0" **Wt:** 225 **Born:** 2/7/1979 **Age:** 28

Year	Team	Lg	G	AB	H	2B	3B	HR	(Hm	Rd)	TB	R	RBI	RC	TBB	IBB	SO	HBP	SH	SF	SB	CS	SB%	GDP	Avg	OBP	Slg
1997	JhsCty	R+	38	120	33	11	1	2	(-	-)	52	15	15	18	7	0	34	6	0	0	0	1	.00	1	.275	.346	.433
1998	NewJrs	A-	48	175	43	4	1	2	(-	-)	55	16	19	15	6	0	49	2	1	3	1	0	1.00	5	.246	.274	.314
1999	NewJrs	A-	46	178	58	12	2	3	(-	-)	83	14	28	27	3	0	39	4	1	1	3	4	.43	5	.326	.349	.466
2000	Peoria	A	49	175	54	16	0	5	(-	-)	85	28	21	30	6	0	35	6	1	2	2	0	1.00	6	.309	.349	.486
2000	Beloit	A	60	221	59	10	0	5	(-	-)	84	22	27	25	8	0	58	3	0	2	2	2	.50	6	.267	.299	.380
2001	Beloit	A	106	397	110	28	2	14	(-	-)	184	52	48	58	13	3	65	8	3	3	0	1	.00	10	.277	.311	.463
2002	Hi Dsrt	A+	12	43	15	2	0	2	(-	-)	23	7	9	9	3	0	14	2	1	0	0	0	-	1	.349	.417	.535
2002	Hntsvl	AA	69	244	63	15	1	7	(-	-)	101	23	38	29	9	0	55	3	1	1	2	3	.40	8	.258	.292	.414
2004	Jupiter	A+	105	399	112	12	2	18	(-	-)	182	51	70	61	22	2	105	12	0	3	6	4	.60	16	.281	.335	.456
2004	Carlina	AA	4	4	0	0	0	0	(-	-)	0	0	0	0	0	0	4	0	0	0	0	0	-	0	.000	.000	.000
2005	SnJos	A+	53	196	70	16	0	13	(-	-)	125	35	45	47	11	0	49	8	0	2	1	3	.25	2	.357	.410	.638
2005	Nrwich	AA	49	176	55	9	0	9	(-	-)	91	30	31	32	8	2	39	4	0	1	1	0	1.00	5	.313	.354	.517
2005	Fresno	AAA	4	14	4	1	0	1	(-	-)	8	3	3	2	1	0	2	1	0	0	0	0	-	1	.286	.375	.571
2006	Conn	AA	20	65	18	3	0	0	(-	-)	21	8	7	8	7	0	16	1	0	1	1	0	1.00	0	.277	.351	.323
2006	Fresno	AAA	24	74	14	0	1	2	(-	-)	22	5	6	6	4	0	18	6	2	1	0	0	-	0	.189	.282	.297
2006	SF	NL	87	286	76	17	2	12	(3	9)	133	27	39	36	9	7	74	7	4	3	1	0	1.00	11	.266	.302	.465

Sandy Alomar Jr.

Bats: R **Throws:** R **Pos:** C-35; PH-11; DH-2   **Ht:** 6'3" **Wt:** 235 **Born:** 6/18/1966 **Age:** 41

Year	Team	Lg	G	AB	H	2B	3B	HR	(Hm	Rd)	TB	R	RBI	RC	TBB	IBB	SO	HBP	SH	SF	SB	CS	SB%	GDP	Avg	OBP	Slg
1988	SD	NL	1	1	0	0	0	0	(0	0)	0	0	0	0	0	0	1	0	0	0	0	0	-	0	.000	.000	.000
1989	SD	NL	7	19	4	1	0	1	(1	0)	8	1	6	2	3	1	3	0	0	0	0	0	-	1	.211	.318	.421
1990	Cle	AL	132	445	129	26	2	9	(5	4)	186	60	66	60	25	2	46	2	5	6	4	1	.80	10	.290	.326	.418
1991	Cle	AL	51	184	40	9	0	0	(0	0)	49	10	7	10	8	1	24	4	2	1	0	4	.00	4	.217	.264	.266
1992	Cle	AL	89	299	75	16	0	2	(1	1)	97	22	26	26	13	3	32	5	3	0	3	3	.50	7	.251	.293	.324
1993	Cle	AL	64	215	58	7	1	6	(3	3)	85	24	32	28	11	0	28	6	1	4	3	1	.75	3	.270	.318	.395
1994	Cle	AL	80	292	84	15	1	14	(4	10)	143	44	43	48	25	2	31	2	0	1	8	4	.67	7	.288	.347	.490
1995	Cle	AL	66	203	61	6	0	10	(4	6)	97	32	35	30	7	0	26	3	4	1	3	1	.75	8	.300	.332	.478
1996	Cle	AL	127	418	110	23	0	11	(3	8)	166	53	50	44	19	0	42	3	2	2	1	0	1.00	16	.263	.299	.397
1997	Cle	AL	125	451	146	37	0	21	(9	12)	246	63	83	78	19	2	48	3	6	1	0	2	.00	16	.324	.354	.545
1998	Cle	AL	117	409	96	26	2	6	(3	3)	144	45	44	33	18	0	45	3	5	3	0	3	.00	15	.235	.270	.352
1999	Cle	AL	37	137	42	13	0	6	(4	2)	73	19	25	23	4	0	23	0	1	2	0	1	.00	1	.307	.322	.533
2000	Cle	AL	97	356	103	16	2	7	(5	2)	144	44	42	45	16	1	41	4	4	4	2	2	.50	9	.289	.324	.404
2001	CWS	AL	70	220	54	8	1	4	(1	3)	76	17	21	20	12	1	17	2	3	2	1	2	.33	6	.245	.288	.345
2002	2 Tms		89	283	79	14	1	7	(5	2)	116	29	37	30	9	0	33	1	1	2	0	0	-	11	.279	.302	.410
2003	CWS	AL	75	194	52	12	0	5	(3	2)	79	22	26	21	4	0	17	0	5	1	0	0	-	4	.268	.281	.407
2004	CWS	AL	50	146	35	4	0	2	(1	1)	45	15	14	12	11	2	13	2	3	2	0	0	-	4	.240	.298	.308
2005	Tex	AL	46	128	35	7	0	0	(0	0)	42	11	14	14	5	0	12	1	3	0	0	0	-	3	.273	.306	.328
2006	2 Tms		46	108	30	8	0	1	(1	0)	41	8	17	13	3	0	14	0	0	2	0	0	-	3	.278	.292	.380
02	CWS	AL	51	167	48	10	1	7	(5	2)	81	21	25	22	5	0	14	1	1	2	0	0	-	5	.287	.309	.485
02	Col	AL	38	116	31	4	0	0	(0	0)	35	8	12	8	4	0	19	0	0	0	0	0	-	6	.267	.292	.302
06	LAD	NL	27	62	20	5	0	0	(0	0)	25	3	9	10	0	0	7	0	0	0	0	0	-	3	.323	.323	.403
06	CWS	AL	19	46	10	3	0	1	(1	0)	16	5	8	3	3	0	7	0	0	2	0	0	-	0	.217	.255	.348
	19 ML YEARS		1369	4508	1233	248	10	112	(53	59)	1837	519	588	537	212	15	496	41	48	34	25	24	.51	132	.274	.310	.407

Moises Alou

Bats: R **Throws:** R **Pos:** RF-81; LF-11; PH-7; DH-1   **Ht:** 6'3" **Wt:** 225 **Born:** 7/3/1966 **Age:** 40

Year	Team	Lg	G	AB	H	2B	3B	HR	(Hm	Rd)	TB	R	RBI	RC	TBB	IBB	SO	HBP	SH	SF	SB	CS	SB%	GDP	Avg	OBP	Slg
1990	2 Tms	NL	16	20	4	0	1	0	(0	0)	6	4	0	1	0	0	3	0	1	0	0	0	-	1	.200	.200	.300
1992	Mon	NL	115	341	96	28	2	9	(6	3)	155	53	56	53	25	0	46	1	5	5	16	2	.89	5	.282	.328	.455
1993	Mon	NL	136	482	138	29	6	18	(10	8)	233	70	85	79	38	9	53	5	3	7	17	6	.74	9	.286	.340	.483
1994	Mon	NL	107	422	143	31	5	22	(9	13)	250	81	78	92	42	10	63	2	0	5	7	6	.54	7	.339	.397	.592
1995	Mon	NL	93	344	94	22	0	14	(4	10)	158	48	58	52	29	6	56	9	0	4	4	3	.57	9	.273	.342	.459
1996	Mon	NL	143	540	152	28	2	21	(14	7)	247	87	96	81	49	7	83	2	0	7	9	4	.69	15	.281	.339	.457
1997	Fla	NL	150	538	157	29	5	23	(12	11)	265	88	115	97	70	9	85	4	0	7	9	5	.64	13	.292	.373	.493
1998	Hou	NL	159	584	182	34	5	38	(19	19)	340	104	124	130	84	11	87	5	0	6	11	3	.79	14	.312	.399	.582
2000	Hou	NL	126	454	161	28	2	30	(17	13)	283	82	114	104	52	4	45	2	0	9	3	3	.50	21	.355	.416	.623
2001	Hou	NL	136	513	170	31	1	27	(15	12)	284	79	108	104	57	14	57	3	0	8	5	1	.83	18	.331	.396	.554
2002	ChC	NL	132	484	133	23	1	15	(7	8)	203	50	61	59	47	4	61	0	0	3	3	0	1.00	16	.275	.337	.419
2003	ChC	NL	151	565	158	35	1	22	(14	8)	261	83	91	94	63	7	67	7	0	3	3	1	.75	16	.280	.357	.462
2004	ChC	NL	155	601	176	36	3	39	(29	10)	335	106	106	114	68	2	80	0	0	6	3	0	1.00	12	.293	.361	.557
2005	SF	NL	123	427	137	21	3	19	(12	7)	221	67	63	74	56	1	43	3	0	4	5	1	.83	11	.321	.400	.518
2006	SF	NL	98	345	104	25	1	22	(13	9)	197	52	74	65	28	2	31	1	0	4	2	1	.67	15	.301	.352	.571
90	Pit	NL	2	5	1	0	0	0	(0	0)	1	0	0	0	0	0	0	0	0	0	0	0	-	1	.200	.200	.200
90	Mon	NL	14	15	3	0	1	0	(0	0)	5	4	0	1	0	0	3	0	1	0	0	0	-	0	.200	.200	.333
	15 ML YEARS		1840	6660	2005	400	38	319	(181	138)	3438	1054	1229	1199	708	86	860	44	9	78	102	36	.74	181	.301	.368	.516

Abe Alvarez

Pitches: L Bats: L Pos: RP-1   Ht: 6'2" Wt: 190 Born: 10/17/1982 Age: 24

			HOW MUCH HE PITCHED						WHAT HE GAVE UP											THE RESULTS						
Year	Team	Lg	G	GS	CG	GF	IP	BFP	H	R	ER	HR	SH	SF	HB	TBB	IBB	SO	WP	Bk	W	L	Pct	ShO	Sv-Op	Hld	ERC	ERA
2006	Pwtckt*	AAA	22	21	0	0	118.0	526	136	79	74	22	6	3	4	40	0	71	2	0	6	9	.400	0	0- -	-	5.45	5.64
2004	Bos	AL	1	1	0	0	5.0	25	8	5	5	2	0	0	0	5	0	2	0	0	0	1	.000	0	0-0	0	15.00	9.00
2005	Bos	AL	2	0	0	1	2.1	13	6	4	4	1	0	0	0	0	0	1	0	0	0	0	-	0	0-0	0	15.72	15.43
2006	Bos	AL	1	0	0	0	3.0	15	5	4	4	2	0	0	0	2	0	2	0	0	0	0	-	0	0-0	0	15.67	12.00
3 ML YEARS			4	1	0	1	10.1	53	19	13	13	5	0	0	0	7	0	5	0	0	0	1	.000	0	0-0	0	15.40	11.32

Alfredo Amezaga

Bats: B Throws: R Pos: CF-75; PH-26; 2B-23; LF-14; SS-11; PR-6; 3B-4; 1B-2; RF-2   Ht: 5'10" Wt: 165 Born: 1/16/1978 Age: 29

			BATTING																		BASERUNNING				AVERAGES		
Year	Team	Lg	G	AB	H	2B	3B	HR	(Hm	Rd)	TB	R	RBI	RC	TBB	IBB	SO	HBP	SH	SF	SB	CS	SB%	GDP	Avg	OBP	Slg
2002	LAA	AL	12	13	7	2	0	0	(0	0)	9	3	2	6	0	0	1	0	0	0	1	0	1.00	1	.538	.538	.692
2003	LAA	AL	37	105	22	3	2	2	(0	2)	35	15	7	7	9	0	23	1	5	0	2	2	.50	2	.210	.278	.333
2004	LAA	AL	73	93	15	2	0	2	(0	2)	23	12	11	5	3	0	24	3	6	0	3	2	.60	2	.161	.212	.247
2005	2 Tms	NL	5	6	1	0	0	0	(0	0)	1	2	0	0	1	0	0	0	0	0	1	0	1.00	0	.167	.286	.167
2006	Fla	NL	132	334	87	9	3	3	(0	3)	111	42	19	32	33	4	46	3	7	1	20	12	.63	5	.260	.332	.332
05	Col	NL	2	3	1	0	0	0	(0	0)	1	1	0	0	0	0	0	0	0	0	0	0	-	0	.333	.333	.333
05	Pit	NL	3	3	0	0	0	0	(0	0)	0	1	0	0	1	0	0	0	0	0	1	0	1.00	0	.000	.250	.000
5 ML YEARS			259	551	132	16	5	7	(0	7)	179	74	39	50	46	4	94	7	18	1	27	16	.63	10	.240	.306	.325

Brian J Anderson

Pitches: L Bats: R Pos: P   Ht: 6'1" Wt: 190 Born: 4/26/1972 Age: 35

			HOW MUCH HE PITCHED						WHAT HE GAVE UP											THE RESULTS						
Year	Team	Lg	G	GS	CG	GF	IP	BFP	H	R	ER	HR	SH	SF	HB	TBB	IBB	SO	WP	Bk	W	L	Pct	ShO	Sv-Op	Hld	ERC	ERA
1993	LAA	AL	4	1	0	3	11.1	45	11	5	5	1	0	0	0	2	0	4	0	0	0	0	-	0	0-0	0	3.08	3.97
1994	LAA	AL	18	18	0	0	101.2	441	120	63	59	13	3	6	5	27	0	47	5	5	7	5	.583	0	0-0	0	5.05	5.22
1995	LAA	AL	18	17	1	0	99.2	433	110	66	65	24	5	3	3	30	2	45	1	3	6	8	.429	0	0-0	0	5.37	5.87
1996	Cle	AL	10	9	0	0	51.1	215	58	29	28	9	2	3	0	14	1	21	2	0	3	1	.750	0	0-0	1	4.96	4.91
1997	Cle	AL	8	8	0	0	48.0	199	55	28	25	7	0	5	0	11	0	22	1	0	4	2	.667	0	0-0	0	4.71	4.69
1998	Ari	NL	32	32	2	0	208.0	845	221	100	100	39	8	3	4	24	2	95	3	6	12	13	.480	1	0-0	0	3.99	4.33
1999	Ari	NL	31	19	2	4	130.0	549	144	69	66	18	4	0	1	28	3	75	0	2	8	2	.800	1	1-2	1	4.23	4.57
2000	Ari	NL	33	32	2	0	213.1	876	226	101	96	38	6	6	3	39	7	104	1	4	11	7	.611	0	0-0	0	4.15	4.05
2001	Ari	NL	29	22	1	1	133.1	571	156	93	77	25	7	4	1	30	2	55	2	1	4	9	.308	0	0-1	0	5.00	5.20
2002	Ari	NL	35	24	0	1	156.0	659	174	86	83	23	6	8	1	32	3	81	2	5	6	11	.353	0	0-0	0	4.28	4.79
2003	2 Tms	NL	32	31	2	0	197.2	821	212	110	83	27	4	12	4	43	3	87	3	1	14	11	.560	1	0-0	0	4.14	3.78
2004	KC	AL	35	26	2	2	166.0	745	217	123	104	33	5	7	1	53	4	70	2	0	6	12	.333	1	0-0	2	6.36	5.64
2005	KC	AL	6	6	0	0	30.2	133	39	24	23	7	0	1	0	4	1	17	0	1	1	2	.333	0	0-0	0	5.36	6.75
03	Cle	AL	25	24	0	0	148.0	623	162	88	61	21	3	10	4	32	3	72	2	1	9	10	.474	0	0-0	0	4.29	3.71
03	KC	AL	7	7	2	0	49.2	198	50	22	22	6	1	2	0	11	0	15	1	0	5	1	.833	1	0-0	0	3.72	3.99
13 ML YEARS			291	245	12	11	1547.0	6532	1743	897	814	264	50	60	23	337	28	723	22	28	82	83	.497	4	1-3	5	4.64	4.74

Brian Anderson

Bats: R Throws: R Pos: CF-134; PH-7   Ht: 6'2" Wt: 215 Born: 3/11/1982 Age: 25

			BATTING																		BASERUNNING				AVERAGES		
Year	Team	Lg	G	AB	H	2B	3B	HR	(Hm	Rd)	TB	R	RBI	RC	TBB	IBB	SO	HBP	SH	SF	SB	CS	SB%	GDP	Avg	OBP	Slg
2003	Gr Falls	R+	13	49	19	2	1	2	(-	-)	29	6	13	13	9	1	10	1	0	0	3	1	.75	1	.388	.492	.592
2004	WinSa	A+	69	254	81	22	4	8	(-	-)	135	43	46	51	29	5	44	3	0	1	10	1	.91	3	.319	.394	.531
2004	Brham	AA	48	185	50	9	3	4	(-	-)	77	26	27	26	19	3	30	3	1	1	3	2	.60	3	.270	.346	.416
2005	Charltt	AAA	118	448	132	24	3	16	(-	-)	210	71	57	77	44	0	115	4	1	4	4	2	.67	11	.295	.360	.469
2005	CWS	AL	13	34	6	1	0	2	(0	2)	13	3	3	2	0	0	12	0	1	0	1	0	1.00	2	.176	.176	.382
2006	CWS	AL	134	365	82	23	1	8	(7	1)	131	46	33	32	30	2	90	5	2	3	4	7	.36	3	.225	.290	.359
2 ML YEARS			147	399	88	24	1	10	(7	3)	144	49	36	34	30	2	102	5	3	3	5	7	.42	5	.221	.281	.361

Drew Anderson

Bats: L Throws: R Pos: PH-5; PR-3; LF-1; RF-1   Ht: 6'2" Wt: 195 Born: 6/9/1981 Age: 26

			BATTING																		BASERUNNING				AVERAGES		
Year	Team	Lg	G	AB	H	2B	3B	HR	(Hm	Rd)	TB	R	RBI	RC	TBB	IBB	SO	HBP	SH	SF	SB	CS	SB%	GDP	Avg	OBP	Slg
2003	Helena	R+	61	214	68	11	3	2	(-	-)	91	33	38	41	35	1	39	4	4	2	9	5	.64	4	.318	.420	.425
2004	Beloit	A	123	456	140	22	5	5	(-	-)	187	64	59	75	45	3	95	6	11	7	12	4	.75	6	.307	.372	.410
2005	BrvdCt	A+	129	508	158	17	7	6	(-	-)	207	69	62	78	39	6	95	3	2	6	19	8	.70	7	.311	.360	.407
2006	Hntsvl	AA	108	402	117	24	4	6	(-	-)	167	60	43	63	39	3	80	5	4	2	17	8	.68	7	.291	.359	.415
2006	Nashv	AAA	16	63	21	5	1	1	(-	-)	31	15	9	11	2	0	12	0	3	1	3	1	.75	0	.333	.348	.492
2006	Mil	NL	9	9	1	0	0	0	(0	0)	1	3	0	0	1	0	4	0	0	0	0	0	-	0	.111	.200	.111

Garret Anderson

Bats: L Throws: L Pos: LF-94; DH-45; PH-2   Ht: 6'3" Wt: 225 Born: 6/30/1972 Age: 35

			BATTING																		BASERUNNING				AVERAGES		
Year	Team	Lg	G	AB	H	2B	3B	HR	(Hm	Rd)	TB	R	RBI	RC	TBB	IBB	SO	HBP	SH	SF	SB	CS	SB%	GDP	Avg	OBP	Slg
1994	LAA	AL	5	13	5	0	0	0	(0	0)	5	0	1	2	0	0	2	0	0	0	0	0	-	0	.385	.385	.385
1995	LAA	AL	106	374	120	19	1	16	(7	9)	189	50	69	63	19	4	65	1	2	4	6	2	.75	8	.321	.352	.505
1996	LAA	AL	150	607	173	33	2	12	(7	5)	246	79	72	68	27	5	84	0	5	3	7	9	.44	22	.285	.314	.405
1997	LAA	AL	154	624	189	36	3	8	(5	3)	255	76	92	80	30	6	70	2	1	5	10	4	.71	20	.303	.334	.409
1998	LAA	AL	156	622	183	41	7	15	(4	11)	283	62	79	80	29	8	80	1	3	3	8	3	.73	13	.294	.325	.455

Year	Team	Lg	G	AB	H	2B	3B	HR	(Hm	Rd)	TB	R	RBI	RC	TBB	IBB	SO	HBP	SH	SF	SB	CS	SB%	GDP	Avg	OBP	Slg
1999	LAA	AL	157	620	188	36	2	21	(10	11)	291	88	80	92	34	8	81	0	0	6	3	4	.43	15	.303	.336	.469
2000	LAA	AL	159	647	185	40	3	35	(20	15)	336	92	117	95	24	5	87	0	1	9	7	6	.54	21	.286	.307	.519
2001	LAA	AL	161	672	194	39	2	28	(13	15)	321	83	123	97	27	4	100	0	0	5	13	6	.68	12	.289	.314	.478
2002	LAA	AL	158	638	195	56	3	29	(13	16)	344	93	123	108	30	11	80	0	0	10	6	4	.60	11	.306	.332	.539
2003	LAA	AL	159	638	201	49	4	29	(12	17)	345	80	116	114	31	10	83	0	0	4	6	3	.67	15	.315	.345	.541
2004	LAA	AL	112	442	133	20	1	14	(4	10)	197	57	75	70	29	6	75	1	0	3	2	1	.67	3	.301	.343	.446
2005	LAA	AL	142	575	163	34	1	17	(5	12)	250	68	96	82	23	8	84	0	0	5	1	1	.50	13	.283	.308	.435
2006	LAA	AL	141	543	152	28	2	17	(8	9)	235	63	85	75	38	11	95	0	0	7	1	0	1.00	8	.280	.323	.433
13 ML YEARS			1760	7015	2081	431	31	241	(108	133)	3297	891	1128	1034	341	86	986	5	12	64	70	43	.62	161	.297	.327	.470

Marlon Anderson

Bats: L **Throws:** R **Pos:** PH-71; 2B-33; LF-15; RF-11; CF-7; DH-3; 1B-2; PR-1   **Ht:** 5'11" **Wt:** 200 **Born:** 1/6/1974 **Age:** 33

Year	Team	Lg	G	AB	H	2B	3B	HR	(Hm	Rd)	TB	R	RBI	RC	TBB	IBB	SO	HBP	SH	SF	SB	CS	SB%	GDP	Avg	OBP	Slg
1998	Phi	NL	17	43	14	3	0	1	(1	0)	20	4	4	7	1	0	6	0	0	1	2	0	1.00	0	.326	.333	.465
1999	Phi	NL	129	452	114	26	4	5	(4	1)	163	48	54	49	24	1	61	2	4	2	13	2	.87	6	.252	.292	.361
2000	Phi	NL	41	162	37	8	1	1	(1	0)	50	10	15	12	12	0	22	0	0	0	2	2	.50	5	.228	.282	.309
2001	Phi	NL	147	522	153	30	2	11	(7	4)	220	69	61	72	35	5	74	2	10	5	8	5	.62	12	.293	.337	.421
2002	Phi	NL	145	539	139	30	6	8	(4	4)	205	64	48	53	42	14	71	5	2	4	5	1	.83	16	.258	.315	.380
2003	TB	NL	145	482	130	27	3	6	(2	4)	181	59	67	70	41	5	60	3	4	5	19	3	.86	6	.270	.328	.376
2004	StL	NL	113	253	60	12	0	8	(2	6)	96	31	28	23	12	1	38	1	0	5	6	2	.75	5	.237	.269	.379
2005	NYM	NL	123	235	62	9	0	7	(3	4)	92	31	19	23	18	0	45	1	4	2	6	1	.86	2	.264	.316	.391
2006	2 Tms	NL	134	279	83	16	4	12	(4	8)	143	43	38	42	25	1	49	1	4	3	4	6	.40	4	.297	.354	.513
06	Was	NL	109	215	59	13	2	5	(0	5)	91	31	23	28	18	1	41	1	3	2	2	4	.33	1	.274	.331	.423
06	LAD	NL	25	64	24	3	2	7	(4	3)	52	12	15	14	7	0	8	0	1	1	2	2	.50	3	.375	.431	.813
9 ML YEARS			994	2967	792	161	20	59	(28	31)	1170	359	334	351	210	27	426	15	28	27	65	22	.75	56	.267	.316	.394

Robert Andino

Bats: R **Throws:** R **Pos:** SS-9; PH-2   **Ht:** 6'0" **Wt:** 170 **Born:** 4/25/1984 **Age:** 23

Year	Team	Lg	G	AB	H	2B	3B	HR	(Hm	Rd)	TB	R	RBI	RC	TBB	IBB	SO	HBP	SH	SF	SB	CS	SB%	GDP	Avg	OBP	Slg
2002	Mrlns	R	9	27	7	0	0	0	(-	-)	7	2	2	3	5	0	6	0	0	1	3	0	1.00	1	.259	.364	.259
2002	Jmstwn	A-	9	36	6	1	1	0	(-	-)	9	2	3	1	1	0	9	0	0	0	1	0	1.00	0	.167	.189	.250
2003	Grnsbr	A	119	416	78	17	2	2	(-	-)	105	45	27	28	46	0	128	0	7	5	6	5	.55	6	.188	.266	.252
2004	Grnsbr	A	76	295	83	10	1	8	(-	-)	119	27	46	40	18	0	83	1	6	4	9	2	.82	5	.281	.321	.403
2004	Jupiter	A+	49	197	55	7	2	0	(-	-)	66	18	15	20	7	0	43	0	3	1	6	2	.75	3	.279	.302	.335
2005	Carlina	AA	127	516	139	30	0	5	(-	-)	184	63	48	64	37	0	111	6	8	4	22	7	.76	11	.269	.323	.357
2006	Albq	AAA	120	498	127	18	6	8	(-	-)	181	70	46	56	33	0	100	4	8	6	13	11	.54	13	.255	.303	.363
2005	Fla	NL	17	44	7	4	0	0	(0	0)	11	4	1	1	5	1	8	0	1	0	1	0	1.00	2	.159	.245	.250
2006	Fla	NL	11	24	4	1	0	0	(0	0)	5	0	2	0	1	0	6	0	1	2	1	0	1.00	0	.167	.185	.208
2 ML YEARS			28	68	11	5	0	0	(0	0)	16	4	3	1	6	1	14	0	2	2	2	0	1.00	2	.162	.224	.235

Steve Andrade

Pitches: R **Bats:** R **Pos:** RP-4   **Ht:** 6'1" **Wt:** 220 **Born:** 2/6/1978 **Age:** 29

Year	Team	Lg	G	GS	CG	GF	IP	BFP	H	R	ER	HR	SH	SF	HB	TBB	IBB	SO	WP	Bk	W	L	Pct	ShO	Sv-Op	Hld	ERC	ERA
2001	Provo	R+	1	0	0	0	2.0	9	3	0	0	0	0	0	0	0	0	5	0	0	0	0	-	0	0--	-	4.47	0.00
2001	CRpds	A	20	0	0	9	29.0	129	33	24	21	3	2	1	2	8	0	31	7	0	2	1	.667	0	0--	-	4.59	6.52
2002	CRpds	A	46	0	0	21	54.1	204	30	7	7	1	0	1	2	16	1	93	12	0	1	1	.500	0	11--	-	1.33	1.16
2003	RCuca	A+	3	0	0	2	3.0	13	0	0	0	0	0	0	1	3	0	7	2	0	0	0	-	0	1--	-	1.55	0.00
2003	Ark	AA	36	0	0	13	51.0	199	26	16	15	2	2	0	1	19	1	74	4	0	5	1	.833	0	7--	-	1.36	2.65
2004	Ark	AA	35	0	0	24	48.0	196	37	16	13	4	0	0	3	12	0	59	4	0	2	2	.500	0	9--	-	2.40	2.44
2004	Salt Lk	AAA	12	0	0	4	13.2	62	15	7	7	1	0	1	1	8	0	17	0	0	0	1	.000	0	3--	-	5.62	4.61
2005	NHam	AA	35	0	0	14	50.1	193	23	12	11	3	2	1	2	16	2	71	4	0	3	2	.600	0	3--	-	1.20	1.97
2006	Omha	AAA	12	0	0	8	23.1	99	21	13	12	3	0	1	1	8	0	22	4	0	2	0	.000	0	0--	-	3.63	4.63
2006	Portlnd	AAA	26	0	0	7	44.1	183	33	13	12	1	1	0	2	22	1	45	9	0	3	0	1.000	0	0--	-	2.74	2.44
2006	KC	AL	4	0	0	2	4.2	23	5	5	5	0	1	0	0	4	0	5	1	0	0	0	-	0	0-0	1	5.35	9.64

Greg Aquino

Pitches: R **Bats:** R **Pos:** RP-42   **Ht:** 6'1" **Wt:** 190 **Born:** 1/11/1978 **Age:** 29

Year	Team	Lg	G	GS	CG	GF	IP	BFP	H	R	ER	HR	SH	SF	HB	TBB	IBB	SO	WP	Bk	W	L	Pct	ShO	Sv-Op	Hld	ERC	ERA
2006	Tucsn*	AAA	9	0	0	3	11.2	43	6	0	0	0	0	0	0	4	0	15	1	1	2	0	1.000	0	1--	-	1.20	0.00
2004	Ari	NL	34	0	0	26	35.1	147	24	15	12	4	2	2	1	17	2	26	4	0	0	2	.000	0	16-19	-	2.87	3.06
2005	Ari	NL	35	0	0	11	31.1	155	42	29	27	7	1	1	4	17	1	34	2	1	0	1	.000	0	1-3	3	8.22	7.76
2006	Ari	NL	42	0	0	12	48.1	220	54	27	24	8	1	0	4	24	2	51	2	0	2	0	1.000	0	0-0	2	5.99	4.47
3 ML YEARS			111	0	0	49	115.0	522	120	71	63	19	4	3	10	58	5	111	8	1	2	3	.400	0	17-22	6	5.52	4.93

Danny Ardoin

Bats: R **Throws:** R **Pos:** C-40   **Ht:** 6'0" **Wt:** 215 **Born:** 7/8/1974 **Age:** 32

Year	Team	Lg	G	AB	H	2B	3B	HR	(Hm	Rd)	TB	R	RBI	RC	TBB	IBB	SO	HBP	SH	SF	SB	CS	SB%	GDP	Avg	OBP	Slg
2006	Mdest*	A+	7	26	2	2	0	0	(-	-)	4	4	0	0	2	0	8	2	0	0	0	0	-	0	.077	.200	.154
2006	ColSpr*	AAA	6	15	4	2	0	0	(-	-)	6	2	2	2	2	0	5	1	1	0	0	0	-	0	.267	.389	.400
2000	Min	AL	15	32	4	1	0	1	(0	1)	8	4	5	2	8	0	10	0	0	0	0	0	-	0	.125	.300	.250

Year	Team	Lg	G	AB	H	2B	3B	HR	(Hm	Rd)	TB	R	RBI	RC	TBB	IBB	SO	HBP	SH	SF	SB	CS	SB%	GDP	Avg	OBP	Slg
2004	Tex	AL	6	8	1	0	0	0	(0	0)	1	1	1	1	3	0	2	0	0	0	0	0	-	0	.125	.364	.125
2005	Col	NL	80	210	48	10	0	6	(3	3)	76	28	22	21	20	2	69	9	7	2	1	1	.50	8	.229	.320	.362
2006	2 Tms		40	122	22	5	1	0	(0	0)	29	14	3	2	9	2	33	3	1	0	0	0	-	3	.180	.254	.238
06	Col	NL	35	109	21	5	1	0	(0	0)	28	12	2	2	8	2	27	2	1	0	0	0	-	2	.193	.261	.257
06	Bal	AL	5	13	1	0	0	0	(0	0)	1	2	1	0	1	0	6	1	0	0	0	0	-	1	.077	.200	.077
4 ML YEARS			141	372	75	16	1	7	(3	4)	114	47	31	26	40	4	114	12	8	2	1	1	.50	11	.202	.298	.306

Joaquin Arias

Bats: R **Throws:** R **Pos:** SS-5; PH-2; 3B-1; PR-1   **Ht:** 6'1" **Wt:** 165 **Born:** 9/21/1984 **Age:** 22

Year	Team	Lg	G	AB	H	2B	3B	HR	(Hm	Rd)	TB	R	RBI	RC	TBB	IBB	SO	HBP	SH	SF	SB	CS	SB%	GDP	Avg	OBP	Slg
2002	Yanks	R	57	203	61	7	6	0	(-	-)	80	29	21	26	12	0	16	0	2	1	2	4	.33	4	.300	.338	.394
2003	Btl Crk	A	130	481	128	12	8	3	(-	-)	165	60	48	53	26	0	44	3	7	3	12	5	.71	7	.266	.306	.343
2004	Stcktn	A+	123	500	150	20	8	4	(-	-)	198	77	62	71	31	2	53	5	2	5	30	14	.68	3	.300	.344	.396
2005	Frisco	AA	120	499	157	23	8	5	(-	-)	211	65	56	72	17	1	46	1	3	6	20	10	.67	5	.315	.335	.423
2006	Okla	AAA	124	493	132	14	10	4	(-	-)	178	56	49	55	19	2	64	4	2	7	26	10	.72	6	.268	.296	.361
2006	Tex	AL	6	11	6	1	0	0	(0	0)	7	4	1	3	1	0	0	0	0	0	0	1	.00	0	.545	.583	.636

Tony Armas Jr.

Pitches: R **Bats:** R **Pos:** SP-30   **Ht:** 6'3" **Wt:** 225 **Born:** 4/29/1978 **Age:** 29

			HOW MUCH HE PITCHED						WHAT HE GAVE UP										THE RESULTS						
Year	Team	Lg	G	GS	CG	GF	IP	BFP	H	R	ER	HR	SH	SF	HB	TBB	IBB	SO	WP	Bk	W	L	Pct	ShO	Sv-Op Hld	ERC	ERA
2006	Nats*	R	1	1	0	0	5.0	24	8	3	3	0	0	0	0	1	0	7	0	0	0	1	.000	0	0-- -	5.85	5.40
2006	Hrsbrg*	AA	1	1	0	0	2.1	12	3	2	2	0	0	0	1	1	0	4	0	0	0	-	.000	0	0-- -	6.63	7.71
1999	Mon	NL	1	1	0	0	6.0	28	8	4	1	0	0	1	0	2	1	2	2	0	0	1	.000	0	0-0 0	4.53	1.50
2000	Mon	NL	17	17	0	0	95.0	403	74	49	46	10	7	3	3	50	2	59	3	0	7	9	.438	0	0-0 0	3.49	4.36
2001	Mon	NL	34	34	0	0	196.2	851	180	101	88	18	15	6	10	91	6	176	9	1	9	14	.391	0	0-0 0	3.95	4.03
2002	Mon	NL	29	29	0	0	164.1	705	149	87	81	22	6	2	7	78	12	131	14	2	12	12	.500	0	0-0 0	4.19	4.44
2003	Mon	NL	5	5	0	0	31.0	124	25	9	9	4	2	1	1	8	0	23	0	0	2	1	.667	0	0-0 0	2.84	2.61
2004	Mon	NL	16	16	0	0	72.0	320	66	41	39	13	2	2	4	45	6	54	0	0	2	4	.333	0	0-0 0	5.26	4.88
2005	Was	NL	19	19	0	0	101.1	452	100	57	56	16	4	1	5	54	4	59	6	2	7	7	.500	0	0-0 0	5.11	4.97
2006	Was	NL	30	30	0	0	154.0	693	167	96	86	19	12	6	13	64	7	97	6	1	9	12	.429	0	0-0 0	5.04	5.03
8 ML YEARS			151	151	0	0	820.1	3576	769	444	406	102	48	23	43	392	38	601	40	6	48	60	.444	0	0-0 0	4.35	4.45

Bronson Arroyo

Pitches: R **Bats:** R **Pos:** SP-35   **Ht:** 6'5" **Wt:** 190 **Born:** 2/24/1977 **Age:** 30

			HOW MUCH HE PITCHED						WHAT HE GAVE UP										THE RESULTS						
Year	Team	Lg	G	GS	CG	GF	IP	BFP	H	R	ER	HR	SH	SF	HB	TBB	IBB	SO	WP	Bk	W	L	Pct	ShO	Sv-Op Hld	ERC	ERA
2000	Pit	NL	20	12	0	1	71.2	338	88	61	51	10	5	2	4	36	6	50	3	1	2	6	.250	0	0-0 0	6.18	6.40
2001	Pit	NL	24	13	1	1	88.1	390	99	54	50	12	4	6	4	34	6	39	4	1	5	7	.417	0	0-0 2	5.09	5.09
2002	Pit	NL	9	4	0	1	26.2	123	30	14	12	1	1	1	0	15	3	22	0	0	2	1	.667	0	0-0 1	4.71	4.05
2003	Bos	AL	6	0	0	2	17.1	66	10	5	4	0	0	0	1	4	2	14	0	0	0	0	-	0	1-1 0	1.14	2.08
2004	Bos	AL	32	29	0	0	178.2	764	171	99	80	17	5	4	20	47	3	142	5	0	10	9	.526	0	0-0 0	3.65	4.03
2005	Bos	AL	35	32	0	1	205.1	878	213	116	103	22	4	4	14	54	3	100	5	1	14	10	.583	0	0-0 0	4.04	4.51
2006	Cin	NL	35	35	3	0	240.2	992	222	98	88	31	9	2	5	64	7	184	6	0	14	11	.560	1	0-0 0	3.37	3.29
7 ML YEARS			161	125	4	6	828.2	3551	833	447	388	93	28	19	48	254	30	551	23	3	47	44	.516	1	1-1 3	3.99	4.21

Miguel Asencio

Pitches: R **Bats:** R **Pos:** RP-2; SP-1   **Ht:** 6'2" **Wt:** 190 **Born:** 9/29/1980 **Age:** 26

			HOW MUCH HE PITCHED						WHAT HE GAVE UP										THE RESULTS						
Year	Team	Lg	G	GS	CG	GF	IP	BFP	H	R	ER	HR	SH	SF	HB	TBB	IBB	SO	WP	Bk	W	L	Pct	ShO	Sv-Op Hld	ERC	ERA
2006	ColSpr*	AAA	38	16	0	7	111.0	490	127	69	62	13	8	5	4	41	0	71	9	0	8	7	.533	0	1-- -	5.10	5.03
2002	KC	AL	31	21	0	7	123.1	557	136	73	70	17	2	6	3	64	2	58	7	0	4	7	.364	0	0-0 0	5.55	5.11
2003	KC	AL	8	8	1	0	48.1	215	54	29	28	4	3	5	3	21	0	27	1	0	2	1	.667	0	0-0 0	5.08	5.21
2006	Col	NL	3	1	0	0	7.2	37	9	8	4	1	0	0	1	4	0	7	0	0	1	0	1.000	0	0-0 0	6.23	4.70
3 ML YEARS			42	30	1	7	179.1	809	199	110	102	22	5	11	7	89	2	92	8	0	7	8	.467	0	0-0 0	5.45	5.12

Ezequiel Astacio

Pitches: R **Bats:** R **Pos:** RP-6   **Ht:** 6'3" **Wt:** 150 **Born:** 11/4/1979 **Age:** 27

			HOW MUCH HE PITCHED						WHAT HE GAVE UP										THE RESULTS						
Year	Team	Lg	G	GS	CG	GF	IP	BFP	H	R	ER	HR	SH	SF	HB	TBB	IBB	SO	WP	Bk	W	L	Pct	ShO	Sv-Op Hld	ERC	ERA
2001	Phillies	R	9	9	0	0	47.0	199	48	16	12	2	2	1	4	10	0	42	1	0	4	2	.667	0	0-- -	3.40	2.30
2002	Lakwd	A	25	25	1	0	152.1	662	159	61	56	9	8	3	12	46	1	100	6	0	10	7	.588	0	0-- -	3.92	3.31
2003	Clrwtr	A+	25	22	2	2	147.2	612	140	60	54	9	1	1	7	29	0	83	2	2	15	5	.750	1	0-- -	2.92	3.29
2004	RdRck	AA	28	28	1	0	176.0	739	155	89	76	12	11	4	8	56	1	185	11	1	13	10	.565	0	0-- -	3.04	3.89
2005	RdRck	AAA	13	12	0	1	65.2	262	53	25	22	6	2	1	8	12	0	57	0	0	4	4	.500	0	1-- -	2.69	3.02
2006	RdRck	AAA	21	17	0	1	92.2	413	95	51	50	15	2	2	4	43	2	76	4	1	8	4	.667	0	0-- -	5.05	4.86
2005	Hou	NL	22	14	0	5	81.0	366	100	56	51	23	2	6	1	25	2	66	4	1	3	6	.333	0	0-0 0	6.38	5.67
2006	Hou	NL	6	0	0	2	5.2	30	7	7	7	2	0	0	0	6	3	6	0	0	2	0	1.000	0	0-0 0	9.34	11.12
2 ML YEARS			28	14	0	7	86.2	396	107	63	58	25	2	6	1	31	5	72	4	1	5	6	.455	0	0-0 0	6.57	6.02

Pedro Astacio

Pitches: R **Bats:** R **Pos:** SP-17   **Ht:** 6'2" **Wt:** 210 **Born:** 11/28/1969 **Age:** 37

Year	Team	Lg	G	GS	CG	GF	IP	BFP	H	R	ER	HR	SH	SF	HB	TBB	IBB	SO	WP	Bk	W	L	Pct	ShO	Sv-Op	Hld	ERC	ERA
2006	Ptomc*	A+	1	1	0	0	3.0	12	3	0	0	0	0	0	0	0	0	2	0	0	0	0	-	0	0- -	-	1.95	0.00
2006	Hrsbrg*	AA	1	1	0	0	4.0	13	1	1	1	1	0	0	0	0	0	2	0	0	0	0	-	0	0- -	-	0.46	2.25
2006	NewOr*	AAA	3	3	0	0	14.0	61	17	10	10	1	1	1	0	3	0	4	0	0	1	1	.500	0	0- -	-	4.31	6.43
1992	LAD	NL	11	11	4	0	82.0	341	80	23	18	1	3	2	2	20	4	43	1	0	5	5	.500	4	0-0	0	2.78	1.98
1993	LAD	NL	31	31	3	0	186.1	777	165	80	74	14	7	8	5	68	5	122	8	9	14	9	.609	2	0-0	0	3.24	3.57
1994	LAD	NL	23	23	3	0	149.0	625	142	77	71	18	6	5	4	47	4	108	4	0	6	8	.429	1	0-0	0	3.71	4.29
1995	LAD	NL	48	11	1	7	104.0	436	103	53	49	12	5	3	4	29	5	80	5	0	7	8	.467	1	0-1	2	3.76	4.24
1996	LAD	NL	35	32	0	0	211.2	885	207	86	81	18	11	5	9	67	9	130	6	2	9	8	.529	0	0-0	0	3.69	3.44
1997	2 Tms	NL	33	31	2	2	202.1	862	200	98	93	24	9	7	9	61	0	166	6	3	12	10	.545	1	0-0	0	3.92	4.14
1998	Col	NL	35	34	0	0	209.1	938	245	160	145	39	12	3	17	74	0	170	2	0	13	14	.481	0	0-0	0	5.91	6.23
1999	Col	NL	34	34	7	0	232.0	1008	258	140	130	38	6	10	11	75	6	210	5	0	17	11	.607	0	0-0	0	5.08	5.04
2000	Col	NL	32	32	3	0	196.1	875	217	119	115	32	7	4	15	77	5	193	8	0	12	9	.571	0	0-0	0	5.42	5.27
2001	2 Tms	NL	26	26	4	0	169.2	733	181	101	96	22	6	5	13	54	3	144	2	0	8	14	.364	1	0-0	0	4.68	5.09
2002	NYM	NL	31	31	3	0	191.2	828	192	106	102	32	8	7	16	63	5	152	1	2	12	11	.522	1	0-0	0	4.57	4.79
2003	NYM	NL	7	7	0	0	36.2	174	47	30	30	8	1	1	3	18	1	20	4	0	3	2	.600	0	0-0	0	7.42	7.36
2004	Bos	AL	5	1	0	1	8.2	43	13	10	10	2	0	0	0	5	0	6	1	0	0	0	-	0	0-0	0	9.09	10.38
2005	2 Tms	NL	24	22	0	1	126.2	540	133	66	66	17	7	4	2	37	4	78	6	1	6	10	.375	0	0-0	0	4.19	4.69
2006	Was	NL	17	17	1	0	90.1	407	109	64	60	14	8	5	1	31	3	42	0	1	5	5	.500	1	0-0	0	5.38	5.98
97	LAD	NL	26	24	2	2	153.2	654	151	75	70	15	9	5	4	47	0	115	4	3	7	9	.438	1	0-0	0	3.67	4.10
97	Col	NL	7	7	0	0	48.2	208	49	23	23	9	0	2	5	14	0	51	2	0	5	1	.833	0	0-0	0	4.72	4.25
01	Col	NL	22	22	4	0	141.0	617	151	91	86	21	5	4	10	50	3	125	2	0	6	13	.316	1	0-0	0	4.94	5.49
01	Hou	NL	4	4	0	0	28.2	116	30	10	10	1	1	1	3	4	0	19	0	0	2	1	.667	0	0-0	0	3.43	3.14
05	Tex	AL	12	12	0	0	67.0	288	79	45	45	13	3	2	1	11	1	45	3	1	2	8	.200	0	0-0	0	4.79	4.68
05	SD	NL	12	10	0	1	59.2	252	54	21	21	4	4	2	1	26	3	33	3	0	4	2	.667	0	0-0	0	3.49	3.17
15 ML YEARS			392	343	31	11	2196.2	9472	2292	1213	1140	291	96	69	111	726	54	1664	59	18	129	124	.510	12	0-1	2	4.46	4.67

Garrett Atkins

Bats: R **Throws:** R **Pos:** 3B-157; 1B-3   **Ht:** 6'3" **Wt:** 215 **Born:** 12/12/1979 **Age:** 27

Year	Team	Lg	G	AB	H	2B	3B	HR	(Hm	Rd)	TB	R	RBI	RC	TBB	IBB	SO	HBP	SH	SF	SB	CS	SB%	GDP	Avg	OBP	Slg
2003	Col	NL	25	69	11	2	0	0	(0	0)	13	6	4	2	3	0	14	1	0	0	0	0	-	1	.159	.205	.188
2004	Col	NL	15	28	10	2	0	1	(1	0)	15	3	8	8	4	0	3	0	0	1	0	0	-	0	.357	.424	.536
2005	Col	NL	138	519	149	31	1	13	(9	4)	221	62	89	74	45	1	72	5	0	4	0	2	.00	18	.287	.347	.426
2006	Col	NL	157	602	198	48	1	29	(15	14)	335	117	120	129	79	6	76	7	0	7	4	0	1.00	24	.329	.409	.556
4 ML YEARS			335	1218	368	83	2	43	(25	18)	584	188	221	213	131	7	165	13	0	12	4	2	.67	43	.302	.373	.479

Rich Aurilia

Bats: R **Throws:** R **Pos:** 3B-52; 1B-47; SS-26; PH-12; 2B-10; DH-1   **Ht:** 6'1" **Wt:** 190 **Born:** 9/2/1971 **Age:** 35

Year	Team	Lg	G	AB	H	2B	3B	HR	(Hm	Rd)	TB	R	RBI	RC	TBB	IBB	SO	HBP	SH	SF	SB	CS	SB%	GDP	Avg	OBP	Slg
1995	SF	NL	9	19	9	3	0	2	(0	2)	18	4	4	7	1	0	2	0	1	1	1	0	1.00	1	.474	.476	.947
1996	SF	NL	105	318	76	7	1	3	(1	2)	94	27	26	29	25	2	52	1	6	2	4	1	.80	1	.239	.295	.296
1997	SF	NL	46	102	28	8	0	5	(1	4)	51	16	19	16	8	0	15	0	1	2	1	1	.50	3	.275	.321	.500
1998	SF	NL	122	413	110	27	2	9	(5	4)	168	54	49	54	31	3	62	2	5	2	3	3	.50	3	.266	.319	.407
1999	SF	NL	152	558	157	23	1	22	(9	13)	248	68	80	79	43	3	71	5	3	5	2	3	.40	16	.281	.336	.444
2000	SF	NL	141	509	138	24	2	20	(12	8)	226	67	79	74	54	2	90	0	4	4	1	2	.33	15	.271	.339	.444
2001	SF	NL	156	636	206	37	5	37	(15	22)	364	114	97	124	47	2	83	0	3	3	1	3	.25	14	.324	.369	.572
2002	SF	NL	133	538	138	35	2	15	(4	11)	222	76	61	61	37	0	90	4	3	7	1	2	.33	15	.257	.305	.413
2003	SF	NL	129	505	140	26	1	13	(6	7)	207	65	58	56	36	0	82	1	0	3	2	2	.50	18	.277	.325	.410
2004	2 Tms		124	399	98	21	2	6	(3	3)	141	49	44	39	37	1	71	4	3	3	1	0	1.00	13	.246	.314	.353
2005	Cin	NL	114	426	120	23	2	14	(11	3)	189	61	68	70	37	2	67	1	1	3	2	0	1.00	8	.282	.338	.444
2006	Cin	NL	122	440	132	25	1	23	(13	10)	228	61	70	72	34	1	51	1	2	4	3	0	1.00	10	.300	.349	.518
04	Sea	AL	73	261	63	13	0	4	(2	2)	88	27	28	25	22	1	43	2	6	1	1	0	1.00	11	.241	.304	.337
04	SD	NL	51	138	35	8	2	2	(1	1)	53	22	16	14	15	0	28	2	1	2	0	0	-	2	.254	.331	.384
12 ML YEARS			1353	4863	1352	259	19	169	(80	89)	2156	662	655	681	390	16	736	19	36	39	22	17	.56	117	.278	.332	.443

Brad Ausmus

Bats: R **Throws:** R **Pos:** C-138; 2B-2; PH-2; 1B-1   **Ht:** 5'11" **Wt:** 190 **Born:** 4/14/1969 **Age:** 38

Year	Team	Lg	G	AB	H	2B	3B	HR	(Hm	Rd)	TB	R	RBI	RC	TBB	IBB	SO	HBP	SH	SF	SB	CS	SB%	GDP	Avg	OBP	Slg
1993	SD	NL	49	160	41	8	1	5	(4	1)	66	18	12	19	6	0	28	0	0	0	2	0	1.00	2	.256	.283	.413
1994	SD	NL	101	327	82	12	1	7	(6	1)	117	45	24	36	30	12	63	1	6	2	5	1	.83	8	.251	.314	.358
1995	SD	NL	103	328	96	16	4	5	(2	3)	135	44	34	49	31	3	56	2	4	4	16	5	.76	6	.293	.353	.412
1996	2 Tms		125	375	83	16	0	5	(2	3)	114	46	35	32	39	1	72	5	6	2	4	8	.33	8	.221	.302	.304
1997	Hou	NL	130	425	113	25	1	4	(1	3)	152	45	44	51	38	4	78	3	6	4	14	6	.70	6	.266	.326	.358
1998	Hou	NL	128	412	111	10	4	6	(2	4)	147	62	45	51	53	11	60	3	3	1	10	3	.77	18	.269	.356	.357
1999	Det	AL	127	458	126	25	6	9	(5	4)	190	62	54	69	51	0	71	14	3	1	12	9	.57	11	.275	.365	.415
2000	Det	AL	150	523	139	25	3	7	(3	4)	191	75	51	68	69	0	79	6	4	2	11	5	.69	19	.266	.357	.365
2001	Hou	NL	128	422	98	23	4	5	(4	1)	144	45	34	38	30	6	64	1	6	2	4	1	.80	13	.232	.284	.341
2002	Hou	NL	130	447	115	19	3	6	(4	2)	158	57	50	44	38	3	71	6	2	3	2	3	.40	30	.257	.322	.353
2003	Hou	NL	143	450	103	12	2	4	(1	3)	131	43	47	44	46	1	66	4	4	5	5	3	.63	8	.229	.303	.291
2004	Hou	NL	129	403	100	14	1	5	(2	3)	131	38	31	34	33	11	56	2	7	3	2	2	.50	13	.248	.306	.325
2005	Hou	NL	134	387	100	19	0	3	(2	1)	128	35	47	42	51	8	48	5	7	1	5	3	.63	17	.258	.351	.331
2006	Hou	NL	139	439	101	16	1	2	(1	1)	125	37	39	36	45	2	71	6	9	3	3	1	.75	21	.230	.308	.285

30

Year	Team	Lg	G	AB	H	2B	3B	HR	(Hm	Rd)	TB	R	RBI	RC	TBB	IBB	SO	HBP	SH	SF	SB	CS	SB%	GDP	Avg	OBP	Slg
																									BATTING	**BASERUNNING**	**AVERAGES**
96	SD	NL	50	149	27	4	0	1	(0	1)	34	16	13	6	13	0	27	3	1	0	1	4	.20	4	.181	.261	.228
96	Det	AL	75	226	56	12	0	4	(2	2)	80	30	22	26	26	1	45	2	5	2	3	4	.43	4	.248	.328	.354
14 ML YEARS			1716	5556	1408	240	31	73	(39	34)	1929	652	547	613	560	62	883	58	67	35	95	50	.66	182	.253	.326	.347

Luis Ayala

Pitches: R **Bats:** R **Pos:** P   **Ht:** 6'2" **Wt:** 185 **Born:** 1/12/1978 **Age:** 29

Year	Team	Lg	G	GS	CG	GF	IP	BFP	H	R	ER	HR	SH	SF	HB	TBB	IBB	SO	WP	Bk	W	L	Pct	ShO	Sv-Op	Hld	ERC	ERA
			HOW MUCH HE PITCHED						**WHAT HE GAVE UP**												**THE RESULTS**							
2003	Mon	NL	65	0	0	24	71.0	288	65	27	23	8	3	1	5	13	3	46	1	0	10	3	.769	0	5-8	19	3.11	2.92
2004	Mon	NL	81	0	0	28	90.1	367	92	30	27	6	2	2	5	15	2	63	3	1	6	12	.333	0	2-7	21	3.32	2.69
2005	Was	NL	68	0	0	18	71.0	293	75	23	21	7	8	3	6	14	4	40	0	0	8	7	.533	0	1-3	22	3.95	2.66
3 ML YEARS			214	0	0	70	232.1	948	232	80	71	21	13	6	16	42	9	149	4	1	24	22	.522	0	8-18	62	3.44	2.75

Erick Aybar

Bats: B **Throws:** R **Pos:** SS-19; PH-9; PR-9; 2B-3; DH-3   **Ht:** 5'10" **Wt:** 170 **Born:** 1/14/1984 **Age:** 23

Year	Team	Lg	G	AB	H	2B	3B	HR	(Hm	Rd)	TB	R	RBI	RC	TBB	IBB	SO	HBP	SH	SF	SB	CS	SB%	GDP	Avg	OBP	Slg
																									BATTING	**BASERUNNING**	**AVERAGES**
2002	Provo	R	67	273	89	15	6	4	(-	-)	128	64	29	50	21	1	43	11	2	1	15	10	.60	4	.326	.395	.469
2003	CRpds	A	125	496	153	30	10	6	(-	-)	221	83	57	80	17	0	54	13	6	3	32	9	.78	6	.308	.346	.446
2004	RCuca	A+	136	573	189	25	11	14	(-	-)	278	102	65	98	26	1	66	13	10	5	51	36	.59	3	.330	.370	.485
2005	Ark	AA	134	535	162	29	10	9	(-	-)	238	101	54	86	29	0	51	14	4	8	49	23	.68	13	.303	.350	.445
2006	Salt Lk	AAA	81	339	96	20	3	6	(-	-)	140	63	45	46	21	2	36	3	1	4	32	18	.64	5	.283	.327	.413
2006	LAA	AL	34	40	10	1	1	0	(0	0)	13	5	2	4	0	0	8	0	0	0	1	0	1.00	1	.250	.250	.325

Willy Aybar

Bats: B **Throws:** R **Pos:** 3B-61; 2B-15; PH-11   **Ht:** 5'11" **Wt:** 200 **Born:** 3/9/1983 **Age:** 24

Year	Team	Lg	G	AB	H	2B	3B	HR	(Hm	Rd)	TB	R	RBI	RC	TBB	IBB	SO	HBP	SH	SF	SB	CS	SB%	GDP	Avg	OBP	Slg
																									BATTING	**BASERUNNING**	**AVERAGES**
2000	Gr Falls	R+	70	266	70	15	1	4	(-	-)	99	39	49	37	36	2	45	0	6	2	5	5	.50	3	.263	.349	.372
2001	Wilmg	A	120	431	102	25	2	4	(-	-)	143	45	48	45	43	3	64	3	3	5	7	9	.44	4	.237	.307	.332
2001	VeroB	A+	2	7	2	0	0	0	(-	-)	2	0	0	0	1	0	2	0	0	0	0	0	-	0	.286	.375	.286
2002	VeroB	A+	108	372	80	18	2	11	(-	-)	135	56	65	52	69	4	54	3	2	4	15	8	.65	7	.215	.339	.363
2003	VeroB	A+	119	445	122	29	3	11	(-	-)	190	47	74	65	41	1	70	3	1	5	9	9	.50	3	.274	.336	.427
2004	Jaxnvl	AA	126	482	133	27	0	15	(-	-)	205	56	77	72	50	4	77	3	0	2	8	10	.44	11	.276	.346	.425
2005	LsVgs	AAA	108	401	119	26	4	5	(-	-)	168	47	60	61	40	0	56	1	1	7	1	6	.14	8	.297	.356	.419
2006	LsVgs	AAA	50	197	62	12	1	10	(-	-)	106	30	41	39	22	1	24	1	0	2	1	3	.25	6	.315	.383	.538
2006	Rchmd	AAA	3	10	3	1	0	0	(-	-)	4	2	1	1	2	0	3	0	0	0	0	0	-	1	.300	.417	.400
2005	LAD	NL	26	86	28	8	0	1	(0	1)	39	12	10	21	18	0	11	1	0	0	3	1	.75	0	.326	.448	.453
2006	2 Tms	NL	79	243	68	18	0	4	(3	1)	98	32	30	33	28	0	36	4	3	0	1	2	.33	7	.280	.364	.403
06	LAD	NL	43	128	32	12	0	3	(2	1)	53	15	22	19	18	0	17	3	2	0	1	0	1.00	5	.250	.356	.414
06	Atl	NL	36	115	36	6	0	1	(1	0)	45	17	8	14	10	0	19	1	1	0	0	2	.00	2	.313	.373	.391
2 ML YEARS			105	329	96	26	0	5	(3	2)	137	44	40	54	46	0	47	5	3	0	4	3	.57	7	.292	.387	.416

Brandon Backe

Pitches: R **Bats:** R **Pos:** SP-8   **Ht:** 6'0" **Wt:** 195 **Born:** 4/5/1978 **Age:** 29

Year	Team	Lg	G	GS	CG	GF	IP	BFP	H	R	ER	HR	SH	SF	HB	TBB	IBB	SO	WP	Bk	W	L	Pct	ShO	Sv-Op	Hld	ERC	ERA
			HOW MUCH HE PITCHED						**WHAT HE GAVE UP**												**THE RESULTS**							
2006	RdRck*	AAA	4	4	0	0	20.1	93	23	12	12	1	2	2	2	13	0	13	1	0	1	2	.333	0	0- -	-	6.05	5.31
2002	TB	AL	9	0	0	4	13.0	61	15	10	10	3	0	0	2	7	0	6	0	0	0	0	-	0	0- -	0	7.37	6.92
2003	TB	AL	28	0	0	8	44.2	192	40	28	27	6	2	1	2	25	1	36	3	0	1	1	.500	0	0-0	5	4.64	5.44
2004	Hou	NL	33	9	0	8	67.0	293	75	33	32	10	5	1	1	27	4	54	1	0	5	3	.625	0	0-0	3	5.18	4.30
2005	Hou	NL	26	25	1	0	149.1	653	151	82	79	19	7	1	4	67	1	97	5	2	10	8	.556	1	0-0	0	4.65	4.76
2006	Hou	NL	8	8	0	0	43.0	189	43	18	18	4	1	2	3	18	0	19	2	0	3	2	.600	0	0-0	0	4.37	3.77
5 ML YEARS			104	42	1	20	317.0	1388	324	171	166	42	15	5	12	144	6	212	11	2	19	14	.576	1	0-0	8	4.83	4.71

Cha Seung Baek

Pitches: R **Bats:** R **Pos:** SP-6   **Ht:** 6'4" **Wt:** 220 **Born:** 5/29/1980 **Age:** 27

Year	Team	Lg	G	GS	CG	GF	IP	BFP	H	R	ER	HR	SH	SF	HB	TBB	IBB	SO	WP	Bk	W	L	Pct	ShO	Sv-Op	Hld	ERC	ERA
			HOW MUCH HE PITCHED						**WHAT HE GAVE UP**												**THE RESULTS**							
1999	Ms	R	8	4	0	1	27.0	112	30	13	11	2	2	0	0	6	0	25	2	3	3	0	1.000	0	0- -	-	3.91	3.67
2000	Wisc	A	24	24	0	0	127.2	547	137	71	56	13	6	2	5	36	0	99	6	0	8	5	.615	0	0- -	-	4.21	3.95
2001	SnBrn	A+	5	4	0	0	21.0	81	17	10	8	2	0	1	2	2	0	16	0	0	1	0	1.000	0	0- -	-	2.34	3.43
2003	InldEm	A+	13	10	0	2	56.2	236	55	27	23	3	4	0	2	9	0	50	1	1	5	1	.833	0	0- -	-	2.77	3.65
2003	SnAnt	AA	9	9	0	0	56.0	229	49	18	16	2	2	0	4	17	1	46	0	0	3	3	.500	0	0- -	-	2.92	2.57
2004	Ms	R	2	2	0	0	7.0	25	3	2	1	0	0	0	0	1	0	5	1	0	0	0	-	0	0- -	-	0.60	1.29
2004	SnAnt	AA	1	1	0	0	5.0	15	2	0	0	0	1	0	0	0	0	5	0	0	0	0	-	0	0- -	-	0.40	0.00
2004	Tacom	AAA	14	14	0	0	72.2	323	85	41	34	7	4	5	2	24	0	56	2	0	5	4	.556	0	0- -	-	4.83	4.21
2005	Tacom	AAA	25	21	0	2	113.2	524	147	87	81	19	5	1	1	36	0	73	6	0	8	8	.500	0	0- -	-	5.87	6.41
2006	Tacom	AAA	24	24	0	0	147.0	602	133	57	49	17	6	1	6	37	0	103	5	0	12	4	.750	0	0- -	-	3.27	3.00
2004	Sea	AL	7	5	0	2	31.0	139	35	23	19	5	0	0	2	11	1	20	2	0	2	4	.333	0	0-0	0	5.26	5.52
2006	Sea	AL	6	6	0	0	34.1	140	26	15	14	6	0	0	2	13	0	23	1	0	4	1	.800	0	0-0	0	3.44	3.67
2 ML YEARS			13	11	0	2	65.1	279	61	38	33	11	0	0	4	24	1	43	3	0	6	5	.545	0	0-0	0	4.28	4.55

Danys Baez

Pitches: R Bats: R Pos: RP-57   Ht: 6'1" Wt: 230 Born: 9/10/1977 Age: 29

			HOW MUCH HE PITCHED						WHAT HE GAVE UP													THE RESULTS							
Year	Team	Lg	G	GS	CG	GF	IP	BFP	H	R	ER	HR	SH	SF	HB	TBB	IBB	SO	WP	Bk	W	L	Pct	ShO	Sv-Op	Hld	ERC	ERA
2001	Cle	AL	43	0	0	8	50.1	202	34	22	14	5	0	1	3	20	4	52	3	0	5	3	.625	0	0-1	14	2.51	2.50
2002	Cle	AL	39	26	1	9	165.1	726	160	84	81	14	2	8	9	82	5	130	6	1	10	11	.476	0	6-8	0	4.35	4.41
2003	Cle	AL	73	0	0	46	75.2	318	65	36	32	9	6	1	4	23	0	66	5	0	2	9	.182	0	25-35	5	3.22	3.81
2004	TB	AL	62	0	0	59	68.0	295	60	31	27	6	5	1	7	29	4	52	3	1	4	4	.500	0	30-33	1	3.73	3.57
2005	TB	AL	67	0	0	64	72.1	308	66	27	23	7	4	2	2	30	0	51	0	0	5	4	.556	0	41-49	5	3.74	2.86
2006	2 Tms	NL	57	0	0	28	59.2	257	60	35	30	3	4	5	7	17	3	39	3	0	5	6	.455	0	9-17	12	3.69	4.53
06	LAD	NL	46	0	0	27	49.2	213	53	29	24	3	4	5	6	11	2	29	3	0	5	5	.500	0	9-16	6	3.90	4.35
06	Atl	NL	11	0	0	1	10.0	44	7	6	6	0	0	0	1	6	1	10	0	0	0	1	.000	0	0-1	6	2.64	5.40
6 ML YEARS			341	26	1	214	491.1	2106	445	235	207	44	21	18	32	201	16	390	20	2	31	37	.456	0	111-143	32	3.72	3.79

Jeff Bajenaru

Pitches: R Bats: R Pos: RP-1   Ht: 6'1" Wt: 200 Born: 3/21/1978 Age: 29

			HOW MUCH HE PITCHED						WHAT HE GAVE UP													THE RESULTS							
Year	Team	Lg	G	GS	CG	GF	IP	BFP	H	R	ER	HR	SH	SF	HB	TBB	IBB	SO	WP	Bk	W	L	Pct	ShO	Sv-Op	Hld	ERC	ERA
2006	Tucsn*	AAA	52	3	0	22	80.0	360	79	47	40	6	3	7	4	40	1	72	6	0	4	3	.571	0	7--	-	4.32	4.50
2004	CWS	AL	9	0	0	4	8.1	44	15	10	10	0	1	0	0	6	1	8	0	0	0	1	.000	0	0-0	0	9.52	10.80
2005	CWS	AL	4	0	0	3	4.1	18	4	3	3	2	0	0	0	0	0	3	1	0	0	0	-	0	0-0	0	3.76	6.23
2006	Ari	NL	1	0	0	0	1.0	7	4	4	4	3	0	0	0	0	0	0	0	0	0	1	.000	0	0-1	0	60.11	36.00
3 ML YEARS			14	0	0	7	13.2	69	23	17	17	5	1	0	0	6	1	11	1	0	0	2	.000	0	0-1	0	10.71	11.20

Jeff Baker

Bats: R Throws: R Pos: RF-10; PH-6; LF-2; 1B-1   Ht: 6'2" Wt: 220 Born: 6/21/1981 Age: 26

			BATTING																		BASERUNNING				AVERAGES		
Year	Team	Lg	G	AB	H	2B	3B	HR	(Hm	Rd)	TB	R	RBI	RC	TBB	IBB	SO	HBP	SH	SF	SB	CS	SB%	GDP	Avg	OBP	Slg
2003	Ashvlle	A	70	263	76	17	0	11	(-	-)	126	44	44	49	30	2	79	9	0	3	4	2	.67	2	.289	.377	.479
2004	Visalia	A+	73	271	88	23	1	11	(-	-)	146	60	64	64	47	0	73	6	0	1	1	0	1.00	5	.325	.434	.539
2004	Tulsa	AA	24	91	27	5	1	4	(-	-)	46	10	20	15	7	1	22	0	0	1	0	0	-	3	.297	.343	.505
2005	ColSpr	AAA	61	228	69	16	1	10	(-	-)	117	40	41	41	16	0	44	1	1	2	3	1	.75	7	.303	.348	.513
2006	ColSpr	AAA	128	482	147	30	4	20	(-	-)	245	71	108	92	46	2	110	5	1	4	7	1	.88	14	.305	.369	.508
2005	Col	NL	12	38	8	4	0	1	(1	0)	15	6	4	4	5	0	12	0	0	0	0	0	-	1	.211	.302	.395
2006	Col	NL	18	57	21	7	2	5	(4	1)	47	13	21	17	1	0	14	0	0	0	2	0	1.00	0	.368	.379	.825
2 ML YEARS			30	95	29	11	2	6	(5	1)	62	19	25	21	6	0	26	0	0	0	2	0	1.00	1	.305	.347	.653

Scott Baker

Pitches: R Bats: R Pos: SP-16   Ht: 6'4" Wt: 210 Born: 9/19/1981 Age: 25

			HOW MUCH HE PITCHED						WHAT HE GAVE UP													THE RESULTS							
Year	Team	Lg	G	GS	CG	GF	IP	BFP	H	R	ER	HR	SH	SF	HB	TBB	IBB	SO	WP	Bk	W	L	Pct	ShO	Sv-Op	Hld	ERC	ERA
2003	QuadC	A	11	11	0	0	50.2	207	45	16	14	4	1	1	2	8	0	47	4	0	3	1	.750	0	0--	-	2.54	2.49
2004	FtMyrs	A+	7	7	0	0	45.0	181	40	13	12	1	0	0	0	6	0	37	1	0	4	2	.667	0	0--	-	2.01	2.40
2004	NwBrit	AA	10	10	2	0	70.1	276	44	23	19	2	0	0	6	13	2	72	0	0	5	3	.625	2	0--	-	1.39	2.43
2004	Roch	AAA	9	9	0	0	54.1	248	65	31	30	3	0	2	4	15	1	36	0	0	1	3	.250	0	0--	-	4.49	4.97
2005	Roch	AAA	22	22	1	0	134.2	544	123	50	45	15	0	3	7	26	1	107	4	0	5	8	.385	1	0--	-	3.12	3.11
2006	Roch	AAA	12	12	1	0	84.1	352	77	26	25	4	8	2	4	25	4	68	5	1	5	4	.556	0	0--	-	2.97	2.67
2005	Min	AL	10	9	0	0	53.2	217	48	21	20	5	2	2	0	14	0	32	0	0	3	3	.500	0	0-0	1	2.97	3.35
2006	Min	AL	16	16	0	0	83.1	377	114	63	59	17	2	4	3	16	1	62	0	0	5	8	.385	0	0-0	0	6.26	6.37
2 ML YEARS			26	25	0	0	137.0	594	162	84	79	22	4	6	3	30	1	94	0	0	8	11	.421	0	0-0	1	4.89	5.19

Paul Bako

Bats: L Throws: R Pos: C-53; PH-3; DH-1   Ht: 6'2" Wt: 215 Born: 6/20/1972 Age: 35

			BATTING																		BASERUNNING				AVERAGES		
Year	Team	Lg	G	AB	H	2B	3B	HR	(Hm	Rd)	TB	R	RBI	RC	TBB	IBB	SO	HBP	SH	SF	SB	CS	SB%	GDP	Avg	OBP	Slg
2006	Wichta*	AA	3	12	2	0	0	0	(-	-)	2	3	2	0	0	0	1	0	0	0	0	0	-	0	.167	.167	.167
1998	Det	AL	96	305	83	12	1	3	(2	1)	106	23	30	34	23	4	82	0	1	4	1	1	.50	3	.272	.319	.348
1999	Hou	NL	73	215	55	14	1	2	(2	0)	77	16	17	26	26	3	57	0	3	3	1	1	.50	4	.256	.332	.358
2000	3 Tms	NL	81	221	50	10	1	2	(2	0)	68	18	20	20	27	10	64	1	1	1	0	0	-	6	.226	.312	.308
2001	Atl	NL	61	137	29	10	1	2	(0	2)	47	19	15	15	20	2	34	0	0	0	1	0	1.00	3	.212	.312	.343
2002	Mil	NL	87	234	55	8	1	4	(2	2)	77	24	20	20	20	3	46	0	3	0	0	2	.00	4	.235	.295	.329
2003	ChC	NL	70	188	43	13	3	0	(0	0)	62	19	17	21	22	3	47	1	1	1	0	1	.00	2	.229	.311	.330
2004	ChC	NL	49	138	28	8	0	1	(1	0)	39	13	10	11	15	3	29	2	1	1	1	0	1.00	4	.203	.288	.283
2005	LAD	NL	13	40	10	2	0	0	(0	0)	12	1	4	6	7	1	12	0	0	0	0	0	-	2	.250	.362	.300
2006	KC	AL	56	153	32	3	0	0	(0	0)	35	7	10	9	11	0	46	0	2	1	0	0	-	3	.209	.261	.229
00	Hou	NL	1	2	0	0	0	0	(0	0)	0	0	0	0	0	0	1	0	0	0	0	0	-	0	.000	.000	.000
00	Fla	NL	56	161	39	6	1	0	(0	0)	47	10	14	16	22	7	48	1	1	1	0	0	-	4	.242	.335	.292
00	Atl	NL	24	58	11	4	0	2	(2	0)	21	8	6	4	5	3	15	0	0	0	0	0	-	2	.190	.254	.362
9 ML YEARS			586	1631	385	80	8	14	(9	5)	523	140	143	162	171	29	417	4	12	11	4	5	.44	29	.236	.308	.321

Rocco Baldelli

Bats: R Throws: R Pos: CF-91; PH-3   Ht: 6'4" Wt: 200 Born: 9/25/1981 Age: 25

									BATTING											BASERUNNING				AVERAGES		
Year	Team	Lg	G	AB	H	2B	3B	HR	(Hm	Rd)	TB	R	RBI	RC	TBB	IBB	SO	HBP	SH	SF	SB	CS	SB%	GDP	Avg	OBP	Slg
2006	Drham*	AAA	12	47	19	5	0	6	(-	-)	24	7	4	9	4	0	10	0	0	0	0	1	.00	1	.404	.451	.511
2003	TB	AL	156	637	184	32	8	11	(2	9)	265	89	78	77	30	4	128	8	3	6	27	10	.73	10	.289	.326	.416
2004	TB	AL	136	518	145	27	3	16	(6	10)	226	79	74	70	30	2	88	8	3	6	17	4	.81	12	.280	.326	.436
2006	TB	AL	92	364	110	24	6	16	(6	10)	194	59	57	65	14	1	70	7	0	2	10	1	.91	2	.302	.339	.533
	3 ML YEARS		384	1519	439	83	17	43	(14	29)	685	227	209	212	74	7	286	23	6	14	54	15	.78	24	.289	.329	.451

Grant Balfour

Pitches: R Bats: R Pos: P   Ht: 6'2" Wt: 195 Born: 12/30/1977 Age: 29

				HOW MUCH HE PITCHED							WHAT HE GAVE UP										THE RESULTS					
Year	Team	Lg	G	GS	CG	GF	IP	BFP	H	R	ER	HR	SH	SF	HB	TBB	IBB	SO	WP	Bk	W	L	Pct	ShO	Sv-Op Hld	ERC	ERA
2006	Reds*	R	2	2	0	0	1.1	7	1	2	2	0	-	-	1	3	-	2	0	0	0	0	-	0	0- -	15.63	13.50
2006	Dayton*	A	2	0	0	0	2.0	6	0	0	0	0	-	-	0	0	-	3	0	0	0	0	-	0	0- -	0.00	0.00
2006	Srsota*	A+	5	0	0	0	5.2	26	8	7	5	0	-	-	1	3	-	7	4	1	0	0	-	0	0- -	7.63	7.94
2001	Min	AL	2	1	0	0	2.2	14	3	4	4	2	0	0	0	3	0	2	0	0	0	0	-	0	0-0 0	13.78	13.50
2003	Min	AL	17	1	0	6	26.0	115	23	12	12	4	2	1	0	14	2	30	0	0	1	0	1.000	0	0-1 1	4.14	4.15
2004	Min	AL	36	0	0	14	39.1	172	35	19	19	4	2	0	2	21	1	42	3	0	4	1	.800	0	0-1 4	4.16	4.35
	3 ML YEARS		55	2	0	20	68.0	301	61	35	35	10	4	1	2	38	3	74	3	0	5	1	.833	0	0-2 5	4.47	4.63

Brian Bannister

Pitches: R Bats: R Pos: SP-6; RP-2   Ht: 6'2" Wt: 200 Born: 2/28/1981 Age: 26

				HOW MUCH HE PITCHED							WHAT HE GAVE UP										THE RESULTS					
Year	Team	Lg	G	GS	CG	GF	IP	BFP	H	R	ER	HR	SH	SF	HB	TBB	IBB	SO	WP	Bk	W	L	Pct	ShO	Sv-Op Hld	ERC	ERA
2003	Bklyn	A-	12	9	0	1	46.0	179	27	12	11	0	3	1	1	18	0	42	4	2	4	1	.800	0	1- -	1.54	2.15
2004	Bnghtn	AA	8	8	0	0	44.1	180	45	23	20	2	2	0	2	17	0	28	4	0	3	3	.500	0	0- -	4.19	4.06
2004	StLuci	A+	20	20	0	0	110.1	462	111	63	53	6	10	4	10	27	1	106	10	1	5	7	.417	0	0- -	3.59	4.32
2005	Bnghtn	AA	18	18	1	0	109.0	428	91	36	31	11	1	1	6	27	0	94	2	1	9	4	.692	1	0- -	2.96	2.56
2005	Norfolk	AAA	8	8	0	0	45.1	197	48	19	16	0	1	4	1	13	0	48	4	0	4	1	.800	0	0- -	3.28	3.18
2006	StLuci	A+	2	2	0	0	12.0	49	10	4	2	0	0	1	1	4	0	9	0	0	1	0	1.000	0	0- -	2.65	1.50
2006	Norfolk	AAA	6	6	1	0	30.1	128	34	15	13	4	1	0	0	5	0	24	1	0	3	3	.500	0	0- -	4.01	3.86
2006	NYM	NL	8	6	0	1	38.0	171	34	18	18	4	1	4	2	22	2	19	2	0	2	1	.667	0	0-0 0	4.27	4.26

Rod Barajas

Bats: R Throws: R Pos: C-94; 1B-5   Ht: 6'2" Wt: 230 Born: 9/5/1975 Age: 31

									BATTING											BASERUNNING				AVERAGES		
Year	Team	Lg	G	AB	H	2B	3B	HR	(Hm	Rd)	TB	R	RBI	RC	TBB	IBB	SO	HBP	SH	SF	SB	CS	SB%	GDP	Avg	OBP	Slg
1999	Ari	NL	5	16	4	1	0	1	(1	0)	8	3	3	2	1	0	1	0	1	0	0	0	-	0	.250	.294	.500
2000	Ari	NL	5	13	3	0	0	1	(1	0)	6	1	3	1	0	0	4	0	0	0	0	0	-	0	.231	.231	.462
2001	Ari	NL	51	106	17	3	0	3	(2	1)	29	9	9	4	4	0	26	0	0	0	0	0	-	0	.160	.191	.274
2002	Ari	NL	70	154	36	10	0	3	(1	2)	55	12	23	15	10	4	25	3	2	3	1	0	1.00	4	.234	.288	.357
2003	Ari	NL	80	220	48	15	0	3	(3	0)	72	19	28	19	14	7	43	1	1	3	0	0	-	6	.218	.265	.327
2004	Tex	AL	108	358	89	26	1	15	(8	7)	162	50	58	43	13	0	63	3	8	7	0	1	.00	3	.249	.276	.453
2005	Tex	AL	120	410	104	24	0	21	(7	14)	191	53	60	56	26	0	70	6	4	3	0	0	-	6	.254	.306	.466
2006	Tex	AL	97	344	88	20	0	11	(6	5)	141	49	41	36	17	0	51	4	5	1	0	0	-	9	.256	.298	.410
	8 ML YEARS		536	1621	389	99	1	58	(29	29)	664	196	225	176	85	11	283	17	21	17	1	1	.50	28	.240	.282	.410

Josh Bard

Bats: B Throws: R Pos: C-78; PH-27; PR-2   Ht: 6'3" Wt: 210 Born: 3/30/1978 Age: 29

									BATTING											BASERUNNING				AVERAGES		
Year	Team	Lg	G	AB	H	2B	3B	HR	(Hm	Rd)	TB	R	RBI	RC	TBB	IBB	SO	HBP	SH	SF	SB	CS	SB%	GDP	Avg	OBP	Slg
2002	Cle	AL	24	90	20	5	0	3	(2	1)	34	9	12	7	4	0	13	0	1	0	0	0	-	6	.222	.255	.378
2003	Cle	AL	91	303	74	13	1	8	(5	3)	113	25	36	34	22	1	53	0	1	3	0	2	.00	9	.244	.293	.373
2004	Cle	AL	7	19	8	2	0	1	(1	0)	13	5	4	6	3	0	0	0	0	1	0	0	-	0	.421	.478	.684
2005	Cle	AL	34	83	16	4	0	1	(0	1)	23	6	9	8	9	0	11	0	1	2	0	0	-	2	.193	.266	.277
2006	2 Tms		100	249	83	20	0	9	(5	4)	130	30	40	44	30	1	42	1	2	2	1	0	1.00	9	.333	.404	.522
06	Bos	AL	7	18	5	1	0	0	(0	0)	6	2	0	2	3	0	3	0	0	0	0	0	-	0	.278	.381	.333
06	SD	NL	93	231	78	19	0	9	(5	4)	124	28	40	42	27	1	39	1	2	2	1	0	1.00	9	.338	.406	.537
	5 ML YEARS		256	744	201	44	1	22	(13	9)	313	75	101	99	68	2	119	1	5	8	1	2	.33	26	.270	.329	.421

Josh Barfield

Bats: R Throws: R Pos: 2B-147; PH-5; PR-4   Ht: 6'0" Wt: 190 Born: 12/17/1982 Age: 24

									BATTING											BASERUNNING				AVERAGES		
Year	Team	Lg	G	AB	H	2B	3B	HR	(Hm	Rd)	TB	R	RBI	RC	TBB	IBB	SO	HBP	SH	SF	SB	CS	SB%	GDP	Avg	OBP	Slg
2001	Idaho	R+	66	277	86	15	4	4	(-	-)	121	51	53	44	16	1	54	3	0	4	12	4	.75	7	.310	.350	.437
2002	FtWyn	A	129	536	164	22	3	8	(-	-)	216	73	57	77	26	0	105	4	3	5	26	8	.76	13	.306	.340	.403
2002	Lk Els	A+	6	23	2	0	0	0	(-	-)	2	2	4	0	1	0	4	0	1	1	0	0	-	1	.087	.120	.087
2003	Lk Els	A+	135	549	185	46	6	16	(-	-)	291	99	128	114	50	3	122	4	1	11	16	4	.80	11	.337	.389	.530
2004	Mobile	AA	138	521	129	28	3	18	(-	-)	217	79	90	71	48	4	119	5	0	7	4	2	.67	6	.248	.313	.417
2005	Portlnd	AAA	137	516	160	25	1	15	(-	-)	232	74	72	90	52	1	108	1	2	7	20	5	.80	10	.310	.370	.450
2006	SD	NL	150	539	151	32	3	13	(6	7)	228	72	58	69	30	7	81	2	2	5	21	5	.81	8	.280	.318	.423

Kevin Barker

Bats: L Throws: L Pos: PH-5; DH-4; PR-3; 1B-2; RF-1   Ht: 6'1" Wt: 235 Born: 7/26/1975 Age: 31

Year	Team	Lg	G	AB	H	2B	3B	HR	(Hm	Rd)	TB	R	RBI	RC	TBB	IBB	SO	HBP	SH	SF	SB	CS	SB%	GDP	Avg	OBP	Slg
2006	Syrcse*	AAA	130	473	130	39	2	18	(-	-)	227	72	76	90	80	7	119	2	0	4	5	3	.63	10	.275	.379	.480
1999	Mil	NL	38	117	33	3	0	3	(1	2)	45	13	23	16	9	1	19	0	0	1	1	0	1.00	0	.282	.331	.385
2000	Mil	NL	40	100	22	5	0	2	(0	2)	33	14	9	14	20	0	21	1	0	1	1	0	1.00	1	.220	.352	.330
2002	SD	NL	7	19	3	0	0	0	(0	0)	3	0	0	0	1	0	6	0	0	0	1	0	1.00	1	.158	.200	.158
2006	Tor	AL	12	17	4	1	0	1	(0	1)	8	3	1	0	1	0	10	0	0	0	0	0	-	0	.235	.278	.471
4 ML YEARS			97	253	62	9	0	6	(1	5)	89	30	33	30	31	1	56	1	0	2	3	0	1.00	2	.245	.328	.352

Clint Barmes

Bats: R Throws: R Pos: SS-125; PH-6; 2B-4; PR-2   Ht: 6'0" Wt: 210 Born: 3/6/1979 Age: 28

Year	Team	Lg	G	AB	H	2B	3B	HR	(Hm	Rd)	TB	R	RBI	RC	TBB	IBB	SO	HBP	SH	SF	SB	CS	SB%	GDP	Avg	OBP	Slg
2003	Col	NL	12	25	8	2	0	0	(0	0)	10	2	2	3	0	0	10	2	0	1	0	0	-	0	.320	.357	.400
2004	Col	NL	20	71	20	3	1	2	(0	2)	31	14	10	12	3	0	10	1	2	0	0	1	.00	2	.282	.320	.437
2005	Col	NL	81	350	101	19	1	10	(7	3)	152	55	46	49	16	1	36	6	4	1	6	4	.60	4	.289	.330	.434
2006	Col	NL	131	478	105	26	4	7	(3	4)	160	57	56	47	22	6	72	9	19	7	5	4	.56	2	.220	.264	.335
4 ML YEARS			244	924	234	50	6	19	(10	9)	353	128	114	111	41	7	128	18	25	9	11	9	.55	8	.253	.295	.382

Chris Barnwell

Bats: R Throws: R Pos: SS-5; 2B-3; 3B-3; PH-2; PR-1   Ht: 5'10" Wt: 180 Born: 3/1/1979 Age: 28

Year	Team	Lg	G	AB	H	2B	3B	HR	(Hm	Rd)	TB	R	RBI	RC	TBB	IBB	SO	HBP	SH	SF	SB	CS	SB%	GDP	Avg	OBP	Slg
2001	Ogden	R+	69	261	80	19	5	0	(-	-)	109	49	37	40	7	2	28	7	3	4	17	2	.89	2	.307	.337	.418
2002	Beloit	A	91	344	78	12	2	1	(-	-)	97	37	40	31	27	0	47	7	5	3	13	5	.72	4	.227	.294	.282
2002	Hi Dsrt	A	35	132	32	7	0	1	(-	-)	42	19	14	12	8	0	14	2	2	1	1	1	.50	2	.242	.294	.318
2003	Hntsvl	AA	102	313	77	7	0	3	(-	-)	93	39	25	32	27	2	47	9	4	2	6	6	.50	12	.246	.322	.297
2004	Hntsvl	AA	138	484	119	24	4	6	(-	-)	169	43	51	53	36	3	76	12	5	6	11	14	.44	3	.246	.310	.349
2005	Hntsvl	AA	15	35	9	2	1	1	(-	-)	16	6	4	4	1	0	7	1	0	0	0	0	-	0	.257	.289	.457
2005	Nashv	AAA	100	261	64	14	1	3	(-	-)	89	30	20	27	18	1	46	3	4	2	5	3	.63	6	.245	.299	.341
2006	Nashv	AAA	106	383	115	18	2	4	(-	-)	149	46	37	61	38	1	60	10	5	4	16	6	.73	11	.300	.375	.389
2006	Mil	NL	13	30	2	0	0	0	(0	0)	2	2	1	0	1	0	6	0	0	0	1	0	1.00	0	.067	.097	.067

Michael Barrett

Bats: R Throws: R Pos: C-102; PH-9; DH-1   Ht: 6'3" Wt: 210 Born: 10/22/1976 Age: 30

Year	Team	Lg	G	AB	H	2B	3B	HR	(Hm	Rd)	TB	R	RBI	RC	TBB	IBB	SO	HBP	SH	SF	SB	CS	SB%	GDP	Avg	OBP	Slg
1998	Mon	NL	8	23	7	2	0	1	(0	1)	12	3	2	5	3	0	6	1	0	0	0	0	-	0	.304	.407	.522
1999	Mon	NL	126	433	127	32	3	8	(5	3)	189	53	52	59	32	4	39	3	0	1	0	2	.00	18	.293	.345	.436
2000	Mon	NL	89	271	58	15	1	1	(0	1)	78	28	22	19	23	5	35	1	1	1	0	1	.00	7	.214	.277	.288
2001	Mon	NL	132	472	118	33	2	6	(3	3)	173	42	38	46	25	2	54	2	4	3	2	1	.67	14	.250	.289	.367
2002	Mon	NL	117	376	99	20	1	12	(4	8)	157	41	49	49	40	7	65	1	6	5	6	3	.67	14	.263	.332	.418
2003	Mon	NL	70	226	47	9	2	10	(5	5)	90	33	30	25	21	7	37	2	2	1	0	0	-	6	.208	.280	.398
2004	ChC	NL	134	456	131	32	6	16	(9	7)	223	55	65	67	33	4	64	5	4	8	1	4	.20	13	.287	.337	.489
2005	ChC	NL	133	424	117	32	3	16	(9	7)	203	48	61	67	40	3	61	7	2	4	0	3	.00	7	.276	.345	.479
2006	ChC	NL	107	375	115	25	3	16	(9	7)	194	54	53	58	33	2	41	5	2	3	0	1	.00	12	.307	.368	.517
9 ML YEARS			916	3056	819	200	21	86	(44	42)	1319	357	372	395	250	34	402	27	21	26	9	15	.38	91	.268	.326	.432

Kevin Barry

Pitches: R Bats: R Pos: RP-18; SP-1   Ht: 6'2" Wt: 235 Born: 8/18/1978 Age: 28

Year	Team	Lg	G	GS	CG	GF	IP	BFP	H	R	ER	HR	SH	SF	HB	TBB	IBB	SO	WP	Bk	W	L	Pct	ShO	Sv-Op	Hld	ERC	ERA
2001	Jmstwn	A-	29	0	0	23	31.1	126	14	5	3	0	0	0	0	18	0	54	0	0	1	0	1.000	0	12-	-	1.41	0.86
2002	MrtlBh	A+	47	0	0	43	50.0	197	37	14	14	2	3	4	1	17	1	67	0	0	4	2	.667	0	26-	-	2.24	2.52
2003	Grnvlle	A	51	0	0	19	56.1	257	54	36	31	1	2	3	3	32	0	68	3	0	4	4	.500	0	5-	-	4.00	4.95
2004	Grnvlle	A	20	0	0	19	24.2	100	15	2	2	0	1	0	2	20	2	31	2	0	2	1	.667	0	4-	-	3.21	0.73
2004	Rchmd	AAA	30	0	0	13	35.2	157	25	15	10	1	0	0	2	25	2	40	0	0	3	3	.500	0	2-	-	2.92	2.52
2005	Missi	AA	3	0	0	0	7.1	31	3	1	1	0	0	0	0	6	0	7	0	0	0	0	-	0	0-	-	1.83	1.23
2005	Rchmd	AAA	32	8	0	12	79.0	336	60	28	25	8	2	2	2	44	4	73	0	0	5	3	.625	0	1-	-	3.40	2.85
2006	Rchmd	AAA	18	15	0	2	95.1	409	87	40	35	5	5	5	2	36	2	73	1	0	4	5	.444	0	0-	-	3.18	3.30
2006	Atl	NL	19	1	0	7	25.2	115	24	16	16	2	3	2	1	14	0	19	0	0	1	1	.500	0	0-1	1	4.21	5.61

Jason Bartlett

Bats: R Throws: R Pos: SS-99   Ht: 6'0" Wt: 180 Born: 10/30/1979 Age: 27

Year	Team	Lg	G	AB	H	2B	3B	HR	(Hm	Rd)	TB	R	RBI	RC	TBB	IBB	SO	HBP	SH	SF	SB	CS	SB%	GDP	Avg	OBP	Slg
2006	Roch*	AAA	58	235	72	23	3	1	(-	-)	104	42	20	35	10	0	28	2	0	3	6	3	.67	1	.306	.336	.443
2004	Min	AL	8	12	1	0	0	0	(0	0)	1	2	1	1	1	0	1	0	1	0	2	0	1.00	0	.083	.154	.083
2005	Min	AL	74	224	54	10	1	3	(2	1)	75	33	16	22	21	0	37	4	2	1	4	0	1.00	6	.241	.316	.335
2006	Min	AL	99	333	103	18	2	2	(0	2)	131	44	32	50	22	1	46	11	1	5	10	5	.67	8	.309	.367	.393
3 ML YEARS			181	569	158	28	3	5	(2	3)	207	79	49	73	44	1	84	15	4	6	16	5	.76	14	.278	.342	.364

Phil Barzilla

Pitches: L Bats: L Pos: RP-1
Ht: 6'0" Wt: 180 Born: 1/25/1979 Age: 28

			HOW MUCH HE PITCHED						WHAT HE GAVE UP										THE RESULTS						
Year	Team	Lg	G	GS	CG	GF	IP	BFP	H	R	ER	HR	SH	SF	HB	TBB	IBB	SO	WP	Bk	W	L	Pct	ShO	Sv-Op Hld	ERC	ERA
2001	Pittsfld	A-	16	14	0	0	78.1	352	87	52	41	1	1	2	1	34	0	56	9	0	4	5	.444	0	0- - -	4.19	4.71
2002	Lxngtn	A	43	0	0	27	85.2	356	66	39	31	2	9	2	3	34	5	62	4	0	6	9	.400	0	4- - -	2.37	3.26
2003	Salem	A	52	0	0	18	93.0	395	86	39	32	1	8	2	5	41	5	51	4	0	8	3	.727	0	5- - -	3.37	3.10
2004	RdRck	AA	17	1	0	2	39.0	166	33	13	11	2	1	1	1	17	2	32	3	0	1	1	.750	0	0- - -	3.03	2.54
2004	NewOr	AAA	27	0	0	11	33.2	165	42	21	16	4	0	0	1	21	1	22	2	0	1	1	.500	0	0- - -	6.54	4.28
2005	CpChr	AA	41	14	0	8	113.0	490	126	49	38	6	6	1	4	30	5	87	6	0	7	7	.500	0	0- - -	3.90	3.03
2005	RdRck	AAA	1	0	0	0	0.0	1	0	0	0	0	0	0	0	0	0	0	1	0	0	0	-	0	0- - -	-	-
2006	RdRck	AAA	25	14	1	3	112.1	497	114	57	48	5	8	2	3	48	2	80	1	1	8	5	.615	1	1- - -	3.88	3.85
2006	Hou	NL	1	0	0	0	0.1	2	1	0	0	0	0	0	0	0	0	0	0	0	0	0	-	0	0-0 0	14.52	0.00

Miguel Batista

Pitches: R Bats: R Pos: SP-33; RP-1
Ht: 6'1" Wt: 195 Born: 2/19/1971 Age: 36

			HOW MUCH HE PITCHED						WHAT HE GAVE UP										THE RESULTS						
Year	Team	Lg	G	GS	CG	GF	IP	BFP	H	R	ER	HR	SH	SF	HB	TBB	IBB	SO	WP	Bk	W	L	Pct	ShO	Sv-Op Hld	ERC	ERA
1992	Pit	NL	1	0	0	1	2.0	13	4	2	2	1	0	0	0	3	0	1	0	0	0	0	-	0	0-0 0	20.26	9.00
1996	Fla	NL	9	0	0	4	11.1	49	9	8	7	0	3	0	0	7	2	6	1	0	0	0	-	0	0-0 0	2.77	5.56
1997	ChC	NL	11	6	0	2	36.1	168	36	24	23	4	4	4	1	24	2	27	2	0	0	5	.000	0	0-0 0	5.09	5.70
1998	Mon	NL	56	13	0	12	135.0	598	141	66	57	12	7	5	6	65	7	92	6	1	3	5	.375	0	0-0 3	4.70	3.80
1999	Mon	NL	39	17	2	3	134.2	606	146	88	73	10	8	11	7	58	2	95	6	0	8	7	.533	1	1-1 0	4.62	4.88
2000	2 Tms		18	9	0	2	65.1	310	85	68	62	19	1	2	2	37	2	37	4	0	2	7	.222	0	0-2 0	8.37	8.54
2001	Ari	NL	48	18	0	6	139.1	581	113	57	52	13	9	3	10	60	2	90	6	0	11	8	.579	0	0-0 4	3.43	3.36
2002	Ari	NL	36	29	1	2	184.2	790	172	99	88	12	5	8	6	70	3	112	9	2	8	9	.471	2	0-0 2	3.45	4.29
2003	Ari	NL	36	29	2	5	193.1	822	197	85	76	13	10	6	8	60	3	142	7	0	10	9	.526	1	0-0 0	3.77	3.54
2004	Tor	AL	38	31	2	7	198.2	867	206	115	106	22	7	6	3	96	1	104	12	0	10	13	.435	1	5-5 0	4.84	4.80
2005	Tor	AL	71	0	0	62	74.2	331	80	39	34	9	2	2	2	27	5	54	3	0	5	8	.385	0	31-39 0	4.39	4.10
2006	Ari	NL	34	33	3	0	206.1	910	231	116	105	18	12	5	6	84	5	110	14	1	11	8	.579	1	0-0 0	4.82	4.58
00	Mon	NL	4	0	0	0	8.1	49	19	14	13	2	1	1	2	3	0	7	0	0	0	1	.000	0	0-2 0	14.73	14.04
00	KC	AL	14	9	0	2	57.0	261	66	54	49	17	0	1	0	34	2	30	4	0	2	6	.250	0	0-0 0	7.50	7.74
	12 ML YEARS		397	185	10	106	1381.2	6045	1420	767	685	133	68	52	51	591	34	870	70	4	68	79	.463	4	37-47 9	4.44	4.46

Tony Batista

Bats: R Throws: R Pos: 3B-50
Ht: 6'0" Wt: 225 Born: 12/9/1973 Age: 33

			BATTING																					BASERUNNING				AVERAGES		
Year	Team	Lg	G	AB	H	2B	3B	HR	(Hm	Rd)	TB	R	RBI	RC	TBB	IBB	SO	HBP	SH	SF					SB	CS	SB% GDP		Avg	OBP	Slg
1996	Oak	AL	74	238	71	10	2	6	(1	5)	103	38	25	37	19	0	49	1	0	2					7	3	.70	2	.298	.350	.433
1997	Oak	AL	68	188	38	10	1	4	(0	4)	62	22	18	14	14	0	31	2	3	0					2	2	.50	8	.202	.265	.330
1998	Ari	NL	106	293	80	16	1	18	(9	9)	152	46	41	46	18	0	52	3	0	4					1	1	.50	7	.273	.318	.519
1999	2 Tms		142	519	144	30	1	31	(10	21)	269	77	100	94	37	4	96	6	3	7					4	0	1.00	12	.277	.330	.518
2000	Tor	AL	154	620	163	32	2	41	(25	16)	322	96	114	94	35	1	121	6	0	3					5	4	.56	15	.263	.307	.519
2001	2 Tms		156	579	138	27	6	25	(14	11)	252	70	87	70	32	1	113	4	0	7					5	2	.71	9	.238	.280	.435
2002	Bal	AL	161	615	150	36	1	31	(14	17)	281	90	87	79	50	9	107	11	0	6					5	4	.56	13	.244	.309	.457
2003	Bal	AL	161	631	148	20	1	26	(10	16)	248	76	99	66	28	4	102	5	0	6					3	5	.57	20	.235	.270	.393
2004	Mon	NL	157	606	146	30	2	32	(13	19)	276	76	110	69	26	4	78	4	4	10					14	6	.70	14	.241	.272	.455
2006	Min		50	178	42	12	0	5	(2	3)	69	24	21	23	15	1	27	2	0	0					0	1	.00	5	.236	.303	.388
99	Ari	NL	44	144	37	5	0	5	(1	4)	57	16	21	21	16	3	17	2	0	2					2	0	1.00	1	.257	.335	.396
99	Tor	AL	98	375	107	25	1	26	(9	17)	212	61	79	66	22	1	79	4	3	5					2	0	1.00	11	.285	.328	.565
01	Tor	AL	72	271	56	11	1	13	(9	4)	108	29	45	27	13	1	66	4	0	3					0	1	.00	2	.207	.251	.399
01	Bal	AL	84	308	82	16	5	12	(5	7)	144	41	42	43	19	0	47	0	0	4					5	1	.83	7	.266	.305	.468
	10 ML YEARS		1229	4467	1120	223	17	219	(98	121)	2034	615	702	585	275	24	776	44	10	45					47	26	.64	105	.251	.298	.455

Rick Bauer

Pitches: R Bats: R Pos: RP-57; SP-1
Ht: 6'6" Wt: 225 Born: 1/10/1977 Age: 30

			HOW MUCH HE PITCHED						WHAT HE GAVE UP										THE RESULTS						
Year	Team	Lg	G	GS	CG	GF	IP	BFP	H	R	ER	HR	SH	SF	HB	TBB	IBB	SO	WP	Bk	W	L	Pct	ShO	Sv-Op Hld	ERC	ERA
2001	Bal	AL	6	6	0	0	33.0	143	35	22	17	7	0	1	1	9	0	16	0	0	0	5	.000	0	0-0 0	4.74	4.64
2002	Bal	AL	56	1	0	15	83.2	358	84	41	37	12	2	2	4	36	4	45	4	0	6	7	.462	0	1-5 12	4.78	3.98
2003	Bal	AL	35	0	0	10	61.1	259	58	36	31	5	1	3	4	24	3	43	6	0	0	0	-	0	0-1 3	3.87	4.55
2004	Bal	AL	23	2	0	7	53.2	230	49	31	28	4	0	0	4	20	0	37	1	0	2	1	.667	0	0-1 0	3.59	4.70
2005	Bal	AL	5	0	0	2	8.1	40	13	9	9	2	0	0	0	4	0	5	0	0	0	0	-	0	0-0 0	9.38	9.72
2006	Tex	AL	58	1	0	19	71.0	302	73	31	28	4	0	5	4	25	0	35	3	0	3	1	.750	0	2-5 7	4.04	3.55
	6 ML YEARS		183	10	0	53	311.0	1332	312	170	150	34	3	11	17	118	7	181	14	0	11	14	.440	0	3-12 22	4.33	4.34

Denny Bautista

Pitches: R Bats: R Pos: SP-8; RP-4
Ht: 6'5" Wt: 190 Born: 8/23/1980 Age: 26

			HOW MUCH HE PITCHED						WHAT HE GAVE UP										THE RESULTS						
Year	Team	Lg	G	GS	CG	GF	IP	BFP	H	R	ER	HR	SH	SF	HB	TBB	IBB	SO	WP	Bk	W	L	Pct	ShO	Sv-Op Hld	ERC	ERA
2006	ColSpr*	AAA	6	6	0	0	36.0	170	46	24	18	2	2	0	4	16	0	35	1	1	1	4	.200	0	0- - -	5.99	4.50
2006	Omha*	AAA	10	10	0	0	44.0	206	52	38	36	3	0	2	1	32	0	28	6	0	2	5	.286	0	0- - -	6.52	7.36
2004	2 Tms	AL	7	5	0	0	29.2	142	44	28	28	3	0	1	3	13	1	19	3	2	0	4	.000	0	0-0 0	7.76	8.49
2005	KC	AL	7	7	0	0	35.2	160	36	23	23	2	1	1	2	17	0	23	3	0	2	2	.500	0	0-0 0	4.27	5.80
2006	2 Tms	AL	12	8	0	3	41.2	194	47	34	26	5	1	2	4	21	0	27	5	0	0	3	.000	0	0-0 0	5.75	5.62
04	Bal	AL	2	0	0	0	2.0	15	6	8	8	1	0	1	1	2	0	1	1	0	0	0	-	0	0-0 0	28.67	36.00
04	KC	AL	5	5	0	0	27.2	127	38	20	20	2	0	0	2	11	1	18	2	2	0	4	.000	0	0-0 0	6.50	6.51

Year	Team	Lg	G	GS	CG	GF	IP	BFP	H	R	ER	HR	SH	SF	HB	TBB	IBB	SO	WP	Bk	W	L	Pct	ShO	Sv-Op	Hld	ERC	ERA
06	KC	AL	8	7	0	0	35.0	161	38	24	22	5	1	2	4	17	0	22	5	0	0	2	.000	0	0-0	0	5.70	5.66
06	Col	NL	4	1	0	3	6.2	33	9	10	4	0	0	0	0	4	0	5	0	0	0	1	.000	0	0-0	0	5.98	5.40
	3 ML YEARS		26	20	0	3	107.0	496	127	85	77	10	2	4	9	51	1	69	11	2	2	9	.182	0	0-0	0	5.76	6.48

Jose Bautista

Bats: R **Throws:** R **Pos:** CF-57; 3B-33; RF-25; PH-7; LF-6; 2B-3   **Ht:** 6'0" **Wt:** 190 **Born:** 10/19/1980 **Age:** 26

							BATTING														BASERUNNING				AVERAGES		
Year	Team	Lg	G	AB	H	2B	3B	HR	(Hm	Rd)	TB	R	RBI	RC	TBB	IBB	SO	HBP	SH	SF	SB	CS	SB%	GDP	Avg	OBP	Slg
2006	Indy*	AAA	29	101	28	9	0	2	(-	-)	43	12	9	17	14	1	19	2	0	2	2	1	.67	3	.277	.370	.426
2004	4 Tms		64	88	18	3	0	0	(0	0)	21	6	2	2	7	0	40	0	1	0	1		.00	1	.205	.263	.239
2005	Pit	NL	11	28	4	1	0	0	(0	0)	5	3	1	0	3	0	7	0	0	0	1	0	1.00	2	.143	.226	.179
2006	Pit	NL	117	400	94	20	3	16	(11	5)	168	58	51	55	46	2	110	16	3	4	2	4	.33	12	.235	.335	.420
04	Bal	AL	16	11	3	0	0	0	(0	0)	3	3	0	1	1	0	3	0	0	0	0	0	-	0	.273	.333	.273
04	TB	AL	12	12	2	0	0	0	(0	0)	2	1	1	0	3	0	7	0	0	0	1		.00	0	.167	.333	.167
04	KC	AL	13	25	5	1	0	0	(0	0)	6	1	1	0	1	0	12	0	0	0	0	0	-	0	.200	.231	.240
04	Pit	NL	23	40	8	2	0	0	(0	0)	10	1	0	1	2	0	18	0	1	0	0	0	-	1	.200	.238	.250
	3 ML YEARS		192	516	116	24	3	16	(11	5)	194	67	54	57	56	2	157	16	4	4	3	5	.38	15	.225	.318	.376

Jason Bay

Bats: R **Throws:** R **Pos:** LF-157; PH-2   **Ht:** 6'2" **Wt:** 205 **Born:** 9/20/1978 **Age:** 28

							BATTING														BASERUNNING				AVERAGES		
Year	Team	Lg	G	AB	H	2B	3B	HR	(Hm	Rd)	TB	R	RBI	RC	TBB	IBB	SO	HBP	SH	SF	SB	CS	SB%	GDP	Avg	OBP	Slg
2003	2 Tms	NL	30	87	25	7	1	4	(2	2)	46	15	14	19	19	0	29	1	0	0	3	1	.75	0	.287	.421	.529
2004	Pit	NL	120	411	116	24	4	26	(15	11)	226	61	82	75	41	2	129	10	5	5	4	6	.40	9	.282	.358	.550
2005	Pit	NL	**162**	599	183	44	6	32	(9	23)	335	110	101	128	95	9	142	6	0	7	21	1	**.95**	12	.306	.402	.559
2006	Pit	NL	159	570	163	29	3	35	(13	22)	303	101	109	103	102	9	156	8	0	9	11	2	.85	15	.286	.396	.532
03	SD	NL	3	8	2	1	0	1	(0	1)	6	2	2	2	1	0	1	1	0	0	0	0	-	0	.250	.400	.750
03	Pit	NL	27	79	23	6	1	3	(2	1)	40	13	12	17	18	0	28	0	0	0	3	1	.75	0	.291	.423	.506
	4 ML YEARS		471	1667	487	104	14	97	(39	58)	910	287	306	325	257	20	456	25	5	21	39	10	.80	36	.292	.390	.546

Jonah Bayliss

Pitches: R **Bats:** R **Pos:** RP-11   **Ht:** 6'2" **Wt:** 200 **Born:** 8/13/1980 **Age:** 26

				HOW MUCH HE PITCHED					WHAT HE GAVE UP											THE RESULTS							
Year	Team	Lg	G	GS	CG	GF	IP	BFP	H	R	ER	HR	SH	SF	HB	TBB	IBB	SO	WP	Bk	W	L	Pct	ShO	Sv-Op	Hld	ERC	ERA
2002	Spkane	A-	15	15	0	0	70.2	311	70	46	42	9	3	3	7	29	0	38	7	2	4	8	.333	0	0--	-	4.66	5.35
2003	Burlgtn	A	26	26	2	0	140.0	618	129	78	60	11	4	2	10	69	0	133	9	0	7	12	.368	1	0--	-	4.10	3.86
2004	Wilmg	A	23	23	0	0	107.0	477	114	69	60	11	9	8	9	42	0	73	6	2	6	6	.500	0	0--	-	4.76	5.05
2005	Wichta	AA	30	0	0	15	57.0	240	43	19	18	5	0	1	2	26	0	63	5	0	1	2	.333	0	8--	-	2.99	2.84
2006	Indy	AAA	46	0	0	36	58.0	241	37	15	14	4	5	1	3	28	6	67	4	0	3	3	.500	0	23--	-	2.29	2.17
2005	KC	AL	11	0	0	7	11.2	48	7	6	6	2	0	0	2	4	0	10	0	0	0	0	-	0	0-0	0	2.80	4.63
2006	Pit	NL	11	0	0	5	14.2	69	13	7	7	1	2	1	1	11	2	15	2	0	1	1	.500	0	0-0	1	4.46	4.30
	2 ML YEARS		22	0	0	12	26.1	117	20	13	13	3	2	1	3	15	2	25	2	0	1	1	.500	0	0-0	1	3.73	4.44

T.J. Beam

Pitches: R **Bats:** R **Pos:** RP-20   **Ht:** 6'7" **Wt:** 215 **Born:** 8/28/1980 **Age:** 26

				HOW MUCH HE PITCHED					WHAT HE GAVE UP											THE RESULTS							
Year	Team	Lg	G	GS	CG	GF	IP	BFP	H	R	ER	HR	SH	SF	HB	TBB	IBB	SO	WP	Bk	W	L	Pct	ShO	Sv-Op	Hld	ERC	ERA
2003	StIsInd	A-	9	5	0	1	33.1	137	25	14	10	4	1	2	0	9	0	31	1	0	2	1	.667	0	1--	-	2.30	2.70
2003	Btl Crk	A	5	5	0	1	21.2	100	27	16	14	3	0	0	2	8	0	19	0	0	2	1	.667	0	0--	-	6.06	5.82
2004	StIsInd	A-	12	12	1	0	66.2	269	61	28	19	4	0	2	3	14	0	69	1	2	2	4	.333	0	0--	-	2.86	2.57
2004	Btl Crk	A	11	7	0	2	41.1	169	34	20	20	8	5	3	0	17	0	54	1	1	2	5	.286	0	0--	-	3.85	4.35
2005	CtnSC	A+	35	2	0	16	59.2	240	45	15	11	2	1	1	0	18	0	78	0	0	3	3	.500	0	2--	-	2.09	1.66
2005	Tampa	A+	12	0	0	5	17.1	72	14	7	6	2	0	0	0	7	1	27	0	0	1	1	.500	0	1--	-	3.06	3.12
2006	Trntn	AA	18	0	0	7	42.0	158	26	5	4	1	1	2	0	12	0	34	0	0	4	0	1.000	0	3--	-	1.48	0.86
2006	Clmbs	AAA	19	0	0	5	31.2	122	16	6	6	1	2	1	0	13	0	37	2	0	2	0	1.000	0	1--	-	1.40	1.71
2006	NYY	AL	20	0	0	5	18.0	85	26	17	17	5	0	0	2	6	2	12	1	1	2	0	1.000	0	0-1	2	8.36	8.50

Colter Bean

Pitches: R **Bats:** L **Pos:** RP-2   **Ht:** 6'6" **Wt:** 255 **Born:** 1/16/1977 **Age:** 30

				HOW MUCH HE PITCHED					WHAT HE GAVE UP											THE RESULTS							
Year	Team	Lg	G	GS	CG	GF	IP	BFP	H	R	ER	HR	SH	SF	HB	TBB	IBB	SO	WP	Bk	W	L	Pct	ShO	Sv-Op	Hld	ERC	ERA
2000	StIsInd	A-	3	0	0	2	2.0	14	3	3	1	0	0	0	0	3	1	2	0	1	0	0	-	0	0--	-	8.06	4.50
2000	Grnsbr	A	18	0	0	9	25.2	109	21	16	14	1	0	0	1	11	0	35	4	0	1	0	1.000	0	0--	-	2.90	4.91
2001	Tampa	A+	32	0	0	10	49.1	193	27	9	8	0	0	0	3	18	2	77	2	0	7	1	.875	0	2--	-	1.39	1.46
2001	Nrwich	AA	1	0	0	1	1.0	5	1	1	1	1	0	0	0	1	0	0	0	0	0	1	.000	0	0--	-	14.27	9.00
2002	Tampa	A+	46	0	0	25	54.2	219	34	17	12	2	3	2	5	21	1	78	1	0	2	2	.500	0	9--	-	1.98	1.98
2002	Nrwich	AA	12	0	0	4	10.2	52	14	8	8	1	1	1	2	6	0	9	0	0	0	2	.000	0	0--	-	7.49	6.75
2003	Trntn	AA	3	0	0	1	4.2	18	2	0	0	0	2	1	0	2	0	9	0	0	0	0	-	0	0--	-	1.08	0.00
2003	Clmbs	AAA	50	0	0	17	69.0	287	53	33	22	5	1	0	5	27	2	70	1	1	4	2	.667	0	4--	-	2.85	2.87
2004	Clmbs	AAA	53	0	0	12	82.2	332	61	24	21	3	0	0	8	23	0	109	2	1	9	3	.750	0	1--	-	2.24	2.29
2005	Clmbs	AAA	65	0	0	20	71.2	314	60	33	24	5	8	2	8	39	7	82	0	0	4	7	.364	0	2--	-	3.79	3.01
2006	Clmbs	AAA	47	6	0	10	88.1	377	61	26	26	3	3	3	3	53	2	116	2	1	9	2	.818	0	0--	-	3.03	2.65
2005	NYY	AL	1	0	0	1	2.0	9	1	1	1	0	0	0	0	2	0	2	0	0	0	0	-	0	0-0	0	2.80	4.50
2006	NYY	AL	2	0	0	1	2.0	10	2	2	2	0	0	1	1	2	0	1	0	0	0	0	-	0	0-0	0	8.25	9.00
	2 ML YEARS		3	0	0	2	4.0	19	3	3	3	0	0	1	1	4	0	3	0	0	0	0	-	0	0-0	0	5.27	6.75

Josh Beckett

Pitches: R **Bats:** R **Pos:** SP-33 **Ht:** 6'5" **Wt:** 220 **Born:** 5/15/1980 **Age:** 27

Year	Team	Lg	G	GS	CG	GF	IP	BFP	H	R	ER	HR	SH	SF	HB	TBB	IBB	SO	WP	Bk	W	L	Pct	ShO	Sv-Op	Hld	ERC	ERA
2001	Fla	NL	4	4	0	0	24.0	99	14	9	4	3	0	0	1	11	0	24	1	0	2	2	.500	0	0-0	0	2.36	1.50
2002	Fla	NL	23	21	0	0	107.2	454	93	56	49	13	5	3	1	44	2	113	5	0	6	7	.462	0	0-0	0	3.50	4.10
2003	Fla	NL	24	23	0	1	142.0	601	132	54	48	9	5	1	2	56	4	152	6	1	9	8	.529	0	0-0	0	3.44	3.04
2004	Fla	NL	26	26	1	0	156.2	654	137	72	66	16	9	3	6	54	3	152	5	0	9	9	.500	1	0-0	0	3.32	3.79
2005	Fla	NL	29	29	0	0	178.2	729	153	75	67	14	8	2	7	58	2	166	5	0	15	8	.652	1	0-0	0	3.06	3.38
2006	Bos	AL	33	33	0	0	204.2	869	191	120	114	36	2	3	10	74	1	158	11	1	16	11	.593	0	0-0	0	4.28	5.01
6 ML YEARS			139	136	3	1	813.2	3406	720	386	348	91	29	12	27	297	12	765	33	2	57	45	.559	2	0-0	0	3.51	3.85

Erik Bedard

Pitches: L **Bats:** L **Pos:** SP-33 **Ht:** 6'1" **Wt:** 190 **Born:** 3/6/1979 **Age:** 28

Year	Team	Lg	G	GS	CG	GF	IP	BFP	H	R	ER	HR	SH	SF	HB	TBB	IBB	SO	WP	Bk	W	L	Pct	ShO	Sv-Op	Hld	ERC	ERA
2002	Bal	AL	2	0	0	0	0.2	4	2	1	1	0	0	0	0	0	0	1	0	0	0	0	-	0	0-0	0	14.52	13.50
2004	Bal	AL	27	26	0	0	137.1	633	149	83	70	13	0	4	7	71	1	121	7	2	6	10	.375	0	0-0	0	5.11	4.59
2005	Bal	AL	24	24	0	0	141.2	606	139	66	63	10	3	6	5	57	1	125	4	1	6	8	.429	0	0-0	0	3.95	4.00
2006	Bal	AL	33	33	0	0	196.1	844	196	92	82	16	6	4	5	69	0	171	6	0	15	11	.577	0	0-0	0	3.83	3.76
4 ML YEARS			86	83	0	0	476.0	2087	486	242	216	39	9	14	17	197	2	418	17	3	27	29	.482	0	0-0	0	4.24	4.08

Joe Beimel

Pitches: L **Bats:** L **Pos:** RP-62 **Ht:** 6'2" **Wt:** 215 **Born:** 4/19/1977 **Age:** 30

Year	Team	Lg	G	GS	CG	GF	IP	BFP	H	R	ER	HR	SH	SF	HB	TBB	IBB	SO	WP	Bk	W	L	Pct	ShO	Sv-Op	Hld	ERC	ERA
2006	LsVgs*	AAA	10	0	0	1	13.0	49	9	2	2	0	1	1	0	4	1	9	1	1	3	0	1.000	0	0--	0	1.62	1.38
2001	Pit	NL	42	15	0	9	115.1	511	131	72	67	12	3	1	6	49	4	58	3	0	7	11	.389	0	0-0	0	5.24	5.23
2002	Pit	NL	53	8	0	8	85.1	389	88	49	44	9	7	3	4	45	12	53	2	0	2	5	.286	0	0-1	5	4.68	4.64
2003	Pit	NL	69	0	0	11	62.1	276	69	35	35	7	3	5	4	33	6	42	0	1	1	3	.250	0	0-5	12	5.62	5.05
2004	Min	AL	3	0	0	0	1.2	15	8	8	8	1	0	0	0	2	0	2	0	0	0	0	-	0	0-0	0	44.44	43.20
2005	TB	AL	7	0	0	3	11.0	51	15	4	4	1	0	0	0	4	1	3	1	0	0	0	-	0	0-0	0	5.80	3.27
2006	LAD	NL	62	0	0	10	70.0	295	70	26	23	7	4	3	0	21	3	30	6	1	2	1	.667	0	2-2	10	3.62	2.96
6 ML YEARS			236	23	0	41	345.2	1537	381	194	181	37	17	12	14	154	26	188	12	2	12	20	.375	0	2-8	27	4.98	4.71

Matt Belisle

Pitches: R **Bats:** B **Pos:** RP-28; SP-2 **Ht:** 6'3" **Wt:** 195 **Born:** 6/6/1980 **Age:** 27

Year	Team	Lg	G	GS	CG	GF	IP	BFP	H	R	ER	HR	SH	SF	HB	TBB	IBB	SO	WP	Bk	W	L	Pct	ShO	Sv-Op	Hld	ERC	ERA
2006	Dayton*	A	2	0	0	0	4.0	16	3	1	0	0	0	0	0	0	0	3	0	0	1	0	1.000	0	1--	1	1.06	0.00
2006	Chatt*	AA	2	1	0	0	3.1	13	3	0	0	0	0	0	0	0	0	4	1	0	0	0	-	0	0--	1	1.57	0.00
2006	Lsvlle*	AAA	8	1	0	2	9.0	32	4	0	0	0	0	0	0	1	0	9	0	0	1	0	1.000	0	0--	1	0.59	0.00
2003	Cin	NL	6	0	0	0	8.2	39	10	5	5	1	2	1	1	2	0	6	0	0	1	1	.500	0	0-1	1	4.73	5.19
2005	Cin	NL	60	5	0	17	85.2	382	101	49	42	11	4	2	6	26	6	59	3	0	4	8	.333	0	1-4	8	5.08	4.41
2006	Cin	NL	30	2	0	5	40.0	180	43	18	16	5	1	2	3	19	1	26	3	0	2	0	1.000	0	0-1	6	5.29	3.60
3 ML YEARS			96	7	0	24	134.1	601	154	72	63	17	7	5	10	47	7	91	6	0	7	9	.438	0	1-6	8	5.12	4.22

David Bell

Bats: R **Throws:** R **Pos:** 3B-143; PH-3 **Ht:** 5'10" **Wt:** 195 **Born:** 9/14/1972 **Age:** 34

Year	Team	Lg	G	AB	H	2B	3B	HR	(Hm	Rd)	TB	R	RBI	RC	TBB	IBB	SO	HBP	SH	SF	SB	CS	SB%	GDP	Avg	OBP	Slg
1995	2 Tms		41	146	36	7	2	2	(1	1)	53	13	19	14	4	0	25	2	0	1	1	2	.33	0	.247	.275	.363
1996	StL	NL	62	145	31	6	0	1	(1	0)	40	12	9	9	10	2	22	1	0	1	1	1	.50	3	.214	.268	.276
1997	StL	NL	66	142	30	7	2	1	(1	0)	44	9	12	11	10	2	28	0	2	1	1	0	1.00	3	.211	.261	.310
1998	3 Tms		132	429	117	30	2	10	(2	8)	181	48	49	53	27	4	65	2	1	5	0	4	.00	11	.273	.315	.422
1999	Sea	AL	157	597	160	31	2	21	(11	10)	258	92	78	87	58	0	90	2	3	7	7	4	.64	7	.268	.331	.432
2000	Sea	AL	133	454	112	24	2	11	(4	7)	173	57	47	54	42	0	66	6	6	4	2	3	.40	11	.247	.316	.381
2001	Sea	AL	135	470	122	28	0	15	(7	8)	195	62	64	58	28	1	59	3	5	4	2	1	.67	8	.260	.303	.415
2002	SF	NL	154	552	144	29	2	20	(7	13)	237	82	73	79	54	2	80	9	6	7	1	2	.33	18	.261	.333	.429
2003	Phi	NL	85	297	58	14	0	4	(1	3)	84	32	37	27	41	1	40	4	0	6	0	0	-	7	.195	.296	.283
2004	Phi	NL	143	533	155	33	1	18	(10	8)	244	67	77	87	57	4	75	6	2	5	1	1	.50	14	.291	.363	.458
2005	Phi	NL	150	557	138	31	1	10	(5	5)	201	53	61	55	47	6	69	5	4	4	0	1	.00	24	.248	.310	.361
2006	2 Tms	NL	145	504	136	27	4	10	(7	3)	201	60	63	67	50	3	68	4	3	5	3	1	.75	18	.270	.337	.399
95	Cle	AL	2	2	0	0	0	0	(0	0)	0	0	0	0	0	0	0	0	0	0	0	0	-	0	.000	.000	.000
95	StL	NL	39	144	36	7	2	2	(1	1)	53	13	19	14	4	0	25	2	0	1	1	2	.33	0	.250	.278	.368
98	StL	NL	4	9	2	1	0	0	(0	0)	3	0	0	1	0	0	3	0	0	0	0	0	-	0	.222	.222	.333
98	Cle	AL	107	340	89	21	2	10	(2	8)	144	37	41	41	22	4	54	2	1	5	0	4	.00	8	.262	.306	.424
98	Sea	AL	21	80	26	8	0	0	(0	0)	34	11	8	11	5	0	8	0	0	0	0	0	-	3	.325	.365	.425
06	Phi	NL	92	324	90	17	2	6	(4	2)	129	39	34	42	32	2	38	3	3	3	1	0	1.00	11	.278	.345	.398
06	Mil	NL	53	180	46	10	2	4	(3	1)	72	21	29	25	18	1	30	1	0	2	2	1	.67	7	.256	.323	.400
12 ML YEARS			1403	4826	1239	267	18	123	(57	66)	1911	587	589	601	428	25	687	44	32	50	19	20	.49	123	.257	.320	.396

Heath Bell

Pitches: R Bats: R Pos: RP-22   Ht: 6'3" Wt: 225 Born: 9/29/1977 Age: 29

Year	Team	Lg	G	GS	CG	GF	IP	BFP	H	R	ER	HR	SH	SF	HB	TBB	IBB	SO	WP	Bk	W	L	Pct	ShO	Sv-Op	Hld	ERC	ERA
2006	Norfolk*	AAA	30	0	0	30	35.0	142	27	7	5	1	3	0	1	8	1	56	5	0	3	3	.500	0	12--	-	1.86	1.29
2004	NYM	NL	17	0	0	2	24.1	94	22	9	9	5	1	0	0	6	0	27	0	0	0	2	.000	0	0-1	1	3.86	3.33
2005	NYM	NL	42	0	0	12	46.2	206	56	30	29	3	4	0	1	13	3	43	0	1	1	3	.250	0	0-0	4	4.42	5.59
2006	NYM	NL	22	0	0	6	37.0	166	51	25	21	6	1	0	0	11	2	35	1	0	0	0	-	0	0-0	0	6.40	5.11
	3 ML YEARS		81	0	0	20	108.0	466	129	64	59	14	6	0	1	30	5	105	1	1	1	5	.167	0	0-1	5	4.96	4.92

Mark Bellhorn

Bats: B Throws: R Pos: 3B-50; PH-42; 1B-18; 2B-11; DH-2; PR-2; RF-1   Ht: 6'1" Wt: 205 Born: 8/23/1974 Age: 32

								BATTING														BASERUNNING				AVERAGES		
Year	Team	Lg	G	AB	H	2B	3B	HR	(Hm	Rd)	TB	R	RBI	RC	TBB	IBB	SO	HBP	SH	SF	SB	CS	SB%	GDP	Avg	OBP	Slg
1997	Oak	AL	68	224	51	9	1	6	(3	3)	80	33	19	29	32	0	70	0	5	0	7	1	.88	1	.228	.324	.357
1998	Oak	AL	11	12	1	1	0	0	(0	0)	2	1	1	1	3	0	4	1	0	0	2	0	1.00	0	.083	.313	.167
2000	Oak	AL	9	13	2	0	0	0	(0	0)	2	2	0	1	2	0	6	0	0	0	0	0	-	0	.154	.267	.154
2001	Oak	AL	38	74	10	1	2	1	(1	0)	18	11	4	3	7	0	37	0	1	0	0	0	-	1	.135	.210	.243
2002	ChC	NL	146	445	115	24	4	27	(15	12)	228	86	56	79	76	3	144	6	2	0	7	5	.58	6	.258	.374	.512
2003	2 Tms		99	249	55	10	1	2	(1	1)	73	27	26	26	50	1	78	3	1	4	5	6	.45	3	.221	.353	.293
2004	Bos	AL	138	523	138	37	3	17	(11	6)	232	93	82	95	88	1	177	5	1	3	6	1	.86	8	.264	.373	.444
2005	2 Tms		94	300	63	20	0	8	(3	5)	107	43	30	28	52	1	112	0	0	3	3	0	1.00	4	.210	.324	.357
2006	SD	NL	115	253	48	11	2	8	(6	2)	87	26	27	24	32	0	90	2	0	1	0	0	-	3	.190	.285	.344
03	ChC	NL	51	139	29	7	1	2	(1	1)	44	15	22	17	29	1	46	1	0	4	3	3	.50	2	.209	.341	.317
03	Col	NL	48	110	26	3	0	0	(0	0)	29	12	4	9	21	0	32	2	1	0	2	3	.40	1	.236	.368	.264
05	Bos	AL	85	283	61	20	0	7	(3	4)	102	41	28	28	49	1	109	0	0	3	3	0	1.00	4	.216	.328	.360
05	NYY	AL	9	17	2	0	0	1	(0	1)	5	2	2	0	3	0	3	0	0	0	0	0	-	0	.118	.250	.294
	9 ML YEARS		718	2093	483	113	13	69	(40	29)	829	322	245	286	342	6	718	17	10	11	30	13	.70	26	.231	.342	.396

Ronnie Belliard

Bats: R Throws: R Pos: 2B-145; PH-3; 3B-1; PR-1   Ht: 5'8" Wt: 195 Born: 4/7/1975 Age: 32

								BATTING														BASERUNNING				AVERAGES		
Year	Team	Lg	G	AB	H	2B	3B	HR	(Hm	Rd)	TB	R	RBI	RC	TBB	IBB	SO	HBP	SH	SF	SB	CS	SB%	GDP	Avg	OBP	Slg
1998	Mil	NL	8	5	1	0	0	0	(0	0)	1	1	0	0	0	0	0	0	0	0	0	0	-	0	.200	.200	.200
1999	Mil	NL	124	457	135	29	4	8	(5	3)	196	60	58	72	64	0	59	0	6	4	4	5	.44	16	.295	.379	.429
2000	Mil	NL	152	571	150	30	9	8	(4	4)	222	83	54	81	82	4	84	3	4	7	7	5	.58	12	.263	.354	.389
2001	Mil	NL	101	364	96	30	3	11	(7	4)	165	69	36	56	35	2	65	5	4	2	5	2	.71	5	.264	.335	.453
2002	Mil	NL	104	289	61	13	0	3	(0	3)	83	30	26	15	18	0	46	1	6	3	2	3	.40	8	.211	.257	.287
2003	Col	NL	116	447	124	31	2	8	(6	2)	183	73	50	71	49	0	71	2	6	1	7	2	.78	7	.277	.351	.409
2004	Cle	AL	152	599	169	48	1	12	(4	8)	255	78	70	87	60	5	98	2	0	2	3	2	.60	18	.282	.348	.426
2005	Cle	AL	145	536	152	36	1	17	(7	10)	241	71	78	71	35	0	72	1	8	7	2	2	.50	17	.284	.325	.450
2006	2 Tms		147	544	148	30	1	13	(5	8)	219	63	67	62	36	2	81	5	3	2	2	3	.40	17	.272	.322	.403
06	Cle	AL	93	350	102	21	0	8	(3	5)	147	43	44	47	21	0	45	4	2	2	2	0	1.00	8	.291	.337	.420
06	StL	NL	54	194	46	9	1	5	(2	3)	72	20	23	15	15	2	36	1	1	0	0	3	.00	9	.237	.295	.371
	9 ML YEARS		1049	3812	1036	247	21	80	(38	42)	1565	528	439	515	379	13	576	19	37	28	32	24	.57	100	.272	.338	.411

Carlos Beltran

Bats: B Throws: R Pos: CF-136; PH-3; DH-1   Ht: 6'1" Wt: 200 Born: 4/24/1977 Age: 30

								BATTING														BASERUNNING				AVERAGES		
Year	Team	Lg	G	AB	H	2B	3B	HR	(Hm	Rd)	TB	R	RBI	RC	TBB	IBB	SO	HBP	SH	SF	SB	CS	SB%	GDP	Avg	OBP	Slg
1998	KC	AL	14	58	16	5	3	0	(0	0)	27	12	7	9	3	0	12	1	0	1	3	0	1.00	2	.276	.317	.466
1999	KC	AL	156	663	194	27	7	22	(12	10)	301	112	108	100	46	2	123	4	0	10	27	8	.77	17	.293	.337	.454
2000	KC	AL	98	372	92	15	4	7	(4	3)	136	49	44	43	35	2	69	0	2	4	13	0	1.00	12	.247	.309	.366
2001	KC	AL	155	617	189	32	12	24	(7	17)	317	106	101	118	52	2	120	5	1	5	31	1	.97	7	.306	.362	.514
2002	KC	AL	162	637	174	44	7	29	(19	10)	319	114	105	117	71	1	135	4	3	7	35	7	.83	12	.273	.346	.501
2003	KC	AL	141	521	160	14	10	26	(10	16)	272	102	100	100	72	4	81	2	0	7	41	4	.91	8	.307	.389	.522
2004	2 Tms		159	599	160	36	9	38	(15	23)	328	121	104	124	92	10	101	7	3	7	42	3	.93	8	.267	.367	.548
2005	NYM	NL	151	582	155	34	2	16	(6	10)	241	83	78	88	56	5	96	2	4	6	17	6	.74	9	.266	.330	.414
2006	NYM	NL	140	510	140	38	1	41	(15	26)	303	127	116	121	95	6	99	4	1	7	18	3	.86	6	.275	.388	.594
04	KC	AL	69	266	74	19	2	15	(8	7)	142	51	51	57	37	7	44	2	1	3	14	3	.82	4	.278	.367	.534
04	Hou	NL	90	333	86	17	7	23	(7	16)	186	70	53	67	55	3	57	5	2	4	28	0	1.00	4	.258	.368	.559
	9 ML YEARS		1176	4559	1280	245	55	203	(88	115)	2244	826	763	837	522	32	836	29	14	54	227	32	.88	81	.281	.355	.492

Adrian Beltre

Bats: R Throws: R Pos: 3B-155; 2B-1; DH-1   Ht: 5'11" Wt: 220 Born: 4/7/1979 Age: 28

								BATTING														BASERUNNING				AVERAGES		
Year	Team	Lg	G	AB	H	2B	3B	HR	(Hm	Rd)	TB	R	RBI	RC	TBB	IBB	SO	HBP	SH	SF	SB	CS	SB%	GDP	Avg	OBP	Slg
1998	LAD	NL	77	195	42	9	0	7	(5	2)	72	18	22	20	14	0	37	3	2	0	3	1	.75	4	.215	.278	.369
1999	LAD	NL	152	538	148	27	5	15	(6	9)	230	84	67	84	61	12	105	6	4	5	18	7	.72	4	.275	.352	.428
2000	LAD	NL	138	510	148	30	2	20	(7	13)	242	71	85	85	56	2	80	2	3	4	12	5	.71	13	.290	.360	.475
2001	LAD	NL	126	475	126	22	4	13	(4	9)	195	59	60	60	28	1	82	5	2	5	13	4	.76	9	.265	.310	.411
2002	LAD	NL	159	587	151	26	5	21	(7	14)	250	70	75	74	37	4	96	4	1	6	7	5	.58	17	.257	.303	.426
2003	LAD	NL	158	559	134	30	2	23	(13	10)	237	50	80	66	37	4	103	5	1	6	2	2	.50	13	.240	.290	.424
2004	LAD	NL	156	598	200	32	0	48	(23	25)	376	104	121	120	53	9	87	2	0	4	7	2	.78	15	.334	.388	.629
2005	Sea	AL	156	603	154	36	1	19	(7	12)	249	69	87	75	38	6	108	5	0	4	3	1	.75	15	.255	.303	.413
2006	Sea	AL	156	620	166	39	4	25	(16	9)	288	88	89	85	47	4	118	10	1	3	11	5	.69	15	.268	.328	.465
	9 ML YEARS		1278	4685	1269	251	23	191	(88	103)	2139	613	686	669	371	42	816	42	14	37	76	32	.70	105	.271	.328	.457

Armando Benitez

Pitches: R Bats: R Pos: RP-41   Ht: 6'4" Wt: 260 Born: 11/3/1972 Age: 34

			HOW MUCH HE PITCHED						WHAT HE GAVE UP										THE RESULTS							
Year	Team	Lg	G	GS	CG	GF	IP	BFP	H	R	ER	HR	SH	SF	HB	TBB	IBB	SO	WP	Bk	W	L	Pct	ShO	Sv-Op	Hld	ERC	ERA
1994	Bal	AL	3	0	0	1	10.0	42	8	1	1	0	0	0	1	4	0	14	0	0	0	0	-	0	0-0	0	2.71	0.90
1995	Bal	AL	44	0	0	18	47.2	221	37	33	30	8	2	3	5	37	2	56	3	1	1	5	.167	0	2-5	6	5.06	5.66
1996	Bal	AL	18	0	0	8	14.1	56	7	6	6	2	0	1	0	6	0	20	1	0	1	0	1.000	0	4-5	1	1.78	3.77
1997	Bal	AL	71	0	0	26	73.1	307	49	22	20	7	2	4	1	43	5	106	1	0	4	5	.444	0	9-10	20	2.92	2.45
1998	Bal	AL	71	0	0	54	68.1	289	48	29	29	10	3	2	4	39	2	87	0	0	5	6	.455	0	22-26	3	3.63	3.82
1999	NYM	NL	77	0	0	42	78.0	312	40	17	16	4	0	0	0	41	4	128	2	0	4	3	.571	0	22-28	17	1.69	1.85
2000	NYM	NL	76	0	0	68	76.0	304	39	24	22	10	2	1	0	38	2	106	0	0	4	4	.500	0	41-46	0	2.08	2.61
2001	NYM	NL	73	0	0	64	76.1	320	59	32	32	12	2	1	1	40	6	93	5	0	6	4	.600	0	43-46	0	3.67	3.77
2002	NYM	NL	62	0	0	52	67.1	275	46	20	17	8	3	2	3	25	0	79	1	0	1	0	1.000	0	33-37	0	2.55	2.27
2003	3 Tms		69	0	0	49	73.0	313	59	27	24	6	0	1	0	41	3	75	3	1	4	4	.500	0	21-29	5	3.45	2.96
2004	Fla	NL	64	0	0	59	69.2	262	36	11	10	6	3	1	0	21	4	62	0	0	2	2	.500	0	47-51	4	1.36	1.29
2005	SF	NL	30	0	0	27	30.0	127	25	17	15	5	0	2	0	16	0	23	0	0	2	3	.400	0	19-23	0	4.20	4.50
2006	SF	NL	41	0	0	33	38.1	171	39	15	15	6	1	3	0	21	2	31	1	0	4	2	.667	0	17-25	1	5.11	3.52
03	NYM	NL	45	0	0	40	49.1	209	41	18	17	5	0	1	0	24	1	50	3	1	3	3	.500	0	21-28	3	3.46	3.10
03	NYY	AL	9	0	0	2	9.1	40	8	4	2	0	0	0	0	6	1	10	0	0	1	1	.500	0	0-0	4	3.40	1.93
03	Sea	AL	15	0	0	7	14.1	64	10	5	5	1	0	0	0	11	1	15	0	0	0	0	-	0	0-1	1	3.40	3.14
13 ML YEARS			699	0	0	501	722.1	2999	492	254	237	84	18	21	15	372	30	880	17	2	38	38	.500	0	280-331	53	2.93	2.95

Gary Bennett

Bats: R Throws: R Pos: C-56; PH-4; 1B-1; PR-1   Ht: 6'0" Wt: 210 Born: 4/17/1972 Age: 35

			BATTING																			BASERUNNING				AVERAGES		
Year	Team	Lg	G	AB	H	2B	3B	HR	(Hm	Rd)	TB	R	RBI	RC	TBB	IBB	SO	HBP	SH	SF	SB	CS	SB%	GDP	Avg	OBP	Slg
1995	Phi	NL	1	1	0	0	0	0	(0	0)	0	0	0	0	0	0	1	0	0	0	0	0	-	0	.000	.000	.000
1996	Phi	NL	6	16	4	0	0	0	(0	0)	4	0	1	1	2	1	6	0	0	0	0	0	-	0	.250	.333	.250
1998	Phi	NL	9	31	9	0	0	0	(0	0)	9	4	3	4	5	0	5	0	0	1	0	0	-	1	.290	.378	.290
1999	Phi	NL	36	88	24	4	0	1	(0	1)	31	7	21	7	4	0	11	0	0	2	0	0	-	7	.273	.298	.352
2000	Phi	NL	31	74	18	5	0	2	(0	2)	29	8	5	12	13	0	15	2	0	0	0	0	-	0	.243	.371	.392
2001	3 Tms		46	131	32	6	1	2	(2	0)	46	15	10	15	12	4	24	1	2	2	0	0	-	0	.244	.308	.351
2002	Col	NL	90	291	77	10	2	4	(2	2)	103	26	26	29	15	2	45	6	2	0	1	3	.25	10	.265	.314	.354
2003	SD	NL	96	307	73	15	0	2	(1	1)	94	26	42	33	24	3	48	2	3	2	3	0	1.00	8	.238	.296	.306
2004	Mil	NL	75	219	49	14	0	3	(3	0)	72	18	20	15	22	3	32	2	0	3	1	0	1.00	9	.224	.297	.329
2005	Was	NL	68	199	44	7	0	1	(1	0)	54	11	21	17	21	3	37	2	3	3	0	1	.00	7	.221	.298	.271
2006	StL	NL	60	157	35	5	0	4	(2	2)	52	13	22	13	11	2	30	0	2	0	0	0	-	3	.223	.274	.331
01	Phi	NL	26	75	16	3	1	1	(1	0)	24	8	6	7	9	1	19	0	1	1	0	0	-	0	.213	.294	.320
01	NYM	NL	1	1	1	0	0	0	(0	0)	1	0	0	1	0	0	0	0	0	0	0	0	-	0	1.000	1.000	1.000
01	Col	NL	19	55	15	3	0	1	(1	0)	21	7	4	7	3	3	5	1	1	1	0	0	-	0	.273	.317	.382
11 ML YEARS			518	1514	365	66	3	19	(11	8)	494	128	171	146	129	18	254	15	12	13	5	4	.56	46	.241	.305	.326

Joaquin Benoit

Pitches: R Bats: R Pos: RP-56   Ht: 6'3" Wt: 220 Born: 7/26/1977 Age: 29

			HOW MUCH HE PITCHED						WHAT HE GAVE UP										THE RESULTS							
Year	Team	Lg	G	GS	CG	GF	IP	BFP	H	R	ER	HR	SH	SF	HB	TBB	IBB	SO	WP	Bk	W	L	Pct	ShO	Sv-Op	Hld	ERC	ERA
2001	Tex	AL	1	1	0	0	5.0	26	8	6	6	3	0	1	0	3	0	4	0	0	0	0	-	0	0-0	0	13.11	10.80
2002	Tex	AL	17	13	0	2	84.2	405	91	51	50	6	4	3	5	58	2	59	7	0	4	5	.444	0	1-1	0	5.52	5.31
2003	Tex	AL	25	17	0	1	105.0	462	99	67	64	23	1	4	3	51	0	87	3	1	8	5	.615	0	0-0	0	5.03	5.49
2004	Tex	AL	28	15	0	2	103.0	456	113	67	65	19	2	10	8	31	0	95	3	0	3	5	.375	0	0-0	0	5.10	5.68
2005	Tex	AL	32	9	0	6	87.0	369	69	39	36	9	2	1	2	38	0	78	1	0	4	4	.500	0	0-5	5	3.15	3.72
2006	Tex	AL	56	0	0	7	79.2	347	68	49	43	5	0	3	3	38	4	85	3	0	1	1	.500	0	0-2	7	3.30	4.86
6 ML YEARS			159	55	0	18	464.1	2065	448	279	264	65	9	22	21	219	6	408	17	1	20	20	.500	0	1-3	12	4.54	5.12

Kris Benson

Pitches: R Bats: R Pos: SP-30   Ht: 6'4" Wt: 205 Born: 11/7/1974 Age: 32

			HOW MUCH HE PITCHED						WHAT HE GAVE UP										THE RESULTS							
Year	Team	Lg	G	GS	CG	GF	IP	BFP	H	R	ER	HR	SH	SF	HB	TBB	IBB	SO	WP	Bk	W	L	Pct	ShO	Sv-Op	Hld	ERC	ERA
1999	Pit	NL	31	31	2	0	196.2	840	184	105	89	16	6	7	6	83	5	139	2	1	11	14	.440	0	0-0	0	3.78	4.07
2000	Pit	NL	32	32	2	0	217.2	936	206	104	93	24	7	6	10	86	5	184	5	0	10	12	.455	1	0-0	0	3.97	3.85
2002	Pit	NL	25	25	0	0	130.1	576	152	76	68	18	5	3	3	50	8	79	3	1	9	6	.600	0	0-0	0	5.31	4.70
2003	Pit	NL	18	18	0	0	105.0	475	127	67	58	14	3	4	1	36	4	68	7	0	5	9	.357	0	0-0	0	5.20	4.97
2004	2 Tms		31	31	1	0	200.1	854	202	106	96	15	8	6	10	61	8	134	5	0	12	12	.500	1	0-0	0	3.71	4.31
2005	NYM	NL	28	28	0	0	174.1	737	171	86	80	24	5	3	4	49	5	95	4	0	10	8	.556	0	0-0	0	3.78	4.13
2006	Bal	AL	30	30	3	0	183.0	781	199	105	98	33	9	13	7	58	2	88	6	0	11	12	.478	0	0-0	0	5.06	4.82
04	Pit	NL	20	20	0	0	132.1	564	137	69	62	7	7	4	6	44	5	83	2	0	8	8	.500	0	0-0	0	3.84	4.22
04	NYM	NL	11	11	1	0	68.0	290	65	37	34	8	1	2	4	17	3	51	3	0	4	4	.500	1	0-0	0	3.45	4.50
7 ML YEARS			195	195	8	0	1207.1	5199	1241	649	582	144	43	42	41	423	37	787	32	2	68	73	.482	0	0-0	0	4.27	4.34

Jason Bergmann

Pitches: R Bats: R Pos: RP-23; SP-6   Ht: 6'4" Wt: 190 Born: 9/25/1981 Age: 25

			HOW MUCH HE PITCHED						WHAT HE GAVE UP										THE RESULTS							
Year	Team	Lg	G	GS	CG	GF	IP	BFP	H	R	ER	HR	SH	SF	HB	TBB	IBB	SO	WP	Bk	W	L	Pct	ShO	Sv-Op	Hld	ERC	ERA
2003	Savann	A	23	22	1	0	109.0	488	108	57	52	8	1	2	11	53	0	82	10	0	6	11	.353	1	0--	-	4.56	4.29
2004	Savann	A	13	13	0	0	65.0	296	67	44	35	6	3	7	7	34	0	58	6	1	3	7	.300	0	0--	-	5.12	4.85
2004	BrvdCt	A+	24	0	0	21	31.2	133	20	7	4	0	1	2	2	18	3	28	2	0	3	2	.600	0	8--	-	2.16	1.14
2004	Hrsbrg	AA	2	0	0	1	4.0	21	7	5	4	3	0	0	0	2	1	3	1	0	0	2	.000	0	0--	-	14.59	9.00
2005	Hrsbrg	AA	21	0	0	8	37.0	154	27	7	5	3	0	0	2	16	1	37	2	0	2	0	1.000	0	5--	-	2.78	1.22

39

	HOW MUCH HE PITCHED						WHAT HE GAVE UP												THE RESULTS							
Year Team Lg	G	GS	CG	GF	IP	BFP	H	R	ER	HR	SH	SF	HB	TBB	IBB	SO	WP	Bk	W	L	Pct	ShO	Sv-Op	Hld	ERC	ERA
2005 NewOr AAA	20	0	0	9	37.0	150	26	15	13	5	3	3	3	13	1	39	1	0	3	2	.600	0	2--	-	2.82	3.16
2006 NewOr AAA	26	4	0	8	60.1	248	54	22	22	5	3	3	1	20	2	62	3	1	8	2	.800	0	4--	-	3.19	3.28
2005 Was NL	15	1	0	4	19.2	85	14	6	6	1	1	1	2	11	1	21	0	0	2	0	1.000	0	0-0	1	3.05	2.75
2006 Was NL	29	6	0	7	64.2	303	81	49	48	12	6	4	6	27	6	54	3	0	0	2	.000	0	0-0	1	6.50	6.68
2 ML YEARS	44	7	0	11	84.1	388	95	55	54	13	7	5	8	38	7	75	3	0	2	2	.500	0	0-0	2	5.63	5.76

Lance Berkman

Bats: B **Throws:** L **Pos:** 1B-112; RF-42; LF-5; PH-5; DH-3   **Ht:** 6'1" **Wt:** 220 **Born:** 2/10/1976 **Age:** 31

	BATTING																	BASERUNNING				AVERAGES		
Year Team Lg	G	AB	H	2B	3B	HR	(Hm	Rd)	TB	R	RBI	RC	TBB	IBB	SO	HBP	SH	SF	SB	CS	SB%	GDP	Avg	OBP	Slg
1999 Hou NL	34	93	22	2	0	4	(2	2)	36	10	15	12	12	0	21	0	0	1	5	1	.83	2	.237	.321	.387
2000 Hou NL	114	353	105	28	1	21	(10	11)	198	76	67	76	56	1	73	1	0	7	6	2	.75	6	.297	.388	.561
2001 Hou NL	156	577	191	55	5	34	(13	21)	358	110	126	144	92	5	121	13	0	6	7	9	.44	8	.331	.430	.620
2002 Hou NL	158	578	169	35	2	42	(20	22)	334	106	128	130	107	20	118	4	0	3	8	4	.67	10	.292	.405	.578
2003 Hou NL	153	538	155	35	6	25	(11	14)	277	110	93	115	107	13	108	9	1	3	5	3	.63	10	.288	.412	.515
2004 Hou NL	160	544	172	40	3	30	(8	22)	308	104	106	126	127	14	101	10	0	6	9	7	.56	11	.316	.450	.566
2005 Hou NL	132	468	137	34	1	24	(13	11)	245	76	82	88	91	12	72	4	0	2	4	1	.80	18	.293	.411	.524
2006 Hou NL	152	536	169	29	0	45	(24	21)	333	95	136	138	98	22	106	4	0	8	3	2	.60	11	.315	.420	.621
8 ML YEARS	1059	3687	1120	258	18	225	(101	124)	2089	687	753	829	690	87	720	45	1	36	47	29	.62	76	.304	.416	.567

Adam Bernero

Pitches: R **Bats:** R **Pos:** SP-3; RP-1   **Ht:** 6'4" **Wt:** 225 **Born:** 11/28/1976 **Age:** 30

	HOW MUCH HE PITCHED						WHAT HE GAVE UP												THE RESULTS							
Year Team Lg	G	GS	CG	GF	IP	BFP	H	R	ER	HR	SH	SF	HB	TBB	IBB	SO	WP	Bk	W	L	Pct	ShO	Sv-Op	Hld	ERC	ERA
2006 S-WB* AAA	5	5	1	0	25.0	89	11	5	5	2	0	0	1	4	0	17	0	0	1	1	.500	0	0--	-	0.97	1.80
2006 Omha* AAA	16	12	1	2	79.1	301	64	27	25	5	1	0	2	23	0	47	0	0	5	3	.625	0	1--	-	2.72	2.84
2000 Det AL	12	4	0	4	34.1	141	33	18	16	3	2	3	1	13	1	20	1	0	1	0	1.000	0	0-0	1	3.94	4.19
2001 Det AL	5	0	0	4	12.1	56	13	13	10	4	0	1	1	4	0	8	1	0	0	0	-	0	0-0	0	5.79	7.30
2002 Det AL	28	11	0	5	101.2	459	128	74	70	17	3	5	6	31	1	69	5	1	4	7	.364	0	0-0	0	5.95	6.20
2003 2 Tms	49	17	0	5	133.1	589	137	90	87	19	5	8	8	54	1	80	3	0	1	14	.067	0	0-2	5	4.77	5.87
2004 Col NL	16	2	0	4	32.1	147	36	20	20	7	0	3	0	17	2	21	0	0	1	1	.500	0	0-1	1	6.03	5.57
2005 Atl NL	36	0	0	12	47.0	216	61	35	34	5	2	3	4	12	3	37	1	0	4	3	.571	0	0-1	4	5.42	6.51
2006 2 Tms	4	3	0	0	15.0	68	22	10	10	3	0	0	0	2	0	12	0	0	1	1	.500	0	0-0	0	6.43	6.00
03 Det AL	18	17	0	0	100.2	447	104	68	68	14	3	6	7	41	0	54	1	0	1	12	.077	0	0-0	0	4.83	6.08
03 Col NL	31	0	0	5	32.2	142	33	22	19	5	2	2	1	13	1	26	2	0	0	2	.000	0	0-2	5	4.58	5.23
06 Phi NL	1	1	0	0	2.0	15	7	8	8	3	0	0	0	2	0	0	0	0	0	1	.000	0	0-0	0	43.36	36.00
06 KC AL	3	2	0	0	13.0	53	15	2	2	0	0	0	0	0	0	12	0	0	1	0	1.000	0	0-0	0	2.72	1.38
7 ML YEARS	150	37	0	34	376.0	1676	430	260	247	58	12	23	20	133	8	247	11	1	11	27	.289	0	0-4	11	5.29	5.91

Angel Berroa

Bats: R **Throws:** R **Pos:** SS-131; PH-2   **Ht:** 6'0" **Wt:** 190 **Born:** 1/27/1978 **Age:** 29

	BATTING																	BASERUNNING				AVERAGES		
Year Team Lg	G	AB	H	2B	3B	HR	(Hm	Rd)	TB	R	RBI	RC	TBB	IBB	SO	HBP	SH	SF	SB	CS	SB%	GDP	Avg	OBP	Slg
2001 KC AL	15	53	16	2	0	0	(0	0)	18	8	4	6	3	0	10	0	0	0	2	0	1.00	2	.302	.339	.340
2002 KC AL	20	75	17	7	1	0	(0	0)	26	8	5	8	7	1	10	1	0	0	3	0	1.00	1	.227	.301	.347
2003 KC AL	158	567	163	28	7	17	(6	11)	256	92	73	82	29	3	100	18	13	8	21	5	.81	13	.287	.338	.451
2004 KC AL	134	512	134	27	6	8	(3	5)	197	72	43	62	23	0	87	12	5	2	14	8	.64	10	.262	.308	.385
2005 KC AL	159	608	164	21	5	11	(6	5)	228	68	55	68	18	3	108	14	10	2	7	5	.58	13	.270	.305	.375
2006 KC AL	132	474	111	18	1	9	(6	3)	158	45	54	32	14	1	88	3	9	3	3	1	.75	21	.234	.259	.333
6 ML YEARS	618	2289	605	103	20	45	(21	24)	883	293	234	258	94	8	403	48	37	15	50	19	.72	60	.264	.305	.386

Rafael Betancourt

Pitches: R **Bats:** R **Pos:** RP-50   **Ht:** 6'2" **Wt:** 200 **Born:** 4/29/1975 **Age:** 32

	HOW MUCH HE PITCHED						WHAT HE GAVE UP												THE RESULTS							
Year Team Lg	G	GS	CG	GF	IP	BFP	H	R	ER	HR	SH	SF	HB	TBB	IBB	SO	WP	Bk	W	L	Pct	ShO	Sv-Op	Hld	ERC	ERA
2006 Akron* AA	1	1	0	0	1.0	4	0	0	0	0	0	0	0	1	0	2	0	0	0	0	-	0	0--	-	0.95	0.00
2003 Cle AL	33	0	0	13	38.0	154	27	11	9	5	1	1	1	13	2	36	1	0	2	2	.500	0	1-3	4	2.54	2.13
2004 Cle AL	68	0	0	21	66.2	286	71	32	29	7	1	2	0	18	6	76	5	1	5	6	.455	0	4-11	12	3.77	3.92
2005 Cle AL	54	0	0	12	67.2	272	57	23	21	5	1	0	0	17	5	73	0	0	4	3	.571	0	1-3	10	2.49	2.79
2006 Cle AL	50	0	0	17	56.2	231	52	25	24	7	2	2	0	11	5	48	0	0	3	4	.429	0	3-6	7	2.84	3.81
4 ML YEARS	205	0	0	63	229.0	943	207	91	83	24	5	5	1	59	15	233	6	1	14	15	.483	0	9-23	33	2.95	3.26

Yuniesky Betancourt

Bats: R **Throws:** R **Pos:** SS-157   **Ht:** 5'10" **Wt:** 190 **Born:** 1/31/1982 **Age:** 25

	BATTING																	BASERUNNING				AVERAGES		
Year Team Lg	G	AB	H	2B	3B	HR	(Hm	Rd)	TB	R	RBI	RC	TBB	IBB	SO	HBP	SH	SF	SB	CS	SB%	GDP	Avg	OBP	Slg
2005 SnAnt AA	52	227	62	10	3	6	(-	-)	93	25	20	28	9	1	18	1	0	2	12	7	.63	2	.273	.301	.410
2005 Tacom AAA	49	183	54	9	6	2	(-	-)	81	13	30	26	6	0	14	2	2	1	5	5	.58	3	.295	.323	.443
2005 Sea AL	60	211	54	11	5	1	(1	0)	78	24	15	21	11	0	24	2	2	2	1	3	.25	2	.256	.296	.370
2006 Sea AL	157	558	161	28	6	8	(2	6)	225	68	47	60	17	0	54	1	7	1	11	8	.58	10	.289	.310	.403
2 ML YEARS	217	769	215	39	11	9	(3	6)	303	92	62	81	28	0	78	3	9	3	12	11	.52	12	.280	.306	.394

Wilson Betemit

Bats: B Throws: R Pos: 3B-79; PH-46; SS-18; 2B-10; DH-1; PR-1   Ht: 6'3" Wt: 200 Born: 7/28/1980 Age: 26

Year	Team	Lg	G	AB	H	2B	3B	HR	(Hm	Rd)	TB	R	RBI	RC	TBB	IBB	SO	HBP	SH	SF	SB	CS	SB%	GDP	Avg	OBP	Slg
2001	Atl	NL	8	3	0	0	0	0	(0	0)	0	1	0	0	2	0	3	0	0	0	1	0	1.00	0	.000	.400	.000
2004	Atl	NL	22	47	8	0	0	0	(0	0)	8	2	3	0	4	0	16	0	0	1	0	1	.00	0	.170	.231	.170
2005	Atl	NL	115	246	75	12	4	4	(0	4)	107	36	20	36	22	4	55	0	4	2	1	3	.25	5	.305	.359	.435
2006	2 Tms		143	373	98	23	0	18	(7	11)	175	49	53	52	36	6	102	0	1	2	3	1	.75	11	.263	.326	.469
06	Atl	NL	88	199	56	16	0	9	(3	6)	99	30	29	35	19	3	57	0	1	0	2	1	.67	4	.281	.344	.497
06	LAD	NL	55	174	42	7	0	9	(4	5)	76	19	24	17	17	3	45	0	0	2	1	0	1.00	7	.241	.306	.437
4 ML YEARS			288	669	181	35	4	22	(7	15)	290	88	76	88	64	10	176	0	5	5	5	5	.50	16	.271	.332	.433

Larry Bigbie

Bats: L Throws: R Pos: LF-11; PH-9; RF-1   Ht: 6'4" Wt: 215 Born: 11/4/1977 Age: 29

Year	Team	Lg	G	AB	H	2B	3B	HR	(Hm	Rd)	TB	R	RBI	RC	TBB	IBB	SO	HBP	SH	SF	SB	CS	SB%	GDP	Avg	OBP	Slg
2006	QuadC*	A	4	14	5	0	0	0	(-	-)	5	2	1	2	2	0	4	0	0	0	0	0	-	1	.357	.438	.357
2006	Sprgfld*	AA	6	14	4	0	0	1	(-	-)	7	3	2	3	5	0	5	0	0	1	0	0	-	1	.286	.450	.500
2006	Memp*	AAA	11	35	5	0	0	0	(-	-)	5	4	0	1	7	0	14	0	0	0	0	1	.00	2	.143	.286	.143
2001	Bal	AL	47	131	30	6	0	2	(0	2)	42	15	11	14	17	1	42	0	1	0	4	1	.80	2	.229	.318	.321
2002	Bal	AL	16	34	6	1	0	0	(0	0)	7	1	3	1	1	0	11	0	0	1	1	0	1.00	1	.176	.194	.206
2003	Bal	AL	83	287	87	15	1	9	(4	5)	131	43	31	47	29	3	60	1	0	2	7	1	.88	2	.303	.365	.456
2004	Bal	AL	139	478	134	23	1	15	(8	7)	204	76	68	65	45	0	113	1	3	4	8	3	.73	7	.280	.341	.427
2005	2 Tms		90	272	65	10	2	5	(3	2)	94	27	23	28	24	1	67	1	5	2	5	3	.63	2	.239	.301	.346
2006	StL	NL	17	25	6	1	0	0	(0	0)	7	2	1	3	3	0	9	0	0	0	0	0	-	1	.240	.321	.280
05	Bal	AL	67	206	51	9	1	5	(3	2)	77	22	21	23	21	1	49	0	5	2	3	3	.50	2	.248	.314	.374
05	Col	NL	23	66	14	1	1	0	(0	0)	17	5	2	5	3	0	18	1	0	0	2	0	1.00	0	.212	.257	.258
6 ML YEARS			392	1227	328	56	4	31	(15	16)	485	164	137	158	119	5	302	2	10	9	25	8	.76	15	.267	.331	.395

Craig Biggio

Bats: R Throws: R Pos: 2B-129; PH-13; DH-5   Ht: 5'11" Wt: 185 Born: 12/14/1965 Age: 41

Year	Team	Lg	G	AB	H	2B	3B	HR	(Hm	Rd)	TB	R	RBI	RC	TBB	IBB	SO	HBP	SH	SF	SB	CS	SB%	GDP	Avg	OBP	Slg
1988	Hou	NL	50	123	26	6	1	3	(1	2)	43	14	5	11	7	2	29	0	1	0	6	1	.86	1	.211	.254	.350
1989	Hou	NL	134	443	114	21	2	13	(6	7)	178	64	60	64	49	8	64	6	6	5	21	3	.88	7	.257	.336	.402
1990	Hou	NL	150	555	153	24	2	4	(2	2)	193	53	42	68	53	1	79	3	9	1	25	11	.69	11	.276	.342	.348
1991	Hou	NL	149	546	161	23	4	4	(0	4)	204	79	46	79	53	3	71	2	5	3	19	6	.76	2	.295	.358	.374
1992	Hou	NL	162	613	170	32	3	6	(3	3)	226	96	39	95	94	9	95	7	5	2	38	15	.72	5	.277	.378	.369
1993	Hou	NL	155	610	175	41	5	21	(8	13)	289	98	64	105	77	7	93	10	4	5	15	17	.47	10	.287	.373	.474
1994	Hou	NL	114	437	139	44	5	6	(4	2)	211	88	56	94	62	1	58	8	2	2	39	4	.91	5	.318	.411	.483
1995	Hou	NL	141	553	167	30	2	22	(6	16)	267	123	77	116	80	1	85	22	11	7	33	8	.80	6	.302	.406	.483
1996	Hou	NL	162	605	174	24	4	15	(7	8)	251	113	75	105	75	0	72	27	8	8	25	7	.78	10	.288	.386	.415
1997	Hou	NL	162	619	191	37	8	22	(7	15)	310	146	81	139	84	6	107	34	0	7	47	10	.82	6	.309	.415	.501
1998	Hou	NL	160	646	210	51	2	20	(10	10)	325	123	88	135	64	6	113	23	1	4	50	8	.86	10	.325	.403	.503
1999	Hou	NL	160	639	188	56	0	16	(10	6)	292	123	73	117	88	9	107	11	5	6	28	14	.67	5	.294	.386	.457
2000	Hou	NL	101	377	101	13	5	8	(2	6)	148	67	35	63	61	3	73	16	7	5	12	2	.86	10	.268	.388	.393
2001	Hou	NL	155	617	180	35	3	20	(10	10)	281	118	70	109	66	4	100	28	0	6	7	4	.64	11	.292	.382	.455
2002	Hou	NL	145	577	146	36	3	15	(7	8)	233	96	58	71	50	2	111	17	9	2	16	2	.89	15	.253	.330	.404
2003	Hou	NL	153	628	166	44	2	15	(6	9)	259	102	62	97	57	3	116	27	3	2	8	4	.67	4	.264	.350	.412
2004	Hou	NL	156	633	178	47	0	24	(13	11)	297	100	63	88	40	0	94	15	9	3	7	2	.78	8	.281	.337	.469
2005	Hou	NL	155	590	156	40	1	26	(19	7)	276	94	69	80	37	2	90	17	4	3	11	1	.92	10	.264	.325	.468
2006	Hou	NL	145	548	135	33	0	21	(15	6)	231	79	62	62	40	1	84	9	5	5	3	2	.60	16	.246	.306	.422
19 ML YEARS			2709	10359	2930	637	52	281	(136	145)	4514	1776	1125	1698	1137	68	1641	282	94	76	410	121	.77	146	.283	.367	.436

Chad Billingsley

Pitches: R Bats: R Pos: SP-16; RP-2   Ht: 6'0" Wt: 245 Born: 7/29/1984 Age: 22

Year	Team	Lg	G	GS	CG	GF	IP	BFP	H	R	ER	HR	SH	SF	HB	TBB	IBB	SO	WP	Bk	W	L	Pct	ShO	Sv-Op	Hld	ERC	ERA
2003	Ogden	R+	11	11	0	0	54.0	225	49	24	17	0	3	2	3	15	0	62	8	0	5	4	.556	0	0--	-	2.66	2.83
2004	VeroB	A+	18	18	0	0	92.0	386	68	32	24	6	6	2	2	49	0	111	3	0	7	4	.636	0	0--	-	3.03	2.35
2004	Jaxnvl	AA	8	8	0	0	42.1	169	32	16	14	1	1	0	1	22	0	47	2	0	4	0	1.000	0	0--	-	2.97	2.98
2005	Jaxnvl	AA	28	26	2	0	146.0	604	116	60	57	12	5	3	4	50	0	162	10	0	13	6	.684	1	0--	-	2.72	3.51
2006	LsVgs	AAA	13	13	0	0	70.2	297	57	32	31	7	2	2	3	32	0	78	4	0	6	3	.667	0	0--	-	3.40	3.95
2006	LAD	NL	18	16	0	0	90.0	403	92	43	38	7	4	0	3	58	3	59	5	0	7	4	.636	0	0-0	-	5.22	3.80

Kurt Birkins

Pitches: L Bats: L Pos: RP-35   Ht: 6'2" Wt: 190 Born: 8/11/1980 Age: 26

Year	Team	Lg	G	GS	CG	GF	IP	BFP	H	R	ER	HR	SH	SF	HB	TBB	IBB	SO	WP	Bk	W	L	Pct	ShO	Sv-Op	Hld	ERC	ERA
2001	Orioles	R	5	4	0	1	22.0	85	13	5	5	2	0	4	2	3	0	24	1	0	2	1	.667	0	0--	-	1.69	2.05
2001	Bluefld	R+	6	6	0	0	37.0	144	28	14	12	2	1	0	2	5	0	42	3	0	4	1	.800	0	0--	-	1.81	2.92
2002	Dlmrva	A	27	25	3	0	143.2	607	140	66	56	10	6	1	10	46	1	102	7	0	9	7	.563	0	0--	-	3.72	3.51
2003	Frdrck	A+	25	25	0	0	126.1	576	152	82	66	10	5	6	13	40	0	79	12	0	8	11	.421	0	0--	-	5.12	4.70
2004	Frdrck	A+	27	6	0	8	68.0	291	70	36	34	9	2	5	2	22	1	55	3	0	5	2	.714	0	2--	-	4.27	4.50
2005	Bowie	AA	26	24	0	0	129.0	552	134	69	56	8	5	2	11	42	0	114	10	0	7	11	.389	0	0--	-	4.14	3.91
2006	Abrdn	A-	2	0	0	0	2.2	10	3	1	1	0	0	1	1	0	0	2	0	0	1	1	.500	0	0--	-	4.72	3.38
2006	Frdrck	A+	1	0	0	0	1.0	3	0	0	0	0	0	0	0	1	0	1	0	0	0	0	-	0	0--	-	1.26	0.00

Year	Team	Lg	G	GS	CG	GF	IP	BFP	H	R	ER	HR	SH	SF	HB	TBB	IBB	SO	WP	Bk	W	L	Pct	ShO	Sv-Op	Hld	ERC	ERA
													WHAT HE GAVE UP											**THE RESULTS**				
2006	Bowie	AA	2	0	0	0	4.0	17	5	4	4	2	0	0	0	1	0	5	0	0	0	1	.000	0	0- -	-	8.20	9.00
2006	Ottawa	AAA	5	5	0	0	25.1	101	20	10	9	2	0	0	1	11	0	19	0	0	1	3	.250	0	0- -	-	3.26	3.20
2006	Bal	AL	35	0	0	4	31.0	136	25	19	17	4	2	2	3	16	0	27	3	0	5	2	.714	0	0-1	4	3.98	4.94

Casey Blake

Bats: R **Throws:** R **Pos:** RF-93; 1B-9; DH-8; PH-1 **Ht:** 6'2" **Wt:** 210 **Born:** 8/23/1973 **Age:** 33

Year	Team	Lg	G	AB	H	2B	3B	HR	(Hm	Rd)	TB	R	RBI	RC	TBB	IBB	SO	HBP	SH	SF	SB	CS	SB%	GDP	Avg	OBP	Slg
							BATTING														**BASERUNNING**				**AVERAGES**		
2006	Lk Cty*	A	1	2	1	0	0	1	(-	-)	4	1	2	2	2	0	0	0	0	0	0	0	-	0	.500	.750	2.000
2006	Akron*	AA	1	3	1	1	0	0	(-	-)	2	0	1	0	0	0	0	0	0	0	0	0	-	0	.333	.333	.667
1999	Tor	AL	14	39	10	2	0	1	(0	1)	15	6	1	4	2	0	7	0	0	0	0	0	-	1	.256	.293	.385
2000	Min	AL	7	16	3	2	0	0	(0	0)	5	1	1	2	3	0	7	1	0	1	0	0	-	0	.188	.333	.313
2001	2 Tms	AL	19	37	9	1	0	1	(0	1)	13	3	4	5	4	1	12	0	0	0	3	0	1.00	0	.243	.317	.351
2002	Min	AL	9	20	4	1	0	0	(0	0)	5	2	1	1	2	0	7	0	0	0	0	0	-	0	.200	.273	.250
2003	Cle	AL	152	557	143	35	0	17	(2	15)	229	80	67	68	38	1	109	10	8	8	7	9	.44	11	.257	.312	.411
2004	Cle	AL	152	587	159	36	3	28	(13	15)	285	93	88	88	68	2	139	9	1	3	5	8	.38	19	.271	.354	.486
2005	Cle	AL	147	523	126	32	1	23	(7	16)	229	72	58	53	43	3	116	10	2	5	4	5	.44	9	.241	.308	.438
2006	Cle	AL	109	401	113	20	1	19	(9	10)	192	63	68	62	45	5	93	4	1	5	6	0	1.00	11	.282	.356	.479
01	Min	AL	13	22	7	1	0	0	(0	0)	8	1	2	4	3	1	8	0	0	0	1	0	1.00	0	.318	.400	.364
01	Bal	AL	6	15	2	0	0	1	(0	1)	5	2	2	1	1	0	4	0	0	0	2	0	1.00	0	.133	.188	.333
	8 ML YEARS		609	2180	567	129	5	89	(31	58)	973	320	288	283	205	12	490	34	12	22	25	22	.53	52	.260	.330	.446

Hank Blalock

Bats: L **Throws:** R **Pos:** 3B-122; DH-29; PH-2 **Ht:** 6'1" **Wt:** 200 **Born:** 11/21/1980 **Age:** 26

Year	Team	Lg	G	AB	H	2B	3B	HR	(Hm	Rd)	TB	R	RBI	RC	TBB	IBB	SO	HBP	SH	SF	SB	CS	SB%	GDP	Avg	OBP	Slg
							BATTING														**BASERUNNING**				**AVERAGES**		
2002	Tex	AL	49	147	31	8	0	3	(2	1)	48	16	17	15	20	1	43	1	2	2	0	0	-	2	.211	.306	.327
2003	Tex	AL	143	567	170	33	3	29	(18	11)	296	89	90	90	44	1	97	1	0	3	2	3	.40	17	.300	.350	.522
2004	Tex	AL	159	624	172	38	3	32	(16	16)	312	107	110	119	75	7	149	6	0	8	2	2	.50	13	.276	.355	.500
2005	Tex	AL	161	647	170	34	0	25	(20	5)	279	80	92	86	51	1	132	3	0	4	1	0	1.00	16	.263	.318	.431
2006	Tex	AL	152	591	157	26	3	16	(8	8)	237	76	89	87	51	6	98	2	0	2	1	0	1.00	15	.266	.325	.401
	5 ML YEARS		664	2576	700	139	9	105	(64	41)	1172	368	398	397	241	16	519	13	2	19	6	5	.55	63	.272	.335	.455

Andres Blanco

Bats: B **Throws:** R **Pos:** SS-25; 2B-7; PR-3; DH-1; PH-1 **Ht:** 5'10" **Wt:** 185 **Born:** 4/11/1984 **Age:** 23

Year	Team	Lg	G	AB	H	2B	3B	HR	(Hm	Rd)	TB	R	RBI	RC	TBB	IBB	SO	HBP	SH	SF	SB	CS	SB%	GDP	Avg	OBP	Slg
							BATTING														**BASERUNNING**				**AVERAGES**		
2006	Omha*	AAA	88	283	67	9	4	2	(-	-)	90	30	20	29	21	0	41	9	5	1	6	4	.60	7	.237	.309	.318
2004	KC	AL	19	60	19	2	2	0	(0	0)	25	9	5	12	5	0	6	1	1	0	1	2	.33	0	.317	.379	.417
2005	KC	AL	26	79	17	0	1	0	(0	0)	19	6	5	3	0	0	5	1	4	2	0	1	.00	3	.215	.220	.241
2006	KC	AL	33	87	21	4	1	0	(0	0)	27	9	9	9	5	0	14	1	3	0	0	1	.00	2	.241	.290	.310
	3 ML YEARS		78	226	57	6	4	0	(0	0)	71	24	19	24	10	0	25	3	8	2	1	4	.20	5	.252	.290	.314

Henry Blanco

Bats: R **Throws:** R **Pos:** C-69; 1B-6; PH-2 **Ht:** 5'11" **Wt:** 220 **Born:** 8/29/1971 **Age:** 35

Year	Team	Lg	G	AB	H	2B	3B	HR	(Hm	Rd)	TB	R	RBI	RC	TBB	IBB	SO	HBP	SH	SF	SB	CS	SB%	GDP	Avg	OBP	Slg
							BATTING														**BASERUNNING**				**AVERAGES**		
1997	LAD	NL	3	5	2	0	0	1	(0	1)	5	1	1	2	0	0	1	0	0	0	0	0	-	0	.400	.400	1.000
1999	Col	NL	88	263	61	12	3	6	(3	3)	97	30	28	32	34	1	38	1	3	2	1	1	.50	4	.232	.320	.369
2000	Mil	NL	93	284	67	24	0	7	(3	4)	112	29	31	33	36	6	60	0	0	4	0	3	.00	9	.236	.318	.394
2001	Mil	NL	104	314	66	18	3	6	(4	2)	108	33	31	30	34	6	72	2	5	2	3	1	.75	10	.210	.290	.344
2002	Atl	NL	81	221	45	9	1	6	(4	2)	74	17	22	15	20	5	51	1	2	5	0	2	.00	5	.204	.267	.335
2003	Atl	NL	55	151	30	8	0	1	(0	1)	41	11	13	13	10	2	21	1	3	1	0	0	-	3	.199	.252	.272
2004	Min	NL	114	315	65	19	1	10	(4	6)	116	36	37	25	21	0	56	3	11	3	0	3	.00	8	.206	.260	.368
2005	ChC	NL	54	161	39	6	0	6	(2	4)	63	16	25	17	11	1	24	0	4	2	0	0	-	6	.242	.287	.391
2006	ChC	NL	74	241	64	15	2	6	(2	4)	101	23	37	26	14	1	38	0	4	2	0	0	-	8	.266	.304	.419
	9 ML YEARS		666	1955	439	111	10	49	(22	27)	717	196	225	193	180	22	361	8	32	21	4	10	.29	53	.225	.290	.367

Joe Blanton

Pitches: R **Bats:** R **Pos:** SP-31; RP-1 **Ht:** 6'3" **Wt:** 240 **Born:** 12/11/1980 **Age:** 26

Year	Team	Lg	G	GS	CG	GF	IP	BFP	H	R	ER	HR	SH	SF	HB	TBB	IBB	SO	WP	Bk	W	L	Pct	ShO	Sv-Op	Hld	ERC	ERA
				HOW MUCH HE PITCHED									**WHAT HE GAVE UP**										**THE RESULTS**				
2004	Oak	AL	3	0	0	1	8.0	30	6	5	5	1	0	0	0	2	0	6	0	0	0	0	-	0	0-0	0	2.52	5.63
2005	Oak	AL	33	33	2	0	201.1	835	178	86	79	23	2	7	5	67	3	116	4	2	12	12	.500	0	0-0	0	3.37	3.53
2006	Oak	AL	32	31	1	0	194.1	856	241	111	104	17	3	9	5	58	4	107	3	0	16	12	.571	1	0-0	0	5.09	4.82
	3 ML YEARS		68	64	3	1	403.2	1721	425	202	188	41	5	16	10	127	7	229	7	2	28	24	.538	1	0-0	0	4.16	4.19

Willie Bloomquist

Bats: R Throws: R Pos: CF-48; SS-17; 2B-15; 3B-12; RF-12; PR-10; PH-5; 1B-4; LF-3; DH-1   Ht: 5'11" Wt: 195 Born: 11/27/1977 Age: 29

Year	Team	Lg	G	AB	H	2B	3B	HR	(Hm	Rd)	TB	R	RBI	RC	TBB	IBB	SO	HBP	SH	SF	SB	CS	SB%	GDP	Avg	OBP	Slg
2002	Sea	AL	12	33	15	4	0	0	(0	0)	19	11	7	10	5	0	2	0	0	0	3	1	.75	0	.455	.526	.576
2003	Sea	AL	89	196	49	7	2	1	(1	0)	63	30	14	18	19	1	39	1	2	2	4	1	.80	6	.250	.317	.321
2004	Sea	AL	93	188	46	10	4	2	(0	2)	62	27	18	18	10	0	48	0	3	0	13	2	.87	2	.245	.283	.330
2005	Sea	AL	82	249	64	15	2	0	(0	0)	83	27	22	26	11	0	38	1	4	2	14	1	.93	5	.257	.289	.333
2006	Sea	AL	102	251	62	6	2	1	(0	1)	75	36	15	27	24	0	40	4	2	2	16	3	.84	3	.247	.320	.299
	5 ML YEARS		378	917	236	42	6	4	(1	3)	302	131	76	99	69	1	167	6	11	6	50	8	.86	16	.257	.312	.329

Geoff Blum

Bats: B Throws: R Pos: SS-49; 3B-34; PH-32; 1B-2; 2B-1; RF-1   Ht: 6'3" Wt: 205 Born: 4/26/1973 Age: 34

Year	Team	Lg	G	AB	H	2B	3B	HR	(Hm	Rd)	TB	R	RBI	RC	TBB	IBB	SO	HBP	SH	SF	SB	CS	SB%	GDP	Avg	OBP	Slg
1999	Mon	NL	45	133	32	7	2	8	(0	8)	67	21	18	22	17	3	25	0	3	0	1	0	1.00	3	.241	.327	.504
2000	Mon	NL	124	343	97	20	2	11	(5	6)	154	40	45	50	26	2	60	3	3	4	1	4	.20	4	.283	.335	.449
2001	Mon	NL	148	453	107	25	0	9	(6	3)	159	57	50	49	43	8	94	10	3	5	9	5	.64	12	.236	.313	.351
2002	Hou	NL	130	368	104	20	4	10	(6	4)	162	45	52	62	49	5	70	1	1	2	2	0	1.00	8	.283	.367	.440
2003	Hou	NL	123	420	110	19	0	10	(6	4)	159	51	52	40	20	1	50	2	2	5	0	0	-	15	.262	.295	.379
2004	TB	AL	112	339	73	21	0	8	(2	6)	118	38	35	29	24	1	58	0	4	2	2	3	.40	4	.215	.266	.348
2005	2 Tms		109	319	73	15	2	6	(1	5)	110	32	25	27	28	0	43	3	0	1	3	3	.50	6	.229	.296	.345
2006	SD	NL	109	276	70	17	1	4	(0	4)	101	27	34	26	17	1	51	0	2	4	0	1	.00	5	.254	.293	.366
05	SD	NL	78	224	54	13	1	5	(1	4)	84	26	22	23	24	0	28	3	0	1	3	2	.60	5	.241	.321	.375
05	CWS	AL	31	95	19	2	1	1	(0	1)	26	6	3	4	4	0	15	0	0	0	0	1	.00	1	.200	.232	.274
	8 ML YEARS		900	2651	666	144	11	66	(26	40)	1030	311	311	305	224	21	451	19	18	23	18	16	.53	57	.251	.312	.389

Hiram Bocachica

Bats: R Throws: R Pos: CF-4; RF-3; PR-2; LF-1   Ht: 5'11" Wt: 195 Born: 3/4/1976 Age: 31

Year	Team	Lg	G	AB	H	2B	3B	HR	(Hm	Rd)	TB	R	RBI	RC	TBB	IBB	SO	HBP	SH	SF	SB	CS	SB%	GDP	Avg	OBP	Slg
2006	Stcktn*	A+	4	14	4	2	0	0	(-	-)	6	3	2	1	0	0	4	2	0	0	0	1	.00	0	.286	.375	.429
2006	Scrmto*	AAA	77	291	95	15	3	19	(-	-)	173	61	60	74	43	1	55	7	0	3	18	3	.86	7	.326	.422	.595
2000	LAD	NL	8	10	3	0	0	0	(0	0)	3	2	0	1	0	0	2	0	0	0	0	0	-	0	.300	.300	.300
2001	LAD	NL	75	133	31	11	1	2	(2	0)	50	15	9	15	9	0	33	1	0	0	4	1	.80	1	.233	.287	.376
2002	2 Tms		83	168	37	7	0	8	(2	6)	68	26	17	13	10	0	41	0	1	0	3	3	.50	3	.220	.264	.405
2003	Det	AL	6	22	1	1	0	0	(0	0)	2	1	0	0	0	0	7	0	0	0	0	0	-	0	.045	.045	.091
2004	Sea	AL	50	90	22	5	0	3	(3	0)	36	9	6	9	12	0	27	1	3	1	5	4	.56	1	.244	.337	.400
2005	Oak	AL	9	19	2	0	0	0	(0	0)	2	2	0	0	0	0	7	0	0	0	0	0	-	0	.105	.105	.105
2006	Oak	AL	8	13	3	0	0	0	(0	0)	3	3	0	1	3	0	4	0	0	0	1	0	1.00	0	.231	.375	.231
02	LAD	NL	49	65	14	3	0	4	(1	3)	29	12	9	6	5	0	19	0	0	0	1	1	.50	1	.215	.271	.446
02	Det	AL	34	103	23	4	0	4	(1	3)	39	14	8	7	5	0	22	0	1	0	2	2	.50	2	.223	.259	.379
	7 ML YEARS		239	455	99	24	1	13	(7	6)	164	58	32	39	34	0	121	2	4	1	13	8	.62	5	.218	.274	.360

T.J. Bohn

Bats: R Throws: R Pos: RF-17; PH-2; LF-1; PR-1   Ht: 6'5" Wt: 210 Born: 1/17/1980 Age: 27

Year	Team	Lg	G	AB	H	2B	3B	HR	(Hm	Rd)	TB	R	RBI	RC	TBB	IBB	SO	HBP	SH	SF	SB	CS	SB%	GDP	Avg	OBP	Slg
2002	Everett	A-	62	212	52	10	0	3	(-	-)	71	28	20	27	29	1	53	3	2	3	7	2	.78	4	.245	.340	.335
2003	Wisc	A	128	471	128	31	2	13	(-	-)	202	75	70	80	70	1	131	8	1	6	16	8	.67	5	.272	.371	.429
2004	InldEm	A+	71	240	68	9	3	7	(-	-)	104	46	37	46	44	2	61	9	2	1	6	4	.60	4	.283	.412	.433
2004	SnAnt	AA	62	220	58	9	4	7	(-	-)	96	24	29	34	22	0	46	3	2	2	6	1	.86	1	.264	.336	.436
2005	SnAnt	AA	113	438	135	30	2	12	(-	-)	205	67	57	77	35	1	96	5	7	1	27	9	.75	8	.308	.365	.468
2005	Tacom	AAA	22	81	26	3	0	1	(-	-)	32	15	7	12	2	0	23	3	0	0	4	0	1.00	5	.321	.360	.395
2006	Ms	R	4	16	4	3	1	0	(-	-)	9	4	1	3	1	0	8	0	0	0	3	0	1.00	0	.250	.294	.563
2006	Tacom	AAA	97	378	107	20	1	9	(-	-)	156	53	43	57	33	2	81	4	2	2	15	3	.83	10	.283	.345	.413
2006	Sea	AL	18	14	2	0	0	1	(0	1)	5	2	0	8	1	2	0	8	0	0	0	0	-	0	.143	.250	.357

Jeremy Bonderman

Pitches: R Bats: R Pos: SP-34   Ht: 6'2" Wt: 220 Born: 10/28/1982 Age: 24

			HOW MUCH HE PITCHED					WHAT HE GAVE UP										THE RESULTS						
Year	Team	Lg	G	GS	CG	GF	IP	BFP	H	R	ER	HR	SH	SF	HB	TBB	IBB	SO	WP	Bk	W	L	Pct	ShO	Sv-Op	Hld	ERC	ERA
2003	Det	AL	33	33	1	0	162.0	727	193	118	100	23	3	6	6	58	2	108	12	2	6	19	.240	0	0-0	0	5.39	5.56
2004	Det	AL	33	32	2	0	184.0	793	168	101	100	24	10	5	10	73	5	168	7	0	11	13	.458	2	0-0	0	3.93	4.89
2005	Det	AL	29	29	4	0	189.0	801	199	101	96	21	3	3	4	57	0	145	5	1	14	13	.519	0	0-0	0	4.20	4.57
2006	Det	AL	34	**34**	0	0	214.0	903	214	104	97	18	3	6	3	64	7	202	3	1	14	8	.636	0	0-0	0	3.58	4.08
	4 ML YEARS		129	123	6	0	749.0	3224	774	424	393	86	19	20	21	252	14	623	27	4	45	53	.459	2	0-0	0	4.20	4.72

Barry Bonds

Bats: L Throws: L Pos: LF-116; PH-10; DH-5   Ht: 6'2" Wt: 230 Born: 7/24/1964 Age: 42

Year	Team	Lg	G	AB	H	2B	3B	HR	(Hm	Rd)	TB	R	RBI	RC	TBB	IBB	SO	HBP	SH	SF	SB	CS	SB%	GDP	Avg	OBP	Slg
1986	Pit	NL	113	413	92	26	3	16	(9	7)	172	72	48	64	65	2	102	2	2	2	36	7	.84	4	.223	.330	.416
1987	Pit	NL	150	551	144	34	9	25	(12	13)	271	99	59	92	54	3	88	3	0	3	32	10	.76	4	.261	.329	.492
1988	Pit	NL	144	538	152	30	5	24	(14	10)	264	97	58	97	72	14	82	2	0	2	17	11	.61	3	.283	.368	.491
1989	Pit	NL	159	580	144	34	6	19	(7	12)	247	96	58	91	93	22	93	1	1	4	32	10	.76	9	.248	.351	.426

									BATTING											BASERUNNING				AVERAGES		
Year	Team	Lg	G	AB	H	2B	3B	HR	(Hm Rd)	TB	R	RBI	RC	TBB	IBB	SO	HBP	SH	SF	SB	CS	SB%	GDP	Avg	OBP	Slg
1990	Pit	NL	151	519	156	32	3	33	(14 19)	293	104	114	121	93	15	83	3	0	6	52	13	.80	8	.301	.406	.565
1991	Pit	NL	153	510	149	28	5	25	(12 13)	262	95	116	113	107	25	73	4	0	13	43	13	.77	8	.292	.410	.514
1992	Pit	NL	140	473	147	36	5	34	(15 19)	295	109	103	134	127	32	69	5	0	7	39	8	.83	9	.311	.456	.624
1993	SF	NL	159	539	181	38	4	46	(21 25)	365	129	123	155	126	43	79	2	0	7	29	12	.71	11	.336	.458	.677
1994	SF	NL	112	391	122	18	1	37	(15 22)	253	89	81	105	74	18	43	6	0	3	29	9	.76	3	.312	.426	.647
1995	SF	NL	144	506	149	30	7	33	(16 17)	292	109	104	125	120	22	83	5	0	4	31	10	.76	12	.294	.431	.577
1996	SF	NL	158	517	159	27	3	42	(23 19)	318	122	129	148	151	30	76	1	0	6	40	7	.85	11	.308	.461	.615
1997	SF	NL	159	532	155	26	5	40	(24 16)	311	123	101	140	145	34	87	8	0	5	37	8	.82	13	.291	.446	.585
1998	SF	NL	156	552	167	44	7	37	(21 16)	336	120	122	141	130	29	92	8	1	6	28	12	.70	15	.303	.438	.609
1999	SF	NL	102	355	93	20	2	34	(16 18)	219	91	83	85	73	9	62	3	0	3	15	2	.88	6	.262	.389	.617
2000	SF	NL	143	480	147	28	4	49	(25 24)	330	129	106	139	117	22	77	3	0	7	11	3	.79	6	.306	.440	.688
2001	SF	NL	153	476	156	32	2	73	(37 36)	411	129	137	191	177	35	93	9	0	2	13	3	.81	5	.328	.515	.863
2002	SF	NL	143	403	149	31	2	46	(19 27)	322	117	110	160	198	68	47	9	0	2	9	2	.82	4	.370	.582	.799
2003	SF	NL	130	390	133	22	1	45	(23 22)	292	111	90	129	148	61	58	10	0	2	7	0	1.00	7	.341	.529	.749
2004	SF	NL	147	373	135	27	3	45	(26 19)	303	129	101	171	232	120	41	9	0	3	6	1	.86	5	.362	.609	.812
2005	SF	NL	14	42	12	1	0	5	(2 3)	28	8	10	9	9	3	6	0	0	1	0	0	-	0	.286	.404	.667
2006	SF	NL	130	367	99	23	0	26	(12 14)	200	74	77	103	115	38	51	10	0	1	3	0	1.00	9	.270	.454	.545
21 ML YEARS			2860	9507	2841	587	77	734	(363 371)	5784	2152	1930	2513	2426	645	1485	103	4	89	509	141	.78	152	.299	.443	.608

Boof Bonser

Pitches: R **Bats:** R **Pos:** SP-18   **Ht:** 6'4" **Wt:** 260 **Born:** 10/14/1981 **Age:** 25

			HOW MUCH HE PITCHED						WHAT HE GAVE UP												THE RESULTS						
Year	Team	Lg	G	GS	CG	GF	IP	BFP	H	R	ER	HR	SH	SF	HB	TBB	IBB	SO	WP	Bk	W	L	Pct	ShO	Sv-Op	Hld	ERC	ERA
2000	SlmKzr	A-	10	9	0	0	33.0	145	21	23	22	2	1	2	1	29	0	41	4	0	1	4	.200	0	0- -	-	3.77	6.00
2001	Hgrstn	A	27	27	0	0	134.0	548	91	40	37	7	2	3	9	61	2	178	10	1	16	4	.800	0	0- -	-	2.53	2.49
2002	SnJos	A+	23	23	0	0	128.1	537	89	44	41	9	1	2	7	70	0	139	7	1	8	6	.571	0	0- -	-	3.01	2.88
2002	Shreve	AA	5	5	0	0	24.1	112	30	15	15	3	0	2	1	14	0	23	0	0	1	2	.333	0	0- -	-	6.76	5.55
2003	Nrwich	AA	24	24	1	0	135.0	579	122	80	60	11	7	7	0	67	0	103	10	0	7	10	.412	1	0- -	-	3.81	4.00
2003	Fresno	AAA	4	4	0	0	23.0	97	17	13	8	4	1	1	0	8	0	28	2	0	1	2	.333	0	0- -	-	2.79	3.13
2004	NwBrit	AA	27	27	0	0	154.1	658	160	89	75	22	2	8	3	56	1	146	4	0	12	9	.571	0	0- -	-	4.58	4.37
2004	Roch	AAA	1	1	0	0	7.0	26	5	1	1	1	0	0	0	1	0	7	0	0	1	0	1.000	0	0- -	-	1.99	1.29
2005	Roch	AAA	28	28	0	0	160.1	684	153	80	71	22	7	8	2	57	0	168	3	0	11	9	.550	0	0- -	-	3.92	3.99
2006	Roch	AAA	14	14	0	0	86.1	361	68	31	27	4	0	1	3	35	0	83	0	0	6	4	.600	0	0- -	-	2.72	2.81
2006	Min	AL	18	18	0	0	100.1	419	104	50	47	18	2	2	1	24	0	84	2	0	7	6	.538	0	0-0	0	4.25	4.22

Chris Booker

Pitches: R **Bats:** R **Pos:** RP-11   **Ht:** 6'3" **Wt:** 235 **Born:** 12/9/1976 **Age:** 30

			HOW MUCH HE PITCHED						WHAT HE GAVE UP												THE RESULTS						
Year	Team	Lg	G	GS	CG	GF	IP	BFP	H	R	ER	HR	SH	SF	HB	TBB	IBB	SO	WP	Bk	W	L	Pct	ShO	Sv-Op	Hld	ERC	ERA
1995	Cubs	R	13	7	0	2	42.1	179	36	22	13	0	0	2	0	16	0	43	4	1	3	2	.600	0	1- -	-	2.48	2.76
1996	Dytona	A+	1	1	0	0	2.1	11	1	1	0	0	0	0	0	3	0	2	1	0	0	0	-	0	0- -	-	3.36	0.00
1996	Wmspt	A-	14	14	0	0	61.0	291	57	51	36	2	0	6	3	51	1	52	7	2	4	6	.400	0	0- -	-	4.97	5.31
1997	Wmspt	A-	24	3	0	11	45.2	201	39	20	17	2	3	4	0	25	0	60	9	0	1	5	.167	0	1- -	-	3.36	3.35
1998	Rckford	A	44	1	0	22	64.0	292	47	32	24	2	3	5	4	53	4	78	8	1	1	2	.333	0	4- -	-	3.80	3.38
1999	Dytona	A+	42	0	0	29	73.0	328	72	45	32	6	2	3	3	37	1	68	5	0	2	5	.286	0	6- -	-	4.36	3.95
2000	Dytona	A+	31	0	0	24	27.2	122	25	12	7	0	2	0	1	14	1	34	2	0	0	2	.000	0	10- -	-	3.25	2.28
2000	WTenn	AA	12	0	0	3	14.2	66	10	8	6	1	0	0	0	12	0	21	0	0	1	0	1.000	0	0- -	-	3.60	3.68
2001	Chatt	AA	16	0	0	4	16.0	72	13	7	7	1	1	0	0	11	0	25	0	0	2	0	1.000	0	1- -	-	3.78	3.94
2001	WTenn	AA	45	0	0	13	52.0	231	39	29	25	7	5	3	1	36	2	76	7	0	2	6	.250	0	1- -	-	4.01	4.33
2003	Reds	R	12	0	0	9	11.2	60	17	11	11	1	1	0	0	8	0	11	1	0	0	2	.000	0	2- -	-	7.77	8.49
2003	Dayton	A	5	0	0	1	5.0	23	4	5	5	3	1	2	0	4	0	6	0	0	0	0	-	0	0- -	-	8.23	9.00
2004	Chatt	AA	28	0	0	12	39.0	168	26	6	6	0	0	0	1	25	4	57	5	0	2	0	1.000	0	5- -	-	2.39	1.38
2004	Lsvlle	AAA	7	0	0	2	12.0	56	10	6	6	2	0	0	0	10	0	9	4	0	1	0	1.000	0	0- -	-	5.24	4.50
2005	Lsvlle	AAA	59	0	0	48	65.0	268	45	20	18	2	0	3	1	28	1	91	3	0	8	4	.667	0	20- -	-	2.15	2.49
2006	Clrwtr	A+	6	0	0	2	10.0	38	7	6	6	2	0	0	0	2	0	20	1	0	0	0	-	0	0- -	-	2.39	5.40
2006	Wichta	AA	4	0	0	1	4.1	20	6	4	2	0	0	0	0	0	0	5	1	0	0	0	-	0	0- -	-	3.62	4.15
2006	S-WB	AAA	6	0	0	1	7.0	26	4	1	1	1	0	0	0	3	0	7	0	0	0	0	-	0	0- -	-	2.41	1.29
2006	Omha	AAA	4	0	0	0	4.2	21	6	4	4	2	0	0	0	3	0	6	0	0	0	0	-	0	0- -	-	10.41	7.71
2006	NewOr	AAA	15	0	0	8	16.0	74	14	7	7	0	2	0	0	13	0	29	0	0	2	2	.500	0	0- -	-	4.14	3.94
2005	KC	AL	3	0	0	1	2.0	15	6	8	7	2	0	0	0	4	0	2	0	0	0	0	-	0	0-0	0	40.92	31.50
2006	2 Tms		11	0	0	2	8.1	38	10	9	9	4	0	0	0	4	0	7	1	0	0	0	-	0	0-0	2	8.66	9.72
06	KC	AL	1	0	0	0	1.0	11	5	6	6	3	0	0	0	3	0	0	0	0	0	0	-	0	0-0	0	94.96	54.00
06	Was	NL	10	0	0	2	7.1	27	5	3	3	1	0	0	0	1	0	7	1	0	0	0	-	0	0-0	2	1.78	3.68
2 ML YEARS			14	0	0	3	10.1	53	16	17	16	6	0	0	0	8	0	9	1	0	0	0	-	0	0-0	2	14.04	13.94

Aaron Boone

Bats: R **Throws:** R **Pos:** 3B-101; PH-4; 2B-1; DH-1   **Ht:** 6'2" **Wt:** 200 **Born:** 3/9/1973 **Age:** 34

									BATTING											BASERUNNING				AVERAGES		
Year	Team	Lg	G	AB	H	2B	3B	HR	(Hm Rd)	TB	R	RBI	RC	TBB	IBB	SO	HBP	SH	SF	SB	CS	SB%	GDP	Avg	OBP	Slg
1997	Cin	NL	16	49	12	1	0	0	(0 0)	13	5	5	3	2	0	5	0	1	0	1	0	1.00	1	.245	.275	.265
1998	Cin	NL	58	181	51	13	2	2	(2 0)	74	24	28	27	15	1	36	5	3	2	6	1	.86	3	.282	.350	.409
1999	Cin	NL	139	472	132	26	5	14	(7 7)	210	56	72	70	30	2	79	8	5	5	17	6	.74	6	.280	.330	.445
2000	Cin	NL	84	291	83	18	0	12	(5 7)	137	44	43	50	24	1	52	10	2	4	6	1	.86	5	.285	.356	.471
2001	Cin	NL	103	381	112	26	2	14	(10 4)	184	54	62	63	29	1	71	8	3	6	6	3	.67	4	.294	.351	.483
2002	Cin	NL	162	606	146	38	2	26	(14 12)	266	83	87	83	56	4	111	10	9	4	32	8	.80	9	.241	.314	.439
2003	2 Tms		160	592	158	32	3	24	(13 11)	268	92	96	89	46	2	104	8	6	2	23	3	.88	13	.267	.327	.453
2005	Cle	AL	143	511	124	19	1	16	(5 11)	193	61	60	52	35	3	92	9	4	6	9	3	.75	16	.243	.299	.378
2006	Cle	AL	104	354	89	19	1	7	(1 6)	131	50	46	46	27	1	62	6	4	1	5	4	.56	4	.251	.314	.370

Year	Team	Lg	G	AB	H	2B	3B	HR	(Hm	Rd)	TB	R	RBI	RC	TBB	IBB	SO	HBP	SH	SF	SB	CS	SB%	GDP	Avg	OBP	Slg
									BATTING												**BASERUNNING**				**AVERAGES**		
03	Cin	NL	106	403	110	19	3	18	(10	8)	189	61	65	65	35	2	74	5	3	0	15	3	.83	6	.273	.339	.469
03	NYY	AL	54	189	48	13	0	6	(3	3)	79	31	31	24	11	0	30	3	3	2	8	0	1.00	7	.254	.302	.418
	9 ML YEARS		969	3437	907	192	16	115	(57	58)	1476	469	499	483	264	15	612	64	37	30	105	29	.78	66	.264	.325	.429

Chris Bootcheck

Pitches: R **Bats:** R **Pos:** RP-7 **Ht:** 6'5" **Wt:** 200 **Born:** 10/24/1978 **Age:** 28

Year	Team	Lg	G	GS	CG	GF	IP	BFP	H	R	ER	HR	SH	SF	HB	TBB	IBB	SO	WP	Bk	W	L	Pct	ShO	Sv-Op	Hld	ERC	ERA
						HOW MUCH HE PITCHED						**WHAT HE GAVE UP**												**THE RESULTS**				
2006	Salt Lk*	AAA	40	5	0	14	65.2	308	84	56	49	10	1	3	6	34	0	43	5	0	4	3	.571	0	1--	-	7.20	6.72
2003	LAA	AL	4	1	0	2	10.1	53	16	13	11	5	0	0	0	6	0	7	0	0	0	1	.000	0	0-0	0	11.53	9.58
2005	LAA	AL	5	2	0	1	18.2	79	19	7	7	1	0	1	0	4	1	8	1	0	0	1	.000	0	1-1	0	3.38	3.38
2006	LAA	AL	7	0	0	5	10.1	54	16	12	12	3	1	0	0	9	0	7	1	0	0	1	.000	0	0-0	0	11.63	10.45
	3 ML YEARS		16	3	0	8	39.1	186	51	32	30	9	1	1	0	19	1	22	2	0	0	3	.000	0	1-1	0	7.11	6.86

Joe Borchard

Bats: B **Throws:** R **Pos:** RF-55; PH-51; LF-15; CF-3; DH-3; PR-2; 1B-1 **Ht:** 6'4" **Wt:** 230 **Born:** 11/25/1978 **Age:** 28

Year	Team	Lg	G	AB	H	2B	3B	HR	(Hm	Rd)	TB	R	RBI	RC	TBB	IBB	SO	HBP	SH	SF	SB	CS	SB%	GDP	Avg	OBP	Slg
									BATTING												**BASERUNNING**				**AVERAGES**		
2002	CWS	AL	16	36	8	0	0	2	(0	2)	14	5	5	5	1	0	14	0	0	0	0	0	-	0	.222	.243	.389
2003	CWS	AL	16	49	9	1	0	1	(0	1)	13	5	5	2	5	0	18	0	0	3	0	1	.00	0	.184	.246	.265
2004	CWS	AL	63	201	35	4	1	9	(6	3)	68	26	20	13	19	1	57	1	1	0	1	0	1.00	4	.174	.249	.338
2005	CWS	AL	7	12	5	2	0	0	(0	0)	7	0	0	2	0	0	4	0	0	0	1	0	1.00	0	.417	.417	.583
2006	2 Tms		114	239	55	7	1	10	(5	5)	94	33	28	26	28	3	69	3	0	0	3	3	.00	5	.230	.319	.393
06	Sea	AL	6	9	2	0	0	0	(0	0)	2	3	0	0	0	0	3	0	0	0	0	1	.00	0	.222	.222	.222
06	Fla	NL	108	230	53	7	1	10	(5	5)	92	30	28	26	28	3	66	3	0	0	0	2	.00	5	.230	.322	.400
	5 ML YEARS		216	537	112	14	2	22	(11	11)	196	69	58	48	53	4	162	4	1	3	1	5	.17	9	.209	.283	.365

Dave Borkowski

Pitches: R **Bats:** R **Pos:** RP-40 **Ht:** 6'1" **Wt:** 230 **Born:** 2/7/1977 **Age:** 30

Year	Team	Lg	G	GS	CG	GF	IP	BFP	H	R	ER	HR	SH	SF	HB	TBB	IBB	SO	WP	Bk	W	L	Pct	ShO	Sv-Op	Hld	ERC	ERA
						HOW MUCH HE PITCHED						**WHAT HE GAVE UP**												**THE RESULTS**				
2006	RdRck*	AAA	6	0	0	5	7.0	27	6	2	2	1	1	0	0	2	0	6	1	0	0	1	.000	0	3--	-	3.35	2.57
1999	Det	AL	17	12	0	2	76.2	351	86	58	52	10	1	2	4	40	0	50	3	0	2	6	.250	0	0-	0	5.75	6.10
2000	Det	AL	2	1	0	0	5.1	34	11	13	13	2	0	1	0	7	1	1	0	0	0	1	.000	0	0-	0	17.78	21.94
2001	Det	AL	15	0	0	7	29.2	135	30	21	21	5	0	2	3	15	3	30	0	0	0	2	.000	0	0-	0	5.28	6.37
2004	Bal	AL	17	8	0	2	56.0	247	65	37	32	6	2	2	3	15	1	45	2	1	3	4	.429	0	0-1	1	4.67	5.14
2006	Hou	NL	40	0	0	12	71.0	299	70	38	37	8	2	2	0	23	7	52	2	0	3	2	.600	0	0-0	1	3.65	4.69
	5 ML YEARS		91	21	0	23	238.2	1066	262	167	155	31	5	9	10	100	12	178	7	1	8	15	.348	0	0-1	2	5.01	5.84

Joe Borowski

Pitches: R **Bats:** R **Pos:** RP-72 **Ht:** 6'2" **Wt:** 225 **Born:** 5/4/1971 **Age:** 36

Year	Team	Lg	G	GS	CG	GF	IP	BFP	H	R	ER	HR	SH	SF	HB	TBB	IBB	SO	WP	Bk	W	L	Pct	ShO	Sv-Op	Hld	ERC	ERA
						HOW MUCH HE PITCHED						**WHAT HE GAVE UP**												**THE RESULTS**				
1995	Bal	AL	6	0	0	3	7.1	30	5	1	1	0	0	0	0	4	0	3	0	0	0	0	-	0	0-0	0	2.32	1.23
1996	Atl	NL	22	0	0	8	26.0	121	33	15	14	4	5	0	1	13	4	15	1	0	2	4	.333	0	0-0	1	6.46	4.85
1997	2 Tms		21	0	0	9	26.0	123	29	13	12	2	1	0	0	20	5	8	0	0	2	3	.400	0	0-0	0	5.74	4.15
1998	NYY	AL	8	0	0	6	9.2	42	11	7	7	0	0	0	0	4	0	7	0	0	1	0	1.000	0	0-0	0	4.27	6.52
2001	ChC	NL	1	1	0	0	1.2	13	6	6	6	1	1	0	0	3	0	1	0	0	0	1	.000	0	0-0	0	39.91	32.40
2002	ChC	NL	73	0	0	25	95.2	391	84	31	29	10	5	3	1	29	6	97	1	0	4	4	.500	0	2-6	12	3.05	2.73
2003	ChC	NL	68	0	0	59	68.1	280	53	23	20	5	4	0	1	19	1	66	0	0	2	2	.500	0	33-37	1	2.26	2.63
2004	ChC	NL	22	0	0	19	21.1	106	27	19	19	3	1	1	0	15	2	17	0	0	2	4	.333	0	9-11	0	6.92	8.02
2005	2 Tms		43	0	0	7	46.1	184	38	23	23	8	1	0	0	12	1	27	1	0	1	5	.167	0	0-4	20	3.04	4.47
2006	Fla	NL	72	0	0	60	69.2	304	63	31	29	7	4	0	2	33	7	64	1	0	3	3	.500	0	36-43	0	3.74	3.75
97	Atl	NL	20	0	0	8	24.0	111	27	11	10	2	1	0	0	16	4	6	0	0	2	2	.500	0	0-0	2	5.51	3.75
97	NYY	AL	1	0	0	1	2.0	12	2	2	2	0	0	0	0	4	1	2	0	0	0	1	.000	0	0-0	0	8.25	9.00
05	ChC	NL	11	0	0	3	11.0	47	12	8	8	5	0	0	0	1	0	11	0	0	0	0	-	0	0-0	1	5.36	6.55
05	TB	AL	32	0	0	4	35.1	137	26	15	15	3	1	0	0	11	1	16	1	0	1	5	.167	0	0-4	19	2.33	3.82
	10 ML YEARS		336	1	0	196	372.0	1594	349	169	160	40	19	4	5	152	26	305	4	0	17	26	.395	0	80-101	36	3.75	3.87

Jason Botts

Bats: B **Throws:** R **Pos:** DH-13; PH-6; LF-1 **Ht:** 6'5" **Wt:** 250 **Born:** 7/26/1980 **Age:** 26

Year	Team	Lg	G	AB	H	2B	3B	HR	(Hm	Rd)	TB	R	RBI	RC	TBB	IBB	SO	HBP	SH	SF	SB	CS	SB%	GDP	Avg	OBP	Slg
									BATTING												**BASERUNNING**				**AVERAGES**		
2000	Rngrs	R	48	163	52	12	6	6	(-	-)	82	36	34	38	26	4	29	10	0	1	4	1	.80	5	.319	.440	.503
2001	Savann	A	114	392	121	24	2	9	(-	-)	176	63	50	77	53	4	88	20	0	1	13	7	.65	10	.309	.416	.449
2001	Charltt	A+	4	12	2	1	0	0	(-	-)	3	1	0	1	4	0	4	0	0	0	0	0	-	0	.167	.375	.250
2002	Charltt	A+	116	401	102	22	5	9	(-	-)	161	67	54	70	75	3	99	14	0	3	7	2	.78	4	.254	.387	.401
2003	Stcktn	A+	76	283	89	14	2	9	(-	-)	134	58	61	58	45	1	59	1	0	1	12	3	.80	8	.314	.409	.473
2003	Frisco	AA	55	194	51	11	4	1	(-	-)	76	26	27	28	21	1	45	3	0	2	6	1	.86	6	.263	.341	.392
2004	Frisco	AA	132	476	141	25	3	24	(-	-)	244	85	92	100	76	4	125	10	1	4	7	4	.64	18	.296	.401	.513
2005	Okla	AAA	133	510	146	31	7	25	(-	-)	266	93	102	100	67	2	152	8	0	4	2	4	.33	13	.286	.375	.522
2006	Rngrs	R	3	12	3	2	0	0	(-	-)	5	1	1	1	2	0	1	0	0	0	0	0	-	0	.250	.357	.417
2006	Frisco	AA	5	16	2	0	0	0	(-	-)	2	3	2	0	3	0	3	0	0	1	0	0	-	1	.125	.250	.125
2006	Okla	AAA	63	220	68	19	1	13	(-	-)	128	43	39	52	31	3	61	4	0	4	6	0	1.00	3	.309	.398	.582

45

Year	Team	Lg	BATTING																					BASERUNNING				AVERAGES		
			G	AB	H	2B	3B	HR	(Hm	Rd)	TB	R	RBI	RC	TBB	IBB	SO	HBP	SH	SF		SB	CS	SB%	GDP		Avg	OBP	Slg
2005	Tex	AL	10	27	8	0	0	0	(0	0)	8	4	3	3	3	0	13	0	0	0		0	0	-	1		.296	.367	.296
2006	Tex	AL	20	50	11	4	0	1	(1	0)	18	8	6	6	8	1	18	0	0	0		0	0	-	0		.220	.317	.360
	2 ML YEARS		30	77	19	4	0	1	(1	0)	26	12	9	9	11	1	31	0	0	0		0	0	-	1		.247	.333	.338

Michael Bourn

Bats: L Throws: R Pos: RF-14; PR-6; PH-2; LF-1   **Ht: 5'11" Wt: 180 Born: 12/27/1982 Age: 24**

Year	Team	Lg	BATTING																					BASERUNNING				AVERAGES		
			G	AB	H	2B	3B	HR	(Hm	Rd)	TB	R	RBI	RC	TBB	IBB	SO	HBP	SH	SF		SB	CS	SB%	GDP		Avg	OBP	Slg
2003	Batvia	A-	35	125	35	0	1	0	(-	-)	37	12	4	21	23	0	28	3	2	0		23	5	.82	2		.280	.404	.296
2004	Lakwd	A	109	413	131	20	14	5	(-	-)	194	92	53	98	85	2	88	2	6	4		57	6	.90	1		.317	.433	.470
2005	Rdng	AA	135	544	146	18	8	6	(-	-)	198	80	44	76	63	5	123	3	4	1		38	12	.76	2		.268	.348	.364
2006	Rdng	AA	80	318	87	5	6	4	(-	-)	116	62	26	48	36	2	67	2	4	1		30	4	.88	3		.274	.350	.365
2006	S-WB	AAA	38	152	43	5	7	1	(-	-)	65	34	15	27	20	0	33	1	0	1		15	1	.94	2		.283	.368	.428
2006	Phi	NL	17	8	1	0	0	0	(0	0)	1	2	0	0	1	0	3	0	2	0		1	2	.33	0		.125	.222	.125

Rob Bowen

Bats: B Throws: R Pos: C-65; PH-32; PR-21; 1B-1; DH-1   **Ht: 6'3" Wt: 225 Born: 2/24/1981 Age: 26**

Year	Team	Lg	BATTING																					BASERUNNING				AVERAGES		
			G	AB	H	2B	3B	HR	(Hm	Rd)	TB	R	RBI	RC	TBB	IBB	SO	HBP	SH	SF		SB	CS	SB%	GDP		Avg	OBP	Slg
2006	Lk Els*	A+	2	7	1	0	0	0	(-	-)	1	0	0	0	0	0	2	0	0	0		0	0	-	0		.143	.143	.143
2003	Min	AL	7	10	1	0	0	0	(0	0)	1	0	1	0	0	0	4	0	0	1		0	0	-	1		.100	.091	.100
2004	Min	AL	17	27	3	0	0	1	(0	1)	6	1	2	2	4	0	10	0	1	0		0	0	-	1		.111	.226	.222
2006	SD	NL	94	94	23	5	0	3	(2	1)	37	22	13	12	13	0	26	1	1	1		0	1	.00	1		.245	.339	.394
	3 ML YEARS		118	131	27	5	0	4	(2	2)	44	23	16	14	17	0	40	1	2	2		0	1	.00	3		.206	.298	.336

Micah Bowie

Pitches: L Bats: L Pos: RP-15   **Ht: 6'4" Wt: 205 Born: 11/10/1974 Age: 32**

Year	Team	Lg	HOW MUCH HE PITCHED						WHAT HE GAVE UP												THE RESULTS							
			G	GS	CG	GF	IP	BFP	H	R	ER	HR	SH	SF	HB	TBB	IBB	SO	WP	Bk	W	L	Pct	ShO	Sv-Op	Hld	ERC	ERA
2006	NewOr*	AAA	31	0	0	8	42.1	187	33	20	18	0	5	0	3	24	0	57	2	0	2	0	1.000	0	1- -		2.99	3.83
1999	2 Tms	NL	14	11	0	2	51.0	265	81	60	58	9	3	3	2	34	2	41	4	2	2	7	.222	0	0-0		9.69	10.24
2002	Oak	AL	13	0	0	4	12.0	55	12	2	2	1	0	0	1	8	1	8	0	0	2	0	1.000	0	0-0	3	5.26	1.50
2003	Oak	AL	6	0	0	3	8.1	38	13	7	7	1	0	0	0	2	0	4	0	0	0	1	.000	0	0-0	0	7.15	7.56
2006	Was	NL	15	0	0	3	19.2	75	11	3	3	1	1	0	0	7	0	11	0	0	0	1	.000	0	0-0	5	1.54	1.37
99	Atl	NL	3	0	0	2	4.0	23	8	6	6	1	0	0	0	4	0	2	0	0	0	1	.000	0	0-0	0	15.43	13.50
99	ChC	NL	11	11	0	0	47.0	242	73	54	52	8	3	3	2	30	2	39	4	2	2	6	.250	0	0-0	0	9.23	9.96
	4 ML YEARS		48	11	0	12	91.0	433	117	72	70	12	4	3	3	51	3	64	4	2	4	9	.308	0	0-0	8	6.80	6.92

Blaine Boyer

Pitches: R Bats: R Pos: RP-2   **Ht: 6'3" Wt: 215 Born: 7/11/1981 Age: 25**

Year	Team	Lg	HOW MUCH HE PITCHED						WHAT HE GAVE UP												THE RESULTS							
			G	GS	CG	GF	IP	BFP	H	R	ER	HR	SH	SF	HB	TBB	IBB	SO	WP	Bk	W	L	Pct	ShO	Sv-Op	Hld	ERC	ERA
2000	Braves	R	11	5	0	2	32.1	140	24	16	9	0	0	0	3	19	0	27	3	2	1	3	.250	0	1- -		3.02	2.51
2001	Danvle	R+	13	12	0	0	50.0	217	48	35	24	4	3	1	5	19	0	57	9	1	4	5	.444	0	0- -		4.03	4.32
2002	Macon	A	43	0	0	22	70.1	302	52	30	24	0	6	3	5	39	0	73	8	2	5	9	.357	0	1- -		2.74	3.07
2003	Rome	A	30	26	1	0	136.2	614	146	70	56	5	1	1	4	58	0	115	10	1	12	8	.600	0	0- -		4.13	3.69
2004	MrtlBh	A+	28	28	0	0	154.0	649	138	63	51	4	15	6	7	49	0	95	7	0	10	10	.500	0	0- -		2.85	2.98
2005	Missi	AA	14	8	0	2	48.1	225	62	28	27	4	3	3	2	18	3	40	0	0	2	4	.333	0	0- -		5.45	5.03
2005	Atl	NL	43	0	0	5	37.2	158	32	13	13	1	1	1	2	17	0	33	2	0	4	2	.667	0	0-2	9	3.21	3.11
2006	Atl	NL	2	0	0	0	0.2	7	4	3	3	0	0	0	0	1	0	0	0	0	0	0	-	0	0-0	1	47.92	40.50
	2 ML YEARS		45	0	0	5	38.1	165	36	16	16	1	1	1	2	18	0	33	2	0	4	2	.667	0	0-2	10	3.73	3.76

Chad Bradford

Pitches: R Bats: R Pos: RP-70   **Ht: 6'5" Wt: 205 Born: 9/14/1974 Age: 32**

Year	Team	Lg	HOW MUCH HE PITCHED						WHAT HE GAVE UP												THE RESULTS							
			G	GS	CG	GF	IP	BFP	H	R	ER	HR	SH	SF	HB	TBB	IBB	SO	WP	Bk	W	L	Pct	ShO	Sv-Op	Hld	ERC	ERA
1998	CWS	AL	29	0	0	8	30.2	125	27	16	11	0	0	0	0	7	0	11	1	1	2	1	.667	0	1-3	9	2.16	3.23
1999	CWS	AL	3	0	0	0	3.2	24	9	8	8	1	0	0	0	5	0	1	0	0	0	0	-	0	0-0	0	21.34	19.64
2000	CWS	AL	12	0	0	5	13.2	52	13	4	3	0	0	0	0	1	1	9	0	0	1	0	1.000	0	0-0	2	2.01	1.98
2001	Oak	AL	35	0	0	19	36.2	154	41	12	11	6	1	0	1	6	0	34	0	0	2	1	.667	0	1-4	4	4.36	2.70
2002	Oak	AL	75	0	0	14	75.1	311	73	29	26	2	2	2	5	14	5	56	0	1	4	2	.667	0	2-5	24	2.77	3.11
2003	Oak	AL	72	0	0	12	77.0	322	67	28	26	7	1	0	7	30	9	62	0	1	7	4	.636	0	2-5	23	3.50	3.04
2004	Oak	AL	68	0	0	16	59.0	251	51	32	29	5	3	1	5	24	9	34	0	0	5	7	.417	0	1-4	14	3.35	4.42
2005	Bos	AL	31	0	0		23.1	104	29	10	10	1	3	1	3	4	1	10	2	0	1	1	.667	0	0-1	8	4.54	3.86
2006	NYM	NL	70	0	0	15	62.0	252	59	22	20	1	4	3	0	13	4	45	0	0	4	2	.667	0	2-3	10	2.48	2.90
	9 ML YEARS		395	0	0	91	381.1	1595	369	161	144	23	14	7	21	104	29	261	4	3	27	18	.600	0	9-25	94	3.26	3.40

Milton Bradley

Bats: B Throws: R Pos: RF-94; DH-1; PH-1; PR-1   Ht: 6'0" Wt: 190 Born: 4/15/1978 Age: 29

Year	Team	Lg	G	AB	H	2B	3B	HR	(Hm	Rd)	TB	R	RBI	RC	TBB	IBB	SO	HBP	SH	SF	SB	CS	SB%	GDP	Avg	OBP	Slg
2006	Stcktn*	A+	2	7	1	0	0	0	(-	-)	1	1	0	0	1	0	1	0	0	0	0	0	-	0	.143	.250	.143
2006	Scrmto*	AAA	6	24	5	0	0	2	(-	-)	11	3	6	3	2	0	10	1	0	0	1	0	1.00	0	.208	.296	.458
2000	Mon	NL	42	154	34	8	1	2	(1	1)	50	20	15	14	14	0	32	1	1	1	2	1	.67	3	.221	.288	.325
2001	2 Tms		77	238	53	17	3	1	(0	1)	79	22	19	21	21	0	65	1	2	0	8	5	.62	7	.223	.288	.332
2002	Cle	AL	98	325	81	18	3	9	(4	5)	132	48	38	40	32	2	58	0	1	0	6	3	.67	12	.249	.317	.406
2003	Cle	AL	101	377	121	34	2	10	(4	6)	189	61	56	77	64	8	73	5	0	5	17	7	.71	10	.321	.421	.501
2004	LAD	NL	141	516	138	24	0	19	(8	11)	219	72	67	70	71	3	123	6	3	1	15	11	.58	12	.267	.362	.424
2005	LAD	NL	75	283	82	14	1	13	(6	7)	137	49	38	40	25	1	47	2	4	1	6	1	.86	6	.290	.350	.484
2006	Oak	AL	96	351	97	14	2	14	(7	7)	157	53	52	60	51	1	65	2	0	1	10	2	.83	13	.276	.370	.447
01	Mon	NL	67	220	49	16	3	1	(0	1)	74	19	19	20	19	0	62	1	2	0	7	4	.64	6	.223	.288	.336
01	Cle	AL	10	18	4	1	0	0	(0	0)	5	3	0	1	2	0	3	0	0	0	1	1	.50	1	.222	.300	.278
7 ML YEARS			630	2244	606	129	12	68	(30	38)	963	325	285	322	278	15	463	17	11	9	64	30	.68	63	.270	.354	.429

Russell Branyan

Bats: L Throws: R Pos: RF-54; 3B-31; PH-9; 1B-2; LF-1; PR-1   Ht: 6'3" Wt: 195 Born: 12/19/1975 Age: 31

Year	Team	Lg	G	AB	H	2B	3B	HR	(Hm	Rd)	TB	R	RBI	RC	TBB	IBB	SO	HBP	SH	SF	SB	CS	SB%	GDP	Avg	OBP	Slg
1998	Cle	AL	1	4	0	0	0	0	(0	0)	0	0	0	0	0	0	2	0	0	0	0	0	-	0	.000	.000	.000
1999	Cle	AL	11	38	8	2	0	1	(0	1)	13	4	6	4	3	0	19	1	0	0	0	0	-	0	.211	.286	.342
2000	Cle	AL	67	193	46	7	2	16	(13	3)	105	32	38	34	22	1	76	4	0	1	0	0	-	2	.238	.327	.544
2001	Cle	AL	113	315	73	16	2	20	(11	9)	153	48	54	50	38	1	132	3	0	5	1	1	.50	2	.232	.316	.486
2002	2 Tms		134	378	86	13	1	24	(5	19)	173	50	56	49	51	3	151	2	0	4	4	3	.57	5	.228	.320	.458
2003	Cin	NL	74	176	38	12	0	9	(7	2)	77	22	26	23	27	0	69	1	0	1	0	0	-	1	.216	.322	.438
2004	Mil	NL	51	158	37	11	1	11	(8	3)	83	21	27	23	20	0	68	2	0	2	1	0	1.00	1	.234	.324	.525
2005	Mil	NL	85	202	52	11	0	12	(3	9)	99	23	31	38	39	10	80	0	1	0	1	0	1.00	3	.257	.378	.490
2006	2 Tms		91	241	55	11	0	18	(9	9)	120	37	36	34	34	1	89	3	1	3	2	0	1.00	1	.228	.327	.498
02	Cle	AL	50	161	33	4	0	8	(1	7)	61	16	17	14	17	0	65	0	0	2	1	2	.33	3	.205	.278	.379
02	Cin	AL	84	217	53	9	1	16	(4	12)	112	34	39	35	34	3	86	2	0	2	3	1	.75	2	.244	.349	.516
06	TB	AL	64	169	34	10	0	12	(7	5)	80	23	27	22	19	0	62	2	1	2	2	0	1.00	1	.201	.286	.473
06	SD	NL	27	72	21	1	0	6	(2	4)	40	14	9	12	15	1	27	1	0	1	0	0	-	0	.292	.416	.556
9 ML YEARS			627	1705	395	83	6	111	(56	55)	823	237	274	255	234	16	686	16	2	16	9	4	.69	15	.232	.327	.483

Ryan Braun

Pitches: R Bats: R Pos: RP-9   Ht: 6'1" Wt: 215 Born: 7/29/1980 Age: 26

Year	Team	Lg	G	GS	CG	GF	IP	BFP	H	R	ER	HR	SH	SF	HB	TBB	IBB	SO	WP	Bk	W	L	Pct	ShO	Sv-Op	Hld	ERC	ERA
2003	Royals	R	18	0	0	13	21.1	90	15	9	7	0	0	0	0	10	0	25	0	0	0	0	-	0	3- -	-	2.06	2.95
2004	Wilmg	A+	51	0	0	42	57.0	248	48	25	14	2	1	0	3	25	4	58	4	0	2	3	.400	0	23- -	-	2.92	2.21
2005	Hi Dsrt	A+	2	0	0	0	4.0	17	3	2	2	0	0	0	0	2	0	6	0	0	1	0	1.000	0	0- -	-	2.40	4.50
2005	Wichta	AA	6	0	0	3	4.2	35	15	10	9	0	0	0	0	7	1	1	1	0	0	1	.000	0	0- -	-	23.82	17.36
2006	Wichta	AA	26	0	0	22	40.2	170	30	11	10	2	3	0	4	16	3	58	2	0	1	6	.143	0	10- -	-	2.56	2.21
2006	Omha	AAA	17	0	0	11	25.0	109	23	9	6	0	2	1	0	13	2	22	0	0	0	2	.000	0	3- -	-	3.23	2.16
2006	KC	AL	9	0	0	2	10.2	46	13	8	8	2	1	1	0	3	0	6	0	0	0	1	.000	0	0-2	0	5.63	6.75

Bill Bray

Pitches: L Bats: L Pos: RP-48   Ht: 6'3" Wt: 215 Born: 6/5/1983 Age: 24

Year	Team	Lg	G	GS	CG	GF	IP	BFP	H	R	ER	HR	SH	SF	HB	TBB	IBB	SO	WP	Bk	W	L	Pct	ShO	Sv-Op	Hld	ERC	ERA
2004	BrvdCt	A+	6	0	0	4	7.1	32	9	5	4	0	0	0	0	1	0	6	0	0	0	2	.000	0	1- -	-	3.51	4.91
2005	Ptomc	A+	8	0	0	5	12.2	49	8	3	3	1	0	0	0	3	0	18	0	0	1	0	1.000	0	3- -	-	1.56	2.13
2005	Hrsbrg	AA	3	0	0	1	5.2	27	10	4	4	1	0	0	0	1	0	6	0	0	1	0	1.000	0	1- -	-	8.61	6.35
2005	NewOr	AAA	23	0	0	12	21.1	99	23	16	12	3	2	2	2	9	3	25	1	0	1	4	.200	0	2- -	-	4.87	5.06
2006	NewOr	AAA	21	0	0	7	31.2	131	26	14	14	5	0	0	2	9	0	45	0	0	4	1	.800	0	5- -	-	3.25	3.98
2006	2 Tms	NL	48	0	0	10	50.2	223	57	27	23	5	2	1	1	18	3	39	0	0	3	2	.600	0	2-3	3	4.58	4.09
06	Was	NL	19	0	0	4	23.0	100	24	11	10	2	1	1	1	9	2	16	0	0	1	1	.500	0	0-0	1	4.25	3.91
06	Cin	NL	29	0	0	6	27.2	123	33	16	13	3	1	0	0	9	1	23	0	0	2	1	.667	0	2-3	2	4.85	4.23

Dewon Brazelton

Pitches: R Bats: R Pos: RP-7; SP-2   Ht: 6'4" Wt: 215 Born: 6/16/1980 Age: 27

Year	Team	Lg	G	GS	CG	GF	IP	BFP	H	R	ER	HR	SH	SF	HB	TBB	IBB	SO	WP	Bk	W	L	Pct	ShO	Sv-Op	Hld	ERC	ERA
2006	Padres*	R	1	1	0	0	2.0	10	1	2	0	0	0	0	0	2	0	2	0	0	0	0	-	0	0- -	-	2.46	0.00
2006	Portlnd*	AAA	17	16	1	0	91.1	392	100	50	46	15	4	4	3	25	0	53	4	0	5	7	.417	1	0- -	-	4.72	4.53
2002	TB	AL	2	2	0	0	13.0	51	12	7	7	3	0	0	2	6	0	5	0	0	0	1	.000	0	0-0	0	6.29	4.85
2003	TB	AL	10	10	0	0	48.1	225	57	49	37	9	2	2	3	23	1	24	1	0	1	6	.143	0	0-0	0	6.29	6.89
2004	TB	AL	22	21	0	0	120.2	535	121	71	64	12	0	6	11	53	2	64	2	1	6	8	.429	0	0-0	0	4.58	4.77
2005	TB	AL	20	8	0	2	71.0	354	87	65	60	12	4	3	4	60	3	43	5	0	1	8	.111	0	0-1	1	8.13	7.61
2006	SD	NL	9	2	0	3	18.0	91	28	25	24	6	1	2	0	9	1	9	1	0	0	2	.000	0	0-0	0	9.69	12.00
5 ML YEARS			63	43	0	5	271.0	1256	305	217	192	42	7	13	20	151	7	145	9	1	8	25	.242	0	0-1	1	6.18	6.38

Yhency Brazoban

Pitches: R **Bats:** R **Pos:** RP-5 **Ht:** 6'0" **Wt:** 240 **Born:** 6/11/1980 **Age:** 27

Year	Team	Lg	G	GS	CG	GF	IP	BFP	H	R	ER	HR	SH	SF	HB	TBB	IBB	SO	WP	Bk	W	L	Pct	ShO	Sv-Op	Hld	ERC	ERA
2004	LAD	NL	31	0	0	10	32.2	133	25	9	9	2	4	0	0	15	2	27	1	0	6	2	.750	0	0-0	5	2.76	2.48
2005	LAD	NL	74	0	0	44	72.2	317	70	46	43	11	7	2	5	32	4	61	1	0	4	10	.286	0	21-27	8	4.60	5.33
2006	LAD	NL	5	0	0	2	5.0	23	7	3	3	0	0	1	0	2	0	4	1	0	0	0	-	0	0-1	0	5.74	5.40
3 ML YEARS			110	0	0	56	110.1	473	102	58	55	13	11	3	5	49	6	92	3	0	10	12	.455	0	21-28	13	4.08	4.49

Craig Breslow

Pitches: L **Bats:** L **Pos:** RP-13 **Ht:** 6'1" **Wt:** 180 **Born:** 8/8/1980 **Age:** 26

Year	Team	Lg	G	GS	CG	GF	IP	BFP	H	R	ER	HR	SH	SF	HB	TBB	IBB	SO	WP	Bk	W	L	Pct	ShO	Sv-Op	Hld	ERC	ERA
2002	Ogden	R+	23	0	0	6	54.1	229	42	15	11	2	3	2	1	24	0	56	7	0	6	2	.750	0	2- -		2.63	1.82
2003	Beloit	A	23	0	0	12	65.0	286	64	43	37	4	4	2	1	27	0	80	1	0	3	4	.429	0	2- -		3.76	5.12
2004	Hi Dsrt	A+	23	0	0	9	41.1	202	54	39	33	5	0	0	2	24	0	41	4	0	1	3	.250	0	0- -		6.95	7.19
2005	Mobile	AA	40	0	0	6	52.1	212	38	16	16	3	4	2	1	17	3	47	2	0	2	1	.667	0	0- -		2.08	2.75
2005	Portlnd	AAA	7	0	0	6	9.0	39	11	4	4	1	1	1	0	1	0	9	0	0	1	0	1.000	0	0- -		4.14	4.00
2006	Pwtckt	AAA	39	0	0	21	67.0	278	49	21	20	3	5	0	4	24	0	77	6	1	7	1	.875	0	7- -		2.33	2.69
2005	SD	NL	14	0	0	3	16.1	78	15	6	4	1	0	1	1	13	0	14	1	0	0	0	-	0	0-0	1	4.98	2.20
2006	Bos	AL	13	0	0	3	12.0	55	12	5	5	0	0	2	1	6	1	12	2	1	0	2	.000	0	0-0	3	3.78	3.75
2 ML YEARS			27	0	0	6	28.1	133	27	11	9	1	0	3	2	19	1	26	3	1	0	2	.000	0	0-0	4	4.46	2.86

Eude Brito

Pitches: L **Bats:** L **Pos:** RP-3; SP-2 **Ht:** 5'11" **Wt:** 160 **Born:** 8/19/1978 **Age:** 28

Year	Team	Lg	G	GS	CG	GF	IP	BFP	H	R	ER	HR	SH	SF	HB	TBB	IBB	SO	WP	Bk	W	L	Pct	ShO	Sv-Op	Hld	ERC	ERA
1999	Phillies	R	12	3	0	3	28.2	144	39	22	16	0	2	2	0	19	0	23	4	1	0	1	.000	0	0- -		6.29	5.02
2000	Phillies	R	9	7	0	1	49.2	206	38	20	14	1	0	1	3	19	0	42	10	0	3	5	.375	0	0- -		2.46	2.54
2000	Batvia	A-	4	3	0	1	18.1	74	16	14	11	0	0	0	1	3	0	11	5	0	1	1	.500	0	0- -		2.11	5.40
2001	Lakwd	A	44	0	0	20	69.1	275	53	28	21	7	5	0	2	14	2	58	3	2	4	3	.571	0	6- -		2.18	2.73
2002	Lakwd	A	11	0	0	9	17.2	73	14	5	5	1	2	0	0	6	0	11	0	0	1	1	.500	0	1- -		2.43	2.55
2002	Clrwtr	A+	20	0	0	11	34.2	158	40	22	22	5	2	1	0	14	1	27	7	0	3	3	.500	0	0- -		5.13	5.71
2003	Clrwtr	A+	36	0	0	19	58.1	252	50	21	20	3	3	4	0	27	1	54	7	0	4	3	.571	0	6- -		3.10	3.09
2004	Rdng	AA	43	7	1	15	97.2	430	95	56	48	10	3	5	4	42	2	84	7	3	8	6	.571	0	4- -		4.13	4.42
2005	S-WB	AAA	28	15	0	3	98.1	431	97	59	53	13	2	5	8	39	0	76	3	3	6	2	.750	0	0- -		4.53	4.85
2006	S-WB	AAA	26	23	2	1	147.2	608	116	60	52	11	3	4	2	55	0	103	7	1	10	8	.556	1	1- -		2.71	3.17
2005	Phi	NL	6	5	0	0	22.0	94	20	9	9	2	0	1	2	11	1	15	0	1	1	2	.333	0	0-0	0	4.32	3.68
2006	Phi	NL	5	2	0	0	18.1	87	21	15	15	2	2	1	1	12	2	9	3	1	1	2	.333	0	0-0	0	6.06	7.36
2 ML YEARS			11	7	0	0	40.1	181	41	24	24	4	2	2	3	23	3	24	3	2	2	4	.333	0	0-0	0	5.09	5.36

Chris Britton

Pitches: R **Bats:** R **Pos:** RP-52 **Ht:** 6'3" **Wt:** 280 **Born:** 12/16/1982 **Age:** 24

Year	Team	Lg	G	GS	CG	GF	IP	BFP	H	R	ER	HR	SH	SF	HB	TBB	IBB	SO	WP	Bk	W	L	Pct	ShO	Sv-Op	Hld	ERC	ERA
2001	Orioles	R	12	3	0	2	32.2	153	35	20	10	3	2	2	5	12	1	20	1	0	2	3	.400	0	0- -		4.63	2.76
2002	Bluefld	A	9	8	0	1	35.2	145	30	21	18	5	1	2	0	10	0	27	0	0	3	0	1.000	0	0- -		3.01	4.54
2004	Dlmrva	A	27	8	1	3	84.0	356	76	38	35	11	2	3	2	31	2	80	2	0	9	4	.692	0	0- -		3.68	3.75
2005	Frdrck	A+	46	0	0	15	78.2	298	47	15	14	5	0	0	1	23	0	110	1	0	6	0	1.000	0	6- -		1.60	1.60
2006	Bowie	AA	13	0	0	4	16.0	67	14	5	5	0	1	0	0	6	1	24	0	0	1	0	1.000	0	2- -		2.54	2.81
2006	Bal	AL	52	0	0	12	53.2	221	46	22	20	4	1	1	0	17	3	41	0	0	0	2	.000	0	1-3	6	2.74	3.35

Doug Brocail

Pitches: R **Bats:** L **Pos:** RP-25 **Ht:** 6'5" **Wt:** 250 **Born:** 5/16/1967 **Age:** 40

Year	Team	Lg	G	GS	CG	GF	IP	BFP	H	R	ER	HR	SH	SF	HB	TBB	IBB	SO	WP	Bk	W	L	Pct	ShO	Sv-Op	Hld	ERC	ERA
2006	Lk Els*	A+	6	2	0	0	6.1	25	3	1	0	0	0	0	0	2	0	12	1	0	0	0	-	0	0- -		0.95	0.00
1992	SD	NL	3	3	0	0	14.0	64	17	10	10	2	2	0	0	5	0	15	0	0	0	0	-	0	0-0	0	5.33	6.43
1993	SD	NL	24	24	0	0	128.1	571	143	75	65	16	10	8	4	42	4	70	4	1	4	13	.235	0	0-0	0	4.60	4.56
1994	SD	NL	12	0	0	4	17.0	78	21	13	11	1	1	1	2	5	3	11	1	1	0	0	-	0	0-1	0	4.79	5.82
1995	Hou	NL	36	7	0	12	77.1	339	87	40	36	10	1	1	4	22	2	39	1	1	6	4	.600	0	1-1	0	4.68	4.19
1996	Hou	NL	23	4	0	4	53.0	231	58	31	27	7	3	2	2	23	1	34	0	0	1	5	.167	0	0-0	1	5.26	4.58
1997	Det	AL	61	4	0	20	78.0	332	74	31	28	10	1	3	3	36	4	60	6	0	3	4	.429	0	2-9	16	4.42	3.23
1998	Det	AL	60	0	0	24	62.2	247	47	23	19	2	2	3	1	18	3	55	6	0	5	2	.714	0	0-1	11	1.99	2.73
1999	Det	AL	70	0	0	22	82.0	326	60	23	23	7	4	2	4	25	1	78	4	1	4	4	.500	0	2-4	23	2.43	2.52
2000	Det	AL	49	0	0	10	50.2	221	57	25	23	5	3	3	1	14	2	41	1	1	5	4	.556	0	0-5	19	4.25	4.09
2004	Tex	AL	43	0	0	14	52.1	232	54	29	24	2	4	2	5	20	1	43	2	1	4	1	.800	0	1-1	4	4.05	4.13
2005	Tex	AL	61	0	0	13	73.1	344	90	48	45	2	3	4	4	34	3	61	4	0	5	3	.625	0	1-5	5	5.15	5.52
2006	SD	NL	25	0	0	6	28.1	119	27	16	15	1	3	1	0	8	2	19	1	0	2	2	.500	0	0-0	0	2.80	4.76
12 ML YEARS			467	42	0	129	717.0	3104	735	364	326	65	37	30	30	252	26	526	30	6	39	42	.481	0	7-26	79	4.06	4.09

Ben Broussard

Bats: L Throws: L Pos: 1B-90; DH-42; PH-28; PR-1 Ht: 6'2" Wt: 220 Born: 9/24/1976 Age: 30

Year	Team	Lg	G	AB	H	2B	3B	HR	(Hm	Rd)	TB	R	RBI	RC	TBB	IBB	SO	HBP	SH	SF	SB	CS	SB%	GDP	Avg	OBP	Slg
2002	Cle	AL	39	112	27	4	0	4	(2	2)	43	10	9	9	7	1	25	1	0	0	0	0	-	3	.241	.292	.384
2003	Cle	AL	116	386	96	21	3	16	(7	9)	171	53	55	53	32	2	75	5	3	3	5	2	.71	6	.249	.312	.443
2004	Cle	AL	139	418	115	28	5	17	(9	8)	204	57	82	79	52	3	95	12	1	2	4	2	.67	7	.275	.370	.488
2005	Cle	AL	142	466	119	30	5	19	(11	8)	216	59	68	60	32	5	98	4	0	3	2	2	.50	4	.255	.307	.464
2006	2 Tms	AL	144	432	125	21	0	21	(12	9)	209	61	63	64	26	3	103	3	0	4	2	1	.67	8	.289	.331	.484
06	Cle	AL	88	268	86	14	0	13	(11	2)	139	44	46	48	17	1	58	1	0	2	0	1	.00	5	.321	.361	.519
06	Sea	AL	56	164	39	7	0	8	(1	7)	70	17	17	16	9	2	45	2	0	2	2	0	1.00	3	.238	.282	.427
5 ML YEARS			580	1814	482	104	13	77	(41	36)	843	240	277	265	149	14	396	25	4	12	13	7	.65	28	.266	.328	.465

Jim Brower

Pitches: R Bats: R Pos: RP-18 Ht: 6'3" Wt: 215 Born: 12/29/1972 Age: 34

Year	Team	Lg	G	GS	CG	GF	IP	BFP	H	R	ER	HR	SH	SF	HB	TBB	IBB	SO	WP	Bk	W	L	Pct	ShO	Sv-Op	Hld	ERC	ERA
2006	Portlnd*	AAA	24	0	0	8	34.1	156	37	21	19	5	0	1	3	18	1	28	1	1	5	2	.714	0	1--	-	5.75	4.98
2006	Albq*	AAA	15	0	0	5	18.1	76	20	9	8	3	0	0	2	3	0	13	2	0	0	1	.000	0	0--	-	4.68	3.93
1999	Cle	AL	9	2	0	1	25.2	113	27	13	13	8	1	1	1	10	1	18	0	0	3	1	.750	0	0-0	0	5.96	4.56
2000	Cle	AL	17	11	0	1	62.0	293	80	45	43	11	1	0	2	31	1	32	3	0	2	3	.400	0	0-0	0	6.95	6.24
2001	Cin	NL	46	10	0	13	129.1	559	119	65	57	17	9	3	5	60	5	94	5	1	7	10	.412	0	1-2	4	4.21	3.97
2002	2 Tms	NL	52	0	0	23	80.1	344	77	40	39	7	2	1	4	32	2	57	1	0	3	2	.600	0	0-1	6	3.94	4.37
2003	SF	NL	51	5	0	13	100.0	411	90	48	44	8	5	4	1	39	2	65	4	0	8	5	.615	0	2-3	3	3.46	3.96
2004	SF	NL	89	0	0	21	93.0	401	90	42	34	6	11	2	4	36	2	63	10	0	7	7	.500	0	1-5	24	3.72	3.29
2005	2 Tms	NL	69	0	0	12	60.1	282	73	36	36	11	2	1	5	32	3	53	4	0	3	3	.500	0	1-3	12	6.86	5.37
2006	2 Tms	NL	18	0	0	4	20.0	106	32	27	27	2	0	1	5	14	1	14	2	0	0	1	.000	0	0-1	1	10.42	12.15
02	Cin	NL	22	0	0	11	39.1	158	38	18	17	2	1	1	0	10	1	24	0	0	2	0	1.000	0	0-0	0	3.08	3.89
02	Mon	NL	30	0	0	12	41.0	186	39	22	22	5	1	0	4	22	1	33	1	0	1	2	.333	0	0-1	6	4.79	4.83
05	SF	NL	32	0	0	8	30.1	144	40	22	22	5	1	1	2	15	0	25	2	0	2	1	.667	0	1-3	5	7.24	6.53
05	Atl	NL	37	0	0	4	30.0	138	33	14	14	6	1	0	3	17	3	28	2	0	1	2	.333	0	0-0	7	6.47	4.20
06	Bal	AL	12	0	0	1	12.1	71	21	19	19	1	0	1	3	13	1	9	2	0	0	1	.000	0	0-1	1	12.48	13.86
06	SD	NL	6	0	0	3	7.2	35	11	8	8	1	0	0	2	1	0	5	0	0	0	0	-	0	0-0	0	7.15	9.39
8 ML YEARS			351	28	0	88	570.2	2509	588	316	293	70	31	13	27	254	17	396	29	1	33	32	.508	0	5-15	47	4.77	4.62

Adrian Brown

Bats: B Throws: R Pos: RF-11; CF-10; PR-6; LF-3 Ht: 6'0" Wt: 190 Born: 2/7/1974 Age: 33

Year	Team	Lg	G	AB	H	2B	3B	HR	(Hm	Rd)	TB	R	RBI	RC	TBB	IBB	SO	HBP	SH	SF	SB	CS	SB%	GDP	Avg	OBP	Slg
2006	Okla*	AAA	36	122	36	4	1	1	(-	-)	45	15	11	20	17	1	18	0	2	1	11	1	.92	7	.295	.379	.369
1997	Pit	NL	48	147	28	6	0	1	(0	1)	37	17	10	10	13	0	18	4	2	1	8	4	.67	3	.190	.273	.252
1998	Pit	NL	41	152	43	4	1	0	(0	0)	49	20	5	16	9	0	18	0	4	0	4	0	1.00	3	.283	.323	.322
1999	Pit	NL	116	226	61	5	2	4	(2	2)	82	34	17	31	33	2	39	1	6	1	5	3	.63	5	.270	.364	.363
2000	Pit	NL	104	308	97	18	3	4	(2	2)	133	64	28	53	29	1	34	0	2	1	13	1	.93	1	.315	.373	.432
2001	Pit	NL	8	31	6	0	0	1	(0	1)	9	3	2	2	3	0	3	0	0	0	2	1	.67	1	.194	.265	.290
2002	Pit	NL	91	208	45	10	2	1	(0	1)	62	20	21	16	19	0	34	1	3	1	10	6	.63	5	.216	.284	.298
2003	Bos	AL	9	15	3	0	0	0	(0	0)	3	1	1	1	1	0	4	0	0	0	2	0	1.00	0	.200	.250	.200
2004	KC	AL	5	11	3	0	0	0	(0	0)	3	0	0	1	0	0	2	0	0	0	0	0	-	0	.273	.273	.273
2006	Tex	AL	25	36	7	1	0	0	(0	0)	8	6	2	0	2	0	9	0	1	1	1	0	1.00	2	.194	.231	.222
9 ML YEARS			447	1134	293	44	8	11	(4	7)	386	166	86	130	109	3	161	6	18	5	45	15	.75	20	.258	.325	.340

Andrew Brown

Pitches: R Bats: R Pos: RP-9 Ht: 6'6" Wt: 230 Born: 2/17/1981 Age: 26

Year	Team	Lg	G	GS	CG	GF	IP	BFP	H	R	ER	HR	SH	SF	HB	TBB	IBB	SO	WP	Bk	W	L	Pct	ShO	Sv-Op	Hld	ERC	ERA
1999	Braves	R	11	11	0	0	42.1	183	40	15	11	4	1	0	3	16	0	57	1	4	1	1	.500	0	0--	-	3.90	2.34
2001	Jmstwn	A-	14	12	0	0	64.1	267	50	29	28	5	0	0	3	31	0	59	5	0	3	4	.429	0	0--	-	3.27	3.92
2002	VeroB	A+	25	24	1	0	127.0	530	97	63	58	13	3	6	8	62	0	129	9	3	10	10	.500	1	0--	-	3.44	4.11
2003	Jaxnvl	AA	1	1	0	0	1.0	3	0	0	0	0	0	0	0	0	0	1	0	0	0	0	-	0	0--	-	0.00	0.00
2004	Akron	AA	17	17	0	0	77.1	335	66	44	40	7	7	7	3	36	1	67	4	0	3	6	.333	0	0--	-	3.53	4.66
2004	Jaxnvl	AA	8	8	0	0	40.1	173	36	23	18	5	3	1	2	14	0	58	3	0	1	3	.250	0	0--	-	3.56	4.02
2004	Buffalo	AAA	1	1	0	0	5.0	21	4	0	0	0	0	0	0	3	0	4	1	0	1	0	1.000	0	0--	-	3.13	0.00
2005	Buffalo	AAA	49	0	0	21	69.2	279	52	28	26	7	0	2	3	19	0	81	4	0	4	2	.667	0	4--	-	2.44	3.36
2006	Buffalo	AAA	39	0	0	17	62.1	276	52	21	18	5	5	3	4	36	1	53	9	0	5	4	.556	0	5--	-	3.87	2.60
2006	Cle	AL	9	0	0	4	10.0	44	6	4	4	0	0	0	1	8	1	7	1	0	0	0	-	0	0-0	0	2.87	3.60

Emil Brown

Bats: R Throws: R Pos: LF-87; RF-54; DH-10; PH-4; PR-1 Ht: 6'2" Wt: 210 Born: 12/29/1974 Age: 32

Year	Team	Lg	G	AB	H	2B	3B	HR	(Hm	Rd)	TB	R	RBI	RC	TBB	IBB	SO	HBP	SH	SF	SB	CS	SB%	GDP	Avg	OBP	Slg
1997	Pit	NL	66	95	17	2	1	2	(1	1)	27	16	6	9	10	1	32	7	0	0	5	1	.83	1	.179	.304	.284
1998	Pit	NL	13	39	10	1	0	0	(0	0)	11	2	3	3	1	0	11	1	0	0	0	0	-	0	.256	.293	.282
1999	Pit	NL	6	14	2	1	0	0	(0	0)	3	0	0	0	0	0	3	0	0	0	0	0	-	0	.143	.143	.214
2000	Pit	NL	50	119	26	5	0	3	(2	1)	40	13	16	11	11	0	34	3	1	1	3	1	.75	3	.218	.299	.336
2001	2 Tms	NL	74	137	26	4	1	3	(2	1)	41	21	13	12	16	1	49	2	0	0	12	4	.75	7	.190	.284	.299
2005	KC	AL	150	545	156	31	5	17	(8	9)	248	75	86	91	48	1	108	8	1	7	10	1	.91	14	.286	.349	.455
2006	KC	AL	147	527	151	41	2	15	(6	9)	241	77	81	79	59	3	95	5	0	10	6	3	.67	15	.287	.358	.457

Year	Team	Lg	G	AB	H	2B	3B	HR	(Hm	Rd)	TB	R	RBI	RC	TBB	IBB	SO	HBP	SH	SF	SB	CS	SB%	GDP	Avg	OBP	Slg
01	SD	NL	13	14	1	0	0	0	(0	0)	1	3	0	0	1	0	7	0	0	0	2	0	1.00	0	.071	.133	.071
01	Pit	NL	61	123	25	4	1	3	(2	1)	40	18	13	12	15	1	42	2	0	0	10	4	.71	2	.203	.300	.325
7 ML YEARS			506	1476	388	85	9	40	(19	21)	611	204	205	205	145	6	332	26	2	18	36	10	.78	35	.263	.336	.414

Jeremy Brown

Bats: R Throws: R Pos: DH-4; PH-3; C-1 Ht: 5'10" Wt: 225 Born: 10/25/1979 Age: 27

Year	Team	Lg	G	AB	H	2B	3B	HR	(Hm	Rd)	TB	R	RBI	RC	TBB	IBB	SO	HBP	SH	SF	SB	CS	SB%	GDP	Avg	OBP	Slg
2002	Vancvr	A	10	28	8	1	0	0	(-	-)	9	7	1	6	10	0	5	1	0	0	1	0	1.00	1	.286	.487	.321
2002	Visalia	A+	55	187	58	14	0	10	(-	-)	102	36	40	46	44	0	49	2	2	1	1	1	.50	5	.310	.444	.545
2003	Mdland	AA	66	233	64	10	1	5	(-	-)	91	37	37	40	41	1	38	3	0	1	3	0	1.00	11	.275	.388	.391
2004	Mdland	AA	122	446	114	27	0	6	(-	-)	159	59	49	64	71	0	80	4	3	2	2	1	.67	20	.256	.361	.357
2005	Mdland	AA	115	394	103	27	1	20	(-	-)	192	65	72	72	52	0	88	11	0	5	0	0	-	17	.261	.359	.487
2006	Scrmto	AAA	77	275	70	14	0	13	(-	-)	123	41	40	40	23	1	60	4	0	4	0	0	-	6	.255	.317	.447
2006	Oak	AL	5	10	3	2	0	0	(0	0)	5	1	0	1	1	0	1	0	0	0	0	0	-	0	.300	.364	.500

Jonathan Broxton

Pitches: R Bats: R Pos: RP-68 Ht: 6'3" Wt: 290 Born: 6/16/1984 Age: 23

Year	Team	Lg	G	GS	CG	GF	IP	BFP	H	R	ER	HR	SH	SF	HB	TBB	IBB	SO	WP	Bk	W	L	Pct	ShO	Sv-Op	Hld	ERC	ERA
2002	Gr Falls	R+	11	6	0	2	29.1	126	22	9	9	0	4	0	3	16	0	33	0	0	2	0	1.000	0	2--	-	2.96	2.76
2003	SoGA	A	9	8	0	0	37.1	161	27	15	13	1	5	3	2	22	0	30	2	2	4	2	.667	0	0--	-	2.96	3.13
2004	VeroB	A+	23	23	1	0	128.1	538	110	49	46	7	7	4	4	43	0	144	6	0	11	6	.647	1	0--	-	2.84	3.23
2005	Jaxnvl	AA	33	13	0	15	96.2	400	79	36	34	4	3	2	1	31	0	107	7	0	5	3	.625	0	5--	-	2.44	3.17
2006	LsVgs	AAA	11	0	0	11	11.1	43	6	0	0	0	0	0	1	3	0	18	1	0	1	0	1.000	0	5--	-	1.24	0.00
2005	LAD	NL	14	0	0	5	13.2	68	13	11	9	0	0	2	1	12	2	22	2	0	1	0	1.000	0	0-1	1	4.65	5.93
2006	LAD	NL	68	0	0	20	76.1	320	61	25	22	7	3	1	1	33	6	97	7	0	4	1	.800	0	3-7	12	2.97	2.59
2 ML YEARS			82	0	0	25	90.0	388	74	36	31	7	3	3	2	45	8	119	9	0	5	1	.833	0	3-8	13	3.23	3.10

Brian Bruney

Pitches: R Bats: R Pos: RP-19 Ht: 6'2" Wt: 245 Born: 2/17/1982 Age: 25

Year	Team	Lg	G	GS	CG	GF	IP	BFP	H	R	ER	HR	SH	SF	HB	TBB	IBB	SO	WP	Bk	W	L	Pct	ShO	Sv-Op	Hld	ERC	ERA
2006	Yanks*	R	3	0	0	0	3.2	17	1	2	2	0	1	0	2	3	0	5	0	0	0	0	-	0	0--	-	2.83	4.91
2006	Tucsn*	AAA	4	0	0	2	2.2	23	10	12	10	2	1	0	0	4	0	4	0	0	0	1	.000	0	0--	-	37.03	33.75
2006	Clmbs*	AAA	11	0	0	5	14.1	60	10	6	5	2	1	0	0	8	0	22	2	0	1	1	.500	0	3--	-	3.31	3.14
2004	Ari	NL	30	0	0	14	31.1	135	20	16	15	2	1	0	1	27	5	34	2	0	3	4	.429	0	0-1	3	3.54	4.31
2005	Ari	NL	47	0	0	21	46.0	230	56	39	38	6	2	1	5	35	2	51	2	0	1	3	.250	0	12-16	4	7.48	7.43
2006	NYY	AL	19	0	0	2	20.2	90	14	2	2	1	0	0	1	15	0	25	2	0	1	1	.500	0	0-0	4	3.37	0.87
3 ML YEARS			96	0	0	37	98.0	455	90	57	55	9	3	1	7	77	7	110	6	0	5	8	.385	0	12-17	11	5.26	5.05

Eric Bruntlett

Bats: R Throws: R Pos: 2B-23; SS-21; PH-21; CF-8; LF-6; RF-5; PR-4; 3B-2 Ht: 6'0" Wt: 190 Born: 3/29/1978 Age: 29

Year	Team	Lg	G	AB	H	2B	3B	HR	(Hm	Rd)	TB	R	RBI	RC	TBB	IBB	SO	HBP	SH	SF	SB	CS	SB%	GDP	Avg	OBP	Slg
2006	RdRck*	AAA	22	73	16	3	1	1	(-	-)	24	11	7	11	17	0	13	2	1	0	3	2	.60	0	.219	.380	.329
2003	Hou	NL	31	54	14	3	0	1	(1	0)	20	3	4	5	0	0	10	0	1	1	0	0	-	1	.259	.255	.370
2004	Hou	NL	45	52	13	2	0	4	(3	1)	27	14	8	9	7	0	13	0	0	2	4	0	1.00	6	.250	.328	.519
2005	Hou	NL	91	109	24	5	2	4	(2	2)	45	19	14	12	10	0	25	1	1	0	7	2	.78	4	.220	.292	.413
2006	Hou	NL	73	119	33	8	0	0	(0	0)	41	11	10	15	13	1	21	1	2	1	3	1	.75	2	.277	.351	.345
4 ML YEARS			240	334	84	18	2	9	(6	3)	133	47	36	41	30	1	69	2	4	4	14	3	.82	7	.251	.314	.398

Taylor Buchholz

Pitches: R Bats: R Pos: SP-19; RP-3 Ht: 6'4" Wt: 220 Born: 10/13/1981 Age: 25

Year	Team	Lg	G	GS	CG	GF	IP	BFP	H	R	ER	HR	SH	SF	HB	TBB	IBB	SO	WP	Bk	W	L	Pct	ShO	Sv-Op	Hld	ERC	ERA
2000	Phillies	R	12	7	0	2	44.0	188	46	22	11	2	0	1	2	14	0	41	3	1	2	3	.400	0	0--	-	3.84	2.25
2001	Lakwd	A	28	26	5	0	176.2	741	165	83	66	8	5	7	11	57	0	136	1	0	9	14	.391	3	0--	-	3.32	3.36
2002	Clrwtr	A	23	23	4	0	158.2	666	140	66	58	11	3	3	7	51	1	129	7	0	10	6	.625	2	0--	-	3.07	3.29
2002	Rdng	AA	4	4	0	0	23.0	102	29	19	19	5	2	1	1	6	0	17	0	0	2	2	.000	0	0--	-	6.14	7.43
2003	Rdng	AA	25	24	1	0	144.2	600	136	62	57	14	3	7	9	33	0	114	3	0	9	11	.450	0	0--	-	3.31	3.55
2004	NewOrl	AAA	20	17	1	0	98.0	425	107	60	57	16	2	8	2	29	0	74	8	0	6	7	.462	0	0--	-	4.69	5.23
2005	RdRck	AAA	20	14	0	4	76.2	323	79	41	41	14	3	2	4	27	0	45	2	0	6	0	1.000	0	0--	-	5.03	4.81
2006	RdRck	AAA	7	7	0	0	44.0	192	47	27	24	2	3	2	1	17	0	37	0	0	1	3	.250	0	0--	-	4.11	4.91
2006	Hou	NL	22	19	1	1	113.0	479	107	80	74	21	5	6	3	34	4	77	5	0	6	10	.375	1	0-0	0	3.97	5.89

John Buck

Bats: R Throws: R Pos: C-112; PH-4 Ht: 6'3" Wt: 220 Born: 7/7/1980 Age: 26

Year	Team	Lg	G	AB	H	2B	3B	HR	(Hm	Rd)	TB	R	RBI	RC	TBB	IBB	SO	HBP	SH	SF	SB	CS	SB%	GDP	Avg	OBP	Slg
2004	KC	AL	71	238	56	9	0	12	(6	6)	101	36	30	26	15	0	79	0	4	1	1	1	.50	6	.235	.280	.424

		BATTING																			BASERUNNING				AVERAGES		
Year	Team	Lg	G	AB	H	2B	3B	HR	(Hm	Rd)	TB	R	RBI	RC	TBB	IBB	SO	HBP	SH	SF	SB	CS	SB%	GDP	Avg	OBP	Slg
2005	KC	AL	118	401	97	21	1	12	(3	9)	156	40	47	43	23	2	94	3	1	2	2	2	.50	9	.242	.287	.389
2006	KC	AL	114	371	91	21	1	11	(6	5)	147	37	50	43	26	2	84	7	4	1	0	2	.00	8	.245	.306	.396
3 ML YEARS			303	1010	244	51	2	35	(15	20)	404	113	127	112	64	4	257	10	9	4	3	5	.38	23	.242	.292	.400

Mark Buehrle

Pitches: L **Bats:** L **Pos:** SP-32   **Ht:** 6'2" **Wt:** 225 **Born:** 3/23/1979 **Age:** 28

			HOW MUCH HE PITCHED						WHAT HE GAVE UP											THE RESULTS						
Year	Team	Lg	G	GS	CG	GF	IP	BFP	H	R	ER	HR	SH	SF	HB	TBB	IBB	SO	WP	Bk	W	L	Pct	ShO	Sv-Op	Hld	ERC	ERA
2000	CWS	AL	28	3	0	6	51.1	225	55	27	24	5	1	0	3	19	1	37	0	0	4	1	.800	0	0-2	3	4.56	4.21
2001	CWS	AL	32	32	4	0	221.1	885	188	89	81	24	9	4	8	48	2	126	1	5	16	8	.667	2	0-0	0	2.79	3.29
2002	CWS	AL	34	34	5	0	239.0	984	236	102	95	25	9	3	3	61	7	134	6	1	19	12	.613	2	0-0	0	3.53	3.58
2003	CWS	AL	35	35	2	0	230.1	978	250	124	106	22	7	7	5	61	2	119	1	0	14	14	.500	0	0-0	0	4.10	4.14
2004	CWS	AL	35	35	4	0	245.1	1016	257	119	106	33	4	6	8	51	2	165	0	0	16	10	.615	1	0-0	0	4.00	3.89
2005	CWS	AL	33	33	3	0	236.2	971	240	99	82	20	7	4	4	40	4	149	2	2	16	8	.667	1	0-0	0	3.21	3.12
2006	CWS	AL	32	32	1	0	204.0	876	247	124	113	36	6	7	6	48	5	98	0	1	12	13	.480	0	0-0	0	5.37	4.99
7 ML YEARS			229	204	19	6	1428.0	5935	1473	684	607	165	43	31	37	328	23	828	10	9	97	66	.595	6	0-2	3	3.81	3.83

Jason Bulger

Pitches: R **Bats:** R **Pos:** RP-2   **Ht:** 6'4" **Wt:** 215 **Born:** 12/6/1978 **Age:** 28

			HOW MUCH HE PITCHED						WHAT HE GAVE UP											THE RESULTS						
Year	Team	Lg	G	GS	CG	GF	IP	BFP	H	R	ER	HR	SH	SF	HB	TBB	IBB	SO	WP	Bk	W	L	Pct	ShO	Sv-Op	Hld	ERC	ERA
2002	Sbend	A	20	20	1	0	94.2	434	111	65	52	5	3	8	7	39	0	84	14	0	4	9	.308	0	0--	-	5.01	4.94
2002	Lancst	A+	2	2	0	0	10.0	44	11	7	6	0	0	1	3	3	0	12	0	1	1	1	.500	0	0--	-	4.88	5.40
2003	Lancst	A+	4	4	0	0	17.1	80	23	13	13	3	7	6	3	5	0	20	0	0	2	1	.667	0	0--	-	6.98	6.75
2004	Lancst	A+	21	0	0	18	23.2	95	14	4	4	0	0	0	3	10	1	31	0	0	0	1	.000	0	11--	-	1.86	1.52
2004	ElPaso	AA	24	0	0	22	25.1	119	24	12	11	0	0	0	2	19	2	25	7	0	3	0	.000	0	8--	-	4.47	3.91
2005	Tucsn	AAA	56	0	0	18	56.0	245	50	28	22	3	3	3	2	27	1	55	3	1	3	6	.333	0	4--	-	3.53	3.54
2006	Salt Lk	AAA	27	0	0	16	34.1	151	30	19	18	0	2	1	4	15	0	44	2	0	2	2	.500	0	4--	-	3.20	4.72
2005	Ari	NL	9	0	0	5	10.0	48	14	6	6	1	1	0	0	5	1	9	0	0	1	0	1.000	0	0-0	0	6.68	5.40
2006	LAA	AL	2	0	0	1	1.2	9	1	3	3	0	0	0	0	3	0	1	1	0	0	0	-	0	0-0	0	6.15	16.20
2 ML YEARS			11	0	0	6	11.2	57	15	9	9	1	1	0	0	8	1	10	1	0	1	0	1.000	0	0-0	0	6.64	6.94

Ambiorix Burgos

Pitches: R **Bats:** R **Pos:** RP-67; SP-1   **Ht:** 6'3" **Wt:** 235 **Born:** 4/19/1984 **Age:** 23

			HOW MUCH HE PITCHED						WHAT HE GAVE UP											THE RESULTS						
Year	Team	Lg	G	GS	CG	GF	IP	BFP	H	R	ER	HR	SH	SF	HB	TBB	IBB	SO	WP	Bk	W	L	Pct	ShO	Sv-Op	Hld	ERC	ERA
2003	Royals	R	9	7	0	1	36.0	161	37	22	16	1	0	1	3	16	0	43	8	1	3	2	.600	0	0--	-	4.17	4.00
2003	Burlgtn	A	2	2	0	0	5.0	24	3	3	3	1	4	8	0	6	0	4	1	0	1	0	1.000	0	0--	-	5.62	5.40
2004	Burlgtn	A	27	26	0	0	133.2	585	109	70	65	13	6	5	13	75	1	172	13	4	7	11	.389	0	0--	-	4.03	4.38
2005	Wichta	AA	12	0	0	6	12.2	54	8	7	7	1	0	0	1	8	0	19	2	0	1	1	.500	0	1--	-	3.11	4.97
2005	KC	AL	59	0	0	17	63.1	278	60	29	28	6	2	1	5	31	1	65	8	2	3	5	.375	0	2-6	11	4.41	3.98
2006	KC	AL	68	1	0	41	73.1	336	83	49	45	16	1	4	6	37	4	72	11	3	4	5	.444	0	18-30	5	6.51	5.52
2 ML YEARS			127	1	0	58	136.2	614	143	78	73	22	3	5	11	68	5	137	19	5	7	10	.412	0	20-36	16	5.51	4.81

Chris Burke

Bats: R **Throws:** R **Pos:** 2B-69; CF-38; LF-19; PH-17; SS-8; RF-7   **Ht:** 5'11" **Wt:** 180 **Born:** 3/11/1980 **Age:** 27

			BATTING																			BASERUNNING				AVERAGES		
Year	Team	Lg	G	AB	H	2B	3B	HR	(Hm	Rd)	TB	R	RBI	RC	TBB	IBB	SO	HBP	SH	SF	SB	CS	SB%	GDP	Avg	OBP	Slg
2006	RdRck*	AAA	2	8	4	1	0	1	(-	-)	8	2	2	3	1	0	1	0	0	0	1	0	1.00	0	.500	.556	1.000
2004	Hou	NL	17	17	1	0	0	0	(0	0)	1	2	0	0	3	0	3	0	0	0	0	0	-	0	.059	.200	.059
2005	Hou	NL	108	318	79	19	2	5	(2	3)	117	49	26	35	23	0	62	6	9	3	11	6	.65	7	.248	.309	.368
2006	Hou	NL	123	366	101	23	1	9	(3	6)	153	58	40	49	27	0	77	14	4	2	11	1	.92	6	.276	.347	.418
3 ML YEARS			248	701	181	42	3	14	(5	9)	271	109	66	84	53	0	142	20	13	5	22	7	.76	13	.258	.326	.387

A.J. Burnett

Pitches: R **Bats:** R **Pos:** SP-21   **Ht:** 6'4" **Wt:** 230 **Born:** 1/3/1977 **Age:** 30

			HOW MUCH HE PITCHED						WHAT HE GAVE UP											THE RESULTS						
Year	Team	Lg	G	GS	CG	GF	IP	BFP	H	R	ER	HR	SH	SF	HB	TBB	IBB	SO	WP	Bk	W	L	Pct	ShO	Sv-Op	Hld	ERC	ERA
2006	Dnedin*	A+	2	2	0	0	8.0	34	9	3	3	0	0	0	1	2	0	6	0	0	0	0	-	0	0--	-	4.10	3.38
2006	NHam*	AA	1	1	0	0	6.0	22	2	2	1	1	0	0	0	3	0	9	0	0	1	0	1.000	0	0--	-	1.63	1.50
2006	Syrcse*	AAA	1	1	0	0	5.0	17	0	0	0	0	0	0	1	1	0	7	1	0	1	0	1.000	0	0--	-	0.18	0.00
1999	Fla	NL	7	7	0	0	41.1	182	37	23	16	3	1	3	0	25	2	33	0	0	4	2	.667	0	0-0	0	4.00	3.48
2000	Fla	NL	13	13	0	0	82.2	364	80	46	44	8	6	3	2	44	3	57	2	0	3	7	.300	0	0-0	0	4.45	4.79
2001	Fla	NL	27	27	2	0	173.1	733	145	82	78	20	6	8	7	83	3	128	7	1	11	12	.478	1	0-0	0	3.76	4.05
2002	Fla	NL	31	29	7	0	204.1	844	153	84	75	12	9	4	9	90	5	203	14	0	12	9	.571	5	0-1	0	2.77	3.30
2003	Fla	NL	4	4	0	0	23.0	98	18	13	12	2	2	1	2	18	2	21	2	0	0	2	.000	0	0-0	0	4.36	4.70
2004	Fla	NL	20	19	1	0	120.0	490	102	50	49	9	3	3	4	38	0	113	7	0	7	6	.538	0	0-0	0	2.95	3.68
2005	Fla	NL	32	32	4	0	209.0	873	184	97	80	12	7	5	7	79	1	198	12	0	12	12	.500	2	0-0	0	3.20	3.44
2006	Tor	AL	21	21	2	0	135.2	577	138	67	60	14	4	3	8	39	3	118	6	1	10	8	.556	1	0-1	0	3.97	3.98
8 ML YEARS			155	152	16	0	989.1	4169	857	462	414	80	38	30	39	416	19	871	50	2	59	58	.504	9	0-1	0	3.44	3.77

Jeromy Burnitz

Bats: L Throws: R Pos: RF-84; PH-29   Ht: 6'0" Wt: 210 Born: 4/15/1969 Age: 38

															BASERUNNING				AVERAGES		
							BATTING																
Year	Team	Lg	G	AB	H	2B	3B	HR	(Hm Rd)	TB	R	RBI	RC	TBB	IBB	SO	HBP	SH	SF	SB	CS	SB%	GDP	Avg	OBP	Slg

Year	Team	Lg	G	AB	H	2B	3B	HR	(Hm	Rd)	TB	R	RBI	RC	TBB	IBB	SO	HBP	SH	SF	SB	CS	SB%	GDP	Avg	OBP	Slg
1993	NYM	NL	86	263	64	10	6	13	(6	7)	125	49	38	42	38	4	66	1	2	2	3	6	.33	2	.243	.339	.475
1994	NYM	NL	45	143	34	4	0	3	(2	1)	47	26	15	17	23	0	45	1	1	0	1	1	.50	2	.238	.347	.329
1995	Cle	AL	9	7	4	1	0	0	(0	0)	5	4	0	2	0	0	0	0	0	0	0	0	-	0	.571	.571	.714
1996	2 Tms		94	200	53	14	0	9	(5	4)	94	38	40	37	33	2	47	4	0	2	4	1	.80	4	.265	.377	.470
1997	Mil	AL	153	494	139	37	8	27	(18	9)	273	85	85	100	75	8	111	5	3	0	20	13	.61	8	.281	.382	.553
1998	Mil	NL	161	609	160	28	1	38	(17	21)	304	92	125	102	70	7	158	4	1	7	7	4	.64	9	.263	.339	.499
1999	Mil	NL	130	467	126	33	2	33	(12	21)	262	87	103	104	91	7	124	16	0	6	7	3	.70	11	.270	.402	.561
2000	Mil	NL	161	564	131	29	2	31	(12	19)	257	91	98	94	99	10	121	14	0	9	6	4	.60	12	.232	.356	.456
2001	Mil	NL	154	562	141	32	4	34	(16	18)	283	104	100	97	80	9	150	5	0	4	0	4	.00	8	.251	.347	.504
2002	NYM	NL	154	479	103	15	0	19	(12	7)	175	65	54	48	58	5	135	10	1	2	10	7	.59	11	.215	.311	.365
2003	2 Tms		126	464	111	22	0	31	(10	21)	226	63	77	61	35	9	112	5	0	1	5	4	.56	5	.239	.299	.487
2004	Col	NL	150	540	153	30	4	37	(24	13)	302	94	110	99	58	7	124	5	0	3	5	6	.45	7	.283	.356	.559
2005	ChC	NL	160	605	156	31	2	24	(17	7)	263	84	87	79	57	3	109	3	1	5	5	4	.56	12	.258	.322	.435
2006	Pit	NL	111	313	72	12	0	16	(11	5)	132	35	49	36	22	4	74	5	0	2	1	1	.50	8	.230	.289	.422
96	Cle	AL	71	128	36	10	0	7	(4	3)	67	30	26	27	25	1	31	2	0	0	2	1	.67	3	.281	.406	.523
96	Mil	AL	23	72	17	4	0	2	(1	1)	27	8	14	10	8	1	16	2	0	2	2	0	1.00	1	.236	.321	.375
03	NYM	NL	65	234	64	18	0	18	(4	14)	136	38	45	41	21	6	55	4	0	0	1	4	.20	4	.274	.344	.581
03	LAD	NL	61	230	47	4	0	13	(6	7)	90	25	32	20	14	3	57	1	0	1	4	0	1.00	1	.204	.252	.391
14 ML YEARS			1694	5710	1447	298	29	315	(162	153)	2748	917	981	918	739	75	1376	78	9	43	74	58	.56	99	.253	.345	.481

Mike Burns

Pitches: R Bats: R Pos: RP-18   Ht: 6'1" Wt: 210 Born: 7/14/1978 Age: 28

Year	Team	Lg	G	GS	CG	GF	IP	BFP	H	R	ER	HR	SH	SF	HB	TBB	IBB	SO	WP	Bk	W	L	Pct	ShO	Sv-Op	Hld	ERC	ERA
2000	Mrtnsvl	R+	12	12	0	0	65.2	281	75	52	33	12	4	2	4	9	0	51	2	1	2	7	.222	0	0- -	-	4.61	4.52
2001	Mich	A	29	21	1	3	132.0	554	131	67	58	10	4	5	13	27	0	108	0	1	7	7	.500	0	1- -	-	3.50	3.95
2002	Mich	A	28	28	3	0	181.0	718	146	59	50	12	5	3	7	29	1	126	8	2	14	9	.609	2	0- -	-	2.11	2.49
2003	RdRck	AA	38	14	0	9	105.2	476	129	80	72	15	4	3	4	30	3	89	4	0	2	13	.133	0	0- -	-	5.22	6.13
2004	RdRck	AA	56	0	0	35	80.2	320	63	18	15	1	0	4	4	15	3	94	1	0	11	3	.786	0	9- -	-	1.78	1.67
2005	RdRck	AAA	25	0	0	24	30.0	116	22	7	7	4	1	0	0	4	0	34	2	0	2	1	.667	0	13- -	-	1.90	2.10
2006	Lsvlle	AAA	40	2	0	7	56.2	225	47	11	11	3	1	2	2	12	0	52	1	0	6	1	.857	0	0- -	-	2.35	1.75
2005	Hou	NL	27	0	0	10	31.0	136	29	18	17	6	1	0	5	8	1	20	1	0	0	0	-	0	0-0	1	4.26	4.94
2006	2 Tms		18	0	0	6	21.0	104	40	17	17	2	1	2	2	4	2	16	1	0	0	0	-	0	0-0	1	9.26	7.29
06	Cin	NL	11	0	0	2	13.1	70	30	13	13	2	1	0	2	3	1	9	1	0	0	0	-	0	0-0	1	13.15	8.78
06	Bos	AL	7	0	0	4	7.2	34	10	4	4	0	0	2	0	1	1	7	0	0	0	0	-	0	0-0	0	3.68	4.70
2 ML YEARS			45	0	0	16	52.0	240	69	35	34	8	2	2	7	12	3	36	2	0	0	0	-	0	0-0	2	6.14	5.88

Pat Burrell

Bats: R Throws: R Pos: LF-126; PH-13; DH-6   Ht: 6'4" Wt: 235 Born: 10/10/1976 Age: 30

Year	Team	Lg	G	AB	H	2B	3B	HR	(Hm	Rd)	TB	R	RBI	RC	TBB	IBB	SO	HBP	SH	SF	SB	CS	SB%	GDP	Avg	OBP	Slg
2000	Phi	NL	111	408	106	27	1	18	(7	11)	189	57	79	69	63	2	139	1	0	2	0	0	-	5	.260	.359	.463
2001	Phi	NL	155	539	139	29	2	27	(10	17)	253	70	89	86	70	7	162	5	0	4	2	1	.67	12	.258	.346	.469
2002	Phi	NL	157	586	165	39	2	37	(18	19)	319	96	116	104	89	9	153	3	0	6	1	0	1.00	16	.282	.376	.544
2003	Phi	NL	146	522	109	31	4	21	(9	12)	211	57	64	57	72	2	142	4	0	1	0	0	-	18	.209	.309	.404
2004	Phi	NL	127	448	115	17	0	24	(14	10)	204	66	84	72	78	7	130	2	0	6	2	0	1.00	10	.257	.365	.455
2005	Phi	NL	154	562	158	27	1	32	(20	12)	283	78	117	109	99	6	160	3	0	5	0	0	-	12	.281	.389	.504
2006	Phi	NL	144	462	119	24	1	29	(12	17)	232	80	95	81	98	5	131	3	0	4	0	0	-	11	.258	.388	.502
7 ML YEARS			994	3527	911	194	11	188	(90	98)	1691	504	644	578	569	38	1017	21	0	28	5	1	.83	84	.258	.362	.479

Brian Burres

Pitches: L Bats: L Pos: RP-11   Ht: 6'1" Wt: 180 Born: 4/8/1981 Age: 26

Year	Team	Lg	G	GS	CG	GF	IP	BFP	H	R	ER	HR	SH	SF	HB	TBB	IBB	SO	WP	Bk	W	L	Pct	ShO	Sv-Op	Hld	ERC	ERA
2001	SlmKzr	A-	14	6	0	2	40.2	174	43	20	14	2	3	2	1	11	0	38	5	0	3	1	.750	0	1- -	-	3.61	3.10
2002	Hgrstn	A	32	16	0	4	119.1	522	114	78	63	15	4	4	9	53	0	119	8	1	3	10	.231	0	1- -	-	4.49	4.75
2003	SnJos	A	39	0	0	16	60.2	276	55	33	26	4	2	4	3	36	3	64	7	0	3	3	.500	0	1- -	-	4.06	3.86
2004	SnJos	A	36	15	0	6	123.2	506	115	49	39	10	4	4	7	30	0	114	6	0	12	1	.923	0	0- -	-	3.24	2.84
2005	Nrwich	AA	26	24	0	1	128.2	563	130	66	60	13	6	3	10	57	0	105	8	1	9	6	.600	0	0- -	-	4.69	4.20
2006	Ottawa	AAA	26	26	1	0	139.0	596	133	63	58	14	6	3	8	57	1	110	8	0	10	6	.625	1	0- -	-	4.14	3.76
2006	Bal	AL	11	0	0	2	8.0	31	6	2	2	1	0	0	0	1	0	6	0	0	0	0	-	0	0-0	4	1.91	2.25

Sean Burroughs

Bats: L Throws: R Pos: 3B-7; PH-2   Ht: 6'2" Wt: 180 Born: 9/12/1980 Age: 26

Year	Team	Lg	G	AB	H	2B	3B	HR	(Hm	Rd)	TB	R	RBI	RC	TBB	IBB	SO	HBP	SH	SF	SB	CS	SB%	GDP	Avg	OBP	Slg
2006	Drham*	AAA	37	131	28	2	0	1	(-	-)	33	8	11	7	9	0	29	1	1	1	1	3	.25	5	.214	.268	.252
2002	SD	NL	63	192	52	5	1	1	(0	1)	62	18	11	15	12	1	30	1	1	0	2	0	1.00	6	.271	.317	.323
2003	SD	NL	146	517	148	27	6	7	(2	5)	208	62	58	68	44	4	75	11	2	4	7	2	.78	13	.286	.352	.402
2004	SD	NL	130	523	156	23	3	2	(0	2)	191	76	47	70	31	4	52	9	1	0	5	4	.56	6	.298	.348	.365
2005	SD	NL	93	284	71	7	2	1	(1	0)	85	20	17	24	24	4	41	5	3	1	4	0	1.00	7	.250	.318	.299
2006	TB	AL	8	21	4	1	0	0	(0	0)	5	3	1	2	4	0	7	0	0	0	1	0	1.00	1	.190	.320	.238
5 ML YEARS			440	1537	431	63	12	11	(3	8)	551	179	134	179	115	13	205	26	7	5	19	6	.76	33	.280	.340	.358

David Bush

Pitches: R **Bats:** R **Pos:** SP-32; RP-2   **Ht:** 6'2" **Wt:** 210 **Born:** 11/9/1979 **Age:** 27

		HOW MUCH HE PITCHED						WHAT HE GAVE UP										THE RESULTS						
Year	Team	Lg	G	GS	CG	GF	IP	BFP	H	R	ER	HR	SH	SF	HB	TBB	IBB	SO	WP	Bk	W	L	Pct	ShO	Sv-Op Hld	ERC	ERA
2004	Tor	AL	16	16	1	0	97.2	412	95	47	40	11	4	4	6	25	2	64	3	0	5	4	.556	1	0-0 0	3.65	3.69
2005	Tor	AL	25	24	2	1	136.1	575	142	73	68	24	3	2	13	29	3	75	2	0	5	11	.313	0	0-0 0	4.28	4.49
2006	Mil	NL	34	32	3	0	210.0	869	201	111	103	26	9	6	18	38	2	166	6	0	12	11	.522	2	0-0 1	3.47	4.41
	3 ML YEARS		75	72	6	1	444.0	1856	438	231	211	57	16	12	37	92	7	305	11	0	22	26	.458	3	0-0 1	3.75	4.28

Freddie Bynum

Bats: L **Throws:** R **Pos:** PH-37; 2B-15; LF-13; RF-8; CF-2; PR-1   **Ht:** 6'1" **Wt:** 185 **Born:** 3/15/1980 **Age:** 27

								BATTING												BASERUNNING				AVERAGES		
Year	Team	Lg	G	AB	H	2B	3B	HR	(Hm	Rd)	TB	R	RBI	RC	TBB	IBB	SO	HBP	SH	SF	SB	CS	SB%	GDP	Avg	OBP	Slg
2000	Vancvr	A-	72	281	72	10	1	1	(-	-)	87	52	26	32	31	0	58	5	3	0	22	12	.65	3	.256	.341	.310
2001	Mdest	A+	120	440	115	19	7	2	(-	-)	154	59	46	54	41	0	95	1	4	1	28	11	.72	8	.261	.325	.350
2002	Visalia	A+	135	539	165	26	5	3	(-	-)	210	83	56	87	64	1	116	7	15	3	41	21	.66	9	.306	.385	.390
2003	Mdland	AA	132	510	134	18	9	5	(-	-)	185	84	58	70	56	4	135	8	12	2	22	8	.73	6	.263	.344	.363
2004	Mdland	AA	65	265	71	13	4	1	(-	-)	95	38	22	34	24	0	56	2	5	1	18	7	.72	1	.268	.332	.358
2004	Scrmto	AAA	66	258	73	11	2	2	(-	-)	94	42	26	36	19	0	61	3	11	0	21	4	.84	8	.283	.339	.364
2005	Scrmto	AAA	102	378	105	16	9	2	(-	-)	145	56	40	55	38	1	83	3	7	2	23	7	.77	3	.278	.347	.384
2006	Iowa	AAA	6	22	5	0	0	0	(-	-)	5	3	3	1	1	0	3	0	0	0	0	0	-	0	.227	.261	.227
2005	Oak	AL	7	7	2	1	0	0	(0	0)	3	0	1	1	0	0	3	0	0	0	0	0	-	0	.286	.286	.429
2006	ChC	NL	71	136	35	5	5	4	(3	1)	62	20	12	18	9	0	44	1	2	0	8	4	.67	2	.257	.308	.456
	2 ML YEARS		78	143	37	6	5	4	(3	1)	65	20	13	19	9	0	47	1	2	0	8	4	.67	2	.259	.307	.455

Marlon Byrd

Bats: R **Throws:** R **Pos:** CF-57; RF-18; PH-9; LF-3; PR-2   **Ht:** 6'0" **Wt:** 235 **Born:** 8/30/1977 **Age:** 29

								BATTING												BASERUNNING				AVERAGES		
Year	Team	Lg	G	AB	H	2B	3B	HR	(Hm	Rd)	TB	R	RBI	RC	TBB	IBB	SO	HBP	SH	SF	SB	CS	SB%	GDP	Avg	OBP	Slg
2006	NewOr*	AAA	46	155	42	9	0	7	(-	-)	72	20	29	27	16	1	31	7	0	1	3	1	.75	1	.271	.363	.465
2002	Phi	NL	10	35	8	2	0	1	(1	0)	13	2	1	0	1	0	8	0	0	0	0	2	.00	1	.229	.250	.371
2003	Phi	NL	135	495	150	28	4	7	(3	4)	207	86	45	72	44	3	94	7	4	3	11	1	.92	8	.303	.366	.418
2004	Phi	NL	106	346	79	13	2	5	(3	2)	111	48	33	35	22	1	68	7	2	1	2	2	.50	10	.228	.287	.321
2005	2 Tms	NL	79	229	61	15	2	2	(0	2)	86	20	26	30	19	1	50	2	5	4	5	1	.83	5	.266	.323	.376
2006	Was	NL	78	197	44	8	1	5	(1	4)	69	28	18	18	22	1	47	6	1	2	3	3	.50	6	.223	.317	.350
05	Phi	NL	5	13	4	0	0	0	(0	0)	4	0	0	2	1	0	3	1	0	0	0	0	-	0	.308	.400	.308
05	Was	NL	74	216	57	15	2	2	(0	2)	82	20	26	28	18	1	47	1	5	4	5	1	.83	5	.264	.318	.380
	5 ML YEARS		408	1302	342	66	9	20	(8	12)	486	184	123	155	108	6	267	22	12	10	21	9	.70	29	.263	.327	.373

Paul Byrd

Pitches: R **Bats:** R **Pos:** SP-31   **Ht:** 6'1" **Wt:** 190 **Born:** 12/3/1970 **Age:** 36

				HOW MUCH HE PITCHED						WHAT HE GAVE UP										THE RESULTS						
Year	Team	Lg	G	GS	CG	GF	IP	BFP	H	R	ER	HR	SH	SF	HB	TBB	IBB	SO	WP	Bk	W	L	Pct	ShO	Sv-Op Hld	ERC	ERA
1995	NYM	NL	17	0	0	6	22.0	91	18	6	5	1	0	2	1	7	1	26	1	2	2	0	1.000	0	0-0 3	2.53	2.05
1996	NYM	NL	38	0	0	14	46.2	204	48	22	22	7	1	1	0	21	4	31	3	0	1	2	.333	0	0-2 3	4.67	4.24
1997	Atl	NL	31	4	0	9	53.0	236	47	34	31	6	2	2	4	28	4	37	3	1	4	4	.500	0	0-0 1	4.15	5.26
1998	2 Tms	NL	9	8	2	0	57.0	233	45	19	17	6	2	1	0	18	1	39	2	0	5	2	.714	1	0-0 0	2.62	2.68
1999	Phi	NL	32	32	1	0	199.2	872	205	119	102	34	5	6	17	70	2	106	11	3	15	11	.577	0	0-0 0	4.87	4.60
2000	Phi	NL	17	15	0	0	83.0	371	89	67	60	17	3	1	3	35	2	53	1	0	2	9	.182	0	0-0 0	5.42	6.51
2001	2 Tms	NL	19	16	1	0	103.1	444	120	54	51	12	4	6	2	26	1	52	2	0	6	7	.462	0	0-0 0	4.62	4.44
2002	KC	AL	33	33	7	0	228.1	935	224	111	99	36	2	13	7	38	1	129	3	1	17	11	.607	2	0-0 0	3.55	3.90
2004	Atl	NL	19	19	0	0	114.1	482	123	57	50	18	3	3	2	19	0	79	1	0	8	7	.533	0	0-0 0	3.98	3.94
2005	LAA	AL	31	31	2	0	204.1	842	216	95	85	22	7	7	7	28	1	102	1	0	12	11	.522	1	0-0 0	3.56	3.74
2006	Cle	AL	31	31	1	0	179.0	805	232	120	97	26	1	6	6	38	3	88	2	0	10	9	.526	0	0-0 0	5.40	4.88
98	Atl	NL	1	0	0	0	2.0	11	4	3	3	0	0	0	0	1	0	1	0	0	0	0	-	0	0-0 0	9.72	13.50
98	Atl	NL	8	8	2	0	55.0	222	41	16	14	6	2	1	0	17	1	38	2	0	5	2	.714	1	0-0 0	2.41	2.29
01	Phi	NL	3	1	0	0	10.0	45	10	9	9	1	2	2	1	4	0	3	1	0	0	1	.000	0	0-0 0	4.36	8.10
01	KC	AL	16	15	1	0	93.1	399	110	45	42	11	2	4	1	22	1	49	1	0	6	6	.500	0	0-0 0	4.65	4.05
	11 ML YEARS		277	189	14	30	1290.2	5515	1367	704	619	185	30	48	49	328	20	742	30	7	82	73	.529	4	0-2 7	4.24	4.32

Tim Byrdak

Pitches: L **Bats:** L **Pos:** RP-16   **Ht:** 5'11" **Wt:** 195 **Born:** 10/31/1973 **Age:** 33

				HOW MUCH HE PITCHED						WHAT HE GAVE UP										THE RESULTS						
Year	Team	Lg	G	GS	CG	GF	IP	BFP	H	R	ER	HR	SH	SF	HB	TBB	IBB	SO	WP	Bk	W	L	Pct	ShO	Sv-Op Hld	ERC	ERA
2006	Abrdn*	A-	1	0	0	0	1.0	5	2	1	1	0	0	0	0	0	0	3	0	0	0	0	-	0	0-- -	7.48	9.00
2006	Frdrck*	A+	1	0	0	0	1.1	8	4	2	2	0	0	0	0	1	0	1	0	0	0	0	-	0	0-- -	20.65	13.50
2006	Bowie*	AA	3	0	0	2	4.0	18	4	1	1	0	0	0	0	2	0	7	0	0	0	0	-	0	0-- -	3.63	2.25
1998	KC	AL	3	0	0	0	1.2	9	5	1	1	1	0	0	0	0	0	1	0	0	0	0	-	0	0-0 0	23.52	5.40
1999	KC	AL	33	0	0	5	24.2	128	32	24	21	5	3	0	1	20	2	17	3	1	0	3	.000	0	1-4 10	8.29	7.66
2000	KC	AL	12	0	0	1	6.1	34	11	8	8	3	0	0	0	4	0	8	1	0	0	0	-	0	0-2 3	13.14	11.37
2005	Bal	AL	41	0	0	3	26.2	131	27	14	12	1	2	1	1	21	1	31	5	0	0	1	.000	0	1-1 11	5.04	4.05
2006	Bal	AL	16	0	0	2	7.0	42	14	10	10	2	2	0	0	8	1	2	1	0	1	0	1.000	0	0-0 3	15.90	12.86
	5 ML YEARS		105	0	0	11	66.1	344	89	57	52	12	7	1	2	53	4	59	10	1	1	5	.167	0	2-7 27	8.37	7.06

Eric Byrnes

Bats: R Throws: R Pos: CF-123; LF-12; RF-10; PH-7; PR-2 Ht: 6'2" Wt: 210 Born: 2/16/1976 Age: 31

Year Team	Lg	G	AB	H	2B	3B	HR	(Hm	Rd)	TB	R	RBI	RC	TBB	IBB	SO	HBP	SH	SF	SB	CS	SB%	GDP	Avg	OBP	Slg
2000 Oak	AL	10	10	3	0	0	0	(0	0)	3	5	0	1	0	0	1	1	0	0	2	1	.67	0	.300	.364	.300
2001 Oak	AL	19	38	9	1	0	3	(2	1)	19	9	5	7	4	0	6	1	0	0	1	0	1.00	0	.237	.326	.500
2002 Oak	AL	90	94	23	4	2	3	(2	1)	40	24	11	10	4	0	17	3	1	2	3	0	1.00	3	.245	.291	.426
2003 Oak	AL	121	414	109	27	9	12	(7	5)	190	64	51	68	42	4	71	2	0	2	10	2	.83	3	.263	.333	.459
2004 Oak	AL	143	569	161	39	3	20	(10	10)	266	91	73	87	46	0	111	12	0	5	17	1	.94	11	.283	.347	.467
2005 3 Tms		126	412	93	24	3	10	(5	5)	153	49	40	41	32	0	71	8	3	1	7	2	.78	7	.226	.294	.371
2006 Ari	NL	143	562	150	37	3	26	(12	14)	271	82	79	78	34	2	88	5	2	3	25	3	.89	12	.267	.313	.482
05 Oak	AL	59	192	51	15	2	7	(3	4)	91	30	24	29	14	0	27	7	1	1	2	2	.50	1	.266	.336	.474
05 Col	NL	15	53	10	2	0	0	(0	0)	12	2	5	4	7	0	11	0	0	0	2	0	1.00	0	.189	.283	.226
05 Bal	AL	52	167	32	7	1	3	(2	1)	50	17	11	8	11	0	33	1	2	0	3	0	1.00	5	.192	.246	.299
7 ML YEARS		652	2099	548	132	20	74	(38	36)	942	324	259	292	162	6	365	32	6	13	65	9	.88	36	.261	.322	.449

Daniel Cabrera

Pitches: R Bats: R Pos: SP-26 Ht: 6'7" Wt: 260 Born: 5/28/1981 Age: 26

Year Team	Lg	G	GS	CG	GF	IP	BFP	H	R	ER	HR	SH	SF	HB	TBB	IBB	SO	WP	Bk	W	L	Pct	ShO	Sv-Op	Hld	ERC	ERA
2006 Bowie*	AA	1	1	0	0	4.0	14	0	1	0	0	0	0	1	1	0	7	2	0	0	0	-	0	0--	-	0.27	0.00
2006 Ottawa*	AAA	4	4	0	0	24.1	103	20	13	11	1	1	1	1	9	0	27	5	0	3	1	.750	0	0--	-	2.71	4.07
2004 Bal	AL	28	27	1	1	147.2	662	145	85	82	14	4	7	2	89	2	76	12	0	12	8	.600	1	1-1	0	4.79	5.00
2005 Bal	AL	29	29	0	0	161.1	716	144	92	81	14	2	3	11	87	2	157	9	1	10	13	.435	0	0-0	0	4.13	4.52
2006 Bal	AL	26	26	2	0	148.0	662	130	82	78	11	5	8	5	104	1	157	17	1	9	10	.474	1	0-0	0	4.55	4.74
3 ML YEARS		83	82	3	1	457.0	2040	419	259	241	39	11	18	18	280	5	390	38	2	31	31	.500	2	1-1	0	4.47	4.75

Fernando Cabrera

Pitches: R Bats: R Pos: RP-51 Ht: 6'4" Wt: 220 Born: 11/16/1981 Age: 25

Year Team	Lg	G	GS	CG	GF	IP	BFP	H	R	ER	HR	SH	SF	HB	TBB	IBB	SO	WP	Bk	W	L	Pct	ShO	Sv-Op	Hld	ERC	ERA
2006 Buffalo*	AAA	4	0	0	1	8.1	35	8	1	1	1	0	0	0	2	0	13	1	0	1	0	1.000	0	0--	-	3.30	1.08
2004 Cle	AL	4	0	0	2	5.1	20	3	3	2	0	0	1	0	1	0	6	0	0	0	0	-	0	0-0	0	0.99	3.38
2005 Cle	AL	15	0	0	6	30.2	124	24	7	5	1	0	0	0	11	1	29	1	1	2	1	.667	0	0-0	1	2.33	1.47
2006 Cle	AL	51	0	0	20	60.2	256	53	36	35	12	1	4	1	32	2	71	5	0	3	3	.500	0	0-4	6	4.72	5.19
3 ML YEARS		70	0	0	28	96.2	400	80	46	42	13	1	5	1	44	3	106	6	1	5	4	.556	0	0-4	7	3.65	3.91

Melky Cabrera

Bats: B Throws: L Pos: LF-116; RF-8; PH-6; CF-4 Ht: 5'11" Wt: 170 Born: 8/11/1984 Age: 22

Year Team	Lg	G	AB	H	2B	3B	HR	(Hm	Rd)	TB	R	RBI	RC	TBB	IBB	SO	HBP	SH	SF	SB	CS	SB%	GDP	Avg	OBP	Slg
2003 StIsInd	A-	67	279	79	10	2	2	(-	-)	99	34	31	37	23	1	36	4	4	1	13	5	.72	6	.283	.345	.355
2004 Tampa	A+	85	333	96	20	3	8	(-	-)	146	48	51	51	23	1	59	5	0	3	3	1	.75	8	.288	.341	.438
2004 Btl Crk	A	42	171	57	16	3	0	(-	-)	79	35	16	31	15	0	23	0	0	2	7	2	.78	2	.333	.383	.462
2005 Trntn	AA	106	426	117	22	3	10	(-	-)	175	57	60	60	28	2	72	4	1	5	11	2	.85	11	.275	.322	.411
2005 Clmbs	AAA	26	101	25	3	0	3	(-	-)	37	15	17	12	9	0	15	0	2	0	2	0	1.00	3	.248	.309	.366
2006 Clmbs	AAA	31	122	47	6	2	4	(-	-)	69	19	24	28	10	0	9	1	0	2	3	1	.75	6	.385	.430	.566
2005 NYY	AL	6	19	4	0	0	0	(0	0)	4	1	0	0	0	0	2	0	0	0	0	0	-	0	.211	.211	.211
2006 NYY	AL	130	460	129	26	2	7	(3	4)	180	75	50	68	56	3	59	2	5	1	12	5	.71	9	.280	.360	.391
2 ML YEARS		136	479	133	26	2	7	(3	4)	184	76	50	68	56	3	61	2	5	1	12	5	.71	9	.278	.355	.384

Miguel Cabrera

Bats: R Throws: R Pos: 3B-157; DH-1 Ht: 6'2" Wt: 210 Born: 4/18/1983 Age: 24

Year Team	Lg	G	AB	H	2B	3B	HR	(Hm	Rd)	TB	R	RBI	RC	TBB	IBB	SO	HBP	SH	SF	SB	CS	SB%	GDP	Avg	OBP	Slg
2003 Fla	NL	87	314	84	21	3	12	(7	5)	147	39	62	51	25	3	84	2	4	1	0	2	.00	12	.268	.325	.468
2004 Fla	NL	160	603	177	31	1	33	(14	19)	309	101	112	92	68	5	148	6	0	8	5	2	.71	20	.294	.366	.512
2005 Fla	NL	158	613	198	43	2	33	(11	22)	344	106	116	108	64	12	125	2	0	6	1	0	1.00	20	.323	.385	.561
2006 Fla	NL	158	576	195	50	2	26	(15	11)	327	112	114	132	86	27	108	10	0	4	9	6	.60	18	.339	.430	.568
4 ML YEARS		563	2106	654	145	8	104	(47	57)	1127	358	404	383	243	47	465	20	4	19	15	10	.60	70	.311	.384	.535

Orlando Cabrera

Bats: R Throws: R Pos: SS-152; PH-1 Ht: 5'9" Wt: 180 Born: 11/2/1974 Age: 32

Year Team	Lg	G	AB	H	2B	3B	HR	(Hm	Rd)	TB	R	RBI	RC	TBB	IBB	SO	HBP	SH	SF	SB	CS	SB%	GDP	Avg	OBP	Slg
1997 Mon	NL	16	18	4	0	0	0	(0	0)	4	4	2	0	1	0	3	0	1	0	1	2	.33	1	.222	.263	.222
1998 Mon	NL	79	261	73	16	5	3	(2	1)	108	44	22	34	18	1	27	0	5	1	6	2	.75	6	.280	.325	.414
1999 Mon	NL	104	382	97	23	5	8	(6	2)	154	48	39	42	18	4	38	3	4	0	2	2	.50	9	.254	.293	.403
2000 Mon	NL	125	422	100	25	1	13	(7	6)	166	47	55	43	25	3	28	1	3	3	4	4	.50	12	.237	.279	.393
2001 Mon	NL	162	626	173	41	6	14	(7	7)	268	64	96	85	43	5	54	4	4	7	19	7	.73	15	.276	.324	.428
2002 Mon	NL	153	563	148	43	1	7	(3	4)	214	64	56	61	48	4	53	2	9	4	25	7	.78	16	.263	.321	.380
2003 Mon	NL	162	626	186	47	2	17	(8	9)	288	95	80	92	52	3	64	1	3	9	24	2	.92	18	.297	.347	.460
2004 2 Tms		161	618	163	38	3	10	(2	8)	237	74	62	67	39	0	54	3	3	10	16	4	.80	17	.264	.306	.383
2005 LAA	AL	141	540	139	28	3	8	(2	6)	197	70	57	61	38	4	50	3	4	2	21	2	.91	10	.257	.309	.365
2006 LAA	AL	153	607	171	45	1	9	(3	6)	245	95	72	77	51	0	58	3	3	11	27	3	.90	12	.282	.335	.404

Year	Team	Lg	G	AB	H	2B	3B	HR	(Hm	Rd)	TB	R	RBI	RC	TBB	IBB	SO	HBP	SH	SF	SB	CS	SB%	GDP	Avg	OBP	Slg
04	Mon	NL	103	390	96	19	2	4	(1	3)	131	41	31	37	28	0	31	2	2	3	12	3	.80	13	.246	.298	.336
04	Bos	AL	58	228	67	19	1	6	(1	5)	106	33	31	30	11	0	23	1	1	1	4	1	.80	4	.294	.320	.465
10 ML YEARS			1256	4663	1254	306	27	89	(40	49)	1881	605	541	562	333	24	429	20	39	47	145	35	.81	116	.269	.317	.403

Matt Cain

Pitches: R **Bats:** R **Pos:** SP-31; RP-1   **Ht:** 6'3" **Wt:** 235 **Born:** 10/1/1984 **Age:** 22

			HOW MUCH HE PITCHED					WHAT HE GAVE UP										THE RESULTS						
Year	Team	Lg	G	GS	CG	GF	IP	BFP	H	R	ER	HR	SH	SF	HB	TBB	IBB	SO	WP	Bk	W	L	Pct	ShO	Sv-Op Hld	ERC	ERA
2002	Giants	R	8	7	0	0	19.1	82	13	10	8	1	0	2	4	11	0	20	3	0	0	1	.000	0	0- - -	3.47	3.72
2003	Hgrstn	A	14	14	0	0	74.0	303	57	24	21	5	0	0	5	24	0	90	1	1	4	4	.500	0	0- - -	2.62	2.55
2004	SnJos	A+	13	13	0	0	72.2	293	58	25	15	5	0	4	4	17	0	89	0	0	7	1	.875	0	0- - -	2.40	1.86
2004	Nrwich	AA	15	15	0	0	86.0	371	73	44	32	7	1	7	3	40	0	72	4	0	6	4	.600	0	0- - -	3.46	3.35
2005	Fresno	AAA	26	26	1	0	145.2	628	118	77	71	22	3	4	5	73	0	176	6	0	10	5	.667	0	0- - -	3.86	4.39
2005	SF	NL	7	7	1	0	46.1	181	24	12	12	4	2	1	0	19	1	30	1	0	2	1	.667	0	0-0 0	1.61	2.33
2006	SF	NL	32	31	1	1	190.2	818	157	93	88	18	11	6	6	87	1	179	9	2	13	12	.520	1	0-0 0	3.35	4.15
2 ML YEARS			39	38	2	1	237.0	999	181	105	100	22	13	7	6	106	2	209	10	2	15	13	.536	1	0-0 0	2.98	3.80

Miguel Cairo

Bats: R **Throws:** R **Pos:** 2B-45; 1B-16; SS-14; 3B-8; PR-5; PH-4; DH-2; LF-1   **Ht:** 6'1" **Wt:** 210 **Born:** 5/4/1974 **Age:** 33

			BATTING												BASERUNNING				AVERAGES		
Year	Team	Lg	G	AB	H	2B	3B	HR	(Hm	Rd)	TB	R	RBI	RC	TBB	IBB	SO	HBP	SH	SF	SB	CS	SB%	GDP	Avg	OBP	Slg
1996	Tor	AL	9	27	6	2	0	0	(0	0)	8	5	1	2	2	0	9	1	0	0	0	0	-	1	.222	.300	.296
1997	ChC	NL	16	29	7	1	0	0	(0	0)	8	7	1	3	2	0	3	1	0	0	0	0	-	0	.241	.313	.276
1998	TB	AL	150	515	138	26	5	5	(3	2)	189	49	46	58	24	0	44	6	11	2	19	8	.70	9	.268	.307	.367
1999	TB	AL	120	465	137	15	5	3	(1	2)	171	61	36	57	24	0	46	7	7	5	22	7	.76	13	.295	.335	.368
2000	TB	AL	119	375	98	18	2	1	(0	1)	123	49	34	42	29	0	34	2	6	5	28	7	.80	7	.261	.314	.328
2001	2 Tms		93	156	46	8	1	3	(2	1)	65	25	16	23	18	1	23	0	7	1	2	1	.67	4	.295	.366	.417
2002	StL	NL	108	184	46	9	2	2	(1	1)	65	28	23	19	13	2	36	3	6	2	1	1	.50	5	.250	.307	.353
2003	StL	NL	92	261	64	15	2	5	(2	3)	98	41	32	25	13	1	30	6	3	7	4	1	.80	6	.245	.289	.375
2004	NYY	AL	122	360	105	17	5	6	(4	2)	150	48	42	50	18	1	49	14	12	4	11	3	.79	7	.292	.346	.417
2005	NYM	NL	100	327	82	18	0	2	(1	1)	106	31	19	29	19	2	31	4	12	5	13	3	.81	5	.251	.296	.324
2006	NYY	AL	81	222	53	12	3	0	(0	0)	71	28	30	26	13	0	31	1	5	3	13	1	.93	4	.239	.280	.320
01	ChC	NL	66	123	35	3	1	2	(1	1)	46	20	9	17	16	1	21	0	7	1	2	1	.67	3	.285	.364	.374
01	StL	NL	27	33	11	5	0	1	(1	0)	19	5	7	6	2	0	2	0	0	0	0	0	-	1	.333	.371	.576
11 ML YEARS			1010	2921	782	141	25	27	(14	13)	1054	372	280	334	175	7	336	45	69	34	113	32	.78	61	.268	.316	.361

Kiko Calero

Pitches: R **Bats:** R **Pos:** RP-70   **Ht:** 6'1" **Wt:** 200 **Born:** 1/9/1975 **Age:** 32

			HOW MUCH HE PITCHED					WHAT HE GAVE UP										THE RESULTS						
Year	Team	Lg	G	GS	CG	GF	IP	BFP	H	R	ER	HR	SH	SF	HB	TBB	IBB	SO	WP	Bk	W	L	Pct	ShO	Sv-Op Hld	ERC	ERA
2003	StL	NL	26	1	0	7	38.1	162	29	12	12	5	1	3	1	20	2	51	3	1	1	1	.500	0	1-4 1	3.44	2.82
2004	StL	NL	41	0	0	4	45.1	168	27	14	14	5	4	0	1	10	1	47	1	0	3	1	.750	0	2-3 12	1.62	2.78
2005	Oak	AL	58	0	0	15	55.2	229	45	20	20	6	1	1	1	18	2	52	2	0	4	1	.800	0	1-2 12	2.80	3.23
2006	Oak	AL	70	0	0	17	58.0	241	50	22	22	4	0	1	0	24	3	67	1	0	3	2	.600	0	2-5 23	3.13	3.41
4 ML YEARS			195	1	0	43	197.1	800	151	68	68	20	6	5	3	72	8	217	7	1	11	5	.688	0	6-14 48	2.73	3.10

Alberto Callaspo

Bats: B **Throws:** R **Pos:** PH-17; SS-4; 2B-3; 3B-2   **Ht:** 5'10" **Wt:** 175 **Born:** 4/19/1983 **Age:** 24

			BATTING												BASERUNNING				AVERAGES		
Year	Team	Lg	G	AB	H	2B	3B	HR	(Hm	Rd)	TB	R	RBI	RC	TBB	IBB	SO	HBP	SH	SF	SB	CS	SB%	GDP	Avg	OBP	Slg
2002	Provo	R	70	299	101	16	10	3	(-	-)	146	70	60	55	17	0	14	2	3	3	13	4	.76	6	.338	.374	.488
2003	CRpds	A	133	514	168	38	4	2	(-	-)	220	86	67	87	42	4	28	3	0	6	20	6	.77	8	.327	.377	.428
2004	Ark	AA	136	550	156	29	2	6	(-	-)	207	76	48	72	47	1	25	0	11	4	15	14	.52	16	.284	.338	.376
2005	Ark	AA	89	350	104	9	0	10	(-	-)	143	53	49	51	28	1	17	1	1	5	9	8	.53	4	.297	.346	.409
2005	Salt Lk	AAA	50	212	67	21	2	1	(-	-)	95	28	31	32	10	1	13	1	2	3	2	5	.29	7	.316	.345	.448
2006	Tucsn	AAA	114	490	165	24	12	7	(-	-)	234	93	68	96	56	3	27	2	2	4	8	5	.62	5	.337	.404	.478
2006	Ari	NL	23	42	10	1	1	0	(0	0)	13	2	6	5	4	0	6	0	0	1	0	1	.00	1	.238	.298	.310

Mike Cameron

Bats: R **Throws:** R **Pos:** CF-141; PH-1   **Ht:** 6'2" **Wt:** 200 **Born:** 1/8/1973 **Age:** 34

			BATTING												BASERUNNING				AVERAGES		
Year	Team	Lg	G	AB	H	2B	3B	HR	(Hm	Rd)	TB	R	RBI	RC	TBB	IBB	SO	HBP	SH	SF	SB	CS	SB%	GDP	Avg	OBP	Slg
2006	Lk Els*	A+	2	6	2	1	0	0	(-	-)	3	1	1	1	1	0	2	0	0	0	0	0	-	0	.333	.429	.500
1995	CWS	AL	28	38	7	2	0	1	(0	1)	12	4	2	3	3	0	15	0	3	0	0	0	-	0	.184	.244	.316
1996	CWS	AL	11	11	1	0	0	0	(0	0)	1	1	0	0	1	0	3	0	0	0	0	1	.00	0	.091	.167	.091
1997	CWS	AL	116	379	98	18	3	14	(10	4)	164	63	55	63	55	1	105	6	2	5	23	2	.92	6	.259	.356	.433
1998	CWS	AL	141	396	83	16	5	8	(5	3)	133	53	43	39	37	0	101	6	1	3	27	11	.71	6	.210	.285	.336
1999	Cin	NL	146	542	139	34	9	21	(12	9)	254	93	66	96	80	2	145	6	5	3	38	12	.76	4	.256	.357	.469
2000	Sea	AL	155	543	145	28	4	19	(5	14)	238	96	78	91	78	0	133	9	7	6	24	7	.77	10	.267	.365	.438
2001	Sea	AL	150	540	144	30	5	25	(7	18)	259	99	110	96	69	3	155	10	1	13	34	5	.87	13	.267	.353	.480
2002	Sea	AL	158	545	130	26	5	25	(7	18)	241	80	80	78	79	3	176	7	4	5	31	8	.79	8	.239	.340	.442
2003	Sea	AL	147	534	135	31	5	18	(11	7)	230	74	76	80	70	1	137	5	1	2	17	7	.71	13	.253	.344	.431
2004	NYM	NL	140	493	114	30	1	30	(11	19)	236	76	76	70	57	2	143	8	1	3	22	6	.79	5	.231	.319	.479

55

Year	Team	Lg	G	AB	H	2B	3B	HR	(Hm	Rd)	TB	R	RBI	RC	TBB	IBB	SO	HBP	SH	SF	SB	CS	SB%	GDP	Avg	OBP	Slg
																									BATTING	BASERUNNING	AVERAGES
2005	NYM	NL	76	308	84	23	2	12	(7	5)	147	47	39	52	29	0	85	4	1	1	13	1	.93	5	.273	.342	.477
2006	SD	NL	141	552	148	34	9	22	(11	11)	266	88	83	98	71	2	142	6	0	5	25	9	.74	8	.268	.355	.482
12 ML YEARS			1409	4881	1228	272	48	195	(86	109)	2181	778	708	766	629	14	1340	66	26	46	254	69	.79	80	.252	.342	.447

Shawn Camp

Pitches: R **Bats:** R **Pos:** RP-75   **Ht:** 6'1" **Wt:** 200 **Born:** 11/18/1975 **Age:** 31

Year	Team	Lg	G	GS	CG	GF	IP	BFP	H	R	ER	HR	SH	SF	HB	TBB	IBB	SO	WP	Bk	W	L	Pct	ShO	Sv-Op	Hld	ERC	ERA
				HOW MUCH HE PITCHED					WHAT HE GAVE UP												THE RESULTS							
2004	KC	AL	42	0	0	12	66.2	286	74	37	29	10	2	3	5	16	1	51	2	1	2	2	.500	0	2-3	5	4.74	3.92
2005	KC	AL	29	0	0	7	49.0	228	69	40	35	4	0	3	4	13	3	28	3	0	1	4	.200	0	0-2	0	6.00	6.43
2006	TB	AL	75	0	0	15	75.0	328	93	43	39	9	2	3	7	19	3	53	4	0	1	4	.636	0	4-6	12	5.48	4.68
3 ML YEARS			146	0	0	34	190.2	842	236	120	103	23	4	9	16	48	7	132	9	1	10	10	.500	0	6-11	17	5.36	4.86

Brett Campbell

Pitches: R **Bats:** R **Pos:** RP-4   **Ht:** 6'0" **Wt:** 170 **Born:** 10/17/1981 **Age:** 25

Year	Team	Lg	G	GS	CG	GF	IP	BFP	H	R	ER	HR	SH	SF	HB	TBB	IBB	SO	WP	Bk	W	L	Pct	ShO	Sv-Op	Hld	ERC	ERA
				HOW MUCH HE PITCHED					WHAT HE GAVE UP												THE RESULTS							
2004	Expos	R	5	0	0	5	7.0	33	6	3	3	0	0	0	0	6	1	11	4	0	0	1	.000	0	1--	-	3.88	3.86
2004	BrvdCt	A+	4	0	0	2	7.0	31	6	3	3	1	0	0	0	4	0	2	1	0	1	0	1.000	0	0--	-	4.16	3.86
2004	Vrmnt	A-	11	0	0	5	22.0	100	24	14	10	3	0	0	0	10	1	25	2	0	0	1	.000	0	0--	-	4.89	4.09
2005	Savann	A	36	0	0	28	48.0	188	28	10	9	2	1	0	2	15	1	50	4	0	4	2	.667	0	19--	-	1.52	1.69
2006	Ptomc	A+	12	0	0	5	15.0	76	21	18	16	3	1	1	3	10	0	13	4	0	0	2	.000	0	1--	-	9.66	9.60
2006	Ptomc	A+	19	0	0	17	22.2	93	22	7	6	3	1	1	2	2	0	27	1	0	3	1	.750	0	8--	-	3.23	2.38
2006	Hrsbrg	AA	13	0	0	11	14.1	69	16	6	5	0	0	0	0	11	3	20	4	0	3	0	.000	0	8--	-	4.93	3.14
2006	NewOr	AAA	15	0	0	8	20.2	85	14	9	9	1	0	0	0	11	1	19	2	0	0	1	.000	0	0--	-	2.47	3.92
2006	Was	NL	4	0	0	2	4.1	19	4	5	5	1	0	0	1	2	0	4	0	0	0	0	-	0	0-0	0	6.01	10.38

Jorge Campillo

Pitches: R **Bats:** R **Pos:** RP-1   **Ht:** 6'1" **Wt:** 190 **Born:** 8/10/1978 **Age:** 28

Year	Team	Lg	G	GS	CG	GF	IP	BFP	H	R	ER	HR	SH	SF	HB	TBB	IBB	SO	WP	Bk	W	L	Pct	ShO	Sv-Op	Hld	ERC	ERA
				HOW MUCH HE PITCHED					WHAT HE GAVE UP												THE RESULTS							
2005	Tacom	AAA	12	12	0	0	66.1	280	63	21	20	5	3	1	0	18	0	43	3	0	4	1	.800	0	0--	-	3.08	2.71
2005	Ms	R	4	4	0	0	11.0	53	18	11	7	0	0	0	0	2	0	10	0	0	0	2	.000	0	0--	-	5.99	5.73
2006	Ms	R	6	5	0	0	13.0	49	13	6	6	0	0	1	1	0	0	15	0	0	0	0	-	0	0--	-	2.42	4.15
2006	InldEm	A+	2	2	0	0	9.0	38	8	4	4	2	0	0	0	2	0	6	0	0	1	1	.500	0	0--	-	3.37	4.00
2006	SnAnt	AA	2	2	0	0	10.2	45	12	4	3	0	1	1	0	2	0	3	1	0	2	0	1.000	0	0--	-	3.25	2.53
2005	Sea	AL	2	1	0	1	2.0	9	1	0	0	0	0	0	0	1	0	1	0	0	0	0	-	0	0-0	0	1.26	0.00
2006	Sea	AL	1	0	0	0	2.1	11	4	4	4	0	0	0	0	0	0	1	0	0	0	0	-	0	0-0	0	5.71	15.43
2 ML YEARS			3	1	0	1	4.1	20	5	4	4	0	0	0	0	1	0	2	0	0	0	0	-	0	0-0	0	3.27	8.31

Andy Cannizaro

Bats: R **Throws:** R **Pos:** SS-10; 2B-2; 3B-2; PR-2; PH-1   **Ht:** 5'10" **Wt:** 170 **Born:** 12/19/1978 **Age:** 28

Year	Team	Lg	G	AB	H	2B	3B	HR	(Hm	Rd)	TB	R	RBI	RC	TBB	IBB	SO	HBP	SH	SF	SB	CS	SB%	GDP	Avg	OBP	Slg
																							BATTING		BASERUNNING	AVERAGES	
2001	StlsInd	A-	67	254	72	9	2	0	(-	-)	85	38	20	33	22	1	21	6	3	3	5	3	.63	15	.283	.351	.335
2002	Tampa	A+	112	366	91	18	1	1	(-	-)	114	52	46	43	38	0	31	14	5	4	3	4	.43	14	.249	.339	.311
2003	Trntn	AA	108	369	102	23	1	1	(-	-)	130	50	39	47	26	1	24	9	8	2	9	4	.69	7	.276	.337	.352
2004	Trntn	AA	85	328	103	18	0	3	(-	-)	130	44	44	52	36	1	31	5	5	5	7	9	.44	7	.314	.385	.396
2005	Trntn	AA	54	202	50	12	0	0	(-	-)	62	28	20	20	11	0	19	4	1	1	5	0	1.00	4	.248	.298	.307
2005	Clmbs	AAA	56	170	43	10	2	1	(-	-)	60	22	18	23	17	0	11	9	6	0	1	1	.50	11	.253	.352	.353
2006	Clmbs	AAA	116	416	115	32	1	3	(-	-)	158	69	32	63	51	0	59	10	7	3	6	5	.55	7	.276	.367	.380
2006	NYY	AL	13	8	2	0	0	1	(0	1)	5	5	1	1	0	0	1	0	0	0	0	0	-	1	.250	.333	.625

Robinson Cano

Bats: L **Throws:** R **Pos:** 2B-118; DH-4; PH-2   **Ht:** 6'0" **Wt:** 190 **Born:** 10/22/1982 **Age:** 24

Year	Team	Lg	G	AB	H	2B	3B	HR	(Hm	Rd)	TB	R	RBI	RC	TBB	IBB	SO	HBP	SH	SF	SB	CS	SB%	GDP	Avg	OBP	Slg
																							BATTING		BASERUNNING	AVERAGES	
2001	Yanks	R	57	200	46	14	2	3	(-	-)	73	37	34	28	28	0	27	3	0	2	11	2	.85	4	.230	.330	.365
2001	StlsInd	A-	2	8	2	0	0	0	(-	-)	2	0	2	0	0	0	2	0	0	0	0	0	-	0	.250	.250	.250
2002	Grnsbr	A	113	474	131	20	9	14	(-	-)	211	67	66	69	29	0	78	3	0	1	2	1	.67	8	.276	.321	.445
2002	StlsInd	A-	22	87	24	5	1	1	(-	-)	34	11	15	11	4	0	8	0	1	0	6	1	.86	1	.276	.308	.391
2003	Tampa	A+	90	366	101	16	3	5	(-	-)	138	50	50	44	17	1	49	4	0	3	1	1	.50	5	.276	.313	.377
2003	Trntn	AA	46	164	46	9	1	1	(-	-)	60	21	13	21	9	0	16	6	2	0	0	0	-	6	.280	.341	.366
2004	Trntn	AA	74	292	88	20	8	7	(-	-)	145	43	44	51	24	1	40	3	0	4	2	4	.33	8	.301	.356	.497
2004	Clmbs	AAA	61	216	56	9	2	6	(-	-)	87	22	30	28	18	1	27	1	3	2	0	1	.00	7	.259	.316	.403
2005	Clmbs	AAA	24	108	36	8	3	4	(-	-)	62	19	24	21	6	3	13	0	0	0	0	0	-	2	.333	.368	.574
2006	Yanks	R	1	5	2	0	0	0	(-	-)	2	0	1	0	0	0	0	0	0	0	0	0	-	0	.400	.400	.400
2006	Trntn	AA	3	10	5	2	0	0	(-	-)	7	1	2	3	3	1	1	0	0	0	0	0	-	0	.500	.615	.700
2005	NYY	AL	132	522	155	34	4	14	(5	9)	239	78	62	59	16	1	68	3	7	3	1	3	.25	16	.297	.320	.458
2006	NYY	AL	122	482	165	41	1	15	(9	6)	253	62	78	74	18	3	54	2	1	5	5	2	.71	19	.342	.365	.525
2 ML YEARS			254	1004	320	75	5	29	(14	15)	492	140	140	133	34	4	122	5	8	8	6	5	.55	35	.319	.342	.490

Jorge Cantu

Bats: R **Throws:** R **Pos:** 2B-103; DH-2; PH-2   **Ht:** 6'1" **Wt:** 185 **Born:** 1/30/1982 **Age:** 25

Year	Team	Lg	G	AB	H	2B	3B	HR	(Hm	Rd)	TB	R	RBI	RC	TBB	IBB	SO	HBP	SH	SF	SB	CS	SB%	GDP	Avg	OBP	Slg
2006	Mont*	AA	8	31	6	0	0	2	(-	-)	12	4	8	2	1	0	9	0	0	1	0	0	-	1	.194	.212	.387
2004	TB	AL	50	173	52	20	1	2	(0	2)	80	25	17	22	9	0	44	2	0	1	0	0	-	5	.301	.341	.462
2005	TB	AL	150	598	171	40	1	28	(16	12)	297	73	117	88	19	1	83	6	0	7	1	0	1.00	24	.286	.311	.497
2006	TB	AL	107	413	103	18	2	14	(7	7)	167	40	62	42	26	2	91	3	0	6	1	1	.50	16	.249	.295	.404
3 ML YEARS			307	1184	326	78	4	44	(23	21)	544	138	196	152	54	3	218	11	0	14	2	1	.67	45	.275	.310	.459

Jose Capellan

Pitches: R **Bats:** R **Pos:** RP-61   **Ht:** 6'4" **Wt:** 235 **Born:** 1/13/1981 **Age:** 26

Year	Team	Lg	G	GS	CG	GF	IP	BFP	H	R	ER	HR	SH	SF	HB	TBB	IBB	SO	WP	Bk	W	L	Pct	ShO	Sv-Op	Hld	ERC	ERA
2006	Hntsvl*	AA	1	1	0	0	1.0	3	0	0	0	0	0	0	0	0	0	2	0	0	0	0	-	0	0--	-	0.00	0.00
2004	Atl	NL	3	2	0	0	8.0	42	14	10	10	2	1	1	0	5	0	4	0	0	0	1	.000	0	0-0	0	11.31	11.25
2005	Mil	NL	17	0	0	7	15.2	67	17	6	5	1	2	2	0	5	0	14	0	0	1	1	.500	0	0-0	3	4.01	2.87
2006	Mil	NL	61	0	0	12	71.2	310	65	37	35	11	8	2	3	31	7	58	3	0	4	2	.667	0	0-2	16	4.04	4.40
3 ML YEARS			81	2	0	19	95.1	419	96	53	50	14	11	5	3	41	7	76	3	0	5	4	.556	0	0-2	19	4.55	4.72

Matt Capps

Pitches: R **Bats:** R **Pos:** RP-85   **Ht:** 6'2" **Wt:** 240 **Born:** 9/3/1983 **Age:** 23

Year	Team	Lg	G	GS	CG	GF	IP	BFP	H	R	ER	HR	SH	SF	HB	TBB	IBB	SO	WP	Bk	W	L	Pct	ShO	Sv-Op	Hld	ERC	ERA
2002	Pirates	R	7	0	0	4	13.0	58	13	2	1	0	0	0	0	6	0	8	1	1	1	0	1.000	0	1--	-	3.50	0.69
2003	Pirates	R	10	10	1	0	62.2	237	40	16	13	1	0	1	5	9	0	54	1	0	5	1	.833	0	0--	-	1.35	1.87
2003	Lynbrg	A+	1	1	0	0	5.0	22	3	3	3	0	7	4	0	4	0	5	0	0	0	0	-	0	0--	-	2.64	5.40
2004	Wmspt	A-	11	11	0	0	65.0	283	84	43	35	7	3	1	2	4	1	33	1	0	3	5	.375	0	0--	-	4.45	4.85
2004	Hickory	A	12	8	0	1	42.0	224	82	55	47	8	0	1	5	16	0	27	0	0	2	3	.400	0	0--	-	11.55	10.07
2005	Hickory	A	35	0	0	27	53.2	213	47	15	15	0	4	2	2	5	2	39	2	0	3	4	.429	0	14--	-	1.79	2.52
2005	Altna	AA	17	0	0	12	20.0	82	21	8	6	2	0	0	0	1	0	26	0	1	0	2	.000	0	7--	-	2.93	2.70
2005	Pit	NL	4	0	0	0	4.0	16	5	2	2	0	0	0	1	0	0	3	0	0	0	0	-	0	0-0	0	4.62	4.50
2006	Pit	NL	85	0	0	15	80.2	329	81	37	34	12	8	2	3	12	5	56	4	0	9	1	.900	0	1-10	13	3.52	3.79
2 ML YEARS			89	0	0	15	84.2	345	86	39	36	12	8	2	4	12	5	59	4	0	9	1	.900	0	1-10	13	3.57	3.83

Chris Capuano

Pitches: L **Bats:** L **Pos:** SP-34   **Ht:** 6'2" **Wt:** 220 **Born:** 8/19/1978 **Age:** 28

Year	Team	Lg	G	GS	CG	GF	IP	BFP	H	R	ER	HR	SH	SF	HB	TBB	IBB	SO	WP	Bk	W	L	Pct	ShO	Sv-Op	Hld	ERC	ERA
2003	Ari	NL	9	5	0	2	33.0	139	27	19	17	3	4	1	6	11	1	23	3	0	2	4	.333	0	0-0	1	3.45	4.64
2004	Mil	NL	17	17	0	0	88.1	385	91	55	49	18	4	1	5	37	1	80	3	1	6	8	.429	0	0-0	0	5.37	4.99
2005	Mil	NL	35	35	0	0	219.0	949	212	105	97	31	14	5	12	91	6	176	3	4	18	12	.600	0	0-0	0	4.44	3.99
2006	Mil	NL	34	34	3	0	221.1	936	229	108	99	29	9	8	9	47	4	174	7	0	11	12	.478	2	0-0	0	3.84	4.03
4 ML YEARS			95	91	3	2	561.2	2409	559	287	262	81	31	15	32	186	12	453	16	5	37	36	.507	2	0-0	1	4.29	4.20

Fausto Carmona

Pitches: R **Bats:** R **Pos:** RP-31; SP-7   **Ht:** 6'4" **Wt:** 220 **Born:** 12/7/1983 **Age:** 23

Year	Team	Lg	G	GS	CG	GF	IP	BFP	H	R	ER	HR	SH	SF	HB	TBB	IBB	SO	WP	Bk	W	L	Pct	ShO	Sv-Op	Hld	ERC	ERA
2002	Burlgtn	R+	13	11	0	2	76.1	326	89	36	28	4	4	4	6	10	0	42	1	3	2	4	.333	0	1--	-	3.93	3.30
2002	MhVlly	A	3	0	0	2	4.0	13	2	0	0	0	0	1	0	1	0	0	0	0	0	0	-	0	0--	-	1.09	0.00
2003	Lk Cty	A	24	24	1	0	148.1	573	117	48	34	10	7	2	3	14	0	83	3	0	17	4	.810	0	0--	-	1.78	2.06
2003	Akron	AA	1	1	0	0	6.0	27	8	3	3	1	0	0	1	0	0	3	0	0	0	0	-	0	0--	-	5.41	4.50
2004	Kinston	A+	12	12	0	0	70.0	297	68	28	22	6	3	0	3	20	0	57	4	0	5	2	.714	0	0--	-	3.52	2.83
2004	Akron	AA	15	15	0	0	87.0	381	114	52	48	3	7	5	2	21	0	63	4	1	4	8	.333	0	0--	-	4.93	4.97
2004	Buffalo	AAA	1	1	0	0	6.0	26	6	4	4	0	0	1	0	3	0	2	0	0	1	0	1.000	0	0--	-	3.79	6.00
2005	Akron	AA	14	14	0	0	90.2	398	100	46	41	7	5	2	8	20	1	57	2	0	6	5	.545	0	0--	-	4.03	4.07
2005	Buffalo	AAA	13	12	1	0	83.0	336	76	32	30	10	4	2	3	15	0	49	2	0	7	4	.636	0	0--	-	3.06	3.25
2006	Buffalo	AAA	6	5	0	0	27.2	118	28	21	17	2	0	3	1	8	0	28	3	0	1	3	.250	0	0--	-	3.64	5.53
2006	Cle	AL	38	7	0	12	74.2	340	88	46	45	9	2	4	7	31	3	58	3	1	1	10	.091	0	0-3	10	5.69	5.42

Chris Carpenter

Pitches: R **Bats:** R **Pos:** SP-32   **Ht:** 6'6" **Wt:** 230 **Born:** 4/27/1975 **Age:** 32

Year	Team	Lg	G	GS	CG	GF	IP	BFP	H	R	ER	HR	SH	SF	HB	TBB	IBB	SO	WP	Bk	W	L	Pct	ShO	Sv-Op	Hld	ERC	ERA
1997	Tor	AL	14	13	1	1	81.1	374	108	55	46	7	1	2	2	37	0	55	7	1	3	7	.300	1	0-0	0	6.38	5.09
1998	Tor	AL	33	24	1	4	175.0	742	177	97	85	18	4	5	5	61	1	136	5	0	12	7	.632	1	0-0	0	4.12	4.37
1999	Tor	AL	24	24	4	0	150.0	663	177	81	73	16	4	6	3	48	1	106	9	1	9	8	.529	1	0-0	0	4.90	4.38
2000	Tor	AL	34	27	2	1	175.1	795	204	130	122	30	3	1	5	83	1	113	3	0	10	12	.455	0	0-0	0	6.04	6.26
2001	Tor	AL	34	34	3	0	215.2	930	229	112	98	29	3	1	16	75	5	157	5	0	11	11	.500	2	0-0	0	4.82	4.09
2002	Tor	AL	13	13	1	0	73.1	327	89	45	43	11	1	4	4	27	0	45	3	0	4	5	.444	0	0-0	0	5.91	5.28
2004	StL	NL	28	28	1	0	182.0	746	169	75	70	24	6	3	8	38	2	152	4	0	15	5	.750	0	0-0	0	3.32	3.46
2005	StL	NL	33	33	7	0	241.2	953	204	82	76	18	7	7	3	51	0	213	5	0	21	5	.808	4	0-0	0	2.49	2.83
2006	StL	NL	32	32	5	0	221.2	896	194	81	76	21	12	4	10	43	3	184	3	0	15	8	.652	3	0-0	0	2.75	3.09
9 ML YEARS			245	228	25	6	1516.0	6426	1551	758	689	174	41	33	56	463	13	1161	44	2	100	68	.595	12	0-0	0	4.11	4.09

Giovanni Carrara

Pitches: R **Bats:** R **Pos:** RP-25   **Ht:** 6'2" **Wt:** 230 **Born:** 3/4/1968 **Age:** 39

			HOW MUCH HE PITCHED						WHAT HE GAVE UP									THE RESULTS						
Year	Team	Lg	G	GS	CG	GF	IP	BFP	H	R	ER	HR	SH	SF	HB	TBB	IBB	SO	WP	Bk	W	L	Pct	ShO	Sv-Op	Hld	ERC	ERA
2006	Indy*	AAA	9	1	0	2	15.0	57	8	5	5	1	1	2	2	5	1	14	0	0	1	1	.500	0	0- -	-	1.77	3.00
2006	LsVgs*	AAA	21	0	0	10	25.1	110	23	13	13	3	1	0	1	12	0	19	1	0	2	1	.667	0	4- -	-	4.13	4.62
1995	Tor	AL	12	7	1	2	48.2	229	64	46	39	10	1	2	1	25	1	27	1	0	2	4	.333	0	0-0	0	7.43	7.21
1996	2 Tms		19	5	0	4	38.0	188	54	36	34	11	1	0	2	25	3	23	1	0	1	1	.500	0	0-1	0	9.71	8.05
1997	Cin	NL	2	2	0	0	10.1	49	14	9	9	4	1	0	0	6	1	5	0	0	0	1	.000	0	0-0	0	9.47	7.84
2000	Col	NL	8	0	0	2	13.1	72	21	19	19	5	0	1	1	11	2	15	0	0	0	1	.000	0	0-1	0	12.21	12.83
2001	LAD	NL	47	3	0	2	85.1	348	73	30	30	12	6	1	1	24	3	70	0	0	6	1	.857	0	0-3	9	3.10	3.16
2002	LAD	NL	63	1	0	13	90.2	387	83	34	33	14	6	2	6	32	4	56	1	0	6	3	.667	0	1-6	14	3.97	3.28
2003	Sea	AL	23	0	0	7	29.0	137	40	22	22	6	1	0	2	14	0	13	0	0	2	0	1.000	0	0-0	4	8.10	6.83
2004	LAD	NL	42	0	0	15	53.2	227	46	15	13	1	4	0	1	20	3	48	1	0	5	2	.714	0	2-3	6	2.60	2.18
2005	LAD	NL	72	0	0	18	75.2	326	65	35	33	6	9	5	6	38	5	56	4	0	7	4	.636	0	0-2	11	3.78	3.93
2006	LAD	NL	25	0	0	9	27.2	116	27	14	14	5	0	0	1	7	0	25	1	0	0	1	.000	0	1-2	2	4.04	4.55
96	Tor	AL	11	0	0	3	15.0	76	23	19	19	5	0	0	0	12	2	10	1	0	0	1	.000	0	0-1	0	11.46	11.40
96	Cin	NL	8	5	0	1	23.0	112	31	17	15	6	1	0	2	13	1	13	0	0	1	0	1.000	0	0-0	0	8.62	5.87
	10 ML YEARS		313	18	1	72	472.1	2079	487	260	246	74	29	11	21	202	22	338	9	0	29	18	.617	0	4-18	46	4.89	4.69

Hector Carrasco

Pitches: R **Bats:** R **Pos:** RP-53; SP-3   **Ht:** 6'2" **Wt:** 220 **Born:** 10/22/1969 **Age:** 37

			HOW MUCH HE PITCHED						WHAT HE GAVE UP									THE RESULTS						
Year	Team	Lg	G	GS	CG	GF	IP	BFP	H	R	ER	HR	SH	SF	HB	TBB	IBB	SO	WP	Bk	W	L	Pct	ShO	Sv-Op	Hld	ERC	ERA
1994	Cin	NL	45	0	0	29	56.1	237	42	17	14	3	5	0	2	30	1	41	3	1	5	6	.455	0	6-0	0	3.01	2.24
1995	Cin	NL	64	0	0	28	87.1	391	86	45	40	1	2	6	2	46	5	64	15	0	2	7	.222	0	5-0	0	3.77	4.12
1996	Cin	NL	56	0	0	10	74.1	325	58	37	31	6	4	4	1	45	5	59	8	1	3	4	.571	0	0-0	0	3.41	3.75
1997	2 Tms		66	0	0	22	86.0	388	80	46	42	7	4	3	8	41	5	76	11	2	2	8	.200	0	0-0	0	4.00	4.40
1998	Min	AL	63	0	0	20	61.2	287	75	30	30	4	0	8	1	31	1	46	8	0	4	2	.667	0	1-0	0	5.47	4.38
1999	Min	AL	39	0	0	10	49.0	204	48	29	26	3	0	1	1	18	0	35	4	0	2	3	.400	0	1-0	0	3.76	4.78
2000	2 Tms		69	1	0	20	78.2	364	90	46	41	8	8	4	4	38	1	64	14	1	5	4	.556	0	1-0	0	5.37	4.69
2001	Min	AL	56	0	0	12	73.2	317	77	40	38	8	6	3	0	30	3	70	7	1	4	3	.571	0	1-0	0	4.42	4.64
2003	Bal	AL	40	0	0	10	38.1	174	40	22	21	5	4	0	2	20	3	27	0	0	2	6	.250	0	1-3	8	5.09	4.93
2005	Was	NL	64	5	0	13	88.1	358	59	23	20	6	4	4	6	38	7	75	6	1	5	4	.556	0	2-4	8	2.41	2.04
2006	LAA	AL	56	3	0	24	100.1	417	93	42	38	10	2	2	5	27	1	72	6	0	7	3	.700	0	1-2	1	3.36	3.41
97	Cin	NL	38	0	0	11	51.1	237	51	25	21	3	3	1	4	25	2	46	3	2	1	2	.333	0	0-0	0	4.14	3.68
97	KC	AL	28	0	0	11	34.2	151	29	21	21	4	1	2	4	16	3	30	8	0	1	6	.143	0	0-0	0	3.79	5.45
00	Min	AL	61	0	0	18	72.0	324	75	38	34	6	6	4	3	33	0	57	14	0	4	3	.571	0	1-0	0	4.52	4.25
00	Bos	AL	8	1	0	2	6.2	40	15	8	7	2	2	0	1	5	1	7	0	1	1	1	.500	0	0-0	0	16.76	9.45
	11 ML YEARS		618	9	0	198	794.0	3462	748	377	341	61	39	35	32	364	32	629	82	7	42	49	.462	0	19-9	17	3.89	3.87

Jamey Carroll

Bats: R **Throws:** R **Pos:** 2B-109; PH-17; SS-10; 3B-8; PR-3   **Ht:** 5'9" **Wt:** 170 **Born:** 2/18/1974 **Age:** 33

			BATTING																		BASERUNNING				AVERAGES		
Year	Team	Lg	G	AB	H	2B	3B	HR	(Hm	Rd)	TB	R	RBI	RC	TBB	IBB	SO	HBP	SH	SF	SB	CS	SB%	GDP	Avg	OBP	Slg
2002	Mon	NL	16	71	22	5	3	1	(1	0)	36	16	6	12	4	0	12	0	4	0	1	0	1.00	1	.310	.347	.507
2003	Mon	NL	105	227	59	10	1	1	(1	0)	74	31	10	18	19	0	39	9	2	2	5	2	.71	10	.260	.323	.326
2004	Mon	NL	102	218	63	14	2	0	(0	0)	81	36	16	28	32	1	21	1	2	3	5	1	.83	3	.289	.378	.372
2005	Was	NL	113	303	76	8	1	0	(0	0)	86	44	22	38	34	1	55	5	13	3	3	4	.43	2	.251	.333	.284
2006	Col	NL	136	463	139	23	5	5	(2	3)	187	84	36	65	56	1	66	3	9	3	10	12	.45	10	.300	.377	.404
	5 ML YEARS		472	1282	359	60	12	7	(4	3)	464	211	90	161	145	3	193	12	37	11	24	19	.56	26	.280	.356	.362

Lance Carter

Pitches: R **Bats:** R **Pos:** RP-10   **Ht:** 6'1" **Wt:** 190 **Born:** 12/18/1974 **Age:** 32

			HOW MUCH HE PITCHED						WHAT HE GAVE UP									THE RESULTS						
Year	Team	Lg	G	GS	CG	GF	IP	BFP	H	R	ER	HR	SH	SF	HB	TBB	IBB	SO	WP	Bk	W	L	Pct	ShO	Sv-Op	Hld	ERC	ERA
2006	LsVgs*	AAA	45	0	0	27	57.1	236	58	25	25	7	0	2	1	16	1	51	1	0	2	4	.333	0	13- -	-	3.97	3.92
1999	KC	AL	6	0	0	3	5.1	21	3	3	3	2	0	0	0	3	0	3	0	0	1	0	.000	0	0-0	0	4.22	5.06
2002	TB	AL	8	0	0	7	20.1	79	15	3	3	2	0	0	0	5	1	14	0	0	2	0	1.000	0	2-2	0	2.12	1.33
2003	TB	AL	62	0	0	55	79.0	328	72	39	38	12	1	6	4	19	6	47	0	0	7	5	.583	0	26-33	2	3.38	4.33
2004	TB	AL	56	0	0	27	80.1	336	77	32	31	12	1	5	1	23	2	36	1	0	3	3	.500	0	0-1	7	3.74	3.47
2005	TB	AL	39	0	0	18	57.0	239	61	31	31	9	1	3	1	15	1	22	0	0	1	2	.333	0	1-4	5	4.45	4.89
2006	LAD	NL	10	0	0	2	11.2	59	17	11	11	1	0	2	0	8	0	5	2	0	0	1	.000	0	0-1	0	7.91	8.49
	6 ML YEARS		181	0	0	112	253.2	1062	245	119	117	38	3	16	6	73	10	127	3	0	13	12	.520	0	29-41	14	3.83	4.15

Sean Casey

Bats: L **Throws:** R **Pos:** 1B-106; PH-8   **Ht:** 6'4" **Wt:** 235 **Born:** 7/2/1974 **Age:** 32

			BATTING																		BASERUNNING				AVERAGES		
Year	Team	Lg	G	AB	H	2B	3B	HR	(Hm	Rd)	TB	R	RBI	RC	TBB	IBB	SO	HBP	SH	SF	SB	CS	SB%	GDP	Avg	OBP	Slg
2006	Altna*	AA	3	11	3	0	0	1	(-	-)	6	1	2	2	1	0	0	0	0	0	0	0	-	1	.273	.333	.545
1997	Cle	AL	6	10	2	0	0	0	(0	0)	2	1	1	1	1	0	2	1	0	0	0	0	-	0	.200	.333	.200
1998	Cin	NL	96	302	82	21	1	7	(3	4)	126	44	52	45	43	3	45	3	0	3	1	1	.50	11	.272	.365	.417
1999	Cin	NL	151	594	197	42	3	25	(11	14)	320	103	99	119	61	13	88	9	0	5	0	2	.00	15	.332	.399	.539
2000	Cin	NL	133	480	151	33	2	20	(9	11)	248	69	85	91	52	4	80	7	0	6	1	0	1.00	16	.315	.385	.517
2001	Cin	NL	145	533	165	40	0	13	(5	8)	244	69	89	86	43	8	63	9	0	3	3	1	.75	16	.310	.369	.458
2002	Cin	NL	120	425	111	25	0	6	(3	3)	154	56	42	45	43	6	47	5	0	3	2	1	.67	11	.261	.334	.362
2003	Cin	NL	147	573	167	19	3	14	(8	6)	234	71	80	84	51	4	58	2	0	3	4	0	1.00	19	.291	.350	.408
2004	Cin	NL	146	571	185	44	2	24	(9	15)	305	101	99	104	46	5	36	10	0	6	2	0	1.00	16	.324	.381	.534

58

Year Team	Lg	G	AB	H	2B	3B	HR	(Hm Rd)	TB	R	RBI	RC	TBB	IBB	SO	HBP	SH	SF	SB	CS	SB%	GDP	Avg	OBP	Slg
2005 Cin	NL	137	529	165	32	0	9	(4 5)	224	75	58	72	48	3	48	5	0	5	2	0	1.00	27	.312	.371	.423
2006 2 Tms		112	397	108	22	0	8	(3 5)	154	47	59	57	33	9	43	7	0	3	0	1	.00	10	.272	.336	.388
06 Pit	NL	59	213	63	15	0	3	(1 2)	87	30	29	33	23	5	22	6	0	2	0	0	-	7	.296	.377	.408
06 Det	AL	53	184	45	7	0	5	(2 3)	67	17	30	24	10	4	21	1	0	1	0	1	.00	3	.245	.286	.364
10 ML YEARS		1193	4414	1333	278	11	126	(55 71)	2011	636	664	704	421	55	510	58	0	37	15	6	.71	141	.302	.368	.456

Alexi Casilla

Bats: B Throws: R Pos: 2B-4; PH-3; PR-3; SS-2; DH-2 Ht: 5'9" Wt: 160 Born: 7/20/1984 Age: 22

Year Team	Lg	G	AB	H	2B	3B	HR	(Hm Rd)	TB	R	RBI	RC	TBB	IBB	SO	HBP	SH	SF	SB	CS	SB%	GDP	Avg	OBP	Slg
2004 Angels	R	45	163	42	1	4	0	(- -)	51	29	10	20	15	0	10	4	2	2	24	8	.75	3	.258	.332	.313
2004 Provo	R	4	12	4	1	1	0	(- -)	7	4	1	4	4	0	1	0	0	1	1	0	1.00	0	.333	.529	.583
2004 CRpds	A	9	29	9	2	1	0	(- -)	13	6	1	5	5	0	4	0	0	0	1	1	.50	0	.310	.412	.448
2005 CRpds	A	78	308	100	11	3	3	(- -)	126	62	17	56	29	0	31	6	3	1	47	12	.80	6	.325	.392	.409
2005 Ark	AA	7	19	4	0	0	0	(- -)	4	4	4	1	2	0	3	0	0	0	1	1	.50	0	.211	.286	.211
2005 Salt Lk	AAA	13	39	10	0	0	0	(- -)	10	3	1	3	3	0	6	0	4	0	1	1	.50	1	.256	.310	.256
2006 FtMyrs	A+	78	323	107	12	6	0	(- -)	131	56	33	57	30	0	36	2	3	1	31	6	.84	8	.331	.390	.406
2006 NwBrit	AA	45	170	50	10	1	1	(- -)	65	28	13	28	18	0	20	4	7	0	19	4	.83	1	.294	.375	.382
2006 Min	AL	9	4	1	0	0	0	(0 0)	1	1	0	1	2	0	1	0	0	0	0	0	-	0	.250	.500	.250

Santiago Casilla

Pitches: R Bats: R Pos: RP-2 Ht: 6'0" Wt: 200 Born: 6/25/1980 Age: 27

Year Team	Lg	G	GS	CG	GF	IP	BFP	H	R	ER	HR	SH	SF	HB	TBB	IBB	SO	WP	Bk	W	L	Pct	ShO	Sv-Op	Hld	ERC	ERA
2006 Scrmto*	AAA	25	0	0	16	33.0	136	25	13	12	2	2	1	2	10	1	32	1	0	2	0	1.000	0	4- -	-	2.33	3.27
2004 Oak	AL	4	0	0	2	5.2	32	5	8	8	3	0	0	1	9	0	5	0	0	0	0	-	0	0-0	0	13.22	12.71
2005 Oak	AL	3	0	0	3	3.0	12	2	1	1	0	0	0	0	1	0	1	1	0	0	0	-	0	0-0	0	1.57	3.00
2006 Oak	AL	2	0	0	1	2.1	10	2	3	3	0	0	0	0	2	0	2	0	0	0	0	-	0	0-0	0	4.61	11.57
3 ML YEARS		9	0	0	6	11.0	54	9	12	12	3	0	0	1	12	0	8	1	0	0	0	-	0	0-0	0	7.66	9.82

Scott Cassidy

Pitches: R Bats: R Pos: RP-42 Ht: 6'2" Wt: 180 Born: 10/3/1975 Age: 31

Year Team	Lg	G	GS	CG	GF	IP	BFP	H	R	ER	HR	SH	SF	HB	TBB	IBB	SO	WP	Bk	W	L	Pct	ShO	Sv-Op	Hld	ERC	ERA
2006 PortInd*	AAA	17	0	0	16	20.0	86	21	6	6	0	2	0	0	6	2	23	0	0	3	1	.750	0	9- -	-	3.07	2.70
2002 Tor	AL	58	0	0	17	66.0	282	52	42	42	12	4	5	7	32	3	48	2	0	1	4	.200	0	0-7	7	4.17	5.73
2005 2 Tms		11	0	0	4	13.0	60	19	13	12	3	2	0	0	3	0	12	0	0	1	1	.500	0	0-0	1	7.11	8.31
2006 SD	NL	42	0	0	14	42.2	182	39	18	12	8	4	1	1	19	2	49	0	0	6	4	.600	0	0-2	4	4.44	2.53
05 Bos	AL	1	0	0	0	0.2	6	4	3	3	0	0	0	0	0	0	0	0	0	0	0	-	0	0-0	0	39.65	40.50
05 SD	NL	10	0	0	4	12.1	54	15	10	9	3	2	0	0	3	0	12	0	0	1	1	.500	0	0-0	1	5.71	6.57
3 ML YEARS		111	0	0	35	121.2	524	110	73	66	23	10	6	8	54	5	109	2	0	8	9	.471	0	0-9	12	4.56	4.88

Vinny Castilla

Bats: R Throws: R Pos: 3B-70; PH-15; 1B-7 Ht: 6'1" Wt: 205 Born: 7/4/1967 Age: 39

Year Team	Lg	G	AB	H	2B	3B	HR	(Hm Rd)	TB	R	RBI	RC	TBB	IBB	SO	HBP	SH	SF	SB	CS	SB%	GDP	Avg	OBP	Slg
2006 ColSpr*	AAA	8	31	12	3	0	0	(- -)	15	6	4	6	2	0	5	1	0	0	0	0	-	0	.387	.441	.484
1991 Atl	NL	12	5	1	0	0	0	(0 0)	1	1	0	0	0	0	2	0	1	0	0	0	-	0	.200	.200	.200
1992 Atl	NL	9	16	4	1	0	0	(0 0)	5	1	1	2	1	1	4	1	0	0	0	0	-	0	.250	.333	.313
1993 Col	NL	105	337	86	9	7	9	(5 4)	136	36	30	34	13	4	45	2	0	5	2	5	.29	10	.255	.283	.404
1994 Col	NL	52	130	43	11	1	3	(1 2)	65	16	18	22	7	1	23	0	1	3	2	1	.67	3	.331	.357	.500
1995 Col	NL	139	527	163	34	2	32	(23 9)	297	82	90	94	30	2	87	4	4	6	2	8	.20	15	.309	.347	.564
1996 Col	NL	160	629	191	34	0	40	(27 13)	345	97	113	110	35	7	88	5	0	4	7	2	.78	20	.304	.343	.548
1997 Col	NL	159	612	186	25	2	40	(19 21)	335	94	113	110	44	9	108	8	0	4	2	4	.33	17	.304	.356	.547
1998 Col	NL	162	645	206	28	4	46	(26 20)	380	108	144	122	40	7	89	6	0	6	5	9	.36	24	.319	.362	.589
1999 Col	NL	158	615	169	24	1	33	(20 13)	294	83	102	93	53	7	75	1	0	5	2	3	.40	15	.275	.331	.478
2000 TB	AL	85	331	73	9	1	4	(2 2)	102	22	42	22	14	3	41	3	0	6	1	2	.33	22	.221	.254	.308
2001 2 Tms		146	538	140	34	1	25	(12 13)	251	69	91	70	35	3	108	4	0	4	1	4	.20	22	.260	.308	.467
2002 Atl	NL	143	543	126	23	2	12	(5 7)	189	56	61	36	22	4	69	7	0	6	4	1	.80	22	.232	.268	.348
2003 Atl	NL	147	542	150	28	3	22	(6 16)	250	65	76	70	26	3	86	3	1	6	1	2	.33	22	.277	.310	.461
2004 Col	NL	148	583	158	43	3	35	(14 21)	312	93	131	88	51	6	113	6	0	8	0	0	-	22	.271	.332	.535
2005 Was	NL	142	494	125	36	1	12	(8 4)	199	53	66	52	43	7	82	7	1	4	4	2	.67	16	.253	.319	.403
2006 2 Tms		87	275	63	10	0	5	(2 3)	88	26	27	18	9	0	49	3	0	4	0	0	-	7	.229	.258	.320
01 TB	AL	24	93	20	6	0	2	(2 0)	32	7	9	7	3	0	22	1	0	0	0	0	-	3	.215	.247	.344
01 Hou	NL	122	445	120	28	1	23	(10 13)	219	62	82	63	32	3	86	3	0	4	1	4	.20	19	.270	.320	.492
06 SD	NL	72	254	59	10	0	4	(2 2)	81	24	23	16	9	0	46	2	0	4	0	0	-	5	.232	.260	.319
06 Col	NL	15	21	4	0	0	1	(0 1)	7	2	4	2	0	0	3	1	0	0	0	0	-	2	.190	.227	.333
16 ML YEARS		1854	6822	1884	349	28	320	(172 148)	3249	902	1105	943	423	64	1069	60	8	71	33	43	.43	224	.276	.321	.476

Jose Castillo

Bats: R Throws: R Pos: 2B-145; PH-6   Ht: 6'0" Wt: 210 Born: 3/19/1981 Age: 26

Year	Team	Lg	G	AB	H	2B	3B	HR	(Hm	Rd)	TB	R	RBI	RC	TBB	IBB	SO	HBP	SH	SF	SB	CS	SB%	GDP	Avg	OBP	Slg
2004	Pit	NL	129	383	98	15	2	8	(3	5)	141	44	39	40	23	5	92	1	5	2	3	2	.60	12	.256	.298	.368
2005	Pit	NL	101	370	99	16	3	11	(2	9)	154	49	53	43	23	3	59	0	1	4	2	3	.40	11	.268	.307	.416
2006	Pit	NL	148	518	131	25	0	14	(10	4)	198	54	65	53	32	8	98	5	1	6	6	4	.60	22	.253	.299	.382
3 ML YEARS			378	1271	328	56	5	33	(15	18)	493	147	157	136	78	16	249	6	7	12	11	9	.55	45	.258	.301	.388

Luis Castillo

Bats: B Throws: R Pos: 2B-142   Ht: 5'11" Wt: 190 Born: 9/12/1975 Age: 31

Year	Team	Lg	G	AB	H	2B	3B	HR	(Hm	Rd)	TB	R	RBI	RC	TBB	IBB	SO	HBP	SH	SF	SB	CS	SB%	GDP	Avg	OBP	Slg
1996	Fla	NL	41	164	43	2	1	1	(0	1)	50	26	8	19	14	0	46	0	2	0	17	4	.81	0	.262	.320	.305
1997	Fla	NL	75	263	63	8	0	0	(0	0)	71	27	8	21	27	0	53	0	1	0	16	10	.62	6	.240	.310	.270
1998	Fla	NL	44	153	31	3	2	1	(0	1)	41	21	10	14	22	0	33	1	1	0	3	0	1.00	1	.203	.307	.268
1999	Fla	NL	128	487	147	23	4	0	(0	0)	178	76	28	78	67	0	85	0	6	3	50	17	.75	3	.302	.384	.366
2000	Fla	NL	136	539	180	17	3	2	(1	1)	209	101	17	95	78	0	86	0	9	0	62	22	.74	11	.334	.418	.388
2001	Fla	NL	134	537	141	16	10	2	(1	1)	183	76	45	67	67	0	90	1	4	3	33	16	.67	6	.263	.344	.341
2002	Fla	NL	146	606	185	18	5	2	(0	2)	219	86	39	84	55	4	76	2	4	1	48	15	.76	7	.305	.364	.361
2003	Fla	NL	152	595	187	19	6	6	(2	4)	236	99	39	87	63	0	60	2	15	1	21	19	.53	7	.314	.381	.397
2004	Fla	NL	150	564	164	12	7	2	(1	1)	196	91	47	84	75	2	68	1	5	4	21	4	.84	15	.291	.373	.348
2005	Fla	NL	122	439	132	12	4	4	(0	4)	164	72	30	61	65	1	32	1	18	1	10	7	.59	11	.301	.391	.374
2006	Min	AL	142	584	173	22	6	3	(3	0)	216	84	49	80	56	0	58	1	9	2	25	11	.69	14	.296	.358	.370
11 ML YEARS			1270	4931	1446	152	48	23	(8	15)	1763	759	320	690	589	7	687	9	74	15	306	125	.71	81	.293	.369	.358

Bernie Castro

Bats: B Throws: R Pos: 2B-29; PH-10; PR-5; LF-2   Ht: 5'10" Wt: 165 Born: 7/14/1979 Age: 27

Year	Team	Lg	G	AB	H	2B	3B	HR	(Hm	Rd)	TB	R	RBI	RC	TBB	IBB	SO	HBP	SH	SF	SB	CS	SB%	GDP	Avg	OBP	Slg
2000	Yanks	R	9	34	15	4	1	0	(-	-)	21	7	6	10	6	0	4	0	0	0	3	1	.75	1	.441	.525	.618
2001	Grnsbr	A	101	389	101	15	7	0	(-	-)	130	71	36	56	54	1	67	1	5	2	67	20	.77	5	.260	.350	.334
2001	StIsInd	A-	15	57	20	1	0	1	(-	-)	24	6	7	12	11	0	12	1	0	0	8	3	.73	0	.351	.464	.421
2002	Mobile	AA	109	419	109	13	3	0	(-	-)	128	61	32	52	52	1	67	3	2	1	53	20	.73	1	.260	.345	.305
2003	Portlnd	AAA	105	424	131	17	5	2	(-	-)	164	57	24	63	25	0	43	1	3	2	49	13	.79	5	.309	.347	.387
2004	Portlnd	AAA	90	308	81	8	1	0	(-	-)	91	38	20	30	22	2	30	0	2	2	17	9	.65	6	.263	.310	.295
2005	Ottawa	AAA	126	502	158	21	5	1	(-	-)	192	81	36	80	42	3	50	0	9	6	41	6	.87	5	.315	.364	.382
2006	NewOr	AAA	69	268	76	5	3	2	(-	-)	93	36	25	35	18	1	34	0	6	0	22	2	.92	7	.284	.329	.347
2005	Bal	AL	24	80	23	3	1	0	(0	0)	28	14	7	13	9	0	10	0	0	0	6	2	.75	0	.288	.360	.350
2006	Was	NL	42	110	25	1	3	0	(0	0)	32	18	10	10	9	0	18	0	1	0	7	2	.78	2	.227	.286	.291
2 ML YEARS			66	190	48	4	4	0	(0	0)	60	32	17	23	18	0	28	0	1	0	13	4	.76	2	.253	.317	.316

Fabio Castro

Pitches: L Bats: L Pos: RP-20   Ht: 5'7" Wt: 175 Born: 1/20/1985 Age: 22

Year	Team	Lg	G	GS	CG	GF	IP	BFP	H	R	ER	HR	SH	SF	HB	TBB	IBB	SO	WP	Bk	W	L	Pct	ShO	Sv-Op	Hld	ERC	ERA
2003	Bristol	R+	19	0	0	10	47.0	190	29	14	9	1	1	1	1	19	1	59	6	2	6	2	.750	0	2--	-	1.69	1.72
2003	Knapol	A	2	2	0	0	11.0	45	8	5	4	0	0	0	0	5	0	16	0	0	2	0	.000	0	0--	-	2.21	3.27
2004	Knapol	A	37	0	0	15	51.0	222	44	20	17	2	0	0	3	23	0	44	2	0	4	0	1.000	0	3--	-	3.26	3.00
2004	WinSa	A+	6	0	0	0	7.2	27	2	2	2	0	0	0	1	2	0	9	1	0	1	1	.500	0	0--	-	0.64	2.35
2005	WinSa	A+	53	0	0	20	79.0	321	58	23	20	7	4	4	3	37	0	75	4	0	5	5	.500	0	6--	-	3.07	2.28
2006	Frisco	AA	5	4	0	0	13.2	62	14	7	3	1	0	0	0	8	0	10	1	0	1	0	1.000	0	0--	-	4.71	1.98
2006	Okla	AAA	1	1	0	0	3.2	17	5	2	2	0	0	0	0	1	0	5	0	0	0	0	-	0	0--	-	4.76	4.91
2006 2 Tms			20	0	0	11	31.2	125	18	9	8	1	2	2	2	13	0	18	0	1	0	1	.000	0	1-2	0	1.76	2.27
06 Tex		AL	4	0	0	2	8.1	37	6	5	4	0	0	0	0	7	0	5	0	0	0	0	-	0	0-0	0	3.47	4.32
06 Phi		NL	16	0	0	9	23.1	88	12	4	4	1	2	2	2	6	0	13	0	1	0	1	.000	0	1-2	0	1.34	1.54

Juan Castro

Bats: R Throws: R Pos: SS-77; 3B-19; PH-11; 2B-1; PR-1   Ht: 5'11" Wt: 195 Born: 6/20/1972 Age: 35

Year	Team	Lg	G	AB	H	2B	3B	HR	(Hm	Rd)	TB	R	RBI	RC	TBB	IBB	SO	HBP	SH	SF	SB	CS	SB%	GDP	Avg	OBP	Slg
1995	LAD	NL	11	4	1	0	0	0	(0	0)	1	0	0	1	1	0	1	0	0	0	0	0	-	0	.250	.400	.250
1996	LAD	NL	70	132	26	5	3	0	(0	0)	37	16	5	8	10	0	27	0	4	0	1	0	1.00	3	.197	.254	.280
1997	LAD	NL	40	75	11	3	1	0	(0	0)	16	3	4	2	7	1	20	0	2	0	0	0	-	2	.147	.220	.213
1998	LAD	NL	89	220	43	7	0	2	(0	2)	56	25	14	12	15	0	37	0	9	2	0	0	-	5	.195	.245	.255
1999	LAD	NL	2	1	0	0	0	0	(0	0)	0	0	0	0	0	0	0	0	0	0	0	0	-	0	.000	.000	.000
2000	Cin	NL	82	224	54	12	2	4	(1	3)	82	20	23	20	14	1	33	0	4	2	0	2	.00	9	.241	.283	.366
2001	Cin	NL	96	242	54	10	0	3	(0	3)	73	27	13	16	13	2	50	0	4	2	0	0	-	9	.223	.261	.302
2002	Cin	NL	54	82	18	3	0	2	(0	2)	27	5	11	11	7	0	18	0	1	1	0	0	-	0	.220	.278	.329
2003	Cin	NL	113	320	81	14	1	9	(4	5)	124	28	33	36	18	1	58	0	7	3	2	3	.40	7	.253	.290	.388
2004	Cin	NL	111	299	73	21	2	5	(3	2)	113	36	26	26	14	1	51	0	2	1	1	0	1.00	11	.244	.277	.378
2005	Min	AL	97	272	70	18	1	5	(2	3)	105	27	33	28	9	1	39	0	9	2	0	1	.00	8	.257	.279	.386
2006 2 Tms			104	251	63	10	3	3	(3	0)	88	18	28	26	11	0	36	0	1	1	1	2	.33	6	.251	.281	.340
06 Min		AL	50	156	36	5	2	1	(1	0)	48	10	14	11	6	0	23	0	1	1	1	1	.50	6	.231	.258	.308
06 Cin		NL	54	95	27	5	1	2	(2	0)	40	8	14	15	5	0	13	0	0	0	0	1	.00	0	.284	.320	.421
12 ML YEARS			869	2122	494	103	13	33	(13	20)	722	205	190	186	119	7	371	0	43	14	5	8	.38	60	.233	.272	.340

Ramon Castro

Bats: R Throws: R Pos: C-37; PH-3   Ht: 6'3" Wt: 235 Born: 3/1/1976 Age: 31

								BATTING												BASERUNNING				AVERAGES		
Year	Team	Lg	G	AB	H	2B	3B	HR	(Hm | Rd)	TB	R	RBI	RC	TBB	IBB	SO	HBP	SH	SF	SB	CS	SB%	GDP	Avg	OBP	Slg
2006	Mets*	R	1	3	2	0	0	0	(- | -)	2	0	2	1	0	0	0	0	0	0	0	0	-	0	.667	.667	.667
1999	Fla	NL	24	67	12	4	0	2	(0 | 2)	22	4	4	6	10	3	14	0	0	1	0	0	-	1	.179	.282	.328
2000	Fla	NL	50	138	33	4	0	2	(0 | 2)	43	10	14	14	16	7	36	1	0	2	0	0	-	1	.239	.318	.312
2001	Fla	NL	7	11	2	0	0	0	(0 | 0)	2	0	1	0	1	0	1	0	0	0	0	0	-	0	.182	.250	.182
2002	Fla	NL	54	101	24	4	0	6	(4 | 2)	46	11	18	14	14	3	24	0	1	3	0	0	-	0	.238	.322	.455
2003	Fla	NL	40	53	15	2	0	5	(4 | 1)	32	6	8	8	4	0	11	0	0	0	0	0	-	0	.283	.333	.604
2004	Fla	NL	32	96	13	3	0	3	(0 | 3)	25	9	8	4	11	2	30	1	0	0	0	0	-	0	.135	.231	.260
2005	NYM	NL	99	209	51	16	0	8	(5 | 3)	91	26	41	30	25	2	58	0	3	3	1	0	1.00	7	.244	.321	.435
2006	NYM	NL	40	126	30	7	0	4	(1 | 3)	49	13	12	11	15	2	40	1	1	1	0	0	-	2	.238	.322	.389
	8 ML YEARS		346	801	180	40	0	30	(14 | 16)	310	79	106	87	96	19	214	3	5	10	1	0	1.00	16	.225	.307	.387

Frank Catalanotto

Bats: L Throws: R Pos: LF-101; DH-20; PH-13; RF-1; PR-1   Ht: 6'0" Wt: 195 Born: 4/27/1974 Age: 33

								BATTING												BASERUNNING				AVERAGES		
Year	Team	Lg	G	AB	H	2B	3B	HR	(Hm | Rd)	TB	R	RBI	RC	TBB	IBB	SO	HBP	SH	SF	SB	CS	SB%	GDP	Avg	OBP	Slg
1997	Det	AL	13	26	8	2	0	0	(0 | 0)	10	2	3	4	3	0	7	0	0	0	0	0	-	0	.308	.379	.385
1998	Det	AL	89	213	60	13	2	6	(3 | 3)	95	23	25	30	12	1	39	4	0	5	3	2	.60	4	.282	.325	.446
1999	Det	AL	100	286	79	19	0	11	(6 | 5)	131	41	35	42	15	1	49	9	0	5	3	4	.43	5	.276	.327	.458
2000	Tex	AL	103	282	82	13	2	10	(6 | 4)	129	55	42	49	33	0	36	6	3	2	6	2	.75	5	.291	.375	.457
2001	Tex	AL	133	463	153	31	5	11	(4 | 7)	227	77	54	88	39	3	55	8	1	1	15	5	.75	5	.330	.391	.490
2002	Tex	AL	68	212	57	16	6	3	(2 | 1)	94	42	23	39	25	0	27	8	3	2	9	5	.64	3	.269	.364	.443
2003	Tor	AL	133	489	146	34	6	13	(7 | 6)	231	83	59	84	35	1	62	6	2	3	2	2	.50	9	.299	.351	.472
2004	Tor	AL	75	249	73	19	1	1	(1 | 0)	97	27	26	34	17	1	33	4	1	3	1	0	1.00	1	.293	.344	.390
2005	Tor	AL	130	419	126	29	5	8	(3 | 5)	189	56	59	80	37	0	53	10	4	5	0	2	.00	9	.301	.367	.451
2006	Tor	AL	128	437	131	36	2	7	(2 | 5)	192	56	56	72	52	0	37	4	2	4	1	3	.25	11	.300	.376	.439
	10 ML YEARS		972	3076	915	212	29	70	(34 | 36)	1395	462	382	522	268	7	398	59	16	30	40	25	.62	58	.297	.362	.454

Ronny Cedeno

Bats: R Throws: R Pos: SS-134; 2B-15; PH-5   Ht: 6'0" Wt: 180 Born: 2/2/1983 Age: 24

								BATTING												BASERUNNING				AVERAGES		
Year	Team	Lg	G	AB	H	2B	3B	HR	(Hm | Rd)	TB	R	RBI	RC	TBB	IBB	SO	HBP	SH	SF	SB	CS	SB%	GDP	Avg	OBP	Slg
2001	Cubs	R	52	206	72	13	4	1	(- | -)	96	36	17	38	13	0	32	5	3	2	17	10	.63	3	.350	.398	.466
2001	Lansng	A	17	56	11	4	1	1	(- | -)	20	9	2	3	2	0	18	1	0	0	0	2	.00	1	.196	.237	.357
2002	Boise	A-	29	110	24	5	2	0	(- | -)	33	17	6	10	9	0	25	0	2	1	8	2	.80	1	.218	.275	.300
2002	Lansng	A	98	376	80	17	4	2	(- | -)	111	44	31	29	22	0	74	8	8	3	14	10	.58	6	.213	.269	.295
2003	Dytona	A+	107	380	80	18	1	4	(- | -)	112	43	36	30	21	0	82	4	12	3	19	6	.76	5	.211	.257	.295
2004	WTenn	AA	116	384	107	19	5	6	(- | -)	154	39	48	51	24	3	74	8	8	8	10	10	.50	10	.279	.328	.401
2005	Iowa	AAA	65	245	87	14	1	8	(- | -)	127	42	36	51	20	2	31	1	7	2	11	3	.79	10	.355	.403	.518
2005	ChC	NL	41	80	24	3	0	1	(0 | 1)	30	13	6	11	5	1	11	2	2	0	1	0	1.00	4	.300	.356	.375
2006	ChC	NL	151	534	131	18	7	6	(4 | 2)	181	51	41	41	17	4	109	3	15	3	8	8	.50	10	.245	.271	.339
	2 ML YEARS		192	614	155	21	7	7	(4 | 3)	211	64	47	52	22	5	120	5	17	3	9	8	.53	14	.252	.283	.344

Matt Cepicky

Bats: L Throws: R Pos: RF-5; PH-4; LF-1   Ht: 6'2" Wt: 215 Born: 11/10/1977 Age: 29

								BATTING												BASERUNNING				AVERAGES		
Year	Team	Lg	G	AB	H	2B	3B	HR	(Hm | Rd)	TB	R	RBI	RC	TBB	IBB	SO	HBP	SH	SF	SB	CS	SB%	GDP	Avg	OBP	Slg
2006	Albq*	AAA	107	320	85	19	2	7	(- | -)	129	39	34	48	44	6	66	0	0	2	2	1	.67	10	.266	.352	.403
2002	Mon	NL	32	74	16	3	0	3	(2 | 1)	28	7	15	8	4	1	21	0	0	0	0	0	-	0	.216	.256	.378
2003	Mon	NL	5	8	2	1	0	0	(0 | 0)	3	0	0	0	0	0	2	0	0	0	0	0	-	0	.250	.250	.375
2004	Mon	NL	32	60	13	4	0	1	(1 | 0)	20	4	3	2	1	0	18	0	0	0	1	0	1.00	1	.217	.230	.333
2005	Was	NL	11	25	6	3	0	0	(0 | 0)	9	1	3	1	1	0	8	0	0	0	0	1	.00	1	.240	.269	.360
2006	Fla	NL	9	18	2	0	0	0	(0 | 0)	2	0	0	0	1	0	4	0	0	0	0	0	-	0	.111	.158	.111
	5 ML YEARS		89	185	39	11	0	4	(3 | 1)	62	12	21	11	7	1	53	0	0	0	1	1	.50	2	.211	.240	.335

Gustavo Chacin

Pitches: L Bats: L Pos: SP-17   Ht: 5'11" Wt: 195 Born: 12/4/1980 Age: 26

							HOW MUCH HE PITCHED		WHAT HE GAVE UP												THE RESULTS					
Year	Team	Lg	G	GS	CG	GF	IP	BFP	H	R	ER	HR	SH	SF	HB	TBB	IBB	SO	WP	Bk	W	L	Pct	ShO	Sv-Op	Hld	ERC	ERA
2006	Dnedin*	A+	1	1	0	0	4.2	24	6	5	5	0	0	0	0	4	0	5	0	0	0	0	-	0	0--	-	6.63	9.64
2006	Syrcse*	AAA	4	4	0	0	10.2	58	22	12	12	1	0	0	0	3	0	11	1	0	0	3	.000	0	0--	-	9.88	10.13
2004	Tor	AL	2	2	0	0	14.0	52	8	4	4	0	0	0	1	3	0	6	0	0	1	1	.500	0	0-0	0	1.24	2.57
2005	Tor	AL	34	34	0	0	203.0	872	213	93	84	20	8	10	8	70	3	121	3	0	13	9	.591	0	0-0	0	4.30	3.72
2006	Tor	AL	17	17	0	0	87.1	384	90	51	49	19	2	0	6	38	2	47	0	0	9	4	.692	0	0-0	0	5.57	5.05
	3 ML YEARS		53	53	0	0	304.1	1308	311	148	137	39	10	10	15	111	5	174	3	0	23	14	.622	0	0-0	0	4.48	4.05

Shawn Chacon

Pitches: R Bats: R Pos: SP-20; RP-6   Ht: 6'3" Wt: 220 Born: 12/23/1977 Age: 29

							HOW MUCH HE PITCHED		WHAT HE GAVE UP												THE RESULTS					
Year	Team	Lg	G	GS	CG	GF	IP	BFP	H	R	ER	HR	SH	SF	HB	TBB	IBB	SO	WP	Bk	W	L	Pct	ShO	Sv-Op	Hld	ERC	ERA
2006	Trntn*	AA	1	1	0	0	5.0	21	4	3	3	0	0	0	0	2	0	3	1	0	0	0	-	0	0--	-	2.31	5.40
2001	Col	NL	27	27	0	0	160.0	711	157	96	90	26	6	3	10	87	10	134	6	0	6	10	.375	0	0-0	0	5.22	5.06
2002	Col	NL	21	21	0	0	119.1	537	122	84	76	25	5	2	7	60	3	67	0	1	5	11	.313	0	0-0	0	5.63	5.73

HOW MUCH HE PITCHED						WHAT HE GAVE UP												THE RESULTS							
Year	Team	Lg	G	GS	CG	GF	IP	BFP	H	R	ER	HR	SH	SF	HB	TBB	IBB	SO	WP	Bk	W	L	Pct	ShO	Sv-Op	Hld	ERC	ERA
2003	Col	NL	23	23	0	0	137.0	596	124	73	70	12	10	5	12	58	4	93	8	0	11	8	.579	0	0-0	0	3.82	4.60
2004	Col	NL	66	0	0	60	63.1	316	71	52	50	12	7	0	5	52	7	52	9	0	1	9	.100	0	35-44	0	7.30	7.11
2005	2 Tms		27	24	0	0	151.2	652	135	59	58	14	9	5	14	66	4	79	6	1	8	10	.444	0	0-0	1	3.89	3.44
2006	2 Tms		26	20	0	0	109.0	516	124	86	77	23	7	7	9	63	3	62	4	1	7	6	.538	0	0-0	0	6.76	6.36
05	Col	NL	13	12	0	0	72.2	322	69	33	33	7	9	4	8	36	4	39	3	0	1	7	.125	0	0-0	0	4.51	4.09
05	NYY	AL	14	12	0	0	79.0	330	66	26	25	7	0	1	6	30	0	40	3	1	7	3	.700	0	0-0	0	3.35	2.85
06	NYY	AL	17	11	0	0	63.0	306	77	54	49	11	3	5	5	36	2	35	3	0	5	3	.625	0	0-0	0	6.86	7.00
06	Pit	NL	9	9	0	0	46.0	210	47	32	28	12	4	2	4	27	1	27	1	1	2	3	.400	0	0-0	0	6.61	5.48
6 ML YEARS			190	115	0	60	740.1	3328	733	450	421	112	44	22	57	386	31	487	33	3	38	54	.413	0	35-44	1	5.12	5.12

Endy Chavez

Bats: L **Throws:** L **Pos:** RF-45; LF-43; CF-39; PH-21; PR-2 **Ht:** 6'0" **Wt:** 165 **Born:** 2/7/1978 **Age:** 29

BATTING																			BASERUNNING				AVERAGES		
Year	Team	Lg	G	AB	H	2B	3B	HR	(Hm | Rd)	TB	R	RBI	RC	TBB	IBB	SO	HBP	SH	SF	SB	CS	SB%	GDP	Avg	OBP	Slg
2001	KC	AL	29	77	16	2	0	0	(0 | 0)	18	4	5	2	3	0	8	0	0	0	2	2	.00	3	.208	.238	.234
2002	Mon	NL	36	125	37	8	5	1	(0 | 1)	58	20	9	14	5	0	16	0	7	1	3	5	.38	0	.296	.321	.464
2003	Mon	NL	141	483	121	25	5	5	(4 | 1)	171	66	47	56	31	3	59	0	9	3	18	7	.72	7	.251	.294	.354
2004	Mon	NL	132	502	139	20	6	5	(4 | 1)	186	65	34	56	30	0	40	1	12	2	32	7	.82	6	.277	.318	.371
2005	2 Tms		98	116	25	4	3	0	(0 | 0)	35	19	11	8	7	0	14	0	7	0	2	2	.50	3	.216	.260	.302
2006	NYM	NL	133	353	108	22	5	4	(2 | 2)	152	48	42	54	24	3	44	0	11	2	12	3	.80	7	.306	.348	.431
05	Was	NL	7	9	2	1	0	0	(0 | 0)	3	2	1	1	3	0	1	0	0	0	0	1	.00	1	.222	.417	.333
05	Phi	NL	91	107	23	3	3	0	(0 | 0)	32	17	10	7	4	0	13	0	7	0	2	1	.67	2	.215	.243	.299
6 ML YEARS			569	1656	446	81	24	15	(10 | 5)	620	222	148	190	100	6	181	1	46	8	67	26	.72	26	.269	.310	.374

Eric Chavez

Bats: L **Throws:** R **Pos:** 3B-134; DH-3 **Ht:** 6'1" **Wt:** 210 **Born:** 12/7/1977 **Age:** 29

BATTING																			BASERUNNING				AVERAGES		
Year	Team	Lg	G	AB	H	2B	3B	HR	(Hm | Rd)	TB	R	RBI	RC	TBB	IBB	SO	HBP	SH	SF	SB	CS	SB%	GDP	Avg	OBP	Slg
1998	Oak	AL	16	45	14	4	1	0	(0 | 0)	20	6	6	7	3	1	5	0	0	0	1	1	.50	1	.311	.354	.444
1999	Oak	AL	115	356	88	21	2	13	(8 | 5)	152	47	50	50	46	4	56	0	0	0	1	1	.50	7	.247	.333	.427
2000	Oak	AL	153	501	139	23	4	26	(15 | 11)	248	89	86	86	62	8	94	1	0	5	2	2	.50	9	.277	.355	.495
2001	Oak	AL	151	552	159	43	0	32	(14 | 18)	298	91	114	99	41	9	99	4	0	7	8	2	.80	7	.288	.338	.540
2002	Oak	AL	153	585	161	31	3	34	(17 | 17)	300	87	109	103	65	13	119	1	0	3	8	3	.73	8	.275	.348	.513
2003	Oak	AL	156	588	166	39	5	29	(12 | 17)	302	94	101	97	62	10	89	1	0	3	8	3	.73	14	.282	.350	.514
2004	Oak	AL	125	475	131	20	0	29	(15 | 14)	238	87	77	84	95	10	99	3	0	4	6	3	.67	21	.276	.397	.501
2005	Oak	AL	160	625	168	40	1	27	(15 | 12)	291	92	101	95	58	4	129	2	0	9	6	0	1.00	9	.269	.329	.466
2006	Oak	AL	137	485	117	24	2	22	(8 | 14)	211	74	72	70	84	6	100	1	0	6	3	0	1.00	19	.241	.351	.435
9 ML YEARS			1166	4212	1143	245	18	212	(104 | 108)	2060	667	716	691	516	65	790	13	0	36	43	15	.74	95	.271	.350	.489

Raul Chavez

Bats: R **Throws:** R **Pos:** C-15; PH-1 **Ht:** 5'11" **Wt:** 180 **Born:** 3/18/1973 **Age:** 34

BATTING																			BASERUNNING				AVERAGES		
Year	Team	Lg	G	AB	H	2B	3B	HR	(Hm | Rd)	TB	R	RBI	RC	TBB	IBB	SO	HBP	SH	SF	SB	CS	SB%	GDP	Avg	OBP	Slg
2006	Bowie*	AA	52	196	50	10	0	2	(- | -)	66	18	21	20	11	1	19	0	3	3	0	0	-	7	.255	.290	.337
1996	Mon	NL	4	5	1	0	0	0	(0 | 0)	1	1	0	0	1	0	1	0	0	0	1	0	1.00	1	.200	.333	.200
1997	Mon	NL	13	26	7	0	0	0	(0 | 0)	7	0	2	2	0	0	5	0	0	1	1	0	1.00	0	.269	.259	.269
1998	Sea	AL	1	1	0	0	0	0	(0 | 0)	0	0	0	0	0	0	0	0	0	0	0	0	-	0	.000	.000	.000
2000	Hou	NL	14	43	11	2	0	1	(0 | 1)	16	3	5	3	3	2	6	0	0	1	0	0	-	5	.256	.298	.372
2002	Hou	NL	2	4	1	1	0	0	(0 | 0)	2	1	0	1	1	0	0	1	0	0	0	0	-	3	.250	.500	.500
2003	Hou	NL	19	37	10	1	1	1	(0 | 1)	16	5	4	4	1	0	6	0	0	0	0	0	-	3	.270	.289	.432
2004	Hou	NL	64	162	34	8	0	0	(0 | 0)	42	9	23	10	10	3	38	0	4	0	0	1	.00	9	.210	.256	.259
2005	Hou	NL	37	99	17	3	0	2	(1 | 1)	26	6	6	2	4	0	18	1	0	1	1	0	1.00	5	.172	.210	.263
2006	Bal	AL	16	28	5	0	0	0	(0 | 0)	5	1	0	0	1	0	4	0	0	0	0	0	-	0	.179	.207	.179
9 ML YEARS			170	405	86	15	1	4	(1 | 3)	115	26	40	22	21	5	78	2	4	3	3	1	.75	23	.212	.253	.284

Bruce Chen

Pitches: L **Bats:** L **Pos:** RP-28; SP-12 **Ht:** 6'1" **Wt:** 215 **Born:** 6/19/1977 **Age:** 30

HOW MUCH HE PITCHED									WHAT HE GAVE UP												THE RESULTS							
Year	Team	Lg	G	GS	CG	GF	IP	BFP	H	R	ER	HR	SH	SF	HB	TBB	IBB	SO	WP	Bk	W	L	Pct	ShO	Sv-Op	Hld	ERC	ERA
1998	Atl	NL	4	4	0	0	20.1	91	23	9	9	3	1	0	1	9	1	17	0	0	2	0	1.000	0	0-0	0	5.55	3.98
1999	Atl	NL	16	7	0	3	51.0	214	38	32	31	11	1	1	2	27	3	45	0	0	2	2	.500	0	0-0	0	4.07	5.47
2000	2 Tms	NL	37	15	0	4	134.0	559	116	54	49	18	8	3	2	46	4	112	4	1	7	4	.636	0	0-0	0	3.35	3.29
2001	2 Tms	NL	27	27	0	0	146.0	634	146	90	79	29	4	7	1	59	4	126	5	0	7	7	.500	0	0-0	0	4.75	4.87
2002	3 Tms	NL	55	6	0	9	77.2	360	85	53	48	16	2	3	2	43	5	80	4	0	2	5	.286	0	0-0	4	5.99	5.56
2003	2 Tms	NL	16	2	0	4	24.1	110	26	16	15	6	3	3	2	10	1	20	0	0	0	1	.000	0	0-0	1	5.81	5.55
2004	Bal	AL	8	7	0	0	47.2	196	39	19	16	7	2	1	0	16	0	32	0	0	1	2	.667	0	0-0	0	3.13	3.02
2005	Bal	AL	34	32	1	0	197.1	832	187	94	84	33	3	3	9	63	0	133	2	1	13	10	.565	0	0-0	0	4.12	3.83
2006	Bal	AL	40	12	0	16	98.2	453	137	81	76	28	3	5	0	35	3	70	1	0	0	7	.000	0	0-0	0	7.73	6.93
00	Atl	NL	22	0	0	4	39.2	176	35	15	11	4	3	2	1	19	2	32	0	1	4	0	1.000	0	0-0	0	3.62	2.50
00	Phi	NL	15	15	0	0	94.1	383	81	39	38	14	5	1	1	27	2	80	4	0	3	4	.429	0	0-0	0	3.22	3.63
01	Phi	NL	16	16	0	0	86.1	381	90	53	48	19	2	4	1	31	4	79	2	0	4	5	.444	0	0-0	0	4.87	5.00
01	NYM	NL	11	11	0	0	59.2	253	56	37	31	10	2	3	0	28	0	47	3	0	3	2	.600	0	0-0	0	4.58	4.68
02	NYM	NL	1	0	0	0	0.2	3	1	0	0	0	0	0	0	0	0	0	0	0	0	0	-	0	0-0	0	4.47	0.00
02	Mon	NL	15	5	0	4	37.1	179	47	29	29	9	0	1	0	23	3	43	3	0	2	3	.400	0	0-0	0	7.69	6.99
02	Cin	NL	39	1	0	5	39.2	178	37	24	19	7	2	3	1	20	2	37	1	0	0	2	.000	0	0-0	4	4.55	4.31

Year	Team	Lg	G	GS	CG	GF	IP	BFP	H	R	ER	HR	SH	SF	HB	TBB	IBB	SO	WP	Bk	W	L	Pct	ShO	Sv-Op	Hld	ERC	ERA
			HOW MUCH HE PITCHED						WHAT HE GAVE UP												THE RESULTS						
03	Hou	NL	11	0	0	2	12.0	60	14	8	8	2	3	2	2	8	1	8	0	0	0	0	-	0	0-0	1	7.11	6.00
03	Bos	AL	5	2	0	2	12.1	50	12	8	7	4	0	1	0	2	0	12	0	0	0	1	.000	0	0-0	4	4.40	5.11
9 ML YEARS			237	112	2	36	797.0	3449	797	448	407	151	27	26	19	308	21	635	16	2	35	37	.486	0	0-0	6	4.70	4.60

Travis Chick

Pitches: R **Bats:** R **Pos:** RP-3   **Ht:** 6'3" **Wt:** 215 **Born:** 6/10/1984 **Age:** 23

Year	Team	Lg	G	GS	CG	GF	IP	BFP	H	R	ER	HR	SH	SF	HB	TBB	IBB	SO	WP	Bk	W	L	Pct	ShO	Sv-Op	Hld	ERC	ERA
			HOW MUCH HE PITCHED						WHAT HE GAVE UP												THE RESULTS						
2002	Mrlns	R	12	8	0	1	45.2	199	40	16	14	1	0	0	4	19	0	39	3	0	3	2	.600	0	1--	-	3.18	2.76
2003	Jmstwn	A+	13	10	0	0	52.0	241	63	41	33	3	1	2	2	26	0	48	3	0	1	2	.333	0	0--	-	5.54	5.71
2004	FtWyn	A+	7	7	0	0	42.1	166	32	12	10	4	5	3	1	9	0	55	1	1	5	0	1.000	0	0--	-	2.19	2.13
2004	Grnsbr	A	28	11	0	6	91.1	384	79	51	41	11	1	2	7	27	0	112	6	0	6	4	.600	0	0--	-	3.33	4.04
2005	Mobile	AA	19	19	1	0	97.1	435	107	65	57	12	5	3	3	40	2	92	6	0	2	9	.182	0	0--	-	4.92	5.27
2005	Chatt	AA	8	8	0	0	46.1	207	47	25	25	5	3	3	0	27	1	21	4	1	2	2	.500	0	0--	-	4.94	4.86
2006	Chatt	AA	16	16	0	0	84.0	366	79	45	43	12	6	4	3	36	0	77	1	2	4	5	.444	0	0--	-	4.26	4.61
2006	SnAnt	AA	11	11	0	0	67.2	289	57	25	24	3	0	1	2	37	0	44	8	0	4	2	.667	0	0--	-	3.54	3.19
2006	Sea	AL	3	0	0	0	5.0	31	7	7	7	0	0	0	0	10	0	2	0	0	0	0	-	0	0-0	0	12.69	12.60

Jason Childers

Pitches: R **Bats:** R **Pos:** RP-5   **Ht:** 6'0" **Wt:** 160 **Born:** 1/13/1975 **Age:** 32

Year	Team	Lg	G	GS	CG	GF	IP	BFP	H	R	ER	HR	SH	SF	HB	TBB	IBB	SO	WP	Bk	W	L	Pct	ShO	Sv-Op	Hld	ERC	ERA
			HOW MUCH HE PITCHED						WHAT HE GAVE UP												THE RESULTS						
1997	Helena	R+	10	0	0	6	16.1	207	14	9	6	2	2	0	0	7	0	25	0	0	1	1	.500	0	2--	-	1.02	3.31
1998	Beloit	A	34	14	1	4	117.0	477	104	48	25	8	6	2	1	22	2	110	7	2	8	6	.571	0	0--	-	2.46	1.92
1999	Ogden	R+	3	3	0	0	13.0	50	10	4	2	1	0	0	1	3	0	14	1	0	0	0	-	0	0--	-	2.51	1.38
1999	Stcktn	A+	12	12	1	0	73.1	314	78	39	29	12	2	2	3	11	0	73	3	1	2	8	.200	0	0--	-	3.91	3.56
2000	Mudvle	A+	28	28	0	0	157.1	646	140	71	61	12	3	3	0	54	0	177	6	0	12	10	.545	0	0--	-	3.15	3.49
2001	Hntsvl	AA	40	2	0	10	87.2	364	76	32	28	7	2	2	2	30	3	85	2	0	7	6	.538	0	2--	-	3.04	2.87
2002	Hntsvl	AA	11	1	0	3	25.2	105	22	6	6	1	1	1	1	12	0	22	2	0	1	1	.500	0	0--	-	3.45	2.10
2002	Indy	AAA	28	2	0	9	52.2	240	57	31	27	6	1	1	1	30	1	29	2	0	2	3	.400	0	0--	-	5.40	4.61
2003	Indy	AAA	46	0	0	24	63.0	255	50	22	16	6	4	0	1	20	2	47	1	0	5	4	.556	0	10--	-	2.67	2.29
2004	Indy	AAA	24	0	0	22	28.2	115	20	4	4	0	1	0	3	9	0	27	0	0	1	0	1.000	0	15--	-	1.98	1.26
2004	Edmtn	AAA	14	0	0	13	14.0	66	15	8	7	1	0	0	0	9	0	13	1	0	0	3	.000	0	5--	-	5.11	4.50
2005	Rchmd	AAA	38	0	0	0	38.2	169	32	14	9	2	4	0	0	20	1	31	2	0	1	2	.333	0	16--	-	3.11	2.09
2006	Drham	AAA	39	0	0	11	52.1	237	58	34	29	8	3	2	1	22	1	39	6	0	2	3	.400	0	2--	-	5.12	4.99
2006	TB	AL	5	0	0	0	7.2	40	12	6	4	1	0	1	0	4	0	5	1	0	0	1	.000	0	0-0	0	7.93	4.70

Randy Choate

Pitches: L **Bats:** L **Pos:** RP-30   **Ht:** 6'1" **Wt:** 195 **Born:** 9/5/1975 **Age:** 31

Year	Team	Lg	G	GS	CG	GF	IP	BFP	H	R	ER	HR	SH	SF	HB	TBB	IBB	SO	WP	Bk	W	L	Pct	ShO	Sv-Op	Hld	ERC	ERA
			HOW MUCH HE PITCHED						WHAT HE GAVE UP												THE RESULTS						
2006	Tucsn*	AAA	43	1	0	19	45.2	184	39	13	11	0	1	1	1	10	1	44	1	0	6	0	1.000	0	8--	-	2.07	2.17
2000	NYY	AL	22	0	0	6	17.0	75	14	10	9	3	0	1	1	9	0	12	1	0	1	0	1.000	0	0-0	2	3.99	4.76
2001	NYY	AL	37	0	0	13	48.1	207	34	21	18	0	2	1	9	27	2	35	3	0	3	1	.750	0	0-0	3	3.03	3.35
2002	NYY	AL	18	0	0	11	22.1	101	18	18	15	1	0	0	3	15	0	17	3	0	0	0	-	0	0-0	4	4.13	6.04
2003	NYY	AL	5	0	0	2	3.2	16	7	3	3	0	0	0	0	1	0	0	0	0	0	0	-	0	0-0	0	9.72	7.36
2004	Ari	NL	74	0	0	17	50.2	232	52	26	26	1	0	4	5	28	11	49	1	1	2	4	.333	0	0-2	11	4.18	4.62
2005	Ari	NL	8	0	0	0	7.0	35	8	7	7	0	0	0	1	5	1	4	1	0	0	0	-	0	0-0	2	5.48	9.00
2006	Ari	NL	30	0	0	3	16.0	75	21	9	7	0	0	0	3	3	0	12	0	0	0	1	.000	0	0-0	5	4.87	3.94
7 ML YEARS			194	0	0	52	165.0	741	154	94	85	5	2	6	22	87	14	129	9	1	5	7	.417	0	0-2	23	4.04	4.64

Shin-Soo Choo

Bats: L **Throws:** L **Pos:** RF-30; LF-9; PH-7; CF-4; DH-1   **Ht:** 5'11" **Wt:** 210 **Born:** 7/13/1982 **Age:** 24

Year	Team	Lg	G	AB	H	2B	3B	HR	(Hm	Rd)	TB	R	RBI	RC	TBB	IBB	SO	HBP	SH	SF	SB	CS	SB%	GDP	Avg	OBP	Slg
			BATTING																		BASERUNNING				AVERAGES		
2001	Ms	R	51	199	60	10	10	4	(-	-)	102	51	35	45	34	2	49	9	0	3	12	4	.75	1	.302	.420	.513
2001	Wisc	A	3	13	6	0	0	0	(-	-)	6	1	3	3	1	0	3	1	0	0	2	0	1.00	0	.462	.533	.462
2002	Wisc	A	119	420	127	24	8	6	(-	-)	185	69	48	81	70	5	98	13	3	1	34	21	.62	2	.302	.417	.440
2002	SnBrn	A+	11	39	12	5	1	1	(-	-)	22	14	9	11	9	1	9	2	1	0	3	0	1.00	0	.308	.460	.564
2003	InldEm	A+	110	412	118	18	13	9	(-	-)	189	62	55	71	44	1	84	9	2	4	18	10	.64	8	.286	.365	.459
2004	SnAnt	AA	132	517	163	17	7	15	(-	-)	239	89	84	97	56	4	97	2	1	3	39	9	.81	6	.315	.382	.462
2005	Tacom	AAA	115	429	121	21	5	11	(-	-)	185	73	54	75	69	0	97	1	2	1	20	10	.67	8	.282	.382	.431
2006	Tacom	AAA	94	375	121	21	3	13	(-	-)	187	71	48	78	45	3	73	2	1	4	26	4	.87	1	.323	.394	.499
2005	Sea	AL	10	18	1	0	0	0	(0	0)	1	1	1	0	3	0	4	0	0	0	0	0	-	0	.056	.190	.056
2006	2 Tms	AL	49	157	44	12	3	3	(2	1)	71	23	22	24	18	2	50	2	1	1	5	3	.63	3	.280	.360	.452
06	Sea	AL	4	11	1	1	0	0	(0	0)	2	0	0	0	0	0	4	1	0	0	0	0	-	1	.091	.167	.182
06	Cle	AL	45	146	43	11	3	3	(2	1)	69	23	22	24	18	2	46	1	1	1	5	3	.63	2	.295	.373	.473
2 ML YEARS			59	175	45	12	3	3	(2	1)	72	24	23	24	21	2	54	2	1	1	5	3	.63	3	.257	.342	.411

Vinnie Chulk

Pitches: R **Bats:** R **Pos:** RP-48 **Ht:** 6'1" **Wt:** 195 **Born:** 12/19/1978 **Age:** 28

Year	Team	Lg	G	GS	CG	GF	IP	BFP	H	R	ER	HR	SH	SF	HB	TBB	IBB	SO	WP	Bk	W	L	Pct	ShO	Sv-Op	Hld	ERC	ERA
2006	Syrcse*	AAA	19	0	0	2	32.0	132	20	8	8	4	2	0	2	14	1	43	2	0	3	2	.600	0	1- -	-	2.55	2.25
2003	Tor	AL	3	0	0	2	5.1	25	6	3	3	0	0	0	0	3	0	2	0	0	0	0	-	0	0-1	0	4.53	5.06
2004	Tor	AL	47	0	0	10	56.0	248	59	30	29	6	1	1	1	27	1	44	2	0	1	3	.250	0	2-5	13	4.83	4.66
2005	Tor	AL	62	0	0	10	72.0	301	68	33	31	9	3	4	1	26	3	39	5	0	0	1	.000	0	0-1	13	3.83	3.88
2006	2 Tms		48	0	0	13	46.1	205	46	29	27	6	0	2	3	20	2	43	4	0	1	3	.250	0	0-2	6	4.53	5.24
06	Tor	AL	20	0	0	8	24.0	107	29	16	14	4	0	1	2	5	0	18	1	0	1	0	1.000	0	0-1	1	5.25	5.25
06	SF	NL	28	0	0	5	22.1	98	17	13	13	2	0	1	1	15	2	25	3	0	0	3	.000	0	0-1	5	3.74	5.24
	4 ML YEARS		160	0	0	35	179.2	779	179	95	90	21	4	7	5	76	6	128	11	0	2	7	.222	0	2-9	32	4.34	4.51

Ryan Church

Bats: L **Throws:** L **Pos:** CF-51; RF-14; PH-12; PR-3; LF-2 **Ht:** 6'1" **Wt:** 220 **Born:** 10/14/1978 **Age:** 28

Year	Team	Lg		G	AB	H	2B	3B	HR	(Hm	Rd)	TB	R	RBI	RC	TBB	IBB	SO	HBP	SH	SF		SB	CS	SB%	GDP		Avg	OBP	Slg
2006	NewOr*	AAA		53	175	43	6	0	7	(-	-)	70	29	29	27	25	2	41	3	0	3		5	1	.83	5		.246	.345	.400
2006	Hrsbrg*	AA		5	19	4	0	0	2	(-	-)	10	3	3	3	3	2	5	0	0	0		1	0	1.00	0		.211	.318	.526
2004	Mon	NL		30	63	11	1	0	1	(0	1)	15	6	6	2	7	1	16	0	1	0		0	0	-	3		.175	.257	.238
2005	Was	NL		102	268	77	15	3	9	(5	4)	125	41	42	34	24	0	70	5	1	3		3	2	.60	6		.287	.353	.466
2006	Was	NL		71	196	54	17	1	10	(6	4)	103	22	35	36	26	0	60	3	3	2		6	1	.86	4		.276	.366	.526
	3 ML YEARS			203	527	142	33	4	20	(11	9)	243	69	83	72	57	1	146	8	5	5		9	3	.75	13		.269	.347	.461

Alex Cintron

Bats: B **Throws:** R **Pos:** SS-41; 2B-26; PH-20; 3B-11; DH-6; PR-2 **Ht:** 6'1" **Wt:** 205 **Born:** 12/17/1978 **Age:** 28

Year	Team	Lg		G	AB	H	2B	3B	HR	(Hm	Rd)	TB	R	RBI	RC	TBB	IBB	SO	HBP	SH	SF		SB	CS	SB%	GDP		Avg	OBP	Slg
2001	Ari	NL		8	7	2	0	1	0	(0	0)	4	0	0	1	0	0	0	0	0	0		0	0	-	0		.286	.286	.571
2002	Ari	NL		38	75	16	6	0	0	(0	0)	22	11	4	5	12	2	13	0	3	0		0	0	-	2		.213	.322	.293
2003	Ari	NL		117	448	142	26	6	13	(6	7)	219	70	51	70	29	0	33	2	5	3		2	3	.40	7		.317	.359	.489
2004	Ari	NL		154	564	148	31	7	4	(1	3)	205	56	49	59	31	2	59	2	12	4		3	3	.50	11		.262	.301	.363
2005	Ari	NL		122	330	90	19	2	8	(5	3)	137	36	48	35	12	3	33	1	2	3		1	2	.33	8		.273	.298	.415
2006	CWS	AL		91	288	82	10	3	5	(3	2)	113	35	41	33	10	0	35	2	1	3		10	3	.77	10		.285	.310	.392
	6 ML YEARS			530	1712	480	92	19	30	(15	15)	700	208	193	203	94	7	173	7	23	13		16	11	.59	38		.280	.318	.409

Jeff Cirillo

Bats: R **Throws:** R **Pos:** PH-47; 3B-42; 1B-14; 2B-12; SS-3 **Ht:** 6'1" **Wt:** 200 **Born:** 9/23/1969 **Age:** 37

Year	Team	Lg		G	AB	H	2B	3B	HR	(Hm	Rd)	TB	R	RBI	RC	TBB	IBB	SO	HBP	SH	SF		SB	CS	SB%	GDP		Avg	OBP	Slg
1994	Mil	AL		39	126	30	9	0	3	(1	2)	48	17	12	14	11	0	16	2	0	0		0	1	.00	4		.238	.309	.381
1995	Mil	AL		125	328	91	19	4	9	(6	3)	145	57	39	55	47	0	42	4	1	4		7	2	.78	8		.277	.371	.442
1996	Mil	AL		158	566	184	46	5	15	(6	9)	285	101	83	105	58	0	69	7	6	6		4	9	.31	14		.325	.391	.504
1997	Mil	AL		154	580	167	46	2	10	(6	4)	247	74	82	91	60	0	74	14	4	3		4	3	.57	13		.288	.367	.426
1998	Mil	NL		156	604	194	31	1	14	(6	8)	269	97	68	103	79	3	88	4	5	2		10	4	.71	26		.321	.402	.445
1999	Mil	NL		157	607	198	35	1	15	(6	9)	280	98	88	111	75	4	83	5	3	7		7	4	.64	15		.326	.401	.461
2000	Col	NL		157	598	195	53	2	11	(9	2)	285	111	115	108	67	4	72	6	1	12		3	4	.43	19		.326	.392	.477
2001	Col	NL		138	528	165	26	4	17	(9	8)	250	72	83	89	43	6	63	5	1	9		12	2	.86	15		.313	.364	.473
2002	Sea	AL		146	485	121	20	0	6	(2	4)	159	51	54	52	31	0	67	9	13	9		8	4	.67	12		.249	.301	.328
2003	Sea	AL		87	258	53	11	0	2	(1	1)	70	24	23	23	24	1	32	5	4	2		1	1	.50	6		.205	.284	.271
2004	SD	NL		33	75	16	3	0	1	(1	0)	22	12	7	6	5	0	14	0	0	1		0	0	-	0		.213	.259	.293
2005	Mil	NL		77	185	52	15	0	4	(1	3)	79	29	23	30	23	0	22	4	7	0		4	2	.67	3		.281	.373	.427
2006	Mil	NL		112	263	84	16	0	3	(1	2)	109	33	23	38	21	0	33	1	3	2		1	1	.50	8		.319	.369	.414
	13 ML YEARS			1539	5203	1550	330	19	110	(54	56)	2248	776	700	825	544	18	675	66	48	57		61	37	.62	143		.298	.368	.432

Brady Clark

Bats: R **Throws:** R **Pos:** CF-114; PH-24; RF-7; LF-3; PR-1 **Ht:** 6'2" **Wt:** 205 **Born:** 4/18/1973 **Age:** 34

Year	Team	Lg		G	AB	H	2B	3B	HR	(Hm	Rd)	TB	R	RBI	RC	TBB	IBB	SO	HBP	SH	SF		SB	CS	SB%	GDP		Avg	OBP	Slg
2000	Cin	NL		11	11	3	1	0	0	(0	0)	4	1	2	1	0	0	2	0	0	0		0	0	-	0		.273	.273	.364
2001	Cin	NL		89	129	34	3	0	6	(4	2)	55	22	18	21	22	1	16	1	4	1		4	1	.80	6		.264	.373	.426
2002	2 Tms	NL		61	78	15	4	0	0	(0	0)	19	9	10	7	7	2	11	1	1	0		1	2	.33	2		.192	.267	.244
2003	Mil	NL		128	315	86	21	1	6	(5	1)	127	33	40	40	21	0	40	9	2	7		13	2	.87	12		.273	.330	.403
2004	Mil	NL		138	353	99	18	1	7	(1	6)	140	41	46	56	53	2	48	9	1	3		15	8	.65	9		.280	.385	.397
2005	Mil	NL		145	599	183	31	1	13	(8	5)	255	94	53	92	47	1	55	18	8	2		10	13	.43	13		.306	.372	.426
2006	Mil	NL		138	415	109	14	2	4	(3	1)	139	51	29	47	43	4	60	14	5	5		3	4	.43	9		.263	.348	.335
02	Cin	NL		51	66	10	3	0	0	(0	0)	13	6	9	5	6	2	9	1	1	0		1	2	.33	2		.152	.233	.197
02	NYM	NL		10	12	5	1	0	0	(0	0)	6	3	1	2	1	0	2	0	0	0		0	0	-	0		.417	.462	.500
	7 ML YEARS			710	1900	529	92	5	36	(21	15)	739	251	198	264	193	10	232	52	21	18		46	30	.61	51		.278	.358	.389

Doug Clark

Bats: L Throws: R Pos: PH-5; LF-1   Ht: 6'2" Wt: 205 Born: 3/5/1976 Age: 31

Year	Team	Lg	G	AB	H	2B	3B	HR	(Hm	Rd)	TB	R	RBI	RC	TBB	IBB	SO	HBP	SH	SF	SB	CS	SB%	GDP	Avg	OBP	Slg
1998	SlmKzr	A-	59	227	76	8	6	3	(-	-)	105	49	41	45	32	0	31	3	1	1	12	8	.60	1	.335	.422	.463
1999	Bkrsfld	A+	118	420	137	17	2	11	(-	-)	191	67	58	81	59	4	89	5	0	0	17	11	.61	5	.326	.415	.455
1999	Shreve	AA	15	50	11	3	0	1	(-	-)	17	6	4	4	4	0	9	0	0	0	0	0	-	2	.220	.278	.340
2000	Shreve	AA	131	492	134	20	7	10	(-	-)	198	68	75	70	43	5	102	5	1	7	12	4	.75	13	.272	.333	.402
2001	Shreve	AA	123	414	114	16	4	6	(-	-)	156	53	51	60	45	4	83	3	6	4	20	5	.80	8	.275	.348	.377
2002	Shreve	AA	44	138	36	6	1	2	(-	-)	50	13	13	17	19	4	35	0	2	1	5	7	.42	4	.261	.348	.362
2002	Fresno	AAA	70	212	57	9	1	5	(-	-)	83	24	19	28	15	2	52	5	1	1	3	3	.50	5	.269	.330	.392
2003	Fresno	AAA	13	21	5	0	0	0	(-	-)	5	4	0	1	2	0	3	0	0	0	0	1	.00	0	.238	.304	.238
2003	Nrwich	AA	113	396	119	23	4	4	(-	-)	162	47	49	63	45	1	67	2	1	4	8	5	.62	8	.301	.371	.409
2004	Nrwich	AA	140	537	157	23	13	10	(-	-)	236	82	71	87	44	1	103	3	1	2	33	8	.80	9	.292	.348	.439
2005	Fresno	AAA	127	472	149	30	5	13	(-	-)	228	81	59	85	35	1	87	5	3	3	29	12	.71	6	.316	.367	.483
2006	Scrmto	AAA	122	494	142	22	2	15	(-	-)	213	93	67	84	57	0	104	8	8	7	25	8	.76	10	.287	.366	.431
2005	SF	NL	8	5	0	0	0	0	(0	0)	0	2	0	0	1	0	2	0	0	0	0	0	-	0	.000	.167	.000
2006	Oak	AL	6	6	1	0	0	0	(0	0)	1	0	0	0	0	0	3	0	0	0	1	0	1.00	0	.167	.167	.167
2 ML YEARS			14	11	1	0	0	0	(0	0)	1	2	0	0	1	0	5	0	0	0	1	0	1.00	0	.091	.167	.091

Howie Clark

Bats: L Throws: R Pos: PH-5; 3B-1; DH-1   Ht: 5'10" Wt: 195 Born: 2/13/1974 Age: 33

Year	Team	Lg	G	AB	H	2B	3B	HR	(Hm	Rd)	TB	R	RBI	RC	TBB	IBB	SO	HBP	SH	SF	SB	CS	SB%	GDP	Avg	OBP	Slg
2006	Ottawa*	AAA	86	308	81	16	1	3	(-	-)	108	41	27	40	36	3	28	2	2	2	2	2	.50	5	.263	.342	.351
2002	Bal	AL	14	53	16	5	0	0	(0	0)	21	3	4	3	3	0	6	2	0	0	0	0	-	5	.302	.362	.396
2003	Tor	AL	38	70	25	3	1	0	(0	0)	30	9	7	13	3	0	6	2	2	0	0	1	.00	3	.357	.400	.429
2004	Tor	AL	40	115	25	6	0	3	(3	0)	40	17	12	11	13	0	15	0	3	2	0	0	-	2	.217	.292	.348
2006	Bal	AL	7	7	1	0	0	0	(0	0)	1	1	0	1	2	0	2	0	1	0	0	0	-	0	.143	.333	.143
4 ML YEARS			99	245	67	14	1	3	(3	0)	92	30	23	28	21	0	29	4	6	2	0	1	.00	10	.273	.338	.376

Tony Clark

Bats: B Throws: R Pos: 1B-53; PH-36   Ht: 6'7" Wt: 245 Born: 6/15/1972 Age: 35

Year	Team	Lg	G	AB	H	2B	3B	HR	(Hm	Rd)	TB	R	RBI	RC	TBB	IBB	SO	HBP	SH	SF	SB	CS	SB%	GDP	Avg	OBP	Slg
2006	Tucsn*	AAA	2	6	2	0	0	1	(-	-)	5	2	1	1	0	0	0	1	0	0	0	0	-	1	.333	.429	.833
1995	Det	AL	27	101	24	5	1	3	(0	3)	40	10	11	11	8	0	30	0	0	0	0	0	-	2	.238	.294	.396
1996	Det	AL	100	376	94	14	0	27	(17	10)	189	56	72	55	29	1	127	0	0	6	0	1	.00	7	.250	.299	.503
1997	Det	AL	159	580	160	28	3	32	(18	14)	290	105	117	107	93	13	144	3	0	5	1	3	.25	11	.276	.376	.500
1998	Det	AL	157	602	175	37	0	34	(18	16)	314	84	103	107	63	5	128	3	0	5	3	3	.50	16	.291	.358	.522
1999	Det	AL	143	536	150	29	0	31	(12	19)	272	74	99	94	64	7	133	6	0	3	2	1	.67	14	.280	.361	.507
2000	Det	AL	60	208	57	14	0	13	(6	7)	110	32	37	35	24	2	51	0	0	0	0	0	-	10	.274	.349	.529
2001	Det	AL	126	428	123	29	3	16	(7	9)	206	67	75	74	62	10	108	1	0	6	0	1	.00	14	.287	.374	.481
2002	Bos	AL	90	275	57	12	1	3	(1	2)	80	25	29	19	21	0	57	1	0	1	0	0	-	11	.207	.265	.291
2003	NYM	NL	125	254	59	13	0	16	(9	7)	120	29	43	29	24	2	73	1	0	1	0	0	-	8	.232	.300	.472
2004	NYY	AL	106	253	56	12	0	16	(5	11)	116	37	49	37	26	3	92	2	0	2	0	0	-	6	.221	.297	.458
2005	Ari	NL	130	349	106	22	2	30	(19	11)	222	47	87	71	37	6	88	1	0	6	0	0	-	10	.304	.366	.636
2006	Ari	NL	79	132	26	4	0	6	(3	3)	48	13	16	10	13	2	40	2	0	0	0	0	-	5	.197	.279	.364
12 ML YEARS			1302	4094	1087	219	10	227	(115	112)	2007	579	738	649	464	51	1071	20	0	35	6	9	.40	114	.266	.341	.490

Brandon Claussen

Pitches: L Bats: R Pos: SP-14   Ht: 6'1" Wt: 200 Born: 5/1/1979 Age: 28

	HOW MUCH HE PITCHED						WHAT HE GAVE UP									THE RESULTS						
Year	Team	Lg	G	GS	CG	GF	IP	BFP	H	R	ER	HR	SH	SF	HB	TBB	IBB	SO	WP	Bk	W	L	Pct	ShO	Sv-Op	Hld	ERC	ERA
2006	Lsvlle*	AAA	5	5	0	0	22.2	105	31	21	21	5	0	2	0	8	0	18	1	0	0	2	.000	0	0- -	-	7.01	8.34
2003	NYY	AL	1	1	0	0	6.1	28	8	2	1	1	0	0	1	0	0	5	0	0	1	0	1.000	0	0-0	0	4.89	1.42
2004	Cin	NL	14	14	0	0	66.0	313	80	50	45	9	5	3	2	35	2	45	3	0	2	8	.200	0	0-0	0	6.11	6.14
2005	Cin	NL	29	29	0	0	166.2	731	178	89	78	24	8	6	7	57	5	121	2	1	10	11	.476	0	0-0	0	4.63	4.21
2006	Cin	NL	14	14	0	0	77.0	351	93	56	53	14	6	2	6	28	1	57	2	0	3	8	.273	0	0-0	0	6.06	6.19
4 ML YEARS			58	58	0	0	316.0	1423	359	197	177	48	19	11	15	121	8	228	7	1	16	27	.372	0	0-0	0	5.28	5.04

Royce Clayton

Bats: R Throws: R Pos: SS-129; PH-10   Ht: 6'0" Wt: 200 Born: 1/2/1970 Age: 37

Year	Team	Lg	G	AB	H	2B	3B	HR	(Hm	Rd)	TB	R	RBI	RC	TBB	IBB	SO	HBP	SH	SF	SB	CS	SB%	GDP	Avg	OBP	Slg
1991	SF	NL	9	26	3	1	0	0	(0	0)	4	0	2	0	1	0	6	0	0	0	0	0	-	1	.115	.148	.154
1992	SF	NL	98	321	72	7	4	4	(3	1)	99	31	24	25	26	3	63	0	3	2	8	4	.67	11	.224	.281	.308
1993	SF	NL	153	549	155	21	5	6	(5	1)	204	54	70	64	38	2	91	5	8	7	11	10	.52	16	.282	.331	.372
1994	SF	NL	108	385	91	14	6	3	(1	2)	126	38	30	40	30	2	74	3	3	2	23	3	.88	7	.236	.295	.327
1995	SF	NL	138	509	124	29	3	5	(2	3)	174	56	58	53	38	1	109	3	4	3	24	9	.73	7	.244	.298	.342
1996	StL	NL	129	491	136	20	4	6	(6	0)	182	64	35	56	33	4	89	1	2	4	33	15	.69	13	.277	.321	.371
1997	StL	NL	154	576	153	39	5	9	(5	4)	229	75	61	67	33	4	109	3	2	5	30	10	.75	19	.266	.306	.398
1998	2 Tms		142	541	136	31	2	9	(2	7)	198	89	53	62	53	1	83	3	6	5	24	11	.69	16	.251	.319	.366
1999	Tex	AL	133	465	134	21	5	14	(6	8)	207	69	52	71	39	1	100	4	9	3	8	6	.57	6	.288	.346	.445
2000	Tex	AL	148	513	124	21	5	9	(5	4)	197	70	54	54	42	1	92	3	12	3	11	7	.61	21	.242	.301	.384
2001	CWS	AL	135	433	114	21	4	9	(6	3)	170	62	60	50	33	2	72	3	9	7	10	7	.59	16	.263	.315	.393
2002	CWS	AL	112	342	86	14	2	7	(4	3)	125	51	35	37	20	0	67	3	4	1	5	1	.83	7	.251	.295	.365
2003	Mil	NL	146	483	110	16	1	11	(5	6)	161	49	39	37	49	10	92	3	4	2	9	3	.75	25	.228	.301	.333

Year	Team	Lg	G	AB	H	2B	3B	HR	(Hm	Rd)	TB	R	RBI	RC	TBB	IBB	SO	HBP	SH	SF	SB	CS	SB%	GDP	Avg	OBP	Slg
																	BATTING				BASERUNNING				AVERAGES		
2004	Col	NL	146	574	160	36	4	8	(6	2)	228	95	54	75	48	0	125	4	24	2	10	5	.67	13	.279	.338	.397
2005	Ari	NL	143	522	141	28	4	2	(1	1)	183	59	44	55	38	0	105	1	10	2	13	3	.81	19	.270	.320	.351
2006	2 Tms	NL	137	454	117	30	1	2	(2	0)	155	49	40	43	30	3	85	5	7	6	14	6	.70	11	.258	.307	.341
98	StL	NL	90	355	83	19	1	4	(1	3)	116	59	29	37	40	1	51	2	3	2	19	6	.76	10	.234	.313	.327
98	Tex	AL	52	186	53	12	1	5	(1	4)	82	30	24	25	13	0	32	1	3	3	5	5	.50	6	.285	.330	.441
06	Was	NL	87	305	82	22	1	0	(0	0)	106	36	27	32	19	3	53	4	5	5	8	3	.73	8	.269	.315	.348
06	Cin	NL	50	149	35	8	0	2	(2	0)	49	13	13	11	11	0	32	1	2	1	6	3	.67	3	.235	.290	.329
16 ML YEARS			2031	7184	1856	349	55	109	(63	46)	2642	911	711	789	551	34	1362	44	110	59	229	99	.70	208	.258	.313	.368

Roger Clemens

Pitches: R Bats: R Pos: SP-19　　　　　　　　　　　**Ht: 6'4" Wt: 235 Born: 8/4/1962 Age: 44**

Year	Team	Lg	G	GS	CG	GF	IP	BFP	H	R	ER	HR	SH	SF	HB	TBB	IBB	SO	WP	Bk	W	L	Pct	ShO	Sv-Op	Hld	ERC	ERA
			HOW MUCH HE PITCHED						WHAT HE GAVE UP												THE RESULTS							
2006	Lxngtn*	A	1	1	0	0	3.0	13	3	1	1	1	0	0	1	0	0	6	0	0	0	0	-	0	0--	-	5.31	3.00
2006	CpChr*	AA	1	1	0	0	6.0	19	2	0	0	0	0	0	0	0	0	11	0	0	1	0	1.000	0	0--	-	0.26	0.00
2006	RdRck*	AAA	1	1	0	0	5.2	25	5	3	3	0	0	0	0	3	0	5	0	0	1	0	1.000	0	0--	-	3.13	4.76
1984	Bos	AL	21	20	5	0	133.1	575	146	67	64	13	2	3	2	29	3	126	4	0	9	4	.692	1	0-0	0	3.81	4.32
1985	Bos	AL	15	15	3	0	98.1	407	83	38	36	5	1	2	3	37	0	74	1	3	7	5	.583	1	0-0	0	2.96	3.29
1986	Bos	AL	33	33	10	0	254.0	997	179	77	70	21	4	6	4	67	0	238	11	3	24	4	.857	1	0-0	0	2.03	2.48
1987	Bos	AL	36	36	18	0	281.2	1157	248	100	93	19	6	4	9	83	4	256	4	3	20	9	.690	7	0-0	0	2.94	2.97
1988	Bos	AL	35	35	14	0	264.0	1063	217	93	86	17	6	3	6	62	4	291	4	7	18	12	.600	8	0-0	0	2.36	2.93
1989	Bos	AL	35	35	8	0	253.1	1044	215	101	88	20	9	5	8	93	5	230	7	0	17	11	.607	3	0-0	0	3.13	3.13
1990	Bos	AL	31	31	7	0	228.1	920	193	59	49	7	7	5	7	54	3	209	6	0	21	6	.778	4	0-0	0	2.33	1.93
1991	Bos	AL	35	35	13	0	271.1	1077	219	93	79	15	6	8	5	65	12	241	6	0	18	10	.643	4	0-0	0	2.23	2.62
1992	Bos	AL	32	32	11	0	246.2	989	203	80	66	11	5	5	9	62	5	208	3	0	18	11	.621	5	0-0	0	2.38	2.41
1993	Bos	AL	29	29	2	0	191.2	808	175	99	95	17	5	7	11	67	4	160	3	1	11	14	.440	1	0-0	0	3.53	4.46
1994	Bos	AL	24	24	3	0	170.2	692	124	62	54	15	2	5	4	71	1	168	4	0	9	7	.563	1	0-0	0	2.72	2.85
1995	Bos	AL	23	23	0	0	140.0	623	141	70	65	15	2	3	14	60	0	132	9	0	10	5	.667	0	0-0	0	4.67	4.18
1996	Bos	AL	34	34	6	0	242.2	1032	216	106	98	19	4	7	4	106	2	257	11	0	10	13	.435	2	0-0	0	3.52	3.63
1997	Tor	AL	34	34	9	0	264.0	1044	204	65	60	9	5	2	12	68	1	292	4	0	21	7	.750	3	0-0	0	2.17	2.05
1998	Tor	AL	33	33	5	0	234.2	961	169	78	69	11	8	2	7	88	0	271	6	0	20	6	.769	3	0-0	0	2.27	2.65
1999	NYY	AL	30	30	1	0	187.2	822	185	101	96	20	10	5	9	90	0	163	8	0	14	10	.583	1	0-0	0	4.59	4.60
2000	NYY	AL	32	32	1	0	204.1	878	184	96	84	26	1	2	10	84	0	188	2	1	13	8	.619	0	0-0	0	3.93	3.70
2001	NYY	AL	33	33	0	0	220.1	918	205	94	86	19	4	4	5	72	1	213	14	0	20	3	.870	0	0-0	0	3.43	3.51
2002	NYY	AL	29	29	0	0	180.0	768	172	94	87	18	5	5	7	63	6	192	14	0	13	6	.684	0	0-0	0	3.72	4.35
2003	NYY	AL	33	33	1	0	211.2	878	199	99	92	24	3	6	5	58	1	190	5	0	17	9	.654	1	0-0	0	3.44	3.91
2004	Hou	NL	33	33	0	0	214.1	878	169	76	71	15	8	7	6	79	5	218	5	0	18	4	.818	0	0-0	0	2.72	2.98
2005	Hou	NL	32	32	1	0	211.1	838	151	51	44	11	9	3	3	62	5	185	3	1	13	8	.619	0	0-0	0	1.96	1.87
2006	Hou	NL	19	19	0	0	113.1	451	89	34	29	7	5	1	4	29	1	102	3	0	7	6	.538	0	0-0	0	2.33	2.30
23 ML YEARS			691	690	118	0	4817.2	19820	4086	1833	1661	354	117	100	154	1549	63	4604	136	20	348	178	.662	46	0-0	0	2.90	3.10

Matt Clement

Pitches: R Bats: R Pos: SP-12　　　　　　　　　　　**Ht: 6'3" Wt: 210 Born: 8/12/1974 Age: 32**

Year	Team	Lg	G	GS	CG	GF	IP	BFP	H	R	ER	HR	SH	SF	HB	TBB	IBB	SO	WP	Bk	W	L	Pct	ShO	Sv-Op	Hld	ERC	ERA
			HOW MUCH HE PITCHED						WHAT HE GAVE UP												THE RESULTS							
2006	RedSx*	R	1	1	0	0	1.0	4	1	0	0	0	0	0	0	0	0	1	1	0	0	0	-	0	0--	-	1.95	0.00
1998	SD	NL	4	2	0	0	13.2	62	15	8	7	0	2	0	1	7	1	13	2	0	2	0	1.000	0	0-0	-	4.14	4.61
1999	SD	NL	31	31	0	0	180.2	803	190	106	90	18	7	6	9	86	2	135	11	0	10	12	.455	0	0-0	0	4.89	4.48
2000	SD	NL	34	34	0	0	205.0	940	194	131	117	22	12	5	16	125	4	170	23	0	13	17	.433	0	0-0	0	4.87	5.14
2001	Fla	NL	31	31	0	0	169.1	760	172	102	95	15	14	3	15	85	2	134	15	0	9	10	.474	0	0-0	0	4.84	5.05
2002	ChC	NL	32	32	3	0	205.0	858	162	84	82	18	11	4	6	85	7	215	7	0	12	11	.522	2	0-0	0	2.96	3.60
2003	ChC	NL	32	32	2	0	201.2	851	169	100	92	22	10	2	14	79	2	171	13	0	14	12	.538	1	0-0	0	3.47	4.11
2004	ChC	NL	30	30	0	0	181.0	775	155	79	74	23	5	4	12	77	4	190	14	1	9	13	.409	0	0-0	0	3.78	3.68
2005	Bos	AL	32	32	1	0	191.0	830	192	102	97	18	2	6	16	68	1	146	13	0	13	6	.684	0	0-0	0	4.22	4.57
2006	Bos	AL	12	12	0	0	65.1	310	77	50	48	8	1	0	6	38	0	43	3	0	5	5	.500	0	0-0	0	6.44	6.61
9 ML YEARS			238	236	6	0	1412.2	6189	1326	762	702	144	64	30	94	650	23	1217	101	1	87	86	.503	3	0-0	0	4.21	4.47

Brent Clevlen

Bats: R Throws: R Pos: CF-13; RF-13; LF-8; PR-5; PH-1　　　　**Ht: 6'2" Wt: 190 Born: 10/27/1983 Age: 23**

Year	Team	Lg	G	AB	H	2B	3B	HR	(Hm	Rd)	TB	R	RBI	RC	TBB	IBB	SO	HBP	SH	SF	SB	CS	SB%	GDP	Avg	OBP	Slg
														BATTING							BASERUNNING				AVERAGES		
2002	Tigers	R	28	103	34	2	3	3	(-	-)	51	14	21	19	8	0	24	0	0	2	2	1	.67	0	.330	.372	.495
2003	W Mich	A	138	481	125	22	7	12	(-	-)	197	67	63	76	72	0	111	4	0	3	6	3	.67	16	.260	.359	.410
2004	Lkland	A+	117	420	94	23	6	6	(-	-)	147	49	50	47	44	1	127	4	0	5	2	1	.67	12	.224	.300	.350
2005	Lkland	A+	130	494	149	28	4	18	(-	-)	239	77	102	95	65	8	118	5	2	2	14	5	.74	16	.302	.387	.484
2006	Erie	AA	109	395	91	17	0	11	(-	-)	141	47	45	48	47	3	138	3	1	5	6	2	.75	9	.230	.313	.357
2006	Det	AL	31	39	11	1	2	3	(0	3)	25	9	6	6	2	0	15	0	1	0	0	0	-	0	.282	.317	.641

JD Closser

Bats: B Throws: R Pos: C-29; PH-4　　　　　　　　　　**Ht: 5'10" Wt: 200 Born: 1/15/1980 Age: 27**

Year	Team	Lg	G	AB	H	2B	3B	HR	(Hm	Rd)	TB	R	RBI	RC	TBB	IBB	SO	HBP	SH	SF	SB	CS	SB%	GDP	Avg	OBP	Slg
														BATTING							BASERUNNING				AVERAGES		
2006	ColSpr*	AAA	70	225	67	15	1	8	(-	-)	108	32	30	43	31	0	38	1	0	1	8	2	.80	6	.298	.384	.480
2004	Col	NL	36	113	36	6	0	1	(0	1)	45	5	10	15	6	0	22	2	3	0	0	0	-	3	.319	.364	.398
2005	Col	NL	92	237	52	12	2	7	(2	5)	89	31	27	24	32	1	48	1	1	1	1	0	1.00	6	.219	.314	.376
2006	Col	NL	32	97	19	3	1	2	(1	1)	30	10	11	8	12	2	23	1	1	1	0	1	.00	1	.196	.288	.309
3 ML YEARS			160	447	107	21	3	10	(3	7)	164	46	48	47	50	3	93	4	5	2	1	1	.50	13	.239	.320	.367

Buck Coats

Bats: L Throws: R Pos: PH-14; CF-3; RF-1; PR-1   Ht: 6'3" Wt: 195 Born: 6/9/1982 Age: 25

								BATTING												BASERUNNING				AVERAGES		
Year	Team	Lg	G	AB	H	2B	3B	HR	(Hm | Rd)	TB	R	RBI	RC	TBB	IBB	SO	HBP	SH	SF	SB	CS	SB%	GDP	Avg	OBP	Slg
2000	Cubs	R	30	98	29	6	3	0	(- | -)	41	20	14	18	12	2	24	4	0	1	7	1	.88	1	.296	.395	.418
2001	Cubs	R	33	123	32	3	3	1	(- | -)	44	11	18	12	4	0	19	2	1	1	3	4	.43	1	.260	.292	.358
2002	Lansng	A	133	501	129	21	4	4	(- | -)	170	65	47	55	31	4	67	4	2	6	14	3	.82	5	.257	.303	.339
2003	Lansng	A	132	488	135	25	7	1	(- | -)	177	64	59	71	64	5	93	4	6	2	32	15	.68	13	.277	.364	.363
2004	Dytona	A	112	414	120	22	4	8	(- | -)	174	64	55	62	32	2	90	1	3	3	28	9	.76	6	.290	.340	.420
2005	WTenn	AA	127	439	124	32	6	1	(- | -)	171	47	49	62	38	1	80	2	1	4	17	5	.77	10	.282	.340	.390
2006	Iowa	AAA	124	450	127	21	0	7	(- | -)	169	60	51	62	38	1	87	4	4	2	17	4	.81	9	.282	.342	.376
2006	ChC	NL	18	18	3	1	0	1	(0 | 1)	7	2	1	0	0	0	6	0	0	0	0	0	-	1	.167	.167	.389

Todd Coffey

Pitches: R Bats: R Pos: RP-81   Ht: 6'5" Wt: 230 Born: 9/9/1980 Age: 26

			HOW MUCH HE PITCHED						WHAT HE GAVE UP											THE RESULTS						
Year	Team	Lg	G	GS	CG	GF	IP	BFP	H	R	ER	HR	SH	SF	HB	TBB	IBB	SO	WP	Bk	W	L	Pct	ShO	Sv-Op	Hld	ERC	ERA
1998	Billings	R+	3	2	0	1	12.0	50	13	4	4	1	2	0	2	1	0	8	0	0	0	0	-	0	0--	-	3.91	3.00
1999	Reds	R	5	2	0	0	16.0	71	9	12	6	1	0	1	1	14	0	14	2	2	1	1	.500	0	0--	-	3.41	3.38
2001	Reds	R	3	2	0	0	12.2	54	11	11	6	1	1	1	1	5	0	15	0	0	0	1	.000	0	0--	-	3.49	4.26
2001	Billings	R+	14	2	0	6	33.1	149	34	21	13	2	1	1	2	15	0	33	2	0	2	2	.500	0	1--	-	4.28	3.51
2002	Dayton	A	38	5	0	11	80.1	344	78	34	32	8	4	5	2	25	5	62	9	4	6	4	.600	0	2--	-	3.51	3.59
2003	Dayton	A	39	0	0	26	56.0	243	61	20	14	1	0	0	2	14	0	53	3	0	3	3	.500	0	9--	-	3.49	2.25
2003	Ptomc	A+	11	0	0	5	23.0	88	16	6	5	0	1	0	1	3	0	21	1	0	0	2	.000	0	2--	-	1.34	1.96
2004	Chatt	AA	40	0	0	34	45.1	176	36	13	12	3	1	0	0	4	1	53	1	1	4	1	.800	0	20--	-	1.67	2.38
2004	Lsvlle	AAA	15	0	0	11	13.2	58	15	8	8	1	0	0	1	2	0	11	1	0	1	0	1.000	0	4--	-	3.71	5.27
2005	Lsvlle	AAA	8	0	0	5	8.2	36	8	5	5	1	1	0	0	2	1	5	0	0	0	0	-	0	3--	-	2.88	5.19
2005	Cin	NL	57	0	0	14	58.0	265	84	33	29	5	3	2	5	11	2	26	1	0	4	1	.800	0	1-2	3	6.11	4.50
2006	Cin	NL	81	0	0	28	78.0	340	85	34	31	7	0	1	2	27	5	60	4	0	6	7	.462	0	8-12	15	4.29	3.58
	2 ML YEARS		138	0	0	42	136.0	605	169	67	60	12	3	3	7	38	7	86	5	0	10	8	.556	0	9-14	18	5.04	3.97

Alvin Colina

Bats: R Throws: R Pos: C-1; PH-1   Ht: 6'3" Wt: 210 Born: 12/26/1981 Age: 25

								BATTING												BASERUNNING				AVERAGES		
Year	Team	Lg	G	AB	H	2B	3B	HR	(Hm	Rd)	TB	R	RBI	RC	TBB	IBB	SO	HBP	SH	SF	SB	CS	SB%	GDP	Avg	OBP	Slg
2000	Rckies	R	35	122	43	7	1	4	(-	-)	64	25	28	25	9	0	26	6	0	2	2	3	.40	2	.352	.417	.525
2001	Tri-Cit	A-	47	164	35	10	0	5	(-	-)	60	12	17	16	12	0	50	4	2	0	0	2	.00	2	.213	.283	.366
2002	Ashvlle	A	59	212	50	8	0	7	(-	-)	79	22	36	26	20	0	57	4	2	1	1	0	1.00	3	.236	.312	.373
2003	Ashvlle	A	72	256	68	20	1	4	(-	-)	102	26	23	34	20	0	53	4	1	0	5	4	.56	5	.266	.329	.398
2004	Visalia	A+	95	334	84	23	0	11	(-	-)	140	43	47	45	24	0	81	6	3	1	0	1	.00	8	.251	.312	.419
2005	Mdest	A+	9	34	9	3	0	0	(-	-)	12	2	3	3	3	0	14	0	0	0	0	1	.00	0	.265	.324	.353
2005	Tulsa	AA	59	207	53	5	0	9	(-	-)	85	23	35	29	20	1	42	4	1	2	0	2	.00	8	.256	.330	.411
2006	Tulsa	AA	92	323	82	14	1	12	(-	-)	134	45	46	43	23	2	77	6	0	2	3	2	.60	13	.254	.314	.415
2006	Col	NL	2	5	1	0	0	0	(0	0)	1	0	1	0	0	0	1	0	0	0	0	0	-	0	.200	.200	.200

Jesus Colome

Pitches: R Bats: R Pos: RP-1   Ht: 6'2" Wt: 205 Born: 12/23/1977 Age: 29

			HOW MUCH HE PITCHED						WHAT HE GAVE UP											THE RESULTS						
Year	Team	Lg	G	GS	CG	GF	IP	BFP	H	R	ER	HR	SH	SF	HB	TBB	IBB	SO	WP	Bk	W	L	Pct	ShO	Sv-Op	Hld	ERC	ERA
2006	Trntn*	AA	3	0	0	1	4.2	20	2	3	1	1	0	0	0	3	0	2	0	0	2	0	1.000	0	0--	-	2.50	1.93
2006	Clmbs*	AAA	25	0	0	9	33.1	150	35	17	14	3	2	1	0	15	0	25	3	0	1	1	.500	0	0--	-	4.37	3.78
2001	TB	AL	30	0	0	9	48.2	209	37	22	18	8	2	2	2	25	4	31	2	0	2	3	.400	0	0-0	6	3.62	3.33
2002	TB	AL	32	0	0	15	41.1	204	56	41	38	6	4	1	2	33	5	33	5	0	2	7	.222	0	0-5	3	8.57	8.27
2003	TB	AL	54	0	0	24	74.0	334	69	37	37	9	2	4	3	46	5	69	7	0	3	7	.300	0	2-8	11	4.76	4.50
2004	TB	AL	33	0	0	9	41.1	169	28	16	15	4	5	0	1	18	1	40	1	1	2	2	.500	0	3-4	8	2.54	3.27
2005	TB	AL	36	0	0	18	45.1	212	54	29	23	7	1	0	2	18	3	28	5	0	2	3	.400	0	0-1	2	5.46	4.57
2006	TB	AL	1	0	0	0	0.1	2	0	1	1	0	0	0	0	1	0	0	0	0	0	0	-	0	0-0	0	7.00	27.00
	6 ML YEARS		186	0	0	75	251.0	1130	244	146	132	34	14	7	10	141	18	201	20	1	11	22	.333	0	5-18	30	4.83	4.73

Bartolo Colon

Pitches: R Bats: R Pos: SP-10   Ht: 5'11" Wt: 250 Born: 5/24/1973 Age: 34

			HOW MUCH HE PITCHED						WHAT HE GAVE UP											THE RESULTS						
Year	Team	Lg	G	GS	CG	GF	IP	BFP	H	R	ER	HR	SH	SF	HB	TBB	IBB	SO	WP	Bk	W	L	Pct	ShO	Sv-Op	Hld	ERC	ERA
2006	RCuca*	A+	1	1	0	0	4.0	14	2	0	0	0	0	0	1	1	0	3	0	0	0	0	-	0	0--	-	1.01	0.00
2006	Salt Lk*	AAA	2	2	0	0	11.2	49	14	8	8	4	1	0	1	2	0	3	0	0	0	1	.000	0	0--	-	6.69	6.17
1997	Cle	AL	19	17	1	0	94.0	427	107	66	59	12	4	1	3	45	1	66	5	0	4	7	.364	0	0-0	0	5.53	5.65
1998	Cle	AL	31	31	6	0	204.0	883	205	91	84	15	10	2	3	79	5	158	4	0	14	9	.609	2	0-0	0	3.87	3.71
1999	Cle	AL	32	32	1	0	205.0	858	185	97	90	24	5	4	7	76	5	161	4	0	18	5	.783	1	0-0	0	3.91	3.95
2000	Cle	AL	30	30	2	0	188.0	807	163	86	81	21	2	3	4	98	4	212	4	0	15	8	.652	1	0-0	0	3.97	3.88
2001	Cle	AL	34	34	1	0	222.1	947	220	106	101	26	8	4	2	90	2	201	4	1	14	12	.538	0	0-0	0	4.24	4.09
2002	2 Tms		33	33	8	0	233.1	966	219	85	76	20	19	6	2	70	5	149	4	0	20	8	.714	3	0-0	0	3.29	2.93
2003	CWS	AL	34	34	9	0	242.0	984	223	107	104	30	5	8	5	67	3	173	8	3	15	13	.536	0	0-0	0	3.47	3.87
2004	LAA	AL	34	34	0	0	208.1	897	215	122	116	38	5	8	3	71	1	158	1	0	18	12	.600	0	0-0	0	4.64	5.01
2005	LAA	AL	33	33	2	0	222.2	906	215	93	86	26	9	4	3	43	0	157	2	1	21	8	.724	0	0-0	0	3.28	3.48
2006	LAA	AL	10	10	0	0	56.1	251	71	39	32	11	4	1	0	11	0	31	1	0	1	5	.167	0	0-0	0	5.61	5.11
02	Cle	AL	16	16	4	0	116.1	467	104	37	33	11	6	3	2	31	1	75	3	0	10	4	.714	2	0-0	0	3.09	2.55
02	Mon	NL	17	17	4	0	117.0	499	115	48	43	9	13	3	0	39	4	74	1	0	10	4	.714	1	0-0	0	3.48	3.31
	10 ML YEARS		290	288	31	0	1876.0	7926	1823	892	829	223	71	41	35	650	26	1466	37	5	140	87	.617	8	0-0	0	3.92	3.98

Roman Colon

Pitches: R **Bats:** R **Pos:** RP-19; SP-1 **Ht:** 6'6" **Wt:** 225 **Born:** 8/13/1979 **Age:** 27

Year	Team	Lg	G	GS	CG	GF	IP	BFP	H	R	ER	HR	SH	SF	HB	TBB	IBB	SO	WP	Bk	W	L	Pct	ShO	Sv-Op	Hld	ERC	ERA
2006	Toledo*	AAA	2	2	0	0	6.2	27	4	5	0	0	0	0	0	2	0	6	1	0	0	0	-	0	0--	-	1.26	0.00
2004	Atl	NL	18	0	0	7	19.0	82	18	9	7	0	1	2	0	8	1	15	0	0	2	1	.667	0	0-1	1	3.05	3.32
2005	2 Tms		35	7	0	7	69.1	306	82	45	43	17	2	3	0	21	1	47	4	1	2	6	.250	0	0-1	2	5.75	5.58
2006	Det	AL	20	1	0	4	38.2	170	46	21	21	6	1	2	1	14	2	25	6	0	2	0	1.000	0	1-1	3	5.56	4.89
05	Atl	NL	23	4	0	6	44.1	191	47	28	26	10	2	2	0	14	1	30	2	1	1	5	.167	0	0-0	2	4.90	5.28
05	Det	AL	12	3	0	1	25.0	115	35	17	17	7	0	1	0	7	0	17	2	0	1	1	.500	0	0-1	0	7.34	6.12
3 ML YEARS			73	8	0	18	127.0	558	146	75	71	23	4	7	1	43	4	87	10	1	6	7	.462	0	1-3	6	5.27	5.03

Clay Condrey

Pitches: R **Bats:** R **Pos:** RP-21 **Ht:** 6'3" **Wt:** 195 **Born:** 11/19/1975 **Age:** 31

Year	Team	Lg	G	GS	CG	GF	IP	BFP	H	R	ER	HR	SH	SF	HB	TBB	IBB	SO	WP	Bk	W	L	Pct	ShO	Sv-Op	Hld	ERC	ERA
2006	S-WB*	AAA	39	0	0	16	51.1	205	41	12	11	1	6	2	3	15	3	28	0	0	4	2	.667	0	6--	-	2.30	1.93
2002	SD	NL	9	3	0	2	26.2	106	20	7	5	1	2	2	2	8	1	16	1	1	1	2	.333	0	0-0	3	2.29	1.69
2003	SD	NL	9	6	0	0	34.0	168	43	32	32	7	3	0	3	21	4	25	0	0	1	2	.333	0	0-0	0	7.50	8.47
2006	Phi	NL	21	0	0	10	28.2	122	35	11	10	3	2	1	0	9	2	16	0	0	2	2	.500	0	0-1	1	5.14	3.14
3 ML YEARS			39	9	0	12	89.1	396	98	50	47	11	7	3	5	38	7	57	1	1	4	6	.400	0	0-1	4	5.05	4.74

Jeff Conine

Bats: R **Throws:** R **Pos:** 1B-73; LF-68; RF-26; PH-10; DH-3; 3B-1 **Ht:** 6'1" **Wt:** 225 **Born:** 6/26/1966 **Age:** 41

Year	Team	Lg	G	AB	H	2B	3B	HR	(Hm	Rd)	TB	R	RBI	RC	TBB	IBB	SO	HBP	SH	SF	SB	CS	SB%	GDP	Avg	OBP	Slg
1990	KC	AL	9	20	5	2	0	0	(0	0)	7	3	2	2	2	0	5	0	0	0	0	0	-	1	.250	.318	.350
1992	KC	AL	28	91	23	5	2	0	(0	0)	32	10	9	10	8	1	23	0	0	0	0	0	-	1	.253	.313	.352
1993	Fla	NL	162	595	174	24	3	12	(5	7)	240	75	79	83	52	2	135	5	0	6	2	2	.50	14	.292	.351	.403
1994	Fla	NL	115	451	144	27	6	18	(8	10)	237	60	82	84	40	4	92	1	0	4	1	2	.33	8	.319	.373	.525
1995	Fla	NL	133	483	146	26	2	25	(13	12)	251	72	105	93	66	5	94	1	0	12	2	0	1.00	13	.302	.379	.520
1996	Fla	NL	157	597	175	32	2	26	(15	11)	289	84	95	99	62	1	121	4	0	7	1	4	.20	17	.293	.360	.484
1997	Fla	NL	151	405	98	13	1	17	(7	10)	164	46	61	55	57	3	89	2	0	2	2	0	1.00	11	.242	.337	.405
1998	KC	AL	93	309	79	26	0	8	(4	4)	129	30	43	40	26	1	68	2	0	6	3	0	1.00	8	.256	.312	.417
1999	Bal	AL	139	444	129	31	1	13	(7	6)	201	54	75	64	30	4	40	3	1	7	0	3	.00	12	.291	.335	.453
2000	Bal	AL	119	409	116	20	2	13	(6	7)	179	53	46	58	36	1	53	2	0	4	4	3	.57	14	.284	.341	.438
2001	Bal	AL	139	524	163	23	2	14	(5	9)	232	75	97	89	64	6	75	5	0	8	12	8	.60	12	.311	.386	.443
2002	Bal	AL	116	451	123	26	4	15	(12	3)	202	44	63	61	25	6	66	2	0	10	8	0	1.00	16	.273	.307	.448
2003	2 Tms		149	577	163	36	3	20	(11	9)	265	88	95	84	50	5	70	5	1	13	5	0	1.00	16	.282	.338	.459
2004	Fla	NL	140	521	146	35	1	14	(9	5)	225	55	83	78	48	3	78	2	2	6	5	5	.50	15	.280	.340	.432
2005	Fla	NL	131	335	102	20	2	3	(1	2)	135	42	33	46	38	2	58	3	2	6	2	0	1.00	12	.304	.374	.403
2006	2 Tms		142	489	131	26	4	10	(6	4)	195	54	66	59	40	4	65	4	1	5	3	2	.60	13	.268	.325	.399
03	Bal	AL	124	493	143	33	3	15	(8	7)	227	75	80	73	37	5	60	5	0	12	5	0	1.00	14	.290	.338	.460
03	Fla	NL	25	84	20	3	0	5	(3	2)	38	13	15	11	13	0	10	0	1	1	0	0	-	2	.238	.337	.452
06	Bal	AL	114	389	103	20	3	9	(6	3)	156	43	49	45	35	2	53	2	1	5	3	2	.60	12	.265	.325	.401
06	Phi	NL	28	100	28	6	1	1	(0	1)	39	11	17	14	5	2	12	2	0	0	0	0	-	1	.280	.327	.390
16 ML YEARS			1923	6701	1917	372	35	208	(109	99)	2983	845	1034	1005	644	44	1132	41	7	96	50	29	.63	177	.286	.348	.445

Jose Contreras

Pitches: R **Bats:** R **Pos:** SP-30 **Ht:** 6'4" **Wt:** 245 **Born:** 12/6/1971 **Age:** 35

Year	Team	Lg	G	GS	CG	GF	IP	BFP	H	R	ER	HR	SH	SF	HB	TBB	IBB	SO	WP	Bk	W	L	Pct	ShO	Sv-Op	Hld	ERC	ERA
2003	NYY	AL	18	9	0	2	71.0	293	52	27	26	4	0	1	5	30	1	72	2	0	7	2	.778	0	0-1	1	2.71	3.30
2004	2 Tms	AL	31	31	0	0	170.1	758	166	114	104	31	3	6	8	84	1	150	17	0	13	9	.591	0	0-0	0	5.05	5.50
2005	CWS	AL	32	32	1	0	204.2	857	177	91	82	23	7	2	9	75	2	154	20	2	15	7	.682	0	0-0	0	3.46	3.61
2006	CWS	AL	30	30	1	0	196.0	833	194	101	93	20	2	8	10	55	4	134	16	0	13	9	.591	1	0-0	0	3.72	4.27
04	NYY	AL	18	18	0	0	95.2	425	93	66	60	22	1	4	6	42	1	82	10	0	8	5	.615	0	0-0	0	5.18	5.64
04	CWS	AL	13	13	0	0	74.2	333	73	48	44	9	2	2	2	42	0	68	7	0	5	4	.556	0	0-0	0	4.87	5.30
4 ML YEARS			111	102	2	2	642.0	2741	589	333	305	78	12	17	32	244	8	510	55	2	48	27	.640	1	0-1	1	3.86	4.28

Aaron Cook

Pitches: R **Bats:** R **Pos:** SP-32 **Ht:** 6'3" **Wt:** 215 **Born:** 2/8/1979 **Age:** 28

Year	Team	Lg	G	GS	CG	GF	IP	BFP	H	R	ER	HR	SH	SF	HB	TBB	IBB	SO	WP	Bk	W	L	Pct	ShO	Sv-Op	Hld	ERC	ERA
2002	Col	NL	9	5	0	1	35.2	154	41	18	18	4	0	0	2	13	0	14	0	0	2	1	.667	0	0-0	1	5.31	4.54
2003	Col	NL	43	16	1	4	124.0	579	160	89	83	8	4	8	7	57	7	43	10	0	4	6	.400	0	0-0	1	5.95	6.02
2004	Col	NL	16	16	1	0	96.2	433	112	47	46	7	5	1	7	39	5	40	6	1	6	4	.600	0	0-0	0	5.05	4.28
2005	Col	NL	13	13	2	0	83.1	357	101	38	34	8	1	3	2	16	2	24	3	0	7	2	.778	0	0-0	0	4.53	3.67
2006	Col	NL	32	32	0	0	212.2	915	242	107	100	17	8	5	7	55	11	92	2	0	9	15	.375	0	0-0	0	4.23	4.23
5 ML YEARS			113	82	4	5	552.1	2438	656	299	281	44	18	15	26	180	25	213	21	1	28	28	.500	0	0-2	2	4.86	4.58

Alex Cora

Bats: L Throws: R Pos: SS-63; 2B-18; 3B-11; PH-9; PR-6; DH-1   Ht: 6'0" Wt: 200 Born: 10/18/1975 Age: 31

								BATTING												BASERUNNING				AVERAGES		
Year	Team	Lg	G	AB	H	2B	3B	HR	(Hm	Rd)	TB	R	RBI	RC	TBB	IBB	SO	HBP	SH	SF	SB	CS	SB%	GDP	Avg	OBP	Slg
1998	LAD	NL	29	33	4	0	1	0	(0	0)	6	1	0	1	2	0	8	1	2	0	0	0	-	0	.121	.194	.182
1999	LAD	NL	11	30	5	1	0	0	(0	0)	6	2	3	0	0	0	4	1	0	0	0	0	-	1	.167	.194	.200
2000	LAD	NL	109	353	84	18	6	4	(2	2)	126	39	32	38	26	4	53	7	6	2	4	1	.80	6	.238	.302	.357
2001	LAD	NL	134	405	88	18	3	4	(2	2)	124	38	29	30	31	6	58	8	3	2	0	2	.00	16	.217	.285	.306
2002	LAD	NL	115	258	75	14	4	5	(4	1)	112	37	28	46	26	4	38	7	2	0	7	2	.78	3	.291	.371	.434
2003	LAD	NL	148	477	119	24	3	4	(3	1)	161	39	34	46	16	3	59	10	9	2	4	2	.67	5	.249	.287	.338
2004	LAD	NL	138	405	107	9	4	10	(4	6)	154	47	47	63	47	10	41	18	12	2	3	4	.43	9	.264	.364	.380
2005	2 Tms	AL	96	250	58	8	4	3	(1	2)	83	25	24	21	11	0	30	5	4	3	7	2	.78	6	.232	.275	.332
2006	Bos	AL	96	235	56	7	2	1	(1	0)	70	31	18	24	19	1	29	6	4	0	6	2	.75	4	.238	.312	.298
05	Cle	AL	49	146	30	5	2	1	(1	0)	42	11	8	9	5	0	18	4	1	1	6	0	1.00	3	.205	.250	.288
05	Bos	AL	47	104	28	3	2	2	(0	2)	41	14	16	12	6	0	12	1	3	2	1	2	.33	3	.269	.310	.394
9 ML YEARS			876	2446	596	99	27	31	(17	14)	842	259	215	269	178	28	320	63	42	11	31	15	.67	50	.244	.310	.344

Roy Corcoran

Pitches: R Bats: R Pos: RP-6   Ht: 5'10" Wt: 170 Born: 5/11/1980 Age: 27

			HOW MUCH HE PITCHED						WHAT HE GAVE UP											THE RESULTS						
Year	Team	Lg	G	GS	CG	GF	IP	BFP	H	R	ER	HR	SH	SF	HB	TBB	IBB	SO	WP	Bk	W	L	Pct	ShO	Sv-Op	Hld	ERC	ERA
2006	Hrsbrg*	AA	21	0	0	20	26.0	99	12	6	1	1	1	0	1	10	1	40	1	0	0	2	.000	0	16--	-	1.29	0.35
2006	NewOr*	AAA	28	0	0	22	33.2	152	24	11	9	0	4	1	2	25	2	37	3	1	2	4	.333	0	11--	-	3.10	2.41
2003	Mon	NL	5	0	0	2	7.1	31	7	2	1	0	0	0	0	3	0	2	1	0	0	0	-	0	0-0	0	3.20	1.23
2004	Mon	NL	5	0	0	3	5.1	28	7	4	4	0	0	0	0	5	0	4	0	0	0	0	-	0	0-0	0	7.12	6.75
2006	Was	NL	6	0	0	2	5.2	34	12	8	7	1	0	1	0	4	0	6	0	0	0	1	.000	0	0-1	0	12.96	11.12
3 ML YEARS			16	0	0	7	18.1	93	26	14	12	1	0	1	0	12	0	12	1	0	0	1	.000	0	0-1	0	7.10	5.89

Tim Corcoran

Pitches: R Bats: R Pos: SP-16; RP-5   Ht: 6'2" Wt: 205 Born: 4/15/1978 Age: 29

			HOW MUCH HE PITCHED						WHAT HE GAVE UP											THE RESULTS						
Year	Team	Lg	G	GS	CG	GF	IP	BFP	H	R	ER	HR	SH	SF	HB	TBB	IBB	SO	WP	Bk	W	L	Pct	ShO	Sv-Op	Hld	ERC	ERA
1997	Mets	R	10	0	0	4	21.0	94	16	8	7	0	2	0	0	15	0	20	4	0	3	0	1.000	0	3--	-	3.15	3.00
1997	Kngspt	R+	7	0	0	3	17.0	71	12	10	8	2	0	2	3	8	2	14	2	1	2	0	1.000	0	0--	-	3.44	4.24
1998	StLuci	A+	4	0	0	2	7.2	35	10	7	7	1	0	0	0	2	0	8	0	0	0	0	-	0	0--	-	5.37	8.22
1998	CptCty	A	20	1	0	10	48.1	203	43	21	14	4	1	1	5	15	0	38	3	0	2	3	.400	0	4--	-	3.43	2.61
1999	CptCty	A	40	3	0	10	75.0	328	62	43	37	5	4	3	9	41	0	89	8	1	0	3	.000	0	3--	-	3.93	4.44
2000	CptCty	A	31	0	0	13	53.1	233	46	28	24	7	0	0	4	27	2	58	11	0	3	5	.375	0	1--	-	4.16	4.05
2001	Frdrck	A+	33	0	0	25	50.1	207	37	16	15	4	5	1	2	19	3	42	5	0	6	5	.545	0	0--	-	2.51	2.68
2001	Bowie	AA	7	0	0	4	11.2	42	4	1	1	0	0	0	0	3	0	13	1	0	1	0	1.000	0	0--	-	0.59	0.77
2002	Bowie	AA	35	0	0	23	49.0	237	61	31	20	5	4	3	4	29	3	48	6	0	5	5	.000	0	1--	-	6.52	3.67
2003	Frdrck	A+	22	3	0	4	47.0	225	57	38	30	3	1	5	0	27	2	41	6	0	2	5	.286	0	0--	-	5.52	5.74
2003	Bowie	AA	26	2	0	14	44.0	188	37	22	20	1	1	0	2	19	2	33	1	0	4	1	.800	0	3--	-	2.87	4.09
2004	Drham	AAA	33	0	0	9	50.2	231	46	22	22	4	1	3	2	33	1	40	2	0	3	3	.500	0	0--	-	4.43	3.91
2004	Mont	AA	6	2	0	3	16.1	66	14	5	5	2	0	0	1	3	0	12	0	0	0	1	.000	0	0--	-	2.86	2.76
2005	Drham	AAA	29	0	0	3	56.0	239	49	22	18	3	0	1	2	22	0	49	4	0	5	1	.833	0	0--	-	3.15	2.89
2006	Drham	AAA	19	3	0	6	37.2	167	30	13	8	2	1	0	0	9	1	32	3	0	5	1	.833	0	1--	-	2.16	1.91
2005	TB	AL	10	1	0	4	22.2	97	19	15	15	1	0	0	1	12	0	13	2	0	0	0	-	0	0-0	0	3.49	5.96
2006	TB	AL	21	16	0	2	90.1	396	92	48	44	10	1	4	4	48	3	59	0	1	5	9	.357	0	0-0	0	5.04	4.38
2 ML YEARS			31	17	0	6	113.0	493	111	63	59	11	1	4	5	60	3	72	2	1	5	9	.357	0	0-0	0	4.72	4.70

Chad Cordero

Pitches: R Bats: R Pos: RP-68   Ht: 6'0" Wt: 200 Born: 3/18/1982 Age: 25

			HOW MUCH HE PITCHED						WHAT HE GAVE UP											THE RESULTS						
Year	Team	Lg	G	GS	CG	GF	IP	BFP	H	R	ER	HR	SH	SF	HB	TBB	IBB	SO	WP	Bk	W	L	Pct	ShO	Sv-Op	Hld	ERC	ERA
2003	Mon	NL	12	0	0	4	11.0	40	4	2	2	1	1	0	0	3	1	12	1	0	1	0	1.000	0	1-1	1	0.86	1.64
2004	Mon	NL	69	0	0	40	82.2	357	68	28	27	8	2	4	1	43	4	83	5	0	7	3	.700	0	14-18	8	3.47	2.94
2005	Was	NL	74	0	0	62	74.1	300	55	24	15	9	2	1	2	17	2	61	0	0	2	4	.333	0	47-54	0	2.22	1.82
2006	Was	NL	68	0	0	59	73.1	307	59	27	26	13	6	2	3	22	5	69	0	0	7	4	.636	0	29-33	3	3.10	3.19
4 ML YEARS			223	0	0	165	241.1	1004	186	81	70	31	11	7	6	85	12	225	6	0	17	11	.607	0	91-106	9	2.81	2.61

Francisco Cordero

Pitches: R Bats: R Pos: RP-77   Ht: 6'2" Wt: 235 Born: 5/11/1975 Age: 32

			HOW MUCH HE PITCHED						WHAT HE GAVE UP											THE RESULTS						
Year	Team	Lg	G	GS	CG	GF	IP	BFP	H	R	ER	HR	SH	SF	HB	TBB	IBB	SO	WP	Bk	W	L	Pct	ShO	Sv-Op	Hld	ERC	ERA
1999	Det	AL	20	0	0	4	19.0	91	19	7	7	2	4	2	0	18	2	19	1	0	2	2	.500	0	0-0	6	6.19	3.32
2000	Tex	AL	56	0	0	13	77.1	365	87	51	46	11	2	6	4	48	3	49	7	0	1	2	.333	0	0-3	4	6.15	5.35
2001	Tex	AL	3	0	0	2	2.1	12	3	1	1	0	0	0	0	2	1	1	1	0	0	1	.000	0	0-0	1	5.73	3.86
2002	Tex	AL	39	0	0	25	45.1	177	33	12	9	2	0	0	2	13	1	41	1	0	2	0	1.000	0	10-12	1	2.11	1.79
2003	Tex	AL	73	0	0	36	82.2	352	70	33	27	4	3	4	2	38	6	90	1	0	5	8	.385	0	15-25	18	3.08	2.94
2004	Tex	AL	67	0	0	63	71.2	304	60	19	17	1	5	1	1	32	2	79	3	2	3	4	.429	0	49-54	0	2.78	2.13
2005	Tex	AL	69	0	0	60	69.0	302	61	28	26	5	4	3	4	30	2	79	0	0	3	1	.750	0	37-45	0	3.47	3.39
2006	2 Tms	AL	77	0	0	47	75.1	322	69	32	31	7	3	5	3	32	2	84	4	0	10	5	.667	0	22-33	16	3.79	3.70
06	Tex	AL	49	0	0	21	48.2	210	49	27	26	5	1	5	3	16	1	54	3	0	7	4	.636	0	6-15	15	4.05	4.81
06	Mil	NL	28	0	0	26	26.2	112	20	5	5	2	2	0	0	16	1	30	1	0	3	1	.750	0	16-18	1	3.30	1.69
8 ML YEARS			404	0	0	250	442.2	1925	402	183	164	32	19	23	16	213	19	442	18	2	26	23	.531	0	133-172	46	3.74	3.33

Bryan Corey

Pitches: R Bats: R Pos: RP-32   Ht: 6'0" Wt: 180 Born: 10/21/1973 Age: 33

Year	Team	Lg	G	GS	CG	GF	IP	BFP	H	R	ER	HR	SH	SF	HB	TBB	IBB	SO	WP	Bk	W	L	Pct	ShO	Sv-Op	Hld	ERC	ERA
2006	Frisco*	AA	13	0	0	11	17.1	76	16	7	4	0	2	0	2	6	1	19	1	0	1	0	1.000	0	7--	-	3.01	2.08
2006	Okla*	AAA	12	0	0	10	15.0	54	8	1	1	0	1	1	1	2	0	16	1	0	0	0	-	0	8--	-	0.97	0.60
2006	Pwtckt*	AAA	3	0	0	0	5.0	25	7	4	4	2	0	0	2	2	0	4	0	0	0	0	-	0	0--	-	11.28	7.20
1998	Ari	NL	3	0	0	2	4.0	20	6	4	4	1	1	0	1	2	0	1	0	0	0	0	-	0	0-0	0	10.40	9.00
2002	LAD	NL	1	0	0	1	1.0	3	0	0	0	0	0	0	0	0	0	0	0	0	0	0	-	0	0-0	0	0.00	0.00
2006	2 Tms	AL	32	0	0	3	39.0	166	35	16	16	1	1	3	2	15	0	28	0	0	2	1	.667	0	0-0	3	3.13	3.69
06	Tex	AL	16	0	0	3	17.1	75	15	5	5	0	1	1	0	8	0	13	0	0	1	1	.500	0	0-0	0	2.82	2.60
06	Bos	AL	16	0	0	0	21.2	91	20	11	11	1	0	2	2	7	0	15	0	0	1	0	1.000	0	0-0	3	3.39	4.57
	3 ML YEARS		36	0	0	6	44.0	189	41	20	20	2	2	3	3	17	0	29	0	0	2	1	.667	0	0-0	3	3.53	4.09

Lance Cormier

Pitches: R Bats: R Pos: RP-20; SP-9   Ht: 6'1" Wt: 200 Born: 8/19/1980 Age: 26

Year	Team	Lg	G	GS	CG	GF	IP	BFP	H	R	ER	HR	SH	SF	HB	TBB	IBB	SO	WP	Bk	W	L	Pct	ShO	Sv-Op	Hld	ERC	ERA
2006	Rome*	A	1	0	0	0	1.0	3	0	0	0	0	0	0	0	0	0	2	0	0	0	0	-	0	0--	-	0.00	0.00
2006	Rchmd*	AAA	9	9	1	0	54.2	235	65	26	24	4	2	2	1	14	1	27	0	0	4	3	.571	1	0--	-	4.50	3.95
2004	Ari	NL	17	5	0	3	45.1	218	62	42	41	13	2	3	2	25	2	24	2	1	1	4	.200	0	0-0	2	8.76	8.14
2005	Ari	NL	67	0	0	13	79.1	356	86	50	45	7	4	1	5	43	5	63	6	0	7	3	.700	0	0-1	13	5.30	5.11
2006	Atl	NL	29	9	0	5	73.2	333	90	44	40	8	1	4	2	39	7	43	2	0	4	5	.444	0	0-0	2	6.13	4.89
	3 ML YEARS		113	14	0	21	198.1	907	238	136	126	28	7	8	9	107	14	130	10	1	12	12	.500	0	0-1	17	6.37	5.72

Rheal Cormier

Pitches: L Bats: L Pos: RP-64   Ht: 5'10" Wt: 195 Born: 4/23/1967 Age: 40

Year	Team	Lg	G	GS	CG	GF	IP	BFP	H	R	ER	HR	SH	SF	HB	TBB	IBB	SO	WP	Bk	W	L	Pct	ShO	Sv-Op	Hld	ERC	ERA
1991	StL	NL	11	10	2	1	67.2	281	74	35	31	5	1	3	2	8	1	38	2	1	4	5	.444	0	0-0	0	3.41	4.12
1992	StL	NL	31	30	3	1	186.0	772	194	83	76	15	11	3	5	33	2	117	4	2	10	10	.500	0	0-0	0	3.42	3.68
1993	StL	NL	38	21	1	4	145.1	619	163	80	70	18	10	4	4	27	3	75	6	0	7	6	.538	0	0-0	0	4.13	4.33
1994	StL	NL	7	7	0	0	39.2	169	40	24	24	6	1	2	3	7	0	26	2	0	3	2	.600	0	0-0	0	3.80	5.45
1995	Bos	AL	48	12	0	3	115.0	488	131	60	52	12	6	2	3	31	2	69	4	0	7	5	.583	0	0-2	9	4.56	4.07
1996	Mon	NL	33	27	1	1	159.2	674	165	80	74	16	4	8	9	41	3	100	8	0	7	10	.412	1	0-0	0	3.93	4.17
1997	Mon	NL	1	1	0	0	1.1	9	4	5	5	1	0	0	0	1	0	0	0	0	0	1	.000	0	0-0	0	27.46	33.75
1999	Bos	AL	60	0	0	7	63.1	275	61	34	26	4	1	3	5	18	2	39	1	0	2	0	1.000	0	0-3	15	3.33	3.69
2000	Bos	AL	64	0	0	12	68.1	293	74	40	35	7	5	2	0	17	2	43	1	0	3	3	.500	0	0-2	9	3.86	4.61
2001	Phi	NL	60	0	0	16	51.1	222	49	26	24	5	3	0	4	17	4	37	1	0	5	6	.455	0	1-6	12	3.67	4.21
2002	Phi	NL	54	0	0	7	60.0	268	61	38	35	6	0	2	4	32	6	49	4	0	5	6	.455	0	0-3	9	4.85	5.25
2003	Phi	NL	65	0	0	21	84.2	327	54	18	16	4	4	0	1	25	2	67	0	1	8	0	1.000	0	1-4	14	1.63	1.70
2004	Phi	NL	84	0	0	8	81.0	330	70	32	32	7	3	1	5	26	6	46	1	0	4	5	.444	0	0-7	28	3.16	3.56
2005	Phi	NL	57	0	0	10	47.1	211	56	33	31	9	2	2	2	16	1	34	3	0	4	2	.667	0	0-2	17	5.71	5.89
2006	2 Tms	NL	64	0	0	13	48.0	205	48	13	13	5	5	0	3	17	3	19	2	0	2	3	.400	0	0-4	14	4.13	2.44
06	Phi	NL	43	0	0	6	34.0	139	27	6	6	2	3	0	3	13	3	13	2	0	2	2	.500	0	0-4	12	2.91	1.59
06	Cin	NL	21	0	0	7	14.0	66	21	7	7	3	2	0	0	4	0	6	0	0	0	1	.000	0	0-0	2	7.48	4.50
	15 ML YEARS		677	108	7	104	1218.2	5143	1244	601	544	120	56	32	50	316	37	759	39	4	71	64	.526	1	2-33	127	3.76	4.02

Manuel Corpas

Pitches: R Bats: R Pos: RP-35   Ht: 6'3" Wt: 170 Born: 12/3/1982 Age: 24

Year	Team	Lg	G	GS	CG	GF	IP	BFP	H	R	ER	HR	SH	SF	HB	TBB	IBB	SO	WP	Bk	W	L	Pct	ShO	Sv-Op	Hld	ERC	ERA
2002	Casper	R	29	0	0	20	33.0	159	37	24	21	4	4	0	2	18	3	42	3	1	2	4	.333	0	2--	-	5.37	5.73
2003	TriCity	A-	15	15	0	0	84.0	375	98	61	54	7	4	6	7	22	1	47	3	0	5	6	.455	0	0--	-	4.60	5.79
2004	Ashvlle	A	43	0	0	20	44.1	199	48	20	15	3	0	0	6	13	1	52	0	1	2	2	.500	0	3--	-	4.29	3.05
2005	Mdest	A+	47	0	0	19	69.0	305	83	33	29	2	2	2	3	14	1	52	3	0	3	2	.600	0	2--	-	4.00	3.78
2006	Tulsa	AA	34	0	0	30	36.2	134	22	7	4	0	3	0	3	4	1	35	1	0	2	1	.667	0	19--	-	1.11	0.98
2006	ColSpr	AAA	8	0	0	5	8.2	32	5	1	1	1	0	0	0	2	0	7	0	0	0	0	-	0	0--	-	1.56	1.04
2006	Col	NL	35	0	0	3	32.1	136	36	13	13	3	0	0	2	8	1	27	2	0	1	2	.333	0	0-2	7	4.39	3.62

Kevin Correia

Pitches: R Bats: R Pos: RP-48   Ht: 6'3" Wt: 200 Born: 8/24/1980 Age: 26

Year	Team	Lg	G	GS	CG	GF	IP	BFP	H	R	ER	HR	SH	SF	HB	TBB	IBB	SO	WP	Bk	W	L	Pct	ShO	Sv-Op	Hld	ERC	ERA
2003	SF	NL	10	7	0	1	39.1	173	41	16	16	6	1	1	4	18	1	28	2	0	3	1	.750	0	0-0	0	5.46	3.66
2004	SF	NL	12	1	0	1	19.0	92	25	20	17	3	3	1	0	10	0	14	0	0	0	1	.000	0	0-0	0	7.12	8.05
2005	SF	NL	16	11	0	1	58.1	264	61	31	30	12	5	1	4	31	2	44	2	0	2	5	.286	0	0-0	0	5.94	4.63
2006	SF	NL	48	0	0	9	69.2	295	64	27	27	5	1	4	3	22	0	57	0	0	2	0	1.000	0	0-1	10	3.25	3.49
	4 ML YEARS		86	19	0	16	186.1	824	191	94	90	26	10	9	12	81	3	143	4	0	7	7	.500	0	0-1	10	4.89	4.35

David Cortes

Pitches: R Bats: R Pos: RP-30   Ht: 5'11" Wt: 225 Born: 10/15/1973 Age: 33

Year	Team	Lg	G	GS	CG	GF	IP	BFP	H	R	ER	HR	SH	SF	HB	TBB	IBB	SO	WP	Bk	W	L	Pct	ShO	Sv-Op	Hld	ERC	ERA
2006	ColSpr*	AAA	18	0	0	8	18.2	87	22	10	10	2	0	0	0	9	1	16	1	0	1	1	.500	0	2- -	0	5.27	4.82
1999	Atl	NL	4	0		4	3.2	18	3	3	2	0	0	0	0	4	0	2	2	0	0	0	-	0	0-0	0	4.78	4.91
2003	Cle	AL	2	0	0	2	3.0	18	8	5	4	1	0	1	0	0	0	1	0	0	0	0	-	0	0-0	0	14.61	12.00
2005	Col	NL	50	0	0	14	52.2	213	50	24	24	9	1	2	1	10	2	36	3	0	2	0	1.000	0	2-3	4	3.50	4.10
2006	Col	NL	30	0	0	16	29.1	124	35	14	14	3	2	2	1	6	1	14	0	0	3	1	.750	0	0-1	3	4.61	4.30
4 ML YEARS			86	0	0	36	88.2	373	96	46	44	13	3	5	2	20	3	53	5	0	5	1	.833	0	2-4	7	4.24	4.47

Shane Costa

Bats: L Throws: R Pos: RF-39; CF-21; PH-7; LF-5; DH-1; PR-1   Ht: 6'0" Wt: 200 Born: 12/12/1981 Age: 25

Year	Team	Lg	G	AB	H	2B	3B	HR	(Hm	Rd)	TB	R	RBI	RC	TBB	IBB	SO	HBP	SH	SF	SB	CS	SB%	GDP	Avg	OBP	Slg
2003	Royals	R	23	88	34	6	4	1	(-	-)	51	22	24	21	6	0	7	4	0	1	4	3	.57	2	.386	.444	.580
2003	Wilmg	A	3	7	1	0	0	0	(-	-)	1	1	0	1	2	0	1	1	0	0	0	0	-	0	.143	.400	.143
2004	Wilmg	A	123	451	139	20	4	7	(-	-)	188	70	59	71	32	1	43	11	0	6	9	4	.69	7	.308	.364	.417
2005	Wichta	AA	75	277	78	18	2	8	(-	-)	124	37	43	46	24	2	23	8	1	6	5	1	.83	10	.282	.349	.448
2005	Omha	AAA	4	16	3	1	0	0	(-	-)	4	1	1	0	0	0	1	0	0	0	0	0	-	0	.188	.188	.250
2006	Wichta	AA	2	8	3	0	0	0	(-	-)	3	0	1	1	0	0	1	0	0	0	0	0	-	0	.375	.375	.375
2006	Omha	AAA	52	199	68	12	4	10	(-	-)	118	35	29	46	13	1	25	7	3	2	4	0	1.00	6	.342	.398	.593
2005	KC	AL	27	81	19	2	0	2	(1	1)	27	13	7	7	5	0	11	1	1	0	0	0	-	3	.235	.287	.333
2006	KC	AL	72	237	65	20	1	3	(1	2)	96	23	23	26	6	2	29	5	2	2	2	0	1.00	5	.274	.304	.405
2 ML YEARS			99	318	84	22	1	5	(2	3)	123	36	30	33	11	2	40	6	3	2	2	0	1.00	8	.264	.300	.387

Chris Coste

Bats: R Throws: R Pos: C-54; PH-11; 1B-2; PR-1   Ht: 6'1" Wt: 200 Born: 2/4/1973 Age: 34

Year	Team	Lg	G	AB	H	2B	3B	HR	(Hm	Rd)	TB	R	RBI	RC	TBB	IBB	SO	HBP	SH	SF	SB	CS	SB%	GDP	Avg	OBP	Slg
2000	Akron	AA	65	240	80	20	4	2	(-	-)	114	32	31	43	15	2	12	4	0	1	1	2	.33	7	.333	.381	.475
2000	Buffalo	AAA	31	96	29	2	0	4	(-	-)	43	15	8	13	3	0	3	1	1	0	0	1	.00	4	.302	.330	.448
2001	Akron	AA	6	24	3	0	0	0	(-	-)	3	1	0	0	1	0	50	0	0	0	0	1	.00	0	.125	.160	.125
2001	Buffalo	AAA	75	271	78	16	2	7	(-	-)	119	31	50	54	15	1	54	4	1	4	0	1	.00	11	.288	.330	.439
2002	Buffalo	AAA	124	478	152	32	1	8	(-	-)	210	59	67	82	34	2	18	13	0	3	0	0	-	14	.318	.377	.439
2003	RedSx	R	11	30	7	2	1	1	(-	-)	14	3	6	5	7	1	37	0	0	0	0	0	-	2	.233	.378	.467
2003	Pwtckt	AAA	29	96	18	5	0	1	(-	-)	26	5	8	5	4	0	5	0	1	1	0	0	-	3	.188	.218	.271
2004	Indy	AAA	78	262	77	21	1	2	(-	-)	106	34	26	38	20	0	85	5	2	2	2	3	.40	6	.294	.353	.405
2005	S-WB	AAA	134	506	148	26	1	20	(-	-)	236	73	89	84	40	0	85	9	0	7	3	4	.43	25	.292	.351	.466
2006	S-WB	AAA	39	147	26	8	0	2	(-	-)	40	12	14	8	9	1	28	3	0	2	1	1	.50	2	.177	.236	.272
2006	Phi	NL	65	198	65	14	0	7	(4	3)	100	25	32	36	10	1	31	5	0	0	0	0	-	6	.328	.376	.505

Humberto Cota

Bats: R Throws: R Pos: C-33; PH-5   Ht: 5'11" Wt: 215 Born: 2/7/1979 Age: 28

Year	Team	Lg	G	AB	H	2B	3B	HR	(Hm	Rd)	TB	R	RBI	RC	TBB	IBB	SO	HBP	SH	SF	SB	CS	SB%	GDP	Avg	OBP	Slg
2001	Pit	NL	7	9	2	0	0	0	(0	0)	2	0	1	0	0	0	5	0	0	0	0	0	-	0	.222	.222	.222
2002	Pit	NL	7	17	5	1	0	0	(0	0)	6	2	0	1	1	1	4	0	0	0	0	0	-	0	.294	.333	.353
2003	Pit	NL	10	16	4	1	0	0	(0	0)	5	1	1	0	1	0	5	0	0	0	0	0	-	0	.250	.294	.313
2004	Pit	NL	36	66	15	1	1	5	(3	2)	33	10	8	7	3	1	20	1	0	0	0	0	-	1	.227	.271	.500
2005	Pit	NL	93	297	72	20	1	7	(5	2)	115	29	43	30	17	2	80	2	1	3	0	0	-	8	.242	.285	.387
2006	Pit	NL	38	100	19	1	0	0	(0	0)	20	5	5	3	8	0	26	0	1	1	0	0	-	3	.190	.248	.200
6 ML YEARS			191	505	117	24	2	12	(8	4)	181	47	58	41	30	4	140	3	2	4	0	0	-	12	.232	.277	.358

Neal Cotts

Pitches: L Bats: L Pos: RP-70   Ht: 6'1" Wt: 195 Born: 3/25/1980 Age: 27

Year	Team	Lg	G	GS	CG	GF	IP	BFP	H	R	ER	HR	SH	SF	HB	TBB	IBB	SO	WP	Bk	W	L	Pct	ShO	Sv-Op	Hld	ERC	ERA
2003	CWS	AL	4	4	0	0	13.1	69	15	12	12	1	1	0	0	17	0	10	0	0	1	1	.500	0	0-0	0	8.43	8.10
2004	CWS	AL	56	1	0	12	65.1	281	61	45	41	13	0	1	3	30	2	58	8	0	4	4	.500	0	0-2	4	4.84	5.65
2005	CWS	AL	69	0	0	12	60.1	248	38	15	13	1	0	3	4	29	5	58	3	0	4	0	1.000	0	0-2	13	2.03	1.94
2006	CWS	AL	70	0	0	14	54.0	251	64	33	31	12	3	1	3	24	6	43	3	0	1	2	.333	0	1-4	14	6.24	5.17
4 ML YEARS			199	5	0	36	193.0	849	178	105	97	27	4	5	10	100	13	169	14	0	10	7	.588	0	1-8	31	4.49	4.52

Craig Counsell

Bats: L Throws: R Pos: SS-88; PH-14; 3B-7; 2B-2; PR-1   Ht: 6'0" Wt: 185 Born: 8/21/1970 Age: 36

Year	Team	Lg	G	AB	H	2B	3B	HR	(Hm	Rd)	TB	R	RBI	RC	TBB	IBB	SO	HBP	SH	SF	SB	CS	SB%	GDP	Avg	OBP	Slg
2006	Tucsn*	AAA	2	11	2	0	0	0	(-	-)	2	2	0	0	1	0	1	0	0	0	0	0	-	0	.182	.250	.182
2006	Lancst*	A+	1	3	3	1	0	0	(-	-)	4	1	0	2	1	0	0	0	0	0	0	0	-	0	1.000	1.000	1.333
1995	Col	NL	3	1	0	0	0	0	(0	0)	0	0	0	0	1	0	0	0	0	0	0	0	-	0	.000	.500	.000
1997	2 Tms	NL	52	164	49	9	2	1	(1	0)	65	20	16	24	18	2	17	3	3	1	1	1	.50	5	.299	.376	.396
1998	Fla	NL	107	335	84	19	5	4	(2	2)	125	43	40	48	51	7	47	4	8	1	3	0	1.00	5	.251	.355	.373
1999	2 Tms	NL	87	174	38	7	0	0	(0	0)	45	24	11	12	14	0	24	0	5	2	1	0	1.00	2	.218	.274	.259
2000	Ari	NL	67	152	48	8	1	2	(0	2)	64	23	11	25	20	0	18	2	1	1	3	3	.50	4	.316	.400	.421
2001	Ari	NL	141	458	126	22	3	4	(4	0)	166	76	38	61	61	3	76	2	6	6	6	8	.43	9	.275	.359	.362

Year	Team	Lg	G	AB	H	2B	3B	HR	(Hm	Rd)	TB	R	RBI	RC	TBB	IBB	SO	HBP	SH	SF	SB	CS	SB%	GDP	Avg	OBP	Slg
								BATTING													BASERUNNING				AVERAGES		
2002	Ari	NL	112	436	123	22	1	2	(0	2)	153	63	51	65	45	3	52	1	4	3	7	5	.58	10	.282	.348	.351
2003	Ari	NL	89	303	71	6	3	3	(3	0)	92	40	21	29	41	0	32	2	3	2	11	4	.73	4	.234	.328	.304
2004	Mil	NL	140	473	114	19	5	2	(1	1)	149	59	23	48	59	9	88	5	5	3	17	4	.81	5	.241	.330	.315
2005	Ari	NL	150	578	148	34	4	9	(5	4)	217	85	42	80	74	4	69	8	2	4	26	7	.79	8	.256	.350	.375
2006	Ari	NL	105	372	95	14	4	4	(3	1)	129	56	30	45	31	0	47	9	2	1	15	8	.65	1	.255	.327	.347
97	Col	NL	1	0	0	0	0	0	(0	0)	0	0	0	0	0	0	0	0	0	0	0	0	-	0	-	-	-
97	Fla	NL	51	164	49	9	2	1	(1	0)	65	20	16	24	18	2	17	3	3	1	1	1	.50	1	.299	.376	.396
99	Fla	NL	37	66	10	1	0	0	(0	0)	11	4	2	1	5	0	10	0	2	0	0	0	-	1	.152	.211	.167
99	LAD	NL	50	108	28	6	0	0	(0	0)	34	20	9	11	9	0	14	0	3	2	1	0	1.00	1	.259	.311	.315
11 ML YEARS			1053	3446	896	160	28	31	(19	12)	1205	489	283	437	419	28	470	36	39	24	90	40	.69	53	.260	.344	.350

Jesse Crain

Pitches: R Bats: R Pos: RP-68   Ht: 6'1" Wt: 205 Born: 7/5/1981 Age: 25

Year	Team	Lg	G	GS	CG	GF	IP	BFP	H	R	ER	HR	SH	SF	HB	TBB	IBB	SO	WP	Bk	W	L	Pct	ShO	Sv-Op	Hld	ERC	ERA
			HOW MUCH HE PITCHED						WHAT HE GAVE UP												THE RESULTS						
2004	Min	AL	22	0	0	3	27.0	109	17	6	6	2	1	0	1	12	1	14	1	0	3	0	1.000	0	0-1	2	2.25	2.00
2005	Min	AL	75	0	0	17	79.2	326	61	28	24	6	9	3	5	29	7	25	2	0	12	5	.706	0	1-4	11	2.66	2.71
2006	Min	AL	68	0	0	24	76.2	325	79	31	30	6	1	2	2	18	2	60	1	0	4	5	.444	0	1-4	10	3.48	3.52
3 ML YEARS			165	0	0	44	183.1	760	157	65	60	14	11	5	8	59	10	99	4	0	19	10	.655	0	2-9	23	2.93	2.95

Carl Crawford

Bats: L Throws: L Pos: LF-148; DH-3; CF-2; PH-1; PR-1   Ht: 6'2" Wt: 220 Born: 8/5/1981 Age: 25

Year	Team	Lg	G	AB	H	2B	3B	HR	(Hm	Rd)	TB	R	RBI	RC	TBB	IBB	SO	HBP	SH	SF	SB	CS	SB%	GDP	Avg	OBP	Slg
								BATTING													BASERUNNING				AVERAGES		
2002	TB	AL	63	259	67	11	6	2	(1	1)	96	23	30	34	9	0	41	3	6	1	9	5	.64	0	.259	.290	.371
2003	TB	AL	151	630	177	18	9	5	(5	0)	228	80	54	80	26	4	102	1	1	3	55	10	.85	5	.281	.309	.362
2004	TB	AL	152	626	185	26	19	11	(6	5)	282	104	55	96	35	2	81	1	4	6	59	15	.80	2	.296	.331	.450
2005	TB	AL	156	644	194	33	15	15	(5	10)	302	101	81	102	27	1	84	5	5	6	46	8	.85	11	.301	.331	.469
2006	TB	AL	151	600	183	20	16	18	(7	11)	289	89	77	113	37	3	85	4	9	2	58	9	.87	8	.305	.348	.482
5 ML YEARS			673	2759	806	108	65	51	(24	27)	1197	397	297	425	134	10	393	14	25	18	227	47	.83	26	.292	.326	.434

Joe Crede

Bats: R Throws: R Pos: 3B-149; PH-2   Ht: 6'2" Wt: 220 Born: 4/26/1978 Age: 29

Year	Team	Lg	G	AB	H	2B	3B	HR	(Hm	Rd)	TB	R	RBI	RC	TBB	IBB	SO	HBP	SH	SF	SB	CS	SB%	GDP	Avg	OBP	Slg
								BATTING													BASERUNNING				AVERAGES		
2000	CWS	AL	7	14	5	1	0	0	(0	0)	6	2	3	2	0	0	3	0	0	1	0	0	-	0	.357	.333	.429
2001	CWS	AL	17	50	11	1	1	0	(0	0)	14	1	7	4	3	0	11	1	0	1	1	0	1.00	1	.220	.273	.280
2002	CWS	AL	53	200	57	10	0	12	(7	5)	103	28	35	31	8	0	40	0	0	1	0	2	.00	1	.285	.311	.515
2003	CWS	AL	151	536	140	31	2	19	(11	8)	232	68	75	69	32	1	75	6	2	4	1	1	.50	11	.261	.308	.433
2004	CWS	AL	144	490	117	25	0	21	(12	9)	205	67	69	58	34	0	81	10	4	5	1	2	.33	14	.239	.299	.418
2005	CWS	AL	132	432	109	21	0	22	(12	10)	196	54	62	62	25	3	66	8	2	4	1	1	.50	7	.252	.303	.454
2006	CWS	AL	150	544	154	31	0	30	(16	14)	275	76	94	84	28	1	58	7	0	7	0	2	.00	18	.283	.323	.506
7 ML YEARS			654	2266	593	120	3	104	(58	46)	1031	296	345	310	130	5	334	32	8	23	4	8	.33	52	.262	.308	.455

Coco Crisp

Bats: B Throws: R Pos: CF-103; PR-4   Ht: 6'0" Wt: 180 Born: 11/1/1979 Age: 27

Year	Team	Lg	G	AB	H	2B	3B	HR	(Hm	Rd)	TB	R	RBI	RC	TBB	IBB	SO	HBP	SH	SF	SB	CS	SB%	GDP	Avg	OBP	Slg
								BATTING													BASERUNNING				AVERAGES		
2006	Pwtckt*	AAA	1	3	1	0	0	0	(-	-)	1	0	2	0	1	0	0	0	0	0	0	0	-	0	.333	.500	.333
2002	Cle	AL	32	127	33	9	2	1	(1	0)	49	16	9	19	11	0	19	0	3	2	4	1	.80	0	.260	.314	.386
2003	Cle	AL	99	414	110	15	6	3	(3	0)	146	55	27	48	23	1	51	0	7	3	15	9	.63	4	.266	.302	.353
2004	Cle	AL	139	491	146	24	2	15	(8	7)	219	78	71	72	36	4	69	0	4	3	20	13	.61	8	.297	.344	.446
2005	Cle	AL	145	594	178	42	4	16	(4	12)	276	86	69	92	44	1	81	0	13	5	15	6	.71	7	.300	.345	.465
2006	Bos	AL	105	413	109	22	2	8	(4	4)	159	58	36	51	31	1	67	1	7	0	22	4	.85	5	.264	.317	.385
5 ML YEARS			520	2039	576	112	16	43	(20	23)	849	293	212	282	145	7	287	1	39	12	76	33	.70	24	.282	.329	.416

Bobby Crosby

Bats: R Throws: R Pos: SS-95; PR-1   Ht: 6'3" Wt: 215 Born: 1/12/1980 Age: 27

Year	Team	Lg	G	AB	H	2B	3B	HR	(Hm	Rd)	TB	R	RBI	RC	TBB	IBB	SO	HBP	SH	SF	SB	CS	SB%	GDP	Avg	OBP	Slg
								BATTING													BASERUNNING				AVERAGES		
2003	Oak	AL	11	12	0	0	0	0	(0	0)	0	1	0	0	1	0	5	1	0	0	0	0	-	0	.000	.143	.000
2004	Oak	AL	151	545	130	34	1	22	(11	11)	232	70	64	60	58	0	141	9	5	6	7	3	.70	20	.239	.319	.426
2005	Oak	AL	84	333	92	25	4	9	(3	6)	152	66	38	47	35	0	54	1	1	1	0	0	-	10	.276	.346	.456
2006	Oak	AL	96	358	82	12	0	9	(3	6)	121	42	40	38	36	1	76	0	2	2	8	1	.89	11	.229	.298	.338
4 ML YEARS			342	1248	304	71	5	40	(17	23)	505	179	142	145	130	1	276	11	8	9	15	4	.79	41	.244	.318	.405

Bubba Crosby

Bats: L Throws: L Pos: RF-31; CF-24; LF-10; PR-9; PH-3; DH-1   Ht: 5'11" Wt: 190 Born: 8/11/1976 Age: 30

Year	Team	Lg	G	AB	H	2B	3B	HR	(Hm	Rd)	TB	R	RBI	RC	TBB	IBB	SO	HBP	SH	SF	SB	CS	SB%	GDP	Avg	OBP	Slg
								BATTING													BASERUNNING				AVERAGES		
2006	Tampa*	A+	3	8	1	0	0	0	(-	-)	1	0	0	0	1	1	2	1	0	0	0	0	-	1	.125	.300	.125
2006	Clmbs*	AAA	22	84	20	5	1	2	(-	-)	33	13	10	13	11	0	16	3	0	0	7	0	1.00	1	.238	.347	.393
2003	LAD	NL	9	12	1	0	0	0	(0	0)	1	0	1	0	0	0	3	0	0	0	0	0	-	0	.083	.083	.083

Year	Team	Lg	G	AB	H	2B	3B	HR	(Hm	Rd)	TB	R	RBI	RC	TBB	IBB	SO	HBP	SH	SF	SB	CS	SB%	GDP	Avg	OBP	Slg
											BATTING										BASERUNNING				AVERAGES		
2004	NYY	AL	55	53	8	2	0	2	(2	0)	16	8	7	7	2	0	13	1	2	0	2	0	1.00	0	.151	.196	.302
2005	NYY	AL	76	98	27	0	1	1	(1	0)	32	15	6	9	4	0	14	0	1	0	4	1	.80	1	.276	.304	.327
2006	NYY	AL	65	87	18	3	1	1	(1	0)	26	9	6	6	4	0	21	2	3	0	3	1	.75	0	.207	.258	.299
4 ML YEARS			205	250	54	5	2	4	(4	0)	75	32	20	22	10	0	51	3	6	0	9	2	.82	1	.216	.255	.300

Francisco Cruceta

Pitches: R **Bats:** R **Pos:** RP-3; SP-1　　　　　　　**Ht:** 6'2" **Wt:** 215 **Born:** 7/4/1981 **Age:** 25

Year	Team	Lg	G	GS	CG	GF	IP	BFP	H	R	ER	HR	SH	SF	HB	TBB	IBB	SO	WP	Bk	W	L	Pct	ShO	Sv-Op	Hld	ERC	ERA
			HOW MUCH HE PITCHED						WHAT HE GAVE UP												THE RESULTS							
2002	SoGA	A	20	20	3	0	112.2	466	98	42	35	7	0	2	4	34	0	111	10	0	8	5	.615	2	0--	-	2.89	2.80
2002	Kinston	A+	7	7	0	0	39.2	169	31	13	11	2	0	1	0	25	1	37	1	1	2	0	1.000	0	0--	-	3.42	2.50
2003	Akron	AA	27	25	6	1	163.1	684	141	70	56	7	3	6	2	66	0	134	3	4	13	9	.591	0	0--	-	3.02	3.09
2004	Akron	AA	15	15	1	0	88.2	381	89	58	52	11	2	3	2	33	0	45	5	1	4	8	.333	0	0--	-	4.26	5.28
2004	Buffalo	AAA	14	14	1	0	83.0	341	78	35	30	6	2	2	0	36	0	62	9	1	6	5	.545	0	0--	-	3.86	3.25
2005	Buffalo	AAA	30	13	1	6	102.1	462	123	65	59	16	2	1	5	32	0	92	9	2	6	4	.600	0	0--	-	5.45	5.19
2005	Tacom	AAA	2	2	0	0	9.0	41	11	6	5	3	0	0	0	3	0	10	3	0	1	1	.500	0	0--	-	6.71	5.00
2006	Tacom	AAA	28	28	1	0	160.1	700	150	81	78	25	4	6	6	76	3	185	18	1	13	9	.591	0	0--	-	4.52	4.38
2004	Cle	AL	2	2	0	0	7.2	39	10	9	8	1	0	1	1	4	0	9	1	0	0	1	.000	0	0-0	0	6.85	9.39
2006	Sea	AL	4	1	0	1	6.2	34	10	8	8	2	0	1	0	6	0	2	1	0	0	0	-	0	0-0	0	11.77	10.80
2 ML YEARS			6	3	0	1	14.1	73	20	17	16	3	0	2	1	10	0	11	2	0	0	1	.000	0	0-0	0	8.99	10.05

Jose Cruz

Bats: B **Throws:** R **Pos:** LF-40; RF-24; PH-21; CF-15; PR-2　　　　　**Ht:** 6'0" **Wt:** 210 **Born:** 4/19/1974 **Age:** 33

Year	Team	Lg	G	AB	H	2B	3B	HR	(Hm	Rd)	TB	R	RBI	RC	TBB	IBB	SO	HBP	SH	SF	SB	CS	SB%	GDP	Avg	OBP	Slg
											BATTING										BASERUNNING				AVERAGES		
1997	2 Tms	AL	104	395	98	19	1	26	(11	15)	197	59	68	63	41	2	117	0	1	5	7	2	.78	5	.248	.315	.499
1998	Tor	AL	105	352	89	14	3	11	(4	7)	142	55	42	55	57	3	99	0	1	0	11	4	.73	0	.253	.354	.403
1999	Tor	AL	106	349	84	19	3	14	(8	6)	151	63	45	57	64	5	91	0	1	0	14	4	.78	6	.241	.358	.433
2000	Tor	AL	162	603	146	32	5	31	(15	16)	281	91	76	91	71	3	129	2	2	3	15	5	.75	11	.242	.323	.466
2001	Tor	AL	146	577	158	38	4	34	(15	19)	306	92	88	101	45	4	138	1	2	2	32	5	.86	8	.274	.326	.530
2002	Tor	AL	124	466	114	26	5	18	(11	7)	204	64	70	71	51	1	106	0	1	4	7	1	.88	8	.245	.317	.438
2003	SF	NL	158	539	135	26	1	20	(9	11)	223	90	68	71	102	6	121	0	2	7	5	8	.38	14	.250	.366	.414
2004	TB	AL	153	545	132	25	8	21	(13	8)	236	76	78	79	76	8	117	2	5	8	11	6	.65	0	.242	.333	.433
2005	3 Tms		115	370	93	24	2	18	(11	7)	175	46	50	55	66	3	101	0	0	1	0	2	.00	10	.251	.364	.473
2006	LAD	NL	86	223	52	16	1	5	(2	3)	85	34	17	27	43	2	54	0	4	3	5	1	.83	3	.233	.353	.381
97	Sea	AL	49	183	49	12	1	12	(7	5)	99	28	34	31	13	0	45	0	1	1	1	0	1.00	1	.268	.315	.541
97	Tor	AL	55	212	49	7	0	14	(4	10)	98	31	34	32	28	2	72	0	0	4	6	2	.75	2	.231	.316	.462
05	Ari	NL	64	202	43	9	0	12	(6	6)	88	23	28	25	42	2	54	0	0	1	0	1	.00	6	.213	.347	.436
05	Bos	AL	4	12	3	1	0	0	(0	0)	4	0	0	1	1	0	4	0	0	0	0	0	-	0	.250	.308	.333
05	LAD	NL	47	156	47	14	2	6	(5	1)	83	23	22	29	23	1	43	0	0	0	0	1	.00	4	.301	.391	.532
10 ML YEARS			1259	4419	1101	239	33	198	(99	99)	2000	670	602	670	616	37	1073	5	18	37	107	38	.74	71	.249	.339	.453

Juan Cruz

Pitches: R **Bats:** R **Pos:** RP-16; SP-15　　　　　　　**Ht:** 6'2" **Wt:** 155 **Born:** 10/15/1978 **Age:** 28

Year	Team	Lg	G	GS	CG	GF	IP	BFP	H	R	ER	HR	SH	SF	HB	TBB	IBB	SO	WP	Bk	W	L	Pct	ShO	Sv-Op	Hld	ERC	ERA
			HOW MUCH HE PITCHED						WHAT HE GAVE UP												THE RESULTS							
2006	Tucsn	AAA	1	1	0	0	3.1	16	4	1	1	0	0	0	1	1	0	4	0	0	0	0	-	0	0--	-	5.10	2.70
2001	ChC	NL	8	8	0	0	44.2	185	40	16	16	4	2	0	2	17	1	39	0	0	3	1	.750	0	0-0	0	3.59	3.22
2002	ChC	NL	45	9	0	14	97.1	431	84	56	43	11	7	8	8	59	4	81	1	0	3	11	.214	0	1-4	3	4.49	3.98
2003	ChC	NL	25	6	0	3	61.0	284	66	44	41	7	7	2	7	28	0	65	4	0	2	7	.222	0	0-1	1	5.23	6.05
2004	Atl	NL	50	0	0	22	72.0	300	59	24	22	7	4	1	2	30	1	70	1	0	6	2	.750	0	0-0	2	3.25	2.75
2005	Oak	AL	28	0	0	14	32.2	159	38	33	27	5	0	2	4	22	4	34	3	0	0	3	.000	0	0-0	0	6.87	7.44
2006	Ari	NL	31	15	0	5	94.2	413	80	45	44	7	5	2	11	47	2	88	2	0	5	6	.455	0	0-0	0	3.82	4.18
6 ML YEARS			187	38	0	58	402.1	1772	367	218	193	41	25	15	34	203	12	377	11	0	19	30	.388	0	1-5	6	4.29	4.32

Nelson Cruz

Bats: R **Throws:** R **Pos:** RF-38; PH-3; CF-2; LF-1; PR-1　　　　　**Ht:** 6'3" **Wt:** 225 **Born:** 7/1/1980 **Age:** 26

Year	Team	Lg	G	AB	H	2B	3B	HR	(Hm	Rd)	TB	R	RBI	RC	TBB	IBB	SO	HBP	SH	SF	SB	CS	SB%	GDP	Avg	OBP	Slg
											BATTING										BASERUNNING				AVERAGES		
2001	As	R	23	88	22	3	1	3	(-	-)	36	11	16	10	4	0	29	0	1	0	6	3	.67	1	.250	.283	.409
2002	Vancvr	A-	63	214	59	14	0	4	(-	-)	85	23	25	29	9	0	58	4	4	1	12	1	.92	2	.276	.316	.397
2003	Kane	A	119	470	112	26	2	20	(-	-)	202	65	85	61	29	2	128	9	1	6	10	5	.67	7	.238	.292	.430
2004	Mdest	A+	66	261	90	27	1	11	(-	-)	152	54	52	59	24	2	73	4	0	1	8	4	.67	2	.345	.407	.582
2004	Mdland	AA	67	262	82	14	2	14	(-	-)	142	51	45	52	26	0	69	1	0	0	8	3	.73	4	.313	.377	.542
2004	Scrmto	AAA	4	13	3	1	0	1	(-	-)	7	4	2	2	1	0	7	0	0	0	0	0	-	0	.231	.286	.538
2005	Hntsvl	AA	68	248	76	19	0	16	(-	-)	143	45	54	55	31	0	71	4	0	3	10	3	.77	6	.306	.388	.577
2006	Nashv	AAA	60	208	56	13	0	11	(-	-)	102	33	27	40	30	2	62	8	0	0	9	4	.69	4	.269	.382	.490
2006	Nashv	AAA	104	371	112	22	1	20	(-	-)	196	68	73	75	42	2	100	6	0	4	17	6	.74	8	.302	.378	.528
2005	Mil	NL	8	5	1	1	0	0	(0	0)	2	1	0	1	2	0	0	0	0	0	0	0	-	0	.200	.429	.400
2006	Tex	AL	41	130	29	3	0	6	(3	3)	50	15	22	18	7	0	32	0	0	1	1	0	1.00	1	.223	.261	.385
2 ML YEARS			49	135	30	4	0	6	(3	3)	52	16	22	19	9	0	32	0	0	1	1	0	1.00	1	.222	.269	.385

Michael Cuddyer

Bats: R Throws: R Pos: RF-142; 1B-6; PH-4; LF-1; DH-1   Ht: 6'2" Wt: 220 Born: 3/27/1979 Age: 28

								BATTING												BASERUNNING				AVERAGES		
Year	Team	Lg	G	AB	H	2B	3B	HR	(Hm	Rd)	TB	R	RBI	RC	TBB	IBB	SO	HBP	SH	SF	SB	CS	SB%	GDP	Avg	OBP	Slg
2001	Min	AL	8	18	4	2	0	0	(0	0)	6	1	1	2	2	0	6	0	0	0	1	0	1.00	1	.222	.300	.333
2002	Min	AL	41	112	29	7	0	4	(2	2)	48	12	13	14	8	0	30	1	1	1	2	0	1.00	3	.259	.311	.429
2003	Min	AL	35	102	25	1	3	4	(1	3)	44	14	8	10	12	0	19	0	0	0	1	1	.50	6	.245	.325	.431
2004	Min	AL	115	339	89	22	1	12	(8	4)	149	49	45	51	37	2	74	3	2	1	5	5	.50	8	.263	.339	.440
2005	Min	AL	126	422	111	25	3	12	(8	4)	178	55	42	43	41	5	93	3	1	3	3	4	.43	19	.263	.330	.422
2006	Min	AL	150	557	158	41	5	24	(15	9)	281	102	109	101	62	5	130	10	0	6	6	0	1.00	11	.284	.362	.504
	6 ML YEARS		475	1550	416	98	12	56	(34	22)	706	233	218	221	162	12	352	17	4	11	18	10	.64	48	.268	.342	.455

Jack Cust

Bats: L Throws: R Pos: PH-3; LF-1   Ht: 6'1" Wt: 230 Born: 1/16/1979 Age: 28

								BATTING												BASERUNNING				AVERAGES		
Year	Team	Lg	G	AB	H	2B	3B	HR	(Hm	Rd)	TB	R	RBI	RC	TBB	IBB	SO	HBP	SH	SF	SB	CS	SB%	GDP	Avg	OBP	Slg
2006	Portlnd*	AAA	138	441	129	23	0	30	(-	-)	242	97	77	119	143	0	124	4	0	3	0	3	.00	10	.293	.467	.549
2001	Ari	NL	3	2	1	0	0	0	(0	0)	1	0	0	1	1	0	0	0	0	0	0	0	-	0	.500	.667	.500
2002	Col	NL	35	65	11	2	0	1	(0	1)	16	8	8	6	12	0	32	0	0	1	0	1	.00	3	.169	.295	.246
2003	Bal	AL	27	73	19	7	0	4	(2	2)	38	7	11	17	10	0	25	1	0	0	0	0	-	0	.260	.357	.521
2004	Bal	AL	1	1	0	0	0	0	(0	0)	0	0	0	0	0	0	1	0	0	0	0	0	-	0	.000	.000	.000
2006	SD	NL	4	3	1	0	0	0	(0	0)	1	1	0	0	0	0	1	0	0	0	0	0	-	0	.333	.333	.333
	5 ML YEARS		70	144	32	9	0	5	(2	3)	56	16	19	24	23	0	59	1	0	1	0	1	.00	3	.222	.331	.389

Casey Daigle

Pitches: R Bats: R Pos: RP-10   Ht: 6'5" Wt: 250 Born: 4/4/1981 Age: 26

			HOW MUCH HE PITCHED						WHAT HE GAVE UP											THE RESULTS							
Year	Team	Lg	G	GS	CG	GF	IP	BFP	H	R	ER	HR	SH	SF	HB	TBB	IBB	SO	WP	Bk	W	L	Pct	ShO	Sv-Op	Hld	ERC	ERA
2000	Msoula	R+	15	15	0	0	82.2	390	88	57	45	4	2	0	9	54	0	56	10	3	3	5	.375	0	0- -	-	5.48	4.90
2001	Sbend	A	28	27	2	0	164.0	727	180	100	75	11	3	9	14	55	0	85	16	4	10	10	.500	1	0- -	-	4.45	4.12
2002	Lancst	A+	21	21	0	0	122.0	137	137	82	69	19	7	8	9	42	0	85	7	2	4	10	.286	0	0- -	-	22.52	5.09
2002	ElPaso	AA	7	7	2	0	44.1	182	46	19	16	5	2	1	3	9	0	29	2	0	3	2	.600	0	0- -	-	3.99	3.25
2003	ElPaso	AA	29	27	1	0	176.1	793	219	108	90	9	7	8	6	51	1	115	14	0	11	11	.500	0	0- -	-	4.73	4.59
2004	Tucsn	AAA	18	15	0	0	100.2	474	154	85	77	21	4	4	5	24	0	51	3	0	4	9	.308	0	0- -	-	7.71	6.88
2005	Tenn	AA	58	2	0	45	64.0	289	75	24	19	3	7	1	1	18	4	50	5	0	9	3	.750	0	19- -	-	3.99	2.67
2006	Tucsn	AAA	42	0	0	15	48.0	219	60	31	25	6	2	1	0	17	0	41	5	0	3	5	.375	0	4- -	-	5.45	4.69
2004	Ari	NL	10	10	0	0	49.0	230	63	41	39	9	3	1	2	27	3	17	1	1	2	3	.400	0	0-0	0	7.30	7.16
2006	Ari	NL	10	0	0	1	12.1	52	14	5	5	1	0	1	0	6	0	7	0	0	0	0	-	0	0-0	2	5.46	3.65
	2 ML YEARS		20	10	0	1	61.1	282	77	46	44	10	3	2	2	33	3	24	1	1	2	3	.400	0	0-0	2	6.92	6.46

Johnny Damon

Bats: L Throws: L Pos: CF-131; DH-16; PH-2; PR-2; 1B-1   Ht: 6'2" Wt: 205 Born: 11/5/1973 Age: 33

								BATTING												BASERUNNING				AVERAGES		
Year	Team	Lg	G	AB	H	2B	3B	HR	(Hm	Rd)	TB	R	RBI	RC	TBB	IBB	SO	HBP	SH	SF	SB	CS	SB%	GDP	Avg	OBP	Slg
1995	KC	AL	47	188	53	11	5	3	(1	2)	83	32	23	29	12	0	22	1	2	3	7	0	1.00	2	.282	.324	.441
1996	KC	AL	145	517	140	22	5	6	(3	3)	190	61	50	64	31	3	64	3	10	5	25	5	.83	4	.271	.313	.368
1997	KC	AL	146	472	130	12	8	8	(3	5)	182	70	48	63	42	2	70	3	6	1	16	10	.62	3	.275	.338	.386
1998	KC	AL	161	642	178	30	10	18	(11	7)	282	104	66	98	58	4	84	4	3	3	26	12	.68	4	.277	.339	.439
1999	KC	AL	145	583	179	39	9	14	(5	9)	278	101	77	108	67	5	50	3	3	4	36	6	.86	13	.307	.379	.477
2000	KC	AL	159	655	214	42	10	16	(10	6)	324	136	88	129	65	4	60	1	8	12	46	9	.84	7	.327	.382	.495
2001	Oak	AL	155	644	165	34	4	9	(2	7)	234	108	49	79	61	1	70	5	5	4	27	12	.69	7	.256	.324	.363
2002	Bos	AL	154	623	178	34	11	14	(5	9)	276	118	63	101	65	5	70	6	3	5	31	6	.84	4	.286	.356	.443
2003	Bos	AL	145	608	166	32	6	12	(5	7)	246	103	67	92	68	4	74	2	6	6	30	6	.83	5	.273	.345	.405
2004	Bos	AL	150	621	189	35	6	20	(9	11)	296	123	94	115	76	1	71	2	0	3	19	8	.70	8	.304	.380	.477
2005	Bos	AL	148	624	197	35	6	10	(3	7)	274	117	75	105	53	3	69	2	0	9	18	1	.95	5	.316	.366	.439
2006	NYY	AL	149	593	169	35	5	24	(13	11)	286	115	80	99	67	1	85	4	2	5	25	10	.71	4	.285	.359	.482
	12 ML YEARS		1704	6770	1958	361	85	154	(70	84)	2951	1188	780	1082	665	33	789	36	48	60	306	85	.78	66	.289	.353	.436

Jeff DaVanon

Bats: B Throws: R Pos: CF-36; PH-34; RF-16; LF-8; DH-3   Ht: 6'0" Wt: 200 Born: 12/8/1973 Age: 33

								BATTING												BASERUNNING				AVERAGES		
Year	Team	Lg	G	AB	H	2B	3B	HR	(Hm	Rd)	TB	R	RBI	RC	TBB	IBB	SO	HBP	SH	SF	SB	CS	SB%	GDP	Avg	OBP	Slg
1999	LAA	AL	7	20	4	0	1	1	(0	1)	9	4	4	2	2	0	7	0	0	0	0	1	.00	0	.200	.273	.450
2001	LAA	AL	40	88	17	2	1	5	(3	2)	36	7	9	9	11	0	29	0	0	1	1	3	.25	1	.193	.280	.409
2002	LAA	AL	16	30	5	3	0	1	(0	1)	11	3	4	4	2	0	6	0	1	0	1	0	1.00	0	.167	.219	.367
2003	LAA	AL	123	330	93	16	1	12	(3	9)	147	56	43	56	42	0	59	1	4	5	17	5	.77	6	.282	.360	.445
2004	LAA	AL	108	285	79	11	4	7	(4	3)	119	41	34	47	46	2	54	0	1	5	18	3	.86	2	.277	.372	.418
2005	LAA	AL	108	225	52	10	1	2	(1	1)	70	42	15	26	39	1	44	2	3	2	11	6	.65	6	.231	.347	.311
2006	Ari	NL	87	221	64	12	4	5	(3	2)	99	38	35	42	31	0	42	0	0	4	10	4	.71	6	.290	.371	.448
	7 ML YEARS		489	1199	314	54	12	33	(15	18)	491	191	144	186	173	3	241	3	9	17	58	22	.73	21	.262	.352	.410

Kyle Davies

Pitches: R Bats: R Pos: SP-14 Ht: 6'2" Wt: 205 Born: 9/9/1983 Age: 23

Year	Team	Lg	G	GS	CG	GF	IP	BFP	H	R	ER	HR	SH	SF	HB	TBB	IBB	SO	WP	Bk	W	L	Pct	ShO	Sv-Op	Hld	ERC	ERA
2001	Braves	R	12	9	1	1	56.0	223	47	17	14	2	1	0	1	8	0	53	2	0	4	2	.667	1	0--	--	1.96	2.25
2001	Macon	A	1	1	0	0	5.2	21	2	0	0	0	0	0	0	1	0	7	1	0	1	0	1.000	0	0--	--	0.48	0.00
2002	Macon	A	2	1	0	0	6.0	28	6	4	4	1	0	1	1	4	0	4	0	0	0	1	.000	0	0--	--	6.48	6.00
2002	Danvle	R+	14	14	0	0	69.1	304	73	39	27	2	1	3	2	23	0	62	1	0	5	3	.625	0	0--	--	3.64	3.50
2003	Rome	A	27	27	1	0	146.1	620	128	52	47	9	1	2	6	53	0	148	7	0	8	8	.500	0	0--	--	3.11	2.89
2004	MrtlBh	A+	14	14	0	0	75.1	313	55	24	22	3	2	3	4	32	0	95	7	0	9	2	.818	0	0--	--	2.53	2.63
2004	Grnvlle	AA	11	10	0	0	62.0	248	40	18	16	9	3	0	2	22	0	73	3	0	4	0	1.000	0	0--	--	2.44	2.32
2004	Rchmd	AAA	1	1	0	0	5.0	23	5	5	5	0	0	1	0	3	0	5	0	0	0	1	.000	0	0--	--	3.99	9.00
2005	Rchmd	AAA	13	13	0	0	73.1	320	66	28	28	6	1	3	0	34	2	62	7	0	5	2	.714	0	0--	--	3.52	3.44
2006	Missi	AA	4	4	0	0	14.0	56	11	8	7	1	0	0	0	5	0	9	1	0	1	1	.500	0	0--	--	2.66	4.50
2006	Rchmd	AAA	2	2	0	0	15.0	54	7	1	1	0	1	0	0	3	0	8	0	0	2	0	1.000	0	0--	--	0.79	0.60
2005	Atl	NL	21	14	0	2	87.2	403	98	51	48	8	3	0	1	49	5	62	4	0	7	6	.538	0	0-1	2	5.25	4.93
2006	Atl	NL	14	14	1	0	63.1	312	90	60	59	14	3	2	3	33	0	51	3	0	3	7	.300	0	0-0	0	8.33	8.38
2 ML YEARS			35	28	1	2	151.0	715	188	111	107	22	6	2	4	82	5	113	7	0	10	13	.435	0	0-1	2	6.50	6.38

Doug Davis

Pitches: L Bats: R Pos: SP-34 Ht: 6'4" Wt: 210 Born: 9/21/1975 Age: 31

Year	Team	Lg	G	GS	CG	GF	IP	BFP	H	R	ER	HR	SH	SF	HB	TBB	IBB	SO	WP	Bk	W	L	Pct	ShO	Sv-Op	Hld	ERC	ERA
1999	Tex	AL	2	0	0	0	2.2	20	12	10	10	3	0	0	0	0	0	3	0	0	0	0	-	0	0-0	0	41.42	33.75
2000	Tex	AL	30	13	1	4	98.2	450	109	61	59	14	6	4	3	58	3	66	5	1	7	6	.538	0	0-3	2	5.93	5.38
2001	Tex	AL	30	30	1	0	186.0	828	220	103	92	14	4	6	3	69	1	115	7	2	11	10	.524	0	0-0	0	4.90	4.45
2002	Tex	AL	10	10	1	0	59.2	262	67	36	33	7	3	3	3	22	0	28	2	2	3	5	.375	1	0-0	0	5.05	4.98
2003	3 Tms		21	20	1	0	109.1	491	123	55	49	16	6	2	1	51	1	62	7	0	7	8	.467	0	0-0	0	5.46	4.03
2004	Mil	NL	34	34	0	0	207.1	880	192	84	78	14	11	5	7	79	3	166	4	1	12	12	.500	0	0-0	0	3.49	3.39
2005	Mil	NL	35	35	2	0	222.2	946	196	103	95	26	12	2	4	93	5	208	3	2	11	11	.500	1	0-0	0	3.62	3.84
2006	Mil	NL	34	34	1	0	203.1	904	206	118	111	19	16	8	5	102	1	159	3	0	11	11	.500	0	0-0	0	4.59	4.91
03	Tex	AL	1	1	0	0	3.0	17	4	4	4	2	0	0	0	4	0	2	0	0	0	0	-	0	0-0	0	15.81	12.00
03	Tor	AL	12	11	0	0	54.0	250	70	33	30	6	3	0	1	26	1	25	6	0	4	6	.400	0	0-0	0	6.39	5.00
03	Mil	NL	8	8	1	0	52.1	224	49	18	15	8	3	2	0	21	0	35	1	0	3	2	.600	0	0-0	0	4.06	2.58
8 ML YEARS			196	176	7	4	1089.2	4781	1125	570	527	113	58	30	26	474	14	807	31	8	62	63	.496	3	0-3	2	4.51	4.35

Jason Davis

Pitches: R Bats: R Pos: RP-39 Ht: 6'6" Wt: 225 Born: 5/8/1980 Age: 27

Year	Team	Lg	G	GS	CG	GF	IP	BFP	H	R	ER	HR	SH	SF	HB	TBB	IBB	SO	WP	Bk	W	L	Pct	ShO	Sv-Op	Hld	ERC	ERA
2006	Buffalo*	AAA	11	0	0	10	16.2	62	8	2	1	0	1	0	0	3	1	15	2	0	0	2	.000	0	4--	--	0.72	0.54
2002	Cle	AL	3	2	0	0	14.2	60	12	3	3	1	1	0	0	4	0	11	0	1	1	0	1.000	0	0-0	0	2.40	1.84
2003	Cle	AL	27	27	1	0	165.1	696	172	101	86	25	7	3	8	47	4	85	9	2	8	11	.421	0	0-0	0	4.44	4.68
2004	Cle	AL	26	19	0	2	114.1	540	148	81	70	13	7	2	4	51	1	72	7	1	2	7	.222	0	0-0	1	6.17	5.51
2005	Cle	AL	11	4	0	2	40.1	182	44	22	21	4	3	3	3	20	0	32	2	0	4	2	.667	0	0-0	0	5.34	4.69
2006	Cle	AL	39	0	0	10	55.1	246	67	28	23	1	3	4	3	14	2	37	3	0	3	2	.600	0	1-3	6	4.20	3.74
5 ML YEARS			106	52	1	14	390.0	1724	443	235	203	44	18	12	18	136	7	237	21	4	18	22	.450	0	1-3	7	4.91	4.68

Rajai Davis

Bats: B Throws: R Pos: PH-16; PR-3; RF-1 Ht: 5'11" Wt: 195 Born: 10/19/1980 Age: 26

Year	Team	Lg	G	AB	H	2B	3B	HR	(Hm	Rd)	TB	R	RBI	RC	TBB	IBB	SO	HBP	SH	SF	SB	CS	SB%	GDP	Avg	OBP	Slg
2001	Pirates	R	26	84	22	1	0	0	(-	-)	23	19	4	11	13	0	26	1	3	1	11	3	.79	0	.262	.364	.274
2001	Wmspt	A-	6	12	1	0	0	0	(-	-)	1	1	0	0	2	0	4	0	0	0	1	0	1.00	0	.083	.214	.083
2002	Pirates	R	58	224	86	16	5	4	(-	-)	124	38	35	54	20	0	25	3	0	3	24	6	.80	3	.384	.436	.554
2002	Wmspt	A-	1	4	0	0	0	0	(-	-)	0	0	0	0	0	0	1	0	0	0	0	0	-	0	.000	.000	.000
2002	Hickory	A+	6	14	6	0	0	0	(-	-)	6	4	3	4	6	0	2	1	1	0	2	2	.50	0	.429	.619	.429
2003	Hickory	A	125	478	146	21	7	6	(-	-)	199	84	54	83	55	0	65	6	8	2	40	13	.75	7	.305	.383	.416
2004	Lynbrg	A+	127	509	160	27	7	5	(-	-)	216	91	38	92	59	2	60	0	4	0	57	15	.79	8	.314	.386	.424
2005	Altna	AA	123	499	140	22	5	4	(-	-)	184	82	34	74	43	2	76	12	6	1	45	9	.83	6	.281	.351	.369
2006	Indy	AAA	100	385	109	17	1	2	(-	-)	134	53	21	50	27	0	59	3	2	0	45	13	.78	3	.283	.335	.348
2006	Pit	NL	20	14	2	1	0	0	(0	0)	3	1	0	0	2	0	3	0	1	0	1	3	.25	0	.143	.250	.214

Zach Day

Pitches: R Bats: R Pos: SP-8 Ht: 6'4" Wt: 215 Born: 6/15/1978 Age: 29

Year	Team	Lg	G	GS	CG	GF	IP	BFP	H	R	ER	HR	SH	SF	HB	TBB	IBB	SO	WP	Bk	W	L	Pct	ShO	Sv-Op	Hld	ERC	ERA
2002	Mon	NL	19	2	0	5	37.1	153	28	18	15	3	1	1	1	15	2	25	1	0	4	1	.800	0	1-2	2	2.66	3.62
2003	Mon	NL	23	23	1	0	131.1	580	132	64	61	8	2	5	10	59	3	61	13	0	9	8	.529	1	0-0	0	4.28	4.18
2004	Mon	NL	19	19	1	0	116.2	496	117	53	51	13	4	1	4	45	7	61	5	0	5	10	.333	1	0-0	0	4.24	3.93
2005	2 Tms	NL	17	8	0	4	47.1	229	61	40	36	6	1	1	1	32	4	23	2	0	1	3	.250	0	0-1	0	7.17	6.85
2006	2 Tms	NL	8	8	0	0	40.0	190	51	32	30	5	1	1	3	21	2	19	1	0	2	5	.286	0	0-0	0	6.68	6.75
05	Was	NL	12	5	0	4	36.0	170	41	29	27	4	1	1	1	25	3	16	1	0	1	2	.333	0	0-1	0	6.18	6.75
05	Col	NL	5	3	0	0	11.1	59	20	11	9	2	0	0	0	7	1	7	1	0	0	1	.000	0	0-0	0	10.55	7.15
06	Col	NL	3	3	0	0	13.1	71	22	17	16	3	0	1	1	10	1	6	0	0	1	2	.333	0	0-0	0	11.21	10.80
06	Was	NL	5	5	0	0	26.2	119	29	15	14	2	1	0	2	11	1	13	1	0	1	3	.250	0	0-0	0	4.68	4.73
5 ML YEARS			86	60	2	9	372.2	1648	389	207	193	35	9	9	19	172	18	189	22	0	21	27	.438	2	1-3	4	4.68	4.66

Jorge de la Rosa

Pitches: L Bats: L Pos: RP-15; SP-13   Ht: 6'1" Wt: 210 Born: 4/5/1981 Age: 26

			HOW MUCH HE PITCHED							WHAT HE GAVE UP										THE RESULTS							
Year	Team	Lg	G	GS	CG	GF	IP	BFP	H	R	ER	HR	SH	SF	HB	TBB	IBB	SO	WP	Bk	W	L	Pct	ShO	Sv-Op	Hld	ERC	ERA
2006	Hntsvl*	AA	6	6	0	0	30.0	120	31	12	8	1	4	0	1	3	0	23	2	0	3	1	.750	0	0--	-	2.88	2.40
2004	Mil	NL	5	5	0	0	22.2	113	29	20	16	1	1	3	1	14	0	5	3	0	0	3	.000	0	0-0	0	6.12	6.35
2005	Mil	NL	38	0	0	13	42.1	208	48	23	21	1	2	2	0	38	4	42	6	0	2	2	.500	0	0-2	5	6.04	4.46
2006	2 Tms		28	13	0	4	79.0	367	81	59	57	14	2	4	2	54	1	67	6	1	5	6	.455	0	0-0	1	6.05	6.49
06	Mil	NL	18	3	0	4	30.1	146	32	30	29	4	1	3	1	22	1	31	4	0	2	2	.500	0	0-0	1	5.90	8.60
06	KC	AL	10	10	0	0	48.2	221	49	29	28	10	1	1	1	32	0	36	2	1	3	4	.429	0	0-0	0	6.14	5.18
3 ML YEARS			71	18	0	17	144.0	688	158	102	94	16	5	9	3	106	5	114	15	1	7	11	.389	0	0-2	6	6.08	5.88

Tomas de la Rosa

Bats: R Throws: R Pos: SS-8; PR-4; PH-3; 2B-2; 3B-2   Ht: 5'10" Wt: 180 Born: 1/28/1978 Age: 29

						BATTING															BASERUNNING				AVERAGES		
Year	Team	Lg	G	AB	H	2B	3B	HR	(Hm	Rd)	TB	R	RBI	RC	TBB	IBB	SO	HBP	SH	SF	SB	CS	SB%	GDP	Avg	OBP	Slg
2006	Giants*	R	7	27	11	1	0	0	(-	-)	12	4	2	5	1	0	2	1	0	1	2	0	1.00	0	.407	.433	.444
2006	Fresno*	AAA	79	300	88	21	2	8	(-	-)	137	43	43	49	23	0	45	5	5	2	8	5	.62	10	.293	.352	.457
2000	Mon	NL	32	66	19	3	1	2	(1	1)	30	7	9	10	7	0	11	1	3	0	2	1	.67	2	.288	.365	.455
2001	Mon	NL	1	1	0	0	0	0	(0	0)	0	0	0	0	0	0	0	0	0	0	0	0	-	0	.000	.000	.000
2006	SF	NL	16	16	5	0	0	0	(0	0)	5	1	1	2	1	0	3	0	0	0	0	0	-	0	.313	.353	.313
3 ML YEARS			49	83	24	3	1	2	(1	1)	35	8	10	12	8	0	14	1	3	0	2	1	.67	2	.289	.359	.422

Yurendell DeCaster

Bats: R Throws: R Pos: PH-2; DH-1; PR-1   Ht: 6'1" Wt: 205 Born: 9/26/1979 Age: 27

						BATTING															BASERUNNING				AVERAGES		
Year	Team	Lg	G	AB	H	2B	3B	HR	(Hm	Rd)	TB	R	RBI	RC	TBB	IBB	SO	HBP	SH	SF	SB	CS	SB%	GDP	Avg	OBP	Slg
1998	DRays	R	56	174	41	4	3	2	(-	-)	57	25	17	20	19	0	48	2	3	2	10	4	.71	3	.236	.315	.328
1999	Princtn	R+	48	183	47	12	0	11	(-	-)	92	37	36	32	20	0	65	6	1	2	4	2	.67	4	.257	.346	.503
2000	CtnWV	A	69	242	58	21	0	7	(-	-)	100	34	28	31	16	0	89	6	2	4	4	1	.80	2	.240	.299	.413
2001	Hickory	A	97	341	99	17	4	19	(-	-)	181	56	74	66	35	2	83	8	0	5	4	4	.50	8	.290	.365	.531
2001	Lynbrg	A+	13	48	5	2	0	0	(-	-)	7	1	4	0	3	0	16	0	0	0	0	0	-	3	.104	.157	.146
2002	Lynbrg	A+	125	432	109	25	3	15	(-	-)	185	54	62	59	30	2	102	8	2	5	1	2	.33	3	.252	.309	.428
2003	Lynbrg	A+	97	330	76	24	1	13	(-	-)	141	50	56	41	22	1	86	4	0	5	3	2	.60	9	.230	.283	.427
2004	Altna	AA	97	330	92	18	1	15	(-	-)	157	54	42	52	22	1	78	5	1	2	4	2	.67	11	.279	.331	.476
2005	Indy	AAA	122	415	116	31	4	11	(-	-)	188	60	61	66	37	1	103	6	2	2	7	5	.58	9	.280	.346	.453
2006	Indy	AAA	119	421	115	22	3	11	(-	-)	176	47	51	58	35	3	100	2	1	3	7	7	.50	16	.273	.330	.418
2006	Pit	NL	3	2	0	0	0	0	(0	0)	0	0	0	0	0	0	2	0	0	0	0	0	-	0	.000	.000	.000

Mike DeJean

Pitches: R Bats: R Pos: RP-2   Ht: 6'2" Wt: 220 Born: 9/28/1970 Age: 36

			HOW MUCH HE PITCHED							WHAT HE GAVE UP										THE RESULTS							
Year	Team	Lg	G	GS	CG	GF	IP	BFP	H	R	ER	HR	SH	SF	HB	TBB	IBB	SO	WP	Bk	W	L	Pct	ShO	Sv-Op	Hld	ERC	ERA
1997	Col	NL	55	0	0	15	67.2	295	74	34	30	4	3	1	3	24	2	38	2	0	5	0	1.000	0	2-4	13	4.29	3.99
1998	Col	NL	59	1	0	9	74.1	307	78	29	25	4	4	4	1	24	1	27	3	0	3	1	.750	0	2-3	11	3.92	3.03
1999	Princtn	R+	56	0	0	17	61.0	288	83	61	57	13	3	3	2	32	8	31	3	0	2	4	.333	0	0-4	9	7.77	8.41
2000	Col	NL	54	0	0	15	53.1	235	54	31	29	9	3	1	0	30	6	34	5	0	4	4	.500	0	0-4	7	5.22	4.89
2001	Mil	NL	75	0	0	19	84.1	371	75	31	26	4	1	4	9	39	7	68	8	0	4	2	.667	0	2-4	8	3.56	2.77
2002	Mil	NL	68	0	0	60	75.0	326	66	28	26	7	4	2	2	39	8	65	7	0	1	5	.167	0	27-30	3	3.74	3.12
2003	2 Tms	NL	76	0	0	45	82.2	365	86	46	43	13	1	3	2	39	7	71	3	0	5	8	.385	0	19-27	10	5.00	4.68
2004	2 Tms		54	0	0	20	61.0	288	70	34	31	2	4	2	8	33	8	60	4	0	0	5	.000	0	0-0	3	5.21	4.57
2005	2 Tms	NL	66	0	0	19	62.1	282	62	33	31	3	3	3	3	30	3	52	5	0	5	4	.556	0	0-3	20	3.98	4.48
2006	Col	NL	2	0	0	1	1.2	8	1	0	0	0	0	0	0	2	0	0	0	0	1	0	1.000	0	0-0	1	3.97	0.00
03	Mil	NL	58	0	0	40	64.2	286	69	38	35	12	0	3	1	27	7	58	3	0	4	7	.364	0	18-26	5	5.02	4.87
03	StL	NL	18	0	0	5	18.0	79	17	8	8	1	1	0	1	12	0	13	0	0	1	1	.500	0	1-1	5	4.89	4.00
04	Bal	NL	37	0	0	12	39.2	197	49	29	27	2	2	2	6	28	6	36	2	0	0	5	.000	0	0-0	1	6.64	6.13
04	NYM	NL	17	0	0	8	21.1	91	21	5	4	0	2	0	2	5	2	24	2	0	0	0	-	0	0-0	2	2.85	1.69
05	NYM	NL	28	0	0	12	25.2	131	36	19	18	3	1	1	1	18	2	17	2	0	3	1	.750	0	0-0	2	7.84	6.31
05	Col	NL	38	0	0	7	36.2	151	26	14	13	0	2	2	2	12	1	35	3	0	2	3	.400	0	0-3	18	1.80	3.19
10 ML YEARS			565	1	0	220	623.1	2765	649	327	298	59	26	23	30	292	50	446	40	0	30	33	.476	0	52-79	82	4.62	4.30

David DeJesus

Bats: L Throws: L Pos: LF-73; CF-61   Ht: 6'0" Wt: 185 Born: 12/20/1979 Age: 27

						BATTING															BASERUNNING				AVERAGES		
Year	Team	Lg	G	AB	H	2B	3B	HR	(Hm	Rd)	TB	R	RBI	RC	TBB	IBB	SO	HBP	SH	SF	SB	CS	SB%	GDP	Avg	OBP	Slg
2006	Omha*	AAA	3	13	5	0	0	0	(-	-)	5	0	2	1	0	0	2	0	0	0	0	0	-	1	.385	.385	.385
2003	KC	AL	12	7	2	0	1	0	(0	0)	4	0	0	2	1	0	2	1	1	0	0	0	-	0	.286	.444	.571
2004	KC	AL	96	363	104	15	3	7	(2	5)	146	58	39	53	33	0	53	9	8	0	8	11	.42	7	.287	.360	.402
2005	KC	AL	122	461	135	31	6	9	(6	3)	205	69	56	77	42	1	76	9	5	6	5	5	.50	6	.293	.359	.445
2006	KC	AL	119	491	145	36	7	8	(4	4)	219	83	56	76	43	4	70	12	2	4	6	3	.67	10	.295	.364	.446
4 ML YEARS			349	1322	386	82	17	24	(12	12)	574	210	151	208	119	5	201	31	16	10	19	19	.50	23	.292	.362	.434

Manny Delcarmen

Pitches: R **Bats:** R **Pos:** RP-50   **Ht:** 6'2" **Wt:** 190 **Born:** 2/16/1982 **Age:** 25

			HOW MUCH HE PITCHED						WHAT HE GAVE UP									THE RESULTS						
Year	Team	Lg	G	GS	CG	GF	IP	BFP	H	R	ER	HR	SF	HB	TBB	IBB	SO	WP	Bk	W	L	Pct	ShO	Sv-Op Hld	ERC	ERA
2001	RedSx	R	11	8	0	2	46.0	192	35	16	13	0	2	1	19	0	62	2	0	4	2	.667	0	1- - -	2.78	2.54
2002	Augsta	A	26	24	0	1	136.0	588	124	77	62	15	6	1	14	56	0	136	3	1	7	8	.467	0	0- - -	4.12	4.10
2003	Srsota	A+	4	3	0	0	23.0	92	16	9	8	1	0	0	3	7	0	16	0	0	1	1	.500	0	0- - -	2.31	3.13
2004	Srsota	A+	19	18	0	0	73.0	323	84	43	38	10	4	3	4	20	1	76	1	0	3	6	.333	0	0- - -	4.85	4.68
2005	Portlnd	AA	31	0	0	8	39.0	168	31	23	14	3	3	0	0	20	1	49	6	0	4	4	.500	0	3- - -	3.12	3.23
2005	Pwtckt	AAA	15	0	0	10	21.0	93	17	3	3	0	0	0	1	13	1	23	1	1	3	1	.750	0	2- - -	3.19	1.29
2006	Pwtckt	AAA	10	0	0	2	17.0	65	9	4	4	0	0	0	1	6	0	19	0	0	0	1	.000	0	0- - -	1.37	2.12
2005	Bos	AL	10	0	0	2	9.0	41	8	3	3	0	0	0	1	7	0	9	0	0	0	0	-	0	0-0 0	4.68	3.00
2006	Bos	AL	50	0	0	11	53.1	243	68	32	30	2	3	1	2	17	2	45	0	0	2	0	1.000	0	0-4 14	4.90	5.06
	2 ML YEARS		60	0	0	13	62.1	284	76	35	33	2	3	1	3	24	2	54	0	0	2	0	1.000	0	0-4 14	4.87	4.76

Carlos Delgado

Bats: L **Throws:** R **Pos:** 1B-141; PH-2; DH-1   **Ht:** 6'3" **Wt:** 240 **Born:** 6/25/1972 **Age:** 35

			BATTING																	BASERUNNING				AVERAGES		
Year	Team	Lg	G	AB	H	2B	3B	HR	(Hm	Rd)	TB	R	RBI	RC	TBB	IBB	SO	HBP	SH	SF	SB	CS	SB%	GDP	Avg	OBP	Slg
1993	Tor	AL	2	1	0	0	0	0	(0	0)	0	0	0	0	1	0	0	0	0	0	0	0	-	0	.000	.500	.000
1994	Tor	AL	43	130	28	2	0	9	(5	4)	57	17	24	20	25	4	46	3	0	1	1	1	.50	5	.215	.352	.438
1995	Tor	AL	37	91	15	3	0	3	(2	1)	27	7	11	5	6	0	26	0	0	2	0	0	-	1	.165	.212	.297
1996	Tor	AL	138	488	132	28	2	25	(12	13)	239	68	92	83	58	2	139	9	0	8	0	0	-	13	.270	.353	.490
1997	Tor	AL	153	519	136	42	3	30	(17	13)	274	79	91	94	64	9	133	8	0	4	0	3	.00	6	.262	.350	.528
1998	Tor	AL	142	530	155	43	1	38	(20	18)	314	94	115	117	73	13	139	11	0	6	3	0	1.00	8	.292	.385	.592
1999	Tor	AL	152	573	156	39	0	44	(17	27)	327	113	134	121	86	7	141	15	0	7	1	1	.50	11	.272	.377	.571
2000	Tor	AL	162	569	196	57	1	41	(30	11)	378	115	137	164	123	18	104	15	0	4	0	1	.00	12	.344	.470	.664
2001	Tor	AL	162	574	160	31	1	39	(13	26)	310	102	102	126	111	22	136	16	0	3	3	0	1.00	9	.279	.408	.540
2002	Tor	AL	143	505	140	34	2	33	(17	16)	277	103	108	117	102	18	126	13	0	8	1	0	1.00	8	.277	.406	.549
2003	Tor	AL	161	570	172	38	1	42	(24	18)	338	117	145	146	109	23	137	19	0	7	0	0	-	9	.302	.426	.593
2004	Tor	AL	128	458	123	26	0	32	(18	14)	245	74	99	88	69	12	115	13	0	11	0	1	.00	11	.269	.372	.535
2005	Fla	NL	144	521	157	41	3	33	(16	17)	303	81	115	110	72	20	121	17	0	6	0	0	-	16	.301	.399	.582
2006	NYM	NL	144	524	139	30	2	38	(18	20)	287	89	114	101	74	11	120	10	0	10	0	0	-	12	.265	.361	.548
	14 ML YEARS		1711	6053	1709	414	16	407	(209	198)	3376	1059	1287	1292	973	159	1483	149	0	77	9	7	.56	121	.282	.390	.558

David Dellucci

Bats: L **Throws:** L **Pos:** PH-69; LF-45; RF-31; DH-2; PR-1   **Ht:** 5'11" **Wt:** 195 **Born:** 10/31/1973 **Age:** 33

			BATTING																	BASERUNNING				AVERAGES		
Year	Team	Lg	G	AB	H	2B	3B	HR	(Hm	Rd)	TB	R	RBI	RC	TBB	IBB	SO	HBP	SH	SF	SB	CS	SB%	GDP	Avg	OBP	Slg
1997	Bal	AL	17	27	6	1	0	1	(0	1)	10	3	3	3	4	1	7	1	0	0	0	0	-	2	.222	.344	.370
1998	Ari	NL	124	416	108	19	12	5	(1	4)	166	43	51	51	33	2	103	3	0	1	3	5	.38	6	.260	.318	.399
1999	Ari	NL	63	109	43	7	1	1	(0	1)	55	27	15	24	11	0	24	3	0	0	2	0	1.00	3	.394	.463	.505
2000	Ari	NL	34	50	15	3	0	0	(0	0)	18	2	2	6	4	0	9	0	0	0	0	2	.00	1	.300	.352	.360
2001	Ari	NL	115	217	60	10	2	10	(5	5)	104	28	40	36	22	4	52	2	0	0	1	2	.67	2	.276	.349	.479
2002	Ari	NL	97	229	56	11	2	7	(2	5)	92	34	29	26	28	5	55	1	0	3	2	4	.33	7	.245	.326	.402
2003	2 Tms		91	216	49	12	3	3	(3	0)	76	26	23	23	23	1	58	5	2	2	12	0	1.00	6	.227	.313	.352
2004	Tex	AL	107	331	80	13	1	17	(9	8)	146	59	61	56	47	3	88	5	1	3	9	4	.69	4	.242	.342	.441
2005	Tex	AL	128	435	109	17	5	29	(14	15)	223	97	65	81	76	0	121	6	0	3	5	3	.63	7	.251	.367	.513
2006	Phi	NL	132	264	77	14	5	13	(6	7)	140	41	39	43	28	6	62	6	0	3	1	3	.25	1	.292	.369	.530
03	Ari	NL	70	165	40	11	3	2	(2	0)	63	18	19	21	19	1	45	3	1	2	9	0	1.00	4	.242	.328	.382
03	NYY	AL	21	51	9	1	0	1	(1	0)	13	8	4	2	4	0	13	2	1	0	3	0	1.00	2	.176	.263	.255
	10 ML YEARS		908	2294	603	107	31	86	(40	46)	1030	360	328	349	276	16	579	31	3	14	36	22	.62	39	.263	.348	.449

Chris Demaria

Pitches: R **Bats:** B **Pos:** RP-10   **Ht:** 6'3" **Wt:** 210 **Born:** 9/28/1980 **Age:** 26

			HOW MUCH HE PITCHED						WHAT HE GAVE UP									THE RESULTS						
Year	Team	Lg	G	GS	CG	GF	IP	BFP	H	R	ER	HR	SH	SF	HB	TBB	IBB	SO	WP	Bk	W	L	Pct	ShO	Sv-Op Hld	ERC	ERA
2002	Wmspt	A-	16	0	0	6	31.0	132	34	20	15	6	1	0	0	4	1	15	0	0	1	1	.500	0	1- - -	3.98	4.35
2003	Wmspt	A-	25	1	0	9	47.0	187	36	15	14	3	1	0	6	10	0	48	3	0	6	3	.667	0	3- - -	2.45	2.68
2004	Hickory	A	40	0	0	27	79.2	321	62	29	26	5	3	1	4	20	0	101	3	0	8	3	.727	0	10- - -	2.31	2.94
2005	Hi Dsrt	A+	48	0	0	60.2	249	57	19	15	8	2	0	2	10	1	73	2	0	4	2	.667	0	19- - -	3.11	2.23
2005	Wichta	AA	10	0	0	6	15.1	60	12	3	3	1	0	0	0	2	0	19	1	0	1	1	.000	0	1- - -	2.43	1.76
2006	Nashv	AAA	38	0	0	11	51.2	218	48	20	17	4	1	0	2	17	0	50	2	0	4	0	1.000	0	1- - -	3.40	2.96
2005	KC	AL	8	0	0	5	9.0	44	14	10	9	3	0	0	0	5	0	11	1	0	1	0	1.000	0	0-0 0	10.57	9.00
2006	Mil	NL	10	0	0	4	13.2	63	10	11	9	4	2	0	2	9	0	11	0	0	0	1	.000	0	0-0 0	5.39	5.93
	2 ML YEARS		18	0	0	9	22.2	107	24	21	18	7	2	0	2	14	0	22	1	0	1	1	.500	0	0-0 0	7.29	7.15

Ryan Dempster

Pitches: R **Bats:** R **Pos:** RP-74   **Ht:** 6'2" **Wt:** 215 **Born:** 5/3/1977 **Age:** 30

			HOW MUCH HE PITCHED						WHAT HE GAVE UP									THE RESULTS						
Year	Team	Lg	G	GS	CG	GF	IP	BFP	H	R	ER	HR	SH	SF	HB	TBB	IBB	SO	WP	Bk	W	L	Pct	ShO	Sv-Op Hld	ERC	ERA
1998	Fla	NL	14	11	0	1	54.2	272	72	47	43	6	5	6	9	38	1	35	5	0	1	5	.167	0	0-1 0	8.14	7.08
1999	Fla	NL	25	25	0	0	147.0	666	146	77	77	21	3	6	6	93	2	126	8	0	7	8	.467	0	0-0 0	5.49	4.71
2000	Fla	NL	33	33	2	0	226.1	974	210	102	92	30	4	5	5	97	7	209	4	0	14	10	.583	1	0-0 0	4.04	3.66
2001	Fla	NL	34	34	2	0	211.1	954	218	123	116	21	15	7	10	112	5	171	5	0	15	12	.556	1	0-0 0	4.91	4.94
2002	2 Tms		33	33	4	0	209.0	915	228	127	125	28	9	6	10	93	2	153	2	0	10	13	.435	0	0-0 0	5.35	5.38
2003	Cin	NL	22	20	0	1	115.2	545	134	89	84	14	9	4	5	70	4	84	3	0	3	7	.300	0	0-0 0	6.11	6.54
2004	ChC	NL	23	0	0	8	20.2	93	16	9	9	1	1	0	2	13	0	18	1	0	1	1	.500	0	2-2 3	3.61	3.92

Year	Team	Lg		HOW MUCH HE PITCHED					WHAT HE GAVE UP													THE RESULTS						
			G	GS	CG	GF	IP	BFP	H	R	ER	HR	SH	SF	HB	TBB	IBB	SO	WP	Bk	W	L	Pct	ShO	Sv-Op	Hld	ERC	ERA
2005	ChC	NL	63	6	0	53	92.0	401	83	35	32	4	5	0	4	49	7	89	4	0	5	3	.625	0	33-35	0	3.69	3.13
2006	ChC	NL	74	0	0	64	75.0	342	77	47	40	5	5	4	3	36	3	67	6	0	1	9	.100	0	24-33	2	4.26	4.80
02	Fla	NL	18	18	3	0	120.1	521	126	66	64	12	7	3	7	55	1	87	0	0	5	8	.385	0	0-0	0	4.95	4.79
02	Cin	NL	15	15	1	0	88.2	394	102	61	61	16	2	3	3	38	1	66	2	0	5	5	.500	0	0-0	0	5.90	6.19
9 ML YEARS			321	162	8	127	1151.2	5162	1184	656	618	130	56	38	54	601	31	952	38	0	57	68	.456	2	59-71	5	4.98	4.83

Chris Denorfia

Bats: R **Throws:** R **Pos:** RF-15; CF-12; PH-12; LF-11; PR-2 **Ht:** 6'0" **Wt:** 195 **Born:** 7/15/1980 **Age:** 26

Year	Team	Lg		BATTING																		BASERUNNING				AVERAGES		
			G	AB	H	2B	3B	HR	(Hm	Rd)	TB	R	RBI	RC	TBB	IBB	SO	HBP	SH	SF	SB	CS	SB%	GDP	Avg	OBP	Slg
2002	Reds	R	57	200	68	9	2	0	(-	-)	81	38	19	38	31	0	23	0	0	2	18	8	.69	8	.340	.425	.405
2002	Dayton	A	3	10	0	0	0	0	(-	-)	0	2	0	0	0	0	3	0	0	0	0	0	-	1	.000	.000	.000
2002	Chatt	AA	3	7	3	2	1	0	(-	-)	7	0	0	3	2	0	1	0	0	0	0	0	-	0	.429	.556	1.000
2003	Ptomc	A+	128	470	111	10	5	4	(-	-)	143	60	39	51	54	0	106	3	11	3	20	7	.74	10	.236	.317	.304
2004	Ptomc	A+	75	269	84	18	4	11	(-	-)	143	52	51	60	48	0	66	1	1	2	10	6	.63	3	.312	.416	.532
2004	Chatt	AA	61	221	55	10	2	6	(-	-)	87	30	27	32	30	1	42	1	3	1	5	2	.71	1	.249	.340	.394
2005	Chatt	AA	46	188	62	17	3	7	(-	-)	106	40	26	39	17	1	38	2	2	0	4	3	.57	1	.330	.391	.564
2005	Lsvlle	AAA	91	323	100	12	6	13	(-	-)	163	50	61	65	41	1	54	4	3	3	8	3	.73	7	.310	.391	.505
2006	Lsvlle	AAA	83	312	109	19	1	7	(-	-)	151	46	45	65	34	4	41	1	1	5	15	1	.94	12	.349	.409	.484
2005	Cin	NL	18	38	10	3	0	1	(1	0)	16	8	2	3	6	0	9	0	0	0	1	0	1.00	1	.263	.364	.421
2006	Cin	NL	49	106	30	6	0	1	(0	1)	39	14	7	13	11	1	21	1	2	0	1	1	.50	1	.283	.356	.368
2 ML YEARS			67	144	40	9	0	2	(1	1)	55	22	9	16	17	1	30	1	2	0	2	1	.67	2	.278	.358	.382

Mark DeRosa

Bats: R **Throws:** R **Pos:** RF-60; 3B-40; 2B-26; SS-7; LF-5; DH-3; 1B-1 **Ht:** 6'1" **Wt:** 205 **Born:** 2/26/1975 **Age:** 32

Year	Team	Lg		BATTING																		BASERUNNING				AVERAGES		
			G	AB	H	2B	3B	HR	(Hm	Rd)	TB	R	RBI	RC	TBB	IBB	SO	HBP	SH	SF	SB	CS	SB%	GDP	Avg	OBP	Slg
2006	Okla*	AAA	3	12	6	1	0	0	(-	-)	7	2	0	3	0	0	1	0	0	0	0	0	-	0	.500	.500	.583
1998	Atl	NL	5	3	1	0	0	0	(0	0)	1	2	0	0	0	0	1	0	0	0	0	0	-	0	.333	.333	.333
1999	Atl	NL	7	8	0	0	0	0	(0	0)	0	0	0	0	0	0	2	0	0	0	0	0	-	0	.000	.000	.000
2000	Atl	NL	22	13	4	1	0	0	(0	0)	5	9	3	2	2	0	1	0	0	0	0	0	-	0	.308	.400	.385
2001	Atl	NL	66	164	47	8	0	3	(3	0)	64	27	20	22	12	6	19	5	1	2	2	1	.67	3	.287	.350	.390
2002	Atl	NL	72	212	63	9	2	5	(3	2)	91	24	23	27	12	3	24	3	2	3	2	3	.40	5	.297	.339	.429
2003	Atl	NL	103	266	70	14	0	6	(3	3)	102	40	22	28	16	0	49	5	0	1	1	0	1.00	6	.263	.316	.383
2004	Atl	NL	118	309	74	16	0	3	(0	3)	99	33	31	24	23	3	53	3	4	6	1	3	.25	6	.239	.293	.320
2005	Tex	AL	66	148	36	5	0	8	(7	1)	65	26	20	20	16	0	35	2	0	0	1	0	1.00	5	.243	.325	.439
2006	Tex	AL	136	520	154	40	2	13	(5	8)	237	78	74	78	44	1	102	6	0	2	4	4	.50	13	.296	.357	.456
9 ML YEARS			595	1643	449	93	4	38	(21	17)	664	239	193	201	125	13	286	24	7	14	11	11	.50	38	.273	.331	.404

Elmer Dessens

Pitches: R **Bats:** R **Pos:** RP-62 **Ht:** 5'11" **Wt:** 200 **Born:** 1/13/1971 **Age:** 36

Year	Team	Lg		HOW MUCH HE PITCHED						WHAT HE GAVE UP												THE RESULTS						
			G	GS	CG	GF	IP	BFP	H	R	ER	HR	SH	SF	HB	TBB	IBB	SO	WP	Bk	W	L	Pct	ShO	Sv-Op	Hld	ERC	ERA
2006	LsVgs*	AAA	1	0	0	0	0.2	6	2	2	1	0	0	0	0	1	0	0	0	0	0	1	.000	0	0- -	-	34.79	13.50
1996	Pit	NL	15	3	0	1	25.0	112	40	23	23	2	3	1	0	4	0	13	0	0	0	2	.000	0	0-0	3	6.77	8.28
1997	Pit	NL	3	0	0	1	3.1	13	2	0	0	0	0	0	1	0	0	2	0	0	0	0	-	0	0-0	1	1.31	0.00
1998	Pit	NL	43	5	0	8	74.2	332	90	50	47	10	4	3	0	25	2	43	1	0	2	6	.250	0	0-1	6	5.19	5.67
2000	Cin	NL	40	16	1	6	147.1	640	170	73	70	10	12	7	3	43	7	85	4	0	11	5	.688	0	1-1	1	4.31	4.28
2001	Cin	NL	34	34	1	0	205.0	862	221	103	102	32	7	7	1	56	1	128	4	1	10	14	.417	1	0-0	0	4.49	4.48
2002	Cin	NL	30	30	0	0	178.0	737	173	70	60	24	7	1	7	49	8	93	3	1	7	8	.467	0	0-0	0	3.82	3.03
2003	Ari	NL	34	30	0	1	175.2	781	212	107	99	22	9	3	4	57	6	113	3	2	8	8	.500	0	0-0	0	5.19	5.07
2004	2 Tms	NL	50	10	0	9	105.0	468	123	61	52	15	4	3	1	31	4	73	2	0	2	6	.250	0	2-5	4	4.83	4.46
2005	LAD	NL	28	7	0	4	65.2	277	63	30	26	6	1	3	1	19	2	37	1	0	1	2	.333	0	0-0	1	3.35	3.56
2006	2 Tms	NL	62	0	0	12	77.0	334	86	43	39	8	5	1	1	22	8	52	3	0	5	8	.385	0	2-7	18	4.17	4.56
04	Ari	NL	38	9	0	7	85.1	386	107	54	45	11	4	3	1	23	4	55	2	0	1	6	.143	0	2-4	4	5.08	4.75
04	LAD	NL	12	1	0	2	19.2	82	16	7	7	4	0	0	0	8	0	18	0	0	1	0	1.000	0	0-1	0	3.74	3.20
06	KC	AL	43	0	0	10	54.0	234	63	31	27	4	3	1	1	13	6	36	2	0	5	7	.417	0	2-7	12	4.08	4.50
06	LAD	NL	19	0	0	2	23.0	100	23	12	12	4	2	0	0	9	2	16	1	0	0	1	.000	0	0-0	6	4.37	4.70
10 ML YEARS			339	135	2	42	1056.2	4556	1180	560	518	129	52	29	19	306	38	639	21	4	46	59	.438	1	5-14	33	4.49	4.41

Joey Devine

Pitches: R **Bats:** R **Pos:** RP-10 **Ht:** 6'1" **Wt:** 225 **Born:** 9/19/1983 **Age:** 23

Year	Team	Lg		HOW MUCH HE PITCHED						WHAT HE GAVE UP												THE RESULTS						
			G	GS	CG	GF	IP	BFP	H	R	ER	HR	SH	SF	HB	TBB	IBB	SO	WP	Bk	W	L	Pct	ShO	Sv-Op	Hld	ERC	ERA
2005	MrtlBh	A+	4	0	0	0	5.0	18	0	0	0	0	0	0	1	3	0	7	0	0	0	0	-	0	1- -	-	0.67	0.00
2005	Missi	AA	18	0	0	15	20.0	92	19	13	6	2	2	0	5	12	1	28	1	0	1	1	.500	0	5- -	-	5.62	2.70
2005	Rchmd	AAA	1	0	0	0	1.0	7	3	2	2	0	0	0	0	1	0	1	0	0	0	0	-	0	0- -	-	19.55	18.00
2006	MrtlBh	A+	13	2	0	1	18.1	79	13	12	12	1	0	0	1	11	1	28	4	0	1	3	.250	0	0- -	-	3.03	5.89
2006	Missi	AA	6	0	0	3	11.0	37	2	1	1	1	2	0	0	4	0	20	0	0	2	0	1.000	0	0- -	-	0.69	0.82
2006	Rchmd	AAA	1	0	0	0	0.0	2	1	1	1	0	0	0	0	1	0	0	0	0	0	0	-	0	0- -	-	-	-
2005	Atl	NL	5	0	0	1	5.0	26	6	7	7	2	0	0	0	5	1	3	0	0	0	1	.000	0	0-0	1	9.97	12.60
2006	Atl	NL	10	0	0	1	6.1	36	8	7	7	1	0	0	1	9	1	10	4	1	0	0	-	0	0-1	0	11.11	9.95
2 ML YEARS			15	0	0	2	11.1	62	14	14	14	3	0	0	1	14	2	13	4	1	0	1	.000	0	0-1	1	10.67	11.12

Einar Diaz

Bats: R **Throws:** R **Pos:** PH-2; C-1   **Ht:** 5'10" **Wt:** 200 **Born:** 12/28/1972 **Age:** 34

							BATTING											BASERUNNING				AVERAGES		
Year	Team	Lg	G	AB	H	2B	3B	HR	(Hm | Rd)	TB	R	RBI	RC	TBB	IBB	SO	HBP	SH	SF	SB	CS	SB%	GDP	Avg	OBP	Slg
2006	LsVgs*	AAA	2	7	3	2	0	0	(- | -)	5	0	2	1	0	0	1	0	0	0	0	0	-	1	.429	.429	.714
2006	Buffalo*	AAA	64	220	48	13	0	3	(- | -)	70	22	29	19	14	0	23	1	6	1	0	1	.00	9	.218	.267	.318
1996	Cle	AL	4	1	0	0	0	0	(0 | 0)	0	0	0	0	0	0	0	0	0	0	0	0	-	0	.000	.000	.000
1997	Cle	AL	5	7	1	1	0	0	(0 | 0)	2	1	1	0	0	0	2	0	0	0	0	0	-	0	.143	.143	.286
1998	Cle	AL	17	48	11	1	0	2	(1 | 1)	18	8	9	5	3	0	2	2	0	3	0	0	-	2	.229	.286	.375
1999	Cle	AL	119	392	110	21	1	3	(2 | 1)	142	43	32	46	23	0	41	5	6	1	11	4	.73	10	.281	.328	.362
2000	Cle	AL	75	250	68	14	2	4	(2 | 2)	98	29	25	30	11	0	29	8	6	0	4	2	.67	7	.272	.323	.392
2001	Cle	AL	134	437	121	34	1	4	(0 | 4)	169	54	56	53	17	0	44	16	8	0	1	2	.33	11	.277	.328	.387
2002	Cle	AL	102	320	66	19	0	2	(1 | 1)	91	34	16	14	17	1	27	6	6	2	0	1	.00	13	.206	.258	.284
2003	Tex	AL	101	334	86	14	1	4	(2 | 2)	114	30	35	31	9	0	32	10	4	4	3	1	.75	12	.257	.294	.341
2004	Mon	NL	55	139	31	6	1	1	(1 | 0)	42	9	11	9	11	3	10	4	2	3	2	0	1.00	6	.223	.293	.302
2005	StL	NL	58	130	27	6	0	1	(1 | 0)	36	14	17	9	5	0	12	2	2	0	0	0	-	8	.208	.248	.277
2006	LAD	NL	3	3	2	0	0	0	(0 | 0)	2	0	0	1	0	0	0	0	0	0	0	0	-	0	.667	.667	.667
	11 ML YEARS		673	2061	523	116	6	21	(10 | 11)	714	222	202	198	96	4	199	53	34	13	21	10	.68	69	.254	.302	.346

Joselo Diaz

Pitches: R **Bats:** R **Pos:** RP-4   **Ht:** 6'0" **Wt:** 240 **Born:** 4/13/1980 **Age:** 27

			HOW MUCH HE PITCHED						WHAT HE GAVE UP										THE RESULTS						
Year	Team	Lg	G	GS	CG	GF	IP	BFP	H	R	ER	HR	SH	SF	HB	TBB	IBB	SO	WP	Bk	W	L	Pct	ShO	Sv-Op	Hld	ERC	ERA
2001	Gr Falls	R+	1	0	0	0	1.0	4	0	0	0	0	0	0	1	0	0	2	0	1	0	0	-	0	0--	-	0.95	0.00
2002	SoGA	A	19	0	0	9	25.2	124	14	12	12	1	1	2	8	25	0	33	4	0	3	1	.750	0	1--	-	4.30	4.21
2003	VeroB	A+	15	11	0	1	61.2	277	39	25	24	2	2	0	5	48	1	69	4	4	5	2	.714	0	1--	-	3.20	3.50
2003	Jaxnvl	AA	5	0	0	1	7.2	31	5	1	0	0	0	0	0	3	0	7	1	0	1	0	1.000	0	0--	-	1.65	0.00
2003	StLuci	A+	11	2	0	3	30.1	137	16	12	10	0	5	1	5	25	0	41	5	2	2	2	.500	0	0--	-	2.89	2.97
2004	Bnghtn	AA	21	19	1	0	83.1	391	84	53	48	3	3	1	12	70	0	90	5	2	4	7	.364	0	0--	-	4.08	5.18
2004	Mont	AA	7	6	0	0	30.0	150	26	19	18	4	1	2	7	27	0	37	3	0	1	3	.250	0	0--	-	6.38	5.40
2005	Mont	AA	18	0	0	9	23.2	115	22	24	24	2	1	1	4	20	0	22	4	0	2	2	.500	0	0--	-	5.97	9.13
2005	Akron	AA	8	0	0	2	15.2	52	5	0	0	0	0	0	0	3	0	19	1	0	0	0	-	0	1--	-	0.48	0.00
2005	Buffalo	AAA	20	0	0	7	34.2	156	27	19	15	4	1	3	4	26	3	44	4	0	1	2	.333	0	2--	-	4.66	3.89
2006	Okla	AAA	28	1	0	12	35.2	157	28	14	13	2	0	2	3	22	0	46	3	0	0	0	-	0	4--	-	3.71	3.28
2006	Frisco	AA	8	4	0	1	28.0	117	16	5	4	0	1	1	3	20	0	29	3	0	2	0	1.000	0	0--	-	2.73	1.29
2006	Omha	AAA	13	0	0	8	18.1	85	14	13	11	3	1	2	2	15	2	16	4	0	2	3	.400	0	0--	-	5.06	5.40
2006	KC	AL	4	0	0	1	6.2	38	10	8	8	2	0	0	1	8	0	3	2	0	0	0	-	0	0-0	0	13.68	10.80

Matt Diaz

Bats: R **Throws:** R **Pos:** LF-95; PH-46; RF-6   **Ht:** 6'1" **Wt:** 205 **Born:** 3/3/1978 **Age:** 29

							BATTING											BASERUNNING				AVERAGES		
Year	Team	Lg	G	AB	H	2B	3B	HR	(Hm | Rd)	TB	R	RBI	RC	TBB	IBB	SO	HBP	SH	SF	SB	CS	SB%	GDP	Avg	OBP	Slg
2003	TB	AL	4	9	1	0	0	0	(0 | 0)	1	2	0	0	1	0	3	0	0	0	0	0	-	0	.111	.200	.111
2004	TB	AL	10	21	4	1	1	1	(1 | 0)	10	3	3	2	1	0	6	2	0	0	0	0	-	0	.190	.292	.476
2005	KC	AL	34	89	25	4	2	1	(0 | 1)	36	7	9	11	4	0	15	2	1	1	0	1	.00	3	.281	.323	.404
2006	Atl	NL	124	297	97	15	4	7	(3 | 4)	141	37	32	40	11	3	49	9	1	4	5	5	.50	9	.327	.364	.475
	4 ML YEARS		172	416	127	20	7	9	(4 | 5)	188	49	44	53	17	3	73	13	2	5	5	6	.45	12	.305	.348	.452

Victor Diaz

Bats: R **Throws:** R **Pos:** LF-4; PH-2   **Ht:** 6'0" **Wt:** 200 **Born:** 12/10/1981 **Age:** 25

							BATTING											BASERUNNING				AVERAGES		
Year	Team	Lg	G	AB	H	2B	3B	HR	(Hm | Rd)	TB	R	RBI	RC	TBB	IBB	SO	HBP	SH	SF	SB	CS	SB%	GDP	Avg	OBP	Slg
2006	Norfolk*	AAA	103	379	85	16	0	8	(- | -)	125	30	38	34	25	2	99	3	2	2	5	5	.50	13	.224	.276	.330
2006	Okla*	AAA	3	13	5	0	0	0	(- | -)	5	1	2	2	1	0	6	0	0	1	0	0	-	0	.385	.400	.385
2004	NYM	NL	15	51	15	3	0	3	(1 | 2)	27	8	8	6	1	0	15	1	0	0	0	0	-	3	.294	.321	.529
2005	NYM	NL	89	280	72	17	3	12	(4 | 8)	131	41	38	35	30	7	82	1	0	2	6	2	.75	13	.257	.329	.468
2006	NYM	NL	6	11	2	1	0	0	(0 | 0)	3	0	2	1	0	0	5	0	0	0	0	0	-	0	.182	.182	.273
	3 ML YEARS		110	342	89	21	3	15	(5 | 10)	161	49	48	42	31	7	102	2	0	2	6	2	.75	16	.260	.324	.471

R.A. Dickey

Pitches: R **Bats:** R **Pos:** SP-1   **Ht:** 6'3" **Wt:** 220 **Born:** 10/29/1974 **Age:** 32

			HOW MUCH HE PITCHED						WHAT HE GAVE UP										THE RESULTS						
Year	Team	Lg	G	GS	CG	GF	IP	BFP	H	R	ER	HR	SH	SF	HB	TBB	IBB	SO	WP	Bk	W	L	Pct	ShO	Sv-Op	Hld	ERC	ERA
2006	Okla*	AAA	22	19	3	1	131.2	560	134	80	72	17	3	8	11	46	0	61	6	2	9	8	.529	1	1--	-	4.64	4.92
2001	Tex	AL	4	0	0	1	12.0	53	13	9	9	3	0	0	0	7	1	4	1	0	0	1	.000	0	0-0	0	6.57	6.75
2003	Tex	AL	38	13	1	6	116.2	513	135	68	66	16	4	3	5	38	5	94	5	2	9	8	.529	1	1-1	3	5.09	5.09
2004	Tex	AL	25	15	0	2	104.1	480	136	77	65	17	3	3	4	33	1	57	5	1	6	7	.462	0	1-1	0	6.08	5.61
2005	Tex	AL	9	4	0	2	29.2	134	29	23	22	4	0	1	2	17	0	15	2	0	1	2	.333	0	0-0	0	5.18	6.67
2006	Tex	AL	1	1	0	0	3.1	18	8	7	7	6	0	0	0	1	0	1	0	0	0	1	.000	0	0-0	0	32.05	18.90
	5 ML YEARS		77	33	1	11	266.0	1198	321	184	169	46	7	7	11	96	7	171	13	3	16	19	.457	1	2-2	3	5.81	5.72

Mike DiFelice

Bats: R Throws: R Pos: C-15; PH-1   Ht: 6'2" Wt: 200 Born: 5/28/1969 Age: 38

Year	Team	Lg	G	AB	H	2B	3B	HR	(Hm	Rd)	TB	R	RBI	RC	TBB	IBB	SO	HBP	SH	SF	SB	CS	SB%	GDP	Avg	OBP	Slg
2006	Brghtn*	AA	39	112	31	7	0	1	(-	-)	41	9	19	17	15	2	24	4	0	3	0	0	-	2	.277	.373	.366
2006	Norfolk*	AAA	1	2	0	0	0	0	(-	-)	0	1	0	0	1	0	0	0	0	0	0	0	-	0	.000	.333	.000
1996	StL	NL	4	7	2	1	0	0	(0	0)	3	0	2	1	0	0	1	0	0	0	0	0	-	0	.286	.286	.429
1997	StL	NL	93	260	62	10	1	4	(1	3)	86	16	30	23	19	0	61	3	6	1	1	1	.50	11	.238	.297	.331
1998	TB	AL	84	248	57	12	3	3	(1	2)	84	17	23	19	15	0	56	1	3	2	0	0	-	12	.230	.274	.339
1999	TB	AL	51	179	55	11	0	6	(5	1)	84	21	27	29	8	0	23	3	0	1	0	0	-	1	.307	.346	.469
2000	TB	AL	60	204	49	13	1	6	(4	2)	82	23	19	21	12	0	40	0	5	2	0	0	-	8	.240	.280	.402
2001	2 Tms		60	170	32	5	1	2	(0	2)	45	14	10	10	8	0	49	4	3	2	1	1	.50	3	.188	.239	.265
2002	StL	NL	70	174	40	11	0	4	(3	1)	63	17	19	17	17	3	42	1	2	3	0	0	-	4	.230	.297	.362
2003	KC	AL	62	189	48	16	1	3	(1	2)	75	29	25	26	9	0	30	4	1	2	1	0	1.00	6	.254	.299	.397
2004	2 Tms		17	25	3	0	1	0	(0	0)	5	3	2	1	3	0	4	0	0	0	0	0	-	3	.120	.214	.200
2005	NYM	NL	11	17	2	0	0	0	(0	0)	2	0	0	0	2	0	5	0	0	1	0	0	-	1	.118	.211	.118
2006	NYM	NL	15	25	2	1	0	0	(0	0)	3	3	1	1	5	0	10	0	0	0	0	0	-	0	.080	.233	.120
01	TB	AL	48	149	31	5	1	2	(0	2)	44	13	9	10	8	0	39	3	2	2	1	1	.50	3	.208	.259	.295
01	Ari	NL	12	21	1	0	0	0	(0	0)	1	1	1	0	0	0	10	1	1	0	0	0	-	0	.048	.091	.048
04	Det	AL	13	22	3	0	1	0	(0	0)	5	3	2	1	3	0	3	0	0	0	0	0	-	3	.136	.240	.227
04	ChC	NL	4	3	0	0	0	0	(0	0)	0	0	0	0	0	0	1	0	0	0	0	0	-	0	.000	.000	.000
11 ML YEARS			527	1498	352	80	8	28	(15	13)	532	143	158	148	98	3	321	16	20	13	3	2	.60	49	.235	.287	.355

Lenny DiNardo

Pitches: L Bats: L Pos: RP-7; SP-6   Ht: 6'4" Wt: 190 Born: 9/19/1979 Age: 27

Year	Team	Lg	G	GS	CG	GF	IP	BFP	H	R	ER	HR	SH	SF	HB	TBB	IBB	SO	WP	Bk	W	L	Pct	ShO	Sv-Op	Hld	ERC	ERA
2006	RedSx*	R	2	2	0	0	4.2	17	2	1	0	0	0	0	0	0	0	4	0	0	0	0	-	0	0--	-	0.38	0.00
2006	PortInd*	AA	1	1	0	0	2.0	14	7	7	7	2	0	0	0	2	0	2	0	0	0	1	.000	0	0--	-	39.43	31.50
2006	Pwtckt*	AAA	2	2	0	0	3.0	15	5	4	4	1	0	0	0	1	0	2	0	0	0	0	-	0	0--	-	9.75	12.00
2004	Bos	AL	22	0	0	6	27.2	130	34	17	13	1	1	1	2	12	1	21	1	0	0	0	-	0	0-0	0	5.17	4.23
2005	Bos	AL	8	1	0	3	14.2	62	13	6	3	1	1	1	0	5	1	15	1	0	0	0	.000	0	0-0	0	2.86	1.84
2006	Bos	AL	13	6	0	0	39.0	190	61	35	34	6	0	1	1	20	1	17	1	0	1	2	.333	0	0-0	1	8.80	7.85
3 ML YEARS			43	7	0	9	81.1	382	108	58	50	8	2	3	3	37	3	53	3	0	1	3	.250	0	0-0	1	6.34	5.53

Greg Dobbs

Bats: L Throws: R Pos: PH-18; 1B-3; RF-3; DH-3; 3B-2   Ht: 6'1" Wt: 205 Born: 7/2/1978 Age: 28

Year	Team	Lg	G	AB	H	2B	3B	HR	(Hm	Rd)	TB	R	RBI	RC	TBB	IBB	SO	HBP	SH	SF	SB	CS	SB%	GDP	Avg	OBP	Slg
2006	Tacom*	AAA	99	379	119	19	3	9	(-	-)	171	60	55	66	37	5	58	2	0	3	14	5	.74	10	.314	.375	.451
2004	Sea	AL	18	53	12	1	0	1	(1	0)	16	4	9	5	1	0	14	1	0	1	0	0	-	0	.226	.250	.302
2005	Sea	AL	59	142	35	7	1	1	(0	1)	47	8	20	16	9	3	25	0	1	2	1	0	1.00	4	.246	.288	.331
2006	Sea	AL	23	27	10	3	1	0	(0	0)	15	4	3	5	0	0	4	1	0	0	0	1	.00	0	.370	.393	.556
3 ML YEARS			100	222	57	11	2	2	(1	1)	78	16	32	26	10	3	43	2	1	3	1	1	.50	4	.257	.291	.351

Scott Dohmann

Pitches: R Bats: R Pos: RP-48   Ht: 6'1" Wt: 200 Born: 2/13/1978 Age: 29

Year	Team	Lg	G	GS	CG	GF	IP	BFP	H	R	ER	HR	SH	SF	HB	TBB	IBB	SO	WP	Bk	W	L	Pct	ShO	Sv-Op	Hld	ERC	ERA
2006	Mdest*	A+	3	3	0	0	4.0	16	2	1	1	0	0	0	1	2	0	5	0	0	0	1	.000	0	0--	-	2.19	2.25
2006	ColSpr*	AAA	10	0	0	2	10.2	39	6	3	3	2	0	0	0	1	0	12	0	0	0	0	-	0	1--	-	1.38	2.53
2004	Col	NL	41	0	0	13	46.0	198	41	22	21	8	2	3	0	19	0	49	3	0	0	3	.000	0	0-4	4	3.94	4.11
2005	Col	NL	32	0	0	10	31.0	143	33	21	21	6	0	0	0	19	1	35	0	0	2	1	.667	0	0-3	7	5.94	6.10
2006	2 Tms		48	0	0	18	48.1	231	59	39	38	9	4	0	4	33	7	44	5	0	2	4	.333	0	1-3	6	7.54	7.08
06	Col	NL	27	0	0	9	24.2	114	26	18	17	4	2	0	2	15	2	22	2	0	1	1	.500	0	1-2	3	5.94	6.20
06	KC	AL	21	0	0	9	23.2	117	33	21	21	5	2	0	2	18	5	22	3	0	1	3	.250	0	0-1	3	9.34	7.99
3 ML YEARS			121	0	0	41	125.1	572	133	82	80	23	6	3	4	71	8	128	8	0	4	8	.333	0	1-10	17	5.77	5.74

Brendan Donnelly

Pitches: R Bats: R Pos: RP-62   Ht: 6'3" Wt: 240 Born: 7/4/1971 Age: 35

Year	Team	Lg	G	GS	CG	GF	IP	BFP	H	R	ER	HR	SH	SF	HB	TBB	IBB	SO	WP	Bk	W	L	Pct	ShO	Sv-Op	Hld	ERC	ERA
2002	LAA	AL	46	0	0	11	49.2	199	32	13	12	2	3	1	2	19	3	54	1	0	1	1	.500	0	1-3	13	1.89	2.17
2003	LAA	AL	63	0	0	15	74.0	307	55	14	13	2	3	1	4	24	1	79	1	0	2	2	.500	0	3-5	29	2.12	1.58
2004	LAA	AL	40	0	0	10	42.0	172	34	14	14	5	2	2	1	15	0	56	0	0	5	2	.714	0	0-0	5	3.12	3.00
2005	LAA	AL	66	0	0	14	65.1	271	60	30	27	9	3	1	2	19	3	53	3	0	9	3	.750	0	0-5	16	3.52	3.72
2006	LAA	AL	62	0	0	17	64.0	278	58	32	28	8	2	2	4	28	3	53	6	0	6	0	1.000	0	0-1	11	4.02	3.94
5 ML YEARS			277	0	0	67	295.0	1227	239	103	94	26	13	7	13	105	10	295	11	0	23	8	.742	0	4-14	74	2.91	2.87

Melvin Dorta

Bats: R Throws: R Pos: PR-6; PH-5; 3B-3; SS-3   Ht: 5'11" Wt: 160 Born: 1/15/1982 Age: 25

Year	Team	Lg	G	AB	H	2B	3B	HR	(Hm	Rd)	TB	R	RBI	RC	TBB	IBB	SO	HBP	SH	SF	SB	CS	SB%	GDP	Avg	OBP	Slg
2001	RedSx	R	21	76	31	6	0	2	(-	-)	43	19	8	20	11	0	5	1	0	0	7	3	.70	0	.408	.489	.566
2001	Augsta	A	36	135	36	4	1	0	(-	-)	42	19	18	13	8	0	16	3	1	1	6	5	.55	2	.267	.320	.311
2002	Srsota	A+	99	378	97	8	1	0	(-	-)	107	46	31	41	49	0	54	3	7	6	9	10	.47	7	.257	.342	.283

Year	Team	Lg	G	AB	H	2B	3B	HR	(Hm	Rd)	TB	R	RBI	RC	TBB	IBB	SO	HBP	SH	SF	SB	CS	SB%	GDP	Avg	OBP	Slg
									BATTING												BASERUNNING				AVERAGES		
2003	Srsota	A+	93	324	70	7	1	0	(-	-)	79	36	27	25	28	0	46	7	9	6	20	9	.69	9	.216	.288	.244
2004	Hrsbrg	AA	72	226	59	11	2	0	(-	-)	74	20	22	25	15	3	24	2	4	2	12	4	.75	6	.261	.310	.327
2005	Hrsbrg	AA	121	408	103	16	0	11	(-	-)	152	56	50	50	35	1	46	3	11	3	22	13	.63	6	.252	.314	.373
2006	Hrsbrg	AA	108	404	104	15	3	5	(-	-)	140	54	30	47	30	1	34	0	5	3	33	10	.77	6	.257	.307	.347
2006	NewOr	AAA	8	30	13	1	0	1	(-	-)	17	6	3	6	1	0	2	0	2	1	3	2	.60	1	.433	.438	.567
2006	Was	NL	15	19	4	1	0	0	(0	0)	5	3	0	0	1	0	2	0	0	0	0	0	.00	0	.211	.250	.263

Octavio Dotel

Pitches: R **Bats:** R **Pos:** RP-14   **Ht:** 6'0" **Wt:** 210 **Born:** 11/25/1973 **Age:** 33

Year	Team	Lg	G	GS	CG	GF	IP	BFP	H	R	ER	HR	SH	SF	HB	TBB	IBB	SO	WP	Bk	W	L	Pct	ShO	Sv-Op	Hld	ERC	ERA
					HOW MUCH HE PITCHED								WHAT HE GAVE UP											THE RESULTS			
2006	Yanks*	R	3	2	0	0	3.0	12	0	0	0	0	0	0	1	1	0	6	0	0	0	0	-	0	0- -	-	0.42	0.00
2006	StlsInd*	A-	1	0	0	0	1.0	5	2	0	0	0	0	0	0	0	0	1	0	0	0	0	-	0	0- -	-	7.48	0.00
2006	Tampa*	A	2	1	0	0	2.0	7	1	0	0	0	1	0	0	0	0	2	1	0	0	0	-	0	0- -	-	0.54	0.00
2006	Trntn*	AA	2	0	0	0	2.0	7	1	0	0	0	1	0	0	0	0	3	0	0	0	0	-	0	0- -	-	0.54	0.00
2006	Clmbs*	AAA	5	0	0	0	5.1	22	6	2	2	1	0	0	1	0	0	8	0	0	0	0	-	0	0- -	-	4.65	3.38
1999	NYM	NL	19	14	0	1	85.1	368	69	52	51	12	3	5	6	49	1	85	3	2	8	3	.727	0	0-0	0	4.30	5.38
2000	Hou	NL	50	16	0	25	125.0	563	127	80	75	26	7	8	7	61	3	142	6	0	3	7	.300	0	16-23	0	5.47	5.40
2001	Hou	NL	61	4	0	20	105.0	438	79	35	31	5	2	2	2	47	2	145	4	0	7	5	.583	0	2-4	14	2.62	2.66
2002	Hou	NL	83	0	0	22	97.1	376	58	21	20	7	3	7	4	27	2	118	2	0	6	4	.600	0	6-10	31	1.61	1.85
2003	Hou	NL	76	0	0	13	87.0	346	53	25	24	9	2	1	3	31	2	97	2	0	6	4	.600	0	4-6	33	2.02	2.48
2004	2 Tms		77	0	0	70	85.1	356	68	38	35	13	4	2	4	33	7	122	4	1	6	6	.500	0	36-45	0	3.31	3.69
2005	Oak	AL	15	0	0	13	15.1	65	10	6	6	2	0	0	0	11	2	16	1	0	1	2	.333	0	7-11	0	3.44	3.52
2006	NYY	AL	14	0	0	7	10.0	59	18	13	12	2	0	1	0	11	1	7	3	0	0	0	-	0	0-0	1	12.97	10.80
04	Hou	NL	32	0	0	29	34.2	146	27	15	12	4	2	1	1	15	4	50	3	1	0	4	.000	0	14-17	0	3.01	3.12
04	Oak	AL	45	0	0	41	50.2	210	41	23	23	9	2	1	3	18	3	72	1	0	6	2	.750	0	22-28	0	3.52	4.09
	8 ML YEARS		395	34	0	171	610.1	2571	482	270	254	76	21	26	26	270	20	732	25	3	37	31	.544	0	71-99	79	3.36	3.75

Ryan Doumit

Bats: B **Throws:** R **Pos:** 1B-28; PH-20; C-11; DH-3   **Ht:** 6'1" **Wt:** 215 **Born:** 4/3/1981 **Age:** 26

Year	Team	Lg	G	AB	H	2B	3B	HR	(Hm	Rd)	TB	R	RBI	RC	TBB	IBB	SO	HBP	SH	SF	SB	CS	SB%	GDP	Avg	OBP	Slg
									BATTING												BASERUNNING				AVERAGES		
1999	Bradtn	R	29	85	24	5	0	1	(-	-)	32	17	7	15	15	0	14	4	0	1	4	2	.67	0	.282	.410	.376
2000	Wmspt	A-	66	246	77	15	5	2	(-	-)	108	25	40	42	23	1	33	4	0	7	2	2	.50	7	.313	.371	.439
2001	Hickory	A	39	148	40	6	0	2	(-	-)	52	14	14	18	10	0	32	4	0	0	2	1	.67	2	.270	.323	.351
2001	Bradtn	R	7	17	4	2	0	0	(-	-)	6	2	3	2	2	1	0	0	0	0	0	0	-	0	.235	.316	.353
2001	Altna	AA	2	4	1	0	0	0	(-	-)	1	0	2	0	1	0	1	0	0	0	0	0	-	0	.250	.400	.250
2002	Hickory	A	68	258	83	14	1	6	(-	-)	117	46	47	44	18	0	40	8	2	5	3	5	.38	6	.322	.377	.453
2003	Lynbrg	A+	127	458	126	38	1	11	(-	-)	199	75	77	75	45	3	79	13	0	8	4	0	1.00	7	.275	.351	.434
2004	Altna	AA	67	221	58	20	0	10	(-	-)	108	31	34	38	21	2	49	8	1	4	0	1	.00	4	.262	.343	.489
2005	Indy	AAA	51	165	57	11	0	12	(-	-)	104	41	35	40	16	3	36	5	0	2	1	3	.25	3	.345	.415	.630
2006	Pirates	R	5	14	0	0	0	0	(-	-)	0	1	0	0	1	0	4	1	0	0	0	0	-	0	.000	.125	.000
2006	Altna	AA	4	15	5	3	0	0	(-	-)	8	4	4	3	0	0	1	2	0	0	0	0	-	0	.333	.412	.533
2006	Indy	AAA	6	22	7	1	1	0	(-	-)	10	3	7	3	2	0	4	0	0	0	0	0	-	0	.318	.375	.455
2005	Pit	NL	75	231	59	13	1	6	(4	2)	92	25	35	32	11	1	48	13	1	1	2	1	.67	5	.255	.324	.398
2006	Pit	NL	61	149	31	9	0	6	(3	3)	58	15	17	17	15	1	42	11	1	2	0	0	-	3	.208	.322	.389
	2 ML YEARS		136	380	90	22	1	12	(7	5)	150	40	52	49	26	2	90	24	2	3	2	1	.67	8	.237	.323	.395

Scott Downs

Pitches: L **Bats:** L **Pos:** RP-54; SP-5   **Ht:** 6'2" **Wt:** 190 **Born:** 3/17/1976 **Age:** 31

Year	Team	Lg	G	GS	CG	GF	IP	BFP	H	R	ER	HR	SH	SF	HB	TBB	IBB	SO	WP	Bk	W	L	Pct	ShO	Sv-Op	Hld	ERC	ERA
					HOW MUCH HE PITCHED								WHAT HE GAVE UP											THE RESULTS			
2000	2 Tms	NL	19	19	0	0	97.0	442	122	62	57	13	2	4	5	40	1	63	1	0	4	3	.571	0	0-0	0	6.19	5.29
2003	Mon	NL	1	1	0	0	3.0	17	5	5	5	2	0	0	0	3	2	4	0	0	0	1	.000	0	0-0	0	15.01	15.00
2004	Mon	NL	12	12	1	0	63.0	284	79	47	36	9	2	1	3	23	2	38	2	0	3	6	.333	1	0-0	0	5.97	5.14
2005	Tor	AL	26	13	0	0	94.0	407	93	49	45	12	0	1	5	34	0	75	3	0	4	3	.571	0	0-0	0	4.25	4.31
2006	Tor	AL	59	5	0	13	77.0	327	73	38	35	9	1	1	2	30	6	61	7	0	6	2	.750	0	1-4	6	3.87	4.09
00	ChC	NL	18	18	0	0	94.0	426	117	59	54	13	2	4	5	37	1	63	1	0	4	3	.571	0	0-0	0	6.07	5.17
00	Mon	NL	1	1	0	0	3.0	16	5	3	3	0	0	0	0	3	0	0	0	0	0	0	-	0	0-0	0	10.34	9.00
	5 ML YEARS		117	50	1	13	334.0	1477	372	201	178	45	5	7	15	130	11	241	13	1	17	15	.531	1	1-4	6	5.10	4.80

Ryan Drese

Pitches: R **Bats:** R **Pos:** SP-2   **Ht:** 6'3" **Wt:** 235 **Born:** 4/5/1976 **Age:** 31

Year	Team	Lg	G	GS	CG	GF	IP	BFP	H	R	ER	HR	SH	SF	HB	TBB	IBB	SO	WP	Bk	W	L	Pct	ShO	Sv-Op	Hld	ERC	ERA
					HOW MUCH HE PITCHED								WHAT HE GAVE UP											THE RESULTS			
2006	Hrsbrg*	AA	3	3	0	0	9.1	45	11	7	4	1	0	2	1	6	1	4	1	0	0	2	.000	0	0- -	-	6.42	3.86
2001	Cle	AL	9	4	0	2	36.2	149	32	15	14	2	1	0	1	15	2	24	0	0	1	2	.333	0	0-0	0	3.27	3.44
2002	Cle	AL	26	26	1	0	137.1	635	176	104	100	15	3	9	6	62	1	102	11	0	10	9	.526	0	0-0	0	6.26	6.55
2003	Tex	AL	11	8	0	0	46.0	223	61	42	35	8	0	5	3	24	1	26	2	0	2	4	.333	0	0-1	1	7.60	6.85
2004	Tex	AL	34	33	2	1	207.2	897	233	104	97	16	6	5	11	58	6	98	1	0	14	10	.583	0	0-0	0	4.32	4.20
2005	2 Tms	NL	23	23	1	0	129.1	583	162	90	83	8	4	5	8	46	2	46	4	0	7	12	.368	0	0-0	0	5.36	5.78
2006	Was	NL	2	2	0	0	8.2	41	9	8	5	0	2	0	0	8	0	5	2	0	0	2	.000	0	0-0	0	5.70	5.19
05	Tex	AL	12	12	1	0	69.2	317	96	52	50	5	2	1	3	24	1	20	1	0	4	6	.400	0	0-0	0	6.16	6.46
05	Was	NL	11	11	0	0	59.2	266	66	38	33	3	2	4	5	22	1	26	3	0	3	6	.333	0	0-0	0	4.48	4.98
	6 ML YEARS		105	96	4	3	565.2	2528	673	363	334	49	16	19	31	213	12	301	20	0	34	39	.466	0	0-0	1	5.22	5.31

J.D. Drew

Bats: L Throws: R Pos: RF-135; PH-10; DH-4   Ht: 6'1" Wt: 200 Born: 11/20/1975 Age: 31

Year	Team	Lg	G	AB	H	2B	3B	HR	(Hm	Rd)	TB	R	RBI	RC	TBB	IBB	SO	HBP	SH	SF	SB	CS	SB%	GDP	Avg	OBP	Slg
1998	StL	NL	14	36	15	3	1	5	(4	1)	35	9	13	12	4	0	10	0	0	1	0	0	-	4	.417	.463	.972
1999	StL	NL	104	368	89	16	6	13	(5	8)	156	72	39	58	50	0	77	6	3	3	19	3	.86	4	.242	.340	.424
2000	StL	NL	135	407	120	17	2	18	(11	7)	195	73	57	80	67	4	99	6	5	1	17	9	.65	3	.295	.401	.479
2001	StL	NL	109	375	121	18	5	27	(15	12)	230	80	73	92	57	4	75	4	3	4	13	3	.81	6	.323	.414	.613
2002	StL	NL	135	424	107	19	1	18	(9	9)	182	61	56	65	57	4	104	8	3	4	8	2	.80	4	.252	.349	.429
2003	StL	NL	100	287	83	13	3	15	(7	8)	147	60	42	58	36	0	48	3	2	0	2	2	.50	6	.289	.374	.512
2004	Atl	NL	145	518	158	28	8	31	(14	17)	295	118	93	121	118	2	116	5	1	3	12	3	.80	7	.305	.436	.569
2005	LAD	NL	72	252	72	12	1	15	(10	5)	131	48	36	49	51	3	50	5	0	3	1	1	.50	3	.286	.412	.520
2006	LAD	NL	146	494	140	34	6	20	(12	8)	246	84	100	92	89	8	106	4	1	6	2	3	.40	4	.283	.393	.498
9 ML YEARS			960	3161	905	160	33	162	(87	75)	1617	605	509	627	529	25	685	41	18	25	74	26	.74	41	.286	.393	.512

Stephen Drew

Bats: L Throws: R Pos: SS-56; PH-6   Ht: 6'1" Wt: 185 Born: 3/16/1983 Age: 24

Year	Team	Lg	G	AB	H	2B	3B	HR	(Hm	Rd)	TB	R	RBI	RC	TBB	IBB	SO	HBP	SH	SF	SB	CS	SB%	GDP	Avg	OBP	Slg
2005	Lancst	A+	38	149	58	16	3	10	(-	-)	110	33	39	47	26	2	25	2	0	0	1	1	.50	1	.389	.486	.738
2005	Tenn	AA	27	101	22	5	0	4	(-	-)	39	11	13	11	12	0	24	0	0	0	2	3	.40	1	.218	.301	.386
2006	Tucsn	AAA	83	342	97	16	3	13	(-	-)	158	55	51	55	33	2	50	0	1	7	3	3	.50	7	.284	.340	.462
2006	Ari	NL	59	209	66	13	7	5	(3	2)	108	27	23	31	14	4	50	0	2	1	2	0	1.00	1	.316	.357	.517

Eric DuBose

Pitches: L Bats: L Pos: RP-2   Ht: 6'3" Wt: 235 Born: 5/15/1976 Age: 31

Year	Team	Lg	G	GS	CG	GF	IP	BFP	H	R	ER	HR	SH	SF	HB	TBB	IBB	SO	WP	Bk	W	L	Pct	ShO	Sv-Op	Hld	ERC	ERA
2006	Bowie*	AA	20	11	2	3	84.0	346	70	33	29	7	3	2	2	34	1	67	2	0	7	1	.875	2	0--	-	3.21	3.11
2006	Ottawa*	AAA	8	8	0	0	39.0	176	44	26	24	3	3	0	0	23	1	30	3	0	3	4	.429	0	0--	-	5.48	5.54
2002	Bal	AL	4	0	0	2	6.0	25	7	2	2	1	0	0	1	1	0	4	0	0	0	0	-	0	0-0	-	5.59	3.00
2003	Bal	AL	17	10	1	3	73.2	305	60	33	31	6	2	3	5	25	2	44	0	1	3	6	.333	0	0-1	1	2.95	3.79
2004	Bal	AL	14	14	0	0	74.2	338	76	55	53	12	1	1	3	44	0	48	5	1	4	6	.400	0	0-0	0	5.60	6.39
2005	Bal	AL	15	3	0	2	29.1	135	28	21	18	4	0	0	1	19	0	17	1	0	2	3	.400	0	0-0	3	5.14	5.52
2006	Bal	AL	2	0	0	0	4.2	23	10	5	5	2	0	0	0	3	0	2	0	0	0	0	-	0	0-0	0	18.77	9.64
5 ML YEARS			52	27	1	7	188.1	826	181	116	109	25	3	4	10	92	2	115	6	2	9	15	.375	0	0-1	4	4.67	5.21

Justin Duchscherer

Pitches: R Bats: R Pos: RP-53   Ht: 6'3" Wt: 200 Born: 11/19/1977 Age: 29

Year	Team	Lg	G	GS	CG	GF	IP	BFP	H	R	ER	HR	SH	SF	HB	TBB	IBB	SO	WP	Bk	W	L	Pct	ShO	Sv-Op	Hld	ERC	ERA
2006	Scrmto*	AAA	2	1	0	0	2.0	7	2	0	0	0	0	0	0	0	0	1	0	0	0	0	-	0	0--	-	2.31	0.00
2001	Tex	AL	5	2	0	1	14.2	76	24	20	20	5	0	0	4	4	0	11	1	0	1	1	.500	0	0-0	0	10.68	12.27
2003	Oak	AL	4	3	0	0	16.1	71	17	7	6	1	1	0	2	3	0	15	0	0	1	1	.500	0	0-0	0	3.58	3.31
2004	Oak	AL	53	0	0	18	96.1	398	85	37	35	13	7	1	5	32	6	59	1	1	7	6	.538	0	0-2	6	3.57	3.27
2005	Oak	AL	65	0	0	24	85.2	338	67	25	21	7	4	2	2	19	3	85	2	0	7	4	.636	0	5-7	10	2.23	2.21
2006	Oak	AL	53	0	0	17	55.2	224	52	18	18	4	1	0	1	9	0	51	3	0	2	1	.667	0	9-11	17	2.73	2.91
5 ML YEARS			180	5	0	60	268.2	1107	245	107	100	30	13	3	14	67	9	221	7	1	18	13	.581	0	14-20	33	3.26	3.35

Brandon Duckworth

Pitches: R Bats: R Pos: SP-8; RP-2   Ht: 6'1" Wt: 215 Born: 1/23/1976 Age: 31

Year	Team	Lg	G	GS	CG	GF	IP	BFP	H	R	ER	HR	SH	SF	HB	TBB	IBB	SO	WP	Bk	W	L	Pct	ShO	Sv-Op	Hld	ERC	ERA
2006	Indy*	AAA	12	12	0	0	74.1	306	67	23	20	4	1	2	3	23	1	57	4	0	8	3	.727	0	0--	-	3.07	2.42
2001	Phi	NL	11	11	0	0	69.0	289	57	29	27	2	7	3	6	29	5	40	2	0	3	2	.600	0	0-0	0	2.98	3.52
2002	Phi	NL	30	29	0	0	163.0	725	167	103	98	26	7	3	7	69	5	167	10	0	8	9	.471	0	0-0	0	4.80	5.41
2003	Phi	NL	24	18	0	2	93.0	398	98	58	51	12	9	1	10	44	3	68	5	0	4	7	.364	0	0-0	0	5.25	4.94
2004	Hou	NL	19	6	0	6	39.1	180	55	30	30	11	3	1	0	13	3	23	3	0	1	2	.333	0	0-0	0	7.56	6.86
2005	Hou	NL	7	2	0	1	16.1	82	24	20	20	4	0	1	5	7	1	10	0	0	0	1	.000	0	0-0	0	9.78	11.02
2006	KC	AL	10	8	0	0	45.2	216	62	36	31	3	1	2	2	24	4	27	4	0	1	5	.167	0	0-0	0	6.58	6.11
6 ML YEARS			101	74	0	9	426.1	1916	463	276	257	58	27	11	30	186	21	335	24	0	17	26	.395	0	0-0	0	5.19	5.43

Chris Duffy

Bats: L Throws: L Pos: CF-77; PH-6; PR-2   Ht: 5'9" Wt: 190 Born: 4/20/1980 Age: 27

Year	Team	Lg	G	AB	H	2B	3B	HR	(Hm	Rd)	TB	R	RBI	RC	TBB	IBB	SO	HBP	SH	SF	SB	CS	SB%	GDP	Avg	OBP	Slg
2001	Wmspt	A-	64	218	70	12	4	1	(-	-)	93	47	23	49	32	1	33	17	4	2	29	5	.85	0	.321	.442	.427
2002	Lynbrg	A+	132	539	162	27	5	10	(-	-)	229	85	52	85	33	1	101	12	10	3	22	7	.76	1	.301	.353	.425
2003	Altna	AA	137	494	135	23	6	1	(-	-)	173	84	42	46	44	6	78	20	8	3	34	12	.74	7	.273	.355	.350
2004	Altna	AA	113	453	140	23	6	8	(-	-)	199	84	41	80	33	2	77	17	6	0	30	8	.79	4	.309	.378	.439
2005	Indy	AAA	78	308	95	13	7	7	(-	-)	143	55	31	52	16	1	57	10	2	4	17	9	.65	4	.308	.358	.464
2006	Indy	AAA	26	106	37	7	2	2	(-	-)	54	18	19	23	10	0	13	2	0	0	13	3	.81	2	.349	.415	.509
2005	Pit	NL	39	126	43	4	2	1	(0	1)	54	22	9	22	7	0	22	2	1	2	22	2	.50	1	.341	.385	.429
2006	Pit	NL	84	314	80	14	3	2	(0	2)	106	46	18	36	19	1	71	10	4	1	26	1	.96	1	.255	.317	.338
2 ML YEARS			123	440	123	18	5	3	(0	3)	160	68	27	58	26	1	93	12	5	2	28	3	.90	2	.280	.336	.364

Zach Duke

Pitches: L Bats: L Pos: SP-34   Ht: 6'2" Wt: 220 Born: 4/19/1983 Age: 24

			HOW MUCH HE PITCHED						WHAT HE GAVE UP									THE RESULTS							
Year	Team	Lg	G	GS	CG	GF	IP	BFP	H	R	ER	HR	SH	SF	HB	TBB	IBB	SO	WP	Bk	W	L	Pct	ShO	Sv-Op	Hld	ERC	ERA
2002	Bradtn	R	11	11	1	0	60.0	236	38	15	13	2	1	1	4	18	0	48	1	0	8	1	.889	1	0--	-	1.71	1.95
2003	Hickory	A	26	26	1	0	141.2	595	124	66	49	7	0	1	5	46	0	113	2	2	8	7	.533	1	0--	-	2.88	3.11
2004	Lynbrg	A+	17	17	1	0	97.0	384	73	24	15	3	8	2	5	20	1	106	1	0	10	5	.667	0	0--	-	1.86	1.39
2004	Altna	AA	9	9	0	0	51.1	205	41	11	9	2	6	2	1	10	0	36	1	1	5	1	.833	0	0--	-	1.97	1.58
2005	Indy	AAA	16	16	1	0	108.0	455	108	39	35	8	5	1	2	23	1	66	1	2	12	3	.800	0	0--	-	3.18	2.92
2005	Pit	NL	14	14	0	0	84.2	341	79	20	17	3	3	1	2	23	2	58	1	0	8	2	.800	0	0-0	0	2.96	1.81
2006	Pit	NL	34	34	2	0	215.1	935	**255**	116	107	17	13	4	7	68	6	117	8	1	10	15	.400	1	0-0	0	4.82	4.47
	2 ML YEARS		48	48	2	0	300.0	1276	334	136	124	20	16	5	9	91	8	175	9	1	18	17	.514	1	0-0	0	4.27	3.72

Chris Duncan

Bats: L Throws: R Pos: LF-49; RF-24; PH-19; 1B-11; DH-1   Ht: 6'5" Wt: 210 Born: 5/5/1981 Age: 26

			BATTING																	BASERUNNING				AVERAGES		
Year	Team	Lg	G	AB	H	2B	3B	HR	(Hm	Rd)	TB	R	RBI	RC	TBB	IBB	SO	HBP	SH	SF	SB	CS	SB%	GDP	Avg	OBP	Slg
1999	JhsCty	R+	55	201	43	8	1	6	(-	-)	71	23	34	23	25	0	62	1	0	3	3	1	.75	4	.214	.300	.353
2000	Peoria	A	122	450	115	34	0	8	(-	-)	173	52	57	56	36	1	111	6	1	0	1	2	.33	11	.256	.319	.384
2001	Ptomc	A+	49	168	30	6	0	3	(-	-)	45	12	16	8	10	0	47	1	1	0	4	4	.50	5	.179	.229	.268
2001	Peoria	A	80	297	91	23	2	13	(-	-)	157	44	59	62	36	2	55	3	0	1	13	3	.81	10	.306	.386	.529
2002	Peoria	A	129	487	132	25	4	16	(-	-)	213	58	75	73	44	4	118	7	1	5	5	5	.50	8	.271	.337	.437
2003	PlmBh	A+	121	425	108	20	0	2	(-	-)	134	26	42	46	44	1	115	1	1	5	4	4	.50	12	.254	.322	.315
2003	Tenn	AA	10	25	5	1	0	1	(-	-)	9	1	3	1	0	0	6	0	0	0	0	0	-	1	.200	.200	.360
2004	Tenn	AA	120	387	112	23	0	16	(-	-)	183	57	65	75	64	8	94	3	0	1	8	4	.67	6	.289	.393	.473
2005	Memp	AAA	128	431	114	21	2	21	(-	-)	202	57	73	75	63	3	104	2	0	4	1	3	.25	14	.265	.358	.469
2006	Memp	AAA	52	181	49	11	0	7	(-	-)	81	23	31	29	25	2	53	0	0	0	1	2	.33	5	.271	.359	.448
2005	StL	NL	9	10	2	1	0	1	(1	0)	6	2	3	1	0	0	5	0	0	1	0	0	-	1	.200	.200	.600
2006	StL	NL	90	280	82	11	3	22	(9	13)	165	60	43	47	30	0	69	2	0	2	0	0	-	4	.293	.363	.589
	2 ML YEARS		99	290	84	12	3	23	(10	13)	171	62	46	48	30	0	74	2	0	2	0	0	-	5	.290	.358	.590

Adam Dunn

Bats: L Throws: R Pos: LF-156; 1B-2; DH-1; PH-1   Ht: 6'6" Wt: 275 Born: 11/9/1979 Age: 27

			BATTING																	BASERUNNING				AVERAGES		
Year	Team	Lg	G	AB	H	2B	3B	HR	(Hm	Rd)	TB	R	RBI	RC	TBB	IBB	SO	HBP	SH	SF	SB	CS	SB%	GDP	Avg	OBP	Slg
2001	Cin	NL	66	244	64	18	1	19	(8	11)	141	54	43	51	38	2	74	4	0	0	4	2	.67	4	.262	.371	.578
2002	Cin	NL	158	535	133	28	2	26	(13	13)	243	84	71	96	128	13	170	9	1	3	19	9	.68	8	.249	.400	.454
2003	Cin	NL	116	381	82	12	1	27	(16	11)	177	70	57	61	74	8	126	10	0	4	8	2	.80	4	.215	.354	.465
2004	Cin	NL	161	568	151	34	0	46	(25	21)	323	105	102	108	108	11	**195**	5	0	0	6	1	.86	8	.266	.388	.569
2005	Cin	NL	160	543	134	35	2	40	(**26**	14)	293	107	101	112	114	14	**168**	12	0	2	4	2	.67	6	.247	.387	.540
2006	Cin	NL	160	561	131	24	0	40	(22	18)	275	99	92	96	112	12	**194**	6	1	3	7	0	1.00	8	.234	.365	.490
	6 ML YEARS		821	2832	695	151	6	198	(110	88)	1452	519	466	524	574	60	927	46	2	12	48	16	.75	38	.245	.380	.513

Scott Dunn

Pitches: R Bats: R Pos: RP-7   Ht: 6'3" Wt: 200 Born: 5/23/1978 Age: 29

			HOW MUCH HE PITCHED						WHAT HE GAVE UP									THE RESULTS							
Year	Team	Lg	G	GS	CG	GF	IP	BFP	H	R	ER	HR	SH	SF	HB	TBB	IBB	SO	WP	Bk	W	L	Pct	ShO	Sv-Op	Hld	ERC	ERA
1999	Billings	R+	9	8	0	0	39.2	178	36	24	19	3	0	1	3	24	0	36	3	2	1	3	.250	0	0--	-	4.47	4.31
2000	Clinton	A	26	26	2	0	147.2	638	123	78	65	9	2	3	4	89	1	159	20	0	11	3	.786	1	0--	-	3.79	3.96
2001	Mudvle	A+	10	10	1	0	59.2	248	45	17	14	2	0	0	1	31	0	73	4	0	5	3	.625	1	0--	-	2.86	2.11
2001	Chatt	AA	17	17	0	0	98.1	450	96	51	45	10	8	2	2	71	0	87	8	0	7	2	.778	0	0--	-	5.37	4.12
2002	Chatt	AA	37	12	0	11	110.1	470	99	57	48	10	4	3	5	54	3	114	6	0	5	7	.417	0	1--	-	4.00	3.92
2003	Chatt	AA	31	0	0	17	40.1	166	31	21	17	3	2	1	0	16	2	54	6	0	3	2	.600	0	8--	-	2.59	3.79
2003	Brham	AA	8	0	0	5	10.2	45	8	2	2	0	1	0	0	5	2	14	0	0	3	1	.750	0	1--	-	2.15	1.69
2003	Ark	AA	3	0	0	2	5.0	16	2	0	0	0	0	0	0	0	0	7	1	0	1	0	1.000	0	-	-	0.38	0.00
2003	Salt Lk	AAA	6	0	0	0	7.2	43	9	10	10	1	0	0	0	10	0	11	1	0	0	0	-	0	0--	-	8.83	11.74
2004	Salt Lk	AAA	46	6	0	9	89.2	393	72	36	32	6	1	3	3	56	0	84	4	0	10	4	.714	0	4--	-	3.73	3.21
2005	Salt Lk	AAA	47	6	0	29	92.0	400	83	44	39	7	6	0	2	41	1	98	4	0	5	7	.417	0	9--	-	3.55	3.82
2006	Drham	AAA	38	1	0	9	66.0	281	57	21	20	2	2	0	1	28	0	70	13	0	4	2	.667	0	-	-	2.98	2.73
2004	LAA	AL	3	0	0	1	3.0	17	7	3	3	0	0	0	0	1	0	2	1	0	0	0	-	0	0-0	0	11.27	9.00
2006	TB	AL	7	0	0	0	7.2	45	17	10	10	2	0	0	2	4	0	4	3	0	1	0	1.000	0	0-1	2	15.78	11.74
	2 ML YEARS		10	0	0	1	10.2	62	24	13	13	2	0	0	2	5	0	6	4	0	1	0	1.000	0	0-1	2	14.46	10.97

Chad Durbin

Pitches: R Bats: R Pos: RP-3   Ht: 6'2" Wt: 200 Born: 12/3/1977 Age: 29

			HOW MUCH HE PITCHED						WHAT HE GAVE UP									THE RESULTS							
Year	Team	Lg	G	GS	CG	GF	IP	BFP	H	R	ER	HR	SH	SF	HB	TBB	IBB	SO	WP	Bk	W	L	Pct	ShO	Sv-Op	Hld	ERC	ERA
2006	Toledo*	AAA	28	28	2	0	185.0	768	169	72	64	17	6	6	12	46	1	149	3	1	11	8	.579	2	0--	-	3.21	3.11
1999	KC	AL	1	0	0	0	2.1	9	1	0	0	0	0	0	0	1	0	3	1	0	0	0	-	0	0-0	0	1.08	0.00
2000	KC	AL	16	16	0	0	72.1	349	91	71	66	14	1	3	0	43	1	37	7	0	2	5	.286	0	0-0	0	7.05	8.21
2001	KC	AL	29	29	2	0	179.0	777	201	109	98	26	2	7	11	58	0	95	6	0	9	16	.360	0	0-0	0	5.15	4.93
2002	KC	AL	2	2	0	0	8.1	43	13	11	11	3	0	0	1	4	0	5	0	0	0	1	.000	0	0-0	0	10.58	11.88
2003	Cle	AL	3	1	0	0	8.2	45	18	12	7	2	0	0	1	3	0	8	2	0	0	1	.000	0	0-0	0	12.37	7.27
2004	2 Tms	AL	24	8	1	5	60.2	291	72	50	47	11	2	2	5	35	3	48	5	0	6	7	.462	0	0-0	1	6.75	6.97
2006	Det	AL	3	0	0	1	6.0	24	6	1	1	1	0	0	0	0	0	3	0	0	0	0	-	0	0-0	0	2.87	1.50
04	Cle	AL	17	8	1	5	51.1	239	63	40	38	10	0	2	4	24	3	38	3	0	5	6	.455	0	0-0	1	6.70	6.66
04	Ari	NL	7	0	0	0	9.1	52	9	10	9	1	2	0	1	11	0	10	2	0	1	1	.500	0	0-0	0	6.92	8.68
	7 ML YEARS		78	56	3	6	337.1	1538	402	254	230	57	5	12	17	144	4	199	21	0	17	30	.362	0	0-0	1	6.04	6.14

Ray Durham

Bats: B Throws: R Pos: 2B-133; PH-5   Ht: 5'8" Wt: 190 Born: 11/30/1971 Age: 35

Year	Team	Lg	G	AB	H	2B	3B	HR	(Hm	Rd)	TB	R	RBI	RC	TBB	IBB	SO	HBP	SH	SF	SB	CS	SB%	GDP	Avg	OBP	Slg
1995	CWS	AL	125	471	121	27	6	7	(1	6)	181	68	51	57	31	2	83	6	5	4	18	5	.78	8	.257	.309	.384
1996	CWS	AL	156	557	153	33	5	10	(3	7)	226	79	65	87	58	4	95	10	7	7	30	4	.88	6	.275	.350	.406
1997	CWS	AL	155	634	172	27	5	11	(3	8)	242	106	53	83	61	0	96	6	2	8	33	16	.67	14	.271	.337	.382
1998	CWS	AL	158	635	181	35	8	19	(10	9)	289	126	67	110	73	3	105	6	6	3	36	9	.80	5	.285	.363	.455
1999	CWS	AL	153	612	181	30	8	13	(7	6)	266	109	60	103	73	1	105	4	3	2	34	11	.76	9	.296	.373	.435
2000	CWS	AL	151	614	172	35	9	17	(5	12)	276	121	75	100	75	0	105	7	5	8	25	13	.66	13	.280	.361	.450
2001	CWS	AL	152	611	163	42	10	20	(9	11)	285	104	65	97	64	3	110	4	6	6	23	10	.70	10	.267	.337	.466
2002	2 Tms	AL	150	564	163	34	6	15	(11	4)	254	114	70	96	73	1	93	7	10	5	26	7	.79	15	.289	.374	.450
2003	SF	NL	110	410	117	30	5	8	(3	5)	181	61	33	56	50	2	82	3	4	2	7	7	.50	4	.285	.366	.441
2004	SF	NL	120	471	133	28	8	17	(8	9)	228	95	65	83	57	3	60	6	4	4	10	4	.71	6	.282	.364	.484
2005	SF	NL	142	497	144	33	0	12	(6	6)	213	67	62	67	48	2	59	7	1	7	6	3	.67	19	.290	.356	.429
2006	SF	NL	137	498	146	30	7	26	(10	16)	268	79	93	93	51	6	61	2	2	2	7	2	.78	17	.293	.360	.538
02	CWS	AL	96	345	103	20	2	9	(6	3)	154	71	48	61	49	0	59	5	8	4	20	5	.80	13	.299	.390	.446
02	Oak	AL	54	219	60	14	4	6	(5	1)	100	43	22	35	24	1	34	2	2	1	6	2	.75	2	.274	.350	.457
12 ML YEARS			1709	6574	1846	384	77	175	(76	99)	2909	1129	759	1032	714	27	1054	68	55	58	255	91	.74	126	.281	.354	.443

Jermaine Dye

Bats: R Throws: R Pos: RF-146; PH-1   Ht: 6'5" Wt: 235 Born: 1/28/1974 Age: 33

Year	Team	Lg	G	AB	H	2B	3B	HR	(Hm	Rd)	TB	R	RBI	RC	TBB	IBB	SO	HBP	SH	SF	SB	CS	SB%	GDP	Avg	OBP	Slg
1996	Atl	NL	98	292	82	16	0	12	(4	8)	134	32	37	36	8	0	67	3	0	3	1	4	.20	11	.281	.304	.459
1997	KC	AL	75	263	62	14	0	7	(3	4)	97	26	22	26	17	0	51	1	1	1	2	1	.67	6	.236	.284	.369
1998	KC	AL	60	214	50	5	1	5	(3	2)	72	24	23	17	11	2	46	1	0	4	2	2	.50	8	.234	.270	.336
1999	KC	AL	158	608	179	44	8	27	(15	12)	320	96	119	106	58	4	119	1	0	6	2	3	.40	17	.294	.354	.526
2000	KC	AL	157	601	193	41	2	33	(15	18)	337	107	118	125	69	6	99	3	0	6	0	1	.00	12	.321	.390	.561
2001	2 Tms	AL	158	599	169	31	1	26	(16	10)	280	91	106	99	57	6	112	7	1	11	9	1	.90	8	.282	.346	.467
2002	Oak	AL	131	488	123	27	1	24	(13	11)	224	74	86	70	52	2	108	10	0	5	2	0	1.00	15	.252	.333	.459
2003	Oak	AL	65	221	38	6	0	4	(3	1)	56	28	20	10	25	2	42	3	0	4	1	0	1.00	11	.172	.261	.253
2004	Oak	AL	137	532	141	29	4	23	(12	11)	247	87	80	69	49	4	128	4	0	5	4	2	.67	16	.265	.329	.464
2005	CWS	AL	145	529	145	29	2	31	(15	16)	271	74	86	80	39	3	99	9	0	2	11	4	.73	15	.274	.333	.512
2006	CWS	AL	146	539	170	27	3	44	(21	23)	335	103	120	116	59	4	118	6	0	7	7	3	.70	15	.315	.385	.622
01	KC	AL	97	367	100	14	0	13	(8	5)	153	50	47	54	30	3	68	6	1	6	7	1	.88	2	.272	.333	.417
01	Oak	AL	61	232	69	17	1	13	(8	5)	127	41	59	45	27	3	44	1	0	5	2	0	1.00	6	.297	.366	.547
11 ML YEARS			1330	4886	1352	269	22	236	(120	116)	2373	742	817	754	444	33	989	48	2	54	41	21	.66	134	.277	.339	.486

Damion Easley

Bats: R Throws: R Pos: PH-41; SS-27; 3B-20; 2B-9; 1B-3; RF-1; DH-1; PR-1   Ht: 5'11" Wt: 190 Born: 11/11/1969 Age: 37

Year	Team	Lg	G	AB	H	2B	3B	HR	(Hm	Rd)	TB	R	RBI	RC	TBB	IBB	SO	HBP	SH	SF	SB	CS	SB%	GDP	Avg	OBP	Slg
1992	LAA	AL	47	151	39	5	0	1	(1	0)	47	14	12	14	8	0	26	3	2	1	9	5	.64	2	.258	.307	.311
1993	LAA	AL	73	230	72	13	2	2	(0	2)	95	33	22	37	28	2	35	3	1	2	6	6	.50	5	.313	.392	.413
1994	LAA	AL	88	316	68	16	1	6	(4	2)	104	41	30	28	29	0	48	4	4	2	5	4	.44	8	.215	.288	.329
1995	LAA	AL	114	357	77	14	2	4	(1	3)	107	35	35	30	32	1	47	6	6	4	5	2	.71	11	.216	.288	.300
1996	2 Tms	AL	49	112	30	2	0	4	(1	3)	44	14	17	16	10	0	25	1	5	1	3	1	.75	0	.268	.331	.393
1997	Det	AL	151	527	139	37	3	22	(12	10)	248	97	72	88	68	3	102	16	4	5	28	13	.68	18	.264	.362	.471
1998	Det	AL	153	594	161	38	2	27	(19	8)	284	84	100	94	39	2	112	16	0	2	15	5	.75	8	.271	.332	.478
1999	Det	AL	151	549	146	30	1	20	(12	8)	238	83	65	82	51	2	124	19	2	6	11	3	.79	15	.266	.346	.434
2000	Det	AL	126	464	120	27	2	14	(5	9)	193	76	58	69	55	1	79	11	4	1	13	4	.76	11	.259	.350	.416
2001	Det	AL	154	585	146	27	7	11	(4	7)	220	77	65	72	52	3	90	13	4	4	10	5	.67	10	.250	.323	.376
2002	Det	AL	85	304	68	14	1	8	(4	4)	108	29	30	29	27	3	43	11	1	3	1	3	.25	4	.224	.307	.355
2003	TB	AL	36	107	20	3	1	1	(0	1)	28	8	7	3	2	0	18	0	1	0	0	0	-	3	.187	.202	.262
2004	Fla	NL	98	223	53	20	1	9	(5	4)	102	26	43	34	24	1	36	8	0	2	4	1	.80	6	.238	.331	.457
2005	Fla	NL	102	267	64	19	1	9	(5	4)	112	37	30	33	26	3	47	4	3	4	4	1	.80	6	.240	.312	.419
2006	Ari	NL	90	189	44	6	1	9	(3	6)	79	24	28	29	21	0	30	5	3	2	1	1	.50	4	.233	.323	.418
96	LAA	AL	28	45	7	1	0	2	(1	1)	14	4	7	4	6	0	12	0	3	0	0	0	-	0	.156	.255	.311
96	Det	AL	21	67	23	1	0	2	(0	2)	30	10	10	12	4	0	13	1	2	1	3	1	.75	0	.343	.384	.448
15 ML YEARS			1517	4975	1247	271	25	147	(76	71)	2009	678	614	658	472	21	862	120	40	39	114	55	.67	111	.251	.328	.404

Adam Eaton

Pitches: R Bats: R Pos: SP-13   Ht: 6'2" Wt: 200 Born: 11/23/1977 Age: 29

Year	Team	Lg	G	GS	CG	GF	IP	BFP	H	R	ER	HR	SH	SF	HB	TBB	IBB	SO	WP	Bk	W	L	Pct	ShO	Sv-Op	Hld	ERC	ERA
2006	Frisco*	AA	2	2	0	0	6.1	24	7	1	1	0	0	0	2	1	0	5	0	0	0	0	-	0	0--	-	4.20	1.42
2006	Okla*	AAA	2	2	0	0	6.0	24	3	1	1	0	0	0	0	2	0	8	0	0	0	0	-	0	0--	-	1.05	1.50
2000	SD	NL	22	22	0	0	135.0	583	134	63	62	14	1	3	2	61	3	90	3	0	7	4	.636	0	0-0	0	4.34	4.13
2001	SD	NL	17	17	2	0	116.2	499	108	61	56	20	3	2	5	40	3	109	3	0	8	5	.615	0	0-0	0	4.01	4.32
2002	SD	NL	6	6	0	0	33.1	142	28	20	20	5	2	2	2	17	0	25	2	0	1	1	.500	0	0-0	0	4.28	5.40
2003	SD	NL	31	31	1	0	183.0	789	173	91	83	20	5	5	7	68	6	146	7	1	9	12	.429	0	0-0	0	3.78	4.08
2004	SD	NL	33	33	0	0	199.1	848	204	113	102	28	12	7	10	52	3	153	5	0	11	14	.440	0	0-0	0	4.10	4.61
2005	SD	NL	24	22	0	2	128.2	568	140	70	61	14	4	6	5	44	6	100	5	0	11	5	.688	0	0-0	0	4.44	4.27
2006	Tex	AL	13	13	0	0	65.0	291	78	38	37	11	1	1	4	24	0	43	0	0	7	4	.636	0	0-0	0	5.98	5.12
7 ML YEARS			146	144	3	2	861.0	3720	865	456	421	112	28	26	35	306	21	666	25	1	54	45	.545	0	0-0	0	4.25	4.40

David Eckstein

Bats: R **Throws:** R **Pos:** SS-120; PH-3   **Ht:** 5'7" **Wt:** 165 **Born:** 1/20/1975 **Age:** 32

								BATTING											BASERUNNING				AVERAGES		
Year	Team	Lg	G	AB	H	2B	3B	HR	(Hm | Rd)	TB	R	RBI	RC	TBB	IBB	SO	HBP	SH	SF	SB	CS	SB%	GDP	Avg	OBP	Slg
2001	LAA	AL	153	582	166	26	2	4	(3 | 1)	208	82	41	80	43	0	60	21	16	2	29	4	.88	11	.285	.355	.357
2002	LAA	AL	152	608	178	22	6	8	(3 | 5)	236	107	63	93	45	0	44	27	14	8	21	13	.62	7	.293	.363	.388
2003	LAA	AL	120	452	114	22	1	3	(1 | 2)	147	59	31	53	36	0	45	15	10	4	16	5	.76	9	.252	.325	.325
2004	LAA	AL	142	566	156	24	1	2	(2 | 0)	188	92	35	60	42	1	49	13	14	2	16	5	.76	11	.276	.339	.332
2005	StL	NL	158	630	185	26	7	8	(3 | 5)	249	90	61	103	58	0	44	13	8	4	11	8	.58	13	.294	.363	.395
2006	StL	NL	123	500	146	18	1	2	(0 | 2)	172	68	23	60	31	0	41	15	3	3	7	6	.54	7	.292	.350	.344
6 ML YEARS			848	3338	945	138	18	27	(12 | 15)	1200	498	254	449	255	1	283	104	65	23	100	41	.71	58	.283	.351	.359

Jim Edmonds

Bats: L **Throws:** L **Pos:** CF-99; PH-10; 1B-6; PR-1   **Ht:** 6'1" **Wt:** 210 **Born:** 6/27/1970 **Age:** 37

								BATTING											BASERUNNING				AVERAGES		
Year	Team	Lg	G	AB	H	2B	3B	HR	(Hm | Rd)	TB	R	RBI	RC	TBB	IBB	SO	HBP	SH	SF	SB	CS	SB%	GDP	Avg	OBP	Slg
1993	LAA	AL	18	61	15	4	1	0	(0 | 0)	21	5	4	4	2	1	16	0	0	0	0	2	.00	1	.246	.270	.344
1994	LAA	AL	94	289	79	13	1	5	(3 | 2)	109	35	37	38	30	3	72	1	1	1	4	2	.67	3	.273	.343	.377
1995	LAA	AL	141	558	162	30	4	33	(16 | 17)	299	120	107	100	51	4	130	5	1	5	1	4	.20	10	.290	.352	.536
1996	LAA	AL	114	431	131	28	3	27	(17 | 10)	246	73	66	88	46	2	101	4	0	2	4	0	1.00	8	.304	.375	.571
1997	LAA	AL	133	502	146	27	0	26	(14 | 12)	251	82	80	90	60	5	80	4	0	5	5	7	.42	8	.291	.368	.500
1998	LAA	AL	154	599	184	42	1	25	(9 | 16)	303	115	91	104	57	7	114	1	1	1	7	5	.58	16	.307	.368	.506
1999	LAA	AL	55	204	51	17	2	5	(3 | 2)	87	34	23	30	28	0	45	0	0	1	5	4	.56	3	.250	.339	.426
2000	StL	NL	152	525	155	25	0	42	(22 | 20)	306	129	108	126	103	3	167	6	1	8	10	3	.77	5	.295	.411	.583
2001	StL	NL	150	500	152	38	1	30	(16 | 14)	282	95	110	113	93	12	136	4	1	10	5	5	.50	8	.304	.410	.564
2002	StL	NL	144	476	148	31	2	28	(17 | 11)	267	96	83	101	86	14	134	8	0	6	4	3	.57	9	.311	.420	.561
2003	StL	NL	137	447	123	32	2	39	(17 | 22)	276	89	89	87	77	6	127	4	1	2	1	3	.25	11	.275	.385	.617
2004	StL	NL	153	498	150	38	3	42	(24 | 18)	320	102	111	115	101	12	150	5	0	8	8	3	.73	4	.301	.418	.643
2005	StL	NL	142	467	123	37	1	29	(15 | 14)	249	88	89	95	91	10	139	4	1	4	5	5	.50	6	.263	.385	.533
2006	StL	NL	110	350	90	18	0	19	(11 | 8)	165	52	70	51	53	7	101	0	0	5	4	0	1.00	11	.257	.350	.471
14 ML YEARS			1697	5907	1709	380	21	350	(184 | 166)	3181	1115	1068	1142	878	86	1512	46	7	58	63	46	.58	103	.289	.382	.539

Mike Edwards

Bats: R **Throws:** R **Pos:** PH-11; 3B-3   **Ht:** 6'1" **Wt:** 200 **Born:** 11/24/1976 **Age:** 30

								BATTING											BASERUNNING				AVERAGES		
Year	Team	Lg	G	AB	H	2B	3B	HR	(Hm | Rd)	TB	R	RBI	RC	TBB	IBB	SO	HBP	SH	SF	SB	CS	SB%	GDP	Avg	OBP	Slg
2006	Indy*	AAA	92	325	84	21	3	3	(- | -)	120	40	29	40	27	0	48	4	0	3	5	4	.56	9	.258	.320	.369
2003	Oak	AL	4	4	1	0	0	0	(0 | 0)	1	0	0	1	2	0	1	0	0	0	0	0	-	0	.250	.500	.250
2005	LAD	NL	88	239	59	9	2	3	(1 | 2)	81	23	15	20	16	0	34	2	1	0	1	1	.50	6	.247	.300	.339
2006	Pit	NL	14	16	3	0	0	0	(0 | 0)	3	1	0	0	1	0	5	0	1	0	0	0	-	1	.188	.235	.188
3 ML YEARS			106	259	63	9	2	3	(1 | 2)	85	24	15	21	19	0	40	2	2	0	1	1	.50	7	.243	.300	.328

Joey Eischen

Pitches: L **Bats:** L **Pos:** RP-22   **Ht:** 6'0" **Wt:** 215 **Born:** 5/25/1970 **Age:** 37

			HOW MUCH HE PITCHED						WHAT HE GAVE UP												THE RESULTS					
Year	Team	Lg	G	GS	CG	GF	IP	BFP	H	R	ER	HR	SH	SF	HB	TBB	IBB	SO	WP	Bk	W	L	Pct	ShO	Sv-Op	Hld	ERC	ERA
1994	Mon	NL	1	0	0	0	0.2	7	4	4	4	0	0	0	1	0	0	1	0	0	0	0	-	0	0-0	0	47.92	54.00
1995	LAD	NL	17	0	0	8	20.1	95	19	9	7	1	0	0	2	11	1	15	1	0	0	0	-	0	0-0	1	3.97	3.10
1996	2 Tms		52	0	0	14	68.1	308	75	36	32	7	3	2	4	34	7	51	4	0	1	2	.333	0	0-2	2	5.15	4.21
1997	Cin	NL	1	0	0	0	1.1	7	2	2	1	0	0	0	0	1	0	2	1	0	0	0	-	0	0-0	0	7.52	6.75
2001	Mon	NL	24	0	0	7	29.2	131	29	17	16	4	1	0	1	16	1	19	1	0	0	0	.000	0	0-2	2	4.89	4.85
2002	Mon	NL	59	0	0	18	53.2	217	43	11	8	1	3	2	2	18	5	51	6	1	6	1	.857	0	2-3	11	2.31	1.34
2003	Mon	NL	70	0	0	15	53.0	221	57	27	18	7	3	0	3	13	1	40	3	0	2	2	.500	0	1-4	15	4.44	3.06
2004	Mon	NL	21	0	0	3	18.1	80	16	10	8	2	1	1	1	8	2	17	0	0	1	0	.000	0	0-1	2	3.53	3.93
2005	Was	NL	57	0	0	14	36.1	168	34	14	13	1	6	2	6	19	7	30	5	1	2	1	.667	0	0-1	8	3.83	3.22
2006	Was	NL	22	0	0	4	14.2	83	18	18	14	2	0	2	1	19	5	18	1	0	0	1	.000	0	0-1	0	8.82	8.59
96 Mon		NL	28	0	0	11	43.1	198	48	25	23	4	3	1	4	20	4	36	1	0	0	0	.000	0	0-0	1	5.07	4.78
96 Det		AL	24	0	0	3	25.0	110	27	11	9	3	0	1	0	14	3	15	3	0	1	1	.500	0	0-2	1	5.30	3.24
10 ML YEARS			324	0	0	83	296.1	1317	297	148	121	25	17	9	21	139	29	244	22	2	11	9	.550	0	3-14	41	4.35	3.67

Scott Elarton

Pitches: R **Bats:** R **Pos:** SP-20   **Ht:** 6'7" **Wt:** 255 **Born:** 2/23/1976 **Age:** 31

			HOW MUCH HE PITCHED						WHAT HE GAVE UP												THE RESULTS					
Year	Team	Lg	G	GS	CG	GF	IP	BFP	H	R	ER	HR	SH	SF	HB	TBB	IBB	SO	WP	Bk	W	L	Pct	ShO	Sv-Op	Hld	ERC	ERA
1998	Hou	NL	28	2	0	7	57.0	227	40	21	21	5	1	1	1	20	0	56	1	0	2	1	.667	0	2-3	2	2.35	3.32
1999	Hou	NL	42	15	0	8	124.0	524	111	55	48	8	7	4	4	43	0	121	3	0	9	5	.643	0	1-4	5	3.16	3.48
2000	Hou	NL	30	30	2	0	192.2	855	198	117	103	29	5	7	6	84	1	131	8	0	17	7	.708	0	0-0	0	4.82	4.81
2001	2 Tms	NL	24	24	0	0	132.2	595	146	105	104	34	7	2	6	59	2	87	5	0	4	10	.286	0	0-0	0	6.21	7.06
2003	Col	NL	11	10	0	0	51.2	253	73	46	36	13	3	4	4	20	3	20	3	0	4	4	.500	0	0-0	0	7.79	6.27
2004	2 Tms	NL	29	29	1	0	158.2	697	164	107	104	33	5	7	4	62	3	103	8	0	3	11	.214	0	0-0	0	5.04	5.90
2005	Cle	AL	31	31	1	0	181.2	774	189	100	93	32	3	10	6	48	1	103	4	1	11	9	.550	0	0-0	0	4.40	4.61
2006	KC	AL	20	20	0	0	114.2	501	117	73	68	26	2	2	6	52	1	49	3	0	4	9	.308	0	0-0	0	5.64	5.34
01 Col		NL	20	20	0	0	109.2	499	126	88	87	26	7	2	6	49	1	76	5	0	4	8	.333	0	0-0	0	6.42	7.14
01 Col		NL	4	4	0	0	23.0	96	20	17	17	8	0	0	0	10	1	11	0	0	0	2	.000	0	0-0	0	5.18	6.65
04 Col		NL	8	8	0	0	41.1	199	57	45	45	8	2	3	0	20	1	23	5	0	0	6	.000	0	0-0	0	7.35	9.80
04 Cle		AL	21	21	1	0	117.1	498	107	62	59	25	3	4	4	42	2	80	3	0	3	5	.375	0	0-0	0	4.28	4.53
8 ML YEARS			215	161	4	15	1013.0	4426	1038	624	577	180	33	37	37	388	11	670	35	1	54	56	.491	1	3-7	7	4.82	5.13

Mark Ellis

Bats: R **Throws:** R **Pos:** 2B-123; PR-2; 1B-1   **Ht:** 5'11" **Wt:** 195 **Born:** 6/6/1977 **Age:** 30

Year	Team	Lg	G	AB	H	2B	3B	HR	(Hm	Rd)	TB	R	RBI	RC	TBB	IBB	SO	HBP	SH	SF	SB	CS	SB%	GDP	Avg	OBP	Slg
2006	Scrmto*	AAA	4	12	2	0	0	0	(-	-)	2	1	2	1	4	0	2	0	0	0	0	0	-	0	.167	.375	.167
2002	Oak	AL	98	345	94	16	4	6	(6	0)	136	58	35	55	44	1	54	4	8	3	4	2	.67	3	.272	.359	.394
2003	Oak	AL	154	553	137	31	5	9	(7	2)	205	78	52	69	48	4	94	7	9	5	6	2	.75	7	.248	.313	.371
2005	Oak	AL	122	434	137	21	5	13	(5	8)	207	76	52	78	44	1	51	4	4	0	1	3	.25	10	.316	.384	.477
2006	Oak	AL	124	441	110	25	1	11	(7	4)	170	64	52	53	40	1	76	8	4	7	4	0	1.00	13	.249	.319	.385
	4 ML YEARS		498	1773	478	93	15	39	(25	14)	718	276	191	255	176	7	275	23	25	15	15	7	.68	33	.270	.341	.405

Jason Ellison

Bats: R **Throws:** R **Pos:** LF-44; PR-21; PH-18; RF-17; CF-4   **Ht:** 5'10" **Wt:** 180 **Born:** 4/4/1978 **Age:** 29

Year	Team	Lg	G	AB	H	2B	3B	HR	(Hm	Rd)	TB	R	RBI	RC	TBB	IBB	SO	HBP	SH	SF	SB	CS	SB%	GDP	Avg	OBP	Slg
2006	Fresno*	AAA	46	192	78	18	2	1	(-	-)	103	41	18	44	14	0	20	3	1	1	7	4	.64	3	.406	.452	.536
2003	SF	NL	7	10	1	0	0	0	(0	0)	1	1	0	0	0	0	1	0	0	0	0	0	-	0	.100	.100	.100
2004	SF	NL	13	4	2	0	0	1	(0	1)	5	4	3	3	0	0	1	0	0	0	2	0	1.00	0	.500	.500	1.250
2005	SF	NL	131	352	93	18	2	4	(2	2)	127	49	24	34	24	1	44	3	6	1	14	6	.70	7	.264	.316	.361
2006	SF	NL	84	81	18	5	1	2	(0	2)	31	14	4	4	5	0	14	1	3	1	2	2	.50	3	.222	.273	.383
	4 ML YEARS		235	447	114	23	3	7	(2	5)	164	68	31	41	29	1	60	4	9	2	18	8	.69	10	.255	.305	.367

Alan Embree

Pitches: L **Bats:** L **Pos:** RP-73   **Ht:** 6'2" **Wt:** 190 **Born:** 1/23/1970 **Age:** 37

			HOW MUCH HE PITCHED						WHAT HE GAVE UP											THE RESULTS							
Year	Team	Lg	G	GS	CG	GF	IP	BFP	H	R	ER	HR	SH	SF	HB	TBB	IBB	SO	WP	Bk	W	L	Pct	ShO	Sv-Op	Hld	ERC	ERA
1992	Cle	AL	4	4	0	0	18.0	81	19	14	14	3	0	2	1	8	0	12	1	1	0	2	.000	0	0-0	0	5.25	7.00
1995	Cle	AL	23	0	0	8	24.2	111	23	16	14	2	2	2	0	16	0	23	1	0	3	2	.600	0	1-1	6	4.51	5.11
1996	Cle	AL	24	0	0	2	31.0	141	30	26	22	10	1	3	0	21	3	33	3	0	1	1	.500	0	0-0	1	6.58	6.39
1997	Atl	NL	66	0	0	15	46.0	190	36	13	13	1	4	1	2	20	2	45	3	1	3	1	.750	0	0-0	16	2.66	2.54
1998	2 Tms	NL	55	0	0	16	53.2	237	56	32	25	7	4	1	1	23	0	43	3	0	4	2	.667	0	1-3	12	4.71	4.19
1999	SF	NL	68	0	0	13	58.2	244	42	22	22	6	3	2	3	26	2	53	3	0	3	2	.600	0	0-3	22	2.86	3.38
2000	SF	NL	63	0	0	21	60.0	263	62	34	33	4	4	5	3	25	2	49	1	0	3	5	.375	0	2-5	9	4.24	4.95
2001	2 Tms		61	0	0	17	54.0	245	65	47	44	14	0	6	3	17	2	59	3	0	1	4	.200	0	0-3	9	6.20	7.33
2002	2 Tms		68	0	0	20	62.0	251	47	19	14	6	1	2	1	20	3	81	1	0	4	6	.400	0	2-7	18	2.48	2.03
2003	Bos	AL	65	0	0	15	55.0	221	49	26	26	5	0	2	0	16	3	45	0	0	4	1	.800	0	1-2	14	3.01	4.25
2004	Bos	AL	71	0	0	11	52.1	217	49	28	24	7	2	2	1	11	1	37	0	0	2	2	.500	0	0-1	20	3.21	4.13
2005	2 Tms	AL	67	0	0	15	52.0	231	62	47	44	10	3	3	2	14	3	38	1	1	2	5	.286	0	1-3	10	5.34	7.62
2006	SD	NL	73	0	0	11	52.1	221	50	21	19	4	2	3	0	15	2	53	0	0	4	3	.571	0	0-0	16	3.13	3.27
98	Atl	NL	20	0	0	5	18.2	87	23	14	9	2	1	1	0	10	0	19	0	0	1	0	1.000	0	0-1	6	6.06	4.34
98	Ari	NL	35	0	0	11	35.0	150	33	18	16	5	3	0	1	13	0	24	3	0	3	2	.600	0	1-2	6	4.03	4.11
01	SF	NL	22	0	0	7	20.0	106	34	26	25	7	0	3	2	10	2	25	1	0	0	2	.000	0	0-1	0	11.29	11.25
01	CWS	AL	39	0	0	10	34.0	139	31	21	19	7	0	3	1	7	0	34	2	0	1	2	.333	0	0-2	9	3.61	5.03
02	SD	NL	36	0	0	13	28.2	118	23	7	3	2	0	0	0	9	2	38	1	0	3	4	.429	0	0-2	10	2.38	0.94
02	Bos	AL	32	0	0	7	33.1	133	24	12	11	4	1	2	1	11	1	43	0	0	1	2	.333	0	2-5	8	2.56	2.97
05	Bos	AL	43	0	0	11	37.2	163	42	33	32	8	1	2	1	11	2	30	1	0	1	4	.200	0	1-3	4	5.14	7.65
05	NYY	AL	24	0	0	4	14.1	68	20	14	12	2	2	1	1	3	1	8	0	1	1	1	.500	0	0-0	6	5.85	7.53
	13 ML YEARS		708	4	0	164	619.2	2653	590	345	314	79	26	34	17	232	23	571	20	3	34	36	.486	0	8-28	153	3.93	4.56

Edwin Encarnacion

Bats: R **Throws:** R **Pos:** 3B-111; PH-6; 1B-2   **Ht:** 6'1" **Wt:** 195 **Born:** 1/7/1983 **Age:** 24

Year	Team	Lg	G	AB	H	2B	3B	HR	(Hm	Rd)	TB	R	RBI	RC	TBB	IBB	SO	HBP	SH	SF	SB	CS	SB%	GDP	Avg	OBP	Slg
2000	Rngrs	R	51	177	55	6	3	0	(-	-)	67	31	36	28	21	1	27	1	3	3	3	1	.75	7	.311	.381	.379
2001	Savann	A	45	170	52	9	2	4	(-	-)	77	23	25	27	12	0	34	2	1	2	3	3	.50	5	.306	.355	.453
2001	Dayton	A	9	37	6	2	0	1	(-	-)	11	2	6	1	1	0	5	0	0	0	0	1	.00	1	.162	.184	.297
2001	Billings	R+	52	211	55	8	2	5	(-	-)	82	27	26	27	15	0	29	0	0	2	8	1	.89	6	.261	.307	.389
2002	Dayton	A	136	517	146	32	4	17	(-	-)	237	80	73	84	40	2	108	7	0	6	25	7	.78	15	.282	.339	.458
2003	Chatt	AA	67	254	69	13	1	5	(-	-)	99	40	36	35	22	0	44	3	0	5	8	3	.73	3	.272	.331	.390
2003	Ptomc	A+	58	215	69	15	1	6	(-	-)	104	40	29	42	24	1	32	1	1	3	7	1	.88	2	.321	.387	.484
2004	Chatt	AA	120	469	132	35	1	13	(-	-)	208	73	76	78	53	3	79	0	1	3	17	3	.85	5	.281	.352	.443
2005	Lsvlle	AAA	78	290	91	23	0	15	(-	-)	159	44	54	62	33	1	53	4	0	3	7	2	.78	8	.314	.388	.548
2006	Lsvlle	AAA	10	36	11	3	0	1	(-	-)	17	6	1	5	2	0	11	0	0	0	0	0	-	1	.306	.342	.472
2005	Cin	NL	69	211	49	16	0	9	(3	6)	92	25	31	24	20	2	60	3	0	0	3	0	1.00	9	.232	.308	.436
2006	Cin	NL	117	406	112	33	1	15	(7	8)	192	60	72	66	41	3	78	13	0	3	6	3	.67	9	.276	.359	.473
	2 ML YEARS		186	617	161	49	1	24	(10	14)	284	85	103	90	61	5	138	16	0	3	9	3	.75	17	.261	.341	.460

Juan Encarnacion

Bats: R **Throws:** R **Pos:** RF-125; CF-32; PH-10; LF-1   **Ht:** 6'3" **Wt:** 215 **Born:** 3/8/1976 **Age:** 31

Year	Team	Lg	G	AB	H	2B	3B	HR	(Hm	Rd)	TB	R	RBI	RC	TBB	IBB	SO	HBP	SH	SF	SB	CS	SB%	GDP	Avg	OBP	Slg
1997	Det	AL	11	33	7	1	1	1	(1	0)	13	3	5	4	3	0	12	2	0	0	3	1	.75	1	.212	.316	.394
1998	Det	AL	40	164	54	9	4	7	(4	3)	92	30	21	31	7	0	31	1	0	3	7	4	.64	2	.329	.354	.561
1999	Det	AL	132	509	130	30	6	19	(6	13)	229	62	74	64	14	1	113	9	4	2	33	12	.73	12	.255	.287	.450
2000	Det	AL	141	547	158	25	6	14	(4	10)	237	75	72	76	29	1	90	7	1	3	16	4	.80	15	.289	.330	.433
2001	Det	AL	120	417	101	19	7	12	(4	8)	170	52	52	48	25	1	93	6	5	4	9	5	.64	9	.242	.292	.408
2002	2 Tms	NL	152	584	158	22	5	24	(8	16)	262	77	85	74	46	0	113	4	3	7	21	9	.70	18	.271	.324	.449
2003	Fla	NL	156	601	162	37	6	19	(9	10)	268	80	94	76	37	0	82	4	5	6	19	8	.70	17	.270	.313	.446

Year	Team	Lg	G	AB	H	2B	3B	HR	(Hm	Rd)	TB	R	RBI	RC	TBB	IBB	SO	HBP	SH	SF	SB	CS	SB%	GDP	Avg	OBP	Slg
																								BASERUNNING		AVERAGES	
2004	2 Tms	NL	135	484	114	30	2	16	(8	8)	196	63	62	60	38	2	86	7	1	2	5	4	.56	11	.236	.299	.405
2005	Fla	NL	141	506	145	27	4	16	(8	8)	226	59	76	79	41	2	104	9	4	3	6	5	.55	9	.287	.349	.447
2006	StL	NL	153	557	155	25	5	19	(10	9)	247	74	79	79	30	6	86	4	1	6	6	5	.55	11	.278	.317	.443
02	Cin	NL	83	321	89	11	2	16	(6	10)	152	43	51	42	26	0	63	1	3	3	9	4	.69	7	.277	.330	.474
02	Fla	NL	69	263	69	11	3	8	(2	6)	110	34	34	32	20	0	50	3	0	4	12	5	.71	11	.262	.317	.418
04	LAD	NL	86	324	76	18	1	13	(6	7)	135	42	43	38	21	0	53	4	0	1	3	3	.50	9	.235	.289	.417
04	Fla	NL	49	160	38	12	1	3	(2	1)	61	21	19	22	17	2	33	3	1	1	2	1	.67	2	.238	.320	.381
10 ML YEARS			1181	4402	1184	225	45	147	(62	85)	1940	575	620	591	270	13	810	53	26	37	125	57	.69	105	.269	.316	.441

Morgan Ensberg

Bats: R **Throws:** R **Pos:** 3B-117; PH-16 **Ht:** 6'2" **Wt:** 220 **Born:** 8/26/1975 **Age:** 31

Year	Team	Lg	G	AB	H	2B	3B	HR	(Hm	Rd)	TB	R	RBI	RC	TBB	IBB	SO	HBP	SH	SF	SB	CS	SB%	GDP	Avg	OBP	Slg
2006	RdRck*	AAA	3	12	6	2	0	2	(-	-)	14	2	7	6	3	0	1	0	0	0	0	0	-	1	.500	.600	1.167
2000	Hou	NL	4	7	2	0	0	0	(0	0)	2	0	0	1	0	0	1	0	0	0	0	0	-	0	.286	.286	.286
2002	Hou	NL	49	132	32	7	2	3	(2	1)	52	14	19	13	18	0	25	3	0	0	2	0	1.00	8	.242	.346	.394
2003	Hou	NL	127	385	112	15	1	25	(16	9)	204	69	60	71	48	1	60	6	1	1	7	2	.78	10	.291	.377	.530
2004	Hou	NL	131	411	113	20	3	10	(9	1)	169	51	66	57	36	1	46	0	5	4	6	4	.60	17	.275	.330	.411
2005	Hou	NL	150	526	149	30	3	36	(20	16)	293	86	101	107	85	9	119	8	0	5	6	7	.46	12	.283	.388	.557
2006	Hou	NL	127	387	91	17	1	23	(16	7)	179	67	58	73	101	7	96	4	0	3	1	4	.20	3	.235	.396	.463
6 ML YEARS			588	1848	499	89	10	97	(63	34)	899	287	304	322	288	18	347	21	6	13	22	17	.56	50	.270	.372	.486

Scott Erickson

Pitches: R **Bats:** R **Pos:** RP-9 **Ht:** 6'4" **Wt:** 230 **Born:** 2/2/1968 **Age:** 39

Year	Team	Lg	G	GS	CG	GF	IP	BFP	H	R	ER	HR	SH	SF	HB	TBB	IBB	SO	WP	Bk	W	L	Pct	ShO	Sv-Op	Hld	ERC	ERA
2006	Clmbs*	AAA	12	0	0	0	17.0	76	11	10	8	1	3	1	0	11	0	11	1	0	1	2	.333	0	0- -	-	2.64	4.24
1990	Min	AL	19	17	1	1	113.0	485	108	49	36	9	5	2	5	51	4	53	3	0	8	4	.667	0	0-0	0	4.07	2.87
1991	Min	AL	32	32	5	0	204.0	851	189	80	72	13	5	7	6	71	3	108	4	0	20	8	.714	3	0-0	0	3.36	3.18
1992	Min	AL	32	32	5	0	212.0	888	197	86	80	18	9	7	8	83	3	101	6	1	13	12	.520	3	0-0	0	3.75	3.40
1993	Min	AL	34	34	1	0	218.2	976	266	138	126	17	10	13	10	71	1	116	5	0	8	19	.296	0	0-0	0	5.05	5.19
1994	Min	AL	23	23	2	0	144.0	654	173	95	87	15	3	4	9	59	0	104	10	0	8	11	.421	1	0-0	0	5.61	5.44
1995	2 Tms	AL	32	31	7	1	196.1	836	213	108	105	18	3	3	5	67	0	106	3	2	13	10	.565	2	0-0	0	4.48	4.81
1996	Bal	AL	34	34	6	0	222.1	968	262	137	124	21	5	5	11	66	4	100	1	0	13	12	.520	2	0-0	0	4.90	5.02
1997	Bal	AL	34	33	3	0	221.2	922	218	100	91	16	3	4	5	61	5	131	11	0	16	7	.696	2	0-0	0	3.40	3.69
1998	Bal	AL	36	36	11	0	251.1	1102	284	125	112	23	7	2	13	69	4	186	4	0	16	13	.552	2	0-0	0	4.40	4.01
1999	Bal	AL	34	34	6	0	230.1	995	244	127	123	27	7	6	11	99	4	106	10	0	15	12	.556	3	0-0	0	4.97	4.81
2000	Bal	AL	16	16	1	0	92.2	446	127	81	81	14	3	5	5	48	0	41	3	0	5	8	.385	0	0-0	0	7.50	7.87
2002	Bal	AL	29	28	3	0	160.2	719	192	109	99	20	3	7	8	68	2	74	5	0	5	12	.294	1	0-0	0	5.80	5.55
2004	2 Tms	AL	6	6	0	0	27.0	136	38	22	20	3	0	3	0	20	0	9	2	0	1	4	.200	0	0-0	0	8.11	6.67
2005	LAD	NL	19	8	0	6	55.1	249	62	37	37	12	3	2	4	25	0	15	1	0	1	4	.200	0	0-0	0	6.26	6.02
2006	NYY	AL	9	0	0	0	11.1	57	13	12	10	2	1	0	3	7	2	2	0	0	0	0	-	0	0-0	2	7.09	7.94
95	Min	AL	15	15	0	0	87.2	390	102	61	58	11	2	1	4	32	0	45	1	0	4	6	.400	0	0-0	0	5.29	5.95
95	Bal	AL	17	16	7	1	108.2	446	111	47	47	7	1	2	1	35	0	61	2	2	9	4	.692	2	0-0	0	3.84	3.89
04	NYM	NL	2	2	0	0	8.0	42	15	9	7	1	0	0	0	4	0	3	1	0	0	1	.000	0	0-0	0	10.35	7.88
04	Tex	AL	4	4	0	0	19.0	94	23	13	13	2	0	3	0	16	0	6	1	0	1	3	.250	0	0-0	0	7.21	6.16
15 ML YEARS			389	364	51	10	2360.2	10284	2586	1306	1203	228	67	70	103	865	32	1252	68	3	142	136	.511	17	0-0	2	4.67	4.59

Darin Erstad

Bats: L **Throws:** L **Pos:** CF-27; 1B-13; PR-1 **Ht:** 6'2" **Wt:** 215 **Born:** 6/4/1974 **Age:** 33

Year	Team	Lg	G	AB	H	2B	3B	HR	(Hm	Rd)	TB	R	RBI	RC	TBB	IBB	SO	HBP	SH	SF	SB	CS	SB%	GDP	Avg	OBP	Slg
2006	RCuca*	A+	7	14	3	0	0	0	(-	-)	3	4	0	1	4	0	2	0	0	0	0	0	-	0	.214	.389	.214
2006	Salt Lk*	AAA	7	30	3	0	0	0	(-	-)	3	0	3	0	1	0	2	0	0	0	1	0	1.00	0	.100	.129	.100
1996	LAA	AL	57	208	59	5	1	4	(1	3)	78	34	20	26	17	1	29	0	1	3	3	3	.50	3	.284	.333	.375
1997	LAA	AL	139	539	161	34	4	16	(8	8)	251	99	77	92	51	4	86	4	5	6	23	8	.74	5	.299	.360	.466
1998	LAA	AL	133	537	159	39	3	19	(9	10)	261	84	82	94	43	7	77	6	1	3	20	6	.77	2	.296	.353	.486
1999	LAA	AL	142	585	148	22	5	13	(7	6)	219	84	53	64	47	3	101	1	2	3	13	7	.65	16	.253	.308	.374
2000	LAA	AL	157	676	240	39	6	25	(11	14)	366	121	100	145	64	9	82	1	2	4	28	8	.78	6	.355	.409	.541
2001	LAA	AL	157	631	163	35	1	9	(3	6)	227	89	63	79	62	7	113	10	1	7	24	10	.71	8	.258	.331	.360
2002	LAA	AL	150	625	177	28	4	10	(6	4)	243	99	73	74	27	4	67	2	5	4	23	3	.88	9	.283	.313	.389
2003	LAA	AL	67	258	65	7	1	4	(1	3)	86	35	17	22	18	1	40	4	2	2	9	1	.90	8	.252	.309	.333
2004	LAA	AL	125	495	146	29	1	7	(3	4)	198	79	69	76	37	1	74	4	3	4	16	1	.94	9	.295	.346	.400
2005	LAA	AL	153	609	166	33	3	7	(4	3)	226	86	66	79	47	3	109	1	4	2	10	3	.77	8	.273	.325	.371
2006	LAA	AL	40	95	21	8	1	0	(0	0)	31	8	5	6	6	0	18	2	1	1	1	1	.50	2	.221	.279	.326
11 ML YEARS			1320	5258	1505	279	30	114	(49	65)	2186	818	625	757	419	40	796	35	27	39	170	51	.77	78	.286	.341	.416

Alex Escobar

Bats: R **Throws:** R **Pos:** CF-23; PH-12; RF-1 **Ht:** 6'1" **Wt:** 190 **Born:** 9/6/1978 **Age:** 28

Year	Team	Lg	G	AB	H	2B	3B	HR	(Hm	Rd)	TB	R	RBI	RC	TBB	IBB	SO	HBP	SH	SF	SB	CS	SB%	GDP	Avg	OBP	Slg
2006	Hrsbrg*	AA	35	122	38	11	0	5	(-	-)	64	21	26	28	20	1	23	8	0	0	2	2	.50	2	.311	.440	.525
2006	Nats*	R	3	7	1	0	0	0	(-	-)	1	1	1	0	2	0	1	0	0	0	0	0	-	0	.143	.333	.143
2001	NYM	NL	18	50	10	1	0	3	(3	0)	20	3	8	5	3	0	19	0	0	0	1	0	1.00	1	.200	.245	.400
2003	Cle	AL	28	99	27	2	0	5	(4	1)	44	16	14	9	7	1	33	1	0	1	1	0	1.00	0	.273	.324	.444

Year	Team	Lg	G	AB	H	2B	3B	HR	(Hm	Rd)	TB	R	RBI	RC	TBB	IBB	SO	HBP	SH	SF	SB	CS	SB%	GDP	Avg	OBP	Slg
												BATTING											**BASERUNNING**			**AVERAGES**	
2004	Cle	AL	46	152	32	8	2	1	(0	1)	47	20	12	17	23	0	42	1	3	0	1	1	.50	1	.211	.318	.309
2006	Was	NL	33	87	31	3	2	4	(2	2)	50	14	18	16	8	0	18	0	0	4	2	0	1.00	3	.356	.394	.575
4 ML YEARS			125	388	100	14	4	13	(9	4)	161	53	52	47	41	1	112	2	3	5	5	1	.83	5	.258	.328	.415

Kelvim Escobar

Pitches: R Bats: R Pos: SP-30　　Ht: 6'1" Wt: 230 Born: 4/11/1976 Age: 31

Year	Team	Lg	G	GS	CG	GF	IP	BFP	H	R	ER	HR	SH	SF	HB	TBB	IBB	SO	WP	Bk	W	L	Pct	ShO	Sv-Op	Hld	ERC	ERA
			HOW MUCH HE PITCHED						**WHAT HE GAVE UP**												**THE RESULTS**							
1997	Tor	AL	27	0	0	23	31.0	139	28	12	10	1	2	0	0	19	2	36	0	0	3	2	.600	0	14-17	1	3.68	2.90
1998	Tor	AL	22	10	0	2	79.2	342	72	37	33	5	0	3	0	35	0	72	0	0	7	3	.700	0	0-1	5	3.41	3.73
1999	Tor	AL	33	30	1	2	174.0	795	203	118	110	19	2	8	10	81	2	129	6	1	14	11	.560	0	0-0	0	5.62	5.69
2000	Tor	AL	43	24	3	8	180.0	794	186	118	107	26	5	4	3	85	3	142	4	0	10	15	.400	1	2-3	3	4.94	5.35
2001	Tor	AL	59	11	1	15	126.0	517	93	51	49	8	2	5	3	52	5	121	2	0	6	8	.429	1	0-0	13	2.54	3.50
2002	Tor	AL	76	0	0	68	78.0	355	75	39	37	10	1	0	5	44	6	85	4	0	5	7	.417	0	38-46	4	4.77	4.27
2003	Tor	AL	41	26	1	12	180.1	797	189	94	86	15	5	5	9	78	3	159	9	0	13	9	.591	1	4-5	0	4.53	4.29
2004	LAA	AL	33	33	0	0	208.1	878	192	91	91	21	3	6	7	76	2	191	9	0	11	12	.478	0	0-0	0	3.65	3.93
2005	LAA	AL	16	7	0	2	59.2	242	45	21	20	4	2	0	2	21	1	63	4	0	3	2	.600	0	1-1	2	2.51	3.02
2006	LAA	AL	30	30	1	0	189.1	789	192	93	76	17	6	3	4	50	2	147	7	0	11	14	.440	0	0-0	0	3.67	3.61
10 ML YEARS			380	171	7	132	1306.1	5648	1275	674	619	126	28	34	43	541	26	1145	45	1	83	83	.500	3	59-73	24	4.08	4.26

Shawn Estes

Pitches: L Bats: R Pos: SP-1　　Ht: 6'2" Wt: 220 Born: 2/18/1973 Age: 34

Year	Team	Lg	G	GS	CG	GF	IP	BFP	H	R	ER	HR	SH	SF	HB	TBB	IBB	SO	WP	Bk	W	L	Pct	ShO	Sv-Op	Hld	ERC	ERA
			HOW MUCH HE PITCHED						**WHAT HE GAVE UP**												**THE RESULTS**							
1995	SF	NL	3	3	0	0	17.1	76	16	14	13	2	0	0	1	5	0	14	4	0	0	3	.000	0	0-0	0	3.37	6.75
1996	SF	NL	11	11	0	0	70.0	305	63	30	28	3	5	0	2	39	3	60	4	0	3	5	.375	0	0-0	0	3.78	3.60
1997	SF	NL	32	32	3	0	201.0	849	162	80	71	12	13	2	8	100	2	181	10	2	19	5	.792	2	0-0	0	3.28	3.18
1998	SF	NL	25	25	1	0	149.1	661	150	89	84	14	15	4	5	80	2	136	6	1	7	12	.368	1	0-0	0	4.71	5.06
1999	SF	NL	32	32	1	0	203.0	914	209	121	111	21	14	3	5	112	2	159	15	1	11	11	.500	1	0-0	0	4.96	4.92
2000	SF	NL	30	30	4	0	190.1	829	194	99	90	11	7	6	3	108	1	136	11	0	15	6	.714	2	0-0	0	4.75	4.26
2001	SF	NL	27	27	0	0	159.0	693	151	78	71	11	5	9	5	77	7	109	10	2	9	8	.529	0	0-0	0	3.96	4.02
2002	2 Tms	NL	29	29	1	0	160.2	713	171	94	91	13	7	6	9	83	9	109	3	1	5	12	.294	1	0-0	0	5.00	5.10
2003	ChC	NL	29	28	1	0	152.1	699	182	113	97	20	11	7	1	83	1	103	6	0	8	11	.421	1	0-0	0	6.15	5.73
2004	Col	NL	34	34	1	0	202.0	904	223	133	131	30	13	8	11	105	5	117	4	2	15	8	.652	0	0-0	0	5.86	5.84
2005	Ari	NL	21	21	2	0	123.2	535	132	70	66	15	10	4	4	45	0	63	4	0	7	8	.467	0	0-0	0	4.65	4.80
2006	SD	NL	1	1	0	0	6.0	27	5	3	3	0	0	0	1	3	0	4	0	0	0	1	.000	0	0-0	0	3.35	4.50
02	NYM	NL	23	23	1	0	132.2	580	133	70	67	12	7	4	5	66	9	92	2	1	4	9	.308	1	0-0	0	4.51	4.55
02	Cin	NL	6	6	0	0	28.0	133	38	24	24	1	0	2	4	17	0	17	1	0	1	3	.250	0	0-0	0	7.52	7.71
12 ML YEARS			274	273	14	0	1634.2	7205	1658	924	856	152	100	49	55	840	36	1191	77	9	99	90	.524	8	0-0	0	4.72	4.71

Johnny Estrada

Bats: B Throws: R Pos: C-108; PH-12　　Ht: 5'11" Wt: 215 Born: 6/27/1976 Age: 31

Year	Team	Lg	G	AB	H	2B	3B	HR	(Hm	Rd)	TB	R	RBI	RC	TBB	IBB	SO	HBP	SH	SF	SB	CS	SB%	GDP	Avg	OBP	Slg
												BATTING											**BASERUNNING**			**AVERAGES**	
2001	Phi	NL	89	298	68	15	0	8	(7	1)	107	26	37	25	16	6	32	4	2	4	0	0	-	15	.228	.273	.359
2002	Phi	NL	10	17	2	1	0	0	(0	0)	3	0	2	0	2	1	2	0	0	0	0	0	-	-	.118	.211	.176
2003	Atl	NL	16	36	11	0	0	0	(0	0)	11	2	2	2	0	0	3	3	0	0	0	0	-	1	.306	.359	.306
2004	Atl	NL	134	462	145	36	0	9	(4	5)	208	56	76	78	39	7	66	11	1	4	0	0	-	18	.314	.378	.450
2005	Atl	NL	105	357	93	26	0	4	(2	2)	131	31	39	36	20	6	38	3	0	3	0	0	-	13	.261	.303	.367
2006	Ari	NL	115	414	125	26	0	11	(7	4)	184	43	71	59	13	7	40	7	1	8	0	0	-	17	.302	.328	.444
6 ML YEARS			469	1584	444	104	0	32	(20	12)	644	158	227	200	90	27	181	28	4	19	0	0	-	64	.280	.327	.407

Seth Etherton

Pitches: R Bats: R Pos: SP-2　　Ht: 6'1" Wt: 200 Born: 10/17/1976 Age: 30

Year	Team	Lg	G	GS	CG	GF	IP	BFP	H	R	ER	HR	SH	SF	HB	TBB	IBB	SO	WP	Bk	W	L	Pct	ShO	Sv-Op	Hld	ERC	ERA
			HOW MUCH HE PITCHED						**WHAT HE GAVE UP**												**THE RESULTS**							
2006	Portlnd*	AAA	9	9	0	0	49.1	207	48	25	24	8	2	1	0	14	0	49	3	0	2	2	.500	0	0--	-	3.87	4.38
2006	Omha*	AAA	10	6	0	3	34.2	158	43	25	25	11	2	1	1	13	0	29	0	0	1	4	.200	0	0--	-	7.19	6.49
2000	LAA	AL	11	11	0	0	60.1	270	68	38	37	16	0	0	1	22	0	32	2	0	5	1	.833	0	0-0	0	5.87	5.52
2003	Cin	AL	7	7	0	0	30.0	145	39	23	23	4	3	3	3	15	1	17	0	0	2	4	.333	0	0-0	0	6.85	6.90
2005	Oak	AL	3	3	0	0	17.2	74	16	13	13	4	0	1	0	5	0	10	1	1	1	1	.500	0	0-0	0	3.84	6.62
2006	KC	AL	2	2	0	0	7.2	40	10	9	8	3	0	2	0	6	0	4	0	0	1	1	.500	0	0-0	0	9.70	9.39
4 ML YEARS			23	23	0	0	115.2	529	133	83	81	27	3	6	4	48	1	63	3	1	9	7	.563	0	0-0	0	6.05	6.30

Andre Ethier

Bats: L Throws: L Pos: LF-109; PH-22; PR-1　　Ht: 6'1" Wt: 210 Born: 4/10/1982 Age: 25

Year	Team	Lg	G	AB	H	2B	3B	HR	(Hm	Rd)	TB	R	RBI	RC	TBB	IBB	SO	HBP	SH	SF	SB	CS	SB%	GDP	Avg	OBP	Slg
												BATTING											**BASERUNNING**			**AVERAGES**	
2003	Vancvr	A-	10	41	16	4	1	1	(-	-)	25	7	7	10	3	1	3	1	0	0	2	1	.67	3	.390	.444	.610
2003	Kane	A	40	162	44	10	0	0	(-	-)	54	23	11	20	19	2	25	2	0	0	2	2	.50	4	.272	.355	.333
2004	Mdest	A+	99	419	131	23	5	7	(-	-)	185	72	53	72	45	0	64	4	1	2	2	5	.29	12	.313	.383	.442
2005	Mdland	AA	131	505	161	30	3	18	(-	-)	251	104	80	97	48	4	93	11	0	8	1	4	.20	18	.319	.385	.497
2005	Scrmto	AAA	4	15	4	1	0	0	(-	-)	5	0	2	1	2	0	3	0	0	0	0	0	-	0	.267	.353	.333
2006	LsVgs	AAA	25	86	30	4	3	1	(-	-)	43	15	12	19	14	0	16	2	0	1	2	1	.67	1	.349	.447	.500
2006	LAD	NL	126	396	122	20	7	11	(9	2)	189	50	55	62	34	2	77	5	0	6	5	5	.50	11	.308	.365	.477

Dana Eveland

Pitches: L **Bats:** L **Pos:** SP-5; RP-4   **Ht:** 6'1" **Wt:** 250 **Born:** 10/29/1983 **Age:** 23

			HOW MUCH HE PITCHED						WHAT HE GAVE UP										THE RESULTS						
Year	Team	Lg	G	GS	CG	GF	IP	BFP	H	R	ER	HR	SH	SF	HB	TBB	IBB	SO	WP	Bk	W	L	Pct	ShO	Sv-Op	Hld	ERC	ERA
2003	Helena	R+	19	0	0	18	26.0	116	30	9	6	1	4	3	2	8	1	41	5	1	2	1	.667	0	14--	-	4.33	2.08
2004	Beloit	A	22	16	1	4	117.1	484	108	48	37	8	4	5	4	24	0	119	2	0	9	6	.600	0	2--	-	2.80	2.84
2004	Hntsvl	AA	4	4	0	0	23.2	98	23	9	6	0	5	1	1	4	0	14	1	0	0	2	.000	0	0--	-	2.54	2.28
2005	Hntsvl	AA	18	18	0	0	109.0	461	96	42	33	4	4	2	4	38	1	98	7	2	10	4	.714	0	0--	-	2.90	2.72
2006	Nashv	AAA	20	19	0	0	105.0	428	71	40	32	4	4	2	9	41	1	110	1	0	6	5	.545	0	0--	-	2.26	2.74
2005	Mil	NL	27	0	0	3	31.2	146	40	21	21	2	0	1	1	18	3	23	1	0	1	1	.500	0	1-2	7	6.16	5.97
2006	Mil	NL	9	5	0	1	27.2	141	39	25	25	4	1	1	5	16	2	32	2	0	0	3	.000	0	0-1	0	8.30	8.13
	2 ML YEARS		36	5	0	4	59.1	287	79	46	46	6	1	2	6	34	5	55	3	0	1	4	.200	0	1-3	7	7.14	6.98

Adam Everett

Bats: R **Throws:** R **Pos:** SS-149; PH-2   **Ht:** 6'0" **Wt:** 170 **Born:** 2/5/1977 **Age:** 30

						BATTING															BASERUNNING				AVERAGES		
Year	Team	Lg	G	AB	H	2B	3B	HR	(Hm	Rd)	TB	R	RBI	RC	TBB	IBB	SO	HBP	SH	SF	SB	CS	SB%	GDP	Avg	OBP	Slg
2001	Hou	NL	9	3	0	0	0	0	(0	0)	0	1	0	0	0	0	1	0	0	0	1	0	1.00	0	.000	.000	.000
2002	Hou	NL	40	88	17	3	0	0	(0	0)	20	11	4	6	12	1	19	1	2	0	3	0	1.00	1	.193	.297	.227
2003	Hou	NL	128	384	98	18	3	8	(5	3)	147	51	51	50	28	6	66	9	11	8	1	.89	7	.256	.320	.380
2004	Hou	NL	104	384	105	15	2	8	(5	3)	148	66	31	51	17	0	56	9	22	3	13	2	.87	4	.273	.317	.385
2005	Hou	NL	152	549	136	27	2	11	(7	4)	200	58	54	61	26	1	103	8	8	4	21	7	.75	5	.248	.290	.364
2006	Hou	NL	150	514	123	28	6	6	(2	4)	181	52	59	50	34	5	71	4	10	4	9	6	.60	5	.239	.290	.352
	6 ML YEARS		583	1925	480	91	13	33	(19	14)	696	239	199	218	117	13	316	31	53	12	55	16	.77	22	.249	.301	.362

Carl Everett

Bats: B **Throws:** R **Pos:** DH-80; PH-11; LF-1; RF-1   **Ht:** 6'0" **Wt:** 220 **Born:** 6/3/1971 **Age:** 36

						BATTING															BASERUNNING				AVERAGES		
Year	Team	Lg	G	AB	H	2B	3B	HR	(Hm	Rd)	TB	R	RBI	RC	TBB	IBB	SO	HBP	SH	SF	SB	CS	SB%	GDP	Avg	OBP	Slg
1993	Fla	NL	11	19	2	0	0	0	(0	0)	2	0	0	0	1	0	9	0	0	0	1	0	1.00	0	.105	.150	.105
1994	Fla	NL	16	51	11	1	0	2	(2	0)	18	7	6	5	3	0	15	0	0	0	4	0	1.00	0	.216	.259	.353
1995	NYM	NL	79	289	75	13	1	12	(9	3)	126	48	54	41	39	2	67	2	1	0	2	5	.29	11	.260	.352	.436
1996	NYM	NL	101	192	46	8	1	1	(1	0)	59	29	16	21	21	2	53	4	1	1	6	0	1.00	4	.240	.326	.307
1997	NYM	NL	142	443	110	28	3	14	(11	3)	186	58	57	58	32	3	102	7	3	2	17	9	.65	3	.248	.308	.420
1998	Hou	NL	133	467	138	34	4	15	(5	10)	225	72	76	74	44	2	102	3	3	2	14	12	.54	11	.296	.359	.482
1999	Hou	NL	123	464	151	31	3	25	(11	14)	265	86	108	105	50	5	94	11	2	8	27	7	.79	5	.325	.398	.571
2000	Bos	AL	137	496	149	32	4	34	(17	17)	291	82	108	106	52	5	113	8	0	5	11	4	.73	4	.300	.373	.587
2001	Bos	AL	102	409	105	24	4	14	(6	8)	179	61	58	59	27	3	104	13	0	0	9	2	.82	3	.257	.323	.438
2002	Tex	AL	105	374	100	16	0	16	(11	5)	164	47	62	60	33	4	77	6	1	4	2	3	.40	7	.267	.333	.439
2003	2 Tms	AL	147	526	151	27	3	28	(15	13)	268	93	92	102	53	6	84	15	4	4	8	4	.67	7	.287	.366	.510
2004	2 Tms	AL	82	281	73	17	1	7	(3	4)	113	29	35	37	16	3	45	10	0	3	1	0	1.00	11	.260	.319	.402
2005	CWS	AL	135	490	123	17	2	23	(15	8)	213	58	87	71	42	2	99	5	0	10	4	5	.44	11	.251	.311	.435
2006	Sea	AL	92	308	70	8	0	11	(6	5)	111	37	33	28	29	2	57	3	0	3	1	3	.25	7	.227	.297	.360
03	Tex	AL	74	270	74	13	3	18	(10	8)	147	53	51	57	31	2	48	5	4	3	4	1	.80	2	.274	.356	.544
03	CWS	AL	73	256	77	14	0	10	(5	5)	121	40	41	45	22	4	36	10	0	1	4	3	.57	5	.301	.377	.473
04	Mon	NL	39	127	32	10	0	2	(1	1)	48	8	14	13	8	2	19	5	0	1	0	0	-	8	.252	.319	.378
04	CWS	AL	43	154	41	7	1	5	(2	3)	65	21	21	24	8	1	26	5	0	2	1	0	1.00	3	.266	.320	.422
	14 ML YEARS		1405	4809	1304	258	26	202	(112	90)	2220	707	792	769	442	39	1021	87	15	42	107	54	.66	84	.271	.341	.462

Scott Eyre

Pitches: L **Bats:** L **Pos:** RP-74   **Ht:** 6'1" **Wt:** 215 **Born:** 5/30/1972 **Age:** 35

			HOW MUCH HE PITCHED						WHAT HE GAVE UP										THE RESULTS						
Year	Team	Lg	G	GS	CG	GF	IP	BFP	H	R	ER	HR	SH	SF	HB	TBB	IBB	SO	WP	Bk	W	L	Pct	ShO	Sv-Op	Hld	ERC	ERA
1997	CWS	AL	11	11	0	0	60.2	267	62	36	34	11	1	2	1	31	1	36	2	0	4	4	.500	0	0-0	0	5.37	5.04
1998	CWS	AL	33	17	0	10	107.0	491	114	78	64	24	2	3	2	64	0	73	7	0	3	8	.273	0	0-0	0	6.31	5.38
1999	CWS	AL	21	0	0	8	25.0	129	38	22	21	6	0	1	1	15	2	17	1	0	1	1	.500	0	0-0	1	9.23	7.56
2000	CWS	AL	13	1	0	3	19.0	93	29	15	14	3	0	2	1	12	0	16	0	0	1	1	.500	0	0-0	0	9.49	6.63
2001	Tor	AL	17	0	0	5	15.2	66	15	6	6	1	0	1	1	7	2	16	2	0	1	2	.333	0	2-3	3	3.96	3.45
2002	2 Tms		70	3	0	6	74.2	333	80	41	37	4	2	4	0	36	8	58	5	0	2	4	.333	0	0-1	18	4.26	4.46
2003	SF	NL	74	0	0	10	57.0	256	60	23	21	4	2	3	1	26	0	35	6	0	2	1	.667	0	1-3	20	4.37	3.32
2004	SF	NL	83	0	0	12	52.2	229	43	26	24	8	3	3	0	27	3	49	3	0	2	2	.500	0	1-5	23	3.67	4.10
2005	SF	NL	86	0	0	15	68.1	277	48	21	20	3	4	3	4	26	0	65	3	0	2	2	.500	0	0-2	32	2.32	2.63
2006	ChC	NL	74	0	0	15	61.1	266	61	25	23	11	2	4	0	30	4	73	6	0	1	3	.250	0	0-3	18	4.94	3.38
02	Tor	AL	49	3	0	3	63.1	283	69	37	35	4	2	4	0	29	7	51	4	0	2	4	.333	0	0-1	12	4.32	4.97
02	SF	NL	21	0	0	3	11.1	50	11	4	2	0	0	0	0	7	1	7	1	0	0	0	-	0	0-0	6	3.91	1.59
	10 ML YEARS		482	32	0	84	541.1	2407	550	293	264	75	16	26	11	274	20	438	35	0	19	28	.404	0	4-17	115	4.90	4.39

Willie Eyre

Pitches: R **Bats:** R **Pos:** RP-42   **Ht:** 6'2" **Wt:** 205 **Born:** 7/21/1978 **Age:** 28

			HOW MUCH HE PITCHED						WHAT HE GAVE UP										THE RESULTS						
Year	Team	Lg	G	GS	CG	GF	IP	BFP	H	R	ER	HR	SH	SF	HB	TBB	IBB	SO	WP	Bk	W	L	Pct	ShO	Sv-Op	Hld	ERC	ERA
1999	Elizab	R+	16	11	1	1	57.2	270	60	38	29	4	2	0	4	34	0	59	7	1	6	3	.667	0	0--	-	5.00	4.53
1999	QuadC	A	2	2	0	0	8.2	51	8	6	6	0	0	1	1	6	0	10	1	0	1	0	1.000	0	0--	-	3.37	6.23
2000	QuadC	A	26	18	1	3	99.2	457	104	64	51	9	2	3	6	56	0	81	9	0	5	7	.417	1	0--	-	5.06	4.61
2001	QuadC	A	17	0	0	6	22.1	87	19	6	6	1	0	0	1	2	0	21	1	0	3	0	1.000	0	4--	-	2.02	2.42
2001	FtMyrs	A+	32	0	0	10	64.1	280	54	27	18	2	2	7	4	33	2	51	5	0	2	5	.286	0	1--	-	3.30	2.52
2002	FtMyrs	A+	19	0	0	6	33.2	136	28	9	9	0	1	1	3	13	1	25	1	0	4	1	.800	0	2--	-	2.62	2.41
2002	NwBrit	AA	28	0	0	9	50.0	209	40	21	18	1	2	3	2	21	0	43	5	0	6	4	.600	0	2--	-	2.78	3.24

Year	Team	Lg	G	GS	CG	GF	IP	BFP	H	R	ER	HR	SH	SF	HB	TBB	IBB	SO	WP	Bk	W	L	Pct	ShO	Sv-Op Hld	ERC	ERA
2003	NwBrit	AA	29	10	1	8	96.1	416	93	42	37	6	2	2	6	38	4	66	5	0	6	5	.545	1	0- -	3.78	3.46
2003	Roch	AAA	6	5	0	1	24.0	116	30	18	16	2	0	1	2	16	0	23	2	1	0	2	.000	0	0- -	6.96	6.00
2004	Roch	AAA	36	21	1	5	136.0	569	131	60	55	13	8	7	4	53	1	91	6	0	6	7	.462	1	4- -	4.02	3.64
2005	Roch	AAA	56	0	0	23	82.2	349	79	30	25	3	3	0	4	28	1	74	4	0	10	3	.769	0	7- -	3.35	2.72
2006	Min	AL	42	0	0	20	59.1	275	75	36	35	8	1	3	6	22	4	26	4	0	1	0	1.000	0	0-0 0	6.07	5.31

Brandon Fahey

Bats: L **Throws:** R **Pos:** LF-53; SS-17; 2B-13; PR-11; PH-4; 3B-1; RF-1; DH-1   **Ht:** 6'2" **Wt:** 160 **Born:** 1/18/1981 **Age:** 26

				BATTING																		BASERUNNING				AVERAGES		
Year	Team	Lg	G	AB	H	2B	3B	HR	(Hm	Rd)	TB	R	RBI	RC	TBB	IBB	SO	HBP	SH	SF		SB	CS	SB%	GDP	Avg	OBP	Slg
2002	Abrdn	A-	63	253	71	10	6	0	(-	-)	93	31	15	30	20	1	34	1	4	2		5	8	.38	1	.281	.333	.368
2003	Frdrck	A+	107	365	85	11	3	1	(-	-)	105	41	22	30	22	0	56	2	13	2		4	2	.67	7	.233	.279	.288
2004	Frdrck	A+	62	181	49	7	0	3	(-	-)	65	20	19	25	22	1	20	2	6	1		3	3	.50	3	.271	.354	.359
2004	Bowie	AA	63	208	49	7	1	1	(-	-)	61	20	15	19	17	0	27	0	7	0		3	1	.75	5	.236	.293	.293
2005	Bowie	AA	139	502	146	21	4	3	(-	-)	184	63	47	70	44	0	71	4	22	6		17	8	.68	12	.291	.349	.367
2006	Ottawa	AAA	20	68	19	1	1	0	(-	-)	22	8	3	10	10	0	5	4	2	0		4	3	.57	1	.279	.402	.324
2006	Bal	AL	91	251	59	8	2	2	(2	0)	77	36	23	27	23	0	48	3	9	0		3	3	.50	2	.235	.307	.307

Brian Falkenborg

Pitches: R **Bats:** R **Pos:** RP-5   **Ht:** 6'6" **Wt:** 225 **Born:** 1/18/1978 **Age:** 29

				HOW MUCH HE PITCHED					WHAT HE GAVE UP											THE RESULTS						
Year	Team	Lg	G	GS	CG	GF	IP	BFP	H	R	ER	HR	SH	SF	HB	TBB	IBB	SO	WP	Bk	W	L	Pct	ShO	Sv-Op Hld	ERC	ERA
2006	Memp*	AAA	47	0	0	39	51.2	219	51	29	24	6	4	3	0	15	0	53	6	0	4	5	.444	0	16- -	3.64	4.18
1999	Bal	AL	2	0	0	0	3.0	12	2	0	0	0	0	0	0	2	0	1	0	0	0	0	-	0	0-0 0	2.79	0.00
2004	LAD	NL	6	0	0	1	14.1	73	19	14	12	2	2	0	3	9	0	11	1	0	1	0	1.000	0	0-0 0	8.19	7.53
2005	SD	NL	10	0	0	3	11.0	54	17	11	10	2	0	0	0	5	1	10	2	0	0	0	-	0	0-0 0	8.14	8.18
2006	StL	NL	5	0	0	3	6.1	25	5	2	2	0	1	0	1	0	0	5	0	0	0	1	.000	0	0-0 0	1.57	2.84
4 ML YEARS			23	0	0	7	34.2	164	43	27	24	4	3	0	4	16	1	27	3	0	1	1	.500	0	0-0 0	6.27	6.23

Kyle Farnsworth

Pitches: R **Bats:** R **Pos:** RP-72   **Ht:** 6'4" **Wt:** 240 **Born:** 4/14/1976 **Age:** 31

				HOW MUCH HE PITCHED					WHAT HE GAVE UP											THE RESULTS						
Year	Team	Lg	G	GS	CG	GF	IP	BFP	H	R	ER	HR	SH	SF	HB	TBB	IBB	SO	WP	Bk	W	L	Pct	ShO	Sv-Op Hld	ERC	ERA
1999	ChC	NL	27	21	1	1	130.0	579	140	80	73	28	6	2	3	52	1	70	7	1	5	9	.357	1	0-0 0	5.39	5.05
2000	ChC	NL	46	5	0	8	77.0	371	90	58	55	14	4	4	4	50	8	74	3	0	2	9	.182	0	1-6 6	6.72	6.43
2001	ChC	NL	76	0	0	24	82.0	339	65	26	25	8	2	2	1	29	2	107	2	2	4	6	.400	0	2-3 24	2.76	2.74
2002	ChC	NL	45	0	0	17	46.2	213	53	47	38	9	2	5	1	24	7	46	1	0	4	6	.400	0	1-7 6	5.89	7.33
2003	ChC	NL	77	0	0	13	76.1	312	53	31	28	6	4	1	0	36	1	92	6	0	3	2	.600	0	0-3 19	2.58	3.30
2004	ChC	NL	72	0	0	25	66.2	298	67	39	35	10	5	0	2	33	1	78	1	0	4	5	.444	0	0-4 18	4.91	4.73
2005	2 Tms		72	0	0	34	70.0	277	44	18	17	5	2	1	3	27	0	87	3	1	1	1	.500	0	16-18 19	2.12	2.19
2006	NYY	AL	72	0	0	24	66.0	289	62	34	32	8	3	2	1	28	3	75	5	1	3	6	.333	0	6-10 19	3.88	4.36
05	Det	AL	46	0	0	16	42.2	174	29	12	11	1	1	1	1	20	0	55	2	0	1	1	.500	0	6-8 15	2.26	2.32
05	Atl	NL	26	0	0	18	27.1	103	15	6	6	4	1	0	2	7	0	32	1	1	0	0	-	0	10-10 4	1.86	1.98
8 ML YEARS			487	26	1	146	614.2	2678	574	333	303	88	28	17	15	279	23	629	28	5	26	44	.371	1	26-51 111	4.22	4.44

Sal Fasano

Bats: R **Throws:** R **Pos:** C-77; PH-3; PR-1   **Ht:** 6'2" **Wt:** 245 **Born:** 8/10/1971 **Age:** 35

					BATTING																BASERUNNING				AVERAGES		
Year	Team	Lg	G	AB	H	2B	3B	HR	(Hm	Rd)	TB	R	RBI	RC	TBB	IBB	SO	HBP	SH	SF		SB	CS	SB%	GDP	Avg	OBP	Slg
2006	Clrwtr*	A+	4	12	1	0	0	0	(-	-)	1	0	1	0	0	0	1	0	0	0		0	0	-	1	.083	.083	.083
2006	Rdng*	AA	1	3	0	0	0	0	(-	-)	0	0	0	0	0	0	0	0	0	0		0	0	-	0	.000	.000	.000
1996	KC	AL	51	143	29	2	0	6	(1	5)	49	20	19	13	14	0	25	2	1	0		1	1	.50	3	.203	.283	.343
1997	KC	AL	13	38	8	2	0	1	(0	1)	13	4	1	2	1	0	12	0	0	0		0	0	-	0	.211	.231	.342
1998	KC	AL	74	216	49	10	0	8	(4	4)	83	21	31	26	10	1	56	16	3	2		1	0	1.00	4	.227	.307	.384
1999	KC	AL	23	60	14	2	0	5	(2	3)	31	11	16	12	7	0	17	7	0	1		0	1	.00	1	.233	.373	.517
2000	Oak	AL	52	126	27	6	0	7	(4	3)	54	21	19	16	14	0	47	3	0	1		0	0	-	3	.214	.306	.429
2001	3 Tms		39	85	17	5	0	3	(3	0)	31	12	9	10	5	0	31	4	2	0		0	0	-	0	.200	.277	.365
2002	LAA	AL	2	1	0	0	0	0	(0	0)	0	0	0	0	0	0	1	0	0	0		0	0	-	0	.000	.000	.000
2005	Bal	AL	64	160	40	3	0	11	(1	10)	76	25	20	17	9	0	41	5	0	0		0	0	-	5	.250	.310	.475
2006	2 Tms		78	189	41	12	0	5	(2	3)	68	12	15	12	7	0	61	6	4	0		0	1	.00	5	.217	.267	.360
01	Oak	AL	11	21	1	0	0	0	(0	0)	1	2	0	0	1	0	12	1	0	0		0	0	-	1	.048	.130	.048
01	KC	AL	3	1	0	0	0	0	(0	0)	0	0	0	0	0	0	0	0	0	0		0	0	-	0	.000	.000	.000
01	Col	NL	25	63	16	5	0	3	(3	0)	30	10	9	10	4	0	19	3	2	0		0	0	-	1	.254	.329	.476
06	Phi	NL	50	140	34	8	0	4	(2	2)	54	9	10	9	5	0	47	3	1	0		0	1	.00	4	.243	.284	.386
06	NYY	AL	28	49	7	4	0	1	(0	1)	14	3	5	3	2	0	14	3	3	0		0	0	-	1	.143	.222	.286
9 ML YEARS			396	1018	225	42	0	46	(17	29)	405	126	130	108	67	1	291	43	10	4		2	3	.40	25	.221	.296	.398

Jeff Fassero

Pitches: L **Bats:** L **Pos:** RP-9; SP-1   **Ht:** 6'1" **Wt:** 215 **Born:** 1/5/1963 **Age:** 44

				HOW MUCH HE PITCHED					WHAT HE GAVE UP											THE RESULTS						
Year	Team	Lg	G	GS	CG	GF	IP	BFP	H	R	ER	HR	SH	SF	HB	TBB	IBB	SO	WP	Bk	W	L	Pct	ShO	Sv-Op Hld	ERC	ERA
1991	Mon	NL	51	0	0	30	55.1	223	39	17	15	1	6	1	0	17	1	42	4	0	2	5	.286	0	8-11 7	1.75	2.44
1992	Mon	NL	70	0	0	22	85.2	368	81	35	27	1	5	2	2	34	6	63	7	1	8	7	.533	0	1-7 12	3.10	2.84
1993	Mon	NL	56	15	1	10	149.2	616	119	50	38	7	7	4	0	54	0	140	5	0	12	5	.706	0	1-3 6	2.48	2.29
1994	Mon	NL	21	21	1	0	138.2	569	119	54	46	13	7	2	1	40	4	119	6	0	8	6	.571	0	0-0 0	2.82	2.99

			HOW MUCH HE PITCHED						WHAT HE GAVE UP												THE RESULTS							
Year	Team	Lg	G	GS	CG	GF	IP	BFP	H	R	ER	HR	SH	SF	HB	TBB	IBB	SO	WP	Bk	W	L	Pct	ShO	Sv-Op	Hld	ERC	ERA
1995	Mon	NL	30	30	1	0	189.0	833	207	102	91	15	**19**	7	2	74	3	164	7	1	13	14	.481	0	0-0	0	4.43	4.33
1996	Mon	NL	34	34	5	0	231.2	967	217	95	85	20	16	5	3	55	3	222	5	2	15	11	.577	0	0-0	0	3.00	3.30
1997	Sea	AL	35	**35**	2	0	234.1	1010	226	108	94	21	7	10	3	84	6	189	13	2	16	9	.640	1	0-0	0	3.60	3.61
1998	Sea	AL	32	32	7	0	224.2	954	223	115	99	33	8	8	10	66	2	176	12	0	13	12	.520	0	0-0	0	4.10	3.97
1999	2 Tms	AL	37	27	0	2	156.1	751	208	135	125	35	2	7	4	83	3	114	9	0	5	14	.263	0	0-0	2	7.69	7.20
2000	Bos	AL	38	23	0	4	130.0	577	153	72	69	16	7	2	1	50	2	97	2	0	8	8	.500	0	0-0	5	5.25	4.78
2001	ChC	NL	82	0	0	30	73.2	308	66	31	28	6	1	2	1	23	5	79	3	0	4	4	.500	0	12-17	25	2.97	3.42
2002	2 Tms	NL	73	0	0	18	69.0	315	81	43	41	9	7	1	3	27	5	56	2	1	8	6	.571	0	0-3	13	5.25	5.35
2003	StL	NL	62	6	0	15	77.2	354	93	51	49	17	3	1	2	34	4	55	2	0	1	7	.125	0	3-6	11	6.34	5.68
2004	2 Tms	NL	41	12	0	2	112.0	508	136	73	68	9	5	7	4	44	5	60	4	1	3	8	.273	0	0-0	2	5.20	5.46
2005	SF	NL	48	6	0	11	91.0	384	92	48	41	7	7	3	0	31	1	60	3	0	4	7	.364	0	0-2	2	3.77	4.05
2006	SF	NL	10	1	0	2	15.0	73	23	13	13	4	1	1	0	8	0	7	2	0	1	1	.500	0	0-0	0	9.62	7.80
99	Sea	AL	30	24	0	1	139.0	669	188	123	114	34	1	6	4	73	3	101	7	0	4	14	.222	0	0-0	2	8.02	7.38
99	Tex	AL	7	3	0	1	17.1	82	20	12	11	1	1	1	0	10	0	13	2	0	1	0	1.000	0	0-0	0	5.21	5.71
02	ChC	NL	57	0	0	17	51.0	240	65	37	35	5	6	1	3	22	5	44	2	1	5	6	.455	0	0-1	6	5.79	6.18
02	StL	NL	16	0	0	1	18.0	75	16	6	6	4	1	0	0	5	0	12	0	0	3	0	1.000	0	0-0	7	3.70	3.00
04	Col	NL	40	12	0	2	111.0	505	136	73	68	9	5	7	4	44	5	59	4	1	3	8	.273	0	0-0	2	5.29	5.51
04	Ari	NL	1	0	0	0	1.0	3	0	0	0	0	0	0	0	0	0	1	0	0	0	0	-	0	0-0	0	0.00	0.00
16 ML YEARS			720	242	17	146	2033.2	8810	2083	1042	929	214	108	62	37	724	50	1643	86	8	121	124	.494	2	25-49	85	4.08	4.11

Ryan Feierabend

Pitches: L Bats: L Pos: SP-2; RP-2   Ht: 6'3" Wt: 190 Born: 8/22/1985 Age: 21

			HOW MUCH HE PITCHED						WHAT HE GAVE UP												THE RESULTS							
Year	Team	Lg	G	GS	CG	GF	IP	BFP	H	R	ER	HR	SH	SF	HB	TBB	IBB	SO	WP	Bk	W	L	Pct	ShO	Sv-Op	Hld	ERC	ERA
2003	Ms	A	6	5	0	1	20.2	89	23	11	6	0	1	1	1	6	0	12	1	1	2	3	.400	0	1--	-	3.79	2.61
2004	Wisc	A	26	26	1	0	161.0	666	158	78	65	17	4	10	7	44	0	106	14	0	9	7	.563	1	0--	-	3.77	3.63
2005	InldEm	A+	29	29	0	0	150.2	689	186	80	65	16	5	1	8	51	0	122	3	0	8	7	.533	0	0--	-	5.38	3.88
2006	SnAnt	AA	28	28	0	0	153.2	654	156	87	73	16	1	6	7	55	1	127	6	1	9	12	.429	0	0--	-	4.27	4.28
2006	Sea	AL	4	2	0	2	17.0	73	15	7	3	1	0	0	0	7	0	11	1	2	0	1	.000	0	0-0	0	3.91	3.71

Scott Feldman

Pitches: R Bats: L Pos: RP-36   Ht: 6'6" Wt: 225 Born: 2/7/1983 Age: 24

			HOW MUCH HE PITCHED						WHAT HE GAVE UP												THE RESULTS							
Year	Team	Lg	G	GS	CG	GF	IP	BFP	H	R	ER	HR	SH	SF	HB	TBB	IBB	SO	WP	Bk	W	L	Pct	ShO	Sv-Op	Hld	ERC	ERA
2003	Rngrs	R	3	1	0	0	6.1	24	4	6	3	0	0	1	1	1	0	7	0	0	1	1	.500	0	0--	-	1.49	4.26
2004	Rngrs	R	4	3	0	0	7.0	24	2	0	0	0	0	0	0	1	0	5	0	0	0	0	-	0	0--	-	0.34	0.00
2005	Bkrsfld	A+	6	0	0	0	9.0	34	5	2	0	0	0	0	1	2	0	11	1	0	0	0	-	0	3--	-	1.28	0.00
2005	Frisco	AA	46	0	0	34	61.0	249	43	18	16	3	3	0	0	23	8	41	5	0	1	2	.333	0	14--	-	1.93	2.36
2006	Okla	AAA	23	0	0	10	27.1	111	20	9	6	2	2	0	3	9	0	24	0	0	2	2	.500	0	4--	-	2.66	1.98
2005	Tex	AL	8	0	0	3	9.1	37	9	1	1	0	0	0	0	2	1	4	0	0	0	1	.000	0	0-0	1	2.48	0.96
2006	Tex	AL	36	0	0	5	41.1	175	42	19	18	4	2	1	4	10	0	30	0	0	0	2	.000	0	0-1	7	3.94	3.92
2 ML YEARS			44	0	0	8	50.2	212	51	20	19	4	2	1	4	12	1	34	0	0	0	3	.000	0	0-1	8	3.66	3.38

Pedro Feliciano

Pitches: L Bats: L Pos: RP-64   Ht: 5'10" Wt: 185 Born: 8/25/1976 Age: 30

			HOW MUCH HE PITCHED						WHAT HE GAVE UP												THE RESULTS							
Year	Team	Lg	G	GS	CG	GF	IP	BFP	H	R	ER	HR	SH	SF	HB	TBB	IBB	SO	WP	Bk	W	L	Pct	ShO	Sv-Op	Hld	ERC	ERA
2006	Norfolk*	AAA	3	0	0	0	4.1	18	4	3	3	1	0	1	0	1	0	5	0	0	0	0	-	0	0--	-	3.75	6.23
2002	NYM	NL	6	0	0	3	6.0	26	9	5	5	0	0	0	0	1	0	4	0	0	0	0	-	0	0-0	0	5.56	7.50
2003	NYM	NL	23	0	0	8	48.1	218	52	21	18	5	0	1	3	21	3	43	3	1	0	0	-	0	0-0	0	4.77	3.35
2004	NYM	NL	22	0	0	3	18.1	82	14	12	11	2	1	1	1	12	0	14	1	0	1	1	.500	0	0-0	2	3.93	5.40
2006	NYM	NL	64	0	0	10	60.1	256	56	15	14	4	4	3	3	20	1	54	1	0	7	2	.778	0	0-3	10	3.34	2.09
4 ML YEARS			115	0	0	24	133.0	582	131	53	48	11	5	5	7	54	4	115	5	1	8	3	.727	0	0-3	12	4.02	3.25

Pedro Feliz

Bats: R Throws: R Pos: 3B-159; LF-3; SS-2   Ht: 6'1" Wt: 210 Born: 4/27/1975 Age: 32

			BATTING																		BASERUNNING				AVERAGES		
Year	Team	Lg	G	AB	H	2B	3B	HR	(Hm	Rd)	TB	R	RBI	RC	TBB	IBB	SO	HBP	SH	SF	SB	CS	SB%	GDP	Avg	OBP	Slg
2000	SF	NL	8	7	2	0	0	0	(0	0)	2	1	0	1	0	0	1	0	0	0	0	0	-	0	.286	.286	.286
2001	SF	NL	94	220	50	9	1	7	(4	3)	82	23	22	20	10	2	50	2	3	3	2	1	.67	5	.227	.264	.373
2002	SF	NL	67	146	37	4	1	2	(1	1)	49	14	13	12	6	1	27	0	0	1	0	0	-	2	.253	.281	.336
2003	SF	NL	95	235	58	9	3	16	(6	10)	121	31	48	34	10	0	53	1	1	2	2	2	.50	7	.247	.278	.515
2004	SF	NL	144	503	130	33	3	22	(11	11)	244	72	84	56	23	1	85	0	0	5	5	2	.71	18	.276	.305	.485
2005	SF	NL	156	569	142	30	4	20	(10	10)	240	69	81	58	38	1	102	1	1	6	0	2	.00	20	.250	.295	.422
2006	SF	NL	160	603	147	35	5	22	(6	16)	258	75	98	71	33	4	112	1	1	6	1	1	.50	18	.244	.281	.428
7 ML YEARS			724	2283	575	120	17	89	(37	52)	996	285	346	252	120	9	430	5	6	23	10	8	.56	70	.252	.288	.436

Jared Fernandez

Pitches: R Bats: R Pos: RP-4   Ht: 6'1" Wt: 235 Born: 2/2/1972 Age: 35

			HOW MUCH HE PITCHED						WHAT HE GAVE UP												THE RESULTS							
Year	Team	Lg	G	GS	CG	GF	IP	BFP	H	R	ER	HR	SH	SF	HB	TBB	IBB	SO	WP	Bk	W	L	Pct	ShO	Sv-Op	Hld	ERC	ERA
2006	Nashv*	AAA	24	15	4	6	129.1	549	141	64	47	9	6	3	3	23	1	76	6	0	6	4	.600	2	3--	-	3.54	3.27
2001	Cin	NL	5	2	0	0	12.1	57	13	9	6	1	0	0	0	6	0	5	1	0	0	0	-	0	0-0	0	5.21	4.38
2002	Cin	NL	14	8	0	2	50.2	231	59	31	25	5	1	2	3	24	1	36	3	0	1	3	.250	0	0-0	0	5.57	4.44
2003	Hou	NL	12	6	0	3	38.1	161	37	17	17	2	1	2	1	12	2	19	3	0	3	3	.500	0	0-0	0	3.38	3.99

	HOW MUCH HE PITCHED							WHAT HE GAVE UP										THE RESULTS						
Year	Team	Lg	G	GS	CG	GF	IP	BFP	H	R	ER	HR	SH	SF	HB	TBB	IBB	SO	WP	Bk	W	L	Pct	ShO	Sv-Op	Hld	ERC	ERA
2004	Hou	NL	2	1	0	0	1.0	14	6	6	6	0	0	1	0	5	0	0	0	0	0	0	-	0	0-0	0	66.63	54.00
2006	Mil	NL	4	0	0	3	6.1	31	11	7	7	2	0	0	0	1	0	1	0	0	0	0	-	0	0-0	0	9.19	9.95
	5 ML YEARS		37	17	0	10	108.2	494	126	70	61	10	4	4	7	48	3	61	7	0	4	7	.364	0	0-0	0	5.34	5.05

Robert Fick

Bats: L **Throws:** R **Pos:** C-26; PH-24; 1B-13; RF-6   **Ht:** 6'1" **Wt:** 205 **Born:** 3/15/1974 **Age:** 33

	BATTING																	BASERUNNING				AVERAGES		
Year	Team	Lg	G	AB	H	2B	3B	HR	(Hm | Rd)	TB	R	RBI	RC	TBB	IBB	SO	HBP	SH	SF	SB	CS	SB%	GDP	Avg	OBP	Slg
2006	Hrsbrg*	AA	16	57	16	1	0	1	(- | -)	20	11	4	8	8	0	8	0	0	0	2	1	.67	1	.281	.369	.351
2006	NewOr*	AAA	2	7	1	0	0	0	(- | -)	1	0	0	0	1	0	2	0	0	0	1	0	1.00	0	.143	.250	.143
1998	Det	AL	7	22	8	1	0	3	(0 | 3)	18	6	7	6	2	0	7	0	0	0	1	0	1.00	1	.364	.417	.818
1999	Det	AL	15	41	9	0	0	3	(1 | 2)	18	6	10	6	7	0	6	0	0	1	1	0	1.00	1	.220	.327	.439
2000	Det	AL	66	163	41	7	2	3	(0 | 3)	61	18	22	21	22	2	39	1	0	2	2	1	.67	4	.252	.340	.374
2001	Det	AL	124	401	109	21	2	19	(8 | 11)	191	62	61	62	39	3	62	4	0	4	0	3	.00	10	.272	.339	.476
2002	Det	AL	148	556	150	36	2	17	(12 | 5)	241	66	63	70	46	4	90	7	0	5	0	1	.00	17	.270	.331	.433
2003	Atl	NL	126	409	110	26	1	11	(4 | 7)	171	52	80	68	42	4	47	2	0	7	1	0	1.00	9	.269	.335	.418
2004	2 Tms		89	226	45	5	2	6	(3 | 3)	72	14	26	22	22	2	36	3	0	2	0	0	-	2	.199	.277	.319
2005	SD	NL	93	230	61	10	2	3	(0 | 3)	84	25	30	29	26	2	33	1	1	2	0	2	.00	4	.265	.340	.365
2006	Was	NL	60	128	34	4	0	2	(1 | 1)	44	14	9	11	10	1	24	1	2	0	1	1	.50	4	.266	.324	.344
04	TB	AL	76	214	43	5	2	6	(3 | 3)	70	12	26	21	20	2	32	2	0	2	0	0	-	2	.201	.273	.327
04	SD	NL	13	12	2	0	0	0	(0 | 0)	2	2	0	1	2	0	4	1	0	0	0	0	-	0	.167	.333	.167
	9 ML YEARS		728	2176	567	110	11	67	(29 | 38)	900	263	308	295	216	18	344	19	3	23	6	8	.43	52	.261	.329	.414

Nate Field

Pitches: R **Bats:** R **Pos:** RP-14   **Ht:** 6'2" **Wt:** 205 **Born:** 12/11/1975 **Age:** 31

	HOW MUCH HE PITCHED								WHAT HE GAVE UP											THE RESULTS						
Year	Team	Lg	G	GS	CG	GF	IP	BFP	H	R	ER	HR	SH	SF	HB	TBB	IBB	SO	WP	Bk	W	L	Pct	ShO	Sv-Op	Hld	ERC	ERA
2006	ColSpr*	AAA	49	0	0	40	49.1	213	63	28	26	7	2	0	1	9	0	55	3	1	3	3	.500	0	25--	-	5.26	4.74
2002	KC	AL	5	0	0	0	5.0	26	8	5	5	2	1	0	0	3	1	3	2	0	0	0	-	0	0-0	0	10.82	9.00
2003	KC	AL	19	0	0	7	21.2	97	19	10	10	3	0	1	1	14	1	19	0	0	1	1	.500	0	0-0	2	4.74	4.15
2004	KC	AL	43	0	0	23	44.1	191	40	25	21	5	1	2	2	19	2	30	2	0	2	3	.400	0	3-5	2	3.82	4.26
2005	KC	AL	7	0	0	3	6.2	35	13	7	7	1	0	0	0	5	2	4	1	0	0	0	-	0	0-0	1	12.38	9.45
2006	Col	NL	14	0	0	1	9.0	40	9	4	4	2	0	0	0	5	1	14	1	0	1	1	.500	0	0-1	4	5.45	4.00
	5 ML YEARS		88	0	0	34	86.2	389	89	51	47	13	2	3	3	46	7	70	6	0	4	5	.444	0	3-6	9	5.14	4.88

Prince Fielder

Bats: L **Throws:** R **Pos:** 1B-152; PH-5; DH-1   **Ht:** 6'0" **Wt:** 260 **Born:** 5/9/1984 **Age:** 23

	BATTING																	BASERUNNING				AVERAGES		
Year	Team	Lg	G	AB	H	2B	3B	HR	(Hm	Rd)	TB	R	RBI	RC	TBB	IBB	SO	HBP	SH	SF	SB	CS	SB%	GDP	Avg	OBP	Slg
2002	Ogden	R+	41	146	57	12	0	10	(-	-)	99	35	40	49	37	1	27	8	0	1	3	4	.43	2	.390	.531	.678
2002	Beloit	A	32	112	27	7	0	3	(-	-)	43	15	11	14	10	0	27	3	0	0	0	0	-	1	.241	.320	.384
2003	Beloit	A	137	502	157	22	2	27	(-	-)	264	81	112	110	71	16	80	15	0	6	2	1	.67	13	.313	.409	.526
2004	Hntsvl	AA	135	497	135	29	1	23	(-	-)	235	70	78	89	65	6	93	11	0	4	11	7	.61	11	.272	.366	.473
2005	Nashv	AAA	103	378	110	21	0	28	(-	-)	215	68	86	83	54	5	93	7	0	2	8	5	.62	11	.291	.388	.569
2005	Mil	NL	39	59	17	4	0	2	(2	0)	27	2	10	10	2	0	17	0	0	1	0	0	-	0	.288	.306	.458
2006	Mil	NL	157	569	154	35	1	28	(11	17)	275	82	81	84	59	5	125	12	0	8	7	2	.78	18	.271	.347	.483
	2 ML YEARS		196	628	171	39	1	30	(13	17)	302	84	91	94	61	5	142	12	0	9	7	2	.78	18	.272	.344	.481

Josh Fields

Bats: R **Throws:** R **Pos:** 3B-6; PH-4; LF-1; DH-1; PR-1   **Ht:** 6'1" **Wt:** 215 **Born:** 12/14/1982 **Age:** 24

	BATTING																	BASERUNNING				AVERAGES		
Year	Team	Lg	G	AB	H	2B	3B	HR	(Hm	Rd)	TB	R	RBI	RC	TBB	IBB	SO	HBP	SH	SF	SB	CS	SB%	GDP	Avg	OBP	Slg
2004	WinSa	A+	66	256	73	12	4	7	(-	-)	114	36	39	38	18	1	74	2	0	3	0	0	-	2	.285	.333	.445
2005	Brham	AA	134	477	120	27	0	16	(-	-)	195	76	79	70	55	2	142	13	9	6	7	6	.54	8	.252	.341	.409
2006	Charltt	AAA	124	462	141	32	4	19	(-	-)	238	85	70	94	54	2	136	3	4	3	28	5	.85	8	.305	.379	.515
2006	CWS	AL	11	20	3	2	0	1	(1	0)	8	4	2	1	5	0	8	0	0	0	0	0	-	0	.150	.320	.400

Chone Figgins

Bats: B **Throws:** R **Pos:** CF-96; 3B-34; LF-16; 2B-9; RF-6; DH-6; PH-4; SS-2; PR-1   **Ht:** 5'7" **Wt:** 180 **Born:** 1/22/1978 **Age:** 29

	BATTING																	BASERUNNING				AVERAGES		
Year	Team	Lg	G	AB	H	2B	3B	HR	(Hm	Rd)	TB	R	RBI	RC	TBB	IBB	SO	HBP	SH	SF	SB	CS	SB%	GDP	Avg	OBP	Slg
2002	LAA	AL	15	12	2	1	0	0	(0	0)	3	6	1	0	0	0	5	0	0	0	2	1	.67	1	.167	.167	.250
2003	LAA	AL	71	240	71	9	4	0	(0	0)	88	34	27	39	20	0	38	0	6	4	13	7	.65	1	.296	.345	.367
2004	LAA	AL	148	577	171	22	17	5	(3	2)	242	83	60	93	49	0	94	0	10	2	34	13	.72	6	.296	.350	.419
2005	LAA	AL	158	642	186	25	10	8	(2	6)	255	113	57	94	64	1	101	0	9	5	62	17	.78	9	.290	.352	.397
2006	LAA	AL	155	604	161	23	8	9	(2	7)	227	93	62	84	65	1	100	2	5	7	52	16	.76	6	.267	.336	.376
	5 ML YEARS		547	2075	591	80	39	22	(7	15)	815	329	207	310	198	2	338	2	30	18	163	54	.75	23	.285	.345	.393

Luis Figueroa

Bats: B **Throws:** R **Pos:** 2B-5; SS-2; PR-1   **Ht:** 5'9" **Wt:** 140 **Born:** 2/16/1974 **Age:** 33

									BATTING										BASERUNNING				AVERAGES		
Year	Team	Lg	G	AB	H	2B	3B	HR	(Hm | Rd)	TB	R	RBI	RC	TBB	IBB	SO	HBP	SH	SF	SB	CS	SB%	GDP	Avg	OBP	Slg
1997	Augsta	A	71	248	56	8	0	0	(- | -)	64	38	21	26	35	0	29	1	9	2	22	6	.79	2	.226	.322	.258
1997	Lynbrg	A+	26	89	25	5	0	0	(- | -)	30	12	2	10	7	0	6	0	0	0	1	2	.33	5	.281	.333	.337
1998	Carlina	AA	117	350	87	9	3	0	(- | -)	102	54	24	47	71	3	46	2	10	2	6	5	.55	12	.249	.376	.291
1999	Altna	AA	131	418	110	15	5	3	(- | -)	144	61	50	54	52	0	44	3	16	3	9	9	.50	7	.263	.347	.344
2000	Altna	AA	94	342	97	10	4	1	(- | -)	118	45	28	47	37	1	32	2	10	1	14	5	.74	8	.284	.356	.345
2000	Nashv	AAA	23	64	16	1	0	3	(- | -)	26	6	8	6	1	0	8	0	0	0	2	1	.67	2	.250	.262	.406
2001	Nashv	AAA	92	347	104	11	1	4	(- | -)	129	45	29	49	31	1	26	1	6	2	8	5	.62	8	.300	.357	.372
2001	Norfolk	AAA	17	58	15	3	1	1	(- | -)	23	7	5	7	5	0	6	0	1	0	0	0	-	1	.259	.317	.397
2002	BrvdCt	A+	15	61	16	1	1	0	(- | -)	19	8	8	5	5	0	2	1	0	0	2	4	.33	3	.262	.328	.311
2002	Hrsbrg	AA	66	250	68	17	3	1	(- | -)	94	47	30	33	25	0	16	2	4	2	6	7	.46	5	.272	.341	.376
2002	Ottawa	AAA	27	82	12	1	1	1	(- | -)	18	6	9	1	3	0	14	1	6	0	0	2	.00	2	.146	.186	.220
2002	Norfolk	AAA	2	4	0	0	0	0	(- | -)	0	0	0	0	0	0	1	0	0	0	0	0	-	0	.000	.000	.000
2003	Tacom	AAA	123	423	119	18	0	3	(- | -)	146	40	50	51	45	2	35	3	1	6	1	5	.17	16	.281	.350	.345
2003	Edmtn	AAA	126	480	152	30	2	2	(- | -)	192	66	44	69	36	1	31	3	5	6	7	7	.50	7	.317	.364	.400
2004	Indy	AAA	116	383	104	14	0	5	(- | -)	133	44	48	42	24	1	24	1	7	3	5	6	.45	6	.272	.314	.347
2004	Nashv	AAA	103	321	95	13	1	6	(- | -)	128	40	44	43	25	0	37	4	0	1	2	2	.50	14	.296	.353	.399
2005	Pwtckt	AAA	109	402	116	22	1	7	(- | -)	161	58	48	54	29	0	28	1	2	5	2	6	.25	10	.289	.334	.400
2006	Syrcse	AAA	93	377	104	22	3	6	(- | -)	150	39	38	49	24	1	35	2	8	6	11	9	.55	9	.276	.318	.398
2001	Pit	NL	4	2	0	0	0	0	(0 | 0)	0	0	0	0	0	0	0	0	0	0	0	0	-	0	.000	.000	.000
2006	Tor	AL	8	9	1	1	0	0	(0 | 0)	2	1	0	0	0	0	2	0	0	0	0	0	-	0	.111	.111	.222
	2 ML YEARS		12	11	1	1	0	0	(0 | 0)	2	1	0	0	0	0	2	0	0	0	0	0	-	0	.091	.091	.182

Steve Finley

Bats: L **Throws:** L **Pos:** CF-130; PH-14; PR-3   **Ht:** 6'2" **Wt:** 195 **Born:** 3/12/1965 **Age:** 42

									BATTING										BASERUNNING				AVERAGES		
Year	Team	Lg	G	AB	H	2B	3B	HR	(Hm | Rd)	TB	R	RBI	RC	TBB	IBB	SO	HBP	SH	SF	SB	CS	SB%	GDP	Avg	OBP	Slg
1989	Bal	AL	81	217	54	5	2	2	(0 | 2)	69	35	25	23	15	1	30	1	6	2	17	3	.85	3	.249	.298	.318
1990	Bal	AL	142	464	119	16	4	3	(1 | 2)	152	46	37	47	32	3	53	2	10	5	22	9	.71	8	.256	.304	.328
1991	Hou	NL	159	596	170	28	10	8	(0 | 8)	242	84	54	80	42	5	65	2	10	6	34	18	.65	8	.285	.331	.406
1992	Hou	NL	162	607	177	29	13	5	(5 | 0)	247	84	55	93	58	6	63	3	16	2	44	9	.83	10	.292	.355	.407
1993	Hou	NL	142	545	145	15	13	8	(1 | 7)	210	69	44	64	28	1	65	3	6	3	19	6	.76	8	.266	.304	.385
1994	Hou	NL	94	373	103	16	5	11	(4 | 7)	162	64	33	54	28	0	52	2	13	1	13	7	.65	3	.276	.329	.434
1995	SD	NL	139	562	167	23	8	10	(4 | 6)	236	104	44	90	59	5	62	3	4	2	36	12	.75	8	.297	.366	.420
1996	SD	NL	161	655	195	45	9	30	(15 | 15)	348	126	95	117	56	5	87	4	1	5	22	8	.73	20	.298	.354	.531
1997	SD	NL	143	560	146	26	5	28	(5 | 23)	266	101	92	84	43	2	92	3	2	7	15	3	.83	10	.261	.313	.475
1998	SD	NL	159	619	154	40	6	14	(8 | 6)	248	92	67	76	45	0	103	3	3	4	12	3	.80	7	.249	.301	.401
1999	Ari	NL	156	590	156	32	10	34	(17 | 17)	310	100	103	105	63	7	94	3	2	5	8	4	.67	4	.264	.336	.525
2000	Ari	NL	152	539	151	27	5	35	(17 | 18)	293	100	96	104	65	7	87	8	2	9	12	6	.67	9	.280	.361	.544
2001	Ari	NL	140	495	136	27	4	14	(8 | 6)	213	66	73	71	47	9	67	1	2	3	11	7	.61	8	.275	.337	.430
2002	Ari	NL	150	505	145	24	4	25	(14 | 11)	252	82	89	94	65	7	73	3	1	3	16	4	.80	10	.287	.370	.499
2003	Ari	NL	147	516	148	24	10	22	(10 | 12)	258	82	70	85	57	4	94	6	0	3	15	8	.65	6	.287	.363	.500
2004	2 Tms	NL	162	628	170	28	1	36	(23 | 13)	308	92	94	86	61	1	82	1	9	7	9	7	.56	14	.271	.333	.490
2005	LAA	NL	112	406	90	20	3	12	(3 | 9)	152	41	54	39	26	3	71	3	1	4	8	4	.67	6	.222	.271	.374
2006	SF	NL	139	426	105	21	12	6	(2 | 4)	168	66	40	52	46	2	55	2	3	4	7	0	1.00	6	.246	.320	.394
	04 Ari	NL	104	404	111	16	1	23	(14 | 9)	198	61	48	52	40	1	52	1	6	5	8	4	.67	9	.275	.338	.490
	04 LAD	NL	58	224	59	12	0	13	(9 | 4)	110	31	46	34	21	0	30	0	3	2	1	3	.25	5	.263	.324	.491
	18 ML YEARS		2540	9303	2531	446	124	303	(137 | 166)	4134	1434	1165	1364	836	68	1295	53	91	75	320	118	.73	150	.272	.333	.444

Jeff Fiorentino

Bats: L **Throws:** R **Pos:** LF-15; PR-3; CF-1; RF-1; DH-1; PH-1   **Ht:** 6'1" **Wt:** 180 **Born:** 4/14/1983 **Age:** 24

									BATTING										BASERUNNING				AVERAGES		
Year	Team	Lg	G	AB	H	2B	3B	HR	(Hm | Rd)	TB	R	RBI	RC	TBB	IBB	SO	HBP	SH	SF	SB	CS	SB%	GDP	Avg	OBP	Slg
2004	Abrdn	A-	14	46	16	7	1	2	(- | -)	31	9	12	14	9	3	4	2	0	0	3	1	.75	0	.348	.474	.674
2004	Dlmrva	A	49	179	54	15	2	10	(- | -)	103	40	36	38	20	1	50	3	0	1	2	2	.50	1	.302	.379	.575
2005	Frdrck	A+	103	413	118	18	4	22	(- | -)	210	70	66	73	34	2	90	4	4	0	12	6	.67	5	.286	.346	.508
2006	Bowie	AA	104	385	106	14	0	13	(- | -)	159	63	62	63	53	1	58	3	6	3	9	3	.75	7	.275	.365	.413
2005	Bal	AL	13	44	11	2	0	1	(1 | 0)	16	7	5	2	2	0	10	0	0	1	1	0	1.00	1	.250	.277	.364
2006	Bal	AL	19	39	10	2	0	0	(0 | 0)	12	8	7	6	7	0	3	1	2	1	1	0	1.00	1	.256	.375	.308
	2 ML YEARS		32	83	21	4	0	1	(1 | 0)	28	15	12	8	9	0	13	1	2	2	2	0	1.00	1	.253	.326	.337

Randy Flores

Pitches: L **Bats:** L **Pos:** RP-65   **Ht:** 6'0" **Wt:** 180 **Born:** 7/31/1975 **Age:** 31

			HOW MUCH HE PITCHED						WHAT HE GAVE UP											THE RESULTS						
Year	Team	Lg	G	GS	CG	GF	IP	BFP	H	R	ER	HR	SH	SF	HB	TBB	IBB	SO	WP	Bk	W	L	Pct	ShO	Sv-Op	Hld	ERC	ERA
2002	2 Tms		28	2	0	9	29.0	140	40	26	24	7	2	2	3	16	3	14	4	0	0	2	.000	0	1-2	2	8.69	7.45
2004	StL	NL	9	1	0	3	14.0	57	13	3	3	0	1	1	3	3	1	7	0	0	1	0	1.000	0	0-0	0	3.15	1.93
2005	StL	NL	50	0	0	6	41.2	174	37	22	16	5	1	3	3	13	0	43	2	0	3	1	.750	0	1-3	11	3.55	3.46
2006	StL	NL	65	0	0	10	41.2	196	49	29	26	5	3	1	1	22	3	40	1	0	1	1	.500	0	0-1	18	5.64	5.62
	02 Tex	AL	20	0	0	5	12.0	52	11	7	6	2	1	2	0	8	2	7	3	0	0	0	-	0	1-2	2	5.07	4.50
	02 Col	NL	8	2	0	4	17.0	88	29	19	18	5	1	0	3	8	1	7	1	0	0	2	.000	0	0-0	0	11.52	9.53
	4 ML YEARS		152	3	0	28	126.1	567	139	80	69	17	7	7	10	54	7	104	7	0	5	4	.556	0	2-6	31	5.27	4.92

Ron Flores

Pitches: L Bats: L Pos: RP-25   Ht: 5'11" Wt: 200 Born: 8/9/1979 Age: 27

Year	Team	Lg	G	GS	CG	GF	IP	BFP	H	R	ER	HR	SH	SF	HB	TBB	IBB	SO	WP	Bk	W	L	Pct	ShO	Sv-Op	Hld	ERC	ERA
2000	Vancvr	A-	13	0	0	1	12.1	57	16	10	7	2	0	1	1	4	0	10	1	0	1	1	.500	0	0- -		6.31	5.11
2001	Mdest	A+	47	0	0	23	66.0	280	53	24	21	4	6	2	1	29	7	71	3	0	5	2	.714	0	6- -		2.75	2.86
2002	Visalia	A+	53	0	0	38	80.1	347	90	41	29	7	5	5	1	16	2	92	1	0	8	6	.571	0	11- -		3.79	3.25
2003	Mdland	AA	39	0	0	17	59.1	237	44	19	19	6	3	4	1	15	3	66	4	0	3	2	.600	0	6- -		2.17	2.88
2003	Scrmto	AAA	12	0	0	0	13.2	60	16	10	10	0	1	0	0	3	1	10	1	0	2	1	.667	0	0- -		3.40	6.59
2004	Scrmto	AAA	55	0	0	13	54.0	241	60	27	23	5	0	1	0	19	4	55	3	0	4	3	.571	0	1- -		4.23	3.83
2005	Scrmto	AAA	52	0	0	16	60.1	257	46	18	16	5	5	1	0	30	7	66	5	0	5	3	.625	0	3- -		2.81	2.39
2006	Scrmto	AAA	26	0	0	6	25.0	114	25	20	18	0	2	1	1	14	1	27	2	0	5	5	.500	0	2- -		3.96	6.48
2005	Oak	AL	11	0	0	4	8.2	34	8	1	1	1	0	0	0	0	0	6	1	0	0	0	-	0	0-0	1	2.22	1.04
2006	Oak	AL	25	0	0	11	29.2	122	28	11	11	3	0	2	0	10	2	20	1	0	1	2	.333	0	1-1	1	3.51	3.34
	2 ML YEARS		36	0	0	15	38.1	156	36	12	12	4	0	2	0	10	2	26	2	0	1	2	.333	0	1-1	2	3.21	2.82

Cliff Floyd

Bats: L Throws: R Pos: LF-92; PH-5   Ht: 6'4" Wt: 230 Born: 12/5/1972 Age: 34

Year	Team	Lg	G	AB	H	2B	3B	HR	(Hm	Rd)	TB	R	RBI	RC	TBB	IBB	SO	HBP	SH	SF	SB	CS	SB%	GDP	Avg	OBP	Slg
2006	Mets*	R	2	6	3	0	0	1	(-	-)	6	2	4	2	1	0	0	0	0	0	0	0	-	0	.500	.571	1.000
2006	Bklyn*	A-	1	2	0	0	0	0	(-	-)	0	0	0	0	1	0	1	0	0	0	0	0	-	1	.000	.333	.000
2006	StLuci*	A+	3	10	4	0	0	2	(-	-)	10	2	4	3	1	1	3	0	0	0	0	0	-	0	.400	.455	1.000
1993	Mon	NL	10	31	7	0	0	1	(0	1)	10	3	2	2	0	0	9	0	0	0	0	0	-	0	.226	.226	.323
1994	Mon	NL	100	334	94	19	4	4	(2	2)	133	43	41	46	24	0	63	3	2	3	10	3	.77	3	.281	.332	.398
1995	Mon	NL	29	69	9	1	0	1	(1	0)	13	6	8	2	7	0	22	1	0	0	3	0	1.00	1	.130	.221	.188
1996	Mon	NL	117	227	55	15	4	6	(3	3)	96	29	26	35	30	1	52	5	1	3	7	1	.88	3	.242	.340	.423
1997	Fla	NL	61	137	32	9	1	6	(2	4)	61	23	19	23	24	0	33	2	1	1	6	2	.75	3	.234	.354	.445
1998	Fla	NL	153	588	166	45	3	22	(10	12)	283	85	90	92	47	7	112	3	0	3	27	14	.66	10	.282	.337	.481
1999	Fla	NL	69	251	76	19	1	11	(4	7)	130	37	49	45	30	5	47	2	0	2	5	6	.45	8	.303	.379	.518
2000	Fla	NL	121	420	126	30	0	22	(13	9)	222	75	91	88	50	5	82	8	0	9	24	3	.89	4	.300	.378	.529
2001	Fla	NL	149	555	176	44	4	31	(16	15)	321	123	103	121	59	19	101	10	0	5	18	3	.86	9	.317	.390	.578
2002	3 Tms		146	520	150	43	0	28	(13	15)	277	86	79	92	76	19	106	10	0	3	15	5	.75	6	.288	.388	.533
2003	NYM	NL	108	365	106	25	2	18	(10	8)	189	57	68	69	51	2	66	3	0	6	3	0	1.00	10	.290	.376	.518
2004	NYM	NL	113	396	103	26	0	18	(7	11)	183	55	63	64	47	6	103	11	0	3	11	4	.73	8	.260	.352	.462
2005	NYM	NL	150	550	150	22	2	34	(21	13)	278	85	98	99	63	13	98	11	0	2	12	2	.86	5	.273	.358	.505
2006	NYM	NL	97	332	81	19	1	11	(5	6)	135	45	44	45	29	3	58	12	0	3	6	0	1.00	5	.244	.324	.407
02	Fla	NL	84	296	85	20	0	18	(7	11)	159	49	57	64	58	18	68	7	0	1	10	5	.67	0	.287	.414	.537
02	Mon	NL	15	53	11	2	0	3	(3	0)	22	7	4	2	3	1	10	1	0	0	1	0	1.00	0	.208	.263	.415
02	Bos	AL	47	171	54	21	0	7	(3	4)	96	30	18	26	15	0	28	2	0	2	4	0	1.00	6	.316	.374	.561
	14 ML YEARS		1423	4775	1331	317	22	213	(107	106)	2331	752	781	823	537	80	952	81	4	43	147	43	.77	75	.279	.359	.488

Gavin Floyd

Pitches: R Bats: R Pos: SP-11   Ht: 6'4" Wt: 220 Born: 1/27/1983 Age: 24

Year	Team	Lg	G	GS	CG	GF	IP	BFP	H	R	ER	HR	SH	SF	HB	TBB	IBB	SO	WP	Bk	W	L	Pct	ShO	Sv-Op	Hld	ERC	ERA
2006	S-WB*	AAA	17	17	2	0	115.0	495	117	57	54	9	5	5	9	38	0	85	7	1	7	4	.636	0	0- -		4.08	4.23
2004	Phi	NL	6	4	0	0	28.1	126	25	11	11	1	1	0	5	16	0	24	1	1	2	0	1.000	0	0-0	0	4.33	3.49
2005	Phi	NL	7	4	0	0	26.0	127	30	31	29	5	1	1	3	16	2	17	2	0	1	2	.333	0	0-0	0	6.82	10.04
2006	Phi	NL	11	11	1	0	54.1	264	70	48	44	14	2	5	3	32	3	34	2	0	4	3	.571	1	0-0	0	8.02	7.29
	3 ML YEARS		24	19	1	0	108.2	517	125	90	84	20	4	6	11	64	5	75	5	1	7	5	.583	1	0-0	0	6.73	6.96

Josh Fogg

Pitches: R Bats: R Pos: SP-31   Ht: 6'0" Wt: 205 Born: 12/13/1976 Age: 30

Year	Team	Lg	G	GS	CG	GF	IP	BFP	H	R	ER	HR	SH	SF	HB	TBB	IBB	SO	WP	Bk	W	L	Pct	ShO	Sv-Op	Hld	ERC	ERA
2001	CWS	AL	11	0	0	4	13.1	53	10	3	3	0	0	1	1	3	1	17	0	0	0	0	-	0	0-0	2	1.73	2.03
2002	Pit	NL	33	33	0	0	194.1	832	199	102	94	28	6	3	8	69	12	113	2	0	12	12	.500	0	0-0	0	4.46	4.35
2003	Pit	NL	26	26	1	0	142.0	625	166	90	83	22	6	4	9	40	0	71	2	0	10	9	.526	0	0-0	0	5.25	5.26
2004	Pit	NL	32	32	0	0	178.1	770	193	98	92	17	9	6	8	66	8	82	4	1	11	10	.524	0	0-0	0	4.59	4.64
2005	Pit	NL	34	28	0	1	169.1	742	196	106	95	27	4	6	6	53	11	85	2	1	6	11	.353	0	0-0	0	5.13	5.05
2006	Col	NL	31	31	1	0	172.0	765	206	115	105	24	6	5	6	60	13	93	3	0	11	9	.550	1	0-0	0	5.36	5.49
	6 ML YEARS		167	150	2	5	869.1	3787	970	514	472	118	31	25	38	291	45	461	13	2	50	51	.495	1	0-0	2	4.88	4.89

Lew Ford

Bats: R Throws: R Pos: LF-64; RF-22; PR-16; CF-13; PH-8; DH-4   Ht: 6'0" Wt: 200 Born: 8/12/1976 Age: 30

Year	Team	Lg	G	AB	H	2B	3B	HR	(Hm	Rd)	TB	R	RBI	RC	TBB	IBB	SO	HBP	SH	SF	SB	CS	SB%	GDP	Avg	OBP	Slg
2006	Roch*	AAA	8	29	8	2	0	0	(-	-)	10	5	2	5	6	0	5	3	0	0	0	1	.00	0	.276	.447	.345
2003	Min	AL	34	73	24	7	1	3	(2	1)	42	16	15	14	8	0	9	1	1	0	2	0	1.00	1	.329	.402	.575
2004	Min	AL	154	569	170	31	4	15	(6	9)	254	89	72	101	67	3	75	13	2	7	20	2	.91	15	.299	.381	.446
2005	Min	AL	147	522	138	30	4	7	(6	1)	197	70	53	70	45	2	85	16	2	5	13	6	.68	9	.264	.338	.377
2006	Min	AL	104	234	53	6	1	4	(2	2)	73	40	18	22	16	0	43	4	1	0	9	1	.90	5	.226	.287	.312
	4 ML YEARS		439	1398	385	74	10	29	(16	13)	566	215	158	209	136	5	212	34	6	12	44	9	.83	30	.275	.351	.405

Bartolome Fortunato

Pitches: R **Bats:** R **Pos:** RP-2   **Ht:** 6'1" **Wt:** 195 **Born:** 8/24/1974 **Age:** 32

			HOW MUCH HE PITCHED						WHAT HE GAVE UP												THE RESULTS						
Year	Team	Lg	G	GS	CG	GF	IP	BFP	H	R	ER	HR	SH	SF	HB	TBB	IBB	SO	WP	Bk	W	L	Pct	ShO	Sv-Op	Hld	ERC	ERA
2000	Princtn	R+	17	5	0	2	46.2	223	56	31	24	4	2	1	4	19	0	51	8	0	3	4	.429	0	1--	-	5.26	4.63
2001	HudVal	A-	16	9	0	2	59.2	266	70	35	34	3	1	0	2	29	0	53	11	0	2	5	.286	0	0--	-	5.33	5.13
2002	Bkrsfld	A+	25	5	0	0	60.2	263	58	31	27	3	4	2	1	25	0	85	3	2	2	4	.333	0	0--	-	3.55	4.01
2002	Orlndo	AA	10	2	0	0	25.2	103	16	7	6	2	1	1	1	11	1	34	1	0	3	0	1.000	0	0--	-	2.20	2.10
2002	Drham	AAA	2	0	0	0	4.1	21	6	3	2	1	0	1	0	2	0	0	0	0	1	0	1.000	0	0--	-	7.56	4.15
2003	Orlndo	AA	35	1	0	8	53.0	227	48	25	18	4	5	2	2	20	1	63	1	0	4	2	.667	0	1--	-	3.37	3.06
2003	Drham	AAA	5	4	0	1	21.2	91	15	11	8	3	1	1	0	11	0	20	1	0	1	2	.333	0	0--	-	3.03	3.32
2004	Drham	AAA	34	0	0	24	44.2	182	28	14	12	4	0	0	0	21	1	54	2	1	4	3	.571	0	9--	-	2.27	2.42
2004	Norfolk	AAA	6	0	0	1	5.1	24	4	2	2	0	0	1	1	3	0	5	0	0	0	0	-	0	0--	-	3.21	3.38
2006	Norfolk	AAA	11	0	0	7	16.2	67	12	6	5	0	0	1	1	4	0	21	2	0	1	0	1.000	0	0--	-	1.67	2.70
2004	2 Tms		18	0	0	6	26.0	112	24	11	11	3	0	0	0	15	0	25	2	0	1	0	1.000	0	1-2	2	4.57	3.81
2006	NYM	NL	2	0	0	0	3.0	18	7	9	9	2	0	0	1	2	0	0	0	0	1	0	1.000	0	0-0	0	23.41	27.00
04	TB	AL	3	0	0	1	7.1	30	10	3	3	1	0	0	0	2	0	5	1	0	0	0	-	0	0-0	0	6.67	3.68
04	NYM	NL	15	0	0	5	18.2	82	14	8	8	2	0	0	0	13	0	20	1	0	1	0	1.000	0	1-2	2	3.85	3.86
2 ML YEARS			20	0	0	6	29.0	130	31	20	20	5	0	0	1	17	0	25	2	0	2	0	1.000	0	1-2	2	6.10	6.21

Casey Fossum

Pitches: L **Bats:** B **Pos:** SP-25   **Ht:** 6'1" **Wt:** 160 **Born:** 1/9/1978 **Age:** 29

			HOW MUCH HE PITCHED						WHAT HE GAVE UP												THE RESULTS						
Year	Team	Lg	G	GS	CG	GF	IP	BFP	H	R	ER	HR	SH	SF	HB	TBB	IBB	SO	WP	Bk	W	L	Pct	ShO	Sv-Op	Hld	ERC	ERA
2001	Bos	AL	13	7	0	3	44.1	197	44	26	24	4	0	1	6	20	1	26	1	1	3	2	.600	0	0-0	0	4.70	4.87
2002	Bos	AL	43	12	0	13	106.2	461	113	56	41	12	2	4	4	30	0	101	3	0	5	4	.556	0	1-1	3	4.14	3.46
2003	Bos	AL	19	14	0	2	79.0	346	82	55	48	9	1	3	4	34	0	63	4	0	6	5	.545	0	1-1	0	4.77	5.47
2004	Ari	NL	27	27	0	0	142.0	652	171	111	105	31	8	4	10	63	5	117	4	2	4	15	.211	0	0-0	0	6.67	6.65
2005	TB	AL	36	25	0	1	162.2	725	170	100	89	21	3	5	18	60	3	128	8	1	8	12	.400	0	0-1	0	4.80	4.92
2006	TB	AL	25	25	0	0	130.0	594	136	89	77	18	2	3	12	63	3	88	4	1	6	6	.500	0	0-0	0	5.25	5.33
6 ML YEARS			163	110	0	19	664.2	2975	716	437	384	95	16	20	54	270	12	523	24	5	32	44	.421	0	2-3	3	5.15	5.20

Keith Foulke

Pitches: R **Bats:** R **Pos:** RP-44   **Ht:** 6'0" **Wt:** 210 **Born:** 10/19/1972 **Age:** 34

			HOW MUCH HE PITCHED						WHAT HE GAVE UP												THE RESULTS						
Year	Team	Lg	G	GS	CG	GF	IP	BFP	H	R	ER	HR	SH	SF	HB	TBB	IBB	SO	WP	Bk	W	L	Pct	ShO	Sv-Op	Hld	ERC	ERA
2006	Lowell*	A-	1	1	0	0	1.0	3	0	0	0	0	0	0	0	0	0	1	0	0	0	0	-	0	0--	-	0.00	0.00
2006	Pwtckt*	AAA	4	2	0	0	5.0	22	4	1	1	0	0	1	0	4	0	5	1	0	0	1	.000	0	0--	-	3.83	1.80
1997	2 Tms		27	8	0	5	73.1	326	88	52	52	13	3	1	4	23	2	54	1	0	4	5	.444	0	3-6	5	5.68	6.38
1998	CWS	AL	54	0	0	18	65.1	267	51	31	30	9	2	2	4	20	3	57	3	1	3	2	.600	0	1-2	13	2.95	4.13
1999	CWS	AL	67	0	0	31	105.1	411	72	28	26	11	3	0	3	21	4	123	1	0	3	3	.500	0	9-13	22	1.80	2.22
2000	CWS	AL	72	0	0	58	88.0	350	66	31	29	9	5	2	2	22	2	91	1	0	3	1	.750	0	34-39	3	2.28	2.97
2001	CWS	AL	72	0	0	69	81.0	322	57	21	21	3	4	1	8	22	1	75	1	0	4	9	.308	0	42-45	0	2.06	2.33
2002	CWS	AL	65	0	0	35	77.2	306	65	26	25	7	2	0	2	13	2	58	1	0	2	4	.333	0	11-14	8	2.38	2.90
2003	Oak	AL	72	0	0	67	86.2	338	57	21	20	10	1	1	7	20	2	88	0	1	9	1	.900	0	43-48	0	2.07	2.08
2004	Bos	AL	72	0	0	61	83.0	333	63	22	20	8	2	4	6	15	5	79	3	0	5	3	.625	0	32-39	0	2.14	2.17
2005	Bos	AL	43	0	0	37	45.2	210	53	30	30	8	2	1	5	18	1	34	0	0	5	5	.500	0	15-19	1	5.93	5.91
2006	Bos	AL	44	0	0	16	49.2	205	52	24	24	9	0	4	2	7	0	36	2	0	3	1	.750	0	0-0	14	4.03	4.35
97	SF	NL	11	8	0	0	44.2	209	60	41	41	9	2	0	4	18	1	33	1	0	1	5	.167	0	0-1	0	7.41	8.26
97	CWS	NL	16	0	0	5	28.2	117	28	11	11	4	1	1	0	5	1	21	0	0	3	0	1.000	0	3-5	5	3.27	3.45
10 ML YEARS			588	8	0	397	755.2	3068	624	286	277	87	24	16	43	181	22	695	13	2	41	34	.547	0	190-225	66	2.81	3.30

Jeff Francis

Pitches: L **Bats:** L **Pos:** SP-32   **Ht:** 6'5" **Wt:** 205 **Born:** 1/8/1981 **Age:** 26

			HOW MUCH HE PITCHED						WHAT HE GAVE UP												THE RESULTS						
Year	Team	Lg	G	GS	CG	GF	IP	BFP	H	R	ER	HR	SH	SF	HB	TBB	IBB	SO	WP	Bk	W	L	Pct	ShO	Sv-Op	Hld	ERC	ERA
2004	Col	NL	7	7	0	0	36.2	164	42	22	21	8	2	1	1	13	1	32	2	0	3	2	.600	0	0-0	0	5.62	5.15
2005	Col	NL	33	33	0	0	183.2	828	228	119	116	26	6	10	8	70	5	128	2	0	14	12	.538	0	0-0	0	5.94	5.68
2006	Col	NL	32	32	1	0	199.0	843	187	101	92	18	7	7	13	69	15	117	0	0	13	11	.542	1	0-0	0	3.63	4.16
3 ML YEARS			72	72	1	0	419.1	1835	457	242	229	52	15	18	22	152	21	277	4	0	30	25	.545	1	0-0	0	4.78	4.91

Frank Francisco

Pitches: R **Bats:** R **Pos:** RP-8   **Ht:** 6'2" **Wt:** 235 **Born:** 9/11/1979 **Age:** 27

			HOW MUCH HE PITCHED						WHAT HE GAVE UP												THE RESULTS						
Year	Team	Lg	G	GS	CG	GF	IP	BFP	H	R	ER	HR	SH	SF	HB	TBB	IBB	SO	WP	Bk	W	L	Pct	ShO	Sv-Op	Hld	ERC	ERA
1999	RedSx	R	12	7	0	1	53.1	253	58	39	27	3	1	1	4	35	0	48	7	3	2	4	.333	0	0--	-	5.52	4.56
2000	RedSx	R	1	0	0	0	1.0	7	2	3	2	0	0	0	0	2	0	1	1	0	0	0	-	0	0--	-	16.69	18.00
2001	Augsta	A	37	0	0	8	68.0	274	40	25	22	3	5	1	6	30	0	90	6	1	4	3	.571	0	2--	-	2.09	2.91
2002	Srsota	A+	16	10	0	2	53.0	217	33	19	15	1	3	5	4	27	0	58	4	0	1	5	.167	0	0--	-	2.28	2.55
2002	WinSa	A+	6	6	0	0	25.2	120	31	23	23	3	1	0	1	18	0	25	4	2	0	4	.000	0	0--	-	7.12	8.06
2002	Trntn	AA	9	0	0	1	16.0	77	10	13	10	0	1	0	2	16	1	18	3	0	2	2	.500	0	0--	-	3.67	5.63
2003	WinSa	A+	16	16	1	0	78.1	332	59	40	31	7	1	4	6	36	0	67	4	1	7	3	.700	1	0--	-	3.16	3.56
2003	Frisco	AA	7	6	0	0	35.1	167	43	33	33	5	0	4	4	18	1	22	0	0	2	3	.400	0	0--	-	6.58	8.41
2004	Frisco	AA	15	0	0	14	17.2	72	7	6	5	1	0	0	2	10	1	30	4	1	1	3	.250	0	6--	-	1.66	2.55
2005	Frisco	AA	4	3	0	0	3.1	16	4	6	3	0	2	2	0	2	0	3	1	1	0	1	.000	0	0--	-	5.10	8.10
2005	Okla	AAA	2	0	0	1	3.0	13	2	1	1	0	0	1	0	2	0	4	0	0	0	0	-	0	1--	-	2.54	3.00
2006	Spkane	A-	4	0	0	1	4.0	15	3	0	0	0	0	0	0	0	0	6	1	0	0	0	-	0	0--	-	1.13	0.00
2006	Frisco	AA	13	0	0	3	14.2	57	10	3	3	1	0	0	0	4	0	22	1	0	0	0	-	0	0--	-	1.83	1.84

Year	Team	Lg	G	GS	CG	GF	IP	BFP	H	R	ER	HR	SH	SF	HB	TBB	IBB	SO	WP	Bk	W	L	Pct	ShO	Sv-Op	Hld	ERC	ERA
							HOW MUCH HE PITCHED						WHAT HE GAVE UP											THE RESULTS				
2004	Tex	AL	45	0	0	7	51.1	216	36	19	19	4	2	1	3	28	2	60	4	1	5	1	.833	0	0-3	10	3.04	3.33
2006	Tex	AL	8	0	0	2	7.1	32	8	4	4	2	0	0	0	2	0	6	1	0	0	1	.000	0	0-0	2	5.17	4.91
	2 ML YEARS		53	0	0	9	58.2	248	44	23	23	6	2	1	3	30	2	66	5	1	5	2	.714	0	0-3	12	3.31	3.53

Julio Franco

Bats: R **Throws:** R **Pos:** PH-66; 1B-27; 3B-3; DH-3; PR-1   **Ht:** 6'1" **Wt:** 210 **Born:** 8/23/1958 **Age:** 48

			BATTING																				BASERUNNING				AVERAGES		
Year	Team	Lg	G	AB	H	2B	3B	HR	(Hm	Rd)	TB	R	RBI	RC	TBB	IBB	SO	HBP	SH	SF	SB	CS	SB%	GDP	Avg	OBP	Slg
1982	Phi	NL	16	29	8	1	0	0	(0	0)	9	3	3	2	2	1	4	0	1	0	0	2	.00	1	.276	.323	.310
1983	Cle	AL	149	560	153	24	8	8	(6	2)	217	68	80	62	27	1	50	2	3	6	32	12	.73	21	.273	.306	.388
1984	Cle	AL	160	658	188	22	5	3	(1	2)	229	82	79	72	43	1	68	6	1	10	19	10	.66	23	.286	.331	.348
1985	Cle	AL	160	636	183	33	4	6	(3	3)	242	97	90	78	54	2	74	4	0	9	13	9	.59	26	.288	.343	.381
1986	Cle	AL	149	599	183	30	5	10	(4	6)	253	80	74	76	32	1	66	0	0	5	10	7	.59	28	.306	.338	.422
1987	Cle	AL	128	495	158	24	3	8	(5	3)	212	86	52	81	57	2	56	3	0	5	32	9	.78	23	.319	.389	.428
1988	Cle	AL	152	613	186	23	6	10	(3	7)	251	88	54	89	56	4	72	2	1	4	25	11	.69	17	.303	.361	.409
1989	Tex	AL	150	548	173	31	5	13	(9	4)	253	80	92	93	66	11	69	1	0	6	21	3	.88	27	.316	.386	.462
1990	Tex	AL	157	582	172	27	1	11	(4	7)	234	96	69	94	82	3	83	2	2	2	31	10	.76	12	.296	.383	.402
1991	Tex	AL	146	589	201	27	3	15	(7	8)	279	108	78	113	65	8	78	3	0	2	36	9	.80	13	.341	.408	.474
1992	Tex	AL	35	107	25	7	0	2	(2	0)	38	19	8	12	15	2	17	0	1	0	1	1	.50	3	.234	.328	.355
1993	Tex	AL	144	532	154	31	3	14	(6	8)	233	85	84	83	62	4	95	1	5	7	9	3	.75	16	.289	.360	.438
1994	CWS	AL	112	433	138	19	2	20	(10	10)	221	72	98	87	62	4	75	5	0	5	8	1	.89	14	.319	.406	.510
1996	Cle	AL	112	432	139	20	1	14	(7	7)	203	72	76	79	61	2	82	3	0	3	8	8	.50	14	.322	.407	.470
1997	2 Tms	AL	120	430	116	16	1	7	(5	2)	155	68	44	58	69	4	116	1	1	4	15	6	.71	17	.270	.369	.360
1999	TB	AL	1	1	0	0	0	0	(0	0)	0	0	0	0	0	0	1	0	0	0	0	0	-	0	.000	.000	.000
2001	Atl	NL	25	90	27	4	0	3	(2	1)	40	13	11	14	10	1	20	1	0	0	0	0	-	3	.300	.376	.444
2002	Atl	NL	125	338	96	13	1	6	(3	3)	129	51	30	39	39	3	75	1	2	3	5	1	.83	13	.284	.357	.382
2003	Atl	NL	103	197	58	12	2	5	(1	4)	89	28	31	31	25	5	43	0	1	0	1	0	1.00	8	.294	.372	.452
2004	Atl	NL	125	320	99	18	3	6	(5	1)	141	37	57	57	36	4	68	1	1	3	4	2	.67	10	.309	.378	.441
2005	Atl	NL	108	233	64	12	1	9	(3	6)	105	30	42	36	27	1	57	1	1	3	4	0	1.00	10	.275	.348	.451
2006	NYM	NL	95	165	45	10	0	2	(0	2)	61	14	26	21	13	2	49	1	0	0	6	1	.86	11	.273	.330	.370
97	Cle	AL	78	289	82	13	1	3	(2	1)	106	46	25	37	38	2	75	0	1	0	8	5	.62	13	.284	.367	.367
97	Mil	AL	42	141	34	3	0	4	(3	1)	49	22	19	21	31	2	41	1	0	4	7	1	.88	4	.241	.373	.348
	22 ML YEARS		2472	8587	2566	404	54	172	(86	86)	3594	1277	1178	1277	903	66	1318	38	19	78	279	106	.72	310	.299	.365	.419

Jeff Francoeur

Bats: R **Throws:** R **Pos:** RF-162; CF-2   **Ht:** 6'4" **Wt:** 220 **Born:** 1/8/1984 **Age:** 23

			BATTING																		BASERUNNING				AVERAGES		
Year	Team	Lg	G	AB	H	2B	3B	HR	(Hm	Rd)	TB	R	RBI	RC	TBB	IBB	SO	HBP	SH	SF	SB	CS	SB%	GDP	Avg	OBP	Slg
2002	Danvle	R+	38	147	48	12	1	8	(-	-)	86	31	31	32	15	0	34	3	0	2	8	5	.62	2	.327	.395	.585
2003	Rome	A	134	524	147	26	9	14	(-	-)	233	78	68	78	30	5	68	7	0	6	14	6	.70	21	.281	.325	.445
2004	MrtlBh	A+	88	334	98	26	0	15	(-	-)	169	56	52	58	22	3	70	7	0	4	10	6	.63	5	.293	.346	.506
2004	Grnville	AA	18	76	15	2	0	3	(-	-)	26	8	9	4	0	0	14	0	0	1	1	0	1.00	6	.197	.197	.342
2005	Missi	AA	84	335	92	28	2	13	(-	-)	163	40	62	54	21	6	76	5	0	6	13	4	.76	7	.275	.322	.487
2005	Atl	NL	70	257	77	20	1	14	(11	3)	141	41	45	50	11	3	58	4	0	2	3	2	.60	4	.300	.336	.549
2006	Atl	NL	162	651	169	24	6	29	(19	10)	292	83	103	91	23	6	132	9	0	3	1	6	.14	16	.260	.293	.449
	2 ML YEARS		232	908	246	44	7	43	(30	13)	433	124	148	141	34	9	190	13	0	5	4	8	.33	20	.271	.305	.477

Kevin Frandsen

Bats: R **Throws:** R **Pos:** 2B-28; PH-10; SS-3; PR-2   **Ht:** 6'0" **Wt:** 175 **Born:** 5/24/1982 **Age:** 25

			BATTING																		BASERUNNING				AVERAGES		
Year	Team	Lg	G	AB	H	2B	3B	HR	(Hm	Rd)	TB	R	RBI	RC	TBB	IBB	SO	HBP	SH	SF	SB	CS	SB%	GDP	Avg	OBP	Slg
2004	SlmKzr	A-	25	98	9	5	0	3	(-	-)	23	22	14	3	9	0	9	3	1	1	0	1	.00	1	.092	.189	.235
2005	SnJos	A+	75	291	102	22	3	2	(-	-)	136	57	40	58	26	0	22	15	2	1	13	11	.54	12	.351	.429	.467
2005	Nrwich	AA	33	129	37	8	0	2	(-	-)	51	22	20	18	4	0	14	6	2	1	7	3	.70	3	.287	.336	.395
2005	Fresno	AAA	20	94	33	10	1	2	(-	-)	51	18	16	18	2	0	5	2	0	0	1	1	.50	6	.351	.378	.543
2006	SnJos	A+	2	7	3	0	0	0	(-	-)	3	1	1	1	0	0	0	2	0	0	0	0	-	0	.429	.556	.429
2006	Fresno	AAA	71	293	89	25	3	3	(-	-)	129	46	30	47	12	0	30	14	7	2	7	4	.64	9	.304	.358	.440
2006	SF	NL	41	93	20	4	0	2	(0	2)	30	12	7	7	3	0	14	6	0	0	0	1	.00	3	.215	.284	.323

Ryan Franklin

Pitches: R **Bats:** R **Pos:** RP-66   **Ht:** 6'3" **Wt:** 190 **Born:** 3/5/1973 **Age:** 34

			HOW MUCH HE PITCHED						WHAT HE GAVE UP											THE RESULTS							
Year	Team	Lg	G	GS	CG	GF	IP	BFP	H	R	ER	HR	SH	SF	HB	TBB	IBB	SO	WP	Bk	W	L	Pct	ShO	Sv-Op	Hld	ERC	ERA
1999	Sea	AL	6	0	0	2	11.1	51	10	6	6	2	0	0	1	8	1	6	0	0	0	0	-	0	0-0	1	5.52	4.76
2001	Sea	AL	38	0	0	14	78.1	335	76	32	31	13	1	2	4	24	4	60	2	0	5	1	.833	0	0-1	5	4.08	3.56
2002	Sea	AL	41	12	0	10	118.2	495	117	62	53	14	5	5	5	22	1	65	0	0	7	5	.583	0	0-1	3	3.40	4.02
2003	Sea	AL	32	32	2	0	212.0	877	199	93	84	34	8	5	9	61	3	99	1	2	11	13	.458	1	0-0	0	3.90	3.57
2004	Sea	AL	32	32	2	0	200.1	870	224	116	109	33	2	11	10	61	1	104	0	3	4	16	.200	1	0-0	0	5.08	4.90
2005	Sea	AL	32	30	2	0	190.2	832	212	110	108	28	3	3	7	62	4	93	3	1	8	15	.348	1	0-0	0	4.89	5.10
2006	2 Tms	NL	66	0	0	19	77.1	343	86	42	39	13	2	4	4	33	10	43	2	0	6	7	.462	0	0-3	8	5.41	4.54
06	Phi	NL	46	0	0	13	53.0	233	59	28	27	10	0	1	4	17	4	25	1	0	1	5	.167	0	0-1	8	5.26	4.58
06	Cin	NL	20	0	0	6	24.1	110	27	14	12	3	2	1	0	16	6	18	1	0	5	2	.714	0	0-2	0	5.67	4.44
	7 ML YEARS		247	106	6	45	888.2	3803	924	461	430	137	21	28	40	271	24	470	8	6	41	57	.418	3	0-5	17	4.46	4.35

Wayne Franklin

Pitches: L **Bats:** L **Pos:** RP-11 | **Ht:** 6'2" **Wt:** 195 **Born:** 3/9/1974 **Age:** 33

Year	Team	Lg	G	GS	CG	GF	IP	BFP	H	R	ER	HR	SH	SF	HB	TBB	IBB	SO	WP	Bk	W	L	Pct	ShO	Sv-Op	Hld	ERC	ERA
							HOW MUCH HE PITCHED					WHAT HE GAVE UP												THE RESULTS				
2006	Rchmd*	AAA	35	1	0	13	53.1	213	39	15	14	2	2	1	0	17	2	52	1	0	2	3	.400	0	4- -	-	1.96	2.36
2000	Hou	NL	25	0	0	4	21.1	103	24	14	13	2	0	2	4	12	1	21	0	1	0	0	-	0	0-0	8	6.01	5.48
2001	Hou	NL	11	0	0	3	12.0	60	17	9	9	4	0	0	0	9	0	9	0	0	0	0	-	0	0-0	1	10.43	6.75
2002	Mil	NL	4	4	0	0	24.0	103	16	8	7	1	1	0	0	17	1	17	0	0	2	1	.667	0	0-0	0	2.96	2.63
2003	Mil	NL	36	34	1	1	194.2	870	201	129	119	36	12	3	10	94	2	116	3	4	10	13	.435	1	0-0	0	5.43	5.50
2004	SF	NL	43	2	0	8	50.2	227	55	37	36	11	4	2	3	22	2	40	0	0	2	1	.667	0	0-1	5	5.77	6.39
2005	NYY	AL	13	0	0	2	12.2	57	11	12	9	1	1	1	1	8	0	10	0	0	0	1	.000	0	0-3	3	4.37	6.39
2006	Atl	NL	11	0	0	3	7.2	35	8	6	6	2	0	2	0	6	2	3	0	0	0	0	-	0	0-0	1	6.98	7.04
7 ML YEARS			143	40	1	21	323.0	1455	332	215	199	57	18	10	18	168	8	216	3	5	14	16	.467	1	0-4	18	5.49	5.54

Jason Frasor

Pitches: R **Bats:** R **Pos:** RP-51 | **Ht:** 5'10" **Wt:** 170 **Born:** 8/9/1977 **Age:** 29

Year	Team	Lg	G	GS	CG	GF	IP	BFP	H	R	ER	HR	SH	SF	HB	TBB	IBB	SO	WP	Bk	W	L	Pct	ShO	Sv-Op	Hld	ERC	ERA
2006	Syrcse*	AAA	18	0	0	6	20.1	92	21	10	9	1	0	0	0	13	0	33	3	0	3	1	.750	0	1- -	-	4.87	3.98
2004	Tor	AL	63	0	0	37	68.1	299	64	31	31	4	3	2	2	36	3	54	4	2	4	6	.400	0	17-19	8	3.97	4.08
2005	Tor	AL	67	0	0	12	74.2	305	67	31	27	8	2	1	3	28	2	62	1	0	3	5	.375	0	1-3	15	3.72	3.25
2006	Tor	AL	51	0	0	12	50.0	215	47	24	24	8	0	3	2	17	1	51	3	0	3	2	.600	0	0-1	12	3.98	4.32
3 ML YEARS			181	0	0	61	193.0	819	178	86	82	20	5	7	7	81	6	167	8	2	10	13	.435	0	18-23	35	3.89	3.82

Ryan Freel

Bats: R **Throws:** R **Pos:** CF-54; RF-42; 2B-13; 3B-13; LF-13; PH-13; PR-5 | **Ht:** 5'10" **Wt:** 180 **Born:** 3/8/1976 **Age:** 31

Year	Team	Lg	G	AB	H	2B	3B	HR	(Hm	Rd)	TB	R	RBI	RC	TBB	IBB	SO	HBP	SH	SF	SB	CS	SB%	GDP	Avg	OBP	Slg
									BATTING												BASERUNNING				AVERAGES		
2001	Tor	AL	9	22	6	1	0	0	(0	0)	7	1	3	3	1	0	4	1	0	0	2	1	.67	0	.273	.333	.318
2003	Cin	NL	43	137	39	6	1	4	(0	4)	59	23	12	17	9	1	13	4	2	1	9	4	.69	2	.285	.344	.431
2004	Cin	NL	143	505	140	21	8	3	(1	2)	186	74	28	73	67	0	88	12	8	0	37	10	.79	7	.277	.375	.368
2005	Cin	NL	103	369	100	19	3	4	(2	2)	137	69	21	55	51	0	59	8	3	0	36	10	.78	9	.271	.371	.371
2006	Cin	NL	132	454	123	30	2	8	(6	2)	181	67	27	59	57	0	98	9	3	0	37	11	.77	5	.271	.363	.399
5 ML YEARS			430	1487	408	77	14	19	(9	10)	570	234	91	207	185	1	262	34	16	1	121	36	.77	23	.274	.367	.383

Choo Freeman

Bats: R **Throws:** R **Pos:** CF-44; PH-41; PR-6; LF-5; RF-2 | **Ht:** 6'2" **Wt:** 200 **Born:** 10/20/1979 **Age:** 27

Year	Team	Lg	G	AB	H	2B	3B	HR	(Hm	Rd)	TB	R	RBI	RC	TBB	IBB	SO	HBP	SH	SF	SB	CS	SB%	GDP	Avg	OBP	Slg
2004	Col	NL	45	90	17	3	2	1	(0	1)	27	15	11	7	14	1	21	0	1	0	1	1	.50	5	.189	.298	.300
2005	Col	NL	18	22	6	1	1	0	(0	0)	9	6	0	2	0	0	5	0	0	0	0	0	-	0	.273	.273	.409
2006	Col	NL	88	173	41	6	3	2	(2	0)	59	24	18	22	14	2	42	1	3	0	5	6	.45	1	.237	.298	.341
3 ML YEARS			151	285	64	10	6	3	(2	1)	95	45	29	31	28	3	68	1	4	0	6	7	.46	6	.225	.296	.333

Emiliano Fruto

Pitches: R **Bats:** R **Pos:** RP-23 | **Ht:** 6'3" **Wt:** 235 **Born:** 6/6/1984 **Age:** 23

Year	Team	Lg	G	GS	CG	GF	IP	BFP	H	R	ER	HR	SH	SF	HB	TBB	IBB	SO	WP	Bk	W	L	Pct	ShO	Sv-Op	Hld	ERC	ERA
2001	Peoria	R	12	12	0	0	61.2	282	73	45	40	3	2	4	3	22	0	51	1	2	5	3	.625	0	0- -	-	4.66	5.84
2002	Wisc	A	33	13	0	9	111.2	500	101	57	44	6	4	5	11	55	1	99	11	4	6	6	.500	0	1- -	-	3.85	3.55
2003	InldEm	A+	42	4	0	25	78.2	347	80	43	33	5	3	3	3	38	5	83	4	1	7	8	.467	0	7- -	-	4.30	3.78
2003	Tacom	AAA	1	0	0	0	4.0	14	1	0	0	0	0	0	0	2	0	2	0	0	0	1	1.000	0	0- -	-	0.81	0.00
2004	SnAnt	AA	43	1	0	13	68.1	322	77	47	43	6	3	3	5	37	0	56	7	1	3	3	.500	0	1- -	-	5.48	5.66
2005	SnAnt	AA	40	0	0	24	66.2	269	56	22	19	6	1	3	1	22	0	63	4	0	2	3	.400	0	12- -	-	3.01	2.57
2005	Tacom	AAA	9	0	0	4	11.0	57	11	17	16	1	1	1	3	11	0	12	2	0	1	2	.333	0	0- -	-	7.54	13.09
2006	Tacom	AAA	28	0	0	22	45.1	193	33	23	16	1	2	2	6	21	0	55	4	0	1	3	.250	0	10- -	-	2.80	3.18
2006	Sea	AL	23	0	0	6	36.0	165	34	24	22	4	0	1	2	24	1	34	4	0	2	2	.500	0	1-2	1	5.05	5.50

Brian Fuentes

Pitches: L **Bats:** L **Pos:** RP-66 | **Ht:** 6'4" **Wt:** 230 **Born:** 8/9/1975 **Age:** 31

Year	Team	Lg	G	GS	CG	GF	IP	BFP	H	R	ER	HR	SH	SF	HB	TBB	IBB	SO	WP	Bk	W	L	Pct	ShO	Sv-Op	Hld	ERC	ERA
2001	Sea	AL	10	0	0	3	11.2	47	6	6	6	2	0	1	3	8	0	10	1	0	1	1	.500	0	0-1	1	4.39	4.63
2002	Col	NL	31	0	0	9	26.2	118	25	14	14	4	0	2	3	13	0	38	1	0	2	0	1.000	0	0-0	0	4.91	4.73
2003	Col	NL	75	0	0	23	75.1	320	64	24	23	7	0	3	6	34	2	82	2	1	3	3	.500	0	4-6	19	3.71	2.75
2004	Col	NL	47	0	0	12	44.2	201	46	30	28	5	7	0	6	19	6	48	3	0	2	4	.333	0	0-11	13	4.50	5.64
2005	Col	NL	78	0	0	55	74.1	321	59	25	24	6	5	1	10	34	4	91	8	0	2	5	.286	0	31-34	0	3.44	2.91
2006	Col	NL	66	0	0	58	65.1	274	50	25	25	8	2	1	6	26	4	73	6	0	3	4	.429	0	30-36	0	3.19	3.44
6 ML YEARS			307	0	0	160	298.0	1281	250	124	120	32	14	8	32	134	16	342	21	1	13	17	.433	0	65-78	39	3.77	3.62

Jeff Fulchino

Pitches: R Bats: R Pos: RP-1   Ht: 6'5" Wt: 250 Born: 11/26/1979 Age: 27

			HOW MUCH HE PITCHED						WHAT HE GAVE UP										THE RESULTS					
Year	Team	Lg	G	GS	CG	GF	IP	BFP	H	R	ER	HR	SH	SF	HB	TBB	IBB	SO	WP	Bk	W	L	Pct	ShO	Sv-Op	Hld	ERC	ERA
2001	Utica	A-	14	13	0	1	60.2	267	48	34	24	2	1	0	8	31	0	33	3	3	3	8	.273	0	0- -	-	3.32	3.56
2002	Kane	A	24	22	0	0	132.2	114	114	67	57	7	5	5	10	51	0	94	9	1	5	5	.500	0	0- -	-	18.04	3.87
2003	Grnsbr	A	5	4	0	0	25.1	113	28	14	11	1	1	1	3	7	0	16	0	2	1	2	.333	0	0- -	-	4.14	3.91
2003	Jupiter	A+	17	16	1	0	78.0	341	76	41	35	1	1	3	10	32	0	47	5	0	2	4	.333	0	0- -	-	3.87	4.04
2004	Jupiter	A+	8	8	0	0	43.0	173	39	17	13	1	3	4	1	16	0	28	3	0	2	2	.500	0	0- -	-	3.20	2.72
2004	Carlina	AA	17	17	0	0	90.2	391	93	45	45	5	5	3	3	37	3	84	3	0	6	5	.545	0	0- -	-	4.06	4.47
2005	Albq	AAA	29	29	0	0	153.0	698	179	102	86	21	13	3	11	67	3	101	9	0	11	7	.611	0	0- -	-	5.79	5.06
2006	Albq	AAA	25	24	0	1	140.0	613	144	82	70	12	7	3	15	56	0	109	9	1	6	10	.375	0	0- -	-	4.62	4.50
2006	Fla	NL	1	0	0	0	0.1	2	0	0	0	0	0	0	0	1	0	0	0	0	0	0	-	0	0-0	0	7.00	0.00

Aaron Fultz

Pitches: L Bats: L Pos: RP-65; SP-1   Ht: 6'0" Wt: 210 Born: 9/4/1973 Age: 33

			HOW MUCH HE PITCHED						WHAT HE GAVE UP										THE RESULTS					
Year	Team	Lg	G	GS	CG	GF	IP	BFP	H	R	ER	HR	SH	SF	HB	TBB	IBB	SO	WP	Bk	W	L	Pct	ShO	Sv-Op	Hld	ERC	ERA
2000	SF	NL	58	0	0	18	69.1	299	67	38	36	8	7	6	3	28	0	62	0	2	5	2	.714	0	1-3	7	4.19	4.67
2001	SF	NL	66	0	0	17	71.0	300	70	40	36	9	3	4	1	21	3	67	1	0	3	1	.750	0	1-2	12	3.75	4.56
2002	SF	NL	43	0	0	12	41.1	185	47	22	22	4	2	1	3	19	3	31	1	0	2	2	.500	0	0-1	4	5.36	4.79
2003	Tex	AL	64	0	0	10	67.1	296	75	43	39	9	4	2	2	27	7	53	1	1	1	3	.250	0	0-0	19	4.99	5.21
2004	Min	AL	55	0	0	16	50.0	216	50	28	28	5	1	4	1	23	2	37	3	0	3	3	.500	0	1-4	5	4.40	5.04
2005	Phi	NL	62	0	0	16	72.1	286	47	21	18	6	4	1	5	23	2	54	0	0	4	0	1.000	0	0-1	2	2.11	2.24
2006	Phi	NL	66	1	0	12	71.1	317	80	39	36	7	3	6	2	28	8	62	5	0	3	1	.750	0	0-2	9	4.64	4.54
	7 ML YEARS		414	1	0	101	442.2	1899	436	231	215	48	24	24	17	169	25	366	11	3	21	12	.636	0	3-13	58	4.06	4.37

Rafael Furcal

Bats: B Throws: R Pos: SS-156; PH-3   Ht: 5'8" Wt: 195 Born: 10/24/1977 Age: 29

			BATTING																		BASERUNNING				AVERAGES		
Year	Team	Lg	G	AB	H	2B	3B	HR	(Hm	Rd)	TB	R	RBI	RC	TBB	IBB	SO	HBP	SH	SF	SB	CS	SB%	GDP	Avg	OBP	Slg
2000	Atl	NL	131	455	134	20	4	4	(1	3)	174	87	37	78	73	0	80	3	9	2	40	14	.74	2	.295	.394	.382
2001	Atl	NL	79	324	89	19	0	4	(3	1)	120	39	30	41	24	1	56	1	4	6	22	6	.79	5	.275	.321	.370
2002	Atl	NL	154	636	175	31	8	8	(4	4)	246	95	47	80	43	0	114	3	9	2	27	15	.64	8	.275	.323	.387
2003	Atl	NL	156	664	194	35	10	15	(4	11)	294	130	61	107	60	2	76	3	3	4	25	2	.93	1	.292	.352	.443
2004	Atl	NL	143	563	157	24	5	14	(5	9)	233	103	59	82	58	4	71	1	5	5	29	6	.83	9	.279	.344	.414
2005	Atl	NL	154	616	175	31	11	12	(9	3)	264	100	58	98	62	3	78	1	5	5	46	10	.82	11	.284	.348	.429
2006	LAD	NL	159	654	196	32	9	15	(12	3)	291	113	63	110	73	3	98	1	5	3	37	13	.74	7	.300	.369	.445
	7 ML YEARS		976	3912	1120	192	47	72	(38	34)	1622	667	355	596	393	13	573	13	40	27	226	66	.77	43	.286	.351	.415

Kason Gabbard

Pitches: L Bats: L Pos: SP-4; RP-3   Ht: 6'3" Wt: 200 Born: 4/8/1982 Age: 25

			HOW MUCH HE PITCHED						WHAT HE GAVE UP										THE RESULTS					
Year	Team	Lg	G	GS	CG	GF	IP	BFP	H	R	ER	HR	SH	SF	HB	TBB	IBB	SO	WP	Bk	W	L	Pct	ShO	Sv-Op	Hld	ERC	ERA
2001	RedSx	R	6	6	0	0	14.1	65	11	11	9	1	0	2	1	9	0	17	3	0	0	1	.000	0	0- -	-	3.56	5.65
2002	Augsta	A	7	7	0	0	38.0	150	31	14	8	0	1	0	2	7	0	31	9	0	0	4	.000	0	0- -	-	1.95	1.89
2003	Srsota	A+	2	2	0	0	7.0	34	13	8	8	0	2	1	0	3	0	4	0	0	0	1	.000	0	0- -	-	9.24	10.29
2004	Srsota	A+	10	7	0	1	43.1	191	43	17	13	2	3	0	4	16	1	30	5	1	3	2	.600	0	1- -	-	3.79	2.70
2004	Portlnd	AA	14	14	0	0	53.0	242	61	42	37	5	1	3	2	26	0	35	4	0	3	6	.333	0	0- -	-	5.44	6.28
2005	Portlnd	AA	27	25	0	0	132.2	580	128	80	68	10	5	4	4	65	1	96	9	1	9	11	.450	0	0- -	-	4.17	4.61
2006	Portlnd	AA	13	13	1	0	73.2	298	51	26	21	4	1	0	6	25	0	68	5	0	9	2	.818	0	0- -	-	2.27	2.57
2006	Pwtckt	AAA	9	8	0	0	51.2	220	51	31	30	8	4	0	0	26	0	48	3	0	1	7	.125	0	0- -	-	4.99	5.23
2006	Bos	AL	7	4	0	1	25.2	111	24	11	10	0	1	0	0	16	0	15	1	1	1	3	.250	0	0-0	0	3.96	3.51

Eric Gagne

Pitches: R Bats: R Pos: RP-2   Ht: 6'0" Wt: 245 Born: 1/7/1976 Age: 31

			HOW MUCH HE PITCHED						WHAT HE GAVE UP										THE RESULTS					
Year	Team	Lg	G	GS	CG	GF	IP	BFP	H	R	ER	HR	SH	SF	HB	TBB	IBB	SO	WP	Bk	W	L	Pct	ShO	Sv-Op	Hld	ERC	ERA
2006	LsVgs*	AAA	2	0	0	2	2.0	7	1	0	0	0	0	0	0	0	0	3	0	0	0	0	-	0	2- -	-	0.54	0.00
1999	LAD	NL	5	5	0	0	30.0	119	18	8	7	3	1	0	0	15	0	30	1	0	1	1	.500	0	0-0	0	2.42	2.10
2000	LAD	NL	20	19	0	0	101.1	464	106	62	58	20	5	3	3	60	1	79	4	0	4	6	.400	0	0-0	0	5.97	5.15
2001	LAD	NL	33	24	0	3	151.2	649	144	90	80	24	6	8	16	46	1	130	3	1	6	7	.462	0	0-0	0	4.22	4.75
2002	LAD	NL	77	0	0	68	82.1	314	55	18	18	6	3	2	2	16	4	114	1	0	4	1	.800	0	52-56	1	1.60	1.97
2003	LAD	NL	77	0	0	67	82.1	306	37	12	11	2	4	0	3	20	2	137	2	0	2	3	.400	0	55-55	0	0.93	1.20
2004	LAD	NL	70	0	0	59	82.1	326	53	24	20	5	4	2	5	22	3	114	2	0	7	3	.700	0	45-47	0	1.72	2.19
2005	LAD	NL	14	0	0	13	13.1	53	10	4	4	2	0	0	0	3	0	22	3	0	1	0	1.000	0	8-8	0	2.38	2.70
2006	LAD	NL	2	0	0	2	2.0	8	0	0	0	0	0	0	1	1	0	3	0	0	0	0	-	0	1-1	0	0.95	0.00
	8 ML YEARS		298	48	0	212	545.1	2239	423	218	198	62	23	15	30	183	11	629	16	1	25	21	.543	0	161-167	1	2.90	3.27

John Gall

Bats: R Throws: R Pos: PH-7; LF-2; 1B-1   Ht: 6'0" Wt: 195 Born: 4/2/1978 Age: 29

			BATTING																		BASERUNNING				AVERAGES		
Year	Team	Lg	G	AB	H	2B	3B	HR	(Hm	Rd)	TB	R	RBI	RC	TBB	IBB	SO	HBP	SH	SF	SB	CS	SB%	GDP	Avg	OBP	Slg
2000	NewJrs	A-	71	259	62	10	0	2	(-	-)	78	28	27	27	25	0	37	1	0	4	16	5	.76	7	.239	.304	.301
2001	Peoria	A	57	205	62	23	0	4	(-	-)	97	27	44	35	16	1	18	4	0	7	0	3	.00	3	.302	.353	.473
2001	Ptomc	A+	84	319	101	25	0	4	(-	-)	138	44	33	50	24	4	40	2	0	1	5	6	.45	9	.317	.369	.433

Year	Team	Lg	G	AB	H	2B	3B	HR	(Hm	Rd)	TB	R	RBI	RC	TBB	IBB	SO	HBP	SH	SF	SB	CS	SB%	GDP	Avg	OBP	Slg
2002	NwHav	AA	135	526	166	45	3	20	(-	-)	277	82	81	99	38	1	75	2	0	3	4	1	.80	26	.316	.362	.527
2003	Memp	AAA	123	461	144	24	1	16	(-	-)	218	62	73	81	39	0	56	2	1	1	5	2	.71	13	.312	.368	.473
2003	Tenn	AA	12	52	17	1	0	3	(-	-)	27	6	12	9	3	0	4	0	0	1	0	1	.00	0	.327	.357	.519
2004	Memp	AAA	135	506	148	34	0	22	(-	-)	248	77	84	89	48	2	68	1	0	8	1	1	.50	19	.292	.350	.490
2005	Memp	AAA	114	374	101	22	0	13	(-	-)	162	61	64	60	45	2	42	1	0	6	9	2	.82	12	.270	.345	.433
2006	Memp	AAA	82	289	83	13	2	6	(-	-)	118	31	34	44	28	0	36	6	0	1	3	4	.43	8	.287	.361	.408
2005	StL	NL	22	37	10	3	0	2	(1	1)	19	5	10	6	1	0	8	0	0	1	0	0	-	0	.270	.282	.514
2006	StL	NL	8	12	3	0	0	0	(0	0)	3	1	1	2	0	0	5	0	0	0	0	0	-	0	.250	.250	.250
2 ML YEARS			30	49	13	3	0	2	(1	1)	22	6	11	8	1	0	13	0	0	1	0	0	-	0	.265	.275	.449

Mike Gallo

Pitches: L **Bats:** L **Pos:** RP-23   **Ht:** 6'0" **Wt:** 175 **Born:** 4/2/1977 **Age:** 30

Year	Team	Lg	G	GS	CG	GF	IP	BFP	H	R	ER	HR	SH	SF	HB	TBB	IBB	SO	WP	Bk	W	L	Pct	ShO	Sv-Op	Hld	ERC	ERA
2006	RdRck*	AAA	33	0	0	8	40.0	175	46	25	25	4	1	3	3	16	2	25	1	0	2	0	1.000	0	0- -	-	5.35	5.63
2003	Hou	NL	32	0	0	6	30.0	121	28	10	10	3	2	3	1	10	2	16	0	0	1	0	1.000	0	0-1	6	3.66	3.00
2004	Hou	NL	69	0	0	5	49.1	223	55	27	26	12	2	1	6	20	7	34	3	0	2	0	1.000	0	0-1	4	6.16	4.74
2005	Hou	NL	36	0	0	5	20.1	87	18	6	6	1	2	1	2	10	2	12	0	0	1	0	.000	0	0-2	8	3.74	2.66
2006	Hou	NL	23	0	0	7	16.1	82	28	11	11	3	2	1	2	7	1	7	4	0	1	2	.333	0	0-1	0	10.15	6.06
4 ML YEARS			160	0	0	23	116.0	513	129	54	53	19	8	6	11	47	12	69	7	0	4	3	.571	0	0-5	18	5.56	4.11

Freddy Garcia

Pitches: R **Bats:** R **Pos:** SP-33   **Ht:** 6'4" **Wt:** 250 **Born:** 6/10/1976 **Age:** 31

Year	Team	Lg	G	GS	CG	GF	IP	BFP	H	R	ER	HR	SH	SF	HB	TBB	IBB	SO	WP	Bk	W	L	Pct	ShO	Sv-Op	Hld	ERC	ERA
1999	Sea	AL	33	33	2	0	201.1	888	205	96	91	18	3	6	10	90	4	170	12	3	17	8	.680	1	0-0	0	4.46	4.07
2000	Sea	AL	21	20	0	0	124.1	538	112	62	54	16	6	1	2	64	4	79	4	2	9	5	.643	0	0-0	0	4.20	3.91
2001	Sea	AL	34	34	4	0	238.2	971	199	88	81	16	8	5	5	69	6	163	3	1	18	6	.750	3	0-0	0	2.61	3.05
2002	Sea	AL	34	34	1	0	223.2	955	227	110	109	30	4	8	6	63	3	181	8	1	16	10	.615	0	0-0	0	3.98	4.39
2003	Sea	AL	33	33	1	0	201.1	862	196	109	101	31	2	8	11	71	2	144	11	0	12	14	.462	0	0-0	0	4.33	4.51
2004	2 Tms	AL	31	31	1	0	210.0	878	192	92	89	22	8	3	7	64	3	184	8	0	13	11	.542	0	0-0	0	3.37	3.81
2005	CWS	AL	33	33	2	0	228.0	943	225	102	98	26	5	5	3	60	2	146	20	1	14	8	.636	0	0-0	0	3.65	3.87
2006	CWS	AL	33	33	1	0	216.1	917	228	116	109	32	1	6	7	48	3	135	4	0	17	9	.654	0	0-0	0	4.09	4.53
04	Sea	AL	15	15	1	0	107.0	446	96	39	38	8	4	1	2	32	1	82	5	0	4	7	.364	0	0-0	0	3.00	3.20
04	CWS	AL	16	16	0	0	103.0	432	96	53	51	14	4	2	5	32	2	102	3	0	9	4	.692	0	0-0	0	3.77	4.46
8 ML YEARS			252	251	12	0	1643.2	6952	1584	775	732	191	37	42	51	529	27	1202	70	8	116	71	.620	4	0-0	0	3.78	4.01

Jose Garcia

Pitches: R **Bats:** R **Pos:** RP-5   **Ht:** 5'11" **Wt:** 165 **Born:** 1/7/1985 **Age:** 22

Year	Team	Lg	G	GS	CG	GF	IP	BFP	H	R	ER	HR	SH	SF	HB	TBB	IBB	SO	WP	Bk	W	L	Pct	ShO	Sv-Op	Hld	ERC	ERA
2005	Mrlns	R	1	1	0	0	2.0	8	1	0	0	0	1	0	0	1	0	3	0	0	0	0	-	0	0- -	-	1.41	0.00
2005	Grnsbr	A	5	4	0	0	28.1	100	11	5	4	1	0	1	1	4	0	39	0	0	3	0	1.000	0	0- -	-	0.67	1.27
2005	Jupiter	A+	1	1	0	0	2.0	10	2	4	4	0	0	1	0	2	0	0	0	3	0	0	-	0	0- -	-	5.48	18.00
2006	Jupiter	A+	12	11	1	0	77.0	306	60	31	16	3	2	1	1	16	0	69	2	1	6	2	.750	0	0- -	-	1.91	1.87
2006	Carlina	AA	14	14	0	0	84.2	359	78	37	32	10	4	4	3	25	2	87	7	0	6	7	.462	0	0- -	-	3.40	3.40
2006	Albq	AAA	1	1	0	0	4.0	21	5	5	5	0	0	0	0	4	1	5	1	0	0	1	.000	0	0- -	-	6.45	11.25
2006	Fla	NL	5	0	0	1	11.0	48	10	6	6	1	0	0	0	5	0	8	0	0	0	0	-	0	0-0	0	3.64	4.91

Nomar Garciaparra

Bats: R **Throws:** R **Pos:** 1B-118; PH-4   **Ht:** 6'0" **Wt:** 190 **Born:** 7/23/1973 **Age:** 33

Year	Team	Lg	G	AB	H	2B	3B	HR	(Hm	Rd)	TB	R	RBI	RC	TBB	IBB	SO	HBP	SH	SF	SB	CS	SB%	GDP	Avg	OBP	Slg
2006	LsVgs*	AAA	2	8	4	2	0	0	(-	-)	6	3	1	2	0	0	0	0	0	0	0	0	-	0	.500	.500	.750
1996	Bos	AL	24	87	21	2	3	4	(3	1)	41	11	16	13	4	0	14	0	1	1	5	0	1.00	6	.241	.272	.471
1997	Bos	AL	153	684	209	44	11	30	(11	19)	365	122	98	122	35	2	92	6	2	7	22	9	.71	9	.306	.342	.534
1998	Bos	AL	143	604	195	37	8	35	(17	18)	353	111	122	117	33	1	62	8	0	7	12	6	.67	20	.323	.362	.584
1999	Bos	AL	135	532	190	42	4	27	(14	13)	321	103	104	125	51	7	39	8	0	4	14	3	.82	11	.357	.418	.603
2000	Bos	AL	140	529	197	51	3	21	(7	14)	317	104	96	127	61	20	50	2	0	7	5	2	.71	8	.372	.434	.599
2001	Bos	AL	21	83	24	3	0	4	(3	1)	39	13	8	13	7	0	9	1	0	1	0	1	.00	1	.289	.352	.470
2002	Bos	AL	156	635	197	56	5	24	(10	14)	335	101	120	113	41	4	63	6	0	11	5	2	.71	17	.310	.352	.528
2003	Bos	AL	156	658	198	37	13	28	(18	10)	345	120	105	114	39	1	61	11	1	10	19	5	.79	10	.301	.345	.524
2004	2 Tms		81	321	99	21	3	9	(6	3)	153	52	41	53	24	2	30	6	1	2	4	1	.80	10	.308	.365	.477
2005	ChC	NL	62	230	65	12	0	9	(5	4)	104	28	30	28	12	0	24	2	0	3	0	0	-	6	.283	.320	.452
2006	LAD	NL	122	469	142	31	2	20	(9	11)	237	82	93	87	42	9	30	8	0	4	3	0	1.00	15	.303	.367	.505
04	Bos	AL	38	156	50	7	3	5	(3	2)	78	24	21	26	8	2	16	4	0	1	2	0	1.00	4	.321	.367	.500
04	ChC	NL	43	165	49	14	0	4	(3	1)	75	28	20	27	16	0	14	2	1	1	2	1	.67	6	.297	.364	.455
11 ML YEARS			1193	4832	1537	336	52	211	(103	108)	2610	847	833	912	349	46	474	58	5	56	89	29	.75	107	.318	.367	.540

Ryan Garko

Bats: R **Throws:** R **Pos:** 1B-45; PH-3; DH-2   **Ht:** 6'2" **Wt:** 225 **Born:** 1/2/1981 **Age:** 26

								BATTING												BASERUNNING				AVERAGES		
Year Team	Lg	G	AB	H	2B	3B	HR	(Hm Rd)	TB	R	RBI	RC	TBB	IBB	SO	HBP	SH	SF	SB	CS	SB%	GDP	Avg	OBP	Slg
2003 MhVlly	A-	45	165	45	8	1	4	(- -)	67	23	16	23	12	0	19	4	2	0	1	1	.50	5	.273	.337	.406
2004 Kinston	A+	65	238	78	17	1	16	(- -)	145	44	57	60	26	3	34	15	0	1	4	1	.80	6	.328	.425	.609
2004 Akron	AA	43	172	57	15	0	6	(- -)	90	29	38	35	14	0	28	6	0	2	1	0	1.00	3	.331	.397	.523
2004 Buffalo	AAA	5	20	7	1	0	0	(- -)	8	2	4	4	2	0	3	0	0	1	0	0	-	0	.350	.391	.400
2005 Buffalo	AAA	127	452	137	25	3	19	(- -)	225	75	77	87	44	2	92	18	2	5	1	3	.25	11	.303	.383	.498
2006 Buffalo	AAA	103	364	90	18	0	15	(- -)	153	43	59	58	45	3	67	19	0	9	4	5	.44	9	.247	.352	.420
2005 Cle	AL	1	1	0	0	0	0	(- -)	0	0	0	0	0	0	1	0	0	0	0	0	-	0	.000	.000	.000
2006 Cle	AL	50	185	54	12	0	7	(4 3)	87	28	45	32	14	0	37	7	0	3	0	0	-	5	.292	.359	.470
2 ML YEARS		51	186	54	12	0	7	(4 3)	87	28	45	32	14	0	38	7	0	3	0	0	-	5	.290	.357	.468

Jon Garland

Pitches: R **Bats:** R **Pos:** SP-32; RP-1   **Ht:** 6'6" **Wt:** 215 **Born:** 9/27/1979 **Age:** 27

			HOW MUCH HE PITCHED					WHAT HE GAVE UP										THE RESULTS						
Year Team	Lg	G	GS	CG	GF	IP	BFP	H	R	ER	HR	SH	SF	HB	TBB	IBB	SO	WP	Bk	W	L	Pct	ShO	Sv-Op	Hld	ERC	ERA
2000 CWS	AL	15	13	0	1	69.2	324	82	55	50	10	0	2	1	40	0	42	4	0	4	8	.333	0	0-0	1	6.26	6.46
2001 CWS	AL	35	16	0	8	117.0	510	123	59	48	16	2	5	4	55	2	61	3	0	6	7	.462	0	1-1	2	5.16	3.69
2002 CWS	AL	33	33	1	0	192.2	827	188	109	98	23	3	4	9	83	1	112	5	0	12	12	.500	1	0-0	0	4.46	4.58
2003 CWS	AL	32	32	0	0	191.2	813	188	103	96	28	4	8	4	74	1	108	8	0	12	13	.480	0	0-0	0	4.38	4.51
2004 CWS	AL	34	33	1	0	217.0	923	223	125	118	34	9	5	4	76	2	113	3	0	12	11	.522	0	0-0	0	4.56	4.89
2005 CWS	AL	32	32	3	0	221.0	901	212	93	86	26	9	8	7	47	3	115	2	0	18	10	.643	3	0-0	0	3.39	3.50
2006 CWS	AL	33	32	1	0	211.1	900	247	112	106	26	5	8	6	41	4	112	4	0	18	7	.720	1	0-0	0	4.50	4.51
7 ML YEARS		214	191	6	9	1220.1	5198	1263	656	602	163	32	40	35	416	13	663	29	0	82	68	.547	5	1-1	3	4.44	4.44

Matt Garza

Pitches: R **Bats:** R **Pos:** SP-9; RP-1   **Ht:** 6'4" **Wt:** 185 **Born:** 11/26/1983 **Age:** 23

			HOW MUCH HE PITCHED					WHAT HE GAVE UP										THE RESULTS						
Year Team	Lg	G	GS	CG	GF	IP	BFP	H	R	ER	HR	SH	SF	HB	TBB	IBB	SO	WP	Bk	W	L	Pct	ShO	Sv-Op	Hld	ERC	ERA
2005 Elizab	R+	4	4	0	0	19.2	79	14	10	8	3	1	0	1	6	0	25	2	0	1	1	.500	0	0- -		2.71	3.66
2005 Beloit	A	10	10	0	0	56.0	236	53	24	22	5	4	1	4	15	0	64	1	0	3	3	.500	0	0- -		3.46	3.54
2006 FtMyrs	A+	8	8	0	0	44.1	77	27	13	7	3	2	2	2	11	0	53	0	0	5	1	.833	0	0- -		4.16	1.42
2006 NwBrit	AA	10	10	0	0	57.1	228	40	22	16	2	1	0	3	14	0	68	3	0	6	2	.750	0	0- -		1.76	2.51
2006 Roch	AAA	5	5	2	0	34.0	126	20	7	7	1	1	0	3	7	0	33	0	0	3	1	.750	1	0- -		1.44	1.85
2006 Min	AL	10	9	0	0	50.0	232	62	33	32	6	0	3	0	23	0	38	1	0	3	6	.333	0	0-0	0	5.82	5.76

Joey Gathright

Bats: L **Throws:** R **Pos:** CF-130; PH-5; PR-3; DH-1   **Ht:** 5'10" **Wt:** 170 **Born:** 4/27/1981 **Age:** 26

								BATTING												BASERUNNING				AVERAGES		
Year Team	Lg	G	AB	H	2B	3B	HR	(Hm Rd)	TB	R	RBI	RC	TBB	IBB	SO	HBP	SH	SF	SB	CS	SB%	GDP	Avg	OBP	Slg
2006 Drham*	AAA	10	31	8	2	0	0	(- -)	10	5	1	5	6	0	3	2	1	0	6	2	.75	0	.258	.410	.323
2004 TB	AL	19	52	13	0	0	0	(0 0)	13	11	1	4	2	0	14	3	0	0	6	1	.86	2	.250	.316	.250
2005 TB	AL	76	203	56	7	3	0	(0 0)	69	29	13	22	10	0	39	2	3	0	20	5	.80	5	.276	.316	.340
2006 2 Tms	AL	134	383	91	12	3	1	(1 0)	112	59	41	46	42	0	75	7	9	4	22	9	.71	3	.238	.321	.292
06 TB	AL	55	154	31	6	0	0	(0 0)	37	25	13	15	20	0	30	3	5	0	12	3	.80	1	.201	.305	.240
06 KC	AL	79	229	60	6	3	1	(1 0)	75	34	28	31	22	0	45	4	4	4	10	6	.63	2	.262	.332	.328
3 ML YEARS		229	638	160	19	6	1	(1 0)	194	99	55	72	54	0	128	12	12	4	48	15	.76	10	.251	.319	.304

Chad Gaudin

Pitches: R **Bats:** R **Pos:** RP-55   **Ht:** 5'11" **Wt:** 165 **Born:** 3/24/1983 **Age:** 24

			HOW MUCH HE PITCHED					WHAT HE GAVE UP										THE RESULTS						
Year Team	Lg	G	GS	CG	GF	IP	BFP	H	R	ER	HR	SH	SF	HB	TBB	IBB	SO	WP	Bk	W	L	Pct	ShO	Sv-Op	Hld	ERC	ERA
2006 Scrmto*	AAA	4	4	0	0	24.1	91	14	6	1	0	1	1	0	8	0	26	0	0	3	0	1.000	0	0- -		1.35	0.37
2003 TB	AL	15	3	0	5	40.0	173	37	18	16	4	0	2	1	16	0	23	1	0	2	0	1.000	0	0-0	0	3.70	3.60
2004 TB	AL	26	4	0	5	42.2	201	59	27	23	4	2	4	4	16	4	30	0	0	1	2	.333	0	0-1	5	6.46	4.85
2005 Tor	AL	5	3	0	0	13.0	74	31	19	19	6	0	1	1	6	0	12	0	0	1	3	.250	0	0-0	0	18.35	13.15
2006 Oak	AL	55	0	0	13	64.0	276	51	24	22	3	0	3	1	42	2	36	2	2	4	2	.667	0	2-3	11	3.62	3.09
4 ML YEARS		101	10	0	23	159.2	724	178	88	80	17	2	10	7	80	6	101	3	2	8	7	.533	0	2-4	16	5.33	4.51

Geoff Geary

Pitches: R **Bats:** R **Pos:** RP-81   **Ht:** 6'0" **Wt:** 175 **Born:** 8/26/1976 **Age:** 30

			HOW MUCH HE PITCHED					WHAT HE GAVE UP										THE RESULTS						
Year Team	Lg	G	GS	CG	GF	IP	BFP	H	R	ER	HR	SH	SF	HB	TBB	IBB	SO	WP	Bk	W	L	Pct	ShO	Sv-Op	Hld	ERC	ERA
2003 Phi	NL	5	0	0	2	6.0	28	8	3	3	0	1	0	0	3	0	3	0	0	0	0	-	0	0-0	0	5.70	4.50
2004 Phi	NL	33	0	0	16	44.2	200	52	29	27	8	1	2	3	16	3	30	2	1	1	0	1.000	0	0-0	0	5.63	5.44
2005 Phi	NL	40	0	0	12	58.0	247	54	29	24	5	2	4	1	21	4	42	3	0	2	1	.667	0	0-1	3	3.38	3.72
2006 Phi	NL	81	0	0	17	91.1	390	103	34	30	6	3	1	6	20	4	60	2	0	7	1	.875	0	1-4	15	4.07	2.96
4 ML YEARS		159	0	0	47	200.0	865	217	95	84	19	7	7	10	60	11	135	7	1	10	2	.833	0	1-5	18	4.25	3.78

Esteban German

Bats: R Throws: R Pos: 2B-26; 3B-24; DH-22; PH-22; LF-14; CF-11; PR-8; 1B-1; SS-1   Ht: 5'9" Wt: 165 Born: 1/26/1978 Age: 29

Year	Team	Lg	G	AB	H	2B	3B	HR	(Hm	Rd)	TB	R	RBI	RC	TBB	IBB	SO	HBP	SH	SF	SB	CS	SB%	GDP	Avg	OBP	Slg
2002	Oak	AL	9	35	7	0	0	0	(0	0)	7	4	0	2	4	0	11	1	0	0	1	0	1.00	0	.200	.300	.200
2003	Oak	AL	5	4	1	0	0	0	(0	0)	1	0	1	1	0	0	1	0	0	0	0	0	-	1	.250	.250	.250
2004	Oak	AL	31	60	15	1	1	0	(0	0)	18	9	7	8	4	0	13	0	1	0	0	1	.00	1	.250	.297	.300
2005	Tex	AL	5	4	3	1	0	0	(0	0)	4	3	1	2	0	0	1	0	0	0	2	0	1.00	0	.750	.750	1.000
2006	KC	AL	106	279	91	18	5	3	(2	1)	128	44	34	55	40	0	49	6	6	0	7	3	.70	8	.326	.422	.459
5 ML YEARS			156	382	117	20	6	3	(2	1)	158	60	43	68	48	0	75	7	7	0	10	4	.71	10	.306	.394	.414

Franklyn German

Pitches: R Bats: R Pos: RP-12   Ht: 6'7" Wt: 260 Born: 1/20/1980 Age: 27

Year	Team	Lg	G	GS	CG	GF	IP	BFP	H	R	ER	HR	SH	SF	HB	TBB	IBB	SO	WP	Bk	W	L	Pct	ShO	Sv-Op	Hld	ERC	ERA
2006	Mrlns*	R	1	1	0	0	1.0	3	0	0	0	0	0	0	0	0	0	1	0	0	0	0	-	0	0--	-	0.00	0.00
2006	Jupiter*	A+	4	4	0	0	4.0	15	2	0	0	0	0	0	0	1	0	1	0	0	0	0	-	0	0--	-	0.94	0.00
2006	Albq*	AAA	8	0	0	1	6.1	34	11	6	6	0	1	0	3	2	1	6	0	0	0	1	.000	0	0--	-	9.15	8.53
2002	Det	AL	7	0	0	1	6.2	25	3	0	0	0	2	0	1	2	1	6	0	0	1	0	1.000	0	1-1	1	1.09	0.00
2003	Det	AL	45	0	0	15	44.2	222	47	32	30	5	2	1	2	45	3	41	8	0	2	4	.333	0	5-7	4	7.06	6.04
2004	Det	AL	16	0	0	5	14.2	73	17	15	12	4	1	0	0	11	1	8	2	0	1	0	1.000	0	0-1	1	7.53	7.36
2005	Det	AL	58	0	0	19	59.0	270	63	26	24	7	2	5	7	34	4	38	4	1	4	0	1.000	0	1-3	4	5.80	3.66
2006	Fla	NL	12	0	0	3	12.0	57	7	4	4	1	1	0	1	14	2	6	0	0	0	0	-	0	0-1	1	4.52	3.00
5 ML YEARS			138	0	0	43	137.0	647	137	77	70	17	8	6	11	106	11	99	14	1	8	4	.667	0	7-13	11	5.99	4.60

Justin Germano

Pitches: R Bats: R Pos: SP-1; RP-1   Ht: 6'3" Wt: 205 Born: 8/6/1982 Age: 24

Year	Team	Lg	G	GS	CG	GF	IP	BFP	H	R	ER	HR	SH	SF	HB	TBB	IBB	SO	WP	Bk	W	L	Pct	ShO	Sv-Op	Hld	ERC	ERA
2000	Padres	R	17	8	0	4	66.2	277	65	36	34	4	3	1	3	9	0	67	5	1	5	5	.500	0	1--	-	2.78	4.59
2001	Eugene	A-	13	13	2	0	80.0	333	77	35	31	5	1	3	4	11	0	74	1	0	6	5	.545	0	0--	-	2.75	3.49
2001	FtWyn	A	13	13	0	0	65.0	293	80	47	36	7	2	3	7	16	1	55	6	0	2	6	.250	0	0--	-	5.22	4.98
2002	FtWyn	A	24	24	1	0	155.2	645	166	63	55	14	2	3	1	19	2	119	4	2	12	5	.706	0	0--	-	3.27	3.18
2002	Lk Els	A+	3	3	0	0	19.0	75	12	3	2	1	0	0	9	5	0	18	1	0	2	0	1.000	0	0--	-	3.33	0.95
2003	Lk Els	A+	19	19	1	0	110.2	482	127	61	52	4	3	2	9	25	1	78	2	0	9	5	.643	0	0--	-	4.06	4.23
2003	Mobile	AA	9	9	1	0	58.0	246	60	34	28	6	3	1	5	13	3	44	0	0	5	2	.286	0	0--	-	3.87	4.34
2004	Mobile	AA	5	5	0	0	32.1	129	31	11	9	3	1	0	1	7	0	20	0	0	2	1	.667	0	0--	-	3.35	2.51
2004	Portlnd	AAA	20	20	2	0	122.2	496	124	48	46	12	5	6	5	25	0	98	3	0	9	5	.643	2	0--	-	3.09	3.38
2005	Portlnd	AAA	19	19	1	0	112.0	479	111	56	46	13	3	1	6	32	1	100	2	0	7	6	.538	1	0--	-	3.85	3.70
2005	Lsvlle	AAA	8	8	0	0	49.1	215	62	27	22	7	1	1	5	5	0	38	2	0	3	2	.600	0	0--	-	5.06	4.01
2006	Lsvlle	AAA	19	18	0	0	117.0	481	124	53	48	11	3	4	9	22	0	67	1	2	8	6	.571	0	0--	-	3.97	3.69
2006	S-WB	AAA	6	6	0	0	38.1	156	40	13	12	2	1	0	1	2	0	25	0	0	2	0	1.000	0	0--	-	2.76	2.82
2004	SD	NL	7	5	0	0	21.1	109	31	24	21	2	3	1	0	14	0	16	0	0	1	2	.333	0	0-0	0	7.69	8.86
2006	Cin	NL	2	1	0	0	6.2	31	8	4	4	1	0	0	1	3	1	8	0	0	0	1	.000	0	0-0	0	6.26	5.40
2 ML YEARS			9	6	0	0	28.0	140	39	28	25	3	3	1	1	17	1	24	0	0	1	3	.250	0	0-0	0	7.35	8.04

Jody Gerut

Bats: L Throws: L Pos: OF   Ht: 6'0" Wt: 190 Born: 9/18/1977 Age: 29

Year	Team	Lg	G	AB	H	2B	3B	HR	(Hm	Rd)	TB	R	RBI	RC	TBB	IBB	SO	HBP	SH	SF	SB	CS	SB%	GDP	Avg	OBP	Slg
2003	Cle	AL	127	480	134	33	2	22	(13	9)	237	66	75	73	35	4	70	7	1	2	4	5	.44	13	.279	.336	.494
2004	Cle	AL	134	481	121	31	5	11	(3	8)	195	72	51	60	54	4	59	7	3	3	13	6	.68	9	.252	.334	.405
2005	3 Tms		59	170	43	11	1	1	(1	0)	59	15	14	18	20	1	20	0	0	1	1	1	.50	4	.253	.330	.347
05	Cle	AL	44	138	38	9	1	1	(1	0)	52	12	12	17	18	1	14	0	0	1	1	1	.50	3	.275	.357	.377
05	ChC	NL	11	14	1	1	0	0	(0	0)	2	1	0	0	2	0	3	0	0	0	0	0	-	0	.071	.188	.143
05	Pit	NL	4	18	4	1	0	0	(0	0)	5	2	2	1	0	0	3	0	0	0	0	0	-	1	.222	.222	.278
3 ML YEARS			320	1131	298	75	8	34	(17	17)	491	153	140	151	109	9	149	14	4	6	18	12	.60	26	.263	.334	.434

Jason Giambi

Bats: L Throws: R Pos: DH-70; 1B-68; PH-4   Ht: 6'3" Wt: 230 Born: 1/8/1971 Age: 36

Year	Team	Lg	G	AB	H	2B	3B	HR	(Hm	Rd)	TB	R	RBI	RC	TBB	IBB	SO	HBP	SH	SF	SB	CS	SB%	GDP	Avg	OBP	Slg
1995	Oak	AL	54	176	45	7	0	6	(3	3)	70	27	25	27	28	0	31	3	1	2	2	1	.67	4	.256	.364	.398
1996	Oak	AL	140	536	156	40	1	20	(6	14)	258	84	79	88	51	3	95	5	1	5	0	1	.00	15	.291	.355	.481
1997	Oak	AL	142	519	152	41	2	20	(14	6)	257	66	81	91	55	3	89	6	0	8	0	1	.00	11	.293	.362	.495
1998	Oak	AL	153	562	166	28	0	27	(12	15)	275	92	110	103	81	7	102	5	0	9	2	2	.50	16	.295	.384	.489
1999	Oak	AL	158	575	181	36	1	33	(17	16)	318	115	123	132	105	6	106	7	0	8	1	1	.50	9	.315	.422	.553
2000	Oak	AL	152	510	170	29	1	43	(23	20)	330	108	137	152	137	6	96	9	0	8	2	0	1.00	9	.333	.476	.647
2001	Oak	AL	154	520	178	47	2	38	(27	11)	343	109	120	153	129	24	83	13	0	9	2	0	1.00	17	.342	.477	.660
2002	NYY	AL	155	560	176	34	1	41	(19	22)	335	120	122	139	109	4	112	15	0	5	2	2	.50	18	.314	.435	.598
2003	NYY	AL	156	535	134	25	0	41	(12	29)	282	97	107	120	129	9	140	21	0	5	2	1	.67	9	.250	.412	.527
2004	NYY	AL	80	264	55	9	0	12	(5	7)	100	33	40	42	47	1	62	8	0	5	0	1	.00	5	.208	.342	.379
2005	NYY	AL	139	417	113	14	0	32	(16	16)	223	74	87	102	108	5	109	19	0	1	0	0	-	10	.271	.440	.535
2006	NYY	AL	139	446	113	25	0	37	(20	17)	249	92	113	106	110	12	106	16	0	7	1	0	1.00	10	.253	.413	.558
12 ML YEARS			1622	5620	1639	335	8	350	(174	176)	3040	1017	1144	1255	1089	80	1131	127	2	70	15	10	.60	132	.292	.413	.541

Jay Gibbons

Bats: L **Throws:** L **Pos:** DH-46; RF-44; PH-1   **Ht:** 6'0" **Wt:** 205 **Born:** 3/2/1977 **Age:** 30

Year	Team	Lg	G	AB	H	2B	3B	HR	(Hm	Rd)	TB	R	RBI	RC	TBB	IBB	SO	HBP	SH	SF	SB	CS	SB%	GDP	Avg	OBP	Slg
2006	Frdrck*	A+	2	8	0	0	0	0	(-	-)	0	1	0	0	0	0	4	0	0	0	0	0	-	0	.000	.000	.000
2006	Bowie*	AA	3	10	4	2	0	0	(-	-)	6	2	0	2	1	0	1	0	0	0	0	0	-	1	.400	.455	.600
2001	Bal	AL	73	225	53	10	0	15	(9	6)	108	27	36	31	17	0	39	4	0	0	0	1	.00	7	.236	.301	.480
2002	Bal	AL	136	490	121	29	1	28	(17	11)	236	71	69	71	45	3	66	2	0	4	1	3	.25	9	.247	.311	.482
2003	Bal	AL	160	625	173	39	2	23	(12	11)	285	80	100	94	49	11	89	3	0	5	0	1	.00	12	.277	.330	.456
2004	Bal	AL	97	346	85	14	1	10	(4	6)	131	36	47	38	29	0	64	1	1	3	1	1	.50	11	.246	.303	.379
2005	Bal	AL	139	488	135	33	3	26	(13	13)	252	72	79	73	28	3	56	1	0	1	0	0	-	15	.277	.317	.516
2006	Bal	AL	90	343	95	23	0	13	(8	5)	157	34	46	50	32	2	48	2	0	1	0	0	-	12	.277	.341	.458
	6 ML YEARS		695	2517	662	148	7	115	(63	52)	1169	320	377	357	200	19	362	13	1	14	2	6	.25	66	.263	.319	.464

Brian Giles

Bats: L **Throws:** L **Pos:** RF-158   **Ht:** 5'10" **Wt:** 205 **Born:** 1/20/1971 **Age:** 36

Year	Team	Lg	G	AB	H	2B	3B	HR	(Hm	Rd)	TB	R	RBI	RC	TBB	IBB	SO	HBP	SH	SF	SB	CS	SB%	GDP	Avg	OBP	Slg
1995	Cle	AL	6	9	5	0	0	0	(0	1)	5	6	3	3	0	0	1	0	0	0	0	0	-	0	.556	.556	.889
1996	Cle	AL	51	121	43	14	1	5	(2	3)	74	26	27	29	19	4	13	0	0	3	3	0	1.00	6	.355	.434	.612
1997	Cle	AL	130	377	101	15	3	17	(7	10)	173	62	61	66	63	2	50	1	3	7	13	3	.81	10	.268	.368	.459
1998	Cle	AL	112	350	94	19	0	16	(10	6)	161	56	66	66	73	8	75	3	1	3	10	5	.67	7	.269	.396	.460
1999	Pit	NL	141	521	164	33	3	39	(24	15)	320	109	115	127	95	7	80	3	0	8	6	2	.75	14	.315	.418	.614
2000	Pit	NL	156	559	176	37	7	35	(16	19)	332	111	123	139	114	13	69	7	0	8	6	0	1.00	15	.315	.432	.594
2001	Pit	NL	160	576	178	37	7	37	(18	19)	340	116	95	131	90	14	67	4	0	4	13	6	.68	10	.309	.404	.590
2002	Pit	NL	153	497	148	37	5	38	(15	23)	309	95	103	128	135	24	74	7	0	5	15	6	.71	10	.298	.450	.622
2003	2 Tms	NL	134	492	147	34	6	20	(12	8)	253	93	88	102	105	12	58	8	0	4	4	3	.57	12	.299	.427	.514
2004	SD	NL	159	609	173	33	7	23	(10	13)	289	97	94	102	89	6	80	4	0	9	10	3	.77	12	.284	.374	.475
2005	SD	NL	158	545	164	38	8	15	(6	9)	263	92	83	112	**119**	9	64	2	0	8	13	5	.72	14	.301	.423	.483
2006	SD	NL	158	604	159	37	1	14	(6	8)	240	87	83	95	104	6	60	5	0	4	9	4	.69	18	.263	.374	.397
03	Pit	NL	105	388	116	30	4	16	(10	6)	202	70	70	79	85	11	48	6	0	2	0	3	.00	8	.299	.430	.521
03	SD	NL	29	104	31	4	2	4	(2	2)	51	23	18	23	20	1	10	2	0	2	4	0	1.00	4	.298	.414	.490
	12 ML YEARS		1518	5260	1552	334	48	260	(126	134)	2762	950	941	1100	1006	105	691	44	4	63	102	37	.73	128	.295	.408	.525

Marcus Giles

Bats: R **Throws:** R **Pos:** 2B-134; PH-8   **Ht:** 5'8" **Wt:** 175 **Born:** 5/18/1978 **Age:** 29

Year	Team	Lg	G	AB	H	2B	3B	HR	(Hm	Rd)	TB	R	RBI	RC	TBB	IBB	SO	HBP	SH	SF	SB	CS	SB%	GDP	Avg	OBP	Slg
2001	Atl	NL	68	244	64	10	2	9	(5	4)	105	36	31	33	28	0	37	0	1	0	2	5	.29	8	.262	.338	.430
2002	Atl	NL	68	213	49	10	1	8	(4	4)	85	27	23	22	25	3	41	2	1	1	1	1	.50	5	.230	.315	.399
2003	Atl	NL	145	551	174	49	2	21	(9	12)	290	101	69	101	59	2	80	11	0	4	14	4	.78	7	.316	.390	.526
2004	Atl	NL	102	379	118	22	2	8	(6	2)	168	61	48	67	36	0	70	9	3	7	17	4	.81	6	.311	.378	.443
2005	Atl	NL	152	577	168	45	4	15	(11	4)	266	104	63	96	64	1	108	5	4	4	16	3	.84	13	.291	.365	.461
2006	Atl	NL	141	550	144	32	2	11	(7	4)	213	87	60	82	62	0	105	6	5	3	10	5	.67	12	.262	.341	.387
	6 ML YEARS		676	2514	717	168	13	72	(42	30)	1127	416	294	401	274	6	441	33	24	19	60	22	.73	51	.285	.361	.448

Hector Gimenez

Bats: B **Throws:** R **Pos:** PH-2   **Ht:** 5'10" **Wt:** 180 **Born:** 9/28/1982 **Age:** 24

Year	Team	Lg	G	AB	H	2B	3B	HR	(Hm	Rd)	TB	R	RBI	RC	TBB	IBB	SO	HBP	SH	SF	SB	CS	SB%	GDP	Avg	OBP	Slg
2002	Lxngtn	A	85	297	78	16	1	11	(-	-)	129	41	42	41	25	1	78	0	1	0	2	3	.40	4	.263	.320	.434
2003	Salem	A+	109	381	94	17	1	7	(-	-)	134	41	54	43	29	1	75	4	1	4	2	0	1.00	7	.247	.304	.352
2004	RdRck	AA	97	331	81	16	3	6	(-	-)	121	38	46	36	18	0	64	2	3	5	2	0	1.00	3	.245	.284	.366
2005	CpChr	AA	121	454	124	19	1	12	(-	-)	181	47	58	59	32	2	88	2	7	3	2	3	.40	8	.273	.322	.399
2006	RdRck	AAA	76	275	75	8	0	8	(-	-)	107	31	37	36	24	3	42	1	0	2	2	3	.40	3	.273	.331	.389
2006	Hou	NL	2	2	0	0	0	0	(0	0)	0	0	0	0	0	0	1	0	0	0	0	0	-	0	.000	.000	.000

Troy Glaus

Bats: R **Throws:** R **Pos:** 3B-145; SS-8; PH-5; DH-4   **Ht:** 6'5" **Wt:** 240 **Born:** 8/3/1976 **Age:** 30

Year	Team	Lg	G	AB	H	2B	3B	HR	(Hm	Rd)	TB	R	RBI	RC	TBB	IBB	SO	HBP	SH	SF	SB	CS	SB%	GDP	Avg	OBP	Slg
1998	LAA	AL	48	165	36	9	0	1	(0	1)	48	19	23	13	15	0	51	0	0	2	1	0	1.00	4	.218	.280	.291
1999	LAA	AL	154	551	132	29	1	29	(12	17)	248	85	79	84	71	1	143	6	1	2	5	1	.83	9	.240	.331	.450
2000	LAA	AL	159	563	160	37	1	47	(24	23)	340	120	102	129	112	6	163	2	0	1	14	11	.56	14	.284	.404	.604
2001	LAA	AL	161	588	147	38	2	41	(22	19)	312	100	108	114	107	7	158	6	0	7	10	3	.77	16	.250	.367	.531
2002	LAA	AL	156	569	142	24	1	30	(13	17)	258	99	111	100	88	4	144	6	0	8	10	3	.77	12	.250	.352	.453
2003	LAA	AL	91	319	79	17	2	16	(9	7)	148	53	50	48	46	4	73	1	0	1	7	2	.78	8	.248	.343	.464
2004	LAA	AL	58	207	52	11	1	18	(9	9)	119	47	42	41	31	3	52	3	0	1	2	3	.40	6	.251	.355	.575
2005	Ari	NL	149	538	139	29	1	37	(20	17)	281	78	97	87	84	2	145	7	0	5	4	2	.67	7	.258	.363	.522
2006	Tor	AL	153	540	136	27	0	38	(25	13)	277	105	104	100	86	6	134	3	0	5	3	2	.60	25	.252	.355	.513
	9 ML YEARS		1129	4040	1023	221	8	257	(134	123)	2031	706	716	700	640	33	1063	34	0	33	56	27	.67	100	.253	.357	.503

Tom Glavine

Pitches: L Bats: L Pos: SP-32   Ht: 6'0" Wt: 185 Born: 3/25/1966 Age: 41

			HOW MUCH HE PITCHED							WHAT HE GAVE UP												THE RESULTS							
Year	Team	Lg	G	GS	CG	GF	IP	BFP	H	R	ER	HR	SH	SF	HB	TBB	IBB	SO	WP	Bk	W	L	Pct	ShO	Sv-Op	Hld	ERC	ERA
1987	Atl	NL	9	9	0	0	50.1	238	55	34	31	5	2	3	3	33	4	20	1	1	2	4	.333	0	0-0	0	5.70	5.54
1988	Atl	NL	34	34	1	0	195.1	844	201	111	99	12	17	11	8	63	7	84	2	2	7	17	.292	0	0-0	0	3.74	4.56
1989	Atl	NL	29	29	6	0	186.0	766	172	88	76	20	11	4	2	40	3	90	2	0	14	8	.636	4	0-0	0	2.99	3.68
1990	Atl	NL	33	33	1	0	214.1	929	232	111	102	18	21	2	1	78	10	129	8	1	10	12	.455	0	0-0	0	4.24	4.28
1991	Atl	NL	34	34	9	0	246.2	989	201	83	70	17	7	6	2	69	6	192	10	2	20	11	.645	1	0-0	0	2.47	2.55
1992	Atl	NL	33	33	7	0	225.0	919	197	81	69	6	2	6	2	70	7	129	5	0	20	8	.714	5	0-0	0	2.61	2.76
1993	Atl	NL	36	36	4	0	239.1	1014	236	91	85	16	10	2	2	90	7	120	4	0	22	6	.786	2	0-0	0	3.70	3.20
1994	Atl	NL	25	25	2	0	165.1	731	173	76	73	10	9	6	1	70	10	140	8	1	13	9	.591	0	0-0	0	4.02	3.97
1995	Atl	NL	29	29	3	0	198.2	822	182	76	68	9	7	5	5	66	0	127	3	0	16	7	.696	1	0-0	0	3.14	3.08
1996	Atl	NL	36	36	1	0	235.1	994	222	91	78	14	15	2	0	85	7	181	4	0	15	10	.600	0	0-0	0	3.29	2.98
1997	Atl	NL	33	33	5	0	240.0	970	197	86	79	20	11	6	4	79	9	152	3	0	14	7	.667	2	0-0	0	2.80	2.96
1998	Atl	NL	33	33	4	0	229.1	934	202	67	63	13	6	2	2	74	2	157	3	0	20	6	.769	3	0-0	0	2.93	2.47
1999	Atl	NL	35	35	2	0	234.0	1023	259	115	107	18	22	10	4	83	14	138	2	0	14	11	.560	0	0-0	0	4.31	4.12
2000	Atl	NL	35	35	4	0	241.0	992	222	101	91	24	9	5	4	65	6	152	0	0	21	9	.700	2	0-0	0	3.19	3.40
2001	Atl	NL	35	35	1	0	219.1	929	213	92	87	24	5	8	2	97	10	116	2	0	16	7	.696	1	0-0	0	4.21	3.57
2002	Atl	NL	36	36	2	0	224.2	936	210	85	74	21	12	6	8	78	8	127	2	0	18	11	.621	1	0-0	0	3.61	2.96
2003	NYM	NL	32	32	0	0	183.1	791	205	94	92	21	7	4	2	66	7	82	2	0	9	14	.391	0	0-0	0	4.77	4.52
2004	NYM	NL	33	33	1	0	212.1	910	204	94	85	20	13	10	0	70	10	109	0	1	11	14	.440	1	0-0	0	3.43	3.60
2005	NYM	NL	33	33	2	0	211.1	901	227	88	83	12	19	3	3	61	5	105	1	0	13	13	.500	1	0-0	0	3.79	3.53
2006	NYM	NL	32	32	0	0	198.0	842	202	94	84	22	11	7	6	62	7	131	1	0	15	7	.682	0	0-0	0	4.01	3.82
20 ML YEARS			635	635	55	0	4149.2	17468	4012	1758	1596	322	216	108	61	1399	139	2481	63	7	290	191	.603	24	0-0	0	3.52	3.46

Ross Gload

Bats: L Throws: L Pos: 1B-49; PH-20; RF-15; PR-8; LF-4; DH-1   Ht: 6'1" Wt: 190 Born: 4/5/1976 Age: 31

			BATTING																	BASERUNNING				AVERAGES		
Year	Team	Lg	G	AB	H	2B	3B	HR	(Hm	Rd)	TB	R	RBI	RC	TBB	IBB	SO	HBP	SH	SF	SB	CS	SB%	GDP	Avg	OBP	Slg
2000	ChC	NL	18	31	6	0	1	1	(0	1)	11	4	3	3	3	0	10	0	0	1	0	0	-	1	.194	.257	.355
2002	Col	NL	26	31	8	1	0	1	(1	0)	12	4	4	3	3	0	7	0	0	0	0	0	-	0	.258	.324	.387
2004	CWS	AL	110	234	75	16	0	7	(3	4)	112	28	44	41	20	1	37	2	1	3	0	3	.00	11	.321	.375	.479
2005	CWS	AL	28	42	7	2	0	0	(0	0)	9	2	5	2	2	0	9	0	0	0	0	0	-	1	.167	.205	.214
2006	CWS	AL	77	156	51	8	2	3	(1	2)	72	22	18	24	6	0	15	1	3	1	6	0	1.00	3	.327	.354	.462
5 ML YEARS			259	494	147	27	3	12	(5	7)	216	60	74	73	34	1	78	3	4	5	6	3	.67	16	.298	.343	.437

Jimmy Gobble

Pitches: L Bats: L Pos: RP-54; SP-6   Ht: 6'3" Wt: 205 Born: 7/19/1981 Age: 25

			HOW MUCH HE PITCHED							WHAT HE GAVE UP												THE RESULTS							
Year	Team	Lg	G	GS	CG	GF	IP	BFP	H	R	ER	HR	SH	SF	HB	TBB	IBB	SO	WP	Bk	W	L	Pct	ShO	Sv-Op	Hld	ERC	ERA
2003	KC	AL	9	9	0	0	52.2	230	56	32	27	8	1	3	4	15	0	31	1	0	4	5	.444	0	0-0	0	4.61	4.61
2004	KC	AL	25	24	1	0	148.0	638	157	94	88	24	4	7	3	43	0	49	4	0	9	8	.529	0	0-0	0	4.47	5.35
2005	KC	AL	28	4	0	11	53.2	249	64	34	34	9	3	1	1	30	4	38	2	0	1	1	.500	0	0-0	4	6.39	5.70
2006	KC	AL	60	6	0	17	84.0	370	95	51	48	12	3	0	1	29	1	80	4	0	4	6	.400	0	2-4	11	4.93	5.14
4 ML YEARS			122	43	1	28	338.1	1487	372	211	197	53	11	11	9	117	5	198	11	0	18	20	.474	0	2-4	15	4.90	5.24

Jonny Gomes

Bats: R Throws: R Pos: DH-101; RF-8; PH-8   Ht: 6'1" Wt: 205 Born: 11/22/1980 Age: 26

			BATTING																	BASERUNNING				AVERAGES		
Year	Team	Lg	G	AB	H	2B	3B	HR	(Hm	Rd)	TB	R	RBI	RC	TBB	IBB	SO	HBP	SH	SF	SB	CS	SB%	GDP	Avg	OBP	Slg
2003	TB	AL	8	15	2	1	0	0	(0	0)	3	1	0	0	0	0	6	1	0	0	0	0	-	0	.133	.188	.200
2004	TB	AL	5	14	1	0	0	0	(0	0)	1	0	1	0	1	0	6	0	0	0	0	0	-	0	.071	.133	.071
2005	TB	AL	101	348	98	13	6	21	(11	10)	186	61	54	62	39	1	113	14	1	5	9	5	.64	9	.282	.372	.534
2006	TB	AL	117	385	83	21	1	20	(7	13)	166	53	59	53	61	2	116	6	0	9	1	5	.17	10	.216	.325	.431
4 ML YEARS			231	762	184	35	7	41	(18	23)	356	115	114	115	101	3	241	21	1	14	10	10	.50	16	.241	.341	.467

Alexis Gomez

Bats: L Throws: L Pos: LF-32; RF-21; PH-11; PR-10; DH-5   Ht: 6'2" Wt: 180 Born: 8/8/1978 Age: 28

			BATTING																	BASERUNNING				AVERAGES		
Year	Team	Lg	G	AB	H	2B	3B	HR	(Hm	Rd)	TB	R	RBI	RC	TBB	IBB	SO	HBP	SH	SF	SB	CS	SB%	GDP	Avg	OBP	Slg
2006	Toledo*	AAA	58	226	65	18	3	11	(-	-)	122	36	36	42	18	2	48	2	3	2	8	4	.67	6	.288	.343	.540
2002	KC	AL	5	10	2	0	0	0	(0	0)	2	0	0	0	0	0	2	0	0	0	0	0	-	0	.200	.200	.200
2004	KC	AL	13	29	8	1	0	0	(0	0)	9	1	4	3	2	0	8	0	0	0	0	0	-	1	.276	.323	.310
2005	Det	AL	9	16	3	0	0	0	(0	0)	3	2	1	1	2	0	2	0	0	0	0	0	-	0	.188	.278	.188
2006	Det	AL	62	103	28	5	2	1	(1	0)	40	17	6	14	6	0	21	1	1	0	4	0	1.00	1	.272	.318	.388
4 ML YEARS			89	158	41	6	2	1	(1	0)	54	20	11	18	10	0	33	1	1	0	4	0	1.00	2	.259	.308	.342

Chris Gomez

Bats: R Throws: R Pos: 1B-27; 2B-15; SS-6; 3B-5; PR-3; PH-2; DH-1   Ht: 6'1" Wt: 190 Born: 6/16/1971 Age: 36

			BATTING																	BASERUNNING				AVERAGES		
Year	Team	Lg	G	AB	H	2B	3B	HR	(Hm	Rd)	TB	R	RBI	RC	TBB	IBB	SO	HBP	SH	SF	SB	CS	SB%	GDP	Avg	OBP	Slg
2006	Abrdn*	A-	1	3	1	0	0	0	(-	-)	1	0	1	0	0	0	1	0	0	0	0	0	-	0	.333	.333	.333
2006	Bowie*	AA	4	16	4	1	0	0	(-	-)	5	4	1	1	1	0	3	0	0	0	0	0	-	1	.250	.294	.313
1993	Det	AL	46	128	32	7	1	0	(0	0)	41	11	11	12	9	0	17	1	3	0	2	2	.50	2	.250	.304	.320
1994	Det	AL	84	296	76	19	0	8	(5	3)	119	32	53	39	33	3	64	3	3	1	5	3	.63	8	.257	.336	.402

Year	Team	Lg	G	AB	H	2B	3B	HR	(Hm	Rd)	TB	R	RBI	RC	TBB	IBB	SO	HBP	SH	SF	SB	CS	SB%	GDP	Avg	OBP	Slg
1995	Det	AL	123	431	96	20	2	11	(5	6)	153	49	50	43	41	0	96	3	3	4	4	1	.80	13	.223	.292	.355
1996	2 Tms		137	456	117	21	1	4	(2	2)	152	53	45	52	57	1	84	7	6	2	3	3	.50	16	.257	.347	.333
1997	SD	NL	150	522	132	19	2	5	(2	3)	170	62	54	52	53	1	114	5	3	3	5	8	.38	16	.253	.326	.326
1998	SD	NL	145	449	120	32	3	4	(3	1)	170	55	39	58	51	7	87	5	7	3	1	3	.25	11	.267	.346	.379
1999	SD	NL	76	234	59	8	1	1	(1	0)	72	20	15	23	27	3	49	1	2	1	1	2	.33	6	.252	.331	.308
2000	SD	NL	33	54	12	0	0	0	(0	0)	12	4	3	4	7	0	5	0	1	1	0	0	-	1	.222	.306	.222
2001	2 Tms		98	301	78	19	0	8	(5	3)	121	37	43	36	17	0	38	2	6	5	4	0	1.00	9	.259	.298	.402
2002	TB	AL	130	461	122	31	3	10	(2	8)	189	51	46	51	21	0	58	7	6	3	1	3	.25	8	.265	.305	.410
2003	Min	AL	58	175	44	9	3	1	(0	1)	62	14	15	15	7	1	13	0	2	1	2	1	.67	10	.251	.279	.354
2004	Bal	AL	109	341	96	11	1	3	(1	2)	118	41	37	48	28	0	41	2	3	3	3	2	.60	4	.282	.337	.346
2005	Bal	AL	89	219	61	11	0	1	(0	1)	75	27	18	24	27	1	17	1	6	1	2	1	.67	14	.279	.359	.342
2006	Bal	AL	55	132	45	7	0	2	(0	2)	58	14	17	22	7	1	11	3	0	0	1	2	.33	7	.341	.387	.439
96	Det		48	128	31	5	0	1	(1	0)	39	21	16	13	18	0	20	1	3	0	1	1	.50	5	.242	.340	.305
96	SD	NL	89	328	86	16	1	3	(1	2)	113	32	29	39	39	1	64	6	3	2	2	2	.50	11	.262	.349	.345
01	SD	NL	40	112	21	3	0	0	(0	0)	24	6	7	4	9	0	14	0	2	2	1	0	1.00	5	.188	.244	.214
01	TB	AL	58	189	57	16	0	8	(5	3)	97	31	36	32	8	0	24	2	4	3	3	0	1.00	4	.302	.332	.513
14 ML YEARS			1333	4199	1090	214	17	58	(26	32)	1512	470	446	479	385	15	694	40	51	28	34	31	.52	125	.260	.326	.360

Adrian Gonzalez

Bats: L Throws: L Pos: 1B-155; PH-1   Ht: 6'2" Wt: 220 Born: 5/8/1982 Age: 25

Year	Team	Lg	G	AB	H	2B	3B	HR	(Hm	Rd)	TB	R	RBI	RC	TBB	IBB	SO	HBP	SH	SF	SB	CS	SB%	GDP	Avg	OBP	Slg
2004	Tex	AL	16	42	10	3	0	1	(1	0)	16	7	7	7	2	0	6	0	0	0	0	0	-	0	.238	.273	.381
2005	Tex	AL	43	150	34	7	1	6	(3	3)	61	17	17	13	10	2	37	0	0	2	0	0	-	3	.227	.272	.407
2006	SD	NL	156	570	173	38	1	24	(10	14)	285	83	82	82	52	9	113	3	1	5	0	1	.00	24	.304	.362	.500
3 ML YEARS			215	762	217	48	2	31	(14	17)	362	107	106	102	64	11	156	3	1	7	0	1	.00	27	.285	.340	.475

Alex Gonzalez

Bats: R Throws: R Pos: SS-111   Ht: 6'0" Wt: 200 Born: 2/15/1977 Age: 30

Year	Team	Lg	G	AB	H	2B	3B	HR	(Hm	Rd)	TB	R	RBI	RC	TBB	IBB	SO	HBP	SH	SF	SB	CS	SB%	GDP	Avg	OBP	Slg
2006	Pwtckt*	AAA	1	3	1	0	0	0	(-	-)	1	0	0	0	0	0	1	1	0	0	0	0	-	0	.333	.500	.333
1998	Fla	NL	25	86	13	2	0	3	(1	2)	24	11	7	5	9	0	30	1	2	0	0	0	-	2	.151	.240	.279
1999	Fla	NL	136	560	155	28	8	14	(7	7)	241	81	59	69	15	0	113	12	1	3	3	5	.38	13	.277	.308	.430
2000	Fla	NL	109	385	77	17	4	7	(5	2)	123	35	42	26	13	0	77	2	5	2	7	1	.88	7	.200	.229	.319
2001	Fla	NL	145	515	129	36	1	9	(5	4)	194	57	48	56	30	6	107	10	3	3	2	2	.50	13	.250	.303	.377
2002	Fla	NL	42	151	34	7	1	2	(1	1)	49	15	18	14	12	1	32	4	3	2	3	1	.75	2	.225	.296	.325
2003	Fla	NL	150	528	135	33	6	18	(7	11)	234	52	77	67	33	13	106	13	3	5	0	4	.00	8	.256	.313	.443
2004	Fla	NL	159	561	130	30	3	23	(13	10)	235	67	79	58	27	9	126	4	3	4	3	1	.75	17	.232	.270	.419
2005	Fla	NL	130	435	115	30	0	5	(2	3)	160	45	45	47	31	10	81	5	4	3	5	3	.63	11	.264	.319	.368
2006	Bos	AL	111	388	99	24	2	9	(4	5)	154	48	50	40	22	1	67	5	7	7	1	0	1.00	6	.255	.299	.397
9 ML YEARS			1007	3609	887	207	25	90	(45	45)	1414	411	425	382	192	40	739	56	31	29	24	17	.59	79	.246	.292	.392

Alex S Gonzalez

Bats: R Throws: R Pos: PH-13; 1B-3; SS-3; 3B-2; LF-1   Ht: 6'0" Wt: 200 Born: 4/8/1973 Age: 34

Year	Team	Lg	G	AB	H	2B	3B	HR	(Hm	Rd)	TB	R	RBI	RC	TBB	IBB	SO	HBP	SH	SF	SB	CS	SB%	GDP	Avg	OBP	Slg
1994	Tor	AL	15	53	8	3	1	0	(0	0)	13	7	1	2	4	0	17	1	1	0	3	0	1.00	0	.151	.224	.245
1995	Tor	AL	111	367	89	19	4	10	(8	2)	146	51	42	47	44	1	114	1	9	4	4	4	.50	7	.243	.322	.398
1996	Tor	AL	147	527	124	30	5	14	(3	11)	206	64	64	61	45	0	127	5	7	3	16	6	.73	12	.235	.300	.391
1997	Tor	AL	126	426	102	23	2	12	(4	8)	165	46	35	50	34	1	94	5	11	2	15	6	.71	9	.239	.302	.387
1998	Tor	AL	158	568	136	28	1	13	(7	6)	205	70	51	56	28	1	121	6	13	3	21	6	.78	13	.239	.281	.361
1999	Tor	AL	38	154	45	13	0	2	(1	1)	64	22	12	23	16	0	23	3	0	0	4	2	.67	4	.292	.370	.416
2000	Tor	AL	141	527	133	31	2	15	(5	10)	213	68	69	64	43	0	113	4	16	1	4	4	.50	14	.252	.313	.404
2001	Tor	AL	154	636	161	25	5	17	(9	8)	247	79	76	72	43	0	149	7	7	10	18	11	.62	16	.253	.303	.388
2002	ChC	NL	142	513	127	27	5	18	(13	5)	218	58	61	59	46	7	136	3	4	2	5	3	.63	11	.248	.312	.425
2003	ChC	NL	152	536	122	37	0	20	(11	9)	219	71	59	57	47	1	123	6	8	4	3	3	.50	17	.228	.295	.408
2004	3 Tms	NL	83	285	64	18	1	7	(2	5)	105	36	27	23	14	0	64	1	4	0	2	2	.50	7	.225	.263	.368
2005	TB	AL	109	349	94	20	1	9	(4	5)	143	47	38	37	26	1	74	3	2	3	2	1	.67	13	.269	.323	.410
2006	Phi	NL	20	36	4	0	0	0	(0	0)	4	4	1	0	2	0	10	0	0	0	0	0	-	0	.111	.158	.111
04	ChC	NL	37	129	28	10	0	3	(0	3)	47	15	8	6	4	0	26	0	2	0	1	1	.50	6	.217	.241	.364
04	Mon	NL	35	133	32	7	0	4	(2	2)	51	19	16	14	8	0	32	1	2	0	1	1	.50	1	.241	.289	.383
04	SD	NL	11	23	4	1	1	0	(0	0)	7	2	3	3	2	0	6	0	0	0	0	0	-	0	.174	.240	.304
13 ML YEARS			1396	4977	1209	274	27	137	(67	70)	1948	623	536	551	392	12	1165	45	82	32	97	48	.67	128	.243	.302	.391

Edgar Gonzalez

Pitches: R Bats: R Pos: RP-6; SP-5   Ht: 6'0" Wt: 225 Born: 2/23/1983 Age: 24

Year	Team	Lg	G	GS	CG	GF	IP	BFP	H	R	ER	HR	SH	SF	HB	TBB	IBB	SO	WP	Bk	W	L	Pct	ShO	Sv-Op	Hld	ERC	ERA
2006	Tucsn*	AAA	24	24	3	0	138.1	577	142	69	60	11	5	3	13	27	0	107	5	0	3	8	.273	1	0- -	-	3.71	3.90
2003	Ari	NL	9	2	0	1	18.1	85	28	10	10	3	1	1	0	7	2	14	2	0	2	1	.667	0	0-1	0	7.81	4.91
2004	Ari	NL	10	10	0	0	46.1	228	72	49	48	15	5	1	5	18	4	31	3	1	0	9	.000	0	0-0	0	9.32	9.32
2005	Ari	NL	1	0	0	0	0.1	5	2	4	4	1	0	0	0	2	0	1	1	0	0	0	-	0	0-0	0	124.7	108.0
2006	Ari	NL	11	5	0	1	42.2	182	45	20	20	7	4	1	3	9	0	28	2	0	3	4	.429	0	0-0	1	4.33	4.22
4 ML YEARS			31	17	0	2	107.2	500	147	83	82	26	10	3	8	36	6	74	8	1	5	14	.263	0	0-1	1	7.39	6.85

Enrique Gonzalez

Pitches: R Bats: R Pos: SP-18; RP-4   Ht: 5'10" Wt: 210 Born: 7/14/1982 Age: 24

Year	Team	Lg	G	GS	CG	GF	IP	BFP	H	R	ER	HR	SH	SF	HB	TBB	IBB	SO	WP	Bk	W	L	Pct	ShO	Sv-Op	Hld	ERC	ERA
2005	Tenn	AA	27	27	2	0	161.1	676	160	76	62	8	6	7	6	52	0	146	9	0	11	8	.579	2	0--	-	3.59	3.46
2006	Tucsn	AAA	10	10	0	0	60.1	251	61	22	15	2	2	1	2	14	0	35	3	0	4	3	.571	0	0--	-	3.19	2.24
2006	Ari	NL	22	18	0	1	106.1	462	114	71	67	14	7	3	4	34	0	66	1	0	3	7	.300	0	0-0	0	4.53	5.67

Geremi Gonzalez

Pitches: R Bats: R Pos: RP-20; SP-4   Ht: 6'0" Wt: 220 Born: 1/8/1975 Age: 32

Year	Team	Lg	G	GS	CG	GF	IP	BFP	H	R	ER	HR	SH	SF	HB	TBB	IBB	SO	WP	Bk	W	L	Pct	ShO	Sv-Op	Hld	ERC	ERA
2006	Norfolk*	AAA	6	6	0	0	35.2	145	31	14	12	1	0	0	1	9	0	30	0	0	1	2	.333	0	0--	-	2.48	3.03
1997	ChC	NL	23	23	1	0	144.0	613	126	73	68	16	4	5	2	69	5	93	1	1	11	9	.550	1	0-0	0	3.79	4.25
1998	ChC	NL	20	20	1	0	110.0	493	124	72	65	13	5	2	3	41	5	70	2	3	7	7	.500	1	0-0	0	4.80	5.32
2003	TB	AL	25	25	2	0	156.1	668	131	71	68	18	3	9	12	69	1	97	3	2	6	11	.353	0	0-0	0	3.74	3.91
2004	TB	AL	11	8	0	1	50.1	235	72	42	39	9	1	3	3	20	0	22	4	0	0	5	.000	0	0-0	0	7.77	6.97
2005	Bos	AL	28	3	0	7	56.0	244	64	39	38	7	0	4	2	16	2	28	1	1	2	1	.667	0	0-0	1	4.71	6.11
2006	2 Tms	NL	24	4	0	3	56.0	260	71	43	36	10	6	3	2	23	2	44	0	0	4	2	.667	0	0-1	0	6.36	5.79
06	NYM	NL	3	3	0	0	14.0	67	21	12	12	4	2	1	0	6	1	8	0	0	0	0	-	0	0-0	0	8.77	7.71
06	Mil	NL	21	1	0	3	42.0	193	50	31	24	6	4	2	2	17	1	36	0	0	4	2	.667	0	0-1	0	5.61	5.14
6 ML YEARS			131	83	4	11	572.2	2513	588	340	314	73	19	26	24	238	15	354	11	7	30	35	.462	2	0-1	1	4.61	4.93

Luis Gonzalez

Bats: L Throws: R Pos: LF-150; PH-3; DH-1   Ht: 6'2" Wt: 200 Born: 9/3/1967 Age: 39

Year	Team	Lg	G	AB	H	2B	3B	HR	(Hm	Rd)	TB	R	RBI	RC	TBB	IBB	SO	HBP	SH	SF	SB	CS	SB%	GDP	Avg	OBP	Slg
1990	Hou	NL	12	21	4	2	0	0	(0	0)	6	1	0	2	2	1	5	0	0	0	0	0	-	0	.190	.261	.286
1991	Hou	NL	137	473	120	28	9	13	(4	9)	205	51	69	64	40	4	101	8	1	4	10	7	.59	9	.254	.320	.433
1992	Hou	NL	122	387	94	19	3	10	(4	6)	149	40	55	44	24	3	52	2	1	2	7	7	.50	9	.243	.289	.385
1993	Hou	NL	154	540	162	34	3	15	(8	7)	247	82	72	90	47	7	83	10	3	10	20	9	.69	9	.300	.361	.457
1994	Hou	NL	112	392	107	29	4	8	(3	5)	168	57	67	57	49	6	57	3	0	6	15	13	.54	10	.273	.353	.429
1995	2 Tms	NL	133	471	130	29	8	13	(6	7)	214	69	69	72	57	8	63	6	1	6	8	6	.43	16	.276	.357	.454
1996	ChC	NL	146	483	131	30	4	15	(6	9)	214	70	79	75	61	8	49	4	1	6	9	6	.60	13	.271	.354	.443
1997	ChC	NL	152	550	142	31	2	10	(4	6)	207	78	68	73	71	7	67	5	0	5	10	7	.59	12	.258	.345	.376
1998	Det	AL	154	547	146	35	5	23	(15	8)	260	84	71	89	57	7	62	8	0	8	12	7	.63	9	.267	.340	.475
1999	Ari	NL	153	614	206	45	4	26	(10	16)	337	112	111	129	66	6	63	7	1	5	9	5	.64	13	.336	.403	.549
2000	Ari	NL	162	618	192	47	2	31	(14	17)	336	106	114	128	78	6	85	12	2	12	2	4	.33	12	.311	.392	.544
2001	Ari	NL	162	609	198	36	7	57	(26	31)	419	128	142	164	100	24	83	14	0	5	1	1	.50	13	.325	.429	.688
2002	Ari	NL	148	524	151	19	3	28	(11	17)	260	90	103	114	97	8	76	5	0	7	9	2	.82	12	.288	.400	.496
2003	Ari	NL	156	579	176	46	4	26	(6	20)	308	92	104	113	94	17	67	3	0	3	5	3	.63	19	.304	.402	.532
2004	Ari	NL	105	379	98	28	5	17	(10	7)	187	69	48	62	68	11	58	2	0	2	2	2	.50	9	.259	.373	.493
2005	Ari	NL	155	579	157	37	0	24	(10	14)	266	90	79	87	78	12	90	11	0	4	4	1	.80	14	.271	.366	.459
2006	Ari	NL	153	586	159	52	2	15	(8	7)	260	93	73	81	69	10	58	7	0	6	0	1	.00	14	.271	.352	.444
95	Hou	NL	56	209	54	10	4	6	(1	5)	90	35	35	26	18	3	30	3	1	3	1	3	.25	8	.258	.322	.431
95	ChC	NL	77	262	76	19	4	7	(5	2)	124	34	34	46	39	5	33	3	0	3	5	5	.50	8	.290	.384	.473
17 ML YEARS			2316	8352	2373	547	65	331	(145	186)	4043	1312	1324	1441	1058	145	1119	107	10	91	121	83	.59	191	.284	.368	.484

Luis A Gonzalez

Bats: R Throws: R Pos: 2B-32; PH-19; 1B-7; RF-6; 3B-3; LF-1   Ht: 5'11" Wt: 205 Born: 6/26/1979 Age: 28

Year	Team	Lg	G	AB	H	2B	3B	HR	(Hm	Rd)	TB	R	RBI	RC	TBB	IBB	SO	HBP	SH	SF	SB	CS	SB%	GDP	Avg	OBP	Slg
2006	ColSpr*	AAA	27	97	26	4	2	2	(-	-)	40	15	10	14	6	1	11	6	0	1	1	0	1.00	10	.268	.345	.412
2004	Col	NL	102	322	94	17	2	12	(4	8)	151	42	40	45	15	1	67	4	9	1	1	5	.17	5	.292	.330	.469
2005	Col	NL	128	404	118	25	0	9	(3	6)	170	51	44	49	20	0	63	6	8	3	3	4	.43	7	.292	.333	.421
2006	Col	NL	61	149	36	9	1	2	(0	2)	53	7	14	11	4	0	27	2	2	1	1	1	.50	3	.242	.269	.356
3 ML YEARS			291	875	248	51	3	23	(7	16)	374	100	98	105	39	1	157	12	19	5	5	10	.33	15	.283	.321	.427

Mike Gonzalez

Pitches: L Bats: R Pos: RP-54   Ht: 6'2" Wt: 220 Born: 5/23/1978 Age: 29

Year	Team	Lg	G	GS	CG	GF	IP	BFP	H	R	ER	HR	SH	SF	HB	TBB	IBB	SO	WP	Bk	W	L	Pct	ShO	Sv-Op	Hld	ERC	ERA
2003	Pit	NL	16	0	0	2	8.1	38	7	7	7	4	1	1	0	6	0	6	1	0	1	0	.000	0	0-0	3	7.18	7.56
2004	Pit	NL	47	0	0	12	43.1	169	32	7	6	2	3	0	1	6	0	55	4	0	3	1	.750	0	1-4	13	1.60	1.25
2005	Pit	NL	51	0	0	15	50.0	212	35	15	15	2	0	2	1	31	2	58	3	0	1	3	.250	0	3-3	15	2.90	2.70
2006	Pit	NL	54	0	0	47	54.0	234	42	13	13	1	3	1	2	31	2	64	0	0	3	4	.429	0	24-24	3	3.00	2.17
4 ML YEARS			168	0	0	76	155.2	653	116	42	41	9	7	4	4	74	4	183	8	0	7	9	.438	0	28-31	34	2.75	2.37

Wiki Gonzalez

Bats: R Throws: R Pos: C-12; PH-1   Ht: 5'11" Wt: 205 Born: 5/17/1974 Age: 33

Year	Team	Lg	G	AB	H	2B	3B	HR	(Hm	Rd)	TB	R	RBI	RC	TBB	IBB	SO	HBP	SH	SF	SB	CS	SB%	GDP	Avg	OBP	Slg
2006	NewOr*	AAA	26	84	25	4	0	4	(-	-)	41	9	16	16	9	1	9	4	0	2	1	0	1.00	3	.298	.384	.488
1999	SD	NL	30	83	21	2	1	3	(1	2)	34	7	12	7	1	0	8	1	0	0	0	0	-	5	.253	.271	.410
2000	SD	NL	95	284	66	15	1	5	(1	4)	98	25	30	30	30	4	31	3	1	1	1	2	.33	5	.232	.311	.345
2001	SD	NL	64	160	44	6	0	8	(5	3)	74	16	27	25	11	1	28	4	0	1	2	0	1.00	3	.275	.335	.463

Year	Team	Lg	G	AB	H	2B	3B	HR	(Hm	Rd)	TB	R	RBI	RC	TBB	IBB	SO	HBP	SH	SF	SB	CS	SB%	GDP	Avg	OBP	Slg
2002	SD	NL	56	164	36	8	1	1	(1	0)	49	16	20	18	27	3	24	1	0	2	0	0	-	10	.220	.330	.299
2003	SD	NL	24	65	13	5	0	0	(0	0)	18	1	10	6	5	1	13	1	1	1	0	0	-	3	.200	.264	.277
2005	Sea	AL	14	45	12	5	0	0	(0	0)	17	7	2	4	2	0	3	0	0	0	0	0	-	1	.267	.298	.378
2006	Was	NL	12	35	8	0	0	0	(0	0)	8	3	2	2	2	0	5	0	0	1	0	0	-	0	.229	.263	.229
7 ML YEARS			295	836	200	41	3	17	(8	9)	298	75	103	92	78	9	112	10	2	6	3	2	.60	27	.239	.310	.356

Tom Gordon

Pitches: R **Bats:** R **Pos:** RP-59   **Ht:** 5'10" **Wt:** 195 **Born:** 11/18/1967 **Age:** 39

			HOW MUCH HE PITCHED						WHAT HE GAVE UP										THE RESULTS						
Year	Team	Lg	G	GS	CG	GF	IP	BFP	H	R	ER	HR	SH	SF	HB	TBB	IBB	SO	WP	Bk	W	L	Pct	ShO	Sv-Op	Hld	ERC	ERA
2006	Clrwtr*	A+	2	2	0	0	4.0	14	1	0	0	0	0	0	0	1	0	5	0	0	0	0	-	0	0- -	-	0.40	0.00
1988	KC	AL	5	2	0	0	15.2	67	16	9	9	1	0	0	0	7	0	18	0	0	0	2	.000	0	0-0	2	4.22	5.17
1989	KC	AL	49	16	1	16	163.0	677	122	67	66	10	4	4	1	86	4	153	12	0	17	9	.654	1	1-7	3	2.97	3.64
1990	KC	AL	32	32	6	0	195.1	858	192	99	81	17	8	2	3	99	1	175	11	0	12	11	.522	1	0-0	4	4.37	3.73
1991	KC	AL	45	14	1	11	158.0	684	129	76	68	16	5	3	4	87	6	167	5	0	9	14	.391	0	1-4	4	3.67	3.87
1992	KC	AL	40	11	0	13	117.2	516	116	67	60	9	2	6	4	55	4	98	5	2	6	10	.375	0	0-2	4	4.17	4.59
1993	KC	AL	48	14	2	18	155.2	651	125	65	62	11	6	6	1	77	5	143	17	0	12	6	.667	0	1-6	2	3.18	3.58
1994	KC	AL	24	24	0	0	155.1	675	136	79	75	15	3	8	3	87	3	126	12	1	11	7	.611	0	0-0	0	4.04	4.35
1995	KC	AL	31	31	2	0	189.0	843	204	110	93	12	7	11	4	89	4	119	9	0	12	12	.500	0	0-0	0	4.59	4.43
1996	Bos	AL	34	34	4	0	215.2	998	249	143	134	28	2	11	4	105	5	171	6	1	12	9	.571	1	0-0	0	5.50	5.59
1997	Bos	AL	42	25	2	16	182.2	774	155	86	76	10	3	4	3	78	1	159	5	0	6	10	.375	1	11-13	0	3.08	3.74
1998	Bos	AL	73	0	0	69	79.1	317	55	24	24	2	2	2	0	25	1	78	9	0	7	4	.636	1	46-47	0	1.72	2.72
1999	Bos	AL	21	0	0	15	17.2	82	17	11	11	2	0	0	1	12	2	24	0	0	2	0	.000	0	11-13	1	5.04	5.60
2001	ChC	NL	47	0	0	40	45.1	187	32	18	17	4	0	0	1	16	1	67	2	0	1	2	.333	0	27-31	6	2.27	3.38
2002	2 Tms	NL	34	0	0	10	42.2	181	42	19	16	3	3	0	1	16	3	48	0	0	1	3	.250	0	0-0	6	3.71	3.38
2003	CWS	AL	66	0	0	35	74.0	310	57	29	26	4	4	3	4	31	3	91	5	0	7	6	.538	0	12-17	7	2.74	3.16
2004	NYY	AL	80	0	0	15	89.2	342	56	23	22	5	5	2	1	23	5	96	3	0	9	4	.692	0	4-10	36	1.50	2.21
2005	NYY	AL	79	0	0	17	80.2	324	59	25	23	8	1	3	0	29	4	69	1	1	5	4	.556	0	2-9	33	2.45	2.57
2006	Phi	NL	59	0	0	53	59.1	253	53	23	22	9	2	1	1	22	4	68	3	0	3	4	.429	0	34-39	0	3.62	3.34
02	ChC	NL	19	0	0	7	23.2	104	27	12	9	1	1	0	1	10	1	31	0	0	1	1	.500	0	0-0	2	4.75	3.42
02	Hou	NL	15	0	0	3	19.0	77	15	7	7	2	2	0	0	6	2	17	0	0	0	2	.000	0	0-0	4	2.53	3.32
18 ML YEARS			809	203	18	328	2036.2	8739	1815	972	885	166	57	66	36	944	56	1870	105	5	130	119	.522	4	150-198	94	3.61	3.91

Tom Gorzelanny

Pitches: L **Bats:** L **Pos:** SP-11   **Ht:** 6'2" **Wt:** 210 **Born:** 7/12/1982 **Age:** 24

			HOW MUCH HE PITCHED						WHAT HE GAVE UP										THE RESULTS						
Year	Team	Lg	G	GS	CG	GF	IP	BFP	H	R	ER	HR	SH	SF	HB	TBB	IBB	SO	WP	Bk	W	L	Pct	ShO	Sv-Op	Hld	ERC	ERA
2003	Wmspt	A-	8	8	0	0	30.1	134	23	6	6	1	1	0	1	10	0	22	1	0	1	2	.333	0	0- -	-	2.02	1.78
2004	Hickory	A	16	15	1	0	93.0	376	63	30	23	9	5	3	2	34	0	106	4	0	7	2	.778	0	0- -	-	2.31	2.23
2004	Lynbrg	A+	10	10	0	0	55.2	240	54	31	30	6	1	1	4	19	0	61	1	0	3	5	.375	0	0- -	-	4.00	4.85
2005	Altna	AA	23	23	1	0	129.2	549	114	50	47	6	3	3	5	46	0	124	4	0	8	5	.615	1	0- -	-	3.00	3.26
2006	Indy	AAA	16	16	0	0	99.2	378	67	28	26	4	2	1	2	27	1	94	3	0	6	5	.545	0	0- -	-	1.74	2.35
2005	Pit	NL	3	1	0	0	6.0	32	10	8	8	1	1	0	0	3	0	3	0	0	0	1	.000	0	0-0	0	8.76	12.00
2006	Pit	NL	11	11	0	0	61.2	267	50	29	26	3	7	4	4	31	2	40	3	0	2	5	.286	0	0-0	0	3.23	3.79
2 ML YEARS			14	12	0	0	67.2	299	60	37	34	4	8	4	4	34	2	43	3	0	2	6	.250	0	0-0	0	3.67	4.52

Mike Gosling

Pitches: L **Bats:** L **Pos:** RP-1   **Ht:** 6'2" **Wt:** 210 **Born:** 9/23/1980 **Age:** 26

			HOW MUCH HE PITCHED						WHAT HE GAVE UP										THE RESULTS						
Year	Team	Lg	G	GS	CG	GF	IP	BFP	H	R	ER	HR	SH	SF	HB	TBB	IBB	SO	WP	Bk	W	L	Pct	ShO	Sv-Op	Hld	ERC	ERA
2006	Lsvlle*	AAA	23	22	0	1	118.0	519	118	68	60	12	5	8	5	53	0	100	9	0	6	8	.429	0	0- -	-	4.45	4.58
2004	Ari	NL	6	4	0	0	25.1	112	26	13	13	5	2	0	2	13	1	14	2	0	1	1	.500	0	0-0	0	5.83	4.62
2005	Ari	NL	13	5	0	5	32.1	154	40	20	16	2	2	0	0	19	2	14	0	0	0	3	.000	0	0-0	0	5.74	4.45
2006	Cin	NL	1	0	0	0	1.1	7	1	2	2	1	0	0	1	1	0	1	0	0	0	0	-	0	0-0	0	12.98	13.50
3 ML YEARS			20	9	0	5	59.0	273	67	35	31	8	4	0	3	33	3	29	2	0	1	4	.200	0	0-0	0	5.94	4.73

John Grabow

Pitches: L **Bats:** L **Pos:** RP-72   **Ht:** 6'2" **Wt:** 210 **Born:** 11/4/1978 **Age:** 28

			HOW MUCH HE PITCHED						WHAT HE GAVE UP										THE RESULTS						
Year	Team	Lg	G	GS	CG	GF	IP	BFP	H	R	ER	HR	SH	SF	HB	TBB	IBB	SO	WP	Bk	W	L	Pct	ShO	Sv-Op	Hld	ERC	ERA
2003	Pit	NL	5	0	0	1	5.0	22	6	3	2	0	0	0	0	0	0	9	0	0	0	0	-	0	0-0	0	2.73	3.60
2004	Pit	NL	68	0	0	10	61.2	286	81	39	35	8	6	1	0	28	7	64	5	0	2	5	.286	0	1-7	11	6.21	5.11
2005	Pit	NL	63	0	0	8	52.0	222	46	31	28	6	2	0	2	25	2	42	1	0	2	3	.400	0	0-1	14	4.00	4.85
2006	Pit	NL	72	0	0	17	69.2	303	68	34	32	7	5	3	3	30	3	66	0	0	4	2	.667	0	0-2	11	4.17	4.13
4 ML YEARS			208	0	0	36	188.1	833	201	107	97	21	13	4	5	83	12	181	6	0	8	10	.444	0	1-10	36	4.72	4.64

Tony Graffanino

Bats: R **Throws:** R **Pos:** 2B-67; 3B-27; 1B-16; SS-13; PH-6; DH-3; PR-2   **Ht:** 6'1" **Wt:** 190 **Born:** 6/6/1972 **Age:** 35

			BATTING																		BASERUNNING				AVERAGES		
Year	Team	Lg	G	AB	H	2B	3B	HR	(Hm	Rd)	TB	R	RBI	RC	TBB	IBB	SO	HBP	SH	SF	SB	CS	SB%	GDP	Avg	OBP	Slg
1996	Atl	NL	22	46	8	1	1	0	(0	0)	11	7	2	3	4	0	13	1	0	0	0	0	-	0	.174	.250	.239
1997	Atl	NL	104	186	48	9	1	8	(5	3)	83	33	20	29	26	1	46	1	3	5	6	4	.60	3	.258	.344	.446
1998	Atl	NL	105	289	61	14	1	5	(3	2)	92	32	22	22	24	0	68	2	1	1	1	4	.20	7	.211	.275	.318
1999	TB	AL	39	130	41	9	4	2	(0	2)	64	20	19	23	9	0	22	1	2	0	3	2	.60	1	.315	.364	.492
2000	2 Tms	AL	70	168	46	6	1	2	(1	1)	60	33	17	23	22	0	27	2	1	1	7	4	.64	2	.274	.363	.357

106

Year	Team	Lg	G	AB	H	2B	3B	HR	(Hm	Rd)	TB	R	RBI	RC	TBB	IBB	SO	HBP	SH	SF	SB	CS	SB%	GDP	Avg	OBP	Slg
																BATTING									**BASERUNNING**		**AVERAGES**
2001	CWS	AL	74	145	44	9	0	2	(1	1)	59	23	15	22	16	0	29	1	4	3	4	1	.80	4	.303	.370	.407
2002	CWS	AL	70	229	60	12	4	6	(4	2)	98	35	31	35	22	1	38	2	4	2	2	1	.67	2	.262	.329	.428
2003	CWS	AL	90	250	65	15	3	7	(4	3)	107	51	23	36	24	1	37	3	3	1	8	0	1.00	1	.260	.331	.428
2004	KC	AL	75	278	73	11	0	3	(0	3)	93	37	26	35	27	0	38	3	4	2	10	2	.83	5	.263	.332	.335
2005	2 Tms	AL	110	379	117	17	3	7	(4	3)	161	68	38	58	31	2	51	4	2	1	7	2	.78	14	.309	.366	.425
2006	2 Tms	AL	129	456	125	33	3	7	(3	4)	185	68	59	67	45	1	68	5	4	1	5	4	.56	10	.274	.345	.406
00	TB	AL	13	20	6	1	0	0	(0	0)	7	8	1	2	1	0	2	1	0	0	0	0	-	1	.300	.364	.350
00	CWS	AL	57	148	40	5	1	2	(1	1)	53	25	16	21	21	0	25	1	1	1	7	4	.64	1	.270	.363	.358
05	KC	AL	59	191	57	5	2	3	(1	2)	75	29	18	32	22	1	28	2	2	0	3	1	.75	6	.298	.377	.393
05	Bos	AL	51	188	60	12	1	4	(3	1)	86	39	20	26	9	1	23	2	0	1	4	1	.80	8	.319	.355	.457
06	KC	AL	69	220	59	16	0	5	(2	3)	90	34	32	31	25	1	31	1	4	0	3	4	.43	4	.268	.346	.409
06	Mil	NL	60	236	66	17	3	2	(1	1)	95	34	27	36	20	0	37	4	0	1	2	0	1.00	6	.280	.345	.403
11 ML YEARS			888	2556	688	136	21	49	(25	24)	1013	407	272	353	250	6	437	25	28	18	53	24	.69	49	.269	.338	.396

Curtis Granderson

Bats: L **Throws:** R **Pos:** CF-157; PH-6; PR-2   **Ht:** 6'1" **Wt:** 185 **Born:** 3/16/1981 **Age:** 26

Year	Team	Lg	G	AB	H	2B	3B	HR	(Hm	Rd)	TB	R	RBI	RC	TBB	IBB	SO	HBP	SH	SF	SB	CS	SB%	GDP	Avg	OBP	Slg
2004	Det	AL	9	25	6	1	1	0	(0	0)	9	2	0	2	3	0	8	0	0	0	0	0	-	1	.240	.321	.360
2005	Det	AL	47	162	44	6	3	8	(5	3)	80	18	20	26	10	0	43	0	2	0	1	1	.50	2	.272	.314	.494
2006	Det	AL	159	596	155	31	9	19	(7	12)	261	90	68	89	66	0	**174**	4	7	6	8	5	.62	4	.260	.335	.438
3 ML YEARS			215	783	205	38	13	27	(12	15)	350	110	88	117	79	0	225	4	9	6	9	6	.60	7	.262	.330	.447

Danny Graves

Pitches: R **Bats:** R **Pos:** RP-13   **Ht:** 6'0" **Wt:** 200 **Born:** 8/7/1973 **Age:** 33

Year	Team	Lg	G	GS	CG	GF	IP	BFP	H	R	ER	HR	SH	SF	HB	TBB	IBB	SO	WP	Bk	W	L	Pct	ShO	Sv-Op	Hld	ERC	ERA
																					THE RESULTS							
2006	Buffalo*	AAA	33	1	0	10	51.2	216	55	26	23	5	1	2	2	13	2	27	3	0	1	1	.500	0	1- -	-	4.01	4.01
1996	Cle	AL	15	0	0	5	29.2	129	29	18	15	2	0	1	0	10	0	22	1	0	2	0	1.000	0	0-1	0	3.37	4.55
1997	2 Tms		15	0	0	3	26.0	134	41	22	16	2	3	2	0	20	1	11	1	0	0	0	-	0	0-0	1	9.10	5.54
1998	Cin	NL	62	0	0	35	81.1	340	76	31	30	6	2	5	2	28	4	44	4	0	2	1	.667	0	8-8	8	3.38	3.32
1999	Cin	NL	75	0	0	56	111.0	454	90	42	38	10	5	2	2	49	4	69	3	0	8	7	.533	0	27-36	0	3.25	3.08
2000	Cin	NL	66	0	0	57	91.1	388	81	31	26	8	6	4	3	42	7	53	3	1	10	5	.667	0	30-35	0	3.64	2.56
2001	Cin	NL	66	0	0	54	80.1	337	83	41	37	7	3	2	4	18	6	49	2	1	6	5	.545	0	32-39	0	3.59	4.15
2002	Cin	NL	68	4	0	54	98.2	412	99	37	35	7	3	6	1	25	9	58	5	0	7	3	.700	0	32-39	0	3.33	3.19
2003	Cin	NL	30	26	2	3	169.0	741	204	108	100	30	6	3	7	41	6	60	2	0	4	15	.211	1	2-2	0	5.32	5.33
2004	Cin	NL	68	0	0	59	68.1	290	77	39	30	12	0	2	2	13	6	40	2	0	1	6	.143	0	41-50	0	4.47	3.95
2005	2 Tms		40	0	0	29	38.2	197	59	35	28	9	3	1	3	20	4	20	3	0	1	1	.500	0	10-12	1	8.99	6.52
2006	Cle	AL	13	0	0	5	14.0	65	18	12	9	3	0	1	0	5	1	3	1	0	2	1	.667	0	0-1	0	6.19	5.79
97	Cle	AL	5	0	0	2	11.1	56	15	8	6	2	0	1	0	9	0	4	0	0	0	0	-	0	0-0	0	8.52	4.76
97	Cin	NL	10	0	0	1	14.2	78	26	14	10	0	3	1	0	11	1	7	1	0	0	0	-	0	0-0	1	9.52	6.14
05	Cin	NL	20	0	0	18	18.1	89	30	18	15	4	2	1	0	12	3	8	3	0	1	1	.500	0	10-12	0	9.50	7.36
05	NYM	NL	20	0	0	11	20.1	98	29	17	13	5	1	0	3	8	1	12	0	0	0	0	-	0	0-0	1	8.51	5.75
11 ML YEARS			518	30	2	360	808.1	3487	857	416	364	96	31	29	26	271	48	429	27	2	43	44	.494	1	182-223	8	4.35	4.05

Andy Green

Bats: R **Throws:** R **Pos:** PH-56; 3B-7; LF-7; 2B-6; SS-2; DH-1; PR-1   **Ht:** 5'9" **Wt:** 180 **Born:** 7/7/1977 **Age:** 29

Year	Team	Lg	G	AB	H	2B	3B	HR	(Hm	Rd)	TB	R	RBI	RC	TBB	IBB	SO	HBP	SH	SF	SB	CS	SB%	GDP	Avg	OBP	Slg
2006	Tucsn*	AAA	18	75	18	3	0	1	(-	-)	24	10	6	7	4	0	14	1	0	0	0	0	-	0	.240	.288	.320
2004	Ari	NL	46	109	22	2	1	1	(1	0)	29	13	4	7	5	0	17	1	3	1	1	1	.50	2	.202	.241	.266
2005	Ari	NL	17	31	7	1	0	0	(0	0)	8	5	2	3	7	0	3	0	0	0	0	0	-	1	.226	.359	.258
2006	Ari	NL	73	86	16	4	0	1	(1	0)	23	15	6	7	13	0	20	0	3	0	1	0	1.00	0	.186	.293	.267
3 ML YEARS			136	226	45	7	1	2	(2	0)	60	33	12	17	25	0	40	1	6	2	2	1	.67	3	.199	.280	.265

Nick Green

Bats: R **Throws:** R **Pos:** 2B-23; SS-20; 3B-17; PR-4; DH-2; PH-2; 1B-1; RF-1   **Ht:** 6'0" **Wt:** 175 **Born:** 9/10/1978 **Age:** 28

Year	Team	Lg	G	AB	H	2B	3B	HR	(Hm	Rd)	TB	R	RBI	RC	TBB	IBB	SO	HBP	SH	SF	SB	CS	SB%	GDP	Avg	OBP	Slg
2006	Drham*	AAA	10	42	10	0	0	1	(-	-)	13	2	2	3	0	0	14	1	1	0	0	0	-	0	.238	.256	.310
2006	Clmbs*	AAA	14	48	10	4	0	0	(-	-)	14	3	4	5	7	0	13	1	1	1	1	0	1.00	0	.208	.316	.292
2004	Atl	NL	95	264	72	15	3	3	(3	0)	102	40	26	36	12	1	63	4	8	2	1	2	.33	0	.273	.312	.386
2005	TB	AL	111	318	76	15	2	5	(2	3)	110	53	29	38	33	0	86	11	10	3	3	1	.75	5	.239	.329	.346
2006	2 Tms	AL	63	114	21	5	0	2	(1	1)	32	12	4	10	11	0	40	1	1	0	1	4	.20	2	.184	.262	.281
06	TB	AL	17	39	3	0	0	0	(0	0)	3	4	0	4	6	0	11	0	0	0	0	3	.00	2	.077	.200	.077
06	NYY	AL	46	75	18	5	0	2	(1	1)	29	8	4	10	5	0	29	1	1	0	1	1	.50	0	.240	.296	.387
3 ML YEARS			269	696	169	35	5	10	(6	4)	244	105	59	84	56	1	189	16	19	5	5	7	.42	7	.243	.312	.351

Sean Green

Pitches: R **Bats:** R **Pos:** RP-24   **Ht:** 6'6" **Wt:** 230 **Born:** 4/20/1979 **Age:** 28

Year	Team	Lg	G	GS	CG	GF	IP	BFP	H	R	ER	HR	SH	SF	HB	TBB	IBB	SO	WP	Bk	W	L	Pct	ShO	Sv-Op	Hld	ERC	ERA
2000	Portlnd	A-	22	0	0	4	28.2	155	45	32	27	2	1	2	5	19	2	17	5	0	0	0	-	0	0- -	-	8.87	8.48
2001	Ashvlle	A	43	0	0	9	58.0	271	66	43	38	4	4	1	4	28	1	37	8	2	3	4	.429	0	0- -	-	5.10	5.90
2002	Salem	A+	52	0	0	17	67.0	319	92	41	29	5	6	4	1	31	8	26	8	0	2	5	.286	0	2- -	-	6.15	3.90

Year	Team	Lg	G	GS	CG	GF	IP	BFP	H	R	ER	HR	SH	SF	HB	TBB	IBB	SO	WP	Bk	W	L	Pct	ShO	Sv-Op	Hld	ERC	ERA
2003	Visalia	A+	46	2	0	17	80.0	370	90	54	43	2	3	1	8	38	2	56	4	0	3	4	.429	0	0--	-	4.82	4.84
2004	Tulsa	AA	52	0	0	19	77.1	330	63	32	26	5	0	1	7	29	1	50	6	0	4	3	.571	0	2--	-	3.01	3.03
2005	SnAnt	AA	21	0	0	19	24.1	100	17	11	8	1	1	0	1	8	1	18	6	0	0	1	.000	0	14--	-	1.93	2.96
2005	Tacom	AAA	33	0	0	14	49.1	217	40	23	20	1	1	2	4	29	0	44	8	0	4	2	.667	0	1--	-	3.47	3.65
2006	Tacom	AAA	15	0	0	12	24.0	96	18	6	6	0	3	0	2	11	1	12	0	0	4	1	.800	0	5--	-	2.69	2.25
2006	Sea	AL	24	0	0	11	32.0	139	34	16	16	2	1	1	2	13	1	15	2	0	0	0	-	0	0-1	3	4.47	4.50

Shawn Green

Bats: L **Throws:** L **Pos:** RF-131; 1B-13; PH-7; DH-1   **Ht:** 6'4" **Wt:** 210 **Born:** 11/10/1972 **Age:** 34

							BATTING															BASERUNNING				AVERAGES		
Year	Team	Lg	G	AB	H	2B	3B	HR	(Hm	Rd)	TB	R	RBI	RC	TBB	IBB	SO	HBP	SH	SF	SB	CS	SB%	GDP	Avg	OBP	Slg
1993	Tor	AL	3	6	0	0	0	0	(0	0)	0	0	0	0	0	0	1	0	0	0	0	0	-	0	.000	.000	.000
1994	Tor	AL	14	33	3	1	0	0	(0	0)	4	1	1	0	1	0	8	0	0	0	1	0	1.00	1	.091	.118	.121
1995	Tor	AL	121	379	109	31	4	15	(5	10)	193	52	54	61	20	3	68	3	0	3	1	2	.33	4	.288	.326	.509
1996	Tor	AL	132	422	118	32	3	11	(7	4)	189	52	45	64	33	3	75	8	0	2	5	1	.83	9	.280	.342	.448
1997	Tor	AL	135	429	123	22	4	16	(10	6)	201	57	53	70	36	4	99	1	1	4	14	3	.82	4	.287	.340	.469
1998	Tor	AL	158	630	175	33	4	35	(21	14)	321	106	100	108	50	2	142	5	1	3	35	12	.74	6	.278	.334	.510
1999	Tor	AL	153	614	190	45	0	42	(20	22)	361	134	123	132	66	4	117	11	0	5	20	7	.74	13	.309	.384	.588
2000	LAD	NL	162	610	164	44	4	24	(15	9)	288	98	99	107	90	9	121	8	0	6	24	5	.83	18	.269	.367	.472
2001	LAD	NL	161	619	184	31	4	49	(19	30)	370	121	125	134	72	10	107	5	0	5	20	4	.83	10	.297	.372	.598
2002	LAD	NL	158	582	166	31	1	42	(18	24)	325	110	114	106	93	22	112	5	0	5	8	5	.62	26	.285	.385	.558
2003	LAD	NL	160	611	171	49	2	19	(10	9)	281	84	85	92	68	2	112	6	0	6	6	2	.75	18	.280	.355	.460
2004	LAD	NL	157	590	157	28	4	28	(16	12)	271	92	86	76	71	6	114	8	0	2	5	2	.71	17	.266	.352	.459
2005	Ari	NL	158	581	166	37	4	22	(12	10)	277	87	73	78	62	6	95	5	0	8	8	4	.67	18	.286	.355	.477
2006	2 Tms	NL	149	530	147	31	3	15	(9	6)	229	73	66	69	45	5	82	10	0	3	4	4	.50	17	.277	.344	.432
06	Ari	NL	115	417	118	22	3	11	(6	5)	179	59	51	57	37	4	64	6	0	2	4	4	.50	9	.283	.348	.429
06	NYM	NL	34	113	29	9	0	4	(3	1)	50	14	15	12	8	1	18	4	0	1	0	0	-	8	.257	.325	.442
	14 ML YEARS		1821	6636	1873	415	34	318	(162	156)	3310	1067	1024	1097	707	76	1253	75	2	52	151	51	.75	161	.282	.355	.499

Khalil Greene

Bats: R **Throws:** R **Pos:** SS-113; PR-9; PH-1   **Ht:** 5'11" **Wt:** 195 **Born:** 10/21/1979 **Age:** 27

							BATTING															BASERUNNING				AVERAGES		
Year	Team	Lg	G	AB	H	2B	3B	HR	(Hm	Rd)	TB	R	RBI	RC	TBB	IBB	SO	HBP	SH	SF	SB	CS	SB%	GDP	Avg	OBP	Slg
2003	SD	NL	20	65	14	4	1	2	(0	2)	26	8	6	4	4	0	19	1	0	0	0	1	.00	3	.215	.271	.400
2004	SD	NL	139	484	132	31	4	15	(3	12)	216	67	65	73	53	10	94	8	1	8	4	2	.67	9	.273	.349	.446
2005	SD	NL	121	436	109	30	2	15	(6	9)	188	51	70	58	25	3	93	6	3	6	5	0	1.00	8	.250	.296	.431
2006	SD	NL	122	412	101	26	2	15	(6	9)	176	56	55	48	39	0	87	7	0	2	5	1	.83	16	.245	.320	.427
	4 ML YEARS		402	1397	356	91	9	47	(15	32)	606	182	196	183	121	13	293	22	4	16	14	4	.78	36	.255	.321	.434

Todd Greene

Bats: R **Throws:** R **Pos:** C-42; PH-18; 1B-5; PR-1   **Ht:** 5'10" **Wt:** 210 **Born:** 5/8/1971 **Age:** 36

							BATTING															BASERUNNING				AVERAGES		
Year	Team	Lg	G	AB	H	2B	3B	HR	(Hm	Rd)	TB	R	RBI	RC	TBB	IBB	SO	HBP	SH	SF	SB	CS	SB%	GDP	Avg	OBP	Slg
1996	LAA	AL	29	79	15	1	0	2	(1	1)	22	9	9	4	4	0	11	1	0	0	2	0	1.00	4	.190	.238	.278
1997	LAA	AL	34	124	36	6	0	9	(5	4)	69	24	24	22	7	1	25	0	0	0	2	0	1.00	1	.290	.328	.556
1998	LAA	AL	29	71	18	4	0	1	(0	1)	25	3	7	7	2	0	20	0	0	0	0	0	-	0	.254	.274	.352
1999	LAA	AL	97	321	78	20	0	14	(7	7)	140	36	42	35	12	0	63	3	0	2	1	4	.20	8	.243	.275	.436
2000	Tor	AL	34	85	20	2	0	5	(2	3)	37	11	10	9	5	0	18	0	0	0	0	0	-	4	.235	.278	.435
2001	NYY	AL	35	96	20	4	0	1	(1	0)	27	9	11	5	3	0	21	1	0	0	0	0	-	3	.208	.240	.281
2002	Tex	AL	42	112	30	5	0	10	(6	4)	65	15	19	11	2	0	23	1	1	2	0	0	-	4	.268	.282	.580
2003	Tex	AL	62	205	47	10	1	10	(4	6)	89	25	20	14	2	0	47	2	0	1	0	0	-	2	.229	.243	.434
2004	Col	NL	75	195	55	14	0	10	(6	4)	99	23	35	28	13	4	38	0	0	1	0	0	-	9	.282	.325	.508
2005	Col	NL	38	126	32	4	0	7	(3	4)	57	10	23	19	7	0	21	1	0	0	0	0	-	5	.254	.299	.452
2006	SF	NL	61	159	46	12	2	2	(0	2)	68	16	17	23	10	3	45	1	0	0	0	0	-	0	.289	.335	.428
	11 ML YEARS		536	1573	397	82	3	71	(35	36)	698	181	217	177	67	8	332	10	1	6	5	4	.56	40	.252	.286	.444

Kevin Gregg

Pitches: R **Bats:** R **Pos:** RP-29; SP-3   **Ht:** 6'6" **Wt:** 235 **Born:** 6/20/1978 **Age:** 29

			HOW MUCH HE PITCHED						WHAT HE GAVE UP												THE RESULTS						
Year	Team	Lg	G	GS	CG	GF	IP	BFP	H	R	ER	HR	SH	SF	HB	TBB	IBB	SO	WP	Bk	W	L	Pct	ShO	Sv-Op	Hld	ERC	ERA
2006	Salt Lk*	AAA	3	2	0	0	10.0	37	5	0	0	0	0	0	0	4	0	8	0	0	1	0	1.000	0	0--	-	1.28	0.00
2003	LAA	AL	5	3	0	0	24.2	97	18	9	9	3	0	0	1	8	0	14	0	0	2	0	1.000	0	0-0	-	2.74	3.28
2004	LAA	AL	55	0	0	23	87.2	377	86	43	41	6	4	5	3	28	3	84	13	1	5	2	.714	0	1-2	3	3.47	4.21
2005	LAA	AL	33	2	0	9	64.1	290	70	37	36	8	1	1	3	29	2	52	5	0	1	2	.333	0	0-1	1	5.08	5.04
2006	LAA	AL	32	3	0	12	78.1	341	88	41	36	10	0	3	2	21	0	71	6	0	3	4	.429	0	0-0	0	4.51	4.14
	4 ML YEARS		125	8	0	44	255.0	1105	262	130	122	27	5	9	9	86	5	221	24	1	11	8	.579	0	1-3	4	4.10	4.31

Zack Greinke

Pitches: R **Bats:** R **Pos:** RP-3   **Ht:** 6'2" **Wt:** 185 **Born:** 10/21/1983 **Age:** 23

			HOW MUCH HE PITCHED						WHAT HE GAVE UP												THE RESULTS						
Year	Team	Lg	G	GS	CG	GF	IP	BFP	H	R	ER	HR	SH	SF	HB	TBB	IBB	SO	WP	Bk	W	L	Pct	ShO	Sv-Op	Hld	ERC	ERA
2006	Wichta*	AA	18	17	1	0	105.2	438	96	53	51	12	2	3	6	27	0	94	6	0	8	3	.727	0	0--	-	3.33	4.34
2004	KC	AL	24	24	0	0	145.0	599	143	64	64	26	3	2	8	26	3	100	1	1	8	11	.421	0	0-0	0	3.85	3.97

Year	Team	Lg	G	GS	CG	GF	IP	BFP	H	R	ER	HR	SH	SF	HB	TBB	IBB	SO	WP	Bk	W	L	Pct	ShO	Sv-Op	Hld	ERC	ERA
2005	KC	AL	33	33	2	0	183.0	829	233	125	118	23	4	4	13	53	0	114	4	2	5	17	.227	0	0-0	0	5.71	5.80
2006	KC	AL	3	0	0	1	6.1	28	7	3	3	1	0	0	0	3	2	5	0	0	1	0	1.000	0	0-0	0	4.93	4.26
3 ML YEARS			60	57	2	1	334.1	1456	383	192	185	50	7	6	21	82	5	219	5	3	14	28	.333	0	0-0	0	4.87	4.98

Ken Griffey Jr.

Bats: L Throws: L Pos: CF-100; PH-6; DH-3   Ht: 6'3" Wt: 220 Born: 11/21/1969 Age: 37

Year	Team	Lg	G	AB	H	2B	3B	HR	(Hm	Rd)	TB	R	RBI	RC	TBB	IBB	SO	HBP	SH	SF	SB	CS	SB%	GDP	Avg	OBP	Slg
1989	Sea	AL	127	455	120	23	0	16	(10	6)	191	61	61	64	44	8	83	2	1	4	16	7	.70	4	.264	.329	.420
1990	Sea	AL	155	597	179	28	7	22	(8	14)	287	91	80	101	63	12	81	2	0	4	16	11	.59	12	.300	.366	.481
1991	Sea	AL	154	548	179	42	1	22	(16	6)	289	76	100	112	71	21	82	1	4	9	18	6	.75	10	.327	.399	.527
1992	Sea	AL	142	565	174	39	4	27	(16	11)	302	83	103	102	44	15	67	5	0	3	10	5	.67	15	.308	.361	.535
1993	Sea	AL	156	582	180	38	3	45	(21	24)	359	113	109	137	96	25	91	6	0	7	17	9	.65	14	.309	.408	.617
1994	Sea	AL	111	433	140	24	4	40	(18	22)	292	94	90	107	56	19	73	2	0	2	11	3	.79	9	.323	.402	.674
1995	Sea	AL	72	260	67	7	0	17	(13	4)	125	52	42	49	52	6	53	0	0	2	4	2	.67	4	.258	.379	.481
1996	Sea	AL	140	545	165	26	2	49	(26	23)	342	125	140	131	78	13	104	7	1	7	16	1	.94	7	.303	.392	.628
1997	Sea	AL	157	608	185	34	3	56	(27	29)	393	125	147	142	76	23	121	8	0	12	15	4	.79	12	.304	.382	.646
1998	Sea	AL	161	633	180	33	3	56	(30	26)	387	120	146	136	76	11	121	7	0	4	20	5	.80	14	.284	.365	.611
1999	Sea	AL	160	606	173	26	3	48	(27	21)	349	123	134	132	91	17	108	7	0	2	24	7	.77	8	.285	.384	.576
2000	Cin	NL	145	520	141	22	3	40	(22	18)	289	100	118	111	94	17	117	9	0	8	6	4	.60	7	.271	.387	.556
2001	Cin	NL	111	364	104	20	2	22	(12	10)	194	57	65	69	44	6	72	4	1	4	2	0	1.00	6	.286	.365	.533
2002	Cin	NL	70	197	52	8	0	8	(4	4)	84	17	23	27	28	6	39	3	0	4	1	2	.33	6	.264	.358	.426
2003	Cin	NL	53	166	41	12	1	13	(5	8)	94	34	26	26	27	5	44	6	1	1	1	0	1.00	3	.247	.370	.566
2004	Cin	NL	83	300	76	18	0	20	(11	9)	154	49	60	56	44	3	67	2	0	2	1	0	1.00	8	.253	.351	.513
2005	Cin	NL	128	491	148	30	0	35	(15	20)	283	85	92	89	54	3	93	3	0	7	0	1	.00	9	.301	.369	.576
2006	Cin	NL	109	428	108	19	0	27	(13	14)	208	62	72	55	39	6	78	2	0	3	0	0	-	13	.252	.316	.486
18 ML YEARS			2234	8298	2412	449	36	563	(294	269)	4622	1467	1608	1646	1077	216	1494	76	8	85	178	67	.73	163	.291	.374	.557

Jason Grilli

Pitches: R Bats: R Pos: RP-51   Ht: 6'5" Wt: 225 Born: 11/11/1976 Age: 30

Year	Team	Lg	G	GS	CG	GF	IP	BFP	H	R	ER	HR	SH	SF	HB	TBB	IBB	SO	WP	Bk	W	L	Pct	ShO	Sv-Op	Hld	ERC	ERA
2000	Fla	NL	1	1	0	0	6.2	35	11	4	4	0	2	0	2	2	0	3	0	0	1	0	1.000	0	0-0	0	7.84	5.40
2001	Fla	NL	6	5	0	1	26.2	115	30	18	18	6	1	0	2	11	0	17	0	0	2	2	.500	0	0-0	0	6.44	6.08
2004	CWS	AL	8	8	1	0	45.0	203	52	38	37	11	2	1	3	20	0	26	2	0	2	3	.400	0	0-0	0	6.67	7.40
2005	Det	AL	3	2	0	0	16.0	63	14	6	6	1	1	1	0	6	0	5	0	0	1	1	.500	0	0-0	0	3.27	3.38
2006	Det	AL	51	0	0	18	62.0	270	61	31	29	6	2	4	5	25	3	31	5	0	2	3	.400	0	0-0	9	4.23	4.21
5 ML YEARS			69	16	1	19	156.1	686	168	97	94	24	8	6	12	64	3	82	7	0	8	9	.471	0	0-0	9	5.32	5.41

Jason Grimsley

Pitches: R Bats: R Pos: RP-19   Ht: 6'3" Wt: 205 Born: 8/7/1967 Age: 39

Year	Team	Lg	G	GS	CG	GF	IP	BFP	H	R	ER	HR	SH	SF	HB	TBB	IBB	SO	WP	Bk	W	L	Pct	ShO	Sv-Op	Hld	ERC	ERA
1989	Phi	NL	4	4	0	0	18.1	91	19	13	12	2	1	0	0	19	1	7	2	0	1	3	.250	0	0-0	0	6.86	5.89
1990	Phi	NL	11	11	0	0	57.1	255	47	21	21	1	2	1	2	43	0	41	6	1	3	2	.600	0	0-0	0	3.98	3.30
1991	Phi	NL	12	12	0	0	61.0	272	54	34	33	4	3	2	3	41	3	42	14	0	1	7	.125	0	0-0	0	4.39	4.87
1993	Cle	AL	10	6	0	1	42.1	194	52	26	25	3	1	0	1	20	1	27	2	0	3	4	.429	0	0-0	1	5.57	5.31
1994	Cle	AL	14	13	1	0	82.2	368	91	47	42	7	4	2	6	34	1	59	6	1	5	2	.714	0	0-0	0	4.89	4.57
1995	Cle	AL	15	2	0	2	34.0	165	37	24	23	4	1	2	2	32	1	25	7	0	0	0	-	0	1-1	0	7.37	6.09
1996	LAA	AL	35	20	2	4	130.1	622	150	110	99	14	4	5	13	74	5	82	11	0	5	7	.417	1	0-0	0	5.98	6.84
1999	NYY	AL	55	0	0	25	75.0	336	66	39	30	7	3	3	4	40	5	49	8	0	7	2	.778	0	1-4	8	3.87	3.60
2000	NYY	AL	63	4	0	18	96.1	428	100	58	54	10	2	6	5	42	1	53	16	0	3	2	.600	0	1-4	4	4.63	5.04
2001	KC	AL	73	0	0	24	80.1	327	71	32	27	8	2	1	2	28	5	61	4	0	1	5	.167	0	0-7	26	3.34	3.02
2002	KC	AL	70	0	0	26	71.1	310	64	32	31	4	1	0	1	37	8	59	8	0	4	7	.364	0	1-3	13	3.51	3.91
2003	KC	AL	76	0	0	5	75.0	346	88	47	43	6	6	5	5	36	5	58	4	0	2	6	.250	0	0-7	28	5.40	5.16
2004	2 Tms		73	0	0	7	63.0	285	61	36	27	4	3	1	3	35	6	39	6	0	5	7	.417	0	0-9	17	4.20	3.86
2005	Bal	AL	22	0	0	9	22.0	93	24	15	14	4	1	0	0	9	2	10	1	0	1	2	.333	0	0-3	5	5.67	5.73
2006	Ari	NL	19	0	0	6	27.2	118	30	15	15	4	3	0	0	8	2	10	1	0	1	2	.333	0	0-0	0	4.33	4.88
04	KC	AL	32	0	0	4	26.2	118	24	11	10	1	1	0	1	15	3	18	4	0	3	3	.500	0	0-3	5	3.62	3.38
04	Bal	AL	41	0	0	3	36.1	167	37	25	17	3	2	1	2	20	3	21	2	0	2	4	.333	0	0-6	12	4.63	4.21
15 ML YEARS			552	72	3	127	936.2	4208	954	549	496	83	36	29	47	498	46	622	96	2	42	58	.420	1	4-38	100	4.74	4.77

Gabe Gross

Bats: L Throws: R Pos: PH-61; CF-33; LF-20; RF-8; PR-1   Ht: 6'3" Wt: 210 Born: 10/21/1979 Age: 27

Year	Team	Lg	G	AB	H	2B	3B	HR	(Hm	Rd)	TB	R	RBI	RC	TBB	IBB	SO	HBP	SH	SF	SB	CS	SB%	GDP	Avg	OBP	Slg
2004	Tor	AL	44	129	27	4	0	3	(2	1)	40	18	16	15	19	0	31	0	0	0	2	2	.50	1	.209	.311	.310
2005	Tor	AL	40	92	23	4	1	1	(1	0)	32	11	7	11	10	0	21	0	0	0	1	1	.50	0	.250	.324	.348
2006	Mil	NL	117	208	57	15	0	9	(5	4)	99	42	38	42	36	3	60	2	3	3	1	0	1.00	3	.274	.382	.476
3 ML YEARS			201	429	107	23	1	13	(8	5)	171	71	61	68	65	3	112	2	3	3	4	3	.57	4	.249	.349	.399

Mark Grudzielanek

Bats: R **Throws:** R **Pos:** 2B-132; SS-4; PH-2   **Ht:** 6'1" **Wt:** 190 **Born:** 6/30/1970 **Age:** 37

										BATTING												BASERUNNING				AVERAGES		
Year	Team	Lg	G	AB	H	2B	3B	HR	(Hm	Rd)	TB	R	RBI	RC	TBB	IBB	SO	HBP	SH	SF	SB	CS	SB%	GDP	Avg	OBP	Slg
1995	Mon	NL	78	269	66	12	2	1	(1	0)	85	27	20	24	14	4	47	7	3	0	8	3	.73	7	.245	.300	.316
1996	Mon	NL	153	657	201	34	4	6	(5	1)	261	99	49	90	26	3	83	9	1	3	33	7	.83	10	.306	.340	.397
1997	Mon	NL	156	**649**	177	**54**	3	4	(1	3)	249	76	51	75	23	0	76	10	3	3	25	9	.74	13	.273	.307	.384
1998	2 Tms	NL	156	589	160	21	1	10	(5	5)	213	62	62	64	26	2	73	11	8	7	18	5	.78	18	.272	.311	.362
1999	LAD	NL	123	488	159	23	5	7	(4	3)	213	72	46	76	31	1	65	10	2	3	6	6	.50	13	.326	.376	.436
2000	LAD	NL	148	617	172	35	6	7	(4	3)	240	101	49	80	45	0	81	9	2	3	12	3	.80	16	.279	.335	.389
2001	LAD	NL	133	539	146	21	3	13	(8	5)	212	83	55	66	28	0	83	11	3	5	4	4	.50	9	.271	.317	.393
2002	LAD	NL	150	536	145	23	0	9	(5	4)	195	56	50	53	22	4	89	3	1	4	4	1	.80	17	.271	.301	.364
2003	ChC	NL	121	481	151	38	1	3	(2	1)	200	73	38	71	30	0	64	11	7	2	6	2	.75	12	.314	.366	.416
2004	ChC	NL	81	257	79	12	1	6	(3	3)	111	32	23	35	15	0	32	1	4	1	1	1	.50	7	.307	.347	.432
2005	StL	NL	137	528	155	30	3	8	(3	5)	215	64	59	68	26	3	81	7	0	2	8	6	.57	14	.294	.334	.407
2006	KC	AL	134	548	163	32	4	7	(5	2)	224	85	52	69	28	4	69	2	3	5	3	2	.60	12	.297	.331	.409
98	Mon	NL	105	396	109	15	1	8	(3	5)	150	51	41	47	21	1	50	9	5	4	11	5	.69	11	.275	.323	.379
98	LAD	NL	51	193	51	6	0	2	(2	0)	63	11	21	17	5	1	23	2	3	3	7	0	1.00	7	.264	.286	.326
12 ML YEARS			1570	6158	1774	335	33	81	(46	35)	2418	830	554	771	314	21	843	91	37	38	128	49	.72	148	.288	.330	.393

Kevin Gryboski

Pitches: R **Bats:** R **Pos:** RP-6   **Ht:** 6'5" **Wt:** 230 **Born:** 11/15/1973 **Age:** 33

			HOW MUCH HE PITCHED						WHAT HE GAVE UP												THE RESULTS							
Year	Team	Lg	G	GS	CG	GF	IP	BFP	H	R	ER	HR	SH	SF	HB	TBB	IBB	SO	WP	Bk	W	L	Pct	ShO	Sv-Op	Hld	ERC	ERA
2006	NewOr*	AAA	52	0	0	18	60.2	269	67	31	25	3	5	0	2	26	3	43	0	0	4	6	.400	0	7--	-	4.48	3.71
2002	Atl	NL	57	0	0	10	51.2	238	50	20	20	6	1	0	5	37	5	33	2	0	2	1	.667	0	0-2	11	5.58	3.48
2003	Atl	NL	64	0	0	9	44.1	191	44	22	19	3	4	0	2	23	6	32	2	0	6	4	.600	0	0-4	12	4.36	3.86
2004	Atl	NL	69	0	0	10	50.2	217	54	22	16	2	1	0	0	23	4	24	5	0	3	2	.600	0	2-4	16	4.22	2.84
2005	2 Tms	NL	42	0	0	9	31.0	154	41	25	19	1	4	2	3	20	5	10	2	0	1	1	.500	0	0-2	5	6.48	5.52
2006	Was	NL	6	0	0	1	5.2	35	14	11	9	3	1	0	1	2	0	4	0	0	0	0	-	0	0-1	0	18.45	14.29
05	Atl	NL	31	0	0	7	21.1	99	24	10	7	0	3	2	2	12	3	8	1	0	0	0	-	0	0-2	2	4.78	2.95
05	Tex	AL	11	0	0	2	9.2	55	17	15	12	1	1	0	1	8	2	2	1	0	1	1	.500	0	0-0	3	10.60	11.17
5 ML YEARS			238	0	0	39	183.1	835	203	100	83	15	11	2	11	105	20	103	11	0	12	8	.600	0	2-13	44	5.39	4.07

Eddie Guardado

Pitches: L **Bats:** R **Pos:** RP-43   **Ht:** 6'0" **Wt:** 205 **Born:** 10/2/1970 **Age:** 36

			HOW MUCH HE PITCHED						WHAT HE GAVE UP												THE RESULTS							
Year	Team	Lg	G	GS	CG	GF	IP	BFP	H	R	ER	HR	SH	SF	HB	TBB	IBB	SO	WP	Bk	W	L	Pct	ShO	Sv-Op	Hld	ERC	ERA
1993	Min	AL	19	16	0	2	94.2	426	123	68	65	13	1	3	1	36	2	46	0	0	3	8	.273	0	0-0	0	6.18	6.18
1994	Min	AL	4	4	0	0	17.0	81	26	16	16	3	1	2	0	4	0	8	0	0	0	2	.000	0	0-0	0	7.01	8.47
1995	Min	AL	51	5	0	10	91.1	410	99	54	52	13	6	5	0	45	2	71	5	1	4	9	.308	0	2-5	5	5.20	5.12
1996	Min	AL	**83**	0	0	17	73.2	313	61	45	43	12	6	4	3	33	4	74	3	0	6	5	.545	0	4-7	18	3.81	5.25
1997	Min	AL	69	0	0	20	46.0	201	45	23	20	7	2	1	2	17	2	54	2	0	0	4	.000	0	1-1	13	4.23	3.91
1998	Min	AL	79	0	0	12	65.2	286	66	34	33	10	3	6	0	28	6	53	2	0	3	1	.750	0	0-4	16	4.42	4.52
1999	Min	AL	63	0	0	13	48.0	197	37	24	24	6	2	1	2	25	4	50	0	0	2	5	.286	0	2-4	15	3.63	4.50
2000	Min	AL	70	0	0	36	61.2	262	55	27	27	14	3	2	1	25	3	52	1	1	7	4	.636	0	9-11	8	4.34	3.94
2001	Min	AL	67	0	0	26	66.2	270	47	27	26	5	5	3	1	23	4	67	4	0	7	1	.875	0	12-14	14	2.13	3.51
2002	Min	AL	68	0	0	62	67.2	270	53	22	22	9	2	2	1	18	2	70	0	0	1	3	.250	0	**45**-51	0	2.66	2.93
2003	Min	AL	66	0	0	60	65.1	260	50	22	21	7	3	2	0	14	2	60	5	0	3	5	.375	0	41-45	0	2.14	2.89
2004	Sea	AL	41	0	0	35	45.1	176	34	14	14	8	0	1	1	14	0	45	0	0	2	2	.500	0	18-25	0	2.69	2.78
2005	Sea	AL	58	0	0	55	56.1	238	52	23	17	7	3	2	0	15	3	48	1	0	2	3	.400	0	36-41	0	3.12	2.72
2006	2 Tms	AL	43	0	0	26	37.0	166	44	19	16	10	3	1	1	13	2	39	0	0	1	3	.250	0	13-18	2	6.26	3.89
06	Sea	AL	28	0	0	15	23.0	108	29	14	14	8	3	0	0	11	1	22	0	0	1	3	.250	0	5-8	2	7.78	5.48
06	Cin	NL	15	0	0	11	14.0	58	15	5	2	2	0	1	1	2	1	17	0	0	0	0	-	0	8-10	0	3.98	1.29
14 ML YEARS			781	25	0	374	836.1	3556	789	418	396	124	40	35	13	310	36	737	23	2	41	55	.427	0	183-226	91	3.97	4.26

Vladimir Guerrero

Bats: R **Throws:** R **Pos:** RF-126; DH-30   **Ht:** 6'3" **Wt:** 235 **Born:** 2/9/1976 **Age:** 31

										BATTING												BASERUNNING				AVERAGES		
Year	Team	Lg	G	AB	H	2B	3B	HR	(Hm	Rd)	TB	R	RBI	RC	TBB	IBB	SO	HBP	SH	SF	SB	CS	SB%	GDP	Avg	OBP	Slg
1996	Mon	NL	9	27	5	0	0	1	(0	1)	8	2	1	1	0	0	3	0	0	0	0	0	-	1	.185	.185	.296
1997	Mon	NL	90	325	98	22	2	11	(5	6)	157	44	40	51	19	2	39	7	0	3	3	4	.43	11	.302	.350	.483
1998	Mon	NL	159	623	202	37	7	38	(19	19)	367	108	109	124	42	13	95	7	0	5	11	9	.55	15	.324	.371	.589
1999	Mon	NL	160	610	193	37	5	42	(23	19)	366	102	131	127	55	14	62	7	0	2	14	7	.67	18	.316	.378	.600
2000	Mon	NL	154	571	197	28	11	44	(25	19)	379	101	123	137	58	**23**	74	8	0	4	9	10	.47	15	.307	.410	.664
2001	Mon	NL	159	599	184	45	4	34	(21	13)	339	107	108	116	60	24	74	8	0	8	37	16	.70	**24**	.307	.377	.566
2002	Mon	NL	161	614	**206**	37	2	39	(20	19)	**364**	106	111	123	84	32	70	6	0	5	40	**20**	.67	20	.336	.417	.593
2003	Mon	NL	112	394	130	20	3	25	(15	10)	231	71	79	83	63	21	53	6	0	4	9	5	.64	18	.330	.426	.586
2004	LAA	AL	156	612	206	39	2	39	(19	20)	**366**	124	126	122	52	14	74	8	0	6	15	3	.83	19	.337	.391	.598
2005	LAA	AL	141	520	165	29	2	32	(19	13)	294	95	108	108	61	**26**	48	8	0	5	13	1	.93	17	.317	.394	.565
2006	LAA	AL	156	607	200	34	1	33	(14	19)	335	92	116	109	50	**25**	68	4	0	4	15	5	.75	16	.329	.382	.552
11 ML YEARS			1457	5502	1786	328	39	338	(180	158)	3206	952	1052	1101	544	194	674	70	0	43	166	80	.67	174	.325	.390	.583

Matt Guerrier

Pitches: R **Bats:** R **Pos:** RP-38; SP-1   **Ht:** 6'3" **Wt:** 194 **Born:** 8/2/1978 **Age:** 28

Year	Team	Lg	HOW MUCH HE PITCHED						WHAT HE GAVE UP												THE RESULTS							
			G	GS	CG	GF	IP	BFP	H	R	ER	HR	SH	SF	HB	TBB	IBB	SO	WP	Bk	W	L	Pct	ShO	Sv-Op	Hld	ERC	ERA
2006	NwBrit*	AA	4	0	0	1	8.2	31	3	1	1	0	0	1	0	3	0	10	0	0	2	0	1.000	0	0--	-	0.76	1.04
2004	Min	AL	9	2	0	5	19.0	84	22	13	12	5	2	0	1	6	0	11	0	0	0	1	.000	0	0-0	0	6.10	5.68
2005	Min	AL	43	0	0	14	71.2	306	71	29	27	6	4	1	3	24	5	46	3	0	0	3	.000	0	0-0	1	3.71	3.39
2006	Min	AL	39	1	0	13	69.2	300	78	29	26	9	3	4	0	21	0	37	6	0	1	0	1.000	0	1-1	2	4.59	3.36
	3 ML YEARS		91	3	0	32	160.1	690	171	71	65	20	9	5	4	51	5	94	9	0	1	4	.200	0	1-1	3	4.36	3.65

Aaron Guiel

Bats: L **Throws:** R **Pos:** RF-30; 1B-15; PH-13; LF-7; CF-5; PR-4; DH-3   **Ht:** 5'10" **Wt:** 200 **Born:** 10/5/1972 **Age:** 34

Year	Team	Lg	BATTING																			BASERUNNING				AVERAGES		
			G	AB	H	2B	3B	HR	(Hm	Rd)	TB	R	RBI	RC	TBB	IBB	SO	HBP	SH	SF	SB	CS	SB%	GDP	Avg	OBP	Slg
2006	Omha*	AAA	52	177	44	14	1	11	(-	-)	93	32	32	38	35	0	45	8	0	4	0	0	-	5	.249	.388	.525
2006	Clmbs*	AAA	16	50	13	2	1	2	(-	-)	23	10	8	9	8	0	10	3	0	1	0	0	-	0	.260	.387	.460
2002	KC	AL	70	240	56	13	0	4	(4	0)	81	30	38	33	19	1	61	4	2	4	1	5	.17	3	.233	.296	.338
2003	KC	AL	99	354	98	30	0	15	(4	11)	173	63	52	59	27	0	63	13	2	5	3	5	.38	3	.277	.346	.489
2004	KC	AL	42	135	21	4	0	5	(2	3)	40	15	13	8	17	0	42	3	1	1	1	1	.50	3	.156	.263	.296
2005	KC	AL	33	109	32	5	0	4	(3	1)	49	18	7	14	6	1	21	5	0	1	1	0	1.00	3	.294	.355	.450
2006	2 Tms	AL	63	132	32	6	0	7	(4	3)	59	25	18	16	14	0	31	5	0	0	2	1	.67	3	.242	.338	.447
06	KC	AL	19	50	11	3	0	3	(3	0)	23	9	7	7	7	0	11	2	0	0	0	0	-	1	.220	.339	.460
06	NYY	AL	44	82	21	3	0	4	(1	3)	36	16	11	9	7	0	20	3	0	0	2	1	.67	2	.256	.337	.439
	5 ML YEARS		307	970	239	58	0	35	(17	18)	402	151	128	130	83	2	218	30	5	11	8	12	.40	15	.246	.322	.414

Carlos Guillen

Bats: B **Throws:** R **Pos:** SS-145; 1B-8; DH-4; PH-2   **Ht:** 6'1" **Wt:** 215 **Born:** 9/30/1975 **Age:** 31

Year	Team	Lg	BATTING																			BASERUNNING				AVERAGES		
			G	AB	H	2B	3B	HR	(Hm	Rd)	TB	R	RBI	RC	TBB	IBB	SO	HBP	SH	SF	SB	CS	SB%	GDP	Avg	OBP	Slg
1998	Sea	AL	10	39	13	1	1	0	(0	0)	16	9	5	7	3	0	9	0	0	0	2	0	1.00	0	.333	.381	.410
1999	Sea	AL	5	19	3	0	0	1	(1	0)	6	2	3	1	1	0	6	0	1	0	0	0	-	1	.158	.200	.316
2000	Sea	AL	90	288	74	15	2	7	(3	4)	114	45	42	36	28	0	53	2	7	3	1	3	.25	6	.257	.324	.396
2001	Sea	AL	140	456	118	21	4	5	(2	3)	162	72	53	56	53	0	89	1	7	6	4	1	.80	9	.259	.333	.355
2002	Sea	AL	134	475	124	24	6	9	(4	5)	187	73	56	46	46	4	91	1	3	3	4	5	.44	8	.261	.326	.394
2003	Sea	AL	109	388	107	19	3	7	(4	3)	153	63	52	53	52	2	64	1	5	5	4	4	.50	12	.276	.359	.394
2004	Det	AL	136	522	166	37	10	20	(7	13)	283	97	97	98	52	3	87	2	3	4	12	5	.71	12	.318	.379	.542
2005	Det	AL	87	334	107	15	4	5	(3	2)	145	48	23	39	24	3	45	2	0	1	2	3	.40	9	.320	.368	.434
2006	Det	AL	153	543	174	41	5	19	(10	9)	282	100	85	106	71	10	87	4	0	4	20	9	.69	16	.320	.400	.519
	9 ML YEARS		864	3064	886	173	35	73	(34	39)	1348	509	416	454	330	22	531	13	26	26	49	30	.62	73	.289	.358	.440

Jose Guillen

Bats: R **Throws:** R **Pos:** RF-68; PH-3   **Ht:** 5'11" **Wt:** 195 **Born:** 5/17/1976 **Age:** 31

Year	Team	Lg	BATTING																			BASERUNNING				AVERAGES		
			G	AB	H	2B	3B	HR	(Hm	Rd)	TB	R	RBI	RC	TBB	IBB	SO	HBP	SH	SF	SB	CS	SB%	GDP	Avg	OBP	Slg
2006	Ptomc*	A+	3	6	3	0	0	2	(-	-)	9	2	3	3	1	0	0	0	0	0	0	0	-	1	.500	.571	1.500
1997	Pit	NL	143	498	133	20	5	14	(5	9)	205	58	70	56	17	0	88	8	0	3	1	2	.33	16	.267	.300	.412
1998	Pit	NL	153	573	153	38	2	14	(10	4)	237	60	84	68	21	0	100	6	1	4	3	5	.38	7	.267	.298	.414
1999	2 Tms		87	288	73	16	0	3	(1	2)	98	42	31	28	20	2	57	7	1	2	1	0	1.00	16	.253	.315	.340
2000	TB	AL	105	316	80	16	5	10	(5	5)	136	40	41	43	18	1	65	13	2	0	3	1	.75	6	.253	.320	.430
2001	TB	AL	41	135	37	5	0	3	(0	3)	51	14	11	15	6	2	26	3	0	1	2	3	.40	2	.274	.317	.378
2002	2 Tms	NL	85	240	57	7	0	8	(3	5)	88	25	31	16	14	1	43	3	1	1	4	5	.44	13	.238	.287	.367
2003	2 Tms		136	485	151	28	2	31	(14	17)	276	77	86	86	24	2	95	14	8	3	1	3	.25	16	.311	.359	.569
2004	LAA	AL	148	565	166	28	3	27	(13	14)	281	88	104	98	37	5	92	15	0	3	5	4	.56	14	.294	.352	.497
2005	Was	NL	148	551	156	32	2	24	(3	21)	264	81	76	72	31	6	102	19	1	9	1	1	.50	14	.283	.338	.479
2006	Was	NL	69	241	52	15	1	9	(4	5)	96	28	40	23	15	4	48	7	0	5	1	0	1.00	8	.216	.276	.398
99	Pit	NL	40	120	32	6	0	1	(0	1)	41	18	18	12	10	1	21	0	1	1	1	0	1.00	7	.267	.321	.342
99	TB	AL	47	168	41	10	0	2	(1	1)	57	24	13	16	10	1	36	7	0	1	0	0	-	9	.244	.312	.339
02	Ari	NL	54	131	30	4	0	4	(3	1)	46	13	15	7	7	1	25	2	0	1	3	4	.43	7	.229	.277	.351
02	Cin	NL	31	109	27	3	0	4	(2	2)	42	12	16	9	7	0	18	1	1	0	1	1	.50	6	.248	.299	.385
03	Cin	NL	91	315	106	21	1	23	(10	13)	198	52	63	64	17	1	63	9	6	2	1	3	.25	8	.337	.385	.629
03	Oak	AL	45	170	45	7	1	8	(4	4)	78	25	23	22	7	1	32	5	2	1	0	0	-	8	.265	.311	.459
	10 ML YEARS		1115	3892	1058	205	20	143	(60	83)	1732	513	574	505	203	23	716	95	14	31	22	24	.48	112	.272	.321	.445

Jeremy Guthrie

Pitches: R **Bats:** R **Pos:** RP-8; SP-1   **Ht:** 6'1" **Wt:** 200 **Born:** 4/8/1979 **Age:** 28

Year	Team	Lg	HOW MUCH HE PITCHED						WHAT HE GAVE UP												THE RESULTS							
			G	GS	CG	GF	IP	BFP	H	R	ER	HR	SH	SF	HB	TBB	IBB	SO	WP	Bk	W	L	Pct	ShO	Sv-Op	Hld	ERC	ERA
2006	Buffalo*	AAA	21	20	2	0	123.1	516	104	50	43	6	4	1	8	48	0	88	6	0	9	5	.643	0	0--	-	3.11	3.14
2004	Cle	AL	6	0	0	2	11.2	49	9	6	6	1	0	0	1	6	0	7	1	0	0	0	-	0	0-0	0	3.58	4.63
2005	Cle	AL	1	0	0	0	6.0	29	9	4	4	2	1	1	0	2	0	3	0	0	0	0	-	0	0-0	0	8.58	6.00
2006	Cle	AL	9	1	0	1	19.1	93	24	15	15	2	0	0	2	15	1	14	3	0	0	0	-	0	0-0	0	7.78	6.98
	3 ML YEARS		16	1	0	4	37.0	171	42	25	25	5	1	3		23	1	24	4	0	0	0	-	0	0-0	0	6.51	6.08

Franklin Gutierrez

Bats: R Throws: R Pos: RF-28; LF-10; CF-7; PH-4; PR-1   Ht: 6'2" Wt: 180 Born: 2/21/1983 Age: 24

								BATTING											BASERUNNING				AVERAGES		
Year	Team	Lg	G	AB	H	2B	3B	HR	(Hm | Rd)	TB	R	RBI	RC	TBB	IBB	SO	HBP	SH	SF	SB	CS	SB%	GDP	Avg	OBP	Slg
2001	Ddgrs	R	56	234	63	16	0	4	(- | -)	91	38	30	31	16	0	39	4	2	2	9	3	.75	1	.269	.324	.389
2002	SoGA	A	92	361	102	18	4	12	(- | -)	164	61	45	59	31	1	88	6	4	6	13	4	.76	5	.283	.344	.454
2002	LsVgs	AAA	2	10	3	2	0	0	(- | -)	5	2	2	1	1	0	4	0	0	0	0	0	-	1	.300	.364	.500
2003	VeroB	A+	110	425	120	28	5	20	(- | -)	218	65	68	77	39	4	111	3	4	3	17	5	.77	9	.282	.345	.513
2003	Jaxnvl	AA	18	67	21	3	2	4	(- | -)	40	12	12	14	7	0	20	1	0	0	3	3	.50	1	.313	.387	.597
2004	Akron	AA	70	262	79	24	2	5	(- | -)	122	38	35	47	23	3	77	9	0	4	6	3	.67	4	.302	.372	.466
2004	Buffalo	AAA	7	27	4	1	0	1	(- | -)	8	4	3	1	1	0	11	0	0	0	0	0	-	0	.148	.179	.296
2005	Akron	AA	95	383	100	25	2	11	(- | -)	162	70	42	56	30	1	77	7	1	5	14	4	.78	7	.261	.322	.423
2005	Buffalo	AAA	19	67	17	6	2	0	(- | -)	27	10	7	8	6	1	13	1	0	1	2	2	.50	1	.254	.320	.403
2006	Buffalo	AAA	90	349	97	27	0	9	(- | -)	151	63	38	59	49	4	84	5	8	2	13	8	.62	2	.278	.373	.433
2005	Cle	AL	7	1	0	0	0	0	(0 | 0)	0	2	0	0	1	0	0	0	0	0	0	0	-	0	.000	.500	.000
2006	Cle	AL	43	136	37	9	0	1	(1 | 0)	49	21	8	12	3	0	28	0	2	0	0	0	-	4	.272	.288	.360
	2 ML YEARS		50	137	37	9	0	1	(1 | 0)	49	23	8	12	4	0	28	0	2	0	0	0	-	4	.270	.291	.358

Angel Guzman

Pitches: R Bats: R Pos: SP-10; RP-5   Ht: 6'3" Wt: 195 Born: 12/14/1981 Age: 25

			HOW MUCH HE PITCHED						WHAT HE GAVE UP											THE RESULTS						
Year	Team	Lg	G	GS	CG	GF	IP	BFP	H	R	ER	HR	SH	SF	HB	TBB	IBB	SO	WP	Bk	W	L	Pct	ShO	Sv-Op	Hld	ERC	ERA
2001	Boise	A	14	14	0	0	76.2	318	68	27	19	2	2	5	0	19	0	63	2	1	9	1	.900	0	0--	-	2.38	2.23
2002	Lansng	A	9	9	1	0	62.0	0	42	18	13	3	0	0	1	16	0	49	5	1	5	2	.714	0	0--	-	-	1.89
2002	Dytona	A	16	15	1	0	94.0	412	99	34	25	2	2	4	4	33	1	74	9	2	6	2	.750	0	0--	-	3.73	2.39
2003	WTenn	AA	15	15	0	0	89.2	366	83	30	28	8	3	2	2	26	0	87	3	1	3	3	.500	0	0--	-	3.33	2.81
2004	Dytona	A	7	7	0	0	30.0	116	27	15	14	2	0	0	1	0	0	40	0	0	3	1	.750	0	0--	-	2.02	4.20
2004	WTenn	AA	4	4	0	0	17.2	74	20	11	11	2	3	0	0	4	0	13	0	0	0	3	.000	0	0--	-	4.31	5.60
2005	Cubs	R	4	4	0	0	12.0	47	10	3	2	0	0	1	0	1	0	17	0	0	0	0	-	0	0--	-	1.79	1.50
2005	Peoria	A	2	2	0	0	6.1	29	10	5	3	1	0	1	0	0	0	7	0	0	0	1	.000	0	0--	-	7.08	4.26
2006	Iowa	AAA	15	15	0	0	75.2	320	72	37	34	5	4	4	2	24	0	77	3	1	4	4	.500	0	0--	-	3.34	4.04
2006	ChC	NL	15	10	0	1	56.0	272	68	48	46	9	5	3	6	37	1	60	8	1	0	6	.000	0	0-0	0	7.41	7.39

Cristian Guzman

Bats: B Throws: R Pos: SS   Ht: 6'0" Wt: 205 Born: 3/21/1978 Age: 29

								BATTING											BASERUNNING				AVERAGES		
Year	Team	Lg	G	AB	H	2B	3B	HR	(Hm	Rd)	TB	R	RBI	RC	TBB	IBB	SO	HBP	SH	SF	SB	CS	SB%	GDP	Avg	OBP	Slg
1999	Min	AL	131	420	95	12	3	1	(1	0)	116	47	26	29	22	0	90	3	7	4	9	7	.56	5	.226	.267	.276
2000	Min	AL	156	631	156	25	20	8	(3	5)	245	89	54	76	46	1	101	2	7	4	28	10	.74	5	.247	.299	.388
2001	Min	AL	118	493	149	28	14	10	(7	3)	235	80	51	79	21	0	78	5	8	0	25	8	.76	6	.302	.337	.477
2002	Min	AL	148	623	170	31	6	9	(6	3)	240	80	59	63	17	2	79	2	8	6	12	13	.48	12	.273	.292	.385
2003	Min	AL	143	534	143	15	14	3	(1	2)	195	78	53	62	30	0	79	5	12	4	18	9	.67	4	.268	.311	.365
2004	Min	AL	145	576	158	31	4	8	(5	3)	221	84	46	66	30	4	64	1	13	4	10	5	.67	15	.274	.309	.384
2005	Was	NL	142	456	100	19	6	4	(0	4)	143	39	31	26	25	6	76	1	8	2	7	4	.64	12	.219	.260	.314
	7 ML YEARS		983	3733	971	161	67	43	(23	20)	1395	497	320	401	191	13	567	19	63	24	109	56	.66	59	.260	.298	.374

Freddy Guzman

Bats: B Throws: R Pos: PR-4; CF-2; PH-2; LF-1; RF-1   Ht: 5'10" Wt: 165 Born: 1/20/1981 Age: 26

								BATTING											BASERUNNING				AVERAGES		
Year	Team	Lg	G	AB	H	2B	3B	HR	(Hm	Rd)	TB	R	RBI	RC	TBB	IBB	SO	HBP	SH	SF	SB	CS	SB%	GDP	Avg	OBP	Slg
2001	Idaho	R+	12	46	16	4	1	0	(-	-)	22	11	5	9	2	0	10	1	1	0	5	0	1.00	0	.348	.388	.478
2002	Lk Els	A+	21	81	21	3	0	1	(-	-)	27	13	6	10	8	0	12	0	0	0	14	4	.78	0	.259	.326	.333
2002	FtWyn	A	47	190	53	7	5	0	(-	-)	70	35	18	29	18	0	37	0	2	0	39	7	.85	0	.279	.341	.368
2002	Eugene	A-	21	80	18	2	1	0	(-	-)	22	14	8	9	7	0	15	2	1	3	16	1	.94	0	.225	.293	.275
2003	Lk Els	A+	70	281	80	12	3	2	(-	-)	104	64	22	47	40	1	60	2	1	2	49	10	.83	1	.285	.375	.370
2003	Mobile	AA	46	177	48	5	2	1	(-	-)	60	30	11	28	26	2	34	1	1	0	38	7	.84	0	.271	.368	.339
2003	Portlnd	AAA	2	10	3	0	0	0	(-	-)	3	1	0	1	0	0	1	0	0	0	3	0	1.00	0	.300	.300	.300
2004	Mobile	AA	35	138	39	5	2	1	(-	-)	51	21	7	20	16	1	28	1	1	1	17	5	.77	2	.283	.359	.370
2004	Portlnd	AAA	66	264	77	12	4	1	(-	-)	100	48	19	45	30	1	46	1	4	1	48	5	.91	1	.292	.365	.379
2006	Portlnd	AAA	30	124	34	7	2	2	(-	-)	51	15	14	19	14	0	19	0	1	0	11	3	.79	3	.274	.348	.411
2006	Okla	AAA	69	252	71	9	2	1	(-	-)	87	45	14	39	36	1	36	2	2	1	31	9	.78	4	.282	.375	.345
2004	SD	NL	20	76	16	3	0	0	(0	0)	19	8	5	4	3	0	13	1	0	0	5	2	.71	0	.211	.250	.250
2006	Tex	AL	9	7	2	0	0	0	(0	0)	2	1	0	1	1	0	1	1	0	0	0	0	-	0	.286	.444	.286
	2 ML YEARS		29	83	18	3	0	0	(0	0)	21	9	5	5	4	0	14	2	0	0	5	2	.71	0	.217	.270	.253

Joel Guzman

Bats: R Throws: R Pos: 3B-6; 1B-1; LF-1; PH-1   Ht: 6'6" Wt: 250 Born: 11/24/1984 Age: 22

								BATTING											BASERUNNING				AVERAGES		
Year	Team	Lg	G	AB	H	2B	3B	HR	(Hm	Rd)	TB	R	RBI	RC	TBB	IBB	SO	HBP	SH	SF	SB	CS	SB%	GDP	Avg	OBP	Slg
2002	Ddgrs	R	10	33	7	2	0	0	(-	-)	9	4	2	3	5	0	8	0	0	0	1	0	1.00	0	.212	.316	.273
2002	Gr Falls	R	43	151	38	8	2	3	(-	-)	59	19	27	20	18	0	54	0	2	0	5	3	.63	4	.252	.331	.391
2003	SoGA	A	58	217	51	13	0	8	(-	-)	88	33	29	22	9	0	62	0	1	2	4	4	.50	4	.235	.263	.406
2003	VeroB	A+	62	240	59	13	1	5	(-	-)	89	30	24	23	11	0	60	0	1	0	0	4	.00	7	.246	.279	.371
2004	VeroB	A+	87	329	101	22	8	14	(-	-)	181	52	51	62	21	4	78	2	2	3	8	5	.62	8	.307	.349	.550
2004	Jaxnvl	AA	46	182	51	11	3	9	(-	-)	95	25	35	31	13	0	44	1	0	4	1	2	.33	4	.280	.325	.522
2005	Jaxnvl	AA	122	442	127	31	2	16	(-	-)	210	63	75	76	42	3	128	5	0	7	7	3	.70	10	.287	.351	.475

Year	Team	Lg	G	AB	H	2B	3B	HR	(Hm	Rd)	TB	R	RBI	RC	TBB	IBB	SO	HBP	SH	SF	SB	CS	SB%	GDP	Avg	OBP	Slg
2006	LsVgs	AAA	85	317	94	16	2	11	(-	-)	147	44	55	53	26	1	72	4	1	4	9	5	.64	11	.297	.353	.464
2006	Drham	AAA	25	88	17	5	0	4	(-	-)	34	7	9	7	4	0	23	0	0	0	0	0	-	5	.193	.228	.386
2006	LAD	NL	8	19	4	0	0	0	(0	0)	4	2	3	3	3	0	2	1	0	0	0	0	-	3	.211	.348	.211

Tony Gwynn

Bats: L **Throws:** R **Pos:** CF-19; PH-14; PR-2   **Ht:** 6'0" **Wt:** 185 **Born:** 10/4/1982 **Age:** 24

Year	Team	Lg	G	AB	H	2B	3B	HR	(Hm	Rd)	TB	R	RBI	RC	TBB	IBB	SO	HBP	SH	SF	SB	CS	SB%	GDP	Avg	OBP	Slg
2003	Beloit	A	61	236	66	8	0	1	(-	-)	77	35	33	34	32	0	31	2	4	5	14	2	.88	3	.280	.364	.326
2004	Hntsvl	AA	138	534	130	20	5	2	(-	-)	166	74	37	57	53	0	95	6	4	1	34	16	.68	4	.243	.318	.311
2005	Hntsvl	AA	133	509	138	21	5	1	(-	-)	172	83	41	73	76	1	75	5	9	2	34	15	.69	11	.271	.370	.338
2006	Nashv	AAA	112	447	134	21	5	4	(-	-)	177	73	42	68	42	1	84	2	0	3	30	11	.73	7	.300	.360	.396
2006	Mil	NL	32	77	20	2	1	0	(0	0)	24	5	4	5	2	0	15	0	0	1	3	1	.75	2	.260	.275	.312

Charlie Haeger

Pitches: R **Bats:** R **Pos:** RP-6; SP-1   **Ht:** 6'1" **Wt:** 200 **Born:** 9/19/1983 **Age:** 23

	HOW MUCH HE PITCHED						WHAT HE GAVE UP												THE RESULTS							
Year Team Lg	G	GS	CG	GF	IP	BFP	H	R	ER	HR	SH	SF	HB	TBB	IBB	SO	WP	Bk	W	L	Pct	ShO	Sv-Op	Hld	ERC	ERA
2001 WhSox R	13	4	0	1	31.0	153	44	29	22	2	1	3	1	17	0	17	4	1	0	3	.000	0	0--	-	6.98	6.39
2002 WhSox R	25	0	0	14	41.0	178	46	25	19	2	2	1	6	13	2	24	1	0	1	4	.200	0	6--	-	4.71	4.17
2004 Bristol R+	10	10	0	0	57.1	271	70	41	33	6	3	5	10	22	1	23	1	0	1	6	.143	0	0--	-	5.95	5.18
2004 Knapol A	5	5	0	0	31.1	137	31	17	7	0	3	4	3	12	0	21	1	0	1	3	.250	0	0--	-	3.59	2.01
2005 WinSa A+	14	13	0	1	81.2	354	82	33	29	3	3	2	5	40	0	64	2	0	8	2	.800	0	0--	-	4.35	3.20
2005 Brham AA	13	13	3	0	85.2	374	84	43	36	1	4	1	5	45	1	48	4	0	6	3	.667	2	0--	-	4.10	3.78
2006 Charltt AAA	26	25	2	1	170.0	716	143	71	58	9	3	3	12	78	3	130	15	0	14	6	.700	0	0--	-	3.41	3.07
2006 CWS AL	7	1	0	4	18.1	79	12	10	7	0	0	0	0	13	0	19	0	0	1	1	.500	0	1-1	0	2.65	3.44

Travis Hafner

Bats: L **Throws:** R **Pos:** DH-122; 1B-4; PH-3   **Ht:** 6'3" **Wt:** 240 **Born:** 6/3/1977 **Age:** 30

Year	Team	Lg	G	AB	H	2B	3B	HR	(Hm	Rd)	TB	R	RBI	RC	TBB	IBB	SO	HBP	SH	SF	SB	CS	SB%	GDP	Avg	OBP	Slg
2002	Tex	AL	23	62	15	4	1	1	(0	1)	24	6	6	7	8	1	15	0	0	0	0	1	.00	0	.242	.329	.387
2003	Cle	AL	91	291	74	19	3	14	(7	7)	141	35	40	42	22	2	81	10	0	1	2	1	.67	7	.254	.327	.485
2004	Cle	AL	140	482	150	41	3	28	(7	21)	281	96	109	103	68	7	111	**17**	0	6	3	2	.60	11	.311	.410	.583
2005	Cle	AL	137	486	148	42	0	33	(14	19)	299	94	108	115	79	7	123	9	0	4	0	0	-	9	.305	.408	.595
2006	Cle	AL	129	454	140	31	1	42	(21	21)	299	100	117	118	100	16	111	7	0	2	0	0	-	10	.308	**.439**	**.659**
	5 ML YEARS		520	1775	527	137	8	118	(49	69)	1034	331	380	385	277	33	441	43	0	13	5	4	.56	37	.297	.402	.583

Jerry Hairston

Bats: R **Throws:** R **Pos:** LF-38; 2B-25; PR-15; CF-12; RF-12; PH-11; SS-3; DH-3; 1B-1; 3B-1   **Ht:** 5'10" **Wt:** 185 **Born:** 5/29/1976 **Age:** 31

Year	Team	Lg	G	AB	H	2B	3B	HR	(Hm	Rd)	TB	R	RBI	RC	TBB	IBB	SO	HBP	SH	SF	SB	CS	SB%	GDP	Avg	OBP	Slg
1998	Bal	AL	6	7	0	0	0	0	(0	0)	0	2	0	0	0	0	1	0	0	0	0	0	-	0	.000	.000	.000
1999	Bal	AL	50	175	47	12	1	4	(1	3)	73	26	17	24	11	0	24	3	4	0	9	4	.69	2	.269	.323	.417
2000	Bal	AL	49	180	46	5	0	5	(2	3)	66	27	19	22	21	0	22	6	5	0	8	5	.62	8	.256	.353	.367
2001	Bal	AL	159	532	124	25	5	8	(5	3)	183	63	47	57	44	0	73	13	9	4	29	11	.73	12	.233	.305	.344
2002	Bal	AL	122	426	114	25	3	5	(2	3)	160	55	32	55	34	0	55	7	8	4	21	6	.78	5	.268	.329	.376
2003	Bal	AL	58	218	59	12	2	2	(1	1)	81	25	21	32	23	0	25	6	10	2	14	5	.74	8	.271	.353	.372
2004	Bal	AL	86	287	87	19	1	2	(0	2)	114	43	24	45	29	1	29	8	6	4	13	8	.62	3	.303	.378	.397
2005	ChC	NL	114	380	99	25	2	4	(3	1)	140	51	30	46	31	0	46	12	7	0	8	9	.47	5	.261	.336	.368
2006	2 Tms		101	170	35	6	1	0	(0	0)	43	25	10	9	13	2	34	2	7	0	5	2	.71	5	.206	.270	.253
06	ChC	NL	38	82	17	3	0	0	(0	0)	20	8	4	5	4	2	14	1	5	0	3	0	1.00	1	.207	.253	.244
06	Tex	AL	63	88	18	3	1	0	(0	0)	23	17	6	4	9	0	20	1	2	0	2	2	.50	4	.205	.286	.261
	9 ML YEARS		745	2375	611	129	15	30	(14	16)	860	317	200	290	206	3	309	57	56	14	107	50	.68	48	.257	.330	.362

Scott Hairston

Bats: R **Throws:** R **Pos:** LF-5; PH-5   **Ht:** 6'0" **Wt:** 200 **Born:** 5/25/1980 **Age:** 27

Year	Team	Lg	G	AB	H	2B	3B	HR	(Hm	Rd)	TB	R	RBI	RC	TBB	IBB	SO	HBP	SH	SF	SB	CS	SB%	GDP	Avg	OBP	Slg
2006	Tucsn*	AAA	98	381	123	22	1	26	(-	-)	225	83	81	90	52	2	78	4	0	3	3	0	1.00	4	.323	.407	.591
2004	Ari	NL	101	339	84	15	6	13	(6	7)	150	39	29	32	21	0	88	1	2	1	3	3	.50	4	.248	.293	.442
2005	Ari	NL	15	20	2	1	0	0	(0	0)	3	0	0	0	0	0	6	0	0	0	0	0	-	1	.100	.100	.150
2006	Ari	NL	9	15	6	2	0	0	(0	0)	8	2	2	2	1	0	5	0	0	0	0	0	-	1	.400	.438	.533
	3 ML YEARS		125	374	92	18	6	13	(6	7)	161	41	31	34	22	0	99	1	2	1	3	3	.50	6	.246	.289	.430

John Halama

Pitches: L **Bats:** L **Pos:** RP-16; SP-1   **Ht:** 6'5" **Wt:** 215 **Born:** 2/22/1972 **Age:** 35

	HOW MUCH HE PITCHED						WHAT HE GAVE UP												THE RESULTS							
Year Team Lg	G	GS	CG	GF	IP	BFP	H	R	ER	HR	SH	SF	HB	TBB	IBB	SO	WP	Bk	W	L	Pct	ShO	Sv-Op	Hld	ERC	ERA
1998 Hou NL	6	6	0	0	32.1	147	37	21	21	0	3	4	2	13	0	21	2	1	1	1	.500	0	0-0	0	4.34	5.85
1999 Sea AL	38	24	1	7	179.0	763	193	88	84	20	5	9	7	56	3	105	4	0	11	10	.524	1	0-0	1	4.47	4.22
2000 Sea AL	30	30	1	0	166.2	736	206	108	94	19	4	6	2	56	0	87	4	1	14	9	.609	1	0-0	0	5.42	5.08
2001 Sea AL	31	17	0	6	110.1	485	132	69	58	14	3	4	6	26	0	50	2	0	10	7	.588	0	0-0	0	5.21	4.73

Year	Team	Lg	G	GS	CG	GF	IP	BFP	H	R	ER	HR	SH	SF	HB	TBB	IBB	SO	WP	Bk	W	L	Pct	ShO	Sv-Op	Hld	ERC	ERA
2002	Sea	AL	31	10	0	12	101.0	438	112	45	40	9	3	2	1	33	5	70	2	1	6	5	.545	0	0-0	2	4.29	3.56
2003	Oak	AL	35	13	0	4	108.2	484	117	68	51	18	7	3	2	36	2	51	3	3	3	5	.375	0	0-0	3	4.61	4.22
2004	TB	AL	34	14	0	7	118.2	513	134	68	62	17	1	3	10	27	3	59	1	1	7	6	.538	0	0-0	0	4.76	4.70
2005	2 Tms		40	4	0	15	65.0	298	79	44	41	6	2	2	7	17	3	37	2	0	1	4	.200	0	0-0	4	4.93	5.68
2006	Bal	AL	17	1	0	7	29.1	132	38	20	20	6	1	1	0	13	2	12	0	0	3	1	.750	0	0-1	0	6.94	6.14
05	Bos	AL	30	1	0	13	43.2	205	56	33	30	5	1	1	7	9	3	26	2	0	1	1	.500	0	0-0	0	5.38	6.18
05	Was	NL	10	3	0	2	21.1	93	23	11	11	1	1	1	0	8	0	11	0	0	0	3	.000	0	0-0	4	4.03	4.64
9 ML YEARS			262	119	2	58	911.0	3996	1048	531	471	113	29	34	37	277	18	492	20	7	56	48	.538	2	0-1	5	4.87	4.65

Bill Hall

Bats: R Throws: R Pos: SS-127; 3B-11; CF-7; PH-5; 2B-4   Ht: 6'0" Wt: 210 Born: 12/28/1979 Age: 27

Year	Team	Lg	G	AB	H	2B	3B	HR	(Hm	Rd)	TB	R	RBI	RC	TBB	IBB	SO	HBP	SH	SF	SB	CS	SB%	GDP	Avg	OBP	Slg
2002	Mil	NL	19	36	7	1	1	1	(0	1)	13	3	5	3	3	0	13	0	0	1	0	1	.00	1	.194	.256	.361
2003	Mil	NL	52	142	37	9	2	5	(2	3)	65	23	20	18	7	0	28	1	4	1	1	2	.33	5	.261	.298	.458
2004	Mil	NL	126	390	93	20	3	9	(5	4)	146	43	53	41	20	1	119	1	2	2	12	6	.67	4	.238	.276	.374
2005	Mil	NL	146	501	146	39	6	17	(12	5)	248	69	62	73	39	2	103	1	2	3	18	6	.75	11	.291	.342	.495
2006	Mil	NL	148	537	145	39	4	35	(18	17)	297	101	85	87	63	6	162	1	3	4	8	9	.47	12	.270	.345	.553
5 ML YEARS			491	1606	428	108	16	67	(37	30)	769	239	225	222	132	9	425	4	11	10	39	24	.62	33	.267	.322	.479

Toby Hall

Bats: R Throws: R Pos: C-82; PH-9; DH-2; 3B-1   Ht: 6'3" Wt: 240 Born: 10/21/1975 Age: 31

Year	Team	Lg	G	AB	H	2B	3B	HR	(Hm	Rd)	TB	R	RBI	RC	TBB	IBB	SO	HBP	SH	SF	SB	CS	SB%	GDP	Avg	OBP	Slg
2000	TB	AL	4	12	2	0	0	1	(0	1)	5	1	1	1	1	0	0	0	0	0	0	0	-	0	.167	.231	.417
2001	TB	AL	49	188	56	16	0	4	(1	3)	84	28	30	25	4	0	16	3	0	1	2	2	.50	5	.298	.321	.447
2002	TB	AL	85	330	85	19	1	6	(2	4)	124	37	42	39	17	3	27	1	2	3	0	1	.00	14	.258	.293	.376
2003	TB	AL	130	463	117	23	0	12	(4	8)	176	50	47	45	23	4	40	7	0	5	0	1	.00	14	.253	.295	.380
2004	TB	AL	119	404	103	21	0	8	(6	2)	148	35	60	42	24	1	41	5	1	7	0	2	.00	20	.255	.300	.366
2005	TB	AL	135	432	124	20	0	5	(1	4)	159	28	48	46	16	1	39	5	3	7	0	2	.00	15	.287	.315	.368
2006	2 Tms		85	278	72	17	0	8	(6	2)	113	17	31	25	10	4	22	2	0	4	0	2	.00	10	.259	.286	.406
06	TB	AL	64	221	51	13	0	8	(6	2)	88	15	23	18	8	2	17	2	0	3	0	2	.00	8	.231	.261	.398
06	LAD	NL	21	57	21	4	0	0	(0	0)	25	2	8	7	2	2	5	0	0	1	0	0	-	2	.368	.383	.439
7 ML YEARS			607	2107	559	116	1	44	(20	24)	809	196	259	223	95	13	185	23	6	27	2	8	.20	78	.265	.301	.384

Roy Halladay

Pitches: R Bats: R Pos: SP-32   Ht: 6'6" Wt: 225 Born: 5/14/1977 Age: 30

Year	Team	Lg	G	GS	CG	GF	IP	BFP	H	R	ER	HR	SH	SF	HB	TBB	IBB	SO	WP	Bk	W	L	Pct	ShO	Sv-Op	Hld	ERC	ERA
1998	Tor	AL	2	2	1	0	14.0	53	9	4	3	2	0	0	0	2	0	13	0	0	1	0	1.000	0	0-0	0	1.61	1.93
1999	Tor	AL	36	18	1	2	149.1	668	156	76	65	19	3	4	4	79	1	82	6	0	8	7	.533	1	1-1	2	5.19	3.92
2000	Tor	AL	19	13	0	4	67.2	349	107	87	80	14	2	3	2	42	0	44	6	1	4	7	.364	0	0-0	0	9.70	10.64
2001	Tor	AL	17	16	1	0	105.1	432	97	41	37	3	3	1	1	25	0	96	4	1	5	3	.625	1	0-0	0	2.61	3.16
2002	Tor	AL	34	34	2	0	239.1	993	223	93	78	10	9	2	7	62	6	168	4	1	19	7	.731	1	0-0	0	2.85	2.93
2003	Tor	AL	36	36	9	0	266.0	1071	253	111	96	26	3	2	9	32	1	204	6	1	22	7	.759	2	0-0	0	2.86	3.25
2004	Tor	AL	21	21	0	0	133.0	561	140	66	62	13	4	3	1	39	1	95	2	2	8	8	.500	1	0-0	0	4.00	4.20
2005	Tor	AL	19	19	5	0	141.2	553	118	39	38	11	2	1	7	18	2	108	2	1	12	4	.750	2	0-0	0	2.26	2.41
2006	Tor	AL	32	32	4	0	220.0	876	208	82	78	19	3	5	5	34	5	132	3	0	16	5	.762	0	0-0	0	2.87	3.19
9 ML YEARS			216	191	24	6	1336.1	5556	1311	599	537	117	29	21	36	333	16	942	33	7	95	48	.664	8	1-1	2	3.41	3.62

Brad Halsey

Pitches: L Bats: L Pos: RP-45; SP-7   Ht: 6'1" Wt: 185 Born: 2/14/1981 Age: 26

Year	Team	Lg	G	GS	CG	GF	IP	BFP	H	R	ER	HR	SH	SF	HB	TBB	IBB	SO	WP	Bk	W	L	Pct	ShO	Sv-Op	Hld	ERC	ERA
2006	Scrmto*	AAA	2	2	0	0	9.1	33	4	1	1	0	0	0	1	1	0	3	0	0	1	0	1.000	0	0--	-	0.73	0.96
2004	NYY	AL	8	7	0	0	32.0	153	41	26	23	4	1	2	2	14	0	25	0	0	1	3	.250	0	0-0	0	6.20	6.47
2005	Ari	NL	28	26	0	1	160.0	700	191	101	82	20	11	5	9	39	3	82	2	1	8	12	.400	0	0-0	0	4.96	4.61
2006	Oak	AL	52	7	0	7	94.1	431	108	53	49	11	3	2	5	46	7	53	7	0	5	4	.556	0	0-0	8	5.50	4.67
3 ML YEARS			88	40	0	8	286.1	1284	340	180	154	35	15	9	16	99	10	160	9	1	14	19	.424	0	0-0	8	5.28	4.84

Cole Hamels

Pitches: L Bats: L Pos: SP-23   Ht: 6'4" Wt: 195 Born: 12/27/1983 Age: 23

Year	Team	Lg	G	GS	CG	GF	IP	BFP	H	R	ER	HR	SH	SF	HB	TBB	IBB	SO	WP	Bk	W	L	Pct	ShO	Sv-Op	Hld	ERC	ERA
2003	Lakwd	A	13	13	1	0	74.2	268	32	8	7	0	3	1	3	25	0	115	3	0	6	1	.857	1	0--	-	1.04	0.84
2003	Clrwtr	A+	5	5	0	0	26.1	115	29	9	8	0	1	2	1	14	0	32	2	0	0	2	.000	0	0--	-	4.77	2.73
2004	Clrwtr	A+	4	4	0	0	16.0	58	10	2	2	0	1	0	1	4	0	24	1	0	1	0	1.000	0	0--	-	1.52	1.13
2005	Clrwtr	A+	3	3	0	0	16.0	62	7	5	4	0	1	1	0	7	0	18	4	0	2	0	1.000	0	0--	-	1.12	2.25
2005	Rdng	AA	3	3	0	0	19.0	77	10	6	5	2	1	0	1	12	0	19	2	0	2	0	1.000	0	0--	-	2.74	2.37
2006	Lakwd	A	1	1	0	0	5.2	19	3	1	1	1	0	0	0	2	0	3	0	0	0	0	-	0	0--	-	2.33	1.59
2006	S-WB	AAA	3	3	1	0	23.0	78	10	1	1	0	0	0	0	1	0	36	0	0	2	0	1.000	1	0--	-	0.49	0.39
2006	Clrwtr	A+	4	4	0	0	20.1	87	16	8	4	0	0	0	0	9	0	29	2	1	1	1	.500	0	0--	-	2.35	1.77
2006	Phi	NL	23	23	0	0	132.1	558	117	66	60	19	6	8	3	48	4	145	5	0	9	8	.529	0	0-0	0	3.61	4.08

Jason Hammel

Pitches: R Bats: R Pos: SP-9   Ht: 6'6" Wt: 200 Born: 9/2/1982 Age: 24

			HOW MUCH HE PITCHED						WHAT HE GAVE UP											THE RESULTS						
Year	Team	Lg	G	GS	CG	GF	IP	BFP	H	R	ER	HR	SH	SF	HB	TBB	IBB	SO	WP	Bk	W	L	Pct	ShO	Sv-Op Hld	ERC	ERA
2002	Princtn	R+	2	0	0	1	5.1	22	7	0	0	0	0	0	0	0	0	5	0	0	0	0	-	0	1- -	3.64	0.00
2002	HudVal	A-	13	10	0	2	51.2	245	71	41	30	0	0	1	4	14	0	38	3	2	1	5	.167	0	1- -	5.10	5.23
2003	CtnSC	A	14	12	1	1	76.2	320	70	32	29	2	3	3	2	27	1	50	4	1	6	2	.750	0	0- -	3.03	3.40
2004	CtnSC	A	18	18	0	0	94.2	405	94	54	34	7	5	5	2	27	0	88	8	0	4	7	.364	0	0- -	3.43	3.23
2004	Bkrsfld	A	11	11	0	0	72.1	275	52	18	15	4	3	1	4	21	0	66	3	0	6	2	.750	0	0- -	2.29	1.87
2005	Mont	AA	12	12	3	0	81.1	322	70	26	24	5	1	2	2	19	0	76	2	1	8	2	.800	0	0- -	2.63	2.66
2005	Drham	AAA	10	10	0	0	54.2	247	57	31	25	8	1	0	3	27	0	48	4	0	3	2	.600	0	0- -	5.24	4.12
2006	Drham	AAA	24	24	1	0	127.2	547	133	71	60	11	7	6	7	36	0	117	5	1	5	9	.357	0	0- -	3.97	4.23
2006	TB	AL	9	9	0	0	44.0	208	61	38	38	7	0	3	1	21	0	32	3	2	0	6	.000	0	0-0 0	7.40	7.77

Robby Hammock

Bats: R Throws: R Pos: 1B-1; PH-1   Ht: 5'10" Wt: 185 Born: 5/13/1977 Age: 30

						BATTING															BASERUNNING				AVERAGES		
Year	Team	Lg	G	AB	H	2B	3B	HR	(Hm	Rd)	TB	R	RBI	RC	TBB	IBB	SO	HBP	SH	SF	SB	CS	SB%	GDP	Avg	OBP	Slg
2006	Tucsn*	AAA	103	369	107	21	1	20	(-	-)	190	57	65	65	24	2	59	7	1	4	2	2	.50	11	.290	.342	.515
2003	Ari	NL	65	195	55	10	2	8	(5	3)	93	30	28	28	17	3	44	2	0	2	3	2	.60	5	.282	.343	.477
2004	Ari	NL	62	195	47	16	2	4	(1	3)	79	22	18	14	13	6	39	0	1	1	3	3	.50	9	.241	.287	.405
2006	Ari	NL	1	2	1	1	0	0	(0	0)	2	1	0	0	0	0	0	0	0	0	0	0	-	0	.500	.500	1.000
	3 ML YEARS		128	392	103	27	4	12	(6	6)	174	53	46	42	30	9	83	2	1	3	6	5	.55	14	.263	.316	.444

Chris Hammond

Pitches: L Bats: L Pos: RP-29   Ht: 6'1" Wt: 210 Born: 1/21/1966 Age: 41

				HOW MUCH HE PITCHED						WHAT HE GAVE UP										THE RESULTS						
Year	Team	Lg	G	GS	CG	GF	IP	BFP	H	R	ER	HR	SH	SF	HB	TBB	IBB	SO	WP	Bk	W	L	Pct	ShO	Sv-Op Hld	ERC	ERA
1990	Cin	NL	3	3	0	0	11.1	56	13	9	8	2	1	0	0	12	1	4	1	3	0	2	.000	0	0-0 -	8.50	6.35
1991	Cin	NL	20	18	0	0	99.2	425	92	51	45	4	6	1	2	48	3	50	3	0	7	7	.500	0	0-0 -	3.63	4.06
1992	Cin	NL	28	26	0	1	147.1	627	149	75	69	13	5	3	3	55	6	79	6	0	7	10	.412	0	0-0 -	4.02	4.21
1993	Fla	NL	32	32	1	0	191.0	826	207	106	99	18	10	2	1	66	2	108	10	5	11	12	.478	0	0-0 -	4.31	4.66
1994	Fla	NL	13	13	1	0	73.1	312	79	30	25	5	5	2	1	23	1	40	3	0	4	4	.500	1	0-0 -	4.03	3.07
1995	Fla	NL	25	24	3	0	161.0	683	157	73	68	17	7	7	9	47	2	126	3	1	9	6	.600	2	0-0 -	3.75	3.80
1996	Fla	NL	38	9	0	5	81.0	368	104	65	59	14	3	4	4	27	3	50	1	0	5	8	.385	0	1-2 4	6.21	6.56
1997	Bos	AL	29	8	0	0	65.1	293	81	45	43	5	0	3	2	27	4	48	2	0	3	4	.429	0	1-2 4	5.47	5.92
1998	Fla	NL	3	3	0	0	13.2	67	20	11	10	3	2	0	1	8	0	8	0	0	0	2	.000	0	0-0 -	9.33	6.59
2002	Atl	NL	63	0	0	6	76.0	311	53	15	8	1	5	2	1	31	9	63	1	0	7	2	.778	0	0-2 17	1.85	0.95
2003	NYY	AL	62	0	0	16	63.0	262	65	23	20	5	5	3	2	11	0	45	1	0	3	2	.600	0	1-4 17	3.36	2.86
2004	Oak	AL	41	0	0	9	53.2	224	56	21	16	4	3	3	3	13	1	34	0	0	4	1	.800	0	1-3 3	3.79	2.68
2005	SD	NL	55	0	0	17	58.2	242	51	25	25	9	1	2	2	14	0	34	0	0	5	1	.833	0	0-3 6	3.17	3.84
2006	Cin	NL	29	0	0	7	28.2	125	36	23	22	5	1	0	0	5	0	23	0	0	1	1	.500	0	0-2 6	5.13	6.91
	14 ML YEARS		441	136	5	67	1123.2	4821	1163	572	517	105	54	32	31	387	32	712	31	9	66	62	.516	3	3-16 58	4.09	4.14

Justin Hampson

Pitches: L Bats: L Pos: RP-4; SP-1   Ht: 6'1" Wt: 200 Born: 5/24/1980 Age: 27

				HOW MUCH HE PITCHED						WHAT HE GAVE UP										THE RESULTS						
Year	Team	Lg	G	GS	CG	GF	IP	BFP	H	R	ER	HR	SH	SF	HB	TBB	IBB	SO	WP	Bk	W	L	Pct	ShO	Sv-Op Hld	ERC	ERA
2000	Portlnd	A-	14	13	0	0	68.2	309	74	43	27	5	3	2	4	27	0	44	1	0	1	8	.111	0	0- -	4.44	3.54
2001	Tri-Cit	A-	15	15	0	0	81.2	354	84	55	41	5	1	5	9	23	0	63	4	0	4	6	.400	0	0- -	3.92	4.52
2002	Ashvlle	A	27	27	1	0	164.1	710	162	87	70	12	5	2	24	58	1	123	7	1	9	8	.529	0	0- -	4.25	3.83
2003	Visalia	A+	26	26	1	0	159.0	684	153	73	65	12	3	3	21	51	1	150	2	2	14	7	.667	0	0- -	3.91	3.68
2003	Tulsa	AA	1	1	0	0	4.0	22	8	6	6	0	0	0	0	3	0	0	0	0	0	1	.000	0	0- -	11.38	13.50
2004	Tulsa	AA	27	27	1	0	170.1	718	176	82	66	8	13	1	8	63	0	104	5	1	10	9	.526	0	0- -	4.09	3.49
2005	ColSpr	AAA	27	26	1	0	144.1	672	167	109	96	18	6	3	11	71	0	93	3	2	5	13	.278	0	0- -	5.83	5.99
2006	ColSpr	AAA	31	13	0	2	121.2	511	121	57	45	10	5	4	5	39	1	95	5	0	8	4	.667	0	0- -	3.83	3.33
2006	Col	NL	5	1	0	0	12.0	60	19	10	10	3	0	0	1	5	0	9	1	0	1	0	1.000	0	0-1 0	9.41	7.50

Mike Hampton

Pitches: L Bats: R Pos: P   Ht: 5'10" Wt: 195 Born: 9/9/1972 Age: 34

				HOW MUCH HE PITCHED						WHAT HE GAVE UP										THE RESULTS						
Year	Team	Lg	G	GS	CG	GF	IP	BFP	H	R	ER	HR	SH	SF	HB	TBB	IBB	SO	WP	Bk	W	L	Pct	ShO	Sv-Op Hld	ERC	ERA
1993	Sea	AL	13	3	0	2	17.0	95	28	20	18	3	1	1	0	17	3	8	1	1	1	3	.250	0	1-1 2	11.09	9.53
1994	Hou	NL	44	0	0	7	41.1	181	46	19	17	4	0	0	2	16	1	24	5	1	2	1	.667	0	0-1 10	4.88	3.70
1995	Hou	NL	24	24	0	0	150.2	641	141	73	56	11	9	5	4	49	3	115	3	1	9	8	.529	0	0-0 0	3.37	3.35
1996	Hou	NL	27	27	2	0	160.1	691	175	79	64	12	10	3	3	49	1	101	7	2	10	10	.500	1	0-0 0	4.11	3.59
1997	Hou	NL	34	34	7	0	223.0	941	217	105	95	16	11	7	2	77	2	139	6	1	15	10	.600	2	0-0 0	3.56	3.83
1998	Hou	NL	32	32	1	0	211.2	917	227	92	79	18	7	7	5	81	1	137	4	2	11	7	.611	1	0-0 0	4.45	3.36
1999	Hou	NL	34	34	3	0	239.0	979	206	86	77	12	10	9	8	101	2	177	9	0	22	4	.846	2	0-0 0	3.25	2.90
2000	NYM	NL	33	33	3	0	217.2	929	194	89	76	10	11	5	8	99	5	151	10	0	15	10	.600	1	0-0 0	3.44	3.14
2001	Col	NL	32	32	2	0	203.0	904	236	138	122	31	8	6	8	85	7	122	6	0	14	13	.519	1	0-0 0	5.69	5.41
2002	Col	NL	30	30	0	0	178.2	838	228	135	122	24	2	9	7	91	4	74	9	2	7	15	.318	0	0-0 0	6.61	6.15
2003	Atl	NL	31	31	1	0	190.0	823	186	91	81	14	10	5	1	78	4	110	10	1	14	8	.636	0	0-0 0	3.77	3.84
2004	Atl	NL	29	29	1	0	172.1	760	198	86	82	15	8	3	6	63	3	87	3	2	13	9	.591	0	0-0 0	4.76	4.28
2005	Atl	NL	12	12	1	0	69.1	284	74	28	27	5	2	1	0	18	0	27	1	0	5	3	.625	1	0-0 0	3.85	3.50
	13 ML YEARS		375	321	21	9	2074.0	8983	2156	1041	916	177	91	61	46	826	36	1272	74	13	138	101	.577	9	1-2 12	4.28	3.97

Tim Hamulack

Pitches: L Bats: R Pos: RP-33 **Ht:** 6'2" **Wt:** 220 **Born:** 11/14/1976 **Age:** 30

		HOW MUCH HE PITCHED				WHAT HE GAVE UP												THE RESULTS							
Year	Team	Lg	G	GS	CG	GF	IP	BFP	H	R	ER	HR	SH	SF	HB	TBB	IBB	SO	WP	Bk	W	L	Pct	ShO	Sv-Op	Hld	ERC	ERA
1996	Astros	R	22	0	0	9	27.0	117	23	9	7	1	0	0	2	13	1	24	1	0	4	1	.800	0	2--	-	3.33	2.33
1997	Astros	R	23	0	0	17	45.0	209	56	31	21	3	0	0	0	18	0	38	2	2	1	1	.500	0	9--	-	5.10	4.20
1998	QuadC	A	52	0	0	14	58.1	259	58	23	21	3	3	2	3	26	3	52	0	2	0	2	.000	0	0--	-	3.93	3.24
1999	Mich	A	25	0	0	12	26.2	114	23	9	9	0	1	2	0	11	0	32	2	1	3	0	1.000	0	0--	-	2.65	3.04
2000	Kissim	A+	41	0	0	20	56.0	256	67	37	31	3	2	1	1	21	1	54	0	0	3	1	.750	0	1--	-	4.69	4.98
2001	BrvdCt	A+	40	0	0	13	71.1	318	83	42	25	3	3	3	2	21	1	39	1	0	2	4	.333	0	1--	-	4.23	3.15
2002	Portlnd	AA	38	1	0	23	78.0	336	73	32	25	6	4	1	0	29	5	53	3	0	8	4	.667	0	6--	-	3.28	2.88
2003	Tacom	AAA	10	0	0	5	14.0	66	16	6	6	1	1	0	0	8	0	12	0	0	1	1	.500	0	0--	-	5.24	3.86
2003	SnAnt	AA	40	0	0	11	47.1	189	32	13	11	0	0	1	3	15	2	54	2	0	1	0	1.000	0	1--	-	1.69	2.09
2004	Pwtckt	AAA	35	0	0	15	29.2	152	44	26	23	4	0	1	2	19	2	25	1	0	7	4	.636	0	2--	-	8.46	6.98
2004	Portlnd	AA	7	0	0	2	15.1	69	16	6	6	0	0	0	0	7	0	16	1	0	2	0	1.000	0	0--	-	3.70	3.52
2005	Bnghtn	AA	21	0	0	14	28.2	112	20	7	4	0	1	0	0	6	1	27	0	0	2	2	.500	0	6--	-	1.37	1.26
2005	Norfolk	AAA	28	0	0	16	35.1	135	20	5	4	1	3	0	1	9	1	34	2	0	3	1	.750	0	6--	-	1.27	1.02
2006	LsVgs	AAA	28	0	0	10	38.0	163	30	9	6	1	1	0	1	26	0	44	2	0	0	1	.000	0	3--	-	3.67	1.42
2005	NYM	NL	6	0	0	2	2.1	14	7	6	6	3	0	1	0	1	1	2	0	0	0	0	-	0	0-0	1	32.83	23.14
2006	LAD	NL	33	0	0	12	34.0	161	36	28	24	7	1	0	2	22	1	34	2	1	0	3	.000	0	0-0	4	6.36	6.35
	2 ML YEARS		39	0	0	14	36.1	175	43	34	30	10	1	1	2	23	2	36	2	1	0	3	.000	0	0-0	5	7.65	7.43

Josh Hancock

Pitches: R Bats: R Pos: RP-62 **Ht:** 6'3" **Wt:** 205 **Born:** 4/11/1978 **Age:** 29

		HOW MUCH HE PITCHED				WHAT HE GAVE UP												THE RESULTS							
Year	Team	Lg	G	GS	CG	GF	IP	BFP	H	R	ER	HR	SH	SF	HB	TBB	IBB	SO	WP	Bk	W	L	Pct	ShO	Sv-Op	Hld	ERC	ERA
2002	Bos	AL	3	1	0	2	7.1	28	5	3	3	1	1	0	0	2	0	6	0	0	0	1	.000	0	0-0	0	2.25	3.68
2003	Phi	NL	2	0	0	0	3.0	11	2	1	1	0	0	0	0	0	0	4	0	0	0	0	-	0	0-0	0	0.91	3.00
2004	2 Tms	NL	16	11	0	2	63.2	293	73	43	36	17	3	2	1	28	2	36	5	0	5	2	.714	0	0-0	0	6.24	5.09
2005	Cin	NL	11	0	0	5	14.0	54	11	4	3	1	0	0	0	1	0	5	0	0	1	0	1.000	0	0-0	0	1.64	1.93
2006	StL	NL	62	0	0	15	77.0	323	70	37	35	9	4	4	1	23	2	50	3	1	3	3	.500	0	1-3	5	3.27	4.09
04	Phi	NL	4	2	0	0	9.0	42	13	9	9	3	0	0	0	3	0	5	0	0	0	1	.000	0	0-0	0	8.40	9.00
04	Cin	NL	12	9	0	2	54.2	251	60	34	27	14	3	2	1	25	2	31	5	0	5	1	.833	0	0-0	0	5.91	4.45
	5 ML YEARS		94	12	0	24	165.0	709	161	88	78	28	8	6	2	54	4	101	8	1	9	6	.600	0	1-3	5	4.07	4.25

Jack Hannahan

Bats: L Throws: R Pos: 1B-1; DH-1; PH-1 **Ht:** 6'2" **Wt:** 205 **Born:** 3/4/1980 **Age:** 27

			BATTING																		BASERUNNING				AVERAGES		
Year	Team	Lg	G	AB	H	2B	3B	HR	(Hm	Rd)	TB	R	RBI	RC	TBB	IBB	SO	HBP	SH	SF	SB	CS	SB%	GDP	Avg	OBP	Slg
2001	Oneont	A-	14	55	16	4	1	0	(-	-)	22	11	8	8	5	0	7	0	0	3	2	1	.67	2	.291	.333	.400
2001	W Mich	A	46	170	54	11	0	1	(-	-)	68	24	27	30	26	0	39	1	0	1	4	2	.67	5	.318	.409	.400
2002	Lkland	A	66	246	67	11	1	6	(-	-)	98	28	42	39	36	2	44	1	0	4	9	3	.75	2	.272	.362	.398
2002	Erie	AA	65	226	54	12	1	3	(-	-)	77	17	20	25	21	0	50	2	0	0	2	1	.67	7	.239	.309	.341
2003	Erie	AA	135	471	121	18	0	9	(-	-)	166	64	45	59	48	6	78	3	5	2	2	0	1.00	13	.257	.328	.352
2004	Erie	AA	108	374	102	21	1	8	(-	-)	149	48	39	59	53	4	60	2	1	1	7	3	.70	9	.273	.365	.398
2005	Erie	AA	7	22	3	0	0	0	(-	-)	3	1	1	0	4	0	8	0	0	0	0	0	-	0	.136	.269	.136
2005	Toledo	AAA	68	238	64	15	0	4	(-	-)	91	31	28	33	25	2	58	3	0	3	6	3	.67	5	.269	.342	.382
2006	Toledo	AAA	119	415	117	27	0	9	(-	-)	171	59	62	70	61	4	114	8	3	7	9	6	.60	5	.282	.379	.412
2006	Det	AL	3	9	0	0	0	0	(0	0)	0	0	0	0	1	0	1	0	0	0	0	0	-	0	.000	.100	.000

Devern Hansack

Pitches: R Bats: R Pos: SP-2 **Ht:** 6'2" **Wt:** 180 **Born:** 2/5/1978 **Age:** 29

			HOW MUCH HE PITCHED					WHAT HE GAVE UP												THE RESULTS							
Year	Team	Lg	G	GS	CG	GF	IP	BFP	H	R	ER	HR	SH	SF	HB	TBB	IBB	SO	WP	Bk	W	L	Pct	ShO	Sv-Op	Hld	ERC	ERA
2002	TriCity	A-	12	10	0	0	50.0	207	44	21	20	6	2	3	2	17	0	37	0	1	3	4	.429	0	0--	-	3.52	3.60
2003	Lxngtn	A	22	16	0	0	91.2	397	100	53	46	10	1	3	1	32	0	76	6	1	10	6	.625	0	0--	-	4.53	4.52
2006	Portlnd	AA	31	18	0	8	132.1	555	122	55	48	14	3	4	8	36	4	124	10	0	8	7	.533	0	1--	-	3.36	3.26
2006	Bos	AL	2	2	1	0	10.0	36	6	3	3	2	0	0	0	1	0	8	0	0	1	1	.500	1	0-0	0	1.59	2.70

Craig Hansen

Pitches: R Bats: R Pos: RP-38 **Ht:** 6'5" **Wt:** 185 **Born:** 11/15/1983 **Age:** 23

			HOW MUCH HE PITCHED					WHAT HE GAVE UP												THE RESULTS							
Year	Team	Lg	G	GS	CG	GF	IP	BFP	H	R	ER	HR	SH	SF	HB	TBB	IBB	SO	WP	Bk	W	L	Pct	ShO	Sv-Op	Hld	ERC	ERA
2005	RedSx	R	2	1	0	0	3.0	11	2	0	0	0	0	0	0	0	0	4	0	0	1	0	1.000	0	0--	-	0.91	0.00
2005	Lxngtn	A	8	0	0	2	9.2	39	9	0	0	0	0	0	0	1	0	10	0	0	0	0	-	0	1--	-	1.97	0.00
2006	Portlnd	AA	5	0	0	1	11.0	45	4	1	1	0	0	0	3	4	0	12	0	0	1	0	1.000	0	0--	-	1.26	0.82
2006	Pwtckt	AAA	14	4	0	1	36.0	152	31	14	11	0	3	0	0	19	0	26	2	0	1	2	.333	0	0--	-	3.16	2.75
2005	Bos	AL	4	0	0	1	3.0	16	6	2	2	1	0	1	0	1	0	3	0	0	0	0	-	0	0-1	0	12.18	6.00
2006	Bos	AL	38	0	0	11	38.0	176	46	32	28	5	3	3	4	15	0	30	1	0	2	2	.500	0	0-2	8	5.93	6.63
	2 ML YEARS		42	0	0	12	41.0	192	52	34	30	6	3	4	4	16	0	33	1	0	2	2	.500	0	0-3	8	6.35	6.59

Aaron Harang

Pitches: R Bats: R Pos: SP-35; RP-1   Ht: 6'7" Wt: 270 Born: 5/9/1978 Age: 29

	HOW MUCH HE PITCHED						WHAT HE GAVE UP											THE RESULTS						
Year	Team	Lg	G	GS	CG	GF	IP	BFP	H	R	ER	HR	SH	SF	HB	TBB	IBB	SO	WP	Bk	W	L	Pct	ShO	Sv-Op	Hld	ERC	ERA
2002	Oak	AL	16	15	0	0	78.1	354	78	44	42	7	3	4	3	45	2	64	1	0	5	4	.556	0	0-0	0	4.76	4.83
2003	2 Tms		16	15	0	1	76.1	327	89	47	45	11	5	1	1	19	0	42	3	1	5	6	.455	0	0-0	0	4.84	5.31
2004	Cin	NL	28	28	1	0	161.0	711	177	90	87	26	13	6	5	53	5	125	7	0	10	9	.526	1	0-0	0	4.81	4.86
2005	Cin	NL	32	32	1	0	211.2	887	217	93	90	22	11	5	8	51	3	163	6	0	11	13	.458	0	0-0	0	3.77	3.83
2006	Cin	NL	36	35	6	0	234.1	993	242	109	98	28	21	8	8	56	8	216	6	1	16	11	.593	2	0-0	0	3.82	3.76
03	Oak	AL	7	6	0	1	30.1	136	41	19	18	5	2	1	0	9	0	16	0	1	1	3	.250	0	0-0	0	6.32	5.34
03	Cin	NL	9	9	0	0	46.0	191	48	28	27	6	3	0	1	10	0	26	3	0	4	3	.571	0	0-0	0	3.94	5.28
	5 ML YEARS		128	125	8	1	761.2	3272	803	383	362	94	53	24	25	224	18	610	23	2	47	43	.522	3	0-0	0	4.21	4.28

Rich Harden

Pitches: R Bats: L Pos: SP-9   Ht: 6'1" Wt: 195 Born: 11/30/1981 Age: 25

	HOW MUCH HE PITCHED						WHAT HE GAVE UP											THE RESULTS						
Year	Team	Lg	G	GS	CG	GF	IP	BFP	H	R	ER	HR	SH	SF	HB	TBB	IBB	SO	WP	Bk	W	L	Pct	ShO	Sv-Op	Hld	ERC	ERA
2006	Scrmto*	AAA	1	1	0	0	2.0	8	1	0	0	0	0	0	0	0	0	3	1	0	0	0	-	0	0- --	-	0.47	0.00
2003	Oak	AL	15	13	0	0	74.2	324	72	38	37	5	2	3	1	40	1	67	6	0	5	4	.556	0	0-0	1	4.28	4.46
2004	Oak	AL	31	31	0	0	189.2	803	171	90	84	16	5	6	3	81	6	167	4	1	11	7	.611	0	0-0	0	3.57	3.99
2005	Oak	AL	22	19	2	0	128.0	514	93	42	36	7	4	2	2	43	0	121	6	0	10	5	.667	1	0-0	1	2.20	2.53
2006	Oak	AL	9	9	0	0	46.2	191	31	22	22	5	0	2	1	26	0	49	0	0	4	0	1.000	0	0-0	0	3.07	4.24
	4 ML YEARS		77	72	2	0	439.0	1832	367	192	179	33	11	13	7	190	7	404	16	1	30	16	.652	1	0-0	1	3.21	3.67

J.J. Hardy

Bats: R Throws: R Pos: SS-32; PH-4   Ht: 6'2" Wt: 190 Born: 8/19/1982 Age: 24

	BATTING																			BASERUNNING				AVERAGES		
Year	Team	Lg	G	AB	H	2B	3B	HR	(Hm | Rd)	TB	R	RBI	RC	TBB	IBB	SO	HBP	SH	SF	SB	CS	SB%	GDP	Avg	OBP	Slg
2001	Brewrs	R	5	20	5	2	1	0	(- | -)	9	6	1	2	1	0	2	0	1	0	0	0	-	0	.250	.286	.450
2001	Ogden	R+	35	125	31	5	0	2	(- | -)	42	20	15	14	15	0	12	0	3	1	1	2	.33	2	.248	.326	.336
2002	Hi Dsrt	A+	84	335	98	19	1	6	(- | -)	137	53	48	47	19	0	38	1	3	6	9	3	.75	3	.293	.327	.409
2002	Hntsvl	AA	38	145	33	7	0	1	(- | -)	43	14	13	11	9	0	19	0	4	2	1	2	.33	4	.228	.269	.297
2003	Hntsvl	AA	114	416	116	26	0	12	(- | -)	178	67	62	70	58	4	54	3	4	4	6	4	.60	11	.279	.368	.428
2004	Indy	AAA	26	101	28	10	0	4	(- | -)	50	17	20	17	9	0	8	0	0	2	0	0	-	1	.277	.330	.495
2005	Mil	NL	124	372	92	22	1	9	(6 | 3)	143	46	50	49	44	7	48	1	8	2	0	0	-	10	.247	.327	.384
2006	Mil	NL	35	128	31	5	0	5	(4 | 1)	51	13	14	13	10	0	23	0	0	1	1	1	.50	4	.242	.295	.398
	2 ML YEARS		159	500	123	27	1	14	(10 | 4)	194	59	64	62	54	7	71	1	8	3	1	1	.50	14	.246	.319	.388

Dan Haren

Pitches: R Bats: R Pos: SP-34   Ht: 6'5" Wt: 220 Born: 9/17/1980 Age: 26

	HOW MUCH HE PITCHED						WHAT HE GAVE UP											THE RESULTS						
Year	Team	Lg	G	GS	CG	GF	IP	BFP	H	R	ER	HR	SH	SF	HB	TBB	IBB	SO	WP	Bk	W	L	Pct	ShO	Sv-Op	Hld	ERC	ERA
2003	StL	NL	14	14	0	0	72.2	320	84	44	41	9	4	2	5	22	0	43	3	0	3	7	.300	0	0-0	0	5.07	5.08
2004	StL	NL	14	5	0	2	46.0	195	45	23	23	4	4	2	2	17	2	32	1	0	3	3	.500	0	0-0	0	3.91	4.50
2005	Oak	AL	34	34	3	0	217.0	897	212	101	90	26	3	5	6	53	5	163	6	0	14	12	.538	0	0-0	0	3.58	3.73
2006	Oak	AL	34	34	2	0	223.0	930	224	109	102	31	3	3	10	45	6	176	10	0	14	13	.519	0	0-0	0	3.72	4.12
	4 ML YEARS		96	87	5	2	558.2	2342	565	277	256	70	14	12	23	137	13	414	20	0	34	35	.493	0	0-0	0	3.85	4.12

Brandon Harper

Bats: R Throws: R Pos: C-14; PH-4; PR-1   Ht: 6'4" Wt: 200 Born: 4/29/1976 Age: 31

	BATTING																			BASERUNNING				AVERAGES		
Year	Team	Lg	G	AB	H	2B	3B	HR	(Hm | Rd)	TB	R	RBI	RC	TBB	IBB	SO	HBP	SH	SF	SB	CS	SB%	GDP	Avg	OBP	Slg
1997	Mrlns	R	2	6	0	0	0	0	(- | -)	0	0	1	0	0	0	1	0	0	0	0	0	-	1	.000	.000	.000
1997	Utica	A-	47	152	39	7	2	2	(- | -)	56	27	22	20	19	2	32	1	0	2	1	1	.50	9	.257	.339	.368
1998	Kane	A	113	412	95	22	2	4	(- | -)	133	34	50	43	42	3	64	4	1	5	1	3	.25	16	.231	.305	.323
1999	BrvdCt	A+	81	280	75	9	0	4	(- | -)	96	35	40	36	30	2	31	3	4	3	1	1	.50	4	.268	.342	.343
2000	BrvdCt	A+	8	27	8	1	0	0	(- | -)	9	8	2	4	7	0	4	0	0	0	0	0	-	0	.296	.441	.333
2000	Portlnd	AA	37	125	26	3	0	5	(- | -)	44	15	17	13	12	0	23	1	0	0	0	0	-	4	.208	.283	.352
2001	BrvdCt	A+	29	101	24	6	0	2	(- | -)	36	14	16	12	12	0	14	2	1	0	0	1	.00	4	.238	.330	.356
2001	Portlnd	AA	76	247	59	13	0	3	(- | -)	81	21	24	28	27	3	52	5	1	3	0	0	-	7	.239	.323	.328
2003	Carlina	AA	67	195	47	12	0	2	(- | -)	65	18	20	24	24	3	34	2	1	2	2	0	1.00	6	.241	.327	.333
2004	Erie	AA	48	166	48	12	0	9	(- | -)	87	26	29	32	16	1	31	6	0	0	2	1	.67	2	.289	.372	.524
2004	Toledo	AAA	21	58	11	0	0	3	(- | -)	20	10	7	6	6	0	10	3	0	1	0	1	.00	2	.190	.294	.345
2005	Toledo	AAA	81	252	62	14	1	6	(- | -)	96	33	34	35	28	1	36	7	0	3	4	0	1.00	8	.246	.334	.381
2006	NewOr	AAA	43	120	35	10	0	2	(- | -)	51	18	11	22	15	0	21	6	1	1	3	1	.75	0	.292	.394	.425
2006	Was	NL	18	41	12	3	0	2	(0 | 2)	21	6	4	7	4	0	4	1	0	1	0	0	-	1	.293	.362	.512

Travis Harper

Pitches: R Bats: L Pos: RP-30   Ht: 6'4" Wt: 190 Born: 5/21/1976 Age: 31

	HOW MUCH HE PITCHED						WHAT HE GAVE UP											THE RESULTS						
Year	Team	Lg	G	GS	CG	GF	IP	BFP	H	R	ER	HR	SH	SF	HB	TBB	IBB	SO	WP	Bk	W	L	Pct	ShO	Sv-Op	Hld	ERC	ERA
2000	TB	AL	6	5	1	0	32.0	141	30	17	17	5	1	1	1	15	0	14	1	0	1	2	.333	1	0-0	0	4.46	4.78
2001	TB	AL	2	2	0	0	7.0	36	15	11	6	5	0	0	0	3	0	2	1	0	0	2	.000	0	0-0	0	19.14	7.71
2002	TB	AL	37	7	0	16	85.2	394	101	54	52	14	5	4	9	27	3	60	2	0	5	9	.357	0	1-2	5	5.49	5.46
2003	TB	AL	61	0	0	14	93.0	388	86	45	39	9	7	3	6	31	6	64	6	0	4	8	.333	0	1-6	15	3.56	3.77
2004	TB	AL	52	0	0	11	78.2	330	69	37	34	8	3	2	7	23	3	59	3	0	6	2	.750	0	0-1	9	3.27	3.89

Year	Team	Lg	G	GS	CG	GF	IP	BFP	H	R	ER	HR	SH	SF	HB	TBB	IBB	SO	WP	Bk	W	L	Pct	ShO	Sv-Op	Hld	ERC	ERA
2005	TB	AL	52	0	0	13	73.1	321	88	57	55	14	5	2	1	24	9	40	2	0	4	6	.400	0	0-3	11	5.55	6.75
2006	TB	AL	30	0	0	7	42.0	196	62	27	23	6	2	1	2	13	1	32	2	1	2	0	1.000	0	0-2	5	7.16	4.93
	7 ML YEARS		240	14	1	61	411.2	1806	451	248	226	61	23	13	26	136	24	271	17	1	22	29	.431	1	2-14	43	4.86	4.94

Brendan Harris

Bats: R **Throws:** R **Pos:** PH-12; 2B-7; SS-5; 3B-3; PR-1   **Ht:** 6'1" **Wt:** 200 **Born:** 8/26/1980 **Age:** 26

Year	Team	Lg	G	AB	H	2B	3B	HR	(Hm	Rd)	TB	R	RBI	RC	TBB	IBB	SO	HBP	SH	SF	SB	CS	SB%	GDP	Avg	OBP	Slg
2006	NewOr*	AAA	59	219	62	14	0	5	(-	-)	91	37	32	37	26	3	56	9	1	2	3	2	.60	5	.283	.379	.416
2006	Lsvlle*	AAA	43	148	48	14	1	5	(-	-)	79	22	28	30	14	0	29	1	1	1	2	0	1.00	4	.324	.384	.534
2004	2 Tms	NL	23	59	10	3	0	1	(0	1)	16	4	3	2	3	0	12	1	0	0	0	0	-	0	.169	.222	.271
2005	Was	NL	4	9	3	1	0	1	(0	1)	7	1	3	3	0	0	0	1	0	0	0	0	-	2	.333	.400	.778
2006	2 Tms	NL	25	42	10	2	0	1	(1	0)	15	5	3	4	4	0	7	1	0	0	0	0	-	2	.238	.319	.357
04	ChC	NL	3	9	2	1	0	0	(0	0)	3	0	1	1	1	0	1	0	0	0	0	0	-	0	.222	.300	.333
04	Mon	NL	20	50	8	2	0	1	(0	1)	13	4	2	1	2	0	11	1	0	0	0	0	-	0	.160	.208	.260
06	Was	NL	17	32	8	2	0	0	(0	0)	10	3	2	3	3	0	3	1	0	0	0	0	-	1	.250	.333	.313
06	Cin	NL	8	10	2	0	0	1	(1	0)	5	2	1	1	1	0	4	0	0	0	0	0	-	1	.200	.273	.500
	3 ML YEARS		52	110	23	6	0	3	(1	2)	38	10	9	9	7	0	19	3	0	0	0	0	-	4	.209	.275	.345

Jeff Harris

Pitches: R **Bats:** R **Pos:** RP-3   **Ht:** 6'1" **Wt:** 190 **Born:** 7/4/1974 **Age:** 32

Year	Team	Lg	G	GS	CG	GF	IP	BFP	H	R	ER	HR	SH	SF	HB	TBB	IBB	SO	WP	Bk	W	L	Pct	ShO	Sv-Op	Hld	ERC	ERA
1995	Elizab	R+	21	0	0	10	33.0	155	42	15	14	2	1	0	4	13	1	27	6	1	1	3	.250	0	0- -	-	5.75	3.82
1996	FtWyn	A	42	0	0	15	89.2	393	90	35	31	4	3	8	4	33	1	85	10	1	8	3	.727	0	3- -	-	3.67	3.11
1997	FtMyrs	A+	24	0	0	6	42.0	173	30	11	10	4	3	1	0	15	2	32	1	0	2	4	.333	0	1- -	-	2.26	2.14
1997	NwBrit	AA	28	0	0	14	42.1	173	30	15	11	2	3	2	3	16	0	44	3	0	2	1	.667	0	0- -	-	2.39	2.34
1998	NwBrit	AA	26	0	0	11	38.0	140	21	7	7	3	1	1	0	5	0	40	0	1	1	0	1.000	0	5- -	-	1.11	1.66
1998	Salt Lk	AAA	25	0	0	18	32.0	157	38	24	21	4	3	3	0	19	4	24	3	0	8	0	1.000	0	3- -	-	5.63	5.91
1999	Salt Lk	AAA	36	0	0	7	45.2	225	61	38	35	7	3	4	3	26	1	20	2	0	4	3	.571	0	0- -	-	7.40	6.90
1999	NwBrit	AA	20	0	0	6	24.1	110	21	5	4	0	3	0	1	14	2	12	1	0	3	1	.750	0	0- -	-	3.16	1.48
2000	NwBrit	AA	24	0	0	12	28.0	129	35	17	15	5	2	2	3	10	0	28	2	0	2	0	1.000	0	0- -	-	6.45	4.82
2004	Tacom	AAA	26	8	1	4	74.2	310	60	37	36	6	1	2	4	26	0	53	4	0	5	3	.625	1	1- -	-	2.89	4.34
2005	SnAnt	AA	11	2	0	4	34.1	136	25	9	8	4	2	1	3	8	1	31	0	0	5	0	1.000	0	0- -	-	2.44	2.10
2005	Tacom	AAA	16	9	0	3	68.0	271	50	22	21	8	3	2	1	17	0	56	0	0	5	2	.714	0	1- -	-	2.28	2.78
2006	Ms	R	4	2	0	0	6.0	24	6	0	0	0	0	0	0	0	0	6	0	0	0	0	-	0	0- -	-	1.95	0.00
2006	Tacom	AAA	15	4	0	1	31.0	144	43	22	19	6	0	0	2	7	0	13	0	0	0	3	.000	0	0- -	-	6.54	5.52
2005	Sea	AL	11	8	0	1	53.2	227	48	27	25	9	0	2	3	20	2	25	0	0	2	5	.286	0	0-0	0	4.02	4.19
2006	Sea	AL	3	0	0	1	3.1	12	3	2	2	0	0	0	0	0	0	1	0	0	0	0	-	0	0-0	1	1.70	5.40
	2 ML YEARS		14	8	0	2	57.0	239	51	29	27	9	0	2	3	20	2	26	0	0	2	5	.286	0	0-0	1	3.87	4.26

Willie Harris

Bats: L **Throws:** R **Pos:** CF-24; PR-20; LF-11; PH-2; 2B-1; RF-1   **Ht:** 5'9" **Wt:** 170 **Born:** 6/22/1978 **Age:** 29

Year	Team	Lg	G	AB	H	2B	3B	HR	(Hm	Rd)	TB	R	RBI	RC	TBB	IBB	SO	HBP	SH	SF	SB	CS	SB%	GDP	Avg	OBP	Slg
2006	Pwtckt*	AAA	60	218	48	6	1	8	(-	-)	80	32	17	28	29	1	56	3	2	1	11	3	.79	4	.220	.319	.367
2001	Bal	AL	24	3	1	0	0	0	(0	0)	4	3	0	0	0	0	7	0	1	0	0	0	-	0	.125	.125	.167
2002	CWS	AL	49	163	38	4	0	2	(2	0)	48	14	12	15	9	0	21	0	3	2	8	0	1.00	3	.233	.270	.294
2003	CWS	AL	79	137	28	3	1	0	(0	0)	33	19	5	11	10	0	28	0	3	0	12	2	.86	1	.204	.259	.241
2004	CWS	AL	129	409	107	15	2	2	(2	0)	132	68	27	53	51	0	79	1	7	3	19	7	.73	4	.262	.343	.323
2005	CWS	AL	56	121	31	2	1	1	(1	0)	38	17	8	15	13	0	25	1	4	0	10	3	.77	1	.256	.333	.314
2006	Bos	AL	47	45	7	2	0	0	(0	0)	9	17	1	1	4	0	11	2	0	1	6	3	.67	0	.156	.250	.200
	6 ML YEARS		369	899	214	27	4	5	(5	0)	264	138	53	95	87	0	171	4	18	6	55	15	.79	9	.238	.306	.294

Corey Hart

Bats: R **Throws:** R **Pos:** RF-37; PH-31; LF-26; CF-6; 1B-2; PR-1   **Ht:** 6'6" **Wt:** 215 **Born:** 3/24/1982 **Age:** 25

Year	Team	Lg	G	AB	H	2B	3B	HR	(Hm	Rd)	TB	R	RBI	RC	TBB	IBB	SO	HBP	SH	SF	SB	CS	SB%	GDP	Avg	OBP	Slg
2006	Nashv*	AAA	26	100	32	10	1	4	(-	-)	56	19	21	23	12	0	25	1	0	2	11	2	.85	1	.320	.391	.560
2004	Mil	NL	1	1	0	0	0	0	(0	0)	0	0	0	0	0	0	1	0	0	0	0	0	-	0	.000	.000	.000
2005	Mil	NL	21	57	11	2	1	2	(2	0)	21	9	7	4	6	0	11	0	0	0	2	0	1.00	6	.193	.270	.368
2006	Mil	NL	87	237	67	13	2	9	(6	3)	111	32	33	30	17	1	58	0	0	2	5	8	.38	7	.283	.328	.468
	3 ML YEARS		109	295	78	15	3	11	(8	3)	132	41	40	34	23	1	70	0	0	2	7	8	.47	13	.264	.316	.447

Chad Harville

Pitches: R **Bats:** R **Pos:** RP-32   **Ht:** 5'9" **Wt:** 185 **Born:** 9/16/1976 **Age:** 30

Year	Team	Lg	G	GS	CG	GF	IP	BFP	H	R	ER	HR	SH	SF	HB	TBB	IBB	SO	WP	Bk	W	L	Pct	ShO	Sv-Op	Hld	ERC	ERA
2006	Drham*	AAA	11	0	0	5	15.0	68	15	5	5	0	0	3	0	8	2	9	4	0	0	0	-	0	1- -	-	3.52	3.00
1999	Oak	AL	15	0	0	8	14.1	69	18	11	11	2	0	0	0	10	1	15	3	1	0	2	.000	0	0-0	0	7.09	6.91
2001	Oak	AL	3	0	0	1	3.0	11	2	0	0	0	0	0	0	0	0	2	1	0	0	0	-	0	0-0	0	0.91	0.00
2003	Oak	AL	21	0	0	5	21.2	104	25	15	14	3	0	1	1	17	1	18	3	0	1	0	1.000	0	1-1	0	7.13	5.82
2004	2 Tms	AL	59	0	0	15	55.2	249	56	36	29	8	2	0	2	27	2	46	5	0	3	2	.600	0	0-4	4	4.81	4.69
2005	2 Tms	AL	45	0	0	20	45.1	203	43	26	24	8	1	2	5	27	1	36	4	0	0	3	.000	0	0-1	2	5.67	4.76
2006	TB	AL	32	0	0	14	41.0	184	44	27	27	5	2	1	0	22	2	30	4	2	0	2	.000	0	1-2	5	5.15	5.93

	HOW MUCH HE PITCHED					WHAT HE GAVE UP												THE RESULTS							
Year Team	Lg	G	GS	CG	GF	IP	BFP	H	R	ER	HR	SH	SF	HB	TBB	IBB	SO	WP	Bk	W	L	Pct	ShO	Sv-Op	Hld	ERC	ERA
04 Oak	AL	3	0	0	1	2.2	11	2	1	1	0	0	0	0	1	0	0	0	0	0	0	-	0	0-0	1	2.01	3.38
04 Hou	NL	56	0	0	14	53.0	238	54	35	28	8	2	0	2	26	2	46	5	0	3	2	.600	0	0-4	3	4.96	4.75
05 Hou	NL	37	0	0	16	38.1	173	36	21	19	7	1	2	4	24	1	33	4	0	0	2	.000	0	0-1	2	5.73	4.46
05 Bos	AL	8	0	0	4	7.0	30	7	5	5	1	0	0	1	3	0	3	0	0	0	1	.000	0	0-0	0	5.33	6.43
6 ML YEARS		175	0	0	63	181.0	820	188	115	105	26	5	4	8	103	7	147	20	3	4	9	.308	0	2-8	8	5.45	5.22

Scott Hatteberg

Bats: L Throws: R Pos: 1B-131; PH-11   Ht: 6'1" Wt: 210 Born: 12/14/1969 Age: 37

	BATTING																			BASERUNNING				AVERAGES		
Year Team	Lg	G	AB	H	2B	3B	HR	(Hm	Rd)	TB	R	RBI	RC	TBB	IBB	SO	HBP	SH	SF	SB	CS	SB%	GDP	Avg	OBP	Slg
1995 Bos	AL	2	2	1	0	0	0	(0	0)	1	1	0	0	0	0	0	0	0	0	0	0	-	1	.500	.500	.500
1996 Bos	AL	10	11	2	1	0	0	(0	0)	3	3	0	1	3	0	2	0	0	0	0	0	-	2	.182	.357	.273
1997 Bos	AL	114	350	97	23	1	10	(5	5)	152	46	44	52	40	2	70	2	2	1	0	1	.00	11	.277	.354	.434
1998 Bos	AL	112	359	99	23	1	12	(4	8)	160	46	43	56	43	3	58	5	0	3	0	0	-	11	.276	.359	.446
1999 Bos	AL	30	80	22	5	0	1	(1	0)	30	12	11	14	18	0	14	1	0	1	0	0	-	2	.275	.410	.375
2000 Bos	AL	92	230	61	15	0	8	(2	6)	100	21	36	36	38	3	39	0	1	2	0	1	.00	8	.265	.367	.435
2001 Bos	AL	94	278	68	19	0	3	(2	1)	96	34	25	32	33	0	26	4	0	1	1	1	.50	7	.245	.332	.345
2002 Oak	AL	136	492	138	22	4	15	(8	7)	213	58	61	77	68	1	56	6	1	1	0	0	-	8	.280	.374	.433
2003 Oak	AL	147	541	137	34	0	12	(6	6)	207	63	61	80	66	0	53	9	3	3	0	1	.00	14	.253	.342	.383
2004 Oak	AL	152	550	156	30	0	15	(8	7)	231	87	82	90	72	5	48	5	3	8	0	0	-	10	.284	.367	.420
2005 Oak	AL	134	464	119	19	0	7	(4	3)	159	52	59	60	51	4	54	4	2	2	0	1	.00	22	.256	.334	.343
2006 Cin	NL	141	456	132	28	0	13	(10	3)	199	62	51	76	74	3	41	3	2	4	2	2	.50	13	.289	.389	.436
12 ML YEARS		1164	3813	1032	219	6	96	(50	46)	1551	485	473	574	506	21	461	39	14	26	3	7	.30	109	.271	.360	.407

John Hattig

Bats: B Throws: R Pos: 3B-10; PH-2; PR-1   Ht: 6'2" Wt: 230 Born: 2/27/1980 Age: 27

	BATTING																			BASERUNNING				AVERAGES		
Year Team	Lg	G	AB	H	2B	3B	HR	(Hm	Rd)	TB	R	RBI	RC	TBB	IBB	SO	HBP	SH	SF	SB	CS	SB%	GDP	Avg	OBP	Slg
1999 RedSx	R	50	163	44	7	3	1	(-	-)	60	28	17	21	16	1	20	1	0	3	1	1	.50	8	.270	.333	.368
2000 Lowell	A-	61	242	70	8	1	0	(-	-)	80	30	28	29	20	1	43	0	1	1	1	1	.50	1	.289	.342	.331
2001 Lowell	A-	11	45	5	0	1	1	(-	-)	10	4	5	1	3	0	7	1	0	0	0	1	1.00	6	.111	.184	.222
2001 Augsta	A	50	179	51	9	1	1	(-	-)	65	25	23	26	22	1	42	3	0	1	4	1	.80	3	.285	.371	.363
2002 Srsota	A+	24	85	21	6	0	0	(-	-)	27	6	6	8	7	0	16	0	0	1	0	0	-	2	.247	.301	.318
2002 Augsta	A	93	347	98	20	0	7	(-	-)	139	46	56	56	52	4	73	2	0	2	1	2	.33	13	.282	.377	.401
2003 Srsota	A+	114	400	118	29	2	6	(-	-)	169	51	70	69	59	3	70	2	1	4	9	7	.56	15	.295	.385	.423
2003 Portlnd	AA	8	32	7	2	0	0	(-	-)	9	3	1	2	2	0	11	0	0	0	0	0	-	2	.219	.265	.281
2004 Portlnd	AA	75	264	78	21	1	12	(-	-)	137	35	53	57	47	3	68	6	0	2	3	3	.50	8	.295	.411	.519
2004 NHam	AA	40	142	42	7	0	10	(-	-)	79	24	30	27	12	1	41	2	0	3	0	1	.00	3	.296	.352	.556
2005 Dnedin	A+	11	44	17	3	0	0	(-	-)	20	8	5	8	3	0	7	0	0	1	0	0	-	2	.386	.417	.455
2005 Syrcse	AAA	26	95	30	7	0	1	(-	-)	40	15	10	16	10	0	16	1	0	0	0	0	-	5	.316	.387	.421
2006 Syrcse	AAA	103	373	103	30	1	4	(-	-)	147	48	36	52	35	3	108	2	3	0	0	0	-	9	.276	.341	.394
2006 Tor	AL	13	24	8	1	0	0	(0	0)	9	2	3	5	5	0	8	0	0	0	0	0	-	1	.333	.448	.375

LaTroy Hawkins

Pitches: R Bats: R Pos: RP-60   Ht: 6'5" Wt: 215 Born: 12/21/1972 Age: 34

	HOW MUCH HE PITCHED						WHAT HE GAVE UP												THE RESULTS							
Year Team	Lg	G	GS	CG	GF	IP	BFP	H	R	ER	HR	SH	SF	HB	TBB	IBB	SO	WP	Bk	W	L	Pct	ShO	Sv-Op	Hld	ERC	ERA
1995 Min	AL	6	6	1	0	27.0	131	39	29	26	3	0	3	1	12	0	9	1	1	2	3	.400	0	0-0	0	7.14	8.67
1996 Min	AL	7	6	0	1	26.1	124	42	24	24	8	1	1	0	9	0	24	1	1	1	1	.500	0	0-0	0	9.49	8.20
1997 Min	AL	20	20	0	0	103.1	478	134	71	67	19	2	2	4	47	0	58	6	3	6	12	.333	0	0-0	0	7.01	5.84
1998 Min	AL	33	33	0	0	190.1	840	227	126	111	27	4	10	5	61	1	105	10	2	7	14	.333	0	0-0	0	5.31	5.25
1999 Min	AL	33	33	1	0	174.1	803	238	136	129	29	1	5	1	60	2	103	9	0	10	14	.417	0	0-0	0	6.55	6.66
2000 Min	AL	66	0	0	38	87.2	370	85	34	33	7	4	1	1	32	1	59	6	0	2	5	.286	0	14-14	7	3.70	3.39
2001 Min	AL	62	0	0	51	51.1	248	59	34	34	3	1	4	1	39	3	36	7	0	1	5	.167	0	28-37	1	6.02	5.96
2002 Min	AL	65	0	0	15	80.1	310	63	23	19	5	2	3	0	15	1	63	5	0	6	0	1.000	0	0-3	13	1.99	2.13
2003 Min	AL	74	0	0	12	77.1	310	69	20	16	4	4	1	1	15	1	75	5	0	9	3	.750	0	2-8	28	2.48	1.86
2004 ChC	NL	77	0	0	50	82.0	333	72	27	24	10	6	2	2	14	5	69	2	0	5	4	.556	0	25-34	4	2.66	2.63
2005 2 Tms	NL	66	0	0	21	56.1	247	58	27	24	7	3	1	0	24	3	43	1	0	2	8	.200	0	6-15	15	4.41	3.83
2006 Bal	AL	60	0	0	12	60.1	261	73	30	30	4	1	2	0	15	3	27	2	0	3	2	.600	0	0-4	16	4.37	4.48
05 ChC	NL	21	0	0	12	19.0	80	18	9	7	4	1	0	0	7	0	13	0	0	1	4	.200	0	4-8	0	4.44	3.32
05 SF	NL	45	0	0	9	37.1	167	40	18	17	3	2	1	0	17	3	30	1	0	1	4	.200	0	2-7	15	4.36	4.10
12 ML YEARS		569	98	2	200	1016.2	4455	1159	581	537	126	29	35	16	343	20	671	55	7	54	71	.432	0	75-115	84	4.85	4.75

Brad Hawpe

Bats: L Throws: L Pos: RF-145; PH-9; PR-1   Ht: 6'3" Wt: 205 Born: 6/22/1979 Age: 28

	BATTING																			BASERUNNING				AVERAGES		
Year Team	Lg	G	AB	H	2B	3B	HR	(Hm	Rd)	TB	R	RBI	RC	TBB	IBB	SO	HBP	SH	SF	SB	CS	SB%	GDP	Avg	OBP	Slg
2004 Col	NL	42	105	26	3	2	3	(1	2)	42	12	9	11	11	3	34	1	0	1	1	1	.50	4	.248	.322	.400
2005 Col	NL	101	305	80	10	3	9	(5	4)	123	38	47	44	43	3	70	0	0	3	2	2	.50	5	.262	.350	.403
2006 Col	NL	150	499	146	33	6	22	(6	16)	257	67	84	85	74	11	123	0	0	2	5	5	.50	8	.293	.383	.515
3 ML YEARS		293	909	252	46	11	34	(12	22)	422	117	140	140	128	17	227	1	0	6	8	8	.50	17	.277	.365	.464

Aaron Heilman

Pitches: R Bats: R Pos: RP-74 Ht: 6'5" Wt: 220 Born: 11/12/1978 Age: 28

Year	Team	Lg	G	GS	CG	GF	IP	BFP	H	R	ER	HR	SH	SF	HB	TBB	IBB	SO	WP	Bk	W	L	Pct	ShO	Sv-Op Hld	ERC	ERA
2003	NYM	NL	14	13	0	0	65.1	315	79	53	49	13	5	3	3	41	2	51	5	0	2	7	.222	0	0-0 0	7.16	6.75
2004	NYM	NL	5	5	0	0	28.0	119	27	17	17	4	1	0	0	13	0	22	0	0	1	3	.250	0	0-0 0	4.54	5.46
2005	NYM	NL	53	7	1	20	108.0	439	87	40	38	6	4	1	6	37	4	106	1	1	5	3	.625	1	5-6 5	2.74	3.17
2006	NYM	NL	74	0	0	14	87.0	356	73	37	35	5	7	2	3	28	2	73	5	0	4	5	.444	0	0-5 27	2.76	3.62
4 ML YEARS			146	25	1	34	288.1	1229	266	147	139	28	17	6	12	119	8	252	11	1	12	18	.400	1	5-11 32	3.82	4.34

Chris Heintz

Bats: R Throws: R Pos: C-2; PH-1 Ht: 6'1" Wt: 210 Born: 8/6/1974 Age: 32

Year	Team	Lg	G	AB	H	2B	3B	HR	(Hm	Rd)	TB	R	RBI	RC	TBB	IBB	SO	HBP	SH	SF	SB	CS	SB%	GDP	Avg	OBP	Slg
1996	Bristol	R+	8	29	10	7	0	2	(-	-)	23	7	8	8	4	0	2	0	0	0	1	1	.50	0	.345	.424	.793
1996	Sbend	A	64	230	61	12	1	1	(-	-)	78	25	22	28	23	0	46	3	1	1	1	1	.50	3	.265	.339	.339
1997	Hickory	A	107	388	110	28	1	2	(-	-)	146	57	54	52	28	0	57	9	2	5	1	3	.25	6	.284	.342	.376
1998	WinSa	A+	130	508	147	21	4	8	(-	-)	200	66	79	68	31	0	87	5	3	9	10	8	.56	17	.289	.331	.394
1999	WinSa	A+	118	417	122	33	2	7	(-	-)	180	55	60	67	40	1	72	4	3	2	6	3	.67	7	.293	.359	.432
2000	Brham	AA	73	239	64	15	1	2	(-	-)	87	27	34	30	21	0	33	0	1	6	4	1	.80	2	.268	.320	.364
2001	Brham	AA	37	119	28	8	0	2	(-	-)	42	14	8	12	10	0	23	2	2	1	0	2	.00	2	.235	.303	.353
2001	Charltt	AA	5	10	1	1	0	0	(-	-)	2	1	1	1	0	0	3	0	0	1	0	0	-	0	.100	.091	.200
2002	NwHav	AA	105	373	117	29	1	7	(-	-)	169	40	45	59	19	3	61	2	2	1	1	0	1.00	13	.314	.349	.453
2003	Altna	AA	78	271	70	12	4	2	(-	-)	96	28	26	31	19	2	24	3	5	1	0	0	-	6	.258	.313	.354
2004	Roch	AAA	86	294	82	14	0	8	(-	-)	120	33	45	39	16	0	40	3	7	5	0	2	.00	6	.279	.318	.408
2005	Roch	AAA	89	329	100	18	2	8	(-	-)	146	38	58	51	22	0	61	0	4	5	0	0	-	5	.304	.343	.444
2006	Roch	AAA	100	374	107	22	0	3	(-	-)	138	46	39	45	23	0	63	0	4	5	4	0	.00	5	.286	.323	.369
2005	Min	AL	8	25	5	3	0	0	(0	0)	8	1	2	2	1	0	6	0	0	0	0	0	-	1	.200	.231	.320
2006	Min	AL	2	1	0	0	0	0	(0	0)	0	0	0	0	0	0	0	0	0	0	0	0	-	0	.000	.000	.000
2 ML YEARS			10	26	5	3	0	0	(0	0)	8	1	2	2	1	0	6	0	0	0	0	0	-	1	.192	.222	.308

Rick Helling

Pitches: R Bats: R Pos: RP-18; SP-2 Ht: 6'3" Wt: 255 Born: 12/15/1970 Age: 36

Year	Team	Lg	G	GS	CG	GF	IP	BFP	H	R	ER	HR	SH	SF	HB	TBB	IBB	SO	WP	Bk	W	L	Pct	ShO	Sv-Op Hld	ERC	ERA
2006	Nashv*	AAA	2	2	0	0	12.0	47	9	5	5	0	0	0	1	2	0	6	0	0	1	0	1.000	0	0- -	1.69	3.75
1994	Tex	AL	9	9	1	0	52.0	228	62	34	34	14	0	0	0	18	0	25	4	1	3	2	.600	1	0-0 0	6.33	5.88
1995	Tex	AL	3	3	0	0	12.1	62	17	11	9	2	0	2	2	8	0	5	0	0	0	2	.000	0	0-0 0	8.81	6.57
1996	2 Tms		11	6	0	2	48.0	198	37	23	23	9	1	1	0	16	0	42	1	1	3	3	.500	0	0-0 1	3.07	4.31
1997	2 Tms		41	16	0	9	131.0	550	108	67	65	17	3	9	6	69	2	99	3	0	5	9	.357	0	0-1 6	4.08	4.47
1998	Tex	AL	33	33	4	0	216.1	922	209	109	106	27	6	10	1	78	6	164	10	0	20	7	.741	2	0-0 0	3.86	4.41
1999	Tex	AL	35	35	3	0	219.1	943	228	127	118	41	5	10	6	85	5	131	8	0	13	11	.542	0	0-0 0	5.03	4.84
2000	Tex	AL	35	35	0	0	217.0	953	212	122	108	29	4	9	9	99	2	146	2	0	16	13	.552	0	0-0 0	4.50	4.48
2001	Tex	AL	34	34	2	0	215.2	941	256	134	124	38	3	10	4	63	2	154	6	0	12	11	.522	1	0-0 0	5.39	5.17
2002	Ari	NL	30	30	0	0	175.2	751	180	94	88	31	10	6	6	48	6	120	7	1	10	12	.455	0	0-0 1	4.29	4.51
2003	2 Tms		35	24	0	5	155.0	665	167	91	89	31	4	2	12	45	0	98	5	1	8	8	.500	0	0-0 1	5.19	5.17
2005	Mil	NL	15	7	0	2	49.0	199	39	13	13	2	0	1	2	18	1	42	1	0	3	1	.750	0	0-0 2	2.66	2.39
2006	Mil	NL	20	2	0	4	35.0	142	25	17	16	6	1	2	0	15	0	32	1	0	0	2	.000	0	0-1 2	3.13	4.11
96	Tex	AL	6	2	0	2	20.1	92	23	17	17	7	0	1	0	9	0	16	1	0	1	2	.333	0	0-0 1	6.80	7.52
96	Fla	NL	5	4	0	0	27.2	106	14	6	6	2	1	0	0	7	0	26	0	1	2	1	.667	0	0-0 0	1.18	1.95
97	Fla	NL	31	8	0	8	76.0	324	61	38	37	12	2	7	4	48	2	53	0	0	2	6	.250	0	0-1 6	4.62	4.38
97	Tex	AL	10	8	0	1	55.0	226	47	29	28	5	1	2	2	21	0	46	3	0	3	3	.500	0	0-0 0	3.37	4.58
03	Bal	AL	24	24	0	0	138.2	603	156	90	88	30	4	2	12	40	0	86	4	1	7	8	.467	0	0-0 0	5.63	5.71
03	Fla	NL	11	0	0	5	16.1	62	11	1	1	1	0	0	0	5	0	12	1	0	1	0	1.000	0	0-0 0	1.93	0.55
12 ML YEARS			301	234	10	22	1526.1	6564	1540	842	793	247	37	62	48	562	24	1058	48	4	93	81	.534	4	0-2 12	4.56	4.68

Wes Helms

Bats: R Throws: R Pos: 1B-88; PH-52; 3B-24; PR-3; LF-1 Ht: 6'4" Wt: 230 Born: 5/12/1976 Age: 31

Year	Team	Lg	G	AB	H	2B	3B	HR	(Hm	Rd)	TB	R	RBI	RC	TBB	IBB	SO	HBP	SH	SF	SB	CS	SB%	GDP	Avg	OBP	Slg
1998	Atl	NL	7	13	4	1	0	1	(0	1)	8	2	2	2	0	0	4	0	0	0	0	0	-	0	.308	.308	.615
2000	Atl	NL	6	5	1	0	0	0	(0	0)	1	0	0	0	0	0	2	0	0	0	0	0	-	0	.200	.200	.200
2001	Atl	NL	100	216	48	10	3	10	(6	4)	94	28	36	27	21	2	56	1	0	1	1	1	.50	3	.222	.293	.435
2002	Atl	NL	85	210	51	16	0	6	(4	2)	85	20	22	15	11	2	57	3	1	6	1	1	.50	5	.243	.283	.405
2003	Mil	NL	134	476	124	21	0	23	(16	7)	214	56	67	66	43	3	131	10	0	7	0	1	.00	10	.261	.330	.450
2004	Mil	NL	92	274	72	13	1	4	(3	1)	99	24	28	28	24	1	60	5	1	2	0	1	.00	10	.263	.331	.361
2005	Mil	NL	95	168	50	13	1	4	(2	2)	77	18	24	26	14	0	30	3	0	3	0	1	.00	7	.298	.356	.458
2006	Fla	NL	140	240	79	19	5	10	(4	6)	138	30	47	45	21	1	55	6	6	5	0	4	.00	7	.329	.390	.575
8 ML YEARS			659	1602	429	93	10	58	(35	23)	716	178	226	209	134	9	395	28	8	24	2	9	.18	42	.268	.331	.447

Todd Helton

Bats: L Throws: L Pos: 1B-145 Ht: 6'2" Wt: 210 Born: 8/20/1973 Age: 33

Year	Team	Lg	G	AB	H	2B	3B	HR	(Hm	Rd)	TB	R	RBI	RC	TBB	IBB	SO	HBP	SH	SF	SB	CS	SB%	GDP	Avg	OBP	Slg
2006	ColSpr*	AAA	2	6	2	0	0	0	(-	-)	2	0	0	0	1	0	1	0	0	0	0	0	-	0	.333	.429	.333
1997	Col	NL	35	93	26	2	1	5	(3	2)	45	13	11	15	8	0	11	0	0	0	0	1	.00	1	.280	.337	.484
1998	Col	NL	152	530	167	37	1	25	(13	12)	281	78	97	101	53	5	54	6	1	5	3	3	.50	15	.315	.380	.530
1999	Col	NL	159	578	185	39	5	35	(23	12)	339	114	113	124	68	6	77	6	0	4	7	6	.54	14	.320	.395	.587

120

								BATTING														BASERUNNING				AVERAGES		
Year	Team	Lg	G	AB	H	2B	3B	HR	(Hm	Rd)	TB	R	RBI	RC	TBB	IBB	SO	HBP	SH	SF	SB	CS	SB%	GDP	Avg	OBP	Slg
2000	Col	NL	160	580	216	59	2	42	(27	15)	405	138	147	169	103	22	61	4	0	10	5	3	.63	12	.372	.463	.698
2001	Col	NL	159	587	197	54	2	49	(27	22)	402	132	146	157	98	15	104	5	1	5	7	5	.58	14	.336	.432	.685
2002	Col	NL	156	553	182	39	4	30	(18	12)	319	107	109	127	99	21	91	5	0	10	5	1	.83	10	.329	.429	.577
2003	Col	NL	160	583	209	49	5	33	(23	10)	367	135	117	160	111	21	72	2	0	7	0	4	.00	19	.358	.458	.630
2004	Col	NL	154	547	190	49	2	32	(21	11)	339	115	96	143	127	19	72	3	0	6	3	0	1.00	12	.347	.469	.620
2005	Col	NL	144	509	163	45	2	20	(13	7)	272	92	79	114	106	22	80	9	1	1	3	0	1.00	14	.320	.445	.534
2006	Col	NL	145	546	165	40	5	15	(8	7)	260	94	81	118	91	15	64	6	0	6	3	2	.60	10	.302	.404	.476
10 ML YEARS			1424	5106	1700	413	29	286	(176	110)	3029	1018	996	1228	864	146	686	46	3	54	36	25	.59	121	.333	.430	.593

Ben Hendrickson

Pitches: R Bats: R Pos: SP-3; RP-1 Ht: 6'4" Wt: 190 Born: 2/4/1981 Age: 26

			HOW MUCH HE PITCHED						WHAT HE GAVE UP										THE RESULTS						
Year	Team	Lg	G	GS	CG	GF	IP	BFP	H	R	ER	HR	SH	SF	HB	TBB	IBB	SO	WP	Bk	W	L	Pct	ShO	Sv-Op Hld	ERC	ERA
2000	Ogden	R+	13	7	0	2	50.2	237	50	37	32	7	1	2	1	29	0	48	12	0	4	3	.571	0	1-- -	4.82	5.68
2001	Beloit	A	25	25	1	0	133.1	576	122	58	42	3	1	1	6	72	0	133	9	1	8	9	.471	0	0-- -	3.83	2.84
2002	Hi Dsrt	A+	14	14	0	0	81.1	338	61	31	23	3	1	2	2	41	0	70	3	0	5	5	.500	0	0-- -	2.83	2.55
2002	Hntsvl	AA	13	13	0	0	69.2	295	57	31	23	2	8	2	3	35	0	50	2	1	4	2	.667	0	0-- -	3.18	2.97
2003	Hntsvl	AA	17	16	0	0	78.1	327	82	35	30	6	3	1	0	28	0	56	3	0	7	6	.538	0	0-- -	4.15	3.45
2004	Indy	AAA	21	21	2	0	125.0	492	114	32	28	6	6	3	1	26	0	93	6	1	11	3	.786	2	0-- -	2.68	2.02
2005	Nashv	AAA	28	27	1	0	155.2	701	176	100	86	17	9	5	6	58	2	122	8	0	6	12	.333	0	0-- -	4.84	4.97
2006	Nashv	AAA	23	23	1	0	139.1	570	121	60	52	9	11	5	5	46	0	97	6	0	9	8	.529	0	0-- -	3.06	3.36
2004	Mil	NL	10	9	0	1	46.1	215	58	33	32	6	2	2	4	20	1	29	1	0	1	8	.111	0	0-0 0	6.28	6.22
2006	Mil	NL	4	3	0	0	12.0	65	21	17	16	0	0	1	0	9	0	8	4	0	0	2	.000	0	0-0 0	9.30	12.00
2 ML YEARS			14	12	0	1	58.1	280	79	50	48	6	2	3	4	29	1	37	5	0	1	10	.091	0	0-0 0	6.90	7.41

Mark Hendrickson

Pitches: L Bats: L Pos: SP-25; RP-6 Ht: 6'9" Wt: 230 Born: 6/23/1974 Age: 33

			HOW MUCH HE PITCHED						WHAT HE GAVE UP										THE RESULTS						
Year	Team	Lg	G	GS	CG	GF	IP	BFP	H	R	ER	HR	SH	SF	HB	TBB	IBB	SO	WP	Bk	W	L	Pct	ShO	Sv-Op Hld	ERC	ERA
2002	Tor	AL	16	4	0	0	36.2	142	25	11	10	1	2	2	2	12	3	21	0	0	3	0	1.000	0	0-1 1	1.90	2.45
2003	Tor	AL	30	30	1	0	158.1	703	207	111	97	24	1	8	0	40	3	76	4	0	9	9	.500	1	0-0 0	5.64	5.51
2004	TB	AL	32	30	2	1	183.1	803	211	113	98	21	4	5	7	46	5	87	5	2	10	15	.400	0	0-0 0	4.51	4.81
2005	TB	AL	31	31	1	0	178.1	796	227	126	117	24	8	7	2	49	1	89	4	1	11	8	.579	1	0-0 0	5.44	5.90
2006	2 Tms		31	25	1	0	164.2	719	173	87	77	17	5	4	4	62	0	99	6	1	6	15	.286	1	0-0 1	4.38	4.21
06	TB	AL	13	13	1	0	89.2	377	81	42	38	10	2	3	2	34	0	51	4	0	4	8	.333	1	0-0 0	3.65	3.81
06	LAD	NL	18	12	0	0	75.0	342	92	45	39	7	3	1	2	28	0	48	2	1	2	7	.222	0	0-0 1	5.29	4.68
5 ML YEARS			140	120	5	1	721.1	3163	843	448	399	87	20	26	15	209	12	372	19	4	39	47	.453	2	0-1 2	4.80	4.98

Sean Henn

Pitches: L Bats: R Pos: RP-3; SP-1 Ht: 6'5" Wt: 200 Born: 4/23/1981 Age: 26

			HOW MUCH HE PITCHED						WHAT HE GAVE UP										THE RESULTS						
Year	Team	Lg	G	GS	CG	GF	IP	BFP	H	R	ER	HR	SH	SF	HB	TBB	IBB	SO	WP	Bk	W	L	Pct	ShO	Sv-Op Hld	ERC	ERA
2001	StlsInd	A-	9	8	0	1	42.0	167	26	15	14	3	0	1	1	15	0	49	4	0	3	1	.750	0	1-- -	1.88	3.00
2003	Tampa	A+	16	16	0	0	72.1	323	69	34	29	3	0	1	0	37	0	52	7	0	4	3	.571	0	0-- -	3.73	3.61
2003	Yanks	R	2	1	0	0	8.0	32	5	3	2	1	0	0	1	3	0	10	1	0	1	1	.500	0	0-- -	2.69	2.25
2004	Trntn	AA	27	27	0	0	163.1	726	173	94	80	11	10	8	6	63	2	118	12	1	6	8	.429	0	0-- -	4.17	4.41
2005	Trntn	AA	4	4	0	0	25.1	101	16	2	2	1	0	0	0	9	0	21	2	0	2	1	.667	0	0-- -	1.67	0.71
2005	Clmbs	AAA	16	16	1	0	86.1	365	79	37	31	5	3	3	4	27	1	64	0	0	5	5	.500	1	0-- -	3.12	3.23
2006	Clmbs	AAA	18	6	0	4	42.2	185	44	19	19	1	3	0	2	20	0	33	1	0	3	1	.750	0	0-- -	4.25	4.01
2005	NYY	AL	3	3	0	0	11.1	61	18	16	14	3	0	0	0	11	0	3	0	0	0	3	.000	0	0-0 0	12.12	11.12
2006	NYY	AL	4	1	0	0	9.1	44	11	5	5	2	0	1	1	5	0	7	0	0	0	1	.000	0	0-0 0	7.09	4.82
2 ML YEARS			7	4	0	0	20.2	105	29	21	19	5	0	1	1	16	0	10	0	0	0	4	.000	0	0-0 0	9.77	8.27

Brad Hennessey

Pitches: R Bats: R Pos: RP-22; SP-12 Ht: 6'2" Wt: 195 Born: 2/7/1980 Age: 27

			HOW MUCH HE PITCHED						WHAT HE GAVE UP										THE RESULTS						
Year	Team	Lg	G	GS	CG	GF	IP	BFP	H	R	ER	HR	SH	SF	HB	TBB	IBB	SO	WP	Bk	W	L	Pct	ShO	Sv-Op Hld	ERC	ERA
2006	Fresno*	AAA	2	2	0	0	10.2	45	11	9	3	1	0	0	0	1	0	7	0	0	0	1	.000	0	0-- -	2.88	2.53
2004	SF	NL	7	7	0	0	34.1	163	42	24	19	2	4	1	0	15	1	25	1	0	2	2	.500	0	0-0 0	4.91	4.98
2005	SF	NL	21	21	0	0	118.1	521	127	63	61	15	2	3	4	52	3	64	3	1	5	8	.385	0	0-0 0	5.00	4.64
2006	SF	NL	34	12	0	9	99.1	428	92	53	47	12	6	2	10	42	1	42	3	0	5	6	.455	0	1-1 2	4.34	4.26
3 ML YEARS			62	40	0	9	252.0	1112	261	140	127	29	12	6	14	109	5	131	7	1	12	16	.429	0	1-1 2	4.72	4.54

Clay Hensley

Pitches: R Bats: R Pos: SP-29; RP-8 Ht: 5'11" Wt: 190 Born: 8/31/1979 Age: 27

			HOW MUCH HE PITCHED						WHAT HE GAVE UP										THE RESULTS						
Year	Team	Lg	G	GS	CG	GF	IP	BFP	H	R	ER	HR	SH	SF	HB	TBB	IBB	SO	WP	Bk	W	L	Pct	ShO	Sv-Op Hld	ERC	ERA
2002	SlmKzr	A-	15	15	1	0	81.2	342	72	31	23	3	2	1	3	25	0	84	6	1	7	0	1.000	0	0-- -	2.77	2.53
2003	Hgrstn	A	12	12	3	0	68.0	280	56	26	24	4	1	0	1	20	0	74	4	0	4	3	.571	2	0-- -	2.50	3.18
2003	SnJos	A+	5	5	0	0	29.1	135	38	20	19	4	3	4	1	9	0	25	0	0	2	3	.400	0	0-- -	5.75	5.83
2003	Lk Els	A+	8	8	0	0	44.1	198	51	24	17	0	0	0	0	14	0	40	3	0	3	4	.429	0	0-- -	3.76	3.45
2004	Mobile	AA	27	27	2	0	159.0	692	167	84	76	14	8	7	8	48	2	125	6	0	11	10	.524	1	0-- -	4.02	4.30
2005	Portlnd	AAA	15	14	0	0	90.1	356	63	31	30	8	3	3	2	22	0	71	1	1	2	2	.500	0	0-- -	1.96	2.99

Year	Team	Lg	G	GS	CG	GF	IP	BFP	H	R	ER	HR	SH	SF	HB	TBB	IBB	SO	WP	Bk	W	L	Pct	ShO	Sv-Op	Hld	ERC	ERA
2005	SD	NL	24	1	0	5	47.2	189	33	12	9	0	1	2	0	17	2	28	2	0	1	1	.500	0	0-0	2	1.70	1.70
2006	SD	NL	37	29	1	2	187.0	787	174	82	77	15	10	3	3	76	7	122	3	0	11	12	.478	1	0-1	1	3.64	3.71
2 ML YEARS			61	30	1	7	234.2	976	207	94	86	15	11	5	3	93	9	150	5	0	12	13	.480	1	0-1	3	3.21	3.30

Matt Herges

Pitches: R Bats: L Pos: RP-66 — Ht: 6'0" Wt: 210 Born: 4/1/1970 Age: 37

Year	Team	Lg	G	GS	CG	GF	IP	BFP	H	R	ER	HR	SH	SF	HB	TBB	IBB	SO	WP	Bk	W	L	Pct	ShO	Sv-Op	Hld	ERC	ERA
1999	LAD	NL	17	0	0	9	24.1	104	24	13	11	5	1	0	1	8	0	18	0	0	0	2	.000	0	0-2	1	4.61	4.07
2000	LAD	NL	59	4	0	17	110.2	461	100	43	39	7	9	4	6	40	5	75	4	0	11	3	.786	0	1-3	4	3.35	3.17
2001	LAD	NL	75	0	0	22	99.1	435	97	39	38	8	4	3	6	46	12	76	2	0	9	8	.529	0	1-8	15	4.20	3.44
2002	Mon	NL	62	0	0	25	64.2	298	80	33	29	10	6	2	2	26	8	50	3	0	2	5	.286	0	6-14	9	5.74	4.04
2003	2 Tms	NL	67	0	0	24	79.0	332	68	27	23	3	2	6	3	29	2	68	1	1	3	2	.600	0	3-6	9	2.87	2.62
2004	SF	NL	70	0	0	43	65.1	301	90	44	38	8	7	4	3	21	4	39	2	0	4	5	.444	0	23-31	5	6.29	5.23
2005	2 Tms	NL	28	0	0	7	29.0	132	35	23	23	6	2	2	1	12	1	9	0	0	1	1	.500	0	0-0	3	6.26	7.14
2006	Fla	NL	66	0	0	21	71.0	328	94	42	34	5	3	1	3	28	5	36	1	0	2	3	.400	0	0-4	9	5.81	4.31
03	SD	NL	40	0	0	21	44.0	192	40	16	14	2	1	5	2	20	2	40	1	0	2	2	.500	0	3-5	4	3.45	2.86
03	SF	NL	27	0	0	3	35.0	140	28	11	9	1	1	1	1	9	0	28	0	1	1	0	1.000	0	0-1	5	2.18	2.31
05	SD	NL	21	0	0	5	21.0	90	23	11	11	2	2	1	0	7	1	6	0	0	1	1	.500	0	0-0	3	4.29	4.71
05	Ari	NL	7	0	0	2	8.0	42	12	12	12	4	0	1	1	5	0	3	0	0	0	0	-	0	0-0	0	12.23	13.50
8 ML YEARS			444	4	0	168	543.1	2391	588	264	235	52	34	22	27	210	37	371	13	1	32	29	.525	0	34-68	55	4.56	3.89

Dustin Hermanson

Pitches: R Bats: R Pos: RP-6 — Ht: 6'2" Wt: 205 Born: 12/21/1972 Age: 34

Year	Team	Lg	G	GS	CG	GF	IP	BFP	H	R	ER	HR	SH	SF	HB	TBB	IBB	SO	WP	Bk	W	L	Pct	ShO	Sv-Op	Hld	ERC	ERA
2006	Charltt*	AAA	14	0	0	6	13.2	54	8	5	5	1	1	0	0	7	0	16	0	0	0	1	.000	0	0--	-	2.24	3.29
1995	SD	NL	26	0	0	6	31.2	151	35	26	24	8	3	0	1	22	1	19	3	0	3	1	.750	0	0-0	1	7.19	6.82
1996	SD	NL	8	0	0	4	13.2	62	18	15	13	3	2	3	0	4	0	11	0	1	1	0	1.000	0	0-0	0	6.37	8.56
1997	Mon	NL	32	28	1	0	158.1	656	134	68	65	15	10	6	1	66	2	136	4	1	8	8	.500	1	0-0	0	3.32	3.69
1998	Mon	NL	32	30	1	0	187.0	768	163	80	65	21	9	3	3	56	3	154	4	3	14	11	.560	0	0-0	1	3.12	3.13
1999	Mon	NL	34	34	0	0	216.1	928	225	110	101	20	16	7	7	69	4	145	4	1	9	14	.391	0	0-0	0	4.03	4.20
2000	Mon	NL	38	30	2	7	198.0	876	226	128	105	26	10	9	4	75	5	94	5	0	12	14	.462	1	4-7	1	5.10	4.77
2001	StL	NL	33	33	0	0	192.1	830	195	106	95	34	7	2	8	73	3	123	6	0	14	13	.519	0	0-0	0	4.80	4.45
2002	Bos	AL	12	1	0	4	22.0	107	35	19	19	3	0	1	0	7	0	13	2	0	1	1	.500	0	0-1	2	7.52	7.77
2003	2 Tms	NL	32	6	0	12	68.2	291	70	32	31	9	4	2	3	24	4	39	3	0	3	3	.500	0	1-6	1	4.38	4.06
2004	SF	NL	47	18	0	26	131.0	565	132	71	66	15	5	7	3	46	5	102	4	0	6	9	.400	0	17-20	1	4.03	4.53
2005	CWS	AL	57	0	0	45	57.1	228	46	17	13	4	3	0	1	17	4	33	3	0	2	4	.333	0	34-39	5	2.48	2.04
2006	CWS	AL	6	0	0	3	6.2	27	6	3	3	2	0	0	1	1	1	5	0	0	0	0	-	0	0-0	0	4.30	4.05
03	StL	NL	23	0	0	10	29.2	129	35	18	18	4	2	1	1	14	2	12	1	0	1	2	.333	0	1-6	1	6.04	5.46
03	SF	NL	9	6	0	2	39.0	162	35	14	13	5	2	1	2	10	2	27	2	0	2	1	.667	0	0-0	0	3.25	3.00
12 ML YEARS			357	180	4	107	1283.0	5489	1285	675	600	160	69	40	32	460	32	874	38	6	73	78	.483	2	56-73	12	4.17	4.21

Jeremy Hermida

Bats: L Throws: R Pos: RF-85; PH-12; CF-9 — Ht: 6'4" Wt: 200 Born: 1/30/1984 Age: 23

Year	Team	Lg	G	AB	H	2B	3B	HR	(Hm	Rd)	TB	R	RBI	RC	TBB	IBB	SO	HBP	SH	SF	SB	CS	SB%	GDP	Avg	OBP	Slg
2002	Mrlns	R	38	134	30	7	3	0	(-	-)	43	15	14	15	15	0	25	3	0	0	5	0	1.00	0	.224	.316	.321
2002	Jmstwn	A-	13	47	15	2	1	0	(-	-)	19	8	7	7	7	0	10	0	0	0	1	3	.25	0	.319	.407	.404
2003	Grnsbr	A	133	468	133	23	5	6	(-	-)	184	73	49	83	80	3	100	2	4	6	28	2	.93	3	.284	.387	.393
2003	Albq	AAA	1	3	0	0	0	0	(-	-)	0	0	0	0	0	0	3	0	0	0	0	0	-	0	.000	.000	.000
2004	Jupiter	A+	91	340	101	17	1	10	(-	-)	150	53	50	60	42	7	73	5	0	6	10	3	.77	3	.297	.377	.441
2005	Carlina	AA	118	386	113	29	2	18	(-	-)	200	77	63	102	111	5	89	7	1	2	23	2	.92	8	.293	.457	.518
2006	Jupiter	A+	6	17	3	1	0	0	(-	-)	4	3	2	1	3	0	7	0	0	0	0	0	-	0	.176	.300	.235
2005	Fla	NL	23	41	12	2	0	4	(4	0)	26	9	11	10	6	1	12	0	0	0	2	0	1.00	1	.293	.383	.634
2006	Fla	NL	99	307	77	19	1	5	(3	2)	113	37	28	38	33	3	70	5	2	1	4	1	.80	6	.251	.332	.368
2 ML YEARS			122	348	89	21	1	9	(7	2)	139	46	39	48	39	4	82	5	2	1	6	1	.86	7	.256	.338	.399

Anderson Hernandez

Bats: B Throws: R Pos: 2B-13; SS-10; PH-4; PR-2 — Ht: 5'9" Wt: 170 Born: 10/30/1982 Age: 24

Year	Team	Lg	G	AB	H	2B	3B	HR	(Hm	Rd)	TB	R	RBI	RC	TBB	IBB	SO	HBP	SH	SF	SB	CS	SB%	GDP	Avg	OBP	Slg
2001	Tigers	R	55	216	57	5	11	0	(-	-)	84	37	18	29	13	0	38	0	3	2	34	8	.81	0	.264	.303	.389
2001	Lkland	A+	7	21	4	0	1	0	(-	-)	6	2	1	0	0	0	8	0	2	0	0	0	-	0	.190	.190	.286
2002	Lkland	A+	123	410	106	13	7	2	(-	-)	139	52	42	43	33	0	102	0	10	5	16	14	.53	2	.259	.310	.339
2003	Lkland	A+	106	380	87	11	4	2	(-	-)	112	47	28	32	27	0	69	0	14	3	15	7	.68	10	.229	.278	.295
2004	Lkland	A+	32	122	36	4	3	0	(-	-)	46	20	11	21	6	0	26	0	2	1	7	0	1.00	2	.295	.326	.377
2004	Erie	AA	101	394	108	19	3	5	(-	-)	148	65	29	51	26	0	89	5	13	2	17	6	.74	5	.274	.326	.376
2005	Bnghtn	AA	66	273	89	14	1	7	(-	-)	126	46	24	43	14	2	58	1	7	1	11	9	.55	0	.326	.360	.462
2005	Norfolk	AAA	66	261	79	6	4	2	(-	-)	99	34	30	38	22	1	46	1	4	4	24	9	.73	2	.303	.354	.379
2006	Norfolk	AAA	102	414	103	11	4	0	(-	-)	122	44	23	36	21	0	70	0	9	0	15	5	.75	4	.249	.285	.295
2006	StLuci	A+	2	9	1	0	0	0	(-	-)	1	0	0	0	0	0	1	0	0	0	0	0	-	0	.111	.111	.111
2005	NYM	NL	6	18	1	0	0	0	(0	0)	1	1	0	0	1	0	4	0	0	0	0	1	.00	0	.056	.105	.056
2006	NYM	NL	25	66	10	1	1	1	(1	0)	16	4	3	0	1	0	12	0	0	3	0	0	-	3	.152	.164	.242
2 ML YEARS			31	84	11	1	1	1	(1	0)	17	5	3	0	2	0	16	0	0	3	0	1	.00	3	.131	.151	.202

Felix Hernandez

Pitches: R Bats: R Pos: SP-31
Ht: 6'3" Wt: 230 Born: 4/8/1986 Age: 21

				HOW MUCH HE PITCHED							WHAT HE GAVE UP												THE RESULTS						
Year	Team	Lg	G	GS	CG	GF	IP	BFP	H	R	ER	HR	SH	SF	HB	TBB	IBB	SO	WP	Bk	W	L	Pct	ShO	Sv-Op	Hld	ERC	ERA
2003	Everett	A-	11	7	0	0	55.0	232	43	17	14	2	5	5	8	24	0	73	7	0	7	2	.778	0	0- -	-	3.19	2.29
2003	Wisc	A	2	2	0	0	14.0	54	9	4	3	1	6	6	0	3	0	18	0	0	0	0	-	0	0- -	-	1.52	1.93
2004	InldEm	A+	16	15	0	1	92.0	387	85	31	28	5	6	2	8	26	0	114	6	0	9	3	.750	0	0- -	-	3.24	2.74
2004	SnAnt	AA	10	10	1	0	57.1	240	47	23	21	3	6	0	4	21	0	58	2	0	5	1	.833	1	0- -	-	2.92	3.30
2005	Tacom	AAA	19	14	1	0	88.0	374	62	24	22	3	1	2	3	48	0	100	2	2	9	4	.692	0	0- -	-	2.69	2.25
2005	Sea	AL	12	12	0	0	84.1	328	61	26	25	5	1	2	2	23	0	77	3	0	4	4	.500	0	0-0	0	2.08	2.67
2006	Sea	AL	31	31	2	0	191.0	816	195	105	96	23	2	3	6	60	2	176	11	0	12	14	.462	1	0-0	0	4.11	4.52
	2 ML YEARS		43	43	2	0	275.1	1144	256	131	121	28	3	5	8	83	2	253	14	0	16	18	.471	1	0-0	0	3.45	3.96

Jose Hernandez

Bats: R Throws: R Pos: PH-44; 1B-19; 3B-11; SS-11; RF-9; PR-4; 2B-3; LF-3
Ht: 6'1" Wt: 190 Born: 7/14/1969 Age: 37

									BATTING												BASERUNNING				AVERAGES		
Year	Team	Lg	G	AB	H	2B	3B	HR	(Hm	Rd)	TB	R	RBI	RC	TBB	IBB	SO	HBP	SH	SF	SB	CS	SB%	GDP	Avg	OBP	Slg
1991	Tex	AL	45	98	18	2	1	0	(0	0)	22	8	4	2	3	0	31	0	6	0	0	1	.00	2	.184	.208	.224
1992	Cle	AL	3	4	0	0	0	0	(0	0)	0	0	0	0	0	0	2	0	0	0	0	0	-	0	.000	.000	.000
1994	ChC	NL	56	132	32	2	3	1	(0	1)	43	18	9	11	8	0	29	1	5	0	2	2	.50	4	.242	.291	.326
1995	ChC	NL	93	245	60	11	4	13	(6	7)	118	37	40	31	13	3	69	0	8	2	1	0	1.00	8	.245	.281	.482
1996	ChC	NL	131	331	80	14	1	10	(4	6)	126	52	41	35	24	4	97	1	5	2	4	0	1.00	10	.242	.293	.381
1997	ChC	NL	121	183	50	8	5	7	(4	3)	89	33	26	26	14	2	42	0	1	1	2	5	.29	5	.273	.323	.486
1998	ChC	NL	149	488	124	23	7	23	(11	12)	230	76	75	67	40	3	140	1	2	2	4	6	.40	12	.254	.311	.471
1999	2 Tms	NL	147	508	135	20	2	19	(6	13)	216	79	62	73	52	6	145	5	2	1	11	3	.79	10	.266	.339	.425
2000	Mil	NL	124	446	109	22	1	11	(8	3)	166	51	59	48	41	3	125	6	0	3	3	7	.30	12	.244	.315	.372
2001	Mil	NL	152	542	135	26	2	25	(9	16)	240	67	78	69	39	8	**185**	2	5	4	5	4	.56	9	.249	.300	.443
2002	Mil	NL	152	525	151	24	2	24	(13	11)	251	72	73	76	52	5	**188**	4	0	1	3	5	.38	19	.288	.356	.478
2003	3 Tms	NL	150	519	117	18	3	13	(7	6)	180	58	57	41	46	0	177	1	0	5	2	1	.67	16	.225	.287	.347
2004	LAD	NL	95	211	61	12	1	13	(5	8)	114	32	29	33	26	6	61	1	0	0	3	1	.75	3	.289	.370	.540
2005	Cle	AL	84	234	54	7	0	6	(3	3)	79	28	31	20	14	0	60	2	3	3	1	3	.25	11	.231	.277	.338
2006	2 Tms	NL	85	152	40	4	1	3	(1	2)	55	12	19	17	12	0	40	0	2	0	0	0	-	4	.263	.317	.362
99	ChC	NL	99	342	93	12	2	15	(5	10)	154	57	43	55	40	3	101	5	1	0	7	2	.78	5	.272	.357	.450
99	Atl	NL	48	166	42	8	0	4	(1	3)	62	22	19	18	12	3	44	0	1	1	4	1	.80	5	.253	.302	.373
03	Col	NL	69	257	61	6	1	8	(4	4)	93	33	27	23	27	0	95	0	0	2	1	1	.50	6	.237	.308	.362
03	ChC	NL	23	69	13	3	1	2	(1	1)	24	6	9	4	3	0	26	0	0	0	0	0	-	1	.188	.222	.348
03	Pit	NL	58	193	43	9	1	3	(2	1)	63	19	21	14	16	0	56	1	0	3	1	0	1.00	9	.223	.282	.326
06	Pit	NL	67	120	32	2	1	2	(0	2)	42	8	12	12	11	0	29	0	1	0	0	0	-	3	.267	.328	.350
06	Phi	NL	18	32	8	2	0	1	(1	0)	13	4	7	5	1	0	11	0	1	0	0	0	-	1	.250	.273	.406
	15 ML YEARS		1587	4618	1166	193	33	168	(77	91)	1929	623	603	549	384	40	1391	24	39	24	41	38	.52	125	.252	.312	.418

Livan Hernandez

Pitches: R Bats: R Pos: SP-34
Ht: 6'2" Wt: 245 Born: 2/20/1975 Age: 32

				HOW MUCH HE PITCHED							WHAT HE GAVE UP												THE RESULTS						
Year	Team	Lg	G	GS	CG	GF	IP	BFP	H	R	ER	HR	SH	SF	HB	TBB	IBB	SO	WP	Bk	W	L	Pct	ShO	Sv-Op	Hld	ERC	ERA
1996	Fla	NL	1	0	0	0	3.0	13	3	0	0	0	0	0	0	2	0	2	0	0	0	0	-	0	0-0	0	4.60	0.00
1997	Fla	NL	17	17	0	0	96.1	405	81	39	34	5	4	7	3	38	1	72	0	0	9	3	.750	0	0-0	0	2.96	3.18
1998	Fla	NL	33	33	9	0	234.1	1040	**265**	133	123	37	8	5	6	104	8	162	4	3	10	12	.455	0	0-0	0	5.58	4.72
1999	2 Tms	NL	30	30	2	0	199.2	886	227	110	103	23	7	6	2	76	5	144	2	2	8	12	.400	0	0-0	0	4.88	4.64
2000	SF	NL	33	33	5	0	240.0	1030	**254**	114	100	22	12	9	4	73	3	165	3	0	17	11	.607	2	0-0	0	4.01	3.75
2001	SF	NL	34	34	2	0	226.2	1008	**266**	143	132	24	12	**12**	3	85	7	138	7	0	13	15	.464	0	0-0	0	5.03	5.24
2002	SF	NL	33	33	5	0	216.0	921	233	113	105	19	14	8	4	71	5	134	1	1	12	**16**	.429	3	0-0	0	4.38	4.38
2003	Mon	NL	33	33	**8**	0	**233.1**	**967**	225	92	83	27	6	4	10	57	3	178	6	1	15	10	.600	0	0-0	0	3.55	3.20
2004	Mon	NL	35	**35**	9	0	**255.0**	**1053**	234	105	102	26	11	4	10	83	9	186	1	0	11	15	.423	2	0-0	0	3.52	3.60
2005	Was	NL	35	**35**	2	0	246.1	1065	**268**	116	109	25	15	9	13	84	**14**	147	3	2	15	10	.600	0	0-0	0	4.54	3.98
2006	2 Tms	NL	34	34	0	0	216.0	959	246	116	116	29	16	8	4	78	6	128	1	0	13	13	.500	0	0-0	0	4.97	4.83
99	Fla	NL	20	20	2	0	136.0	612	161	78	72	17	3	4	2	55	3	97	2	1	5	9	.357	0	0-0	0	5.37	4.76
99	SF	NL	10	10	0	0	63.2	274	66	32	31	6	4	2	0	21	2	47	0	1	3	3	.500	0	0-0	0	3.88	4.38
06	Was	NL	24	24	0	0	146.2	661	176	94	87	22	10	7	2	52	4	89	0	0	9	8	.529	0	0-0	0	5.38	5.34
06	Ari	NL	10	10	0	0	69.1	298	70	31	29	7	6	1	2	26	2	39	1	0	4	5	.444	0	0-0	0	4.13	3.76
	11 ML YEARS		318	317	42	0	2166.2	9347	2302	1090	1007	237	105	72	59	751	61	1456	28	9	123	117	.513	7	0-0	0	4.38	4.18

Orlando Hernandez

Pitches: R Bats: R Pos: SP-29
Ht: 6'2" Wt: 220 Born: 10/11/1969 Age: 37

				HOW MUCH HE PITCHED							WHAT HE GAVE UP												THE RESULTS						
Year	Team	Lg	G	GS	CG	GF	IP	BFP	H	R	ER	HR	SH	SF	HB	TBB	IBB	SO	WP	Bk	W	L	Pct	ShO	Sv-Op	Hld	ERC	ERA
1998	NYY	AL	21	21	3	0	141.0	574	113	53	49	11	3	5	6	52	1	131	5	2	12	4	.750	1	0-0	0	2.96	3.13
1999	NYY	AL	33	33	2	0	214.1	910	187	100	98	24	3	**11**	8	87	2	157	4	0	17	9	.654	1	0-0	0	3.60	4.12
2000	NYY	AL	29	29	3	0	195.2	820	186	104	98	34	4	5	6	51	2	141	1	0	12	13	.480	0	0-0	0	3.82	4.51
2001	NYY	AL	17	16	0	0	94.2	414	90	51	51	19	2	2	5	42	1	77	0	0	4	7	.364	0	0-0	0	4.87	4.85
2002	NYY	AL	24	22	0	1	146.0	606	131	63	59	17	1	5	8	36	2	113	8	0	8	5	.615	0	1-1	1	3.20	3.64
2004	NYY	AL	15	15	0	0	84.2	359	73	31	31	9	0	1	5	36	0	84	3	0	8	2	.800	0	0-0	0	3.71	3.30
2005	CWS	AL	24	22	0	1	128.1	568	137	77	73	18	3	5	12	50	1	91	3	2	9	9	.500	0	1-1	1	5.12	5.12
2006	2 Tms	NL	29	29	1	0	162.1	699	155	90	84	22	7	5	12	61	5	164	1	**3**	11	11	.500	0	0-0	0	4.23	4.66
06	Ari	NL	9	9	0	0	45.2	204	52	32	31	8	2	0	4	20	3	52	0	0	2	4	.333	0	0-0	0	6.00	6.11
06	NYM	NL	20	20	1	0	116.2	495	103	58	53	14	5	5	8	41	2	112	1	**3**	9	7	.563	0	0-0	0	3.60	4.09
	8 ML YEARS		192	187	9	2	1167.0	4950	1072	577	543	154	23	39	62	415	14	958	25	7	81	60	.574	2	2-2	2	3.86	4.19

Ramon Hernandez

Bats: R **Throws:** R **Pos:** C-135; PH-8; DH-6; 1B-2   **Ht:** 6'0" **Wt:** 225 **Born:** 5/20/1976 **Age:** 31

Year	Team	Lg	G	AB	H	2B	3B	HR	(Hm	Rd)	TB	R	RBI	RC	TBB	IBB	SO	HBP	SH	SF	SB	CS	SB%	GDP	Avg	OBP	Slg
1999	Oak	AL	40	136	38	7	0	3	(1	2)	54	13	21	20	18	0	11	1	1	2	1	0	1.00	5	.279	.363	.397
2000	Oak	AL	143	419	101	19	0	14	(7	7)	162	52	62	49	38	1	64	7	10	5	1	0	1.00	14	.241	.311	.387
2001	Oak	AL	136	453	115	25	0	15	(5	10)	185	55	60	58	37	3	68	6	9	4	1	1	.50	10	.254	.316	.408
2002	Oak	AL	136	403	94	20	0	7	(3	4)	135	51	42	41	43	1	64	5	3	3	0	0	-	11	.233	.313	.335
2003	Oak	AL	140	483	132	24	1	21	(9	12)	221	70	78	69	33	2	79	12	2	6	0	0	-	14	.273	.331	.458
2004	SD	NL	111	384	106	23	0	18	(10	8)	183	45	63	50	35	0	45	5	4	4	1	0	1.00	16	.276	.341	.477
2005	SD	NL	99	369	107	19	2	12	(5	7)	166	36	58	44	18	0	40	1	1	3	1	0	1.00	15	.290	.322	.450
2006	Bal	AL	144	501	138	29	2	23	(17	6)	240	66	91	82	43	2	79	11	0	5	1	0	1.00	13	.275	.343	.479
8 ML YEARS			949	3148	831	166	5	113	(57	56)	1346	388	475	413	265	9	450	48	30	32	6	1	.86	97	.264	.328	.428

Roberto Hernandez

Pitches: R **Bats:** R **Pos:** RP-68   **Ht:** 6'4" **Wt:** 245 **Born:** 11/11/1964 **Age:** 42

Year	Team	Lg	G	GS	CG	GF	IP	BFP	H	R	ER	HR	SH	SF	HB	TBB	IBB	SO	WP	Bk	W	L	Pct	ShO	Sv-Op	Hld	ERC	ERA
1991	CWS	AL	9	3	0	1	15.0	69	18	15	13	1	0	0	0	7	0	6	1	0	1	0	1.000	0	0-0	0	5.19	7.80
1992	CWS	AL	43	0	0	27	71.0	277	45	15	13	4	0	3	4	20	1	68	2	0	7	3	.700	0	12-16	6	1.74	1.65
1993	CWS	AL	70	0	0	67	78.2	314	66	21	20	6	2	2	0	20	1	71	2	0	3	4	.429	0	38-44	0	2.54	2.29
1994	CWS	AL	45	0	0	43	47.2	206	44	29	26	5	0	1	1	19	1	50	1	0	4	4	.500	0	14-20	0	3.66	4.91
1995	CWS	AL	60	0	0	57	59.2	272	63	30	26	9	4	0	3	28	4	84	1	0	3	7	.300	0	32-42	0	5.04	3.92
1996	CWS	AL	72	0	0	61	84.2	355	65	21	18	2	2	2	0	38	5	85	6	0	6	5	.545	0	38-46	0	2.40	1.91
1997	2 Tms		74	0	0	50	80.2	340	67	24	22	7	2	1	1	38	5	82	3	0	10	3	.769	0	31-39	9	3.30	2.45
1998	TB	AL	67	0	0	58	71.1	310	55	33	32	5	4	0	5	41	4	55	1	0	2	6	.250	0	26-35	0	3.43	4.04
1999	TB	AL	72	0	0	66	73.1	321	68	27	25	1	2	3	4	33	1	69	3	0	2	3	.400	0	43-47	0	3.40	3.07
2000	TB	AL	68	0	0	58	73.1	315	76	33	26	9	7	3	3	23	1	61	2	1	4	7	.364	0	32-40	1	4.24	3.19
2001	KC	AL	63	0	0	55	67.2	287	69	34	31	7	1	0	1	26	3	46	6	0	5	6	.455	0	28-34	0	4.23	4.12
2002	KC	AL	53	0	0	42	52.0	227	62	29	25	6	4	1	3	12	2	39	3	0	1	3	.250	0	26-33	0	4.79	4.33
2003	Atl	NL	66	0	0	12	60.0	282	61	36	29	10	4	0	3	43	7	45	0	0	5	3	.625	0	0-4	19	5.95	4.35
2004	Phi	NL	63	0	0	11	56.2	260	66	39	30	9	7	1	1	29	3	44	3	0	3	5	.375	0	0-4	9	5.94	4.76
2005	NYM	NL	67	0	0	20	69.2	291	57	20	20	5	9	2	2	28	4	61	4	0	8	6	.571	0	4-10	18	2.93	2.58
2006	2 Tms		68	0	0	19	63.2	285	61	32	22	5	5	1	1	32	8	48	5	0	0	3	.000	0	2-5	12	3.84	3.11
97	CWS	AL	46	0	0	43	48.0	203	38	15	13	5	1	1	1	24	4	47	2	0	5	1	.833	0	27-31	0	3.30	2.44
97	SF	NL	28	0	0	7	32.2	137	29	9	9	2	1	0	0	14	1	35	1	0	5	2	.714	0	4-8	9	3.29	2.48
06	Pit	NL	46	0	0	14	43.0	202	46	24	14	3	2	1	1	24	7	33	3	0	0	3	.000	0	2-5	9	4.50	2.93
06	NYM	NL	22	0	0	5	20.2	83	15	8	8	2	3	0	0	8	1	15	2	0	0	0	-	0	0-0	3	2.52	3.48
16 ML YEARS			960	3	0	647	1025.0	4411	943	438	378	91	53	20	32	437	50	914	43	1	64	68	.485	0	326-419	74	3.68	3.32

Runelvys Hernandez

Pitches: R **Bats:** R **Pos:** SP-21   **Ht:** 6'1" **Wt:** 250 **Born:** 4/27/1978 **Age:** 29

Year	Team	Lg	G	GS	CG	GF	IP	BFP	H	R	ER	HR	SH	SF	HB	TBB	IBB	SO	WP	Bk	W	L	Pct	ShO	Sv-Op	Hld	ERC	ERA
2006	Omha*	AAA	12	11	1	0	64.2	278	65	35	33	6	0	1	1	27	1	43	3	0	5	6	.455	0	0- -	-	4.21	4.59
2002	KC	AL	12	12	0	0	74.1	316	79	36	36	8	1	3	1	22	0	45	2	0	4	4	.500	0	0-0	-	4.16	4.36
2003	KC	AL	16	16	0	0	91.2	397	87	51	47	9	1	4	6	37	0	48	2	1	7	5	.583	0	0-0	-	4.05	4.61
2005	KC	AL	29	29	0	0	159.2	706	172	101	98	18	1	6	7	70	0	88	4	0	8	14	.364	0	0-0	-	4.99	5.52
2006	KC	AL	21	21	1	0	109.2	508	145	87	79	22	3	8	6	48	0	50	3	2	6	10	.375	1	0-0	-	7.35	6.48
4 ML YEARS			78	78	1	0	435.1	1927	483	275	260	57	6	21	20	177	0	231	11	3	25	33	.431	1	0-0	-	5.20	5.38

Aaron Hill

Bats: R **Throws:** R **Pos:** 2B-112; SS-63; DH-1   **Ht:** 5'11" **Wt:** 195 **Born:** 3/21/1982 **Age:** 25

Year	Team	Lg	G	AB	H	2B	3B	HR	(Hm	Rd)	TB	R	RBI	RC	TBB	IBB	SO	HBP	SH	SF	SB	CS	SB%	GDP	Avg	OBP	Slg
2003	Auburn	A-	33	122	44	4	0	4	(-	-)	60	22	34	28	16	2	20	6	0	4	1	1	.50	2	.361	.446	.492
2003	Dnedin	A+	32	119	34	7	0	0	(-	-)	41	26	11	15	11	0	10	1	0	3	1	0	1.00	3	.286	.343	.345
2004	NHam	AA	135	480	134	26	2	11	(-	-)	197	78	80	79	63	2	61	11	0	11	3	2	.60	12	.279	.368	.410
2005	Syrcse	AAA	38	156	47	11	0	5	(-	-)	73	22	18	25	4	0	17	6	0	2	2	0	1.00	5	.301	.339	.468
2005	Tor	AL	105	361	99	25	3	3	(3	0)	139	49	40	50	34	0	41	5	3	4	2	1	.67	5	.274	.342	.385
2006	Tor	AL	155	546	159	28	3	6	(4	2)	211	70	50	68	42	5	66	9	4	5	5	2	.71	15	.291	.349	.386
2 ML YEARS			260	907	258	53	6	9	(7	2)	350	119	90	118	76	5	107	14	7	9	7	3	.70	20	.284	.346	.386

Rich Hill

Pitches: L **Bats:** L **Pos:** SP-16; RP-1   **Ht:** 6'5" **Wt:** 205 **Born:** 3/11/1980 **Age:** 27

Year	Team	Lg	G	GS	CG	GF	IP	BFP	H	R	ER	HR	SH	SF	HB	TBB	IBB	SO	WP	Bk	W	L	Pct	ShO	Sv-Op	Hld	ERC	ERA
2002	Boise	A-	6	5	0	1	14.0	71	15	19	13	0	0	0	1	14	0	12	4	0	0	2	.000	0	0- -	-	6.27	8.36
2003	Lansng	A	15	4	0	2	29.1	138	14	12	9	0	3	1	3	36	0	50	9	0	0	1	1.000	0	0- -	-	3.86	2.76
2003	Boise	A-	14	14	0	0	68.1	293	57	40	33	5	0	0	9	32	0	99	5	1	1	6	.143	0	0- -	-	3.79	4.35
2004	Dytona	A+	28	19	0	0	109.1	488	88	64	49	9	4	2	19	72	0	136	12	5	7	6	.538	0	0- -	-	4.61	4.03
2005	WTenn	AA	10	10	0	0	57.2	236	42	22	21	9	1	0	2	21	0	90	0	0	4	3	.571	0	0- -	-	2.96	3.28
2005	Peoria	A	1	1	0	0	8.0	29	5	2	1	0	0	0	0	0	0	12	0	0	1	0	1.000	0	0- -	-	0.81	1.13
2005	Iowa	AAA	11	10	1	0	65.0	262	53	28	26	11	0	1	4	14	0	92	2	0	6	1	.857	0	0- -	-	3.05	3.60
2006	Iowa	AAA	15	15	0	0	100.0	380	62	22	20	3	5	2	5	21	0	135	2	0	7	1	.875	0	0- -	-	1.42	1.80
2005	ChC	NL	10	4	0	1	23.2	115	25	24	24	3	1	0	1	17	1	21	0	0	0	2	.000	0	0-0	-	5.81	9.13
2006	ChC	NL	17	16	2	1	99.1	417	83	51	46	16	8	3	2	39	1	90	3	0	6	7	.462	1	0-0	-	3.59	4.17
2 ML YEARS			27	20	2	2	123.0	532	108	75	70	19	9	3	3	56	2	111	3	0	6	9	.400	0	0-0	-	4.01	5.12

Shawn Hill

Pitches: R Bats: R Pos: SP-6   Ht: 6'2" Wt: 185 Born: 4/28/1981 Age: 26

			HOW MUCH HE PITCHED					WHAT HE GAVE UP										THE RESULTS					
Year	Team	Lg	G	GS	CG	GF	IP	BFP	H	R	ER	HR	SH	SF	HB	TBB	IBB	SO	WP	Bk	W	L	Pct	ShO	Sv-Op Hld	ERC	ERA
2000	Expos	R	7	7	0	0	24.1	117	25	17	13	0	0	1	6	10	0	20	3	1	1	3	.250	0	0- - -	4.22	4.81
2001	Vrmnt	A-	7	7	0	0	35.2	144	22	12	9	0	1	0	7	8	0	23	2	0	2	2	.500	0	0- - -	1.60	2.27
2002	Clinton	A	25	25	0	0	146.2	149	149	75	56	7	3	6	11	35	2	99	11	1	12	7	.632	0	0- - -	16.16	3.44
2003	BrvdCt	A+	22	21	2	0	126.2	525	118	47	36	3	6	7	10	26	0	66	1	0	9	4	.692	1	0- - -	2.76	2.56
2003	Hrsbrg	AA	4	4	0	0	20.1	95	23	12	8	0	0	1	1	11	1	12	0	0	3	1	.750	0	0- - -	4.63	3.54
2004	Hrsbrg	AA	17	17	2	0	87.2	357	90	39	33	4	4	0	5	20	0	53	2	1	5	7	.417	0	0- - -	3.55	3.39
2006	Hrsbrg	AA	10	10	0	0	50.1	201	46	20	15	2	0	0	2	5	0	32	1	0	3	3	.500	0	0- - -	2.28	2.68
2006	NewOr	AAA	1	1	0	0	5.0	25	6	2	2	0	0	0	2	2	0	2	0	0	0	0	-	0	0- - -	5.88	3.60
2004	Mon	NL	3	3	0	0	9.0	51	17	16	16	1	0	2	1	7	0	10	0	0	1	2	.333	0	0-0 0	12.14	16.00
2006	Was	NL	6	6	0	0	36.2	163	43	20	19	2	2	1	3	12	2	16	1	0	1	3	.250	0	0-0 0	4.70	4.66
	2 ML YEARS		9	9	0	0	45.2	214	60	36	35	3	2	3	4	19	2	26	1	0	2	5	.286	0	0-0 0	6.02	6.90

Shea Hillenbrand

Bats: R Throws: R Pos: 1B-77; DH-44; 3B-25; PH-6   Ht: 6'1" Wt: 210 Born: 7/27/1975 Age: 31

			BATTING																		BASERUNNING				AVERAGES		
Year	Team	Lg	G	AB	H	2B	3B	HR	(Hm	Rd)	TB	R	RBI	RC	TBB	IBB	SO	HBP	SH	SF	SB	CS	SB%	GDP	Avg	OBP	Slg
2001	Bos	AL	139	468	123	20	2	12	(5	7)	183	52	49	49	13	3	61	7	1	4	3	4	.43	12	.263	.291	.391
2002	Bos	AL	156	634	186	43	4	18	(5	13)	291	94	83	88	25	4	95	12	0	5	4	2	.67	18	.293	.330	.459
2003	2 Tms		134	515	144	35	1	20	(11	9)	241	60	97	66	24	4	70	6	4	9	1	0	1.00	22	.280	.314	.468
2004	Ari	NL	148	562	174	36	3	15	(9	6)	261	68	80	82	24	2	49	12	0	6	2	0	1.00	18	.310	.348	.464
2005	Tor	AL	152	594	173	36	2	18	(13	5)	267	91	82	88	26	2	79	22	0	3	5	1	.83	21	.291	.343	.449
2006	2 Tms		141	530	147	27	1	21	(9	12)	239	73	68	61	21	2	80	9	0	6	1	2	.33	22	.277	.313	.451
03	Bos	AL	49	185	56	17	0	3	(0	3)	82	20	38	27	7	1	26	4	0	4	1	0	1.00	9	.303	.335	.443
03	Ari	NL	85	330	88	18	1	17	(11	6)	159	40	59	39	17	3	44	2	0	5	0	0	-	13	.267	.302	.482
06	Tor	AL	81	296	89	15	1	12	(5	7)	142	40	39	38	14	2	40	6	0	3	1	2	.33	15	.301	.342	.480
06	SF	NL	60	234	58	12	0	9	(4	5)	97	33	29	23	7	0	40	3	0	3	0	0	-	7	.248	.275	.415
	6 ML YEARS		870	3303	947	197	13	104	(52	52)	1482	438	459	434	133	17	434	68	1	33	16	9	.64	113	.287	.325	.449

Eric Hinske

Bats: L Throws: R Pos: RF-40; DH-21; PH-20; 1B-16; 3B-10; LF-6; PR-6   Ht: 6'2" Wt: 235 Born: 8/5/1977 Age: 29

			BATTING																		BASERUNNING				AVERAGES		
Year	Team	Lg	G	AB	H	2B	3B	HR	(Hm	Rd)	TB	R	RBI	RC	TBB	IBB	SO	HBP	SH	SF	SB	CS	SB%	GDP	Avg	OBP	Slg
2002	Tor	AL	151	566	158	38	2	24	(15	9)	272	99	84	103	77	5	138	2	0	5	13	1	.93	12	.279	.365	.481
2003	Tor	AL	124	449	109	45	3	12	(4	8)	196	74	63	66	59	1	104	1	0	5	12	2	.86	11	.243	.329	.437
2004	Tor	AL	155	570	140	23	3	15	(6	9)	214	66	69	60	54	2	109	4	0	6	12	8	.60	14	.246	.312	.375
2005	Tor	AL	147	477	125	31	2	15	(7	8)	205	79	68	71	46	4	121	8	0	6	8	4	.67	8	.262	.333	.430
2006	2 Tms		109	277	75	17	2	13	(7	6)	135	43	34	39	35	2	79	0	0	0	2	2	.50	8	.271	.353	.487
06	Tor	AL	78	197	52	9	2	12	(6	6)	101	35	29	29	27	2	49	0	0	0	1	1	.50	6	.264	.353	.513
06	Bos	AL	31	80	23	8	0	1	(1	0)	34	8	5	10	8	0	30	0	0	0	1	1	.50	2	.288	.352	.425
	5 ML YEARS		686	2339	607	154	12	79	(39	40)	1022	361	318	339	271	14	551	15	0	22	47	17	.73	53	.260	.337	.437

Jason Hirsh

Pitches: R Bats: R Pos: SP-9   Ht: 6'8" Wt: 250 Born: 2/20/1982 Age: 25

			HOW MUCH HE PITCHED					WHAT HE GAVE UP										THE RESULTS					
Year	Team	Lg	G	GS	CG	GF	IP	BFP	H	R	ER	HR	SH	SF	HB	TBB	IBB	SO	WP	Bk	W	L	Pct	ShO	Sv-Op Hld	ERC	ERA
2003	TriCity	A	10	8	0	0	32.1	126	22	10	7	0	0	1	2	7	0	33	1	0	3	1	.750	0	0- - -	1.52	1.95
2004	Salem	A	26	23	0	1	130.1	557	128	66	58	8	9	7	9	57	0	96	5	0	11	7	.611	0	0- - -	4.24	4.01
2005	CpChr	AA	29	29	1	0	172.1	696	137	63	55	12	4	7	12	42	0	165	7	1	13	8	.619	1	0- - -	2.49	2.87
2006	RdRck	AAA	23	23	1	0	137.1	527	94	37	32	5	3	1	8	51	0	118	2	0	13	2	.867	1	0- - -	2.30	2.10
2006	Hou	NL	9	9	0	0	44.2	206	48	32	30	10	0	1	3	22	2	29	4	0	3	4	.429	0	0-0 0	6.11	6.04

James Hoey

Pitches: R Bats: R Pos: RP-12   Ht: 6'6" Wt: 200 Born: 12/30/1982 Age: 24

			HOW MUCH HE PITCHED					WHAT HE GAVE UP										THE RESULTS					
Year	Team	Lg	G	GS	CG	GF	IP	BFP	H	R	ER	HR	SH	SF	HB	TBB	IBB	SO	WP	Bk	W	L	Pct	ShO	Sv-Op Hld	ERC	ERA
2003	Bluefld	R+	11	8	0	0	42.0	177	33	19	13	3	0	0	6	19	0	20	2	0	2	3	.400	0	0- - -	3.53	2.79
2004	Abrdn	A-	2	2	0	0	6.2	34	12	8	7	1	0	1	0	1	0	6	0	0	0	1	.000	0	0- - -	7.91	9.45
2005	Abrdn	A-	9	0	0	2	15.0	66	11	10	8	1	2	1	3	10	0	15	1	0	1	1	.500	0	0- - -	4.24	4.80
2006	Dlmrva	A	27	0	0	23	28.1	113	17	8	8	2	5	1	0	10	2	46	1	0	2	1	.667	0	18- - -	1.61	2.54
2006	Frdrck	A+	14	0	0	14	14.0	63	13	3	1	0	0	0	1	5	0	16	1	0	0	0	-	0	11- - -	2.91	0.64
2006	Bowie	AA	8	0	0	6	9.0	41	9	5	4	1	0	1	0	3	0	11	0	0	0	0	-	0	4- - -	3.59	4.00
2006	Bal	AL	12	0	0	2	9.2	49	14	11	11	1	1	2	2	5	0	6	0	1	0	1	.000	0	0-1 4	8.22	10.24

Trevor Hoffman

Pitches: R Bats: R Pos: RP-65   Ht: 6'0" Wt: 215 Born: 10/13/1967 Age: 39

			HOW MUCH HE PITCHED					WHAT HE GAVE UP										THE RESULTS					
Year	Team	Lg	G	GS	CG	GF	IP	BFP	H	R	ER	HR	SH	SF	HB	TBB	IBB	SO	WP	Bk	W	L	Pct	ShO	Sv-Op Hld	ERC	ERA
1993	2 Tms	NL	67	0	0	26	90.0	391	80	43	39	10	4	5	1	39	13	79	5	0	4	6	.400	0	5-8 15	3.40	3.90
1994	SD	NL	47	0	0	41	56.0	225	39	16	16	4	1	2	0	20	6	68	3	0	4	4	.500	0	20-23 1	2.02	2.57
1995	SD	NL	55	0	0	51	53.1	218	48	25	23	10	0	0	0	14	3	52	1	0	7	4	.636	0	31-38 0	3.48	3.88
1996	SD	NL	70	0	0	62	88.0	348	50	23	22	6	2	2	2	31	5	111	2	0	9	5	.643	0	42-49 0	1.58	2.25
1997	SD	NL	70	0	0	59	81.1	322	59	25	24	9	2	1	0	24	4	111	7	0	6	4	.600	0	37-44 0	2.27	2.66

Year	Team	Lg	G	GS	CG	GF	IP	BFP	H	R	ER	HR	SH	SF	HB	TBB	IBB	SO	WP	Bk	W	L	Pct	ShO	Sv-Op	Hld	ERC	ERA
1998	SD	NL	66	0	0	54	73.0	274	41	12	12	2	3	0	1	21	2	86	8	0	4	2	.667	0	53-54	0	1.32	1.48
1999	SD	NL	64	0	0	54	67.1	263	48	23	16	5	1	3	0	15	2	73	4	0	2	3	.400	0	40-43	0	1.78	2.14
2000	SD	NL	70	0	0	59	72.1	291	61	29	24	7	3	5	0	11	4	85	4	0	4	7	.364	0	43-50	0	2.18	2.99
2001	SD	NL	62	0	0	55	60.1	248	48	25	23	10	2	2	1	21	2	63	3	0	3	4	.429	0	43-46	0	3.20	3.43
2002	SD	NL	61	0	0	52	59.1	245	52	20	18	2	2	2	1	18	2	69	3	0	2	5	.286	0	38-41	0	2.63	2.73
2003	SD	NL	9	0	0	7	9.0	36	7	2	2	1	0	0	0	3	0	11	0	0	0	0	-	0	0-0	0	2.76	2.00
2004	SD	NL	55	0	0	51	54.2	209	42	14	14	5	2	0	0	8	1	53	2	0	3	3	.500	0	41-45	0	1.92	2.30
2005	SD	NL	60	0	0	54	57.2	240	52	23	19	3	2	3	1	12	1	54	1	0	1	6	.143	0	43-46	0	2.49	2.97
2006	SD	NL	65	0	0	50	63.0	248	48	16	15	6	0	0	1	13	1	50	2	0	0	2	.000	0	46-51	0	2.14	2.14
93	Fla	NL	28	0	0	13	35.2	152	24	13	13	5	2	1	0	19	7	26	3	0	2	2	.500	0	2-3	8	2.71	3.28
93	SD	NL	39	0	0	13	54.1	239	56	30	26	5	2	4	1	20	6	53	2	0	2	4	.333	0	3-5	7	3.88	4.31
14 ML YEARS			821	0	0	682	885.1	3558	675	296	267	80	24	25	8	250	46	965	45	0	49	55	.471	0	482-538	16	2.29	2.71

Todd Hollandsworth

Bats: L Throws: L Pos: PH-35; RF-34; LF-31; CF-2; PR-2; DH-1 **Ht: 6'2" Wt: 225 Born: 4/20/1973 Age: 34**

Year	Team	Lg	G	AB	H	2B	3B	HR	(Hm	Rd)	TB	R	RBI	RC	TBB	IBB	SO	HBP	SH	SF	SB	CS	SB%	GDP	Avg	OBP	Slg
1995	LAD	NL	41	103	24	2	0	5	(3	2)	41	16	13	13	10	2	29	1	0	1	2	1	.67	1	.233	.304	.398
1996	LAD	NL	149	478	139	26	4	12	(2	10)	209	64	59	76	41	1	93	2	3	2	21	6	.78	2	.291	.348	.437
1997	LAD	NL	106	296	73	20	2	4	(1	3)	109	39	31	28	17	2	60	0	2	2	5	5	.50	8	.247	.286	.368
1998	LAD	NL	55	175	47	6	4	3	(1	2)	70	23	20	21	9	0	42	1	2	0	4	3	.57	2	.269	.308	.400
1999	LAD	NL	92	261	74	12	2	9	(5	4)	117	39	32	41	24	1	61	1	0	1	5	2	.71	2	.284	.345	.448
2000	2 Tms	NL	137	428	115	20	0	19	(13	6)	192	81	47	63	41	3	99	1	0	1	18	7	.72	6	.269	.333	.449
2001	Col	NL	33	117	43	15	1	6	(3	3)	78	21	19	30	8	2	20	0	0	0	5	0	1.00	1	.368	.408	.667
2002	2 Tms	NL	134	430	122	27	1	16	(11	5)	199	55	67	67	40	4	98	1	3	3	8	8	.50	8	.284	.344	.463
2003	Fla	NL	93	228	58	23	3	3	(1	2)	96	32	20	26	22	4	55	0	2	2	2	3	.40	2	.254	.317	.421
2004	ChC	NL	57	148	47	6	2	8	(3	5)	81	28	22	27	17	3	26	1	1	0	1	1	.50	2	.318	.392	.547
2005	2 Tms	NL	131	303	74	17	2	6	(4	4)	113	26	36	28	23	1	66	1	1	2	4	5	.44	5	.244	.298	.373
2006	2 Tms	NL	90	224	55	18	1	7	(3	4)	96	27	35	30	10	1	52	0	0	2	0	2	.00	3	.246	.275	.429
00	LAD	NL	81	261	61	12	0	8	(6	2)	97	42	24	31	30	2	61	1	0	1	11	4	.73	4	.234	.314	.372
00	Col	NL	56	167	54	8	0	11	(7	4)	95	39	23	32	11	1	38	0	0	0	7	3	.70	4	.323	.365	.569
02	Col	NL	95	298	88	21	1	11	(9	2)	144	39	48	45	26	4	71	1	1	2	7	8	.47	8	.295	.352	.483
02	Tex	AL	39	132	34	6	0	5	(2	3)	55	16	19	22	14	0	27	0	2	1	1	0	1.00	0	.258	.327	.417
05	ChC	NL	107	268	68	17	2	5	(2	3)	104	23	35	27	18	1	53	1	1	2	4	4	.50	2	.254	.301	.388
05	Atl	NL	24	35	6	0	0	1	(0	1)	9	3	1	1	5	0	13	0	0	0	0	1	.00	1	.171	.275	.257
06	Cle	AL	56	156	37	12	1	6	(3	3)	69	21	27	21	4	1	33	0	0	2	0	1	.00	2	.237	.253	.442
06	Cin	NL	34	68	18	6	0	1	(0	1)	27	6	8	9	6	0	19	0	0	0	0	1	.00	1	.265	.324	.397
12 ML YEARS			1118	3191	871	192	22	98	(48	50)	1401	451	401	450	262	24	701	9	14	16	75	43	.64	44	.273	.328	.439

Matt Holliday

Bats: R Throws: R Pos: LF-153; DH-1; PH-1 **Ht: 6'4" Wt: 235 Born: 1/15/1980 Age: 27**

Year	Team	Lg	G	AB	H	2B	3B	HR	(Hm	Rd)	TB	R	RBI	RC	TBB	IBB	SO	HBP	SH	SF	SB	CS	SB%	GDP	Avg	OBP	Slg
2004	Col	NL	121	400	116	31	3	14	(10	4)	195	65	57	61	31	0	86	6	1	1	3	3	.50	10	.290	.349	.488
2005	Col	NL	125	479	147	24	7	19	(12	7)	242	68	87	88	36	1	79	7	0	4	14	3	.82	11	.307	.361	.505
2006	Col	NL	155	602	196	45	5	34	(22	12)	353	119	114	112	47	3	110	15	0	3	10	5	.67	22	.326	.387	.586
3 ML YEARS			401	1481	459	100	15	67	(44	23)	790	252	258	261	114	4	275	28	1	8	27	11	.71	43	.310	.368	.533

Damon Hollins

Bats: R Throws: L Pos: RF-78; CF-33; LF-18; PH-8; PR-6; DH-2 **Ht: 5'11" Wt: 180 Born: 6/12/1974 Age: 33**

Year	Team	Lg	G	AB	H	2B	3B	HR	(Hm	Rd)	TB	R	RBI	RC	TBB	IBB	SO	HBP	SH	SF	SB	CS	SB%	GDP	Avg	OBP	Slg
1998	2 Tms	NL	8	15	3	0	0	0	(0	0)	3	1	2	0	0	0	3	0	0	0	0	1	.00	0	.200	.200	.200
2004	Atl	NL	7	22	8	2	0	0	(0	0)	10	3	5	2	0	0	4	0	1	0	0	0	-	0	.364	.364	.455
2005	TB	AL	120	342	85	17	1	13	(5	8)	143	44	46	41	23	0	63	1	1	2	8	1	.89	8	.249	.296	.418
2006	TB	AL	121	333	76	20	0	15	(7	8)	141	37	33	32	19	1	64	0	2	1	3	3	.50	4	.228	.269	.423
98	Atl	NL	3	6	1	0	0	0	(0	0)	1	0	0	0	0	0	1	0	0	0	0	0	-	0	.167	.167	.167
98	LAD	NL	5	9	2	0	0	0	(0	0)	2	1	2	0	0	0	2	0	0	0	0	1	.00	0	.222	.222	.222
4 ML YEARS			256	712	172	39	1	28	(12	16)	297	85	86	75	42	1	134	1	4	3	11	5	.69	12	.242	.284	.417

Mike Holtz

Pitches: L Bats: L Pos: RP-3 **Ht: 5'9" Wt: 180 Born: 10/10/1972 Age: 34**

Year	Team	Lg	G	GS	CG	GF	IP	BFP	H	R	ER	HR	SH	SF	HB	TBB	IBB	SO	WP	Bk	W	L	Pct	ShO	Sv-Op	Hld	ERC	ERA
2006	Pwtckt*	AAA	14	0	0	7	18.2	74	10	4	4	2	0	0	2	7	0	29	1	0	0	0	-	0	3- -	-	2.05	1.93
1996	LAA	AL	30	0	0	8	29.1	127	21	11	8	1	1	1	3	19	2	31	1	0	3	3	.500	0	0-0	5	3.29	2.45
1997	LAA	AL	66	0	0	11	43.1	187	38	21	16	7	1	2	2	15	4	40	1	0	3	4	.429	0	2-8	14	3.52	3.32
1998	LAA	AL	53	0	0	9	30.1	137	38	16	16	0	1	2	1	15	1	29	4	0	2	2	.500	0	1-2	13	5.39	4.75
1999	LAA	AL	28	0	0	9	22.1	106	26	20	20	3	1	0	2	15	1	17	3	0	2	3	.400	0	0-0	1	6.85	8.06
2000	LAA	AL	61	0	0	6	41.0	176	37	26	23	4	4	3	2	18	2	40	1	0	3	3	.500	0	0-0	10	3.79	5.05
2001	LAA	AL	63	0	0	11	37.0	167	40	24	20	5	3	1	2	15	4	38	5	0	1	2	.333	0	0-1	15	4.77	4.86
2002	2 Tms	AL	49	0	0	12	35.0	178	42	25	21	5	4	1	2	30	3	26	3	0	2	2	.500	0	0-4	5	7.50	5.40
2006	Bos	AL	3	0	0	1	1.2	13	3	3	3	0	1	0	1	4	0	2	0	0	0	0	-	0	0-0	1	19.88	16.20
02	Oak	AL	16	0	0	7	14.0	72	24	11	10	3	0	0	1	9	0	7	0	0	0	1	-	0	0-1	1	10.72	6.43
02	SD	NL	33	0	0	5	21.0	101	18	14	11	2	0	3	1	21	3	19	3	0	2	2	.500	0	0-3	4	5.49	4.71
8 ML YEARS			353	0	0	67	240.0	1091	245	146	127	25	12	12	15	131	17	223	18	0	16	19	.457	0	3-15	64	4.91	4.76

Kevin Hooper

Bats: R **Throws:** R **Pos:** PH-4; 2B-3; 3B-2; PR-2; DH-1   **Ht:** 5'10" **Wt:** 160 **Born:** 12/7/1976 **Age:** 30

Year	Team	Lg	G	AB	H	2B	3B	HR	(Hm	Rd)	TB	R	RBI	RC	TBB	IBB	SO	HBP	SH	SF	SB	CS	SB%	GDP	Avg	OBP	Slg
1999	Utica	A-	73	289	81	18	6	0	(-	-)	111	52	22	45	39	0	35	4	2	3	14	8	.64	2	.280	.370	.384
2000	Kane	A	123	457	114	25	6	3	(-	-)	160	73	38	67	73	2	83	6	9	1	17	2	.89	6	.249	.359	.350
2001	Kane	A	17	65	19	2	0	0	(-	-)	21	11	4	9	11	0	13	0	0	1	3	1	.75	0	.292	.390	.323
2001	Portlnd	AA	117	468	144	19	6	2	(-	-)	181	70	39	77	59	4	78	7	7	2	24	12	.67	8	.308	.392	.387
2002	Calgry	AAA	117	452	130	21	3	2	(-	-)	163	70	38	58	34	0	51	4	6	2	17	10	.63	7	.288	.341	.361
2003	Albq	AAA	130	493	131	9	4	1	(-	-)	151	77	54	55	35	3	62	10	9	4	25	9	.74	5	.266	.325	.306
2004	Albq	AAA	39	155	43	3	2	0	(-	-)	50	21	17	17	14	0	24	0	5	1	6	5	.55	1	.277	.335	.323
2004	Clmbs	AAA	29	87	17	1	0	0	(-	-)	18	6	4	3	5	0	11	0	3	0	3	1	.75	1	.195	.239	.207
2004	Omha	AAA	27	92	15	2	0	0	(-	-)	17	12	4	3	9	0	14	1	3	0	2	2	.50	1	.163	.245	.185
2005	Toledo	AAA	85	313	75	13	2	1	(-	-)	95	41	27	31	22	1	37	2	10	3	16	4	.80	4	.240	.291	.304
2006	Toledo	AAA	121	504	139	15	4	1	(-	-)	165	66	29	53	23	0	71	3	15	4	24	12	.67	4	.276	.309	.327
2005	Det	AL	6	5	1	0	0	0	(0	0)	1	0	0	1	0	0	1	0	2	0	0	0	-	0	.200	.200	.200
2006	Det	AL	8	3	0	0	0	0	(0	0)	0	1	0	0	1	0	1	0	1	0	0	0	-	0	.000	.250	.000
	2 ML YEARS		14	8	1	0	0	0	(0	0)	1	1	0	1	1	0	2	0	3	0	0	0	-	0	.125	.222	.125

Paul Hoover

Bats: R **Throws:** R **Pos:** C-3; PH-1   **Ht:** 6'1" **Wt:** 200 **Born:** 4/14/1976 **Age:** 31

Year	Team	Lg	G	AB	H	2B	3B	HR	(Hm	Rd)	TB	R	RBI	RC	TBB	IBB	SO	HBP	SH	SF	SB	CS	SB%	GDP	Avg	OBP	Slg
2006	Albq*	AAA	92	302	84	21	1	6	(-	-)	125	38	41	46	33	1	71	3	1	4	3	2	.60	8	.278	.351	.414
2001	TB	AL	3	4	1	0	0	0	(0	0)	1	1	0	0	0	0	1	0	0	0	0	0	-	0	.250	.250	.250
2002	TB	AL	5	17	3	0	0	0	(0	0)	3	1	2	1	0	0	5	0	0	0	0	0	-	0	.176	.176	.176
2006	Fla	NL	4	5	2	0	0	0	(0	0)	2	0	1	1	0	0	0	0	0	0	0	0	-	0	.400	.400	.400
	3 ML YEARS		12	26	6	0	0	0	(0	0)	6	2	3	2	0	0	6	0	0	0	0	0	-	0	.231	.231	.231

Norris Hopper

Bats: R **Throws:** R **Pos:** RF-13; PH-8; CF-2; PR-2; LF-1   **Ht:** 5'10" **Wt:** 200 **Born:** 3/24/1979 **Age:** 28

Year	Team	Lg	G	AB	H	2B	3B	HR	(Hm	Rd)	TB	R	RBI	RC	TBB	IBB	SO	HBP	SH	SF	SB	CS	SB%	GDP	Avg	OBP	Slg
1998	Royals	R	40	133	41	2	1	0	(-	-)	45	19	11	19	13	0	12	0	2	2	11	2	.85	1	.308	.365	.338
1999	Royals	R	46	179	46	3	2	0	(-	-)	53	33	13	21	19	0	20	0	2	4	22	5	.81	2	.257	.322	.296
1999	CtnWV	A	5	22	11	0	2	0	(-	-)	15	3	2	6	0	0	1	0	0	0	1	0	1.00	0	.500	.500	.682
2000	CtnWV	A	116	454	127	20	6	0	(-	-)	159	70	29	63	51	0	55	4	4	1	24	10	.71	10	.280	.357	.350
2001	Wilmg	A+	110	389	96	6	2	1	(-	-)	109	38	38	38	32	2	60	5	11	0	16	4	.80	15	.247	.312	.280
2002	Wilmg	A+	125	514	140	12	3	1	(-	-)	161	78	46	57	31	1	55	8	22	3	22	9	.71	15	.272	.323	.313
2003	Wichta	AA	115	424	127	14	2	0	(-	-)	145	56	40	54	27	1	58	4	16	1	24	10	.71	10	.300	.346	.342
2004	Wichta	AA	98	363	101	5	3	0	(-	-)	112	48	40	43	33	0	44	5	10	2	17	7	.71	10	.278	.345	.309
2005	Chatt	AA	116	451	140	15	4	1	(-	-)	166	70	37	63	27	2	38	4	4	1	25	7	.78	12	.310	.354	.368
2006	Chatt	AA	13	46	13	2	1	0	(-	-)	17	7	10	7	6	1	3	0	0	0	3	0	1.00	6	.283	.365	.370
2006	Lsvlle	AAA	98	383	133	11	3	0	(-	-)	150	47	26	60	20	0	25	0	5	2	25	7	.78	7	.347	.378	.392
2006	Cin	NL	21	39	14	1	0	1	(1	0)	18	6	5	8	6	0	4	0	1	1	2	2	.50	1	.359	.435	.462

J.R. House

Bats: R **Throws:** R **Pos:** C-3; 1B-2   **Ht:** 5'10" **Wt:** 200 **Born:** 11/11/1979 **Age:** 27

Year	Team	Lg	G	AB	H	2B	3B	HR	(Hm	Rd)	TB	R	RBI	RC	TBB	IBB	SO	HBP	SH	SF	SB	CS	SB%	GDP	Avg	OBP	Slg
2006	CpChr*	AA	97	379	123	23	2	10	(-	-)	180	58	69	69	32	5	44	4	0	8	2	2	.50	9	.325	.376	.475
2006	RdRck*	AAA	31	114	47	15	0	5	(-	-)	77	25	36	31	9	1	15	1	0	4	0	0	-	4	.412	.445	.675
2003	Pit	NL	1	1	1	0	0	0	(0	0)	1	0	0	1	0	0	0	0	0	0	0	0	-	0	1.000	1.000	1.000
2004	Pit	NL	5	9	1	1	0	0	(0	0)	2	1	0	0	0	0	2	0	0	0	0	0	-	1	.111	.111	.222
2006	Hou	NL	4	9	0	0	0	0	(0	0)	0	0	0	0	0	0	2	0	0	0	0	0	-	1	.000	.000	.000
	3 ML YEARS		10	19	2	1	0	0	(0	0)	3	1	0	1	0	0	4	0	0	0	0	0	-	2	.105	.105	.158

Ryan Howard

Bats: L **Throws:** L **Pos:** 1B-159; PH-2   **Ht:** 6'4" **Wt:** 250 **Born:** 11/19/1979 **Age:** 27

Year	Team	Lg	G	AB	H	2B	3B	HR	(Hm	Rd)	TB	R	RBI	RC	TBB	IBB	SO	HBP	SH	SF	SB	CS	SB%	GDP	Avg	OBP	Slg
2004	Phi	NL	19	39	11	5	0	2	(1	1)	22	5	5	7	2	0	13	1	0	0	0	0	-	2	.282	.333	.564
2005	Phi	NL	88	312	90	17	2	22	(11	11)	177	52	63	50	33	8	100	1	0	2	0	1	.00	6	.288	.356	.567
2006	Phi	NL	159	581	182	25	1	58	(29	29)	383	104	149	138	108	37	181	9	0	6	0	0	-	7	.313	.425	.659
	3 ML YEARS		266	932	283	47	3	82	(41	41)	582	161	217	195	143	45	294	11	0	8	0	1	.00	15	.304	.399	.624

J.P. Howell

Pitches: L **Bats:** L **Pos:** SP-8   **Ht:** 6'0" **Wt:** 175 **Born:** 4/25/1983 **Age:** 24

			HOW MUCH HE PITCHED						WHAT HE GAVE UP											THE RESULTS						
Year	Team	Lg	G	GS	CG	GF	IP	BFP	H	R	ER	HR	SH	SF	HB	TBB	IBB	SO	WP	Bk	W	L	Pct	ShO	Sv-Op Hld	ERC	ERA
2004	Idaho	R+	6	4	0	0	26.0	101	16	9	8	1	0	0	2	12	0	38	9	0	3	1	.750	0	0- -	2.33	2.77
2005	Hi Dsrt	A+	8	8	0	0	46.0	195	33	16	10	2	0	0	3	24	0	48	5	1	3	1	.750	0	0- -	2.86	1.96
2005	Wichta	AA	3	3	0	0	18.0	71	12	5	5	2	0	0	1	5	0	23	2	0	2	0	1.000	0	0- -	2.18	2.50
2005	Omha	AAA	7	7	0	0	37.2	172	40	19	17	1	2	0	1	19	0	29	3	0	3	1	.750	0	0- -	4.30	4.06
2006	Omha	AAA	8	8	0	0	36.0	180	39	19	19	3	4	0	0	14	0	33	3	0	3	2	.600	0	0- -	3.76	4.75
2006	Drham	AAA	10	10	0	0	55.0	226	53	18	16	2	2	1	4	15	0	49	0	0	5	3	.625	0	0- -	3.34	2.62

Year	Team	Lg	G	GS	CG	GF	IP	BFP	H	R	ER	HR	SH	SF	HB	TBB	IBB	SO	WP	Bk	W	L	Pct	ShO	Sv-Op	Hld	ERC	ERA
2005	KC	AL	15	15	0	0	72.2	328	73	55	50	9	3	3	6	39	0	54	7	0	3	5	.375	0	0-0	0	5.18	6.19
2006	TB	AL	8	8	0	0	42.1	187	52	25	24	4	0	2	3	14	0	33	1	0	1	3	.250	0	0-0	0	5.51	5.10
2 ML YEARS			23	23	0	0	115.0	515	125	80	74	13	3	5	9	53	0	87	8	0	4	8	.333	0	0-0	0	5.30	5.79

Bob Howry

Pitches: R Bats: L Pos: RP-84   **Ht: 6'5" Wt: 220 Born: 8/4/1973 Age: 33**

			HOW MUCH HE PITCHED						WHAT HE GAVE UP												THE RESULTS							
Year	Team	Lg	G	GS	CG	GF	IP	BFP	H	R	ER	HR	SH	SF	HB	TBB	IBB	SO	WP	Bk	W	L	Pct	ShO	Sv-Op	Hld	ERC	ERA
1998	CWS	AL	44	0	0	15	54.1	217	37	20	19	7	2	3	2	19	2	51	2	0	0	3	.000	0	9-11	19	2.50	3.15
1999	CWS	AL	69	0	0	54	67.2	298	58	34	27	8	3	1	3	38	3	80	3	1	5	3	.625	0	28-34	1	4.11	3.59
2000	CWS	AL	65	0	0	29	71.0	289	54	26	25	6	2	4	4	29	2	60	2	0	2	4	.333	0	7-12	14	2.96	3.17
2001	CWS	AL	69	0	0	23	78.2	346	85	41	41	11	4	3	4	30	9	64	6	0	4	5	.444	0	5-11	21	4.78	4.69
2002	2 Tms	AL	67	0	0	26	68.2	292	67	37	32	9	4	6	5	21	4	45	2	0	3	5	.375	0	0-1	15	4.00	4.19
2003	Bos	AL	4	0	0	3	4.1	27	11	6	6	1	0	1	0	3	1	4	0	0	0	0	-	0	0-1	0	16.51	12.46
2004	Cle	AL	37	0	0	6	42.2	178	37	14	13	5	1	1	2	12	0	39	0	0	4	2	.667	0	0-2	8	3.15	2.74
2005	Cle	AL	79	0	0	24	73.0	277	49	23	20	4	3	2	0	16	1	48	0	0	7	4	.636	0	3-5	29	1.58	2.47
2006	ChC	NL	84	0	0	26	76.2	314	70	28	27	8	5	3	3	17	4	71	1	0	4	5	.444	0	5-9	21	3.03	3.17
02 CWS		AL	47	0	0	17	50.2	209	45	22	22	7	1	4	3	17	2	31	1	0	2	2	.500	0	0-0	10	3.72	3.91
02 Bos		AL	20	0	0	9	18.0	83	22	15	10	2	3	2	2	4	2	14	1	0	1	3	.250	0	0-1	5	4.79	5.00
9 ML YEARS			518	0	0	206	537.0	2238	468	229	210	59	24	24	23	185	26	462	16	1	29	31	.483	0	57-86	128	3.33	3.52

Jon Huber

Pitches: R Bats: R Pos: RP-16   **Ht: 6'2" Wt: 195 Born: 7/7/1981 Age: 25**

			HOW MUCH HE PITCHED						WHAT HE GAVE UP												THE RESULTS							
Year	Team	Lg	G	GS	CG	GF	IP	BFP	H	R	ER	HR	SH	SF	HB	TBB	IBB	SO	WP	Bk	W	L	Pct	ShO	Sv-Op	Hld	ERC	ERA
2000	Padres	R	14	10	0	0	45.0	223	54	49	33	1	3	3	1	32	0	39	6	0	1	4	.200	0	0--	-	5.78	6.60
2001	Idaho	R+	15	15	0	0	73.0	344	77	61	49	7	4	4	7	48	0	75	10	0	5	9	.357	0	0--	-	5.77	6.04
2002	FtWyn	A	28	26	2	0	146.0	168	168	99	83	7	6	1	7	59	0	86	11	3	8	12	.400	0	0--	-	20.19	5.12
2003	FtWyn	A	7	7	0	0	38.1	157	31	18	16	2	1	4	4	11	0	34	0	0	1	1	.500	0	0--	-	2.74	3.76
2003	Lk Els	A+	12	11	0	0	57.1	265	69	41	33	2	1	2	1	31	1	43	2	1	3	5	.375	0	0--	-	5.38	5.18
2004	Lk Els	A+	20	20	0	0	107.0	466	107	53	44	9	5	4	4	44	0	100	7	0	8	6	.571	0	0--	-	4.15	3.70
2004	InldEm	A+	7	5	0	1	32.1	157	42	24	22	4	0	1	3	14	0	38	0	0	4	1	.800	0	0--	-	6.37	6.12
2005	SnAnt	AA	26	26	1	0	148.0	640	159	87	78	11	4	3	6	49	1	112	7	2	7	8	.467	1	0--	-	4.21	4.74
2006	SnAnt	AA	21	0	0	21	24.0	105	30	13	13	0	2	3	1	4	1	19	0	0	0	3	.000	0	11--	-	3.91	4.88
2006	Tacom	AAA	29	0	0	24	41.1	179	46	14	12	3	0	2	3	10	0	38	4	0	3	1	.750	0	12--	-	4.18	2.61
2006	Sea	AL	16	0	0	4	16.2	66	10	3	2	0	2	0	0	6	1	11	0	0	2	1	.667	0	0-0	6	1.37	1.08

Justin Huber

Bats: R Throws: R Pos: DH-3; PH-2   **Ht: 6'2" Wt: 195 Born: 7/1/1982 Age: 24**

			BATTING																BASERUNNING				AVERAGES		
Year	Team	Lg	G	AB	H	2B	3B	HR	(Hm Rd)	TB	R	RBI	RC	TBB	IBB	SO	HBP	SH	SF	SB	CS	SB%	GDP	Avg	OBP	Slg
2001	StLuci	A+	2	6	0	0	0	0	(- -)	0	0	0	0	0	0	4	0	0	0	0	0	-	0	.000	.000	.000
2001	Kngspt	R+	47	159	50	11	1	7	(- -)	84	24	31	36	17	0	42	13	1	4	4	2	.67	4	.314	.415	.528
2001	Bklyn	A-	3	9	0	0	0	0	(- -)	0	0	0	0	0	0	4	0	0	0	0	0	-	1	.000	.000	.000
2002	Clmbia	A-	95	330	96	22	2	11	(- -)	155	49	78	67	45	10	81	23	0	4	1	2	.33	5	.291	.408	.470
2002	StLuci	A+	28	100	27	2	1	3	(- -)	40	15	15	16	11	0	18	6	0	2	0	0	-	3	.270	.370	.400
2003	StLuci	A+	50	183	52	15	0	9	(- -)	94	26	36	35	17	0	30	9	0	2	1	1	.50	9	.284	.370	.514
2003	Bnghtn	AA	55	193	51	13	0	6	(- -)	82	16	36	29	19	0	54	7	3	1	0	2	.00	4	.264	.350	.425
2004	StLuci	A+	14	49	12	2	0	2	(- -)	20	10	8	7	5	0	8	1	0	0	1	0	1.00	0	.245	.327	.408
2004	Bnghtn	AA	70	236	64	16	1	11	(- -)	115	44	33	50	46	4	57	12	0	1	2	2	.50	5	.271	.414	.487
2004	Norfolk	AAA	5	16	5	2	0	0	(- -)	7	3	3	3	3	0	3	0	0	0	0	0	-	0	.313	.421	.438
2005	Wichta	AA	88	335	115	22	3	16	(- -)	191	68	74	82	51	2	70	5	0	5	7	3	.70	11	.343	.432	.570
2005	Omha	AAA	32	113	31	6	1	7	(- -)	60	19	23	23	16	1	33	2	0	0	3	0	1.00	3	.274	.374	.531
2006	Omha	AAA	100	352	98	22	2	15	(- -)	169	47	44	61	40	2	94	4	1	1	2	2	.50	11	.278	.358	.480
2005	KC	AL	25	78	17	3	0	0	(0 0)	20	6	6	4	5	0	20	1	0	1	0	0	-	1	.218	.271	.256
2006	KC	AL	5	10	2	1	0	0	(0 0)	3	1	1	1	1	0	4	0	0	0	1	0	1.00	0	.200	.273	.300
2 ML YEARS			30	88	19	4	0	0	(0 0)	23	7	7	5	6	0	24	1	0	1	1	0	1.00	1	.216	.271	.261

Ken Huckaby

Bats: R Throws: R Pos: C-8; PR-1   **Ht: 6'1" Wt: 200 Born: 1/27/1971 Age: 36**

			BATTING																BASERUNNING				AVERAGES		
Year	Team	Lg	G	AB	H	2B	3B	HR	(Hm Rd)	TB	R	RBI	RC	TBB	IBB	SO	HBP	SH	SF	SB	CS	SB%	GDP	Avg	OBP	Slg
2006	Pwtckt*	AAA	88	288	63	10	0	2	(- -)	79	18	23	18	9	0	72	0	4	4	4	0	1.00	9	.219	.239	.274
2001	Ari	NL	1	1	0	0	0	0	(0 0)	0	0	0	0	0	0	1	0	0	0	0	0	-	0	.000	.000	.000
2002	Tor	AL	88	273	67	6	1	3	(1 2)	84	29	22	19	9	1	44	0	1	0	0	0	-	10	.245	.270	.308
2003	Tor	AL	5	11	2	1	0	0	(0 0)	3	1	2	1	0	0	2	0	0	0	0	0	-	1	.182	.182	.273
2004	2 Tms	AL	24	50	7	3	0	0	(0 0)	10	4	0	0	5	0	12	0	0	0	0	0	-	1	.140	.218	.200
2005	Tor	AL	35	87	18	4	0	0	(0 0)	22	8	6	3	5	0	19	0	4	0	0	0	-	4	.207	.250	.253
2006	Bos	AL	8	5	1	0	0	0	(0 0)	1	0	1	0	0	0	0	0	0	0	0	0	-	1	.200	.200	.200
04 Tex		AL	16	38	5	2	0	0	(0 0)	7	3	0	0	5	0	12	0	0	0	0	0	-	1	.132	.233	.184
04 Bal		AL	8	12	2	1	0	0	(0 0)	3	1	0	0	0	0	0	0	0	0	0	0	-	0	.167	.167	.250
6 ML YEARS			161	427	95	14	1	3	(1 2)	120	42	31	23	19	1	78	0	5	0	0	0	-	16	.222	.256	.281

Luke Hudson

Pitches: R Bats: R Pos: SP-15; RP-11   Ht: 6'3" Wt: 195 Born: 5/2/1977 Age: 30

			HOW MUCH HE PITCHED						WHAT HE GAVE UP													THE RESULTS							
Year	Team	Lg	G	GS	CG	GF	IP	BFP	H	R	ER	HR	SH	SF	HB	TBB	IBB	SO	WP	Bk	W	L	Pct	ShO	Sv-Op	Hld	ERC	ERA
2006	Omha*	AAA	13	2	0	6	35.1	145	30	14	11	0	1	2	2	7	1	21	1	0	2	0	1.000	0	1--	-	2.04	2.80
2002	Cin	NL	3	0	0	0	6.0	28	5	5	3	1	0	0	0	6	0	7	2	0	0	0	-	0	0-0	1	6.15	4.50
2004	Cin	NL	9	9	0	0	48.1	204	36	16	13	3	2	2	2	25	1	38	5	0	4	2	.667	0	0-0	0	3.01	2.42
2005	Cin	NL	19	16	0	1	84.2	380	83	62	60	14	5	4	11	50	2	53	5	0	6	9	.400	0	0-0	0	5.88	6.38
2006	KC	AL	26	15	0	1	102.0	440	109	62	58	7	0	3	4	38	1	64	6	0	7	6	.538	0	0-1	1	4.34	5.12
4 ML YEARS			57	40	0	2	241.0	1052	233	145	134	25	7	9	17	119	4	162	18	0	17	17	.500	0	0-1	2	4.62	5.00

Orlando Hudson

Bats: B Throws: R Pos: 2B-157; PH-4   Ht: 6'0" Wt: 185 Born: 12/12/1977 Age: 29

			BATTING																		BASERUNNING				AVERAGES		
Year	Team	Lg	G	AB	H	2B	3B	HR	(Hm	Rd)	TB	R	RBI	RC	TBB	IBB	SO	HBP	SH	SF	SB	CS	SB%	GDP	Avg	OBP	Slg
2002	Tor	AL	54	192	53	10	5	4	(2	2)	85	20	23	30	11	0	27	2	0	2	0	1	.00	6	.276	.319	.443
2003	Tor	AL	142	474	127	21	6	9	(5	4)	187	54	57	64	39	1	87	5	0	3	5	4	.56	13	.268	.328	.395
2004	Tor	AL	135	489	132	32	7	12	(5	7)	214	73	58	71	51	0	98	4	3	4	7	3	.70	12	.270	.341	.438
2005	Tor	AL	131	461	125	25	5	10	(4	6)	190	62	63	59	30	1	65	3	0	7	7	1	.88	10	.271	.315	.412
2006	Ari	NL	157	579	166	34	9	15	(7	8)	263	87	67	89	61	5	78	2	4	4	9	6	.60	17	.287	.354	.454
5 ML YEARS			619	2195	603	122	32	50	(23	27)	939	296	268	313	192	7	355	16	7	20	28	15	.65	58	.275	.335	.428

Tim Hudson

Pitches: R Bats: R Pos: SP-35   Ht: 6'1" Wt: 170 Born: 7/14/1975 Age: 31

			HOW MUCH HE PITCHED						WHAT HE GAVE UP													THE RESULTS							
Year	Team	Lg	G	GS	CG	GF	IP	BFP	H	R	ER	HR	SH	SF	HB	TBB	IBB	SO	WP	Bk	W	L	Pct	ShO	Sv-Op	Hld	ERC	ERA
1999	Oak	AL	21	21	1	0	136.1	580	121	56	49	8	1	2	4	62	2	132	6	0	11	2	.846	0	0-0	0	3.50	3.23
2000	Oak	AL	32	32	2	0	202.1	847	169	100	93	24	5	7	7	82	5	169	7	0	20	6	.769	2	0-0	0	3.43	4.14
2001	Oak	AL	35	35	3	0	235.0	980	216	100	88	20	12	8	6	71	5	181	9	1	18	9	.667	0	0-0	0	3.22	3.37
2002	Oak	AL	34	34	4	0	238.1	983	237	87	79	19	6	5	8	62	9	152	7	1	15	9	.625	2	0-0	0	3.51	2.98
2003	Oak	AL	34	34	3	0	240.0	967	197	84	72	15	11	2	10	61	9	162	6	0	16	7	.696	2	0-0	0	2.47	2.70
2004	Oak	AL	27	27	3	0	188.2	793	194	82	74	8	7	4	12	44	3	103	4	1	12	6	.667	2	0-0	0	3.44	3.53
2005	Atl	NL	29	29	2	0	192.0	817	194	79	75	20	9	1	9	65	5	115	4	0	14	9	.609	0	0-0	0	4.12	3.52
2006	Atl	NL	35	35	2	0	218.1	959	235	129	118	25	8	3	9	79	10	141	7	0	13	12	.520	1	0-0	0	4.54	4.86
8 ML YEARS			247	247	20	0	1651.0	6926	1563	717	648	139	59	32	65	526	48	1155	50	3	119	60	.665	9	0-0	0	3.49	3.53

Aubrey Huff

Bats: L Throws: R Pos: 3B-90; RF-37; PH-9; 1B-3; DH-3   Ht: 6'4" Wt: 230 Born: 12/20/1976 Age: 30

			BATTING																		BASERUNNING				AVERAGES		
Year	Team	Lg	G	AB	H	2B	3B	HR	(Hm	Rd)	TB	R	RBI	RC	TBB	IBB	SO	HBP	SH	SF	SB	CS	SB%	GDP	Avg	OBP	Slg
2006	Visalia*	A+	2	8	2	1	0	0	(-	-)	3	2	1	1	1	0	2	0	0	1	0	0	-	6	.250	.333	.375
2000	TB	AL	39	122	35	7	0	4	(3	1)	54	12	14	15	5	1	18	1	0	1	0	0	-	6	.287	.318	.443
2001	TB	AL	111	411	102	25	1	8	(5	3)	153	42	45	37	23	2	72	0	0	0	1	3	.25	18	.248	.288	.372
2002	TB	AL	113	454	142	25	0	23	(17	6)	236	67	59	66	37	7	55	1	0	2	4	1	.80	17	.313	.364	.520
2003	TB	AL	162	636	198	47	3	34	(15	19)	353	91	107	112	53	17	80	8	0	9	2	3	.40	19	.311	.367	.555
2004	TB	AL	157	600	178	27	2	29	(16	13)	296	92	104	96	56	6	74	6	0	5	5	1	.83	10	.297	.360	.493
2005	TB	AL	154	575	150	26	2	21	(9	13)	246	70	92	77	49	13	88	5	0	7	8	7	.53	12	.261	.321	.418
2006	2 Tms		131	454	121	25	2	21	(9	12)	213	57	66	55	50	6	64	7	0	6	0	0	-	11	.267	.344	.469
06	TB	AL	63	230	65	15	1	8	(4	4)	106	26	28	28	24	3	25	0	0	2	0	0	-	4	.283	.348	.461
06	Hou	NL	68	224	56	10	1	13	(5	8)	107	31	38	27	26	3	39	7	0	4	0	0	-	7	.250	.341	.478
7 ML YEARS			867	3252	926	182	10	141	(74	67)	1551	431	487	458	273	52	451	28	0	30	20	15	.57	93	.285	.342	.477

Travis Hughes

Pitches: R Bats: R Pos: RP-8   Ht: 6'5" Wt: 235 Born: 5/25/1978 Age: 29

			HOW MUCH HE PITCHED						WHAT HE GAVE UP													THE RESULTS							
Year	Team	Lg	G	GS	CG	GF	IP	BFP	H	R	ER	HR	SH	SF	HB	TBB	IBB	SO	WP	Bk	W	L	Pct	ShO	Sv-Op	Hld	ERC	ERA
2006	NewOr*	AAA	51	0	0	24	73.2	309	50	30	19	3	4	1	3	41	4	87	4	0	2	6	.250	0	4--	-	2.62	2.32
2004	Tex	AL	2	0	0	1	1.1	10	4	2	2	0	0	0	0	2	0	4	0	0	0	0	-	0	0-0	0	22.07	13.50
2005	Was	NL	14	0	0	0	13.0	66	18	8	8	4	1	0	1	8	1	8	0	0	1	1	.500	0	0-1	0	9.47	5.54
2006	Was	NL	8	0	0	2	11.1	54	13	8	8	2	2	1	3	6	1	4	1	0	0	0	-	0	0-0	0	7.17	6.35
3 ML YEARS			24	0	0	3	25.2	128	35	18	18	6	3	1	4	16	2	16	1	0	1	1	.500	0	0-1	0	9.06	6.31

Philip Humber

Pitches: R Bats: R Pos: RP-2   Ht: 6'4" Wt: 210 Born: 12/21/1982 Age: 24

			HOW MUCH HE PITCHED						WHAT HE GAVE UP													THE RESULTS							
Year	Team	Lg	G	GS	CG	GF	IP	BFP	H	R	ER	HR	SH	SF	HB	TBB	IBB	SO	WP	Bk	W	L	Pct	ShO	Sv-Op	Hld	ERC	ERA
2005	StLuci	A+	14	14	0	0	70.1	303	74	41	39	6	1	3	8	18	0	65	2	0	2	6	.250	0	0--	-	4.16	4.99
2005	Bnghtn	AA	1	1	0	0	4.0	18	4	3	3	0	0	0	0	2	0	2	0	0	0	1	1.000	0	0--	-	3.63	6.75
2006	Mets	R	1	1	0	0	4.0	20	7	3	3	0	0	0	1	1	0	7	1	0	0	0	-	0	0--	-	8.49	6.75
2006	StLuci	A+	7	7	0	0	38.0	151	24	12	10	4	2	3	3	9	0	36	1	0	3	1	.750	0	0--	-	1.88	2.37
2006	Bnghtn	AA	6	6	0	0	34.1	141	25	12	11	4	1	1	2	10	0	36	0	0	2	2	.500	0	0--	-	2.50	2.88
2006	NYM	NL	2	0	0	1	2.0	7	0	0	0	0	0	0	0	1	0	2	0	0	0	0	-	0	0-0	0	0.27	0.00

Torii Hunter

Bats: R Throws: R Pos: CF-143; DH-4   Ht: 6'2" Wt: 215 Born: 7/18/1975 Age: 31

Year	Team	Lg	G	AB	H	2B	3B	HR	(Hm	Rd)	TB	R	RBI	RC	TBB	IBB	SO	HBP	SH	SF	SB	CS	SB%	GDP	Avg	OBP	Slg
1997	Min	AL	1	0	0	0	0	0	(0	0)	0	0	0	0	0	0	0	0	0	0	0	0	-	0	-	-	-
1998	Min	AL	6	17	4	1	0	0	(0	0)	5	0	2	1	2	0	6	0	0	0	0	1	.00	1	.235	.316	.294
1999	Min	AL	135	384	98	17	2	9	(2	7)	146	52	35	44	26	1	72	6	1	5	10	6	.63	9	.255	.309	.380
2000	Min	AL	99	336	94	14	7	5	(4	1)	137	44	44	39	18	2	68	2	0	2	4	3	.57	13	.280	.318	.408
2001	Min	AL	148	564	147	32	5	27	(13	14)	270	82	92	79	29	0	125	8	1	1	9	6	.60	12	.261	.306	.479
2002	Min	AL	148	561	162	37	4	29	(13	16)	294	89	94	85	35	3	118	5	0	3	23	8	.74	17	.289	.334	.524
2003	Min	AL	154	581	145	31	4	26	(12	14)	262	83	102	76	50	7	106	5	0	6	6	7	.46	15	.250	.312	.451
2004	Min	AL	138	520	141	37	0	23	(9	14)	247	79	81	69	40	4	101	7	0	2	21	7	.75	23	.271	.330	.475
2005	Min	AL	98	372	100	24	1	14	(6	8)	168	63	56	53	34	3	65	6	0	4	23	7	.77	8	.269	.337	.452
2006	Min	AL	147	557	155	21	2	31	(15	16)	273	86	98	81	45	2	108	5	0	4	12	6	.67	19	.278	.336	.490
10 ML YEARS			1074	3892	1046	214	25	164	(74	90)	1802	578	604	527	279	22	769	44	2	27	108	51	.68	117	.269	.323	.463

Adam Hyzdu

Bats: R Throws: R Pos: RF-1; PR-1   Ht: 6'2" Wt: 220 Born: 12/6/1971 Age: 35

Year	Team	Lg	G	AB	H	2B	3B	HR	(Hm	Rd)	TB	R	RBI	RC	TBB	IBB	SO	HBP	SH	SF	SB	CS	SB%	GDP	Avg	OBP	Slg
2006	Okla*	AAA	128	439	119	25	4	19	(-	-)	209	64	80	82	74	1	102	1	0	10	7	4	.64	8	.271	.370	.476
2000	Pit	NL	12	18	7	2	0	1	(0	1)	12	2	4	4	0	0	4	0	0	0	0	0	-	0	.389	.389	.667
2001	Pit	NL	51	72	15	1	0	5	(0	5)	31	7	9	8	4	0	18	1	0	0	0	1	.00	1	.208	.260	.431
2002	Pit	NL	59	155	36	6	0	11	(6	5)	75	24	34	27	21	0	44	1	0	2	0	0	-	1	.232	.324	.484
2003	Pit	NL	51	63	13	5	0	1	(0	1)	21	16	8	6	10	0	21	1	0	1	0	0	-	2	.206	.320	.333
2004	Bos	AL	17	10	3	2	0	1	(0	1)	8	3	2	2	1	0	2	0	0	0	0	0	-	0	.300	.364	.800
2005	2 Tms		29	36	7	2	0	0	(0	0)	9	2	4	1	5	0	7	0	1	1	1	0	1.00	1	.194	.286	.250
2006	Tex	AL	2	4	1	0	0	0	(0	0)	1	0	0	0	0	0	2	0	0	0	0	0	-	0	.250	.250	.250
05	SD	NL	17	20	3	1	0	0	(0	0)	4	1	4	1	3	0	4	0	1	1	1	0	1.00	1	.150	.250	.200
05	Bos	AL	12	16	4	1	0	0	(0	0)	5	1	0	0	2	0	3	0	0	0	0	0	-	0	.250	.333	.313
7 ML YEARS			221	358	82	18	0	19	(6	13)	157	54	61	48	41	0	98	3	1	4	1	1	.50	5	.229	.310	.439

Chris Iannetta

Bats: R Throws: R Pos: C-21   Ht: 5'11" Wt: 195 Born: 4/8/1983 Age: 24

Year	Team	Lg	G	AB	H	2B	3B	HR	(Hm	Rd)	TB	R	RBI	RC	TBB	IBB	SO	HBP	SH	SF	SB	CS	SB%	GDP	Avg	OBP	Slg
2004	Ashvlle	A	36	121	38	5	1	5	(-	-)	60	23	17	28	27	0	29	4	0	0	0	1	.00	3	.314	.454	.496
2005	Mdest	A+	74	261	72	17	3	11	(-	-)	128	51	58	50	45	1	61	2	0	4	1	2	.33	9	.276	.381	.490
2005	Tulsa	AA	19	60	14	3	1	2	(-	-)	25	7	11	8	8	0	15	1	0	1	0	0	-	5	.233	.329	.417
2006	Tulsa	AA	44	156	50	10	2	11	(-	-)	97	38	26	39	24	0	26	3	1	1	1	0	1.00	3	.321	.418	.622
2006	ColSpr	AAA	47	151	53	11	2	3	(-	-)	77	23	22	35	24	0	29	3	1	1	0	0	-	9	.351	.447	.510
2006	Col	NL	21	77	20	4	0	2	(0	2)	30	12	10	9	13	2	17	1	1	1	0	1	.00	1	.260	.370	.390

Raul Ibanez

Bats: L Throws: R Pos: LF-158; DH-1   Ht: 6'2" Wt: 220 Born: 6/2/1972 Age: 35

Year	Team	Lg	G	AB	H	2B	3B	HR	(Hm	Rd)	TB	R	RBI	RC	TBB	IBB	SO	HBP	SH	SF	SB	CS	SB%	GDP	Avg	OBP	Slg
1996	Sea	AL	4	5	0	0	0	0	(0	0)	0	0	0	0	0	0	1	1	0	0	0	0	-	0	.000	.167	.000
1997	Sea	AL	11	26	4	0	1	1	(1	0)	9	3	4	1	0	0	6	0	0	0	0	0	-	0	.154	.154	.346
1998	Sea	AL	37	98	25	7	1	2	(1	1)	40	12	12	10	5	0	22	0	0	0	0	0	-	4	.255	.291	.408
1999	Sea	AL	87	209	54	7	0	9	(3	6)	88	23	27	28	17	1	32	0	0	1	5	1	.83	4	.258	.313	.421
2000	Sea	AL	92	140	32	8	0	2	(2	0)	46	21	15	15	14	1	25	1	0	1	2	0	1.00	1	.229	.301	.329
2001	KC	AL	104	279	78	11	5	13	(5	8)	138	44	54	46	32	2	51	0	0	1	0	2	.00	6	.280	.353	.495
2002	KC	AL	137	497	146	37	6	24	(14	10)	267	70	103	89	40	5	76	2	1	4	5	3	.63	11	.294	.346	.537
2003	KC	AL	157	608	179	33	5	18	(8	10)	276	95	90	91	49	5	81	3	1	10	8	4	.67	10	.294	.345	.454
2004	Sea	AL	123	481	146	31	1	16	(9	7)	227	67	62	67	36	5	72	3	0	4	1	2	.33	10	.304	.353	.472
2005	Sea	AL	162	614	172	32	2	20	(9	11)	268	92	89	99	71	6	99	2	0	3	9	4	.69	12	.280	.355	.436
2006	Sea	AL	159	626	181	33	5	33	(17	16)	323	103	123	114	65	15	115	1	0	7	2	4	.33	13	.289	.353	.516
11 ML YEARS			1073	3583	1017	199	26	138	(69	69)	1682	530	579	560	329	40	580	13	2	31	32	20	.62	71	.284	.344	.469

Kei Igawa

Pitches: L Bats: L Pos: P   Ht: 6'1" Wt: 211 Born: 7/13/1979 Age: 27

	HOW MUCH HE PITCHED						WHAT HE GAVE UP										THE RESULTS							
Year	Team	Lg	G	GS	CG	GF	IP	BFP	H	R	ER	HR	SH	SF	HB	TBB	IBB	SO	WP	Bk	W	L	Pct	ShO	Sv-Op	Hld	ERC	ERA
1999	Hnshn	Jap	7	3	0	1	15.1	80	23	11	11	1	-	-	1	13	-	14	0	0	1	1	.500	0	0- -	-	9.21	6.46
2000	Hnshn	Jap	9	5	0	1	39.1	172	36	16	16	5	-	-	0	19	-	37	7	0	1	3	.250	0	0- -	-	4.05	3.66
2001	Hnshn	Jap	29	28	3	0	192.0	829	174	76	57	11	-	-	3	89	-	171	6	0	9	13	.409	2	0- -	-	3.54	2.67
2002	Hnshn	Jap	31	29	8	2	209.2	830	163	63	58	15	-	-	7	53	-	206	8	0	14	9	.609	4	0- -	-	2.35	2.49
2003	Hnshn	Jap	29	29	8	0	206.0	839	184	72	64	15	0	0	3	58	3	179	5	0	20	5	.800	2	0- -	-	2.94	2.80
2004	Hnshn	Jap	29	29	6	0	200.1	840	190	95	83	29	11	2	6	54	0	228	5	0	14	11	.560	3	0- -	-	3.67	3.73
2005	Hnshn	Jap	27	27	2	0	172.1	778	199	91	74	23	-	-	1	60	-	145	4	0	13	9	.591	1	0- -	-	4.90	3.86
2006	Hnshn	Jap	28	28	7	0	200.0	820	174	77	69	17	-	-	6	46	-	184	4	0	13	9	.591	2	0- -	-	2.60	3.11

Tadahito Iguchi

Bats: R Throws: R Pos: 2B-136; PR-2; DH-1   Ht: 5'10" Wt: 200 Born: 12/4/1974 Age: 32

								BATTING													BASERUNNING				AVERAGES		
Year	Team	Lg	G	AB	H	2B	3B	HR	(Hm	Rd)	TB	R	RBI	RC	TBB	IBB	SO	HBP	SH	SF	SB	CS	SB%	GDP	Avg	OBP	Slg
1997	Fk Dai	Jap	76	217	44	6	3	8	(-	-)	80	31	23	25	24	-	67	8	2	1	3	3	.50	4	.203	.304	.369
1998	Fk Dai	Jap	135	421	93	18	4	21	(-	-)	182	58	66	53	28	-	121	8	15	4	12	6	.67	6	.221	.280	.432
1999	Fk Dai	Jap	116	370	83	15	1	14	(-	-)	142	38	47	47	38	-	113	9	4	3	14	7	.67	13	.224	.310	.384
2000	Fk Dai	Jap	54	162	40	9	2	7	(-	-)	74	21	23	24	15	-	29	2	5	1	5	2	.71	5	.247	.317	.457
2001	Fk Dai	Jap	140	552	144	26	1	30	(-	-)	262	104	97	99	61	-	117	12	9	2	44	9	.83	14	.261	.346	.475
2002	Fk Dai	Jap	114	428	111	14	1	18	(-	-)	181	64	53	60	27	-	84	10	5	2	21	7	.75	8	.259	.317	.423
2003	Fk Dai	Jap	135	515	175	37	1	27	(-	-)	295	112	109	134	81	-	81	14	1	6	42	6	.88	10	.340	.438	.573
2004	Fk Dai	Jap	124	510	170	34	2	24	(-	-)	280	96	89	110	47	-	90	9	0	8	18	5	.78	14	.333	.394	.549
2005	CWS	AL	135	511	142	25	6	15	(7	8)	224	74	71	74	47	0	114	6	11	6	15	5	.75	16	.278	.342	.438
2006	CWS	AL	138	555	156	24	0	18	(12	6)	234	97	67	87	59	0	110	3	8	2	11	5	.69	7	.281	.352	.422
	2 ML YEARS		273	1066	298	49	6	33	(19	14)	458	171	138	161	106	0	224	9	19	8	26	10	.72	23	.280	.347	.430

Omar Infante

Bats: R Throws: R Pos: 2B-37; DH-16; SS-10; 3B-7; PH-7; PR-6; CF-4   Ht: 6'0" Wt: 180 Born: 12/26/1981 Age: 25

								BATTING													BASERUNNING				AVERAGES		
Year	Team	Lg	G	AB	H	2B	3B	HR	(Hm	Rd)	TB	R	RBI	RC	TBB	IBB	SO	HBP	SH	SF	SB	CS	SB%	GDP	Avg	OBP	Slg
2002	Det	AL	18	72	24	3	0	1	(0	1)	30	4	6	12	3	0	10	0	0	0	0	1	.00	0	.333	.360	.417
2003	Det	AL	69	221	49	6	1	0	(0	0)	57	24	8	16	18	0	37	0	3	2	6	3	.67	1	.222	.278	.258
2004	Det	AL	142	503	133	27	9	16	(7	9)	226	69	55	69	40	3	112	1	7	5	13	7	.65	4	.264	.317	.449
2005	Det	AL	121	406	90	28	2	9	(3	6)	149	36	43	38	16	0	73	2	8	2	8	0	1.00	5	.222	.254	.367
2006	Det	AL	78	224	62	11	4	4	(0	4)	93	35	25	26	14	0	45	3	2	2	3	2	.60	5	.277	.325	.415
	5 ML YEARS		428	1426	358	75	16	30	(10	20)	555	168	137	161	91	3	277	6	20	11	30	13	.70	15	.251	.297	.389

Brandon Inge

Bats: R Throws: R Pos: 3B-159   Ht: 5'11" Wt: 190 Born: 5/19/1977 Age: 30

								BATTING													BASERUNNING				AVERAGES		
Year	Team	Lg	G	AB	H	2B	3B	HR	(Hm	Rd)	TB	R	RBI	RC	TBB	IBB	SO	HBP	SH	SF	SB	CS	SB%	GDP	Avg	OBP	Slg
2001	Det	AL	79	189	34	11	0	0	(0	0)	45	13	15	6	9	0	41	0	2	2	1	4	.20	2	.180	.215	.238
2002	Det	AL	95	321	65	15	3	7	(3	4)	107	27	24	24	24	0	101	4	1	1	1	3	.25	7	.202	.266	.333
2003	Det	AL	104	330	67	15	3	8	(4	4)	112	32	30	23	24	0	79	5	4	3	4	4	.50	9	.203	.265	.339
2004	Det	AL	131	408	117	15	7	13	(9	4)	185	43	64	63	32	0	72	4	8	6	5	4	.56	4	.287	.340	.453
2005	Det	AL	160	616	161	31	9	16	(10	6)	258	75	72	82	63	1	140	3	6	6	7	6	.54	14	.261	.330	.419
2006	Det	AL	159	542	137	29	2	27	(12	15)	251	83	83	79	43	2	128	7	4	5	7	4	.64	12	.253	.313	.463
	6 ML YEARS		728	2406	581	116	24	71	(38	33)	958	273	288	277	195	3	561	23	25	23	25	25	.50	48	.241	.302	.398

Joe Inglett

Bats: L Throws: R Pos: 2B-53; PH-7; LF-6; CF-3; SS-1; DH-1; PR-1   Ht: 5'10" Wt: 180 Born: 6/29/1978 Age: 29

								BATTING													BASERUNNING				AVERAGES		
Year	Team	Lg	G	AB	H	2B	3B	HR	(Hm	Rd)	TB	R	RBI	RC	TBB	IBB	SO	HBP	SH	SF	SB	CS	SB%	GDP	Avg	OBP	Slg
2000	MhVlly	A-	56	202	58	12	4	2	(-	-)	84	37	37	34	31	1	30	5	0	0	4	5	.44	1	.287	.395	.416
2001	Clmbs	A	62	237	71	9	2	2	(-	-)	90	34	33	34	24	0	22	0	0	2	5	3	.63	7	.300	.361	.380
2002	Clmbs	A	60	235	73	18	5	2	(-	-)	107	44	46	43	28	1	25	4	1	3	5	3	.63	5	.311	.389	.455
2002	Kinston	A	66	238	67	12	0	0	(-	-)	79	24	29	32	29	3	38	2	0	2	5	2	.71	3	.282	.362	.332
2003	Kinston	A	28	85	28	10	1	0	(-	-)	40	21	15	20	20	0	14	1	0	2	1	0	1.00	2	.329	.454	.471
2003	Akron	AA	71	276	78	16	1	4	(-	-)	108	41	25	44	37	0	36	6	1	2	1	2	.33	8	.283	.377	.391
2004	Akron	AA	66	266	85	19	7	1	(-	-)	121	49	20	47	31	2	28	1	2	0	3	5	.38	1	.320	.393	.455
2005	Buffalo	AAA	95	327	108	20	9	2	(-	-)	152	57	40	58	17	1	41	9	10	3	13	6	.68	7	.330	.376	.465
2006	Akron	AA	18	64	33	9	0	3	(-	-)	51	20	9	25	11	0	4	0	2	0	7	3	.70	0	.516	.587	.797
2006	Buffalo	AAA	40	157	47	7	2	1	(-	-)	61	21	13	23	13	0	24	2	8	1	3	2	.60	6	.299	.358	.389
2006	Cle	AL	64	201	57	8	3	2	(1	1)	77	26	21	28	14	0	39	1	5	1	5	1	.83	1	.284	.332	.383

Hirotoshi Ishii

Pitches: L Bats: L Pos: P   Ht: 6'0" Wt: 176 Born: 9/14/1977 Age: 29

			HOW MUCH HE PITCHED						WHAT HE GAVE UP										THE RESULTS						
Year	Team	Lg	G	GS	CG	GF	IP	BFP	H	R	ER	HR	SH	SF	HB	TBB	IBB	SO	WP	Bk	W	L	Pct	ShO	Sv-Op	Hld	ERC	ERA
1996	Yakult	Jap	13	1	0	4	8.0	41	6	3	3	1	0	0	0	13	0	9	1	0	1	0	1.000	0	0--	-	6.73	3.38
1997	Yakult	Jap	1	0	0	1	2.0	13	2	2	2	1	0	0	0	6	0	2	0	0	0	0	-	0	0--	-	21.70	9.00
1999	Yakult	Jap	25	0	0	8	28.2	141	32	21	20	6	4	2	0	27	0	21	2	0	0	1	.000	0	0--	-	8.05	6.28
2000	Yakult	Jap	45	3	0	9	76.1	318	66	29	28	7	10	2	3	36	3	68	5	0	4	3	.571	0	0--	-	3.76	3.30
2001	Yakult	Jap	39	0	0	13	39.2	175	31	23	15	6	3	2	2	23	1	40	4	0	2	3	.400	0	1--	-	3.99	3.40
2002	Yakult	Jap	69	0	0	20	89.2	341	63	15	15	7	7	1	1	12	2	109	3	0	6	2	.750	0	5--	-	1.57	1.51
2003	Yakult	Jap	36	0	0	9	45.1	182	37	10	10	4	3	1	2	10	4	61	2	0	6	1	.857	0	1--	-	2.41	1.99
2004	Yakult	Jap	38	0	0	8	52.2	201	38	12	12	5	3	0	0	10	1	69	2	0	4	2	.667	0	5--	-	1.88	2.05
2005	Yakult	Jap	61	0	0	-	73.2	287	51	16	16	6	-	-	2	15	-	91	0	0	4	3	.571	0	37--	-	1.79	1.95
2006	Yakult	Jap	11	0	0	9	10.1	43	8	5	5	2	-	-	0	4	-	14	0	0	0	0	-	0	6--	-	3.34	4.35

Travis Ishikawa

Bats: L Throws: L Pos: 1B-10; PH-3   Ht: 6'3" Wt: 210 Born: 9/24/1983 Age: 23

Year	Team	Lg	G	AB	H	2B	3B	HR	(Hm	Rd)	TB	R	RBI	RC	TBB	IBB	SO	HBP	SH	SF	SB	CS	SB%	GDP	Avg	OBP	Slg
2002	Giants	R	19	68	19	4	2	1	(-	-)	30	10	10	12	7	1	20	2	0	0	7	0	1.00	1	.279	.364	.441
2002	SlmKzr	A-	23	88	27	2	1	1	(-	-)	34	14	17	12	5	0	22	1	1	1	1	1	.50	2	.307	.347	.386
2003	Hgrstn	A	57	194	40	5	0	3	(-	-)	54	20	22	19	33	5	69	3	1	1	3	4	.43	7	.206	.329	.278
2003	SlmKzr	A-	66	248	63	17	4	3	(-	-)	97	53	31	40	44	0	77	5	0	1	0	0	-	2	.254	.376	.391
2004	Hgrstn	A	97	355	91	19	2	15	(-	-)	159	59	54	59	45	0	110	11	1	1	10	5	.67	8	.256	.357	.448
2004	SnJos	A+	16	56	13	7	0	1	(-	-)	23	10	10	9	10	2	16	1	0	1	0	0	-	1	.232	.353	.411
2005	SnJos	A+	127	432	122	28	7	22	(-	-)	230	87	79	90	70	3	129	7	2	5	1	4	.20	1	.282	.387	.532
2006	Nrwich	AA	86	298	69	13	4	10	(-	-)	120	33	42	40	35	3	88	3	1	3	0	0	-	4	.232	.316	.403
2006	SF	NL	12	24	7	3	1	0	(0	0)	12	1	4	4	1	0	6	0	0	0	0	0	-	1	.292	.320	.500

Jason Isringhausen

Pitches: R Bats: R Pos: RP-59   Ht: 6'3" Wt: 230 Born: 9/7/1972 Age: 34

			HOW MUCH HE PITCHED					WHAT HE GAVE UP										THE RESULTS						
Year	Team	Lg	G	GS	CG	GF	IP	BFP	H	R	ER	HR	SH	SF	HB	TBB	IBB	SO	WP	Bk	W	L	Pct	ShO	Sv-Op	Hld	ERC	ERA
1995	NYM	NL	14	14	1	0	93.0	385	88	29	29	6	3	3	2	31	2	55	4	1	9	2	.818	0	0-0	0	3.40	2.81
1996	NYM	NL	27	27	2	0	171.2	766	190	103	91	13	7	9	8	73	5	114	14	0	6	14	.300	1	0-0	0	4.75	4.77
1997	NYM	NL	6	6	0	0	29.2	145	40	27	25	3	1	2	1	22	0	25	3	0	2	2	.500	0	0-0	0	7.99	7.58
1999	2 Tms		33	5	0	20	64.2	286	64	35	34	9	0	1	2	34	4	51	5	0	1	4	.200	0	9-9	0	4.86	4.73
2000	Oak	AL	66	0	0	57	69.0	304	67	34	29	6	2	1	3	32	5	57	5	1	6	4	.600	0	33-40	0	4.09	3.78
2001	Oak	AL	65	0	0	54	71.1	293	54	24	21	5	3	1	0	23	5	74	2	0	4	3	.571	0	34-43	0	2.18	2.65
2002	StL	NL	60	0	0	51	65.1	257	46	22	18	0	4	3	1	18	1	68	0	0	3	2	.600	0	32-37	0	1.61	2.48
2003	StL	NL	40	0	0	31	42.0	174	31	14	11	2	1	0	0	18	1	41	6	0	0	1	.000	0	22-25	1	2.40	2.36
2004	StL	NL	74	0	0	66	75.1	308	55	27	24	5	6	1	2	23	4	71	1	0	4	2	.667	0	47-54	0	2.09	2.87
2005	StL	NL	63	0	0	52	59.0	245	43	14	14	4	3	1	1	27	5	51	2	0	1	2	.333	0	39-43	1	2.56	2.14
2006	StL	NL	59	0	0	51	58.1	257	47	25	23	10	1	3	3	38	3	52	3	0	4	8	.333	0	33-43	0	4.63	3.55
99	NYM	NL	13	5	0	2	39.1	179	43	29	28	7	0	1	1	22	2	31	3	0	1	3	.250	0	1-1	0	5.93	6.41
99	Oak	AL	20	0	0	18	25.1	107	21	6	6	2	0	0	1	12	2	20	2	0	0	1	.000	0	8-8	0	3.33	2.13
11 ML YEARS			507	52	3	382	799.1	3420	725	354	319	63	31	25	23	339	35	659	45	2	40	44	.476	1	249-294	2	3.54	3.59

Akinori Iwamura

Bats: L Throws: R Pos: 3B   Ht: 5'9" Wt: 176 Born: 2/9/1979 Age: 28

Year	Team	Lg	G	AB	H	2B	3B	HR	(Hm	Rd)	TB	R	RBI	RC	TBB	IBB	SO	HBP	SH	SF	SB	CS	SB%	GDP	Avg	OBP	Slg
1998	Yakult	Jap	1	3	0	0	0	0	(-	-)	0	0	0	0	0	-	2	0	0	0	0	0	-	0	.000	.000	.000
1999	Yakult	Jap	83	252	74	11	4	11	(-	-)	126	28	35	44	18	-	46	1	0	2	7	1	.88	2	.294	.341	.500
2000	Yakult	Jap	130	436	121	13	9	18	(-	-)	206	67	66	74	39	-	103	4	9	1	13	1	.93	7	.278	.342	.472
2001	Yakult	Jap	136	520	149	24	4	19	(-	-)	238	79	81	80	32	-	111	3	5	4	15	6	.71	6	.287	.329	.458
2002	Yakult	Jap	140	510	163	35	2	23	(-	-)	271	67	75	104	58	6	114	3	2	4	5	4	.56	10	.320	.390	.531
2003	Yakult	Jap	60	232	61	6	2	12	(-	-)	107	43	31	36	22	3	55	1	2	1	5	1	.83	3	.263	.328	.461
2004	Yakult	Jap	138	533	160	19	0	44	(-	-)	311	99	103	117	70	3	173	4	0	4	8	3	.73	5	.300	.383	.583
2005	Yakult	Jap	143	545	173	31	4	29	(-	-)	299	82	101	114	62	-	145	2	0	5	5	3	.63	2	.317	.386	.549
2006	Yakult	Jap	140	529	165	27	2	32	(-	-)	292	84	74	-	67	-	124	1	1	3	8	1	.89	-	.312	.385	.552

Cesar Izturis

Bats: B Throws: R Pos: 3B-28; SS-23; PH-5; 2B-1   Ht: 5'7" Wt: 190 Born: 2/10/1980 Age: 27

Year	Team	Lg	G	AB	H	2B	3B	HR	(Hm	Rd)	TB	R	RBI	RC	TBB	IBB	SO	HBP	SH	SF	SB	CS	SB%	GDP	Avg	OBP	Slg
2006	LsVgs*	AAA	15	59	16	3	0	0	(-	-)	19	9	3	8	10	0	3	0	0	1	0	0	-	1	.271	.371	.322
2001	Tor	AL	46	134	36	6	2	2	(1	1)	52	19	9	16	2	0	15	0	4	0	8	1	.89	0	.269	.279	.388
2002	LAD	NL	135	439	102	24	2	1	(0	1)	133	43	31	26	14	1	39	0	10	5	7	7	.50	12	.232	.253	.303
2003	LAD	NL	158	558	140	21	6	1	(0	1)	176	47	40	42	25	8	70	0	7	3	10	5	.67	9	.251	.282	.315
2004	LAD	NL	159	670	193	32	9	4	(1	3)	255	90	62	95	43	2	70	0	12	3	25	9	.74	6	.288	.330	.381
2005	LAD	NL	106	444	114	19	2	2	(1	1)	143	48	31	37	25	1	51	4	4	1	8	8	.50	11	.257	.302	.322
2006	2 Tms	NL	54	192	47	9	1	1	(1	0)	61	14	18	14	12	3	14	2	1	1	1	4	.20	4	.245	.295	.318
06	LAD	NL	32	119	30	7	1	1	(1	0)	42	10	12	10	7	3	6	2	0	1	1	3	.25	1	.252	.302	.353
06	ChC	NL	22	73	17	2	0	0	(0	0)	19	4	6	4	5	0	8	0	1	0	0	1	.00	3	.233	.282	.260
6 ML YEARS			658	2437	632	111	22	11	(4	7)	820	261	191	230	121	15	259	6	38	13	59	34	.63	42	.259	.295	.336

Maicer Izturis

Bats: B Throws: R Pos: 3B-87; SS-10; PR-8; 2B-4; PH-3; DH-1   Ht: 5'8" Wt: 160 Born: 9/12/1980 Age: 26

Year	Team	Lg	G	AB	H	2B	3B	HR	(Hm	Rd)	TB	R	RBI	RC	TBB	IBB	SO	HBP	SH	SF	SB	CS	SB%	GDP	Avg	OBP	Slg
2006	Salt Lk*	AAA	9	36	11	5	1	0	(-	-)	18	5	5	7	5	0	5	0	0	2	1	0	1.00	1	.306	.372	.500
2004	Mon	NL	32	107	22	5	2	1	(1	0)	34	10	4	8	10	1	20	2	2	0	4	0	1.00	1	.206	.286	.318
2005	LAA	AL	77	191	47	8	4	1	(0	1)	66	18	15	25	17	2	21	0	1	1	9	3	.75	5	.246	.306	.346
2006	LAA	AL	104	352	103	21	3	5	(1	4)	145	64	44	56	38	1	35	3	5	1	14	6	.70	7	.293	.365	.412
3 ML YEARS			213	650	172	34	9	7	(2	5)	245	92	63	89	65	4	76	5	8	2	27	9	.75	13	.265	.335	.377

Conor Jackson

Bats: R **Throws:** R **Pos:** 1B-129; PH-11; DH-1   **Ht:** 6'2" **Wt:** 225 **Born:** 5/7/1982 **Age:** 25

									BATTING												BASERUNNING				AVERAGES		
Year	Team	Lg	G	AB	H	2B	3B	HR	(Hm	Rd)	TB	R	RBI	RC	TBB	IBB	SO	HBP	SH	SF	SB	CS	SB%	GDP	Avg	OBP	Slg
2003	Yakima	A-	68	257	82	35	1	6	(-	-)	137	44	60	57	36	4	41	5	0	2	3	0	1.00	7	.319	.410	.533
2004	Lancst	A+	67	258	89	19	2	11	(-	-)	145	64	54	64	45	1	36	3	0	7	4	3	.57	3	.345	.438	.562
2004	ElPaso	AA	60	226	68	13	2	6	(-	-)	103	33	37	39	24	0	36	2	0	4	3	3	.50	4	.301	.367	.456
2005	Tucsn	AAA	93	333	118	38	2	8	(-	-)	184	66	73	85	69	1	32	0	0	7	3	2	.60	8	.354	.457	.553
2005	Ari	NL	40	85	17	3	0	2	(2	0)	26	8	8	6	12	0	11	1	0	1	0	0	-	6	.200	.303	.306
2006	Ari	NL	140	485	141	26	1	15	(8	7)	214	75	79	77	54	2	73	9	1	7	1	0	1.00	18	.291	.368	.441
	2 ML YEARS		180	570	158	29	1	17	(10	7)	240	83	87	83	66	2	84	10	1	8	1	0	1.00	24	.277	.358	.421

Damian Jackson

Bats: R **Throws:** R **Pos:** CF-22; SS-16; PH-13; 2B-11; PR-8; 3B-6; LF-2; RF-2   **Ht:** 5'11" **Wt:** 185 **Born:** 8/16/1973 **Age:** 33

									BATTING												BASERUNNING				AVERAGES		
Year	Team	Lg	G	AB	H	2B	3B	HR	(Hm	Rd)	TB	R	RBI	RC	TBB	IBB	SO	HBP	SH	SF	SB	CS	SB%	GDP	Avg	OBP	Slg
1996	Cle	AL	5	10	3	2	0	0	(0	0)	5	2	1	2	1	0	4	0	0	0	0	0	-	0	.300	.364	.500
1997	2 Tms		20	36	7	2	1	1	(0	1)	14	8	2	4	4	1	8	1	1	0	2	1	.67	1	.194	.293	.389
1998	Cin	NL	13	38	12	5	0	0	(0	0)	17	4	7	7	6	0	4	0	0	1	2	0	1.00	1	.316	.400	.447
1999	SD	NL	133	388	87	20	2	9	(6	3)	138	56	39	50	53	3	105	3	0	3	34	10	.77	2	.224	.320	.356
2000	SD	NL	138	470	120	27	6	6	(5	1)	177	68	37	66	62	2	108	3	4	2	28	6	.82	7	.255	.345	.377
2001	SD	NL	122	440	106	21	6	4	(1	3)	151	67	38	51	44	2	128	6	2	3	23	6	.79	6	.241	.316	.343
2002	Det	AL	81	245	63	20	1	1	(0	1)	88	31	25	32	21	0	36	3	2	3	12	3	.80	3	.257	.320	.359
2003	Bos	AL	109	161	42	7	0	1	(0	1)	52	34	13	12	8	0	28	0	2	1	16	8	.67	4	.261	.294	.323
2004	2 Tms		21	30	3	2	0	1	(1	0)	8	2	3	1	4	2	12	0	0	0	0	0	-	0	.100	.206	.267
2005	SD	NL	118	275	70	9	6	5	(3	2)	94	44	23	31	30	1	45	4	3	1	15	2	.88	4	.255	.335	.342
2006	Was	NL	67	116	23	6	1	4	(2	2)	43	16	10	12	12	0	39	4	3	0	1	3	.25	1	.198	.295	.371
97	Cle	AL	8	9	1	0	0	0	(0	0)	1	2	0	0	0	0	1	1	0	0	1	0	1.00	0	.111	.200	.111
97	Cin	AL	12	27	6	2	1	1	(0	1)	13	6	2	4	4	1	7	0	1	0	1	1	.50	1	.222	.323	.481
04	ChC	NL	7	15	1	0	0	1	(1	0)	4	1	1	0	3	2	6	0	0	0	0	0	-	0	.067	.222	.267
04	KC	AL	14	15	2	2	0	0	(0	0)	4	1	2	1	1	0	6	0	0	0	0	0	-	0	.133	.188	.267
	11 ML YEARS		827	2209	536	121	17	32	(18	14)	787	332	198	268	245	11	517	24	17	14	133	39	.77	28	.243	.323	.356

Edwin Jackson

Pitches: R **Bats:** R **Pos:** RP-22; SP-1   **Ht:** 6'3" **Wt:** 190 **Born:** 9/9/1983 **Age:** 23

			HOW MUCH HE PITCHED						WHAT HE GAVE UP											THE RESULTS					
Year	Team	Lg	G	GS	CG	GF	IP	BFP	H	R	ER	HR	SH	SF	HB	TBB	IBB	SO	WP	Bk	W	L	Pct	ShO	Sv-Op Hld	ERC	ERA
2006	Drham*	AAA	22	13	0	8	73.0	337	84	55	45	7	1	6	3	35	0	66	6	0	3	7	.300	0	5-- -	5.34	5.55
2003	LAD	NL	4	3	0	0	22.0	91	17	6	6	2	1	1	1	11	1	19	3	0	2	1	.667	0	0-0 -	3.36	2.45
2004	LAD	NL	8	5	0	1	24.2	113	31	20	20	7	1	0	0	11	1	16	0	0	2	1	.667	0	0-0 -	7.21	7.30
2005	LAD	NL	7	6	0	0	28.2	134	31	22	20	2	0	2	1	17	0	13	2	1	2	2	.500	0	0-0 -	5.13	6.28
2006	TB	AL	23	1	0	7	36.1	174	42	27	22	2	2	2	1	25	0	27	3	1	0	0	-	0	0-0 -	5.86	5.45
	4 ML YEARS		42	15	0	8	111.2	512	121	75	68	13	4	5	3	64	2	75	8	2	6	4	.600	0	0-0 -	5.46	5.48

Zach Jackson

Pitches: L **Bats:** L **Pos:** SP-7; RP-1   **Ht:** 6'5" **Wt:** 220 **Born:** 5/13/1983 **Age:** 24

			HOW MUCH HE PITCHED						WHAT HE GAVE UP											THE RESULTS					
Year	Team	Lg	G	GS	CG	GF	IP	BFP	H	R	ER	HR	SH	SF	HB	TBB	IBB	SO	WP	Bk	W	L	Pct	ShO	Sv-Op Hld	ERC	ERA
2004	Auburn	A-	4	4	0	0	15.0	69	20	9	9	1	0	1	0	6	0	11	1	0	0	0	-	0	0-- -	5.80	5.40
2005	Dnedin	A+	10	10	0	0	59.1	240	56	25	19	3	2	3	0	6	0	48	0	0	8	1	.889	0	0-- -	2.31	2.88
2005	NHam	AA	9	9	0	0	54.0	227	57	27	24	3	3	3	3	12	0	43	0	0	4	3	.571	0	0-- -	3.64	4.00
2005	Syrcse	AAA	8	8	0	0	47.1	216	61	33	27	3	3	1	2	21	1	33	1	0	4	4	.500	0	0-- -	5.93	5.13
2006	Nashv	AAA	18	18	1	0	107.0	458	106	55	49	11	2	1	7	44	0	58	4	0	4	6	.400	0	0-- -	4.45	4.12
2006	Mil	NL	8	7	0	1	38.1	178	48	26	23	6	1	1	4	14	0	22	1	0	2	2	.500	0	0-0 0	6.26	5.40

Mike Jacobs

Bats: L **Throws:** R **Pos:** 1B-124; PH-12; DH-1   **Ht:** 6'2" **Wt:** 200 **Born:** 10/30/1980 **Age:** 26

									BATTING												BASERUNNING				AVERAGES		
Year	Team	Lg	G	AB	H	2B	3B	HR	(Hm	Rd)	TB	R	RBI	RC	TBB	IBB	SO	HBP	SH	SF	SB	CS	SB%	GDP	Avg	OBP	Slg
1999	Mets	R	44	147	49	12	0	4	(-	-)	73	18	30	29	14	2	30	1	0	5	2	0	1.00	3	.333	.383	.497
2000	Clmbia	A	18	56	12	5	0	0	(-	-)	17	1	8	4	6	1	19	0	0	0	1	1	.50	2	.214	.290	.304
2000	Kngspt	R+	59	204	55	15	4	7	(-	-)	99	28	40	39	33	1	62	1	1	2	6	1	.86	3	.270	.371	.485
2001	Bklyn	A-	19	66	19	5	0	1	(-	-)	27	12	15	10	6	0	11	3	0	2	1	1	.50	1	.288	.364	.409
2001	Clmbia	A	46	180	50	13	0	2	(-	-)	69	18	26	23	13	0	46	1	1	1	0	1	.00	4	.278	.328	.383
2002	StLuci	A+	118	467	117	26	1	11	(-	-)	178	62	64	53	25	5	95	4	0	5	2	3	.40	11	.251	.291	.381
2003	Bnghtn	AA	119	407	134	36	1	17	(-	-)	223	56	81	81	28	7	80	7	0	8	0	3	.00	11	.329	.376	.548
2004	Norfolk	AAA	27	96	17	3	0	2	(-	-)	26	8	6	6	9	2	30	0	0	1	0	0	-	1	.177	.245	.271
2005	Bnghtn	AA	117	433	139	37	2	25	(-	-)	255	66	93	93	35	6	94	7	1	6	1	2	.33	11	.321	.376	.589
2005	NYM	NL	30	100	31	7	0	11	(6	5)	71	19	23	21	10	0	22	1	0	1	0	0	-	5	.310	.375	.710
2006	Fla	NL	136	469	123	37	1	20	(12	8)	222	54	77	66	45	2	105	1	0	5	3	0	1.00	16	.262	.325	.473
	2 ML YEARS		166	569	154	44	1	31	(18	13)	293	73	100	87	55	2	127	2	0	6	3	0	1.00	21	.271	.334	.515

Chuck James

Pitches: L Bats: L Pos: SP-18; RP-7 · · · · · · · · · · · · · · · · Ht: 6'0" Wt: 190 Born: 11/9/1981 Age: 25

			HOW MUCH HE PITCHED						WHAT HE GAVE UP										THE RESULTS						
Year	Team	Lg	G	GS	CG	GF	IP	BFP	H	R	ER	HR	SH	SF	HB	TBB	IBB	SO	WP	Bk	W	L	Pct	ShO	Sv-Op Hld	ERC	ERA
2003	Danvle	R+	11	11	0	0	50.1	196	26	9	7	1	2	0	0	19	0	68	2	0	2	1	.667	0	0-- -	1.30	1.25
2004	Rome	A	26	22	1	2	132.0	536	92	41	33	6	9	9	7	48	1	156	3	0	10	5	.667	0	0-- -	2.20	2.25
2005	MrtlBh	A+	7	7	0	0	41.2	153	20	6	5	1	0	0	0	8	0	59	2	0	3	3	.500	0	0-- -	0.87	1.08
2005	Missi	AA	16	16	0	0	86.0	338	62	25	20	4	6	0	2	18	0	104	4	0	9	1	.900	0	0-- -	1.73	2.09
2005	Rchmd	AAA	6	6	0	0	33.2	132	21	13	13	4	0	1	1	10	0	30	2	0	1	3	.250	0	0-- -	1.99	3.48
2006	Rome	A	1	1	0	0	1.0	3	0	0	0	0	0	0	0	0	0	1	0	0	0	0	-	0	0-- -	0.00	0.00
2006	Rchmd	AAA	7	6	0	0	33.2	135	30	10	10	3	1	1	0	6	0	25	1	0	1	0	1.000	0	0-- -	2.59	2.67
2005	Atl	NL	2	0	0	0	5.2	23	4	1	1	0	0	0	0	3	0	5	1	0	0	0	-	0	0-0 0	2.41	1.59
2006	Atl	NL	25	18	0	0	119.0	504	101	54	50	20	8	7	6	47	2	91	2	0	11	4	.733	0	0-0 0	3.84	3.78
	2 ML YEARS		27	18	0	0	124.2	527	105	55	51	20	8	7	6	50	2	96	3	0	11	4	.733	0	0-0 0	3.77	3.68

Casey Janssen

Pitches: R Bats: R Pos: SP-17; RP-2 · · · · · · · · · · · · · · · · Ht: 6'4" Wt: 205 Born: 9/17/1981 Age: 25

			HOW MUCH HE PITCHED						WHAT HE GAVE UP										THE RESULTS						
Year	Team	Lg	G	GS	CG	GF	IP	BFP	H	R	ER	HR	SH	SF	HB	TBB	IBB	SO	WP	Bk	W	L	Pct	ShO	Sv-Op Hld	ERC	ERA
2004	Auburn	A-	10	10	0	0	51.2	208	47	21	20	2	0	0	2	10	0	45	2	0	3	1	.750	0	0-- -	2.61	3.48
2005	Lansng	A	7	7	0	0	46.0	163	27	8	7	0	0	3	1	4	0	38	1	0	4	0	1.000	0	0-- -	0.95	1.37
2005	Dnedin	A+	10	10	0	0	59.2	228	46	16	15	2	1	1	2	12	0	51	1	0	6	1	.857	0	0-- -	1.98	2.26
2005	NHam	AA	9	9	0	0	43.0	177	49	20	14	3	1	0	2	4	0	47	2	0	3	3	.500	0	0-- -	3.69	2.93
2006	Syrcse	AAA	9	9	0	0	42.2	178	47	23	23	3	1	1	2	8	0	32	2	0	1	5	.167	0	0-- -	3.86	4.85
2006	Tor	AL	19	17	0	1	94.0	407	103	58	53	12	2	2	7	21	3	44	3	2	6	10	.375	0	0-0 0	4.32	5.07

Kevin Jarvis

Pitches: R Bats: L Pos: RP-5; SP-4 · · · · · · · · · · · · · · · · Ht: 6'2" Wt: 200 Born: 8/1/1969 Age: 37

			HOW MUCH HE PITCHED						WHAT HE GAVE UP										THE RESULTS						
Year	Team	Lg	G	GS	CG	GF	IP	BFP	H	R	ER	HR	SH	SF	HB	TBB	IBB	SO	WP	Bk	W	L	Pct	ShO	Sv-Op Hld	ERC	ERA
2006	Tucsn*	AAA	15	13	0	1	83.2	347	76	40	32	7	3	2	3	22	0	58	1	0	3	6	.333	0	0-- -	3.07	3.44
1994	Cin	NL	6	3	0	0	17.2	79	22	14	14	4	1	0	0	5	0	10	1	0	1	1	.500	0	0-0 0	5.91	7.13
1995	Cin	NL	19	11	1	2	79.0	354	91	56	50	13	2	5	3	32	2	33	2	0	3	4	.429	1	0-0 0	5.60	5.70
1996	Cin	NL	24	20	2	2	120.1	552	152	93	80	17	6	2	2	43	5	63	3	0	8	9	.471	1	0-0 0	5.68	5.98
1997	3 Tms		32	5	0	13	68.0	329	99	62	58	17	2	1	1	29	0	48	4	0	0	4	.000	0	1-1 0	8.21	7.68
1999	Oak	AL	4	1	0	0	14.0	75	28	19	18	6	0	1	1	6	0	11	0	0	1	0	1.000	0	0-0 0	14.40	11.57
2000	Col	NL	24	19	0	0	115.0	505	138	83	76	26	6	2	4	33	3	60	2	0	3	4	.429	0	0-0 0	5.86	5.95
2001	SD	NL	32	32	1	0	193.1	809	189	107	103	37	7	4	5	49	4	133	1	0	12	11	.522	1	0-0 0	4.05	4.79
2002	SD	NL	7	7	0	0	35.0	146	36	19	17	5	0	1	1	10	1	24	2	0	2	4	.333	0	0-0 0	4.24	4.37
2003	SD	NL	16	16	0	0	92.0	413	113	65	60	15	2	5	2	32	5	49	2	0	4	8	.333	0	0-0 0	5.68	5.87
2004	2 Tms		10	0	0	2	15.0	78	26	18	18	5	1	0	0	9	2	7	2	0	1	0	1.000	0	0-0 0	11.60	10.80
2005	StL	NL	4	0	0	1	3.1	17	3	5	5	1	0	0	2	3	0	2	0	0	1	0	1.000	0	0-1 0	10.36	13.50
2006	2 Tms		9	4	0	2	28.0	135	40	27	24	3	1	3	2	11	1	13	2	0	0	2	.000	0	0-0 0	6.85	7.71
97	Cin	NL	9	0	0	3	13.1	70	21	16	15	4	1	0	1	7	0	12	2	0	0	1	.000	0	1-1 0	9.98	10.13
97	Min	AL	6	2	0	1	13.0	70	23	18	18	4	0	0	0	8	0	9	2	0	0	0	-	0	0-0 0	11.69	12.46
97	Det	AL	17	3	0	9	41.2	189	55	28	25	9	1	1	0	14	0	27	0	0	0	3	.000	0	0-0 0	6.64	5.40
04	Sea	AL	8	0	0	2	13.0	63	20	12	12	4	0	0	0	5	0	7	2	0	1	0	1.000	0	0-0 0	9.03	8.31
04	Col	NL	2	0	0	0	2.0	15	6	6	6	1	1	0	0	4	2	0	0	0	0	0	-	0	0-0 0	30.23	27.00
06	Ari	NL	5	1	0	1	11.1	58	18	15	15	2	0	2	1	5	0	6	2	0	0	1	.000	0	0-0 0	8.76	11.91
06	Bos	AL	4	3	0	1	16.2	77	22	12	9	1	1	1	1	6	1	7	0	0	0	1	.000	0	0-0 0	5.62	4.86
	12 ML YEARS		187	118	4	22	780.2	3492	937	568	523	149	28	24	23	262	23	453	21	0	34	49	.410	3	1-2 0	5.72	6.03

Geoff Jenkins

Bats: L Throws: R Pos: RF-133; PH-15 · · · · · · · · · · · · · · · · Ht: 6'1" Wt: 210 Born: 7/21/1974 Age: 32

			BATTING																BASERUNNING				AVERAGES		
Year	Team	Lg	G	AB	H	2B	3B	HR	(Hm | Rd)	TB	R	RBI	RC	TBB	IBB	SO	HBP	SH	SF	SB	CS	SB%	GDP	Avg	OBP	Slg
1998	Mil	NL	84	262	60	12	1	9	(4 | 5)	101	33	28	26	20	4	61	2	0	1	1	3	.25	7	.229	.288	.385
1999	Mil	NL	135	447	140	43	3	21	(10 | 11)	252	70	82	88	35	7	87	7	3	1	5	1	.83	10	.313	.371	.564
2000	Mil	NL	135	512	155	36	4	34	(15 | 19)	301	100	94	104	33	6	135	15	0	4	11	1	.92	9	.303	.360	.588
2001	Mil	NL	105	397	105	21	1	20	(11 | 9)	188	60	63	60	36	7	120	8	0	5	4	2	.67	11	.264	.334	.474
2002	Mil	NL	67	243	59	17	1	10	(4 | 6)	108	35	29	28	22	1	60	6	0	1	1	2	.33	8	.243	.320	.444
2003	Mil	NL	124	487	144	30	2	28	(16 | 12)	262	81	95	90	58	10	120	6	0	3	0	0	-	12	.296	.375	.538
2004	Mil	NL	157	617	163	36	4	27	(13 | 14)	292	88	93	76	46	10	152	12	0	6	3	1	.75	19	.264	.325	.473
2005	Mil	NL	148	538	157	42	1	25	(10 | 15)	276	87	86	87	56	9	138	6	0	5	0	0	-	13	.292	.375	.513
2006	Mil	NL	147	484	131	26	1	17	(8 | 9)	210	62	70	76	56	8	129	11	0	4	4	1	.80	9	.271	.357	.434
	9 ML YEARS		1102	3987	1114	263	20	191	(91 | 100)	1990	616	640	635	362	62	1002	86	3	30	29	11	.73	98	.279	.350	.499

Bobby Jenks

Pitches: R Bats: R Pos: RP-67 · · · · · · · · · · · · · · · · Ht: 6'3" Wt: 280 Born: 3/14/1981 Age: 26

			HOW MUCH HE PITCHED						WHAT HE GAVE UP										THE RESULTS						
Year	Team	Lg	G	GS	CG	GF	IP	BFP	H	R	ER	HR	SH	SF	HB	TBB	IBB	SO	WP	Bk	W	L	Pct	ShO	Sv-Op Hld	ERC	ERA
2000	Butte	R+	14	12	0	0	52.2	263	61	57	46	2	2	4	5	44	0	42	19	2	1	7	.125	0	0-- -	6.62	7.86
2001	CRpds	A	21	21	0	0	99.0	451	90	74	58	10	2	4	12	64	0	98	13	1	3	7	.300	0	0-- -	5.05	5.27
2001	Ark	AA	2	2	0	0	10.0	43	8	5	4	0	0	0	2	5	0	10	3	0	1	0	1.000	0	0-- -	3.48	3.60
2002	Ark	AA	10	10	1	0	58.0	267	49	34	30	2	2	3	2	44	0	58	2	1	6	3	.333	0	0-- -	4.15	4.66
2002	RCuca	A+	11	10	1	0	65.1	292	50	42	35	4	4	5	4	46	0	64	11	2	3	5	.375	1	0-- -	3.86	4.82
2003	Ark	AA	16	16	0	0	83.0	356	56	23	20	2	1	3	1	51	0	103	6	0	7	2	.778	0	0-- -	2.62	2.17
2003	Angels	R	1	1	0	0	4.0	14	2	0	0	0	0	0	0	0	0	5	0	0	0	0	-	0	0-- -	0.54	0.00

Year	Team	Lg	G	GS	CG	GF	IP	BFP	H	R	ER	HR	SH	SF	HB	TBB	IBB	SO	WP	Bk	W	L	Pct	ShO	Sv-Op	Hld	ERC	ERA
2004	Salt Lk	AAA	3	3	0	0	12.1	62	19	15	12	1	0	0	1	6	0	13	0	0	0	1	.000	0	0--	-	7.88	8.76
2004	RCuca	A+	1	1	0	0	3.2	23	5	8	8	0	0	2	1	7	0	3	0	0	0	1	.000	0	0--	-	13.40	19.64
2004	Angels	R	1	1	0	0	3.1	15	2	3	3	0	0	0	0	3	0	5	1	0	0	0	-	0	0--	-	2.96	8.10
2005	Brham	AA	35	0	0	32	41.0	177	34	17	13	1	1	2	4	20	1	48	6	0	1	2	.333	0	19--	-	3.27	2.85
2005	CWS	AL	32	0	0	18	39.1	168	34	15	12	3	1	0	1	15	3	50	4	0	1	1	.500	0	6-8	3	3.02	2.75
2006	CWS	AL	67	0	0	58	69.2	300	66	32	31	5	4	2	2	31	10	80	3	0	3	4	.429	0	41-45	3	3.65	4.00
2 ML YEARS			99	0	0	76	109.0	468	100	47	43	8	5	2	3	46	13	130	7	0	4	5	.444	0	47-53	3	3.42	3.55

Jason Jennings

Pitches: R Bats: L Pos: SP-32   Ht: 6'2" Wt: 235 Born: 7/17/1978 Age: 28

Year	Team	Lg	G	GS	CG	GF	IP	BFP	H	R	ER	HR	SH	SF	HB	TBB	IBB	SO	WP	Bk	W	L	Pct	ShO	Sv-Op	Hld	ERC	ERA
2001	Col	NL	7	7	1	0	39.1	174	42	21	20	2	1	1	1	19	0	26	1	0	4	1	.800	1	0-0	-	4.58	4.58
2002	Col	NL	32	32	0	0	185.1	808	201	102	93	26	9	3	8	70	2	127	10	0	16	8	.667	0	0-0	0	4.98	4.52
2003	Col	NL	32	32	1	0	181.1	820	212	115	103	20	11	6	5	88	7	119	6	0	12	13	.480	0	0-0	0	5.60	5.11
2004	Col	NL	33	33	0	0	201.0	925	241	125	123	27	9	3	7	101	14	133	6	1	11	12	.478	0	0-0	0	5.99	5.51
2005	Col	NL	20	20	1	0	122.0	551	130	73	68	11	6	3	5	62	4	75	8	0	6	9	.400	0	0-0	0	4.91	5.02
2006	Col	NL	32	32	3	0	212.0	902	206	94	89	17	8	6	3	85	7	142	10	0	9	13	.409	2	0-0	0	3.83	3.78
6 ML YEARS			156	156	6	0	941.0	4180	1032	530	496	103	44	22	29	425	34	622	41	1	58	56	.509	3	0-0	0	5.01	4.74

Derek Jeter

Bats: R Throws: R Pos: SS-150; DH-5   Ht: 6'3" Wt: 195 Born: 6/26/1974 Age: 33

Year	Team	Lg	G	AB	H	2B	3B	HR	(Hm	Rd)	TB	R	RBI	RC	TBB	IBB	SO	HBP	SH	SF	SB	CS	SB%	GDP	Avg	OBP	Slg
1995	NYY	AL	15	48	12	4	1	0	(0	0)	18	5	7	5	3	0	11	0	0	0	0	0	-	0	.250	.294	.375
1996	NYY	AL	157	582	183	25	6	10	(3	7)	250	104	78	92	48	1	102	9	6	9	14	7	.67	13	.314	.370	.430
1997	NYY	AL	159	654	190	31	7	10	(5	5)	265	116	70	99	74	0	125	10	8	2	23	12	.66	14	.291	.370	.405
1998	NYY	AL	149	626	203	25	8	19	(9	10)	301	127	84	115	57	1	119	5	3	3	30	6	.83	13	.324	.384	.481
1999	NYY	AL	158	627	219	37	9	24	(15	9)	346	134	102	146	91	5	116	12	3	6	19	8	.70	12	.349	.438	.552
2000	NYY	AL	148	593	201	31	4	15	(8	7)	285	119	73	118	68	4	99	12	3	3	22	4	.85	14	.339	.416	.481
2001	NYY	AL	150	614	191	35	3	21	(13	8)	295	110	74	112	56	3	99	10	5	1	27	3	.90	13	.311	.377	.480
2002	NYY	AL	157	644	191	26	0	18	(10	8)	271	124	75	108	73	2	114	7	3	3	32	3	.91	14	.297	.373	.421
2003	NYY	AL	119	482	156	25	3	10	(7	3)	217	87	52	86	43	2	88	13	3	1	11	5	.69	10	.324	.393	.450
2004	NYY	AL	154	643	188	44	1	23	(11	12)	303	111	78	100	46	1	99	14	16	2	23	4	.85	19	.292	.352	.471
2005	NYY	AL	159	654	202	25	5	19	(12	7)	294	122	70	105	77	3	117	11	7	3	14	5	.74	15	.309	.389	.450
2006	NYY	AL	154	623	214	39	3	14	(8	6)	301	118	97	132	69	4	102	12	7	4	34	5	.87	13	.343	.417	.483
12 ML YEARS			1679	6790	2150	347	50	183	(99	84)	3146	1277	860	1218	705	26	1191	115	64	37	249	62	.80	150	.317	.388	.463

Cesar Jimenez

Pitches: L Bats: L Pos: RP-3; SP-1   Ht: 5'11" Wt: 180 Born: 11/12/1984 Age: 22

Year	Team	Lg	G	GS	CG	GF	IP	BFP	H	R	ER	HR	SH	SF	HB	TBB	IBB	SO	WP	Bk	W	L	Pct	ShO	Sv-Op	Hld	ERC	ERA
2002	Ms	R	1	0	0	0	2.2	11	3	2	1	0	1	0	0	0	0	3	0	0	0	0	-	0	0--	-	2.52	3.38
2002	Everett	A	8	0	0	2	20.0	81	12	7	6	2	3	1	3	5	0	25	1	0	2	1	.667	0	0--	-	1.97	2.70
2003	Wisc	A	28	20	0	3	126.1	552	134	61	41	7	8	6	2	46	2	76	10	0	8	11	.421	0	0--	-	3.96	2.92
2004	InldEm	A+	43	2	0	26	86.1	360	80	28	22	3	3	1	5	19	0	81	6	3	6	7	.462	0	6--	-	2.76	2.29
2005	SnAnt	AA	45	1	0	19	68.2	288	64	21	20	3	4	2	2	24	0	54	4	0	3	5	.375	0	4--	-	3.26	2.62
2005	Tacom	AAA	4	0	0	2	7.2	33	9	8	8	5	0	1	0	1	0	9	0	0	0	0	-	0	0--	-	7.56	9.39
2006	SnAnt	AA	3	3	0	0	16.1	62	10	5	5	0	0	0	1	5	0	10	1	0	0	2	.000	0	0--	-	1.55	2.76
2006	Tacom	AAA	24	19	1	3	107.1	468	107	54	52	8	4	3	4	55	1	66	5	1	5	10	.333	1	3--	-	4.54	4.36
2006	Sea	AL	4	1	0	1	7.1	38	13	12	12	4	0	0	0	4	0	3	2	0	0	0	-	0	0-0	0	14.01	14.73

D'Angelo Jimenez

Bats: B Throws: R Pos: 2B-18; 3B-5; PH-4; SS-3   Ht: 6'0" Wt: 215 Born: 12/21/1977 Age: 29

Year	Team	Lg	G	AB	H	2B	3B	HR	(Hm	Rd)	TB	R	RBI	RC	TBB	IBB	SO	HBP	SH	SF	SB	CS	SB%	GDP	Avg	OBP	Slg
2006	Scrmto*	AAA	35	125	38	8	1	4	(-	-)	60	30	23	25	24	0	14	0	1	1	2	4	.33	3	.304	.413	.480
1999	NYY	AL	7	20	8	2	0	0	(0	0)	10	3	4	5	3	0	4	0	0	0	0	0	-	0	.400	.478	.500
2001	SD	NL	86	308	85	19	0	3	(2	1)	113	45	33	39	39	4	68	0	0	2	5	3	.40	9	.276	.355	.367
2002	2 Tms		114	429	108	15	7	4	(3	1)	149	61	44	54	50	1	73	1	0	2	6	3	.67	11	.252	.330	.347
2003	2 Tms		146	561	153	24	7	14	(6	8)	233	69	57	78	66	1	89	2	6	4	11	7	.61	7	.273	.349	.415
2004	Cin	NL	152	563	152	28	3	12	(6	6)	222	76	67	87	82	1	99	2	3	2	13	7	.65	15	.270	.364	.394
2005	Cin	NL	35	105	24	7	0	0	(0	0)	31	14	5	10	14	0	23	0	0	0	2	1	.67	1	.229	.319	.295
2006	2 Tms	AL	28	71	13	3	0	1	(0	1)	19	8	8	7	16	2	13	0	1	0	0	0	-	3	.183	.333	.268
02	SD	NL	87	321	77	11	4	3	(2	1)	105	39	33	34	34	1	63	0	0	2	4	2	.67	10	.240	.311	.327
02	CWS	AL	27	108	31	4	3	1	(1	0)	44	22	11	20	16	0	10	1	0	0	2	1	.67	1	.287	.384	.407
03	CWS	AL	73	271	69	11	5	7	(3	4)	111	35	26	35	32	1	46	0	4	1	4	3	.57	3	.255	.332	.410
03	Cin	NL	73	290	84	13	2	7	(3	4)	122	34	31	43	34	0	43	2	2	3	7	4	.64	4	.290	.365	.421
06	Tex	AL	20	57	12	3	0	1	(0	1)	18	7	8	7	10	0	6	0	1	0	0	0	-	2	.211	.328	.316
06	Oak	AL	8	14	1	0	0	0	(0	0)	1	1	0	0	6	2	7	0	0	0	0	0	-	1	.071	.350	.071
7 ML YEARS			568	2057	543	98	17	34	(17	17)	777	276	218	280	270	9	369	5	10	10	34	21	.62	46	.264	.349	.378

Ubaldo Jimenez

Pitches: R Bats: R Pos: SP-1; RP-1   Ht: 6'4" Wt: 200 Born: 1/22/1984 Age: 23

Year	Team	Lg	G	GS	CG	GF	IP	BFP	H	R	ER	HR	SH	SF	HB	TBB	IBB	SO	WP	Bk	W	L	Pct	ShO	Sv-Op	Hld	ERC	ERA
2002	Casper	R	14	14	0	0	62.0	288	72	46	45	6	1	3	5	29	1	65	2	3	3	5	.375	0	0- -	-	5.51	6.53
2003	Ashvlle	A	27	27	0	0	153.2	646	129	67	59	11	2	1	14	67	0	138	9	0	10	6	.625	0	0- -	-	3.56	3.46
2003	Visalia	A+	1	0	0	1	5.0	18	3	0	0	0	0	0	0	1	0	7	0	0	1	0	1.000	0	0- -	-	1.17	0.00
2004	Visalia	A+	9	9	1	0	44.1	176	29	15	11	1	2	1	3	12	0	61	1	0	4	1	.800	0	0- -	-	1.65	2.23
2005	Mdest	A+	14	14	0	0	72.1	319	61	35	32	5	0	1	5	40	1	78	4	0	5	3	.625	0	0- -	-	3.78	3.98
2005	Tulsa	AA	12	11	0	0	63.0	279	58	40	38	12	0	5	4	31	0	53	7	0	2	5	.286	0	0- -	-	4.85	5.43
2006	Tulsa	AA	13	13	1	0	73.1	299	49	21	20	2	2	1	4	40	1	86	3	1	9	2	.818	1	0- -	-	2.63	2.45
2006	ColSpr	AAA	13	13	0	0	78.1	349	74	49	44	7	1	3	7	43	1	64	10	1	5	2	.714	0	0- -	-	4.63	5.06
2006	Col	NL	2	1	0	0	7.2	30	5	4	3	1	0	0	0	3	0	3	0	0	0	0	-	0	0-0	0	2.48	3.52

Charlton Jimerson

Bats: R Throws: R Pos: RF-9; PH-6; PR-6; CF-1   Ht: 6'3" Wt: 210 Born: 9/22/1979 Age: 27

									BATTING										BASERUNNING		AVERAGES					
Year	Team	Lg	G	AB	H	2B	3B	HR	(Hm | Rd)	TB	R	RBI	RC	TBB	IBB	SO	HBP	SH	SF	SB	CS	SB%	GDP	Avg	OBP	Slg
2001	Pittsfld	A-	51	197	46	12	1	9	(- | -)	87	35	31	28	18	1	79	2	1	0	15	4	.79	4	.234	.304	.442
2002	Lxngtn	A	125	439	100	22	4	14	(- | -)	172	65	57	55	36	0	168	7	2	2	34	9	.79	7	.228	.295	.392
2003	Salem	A+	97	336	89	19	3	12	(- | -)	150	53	55	52	25	1	109	2	1	3	27	4	.87	4	.265	.317	.446
2004	RdChr	AA	131	488	116	22	5	18	(- | -)	202	78	53	64	31	5	163	5	3	1	39	6	.87	8	.238	.290	.414
2005	CpChr	AA	115	425	110	24	3	16	(- | -)	188	67	44	62	29	4	145	8	3	2	27	10	.73	0	.259	.317	.442
2005	RdRck	AAA	7	23	7	1	0	0	(- | -)	8	1	1	3	0	0	7	0	1	1	1	0	1.00	0	.304	.292	.348
2006	RdRck	AAA	123	470	116	27	6	18	(- | -)	209	56	45	62	23	3	183	4	3	1	28	8	.78	2	.247	.287	.445
2005	Hou	NL	1	0	0	0	0	0	(0 | 0)	0	0	0	0	0	0	0	0	0	0	0	0	-	0	-	-	-
2006	Hou	NL	17	6	2	0	0	1	(0 | 1)	5	2	1	1	0	0	3	0	0	0	2	0	1.00	0	.333	.333	.833
	2 ML YEARS		18	6	2	0	0	1	(0 | 1)	5	2	1	1	0	0	3	0	0	0	2	0	1.00	0	.333	.333	.833

Kenji Johjima

Bats: R Throws: R Pos: C-144; PH-5   Ht: 6'0" Wt: 200 Born: 6/8/1976 Age: 31

									BATTING										BASERUNNING		AVERAGES					
Year	Team	Lg	G	AB	H	2B	3B	HR	(Hm | Rd)	TB	R	RBI	RC	TBB	IBB	SO	HBP	SH	SF	SB	CS	SB%	GDP	Avg	OBP	Slg
1995	Fk Dai	Jap	12	12	2	0	0	0	(- | -)	2	2	1	0	1	-	4	0	0	0	0	0	-	0	.167	.231	.167
1996	Fk Dai	Jap	17	58	14	2	0	4	(- | -)	28	5	9	8	3	-	9	1	0	0	1	0	1.00	1	.241	.290	.483
1997	Fk Dai	Jap	120	432	133	24	2	15	(-	-)	206	49	68	72	22	-	62	5	4	7	2	.75	15	.308	.343	.477
1998	Fk Dai	Jap	122	395	99	19	0	16	(- | -)	166	53	58	54	27	-	67	8	6	4	5	2	.71	18	.251	.309	.420
1999	Fk Dai	Jap	135	493	151	33	1	17	(- | -)	237	65	77	85	31	-	61	8	6	1	6	2	.75	13	.306	.356	.481
2000	Fk Dai	Jap	84	303	94	22	2	9	(-	-)	147	38	50	57	27	-	48	6	5	1	2	.83	13	.310	.377	.485
2001	Fk Dai	Jap	140	534	138	18	0	31	(- | -)	249	63	95	78	31	-	55	6	5	2	9	4	.69	17	.258	.305	.466
2002	Fk Dai	Jap	115	416	122	18	0	25	(- | -)	215	60	74	75	30	5	41	8	3	6	8	7	.53	11	.293	.348	.517
2003	Fk Dai	Jap	140	551	182	39	2	34	(-	-)	327	101	119	128	53	10	50	15	2	7	4	.69	22	.330	.399	.593
2004	Fk Dai	Jap	116	426	144	25	1	36	(- | -)	279	91	91	113	49	5	45	22	0	1	6	5	.55	16	.338	.432	.655
2005	Fk Dai	Jap	116	411	127	22	4	24	(- | -)	229	70	57	86	33	-	32	17	0	3	3	4	.43	-	.309	.381	.557
2006	Sea	AL	144	506	147	25	1	18	(6 | 12)	228	61	76	79	20	1	46	13	0	3	3	1	.75	15	.291	.332	.451

Ben Johnson

Bats: R Throws: R Pos: LF-22; CF-17; PR-13; PH-12; RF-4   Ht: 6'1" Wt: 220 Born: 6/18/1981 Age: 26

									BATTING										BASERUNNING		AVERAGES					
Year	Team	Lg	G	AB	H	2B	3B	HR	(Hm | Rd)	TB	R	RBI	RC	TBB	IBB	SO	HBP	SH	SF	SB	CS	SB%	GDP	Avg	OBP	Slg
1999	JhsCty	R+	57	203	67	9	1	10	(- | -)	108	38	51	46	29	1	57	5	1	2	14	6	.70	0	.330	.423	.532
2000	Peoria	A	93	330	80	22	1	13	(- | -)	143	58	46	55	53	0	78	5	0	3	17	6	.74	8	.242	.353	.433
2000	FtWyn	A	29	109	21	6	2	3	(- | -)	40	11	13	9	7	1	25	3	2	0	0	3	.00	5	.193	.261	.367
2001	Lk Els	A+	136	503	139	35	6	12	(- | -)	222	79	63	84	54	1	141	11	1	2	22	7	.76	15	.276	.358	.441
2002	Mobile	AA	131	456	110	23	4	10	(- | -)	171	58	55	61	65	1	127	3	0	4	11	9	.55	9	.241	.337	.375
2003	Mobile	AA	44	127	23	5	0	1	(- | -)	31	8	7	7	10	0	36	2	1	0	0	1	.00	0	.181	.252	.244
2003	Lk Els	A+	52	184	49	9	0	8	(- | -)	82	30	29	31	20	0	49	5	1	0	6	1	.86	6	.266	.354	.446
2004	Mobile	AA	136	475	119	28	6	23	(- | -)	228	80	85	78	55	3	136	7	2	5	5	6	.45	0	.251	.334	.480
2005	Portlnd	AAA	107	414	129	27	0	25	(- | -)	231	79	83	90	51	0	88	6	0	1	6	1	.86	7	.312	.394	.558
2006	Portlnd	AAA	51	198	52	11	1	7	(- | -)	86	35	22	32	23	0	55	3	0	3	7	1	.88	3	.263	.344	.434
2005	SD	NL	31	75	16	8	1	3	(1 | 2)	35	10	13	8	11	1	23	0	1	1	0	2	.00	4	.213	.310	.467
2006	SD	NL	58	120	30	5	2	4	(4 | 0)	51	19	12	10	14	2	36	1	0	0	3	0	1.00	3	.250	.333	.425
	2 ML YEARS		89	195	46	13	3	7	(5 | 2)	86	29	25	18	25	3	59	1	1	1	3	2	.60	7	.236	.324	.441

Dan Johnson

Bats: L Throws: R Pos: 1B-85; PH-9; DH-1; PR-1   Ht: 6'2" Wt: 225 Born: 8/10/1979 Age: 27

									BATTING										BASERUNNING		AVERAGES					
Year	Team	Lg	G	AB	H	2B	3B	HR	(Hm | Rd)	TB	R	RBI	RC	TBB	IBB	SO	HBP	SH	SF	SB	CS	SB%	GDP	Avg	OBP	Slg
2001	Vancvr	A-	69	247	70	12	1	8	(- | -)	122	36	41	44	27	2	63	2	0	4	0	0	-	6	.283	.354	.494
2002	Mdest	A+	126	426	125	23	1	21	(- | -)	213	56	85	82	57	4	87	0	1	8	4	1	.80	8	.293	.371	.500
2003	Mdland	AA	139	538	156	26	4	27	(- | -)	271	90	114	102	68	16	82	2	0	11	7	4	.64	14	.290	.365	.504
2003	Scrmto	AAA	1	4	1	1	0	0	(- | -)	2	0	0	0	0	0	0	0	0	0	0	0	-	0	.250	.250	.500
2004	Scrmto	AAA	142	536	160	29	5	29	(- | -)	286	95	111	118	89	2	93	9	0	6	0	1	.00	15	.299	.403	.534
2005	Scrmto	AAA	47	182	59	17	0	8	(- | -)	100	36	41	42	32	1	24	1	0	2	0	1	.00	1	.324	.424	.549
2006	Scrmto	AAA	46	172	54	13	1	7	(- | -)	90	34	44	39	32	2	17	3	0	2	0	1	.00	6	.314	.426	.523
2005	Oak	AL	109	375	103	21	0	15	(2 | 13)	169	54	58	56	50	1	52	1	0	8	0	0	.00	11	.275	.355	.451
2006	Oak	AL	91	286	67	13	1	9	(4 | 5)	109	30	37	33	40	2	45	0	0	5	0	0	-	6	.234	.323	.381
	2 ML YEARS		200	661	170	34	1	24	(6 | 18)	278	84	95	89	90	3	97	1	0	13	0	0	.00	17	.257	.341	.421

Jason Johnson

Pitches: R **Bats:** R **Pos:** SP-20; RP-4   **Ht:** 6'6" **Wt:** 225 **Born:** 10/27/1973 **Age:** 33

Year	Team	Lg	G	GS	CG	GF	IP	BFP	H	R	ER	HR	SH	SF	HB	TBB	IBB	SO	WP	Bk	W	L	Pct	ShO	Sv-Op	Hld	ERC	ERA
2006	Wilmg*	A+	1	1	0	0	7.0	31	10	4	4	0	0	0	0	0	0	1	1	0	1	0	1.000	0	0- -	-	4.07	5.14
2006	Pwtckt*	AAA	3	3	1	0	19.0	77	15	7	7	1	1	1	0	6	0	12	0	0	1	0	1.000	0	0- -	-	2.35	3.32
2006	Lsvlle*	AAA	1	1	0	0	5.0	23	6	6	5	1	0	0	0	1	0	2	1	0	0	1	.000	0	0- -	-	4.76	9.00
1997	Pit	NL	3	0	0	0	6.0	27	10	4	4	2	0	1	0	1	0	3	0	0	0	0	-	0	0-0	0	9.59	6.00
1998	TB	AL	13	13	0	0	60.0	274	74	38	38	9	1	1	3	27	0	36	2	0	2	5	.286	0	0-0	0	6.35	5.70
1999	Bal	AL	22	21	0	0	115.1	515	120	74	70	16	2	4	3	55	0	71	5	1	8	7	.533	0	0-0	0	4.99	5.46
2000	Bal	AL	25	13	0	3	107.2	501	119	95	84	21	3	5	4	61	2	79	3	0	1	10	.091	0	0-0	2	6.18	7.02
2001	Bal	AL	32	32	2	0	196.0	856	194	109	89	28	6	6	13	77	3	114	9	0	10	12	.455	0	0-0	0	4.53	4.09
2002	Bal	AL	22	22	1	0	131.1	561	141	68	67	19	0	3	6	41	2	97	4	0	5	14	.263	0	0-0	0	4.70	4.59
2003	Bal	AL	32	32	0	0	189.2	858	216	100	88	22	3	1	10	80	8	118	7	0	10	10	.500	0	0-0	0	5.21	4.18
2004	Det	AL	33	33	2	0	196.2	859	222	121	112	22	1	10	5	60	3	125	7	1	8	15	.348	1	0-0	0	4.58	5.13
2005	Det	AL	33	33	1	0	210.0	888	233	117	106	23	9	7	6	49	4	93	17	0	8	13	.381	0	0-0	0	4.24	4.54
2006	3 Tms		24	20	0	0	115.0	527	160	86	78	14	1	8	5	35	0	54	8	0	3	12	.200	0	0-0	0	6.43	6.10
	06 Cle	AL	14	14	0	0	77.0	348	108	55	51	10	1	6	2	22	0	32	6	0	3	8	.273	0	0-0	0	6.47	5.96
	06 Bos	AL	6	6	0	0	29.1	141	41	26	24	3	0	2	2	13	0	18	2	0	0	4	.000	0	0-0	0	6.94	7.36
	06 Cin	NL	4	0	0	0	8.2	38	11	5	3	1	0	0	1	0	0	4	0	0	0	0	-	0	0-0	0	4.45	3.12
	10 ML YEARS		239	219	6	3	1327.2	5866	1489	812	736	176	26	46	55	486	22	790	62	2	55	98	.359	1	0-0	2	5.03	4.99

Jim Johnson

Pitches: R **Bats:** R **Pos:** SP-1   **Ht:** 6'5" **Wt:** 213 **Born:** 6/27/1983 **Age:** 24

Year	Team	Lg	G	GS	CG	GF	IP	BFP	H	R	ER	HR	SH	SF	HB	TBB	IBB	SO	WP	Bk	W	L	Pct	ShO	Sv-Op	Hld	ERC	ERA
2001	Orioles	R	7	4	0	0	18.2	81	17	10	8	3	1	0	2	7	1	19	1	0	1	1	.000	0	0- -	-	4.21	3.86
2002	Bluefld	R+	11	9	0	0	55.2	231	52	36	27	5	2	2	3	16	2	36	1	1	4	2	.667	0	0- -	-	3.41	4.37
2003	Bluefld	R+	11	11	0	0	51.1	237	62	24	21	2	0	2	4	18	0	46	4	1	3	2	.600	0	0- -	-	4.81	3.68
2004	Dlmrva	A	20	17	0	1	106.2	443	97	44	39	9	5	5	9	30	1	93	6	0	8	7	.533	0	0- -	-	3.37	3.29
2004	Frdrck	A+	1	1	0	0	3.0	15	6	4	3	0	2	0	0	1	0	6	1	0	0	0	-	0	0- -	-	9.61	9.00
2005	Frdrck	A+	28	27	2	1	159.2	685	139	77	62	11	4	1	19	64	2	168	5	1	12	9	.571	0	1- -	-	3.60	3.49
2005	Bowie	AA	1	1	0	0	7.0	25	3	0	0	0	1	0	1	2	0	6	0	0	0	0	-	0	0- -	-	1.16	0.00
2006	Bowie	AA	27	26	0	0	156.0	690	165	80	77	13	4	3	11	57	1	124	6	0	13	6	.684	0	0- -	-	4.38	4.44
2006	Bal	AL	1	1	0	0	3.0	21	9	8	8	1	0	1	1	3	0	0	0	0	0	1	.000	0	0-0	0	26.81	24.00

Josh Johnson

Pitches: R **Bats:** L **Pos:** SP-24; RP-7   **Ht:** 6'7" **Wt:** 240 **Born:** 1/31/1984 **Age:** 23

Year	Team	Lg	G	GS	CG	GF	IP	BFP	H	R	ER	HR	SH	SF	HB	TBB	IBB	SO	WP	Bk	W	L	Pct	ShO	Sv-Op	Hld	ERC	ERA
2002	Mrlns	R	4	3	0	0	15.0	58	8	3	1	0	0	0	2	3	0	11	0	0	2	0	1.000	0	0- -	-	1.18	0.60
2002	Jmstwn	A-	2	2	0	0	8.0	47	15	15	11	0	0	0	1	7	0	5	0	0	0	2	.000	0	0- -	-	11.13	12.38
2003	Grnsbr	A	17	17	0	0	82.1	354	69	44	33	5	6	3	9	29	0	59	2	0	4	7	.364	0	0- -	-	3.09	3.61
2004	Jupiter	A+	23	22	1	0	114.1	518	124	63	43	4	4	12	3	47	1	103	12	0	5	12	.294	0	0- -	-	4.09	3.38
2005	Carlina	AA	26	26	1	0	139.2	608	139	67	60	4	9	2	4	50	4	113	9	1	12	4	.750	0	0- -	-	3.39	3.87
2005	Fla	NL	4	1	0	0	12.1	55	11	5	5	1	0	1	0	10	0	10	0	0	0	0	-	0	0-0	0	4.82	3.65
2006	Fla	NL	31	24	0	1	157.0	659	136	63	54	14	11	0	4	68	6	133	3	1	12	7	.632	0	0-1	0	3.48	3.10
	2 ML YEARS		35	25	0	1	169.1	714	147	68	59	14	12	0	5	78	6	143	3	1	12	7	.632	0	0-1	0	3.57	3.14

Nick Johnson

Bats: L **Throws:** L **Pos:** 1B-147; PH-2   **Ht:** 6'3" **Wt:** 225 **Born:** 9/19/1978 **Age:** 28

Year	Team	Lg	G	AB	H	2B	3B	HR	(Hm	Rd)	TB	R	RBI	RC	TBB	IBB	SO	HBP	SH	SF	SB	CS	SB%	GDP	Avg	OBP	Slg
2001	NYY	AL	23	67	13	2	0	2	(1	1)	21	6	8	6	7	0	15	4	0	0	0	0	-	3	.194	.308	.313
2002	NYY	AL	129	378	92	15	0	15	(7	8)	152	56	58	59	48	5	98	12	3	0	1	3	.25	11	.243	.347	.402
2003	NYY	AL	96	324	92	19	0	14	(8	6)	153	60	47	65	70	4	57	8	3	1	5	2	.71	9	.284	.422	.472
2004	Mon	NL	73	251	63	16	0	7	(4	3)	100	35	33	36	40	2	58	3	0	1	6	3	.67	5	.251	.359	.398
2005	Was	NL	131	453	131	35	3	15	(7	8)	217	66	74	83	80	8	87	12	0	2	3	8	.27	15	.289	.408	.479
2006	Was	NL	147	500	145	46	0	23	(10	13)	260	100	77	104	110	15	99	13	2	3	10	3	.77	12	.290	.428	.520
	6 ML YEARS		599	1973	536	133	3	76	(37	39)	903	323	297	353	355	34	414	52	8	7	25	19	.57	55	.272	.395	.458

Randy Johnson

Pitches: L **Bats:** R **Pos:** SP-33   **Ht:** 6'10" **Wt:** 230 **Born:** 9/10/1963 **Age:** 43

Year	Team	Lg	G	GS	CG	GF	IP	BFP	H	R	ER	HR	SH	SF	HB	TBB	IBB	SO	WP	Bk	W	L	Pct	ShO	Sv-Op	Hld	ERC	ERA
1988	Mon	NL	4	4	1	0	26.0	109	23	8	7	3	0	0	0	7	0	25	3	0	3	0	1.000	0	0-0	0	2.96	2.42
1989	2 Tms		29	28	2	1	160.2	715	147	100	86	13	10	13	3	96	2	130	7	7	7	13	.350	0	0-0	0	4.26	4.82
1990	Sea	AL	33	33	5	0	219.2	944	174	103	89	26	7	6	5	120	2	194	4	2	14	11	.560	2	0-0	0	3.68	3.65
1991	Sea	AL	33	33	2	0	201.1	889	151	96	89	15	9	8	12	152	0	228	12	2	13	10	.565	1	0-0	0	4.15	3.98
1992	Sea	AL	31	31	6	0	210.1	922	154	104	88	13	3	8	18	144	1	241	13	1	12	14	.462	2	0-0	0	3.75	3.77
1993	Sea	AL	35	34	10	1	255.1	1043	185	97	92	22	8	7	16	99	1	308	8	2	19	8	.704	3	1-1	0	2.73	3.24
1994	Sea	AL	23	23	9	0	172.0	694	132	65	61	14	3	1	6	72	2	204	5	0	13	6	.684	4	0-0	0	2.99	3.19
1995	Sea	AL	30	30	6	0	214.1	866	159	65	59	12	2	1	6	65	1	294	5	2	18	2	.900	3	0-0	0	2.18	2.48
1996	Sea	AL	14	8	0	2	61.1	256	48	27	25	8	1	0	2	25	0	85	3	1	5	0	1.000	0	1-2	0	3.24	3.67
1997	Sea	AL	30	29	5	0	213.0	850	147	60	54	20	4	1	10	77	2	291	4	0	20	4	.833	2	0-0	0	2.47	2.28
1998	2 Tms		34	34	10	0	244.1	1014	203	102	89	23	5	2	14	86	1	329	7	2	19	11	.633	6	0-0	0	3.16	3.28
1999	Ari	NL	35	35	12	0	271.2	1079	207	86	75	30	4	3	9	70	3	364	4	2	17	9	.654	2	0-0	0	2.49	2.48
2000	Ari	NL	35	35	8	0	248.2	1001	202	89	73	23	14	5	6	76	1	347	5	2	19	7	.731	3	0-0	0	2.80	2.64

| | | | HOW MUCH HE PITCHED | | | | | | WHAT HE GAVE UP | | | | | | | | | | | | THE RESULTS | | | | | | | |
Year	Team	Lg	G	GS	CG	GF	IP	BFP	H	R	ER	HR	SH	SF	HB	TBB	IBB	SO	WP	Bk	W	L	Pct	ShO	Sv-Op	Hld	ERC	ERA
2001	Ari	NL	35	34	3	1	249.2	994	181	74	69	19	10	5	18	71	2	372	8	1	21	6	.778	2	0-0	0	2.35	2.49
2002	Ari	NL	35	35	8	0	260.0	1035	197	78	67	26	4	2	13	71	1	334	3	2	24	5	.828	4	0-0	0	2.54	2.32
2003	Ari	NL	18	18	1	0	114.0	489	125	61	54	16	4	3	8	27	3	125	1	1	6	8	.429	1	0-0	0	4.52	4.26
2004	Ari	NL	35	35	4	0	245.2	964	177	88	71	18	7	5	10	44	1	290	3	1	16	14	.533	2	0-0	0	1.82	2.60
2005	NYY	AL	34	34	4	0	225.2	920	207	102	95	32	5	5	12	47	2	211	3	1	17	8	.680	0	0-0	0	3.38	3.79
2006	NYY	AL	33	33	2	0	205.0	860	194	125	114	28	6	7	10	60	1	172	3	2	17	11	.607	0	0-0	0	3.80	5.00
89	Mon	NL	7	6	0	1	29.2	143	29	25	22	2	3	4	0	26	1	26	2	2	0	4	.000	0	0-0	0	5.42	6.67
89	Sea	AL	22	22	2	0	131.0	572	118	75	64	11	7	9	3	70	1	104	5	5	7	9	.438	0	0-0	0	4.01	4.40
98	Sea	AL	23	23	6	0	160.0	685	146	90	77	19	5	1	11	60	0	213	7	2	9	10	.474	2	0-0	0	3.88	4.33
98	Hou	NL	11	11	4	0	84.1	329	57	12	12	4	0	1	3	26	1	116	0	0	10	1	.909	4	0-0	0	1.93	1.28
19 ML YEARS			556	546	98	5	3798.2	15644	3013	1530	1357	361	106	82	178	1409	26	4544	101	31	280	147	.656	37	2-3	0	3.01	3.22

Reed Johnson

Bats: R Throws: R Pos: LF-100; RF-30; CF-16; PH-8; PR-7; DH-1   Ht: 5'10" Wt: 180 Born: 12/8/1976 Age: 30

| | | | BATTING | | | | | | | | | | | | | | | | | BASERUNNING | | | | AVERAGES | | |
Year	Team	Lg	G	AB	H	2B	3B	HR	(Hm	Rd)	TB	R	RBI	RC	TBB	IBB	SO	HBP	SH	SF	SB	CS	SB%	GDP	Avg	OBP	Slg
2003	Tor	AL	114	412	121	21	2	10	(6	4)	176	79	52	64	20	1	67	20	1	4	5	3	.63	10	.294	.353	.427
2004	Tor	AL	141	537	145	25	2	10	(8	2)	204	68	61	85	28	2	98	12	3	2	6	3	.67	17	.270	.320	.380
2005	Tor	AL	142	398	107	21	6	8	(4	4)	164	55	58	57	22	1	82	16	2	1	5	6	.45	8	.269	.332	.412
2006	Tor	AL	134	461	147	34	2	12	(4	8)	221	86	49	76	33	4	81	21	1	1	8	2	.80	9	.319	.390	.479
4 ML YEARS			531	1808	520	101	12	40	(22	18)	765	288	220	262	103	8	328	69	7	8	24	14	.63	44	.288	.348	.423

Tyler Johnson

Pitches: L Bats: B Pos: RP-56   Ht: 6'2" Wt: 180 Born: 6/7/1981 Age: 26

| | | | HOW MUCH HE PITCHED | | | | | | WHAT HE GAVE UP | | | | | | | | | | | | THE RESULTS | | | | | | |
Year	Team	Lg	G	GS	CG	GF	IP	BFP	H	R	ER	HR	SH	SF	HB	TBB	IBB	SO	WP	Bk	W	L	Pct	ShO	Sv-Op	Hld	ERC	ERA
2001	JhsCty	R+	9	9	0	0	40.2	170	26	17	12	1	0	0	3	21	0	58	9	5	1	1	.500	0	0- -	2.36	2.66
2001	Peoria	A	3	3	0	0	13.2	66	14	9	6	1	0	0	0	10	0	15	2	1	0	1	.000	0	0- -	5.11	3.95
2002	Peoria	A	22	18	0	1	121.1	502	96	35	27	7	4	0	4	42	1	132	8	4	15	3	.833	0	0- -	2.58	2.00
2003	PlmBh	A+	22	10	0	3	79.0	354	79	29	27	2	10	2	1	38	2	81	8	0	5	5	.500	0	0- -	3.76	3.08
2003	Tenn	AA	20	0	0	6	27.1	113	16	7	5	1	4	2	3	15	1	39	0	0	1	1	.500	0	0- -	2.40	1.65
2004	Tenn	AA	53	0	0	21	56.1	254	48	32	30	4	0	0	3	37	1	77	8	0	2	2	.500	0	4- -	4.16	4.79
2005	Memp	AAA	57	0	0	15	59.0	254	51	31	28	6	1	0	3	26	2	77	2	0	2	1	.667	0	7- -	3.61	4.27
2006	Memp	AAA	8	0	0	0	8.1	42	12	8	8	1	0	0	0	4	3	8	1	0	0	0	-	0	0- -	6.19	8.64
2005	StL	NL	5	0	0	0	2.2	13	3	0	0	0	0	0	0	3	0	4	0	0	0	0	-	0	0-1	1	7.28	0.00
2006	StL	NL	56	0	0	12	36.1	164	33	21	20	5	1	1	4	23	2	37	2	0	2	4	.333	0	0-2	11	5.16	4.95
2 ML YEARS			61	0	0	13	39.0	177	36	21	20	5	1	1	4	26	2	41	2	0	2	4	.333	0	0-3	12	5.30	4.62

Adam Jones

Bats: R Throws: R Pos: CF-26; PR-4; PH-2   Ht: 6'2" Wt: 200 Born: 8/1/1985 Age: 21

| | | | BATTING | | | | | | | | | | | | | | | | | BASERUNNING | | | | AVERAGES | | |
Year	Team	Lg	G	AB	H	2B	3B	HR	(Hm	Rd)	TB	R	RBI	RC	TBB	IBB	SO	HBP	SH	SF	SB	CS	SB%	GDP	Avg	OBP	Slg
2003	Ms	R	28	109	31	5	1	0	(-	-)	38	18	8	16	5	0	19	10	3	1	5	1	.83	1	.284	.368	.349
2003	Everett	A-	3	13	6	1	0	0	(-	-)	7	2	4	3	1	0	3	0	0	1	0	0	-	1	.462	.467	.538
2004	Wisc	A	130	510	136	23	7	11	(-	-)	206	76	72	67	33	0	124	5	4	7	8	4	.67	13	.267	.314	.404
2005	InldEm	A+	68	271	80	20	5	8	(-	-)	134	43	46	50	29	0	64	8	2	5	4	5	.44	4	.295	.374	.494
2005	SnAnt	AA	63	228	68	10	3	7	(-	-)	105	33	20	39	22	1	48	3	2	2	9	4	.69	4	.298	.365	.461
2006	Tacom	AAA	96	380	109	19	4	16	(-	-)	184	69	62	65	28	1	78	6	1	1	13	4	.76	12	.287	.345	.484
2006	Sea	AL	32	74	16	4	0	1	(0	1)	23	6	8	4	2	0	22	0	0	0	3	1	.75	3	.216	.237	.311

Andruw Jones

Bats: R Throws: R Pos: CF-153; DH-2; PH-2   Ht: 6'1" Wt: 210 Born: 4/23/1977 Age: 30

| | | | BATTING | | | | | | | | | | | | | | | | | BASERUNNING | | | | AVERAGES | | |
Year	Team	Lg	G	AB	H	2B	3B	HR	(Hm	Rd)	TB	R	RBI	RC	TBB	IBB	SO	HBP	SH	SF	SB	CS	SB%	GDP	Avg	OBP	Slg
1996	Atl	NL	31	106	23	7	1	5	(3	2)	47	11	13	13	7	0	29	0	0	0	3	0	1.00	1	.217	.265	.443
1997	Atl	NL	153	399	92	18	1	18	(5	13)	166	60	70	54	56	2	107	4	5	3	20	11	.65	11	.231	.329	.416
1998	Atl	NL	159	582	158	33	8	31	(16	15)	300	89	90	97	40	8	129	4	1	4	27	4	.87	10	.271	.321	.515
1999	Atl	NL	162	592	163	35	5	26	(10	16)	286	97	84	103	76	11	103	9	0	2	24	12	.67	12	.275	.365	.483
2000	Atl	NL	161	656	199	36	6	36	(15	21)	355	122	104	127	59	0	100	9	0	5	21	6	.78	12	.303	.366	.541
2001	Atl	NL	161	625	157	25	2	34	(16	18)	288	104	104	90	56	3	142	3	0	9	11	4	.73	10	.251	.312	.461
2002	Atl	NL	154	560	148	34	0	35	(18	17)	287	91	94	94	83	4	135	10	0	6	8	3	.73	14	.264	.366	.513
2003	Atl	NL	156	595	165	28	2	36	(16	20)	305	101	116	92	53	2	125	5	0	6	4	3	.57	18	.277	.338	.513
2004	Atl	NL	154	570	149	34	4	29	(13	16)	278	85	91	75	71	9	147	3	0	2	6	6	.50	24	.261	.345	.488
2005	Atl	NL	160	586	154	24	3	51	(21	30)	337	95	128	91	64	13	112	15	0	7	5	3	.63	19	.263	.347	.575
2006	Atl	NL	156	565	148	29	0	41	(19	22)	300	107	129	108	82	9	127	13	0	9	4	1	.80	13	.262	.363	.531
11 ML YEARS			1607	5836	1556	303	32	342	(152	190)	2949	962	1023	944	647	61	1256	75	6	53	133	53	.72	144	.267	.345	.505

Chipper Jones

Bats: B Throws: R Pos: 3B-105; PH-4; DH-2   Ht: 6'4" Wt: 230 Born: 4/24/1972 Age: 35

| | | | BATTING | | | | | | | | | | | | | | | | | BASERUNNING | | | | AVERAGES | | |
Year	Team	Lg	G	AB	H	2B	3B	HR	(Hm	Rd)	TB	R	RBI	RC	TBB	IBB	SO	HBP	SH	SF	SB	CS	SB%	GDP	Avg	OBP	Slg
2006	Missi*	AA	2	6	1	0	0	0	(-	-)	1	1	0	0	0	0	2	0	0	0	0	0	-	0	.167	.167	.167
1993	Atl	NL	8	3	2	1	0	0	(0	0)	3	2	0	2	1	0	1	0	0	0	0	0	-	0	.667	.750	1.000
1995	Atl	NL	140	524	139	22	3	23	(15	8)	236	87	86	84	73	1	99	0	1	4	8	4	.67	10	.265	.353	.450
1996	Atl	NL	157	598	185	32	5	30	(18	12)	317	114	110	123	87	0	88	0	1	7	14	1	.93	14	.309	.393	.530

Year	Team	Lg	G	AB	H	2B	3B	HR	(Hm	Rd)	TB	R	RBI	RC	TBB	IBB	SO	HBP	SH	SF	SB	CS	SB%	GDP	Avg	OBP	Slg
1997	Atl	NL	157	597	176	41	3	21	(7	14)	286	100	111	104	76	8	88	0	0	6	20	5	.80	19	.295	.371	.479
1998	Atl	NL	160	601	188	29	5	34	(17	17)	329	123	107	129	96	1	93	1	1	8	16	6	.73	17	.313	.404	.547
1999	Atl	NL	157	567	181	41	1	45	(25	20)	359	116	110	150	126	18	94	2	0	5	25	3	.89	20	.319	.441	.633
2000	Atl	NL	156	579	180	38	1	36	(18	18)	328	118	111	128	95	10	64	2	0	10	14	7	.67	14	.311	.404	.566
2001	Atl	NL	159	572	189	33	5	38	(19	19)	346	113	102	136	98	20	82	2	0	5	9	10	.47	13	.330	.427	.605
2002	Atl	NL	158	548	179	35	1	26	(17	9)	294	90	100	119	107	23	89	2	0	5	8	2	.80	18	.327	.435	.536
2003	Atl	NL	153	555	169	33	2	27	(16	11)	287	103	106	110	94	13	83	1	0	6	2	2	.50	10	.305	.402	.517
2004	Atl	NL	137	472	117	20	1	30	(19	11)	229	69	96	82	84	8	96	4	0	7	2	0	1.00	15	.248	.362	.485
2005	Atl	NL	109	358	106	30	0	21	(9	12)	199	66	72	78	72	5	56	0	0	2	5	1	.83	9	.296	.412	.556
2006	Atl	NL	110	411	133	28	3	26	(12	14)	245	87	86	94	61	4	73	1	0	4	6	1	.86	12	.324	.409	.596
13 ML YEARS			1761	6385	1944	383	30	357	(192	165)	3458	1188	1197	1339	1070	111	1006	15	3	70	129	42	.75	171	.304	.402	.542

Greg Jones

Pitches: R **Bats:** R **Pos:** RP-5   **Ht:** 6'2" **Wt:** 195 **Born:** 11/15/1976 **Age:** 30

	HOW MUCH HE PITCHED						WHAT HE GAVE UP												THE RESULTS							
Year	Team	Lg	G	GS	CG	GF	IP	BFP	H	R	ER	HR	SH	SF	HB	TBB	IBB	SO	WP	Bk	W	L	Pct	ShO	Sv-Op	Hld	ERC	ERA
2006	Salt Lk*	AAA	47	0	0	44	55.0	233	52	28	26	7	1	6	1	19	2	45	10	0	5	6	.455	0	17- -	-	3.75	4.25
2003	LAA	AL	18	0	0	7	27.2	127	29	15	15	3	0	0	2	14	0	28	5	0	0	0	-	0	0-0	0	5.05	4.88
2005	LAA	AL	6	0	0	6	5.1	24	7	4	4	2	0	0	0	2	0	6	0	0	0	0	-	0	0-0	0	8.19	6.75
2006	LAA	AL	5	0	0	2	6.0	28	8	5	4	1	0	3	0	2	0	1	0	0	0	0	-	0	0-0	0	6.14	6.00
3 ML YEARS			29	0	0	15	39.0	179	44	24	23	6	0	3	2	18	0	35	5	0	0	0	-	0	0-0	2	5.63	5.31

Jacque Jones

Bats: L **Throws:** L **Pos:** RF-143; PH-10   **Ht:** 5'10" **Wt:** 200 **Born:** 4/25/1975 **Age:** 32

									BATTING											BASERUNNING				AVERAGES		
Year	Team	Lg	G	AB	H	2B	3B	HR	(Hm	Rd)	TB	R	RBI	RC	TBB	IBB	SO	HBP	SH	SF	SB	CS	SB%	GDP	Avg	OBP	Slg
1999	Min	AL	95	322	93	24	2	9	(5	4)	148	54	44	46	17	1	63	4	1	3	3	4	.43	7	.289	.329	.460
2000	Min	AL	154	523	149	26	5	19	(11	8)	242	66	76	70	26	4	111	0	1	0	7	5	.58	17	.285	.319	.463
2001	Min	AL	149	475	131	25	0	14	(5	9)	198	57	49	63	39	2	92	3	2	0	12	9	.57	10	.276	.335	.417
2002	Min	AL	149	577	173	37	2	27	(6	21)	295	96	85	100	37	2	129	2	4	6	6	7	.46	8	.300	.341	.511
2003	Min	AL	136	517	157	33	1	16	(7	9)	240	76	69	73	21	2	105	4	1	5	13	1	.93	10	.304	.333	.464
2004	Min	AL	151	555	141	22	1	24	(9	15)	237	69	80	73	40	2	117	10	2	1	13	10	.57	12	.254	.315	.427
2005	Min	AL	142	523	130	22	4	23	(9	14)	229	74	73	72	51	12	120	5	2	4	13	4	.76	17	.249	.319	.438
2006	ChC	NL	149	533	152	31	1	27	(12	15)	266	73	81	82	35	6	116	5	2	2	9	1	.90	17	.285	.334	.499
8 ML YEARS			1125	4025	1126	220	16	159	(64	95)	1855	565	557	579	266	31	853	33	15	21	76	41	.65	98	.280	.328	.461

Todd Jones

Pitches: R **Bats:** B **Pos:** RP-62   **Ht:** 6'3" **Wt:** 230 **Born:** 4/24/1968 **Age:** 39

	HOW MUCH HE PITCHED						WHAT HE GAVE UP												THE RESULTS							
Year	Team	Lg	G	GS	CG	GF	IP	BFP	H	R	ER	HR	SH	SF	HB	TBB	IBB	SO	WP	Bk	W	L	Pct	ShO	Sv-Op	Hld	ERC	ERA
1993	Hou	NL	27	0	0	8	37.1	150	28	14	13	4	2	1	1	15	2	25	1	1	1	2	.333	0	2-3	6	2.90	3.13
1994	Hou	NL	48	0	0	20	72.2	288	52	23	22	3	3	1	1	26	4	63	1	0	5	2	.714	0	5-9	8	2.10	2.72
1995	Hou	NL	68	0	0	40	99.2	442	89	38	34	8	5	4	6	52	17	96	5	0	6	5	.545	0	15-20	3	3.70	3.07
1996	Hou	NL	51	0	0	37	57.1	263	61	30	28	5	2	1	5	32	6	44	3	0	6	3	.667	0	17-23	1	5.16	4.40
1997	Det	AL	68	0	0	51	70.0	301	60	29	24	3	1	4	1	35	2	70	7	0	5	4	.556	0	31-36	5	3.27	3.09
1998	Det	AL	65	0	0	53	63.1	279	58	38	35	7	2	6	2	36	4	57	5	0	1	4	.200	0	28-32	5	4.37	4.97
1999	Det	AL	65	0	0	62	66.1	287	64	30	28	7	3	1	1	35	1	64	2	0	4	4	.500	0	30-35	4	4.55	3.80
2000	Det	AL	67	0	0	60	64.0	271	67	28	25	6	1	1	1	25	1	67	2	0	2	4	.333	0	**42-46**	4	4.43	3.52
2001	2 Tms	AL	69	0	0	36	68.0	314	87	39	32	9	3	3	0	29	1	54	3	0	5	5	.500	0	13-21	10	6.03	4.24
2002	Col	NL	79	0	0	20	82.1	352	84	43	43	10	6	3	3	28	3	73	1	0	1	4	.200	0	1-3	30	4.22	4.70
2003	2 Tms		59	1	0	14	68.2	326	93	58	54	10	3	3	1	31	2	59	0	0	3	5	.375	0	0-5	4	6.73	7.08
2004	2 Tms	NL	78	0	0	16	82.1	358	84	39	38	7	5	6	6	33	5	59	2	0	11	5	.688	0	2-8	27	4.32	4.15
2005	Fla	NL	68	0	0	55	73.0	289	61	19	17	2	6	1	3	14	2	62	2	0	1	5	.167	0	40-45	1	2.15	2.10
2006	Det	AL	62	0	0	56	64.0	272	70	31	28	4	3	1	3	11	3	28	2	0	2	6	.250	0	37-43	0	3.53	3.94
01	Det	AL	45	0	0	28	48.2	225	60	31	25	6	2	3	0	22	1	39	3	0	4	5	.444	0	11-17	3	5.74	4.62
01	Min	AL	24	0	0	8	19.1	89	27	8	7	3	1	0	0	7	0	15	0	0	1	0	1.000	0	2-4	7	6.80	3.26
03	Col	NL	33	1	0	7	39.1	193	61	39	36	8	3	2	1	18	0	28	0	0	1	2	.200	0	0-5	3	8.77	8.24
03	Bos	AL	26	0	0	7	29.1	133	32	19	18	2	0	1	0	13	2	31	0	0	2	1	.667	0	0-0	1	4.30	5.52
04	Cin	NL	51	0	0	10	57.0	235	49	25	24	4	2	5	1	25	2	37	2	0	8	2	.800	0	1-6	22	3.37	3.79
04	Phi	NL	27	0	0	6	25.1	123	35	14	14	3	3	1	5	8	3	22	0	3	3	3	.500	0	1-2	5	6.65	4.97
14 ML YEARS			874	1	0	528	969.0	4192	958	459	421	85	45	36	34	402	53	821	36	1	53	58	.477	0	263-329	100	4.05	3.91

Brian Jordan

Bats: R **Throws:** R **Pos:** 1B-25; PH-22; LF-3; CF-2; RF-1; PR-1   **Ht:** 6'1" **Wt:** 225 **Born:** 3/29/1967 **Age:** 40

									BATTING											BASERUNNING				AVERAGES		
Year	Team	Lg	G	AB	H	2B	3B	HR	(Hm	Rd)	TB	R	RBI	RC	TBB	IBB	SO	HBP	SH	SF	SB	CS	SB%	GDP	Avg	OBP	Slg
2006	Rome*	A	1	1	0	0	0	0	(-	-)	0	0	0	0	3	0	1	0	0	0	0	0	-	0	.000	.750	.000
2006	Rchmd*	AAA	4	15	5	1	0	2	(-	-)	12	3	4	4	1	0	7	0	0	0	0	0	-	0	.333	.375	.800
1992	StL	NL	55	193	40	9	4	5	(3	2)	72	17	22	16	10	1	48	1	0	0	7	2	.78	6	.207	.250	.373
1993	StL	NL	67	223	69	10	6	10	(4	6)	121	33	44	39	12	0	35	4	0	3	6	6	.50	6	.309	.351	.543
1994	StL	NL	53	178	46	8	2	5	(4	1)	73	14	15	22	16	0	40	1	0	2	4	3	.57	6	.258	.320	.410
1995	StL	NL	131	490	145	20	4	22	(8	14)	239	83	81	80	22	4	79	11	0	2	24	9	.73	5	.296	.339	.488
1996	StL	NL	140	513	159	36	1	17	(3	14)	248	82	104	88	29	4	84	7	2	9	22	5	.81	6	.310	.349	.483
1997	StL	NL	47	145	34	5	0	0	(0	0)	39	17	10	13	10	1	21	6	0	0	6	1	.86	4	.234	.311	.269
1998	StL	NL	150	564	178	34	7	25	(9	16)	301	100	91	104	40	1	66	9	0	4	17	5	.77	18	.316	.368	.534
1999	Atl	NL	153	576	163	28	4	23	(11	12)	268	100	115	92	51	2	81	9	0	4	13	8	.62	9	.283	.346	.465
2000	Atl	NL	133	489	129	26	0	17	(7	10)	206	71	77	66	38	1	80	5	0	5	10	2	.83	12	.264	.320	.421

Year	Team	Lg	G	AB	H	2B	3B	HR	(Hm	Rd)	TB	R	RBI	RC	TBB	IBB	SO	HBP	SH	SF	SB	CS	SB%	GDP	Avg	OBP	Slg
												BATTING									BASERUNNING				AVERAGES		
2001	Atl	NL	148	560	165	32	3	25	(14	11)	278	82	97	87	31	3	88	6	0	8	3	2	.60	18	.295	.334	.496
2002	LAD	NL	128	471	134	27	3	18	(7	11)	221	65	80	72	34	3	86	6	0	4	2	2	.50	10	.285	.338	.469
2003	LAD	NL	66	224	67	9	0	6	(3	3)	94	28	28	34	23	3	30	4	0	2	1	1	.50	3	.299	.372	.420
2004	Tex	AL	61	212	47	13	1	5	(4	1)	77	27	23	14	16	2	35	1	0	4	2	2	.50	7	.222	.275	.363
2005	Atl	NL	76	231	57	8	2	3	(2	1)	78	25	24	24	14	0	46	3	0	3	2	0	1.00	6	.247	.295	.338
2006	Atl	NL	48	91	21	2	0	3	(0	3)	32	11	10	7	7	0	23	1	0	2	0	0	-	3	.231	.287	.352
15 ML YEARS			1456	5160	1454	267	37	184	(85	99)	2347	755	821	758	353	25	842	74	2	57	119	48	.71	118	.282	.333	.455

Jorge Julio

Pitches: R Bats: R Pos: RP-62 Ht: 6'1" Wt: 235 Born: 3/3/1979 Age: 28

Year	Team	Lg	G	GS	CG	GF	IP	BFP	H	R	ER	HR	SH	SF	HB	TBB	IBB	SO	WP	Bk	W	L	Pct	ShO	Sv-Op	Hld	ERC	ERA
				HOW MUCH HE PITCHED						WHAT HE GAVE UP											THE RESULTS						
2001	Bal	AL	18	0	0	8	21.1	99	25	13	9	2	2	0	1	9	0	22	1	0	1	1	.500	0	0-1	3	5.17	3.80
2002	Bal	AL	67	0	0	61	68.0	289	55	22	15	5	1	1	2	27	3	55	8	0	5	6	.455	0	25-31	1	2.83	1.99
2003	Bal	AL	64	0	0	51	61.2	273	60	36	30	10	2	1	2	34	4	52	0	0	0	7	.000	0	36-44	2	5.05	4.38
2004	Bal	AL	65	0	0	50	69.0	306	59	35	35	11	2	3	3	39	4	70	7	0	2	5	.286	0	22-26	2	4.35	4.57
2005	Bal	AL	67	0	0	19	71.2	313	76	50	47	14	1	3	2	24	4	58	10	0	3	5	.375	0	0-2	12	4.82	5.90
2006	2 Tms	NL	62	0	0	44	66.0	285	52	35	31	10	1	0	1	35	2	88	9	0	2	4	.333	0	16-20	1	3.72	4.23
06	NYM	NL	18	0	0	12	21.1	96	21	15	12	4	0	0	1	10	1	33	2	0	1	2	.333	0	1-1	0	4.90	5.06
06	Ari	NL	44	0	0	32	44.2	189	31	20	19	6	1	0	0	25	1	55	7	0	1	2	.333	0	15-19	1	3.18	3.83
6 ML YEARS			343	0	0	233	357.2	1565	327	191	167	52	9	8	11	168	17	345	35	0	13	28	.317	0	99-124	21	4.18	4.20

Gabe Kapler

Bats: R Throws: R Pos: RF-37; LF-21; CF-14; PR-11; PH-6; DH-1 Ht: 6'2" Wt: 210 Born: 7/31/1975 Age: 31

Year	Team	Lg	G	AB	H	2B	3B	HR	(Hm	Rd)	TB	R	RBI	RC	TBB	IBB	SO	HBP	SH	SF	SB	CS	SB%	GDP	Avg	OBP	Slg
												BATTING									BASERUNNING				AVERAGES		
2006	Portlnd*	AA	3	10	4	3	1	0	(-	-)	9	2	2	3	1	0	2	0	0	0	0	0	-	0	.400	.455	.900
2006	Pwtckt*	AAA	4	15	3	1	0	0	(-	-)	4	0	2	0	1	0	4	0	0	0	0	0	-	0	.200	.250	.267
1998	Det	AL	7	25	5	0	1	0	(0	0)	7	3	0	2	1	0	4	0	0	0	2	0	1.00	0	.200	.231	.280
1999	Det	AL	130	416	102	22	4	18	(12	6)	186	60	49	59	42	0	74	2	4	4	11	5	.69	7	.245	.315	.447
2000	Tex	AL	116	444	134	32	1	14	(11	3)	210	59	66	72	42	2	57	0	2	3	8	4	.67	12	.302	.360	.473
2001	Tex	AL	134	483	129	29	1	17	(11	6)	211	77	72	77	61	2	70	3	2	7	23	6	.79	10	.267	.348	.437
2002	2 Tms		112	315	88	16	4	2	(1	1)	118	37	34	44	16	0	53	1	7	3	11	4	.73	5	.279	.313	.375
2003	2 Tms		107	225	61	13	1	4	(2	2)	88	39	27	28	22	1	41	0	0	0	6	2	.75	8	.271	.336	.391
2004	Bos	AL	136	290	79	14	1	6	(3	3)	113	51	33	32	15	0	49	2	1	2	5	4	.56	5	.272	.311	.390
2005	Bos	AL	36	97	24	7	0	1	(0	1)	34	15	9	7	3	0	15	2	1	1	1	0	1.00	1	.247	.282	.351
2006	Bos	AL	72	130	33	7	0	2	(1	1)	46	21	12	14	14	0	15	3	0	0	1	1	.50	5	.254	.340	.354
02	Tex	AL	72	196	51	12	1	0	(0	0)	65	25	17	20	8	0	30	0	7	3	5	2	.71	3	.260	.285	.332
02	Col	NL	40	119	37	4	3	2	(1	1)	53	12	17	24	8	0	23	1	0	0	6	2	.75	2	.311	.359	.445
03	Col	NL	39	67	15	2	0	0	(0	0)	17	10	4	5	8	1	18	0	0	0	2	0	1.00	3	.224	.307	.254
03	Bos	AL	68	158	46	11	1	4	(2	2)	71	29	23	23	14	0	23	0	0	0	4	2	.67	5	.291	.349	.449
9 ML YEARS			850	2425	655	140	13	64	(41	23)	1013	362	302	335	216	5	378	13	17	20	68	26	.72	53	.270	.331	.418

Steve Karsay

Pitches: R Bats: R Pos: RP-9 Ht: 6'3" Wt: 215 Born: 3/24/1972 Age: 35

Year	Team	Lg	G	GS	CG	GF	IP	BFP	H	R	ER	HR	SH	SF	HB	TBB	IBB	SO	WP	Bk	W	L	Pct	ShO	Sv-Op	Hld	ERC	ERA
				HOW MUCH HE PITCHED						WHAT HE GAVE UP											THE RESULTS						
2006	Buffalo*	AAA	8	0	0	3	18.0	67	12	6	4	2	0	1	1	0	14	1	0	1	1	.500	0	0- -	-	1.52	2.00
1993	Oak	AL	8	8	0	0	49.0	210	49	23	22	4	0	2	2	16	1	33	1	0	3	3	.500	0	0-0	0	3.78	4.04
1994	Oak	AL	4	4	1	0	28.0	115	26	8	8	1	2	1	1	8	0	15	0	0	1	1	.500	0	0-0	0	3.01	2.57
1997	Oak	AL	24	24	0	0	132.2	609	166	92	85	20	2	5	9	47	3	92	7	0	3	12	.200	0	0-0	0	5.97	5.77
1998	Cle	AL	11	1	0	4	24.1	111	31	16	16	3	1	2	2	6	1	13	2	0	0	2	.000	0	0-0	2	5.40	5.92
1999	Cle	AL	50	3	0	13	78.2	324	71	29	26	6	2	3	2	30	3	68	5	0	10	2	.833	0	1-3	9	3.45	2.97
2000	Cle	AL	72	0	0	46	76.2	329	79	33	32	5	2	2	3	25	4	66	0	0	5	9	.357	0	20-29	11	3.79	3.76
2001	2 Tms		74	0	0	29	88.0	356	73	27	23	5	6	4	1	25	10	83	3	0	3	5	.375	0	8-12	12	2.36	2.35
2002	NYY	AL	78	0	0	38	88.1	379	87	33	32	7	7	3	2	30	14	65	3	0	6	4	.600	0	12-16	14	3.42	3.26
2004	NYY	AL	7	0	0	6	6.2	27	5	3	2	2	0	2	0	2	0	4	1	0	0	0	-	0	0-0	0	3.50	2.70
2005	2 Tms		20	0	0	10	21.2	106	36	19	17	2	0	2	2	7	1	14	1	0	0	1	.000	0	0-0	2	7.61	7.06
2006	Oak	AL	9	0	0	5	9.1	43	13	6	6	4	1	1	1	3	1	5	0	0	1	0	1.000	0	0-0	2	9.34	5.79
01	Cle	AL	31	0	0	8	43.1	166	29	6	6	1	3	0	0	8	2	44	2	0	0	1	.000	0	1-1	8	1.33	1.25
01	Atl	NL	43	0	0	21	44.2	190	44	21	17	4	3	3	1	17	8	39	1	0	3	4	.429	0	7-11	4	3.68	3.43
05	NYY	AL	6	0	0	2	6.0	29	10	5	4	0	0	2	1	5	1	5	0	0	0	0	-	0	0-0	0	6.72	6.00
05	Tex	AL	14	0	0	8	15.2	77	26	14	13	2	0	1	0	5	0	9	1	0	0	1	.000	0	0-0	2	7.93	7.47
11 ML YEARS			357	40	1	151	603.1	2609	636	289	269	59	23	27	23	199	38	458	23	0	32	39	.451	0	41-60	52	4.14	4.01

Jeff Karstens

Pitches: R Bats: R Pos: SP-6; RP-2 Ht: 6'3" Wt: 175 Born: 9/24/1982 Age: 24

Year	Team	Lg	G	GS	CG	GF	IP	BFP	H	R	ER	HR	SH	SF	HB	TBB	IBB	SO	WP	Bk	W	L	Pct	ShO	Sv-Op	Hld	ERC	ERA
				HOW MUCH HE PITCHED						WHAT HE GAVE UP											THE RESULTS						
2003	StsIsInd	A-	14	10	0	2	67.1	275	63	22	19	2	6	5	2	16	1	53	3	0	4	2	.667	0	0- -	-	2.78	2.54
2004	Tampa	A+	24	24	1	0	138.2	582	151	70	62	11	7	8	4	31	3	116	2	1	6	9	.400	1	0- -	-	3.87	4.02
2005	Trntn	AA	28	27	0	0	169.0	742	192	91	78	16	3	5	3	42	1	147	8	1	12	11	.522	0	0- -	-	4.17	4.15
2006	Trntn	AA	11	11	0	0	74.0	296	54	20	19	4	2	3	3	14	1	67	5	0	6	0	1.000	0	0- -	-	1.75	2.31
2006	Clmbs	AAA	14	14	1	0	73.2	326	80	42	35	9	1	3	1	30	1	48	1	1	5	5	.500	0	0- -	-	4.77	4.28
2006	NYY	AL	8	6	0	2	42.2	179	40	20	18	6	0	2	1	11	2	16	3	1	2	1	.667	0	0-0	0	3.42	3.80

Scott Kazmir

Pitches: L Bats: L Pos: SP-24   Ht: 6'0" Wt: 190 Born: 1/24/1984 Age: 23

Year	Team	Lg	G	GS	CG	GF	IP	BFP	H	R	ER	HR	SH	SF	HB	TBB	IBB	SO	WP	Bk	W	L	Pct	ShO	Sv-Op Hld	ERC	ERA
			HOW MUCH HE PITCHED						**WHAT HE GAVE UP**											**THE RESULTS**					
2004	TB	AL	8	7	0	0	33.1	152	33	22	21	4	0	0	2	21	0	41	3	0	2	3	.400	0	0-0 0	5.36	5.67
2005	TB	AL	32	32	0	0	186.0	818	172	90	78	12	6	9	10	**100**	3	174	7	1	10	9	.526	0	0-0 0	4.13	3.77
2006	TB	AL	24	24	1	0	144.2	610	132	59	52	15	0	5	2	52	3	163	6	0	10	8	.556	1	0-0 0	3.47	3.24
3 ML YEARS			64	63	1	0	364.0	1580	337	171	151	31	6	14	14	173	6	378	16	1	22	20	.524	1	0-0 0	3.98	3.73

Austin Kearns

Bats: R Throws: R Pos: RF-144; PH-7; CF-5   Ht: 6'3" Wt: 235 Born: 5/20/1980 Age: 27

Year	Team	Lg	G	AB	H	2B	3B	HR	(Hm	Rd)	TB	R	RBI	RC	TBB	IBB	SO	HBP	SH	SF	SB	CS	SB%	GDP	Avg	OBP	Slg
			BATTING																		**BASERUNNING**				**AVERAGES**		
2002	Cin	NL	107	372	117	24	3	13	(7	6)	186	66	56	70	54	3	81	6	0	3	6	3	.67	11	.315	.407	.500
2003	Cin	NL	82	292	77	11	0	15	(8	7)	133	39	58	52	41	1	68	5	0	0	5	2	.71	7	.264	.364	.455
2004	Cin	NL	64	217	50	10	2	9	(3	6)	91	28	32	26	28	0	71	1	0	0	2	1	.67	8	.230	.321	.419
2005	Cin	NL	112	387	93	26	1	18	(9	9)	175	62	67	55	48	2	107	8	0	5	0	0	-	8	.240	.333	.452
2006	2 Tms	NL	150	537	142	33	2	24	(12	12)	251	86	86	81	76	4	135	10	1	5	9	4	.69	18	.264	.363	.467
06 Cin		NL	87	325	89	21	1	16	(8	8)	160	53	50	46	35	2	85	5	0	3	7	1	.88	14	.274	.351	.492
06 Was		NL	63	212	53	12	1	8	(4	4)	91	33	36	35	41	2	50	5	1	2	2	3	.40	4	.250	.381	.429
5 ML YEARS			515	1805	479	104	8	79	(39	40)	836	281	299	284	247	10	462	30	1	13	22	10	.69	52	.265	.361	.463

Randy Keisler

Pitches: L Bats: L Pos: RP-11   Ht: 6'3" Wt: 190 Born: 2/24/1976 Age: 31

Year	Team	Lg	G	GS	CG	GF	IP	BFP	H	R	ER	HR	SH	SF	HB	TBB	IBB	SO	WP	Bk	W	L	Pct	ShO	Sv-Op Hld	ERC	ERA
			HOW MUCH HE PITCHED						**WHAT HE GAVE UP**											**THE RESULTS**					
2006	Scrmto*	AAA	25	16	0	1	103.1	462	107	53	44	2	6	4	6	47	3	82	6	0	9	5	.643	0	0- -	4.04	3.83
2000	NYY	AL	4	1	0	0	10.2	52	16	14	14	1	0	0	0	8	0	6	0	0	1	0	1.000	0	0-0 0	9.10	11.81
2001	NYY	AL	10	10	0	0	50.2	236	52	36	35	12	0	0	0	34	0	36	0	0	1	2	.333	0	0-0 0	6.33	6.22
2003	SD	NL	2	2	0	0	6.0	33	7	9	8	3	0	1	1	7	0	5	0	1	0	1	.000	0	0-0 0	12.82	12.00
2005	Cin	NL	24	4	0	7	56.0	262	64	45	39	10	1	1	1	28	2	43	2	0	2	1	.667	0	0-0 0	5.77	6.27
2006	Oak	AL	11	0	0	2	10.0	42	14	5	5	3	0	0	0	2	1	5	0	0	0	0	-	0	0-0 1	7.51	4.50
5 ML YEARS			51	17	0	9	133.1	625	153	109	101	29	1	2	2	79	3	95	2	1	4	4	.500	0	0-0 1	6.65	6.82

Matt Kemp

Bats: R Throws: R Pos: CF-29; LF-11; RF-10; PH-8; PR-3   Ht: 6'2" Wt: 230 Born: 9/23/1984 Age: 22

Year	Team	Lg	G	AB	H	2B	3B	HR	(Hm	Rd)	TB	R	RBI	RC	TBB	IBB	SO	HBP	SH	SF	SB	CS	SB%	GDP	Avg	OBP	Slg
			BATTING																		**BASERUNNING**				**AVERAGES**		
2003	Ddgrs	R	42	159	43	5	2	1	(-	-)	55	11	17	16	7	1	25	0	0	2	2	1	.67	1	.270	.298	.346
2004	Clmbs	A	111	423	122	22	8	17	(-	-)	211	67	66	69	24	1	100	5	1	5	8	7	.53	10	.288	.330	.499
2004	VeroB	A+	11	37	13	5	0	1	(-	-)	21	5	9	8	4	0	12	0	0	1	2	1	.67	0	.351	.405	.568
2005	VeroB	A+	109	418	128	21	4	27	(-	-)	238	76	90	84	25	2	92	5	1	5	23	6	.79	8	.306	.349	.569
2006	Jaxnvl	AA	48	199	65	15	2	7	(-	-)	105	38	34	43	20	4	38	5	0	0	11	2	.85	10	.327	.402	.528
2006	LsVgs	AAA	44	182	67	14	6	3	(-	-)	102	37	36	43	17	0	26	2	1	0	14	3	.82	4	.368	.428	.560
2006	LAD	NL	52	154	39	7	1	7	(4	3)	69	30	23	20	9	1	53	0	0	3	6	0	1.00	1	.253	.289	.448

Jason Kendall

Bats: R Throws: R Pos: C-141; PH-2   Ht: 6'0" Wt: 205 Born: 6/26/1974 Age: 33

Year	Team	Lg	G	AB	H	2B	3B	HR	(Hm	Rd)	TB	R	RBI	RC	TBB	IBB	SO	HBP	SH	SF	SB	CS	SB%	GDP	Avg	OBP	Slg
			BATTING																		**BASERUNNING**				**AVERAGES**		
1996	Pit	NL	130	414	124	23	5	3	(2	1)	166	54	42	63	35	11	30	15	3	4	5	2	.71	7	.300	.372	.401
1997	Pit	NL	144	486	143	36	4	8	(5	3)	211	71	49	86	49	2	53	31	1	5	18	6	.75	11	.294	.391	.434
1998	Pit	NL	149	535	175	36	3	12	(6	6)	253	95	75	110	51	3	51	**31**	2	8	26	5	.84	6	.327	.411	.473
1999	Pit	NL	78	280	93	20	3	8	(5	3)	143	61	41	63	38	3	32	12	0	4	22	3	.88	8	.332	.428	.511
2000	Pit	NL	152	579	185	33	6	14	(7	7)	272	112	58	112	79	3	79	15	1	4	22	12	.65	13	.320	.412	.470
2001	Pit	NL	157	606	161	22	2	10	(3	7)	217	84	53	68	44	4	48	20	0	2	13	14	.48	18	.266	.335	.358
2002	Pit	NL	145	545	154	25	3	3	(1	2)	194	59	44	66	49	1	29	9	0	2	15	8	.65	11	.283	.350	.356
2003	Pit	NL	150	587	191	29	3	6	(3	3)	244	84	58	97	49	3	40	25	1	3	8	7	.53	9	.325	.399	.416
2004	Pit	NL	147	574	183	32	0	3	(2	1)	224	86	51	95	60	2	41	19	1	4	11	8	.58	12	.319	.399	.390
2005	Oak	AL	150	601	163	28	1	0	(0	0)	193	70	53	79	50	0	39	20	0	5	8	3	.73	**26**	.271	.345	.321
2006	Oak	AL	143	552	163	23	0	1	(1	0)	189	76	50	80	53	2	54	12	4	5	11	5	.69	19	.295	.367	.342
11 ML YEARS			1545	5759	1735	307	30	68	(35	33)	2306	852	574	919	557	34	496	209	13	46	159	73	.69	140	.301	.381	.400

Howie Kendrick

Bats: R Throws: R Pos: 1B-44; 2B-28; DH-2; 3B-1; PR-1   Ht: 5'10" Wt: 195 Born: 7/12/1983 Age: 23

Year	Team	Lg	G	AB	H	2B	3B	HR	(Hm	Rd)	TB	R	RBI	RC	TBB	IBB	SO	HBP	SH	SF	SB	CS	SB%	GDP	Avg	OBP	Slg
			BATTING																		**BASERUNNING**				**AVERAGES**		
2002	Angels	R	42	157	50	6	4	0	(-	-)	64	24	13	24	7	0	11	6	1	1	12	6	.67	2	.318	.368	.408
2003	Provo	R	63	234	86	20	3	3	(-	-)	121	65	36	53	24	1	28	6	3	3	8	3	.73	5	.368	.434	.517
2004	CRpds	A	75	313	115	24	6	10	(-	-)	181	66	49	69	12	2	41	6	3	3	15	6	.71	2	.367	.398	.578
2005	RCuca	A+	63	279	107	23	6	12	(-	-)	178	69	47	70	14	0	42	7	0	4	13	4	.76	5	.384	.421	.638
2005	Ark	AA	44	190	65	20	2	7	(-	-)	110	35	42	41	6	0	20	7	0	1	12	4	.75	7	.342	.382	.579
2006	Salt Lk	AAA	69	290	107	25	6	13	(-	-)	183	57	62	70	12	1	48	8	1	1	11	3	.79	2	.369	.408	.631
2006	LAA	AL	72	267	76	21	1	4	(2	2)	111	25	30	32	9	2	44	4	0	3	6	0	1.00	5	.285	.314	.416

Adam Kennedy

Bats: L Throws: R Pos: 2B-133; PH-10; DH-1 Ht: 6'0" Wt: 185 Born: 1/10/1976 Age: 31

									BATTING												BASERUNNING				AVERAGES		
Year	Team	Lg	G	AB	H	2B	3B	HR	(Hm	Rd)	TB	R	RBI	RC	TBB	IBB	SO	HBP	SH	SF	SB	CS	SB%	GDP	Avg	OBP	Slg
1999	StL	NL	33	102	26	10	1	1	(1	0)	41	12	16	12	3	0	8	2	1	2	0	1	.00	1	.255	.284	.402
2000	LAA	AL	156	598	159	33	11	9	(7	2)	241	82	72	72	28	5	73	3	8	4	22	8	.73	10	.266	.300	.403
2001	LAA	AL	137	478	129	25	3	6	(4	2)	178	48	40	57	27	3	71	11	7	9	12	7	.63	7	.270	.318	.372
2002	LAA	AL	144	474	148	32	6	7	(6	1)	213	65	52	70	19	1	80	7	5	4	17	4	.81	5	.312	.345	.449
2003	LAA	AL	143	449	121	17	1	13	(8	5)	179	71	49	61	45	4	73	9	2	5	22	9	.71	7	.269	.344	.399
2004	LAA	AL	144	468	130	20	5	10	(5	5)	190	70	48	60	41	7	92	13	9	2	15	5	.75	10	.278	.351	.406
2005	LAA	AL	129	416	125	23	0	2	(1	1)	154	49	37	62	29	1	64	7	5	3	19	4	.83	5	.300	.354	.370
2006	LAA	AL	139	451	123	26	6	4	(3	1)	173	50	55	62	39	5	72	5	3	5	16	10	.62	15	.273	.334	.384
	8 ML YEARS		1025	3436	961	186	33	52	(35	17)	1369	447	369	456	231	26	533	57	40	34	123	48	.72	60	.280	.332	.398

Joe Kennedy

Pitches: L Bats: R Pos: RP-39 Ht: 6'4" Wt: 245 Born: 5/24/1979 Age: 28

			HOW MUCH HE PITCHED						WHAT HE GAVE UP												THE RESULTS						
Year	Team	Lg	G	GS	CG	GF	IP	BFP	H	R	ER	HR	SH	SF	HB	TBB	IBB	SO	WP	Bk	W	L	Pct	ShO	Sv-Op	Hld	ERC	ERA
2006 Scrmto*	AAA		3	1	0	0	4.0	15	2	0	0	0	0	0	1	1	0	2	0	0	0	0	-	0	0- -	-	1.51	0.00
2001	TB	AL	20	20	0	0	117.2	498	122	63	58	16	2	5	3	34	0	78	5	1	7	8	.467	0	0-0	0	4.23	4.44
2002	TB	AL	30	30	5	0	196.2	840	204	114	99	23	2	9	16	55	0	109	4	0	8	11	.421	1	0-0	0	4.29	4.53
2003	TB	AL	32	22	1	7	133.2	619	167	101	91	19	1	8	11	47	1	77	3	1	3	12	.200	1	1-2	1	5.92	6.13
2004	Col	NL	27	27	1	0	162.1	705	163	68	66	17	9	6	8	67	12	117	5	0	9	7	.563	0	0-0	0	4.29	3.66
2005 2 Tms			35	24	0	3	152.2	704	192	114	102	20	4	6	7	64	6	97	8	1	8	13	.381	0	0-2	0	6.04	6.01
2006	Oak	AL	39	0	0	8	35.0	148	34	10	9	1	0	0	1	13	3	29	2	0	4	1	.800	0	1-3	14	3.32	2.31
05 Col	NL		16	16	0	0	92.0	442	128	81	72	12	4	5	6	44	4	52	7	1	4	8	.333	0	0-0	0	7.24	7.04
05 Oak	AL		19	8	0	3	60.2	262	64	33	30	8	0	1	1	20	2	45	1	0	4	5	.444	0	0-2	0	4.33	4.45
	6 ML YEARS		183	123	7	18	798.0	3514	882	470	425	96	18	34	46	280	22	507	27	3	39	52	.429	2	2-7	15	4.83	4.79

Logan Kensing

Pitches: R Bats: R Pos: RP-37 Ht: 6'1" Wt: 185 Born: 7/3/1982 Age: 24

			HOW MUCH HE PITCHED						WHAT HE GAVE UP												THE RESULTS						
Year	Team	Lg	G	GS	CG	GF	IP	BFP	H	R	ER	HR	SH	SF	HB	TBB	IBB	SO	WP	Bk	W	L	Pct	ShO	Sv-Op	Hld	ERC	ERA
2006 Albq*	AAA		13	0	0	5	18.0	66	11	6	6	2	0	0	6	5	0	18	1	0	1	1	.500	0	2- -	-	1.86	3.00
2004	Fla	NL	5	3	0	2	13.2	66	19	15	15	5	0	1	1	9	0	7	2	0	0	3	.000	0	0-0	0	10.74	9.88
2005	Fla	NL	3	0	0	0	5.2	31	11	7	7	2	0	1	0	3	0	4	0	0	0	0	-	0	0-0	1	12.96	11.12
2006	Fla	NL	37	0	0	10	37.2	161	30	19	19	6	3	0	3	19	2	45	0	0	1	3	.250	0	1-7	14	4.02	4.54
	3 ML YEARS		45	3	0	12	57.0	258	60	41	41	13	3	2	4	31	2	56	2	0	1	6	.143	0	1-7	15	6.26	6.47

Jeff Kent

Bats: R Throws: R Pos: 2B-108; 1B-9; PH-2 Ht: 6'1" Wt: 210 Born: 3/7/1968 Age: 39

									BATTING												BASERUNNING				AVERAGES		
Year	Team	Lg	G	AB	H	2B	3B	HR	(Hm	Rd)	TB	R	RBI	RC	TBB	IBB	SO	HBP	SH	SF	SB	CS	SB%	GDP	Avg	OBP	Slg
1992 2 Tms			102	305	73	21	2	11	(4	7)	131	52	50	40	27	0	76	7	0	4	2	3	.40	5	.239	.312	.430
1993 NYM	NL		140	496	134	24	0	21	(9	12)	221	65	80	68	30	2	88	8	6	4	4	4	.50	11	.270	.320	.446
1994 NYM	NL		107	415	121	24	5	14	(10	4)	197	53	68	64	23	3	84	10	1	3	1	4	.20	7	.292	.341	.475
1995 NYM	NL		125	472	131	22	3	20	(11	9)	219	65	65	69	29	3	89	8	1	4	3	3	.50	9	.278	.327	.464
1996 2 Tms			128	437	124	27	1	12	(4	8)	189	61	55	61	31	1	78	2	1	6	6	4	.60	8	.284	.330	.432
1997 SF	NL		155	580	145	38	2	29	(13	16)	274	90	121	86	48	6	133	13	0	10	11	3	.79	14	.250	.316	.472
1998 SF	NL		137	526	156	37	3	31	(17	14)	292	94	128	100	48	4	110	9	1	10	9	4	.69	16	.297	.359	.555
1999 SF	NL		138	511	148	40	2	23	(11	12)	261	86	101	93	61	3	112	5	0	8	13	6	.68	12	.290	.366	.511
2000 SF	NL		159	587	196	41	7	33	(14	19)	350	114	125	138	90	6	107	9	0	9	12	9	.57	17	.334	.424	.596
2001 SF	NL		159	607	181	49	6	22	(8	14)	308	84	106	112	65	4	96	11	0	13	7	6	.54	11	.298	.369	.507
2002 SF	NL		152	623	195	42	2	37	(11	26)	352	102	108	105	52	3	101	4	0	3	5	1	.83	20	.313	.368	.565
2003 Hou	NL		130	505	150	39	1	22	(9	13)	257	77	93	92	39	2	85	5	0	3	6	2	.75	13	.297	.351	.509
2004 Hou	NL		145	540	156	34	8	27	(14	13)	287	96	107	87	49	3	96	6	0	11	7	3	.70	23	.289	.348	.531
2005 LAD	NL		149	553	160	36	0	29	(15	14)	283	100	105	105	72	8	85	8	0	4	6	2	.75	19	.289	.377	.512
2006 LAD	NL		115	407	119	27	3	14	(10	4)	194	61	68	71	55	8	69	8	0	3	1	2	.33	9	.292	.385	.477
92 Tor	AL		65	192	46	13	1	8	(2	6)	85	36	35	28	20	0	47	6	0	4	2	1	.67	3	.240	.324	.443
92 NYM	NL		37	113	27	8	1	3	(2	1)	46	16	15	12	7	0	29	1	0	0	0	2	.00	2	.239	.289	.407
96 NYM	NL		89	335	97	20	1	9	(2	7)	146	45	39	46	21	1	56	1	1	3	4	3	.57	7	.290	.331	.436
96 Cle	AL		39	102	27	7	0	3	(2	1)	43	16	16	15	10	0	22	1	0	3	2	1	.67	1	.265	.328	.422
	15 ML YEARS		2041	7564	2189	501	45	345	(160	185)	3815	1200	1380	1291	719	56	1409	113	10	95	93	56	.62	194	.289	.356	.504

Bobby Keppel

Pitches: R Bats: R Pos: SP-6; RP-2 Ht: 6'5" Wt: 205 Born: 6/11/1982 Age: 25

			HOW MUCH HE PITCHED						WHAT HE GAVE UP												THE RESULTS						
Year	Team	Lg	G	GS	CG	GF	IP	BFP	H	R	ER	HR	SH	SF	HB	TBB	IBB	SO	WP	Bk	W	L	Pct	ShO	Sv-Op	Hld	ERC	ERA
2000 Kngspt	R+		8	6	0	0	29.0	136	31	22	22	1	0	4	4	13	0	29	6	0	1	2	.333	0	0- -	-	4.54	6.83
2001 CptCty	A		26	20	1	3	124.1	516	118	58	43	6	2	2	14	25	1	87	7	0	6	7	.462	0	0- -	-	3.13	3.11
2002 StLuci	A		27	26	1	0	152.0	656	162	83	73	13	5	7	16	43	0	109	12	1	9	7	.563	2	0- -	-	4.34	4.32
2003 Bnghtn	AA		18	17	2	0	94.2	388	92	36	32	6	5	1	6	27	0	46	3	1	7	4	.636	2	0- -	-	3.60	3.04
2003 Bklyn	A-		3	3	0	0	14.1	57	10	5	4	0	0	0	2	2	0	13	0	0	2	0	1.000	0	0- -	-	1.55	2.51
2004 StLuci	A		2	2	0	0	10.0	37	7	2	1	0	1	0	0	2	0	6	0	0	1	1	.500	0	0- -	-	1.47	0.90
2004 Norfolk	AAA		17	16	1	0	93.2	402	111	51	49	8	8	6	9	22	1	42	2	1	3	7	.300	0	0- -	-	4.88	4.71
2005 Norfolk	AAA		5	5	0	0	27.1	112	24	11	10	0	0	4	0	6	0	19	1	0	2	1	.667	0	0- -	-	2.68	3.29
2006 Omha	AAA		25	14	0	2	98.1	432	126	73	62	12	2	4	1	28	1	43	8	1	6	7	.462	0	1- -	-	5.54	5.67
2006 KC	AL		8	6	0	0	34.1	157	45	21	21	6	1	2	1	15	2	20	0	0	0	4	.000	0	0-0	0	6.85	5.50

Jeff Keppinger

Bats: R **Throws:** R **Pos:** 3B-12; 1B-4; PR-4; DH-3; PH-2; 2B-1; LF-1   **Ht:** 6'0" **Wt:** 180 **Born:** 4/21/1980 **Age:** 27

									BATTING											BASERUNNING				AVERAGES		
Year	Team	Lg	G	AB	H	2B	3B	HR	(Hm	Rd)	TB	R	RBI	RC	TBB	IBB	SO	HBP	SH	SF	SB	CS	SB%	GDP	Avg	OBP	Slg
2002	Hickory	A	126	478	132	23	4	10	(-	-)	193	75	73	67	47	0	33	6	2	7	6	2	.75	13	.276	.344	.404
2003	Lynbrg	A+	92	342	111	21	2	3	(-	-)	145	55	51	51	23	0	28	1	3	4	3	2	.60	10	.325	.365	.424
2004	Altna	AA	82	323	108	17	2	1	(-	-)	132	45	33	49	27	1	17	0	2	2	10	6	.63	13	.334	.384	.409
2004	Bnghtn	AA	14	47	17	3	1	0	(-	-)	22	14	5	9	6	1	2	0	0	1	2	1	.67	2	.362	.426	.468
2004	Norfolk	AAA	6	19	6	1	0	0	(-	-)	7	1	2	3	4	0	2	1	0	0	0	0	-	2	.316	.458	.368
2005	Norfolk	AAA	64	255	86	15	3	3	(-	-)	116	40	29	44	16	1	13	1	5	1	5	1	.83	6	.337	.377	.455
2006	Norfolk	AAA	87	323	97	13	0	2	(-	-)	116	36	26	43	28	0	21	0	12	3	4	4	.00	7	.300	.353	.359
2006	Omha	AAA	32	127	45	6	1	2	(-	-)	59	21	17	24	12	0	9	0	2	1	0	0	-	5	.354	.407	.465
2004	NYM	NL	33	116	33	2	0	3	(3	0)	44	9	9	12	6	0	7	0	0	1	2	1	.67	6	.284	.317	.379
2006	KC	AL	22	60	16	2	0	2	(0	2)	24	11	8	8	5	1	6	0	2	0	0	0	-	2	.267	.323	.400
	2 ML YEARS		55	176	49	4	0	5	(3	2)	68	20	17	20	11	1	13	0	2	1	2	1	.67	8	.278	.319	.386

Bobby Kielty

Bats: B **Throws:** R **Pos:** LF-44; RF-31; PH-6; DH-3; PR-2   **Ht:** 6'1" **Wt:** 220 **Born:** 8/5/1976 **Age:** 30

									BATTING											BASERUNNING				AVERAGES		
Year	Team	Lg	G	AB	H	2B	3B	HR	(Hm	Rd)	TB	R	RBI	RC	TBB	IBB	SO	HBP	SH	SF	SB	CS	SB%	GDP	Avg	OBP	Slg
2006	Scrmto*	AAA	10	36	8	0	0	1	(-	-)	11	5	4	4	7	0	12	0	0	0	0	0	-	2	.222	.349	.306
2001	Min	AL	37	104	26	8	0	2	(1	1)	40	8	14	13	8	2	25	1	0	5	3	0	1.00	2	.250	.297	.385
2002	Min	AL	112	289	84	14	3	12	(8	4)	140	49	46	59	52	4	66	5	0	2	4	1	.80	4	.291	.405	.484
2003	2 Tms	AL	137	427	104	26	1	13	(6	7)	171	71	57	68	71	6	92	7	0	4	8	3	.73	11	.244	.358	.400
2004	Oak	AL	83	238	51	14	1	7	(6	1)	88	29	31	29	35	0	47	3	1	1	1	0	1.00	5	.214	.321	.370
2005	Oak	AL	116	377	99	20	0	10	(6	4)	149	55	57	53	50	3	67	2	2	3	3	2	.60	14	.263	.350	.395
2006	Oak	AL	81	270	73	20	1	8	(5	3)	119	35	36	40	22	0	49	2	2	1	2	0	1.00	9	.270	.329	.441
	03 Min	AL	75	238	60	13	0	9	(4	5)	100	40	32	41	42	2	56	3	0	1	6	2	.75	5	.252	.370	.420
	03 Tor	AL	62	189	44	13	1	4	(2	2)	71	31	25	27	29	4	36	4	0	3	2	1	.67	6	.233	.342	.376
	6 ML YEARS		566	1705	437	102	6	52	(32	20)	707	247	241	262	238	15	346	20	5	15	21	6	.78	45	.256	.351	.415

Byung-Hyun Kim

Pitches: R **Bats:** R **Pos:** SP-27   **Ht:** 5'9" **Wt:** 175 **Born:** 1/19/1979 **Age:** 28

			HOW MUCH HE PITCHED						WHAT HE GAVE UP											THE RESULTS						
Year	Team	Lg	G	GS	CG	GF	IP	BFP	H	R	ER	HR	SH	SF	HB	TBB	IBB	SO	WP	Bk	W	L	Pct	ShO	Sv-Op	Hld	ERC	ERA
2006	ColSpr*	AAA	3	3	0	0	13.0	63	18	11	9	0	0	0	1	4	0	11	1	0	0	1	.000	0	0--	-	5.23	6.23
1999	Ari	NL	25	0	0	10	27.1	121	20	15	14	2	1	0	5	20	2	31	4	1	1	2	.333	0	1-4	3	4.35	4.61
2000	Ari	NL	61	1	0	30	70.2	320	52	39	35	9	2	3	9	46	5	111	3	2	6	6	.500	0	14-20	5	4.04	4.46
2001	Ari	NL	78	0	0	44	98.0	392	58	32	32	10	5	0	8	44	3	113	5	1	5	6	.455	0	19-23	11	2.45	2.94
2002	Ari	NL	72	0	0	66	84.0	343	64	20	19	5	1	2	6	26	2	92	2	0	8	3	.727	0	36-42	2	2.45	2.04
2003	2 Tms		56	12	0	35	122.1	517	104	55	45	12	6	2	12	33	3	102	1	0	9	10	.474	0	16-19	1	3.02	3.31
2004	Bos	AL	7	3	0	2	17.1	77	17	15	12	1	0	2	2	7	1	6	1	0	1	1	.667	0	0-0	0	3.98	6.23
2005	Col	NL	40	22	0	3	148.0	667	156	82	80	17	8	7	14	71	8	115	11	1	5	12	.294	0	0-2	1	5.13	4.86
2006	Col	NL	27	27	0	0	155.0	689	179	103	96	18	8	5	8	61	8	129	5	1	8	12	.400	0	0-0	0	5.25	5.57
	03 Ari	NL	7	7	0	0	43.0	181	34	17	17	6	3	0	4	15	0	33	0	0	1	5	.167	0	0-0	0	3.32	3.56
	03 Bos	AL	49	5	0	35	79.1	336	70	38	28	6	3	2	8	18	3	69	1	0	8	5	.615	0	16-19	1	2.87	3.18
	8 ML YEARS		366	65	0	190	722.2	3126	650	361	333	74	31	21	64	308	32	699	32	6	44	52	.458	0	86-110	21	3.91	4.15

Sun-Woo Kim

Pitches: R **Bats:** R **Pos:** RP-7; SP-1   **Ht:** 6'1" **Wt:** 190 **Born:** 9/4/1977 **Age:** 29

			HOW MUCH HE PITCHED						WHAT HE GAVE UP											THE RESULTS						
Year	Team	Lg	G	GS	CG	GF	IP	BFP	H	R	ER	HR	SH	SF	HB	TBB	IBB	SO	WP	Bk	W	L	Pct	ShO	Sv-Op	Hld	ERC	ERA
2006	ColSpr*	AAA	21	21	2	0	124.2	539	149	77	70	14	3	5	7	36	0	71	9	0	8	6	.571	2	0--	-	5.22	5.05
2001	Bos	AL	20	2	0	7	41.2	201	54	27	27	1	3	0	4	21	5	27	5	0	0	2	.000	0	0-0	1	5.72	5.83
2002	2 Tms		19	5	0	7	49.1	208	52	26	26	5	0	2	2	14	2	29	2	0	3	0	1.000	0	0-0	4	4.10	4.74
2003	Mon	NL	4	3	0	1	14.0	72	24	13	13	6	0	0	1	8	0	5	0	0	0	1	.000	0	0-0	0	14.93	8.36
2004	Mon	NL	43	17	0	3	135.2	603	145	80	69	17	5	3	13	55	11	87	6	0	4	6	.400	0	0-0	0	4.96	4.58
2005	2 Tms	NL	24	10	1	3	82.2	363	97	46	45	10	5	3	3	21	2	55	4	0	6	3	.667	1	0-0	4	4.71	4.90
2006	2 Tms	NL	8	1	0	1	13.2	73	24	19	19	5	0	3	1	8	0	8	3	0	0	1	.000	0	0-0	0	12.56	12.51
	02 Bos	AL	15	2	0	7	29.0	128	34	24	24	5	0	2	1	7	0	18	2	0	2	0	1.000	0	0-0	2	5.01	7.45
	02 Mon	NL	4	3	0	0	20.1	80	18	2	2	0	0	0	1	7	2	11	0	0	1	0	1.000	0	0-0	2	2.82	0.89
	05 Was	NL	12	2	0	3	29.1	135	41	20	20	3	1	2	2	8	2	17	1	0	1	2	.333	0	0-0	1	6.12	6.14
	05 Col	NL	12	8	1	0	53.1	228	56	26	25	7	4	1	1	13	0	38	3	0	5	1	.833	1	0-0	3	3.54	4.22
	06 Col	NL	6	0	0	1	7.0	45	17	15	15	2	0	2	1	8	0	4	1	0	0	0	-	0	0-0	0	20.92	19.29
	06 Cin	NL	2	1	0	0	6.2	28	7	4	4	3	0	1	0	0	0	4	2	0	0	1	.000	0	0-0	0	4.55	5.40
	6 ML YEARS		118	38	1	22	337.0	1520	396	211	199	44	13	12	27	127	20	211	20	0	13	13	.500	1	0-0	5	5.48	5.31

Ray King

Pitches: L **Bats:** L **Pos:** RP-67   **Ht:** 6'1" **Wt:** 240 **Born:** 1/15/1974 **Age:** 33

			HOW MUCH HE PITCHED						WHAT HE GAVE UP											THE RESULTS						
Year	Team	Lg	G	GS	CG	GF	IP	BFP	H	R	ER	HR	SH	SF	HB	TBB	IBB	SO	WP	Bk	W	L	Pct	ShO	Sv-Op	Hld	ERC	ERA
1999	ChC	NL	10	0	0	0	10.2	50	11	8	7	2	1	0	1	10	0	5	1	0	0	0	-	0	0-0	2	8.10	5.91
2000	Mil	NL	36	0	0	8	28.2	111	18	7	4	1	0	1	0	10	1	19	1	0	3	2	.600	0	0-1	5	1.64	1.26
2001	Mil	NL	82	0	0	19	55.0	234	49	22	22	5	3	2	1	25	7	49	2	0	0	4	.000	0	1-4	18	3.51	3.60
2002	Mil	NL	76	0	0	15	65.0	273	61	24	24	5	5	2	3	24	6	50	0	1	3	2	.600	0	0-1	15	3.55	3.05
2003	Atl	NL	80	0	0	9	59.0	247	46	30	23	3	1	2	1	27	2	43	4	0	3	4	.429	0	0-1	18	2.79	3.51
2004	StL	NL	86	0	0	9	62.0	248	43	19	18	1	2	1	3	24	0	40	2	0	5	2	.714	0	0-1	31	2.13	2.61

Year	Team	Lg	G	GS	CG	GF	IP	BFP	H	R	ER	HR	SH	SF	HB	TBB	IBB	SO	WP	Bk	W	L	Pct	ShO	Sv-Op	Hld	ERC	ERA
2005	StL	NL	77	0	0	18	40.0	177	46	17	15	4	0	1	3	16	0	23	1	0	4	4	.500	0	0-6	16	5.37	3.38
2006	Col	NL	67	0	0	7	44.2	199	56	26	22	6	3	3	2	20	0	23	3	0	1	4	.200	0	1-2	15	6.51	4.43
8 ML YEARS			514	0	0	85	365.0	1539	330	153	133	27	15	12	14	156	16	252	14	1	19	22	.463	0	2-16	120	3.61	3.28

Josh Kinney

Pitches: R Bats: R Pos: RP-21   Ht: 6'1" Wt: 195 Born: 3/31/1979 Age: 28

Year	Team	Lg	G	GS	CG	GF	IP	BFP	H	R	ER	HR	SH	SF	HB	TBB	IBB	SO	WP	Bk	W	L	Pct	ShO	Sv-Op	Hld	ERC	ERA
2001	NewJrs	A-	3	0	0	0	5.2	18	2	0	0	0	0	0	0	0	0	5	0	0	2	0	1.000	0	0--	-	0.30	0.00
2001	Peoria	A	27	0	0	5	41.0	192	47	24	20	1	4	2	7	15	0	35	4	1	1	4	.200	0	0--	-	4.75	4.39
2002	Ptomc	A+	44	0	0	28	55.0	239	52	21	14	2	2	1	3	23	1	42	6	0	1	3	.250	0	7--	-	3.55	2.29
2003	PlmBh	A+	31	0	0	10	41.1	167	38	7	7	0	2	0	0	10	4	35	5	0	3	0	1.000	0	3--	-	2.31	1.52
2003	Tenn	AA	29	0	0	12	39.2	147	19	4	3	2	1	0	0	12	0	48	1	0	2	1	.667	0	2--	-	1.18	0.68
2004	Tenn	AA	50	0	0	25	55.2	270	67	40	34	6	0	0	3	34	0	48	6	0	3	8	.273	0	4--	-	6.30	5.50
2004	PlmBh	A+	7	0	0	7	8.1	39	8	6	4	1	0	0	1	6	2	12	0	0	0	1	.000	0	0--	-	5.33	4.32
2005	Sprgfld	AA	32	0	0	22	42.0	165	28	9	6	2	0	2	0	12	0	42	1	0	5	2	.714	0	11--	-	1.67	1.29
2005	Memp	AAA	26	0	0	8	25.2	135	40	21	21	4	0	1	2	19	1	25	4	0	1	2	.333	0	0--	-	9.84	7.36
2006	Memp	AAA	51	0	0	17	71.0	286	46	16	12	2	4	1	5	29	4	76	12	0	2	2	.500	0	3--	-	2.03	1.52
2006	StL	NL	21	0	0	4	25.0	99	17	9	9	3	0	0	1	8	0	22	0	0	0	0	-	0	0-0	2	2.40	3.24

Ian Kinsler

Bats: R Throws: R Pos: 2B-119; PH-1   Ht: 6'0" Wt: 200 Born: 6/22/1982 Age: 25

Year	Team	Lg	G	AB	H	2B	3B	HR	(Hm	Rd)	TB	R	RBI	RC	TBB	IBB	SO	HBP	SH	SF	SB	CS	SB%	GDP	Avg	OBP	Slg
2003	Spkane	A-	51	188	52	10	6	1	(-	-)	77	32	15	30	20	0	34	4	0	4	11	3	.79	5	.277	.352	.410
2004	Clinton	A	59	224	90	30	1	11	(-	-)	155	52	52	66	25	3	36	1	2		16	5	.76	7	.402	.465	.692
2004	Frisco	AA	71	277	83	21	1	9	(-	-)	133	51	46	55	32	1	47	15	1	1	7	4	.64	5	.300	.400	.480
2005	Okla	AAA	131	530	145	28	2	23	(-	-)	246	102	94	90	53	0	89	9	2	3	19	5	.79	21	.274	.348	.464
2006	Okla	AAA	10	39	10	3	0	2	(-	-)	19	7	6	5	2	0	5	0	0	0	1	1	.50	1	.256	.293	.487
2006	Tex	AL	120	423	121	27	1	14	(10	4)	192	65	55	65	40	1	64	3	1	7	11	4	.73	12	.286	.347	.454

Ryan Klesko

Bats: L Throws: L Pos: PH-6   Ht: 6'3" Wt: 220 Born: 6/12/1971 Age: 36

Year	Team	Lg	G	AB	H	2B	3B	HR	(Hm	Rd)	TB	R	RBI	RC	TBB	IBB	SO	HBP	SH	SF	SB	CS	SB%	GDP	Avg	OBP	Slg
2006	Lk Els*	A+	8	22	6	2	0	0	(0	0)	8	2	1	3	5	0	5	1	0	0	0	0	-	1	.273	.407	.364
1992	Atl	NL	13	14	0	0	0	0	(0	0)	0	0	0	1	0	0	5	1	0	0	0	0	-	0	.000	.067	.000
1993	Atl	NL	22	17	6	1	0	2	(2	0)	13	3	5	5	3	1	4	0	0	0	0	0	-	0	.353	.450	.765
1994	Atl	NL	92	245	68	13	3	17	(7	10)	138	42	47	45	26	3	48	1	0	4	1	0	1.00	8	.278	.344	.563
1995	Atl	NL	107	329	102	25	2	23	(15	8)	200	48	70	73	47	10	72	2	0	3	5	4	.56	8	.310	.396	.608
1996	Atl	NL	153	528	149	21	4	34	(20	14)	280	90	93	99	68	10	129	2	0	4	6	3	.67	10	.282	.364	.530
1997	Atl	NL	143	467	122	23	6	24	(10	14)	229	67	84	73	48	5	130	4	1	2	4	4	.50	12	.261	.334	.490
1998	Atl	NL	129	427	117	29	1	18	(8	10)	202	69	70	72	56	5	66	3	0	4	5	3	.63	9	.274	.359	.473
1999	Atl	NL	133	404	120	28	2	21	(12	9)	215	55	80	80	53	8	69	2	0	7	5	2	.71	6	.297	.376	.532
2000	SD	NL	145	494	140	33	2	26	(9	17)	255	88	92	101	91	9	81	1	0	4	23	7	.77	10	.283	.393	.516
2001	SD	NL	146	538	154	34	6	30	(15	15)	290	105	113	111	88	7	89	3	0	9	23	4	.85	16	.286	.384	.539
2002	SD	NL	146	540	162	39	1	29	(11	18)	290	90	95	111	76	11	86	4	1	4	6	2	.75	7	.300	.388	.537
2003	SD	NL	121	397	100	18	0	21	(8	13)	181	47	67	59	65	5	83	3	0	9	2	5	.29	11	.252	.354	.456
2004	SD	NL	127	402	117	32	2	9	(3	6)	180	58	66	76	73	6	67	1	1	3	3	2	.60	8	.291	.399	.448
2005	SD	NL	137	443	110	19	1	18	(10	8)	185	61	58	64	75	2	80	1	0	1	3	4	.43	6	.248	.358	.418
2006	SD	NL	6	4	3	1	0	0	(0	0)	4	0	2	3	2	0	0	0	0	0	0	0	-	0	.750	.833	1.000
15 ML YEARS			1620	5249	1470	316	30	272	(130	142)	2662	823	943	972	771	82	1009	28	3	54	86	40	.68	111	.280	.372	.507

Steve Kline

Pitches: L Bats: B Pos: RP-72   Ht: 6'1" Wt: 210 Born: 8/22/1972 Age: 34

Year	Team	Lg	G	GS	CG	GF	IP	BFP	H	R	ER	HR	SH	SF	HB	TBB	IBB	SO	WP	Bk	W	L	Pct	ShO	Sv-Op	Hld	ERC	ERA
1997	2 Tms		46	1	0	7	52.2	248	73	37	35	10	4	2	2	23	4	37	4	1	4	4	.500	0	0-3	5	7.39	5.98
1998	Mon	NL	78	0	0	18	71.2	319	62	25	22	4	1	2	3	41	7	76	5	0	3	6	.333	0	1-2	18	3.60	2.76
1999	Mon	NL	82	0	0	18	69.2	297	56	32	29	8	3	1	3	33	6	69	2	0	7	4	.636	0	0-2	16	3.40	3.75
2000	Mon	NL	83	0	0	42	82.1	349	88	36	32	8	2	1	3	27	2	64	4	0	1	5	.167	0	14-18	12	4.37	3.50
2001	StL	NL	89	0	0	26	75.0	303	53	16	15	3	4	5	4	29	7	54	1	0	3	3	.500	0	9-10	17	2.20	1.80
2002	StL	NL	66	0	0	17	58.1	241	54	23	22	3	2	2	1	21	2	41	1	0	2	1	.667	0	6-8	21	3.28	3.39
2003	StL	NL	78	0	0	22	63.2	274	56	29	27	5	3	2	3	30	5	31	2	0	5	5	.500	0	3-7	18	3.59	3.82
2004	StL	NL	67	0	0	22	50.1	202	37	12	10	3	3	1	4	17	4	35	1	0	2	2	.500	0	3-4	15	2.43	1.79
2005	Bal	AL	67	0	0	23	61.0	264	59	34	29	11	2	2	4	30	5	36	4	3	2	4	.333	0	0-3	9	4.75	4.28
2006	SF	NL	72	0	0	17	51.2	227	53	24	21	3	6	1	1	26	3	33	1	0	4	3	.571	0	1-1	18	4.35	3.66
97	Cle	AL	20	1	0	0	26.1	130	42	19	17	6	1	0	1	13	1	17	3	1	3	1	.750	0	0-2	4	9.58	5.81
97	Mon	NL	26	0	0	7	26.1	118	31	18	18	4	3	2	1	10	3	20	1	0	1	3	.250	0	0-1	1	5.39	6.15
10 ML YEARS			728	1	0	212	636.1	2724	591	268	242	58	30	19	24	277	45	476	25	4	33	37	.471	0	37-58	149	3.82	3.42

Justin Knoedler

Bats: R **Throws:** R **Pos:** C-5; PH-1 **Ht:** 6'2" **Wt:** 210 **Born:** 7/17/1980 **Age:** 26

Year	Team	Lg		G	AB	H	2B	3B	HR	(Hm	Rd)	TB	R	RBI	RC	TBB	IBB	SO	HBP	SH	SF		SB	CS	SB%	GDP		Avg	OBP	Slg
2006	Conn*	AA		21	71	15	6	0	1	(-	-)	24	7	8	6			24					1	1	.50	1		.211	.263	.338
2006	Fresno*	AAA		71	233	59	13	4	4	(-	-)	92	32	27	31	22	0	58	1	4	1		4	0	1.00	4		.253	.319	.395
2004	SF	NL		1	1	0	0	0	0	(0	0)	0	0	0	0	0	0	0	0	0	0		0	0	-	0		.000	.000	.000
2005	SF	NL		8	10	1	0	0	0	(0	0)	1	0	0	0	0	0	1	1	0	0		0	0	-	0		.100	.182	.100
2006	SF	NL		5	7	1	0	0	0	(0	0)	1	0	0	0	0	0	1	0	0	0		0	0	-	0		.143	.143	.143
	3 ML YEARS			14	18	2	0	0	0	(0	0)	2	0	0	0	0	0	2	1	0	0		0	0	-	0		.111	.158	.111

Jon Knott

Bats: R **Throws:** R **Pos:** PH-3 **Ht:** 6'3" **Wt:** 220 **Born:** 8/4/1978 **Age:** 28

Year	Team	Lg		G	AB	H	2B	3B	HR	(Hm	Rd)	TB	R	RBI	RC	TBB	IBB	SO	HBP	SH	SF		SB	CS	SB%	GDP		Avg	OBP	Slg
2002	FtWyn	A		37	126	42	12	3	3	(-	-)	69	19	18	27	17	1	33	1	0	2		2	1	.67	1		.333	.411	.548
2002	Lk Els	A+		93	367	125	33	8	6	(-	-)	192	55	73	75	46	2	68	3	0	4		5	4	.56	7		.341	.414	.523
2003	Mobile	AA		127	432	109	32	0	27	(-	-)	222	83	82	88	82	1	117	17	0	6		5	3	.63	1		.252	.387	.514
2003	Portlnd	AAA		7	26	9	1	0	1	(-	-)	13	5	5	5	4	0	3	0	0	0		0	0	-	1		.346	.433	.500
2004	Portlnd	AAA		113	435	126	22	3	26	(-	-)	232	79	85	83	58	0	110	7	0	8		5	3	.63	12		.290	.376	.533
2005	Portlnd	AAA		134	503	126	34	4	25	(-	-)	243	81	78	85	55	0	112	11	0	8		1	0	1.00	17		.250	.333	.483
2006	Portlnd	AAA		136	479	134	32	6	32	(-	-)	274	80	113	97	52	0	103	6	0	7		3	3	.50	22		.280	.353	.572
2004	SD	NL		9	14	3	2	0	0	(0	0)	5	1	1	1	1	0	5	0	0	0		0	0	-	0		.214	.267	.357
2006	SD	NL		3	3	0	0	0	0	(0	0)	0	0	0	0	0	0	1	0	0	0		0	0	-	0		.000	.000	.000
	2 ML YEARS			12	17	3	2	0	0	(0	0)	5	1	1	1	1	0	6	0	0	0		0	0	-	0		.176	.222	.294

Dan Kolb

Pitches: R **Bats:** R **Pos:** RP-53 **Ht:** 6'4" **Wt:** 210 **Born:** 3/29/1975 **Age:** 32

Year	Team	Lg		G	GS	CG	GF	IP	BFP		H	R	ER	HR	SH	SF	HB	TBB	IBB	SO	WP	Bk		W	L	Pct	ShO	Sv-Op	Hld		ERC	ERA
1999	Tex	AL		16	0	0	6	31.0	139		33	18	16	2	0	0	1	15	0	15	2	0		2	1	.667	0	0-0	0		4.63	4.65
2000	Tex	AL		1	0	0	0	0.2	9		5	5	5	0	0	1	0	2	0	0	0	0		0	0	-	0	0-0	0		69.84	67.50
2001	Tex	AL		17	0	0	1	15.1	70		15	8	8	2	1	1	0	10	1	15	3	0		0	0	-	0	0-0	7		5.03	4.70
2002	Tex	AL		34	0	0	14	32.0	145		27	17	15	1	1	2	1	22	2	20	6	0		3	6	.333	0	1-4	2		3.74	4.22
2003	Mil	NL		37	0	0	25	41.1	175		34	10	9	2	1	0	1	19	3	39	1	0		1	2	.333	0	21-23	4		2.96	1.96
2004	Mil	NL		64	0	0	48	57.1	236		50	22	19	3	3	1	3	15	1	21	2	0		0	4	.000	0	39-44	1		2.73	2.98
2005	Atl	NL		65	0	0	34	57.2	270		78	39	38	5	2	1	1	29	5	39	5	0		3	8	.273	0	11-18	6		6.52	5.93
2006	Mil	NL		53	0	0	18	48.1	213		53	28	26	4	1	3	1	20	1	26	5	0		2	2	.500	0	1-3	6		4.63	4.84
	8 ML YEARS			287	0	0	146	283.2	1257		295	147	136	19	9	9	8	132	13	175	24	0		11	23	.324	0	73-92	26		4.35	4.31

Shane Komine

Pitches: R **Bats:** R **Pos:** SP-2 **Ht:** 5'9" **Wt:** 175 **Born:** 10/18/1980 **Age:** 26

Year	Team	Lg		G	GS	CG	GF	IP	BFP		H	R	ER	HR	SH	SF	HB	TBB	IBB	SO	WP	Bk		W	L	Pct	ShO	Sv-Op	Hld		ERC	ERA
2002	Visalia	A+		18	0	0	2	25.2	120		23	20	17	2	3	0	1	20	3	22	3	0		1	3	.250	0	0--	-		4.67	5.96
2003	Kane	A		8	8	1	0	54.1	216		45	12	11	1	0	3	2	9	0	50	0	1		6	0	1.000	0	0--	-		1.97	1.82
2003	Mdland	AA		19	18	1	0	103.1	442		108	51	43	6	5	6	1	30	2	75	4	1		4	6	.400	1	0--	-		3.59	3.75
2004	Mdland	AA		17	17	0	0	94.1	409		103	56	50	10	5	5	3	28	0	65	6	1		4	5	.444	0	0--	-		4.34	4.77
2005	As	R		4	4	0	0	8.1	42		10	10	10	0	0	1	1	7	0	11	1	2		0	1	.000	0	0--	-		6.68	9.72
2005	Stcktn	A+		2	2	0	0	8.2	39		10	4	4	0	0	0	2	3	0	11	3	0		0	0	-	0	0--	-		5.02	4.15
2005	Mdland	AA		5	5	0	0	31.1	128		27	12	11	5	0	0	2	7	0	31	1	0		2	1	.667	0	0--	-		3.27	3.16
2006	Scrmto	AAA		24	22	1	0	140.0	591		145	67	63	13	2	2	6	38	2	116	11	1		11	8	.579	1	0--	-		3.91	4.05
2006	Oak	AL		2	2	0	0	9.0	45		10	5	5	3	0	0	0	8	1	1	0	0		0	0	-	0	0-0	0		8.41	5.00

Paul Konerko

Bats: R **Throws:** R **Pos:** 1B-140; DH-12; PH-1 **Ht:** 6'2" **Wt:** 220 **Born:** 3/5/1976 **Age:** 31

Year	Team	Lg		G	AB	H	2B	3B	HR	(Hm	Rd)	TB	R	RBI	RC	TBB	IBB	SO	HBP	SH	SF		SB	CS	SB%	GDP		Avg	OBP	Slg
1997	LAD	NL		6	7	1	0	0	0	(0	0)	1	0	0	0	1	0	2	0	0	0		0	0	-	1		.143	.250	.143
1998	2 Tms			75	217	47	4	0	7	(5	2)	72	21	29	17	16	0	40	3	0	3		0	1	.00	10		.217	.276	.332
1999	CWS	AL		142	513	151	31	4	24	(16	8)	262	71	81	86	45	0	68	2	1	3		1	0	1.00	19		.294	.352	.511
2000	CWS	AL		143	524	156	31	1	21	(10	11)	252	84	97	86	47	0	72	10	0	5		1	0	1.00	22		.298	.363	.481
2001	CWS	AL		156	582	164	35	0	32	(13	19)	295	92	99	99	47	6	89	9	0	5		1	0	1.00	17		.282	.349	.507
2002	CWS	AL		151	570	173	30	0	27	(13	14)	284	81	104	96	44	2	72	9	0	7		0	0	-	17		.304	.359	.498
2003	CWS	AL		137	444	104	19	0	18	(9	9)	177	49	65	42	43	7	50	4	0	4		0	0	-	**28**		.234	.305	.399
2004	CWS	AL		155	563	156	22	0	41	(**29**	12)	301	84	117	106	69	5	107	6	0	5		1	0	1.00	23		.277	.359	.535
2005	CWS	AL		158	575	163	24	0	40	(23	17)	307	98	100	106	81	10	109	5	0	3		0	0	-	9		.283	.375	.534
2006	CWS	AL		152	566	177	30	0	35	(21	14)	312	97	113	110	60	3	104	8	0	9		1	0	1.00	25		.313	.381	.551
98	LAD	NL		49	144	31	1	0	4	(2	2)	44	14	16	10	10	0	30	2	0	2		0	1	.00	5		.215	.272	.306
98	Cin	NL		26	73	16	3	0	3	(0	3)	28	7	13	7	6	0	10	1	0	1		0	0	-	5		.219	.284	.384
	10 ML YEARS			1275	4561	1292	226	5	245	(142	103)	2263	677	805	748	460	33	713	56	1	44		5	1	.83	171		.283	.353	.496

Mike Koplove

Pitches: R Bats: R Pos: RP-2   Ht: 5'11" Wt: 175 Born: 8/30/1976 Age: 30

Year	Team	Lg	G	GS	CG	GF	IP	BFP	H	R	ER	HR	SH	SF	HB	TBB	IBB	SO	WP	Bk	W	L	Pct	ShO	Sv-Op	Hld	ERC	ERA
2006	Tucsn*	AAA	48	0	0	9	65.0	270	63	31	26	4	3	0	1	24	1	49	2	0	5	0	1.000	0	0--	-	3.66	3.60
2001	Ari	NL	9	0	0	1	10.0	50	8	7	4	1	1	0	2	9	1	14	1	0	1	0	.000	0	0-0	1	5.25	3.60
2002	Ari	NL	55	0	0	15	61.2	249	47	24	23	2	4	1	0	23	4	46	1	0	6	1	.857	0	0-0	10	2.23	3.36
2003	Ari	NL	31	0	0	5	37.2	157	31	11	9	3	2	2	5	10	1	27	1	0	3	0	1.000	0	0-1	5	2.93	2.15
2004	Ari	NL	76	0	0	24	86.2	371	86	42	39	7	8	1	5	37	10	55	4	0	4	4	.500	0	2-8	19	4.14	4.05
2005	Ari	NL	44	0	0	11	49.2	217	48	31	28	6	1	3	6	20	3	28	1	1	2	1	.667	0	0-2	9	4.45	5.07
2006	Ari	NL	2	0	0	1	3.0	15	5	1	1	0	1	0	0	2	0	1	0	0	0	0	-	0	0-0	0	8.83	3.00
	6 ML YEARS		217	0	0	56	248.2	1059	225	116	104	19	17	7	18	101	19	171	8	1	15	7	.682	0	2-11	44	3.60	3.76

John Koronka

Pitches: L Bats: L Pos: SP-23   Ht: 6'1" Wt: 180 Born: 7/3/1980 Age: 26

Year	Team	Lg	G	GS	CG	GF	IP	BFP	H	R	ER	HR	SH	SF	HB	TBB	IBB	SO	WP	Bk	W	L	Pct	ShO	Sv-Op	Hld	ERC	ERA
1998	Billings	R+	12	3	0	3	31.1	167	47	43	28	2	1	3	3	26	0	36	4	1	0	3	.000	0	0--	-	9.06	8.04
1999	Reds	R	7	7	0	0	37.1	151	25	11	7	1	1	1	3	14	0	27	1	1	3	3	.500	0	0--	-	2.11	1.69
1999	Billings	R+	7	7	0	0	40.1	179	41	26	25	1	2	2	2	17	0	34	1	0	2	3	.400	0	0--	-	3.84	5.58
2000	Clinton	A	20	18	4	0	104.0	473	123	65	50	7	2	3	0	38	2	74	4	0	4	13	.235	0	0--	-	4.58	4.33
2001	Dayton	A	5	5	0	0	24.0	103	23	12	2	0	0	0	2	8	0	25	0	0	3	1	.750	0	0--	-	3.20	0.75
2001	Mudvle	A+	12	12	0	0	71.0	330	78	44	39	10	1	1	2	39	0	66	3	3	5	2	.714	0	0--	-	5.59	4.94
2001	Chatt	AA	9	9	0	0	55.0	255	62	37	35	7	4	1	1	28	0	44	1	1	1	5	.167	0	0--	-	5.43	5.73
2002	Stcktn	A+	12	12	0	0	73.1	314	59	36	25	4	0	2	3	35	0	69	3	1	11	0	1.000	0	0--	-	3.12	3.07
2002	Chatt	AA	16	15	0	0	95.2	448	109	56	53	10	5	4	1	52	1	69	4	1	2	8	.200	0	0--	-	5.40	4.99
2003	Chatt	AA	25	25	0	0	155.2	704	177	88	76	8	0	3	5	60	1	115	7	5	7	13	.350	0	0--	-	4.47	4.39
2003	WTenn	AA	1	1	0	0	7.0	25	3	0	0	0	1	2	0	1	0	3	0	0	0	0	-	0	0--	-	0.60	0.00
2004	Iowa	AAA	29	23	2	1	153.1	689	164	86	74	19	8	9	5	65	3	116	6	5	12	9	.571	2	0--	-	4.76	4.34
2005	Iowa	AAA	23	21	0	0	136.0	591	135	65	64	12	9	2	3	48	0	96	6	3	9	11	.450	0	0--	-	3.79	4.24
2006	Okla	AAA	3	3	0	0	19.2	83	19	9	9	2	1	0	2	7	0	17	1	0	0	1	.000	0	0--	-	4.25	4.12
2005	ChC	NL	4	3	0	1	15.2	76	19	13	13	2	1	0	0	8	0	10	1	2	1	2	.333	0	0-0	0	5.68	7.47
2006	Tex	AL	23	23	0	0	125.0	554	145	80	79	17	1	7	5	47	2	61	4	1	7	7	.500	0	0-0	0	5.37	5.69
	2 ML YEARS		27	26	0	1	140.2	630	164	93	92	19	2	7	5	55	2	71	5	3	8	9	.471	0	0-0	0	5.40	5.89

Corey Koskie

Bats: L Throws: R Pos: 3B-70; PH-6   Ht: 6'3" Wt: 220 Born: 6/28/1973 Age: 34

Year	Team	Lg	G	AB	H	2B	3B	HR	(Hm	Rd)	TB	R	RBI	RC	TBB	IBB	SO	HBP	SH	SF	SB	CS	SB%	GDP	Avg	OBP	Slg
1998	Min	AL	11	29	4	0	0	1	(1	0)	7	2	2	1	2	0	10	0	0	0	0	0	-	0	.138	.194	.241
1999	Min	AL	117	342	106	21	0	11	(4	7)	160	42	58	61	40	4	72	5	2	3	4	4	.50	6	.310	.387	.468
2000	Min	AL	146	474	142	32	4	9	(1	8)	209	79	65	84	77	7	104	4	1	3	5	4	.56	15	.300	.400	.441
2001	Min	AL	153	562	155	37	2	26	(11	15)	274	100	103	99	68	9	118	12	0	7	27	6	.82	16	.276	.362	.488
2002	Min	AL	140	490	131	37	3	15	(6	9)	219	71	69	72	72	4	127	9	0	5	10	11	.48	14	.267	.368	.447
2003	Min	AL	131	469	137	29	2	14	(8	6)	212	76	69	84	77	5	113	7	0	9	11	5	.69	5	.292	.393	.452
2004	Min	AL	118	422	106	24	2	25	(16	9)	209	68	71	67	49	10	103	12	0	5	9	3	.75	6	.251	.342	.495
2005	Tor	AL	97	354	88	20	0	11	(5	6)	141	49	36	41	44	3	90	4	0	2	4	1	.80	10	.249	.337	.398
2006	Mil	NL	76	257	67	23	0	12	(8	4)	126	29	33	40	29	3	58	3	0	0	1	2	.33	7	.261	.343	.490
	9 ML YEARS		989	3399	936	223	13	124	(60	64)	1557	516	506	549	458	45	795	56	3	34	71	36	.66	75	.275	.367	.458

Casey Kotchman

Bats: L Throws: L Pos: 1B-26; PH-3   Ht: 6'3" Wt: 215 Born: 2/22/1983 Age: 24

Year	Team	Lg	G	AB	H	2B	3B	HR	(Hm	Rd)	TB	R	RBI	RC	TBB	IBB	SO	HBP	SH	SF	SB	CS	SB%	GDP	Avg	OBP	Slg
2006	Salt Lk*	AAA	3	7	0	0	0	0	(-	-)	0	0	1	0	1	0	1	0	0	0	0	0	-	1	.000	.125	.000
2004	LAA	AL	38	116	26	6	0	0	(0	0)	32	7	15	14	7	3	11	4	0	1	3	0	1.00	3	.224	.289	.276
2005	LAA	AL	47	126	35	5	0	7	(5	2)	61	16	22	21	15	0	18	0	1	1	1	1	.50	3	.278	.352	.484
2006	LAA	AL	29	79	12	2	0	1	(0	1)	17	6	6	1	7	0	13	0	2	0	0	1	.00	2	.152	.221	.215
	3 ML YEARS		114	321	73	13	0	8	(5	3)	110	29	43	36	29	3	42	4	3	2	4	2	.67	8	.227	.298	.343

Mark Kotsay

Bats: L Throws: L Pos: CF-127; 1B-4; PH-3; DH-1; PR-1   Ht: 6'0" Wt: 205 Born: 12/2/1975 Age: 31

Year	Team	Lg	G	AB	H	2B	3B	HR	(Hm	Rd)	TB	R	RBI	RC	TBB	IBB	SO	HBP	SH	SF	SB	CS	SB%	GDP	Avg	OBP	Slg
1997	Fla	NL	14	52	10	1	1	0	(0	0)	13	5	4	3	4	0	7	0	1	0	3	0	1.00	1	.192	.250	.250
1998	Fla	NL	154	578	161	25	7	11	(5	6)	233	72	68	70	34	2	61	1	7	3	10	5	.67	17	.279	.318	.403
1999	Fla	NL	148	495	134	23	9	8	(5	3)	199	57	50	58	29	5	50	0	2	9	7	6	.54	11	.271	.306	.402
2000	Fla	NL	152	530	158	31	5	12	(5	7)	235	87	59	78	42	2	46	0	2	4	19	9	.68	17	.298	.347	.443
2001	SD	NL	119	406	118	29	1	10	(3	7)	179	67	58	65	48	1	58	2	1	3	13	5	.72	11	.291	.366	.441
2002	SD	NL	153	578	169	27	7	17	(11	6)	261	82	61	92	59	0	89	3	2	4	11	9	.55	10	.292	.359	.452
2003	SD	NL	128	482	128	28	4	7	(1	6)	185	64	38	59	56	3	82	1	1	1	6	3	.67	8	.266	.343	.384
2004	Oak	AL	148	606	190	37	3	15	(4	11)	278	78	63	94	55	5	70	2	5	5	8	5	.62	6	.314	.370	.459
2005	Oak	AL	139	582	163	35	1	15	(4	11)	245	75	82	86	40	3	51	1	2	4	5	5	.50	13	.280	.325	.421
2006	Oak	AL	129	502	138	29	3	7	(1	6)	194	57	59	63	44	1	55	2	4	6	4	3	.67	18	.275	.332	.386
	10 ML YEARS		1284	4811	1369	265	41	102	(44	58)	2022	644	540	668	411	22	569	12	27	39	88	50	.64	112	.285	.340	.420

Kevin Kouzmanoff

Bats: R Throws: R Pos: DH-14; 3B-2; PH-1   Ht: 6'1" Wt: 210 Born: 7/25/1981 Age: 25

Year	Team	Lg	G	AB	H	2B	3B	HR	(Hm	Rd)	TB	R	RBI	RC	TBB	IBB	SO	HBP	SH	SF	SB	CS	SB%	GDP	Avg	OBP	Slg
2003	MhVlly	A-	54	206	56	8	1	8	(-	-)	90	31	33	32	21	1	36	3	0	4	2	1	.67	6	.272	.342	.437
2004	Lk Cty	A	123	473	156	35	5	16	(-	-)	249	74	87	97	44	0	75	9	0	5	5	4	.56	17	.330	.394	.526
2004	Akron	AA	7	24	5	1	1	1	(-	-)	11	3	6	3	2	0	5	0	0	1	0	0	-	0	.208	.259	.458
2005	Kinston	A+	68	254	86	20	4	12	(-	-)	150	47	58	58	24	1	51	5	0	4	3	1	.75	6	.339	.401	.591
2005	MhVlly	A-	3	7	1	0	0	0	(-	-)	1	0	0	0	1	0	2	0	0	0	0	0	-	0	.143	.250	.143
2006	Akron	AA	67	244	95	19	1	15	(-	-)	161	46	55	66	23	6	34	6	0	3	2	3	.40	5	.389	.449	.660
2006	Buffalo	AAA	27	102	36	9	0	7	(-	-)	66	22	20	25	10	0	12	1	0	2	2	1	.67	1	.353	.409	.647
2006	Cle	AL	16	56	12	2	0	3	(0	3)	23	4	11	7	5	0	12	0	0	0	0	0	-	3	.214	.279	.411

Marc Kroon

Pitches: R Bats: R Pos: P   Ht: 6'2" Wt: 190 Born: 4/2/1973 Age: 34

Year	Team	Lg	G	GS	CG	GF	IP	BFP	H	R	ER	HR	SH	SF	HB	TBB	IBB	SO	WP	Bk	W	L	Pct	ShO	Sv-Op	Hld	ERC	ERA
2006	Yokha*	Jap	47	0	0	42	48.0	190	38	16	16	4	-	-	1	8	-	70	4	0	2	5	.286	0	27--	-	2.01	3.00
1995	SD	NL	2	0	0	1	1.2	7	1	2	2	0	0	0	0	2	0	2	0	0	0	1	.000	0	0-0	0	4.62	10.80
1997	SD	NL	12	0	0	2	11.1	56	14	9	9	2	0	0	1	5	0	12	1	0	0	1	.000	0	0-0	1	6.21	7.15
1998	2 Tms	NL	6	0	0	4	7.2	38	7	8	8	0	0	0	1	9	0	6	2	1	0	0	-	0	0-0	0	6.49	9.39
2004	Col	NL	6	0	0	1	6.0	32	7	4	4	1	1	1	0	10	0	3	1	0	0	0	-	0	0-0	0	12.08	6.00
98	SD	NL	2	0	0	2	2.1	8	0	0	0	0	0	0	0	1	0	2	0	0	0	0	-	0	0-0	0	0.20	0.00
98	Cin	NL	4	0	0	2	5.1	30	7	8	8	0	0	0	1	8	0	4	2	1	0	0	-	0	0-0	0	11.01	13.50
	4 ML YEARS		26	0	0	8	26.2	133	29	23	23	3	1	1	2	26	0	23	4	1	0	2	.000	0	0-0	1	7.45	7.76

Jason Kubel

Bats: L Throws: R Pos: LF-30; DH-29; PH-15; RF-7   Ht: 5'11" Wt: 200 Born: 5/25/1982 Age: 25

Year	Team	Lg	G	AB	H	2B	3B	HR	(Hm	Rd)	TB	R	RBI	RC	TBB	IBB	SO	HBP	SH	SF	SB	CS	SB%	GDP	Avg	OBP	Slg
2000	Twins	R	23	78	22	3	2	0	(-	-)	29	17	13	11	10	0	9	1	1	1	0	0	-	1	.282	.367	.372
2001	Twins	R	37	124	41	10	4	1	(-	-)	62	14	30	25	19	3	14	2	0	2	3	2	.60	3	.331	.422	.500
2002	QuadC	A	115	424	136	26	4	17	(-	-)	221	60	69	77	41	2	48	1	2	3	3	5	.38	11	.321	.380	.521
2003	FtMyrs	A+	116	420	125	20	4	5	(-	-)	168	56	82	61	48	8	54	1	0	13	4	6	.40	11	.298	.361	.400
2004	NwBrit	AA	37	138	52	14	4	6	(-	-)	92	25	29	36	19	1	19	1	0	1	0	2	.00	3	.377	.453	.667
2004	Roch	AAA	90	350	120	28	0	16	(-	-)	196	71	71	76	34	2	40	1	1	4	16	3	.84	2	.343	.398	.560
2006	Roch	AAA	30	120	34	7	2	4	(-	-)	57	18	22	20	12	3	23	0	0	2	2	0	1.00	5	.283	.343	.475
2004	Min	AL	23	60	18	2	0	2	(0	2)	26	10	7	13	6	0	9	0	0	1	1	1	.50	0	.300	.358	.433
2006	Min	AL	73	220	53	8	0	8	(3	5)	85	23	26	20	12	0	45	0	2	1	2	0	1.00	13	.241	.279	.386
	2 ML YEARS		96	280	71	10	0	10	(3	7)	111	33	33	33	18	0	54	0	2	2	3	1	.75	13	.254	.297	.396

Hong-Chih Kuo

Pitches: L Bats: L Pos: RP-23; SP-5   Ht: 6'0" Wt: 235 Born: 7/23/1981 Age: 25

Year	Team	Lg	G	GS	CG	GF	IP	BFP	H	R	ER	HR	SH	SF	HB	TBB	IBB	SO	WP	Bk	W	L	Pct	ShO	Sv-Op	Hld	ERC	ERA
2000	SnBrn	A+	1	1	0	0	3.0	9	0	0	0	0	0	0	1	0	0	7	0	0	0	0	-	0	0--	-	0.14	0.00
2001	Ddgrs	R	7	6	0	0	19.1	75	13	5	5	0	0	0	2	4	0	21	0	0	0	0	-	0	0--	-	1.58	2.33
2002	Ddgrs	R	3	3	0	0	6.0	23	4	3	3	0	0	1	0	1	0	9	0	0	0	0	-	0	0--	-	1.23	4.50
2002	VeroB	A+	4	4	0	0	8.0	37	11	6	6	0	0	0	3	2	0	8	1	0	0	1	.000	0	0--	-	6.78	6.75
2004	Clmbs	A	3	0	0	1	6.0	30	8	3	3	0	0	0	1	4	0	10	1	0	1	0	1.000	0	0--	-	7.07	4.50
2005	VeroB	A+	11	3	0	0	26.0	107	19	7	6	2	0	1	2	10	0	42	1	0	1	1	.500	0	0--	-	2.73	2.08
2005	Jaxnvl	AA	17	0	0	9	28.1	118	22	7	6	1	0	1	0	11	1	44	3	0	1	1	.500	0	3--	-	2.34	1.91
2006	LsVgs	AAA	23	9	0	5	53.0	223	52	24	18	5	0	1	0	22	1	63	1	0	4	3	.571	0	1--	-	4.06	3.06
2005	LAD	NL	9	0	0	0	5.1	26	5	4	4	1	0	0	0	5	1	10	0	1	0	0	-	0	0-1	3	6.10	6.75
2006	LAD	NL	28	5	0	6	59.2	258	54	30	28	3	2	1	1	33	5	71	2	0	1	5	.167	0	0-0	2	3.76	4.22
	2 ML YEARS		37	5	0	6	65.0	284	59	34	32	4	2	1	1	38	6	81	2	1	1	6	.143	0	0-1	5	3.94	4.43

Hiroki Kuroda

Pitches: R Bats: R Pos: P   Ht: 6'2" Wt: 174 Born: 2/10/1975 Age: 32

Year	Team	Lg	G	GS	CG	GF	IP	BFP	H	R	ER	HR	SH	SF	HB	TBB	IBB	SO	WP	Bk	W	L	Pct	ShO	Sv-Op	Hld	ERC	ERA
1997	Hrshm	Jap	23	23	4	0	135.0	601	147	72	66	17	-	-	4	63	-	64	8	1	6	9	.400	1	0--	-	5.21	4.40
1998	Hrshm	Jap	18	6	0	3	45.0	199	53	34	33	5	-	-	1	24	-	25	1	0	1	4	.200	0	0--	-	6.14	6.60
1999	Hrshm	Jap	21	16	2	1	87.2	406	106	70	66	20	-	-	3	39	-	55	4	0	5	8	.385	0	0--	-	6.58	6.78
2000	Hrshm	Jap	29	21	7	3	144.0	623	147	73	69	21	-	-	1	61	-	116	3	0	9	6	.600	1	0--	-	4.69	4.31
2001	Hrshm	Jap	27	27	13	0	190.0	786	175	72	64	19	-	-	8	45	-	146	7	0	12	8	.600	3	0--	-	3.17	3.03
2002	Hrshm	Jap	23	23	8	0	164.1	671	166	69	67	16	-	-	1	34	-	144	0	0	10	10	.500	2	0--	-	3.44	3.67
2003	Hrshm	Jap	28	28	8	0	205.2	827	197	77	71	18	-	-	3	45	2	137	5	1	13	9	.591	1	0--	-	3.20	3.11
2004	Hrshm	Jap	21	21	7	0	147.0	639	187	81	76	17	6	6	2	29	1	138	1	0	7	9	.438	1	0--	-	5.02	4.65
2005	Hrshm	Jap	29	29	11	0	212.2	863	183	76	75	17	-	-	7	42	-	165	7	0	15	12	.556	1	0--	-	2.55	3.17
2006	Hrshm	Jap	25	25	7	29	189.0	757	169	49	39	12	-	-	7	21	-	143	5	0	13	6	.684	2	0--	-	2.19	1.86

John Lackey

Pitches: R Bats: R Pos: SP-33   Ht: 6'6" Wt: 235 Born: 10/23/1978 Age: 28

			HOW MUCH HE PITCHED						WHAT HE GAVE UP												THE RESULTS							
Year	Team	Lg	G	GS	CG	GF	IP	BFP	H	R	ER	HR	SH	SF	HB	TBB	IBB	SO	WP	Bk	W	L	Pct	ShO	Sv-Op	Hld	ERC	ERA
2002	LAA	AL	18	18	1	0	108.1	465	113	52	44	10	0	4	4	33	0	69	7	2	9	4	.692	0	0-0	0	4.03	3.66
2003	LAA	AL	33	33	2	0	204.0	885	223	117	105	31	2	6	10	66	4	151	11	1	10	16	.385	2	0-0	0	4.88	4.63
2004	LAA	AL	33	32	1	0	198.1	855	215	108	103	22	9	4	8	60	4	144	11	1	14	13	.519	1	0-0	0	4.39	4.67
2005	LAA	AL	33	33	1	0	209.0	892	208	85	80	13	1	2	11	71	3	199	18	0	14	5	.737	0	0-0	0	3.76	3.44
2006	LAA	AL	33	33	3	0	217.2	922	203	98	86	14	8	6	9	72	4	190	16	0	13	11	.542	2	0-0	0	3.31	3.56
5 ML YEARS			150	149	8	0	937.1	4019	962	460	418	90	20	22	42	302	15	753	63	4	60	49	.550	5	0-0	0	4.05	4.01

Gerald Laird

Bats: R Throws: R Pos: C-71; PR-8; RF-1; DH-1; PH-1   Ht: 6'1" Wt: 225 Born: 11/13/1979 Age: 27

			BATTING																	BASERUNNING				AVERAGES		
Year	Team	Lg	G	AB	H	2B	3B	HR	(Hm	Rd)	TB	R	RBI	RC	TBB	IBB	SO	HBP	SH	SF	SB	CS	SB%	GDP	Avg	OBP	Slg
2003	Tex	AL	19	44	12	2	1	1	(0	1)	19	9	4	5	5	0	11	1	0	0	0	0	-	2	.273	.360	.432
2004	Tex	AL	49	147	33	6	0	1	(1	0)	42	20	16	11	12	0	35	2	4	3	0	1	.00	5	.224	.287	.286
2005	Tex	AL	13	40	9	2	0	1	(0	1)	14	7	4	4	2	0	7	0	0	0	0	0	-	1	.225	.262	.350
2006	Tex	AL	78	243	72	20	1	7	(3	4)	115	46	22	24	12	0	54	2	1	2	3	1	.75	7	.296	.332	.473
4 ML YEARS			159	474	126	30	2	10	(4	6)	190	82	46	44	31	0	107	5	5	5	3	2	.60	15	.266	.315	.401

Tim Laker

Bats: R Throws: R Pos: C-4   Ht: 6'3" Wt: 225 Born: 11/27/1969 Age: 37

			BATTING																	BASERUNNING				AVERAGES		
Year	Team	Lg	G	AB	H	2B	3B	HR	(Hm	Rd)	TB	R	RBI	RC	TBB	IBB	SO	HBP	SH	SF	SB	CS	SB%	GDP	Avg	OBP	Slg
2006	Buffalo*	AAA	54	188	39	14	0	0	(-	-)	53	24	12	14	13	0	50	2	2	1	0	0	-	5	.207	.265	.282
1992	Mon	NL	28	46	10	3	0	0	(0	0)	13	8	4	2	2	0	14	0	0	0	1	1	.50	1	.217	.250	.283
1993	Mon	NL	43	86	17	2	1	0	(0	0)	21	3	7	4	2	0	16	1	3	1	2	0	1.00	2	.198	.222	.244
1995	Mon	NL	64	141	33	8	1	3	(1	2)	52	17	20	14	14	4	38	1	1	1	0	1	.00	5	.234	.306	.369
1997	Bal	AL	7	14	0	0	0	0	(0	0)	0	0	1	0	2	0	9	0	1	1	0	0	-	0	.000	.118	.000
1998	2 Tms		17	29	10	1	0	1	(0	1)	14	3	2	5	2	0	4	0	0	1	0	1	.00	1	.345	.375	.483
1999	Pit	NL	6	9	3	0	0	0	(0	0)	3	0	0	1	0	0	2	0	0	0	0	0	-	0	.333	.333	.333
2001	Cle	AL	16	33	6	0	0	1	(0	1)	9	5	5	3	6	0	8	0	1	0	0	0	-	0	.182	.308	.273
2003	Cle	AL	52	162	39	11	0	3	(1	2)	59	17	21	18	9	1	38	0	5	0	2	2	.50	4	.241	.281	.364
2004	Cle	AL	44	117	25	2	0	3	(0	3)	36	12	17	10	7	1	28	1	2	1	0	0	-	5	.214	.262	.308
2005	TB	AL	1	1	0	0	0	0	(0	0)	0	0	0	0	0	0	1	0	0	0	0	0	-	0	.000	.000	.000
2006	Cle	AL	4	13	4	1	0	0	(0	0)	5	1	2	2	0	0	4	0	0	0	0	0	-	0	.308	.308	.385
98	TB	AL	3	5	1	0	0	0	(0	0)	1	1	0	0	1	0	1	0	0	0	0	1	.00	1	.200	.333	.200
98	Pit	NL	14	24	9	1	0	1	(0	1)	13	2	2	5	1	0	3	0	0	1	0	0	-	0	.375	.385	.542
11 ML YEARS			282	651	147	28	2	11	(2	9)	212	66	79	59	44	6	162	3	13	5	5	5	.50	19	.226	.276	.326

Mike Lamb

Bats: L Throws: R Pos: 1B-68; 3B-36; PH-36; 2B-2   Ht: 6'1" Wt: 190 Born: 8/9/1975 Age: 31

			BATTING																	BASERUNNING				AVERAGES		
Year	Team	Lg	G	AB	H	2B	3B	HR	(Hm	Rd)	TB	R	RBI	RC	TBB	IBB	SO	HBP	SH	SF	SB	CS	SB%	GDP	Avg	OBP	Slg
2000	Tex	AL	138	493	137	25	2	6	(4	2)	184	65	47	59	34	6	60	4	5	2	0	2	.00	10	.278	.328	.373
2001	Tex	AL	76	284	87	18	0	4	(1	3)	117	42	35	40	14	1	27	5	1	2	2	1	.67	6	.306	.348	.412
2002	Tex	AL	115	314	89	13	0	9	(7	2)	129	54	33	46	33	5	48	3	2	3	0	0	-	7	.283	.354	.411
2003	Tex	AL	28	38	5	0	0	0	(0	0)	5	3	2	0	2	0	7	1	0	1	1	0	1.00	1	.132	.190	.132
2004	Hou	NL	112	278	80	14	3	14	(8	6)	142	38	58	51	31	3	63	0	0	3	1	1	.50	4	.288	.356	.511
2005	Hou	NL	125	322	76	13	5	12	(4	8)	135	41	53	38	22	1	65	1	0	4	1	1	.50	10	.236	.284	.419
2006	Hou	NL	126	381	117	22	3	12	(5	7)	181	70	45	52	35	6	55	0	0	5	2	4	.33	10	.307	.361	.475
7 ML YEARS			720	2110	591	105	13	57	(29	28)	893	313	273	286	171	22	325	14	8	20	7	9	.44	48	.280	.335	.423

Jason Lane

Bats: R Throws: L Pos: RF-89; PH-21; LF-6; CF-5; 1B-1   Ht: 6'2" Wt: 220 Born: 12/22/1976 Age: 30

			BATTING																	BASERUNNING				AVERAGES		
Year	Team	Lg	G	AB	H	2B	3B	HR	(Hm	Rd)	TB	R	RBI	RC	TBB	IBB	SO	HBP	SH	SF	SB	CS	SB%	GDP	Avg	OBP	Slg
2006	RdRck*	AAA	12	46	12	2	0	1	(-	-)	17	7	11	6	5	0	16	1	0	3	1	0	1.00	4	.261	.327	.370
2002	Hou	NL	44	69	20	3	1	4	(2	2)	37	12	10	11	10	1	12	0	0	1	1	1	.50	0	.290	.375	.536
2003	Hou	NL	18	27	8	2	0	4	(4	0)	22	5	10	6	0	0	2	0	0	0	0	0	-	0	.296	.296	.815
2004	Hou	NL	107	136	37	10	2	4	(4	0)	63	21	19	23	16	0	33	1	1	2	1	0	1.00	2	.272	.348	.463
2005	Hou	NL	145	517	130	34	4	26	(14	12)	258	65	78	72	32	1	105	7	0	5	6	2	.75	10	.267	.316	.499
2006	Hou	NL	112	288	58	10	0	15	(8	7)	113	44	45	39	49	0	75	2	2	4	1	2	.33	6	.201	.318	.392
5 ML YEARS			426	1037	261	59	7	53	(32	21)	493	147	162	151	107	2	227	10	3	12	9	5	.64	18	.252	.324	.475

Ryan Langerhans

Bats: L Throws: L Pos: LF-104; CF-24; PH-13; RF-2; PR-1   Ht: 6'3" Wt: 205 Born: 2/20/1980 Age: 27

			BATTING																	BASERUNNING				AVERAGES		
Year	Team	Lg	G	AB	H	2B	3B	HR	(Hm	Rd)	TB	R	RBI	RC	TBB	IBB	SO	HBP	SH	SF	SB	CS	SB%	GDP	Avg	OBP	Slg
2002	Atl	NL	1	1	0	0	0	0	(0	0)	0	0	0	0	0	0	0	0	0	0	0	0	-	0	.000	.000	.000
2003	Atl	NL	16	15	4	0	0	0	(0	0)	4	2	0	1	0	0	6	0	0	0	0	0	-	1	.267	.267	.267
2005	Atl	NL	128	326	87	22	3	8	(3	5)	139	48	42	53	37	3	75	5	2	3	0	2	.00	2	.267	.348	.426
2006	Atl	NL	131	315	76	16	3	7	(3	4)	119	46	28	45	50	8	91	3	0	1	1	2	.33	9	.241	.350	.378
4 ML YEARS			276	657	167	38	6	15	(6	9)	262	96	70	99	87	11	172	8	2	4	1	4	.20	12	.254	.347	.399

Juan Lara

Pitches: L **Bats:** R **Pos:** RP-9   **Ht:** 6'2" **Wt:** 190 **Born:** 1/26/1981 **Age:** 26

			HOW MUCH HE PITCHED						WHAT HE GAVE UP										THE RESULTS						
Year	Team	Lg	G	GS	CG	GF	IP	BFP	H	R	ER	HR	SH	SF	HB	TBB	IBB	SO	WP	Bk	W	L	Pct	ShO	Sv-Op Hld	ERC	ERA
2002	Burlgtn	R	14	14	0	0	65.0	283	67	42	36	4	3	1	7	28	0	50	0	2	2	6	.250	0	0- -	4.64	4.98
2003	MhVlly	A-	12	12	0	0	61.2	261	54	29	24	4	4	1	8	18	1	54	6	0	3	3	.500	0	0- -	3.20	3.50
2003	Lk Cty	A	16	3	0	6	45.0	215	51	31	25	7	1	2	3	26	0	37	6	1	1	4	.200	0	1- -	6.16	5.00
2004	Kinston	A	35	8	0	12	84.1	393	106	60	53	6	3	3	4	38	1	74	6	2	4	3	.571	0	1- -	5.71	5.66
2005	Kinston	A+	26	0	0	7	42.1	183	40	22	19	4	1	0	0	15	1	46	6	0	0	1	.000	0	0- -	3.42	4.04
2005	Akron	AA	18	0	0	8	23.2	112	27	15	12	1	2	2	1	14	3	16	3	1	1	2	.333	0	5- -	5.05	4.56
2006	Akron	AA	40	0	0	17	46.2	197	32	14	14	2	5	0	2	21	1	48	0	0	4	2	.667	0	7- -	2.29	2.70
2006	Buffalo	AAA	13	0	0	6	15.0	65	17	6	5	1	0	0	1	3	0	15	1	0	1	1	.500	0	1- -	4.03	3.00
2006	Cle	AL	9	0	0	1	5.0	19	4	2	1	0	0	0	0	1	0	2	0	0	0	0	-	0	0-1	1.82	1.80

Adam LaRoche

Bats: L **Throws:** L **Pos:** 1B-142; PH-12   **Ht:** 6'3" **Wt:** 185 **Born:** 11/6/1979 **Age:** 27

			BATTING																			BASERUNNING				AVERAGES		
Year	Team	Lg	G	AB	H	2B	3B	HR	(Hm	Rd)	TB	R	RBI	RC	TBB	IBB	SO	HBP	SH	SF	SB	CS	SB%	GDP	Avg	OBP	Slg
2004	Atl	NL	110	324	90	27	1	13	(7	6)	158	45	45	43	27	1	78	1	2	2	0	0	-	10	.278	.333	.488
2005	Atl	NL	141	451	117	28	0	20	(11	9)	205	53	78	63	39	7	87	4	2	4	0	2	.00	15	.259	.320	.455
2006	Atl	NL	149	492	140	38	1	32	(11	21)	276	89	90	83	55	5	128	2	1	7	0	2	.00	9	.285	.354	.561
3 ML YEARS			400	1267	347	93	2	65	(29	36)	639	187	213	189	121	13	293	7	5	15	0	4	.00	34	.274	.337	.504

Jason LaRue

Bats: R **Throws:** R **Pos:** C-63; PH-9; PR-1   **Ht:** 5'11" **Wt:** 205 **Born:** 3/19/1974 **Age:** 33

			BATTING																			BASERUNNING				AVERAGES		
Year	Team	Lg	G	AB	H	2B	3B	HR	(Hm	Rd)	TB	R	RBI	RC	TBB	IBB	SO	HBP	SH	SF	SB	CS	SB%	GDP	Avg	OBP	Slg
2006	Srsota*	A+	3	12	2	0	0	0	(-	-)	2	1	1	0	1	0	3	0	0	0	0	0	-	1	.167	.231	.167
2006	Lsvlle*	AAA	2	8	2	1	0	0	(-	-)	3	1	0	0	0	0	1	0	0	0	0	0	-	0	.250	.250	.375
1999	Cin	NL	36	90	19	7	0	3	(1	2)	35	12	10	10	11	1	32	2	0	0	4	1	.80	4	.211	.311	.389
2000	Cin	NL	31	98	23	3	0	5	(1	4)	41	12	12	12	5	2	19	4	0	0	0	0	-	1	.235	.299	.418
2001	Cin	NL	121	364	86	21	2	12	(3	9)	147	39	43	42	27	4	106	9	1	2	3	3	.50	11	.236	.303	.404
2002	Cin	NL	113	353	88	17	1	12	(5	7)	143	42	52	44	27	6	117	13	2	2	1	2	.33	13	.249	.324	.405
2003	Cin	NL	118	379	87	23	1	16	(12	4)	160	52	50	47	33	4	111	20	1	4	3	3	.50	9	.230	.321	.422
2004	Cin	NL	114	390	98	24	2	14	(3	11)	168	46	55	53	26	5	108	24	2	3	0	2	.00	7	.251	.334	.431
2005	Cin	NL	110	361	94	27	0	14	(6	8)	163	38	60	63	41	7	101	13	5	2	0	0	-	8	.260	.355	.452
2006	Cin	NL	72	191	37	5	0	8	(5	3)	66	22	21	17	27	9	51	8	3	1	1	0	1.00	3	.194	.317	.346
8 ML YEARS			715	2226	532	127	6	84	(36	48)	923	263	303	288	197	38	645	93	14	14	12	11	.52	56	.239	.325	.415

Brian Lawrence

Pitches: R **Bats:** R **Pos:** P   **Ht:** 6'0" **Wt:** 195 **Born:** 5/14/1976 **Age:** 31

			HOW MUCH HE PITCHED						WHAT HE GAVE UP											THE RESULTS						
Year	Team	Lg	G	GS	CG	GF	IP	BFP	H	R	ER	HR	SH	SF	HB	TBB	IBB	SO	WP	Bk	W	L	Pct	ShO	Sv-Op Hld	ERC	ERA
2001	SD	NL	27	15	1	5	114.2	484	107	53	44	10	4	3	5	34	5	84	1	0	5	5	.500	0	0-0 0	3.30	3.45
2002	SD	NL	35	31	2	0	210.0	894	230	97	86	16	8	4	11	52	6	149	2	1	12	12	.500	2	0-0 1	4.05	3.69
2003	SD	NL	33	33	1	0	210.2	884	206	106	98	27	11	6	11	57	8	116	4	0	10	15	.400	0	0-0 0	3.81	4.19
2004	SD	NL	34	34	2	0	203.0	870	226	101	93	26	11	9	7	55	7	121	2	0	15	14	.517	1	0-0 0	4.53	4.12
2005	SD	NL	33	33	1	0	195.2	852	211	106	105	18	3	7	11	57	7	109	3	1	7	15	.318	0	0-0 0	4.17	4.83
5 ML YEARS			162	146	7	5	934.0	3984	980	463	426	97	37	29	45	255	33	579	12	2	49	61	.445	3	0-0 1	4.03	4.10

Matt Lawton

Bats: L **Throws:** R **Pos:** CF-5; RF-2; PR-2; LF-1; DH-1; PH-1   **Ht:** 5'10" **Wt:** 190 **Born:** 11/30/1971 **Age:** 35

			BATTING																			BASERUNNING				AVERAGES		
Year	Team	Lg	G	AB	H	2B	3B	HR	(Hm	Rd)	TB	R	RBI	RC	TBB	IBB	SO	HBP	SH	SF	SB	CS	SB%	GDP	Avg	OBP	Slg
1995	Min	AL	21	60	19	4	1	1	(1	0)	28	11	12	11	7	0	11	3	0	0	1	1	.50	1	.317	.414	.467
1996	Min	AL	79	252	65	7	1	6	(1	5)	92	34	42	31	28	1	28	4	0	2	4	4	.50	6	.258	.339	.365
1997	Min	AL	142	460	114	29	3	14	(8	6)	191	74	60	73	76	3	81	10	1	1	7	4	.64	7	.248	.366	.415
1998	Min	AL	152	557	155	36	6	21	(11	10)	266	91	77	105	86	6	64	15	0	4	16	8	.67	10	.278	.387	.478
1999	Min	AL	118	406	105	18	0	7	(2	5)	144	58	54	57	57	7	42	6	0	7	26	4	.87	11	.259	.353	.355
2000	Min	AL	156	561	151	44	2	13	(8	5)	258	84	88	109	91	8	63	7	0	5	23	7	.77	10	.305	.405	.460
2001	2 Tms		151	559	155	36	1	13	(5	8)	232	95	64	92	85	6	80	11	0	2	29	8	.78	16	.277	.382	.415
2002	Cle	AL	114	416	98	19	2	15	(8	7)	166	71	57	59	59	0	34	8	1	0	8	9	.47	13	.236	.342	.399
2003	Cle	AL	99	374	93	19	0	15	(6	9)	157	57	53	57	47	0	47	7	0	1	10	3	.77	8	.249	.343	.420
2004	Cle	AL	150	591	164	25	0	20	(10	10)	249	109	70	86	74	3	84	11	0	4	23	9	.72	21	.277	.366	.421
2005	3 Tms		141	500	127	30	1	13	(8	5)	198	67	53	69	69	0	77	12	0	4	18	9	.67	10	.254	.356	.396
2006	Sea	AL	11	27	7	0	0	0	(0	0)	7	5	1	4	2	0	2	0	0	0	0	0	-	0	.259	.310	.259
01	Min	AL	103	376	110	25	0	10	(4	6)	165	71	51	66	63	6	46	3	0	2	19	6	.76	14	.293	.396	.439
01	NYM	NL	48	183	45	11	1	3	(1	2)	67	24	13	26	22	0	34	8	0	0	10	2	.83	2	.246	.352	.366
05	Pit	NL	101	374	102	28	1	10	(6	4)	162	53	44	61	58	0	61	9	0	4	16	9	.64	7	.273	.380	.433
05	ChC	NL	19	78	19	2	0	1	(0	1)	24	8	5	5	4	0	8	1	0	0	1	0	1.00	1	.244	.289	.308
05	NYY	AL	21	48	6	0	0	2	(1	1)	12	6	4	3	7	0	8	2	0	0	1	0	1.00	0	.125	.263	.250
12 ML YEARS			1334	4763	1273	267	17	138	(68	70)	1988	756	631	753	681	34	613	94	2	30	165	66	.71	113	.267	.368	.417

Brandon League

Pitches: R **Bats:** R **Pos:** RP-33   **Ht:** 6'2" **Wt:** 195 **Born:** 3/16/1983 **Age:** 24

			HOW MUCH HE PITCHED						WHAT HE GAVE UP											THE RESULTS							
Year	Team	Lg	G	GS	CG	GF	IP	BFP	H	R	ER	HR	SH	SF	HB	TBB	IBB	SO	WP	Bk	W	L	Pct	ShO	Sv-Op	Hld	ERC	ERA
2006	Syrcse*	AAA	31	1	0	14	54.2	227	57	19	13	0	1	0	2	15	1	43	2	0	3	2	.600	0	8--	-	3.34	2.14
2004	Tor	AL	3	0	0	0	4.2	18	3	0	0	0	0	0	0	1	0	2	0	0	0	0	1.000	0	0-0	1	1.26	0.00
2005	Tor	AL	20	0	0	4	35.2	162	42	27	26	8	0	1	2	20	1	17	5	0	1	0	1.000	0	0-0	1	7.24	6.56
2006	Tor	AL	33	0	0	8	42.2	173	34	17	12	3	2	0	3	9	2	29	0	0	1	2	.333	0	1-4	12	2.30	2.53
	3 ML YEARS		56	0	0	12	83.0	353	79	44	38	11	2	1	5	30	3	48	5	0	3	2	.600	0	1-4	14	4.10	4.12

Matthew LeCroy

Bats: R **Throws:** R **Pos:** PH-22; C-13; 1B-6; DH-2   **Ht:** 6'2" **Wt:** 230 **Born:** 12/13/1975 **Age:** 31

			BATTING																	BASERUNNING				AVERAGES		
Year	Team	Lg	G	AB	H	2B	3B	HR	(Hm	Rd)	TB	R	RBI	RC	TBB	IBB	SO	HBP	SH	SF	SB	CS	SB%	GDP	Avg	OBP	Slg
2006	NewOr*	AAA	5	15	4	1	0	0	(-	-)	5	0	2	1	0	0	4	0	0	0	0	0	-	1	.267	.267	.333
2000	Min	AL	56	167	29	10	0	5	(2	3)	54	18	17	12	17	2	38	2	1	3	0	0	-	6	.174	.254	.323
2001	Min	AL	15	40	17	5	0	3	(0	3)	31	6	12	11	0	0	8	1	0	1	0	1	.00	0	.425	.429	.775
2002	Min	AL	63	181	47	11	1	7	(2	5)	81	19	27	24	13	1	38	0	0	2	0	2	.00	5	.260	.306	.448
2003	Min	AL	107	345	99	19	0	17	(9	8)	169	39	64	60	25	1	82	4	0	0	0	1	.00	8	.287	.342	.490
2004	Min	AL	88	264	71	14	0	9	(5	4)	112	25	39	32	16	0	60	5	0	2	0	0	-	7	.269	.321	.424
2005	Min	AL	101	304	79	5	0	17	(10	7)	135	33	50	48	41	2	85	4	0	1	0	0	-	7	.260	.354	.444
2006	Was	NL	39	67	16	3	0	2	(0	2)	25	5	9	9	11	0	17	1	0	1	0	0	-	2	.239	.350	.373
	7 ML YEARS		469	1368	358	67	1	60	(28	32)	607	145	218	196	123	6	328	17	1	10	0	4	.00	35	.262	.328	.444

Ricky Ledee

Bats: L **Throws:** L **Pos:** PH-60; LF-9; RF-5   **Ht:** 6'1" **Wt:** 225 **Born:** 11/22/1973 **Age:** 33

			BATTING																	BASERUNNING				AVERAGES		
Year	Team	Lg	G	AB	H	2B	3B	HR	(Hm	Rd)	TB	R	RBI	RC	TBB	IBB	SO	HBP	SH	SF	SB	CS	SB%	GDP	Avg	OBP	Slg
2006	Jaxnvl*	AA	3	10	1	0	0	0	(-	-)	1	0	1	0	2	0	5	0	0	0	0	0	-	0	.100	.250	.100
2006	Norfolk*	AAA	4	12	1	0	0	0	(-	-)	1	1	1	0	0	0	2	0	0	0	0	0	-	0	.083	.083	.083
1998	NYY	AL	42	79	19	5	2	1	(0	1)	31	13	12	9	7	0	29	0	0	1	3	1	.75	1	.241	.299	.392
1999	NYY	AL	88	250	69	13	5	9	(4	5)	119	45	40	41	28	5	73	0	0	2	4	3	.57	2	.276	.346	.476
2000	3 Tms	AL	137	467	110	19	5	13	(6	7)	178	59	77	56	59	4	98	2	0	3	13	6	.68	17	.236	.322	.381
2001	Tex	AL	78	242	56	21	1	2	(1	1)	85	33	36	26	23	0	58	1	1	3	3	3	.50	3	.231	.303	.351
2002	Phi	NL	96	203	46	13	1	8	(4	4)	85	33	23	24	35	0	50	1	1	1	1	2	.33	3	.227	.342	.419
2003	Phi	NL	121	255	63	15	2	13	(6	7)	121	37	46	36	34	5	59	0	1	1	0	0	-	4	.247	.334	.475
2004	2 Tms	NL	104	176	41	9	0	7	(3	4)	71	25	30	24	27	2	47	1	0	1	3	0	1.00	6	.233	.337	.403
2005	LAD	NL	102	237	66	16	1	7	(5	2)	105	31	39	34	20	1	55	3	0	6	0	0	-	5	.278	.335	.443
2006	2 Tms	NL	70	85	16	6	0	2	(1	1)	28	8	9	5	6	0	16	0	0	0	1	0	1.00	3	.188	.242	.329
00	NYY	AL	62	191	46	11	1	7	(2	5)	80	23	31	26	26	2	39	1	0	2	7	3	.70	7	.241	.332	.419
00	Cle	AL	17	63	14	2	1	2	(2	0)	24	13	8	7	8	0	9	0	0	0	0	0	-	3	.222	.310	.381
00	Tex	AL	58	213	50	6	3	4	(2	2)	74	23	38	23	25	2	50	1	0	1	6	3	.67	7	.235	.317	.347
04	Phi	NL	73	123	35	7	0	7	(3	4)	63	19	26	23	22	2	27	0	0	0	2	0	1.00	5	.285	.393	.512
04	SF	NL	31	53	6	2	0	0	(0	0)	8	6	4	1	5	0	20	1	0	1	1	0	1.00	1	.113	.200	.151
06	LAD	NL	43	53	13	5	0	1	(0	1)	21	4	8	5	2	0	10	0	0	0	1	0	1.00	3	.245	.273	.396
06	NYM	NL	27	32	3	1	0	1	(1	0)	7	4	1	0	4	0	6	0	0	0	0	0	-	0	.094	.194	.219
	9 ML YEARS		838	1994	486	117	17	62	(30	32)	823	284	312	255	239	17	485	10	3	18	28	15	.65	44	.244	.325	.413

Wil Ledezma

Pitches: L **Bats:** L **Pos:** RP-17; SP-7   **Ht:** 6'4" **Wt:** 210 **Born:** 1/21/1981 **Age:** 26

			HOW MUCH HE PITCHED						WHAT HE GAVE UP											THE RESULTS							
Year	Team	Lg	G	GS	CG	GF	IP	BFP	H	R	ER	HR	SH	SF	HB	TBB	IBB	SO	WP	Bk	W	L	Pct	ShO	Sv-Op	Hld	ERC	ERA
2006	Toledo*	AAA	12	12	0	0	71.1	290	60	22	20	6	7	2	3	23	1	66	0	0	4	3	.571	0	0--	-	3.02	2.52
2003	Det	AL	34	8	0	13	84.0	376	99	55	54	12	1	4	3	35	3	49	2	0	3	7	.300	0	0-1	1	5.67	5.79
2004	Det	AL	15	8	0	1	53.1	225	55	28	26	3	0	3	2	18	0	29	3	1	4	3	.571	0	0-1	0	3.94	4.39
2005	Det	AL	10	10	0	0	49.2	234	61	46	39	10	3	4	2	24	0	30	2	2	2	4	.333	0	0-0	0	6.66	7.07
2006	Det	AL	24	7	0	2	60.1	264	60	28	24	5	2	1	2	23	0	39	2	0	3	3	.500	0	0-1	2	3.92	3.58
	4 ML YEARS		83	33	0	16	247.1	1099	275	157	143	30	6	12	9	100	3	147	9	3	12	17	.414	0	0-3	3	5.03	5.20

Carlos Lee

Bats: R **Throws:** R **Pos:** LF-149; DH-12; PH-1   **Ht:** 6'2" **Wt:** 240 **Born:** 6/20/1976 **Age:** 31

			BATTING																	BASERUNNING				AVERAGES		
Year	Team	Lg	G	AB	H	2B	3B	HR	(Hm	Rd)	TB	R	RBI	RC	TBB	IBB	SO	HBP	SH	SF	SB	CS	SB%	GDP	Avg	OBP	Slg
1999	CWS	AL	127	492	144	32	2	16	(10	6)	228	66	84	68	13	0	72	4	1	7	4	2	.67	11	.293	.312	.463
2000	CWS	AL	152	572	172	29	2	24	(12	12)	277	107	92	91	38	1	94	3	1	5	13	4	.76	17	.301	.345	.484
2001	CWS	AL	150	558	150	33	3	24	(12	12)	261	75	84	81	38	2	85	6	1	2	17	7	.71	15	.269	.321	.468
2002	CWS	AL	140	492	130	26	2	26	(14	12)	238	82	80	86	75	4	73	2	0	7	1	4	.20	5	.264	.359	.484
2003	CWS	AL	158	623	181	35	1	31	(18	13)	311	100	113	105	37	2	91	4	0	7	18	4	.82	20	.291	.331	.499
2004	CWS	AL	153	591	180	37	0	31	(17	14)	310	103	99	112	54	3	86	7	0	6	11	5	.69	10	.305	.366	.525
2005	Mil	NL	162	618	164	41	0	32	(15	17)	301	85	114	98	57	7	87	2	0	11	13	4	.76	8	.265	.324	.487
2006	2 Tms		161	624	187	37	1	37	(15	22)	337	102	116	113	58	6	65	2	0	11	19	2	.90	22	.300	.355	.540
06	Mil	NL	102	388	111	18	0	28	(10	18)	213	60	81	75	38	4	39	2	0	7	12	2	.86	13	.286	.347	.549
06	Tex	AL	59	236	76	19	1	9	(5	4)	124	42	35	38	20	2	26	0	0	4	7	0	1.00	9	.322	.369	.525
	8 ML YEARS		1203	4570	1308	270	11	221	(113	108)	2263	720	782	754	370	25	653	30	3	56	96	32	.75	108	.286	.340	.495

Cliff Lee

Pitches: L Bats: L Pos: SP-33   Ht: 6'3" Wt: 190 Born: 8/30/1978 Age: 28

Year	Team	Lg	G	GS	CG	GF	IP	BFP	H	R	ER	HR	SH	SF	HB	TBB	IBB	SO	WP	Bk	W	L	Pct	ShO	Sv-Op Hld	ERC	ERA
2002	Cle	AL	2	2	0	0	10.1	44	6	2	2	0	1	0	0	8	1	6	0	1	0	1	.000	0	0-0 0	2.38	1.74
2003	Cle	AL	9	9	0	0	52.1	210	41	28	21	7	1	1	2	20	1	44	3	0	3	3	.500	0	0-0 0	3.29	3.61
2004	Cle	AL	33	33	0	0	179.0	802	188	113	108	30	2	6	11	81	1	161	6	0	14	8	.636	0	0-0 0	5.31	5.43
2005	Cle	AL	32	32	1	0	202.0	838	194	91	85	22	5	7	0	52	1	143	4	0	18	5	.783	0	0-0 0	3.35	3.79
2006	Cle	AL	33	33	1	0	200.2	882	224	114	98	29	3	6	8	58	3	129	3	0	14	11	.560	0	0-0 0	4.69	4.40
5 ML YEARS			109	109	2	0	644.1	2776	653	348	314	88	12	20	21	219	7	483	16	1	49	28	.636	0	0-0 0	4.27	4.39

Derrek Lee

Bats: R Throws: R Pos: 1B-47; PH-4; DH-1   Ht: 6'5" Wt: 245 Born: 9/6/1975 Age: 31

Year	Team	Lg	G	AB	H	2B	3B	HR	(Hm	Rd)	TB	R	RBI	RC	TBB	IBB	SO	HBP	SH	SF	SB	CS	SB%	GDP	Avg	OBP	Slg
2006	Iowa*	AAA	1	4	1	0	0	0	(-	-)	1	0	1	0	0	0	0	0	0	0	0	0	-	0	.250	.250	.250
1997	SD	NL	22	54	14	3	0	1	(0	1)	20	9	4	8	9	0	24	0	0	0	0	0	-	1	.259	.365	.370
1998	Fla	NL	141	454	106	29	1	17	(4	13)	188	62	74	59	47	1	120	10	0	2	5	2	.71	12	.233	.318	.414
1999	Fla	NL	70	218	45	9	1	5	(0	5)	71	21	20	18	17	1	70	0	0	1	2	1	.67	3	.206	.263	.326
2000	Fla	NL	158	477	134	18	3	28	(9	19)	242	70	70	84	63	6	123	4	0	2	0	3	.00	14	.281	.368	.507
2001	Fla	NL	158	561	158	37	4	21	(8	13)	266	83	75	88	50	1	126	8	0	6	4	2	.67	18	.282	.346	.474
2002	Fla	NL	162	581	157	35	7	27	(9	18)	287	95	86	96	98	8	164	5	0	4	19	9	.68	14	.270	.378	.494
2003	Fla	NL	155	539	146	31	2	31	(11	20)	274	91	92	99	88	7	131	10	0	6	21	8	.72	9	.271	.379	.508
2004	ChC	NL	161	605	168	39	1	32	(18	14)	305	90	98	101	68	4	128	8	2	5	12	5	.71	14	.278	.356	.504
2005	ChC	NL	158	594	199	50	3	46	(24	22)	393	120	107	135	85	23	109	5	0	7	15	3	.83	12	.335	.418	.662
2006	ChC	NL	50	175	50	9	0	8	(5	3)	83	30	30	27	25	1	41	0	0	4	8	4	.67	11	.286	.368	.474
10 ML YEARS			1235	4258	1177	260	22	216	(88	128)	2129	671	656	715	550	52	1036	50	2	37	86	37	.70	108	.276	.363	.500

Seung-Yeop Lee

Bats: L Throws: L Pos: 1B   Ht: 6'1" Wt: 187 Born: 8/18/1976 Age: 30

Year	Team	Lg	G	AB	H	2B	3B	HR	(Hm	Rd)	TB	R	RBI	RC	TBB	IBB	SO	HBP	SH	SF	SB	CS	SB%	GDP	Avg	OBP	Slg
2004	Chiba	Jap	100	333	80	20	4	14	(-	-)	150	50	50	51	42	0	88	3	1	3	1	2	.33	6	.240	.328	.450
2005	Chiba	Jap	117	408	106	25	2	30	(-	-)	225	64	82	71	33	3	79	1	0	3	5	4	.56	9	.260	.315	.551
2006	Yomiuri	Jap	143	524	169	30	0	41	(-	-)	322	101	108	-	56	3	126	5	0	7	5	1	.83	-	.323	.389	.615

Travis Lee

Bats: L Throws: L Pos: 1B-112; PH-2; PR-1   Ht: 6'3" Wt: 225 Born: 5/26/1975 Age: 32

Year	Team	Lg	G	AB	H	2B	3B	HR	(Hm	Rd)	TB	R	RBI	RC	TBB	IBB	SO	HBP	SH	SF	SB	CS	SB%	GDP	Avg	OBP	Slg
1998	Ari	NL	146	562	151	20	2	22	(12	10)	241	71	72	83	67	5	123	0	0	1	8	1	.89	13	.269	.346	.429
1999	Ari	NL	120	375	89	16	2	9	(7	2)	136	57	50	49	58	4	50	0	0	3	17	3	.85	10	.237	.337	.363
2000	2 Tms	NL	128	404	95	24	1	9	(2	7)	148	53	54	53	65	1	79	2	0	2	8	1	.89	12	.235	.342	.366
2001	Phi	NL	157	555	143	34	2	20	(11	9)	241	75	90	81	71	5	109	4	1	9	3	4	.43	15	.258	.341	.434
2002	Phi	NL	153	536	142	26	2	13	(8	5)	211	55	70	65	54	10	104	0	0	2	5	3	.63	12	.265	.331	.394
2003	TB	AL	145	542	149	37	3	19	(9	10)	249	75	70	77	64	4	97	0	1	6	6	2	.75	13	.275	.348	.459
2004	NYY	AL	7	19	2	1	0	0	(0	0)	3	1	2	0	1	1	3	0	0	0	0	0	-	2	.105	.150	.158
2005	TB	AL	129	404	110	22	2	12	(5	7)	172	54	49	51	35	4	66	1	0	1	7	4	.64	7	.272	.331	.426
2006	TB	AL	114	343	77	11	2	11	(5	6)	125	35	31	32	42	1	73	2	0	1	5	2	.71	8	.224	.312	.364
00	Ari	NL	72	224	52	13	0	8	(1	7)	89	34	40	27	25	1	46	0	0	1	5	1	.83	6	.232	.308	.397
00	Phi	NL	56	180	43	11	1	1	(1	0)	59	19	14	26	40	0	33	2	0	1	3	0	1.00	6	.239	.381	.328
9 ML YEARS			1099	3740	958	191	16	115	(59	56)	1526	476	488	491	457	35	704	9	2	25	59	20	.75	92	.256	.337	.408

Justin Lehr

Pitches: R Bats: R Pos: RP-16   Ht: 6'2" Wt: 215 Born: 8/3/1977 Age: 29

Year	Team	Lg	G	GS	CG	GF	IP	BFP	H	R	ER	HR	SH	SF	HB	TBB	IBB	SO	WP	Bk	W	L	Pct	ShO	Sv-Op Hld	ERC	ERA
2006	Nashv*	AAA	19	17	0	0	112.0	469	120	53	49	15	0	4	3	31	1	90	6	0	4	7	.364	0	0-- -	4.43	3.94
2004	Oak	AL	27	0	0	11	32.2	144	35	19	19	3	1	2	2	14	2	16	2	0	1	1	.500	0	0-1 5	4.73	5.23
2005	Mil	NL	23	0	0	9	34.2	154	32	19	15	4	2	1	1	18	2	23	1	1	1	1	.500	0	0-1 3	4.17	3.89
2006	Mil	NL	16	0	0	4	15.2	75	24	16	15	2	1	1	1	7	1	12	1	0	2	1	.667	0	0-0 0	8.17	8.62
3 ML YEARS			66	0	0	24	83.0	373	91	54	49	9	4	4	4	39	5	51	4	1	4	3	.571	0	0-2 8	5.08	5.31

Justin Leone

Bats: R Throws: R Pos: PH-1   Ht: 6'1" Wt: 210 Born: 3/9/1977 Age: 30

Year	Team	Lg	G	AB	H	2B	3B	HR	(Hm	Rd)	TB	R	RBI	RC	TBB	IBB	SO	HBP	SH	SF	SB	CS	SB%	GDP	Avg	OBP	Slg
1999	Everett	A-	62	205	54	14	2	6	(-	-)	90	34	35	32	32	0	49	2	1	5	5	3	.63	5	.263	.361	.439
2000	Wisc	A	115	374	100	32	3	18	(-	-)	192	77	63	80	79	1	107	11	2	3	9	2	.82	3	.267	.407	.513
2001	SnBrn	A+	130	485	113	27	4	22	(-	-)	214	70	69	66	57	2	158	5	6	3	4	3	.57	8	.233	.318	.441
2002	SnBrn	A+	98	358	89	20	5	18	(-	-)	173	64	58	61	57	1	98	5	0	2	6	0	1.00	9	.249	.358	.483
2003	SnAnt	AA	135	455	131	38	7	21	(-	-)	246	103	94	98	92	10	104	3	0	8	20	6	.77	7	.288	.405	.541
2004	Tacom	AAA	68	253	68	10	5	21	(-	-)	151	56	51	47	26	0	82	4	1	2	5	6	.45	4	.269	.344	.597
2005	Tacom	AAA	87	313	76	19	2	7	(-	-)	120	51	38	46	51	1	93	2	2	2	5	2	.71	14	.243	.351	.383
2006	Portlnd	AAA	124	453	118	20	0	20	(-	-)	198	66	73	73	61	2	106	6	0	4	4	4	.50	18	.260	.353	.437

									BATTING														BASERUNNING				AVERAGES		
Year	Team	Lg	G	AB	H	2B	3B	HR	(Hm	Rd)	TB	R	RBI	RC	TBB	IBB	SO	HBP	SH	SF		SB	CS	SB%	GDP		Avg	OBP	Slg
2004	Sea	AL	31	102	22	5	0	6	(2	4)	45	15	13	14	9	0	32	3	1	0		1	0	1.00	0		.216	.298	.441
2006	SD	NL	1	1	0	0	0	0	(0	0)	0	0	0	0	0	0	0	0	0	0		0	0	-	0		.000	.000	.000
	2 ML YEARS		32	103	22	5	0	6	(2	4)	45	15	13	14	9	0	32	3	1	0		1	0	1.00	0		.214	.296	.437

Anthony Lerew

Pitches: R Bats: L Pos: RP-1   **Ht:** 6'3" **Wt:** 220 **Born:** 10/28/1982 **Age:** 24

					HOW MUCH HE PITCHED				WHAT HE GAVE UP											THE RESULTS						
Year	Team	Lg	G	GS	CG	GF	IP	BFP	H	R	ER	HR	SH	SF	HB	TBB	IBB	SO	WP	Bk	W	L	Pct	ShO	Sv-Op	Hld	ERC	ERA
2001	Braves	R	12	7	0	1	49.0	204	43	25	16	3	0	1	0	14	0	40	4	2	1	2	.333	0	0--	-	2.68	2.94
2002	Danvle	R+	14	14	0	0	83.0	334	60	23	16	2	3	2	5	25	0	75	0	0	8	3	.727	0	0--	-	2.03	1.73
2003	Rome	A	25	25	0	0	143.2	586	112	45	38	7	8	6	3	43	2	127	0	0	7	6	.538	0	0--	-	2.26	2.38
2004	MrtlBh	A+	27	27	0	0	144.0	623	145	75	60	12	7	5	3	46	0	125	6	0	8	9	.471	0	0--	-	3.70	3.75
2005	Missi	AA	14	14	1	0	75.2	329	70	34	33	6	4	1	2	32	1	64	0	0	6	2	.750	0	0--	-	3.63	3.93
2005	Rchmd	AAA	13	13	0	0	72.1	303	63	34	28	9	3	2	3	23	0	53	1	0	4	4	.500	0	0--	-	3.35	3.48
2006	Rchmd	AA	9	8	0	0	48.2	205	43	18	11	1	3	2	2	13	0	37	1	0	4	2	.667	0	0--	-	2.52	2.03
2006	Rchmd	AAA	16	15	1	0	71.0	345	92	63	59	12	4	5	8	36	0	69	7	0	3	5	.375	0	0--	-	7.27	7.48
2005	Atl	NL	7	0	0	4	8.0	37	9	5	5	1	1	0	0	5	2	5	0	0	0	0	-	0	0-1	0	5.47	5.63
2006	Atl	NL	1	0	0	0	2.0	15	5	5	5	0	0	0	1	3	0	1	0	0	0	0	-	0	0-0	0	20.57	22.50
	2 ML YEARS		8	0	0	4	10.0	52	14	10	10	1	1	0	1	8	2	6	0	0	0	0	-	0	0-1	0	8.20	9.00

Jon Lester

Pitches: L Bats: L Pos: SP-15   **Ht:** 6'2" **Wt:** 190 **Born:** 1/7/1984 **Age:** 23

					HOW MUCH HE PITCHED				WHAT HE GAVE UP											THE RESULTS						
Year	Team	Lg	G	GS	CG	GF	IP	BFP	H	R	ER	HR	SH	SF	HB	TBB	IBB	SO	WP	Bk	W	L	Pct	ShO	Sv-Op	Hld	ERC	ERA
2002	RedSx	R	1	1	0	0	0.2	8	5	6	1	0	0	0	0	1	0	1	0	0	0	1	.000	0	0--	-	61.66	13.50
2003	Augsta	A	24	21	0	2	106.0	452	102	54	43	7	6	4	8	44	0	71	2	0	6	9	.400	0	0--	-	4.07	3.65
2004	Srsota	A+	21	20	0	0	90.1	390	82	46	43	2	0	0	3	37	0	97	1	1	7	6	.538	0	0--	-	3.14	4.28
2004	RedSx	R	1	1	0	0	1.0	5	0	0	0	0	0	0	0	2	0	1	1	0	0	0	-	0	0--	-	3.47	0.00
2005	Portlnd	AA	26	26	3	0	148.1	603	114	52	43	10	6	4	4	57	3	163	10	1	11	6	.647	1	0--	-	2.68	2.61
2006	Pwtckt	AAA	11	11	0	0	46.2	207	43	17	14	5	2	1	0	25	0	43	0	0	3	4	.429	0	0--	-	4.14	2.70
2006	Bos	AL	15	15	0	0	81.1	367	91	43	43	7	2	8	5	43	1	60	5	0	7	2	.778	0	0-0	0	5.52	4.76

Colby Lewis

Pitches: R Bats: R Pos: RP-2   **Ht:** 6'4" **Wt:** 230 **Born:** 8/2/1979 **Age:** 27

					HOW MUCH HE PITCHED				WHAT HE GAVE UP											THE RESULTS						
Year	Team	Lg	G	GS	CG	GF	IP	BFP	H	R	ER	HR	SH	SF	HB	TBB	IBB	SO	WP	Bk	W	L	Pct	ShO	Sv-Op	Hld	ERC	ERA
2006	Toledo*	AAA	24	24	1	0	147.2	662	154	70	65	13	5	4	7	36	0	104	1	0	6	7	.462	1	0--	-	3.57	3.96
2002	Tex	AL	15	4	0	4	34.1	168	42	26	24	4	2	0	2	26	2	28	3	1	1	3	.250	0	0-2	1	7.22	6.29
2003	Tex	AL	26	26	0	0	127.0	594	163	104	103	23	2	2	5	70	1	88	5	0	10	9	.526	0	0-0	0	7.38	7.30
2004	Tex	AL	3	3	0	0	15.1	71	13	7	7	1	0	0	1	13	0	11	0	0	1	1	.500	0	0-0	0	4.98	4.11
2006	Det	AL	2	0	0	1	3.0	18	8	1	1	1	0	0	0	1	0	5	0	0	0	0	-	0	0-0	0	17.35	3.00
	4 ML YEARS		46	33	0	5	179.2	851	226	138	135	29	4	2	8	110	3	132	8	1	12	13	.480	0	0-2	1	7.29	6.76

Fred Lewis

Bats: L Throws: R Pos: LF-6; PR-6; PH-3; CF-1   **Ht:** 6'2" **Wt:** 190 **Born:** 12/9/1980 **Age:** 26

									BATTING														BASERUNNING				AVERAGES		
Year	Team	Lg	G	AB	H	2B	3B	HR	(Hm	Rd)	TB	R	RBI	RC	TBB	IBB	SO	HBP	SH	SF		SB	CS	SB%	GDP		Avg	OBP	Slg
2002	SlmKzr	A-	58	239	77	9	3	1	(-	-)	95	43	23	39	26	1	58	3	1	0		9	6	.60	1		.322	.396	.397
2003	Hgrstn	A	114	420	105	17	8	1	(-	-)	141	61	27	58	68	1	112	6	6	2		30	15	.67	5		.250	.361	.336
2004	SnJos	A+	115	439	132	20	11	8	(-	-)	198	88	57	92	84	1	109	12	3	3		33	14	.70	5		.301	.424	.451
2004	Fresno	AA	6	23	7	1	0	1	(-	-)	11	3	2	4	5	0	5	0	1	0		1	0	.50	1		.304	.429	.478
2005	Nrwich	AA	137	512	140	28	7	7	(-	-)	203	79	47	79	69	2	124	3	6	4		30	13	.70	9		.273	.361	.396
2006	Fresno	AAA	120	439	121	20	11	12	(-	-)	199	85	56	79	68	2	105	4	2	4		18	8	.69	13		.276	.375	.453
2006	SF	NL	13	11	5	1	0	0	(0	0)	6	5	2	4	0	0	3	0	0	0		0	0	-	0		.455	.455	.545

Brad Lidge

Pitches: R Bats: R Pos: RP-78   **Ht:** 6'5" **Wt:** 210 **Born:** 12/23/1976 **Age:** 30

					HOW MUCH HE PITCHED				WHAT HE GAVE UP											THE RESULTS						
Year	Team	Lg	G	GS	CG	GF	IP	BFP	H	R	ER	HR	SH	SF	HB	TBB	IBB	SO	WP	Bk	W	L	Pct	ShO	Sv-Op	Hld	ERC	ERA
2002	Hou	NL	6	1	0	2	8.2	48	12	6	6	0	1	0	2	9	1	12	0	0	1	0	1.000	0	0-0	0	8.90	6.23
2003	Hou	NL	78	0	0	9	85.0	349	60	36	34	6	2	3	5	42	7	97	4	1	6	3	.667	0	1-6	28	2.82	3.60
2004	Hou	NL	80	0	0	44	94.2	369	57	21	20	8	3	2	6	30	5	157	3	1	6	5	.545	0	29-33	17	1.85	1.90
2005	Hou	NL	70	0	0	65	70.2	291	58	21	18	5	4	1	3	23	1	103	8	0	4	4	.500	0	42-46	0	2.79	2.29
2006	Hou	NL	78	0	0	52	75.0	340	69	47	44	10	6	2	6	36	4	104	11	0	1	5	.167	0	32-38	6	4.25	5.28
	5 ML YEARS		312	1	0	172	334.0	1397	256	131	122	29	16	8	22	140	18	473	26	2	18	17	.514	0	104-123	51	2.97	3.29

Cory Lidle

Pitches: R Bats: R Pos: SP-30; RP-1   **Ht:** 5'11" **Wt:** 190 **Born:** 3/22/1972 **Age:** 35

					HOW MUCH HE PITCHED				WHAT HE GAVE UP											THE RESULTS						
Year	Team	Lg	G	GS	CG	GF	IP	BFP	H	R	ER	HR	SH	SF	HB	TBB	IBB	SO	WP	Bk	W	L	Pct	ShO	Sv-Op	Hld	ERC	ERA
1997	NYM	NL	54	2	0	20	81.2	345	86	38	32	7	4	4	3	20	4	54	2	0	7	2	.778	0	2-3	9	3.75	3.53
1999	TB	AL	5	1	0	1	5.0	24	8	4	4	0	0	0	0	2	0	4	0	0	1	0	1.000	0	0-0	0	6.98	7.20
2000	TB	AL	31	11	0	5	96.2	424	114	61	54	13	3	1	5	29	3	62	6	0	4	6	.400	0	0-0	2	5.06	5.03

Year	Team	Lg	G	GS	CG	GF	IP	BFP	H	R	ER	HR	SH	SF	HB	TBB	IBB	SO	WP	Bk	W	L	Pct	ShO	Sv-Op	Hld	ERC	ERA
2001	Oak	AL	29	29	1	0	188.0	762	170	84	75	23	2	1	10	47	7	118	5	0	13	6	.684	0	0-0	0	3.35	3.59
2002	Oak	AL	31	30	2	0	192.0	796	191	90	83	17	5	6	6	39	3	111	6	1	8	10	.444	2	0-0	0	3.31	3.89
2003	Tor	AL	31	31	2	0	192.2	840	216	**133**	**123**	24	5	5	5	60	3	112	9	0	12	15	.444	0	0-0	0	4.67	5.75
2004	2 Tms		34	34	5	0	211.1	911	224	123	115	27	14	6	10	61	5	126	8	0	12	12	.500	**3**	0-0	0	4.31	4.90
2005	Phi		31	31	1	0	184.2	792	210	105	93	18	11	8	6	40	5	121	6	0	13	11	.542	0	0-0	0	4.19	4.53
2006	2 Tms		31	30	0	0	170.2	745	181	100	92	30	5	4	11	58	4	130	5	0	12	10	.545	0	0-0	0	4.96	4.85
04	Cin	NL	24	24	3	0	149.0	656	170	95	88	24	12	4	5	44	4	93	8	0	7	10	.412	1	0-0	0	4.96	5.32
04		NL	10	10	2	0	62.1	255	54	28	27	3	2	2	5	17	1	33	0	0	5	2	.714	2	0-0	0	2.86	3.90
06	Phi	NL	21	21	0	0	125.1	542	132	74	66	19	4	4	8	39	3	98	4	0	8	7	.533	0	0-0	0	4.62	4.74
06	NYY	AL	10	9	0	0	45.1	203	49	26	26	11	1	0	3	19	1	32	1	0	4	3	.571	0	0-0	0	5.92	5.16
9 ML YEARS			277	199	11	26	1322.2	5639	1400	738	671	159	49	35	54	356	34	838	47	1	82	72	.532	5	2-3	11	4.16	4.57

Jon Lieber

Pitches: R Bats: L Pos: SP-27   Ht: 6'2" Wt: 235 Born: 4/2/1970 Age: 37

Year	Team	Lg	G	GS	CG	GF	IP	BFP	H	R	ER	HR	SH	SF	HB	TBB	IBB	SO	WP	Bk	W	L	Pct	ShO	Sv-Op	Hld	ERC	ERA
2006	Phillies*	R	1	1	0	0	3.0	14	4	1	1	0	0	0	1	0	0	1	0	0	0	0	-	0	0--	-	4.83	3.00
2006	Clrwtr*	A+	2	2	0	0	11.1	52	19	10	9	1	0	1	1	0	0	6	0	0	0	2	.000	0	0--	-	6.84	7.15
1994	Pit	NL	17	17	1	0	108.2	460	116	62	45	12	3	3	1	25	3	71	2	3	6	7	.462	0	0-0	0	3.83	3.73
1995	Pit	NL	21	12	0	3	72.2	327	103	56	51	7	5	4	4	14	0	45	3	0	4	7	.364	0	0-1	3	5.96	6.32
1996	Pit	NL	51	15	0	6	142.0	600	156	70	63	19	7	2	3	28	2	94	0	0	9	5	.643	0	1-4	9	4.12	3.99
1997	Pit	NL	33	32	1	0	188.1	799	193	102	94	23	6	7	1	51	8	160	3	1	11	14	.440	0	0-0	0	3.78	4.49
1998	Pit	NL	29	28	2	1	171.0	731	182	93	78	23	7	4	3	40	4	138	0	3	8	14	.364	1	1-1	0	4.00	4.11
1999	ChC	NL	31	31	3	0	203.1	875	226	107	92	28	7	11	1	46	6	186	2	2	10	11	.476	1	0-0	0	4.19	4.07
2000	ChC	NL	35	**35**	6	0	**251.0**	1047	248	130	123	36	9	7	10	54	3	192	2	2	12	11	.522	1	0-0	0	3.70	4.41
2001	ChC	NL	34	34	5	0	232.1	958	226	104	98	25	13	9	7	41	4	148	4	1	20	6	.769	1	0-0	0	3.19	3.80
2002	ChC	NL	21	21	3	0	141.0	582	153	64	58	15	10	6	1	12	2	87	0	0	6	8	.429	0	0-0	0	3.33	3.70
2004	NYY	AL	27	27	0	0	176.2	749	216	95	85	20	3	7	2	18	2	102	7	0	14	8	.636	0	0-0	0	4.26	4.33
2005	Phi	NL	35	**35**	1	0	218.1	912	223	107	102	33	13	5	5	41	6	149	3	0	17	13	.567	0	0-0	0	3.72	4.20
2006	Phi	NL	27	27	2	0	168.0	714	196	100	92	27	6	4	6	24	3	100	3	0	9	11	.450	1	0-0	0	4.53	4.93
12 ML YEARS			361	314	24	10	2073.1	8754	2238	1090	981	268	89	71	44	394	43	1472	29	12	126	115	.523	4	2-6	12	3.92	4.26

Mike Lieberthal

Bats: R Throws: R Pos: C-60; PH-7   Ht: 6'0" Wt: 190 Born: 1/18/1972 Age: 35

			BATTING																		BASERUNNING				AVERAGES		
Year	Team	Lg	G	AB	H	2B	3B	HR	(Hm	Rd)	TB	R	RBI	RC	TBB	IBB	SO	HBP	SH	SF	SB	CS	SB%	GDP	Avg	OBP	Slg
2006	Rdng*	AA	2	6	1	0	0	0	(-	-)	1	0	2	0	0	0	0	0	0	0	0	0	-	0	.167	.167	.167
2006	S-WB*	AAA	2	6	4	1	0	0	(-	-)	5	3	2	2	0	0	0	1	0	0	0	0	-	0	.667	.714	.833
1994	Phi	NL	24	79	21	3	1	1	(1	0)	29	6	5	8	3	0	5	1	1	0	0	0	-	4	.266	.301	.367
1995	Phi	NL	16	47	12	2	0	0	(0	0)	14	1	4	5	5	0	5	0	2	0	0	0	-	4	.255	.327	.298
1996	Phi	NL	50	166	42	8	0	7	(4	3)	71	21	23	21	10	0	30	2	0	4	0	0	-	4	.253	.297	.428
1997	Phi	NL	134	455	112	27	1	20	(11	9)	201	59	77	62	44	1	76	4	0	7	3	4	.43	10	.246	.314	.442
1998	Phi	NL	86	313	80	15	3	8	(5	3)	125	39	45	39	17	1	44	7	0	5	2	1	.67	4	.256	.304	.399
1999	Phi	NL	145	510	153	33	1	31	(10	21)	281	84	96	96	44	7	86	11	1	8	0	0	-	15	.300	.363	.551
2000	Phi	NL	108	389	108	30	0	15	(8	7)	183	55	71	62	40	3	53	6	0	3	2	0	1.00	12	.278	.352	.470
2001	Phi	NL	34	121	28	8	0	2	(0	2)	42	21	11	13	12	2	21	3	0	0	0	0	-	2	.231	.316	.347
2002	Phi	NL	130	476	133	29	2	15	(7	8)	211	46	52	56	38	2	58	14	0	2	0	1	.00	16	.279	.344	.443
2003	Phi	NL	131	508	159	30	1	13	(6	7)	230	68	81	81	38	2	59	12	0	3	0	0	-	14	.313	.373	.453
2004	Phi	NL	131	476	129	31	1	17	(8	9)	213	58	61	49	37	2	69	11	1	4	1	1	.50	19	.271	.335	.447
2005	Phi	NL	118	392	103	25	0	12	(6	6)	164	48	47	49	35	14	35	11	0	5	0	0	-	6	.263	.336	.418
2006	Phi	NL	67	209	57	14	0	9	(5	4)	98	22	36	28	8	0	19	6	5	2	0	0	-	5	.273	.316	.469
13 ML YEARS			1174	4141	1137	255	10	150	(71	79)	1862	528	609	569	331	34	560	88	10	43	8	7	.53	112	.275	.338	.450

Ted Lilly

Pitches: L Bats: L Pos: SP-32   Ht: 6'1" Wt: 190 Born: 1/4/1976 Age: 31

Year	Team	Lg	G	GS	CG	GF	IP	BFP	H	R	ER	HR	SH	SF	HB	TBB	IBB	SO	WP	Bk	W	L	Pct	ShO	Sv-Op	Hld	ERC	ERA
1999	Mon	NL	9	3	0	1	23.2	110	30	20	20	7	0	1	3	9	0	28	1	0	0	1	.000	0	0-0	0	7.76	7.61
2000	NYY	AL	7	0	0	1	8.0	39	8	6	5	1	0	0	0	5	0	11	1	1	0	0	-	0	0-0	0	4.76	5.63
2001	NYY	AL	26	21	0	2	120.2	537	126	81	72	20	2	5	7	51	1	112	9	2	5	6	.455	0	0-0	0	5.10	5.37
2002	2 Tms	AL	22	16	2	1	100.0	413	80	43	41	15	0	3	6	31	3	77	6	1	5	7	.417	1	0-0	0	3.14	3.69
2003	Oak	AL	32	31	0	0	178.1	773	179	92	86	24	3	4	5	58	3	147	5	**4**	12	10	.545	0	0-0	0	4.06	4.34
2004	Tor	AL	32	32	0	0	197.1	845	171	92	89	26	3	3	6	89	2	168	6	**4**	12	10	.545	1	0-0	0	3.84	4.06
2005	Tor	AL	25	25	0	0	126.1	566	135	79	78	23	3	5	3	58	1	96	2	2	10	11	.476	0	0-0	0	5.38	5.56
2006	Tor	AL	32	32	0	0	181.2	797	179	98	87	28	4	2	4	81	6	160	7	**4**	15	13	.536	0	0-0	0	4.57	4.31
02	NYY	AL	16	11	2	1	76.2	314	57	31	29	10	0	3	5	24	3	59	6	0	3	6	.333	1	0-0	0	2.74	3.40
02	Oak	AL	6	5	0	0	23.1	99	23	12	12	5	0	0	1	7	0	18	0	1	2	1	.667	0	0-0	0	4.56	4.63
8 ML YEARS			185	160	4	5	936.0	4080	908	511	478	144	15	23	34	382	16	799	37	18	59	58	.504	2	0-0	0	4.40	4.60

Jose Lima

Pitches: R Bats: R Pos: SP-4   Ht: 6'2" Wt: 210 Born: 9/30/1972 Age: 34

Year	Team	Lg	G	GS	CG	GF	IP	BFP	H	R	ER	HR	SH	SF	HB	TBB	IBB	SO	WP	Bk	W	L	Pct	ShO	Sv-Op	Hld	ERC	ERA
2006	Norfolk*	AAA	25	20	0	1	140.0	572	140	64	61	15	10	6	6	20	0	88	2	0	7	8	.467	0	0--	-	3.31	3.92
1994	Det	AL	3	1	0	1	6.2	34	11	10	10	2	0	0	0	3	1	7	1	0	0	1	.000	0	0-0	0	9.61	13.50
1995	Det	AL	15	15	0	0	73.2	320	85	52	50	10	2	1	4	18	4	37	5	0	3	9	.250	0	0-0	0	4.73	6.11
1996	Det	AL	39	4	0	15	72.2	329	87	48	46	13	5	3	5	22	4	59	3	0	5	6	.455	0	3-7	6	5.53	5.70

HOW MUCH HE PITCHED / WHAT HE GAVE UP / THE RESULTS

Year	Team	Lg	G	GS	CG	GF	IP	BFP	H	R	ER	HR	SH	SF	HB	TBB	IBB	SO	WP	Bk	W	L	Pct	ShO	Sv-Op	Hld	ERC	ERA
1997	Hou	NL	52	1	0	15	75.0	321	79	45	44	9	6	3	5	16	2	63	2	0	1	6	.143	0	2-2	3	3.96	5.28
1998	Hou	NL	33	33	3	0	233.1	950	229	100	96	34	11	5	7	32	1	169	4	0	16	8	.667	1	0-0	0	3.36	3.70
1999	Hou	NL	35	35	3	0	246.1	1024	256	108	98	30	5	7	2	44	2	187	8	0	21	10	.677	0	0-0	0	3.58	3.58
2000	Hou	NL	33	33	0	0	196.1	895	251	152	145	48	12	12	2	68	3	124	3	0	7	16	.304	0	0-0	0	6.59	6.65
2001	2 Tms		32	27	2	3	165.2	719	197	114	102	35	5	9	9	38	3	84	4	0	6	12	.333	0	0-0	0	5.53	5.54
2002	Det	AL	20	12	0	3	68.1	304	86	60	59	12	1	6	2	21	0	33	2	0	4	6	.400	0	0-0	0	5.97	7.77
2003	KC	AL	14	14	0	0	73.1	321	80	40	40	7	1	3	5	26	0	32	2	2	8	3	.727	0	0-0	0	4.69	4.91
2004	LAD	NL	36	24	0	3	170.1	702	178	81	77	33	9	1	1	34	6	93	3	0	13	5	.722	0	0-0	1	4.18	4.07
2005	KC	AL	32	32	1	0	168.2	780	219	140	131	31	5	7	9	61	1	80	5	0	5	16	.238	0	0-0	0	6.54	6.99
2006	NYM	NL	4	4	0	0	17.1	91	25	22	19	3	2	1	2	10	0	12	1	1	0	4	.000	0	0-0	0	8.30	9.87
01	Hou	NL	14	9	0	3	53.0	249	77	48	43	12	4	4	5	16	1	41	3	0	1	2	.333	0	0-0	0	7.90	7.30
01	Det	AL	18	18	2	0	112.2	470	120	66	59	23	1	5	4	22	2	43	1	0	5	10	.333	0	0-0	0	4.49	4.71
13 ML YEARS			348	235	9	40	1567.2	6790	1783	972	917	267	64	58	53	393	27	980	43	3	89	102	.466	1	5-9	10	4.86	5.26

Adam Lind

Bats: L **Throws:** L **Pos:** DH-14; PH-3; LF-2 **Ht:** 6'2" **Wt:** 195 **Born:** 7/17/1983 **Age:** 23

BATTING / BASERUNNING / AVERAGES

Year	Team	Lg	G	AB	H	2B	3B	HR	(Hm	Rd)	TB	R	RBI	RC	TBB	IBB	SO	HBP	SH	SF	SB	CS	SB%	GDP	Avg	OBP	Slg
2004	Auburn	A-	70	266	83	23	0	7	(-	-)	127	43	50	48	24	0	36	2	1	2	1	0	1.00	7	.312	.371	.477
2005	Dnedin	A+	126	495	155	42	4	12	(-	-)	241	80	84	92	49	7	77	4	0	6	2	1	.67	12	.313	.375	.487
2006	NHam	AA	91	348	108	24	0	19	(-	-)	189	43	71	66	25	2	87	2	0	3	2	1	.67	5	.310	.357	.543
2006	Syrcse	AAA	34	109	43	7	0	5	(-	-)	65	20	18	32	23	5	18	2	0	3	1	0	1.00	2	.394	.496	.596
2006	Tor	AL	18	60	22	8	0	2	(0	2)	36	8	8	13	5	0	12	0	0	0	0	0	-	0	.367	.415	.600

Todd Linden

Bats: B **Throws:** R **Pos:** LF-40; PH-21; RF-12; PR-5 **Ht:** 6'3" **Wt:** 220 **Born:** 6/30/1980 **Age:** 27

BATTING / BASERUNNING / AVERAGES

Year	Team	Lg	G	AB	H	2B	3B	HR	(Hm	Rd)	TB	R	RBI	RC	TBB	IBB	SO	HBP	SH	SF	SB	CS	SB%	GDP	Avg	OBP	Slg
2006	Fresno*	AAA	52	187	52	11	3	5	(-	-)	84	31	23	35	29	1	44	4	0	1	5	0	1.00	3	.278	.385	.449
2003	SF	NL	18	38	8	1	0	1	(0	1)	12	2	6	5	1	0	8	0	0	0	0	0	-	0	.211	.231	.316
2004	SF	NL	16	32	5	1	0	0	(0	0)	6	6	1	1	5	0	7	1	2	0	0	0	-	0	.156	.289	.188
2005	SF	NL	60	171	37	8	0	4	(2	2)	57	20	13	12	10	0	54	5	1	0	3	0	1.00	5	.216	.280	.333
2006	SF	NL	61	77	21	4	2	2	(0	2)	35	15	5	10	9	0	20	1	2	0	1	0	1.00	1	.273	.356	.455
4 ML YEARS			155	318	71	14	2	7	(2	5)	110	43	25	28	25	0	89	7	5	0	4	0	1.00	9	.223	.294	.346

Scott Linebrink

Pitches: R **Bats:** R **Pos:** RP-73 **Ht:** 6'2" **Wt:** 200 **Born:** 8/4/1976 **Age:** 30

HOW MUCH HE PITCHED / WHAT HE GAVE UP / THE RESULTS

Year	Team	Lg	G	GS	CG	GF	IP	BFP	H	R	ER	HR	SH	SF	HB	TBB	IBB	SO	WP	Bk	W	L	Pct	ShO	Sv-Op	Hld	ERC	ERA
2000	2 Tms	NL	11	0	0	4	12.0	63	18	8	8	4	0	0	3	8	0	6	0	0	0	0	-	0	0-0	0	11.88	6.00
2001	Hou	NL	9	0	0	2	10.1	44	6	4	3	0	1	1	2	6	0	9	1	0	0	0	-	0	0-0	0	2.54	2.61
2002	Hou	NL	22	0	0	4	24.1	120	31	21	19	2	0	2	1	13	4	24	0	0	0	0	-	0	0-1	1	5.70	7.03
2003	2 Tms	NL	52	6	0	8	92.1	397	93	37	34	9	4	6	6	36	4	68	11	0	3	2	.600	0	0-0	6	4.32	3.31
2004	SD	NL	73	0	0	7	84.0	326	61	22	20	8	2	3	3	26	2	83	3	0	7	3	.700	0	0-5	28	2.48	2.14
2005	SD	NL	73	0	0	17	73.2	288	55	17	15	4	2	0	0	23	4	70	3	0	8	1	.889	0	1-6	26	2.15	1.83
2006	SD	NL	73	0	0	11	75.2	314	70	31	30	9	1	2	1	22	3	68	2	0	7	4	.636	0	2-11	36	3.36	3.57
00	SF	NL	3	0	0	1	2.1	16	7	3	3	1	0	0	0	2	0	0	0	0	0	0	-	0	0-0	0	24.13	11.57
00	Hou	NL	8	0	0	3	9.2	47	11	5	5	3	0	0	3	6	0	6	0	0	0	0	-	0	0-0	0	9.21	4.66
03	Hou	NL	9	6	0	2	31.2	140	38	15	15	4	2	1	3	14	1	17	5	0	1	1	.500	0	0-0	0	6.27	4.26
03	SD	NL	43	0	0	6	60.2	257	55	22	19	5	2	5	3	22	3	51	6	0	2	1	.667	0	0-0	6	3.41	2.82
7 ML YEARS			313	6	0	53	372.1	1552	334	140	129	36	10	14	16	134	17	328	20	0	25	10	.714	0	3-22	97	3.48	3.12

Francisco Liriano

Pitches: L **Bats:** L **Pos:** SP-16; RP-12 **Ht:** 6'2" **Wt:** 200 **Born:** 10/26/1983 **Age:** 23

HOW MUCH HE PITCHED / WHAT HE GAVE UP / THE RESULTS

Year	Team	Lg	G	GS	CG	GF	IP	BFP	H	R	ER	HR	SH	SF	HB	TBB	IBB	SO	WP	Bk	W	L	Pct	ShO	Sv-Op	Hld	ERC	ERA
2001	Giants	R	13	12	0	0	62.0	261	51	26	25	3	1	0	1	24	0	67	6	3	5	4	.556	0	0- -	-	2.75	3.63
2001	SlmKzr	A-	2	2	0	0	9.0	35	7	5	5	2	0	0	0	1	0	12	0	0	0	0	-	0	0- -	-	2.47	5.00
2002	Hgrstn	A	16	16	0	0	80.0	332	61	45	31	6	4	3	0	31	0	85	4	0	3	6	.333	0	0- -	-	2.56	3.49
2003	SnJos	A+	1	1	0	0	0.2	9	5	4	4	0	3	1	0	2	0	0	1	0	1	0	1.000	0	0- -	-	69.84	54.00
2003	Giants	R	4	4	0	0	8.1	36	5	4	4	1	0	0	0	6	0	9	1	1	0	1	.000	0	0- -	-	3.20	4.32
2004	FtMyrs	A+	21	21	0	0	117.0	512	118	56	52	6	4	1	4	43	2	125	6	2	6	7	.462	0	0- -	-	3.54	4.00
2004	NwBrit	AA	7	7	0	0	39.2	181	45	14	14	4	3	1	2	17	0	49	3	0	3	2	.600	0	0- -	-	5.11	3.18
2005	NwBrit	AA	13	13	0	0	76.2	326	70	36	31	6	0	0	2	26	0	92	3	1	3	5	.375	0	0- -	-	3.27	3.64
2005	Roch	AAA	14	14	0	0	91.0	353	56	25	18	4	0	2	0	24	0	112	2	1	9	2	.818	0	0- -	-	1.44	1.78
2005	Min	AL	6	4	0	2	23.2	93	19	15	15	4	0	0	0	7	0	33	0	0	1	2	.333	0	0-0	0	3.15	5.70
2006	Min	AL	28	16	0	2	121.0	473	89	31	29	9	4	2	1	32	0	144	9	1	12	3	.800	0	1-1	1	2.12	2.16
2 ML YEARS			34	20	0	4	144.2	566	108	46	44	13	4	2	1	39	0	177	9	1	13	5	.722	0	1-1	1	2.28	2.74

Wes Littleton

Pitches: R Bats: R Pos: RP-33   **Ht:** 6'2" **Wt:** 210 **Born:** 9/2/1982 **Age:** 24

Year	Team	Lg	G	GS	CG	GF	IP	BFP	H	R	ER	HR	SH	SF	HB	TBB	IBB	SO	WP	Bk	W	L	Pct	ShO	Sv-Op Hld	ERC	ERA
2003	Spkane	A-	12	8	0	2	52.0	192	36	9	9	2	1	0	1	8	0	47	2	1	6	0	1.000	0	0- - -	1.53	1.56
2004	Stcktn	A+	30	23	0	1	141.0	600	139	76	65	7	8	15	11	56	0	72	14	0	8	10	.444	0	0- - -	4.04	4.15
2005	Frisco	AA	48	0	0	27	81.2	369	93	37	36	9	2	4	3	24	7	71	3	1	2	3	.400	0	3- - -	4.35	3.97
2006	Frisco	AA	17	0	0	6	27.1	104	13	3	2	1	0	0	2	7	0	25	1	0	3	0	1.000	0	3- - -	1.15	0.66
2006	Okla	AAA	13	0	0	6	16.2	66	14	4	4	3	1	0	0	5	0	15	0	0	4	1	.800	0	2- - -	3.45	2.16
2006	Tex	AL	33	0	0	6	36.1	138	23	7	7	2	0	1	2	13	0	17	0	0	2	1	.667	0	1-1 7	2.10	1.73

Bobby Livingston

Pitches: L Bats: L Pos: RP-3   **Ht:** 6'3" **Wt:** 195 **Born:** 9/3/1982 **Age:** 24

Year	Team	Lg	G	GS	CG	GF	IP	BFP	H	R	ER	HR	SH	SF	HB	TBB	IBB	SO	WP	Bk	W	L	Pct	ShO	Sv-Op Hld	ERC	ERA
2002	Everett	A-	15	14	0	1	80.1	338	80	33	27	2	1	2	7	14	0	76	4	2	6	5	.545	0	0- - -	2.99	3.02
2003	Wisc	A	26	26	1	0	178.0	733	176	72	54	10	7	7	12	28	0	105	1	3	15	7	.682	0	0- - -	3.07	2.73
2004	InldEm	A+	28	27	1	0	186.2	762	187	90	74	15	8	4	7	30	0	141	4	0	12	6	.667	1	0- - -	3.21	3.57
2005	SnAnt	AA	18	18	0	0	116.1	467	103	45	37	7	7	5	2	27	0	78	2	1	8	4	.667	0	0- - -	2.68	2.86
2005	Tacom	AAA	10	10	0	0	51.2	224	53	31	27	2	3	1	1	15	0	41	1	0	6	2	.750	0	0- - -	3.36	4.70
2006	Tacom	AAA	23	22	0	1	135.1	583	165	74	69	18	1	9	2	36	2	69	2	2	8	11	.421	0	0- - -	5.19	4.59
2006	Sea	AL	3	0	0	1	5.0	32	9	10	10	2	0	0	2	6	1	3	0	0	0	0	-	0	0-0 0	17.47	18.00

Paul Lo Duca

Bats: R Throws: R Pos: C-118; PH-4; DH-3   **Ht:** 5'10" **Wt:** 185 **Born:** 4/12/1972 **Age:** 35

											BATTING											BASERUNNING				AVERAGES		
Year	Team	Lg	G	AB	H	2B	3B	HR	(Hm	Rd)	TB	R	RBI	RC	TBB	IBB	SO	HBP	SH	SF	SB	CS	SB%	GDP	Avg	OBP	Slg
1998	LAD	NL	6	14	4	1	0	0	(0	0)	5	2	1	1	0	0	1	0	0	0	0	0	-	0	.286	.286	.357
1999	LAD	NL	36	95	22	1	0	3	(1	2)	32	11	11	9	10	4	9	2	1	2	1	2	.33	3	.232	.312	.337
2000	LAD	NL	34	65	16	2	0	2	(0	2)	24	6	8	6	6	0	8	0	2	2	0	2	.00	2	.246	.301	.369
2001	LAD	NL	125	460	147	28	0	25	(11	14)	250	71	90	89	39	2	30	6	5	9	2	4	.33	11	.320	.374	.543
2002	LAD	NL	149	580	163	38	1	10	(5	5)	233	74	64	73	34	2	31	10	4	4	3	1	.75	20	.281	.330	.402
2003	LAD	NL	147	568	155	34	2	7	(4	3)	214	64	52	67	44	6	54	10	7	1	0	2	.00	21	.273	.335	.377
2004	2 Tms	NL	143	535	153	29	2	13	(8	5)	225	68	80	78	36	0	49	9	8	6	4	5	.44	22	.286	.338	.421
2005	Fla	NL	132	445	126	23	1	6	(2	4)	169	45	57	50	34	5	31	4	5	8	4	3	.57	16	.283	.334	.380
2006	NYM	NL	124	512	163	39	1	5	(2	3)	219	80	49	71	24	0	38	6	7	2	3	0	1.00	15	.318	.355	.428
04	LAD	NL	91	349	105	18	1	10	(6	4)	155	41	49	51	22	0	27	6	2	2	2	4	.33	15	.301	.351	.444
04	Fla	NL	52	186	48	11	1	3	(2	1)	70	27	31	27	14	0	22	3	6	4	2	1	.67	7	.258	.314	.376
9 ML YEARS			896	3274	949	195	7	71	(33	38)	1371	421	412	444	227	19	251	47	39	34	17	19	.47	110	.290	.341	.419

Esteban Loaiza

Pitches: R Bats: R Pos: SP-26   **Ht:** 6'3" **Wt:** 215 **Born:** 12/31/1971 **Age:** 35

Year	Team	Lg	G	GS	CG	GF	IP	BFP	H	R	ER	HR	SH	SF	HB	TBB	IBB	SO	WP	Bk	W	L	Pct	ShO	Sv-Op Hld	ERC	ERA
2006	Scrmto*	AAA	2	1	0	0	7.2	36	11	5	5	0	1	0	1	2	0	4	0	0	1	1	.500	0	0- - -	5.82	5.87
1995	Pit	NL	32	31	1	0	172.2	762	205	115	99	21	10	9	5	55	3	85	6	1	8	9	.471	0	0-0 0	5.10	5.16
1996	Pit	NL	10	10	1	0	52.2	236	65	32	29	11	3	1	2	19	2	32	0	0	2	3	.400	1	0-0 0	6.30	4.96
1997	Pit	NL	33	32	1	0	196.1	851	214	99	90	17	10	7	12	56	9	122	2	3	11	11	.500	2	0-0 0	4.20	4.13
1998	2 Tms		35	28	1	3	171.0	751	199	107	98	28	7	12	5	52	4	108	4	2	9	11	.450	1	0-1 0	5.19	5.16
1999	Tex	AL	30	15	0	4	120.1	517	128	65	61	10	7	4	0	40	2	77	2	0	9	5	.643	0	0-0 0	4.03	4.56
2000	2 Tms		34	31	1	2	199.1	871	228	112	101	29	4	5	13	57	1	137	1	0	10	13	.435	1	1-1 0	5.07	4.56
2001	Tor	AL	36	30	1	1	190.0	837	239	113	106	27	6	4	9	40	1	110	1	1	11	11	.500	1	0-0 0	5.30	5.02
2002	Tor	AL	25	25	3	0	151.1	670	192	102	96	18	1	6	4	38	3	87	1	0	9	10	.474	1	0-0 0	5.26	5.71
2003	CWS	AL	34	34	1	0	226.1	922	196	75	73	17	7	6	10	56	2	207	3	1	21	9	.700	1	0-0 0	2.79	2.90
2004	2 Tms		31	27	2	1	183.0	818	217	124	116	32	1	10	3	71	5	117	4	0	10	7	.588	1	0-0 0	5.72	5.70
2005	Was	AL	34	34	0	0	217.0	912	227	93	91	18	9	3	5	55	3	173	6	0	12	10	.545	0	0-0 0	3.74	3.77
2006	Oak	AL	26	26	2	0	154.2	679	179	92	84	17	5	8	5	40	3	97	2	0	11	9	.550	1	0-0 0	4.53	4.89
98	Pit	NL	21	14	0	3	91.2	394	96	50	46	13	5	7	3	30	1	53	1	2	6	5	.545	0	0-1 0	4.48	4.52
98	Tex	AL	14	14	1	0	79.1	357	103	57	52	15	2	5	2	22	3	55	3	0	3	6	.333	0	0-0 0	6.04	5.90
00	Tex	AL	20	17	0	2	107.1	480	133	67	64	21	2	4	3	31	1	75	1	0	5	6	.455	0	1-1 0	5.81	5.37
00	Tor	AL	14	14	1	0	92.0	391	95	45	37	8	2	1	10	26	0	62	0	0	5	7	.417	1	0-0 0	4.22	3.62
04	CWS	AL	21	21	2	0	140.2	604	156	81	76	23	1	5	1	45	3	83	2	0	9	5	.643	1	0-0 0	4.89	4.86
04	NYY	AL	10	6	0	1	42.1	214	61	43	40	9	0	5	2	26	2	34	2	0	1	2	.333	0	0-0 0	8.70	8.50
12 ML YEARS			360	323	14	11	2034.2	8826	2289	1129	1044	245	70	75	73	579	38	1352	32	8	123	108	.532	6	1-2 0	4.60	4.62

Kameron Loe

Pitches: R Bats: R Pos: SP-15   **Ht:** 6'7" **Wt:** 240 **Born:** 9/10/1981 **Age:** 25

Year	Team	Lg	G	GS	CG	GF	IP	BFP	H	R	ER	HR	SH	SF	HB	TBB	IBB	SO	WP	Bk	W	L	Pct	ShO	Sv-Op Hld	ERC	ERA
2006	Frisco*	AA	2	2	0	0	7.0	32	8	5	4	1	0	0	0	4	0	4	0	0	0	1	.000	0	0- - -	6.01	5.14
2006	Okla*	AAA	13	3	0	7	22.2	115	32	24	23	3	1	2	1	13	0	21	4	0	1	2	.333	0	1- - -	7.53	9.13
2004	Tex	AL	2	1	0	0	6.2	29	6	5	4	0	0	0	1	6	0	3	0	0	0	0	-	0	0-0 0	5.87	5.40
2005	Tex	AL	48	8	0	13	92.0	392	89	43	35	7	5	1	2	31	6	45	2	0	9	6	.600	0	1-4 4	3.45	3.42
2006	Tex	AL	15	15	1	0	78.1	358	105	54	51	10	1	3	1	22	0	34	3	0	3	6	.333	1	0-0 0	5.79	5.86
3 ML YEARS			65	24	1	13	177.0	779	200	102	90	17	6	4	4	59	6	82	5	0	12	12	.500	1	1-4 4	4.54	4.58

Adam Loewen

Pitches: L **Bats:** L **Pos:** SP-19; RP-3 **Ht:** 6'5" **Wt:** 235 **Born:** 4/9/1984 **Age:** 23

		HOW MUCH HE PITCHED						WHAT HE GAVE UP											THE RESULTS						
Year	Team	Lg	G	GS	CG	GF	IP	BFP	H	R	ER	HR	SH	SF	HB	TBB	IBB	SO	WP	Bk	W	L	Pct	ShO	Sv-Op	Hld	ERC	ERA
2003	Abrdn	A-	7	7	0	0	23.1	91	13	7	7	0	0	0	4	9	0	25	2	0	0	2	.000	0	0- -	-	1.84	2.70
2004	Dlmrva	A	20	19	1	0	85.1	376	77	47	39	3	2	4	4	58	0	82	8	4	4	5	.444	0	0- -	-	4.43	4.11
2004	Frdrck	A+	2	2	1	0	8.0	37	7	6	6	2	1	0	0	9	0	3	0	0	0	2	.000	0	0- -	-	8.07	6.75
2005	Frdrck	A+	28	27	1	0	142.0	631	130	77	65	8	4	1	14	86	0	146	15	1	10	8	.556	0	0- -	-	4.54	4.12
2006	Bowie	AA	9	8	0	0	49.2	215	46	17	15	3	2	1	2	26	0	55	6	2	4	2	.667	0	0- -	-	4.08	2.72
2006	Ottawa	AAA	3	3	0	0	21.1	73	10	3	3	0	0	0	0	3	0	21	1	0	2	0	1.000	0	0- -	-	0.72	1.27
2006	Bal	AL	22	19	0	1	112.1	504	111	72	67	8	1	4	8	62	0	98	3	1	6	6	.500	0	0-0	1	4.70	5.37

Kenny Lofton

Bats: L **Throws:** L **Pos:** CF-120; PR-6; PH-3; DH-2 **Ht:** 5'11" **Wt:** 190 **Born:** 5/31/1967 **Age:** 40

						BATTING														BASERUNNING				AVERAGES		
Year	Team	Lg	G	AB	H	2B	3B	HR	(Hm	Rd)	TB	R	RBI	RC	TBB	IBB	SO	HBP	SH	SF	SB	CS	SB%	GDP	Avg	OBP	Slg
1991	Hou	NL	20	74	15	1	0	0	(0	0)	16	9	0	4	5	0	19	0	0	0	2	1	.67	0	.203	.253	.216
1992	Cle	AL	148	576	164	15	8	5	(3	2)	210	96	42	88	68	3	54	2	4	1	66	12	.85	7	.285	.362	.365
1993	Cle	AL	148	569	185	28	8	1	(1	0)	232	116	42	107	81	6	83	1	2	4	70	14	.83	8	.325	.408	.408
1994	Cle	AL	112	459	160	32	9	12	(10	2)	246	105	57	105	52	5	56	2	4	6	60	12	.83	5	.349	.412	.536
1995	Cle	AL	118	481	149	22	13	7	(5	2)	218	93	53	83	40	6	49	1	4	3	54	15	.78	6	.310	.362	.453
1996	Cle	AL	154	662	210	35	4	14	(7	7)	295	132	67	118	61	3	82	0	7	6	75	17	.82	7	.317	.372	.446
1997	Atl	NL	122	493	164	20	6	5	(3	2)	211	90	48	84	64	5	83	2	2	3	27	20	.57	10	.333	.409	.428
1998	Cle	AL	154	600	169	31	6	12	(6	6)	248	101	64	103	87	1	80	2	3	6	54	10	.84	7	.282	.371	.413
1999	Cle	AL	120	465	140	28	6	7	(1	6)	201	110	39	89	79	2	84	6	5	5	25	6	.81	6	.301	.405	.432
2000	Cle	AL	137	543	151	23	5	15	(10	5)	229	107	73	91	79	3	72	4	6	8	30	7	.81	11	.278	.369	.422
2001	Cle	AL	133	517	135	21	4	14	(9	5)	206	91	66	67	47	1	69	2	5	5	16	8	.67	8	.261	.322	.398
2002	2 Tms		139	532	139	30	9	11	(3	8)	220	98	51	83	72	0	73	1	5	1	29	11	.73	1	.261	.350	.414
2003	2 Tms	NL	140	547	162	32	8	12	(5	7)	246	97	46	79	46	3	51	4	7	6	30	9	.77	6	.296	.352	.450
2004	NYY	AL	83	276	76	10	7	3	(2	1)	109	51	18	36	31	1	27	1	1	4	7	3	.70	4	.275	.346	.395
2005	Phi	NL	110	367	123	15	5	2	(1	1)	154	67	36	62	32	2	41	2	5	0	22	3	.88	3	.335	.392	.420
2006	LAD	NL	129	469	141	15	12	3	(2	1)	189	79	41	68	45	1	42	0	6	2	32	5	.86	16	.301	.360	.403
02	CWS	AL	93	352	91	20	6	8	(3	5)	147	68	42	57	49	0	51	0	4	1	22	8	.73	0	.259	.348	.418
02	SF	NL	46	180	48	10	3	3	(0	3)	73	30	9	26	23	0	22	1	1	0	7	3	.70	1	.267	.353	.406
03	Pit	NL	84	339	94	19	4	9	(4	5)	148	58	26	42	28	1	29	2	2	3	18	5	.78	2	.277	.333	.437
03	ChC	NL	56	208	68	13	4	3	(1	2)	98	39	20	37	18	2	22	2	5	3	12	4	.75	4	.327	.381	.471
16 ML YEARS			1967	7630	2283	358	110	123	(67	56)	3230	1442	743	1267	889	42	965	30	66	60	599	153	.80	105	.299	.372	.423

Boone Logan

Pitches: L **Bats:** R **Pos:** RP-21 **Ht:** 6'5" **Wt:** 200 **Born:** 8/13/1984 **Age:** 22

			HOW MUCH HE PITCHED						WHAT HE GAVE UP											THE RESULTS						
Year	Team	Lg	G	GS	CG	GF	IP	BFP	H	R	ER	HR	SH	SF	HB	TBB	IBB	SO	WP	Bk	W	L	Pct	ShO	Sv-Op	Hld	ERC	ERA
2003	Gr Falls	R+	16	14	0	0	67.0	321	76	60	49	4	3	4	11	31	0	48	8	1	3	3	.500	0	0- -	-	5.28	6.58
2004	Gr Falls	R+	18	9	0	2	64.1	297	74	48	40	7	2	2	4	31	0	48	8	2	3	7	.300	0	1- -	-	5.57	5.60
2005	Gr Falls	R+	21	0	0	5	35.1	141	34	15	13	1	0	2	3	4	0	29	4	0	1	1	.500	0	2- -	-	2.72	3.31
2005	WinSa	A+	4	0	0	1	5.1	27	7	3	3	2	0	1	0	4	0	5	0	0	0	0	-	0	0- -	-	9.71	5.06
2006	Charltt	AAA	38	0	0	24	42.2	181	35	18	16	1	1	1	9	12	3	57	3	0	3	1	.750	0	11- -	-	2.81	3.38
2006	CWS	AL	21	0	0	4	17.1	93	21	18	16	2	1	1	3	15	2	15	1	0	0	0	-	0	1-2	2	7.56	8.31

Nook Logan

Bats: B **Throws:** R **Pos:** CF-26; PH-2 **Ht:** 6'3" **Wt:** 180 **Born:** 11/28/1979 **Age:** 27

						BATTING														BASERUNNING				AVERAGES		
Year	Team	Lg	G	AB	H	2B	3B	HR	(Hm	Rd)	TB	R	RBI	RC	TBB	IBB	SO	HBP	SH	SF	SB	CS	SB%	GDP	Avg	OBP	Slg
2006	Toledo*	AAA	19	65	12	2	1	0	(-	-)	16	9	4	4	9	0	18	0	2	0	3	2	.60	0	.185	.284	.246
2006	Erie*	AA	20	77	19	2	1	0	(-	-)	23	14	2	9	11	0	23	0	0	0	9	3	.75	1	.247	.341	.299
2004	Det	AL	47	133	37	5	2	0	(0	0)	46	12	10	15	13	0	24	0	5	1	8	2	.80	1	.278	.340	.346
2005	Det	AL	129	322	83	12	5	1	(0	1)	108	47	17	33	21	3	52	1	12	0	23	6	.79	5	.258	.305	.335
2006	Was	NL	27	90	27	3	1	1	(0	1)	35	13	8	10	6	1	20	0	1	2	2	1	.67	0	.300	.337	.389
3 ML YEARS			203	545	147	20	8	2	(0	2)	189	72	35	58	40	4	96	1	18	3	33	9	.79	6	.270	.319	.347

Kyle Lohse

Pitches: R **Bats:** R **Pos:** SP-19; RP-15 **Ht:** 6'2" **Wt:** 200 **Born:** 10/4/1978 **Age:** 28

			HOW MUCH HE PITCHED						WHAT HE GAVE UP											THE RESULTS						
Year	Team	Lg	G	GS	CG	GF	IP	BFP	H	R	ER	HR	SH	SF	HB	TBB	IBB	SO	WP	Bk	W	L	Pct	ShO	Sv-Op	Hld	ERC	ERA
2006	Roch*	AAA	4	4	2	0	24.0	94	15	6	4	1	1	2	0	6	0	12	0	0	2	1	.667	0	0- -	-	1.42	1.50
2001	Min	AL	19	16	0	2	90.1	402	102	60	57	16	1	5	8	29	0	64	5	0	4	7	.364	0	0-0	0	5.43	5.68
2002	Min	AL	32	31	1	0	180.2	783	181	92	85	26	3	3	9	70	2	124	8	0	13	8	.619	1	0-1	0	4.55	4.23
2003	Min	AL	33	33	2	0	201.0	850	211	107	103	28	8	5	5	45	1	130	10	1	14	11	.560	1	0-0	0	4.00	4.61
2004	Min	AL	35	34	1	1	194.0	883	240	128	115	28	5	7	7	76	5	111	6	0	9	13	.409	1	0-0	0	5.89	5.34
2005	Min	AL	31	30	0	1	178.2	769	211	85	83	22	3	7	9	44	5	86	4	1	9	13	.409	0	0-0	0	4.91	4.18
2006	2 Tms		34	19	0	6	126.2	567	150	83	82	15	8	5	6	44	4	97	3	1	5	10	.333	0	0-0	0	5.20	5.83
06	Min	AL	22	8	0	5	63.2	295	80	50	50	8	1	3	6	25	2	46	1	1	2	5	.286	0	0-0	0	6.10	7.07
06	Cin	NL	12	11	0	1	63.0	272	70	33	32	7	7	2	0	19	2	51	2	0	3	5	.375	0	0-0	0	4.34	4.57
6 ML YEARS			184	163	4	10	971.1	4254	1095	555	525	135	28	32	44	308	17	612	36	3	54	62	.466	3	0-1	0	4.93	4.86

George Lombard

Bats: L **Throws:** R **Pos:** PH-12; RF-5; LF-3; PR-2 **Ht:** 6'0" **Wt:** 210 **Born:** 9/14/1975 **Age:** 31

Year	Team	Lg	G	AB	H	2B	3B	HR	(Hm	Rd)	TB	R	RBI	RC	TBB	IBB	SO	HBP	SH	SF	SB	CS	SB%	GDP	Avg	OBP	Slg
2006	Nats*	R	6	17	3	1	0	0	(-	-)	4	1	1	2	6	0	3	1	0	0	1	0	1.00	0	.176	.417	.235
2006	NewOr*	AAA	62	189	57	10	1	10	(-	-)	99	35	24	41	23	3	49	5	3	0	18	2	.90	1	.302	.392	.524
1998	Atl	NL	6	6	2	0	0	1	(0	1)	5	2	1	2	0	0	1	0	0	0	1	0	1.00	0	.333	.333	.833
1999	Atl	NL	6	6	2	0	0	0	(0	0)	2	1	0	1	1	0	2	0	0	0	2	0	1.00	0	.333	.429	.333
2000	Atl	NL	27	39	4	0	0	0	(0	0)	4	8	2	0	1	0	14	1	0	0	4	0	1.00	2	.103	.146	.103
2002	Det	AL	72	241	58	11	3	5	(2	3)	90	34	13	26	20	1	78	1	7	1	13	2	.87	0	.241	.300	.373
2003	TB	AL	13	37	8	1	0	1	(0	1)	12	8	4	2	0	0	6	1	0	0	1	0	1.00	0	.216	.237	.324
2006	Was	NL	20	21	3	0	0	1	(0	1)	6	2	1	1	5	0	10	0	0	0	2	0	1.00	0	.143	.308	.286
	6 ML YEARS		144	350	77	12	3	8	(2	6)	119	55	21	32	27	1	111	3	7	1	23	2	.92	2	.220	.281	.340

James Loney

Bats: L **Throws:** L **Pos:** 1B-39; PH-10; RF-2; PR-1 **Ht:** 6'2" **Wt:** 220 **Born:** 5/7/1984 **Age:** 23

Year	Team	Lg	G	AB	H	2B	3B	HR	(Hm	Rd)	TB	R	RBI	RC	TBB	IBB	SO	HBP	SH	SF	SB	CS	SB%	GDP	Avg	OBP	Slg
2002	Gr Falls	R+	47	170	63	22	3	5	(-	-)	106	33	30	45	25	1	18	2	0	0	5	4	.56	4	.371	.457	.624
2002	VeroB	A+	17	67	20	6	0	0	(-	-)	26	6	5	9	6	0	10	0	1	0	0	0	-	2	.299	.356	.388
2003	VeroB	A+	125	468	129	31	3	7	(-	-)	187	64	46	66	43	5	80	1	3	1	9	4	.69	13	.276	.337	.400
2004	Jaxnvl	AA	104	395	94	19	2	4	(-	-)	129	39	35	43	42	6	75	3	0	2	5	5	.50	7	.238	.314	.327
2005	Jaxnvl	AA	138	504	143	31	2	11	(-	-)	211	74	65	78	59	8	87	2	1	6	1	4	.20	13	.284	.357	.419
2006	LsVgs	AAA	98	366	139	33	2	8	(-	-)	200	64	67	82	32	7	34	2	0	6	9	5	.64	11	.380	.426	.546
2006	LAD	NL	48	102	29	6	5	4	(1	3)	57	20	18	17	8	1	10	1	0	0	1	0	1.00	8	.284	.342	.559

Terrence Long

Bats: L **Throws:** L **Pos:** RF-7; LF-2; CF-2; DH-1; PH-1 **Ht:** 6'1" **Wt:** 200 **Born:** 2/29/1976 **Age:** 31

Year	Team	Lg	G	AB	H	2B	3B	HR	(Hm	Rd)	TB	R	RBI	RC	TBB	IBB	SO	HBP	SH	SF	SB	CS	SB%	GDP	Avg	OBP	Slg
2006	Lsvlle*	AAA	15	48	11	3	0	0	(-	-)	14	2	6	3	2	0	10	0	0	0	0	0	-	1	.229	.260	.292
2006	Clmbs*	AAA	69	260	72	13	1	10	(-	-)	117	29	38	39	19	2	53	1	0	0	0	0	-	5	.277	.329	.450
1999	NYM	NL	3	3	0	0	0	0	(0	0)	0	0	0	0	0	0	2	0	0	0	0	0	-	0	.000	.000	.000
2000	Oak	AL	138	584	168	34	4	18	(9	9)	264	104	80	85	43	1	77	1	0	3	5	0	1.00	18	.288	.336	.452
2001	Oak	AL	162	629	178	37	4	12	(6	6)	259	90	85	84	52	8	103	0	0	6	9	3	.75	17	.283	.335	.412
2002	Oak	AL	162	587	141	32	4	16	(9	7)	229	71	67	61	48	6	96	2	0	3	3	6	.33	17	.240	.298	.390
2003	Oak	AL	140	486	119	22	2	14	(8	6)	187	64	61	61	31	4	67	3	0	2	4	1	.80	9	.245	.293	.385
2004	SD	NL	136	288	85	19	4	3	(1	2)	121	31	28	30	19	4	51	1	0	5	3	2	.60	13	.295	.335	.420
2005	KC	AL	137	455	127	21	3	6	(2	4)	172	62	53	57	30	0	56	0	0	4	3	3	.50	15	.279	.321	.378
2006	NYY	AL	12	36	6	1	0	0	(0	0)	7	6	2	2	4	0	8	0	0	0	0	0	-	0	.167	.250	.194
	8 ML YEARS		890	3068	824	166	21	69	(35	34)	1239	428	376	380	227	23	460	7	0	23	27	15	.64	90	.269	.318	.404

Braden Looper

Pitches: R **Bats:** R **Pos:** RP-69 **Ht:** 6'3" **Wt:** 220 **Born:** 10/28/1974 **Age:** 32

Year	Team	Lg	G	GS	CG	GF	IP	BFP	H	R	ER	HR	SH	SF	HB	TBB	IBB	SO	WP	Bk	W	L	Pct	ShO	Sv-Op	Hld	ERC	ERA
1998	StL	NL	4	0	0	3	3.1	16	5	4	2	1	0	1	0	1	0	4	1	0	0	1	.000	0	0-2	0	8.14	5.40
1999	Fla	NL	72	0	0	22	83.0	370	96	43	35	7	5	5	1	31	5	50	2	2	3	3	.500	0	0-4	8	4.67	3.80
2000	Fla	NL	73	0	0	23	67.1	311	71	41	33	3	3	2	5	36	6	29	5	0	5	1	.833	0	2-5	18	4.55	4.41
2001	Fla	NL	71	0	0	21	71.0	295	63	28	28	8	0	3	2	30	3	52	0	0	3	3	.500	0	3-6	16	3.77	3.55
2002	Fla	NL	78	0	0	40	86.0	349	73	31	30	8	3	0	1	28	3	55	1	0	2	5	.286	0	13-16	16	2.98	3.14
2003	Fla	NL	74	0	0	64	80.2	347	82	34	33	4	3	3	1	29	1	56	2	0	6	4	.600	0	28-34	0	3.67	3.68
2004	NYM	NL	71	0	0	60	83.1	346	86	28	25	5	2	2	3	16	3	60	1	0	2	5	.286	0	29-34	0	3.28	2.70
2005	NYM	NL	60	0	0	54	59.1	271	65	31	26	7	4	0	5	22	3	27	1	0	4	7	.364	0	28-36	0	4.75	3.94
2006	StL	NL	69	0	0	28	73.1	308	76	30	29	3	7	5	2	20	5	41	0	0	9	3	.750	0	0-2	15	3.41	3.56
	9 ML YEARS		572	0	0	315	607.1	2613	617	270	241	46	27	21	20	213	29	374	13	2	34	32	.515	0	103-139	73	3.85	3.57

Felipe Lopez

Bats: B **Throws:** R **Pos:** SS-155; PH-3 **Ht:** 6'1" **Wt:** 185 **Born:** 5/12/1980 **Age:** 27

Year	Team	Lg	G	AB	H	2B	3B	HR	(Hm	Rd)	TB	R	RBI	RC	TBB	IBB	SO	HBP	SH	SF	SB	CS	SB%	GDP	Avg	OBP	Slg
2001	Tor	AL	49	177	46	5	4	5	(3	2)	74	21	23	22	12	1	39	0	1	2	4	3	.57	2	.260	.304	.418
2002	Tor	AL	85	282	64	15	3	8	(5	3)	109	35	34	32	23	1	90	1	2	1	5	4	.56	4	.227	.287	.387
2003	Cin	NL	59	197	42	7	2	2	(0	2)	59	28	13	21	28	1	59	1	2	1	8	5	.62	2	.213	.313	.299
2004	Cin	NL	79	264	64	18	2	7	(4	3)	107	35	31	34	25	0	81	3	2	1	1	1	.50	1	.242	.314	.405
2005	Cin	NL	148	580	169	34	5	23	(16	7)	282	97	85	95	57	2	111	1	3	7	15	7	.68	8	.291	.352	.486
2006	2 Tms	NL	156	617	169	27	3	11	(5	6)	235	98	52	84	81	1	126	2	11	3	44	12	.79	10	.274	.358	.381
06	Cin	NL	85	343	92	14	1	9	(5	4)	135	55	30	48	47	1	66	0	3	1	23	6	.79	6	.268	.355	.394
06	Was	NL	71	274	77	13	2	2	(0	2)	100	43	22	36	34	0	60	2	8	2	21	6	.78	4	.281	.362	.365
	6 ML YEARS		576	2117	554	106	19	56	(32	24)	866	314	238	288	226	6	506	8	21	15	77	32	.71	27	.262	.333	.409

Javier Lopez

Pitches: L Bats: L Pos: RP-27

Ht: 6'4" **Wt:** 220 **Born:** 7/11/1977 **Age:** 29

			HOW MUCH HE PITCHED					WHAT HE GAVE UP											THE RESULTS							
Year	Team	Lg	G	GS	CG	GF	IP	BFP	H	R	ER	HR	SH	SF	HB	TBB	IBB	SO	WP	Bk	W	L	Pct	ShO	Sv-Op	Hld	ERC	ERA
2006	Charltt*	AAA	26	0	0	21	33.0	126	28	2	2	1	0	0	1	6	0	26	1	0	2	1	.667	0	12--	-	2.29	0.55
2006	Pwtckt*	AAA	13	0	0	10	16.2	78	20	10	9	1	1	1	1	8	1	12	1	0	0	0	-	0	4--	-	5.31	4.86
2003	Col	NL	75	0	0	11	58.1	242	58	25	24	5	1	0	4	12	2	40	1	3	4	1	.800	0	1-2	15	3.44	3.70
2004	Col	NL	64	0	0	10	40.2	187	45	34	34	1	1	0	3	26	4	20	3	0	1	2	.333	0	0-1	12	5.28	7.52
2005	2 Tms	NL	32	0	0	6	16.1	87	26	20	20	2	1	0	1	11	3	12	0	0	1	1	.500	0	2-4	6	8.82	11.02
2006	Bos	AL	27	0	0	8	16.2	69	13	10	5	1	0	1	2	10	1	11	0	0	1	0	1.000	0	1-1	6	3.96	2.70
05	Col	NL	3	0	0	1	2.0	13	7	5	5	0	0	0	0	0	0	1	0	0	0	0	-	0	0-1	0	18.39	22.50
05	Ari	NL	29	0	0	5	14.1	74	19	15	15	2	1	0	1	11	3	11	0	0	1	1	.500	0	2-3	6	7.63	9.42
	4 ML YEARS		198	0	0	35	132.0	585	142	89	83	9	3	1	10	59	10	83	4	3	7	4	.636	0	4-8	39	4.69	5.66

Javy Lopez

Bats: R Throws: R Pos: DH-53; C-38; PH-5

Ht: 6'3" **Wt:** 220 **Born:** 11/5/1970 **Age:** 36

					BATTING																BASERUNNING				AVERAGES		
Year	Team	Lg	G	AB	H	2B	3B	HR	(Hm	Rd)	TB	R	RBI	RC	TBB	IBB	SO	HBP	SH	SF	SB	CS	SB%	GDP	Avg	OBP	Slg
2006	Bowie*	AA	2	7	2	1	0	1	(-	-)	6	1	1	2	1	0	1	0	0	0	0	0	-	1	.286	.375	.857
1992	Atl	NL	9	16	6	2	0	0	(0	0)	8	3	2	3	0	0	1	0	0	0	0	0	-	0	.375	.375	.500
1993	Atl	NL	8	16	6	1	1	1	(0	1)	12	1	2	4	0	0	2	1	0	0	0	0	-	0	.375	.412	.750
1994	Atl	NL	80	277	68	9	0	13	(4	9)	116	27	35	31	17	0	61	5	2	2	0	2	.00	12	.245	.299	.419
1995	Atl	NL	100	333	105	11	4	14	(8	6)	166	37	51	51	14	0	57	2	0	3	0	1	.00	13	.315	.344	.498
1996	Atl	NL	138	489	138	19	1	23	(10	13)	228	56	69	66	28	5	84	3	1	5	1	6	.14	17	.282	.322	.466
1997	Atl	NL	123	414	122	28	1	23	(11	12)	221	52	68	76	40	10	82	5	1	4	1	1	.50	9	.295	.361	.534
1998	Atl	NL	133	489	139	21	1	34	(18	16)	264	73	106	79	30	1	85	6	1	8	5	3	.63	22	.284	.328	.540
1999	Atl	NL	65	246	78	18	1	11	(1	10)	131	34	45	45	20	2	41	3	0	0	0	3	.00	6	.317	.375	.533
2000	Atl	NL	134	481	138	21	1	24	(12	12)	233	60	89	72	35	3	80	4	0	5	0	0	-	20	.287	.337	.484
2001	Atl	NL	128	438	117	16	1	17	(10	7)	186	45	66	58	28	3	82	10	1	5	1	0	1.00	13	.267	.322	.425
2002	Atl	NL	109	347	81	15	0	11	(1	10)	129	31	52	40	26	8	63	8	0	4	0	1	.00	15	.233	.299	.372
2003	Atl	NL	129	457	150	29	3	43	(26	17)	314	89	109	102	33	5	90	4	0	1	0	1	.00	10	.328	.378	.687
2004	Bal	AL	150	579	183	33	3	23	(14	9)	291	83	86	90	47	4	97	6	0	6	0	1	.00	16	.316	.370	.503
2005	Bal	AL	103	395	110	24	1	15	(12	3)	181	47	49	56	19	2	68	7	0	2	0	1	.00	10	.278	.322	.458
2006	2 Tms	AL	94	342	86	20	1	8	(5	3)	132	36	35	34	20	0	76	2	0	0	0	0	-	10	.251	.297	.386
06	Bal	AL	76	279	74	15	1	8	(5	3)	115	30	31	34	18	0	60	2	0	0	0	0	-	5	.265	.314	.412
06	Bos	AL	18	63	12	5	0	0	(0	0)	17	6	4	0	2	0	16	0	0	0	0	0	-	5	.190	.215	.270
	15 ML YEARS		1503	5319	1527	267	19	260	(132	128)	2612	674	864	807	357	43	969	66	6	45	8	19	.30	172	.287	.337	.491

Jose Lopez

Bats: R Throws: R Pos: 2B-150; PH-1; PR-1

Ht: 6'0" **Wt:** 200 **Born:** 11/24/1983 **Age:** 23

					BATTING																BASERUNNING				AVERAGES		
Year	Team	Lg	G	AB	H	2B	3B	HR	(Hm	Rd)	TB	R	RBI	RC	TBB	IBB	SO	HBP	SH	SF	SB	CS	SB%	GDP	Avg	OBP	Slg
2004	Sea	AL	57	207	48	13	0	5	(4	1)	76	28	22	20	8	0	31	1	1	1	0	1	.00	1	.232	.263	.367
2005	Sea	AL	54	190	47	19	0	2	(1	1)	72	18	25	24	6	0	25	4	1	2	4	2	.67	5	.247	.282	.379
2006	Sea	AL	151	603	170	28	8	10	(4	6)	244	78	79	84	26	1	80	9	12	5	5	2	.71	17	.282	.319	.405
	3 ML YEARS		262	1000	265	60	8	17	(9	8)	392	124	126	128	40	1	136	14	14	8	9	5	.64	23	.265	.300	.392

Rodrigo Lopez

Pitches: R Bats: R Pos: SP-29; RP-7

Ht: 6'1" **Wt:** 185 **Born:** 12/14/1975 **Age:** 31

			HOW MUCH HE PITCHED						WHAT HE GAVE UP											THE RESULTS							
Year	Team	Lg	G	GS	CG	GF	IP	BFP	H	R	ER	HR	SH	SF	HB	TBB	IBB	SO	WP	Bk	W	L	Pct	ShO	Sv-Op	Hld	ERC	ERA
2000	SD	NL	6	6	0	0	24.2	120	40	24	24	5	0	1	0	13	0	17	0	0	0	3	.000	0	0-0	0	9.78	8.76
2002	Bal	AL	33	28	1	0	196.2	809	172	83	78	23	2	4	5	62	4	136	2	1	15	9	.625	0	0-0	0	3.27	3.57
2003	Bal	AL	26	26	3	0	147.0	663	188	101	95	24	3	7	10	43	6	103	2	1	7	10	.412	1	0-0	0	6.00	5.82
2004	Bal	AL	37	23	1	3	170.2	714	164	71	68	21	5	2	2	54	2	121	4	1	14	9	.609	1	0-1	4	3.74	3.59
2005	Bal	AL	35	35	0	0	209.1	918	232	126	114	28	3	5	7	63	1	118	5	1	15	12	.556	0	0-0	0	4.62	4.90
2006	Bal	AL	36	29	0	2	189.0	847	234	129	124	32	5	5	4	59	2	136	6	1	9	18	.333	0	0-0	0	5.68	5.90
	6 ML YEARS		173	147	5	5	937.1	4071	1030	534	503	133	18	24	28	294	15	631	19	5	60	61	.496	2	0-1	4	4.69	4.83

Mark Loretta

Bats: R Throws: R Pos: 2B-138; 1B-11; PH-7; DH-6

Ht: 6'0" **Wt:** 185 **Born:** 8/14/1971 **Age:** 35

					BATTING																BASERUNNING				AVERAGES		
Year	Team	Lg	G	AB	H	2B	3B	HR	(Hm	Rd)	TB	R	RBI	RC	TBB	IBB	SO	HBP	SH	SF	SB	CS	SB%	GDP	Avg	OBP	Slg
1995	Mil	AL	19	50	13	3	0	1	(0	1)	19	13	3	6	4	0	7	1	1	0	1	1	.50	1	.260	.327	.380
1996	Mil	AL	73	154	43	3	0	1	(0	1)	49	20	13	16	14	0	15	0	2	0	2	1	.67	7	.279	.339	.318
1997	Mil	AL	132	418	120	17	5	5	(2	3)	162	56	47	56	47	2	60	2	5	10	5	5	.50	15	.287	.354	.388
1998	Mil	NL	140	434	137	29	4	6	(3	3)	184	55	54	68	42	1	47	7	4	4	9	6	.60	14	.316	.382	.424
1999	Mil	NL	153	587	170	34	5	5	(2	3)	229	93	67	82	52	1	59	10	9	6	4	1	.80	14	.290	.354	.390
2000	Mil	NL	91	352	99	21	1	7	(3	4)	143	49	40	48	37	2	38	1	8	1	0	3	.00	9	.281	.350	.406
2001	Mil	NL	102	384	111	14	2	2	(0	2)	135	40	29	48	28	0	46	7	7	3	1	2	.33	6	.289	.346	.352
2002	2 Tms	NL	107	283	86	18	0	4	(2	2)	116	33	27	50	32	1	37	5	6	3	1	1	.50	7	.304	.381	.410
2003	SD	NL	154	589	185	28	4	13	(10	3)	260	74	72	93	54	2	62	3	3	4	5	4	.56	17	.314	.372	.441
2004	SD	NL	154	620	208	47	2	16	(11	5)	307	108	76	112	58	3	45	9	4	16	5	3	.63	10	.335	.391	.495
2005	SD	NL	105	404	113	16	1	3	(1	2)	140	54	38	53	45	4	34	8	2	4	8	4	.67	11	.280	.360	.347
2006	Bos	AL	155	635	181	33	0	5	(1	4)	229	75	59	80	49	1	63	12	2	5	4	1	.80	16	.285	.345	.361
02	Mil	NL	86	217	58	14	0	2	(1	1)	78	23	19	33	23	1	32	5	6	1	0	0	-	6	.267	.350	.359
02	Hou	NL	21	66	28	4	0	2	(1	1)	38	10	8	17	9	0	5	0	0	2	1	1	.50	1	.424	.481	.576
	12 ML YEARS		1385	4910	1466	263	20	68	(38	30)	1973	670	525	712	462	17	513	65	53	56	45	32	.58	127	.299	.363	.402

Derek Lowe

Pitches: R **Bats:** R **Pos:** SP-34; RP-1   **Ht:** 6'6" **Wt:** 230 **Born:** 6/1/1973 **Age:** 34

Year	Team	Lg	G	GS	CG	GF	IP	BFP	H	R	ER	HR	SH	SF	HB	TBB	IBB	SO	WP	Bk	W	L	Pct	ShO	Sv-Op	Hld	ERC	ERA
1997	2 Tms	AL	20	9	0	1	69.0	298	74	49	47	11	4	2	4	23	3	52	2	0	2	6	.250	0	0-2	1	4.88	6.13
1998	Bos	AL	63	10	0	8	123.0	527	126	65	55	5	4	5	4	42	5	77	8	0	3	9	.250	0	4-9	12	3.64	4.02
1999	Bos	AL	74	0	0	32	109.1	436	84	35	32	7	1	2	4	25	1	80	1	0	6	3	.667	0	15-20	22	2.14	2.63
2000	Bos	AL	74	0	0	**64**	91.1	379	90	27	26	6	4	1	2	22	5	79	1	1	4	4	.500	0	**42-47**	0	3.17	2.56
2001	Bos	AL	67	3	0	50	91.2	404	103	39	36	7	5	1	5	29	9	82	4	0	5	10	.333	0	24-30	4	4.31	3.53
2002	Bos	AL	32	32	1	0	219.2	854	166	65	63	12	5	2	12	48	0	127	5	0	21	8	.724	1	0-0	0	2.13	2.58
2003	Bos	AL	33	33	1	0	203.1	886	216	113	101	17	3	5	11	72	4	110	3	0	17	7	.708	0	0-0	0	4.32	4.47
2004	Bos	AL	33	33	0	0	182.2	839	224	138	110	15	8	4	8	71	2	105	3	0	14	12	.538	0	0-0	0	5.31	5.42
2005	LAD	NL	35	**35**	2	0	222.0	934	223	113	89	28	12	5	5	55	1	146	3	2	12	15	.444	2	0-0	0	3.75	3.61
2006	LAD	NL	35	34	1	1	218.0	913	221	97	88	14	7	2	5	55	2	123	3	2	**16**	8	.667	0	0-0	0	3.42	3.63
97	Sea	AL	12	9	0	1	53.0	234	59	43	41	11	2	1	2	20	2	39	2	0	2	4	.333	0	0-0	0	5.55	6.96
97	Sea	AL	8	0	0	0	16.0	64	15	6	6	0	2	1	2	3	1	13	0	0	0	2	.000	0	0-2	1	2.78	3.38
	10 ML YEARS		466	189	5	156	1530.0	6470	1527	741	647	122	53	29	60	442	32	981	33	5	100	82	.549	3	85-108	39	3.62	3.81

Mark Lowe

Pitches: R **Bats:** R **Pos:** RP-15   **Ht:** 6'3" **Wt:** 190 **Born:** 6/7/1983 **Age:** 24

Year	Team	Lg	G	GS	CG	GF	IP	BFP	H	R	ER	HR	SH	SF	HB	TBB	IBB	SO	WP	Bk	W	L	Pct	ShO	Sv-Op	Hld	ERC	ERA
2004	Everett	A-	18	3	0	12	38.1	173	42	22	21	4	2	1	4	14	0	38	2	1	1	2	.333	0	7- -	-	4.88	4.93
2005	Wisc	A	22	22	0	0	103.2	468	107	72	63	12	1	2	11	49	0	72	5	0	6	6	.500	0	0- -	-	5.09	5.47
2006	InldEm	A+	13	2	0	5	29.1	118	14	10	6	0	0	0	1	11	0	46	1	1	1	0	1.000	0	2- -	-	1.13	1.84
2006	SnAnt	AA	11	0	0	9	16.2	63	14	4	4	1	0	0	3	0	14	0	0	0	2	.000	0	4- -	-	2.32	2.16
2006	Sea	AL	15	0	0	3	18.2	75	12	4	4	1	1	0	2	9	1	20	1	0	1	0	1.000	0	0-0	6	2.61	1.93

Mike Lowell

Bats: R **Throws:** R **Pos:** 3B-153; PH-2   **Ht:** 6'3" **Wt:** 210 **Born:** 2/24/1974 **Age:** 33

Year	Team	Lg	G	AB	H	2B	3B	HR	(Hm	Rd)	TB	R	RBI	RC	TBB	IBB	SO	HBP	SH	SF	SB	CS	SB%	GDP	Avg	OBP	Slg
1998	NYY	AL	8	15	4	0	0	0	(0	0)	4	1	0	1	0	0	1	0	0	0	0	0	-	0	.267	.267	.267
1999	Fla	NL	97	308	78	15	0	12	(7	5)	129	32	47	40	26	1	69	5	0	5	0	0	-	8	.253	.317	.419
2000	Fla	NL	140	508	137	38	0	22	(11	11)	241	73	91	86	54	4	75	9	0	11	4	0	1.00	4	.270	.344	.474
2001	Fla	NL	146	551	156	37	0	18	(12	6)	247	65	100	84	43	3	79	10	0	10	1	2	.33	9	.283	.340	.448
2002	Fla	NL	160	597	165	44	0	24	(13	11)	281	88	92	84	65	5	92	4	0	11	4	3	.57	16	.276	.346	.471
2003	Fla	NL	130	492	136	27	1	32	(14	18)	261	76	105	88	56	6	78	3	0	6	3	1	.75	14	.276	.350	.530
2004	Fla	NL	158	598	175	44	1	27	(14	13)	302	87	85	96	64	8	77	6	0	3	5	1	.83	17	.293	.365	.505
2005	Fla	NL	150	500	118	36	1	8	(5	3)	180	56	58	46	46	1	58	2	1	9	4	0	1.00	14	.236	.298	.360
2006	Bos	AL	153	573	163	47	1	20	(9	11)	272	79	80	77	47	5	61	4	0	7	2	2	.50	22	.284	.339	.475
	9 ML YEARS		1142	4142	1132	288	4	163	(85	78)	1917	557	658	602	401	33	590	43	1	62	23	9	.72	104	.273	.339	.463

Noah Lowry

Pitches: L **Bats:** R **Pos:** SP-27   **Ht:** 6'2" **Wt:** 200 **Born:** 10/10/1980 **Age:** 26

Year	Team	Lg	G	GS	CG	GF	IP	BFP	H	R	ER	HR	SH	SF	HB	TBB	IBB	SO	WP	Bk	W	L	Pct	ShO	Sv-Op	Hld	ERC	ERA
2006	SnJos*	A+	1	1	0	0	4.2	21	5	0	0	0	0	0	0	1	0	9	0	0	0	0	-	0	0- -	-	2.83	0.00
2006	Fresno*	AAA	1	1	0	0	6.0	25	5	3	3	1	0	0	0	1	0	6	0	0	0	0	-	0	0- -	-	2.53	4.50
2003	SF	NL	4	0	0	3	6.1	24	1	0	0	0	0	0	1	2	0	5	0	0	0	0	-	0	0-0	0	0.50	0.00
2004	SF	NL	16	14	2	0	92.0	383	91	41	39	10	2	1	0	28	1	72	2	0	6	0	1.000	1	0-0	0	3.73	3.82
2005	SF	NL	33	33	0	0	204.2	875	193	92	86	21	13	3	7	76	1	172	2	0	13	13	.500	0	0-0	0	3.78	3.78
2006	SF	NL	27	27	1	0	159.1	689	166	89	84	21	11	7	6	56	2	84	2	1	7	10	.412	1	0-0	0	4.49	4.74
	4 ML YEARS		80	74	3	3	462.1	1971	451	222	209	52	26	11	14	162	4	333	6	1	26	23	.531	2	0-0	0	3.94	4.07

Julio Lugo

Bats: R **Throws:** R **Pos:** SS-81; 2B-29; 3B-16; PH-10; RF-2; LF-1; PR-1   **Ht:** 6'1" **Wt:** 175 **Born:** 11/16/1975 **Age:** 31

Year	Team	Lg	G	AB	H	2B	3B	HR	(Hm	Rd)	TB	R	RBI	RC	TBB	IBB	SO	HBP	SH	SF	SB	CS	SB%	GDP	Avg	OBP	Slg
2000	Hou	NL	116	420	119	22	5	10	(6	4)	181	78	40	62	37	0	93	4	3	1	22	9	.71	9	.283	.346	.431
2001	Hou	NL	140	513	135	20	3	10	(6	4)	191	93	37	63	46	0	116	5	15	7	12	11	.52	7	.263	.326	.372
2002	Hou	NL	88	322	84	15	1	8	(6	2)	125	45	35	43	28	3	74	2	4	2	9	3	.75	6	.261	.322	.388
2003	2 Tms		139	498	135	16	4	15	(5	10)	204	64	55	68	44	1	100	4	7	3	12	4	.75	7	.271	.333	.410
2004	TB	AL	157	581	160	41	4	7	(3	4)	230	83	75	86	54	1	106	5	7	8	21	5	.81	8	.275	.338	.396
2005	TB	AL	158	616	182	36	6	6	(0	6)	248	89	57	94	61	0	72	6	3	4	39	11	.78	5	.295	.362	.403
2006	2 Tms		122	435	121	22	2	12	(7	5)	183	69	37	61	39	0	76	4	5	3	24	9	.73	9	.278	.341	.421
03	Hou	NL	22	65	16	3	0	0	(0	0)	19	6	2	7	9	1	12	0	0	0	2	1	.67	2	.246	.338	.292
03	TB	AL	117	433	119	13	4	15	(5	10)	185	58	53	61	35	0	88	4	7	3	10	3	.77	5	.275	.333	.427
06	TB	AL	73	289	89	17	1	12	(7	5)	144	53	27	52	27	0	47	3	3	0	18	4	.82	7	.308	.373	.498
06	LAD	NL	49	146	32	5	1	0	(0	0)	39	16	10	9	12	0	29	1	2	3	6	5	.55	2	.219	.278	.267
	7 ML YEARS		920	3385	936	172	25	68	(33	35)	1362	521	336	477	309	4	637	30	44	28	139	52	.73	51	.277	.340	.402

Ruddy Lugo

Pitches: R **Bats:** R **Pos:** RP-64   **Ht:** 6'0" **Wt:** 190 **Born:** 5/22/1980 **Age:** 27

			HOW MUCH HE PITCHED						WHAT HE GAVE UP												THE RESULTS							
Year	Team	Lg	G	GS	CG	GF	IP	BFP	H	R	ER	HR	SH	SF	HB	TBB	IBB	SO	WP	Bk	W	L	Pct	ShO	Sv-Op	Hld	ERC	ERA
1999	Ogden	R+	6	6	0	0	24.0	117	35	23	21	2	1	0	1	12	0	26	1	0	1	2	.333	0	0- -	-	7.33	7.88
2000	Ogden	R+	16	16	1	0	91.2	397	82	48	35	7	3	6	12	52	1	88	7	0	5	5	.500	0	0- -	-	4.64	3.44
2001	Beloit	A	10	0	0	8	15.0	60	10	1	1	0	1	0	1	6	0	20	0	0	1	0	1.000	0	5- -	-	2.01	0.60
2001	Wilmg	A	16	0	0	7	31.0	133	29	14	13	2	2	4	2	13	0	23	2	0	0	2	.000	0	2- -	-	3.83	3.77
2002	VeroB	A	22	9	1	6	87.0	347	68	28	23	5	1	3	3	26	0	77	7	0	8	2	.800	1	1- -	-	2.46	2.38
2002	Jaxnvl	AA	11	2	0	2	33.1	144	34	15	15	3	4	0	3	13	5	23	4	0	3	1	.750	0	1- -	-	4.26	4.05
2003	RdRck	AA	41	15	1	10	118.1	539	133	93	79	12	6	6	5	53	5	112	3	0	4	15	.211	0	1- -	-	5.03	6.01
2004	Jupiter	A+	31	0	0	28	39.2	180	42	31	23	4	0	0	4	15	4	33	3	0	1	7	.125	0	11- -	-	4.44	5.22
2004	Carlina	AA	8	1	0	2	14.2	67	16	10	8	3	0	1	1	9	0	6	0	0	0	1	.000	0	0- -	-	6.77	4.91
2005	Visalia	A+	1	0	0	1	2.0	13	7	4	3	0	0	0	0	1	0	0	0	0	0	0	-	0	0- -	-	22.64	13.50
2005	Mont	AA	26	0	0	13	40.1	172	25	12	5	1	0	0	1	23	0	48	8	0	1	1	.500	0	2- -	-	2.22	1.12
2006	Visalia	A+	4	0	0	1	4.0	21	6	4	3	0	0	0	0	2	0	5	0	0	0	0	-	0	1- -	-	6.14	6.75
2006	TB	AL	64	0	0	24	85.0	363	75	39	36	4	1	7	5	37	0	48	3	0	2	4	.333	0	0-0	8	3.44	3.81

Hector Luna

Bats: R **Throws:** R **Pos:** 2B-61; SS-24; LF-17; PH-9; 1B-6; 3B-4; DH-3; PR-3; RF-2   **Ht:** 6'1" **Wt:** 170 **Born:** 2/1/1980 **Age:** 27

						BATTING														BASERUNNING				AVERAGES		
Year	Team	Lg	G	AB	H	2B	3B	HR	(Hm	Rd)	TB	R	RBI	RC	TBB	IBB	SO	HBP	SH	SF	SB	CS	SB%	GDP	Avg	OBP	Slg
2004	StL	NL	83	173	43	7	2	3	(1	2)	63	25	22	20	13	0	37	2	1	3	6	3	.67	2	.249	.304	.364
2005	StL	NL	64	137	39	10	2	1	(0	1)	56	26	18	19	9	0	25	4	2	1	10	2	.83	4	.285	.344	.409
2006	2 Tms		113	350	100	21	2	6	(1	5)	143	41	38	46	27	1	60	1	0	1	5	4	.56	7	.286	.338	.409
06	StL	NL	76	223	65	14	1	4	(1	3)	93	27	21	32	21	1	34	1	0	0	5	3	.63	3	.291	.355	.417
06	Cle	AL	37	127	35	7	1	2	(0	2)	50	14	17	14	6	0	26	0	0	1	0	1	.00	4	.276	.306	.394
	3 ML YEARS		260	660	182	38	6	10	(2	8)	262	92	78	85	49	1	122	7	3	5	21	9	.70	13	.276	.330	.397

Brandon Lyon

Pitches: R **Bats:** R **Pos:** RP-68   **Ht:** 6'1" **Wt:** 195 **Born:** 8/10/1979 **Age:** 27

			HOW MUCH HE PITCHED						WHAT HE GAVE UP												THE RESULTS							
Year	Team	Lg	G	GS	CG	GF	IP	BFP	H	R	ER	HR	SH	SF	HB	TBB	IBB	SO	WP	Bk	W	L	Pct	ShO	Sv-Op	Hld	ERC	ERA
2001	Tor	AL	11	11	0	0	63.0	261	63	31	30	6	2	6	1	15	0	35	0	1	5	4	.556	0	0-0	0	3.50	4.29
2002	Tor	AL	15	10	0	0	62.0	279	78	47	45	14	3	2	2	19	2	30	2	0	1	4	.200	0	0-1	0	6.24	6.53
2003	Bos	AL	49	0	0	31	59.0	273	73	33	27	6	1	4	2	19	5	50	0	0	4	6	.400	0	9-12	2	4.96	4.12
2005	Ari	NL	32	0	0	22	29.1	144	44	25	21	6	2	1	2	10	2	17	1	1	0	2	.000	0	14-15	1	7.72	6.44
2006	Ari	NL	68	0	0	22	69.1	293	68	32	30	7	3	4	0	22	7	46	1	0	2	4	.333	0	0-7	23	3.49	3.89
	5 ML YEARS		175	21	0	75	282.2	1250	326	168	153	39	11	17	7	85	16	178	4	2	12	20	.375	0	23-35	26	4.78	4.87

Chris Mabeus

Pitches: R **Bats:** R **Pos:** RP-1   **Ht:** 6'3" **Wt:** 235 **Born:** 2/11/1979 **Age:** 28

			HOW MUCH HE PITCHED						WHAT HE GAVE UP												THE RESULTS							
Year	Team	Lg	G	GS	CG	GF	IP	BFP	H	R	ER	HR	SH	SF	HB	TBB	IBB	SO	WP	Bk	W	L	Pct	ShO	Sv-Op	Hld	ERC	ERA
2001	Vancvr	A-	20	8	0	6	62.0	273	75	34	31	3	1	4	0	18	0	28	3	1	2	5	.286	0	2- -	-	4.44	4.50
2002	Mdest	A+	37	1	0	7	84.2	371	97	39	38	3	2	2	0	32	4	69	6	1	3	1	.750	0	1- -	-	4.29	4.04
2003	Mdest	A+	18	0	0	15	23.2	99	19	6	4	1	0	1	0	6	0	30	1	0	2	0	1.000	0	2- -	-	2.04	1.52
2003	Mdland	AA	32	0	0	26	38.1	162	37	20	15	1	4	4	0	9	2	40	1	0	1	3	.250	0	13- -	-	2.62	3.52
2004	Mdland	AA	20	0	0	18	22.2	94	23	5	5	0	0	0	0	2	1	27	4	0	4	0	1.000	0	11- -	-	2.21	1.99
2004	Scrmto	AAA	38	0	0	4	51.0	211	45	18	17	6	0	0	1	12	1	61	0	2	7	2	.778	0	4- -	-	2.92	3.00
2005	Scrmto	AAA	42	0	0	18	62.0	274	61	31	29	4	5	5	2	24	5	72	3	0	9	2	.818	0	1- -	-	3.57	4.21
2006	Scrmto	AAA	12	0	0	3	19.2	84	16	11	10	1	0	1	0	10	1	20	2	1	0	1	.000	0	0- -	-	3.03	4.58
2006	Nashv	AAA	6	0	0	5	6.1	32	7	8	4	1	0	1	1	5	0	6	0	0	1	0	1.000	0	0- -	-	7.30	5.68
2006	Hntsvl	AA	18	1	0	6	22.1	103	21	15	15	1	1	0	0	20	2	15	2	0	1	2	.333	0	0- -	-	5.21	6.04
2006	Mil	NL	1	0	0	0	1.2	12	4	4	4	1	0	0	0	3	0	2	3	0	0	0	-	0	0-0	0	26.50	21.60

John Mabry

Bats: L **Throws:** R **Pos:** 1B-51; PH-49; RF-7; LF-5; 3B-2; DH-2   **Ht:** 6'4" **Wt:** 210 **Born:** 10/17/1970 **Age:** 36

						BATTING														BASERUNNING				AVERAGES		
Year	Team	Lg	G	AB	H	2B	3B	HR	(Hm	Rd)	TB	R	RBI	RC	TBB	IBB	SO	HBP	SH	SF	SB	CS	SB%	GDP	Avg	OBP	Slg
1994	StL	NL	6	23	7	3	0	0	(0	0)	10	2	3	4	2	0	4	0	0	0	0	0	-	0	.304	.360	.435
1995	StL	NL	129	388	119	21	1	5	(2	3)	157	35	41	53	24	5	45	2	0	4	0	3	.00	6	.307	.347	.405
1996	StL	NL	151	543	161	30	2	13	(3	10)	234	63	74	74	37	11	84	3	3	5	3	2	.60	21	.297	.342	.431
1997	StL	NL	116	388	110	19	0	5	(5	0)	144	40	36	49	39	9	77	3	2	2	0	1	.00	11	.284	.352	.371
1998	StL	NL	142	377	94	22	0	9	(4	5)	143	41	46	42	30	6	76	1	3	2	0	2	.00	6	.249	.305	.379
1999	Sea	AL	87	262	64	14	0	9	(5	4)	105	34	33	30	20	1	60	0	2	1	2	1	.67	6	.244	.297	.401
2000	2 Tms		95	226	53	13	0	8	(3	5)	90	35	32	25	15	0	69	2	0	1	0	1	.00	4	.235	.287	.398
2001	2 Tms	NL	87	154	32	7	0	6	(2	4)	57	14	20	16	13	1	46	1	0	2	1	0	1.00	6	.208	.287	.370
2002	2 Tms		110	214	59	13	1	11	(8	3)	107	28	43	34	15	2	42	1	0	4	1	1	.50	7	.276	.321	.500
2003	Sea	AL	64	104	22	6	0	3	(1	2)	37	12	16	11	15	2	21	3	0	0	0	0	-	3	.212	.328	.356
2004	StL	NL	87	240	71	11	0	13	(7	6)	121	32	40	37	26	5	63	1	5	3	0	1	.00	6	.296	.363	.504
2005	StL	NL	112	246	59	15	1	8	(2	6)	100	26	25	29	20	1	63	0	6	2	0	0	-	6	.240	.295	.407
2006	ChC	NL	107	210	43	8	1	5	(2	3)	68	16	25	24	23	0	57	1	0	3	0	0	-	5	.205	.283	.324
00	Sea	AL	47	103	25	5	0	1	(0	1)	33	18	7	11	10	0	31	2	0	0	0	1	.00	1	.243	.322	.320
00	SD	NL	48	123	28	8	0	7	(3	4)	57	17	25	14	5	0	38	0	0	1	0	0	-	3	.228	.256	.463
01	StL	NL	5	7	0	0	0	0	(0	0)	0	0	0	0	0	0	2	0	0	0	0	0	-	0	.000	.000	.000
01	Fla	NL	82	147	32	7	0	6	(2	4)	57	14	20	16	13	1	44	1	0	2	1	0	1.00	6	.218	.299	.388

Year	Team	Lg	G	AB	H	2B	3B	HR	(Hm	Rd)	TB	R	RBI	RC	TBB	IBB	SO	HBP	SH	SF	SB	CS	SB%	GDP	Avg	OBP	Slg
02	Phi	NL	21	21	6	0	0	0	(0	0)	6	1	3	3	1	1	5	0	0	1	0	0	-	0	.286	.304	.286
02	Oak	AL	89	193	53	13	1	11	(8	3)	101	27	40	31	14	1	37	1	0	3	1	1	.50	7	.275	.322	.523
13 ML YEARS			1293	3375	894	182	6	95	(44	51)	1373	378	441	424	279	43	707	22	21	29	7	12	.37	87	.265	.323	.407

Mike MacDougal

Pitches: R Bats: B Pos: RP-29   Ht: 6'4" Wt: 185 Born: 3/5/1977 Age: 30

			HOW MUCH HE PITCHED					WHAT HE GAVE UP											THE RESULTS						
Year	Team	Lg	G	GS	CG	GF	IP	BFP	H	R	ER	HR	SH	SF	HB	TBB	IBB	SO	WP	Bk	W	L	Pct	ShO	Sv-Op	Hld	ERC	ERA
2006	Wichta*	AA	1	1	0	0	1.0	3	0	0	0	0	0	0	0	0	0	1	0	0	0	0	-	0	0- -	-	0.00	0.00
2006	Omha*	AAA	8	4	0	3	7.2	31	4	4	4	0	0	1	0	5	0	6	0	0	0	1	1.000	0	1- -	-	1.92	4.70
2001	KC	AL	3	3	0	0	15.1	67	18	10	8	2	0	1	4	0	7	3	0	1	1	.500	0	0-0	0	5.04	4.70
2002	KC	AL	6	0	0	1	9.0	38	5	5	5	0	0	0	0	7	1	10	1	0	0	1	.000	0	0-0	0	2.26	5.00
2003	KC	AL	68	0	0	61	64.0	285	64	36	29	4	3	2	8	32	0	57	6	0	3	5	.375	0	27-35	1	4.76	4.08
2004	KC	AL	13	0	0	8	11.1	61	16	8	7	2	0	0	1	9	0	14	2	0	1	1	.500	0	1-3	0	9.04	5.56
2005	KC	AL	68	0	0	53	70.1	298	69	32	26	6	1	1	3	24	2	72	6	1	5	6	.455	0	21-25	0	3.80	3.33
2006	2 Tms	AL	29	0	0	7	29.0	110	21	5	5	1	1	0	1	6	0	21	1	0	1	1	.500	0	1-2	11	1.80	1.55
06	KC	AL	4	0	0	3	4.0	13	2	0	0	0	0	0	0	0	0	2	0	0	0	0	-	0	1-1	0	0.58	0.00
06	CWS	AL	25	0	0	4	25.0	97	19	5	5	1	1	0	1	6	0	19	1	0	1	1	.500	0	0-1	11	2.10	1.80
6 ML YEARS			187	3	0	130	199.0	859	193	96	80	15	5	3	14	82	3	181	19	1	11	15	.423	0	50-65	12	4.07	3.62

Rob Mackowiak

Bats: L Throws: R Pos: CF-63; LF-28; PH-24; RF-21; 3B-6; DH-2; PR-2   Ht: 6'0" Wt: 200 Born: 6/20/1976 Age: 31

			BATTING																		BASERUNNING				AVERAGES		
Year	Team	Lg	G	AB	H	2B	3B	HR	(Hm	Rd)	TB	R	RBI	RC	TBB	IBB	SO	HBP	SH	SF	SB	CS	SB%	GDP	Avg	OBP	Slg
2001	Pit	NL	62	214	57	15	2	4	(3	1)	88	30	21	28	15	5	52	3	2	3	4	3	.57	3	.266	.319	.411
2002	Pit	NL	136	385	94	22	0	16	(9	7)	164	57	48	57	42	5	120	7	3	2	9	3	.75	0	.244	.328	.426
2003	Pit	NL	77	174	47	4	4	6	(1	5)	77	20	19	27	15	2	53	4	0	0	6	0	1.00	1	.270	.342	.443
2004	Pit	NL	155	491	121	22	6	17	(11	6)	206	65	75	73	50	2	114	6	1	7	13	4	.76	3	.246	.319	.420
2005	Pit	NL	142	463	126	21	3	9	(7	2)	180	57	58	59	43	4	100	3	2	1	8	4	.67	7	.272	.337	.389
2006	CWS	AL	112	255	74	12	1	5	(2	3)	103	31	23	35	28	3	59	3	2	2	5	2	.71	1	.290	.365	.404
6 ML YEARS			705	1982	519	96	16	57	(33	24)	818	260	244	279	193	21	498	26	10	15	45	16	.74	15	.262	.333	.413

Greg Maddux

Pitches: R Bats: R Pos: SP-34   Ht: 6'0" Wt: 180 Born: 4/14/1966 Age: 41

			HOW MUCH HE PITCHED					WHAT HE GAVE UP											THE RESULTS						
Year	Team	Lg	G	GS	CG	GF	IP	BFP	H	R	ER	HR	SH	SF	HB	TBB	IBB	SO	WP	Bk	W	L	Pct	ShO	Sv-Op	Hld	ERC	ERA
1986	ChC	NL	6	5	1	1	31.0	144	44	20	19	3	1	0	1	11	2	20	2	0	2	4	.333	0	0-0	0	6.45	5.52
1987	ChC	NL	30	27	1	2	155.2	701	181	111	97	17	7	1	4	74	13	101	4	7	6	14	.300	1	0-0	0	5.42	5.61
1988	ChC	NL	34	34	9	0	249.0	1047	230	97	88	13	11	2	9	81	16	140	3	6	18	8	.692	3	0-0	0	3.09	3.18
1989	ChC	NL	35	35	7	0	238.1	1002	222	90	78	13	18	6	6	82	13	135	5	3	19	12	.613	1	0-0	0	3.20	2.95
1990	ChC	NL	35	35	8	0	237.0	1011	242	116	91	11	18	5	4	71	10	144	3	3	15	15	.500	2	0-0	0	3.41	3.46
1991	ChC	NL	37	37	7	0	263.0	1070	232	113	98	18	16	3	6	66	9	198	6	3	15	11	.577	2	0-0	0	2.73	3.35
1992	ChC	NL	35	35	9	0	268.0	1061	201	68	65	7	15	3	14	70	7	199	5	0	20	11	.645	4	0-0	0	2.01	2.18
1993	Atl	NL	36	36	8	0	267.0	1064	228	85	70	14	15	7	6	52	7	197	5	1	20	10	.667	1	0-0	0	2.32	2.36
1994	Atl	NL	25	25	10	0	202.0	774	150	44	35	4	6	5	6	31	3	156	3	1	16	6	.727	3	0-0	0	1.59	1.56
1995	Atl	NL	28	28	10	0	209.2	785	147	39	38	8	9	1	4	23	3	181	1	0	19	2	.905	3	0-0	0	1.41	1.63
1996	Atl	NL	35	35	5	0	245.0	978	225	85	74	11	8	5	3	28	11	172	4	0	15	11	.577	0	0-0	0	2.22	2.72
1997	Atl	NL	33	33	5	0	232.2	893	200	58	57	9	11	7	6	20	6	177	0	0	19	4	.826	2	0-0	0	1.95	2.20
1998	Atl	NL	34	34	9	0	251.0	987	201	75	62	13	15	5	7	45	10	204	4	0	18	9	.667	5	0-0	0	2.01	2.22
1999	Atl	NL	33	33	4	0	219.1	940	258	103	87	16	15	5	4	37	8	136	1	0	19	9	.679	0	0-0	0	3.95	3.57
2000	Atl	NL	35	35	6	0	249.1	1012	225	91	83	19	8	5	10	42	12	190	1	2	19	9	.679	3	0-0	0	2.60	3.00
2001	Atl	NL	34	34	3	0	233.0	927	220	86	79	20	12	11	7	27	10	173	2	0	17	11	.607	3	0-0	0	2.70	3.05
2002	Atl	NL	34	34	0	0	199.1	820	194	67	58	14	13	4	4	45	7	118	1	0	16	6	.727	0	0-0	0	3.11	2.62
2003	Atl	NL	36	36	1	0	218.1	901	225	112	96	24	10	9	8	33	7	124	3	0	16	11	.593	0	0-0	0	3.44	3.96
2004	ChC	NL	33	33	2	0	212.2	872	218	103	95	35	12	8	9	33	4	151	2	0	16	11	.593	1	0-0	0	3.86	4.02
2005	ChC	NL	35	35	3	0	225.0	936	239	112	106	29	19	6	7	36	4	136	8	0	13	15	.464	0	0-0	0	3.77	4.24
2006	2 Tms	NL	34	34	0	0	210.0	862	219	109	98	20	11	5	0	37	7	117	0	0	15	14	.517	0	0-0	0	3.39	4.20
06	ChC	NL	22	22	0	0	136.1	572	153	78	71	14	7	3	0	23	3	81	0	0	9	11	.450	0	0-0	0	3.83	4.69
06	LAD	NL	12	12	0	0	73.2	290	66	31	27	6	4	2	0	14	4	36	0	0	6	3	.667	0	0-0	0	2.61	3.30
21 ML YEARS			677	673	108	3	4616.1	18787	4301	1784	1574	318	250	103	125	944	169	3169	63	26	333	203	.621	35	0-0	0	2.83	3.07

Ryan Madson

Pitches: R Bats: L Pos: RP-33; SP-17   Ht: 6'6" Wt: 195 Born: 8/28/1980 Age: 26

			HOW MUCH HE PITCHED					WHAT HE GAVE UP											THE RESULTS						
Year	Team	Lg	G	GS	CG	GF	IP	BFP	H	R	ER	HR	SH	SF	HB	TBB	IBB	SO	WP	Bk	W	L	Pct	ShO	Sv-Op	Hld	ERC	ERA
2003	Phi	NL	1	0	0	0	2.0	6	0	0	0	0	0	0	0	0	0	0	0	0	0	0	-	0	0-0	0	0.00	0.00
2004	Phi	NL	52	1	0	14	77.0	312	68	23	20	6	1	1	5	19	4	55	7	0	9	3	.750	0	1-2	7	2.95	2.34
2005	Phi	NL	78	0	0	10	87.0	365	84	44	40	11	5	5	6	25	6	79	6	1	6	5	.545	0	0-7	32	3.83	4.14
2006	Phi	NL	50	17	0	8	134.1	620	176	92	85	20	9	3	10	50	4	99	12	0	11	9	.550	0	2-4	6	6.50	5.69
4 ML YEARS			181	18	0	32	300.1	1303	328	159	145	37	15	9	21	94	14	233	25	1	26	17	.605	0	3-13	45	4.67	4.35

Ron Mahay

Pitches: L **Bats:** L **Pos:** RP-62   **Ht:** 6'2" **Wt:** 190 **Born:** 6/28/1971 **Age:** 36

Year	Team	Lg	G	GS	CG	GF	IP	BFP	H	R	ER	HR	SH	SF	HB	TBB	IBB	SO	WP	Bk	W	L	Pct	ShO	Sv-Op	Hld	ERC	ERA
2006	Okla*	AAA	5	0	0	3	6.1	24	5	4	1	0	1	1	0	0	0	11	0	0	0	1	.000	0	2--	-	1.24	1.42
1997	Bos	AL	28	0	0	7	25.0	105	19	7	7	3	1	0	0	11	0	22	3	0	3	0	1.000	0	0-2	6	3.01	2.52
1998	Bos	AL	29	0	0	6	26.0	120	26	16	10	2	0	4	2	15	1	14	3	0	1	1	.500	0	1-2	7	4.76	3.46
1999	Oak	AL	6	1	0	2	19.1	68	8	4	4	2	0	0	0	3	0	15	0	0	2	0	1.000	0	1-1	0	0.88	1.86
2000	2 Tms		23	2	0	7	41.1	199	57	35	33	10	1	2	0	25	1	32	4	0	1	1	.500	0	0-0	2	8.55	7.19
2001	ChC	NL	17	0	0	4	20.2	86	14	6	6	4	0	0	0	15	1	24	1	0	0	0	-	0	0-0	2	4.32	2.61
2002	ChC	NL	11	0	0	1	14.2	65	13	14	14	6	0	0	0	8	0	14	0	0	2	0	1.000	0	0-0	0	6.11	8.59
2003	Tex	AL	35	0	0	5	45.1	189	33	19	16	3	0	0	0	20	7	38	4	0	3	3	.500	0	0-3	9	2.31	3.18
2004	Tex	AL	60	0	0	12	67.0	290	60	23	19	5	4	0	2	29	5	54	2	0	3	0	1.000	0	0-2	14	3.39	2.55
2005	Tex	AL	30	0	0	9	35.2	167	47	28	27	8	0	1	0	16	1	30	2	0	0	2	.000	0	1-1	6	7.10	6.81
2006	Tex	AL	62	0	0	14	57.0	246	54	30	25	7	1	1	0	28	2	56	1	0	1	3	.250	0	0-1	9	4.28	3.95
00	Oak	AL	5	2	0	1	16.0	82	26	18	16	4	1	1	0	9	0	5	2	0	0	1	.000	0	0-0	0	9.97	9.00
00	Fla	NL	18	0	0	6	25.1	117	31	17	17	6	0	1	0	16	1	27	2	0	1	0	1.000	0	0-0	2	7.67	6.04
	10 ML YEARS		301	3	0	67	352.0	1535	331	182	161	50	7	8	4	170	18	299	20	0	16	10	.615	0	3-12	55	4.31	4.12

Paul Maholm

Pitches: L **Bats:** L **Pos:** SP-30   **Ht:** 6'2" **Wt:** 230 **Born:** 6/25/1982 **Age:** 25

Year	Team	Lg	G	GS	CG	GF	IP	BFP	H	R	ER	HR	SH	SF	HB	TBB	IBB	SO	WP	Bk	W	L	Pct	ShO	Sv-Op	Hld	ERC	ERA
2003	Wmspt	A-	8	8	0	0	34.1	138	25	11	7	1	1	1	0	10	0	32	1	0	2	1	.667	0	0--	-	1.83	1.83
2004	Lynbrg	A+	8	8	0	0	44.0	186	39	11	9	2	2	2	1	15	0	28	3	0	1	3	.250	0	0--	-	2.91	1.84
2004	Pirates	R	1	0	0	1	4.0	18	5	1	1	0	0	0	0	1	0	2	0	0	0	0	-	0	0--	-	4.05	2.25
2004	Hickory	A	3	3	0	0	12.1	64	17	14	13	2	1	0	3	10	0	12	4	1	0	2	.000	0	0--	-	10.10	9.49
2005	Altna	AA	16	16	0	0	81.2	344	73	32	29	5	10	2	3	26	3	75	3	0	6	2	.750	0	0--	-	2.98	3.20
2005	Indy	AAA	6	6	0	0	35.2	159	40	19	14	2	0	0	1	12	0	21	1	0	1	1	.500	0	0--	-	4.22	3.53
2005	Pit	NL	6	6	0	0	41.1	168	31	10	10	2	0	0	3	17	0	26	0	0	3	1	.750	0	0-0	0	2.79	2.18
2006	Pit	NL	30	30	0	0	176.0	788	202	98	93	19	7	4	12	81	6	117	3	1	8	10	.444	0	0-0	0	5.58	4.76
	2 ML YEARS		36	36	0	0	217.1	956	233	108	103	21	7	4	15	98	6	143	3	1	11	11	.500	0	0-0	0	5.01	4.27

Mitch Maier

Bats: L **Throws:** R **Pos:** LF-2; RF-2; DH-1; PR-1   **Ht:** 6'2" **Wt:** 210 **Born:** 6/30/1982 **Age:** 25

Year	Team	Lg	G	AB	H	2B	3B	HR	(Hm	Rd)	TB	R	RBI	RC	TBB	IBB	SO	HBP	SH	SF	SB	CS	SB%	GDP	Avg	OBP	Slg
2003	Royals	R	51	203	71	14	6	2	(-	-)	103	41	45	41	18	0	25	2	0	3	7	3	.70	4	.350	.403	.507
2004	Burlgtn	A	82	317	95	24	3	4	(-	-)	137	41	36	52	27	4	51	0	0	1	34	10	.77	3	.300	.354	.432
2004	Wilmg	A+	51	174	46	9	2	3	(-	-)	68	25	17	24	15	0	29	2	1	2	9	2	.82	3	.264	.326	.391
2005	Hi Dsrt	A+	50	211	71	26	1	8	(-	-)	123	42	32	44	12	1	43	1	0	3	6	1	.86	5	.336	.370	.583
2005	Wichta	AA	80	322	82	21	5	7	(-	-)	134	55	49	40	15	1	47	2	0	3	10	3	.77	4	.255	.289	.416
2006	Wichta	AA	138	543	166	35	7	14	(-	-)	257	95	92	92	41	1	96	7	3	9	13	12	.52	8	.306	.357	.473
2006	KC	AL	5	13	2	0	0	0	(0	0)	2	3	0	0	2	0	4	0	0	0	0	0	-	1	.154	.267	.154

John Maine

Pitches: R **Bats:** R **Pos:** SP-15; RP-1   **Ht:** 6'4" **Wt:** 205 **Born:** 5/8/1981 **Age:** 26

Year	Team	Lg	G	GS	CG	GF	IP	BFP	H	R	ER	HR	SH	SF	HB	TBB	IBB	SO	WP	Bk	W	L	Pct	ShO	Sv-Op	Hld	ERC	ERA
2006	StLuci*	A+	1	1	0	0	5.0	20	3	0	0	0	0	0	0	2	0	7	0	0	1	0	1.000	0	0--	-	1.51	0.00
2006	Norfolk*	AAA	10	10	0	0	56.2	241	55	25	22	2	1	2	0	20	0	48	2	0	3	5	.375	0	0--	-	3.27	3.49
2004	Bal	AL	1	1	0	0	3.2	19	7	4	4	1	0	0	0	3	0	1	1	0	0	1	.000	0	0-0	0	14.87	9.82
2005	Bal	AL	10	8	0	1	40.0	184	39	30	28	8	0	2	1	24	0	24	0	1	2	3	.400	0	0-0	0	5.47	6.30
2006	NYM	NL	16	15	1	1	90.0	365	69	40	36	15	3	1	2	33	1	71	3	0	6	5	.545	1	0-0	0	3.22	3.60
	3 ML YEARS		27	24	1	2	133.2	568	115	74	68	24	3	3	3	60	1	96	4	1	8	9	.471	1	0-0	0	4.12	4.58

Gary Majewski

Pitches: R **Bats:** R **Pos:** RP-65   **Ht:** 6'1" **Wt:** 215 **Born:** 2/26/1980 **Age:** 27

Year	Team	Lg	G	GS	CG	GF	IP	BFP	H	R	ER	HR	SH	SF	HB	TBB	IBB	SO	WP	Bk	W	L	Pct	ShO	Sv-Op	Hld	ERC	ERA
2006	Lsvlle*	AAA	4	1	0	0	3.2	16	4	2	0	0	0	0	0	1	0	3	0	0	0	0	-	0	0--	-	3.30	0.00
2004	Mon	NL	16	0	0	7	21.0	95	28	15	9	2	1	1	2	5	1	12	0	0	1	1	.000	0	1-2	0	5.68	3.86
2005	Was	NL	79	0	0	24	86.0	376	80	32	28	2	5	4	7	37	6	50	1	0	4	4	.500	0	1-5	24	3.43	2.93
2006	2 Tms	NL	65	0	0	21	70.1	316	79	38	36	5	1	3	4	29	3	43	6	0	4	4	.500	0	0-7	8	4.76	4.61
06	Was	NL	46	0	0	14	55.1	237	49	24	22	4	1	0	1	25	1	34	6	0	3	2	.600	0	0-5	6	3.48	3.58
06	Cin	NL	19	0	0	7	15.0	79	30	14	14	1	0	3	3	4	2	9	0	0	1	2	.333	0	0-2	2	10.33	8.40
	3 ML YEARS		160	0	0	52	177.1	787	187	85	73	9	7	8	13	71	10	105	7	0	8	9	.471	0	2-14	32	4.20	3.70

Carlos Maldonado

Bats: R **Throws:** R **Pos:** C-8   **Ht:** 6'1" **Wt:** 245 **Born:** 1/3/1979 **Age:** 28

Year	Team	Lg	G	AB	H	2B	3B	HR	(Hm	Rd)	TB	R	RBI	RC	TBB	IBB	SO	HBP	SH	SF	SB	CS	SB%	GDP	Avg	OBP	Slg
1996	Peoria	R	29	100	22	0	0	2	(-	-)	28	10	18	7	6	0	10	1	1	4	0	1	.00	7	.220	.261	.280
1997	Wisc	A	97	316	60	8	2	0	(-	-)	72	15	25	15	17	1	33	3	8	3	2	3	.40	8	.190	.236	.228
1998	Wisc	A	7	23	4	0	0	0	(-	-)	4	4	1	0	2	0	1	0	0	0	0	0	-	1	.174	.240	.174
1998	Everett	A-	42	150	43	10	0	5	(-	-)	68	19	24	23	10	0	17	2	0	2	1	0	1.00	5	.287	.335	.453

Year	Team	Lg	G	AB	H	2B	3B	HR	(Hm	Rd)	TB	R	RBI	RC	TBB	IBB	SO	HBP	SH	SF	SB	CS	SB%	GDP	Avg	OBP	Slg
1998	Tacom	AAA	3	9	0	0	0	0	(-	-)	0	0	0	0	0	0	1	0	0	0	0	0	-	0	.000	.000	.000
1999	Wisc	A	92	302	93	13	0	0	(-	-)	106	35	33	45	43	1	32	0	2	2	4	6	.40	10	.308	.392	.351
2000	RdRck	AA	116	423	114	24	2	5	(-	-)	157	46	52	54	35	3	71	5	5	6	5	4	.56	15	.270	.328	.371
2001	RdRck	AA	76	262	75	14	0	4	(-	-)	101	29	33	38	27	0	55	3	0	3	1	2	.33	11	.286	.356	.385
2002	NewOrl	AAA	12	29	5	0	0	0	(-	-)	5	1	2	0	1	0	7	0	0	0	0	0	-	0	.172	.200	.172
2002	RdRck	AA	47	123	31	8	0	4	(-	-)	51	13	20	20	22	0	23	0	0	4	0	0	-	3	.252	.356	.415
2003	Brham	AA	120	408	107	24	1	6	(-	-)	151	50	63	55	43	1	50	6	3	9	1	1	.50	13	.262	.335	.370
2004	Brham	AA	108	388	103	30	1	12	(-	-)	171	48	68	63	52	1	81	3	1	4	0	3	.00	10	.265	.353	.441
2005	Altna	AA	82	278	70	14	0	7	(-	-)	105	27	34	38	35	0	63	2	5	1	0	1	.00	10	.252	.339	.378
2006	Altna	AA	5	18	5	2	0	0	(-	-)	7	1	0	1	0	0	6	0	0	0	0	0	-	0	.278	.278	.389
2006	Indy	AAA	103	336	95	18	0	6	(-	-)	131	37	47	50	36	3	67	3	5	4	2	0	1.00	11	.283	.354	.390
2006	Pit	NL	8	19	2	0	0	0	(0	0)	2	0	0	0	1	1	10	0	0	0	1	0	1.00	0	.105	.150	.105

Julio Manon

Pitches: R Bats: R Pos: RP-22   Ht: 6'0" Wt: 200 Born: 6/10/1973 Age: 34

Year	Team	Lg	G	GS	CG	GF	IP	BFP	H	R	ER	HR	SH	SF	HB	TBB	IBB	SO	WP	Bk	W	L	Pct	ShO	Sv-Op	Hld	ERC	ERA
1993	Cards	R	15	4	0	1	33.1	151	44	21	19	2	0	3	0	12	0	22	5	4	2	3	.400	0	0--	-	5.52	5.13
1994	JhsCty	R+	5	0	0	2	8.2	43	11	8	8	2	0	0	0	5	0	7	0	0	1	2	.333	0	0--	-	7.16	8.31
1994	Cards	R	14	0	0	4	16.0	69	20	9	9	0	0	0	0	1	0	18	1	2	0	1	.000	0	1--	-	3.36	5.06
1995	Hntgtn	R+	16	8	2	3	74.0	319	75	34	30	4	0	3	2	30	2	77	10	0	3	4	.429	0	1--	-	3.94	3.65
1997	CtnSC	A	27	9	0	4	88.2	392	95	53	44	8	5	3	3	22	1	98	7	0	3	5	.375	0	0--	-	3.76	4.47
1998	StPete	A+	38	0	0	14	55.2	219	41	25	23	7	0	0	2	19	1	73	4	1	5	5	.500	0	1--	-	2.83	3.72
1998	Orlndo	AA	13	0	0	5	20.2	96	22	19	14	3	0	1	0	9	0	22	3	0	0	2	.000	0	0--	-	4.63	6.10
1999	Orlndo	AA	30	5	0	8	67.0	303	80	43	38	9	0	1	2	23	0	53	3	0	3	3	.500	0	0--	-	5.27	5.10
2000	Expos	R	4	0	0	1	10.1	36	4	1	1	0	2	0	1	2	0	10	0	0	2	0	1.000	0	0--	-	0.78	0.87
2000	Hrsbrg	AA	14	4	0	4	31.1	136	32	19	18	7	1	2	2	8	0	25	1	0	2	1	.667	0	1--	-	4.62	5.17
2001	Hrsbrg	AA	10	7	0	3	52.0	207	50	20	18	6	1	1	0	16	0	44	1	0	4	3	.571	0	1--	-	3.83	3.12
2001	Ottawa	AAA	15	14	0	1	84.0	339	71	31	29	11	2	0	0	34	0	67	2	0	1	4	.200	0	0--	-	3.60	3.11
2002	Ottawa	AAA	28	13	2	9	105.1	436	83	42	41	8	5	2	2	45	0	81	3	0	8	6	.571	1	2--	-	2.97	3.50
2002	Hrsbrg	AA	6	6	0	0	39.0	158	37	13	13	3	1	1	1	4	0	51	1	0	5	1	.833	0	0--	-	2.60	3.00
2003	Edmtn	AAA	35	0	0	32	42.0	180	33	12	10	4	0	0	0	19	1	48	2	0	3	1	.750	0	14--	-	2.95	2.14
2006	Ottawa	AAA	47	0	0	45	50.2	201	35	13	12	4	1	3	0	20	4	61	0	0	0	2	.000	0	30--	-	2.25	2.13
2003	Mon	NL	23	0	0	7	28.1	125	26	13	13	3	2	2	1	17	1	15	0	0	1	2	.333	0	1-1	6	4.57	4.13
2006	Bal	AL	22	0	0	8	20.0	103	23	13	12	5	1	0	2	16	1	22	1	0	0	0	-	0	0-1	2	7.94	5.40
	2 ML YEARS		45	0	0	15	48.1	228	49	26	25	8	3	2	3	33	2	37	1	0	1	3	.250	0	1-2	8	5.92	4.66

Shaun Marcum

Pitches: R Bats: R Pos: SP-14; RP-7   Ht: 6'0" Wt: 190 Born: 12/14/1981 Age: 25

Year	Team	Lg	G	GS	CG	GF	IP	BFP	H	R	ER	HR	SH	SF	HB	TBB	IBB	SO	WP	Bk	W	L	Pct	ShO	Sv-Op	Hld	ERC	ERA
2003	Auburn	A-	21	0	0	13	34.0	125	15	6	5	1	1	1	1	7	0	47	2	0	1	0	1.000	0	8--	-	0.86	1.32
2004	CtnWV	A	13	13	1	0	79.0	317	64	32	28	7	6	3	0	16	0	83	1	0	7	4	.636	1	0--	-	2.24	3.19
2004	Dnedin	A+	12	12	0	0	69.1	286	74	30	24	6	6	3	3	4	0	72	0	0	3	2	.600	0	0--	-	3.16	3.12
2005	NHam	AA	9	9	1	0	53.1	214	44	15	15	5	2	2	2	10	0	40	1	0	7	1	.875	1	0--	-	2.45	2.53
2005	Syrcse	AAA	18	18	0	0	103.2	441	112	59	57	17	1	2	4	18	2	90	2	0	6	4	.600	0	0--	-	4.13	4.95
2006	Syrcse	AAA	18	5	0	4	52.2	211	48	20	20	6	1	1	1	9	0	60	1	0	4	0	1.000	0	0--	-	2.91	3.42
2005	Tor	AL	5	0	0	3	8.0	32	6	0	0	0	0	0	0	4	0	4	0	0	0	0	-	0	0-0	-	2.58	0.00
2006	Tor	AL	21	14	0	3	78.1	357	87	44	44	14	1	2	4	38	3	65	1	0	3	4	.429	0	0-0	-	5.80	5.06
	2 ML YEARS		26	14	0	6	86.1	389	93	44	44	14	1	2	4	42	3	69	1	0	3	4	.429	0	0-0	-	5.48	4.59

Nick Markakis

Bats: L Throws: L Pos: RF-127; LF-26; CF-9; PR-4; PH-3; DH-1   Ht: 6'2" Wt: 195 Born: 11/17/1983 Age: 23

Year	Team	Lg	G	AB	H	2B	3B	HR	(Hm	Rd)	TB	R	RBI	RC	TBB	IBB	SO	HBP	SH	SF	SB	CS	SB%	GDP	Avg	OBP	Slg
2003	Abrdn	A-	59	205	58	14	3	1	(-	-)	81	22	28	33	30	1	33	1	1	3	5	5	.72	6	.283	.372	.395
2004	Dlmrva	A	96	355	106	22	3	11	(-	-)	167	57	64	65	42	1	66	2	2	5	12	3	.80	6	.299	.371	.470
2005	Frdrck	A+	91	350	105	25	1	12	(-	-)	168	59	62	65	43	4	65	4	0	4	2	1	.67	6	.300	.379	.480
2005	Bowie	AA	33	124	42	16	2	3	(-	-)	71	19	30	28	18	0	30	0	0	1	0	1	.00	5	.339	.420	.573
2006	Bal	AL	147	491	143	25	2	16	(9	7)	220	72	62	67	43	3	72	3	3	2	2	0	1.00	15	.291	.351	.448

Carlos Marmol

Pitches: R Bats: R Pos: SP-13; RP-6   Ht: 6'2" Wt: 180 Born: 10/14/1982 Age: 24

Year	Team	Lg	G	GS	CG	GF	IP	BFP	H	R	ER	HR	SH	SF	HB	TBB	IBB	SO	WP	Bk	W	L	Pct	ShO	Sv-Op	Hld	ERC	ERA
2002	Cubs	R	1	0	0	1	1.0	5	1	0	0	0	0	0	0	1	0	1	0	1	0	0	-	0	0--	-	5.48	0.00
2003	Cubs	R	14	9	0	0	62.1	288	54	38	29	5	2	2	7	37	0	74	6	2	3	5	.375	0	0--	-	4.21	4.19
2004	Lansng	A	26	24	0	1	154.2	635	131	64	55	15	9	6	14	53	0	154	5	2	14	8	.636	0	0--	-	3.44	3.20
2005	Dytona	A+	13	13	0	0	72.1	315	60	30	24	7	1	1	3	37	1	71	5	1	6	2	.750	0	0--	-	3.63	2.99
2005	WTenn	AA	14	14	0	0	81.1	349	70	33	33	10	6	2	8	40	0	70	1	1	3	4	.429	0	0--	-	4.28	3.65
2006	WTenn	AA	11	11	0	0	58.0	234	42	18	15	1	4	1	1	25	0	67	3	1	3	2	.600	0	0--	-	2.32	2.33
2006	Iowa	AAA	2	0	0	0	3.0	13	4	3	3	1	0	0	0	1	0	1	0	0	0	0	-	0	0--	-	5.24	9.00
2006	ChC	NL	19	13	0	1	77.0	356	71	54	52	14	6	2	5	59	2	59	3	1	5	7	.417	0	0-0	0	6.01	6.08

Mike Maroth

Pitches: L **Bats:** L **Pos:** SP-9; RP-4   **Ht:** 6'0" **Wt:** 190 **Born:** 8/17/1977 **Age:** 29

			HOW MUCH HE PITCHED						WHAT HE GAVE UP										THE RESULTS						
Year	Team	Lg	G	GS	CG	GF	IP	BFP	H	R	ER	HR	SH	SF	HB	TBB	IBB	SO	WP	Bk	W	L	Pct	ShO	Sv-Op	Hld	ERC	ERA
2006	Toledo*	AAA	4	4	0	0	20.0	81	18	10	10	4	1	1	1	4	0	11	0	0	3	0	1.000	0	0--	-	3.62	4.50
2002	Det	AL	21	21	0	0	128.2	538	136	68	64	7	5	3	2	36	1	58	4	0	6	10	.375	0	0-0	0	3.73	4.48
2003	Det	AL	33	33	1	0	193.1	847	231	131	123	34	9	8	8	50	2	87	7	0	9	21	.300	0	0-0	0	5.36	5.73
2004	Det	AL	33	33	2	0	217.0	928	244	112	104	25	11	4	7	59	1	108	10	1	11	13	.458	1	0-0	0	4.57	4.31
2005	Det	AL	34	34	0	0	209.0	889	235	123	110	30	3	11	9	51	1	115	5	0	14	14	.500	0	0-0	0	4.71	4.74
2006	Det	AL	13	9	0	2	53.2	234	64	26	25	11	0	0	1	16	1	24	0	0	5	2	.714	0	0-0	0	5.67	4.19
	5 ML YEARS		134	130	3	2	801.2	3436	910	460	426	107	28	26	27	212	6	392	26	1	45	60	.429	1	0-0	0	4.73	4.78

Jason Marquis

Pitches: R **Bats:** L **Pos:** SP-33   **Ht:** 6'1" **Wt:** 210 **Born:** 8/21/1978 **Age:** 28

			HOW MUCH HE PITCHED						WHAT HE GAVE UP										THE RESULTS						
Year	Team	Lg	G	GS	CG	GF	IP	BFP	H	R	ER	HR	SH	SF	HB	TBB	IBB	SO	WP	Bk	W	L	Pct	ShO	Sv-Op	Hld	ERC	ERA
2000	Atl	NL	15	0	0	7	23.1	103	23	16	13	4	1	1	1	12	1	17	1	0	1	0	1.000	0	0-1	1	5.13	5.01
2001	Atl	NL	38	16	0	9	129.1	556	113	62	50	14	6	5	4	59	4	98	1	2	5	6	.455	0	0-2	2	3.70	3.48
2002	Atl	NL	22	22	0	0	114.1	507	127	66	64	19	4	3	3	49	3	84	4	0	8	9	.471	0	0-0	0	5.43	5.04
2003	Atl	NL	21	2	0	10	40.2	182	43	27	25	3	0	3	2	18	2	19	2	0	0	-	-	0	1-1	0	4.45	5.53
2004	StL	NL	32	32	0	0	201.1	874	215	90	83	26	5	6	10	70	1	138	6	0	15	7	.682	0	0-0	0	4.69	3.71
2005	StL	NL	33	32	3	0	207.0	868	206	110	95	29	4	3	5	69	2	100	10	3	13	14	.481	1	0-0	0	4.23	4.13
2006	StL	NL	33	33	0	0	194.1	870	221	136	130	35	12	3	16	75	2	96	2	1	14	16	.467	0	0-0	0	5.79	6.02
	7 ML YEARS		194	137	3	26	910.1	3960	948	507	460	130	32	24	41	352	15	552	26	6	56	52	.519	1	1-4	3	4.76	4.55

Eli Marrero

Bats: R **Throws:** R **Pos:** PH-32; 1B-8; C-7; LF-6; RF-5; CF-2; 3B-1   **Ht:** 6'1" **Wt:** 180 **Born:** 11/17/1973 **Age:** 33

			BATTING																		BASERUNNING				AVERAGES		
Year	Team	Lg	G	AB	H	2B	3B	HR	(Hm	Rd)	TB	R	RBI	RC	TBB	IBB	SO	HBP	SH	SF	SB	CS	SB%	GDP	Avg	OBP	Slg
1997	StL	NL	17	45	11	2	0	2	(0	2)	19	4	7	6	2	1	13	0	0	1	4	0	1.00	1	.244	.271	.422
1998	StL	NL	83	254	62	18	1	4	(2	2)	94	28	20	30	28	5	42	0	1	1	6	2	.75	5	.244	.318	.370
1999	StL	NL	114	317	61	13	1	6	(3	3)	94	32	34	18	18	4	56	1	4	3	11	2	.85	14	.192	.236	.297
2000	StL	NL	53	102	23	3	1	5	(2	3)	43	21	17	14	9	0	16	3	0	2	5	0	1.00	3	.225	.302	.422
2001	StL	NL	86	203	54	11	3	6	(2	4)	89	37	23	27	15	2	36	0	3	3	6	3	.67	4	.266	.312	.438
2002	StL	NL	131	397	104	19	1	18	(9	9)	179	63	66	59	40	11	72	0	5	4	14	2	.88	5	.262	.327	.451
2003	StL	NL	41	107	24	4	2	2	(1	1)	38	10	20	15	7	0	18	0	0	2	1	0	1.00	0	.224	.267	.355
2004	Atl	NL	90	250	80	18	1	10	(6	4)	130	37	40	50	23	1	50	1	2	4	4	1	.80	4	.320	.374	.520
2005	2 Tms	NL	54	138	25	7	2	7	(2	5)	57	19	19	8	11	0	38	1	1	5	1	0	1.00	3	.181	.239	.413
2006	2 Tms	NL	55	93	19	4	0	6	(2	4)	41	11	15	14	15	1	31	2	2	1	5	0	1.00	1	.204	.324	.441
05	KC	AL	32	88	14	4	0	4	(1	3)	30	11	9	2	7	0	18	1	1	3	1	0	1.00	2	.159	.222	.341
05	Bal	AL	22	50	11	3	2	3	(1	2)	27	8	10	6	4	0	20	0	0	2	0	0	-	1	.220	.268	.540
06	Col	NL	30	60	13	3	0	4	(2	2)	28	7	10	10	11	1	16	1	0	0	3	0	1.00	1	.217	.347	.467
06	NYM	NL	25	33	6	1	0	2	(0	2)	13	4	5	4	4	0	15	1	2	1	2	0	1.00	0	.182	.282	.394
	10 ML YEARS		724	1906	463	99	12	66	(29	37)	784	262	261	241	168	25	372	8	18	26	56	11	.84	40	.243	.303	.411

Sean Marshall

Pitches: L **Bats:** L **Pos:** SP-24   **Ht:** 6'7" **Wt:** 205 **Born:** 8/30/1982 **Age:** 24

			HOW MUCH HE PITCHED						WHAT HE GAVE UP										THE RESULTS						
Year	Team	Lg	G	GS	CG	GF	IP	BFP	H	R	ER	HR	SH	SF	HB	TBB	IBB	SO	WP	Bk	W	L	Pct	ShO	Sv-Op	Hld	ERC	ERA
2003	Boise	A-	14	14	0	0	73.2	66	66	31	21	1	3	5	5	23	0	88	8	0	5	6	.455	0	0--	-	15.42	2.57
2003	Lansng	A	1	1	0	0	7.0	26	5	1	0	0	0	0	0	0	0	11	0	0	1	0	1.000	0	0--	-	1.04	0.00
2004	Lansng	A	7	7	1	0	48.2	175	29	7	6	1	2	0	4	4	0	51	4	0	2	0	1.000	1	0--	-	0.97	1.11
2004	WTenn	AA	6	6	0	0	29.0	131	36	20	19	2	2	2	2	12	0	23	3	0	2	2	.500	0	0--	-	5.71	5.90
2005	Dytona	A+	12	12	1	0	69.0	296	63	24	21	7	1	0	1	26	0	61	7	1	4	4	.500	0	0--	-	3.51	2.74
2005	WTenn	AA	4	4	0	0	25.0	96	16	7	7	1	1	0	1	5	0	24	2	1	0	1	.000	0	0--	-	1.46	2.52
2006	Iowa	AAA	4	4	0	0	21.2	92	17	10	8	1	1	0	0	14	0	21	5	0	0	2	.000	0	0--	-	3.54	3.32
2006	ChC	NL	24	24	0	0	125.2	563	132	85	78	20	7	1	7	59	3	77	6	0	6	9	.400	0	0-0	0	5.27	5.59

Andy Marte

Bats: R **Throws:** R **Pos:** 3B-50   **Ht:** 6'1" **Wt:** 190 **Born:** 10/21/1983 **Age:** 23

			BATTING																		BASERUNNING				AVERAGES		
Year	Team	Lg	G	AB	H	2B	3B	HR	(Hm	Rd)	TB	R	RBI	RC	TBB	IBB	SO	HBP	SH	SF	SB	CS	SB%	GDP	Avg	OBP	Slg
2001	Danvle	R+	37	125	25	6	0	1	(-	-)	34	12	12	12	20	0	45	0	1	2	3	0	1.00	3	.200	.306	.272
2002	Macon	A	126	488	137	32	4	21	(-	-)	240	69	105	83	41	3	114	6	0	7	2	1	.67	6	.281	.339	.492
2003	MrtlBh	A+	130	463	132	35	1	16	(-	-)	217	69	63	85	67	8	109	2	0	9	5	2	.71	13	.285	.372	.469
2004	Grnville	AA	107	387	104	28	1	23	(-	-)	203	52	68	75	58	4	105	2	0	3	1	1	.50	8	.269	.364	.525
2004	Braves	R	3	15	7	4	0	1	(-	-)	14	4	6	5	2	0	2	0	0	0	0	0	-	0	.467	.529	.933
2005	Rchmd	AAA	109	389	107	26	2	20	(-	-)	197	51	74	75	64	2	83	0	0	7	0	3	.00	8	.275	.372	.506
2006	Buffalo	AAA	96	357	93	23	0	15	(-	-)	161	49	46	54	34	1	81	0	0	3	1	0	1.00	11	.261	.322	.451
2005	Atl	NL	24	57	8	2	1	0	(0	0)	12	3	4	1	7	0	13	0	0	2	0	1	.00	2	.140	.227	.211
2006	Cle	AL	50	164	37	15	1	5	(3	2)	69	20	23	21	13	0	38	1	0	0	0	0	-	3	.226	.287	.421
	2 ML YEARS		74	221	45	17	2	5	(3	2)	81	23	27	22	20	0	51	1	0	2	0	1	.00	5	.204	.270	.367

Damaso Marte

Pitches: L **Bats:** L **Pos:** RP-75   **Ht:** 6'2" **Wt:** 210 **Born:** 2/14/1975 **Age:** 32

			HOW MUCH HE PITCHED						WHAT HE GAVE UP										THE RESULTS						
Year	Team	Lg	G	GS	CG	GF	IP	BFP	H	R	ER	HR	SH	SF	HB	TBB	IBB	SO	WP	Bk	W	L	Pct	ShO	Sv-Op	Hld	ERC	ERA
1999	Sea	AL	5	0	0	2	8.2	47	16	9	9	3	0	0	6	6	0	3	0	0	0	1	.000	0	0-0	0	13.32	9.35
2001	Pit	NL	23	0	0	4	36.1	154	34	21	19	5	1	2	3	12	3	39	1	0	0	1	.000	0	0-0	0	3.93	4.71
2002	CWS	AL	68	0	0	22	60.1	240	44	19	19	5	1	1	4	18	2	72	3	1	1	1	.500	0	10-12	14	2.42	2.83
2003	CWS	AL	71	0	0	25	79.2	314	50	16	14	3	3	3	3	34	6	87	1	0	4	2	.667	0	11-18	14	1.96	1.58
2004	CWS	AL	74	0	0	24	73.2	303	56	28	28	10	2	6	3	34	4	68	3	0	6	5	.545	0	6-12	21	3.39	3.42
2005	CWS	AL	66	0	0	15	45.1	213	45	21	19	5	1	0	3	33	4	54	1	1	3	4	.429	0	4-8	22	5.51	3.77
2006	Pit	NL	75	0	0	15	58.1	255	51	30	24	5	8	3	4	31	6	63	3	1	1	7	.125	0	0-4	13	3.88	3.70
	7 ML YEARS		382	0	0	107	362.1	1526	296	144	132	36	16	15	20	168	25	386	12	3	15	21	.417	0	31-54	84	3.46	3.28

Russell Martin

Bats: R **Throws:** R **Pos:** C-117; PH-3; DH-1   **Ht:** 5'10" **Wt:** 210 **Born:** 2/15/1983 **Age:** 24

			BATTING																				BASERUNNING				AVERAGES		
Year	Team	Lg	G	AB	H	2B	3B	HR	(Hm	Rd)	TB	R	RBI	RC	TBB	IBB	SO	HBP	SH	SF	SB	CS	SB%	GDP	Avg	OBP	Slg
2002	Ddgrs	R	41	126	36	3	3	0	(-	-)	45	22	10	22	23	0	18	4	2	0	7	1	.88	4	.286	.412	.357
2003	SoGA	A	25	98	28	4	1	3	(-	-)	43	15	14	15	9	0	11	0	1	1	5	2	.71	1	.286	.343	.439
2003	Ogden	R+	52	188	51	13	0	6	(-	-)	82	25	36	32	26	1	26	4	2	2	3	1	.75	6	.271	.368	.436
2004	VeroB	A+	122	416	104	24	1	15	(-	-)	175	74	64	71	71	1	54	10	0	8	9	5	.64	10	.250	.366	.421
2005	Jaxnvl	AA	129	409	127	17	1	9	(-	-)	173	83	61	82	78	0	69	10	5	3	15	7	.68	14	.311	.430	.423
2006	LsVgs	AAA	23	74	22	9	0	0	(-	-)	31	14	9	12	13	0	11	0	1	3	0	2	.00	1	.297	.389	.419
2006	LAD	NL	121	415	117	26	4	10	(8	2)	181	65	65	58	45	8	57	4	1	3	10	5	.67	17	.282	.355	.436

Tom Martin

Pitches: L **Bats:** L **Pos:** RP-68   **Ht:** 6'1" **Wt:** 205 **Born:** 5/21/1970 **Age:** 37

			HOW MUCH HE PITCHED						WHAT HE GAVE UP										THE RESULTS						
Year	Team	Lg	G	GS	CG	GF	IP	BFP	H	R	ER	HR	SH	SF	HB	TBB	IBB	SO	WP	Bk	W	L	Pct	ShO	Sv-Op	Hld	ERC	ERA
1997	Hou	NL	55	0	0	18	56.0	236	52	13	13	2	6	1	1	23	2	36	3	0	5	3	.625	0	2-3	7	3.34	2.09
1998	Cle	AL	14	0	0	1	14.2	85	29	21	21	3	1	1	0	12	0	9	2	0	1	1	.500	0	0-0	3	13.19	12.89
1999	Cle	AL	6	0	0	0	9.1	44	13	9	9	2	0	1	0	3	1	8	0	0	0	1	.000	0	0-0	6	6.64	8.68
2000	Cle	AL	31	0	0	7	33.1	143	32	16	15	3	0	1	1	15	2	21	1	0	1	0	1.000	0	0-0	5	4.05	4.05
2001	NYM	NL	14	0	0	2	17.0	85	23	22	19	4	1	1	1	10	2	12	0	1	1	0	1.000	0	0-0	1	8.02	10.06
2002	TB	AL	2	0	0	2	1.2	11	5	3	3	0	0	0	0	1	0	1	0	0	0	0	-	0	0-0	0	17.54	16.20
2003	LAD	NL	80	0	0	13	51.0	210	36	21	20	6	0	2	2	24	4	51	1	0	1	2	.333	0	0-1	28	2.94	3.53
2004	2 Tms	NL	76	0	0	11	45.1	204	49	20	20	7	5	4	3	19	3	30	1	0	2	0	.000	0	1-4	12	5.14	3.97
2005	Atl	NL	4	0	0	1	2.1	14	6	5	5	1	0	0	0	2	0	0	0	0	0	0	-	0	0-0	0	22.06	19.29
2006	Col	NL	68	0	0	9	60.1	266	62	37	34	4	1	1	4	25	5	46	1	0	2	0	1.000	0	0-11	41	4.16	5.07
	04	LAD	NL	47	0	0	9	28.1	132	32	13	13	3	3	2	3	14	1	18	1	0	0	1	.000	0	1-1	5	5.58	4.13
	04	Atl	NL	29	0	0	2	17.0	72	17	7	7	4	2	2	0	5	2	12	0	0	1	0	.000	0	0-3	7	4.36	3.71
	10 ML YEARS		350	0	0	64	291.0	1298	307	167	159	32	14	12	12	134	19	214	9	0	11	9	.550	0	3-9	62	4.75	4.92

Carlos Martinez

Pitches: R **Bats:** R **Pos:** RP-12   **Ht:** 6'1" **Wt:** 170 **Born:** 2/21/1986 **Age:** 21

			HOW MUCH HE PITCHED						WHAT HE GAVE UP										THE RESULTS						
Year	Team	Lg	G	GS	CG	GF	IP	BFP	H	R	ER	HR	SH	SF	HB	TBB	IBB	SO	WP	Bk	W	L	Pct	ShO	Sv-Op	Hld	ERC	ERA
2002	Mrlns	R	22	0	0	19	32.1	130	26	8	4	1	3	1	0	6	0	23	2	0	1	2	.333	0	7--	-	1.83	1.11
2003	Mrlns	R	3	0	0	3	6.1	20	1	0	0	0	0	0	0	1	0	2	0	0	1	0	1.000	0	1--	-	0.18	0.00
2003	Jmstwn	A-	1	0	0	1	1.2	9	2	1	1	0	0	0	0	1	0	4	1	0	0	1	.000	0	0--	-	4.47	5.40
2003	Grnsbr	A	15	0	0	5	18.1	80	18	7	6	1	1	1	2	4	0	15	0	0	0	3	.000	0	1--	-	3.26	2.95
2004	Grnsbr	A	40	0	0	21	48.1	203	43	21	17	8	0	0	1	12	0	37	2	1	2	3	.400	0	6--	-	3.29	3.17
2005	Jupiter	A+	47	0	0	37	60.2	257	52	25	21	5	3	2	3	22	1	65	1	0	4	5	.444	0	22--	-	3.16	3.12
2005	Albq	AAA	2	0	0	0	2.0	10	4	2	2	1	0	0	0	0	0	0	0	0	0	0	-	0	0--	-	11.88	9.00
2005	Carlna	AA	1	0	0	1	1.0	5	1	1	1	0	0	0	0	1	0	1	0	0	0	0	-	0	1--	-	5.48	9.00
2006	Jupiter	A+	2	1	0	0	2.0	8	0	0	0	0	0	0	0	1	0	0	0	0	0	0	-	0	0--	-	0.24	0.00
2006	Fla	NL	12	0	0	4	10.1	44	9	2	2	0	0	2	0	6	0	11	0	0	0	1	.000	0	0-0	5	3.42	1.74

Pedro Martinez

Pitches: R **Bats:** R **Pos:** SP-23   **Ht:** 5'11" **Wt:** 180 **Born:** 10/25/1971 **Age:** 35

			HOW MUCH HE PITCHED						WHAT HE GAVE UP										THE RESULTS						
Year	Team	Lg	G	GS	CG	GF	IP	BFP	H	R	ER	HR	SH	SF	HB	TBB	IBB	SO	WP	Bk	W	L	Pct	ShO	Sv-Op	Hld	ERC	ERA
1992	LAD	NL	2	1	0	1	8.0	31	6	2	2	0	0	0	0	1	0	8	0	0	0	1	.000	0	0-0	0	1.38	2.25
1993	LAD	NL	65	2	0	20	107.0	444	76	34	31	5	0	5	4	57	4	119	3	1	10	5	.667	0	2-3	14	2.79	2.61
1994	Mon	NL	24	23	1	1	144.2	584	115	58	55	11	2	3	11	45	3	142	6	0	11	5	.688	1	1-1	0	2.81	3.42
1995	Mon	NL	30	30	2	0	194.2	784	158	79	76	21	7	3	11	66	1	174	5	2	14	10	.583	2	0-0	0	3.19	3.51
1996	Mon	NL	33	33	4	0	216.2	901	189	100	89	19	9	6	3	70	3	222	6	0	13	10	.565	1	0-0	0	3.02	3.70
1997	Mon	NL	31	31	13	0	241.1	947	158	65	51	16	9	1	9	67	5	305	3	1	17	8	.680	4	0-0	0	1.79	1.90
1998	Bos	AL	33	33	3	0	233.2	951	188	82	75	26	4	7	8	67	3	251	9	0	19	7	.731	2	0-0	0	2.78	2.89
1999	Bos	AL	31	29	5	1	213.1	835	160	56	49	9	3	6	9	37	1	313	6	0	23	4	.852	1	0-0	0	1.79	2.07
2000	Bos	AL	29	29	7	0	217.0	817	128	44	42	17	2	1	14	32	0	284	1	0	18	6	.750	4	0-0	0	1.39	1.74
2001	Bos	AL	18	18	1	0	116.2	456	84	33	31	5	2	0	6	25	0	163	4	0	7	3	.700	0	0-0	0	1.84	2.39
2002	Bos	AL	30	30	2	0	199.1	787	144	62	50	13	2	4	15	40	1	239	3	0	20	4	.833	1	0-0	0	1.98	2.26
2003	Bos	AL	29	29	3	0	186.2	749	147	52	46	7	4	4	9	47	0	206	5	0	14	4	.778	0	0-0	0	2.22	2.22
2004	Bos	AL	33	33	1	0	217.0	903	193	99	94	26	5	9	16	61	0	227	2	0	16	9	.640	1	0-0	0	3.44	3.90
2005	NYM	NL	31	31	4	0	217.0	843	159	69	68	19	9	2	4	47	3	208	4	0	15	8	.652	1	0-0	0	2.03	2.82
2006	NYM	NL	23	23	0	0	132.2	550	108	72	66	19	6	5	10	39	2	137	2	1	9	8	.529	0	0-0	0	3.18	4.48
	15 ML YEARS		442	375	46	23	2645.2	10582	2013	907	825	213	64	56	129	701	26	2998	59	5	206	92	.691	17	3-4	14	2.38	2.81

Ramon Martinez

Bats: R Throws: R Pos: 2B-39; 3B-20; PH-18; SS-12; PR-5; 1B-1; RF-1   Ht: 6'0" Wt: 190 Born: 10/10/1972 Age: 34

									BATTING											BASERUNNING				AVERAGES		
Year	Team	Lg	G	AB	H	2B	3B	HR	(Hm	Rd)	TB	R	RBI	RC	TBB	IBB	SO	HBP	SH	SF	SB	CS	SB%	GDP	Avg	OBP	Slg
1998	SF	NL	19	19	6	1	0	0	(0	0)	7	4	0	4	4	0	2	0	1	0	0	0	-	0	.316	.435	.368
1999	SF	NL	61	144	38	6	0	5	(3	2)	59	21	19	19	14	0	17	0	6	1	1	2	.33	2	.264	.327	.410
2000	SF	NL	88	189	57	13	2	6	(4	2)	92	30	25	31	15	1	22	1	4	1	3	2	.60	6	.302	.354	.487
2001	SF	NL	128	391	99	18	3	5	(1	4)	138	48	37	44	38	6	52	5	6	6	1	2	.33	11	.253	.323	.353
2002	SF	NL	72	181	49	10	2	4	(4	0)	75	26	25	33	14	2	26	4	0	1	2	0	1.00	1	.271	.335	.414
2003	ChC	NL	108	293	83	16	1	3	(3	0)	110	30	34	34	24	1	50	2	6	8	0	1	.00	8	.283	.333	.375
2004	ChC	NL	102	260	64	15	1	3	(1	2)	90	22	30	28	26	3	40	1	7	4	1	0	1.00	5	.246	.313	.346
2005	2 Tms		52	112	31	3	0	1	(1	0)	37	11	14	14	6	0	11	1	4	4	0	0	-	2	.277	.309	.330
2006	LAD	NL	82	176	49	7	1	2	(1	1)	64	20	24	22	15	1	20	1	2	0	0	0	-	9	.278	.339	.364
05	Det	AL	19	56	15	1	0	0	(0	0)	16	4	5	7	3	0	4	0	2	1	0	0	-	1	.268	.300	.286
05	Phi	NL	33	56	16	2	0	1	(1	0)	21	7	9	7	3	0	7	1	2	3	0	0	-	1	.286	.317	.375
9 ML YEARS			712	1765	476	89	10	29	(18	11)	672	212	208	229	156	14	240	15	36	25	8	7	.53	44	.270	.330	.381

Victor Martinez

Bats: B Throws: R Pos: C-133; 1B-22; PH-4; DH-3   Ht: 6'2" Wt: 195 Born: 12/23/1978 Age: 28

									BATTING											BASERUNNING				AVERAGES		
Year	Team	Lg	G	AB	H	2B	3B	HR	(Hm	Rd)	TB	R	RBI	RC	TBB	IBB	SO	HBP	SH	SF	SB	CS	SB%	GDP	Avg	OBP	Slg
2002	Cle	AL	12	32	9	1	0	1	(1	0)	13	2	5	5	3	0	2	0	0	1	0	0	-	1	.281	.333	.406
2003	Cle	AL	49	159	46	4	0	1	(0	1)	53	15	16	17	13	0	21	1	0	1	1	1	.50	8	.289	.345	.333
2004	Cle	AL	141	520	147	38	1	23	(8	15)	256	77	108	90	60	11	69	5	0	6	0	1	.00	16	.283	.359	.492
2005	Cle	AL	147	547	167	33	0	20	(10	10)	260	73	80	90	63	9	78	5	0	7	0	1	.00	16	.305	.378	.475
2006	Cle	AL	153	572	181	37	0	16	(4	12)	266	82	93	96	71	8	78	3	0	6	0	0	-	27	.316	.391	.465
5 ML YEARS			502	1830	550	113	1	61	(23	38)	848	249	302	298	210	28	248	14	0	21	1	3	.25	68	.301	.373	.463

Nick Masset

Pitches: R Bats: R Pos: RP-8   Ht: 6'4" Wt: 190 Born: 5/17/1982 Age: 25

				HOW MUCH HE PITCHED						WHAT HE GAVE UP								THE RESULTS						
Year	Team	Lg	G	GS	CG	GF	IP	BFP	H	R	ER	HR	SH	SF	HB	TBB	IBB	SO	WP	Bk	W	L	Pct	ShO	Sv-Op	Hld	ERC	ERA
2001	Rngrs	R	15	14	0	0	31.0	131	34	21	15	2	0	1	2	7	0	32	1	0	0	6	.000	0	0--	-	4.00	4.35
2002	Savann	A	33	16	0	4	120.1	539	129	75	61	11	4	9	9	47	1	93	11	1	5	8	.385	0	0--	-	4.62	4.56
2003	Clinton	A	30	20	0	6	123.2	557	144	75	56	7	6	6	9	43	0	63	8	3	7	7	.500	0	2--	-	4.74	4.08
2004	Stcktn	A+	16	11	0	0	77.0	323	71	38	30	6	2	3	6	19	0	43	4	0	6	5	.545	0	0--	-	3.19	3.51
2004	Frisco	AA	2	1	0	0	10.0	37	8	2	2	0	0	1	2	4	0	8	1	0	1	0	1.000	0	0--	-	3.63	1.80
2005	Frisco	AA	29	27	1	1	157.1	706	197	124	108	19	3	4	9	61	1	105	9	2	7	12	.368	0	0--	-	6.04	6.18
2006	Frisco	AA	8	8	0	0	48.0	203	38	16	11	0	3	0	2	20	0	44	1	2	2	2	.500	0	0--	-	2.47	2.06
2006	Okla	AAA	24	7	1	8	67.1	306	79	48	36	4	3	2	3	28	1	65	3	0	4	5	.444	0	3--	-	4.96	4.81
2006	Tex	AL	8	0	0	7	8.2	36	9	4	4	0	0	2	2	2	0	4	0	0	0	0	-	0	0-0	0	4.05	4.15

Tom Mastny

Pitches: R Bats: R Pos: RP-15   Ht: 6'6" Wt: 220 Born: 2/4/1981 Age: 26

				HOW MUCH HE PITCHED						WHAT HE GAVE UP								THE RESULTS						
Year	Team	Lg	G	GS	CG	GF	IP	BFP	H	R	ER	HR	SH	SF	HB	TBB	IBB	SO	WP	Bk	W	L	Pct	ShO	Sv-Op	Hld	ERC	ERA
2003	Auburn	A-	14	14	0	0	63.2	251	56	19	16	1	0	0	3	12	0	68	2	1	8	0	1.000	0	0--	-	2.37	2.26
2004	CtnWV	A	27	27	0	0	149.0	592	123	44	36	4	9	5	3	41	0	141	7	0	10	3	.769	0	0--	-	2.37	2.17
2005	Kinston	A+	29	11	0	0	88.0	361	78	28	23	4	6	1	5	26	0	94	2	0	7	3	.700	0	2--	-	2.97	2.35
2005	Akron	AA	5	3	0	1	20.2	87	18	7	5	0	0	0	2	5	0	18	1	0	1	1	.500	0	0--	-	2.45	2.18
2006	Akron	AA	12	1	0	6	24.2	100	15	5	3	0	1	1	1	8	1	30	1	0	0	1	.000	0	1--	-	1.39	1.09
2006	Buffalo	AAA	24	0	0	7	38.0	158	25	11	11	0	2	0	4	16	2	46	2	0	2	1	.667	0	0--	-	2.00	2.61
2006	Cle	AL	15	0	0	12	16.1	73	17	10	10	1	1	2	1	8	1	14	0	0	0	1	.000	0	5-7	0	4.53	5.51

Henry Mateo

Bats: B Throws: R Pos: PH-16; SS-3; 3B-2; CF-1; PR-1   Ht: 6'0" Wt: 175 Born: 10/14/1976 Age: 30

									BATTING											BASERUNNING				AVERAGES		
Year	Team	Lg	G	AB	H	2B	3B	HR	(Hm	Rd)	TB	R	RBI	RC	TBB	IBB	SO	HBP	SH	SF	SB	CS	SB%	GDP	Avg	OBP	Slg
2006	NewOr*	AAA	113	433	110	21	6	2	(-	-)	149	55	35	53	38	1	78	4	12	3	33	11	.75	10	.254	.318	.344
2001	Mon	NL	5	9	3	1	0	0	(0	0)	4	1	0	1	0	0	1	0	0	0	0	0	-	0	.333	.333	.444
2002	Mon	NL	22	23	4	0	1	0	(0	0)	6	1	0	1	2	1	6	0	0	0	2	0	1.00	0	.174	.240	.261
2003	Mon	NL	100	154	37	3	1	0	(0	0)	42	29	7	16	11	0	38	3	1	0	11	1	.92	0	.240	.304	.273
2004	Mon	NL	40	44	12	2	0	0	(0	0)	14	3	0	1	1	0	9	0	1	0	2	3	.40	1	.273	.289	.318
2005	Was	NL	1	1	0	0	0	0	(0	0)	0	0	0	0	1	0	0	0	0	0	0	0	-	0	.000	.500	.000
2006	Was	NL	22	26	4	2	0	1	(0	1)	9	5	3	2	2	0	3	0	1	0	0	0	-	1	.154	.214	.346
6 ML YEARS			190	257	60	8	2	1	(0	1)	75	39	10	21	17	1	57	3	3	0	15	4	.79	2	.233	.289	.292

Juan Mateo

Pitches: R Bats: R Pos: SP-10; RP-1   Ht: 6'2" Wt: 180 Born: 12/17/1982 Age: 24

				HOW MUCH HE PITCHED						WHAT HE GAVE UP								THE RESULTS						
Year	Team	Lg	G	GS	CG	GF	IP	BFP	H	R	ER	HR	SH	SF	HB	TBB	IBB	SO	WP	Bk	W	L	Pct	ShO	Sv-Op	Hld	ERC	ERA
2003	Cubs	R	18	0	0	11	36.1	167	42	25	18	2	3	2	2	14	0	35	0	0	4	1	.800	0	2--	-	4.67	4.46
2004	Lansng	A	53	1	0	26	74.0	305	61	28	27	3	1	1	1	19	1	60	3	0	4	1	.800	0	9--	-	2.22	3.28
2005	Dytona	A+	32	16	1	11	109.1	456	99	47	39	9	2	3	3	27	2	123	2	0	10	5	.667	1	2--	-	2.89	3.21
2006	WTenn	AA	18	17	0	0	92.2	378	78	32	29	6	5	3	3	26	0	70	4	0	7	4	.636	0	0--	-	2.68	2.82
2006	ChC	NL	11	10	0	0	45.2	210	51	31	27	6	5	2	3	23	1	35	1	0	1	3	.250	0	0-0	0	5.63	5.32

Julio Mateo

Pitches: R Bats: R Pos: RP-48   Ht: 6'0" Wt: 220 Born: 8/2/1977 Age: 29

			HOW MUCH HE PITCHED						WHAT HE GAVE UP									THE RESULTS						
Year	Team	Lg	G	GS	CG	GF	IP	BFP	H	R	ER	HR	SH	SF	HB	TBB	IBB	SO	WP	Bk	W	L	Pct	ShO	Sv-Op	Hld	ERC	ERA
2002	Sea	AL	12	0	0	7	21.0	94	20	10	10	2	0	0	1	12	0	15	1	0	0	0	-	0	0-0	2	4.63	4.29
2003	Sea	AL	50	0	0	17	85.2	338	69	32	30	14	2	4	5	13	1	71	1	1	4	0	1.000	0	1-1	2	2.71	3.15
2004	Sea	AL	45	0	0	9	57.2	248	56	30	30	11	0	4	5	16	3	43	2	0	1	2	.333	0	1-4	6	4.26	4.68
2005	Sea	AL	55	1	0	7	88.1	364	79	32	30	12	5	2	7	17	6	52	1	0	3	6	.333	0	0-2	8	3.12	3.06
2006	Sea	AL	48	0	0	13	53.2	241	62	27	25	6	2	5	3	22	8	31	1	0	9	4	.692	0	0-3	7	5.10	4.19
	5 ML YEARS		210	1	0	53	306.1	1285	286	131	125	45	9	15	21	80	18	212	6	1	17	12	.586	0	2-10	25	3.65	3.67

Mike Matheny

Bats: R Throws: R Pos: C-46; PH-1   Ht: 6'3" Wt: 225 Born: 9/22/1970 Age: 36

									BATTING													BASERUNNING				AVERAGES		
Year	Team	Lg	G	AB	H	2B	3B	HR	(Hm	Rd)	TB	R	RBI	RC	TBB	IBB	SO	HBP	SH	SF	SB	CS	SB%	GDP	Avg	OBP	Slg
1994	Mil	AL	28	53	12	3	0	1	(1	0)	18	3	2	5	3	0	13	2	1	0	0	1	.00	1	.226	.293	.340
1995	Mil	AL	80	166	41	9	1	0	(0	0)	52	13	21	16	12	0	28	2	1	0	2	1	.67	3	.247	.306	.313
1996	Mil	AL	106	313	64	15	2	8	(5	3)	107	31	46	23	14	0	80	3	7	4	3	2	.60	9	.204	.243	.342
1997	Mil	AL	123	320	78	16	1	4	(2	2)	108	29	32	30	17	0	68	7	9	3	0	1	.00	9	.244	.294	.338
1998	Mil	NL	108	320	76	13	0	6	(4	2)	107	24	27	28	11	0	63	7	3	0	1	0	1.00	6	.238	.278	.334
1999	Tor	AL	57	163	35	6	0	3	(1	2)	50	16	17	13	12	0	37	1	2	1	0	0	-	3	.215	.271	.307
2000	StL	NL	128	417	109	22	1	6	(2	4)	151	43	47	46	32	8	96	4	7	4	0	0	-	11	.261	.317	.362
2001	StL	NL	121	381	83	12	0	7	(4	3)	116	40	42	29	28	5	76	4	8	3	0	1	.00	11	.218	.276	.304
2002	StL	NL	110	315	77	12	1	3	(1	2)	100	31	35	36	32	6	49	2	8	6	1	3	.25	3	.244	.313	.317
2003	StL	NL	141	441	111	18	2	8	(4	4)	157	43	47	52	44	16	81	2	8	3	1	1	.50	11	.252	.320	.356
2004	StL	NL	122	385	95	22	1	5	(4	1)	134	28	50	32	23	7	83	3	5	3	0	2	.00	12	.247	.292	.348
2005	SF	NL	134	443	107	34	0	13	(8	5)	180	42	59	52	29	10	91	6	3	4	0	2	.00	11	.242	.295	.406
2006	SF	NL	47	160	37	8	0	3	(0	3)	54	10	18	13	9	2	30	2	3	3	0	0	-	7	.231	.276	.338
	13 ML YEARS		1305	3877	925	190	9	67	(36	31)	1334	353	443	375	266	54	795	45	65	34	8	14	.36	97	.239	.293	.344

Scott Mathieson

Pitches: R Bats: R Pos: SP-8; RP-1   Ht: 6'3" Wt: 190 Born: 2/27/1984 Age: 23

			HOW MUCH HE PITCHED						WHAT HE GAVE UP									THE RESULTS						
Year	Team	Lg	G	GS	CG	GF	IP	BFP	H	R	ER	HR	SH	SF	HB	TBB	IBB	SO	WP	Bk	W	L	Pct	ShO	Sv-Op	Hld	ERC	ERA
2002	Phillies	R	7	2	0	1	16.2	81	24	11	10	0	1	1	2	6	0	14	0	1	0	2	.000	0	0- -	-	6.11	5.40
2003	Phillies	R	11	11	0	0	58.2	257	59	42	36	5	1	3	1	13	0	51	4	0	2	7	.222	0	0- -	-	3.19	5.52
2003	Batvia	A-	2	0	0	1	6.0	18	0	0	0	0	0	0	0	0	0	7	0	0	0	0	-	0	1- -	-	0.00	0.00
2004	Lakwd	A	25	25	1	0	131.1	572	130	73	63	7	6	7	9	50	0	112	9	0	8	9	.471	0	0- -	-	3.86	4.32
2005	Clrwtr	A+	23	23	1	0	121.2	510	111	62	56	17	4	5	5	34	0	118	7	0	3	8	.273	0	0- -	-	3.52	4.14
2006	Rdng	AA	14	14	0	0	92.2	375	73	35	33	8	3	5	7	29	1	99	1	0	7	2	.778	0	0- -	-	2.85	3.21
2006	S-WB	AAA	5	5	0	0	34.1	138	26	16	15	2	1	1	1	10	0	36	3	0	3	1	.750	0	0- -	-	2.26	3.93
2006	Phi	NL	9	8	0	0	37.1	177	48	36	31	8	5	1	1	16	1	28	2	1	1	4	.200	0	0-0	0	6.71	7.47

Jeff Mathis

Bats: R Throws: R Pos: C-20; DH-2; PH-2; PR-1   Ht: 6'0" Wt: 185 Born: 3/31/1983 Age: 24

									BATTING													BASERUNNING				AVERAGES		
Year	Team	Lg	G	AB	H	2B	3B	HR	(Hm	Rd)	TB	R	RBI	RC	TBB	IBB	SO	HBP	SH	SF	SB	CS	SB%	GDP	Avg	OBP	Slg
2001	Angels	R	7	23	7	1	0	0	(-	-)	8	1	3	3	2	0	4	0	0	1	0	0	-	1	.304	.346	.348
2001	Provo	R+	22	77	23	6	3	0	(-	-)	35	14	18	15	11	0	13	2	0	3	1	0	1.00	1	.299	.387	.455
2002	CRpds	A	128	491	141	41	3	10	(-	-)	218	75	73	78	40	3	75	8	2	8	7	4	.64	6	.287	.346	.444
2003	RCuca	A+	98	378	122	28	3	11	(-	-)	189	74	54	72	35	0	74	5	0	4	5	3	.63	4	.323	.384	.500
2003	Ark	AA	24	95	27	11	0	2	(-	-)	44	19	14	16	12	1	16	1	1	2	1	2	.33	2	.284	.364	.463
2004	Ark	AA	117	432	98	24	3	14	(-	-)	170	57	55	55	49	1	101	5	4	4	2	1	.67	5	.227	.310	.394
2005	Salt Lk	AAA	112	427	118	26	3	21	(-	-)	213	78	73	73	42	1	85	1	5	4	4	3	.57	7	.276	.340	.499
2006	Salt Lk	AAA	99	384	111	33	3	5	(-	-)	165	62	45	57	26	1	75	2	0	5	3	1	.75	6	.289	.333	.430
2005	LAA	AL	5	3	1	0	0	0	(0	0)	1	1	0	0	0	0	1	0	0	0	0	0	-	0	.333	.333	.333
2006	LAA	AL	23	55	8	2	0	2	(1	1)	16	9	6	4	7	1	14	0	0	1	0	0	-	0	.145	.238	.291
	2 ML YEARS		28	58	9	2	0	2	(1	1)	17	10	6	4	7	1	15	0	0	1	0	0	-	0	.155	.242	.293

Luis Matos

Bats: R Throws: R Pos: LF-32; PH-20; RF-13; CF-12; PR-6; DH-1   Ht: 6'0" Wt: 215 Born: 10/30/1978 Age: 28

									BATTING													BASERUNNING				AVERAGES		
Year	Team	Lg	G	AB	H	2B	3B	HR	(Hm	Rd)	TB	R	RBI	RC	TBB	IBB	SO	HBP	SH	SF	SB	CS	SB%	GDP	Avg	OBP	Slg
2006	Frdrck*	A+	2	9	3	0	0	1	(-	-)	6	1	2	2	0	0	1	0	0	0	1	0	1.00	0	.333	.333	.667
2000	Bal	AL	72	182	41	6	3	1	(1	0)	56	21	17	15	12	0	30	3	2	2	13	4	.76	7	.225	.281	.308
2001	Bal	AL	31	98	21	7	0	4	(1	3)	40	16	12	14	11	0	30	1	2	0	7	0	1.00	1	.214	.300	.408
2002	Bal	AL	17	31	4	1	0	0	(0	0)	5	0	1	0	1	0	6	0	1	0	1	0	1.00	1	.129	.156	.161
2003	Bal	AL	109	439	133	23	3	13	(6	7)	201	70	45	66	28	0	90	7	10	2	15	7	.68	9	.303	.353	.458
2004	Bal	AL	89	330	74	18	0	6	(2	4)	110	36	28	27	19	2	60	5	3	2	12	4	.75	7	.224	.275	.333
2005	Bal	AL	121	389	109	20	2	4	(3	1)	145	53	32	51	27	0	58	10	3	4	17	9	.65	4	.280	.340	.373
2006	2 Tms		69	136	28	9	1	2	(2	0)	45	16	5	8	10	0	23	2	1	0	7	0	1.00	3	.206	.270	.331
	06 Bal	AL	55	121	25	7	1	2	(2	0)	40	14	5	7	10	0	21	2	1	0	7	0	1.00	3	.207	.278	.331
	06 Was	NL	14	15	3	2	0	0	(0	0)	5	2	0	1	0	0	2	0	0	0	0	0	-	0	.200	.200	.333
	7 ML YEARS		508	1605	410	84	9	30	(15	15)	602	212	140	181	108	2	297	28	22	10	72	24	.75	32	.255	.312	.375

Hideki Matsui

Bats: L Throws: R Pos: LF-36; DH-13; PH-2   Ht: 6'2" Wt: 230 Born: 6/12/1974 Age: 33

Year	Team	Lg	G	AB	H	2B	3B	HR	(Hm	Rd)	TB	R	RBI	RC	TBB	IBB	SO	HBP	SH	SF	SB	CS	SB%	GDP	Avg	OBP	Slg
2003	NYY	AL	**163**	623	179	42	1	16	(9	7)	271	82	106	96	63	5	86	3	0	6	2	2	.50	25	.287	.353	.435
2004	NYY	AL	**162**	584	174	34	2	31	(18	13)	305	109	108	117	88	2	103	3	0	5	3	0	1.00	11	.298	.390	.522
2005	NYY	AL	**162**	629	192	45	3	23	(15	8)	312	108	116	109	63	7	78	3	0	8	2	2	.50	16	.305	.367	.496
2006	NYY	AL	51	172	52	9	0	8	(1	7)	85	32	29	30	27	2	23	0	0	2	1	0	1.00	6	.302	.393	.494
	4 ML YEARS		538	2008	597	130	6	78	(43	35)	973	331	359	352	241	16	290	9	0	21	8	4	.67	58	.297	.372	.485

Kaz Matsui

Bats: B Throws: R Pos: 2B-52; PH-14; SS-3; PR-2   Ht: 5'10" Wt: 185 Born: 10/23/1975 Age: 31

Year	Team	Lg	G	AB	H	2B	3B	HR	(Hm	Rd)	TB	R	RBI	RC	TBB	IBB	SO	HBP	SH	SF	SB	CS	SB%	GDP	Avg	OBP	Slg
2006	StLuci*	A+	2	7	2	0	0	0	(-	-)	2	1	0	0	1	0	0	0	0	0	0	0	-	0	.286	.375	.286
2006	Norfolk*	AAA	4	12	4	2	0	0	(-	-)	6	2	1	1	0	0	2	0	1	0	0	0	-	0	.333	.333	.500
2006	ColSpr*	AAA	31	115	32	4	0	3	(-	-)	45	26	16	16	9	0	20	1	1	3	3	1	.75	0	.278	.328	.391
2004	NYM	NL	114	460	125	32	2	7	(4	3)	182	65	44	63	40	4	97	2	5	2	14	3	.82	3	.272	.331	.396
2005	NYM	NL	87	267	68	9	4	3	(1	2)	94	31	24	27	14	1	43	5	5	4	6	1	.86	2	.255	.300	.352
2006	2 Tms	NL	70	243	65	12	3	3	(0	3)	92	32	26	28	16	1	46	0	4	2	10	1	.91	1	.267	.310	.379
06	NYM	NL	38	130	26	6	0	1	(0	1)	35	10	7	5	6	1	19	0	3	0	2	0	1.00	1	.200	.235	.269
06	Col	NL	32	113	39	6	3	2	(0	2)	57	22	19	23	10	0	27	0	1	2	8	1	.89	0	.345	.392	.504
	3 ML YEARS		271	970	258	53	9	13	(5	8)	368	128	94	118	70	6	186	7	14	8	30	5	.86	6	.266	.318	.379

Daisuke Matsuzaka

Pitches: R Bats: R Pos: P   Ht: 5'11" Wt: 187 Born: 9/13/1980 Age: 26

Year	Team	Lg	G	GS	CG	GF	IP	BFP	H	R	ER	HR	SH	SF	HB	TBB	IBB	SO	WP	Bk	W	L	Pct	ShO	Sv-Op	Hld	ERC	ERA
1999	Seibu	Jap	25	18	6	1	180.0	743	124	55	52	14	-	-	8	87	-	151	5	-	16	5	.762	2	0- -	-	2.77	2.60
2000	Seibu	Jap	27	18	6	2	167.2	727	132	85	74	12	-	-	4	95	-	144	2	-	14	7	.667	2	1- -	-	3.40	3.97
2001	Seibu	Jap	33	20	12	1	240.1	1004	184	104	96	27	-	-	8	117	-	214	9	-	15	15	.500	2	0- -	-	3.38	3.60
2002	Seibu	Jap	14	9	2	0	73.1	302	60	30	30	13	-	-	7	15	-	78	2	-	6	2	.750	0	0- -	-	3.14	3.68
2003	Seibu	Jap	29	19	8	1	194.0	801	165	71	61	13	-	-	9	63	3	215	4	0	16	7	.696	2	0- -	-	2.94	2.83
2004	Seibu	Jap	23	23	10	0	143.1	605	127	50	47	6	-	-	6	42	-	127	5	-	10	6	.625	0	0- -	-	2.82	2.95
2005	Seibu	Jap	28	28	15	0	215.0	974	172	63	55	13	-	-	10	49	-	226	9	0	14	13	.519	3	0- -	-	1.99	2.30
2006	Seibu	Jap	25	25	14	0	186.1	731	138	50	44	13	-	-	3	34	-	200	5	0	17	5	.773	2	0- -	-	1.77	2.13

Gary Matthews Jr.

Bats: B Throws: R Pos: CF-142; RF-3; PH-2; DH-1   Ht: 6'3" Wt: 225 Born: 8/25/1974 Age: 32

Year	Team	Lg	G	AB	H	2B	3B	HR	(Hm	Rd)	TB	R	RBI	RC	TBB	IBB	SO	HBP	SH	SF	SB	CS	SB%	GDP	Avg	OBP	Slg
2006	Okla*	AAA	6	21	9	2	0	0	(-	-)	11	10	1	6	4	1	0	1	0	0	2	0	1.00	1	.429	.538	.524
1999	SD	NL	23	36	8	0	0	0	(0	0)	8	4	7	4	9	0	9	0	0	0	2	0	1.00	1	.222	.378	.222
2000	ChC	NL	80	158	30	1	2	4	(2	2)	47	24	14	13	15	1	28	1	1	0	3	0	1.00	2	.190	.264	.297
2001	2 Tms	NL	152	405	92	15	2	14	(4	10)	153	63	44	51	60	2	100	1	5	1	8	5	.62	8	.227	.328	.378
2002	2 Tms		111	345	95	25	3	7	(6	1)	147	54	38	55	43	1	69	1	5	4	15	5	.75	4	.275	.354	.426
2003	2 Tms		144	468	116	31	2	6	(3	3)	169	71	42	51	43	0	95	2	0	0	12	8	.60	8	.248	.314	.361
2004	Tex	AL	87	280	77	17	1	11	(7	4)	129	37	36	48	33	5	64	1	0	3	5	1	.83	1	.275	.350	.461
2005	Tex	AL	131	475	121	25	5	17	(8	9)	207	72	55	63	47	1	90	0	1	3	9	2	.82	11	.255	.320	.436
2006	Tex	AL	147	620	194	44	6	19	(11	8)	307	102	79	109	58	5	99	4	0	8	10	7	.59	8	.313	.371	.495
01	ChC	NL	106	258	56	9	1	9	(2	7)	94	41	30	31	38	2	55	1	5	0	5	3	.63	4	.217	.320	.364
01	Pit	NL	46	147	36	6	1	5	(2	3)	59	22	14	20	22	0	45	0	0	1	3	2	.60	4	.245	.341	.401
02	NYM	NL	2	1	0	0	0	0	(0	0)	0	0	0	0	0	0	0	0	0	0	0	0	-	0	.000	.000	.000
02	Bal	AL	109	344	95	25	3	7	(6	1)	147	54	38	55	43	1	69	1	5	4	15	5	.75	4	.276	.355	.427
03	Bal	AL	41	162	33	12	1	2	(2	0)	53	21	20	15	9	0	29	1	0	0	0	3	.00	4	.204	.250	.327
03	SD	NL	103	306	83	19	1	4	(1	3)	116	50	22	36	34	0	66	1	0	0	12	5	.71	4	.271	.346	.379
	8 ML YEARS		875	2787	733	158	21	78	(41	37)	1167	427	315	394	308	15	554	10	12	19	64	28	.70	43	.263	.336	.419

Joe Mauer

Bats: L Throws: R Pos: C-120; DH-17; PH-4   Ht: 6'4" Wt: 220 Born: 4/19/1983 Age: 24

Year	Team	Lg	G	AB	H	2B	3B	HR	(Hm	Rd)	TB	R	RBI	RC	TBB	IBB	SO	HBP	SH	SF	SB	CS	SB%	GDP	Avg	OBP	Slg
2004	Min	AL	35	107	33	8	1	6	(4	2)	61	18	17	21	11	0	14	1	0	3	1	0	1.00	1	.308	.369	.570
2005	Min	AL	131	489	144	26	2	9	(4	5)	201	61	55	78	61	12	64	1	0	3	13	1	.93	9	.294	.372	.411
2006	Min	AL	140	521	181	36	4	13	(3	10)	264	86	84	103	79	21	54	1	0	7	8	3	.73	24	**.347**	.429	.507
	3 ML YEARS		306	1117	358	70	7	28	(11	17)	526	165	156	202	151	33	132	3	0	13	22	4	.85	34	.321	.399	.471

Joe Mays

Pitches: R Bats: B Pos: SP-10; RP-3   Ht: 6'1" Wt: 200 Born: 12/10/1975 Age: 31

Year	Team	Lg	G	GS	CG	GF	IP	BFP	H	R	ER	HR	SH	SF	HB	TBB	IBB	SO	WP	Bk	W	L	Pct	ShO	Sv-Op	Hld	ERC	ERA
2006	Lsvlle*	AAA	10	10	1	0	67.1	273	68	27	23	4	4	1	0	13	0	40	0	0	6	3	.667	0	0- -	-	3.13	3.07
1999	Min	AL	49	20	2	8	171.0	746	179	92	83	24	7	6	2	67	2	115	6	0	6	11	.353	1	0-0	2	4.62	4.37
2000	Min	AL	31	28	2	1	160.1	723	193	105	99	20	3	5	2	67	1	102	11	0	7	15	.318	1	0-0	0	5.59	5.56
2001	Min	AL	34	34	4	0	233.2	957	205	87	82	25	8	8	5	64	2	123	11	0	17	13	.567	2	0-0	0	3.05	3.16
2002	Min	AL	17	17	1	0	95.1	418	113	60	57	14	2	2	2	25	0	38	6	0	4	8	.333	1	0-0	0	4.99	5.38

			HOW MUCH HE PITCHED						WHAT HE GAVE UP										THE RESULTS						
Year	Team	Lg	G	GS	CG	GF	IP	BFP	H	R	ER	HR	SH	SF	HB	TBB	IBB	SO	WP	Bk	W	L	Pct	ShO	Sv-Op	Hld	ERC	ERA
2003	Min	AL	31	21	0	4	130.0	576	159	92	91	21	3	3	4	39	2	50	3	0	8	8	.500	0	0-1	1	5.55	6.30
2005	Min	AL	31	26	1	1	156.0	690	203	109	98	23	5	3	3	41	1	59	4	0	6	10	.375	0	0-0	0	5.78	5.65
2006	2 Tms		13	10	0	0	50.2	250	78	56	49	11	2	2	0	26	2	25	6	0	0	5	.000	0	0-0	0	8.86	8.70
06	KC	AL	6	6	0	0	23.2	120	38	33	27	7	1	2	0	14	0	9	3	0	0	4	.000	0	0-0	0	10.54	10.27
06	Cin	NL	7	4	0	0	27.0	130	40	23	22	4	1	0	0	12	2	16	3	0	0	1	.000	0	0-0	0	7.45	7.33
	7 ML YEARS		206	156	10	14	997.0	4360	1130	601	559	138	30	29	18	329	10	512	47	0	48	70	.407	6	0-1	3	4.91	5.05

Paul McAnulty

Bats: L **Throws:** R **Pos:** PH-15; RF-1; PR-1   **Ht:** 5'10" **Wt:** 220 **Born:** 2/24/1981 **Age:** 26

			BATTING																		BASERUNNING				AVERAGES		
Year	Team	Lg	G	AB	H	2B	3B	HR	(Hm	Rd)	TB	R	RBI	RC	TBB	IBB	SO	HBP	SH	SF	SB	CS	SB%	GDP	Avg	OBP	Slg
2002	Idaho	R+	67	235	89	29	0	8	(-	-)	142	56	51	68	49	2	43	4	0	3	7	2	.78	5	.379	.488	.604
2003	FtWyn	A	133	455	124	27	0	7	(-	-)	172	48	73	71	67	2	82	9	2	9	5	3	.63	7	.273	.370	.378
2004	Lk Els	A+	133	495	147	36	3	23	(-	-)	258	98	87	107	88	3	106	4	0	4	3	1	.75	5	.297	.404	.521
2005	Mobile	AA	79	298	84	17	2	10	(-	-)	135	39	42	52	34	3	66	7	0	3	5	2	.71	3	.282	.365	.453
2005	PortInd	AAA	38	151	52	15	0	6	(-	-)	85	27	27	33	16	0	29	0	0	1	0	0	-	3	.344	.405	.563
2006	PortInd	AAA	125	478	148	34	5	19	(-	-)	249	76	79	98	62	2	79	4	0	8	1	2	.33	14	.310	.388	.521
2005	SD	NL	22	24	5	0	0	0	(0	0)	5	4	0	1	3	1	7	1	1	0	1	0	1.00	0	.208	.321	.208
2006	SD	NL	16	13	3	1	0	1	(1	0)	7	3	3	3	2	0	4	0	0	0	0	0	-	0	.231	.333	.538
	2 ML YEARS		38	37	8	1	0	1	(1	0)	12	7	3	4	5	1	11	1	1	0	1	0	1.00	0	.216	.326	.324

Macay McBride

Pitches: L **Bats:** L **Pos:** RP-71   **Ht:** 5'11" **Wt:** 210 **Born:** 10/24/1982 **Age:** 24

			HOW MUCH HE PITCHED						WHAT HE GAVE UP											THE RESULTS						
Year	Team	Lg	G	GS	CG	GF	IP	BFP	H	R	ER	HR	SH	SF	HB	TBB	IBB	SO	WP	Bk	W	L	Pct	ShO	Sv-Op	Hld	ERC	ERA
2001	Braves	R	13	11	0	0	55.0	239	51	30	23	2	2	4		23	1	67	8	0	4	4	.500	0	0--		3.26	3.76
2002	Macon	A	25	25	2	0	157.1	639	119	49	37	6	2	3	4	48	1	138	13	1	12	8	.600	1	0--		2.06	2.12
2003	MrtlBh	A+	27	27	1	0	164.2	707	164	63	54	5	0	0	4	49	0	139	4	0	9	8	.529	0	0--		3.22	2.95
2004	Grnville	AA	38	12	0	5	103.1	469	113	59	51	9	5	5	0	46	0	102	5	0	1	7	.125	0	0--		4.58	4.44
2005	Missi	AA	6	3	0	1	24.2	107	21	11	10	2	1	0	0	12	1	16	1	0	3	1	.750	0	0--		3.32	3.65
2005	Rchmd	AAA	25	1	0	6	43.2	202	49	27	21	5	7	1	2	22	2	47	0	0	1	5	.167	0	2--		5.34	4.33
2006	Missi	AA	4	2	0	0	4.2	23	8	5	5	1	1	0	0	1	0	6	1	0	0	0	-	0	0--		8.45	9.64
2006	Rchmd	AAA	3	0	0	0	3.0	11	1	0	0	0	1	0	0	1	0	3	0	0	0	0	-	0	0--		0.69	0.00
2005	Atl	NL	23	0	0	4	14.0	68	18	11	9	0	1	0	1	7	0	22	2	0	1	0	1.000	0	1-1	6	5.12	5.79
2006	Atl	NL	71	0	0	13	56.2	249	53	28	23	2	2	0	1	32	4	46	3	0	4	1	.800	0	1-2	10	3.85	3.65
	2 ML YEARS		94	0	0	17	70.2	317	71	39	32	2	3	1	1	39	4	68	5	0	5	1	.833	0	2-3	16	4.09	4.08

Brian McCann

Bats: L **Throws:** R **Pos:** C-124; PH-9   **Ht:** 6'3" **Wt:** 210 **Born:** 2/20/1984 **Age:** 23

			BATTING																		BASERUNNING				AVERAGES		
Year	Team	Lg	G	AB	H	2B	3B	HR	(Hm	Rd)	TB	R	RBI	RC	TBB	IBB	SO	HBP	SH	SF	SB	CS	SB%	GDP	Avg	OBP	Slg
2002	Braves	R	29	100	22	5	0	2	(-	-)	33	9	11	10	10	0	22	1	0	1	0	0	-	0	.220	.295	.330
2003	Rome	A	115	424	123	31	3	12	(-	-)	196	40	71	65	24	2	73	2	0	3	7	4	.64	5	.290	.329	.462
2004	MrtlBh	A+	111	385	107	35	0	16	(-	-)	190	45	66	63	31	4	54	4	0	1	2	2	.50	6	.278	.337	.494
2005	Missi	AA	48	166	44	13	2	6	(-	-)	79	27	26	29	25	3	26	2	0	5	2	3	.40	2	.265	.359	.476
2006	Rome	A	2	7	2	0	0	0	(-	-)	2	0	0	0	1	0	0	0	0	0	0	0	-	0	.286	.375	.286
2005	Atl	NL	59	180	50	7	0	5	(2	3)	72	20	23	25	18	5	26	1	4	1	1	1	.50	5	.278	.345	.400
2006	Atl	NL	130	442	147	34	0	24	(10	14)	253	61	93	94	41	8	54	3	0	6	2	0	1.00	12	.333	.388	.572
	2 ML YEARS		189	622	197	41	0	29	(12	17)	325	81	116	119	59	13	80	4	4	7	3	1	.75	17	.317	.376	.523

Brandon McCarthy

Pitches: R **Bats:** R **Pos:** RP-51; SP-2   **Ht:** 6'7" **Wt:** 195 **Born:** 7/7/1983 **Age:** 23

			HOW MUCH HE PITCHED						WHAT HE GAVE UP											THE RESULTS						
Year	Team	Lg	G	GS	CG	GF	IP	BFP	H	R	ER	HR	SH	SF	HB	TBB	IBB	SO	WP	Bk	W	L	Pct	ShO	Sv-Op	Hld	ERC	ERA
2002	WhSox	R	14	14	0	0	78.1	328	78	40	24	6	2	1	2	15	1	79	5	3	4	4	.500	0	0--		3.13	2.76
2003	Gr Falls	R+	16	15	1	0	101.0	423	105	49	41	7	2	0	3	15	0	125	3	3	9	4	.692	0	0--		3.18	3.65
2004	Knapol	A-	15	15	3	0	94.0	383	80	41	38	10	1	2	7	21	0	113	3	2	8	5	.615	1	0--		2.94	3.64
2004	WinSa	A+	8	8	0	0	52.0	190	31	12	12	3	2	1	1	3	0	60	1	2	6	0	1.000	0	0--		1.06	2.08
2004	Brham	A	4	4	0	0	26.0	107	23	10	10	2	0	1	2	6	1	29	1	0	3	1	.750	0	0--		2.90	3.46
2005	Charltt	AAA	20	19	1	1	119.1	494	104	53	52	16	3	1	2	32	0	130	5	1	7	7	.500	1	0--		3.11	3.92
2005	CWS	AL	12	10	0	0	67.0	277	62	30	30	13	1	1	2	17	0	48	1	1	3	2	.600	0	0-0	0	3.83	4.03
2006	CWS	AL	53	2	0	13	84.2	354	77	44	44	17	3	1	0	33	9	69	5	0	4	7	.364	0	0-1	11	4.10	4.68
	2 ML YEARS		65	12	0	13	151.2	631	139	74	74	30	4	2	2	50	9	117	6	1	7	9	.438	0	0-1	11	3.98	4.39

Seth McClung

Pitches: R **Bats:** R **Pos:** RP-24; SP-15   **Ht:** 6'6" **Wt:** 250 **Born:** 2/7/1981 **Age:** 26

			HOW MUCH HE PITCHED						WHAT HE GAVE UP											THE RESULTS						
Year	Team	Lg	G	GS	CG	GF	IP	BFP	H	R	ER	HR	SH	SF	HB	TBB	IBB	SO	WP	Bk	W	L	Pct	ShO	Sv-Op	Hld	ERC	ERA
2006	Drham*	AAA	14	0	0	12	16.1	70	16	5	4	1	0	0	2	2	0	26	0	0	1	0	1.000	0	5--		2.99	2.20
2003	TB	AL	12	5	0	2	38.2	167	33	23	23	6	1	1	3	25	1	25	2	0	4	1	.800	0	0-0	1	5.11	5.35
2005	TB	AL	34	17	0	3	109.1	500	106	85	80	20	0	5	7	62	1	92	6	0	7	11	.389	0	0-1	2	5.36	6.59
2006	TB	AL	39	15	0	20	103.0	489	120	77	72	14	1	9	3	68	5	59	7	0	6	12	.333	0	6-7	0	6.44	6.29
	3 ML YEARS		85	37	0	25	251.0	1156	259	185	175	40	2	15	13	155	7	176	15	0	17	24	.415	0	6-8	3	5.76	6.27

Quinton McCracken

Bats: B **Throws:** R **Pos:** PH-31; LF-7; CF-6; PR-3; RF-2   **Ht:** 5'8" **Wt:** 185 **Born:** 8/16/1970 **Age:** 36

						BATTING													BASERUNNING				AVERAGES		
Year	Team	Lg	G	AB	H	2B	3B	HR	(Hm | Rd)	TB	R	RBI	RC	TBB	IBB	SO	HBP	SH	SF	SB	CS	SB%	GDP	Avg	OBP	Slg
2006	Srsota*	A+	4	16	8	0	1	0	(- | -)	10	3	0	4	0	0	0	0	0	0	0	0	-	0	.500	.500	.625
2006	Roch*	AAA	31	109	31	4	0	1	(- | -)	38	10	11	13	9	0	17	0	1	0	2	1	.67	4	.284	.339	.349
1995	Col	NL	3	1	0	0	0	0	(0 | 0)	0	0	0	0	0	0	1	0	0	0	0	0	-	0	.000	.000	.000
1996	Col	NL	124	283	82	13	6	3	(2 | 1)	116	50	40	43	32	4	62	1	12	1	17	6	.74	5	.290	.363	.410
1997	Col	NL	147	325	95	11	1	3	(1 | 2)	117	69	36	47	42	0	62	1	6	1	28	11	.72	6	.292	.374	.360
1998	TB	AL	155	614	179	38	7	7	(5 | 2)	252	77	59	83	41	1	107	3	9	8	19	10	.66	12	.292	.335	.410
1999	TB	AL	40	148	37	6	1	1	(1 | 0)	48	20	18	13	14	0	23	1	1	1	6	5	.55	7	.250	.317	.324
2000	TB	AL	15	31	4	0	0	0	(0 | 0)	4	5	2	0	6	0	4	0	0	0	0	1	.00	3	.129	.270	.129
2001	Min	AL	24	64	14	2	2	0	(0 | 0)	20	7	3	5	5	0	13	0	1	0	0	1	.00	2	.219	.275	.313
2002	Ari	NL	123	349	108	27	8	3	(1 | 2)	160	60	40	62	32	0	68	2	13	4	5	4	.56	3	.309	.367	.458
2003	Ari	NL	115	203	46	5	2	0	(0 | 0)	55	17	18	16	15	2	34	0	5	3	5	1	.83	4	.227	.276	.271
2004	2 Tms		74	176	48	11	1	2	(2 | 0)	67	26	13	20	15	0	27	0	3	1	3	5	.38	3	.273	.328	.381
2005	Ari	NL	134	215	51	4	3	1	(1 | 0)	64	23	13	20	23	4	35	1	6	1	4	0	1.00	4	.237	.313	.298
2006	Cin	NL	45	53	11	1	1	1	(0 | 1)	17	5	2	3	4	0	9	0	3	0	2	0	1.00	1	.208	.263	.321
04	Sea	AL	19	20	3	0	0	0	(0 | 0)	3	6	0	0	2	0	4	0	1	0	1	1	.50	1	.150	.227	.150
04	Ari	NL	55	156	45	11	1	2	(2 | 0)	64	20	13	20	13	0	23	0	2	1	2	4	.33	2	.288	.341	.410
	12 ML YEARS		999	2462	675	118	32	21	(13 | 8)	920	359	244	312	229	11	445	9	59	20	89	44	.67	50	.274	.336	.374

John McDonald

Bats: R **Throws:** R **Pos:** SS-90; 2B-10; PH-6; PR-3; 3B-2; DH-1   **Ht:** 5'11" **Wt:** 185 **Born:** 9/24/1974 **Age:** 32

						BATTING													BASERUNNING				AVERAGES		
Year	Team	Lg	G	AB	H	2B	3B	HR	(Hm | Rd)	TB	R	RBI	RC	TBB	IBB	SO	HBP	SH	SF	SB	CS	SB%	GDP	Avg	OBP	Slg
1999	Cle	AL	18	21	7	0	0	0	(0 | 0)	7	2	0	1	0	0	3	0	0	0	0	1	.00	1	.333	.333	.333
2000	Cle	AL	9	9	4	0	0	0	(0 | 0)	4	0	0	2	0	0	1	0	0	0	0	0	-	0	.444	.444	.444
2001	Cle	AL	17	22	2	1	0	0	(0 | 0)	3	1	0	0	1	0	7	1	1	0	0	0	-	0	.091	.167	.136
2002	Cle	AL	93	264	66	11	3	1	(0 | 1)	86	35	12	24	10	0	50	5	7	2	3	0	1.00	4	.250	.288	.326
2003	Cle	AL	82	214	46	9	1	1	(0 | 1)	60	21	14	18	11	0	31	2	4	2	3	3	.50	4	.215	.258	.280
2004	Cle	AL	66	93	19	5	1	2	(0 | 2)	32	17	7	6	4	0	11	0	3	0	0	0	-	2	.204	.237	.344
2005	2 Tms		68	166	46	6	1	0	(0 | 0)	54	18	16	19	11	0	24	2	3	2	6	1	.86	6	.277	.326	.325
2006	Tor	AL	104	260	58	7	3	3	(1 | 2)	80	35	23	20	6	0	41	2	6	2	7	2	.78	8	.223	.271	.308
05	Tor	AL	37	93	27	3	0	0	(0 | 0)	30	8	12	13	6	0	12	2	3	2	5	0	1.00	3	.290	.340	.323
05	Det	AL	31	73	19	3	1	0	(0 | 0)	24	10	4	6	5	0	12	0	0	0	1	1	.50	3	.260	.308	.329
	8 ML YEARS		457	1049	248	39	9	7	(1 | 6)	326	129	72	90	53	0	168	12	24	8	19	7	.73	26	.236	.279	.311

Joe McEwing

Bats: R **Throws:** R **Pos:** PH-6; 2B-2   **Ht:** 5'11" **Wt:** 170 **Born:** 10/19/1972 **Age:** 34

						BATTING													BASERUNNING				AVERAGES		
Year	Team	Lg	G	AB	H	2B	3B	HR	(Hm | Rd)	TB	R	RBI	RC	TBB	IBB	SO	HBP	SH	SF	SB	CS	SB%	GDP	Avg	OBP	Slg
2006	RdRck*	AAA	112	422	133	21	1	10	(- | -)	186	64	46	67	23	1	65	3	7	5	16	7	.70	5	.315	.351	.441
1998	StL	NL	10	20	4	1	0	0	(0 | 0)	5	5	1	1	1	0	3	1	1	0	0	1	.00	0	.200	.273	.250
1999	StL	NL	152	513	141	28	4	9	(5 | 4)	204	65	44	70	41	8	87	6	9	5	7	4	.64	3	.275	.333	.398
2000	NYM	NL	87	153	34	14	1	2	(1 | 1)	56	20	19	14	5	0	29	1	8	2	3	1	.75	2	.222	.248	.366
2001	NYM	NL	116	283	80	17	3	8	(3 | 5)	127	41	30	44	17	0	57	10	6	3	8	5	.62	2	.283	.342	.449
2002	NYM	NL	105	196	39	8	1	3	(2 | 1)	58	22	26	14	9	0	50	3	3	3	4	4	.50	0	.199	.242	.296
2003	NYM	NL	119	278	67	11	0	1	(0 | 1)	81	31	16	26	25	4	57	3	6	1	3	0	1.00	6	.241	.309	.291
2004	NYM	NL	75	138	35	3	1	1	(1 | 0)	43	17	16	17	9	4	32	0	6	1	4	1	.80	2	.254	.297	.312
2005	KC	AL	83	180	43	7	0	1	(0 | 1)	53	16	6	11	6	0	35	0	5	0	4	4	.50	5	.239	.263	.294
2006	Hou	NL	7	6	0	0	0	0	(0 | 0)	0	0	0	0	0	0	2	0	0	0	0	0	-	0	.000	.000	.000
	9 ML YEARS		754	1767	443	89	10	25	(12 | 13)	627	217	158	197	113	16	352	24	44	15	33	20	.62	18	.251	.302	.355

Dustin McGowan

Pitches: R **Bats:** R **Pos:** RP-13; SP-3   **Ht:** 6'2" **Wt:** 215 **Born:** 3/24/1982 **Age:** 25

			HOW MUCH HE PITCHED					WHAT HE GAVE UP										THE RESULTS						
Year	Team	Lg	G	GS	CG	GF	IP	BFP	H	R	ER	HR	SH	SF	HB	TBB	IBB	SO	WP	Bk	W	L	Pct	ShO	Sv-Op	Hld	ERC	ERA
2000	MdHat	R+	8	8	0	0	25.0	126	26	21	18	2	1	5	3	25	0	19	8	0	0	3	.000	0	0- -	-	7.09	6.48
2001	Auburn	A-	15	14	0	0	67.0	307	57	33	28	1	1	2	4	49	0	80	16	0	3	6	.333	0	0- -	-	4.05	3.76
2002	CtnWV	A	28	28	1	0	148.1	647	143	77	69	10	6	3	5	59	0	163	12	0	11	10	.524	0	0- -	-	3.71	4.19
2003	Dnedin	A+	14	14	1	0	75.2	314	62	29	24	1	2	0	4	25	0	66	9	0	5	6	.455	1	0- -	-	2.47	2.85
2003	NwHav	AA	14	14	1	0	76.2	327	78	28	27	1	5	1	4	19	0	72	5	1	7	0	1.000	0	0- -	-	3.15	3.17
2004	NHam	AA	6	6	0	0	31.0	132	24	14	14	4	0	0	0	15	0	29	2	0	2	0	1.000	0	0- -	-	3.30	4.06
2005	Dnedin	A+	5	5	0	0	21.0	89	21	12	10	2	1	0	2	5	0	20	0	1	0	1	.000	0	0- -	-	3.79	4.29
2005	NHam	AA	6	6	0	0	35.0	150	35	16	13	6	1	3	1	10	0	33	1	0	0	2	.000	0	0- -	-	4.16	3.34
2006	Syrcse	AAA	23	13	0	5	84.0	369	77	45	41	7	1	2	3	39	0	86	10	0	4	5	.444	0	1- -	-	3.82	4.39
2005	Tor	AL	13	7	0	2	45.1	205	49	34	32	7	0	4	7	17	0	34	7	0	1	3	.250	0	0-0	1	5.47	6.35
2006	Tor	AL	16	3	0	3	27.1	143	35	27	22	2	0	1	2	25	2	22	3	1	1	2	.333	0	0-1	1	7.72	7.24
	2 ML YEARS		29	10	0	5	72.2	348	84	61	54	9	0	5	9	42	2	56	10	1	2	5	.286	0	0-1	2	6.32	6.69

Marty McLeary

Pitches: R **Bats:** R **Pos:** RP-3; SP-2   **Ht:** 6'3" **Wt:** 225 **Born:** 10/26/1974 **Age:** 32

			HOW MUCH HE PITCHED					WHAT HE GAVE UP										THE RESULTS						
Year	Team	Lg	G	GS	CG	GF	IP	BFP	H	R	ER	HR	SH	SF	HB	TBB	IBB	SO	WP	Bk	W	L	Pct	ShO	Sv-Op	Hld	ERC	ERA
1997	Lowell	A-	13	13	0	0	62.1	275	53	38	26	2	3	5	5	36	1	43	6	2	3	6	.333	0	0- -	-	3.71	3.75
1998	Mich	A	37	7	0	11	88.2	396	99	58	41	4	1	3	5	35	2	54	5	1	5	7	.417	0	0- -	-	4.49	4.16
1999	Srsota	A+	8	0	0	0	12.2	73	29	20	17	1	2	1	1	7	0	11	0	0	1	0	1.000	0	0- -	-	13.60	12.08

Year	Team	Lg	G	GS	CG	GF	IP	BFP	H	R	ER	HR	SH	SF	HB	TBB	IBB	SO	WP	Bk	W	L	Pct	ShO	Sv-Op Hld	ERC	ERA
1999	Augsta	A	35	9	0	16	80.2	338	73	34	28	8	3	2	4	25	1	90	5	2	5	6	.455	0	3- -	3.37	3.12
2000	Trntn	AA	43	8	0	22	96.2	449	114	66	49	5	2	6	2	53	3	53	8	1	2	9	.182	0	5- -	5.35	4.56
2001	Trntn	AA	35	0	0	14	54.2	252	58	30	21	2	4	1	5	30	5	42	2	0	9	6	.600	0	2- -	4.69	3.46
2001	Pwtckt	AAA	18	0	0	7	30.0	127	28	13	10	4	2	1	1	15	1	20	1	0	1	2	.333	0	0- -	4.58	3.00
2002	Trntn	AA	11	0	0	7	16.2	76	20	12	9	0	1	2	1	8	2	10	2	0	0	2	.000	0	0- -	4.85	4.86
2002	Pwtckt	AAA	18	1	0	6	35.2	168	44	30	29	6	1	1	2	23	0	19	6	0	1	1	.500	0	0- -	7.50	7.32
2003	Carlina	AA	11	2	0	1	30.0	124	22	8	6	1	0	0	3	15	0	22	3	0	1	1	.500	0	0- -	3.03	1.80
2003	Albq	AAA	20	1	0	4	33.1	160	40	22	16	3	1	2	3	18	1	17	3	0	1	1	.500	0	0- -	5.95	4.32
2004	Portlnd	AAA	44	7	0	23	84.1	357	65	30	28	4	3	0	5	42	1	81	5	1	5	4	.556	0	13- -	3.06	2.99
2005	Portlnd	AAA	41	12	1	10	110.0	503	122	68	58	10	4	2	5	51	1	104	5	0	5	8	.385	1	0- -	4.98	4.75
2006	Indy	AAA	35	13	0	8	104.0	434	96	32	31	6	4	0	1	33	2	115	3	0	3	4	.429	0	2- -	3.06	2.68
2004	SD	NL	3	0	0	2	3.2	20	7	6	6	2	1	1	0	2	0	4	0	0	0	0	-	0	0-0	14.71	14.73
2006	Pit	NL	5	2	0	1	17.2	73	17	5	4	1	0	1	0	6	1	8	1	0	2	0	1.000	0	0-0	3.33	2.04
	2 ML YEARS		8	2	0	3	21.1	93	24	11	10	3	1	2	0	8	1	12	1	0	2	0	1.000	0	0-0	4.96	4.22

Nate McLouth

Bats: L **Throws:** R **Pos:** CF-42; RF-39; PH-34; PR-6; LF-3 **Ht:** 5'11" **Wt:** 185 **Born:** 10/28/1981 **Age:** 25

						BATTING														BASERUNNING				AVERAGES		
Year	Team	Lg	G	AB	H	2B	3B	HR	(Hm | Rd)	TB	R	RBI	RC	TBB	IBB	SO	HBP	SH	SF	SB	CS	SB%	GDP	Avg	OBP	Slg
2001	Hickory	A	96	351	100	17	5	12	(- | -)	163	59	54	65	43	6	54	7	2	3	21	5	.81	5	.285	.371	.464
2002	Lynbrg	A+	114	393	96	23	4	9	(- | -)	154	58	46	55	41	3	48	8	6	5	20	7	.74	12	.244	.324	.392
2003	Lynbrg	A+	117	440	132	27	2	6	(- | -)	181	85	33	80	55	2	68	7	5	1	40	4	.91	4	.300	.386	.411
2004	Altna	AA	133	515	166	40	4	8	(- | -)	238	93	73	98	48	2	62	8	14	7	31	7	.82	6	.322	.384	.462
2005	Indy	AAA	110	397	118	20	3	5	(- | -)	159	64	39	66	39	1	58	7	5	7	34	8	.81	10	.297	.364	.401
2005	Pit	NL	41	109	28	6	0	5	(2 | 3)	49	20	12	9	3	0	20	5	2	1	2	0	1.00	3	.257	.305	.450
2006	Pit	NL	106	270	63	16	2	7	(3 | 4)	104	50	16	25	18	0	59	5	3	1	10	1	.91	7	.233	.293	.385
	2 ML YEARS		147	379	91	22	2	12	(5 | 7)	153	70	28	34	21	0	79	10	5	2	12	1	.92	10	.240	.296	.404

Dallas McPherson

Bats: L **Throws:** R **Pos:** 3B-31; PH-8; 1B-6; DH-2 **Ht:** 6'4" **Wt:** 230 **Born:** 7/23/1980 **Age:** 26

						BATTING														BASERUNNING				AVERAGES		
Year	Team	Lg	G	AB	H	2B	3B	HR	(Hm | Rd)	TB	R	RBI	RC	TBB	IBB	SO	HBP	SH	SF	SB	CS	SB%	GDP	Avg	OBP	Slg
2006	Salt Lk*	AAA	56	208	52	11	5	17	(- | -)	124	35	45	39	15	0	88	4	0	4	3	1	.75	0	.250	.307	.596
2004	LAA	AL	16	40	9	1	0	3	(2 | 1)	19	5	6	5	3	0	17	0	0	0	1	0	1.00	0	.225	.279	.475
2005	LAA	AL	61	205	50	14	2	8	(6 | 2)	92	29	26	28	14	0	64	1	0	0	3	3	.50	5	.244	.295	.449
2006	LAA	AL	40	115	30	4	0	7	(3 | 4)	55	16	13	16	6	0	40	0	0	0	1	0	1.00	3	.261	.298	.478
	3 ML YEARS		117	360	89	19	2	18	(11 | 7)	166	50	45	49	23	0	121	1	0	0	5	3	.63	8	.247	.294	.461

Brian Meadows

Pitches: R **Bats:** R **Pos:** RP-53 **Ht:** 6'3" **Wt:** 240 **Born:** 11/21/1975 **Age:** 31

Year	Team	Lg	G	GS	CG	GF	IP	BFP	H	R	ER	HR	SH	SF	HB	TBB	IBB	SO	WP	Bk	W	L	Pct	ShO	Sv-Op Hld	ERC	ERA
1998	Fla	NL	31	31	1	0	174.1	772	222	106	101	20	14	4	3	46	3	88	5	1	11	13	.458	0	0-0	5.29	5.21
1999	Fla	NL	31	31	0	0	178.1	795	214	117	111	31	16	8	5	57	5	72	4	1	11	15	.423	0	0-0	5.51	5.60
2000	2 Tms		33	32	2	0	196.1	869	234	119	112	32	7	5	8	64	6	79	3	0	13	10	.565	0	0-0	5.52	5.13
2001	KC	AL	10	10	0	0	50.1	224	73	41	39	12	1	2	1	12	2	21	1	0	1	6	.143	0	0-0	7.47	6.97
2002	Pit	NL	11	11	0	0	62.2	259	62	29	27	7	2	0	1	14	8	31	2	0	1	6	.143	0	0-0	3.29	3.88
2003	Pit	NL	34	7	0	11	76.1	329	91	45	40	8	2	1	1	11	2	38	4	0	2	1	.667	0	1-1	4.12	4.72
2004	Pit	NL	68	0	0	15	78.0	323	76	40	31	7	6	5	0	19	7	46	5	0	2	4	.333	0	1-2 13	3.13	3.58
2005	Pit	NL	65	0	0	9	74.2	326	84	42	38	8	3	9	0	21	7	44	3	0	3	1	.750	0	2-4 15	4.58	4.58
2006	TB		53	0	0	27	69.2	311	90	43	40	14	1	6	0	15	4	35	2	0	3	6	.333	0	8-10 4	5.58	5.17
00	SD	NL	22	22	0	0	124.2	565	150	80	74	24	7	2	8	50	6	53	3	0	7	8	.467	0	0-0	6.23	5.34
00	KC	AL	11	10	2	0	71.2	304	84	39	38	8	0	3	0	14	0	26	0	0	6	2	.750	0	0-0	4.35	4.77
	9 ML YEARS		336	122	3	62	960.2	4208	1146	582	539	139	52	40	19	259	44	454	29	2	47	62	.431	0	10-15 29	4.99	5.05

Gil Meche

Pitches: R **Bats:** R **Pos:** SP-32 **Ht:** 6'3" **Wt:** 220 **Born:** 9/8/1978 **Age:** 28

Year	Team	Lg	G	GS	CG	GF	IP	BFP	H	R	ER	HR	SH	SF	HB	TBB	IBB	SO	WP	Bk	W	L	Pct	ShO	Sv-Op Hld	ERC	ERA
1999	Sea	AL	16	15	0	0	85.2	375	73	48	45	9	5	3	2	57	1	47	1	0	8	4	.667	0	0-0	4.47	4.73
2000	Sea	AL	15	15	1	0	85.2	363	75	37	36	7	5	4	1	40	0	60	2	0	4	4	.500	1	0-0	3.60	3.78
2003	Sea	AL	32	32	1	0	186.1	785	187	97	95	30	3	5	3	63	2	130	7	0	15	13	.536	0	0-0	4.39	4.59
2004	Sea	AL	23	23	1	0	127.2	565	139	73	71	21	1	5	3	47	0	99	4	0	7	7	.500	1	0-0	5.06	5.01
2005	Sea	AL	29	26	0	2	143.1	638	153	92	81	18	1	5	2	72	1	83	4	0	10	8	.556	0	0-0	5.15	5.09
2006	Sea	AL	32	32	1	0	186.2	811	183	106	93	24	3	2	8	84	2	156	4	2	11	8	.579	0	0-0	4.56	4.48
	6 ML YEARS		147	143	4	2	815.1	3537	810	453	421	109	18	22	21	363	6	575	22	2	55	44	.556	2	0-0	4.59	4.65

Brandon Medders

Pitches: R **Bats:** R **Pos:** RP-60 **Ht:** 6'1" **Wt:** 190 **Born:** 1/26/1980 **Age:** 27

Year	Team	Lg	G	GS	CG	GF	IP	BFP	H	R	ER	HR	SH	SF	HB	TBB	IBB	SO	WP	Bk	W	L	Pct	ShO	Sv-Op Hld	ERC	ERA
2001	Lancst	A+	31	0	0	15	41.0	164	26	8	6	1	2	1	2	15	3	53	2	1	2	3	.333	0	3- -	1.70	1.32
2002	Lancst	A+	43	12	0	25	98.2	443	111	73	59	9	2	3	8	36	1	104	10	3	4	8	.333	0	15- -	4.87	5.38
2003	ElPaso	AA	56	0	0	37	69.1	299	65	37	34	3	10	5	0	26	6	72	3	1	5	3	.625	0	7- -	3.04	4.41
2004	Tucsn	AAA	11	0	0	3	12.2	57	15	7	6	3	1	0	0	4	1	17	0	0	0	0	-	0	0- -	5.54	4.26

Year	Team	Lg	G	GS	CG	GF	IP	BFP	H	R	ER	HR	SH	SF	HB	TBB	IBB	SO	WP	Bk	W	L	Pct	ShO	Sv-Op	Hld	ERC	ERA
2005	Tucsn	AAA	36	0	0	24	36.1	158	31	11	10	3	2	1	1	18	3	44	6	0	3	2	.600	0	8- -	-	3.43	2.48
2006	Tucsn	AAA	5	0	0	1	6.0	22	4	2	1	0	1	0	0	1	0	9	0	1	1	0	1.000	0	0- -	-	1.29	1.50
2005	Ari	NL	27	0	0	10	30.1	122	21	6	6	2	0	2	1	11	0	31	1	0	4	1	.800	0	0-0	2	2.25	1.78
2006	Ari	NL	60	0	0	13	71.2	316	76	37	29	5	3	2	2	28	3	47	2	0	5	3	.625	0	0-1	10	4.17	3.64
2 ML YEARS			87	0	0	23	102.0	438	97	43	35	7	3	4	3	39	3	78	3	0	9	4	.692	0	0-1	12	3.56	3.09

Adam Melhuse

Bats: B Throws: R Pos: C-24; PH-19; DH-13; 3B-3; 1B-2; PR-2   Ht: 6'2" Wt: 210 Born: 3/27/1972 Age: 35

Year	Team	Lg	G	AB	H	2B	3B	HR	(Hm	Rd)	TB	R	RBI	RC	TBB	IBB	SO	HBP	SH	SF	SB	CS	SB%	GDP	Avg	OBP	Slg
2000	2 Tms	NL	24	24	4	0	1	0	(0	0)	6	3	4	2	3	0	6	0	0	0	0	0	-	1	.167	.259	.250
2001	Col	NL	40	71	13	2	0	1	(0	1)	18	5	8	4	6	0	18	0	0	2	1	0	1.00	1	.183	.241	.254
2003	Oak	AL	40	77	23	7	0	5	(2	3)	45	13	14	15	9	0	19	0	0	0	0	0	-	2	.299	.372	.584
2004	Oak	AL	69	214	55	11	0	11	(3	8)	99	23	31	21	16	1	47	0	1	0	0	1	.00	4	.257	.309	.463
2005	Oak	AL	39	97	24	7	0	2	(1	1)	37	11	12	12	5	0	28	0	0	0	0	0	-	2	.247	.284	.381
2006	Oak	AL	49	128	28	8	0	4	(2	2)	48	10	18	10	9	1	34	1	0	1	0	1	.00	6	.219	.273	.375
00	LAD	NL	1	1	0	0	0	0	(0	0)	0	0	0	0	0	0	1	0	0	0	0	0	-	0	.000	.000	.000
00	Col	NL	23	23	4	0	1	0	(0	0)	6	3	4	2	3	0	5	0	0	0	0	0	-	1	.174	.269	.261
6 ML YEARS			261	611	147	35	1	23	(8	15)	253	65	87	64	48	2	152	1	1	3	1	2	.33	16	.241	.296	.414

Kevin Mench

Bats: R Throws: R Pos: RF-57; LF-55; DH-14; PH-6; PR-1   Ht: 6'0" Wt: 225 Born: 1/7/1978 Age: 29

Year	Team	Lg	G	AB	H	2B	3B	HR	(Hm	Rd)	TB	R	RBI	RC	TBB	IBB	SO	HBP	SH	SF	SB	CS	SB%	GDP	Avg	OBP	Slg
2002	Tex	AL	110	366	95	20	2	15	(8	7)	164	52	60	59	31	0	83	8	2	5	1	1	.50	4	.260	.327	.448
2003	Tex	AL	38	125	40	12	0	2	(1	1)	58	15	11	23	10	0	17	3	0	1	1	1	.50	2	.320	.381	.464
2004	Tex	AL	125	438	122	30	3	26	(14	12)	236	69	71	72	33	2	63	6	0	4	0	0	-	6	.279	.335	.539
2005	Tex	AL	150	557	147	33	3	25	(13	12)	261	71	73	75	50	4	68	5	0	3	4	3	.57	6	.264	.328	.469
2006	2 Tms		127	446	120	24	2	13	(9	4)	187	45	68	57	27	5	59	4	0	5	1	0	1.00	8	.269	.313	.419
06	Tex	AL	87	320	91	18	1	12	(8	4)	147	36	50	48	23	5	42	4	0	2	1	0	1.00	4	.284	.338	.459
06	Mil	NL	40	126	29	6	1	1	(1	0)	40	9	18	9	4	0	17	0	0	3	0	0	-	4	.230	.248	.317
5 ML YEARS			550	1932	524	119	10	81	(45	36)	906	252	283	286	151	11	290	26	2	18	7	5	.58	26	.271	.330	.469

Kent Mercker

Pitches: L Bats: L Pos: RP-37   Ht: 6'2" Wt: 205 Born: 2/1/1968 Age: 39

Year	Team	Lg	G	GS	CG	GF	IP	BFP	H	R	ER	HR	SH	SF	HB	TBB	IBB	SO	WP	Bk	W	L	Pct	ShO	Sv-Op	Hld	ERC	ERA
1989	Atl	NL	2	1	0	1	4.1	26	8	6	6	0	0	0	0	6	0	4	0	0	0	0	-	0	0-0	0	13.19	12.46
1990	Atl	NL	36	0	0	28	48.1	211	43	22	17	6	1	2	2	24	3	39	2	0	4	7	.364	0	7-10	0	4.04	3.17
1991	Atl	NL	50	4	0	28	73.1	306	56	23	21	5	2	2	1	35	3	62	4	1	5	3	.625	0	6-8	3	2.88	2.58
1992	Atl	NL	53	0	0	18	68.1	289	51	27	26	4	4	1	3	35	1	49	6	0	3	2	.600	0	6-9	6	2.99	3.42
1993	Atl	NL	43	6	0	9	66.0	283	52	24	21	2	0	0	2	36	3	59	5	1	3	1	.750	0	0-3	3	3.02	2.86
1994	Atl	NL	20	17	2	0	112.1	461	90	46	43	16	4	3	0	45	3	111	4	1	9	4	.692	1	0-0	0	3.27	3.45
1995	Atl	NL	29	26	0	1	143.0	622	140	73	66	16	8	7	3	61	2	102	6	2	7	8	.467	0	0-0	0	4.19	4.15
1996	2 Tms	AL	24	12	0	2	69.2	329	83	60	54	13	6	3	3	38	2	29	3	1	4	6	.400	0	0-0	2	6.56	6.98
1997	Cin	NL	28	25	0	0	144.2	616	135	65	63	16	8	4	2	62	6	75	2	1	8	11	.421	0	0-0	0	3.91	3.92
1998	StL	NL	30	29	0	1	161.2	716	199	99	91	11	10	9	3	53	4	72	6	4	11	11	.500	0	0-0	0	4.96	5.07
1999	2 Tms	NL	30	23	0	2	129.1	589	148	85	69	16	8	4	3	64	3	81	3	1	8	5	.615	0	0-0	0	5.54	4.80
2000	LAA	AL	21	7	0	2	48.1	225	57	35	35	12	3	1	2	29	3	30	2	0	1	3	.250	0	0-0	1	7.35	6.52
2002	Col	NL	58	0	0	8	44.0	208	55	33	30	12	0	0	2	22	2	37	1	0	3	1	.750	0	0-3	9	7.45	6.14
2003	2 Tms	NL	67	0	0	15	55.1	242	46	16	12	6	6	1	0	32	4	48	4	1	0	2	.000	0	1-5	11	3.72	1.95
2004	ChC	NL	71	0	0	7	53.0	223	39	15	15	4	0	3	3	27	2	51	4	1	3	1	.750	0	0-3	16	3.07	2.55
2005	Cin	NL	78	0	0	23	61.2	265	64	27	25	8	4	2	3	19	4	45	1	0	3	1	.750	0	4-7	20	4.23	3.65
2006	Cin	NL	37	0	0	7	28.1	123	28	15	13	6	3	1	0	11	1	17	1	1	1	1	.500	0	1-3	6	4.63	4.13
96	Bal	AL	14	12	0	0	58.0	283	73	56	50	12	3	4	3	35	1	22	3	1	3	6	.333	0	0-0	0	7.45	7.76
96	Cle	AL	10	0	0	2	11.2	46	10	4	4	1	0	2	0	3	1	7	0	0	1	0	1.000	0	0-0	2	2.65	3.09
99	StL	NL	25	18	0	2	103.2	476	125	73	59	16	8	3	2	51	3	64	3	1	6	5	.545	0	0-0	0	6.15	5.12
99	Bos	AL	5	5	0	0	25.2	113	23	12	10	0	0	1	1	13	0	17	0	0	2	0	1.000	0	0-0	0	3.29	3.51
03	Cin	NL	49	0	0	8	38.1	169	31	10	10	5	6	0	0	25	2	41	2	1	0	2	.000	0	0-3	10	4.09	2.35
03	Atl	NL	18	0	0	7	17.0	73	15	3	2	1	0	1	0	7	2	7	2	0	0	0	-	0	1-2	1	2.95	1.06
17 ML YEARS			677	150	2	152	1311.2	5734	1294	671	607	153	64	46	32	599	46	911	54	15	73	67	.521	1	25-51	78	4.39	4.16

Cla Meredith

Pitches: R Bats: R Pos: RP-45   Ht: 6'0" Wt: 180 Born: 6/4/1983 Age: 24

Year	Team	Lg	G	GS	CG	GF	IP	BFP	H	R	ER	HR	SH	SF	HB	TBB	IBB	SO	WP	Bk	W	L	Pct	ShO	Sv-Op	Hld	ERC	ERA
2004	Augsta	A	13	0	0	10	15.1	57	8	0	0	0	0	0	2	3	0	18	0	0	1	0	1.000	0	6- -	-	1.18	0.00
2004	Srsota	A+	16	0	0	16	16.1	68	15	4	4	0	0	1	0	3	0	16	0	0	0	2	.000	0	12- -	-	2.36	2.20
2005	Wilmg	A+	1	0	0	1	1.0	4	1	0	0	0	0	0	0	0	0	2	0	0	0	0	-	0	0- -	-	1.95	0.00
2005	Portlnd	AA	12	0	0	11	15.0	53	5	0	0	0	1	0	1	3	1	12	0	1	1	0	1.000	0	9- -	-	0.56	0.00
2005	Pwtckt	AAA	40	0	0	25	48.1	220	63	30	30	6	1	0	1	12	2	42	0	0	2	5	.286	0	10- -	-	5.31	5.59
2006	Pwtckt	AAA	8	0	0	2	13.2	60	16	9	8	1	1	1	0	5	0	14	0	0	0	0	-	0	0- -	-	4.77	5.27
2006	Portlnd	AAA	24	0	0	8	32.1	123	26	5	5	2	2	0	0	4	1	24	0	0	3	0	1.000	0	2- -	-	1.86	1.39
2005	Bos	AL	3	0	0	0	2.1	18	6	7	7	1	0	0	1	4	0	0	1	0	0	0	-	0	0-0	0	27.60	27.00
2006	SD	NL	45	0	0	11	50.2	185	30	6	6	3	1	0	2	6	3	37	0	2	5	1	.833	0	0-2	16	1.19	1.07
2 ML YEARS			48	0	0	11	53.0	203	36	13	13	4	1	0	3	10	3	37	1	2	5	1	.833	0	0-2	16	1.72	2.21

Lou Merloni

Bats: R **Throws:** R **Pos:** 2B-3; 3B-3; SS-3; PH-1   **Ht:** 5'10" **Wt:** 200 **Born:** 4/6/1971 **Age:** 36

									BATTING												BASERUNNING				AVERAGES		
Year	Team	Lg	G	AB	H	2B	3B	HR	(Hm	Rd)	TB	R	RBI	RC	TBB	IBB	SO	HBP	SH	SF	SB	CS	SB%	GDP	Avg	OBP	Slg
2006	Buffalo*	AAA	91	330	94	22	0	7	(-	-)	137	33	38	51	29	2	49	11	3	1	0	2	.00	9	.285	.361	.415
1998	Bos	AL	39	96	27	6	0	1	(1	0)	36	10	15	13	7	1	20	2	1	0	1	0	1.00	1	.281	.343	.375
1999	Bos	AL	43	126	32	7	0	1	(0	1)	42	18	13	12	8	0	16	2	3	1	0	0	-	6	.254	.307	.333
2000	Bos	AL	40	128	41	11	2	0	(0	0)	56	10	18	17	4	1	22	1	4	2	1	0	1.00	8	.320	.341	.438
2001	Bos	AL	52	146	39	10	0	3	(0	3)	58	21	13	16	6	0	31	3	2	2	2	1	.67	5	.267	.306	.397
2002	Bos	AL	84	194	48	12	2	4	(1	3)	76	28	18	26	20	0	35	5	2	1	1	2	.33	4	.247	.332	.392
2003	2 Tms		80	181	48	8	2	1	(1	0)	63	24	18	22	26	2	41	1	2	3	2	3	.40	3	.265	.355	.348
2004	Cle	AL	71	190	55	12	1	4	(1	3)	81	25	28	28	14	1	41	3	4	3	1	2	.33	9	.289	.343	.426
2005	LAA	AL	5	5	0	0	0	0	(0	0)	0	1	1	0	1	0	2	0	0	1	0	0	-	0	.000	.143	.000
2006	Cle	AL	9	19	4	1	0	0	(0	0)	5	1	1	1	2	0	5	0	2	0	1	0	1.00	1	.211	.286	.263
03	SD	NL	65	151	41	7	2	1	(1	0)	55	20	17	19	22	2	33	1	2	3	2	3	.40	3	.272	.362	.364
03	Bos	AL	15	30	7	1	0	0	(0	0)	8	4	1	3	4	0	8	0	0	0	0	0	-	0	.233	.324	.267
9 ML YEARS			423	1085	294	67	7	14	(4	10)	417	138	125	135	88	5	213	17	20	13	9	8	.53	38	.271	.332	.384

Jose Mesa

Pitches: R **Bats:** R **Pos:** RP-79   **Ht:** 6'3" **Wt:** 235 **Born:** 5/22/1966 **Age:** 41

			HOW MUCH HE PITCHED						WHAT HE GAVE UP											THE RESULTS							
Year	Team	Lg	G	GS	CG	GF	IP	BFP	H	R	ER	HR	SH	SF	HB	TBB	IBB	SO	WP	Bk	W	L	Pct	ShO	Sv-Op	Hld	ERC	ERA
1987	Bal	AL	6	5	0	0	31.1	143	38	23	21	7	0	0	0	15	0	17	4	0	1	3	.250	0	0-0	1	6.67	6.03
1990	Bal	AL	7	7	0	0	46.2	202	37	20	20	2	2	2	1	27	2	24	1	1	3	2	.600	0	0-0	0	3.21	3.86
1991	Bal	AL	23	23	2	0	123.2	566	151	86	82	11	5	4	3	62	2	64	3	0	6	11	.353	1	0-0	0	5.85	5.97
1992	2 Tms	AL	28	27	1	1	160.2	700	169	86	82	14	2	5	4	70	1	62	2	0	7	12	.368	1	0-0	0	4.57	4.59
1993	Cle	AL	34	33	3	0	208.2	897	232	122	114	21	9	9	7	62	2	118	8	2	10	12	.455	0	0-0	0	4.48	4.92
1994	Cle	AL	51	0	0	22	73.0	315	71	33	31	3	3	4	3	26	7	63	3	0	7	5	.583	0	2-6	8	3.31	3.82
1995	Cle	AL	62	0	0	57	64.0	250	49	9	8	3	4	2	0	17	2	58	5	0	3	0	1.000	0	46-48	0	2.06	1.13
1996	Cle	AL	69	0	0	60	72.1	304	69	32	30	6	2	2	3	28	4	64	4	0	2	7	.222	0	39-44	0	3.81	3.73
1997	Cle	AL	66	0	0	38	82.1	356	83	28	22	7	2	2	3	28	3	69	1	0	4	4	.500	0	16-21	9	3.83	2.40
1998	2 Tms	AL	76	0	0	36	84.2	383	91	50	43	8	6	2	4	38	5	63	10	0	8	7	.533	0	1-4	13	4.68	4.57
1999	Sea	AL	68	0	0	60	68.2	325	84	42	38	11	2	4	4	40	4	42	7	0	3	6	.333	0	33-38	1	6.83	4.98
2000	Sea	AL	66	0	0	29	80.2	372	89	48	48	11	2	6	5	41	0	84	3	0	4	6	.400	0	1-3	11	5.60	5.36
2001	Phi	NL	71	0	0	59	69.1	291	65	26	18	4	2	3	2	20	2	59	2	1	3	3	.500	0	42-46	1	3.07	2.34
2002	Phi	NL	74	0	0	64	75.2	331	65	26	25	5	6	1	4	39	7	64	9	0	4	6	.400	0	45-54	0	3.51	2.97
2003	Phi	NL	61	0	0	47	58.0	273	71	44	42	7	1	0	1	31	2	45	1	0	5	7	.417	0	24-28	2	6.07	6.52
2004	Pit	NL	70	0	0	65	69.1	295	78	26	25	6	4	2	1	20	3	37	1	0	5	2	.714	0	43-48	0	4.31	3.25
2005	Pit	NL	55	0	0	48	56.2	257	61	30	30	7	8	6	3	26	3	37	2	0	2	8	.200	0	27-34	1	4.99	4.76
2006	Col	NL	79	0	0	26	72.1	315	73	32	31	9	2	2	5	36	6	39	4	1	1	5	.167	0	1-8	19	4.98	3.86
92	Bal	AL	13	12	0	1	67.2	300	77	41	39	9	0	3	2	27	1	22	2	0	3	8	.273	0	0-0	0	5.25	5.19
92	Cle	AL	15	15	1	0	93.0	400	92	45	43	5	2	2	2	43	0	40	0	0	4	4	.500	1	0-0	0	4.09	4.16
98	Cle	AL	44	0	0	18	54.0	244	61	36	31	7	2	2	4	20	3	35	2	0	3	4	.429	0	1-3	7	5.07	5.17
98	SF	NL	32	0	0	18	30.2	139	30	14	12	1	4	0	0	18	2	28	8	0	5	3	.625	0	0-1	6	3.99	3.52
18 ML YEARS			966	95	6	612	1498.0	6575	1576	763	710	142	62	56	53	626	55	1009	72	5	78	106	.424	2	320-382	66	4.50	4.27

Randy Messenger

Pitches: R **Bats:** R **Pos:** RP-59   **Ht:** 6'6" **Wt:** 245 **Born:** 8/13/1981 **Age:** 25

			HOW MUCH HE PITCHED						WHAT HE GAVE UP											THE RESULTS							
Year	Team	Lg	G	GS	CG	GF	IP	BFP	H	R	ER	HR	SH	SF	HB	TBB	IBB	SO	WP	Bk	W	L	Pct	ShO	Sv-Op	Hld	ERC	ERA
1999	Mrlns	R	13	2	0	6	26.1	126	28	25	22	1	0	1	3	19	0	23	1	0	0	3	.000	0	2- -	-	5.68	7.52
2000	Mrlns	R	12	12	0	0	59.2	267	66	37	32	6	1	1	3	22	0	29	7	2	2	2	.500	0	0- -	-	4.70	4.83
2001	BrvdCt	A+	18	18	0	0	92.2	412	99	55	42	3	1	3	5	35	0	42	3	0	7	4	.636	0	0- -	-	4.04	4.08
2001	Kane	A	14	0	0	7	18.1	82	22	13	8	0	3	2	1	5	0	14	0	0	2	1	.667	0	0- -	-	4.39	3.93
2002	Jupiter	A+	28	27	1	0	156.2	706	178	94	76	4	5	4	7	58	0	96	4	2	11	8	.579	0	0- -	-	4.28	4.37
2003	Carlina	AA	29	23	0	3	113.2	529	137	83	69	7	2	0	3	51	1	78	9	0	5	7	.417	0	0- -	-	5.15	5.46
2004	Carlina	AA	58	0	0	45	69.2	305	67	21	20	4	1	2	0	29	3	71	4	0	6	3	.667	0	21- -	-	3.47	2.58
2005	Albq	AAA	39	0	0	15	48.2	209	46	25	21	5	1	1	2	17	1	35	1	0	4	2	.667	0	7- -	-	3.68	3.88
2006	Jupiter	A+	1	0	0	0	1.0	4	1	0	0	0	0	0	0	0	0	1	0	0	0	0	-	0	0- -	-	1.95	0.00
2006	Albq	AAA	4	0	0	1	3.0	12	1	3	3	0	1	0	0	3	0	1	0	0	0	0	-	0	0- -	-	2.24	9.00
2005	Fla	NL	29	0	0	8	37.0	178	39	22	22	5	2	3	0	30	7	29	1	0	0	0	-	0	0-0	2	5.91	5.35
2006	Fla	NL	59	0	0	10	60.1	275	72	42	38	8	5	2	1	24	2	45	3	0	2	7	.222	0	0-1	9	5.38	5.67
2 ML YEARS			88	0	0	18	97.1	453	111	64	60	13	7	5	1	54	9	74	4	0	2	7	.222	0	0-1	11	5.59	5.55

Drew Meyer

Bats: L **Throws:** R **Pos:** 2B-3; SS-1; RF-1; PH-1   **Ht:** 5'10" **Wt:** 200 **Born:** 8/29/1981 **Age:** 25

									BATTING												BASERUNNING				AVERAGES		
Year	Team	Lg	G	AB	H	2B	3B	HR	(Hm	Rd)	TB	R	RBI	RC	TBB	IBB	SO	HBP	SH	SF	SB	CS	SB%	GDP	Avg	OBP	Slg
2002	Savann	A	54	214	52	5	4	1	(-	-)	68	15	24	18	10	0	53	0	11	2	7	6	.54	2	.243	.274	.318
2002	Tulsa	AA	4	14	3	0	0	0	(-	-)	3	0	0	0	1	0	5	0	0	0	0	0	-	0	.214	.267	.214
2003	Stcktn	A+	94	398	112	16	9	5	(-	-)	161	59	53	56	32	1	92	0	9	7	24	10	.71	6	.281	.330	.405
2003	Frisco	AA	26	98	31	1	1	0	(-	-)	34	14	6	15	11	1	23	0	2	0	9	1	.90	1	.316	.385	.347
2004	Frisco	AA	59	232	56	6	2	2	(-	-)	72	35	13	23	22	1	43	1	1	1	4	2	.67	2	.241	.309	.310
2004	DBcks	R	15	62	24	2	0	0	(-	-)	26	15	5	11	3	0	8	0	0	0	4	1	.80	2	.387	.415	.419
2005	Frisco	AA	83	321	103	14	4	3	(-	-)	134	49	45	53	26	3	55	3	3	5	12	2	.86	3	.321	.372	.417
2005	Okla	AAA	42	178	44	11	4	0	(-	-)	63	25	19	19	14	0	43	0	2	1	5	2	.71	6	.247	.301	.354
2006	Okla	AAA	95	364	83	14	4	2	(-	-)	111	37	28	29	27	0	91	0	8	4	9	11	.45	10	.228	.278	.305
2006	Tex	AL	5	14	3	0	0	0	(0	0)	3	1	0	1	0	0	8	0	1	0	0	0	-	0	.214	.214	.214

Dan Miceli

Pitches: R Bats: R Pos: RP-33   Ht: 6'0" Wt: 225 Born: 9/9/1970 Age: 36

				HOW MUCH HE PITCHED						WHAT HE GAVE UP												THE RESULTS						
Year	Team	Lg	G	GS	CG	GF	IP	BFP	H	R	ER	HR	SH	SF	HB	TBB	IBB	SO	WP	Bk	W	L	Pct	ShO	Sv-Op	Hld	ERC	ERA
2006	Mont*	AA	4	0	0	1	5.0	18	3	0	0	0	0	0	0	1	0	5	0	0	0	0	-	0	1--	-	1.17	0.00
1993	Pit	NL	9	0	0	1	5.1	25	6	3	3	0	0	0	0	3	0	4	0	1	0	0	-	0	0-0	0	4.53	5.06
1994	Pit	NL	28	0	0	9	27.1	121	28	19	18	5	1	2	2	11	2	27	2	0	2	1	.667	0	2-3	4	4.98	5.93
1995	Pit	NL	58	0	0	51	58.0	264	61	30	30	7	2	4	4	28	5	56	4	0	4	4	.500	0	21-27	2	4.93	4.66
1996	Pit	NL	44	9	0	17	85.2	398	99	65	55	15	3	7	3	45	5	66	9	0	2	10	.167	0	1-1	4	6.09	5.78
1997	Det	AL	71	0	0	24	82.2	357	77	49	46	13	5	3	1	38	4	79	3	0	3	2	.600	0	3-8	11	4.30	5.01
1998	SD	NL	67	0	0	18	72.2	302	64	28	26	6	3	2	2	27	4	70	5	1	10	5	.667	0	2-8	20	3.20	3.22
1999	SD	NL	66	0	0	28	68.2	296	67	39	34	7	4	2	2	36	5	59	2	0	4	5	.444	0	2-4	9	4.57	4.46
2000	Fla	NL	45	0	0	9	48.2	207	45	23	23	4	1	1	1	18	2	40	3	0	6	4	.600	0	0-3	11	3.42	4.25
2001	2 Tms	NL	51	0	0	15	45.0	199	47	29	24	7	2	2	0	16	2	48	4	0	2	5	.286	0	1-4	8	4.34	4.80
2002	Tex	AL	9	0	0	5	8.1	42	13	8	8	1	0	0	0	3	0	5	0	1	0	2	.000	0	0-1	0	7.11	8.64
2003	4 Tms		57	0	0	16	70.1	294	59	27	25	13	3	0	2	25	3	58	4	1	2	4	.333	0	1-2	5	3.60	3.20
2004	Hou	NL	74	0	0	15	77.2	336	74	34	31	10	5	3	2	27	12	83	4	0	6	6	.500	0	2-8	24	3.58	3.59
2005	Col	NL	19	0	0	3	18.1	86	19	12	12	1	2	0	1	13	0	19	0	0	1	2	.333	0	0-2	5	5.37	5.89
2006	TB	AL	33	0	0	14	32.0	142	25	17	14	4	3	3	1	20	3	18	3	0	1	2	.333	0	4-7	6	3.79	3.94
01	Fla	NL	29	0	0	9	24.2	114	29	21	19	5	1	1	0	11	2	31	3	0	0	5	.000	0	0-3	8	5.80	6.93
01	Col	NL	22	0	0	6	20.1	85	18	8	5	2	1	1	0	5	0	17	1	0	2	0	1.000	0	1-1	0	2.77	2.21
03	Col	NL	14	0	0	1	20.2	95	24	13	13	7	1	0	1	9	1	18	1	0	0	2	.000	0	0-0	1	7.07	5.66
03	Cle	AL	13	0	0	4	15.0	61	9	4	2	1	0	0	0	6	1	19	1	0	1	1	.500	0	0-1	0	1.70	1.20
03	NYY	AL	7	0	0	3	4.2	22	4	3	3	2	0	0	0	3	0	1	0	0	0	0	-	0	1-1	1	6.21	5.79
03	Hou	NL	23	0	0	8	30.0	116	22	7	7	3	2	0	1	7	1	20	2	1	1	1	.500	0	0-0	3	2.22	2.10
	14 ML YEARS		631	9	0	225	700.2	3069	684	383	349	93	34	29	20	310	47	632	43	4	43	52	.453	0	39-78	109	4.32	4.48

Jason Michaels

Bats: R Throws: R Pos: LF-117; PH-4; DH-2; RF-1; PR-1   Ht: 6'0" Wt: 205 Born: 5/4/1976 Age: 31

							BATTING														BASERUNNING				AVERAGES		
Year	Team	Lg	G	AB	H	2B	3B	HR	(Hm	Rd)	TB	R	RBI	RC	TBB	IBB	SO	HBP	SH	SF	SB	CS	SB%	GDP	Avg	OBP	Slg
2006	Buffalo*	AAA	2	7	3	0	0	1	(-	-)	6	1	1	2	0	0	0	0	0	0	0	0	-	1	.429	.429	.857
2001	Phi	NL	6	6	1	0	0	0	(0	0)	1	0	1	0	0	0	2	0	0	0	0	0	-	0	.167	.167	.167
2002	Phi	NL	81	105	28	10	3	2	(0	2)	50	16	11	14	13	1	33	1	0	2	1	1	.50	1	.267	.347	.476
2003	Phi	NL	76	109	36	11	0	5	(1	4)	62	20	17	19	15	1	22	1	0	0	0	0	-	3	.330	.416	.569
2004	Phi	NL	115	299	82	12	0	10	(5	5)	124	44	40	47	42	1	80	2	0	3	2	2	.50	3	.274	.364	.415
2005	Phi	NL	105	289	88	16	2	4	(1	3)	120	54	31	47	44	1	45	4	2	4	3	3	.50	3	.304	.399	.415
2006	Cle	AL	123	494	132	32	1	9	(4	5)	193	77	55	62	43	0	101	3	2	6	9	5	.64	6	.267	.326	.391
	6 ML YEARS		506	1302	367	81	6	30	(11	19)	550	211	155	189	157	4	283	11	4	15	15	11	.58	16	.282	.360	.422

Chris Michalak

Pitches: L Bats: L Pos: SP-6; RP-2   Ht: 6'2" Wt: 195 Born: 1/4/1971 Age: 36

				HOW MUCH HE PITCHED						WHAT HE GAVE UP												THE RESULTS						
Year	Team	Lg	G	GS	CG	GF	IP	BFP	H	R	ER	HR	SH	SF	HB	TBB	IBB	SO	WP	Bk	W	L	Pct	ShO	Sv-Op	Hld	ERC	ERA
2006	Lsvlle*	AAA	23	22	0	0	132.1	552	142	56	44	17	4	0	9	28	0	61	2	3	9	5	.643	0	0--	-	4.31	2.99
1998	Ari	NL	5	0	0	2	5.1	29	9	7	7	1	0	1	0	4	0	5	0	0	0	0	-	0	0-0	0	10.59	11.81
2001	2 Tms	AL	35	18	0	4	136.2	610	157	74	67	19	3	4	13	55	5	67	1	6	8	9	.471	0	1-2	0	5.68	4.41
2002	Tex	AL	13	0	0	4	14.1	71	20	7	7	1	0	1	1	10	2	5	1	0	0	2	.000	0	0-0	2	7.62	4.40
2006	Cin	NL	8	6	0	0	35.0	162	42	21	19	6	5	0	3	16	2	10	1	1	2	4	.333	0	0-0	0	6.32	4.89
01	Tor	AL	24	18	0	2	115.0	517	133	66	59	14	3	4	12	49	5	57	0	5	6	7	.462	0	0-0	0	5.73	4.62
01	Tex	AL	11	0	0	2	21.2	93	24	8	8	5	0	0	1	6	0	10	1	1	2	2	.500	0	1-2	0	5.39	3.32
	4 ML YEARS		61	24	0	10	191.1	872	228	109	100	27	8	6	17	85	9	87	3	7	10	15	.400	0	1-2	2	6.07	4.70

Doug Mientkiewicz

Bats: L Throws: R Pos: 1B-90; PH-3   Ht: 6'2" Wt: 205 Born: 6/19/1974 Age: 33

							BATTING														BASERUNNING				AVERAGES		
Year	Team	Lg	G	AB	H	2B	3B	HR	(Hm	Rd)	TB	R	RBI	RC	TBB	IBB	SO	HBP	SH	SF	SB	CS	SB%	GDP	Avg	OBP	Slg
1998	Min	AL	8	25	5	1	0	0	(0	0)	6	1	2	2	4	0	3	0	0	0	1	1	.50	0	.200	.310	.240
1999	Min	AL	118	327	75	21	3	2	(0	2)	108	34	32	34	43	3	51	4	3	2	1	1	.50	13	.229	.324	.330
2000	Min	AL	3	14	6	0	0	0	(0	0)	6	0	4	2	0	0	0	0	0	1	0	0	-	1	.429	.400	.429
2001	Min	AL	151	543	166	39	1	15	(11	4)	252	77	74	96	67	6	92	9	0	7	2	6	.25	10	.306	.387	.464
2002	Min	AL	143	467	122	29	1	10	(6	4)	183	60	64	76	74	8	69	6	0	7	1	2	.33	7	.261	.365	.392
2003	Min	AL	142	487	146	38	1	11	(6	5)	219	67	65	89	74	4	55	5	2	6	4	1	.80	9	.300	.393	.450
2004	2 Tms	AL	127	391	93	24	1	6	(1	5)	137	47	35	46	48	2	56	4	2	2	2	3	.40	12	.238	.326	.350
2005	NYM	NL	87	275	66	13	0	11	(3	8)	112	36	29	28	32	7	39	2	2	2	0	1	.00	11	.240	.322	.407
2006	KC	AL	91	314	89	24	2	4	(1	3)	129	37	43	48	35	1	50	5	1	5	3	0	1.00	6	.283	.359	.411
04	Min	AL	78	284	70	18	0	5	(1	4)	103	34	25	34	38	2	38	3	2	1	2	2	.50	9	.246	.340	.363
04	Bos	AL	49	107	23	6	1	1	(0	1)	34	13	10	12	10	0	18	1	0	1	0	1	.00	3	.215	.286	.318
	9 ML YEARS		870	2843	768	189	9	59	(28	31)	1152	359	348	421	377	31	415	35	10	32	14	15	.48	69	.270	.359	.405

Aaron Miles

Bats: B Throws: R Pos: 2B-88; SS-39; PH-19; 3B-1   Ht: 5'8" Wt: 175 Born: 12/15/1976 Age: 30

							BATTING														BASERUNNING				AVERAGES		
Year	Team	Lg	G	AB	H	2B	3B	HR	(Hm	Rd)	TB	R	RBI	RC	TBB	IBB	SO	HBP	SH	SF	SB	CS	SB%	GDP	Avg	OBP	Slg
2003	CWS	AL	8	12	4	3	0	0	(0	0)	7	3	2	3	0	0	0	0	0	0	0	0	-	0	.333	.333	.583
2004	Col	NL	134	522	153	15	3	6	(4	2)	192	75	47	70	29	0	53	2	7	6	12	7	.63	12	.293	.329	.368

Year	Team	Lg	G	AB	H	2B	3B	HR	Hm	Rd	TB	R	RBI	RC	TBB	IBB	SO	HBP	SH	SF	SB	CS	SB%	GDP	Avg	OBP	Slg
2005	Col	NL	99	324	91	12	3	2	(0	2)	115	37	28	42	8	1	38	4	10	1	4	2	.67	6	.281	.306	.355
2006	StL	NL	135	426	112	20	5	2	(1	1)	148	48	30	49	38	9	42	2	2	3	2	1	.67	8	.263	.324	.347
4 ML YEARS			376	1284	360	50	11	10	(5	5)	462	163	107	164	75	10	133	8	19	10	18	10	.64	26	.280	.322	.360

Kevin Millar

Bats: R Throws: R Pos: 1B-98; DH-29; PH-7   Ht: 6'0" Wt: 215 Born: 9/24/1971 Age: 35

Year	Team	Lg	G	AB	H	2B	3B	HR	Hm	Rd	TB	R	RBI	RC	TBB	IBB	SO	HBP	SH	SF	SB	CS	SB%	GDP	Avg	OBP	Slg
1998	Fla	NL	2	2	1	0	0	0	(0	0)	1	1	0	1	1	0	0	0	0	0	0	0	-	0	.500	.667	.500
1999	Fla	NL	105	351	100	17	4	9	(3	6)	152	48	67	57	40	2	64	7	1	8	1	0	1.00	8	.285	.362	.433
2000	Fla	NL	123	259	67	14	3	14	(6	8)	129	36	42	47	36	0	47	8	0	2	0	0	-	5	.259	.364	.498
2001	Fla	NL	144	449	141	39	5	20	(13	7)	250	62	85	89	39	2	70	5	0	2	0	0	-	8	.314	.374	.557
2002	Fla	NL	126	438	134	41	0	16	(11	5)	223	58	57	63	40	0	74	5	0	6	0	2	.00	15	.306	.366	.509
2003	Bos	AL	148	544	150	30	1	25	(10	15)	257	83	96	87	60	5	108	5	0	9	3	2	.60	14	.276	.348	.472
2004	Bos	AL	150	508	151	36	0	18	(12	6)	241	74	74	90	57	0	91	17	0	6	1	1	.50	16	.297	.383	.474
2005	Bos	AL	134	449	122	28	1	9	(8	1)	179	57	50	58	54	0	74	8	0	8	1	1	.00	12	.272	.355	.399
2006	Bal	AL	132	430	117	26	0	15	(7	8)	188	64	64	67	59	3	74	12	0	2	1	1	.50	14	.272	.374	.437
9 ML YEARS			1064	3430	983	231	14	126	(70	56)	1620	483	535	559	386	12	602	67	1	43	6	7	.46	91	.287	.366	.472

Lastings Milledge

Bats: R Throws: R Pos: LF-26; RF-24; PH-7; PR-1   Ht: 6'1" Wt: 185 Born: 4/5/1985 Age: 22

Year	Team	Lg	G	AB	H	2B	3B	HR	Hm	Rd	TB	R	RBI	RC	TBB	IBB	SO	HBP	SH	SF	SB	CS	SB%	GDP	Avg	OBP	Slg
2003	Kngspt	R+	7	26	6	2	0	0	(-	-)	8	4	2	4	3	0	4	3	0	1	5	1	.83	0	.231	.364	.308
2004	StLuci	A+	22	81	19	6	2	2	(-	-)	35	6	8	11	9	0	21	1	2	0	3	2	.60	3	.235	.319	.432
2004	CptCty	A	65	261	88	22	1	13	(-	-)	151	66	58	60	17	1	53	12	1	3	23	6	.79	3	.337	.399	.579
2005	StLuci	A+	62	232	70	15	0	4	(-	-)	97	48	22	38	19	1	41	13	4	1	18	13	.58	5	.302	.385	.418
2005	Bnghtn	AA	48	193	65	17	0	4	(-	-)	94	33	24	36	14	1	47	4	2	1	11	5	.69	1	.337	.392	.487
2006	Norfolk	AAA	84	307	85	21	4	7	(-	-)	135	52	36	55	43	1	67	14	1	2	13	10	.57	1	.277	.388	.440
2006	NYM	NL	56	166	40	7	2	4	(2	2)	63	14	22	21	12	4	39	5	1	1	1	2	.33	4	.241	.310	.380

Andrew Miller

Pitches: L Bats: L Pos: RP-8   Ht: 6'6" Wt: 210 Born: 5/21/1985 Age: 22

			HOW MUCH HE PITCHED					WHAT HE GAVE UP												THE RESULTS							
Year	Team	Lg	G	GS	CG	GF	IP	BFP	H	R	ER	HR	SH	SF	HB	TBB	IBB	SO	WP	Bk	W	L	Pct	ShO	Sv-Op	Hld	ERC	ERA
2006	Lkland	A+	3	0	0	0	5.0	19	2	0	0	0	0	0	1	1	0	9	1	0	0	0	-	0	0--	-	0.95	0.00
2006	Det	AL	8	0	0	3	10.1	51	8	9	7	0	0	0	2	10	0	6	1	0	0	1	.000	0	0-0	1	4.79	6.10

Corky Miller

Bats: R Throws: R Pos: C-1   Ht: 6'1" Wt: 245 Born: 3/18/1976 Age: 31

Year	Team	Lg	G	AB	H	2B	3B	HR	Hm	Rd	TB	R	RBI	RC	TBB	IBB	SO	HBP	SH	SF	SB	CS	SB%	GDP	Avg	OBP	Slg
2006	Tacom*	AAA	2	6	2	0	0	0	(-	-)	2	1	0	0	1	0	1	0	0	0	0	0	-	0	.333	.429	.333
2006	Pwtckt*	AAA	63	198	51	11	0	13	(-	-)	101	29	36	36	22	1	43	6	0	4	0	0	-	6	.258	.343	.510
2001	Cin	NL	17	49	9	2	0	3	(1	2)	20	5	7	6	4	0	16	2	0	2	1	0	1.00	1	.184	.263	.408
2002	Cin	NL	39	114	29	10	0	3	(2	1)	48	9	15	15	9	2	20	4	1	1	0	0	-	7	.254	.328	.421
2003	Cin	NL	14	30	8	0	0	0	(0	0)	8	4	1	5	5	0	7	2	0	1	0	0	-	1	.267	.395	.267
2004	Cin	NL	13	39	1	0	0	0	(0	0)	1	2	3	0	6	0	12	3	0	1	0	0	-	3	.026	.204	.026
2005	Min	AL	5	12	0	0	0	0	(0	0)	0	0	0	0	0	0	2	0	0	0	0	0	-	0	.000	.000	.000
2006	Bos	AL	1	4	0	0	0	0	(0	0)	0	0	0	0	0	0	1	0	0	0	0	0	-	0	.000	.000	.000
6 ML YEARS			89	248	47	12	0	6	(3	3)	77	20	26	26	24	2	58	11	1	5	1	0	1.00	12	.190	.285	.310

Damian Miller

Bats: R Throws: R Pos: C-98; PH-3   Ht: 6'3" Wt: 220 Born: 10/13/1969 Age: 37

Year	Team	Lg	G	AB	H	2B	3B	HR	Hm	Rd	TB	R	RBI	RC	TBB	IBB	SO	HBP	SH	SF	SB	CS	SB%	GDP	Avg	OBP	Slg
1997	Min	AL	25	66	18	1	0	2	(1	1)	25	5	13	7	2	0	12	0	0	3	0	0	-	2	.273	.282	.379
1998	Ari	NL	57	168	48	14	2	3	(2	1)	75	17	14	25	11	2	43	2	2	0	1	0	1.00	2	.286	.337	.446
1999	Ari	NL	86	296	80	19	0	11	(3	8)	132	35	47	40	19	3	78	2	0	3	0	0	-	6	.270	.316	.446
2000	Ari	NL	100	324	89	24	0	10	(6	4)	143	43	44	49	36	4	74	1	1	2	2	2	.50	6	.275	.347	.441
2001	Ari	NL	123	380	103	19	0	13	(9	4)	161	45	47	52	35	9	80	4	4	2	0	1	.00	9	.271	.337	.424
2002	Ari	NL	101	297	74	22	0	11	(4	7)	129	40	42	35	38	5	88	3	2	0	0	0	-	14	.249	.340	.434
2003	ChC	NL	114	352	82	19	1	9	(6	3)	130	34	36	36	39	6	91	1	7	1	1	0	1.00	15	.233	.310	.369
2004	Oak	AL	110	397	108	25	0	9	(5	4)	160	39	58	54	39	0	87	2	2	2	0	1	.00	19	.272	.339	.403
2005	Mil	NL	114	385	105	25	1	9	(3	6)	159	50	43	39	37	6	94	4	2	3	0	1	.00	16	.273	.340	.413
2006	Mil	NL	101	331	83	28	0	6	(3	3)	129	34	38	38	33	7	86	4	3	5	0	0	-	11	.251	.322	.390
10 ML YEARS			931	2996	790	196	4	83	(44	39)	1243	342	382	375	289	42	733	23	23	21	4	5	.44	100	.264	.331	.415

Matt Miller

Pitches: R Bats: R Pos: RP-14   Ht: 6'3" Wt: 215 Born: 11/23/1971 Age: 35

			HOW MUCH HE PITCHED						WHAT HE GAVE UP												THE RESULTS							
Year	Team	Lg	G	GS	CG	GF	IP	BFP	H	R	ER	HR	SH	SF	HB	TBB	IBB	SO	WP	Bk	W	L	Pct	ShO	Sv-Op	Hld	ERC	ERA
2006	Akron*	AA	2	0	0	0	2.0	8	2	0	0	0	0	0	0	1	0	0	0	0	0	0	-	0	0--	-	4.15	0.00
2006	Buffalo*	AAA	1	1	0	0	1.0	4	0	0	0	0	0	0	0	0	0	2	0	0	0	0	-	0	0--	-	0.00	0.00
2003	Col	NL	4	0	0	2	4.1	18	5	1	1	0	0	0	0	2	0	5	0	0	0	0	-	0	0-0	0	4.86	2.08
2004	Cle	AL	57	0	0	13	55.1	226	42	22	19	1	2	1	6	23	8	55	1	1	4	1	.800	0	1-2	7	2.56	3.09
2005	Cle	AL	23	0	0	4	29.2	118	22	6	6	1	0	1	3	10	3	23	1	1	0	1	.000	0	1-2	4	2.37	1.82
2006	Cle	AL	14	0	0	3	15.2	65	11	6	6	2	0	2	2	9	0	12	0	0	1	0	1.000	0	0-0	1	3.98	3.45
	4 ML YEARS		98	0	0	22	105.0	427	80	35	32	4	2	4	11	44	11	95	2	2	6	1	.857	0	2-4	12	2.79	2.74

Trever Miller

Pitches: L Bats: R Pos: RP-70   Ht: 6'3" Wt: 200 Born: 5/29/1973 Age: 34

			HOW MUCH HE PITCHED						WHAT HE GAVE UP												THE RESULTS							
Year	Team	Lg	G	GS	CG	GF	IP	BFP	H	R	ER	HR	SH	SF	HB	TBB	IBB	SO	WP	Bk	W	L	Pct	ShO	Sv-Op	Hld	ERC	ERA
2006	RdRck*	AAA	2	2	0	0	2.0	6	0	0	0	0	0	0	0	0	0	3	0	0	0	0	-	0	0--	-	0.00	0.00
1996	Det	AL	5	4	0	0	16.2	88	28	17	17	3	2	2	2	9	0	8	0	0	0	4	.000	0	0-0	0	10.15	9.18
1998	Hou	NL	37	1	0	15	53.1	235	57	21	18	4	0	0	1	20	1	30	1	0	2	0	1.000	0	1-2	1	4.18	3.04
1999	Hou	NL	47	0	0	11	49.2	232	58	29	28	6	2	2	5	29	1	37	4	0	3	2	.600	0	1-1	4	6.48	5.07
2000	2 Tms	NL	16	0	0	2	16.1	90	27	22	19	3	1	1	2	12	1	11	1	0	0	0	-	0	0-0	0	10.68	10.47
2003	Tor	AL	79	0	0	18	52.2	233	46	30	27	7	1	0	5	28	3	44	2	0	2	2	.500	0	4-5	16	4.38	4.61
2004	TB	AL	60	0	0	15	49.0	208	48	21	17	3	3	0	3	19	1	43	2	0	1	1	.500	0	1-3	9	3.45	3.12
2005	TB	AL	61	0	0	13	44.1	206	45	23	20	4	3	5	7	29	6	35	2	0	2	2	.500	0	0-3	11	5.57	4.06
2006	Hou	NL	70	0	0	14	50.2	207	42	17	17	7	1	2	4	13	2	56	1	0	2	3	.400	0	1-3	12	3.11	3.02
00	Phi	NL	14	0	0	2	14.0	72	19	16	13	3	1	1	1	9	1	10	1	0	0	0	-	0	0-0	0	8.14	8.36
00	LAD	NL	2	0	0	0	2.1	18	8	6	6	0	0	0	1	3	0	1	0	0	0	0	-	0	0-0	0	28.18	23.14
	8 ML YEARS		375	5	0	88	332.2	1499	351	180	163	37	13	12	29	155	18	264	13	0	12	14	.462	0	8-17	53	5.00	4.41

Wade Miller

Pitches: R Bats: R Pos: SP-5   Ht: 6'2" Wt: 210 Born: 9/13/1976 Age: 30

			HOW MUCH HE PITCHED						WHAT HE GAVE UP												THE RESULTS							
Year	Team	Lg	G	GS	CG	GF	IP	BFP	H	R	ER	HR	SH	SF	HB	TBB	IBB	SO	WP	Bk	W	L	Pct	ShO	Sv-Op	Hld	ERC	ERA
2006	Peoria*	A	5	5	0	0	18.0	73	17	5	5	0	0	1	0	5	0	15	0	0	0	0	-	0	0--	-	2.72	2.50
2006	WTenn*	AA	1	1	0	0	6.0	22	3	1	1	0	0	0	0	1	0	4	0	0	1	0	1.000	0	0--	-	0.80	1.50
2006	Iowa*	AAA	2	2	0	0	11.0	51	18	8	8	2	1	0	0	3	0	9	0	0	1	0	1.000	0	0--	-	8.43	6.55
1999	Hou	NL	5	1	0	2	10.1	52	17	11	11	4	0	0	0	5	0	8	0	0	0	1	.000	0	0-0	0	11.07	9.58
2000	Hou	NL	16	16	0	2	105.0	453	104	66	60	14	3	1	3	42	1	89	1	0	6	6	.500	0	0-0	0	4.37	5.14
2001	Hou	NL	32	32	1	0	212.0	873	183	91	80	31	7	5	4	76	3	183	8	0	16	8	.667	0	0-0	0	3.57	3.40
2002	Hou	NL	26	26	1	0	164.2	688	151	63	60	14	8	5	6	62	9	144	4	0	15	4	.789	1	0-0	0	3.54	3.28
2003	Hou	NL	33	33	1	0	187.1	797	168	96	86	17	8	7	10	77	1	161	4	0	14	13	.519	0	0-0	0	3.70	4.13
2004	Hou	NL	15	15	0	0	88.2	383	76	35	33	11	5	1	0	44	0	74	1	0	7	7	.500	0	0-0	0	3.78	3.35
2005	Bos	AL	16	16	0	0	91.0	414	96	53	50	8	1	4	3	47	0	64	6	0	4	4	.500	0	0-0	0	4.84	4.95
2006	ChC	NL	5	5	0	0	21.2	103	19	12	11	4	2	0	1	18	1	20	1	0	0	2	.000	0	0-0	0	5.73	4.57
	8 ML YEARS		148	144	5	2	880.2	3763	814	427	391	103	34	23	27	371	15	743	25	0	62	45	.579	1	0-0	0	3.97	4.00

Kevin Millwood

Pitches: R Bats: R Pos: SP-34   Ht: 6'4" Wt: 230 Born: 12/24/1974 Age: 32

			HOW MUCH HE PITCHED						WHAT HE GAVE UP												THE RESULTS							
Year	Team	Lg	G	GS	CG	GF	IP	BFP	H	R	ER	HR	SH	SF	HB	TBB	IBB	SO	WP	Bk	W	L	Pct	ShO	Sv-Op	Hld	ERC	ERA
1997	Atl	NL	12	8	0	2	51.1	227	55	26	23	1	3	5	2	21	1	42	1	0	5	3	.625	0	0-0	0	4.03	4.03
1998	Atl	NL	31	29	3	1	174.1	748	175	86	79	18	8	3	3	56	3	163	6	1	17	8	.680	1	0-0	1	3.81	4.08
1999	Atl	NL	33	33	2	0	228.0	906	168	80	68	24	9	3	4	59	2	205	5	0	18	7	.720	0	0-0	0	2.26	2.68
2000	Atl	NL	36	35	0	0	212.2	903	213	115	110	26	8	5	3	62	2	168	4	0	10	13	.435	0	0-0	0	3.83	4.66
2001	Atl	NL	21	21	0	0	121.0	515	121	66	58	20	7	2	1	40	6	84	5	1	7	7	.500	0	0-0	0	4.20	4.31
2002	Atl	NL	35	34	1	0	217.0	895	186	83	78	16	9	4	8	65	7	178	4	0	18	8	.692	1	0-0	0	2.85	3.24
2003	Phi	NL	35	35	5	0	222.0	930	210	103	99	19	12	5	4	68	6	169	2	0	14	12	.538	3	0-0	0	3.35	4.01
2004	Phi	NL	25	25	0	0	141.0	628	155	81	76	14	11	2	7	51	5	125	4	0	9	6	.600	0	0-0	0	4.57	4.85
2005	Cle	AL	30	30	1	0	192.0	799	182	72	61	20	6	4	4	52	0	146	2	0	9	11	.450	0	0-0	0	3.40	2.86
2006	Tex	AL	34	34	2	0	215.0	907	228	114	108	23	8	3	4	53	4	157	6	0	16	12	.571	0	0-0	0	3.92	4.52
	10 ML YEARS		292	284	14	3	1774.1	7458	1693	826	760	181	81	36	40	527	36	1437	39	2	123	87	.586	5	0-0	1	3.48	3.85

Eric Milton

Pitches: L Bats: L Pos: SP-26   Ht: 6'3" Wt: 205 Born: 8/4/1975 Age: 31

			HOW MUCH HE PITCHED						WHAT HE GAVE UP												THE RESULTS							
Year	Team	Lg	G	GS	CG	GF	IP	BFP	H	R	ER	HR	SH	SF	HB	TBB	IBB	SO	WP	Bk	W	L	Pct	ShO	Sv-Op	Hld	ERC	ERA
1998	Min	AL	32	32	1	0	172.1	772	195	113	108	25	2	6	2	70	0	107	1	0	8	14	.364	0	0-0	0	5.21	5.64
1999	Min	AL	34	34	4	0	206.1	858	190	111	103	28	3	6	3	63	2	163	2	0	7	11	.389	2	0-0	0	3.56	4.49
2000	Min	AL	33	33	0	0	200.0	849	205	123	108	35	4	6	7	44	0	160	5	0	13	10	.565	0	0-0	0	4.09	4.86
2001	Min	AL	35	34	2	0	220.2	944	222	109	106	35	8	6	5	61	0	157	2	0	15	7	.682	1	0-0	0	4.05	4.32
2002	Min	AL	29	29	2	0	171.0	707	173	96	92	24	0	4	3	30	0	121	4	0	13	9	.591	1	0-0	0	3.59	4.84
2003	Min	AL	3	3	0	0	17.0	66	15	5	5	2	0	1	0	7	0	7	0	0	1	0	1.000	0	0-0	0	2.29	2.65
2004	Phi	NL	34	34	0	0	201.0	862	196	110	106	43	11	6	1	75	6	161	3	0	14	6	.700	0	0-0	0	4.57	4.75
2005	Cin	NL	34	34	0	0	186.1	855	237	141	134	40	6	6	7	52	2	123	8	0	8	15	.348	0	0-0	0	6.03	6.47
2006	Cin	NL	26	26	0	0	152.2	662	163	94	88	29	6	3	5	42	4	90	2	0	8	8	.500	0	0-0	0	4.62	5.19
	9 ML YEARS		260	259	9	0	1527.1	6575	1596	902	850	261	40	44	33	438	14	1089	27	0	87	80	.521	4	0-0	0	4.40	5.01

Zach Miner

Pitches: R Bats: R Pos: SP-16; RP-11   Ht: 6'3" Wt: 200 Born: 3/12/1982 Age: 25

			HOW MUCH HE PITCHED						WHAT HE GAVE UP										THE RESULTS					
Year	Team	Lg	G	GS	CG	GF	IP	BFP	H	R	ER	HR	SH	SF	HB	TBB	IBB	SO	WP	Bk	W	L	Pct	ShO	Sv-Op Hld	ERC	ERA
2001	Jmstwn	A-	15	15	0	0	90.2	358	76	26	19	6	2	0	4	16	0	68	4	1	3	4	.429	0	0- - -	2.39	1.89
2002	Macon	A	29	28	1	0	159.0	663	143	73	58	10	6	5	12	51	1	131	9	1	8	9	.471	1	0- - -	3.29	3.28
2003	MrtlBh	A+	27	27	2	0	153.2	652	150	74	63	10	6	5	7	61	1	88	4	1	6	10	.375	0	0- - -	3.93	3.69
2004	Grnvlle	AA	27	22	1	1	129.1	552	132	87	75	14	9	9	5	55	0	111	1	1	6	10	.375	0	0- - -	4.65	5.22
2005	Missi	AA	4	2	0	1	16.2	73	21	10	8	0	0	1	0	5	0	18	2	0	0	1	.000	0	1- - -	4.49	4.32
2005	Rchmd	AAA	17	17	0	0	89.1	402	97	47	42	6	1	1	2	45	1	63	3	0	1	7	.125	0	0- - -	4.81	4.23
2005	Toledo	AAA	6	6	0	0	34.1	147	28	10	9	4	2	1	2	20	0	20	0	0	3	1	.750	0	0- - -	4.20	2.36
2006	Toledo	AAA	9	9	1	0	51.0	206	43	18	16	2	0	0	0	21	0	40	1	0	6	0	1.000	0	0- - -	2.99	2.82
2006	Det	AL	27	16	1	4	93.0	398	100	53	50	11	2	2	0	32	1	59	1	0	7	6	.538	0	0-0 -	4.44	4.84

Doug Mirabelli

Bats: R Throws: R Pos: C-66; PH-9; DH-1; PR-1   Ht: 6'1" Wt: 220 Born: 10/18/1970 Age: 36

			BATTING																			BASERUNNING				AVERAGES		
Year	Team	Lg	G	AB	H	2B	3B	HR	(Hm	Rd)	TB	R	RBI	RC	TBB	IBB	SO	HBP	SH	SF	SB	CS	SB%	GDP	Avg	OBP	Slg
1996	SF	NL	9	18	4	1	0	0	(0	0)	5	2	1	2	3	0	4	0	0	0	0	0	-	0	.222	.333	.278
1997	SF	NL	6	7	1	0	0	0	(0	0)	1	0	0	0	1	0	3	0	0	0	0	0	-	0	.143	.250	.143
1998	SF	NL	10	17	4	2	0	1	(1	0)	9	2	4	3	2	0	6	0	0	0	0	0	-	0	.235	.316	.529
1999	SF	NL	33	87	22	6	0	1	(1	0)	31	10	10	10	9	1	25	1	0	1	0	0	-	1	.253	.327	.356
2000	SF	NL	82	230	53	10	2	6	(2	4)	85	23	28	30	36	2	57	2	3	2	1	0	1.00	6	.230	.337	.370
2001	2 Tms		77	190	43	10	0	11	(5	6)	86	20	29	29	27	2	57	4	1	2	0	0	-	3	.226	.332	.453
2002	Bos	AL	57	151	34	7	0	7	(5	2)	62	17	25	19	17	0	33	3	0	2	0	0	-	6	.225	.312	.411
2003	Bos	AL	62	163	42	13	0	6	(3	3)	73	23	18	15	11	0	36	1	0	1	0	0	-	3	.258	.307	.448
2004	Bos	AL	59	160	45	12	0	9	(3	6)	84	27	32	32	19	0	46	3	0	0	0	0	-	5	.281	.368	.525
2005	Bos	AL	50	136	31	7	0	6	(4	2)	56	16	18	19	14	0	48	2	0	0	2	0	1.00	2	.228	.309	.412
2006	2 Tms		73	183	35	7	0	6	(3	3)	60	13	25	17	15	0	59	4	0	0	0	0	-	2	.191	.267	.328
01	Tex	AL	23	49	5	2	0	2	(1	1)	13	4	3	3	10	0	21	0	0	0	0	0	-	1	.102	.254	.265
01	Bos	AL	54	141	38	8	0	9	(4	5)	73	16	26	26	17	2	36	4	1	2	0	0	-	2	.270	.360	.518
06	SD	NL	14	22	4	1	0	0	(0	0)	5	1	0	1	4	0	5	0	0	0	0	0	-	0	.182	.308	.227
06	Bos	AL	59	161	31	6	0	6	(3	3)	55	12	25	16	11	0	54	4	0	0	0	0	-	2	.193	.261	.342
11 ML YEARS			518	1342	314	75	2	53	(27	26)	552	153	190	176	154	5	374	20	4	8	3	0	1.00	28	.234	.320	.411

Patrick Misch

Pitches: L Bats: R Pos: RP-1   Ht: 6'2" Wt: 195 Born: 8/18/1981 Age: 25

			HOW MUCH HE PITCHED						WHAT HE GAVE UP										THE RESULTS					
Year	Team	Lg	G	GS	CG	GF	IP	BFP	H	R	ER	HR	SH	SF	HB	TBB	IBB	SO	WP	Bk	W	L	Pct	ShO	Sv-Op Hld	ERC	ERA
2003	SlmKzr	A-	14	14	0	0	86.0	350	78	33	21	3	3	4	7	20	0	61	1	0	7	5	.583	0	0- - -	2.88	2.20
2004	Nrwich	AA	26	26	4	0	159.0	623	138	61	54	13	10	6	3	35	0	123	4	1	7	6	.538	3	0- - -	2.75	3.06
2005	Fresno	AAA	19	19	1	0	102.0	476	135	80	72	18	11	4	6	40	0	69	2	1	3	9	.250	0	0- - -	6.84	6.35
2005	Nrwich	AA	9	9	1	0	61.1	248	63	25	24	7	3	2	3	7	0	43	0	0	4	2	.667	1	0- - -	3.46	3.52
2006	Conn	AA	18	17	0	0	103.2	420	95	32	26	7	1	2	8	24	0	79	0	1	5	4	.556	0	0- - -	3.14	2.26
2006	Fresno	AAA	10	10	1	0	65.0	275	74	32	29	7	5	2	0	11	0	57	1	1	4	2	.667	0	0- - -	3.97	4.02
2006	SF	NL	1	0	0	0	1.0	5	2	0	0	0	0	0	0	0	0	1	0	0	0	0	-	0	0-0 0	7.48	0.00

Sergio Mitre

Pitches: R Bats: R Pos: RP-8; SP-7   Ht: 6'4" Wt: 210 Born: 2/16/1981 Age: 26

			HOW MUCH HE PITCHED						WHAT HE GAVE UP										THE RESULTS					
Year	Team	Lg	G	GS	CG	GF	IP	BFP	H	R	ER	HR	SH	SF	HB	TBB	IBB	SO	WP	Bk	W	L	Pct	ShO	Sv-Op Hld	ERC	ERA
2006	Mrlns*	R	1	1	0	0	1.0	3	0	0	0	0	0	0	0	1	0	0	0	0	0	0	-	0	0- - -	1.26	0.00
2003	ChC	NL	3	2	0	1	8.2	43	15	8	8	1	0	1	0	4	1	3	0	0	0	1	.000	0	0-0 0	9.02	8.31
2004	ChC	NL	12	9	0	2	51.2	244	71	38	38	6	3	0	4	20	1	37	5	1	2	4	.333	0	0-0 0	6.69	6.62
2005	ChC	NL	21	7	1	7	60.1	268	62	37	36	11	1	3	3	23	2	37	5	0	2	5	.286	1	0-0 0	4.81	5.37
2006	Fla	NL	15	7	0	3	41.0	189	44	28	26	7	2	1	6	20	3	31	1	0	1	5	.167	0	0-1 2	5.87	5.71
4 ML YEARS			51	25	1	13	161.2	744	192	111	108	25	6	5	13	67	7	108	11	1	5	15	.250	1	0-1 2	5.88	6.01

Brian Moehler

Pitches: R Bats: R Pos: SP-21; RP-8   Ht: 6'3" Wt: 235 Born: 12/31/1971 Age: 35

			HOW MUCH HE PITCHED						WHAT HE GAVE UP										THE RESULTS					
Year	Team	Lg	G	GS	CG	GF	IP	BFP	H	R	ER	HR	SH	SF	HB	TBB	IBB	SO	WP	Bk	W	L	Pct	ShO	Sv-Op Hld	ERC	ERA
2006	Mrlns*	R	1	1	0	0	5.0	23	8	2	2	0	0	0	0	4	0	4	0	0	0	1	.000	0	0- - -	5.03	3.60
1996	Det	AL	2	2	0	0	10.1	51	11	10	5	1	1	0	0	8	1	2	1	0	0	1	.000	0	0-0 0	5.49	4.35
1997	Det	AL	31	31	2	0	175.1	770	198	97	91	22	1	8	5	61	1	97	3	0	11	12	.478	1	0-0 0	4.92	4.67
1998	Det	AL	33	33	4	0	221.1	912	220	103	96	30	3	3	2	56	1	123	4	0	14	13	.519	3	0-0 0	3.79	3.90
1999	Det	AL	32	32	2	0	196.1	859	229	116	110	22	8	5	7	59	5	106	4	0	10	16	.385	2	0-0 0	4.85	5.04
2000	Det	AL	29	29	2	0	178.0	776	222	99	89	20	3	4	2	40	0	103	2	1	12	9	.571	0	0-0 0	4.95	4.50
2001	Det	AL	1	1	0	0	8.0	30	6	3	3	0	0	0	0	1	0	2	0	0	0	0	-	0	0-0 0	1.43	3.38
2002	2 Tms		13	12	0	0	63.0	278	78	39	34	11	4	2	1	13	0	31	0	0	3	5	.375	0	0-0 0	5.20	4.86
2003	Hou	NL	3	3	0	0	13.2	66	22	12	12	4	1	1	0	6	0	5	0	0	0	0	-	0	0-0 0	9.97	7.90
2005	Fla	NL	37	25	0	0	158.1	696	198	82	80	16	13	4	5	42	9	95	1	0	6	12	.333	1	0-0 0	5.07	4.55
2006	Fla	NL	29	21	0	2	122.0	556	164	95	89	19	7	2	5	38	3	58	2	1	7	11	.389	0	0-1 2	6.36	6.57
02	Det	AL	3	3	0	0	19.2	77	17	5	5	3	1	1	0	2	0	13	0	0	1	1	.500	0	0-0 0	2.54	2.29
02	Cin	NL	10	9	0	0	43.1	201	61	34	29	8	3	1	1	11	0	18	0	0	2	4	.333	0	0-0 0	6.56	6.02
10 ML YEARS			210	189	10	6	1146.1	4994	1348	656	609	145	41	29	27	324	20	622	17	2	63	79	.444	6	0-1 1	4.90	4.78

Chad Moeller

Bats: R Throws: R Pos: C-29   Ht: 6'3" Wt: 215 Born: 2/18/1975 Age: 32

Year	Team	Lg	G	AB	H	2B	3B	HR	(Hm	Rd)	TB	R	RBI	RC	TBB	IBB	SO	HBP	SH	SF	SB	CS	SB%	GDP	Avg	OBP	Slg
2006	Nashv*	AAA	41	132	29	6	0	2	(-	-)	41	10	18	13	15	1	28	3	1	3	0	2	.00	4	.220	.307	.311
2000	Min	AL	48	128	27	3	1	1	(1	0)	35	13	9	8	9	0	33	0	1	1	1	0	1.00	4	.211	.261	.273
2001	Ari	NL	25	56	13	0	1	1	(1	0)	18	8	2	5	6	1	12	0	1	0	0	0	-	2	.232	.306	.321
2002	Ari	NL	37	105	30	11	1	2	(2	0)	49	10	16	17	17	3	23	0	1	0	0	1	.00	6	.286	.385	.467
2003	Ari	NL	78	239	64	17	1	7	(2	5)	104	29	29	28	23	11	59	2	3	2	1	2	.33	7	.268	.335	.435
2004	Mil	NL	101	317	66	13	1	5	(3	2)	96	25	27	14	21	1	74	4	6	1	0	1	.00	12	.208	.265	.303
2005	Mil	NL	66	199	41	9	1	7	(5	2)	73	23	23	14	13	1	48	1	2	1	0	0	-	9	.206	.257	.367
2006	Mil	NL	29	98	18	3	0	2	(2	0)	27	9	5	3	4	0	26	2	0	0	0	0	-	3	.184	.231	.276
	7 ML YEARS		384	1142	259	56	6	25	(16	9)	402	117	111	89	93	17	275	9	14	5	2	4	.33	43	.227	.289	.352

Dustan Mohr

Bats: R Throws: R Pos: CF-13; LF-7; RF-5; PH-3; PR-1   Ht: 6'1" Wt: 210 Born: 6/19/1976 Age: 31

Year	Team	Lg	G	AB	H	2B	3B	HR	(Hm	Rd)	TB	R	RBI	RC	TBB	IBB	SO	HBP	SH	SF	SB	CS	SB%	GDP	Avg	OBP	Slg
2006	Toledo*	AAA	54	187	49	11	4	6	(-	-)	86	21	25	28	22	0	70	0	2	1	1	4	.20	2	.262	.338	.460
2006	Pwtckt*	AAA	22	65	11	2	0	1	(-	-)	16	10	6	8	21	3	23	0	0	1	0	0	-	0	.169	.368	.246
2001	Min	AL	20	51	12	2	0	0	(0	0)	14	6	4	4	5	0	17	0	0	1	1	1	.50	0	.235	.298	.275
2002	Min	AL	120	383	103	23	2	12	(3	9)	166	55	45	51	31	3	86	1	2	0	6	3	.67	5	.269	.325	.433
2003	Min	AL	121	348	87	22	0	10	(4	6)	139	50	36	37	33	0	106	1	2	3	5	2	.71	10	.250	.314	.399
2004	SF	NL	117	263	72	20	1	7	(3	4)	115	52	28	43	46	3	64	8	4	3	0	3	.00	5	.274	.394	.437
2005	Col	NL	98	266	57	10	3	17	(13	4)	124	34	38	27	23	2	94	2	0	2	1	2	.33	3	.214	.280	.466
2006	Bos	AL	21	40	7	1	0	2	(2	0)	14	5	3	2	3	0	20	0	0	0	0	0	-	0	.175	.233	.350
	6 ML YEARS		497	1351	338	78	6	48	(25	23)	572	202	154	164	141	8	387	12	8	9	13	11	.54	23	.250	.325	.423

Bengie Molina

Bats: R Throws: R Pos: C-99; DH-16; PH-3   Ht: 5'11" Wt: 225 Born: 7/20/1974 Age: 32

Year	Team	Lg	G	AB	H	2B	3B	HR	(Hm	Rd)	TB	R	RBI	RC	TBB	IBB	SO	HBP	SH	SF	SB	CS	SB%	GDP	Avg	OBP	Slg
1998	LAA	AL	2	1	0	0	0	0	(0	0)	0	0	0	0	0	0	0	0	0	0	0	0	-	0	.000	.000	.000
1999	LAA	AL	31	101	26	5	0	1	(0	1)	34	8	10	9	6	0	6	2	0	0	0	1	.00	5	.257	.312	.337
2000	LAA	AL	130	473	133	20	2	14	(11	3)	199	59	71	60	23	0	33	6	4	7	1	0	1.00	17	.281	.318	.421
2001	LAA	AL	96	325	85	11	0	6	(6	0)	114	31	40	34	16	3	51	8	2	4	0	1	.00	8	.262	.309	.351
2002	LAA	AL	122	428	105	18	0	5	(2	3)	138	34	47	33	15	3	34	4	6	6	0	0	-	15	.245	.274	.322
2003	LAA	AL	119	409	115	24	0	14	(7	7)	181	37	71	57	13	2	31	2	2	4	1	1	.50	17	.281	.304	.443
2004	LAA	AL	97	337	93	13	0	10	(5	5)	136	36	54	44	18	1	35	2	2	4	0	1	.00	18	.276	.313	.404
2005	LAA	AL	119	410	121	17	0	15	(8	7)	183	45	69	53	27	2	41	1	5	6	0	2	.00	14	.295	.336	.446
2006	Tor	AL	117	433	123	20	1	19	(12	7)	202	44	57	58	19	1	47	4	0	2	1	1	.50	15	.284	.319	.467
	9 ML YEARS		833	2917	801	128	3	84	(51	33)	1187	294	419	348	137	12	278	29	21	33	3	7	.30	109	.275	.310	.407

Jose Molina

Bats: R Throws: R Pos: C-76; 1B-3; PH-1; PR-1   Ht: 6'2" Wt: 220 Born: 6/3/1975 Age: 32

Year	Team	Lg	G	AB	H	2B	3B	HR	(Hm	Rd)	TB	R	RBI	RC	TBB	IBB	SO	HBP	SH	SF	SB	CS	SB%	GDP	Avg	OBP	Slg
1999	ChC	NL	10	19	5	1	0	0	(0	0)	6	3	1	2	2	1	4	0	0	0	0	0	-	0	.263	.333	.316
2001	LAA	AL	15	37	10	3	0	2	(0	2)	19	8	4	6	3	0	8	0	2	0	0	0	-	2	.270	.325	.514
2002	LAA	AL	29	70	19	3	0	0	(0	0)	22	5	5	4	5	0	15	0	4	2	0	2	.00	2	.271	.312	.314
2003	LAA	AL	53	114	21	4	0	0	(0	0)	25	12	6	5	1	0	26	3	4	1	0	0	-	1	.184	.210	.219
2004	LAA	AL	73	203	53	10	2	3	(1	2)	76	26	25	19	10	0	52	0	5	0	4	1	.80	7	.261	.296	.374
2005	LAA	AL	75	184	42	4	0	6	(2	4)	64	14	25	19	13	0	41	2	4	0	2	0	1.00	5	.228	.286	.348
2006	LAA	AL	78	225	54	17	0	4	(0	4)	83	18	22	21	9	0	49	2	7	2	1	0	1.00	6	.240	.273	.369
	7 ML YEARS		333	852	204	42	2	15	(3	12)	295	86	88	76	43	1	195	7	26	5	7	3	.70	23	.239	.280	.346

Yadier Molina

Bats: R Throws: R Pos: C-127; 1B-4; PH-2   Ht: 5'11" Wt: 225 Born: 7/13/1982 Age: 24

Year	Team	Lg	G	AB	H	2B	3B	HR	(Hm	Rd)	TB	R	RBI	RC	TBB	IBB	SO	HBP	SH	SF	SB	CS	SB%	GDP	Avg	OBP	Slg
2004	StL	NL	51	135	36	6	0	2	(1	1)	48	12	15	15	13	3	20	0	2	1	0	1	.00	4	.267	.329	.356
2005	StL	NL	114	385	97	15	1	8	(6	2)	138	36	49	46	23	3	30	2	8	3	2	3	.40	10	.252	.295	.358
2006	StL	NL	129	417	90	26	0	6	(2	4)	134	29	49	35	26	2	41	8	8	2	1	2	.33	15	.216	.274	.321
	3 ML YEARS		294	937	223	47	1	16	(9	7)	320	77	113	96	62	8	91	10	18	6	3	6	.33	29	.238	.291	.342

Craig Monroe

Bats: R Throws: R Pos: LF-113; DH-30; CF-8; PH-2   Ht: 6'1" Wt: 205 Born: 2/27/1977 Age: 30

Year	Team	Lg	G	AB	H	2B	3B	HR	(Hm	Rd)	TB	R	RBI	RC	TBB	IBB	SO	HBP	SH	SF	SB	CS	SB%	GDP	Avg	OBP	Slg
2001	Tex	AL	27	52	11	1	0	2	(1	1)	18	8	5	6	6	0	18	0	0	0	2	0	1.00	1	.212	.293	.346
2002	Det	AL	13	25	3	1	0	1	(0	1)	7	3	1	0	0	0	5	1	0	0	0	2	.00	1	.120	.154	.280
2003	Det	AL	128	425	102	18	1	23	(10	13)	191	51	70	61	27	2	89	2	1	3	4	2	.67	10	.240	.287	.449
2004	Det	AL	128	447	131	27	3	18	(9	9)	218	65	72	66	29	1	79	2	0	3	3	4	.43	8	.293	.337	.488
2005	Det	AL	157	567	157	30	3	20	(9	11)	253	69	89	77	40	4	95	3	1	12	8	3	.73	16	.277	.322	.446
2006	Det	AL	147	541	138	35	2	28	(12	16)	261	89	92	76	37	3	126	1	0	6	2	2	.50	14	.255	.301	.482
	6 ML YEARS		600	2057	542	112	9	92	(41	51)	948	285	329	286	139	10	412	9	2	24	19	13	.59	50	.263	.310	.461

Agustin Montero

Pitches: R Bats: R Pos: RP-11   Ht: 6'3" Wt: 210 Born: 8/26/1977 Age: 29

			HOW MUCH HE PITCHED								WHAT HE GAVE UP									THE RESULTS							
Year	Team	Lg	G	GS	CG	GF	IP	BFP	H	R	ER	HR	SH	SF	HB	TBB	IBB	SO	WP	Bk	W	L	Pct	ShO	Sv-Op	Hld	ERC	ERA
1997	As	R	14	13	0	1	72.2	327	72	38	29	3	0	0	8	31	0	88	9	9	3	2	.600	0	0- -	-	4.05	3.59
1997	SoOre	A-	2	0	0	1	2.2	15	4	2	2	0	0	0	2	3	0	1	0	0	0	0	-	0	0- -	-	14.16	6.75
1998	SoOre	A-	14	3	0	6	37.1	191	47	42	36	5	2	3	4	26	0	28	6	2	2	3	.400	0	0- -	-	7.36	8.68
2000	VeroB	A+	3	0	0	1	3.0	17	2	2	2	0	0	0	0	6	0	4	2	0	0	0	-	0	0- -	-	7.34	6.00
2000	SnBrn	A+	7	0	0	3	8.1	52	13	14	9	0	0	1	2	12	0	10	2	0	0	2	.000	0	0- -	-	11.98	9.72
2000	Gr Falls	R+	11	0	0	3	18.1	85	16	10	8	1	0	0	2	12	0	21	3	0	2	1	.667	0	0- -	-	4.32	3.93
2000	Yakima	A-	7	0	0	3	13.1	64	12	9	9	0	1	0	5	7	1	21	3	0	1	0	1.000	0	0- -	-	4.39	6.08
2001	Wilmg	A	18	0	0	9	27.1	113	13	11	10	1	0	1	5	19	1	30	5	1	2	1	.667	0	1- -	-	2.66	3.29
2001	VeroB	A+	16	0	0	7	31.1	134	29	14	12	7	1	1	3	13	0	23	1	0	1	0	1.000	0	1- -	-	5.08	3.45
2002	VeroB	A+	7	0	0	1	13.0	53	10	5	5	1	1	0	1	4	0	14	2	3	1	0	1.000	0	0- -	-	2.66	3.46
2002	Jaxnvl	AA	31	0	0	11	41.0	187	38	21	18	5	3	1	8	29	6	25	5	0	1	3	.250	0	0- -	-	5.78	3.95
2003	Jaxnvl	AA	16	0	0	5	26.2	113	24	10	9	1	1	2	0	13	1	22	2	0	2	1	.667	0	0- -	-	3.41	3.04
2003	LsVgs	AAA	35	0	0	9	50.2	233	57	32	28	4	4	4	3	31	3	30	1	2	2	2	.500	0	1- -	-	5.74	4.97
2004	LsVgs	AAA	42	0	0	24	45.2	228	55	47	39	9	0	0	9	26	1	38	9	2	1	4	.200	0	3- -	-	7.41	7.69
2004	Jaxnvl	AA	21	0	0	13	30.0	128	20	10	8	1	0	0	2	16	0	36	4	1	2	0	1.000	0	4- -	-	2.54	2.40
2005	Frisco	AA	40	0	0	18	61.0	284	64	40	37	9	3	3	2	33	1	69	10	1	2	4	.333	0	2- -	-	5.23	5.46
2005	Okla	AAA	4	0	0	1	5.0	24	6	3	3	0	1	0	1	3	0	4	0	0	0	0	-	0	0- -	-	6.15	5.40
2006	Charltt	AAA	39	0	0	8	59.1	246	54	33	32	8	0	1	4	20	4	55	7	0	2	3	.400	0	1- -	-	3.82	4.85
2006	CWS	AL	11	0	0	6	14.0	59	15	10	8	3	0	3	0	2	0	7	2	0	1	0	1.000	0	0-0	2	4.11	5.14

Miguel Montero

Bats: L Throws: R Pos: C-5; PH-1   Ht: 5'11" Wt: 195 Born: 7/9/1983 Age: 23

									BATTING												BASERUNNING				AVERAGES		
Year	Team	Lg	G	AB	H	2B	3B	HR	(Hm	Rd)	TB	R	RBI	RC	TBB	IBB	SO	HBP	SH	SF	SB	CS	SB%	GDP	Avg	OBP	Slg
2002	Msoula	R	50	152	40	10	1	3	(-	-)	61	21	14	22	17	0	26	3	1	3	2	1	.67	5	.263	.343	.401
2003	Msoula	R	59	196	59	10	2	4	(-	-)	85	24	32	30	9	2	15	8	0	3	2	3	.40	6	.301	.352	.434
2004	Sbend	A	115	403	106	22	2	11	(-	-)	165	47	59	58	36	0	74	6	0	4	8	2	.80	5	.263	.330	.409
2005	Lancst	A+	85	355	124	24	1	24	(-	-)	222	73	82	85	26	0	52	10	2	6	1	2	.33	5	.349	.403	.625
2005	Tenn	AA	30	108	27	1	2	2	(-	-)	38	13	13	12	7	0	26	3	1	1	1	0	1.00	2	.250	.311	.352
2006	Tenn	AA	81	289	78	18	0	10	(-	-)	126	24	46	47	39	3	44	5	0	4	0	3	.00	3	.270	.362	.436
2006	Tucsn	AAA	36	134	43	5	0	7	(-	-)	69	21	29	27	14	0	21	4	0	2	1	1	.50	4	.321	.396	.515
2006	Ari	NL	6	16	4	1	0	0	(0	0)	5	0	3	2	1	0	3	0	0	0	0	0	-	0	.250	.294	.313

Scott Moore

Bats: L Throws: R Pos: 1B-6; PH-6; 3B-5   Ht: 6'2" Wt: 180 Born: 11/17/1983 Age: 23

									BATTING												BASERUNNING				AVERAGES		
Year	Team	Lg	G	AB	H	2B	3B	HR	(Hm	Rd)	TB	R	RBI	RC	TBB	IBB	SO	HBP	SH	SF	SB	CS	SB%	GDP	Avg	OBP	Slg
2002	Tigers	R	40	133	39	6	2	4	(-	-)	61	18	25	21	10	1	31	3	0	3	1	2	.33	2	.293	.349	.459
2003	W Mich	A	107	372	89	16	6	6	(-	-)	135	40	45	45	41	0	110	7	0	1	2	4	.33	9	.239	.325	.363
2004	Lkland	A+	118	391	87	13	4	14	(-	-)	150	52	56	51	49	1	125	10	0	3	2	4	.33	10	.223	.322	.384
2005	Dytona	A+	128	466	131	31	2	20	(-	-)	226	77	82	85	55	4	134	6	0	9	22	7	.76	7	.281	.358	.485
2006	WTenn	AA	132	463	128	28	0	22	(-	-)	222	52	75	82	55	7	126	8	1	5	12	7	.63	7	.276	.360	.479
2006	Iowa	AAA	1	4	1	1	0	0	(-	-)	2	1	0	0	0	0	1	0	0	0	0	0	-	0	.250	.250	.500
2006	ChC	NL	16	38	10	2	0	2	(1	1)	18	6	5	5	2	0	10	1	1	0	0	0	-	1	.263	.317	.474

Melvin Mora

Bats: R Throws: R Pos: 3B-154; 2B-1; DH-1   Ht: 5'11" Wt: 200 Born: 2/2/1972 Age: 35

									BATTING												BASERUNNING				AVERAGES		
Year	Team	Lg	G	AB	H	2B	3B	HR	(Hm	Rd)	TB	R	RBI	RC	TBB	IBB	SO	HBP	SH	SF	SB	CS	SB%	GDP	Avg	OBP	Slg
1999	NYM	NL	66	31	5	0	0	0	(0	0)	5	6	1	2	4	0	7	1	3	0	2	1	.67	0	.161	.278	.161
2000	2 Tms		132	414	114	22	5	8	(5	3)	170	60	47	56	35	3	80	6	4	5	12	11	.52	5	.275	.337	.411
2001	Bal	AL	128	436	109	28	0	7	(6	1)	158	49	48	55	41	2	91	14	5	7	11	4	.73	6	.250	.329	.362
2002	Bal	AL	149	557	130	30	4	19	(8	11)	225	86	64	78	70	2	108	20	1	4	16	10	.62	7	.233	.338	.404
2003	Bal	AL	96	344	109	17	1	15	(8	7)	173	68	48	67	49	0	71	12	6	2	6	3	.67	3	.317	.418	.503
2004	Bal	AL	140	550	187	41	0	27	(15	12)	309	111	104	115	66	0	95	11	6	3	11	6	.65	10	.340	.419	.562
2005	Bal	AL	149	593	168	30	1	27	(13	14)	281	86	88	88	50	0	112	10	8	3	7	4	.64	9	.283	.348	.474
2006	Bal	AL	155	624	171	25	0	16	(8	8)	244	96	83	93	54	1	99	14	6	7	11	1	.92	9	.274	.342	.391
00	NYM	NL	79	215	56	13	2	6	(4	2)	91	35	30	29	18	3	48	2	2	5	7	3	.70	3	.260	.317	.423
00	Bal	AL	53	199	58	9	3	2	(1	1)	79	25	17	27	17	0	32	4	2	0	5	8	.38	2	.291	.359	.397
8 ML YEARS			1015	3549	993	193	11	119	(63	56)	1565	562	483	554	369	8	663	88	39	31	76	40	.66	49	.280	.359	.441

Kendry Morales

Bats: B Throws: R Pos: 1B-56; PH-5   Ht: 6'1" Wt: 220 Born: 6/20/1983 Age: 24

									BATTING												BASERUNNING				AVERAGES		
Year	Team	Lg	G	AB	H	2B	3B	HR	(Hm	Rd)	TB	R	RBI	RC	TBB	IBB	SO	HBP	SH	SF	SB	CS	SB%	GDP	Avg	OBP	Slg
2005	RCuca	A+	22	90	31	3	0	5	(-	-)	49	18	17	19	6	0	11	3	0	1	0	0	-	3	.344	.400	.544
2005	Ark	AA	74	281	86	12	0	17	(-	-)	149	47	54	51	17	1	43	2	0	1	2	0	1.00	6	.306	.349	.530
2006	Salt Lk	AAA	66	256	82	13	1	12	(-	-)	133	41	52	45	14	0	40	2	0	1	0	3	.00	6	.320	.359	.520
2006	LAA	AL	57	197	46	10	1	5	(1	4)	73	21	22	19	17	1	28	0	0	1	1	1	.50	11	.234	.293	.371

Shinji Mori

Pitches: R Bats: L Pos: P   Ht: 6'2" Wt: 194 Born: 9/12/1974 Age: 32

Year	Team	Lg	G	GS	CG	GF	IP	BFP	H	R	ER	HR	SH	SF	HB	TBB	IBB	SO	WP	Bk	W	L	Pct	ShO	Sv-Op	Hld	ERC	ERA
1997	Seibu	Jap	38	3	0	27	57.2	251	61	24	21	4	-	-	0	20	-	61	3	0	6	2	.750	0	9- -	-	3.93	3.28
1998	Seibu	Jap	52	9	1	27	111.0	490	112	53	47	9	-	-	0	55	-	110	8	0	8	8	.500	0	5- -	-	4.36	3.81
1999	Seibu	Jap	41	13	0	10	113.1	505	116	62	58	11	-	-	2	54	-	128	10	1	5	8	.385	0	0- -	-	4.52	4.61
2000	Seibu	Jap	58	0	0	56	78.2	299	51	16	16	6	-	-	0	20	-	101	4	0	5	6	.455	0	23- -	-	1.69	1.83
2001	Seibu	Jap	28	0	0	9	46.0	194	38	21	20	9	-	-	0	16	-	52	5	0	5	4	.556	0	1- -	-	3.44	3.91
2002	Seibu	Jap	71	0	0	18	78.1	327	61	25	18	4	-	-	0	29	-	102	9	1	6	7	.462	0	1- -	-	2.42	2.07
2003	Seibu	Jap	61	0	0	11	70.0	287	55	19	18	6	-	-	2	22	-	92	5	0	7	3	.700	0	2- -	-	2.61	2.31
2004	Seibu	Jap	34	2	0	13	49.0	235	50	35	25	5	1	2	0	38	1	49	2	0	0	4	.000	0	4- -	-	5.55	4.59
2005	Seibu	Jap	48	-	0	-	49.0	210	44	24	23	5	-	-	3	19	-	60	0	0	2	2	.500	0	5- -	-	3.69	4.22

Juan Morillo

Pitches: R Bats: R Pos: SP-1   Ht: 6'3" Wt: 190 Born: 11/5/1983 Age: 23

Year	Team	Lg	G	GS	CG	GF	IP	BFP	H	R	ER	HR	SH	SF	HB	TBB	IBB	SO	WP	Bk	W	L	Pct	ShO	Sv-Op	Hld	ERC	ERA
2003	Casper	R+	15	15	0	0	64.0	320	85	73	42	6	4	4	5	40	0	44	7	0	1	6	.143	0	0- -	-	7.14	5.91
2004	Tri-Cit	A-	14	14	0	0	66.1	295	56	34	22	0	1	1	4	41	0	73	3	0	3	2	.600	0	0- -	-	3.52	2.98
2005	Ashvlle	A	7	7	0	0	33.2	154	40	24	17	2	0	0	1	13	0	43	3	0	1	3	.250	0	0- -	-	4.82	4.54
2005	Mdest	A+	20	20	0	0	112.1	509	107	69	55	10	3	2	8	65	0	101	13	1	6	5	.545	0	0- -	-	4.68	4.41
2006	Tulsa	AA	27	27	1	0	140.1	618	128	82	72	13	11	3	8	80	1	132	12	0	12	8	.600	0	0- -	-	4.45	4.62
2006	Col	NL	1	1	0	0	4.0	24	8	7	7	3	1	0	1	3	0	4	0	0	0	0	-	0	0-0	0	20.26	15.75

Justin Morneau

Bats: L Throws: R Pos: 1B-153; DH-4; PH-1   Ht: 6'4" Wt: 225 Born: 5/15/1981 Age: 26

Year	Team	Lg	G	AB	H	2B	3B	HR	(Hm	Rd)	TB	R	RBI	RC	TBB	IBB	SO	HBP	SH	SF	SB	CS	SB%	GDP	Avg	OBP	Slg
2003	Min	AL	40	106	24	4	0	4	(1	3)	40	14	16	11	9	1	30	0	0	0	0	0	-	4	.226	.287	.377
2004	Min	AL	74	280	76	17	4	19	(9	10)	150	39	58	48	28	8	54	2	0	2	0	0	-	4	.271	.340	.536
2005	Min	AL	141	490	117	23	4	22	(9	13)	214	62	79	58	44	8	94	4	0	5	0	2	.00	12	.239	.304	.437
2006	Min	AL	157	592	190	37	1	34	(17	17)	331	97	130	118	53	9	93	5	0	11	3	3	.50	10	.321	.375	.559
4 ML YEARS			412	1468	407	81	5	79	(36	43)	735	212	283	235	134	26	271	11	0	18	3	5	.38	30	.277	.338	.501

Matt Morris

Pitches: R Bats: R Pos: SP-33   Ht: 6'5" Wt: 220 Born: 8/9/1974 Age: 32

Year	Team	Lg	G	GS	CG	GF	IP	BFP	H	R	ER	HR	SH	SF	HB	TBB	IBB	SO	WP	Bk	W	L	Pct	ShO	Sv-Op	Hld	ERC	ERA
1997	StL	NL	33	33	3	0	217.0	900	208	88	77	12	11	7	7	69	2	149	5	3	12	9	.571	0	0-0	0	3.41	3.19
1998	StL	NL	17	17	2	0	113.2	468	101	37	32	8	6	1	3	42	6	79	3	0	7	5	.583	1	0-0	0	3.25	2.53
2000	StL	NL	31	0	0	12	53.0	226	53	22	21	3	3	1	2	17	1	34	0	0	3	3	.500	0	4-7	7	3.58	3.57
2001	StL	NL	34	34	2	0	216.1	909	218	86	76	13	14	5	13	54	3	185	5	1	22	8	.733	1	0-0	0	3.50	3.16
2002	StL	NL	32	32	1	0	210.1	890	210	86	80	16	7	8	6	64	3	171	3	0	17	9	.654	1	0-0	0	3.63	3.42
2003	StL	NL	27	27	5	0	172.1	703	164	76	72	20	5	3	4	39	1	120	3	0	11	8	.579	3	0-0	0	3.37	3.76
2004	StL	NL	32	32	3	0	202.0	850	205	116	106	35	5	6	5	56	3	131	3	1	15	10	.600	2	0-0	0	4.30	4.72
2005	StL	NL	31	31	2	0	192.2	818	209	101	88	22	10	5	8	37	3	117	1	1	14	10	.583	0	0-0	0	3.95	4.11
2006	SF	NL	33	33	2	0	207.2	903	218	123	115	22	9	5	14	63	9	117	1	3	10	15	.400	0	0-0	0	4.19	4.98
9 ML YEARS			270	239	20	12	1585.0	6667	1586	735	667	151	78	40	63	441	31	1103	24	9	111	77	.590	8	4-7	7	3.72	3.79

Mike Morse

Bats: R Throws: R Pos: RF-7; PH-7; 3B-5; DH-4; 1B-2; LF-2; SS-1   Ht: 6'4" Wt: 225 Born: 3/22/1982 Age: 25

Year	Team	Lg	G	AB	H	2B	3B	HR	(Hm	Rd)	TB	R	RBI	RC	TBB	IBB	SO	HBP	SH	SF	SB	CS	SB%	GDP	Avg	OBP	Slg
2000	WhSox	R	45	180	46	6	1	2	(-	-)	60	32	24	20	15	0	29	1	0	5	5	2	.71	6	.256	.308	.333
2001	Bristol	R+	56	176	41	7	3	4	(-	-)	66	23	26	23	17	1	54	9	0	0	6	2	.75	4	.233	.332	.375
2002	Knapol	A-	113	417	107	30	4	2	(-	-)	151	43	56	48	25	0	73	8	7	2	7	6	.54	16	.257	.310	.362
2003	WinSa	A+	122	432	106	30	2	10	(-	-)	170	45	55	51	25	0	91	7	2	2	4	4	.50	12	.245	.296	.394
2004	Brham	AA	54	209	60	9	5	11	(-	-)	112	30	38	36	15	1	46	1	0	1	0	3	.00	4	.287	.336	.536
2004	SnAnt	AA	41	157	43	10	1	6	(-	-)	73	18	33	23	9	0	27	4	1	2	0	2	.00	8	.274	.326	.465
2005	Tacom	AAA	49	182	46	12	2	4	(-	-)	74	20	23	24	16	1	36	2	1	2	1	0	1.00	6	.253	.317	.407
2006	Tacom	AAA	57	206	51	15	1	5	(-	-)	83	23	34	25	14	1	46	3	1	4	0	1	.00	7	.248	.300	.403
2005	Sea	AL	72	230	64	10	1	3	(3	0)	85	27	23	28	18	0	50	8	0	2	3	1	.75	9	.278	.349	.370
2006	Sea	AL	21	43	16	5	0	0	(0	0)	21	5	11	9	3	0	7	0	0	2	1	0	1.00	2	.372	.396	.488
2 ML YEARS			93	273	80	15	1	3	(3	0)	106	32	34	37	21	0	57	8	0	4	4	1	.80	11	.293	.356	.388

Dustin Moseley

Pitches: R Bats: R Pos: SP-2; RP-1   Ht: 6'4" Wt: 190 Born: 12/26/1981 Age: 25

Year	Team	Lg	G	GS	CG	GF	IP	BFP	H	R	ER	HR	SH	SF	HB	TBB	IBB	SO	WP	Bk	W	L	Pct	ShO	Sv-Op	Hld	ERC	ERA
2001	Dayton	A	25	25	0	0	148.0	638	158	83	69	10	4	1	8	42	0	108	3	2	10	8	.556	0	0- -	-	3.98	4.20
2002	Stcktn	A+	14	14	2	0	88.2	350	60	28	27	3	2	0	8	21	0	80	2	3	6	3	.667	2	0- -	-	1.78	2.74
2002	Chatt	AA	13	13	0	0	80.2	361	91	47	37	5	6	3	4	37	0	52	2	0	5	6	.455	0	0- -	-	5.02	4.13
2003	Chatt	AA	18	18	0	0	112.2	480	116	55	48	10	3	3	7	28	0	73	2	0	5	6	.455	0	0- -	-	3.80	3.83
2003	Lsvlle	AAA	8	8	0	0	50.0	207	46	19	15	5	1	3	1	14	0	27	2	1	2	3	.400	0	0- -	-	3.26	2.70
2004	Chatt	AA	8	8	0	0	47.1	181	33	16	14	4	1	1	2	10	0	40	0	3	3	2	.600	0	0- -	-	1.96	2.66

Year	Team	Lg	G	GS	CG	GF	IP	BFP	H	R	ER	HR	SH	SF	HB	TBB	IBB	SO	WP	Bk	W	L	Pct	ShO	Sv-Op	Hld	ERC	ERA
			HOW MUCH HE PITCHED						**WHAT HE GAVE UP**												**THE RESULTS**							
2004	Lsvlle	AAA	12	12	0	0	71.2	312	78	38	37	7	4	5	4	34	0	48	2	0	2	4	.333	0	0- --		5.30	4.65
2005	Salt Lk	AAA	17	17	0	0	82.1	371	102	51	46	11	1	8	5	30	1	38	1	2	4	6	.400	0	0- --		5.89	5.03
2006	Salt Lk	AAA	26	26	3	0	149.2	646	164	89	78	18	3	5	8	51	0	114	7	2	13	8	.619	0	0- --		4.84	4.69
2006	LAA	AL	3	2	0	1	11.0	54	22	11	11	3	0	1	0	2	0	3	0	0	1	0	1.000	0	0-0	0	11.45	9.00

Guillermo Mota

Pitches: R **Bats:** R **Pos:** RP-52 **Ht:** 6'4" **Wt:** 210 **Born:** 7/25/1973 **Age:** 33

Year	Team	Lg	G	GS	CG	GF	IP	BFP	H	R	ER	HR	SH	SF	HB	TBB	IBB	SO	WP	Bk	W	L	Pct	ShO	Sv-Op	Hld	ERC	ERA
			HOW MUCH HE PITCHED						**WHAT HE GAVE UP**												**THE RESULTS**							
1999	Mon	NL	51	0	0	18	55.1	243	54	24	18	5	3	3	2	25	3	27	1	1	2	4	.333	0	0-1	3	4.10	2.93
2000	Mon	NL	29	0	0	7	30.0	126	27	21	20	3	1	1	2	12	0	24	1	1	1	1	.500	0	0-0	5	3.86	6.00
2001	Mon	NL	53	0	0	12	49.2	212	51	30	29	9	3	2	1	18	1	31	1	0	1	3	.250	0	0-3	12	4.77	5.26
2002	LAD	NL	43	0	0	11	60.2	256	45	30	28	4	3	1	2	27	6	49	3	0	1	3	.250	0	0-1	4	2.57	4.15
2003	LAD	NL	76	0	0	18	105.0	410	78	23	23	7	3	1	1	26	4	99	0	0	6	3	.667	0	1-3	13	2.01	1.97
2004	2 Tms	NL	78	0	0	18	96.2	393	75	33	33	8	5	3	4	37	6	85	5	0	9	8	.529	0	4-8	30	2.82	3.07
2005	Fla	NL	56	0	0	24	67.0	293	65	38	35	5	1	3	1	32	7	60	4	0	2	2	.500	0	2-4	14	3.90	4.70
2006	2 Tms	NL	52	0	0	17	55.2	241	55	29	28	11	0	3	0	24	4	46	2	0	4	3	.571	0	0-0	9	4.71	4.53
04	LAD	NL	52	0	0	11	63.0	259	51	15	15	4	4	2	2	27	5	52	5	0	8	4	.667	0	1-1	17	2.98	2.14
04	Fla	NL	26	0	0	7	33.2	134	24	18	18	4	1	1	2	10	1	33	0	0	1	4	.200	0	3-7	13	2.51	4.81
06	Cle	AL	34	0	0	13	37.2	173	45	27	26	9	0	3	0	19	3	27	2	0	1	3	.250	0	0-0	5	6.62	6.21
06	NYM	NL	18	0	0	4	18.0	68	10	2	2	2	0	0	0	5	1	19	0	0	3	0	1.000	0	0-0	4	1.51	1.00
8 ML YEARS			438	0	0	125	520.0	2174	450	228	214	52	19	17	13	201	31	421	17	2	26	27	.491	0	7-20	90	3.31	3.70

Chad Mottola

Bats: R **Throws:** R **Pos:** LF-3; RF-2; DH-2; PH-2; PR-2 **Ht:** 6'3" **Wt:** 235 **Born:** 10/15/1971 **Age:** 35

Year	Team	Lg	G	AB	H	2B	3B	HR	(Hm	Rd)	TB	R	RBI	RC	TBB	IBB	SO	HBP	SH	SF	SB	CS	SB%	GDP	Avg	OBP	Slg
						BATTING															**BASERUNNING**				**AVERAGES**		
2006	Syrcse*	AAA	110	431	114	27	2	16	(-	-)	193	48	65	63	30	1	103	2	0	1	8	0	1.00	9	.265	.315	.448
1996	Cin	NL	35	79	17	3	0	3	(1	2)	29	10	6	7	6	1	16	0	0	0	2	2	.50	0	.215	.271	.367
2000	Tor	AL	3	9	2	0	0	0	(0	0)	2	1	2	0	0	0	4	1	0	0	0	0	-	0	.222	.300	.222
2001	Fla	NL	5	7	0	0	0	0	(0	0)	0	1	1	0	2	0	2	0	0	1	0	0	-	0	.000	.200	.000
2004	Bal	AL	6	14	2	1	0	1	(0	1)	6	2	3	2	2	0	3	0	0	0	0	0	-	1	.143	.250	.429
2006	Tor	AL	10	16	4	2	0	0	(0	0)	6	3	0	0	0	0	3	0	0	0	0	0	-	0	.250	.250	.375
5 ML YEARS			59	125	25	6	0	4	(1	3)	43	17	12	9	10	1	28	1	0	1	2	2	.50	1	.200	.263	.344

Jamie Moyer

Pitches: L **Bats:** L **Pos:** SP-33 **Ht:** 6'0" **Wt:** 180 **Born:** 11/18/1962 **Age:** 44

Year	Team	Lg	G	GS	CG	GF	IP	BFP	H	R	ER	HR	SH	SF	HB	TBB	IBB	SO	WP	Bk	W	L	Pct	ShO	Sv-Op	Hld	ERC	ERA
			HOW MUCH HE PITCHED						**WHAT HE GAVE UP**												**THE RESULTS**							
1986	ChC	NL	16	16	1	0	87.1	395	107	52	49	10	3	3	3	42	1	45	3	3	7	4	.636	1	0-0	0	6.13	5.05
1987	ChC	NL	35	33	1	1	201.0	899	210	127	114	28	14	7	5	97	9	147	11	2	12	15	.444	0	0-0	0	4.96	5.10
1988	ChC	NL	34	30	3	1	202.0	855	212	84	78	20	14	4	4	55	7	121	4	0	9	15	.375	1	0-2	0	3.89	3.48
1989	Tex	AL	15	15	1	0	76.0	337	84	51	41	10	1	4	2	33	0	44	1	0	4	9	.308	0	0-0	0	5.20	4.86
1990	Tex	AL	33	10	1	6	102.1	447	115	59	53	6	1	7	4	39	4	58	1	0	2	6	.250	0	0-0	1	4.57	4.66
1991	StL	NL	8	7	0	1	31.1	142	38	21	20	5	4	2	1	16	0	20	2	1	0	5	.000	0	0-0	0	6.58	5.74
1993	Bal	AL	25	25	3	0	152.0	630	154	63	58	11	3	1	6	38	2	90	1	1	12	9	.571	1	0-0	0	3.58	3.43
1994	Bal	AL	23	23	0	0	149.0	631	158	81	79	23	5	2	2	38	3	87	1	0	5	7	.417	0	0-0	0	4.24	4.77
1995	Bal	AL	27	18	0	3	115.2	483	117	70	67	18	5	3	3	30	0	65	0	0	8	6	.571	0	0-0	0	4.11	5.21
1996	2 Tms	AL	34	21	0	1	160.2	703	177	86	71	23	7	6	2	46	5	79	3	1	13	3	.813	0	0-0	1	4.42	3.98
1997	Sea	AL	30	30	2	0	188.2	787	187	82	81	21	6	1	7	43	2	113	3	0	17	5	.773	0	0-0	0	3.56	3.86
1998	Sea	AL	34	34	4	0	234.1	974	234	99	92	23	4	3	10	42	2	158	3	1	15	9	.625	3	0-0	0	3.34	3.53
1999	Sea	AL	32	32	4	0	228.0	945	235	108	98	23	6	2	9	48	1	137	3	0	14	8	.636	0	0-0	0	3.71	3.87
2000	Sea	AL	26	26	0	0	154.0	678	173	103	94	22	3	3	3	53	2	98	4	1	13	10	.565	0	0-0	0	4.91	5.49
2001	Sea	AL	33	33	1	0	209.2	851	187	84	80	24	5	11	10	44	4	119	1	0	20	6	.769	0	0-0	0	3.03	3.43
2002	Sea	AL	34	34	4	0	230.2	931	198	89	85	28	5	7	9	50	4	147	3	0	13	8	.619	2	0-0	0	2.89	3.32
2003	Sea	AL	33	33	1	0	215.0	897	199	83	78	19	7	6	8	66	3	129	0	0	21	7	.750	0	0-0	0	3.37	3.27
2004	Sea	AL	34	33	1	1	202.0	888	217	127	117	44	9	6	11	63	3	125	1	0	7	13	.350	0	0-0	0	5.13	5.21
2005	Sea	AL	32	32	1	0	200.0	868	225	99	95	23	6	6	8	52	2	102	3	1	13	7	.650	0	0-0	0	4.46	4.28
2006	2 Tms		33	33	2	0	211.1	894	228	110	101	33	5	9	5	51	5	108	3	1	11	14	.440	1	0-0	0	4.36	4.30
96	Bos	AL	23	10	0	1	90.0	405	111	50	45	14	4	3	1	27	2	50	2	1	7	1	.875	0	0-0	1	5.37	4.50
96	Sea	AL	11	11	0	0	70.2	298	66	36	26	9	3	3	1	19	3	29	1	0	6	2	.750	0	0-0	0	3.31	3.31
06	Sea	AL	25	25	2	0	160.0	685	179	85	78	25	3	7	3	44	3	82	3	1	6	12	.333	1	0-0	0	4.74	4.39
06	Phi	NL	8	8	0	0	51.1	209	49	25	23	8	2	2	2	7	2	26	0	0	5	2	.714	0	0-0	0	3.24	4.03
20 ML YEARS			571	518	30	14	3351.0	14235	3455	1678	1551	414	113	93	112	946	59	1992	51	11	216	166	.565	9	0-2	2	4.06	4.17

Peter Moylan

Pitches: R **Bats:** R **Pos:** RP-15 **Ht:** 6'3" **Wt:** 220 **Born:** 12/2/1978 **Age:** 28

Year	Team	Lg	G	GS	CG	GF	IP	BFP	H	R	ER	HR	SH	SF	HB	TBB	IBB	SO	WP	Bk	W	L	Pct	ShO	Sv-Op	Hld	ERC	ERA
			HOW MUCH HE PITCHED						**WHAT HE GAVE UP**												**THE RESULTS**							
1996	Twins	R	13	0	0	4	28.2	128	34	16	13	3	1	2	3	9	0	16	4	0	1	1	.500	0	1- --		5.31	4.08
1997	Twins	R	12	7	0	2	40.0	178	46	21	18	0	0	1	4	10	0	40	3	0	4	2	.667	0	0- --		3.93	4.05
2006	Rchmd	AAA	35	0	0	11	56.2	275	61	43	40	4	4	1	8	38	6	54	6	0	1	7	.125	0	1- --		5.64	6.35
2006	Atl	NL	15	0	0	5	15.0	68	18	8	8	1	1	0	0	5	1	14	0	0	0	0	-	0	0-0	0	4.47	4.80

Bill Mueller

Bats: B Throws: R Pos: 3B-30; PH-2   **Ht: 5'10" Wt: 180 Born: 3/17/1971 Age: 36**

Year	Team	Lg	G	AB	H	2B	3B	HR	(Hm	Rd)	TB	R	RBI	RC	TBB	IBB	SO	HBP	SH	SF	SB	CS	SB%	GDP	Avg	OBP	Slg
1996	SF	NL	55	200	66	15	1	0	(0	0)	83	31	19	35	24	0	26	1	1	2	0	0	-	1	.330	.401	.415
1997	SF	NL	128	390	114	26	3	7	(5	2)	167	51	44	62	48	1	71	3	6	6	4	3	.57	10	.292	.369	.428
1998	SF	NL	145	534	157	27	0	9	(1	8)	211	93	59	83	79	1	83	1	3	5	3	3	.50	12	.294	.383	.395
1999	SF	NL	116	414	120	24	0	2	(1	1)	150	61	36	62	65	1	52	3	8	2	4	2	.67	11	.290	.388	.362
2000	SF	NL	153	560	150	29	4	10	(3	7)	217	97	55	72	52	0	62	6	7	6	4	2	.67	16	.268	.333	.388
2001	ChC	NL	70	210	62	12	1	6	(3	3)	94	38	23	39	37	3	19	3	4	3	1	1	.50	4	.295	.403	.448
2002	2 Tms		111	366	96	19	4	7	(4	3)	144	51	38	56	52	2	42	0	4	5	0	0	-	9	.262	.350	.393
2003	Bos	AL	146	524	171	45	5	19	(6	13)	283	85	85	102	59	2	77	7	4	6	1	4	.20	11	.326	.398	.540
2004	Bos	AL	110	399	113	27	1	12	(9	3)	178	75	57	61	51	1	56	4	0	6	2	2	.50	8	.283	.365	.446
2005	Bos	AL	150	519	153	34	3	10	(6	4)	223	69	62	82	59	3	74	6	0	6	0	0	-	22	.295	.369	.430
2006	LAD	NL	32	107	27	7	0	3	(0	3)	43	12	15	16	17	3	9	1	0	1	1	1	.50	1	.252	.357	.402
02	ChC	NL	103	353	94	19	4	7	(4	3)	142	51	37	56	51	2	41	0	4	5	0	0	-	8	.266	.355	.402
02	SF	NL	8	13	2	0	0	0	(0	0)	2	0	1	0	1	0	1	0	0	0	0	0	-	1	.154	.214	.154
11 ML YEARS			1216	4223	1229	265	22	85	(38	47)	1793	663	493	670	543	17	571	35	37	48	20	18	.53	105	.291	.373	.425

Edward Mujica

Pitches: R Bats: R Pos: RP-10   **Ht: 6'2" Wt: 220 Born: 5/10/1984 Age: 23**

			HOW MUCH HE PITCHED					WHAT HE GAVE UP										THE RESULTS						
Year	Team	Lg	G	GS	CG	GF	IP	BFP	H	R	ER	HR	SH	SF	HB	TBB	IBB	SO	WP	Bk	W	L	Pct	ShO	Sv-Op Hld	ERC	ERA
2003	Burlgtn	A+	14	10	0	3	55.2	231	57	31	27	3	2	1	1	20	0	41	2	1	2	6	.250	0	0- - -	3.96	4.37
2004	Lk Cty	A	26	19	1	3	124.0	525	130	77	64	18	5	7	13	32	1	89	6	4	7	7	.500	0	2- - -	4.61	4.65
2005	Kinston	A+	25	0	0	25	26.0	96	17	6	6	3	1	0	1	2	0	32	1	0	1	0	1.000	0	14- - -	1.51	2.08
2005	Akron	AA	27	0	0	18	34.1	141	36	11	11	2	4	0	0	5	0	33	3	1	2	1	.667	0	10- - -	3.09	2.88
2006	Akron	AA	12	0	0	10	19.0	77	11	1	0	0	2	0	1	9	1	17	1	0	1	0	1.000	0	8- - -	1.68	0.00
2006	Buffalo	AAA	22	0	0	16	32.2	130	31	10	9	1	4	0	1	5	0	29	1	0	3	1	.750	0	5- - -	2.61	2.48
2006	Cle	AL	10	0	0	2	18.1	78	25	6	6	1	0	2	1	0	0	12	0	0	0	1	.000	0	0-0 0	4.50	2.95

Mark Mulder

Pitches: L Bats: L Pos: SP-17   **Ht: 6'6" Wt: 215 Born: 8/5/1977 Age: 29**

			HOW MUCH HE PITCHED					WHAT HE GAVE UP										THE RESULTS						
Year	Team	Lg	G	GS	CG	GF	IP	BFP	H	R	ER	HR	SH	SF	HB	TBB	IBB	SO	WP	Bk	W	L	Pct	ShO	Sv-Op Hld	ERC	ERA
2006	QuadC*	A	1	1	0	0	5.0	18	2	2	1	1	0	0	0	2	0	1	0	0	0	0	-	0	0- - -	1.76	1.80
2006	Memp*	AAA	2	2	0	0	8.0	43	11	9	8	2	0	0	0	9	0	5	0	0	0	1	.000	0	0- - -	11.06	9.00
2000	Oak	AL	27	27	0	0	154.0	705	191	106	93	22	3	8	4	69	3	88	6	0	9	10	.474	0	0-0 0	6.14	5.44
2001	Oak	AL	34	34	6	0	229.1	927	214	92	88	16	8	3	5	51	4	153	4	0	21	8	.724	4	0-0 0	2.95	3.45
2002	Oak	AL	30	30	2	0	207.1	862	182	88	80	21	6	4	11	55	3	159	7	1	19	7	.731	1	0-0 0	3.06	3.47
2003	Oak	AL	26	26	9	0	186.2	747	180	66	65	15	7	2	2	40	2	128	7	0	15	9	.625	2	0-0 0	3.17	3.13
2004	Oak	AL	33	33	5	0	225.2	952	223	119	111	25	7	6	12	83	1	140	10	0	17	8	.680	1	0-0 0	4.27	4.43
2005	StL	NL	32	32	3	0	205.0	868	212	90	83	19	9	4	9	70	1	111	9	0	16	8	.667	2	0-0 0	4.25	3.64
2006	StL	NL	17	17	0	0	93.1	430	124	77	74	19	10	1	5	35	1	50	3	0	6	7	.462	0	0-0 0	7.04	7.14
7 ML YEARS			199	199	25	0	1301.1	5491	1326	638	594	137	50	28	48	403	15	829	46	1	103	57	.644	10	0-0 0	4.05	4.11

Terry Mulholland

Pitches: L Bats: R Pos: RP-5   **Ht: 6'3" Wt: 225 Born: 3/9/1963 Age: 44**

			HOW MUCH HE PITCHED					WHAT HE GAVE UP										THE RESULTS						
Year	Team	Lg	G	GS	CG	GF	IP	BFP	H	R	ER	HR	SH	SF	HB	TBB	IBB	SO	WP	Bk	W	L	Pct	ShO	Sv-Op Hld	ERC	ERA
2006	Tucsn*	AAA	3	1	0	1	10.2	40	9	4	4	0	0	2	0	3	0	5	0	0	1	1	.500	0	0- - -	2.41	3.38
1986	SF	NL	15	10	0	1	54.2	245	51	33	30	3	5	1	1	35	2	27	6	0	1	7	.125	0	0-0 0	4.31	4.94
1988	SF	NL	9	6	2	1	46.0	191	50	20	19	3	5	0	1	7	0	18	1	0	2	1	.667	1	0-0 1	3.46	3.72
1989	2 Tms	NL	25	18	2	4	115.1	513	137	66	63	8	7	1	4	36	3	66	3	0	4	7	.364	1	0-0 1	4.64	4.92
1990	Phi	NL	33	26	6	2	180.2	746	172	78	67	15	7	12	2	42	7	75	7	2	9	10	.474	1	0-1 0	3.04	3.34
1991	Phi	NL	34	34	8	0	232.0	956	231	100	93	15	11	6	3	49	2	142	3	0	16	13	.552	3	0-0 0	3.15	3.61
1992	Phi	NL	32	32	12	0	229.0	937	227	101	97	14	10	7	3	46	3	125	3	0	13	11	.542	2	0-0 0	3.07	3.81
1993	Phi	NL	29	28	7	0	191.0	786	177	80	69	20	5	4	3	40	2	116	5	0	12	9	.571	2	0-0 0	2.99	3.25
1994	NYY	AL	24	19	2	4	120.2	542	150	94	87	24	3	4	3	37	1	72	5	0	6	7	.462	0	0-0 0	5.92	6.49
1995	SF	NL	29	24	2	2	149.0	666	190	112	96	25	11	6	4	38	1	65	4	0	5	13	.278	0	0-0 0	5.67	5.80
1996	2 Tms	NL	33	33	3	0	202.2	871	232	112	105	22	11	8	5	49	4	86	6	0	13	11	.542	0	0-0 0	4.41	4.66
1997	2 Tms	NL	40	27	1	5	186.2	794	190	100	88	24	17	4	11	51	3	99	3	0	6	13	.316	0	0-0 1	4.09	4.24
1998	ChC	NL	70	6	0	14	112.0	476	100	49	36	7	5	3	4	39	7	72	4	0	6	5	.545	0	3-5 19	3.04	2.89
1999	2 Tms	NL	42	24	0	7	170.1	736	201	95	83	21	9	4	1	45	6	83	3	0	10	8	.556	0	1-1 4	4.73	4.39
2000	Atl	NL	54	20	1	14	156.2	702	198	96	89	24	10	5	4	41	7	78	0	0	9	9	.500	0	1-3 2	5.43	5.11
2001	2 Tms	NL	41	4	0	8	65.2	285	78	35	34	12	1	1	2	17	1	42	1	0	1	1	.500	0	0-0 7	5.34	4.66
2002	2 Tms	NL	37	3	0	17	79.0	357	101	56	50	15	2	6	6	23	3	38	1	0	3	2	.600	0	0-0 2	6.09	5.70
2003	Cle	AL	45	3	0	14	99.0	445	117	60	54	17	6	6	6	37	6	42	1	0	3	4	.429	0	0-2 2	5.75	4.91
2004	Min	AL	39	15	0	9	123.1	549	163	76	71	17	7	7	5	33	3	60	2	0	5	9	.357	0	0-0 0	5.94	5.18
2005	Min	AL	49	0	0	26	59.0	246	61	30	28	6	5	1	2	17	4	18	3	1	0	2	.000	0	0-1 3	3.96	4.27
2006	Ari	NL	5	0	0	1	3.0	17	7	3	3	1	2	0	0	1	0	1	0	0	0	0	-	0	0-1 1	14.72	9.00
89	SF	NL	5	1	0	2	11.0	51	15	5	5	0	0	0	4	0	0	6	0	0	0	0	-	0	0-0 1	5.23	4.09
89	Phi	NL	20	17	2	2	104.1	462	122	61	58	8	7	1	4	32	3	60	3	0	4	7	.364	1	0-0 0	4.58	5.00
96	Phi	NL	21	21	3	0	133.1	571	157	74	69	17	6	5	3	21	1	52	5	0	8	7	.533	0	0-0 0	4.36	4.66
96	Sea	AL	12	12	0	0	69.1	300	75	38	36	5	5	3	2	28	3	34	1	0	5	4	.556	0	0-0 0	4.49	4.67
97	ChC	NL	25	25	1	0	157.0	668	162	79	71	20	13	3	9	45	2	74	2	0	6	12	.333	0	0-0 0	4.24	4.07
97	SF	NL	15	2	0	5	29.2	126	28	21	17	4	4	1	2	6	1	25	1	0	0	1	.000	0	0-0 1	3.34	5.16
99	ChC	NL	26	16	0	4	110.0	485	137	71	63	16	6	3	1	32	4	44	2	0	6	6	.500	0	0-0 0	5.42	5.15
99	Atl	NL	16	8	0	3	60.1	251	64	24	20	5	3	1	0	13	2	39	1	0	4	2	.667	0	1-1 3	3.55	2.98
01	Pit	NL	22	1	0	3	36.1	150	38	15	15	5	1	1	1	10	1	17	1	0	0	0	-	0	0-0 3	4.32	3.72

Year	Team	Lg	G	GS	CG	GF	IP	BFP	H	R	ER	HR	SH	SF	HB	TBB	IBB	SO	WP	Bk	W	L	Pct	ShO	Sv-Op	Hld	ERC	ERA
01	LAD	NL	19	3	0	5	29.1	135	40	20	19	7	0	0	1	7	0	25	0	0	1	1	.500	0	0-0	4	6.67	5.83
02	LAD	NL	21	0	0	12	32.0	147	45	29	26	10	0	2	2	7	0	17	1	0	0	0	-	0	0-0	0	7.68	7.31
02	Cle	AL	16	3	0	5	47.0	210	56	27	24	5	2	4	4	14	3	21	0	0	3	2	.600	0	0-0	0	5.05	4.60
20 ML YEARS			685	332	46	128	2575.2	11060	2833	1396	1262	293	133	84	70	681	65	1325	64	3	124	142	.466	10	5-14	45	4.27	4.41

Eric Munson

Bats: L **Throws:** R **Pos:** C-37; PH-15; 1B-4; DH-1   **Ht:** 6'3" **Wt:** 220 **Born:** 10/3/1977 **Age:** 29

Year	Team	Lg	G	AB	H	2B	3B	HR	(Hm	Rd)	TB	R	RBI	RC	TBB	IBB	SO	HBP	SH	SF	SB	CS	SB%	GDP	Avg	OBP	Slg
2006	RdRck*	AAA	9	32	8	1	0	2	(-	-)	15	6	8	5	3	0	4	2	0	0	0	0	-	1	.250	.351	.469
2000	Det	AL	3	5	0	0	0	0	(0	0)	0	0	1	0	0	0	1	0	0	0	0	0	-	0	.000	.000	.000
2001	Det	AL	17	66	10	3	1	1	(1	0)	18	4	6	2	3	0	21	0	0	0	0	1	.00	2	.152	.188	.273
2002	Det	AL	18	59	11	0	0	2	(0	2)	17	3	5	3	6	0	11	1	0	1	0	0	-	1	.186	.269	.288
2003	Det	AL	99	313	75	9	0	18	(7	11)	138	28	50	45	35	1	61	1	1	7	3	0	1.00	4	.240	.312	.441
2004	Det	AL	109	321	68	14	2	19	(13	6)	143	36	49	48	29	3	90	6	1	0	1	1	.50	1	.212	.289	.445
2005	TB	AL	11	18	3	1	0	0	(0	0)	4	2	2	2	4	0	3	1	0	1	0	0	-	2	.167	.333	.222
2006	Hou	NL	53	141	28	6	0	5	(2	3)	49	10	19	12	11	1	32	3	0	1	0	0	-	2	.199	.269	.348
7 ML YEARS			310	923	195	33	3	45	(23	22)	369	83	132	112	88	5	219	12	2	10	4	2	.67	12	.211	.286	.400

Scott Munter

Pitches: R **Bats:** R **Pos:** RP-27   **Ht:** 6'6" **Wt:** 260 **Born:** 3/7/1980 **Age:** 27

Year	Team	Lg	G	GS	CG	GF	IP	BFP	H	R	ER	HR	SH	SF	HB	TBB	IBB	SO	WP	Bk	W	L	Pct	ShO	Sv-Op	Hld	ERC	ERA
2001	SlmKzr	A-	15	0	0	1	35.0	159	42	26	23	3	0	1	1	12	0	28	3	0	1	2	.333	0	0--	-	4.91	5.91
2001	Hgrstn	A	1	1	0	0	5.1	21	5	3	2	0	1	1	0	1	0	2	0	0	1	0	1.000	0	0--	-	2.40	3.38
2002	SnJos	A	3	0	0	0	4.1	29	12	5	5	0	0	2	0	4	0	2	0	0	0	0	-	0	0--	-	17.37	10.38
2002	SlmKzr	A-	10	4	0	1	29.2	142	33	24	23	0	1	3	2	20	0	20	3	1	1	1	.500	0	0--	-	5.22	6.98
2003	Hgrstn	A	40	0	0	18	68.2	296	61	28	18	3	3	0	2	28	0	47	7	1	3	5	.375	0	5--	-	3.16	2.36
2004	Nrwich	AA	42	0	0	19	65.0	280	63	19	17	4	1	0	2	22	5	30	9	0	2	4	.333	0	3--	-	3.35	2.35
2004	Fresno	AAA	13	0	0	6	15.2	71	20	8	6	1	0	0	0	4	0	5	1	0	1	1	.500	0	1--	-	4.69	3.45
2005	Fresno	AAA	12	0	0	5	12.1	58	17	8	7	0	1	2	0	4	0	5	1	0	1	3	.250	0	1--	-	5.05	5.11
2006	Nrwich	AA	28	0	0	10	40.0	177	45	24	21	1	3	3	2	15	0	22	1	0	1	4	.200	0	1--	-	4.34	4.73
2005	SF	NL	45	0	0	7	38.2	159	40	15	11	1	2	1	1	12	1	11	1	0	2	0	1.000	0	0-3	12	3.62	2.56
2006	SF	NL	27	0	0	11	22.2	110	30	22	22	1	7	1	2	18	2	7	0	0	0	1	.000	0	0-0	5	7.75	8.74
2 ML YEARS			72	0	0	18	61.1	269	70	37	33	2	9	2	3	30	3	18	1	0	2	1	.667	0	0-3	17	5.05	4.84

David Murphy

Bats: L **Throws:** L **Pos:** CF-8; LF-6; PR-5; RF-2; PH-2; DH-1   **Ht:** 6'4" **Wt:** 190 **Born:** 10/18/1981 **Age:** 25

Year	Team	Lg	G	AB	H	2B	3B	HR	(Hm	Rd)	TB	R	RBI	RC	TBB	IBB	SO	HBP	SH	SF	SB	CS	SB%	GDP	Avg	OBP	Slg
2003	Lowell	A	21	78	27	4	0	0	(-	-)	31	13	13	16	16	2	9	0	0	1	4	1	.80	1	.346	.453	.397
2003	Srsota	A	45	153	37	5	1	1	(-	-)	47	18	18	17	20	1	33	0	0	0	6	2	.75	3	.242	.329	.307
2004	RedSx	R	5	18	5	1	0	0	(-	-)	6	3	1	2	1	0	2	0	0	0	1	0	1.00	1	.278	.316	.333
2004	Srsota	A	73	272	71	11	0	4	(-	-)	94	35	38	30	25	4	46	0	0	0	3	5	.38	5	.261	.323	.346
2005	Portlnd	AA	135	484	133	25	4	14	(-	-)	208	71	75	73	46	3	83	1	1	3	13	6	.68	11	.275	.337	.430
2006	Portlnd	AA	42	172	47	17	1	3	(-	-)	75	22	25	24	11	0	29	0	0	1	4	2	.67	3	.273	.315	.436
2006	Pwtckt	AAA	84	318	85	23	5	8	(-	-)	142	45	44	52	45	8	53	0	0	3	3	3	.50	13	.267	.355	.447
2006	Bos	AL	20	22	5	1	0	1	(0	1)	9	4	2	2	4	0	4	0	0	0	0	0	-	1	.227	.346	.409

Tommy Murphy

Bats: B **Throws:** R **Pos:** CF-29; RF-12; PR-11; LF-2; PH-2; DH-1   **Ht:** 6'0" **Wt:** 185 **Born:** 8/27/1979 **Age:** 27

Year	Team	Lg	G	AB	H	2B	3B	HR	(Hm	Rd)	TB	R	RBI	RC	TBB	IBB	SO	HBP	SH	SF	SB	CS	SB%	GDP	Avg	OBP	Slg
2000	Boise	A-	55	213	48	18	1	2	(-	-)	74	38	25	22	15	0	52	5	1	1	14	7	.67	1	.225	.291	.347
2001	CRpds	A	74	280	57	15	3	4	(-	-)	90	32	31	21	16	1	94	6	3	6	7	10	.41	5	.204	.259	.321
2001	RCuca	A+	50	200	38	8	0	0	(-	-)	46	16	11	7	5	0	69	1	1	0	7	3	.70	4	.190	.214	.230
2002	CRpds	A	128	485	131	20	2	3	(-	-)	164	72	48	58	40	0	115	1	7	5	31	11	.74	8	.270	.324	.338
2003	RCuca	A+	132	565	151	25	6	11	(-	-)	221	74	43	71	31	0	138	8	7	3	24	12	.67	7	.267	.313	.391
2004	Ark	AA	129	477	124	24	6	7	(-	-)	181	77	45	62	36	1	113	1	9	5	27	5	.84	9	.260	.310	.379
2005	Ark	AA	135	500	144	24	11	17	(-	-)	241	85	76	86	43	2	97	5	2	7	26	12	.68	11	.288	.346	.482
2006	Salt Lk	AAA	73	285	86	16	3	7	(-	-)	129	43	36	42	19	2	62	3	2	1	6	13	.32	1	.302	.351	.453
2006	LAA	AL	48	70	16	4	1	1	(1	0)	25	12	6	7	5	0	21	0	1	1	4	1	.80	0	.229	.276	.357

Matt Murton

Bats: R **Throws:** R **Pos:** LF-133; PH-12; PR-1   **Ht:** 6'1" **Wt:** 220 **Born:** 10/3/1981 **Age:** 25

Year	Team	Lg	G	AB	H	2B	3B	HR	(Hm	Rd)	TB	R	RBI	RC	TBB	IBB	SO	HBP	SH	SF	SB	CS	SB%	GDP	Avg	OBP	Slg
2003	Lowell	A-	53	189	54	11	2	2	(-	-)	75	30	29	32	27	0	39	4	0	7	9	3	.75	5	.286	.374	.397
2004	Srsota	A+	102	376	113	16	4	11	(-	-)	170	60	55	65	42	4	61	3	0	4	5	4	.56	7	.301	.372	.452
2004	Dytona	A+	24	79	20	1	1	2	(-	-)	29	13	8	10	8	1	10	1	0	1	2	0	1.00	3	.253	.326	.367
2005	WTenn	AA	78	313	107	17	4	8	(-	-)	156	46	46	64	29	3	42	4	3	1	18	5	.78	10	.342	.403	.498
2005	Iowa	AAA	9	34	12	2	0	1	(-	-)	17	4	3	7	4	0	8	0	0	0	2	2	.50	2	.353	.421	.500
2005	ChC	NL	51	140	45	3	2	7	(2	5)	73	19	14	19	16	4	22	0	2	2	2	1	.67	4	.321	.386	.521
2006	ChC	NL	144	455	135	22	3	13	(7	6)	202	70	62	68	45	1	62	5	1	2	5	2	.71	16	.297	.365	.444
2 ML YEARS			195	595	180	25	5	20	(9	11)	275	89	76	87	61	5	84	5	3	4	7	3	.70	20	.303	.370	.462

Mike Mussina

Pitches: R **Bats:** L **Pos:** SP-32   **Ht:** 6'2" **Wt:** 190 **Born:** 12/8/1968 **Age:** 38

				HOW MUCH HE PITCHED					WHAT HE GAVE UP											THE RESULTS							
Year	Team	Lg	G	GS	CG	GF	IP	BFP	H	R	ER	HR	SH	SF	HB	TBB	IBB	SO	WP	Bk	W	L	Pct	ShO	Sv-Op	Hld	ERC	ERA
1991	Bal	AL	12	12	2	0	87.2	349	77	31	28	7	3	2	1	21	0	52	3	1	4	5	.444	0	0-0	0	2.80	2.87
1992	Bal	AL	32	32	8	0	241.0	957	212	70	68	16	13	6	2	48	2	130	6	0	18	5	.783	4	0-0	0	2.54	2.54
1993	Bal	AL	25	25	3	0	167.2	693	163	84	83	20	6	4	3	44	2	117	5	0	14	6	.700	2	0-0	0	3.61	4.46
1994	Bal	AL	24	24	3	0	176.1	712	163	63	60	19	3	9	1	42	1	99	0	0	16	5	.762	0	0-0	0	3.16	3.06
1995	Bal	AL	32	32	7	0	221.2	882	187	86	81	24	2	2	1	50	4	158	2	0	19	9	.679	4	0-0	0	2.66	3.29
1996	Bal	AL	36	36	4	0	243.1	1039	264	137	130	31	4	4	3	69	0	204	3	0	19	11	.633	1	0-0	0	4.36	4.81
1997	Bal	AL	33	33	4	0	224.2	905	197	87	80	27	3	2	3	54	3	218	5	0	15	8	.652	1	0-0	0	3.00	3.20
1998	Bal	AL	29	29	4	0	206.1	835	189	85	80	22	6	3	4	41	3	175	10	0	13	10	.565	2	0-0	0	2.96	3.49
1999	Bal	AL	31	31	4	0	203.1	842	207	88	79	16	9	7	1	52	0	172	2	0	18	7	.720	0	0-0	0	3.54	3.50
2000	Bal	AL	34	34	6	0	237.2	987	236	105	100	28	8	6	3	46	0	210	3	0	11	15	.423	1	0-0	0	3.37	3.79
2001	NYY	AL	34	34	4	0	228.2	909	202	87	80	20	5	6	4	42	2	214	6	0	17	11	.607	3	0-0	0	2.65	3.15
2002	NYY	AL	33	33	2	0	215.2	886	208	103	97	27	5	5	5	48	1	182	7	0	18	10	.643	2	0-0	0	3.46	4.05
2003	NYY	AL	31	31	2	0	214.2	855	192	86	81	21	1	4	3	40	4	195	4	0	17	8	.680	1	0-0	0	2.75	3.40
2004	NYY	AL	27	27	1	0	164.2	697	178	91	84	22	5	4	2	40	1	132	5	0	12	9	.571	0	0-0	0	4.19	4.59
2005	NYY	AL	30	30	2	0	179.2	766	199	93	88	23	6	4	7	47	0	142	2	0	13	8	.619	2	0-0	0	4.55	4.41
2006	NYY	AL	32	32	1	0	197.1	804	184	88	77	22	1	1	5	35	1	172	3	0	15	7	.682	0	0-0	0	3.01	3.51
16 ML YEARS			475	475	57	0	3210.1	13118	3058	1384	1296	345	80	69	48	719	24	2572	66	1	239	134	.641	23	0-0	0	3.26	3.63

Brett Myers

Pitches: R **Bats:** R **Pos:** SP-31   **Ht:** 6'4" **Wt:** 240 **Born:** 8/17/1980 **Age:** 26

				HOW MUCH HE PITCHED					WHAT HE GAVE UP											THE RESULTS							
Year	Team	Lg	G	GS	CG	GF	IP	BFP	H	R	ER	HR	SH	SF	HB	TBB	IBB	SO	WP	Bk	W	L	Pct	ShO	Sv-Op	Hld	ERC	ERA
2002	Phi	NL	12	12	1	0	72.0	307	73	38	34	11	6	2	6	29	1	34	2	1	4	5	.444	0	0-0	0	5.04	4.25
2003	Phi	NL	32	32	1	0	193.0	848	205	99	95	20	6	3	9	76	8	143	9	0	14	9	.609	1	0-0	0	4.56	4.43
2004	Phi	NL	32	31	1	1	176.0	778	196	113	108	31	9	3	6	62	4	116	5	0	11	11	.500	1	0-0	0	5.17	5.52
2005	Phi	NL	34	34	2	0	215.1	905	193	94	89	31	9	3	11	68	2	208	4	4	13	8	.619	0	0-0	0	3.64	3.72
2006	Phi	NL	31	31	1	0	198.0	833	194	93	86	29	7	4	3	63	3	189	3	0	12	7	.632	0	0-0	0	4.02	3.91
5 ML YEARS			141	140	6	1	854.1	3671	861	437	412	122	37	15	35	298	18	690	23	5	54	40	.574	2	0-0	0	4.36	4.34

Mike Myers

Pitches: L **Bats:** L **Pos:** RP-62   **Ht:** 6'3" **Wt:** 220 **Born:** 6/26/1969 **Age:** 38

				HOW MUCH HE PITCHED					WHAT HE GAVE UP											THE RESULTS							
Year	Team	Lg	G	GS	CG	GF	IP	BFP	H	R	ER	HR	SH	SF	HB	TBB	IBB	SO	WP	Bk	W	L	Pct	ShO	Sv-Op	Hld	ERC	ERA
1995	2 Tms		13	0	0	5	8.1	42	11	7	7	1	0	1	2	7	0	4	0	0	1	0	1.000	0	0-1	1	9.61	7.56
1996	Det	AL	83	0	0	25	64.2	298	70	41	36	6	2	1	4	34	8	69	2	0	1	5	.167	0	6-8	17	4.97	5.01
1997	Det	AL	88	0	0	23	53.2	246	58	36	34	12	4	3	2	25	2	50	0	0	0	4	.000	0	2-5	18	5.70	5.70
1998	Mil	NL	70	0	0	14	50.0	211	44	19	15	5	4	2	6	22	1	40	2	1	2	2	.500	0	1-3	23	4.14	2.70
1999	Mil	NL	71	0	0	14	41.1	179	46	24	24	7	5	0	3	13	1	35	1	0	2	1	.667	0	0-3	14	5.24	5.23
2000	Col	NL	78	0	0	22	45.1	177	24	10	10	2	1	0	2	24	3	41	1	0	0	1	.000	0	1-2	15	1.94	1.99
2001	Col	NL	73	0	0	14	40.0	169	32	17	16	2	1	1	1	24	7	36	0	0	2	3	.400	0	0-2	10	3.29	3.60
2002	Ari	NL	69	0	0	15	37.0	171	39	18	18	2	3	1	8	17	0	31	0	0	4	3	.571	0	4-9	17	5.13	4.38
2003	Ari	NL	64	0	0	17	36.1	172	38	23	23	4	1	0	5	21	1	21	1	0	0	1	.000	0	0-3	6	5.54	5.70
2004	2 Tms	AL	75	0	0	15	42.2	192	45	22	22	5	2	1	2	23	5	32	2	0	5	1	.833	0	0-0	10	5.11	4.64
2005	Bos	AL	65	0	0	11	37.1	151	30	14	13	3	1	1	2	13	2	21	0	0	3	1	.750	0	0-1	9	2.90	3.13
2006	NYY	AL	62	0	0	6	30.2	132	29	14	11	3	0	0	3	10	1	22	1	0	1	2	.333	0	0-1	18	3.78	3.23
95	Fla	NL	2	0	0	2	2.0	9	1	0	0	0	0	0	0	3	0	0	0	0	0	0	-	0	0-0	0	5.03	0.00
95	Det	AL	11	0	0	3	6.1	33	10	7	7	1	0	1	2	4	0	4	0	0	1	0	1.000	0	0-1	1	11.13	9.95
04	Sea	AL	50	0	0	10	27.2	126	29	15	15	3	2	1	2	17	4	23	1	0	4	1	.800	0	0-0	8	5.40	4.88
04	Bos	AL	25	0	0	5	15.0	66	16	7	7	2	0	0	0	6	1	9	1	0	1	0	1.000	0	0-0	2	4.55	4.20
12 ML YEARS			811	0	0	181	487.1	2140	466	245	229	52	24	11	40	233	31	402	10	1	21	24	.467	0	14-38	158	4.43	4.23

Xavier Nady

Bats: R **Throws:** R **Pos:** RF-99; 1B-35; PH-4   **Ht:** 6'2" **Wt:** 205 **Born:** 11/14/1978 **Age:** 28

							BATTING														BASERUNNING				AVERAGES		
Year	Team	Lg	G	AB	H	2B	3B	HR	(Hm	Rd)	TB	R	RBI	RC	TBB	IBB	SO	HBP	SH	SF	SB	CS	SB%	GDP	Avg	OBP	Slg
2006	Norfolk*	AAA	3	11	4	1	0	0	(-	-)	5	2	3	2	1	0	3	0	0	0	0	0	-	0	.364	.417	.455
2000	SD	NL	1	1	1	0	0	0	(0	0)	1	1	0	1	0	0	0	0	0	0	0	0	-	0	1.000	1.000	1.000
2003	SD	NL	110	371	99	17	1	9	(5	4)	145	50	39	39	24	0	74	6	2	1	6	2	.75	14	.267	.321	.391
2004	SD	NL	34	77	19	4	0	3	(1	2)	32	7	9	8	5	0	13	1	1	0	0	0	-	4	.247	.301	.416
2005	SD	NL	124	326	85	15	2	13	(5	8)	143	40	43	37	22	1	67	7	1	0	2	1	.67	5	.261	.321	.439
2006	2 Tms	NL	130	468	131	28	1	17	(10	7)	212	57	63	62	30	7	85	11	2	1	3	3	.50	12	.280	.337	.453
06	NYM	NL	75	265	70	15	1	14	(10	4)	129	37	40	35	19	4	51	6	1	1	2	1	.67	7	.264	.326	.487
06	Pit	NL	55	203	61	13	0	3	(0	3)	83	20	23	27	11	3	34	5	1	0	1	2	.33	5	.300	.352	.409
5 ML YEARS			399	1243	335	64	4	42	(21	21)	533	155	154	147	81	8	239	25	6	2	11	6	.65	35	.270	.326	.429

Clint Nageotte

Pitches: R **Bats:** R **Pos:** RP-1   **Ht:** 6'3" **Wt:** 225 **Born:** 10/25/1980 **Age:** 26

				HOW MUCH HE PITCHED					WHAT HE GAVE UP											THE RESULTS							
Year	Team	Lg	G	GS	CG	GF	IP	BFP	H	R	ER	HR	SH	SF	HB	TBB	IBB	SO	WP	Bk	W	L	Pct	ShO	Sv-Op	Hld	ERC	ERA
2006	Ms*	R	2	2	0	0	5.0	20	4	1	1	0	0	0	0	2	0	2	0	0	0	0	-	0	0--	-	2.46	1.80
2006	Tacom*	AAA	19	19	0	0	89.1	412	102	63	57	6	0	5	6	53	0	51	8	0	7	7	.500	0	0--	-	5.80	5.74
2004	Sea	AL	12	5	0	4	36.2	185	48	31	30	3	4	2	4	27	1	24	3	0	1	6	.143	0	0-0	0	7.59	7.36

Year	Team	Lg	G	GS	CG	GF	IP	BFP	H	R	ER	HR	SH	SF	HB	TBB	IBB	SO	WP	Bk	W	L	Pct	ShO	Sv-Op	Hld	ERC	ERA
							HOW MUCH HE PITCHED						**WHAT HE GAVE UP**											**THE RESULTS**					
2005	Sea	AL	3	0	0	0	4.0	19	6	3	3	0	0	0	1	1	0	1	0	0	0	0	-	0	0-0	0	6.85	6.75
2006	Sea	AL	1	0	0	0	1.0	7	2	3	3	1	0	0	0	2	1	1	0	0	0	0	-	0	0-0	0	26.37	27.00
	3 ML YEARS		16	5	0	4	41.2	211	56	37	36	4	4	2	5	30	2	26	3	0	1	6	.143	0	0-0	0	7.90	7.78

Mike Napoli

Bats: R **Throws:** R **Pos:** C-94; PH-9; DH-1; PR-1   **Ht:** 6'0" **Wt:** 205 **Born:** 10/31/1981 **Age:** 25

Year	Team	Lg	G	AB	H	2B	3B	HR	(Hm	Rd)	TB	R	RBI	RC	TBB	IBB	SO	HBP	SH	SF	SB	CS	SB%	GDP	Avg	OBP	Slg
						BATTING															**BASERUNNING**				**AVERAGES**		
2000	Butte	R+	10	26	6	2	0	0	(-	-)	8	3	3	4	8	1	8	0	1	1	1	0	1.00	2	.231	.400	.308
2001	RCuca	A+	7	20	4	0	0	1	(-	-)	7	3	4	3	8	0	11	0	0	0	0	0	-	0	.200	.429	.350
2001	CRpds	A	43	155	36	10	1	5	(-	-)	63	23	18	23	24	0	54	2	1	1	3	2	.60	1	.232	.341	.406
2002	CRpds	A	106	362	91	19	1	10	(-	-)	142	57	50	56	62	1	104	4	0	6	6	5	.55	9	.251	.362	.392
2003	RCuca	A+	47	165	44	10	1	4	(-	-)	68	28	26	28	23	1	32	4	0	3	5	0	1.00	3	.267	.364	.412
2004	RCuca	A+	132	482	136	29	4	29	(-	-)	260	94	118	105	88	5	166	6	1	8	9	5	.64	6	.282	.394	.539
2005	Ark	AA	131	439	104	22	2	31	(-	-)	223	96	99	88	88	1	140	9	0	5	12	4	.75	8	.237	.372	.508
2006	Salt Lk	AAA	21	78	19	6	0	3	(-	-)	34	12	10	12	8	0	29	4	0	0	1	1	.50	0	.244	.344	.436
2006	LAA	AL	99	268	61	13	0	16	(10	6)	122	47	42	40	51	0	90	5	0	1	2	3	.40	2	.228	.360	.455

Chris Narveson

Pitches: L **Bats:** L **Pos:** RP-4; SP-1   **Ht:** 6'3" **Wt:** 205 **Born:** 12/20/1981 **Age:** 25

Year	Team	Lg	G	GS	CG	GF	IP	BFP	H	R	ER	HR	SH	SF	HB	TBB	IBB	SO	WP	Bk	W	L	Pct	ShO	Sv-Op	Hld	ERC	ERA
							HOW MUCH HE PITCHED							**WHAT HE GAVE UP**										**THE RESULTS**					
2000	JhsCty	R+	12	12	0	0	55.0	247	57	33	20	7	1	1	3	25	0	63	3	0	2	4	.333	0	0--	-	4.87	3.27
2001	Peoria	A	8	8	0	0	50.0	190	32	14	11	3	2	1	3	11	0	53	0	0	3	3	.500	0	0--	-	1.66	1.98
2001	Ptomc	A+	11	11	1	0	66.2	263	52	22	19	4	2	3	0	13	1	53	3	0	4	3	.571	0	0--	-	1.93	2.57
2002	JhsCty	R+	6	6	0	0	18.1	83	23	12	10	2	0	1	1	6	0	16	0	0	0	2	.000	0	0--	-	5.56	4.91
2002	Peoria	A	9	9	0	0	42.1	184	49	24	21	5	0	3	0	8	0	36	3	0	2	1	.667	0	0--	-	4.14	4.46
2003	PlmBh	A+	15	14	1	0	91.1	369	83	34	29	4	3	2	2	19	0	65	4	0	7	7	.500	0	0--	-	2.61	2.86
2003	Tenn	AA	10	10	0	0	57.0	247	56	21	19	6	4	3	0	26	2	34	4	1	4	3	.571	0	0--	-	4.19	3.00
2004	Tulsa	AA	4	4	0	0	20.0	87	16	14	7	1	1	3	2	13	0	14	2	0	0	3	.000	0	0--	-	4.04	3.15
2004	Tenn	AA	23	23	0	0	127.2	538	114	64	59	11	11	4	5	51	0	121	7	0	5	10	.333	0	0--	-	3.57	4.16
2005	Pwtckt	AAA	21	20	0	1	111.1	477	109	62	59	15	4	1	10	46	0	66	4	1	4	5	.444	0	0--	-	4.75	4.77
2005	Memp	AAA	2	2	0	0	6.2	37	11	9	9	2	0	1	1	7	0	8	0	0	0	1	.000	0	0--	-	14.45	12.15
2006	PlmBh	A+	3	3	0	0	17.0	62	9	4	4	2	1	0	1	1	0	13	0	0	0	0	-	0	0--	-	0.99	2.12
2006	Memp	AAA	15	15	0	0	80.0	332	70	26	25	9	1	2	2	33	2	58	3	0	8	5	.615	0	0--	-	3.66	2.81
2006	StL	NL	5	1	0	1	9.1	40	6	5	5	1	0	0	1	5	0	12	1	1	0	0	-	0	0-0	0	3.06	4.82

Joe Nathan

Pitches: R **Bats:** R **Pos:** RP-64   **Ht:** 6'4" **Wt:** 220 **Born:** 11/22/1974 **Age:** 32

Year	Team	Lg	G	GS	CG	GF	IP	BFP	H	R	ER	HR	SH	SF	HB	TBB	IBB	SO	WP	Bk	W	L	Pct	ShO	Sv-Op	Hld	ERC	ERA
							HOW MUCH HE PITCHED							**WHAT HE GAVE UP**										**THE RESULTS**					
1999	SF	NL	19	14	0	2	90.1	395	84	45	42	17	2	0	1	46	0	54	2	0	7	4	.636	0	1-1	0	4.78	4.18
2000	SF	NL	20	15	0	0	93.1	426	89	63	54	12	5	5	4	63	4	61	5	0	5	2	.714	0	0-1	0	5.23	5.21
2002	SF	NL	4	0	0	3	3.2	12	1	0	0	0	0	0	0	0	0	2	0	0	0	0	-	0	0-0	0	0.17	0.00
2003	SF	NL	78	0	0	9	79.0	316	51	26	26	7	2	4	3	33	3	83	4	1	12	4	.750	0	0-3	20	2.34	2.96
2004	Min	AL	73	0	0	63	72.1	284	48	14	13	3	2	0	2	23	3	89	5	0	1	2	.333	0	44-47	0	1.78	1.62
2005	Min	AL	69	0	0	58	70.0	276	46	22	21	5	1	2	0	22	1	94	2	0	7	4	.636	0	43-48	0	1.83	2.70
2006	Min	AL	64	0	0	61	68.1	262	38	12	12	3	3	2	1	16	4	95	3	0	7	0	1.000	0	36-38	0	1.18	1.58
	7 ML YEARS		327	29	0	196	477.0	1971	357	182	168	47	15	13	11	203	15	478	21	1	39	16	.709	0	124-138	20	2.86	3.17

Dioner Navarro

Bats: B **Throws:** R **Pos:** C-78; PH-5   **Ht:** 5'10" **Wt:** 190 **Born:** 2/9/1984 **Age:** 23

Year	Team	Lg	G	AB	H	2B	3B	HR	(Hm	Rd)	TB	R	RBI	RC	TBB	IBB	SO	HBP	SH	SF	SB	CS	SB%	GDP	Avg	OBP	Slg
						BATTING															**BASERUNNING**				**AVERAGES**		
2006	LsVgs*	AAA	11	40	7	2	0	0	(-	-)	9	3	2	1	3	0	7	0	0	0	1	0	1.00	1	.175	.233	.225
2004	NYY	AL	5	7	3	0	0	0	(0	0)	3	2	1	1	0	0	0	0	0	0	0	0	-	1	.429	.429	.429
2005	LAD	NL	50	176	48	9	0	3	(3	0)	66	21	14	18	20	1	21	2	1	0	0	0	-	3	.273	.354	.375
2006	2 Tms		81	268	68	9	0	6	(4	2)	95	28	28	27	31	6	51	1	1	1	2	1	.67	4	.254	.332	.354
06	LAD	NL	25	75	21	2	0	2	(1	1)	29	5	8	8	11	4	18	0	0	0	1	0	1.00	1	.280	.372	.387
06	TB	AL	56	193	47	7	0	4	(3	1)	66	23	20	19	20	2	33	1	1	1	1	1	.50	6	.244	.316	.342
	3 ML YEARS		136	451	119	18	0	9	(7	2)	164	51	43	46	51	7	72	3	2	1	2	1	.67	11	.264	.342	.364

Oswaldo Navarro

Bats: B **Throws:** R **Pos:** PH-3; SS-2   **Ht:** 6'0" **Wt:** 155 **Born:** 10/2/1984 **Age:** 22

Year	Team	Lg	G	AB	H	2B	3B	HR	(Hm	Rd)	TB	R	RBI	RC	TBB	IBB	SO	HBP	SH	SF	SB	CS	SB%	GDP	Avg	OBP	Slg
						BATTING															**BASERUNNING**				**AVERAGES**		
2003	Everett	A-	61	233	60	12	1	0	(-	-)	74	42	23	25	10	0	39	5	0	0	16	3	.84	4	.258	.302	.318
2004	Wisc	A	40	109	23	4	0	0	(-	-)	27	13	7	9	11	0	19	2	1	0	4	1	.80	9	.211	.295	.248
2004	Everett	A-	68	267	73	27	1	1	(-	-)	105	38	30	38	21	0	59	3	3	2	17	4	.81	3	.273	.331	.393
2005	Wisc	A	120	450	121	29	0	9	(-	-)	177	57	69	62	39	0	60	6	4	10	11	7	.61	9	.269	.329	.393
2006	SnAnt	AA	79	266	71	13	1	1	(-	-)	89	27	24	36	39	1	57	5	3	0	7	6	.54	5	.267	.371	.335
2006	Tacom	AAA	55	183	45	9	0	2	(-	-)	60	15	21	20	19	0	33	1	2	4	1	2	.33	6	.246	.314	.328
2006	Sea	AL	4	3	2	0	0	0	(0	0)	2	0	0	0	0	0	1	0	1	0	0	0	-	0	.667	.667	.667

Jeff Nelson

Pitches: R **Bats:** R **Pos:** RP-6   **Ht:** 6'8" **Wt:** 225 **Born:** 11/17/1966 **Age:** 40

			HOW MUCH HE PITCHED						WHAT HE GAVE UP									THE RESULTS						
Year	Team	Lg	G	GS	CG	GF	IP	BFP	H	R	ER	HR	SH	SF	HB	TBB	IBB	SO	WP	Bk	W	L	Pct	ShO	Sv-Op	Hld	ERC	ERA
2006	Charltt*	AAA	4	0	0	0	5.1	23	4	1	0	0	0	0	1	4	0	7	0	0	1	0	1.000	0	0--	-	4.24	0.00
1992	Sea	AL	66	0	0	27	81.0	352	71	34	31	7	9	3	6	44	12	46	2	0	1	7	.125	0	6-14	6	3.93	3.44
1993	Sea	AL	71	0	0	13	60.0	269	57	30	29	5	2	4	8	34	10	61	2	0	5	3	.625	0	1-11	17	4.62	4.35
1994	Sea	AL	28	0	0	7	42.1	185	35	18	13	3	1	1	8	20	4	44	2	0	0	0	-	0	0-0	2	3.77	2.76
1995	Sea	AL	62	0	0	24	78.2	318	58	21	19	4	5	3	6	27	5	96	1	0	7	3	.700	0	2-4	14	2.39	2.17
1996	NYY	AL	73	0	0	27	74.1	328	75	38	36	6	3	1	2	36	1	91	4	0	4	4	.500	0	2-4	10	4.41	4.36
1997	NYY	AL	77	0	0	22	78.2	327	53	32	25	7	7	2	4	37	12	81	4	0	3	7	.300	0	2-8	22	2.48	2.86
1998	NYY	AL	45	0	0	13	40.1	192	44	18	17	1	1	3	8	22	4	35	2	0	5	3	.625	0	3-6	10	5.13	3.79
1999	NYY	AL	39	0	0	8	30.1	139	27	14	14	2	2	2	3	22	2	35	2	1	2	1	.667	0	1-2	10	4.76	4.15
2000	NYY	AL	73	0	0	13	69.2	296	44	24	19	2	6	2	2	45	1	71	4	0	8	4	.667	0	0-4	15	2.61	2.45
2001	Sea	AL	69	0	0	16	65.1	273	30	21	20	3	2	0	6	44	1	88	2	0	4	3	.571	0	4-5	26	2.20	2.76
2002	Sea	AL	41	0	0	12	45.2	199	36	20	20	4	2	4	3	27	3	55	5	0	3	2	.600	0	2-4	12	3.70	3.94
2003	2 Tms	AL	70	0	0	28	55.1	240	51	25	23	4	4	2	4	24	3	68	3	1	4	2	.667	0	8-14	14	3.76	3.74
2004	Tex	AL	29	0	0	9	23.2	103	17	16	14	3	1	1	0	19	0	22	2	0	1	2	.333	0	1-1	9	4.35	5.32
2005	Sea	AL	49	0	0	15	36.2	166	32	17	16	3	4	1	4	22	0	34	1	1	1	3	.250	0	1-4	9	4.38	3.93
2006	CWS	AL	6	0	0	3	2.2	15	3	1	1	0	0	0	1	5	1	2	0	0	1	0	.000	0	0-1	1	13.90	3.38
03	Sea	AL	46	0	0	25	37.2	159	34	16	14	3	4	2	2	14	1	47	2	1	3	2	.600	0	7-11	6	3.48	3.35
03	NYY	AL	24	0	0	3	17.2	81	17	9	9	1	0	0	2	10	2	21	1	0	1	0	1.000	0	1-3	8	4.37	4.58
	15 ML YEARS		798	0	0	237	784.2	3402	633	329	297	55	49	29	64	428	59	829	36	3	48	45	.516	0	33-82	176	3.55	3.41

Joe Nelson

Pitches: R **Bats:** R **Pos:** RP-43   **Ht:** 6'1" **Wt:** 210 **Born:** 10/25/1974 **Age:** 32

			HOW MUCH HE PITCHED						WHAT HE GAVE UP									THE RESULTS						
Year	Team	Lg	G	GS	CG	GF	IP	BFP	H	R	ER	HR	SH	SF	HB	TBB	IBB	SO	WP	Bk	W	L	Pct	ShO	Sv-Op	Hld	ERC	ERA
2006	Omha*	AAA	24	0	0	19	32.0	126	19	9	7	4	3	2	4	12	2	39	2	0	2	2	.500	0	7--	-	2.47	1.97
2001	Atl	NL	2	0	0	0	2.0	16	7	9	8	1	0	1	1	2	0	0	0	0	0	0	-	0	0-0	0	33.03	36.00
2004	Bos	AL	3	0	0	1	2.2	17	4	5	5	0	1	0	2	3	0	5	0	0	0	0	-	0	0-0	0	12.43	16.88
2006	KC	AL	43	0	0	20	44.2	193	37	22	22	5	3	1	1	24	4	44	1	0	1	1	.500	0	9-10	5	3.67	4.43
	3 ML YEARS		48	0	0	21	49.1	226	48	36	35	6	4	2	4	29	4	49	1	0	1	1	.500	0	9-10	5	4.97	6.39

John Nelson

Bats: R **Throws:** R **Pos:** PH-4; PR-3; 1B-1; SS-1   **Ht:** 6'1" **Wt:** 190 **Born:** 3/3/1979 **Age:** 28

			BATTING																BASERUNNING				AVERAGES		
Year	Team	Lg	G	AB	H	2B	3B	HR	(Hm | Rd)	TB	R	RBI	RC	TBB	IBB	SO	HBP	SH	SF	SB	CS	SB%	GDP	Avg	OBP	Slg
2001	NewJrs	A-	66	252	60	16	3	8	(- | -)	106	43	26	39	35	3	76	3	4	5	14	3	.82	3	.238	.332	.421
2002	Peoria	A	132	481	132	28	5	16	(- | -)	218	85	63	81	54	3	123	3	5	4	16	3	.84	8	.274	.349	.453
2003	Tenn	AA	136	506	120	22	1	5	(- | -)	159	60	42	50	44	3	117	3	2	1	10	5	.67	14	.237	.301	.314
2004	Tenn	AA	63	206	62	16	3	8	(- | -)	108	41	29	43	31	0	56	2	2	1	6	2	.75	0	.301	.396	.524
2005	Memp	AAA	128	427	103	27	1	14	(- | -)	174	56	49	59	51	4	141	4	1	2	2	3	.40	4	.241	.326	.407
2006	Memp	AAA	125	423	91	16	2	21	(- | -)	174	55	48	54	42	0	153	5	1	4	12	2	.86	4	.215	.291	.411
2006	StL	NL	8	5	0	0	0	0	(0 | 0)	0	2	0	0	0	0	4	0	0	0	0	0	-	0	.000	.000	.000

Pat Neshek

Pitches: R **Bats:** B **Pos:** RP-32   **Ht:** 6'3" **Wt:** 205 **Born:** 9/4/1980 **Age:** 26

			HOW MUCH HE PITCHED						WHAT HE GAVE UP									THE RESULTS						
Year	Team	Lg	G	GS	CG	GF	IP	BFP	H	R	ER	HR	SH	SF	HB	TBB	IBB	SO	WP	Bk	W	L	Pct	ShO	Sv-Op	Hld	ERC	ERA
2002	Elizab	R+	23	0	0	22	27.1	102	13	6	3	0	1	0	2	6	0	41	1	0	1	2	.000	0	15--	-	0.97	0.99
2003	QuadC	A	28	0	0	24	34.1	136	20	3	2	0	3	0	1	11	2	53	1	0	3	2	.600	0	14--	-	1.29	0.52
2003	FtMyrs	A+	20	0	0	15	29.1	117	22	8	7	2	1	0	1	6	1	29	0	1	4	1	.800	0	2--	-	1.94	2.15
2003	NwBrit	AA	5	1	0	2	7.2	34	7	5	5	2	0	0	1	3	0	5	0	0	1	1	.500	0	1--	-	5.12	5.87
2004	NwBrit	AA	26	0	0	15	35.1	158	34	15	15	2	1	0	1	18	5	38	1	0	2	1	.667	0	2--	-	3.77	3.82
2004	FtMyrs	A+	16	0	0	15	18.1	73	16	7	6	2	0	0	0	2	0	19	0	0	1	0	1.000	0	10--	-	2.33	2.95
2005	NwBrit	AA	55	0	0	48	82.1	335	69	25	20	9	4	2	2	21	3	95	3	0	6	4	.600	0	24--	-	2.75	2.19
2006	Roch	AAA	33	0	0	23	60.0	234	41	13	13	7	2	0	1	14	4	87	2	0	6	2	.750	0	14--	-	1.92	1.95
2006	Min	AL	32	0	0	3	37.0	138	23	9	9	6	0	1	0	6	0	53	0	0	4	2	.667	0	0-2	10	1.68	2.19

Phil Nevin

Bats: R **Throws:** R **Pos:** DH-54; 1B-44; PH-27; LF-8; RF-2; C-1   **Ht:** 6'3" **Wt:** 220 **Born:** 1/19/1971 **Age:** 36

			BATTING																BASERUNNING				AVERAGES		
Year	Team	Lg	G	AB	H	2B	3B	HR	(Hm | Rd)	TB	R	RBI	RC	TBB	IBB	SO	HBP	SH	SF	SB	CS	SB%	GDP	Avg	OBP	Slg
1995	2 Tms		47	156	28	4	1	2	(2 | 0)	40	13	13	10	18	1	40	4	1	0	1	0	1.00	5	.179	.281	.256
1996	Det	AL	38	120	35	5	0	8	(3 | 5)	64	15	19	21	8	0	39	1	0	1	1	0	1.00	1	.292	.338	.533
1997	Det	AL	93	251	59	16	1	9	(4 | 5)	104	32	35	31	25	1	68	1	0	1	0	1	.00	5	.235	.306	.414
1998	LAA	AL	75	237	54	8	1	8	(3 | 5)	88	27	27	25	17	0	67	5	0	2	0	0	-	6	.228	.291	.371
1999	SD	NL	128	383	103	27	0	24	(12 | 12)	202	52	85	71	51	1	82	1	1	5	1	0	1.00	7	.269	.352	.527
2000	SD	NL	143	538	163	34	1	31	(13 | 18)	292	87	107	102	59	9	121	4	0	4	2	0	1.00	17	.303	.374	.543
2001	SD	NL	149	546	167	31	0	41	(19 | 22)	321	97	126	116	71	7	147	4	0	3	4	4	.50	13	.306	.388	.588
2002	SD	NL	107	407	116	16	0	12	(5 | 7)	168	53	57	52	38	4	87	1	0	4	0	0	1.00	12	.285	.344	.413
2003	SD	NL	59	226	63	8	0	13	(6 | 7)	110	30	46	37	21	1	44	0	0	1	2	0	1.00	9	.279	.339	.487
2004	SD	NL	147	547	158	31	1	26	(12 | 14)	269	78	105	97	66	5	121	5	0	0	0	0	-	16	.289	.368	.492
2005	2 Tms		102	380	90	16	1	12	(6 | 6)	144	46	55	37	27	0	77	4	0	3	0	0	1.00	8	.237	.287	.379
2006	3 Tms		129	397	95	13	0	22	(11 | 11)	174	54	68	55	48	1	106	2	1	2	0	0	-	13	.239	.323	.438
95	Hou	NL	18	60	7	1	0	0	(0 | 0)	8	4	1	0	7	1	13	1	1	0	1	0	1.00	2	.117	.221	.133
95	Det	AL	29	96	21	3	1	2	(2 | 0)	32	9	12	10	11	0	27	3	0	0	0	0	-	3	.219	.318	.333

Year	Team	Lg	G	AB	H	2B	3B	HR	(Hm	Rd)	TB	R	RBI	RC	TBB	IBB	SO	HBP	SH	SF	SB	CS	SB%	GDP	Avg	OBP	Slg
05	SD	NL	73	281	72	11	1	9	(4	5)	112	31	47	34	19	0	67	1	0	5	1	0	1.00	2	.256	.301	.399
05	Tex	AL	29	99	18	5	0	3	(2	1)	32	15	8	3	8	0	30	1	0	0	2	0	1.00	6	.182	.250	.323
06	Tex	AL	46	176	38	8	0	9	(6	3)	73	26	31	22	21	0	39	2	0	0	0	0	-	9	.216	.307	.415
06	ChC	NL	67	179	49	4	0	12	(5	7)	89	26	33	29	17	0	52	0	0	1	0	0	-	4	.274	.335	.497
06	Min	AL	16	42	8	1	0	1	(0	1)	12	2	4	4	10	1	15	0	1	1	0	0	-	0	.190	.340	.286
12 ML YEARS			1217	4188	1131	209	6	208	(96	112)	1976	584	743	654	449	30	1019	30	3	33	18	5	.78	112	.270	.343	.472

David Newhan

Bats: L **Throws:** R **Pos:** CF-19; LF-17; RF-3; 1B-1; DH-1; PR-1 **Ht:** 5'10" **Wt:** 170 **Born:** 9/7/1973 **Age:** 33

Year	Team	Lg	G	AB	H	2B	3B	HR	(Hm	Rd)	TB	R	RBI	RC	TBB	IBB	SO	HBP	SH	SF	SB	CS	SB%	GDP	Avg	OBP	Slg
2006	Bowie*	AA	6	17	4	0	1	0	(-	-)	6	4	3	3	4	0	3	1	0	0	1	0	1.00	1	.235	.409	.353
1999	SD	NL	32	43	6	1	0	2	(1	1)	13	7	6	1	1	0	11	0	0	0	2	1	.67	0	.140	.159	.302
2000	2 Tms	NL	24	37	6	1	0	1	(1	0)	10	8	2	2	8	1	13	0	0	0	0	0	-	2	.162	.301	.270
2001	Phi	NL	7	6	2	1	0	0	(0	0)	3	2	1	1	1	0	0	0	0	1	0	0	-	0	.333	.375	.500
2004	Bal	AL	95	373	116	15	7	8	(3	5)	169	66	54	70	27	0	72	4	5	3	11	1	.92	4	.311	.361	.453
2005	Bal	AL	96	218	44	9	0	5	(1	4)	68	31	21	19	22	1	45	2	5	2	9	2	.82	2	.202	.279	.312
2006	Bal	AL	39	131	33	4	0	4	(3	1)	49	14	18	10	7	1	22	2	0	3	4	2	.67	4	.252	.294	.374
00	SD	NL	14	20	3	1	0	1	(1	0)	7	5	2	2	6	1	7	0	0	0	0	0	-	0	.150	.346	.350
00	Phi	NL	10	17	3	0	0	0	(0	0)	3	3	0	0	2	0	6	0	0	0	0	0	-	2	.176	.263	.176
6 ML YEARS			293	808	207	31	7	20	(9	11)	312	128	102	103	66	3	163	8	10	9	26	6	.81	12	.256	.315	.386

Lance Niekro

Bats: R **Throws:** R **Pos:** 1B-58; PH-10 **Ht:** 6'3" **Wt:** 225 **Born:** 1/29/1979 **Age:** 28

Year	Team	Lg	G	AB	H	2B	3B	HR	(Hm	Rd)	TB	R	RBI	RC	TBB	IBB	SO	HBP	SH	SF	SB	CS	SB%	GDP	Avg	OBP	Slg
2006	Fresno*	AAA	36	144	46	7	0	14	(-	-)	95	27	34	31	7	1	23	0	0	1	0	0	-	5	.319	.349	.660
2003	SF	NL	5	5	1	1	0	0	(0	0)	2	2	2	1	0	0	1	0	0	0	0	0	-	0	.200	.200	.400
2005	SF	NL	113	278	70	16	3	12	(5	7)	128	32	46	35	17	0	53	2	0	5	0	2	.00	11	.252	.295	.460
2006	SF	NL	66	199	49	9	2	5	(3	2)	77	27	31	22	11	0	32	0	0	0	0	0	-	7	.246	.286	.387
3 ML YEARS			184	482	120	26	5	17	(8	9)	207	61	79	58	28	0	86	2	0	5	0	2	.00	18	.249	.290	.429

Fernando Nieve

Pitches: R **Bats:** R **Pos:** RP-29; SP-11 **Ht:** 6'0" **Wt:** 195 **Born:** 7/15/1982 **Age:** 24

Year	Team	Lg	G	GS	CG	GF	IP	BFP	H	R	ER	HR	SH	SF	HB	TBB	IBB	SO	WP	Bk	W	L	Pct	ShO	Sv-Op	Hld	ERC	ERA
2001	Mrtnsvl	R+	12	8	1	0	38.0	161	27	20	16	2	0	0	3	21	0	49	3	1	4	2	.667	0	0--	-	3.08	3.79
2002	Mrtnsvl	R+	13	13	0	0	67.2	280	46	23	18	5	1	2	2	27	0	60	1	0	4	1	.800	0	0--	-	2.28	2.39
2002	Lxngtn	A	1	1	0	0	3.0	18	6	5	2	0	0	0	1	0	0	2	0	0	1	0	1.000	0	0--	-	7.91	6.00
2003	Lxngtn	A	28	28	1	0	150.1	638	133	69	61	10	4	8	0	65	0	144	7	1	14	9	.609	0	0--	-	3.33	3.65
2004	Salem	A	24	24	2	0	149.0	599	136	52	49	9	10	6	1	40	0	117	5	0	10	6	.625	2	0--	-	2.95	2.96
2004	RdRck	AA	3	3	0	0	17.1	69	12	4	3	0	1	0	1	8	0	17	0	0	2	0	1.000	0	0--	-	2.35	1.56
2005	CpChr	AA	14	14	0	0	85.0	341	62	27	25	7	2	3	3	29	0	96	4	0	4	3	.571	0	0--	-	2.48	2.65
2005	RdRck	AAA	13	13	2	0	82.0	372	92	45	44	10	2	5	5	33	2	75	3	0	4	4	.500	2	0--	-	5.09	4.83
2006	RdRck	AAA	4	0	0	2	5.1	19	2	0	0	0	0	0	0	0	0	7	0	0	0	0	-	0	2--	-	0.30	0.00
2006	Hou	NL	40	11	0	11	96.1	411	87	46	45	18	5	3	2	41	5	70	1	0	3	3	.500	0	0-0	0	4.24	4.20

Wil Nieves

Bats: R **Throws:** R **Pos:** C-6 **Ht:** 5'11" **Wt:** 190 **Born:** 9/25/1977 **Age:** 29

Year	Team	Lg	G	AB	H	2B	3B	HR	(Hm	Rd)	TB	R	RBI	RC	TBB	IBB	SO	HBP	SH	SF	SB	CS	SB%	GDP	Avg	OBP	Slg
2006	Clmbs*	AAA	88	321	83	13	0	5	(-	-)	111	29	34	34	18	0	29	1	6	2	2	1	.67	13	.259	.298	.346
2002	SD	NL	28	72	13	3	1	0	(0	0)	18	2	3	4	4	4	15	0	0	0	1	0	1.00	1	.181	.224	.250
2005	NYY	AL	3	4	0	0	0	0	(0	0)	0	0	0	0	0	0	1	0	0	0	0	0	-	0	.000	.000	.000
2006	NYY	AL	6	6	0	0	0	0	(0	0)	0	0	0	0	0	0	1	0	0	0	0	0	-	0	.000	.000	.000
3 ML YEARS			37	82	13	3	1	0	(0	0)	18	2	3	4	4	4	17	0	0	0	1	0	1.00	1	.159	.198	.220

Dustin Nippert

Pitches: R **Bats:** R **Pos:** SP-2 **Ht:** 6'8" **Wt:** 225 **Born:** 5/6/1981 **Age:** 26

Year	Team	Lg	G	GS	CG	GF	IP	BFP	H	R	ER	HR	SH	SF	HB	TBB	IBB	SO	WP	Bk	W	L	Pct	ShO	Sv-Op	Hld	ERC	ERA
2002	Msoula	R+	17	11	0	2	54.2	215	42	12	10	2	0	0	0	9	0	77	4	0	4	2	.667	0	0--	-	1.66	1.65
2003	Sbend	A	17	17	0	0	95.2	385	66	32	30	4	0	4	2	32	3	96	5	0	6	4	.600	0	0--	-	1.98	2.82
2004	ElPaso	AA	14	14	0	0	71.2	332	77	45	29	0	6	3	4	40	1	73	4	0	2	5	.286	0	0--	-	4.48	3.64
2005	Tenn	AA	18	18	3	0	118.1	489	95	33	31	4	6	2	7	42	1	97	3	0	8	3	.727	2	0--	-	2.64	2.36
2006	Tucsn	AAA	25	24	1	0	140.1	621	161	85	76	11	2	7	4	52	0	130	7	0	13	8	.619	0	0--	-	4.78	4.87
2005	Ari	NL	3	3	0	0	14.2	68	10	9	9	1	0	0	0	13	0	11	1	0	1	0	1.000	0	0-0	0	4.09	5.52
2006	Ari	NL	2	2	0	0	10.0	51	15	13	13	5	1	0	0	7	0	9	0	0	0	2	.000	0	0-0	0	12.21	11.70
2 ML YEARS			5	5	0	0	24.2	119	25	22	22	6	1	0	1	20	0	20	1	0	1	2	.333	0	0-0	0	7.10	8.03

Laynce Nix

Bats: L **Throws:** L **Pos:** CF-18; PH-1 **Ht:** 6'0" **Wt:** 200 **Born:** 10/30/1980 **Age:** 26

Year	Team	Lg	G	AB	H	2B	3B	HR	(Hm	Rd)	TB	R	RBI	RC	TBB	IBB	SO	HBP	SH	SF	SB	CS	SB%	GDP	Avg	OBP	Slg
2006	Okla*	AAA	77	286	77	14	1	10	(-	-)	123	39	55	41	18	1	77	6	1	3	4	1	.80	2	.269	.323	.430
2006	Nashv*	AAA	18	68	28	5	1	7	(-	-)	56	16	13	21	4	1	18	1	0	0	0	0	-	0	.412	.452	.824
2003	Tex	AL	53	184	47	10	0	8	(7	1)	81	25	30	25	9	0	53	0	1	1	3	0	1.00	1	.255	.289	.440
2004	Tex	AL	115	371	92	20	4	14	(9	5)	162	58	46	44	23	4	113	2	1	3	1	1	.50	6	.248	.293	.437
2005	Tex	AL	63	229	55	12	3	6	(3	3)	91	28	32	26	9	3	45	0	0	2	2	0	1.00	3	.240	.267	.397
2006	2 Tms		19	67	11	2	0	1	(1	0)	16	3	10	3	0	0	28	2	0	1	0	0	-	1	.164	.186	.239
06	Tex		9	32	3	1	0	0	(0	0)	4	1	4	0	0	0	17	1	0	1	0	0	-	0	.094	.118	.125
06	Mil	NL	10	35	8	1	0	1	(1	0)	12	2	6	3	0	0	11	1	0	0	0	0	-	0	.229	.250	.343
4 ML YEARS			250	851	205	44	7	29	(20	9)	350	114	118	98	41	7	239	4	2	7	6	1	.86	11	.241	.277	.411

Trot Nixon

Bats: L **Throws:** L **Pos:** RF-110; PH-14 **Ht:** 6'2" **Wt:** 210 **Born:** 4/11/1974 **Age:** 33

Year	Team	Lg	G	AB	H	2B	3B	HR	(Hm	Rd)	TB	R	RBI	RC	TBB	IBB	SO	HBP	SH	SF	SB	CS	SB%	GDP	Avg	OBP	Slg
2006	Pwtckt*	AAA	3	12	2	1	0	0	(-	-)	3	2	0	0	0	0	0	0	0	0	0	0	-	0	.167	.167	.250
1996	Bos	AL	2	4	2	1	0	0	(0	0)	3	2	0	1	0	0	1	0	0	0	1	0	1.00	0	.500	.500	.750
1998	Bos	AL	13	27	7	1	0	0	(0	0)	8	3	0	2	1	0	3	0	0	0	0	0	-	0	.259	.286	.296
1999	Bos	AL	124	381	103	22	5	15	(3	12)	180	67	52	66	53	1	75	3	2	8	3	1	.75	7	.270	.357	.472
2000	Bos	AL	123	427	118	27	8	12	(4	8)	197	66	60	74	63	2	85	2	5	5	8	1	.89	11	.276	.368	.461
2001	Bos	AL	148	535	150	31	4	27	(14	13)	270	100	88	102	79	1	113	7	6	6	7	4	.64	8	.280	.376	.505
2002	Bos	AL	152	532	136	36	3	24	(8	16)	250	81	94	85	65	2	109	5	3	7	4	2	.67	7	.256	.338	.470
2003	Bos	AL	134	441	135	24	6	28	(10	18)	255	81	87	90	65	4	96	3	1	3	4	2	.67	3	.306	.396	.578
2004	Bos	AL	48	149	47	9	1	6	(3	3)	76	24	23	24	15	1	24	1	0	2	0	0	-	3	.315	.377	.510
2005	Bos	AL	124	408	112	29	1	13	(5	8)	182	64	67	70	53	3	59	3	0	6	2	1	.67	7	.275	.357	.446
2006	Bos	AL	114	381	102	24	0	8	(1	7)	150	59	52	55	60	1	56	7	0	5	0	2	.00	10	.268	.373	.394
10 ML YEARS			982	3285	912	204	28	133	(48	85)	1571	547	523	569	454	15	621	31	17	42	29	13	.69	56	.278	.366	.478

Ricky Nolasco

Pitches: R **Bats:** R **Pos:** SP-22; RP-13 **Ht:** 6'2" **Wt:** 220 **Born:** 12/13/1982 **Age:** 24

Year	Team	Lg	G	GS	CG	GF	IP	BFP	H	R	ER	HR	SH	SF	HB	TBB	IBB	SO	WP	Bk	W	L	Pct	ShO	Sv-Op	Hld	ERC	ERA
2001	Cubs	R	5	4	0	0	18.0	69	11	3	3	0	0	0	1	5	0	23	1	0	1	0	1.000	0	0--	-	1.45	1.50
2002	Boise	A	15	1	5	0	90.2	379	72	32	25	1	8	1	9	25	0	92	5	0	7	2	.778	0	0--	-	2.27	2.48
2003	Dytona	A+	26	26	1	0	149.0	620	129	58	49	7	5	4	8	48	0	136	12	1	11	5	.688	0	0--	-	2.91	2.96
2004	WTenn	AA	19	19	0	0	107.0	454	104	50	44	13	7	4	6	37	3	115	5	1	6	4	.600	0	0--	-	4.08	3.70
2004	Iowa	AAA	9	9	0	0	41.0	173	68	42	42	7	4	3	5	16	1	28	2	0	2	3	.400	0	0--	-	11.21	9.22
2005	WTenn	AA	27	27	1	0	161.2	687	151	57	52	13	11	2	11	46	1	173	4	2	14	3	.824	0	0--	-	3.35	2.89
2006	Fla	NL	35	22	0	0	140.0	613	157	86	75	20	8	6	10	41	5	99	7	0	11	11	.500	0	0-0	2	4.89	4.82

Greg Norton

Bats: B **Throws:** R **Pos:** DH-31; RF-28; 1B-25; PH-18; LF-3 **Ht:** 6'1" **Wt:** 200 **Born:** 7/6/1972 **Age:** 34

Year	Team	Lg	G	AB	H	2B	3B	HR	(Hm	Rd)	TB	R	RBI	RC	TBB	IBB	SO	HBP	SH	SF	SB	CS	SB%	GDP	Avg	OBP	Slg
2006	Drham*	AAA	3	9	1	0	0	0	(-	-)	1	0	1	0	1	0	3	0	0	0	0	0	-	0	.111	.200	.111
1996	CWS	AL	11	23	5	0	0	2	(0	2)	11	4	3	3	4	0	6	0	0	0	0	1	.00	0	.217	.333	.478
1997	CWS	AL	18	34	9	2	2	0	(0	0)	15	5	1	5	2	0	8	0	1	0	0	0	-	0	.265	.306	.441
1998	CWS	AL	105	299	71	17	2	9	(6	3)	119	38	36	33	26	1	77	2	1	2	3	3	.50	11	.237	.301	.398
1999	CWS	AL	132	436	111	26	0	16	(5	11)	185	62	50	66	69	3	93	2	1	2	4	4	.50	11	.255	.358	.424
2000	CWS	AL	71	201	49	6	1	6	(4	2)	75	25	28	27	26	0	47	2	0	2	1	0	1.00	2	.244	.333	.373
2001	Col	NL	117	225	60	13	2	13	(7	6)	116	30	40	36	19	2	65	0	0	2	1	0	1.00	6	.267	.321	.516
2002	Col	NL	113	168	37	8	1	7	(3	4)	68	19	37	22	24	0	52	0	1	2	2	3	.40	4	.220	.314	.405
2003	Col	NL	114	179	47	15	0	6	(2	4)	80	19	31	26	16	0	47	1	0	1	2	1	.67	4	.263	.325	.447
2004	Det	AL	41	86	15	1	0	2	(1	1)	22	9	2	1	12	1	21	0	1	0	0	0	-	3	.174	.276	.256
2006	TB	AL	98	294	87	15	0	17	(9	8)	153	47	45	53	35	2	69	3	1	2	1	5	.17	2	.296	.374	.520
10 ML YEARS			820	1945	491	103	8	78	(37	41)	844	258	273	272	233	9	485	10	6	13	14	17	.45	43	.252	.333	.434

Roberto Novoa

Pitches: R **Bats:** R **Pos:** RP-66 **Ht:** 6'5" **Wt:** 200 **Born:** 8/15/1979 **Age:** 27

Year	Team	Lg	G	GS	CG	GF	IP	BFP	H	R	ER	HR	SH	SF	HB	TBB	IBB	SO	WP	Bk	W	L	Pct	ShO	Sv-Op	Hld	ERC	ERA
2006	Iowa*	AAA	4	0	0	2	6.2	25	3	2	2	0	0	0	3	0	3	0	0	1	0	1.000	0	1--	-	1.22	2.70
2004	Det	AL	16	0	0	2	21.0	94	25	15	13	4	1	4	2	6	0	15	1	0	1	1	.500	0	0-1	3	5.79	5.57
2005	ChC	NL	49	0	0	11	44.2	205	47	22	22	4	2	0	0	25	6	47	4	1	4	5	.444	0	0-5	14	4.60	4.43
2006	ChC	NL	66	0	0	10	76.0	336	77	47	36	15	2	6	6	32	5	53	4	0	2	1	.667	0	0-0	4	5.16	4.26
3 ML YEARS			131	0	0	23	141.2	635	149	84	71	23	5	6	8	63	11	115	9	1	7	7	.500	0	0-6	21	5.08	4.51

Abraham Nunez

Bats: B **Throws:** R **Pos:** 3B-74; PH-41; 2B-6; SS-3; PR-2   **Ht:** 5'11" **Wt:** 190 **Born:** 3/16/1976 **Age:** 31

Year	Team	Lg	G	AB	H	2B	3B	HR	(Hm	Rd)	TB	R	RBI	RC	TBB	IBB	SO	HBP	SH	SF	SB	CS	SB%	GDP	Avg	OBP	Slg
1997	Pit	NL	19	40	9	2	2	0	(0	0)	15	3	6	4	3	0	10	1	0	1	1	0	1.00	1	.225	.289	.375
1998	Pit	NL	24	52	10	2	0	1	(0	1)	15	6	2	6	12	0	14	0	3	0	4	2	.67	1	.192	.344	.288
1999	Pit	NL	90	259	57	8	0	0	(0	0)	65	25	17	22	28	0	54	1	13	0	9	1	.90	2	.220	.299	.251
2000	Pit	NL	40	91	20	1	0	1	(0	1)	24	10	8	6	8	1	14	0	0	0	0	0	-	3	.220	.283	.264
2001	Pit	NL	115	301	79	11	4	1	(0	1)	101	30	21	36	28	1	53	1	4	1	8	2	.80	5	.262	.326	.336
2002	Pit	NL	112	253	59	14	1	2	(2	0)	81	28	15	25	27	1	44	2	3	1	3	4	.43	2	.233	.311	.320
2003	Pit	NL	118	311	77	8	7	4	(2	2)	111	37	35	28	26	1	53	3	9	2	9	3	.75	8	.248	.310	.357
2004	Pit	NL	112	182	43	9	0	2	(1	1)	58	17	13	12	10	0	36	0	2	1	1	3	.25	8	.236	.275	.319
2005	StL	NL	139	421	120	13	2	5	(3	2)	152	64	44	54	37	4	63	0	9	0	1	0	1.00	6	.285	.343	.361
2006	Phi	NL	123	322	68	10	2	2	(2	0)	88	42	32	27	41	8	58	2	3	1	1	0	1.00	7	.211	.303	.273
10 ML YEARS			892	2232	542	78	18	18	(10	8)	710	262	193	220	220	16	399	10	46	7	36	16	.69	38	.243	.313	.318

Leo Nunez

Pitches: R **Bats:** R **Pos:** RP-7   **Ht:** 6'1" **Wt:** 165 **Born:** 8/14/1983 **Age:** 23

Year	Team	Lg	G	GS	CG	GF	IP	BFP	H	R	ER	HR	SH	SF	HB	TBB	IBB	SO	WP	Bk	W	L	Pct	ShO	Sv-Op	Hld	ERC	ERA
2001	Pirates	R	10	7	1	0	53.1	231	62	28	26	4	3	3	3	9	0	34	4	0	2	2	.500	1	0- -	-	4.08	4.39
2002	Pirates	R	11	11	0	0	60.1	240	54	23	23	5	2	0	5	5	0	52	1	0	4	2	.667	0	0- -	-	2.55	3.43
2002	Hickory	A	1	1	0	0	4.0	20	5	0	0	0	0	0	0	3	0	1	0	0	0	0	-	0	0- -	-	5.98	0.00
2003	Hickory	A	13	7	0	4	48.1	218	59	34	30	6	8	6	5	14	0	37	4	2	2	1	.667	0	0- -	-	5.52	5.59
2003	Wmspt	A-	8	8	0	0	38.1	158	31	14	13	0	0	1	0	12	0	41	0	0	4	3	.571	0	0- -	-	2.08	3.05
2004	Hickory	A	27	20	3	3	144.0	599	121	53	49	16	4	6	9	46	0	140	5	1	10	4	.714	0	1- -	-	3.21	3.06
2005	Hi Dsrt	A+	8	0	0	0	13.0	65	23	15	13	2	2	0	0	3	2	15	3	0	0	0	-	0	0- -	-	8.06	9.00
2005	Wichta	AA	12	0	0	11	13.0	49	8	3	1	1	0	0	0	2	0	14	1	0	1	0	1.000	0	4- -	-	1.32	0.69
2006	Wichta	AA	15	0	0	13	21.0	92	18	10	10	3	0	0	1	12	1	22	3	0	1	2	.333	0	3- -	-	4.37	4.29
2006	Omha	AAA	23	0	0	17	38.0	158	37	11	9	5	0	0	0	13	2	33	1	0	2	2	.500	0	5- -	-	3.91	2.13
2005	KC	AL	41	0	0	10	53.2	246	73	45	45	9	1	2	3	18	2	32	1	0	3	2	.600	0	0-1	2	6.76	7.55
2006	KC	AL	7	0	0	5	13.1	58	15	7	7	2	0	1	2	5	0	7	0	0	0	0	-	0	0-0	0	5.98	4.73
2 ML YEARS			48	0	0	15	67.0	304	88	52	52	11	1	3	5	23	2	39	1	0	3	2	.600	0	0-1	2	6.60	6.99

Mike O'Connor

Pitches: L **Bats:** L **Pos:** SP-20; RP-1   **Ht:** 6'3" **Wt:** 170 **Born:** 8/17/1980 **Age:** 26

Year	Team	Lg	G	GS	CG	GF	IP	BFP	H	R	ER	HR	SH	SF	HB	TBB	IBB	SO	WP	Bk	W	L	Pct	ShO	Sv-Op	Hld	ERC	ERA
2002	Vrmnt	A-	21	0	0	11	43.0	177	25	17	15	2	1	3	1	27	2	66	4	0	2	3	.400	0	4- -	-	2.41	3.14
2003	Savann	A	42	0	0	24	70.0	301	56	36	30	6	2	1	3	35	1	83	6	1	8	3	.727	0	1- -	-	3.37	3.86
2004	BrvdCt	A+	26	14	0	0	103.0	438	98	51	47	5	4	6	4	42	0	104	6	2	8	8	.500	0	0- -	-	3.68	4.11
2005	Ptomc	A+	26	26	2	0	167.2	695	144	73	66	14	6	4	3	48	0	158	11	1	10	11	.476	1	0- -	-	2.81	3.54
2006	NewOr	AAA	6	6	0	0	26.1	109	21	10	8	2	0	1	2	11	1	28	0	0	1	0	1.000	0	0- -	-	3.18	2.73
2006	Was	NL	21	20	0	0	105.0	455	96	61	56	15	6	4	7	45	5	59	8	0	3	8	.273	0	0-0	0	4.19	4.80

Eric O'Flaherty

Pitches: L **Bats:** L **Pos:** RP-15   **Ht:** 6'2" **Wt:** 195 **Born:** 2/5/1985 **Age:** 22

Year	Team	Lg	G	GS	CG	GF	IP	BFP	H	R	ER	HR	SH	SF	HB	TBB	IBB	SO	WP	Bk	W	L	Pct	ShO	Sv-Op	Hld	ERC	ERA
2003	Ms	R	13	1	0	5	27.2	110	17	10	6	1	2	1	2	7	1	20	0	0	3	0	1.000	0	0- -	-	1.49	1.95
2003	Everett	A-	3	1	0	0	10.2	41	8	5	4	1	0	2	2	3	0	7	1	0	1	0	1.000	0	0- -	-	3.23	3.38
2004	Wisc	A	12	10	0	0	57.1	274	83	43	39	3	4	3	3	23	1	38	12	0	3	3	.500	0	0- -	-	6.56	6.12
2005	Wisc	A	45	0	0	31	69.2	305	73	35	29	2	3	0	3	30	1	51	7	1	4	4	.500	0	13- -	-	4.12	3.75
2006	InldEm	A+	16	0	0	0	28.2	118	31	11	11	1	2	1	3	6	0	33	0	0	0	1	.000	0	1- -	-	3.92	3.45
2006	SnAnt	AA	25	0	0	14	39.1	171	45	10	5	0	2	0	4	15	1	36	0	2	2	2	.500	0	7- -	-	4.61	1.14
2006	Tacom	AAA	2	0	0	0	3.2	15	3	0	0	0	0	0	0	1	0	4	0	0	1	0	1.000	0	0- -	-	2.00	0.00
2006	Sea	AL	15	0	0	5	11.0	57	18	9	5	2	1	0	0	6	3	6	2	0	0	0	-	0	0-0	1	8.63	4.09

Tomo Ohka

Pitches: R **Bats:** R **Pos:** SP-18   **Ht:** 6'1" **Wt:** 200 **Born:** 3/18/1976 **Age:** 31

Year	Team	Lg	G	GS	CG	GF	IP	BFP	H	R	ER	HR	SH	SF	HB	TBB	IBB	SO	WP	Bk	W	L	Pct	ShO	Sv-Op	Hld	ERC	ERA
2006	Brewrs*	R	1	1	0	0	3.0	17	7	4	2	0	0	0	1	0	0	0	0	0	0	1	.000	0	0- -	-	11.27	6.00
2006	BrvdCt*	A+	2	2	0	0	10.2	45	12	2	0	0	0	0	0	1	0	10	0	0	1	0	1.000	0	0- -	-	2.84	0.00
1999	Bos	AL	8	2	0	3	13.0	65	21	12	9	2	0	1	0	6	0	8	0	0	1	2	.333	0	0-0	0	8.56	6.23
2000	Bos	AL	13	12	0	1	69.1	297	70	25	24	7	1	2	2	26	0	40	3	0	3	6	.333	0	0-0	0	4.19	3.12
2001	2 Tms		22	21	0	1	107.0	469	134	70	65	15	2	2	3	29	0	68	2	1	3	9	.250	0	0-0	0	5.52	5.47
2002	Mon	NL	32	31	2	1	192.2	806	194	83	68	19	13	6	7	45	7	118	2	1	13	8	.619	0	0-0	0	3.55	3.18
2003	Mon	NL	34	34	2	0	199.0	864	233	106	92	24	8	3	9	45	11	118	0	0	10	12	.455	0	0-0	0	4.59	4.16
2004	Mon	NL	15	15	0	0	84.2	367	98	40	32	11	4	2	1	20	1	38	3	0	3	7	.300	0	0-0	0	4.53	3.40
2005	2 Tms	NL	32	29	1	0	180.1	774	189	88	81	22	7	4	3	55	5	98	8	0	11	9	.550	1	0-0	1	4.13	4.04
2006	Mil	NL	18	18	0	0	97.0	421	98	58	52	12	8	4	5	35	1	50	4	0	4	5	.444	0	0-0	0	4.32	4.82
01	Bos	AL	12	11	0	1	52.1	241	69	40	36	7	1	1	2	19	0	37	1	1	2	5	.286	0	0-0	0	6.24	6.19
01	Mon	NL	10	10	0	0	54.2	228	65	30	29	8	1	1	1	10	0	31	1	0	1	4	.200	0	0-0	0	4.83	4.77
05	Was	NL	10	9	0	0	54.2	231	44	23	20	6	6	1	1	27	1	17	3	0	4	3	.571	0	0-0	0	3.54	3.33
05	Mil	NL	22	20	1	0	126.1	543	145	65	61	16	1	3	2	28	4	81	5	0	7	6	.538	1	0-0	1	4.39	4.35
8 ML YEARS			174	162	5	6	943.0	4063	1037	482	423	112	43	24	30	261	25	538	30	2	48	58	.453	1	0-0	1	4.37	4.04

Will Ohman

Pitches: L **Bats:** L **Pos:** RP-78 **Ht:** 6'2" **Wt:** 195 **Born:** 8/13/1977 **Age:** 29

Year	Team	Lg	G	GS	CG	GF	IP	BFP	H	R	ER	HR	SH	SF	HB	TBB	IBB	SO	WP	Bk	W	L	Pct	ShO	Sv-Op	Hld	ERC	ERA
2000	ChC	NL	6	0	0	2	3.1	17	4	3	3	0	0	0	0	4	1	2	1	0	1	0	1.000	0	0-0	1	7.25	8.10
2001	ChC	NL	11	0	0	0	11.2	54	14	10	10	2	0	0	0	6	0	12	2	0	0	1	.000	0	0-0	1	6.26	7.71
2005	ChC	NL	69	0	0	13	43.1	187	32	14	14	6	1	0	3	24	3	45	6	1	2	2	.500	0	0-3	13	3.62	2.91
2006	ChC	NL	78	0	0	14	65.1	286	51	30	30	6	0	2	5	34	2	74	4	0	1	1	.500	0	0-0	9	3.44	4.13
	4 ML YEARS		164	0	0	29	123.2	544	101	57	57	14	1	2	8	68	6	133	13	1	4	4	.500	0	0-3	24	3.85	4.15

Miguel Ojeda

Bats: R **Throws:** R **Pos:** C-29; PH-5 **Ht:** 6'1" **Wt:** 230 **Born:** 1/29/1975 **Age:** 32

Year	Team	Lg	G	AB	H	2B	3B	HR	(Hm	Rd)	TB	R	RBI	RC	TBB	IBB	SO	HBP	SH	SF	SB	CS	SB%	GDP	Avg	OBP	Slg
2006	Okla*	AAA	14	47	16	2	0	0	(-	-)	18	8	4	8	6	1	8	0	0	0	0	0	-	2	.340	.415	.383
2006	ColSpr*	AAA	17	52	15	4	1	2	(-	-)	27	11	4	12	12	0	10	0	1	1	1	0	1.00	2	.288	.415	.519
2003	SD	NL	61	141	33	6	0	4	(3	1)	51	13	22	20	18	2	26	3	0	1	1	1	.50	2	.234	.331	.362
2004	SD	NL	62	156	40	3	0	8	(1	7)	67	23	26	24	15	1	34	1	0	2	0	0	-	1	.256	.322	.429
2005	2 Tms		59	102	15	3	1	1	(1	0)	23	8	9	4	15	2	24	0	3	0	1	2	.33	2	.147	.256	.225
2006	2 Tms		30	87	21	5	0	2	(1	1)	32	5	15	10	8	2	19	0	0	0	0	0	-	6	.241	.305	.368
05	SD	NL	43	73	10	3	1	0	(0	0)	15	6	6	1	9	2	21	0	1	0	1	1	.50	2	.137	.232	.205
05	Sea	AL	16	29	5	0	0	1	(1	0)	8	2	3	3	6	0	3	0	2	0	0	1	.00	0	.172	.314	.276
06	Col	NL	25	74	17	3	0	2	(1	1)	26	5	11	8	8	2	16	0	0	0	0	0	-	6	.230	.305	.351
06	Tex	AL	5	13	4	2	0	0	(0	0)	6	0	4	2	0	0	3	0	0	0	0	0	-	0	.308	.308	.462
	4 ML YEARS		212	486	109	17	1	15	(6	9)	173	49	72	58	56	7	103	4	3	3	2	3	.40	11	.224	.308	.356

Darren Oliver

Pitches: L **Bats:** R **Pos:** RP-45 **Ht:** 6'2" **Wt:** 220 **Born:** 10/6/1970 **Age:** 36

Year	Team	Lg	G	GS	CG	GF	IP	BFP	H	R	ER	HR	SH	SF	HB	TBB	IBB	SO	WP	Bk	W	L	Pct	ShO	Sv-Op	Hld	ERC	ERA
1993	Tex	AL	2	0	0	0	3.1	14	2	1	1	1	0	0	0	1	1	4	0	0	0	0	-	0	0-0	0	2.15	2.70
1994	Tex	AL	43	0	0	10	50.0	226	40	24	19	4	6	0	6	35	4	50	2	2	4	0	1.000	0	2-3	9	4.29	3.42
1995	Tex	AL	17	7	0	2	49.0	222	47	25	23	3	5	1	1	32	1	39	4	0	4	2	.667	0	0-0	0	4.59	4.22
1996	Tex	AL	30	30	1	0	173.2	777	190	97	90	20	2	7	10	76	3	112	5	1	14	6	.700	1	0-0	0	5.10	4.66
1997	Tex	AL	32	32	3	0	201.1	887	213	111	94	29	2	5	11	82	3	104	7	0	13	12	.520	1	0-0	0	4.98	4.20
1998	2 Tms		29	29	2	0	160.1	749	204	115	102	18	8	8	10	66	2	87	7	4	10	11	.476	0	0-0	0	6.01	5.73
1999	StL	NL	30	30	2	0	196.1	842	197	96	93	16	11	4	11	74	4	119	6	2	9	9	.500	1	0-0	0	4.11	4.26
2000	Tex	AL	21	21	0	0	108.0	501	151	95	89	16	5	4	4	42	3	49	4	1	2	9	.182	0	0-0	0	7.04	7.42
2001	Tex	AL	28	28	1	0	154.0	696	189	109	103	23	1	5	6	65	0	104	8	2	11	11	.500	0	0-0	0	6.14	6.02
2002	Bos	AL	14	9	1	0	58.0	258	70	30	30	7	1	3	6	27	0	32	1	0	4	5	.444	1	0-0	0	6.49	4.66
2003	Col	NL	33	32	1	0	180.1	786	201	108	101	21	4	5	8	61	3	88	0	0	13	11	.542	0	0-0	0	4.80	5.04
2004	2 Tms	NL	27	10	0	5	72.2	314	87	50	48	14	4	3	1	21	1	46	1	0	3	3	.500	0	0-0	0	5.59	5.94
2006	NYM	NL	45	0	0	10	81.0	333	70	33	31	13	2	4	3	21	2	60	1	0	4	1	.800	0	0-0	3	3.27	3.44
98	Tex	AL	19	19	2	0	103.1	493	140	84	75	11	3	6	10	43	1	58	6	1	6	7	.462	0	0-0	0	6.68	6.53
98	StL	NL	10	10	0	0	57.0	256	64	31	27	7	5	2	0	23	1	29	1	3	4	4	.500	0	0-0	0	4.85	4.26
04	Fla	NL	18	8	0	3	58.2	260	75	44	42	13	4	3	1	17	1	33	1	0	2	3	.400	0	0-0	0	6.30	6.44
04	Hou	NL	9	2	0	2	14.0	54	12	6	6	1	0	0	0	4	0	13	0	0	1	0	1.000	0	0-0	0	2.89	3.86
	13 ML YEARS		351	228	11	27	1488.0	6605	1661	894	824	185	51	49	77	603	27	894	46	12	91	80	.532	4	2-3	12	5.17	4.98

Miguel Olivo

Bats: R **Throws:** R **Pos:** C-124; PH-12; 1B-5 **Ht:** 6'0" **Wt:** 220 **Born:** 7/15/1978 **Age:** 28

Year	Team	Lg	G	AB	H	2B	3B	HR	(Hm	Rd)	TB	R	RBI	RC	TBB	IBB	SO	HBP	SH	SF	SB	CS	SB%	GDP	Avg	OBP	Slg
2002	CWS	AL	6	19	4	1	0	1	(0	1)	8	2	5	4	2	0	5	0	0	0	0	0	-	1	.211	.286	.421
2003	CWS	AL	114	317	75	19	1	6	(4	2)	114	37	27	32	19	0	80	4	4	2	6	4	.60	3	.237	.287	.360
2004	2 Tms	AL	96	301	70	15	4	13	(8	5)	132	46	40	33	20	2	84	3	4	1	7	6	.54	4	.233	.286	.439
2005	2 Tms		91	267	58	11	1	9	(5	4)	98	30	34	23	8	2	80	3	1	2	7	2	.78	7	.217	.246	.367
2006	Fla	NL	127	430	113	22	3	16	(7	9)	189	52	58	49	9	4	103	7	3	3	2	3	.40	9	.263	.287	.440
04	CWS	AL	46	141	38	7	2	7	(4	3)	70	21	26	21	10	1	29	0	4	1	5	4	.56	2	.270	.316	.496
04	Sea	AL	50	160	32	8	2	6	(4	2)	62	25	14	12	10	1	55	3	0	0	2	2	.50	2	.200	.260	.388
05	Sea	AL	54	152	23	4	0	5	(4	1)	42	14	18	6	4	0	49	0	0	1	1	1	.50	3	.151	.172	.276
05	SD	NL	37	115	35	7	1	4	(1	3)	56	16	16	17	4	2	31	3	1	1	6	1	.86	4	.304	.341	.487
	5 ML YEARS		434	1334	320	68	9	45	(24	21)	541	167	164	141	58	8	352	17	12	8	22	15	.59	24	.240	.279	.406

Ray Olmedo

Bats: B **Throws:** R **Pos:** PH-18; 2B-5; SS-4; 3B-3; PR-3; RF-1 **Ht:** 5'11" **Wt:** 155 **Born:** 5/31/1981 **Age:** 26

Year	Team	Lg	G	AB	H	2B	3B	HR	(Hm	Rd)	TB	R	RBI	RC	TBB	IBB	SO	HBP	SH	SF	SB	CS	SB%	GDP	Avg	OBP	Slg
2006	Lsvlle*	AAA	100	383	108	20	3	3	(-	-)	143	47	29	53	34	1	71	3	8	2	17	6	.74	11	.282	.344	.373
2003	Cin	NL	79	230	55	6	1	0	(0	0)	63	24	17	19	13	0	46	0	7	0	1	1	.50	4	.239	.280	.274
2004	Cin	NL	8	1	0	0	0	0	(0	0)	0	0	0	0	1	0	0	0	0	0	0	0	-	0	.000	.500	.000
2005	Cin	NL	54	77	17	4	1	1	(1	0)	26	10	4	6	6	0	22	1	3	1	4	0	1.00	1	.221	.282	.338
2006	Cin	NL	30	44	9	2	0	1	(0	1)	14	5	4	4	4	0	4	0	0	0	1	0	1.00	0	.205	.271	.318
	4 ML YEARS		171	352	81	12	2	2	(1	1)	103	39	25	29	24	0	72	1	10	1	6	1	.86	5	.230	.280	.293

190

Scott Olsen

Pitches: L **Bats:** L **Pos:** SP-31   **Ht:** 6'4" **Wt:** 200 **Born:** 1/12/1984 **Age:** 23

			HOW MUCH HE PITCHED						WHAT HE GAVE UP											THE RESULTS						
Year	Team	Lg	G	GS	CG	GF	IP	BFP	H	R	ER	HR	SH	SF	HB	TBB	IBB	SO	WP	Bk	W	L	Pct	ShO	Sv-Op Hld	ERC	ERA
2002	Mrlns	R	13	11	0	0	51.2	211	39	18	17	0	1	1	5	17	0	50	5	2	2	3	.400	0	0- - -	2.25	2.96
2003	Grnsbr	A	25	24	0	1	128.1	545	101	51	40	4	1	1	7	59	0	129	7	0	7	9	.438	0	0- - -	2.87	2.81
2004	Jupiter	A+	25	25	1	0	136.1	589	127	57	45	8	5	5	4	53	0	158	7	0	7	6	.538	1	0- - -	3.43	2.97
2005	Carlina	AA	14	14	1	0	80.1	343	75	38	35	7	3	5	3	27	1	94	6	0	6	4	.600	1	0- - -	3.46	3.92
2006	Albq	AAA	1	1	0	0	6.1	25	5	1	0	0	0	0	0	3	0	5	1	0	0	0	-	0	0- - -	2.74	0.00
2005	Fla	NL	5	4	0	0	20.1	91	21	13	9	5	0	0	0	10	0	21	1	0	1	1	.500	0	0-0 0	5.66	3.98
2006	Fla	NL	31	31	0	0	180.2	761	160	94	81	23	7	2	7	75	1	166	8	0	12	10	.545	0	0-0 0	3.88	4.04
	2 ML YEARS		36	35	0	0	201.0	852	181	107	90	28	7	2	7	85	1	187	9	0	13	11	.542	0	0-0 0	4.05	4.03

Ryan O'Malley

Pitches: L **Bats:** R **Pos:** SP-2   **Ht:** 6'1" **Wt:** 200 **Born:** 4/9/1980 **Age:** 27

			HOW MUCH HE PITCHED						WHAT HE GAVE UP											THE RESULTS						
Year	Team	Lg	G	GS	CG	GF	IP	BFP	H	R	ER	HR	SH	SF	HB	TBB	IBB	SO	WP	Bk	W	L	Pct	ShO	Sv-Op Hld	ERC	ERA
2002	Boise	A	23	0	0	5	39.1	162	32	16	11	3	3	3	0	15	1	26	2	1	3	1	.750	0	1- - -	2.82	2.52
2003	Lansng	A	40	3	0	10	81.1	342	85	34	26	3	6	0	3	17	1	55	5	0	6	4	.600	0	0- - -	3.28	2.88
2004	Dytona	A	16	1	0	3	30.2	123	27	9	9	1	0	0	1	6	1	28	2	0	4	1	.800	0	0- - -	2.36	2.64
2004	WTenn	AA	16	7	0	3	55.2	233	49	25	23	6	4	2	4	20	1	37	2	0	2	3	.400	0	0- - -	3.61	3.72
2004	Iowa	AAA	8	3	0	4	15.2	69	23	15	15	5	2	1	0	6	0	8	0	0	0	2	.000	0	0- - -	9.40	8.62
2005	WTenn	AA	31	9	0	5	78.1	344	78	41	34	7	3	2	2	25	1	55	3	0	3	3	.500	0	0- - -	3.61	3.91
2005	Iowa	AAA	7	4	0	0	27.0	131	40	19	19	6	2	1	1	11	2	26	0	0	3	2	.600	0	0- - -	8.03	6.33
2006	Iowa	AAA	26	19	0	1	123.2	521	135	62	56	9	3	7	5	30	1	71	1	0	7	7	.500	0	0- - -	3.99	4.08
2006	ChC	NL	2	2	0	0	12.2	55	10	3	3	0	0	0	1	7	0	4	0	0	1	1	.500	0	0-0 0	3.08	2.13

Luis Ordaz

Bats: R **Throws:** R **Pos:** SS-1   **Ht:** 5'11" **Wt:** 170 **Born:** 8/12/1975 **Age:** 31

			BATTING																BASERUNNING				AVERAGES		
Year	Team	Lg	G	AB	H	2B	3B	HR	(Hm | Rd)	TB	R	RBI	RC	TBB	IBB	SO	HBP	SH	SF	SB	CS	SB%	GDP	Avg	OBP	Slg
2006	Drham*	AAA	17	59	20	4	1	1	(- | -)	29	5	6	10	1	0	3	0	1	1	1	0	1.00	3	.339	.344	.492
1997	StL	NL	12	22	6	1	0	0	(0 | 0)	7	3	1	3	1	0	2	0	0	0	3	0	1.00	0	.273	.304	.318
1998	StL	NL	57	153	31	5	0	0	(0 | 0)	36	9	8	9	12	1	18	0	4	0	2	0	1.00	3	.203	.261	.235
1999	StL	NL	10	9	1	0	0	0	(0 | 0)	1	3	2	0	1	0	2	0	1	0	1	0	1.00	0	.111	.200	.111
2000	KC	AL	65	104	23	2	0	0	(0 | 0)	25	17	11	5	5	0	10	1	4	3	4	2	.67	6	.221	.257	.240
2001	KC	AL	28	56	14	3	0	0	(0 | 0)	17	8	4	5	3	0	8	1	2	1	0	0	-	1	.250	.295	.304
2002	KC	AL	33	94	21	2	0	0	(0 | 0)	23	11	4	7	12	0	13	0	4	1	2	3	.40	2	.223	.308	.245
2006	TB	AL	1	2	0	0	0	0	(0 | 0)	0	0	0	0	0	0	0	0	0	0	0	0	-	0	.000	.000	.000
	7 ML YEARS		206	440	96	13	0	0	(0 | 0)	109	51	30	29	34	1	53	2	15	5	12	5	.71	12	.218	.274	.248

Magglio Ordonez

Bats: R **Throws:** R **Pos:** RF-148; DH-6; PH-3   **Ht:** 6'0" **Wt:** 215 **Born:** 1/28/1974 **Age:** 33

			BATTING																BASERUNNING				AVERAGES		
Year	Team	Lg	G	AB	H	2B	3B	HR	(Hm | Rd)	TB	R	RBI	RC	TBB	IBB	SO	HBP	SH	SF	SB	CS	SB%	GDP	Avg	OBP	Slg
1997	CWS	AL	21	69	22	6	0	4	(2 | 2)	40	12	11	12	2	0	8	0	1	0	1	2	.33	1	.319	.338	.580
1998	CWS	AL	145	535	151	25	2	14	(8 | 6)	222	70	65	67	28	1	53	9	2	4	9	7	.56	19	.282	.326	.415
1999	CWS	AL	157	624	188	34	3	30	(16 | 14)	318	100	117	102	47	4	64	1	0	5	13	6	.68	24	.301	.349	.510
2000	CWS	AL	153	588	185	34	3	32	(21 | 11)	321	102	126	112	60	3	64	2	0	15	18	4	.82	28	.315	.371	.546
2001	CWS	AL	160	593	181	40	1	31	(17 | 14)	316	97	113	117	70	7	70	5	0	3	25	7	.78	14	.305	.382	.533
2002	CWS	AL	153	590	189	47	1	38	(24 | 14)	352	116	135	119	53	2	77	7	0	3	7	5	.58	21	.320	.381	.597
2003	CWS	AL	160	606	192	46	3	29	(17 | 12)	331	95	99	109	57	1	73	7	0	4	9	5	.64	20	.317	.380	.546
2004	CWS	AL	52	202	59	8	2	9	(4 | 5)	98	32	37	39	16	2	22	3	0	1	0	2	.00	4	.292	.351	.485
2005	Det	AL	82	305	92	17	0	8	(2 | 6)	133	38	46	51	30	1	35	1	0	7	0	0	-	8	.302	.359	.436
2006	Det	AL	155	593	177	32	1	24	(8 | 16)	283	82	104	97	45	3	87	4	0	4	1	4	.20	13	.298	.350	.477
	10 ML YEARS		1238	4705	1436	289	16	219	(119 | 100)	2414	744	853	825	408	24	553	39	3	46	83	42	.66	152	.305	.362	.513

Pete Orr

Bats: L **Throws:** R **Pos:** PH-62; 2B-32; 3B-10; PR-7   **Ht:** 6'1" **Wt:** 185 **Born:** 6/8/1979 **Age:** 28

			BATTING																BASERUNNING				AVERAGES		
Year	Team	Lg	G	AB	H	2B	3B	HR	(Hm | Rd)	TB	R	RBI	RC	TBB	IBB	SO	HBP	SH	SF	SB	CS	SB%	GDP	Avg	OBP	Slg
2000	Jmstwn	A-	69	265	64	8	1	2	(- | -)	80	40	15	27	24	0	51	6	0	4	9	5	.64	4	.242	.314	.302
2001	MrtlBh	A+	92	317	74	10	1	4	(- | -)	98	38	23	31	19	0	70	11	3	1	17	6	.74	3	.233	.299	.309
2002	MrtlBh	A+	17	51	20	0	2	0	(- | -)	24	8	8	10	3	0	6	1	1	0	3	0	1.00	1	.392	.436	.471
2002	Grnville	AA	89	305	76	10	2	2	(- | -)	96	36	36	33	21	2	47	3	7	2	23	4	.85	8	.249	.302	.315
2003	Grnville	AA	98	257	58	10	2	2	(- | -)	78	22	31	26	25	3	48	3	4	3	14	5	.74	3	.226	.299	.304
2004	Rchmd	AAA	115	460	147	16	10	1	(- | -)	186	69	35	66	20	0	59	2	7	2	24	11	.69	7	.320	.349	.404
2005	Atl	NL	112	150	45	8	1	1	(0 | 1)	58	32	8	18	6	0	23	1	5	0	7	1	.88	2	.300	.331	.387
2006	Atl	NL	102	154	39	3	4	1	(1 | 0)	53	22	8	16	5	1	30	0	5	0	2	4	.33	1	.253	.277	.344
	2 ML YEARS		214	304	84	11	5	2	(1 | 1)	111	54	16	34	11	1	53	1	10	0	9	5	.64	3	.276	.304	.365

David Ortiz

Bats: L **Throws:** L **Pos:** DH-138; 1B-10; PH-3   **Ht:** 6'4" **Wt:** 230 **Born:** 11/18/1975 **Age:** 31

Year Team	Lg	G	AB	H	2B	3B	HR	(Hm	Rd)	TB	R	RBI	RC	TBB	IBB	SO	HBP	SH	SF	SB	CS	SB%	GDP	Avg	OBP	Slg
1997 Min	AL	15	49	16	3	0	1	(0	1)	22	10	6	7	2	0	19	0	0	0	0	0	-	1	.327	.353	.449
1998 Min	AL	86	278	77	20	0	9	(2	7)	124	47	46	46	39	3	72	5	0	4	1	0	1.00	8	.277	.371	.446
1999 Min	AL	10	20	0	0	0	0	(0	0)	0	1	0	0	5	0	12	0	0	0	0	0	-	2	.000	.200	.000
2000 Min	AL	130	415	117	36	1	10	(7	3)	185	59	63	66	57	2	81	0	0	6	1	0	1.00	13	.282	.364	.446
2001 Min	AL	89	303	71	17	1	18	(6	12)	144	46	48	46	40	8	68	1	1	2	1	0	1.00	6	.234	.324	.475
2002 Min	AL	125	412	112	32	1	20	(5	15)	206	52	75	62	43	0	87	3	0	8	1	2	.33	5	.272	.339	.500
2003 Bos	AL	128	448	129	39	2	31	(17	14)	265	79	101	80	58	8	83	1	0	2	0	0	-	9	.288	.369	.592
2004 Bos	AL	150	582	175	47	3	41	(17	24)	351	94	139	127	75	8	133	4	0	8	0	0	-	12	.301	.380	.603
2005 Bos	AL	159	601	180	40	1	47	(20	27)	363	119	148	137	102	9	124	1	0	9	1	0	1.00	13	.300	.397	.604
2006 Bos	AL	151	558	160	29	2	54	(22	32)	355	115	137	129	119	23	117	4	0	5	1	0	1.00	12	.287	.413	.636
10 ML YEARS		1043	3666	1037	263	11	231	(96	135)	2015	622	763	700	540	61	796	19	1	44	6	2	.75	81	.283	.374	.550

Ramon Ortiz

Pitches: R **Bats:** R **Pos:** SP-33   **Ht:** 6'0" **Wt:** 175 **Born:** 5/23/1973 **Age:** 34

Year Team	Lg	G	GS	CG	GF	IP	BFP	H	R	ER	HR	SH	SF	HB	TBB	IBB	SO	WP	Bk	W	L	Pct	ShO	Sv-Op	Hld	ERC	ERA
1999 LAA	AL	9	9	0	0	48.1	218	50	35	35	7	0	2	2	25	0	44	2	2	2	3	.400	0	0-0	0	5.23	6.52
2000 LAA	AL	18	18	2	0	111.1	472	96	69	63	18	4	4	2	55	0	73	7	4	8	6	.571	0	0-0	0	4.24	5.09
2001 LAA	AL	32	32	2	0	208.2	916	223	114	101	25	9	6	12	76	6	135	7	0	13	11	.542	0	0-0	0	4.65	4.36
2002 LAA	AL	32	32	4	0	217.1	896	188	97	91	40	2	5	5	68	0	162	7	3	15	9	.625	1	0-0	0	3.64	3.77
2003 LAA	AL	32	32	1	0	180.0	814	209	121	104	28	3	7	12	63	0	94	4	0	16	13	.552	0	0-0	0	5.44	5.20
2004 LAA	AL	34	14	0	13	128.0	543	139	64	63	18	2	3	4	38	4	82	5	3	5	7	.417	0	0-0	0	4.61	4.43
2005 Cin	NL	30	30	1	0	171.1	755	206	110	102	34	7	8	7	51	1	96	4	1	9	11	.450	0	0-0	0	5.78	5.36
2006 Was	NL	33	33	0	0	190.2	871	230	127	118	31	10	4	18	64	14	104	4	3	11	16	.407	0	0-0	0	5.71	5.57
8 ML YEARS		220	200	10	13	1255.2	5485	1341	737	677	201	37	39	62	440	25	790	40	16	79	76	.510	1	0-0	0	4.87	4.85

Russ Ortiz

Pitches: R **Bats:** R **Pos:** RP-15; SP-11   **Ht:** 6'1" **Wt:** 220 **Born:** 6/5/1974 **Age:** 33

Year Team	Lg	G	GS	CG	GF	IP	BFP	H	R	ER	HR	SH	SF	HB	TBB	IBB	SO	WP	Bk	W	L	Pct	ShO	Sv-Op	Hld	ERC	ERA
2006 Tucsn*	AAA	4	4	0	0	20.2	90	22	7	6	1	3	0	0	5	0	10	0	0	1	0	1.000	0	0--	-	3.34	2.61
1998 SF	NL	22	13	0	3	88.1	394	90	51	49	11	5	4	4	46	1	75	3	0	4	4	.500	0	0-0	1	5.05	4.99
1999 SF	NL	33	33	3	0	207.2	922	189	109	88	24	11	6	6	125	5	164	13	0	18	9	.667	0	0-0	0	4.56	3.81
2000 SF	NL	33	32	0	0	195.2	871	192	117	109	28	10	6	7	112	0	167	8	0	14	12	.538	0	0-0	0	5.17	5.01
2001 SF	NL	33	33	1	0	218.2	911	187	90	80	13	10	4	0	91	3	169	8	1	17	9	.654	1	0-0	0	3.08	3.29
2002 SF	NL	33	33	2	0	214.1	911	191	89	86	15	15	6	4	94	5	137	5	0	14	10	.583	0	0-0	0	3.46	3.61
2003 Atl	NL	34	34	1	0	212.1	912	177	101	90	17	6	7	4	102	7	149	5	0	21	7	.750	1	0-0	0	3.32	3.81
2004 Atl	NL	34	34	0	0	204.2	896	197	98	94	23	10	7	3	112	7	143	4	1	15	9	.625	1	0-0	0	4.60	4.13
2005 Ari	NL	22	22	0	0	115.0	551	147	92	88	18	5	8	4	65	3	46	5	0	5	11	.313	0	0-0	0	6.96	6.89
2006 2 Tms		26	11	0	5	63.0	303	86	60	57	18	1	1	3	40	1	44	2	0	0	8	.000	0	0-0	0	9.39	8.14
06 Ari	NL	6	6	0	0	22.2	113	27	21	19	3	1	0	1	22	1	21	0	0	0	5	.000	0	0-0	0	8.19	7.54
06 Bal	AL	20	5	0	5	40.1	190	59	39	38	15	0	1	2	18	0	23	2	0	0	3	.000	0	0-0	0	9.99	8.48
9 ML YEARS		270	245	9	8	1519.2	6671	1456	807	741	167	73	49	35	787	33	1094	53	2	108	79	.578	3	0-0	1	4.45	4.39

Dan Ortmeier

Bats: B **Throws:** R **Pos:** PH-7; RF-3; DH-2; PR-1   **Ht:** 6'4" **Wt:** 215 **Born:** 5/11/1981 **Age:** 26

Year Team	Lg	G	AB	H	2B	3B	HR	(Hm	Rd)	TB	R	RBI	RC	TBB	IBB	SO	HBP	SH	SF	SB	CS	SB%	GDP	Avg	OBP	Slg
2002 SlmKzr	A-	49	195	57	9	1	5	(-	-)	83	32	31	31	18	1	37	1	0	2	3	0	1.00	5	.292	.352	.426
2003 SnJos	A+	115	408	124	32	6	8	(-	-)	192	62	56	74	39	4	89	11	0	2	13	6	.68	13	.304	.378	.471
2004 Nrwich	AA	106	377	95	23	6	10	(-	-)	160	55	48	62	47	4	110	12	0	2	18	2	.90	5	.252	.352	.424
2005 Nrwich	AA	135	503	138	23	6	20	(-	-)	233	85	79	89	48	1	115	21	0	3	35	12	.74	2	.274	.360	.463
2006 Nrwich	AA	47	167	42	9	1	2	(-	-)	59	17	11	20	17	1	38	3	0	2	7	4	.64	4	.251	.328	.353
2006 Fresno	AAA	68	262	64	14	3	6	(-	-)	102	37	33	30	16	1	40	3	0	2	8	6	.57	2	.244	.293	.389
2005 SF	NL	15	22	3	0	0	0	(0	0)	3	1	1	1	3	0	5	1	0	0	1	0	1.00	2	.136	.269	.136
2006 SF	NL	9	12	3	1	0	0	(0	0)	4	0	2	2	0	0	4	0	0	0	0	0	-	0	.250	.250	.333
2 ML YEARS		24	34	6	1	0	0	(0	0)	7	1	3	3	3	0	9	1	0	0	1	0	1.00	2	.176	.263	.206

Chad Orvella

Pitches: R **Bats:** R **Pos:** RP-22   **Ht:** 5'11" **Wt:** 190 **Born:** 10/1/1980 **Age:** 26

Year Team	Lg	G	GS	CG	GF	IP	BFP	H	R	ER	HR	SH	SF	HB	TBB	IBB	SO	WP	Bk	W	L	Pct	ShO	Sv-Op	Hld	ERC	ERA
2003 HudVal	A-	10	0	0	9	12.1	44	6	0	0	0	0	1	2	0	1	0	15	0	0	0	0	-	0	8--	-	0.63	0.00
2004 CtnSC	A	22	0	0	10	47.1	175	28	9	7	4	0	0	1	5	0	76	0	0	1	0	1.000	0	4--	-	1.23	1.33
2004 Bkrsfld	A+	15	0	0	13	17.2	70	13	7	6	2	0	0	1	4	1	24	1	0	0	1	.000	0	4--	-	2.28	3.06
2004 Mont	AA	6	0	0	6	7.0	21	0	0	0	0	0	0	1	0	0	14	0	0	0	0	-	0	4--	-	0.03	0.00
2004 Drham	AAA	2	0	0	0	1.2	7	1	1	1	1	0	0	1	1	0	2	1	0	0	0	-	0	0--	-	10.27	5.40
2005 Mont	AA	16	0	0	15	25.0	96	15	1	1	0	1	0	0	6	0	29	1	0	0	0	-	0	9--	-	1.19	0.36
2006 Drham	AAA	27	0	0	12	38.2	154	31	11	8	2	1	0	1	9	0	55	3	0	4	0	1.000	0	1--	-	2.24	1.86
2005 TB	AL	37	0	0	9	50.0	220	47	26	20	4	1	4	1	23	2	43	0	0	3	3	.500	0	1-2	14	3.77	3.60
2006 TB	AL	22	0	0	5	24.1	130	36	23	20	6	2	1	3	20	0	17	1	0	1	5	.167	0	0-3	1	10.81	7.40
2 ML YEARS		59	0	0	14	74.1	350	83	49	40	10	3	5	4	43	2	60	1	0	4	8	.333	0	1-5	15	5.84	4.84

Franquelis Osoria

Pitches: R **Bats:** R **Pos:** RP-12   **Ht:** 5'11" **Wt:** 200 **Born:** 9/12/1981 **Age:** 25

			HOW MUCH HE PITCHED					WHAT HE GAVE UP									THE RESULTS						
Year	Team	Lg	G	GS	CG	GF	IP	BFP	H	R	ER	HR	SH	SF	HB	TBB	IBB	SO	WP	Bk	W	L	Pct	ShO	Sv-Op Hld	ERC	ERA
2002	VeroB	A+	3	0	0	1	7.1	28	4	2	2	0	0	0	1	2	0	10	0	0	0	1	.000	0	0- -	1.41	2.45
2002	SoGA	A	21	1	0	7	43.1	183	40	22	16	1	2	1	2	13	1	30	3	0	2	2	.500	0	1- -	2.87	3.32
2003	VeroB	A+	33	3	0	20	75.0	313	69	34	25	4	5	5	5	19	5	53	5	1	3	6	.333	0	6- -	2.92	3.00
2004	Jaxnvl	AA	51	0	0	24	81.0	332	71	36	33	2	2	0	5	18	4	73	3	0	8	5	.615	0	5- -	2.42	3.67
2004	LsVgs	AAA	4	0	0	0	8.1	39	13	6	6	0	1	1	1	1	0	3	0	0	0	0	-	0	0- -	5.94	6.48
2005	LsVgs	AAA	40	0	0	21	55.0	241	63	18	16	3	1	1	4	13	6	35	3	0	6	4	.600	0	9- -	4.00	2.62
2006	LsVgs	AAA	44	0	0	16	51.2	254	81	31	25	2	2	2	6	21	3	28	5	0	2	2	.500	0	2- -	7.50	4.35
2005	LAD	NL	24	0	0	6	29.2	122	28	14	13	3	3	0	3	8	0	15	0	0	0	2	.000	0	0-2 3	3.78	3.94
2006	LAD	NL	12	0	0	1	17.2	86	27	14	14	4	1	0	1	9	1	13	0	0	0	2	.000	0	0-0 0	9.30	7.13
	2 ML YEARS		36	0	0	7	47.1	208	55	28	27	7	4	0	4	17	1	28	0	0	0	4	.000	0	0-2 3	5.67	5.13

Roy Oswalt

Pitches: R **Bats:** R **Pos:** SP-32; RP-1   **Ht:** 6'0" **Wt:** 185 **Born:** 8/29/1977 **Age:** 29

			HOW MUCH HE PITCHED					WHAT HE GAVE UP									THE RESULTS						
Year	Team	Lg	G	GS	CG	GF	IP	BFP	H	R	ER	HR	SH	SF	HB	TBB	IBB	SO	WP	Bk	W	L	Pct	ShO	Sv-Op Hld	ERC	ERA
2001	Hou	NL	28	24	3	4	141.2	575	126	48	43	13	4	4	6	24	2	144	0	0	14	3	.824	1	0-0 0	2.68	2.73
2002	Hou	NL	35	34	0	0	233.0	956	215	86	78	17	12	7	5	62	4	208	3	0	19	9	.679	0	0-0 0	3.05	3.01
2003	Hou	NL	21	21	0	0	127.1	514	116	48	42	15	7	1	5	29	0	108	1	0	10	5	.667	0	0-0 0	3.26	2.97
2004	Hou	NL	36	35	2	0	237.0	983	233	100	92	17	11	4	11	62	5	206	5	1	20	10	.667	2	0-0 0	3.46	3.49
2005	Hou	NL	35	35	4	0	241.2	1002	243	85	79	18	12	7	8	48	3	184	5	1	20	12	.625	1	0-0 0	3.27	2.94
2006	Hou	NL	33	32	2	1	220.2	896	220	76	73	18	12	4	6	38	4	166	1	1	15	8	.652	0	0-0 0	3.19	**2.98**
	6 ML YEARS		188	177	11	5	1201.1	4926	1153	443	407	98	58	27	41	263	18	1016	15	3	98	47	.676	4	0-0 0	3.18	3.05

Akinori Otsuka

Pitches: R **Bats:** R **Pos:** RP-63   **Ht:** 6'0" **Wt:** 210 **Born:** 1/13/1972 **Age:** 35

			HOW MUCH HE PITCHED					WHAT HE GAVE UP									THE RESULTS						
Year	Team	Lg	G	GS	CG	GF	IP	BFP	H	R	ER	HR	SH	SF	HB	TBB	IBB	SO	WP	Bk	W	L	Pct	ShO	Sv-Op Hld	ERC	ERA
2004	SD	NL	73	0	0	18	77.1	312	56	16	15	6	4	0	0	26	6	87	0	0	7	2	.778	0	2-7 34	2.14	1.75
2005	SD	NL	66	0	0	17	62.2	276	55	28	25	3	5	0	2	34	8	60	1	0	2	8	.200	0	1-7 22	3.44	3.59
2006	Tex	AL	63	0	0	48	59.2	232	53	17	14	3	0	1	0	11	0	47	3	0	2	4	.333	0	32-36 7	2.46	2.11
	3 ML YEARS		202	0	0	83	199.2	820	164	61	54	12	9	1	2	71	14	194	4	0	11	14	.440	0	35-50 63	2.64	2.43

Lyle Overbay

Bats: L **Throws:** L **Pos:** 1B-145; DH-11; PH-2   **Ht:** 6'2" **Wt:** 235 **Born:** 1/28/1977 **Age:** 30

			BATTING																	BASERUNNING				AVERAGES		
Year	Team	Lg	G	AB	H	2B	3B	HR	(Hm	Rd)	TB	R	RBI	RC	TBB	IBB	SO	HBP	SH	SF	SB	CS	SB%	GDP	Avg	OBP	Slg
2001	Ari	NL	2	2	1	0	0	0	(0	0)	1	0	0	0	0	0	1	0	0	0	0	0	-	0	.500	.500	.500
2002	Ari	NL	10	10	1	0	0	0	(0	0)	1	0	1	0	0	0	5	0	0	0	0	0	-	0	.100	.100	.100
2003	Ari	NL	86	254	70	20	0	4	(2	2)	102	23	28	34	35	7	67	2	0	2	1	0	1.00	8	.276	.365	.402
2004	Mil	NL	159	579	174	53	1	16	(6	10)	277	83	87	94	81	9	128	2	0	6	2	1	.67	11	.301	.385	.478
2005	Mil	NL	158	537	148	34	1	19	(10	9)	241	80	72	84	78	8	98	2	1	4	1	0	1.00	17	.276	.367	.449
2006	Tor	AL	157	581	181	46	1	22	(17	5)	295	82	92	89	55	7	96	2	0	2	5	3	.63	19	.312	.372	.508
	6 ML YEARS		572	1963	575	153	3	61	(35	26)	917	268	280	301	249	31	395	8	1	14	9	4	.69	55	.293	.372	.467

Henry Owens

Pitches: R **Bats:** R **Pos:** RP-3   **Ht:** 6'3" **Wt:** 230 **Born:** 4/23/1979 **Age:** 28

			HOW MUCH HE PITCHED					WHAT HE GAVE UP									THE RESULTS						
Year	Team	Lg	G	GS	CG	GF	IP	BFP	H	R	ER	HR	SH	SF	HB	TBB	IBB	SO	WP	Bk	W	L	Pct	ShO	Sv-Op Hld	ERC	ERA
2001	Pirates	R	6	0	0	5	7.0	28	5	1	1	0	0	0	0	2	0	8	0	0	1	0	1.000	0	1- -	1.62	1.29
2002	Wmspt	A-	23	0	0	15	44.2	177	23	18	13	4	0	1	3	16	0	63	8	0	0	3	.000	0	7- -	1.65	2.62
2003	Hickory	A	22	0	0	17	34.0	143	21	14	11	1	1	0	6	17	0	52	7	0	2	1	.667	0	9- -	2.60	2.91
2003	Lynbrg	A+	13	0	0	11	14.2	65	9	6	4	0	2	0	1	11	0	21	0	0	1	2	.333	0	5- -	2.77	2.45
2004	Lynbrg	A+	39	0	0	27	54.2	240	46	26	26	4	0	0	4	26	1	49	10	0	3	4	.429	0	4- -	3.47	4.28
2005	StLuci	A+	38	1	0	16	54.1	240	49	29	19	2	0	1	5	24	2	74	7	0	2	5	.286	0	4- -	3.46	3.15
2006	Bnghtn	AA	37	0	0	36	40.0	154	19	9	7	1	1	0	3	10	1	74	5	0	2	2	.500	0	20- -	1.07	1.58
2006	NYM	NL	3	0	0	1	4.0	19	4	4	4	0	0	1	0	4	0	2	0	0	0	0	-	0	0-0 0	5.79	9.00

Jerry Owens

Bats: L **Throws:** L **Pos:** PR-7; DH-5; CF-4; PH-2; RF-1   **Ht:** 6'3" **Wt:** 195 **Born:** 2/16/1981 **Age:** 26

			BATTING																	BASERUNNING				AVERAGES		
Year	Team	Lg	G	AB	H	2B	3B	HR	(Hm	Rd)	TB	R	RBI	RC	TBB	IBB	SO	HBP	SH	SF	SB	CS	SB%	GDP	Avg	OBP	Slg
2003	Vrmnt	A-	2	8	1	0	0	0	(-	-)	1	0	0	0	0	0	2	0	0	0	1	0	1.00	0	.125	.125	.125
2004	Savann	A	108	418	122	17	2	1	(-	-)	146	69	37	59	46	1	59	3	1	2	30	13	.70	3	.292	.365	.349
2005	Brham	AA	130	522	173	21	6	2	(-	-)	212	99	52	87	52	4	72	2	9	2	38	20	.66	5	.331	.393	.406
2006	Charltt	AAA	112	439	115	15	5	4	(-	-)	152	75	48	57	45	2	61	1	5	3	40	12	.77	5	.262	.330	.346
2006	CWS	AL	12	9	3	1	0	0	(0	0)	4	4	0	1	0	0	2	0	0	0	1	0	1.00	0	.333	.333	.444

Pablo Ozuna

Bats: R **Throws:** R **Pos:** LF-39; 3B-17; PR-16; PH-12; DH-7; 2B-6; RF-1   **Ht:** 5'11" **Wt:** 195 **Born:** 8/25/1974 **Age:** 32

								BATTING													BASERUNNING				AVERAGES		
Year	Team	Lg	G	AB	H	2B	3B	HR	(Hm	Rd)	TB	R	RBI	RC	TBB	IBB	SO	HBP	SH	SF	SB	CS	SB%	GDP	Avg	OBP	Slg
2000	Fla	NL	14	24	8	1	0	0	(0	0)	9	2	0	3	0	0	2	0	2	0	1	0	1.00	0	.333	.333	.375
2002	Fla	NL	34	47	13	2	2	0	(0	0)	19	4	3	4	1	0	3	1	0	1	1	1	.50	2	.277	.300	.404
2003	Col	NL	17	40	8	1	0	0	(0	0)	9	5	2	4	2	0	6	2	1	0	3	0	1.00	1	.200	.273	.225
2005	CWS	AL	70	203	56	7	2	0	(0	0)	67	27	11	20	7	0	26	4	3	0	14	7	.67	5	.276	.313	.330
2006	CWS	AL	79	189	62	12	2	2	(2	0)	84	25	17	30	7	0	16	4	3	0	6	6	.50	3	.328	.365	.444
5 ML YEARS			214	503	147	23	6	2	(2	0)	188	63	33	61	17	0	53	11	9	1	25	14	.64	11	.292	.329	.374

Vicente Padilla

Pitches: R **Bats:** R **Pos:** SP-33   **Ht:** 6'2" **Wt:** 220 **Born:** 9/27/1977 **Age:** 29

			HOW MUCH HE PITCHED						WHAT HE GAVE UP											THE RESULTS					
Year	Team	Lg	G	GS	CG	GF	IP	BFP	H	R	ER	HR	SH	SF	HB	TBB	IBB	SO	WP	Bk	W	L	Pct	ShO	Sv-Op	Hld	ERC	ERA
1999	Ari	NL	5	0	0	2	2.2	19	7	5	5	1	1	0	0	3	0	0	0	0	0	1	.000	0	0-1	1	20.65	16.88
2000	2 Tms	NL	55	0	0	16	65.1	291	72	33	27	3	5	3	1	28	7	51	1	0	4	7	.364	0	2-7	15	4.22	3.72
2001	Phi	NL	23	0	0	5	34.0	144	36	18	16	1	0	0	0	12	0	29	1	0	3	1	.750	0	0-3	1	3.80	4.24
2002	Phi	NL	32	32	1	0	206.0	862	198	83	75	16	10	3	15	53	5	128	6	2	14	11	.560	1	0-0	0	3.42	3.28
2003	Phi	NL	32	32	1	0	208.2	876	196	94	84	22	11	7	16	62	4	133	3	2	14	12	.538	1	0-0	0	3.68	3.62
2004	Phi	NL	20	20	0	0	115.1	503	119	63	58	16	7	5	10	36	6	82	2	0	7	7	.500	0	0-0	0	4.42	4.53
2005	Phi	NL	27	27	0	0	147.0	654	146	79	77	22	7	3	8	74	9	103	1	0	9	12	.429	0	0-0	0	4.94	4.71
2006	Tex	AL	33	33	0	0	200.0	872	206	108	100	21	6	6	17	70	2	156	4	2	15	10	.600	0	0-0	0	4.41	4.50
00	Ari	NL	27	0	0	12	35.0	143	32	10	9	0	0	1	0	10	2	30	0	0	2	1	.667	0	0-1	7	2.48	2.31
00	Phi	NL	28	0	0	4	30.1	148	40	23	18	3	5	2	1	18	5	21	1	0	2	6	.250	0	2-6	8	6.52	5.34
8 ML YEARS			227	144	2	23	979.0	4221	980	483	442	102	47	27	67	338	33	682	18	6	66	61	.520	2	2-11	17	4.12	4.06

Angel Pagan

Bats: B **Throws:** R **Pos:** LF-39; PH-23; RF-21; CF-1   **Ht:** 6'1" **Wt:** 180 **Born:** 7/2/1981 **Age:** 25

								BATTING													BASERUNNING				AVERAGES		
Year	Team	Lg	G	AB	H	2B	3B	HR	(Hm	Rd)	TB	R	RBI	RC	TBB	IBB	SO	HBP	SH	SF	SB	CS	SB%	GDP	Avg	OBP	Slg
2000	Kngspt	R	19	72	26	5	1	0	(-	-)	33	13	8	14	6	0	8	0	0	0	6	1	.86	1	.361	.410	.458
2001	CptCty	A	15	57	17	1	1	0	(-	-)	20	4	5	7	6	0	5	0	1	0	3	2	.60	3	.298	.365	.351
2001	Bklyn	A-	62	238	75	10	2	0	(-	-)	89	46	15	36	22	0	30	7	3	1	30	18	.63	1	.315	.388	.374
2002	CptCty	A	108	458	128	14	5	1	(-	-)	155	79	36	54	32	0	87	0	4	3	52	21	.71	1	.279	.325	.338
2002	StLuci	A	16	67	23	2	1	1	(-	-)	30	12	7	13	7	1	9	0	1	0	10	2	.83	5	.343	.405	.448
2003	StLuci	A	113	441	110	15	5	1	(-	-)	138	64	33	46	35	1	80	2	11	1	35	15	.70	5	.249	.307	.313
2004	Bnghtn	AA	112	449	129	25	8	4	(-	-)	182	71	63	69	42	0	96	1	4	5	29	5	.85	6	.287	.346	.405
2004	Norfolk	AAA	12	45	13	3	3	0	(-	-)	22	13	1	8	4	0	8	0	0	0	4	1	.80	0	.289	.347	.489
2005	Norfolk	AAA	129	516	140	20	10	8	(-	-)	204	69	40	71	49	2	111	1	9	4	27	15	.64	7	.271	.333	.395
2006	Cubs	R	3	9	1	0	0	0	(-	-)	1	1	0	0	2	0	3	0	0	0	1	0	1.00	0	.111	.273	.111
2006	Iowa	AAA	4	15	4	1	0	0	(-	-)	5	2	0	1	1	0	4	0	0	0	1	0	1.00	0	.267	.313	.333
2006	ChC	NL	77	170	42	6	2	5	(4	1)	67	28	18	21	15	0	28	0	0	1	4	2	.67	3	.247	.306	.394

Orlando Palmeiro

Bats: L **Throws:** L **Pos:** PH-88; LF-12; RF-11   **Ht:** 5'11" **Wt:** 185 **Born:** 1/19/1969 **Age:** 38

								BATTING													BASERUNNING				AVERAGES		
Year	Team	Lg	G	AB	H	2B	3B	HR	(Hm	Rd)	TB	R	RBI	RC	TBB	IBB	SO	HBP	SH	SF	SB	CS	SB%	GDP	Avg	OBP	Slg
1995	LAA	AL	15	20	7	0	0	0	(0	0)	7	3	1	3	1	0	1	0	0	0	0	0	-	0	.350	.381	.350
1996	LAA	AL	50	87	25	6	1	0	(0	0)	33	6	6	12	8	1	13	2	1	0	0	1	.00	1	.287	.361	.379
1997	LAA	AL	74	134	29	2	2	0	(0	0)	35	19	8	10	17	1	11	1	3	1	2	2	.50	4	.216	.307	.261
1998	LAA	AL	75	165	53	7	2	0	(0	0)	64	28	21	26	20	1	11	0	7	0	5	4	.56	2	.321	.395	.388
1999	LAA	AL	109	317	88	12	1	1	(0	1)	105	46	23	41	39	1	30	6	6	3	5	5	.50	4	.278	.364	.331
2000	LAA	AL	108	243	73	20	2	0	(0	0)	97	38	25	42	38	0	20	2	10	3	4	1	.80	4	.300	.395	.399
2001	LAA	AL	104	230	56	10	1	2	(0	2)	74	29	23	25	25	2	24	3	7	5	6	6	.50	3	.243	.319	.322
2002	LAA	AL	110	263	79	12	1	0	(0	0)	93	35	31	39	30	1	22	0	4	3	7	2	.78	7	.300	.368	.354
2003	StL	NL	141	317	86	13	1	3	(1	2)	110	37	33	37	32	3	31	2	7	6	3	3	.50	1	.271	.336	.347
2004	Hou	NL	102	133	32	5	0	3	(1	2)	46	19	12	18	18	1	19	3	2	0	2	1	.67	1	.241	.344	.346
2005	Hou	NL	114	204	58	17	2	3	(1	2)	88	22	20	29	15	1	23	4	5	3	3	1	.75	4	.284	.341	.431
2006	Hou	NL	103	119	30	6	1	0	(0	0)	38	12	17	13	6	0	17	1	2	0	0	1	.00	2	.252	.294	.319
12 ML YEARS			1105	2232	616	110	14	12	(3	9)	790	294	220	295	249	12	222	24	54	24	37	27	.58	33	.276	.352	.354

Jonathan Papelbon

Pitches: R **Bats:** R **Pos:** RP-59   **Ht:** 6'4" **Wt:** 230 **Born:** 11/23/1980 **Age:** 26

			HOW MUCH HE PITCHED						WHAT HE GAVE UP											THE RESULTS					
Year	Team	Lg	G	GS	CG	GF	IP	BFP	H	R	ER	HR	SH	SF	HB	TBB	IBB	SO	WP	Bk	W	L	Pct	ShO	Sv-Op	Hld	ERC	ERA
2003	Lowell	A-	13	6	0	1	32.2	154	43	23	23	2	2	1	4	9	0	36	3	0	1	2	.333	0	0--	-	5.47	6.34
2004	Srsota	A+	24	24	2	0	129.2	529	97	43	38	6	6	3	7	43	2	153	3	0	12	7	.632	0	0--	-	2.33	2.64
2005	Portlnd	AA	14	14	0	0	87.0	343	59	28	24	9	4	3	5	23	3	83	2	1	5	2	.714	0	0--	-	2.11	2.48
2005	Pwtckt	AAA	7	4	0	3	27.2	107	21	9	9	2	2	0	1	3	0	27	0	0	1	2	.333	0	1--	-	1.76	2.93
2005	Bos	AL	17	3	0	4	34.0	148	33	11	10	4	1	0	3	17	2	34	1	0	3	1	.750	0	0-1	4	4.82	2.65
2006	Bos	AL	59	0	0	49	68.1	257	40	8	7	3	1	2	1	13	2	75	2	0	4	2	.667	0	35-41	1	1.22	0.92
2 ML YEARS			76	3	0	53	102.1	405	73	19	17	7	2	2	4	30	4	109	3	0	7	3	.700	0	35-42	5	2.12	1.50

Chan Ho Park

Pitches: R **Bats:** R **Pos:** SP-21; RP-3   **Ht:** 6'2" **Wt:** 210 **Born:** 6/30/1973 **Age:** 34

Year	Team	Lg	G	GS	CG	GF	IP	BFP	H	R	ER	HR	SH	SF	HB	TBB	IBB	SO	WP	Bk	W	L	Pct	ShO	Sv-Op	Hld	ERC	ERA
							HOW MUCH HE PITCHED				WHAT HE GAVE UP												THE RESULTS					
1994	LAD	NL	2	0	0	1	4.0	23	5	5	5	1	0	0	1	5	0	6	0	0	0	0	-	0	0-0	0	11.69	11.25
1995	LAD	NL	2	1	0	0	4.0	16	2	2	2	1	0	0	0	2	0	7	0	1	0	0	-	0	0-0	0	2.70	4.50
1996	LAD	NL	48	10	0	7	108.2	477	82	48	44	7	8	1	4	71	3	119	4	3	5	5	.500	0	0-0	4	3.50	3.64
1997	LAD	NL	32	29	2	1	192.0	792	149	80	72	24	9	5	8	70	1	166	4	1	14	8	.636	0	0-0	0	3.04	3.38
1998	LAD	NL	34	34	2	0	220.2	946	199	101	91	16	11	10	11	97	1	191	6	2	15	9	.625	0	0-0	0	3.69	3.71
1999	LAD	NL	33	33	0	0	194.1	883	208	120	113	31	10	5	14	100	4	174	11	1	13	11	.542	0	0-0	0	5.68	5.23
2000	LAD	NL	34	34	3	0	226.0	963	173	92	82	21	12	5	12	124	2	217	13	0	18	10	.643	1	0-0	0	3.51	3.27
2001	LAD	NL	36	35	2	0	234.0	981	183	98	91	23	16	7	20	91	1	218	3	3	15	11	.577	1	0-0	0	3.15	3.50
2002	Tex	AL	25	25	0	0	145.2	666	154	95	93	20	4	3	17	78	2	121	9	0	9	8	.529	0	0-0	0	5.75	5.75
2003	Tex	AL	7	7	0	0	29.2	146	34	26	25	5	1	3	6	25	0	16	1	1	1	3	.250	0	0-0	0	8.56	7.58
2004	Tex	AL	16	16	0	0	95.2	428	105	63	58	22	4	4	13	33	0	63	1	1	4	7	.364	0	0-0	0	5.97	5.46
2005	2 Tms		30	29	0	0	155.1	715	180	103	99	11	7	3	10	80	1	113	6	0	12	8	.600	0	0-0	0	5.52	5.74
2006	SD	NL	24	21	1	0	136.2	606	146	81	73	20	10	4	10	44	7	96	5	0	7	7	.500	1	0-0	0	4.62	4.81
05	Tex	AL	20	20	0	0	109.2	502	130	70	69	8	5	2	6	54	1	80	3	0	8	5	.615	0	0-0	0	5.58	5.66
05	SD	NL	10	9	0	0	45.2	213	50	33	30	3	2	1	4	26	0	33	3	0	4	3	.571	0	0-0	0	5.36	5.91
13 ML YEARS			323	274	10	9	1746.2	7642	1620	914	848	202	92	50	126	820	24	1507	63	13	113	87	.565	3	0-0	4	4.32	4.37

Chad Paronto

Pitches: R **Bats:** R **Pos:** RP-65   **Ht:** 6'5" **Wt:** 250 **Born:** 7/28/1975 **Age:** 31

Year	Team	Lg	G	GS	CG	GF	IP	BFP	H	R	ER	HR	SH	SF	HB	TBB	IBB	SO	WP	Bk	W	L	Pct	ShO	Sv-Op	Hld	ERC	ERA
							HOW MUCH HE PITCHED				WHAT HE GAVE UP												THE RESULTS					
2006	Rchmd*	AAA	12	0	0	9	17.2	72	17	3	2	1	0	0	1	3	0	15	0	0	1	1	.500	0	4--	1	2.96	1.02
2001	Bal	AL	24	0	0	9	27.0	128	33	24	15	5	1	1	1	11	0	16	1	0	1	3	.250	0	0-1	5	5.98	5.00
2002	Cle	AL	29	0	0	11	35.2	154	34	19	16	3	0	4	2	11	1	23	2	0	0	2	.000	0	0-0	0	3.45	4.04
2003	Cle	AL	6	0	0	5	6.2	29	7	8	7	1	1	1	0	3	0	6	0	0	0	2	.000	0	0-0	0	5.90	9.45
2006	Atl	NL	65	0	0	11	56.2	237	53	23	20	5	4	1	3	19	3	41	3	0	2	3	.400	0	0-2	8	3.56	3.18
4 ML YEARS			124	0	0	36	126.0	548	127	74	58	14	6	7	6	44	4	86	6	0	3	10	.231	0	0-3	13	4.10	4.14

Corey Patterson

Bats: L **Throws:** R **Pos:** CF-134; PR-4; PH-2   **Ht:** 5'9" **Wt:** 175 **Born:** 8/13/1979 **Age:** 27

Year	Team	Lg	G	AB	H	2B	3B	HR	(Hm	Rd)	TB	R	RBI	RC	TBB	IBB	SO	HBP	SH	SF	SB	CS	SB%	GDP	Avg	OBP	Slg
								BATTING													BASERUNNING				AVERAGES		
2000	ChC	NL	11	42	7	1	0	2	(1	1)	14	9	2	3	3	0	14	1	1	0	1	1	.50	0	.167	.239	.333
2001	ChC	NL	59	131	29	3	0	4	(1	3)	44	26	14	13	6	0	33	3	2	3	4	0	1.00	1	.221	.266	.336
2002	ChC	NL	153	592	150	30	5	14	(7	7)	232	71	54	61	19	1	142	8	4	5	18	3	.86	8	.253	.284	.392
2003	ChC	NL	83	329	98	17	7	13	(7	6)	168	49	55	55	15	2	77	1	0	2	16	5	.76	5	.298	.329	.511
2004	ChC	NL	157	631	168	30	6	24	(14	10)	285	91	72	87	45	7	168	5	5	1	32	9	.78	7	.266	.320	.452
2005	ChC	NL	126	451	97	15	3	13	(9	4)	157	47	34	32	23	3	118	1	5	1	15	5	.75	5	.215	.254	.348
2006	Bal	AL	135	463	128	19	5	16	(9	7)	205	75	53	66	21	5	94	5	8	1	45	9	.83	0	.276	.314	.443
7 ML YEARS			724	2639	677	118	26	86	(48	38)	1105	368	284	317	132	18	646	24	25	13	131	32	.80	26	.257	.297	.419

John Patterson

Pitches: R **Bats:** R **Pos:** SP-8   **Ht:** 6'5" **Wt:** 210 **Born:** 1/30/1978 **Age:** 29

Year	Team	Lg	G	GS	CG	GF	IP	BFP	H	R	ER	HR	SH	SF	HB	TBB	IBB	SO	WP	Bk	W	L	Pct	ShO	Sv-Op	Hld	ERC	ERA
							HOW MUCH HE PITCHED				WHAT HE GAVE UP												THE RESULTS					
2006	Ptomc*	A+	2	2	0	0	8.2	42	12	7	5	1	0	1	1	2	0	11	1	0	0	1	.000	0	0--	0	5.94	5.19
2006	NewOr*	AAA	1	1	0	0	4.2	20	4	2	1	1	0	0	0	2	0	3	0	0	0	0	-	0	0--	0	4.09	1.93
2002	Ari	NL	7	5	0	1	30.2	123	27	11	11	7	0	0	1	7	0	31	2	0	2	0	1.000	0	0-0	0	3.76	3.23
2003	Ari	NL	16	8	0	3	55.0	252	61	39	37	7	1	2	2	30	5	43	4	0	1	4	.200	0	1-1	0	5.50	6.05
2004	Mon	NL	19	19	0	0	98.1	445	100	58	55	18	4	2	8	46	4	99	0	0	4	7	.364	0	0-0	0	5.26	5.03
2005	Was	NL	31	31	2	0	198.1	817	172	71	69	19	5	4	5	65	11	185	9	1	9	7	.563	1	0-0	0	3.09	3.13
2006	Was	NL	8	8	0	0	40.2	170	36	21	20	4	2	4	3	9	1	42	0	0	1	2	.333	0	0-0	0	2.95	4.43
5 ML YEARS			81	71	2	4	423.0	1807	396	200	192	55	12	12	19	157	21	400	15	1	17	20	.459	1	1-1	0	3.91	4.09

Josh Paul

Bats: R **Throws:** R **Pos:** C-52; PR-7; PH-3; LF-1   **Ht:** 6'1" **Wt:** 220 **Born:** 5/19/1975 **Age:** 32

Year	Team	Lg	G	AB	H	2B	3B	HR	(Hm	Rd)	TB	R	RBI	RC	TBB	IBB	SO	HBP	SH	SF	SB	CS	SB%	GDP	Avg	OBP	Slg
								BATTING													BASERUNNING				AVERAGES		
1999	CWS	AL	6	18	4	1	0	0	(0	0)	5	2	1	1	0	0	4	0	0	0	0	0	-	0	.222	.222	.278
2000	CWS	AL	36	71	20	3	2	1	(1	0)	30	15	8	9	5	0	17	1	2	0	1	0	1.00	3	.282	.338	.423
2001	CWS	AL	57	139	37	11	0	3	(0	3)	57	20	18	19	13	0	25	0	1	1	6	2	.75	3	.266	.327	.410
2002	CWS	AL	33	104	25	4	0	0	(0	0)	29	11	11	12	9	0	22	1	2	2	2	0	1.00	1	.240	.302	.279
2003	2 Tms		16	23	6	0	0	0	(0	0)	6	6	4	5	3	0	6	0	1	0	0	0	-	0	.261	.346	.261
2004	LAA	AL	46	70	17	3	0	2	(0	2)	26	11	10	9	7	0	17	0	3	1	2	1	.67	2	.243	.308	.371
2005	LAA	AL	34	37	7	1	0	2	(2	0)	14	4	4	3	2	0	9	1	0	0	0	0	-	0	.189	.231	.378
2006	TB	AL	58	146	38	9	0	1	(0	1)	50	15	8	16	14	0	39	1	3	1	1	2	.33	2	.260	.327	.342
03	CWS	AL	13	17	6	0	0	0	(0	0)	6	6	4	5	3	0	3	0	0	0	0	0	-	0	.353	.450	.353
03	ChC	NL	3	6	0	0	0	0	(0	0)	0	0	0	0	0	0	3	0	1	0	0	0	-	0	.000	.000	.000
8 ML YEARS			286	608	154	32	2	9	(3	6)	217	84	64	74	53	0	139	3	13	5	12	5	.71	12	.253	.314	.357

David Pauley

Pitches: R Bats: R Pos: SP-3   Ht: 6'2" Wt: 185 Born: 6/17/1983 Age: 24

			HOW MUCH HE PITCHED						WHAT HE GAVE UP												THE RESULTS						
Year	Team	Lg	G	GS	CG	GF	IP	BFP	H	R	ER	HR	SH	SF	HB	TBB	IBB	SO	WP	Bk	W	L	Pct	ShO	Sv-Op	Hld	ERC	ERA
2001	Idaho	R+	15	15	0	0	68.2	315	88	57	46	8	1	3	1	24	0	53	6	0	4	9	.308	0	0--	-	5.64	6.03
2002	Eugene	A	15	15	0	0	80.0	335	81	32	25	6	3	4	6	18	1	62	7	0	6	1	.857	0	0--	-	3.60	2.81
2003	FtWyn	A	22	21	0	1	117.2	495	109	51	43	9	2	2	8	38	0	117	5	0	7	7	.500	0	1--	-	3.50	3.29
2004	Lk Els	A+	27	26	0	0	153.1	665	155	89	71	8	8	9	8	60	0	128	6	0	7	12	.368	0	0--	-	3.98	4.17
2005	Portlnd	AA	27	27	1	0	156.0	666	169	86	66	18	5	5	5	34	3	104	6	0	9	7	.563	0	0--	-	4.00	3.81
2006	Portlnd	AA	10	10	0	0	60.1	245	54	20	16	6	5	3	2	17	1	47	0	0	2	3	.400	0	0--	-	3.22	2.39
2006	Pwtckt	AAA	9	9	0	0	50.1	227	60	40	31	10	3	3	5	18	0	25	1	0	1	3	.250	0	0--	-	6.26	5.54
2006	Bos	AL	3	3	0	0	16.0	82	31	14	14	1	0	0	2	6	1	10	0	0	0	2	.000	0	0-0	0	10.41	7.88

Ronny Paulino

Bats: R Throws: R Pos: C-124; PH-8   Ht: 6'2" Wt: 240 Born: 4/21/1981 Age: 26

			BATTING																		BASERUNNING				AVERAGES		
Year	Team	Lg	G	AB	H	2B	3B	HR	(Hm	Rd)	TB	R	RBI	RC	TBB	IBB	SO	HBP	SH	SF	SB	CS	SB%	GDP	Avg	OBP	Slg
1998	Pirates	R	53	170	40	5	0	4	(-	-)	57	18	26	19	17	-	27	4	0	1	6	4	.60	-	.235	.318	.335
1999	Bradtn	R	29	83	21	2	4	1	(-	-)	34	6	13	11	8	0	19	1	1	2	1	2	.33	0	.253	.319	.410
2000	Hickory	A	88	301	87	16	2	6	(-	-)	125	38	39	45	27	0	71	4	0	1	3	2	.60	9	.289	.354	.415
2001	Lynbrg	A+	103	352	102	16	1	6	(-	-)	138	30	51	52	36	0	76	2	3	7	4	1	.80	11	.290	.353	.392
2002	Lynbrg	A+	119	442	116	26	2	12	(-	-)	182	63	55	61	39	2	87	1	2	4	2	1	.67	15	.262	.321	.412
2003	Altna	AA	46	159	36	6	1	6	(-	-)	62	19	19	17	12	1	35	1	3	1	0	2	.00	4	.226	.283	.390
2003	Lynbrg	A+	23	81	19	3	0	1	(-	-)	25	8	12	8	8	0	8	1	0	1	1	0	1.00	6	.235	.308	.309
2004	Altna	AA	99	369	105	23	2	15	(-	-)	177	54	60	62	32	1	62	3	1	3	3	2	.60	7	.285	.344	.480
2005	Altna	AA	43	168	49	6	0	6	(-	-)	73	24	20	26	15	1	30	0	1	0	3	0	1.00	3	.292	.350	.435
2005	Indy	AAA	77	273	86	18	2	13	(-	-)	147	49	42	54	26	1	48	0	1	2	3	0	1.00	11	.315	.372	.538
2006	Indy	AAA	8	29	7	3	0	0	(-	-)	10	2	4	3	3	0	8	0	0	0	1	0	1.00	2	.241	.313	.345
2005	Pit	NL	2	4	2	0	0	0	(0	0)	2	1	0	1	1	0	0	0	0	0	0	0	-	0	.500	.600	.500
2006	Pit	NL	129	442	137	19	0	6	(2	4)	174	37	55	60	34	5	79	2	1	2	0	0	-	17	.310	.360	.394
	2 ML YEARS		131	446	139	19	0	6	(2	4)	176	38	55	61	35	5	79	2	1	2	0	0	-	17	.312	.363	.395

Carl Pavano

Pitches: R Bats: R Pos: P   Ht: 6'5" Wt: 240 Born: 1/8/1976 Age: 31

			HOW MUCH HE PITCHED						WHAT HE GAVE UP												THE RESULTS						
Year	Team	Lg	G	GS	CG	GF	IP	BFP	H	R	ER	HR	SH	SF	HB	TBB	IBB	SO	WP	Bk	W	L	Pct	ShO	Sv-Op	Hld	ERC	ERA
2006	Tampa*	A+	3	3	0	0	11.2	41	10	6	3	2	0	0	1	3	0	10	0	0	0	2	.000	0	0--	-	4.26	2.31
2006	Trntn*	AA	3	3	0	0	11.0	41	6	2	2	0	0	0	1	0	0	12	0	0	1	0	1.000	0	0--	-	0.76	1.64
2006	Clmbs*	AAA	1	1	0	0	6.0	23	8	2	2	0	1	0	0	1	0	5	0	0	1	0	1.000	0	0--	-	5.01	3.00
1998	Mon	NL	24	23	0	0	134.2	580	130	70	63	18	5	6	8	43	1	83	1	0	6	9	.400	0	0-0	0	3.97	4.21
1999	Mon	NL	19	18	1	0	104.0	457	117	66	65	8	5	2	4	35	1	70	1	3	6	8	.429	1	0-0	0	4.51	5.63
2000	Mon	NL	15	15	0	0	97.0	408	89	40	33	8	4	3	8	34	1	64	1	1	8	4	.667	0	0-0	0	3.67	3.06
2001	Mon	NL	8	8	0	0	42.2	199	59	33	30	7	2	1	2	16	1	36	0	1	1	6	.143	0	0-0	0	6.99	6.33
2002	2 Tms	NL	37	22	0	2	136.0	619	174	88	78	19	4	4	10	45	8	92	3	2	6	10	.375	0	0-0	3	5.98	5.16
2003	Fla	NL	33	32	2	1	201.0	846	204	99	96	19	9	10	7	49	10	133	3	2	12	13	.480	0	0-0	0	3.57	4.30
2004	Fla	NL	31	31	2	0	222.1	909	212	80	74	16	7	4	11	49	13	139	2	3	18	8	.692	2	0-0	0	3.10	3.00
2005	NYY	NL	17	17	1	0	100.0	442	129	66	53	17	4	3	6	31	1	56	2	1	4	6	.400	1	0-0	0	5.74	4.77
02	Mon	NL	15	14	0	0	74.1	350	98	55	52	14	2	2	7	31	5	51	2	1	3	8	.273	0	0-0	0	7.07	6.30
02	Fla	NL	22	8	0	2	61.2	269	76	33	26	5	2	2	3	14	3	41	1	1	3	2	.600	0	0-0	3	4.74	3.79
	8 ML YEARS		184	166	6	3	1037.2	4460	1114	542	492	112	40	33	58	289	36	673	13	13	61	64	.488	4	0-0	3	4.25	4.27

Jay Payton

Bats: R Throws: R Pos: LF-62; CF-46; RF-45; DH-4; PH-1   Ht: 5'10" Wt: 185 Born: 11/22/1972 Age: 34

			BATTING																		BASERUNNING				AVERAGES		
Year	Team	Lg	G	AB	H	2B	3B	HR	(Hm	Rd)	TB	R	RBI	RC	TBB	IBB	SO	HBP	SH	SF	SB	CS	SB%	GDP	Avg	OBP	Slg
1998	NYM	NL	15	22	7	1	0	0	(0	0)	8	2	0	3	1	0	4	1	0	0	0	0	-	0	.318	.348	.364
1999	NYM	NL	13	8	2	1	0	0	(0	0)	3	1	1	0	0	0	2	1	0	0	1	2	.33	0	.250	.333	.375
2000	NYM	NL	149	488	142	23	1	17	(9	8)	218	63	62	68	30	0	60	3	0	8	5	11	.31	9	.291	.331	.447
2001	NYM	NL	104	361	92	16	1	8	(6	2)	134	44	34	37	18	1	52	5	0	2	4	3	.57	11	.255	.298	.371
2002	2 Tms	NL	134	445	135	20	7	16	(9	7)	217	69	59	71	29	0	54	4	2	1	7	4	.64	11	.303	.351	.488
2003	Col	NL	157	600	181	32	5	28	(13	15)	307	93	89	95	43	3	77	7	5	3	6	4	.60	27	.302	.354	.512
2004	Col	NL	143	458	119	17	4	8	(0	8)	168	57	55	61	43	2	56	4	2	4	2	0	1.00	12	.260	.326	.367
2005	2 Tms	AL	124	408	109	16	1	18	(11	7)	181	62	63	56	24	2	47	0	0	3	0	1	.00	8	.267	.306	.444
2006	Oak	AL	142	557	165	32	3	10	(5	5)	233	78	59	76	22	1	52	4	0	5	8	4	.67	12	.296	.325	.418
02	NYM	NL	87	275	78	6	3	8	(4	4)	114	33	31	38	21	0	34	1	2	1	4	1	.80	8	.284	.336	.415
02	Col	NL	47	170	57	14	4	8	(5	3)	103	36	28	33	8	0	20	3	0	0	3	3	.50	3	.335	.376	.606
05	Bos	AL	55	133	35	7	0	5	(2	3)	57	24	21	16	10	0	14	0	0	1	0	0	-	4	.263	.313	.429
05	Oak	AL	69	275	74	9	1	13	(9	4)	124	38	42	40	14	2	33	0	0	2	0	1	.00	4	.269	.302	.451
	9 ML YEARS		981	3347	952	158	22	105	(53	52)	1469	469	422	467	210	9	404	28	9	26	33	29	.53	90	.284	.330	.439

Jake Peavy

Pitches: R Bats: R Pos: SP-32   Ht: 6'1" Wt: 180 Born: 5/31/1981 Age: 26

			HOW MUCH HE PITCHED						WHAT HE GAVE UP												THE RESULTS						
Year	Team	Lg	G	GS	CG	GF	IP	BFP	H	R	ER	HR	SH	SF	HB	TBB	IBB	SO	WP	Bk	W	L	Pct	ShO	Sv-Op	Hld	ERC	ERA
2002	SD	NL	17	17	0	0	97.2	430	106	54	49	11	5	2	3	33	4	90	4	1	6	7	.462	0	0-0	0	4.41	4.52
2003	SD	NL	32	32	0	0	194.2	827	173	94	89	33	7	5	6	82	3	156	2	0	12	11	.522	0	0-0	0	4.13	4.11
2004	SD	NL	27	27	0	0	166.1	694	146	49	42	13	5	6	11	53	4	173	1	1	15	6	.714	0	0-0	0	3.18	2.27

Year	Team	Lg	G	GS	CG	GF	IP	BFP	H	R	ER	HR	SH	SF	HB	TBB	IBB	SO	WP	Bk	W	L	Pct	ShO	Sv-Op	Hld	ERC	ERA
2005	SD	NL	30	30	3	0	203.0	812	162	70	65	18	4	5	7	50	3	216	3	1	13	7	.650	3	0-0	0	2.49	2.88
2006	SD	NL	32	32	2	0	202.1	846	187	93	92	23	5	1	6	62	11	215	4	0	11	14	.440	0	0-0	0	3.42	4.09
	5 ML YEARS		138	138	5	0	864.0	3609	774	360	337	98	26	19	33	280	25	850	14	3	57	45	.559	3	0-0	0	3.41	3.51

Dustin Pedroia

Bats: R Throws: R Pos: 2B-27; SS-6; PH-2 **Ht: 5'9" Wt: 180 Born: 8/17/1983 Age: 23**

Year	Team	Lg	G	AB	H	2B	3B	HR	(Hm	Rd)	TB	R	RBI	RC	TBB	IBB	SO	HBP	SH	SF	SB	CS	SB%	GDP	Avg	OBP	Slg
2004	Augsta	A	12	50	20	5	0	1	(-	-)	28	11	5	13	6	0	3	1	0	0	2	0	1.00	1	.400	.474	.560
2004	Srsota	A+	30	107	36	8	3	2	(-	-)	56	23	14	23	13	0	4	4	1	3	0	2	.00	3	.336	.417	.523
2005	Portlnd	AA	66	256	83	19	2	8	(-	-)	130	39	40	54	34	2	26	4	2	2	7	3	.70	7	.324	.409	.508
2005	Pwtckt	AAA	51	204	52	9	1	5	(-	-)	78	39	24	31	24	0	17	9	1	2	1	0	1.00	6	.255	.356	.382
2006	Pwtckt	AAA	111	423	129	30	3	5	(-	-)	180	55	50	72	48	0	27	9	9	4	1	4	.20	9	.305	.384	.426
2006	Bos	AL	31	89	17	4	0	2	(1	1)	27	5	7	3	7	0	7	1	1	0	0	1	.00	1	.191	.258	.303

Mike Pelfrey

Pitches: R Bats: R Pos: SP-4 **Ht: 6'7" Wt: 210 Born: 1/14/1984 Age: 23**

Year	Team	Lg	G	GS	CG	GF	IP	BFP	H	R	ER	HR	SH	SF	HB	TBB	IBB	SO	WP	Bk	W	L	Pct	ShO	Sv-Op	Hld	ERC	ERA
2006	StLuci	A+	4	4	0	0	22.0	80	17	5	4	1	0	1	1	2	0	26	3	0	2	1	.667	0	0--	-	1.80	1.64
2006	Bnghtn	AA	12	12	0	0	66.1	280	60	23	20	2	2	2	4	26	1	77	2	0	4	2	.667	0	0--	-	3.28	2.71
2006	Norfolk	AAA	2	2	0	0	8.0	32	4	2	2	1	0	0	0	5	0	6	0	0	1	0	1.000	0	0--	-	2.51	2.25
2006	NYM	NL	4	4	0	0	21.1	99	25	14	13	1	1	1	3	12	0	13	2	0	2	1	.667	0	0-0	0	6.05	5.48

Brayan Pena

Bats: B Throws: R Pos: C-15; PH-10; 3B-1; PR-1 **Ht: 5'11" Wt: 220 Born: 1/7/1982 Age: 25**

Year	Team	Lg	G	AB	H	2B	3B	HR	(Hm	Rd)	TB	R	RBI	RC	TBB	IBB	SO	HBP	SH	SF	SB	CS	SB%	GDP	Avg	OBP	Slg
2001	Danvle	R+	64	235	87	16	2	1	(-	-)	110	39	33	50	31	2	2	0	1	2	3	1	.75	5	.370	.464	.468
2002	Macon	A	81	271	62	10	0	3	(-	-)	81	26	25	23	22	1	37	2	3	2	0	3	.00	5	.229	.290	.299
2002	MrtlBh	A+	6	19	4	1	0	0	(-	-)	5	3	1	1	3	0	4	0	0	0	0	0	-	0	.211	.318	.263
2003	MrtlBh	A+	82	286	84	14	1	2	(-	-)	106	24	27	33	11	0	28	1	6	2	2	5	.29	8	.294	.320	.371
2004	Grnville	AA	77	277	87	10	4	2	(-	-)	111	30	30	39	15	2	29	1	4	2	3	4	.43	6	.314	.349	.401
2005	Rchmd	AAA	81	282	92	21	2	0	(-	-)	117	27	25	47	28	2	19	0	6	3	3	1	.75	15	.326	.383	.415
2006	Rchmd	AAA	87	325	98	18	1	1	(-	-)	121	32	33	42	21	1	28	1	1	4	6	6	.50	7	.302	.342	.372
2005	Atl	NL	18	39	7	2	0	0	(0	0)	9	2	4	0	1	1	7	0	0	0	0	0	-	1	.179	.200	.231
2006	Atl	NL	23	41	11	2	0	1	(0	1)	16	9	5	4	2	0	5	0	0	0	0	0	-	2	.268	.302	.390
	2 ML YEARS		41	80	18	4	0	1	(0	1)	25	11	9	4	3	1	12	0	0	0	0	0	-	3	.225	.253	.313

Carlos Pena

Bats: L Throws: L Pos: 1B-17; LF-1; PH-1; PR-1 **Ht: 6'2" Wt: 210 Born: 5/17/1978 Age: 29**

Year	Team	Lg	G	AB	H	2B	3B	HR	(Hm	Rd)	TB	R	RBI	RC	TBB	IBB	SO	HBP	SH	SF	SB	CS	SB%	GDP	Avg	OBP	Slg
2006	Pwtckt*	AAA	11	37	17	3	0	4	(-	-)	32	7	8	14	5	1	5	1	0	1	0	0	-	0	.459	.523	.865
2006	Clmbs*	AAA	105	381	99	17	0	19	(-	-)	173	65	66	70	63	3	89	9	0	9	4	0	1.00	3	.260	.370	.454
2001	Tex	AL	22	62	16	4	1	3	(2	1)	31	6	12	11	10	0	17	0	0	0	0	0	-	1	.258	.361	.500
2002	2 Tms	AL	115	397	96	17	4	19	(10	9)	178	43	52	56	41	0	111	3	0	2	2	2	.50	7	.242	.316	.448
2003	Det	AL	131	452	112	21	6	18	(8	10)	199	51	50	61	53	1	123	6	1	4	5	4	.44	6	.248	.332	.440
2004	Det	AL	142	481	116	22	4	27	(10	17)	227	89	82	73	70	2	146	3	2	5	7	1	.88	11	.241	.338	.472
2005	Det	AL	79	260	61	9	0	18	(14	4)	124	37	44	40	31	2	95	4	0	0	0	1	.00	3	.235	.325	.477
2006	Bos	AL	18	33	9	2	0	1	(1	0)	14	3	3	3	4	0	10	0	0	0	0	0	-	1	.273	.351	.424
02	Oak	AL	40	124	27	4	0	7	(5	2)	52	12	16	17	15	0	38	1	0	0	0	0	-	2	.218	.305	.419
02	Det	AL	75	273	69	13	4	12	(5	7)	126	31	36	39	26	0	73	2	0	1	2	2	.50	5	.253	.321	.462
	6 ML YEARS		507	1685	410	75	15	86	(45	41)	773	229	243	244	209	5	502	16	3	11	13	9	.59	29	.243	.331	.459

Tony Pena

Pitches: R Bats: R Pos: RP-25 **Ht: 6'1" Wt: 220 Born: 1/9/1982 Age: 25**

Year	Team	Lg	G	GS	CG	GF	IP	BFP	H	R	ER	HR	SH	SF	HB	TBB	IBB	SO	WP	Bk	W	L	Pct	ShO	Sv-Op	Hld	ERC	ERA
2002	Msoula	R+	4	4	0	0	20.0	89	26	15	14	0	1	1	3	3	0	14	4	1	1	2	.333	0	0--	-	4.68	6.30
2003	Sbend	A	27	27	0	0	160.1	652	149	59	51	3	1	1	7	30	0	119	8	4	9	5	.643	0	0--	-	2.55	2.86
2004	ElPaso	AA	7	7	0	0	43.0	174	47	27	26	4	0	0	1	5	0	36	0	0	3	3	.500	0	0--	-	3.62	5.44
2005	Tenn	AA	25	25	2	0	148.1	651	165	86	73	17	4	4	10	40	1	95	5	0	7	13	.350	1	0--	-	4.52	4.43
2006	Tenn	AA	17	0	0	3	20.1	35	18	2	2	0	1	0	1	5	0	17	1	0	2	0	1.000	0	6--	-	6.56	0.89
2006	Tucsn	AAA	24	0	0	17	26.1	81	17	6	5	1	1	0	2	2	0	21	1	0	3	1	.750	0	7--	-	1.57	1.71
2006	Ari	NL	25	0	0	6	30.2	135	36	21	19	6	2	1	0	8	0	21	1	0	3	4	.429	0	1-1	2	5.12	5.58

Tony F Pena

Bats: R **Throws:** R **Pos:** SS-22; PH-12; PR-11; 3B-1   **Ht:** 6'1" **Wt:** 180 **Born:** 3/23/1981 **Age:** 26

Year	Team	Lg	G	AB	H	2B	3B	HR	(Hm	Rd)	TB	R	RBI	RC	TBB	IBB	SO	HBP	SH	SF	SB	CS	SB%	GDP	Avg	OBP	Slg
2000	Danvle	R	55	215	46	5	0	2	(-	-)	57	22	20	12	5	0	53	0	2	2	6	2	.75	8	.214	.230	.265
2001	Jmstwn	A	72	264	65	12	2	0	(-	-)	81	26	18	22	10	0	48	2	3	1	8	6	.57	7	.246	.278	.307
2002	Macon	A	118	405	101	9	5	2	(-	-)	126	42	36	32	14	0	68	5	8	2	11	15	.42	6	.249	.282	.311
2003	MrtlBh	A	120	405	105	14	1	4	(-	-)	133	43	30	40	24	1	82	2	7	0	17	12	.59	9	.259	.304	.328
2004	Grnville	AA	130	495	126	22	0	11	(-	-)	181	65	34	51	16	0	108	4	9	3	25	13	.66	6	.255	.282	.366
2005	Rchmd	AAA	138	490	122	25	4	5	(-	-)	170	49	40	47	21	0	113	5	6	4	17	15	.53	7	.249	.285	.347
2006	Atl	NL	40	44	10	2	0	1	(1	0)	15	12	3	3	2	1	10	0	0	0	0	0	-	1	.227	.261	.341

Wily Mo Pena

Bats: R **Throws:** R **Pos:** RF-39; CF-27; LF-18; PH-7; DH-4; PR-1   **Ht:** 6'3" **Wt:** 245 **Born:** 1/23/1982 **Age:** 25

Year	Team	Lg	G	AB	H	2B	3B	HR	(Hm	Rd)	TB	R	RBI	RC	TBB	IBB	SO	HBP	SH	SF	SB	CS	SB%	GDP	Avg	OBP	Slg
2006	Lowell*	A-	2	6	1	0	0	0	(-	-)	1	1	0	0	0	0	1	0	0	0	0	0	-	0	.167	.167	.167
2006	Pwtckt*	AAA	12	41	10	1	0	2	(-	-)	17	8	7	7	7	1	10	3	0	1	0	0	-	2	.244	.385	.415
2002	Cin	NL	13	18	4	0	0	1	(1	0)	7	1	1	1	0	0	11	0	0	0	0	0	-	0	.222	.222	.389
2003	Cin	NL	80	165	36	6	1	5	(1	4)	59	20	16	14	12	2	53	3	1	0	3	2	.60	2	.218	.283	.358
2004	Cin	NL	110	336	87	10	1	26	(13	13)	177	45	66	54	22	1	108	6	0	0	5	2	.71	7	.259	.316	.527
2005	Cin	NL	99	311	79	17	0	19	(11	8)	153	42	51	40	20	0	116	3	0	1	2	1	.67	7	.254	.304	.492
2006	Bos	AL	84	276	83	15	2	11	(5	6)	135	36	42	39	20	0	90	3	0	5	0	1	.00	7	.301	.349	.489
5 ML YEARS			386	1106	289	48	4	62	(31	31)	531	144	176	148	74	3	378	15	1	6	10	6	.63	23	.261	.315	.480

Hayden Penn

Pitches: R **Bats:** R **Pos:** SP-6   **Ht:** 6'3" **Wt:** 195 **Born:** 10/13/1984 **Age:** 22

Year	Team	Lg	G	GS	CG	GF	IP	BFP	H	R	ER	HR	SH	SF	HB	TBB	IBB	SO	WP	Bk	W	L	Pct	ShO	Sv-Op	Hld	ERC	ERA
2003	Orioles	R	1	1	0	0	3.1	14	3	1	1	0	1	1	0	1	0	4	0	0	0	0	-	0	0--	-	2.46	2.70
2003	Bluefld	R+	12	11	0	0	52.1	234	58	27	25	4	0	0	4	19	0	38	3	0	1	4	.200	0	0--	-	4.64	4.30
2004	Frdrck	A+	13	6	0	2	43.1	179	30	18	16	4	2	1	3	19	1	41	4	0	4	1	.800	0	1--	-	2.76	3.32
2004	Frdrck	A+	13	13	0	0	73.1	299	59	33	31	7	1	1	2	20	0	61	1	0	6	5	.545	0	0--	-	2.61	3.80
2004	Bowie	AA	4	4	0	0	20.1	92	22	12	11	0	0	0	1	9	0	20	0	0	3	0	1.000	0	0--	-	4.09	4.87
2005	Bowie	AA	20	19	1	0	110.1	469	101	51	47	11	1	8	1	37	0	120	6	0	7	6	.538	0	0--	-	3.33	3.83
2006	Bowie	AA	1	1	0	0	2.0	10	3	2	2	1	0	0	0	2	0	1	0	0	0	0	-	0	0--	-	15.00	9.00
2006	Ottawa	AAA	14	14	2	0	87.2	351	71	25	22	5	1	2	0	27	1	85	2	0	7	4	.636	1	0--	-	2.48	2.26
2005	Bal	AL	8	8	0	0	38.1	178	46	30	27	6	1	0	0	21	3	18	3	1	3	2	.600	0	0-0	0	6.17	6.34
2006	Bal	AL	6	6	0	0	19.2	112	38	33	33	8	0	0	2	13	0	8	0	0	0	4	.000	0	0-0	0	14.68	15.10
2 ML YEARS			14	14	0	0	58.0	290	84	63	60	14	1	0	2	34	3	26	3	1	3	6	.333	0	0-0	0	8.85	9.31

Brad Penny

Pitches: R **Bats:** R **Pos:** SP-33; RP-1   **Ht:** 6'4" **Wt:** 260 **Born:** 5/24/1978 **Age:** 29

Year	Team	Lg	G	GS	CG	GF	IP	BFP	H	R	ER	HR	SH	SF	HB	TBB	IBB	SO	WP	Bk	W	L	Pct	ShO	Sv-Op	Hld	ERC	ERA
2000	Fla	NL	23	22	0	0	119.2	529	120	70	64	13	6	2	5	60	4	80	4	1	8	7	.533	0	0-0	0	4.70	4.81
2001	Fla	NL	31	31	1	0	205.0	833	183	92	84	15	8	2	7	54	3	154	2	0	10	10	.500	1	0-0	0	2.96	3.69
2002	Fla	NL	24	24	1	0	129.1	574	148	76	67	18	6	4	1	50	7	93	4	0	8	7	.533	1	0-0	0	5.08	4.66
2003	Fla	NL	32	32	0	0	196.1	811	195	96	90	21	7	5	3	56	6	138	3	4	14	10	.583	0	0-0	0	3.73	4.13
2004	2 Tms	NL	24	24	0	0	143.0	590	130	55	50	12	3	3	3	45	6	111	5	0	9	10	.474	0	0-0	0	3.20	3.15
2005	LAD	NL	29	29	1	0	175.1	738	185	78	76	17	7	1	3	41	2	122	3	0	7	9	.438	0	0-0	0	3.77	3.90
2006	LAD	NL	34	33	0	0	189.0	813	206	94	91	19	8	3	9	54	4	148	6	0	16	9	.640	0	0-0	1	4.32	4.33
04 Fla		NL	21	21	0	0	131.1	545	124	50	46	10	3	3	3	39	6	105	5	0	8	8	.500	0	0-0	0	3.26	3.15
04 LAD		NL	3	3	0	0	11.2	45	6	5	4	2	0	0	0	6	0	6	0	0	1	2	.333	0	0-0	0	2.51	3.09
7 ML YEARS			197	195	3	0	1157.2	4888	1167	561	522	115	45	20	31	360	32	846	27	5	72	62	.537	2	0-0	1	3.86	4.06

Jhonny Peralta

Bats: R **Throws:** R **Pos:** SS-147; PH-2; DH-1   **Ht:** 6'1" **Wt:** 195 **Born:** 5/28/1982 **Age:** 25

Year	Team	Lg	G	AB	H	2B	3B	HR	(Hm	Rd)	TB	R	RBI	RC	TBB	IBB	SO	HBP	SH	SF	SB	CS	SB%	GDP	Avg	OBP	Slg
2003	Cle	AL	77	242	55	10	1	4	(3	1)	79	24	21	24	20	0	65	4	2	2	1	3	.25	5	.227	.295	.326
2004	Cle	AL	8	25	6	1	0	0	(0	0)	7	2	2	2	3	0	6	0	0	0	0	1	.00	0	.240	.321	.280
2005	Cle	AL	141	504	147	35	4	24	(14	10)	262	82	78	87	58	3	128	3	1	4	0	2	.00	12	.292	.366	.520
2006	Cle	AL	149	569	146	28	3	13	(7	6)	219	84	68	66	56	0	152	1	3	3	0	1	.00	19	.257	.323	.385
4 ML YEARS			375	1340	354	74	8	41	(24	17)	567	192	169	179	137	3	351	8	6	9	1	7	.13	36	.264	.334	.423

Joel Peralta

Pitches: R **Bats:** R **Pos:** RP-64   **Ht:** 5'11" **Wt:** 180 **Born:** 3/23/1976 **Age:** 31

Year	Team	Lg	G	GS	CG	GF	IP	BFP	H	R	ER	HR	SH	SF	HB	TBB	IBB	SO	WP	Bk	W	L	Pct	ShO	Sv-Op	Hld	ERC	ERA
2000	Butte	R+	10	1	0	8	19.0	91	24	15	14	2	1	2	2	10	1	17	2	1	2	1	.667	0	1--	-	6.53	6.63
2000	Boise	A-	4	0	0	1	8.1	42	12	6	6	0	0	1	1	5	0	9	0	0	0	0	-	0	0--	-	7.20	6.48
2001	CRpds	A	41	0	0	39	42.1	159	27	13	10	3	2	1	4	5	0	53	0	0	0	0	-	0	23--	-	1.54	2.13
2001	Ark	AA	9	0	0	9	10.0	50	15	10	7	2	0	1	2	5	0	14	0	1	0	1	.000	0	2--	-	9.56	6.30
2002	Ark	AA	12	0	0	4	17.2	88	25	15	13	5	0	2	1	10	0	11	2	0	0	0	-	0	0--	-	9.09	6.62
2002	CRpds	A	41	0	0	39	47.1	181	28	7	5	2	0	0	2	11	3	53	6	1	5	0	1.000	0	21--	-	1.35	0.95

Year	Team	Lg	G	GS	CG	GF	IP	BFP	H	R	ER	HR	SH	SF	HB	TBB	IBB	SO	WP	Bk	W	L	Pct	ShO	Sv-Op	Hld	ERC	ERA
2003	Ark	AA	47	0	0	43	52.1	208	39	13	13	3	2	2	5	12	2	48	3	0	5	4	.556	0	20- -	-	2.19	2.24
2003	Salt Lk	AAA	1	0	0	0	0.0	1	0	0	0	0	0	0	0	1	0	0	0	0	0	0	-	0	0- -	-	-	-
2004	Salt Lk	AAA	39	0	0	21	56.0	250	64	33	31	6	0	0	2	18	0	68	5	0	4	2	.667	0	1- -	-	4.70	4.98
2004	Angels	R	2	0	0	0	4.1	14	1	1	1	0	0	0	0	0	0	9	0	0	0	0	-	0	0- -	-	0.12	2.08
2004	RCuca	A+	1	0	0	1	2.0	12	5	2	2	1	0	0	0	1	0	1	0	0	0	0	-	0	0- -	-	18.76	9.00
2005	Salt Lk	AAA	19	0	0	20	20.0	77	11	6	6	0	0	2	3	6	0	18	0	0	4	1	.800	0	10- -	-	1.52	2.70
2006	Omha	AAA	6	0	0	3	7.2	32	8	2	2	1	0	0	2	3	0	8	1	0	1	0	1.000	0	2- -	-	6.20	2.35
2005	LAA	AL	28	0	0	10	34.2	145	28	15	15	6	2	1	0	14	2	30	2	0	1	0	1.000	0	0-0	-	3.40	3.89
2006	KC	AL	64	0	0	21	73.2	304	74	37	36	10	1	3	2	17	2	57	5	0	1	3	.250	0	1-3	17	3.80	4.40
2 ML YEARS			92	0	0	31	108.1	449	102	52	51	16	3	4	2	31	4	87	7	0	2	3	.400	0	1-3	17	3.67	4.24

Antonio Perez

Bats: R **Throws:** R **Pos:** 3B-27; DH-20; PR-19; PH-5; SS-4; 2B-2   **Ht:** 5'11" **Wt:** 175 **Born:** 1/26/1980 **Age:** 27

Year	Team	Lg	G	AB	H	2B	3B	HR	(Hm	Rd)	TB	R	RBI	RC	TBB	IBB	SO	HBP	SH	SF	SB	CS	SB%	GDP	Avg	OBP	Slg
2003	TB	AL	48	125	31	6	1	2	(0	2)	45	19	12	19	18	0	34	1	2	1	4	1	.80	1	.248	.345	.360
2004	LAD	NL	13	13	3	1	0	0	(0	0)	4	5	0	1	0	0	5	1	0	0	1	0	1.00	0	.231	.286	.308
2005	LAD	NL	98	259	77	13	2	3	(1	2)	103	28	23	40	21	1	61	5	1	1	11	4	.73	4	.297	.360	.398
2006	Oak	AL	57	98	10	5	1	1	(0	1)	20	10	8	2	10	0	44	0	1	0	0	1	.00	0	.102	.185	.204
4 ML YEARS			216	495	121	25	4	6	(1	5)	172	62	43	62	49	1	144	7	4	2	16	6	.73	5	.244	.320	.347

Beltran Perez

Pitches: R **Bats:** R **Pos:** RP-5; SP-3   **Ht:** 6'2" **Wt:** 180 **Born:** 10/24/1981 **Age:** 25

Year	Team	Lg	G	GS	CG	GF	IP	BFP	H	R	ER	HR	SH	SF	HB	TBB	IBB	SO	WP	Bk	W	L	Pct	ShO	Sv-Op	Hld	ERC	ERA
2000	DBcks	R	11	4	0	0	48.0	221	61	37	31	1	2	2	2	25	1	47	0	1	5	1	.833	0	0- -	-	5.80	5.81
2000	Hi Dsrt	A+	2	2	0	0	10.0	43	8	4	4	3	0	0	0	5	0	11	0	1	0	1	.000	0	0- -	-	4.63	3.60
2001	Sbend	A	27	27	2	0	160.0	651	142	59	50	10	5	3	6	35	0	157	5	3	12	4	.750	0	0- -	-	2.70	2.81
2002	ElPaso	AA	20	19	1	0	97.0	434	114	70	59	10	4	1	4	33	2	77	4	1	3	8	.273	0	0- -	-	4.97	5.47
2002	Lancst	A+	5	5	0	0	32.1	127	21	11	9	1	2	2	2	3	0	30	1	0	3	2	.600	0	0- -	-	1.23	2.51
2003	ElPaso	AA	29	20	0	2	147.2	656	180	94	87	13	7	8	6	54	1	88	11	0	2	11	.154	0	0- -	-	5.37	5.30
2004	ElPaso	AA	37	8	0	8	104.0	454	102	56	51	14	2	1	6	46	1	77	2	0	2	6	.250	0	3- -	-	4.63	4.41
2005	VeroB	A+	19	0	0	9	33.1	146	31	15	14	3	1	1	2	15	0	33	1	0	3	2	.600	0	0- -	-	4.01	3.78
2005	Jaxnvl	AA	17	1	0	6	31.0	128	22	11	10	1	1	0	1	16	2	32	2	0	2	3	.400	0	3- -	-	2.57	2.90
2006	Hrsbrg	AA	31	16	1	6	121.2	532	127	53	42	8	5	4	7	40	5	107	4	0	8	6	.571	0	1- -	-	3.91	3.11
2006	Was	NL	8	3	0	1	21.0	87	16	9	9	3	2	0	0	13	2	9	0	0	2	1	.667	0	0-0	0	3.92	3.86

Eduardo Perez

Bats: R **Throws:** R **Pos:** 1B-34; DH-33; PH-25; RF-5   **Ht:** 6'4" **Wt:** 240 **Born:** 9/11/1969 **Age:** 37

Year	Team	Lg	G	AB	H	2B	3B	HR	(Hm	Rd)	TB	R	RBI	RC	TBB	IBB	SO	HBP	SH	SF	SB	CS	SB%	GDP	Avg	OBP	Slg
1993	LAA	AL	52	180	45	6	2	4	(2	2)	67	16	30	18	9	0	39	2	0	1	5	4	.56	4	.250	.292	.372
1994	LAA	AL	38	129	27	7	0	5	(3	2)	49	10	16	13	12	1	29	0	1	1	3	0	1.00	5	.209	.275	.380
1995	LAA	AL	29	71	12	4	1	1	(0	1)	21	9	7	6	12	0	9	2	0	1	0	2	.00	1	.169	.302	.296
1996	Cin	NL	18	36	8	0	0	3	(3	0)	17	8	5	5	5	1	9	0	0	0	0	0	-	2	.222	.317	.472
1997	Cin	NL	106	297	75	18	0	16	(7	9)	141	44	52	45	29	1	76	2	0	2	5	1	.83	6	.253	.321	.475
1998	Cin	NL	84	172	41	4	0	4	(1	3)	57	20	30	19	21	2	45	2	1	2	0	1	.00	2	.238	.325	.331
1999	StL	NL	21	32	11	2	0	1	(0	1)	16	6	9	8	7	0	6	0	0	0	0	0	-	0	.344	.462	.500
2000	StL	NL	35	91	27	4	0	3	(0	3)	40	9	10	14	5	0	19	3	2	1	1	0	1.00	2	.297	.350	.440
2002	StL	NL	96	154	31	9	0	10	(4	6)	70	22	26	17	17	0	36	3	1	2	0	0	-	7	.201	.290	.455
2003	StL	NL	105	253	72	16	0	11	(5	6)	121	47	41	38	29	1	53	4	1	2	5	2	.71	7	.285	.365	.478
2004	TB	AL	13	38	8	2	0	1	(1	0)	13	2	7	6	4	0	9	0	0	0	0	0	-	1	.211	.286	.342
2005	TB	AL	77	161	41	6	0	11	(5	6)	80	23	28	31	26	0	30	3	0	0	2	0	.00	6	.255	.368	.497
2006	2 Tms		80	186	47	10	0	9	(4	5)	84	22	33	28	18	2	33	3	0	3	0	1	.00	8	.253	.324	.452
06	Cle	AL	37	99	30	9	0	8	(3	5)	63	16	22	19	5	0	11	2	0	2	0	0	-	5	.303	.343	.636
06	Sea	AL	43	87	17	1	0	1	(1	0)	21	6	11	9	13	2	22	1	0	1	0	1	.00	3	.195	.304	.241
13 ML YEARS			754	1800	445	88	3	79	(35	44)	776	238	294	248	194	8	393	24	6	15	19	13	.59	53	.247	.326	.431

Juan Perez

Pitches: L **Bats:** R **Pos:** RP-7   **Ht:** 6'0" **Wt:** 170 **Born:** 9/3/1978 **Age:** 28

Year	Team	Lg	G	GS	CG	GF	IP	BFP	H	R	ER	HR	SH	SF	HB	TBB	IBB	SO	WP	Bk	W	L	Pct	ShO	Sv-Op	Hld	ERC	ERA
2000	RedSx	R	9	5	0	2	34.1	139	24	12	9	2	0	0	1	13	0	43	0	0	3	1	.750	0	1- -	-	2.27	2.36
2001	Augsta	A	26	25	0	1	125.2	525	118	69	50	14	2	7	3	42	0	113	9	0	8	8	.500	0	0- -	-	3.69	3.58
2002	Srsota	AA	16	14	0	0	66.2	286	71	34	28	4	2	4	2	19	0	39	4	0	0	6	.000	0	0- -	-	3.82	3.78
2003	Srsota	A+	33	0	0	24	38.0	165	34	15	10	0	2	3	0	12	2	37	4	0	3	4	.429	0	18- -	-	2.32	2.37
2003	Portlnd	AA	18	0	0	6	30.2	136	37	19	13	4	1	3	0	11	1	24	2	0	3	3	.500	0	0- -	-	5.31	3.82
2004	Portlnd	AA	46	0	0	18	78.1	345	72	46	36	12	1	4	7	37	5	79	7	0	5	1	.833	0	6- -	-	4.20	4.14
2005	Pwtckt	AAA	40	1	0	18	62.0	274	61	31	31	7	5	1	5	29	0	74	5	2	4	5	.444	0	1- -	-	4.69	4.50
2006	Norfolk	AAA	43	0	0	12	63.0	284	65	24	20	4	2	2	2	34	0	55	4	0	0	1	.000	0	0- -	-	4.65	2.86
2006	Indy	AAA	4	0	0	0	7.0	30	3	0	0	0	0	0	0	3	1	6	0	0	0	0	-	0	0- -	-	0.86	0.00
2006	Pit	NL	7	0	0	0	3.1	17	5	3	3	1	0	1	2	4	0	3	0	0	0	1	.000	0	0-0	0	11.77	8.10

Neifi Perez

Bats: B Throws: R Pos: 2B-67; SS-28; PH-15; 3B-11; PR-2   Ht: 6'0" Wt: 195 Born: 6/2/1973 Age: 34

Year	Team	Lg	G	AB	H	2B	3B	HR	(Hm	Rd)	TB	R	RBI	RC	TBB	IBB	SO	HBP	SH	SF	SB	CS	SB%	GDP	Avg	OBP	Slg
1996	Col	NL	17	45	7	2	0	0	(0	0)	9	4	3	0	0	0	8	0	1	0	2	2	.50	2	.156	.156	.200
1997	Col	NL	83	313	91	13	10	5	(3	2)	139	46	31	46	21	4	43	1	5	4	4	3	.57	3	.291	.333	.444
1998	Col	NL	**162**	647	177	25	9	9	(6	3)	247	80	59	77	38	0	70	1	**22**	4	5	6	.45	8	.274	.313	.382
1999	Col	NL	157	**690**	193	27	**11**	12	(8	4)	278	108	70	87	28	0	54	1	9	4	13	5	.72	4	.280	.307	.403
2000	Col	NL	162	651	187	39	11	6	(7	3)	278	92	71	85	30	6	63	0	7	11	3	6	.33	9	.287	.314	.427
2001	2 Tms		136	581	162	26	9	8	(7	1)	230	83	59	69	26	1	68	1	11	4	9	6	.60	10	.279	.309	.396
2002	KC	AL	145	554	131	20	4	3	(1	2)	168	65	37	37	20	2	53	0	5	6	8	9	.47	11	.236	.260	.303
2003	SF	NL	120	328	84	19	4	1	(1	0)	114	27	31	29	14	3	23	0	9	2	3	2	.60	10	.256	.285	.348
2004	2 Tms		126	381	97	17	1	4	(2	2)	128	40	39	39	24	3	41	0	11	4	1	1	.50	8	.255	.296	.336
2005	ChC	NL	154	572	157	33	1	9	(4	5)	219	59	54	58	18	3	47	3	12	4	8	4	.67	22	.274	.298	.383
2006	2 Tms		108	301	73	14	1	2	(1	1)	95	31	29	27	8	2	25	0	4	3	1	1	.50	5	.243	.260	.316
01	Col	NL	87	382	114	19	8	7	(7	0)	170	65	47	53	16	1	49	0	4	1	6	2	.75	8	.298	.326	.445
01	KC	AL	49	199	48	7	1	1	(0	1)	60	18	12	16	10	0	19	1	7	3	3	4	.43	2	.241	.277	.302
04	SF	NL	103	319	74	12	1	2	(0	2)	94	28	33	26	21	3	35	0	9	4	0	1	.00	7	.232	.276	.295
04	ChC	NL	23	62	23	5	0	2	(2	0)	34	12	6	13	3	0	6	0	2	0	1	0	1.00	1	.371	.400	.548
06	ChC	NL	87	236	60	13	1	2	(1	1)	81	27	24	24	5	2	21	0	2	3	0	1	.00	3	.254	.266	.343
06	Det	AL	21	65	13	1	0	0	(0	0)	14	4	5	3	3	0	4	0	2	0	1	0	1.00	1	.200	.235	.215
11 ML YEARS			1370	5063	1359	235	61	63	(40	23)	1905	635	483	554	227	24	495	7	96	46	57	45	.56	92	.268	.298	.376

Odalis Perez

Pitches: L Bats: L Pos: SP-20; RP-12   Ht: 6'0" Wt: 220 Born: 6/11/1977 Age: 30

Year	Team	Lg	G	GS	CG	GF	IP	BFP	H	R	ER	HR	SH	SF	HB	TBB	IBB	SO	WP	Bk	W	L	Pct	ShO	Sv-Op	Hld	ERC	ERA
1998	Atl	NL	10	0	0	0	10.2	45	10	5	5	1	0	0	0	4	0	5	0	0	0	1	.000	0	0-1	5	3.60	4.22
1999	Atl	NL	18	17	0	0	93.0	424	100	65	62	12	3	4	1	53	2	82	5	3	4	6	.400	0	0-0	0	5.42	6.00
2001	Atl	NL	24	16	0	1	95.1	418	108	55	52	7	3	3	1	39	0	71	2	3	7	8	.467	0	0-0	0	4.79	4.91
2002	LAD	NL	32	32	4	0	222.1	869	182	76	74	21	13	7	4	38	5	155	2	3	15	10	.600	2	0-0	0	**2.31**	3.00
2003	LAD	NL	30	30	0	0	185.1	772	191	98	93	28	5	3	3	46	4	141	2	1	12	12	.500	0	0-0	0	4.07	4.52
2004	LAD	NL	31	31	0	0	196.1	787	180	76	71	26	**16**	3	3	44	4	128	2	2	7	6	.538	0	0-0	0	3.26	3.25
2005	LAD	NL	19	19	0	0	108.2	453	109	59	55	13	8	1	0	28	2	74	3	0	7	8	.467	0	0-0	0	3.65	4.56
2006	2 Tms		32	32	0	6	126.1	573	169	93	87	18	4	7	3	31	2	81	6	2	6	8	.429	0	0-1	0	5.77	6.20
06	Atl	NL	20	8	0	6	59.1	275	89	49	45	9	1	2	2	13	1	33	4	1	4	4	.500	0	0-1	0	6.85	6.83
06	KC	AL	12	12	0	0	67.0	298	80	44	42	9	3	5	1	18	1	48	2	1	2	4	.333	0	0-0	0	4.86	5.64
8 ML YEARS			196	165	4	7	1038.0	4341	1049	527	499	126	52	28	15	283	19	737	22	14	58	59	.496	2	0-2	5	3.84	4.33

Oliver Perez

Pitches: L Bats: L Pos: SP-22   Ht: 6'3" Wt: 210 Born: 8/15/1981 Age: 25

Year	Team	Lg	G	GS	CG	GF	IP	BFP	H	R	ER	HR	SH	SF	HB	TBB	IBB	SO	WP	Bk	W	L	Pct	ShO	Sv-Op	Hld	ERC	ERA
2006	Indy*	AAA	6	6	0	0	32.0	136	28	21	20	6	2	1	2	11	0	34	1	0	1	3	.250	0	0- -	-	3.95	5.63
2006	Norfolk*	AAA	4	4	0	0	19.1	86	18	13	13	4	0	1	1	12	0	26	2	0	1	2	.333	0	0- -	-	5.68	6.05
2002	SD	NL	16	15	0	0	90.0	387	71	37	35	13	5	3	5	48	1	94	3	0	4	5	.444	0	0-0	0	3.93	3.50
2003	2 Tms		24	24	0	0	126.2	579	129	80	77	22	5	2	4	77	3	141	7	1	4	10	.286	0	0-0	0	5.66	5.47
2004	Pit	NL	30	30	2	0	196.0	805	145	71	65	22	9	5	9	81	2	239	2	1	12	10	.545	1	0-0	0	2.99	2.98
2005	Pit	NL	20	20	0	0	103.0	471	102	68	67	23	5	4	6	70	1	97	3	0	7	5	.583	0	0-0	0	6.44	5.85
2006	2 Tms		22	22	1	0	112.2	529	129	90	82	20	5	**10**	6	68	0	102	5	1	3	13	.188	1	0-0	0	6.62	6.55
03	SD	NL	19	19	0	0	103.2	473	103	65	62	20	4	2	3	65	2	117	6	1	4	7	.364	0	0-0	0	5.74	5.38
03	Pit	NL	5	5	0	0	23.0	106	26	15	15	2	1	0	1	12	1	24	1	0	0	3	.000	0	0-0	0	5.29	5.87
06	Pit	NL	15	15	0	0	76.0	364	88	64	56	13	5	8	3	51	0	61	4	1	2	10	.167	0	0-0	0	6.85	6.63
06	NYM	NL	7	7	1	0	36.2	165	41	26	26	7	0	2	3	17	0	41	1	0	1	3	.250	1	0-0	0	6.16	6.38
5 ML YEARS			112	111	3	0	628.1	2771	576	346	326	100	29	24	30	344	7	673	20	3	30	43	.411	2	0-0	0	4.81	4.67

Rafael Perez

Pitches: L Bats: L Pos: RP-18   Ht: 6'3" Wt: 185 Born: 5/15/1982 Age: 25

Year	Team	Lg	G	GS	CG	GF	IP	BFP	H	R	ER	HR	SH	SF	HB	TBB	IBB	SO	WP	Bk	W	L	Pct	ShO	Sv-Op	Hld	ERC	ERA
2003	Burlgtn	R+	13	12	0	0	69.0	277	56	23	13	1	2	0	5	16	0	63	4	0	9	3	.750	0	0- -	-	2.22	1.70
2004	Lk Cty	A	23	22	0	0	115.0	503	121	75	62	9	7	4	8	47	0	99	12	3	7	6	.538	0	0- -	-	4.59	4.85
2004	Kinston	A+	1	1	0	0	4.2	25	10	6	6	1	0	0	0	2	1	3	0	0	0	0	-	0	0- -	-	12.56	11.57
2005	Kinston	A+	14	14	0	0	77.2	315	54	33	29	6	0	2	2	32	0	48	7	0	8	5	.615	0	0- -	-	2.48	3.36
2005	Akron	AA	15	8	0	3	66.2	268	53	22	13	5	4	3	2	12	0	46	3	0	4	3	.571	0	1- -	-	2.11	1.76
2006	Akron	AA	12	12	1	0	67.1	274	53	25	21	3	3	3	3	22	1	53	7	0	4	5	.444	1	0- -	-	2.48	2.81
2006	Buffalo	AAA	13	0	0	4	27.1	112	20	11	8	0	3	0	2	8	1	33	6	0	0	3	.000	0	0- -	-	1.85	2.63
2006	Cle	AL	18	0	0	5	12.1	56	10	6	6	2	1	0	0	6	1	15	4	1	0	0	-	0	0-1	1	3.37	4.38

Timo Perez

Bats: L Throws: L Pos: PH-15; RF-4; LF-3; DH-1; PR-1   Ht: 5'9" Wt: 180 Born: 4/8/1975 Age: 32

Year	Team	Lg	G	AB	H	2B	3B	HR	(Hm	Rd)	TB	R	RBI	RC	TBB	IBB	SO	HBP	SH	SF	SB	CS	SB%	GDP	Avg	OBP	Slg
2006	Memp*	AAA	75	268	79	16	2	13	(-	-)	138	42	41	48	21	0	27	2	4	1	4	2	.67	3	.295	.349	.515
2000	NYM	NL	24	49	14	4	1	1	(0	1)	23	11	3	8	3	0	5	1	0	1	1	1	.50	0	.286	.333	.469
2001	NYM	NL	85	239	59	9	1	5	(3	2)	85	26	22	23	12	0	25	2	6	1	1	6	.14	1	.247	.287	.356
2002	NYM	NL	136	444	131	27	6	8	(3	5)	194	52	47	63	23	2	36	2	10	2	10	6	.63	10	.295	.331	.437
2003	NYM	NL	127	346	93	21	0	4	(1	3)	126	32	42	37	18	1	29	2	7	9	5	6	.45	5	.269	.301	.364

	BATTING																			BASERUNNING				AVERAGES		
Year	Team	Lg	G	AB	H	2B	3B	HR	(Hm	Rd)	TB	R	RBI	RC	TBB	IBB	SO	HBP	SH	SF	SB	CS	SB%	GDP	Avg	OBP	Slg
2004	CWS	AL	103	293	72	12	0	5	(2	3)	99	38	40	39	15	0	29	2	9	2	3	1	.75	9	.246	.285	.338
2005	CWS	AL	76	179	39	8	0	2	(1	1)	53	13	15	13	12	1	25	0	4	1	2	2	.50	3	.218	.266	.296
2006	StL	NL	23	31	6	1	0	1	(0	1)	10	3	3	3	3	1	4	1	0	0	0	0	-	0	.194	.286	.323
7 ML YEARS			574	1581	414	82	8	26	(9	17)	590	175	172	186	86	5	153	10	36	16	22	22	.50	28	.262	.301	.373

Tomas Perez

Bats: B Throws: R Pos: 3B-40; SS-36; 2B-22; PR-8; RF-4; PH-3; 1B-1; LF-1 **Ht: 5'11" Wt: 195 Born: 12/29/1973 Age: 33**

	BATTING																			BASERUNNING				AVERAGES		
Year	Team	Lg	G	AB	H	2B	3B	HR	(Hm	Rd)	TB	R	RBI	RC	TBB	IBB	SO	HBP	SH	SF	SB	CS	SB%	GDP	Avg	OBP	Slg
1995	Tor	AL	41	98	24	3	1	1	(1	0)	32	12	8	7	7	0	18	0	0	1	1	0	.00	6	.245	.292	.327
1996	Tor	AL	91	295	74	13	4	1	(1	0)	98	24	19	28	25	0	29	1	6	1	1	2	.33	10	.251	.311	.332
1997	Tor	AL	40	123	24	3	2	0	(0	0)	31	9	9	8	11	0	28	1	3	0	1	1	.50	2	.195	.267	.252
1998	Tor	AL	6	9	1	0	0	0	(0	0)	1	1	0	0	1	0	3	0	1	0	0	0	-	1	.111	.200	.111
2000	Phi	NL	45	140	31	7	1	1	(0	1)	43	17	13	11	11	2	30	0	1	0	1	1	.50	3	.221	.278	.307
2001	Phi	NL	62	135	41	7	1	3	(2	1)	59	11	19	20	7	1	22	2	1	0	0	1	.00	2	.304	.347	.437
2002	Phi	NL	92	212	53	13	1	5	(2	3)	83	22	20	20	21	6	40	1	2	1	1	0	1.00	5	.250	.319	.392
2003	Phi	NL	125	298	79	18	1	5	(2	3)	114	39	33	29	23	11	54	0	4	2	0	1	.00	7	.265	.316	.383
2004	Phi	NL	86	176	38	13	2	6	(4	2)	73	22	21	20	9	2	44	1	3	1	0	0	-	2	.216	.257	.415
2005	Phi	NL	94	159	37	7	0	0	(0	0)	44	17	22	14	11	2	27	2	3	1	1	0	1.00	6	.233	.289	.277
2006	TB	AL	99	241	51	12	0	2	(2	0)	69	31	16	11	5	0	44	0	4	4	1	0	1.00	3	.212	.224	.286
11 ML YEARS			781	1886	453	96	13	24	(14	10)	647	205	180	168	131	24	339	8	28	11	6	7	.46	47	.240	.291	.343

Glen Perkins

Pitches: L Bats: L Pos: RP-4 **Ht: 5'11" Wt: 200 Born: 3/2/1983 Age: 24**

	HOW MUCH HE PITCHED						WHAT HE GAVE UP											THE RESULTS							
Year	Team	Lg	G	GS	CG	GF	IP	BFP	H	R	ER	HR	SH	SF	HB	TBB	IBB	SO	WP	Bk	W	L	Pct	ShO	Sv-Op	Hld	ERC	ERA
2004	Elizab	R+	3	3	0	0	12.0	50	8	3	3	0	1	2	0	4	0	22	0	0	1	0	1.000	0	0- -	-	1.51	2.25
2004	QuadC	A	9	9	0	0	48.1	183	33	9	7	2	6	1	3	12	0	49	0	0	2	1	.667	0	0- -	-	1.89	1.30
2005	FtMyrs	A+	10	9	2	0	55.0	220	41	14	13	2	1	3	1	13	1	66	2	0	3	2	.600	1	0- -	-	1.81	2.13
2005	NwBrit	AA	14	14	0	0	79.0	352	80	45	43	4	3	2	8	35	1	67	3	1	4	4	.500	1	0- -	-	4.32	4.90
2006	NwBrit	AA	23	23	2	0	117.1	503	109	60	51	11	1	3	6	45	0	131	3	1	4	11	.267	1	0- -	-	3.76	3.91
2006	Roch	AAA	1	1	0	0	4.1	23	6	1	1	0	0	0	0	5	0	3	0	0	0	1	.000	0	0- -	-	8.88	2.08
2006	Min	AL	4	0	0	1	5.2	20	3	1	1	0	0	0	0	0	0	6	0	0	0	0	-	0	0-0	-	0.60	1.59

Roberto Petagine

Bats: L Throws: L Pos: PH-23; 1B-9 **Ht: 6'1" Wt: 170 Born: 6/2/1971 Age: 36**

	BATTING																			BASERUNNING				AVERAGES		
Year	Team	Lg	G	AB	H	2B	3B	HR	(Hm	Rd)	TB	R	RBI	RC	TBB	IBB	SO	HBP	SH	SF	SB	CS	SB%	GDP	Avg	OBP	Slg
2006	Tacom*	AAA	4	6	1	0	0	0	(-	-)	1	1	0	1	4	0	1	0	0	0	0	0	-	0	.167	.500	.167
1994	Hou	NL	8	7	0	0	0	0	(0	0)	0	0	0	0	1	0	3	0	0	0	0	0	-	0	.000	.125	.000
1995	SD	NL	89	124	29	8	0	3	(2	1)	46	15	17	18	26	2	41	0	2	0	0	0	-	2	.234	.367	.371
1996	NYM	NL	50	99	23	3	0	4	(2	2)	38	10	17	10	9	1	27	3	1	1	0	2	.00	4	.232	.313	.384
1997	NYM	NL	12	15	1	0	0	0	(0	0)	1	2	2	0	3	0	6	0	0	0	0	0	-	0	.067	.222	.067
1998	Cin	NL	34	62	16	2	1	3	(1	2)	29	14	7	12	16	0	11	0	0	2	1	0	1.00	0	.258	.400	.468
2005	Bos	AL	18	32	9	2	0	1	(1	0)	14	4	9	4	4	0	5	0	0	0	0	0	-	3	.281	.361	.438
2006	Sea	AL	31	27	5	2	0	1	(1	0)	10	3	2	1	4	0	10	1	0	0	0	0	-	0	.185	.313	.370
7 ML YEARS			242	366	83	17	1	12	(7	5)	138	48	54	45	63	3	103	4	3	3	1	2	.33	11	.227	.344	.377

Yusmeiro Petit

Pitches: R Bats: R Pos: RP-14; SP-1 **Ht: 6'0" Wt: 180 Born: 11/22/1984 Age: 22**

	HOW MUCH HE PITCHED						WHAT HE GAVE UP											THE RESULTS							
Year	Team	Lg	G	GS	CG	GF	IP	BFP	H	R	ER	HR	SH	SF	HB	TBB	IBB	SO	WP	Bk	W	L	Pct	ShO	Sv-Op	Hld	ERC	ERA
2003	Kngspt	R+	12	12	0	0	62.0	230	47	19	16	2	1	2	4	8	0	65	1	0	3	3	.500	0	0- -	-	1.83	2.32
2003	Bklyn	A-	2	2	0	0	12.1	45	5	3	3	0	0	1	0	2	0	20	0	0	1	0	1.000	0	0- -	-	0.71	2.19
2004	CptCty	A	15	15	0	0	83.0	319	47	29	22	8	2	1	4	22	0	122	4	0	9	2	.818	0	0- -	-	1.61	2.39
2004	StLuci	A+	9	9	1	0	44.1	177	27	9	6	0	4	1	3	14	1	62	0	1	2	3	.400	1	0- -	-	1.48	1.22
2004	Bnghtn	AA	2	2	0	0	12.0	49	10	6	6	0	1	0	0	5	0	16	0	0	1	1	.500	0	0- -	-	2.65	4.50
2005	Bnghtn	AA	21	21	2	0	117.2	456	90	41	38	15	3	2	2	18	1	130	0	0	9	3	.750	0	0- -	-	2.17	2.91
2005	Norfolk	AAA	3	3	0	0	14.2	71	24	16	15	5	1	0	0	6	0	14	0	0	0	3	.000	0	0- -	-	10.43	9.20
2006	Albq	AAA	17	17	0	0	96.2	404	101	53	46	14	4	2	1	20	1	68	2	0	4	6	.400	0	0- -	-	3.89	4.28
2006	Fla	NL	15	1	0	5	26.1	129	46	28	28	7	1	1	0	9	1	20	0	0	1	1	.500	0	0-0	-	10.07	9.57

Andy Pettitte

Pitches: L Bats: L Pos: SP-35; RP-1 **Ht: 6'5" Wt: 225 Born: 6/15/1972 Age: 35**

	HOW MUCH HE PITCHED						WHAT HE GAVE UP											THE RESULTS							
Year	Team	Lg	G	GS	CG	GF	IP	BFP	H	R	ER	HR	SH	SF	HB	TBB	IBB	SO	WP	Bk	W	L	Pct	ShO	Sv-Op	Hld	ERC	ERA
1995	NYY	AL	31	26	3	1	175.0	745	183	86	81	15	4	5	1	63	3	114	8	1	12	9	.571	0	0-0	-	4.13	4.17
1996	NYY	AL	35	34	2	1	221.0	929	229	105	95	23	7	3	3	72	2	162	6	1	21	8	.724	0	0-0	-	4.14	3.87
1997	NYY	AL	35	35	4	0	240.1	986	233	86	77	7	6	2	3	65	0	166	7	0	18	7	.720	1	0-0	-	3.05	2.88
1998	NYY	AL	33	32	5	0	216.1	932	226	110	102	20	6	7	6	87	1	146	5	0	16	11	.593	0	0-0	-	4.46	4.24
1999	NYY	AL	31	31	0	0	191.2	851	216	105	100	20	6	6	3	89	3	121	3	1	14	11	.560	0	0-0	-	5.22	4.70
2000	NYY	AL	32	32	3	0	204.2	903	219	111	99	17	7	4	4	80	4	125	2	3	19	9	.679	1	0-0	-	4.32	4.35
2001	NYY	AL	31	31	2	0	200.2	858	224	103	89	14	8	7	6	41	3	164	2	2	15	10	.600	0	0-0	-	3.82	3.99
2002	NYY	AL	22	22	3	0	134.2	570	144	58	49	6	3	2	4	32	2	97	2	1	13	5	.722	1	0-0	-	3.55	3.27
2003	NYY	AL	33	33	1	0	208.1	896	227	109	93	21	5	5	1	50	3	180	5	0	21	8	.724	0	0-0	-	3.89	4.02

201

			HOW MUCH HE PITCHED						WHAT HE GAVE UP										THE RESULTS							
Year	Team	Lg	G	GS	CG	GF	IP	BFP	H	R	ER	HR	SH	SF	HB	TBB	IBB	SO	WP	Bk	W	L	Pct	ShO	Sv-Op	Hld	ERC	ERA
2004	Hou	NL	15	15	0	0	83.0	346	71	37	36	8	1	0	0	31	2	79	4	0	6	4	.600	0	0-0	0	3.12	3.90
2005	Hou	NL	33	33	0	0	222.1	875	188	66	59	17	10	4	3	41	0	171	2	0	17	9	.654	0	0-0	0	2.40	2.39
2006	Hou	NL	36	**35**	2	1	214.1	929	238	114	100	27	14	5	2	70	9	178	2	1	14	13	.519	1	0-0	0	4.58	4.20
12 ML YEARS			367	359	25	3	2312.1	9820	2398	1090	980	195	77	50	36	721	32	1703	48	10	186	104	.641	4	0-0	0	3.89	3.81

Andy Phillips

Bats: R **Throws:** R **Pos:** 1B-94; PR-12; 3B-10; PH-8; DH-4; 2B-1   **Ht:** 6'0" **Wt:** 205 **Born:** 4/6/1977 **Age:** 30

			BATTING																BASERUNNING				AVERAGES		
Year	Team	Lg	G	AB	H	2B	3B	HR	(Hm | Rd)	TB	R	RBI	RC	TBB	IBB	SO	HBP	SH	SF	SB	CS	SB%	GDP	Avg	OBP	Slg
2004	NYY	AL	5	8	2	0	0	1	(0 | 1)	5	1	2	1	0	0	1	0	0	0	0	0	-	1	.250	.250	.625
2005	NYY	AL	27	40	6	4	0	1	(1 | 0)	13	7	4	2	1	0	13	0	0	0	0	0	-	1	.150	.171	.325
2006	NYY	AL	110	246	59	11	3	7	(5 | 2)	97	30	29	22	15	0	56	0	0	2	3	2	.60	9	.240	.281	.394
3 ML YEARS			142	294	67	15	3	9	(6 | 3)	115	38	35	25	16	0	70	0	0	2	3	2	.60	11	.228	.266	.391

Brandon Phillips

Bats: R **Throws:** R **Pos:** 2B-142; PH-5; SS-3; PR-2   **Ht:** 6'0" **Wt:** 195 **Born:** 6/28/1981 **Age:** 26

			BATTING																BASERUNNING				AVERAGES		
Year	Team	Lg	G	AB	H	2B	3B	HR	(Hm | Rd)	TB	R	RBI	RC	TBB	IBB	SO	HBP	SH	SF	SB	CS	SB%	GDP	Avg	OBP	Slg
2002	Cle	AL	11	31	8	3	1	0	(0 | 0)	13	5	4	5	3	0	6	1	1	0	0	0	-	0	.258	.343	.419
2003	Cle	AL	112	370	77	18	1	6	(3 | 3)	115	36	33	22	14	0	77	3	5	1	4	5	.44	12	.208	.242	.311
2004	Cle	AL	6	22	4	2	0	0	(0 | 0)	6	1	1	0	2	0	5	0	0	0	0	2	.00	1	.182	.250	.273
2005	Cle	AL	6	9	0	0	0	0	(0 | 0)	0	1	0	0	0	0	4	0	0	0	0	0	-	0	.000	.000	.000
2006	Cin	NL	149	536	148	28	1	17	(9 | 8)	229	65	75	74	35	3	88	6	4	6	25	2	.93	19	.276	.324	.427
5 ML YEARS			284	968	237	51	3	23	(12 | 11)	363	108	113	101	54	3	180	10	10	7	29	9	.76	32	.245	.290	.375

Jason Phillips

Bats: R **Throws:** R **Pos:** C-9; DH-8; 1B-6; PH-6   **Ht:** 6'1" **Wt:** 210 **Born:** 9/27/1976 **Age:** 30

			BATTING																BASERUNNING				AVERAGES		
Year	Team	Lg	G	AB	H	2B	3B	HR	(Hm | Rd)	TB	R	RBI	RC	TBB	IBB	SO	HBP	SH	SF	SB	CS	SB%	GDP	Avg	OBP	Slg
2006	Syrcse*	AAA	70	249	68	11	0	7	(- | -)	100	31	40	35	22	3	43	4	5	1	1	1	.50	12	.273	.341	.402
2001	NYM	NL	6	7	1	1	0	0	(0 | 0)	2	2	0	0	0	0	1	0	0	0	0	0	-	0	.143	.143	.286
2002	NYM	NL	11	19	7	0	0	1	(0 | 1)	10	4	3	3	1	0	1	1	0	0	0	0	-	1	.368	.409	.526
2003	NYM	NL	119	403	120	25	0	11	(7 | 4)	178	45	58	65	39	3	50	10	0	1	0	1	.00	21	.298	.373	.442
2004	NYM	NL	128	362	79	18	0	7	(2 | 5)	118	34	34	30	35	4	42	8	2	5	0	1	.00	11	.218	.298	.326
2005	LAD	NL	121	399	95	20	0	10	(6 | 4)	145	38	55	42	25	4	50	4	2	4	0	1	.00	16	.238	.287	.363
2006	Tor	AL	25	48	12	6	0	0	(0 | 0)	18	4	6	3	1	0	5	1	0	1	0	1	.00	2	.250	.275	.375
6 ML YEARS			410	1238	314	70	0	29	(15 | 14)	471	127	156	143	101	11	149	24	4	12	0	4	.00	51	.254	.319	.380

Paul Phillips

Bats: R **Throws:** R **Pos:** C-13; 1B-5; PH-3; DH-2; PR-2   **Ht:** 5'11" **Wt:** 205 **Born:** 4/15/1977 **Age:** 30

			BATTING																BASERUNNING				AVERAGES		
Year	Team	Lg	G	AB	H	2B	3B	HR	(Hm | Rd)	TB	R	RBI	RC	TBB	IBB	SO	HBP	SH	SF	SB	CS	SB%	GDP	Avg	OBP	Slg
2006	Omha*	AAA	91	345	84	11	1	9	(- | -)	124	43	39	37	22	3	37	1	1	6	0	0	-	15	.243	.286	.359
2004	KC	AL	4	5	1	0	0	0	(0 | 0)	1	2	0	0	0	0	1	0	0	0	0	0	-	0	.200	.333	.200
2005	KC	AL	23	67	18	4	1	1	(0 | 1)	27	6	9	8	0	0	5	0	0	0	0	0	-	0	.269	.269	.403
2006	KC	AL	23	65	18	3	0	1	(0 | 1)	24	8	5	8	1	0	8	0	2	1	0	0	-	0	.277	.284	.369
3 ML YEARS			50	137	37	7	1	2	(0 | 2)	52	16	14	16	1	0	14	1	2	1	0	0	-	4	.270	.279	.380

Mike Piazza

Bats: R **Throws:** R **Pos:** C-99; PH-19; DH-8   **Ht:** 6'3" **Wt:** 215 **Born:** 9/4/1968 **Age:** 38

			BATTING																BASERUNNING				AVERAGES		
Year	Team	Lg	G	AB	H	2B	3B	HR	(Hm | Rd)	TB	R	RBI	RC	TBB	IBB	SO	HBP	SH	SF	SB	CS	SB%	GDP	Avg	OBP	Slg
1992	LAD	NL	21	69	16	3	0	1	(1 | 0)	22	5	7	6	4	0	12	1	0	0	0	0	-	1	.232	.284	.319
1993	LAD	NL	149	547	174	24	2	35	(21 | 14)	307	81	112	107	46	6	86	3	0	6	3	4	.43	10	.318	.370	.561
1994	LAD	NL	107	405	129	18	0	24	(13 | 11)	219	64	92	74	33	10	65	1	0	2	1	3	.25	11	.319	.370	.541
1995	LAD	NL	112	434	150	17	0	32	(9 | 23)	263	82	93	96	39	10	80	1	0	1	1	0	1.00	10	.346	.400	.606
1996	LAD	NL	148	547	184	16	0	36	(14 | 22)	308	87	105	117	81	21	93	1	0	2	0	3	.00	21	.336	.422	.563
1997	LAD	NL	152	556	201	32	1	40	(22 | 18)	355	104	124	137	69	11	77	3	0	5	5	1	.83	19	.362	.431	.638
1998	3 Tms	NL	151	561	184	38	1	32	(15 | 17)	320	88	111	116	58	14	80	2	0	5	1	0	1.00	15	.328	.390	.570
1999	NYM	NL	141	534	162	25	0	40	(18 | 22)	307	100	124	99	51	11	70	1	0	7	2	2	.50	27	.303	.361	.575
2000	NYM	NL	136	482	156	26	0	38	(17 | 21)	296	90	113	107	58	10	69	3	0	2	4	2	.67	15	.324	.398	.614
2001	NYM	NL	141	503	151	29	0	36	(16 | 20)	288	81	94	100	67	19	87	2	0	1	0	2	.00	20	.300	.384	.573
2002	NYM	NL	135	478	134	23	2	33	(12 | 21)	260	69	98	82	57	9	82	3	0	3	0	3	.00	26	.280	.359	.544
2003	NYM	NL	68	234	67	13	0	11	(4 | 7)	113	37	34	42	35	3	40	1	0	3	0	0	-	11	.286	.377	.483
2004	NYM	NL	129	455	121	21	0	20	(12 | 8)	202	47	54	63	68	14	78	2	0	3	0	0	-	14	.266	.362	.444
2005	NYM	NL	113	398	100	23	0	19	(9 | 10)	180	41	62	55	41	6	67	3	0	0	0	0	-	7	.251	.326	.452
2006	SD	NL	126	399	113	19	1	22	(10 | 12)	200	39	68	56	34	2	66	3	0	3	0	0	-	13	.283	.342	.501
98	LAD	NL	37	149	42	5	0	9	(5 | 4)	74	20	30	23	11	4	27	0	0	1	0	0	-	3	.282	.329	.497
98	Fla	NL	5	18	5	0	1	0	(0 | 0)	7	1	5	2	0	0	0	0	0	1	0	0	-	0	.278	.263	.389
98	NYM	NL	109	394	137	33	0	23	(10 | 13)	239	67	76	91	47	10	53	2	0	3	1	0	1.00	12	.348	.417	.607
15 ML YEARS			1829	6602	2042	327	7	419	(193 | 226)	3640	1015	1291	1257	741	146	1052	30	0	43	17	20	.46	220	.309	.379	.551

Jorge Piedra

Bats: L Throws: L Pos: PH-35; DH-5; LF-2; RF-2; CF-1   Ht: 6'0" Wt: 200 Born: 4/17/1979 Age: 28

								BATTING												BASERUNNING				AVERAGES		
Year	Team	Lg	G	AB	H	2B	3B	HR	(Hm | Rd)	TB	R	RBI	RC	TBB	IBB	SO	HBP	SH	SF	SB	CS	SB%	GDP	Avg	OBP	Slg
2006	ColSpr*	AAA	41	138	33	8	0	6	(- | -)	59	15	18	18	15	3	31	1	0	2	0	2	.00	2	.239	.314	.428
2004	Col	NL	38	91	27	8	0	3	(1 | 2)	44	15	10	11	5	0	19	1	1	0	0	1	.00	1	.297	.340	.484
2005	Col	NL	61	112	35	8	1	6	(3 | 3)	63	19	16	19	10	0	15	1	0	1	2	1	.67	2	.313	.371	.563
2006	Col	NL	43	59	10	2	0	3	(1 | 2)	21	4	10	1	3	0	22	1	0	0	1	0	1.00	2	.169	.222	.356
	3 ML YEARS		142	262	72	18	1	12	(5 | 7)	128	38	36	31	18	0	56	3	1	1	3	2	.60	5	.275	.327	.489

Juan Pierre

Bats: L Throws: L Pos: CF-162   Ht: 6'0" Wt: 180 Born: 8/14/1977 Age: 29

								BATTING												BASERUNNING				AVERAGES		
Year	Team	Lg	G	AB	H	2B	3B	HR	(Hm | Rd)	TB	R	RBI	RC	TBB	IBB	SO	HBP	SH	SF	SB	CS	SB%	GDP	Avg	OBP	Slg
2000	Col	NL	51	200	62	2	0	0	(0 | 0)	64	26	20	23	13	0	15	1	4	1	7	6	.54	2	.310	.353	.320
2001	Col	NL	156	617	202	26	11	2	(0 | 2)	256	108	55	101	41	1	29	10	14	1	46	17	.73	6	.327	.378	.415
2002	Col	NL	152	592	170	20	5	1	(0 | 1)	203	90	35	79	31	0	52	9	8	0	47	12	.80	7	.287	.332	.343
2003	Fla	NL	162	668	204	28	7	1	(1 | 0)	249	100	41	92	55	1	35	5	15	3	65	20	.76	9	.305	.361	.373
2004	Fla	NL	162	678	221	22	12	3	(1 | 2)	276	100	49	101	45	1	35	8	15	2	45	24	.65	9	.326	.374	.407
2005	Fla	NL	162	656	181	19	13	2	(1 | 1)	232	96	47	76	41	1	45	9	10	2	57	17	.77	10	.276	.326	.354
2006	ChC	NL	162	699	204	32	13	3	(1 | 2)	271	87	40	84	32	0	38	8	10	1	58	20	.74	6	.292	.330	.388
	7 ML YEARS		1007	4110	1244	149	61	12	(4 | 8)	1551	607	287	556	258	4	249	50	76	10	325	116	.74	49	.303	.350	.377

A.J. Pierzynski

Bats: L Throws: R Pos: C-132; PH-12   Ht: 6'3" Wt: 235 Born: 12/30/1976 Age: 30

								BATTING												BASERUNNING				AVERAGES		
Year	Team	Lg	G	AB	H	2B	3B	HR	(Hm | Rd)	TB	R	RBI	RC	TBB	IBB	SO	HBP	SH	SF	SB	CS	SB%	GDP	Avg	OBP	Slg
1998	Min	AL	7	10	3	0	0	0	(0 | 0)	3	1	1	2	1	0	2	1	0	1	0	0	-	0	.300	.385	.300
1999	Min	AL	9	22	6	2	0	0	(0 | 0)	8	3	3	3	1	0	4	1	0	0	0	0	-	0	.273	.333	.364
2000	Min	AL	33	88	27	5	1	2	(1 | 1)	40	12	11	14	5	0	14	2	0	1	1	0	1.00	1	.307	.354	.455
2001	Min	AL	114	381	110	33	2	7	(3 | 4)	168	51	55	50	16	4	57	4	1	3	1	7	.13	7	.289	.322	.441
2002	Min	AL	130	440	132	31	6	6	(2 | 4)	193	54	49	60	13	1	61	11	2	3	1	2	.33	14	.300	.334	.439
2003	Min	AL	137	487	152	35	3	11	(6 | 5)	226	63	74	80	24	12	55	15	2	5	3	1	.75	13	.312	.360	.464
2004	SF	NL	131	471	128	28	2	11	(3 | 8)	193	45	77	58	19	4	27	15	2	3	0	1	.00	28	.272	.319	.410
2005	CWS	AL	128	460	118	21	0	18	(12 | 6)	193	61	56	55	23	5	68	12	1	1	0	2	.00	13	.257	.308	.420
2006	CWS	AL	140	509	150	24	0	16	(9 | 7)	222	65	64	68	22	6	72	8	3	1	1	0	1.00	10	.295	.333	.436
	9 ML YEARS		829	2868	826	179	14	71	(36 | 35)	1246	355	390	390	124	32	360	69	11	18	7	13	.35	86	.288	.331	.434

Joel Pineiro

Pitches: R Bats: R Pos: SP-25; RP-15   Ht: 6'1" Wt: 200 Born: 9/25/1978 Age: 28

				HOW MUCH HE PITCHED						WHAT HE GAVE UP										THE RESULTS					
Year	Team	Lg	G	GS	CG	GF	IP	BFP	H	R	ER	HR	SH	SF	HB	TBB	IBB	SO	WP	Bk	W	L	Pct	ShO	Sv-Op Hld	ERC	ERA
2000	Sea	AL	8	1	0	5	19.1	94	25	13	12	3	0	2	0	13	0	10	0	0	1	0	1.000	0	0-0 0	7.44	5.59
2001	Sea	AL	17	11	0	1	75.1	289	50	24	17	2	1	2	3	21	0	56	2	0	6	2	.750	0	0-0 2	1.71	2.03
2002	Sea	AL	37	28	2	4	194.1	812	189	75	70	24	5	7	7	54	1	136	8	0	14	7	.667	1	0-0 3	3.77	3.24
2003	Sea	AL	32	32	3	0	211.2	890	192	94	89	19	3	9	6	76	3	151	5	0	16	11	.593	2	0-0 0	3.43	3.78
2004	Sea	AL	21	21	1	0	140.2	596	144	77	73	21	1	5	4	43	1	111	4	0	6	11	.353	0	0-0 0	4.32	4.67
2005	Sea	AL	30	30	2	0	189.0	822	224	118	118	23	5	7	6	56	4	107	7	1	7	11	.389	0	0-0 0	5.05	5.62
2006	Sea	AL	40	25	1	6	165.2	753	209	123	117	23	1	6	10	64	13	87	4	1	8	13	.381	0	1-2 4	6.05	6.36
	7 ML YEARS		185	148	9	16	996.0	4256	1033	524	496	115	16	38	36	327	22	658	30	2	58	55	.513	3	1-2 9	4.26	4.48

Renyel Pinto

Pitches: L Bats: L Pos: RP-27   Ht: 6'4" Wt: 195 Born: 7/8/1982 Age: 24

				HOW MUCH HE PITCHED						WHAT HE GAVE UP										THE RESULTS					
Year	Team	Lg	G	GS	CG	GF	IP	BFP	H	R	ER	HR	SH	SF	HB	TBB	IBB	SO	WP	Bk	W	L	Pct	ShO	Sv-Op Hld	ERC	ERA
2000	Cubs	R	9	4	1	0	30.0	152	42	29	21	3	2	0	5	16	0	23	6	3	0	2	.000	0	0- -	7.65	6.30
2001	Lansng	A	20	20	0	0	88.0	393	94	64	51	9	4	4	3	44	1	69	5	3	4	8	.333	0	0- -	5.04	5.22
2002	Lansng	A	17	16	0	0	98.0	400	79	39	36	9	0	6	8	28	0	92	3	0	7	5	.583	0	0- -	2.88	3.31
2002	Dytona	A+	7	7	1	0	32.2	149	45	23	20	5	1	1	3	11	0	24	3	2	3	3	.500	0	0- -	7.11	5.51
2003	Dytona	A+	20	19	0	0	114.2	476	91	47	41	4	6	4	9	45	1	104	6	3	8	8	.273	0	0- -	2.81	3.22
2004	WTenn	AA	25	25	0	0	141.2	587	107	50	46	10	8	5	6	72	0	179	9	1	11	8	.579	0	0- -	3.20	2.92
2004	Iowa	AAA	2	2	0	0	9.1	43	9	9	8	2	0	0	0	8	0	9	1	0	1	1	.500	0	0- -	6.84	7.71
2005	WTenn	AA	22	21	0	0	129.2	528	101	43	39	3	5	2	9	58	0	123	3	0	10	3	.769	1	0- -	2.92	2.71
2005	Iowa	AAA	6	6	0	0	22.2	121	31	30	24	3	4	2	2	24	0	24	0	0	1	2	.333	0	0- -	10.01	9.53
2006	Albq	AAA	18	18	1	0	95.1	418	82	40	36	8	4	1	13	47	1	96	7	0	8	2	.800	0	0- -	4.06	3.40
2006	Fla	NL	27	0	0	7	29.2	135	20	12	10	3	0	1	1	27	0	36	4	0	0	0	-	0	1-1 3	4.33	3.03

Scott Podsednik

Bats: L Throws: L Pos: LF-135; PH-13; DH-2; PR-2   Ht: 6'1" Wt: 190 Born: 3/18/1976 Age: 31

								BATTING												BASERUNNING				AVERAGES		
Year	Team	Lg	G	AB	H	2B	3B	HR	(Hm | Rd)	TB	R	RBI	RC	TBB	IBB	SO	HBP	SH	SF	SB	CS	SB%	GDP	Avg	OBP	Slg
2001	Sea	AL	5	6	1	0	0	1	(0 | 1)	4	3	1	3	0	0	1	0	0	0	0	0	-	1	.167	.167	.500
2002	Sea	AL	14	20	4	0	0	1	(0 | 1)	7	2	5	3	4	0	6	0	0	1	0	0	-	1	.200	.320	.350
2003	Mil	NL	154	558	175	29	8	9	(7 | 2)	247	100	58	101	56	2	91	4	8	2	43	10	.81	11	.314	.379	.443
2004	Mil	NL	154	640	156	27	7	12	(3 | 9)	233	85	39	76	58	2	105	7	6	1	70	13	.84	7	.244	.313	.364

203

Year	Team	Lg	G	AB	H	2B	3B	HR	(Hm	Rd)	TB	R	RBI	RC	TBB	IBB	SO	HBP	SH	SF	SB	CS	SB%	GDP	Avg	OBP	Slg
2005	CWS	AL	129	507	147	28	1	0	(0	0)	177	80	25	64	47	0	75	3	6	5	59	23	.72	7	.290	.351	.349
2006	CWS	AL	139	524	137	27	6	3	(2	1)	185	86	45	65	54	1	96	2	8	4	40	19	.68	7	.261	.330	.353
6 ML YEARS			595	2255	620	111	23	25	(12	13)	852	354	175	309	219	5	374	16	28	13	212	65	.77	34	.275	.342	.378

Placido Polanco

Bats: R Throws: R Pos: 2B-108; PH-3   Ht: 5'10" Wt: 195 Born: 10/10/1975 Age: 31

Year	Team	Lg	G	AB	H	2B	3B	HR	(Hm	Rd)	TB	R	RBI	RC	TBB	IBB	SO	HBP	SH	SF	SB	CS	SB%	GDP	Avg	OBP	Slg
1998	StL	NL	45	114	29	3	2	1	(1	0)	39	10	11	12	5	0	9	1	2	0	2	0	1.00	1	.254	.292	.342
1999	StL	NL	88	220	61	9	3	1	(0	1)	79	24	19	23	15	1	24	0	3	2	1	3	.25	7	.277	.321	.359
2000	StL	NL	118	323	102	12	3	5	(2	3)	135	50	39	44	16	0	26	1	7	3	4	4	.50	8	.316	.347	.418
2001	StL	NL	144	564	173	26	4	3	(1	2)	216	87	38	70	25	0	43	6	14	1	12	3	.80	22	.307	.342	.383
2002	2 Tms	NL	147	548	158	32	2	9	(8	1)	221	75	49	64	26	1	41	8	13	0	5	3	.63	15	.288	.330	.403
2003	Phi	NL	122	492	142	30	3	14	(7	7)	220	87	63	74	42	1	38	8	8	4	14	2	.88	16	.289	.352	.447
2004	Phi	NL	126	503	150	21	0	17	(10	7)	222	74	55	71	27	0	39	12	7	6	7	4	.64	13	.298	.345	.441
2005	2 Tms	NL	129	501	166	27	2	9	(6	3)	224	84	56	86	33	0	25	11	2	4	4	3	.57	12	.331	.383	.447
2006	Det	AL	110	461	136	18	1	4	(2	2)	168	58	52	65	17	0	27	7	8	2	1	2	.33	18	.295	.329	.364
02	StL	NL	94	342	97	19	1	5	(5	0)	133	47	27	38	12	1	27	4	9	0	3	1	.75	12	.284	.316	.389
02	Phi	NL	53	206	61	13	1	4	(3	1)	88	28	22	26	14	0	14	4	4	0	2	2	.50	3	.296	.353	.427
05	Phi	NL	43	158	50	7	0	3	(2	1)	66	26	20	26	12	0	9	3	0	0	0	0	-	3	.316	.376	.418
05	Det	AL	86	343	116	20	2	6	(4	2)	158	58	36	60	21	0	16	8	2	4	4	3	.57	9	.338	.386	.461
9 ML YEARS			1029	3726	1117	178	20	63	(37	26)	1524	549	382	509	206	3	272	54	64	22	50	24	.68	112	.300	.344	.409

Cliff Politte

Pitches: R Bats: R Pos: RP-30   Ht: 5'10" Wt: 195 Born: 2/27/1974 Age: 33

Year	Team	Lg	G	GS	CG	GF	IP	BFP	H	R	ER	HR	SH	SF	HB	TBB	IBB	SO	WP	Bk	W	L	Pct	ShO	Sv-Op	Hld	ERC	ERA
2006	Charltt*	AAA	3	2	0	0	4.2	20	5	1	1	0	0	0	0	1	0	5	1	0	0	0	-	0	0- -	-	3.00	1.93
1998	StL	NL	8	8	0	0	37.0	172	45	32	26	6	3	1	1	18	0	22	2	1	2	3	.400	0	0-0	0	6.28	6.32
1999	Phi	NL	13	0	0	0	17.2	85	19	14	14	2	1	0	0	15	0	15	2	0	1	0	1.000	0	0-0	1	6.47	7.13
2000	Phi	NL	12	8	0	1	59.0	251	55	24	24	8	1	1	0	27	1	50	3	0	4	3	.571	0	0-0	0	4.20	3.66
2001	Phi	NL	23	0	0	7	26.0	109	24	8	7	2	1	3	1	8	3	23	1	0	2	3	.400	0	0-0	1	3.11	2.42
2002	2 Tms		68	0	0	20	73.2	304	57	33	30	5	3	1	2	28	2	72	2	0	3	3	.500	0	1-4	25	2.64	3.67
2003	Tor	AL	54	0	0	30	49.1	216	52	32	31	11	1	3	1	17	4	40	1	0	1	5	.167	0	12-18	8	4.93	5.66
2004	CWS	AL	54	0	0	9	51.1	225	52	26	25	6	0	2	2	22	5	48	2	0	3	0	.000	0	1-1	19	4.38	4.38
2005	CWS	AL	68	0	0	14	67.1	262	42	15	15	7	2	4	3	21	4	57	1	0	7	1	.875	0	1-2	23	1.97	2.00
2006	CWS	AL	30	0	0	13	30.0	151	47	30	29	9	0	2	1	15	7	15	0	0	2	2	.500	0	0-2	4	9.39	8.70
02	Phi	NL	13	0	0	7	16.1	77	19	10	7	0	1	0	1	9	1	15	1	0	2	0	1.000	0	0-1	0	4.89	3.86
02	Tor	AL	55	0	0	13	57.1	227	38	23	23	5	2	1	1	19	1	57	1	0	1	3	.250	0	1-3	25	2.06	3.61
9 ML YEARS			330	16	0	94	411.1	1775	393	214	201	56	12	17	11	171	26	342	14	1	22	23	.489	0	15-27	81	4.14	4.40

Sidney Ponson

Pitches: R Bats: R Pos: SP-16; RP-3   Ht: 6'1" Wt: 250 Born: 11/2/1976 Age: 30

Year	Team	Lg	G	GS	CG	GF	IP	BFP	H	R	ER	HR	SH	SF	HB	TBB	IBB	SO	WP	Bk	W	L	Pct	ShO	Sv-Op	Hld	ERC	ERA
1998	Bal	AL	31	20	0	5	135.0	588	157	82	79	19	3	4	3	42	2	85	4	1	8	9	.471	0	1-2	0	5.07	5.27
1999	Bal	AL	32	32	6	0	210.0	897	227	118	110	35	4	7	1	80	2	112	4	0	12	12	.500	0	0-0	0	5.08	4.71
2000	Bal	AL	32	32	6	0	222.0	953	223	125	119	30	3	3	1	83	0	152	5	0	9	13	.409	1	0-0	0	4.26	4.82
2001	Bal	AL	23	23	3	0	138.1	605	161	83	76	21	3	2	6	37	0	84	2	0	5	10	.333	1	0-0	0	5.04	4.94
2002	Bal	AL	28	28	3	0	176.0	736	172	84	80	26	2	3	2	63	1	120	3	0	7	9	.438	0	0-0	0	4.24	4.09
2003	2 Tms		31	31	4	0	216.0	898	211	94	90	16	6	5	5	61	5	134	9	0	17	12	.586	0	0-0	0	3.41	3.75
2004	Bal	AL	33	33	5	0	215.2	954	265	136	127	23	6	3	8	69	3	115	8	2	11	15	.423	2	0-0	0	5.33	5.30
2005	Bal	AL	23	23	1	0	130.1	595	177	97	90	16	2	8	3	48	1	68	10	0	7	11	.389	0	0-0	0	6.45	6.21
2006	2 Tms		19	16	0	1	85.0	384	108	62	59	10	4	0	4	36	1	48	2	0	4	5	.444	0	0-0	0	6.25	6.25
03	Bal	AL	21	21	4	0	148.0	622	147	65	62	10	2	3	4	43	2	100	6	0	14	6	.700	0	0-0	0	3.50	3.77
03	SF	NL	10	10	0	0	68.0	276	64	29	28	6	4	2	1	18	3	34	3	0	3	6	.333	0	0-0	0	3.23	3.71
06	StL	NL	14	13	0	0	68.2	303	82	42	40	7	4	0	4	29	1	33	2	0	4	4	.500	0	0-0	0	5.74	5.24
06	NYY	AL	5	3	0	1	16.1	81	26	20	19	3	0	0	0	7	0	15	0	0	0	1	.000	0	0-0	0	8.48	10.47
9 ML YEARS			252	238	28	6	1528.1	6610	1701	881	830	196	33	35	33	519	15	918	47	3	80	96	.455	4	1-2	0	4.82	4.89

Jorge Posada

Bats: B Throws: R Pos: C-134; PH-19; DH-2; 1B-1   Ht: 6'2" Wt: 205 Born: 8/17/1971 Age: 35

Year	Team	Lg	G	AB	H	2B	3B	HR	(Hm	Rd)	TB	R	RBI	RC	TBB	IBB	SO	HBP	SH	SF	SB	CS	SB%	GDP	Avg	OBP	Slg
1995	NYY	AL	1	0	0	0	0	0	(0	0)	0	0	0	0	0	0	0	0	0	0	0	0	-	0	-	-	-
1996	NYY	AL	8	14	1	0	0	0	(0	0)	1	1	0	0	1	0	6	0	0	0	0	0	-	1	.071	.133	.071
1997	NYY	AL	60	188	47	12	0	6	(2	4)	77	29	25	29	30	2	33	3	1	2	1	2	.33	2	.250	.359	.410
1998	NYY	AL	111	358	96	23	0	17	(6	11)	170	56	63	56	47	7	92	0	0	4	0	1	.00	14	.268	.350	.475
1999	NYY	AL	112	379	93	19	2	12	(4	8)	152	50	57	52	53	2	91	3	0	2	1	0	1.00	9	.245	.341	.401
2000	NYY	AL	151	505	145	35	1	28	(18	10)	266	92	86	110	107	10	151	8	0	4	2	2	.50	11	.287	.417	.527
2001	NYY	AL	138	484	134	28	1	22	(14	8)	230	59	95	80	62	10	132	6	0	5	2	6	.25	10	.277	.363	.475
2002	NYY	AL	143	511	137	40	1	20	(12	8)	239	79	99	92	81	9	143	3	0	3	1	0	1.00	23	.268	.370	.468
2003	NYY	AL	142	481	135	24	0	30	(15	15)	249	83	101	98	93	6	110	10	0	4	2	4	.33	13	.281	.405	.518
2004	NYY	AL	137	449	122	31	0	21	(11	10)	216	72	81	78	88	5	92	9	0	1	1	3	.25	24	.272	.400	.481
2005	NYY	AL	142	474	124	23	0	19	(11	8)	204	67	71	71	66	5	94	2	0	4	1	0	1.00	8	.262	.352	.430
2006	NYY	AL	143	465	129	27	2	23	(11	12)	229	65	93	89	64	1	97	11	0	5	3	0	1.00	10	.277	.374	.492
12 ML YEARS			1288	4308	1163	262	7	198	(104	94)	2033	653	771	755	692	57	1041	55	1	34	14	18	.44	125	.270	.375	.472

204

Martin Prado

Bats: R **Throws:** R **Pos:** 2B-11; PH-9; 3B-8; PR-1   **Ht:** 6'1" **Wt:** 170 **Born:** 10/27/1983 **Age:** 23

Year	Team	Lg	G	AB	H	2B	3B	HR	(Hm	Rd)	TB	R	RBI	RC	TBB	IBB	SO	HBP	SH	SF	SB	CS	SB%	GDP	Avg	OBP	Slg
2003	Braves	R	59	220	63	2	6	0	(-	-)	77	28	23	28	24	0	30	1	5	1	9	9	.50	4	.286	.358	.350
2004	Rome	A	107	429	135	25	6	3	(-	-)	181	68	38	66	30	0	47	3	4	1	14	10	.58	10	.315	.363	.422
2005	MrtlBh	A+	75	297	91	13	3	4	(-	-)	122	44	34	44	24	0	48	0	0	5	9	6	.60	7	.306	.353	.411
2005	Missi	AA	39	143	40	7	1	1	(-	-)	52	17	11	19	17	1	17	0	1	1	3	3	.50	5	.280	.354	.364
2006	Missi	AA	43	176	49	6	2	1	(-	-)	62	17	15	21	14	0	35	0	0	1	2	2	.50	5	.278	.330	.352
2006	Rchmd	AAA	60	241	68	12	1	2	(-	-)	88	30	23	28	12	0	28	0	2	2	2	2	.50	8	.282	.314	.365
2006	Atl	NL	24	42	11	1	1	1	(1	0)	17	3	9	9	5	0	7	0	2	0	0	0	-	2	.262	.340	.405

Todd Pratt

Bats: R **Throws:** R **Pos:** C-54; PH-9   **Ht:** 6'3" **Wt:** 240 **Born:** 2/9/1967 **Age:** 40

Year	Team	Lg	G	AB	H	2B	3B	HR	(Hm	Rd)	TB	R	RBI	RC	TBB	IBB	SO	HBP	SH	SF	SB	CS	SB%	GDP	Avg	OBP	Slg
1992	Phi	NL	16	46	13	1	0	2	(2	0)	20	6	10	6	4	0	12	0	0	0	0	0	-	2	.283	.340	.435
1993	Phi	NL	33	87	25	6	0	5	(4	1)	46	8	13	15	5	0	19	1	1	1	0	0	-	2	.287	.330	.529
1994	Phi	NL	28	102	20	6	1	2	(1	1)	34	10	9	9	12	0	29	0	0	0	0	1	.00	3	.196	.281	.333
1995	ChC	NL	25	60	8	2	0	0	(0	0)	10	3	4	1	6	1	21	0	0	0	0	0	-	1	.133	.209	.167
1997	NYM	NL	39	106	30	6	0	2	(1	1)	42	12	19	16	13	0	32	2	0	0	0	1	.00	1	.283	.372	.396
1998	NYM	NL	41	69	19	9	1	2	(1	1)	36	9	18	11	2	0	20	0	0	0	0	0	-	0	.275	.296	.522
1999	NYM	NL	71	140	41	4	0	3	(1	2)	54	18	21	22	15	0	32	3	0	2	2	0	1.00	1	.293	.369	.386
2000	NYM	NL	80	160	44	6	0	8	(2	6)	74	33	25	28	22	1	31	5	2	1	0	0	-	5	.275	.378	.463
2001	2 Tms	NL	80	173	32	8	0	4	(0	4)	52	18	11	18	34	3	61	3	1	1	1	0	1.00	6	.185	.327	.301
2002	Phi	NL	39	106	33	11	0	3	(2	1)	53	14	16	21	24	6	28	4	0	2	2	0	1.00	3	.311	.449	.500
2003	Phi	NL	43	125	34	10	1	4	(3	1)	58	16	20	25	22	0	38	6	1	2	0	0	-	3	.272	.400	.464
2004	Phi	NL	45	128	33	5	0	3	(2	1)	47	16	16	18	18	0	38	1	1	1	0	0	-	5	.258	.351	.367
2005	Phi	NL	60	175	44	4	0	7	(7	0)	69	17	23	22	19	5	50	2	0	0	0	0	-	3	.251	.332	.394
2006	Atl	NL	62	135	28	6	0	4	(1	3)	46	14	19	13	12	0	43	1	1	3	1	0	1.00	4	.207	.272	.341
01	NYM	NL	45	80	13	5	0	2	(0	2)	24	6	4	7	15	1	36	2	0	1	1	0	1.00	4	.163	.306	.300
01	Phi	NL	35	93	19	3	0	2	(0	2)	28	12	7	11	19	2	25	1	1	0	0	0	-	2	.204	.345	.301
	14 ML YEARS		662	1612	404	84	3	49	(27	22)	641	194	224	225	208	16	454	28	7	14	6	2	.75	39	.251	.344	.398

Curtis Pride

Bats: L **Throws:** R **Pos:** PH-10; LF-8; RF-3; DH-3; PR-1   **Ht:** 6'0" **Wt:** 210 **Born:** 12/17/1968 **Age:** 38

Year	Team	Lg	G	AB	H	2B	3B	HR	(Hm	Rd)	TB	R	RBI	RC	TBB	IBB	SO	HBP	SH	SF	SB	CS	SB%	GDP	Avg	OBP	Slg
2006	Salt Lk*	AAA	87	273	85	18	0	8	(-	-)	127	54	44	59	54	3	75	1	1	2	21	6	.78	10	.311	.424	.465
1993	Mon	NL	10	9	4	1	1	1	(0	0)	10	3	5	5	0	0	3	0	0	0	1	0	1.00	0	.444	.444	1.111
1995	Mon	NL	48	63	11	1	0	0	(0	0)	12	10	2	3	5	0	16	0	1	0	3	2	.60	2	.175	.235	.190
1996	Det	AL	95	267	80	17	5	10	(5	5)	137	52	31	52	31	1	63	0	3	0	11	6	.65	2	.300	.372	.513
1997	2 Tms	AL	81	164	35	4	4	3	(3	0)	56	22	20	19	24	1	46	1	2	1	6	4	.60	4	.213	.316	.341
1998	Atl	NL	70	107	27	6	1	3	(1	2)	44	19	9	15	9	0	29	3	1	1	4	0	1.00	2	.252	.325	.411
2000	Bos	AL	9	20	5	1	0	0	(0	0)	6	4	0	2	1	0	7	0	0	0	0	0	-	0	.250	.286	.300
2001	Mon	NL	36	76	19	3	1	1	(0	1)	27	8	9	9	9	0	22	2	0	0	3	2	.60	4	.250	.345	.355
2003	NYY	AL	4	12	1	0	0	1	(1	0)	4	1	1	0	0	0	2	0	0	0	0	0	-	1	.083	.083	.333
2004	LAA	AL	35	40	10	3	0	0	(0	0)	13	5	3	3	0	0	11	1	1	0	1	0	1.00	1	.250	.268	.325
2005	LAA	AL	11	11	1	1	0	0	(0	0)	2	2	0	0	0	0	4	0	0	0	0	0	-	0	.091	.091	.182
2006	LAA	AL	22	27	6	2	0	1	(0	1)	11	6	2	4	6	0	8	0	0	0	0	0	-	2	.222	.364	.407
97	Det	AL	79	162	34	4	4	2	(2	0)	52	21	19	17	24	1	45	1	2	1	6	4	.60	4	.210	.314	.321
97	Bos	AL	2	2	1	0	0	1	(1	0)	4	1	1	2	0	0	1	0	0	0	0	0	-	0	.500	.500	2.000
	11 ML YEARS		421	796	199	39	12	20	(10	9)	322	132	82	112	85	2	211	7	8	2	29	14	.67	17	.250	.327	.405

Mark Prior

Pitches: R **Bats:** R **Pos:** SP-9   **Ht:** 6'5" **Wt:** 230 **Born:** 9/7/1980 **Age:** 26

Year	Team	Lg	G	GS	CG	GF	IP	BFP	H	R	ER	HR	SH	SF	HB	TBB	IBB	SO	WP	Bk	W	L	Pct	ShO	Sv-Op Hld	ERC	ERA
2006	Peoria*	A	2	2	0	0	7.0	29	7	4	3	1	0	0	0	0	0	8	0	0	0	2	.000	0	0- -	2.62	3.86
2006	WTenn*	AA	1	1	0	0	5.0	21	4	3	3	1	0	0	0	2	0	4	0	0	1	0	1.000	0	0- -	3.57	5.40
2006	Iowa*	AAA	1	1	0	0	6.2	24	4	1	0	0	0	0	0	1	0	10	0	0	0	0	-	0	0- -	1.06	0.00
2002	ChC	NL	19	19	1	0	116.2	486	98	45	43	14	3	4	7	38	0	147	1	0	6	6	.500	1	0-0 0	3.27	3.32
2003	ChC	NL	30	30	3	0	211.1	863	183	67	57	15	9	2	9	50	4	245	9	0	18	6	.750	1	0-0 0	2.69	2.43
2004	ChC	NL	21	21	0	0	118.2	510	112	53	53	14	8	4	3	48	2	139	2	1	6	4	.600	0	0-0 0	3.97	4.02
2005	ChC	NL	27	27	1	0	166.2	701	143	68	68	25	5	3	4	59	2	188	4	1	11	7	.611	0	0-0 0	3.49	3.67
2006	ChC	NL	9	9	0	0	43.2	211	46	39	35	9	2	2	8	28	2	38	5	0	1	6	.143	0	0-0 0	6.84	7.21
	5 ML YEARS		106	106	5	0	657.0	2771	582	277	256	77	27	15	31	223	10	757	21	2	42	29	.592	1	0-0 0	3.47	3.51

Scott Proctor

Pitches: R **Bats:** R **Pos:** RP-83   **Ht:** 6'1" **Wt:** 200 **Born:** 1/2/1977 **Age:** 30

Year	Team	Lg	G	GS	CG	GF	IP	BFP	H	R	ER	HR	SH	SF	HB	TBB	IBB	SO	WP	Bk	W	L	Pct	ShO	Sv-Op Hld	ERC	ERA
2004	NYY	AL	26	0	0	12	25.0	118	29	18	15	5	0	2	0	14	0	21	1	1	2	1	.667	0	0-0 2	6.32	5.40
2005	NYY	AL	29	1	0	11	44.2	199	46	32	30	10	0	1	2	17	4	36	4	0	1	0	1.000	0	0-0 0	4.98	6.04
2006	NYY	AL	83	0	0	12	102.1	426	89	41	40	12	2	6	2	33	6	89	2	0	6	4	.600	0	1-8 26	3.15	3.52
	3 ML YEARS		138	1	0	35	172.0	743	164	91	85	27	2	9	4	64	10	146	7	1	9	5	.643	0	1-8 28	4.04	4.45

Albert Pujols

Bats: R Throws: R Pos: 1B-143; PH-1   Ht: 6'3" Wt: 225 Born: 1/16/1980 Age: 27

Year	Team	Lg	G	AB	H	2B	3B	HR	(Hm	Rd)	TB	R	RBI	RC	TBB	IBB	SO	HBP	SH	SF	SB	CS	SB%	GDP	Avg	OBP	Slg
2001	StL	NL	161	590	194	47	4	37	(18	19)	360	112	130	132	69	6	93	9	1	7	1	3	.25	21	.329	.403	.610
2002	StL	NL	157	590	185	40	2	34	(14	20)	331	118	127	121	72	13	69	9	0	4	2	4	.33	20	.314	.394	.561
2003	StL	NL	157	591	212	51	1	43	(21	22)	394	137	124	160	79	12	65	10	0	5	5	1	.83	13	.359	.439	.667
2004	StL	NL	154	592	196	51	2	46	(18	28)	389	133	123	143	84	12	52	7	0	9	5	5	.50	21	.331	.415	.657
2005	StL	NL	161	591	195	38	2	41	(23	18)	360	129	117	139	97	27	65	9	0	3	16	2	.89	19	.330	.430	.609
2006	StL	NL	143	535	177	33	1	49	(24	25)	359	119	137	146	92	28	50	4	0	3	7	2	.78	20	.331	.431	.671
6 ML YEARS			933	3489	1159	260	12	250	(118	132)	2193	748	758	841	493	98	394	48	1	31	36	17	.68	114	.332	.419	.629

Nick Punto

Bats: B Throws: R Pos: 3B-89; SS-26; 2B-17; PR-6; CF-2; DH-2; PH-2; LF-1   Ht: 5'9" Wt: 185 Born: 11/8/1977 Age: 29

Year	Team	Lg	G	AB	H	2B	3B	HR	(Hm	Rd)	TB	R	RBI	RC	TBB	IBB	SO	HBP	SH	SF	SB	CS	SB%	GDP	Avg	OBP	Slg
2001	Phi	NL	4	5	2	0	0	0	(0	0)	2	0	0	1	0	0	0	0	0	0	0	0	-	0	.400	.400	.400
2002	Phi	NL	9	6	1	0	0	0	(0	0)	1	0	0	0	0	0	3	0	1	0	0	0	-	0	.167	.167	.167
2003	Phi	NL	64	92	20	2	0	1	(0	1)	25	14	4	7	7	1	22	0	0	0	2	1	.67	0	.217	.273	.272
2004	Min	AL	38	91	23	0	0	2	(2	0)	29	17	12	15	12	0	19	0	0	0	6	0	1.00	2	.253	.340	.319
2005	Min	AL	112	394	94	18	4	1	(3	1)	123	45	26	35	36	0	86	0	7	2	13	8	.62	9	.239	.301	.335
2006	Min	AL	135	459	133	21	7	1	(0	1)	171	73	45	59	47	0	68	1	10	7	17	5	.77	8	.290	.352	.373
6 ML YEARS			362	1047	273	41	11	8	(5	3)	360	149	87	117	102	1	198	1	18	9	38	14	.73	19	.261	.324	.344

J.J. Putz

Pitches: R Bats: R Pos: RP-72   Ht: 6'5" Wt: 250 Born: 2/22/1977 Age: 30

Year	Team	Lg	G	GS	CG	GF	IP	BFP	H	R	ER	HR	SH	SF	HB	TBB	IBB	SO	WP	Bk	W	L	Pct	ShO	Sv-Op	Hld	ERC	ERA
2003	Sea	AL	3	0	0	0	3.2	18	4	2	2	0	0	0	0	3	0	3	0	0	0	0	-	0	0-0	0	5.31	4.91
2004	Sea	AL	54	0	0	30	63.0	275	66	35	33	10	3	2	5	24	4	47	1	0	3	0	.000	0	9-13	3	4.97	4.71
2005	Sea	AL	64	0	0	20	60.0	259	58	27	24	8	3	3	2	23	2	45	2	0	6	5	.545	0	1-4	21	4.11	3.60
2006	Sea	AL	72	0	0	57	78.1	303	59	20	20	4	1	2	2	13	1	104	1	0	4	1	.800	0	36-43	5	1.78	2.30
4 ML YEARS			193	0	0	107	205.0	855	187	84	79	22	7	7	9	63	7	199	4	0	10	9	.526	0	46-60	29	3.42	3.47

Chad Qualls

Pitches: R Bats: R Pos: RP-81   Ht: 6'5" Wt: 220 Born: 8/17/1978 Age: 28

Year	Team	Lg	G	GS	CG	GF	IP	BFP	H	R	ER	HR	SH	SF	HB	TBB	IBB	SO	WP	Bk	W	L	Pct	ShO	Sv-Op	Hld	ERC	ERA
2004	Hou	NL	25	0	0	4	33.0	141	34	13	13	3	0	1	4	8	1	24	0	0	4	0	1.000	0	1-2	9	4.02	3.55
2005	Hou	NL	77	0	0	19	79.2	329	73	33	29	7	4	3	6	23	2	60	1	0	6	4	.600	0	0-0	22	3.42	3.28
2006	Hou	NL	81	0	0	13	88.2	356	76	38	37	10	4	4	6	28	6	56	0	0	7	3	.700	0	0-6	23	3.36	3.76
3 ML YEARS			183	0	0	36	201.1	826	183	84	79	20	8	8	16	59	9	140	1	0	17	7	.708	0	1-8	54	3.49	3.53

Carlos Quentin

Bats: R Throws: R Pos: RF-44; PH-13; LF-2   Ht: 6'1" Wt: 225 Born: 8/28/1982 Age: 24

Year	Team	Lg	G	AB	H	2B	3B	HR	(Hm	Rd)	TB	R	RBI	RC	TBB	IBB	SO	HBP	SH	SF	SB	CS	SB%	GDP	Avg	OBP	Slg
2004	Lancst	A	65	242	75	14	1	15	(-	-)	136	64	51	60	25	1	33	27	0	3	5	1	.83	10	.310	.428	.562
2004	ElPaso	AA	60	210	75	19	1	6	(-	-)	112	39	38	47	18	1	23	16	0	2	0	6	.00	6	.357	.443	.533
2005	Tucsn	AAA	136	452	136	28	4	21	(-	-)	235	98	89	106	72	0	71	29	0	8	9	1	.90	14	.301	.422	.520
2006	Tucsn	AAA	85	318	92	30	3	9	(-	-)	155	66	52	71	45	1	46	31	0	2	5	0	1.00	13	.289	.424	.487
2006	Ari	NL	57	166	42	13	3	9	(3	6)	88	23	32	29	15	2	34	8	1	1	1	0	1.00	6	.253	.342	.530

Robb Quinlan

Bats: R Throws: R Pos: 1B-54; 3B-18; LF-11; PH-7; RF-5; PR-2; DH-1   Ht: 6'1" Wt: 200 Born: 3/17/1977 Age: 30

Year	Team	Lg	G	AB	H	2B	3B	HR	(Hm	Rd)	TB	R	RBI	RC	TBB	IBB	SO	HBP	SH	SF	SB	CS	SB%	GDP	Avg	OBP	Slg
2003	LAA	AL	38	94	27	4	2	0	(0	0)	35	13	4	8	6	0	16	0	1	0	1	2	.33	3	.287	.330	.372
2004	LAA	AL	56	160	55	14	0	5	(3	2)	84	23	23	33	14	0	26	2	0	1	3	1	.75	1	.344	.401	.525
2005	LAA	AL	54	134	31	8	0	5	(3	2)	54	17	14	11	7	0	26	1	0	1	0	1	.00	4	.231	.273	.403
2006	LAA	AL	86	234	75	11	1	9	(3	6)	115	28	32	36	7	1	28	2	0	1	2	1	.67	6	.321	.344	.491
4 ML YEARS			234	622	188	37	3	19	(9	10)	288	81	73	88	34	1	96	5	1	3	6	5	.55	14	.302	.342	.463

Omar Quintanilla

Bats: L Throws: R Pos: SS-8; 2B-3; PH-1   Ht: 5'9" Wt: 190 Born: 10/24/1981 Age: 25

Year	Team	Lg	G	AB	H	2B	3B	HR	(Hm	Rd)	TB	R	RBI	RC	TBB	IBB	SO	HBP	SH	SF	SB	CS	SB%	GDP	Avg	OBP	Slg
2003	Vancvr	A-	32	129	44	5	4	0	(-	-)	57	22	14	24	12	0	20	1	1	0	7	1	.88	3	.341	.401	.442
2003	Mdest	A+	8	36	15	3	0	2	(-	-)	24	9	6	9	3	0	6	0	0	0	0	0	-	1	.417	.462	.667
2004	Mdest	A+	108	452	142	32	5	11	(-	-)	217	75	72	80	37	1	54	5	6	3	1	3	.25	11	.314	.370	.480
2004	Mdland	AA	23	94	33	10	0	2	(-	-)	49	20	20	20	10	0	9	1	0	0	2	0	1.00	1	.351	.419	.521
2005	Mdland	AA	78	294	86	14	2	4	(-	-)	116	46	25	41	23	1	40	2	1	1	2	3	.40	5	.293	.347	.395
2005	ColSpr	AAA	13	52	18	3	2	1	(-	-)	28	14	7	10	3	0	8	0	1	1	0	0	-	1	.346	.375	.538
2006	ColSpr	AAA	82	308	85	23	2	4	(-	-)	124	48	29	45	28	0	55	4	7	2	4	1	.80	6	.276	.342	.403

Year	Team	Lg	G	AB	H	2B	3B	HR	(Hm	Rd)	TB	R	RBI	RC	TBB	IBB	SO	HBP	SH	SF	SB	CS	SB%	GDP	Avg	OBP	Slg
2005	Col	NL	39	128	28	1	1	0	(0	0)	31	16	7	9	9	0	15	0	6	0	2	1	.67	3	.219	.270	.242
2006	Col	NL	11	34	6	1	1	0	(0	0)	9	3	3	2	3	1	9	0	0	1	1	1	.50	1	.176	.243	.265
2 ML YEARS			50	162	34	2	2	0	(0	0)	40	19	10	11	12	1	24	0	7	0	3	2	.60	4	.210	.264	.247

Humberto Quintero

Bats: R **Throws:** R **Pos:** C-10; PH-1 **Ht:** 5'9" **Wt:** 215 **Born:** 8/2/1979 **Age:** 27

Year	Team	Lg	G	AB	H	2B	3B	HR	(Hm	Rd)	TB	R	RBI	RC	TBB	IBB	SO	HBP	SH	SF	SB	CS	SB%	GDP	Avg	OBP	Slg
2006	RdRck*	AAA	82	292	87	21	2	4	(-	-)	124	39	37	46	19	0	48	7	1	3	4	0	1.00	16	.298	.352	.425
2003	SD	NL	12	23	5	0	0	0	(0	0)	5	1	2	2	1	1	6	0	0	0	0	0	-	0	.217	.250	.217
2004	SD	NL	23	72	18	3	0	2	(1	1)	27	7	10	6	5	0	16	0	0	1	0	2	.00	5	.250	.295	.375
2005	Hou	NL	18	54	10	1	0	1	(1	0)	14	6	8	2	1	1	10	0	2	0	0	0	-	3	.185	.200	.259
2006	Hou	NL	11	21	7	2	0	0	(0	0)	9	2	2	1	1	0	3	0	0	0	0	0	-	2	.333	.364	.429
4 ML YEARS			64	170	40	6	0	3	(2	1)	55	16	22	11	8	2	35	0	2	1	0	2	.00	10	.235	.268	.324

Guillermo Quiroz

Bats: R **Throws:** R **Pos:** C-1 **Ht:** 6'1" **Wt:** 200 **Born:** 11/29/1981 **Age:** 25

Year	Team	Lg	G	AB	H	2B	3B	HR	(Hm	Rd)	TB	R	RBI	RC	TBB	IBB	SO	HBP	SH	SF	SB	CS	SB%	GDP	Avg	OBP	Slg
2006	SnAnt*	AA	16	64	12	3	0	3	(-	-)	24	5	9	5	3	0	15	1	0	0	0	0	-	2	.188	.235	.375
2006	Tacom*	AAA	38	138	42	8	0	3	(-	-)	59	15	28	22	11	1	29	2	0	2	0	0	-	5	.304	.359	.428
2004	Tor	AL	17	52	11	2	0	0	(0	0)	13	2	6	4	2	0	8	2	0	1	1	0	1.00	1	.212	.263	.250
2005	Tor	AL	12	36	7	2	0	0	(0	0)	9	3	4	3	2	0	13	1	0	0	0	0	-	0	.194	.256	.250
2006	Sea	AL	1	2	0	0	0	0	(0	0)	0	0	0	0	0	0	2	0	0	0	0	0	-	0	.000	.000	.000
3 ML YEARS			30	90	18	4	0	0	(0	0)	22	5	10	7	4	0	23	3	0	1	1	0	1.00	1	.200	.255	.244

Josh Rabe

Bats: R **Throws:** R **Pos:** DH-12; LF-10; PR-7; RF-1; PH-1 **Ht:** 6'3" **Wt:** 215 **Born:** 10/15/1978 **Age:** 28

Year	Team	Lg	G	AB	H	2B	3B	HR	(Hm	Rd)	TB	R	RBI	RC	TBB	IBB	SO	HBP	SH	SF	SB	CS	SB%	GDP	Avg	OBP	Slg
2000	Elizab	R+	44	154	34	5	0	3	(-	-)	48	33	11	19	25	0	34	4	0	0	2	0	1.00	6	.221	.344	.312
2001	QuadC	A	119	397	112	25	3	6	(-	-)	161	58	44	57	32	0	64	8	4	3	9	7	.56	9	.282	.345	.406
2002	FtMyrs	A	85	297	101	23	2	5	(-	-)	143	60	40	64	44	2	36	3	2	3	16	4	.80	10	.340	.427	.481
2002	NwBrit	AA	46	183	43	10	0	1	(-	-)	56	21	18	16	10	0	30	2	1	0	4	1	.80	5	.235	.282	.306
2003	NwBrit	AA	94	366	111	15	2	11	(-	-)	163	63	72	63	30	1	63	6	0	5	19	3	.86	10	.303	.361	.445
2003	Roch	AAA	38	131	31	6	0	5	(-	-)	52	15	11	16	11	0	22	1	1	0	2	1	.67	7	.237	.301	.397
2004	Roch	AAA	122	429	113	27	0	7	(-	-)	161	54	45	60	40	3	76	6	3	3	26	5	.84	9	.263	.333	.375
2005	Roch	AAA	90	285	68	17	0	11	(-	-)	118	50	49	39	29	0	57	3	2	2	5	2	.71	7	.239	.313	.414
2006	Roch	AAA	93	355	106	20	1	6	(-	-)	146	51	47	56	35	1	37	3	0	5	7	4	.64	5	.299	.362	.411
2006	Min	AL	24	49	14	1	0	3	(2	1)	24	8	7	6	2	0	11	0	0	0	0	1	.00	3	.286	.314	.490

Mike Rabelo

Bats: B **Throws:** R **Pos:** DH-1; PH-1 **Ht:** 6'1" **Wt:** 200 **Born:** 1/17/1980 **Age:** 27

Year	Team	Lg	G	AB	H	2B	3B	HR	(Hm	Rd)	TB	R	RBI	RC	TBB	IBB	SO	HBP	SH	SF	SB	CS	SB%	GDP	Avg	OBP	Slg
2001	Oneont	A-	53	194	63	4	2	0	(-	-)	71	27	32	31	23	0	45	4	0	1	1	2	.33	4	.325	.405	.366
2002	W Mich	A	123	410	80	13	1	2	(-	-)	101	42	41	30	42	0	91	8	5	2	3	1	.75	21	.195	.281	.246
2003	W Mich	A	123	394	108	16	0	5	(-	-)	139	41	40	49	31	3	62	3	5	5	9	4	.69	13	.274	.328	.353
2004	Lkland	A+	92	327	94	20	2	0	(-	-)	118	36	38	43	25	1	56	7	1	2	3	2	.60	9	.287	.349	.361
2004	Erie	AA	5	20	2	0	0	0	(-	-)	2	0	2	0	1	0	4	1	0	0	0	0	-	0	.100	.182	.100
2005	Erie	AA	77	282	77	18	1	2	(-	-)	103	33	26	36	18	1	42	9	3	2	0	1	.00	6	.273	.334	.365
2006	Erie	AA	62	213	59	13	1	6	(-	-)	92	31	28	34	19	0	38	9	1	0	2	1	.67	7	.277	.361	.432
2006	Toledo	AAA	38	137	37	12	0	3	(-	-)	58	19	22	20	11	0	33	3	0	2	1	1	.50	3	.270	.333	.423
2006	Det	AL	1	1	0	0	0	0	(0	0)	0	0	0	0	0	0	1	0	0	0	0	0	-	0	.000	.000	.000

Brad Radke

Pitches: R **Bats:** R **Pos:** SP-28 **Ht:** 6'2" **Wt:** 185 **Born:** 10/27/1972 **Age:** 34

	HOW MUCH HE PITCHED							WHAT HE GAVE UP												THE RESULTS						
Year	Team	Lg	G	GS	CG	GF	IP	BFP	H	R	ER	HR	SH	SF	HB	TBB	IBB	SO	WP	Bk	W	L	Pct	ShO	Sv-Op Hld	ERC	ERA
1995	Min	AL	29	28	2	0	181.0	772	195	112	107	32	2	9	4	47	0	75	4	0	11	14	.440	1	0-0 0	4.58	5.32
1996	Min	AL	35	35	3	0	232.0	973	231	125	115	40	5	6	4	57	2	148	1	0	11	16	.407	1	0-0 0	3.97	4.46
1997	Min	AL	35	35	4	0	239.2	989	238	114	103	28	2	9	3	48	1	174	1	1	20	10	.667	1	0-0 0	3.41	3.87
1998	Min	AL	32	32	5	0	213.2	904	238	109	102	23	9	9	3	43	1	146	3	1	12	14	.462	1	0-0 0	4.18	4.30
1999	Min	AL	33	33	4	0	218.2	910	239	97	91	28	5	5	1	44	0	121	4	0	12	14	.462	1	0-0 0	4.07	3.75
2000	Min	AL	34	34	4	0	226.2	978	261	119	112	27	7	4	5	51	1	141	5	0	12	16	.429	1	0-0 0	4.44	4.45
2001	Min	AL	33	33	6	0	226.0	919	235	105	99	24	10	6	10	26	0	137	4	1	15	11	.577	2	0-0 0	3.45	3.94
2002	Min	AL	21	21	2	0	118.1	490	124	64	62	12	2	5	7	20	0	62	0	0	9	5	.643	1	0-0 0	3.73	4.72
2003	Min	AL	33	33	3	0	212.1	888	242	111	106	32	12	4	5	28	2	120	0	0	14	10	.583	1	0-0 0	4.24	4.49
2004	Min	AL	34	34	1	0	219.2	901	229	92	85	23	5	5	6	26	1	143	2	0	11	8	.579	1	0-0 0	3.35	3.48
2005	Min	AL	31	31	3	0	200.2	831	214	98	90	33	4	10	7	23	1	117	2	0	9	12	.429	1	0-0 0	3.86	4.04
2006	Min	AL	28	28	0	0	162.1	689	197	87	78	24	5	10	1	32	3	83	2	0	12	9	.571	0	0-0 0	4.91	4.32
12 ML YEARS			378	377	37	0	2451.0	10244	2643	1233	1150	326	68	76	62	445	12	1467	28	3	148	139	.516	10	0-0 0	3.99	4.22

Aramis Ramirez

Bats: R Throws: R Pos: 3B-156; PH-2   Ht: 6'1" Wt: 215 Born: 6/25/1978 Age: 29

Year	Team	Lg	G	AB	H	2B	3B	HR	(Hm	Rd)	TB	R	RBI	RC	TBB	IBB	SO	HBP	SH	SF	SB	CS	SB%	GDP	Avg	OBP	Slg
1998	Pit	NL	72	251	59	9	1	6	(3	3)	88	23	24	26	18	0	72	4	1	1	0	1	.00	3	.235	.296	.351
1999	Pit	NL	18	56	10	2	1	0	(0	0)	14	2	7	4	6	0	9	0	1	1	0	0	-	0	.179	.254	.250
2000	Pit	NL	73	254	65	15	2	6	(4	2)	102	19	35	28	10	0	36	5	1	4	0	0	-	9	.256	.293	.402
2001	Pit	NL	158	603	181	40	0	34	(16	18)	323	83	112	108	40	4	100	8	0	4	5	4	.56	9	.300	.350	.536
2002	Pit	NL	142	522	122	26	0	18	(7	11)	202	51	71	49	29	3	95	8	0	11	2	0	1.00	17	.234	.279	.387
2003	2 Tms	NL	159	607	165	32	2	27	(10	17)	282	75	106	88	42	3	99	10	0	11	2	2	.50	21	.272	.324	.465
2004	ChC	NL	145	547	174	32	1	36	(22	14)	316	99	103	100	49	6	62	3	0	7	0	2	.00	25	.318	.373	.578
2005	ChC	NL	123	463	140	30	0	31	(11	20)	263	72	92	79	35	4	60	6	0	2	0	1	.00	15	.302	.358	.568
2006	ChC	NL	157	594	173	38	4	38	(14	24)	333	93	119	109	50	4	63	9	0	7	2	1	.67	15	.291	.352	.561
03	Pit	NL	96	375	105	25	1	12	(6	6)	168	44	67	49	25	3	68	7	0	8	1	1	.50	17	.280	.330	.448
03	ChC	NL	63	232	60	7	1	15	(4	11)	114	31	39	39	17	0	31	3	0	3	1	1	.50	4	.259	.314	.491
9 ML YEARS			1047	3897	1089	224	11	196	(87	109)	1923	517	669	591	279	24	596	53	3	48	11	11	.50	114	.279	.332	.493

Elizardo Ramirez

Pitches: R Bats: L Pos: SP-19; RP-2   Ht: 6'0" Wt: 180 Born: 1/28/1983 Age: 24

Year	Team	Lg	G	GS	CG	GF	IP	BFP	H	R	ER	HR	SH	SF	HB	TBB	IBB	SO	WP	Bk	W	L	Pct	ShO	Sv-Op	Hld	ERC	ERA
2006	Dayton*	A	1	1	0	0	6.0	24	6	3	3	1	0	0	0	0	0	3	0	0	0	0	-	0	0--	-	2.87	4.50
2006	Lsvlle*	AAA	4	4	0	0	20.0	84	22	9	9	2	0	0	1	2	0	19	1	0	0	1	.000	0	0--	-	3.61	4.05
2004	Phi	NL	7	0	0	5	15.0	67	17	8	8	3	0	1	1	5	1	9	1	0	0	0	-	0	0-0	0	5.44	4.80
2005	Cin	NL	6	4	0	1	22.1	110	33	22	21	5	2	0	2	10	2	9	2	0	0	3	.000	0	0-0	0	8.45	8.46
2006	Cin	NL	21	19	0	1	104.0	465	123	70	62	14	5	3	8	29	2	69	0	3	4	9	.308	0	0-0	0	5.13	5.37
3 ML YEARS			34	23	0	7	141.1	642	173	100	91	22	7	4	11	44	5	87	3	3	4	12	.250	0	0-0	0	5.66	5.79

Hanley Ramirez

Bats: R Throws: R Pos: SS-154; PR-3; PH-2   Ht: 6'3" Wt: 195 Born: 12/23/1983 Age: 23

Year	Team	Lg	G	AB	H	2B	3B	HR	(Hm	Rd)	TB	R	RBI	RC	TBB	IBB	SO	HBP	SH	SF	SB	CS	SB%	GDP	Avg	OBP	Slg
2002	RedSx	R	45	164	56	11	3	6	(-	-)	91	29	26	35	16	1	15	2	0	2	8	6	.57	5	.341	.402	.555
2002	Lowell	A-	22	97	36	9	2	1	(-	-)	52	17	19	19	4	0	14	2	0	2	4	3	.57	2	.371	.400	.536
2003	Augsta	A	111	422	116	24	3	8	(-	-)	170	69	50	59	32	0	73	2	5	3	36	13	.73	12	.275	.327	.403
2004	Srsota	A+	62	239	74	8	4	1	(-	-)	93	33	24	35	17	1	39	4	2	1	12	7	.63	2	.310	.364	.389
2004	RedSx	R	6	20	8	0	1	0	(-	-)	10	5	7	5	2	0	3	2	0	2	1	0	1.00	1	.400	.462	.500
2004	PortInd	AA	32	129	40	7	2	5	(-	-)	66	26	15	24	10	0	26	0	0	0	12	3	.80	7	.310	.360	.512
2005	PortInd	AA	122	465	126	21	7	6	(-	-)	179	66	52	63	39	1	62	7	6	3	26	13	.67	12	.271	.335	.385
2005	Bos	AL	2	2	0	0	0	0	(0	0)	0	0	0	0	0	0	2	0	0	0	0	0	-	0	.000	.000	.000
2006	Fla	NL	158	633	185	46	11	17	(9	8)	304	119	59	101	56	0	128	4	5	2	51	15	.77	7	.292	.353	.480
2 ML YEARS			160	635	185	46	11	17	(9	8)	304	119	59	101	56	0	130	4	5	2	51	15	.77	7	.291	.352	.479

Horacio Ramirez

Pitches: L Bats: L Pos: SP-14   Ht: 6'1" Wt: 210 Born: 11/24/1979 Age: 27

Year	Team	Lg	G	GS	CG	GF	IP	BFP	H	R	ER	HR	SH	SF	HB	TBB	IBB	SO	WP	Bk	W	L	Pct	ShO	Sv-Op	Hld	ERC	ERA
2006	Rome*	A	1	1	0	0	4.2	20	5	2	2	1	0	0	0	3	0	1	0	0	0	0	-	0	0--	-	6.93	3.86
2006	Rchmd*	AAA	3	3	0	0	12.2	56	18	8	8	1	0	0	0	1	0	10	0	0	1	1	.500	0	0--	-	5.01	5.68
2003	Atl	NL	29	29	1	0	182.1	781	181	91	81	21	12	3	6	72	10	100	5	1	12	4	.750	0	0-0	0	4.21	4.00
2004	Atl	NL	10	9	1	0	60.1	259	51	24	16	7	2	1	0	30	5	31	0	2	2	4	.333	0	0-0	0	3.55	2.39
2005	Atl	NL	33	32	1	0	202.1	847	214	108	104	31	13	5	2	67	4	80	4	1	11	9	.550	1	0-0	0	4.66	4.63
2006	Atl	NL	14	14	0	0	76.1	337	85	42	38	6	3	3	4	31	2	37	0	1	5	5	.500	0	0-0	0	4.82	4.48
4 ML YEARS			86	84	3	0	521.1	2224	531	265	239	65	30	12	12	200	21	248	9	5	30	22	.577	1	0-0	0	4.39	4.13

Manny Ramirez

Bats: R Throws: R Pos: LF-123; DH-5; PH-2   Ht: 6'0" Wt: 200 Born: 5/30/1972 Age: 35

Year	Team	Lg	G	AB	H	2B	3B	HR	(Hm	Rd)	TB	R	RBI	RC	TBB	IBB	SO	HBP	SH	SF	SB	CS	SB%	GDP	Avg	OBP	Slg
1993	Cle	AL	22	53	9	1	0	2	(0	2)	16	5	5	2	2	0	8	0	0	0	0	0	-	3	.170	.200	.302
1994	Cle	AL	91	290	78	22	0	17	(9	8)	151	51	60	53	42	4	72	0	0	4	4	2	.67	6	.269	.357	.521
1995	Cle	AL	137	484	149	26	1	31	(12	19)	270	85	107	103	75	6	112	5	2	5	6	6	.50	13	.308	.402	.558
1996	Cle	AL	152	550	170	45	3	33	(19	14)	320	94	112	120	85	8	104	3	0	9	8	5	.62	18	.309	.399	.582
1997	Cle	AL	150	561	184	40	0	26	(14	12)	302	99	88	117	79	5	115	7	0	4	2	3	.40	19	.328	.415	.538
1998	Cle	AL	150	571	168	35	2	45	(25	20)	342	108	145	121	76	6	121	6	0	10	5	3	.63	18	.294	.377	.599
1999	Cle	AL	147	522	174	34	3	44	(21	23)	346	131	165	141	96	9	131	13	0	7	2	4	.33	12	.333	.442	.663
2000	Cle	AL	118	439	154	34	2	38	(22	16)	306	92	122	127	86	9	117	3	0	4	1	1	.50	9	.351	.457	.697
2001	Bos	AL	142	529	162	33	2	41	(21	20)	322	93	125	122	81	25	147	8	0	2	0	0	-	9	.306	.405	.609
2002	Bos	AL	120	436	152	31	0	33	(18	15)	282	84	107	125	73	14	85	8	0	1	0	0	-	13	.349	.450	.647
2003	Bos	AL	154	569	185	36	1	37	(18	19)	334	117	104	128	97	28	94	8	0	5	3	1	.75	22	.325	.427	.587
2004	Bos	AL	152	568	175	44	0	43	(23	20)	348	108	130	124	82	15	124	6	0	7	2	4	.33	17	.308	.397	.613
2005	Bos	AL	152	554	162	30	1	45	(22	23)	329	112	144	134	80	9	119	10	0	6	1	0	1.00	20	.292	.388	.594
2006	Bos	AL	130	449	144	27	1	35	(16	19)	278	79	102	114	100	16	102	1	0	8	0	1	.00	13	.321	.439	.619
14 ML YEARS			1817	6575	2066	438	16	470	(240	230)	3946	1258	1516	1531	1054	154	1451	78	2	74	34	31	.52	192	.314	.411	.600

Ramon Ramirez

Pitches: R Bats: R Pos: RP-61   Ht: 5'11" Wt: 190 Born: 8/31/1981 Age: 25

			HOW MUCH HE PITCHED						WHAT HE GAVE UP										THE RESULTS						
Year	Team	Lg	G	GS	CG	GF	IP	BFP	H	R	ER	HR	SH	SF	HB	TBB	IBB	SO	WP	Bk	W	L	Pct	ShO	Sv-Op Hld	ERC	ERA
2003	Tampa	A+	14	14	0	0	74.1	327	88	47	43	7	1	2	2	20	2	70	3	1	2	8	.200	0	0-- -	4.60	5.21
2003	Trntn	AA	4	3	0	0	21.1	88	18	8	4	3	0	1	0	8	1	21	0	1	1	1	.500	0	0-- -	3.35	1.69
2003	Clmbs	AAA	2	1	0	0	6.0	25	5	5	3	1	0	0	0	1	0	5	0	0	0	1	.000	0	0-- -	2.53	4.50
2004	Clmbs	AAA	4	4	0	0	18.0	87	25	19	17	3	0	3	0	8	1	17	1	0	0	3	.000	0	0-- -	6.87	8.50
2004	Trntn	AA	18	18	2	0	115.0	45	116	60	59	11	6	4	3	32	0	128	9	3	4	6	.400	0	0-- -	45.67	4.62
2005	Clmbs	AAA	6	6	0	0	27.0	115	32	16	16	3	0	4	1	9	0	26	1	0	1	3	.250	0	0-- -	5.37	5.33
2005	Trntn	AA	15	15	0	0	89.0	375	79	44	38	10	1	3	1	35	0	82	4	1	6	5	.545	0	0-- -	3.56	3.84
2005	Tulsa	AA	9	3	0	2	25.1	110	27	17	15	6	1	1	1	8	0	23	3	0	2	1	.667	0	0-- -	5.24	5.33
2006	ColSpr	AAA	1	0	0	1	1.0	3	0	0	0	0	0	0	0	0	0	1	0	0	0	0	-	0	0-- -	0.00	0.00
2006	Col	NL	61	0	0	14	67.2	285	58	28	26	5	2	3	1	27	3	61	2	0	4	3	.571	0	0-2 10	3.09	3.46

Santiago Ramirez

Pitches: R Bats: R Pos: RP-4   Ht: 5'11" Wt: 210 Born: 8/15/1978 Age: 28

			HOW MUCH HE PITCHED						WHAT HE GAVE UP										THE RESULTS						
Year	Team	Lg	G	GS	CG	GF	IP	BFP	H	R	ER	HR	SH	SF	HB	TBB	IBB	SO	WP	Bk	W	L	Pct	ShO	Sv-Op Hld	ERC	ERA
1999	Mrtnsvl	R+	25	0	0	45	31.0	127	26	9	5	1	1	0	0	14	1	35	7	1	2	1	.667	0	17-- -	2.98	1.45
2000	Mich	A	23	0	0	12	29.2	146	27	28	20	6	1	0	3	32	1	22	3	1	3	3	.500	0	5-- -	7.67	6.07
2000	Auburn	A-	20	9	0	9	53.0	228	36	34	25	3	0	2	4	39	1	57	9	1	3	6	.333	0	2-- -	3.62	4.25
2001	Lxngtn	A	45	0	0	23	79.1	328	69	35	32	2	4	2	3	28	1	85	8	1	8	2	.800	0	4-- -	2.86	3.63
2002	RdRck	AA	33	0	0	18	63.1	262	45	19	18	3	2	2	6	26	3	73	1	0	5	2	.714	0	4-- -	2.52	2.56
2002	NewOrl	AAA	18	0	0	5	21.1	91	17	8	8	2	0	0	3	11	0	15	3	1	2	0	1.000	0	1-- -	4.00	3.38
2003	NewOrl	AAA	10	0	0	4	12.2	56	7	7	6	1	0	4	4	9	0	7	1	0	4	0	1.000	0	0-- -	3.89	4.26
2003	RdRck	AA	6	1	0	2	5.1	22	5	0	0	0	0	0	0	4	0	3	1	0	0	0	-	0	0-- -	4.84	0.00
2004	RdRck	AA	55	0	0	50	78.2	345	71	24	23	1	0	1	1	38	6	83	3	0	6	4	.600	0	32-- -	3.10	2.63
2005	Omha	AAA	50	1	0	41	67.1	307	81	43	39	11	4	2	1	21	3	53	2	1	5	5	.500	0	17-- -	5.18	5.21
2006	NewOr	AAA	19	0	0	14	27.1	97	16	3	3	1	1	0	0	4	1	28	0	0	2	1	.667	0	7-- -	1.12	0.99
2006	Was	NL	4	0	0	1	3.1	18	6	3	3	1	0	0	0	2	0	1	0	0	0	0	-	0	0-0 1	11.76	8.10

Joe Randa

Bats: R Throws: R Pos: 3B-42; PH-34; 1B-15; DH-3   Ht: 5'11" Wt: 190 Born: 12/18/1969 Age: 37

			BATTING																BASERUNNING				AVERAGES		
Year	Team	Lg	G	AB	H	2B	3B	HR	(Hm	Rd)	TB	R	RBI	RC	TBB	IBB	SO	HBP	SH	SF	SB	CS	SB%	GDP	Avg	OBP	Slg
2006	Indy*	AAA	2	8	4	0	0	0	(-	-)	4	1	0	2	1	0	1	0	0	0	0	0	-	0	.500	.556	.500
1995	KC	AL	34	70	12	2	0	1	(1	0)	17	6	5	3	6	0	17	0	0	0	0	1	.00	2	.171	.237	.243
1996	KC	AL	110	337	102	24	1	6	(2	4)	146	36	47	50	26	4	47	1	2	4	13	4	.76	10	.303	.351	.433
1997	Pit	NL	126	443	134	27	9	7	(5	2)	200	58	60	72	41	1	64	6	4	5	4	2	.67	10	.302	.366	.451
1998	Det	AL	138	460	117	21	2	9	(3	6)	169	56	50	54	41	1	70	7	3	3	8	7	.53	9	.254	.323	.367
1999	KC	AL	156	628	197	36	8	16	(7	9)	297	92	84	103	50	4	80	3	1	7	5	4	.56	15	.314	.363	.473
2000	KC	AL	158	612	186	29	4	15	(9	6)	268	88	106	88	36	3	66	6	1	10	6	3	.67	19	.304	.343	.438
2001	KC	AL	151	581	147	34	2	13	(8	5)	224	59	83	67	42	2	80	6	1	6	3	2	.60	15	.253	.307	.386
2002	KC	AL	151	549	155	36	5	11	(6	5)	234	63	80	77	46	1	69	9	2	11	2	1	.67	13	.282	.341	.426
2003	KC	AL	131	502	146	31	1	16	(9	7)	227	80	72	79	41	0	61	7	9	7	1	0	1.00	11	.291	.348	.452
2004	KC	AL	128	485	139	31	2	8	(1	7)	198	65	56	67	44	1	77	6	0	8	0	1	.00	11	.287	.343	.408
2005	2 Tms	NL	150	555	153	43	2	17	(11	6)	251	71	68	71	47	3	81	4	0	3	0	1	.00	11	.276	.335	.452
2006	Pit	NL	89	206	55	13	0	4	(1	3)	80	23	28	21	16	2	26	0	2	3	0	0	-	12	.267	.316	.388
05	Cin	NL	92	332	96	26	1	13	(9	4)	163	44	48	50	33	2	52	2	0	1	0	0	-	6	.289	.356	.491
05	SD	NL	58	223	57	17	1	4	(2	2)	88	27	20	21	14	1	29	2	0	2	0	1	.00	5	.256	.303	.395
12 ML YEARS			1522	5428	1543	327	36	123	(63	60)	2311	697	739	752	432	22	738	55	25	67	42	26	.62	139	.284	.339	.426

Darrell Rasner

Pitches: R Bats: R Pos: SP-3; RP-3   Ht: 6'3" Wt: 210 Born: 1/13/1981 Age: 26

			HOW MUCH HE PITCHED						WHAT HE GAVE UP										THE RESULTS						
Year	Team	Lg	G	GS	CG	GF	IP	BFP	H	R	ER	HR	SH	SF	HB	TBB	IBB	SO	WP	Bk	W	L	Pct	ShO	Sv-Op Hld	ERC	ERA
2002	Vrmnt	A-	10	10	0	0	43.2	189	44	27	21	7	0	0	3	18	0	49	4	0	2	5	.286	0	0-- -	3.93	4.33
2003	Savann	A	22	22	2	0	105.1	458	106	53	49	8	5	2	7	36	0	90	9	1	7	7	.500	0	0-- -	3.94	4.19
2004	BrvdCt	A+	22	21	0	0	119.1	522	133	55	42	6	10	4	8	31	0	88	1	1	6	5	.545	0	0-- -	4.04	3.17
2004	Hrsbrg	AA	5	5	0	0	29.2	119	21	4	4	1	3	2	2	9	1	15	0	0	1	1	.500	0	0-- -	2.01	1.21
2005	Hrsbrg	AA	27	26	1	0	150.1	630	150	66	60	10	7	5	10	29	2	96	2	0	6	7	.462	0	0-- -	3.26	3.59
2006	Clmbs	AAA	10	10	0	0	58.2	242	60	22	18	4	1	1	1	11	0	47	0	0	4	0	1.000	0	0-- -	3.25	2.76
2006	Yanks	R	2	2	0	0	6.0	23	5	3	3	0	0	0	0	1	0	6	1	0	0	0	-	0	0-- -	1.84	4.50
2006	Tampa	A+	2	2	0	0	7.0	36	12	3	2	0	0	0	1	3	0	6	0	0	0	0	-	0	0-- -	8.38	2.57
2005	Was	NL	5	1	0	1	7.1	31	5	3	3	0	1	0	2	2	1	4	0	0	0	1	.000	0	0-0 0	2.03	3.68
2006	NYY	AL	6	3	0	1	20.1	83	18	10	10	2	1	0	1	5	0	11	1	0	3	1	.750	0	0-0 0	3.07	4.43
2 ML YEARS			11	4	0	2	27.2	114	23	13	13	2	2	0	3	7	1	15	1	0	3	2	.600	0	0-0 0	2.79	4.23

Jon Rauch

Pitches: R Bats: R Pos: RP-85   Ht: 6'11" Wt: 260 Born: 9/27/1978 Age: 28

			HOW MUCH HE PITCHED						WHAT HE GAVE UP										THE RESULTS						
Year	Team	Lg	G	GS	CG	GF	IP	BFP	H	R	ER	HR	SH	SF	HB	TBB	IBB	SO	WP	Bk	W	L	Pct	ShO	Sv-Op Hld	ERC	ERA
2002	CWS	AL	8	6	0	1	28.2	130	28	26	21	7	0	1	2	14	2	19	1	1	2	1	.667	0	0-0 0	5.41	6.59
2004	2 Tms		11	4	0	1	32.0	131	30	10	10	1	2	1	0	11	2	22	2	0	4	1	.800	0	0-0 0	3.05	2.81
2005	Was	NL	15	1	0	4	30.0	124	24	12	12	3	1	1	1	11	2	23	2	0	2	4	.333	0	0-0 0	2.90	3.60
2006	Was	NL	85	0	0	19	91.1	383	78	37	34	13	1	6	2	36	6	86	1	0	4	5	.444	0	2-5 18	3.52	3.35

	HOW MUCH HE PITCHED						WHAT HE GAVE UP												THE RESULTS						
Year Team Lg	G	GS	CG	GF	IP	BFP	H	R	ER	HR	SH	SF	HB	TBB	IBB	SO	WP	Bk	W	L	Pct	ShO	Sv-Op	Hld	ERC	ERA
04 CWS AL	2	2	0	0	8.2	43	16	6	6	0	1	1	0	4	0	4	1	0	1	1	.500	0	0-0	-	9.15	6.23
04 Mon NL	9	2	0	1	23.1	88	14	4	4	1	1	0	0	7	2	18	1	0	3	0	1.000	0	0-0	-	1.44	1.54
4 ML YEARS	119	11	0	25	182.0	768	160	85	77	24	4	9	5	72	12	150	9	2	12	11	.522	0	2-5	18	3.62	3.81

Chris Ray

Pitches: R **Bats:** R **Pos:** RP-61 **Ht:** 6'3" **Wt:** 225 **Born:** 1/12/1982 **Age:** 25

	HOW MUCH HE PITCHED						WHAT HE GAVE UP												THE RESULTS						
Year Team Lg	G	GS	CG	GF	IP	BFP	H	R	ER	HR	SH	SF	HB	TBB	IBB	SO	WP	Bk	W	L	Pct	ShO	Sv-Op	Hld	ERC	ERA
2003 Abrdn A-	9	8	0	0	38.1	161	32	15	12	0	0	0	4	10	0	44	0	0	2	0	1.000	0	0- -	-	2.36	2.82
2004 Dlmrva A	10	9	0	0	50.0	210	43	21	19	3	3	4	5	17	0	46	1	1	2	3	.400	0	0- -	-	3.21	3.42
2004 Frdrck A+	14	14	1	0	73.1	322	82	31	31	6	5	2	1	20	0	74	3	0	6	3	.667	1	0- -	-	4.07	3.80
2005 Bowie AA	31	0	0	28	37.1	136	17	5	4	3	1	2	3	7	0	40	1	0	1	2	.333	0	18- -	-	1.15	0.96
2005 Bal AL	41	0	0	8	40.2	174	34	15	12	5	1	1	1	18	3	43	0	1	1	3	.250	0	0-4	8	3.43	2.66
2006 Bal AL	61	0	0	56	66.0	267	45	22	20	10	2	4	1	27	2	51	2	0	4	4	.500	0	33-38	0	2.77	2.73
2 ML YEARS	102	0	0	64	106.2	441	79	37	32	15	3	5	2	45	5	94	2	1	5	7	.417	0	33-42	8	3.02	2.70

Ken Ray

Pitches: R **Bats:** R **Pos:** RP-69 **Ht:** 6'2" **Wt:** 200 **Born:** 11/27/1974 **Age:** 32

	HOW MUCH HE PITCHED						WHAT HE GAVE UP												THE RESULTS						
Year Team Lg	G	GS	CG	GF	IP	BFP	H	R	ER	HR	SH	SF	HB	TBB	IBB	SO	WP	Bk	W	L	Pct	ShO	Sv-Op	Hld	ERC	ERA
1993 Royals R	13	7	0	3	47.1	204	44	21	12	1	1	3	0	17	0	45	6	0	2	3	.400	0	0- -	-	2.91	2.28
1994 Rckford A	27	18	0	6	128.2	516	94	34	26	5	4	1	0	56	2	128	18	2	10	4	.714	0	3- -	-	2.44	1.82
1995 Wilmg A+	13	13	1	0	77.0	320	74	32	23	3	3	3	1	22	2	63	17	2	6	4	.600	0	0- -	-	3.04	2.69
1995 Wichta AA	14	14	0	0	75.1	342	83	55	50	7	1	0	1	46	0	53	8	1	4	5	.444	0	0- -	-	5.62	5.97
1996 Wichta AA	22	22	1	0	120.2	553	151	94	82	17	5	6	1	57	1	79	15	1	4	12	.250	0	0- -	-	6.26	6.12
1997 Omha AAA	25	21	2	1	113.0	516	131	86	80	21	2	5	4	63	2	96	8	1	5	12	.294	0	0- -	-	6.59	6.37
1998 Wichta AA	24	21	0	0	117.2	530	149	79	68	7	5	5	3	47	2	71	1	0	10	5	.667	0	0- -	-	5.48	5.20
1999 Wichta AA	14	0	0	13	21.1	90	23	12	12	2	1	0	1	10	0	18	1	1	0	0	-	0	7- -	-	5.29	5.06
1999 Omha AAA	27	0	0	23	43.1	184	41	27	25	9	1	2	1	12	1	36	3	0	1	0	1.000	0	8- -	-	3.98	5.19
2000 Fresno AAA	7	0	0	1	9.2	49	13	10	8	4	1	1	0	8	0	8	2	0	0	0	-	0	0- -	-	10.92	7.45
2003 Hi Dsrt A+	7	0	0	2	14.0	70	22	13	12	4	0	1	0	6	0	18	0	0	1	1	.500	0	0- -	-	9.14	7.71
2003 Hntsvl AA	31	0	0	15	61.1	262	65	25	20	6	5	2	3	25	0	49	1	0	2	1	.667	0	4- -	-	4.80	2.93
2004 WinSa A+	29	18	0	2	123.2	510	124	63	56	12	3	6	4	43	2	99	5	0	12	8	.600	0	1- -	-	4.15	4.08
2005 Rchmd AAA	17	10	0	3	67.0	298	68	34	29	6	7	4	4	35	1	40	2	0	2	4	.333	0	0- -	-	4.84	3.90
1999 KC AL	13	0	0	4	11.1		23	12	11	2	0	0	1	6	0	0	0	0	1	0	1.000	0	0-0	1	-	8.74
2006 Atl NL	69	0	0	29	67.2	299	66	36	34	9	4	2	0	38	4	50	0	0	1	1	.500	0	5-8	7	4.75	4.52
2 ML YEARS	82	0	0	33	79.0	299	89	48	45	11	4	2	1	44	4	50	0	0	2	1	.667	0	5-8	8	7.06	5.13

Britt Reames

Pitches: R **Bats:** R **Pos:** RP-6 **Ht:** 5'11" **Wt:** 180 **Born:** 8/19/1973 **Age:** 33

	HOW MUCH HE PITCHED						WHAT HE GAVE UP												THE RESULTS						
Year Team Lg	G	GS	CG	GF	IP	BFP	H	R	ER	HR	SH	SF	HB	TBB	IBB	SO	WP	Bk	W	L	Pct	ShO	Sv-Op	Hld	ERC	ERA
2006 Indy* AAA	14	11	0	0	64.1	274	62	22	20	3	4	1	0	14	2	43	2	0	4	2	.667	0	0- -	-	2.67	2.80
2000 StL NL	8	7	0	0	40.2	170	30	17	13	4	0	1	0	23	1	31	2	1	2	1	.667	0	0-0	0	3.39	2.88
2001 Mon NL	41	13	0	3	95.0	432	101	68	59	16	7	2	5	48	3	86	2	0	4	8	.333	0	0-1	6	5.52	5.59
2002 Mon NL	42	6	0	7	68.0	308	70	42	38	8	3	1	3	38	6	76	2	0	1	4	.200	0	0-1	6	5.04	5.03
2003 Mon NL	2	0	0	0	1.1	10	4	4	4	0	0	0	0	2	0	1	0	0	0	0	-	0	0-0	0	22.07	27.00
2005 Oak AL	2	0	0	0	5.2	29	10	6	6	2	0	1	1	2	0	4	1	0	0	0	-	0	0-0	0	12.07	9.53
2006 Pit NL	6	0	0	5	7.1	37	11	8	8	2	0	1	0	5	1	6	1	0	0	0	-	0	0-0	0	9.74	9.82
6 ML YEARS	101	26	0	15	218.0	986	226	145	128	32	10	6	10	118	11	204	8	1	7	13	.350	0	0-2	12	5.31	5.28

Mark Redman

Pitches: L **Bats:** L **Pos:** SP-29 **Ht:** 6'5" **Wt:** 245 **Born:** 1/5/1974 **Age:** 33

	HOW MUCH HE PITCHED						WHAT HE GAVE UP												THE RESULTS						
Year Team Lg	G	GS	CG	GF	IP	BFP	H	R	ER	HR	SH	SF	HB	TBB	IBB	SO	WP	Bk	W	L	Pct	ShO	Sv-Op	Hld	ERC	ERA
2006 Wichta* AA	2	2	0	0	10.0	39	6	2	1	0	0	0	1	1	0	9	0	0	0	0	-	0	0- -	-	1.08	0.90
1999 Min AL	5	1	0	0	12.2	65	17	13	12	3	0	0	1	7	0	11	0	0	1	0	1.000	0	0-0	0	7.86	8.53
2000 Min AL	32	24	0	3	151.1	651	168	81	80	22	3	2	3	45	0	117	6	0	12	9	.571	0	0-0	0	4.73	4.76
2001 2 Tms AL	11	11	0	0	58.0	261	68	32	29	7	2	0	1	23	0	33	6	0	2	6	.250	0	0-0	0	5.26	4.50
2002 Det AL	30	30	3	0	203.0	858	211	107	95	15	5	8	6	51	2	109	11	1	8	15	.348	0	0-0	0	3.64	4.21
2003 Fla NL	29	29	3	0	190.2	802	172	82	76	16	10	5	5	61	3	151	8	2	14	9	.609	0	0-0	0	3.17	3.59
2004 Oak AL	32	32	2	0	191.0	832	218	100	100	28	5	7	6	68	6	102	6	1	11	12	.478	0	0-0	0	5.23	4.71
2005 Pit NL	30	30	2	0	178.1	751	188	100	97	18	11	5	2	56	3	101	7	3	5	15	.250	1	0-0	0	4.15	4.90
2006 KC AL	29	29	2	0	167.0	740	202	110	106	19	6	4	8	63	1	76	12	2	11	10	.524	1	0-0	0	5.63	5.71
01 Min AL	9	9	0	0	49.0	219	57	26	23	6	1	0	1	19	0	29	6	0	2	4	.333	0	0-0	0	5.11	4.22
01 Det AL	2	2	0	0	9.0	42	11	6	6	1	1	0	1	4	0	4	0	0	0	2	.000	0	0-0	0	6.12	6.00
8 ML YEARS	198	186	12	3	1152.0	4960	1244	635	595	128	42	31	32	374	15	700	56	9	64	76	.457	2	0-0	0	4.43	4.65

Mike Redmond

Bats: R **Throws:** R **Pos:** C-43; PH-3; DH-2 **Ht:** 5'11" **Wt:** 200 **Born:** 5/5/1971 **Age:** 36

	BATTING																		BASERUNNING				AVERAGES		
Year Team Lg	G	AB	H	2B	3B	HR	(Hm	Rd)	TB	R	RBI	RC	TBB	IBB	SO	HBP	SH	SF	SB	CS	SB%	GDP	Avg	OBP	Slg
1998 Fla NL	37	118	39	9	0	2	(1	1)	54	10	12	18	5	2	16	2	4	0	0	0	-	6	.331	.368	.458
1999 Fla NL	84	242	73	9	0	1	(0	1)	85	22	27	33	26	2	34	5	5	0	0	0	-	8	.302	.381	.351
2000 Fla NL	87	210	53	8	1	0	(0	0)	63	17	15	20	13	3	19	8	1	3	0	0	-	5	.252	.316	.300

210

Year	Team	Lg	G	AB	H	2B	3B	HR	(Hm	Rd)	TB	R	RBI	RC	TBB	IBB	SO	HBP	SH	SF	SB	CS	SB%	GDP	Avg	OBP	Slg
2001	Fla	NL	48	141	44	4	0	4	(3	1)	60	19	14	21	13	4	13	2	1	1	0	0	-	6	.312	.376	.426
2002	Fla	NL	89	256	78	15	0	2	(1	1)	99	19	28	37	21	8	34	8	2	3	0	2	.00	4	.305	.372	.387
2003	Fla	NL	59	125	30	7	1	0	(0	0)	39	12	11	10	7	0	16	5	2	2	0	0	-	2	.240	.302	.312
2004	Fla	NL	81	246	63	15	0	2	(0	2)	84	19	25	27	14	0	28	8	3	2	1	0	1.00	10	.256	.315	.341
2005	Min	AL	45	148	46	9	0	1	(0	1)	58	17	26	23	6	0	14	3	2	0	0	0	-	9	.311	.350	.392
2006	Min	AL	47	179	61	13	0	0	(0	0)	74	20	23	22	4	0	18	4	1	2	0	0	-	9	.341	.365	.413
9 ML YEARS			577	1665	487	89	2	12	(5	7)	616	155	181	211	109	19	192	45	21	13	1	2	.33	59	.292	.350	.370

Eric Reed

Bats: L **Throws:** L **Pos:** CF-31; PR-13; PH-6; LF-1   **Ht:** 5'11" **Wt:** 170 **Born:** 12/2/1980 **Age:** 26

Year	Team	Lg	G	AB	H	2B	3B	HR	(Hm	Rd)	TB	R	RBI	RC	TBB	IBB	SO	HBP	SH	SF	SB	CS	SB%	GDP	Avg	OBP	Slg
2002	Jmstwn	A	60	250	77	5	1	0	(-	-)	84	35	17	31	17	1	30	0	1	3	19	10	.66	3	.308	.348	.336
2002	Kane	A	12	50	18	1	0	0	(-	-)	19	11	2	8	3	0	11	0	2	0	7	1	.88	1	.360	.396	.380
2003	Jupiter	A+	134	514	154	15	8	0	(-	-)	185	86	25	76	52	4	83	3	19	0	53	18	.75	4	.300	.367	.360
2004	Carlina	AA	55	222	68	9	6	3	(-	-)	98	32	14	36	14	1	55	0	1	2	24	6	.80	2	.306	.345	.441
2005	Carlina	AA	71	271	69	9	0	1	(-	-)	81	35	15	27	17	1	62	4	3	3	23	8	.74	2	.255	.305	.299
2005	Albq	AAA	39	171	53	5	4	1	(-	-)	69	19	20	24	3	0	31	4	2	1	17	7	.71	1	.310	.335	.404
2006	Albq	AAA	95	390	118	20	9	5	(-	-)	171	68	39	60	24	1	94	2	1	3	20	9	.69	7	.303	.344	.438
2006	Fla	NL	42	41	4	0	0	0	(0	0)	4	6	0	0	2	1	10	2	2	0	3	1	.75	1	.098	.178	.098

Jeremy Reed

Bats: L **Throws:** L **Pos:** CF-64; PH-4; PR-1   **Ht:** 6'0" **Wt:** 200 **Born:** 6/15/1981 **Age:** 26

Year	Team	Lg	G	AB	H	2B	3B	HR	(Hm	Rd)	TB	R	RBI	RC	TBB	IBB	SO	HBP	SH	SF	SB	CS	SB%	GDP	Avg	OBP	Slg
2004	Sea	AL	18	58	23	4	0	0	(0	0)	27	11	5	11	7	1	4	1	0	0	3	1	.75	2	.397	.470	.466
2005	Sea	AL	141	488	124	33	3	3	(0	3)	172	61	45	49	48	1	74	2	4	2	12	11	.52	10	.254	.322	.352
2006	Sea	AL	67	212	46	6	5	6	(1	5)	80	27	17	13	11	1	31	2	2	2	2	3	.40	5	.217	.260	.377
3 ML YEARS			226	758	193	43	8	9	(1	8)	279	99	67	73	66	3	109	5	6	4	17	15	.53	17	.255	.317	.368

Kevin Reese

Bats: L **Throws:** L **Pos:** PH-6; LF-2; RF-2; PR-2   **Ht:** 5'11" **Wt:** 195 **Born:** 3/11/1978 **Age:** 29

Year	Team	Lg	G	AB	H	2B	3B	HR	(Hm	Rd)	TB	R	RBI	RC	TBB	IBB	SO	HBP	SH	SF	SB	CS	SB%	GDP	Avg	OBP	Slg
2000	Idaho	R+	53	201	72	14	4	2	(-	-)	100	51	36	51	43	2	30	3	0	2	12	3	.80	5	.358	.474	.498
2001	FtWyn	A	125	459	151	30	6	13	(-	-)	232	84	73	96	54	3	62	5	2	4	30	10	.75	5	.329	.402	.505
2002	Nrwich	AA	138	514	149	24	6	4	(-	-)	197	80	45	82	77	1	87	4	5	2	22	14	.61	6	.290	.385	.383
2003	Clmbs	AAA	15	55	12	1	0	1	(-	-)	16	11	3	5	6	0	8	0	2	0	1	0	1.00	1	.218	.295	.291
2003	Trntn	AA	86	309	84	13	2	4	(-	-)	113	42	21	42	25	1	58	2	4	2	27	5	.84	4	.272	.328	.366
2004	Trntn	AA	78	329	98	37	4	6	(-	-)	161	57	40	57	23	1	48	3	2	1	13	5	.72	5	.298	.348	.489
2004	Clmbs	AAA	53	217	70	13	3	8	(-	-)	113	41	28	40	12	0	34	5	5	1	4	4	.50	5	.323	.370	.521
2005	Clmbs	AAA	133	540	149	38	7	14	(-	-)	243	92	69	93	63	5	86	10	2	5	16	5	.76	10	.276	.359	.450
2006	Clmbs	AAA	53	212	60	8	2	5	(-	-)	87	30	21	31	15	1	37	10	0	3	4	6	.40	5	.283	.354	.410
2005	NYY	AL	2	1	0	0	0	0	(0	0)	0	0	0	0	1	0	1	0	0	0	0	0	-	0	.000	.000	.000
2006	NYY	AL	10	12	5	0	0	0	(0	0)	5	2	1	3	1	0	1	1	0	0	1	0	1.00	0	.417	.500	.417
2 ML YEARS			12	13	5	0	0	0	(0	0)	5	2	1	3	2	0	2	1	0	0	1	0	1.00	0	.385	.500	.385

Chris Reitsma

Pitches: R **Bats:** R **Pos:** RP-27   **Ht:** 6'5" **Wt:** 235 **Born:** 12/31/1977 **Age:** 29

			HOW MUCH HE PITCHED					WHAT HE GAVE UP												THE RESULTS						
Year	Team	Lg	G	GS	CG	GF	IP	BFP	H	R	ER	HR	SH	SF	HB	TBB	IBB	SO	WP	Bk	W	L	Pct	ShO	Sv-Op	Hld	ERC	ERA
2001	Cin	NL	36	29	0	1	182.0	800	209	121	107	23	13	8	5	49	6	96	5	0	7	15	.318	0	0-0	1	4.59	5.29
2002	Cin	NL	32	21	1	6	138.1	598	144	73	56	17	4	4	5	45	5	84	4	0	6	12	.333	1	0-0	0	4.24	3.64
2003	Cin	NL	57	3	0	36	84.0	351	92	41	40	14	4	1	0	19	6	53	2	0	9	5	.643	0	12-18	3	4.33	4.29
2004	Atl	NL	84	0	0	12	79.2	344	89	38	36	9	2	6	3	20	3	60	1	0	6	4	.600	0	2-9	31	4.32	4.07
2005	Atl	NL	76	0	0	37	73.1	307	79	32	32	3	1	2	0	14	3	42	2	0	3	6	.333	0	15-24	13	3.22	3.93
2006	Atl	NL	27	0	0	16	28.0	142	46	27	27	7	3	1	3	8	3	13	0	0	1	2	.333	0	8-12	3	8.85	8.68
6 ML YEARS			312	53	1	108	585.1	2542	659	332	298	73	27	22	16	155	26	348	14	0	32	44	.421	1	37-63	51	4.44	4.58

Mike Remlinger

Pitches: L **Bats:** L **Pos:** RP-36   **Ht:** 6'1" **Wt:** 215 **Born:** 3/23/1966 **Age:** 41

			HOW MUCH HE PITCHED					WHAT HE GAVE UP												THE RESULTS						
Year	Team	Lg	G	GS	CG	GF	IP	BFP	H	R	ER	HR	SH	SF	HB	TBB	IBB	SO	WP	Bk	W	L	Pct	ShO	Sv-Op	Hld	ERC	ERA
1991	SF	NL	8	6	1	1	35.0	155	36	17	17	5	1	1	0	20	1	19	2	1	2	1	.667	1	0-0	0	5.30	4.37
1994	NYM	NL	10	9	0	0	54.2	252	55	30	28	9	2	3	1	35	4	33	3	0	1	5	.167	0	0-0	1	5.46	4.61
1995	2 Tms	NL	7	0	0	4	6.2	34	9	6	5	1	1	0	0	5	0	7	0	0	0	1	.000	0	0-0	1	7.94	6.75
1996	Cin	NL	19	4	0	2	27.1	125	24	17	17	4	3	1	3	19	2	19	2	2	0	1	.000	0	0-0	1	5.23	5.60
1997	Cin	NL	69	12	2	10	124.0	525	100	61	57	11	6	4	7	60	6	145	12	2	8	8	.500	0	2-2	14	3.43	4.14
1998	Cin	NL	35	28	1	0	164.1	727	164	96	88	23	12	7	5	87	1	144	11	1	8	15	.348	1	0-0	0	5.04	4.82
1999	Atl	NL	73	0	0	14	83.2	346	66	24	22	9	2	1	1	35	5	81	5	0	10	1	.909	0	1-3	21	3.03	2.37
2000	Atl	NL	71	0	0	18	72.2	311	55	29	28	6	3	2	3	37	1	72	3	0	5	3	.625	0	12-16	23	3.15	3.47
2001	Atl	NL	74	0	0	6	75.0	313	67	25	23	4	9	0	2	23	4	93	4	0	3	3	.500	0	1-5	31	3.27	2.76
2002	Atl	NL	73	0	0	7	68.0	275	48	17	15	3	4	0	1	28	3	69	0	0	7	3	.700	0	0-5	30	2.24	1.99
2003	ChC	NL	73	0	0	26	69.0	301	54	30	28	11	2	2	7	39	4	83	2	0	6	5	.545	0	0-1	17	3.88	3.65
2004	ChC	NL	48	0	0	6	36.2	156	33	16	14	7	3	4	1	16	3	35	1	0	1	2	.333	0	2-6	13	3.53	3.44

HOW MUCH HE PITCHED					WHAT HE GAVE UP												THE RESULTS							
Year Team Lg	G	GS	CG	GF	IP	BFP	H	R	ER	HR	SH	SF	HB	TBB	IBB	SO	WP	Bk	W	L	Pct	ShO	Sv-Op	Hld	ERC	ERA
2005 2 Tms	43	0	0	9	39.2	182	46	33	29	7	3	0	2	17	2	35	2	0	0	3	.000	0	0-1	5	5.76	6.58
2006 Atl NL	36	0	0	7	22.1	104	27	11	10	2	1	0	2	9	2	19	1	0	2	4	.333	0	2-5	2	5.34	4.03
95 NYM NL	5	0	0	4	5.2	27	7	5	4	1	1	0	0	2	0	6	0	0	0	1	.000	0	0-1	0	5.47	6.35
95 Cin NL	2	0	0	0	1.0	7	2	1	1	0	0	0	0	3	0	1	0	0	0	0	-	0	0-0	0	24.60	9.00
05 ChC NL	35	0	0	7	33.0	141	31	19	18	5	3	0	2	12	2	30	0	0	0	3	.000	0	0-1	5	4.10	4.91
05 Bos AL	8	0	0	2	6.2	41	15	14	11	2	0	0	0	5	0	5	2	0	0	0	-	0	0-0	0	15.53	14.85
14 ML YEARS	639	59	4	110	879.0	3806	784	412	381	103	43	25	30	430	38	854	48	6	53	55	.491	2	20-45	158	4.00	3.90

Edgar Renteria

Bats: R **Throws:** R **Pos:** SS-146; PH-2; DH-1   **Ht:** 6'1" **Wt:** 200 **Born:** 8/7/1975 **Age:** 31

BATTING																		BASERUNNING				AVERAGES		
Year Team Lg	G	AB	H	2B	3B	HR	(Hm	Rd)	TB	R	RBI	RC	TBB	IBB	SO	HBP	SH	SF	SB	CS	SB%	GDP	Avg	OBP	Slg
1996 Fla NL	106	431	133	18	3	5	(2	3)	172	68	31	62	33	0	68	2	2	3	16	2	.89	12	.309	.358	.399
1997 Fla NL	154	617	171	21	3	4	(3	1)	210	90	52	68	45	1	108	4	19	6	32	15	.68	17	.277	.327	.340
1998 Fla NL	133	517	146	18	2	3	(2	1)	177	79	31	61	48	1	78	4	9	2	41	22	.65	13	.282	.347	.342
1999 StL NL	154	585	161	36	2	11	(6	5)	234	92	63	81	53	0	82	2	6	7	37	8	.82	16	.275	.334	.400
2000 StL NL	150	562	156	32	1	16	(4	12)	238	94	76	80	63	3	77	1	8	9	21	13	.62	19	.278	.346	.423
2001 StL NL	141	493	128	19	3	10	(3	7)	183	54	57	57	39	4	73	3	8	6	17	4	.81	15	.260	.314	.371
2002 StL NL	152	544	166	36	2	11	(4	7)	239	77	83	94	49	7	57	4	7	5	22	7	.76	17	.305	.364	.439
2003 StL NL	157	587	194	47	1	13	(4	9)	282	96	100	103	65	12	54	1	3	7	34	7	.83	21	.330	.394	.480
2004 StL NL	149	586	168	37	0	10	(7	3)	235	84	72	74	39	5	78	1	6	10	17	11	.61	14	.287	.327	.401
2005 Bos AL	153	623	172	36	4	8	(3	5)	240	100	70	82	55	0	100	3	6	5	9	4	.69	15	.276	.335	.385
2006 Atl NL	149	598	175	40	2	14	(4	10)	261	100	70	89	62	0	89	3	8	2	17	6	.74	17	.293	.361	.436
11 ML YEARS	1598	6143	1770	340	23	105	(42	63)	2471	934	705	851	551	33	864	28	82	62	263	99	.73	176	.288	.346	.402

Jason Repko

Bats: R **Throws:** R **Pos:** CF-40; RF-14; LF-13; PH-11; PR-11   **Ht:** 5'10" **Wt:** 190 **Born:** 12/27/1980 **Age:** 26

BATTING																		BASERUNNING				AVERAGES		
Year Team Lg	G	AB	H	2B	3B	HR	(Hm	Rd)	TB	R	RBI	RC	TBB	IBB	SO	HBP	SH	SF	SB	CS	SB%	GDP	Avg	OBP	Slg
1999 Gr Falls R+	49	207	63	9	9	8	(-	-)	114	51	32	42	21	0	43	3	1	1	12	5	.71	1	.304	.375	.551
2000 Yakima A-	8	17	5	2	0	0	(-	-)	7	3	1	2	1	0	7	0	0	0	0	0	-	0	.294	.333	.412
2001 Wilmg A	88	337	74	17	4	4	(-	-)	111	36	32	29	15	0	68	3	6	3	17	8	.68	2	.220	.257	.329
2002 VeroB A+	120	470	128	29	5	9	(-	-)	194	73	53	64	25	1	92	8	8	2	29	13	.69	3	.272	.319	.413
2003 Jaxnvl AA	119	416	100	14	5	10	(-	-)	154	62	23	53	42	0	89	6	9	3	21	8	.72	1	.240	.317	.370
2004 Jaxnvl AA	46	189	55	11	2	6	(-	-)	88	26	19	30	13	1	43	2	2	1	10	5	.67	1	.291	.341	.466
2004 LsVgs AAA	75	302	94	26	4	7	(-	-)	149	55	41	53	18	2	57	3	2	1	13	5	.72	4	.311	.355	.493
2005 LsVgs AAA	8	31	12	0	0	3	(-	-)	21	6	6	7	0	0	4	0	1	0	1	0	1.00	0	.387	.387	.677
2006 LsVgs AAA	9	29	8	2	0	0	(-	-)	10	2	2	4	3	0	6	2	0	0	1	0	1.00	1	.276	.382	.345
2005 LAD NL	129	276	61	15	3	8	(4	4)	106	43	30	28	16	1	80	7	2	0	5	0	1.00	7	.221	.281	.384
2006 LAD NL	69	130	33	5	1	3	(1	2)	49	21	16	21	15	1	24	3	2	0	10	4	.71	2	.254	.345	.377
2 ML YEARS	198	406	94	20	4	11	(5	6)	155	64	46	49	31	2	104	10	4	0	15	4	.79	9	.232	.302	.382

Chris Resop

Pitches: R **Bats:** R **Pos:** RP-22   **Ht:** 6'3" **Wt:** 220 **Born:** 11/4/1982 **Age:** 24

HOW MUCH HE PITCHED							WHAT HE GAVE UP												THE RESULTS							
Year Team Lg	G	GS	CG	GF	IP	BFP	H	R	ER	HR	SH	SF	HB	TBB	IBB	SO	WP	Bk	W	L	Pct	ShO	Sv-Op	Hld	ERC	ERA
2003 Grnsbr A	11	0	0	2	12.2	54	11	7	7	1	4	5	0	5	0	15	1	0	0	1	.000	0	0- -	-	3.13	4.97
2004 Grnsbr A	41	0	0	36	41.2	158	26	11	9	1	0	0	2	7	0	68	2	1	3	1	.750	0	13- -	-	1.31	1.94
2005 Carlina AA	43	0	0	40	49.0	210	47	15	14	2	1	1	0	16	1	56	4	0	3	2	.600	0	24- -	-	3.06	2.57
2006 Albq AAA	40	0	0	5	49.2	210	49	21	21	4	4	0	1	15	2	43	1	1	4	0	1.000	0	2- -	-	3.50	3.81
2005 Fla NL	15	0	0	6	17.0	80	22	16	16	1	0	2	1	9	0	15	3	0	2	0	1.000	0	0-0	0	6.35	8.47
2006 Fla NL	22	0	0	10	21.1	101	26	9	8	1	0	0	1	16	5	10	0	0	1	2	.333	0	0-1	2	6.30	3.38
2 ML YEARS	37	0	0	16	38.1	181	48	25	24	2	0	2	2	25	5	25	3	0	3	2	.600	0	0-1	2	6.33	5.63

Mike Restovich

Bats: R **Throws:** R **Pos:** PH-9; RF-2; LF-1   **Ht:** 6'4" **Wt:** 250 **Born:** 1/3/1979 **Age:** 28

BATTING																		BASERUNNING				AVERAGES		
Year Team Lg	G	AB	H	2B	3B	HR	(Hm	Rd)	TB	R	RBI	RC	TBB	IBB	SO	HBP	SH	SF	SB	CS	SB%	GDP	Avg	OBP	Slg
2006 Iowa* AAA	120	443	130	29	4	27	(-	-)	248	75	85	92	52	6	121	7	0	4	2	1	.67	9	.293	.374	.560
2002 Min AL	8	13	4	0	1	0	(0	1)	7	3	1	0	1	0	4	0	0	0	1	0	1.00	0	.308	.357	.538
2003 Min AL	24	53	15	3	2	0	(0	0)	22	10	4	8	10	0	12	1	0	0	0	0	-	3	.283	.406	.415
2004 Min AL	29	47	12	3	0	2	(1	1)	21	9	6	6	4	0	10	0	0	0	0	0	-	0	.255	.314	.447
2005 2 Tms NL	66	115	27	5	1	3	(1	2)	43	15	8	10	11	0	29	0	0	0	0	0	-	5	.235	.302	.374
2006 ChC NL	10	12	2	1	0	0	(0	0)	3	0	1	0	1	0	5	0	0	0	0	0	-	0	.167	.231	.250
05 Col NL	14	31	9	2	0	1	(1	0)	14	5	3	5	3	0	5	0	0	0	0	0	-	2	.290	.353	.452
05 Pit NL	52	84	18	3	1	2	(0	2)	29	10	5	5	8	0	24	0	0	0	0	0	-	3	.214	.283	.345
5 ML YEARS	137	240	60	12	3	6	(2	4)	96	37	20	25	27	0	60	1	0	0	1	0	1.00	10	.250	.328	.400

Anthony Reyes

Pitches: R **Bats:** R **Pos:** SP-17   **Ht:** 6'2" **Wt:** 215 **Born:** 10/16/1981 **Age:** 25

HOW MUCH HE PITCHED							WHAT HE GAVE UP												THE RESULTS							
Year Team Lg	G	GS	CG	GF	IP	BFP	H	R	ER	HR	SH	SF	HB	TBB	IBB	SO	WP	Bk	W	L	Pct	ShO	Sv-Op	Hld	ERC	ERA
2004 PlmBh A+	7	7	0	0	36.2	159	41	21	19	5	0	0	1	7	0	38	3	1	3	0	1.000	0	0- -	-	4.17	4.66
2004 Tenn AA	12	12	0	0	74.1	298	62	27	24	3	6	1	5	13	1	102	3	1	6	2	.750	0	0- -	-	2.24	2.91
2005 Memp AAA	23	23	2	0	128.2	525	105	55	52	13	5	4	4	34	0	136	3	0	7	6	.538	1	0- -	-	2.69	3.64

Year	Team	Lg	G	GS	CG	GF	IP	BFP	H	R	ER	HR	SH	SF	HB	TBB	IBB	SO	WP	Bk	W	L	Pct	ShO	Sv-Op	Hld	ERC	ERA
2006	Memp	AAA	13	13	0	0	84.0	333	70	27	24	9	3	1	2	11	0	82	7	1	6	1	.857	0	0--	-	2.31	2.57
2005	StL	NL	4	1	0	0	13.1	51	6	4	4	2	1	1	0	4	1	12	2	0	1	1	.500	0	0-0	0	1.32	2.70
2006	StL	NL	17	17	1	0	85.1	370	84	48	48	17	5	3	7	34	0	72	2	0	5	8	.385	0	0-0	0	5.08	5.06
2 ML YEARS			21	18	1	0	98.2	421	90	52	52	19	6	4	7	38	1	84	4	0	6	9	.400	0	0-0	0	4.46	4.74

Dennys Reyes

Pitches: L Bats: R Pos: RP-66   Ht: 6'3" Wt: 245 Born: 4/19/1977 Age: 30

Year	Team	Lg	G	GS	CG	GF	IP	BFP	H	R	ER	HR	SH	SF	HB	TBB	IBB	SO	WP	Bk	W	L	Pct	ShO	Sv-Op	Hld	ERC	ERA
2006	Roch*	AAA	4	3	0	0	18.0	66	11	1	1	0	1	1	1	3	0	13	0	0	1	0	1.000	0	0--	-	1.24	0.50
1997	LAD	NL	14	5	0	0	47.0	207	51	21	20	4	5	1	1	18	3	36	2	1	2	3	.400	0	0-0	0	4.34	3.83
1998	2 Tms	NL	19	10	0	4	67.1	300	62	36	34	3	7	2	1	47	5	77	6	1	3	5	.375	0	0-0	0	4.37	4.54
1999	Cin	NL	65	1	0	12	61.2	277	53	30	26	5	4	3	3	39	1	72	5	1	2	2	.500	0	2-3	14	4.16	3.79
2000	Cin	NL	62	0	0	15	43.2	200	43	31	22	5	3	3	1	29	0	36	6	0	2	1	.667	0	0-1	10	5.24	4.53
2001	Cin	NL	35	6	0	2	53.0	246	51	35	29	5	2	2	1	35	1	52	5	0	2	6	.250	0	0-0	6	4.77	4.92
2002	2 Tms	NL	58	5	0	15	82.2	378	98	52	49	10	3	2	0	45	4	59	10	1	4	4	.500	0	0-0	0	5.90	5.33
2003	2 Tms	NL	15	0	0	4	12.2	63	15	16	15	2	1	2	0	10	1	16	5	0	0	0	-	0	0-0	2	6.96	10.66
2004	KC	AL	40	12	0	5	108.0	483	114	64	57	12	5	4	5	50	3	91	6	2	4	8	.333	0	0-1	5	4.81	4.75
2005	SD	NL	36	1	0	9	43.2	215	57	30	25	3	1	0	1	32	2	35	3	1	3	2	.600	0	0-1	0	7.06	5.15
2006	Min	AL	66	0	0	8	50.2	194	35	8	5	3	1	0	0	15	2	49	4	0	5	0	1.000	0	0-1	16	1.90	0.89
98	LAD	NL	11	3	0	4	28.2	130	27	17	15	1	3	1	0	20	4	33	1	1	0	4	.000	0	0-0	0	4.16	4.71
98	Cin	NL	8	7	0	0	38.2	170	35	19	19	2	4	1	1	27	1	44	5	0	3	1	.750	0	0-0	0	4.54	4.42
02	Col	NL	43	0	0	13	40.1	182	43	19	19	1	2	2	0	24	3	30	4	0	0	1	.000	0	0-0	4	4.55	4.24
02	Tex	AL	15	5	0	2	42.1	196	55	33	30	9	1	0	0	21	1	29	6	1	4	3	.571	0	0-0	0	7.24	6.38
03	Pit	NL	12	0	0	4	10.1	50	10	13	12	1	1	2	0	9	1	11	5	0	0	0	-	0	0-0	2	5.43	10.45
03	Ari	NL	3	0	0	0	2.1	13	5	3	3	1	0	0	0	1	0	5	0	0	0	0	-	0	0-0	0	14.73	11.57
10 ML YEARS			410	40	0	74	570.1	2563	579	323	282	52	34	20	12	320	22	523	52	7	27	31	.466	0	2-7	57	4.75	4.45

Jose Reyes

Bats: B Throws: R Pos: SS-149; PH-3; PR-2   Ht: 6'0" Wt: 175 Born: 6/11/1983 Age: 24

Year	Team	Lg	G	AB	H	2B	3B	HR	(Hm	Rd)	TB	R	RBI	RC	TBB	IBB	SO	HBP	SH	SF	SB	CS	SB%	GDP	Avg	OBP	Slg
2003	NYM	NL	69	274	84	12	4	5	(1	4)	119	47	32	46	13	0	36	0	2	3	13	3	.81	1	.307	.334	.434
2004	NYM	NL	53	220	56	12	2	2	(1	1)	82	33	14	25	5	0	31	0	4	0	19	2	.90	1	.255	.271	.373
2005	NYM	NL	161	696	190	24	17	7	(2	5)	269	99	58	84	27	0	78	2	4	4	60	15	.80	7	.273	.300	.386
2006	NYM	NL	153	647	194	30	17	19	(9	10)	315	122	81	121	53	6	81	1	2	0	64	17	.79	6	.300	.354	.487
4 ML YEARS			436	1837	524	82	40	33	(13	20)	785	301	185	276	98	6	226	3	12	7	156	37	.81	15	.285	.321	.427

Jose A Reyes

Bats: B Throws: R Pos: PH-3; C-2   Ht: 5'11" Wt: 180 Born: 2/26/1983 Age: 24

Year	Team	Lg	G	AB	H	2B	3B	HR	(Hm	Rd)	TB	R	RBI	RC	TBB	IBB	SO	HBP	SH	SF	SB	CS	SB%	GDP	Avg	OBP	Slg
2002	Cubs	R	19	50	9	0	1	0	(-	-)	11	4	7	3	6	0	13	1	0	1	3	1	.75	1	.180	.276	.220
2002	WTenn	AA	1	5	2	0	0	0	(-	-)	2	0	0	0	0	0	3	0	0	0	0	0	-	0	.400	.400	.400
2003	Boise	A	11	36	10	0	0	0	(-	-)	10	4	5	2	1	0	4	0	1	0	0	1	.00	0	.278	.297	.278
2003	Lansng	A	70	234	56	9	0	0	(-	-)	65	18	20	20	16	0	37	3	2	1	2	1	.67	3	.239	.295	.278
2004	Dytona	A	80	261	59	12	1	2	(-	-)	79	27	17	20	13	0	54	5	4	0	1	4	.20	6	.226	.276	.303
2005	WTenn	AA	97	319	82	10	0	3	(-	-)	101	27	50	34	27	10	48	1	5	3	6	3	.67	16	.257	.314	.317
2006	WTenn	AA	47	144	33	3	0	0	(-	-)	36	15	11	9	9	1	25	0	3	0	0	1	.00	6	.229	.275	.250
2006	Iowa	AAA	37	108	27	6	0	0	(-	-)	33	10	11	12	14	0	11	2	2	0	0	1	.00	5	.250	.347	.306
2006	ChC	NL	4	5	1	0	0	0	(0	0)	1	0	2	1	0	0	3	0	0	0	0	0	-	0	.200	.200	.200

John Rheinecker

Pitches: L Bats: L Pos: SP-13; RP-8   Ht: 6'2" Wt: 230 Born: 5/29/1979 Age: 28

Year	Team	Lg	G	GS	CG	GF	IP	BFP	H	R	ER	HR	SH	SF	HB	TBB	IBB	SO	WP	Bk	W	L	Pct	ShO	Sv-Op	Hld	ERC	ERA
2001	Vancvr	A-	6	5	0	0	22.2	86	13	5	4	0	1	0	0	4	0	17	1	0	0	1	.000	0	0--	-	0.99	1.59
2001	Mdest	A+	2	2	0	0	10.0	45	10	7	7	1	1	0	0	5	1	5	1	0	0	1	.000	0	0--	-	4.20	6.30
2002	Visalia	A+	9	9	0	0	50.2	203	41	16	13	2	0	0	3	10	0	62	1	0	3	0	1.000	0	0--	-	2.18	2.31
2002	Mdland	AA	20	20	1	0	128.0	540	137	63	48	7	3	6	7	24	1	100	6	1	7	7	.500	1	0--	-	3.53	3.38
2003	Mdland	AA	23	23	1	0	142.1	640	186	90	75	13	3	4	7	32	1	89	3	1	9	6	.600	1	0--	-	5.24	4.74
2003	Scrmto	AAA	6	6	0	0	38.0	171	47	19	16	1	0	2	0	12	1	26	0	1	1	0	1.000	0	0--	-	4.70	3.79
2004	Scrmto	AAA	28	27	0	0	172.1	757	192	102	85	22	9	5	15	51	3	129	8	0	11	9	.550	0	0--	-	4.84	4.44
2005	Scrmto	AAA	7	7	0	0	45.2	179	29	15	9	0	0	2	3	14	0	24	0	0	4	0	1.000	0	0--	-	1.59	1.77
2006	Okla	AAA	15	15	2	0	93.0	378	93	33	26	5	2	0	2	24	0	68	3	0	4	5	.444	2	0--	-	3.42	2.52
2006	Tex	AL	21	13	0	0	70.2	322	104	46	46	6	1	1	3	19	0	28	0	0	4	6	.400	0	0-0	1	6.57	5.86

Arthur Rhodes

Pitches: L Bats: L Pos: RP-55   Ht: 6'2" Wt: 210 Born: 10/24/1969 Age: 37

Year	Team	Lg	G	GS	CG	GF	IP	BFP	H	R	ER	HR	SH	SF	HB	TBB	IBB	SO	WP	Bk	W	L	Pct	ShO	Sv-Op	Hld	ERC	ERA
1991	Bal	AL	8	8	0	0	36.0	174	47	35	32	4	1	3	0	23	0	23	2	0	0	3	.000	0	0-0	0	7.00	8.00
1992	Bal	AL	15	15	2	0	94.1	394	87	39	38	6	5	1	1	38	2	77	2	1	7	5	.583	1	0-0	0	3.48	3.63
1993	Bal	AL	17	17	0	0	85.2	387	91	62	62	16	2	3	1	49	1	49	2	0	5	6	.455	0	0-0	0	5.88	6.51
1994	Bal	AL	10	10	3	0	52.2	238	51	34	34	8	2	3	2	30	1	47	3	0	3	5	.375	2	0-0	0	5.03	5.81

213

Year	Team	Lg	G	GS	CG	GF	IP	BFP	H	R	ER	HR	SH	SF	HB	TBB	IBB	SO	WP	Bk	W	L	Pct	ShO	Sv-Op	Hld	ERC	ERA
1995	Bal	AL	19	9	0	3	75.1	336	68	53	52	13	4	0	0	48	1	77	3	1	2	5	.286	0	0-1	0	4.97	6.21
1996	Bal	AL	28	2	0	5	53.0	224	48	28	24	6	1	1	0	23	3	62	0	0	9	1	.900	0	1-1	2	3.72	4.08
1997	Bal	AL	53	0	0	6	95.1	378	75	32	32	9	0	4	4	26	5	102	2	0	10	3	.769	0	1-2	9	2.58	3.02
1998	Bal	AL	45	0	0	10	77.0	321	65	30	30	8	2	5	1	34	2	83	1	1	4	4	.500	0	4-8	10	3.47	3.51
1999	Bal	AL	43	0	0	11	53.0	244	43	37	32	9	2	2	0	45	6	59	4	0	3	4	.429	0	3-5	5	5.07	5.43
2000	Sea	AL	72	0	0	9	69.1	281	51	34	33	6	1	2	0	29	3	77	4	0	5	8	.385	0	0-7	24	2.62	4.28
2001	Sea	AL	71	0	0	16	68.0	258	46	14	13	5	1	0	1	12	0	83	3	0	8	0	1.000	0	3-7	32	1.61	1.72
2002	Sea	AL	66	0	0	9	69.2	257	45	18	18	4	2	1	0	13	1	81	2	0	10	4	.714	0	2-7	27	1.46	2.33
2003	Sea	AL	67	0	0	14	54.0	228	53	25	25	4	2	0	1	18	2	48	2	0	3	3	.500	0	3-6	18	3.57	4.17
2004	Oak	AL	37	0	0	25	38.2	182	46	23	22	9	3	1	0	21	4	34	2	0	3	3	.500	0	9-14	3	6.54	5.12
2005	Cle	AL	47	0	0	8	43.1	175	33	13	10	2	0	2	1	12	2	43	0	0	3	1	.750	0	0-3	16	2.06	2.08
2006	Phi	NL	55	0	0	10	45.2	214	47	27	27	2	1	0	2	30	7	48	7	0	0	5	.000	0	4-7	23	4.63	5.32
16 ML YEARS			653	61	5	126	1011.0	4291	896	504	484	111	29	28	14	451	40	993	39	3	75	60	.556	3	30-68	169	3.70	4.31

Shawn Riggans

Bats: R Throws: R Pos: C-8; PH-2 Ht: 6'2" Wt: 190 Born: 7/25/1980 Age: 26

Year	Team	Lg	G	AB	H	2B	3B	HR	(Hm	Rd)	TB	R	RBI	RC	TBB	IBB	SO	HBP	SH	SF	SB	CS	SB%	GDP	Avg	OBP	Slg
2001	Princtn	A+	15	58	20	4	0	8	(-	-)	48	15	17	18	9	0	18	0	0	0	1	0	1.00	0	.345	.433	.828
2002	HudVal	A-	73	266	70	13	0	9	(-	-)	110	34	48	39	32	1	72	1	2	1	2	2	.50	0	.263	.343	.414
2003	CtnSC	A	68	232	65	17	0	3	(-	-)	91	33	34	32	19	0	35	4	1	4	3	4	.43	8	.280	.340	.392
2003	Orlndo	AA	22	62	17	6	0	1	(-	-)	26	7	11	8	4	0	14	1	0	2	0	0	-	0	.274	.319	.419
2004	Bkrsfld	A+	34	127	44	11	0	5	(-	-)	70	20	22	28	15	0	23	1	0	1	0	1	.00	3	.346	.417	.551
2004	Mont	AA	10	36	8	1	0	2	(-	-)	15	3	7	4	2	0	14	1	0	0	0	0	-	2	.222	.282	.417
2005	Mont	AA	89	313	97	21	0	8	(-	-)	142	40	53	53	26	0	69	4	2	5	1	2	.33	11	.310	.365	.454
2006	Drham	AAA	115	417	122	26	2	11	(-	-)	185	43	54	64	27	1	88	5	2	2	2	2	.50	11	.293	.341	.444
2006	TB	AL	10	29	5	1	0	0	(0	0)	6	3	1	0	4	0	7	0	0	0	0	0	-	1	.172	.273	.207

Juan Rincon

Pitches: R Bats: R Pos: RP-75 Ht: 5'11" Wt: 205 Born: 1/23/1979 Age: 28

Year	Team	Lg	G	GS	CG	GF	IP	BFP	H	R	ER	HR	SH	SF	HB	TBB	IBB	SO	WP	Bk	W	L	Pct	ShO	Sv-Op	Hld	ERC	ERA
2001	Min	AL	4	0	0	1	5.2	28	7	5	4	1	1	0	0	5	0	4	0	0	0	0	-	0	0-0	0	8.33	6.35
2002	Min	AL	10	3	0	0	28.2	135	44	23	20	5	0	1	0	9	0	21	2	0	0	2	.000	0	0-1	0	7.62	6.28
2003	Min	AL	58	0	0	20	85.2	370	74	38	35	5	2	5	4	38	7	63	7	0	5	6	.455	0	0-1	5	3.21	3.68
2004	Min	AL	77	0	0	18	82.0	327	52	27	24	5	3	3	2	32	1	106	2	0	11	6	.647	0	2-6	16	2.00	2.63
2005	Min	AL	75	0	0	18	77.0	319	63	26	21	2	4	1	3	30	3	84	5	1	6	6	.500	0	0-5	25	2.68	2.45
2006	Min	AL	75	0	0	22	74.1	315	76	30	24	2	5	1	3	24	3	65	2	0	3	1	.750	0	1-3	26	3.53	2.91
6 ML YEARS			299	3	0	79	353.1	1494	316	149	128	20	15	11	12	138	14	343	18	1	25	21	.543	0	3-16	72	3.24	3.26

Ricardo Rincon

Pitches: L Bats: L Pos: RP-5 Ht: 5'9" Wt: 190 Born: 4/13/1970 Age: 37

Year	Team	Lg	G	GS	CG	GF	IP	BFP	H	R	ER	HR	SH	SF	HB	TBB	IBB	SO	WP	Bk	W	L	Pct	ShO	Sv-Op	Hld	ERC	ERA
1997	Pit	NL	62	0	0	23	60.0	254	51	26	23	5	5	1	2	24	6	71	2	3	4	8	.333	0	4-6	18	3.10	3.45
1998	Pit	NL	60	0	0	27	65.0	272	50	31	21	6	1	2	0	29	2	64	2	0	0	2	.000	0	14-17	11	2.88	2.91
1999	Cle	AL	59	0	0	14	44.2	193	41	22	22	6	2	1	1	24	5	30	2	1	2	3	.400	0	0-2	11	4.38	4.43
2000	Cle	AL	35	0	0	4	20.0	90	17	7	6	1	0	0	1	13	1	20	1	0	2	0	1.000	0	0-0	10	3.89	2.70
2001	Cle	AL	67	0	0	19	54.0	223	44	18	17	3	2	3	0	21	5	50	1	0	2	1	.667	0	2-4	12	2.62	2.83
2002	2 Tms	AL	71	0	0	9	56.0	222	47	28	26	4	2	4	1	11	1	49	0	0	1	4	.200	0	1-5	27	2.36	4.18
2003	Oak	AL	64	0	0	16	55.1	241	45	21	20	4	8	2	3	32	4	40	0	0	8	4	.667	0	0-3	13	3.62	3.25
2004	Oak	AL	67	0	0	10	44.0	201	45	22	18	3	1	1	1	22	4	40	4	0	1	1	.500	0	0-4	18	4.16	3.68
2005	Oak	AL	67	0	0	4	37.1	162	34	19	18	7	2	1	1	20	4	27	1	0	1	1	.500	0	0-2	16	4.73	4.34
2006	StL	NL	5	0	0	1	3.1	21	6	4	4	1	0	0	1	4	0	6	0	0	0	0	-	0	0-0	2	16.33	10.80
02	Cle	AL	46	0	0	6	35.2	150	36	21	19	3	2	2	1	8	1	30	0	0	1	4	.200	0	0-3	11	3.38	4.79
02	Oak	AL	25	0	0	3	20.1	72	11	7	7	1	0	2	0	3	0	19	0	0	0	0	-	0	1-2	16	1.06	3.10
10 ML YEARS			557	0	0	127	439.2	1879	380	198	175	40	23	15	11	200	32	397	13	4	21	24	.467	0	21-43	138	3.45	3.58

Royce Ring

Pitches: L Bats: L Pos: RP-11 Ht: 6'0" Wt: 220 Born: 12/21/1980 Age: 26

Year	Team	Lg	G	GS	CG	GF	IP	BFP	H	R	ER	HR	SH	SF	HB	TBB	IBB	SO	WP	Bk	W	L	Pct	ShO	Sv-Op	Hld	ERC	ERA
2002	WhSox	R	3	0	0	2	5.0	17	2	0	0	0	0	0	0	0	0	9	0	0	0	0	-	0	0--	-	0.35	0.00
2002	WinSa	A+	21	0	0	13	23.0	100	20	11	10	2	2	2	0	11	2	22	1	0	2	0	1.000	0	5--	-	3.35	3.91
2003	Brham	AA	36	0	0	32	35.2	154	33	11	10	1	0	1	3	14	1	44	3	0	1	4	.200	0	19--	-	3.39	2.52
2003	Bnghtn	AA	18	0	0	15	21.2	89	13	4	4	2	2	1	1	11	0	18	1	0	3	1	.750	0	7--	-	2.49	1.66
2004	Norfolk	AAA	29	0	0	10	34.2	153	37	15	14	5	0	0	1	12	1	22	1	0	3	1	.750	0	0--	-	4.40	3.63
2004	Bnghtn	AA	19	0	0	8	28.2	122	25	13	12	5	0	0	1	11	1	23	0	0	2	2	.500	0	2--	-	3.85	3.77
2005	Norfolk	AAA	33	0	0	11	38.2	163	34	16	14	2	4	0	3	13	1	26	2	0	3	0	1.000	0	2--	-	3.10	3.26
2006	Norfolk	AAA	36	0	0	26	39.1	165	30	14	13	2	2	2	3	15	2	40	1	1	2	2	.500	0	11--	-	2.59	2.97
2005	NYM	NL	15	0	0	2	10.2	51	10	6	6	0	1	0	0	10	1	8	0	0	0	2	.000	0	0-0	3	4.80	5.06
2006	NYM	NL	11	0	0	2	12.2	48	7	3	3	2	0	0	0	3	0	8	0	0	0	0	-	0	0-0	2	1.60	2.13
2 ML YEARS			26	0	0	4	23.1	99	17	9	9	2	1	0	0	13	1	16	0	0	0	2	.000	0	0-0	5	3.02	3.47

Alex Rios

Bats: R **Throws:** R **Pos:** RF-124; PH-8; CF-6; PR-3   Ht: 6'5" **Wt:** 195 **Born:** 2/18/1981 **Age:** 26

												BATTING												BASERUNNING				AVERAGES		
Year	Team	Lg	G	AB	H	2B	3B	HR	(Hm	Rd)	TB	R	RBI	RC	TBB	IBB	SO	HBP	SH	SF		SB	CS	SB%	GDP	Avg	OBP	Slg
2006 Syrcse*	AAA		3	10	3	1	0	0	(-	-)	4	0	1	1	1	0	3	0	0	0		0	0	-	0	.300	.364	.400
2004 Tor	AL		111	426	122	24	7	1	(0	1)	163	55	28	49	31	0	84	2	1	0		15	3	.83	14	.286	.338	.383
2005 Tor	AL		146	481	126	23	6	10	(5	5)	191	71	59	56	28	1	101	5	0	5		14	9	.61	14	.262	.306	.397
2006 Tor	AL		128	450	136	33	6	17	(12	5)	232	68	82	83	35	1	89	3	0	10		15	6	.71	10	.302	.349	.516
3 ML YEARS			385	1357	384	80	19	28	(17	11)	586	194	169	188	94	2	274	10	1	15		44	18	.71	38	.283	.331	.432

David Riske

Pitches: R **Bats:** R **Pos:** RP-41   Ht: 6'2" **Wt:** 180 **Born:** 10/23/1976 **Age:** 30

						HOW MUCH HE PITCHED				WHAT HE GAVE UP											THE RESULTS						
Year	Team	Lg	G	GS	CG	GF	IP	BFP	H	R	ER	HR	SH	SF	HB	TBB	IBB	SO	WP	Bk	W	L	Pct	ShO	Sv-Op Hld	ERC	ERA
2006 Pwtckt*	AAA		5	2	0	0	5.0	26	5	3	3	0	0	0	1	5	0	8	0	0	0	1	.000	0	0-- -	6.25	5.40
1999 Cle	AL		12	0	0	3	14.0	68	20	15	13	2	1	1	0	6	0	16	0	0	1	1	.500	0	0-1 0	6.96	8.36
2001 Cle	AL		26	0	0	6	27.1	118	20	7	6	3	0	1	2	18	3	29	1	0	2	0	1.000	0	1-1 3	3.81	1.98
2002 Cle	AL		51	0	0	17	51.1	237	49	32	30	8	4	3	4	35	4	65	1	0	2	2	.500	0	1-1 5	5.55	5.26
2003 Cle	AL		68	0	0	24	74.2	293	52	21	19	9	4	1	3	20	3	82	1	0	2	2	.500	0	8-13 17	2.26	2.29
2004 Cle	AL		72	0	0	27	77.1	336	69	32	32	11	3	2	2	41	4	78	3	0	7	3	.700	0	5-12 9	4.32	3.72
2005 Cle	AL		58	0	0	33	72.2	288	55	28	25	11	3	1	4	15	0	48	0	0	3	4	.429	0	1-1 0	2.59	3.10
2006 2 Tms	AL		41	0	0	12	44.0	189	40	20	19	6	1	2	3	17	1	28	0	0	1	2	.333	0	0-1 2	3.98	3.89
06 Bos	AL		8	0	0	2	9.2	42	8	4	4	2	1	0	2	3	0	5	0	0	0	1	.000	0	0-0 0	4.23	3.72
06 CWS	AL		33	0	0	10	34.1	147	32	16	15	4	0	2	1	14	1	23	0	0	1	1	.500	0	0-1 2	3.91	3.93
7 ML YEARS			328	0	0	122	361.1	1529	305	155	144	50	16	11	18	152	15	346	6	0	18	14	.563	0	16-30 36	3.69	3.59

Juan Rivera

Bats: R **Throws:** R **Pos:** LF-56; RF-33; CF-20; DH-18; PH-4; PR-1   Ht: 6'2" **Wt:** 205 **Born:** 7/3/1978 **Age:** 28

												BATTING											BASERUNNING				AVERAGES		
Year	Team	Lg	G	AB	H	2B	3B	HR	(Hm	Rd)	TB	R	RBI	RC	TBB	IBB	SO	HBP	SH	SF		SB	CS	SB%	GDP	Avg	OBP	Slg
2006 Salt Lk*	AAA		2	9	5	3	0	1	(-	-)	11	3	6	4	1	0	0	0	0	0		0	0	-	1	.556	.600	1.222
2001 NYY	AL		3	4	0	0	0	0	(0	0)	0	0	0	0	0	0	0	0	0	0		0	0	-	0	.000	.000	.000
2002 NYY	AL		28	83	22	5	0	1	(0	1)	30	9	6	8	6	0	10	0	1	1		1	1	.50	4	.265	.311	.361
2003 NYY	AL		57	173	46	14	0	7	(4	3)	81	22	26	23	10	1	27	0	1	1		0	0	-	8	.266	.304	.468
2004 Mon	NL		134	391	120	24	1	12	(6	6)	182	48	49	60	34	7	45	1	0	0		6	2	.75	11	.307	.364	.465
2005 LAA	AL		106	350	95	17	1	15	(8	7)	159	46	59	49	23	0	44	0	2	1		1	9	.10	15	.271	.316	.454
2006 LAA	AL		124	448	139	27	0	23	(12	11)	235	65	85	80	33	0	59	7	0	6		0	4	.00	14	.310	.362	.525
6 ML YEARS			452	1449	422	87	2	58	(30	28)	687	190	225	220	106	8	185	8	4	9		8	16	.33	52	.291	.341	.474

Mariano Rivera

Pitches: R **Bats:** R **Pos:** RP-63   Ht: 6'2" **Wt:** 195 **Born:** 11/29/1969 **Age:** 37

						HOW MUCH HE PITCHED				WHAT HE GAVE UP											THE RESULTS						
Year	Team	Lg	G	GS	CG	GF	IP	BFP	H	R	ER	HR	SH	SF	HB	TBB	IBB	SO	WP	Bk	W	L	Pct	ShO	Sv-Op Hld	ERC	ERA
1995 NYY	AL		19	10	0	2	67.0	301	71	43	41	11	0	2	2	30	0	51	0	1	5	3	.625	0	0-1 0	5.14	5.51
1996 NYY	AL		61	0	0	14	107.2	425	73	25	25	1	2	1	2	34	3	130	1	0	8	3	.727	0	5-8 27	1.65	2.09
1997 NYY	AL		66	0	0	56	71.2	301	65	17	15	5	3	4	0	20	6	68	2	0	6	4	.600	0	43-52 0	2.73	1.88
1998 NYY	AL		54	0	0	49	61.1	246	48	13	13	3	2	3	1	17	1	36	0	0	3	0	1.000	0	36-41 0	2.21	1.91
1999 NYY	AL		66	0	0	63	69.0	268	43	15	14	2	0	2	3	18	3	52	2	1	4	3	.571	0	45-49 0	1.47	1.83
2000 NYY	AL		66	0	0	61	75.2	311	58	26	24	4	5	2	0	25	3	58	2	0	7	4	.636	0	36-41 0	2.20	2.85
2001 NYY	AL		71	0	0	66	80.2	310	61	24	21	5	4	1	1	12	2	83	1	0	4	6	.400	0	50-57 0	1.74	2.34
2002 NYY	AL		45	0	0	37	46.0	187	35	16	14	3	2	0	2	11	2	41	1	1	1	4	.200	0	28-32 2	2.08	2.74
2003 NYY	AL		64	0	0	57	70.2	277	61	15	13	3	1	2	4	10	1	63	0	0	5	2	.714	0	40-46 0	2.29	1.66
2004 NYY	AL		74	0	0	69	78.2	316	65	17	17	3	2	0	5	20	3	66	0	0	4	2	.667	0	53-57 0	2.45	1.94
2005 NYY	AL		71	0	0	59	78.1	306	50	18	12	2	0	1	4	18	0	80	0	0	7	4	.636	0	43-47 0	1.48	1.38
2006 NYY	AL		63	0	0	59	75.0	293	61	16	15	3	1	2	5	11	4	55	0	0	5	5	.500	0	34-37 0	2.03	1.80
12 ML YEARS			720	10	0	600	881.2	3541	691	245	224	45	22	20	29	226	28	783	9	3	59	40	.596	0	413-468 29	2.19	2.29

Mike Rivera

Bats: R **Throws:** R **Pos:** C-44; PH-3; PR-1   Ht: 6'0" **Wt:** 210 **Born:** 9/8/1976 **Age:** 30

												BATTING											BASERUNNING				AVERAGES		
Year	Team	Lg	G	AB	H	2B	3B	HR	(Hm	Rd)	TB	R	RBI	RC	TBB	IBB	SO	HBP	SH	SF		SB	CS	SB%	GDP	Avg	OBP	Slg
2006 Nashv*	AAA		60	213	63	11	0	10	(-	-)	104	30	46	35	13	3	40	4	0	6		3	3	.50	5	.296	.339	.488
2001 Det	AL		4	12	4	2	0	0	(0	0)	6	2	1	2	0	0	2	0	0	0		0	0	-	0	.333	.333	.500
2002 Det	AL		39	132	30	8	1	1	(0	1)	43	11	11	8	4	0	35	1	0	1		0	0	-	5	.227	.254	.326
2003 SD	NL		19	53	9	1	0	1	(0	1)	13	2	2	0	5	0	11	0	0	0		0	0	-	4	.170	.241	.245
2006 Mil	NL		46	142	38	9	0	6	(3	3)	65	16	24	19	10	5	21	3	1	2		0	0	-	3	.268	.325	.458
4 ML YEARS			108	339	81	20	1	8	(3	5)	127	31	38	29	19	5	69	4	1	3		0	0	-	12	.239	.285	.375

Rene Rivera

Bats: R **Throws:** R **Pos:** C-35   Ht: 5'10" **Wt:** 210 **Born:** 7/31/1983 **Age:** 23

												BATTING											BASERUNNING				AVERAGES		
Year	Team	Lg	G	AB	H	2B	3B	HR	(Hm	Rd)	TB	R	RBI	RC	TBB	IBB	SO	HBP	SH	SF		SB	CS	SB%	GDP	Avg	OBP	Slg
2006 Tacom*	AAA		1	3	2	1	0	0	(-	-)	3	1	0	1	0	0	1	0	0	0		0	0	-	0	.667	.667	1.000
2004 Sea	AL		2	3	0	0	0	0	(0	0)	0	0	0	0	0	0	1	0	0	0		0	0	-	0	.000	.000	.000

Year	Team	Lg	G	AB	H	2B	3B	HR	(Hm	Rd)	TB	R	RBI	RC	TBB	IBB	SO	HBP	SH	SF	SB	CS	SB%	GDP	Avg	OBP	Slg
2005	Sea	AL	16	48	19	3	0	1	(0	1)	25	3	6	8	1	0	11	0	1	0	0	0	-	0	.396	.408	.521
2006	Sea	AL	35	99	15	4	0	2	(1	1)	25	8	4	4	3	0	29	1	3	0	1	0	1.00	2	.152	.184	.253
	3 ML YEARS		53	150	34	7	0	3	(1	2)	50	11	10	12	4	0	41	1	4	0	1	0	1.00	2	.227	.252	.333

Saul Rivera

Pitches: R **Bats:** R **Pos:** RP-54   **Ht:** 5'11" **Wt:** 150 **Born:** 12/7/1977 **Age:** 29

			HOW MUCH HE PITCHED					WHAT HE GAVE UP										THE RESULTS						
Year	Team	Lg	G	GS	CG	GF	IP	BFP	H	R	ER	HR	SH	SF	HB	TBB	IBB	SO	WP	Bk	W	L	Pct	ShO	Sv-Op Hld	ERC	ERA
1998	Elizab	R+	23	0	0	21	36.0	147	19	10	9	4	2	0	0	19	2	65	1	0	3	3	.500	0	7-- -	2.06	2.25
1999	QuadC	A	60	0	0	54	69.2	283	42	12	11	0	2	0	0	36	5	102	2	0	4	1	.800	0	23-- -	1.73	1.42
2000	FtMyrs	A+	29	0	0	22	37.2	166	34	15	15	0	2	0	0	19	3	45	6	1	8	1	.889	0	5-- -	3.02	3.58
2000	NwBrit	AA	22	0	0	7	37.0	163	28	16	16	0	2	1	2	22	0	47	8	0	1	0	1.000	0	0-- -	2.91	3.89
2001	NwBrit	AA	33	0	0	27	42.2	181	35	16	15	3	2	1	1	18	1	55	1	0	5	2	.714	0	13-- -	3.00	3.16
2001	Twins	R	3	0	0	0	3.0	13	2	0	0	0	0	0	0	1	0	4	0	0	0	0	-	0	0-- -	1.45	0.00
2002	Bnghtn	AA	30	0	0	24	38.2	165	25	18	13	2	1	3	1	23	2	32	1	0	2	3	.400	0	13-- -	2.56	3.03
2002	Hrsbrg	AA	15	0	0	9	19.0	89	21	8	7	0	3	0	4	9	1	15	2	1	0	2	.000	0	3-- -	4.90	3.32
2004	Hrsbrg	AA	18	0	0	12	21.0	101	27	22	18	3	0	0	1	12	2	15	1	1	0	2	.000	0	3-- -	6.85	7.71
2004	Hntsvl	AA	26	0	0	10	33.1	146	30	11	6	0	2	0	0	16	1	25	0	0	2	1	.667	0	1-- -	3.21	1.62
2005	Hrsbrg	AA	40	0	0	29	76.2	326	72	30	21	3	7	0	3	20	6	70	3	0	3	3	.500	0	9-- -	2.77	2.47
2006	NewOr	AAA	12	0	0	3	28.1	125	25	7	5	1	3	0	4	12	1	25	4	0	1	1	.500	0	1-- -	3.48	1.59
2006	Was	NL	54	0	0	16	60.1	277	59	28	23	4	4	1	4	32	6	41	3	0	3	0	1.000	0	1-3 9	4.17	3.43

Sendy Rleal

Pitches: R **Bats:** R **Pos:** RP-42   **Ht:** 6'1" **Wt:** 180 **Born:** 6/21/1980 **Age:** 27

			HOW MUCH HE PITCHED					WHAT HE GAVE UP										THE RESULTS						
Year	Team	Lg	G	GS	CG	GF	IP	BFP	H	R	ER	HR	SH	SF	HB	TBB	IBB	SO	WP	Bk	W	L	Pct	ShO	Sv-Op Hld	ERC	ERA
2000	Bluefld	A	13	12	0	1	61.0	265	61	26	23	5	1	3	8	25	0	55	3	1	6	2	.750	0	0-- -	4.61	3.39
2000	Dlmrva	A	1	1	0	0	3.1	18	3	5	4	0	0	0	1	3	0	4	0	0	1	0	1.000	0	0-- -	5.31	10.80
2001	Dlmrva	A	20	20	1	0	103.1	420	79	50	41	9	0	5	7	27	0	83	6	2	3	6	.333	0	0-- -	2.47	3.57
2002	Dlmrva	A	28	1	0	7	41.1	188	53	28	28	4	4	1	1	15	0	34	7	0	1	0	1.000	0	1-- -	5.67	6.10
2003	Frdrck	A+	44	0	0	27	57.0	228	35	20	20	8	4	2	1	23	7	59	6	1	3	5	.375	0	11-- -	2.22	3.16
2004	Bowie	AA	39	0	0	21	47.1	197	41	16	14	7	1	0	3	12	0	60	2	0	4	0	1.000	0	3-- -	3.29	2.66
2005	Bowie	AA	56	0	0	38	70.2	276	46	19	16	4	8	3	1	18	3	75	2	0	4	4	.500	0	16-- -	1.58	2.04
2006	Ottawa	AAA	19	0	0	6	23.0	100	29	18	17	4	2	1	0	5	0	14	0	2	2	2	.500	0	0-- -	5.42	6.65
2006	Bal	AL	42	0	0	14	46.2	203	48	25	23	10	2	3	0	23	1	19	0	0	1	1	.500	0	0-1 3	5.54	4.44

Chris Roberson

Bats: B **Throws:** R **Pos:** LF-30; RF-21; PR-16; PH-15   **Ht:** 6'2" **Wt:** 180 **Born:** 8/23/1979 **Age:** 27

									BATTING											BASERUNNING				AVERAGES		
Year	Team	Lg	G	AB	H	2B	3B	HR	(Hm	Rd)	TB	R	RBI	RC	TBB	IBB	SO	HBP	SH	SF	SB	CS	SB%	GDP	Avg	OBP	Slg
2001	Phillies	R	38	133	33	8	1	0	(-	-)	43	17	13	16	16	0	30	2	5	1	6	2	.75	3	.248	.336	.323
2002	Batvia	A-	62	214	59	8	3	2	(-	-)	79	29	24	33	26	0	51	10	1	2	17	8	.68	2	.276	.377	.369
2003	Lakwd	A	132	470	110	19	5	2	(-	-)	145	64	32	59	57	1	108	12	8	1	59	16	.79	9	.234	.331	.309
2004	Clrwtr	A+	83	313	96	13	6	9	(-	-)	148	52	38	53	27	0	71	5	0	0	16	12	.57	5	.307	.371	.473
2005	Rdng	AA	139	553	172	24	8	15	(-	-)	257	90	70	96	40	2	112	9	5	4	34	14	.71	6	.311	.365	.465
2006	S-WB	AAA	74	284	83	14	2	1	(-	-)	104	44	17	40	23	0	57	3	4	2	25	9	.74	7	.292	.349	.366
2006	Phi	NL	57	41	8	0	1	0	(0	0)	10	9	1	2	0	0	9	1	1	0	3	0	1.00	0	.195	.214	.244

Brian Roberts

Bats: B **Throws:** R **Pos:** 2B-137; PH-3; DH-1   **Ht:** 5'9" **Wt:** 175 **Born:** 10/9/1977 **Age:** 29

									BATTING											BASERUNNING				AVERAGES		
Year	Team	Lg	G	AB	H	2B	3B	HR	(Hm	Rd)	TB	R	RBI	RC	TBB	IBB	SO	HBP	SH	SF	SB	CS	SB%	GDP	Avg	OBP	Slg
2006	Bowie*	AA	2	5	1	0	0	0	(-	-)	1	0	0	0	2	0	0	0	0	0	0	0	-	0	.200	.429	.200
2001	Bal	AL	75	273	69	12	3	2	(0	2)	93	42	17	27	13	0	36	0	3	3	12	3	.80	5	.253	.284	.341
2002	Bal	AL	38	128	29	6	0	1	(1	0)	38	18	11	12	15	0	21	1	3	2	9	2	.82	3	.227	.308	.297
2003	Bal	AL	112	460	124	22	4	5	(3	2)	169	65	41	62	46	1	58	1	4	1	23	6	.79	9	.270	.337	.367
2004	Bal	AL	159	641	175	50	2	4	(0	4)	241	107	53	91	71	1	95	1	15	6	29	12	.71	3	.273	.344	.376
2005	Bal	AL	143	561	176	45	7	18	(9	9)	289	92	73	106	67	5	83	3	5	4	27	10	.73	6	.314	.387	.515
2006	Bal	AL	138	563	161	34	3	10	(6	4)	231	85	55	74	55	4	66	0	6	5	36	7	.84	16	.286	.347	.410
	6 ML YEARS		665	2626	734	169	19	40	(19	21)	1061	409	250	372	267	11	359	6	36	21	136	40	.77	40	.280	.345	.404

Dave Roberts

Bats: L **Throws:** L **Pos:** LF-116; CF-13; PH-6; PR-2   **Ht:** 5'10" **Wt:** 180 **Born:** 5/31/1972 **Age:** 35

									BATTING											BASERUNNING				AVERAGES		
Year	Team	Lg	G	AB	H	2B	3B	HR	(Hm	Rd)	TB	R	RBI	RC	TBB	IBB	SO	HBP	SH	SF	SB	CS	SB%	GDP	Avg	OBP	Slg
2006	Lk Els*	A+	1	3	1	0	0	0	(-	-)	1	0	0	0	0	0	2	0	0	0	0	0	-	0	.333	.333	.333
1999	Cle	AL	41	143	34	4	0	2	(1	1)	44	26	12	14	9	0	16	0	3	1	11	3	.79	4	.238	.281	.308
2000	Cle	AL	19	10	2	0	0	0	(0	0)	2	1	0	1	2	0	2	0	1	0	1	1	.50	0	.200	.333	.200
2001	Cle	AL	15	12	4	1	0	0	(0	0)	5	3	2	2	1	0	2	0	0	0	0	1	.00	1	.333	.385	.417
2002	LAD	NL	127	422	117	14	7	3	(0	3)	154	63	34	67	48	0	51	2	6	1	45	10	.82	1	.277	.353	.365
2003	LAD	NL	107	388	97	6	5	2	(1	1)	119	56	16	43	43	1	39	4	5	0	40	14	.74	0	.250	.331	.307
2004	2 Tms		113	319	81	14	7	4	(2	2)	121	64	35	52	38	0	48	5	3	6	38	3	.93	4	.254	.337	.379
2005	SD	NL	115	411	113	19	10	8	(5	3)	176	65	38	59	53	3	59	1	11	4	23	12	.66	9	.275	.356	.428
2006	SD	NL	129	499	146	18	13	2	(1	1)	196	80	44	81	51	2	61	4	7	5	49	6	.89	5	.293	.360	.393

Year	Team	Lg	G	AB	H	2B	3B	HR	(Hm	Rd)	TB	R	RBI	RC	TBB	IBB	SO	HBP	SH	SF	SB	CS	SB%	GDP	Avg	OBP	Slg
04	LAD	NL	68	233	59	4	7	2	(1	1)	83	45	21	41	28	0	31	4	2	3	33	1	.97	2	.253	.340	.356
04	Bos	AL	45	86	22	10	0	2	(1	1)	38	19	14	11	10	0	17	1	1	3	5	2	.71	2	.256	.330	.442
8 ML YEARS			666	2204	594	76	42	21	(10	11)	817	358	181	319	245	6	278	16	36	17	207	50	.81	19	.270	.344	.371

Ryan Roberts

Bats: R Throws: R Pos: 2B-7; PH-2; DH-1; PR-1 **Ht: 5'11" Wt: 190 Born: 9/19/1980 Age: 26**

Year	Team	Lg	G	AB	H	2B	3B	HR	(Hm	Rd)	TB	R	RBI	RC	TBB	IBB	SO	HBP	SH	SF	SB	CS	SB%	GDP	Avg	OBP	Slg
2003	Auburn	A-	66	248	69	10	3	8	(-	-)	109	52	36	43	35	0	63	4	0	2	7	3	.70	10	.278	.374	.440
2004	CtnWV	A	64	226	64	9	0	13	(-	-)	112	38	39	53	55	1	50	9	0	1	0	0	-	6	.283	.440	.496
2004	Dnedin	A+	59	205	49	1	1	7	(-	-)	73	29	25	28	36	2	51	1	0	4	0	3	.00	8	.239	.350	.356
2005	Dnedin	A+	42	164	47	9	0	9	(-	-)	83	33	35	33	24	0	27	2	0	2	6	1	.86	5	.287	.380	.506
2005	NHam	AA	92	338	92	19	3	15	(-	-)	162	54	44	64	55	5	94	4	1	1	5	1	.83	6	.272	.379	.479
2006	Syrcse	AAA	98	362	99	28	1	10	(-	-)	159	44	49	54	30	0	86	2	6	3	5	3	.63	5	.273	.330	.439
2006	Tor	AL	9	13	1	0	0	0	(0	1)	4	1	1	0	1	0	4	0	0	0	0	0	-	1	.077	.143	.308

Nate Robertson

Pitches: L Bats: R Pos: SP-32 **Ht: 6'2" Wt: 225 Born: 9/3/1977 Age: 29**

Year	Team	Lg	G	GS	CG	GF	IP	BFP	H	R	ER	HR	SH	SF	HB	TBB	IBB	SO	WP	Bk	W	L	Pct	ShO	Sv-Op	Hld	ERC	ERA
2002	Fla	NL	6	1	0	1	8.1	46	15	11	11	3	0	0	2	4	1	3	0	0	0	1	.000	0	0-0	0	12.69	11.88
2003	Det	AL	8	8	0	0	44.2	203	55	27	27	6	0	0	0	23	2	33	3	0	1	2	.333	0	0-0	0	6.24	5.44
2004	Det	AL	34	32	1	1	196.2	852	210	116	107	30	12	4	4	66	1	155	5	1	12	10	.545	0	1-1	0	4.65	4.90
2005	Det	AL	32	32	2	0	196.2	846	202	113	98	28	3	11	7	65	2	122	6	1	7	16	.304	0	0-0	0	4.38	4.48
2006	Det	AL	32	32	1	0	208.2	881	206	98	89	29	4	7	8	67	2	137	6	0	13	13	.500	0	0-0	0	4.14	3.84
5 ML YEARS			112	105	4	2	655.0	2828	688	365	332	96	19	22	21	225	8	450	20	2	33	42	.440	0	1-1	0	4.60	4.56

Kerry Robinson

Bats: L Throws: L Pos: CF-15; LF-1; RF-1; PH-1; PR-1 **Ht: 6'0" Wt: 175 Born: 10/3/1973 Age: 33**

Year	Team	Lg	G	AB	H	2B	3B	HR	(Hm	Rd)	TB	R	RBI	RC	TBB	IBB	SO	HBP	SH	SF	SB	CS	SB%	GDP	Avg	OBP	Slg
2006	Omha*	AAA	100	396	123	24	3	2	(-	-)	159	68	40	59	33	0	36	4	4	0	17	14	.55	10	.311	.370	.402
1998	TB	AL	2	3	0	0	0	0	(0	0)	0	0	0	0	0	0	1	0	0	0	0	0	-	0	.000	.000	.000
1999	Cin	NL	9	1	0	0	0	0	(0	0)	0	4	0	0	0	0	1	0	0	0	0	1	.00	0	.000	.000	.000
2001	StL	NL	114	186	53	6	1	1	(1	0)	64	34	15	24	12	0	20	2	4	3	11	2	.85	1	.285	.334	.344
2002	StL	NL	124	181	47	7	4	1	(0	1)	65	27	15	20	11	3	29	1	4	0	7	4	.64	1	.260	.301	.359
2003	StL	NL	116	208	52	6	3	1	(1	0)	67	19	16	21	8	3	27	1	4	0	6	1	.86	3	.250	.281	.322
2004	SD	NL	80	92	27	4	0	0	(0	0)	31	20	5	10	5	0	8	1	1	2	11	4	.73	0	.293	.330	.337
2006	KC	AL	18	64	17	2	1	0	(0	0)	21	8	5	5	1	0	7	0	2	0	1	1	.50	1	.266	.277	.328
7 ML YEARS			463	735	196	25	9	3	(2	1)	248	112	56	80	37	6	93	4	13	6	36	13	.73	6	.267	.303	.337

Oscar Robles

Bats: L Throws: R Pos: 2B-13; PH-11; 3B-6; PR-2 **Ht: 5'10" Wt: 185 Born: 4/9/1976 Age: 31**

Year	Team	Lg	G	AB	H	2B	3B	HR	(Hm	Rd)	TB	R	RBI	RC	TBB	IBB	SO	HBP	SH	SF	SB	CS	SB%	GDP	Avg	OBP	Slg
1994	Astros	R	55	165	54	5	1	0	(-	-)	61	40	19	30	32	0	17	2	10	0	14	9	.61	5	.327	.442	.370
1995	Auburn	A-	58	216	62	9	1	0	(-	-)	73	49	19	34	39	1	15	0	1	1	8	2	.80	5	.287	.395	.338
1996	Kissim	A+	125	427	115	13	2	0	(-	-)	132	57	29	60	74	3	37	6	8	2	10	8	.56	13	.269	.383	.309
1997	NewOrl	AAA	2	3	1	0	0	0	(-	-)	1	0	0	0	1	0	1	0	0	0	0	0	-	0	.333	.500	.333
1997	Kissim	A+	66	236	53	4	0	0	(-	-)	57	39	21	24	43	0	28	1	8	2	0	1	.00	4	.225	.344	.242
1998	Jacksn	AA	4	5	1	0	0	0	(-	-)	1	0	0	0	1	1	1	0	1	0	0	0	-	0	.200	.333	.200
1998	Kissim	A+	66	207	56	7	1	0	(-	-)	65	31	24	31	38	0	14	3	2	1	6	2	.75	1	.271	.390	.314
2006	LsVgs	AAA	86	275	79	10	0	0	(-	-)	89	29	28	36	36	1	20	0	2	3	0	1	.00	6	.287	.366	.324
2005	LAD	NL	110	364	99	18	1	5	(2	3)	134	44	34	41	31	0	33	2	1	1	0	8	.00	8	.272	.332	.368
2006	LAD	NL	29	33	5	0	1	0	(0	0)	7	6	0	1	5	0	5	0	1	0	0	0	-	0	.152	.263	.212
2 ML YEARS			139	397	104	18	2	5	(2	3)	141	50	34	42	36	0	38	2	2	1	0	8	.00	8	.262	.326	.355

Fernando Rodney

Pitches: R Bats: R Pos: RP-63 **Ht: 5'11" Wt: 220 Born: 3/18/1977 Age: 30**

Year	Team	Lg	G	GS	CG	GF	IP	BFP	H	R	ER	HR	SH	SF	HB	TBB	IBB	SO	WP	Bk	W	L	Pct	ShO	Sv-Op	Hld	ERC	ERA
2002	Det	AL	20	0	0	10	18.0	89	25	15	12	2	2	1	0	10	2	10	0	1	1	3	.250	0	0-4	0	6.77	6.00
2003	Det	AL	27	0	0	11	29.2	143	35	20	20	2	3	3	1	17	1	33	0	0	1	3	.250	0	3-6	3	5.46	6.07
2005	Det	AL	39	0	0	26	44.0	185	39	14	14	5	2	0	2	17	3	42	2	0	2	3	.400	0	9-15	3	3.59	2.86
2006	Det	AL	63	0	0	30	71.2	304	51	36	28	6	2	0	8	34	4	65	3	0	7	4	.636	0	7-11	18	3.01	3.52
4 ML YEARS			149	0	0	77	163.1	721	150	85	74	15	9	4	11	78	10	150	5	1	11	13	.458	0	19-36	24	3.98	4.08

Alex Rodriguez

Bats: R Throws: R Pos: 3B-151; DH-3; PH-3   Ht: 6'3" Wt: 225 Born: 7/27/1975 Age: 31

Year	Team	Lg	G	AB	H	2B	3B	HR	(Hm	Rd)	TB	R	RBI	RC	TBB	IBB	SO	HBP	SH	SF	SB	CS	SB%	GDP	Avg	OBP	Slg
1994	Sea	AL	17	54	11	0	0	0	(0	0)	11	4	2	3	3	0	20	0	1	1	3	0	1.00	0	.204	.241	.204
1995	Sea	AL	48	142	33	6	2	5	(1	4)	58	15	19	15	6	0	42	0	1	0	4	2	.67	0	.232	.264	.408
1996	Sea	AL	146	601	215	54	1	36	(18	18)	379	141	123	144	59	1	104	4	6	7	15	4	.79	15	.358	.414	.631
1997	Sea	AL	141	587	176	40	3	23	(16	7)	291	100	84	100	41	1	99	5	4	1	29	6	.83	14	.300	.350	.496
1998	Sea	AL	161	686	213	35	5	42	(18	24)	384	123	124	135	45	0	121	10	3	4	46	13	.78	12	.310	.360	.560
1999	Sea	AL	129	502	143	25	0	42	(20	22)	294	110	111	102	56	2	109	5	1	8	21	7	.75	12	.285	.357	.586
2000	Sea	AL	148	554	175	34	2	41	(13	28)	336	134	132	138	100	5	121	7	0	11	15	4	.79	10	.316	.420	.606
2001	Tex	AL	162	632	201	34	1	52	(26	26)	393	133	135	148	75	6	131	16	0	9	18	3	.86	17	.318	.399	.622
2002	Tex	AL	162	624	187	27	2	57	(34	23)	389	125	142	152	87	12	122	10	0	4	9	4	.69	14	.300	.392	.623
2003	Tex	AL	161	607	181	30	6	47	(26	21)	364	124	118	131	87	10	126	15	0	6	17	3	.85	16	.298	.396	.600
2004	NYY	AL	155	601	172	24	2	36	(17	19)	308	112	106	112	80	6	131	10	0	7	28	4	.88	18	.286	.375	.512
2005	NYY	AL	162	605	194	29	1	48	(26	22)	369	124	130	137	91	8	139	16	0	3	21	6	.78	8	.321	.421	.610
2006	NYY	AL	154	572	166	26	1	35	(20	15)	299	113	121	112	90	8	139	8	0	4	15	4	.79	22	.290	.392	.523
13 ML YEARS			1746	6767	2067	364	26	464	(235	229)	3875	1358	1347	1429	820	59	1404	106	16	65	241	60	.80	158	.305	.386	.573

Eddy Rodriguez

Pitches: R Bats: R Pos: RP-9   Ht: 6'1" Wt: 215 Born: 8/8/1981 Age: 25

Year	Team	Lg	G	GS	CG	GF	IP	BFP	H	R	ER	HR	SH	SF	HB	TBB	IBB	SO	WP	Bk	W	L	Pct	ShO	Sv-Op	Hld	ERC	ERA
2000	Orioles	R	18	0	0	14	27.0	116	17	8	6	0	3	0	2	19	1	31	0	0	2	1	.667	0	6--	-	2.74	2.00
2000	Dlmrva	A	4	0	0	1	5.0	21	5	1	1	1	0	0	0	2	0	3	0	0	0	0	-	0	0--	-	4.93	1.80
2001	Dlmrva	A	41	0	0	6	61.0	261	58	27	23	4	0	1	2	23	0	64	4	0	5	3	.625	0	1--	-	3.59	3.39
2001	Bowie	AA	5	0	0	3	8.2	37	7	2	2	0	1	1	0	6	1	10	0	0	1	1	.500	0	2--	-	3.31	2.08
2002	Frdrck	A+	38	0	0	30	48.1	196	28	14	12	3	2	4	4	20	3	58	2	0	0	3	.000	0	11--	-	1.93	2.23
2002	Bowie	AA	6	0	0	4	8.0	38	6	6	5	1	0	0	1	7	0	7	1	0	0	0	-	0	1--	-	5.09	5.63
2003	Bowie	AA	56	0	0	43	73.0	309	49	26	19	3	4	2	6	35	2	66	3	0	3	4	.429	0	13--	-	2.45	2.34
2004	Ottawa	AAA	28	0	0	17	31.2	152	34	19	18	4	0	1	3	18	0	31	1	0	1	0	1.000	0	3--	-	5.56	5.12
2005	Ottawa	AAA	50	0	0	22	62.0	272	57	30	26	2	1	2	3	36	4	51	4	0	2	3	.400	0	3--	-	3.96	3.77
2006	Ottawa	AAA	42	0	0	23	47.1	195	33	13	9	0	1	1	1	18	0	55	1	0	3	1	.750	0	12--	-	1.85	1.71
2004	Bal	AL	29	0	0	10	43.1	193	36	23	23	5	1	1	5	30	5	37	2	1	1	0	1.000	0	0-0	0	4.73	4.78
2006	Bal	AL	9	0	0	6	15.0	72	17	14	12	5	0	2	0	10	0	11	1	0	1	1	.500	0	0-0	0	7.72	7.20
2 ML YEARS			38	0	0	16	58.1	265	53	37	35	10	1	3	5	40	5	48	3	1	2	1	.667	0	0-0	0	5.49	5.40

Felix Rodriguez

Pitches: R Bats: R Pos: RP-31   Ht: 6'1" Wt: 210 Born: 9/9/1972 Age: 34

Year	Team	Lg	G	GS	CG	GF	IP	BFP	H	R	ER	HR	SH	SF	HB	TBB	IBB	SO	WP	Bk	W	L	Pct	ShO	Sv-Op	Hld	ERC	ERA
2006	Ptomc*	A+	1	1	0	0	1.0	5	2	2	1	0	0	0	0	0	0	0	0	0	0	0	-	0	0--	-	16.28	9.00
2006	NewOr*	AAA	8	0	0	1	10.1	55	14	10	9	1	1	0	1	10	1	7	3	1	0	0	-	0	0--	-	8.81	7.84
1995	LAD	NL	11	0	0	5	10.2	45	11	3	3	2	0	0	0	5	0	5	0	0	1	1	.500	0	0-1	0	5.43	2.53
1997	Cin	NL	26	1	0	13	46.0	212	48	23	22	2	0	1	6	28	2	34	4	1	0	0	-	0	0-0	0	5.22	4.30
1998	Ari	NL	43	0	0	23	44.0	207	44	31	30	5	4	3	1	29	1	36	5	2	0	2	.000	0	5-8	0	5.11	6.14
1999	SF	NL	47	0	0	26	66.1	292	67	32	28	6	2	3	2	29	2	55	2	0	2	3	.400	0	0-1	3	4.25	3.80
2000	SF	NL	76	0	0	19	81.2	346	65	29	24	5	2	3	3	42	2	95	3	1	4	2	.667	0	3-8	30	3.26	2.64
2001	SF	NL	80	0	0	13	80.1	314	53	16	15	5	1	3	1	27	2	91	1	0	9	1	.900	0	0-3	32	1.92	1.68
2002	SF	NL	71	0	0	12	69.0	288	53	33	32	5	2	3	4	29	1	58	4	0	8	6	.571	0	0-6	24	2.92	4.17
2003	SF	NL	68	0	0	24	61.0	265	59	21	21	5	3	1	4	29	2	46	5	1	2	3	.800	0	2-3	19	4.33	3.10
2004	2 Tms	NL	76	0	0	13	65.2	289	61	25	24	8	4	1	5	29	4	59	4	0	5	8	.385	0	1-4	20	4.15	3.29
2005	NYY	NL	34	0	0	10	32.1	147	33	18	18	2	0	0	2	20	0	18	3	0	0	0	-	0	0-0	3	5.07	5.01
2006	Was	NL	31	0	0	9	29.1	139	32	25	25	5	2	3	4	16	3	15	1	2	1	1	.500	0	0-0	3	6.04	7.67
04	SF	NL	53	0	0	8	44.2	199	43	18	17	7	3	1	4	19	2	31	4	0	3	5	.375	0	0-3	13	4.58	3.43
04	Phi	NL	23	0	0	5	21.0	90	18	7	7	1	1	0	1	10	2	28	0	0	2	3	.400	0	1-1	7	3.25	3.00
11 ML YEARS			563	1	0	167	586.1	2544	526	256	242	50	20	21	32	283	19	512	32	7	38	26	.594	0	11-34	134	3.88	3.71

Francisco Rodriguez

Pitches: R Bats: R Pos: RP-69   Ht: 6'0" Wt: 180 Born: 1/7/1982 Age: 25

Year	Team	Lg	G	GS	CG	GF	IP	BFP	H	R	ER	HR	SH	SF	HB	TBB	IBB	SO	WP	Bk	W	L	Pct	ShO	Sv-Op	Hld	ERC	ERA
2002	LAA	AL	5	0	0	4	5.2	21	3	0	0	0	0	0	0	2	1	13	0	0	0	0	-	0	-	0	1.52	0.00
2003	LAA	AL	59	0	0	23	86.0	334	50	30	29	12	2	4	2	35	5	95	7	0	8	3	.727	0	2-6	7	2.25	3.03
2004	LAA	AL	69	0	0	29	84.0	335	61	21	17	2	2	1	1	33	1	123	5	0	4	1	.800	0	12-19	27	1.64	1.82
2005	LAA	AL	66	0	0	58	67.1	279	45	20	20	7	1	1	0	32	3	91	8	0	2	5	.286	0	45-50	0	2.52	2.67
2006	LAA	AL	69	0	0	58	73.0	296	52	16	14	6	3	0	1	28	5	98	10	0	2	3	.400	0	47-51	0	2.35	1.73
5 ML YEARS			268	0	0	172	316.0	1265	201	87	80	27	8	6	5	130	15	420	30	0	16	12	.571	0	106-126	34	2.15	2.28

Ivan Rodriguez

Bats: R Throws: R Pos: C-123; 1B-7; DH-5; PH-3; 2B-1   Ht: 5'9" Wt: 195 Born: 11/30/1971 Age: 35

Year	Team	Lg	G	AB	H	2B	3B	HR	(Hm	Rd)	TB	R	RBI	RC	TBB	IBB	SO	HBP	SH	SF	SB	CS	SB%	GDP	Avg	OBP	Slg
1991	Tex	AL	88	280	74	16	0	3	(3	0)	99	24	27	23	5	0	42	0	2	1	0	1	.00	10	.264	.276	.354
1992	Tex	AL	123	420	109	16	1	8	(4	4)	151	39	37	41	24	2	73	1	7	2	0	0	.00	7	.260	.300	.360
1993	Tex	AL	137	473	129	28	4	10	(7	3)	195	56	66	57	29	3	70	4	5	8	8	7	.53	16	.273	.315	.412
1994	Tex	AL	99	363	108	19	1	16	(7	9)	177	56	57	61	31	5	42	7	0	4	6	3	.67	10	.298	.360	.488
1995	Tex	AL	130	492	149	32	2	12	(5	7)	221	56	67	68	16	2	48	4	0	5	0	2	.00	11	.303	.327	.449

Year	Team	Lg	G	AB	H	2B	3B	HR	(Hm	Rd)	TB	R	RBI	RC	TBB	IBB	SO	HBP	SH	SF	SB	CS	SB%	GDP	Avg	OBP	Slg
1996	Tex	AL	153	639	192	47	3	19	(10	9)	302	116	86	99	38	7	55	4	0	4	5	0	1.00	15	.300	.342	.473
1997	Tex	AL	150	597	187	34	4	20	(12	8)	289	98	77	98	38	7	89	8	1	4	7	3	.70	18	.313	.360	.484
1998	Tex	AL	145	579	186	40	4	21	(12	9)	297	88	91	100	32	4	88	3	0	3	9	0	1.00	18	.321	.358	.513
1999	Tex	AL	144	600	199	29	1	35	(12	23)	335	116	113	104	24	2	64	1	0	5	25	12	.68	31	.332	.356	.558
2000	Tex	AL	91	363	126	27	4	27	(16	11)	242	66	83	78	19	5	48	1	0	6	5	5	.50	17	.347	.375	.667
2001	Tex	AL	111	442	136	24	2	25	(16	9)	239	70	65	77	23	3	73	4	0	1	10	3	.77	13	.308	.347	.541
2002	Tex	AL	108	408	128	32	2	19	(15	4)	221	67	60	63	25	2	71	2	1	4	5	4	.56	13	.314	.353	.542
2003	Fla	NL	144	511	152	36	3	16	(8	8)	242	90	85	91	55	6	92	6	1	5	10	6	.63	18	.297	.369	.474
2004	Det	AL	135	527	176	32	2	19	(7	12)	269	72	86	98	41	6	91	3	0	4	7	4	.64	16	.334	.383	.510
2005	Det	AL	129	504	139	33	5	14	(8	6)	224	71	50	44	11	2	93	2	1	7	7	3	.70	19	.276	.290	.444
2006	Det	AL	136	547	164	28	4	13	(5	8)	239	74	69	82	26	4	86	1	4	2	8	3	.73	16	.300	.332	.437
16 ML YEARS			2023	7745	2354	473	42	277	(147	130)	3742	1159	1119	1184	437	60	1125	51	22	65	112	56	.67	256	.304	.342	.483

John Rodriguez

Bats: L **Throws:** L **Pos:** PH-57; LF-41; RF-15; DH-1   **Ht:** 6'0" **Wt:** 205 **Born:** 1/20/1978 **Age:** 29

Year	Team	Lg	G	AB	H	2B	3B	HR	(Hm	Rd)	TB	R	RBI	RC	TBB	IBB	SO	HBP	SH	SF	SB	CS	SB%	GDP	Avg	OBP	Slg
1997	Yanks	R	46	157	47	10	2	3	(-	-)	70	31	23	32	30	1	32	0	0	3	7	0	1.00	3	.299	.405	.446
1998	Grnsbr	A	119	408	103	18	4	10	(-	-)	159	64	49	63	64	1	93	4	0	3	14	3	.82	7	.252	.357	.390
1999	Tampa	A+	71	269	82	14	3	8	(-	-)	126	37	43	51	41	7	52	3	1	3	2	5	.29	5	.305	.399	.468
1999	Yanks	R	3	7	2	0	1	0	(-	-)	4	1	1	2	3	0	0	0	0	0	0	0	-	0	.286	.500	.571
2000	Nrwich	AA	17	56	11	4	0	1	(-	-)	18	4	10	6	8	0	22	1	0	0	0	0	-	1	.196	.308	.321
2000	Tampa	A+	105	362	97	14	2	16	(-	-)	163	59	44	59	40	5	81	8	1	0	3	2	.60	0	.268	.354	.450
2001	Nrwich	AA	103	393	112	31	1	22	(-	-)	211	64	66	72	26	2	117	11	3	2	2	3	.40	7	.285	.345	.537
2001	Yanks	R	2	6	5	0	0	0	(-	-)	5	2	2	2	0	0	0	0	0	0	0	0	-	0	.833	.833	.833
2002	Nrwich	AA	103	354	76	18	3	15	(-	-)	145	51	63	48	35	2	94	11	1	4	13	3	.81	4	.215	.302	.410
2003	Clmbs	AAA	79	232	61	9	2	10	(-	-)	104	35	33	37	24	1	50	1	3	1	6	0	1.00	2	.263	.333	.448
2004	Clmbs	AAA	112	378	111	26	10	16	(-	-)	205	78	68	79	48	7	84	8	1	3	10	3	.77	4	.294	.382	.542
2005	Buffalo	AAA	46	170	42	13	3	5	(-	-)	76	25	23	27	15	1	40	6	1	4	5	0	1.00	1	.247	.323	.447
2005	Memp	AAA	34	120	41	5	0	17	(-	-)	97	24	47	36	13	3	28	3	1	0	1	1	.50	2	.342	.419	.808
2006	Memp	AAA	20	64	17	4	1	3	(-	-)	32	10	7	12	11	2	18	0	1	0	0	0	-	1	.266	.373	.500
2005	StL	NL	56	149	44	6	0	5	(2	3)	65	15	24	24	19	4	45	3	3	2	2	0	1.00	0	.295	.382	.436
2006	StL	NL	102	183	55	12	3	2	(1	1)	79	31	19	29	21	1	45	3	1	4	0	0	-	9	.301	.374	.432
2 ML YEARS			158	332	99	18	3	7	(3	4)	144	46	43	53	40	5	90	6	4	6	2	0	1.00	9	.298	.378	.434

Luis Rodriguez

Bats: B **Throws:** R **Pos:** 3B-29; PH-21; 2B-14; SS-2; DH-2; PR-2; 1B-1   **Ht:** 5'9" **Wt:** 190 **Born:** 6/27/1980 **Age:** 27

Year	Team	Lg	G	AB	H	2B	3B	HR	(Hm	Rd)	TB	R	RBI	RC	TBB	IBB	SO	HBP	SH	SF	SB	CS	SB%	GDP	Avg	OBP	Slg
1998	Twins	R	52	180	50	11	1	1	(-	-)	66	33	15	27	22	2	17	0	1	2	14	3	.82	4	.278	.353	.367
1999	QuadC	A	119	434	117	20	0	3	(-	-)	146	63	50	58	53	0	49	4	13	9	8	4	.67	10	.270	.348	.336
2000	QuadC	A	106	342	77	11	2	0	(-	-)	92	35	28	32	40	1	29	5	19	2	4	5	.44	10	.225	.314	.269
2001	FtMyrs	A+	125	463	127	21	3	4	(-	-)	166	71	64	74	82	2	42	6	14	5	11	8	.58	14	.274	.387	.359
2002	NwBrit	AA	129	455	117	18	2	8	(-	-)	163	60	40	64	61	1	44	5	32	4	3	2	.60	8	.257	.349	.358
2003	Roch	AAA	131	518	153	35	2	1	(-	-)	195	65	44	72	46	2	46	3	9	3	6	8	.43	15	.295	.354	.376
2004	Roch	AAA	126	482	138	33	1	5	(-	-)	188	72	51	71	53	1	49	1	18	6	3	3	.50	17	.286	.354	.390
2005	Roch	AAA	40	138	42	10	0	1	(-	-)	55	19	17	21	16	0	14	1	2	0	0	1	.00	3	.304	.381	.399
2005	Min	AL	79	175	47	10	2	2	(1	1)	67	21	20	27	18	0	23	1	6	3	2	2	.50	4	.269	.335	.383
2006	Min	AL	59	115	27	4	0	2	(1	1)	37	11	6	8	14	1	16	0	2	1	0	0	-	3	.235	.315	.322
2 ML YEARS			138	290	74	14	2	4	(2	2)	104	32	26	35	32	1	39	1	8	4	2	2	.50	7	.255	.327	.359

Wandy Rodriguez

Pitches: L **Bats:** B **Pos:** SP-24; RP-6   **Ht:** 5'11" **Wt:** 160 **Born:** 1/18/1979 **Age:** 28

			HOW MUCH HE PITCHED					WHAT HE GAVE UP										THE RESULTS						
Year	Team	Lg	G	GS	CG	GF	IP	BFP	H	R	ER	HR	SH	SF	HB	TBB	IBB	SO	WP	Bk	W	L	Pct	ShO	Sv-Op Hld	ERC	ERA
2001	Mrtnsvl	R+	12	12	1	0	74.0	296	54	19	13	6	2	3	4	20	0	67	4	1	4	3	.571	0	0- - -	2.27	1.58
2002	Lxngtn	A	28	28	0	0	159.1	689	167	74	67	12	8	5	13	44	0	137	8	2	11	4	.733	0	0- - -	3.99	3.78
2003	Salem	A+	20	20	1	0	111.0	476	102	51	43	9	7	8	6	41	1	72	1	1	8	7	.533	1	0- - -	3.54	3.49
2004	RdRck	AA	26	25	1	0	142.2	644	159	77	71	15	6	6	7	57	1	115	2	6	11	6	.647	0	0- - -	4.89	4.48
2005	RdRck	AAA	8	8	0	0	46.1	198	43	20	19	7	0	1	4	16	0	44	1	0	4	2	.667	0	0- - -	4.16	3.69
2005	CpChr	AA	1	1	0	0	3.1	15	3	1	1	0	0	0	0	2	1	3	0	0	0	0	-	0	0- - -	2.96	2.70
2006	RdRck	AAA	5	5	0	0	26.0	124	32	21	20	2	0	2	4	13	1	13	1	0	2	2	.500	0	0- - -	6.22	6.92
2005	Hou	NL	25	22	0	0	128.2	560	135	82	79	19	3	3	8	53	2	80	3	3	10	10	.500	0	0-0 - -	5.08	5.53
2006	Hou	NL	30	24	0	1	135.2	611	154	96	85	17	7	4	6	63	7	98	6	0	9	10	.474	0	0-0 - -	5.45	5.64
2 ML YEARS			55	46	0	1	264.1	1171	289	178	164	36	10	7	14	116	9	178	9	3	19	20	.487	0	0-0 - -	5.27	5.58

Brian Rogers

Pitches: R **Bats:** R **Pos:** RP-10   **Ht:** 6'4" **Wt:** 190 **Born:** 7/17/1982 **Age:** 24

			HOW MUCH HE PITCHED					WHAT HE GAVE UP										THE RESULTS						
Year	Team	Lg	G	GS	CG	GF	IP	BFP	H	R	ER	HR	SH	SF	HB	TBB	IBB	SO	WP	Bk	W	L	Pct	ShO	Sv-Op Hld	ERC	ERA
2003	Oneont	A-	12	12	0	0	56.2	237	49	23	21	2	2	3	4	18	0	66	1	0	3	2	.600	0	0- - -	2.79	3.34
2004	W Mich	A	25	25	0	0	142.1	627	163	76	72	9	6	11	10	44	1	120	8	0	6	8	.429	0	0- - -	4.55	4.55
2005	Lkland	A+	52	1	0	10	65.2	269	50	16	15	2	1	2	3	21	1	65	6	0	4	1	.800	0	2- - -	2.22	2.06
2006	Altna	AA	2	0	0	1	4.0	15	2	0	0	0	0	0	0	2	1	5	0	0	0	0	-	0	1- - -	1.26	0.00
2006	Erie	AA	37	0	0	10	64.0	250	49	19	17	7	1	1	1	14	1	69	3	0	3	2	.600	0	1- - -	2.31	2.39
2006	Indy	AAA	7	0	0	3	8.1	27	2	1	1	1	0	0	0	1	0	8	1	0	1	1	.500	0	1- - -	0.47	1.08
2006	Pit	NL	10	0	0	4	8.2	38	11	8	8	2	1	0	2	2	0	7	1	0	0	0	-	0	0-0 - -	6.65	8.31

Eddie Rogers

Bats: R **Throws:** R **Pos:** PR-5; 2B-4; 3B-4; PH-4; LF-3; SS-1; RF-1; DH-1   **Ht:** 6'3" **Wt:** 190 **Born:** 8/29/1978 **Age:** 28

Year	Team	Lg	G	AB	H	2B	3B	HR	(Hm	Rd)	TB	R	RBI	RC	TBB	IBB	SO	HBP	SH	SF	SB	CS	SB%	GDP	Avg	OBP	Slg
2006	Ottawa*	AAA	86	339	101	18	1	5	(-	-)	136	40	30	44	13	1	52	1	4	2	12	7	.63	6	.298	.324	.401
2002	Bal	AL	5	3	0	0	0	0	(0	0)	0	0	0	0	0	0	0	0	0	0	0	0	-	1	.000	.000	.000
2005	Bal	AL	8	1	1	0	0	1	(1	0)	4	4	2	0	0	0	0	0	0	0	0	2	.00	0	1.000	1.000	4.000
2006	Bal	AL	17	25	5	0	0	0	(0	0)	5	1	2	2	0	0	3	0	0	1	0	0	-	0	.200	.192	.200
	3 ML YEARS		30	29	6	0	0	1	(1	0)	9	5	4	2	0	0	3	0	0	1	0	2	.00	1	.207	.200	.310

Kenny Rogers

Pitches: L **Bats:** L **Pos:** SP-33; RP-1   **Ht:** 6'1" **Wt:** 190 **Born:** 11/10/1964 **Age:** 42

			HOW MUCH HE PITCHED						WHAT HE GAVE UP										THE RESULTS							
Year	Team	Lg	G	GS	CG	GF	IP	BFP	H	R	ER	HR	SH	SF	HB	TBB	IBB	SO	WP	Bk	W	L	Pct	ShO	Sv-Op	Hld	ERC	ERA
1989	Tex	AL	73	0	0	24	73.2	314	60	28	24	2	6	3	4	42	9	63	6	0	3	4	.429	0	2-5	15	3.26	2.93
1990	Tex	AL	69	3	0	46	97.2	428	93	40	34	6	7	4	1	42	5	74	5	0	10	6	.625	0	15-23	6	3.53	3.13
1991	Tex	AL	63	9	0	20	109.2	511	121	80	66	14	9	5	6	61	7	73	3	1	10	10	.500	0	5-6	11	5.57	5.42
1992	Tex	AL	81	0	0	38	78.2	337	80	32	27	7	4	1	0	26	8	70	4	1	3	6	.333	0	6-10	16	3.63	3.09
1993	Tex	AL	35	33	5	0	208.1	885	210	108	95	18	7	5	4	71	2	140	6	5	16	10	.615	0	0-0	1	3.88	4.10
1994	Tex	AL	24	24	6	0	167.1	714	169	93	83	24	3	6	3	52	1	120	3	1	11	8	.579	2	0-0	0	4.12	4.46
1995	Tex	AL	31	31	3	0	208.0	877	192	87	78	26	3	5	2	76	1	140	8	1	17	7	.708	1	0-0	0	3.72	3.38
1996	NYY	AL	30	30	2	0	179.0	786	179	97	93	16	6	3	8	83	2	92	5	0	12	8	.600	1	0-0	0	4.43	4.68
1997	NYY	AL	31	22	1	4	145.0	651	161	100	91	18	2	4	7	62	1	78	2	2	6	7	.462	0	0-0	1	5.18	5.65
1998	Oak	AL	34	34	7	0	238.2	970	215	96	84	19	4	5	7	67	0	138	5	2	16	8	.667	1	0-0	0	3.13	3.17
1999	2 Tms	AL	31	31	5	0	195.1	845	206	101	91	16	7	7	13	69	1	126	4	1	10	4	.714	1	0-0	0	4.38	4.19
2000	Tex	AL	34	34	2	0	227.1	998	257	126	115	20	3	4	11	78	2	127	1	1	13	13	.500	0	0-0	0	4.72	4.55
2001	Tex	AL	20	20	0	0	120.2	552	150	88	83	18	1	6	8	49	2	74	4	1	5	7	.417	0	0-0	0	6.22	6.19
2002	Tex	AL	33	33	2	0	210.2	892	212	101	90	21	3	1	6	70	1	107	5	1	13	8	.619	1	0-0	0	3.99	3.84
2003	Min	AL	33	31	0	0	195.0	851	227	108	99	22	9	3	11	50	5	116	6	4	13	8	.619	0	0-0	0	4.73	4.57
2004	Tex	AL	35	35	2	0	211.2	935	248	117	112	24	7	4	9	66	0	126	2	1	18	9	.667	1	0-0	0	4.99	4.76
2005	Tex	AL	30	30	1	0	195.1	828	205	86	75	15	5	6	8	53	1	87	0	0	14	8	.636	1	0-0	0	3.87	3.46
2006	Det	AL	34	33	0	1	204.0	849	195	97	87	23	1	7	9	62	2	99	5	0	17	8	.680	0	0-0	0	3.76	3.84
	99 Oak	AL	19	19	3	0	119.1	528	135	66	57	8	4	6	9	41	0	68	3	1	5	3	.625	0	0-0	0	4.68	4.30
	99 NYM	NL	12	12	2	0	76.0	317	71	35	34	8	3	1	4	28	1	58	1	0	5	1	.833	1	0-0	0	3.91	4.03
	18 ML YEARS		721	433	36	133	3066.0	13223	3180	1585	1427	309	87	79	117	1079	50	1850	74	22	207	139	.598	9	28-44	50	4.25	4.19

Scott Rolen

Bats: R **Throws:** R **Pos:** 3B-142   **Ht:** 6'4" **Wt:** 240 **Born:** 4/4/1975 **Age:** 32

Year	Team	Lg	G	AB	H	2B	3B	HR	(Hm	Rd)	TB	R	RBI	RC	TBB	IBB	SO	HBP	SH	SF	SB	CS	SB%	GDP	Avg	OBP	Slg
1996	Phi	NL	37	130	33	7	0	4	(2	2)	52	10	18	16	13	0	27	1	0	2	0	2	.00	4	.254	.322	.400
1997	Phi	NL	156	561	159	35	3	21	(11	10)	263	93	92	103	76	4	138	13	0	7	16	6	.73	6	.283	.377	.469
1998	Phi	NL	160	601	174	45	4	31	(19	12)	320	120	110	124	93	6	141	11	0	6	14	7	.67	10	.290	.391	.532
1999	Phi	NL	112	421	113	28	1	26	(9	17)	221	74	77	83	67	2	114	3	0	6	12	2	.86	8	.268	.368	.525
2000	Phi	NL	128	483	144	32	6	26	(12	14)	266	88	89	97	51	9	99	5	0	2	8	1	.89	4	.298	.370	.551
2001	Phi	NL	151	554	160	39	1	25	(12	13)	276	96	107	108	74	6	127	13	0	12	16	5	.76	6	.289	.378	.498
2002	2 Tms	NL	155	580	154	29	8	31	(14	17)	292	89	110	98	72	4	102	12	0	3	8	4	.67	22	.266	.357	.503
2003	StL	NL	154	559	160	49	1	28	(12	16)	295	98	104	104	82	5	104	9	0	7	13	3	.81	19	.286	.382	.528
2004	StL	NL	142	500	157	32	4	34	(10	24)	299	109	124	124	72	5	92	13	1	7	4	3	.57	8	.314	.409	.598
2005	StL	NL	56	196	46	12	1	5	(2	3)	75	28	28	22	25	1	28	1	0	1	1	2	.33	3	.235	.323	.383
2006	StL	NL	142	521	154	48	1	22	(12	10)	270	94	95	89	56	7	69	9	0	8	7	4	.64	10	.296	.369	.518
	02 Phi	NL	100	375	97	21	4	17	(8	9)	177	52	66	60	52	2	68	8	0	3	5	2	.71	12	.259	.358	.472
	02 StL	NL	55	205	57	8	4	14	(6	8)	115	37	44	38	20	2	34	4	0	0	3	2	.60	10	.278	.354	.561
	11 ML YEARS		1393	5106	1454	356	30	253	(115	138)	2629	899	954	968	681	49	1041	90	1	61	99	39	.72	100	.285	.375	.515

Jimmy Rollins

Bats: B **Throws:** R **Pos:** SS-157; PH-2   **Ht:** 5'8" **Wt:** 170 **Born:** 11/27/1978 **Age:** 28

Year	Team	Lg	G	AB	H	2B	3B	HR	(Hm	Rd)	TB	R	RBI	RC	TBB	IBB	SO	HBP	SH	SF	SB	CS	SB%	GDP	Avg	OBP	Slg
2000	Phi	NL	14	53	17	1	1	0	(0	0)	20	5	5	8	2	0	7	0	0	5	3	0	1.00	5	.321	.345	.377
2001	Phi	NL	158	656	180	29	12	14	(8	6)	275	97	54	96	48	2	108	2	9	5	46	8	.85	5	.274	.323	.419
2002	Phi	NL	154	637	156	33	10	11	(3	8)	242	82	60	72	54	3	103	4	6	4	31	13	.70	14	.245	.306	.380
2003	Phi	NL	156	628	165	42	6	8	(5	3)	243	85	62	76	54	4	113	0	5	2	20	12	.63	9	.263	.320	.387
2004	Phi	NL	154	657	190	43	12	14	(8	6)	299	119	73	108	57	3	73	3	6	2	30	9	.77	4	.289	.348	.455
2005	Phi	NL	158	677	196	38	11	12	(5	7)	292	115	54	100	47	8	71	4	2	2	41	6	.87	9	.290	.338	.431
2006	Phi	NL	158	689	191	45	9	25	(15	10)	329	127	83	114	57	2	80	5	0	7	36	4	.90	12	.277	.334	.478
	7 ML YEARS		952	3997	1095	231	61	84	(44	40)	1700	630	391	574	319	22	555	18	28	22	207	52	.80	53	.274	.329	.425

Davis Romero

Pitches: L **Bats:** L **Pos:** RP-7   **Ht:** 5'10" **Wt:** 170 **Born:** 3/30/1983 **Age:** 24

			HOW MUCH HE PITCHED						WHAT HE GAVE UP										THE RESULTS							
Year	Team	Lg	G	GS	CG	GF	IP	BFP	H	R	ER	HR	SH	SF	HB	TBB	IBB	SO	WP	Bk	W	L	Pct	ShO	Sv-Op	Hld	ERC	ERA
2002	MdHat	R	27	4	0	4	50.1	217	49	38	29	7	1	1	0	18	0	76	2	3	3	2	.600	0	2--	-	3.96	5.19
2003	Auburn	A-	30	0	0	10	41.2	165	31	13	11	1	0	1	0	8	1	53	5	0	4	1	.800	0	2--	-	1.57	2.38
2004	CtnWV	A	32	14	0	7	103.1	414	77	36	29	6	6	6	2	30	0	108	4	3	5	4	.556	0	1--	-	2.16	2.53
2005	Dnedin	A+	34	18	0	4	124.2	541	133	60	48	10	3	2	1	34	0	136	5	1	9	6	.600	0	1--	-	3.76	3.47

Year	Team	Lg	G	GS	CG	GF	IP	BFP	H	R	ER	HR	SH	SF	HB	TBB	IBB	SO	WP	Bk	W	L	Pct	ShO	Sv-Op	Hld	ERC	ERA
			HOW MUCH HE PITCHED						**WHAT HE GAVE UP**												**THE RESULTS**							
2006	NHam	AA	12	12	1	0	73.2	292	57	27	24	3	2	1	2	19	1	70	2	0	6	5	.545	1	0--	-	2.12	2.93
2006	Syrcse	AAA	18	3	0	8	44.2	191	46	25	19	3	4	1	5	7	0	36	0	2	4	4	.500	0	1--	-	3.44	3.83
2006	Tor	AL	7	0	0	1	16.1	71	19	7	7	1	0	0	1	6	1	10	0	1	1	0	1.000	0	0-0	0	4.89	3.86

J.C. Romero

Pitches: L Bats: B Pos: RP-65   Ht: 5'11" Wt: 205 Born: 6/4/1976 Age: 31

Year	Team	Lg	G	GS	CG	GF	IP	BFP	H	R	ER	HR	SH	SF	HB	TBB	IBB	SO	WP	Bk	W	L	Pct	ShO	Sv-Op	Hld	ERC	ERA
			HOW MUCH HE PITCHED						**WHAT HE GAVE UP**												**THE RESULTS**							
1999	Min	AL	5	0	0	3	9.2	39	13	4	4	0	0	0	0	0	0	4	0	0	0	0	-	0	0-0	0	3.95	3.72
2000	Min	AL	12	11	0	0	57.2	268	72	51	45	8	4	2	1	30	0	50	2	1	2	7	.222	0	0-0	0	6.48	7.02
2001	Min	AL	14	11	0	1	65.0	286	71	48	45	10	3	2	1	24	1	39	1	0	1	4	.200	0	0-0	0	4.89	6.23
2002	Min	AL	81	0	0	15	81.0	332	62	17	17	3	1	0	4	36	4	76	9	0	9	2	.818	0	1-5	33	2.74	1.89
2003	Min	AL	73	0	0	17	63.0	295	66	37	35	7	4	0	6	42	7	50	9	2	2	0	1.000	0	0-4	22	5.72	5.00
2004	Min	AL	74	0	0	12	74.1	319	61	32	29	4	3	1	5	38	6	69	5	0	7	4	.636	0	1-8	16	3.33	3.51
2005	Min	AL	68	0	0	11	57.0	264	50	26	22	6	5	1	6	39	8	48	1	1	4	3	.571	0	0-1	11	4.62	3.47
2006	LAA	AL	65	0	0	16	48.1	226	57	40	36	3	1	5	1	28	2	31	1	0	1	2	.333	0	0-1	7	5.54	6.70
	8 ML YEARS		392	22	0	75	456.0	2029	452	255	233	41	21	11	24	237	28	367	28	4	26	22	.542	0	2-19	89	4.54	4.60

Matt Roney

Pitches: R Bats: R Pos: RP-3   Ht: 6'3" Wt: 245 Born: 1/10/1980 Age: 27

Year	Team	Lg	G	GS	CG	GF	IP	BFP	H	R	ER	HR	SH	SF	HB	TBB	IBB	SO	WP	Bk	W	L	Pct	ShO	Sv-Op	Hld	ERC	ERA
			HOW MUCH HE PITCHED						**WHAT HE GAVE UP**												**THE RESULTS**							
1998	Rckies	R	9	9	1	0	40.1	187	50	31	26	1	1	0	3	11	0	49	4	2	1	1	.500	1	0--	-	4.49	5.80
2000	Portlnd	A-	15	15	0	0	80.1	360	75	35	28	6	1	1	7	44	0	85	8	2	7	5	.583	0	0--	-	4.42	3.14
2001	Ashvlle	A	23	23	1	0	121.0	540	131	74	67	16	2	5	13	43	0	115	6	1	8	10	.444	1	0--	-	5.02	4.98
2002	Ashvlle	A	14	14	1	0	82.2	349	82	39	32	7	3	2	5	25	1	88	1	1	4	6	.400	1	0--	-	3.80	3.48
2002	Carlina	AA	13	13	0	0	70.2	312	73	52	48	6	1	1	2	33	0	61	2	1	3	6	.333	0	0--	-	4.54	6.11
2004	Erie	AA	22	22	3	0	133.1	590	163	79	73	20	6	7	7	33	0	89	1	0	9	9	.500	1	0--	-	5.32	4.93
2004	Toledo	AAA	5	5	0	0	30.1	124	30	13	13	3	2	2	3	10	0	18	1	0	2	1	.667	0	0--	-	4.39	3.86
2005	Erie	AA	11	0	0	4	21.2	85	13	3	3	1	2	0	4	6	1	23	0	0	0	1	.000	0	1--	-	1.91	1.25
2005	Toledo	AAA	14	0	0	6	28.1	116	23	3	3	0	1	0	2	11	3	27	0	0	1	1	.500	0	3--	-	2.52	0.95
2005	Okla	AAA	24	0	0	12	32.2	141	34	11	11	3	1	4	3	8	1	32	1	0	4	1	.800	0	1--	-	3.92	3.03
2006	Scrmto	AAA	47	0	0	22	58.0	251	58	26	19	4	2	3	4	19	1	65	0	0	4	3	.571	0	6--	-	3.79	2.95
2003	Det	AL	45	11	0	12	100.2	449	102	67	61	17	4	4	4	48	4	47	2	2	1	9	.100	0	0-2	6	5.03	5.45
2006	Oak	AL	3	0	0	2	4.0	18	5	2	2	0	1	1	0	1	1	0	0	0	1	0	1.000	0	0-0	0	3.63	4.50
	2 ML YEARS		48	11	0	14	104.2	467	107	69	63	17	5	5	4	49	5	47	2	2	1	10	.091	0	0-2	6	4.98	5.42

Francisco Rosario

Pitches: R Bats: R Pos: RP-16; SP-1   Ht: 6'1" Wt: 215 Born: 9/28/1980 Age: 26

Year	Team	Lg	G	GS	CG	GF	IP	BFP	H	R	ER	HR	SH	SF	HB	TBB	IBB	SO	WP	Bk	W	L	Pct	ShO	Sv-Op	Hld	ERC	ERA
			HOW MUCH HE PITCHED						**WHAT HE GAVE UP**												**THE RESULTS**							
2001	MdHat	R+	16	15	0	0	75.2	344	79	61	47	8	1	4	9	38	0	55	6	6	3	7	.300	0	0--	-	5.28	5.59
2002	CtnWV	A	13	13	1	0	66.2	265	50	22	19	5	2	2	4	14	0	78	2	0	6	1	.857	0	0--	-	2.15	2.57
2002	Dnedin	A+	13	12	0	0	63.0	248	33	10	9	3	1	1	3	25	0	65	1	2	3	3	.500	0	0--	-	1.58	1.29
2004	Dnedin	A+	6	6	0	0	17.1	80	16	12	9	2	0	2	0	11	0	16	1	0	1	1	.500	0	0--	-	4.51	4.67
2004	NHam	AA	12	12	0	0	48.0	199	48	25	23	6	1	3	2	16	0	45	1	0	2	4	.333	0	0--	-	4.31	4.31
2005	Syrcse	AAA	30	18	0	4	116.1	489	111	59	51	16	5	1	10	42	1	80	5	1	2	7	.222	0	2--	-	4.38	3.95
2006	Syrcse	AAA	14	8	0	2	42.0	168	29	14	13	2	1	1	5	13	0	50	2	0	0	3	.000	0	1--	-	2.28	2.79
2006	Tor	AL	17	1	0	4	23.0	108	24	17	17	4	0	0	1	16	2	21	3	0	1	2	.333	0	0-0	1	6.12	6.65

Mike Rose

Bats: B Throws: R Pos: PH-6; C-4   Ht: 6'1" Wt: 225 Born: 8/25/1976 Age: 30

Year	Team	Lg	G	AB	H	2B	3B	HR	(Hm	Rd)	TB	R	RBI	RC	TBB	IBB	SO	HBP	SH	SF	SB	CS	SB%	GDP	Avg	OBP	Slg
			BATTING																		**BASERUNNING**				**AVERAGES**		
2006	Drham*	AAA	20	67	7	1	0	2	(-	-)	14	4	5	0	5	0	21	0	0	1	0	0	-	0	.104	.164	.209
2006	Memp*	AAA	82	271	71	19	0	15	(-	-)	135	38	36	50	40	2	83	2	3	0	2	1	.67	7	.262	.361	.498
2004	Oak	AL	2	2	0	0	0	0	(0	0)	0	1	0	0	0	0	2	0	0	0	0	0	-	0	.000	.000	.000
2005	LAD	NL	15	43	9	2	0	1	(0	1)	14	2	1	1	3	0	6	0	0	0	0	0	-	3	.209	.261	.326
2006	StL	NL	10	9	2	0	0	0	(0	0)	2	0	1	0	0	0	4	0	0	0	0	0	-	0	.222	.222	.222
	3 ML YEARS		27	54	11	2	0	1	(0	1)	16	3	2	1	3	0	12	0	0	0	0	0	-	3	.204	.246	.296

Cody Ross

Bats: R Throws: L Pos: LF-41; RF-34; PH-22; CF-21   Ht: 5'9" Wt: 205 Born: 12/23/1980 Age: 26

Year	Team	Lg	G	AB	H	2B	3B	HR	(Hm	Rd)	TB	R	RBI	RC	TBB	IBB	SO	HBP	SH	SF	SB	CS	SB%	GDP	Avg	OBP	Slg
			BATTING																		**BASERUNNING**				**AVERAGES**		
2006	Lsvlle*	AAA	15	50	17	1	0	3	(-	-)	27	11	6	12	13	0	12	1	0	0	0	2	.00	4	.340	.484	.540
2003	Det	AL	6	19	4	1	0	1	(1	0)	8	1	5	4	1	0	3	1	1	0	0	0	-	0	.211	.286	.421
2005	LAD	NL	14	25	4	1	0	0	(0	0)	5	1	1	0	1	0	10	0	0	0	0	0	-	1	.160	.192	.200
2006	3 Tms	NL	101	269	61	12	2	13	(6	7)	116	34	46	36	22	0	65	4	1	2	1	1	.50	8	.227	.293	.431
06	LAD	NL	8	14	7	1	1	2	(0	2)	16	4	9	6	0	0	2	0	0	0	1	0	1.00	0	.500	.500	1.143
06	Cin	NL	2	5	1	0	0	0	(0	0)	1	0	0	1	0	0	2	0	0	0	0	0	-	0	.200	.200	.200
06	Fla	NL	91	250	53	11	1	11	(6	5)	99	30	37	29	22	0	61	4	1	2	0	1	.00	8	.212	.284	.396
	3 ML YEARS		121	313	69	14	2	14	(7	7)	129	36	52	40	24	0	78	5	2	2	1	1	.50	9	.220	.285	.412

Dave Ross

Bats: R **Throws:** R **Pos:** C-75; PH-16   **Ht:** 6'2" **Wt:** 225 **Born:** 3/19/1977 **Age:** 30

Year	Team	Lg	G	AB	H	2B	3B	HR	(Hm	Rd)	TB	R	RBI	RC	TBB	IBB	SO	HBP	SH	SF	SB	CS	SB%	GDP	Avg	OBP	Slg
2006	Chatt*	AA	2	6	2	0	0	0	(-	-)	2	0	2	1	2	0	2	0	0	0	0	0	-	0	.333	.500	.333
2002	LAD	NL	8	10	2	1	0	1	(0	1)	6	2	2	2	2	0	4	1	0	0	0	0	-	0	.200	.385	.600
2003	LAD	NL	40	124	32	7	0	10	(5	5)	69	19	18	18	13	0	42	2	0	1	0	0	-	4	.258	.336	.556
2004	LAD	NL	70	165	28	3	1	5	(2	3)	48	13	15	11	15	1	62	5	0	5	0	0	-	3	.170	.253	.291
2005	2 Tms	NL	51	125	30	8	1	3	(2	1)	49	11	15	13	6	0	28	2	2	3	0	0	-	3	.240	.279	.392
2006	Cin	NL	90	247	63	15	1	21	(13	8)	143	37	52	43	37	7	75	3	4	5	0	0	-	4	.255	.353	.579
05	Pit	NL	40	108	24	8	0	3	(2	1)	41	9	15	9	6	0	24	1	1	3	0	0	-	3	.222	.263	.380
05	SD	NL	11	17	6	0	1	0	(0	0)	8	2	0	4	0	0	4	1	1	0	0	0	-	0	.353	.389	.471
5 ML YEARS			259	671	155	34	3	40	(22	18)	315	82	102	87	73	8	211	13	6	14	0	0	-	14	.231	.313	.469

Vinny Rottino

Bats: R **Throws:** R **Pos:** PH-4; 3B-3; LF-2; C-1   **Ht:** 6'0" **Wt:** 195 **Born:** 4/7/1980 **Age:** 27

Year	Team	Lg	G	AB	H	2B	3B	HR	(Hm	Rd)	TB	R	RBI	RC	TBB	IBB	SO	HBP	SH	SF	SB	CS	SB%	GDP	Avg	OBP	Slg
2003	Helena	R+	64	222	69	10	0	1	(-	-)	82	42	20	37	28	1	25	8	1	2	5	2	.71	4	.311	.404	.369
2004	Beloit	A	140	529	161	25	9	17	(-	-)	255	78	124	92	40	3	71	4	1	10	5	1	.83	12	.304	.352	.482
2005	Hntsvl	AA	120	469	139	20	6	6	(-	-)	189	63	52	69	40	1	68	2	0	5	2	1	.67	14	.296	.351	.403
2005	Nashv	AAA	9	29	10	1	0	1	(-	-)	14	4	2	5	3	0	6	0	0	0	0	1	.00	1	.345	.406	.483
2006	Nashv	AAA	117	398	125	25	2	7	(-	-)	175	55	42	69	40	2	74	5	4	5	12	7	.63	9	.314	.379	.440
2006	Mil	NL	9	14	3	1	0	0	(0	0)	4	1	1	1	1	0	2	0	0	0	1	0	1.00	0	.214	.267	.286

Mike Rouse

Bats: L **Throws:** R **Pos:** 2B-7; PH-1   **Ht:** 5'11" **Wt:** 200 **Born:** 4/25/1980 **Age:** 27

Year	Team	Lg	G	AB	H	2B	3B	HR	(Hm	Rd)	TB	R	RBI	RC	TBB	IBB	SO	HBP	SH	SF	SB	CS	SB%	GDP	Avg	OBP	Slg
2001	Dnedin	A+	48	180	49	17	2	5	(-	-)	85	27	24	28	13	0	45	2	6	1	3	1	.75	2	.272	.327	.472
2002	Tenn	AA	71	231	60	11	0	9	(-	-)	98	35	43	35	29	1	47	2	4	4	7	6	.54	3	.260	.342	.424
2003	Mdland	AA	129	457	137	33	3	3	(-	-)	185	75	53	80	63	2	83	9	13	4	7	2	.78	16	.300	.392	.405
2003	Scrmto	AAA	2	7	3	0	0	0	(-	-)	3	2	1	1	0	0	0	0	0	0	0	0	-	0	.429	.429	.429
2004	Scrmto	AAA	99	323	89	11	2	10	(-	-)	134	53	40	54	50	0	68	5	11	2	0	4	.00	5	.276	.379	.415
2005	Scrmto	AAA	130	469	126	30	3	7	(-	-)	183	69	72	70	59	0	115	7	17	2	2	4	.33	6	.269	.358	.390
2006	Scrmto	AAA	99	345	89	21	1	6	(-	-)	130	59	47	49	42	0	67	6	7	2	4	1	.80	8	.258	.347	.377
2006	Oak	AL	8	24	7	3	0	0	(0	0)	10	2	2	3	1	0	4	1	0	0	1	0	1.00	1	.292	.346	.417

Aaron Rowand

Bats: R **Throws:** R **Pos:** CF-107; PH-3   **Ht:** 6'0" **Wt:** 200 **Born:** 8/29/1977 **Age:** 29

Year	Team	Lg	G	AB	H	2B	3B	HR	(Hm	Rd)	TB	R	RBI	RC	TBB	IBB	SO	HBP	SH	SF	SB	CS	SB%	GDP	Avg	OBP	Slg
2001	CWS	AL	63	123	36	5	0	4	(3	1)	53	21	20	22	15	0	28	4	5	1	5	1	.83	2	.293	.385	.431
2002	CWS	AL	126	302	78	16	2	7	(5	2)	119	41	29	37	12	1	54	6	9	2	0	1	.00	8	.258	.298	.394
2003	CWS	AL	93	157	45	8	0	6	(5	1)	71	22	24	28	7	0	21	3	2	1	0	0	-	1	.287	.327	.452
2004	CWS	AL	140	487	151	38	2	24	(12	12)	265	94	69	92	30	1	91	10	5	2	17	5	.77	5	.310	.361	.544
2005	CWS	AL	157	578	156	30	5	13	(8	5)	235	77	69	78	32	3	116	21	5	4	16	5	.76	17	.270	.329	.407
2006	Phi	NL	109	405	106	24	3	12	(6	6)	172	59	47	47	18	2	76	18	2	2	10	4	.71	13	.262	.321	.425
6 ML YEARS			688	2052	572	121	12	66	(39	27)	915	314	258	304	114	7	386	62	28	12	48	16	.75	46	.279	.334	.446

Carlos Ruiz

Bats: R **Throws:** R **Pos:** C-24; PH-3; PR-3   **Ht:** 5'10" **Wt:** 200 **Born:** 1/22/1979 **Age:** 28

Year	Team	Lg	G	AB	H	2B	3B	HR	(Hm	Rd)	TB	R	RBI	RC	TBB	IBB	SO	HBP	SH	SF	SB	CS	SB%	GDP	Avg	OBP	Slg
2000	Phillies	R	38	130	36	7	1	1	(-	-)	48	11	22	17	9	0	9	2	0	2	3	0	1.00	5	.277	.329	.369
2001	Lakwd	A	73	249	65	14	3	4	(-	-)	97	21	32	28	10	0	27	1	1	2	5	4	.56	5	.261	.290	.390
2002	Clrwtr	A+	92	342	73	18	3	5	(-	-)	112	35	32	30	18	1	30	6	2	1	3	1	.75	16	.213	.264	.327
2003	Clrwtr	A+	15	54	17	0	0	2	(-	-)	23	5	9	7	2	0	5	0	0	0	2	2	.50	5	.315	.339	.426
2003	Rdng	AA	52	169	45	6	0	2	(-	-)	57	22	16	19	12	0	15	3	1	3	1	1	.50	10	.266	.321	.337
2004	Rdng	AA	101	349	99	15	2	17	(-	-)	169	45	50	58	22	1	37	8	1	3	8	4	.67	15	.284	.338	.484
2005	S-WB	AAA	100	347	104	25	9	4	(-	-)	159	50	40	57	30	2	48	3	1	7	4	5	.44	14	.300	.354	.458
2006	S-WB	AAA	100	368	113	25	0	16	(-	-)	186	56	69	73	42	6	56	9	1	3	4	3	.57	13	.307	.389	.505
2006	Phi	NL	27	69	18	1	1	3	(2	1)	30	5	10	10	5	2	8	1	2	1	0	0	-	3	.261	.316	.435

Josh Rupe

Pitches: R **Bats:** R **Pos:** RP-16   **Ht:** 6'2" **Wt:** 210 **Born:** 8/18/1982 **Age:** 24

			HOW MUCH HE PITCHED					WHAT HE GAVE UP											THE RESULTS						
Year	Team	Lg	G	GS	CG	GF	IP	BFP	H	R	ER	HR	SH	SF	HB	TBB	IBB	SO	WP	Bk	W	L	Pct	ShO	Sv-Op Hld	ERC	ERA
2002	Bristol	R+	17	2	0	3	37.2	185	38	23	22	4	1	0	4	22	1	41	6	1	3	3	.500	0	0- -	-	4.91	5.26
2003	Knapol	A-	26	7	2	11	65.2	283	50	27	22	0	1	1	2	36	2	69	2	0	5	5	.500	0	6- -	-	2.68	3.02
2003	Clinton	A	6	5	0	0	27.2	119	29	14	12	1	0	0	3	7	0	23	2	0	4	1	.800	0	0- -	-	3.75	3.90
2004	Stcktn	A+	4	3	0	1	18.1	71	12	4	2	0	1	1	3	4	0	14	2	0	2	0	1.000	0	0- -	-	1.72	0.98
2004	Spkane	A-	4	3	0	0	18.0	71	14	3	3	1	1	0	2	3	0	19	0	0	2	0	1.000	0	0- -	-	2.23	1.50
2004	Frisco	AA	7	6	0	0	37.0	168	41	23	18	5	1	4	5	16	1	16	2	0	2	2	.500	0	0- -	-	5.65	4.38
2005	Frisco	AA	11	10	0	0	65.0	285	64	29	27	7	1	1	3	26	0	55	2	0	4	3	.571	0	0- -	-	4.18	3.74
2005	Okla	AAA	17	17	0	0	93.2	435	116	75	65	12	6	3	8	38	1	62	4	1	6	7	.462	0	0- -	-	6.03	6.25

Year	Team	Lg	G	GS	CG	GF	IP	BFP	H	R	ER	HR	SH	SF	HB	TBB	IBB	SO	WP	Bk	W	L	Pct	ShO	Sv-Op	Hld	ERC	ERA
2006	Frisco	AA	6	0	0	0	6.0	30	7	7	7	2	1	0	0	4	0	3	0	0	0	0	-	0	0--	-	7.66	10.50
2006	Okla	AAA	12	0	0	6	13.1	57	13	6	5	0	0	0	2	6	0	4	0	0	1	1	.500	0	2--	-	4.17	3.38
2005	Tex	AL	4	1	0	1	9.2	39	7	4	3	0	1	0	2	4	0	6	1	0	1	0	1.000	0	0-0	-	2.91	2.79
2006	Tex	AL	16	0	0	3	29.0	126	33	11	11	2	1	0	1	9	0	14	2	0	0	1	.000	0	0-1	1	4.45	3.41
	2 ML YEARS		20	1	0	4	38.2	165	40	15	14	2	2	0	3	13	0	20	3	0	1	1	.500	0	0-1	1	4.06	3.26

Glendon Rusch

Pitches: L Bats: L Pos: RP-16; SP-9   **Ht: 6'1" Wt: 225 Born: 11/7/1974 Age: 32**

Year	Team	Lg	G	GS	CG	GF	IP	BFP	H	R	ER	HR	SH	SF	HB	TBB	IBB	SO	WP	Bk	W	L	Pct	ShO	Sv-Op	Hld	ERC	ERA
2006	Iowa*	AAA	1	1	0	0	4.0	14	2	1	1	0	1	0	0	0	0	2	0	0	0	0	-	0	0--	-	0.54	2.25
1997	KC	AL	30	27	1	0	170.1	758	206	111	104	28	8	7	7	52	0	116	0	1	6	9	.400	0	0--	-	5.56	5.50
1998	KC	AL	29	24	1	2	154.2	686	191	104	101	22	1	2	4	50	0	94	1	0	6	15	.286	1	1-1	0	5.62	5.88
1999	2 Tms		4	0	0	2	5.0	26	8	7	7	1	0	0	1	3	0	4	0	0	1	0	1.000	0	0-0	0	10.75	12.60
2000	NYM	NL	31	30	2	0	190.2	802	196	91	85	18	10	7	6	44	2	157	2	0	11	11	.500	0	0-0	0	3.64	4.01
2001	NYM	NL	33	33	1	0	179.0	785	216	101	92	23	11	5	7	43	2	156	3	2	8	12	.400	0	0-0	0	4.97	4.63
2002	Mil	NL	34	34	4	0	210.2	913	227	118	110	30	14	5	5	76	1	140	6	0	10	16	.385	1	0-0	0	4.80	4.70
2003	Mil	NL	32	19	1	1	123.1	573	171	93	88	11	5	2	4	45	3	93	3	0	1	12	.077	0	1-1	7	6.27	6.42
2004	ChC	NL	32	16	0	5	129.2	545	127	54	50	10	8	2	4	33	1	90	1	1	6	2	.750	0	2-2	3	3.33	3.47
2005	ChC	NL	46	19	1	6	145.1	655	175	79	73	14	13	9	1	53	8	111	1	1	9	8	.529	1	0-1	3	4.97	4.52
2006	ChC	NL	25	9	0	5	66.1	311	86	57	55	21	7	1	1	33	2	59	0	0	3	8	.273	0	0-0	0	8.09	7.46
99	KC	AL	3	0	0	1	4.0	23	7	7	7	1	0	0	1	3	0	4	0	0	0	1	.000	0	0-0	0	12.89	15.75
99	NYM	NL	1	0	0	1	1.0	3	1	0	0	0	0	0	0	0	0	0	0	0	1	0	1.000	0	0-0	0	2.79	0.00
	10 ML YEARS		296	211	11	21	1375.0	6054	1603	815	765	178	77	40	40	432	19	1020	17	5	60	94	.390	3	4-5	13	5.00	5.01

B.J. Ryan

Pitches: L Bats: L Pos: RP-65   **Ht: 6'6" Wt: 260 Born: 12/28/1975 Age: 31**

Year	Team	Lg	G	GS	CG	GF	IP	BFP	H	R	ER	HR	SH	SF	HB	TBB	IBB	SO	WP	Bk	W	L	Pct	ShO	Sv-Op	Hld	ERC	ERA
1999	2 Tms		14	0	0	3	20.1	82	13	7	7	0	0	0	0	13	1	29	1	0	1	0	1.000	0	0-0	0	2.42	3.10
2000	Bal	AL	42	0	0	9	42.2	193	36	29	28	7	1	1	0	31	1	41	2	1	2	3	.400	0	0-3	7	4.87	5.91
2001	Bal	AL	61	0	0	9	53.0	237	47	31	25	6	1	2	2	30	4	54	0	0	2	4	.333	0	2-4	14	4.13	4.25
2002	Bal	AL	67	0	0	13	57.2	252	51	31	30	7	3	0	4	33	4	56	4	0	2	1	.667	0	1-2	12	4.48	4.68
2003	Bal	AL	76	0	0	17	50.1	219	42	19	19	1	1	3	3	27	0	63	2	0	4	1	.800	0	0-2	19	3.33	3.40
2004	Bal	AL	76	0	0	19	87.0	361	64	24	22	4	3	2	1	35	9	122	0	0	4	6	.400	0	3-7	21	2.20	2.28
2005	Bal	AL	69	0	0	61	70.1	290	54	20	19	4	1	1	2	26	2	100	5	0	1	4	.200	0	36-41	0	2.50	2.43
2006	Tor	AL	65	0	0	57	72.1	270	42	12	11	3	1	1	0	20	1	86	4	0	2	2	.500	0	38-42	1	1.39	1.37
99	Cin	NL	1	0	0	0	2.0	9	4	1	1	0	0	0	0	1	0	1	0	0	0	0	-	0	0-0	0	12.01	4.50
99	Bal	AL	13	0	0	3	18.1	73	9	6	6	0	0	0	0	12	1	28	1	0	1	0	1.000	0	0-0	0	1.73	2.95
	8 ML YEARS		470	0	0	188	453.2	1904	349	173	161	32	11	11	12	215	22	551	18	1	18	21	.462	0	80-101	74	2.94	3.19

Jae Kuk Ryu

Pitches: R Bats: R Pos: RP-9; SP-1   **Ht: 6'3" Wt: 220 Born: 5/30/1983 Age: 24**

Year	Team	Lg	G	GS	CG	GF	IP	BFP	H	R	ER	HR	SH	SF	HB	TBB	IBB	SO	WP	Bk	W	L	Pct	ShO	Sv-Op	Hld	ERC	ERA
2001	Cubs	R	4	3	0	0	14.2	61	11	2	1	0	0	0	0	5	0	20	2	0	1	0	1.000	0	0--	-	1.87	0.61
2002	Boise	A	10	10	0	0	53.0	234	45	28	21	1	1	2	4	25	0	56	8	1	6	1	.857	0	0--	-	3.14	3.57
2002	Lansng	A	5	4	0	0	19.0	91	26	16	15	1	3	0	2	8	0	21	5	0	1	2	.333	0	0--	-	6.39	7.11
2003	Dytona	A	4	4	0	0	20.2	79	14	14	7	1	1	0	2	11	0	22	2	0	0	1	.000	0	0--	-	3.21	3.05
2003	Lansng	A	11	11	0	0	72.0	292	59	19	14	2	2	4	5	19	0	57	10	1	6	1	.857	0	0--	-	2.43	1.75
2003	WTenn	AA	11	11	1	0	58.0	261	63	37	35	3	4	2	5	25	0	45	2	1	2	5	.286	0	0--	-	4.66	5.43
2004	Cubs	R	2	2	0	0	4.0	16	4	2	2	1	0	0	0	0	0	5	0	0	0	0	-	0	0--	-	3.33	4.50
2004	Boise	A	5	0	0	0	7.0	33	7	3	2	0	0	0	0	5	0	7	4	0	0	2	.000	0	0--	-	4.40	2.57
2004	WTenn	AA	14	0	0	1	18.1	88	22	8	6	0	0	0	1	10	3	19	2	0	1	0	1.000	0	0--	-	4.79	2.95
2004	Iowa	AAA	1	0	0	0	0.2	5	2	4	3	1	0	0	0	1	0	0	0	0	0	0	-	0	0--	-	41.86	40.50
2005	WTenn	AA	27	27	1	0	169.2	686	154	67	63	12	15	4	6	49	1	133	9	0	11	8	.579	1	0--	-	3.18	3.34
2006	Iowa	AAA	24	23	1	0	139.1	582	123	54	50	12	4	3	4	51	1	114	8	0	8	8	.500	0	0--	-	3.33	3.23
2006	ChC	NL	10	1	0	4	15.0	77	23	14	14	7	3	0	2	6	1	17	1	0	0	1	.000	0	0-0	0	10.72	8.40

Kirk Saarloos

Pitches: R Bats: R Pos: RP-19; SP-16   **Ht: 6'0" Wt: 185 Born: 5/23/1979 Age: 28**

Year	Team	Lg	G	GS	CG	GF	IP	BFP	H	R	ER	HR	SH	SF	HB	TBB	IBB	SO	WP	Bk	W	L	Pct	ShO	Sv-Op	Hld	ERC	ERA
2002	Hou	NL	17	17	1	0	85.1	372	100	59	57	12	5	2	6	27	5	54	1	0	6	7	.462	1	0-0	0	5.35	6.01
2003	Hou	NL	36	4	0	11	49.1	218	55	31	27	4	1	1	3	17	3	43	0	0	2	1	.667	0	0-0	4	4.51	4.93
2004	Oak	AL	6	5	0	0	24.1	112	27	13	12	4	2	1	2	12	0	10	0	0	2	1	.667	0	0-0	0	5.91	4.44
2005	Oak	AL	29	27	2	0	159.2	682	170	75	74	11	3	3	11	54	8	53	1	0	10	9	.526	1	0-0	0	4.27	4.17
2006	Oak	AL	35	16	0	7	121.1	548	149	70	64	19	2	6	3	53	3	52	3	0	7	7	.500	0	2-3	6	6.17	4.75
	5 ML YEARS		123	69	3	19	440.0	1932	501	248	234	50	13	13	25	163	19	212	5	0	27	25	.519	2	2-3	4	5.10	4.79

C.C. Sabathia

Pitches: L Bats: L Pos: SP-28   Ht: 6'7" Wt: 290 Born: 7/21/1980 Age: 26

		HOW MUCH HE PITCHED						WHAT HE GAVE UP											THE RESULTS						
Year	Team	Lg	G	GS	CG	GF	IP	BFP	H	R	ER	HR	SH	SF	HB	TBB	IBB	SO	WP	Bk	W	L	Pct	ShO	Sv-Op Hld	ERC	ERA
2006	Buffalo*	AAA	1	1	0	0	5.0	22	6	2	1	0	1	0	0	1	0	5	1	0	1	0	1.000	0	0-- -	3.60	1.80
2001	Cle	AL	33	33	0	0	180.1	763	149	93	88	19	3	5	7	95	1	171	7	3	17	5	.773	0	0-0 0	3.86	4.39
2002	Cle	AL	33	33	2	0	210.0	891	198	109	102	17	5	10	1	88	2	149	6	3	13	11	.542	0	0-0 0	3.74	4.37
2003	Cle	AL	30	30	2	0	197.2	832	190	85	79	19	10	4	6	66	3	141	4	2	13	9	.591	1	0-0 0	3.70	3.60
2004	Cle	AL	30	30	1	0	188.0	787	176	90	86	20	3	6	7	72	3	139	1	1	11	10	.524	1	0-0 0	3.91	4.12
2005	Cle	AL	31	31	1	0	196.2	823	185	92	88	19	6	3	7	62	1	161	7	0	15	10	.600	0	0-0 0	3.55	4.03
2006	Cle	AL	28	28	6	0	192.2	802	182	83	69	17	8	5	7	44	3	172	3	0	12	11	.522	2	0-0 0	3.13	3.22
6 ML YEARS			185	185	12	0	1165.1	4898	1080	552	512	111	35	33	35	427	13	933	28	9	81	56	.591	4	0-0 0	3.64	3.95

Billy Sadler

Pitches: R Bats: R Pos: RP-5   Ht: 6'0" Wt: 190 Born: 9/21/1981 Age: 25

		HOW MUCH HE PITCHED						WHAT HE GAVE UP											THE RESULTS						
Year	Team	Lg	G	GS	CG	GF	IP	BFP	H	R	ER	HR	SH	SF	HB	TBB	IBB	SO	WP	Bk	W	L	Pct	ShO	Sv-Op Hld	ERC	ERA
2003	Hgrstn	A	12	0	0	6	15.0	72	15	8	8	4	0	0	2	13	0	10	0	0	0	0	-	0	1-- -	8.17	4.80
2004	SnJos	A+	30	3	0	3	56.0	241	29	17	15	1	1	1	4	40	0	16	3	2	2	2	.500	0	0-- -	2.34	2.41
2004	Nrwich	AA	17	0	0	6	30.1	134	22	16	13	3	0	0	3	18	0	24	8	0	0	3	.000	0	0-- -	3.60	3.86
2005	Nrwich	AA	47	0	0	22	84.1	350	64	34	31	4	4	2	12	33	0	81	9	0	6	5	.545	0	5-- -	2.98	3.31
2006	Nrwich	AA	44	0	0	34	45.2	190	23	14	13	1	2	0	2	29	2	67	2	0	4	3	.571	0	20-- -	1.93	2.56
2006	Fresno	AAA	7	0	0	5	10.0	34	5	2	2	1	0	0	0	2	0	12	1	0	2	0	1.000	0	1-- -	1.27	1.80
2006	SF	NL	5	0	0	2	4.0	20	5	3	3	2	0	0	1	2	0	6	0	0	0	0	-	0	0-0 0	10.38	6.75

Olmedo Saenz

Bats: R Throws: R Pos: PH-66; 1B-30; 3B-16; DH-3   Ht: 5'11" Wt: 220 Born: 10/8/1970 Age: 36

		BATTING																BASERUNNING				AVERAGES		
Year	Team	Lg	G	AB	H	2B	3B	HR	(Hm Rd)	TB	R	RBI	RC	TBB	IBB	SO	HBP	SH	SF	SB	CS	SB%	GDP	Avg	OBP	Slg
1994	CWS	AL	5	14	2	0	1	0	(0 0)	4	2	0	0	0	0	5	0	1	0	0	0	-	1	.143	.143	.286
1999	Oak	AL	97	255	70	18	0	11	(8 3)	121	41	41	44	22	1	47	15	0	3	1	1	.50	6	.275	.363	.475
2000	Oak	AL	76	214	67	12	3	6	(3 6)	110	40	33	42	25	2	40	7	0	1	1	0	1.00	6	.313	.401	.514
2001	Oak	AL	106	305	67	21	1	9	(6 3)	117	33	32	32	19	1	64	13	1	3	0	1	.00	9	.220	.291	.384
2002	Oak	AL	68	156	43	10	1	6	(3 3)	73	15	18	23	13	1	31	7	0	2	1	1	.50	2	.276	.354	.468
2004	LAD	NL	77	111	31	1	0	8	(3 5)	56	17	22	18	12	1	33	2	0	3	0	0	-	4	.279	.352	.505
2005	LAD	NL	109	319	84	24	0	15	(9 6)	153	39	63	50	27	1	63	3	0	2	0	1	.00	12	.263	.325	.480
2006	LAD	NL	103	179	53	15	0	11	(6 5)	101	30	48	33	14	1	47	7	0	4	0	0	-	4	.296	.363	.564
8 ML YEARS			641	1553	417	101	5	69	(38 31)	735	217	257	242	132	8	330	54	2	18	3	4	.43	44	.269	.343	.473

Kazumi Saito

Pitches: R Bats: R Pos: P   Ht: 6'4" Wt: 198 Born: 11/30/1977 Age: 29

		HOW MUCH HE PITCHED						WHAT HE GAVE UP											THE RESULTS						
Year	Team	Lg	G	GS	CG	GF	IP	BFP	H	R	ER	HR	SH	SF	HB	TBB	IBB	SO	WP	Bk	W	L	Pct	ShO	Sv-Op Hld	ERC	ERA
1997	Fk Dai	Jap	1	0	0	0	0.2	6	2	2	2	0	-	-	1	1	-	1	0	0	0	0	-	0	0-- -	29.63	27.00
1998	Fk Dai	Jap	1	0	0	1	3.2	19	6	3	3	0	-	-	1	3	-	1	0	0	0	0	-	0	0-- -	10.99	7.36
1999	Fk Dai	Jap	1	0	0	0	1.0	6	1	2	2	0	-	-	1	0	-	3	1	1	0	0	-	0	0-- -	4.47	18.00
2000	Fk Dai	Jap	22	16	0	0	89.1	399	92	44	41	9	-	-	1	46	-	77	10	1	5	2	.714	0	0-- -	4.74	4.13
2001	Fk Dai	Jap	7	3	1	2	22.1	104	28	11	11	4	-	-	1	11	-	16	1	0	1	0	1.000	0	0-- -	6.84	4.43
2002	Fk Dai	Jap	10	10	0	0	70.1	282	53	24	23	4	-	-	3	21	-	63	3	0	4	1	.800	0	0-- -	2.32	2.94
2003	Fk Dai	Jap	26	26	5	0	194.0	801	174	62	61	19	11	3	8	66	3	160	4	0	20	3	.870	1	0-- -	3.47	2.83
2004	Fk Dai	Jap	22	22	3	0	138.0	612	139	100	96	22	15	4	6	59	3	120	6	0	10	7	.588	0	0-- -	4.74	6.26
2005	Fk Dai	Jap	22	-	4	0	157.0	647	135	54	51	14	-	-	10	41	-	129	5	0	16	1	.941	1	0-- -	2.96	2.92
2006	Fk Dai	Jap	26	26	8	0	201.0	796	147	50	39	10	-	-	8	46	-	205	2	0	18	5	.783	5	0-- -	1.77	1.75

Takashi Saito

Pitches: R Bats: R Pos: RP-72   Ht: 6'2" Wt: 200 Born: 2/14/1970 Age: 37

		HOW MUCH HE PITCHED						WHAT HE GAVE UP											THE RESULTS						
Year	Team	Lg	G	GS	CG	GF	IP	BFP	H	R	ER	HR	SH	SF	HB	TBB	IBB	SO	WP	Bk	W	L	Pct	ShO	Sv-Op Hld	ERC	ERA
1992	Yokha	Jap	6	2	0	1	16.0	76	18	16	15	2	-	-	0	10	-	21	2	0	0	2	.000	0	0-- -	5.78	8.44
1993	Yokha	Jap	29	21	2	1	149.0	627	127	66	63	15	-	-	6	61	-	125	7	0	8	10	.444	0	0-- -	3.48	3.81
1994	Yokha	Jap	28	20	7	0	181.0	769	175	70	63	5	-	-	8	69	-	169	2	0	9	12	.429	3	0-- -	3.53	3.13
1995	Yokha	Jap	26	24	2	0	162.0	682	166	79	71	13	-	-	6	45	-	132	1	0	8	9	.471	0	0-- -	3.78	3.94
1996	Yokha	Jap	28	16	11	0	196.2	801	157	80	72	31	-	-	11	63	-	206	4	1	10	10	.500	2	0-- -	3.30	3.29
1998	Yokha	Jap	34	17	1	4	143.2	572	131	49	47	9	-	-	2	23	-	101	2	0	13	5	.722	0	1-- -	2.55	2.94
1999	Yokha	Jap	26	21	5	0	184.2	754	178	83	81	32	-	-	6	31	-	125	1	1	14	3	.824	2	0-- -	3.58	3.95
2000	Yokha	Jap	19	18	1	0	115.2	493	123	74	71	17	-	-	3	36	-	97	1	0	6	10	.375	1	0-- -	4.57	5.52
2001	Yokha	Jap	50	0	0	43	64.0	251	51	12	12	6	-	-	0	14	-	60	0	0	7	1	.875	0	27-- -	2.33	1.69
2002	Yokha	Jap	39	0	0	34	47.2	197	37	17	13	5	-	-	4	15	-	46	0	0	1	2	.333	0	20-- -	2.88	2.45
2003	Yokha	Jap	17	16	1	0	103.1	439	103	59	48	16	-	-	9	22	1	72	1	0	6	7	.462	0	0-- -	3.98	4.18
2004	Yokha	Jap	16	7	0	3	44.1	211	64	41	38	12	2	3	2	13	-	37	1	1	2	5	.286	0	0-- -	7.74	7.71
2005	Yokha	Jap	21	16	0	1	106.0	458	111	50	45	12	-	-	7	29	-	93	2	0	3	4	.429	0	0-- -	4.17	3.82
2006	LAD	NL	72	0	0	48	78.1	303	48	19	18	3	3	4	2	23	3	107	2	0	6	2	.750	0	24-26 7	1.52	2.07

Juan Salas

Pitches: R Bats: R Pos: RP-8   Ht: 6'2" Wt: 210 Born: 11/7/1978 Age: 28

Year	Team	Lg	G	GS	CG	GF	IP	BFP	H	R	ER	HR	SH	SF	HB	TBB	IBB	SO	WP	Bk	W	L	Pct	ShO	Sv-Op	Hld	ERC	ERA
2004	Princtn	A+	8	0	0	3	9.1	44	10	7	5	2	0	0	0	6	1	6	0	1	1	0	1.000	0	0--	-	6.05	4.82
2005	Visalia	A+	25	0	0	11	38.1	164	30	19	15	6	2	1	5	18	1	47	6	1	2	1	.667	0	1--	-	4.03	3.52
2005	Mont	AA	15	0	0	6	22.0	104	25	12	9	2	0	1	2	12	0	18	5	1	1	0	1.000	0	1--	-	5.68	3.68
2006	Mont	AA	23	0	0	22	34.2	133	13	4	0	0	0	0	1	14	0	52	0	0	3	0	1.000	0	14--	-	0.94	0.00
2006	Drham	AAA	27	0	0	10	28.2	113	15	5	5	3	0	0	1	11	0	33	1	0	1	1	.500	0	3--	-	1.75	1.57
2006	TB	AL	8	0	0	2	10.0	48	13	7	6	1	0	1	0	3	0	8	3	0	0	0	-	0	0-1	1	5.03	5.40

Jeff Salazar

Bats: L Throws: L Pos: CF-14; PH-6; RF-1   Ht: 6'0" Wt: 190 Born: 11/24/1980 Age: 26

Year	Team	Lg	G	AB	H	2B	3B	HR	(Hm	Rd)	TB	R	RBI	RC	TBB	IBB	SO	HBP	SH	SF	SB	CS	SB%	GDP	Avg	OBP	Slg
2002	Tri-Cit	A-	72	268	63	5	4	4	(-	-)	88	38	21	35	47	0	43	2	9	2	10	6	.63	2	.235	.351	.328
2003	Ashvlle	A-	129	486	138	23	4	29	(-	-)	256	109	98	102	77	8	74	7	4	4	28	14	.67	5	.284	.387	.527
2003	Visalia	A+	1	5	0	0	0	0	(-	-)	0	1	0	0	0	0	0	0	0	0	0	0	-	0	.000	.000	.000
2004	Visalia	A+	75	314	109	18	9	13	(-	-)	184	79	44	77	38	3	33	2	2	2	17	2	.89	4	.347	.419	.586
2004	Tulsa	AA	58	224	50	13	2	1	(-	-)	70	39	17	27	35	0	31	2	7	2	10	3	.77	1	.223	.331	.313
2005	Tulsa	AA	69	266	74	13	2	6	(-	-)	109	47	35	45	44	4	49	2	4	3	12	8	.60	1	.278	.381	.410
2005	ColSpr	AAA	59	236	62	17	3	6	(-	-)	103	42	26	38	32	0	58	0	3	1	5	2	.71	1	.263	.349	.436
2006	ColSpr	AAA	85	328	87	14	7	9	(-	-)	142	62	39	54	46	1	64	2	3	2	12	5	.71	0	.265	.357	.433
2006	Col	NL	19	53	15	4	0	1	(1	0)	22	13	8	11	11	2	16	1	1	1	2	0	1.00	0	.283	.409	.415

Tim Salmon

Bats: R Throws: R Pos: DH-54; PH-18; RF-3; LF-1; PR-1   Ht: 6'3" Wt: 235 Born: 8/24/1968 Age: 38

Year	Team	Lg	G	AB	H	2B	3B	HR	(Hm	Rd)	TB	R	RBI	RC	TBB	IBB	SO	HBP	SH	SF	SB	CS	SB%	GDP	Avg	OBP	Slg
1992	LAA	AL	23	79	14	1	0	2	(1	1)	21	8	6	6	11	1	23	1	0	1	1	1	.50	1	.177	.283	.266
1993	LAA	AL	142	515	146	35	1	31	(23	8)	276	93	95	104	82	5	135	5	0	8	5	6	.45	6	.283	.382	.536
1994	LAA	AL	100	373	107	18	2	23	(12	11)	198	67	70	75	54	2	102	5	0	3	1	3	.25	3	.287	.382	.531
1995	LAA	AL	143	537	177	34	3	34	(15	19)	319	111	105	130	91	2	111	6	0	4	5	5	.50	9	.330	.429	.594
1996	LAA	AL	156	581	166	27	4	30	(18	12)	291	90	98	113	93	7	125	4	0	3	4	2	.67	8	.286	.386	.501
1997	LAA	AL	157	582	172	28	1	33	(17	16)	301	95	129	117	95	5	142	7	0	11	9	12	.43	7	.296	.394	.517
1998	LAA	AL	136	463	139	28	1	26	(13	13)	247	84	88	103	90	5	100	3	0	10	0	1	.00	4	.300	.410	.533
1999	LAA	AL	98	353	94	24	2	17	(7	10)	173	60	69	66	63	2	82	0	0	6	4	1	.80	7	.266	.372	.490
2000	LAA	AL	158	568	165	36	2	34	(17	17)	307	108	97	120	104	5	139	6	0	2	0	2	.00	14	.290	.404	.540
2001	LAA	AL	137	475	108	21	1	17	(11	6)	182	63	49	72	96	4	121	8	0	2	9	3	.75	11	.227	.365	.383
2002	LAA	AL	138	483	138	37	1	22	(10	12)	243	84	88	98	71	3	102	7	0	7	6	3	.67	6	.286	.380	.503
2003	LAA	AL	148	528	145	35	4	19	(10	9)	245	78	72	91	77	3	93	10	0	6	3	1	.75	12	.275	.374	.464
2004	LAA	AL	60	186	47	7	0	2	(1	1)	60	15	23	21	14	0	41	2	0	4	1	0	1.00	2	.253	.306	.323
2006	LAA	AL	76	211	56	8	2	9	(5	4)	95	30	27	27	29	1	44	3	0	1	0	2	.00	8	.265	.361	.450
	14 ML YEARS		1672	5934	1674	339	24	299	(160	139)	2958	986	1016	1143	970	45	1360	67	0	68	48	42	.53	98	.282	.385	.498

Chris Sampson

Pitches: R Bats: R Pos: RP-9; SP-3   Ht: 6'1" Wt: 190 Born: 5/23/1978 Age: 29

Year	Team	Lg	G	GS	CG	GF	IP	BFP	H	R	ER	HR	SH	SF	HB	TBB	IBB	SO	WP	Bk	W	L	Pct	ShO	Sv-Op	Hld	ERC	ERA
2003	Lxngtn	A	22	14	0	2	81.0	332	66	17	13	2	1	0	5	14	0	66	0	0	4	3	.571	0	1--	-	1.98	1.44
2003	Salem	A+	9	0	0	5	10.2	51	14	8	7	0	2	0	1	5	2	6	0	0	1	1	.500	0	1--	-	5.36	5.91
2004	Salem	A+	27	27	2	0	151.2	626	179	72	64	8	6	8	9	26	0	101	2	0	7	11	.389	2	0--	-	4.29	3.80
2004	RdRck	AA	1	0	0	0	2.0	9	3	0	0	0	0	0	0	0	1	0	0	0	0	0	-	0	0--	-	4.47	0.00
2005	CpChr	AA	32	19	2	9	150.0	618	147	67	52	11	4	4	4	19	2	92	2	0	4	12	.250	1	4--	-	2.79	3.12
2006	RdRck	AAA	27	18	2	8	125.2	501	110	48	35	12	7	5	3	14	0	68	2	0	12	3	.800	0	4--	-	2.38	2.51
2006	Hou	NL	12	3	0	0	34.0	130	25	10	8	3	1	1	1	5	1	15	0	0	2	1	.667	0	0-0	0	1.84	2.12

Brian Sanches

Pitches: R Bats: R Pos: RP-18   Ht: 6'0" Wt: 190 Born: 8/8/1978 Age: 28

Year	Team	Lg	G	GS	CG	GF	IP	BFP	H	R	ER	HR	SH	SF	HB	TBB	IBB	SO	WP	Bk	W	L	Pct	ShO	Sv-Op	Hld	ERC	ERA
1999	Spkane	A-	9	9	0	0	34.0	146	32	19	18	2	0	0	1	12	0	51	0	0	1	1	.500	0	0--	-	3.35	4.76
2000	Wilmg	A+	28	27	2	0	158.0	665	132	77	62	9	5	7	15	69	0	122	11	3	6	12	.333	1	0--	-	3.45	3.53
2001	Wichta	AA	29	21	0	3	134.0	610	152	96	89	12	7	3	13	61	4	95	12	1	7	9	.438	0	0--	-	5.37	5.98
2002	Wichta	AA	33	15	0	7	116.2	498	111	60	57	8	5	3	6	43	5	101	7	1	10	6	.625	0	0--	-	3.61	4.40
2003	Wichta	AA	38	6	0	13	85.0	351	84	38	30	8	4	4	3	17	2	72	3	2	1	5	.167	0	2--	-	3.31	3.18
2004	Rdng	AA	41	0	0	14	69.2	292	55	22	21	10	2	1	3	25	1	60	1	0	4	2	.667	0	3--	-	3.15	2.71
2004	S-WB	AAA	4	0	0	1	6.0	30	9	5	5	1	0	0	0	3	0	4	0	0	0	0	-	0	0--	-	7.95	7.50
2005	S-WB	AAA	51	2	0	13	83.0	352	81	36	34	9	1	4	9	27	2	75	1	0	5	3	.625	0	1--	-	4.18	3.69
2006	S-WB	AAA	36	0	0	28	43.2	164	24	9	9	2	2	2	1	13	1	52	1	1	3	2	.600	0	19--	-	1.40	1.85
2006	Phi	NL	18	0	0	5	21.1	98	23	14	14	5	0	0	0	13	3	22	0	1	0	0	-	0	0-0	0	6.18	5.91

Angel Sanchez

Bats: R **Throws:** R **Pos:** 2B-4; SS-4 **Ht:** 6'2" **Wt:** 185 **Born:** 9/20/1983 **Age:** 23

Year	Team	Lg	G	AB	H	2B	3B	HR	(Hm	Rd)	TB	R	RBI	RC	TBB	IBB	SO	HBP	SH	SF	SB	CS	SB%	GDP	Avg	OBP	Slg
2001	Royals	R	30	95	23	4	0	0	(-	-)	27	10	6	8	6	0	28	0	2	0	3	1	.75	2	.242	.287	.284
2002	Royals	R	49	175	44	4	0	0	(-	-)	48	21	12	16	10	0	24	4	5	3	9	2	.82	1	.251	.302	.274
2003	Burlgtn	A	106	408	110	8	1	2	(-	-)	126	54	35	44	28	0	52	4	6	3	14	5	.74	10	.270	.321	.309
2004	Burlgtn	A	90	337	85	12	1	2	(-	-)	105	34	24	33	15	0	47	9	9	2	16	7	.70	5	.252	.300	.312
2005	Hi Dsrt	A+	133	585	183	33	4	5	(-	-)	239	102	70	88	39	0	54	3	7	5	10	5	.67	11	.313	.356	.409
2006	Wichta	AA	133	542	153	24	1	4	(-	-)	191	105	57	68	44	0	63	7	11	8	8	9	.47	12	.282	.339	.352
2006	KC	AL	8	27	6	0	0	0	(0	0)	6	2	1	0	0	0	4	0	0	1	0	0	-	0	.222	.214	.222

Anibal Sanchez

Pitches: R **Bats:** R **Pos:** SP-17; RP-1 **Ht:** 6'0" **Wt:** 180 **Born:** 2/27/1984 **Age:** 23

			HOW MUCH HE PITCHED					WHAT HE GAVE UP										THE RESULTS						
Year	Team	Lg	G	GS	CG	GF	IP	BFP	H	R	ER	HR	SH	SF	HB	TBB	IBB	SO	WP	Bk	W	L	Pct	ShO	Sv-Op Hld	ERC	ERA
2004	Lowell	A	15	15	0	0	76.1	310	43	24	15	3	3	4	6	29	0	101	2	1	3	4	.429	0	0-- -	1.67	1.77
2005	Wilmg	A+	14	14	0	0	78.2	313	53	25	21	7	0	5	3	24	0	95	5	0	6	1	.857	0	0-- -	2.11	2.40
2005	Portlnd	AA	11	11	0	0	57.1	241	53	28	22	5	1	2	5	16	2	63	4	1	3	5	.375	0	0-- -	3.40	3.45
2006	Carlina	AA	15	15	2	0	85.2	366	82	41	30	7	3	0	2	27	1	92	4	0	3	6	.333	1	0-- -	3.40	3.15
2006	Fla	NL	18	17	2	0	114.1	469	90	39	36	9	3	1	4	46	1	72	4	1	10	3	.769	1	0-0 0	2.96	2.83

Duaner Sanchez

Pitches: R **Bats:** R **Pos:** RP-49 **Ht:** 6'2" **Wt:** 210 **Born:** 10/14/1979 **Age:** 27

			HOW MUCH HE PITCHED					WHAT HE GAVE UP										THE RESULTS						
Year	Team	Lg	G	GS	CG	GF	IP	BFP	H	R	ER	HR	SH	SF	HB	TBB	IBB	SO	WP	Bk	W	L	Pct	ShO	Sv-Op Hld	ERC	ERA
2002	2 Tms	NL	9	0	0	5	6.0	31	6	6	6	2	0	0	0	7	0	6	0	0	0	0	-	0	0-1 1	9.19	9.00
2003	Pit	NL	6	0	0	2	6.0	34	15	11	11	2	0	1	2	1	0	3	0	0	1	0	1.000	0	0-0 0	17.96	16.50
2004	LAD	NL	67	0	0	27	80.0	342	81	34	30	9	2	3	6	27	2	44	6	0	3	1	.750	0	0-1 4	4.31	3.38
2005	LAD	NL	79	0	0	31	82.0	353	75	36	34	8	10	1	3	36	6	71	7	1	4	7	.364	0	8-12 13	3.76	3.73
2006	NYM	NL	49	0	0	15	55.1	229	43	19	16	3	4	4	4	24	6	44	1	0	5	1	.833	0	0-1 14	2.85	2.60
02	Ari	NL	6	0	0	3	3.2	19	3	2	2	1	0	0	0	5	0	4	0	0	0	0	-	0	0-1 1	8.32	4.91
02	Pit	NL	3	0	0	2	2.1	12	3	4	4	1	0	0	0	2	0	2	0	0	0	0	-	0	0-0 0	10.55	15.43
	5 ML YEARS		210	0	0	80	229.1	989	220	106	97	24	16	9	15	95	14	168	14	1	13	9	.591	0	8-15 32	4.13	3.81

Freddy Sanchez

Bats: R **Throws:** R **Pos:** 3B-99; SS-28; 2B-23; PH-17 **Ht:** 5'10" **Wt:** 185 **Born:** 12/21/1977 **Age:** 29

Year	Team	Lg	G	AB	H	2B	3B	HR	(Hm	Rd)	TB	R	RBI	RC	TBB	IBB	SO	HBP	SH	SF	SB	CS	SB%	GDP	Avg	OBP	Slg
2002	Bos	AL	12	16	3	0	0	0	(0	0)	3	3	2	1	2	0	3	0	0	0	0	0	-	0	.188	.278	.188
2003	Bos	AL	20	34	8	2	0	0	(0	0)	10	6	2	1	0	0	8	0	0	0	0	0	-	0	.235	.235	.294
2004	Pit	NL	9	19	3	0	0	0	(0	0)	3	2	2	2	0	0	3	0	1	0	0	0	-	0	.158	.158	.158
2005	Pit	NL	132	453	132	26	4	5	(3	2)	181	54	35	57	27	1	36	5	4	3	2	2	.50	6	.291	.336	.400
2006	Pit	NL	157	582	200	53	2	6	(2	4)	275	85	85	101	31	6	52	7	3	9	3	2	.60	12	**.344**	.378	.473
	5 ML YEARS		330	1104	346	81	6	11	(5	6)	472	150	126	162	60	7	102	12	8	12	5	4	.56	18	.313	.352	.428

Jonathan Sanchez

Pitches: L **Bats:** L **Pos:** RP-23; SP-4 **Ht:** 6'2" **Wt:** 165 **Born:** 11/19/1982 **Age:** 24

			HOW MUCH HE PITCHED					WHAT HE GAVE UP										THE RESULTS						
Year	Team	Lg	G	GS	CG	GF	IP	BFP	H	R	ER	HR	SH	SF	HB	TBB	IBB	SO	WP	Bk	W	L	Pct	ShO	Sv-Op Hld	ERC	ERA
2004	Giants	R	9	3	0	3	26.0	109	22	9	8	0	0	1	2	9	1	27	1	0	5	0	1.000	0	1-- -	2.60	2.77
2004	SlmKzr	A-	6	6	0	0	22.1	102	16	13	12	3	2	1	1	19	0	34	0	1	2	1	.667	0	0-- -	4.62	4.84
2005	Augsta	A	25	25	0	0	125.2	538	122	59	57	8	3	5	7	39	0	166	7	0	5	7	.417	0	0-- -	3.50	4.08
2006	Conn	AA	13	13	0	4	31.1	116	14	7	4	0	2	1	2	9	0	46	2	0	2	1	.667	0	2-- -	1.01	1.15
2006	Fresno	AAA	6	6	0	0	23.2	97	13	10	10	1	0	2	2	13	0	28	1	0	2	2	.500	0	0-- -	2.22	3.80
2006	SF	NL	27	4	0	4	40.0	185	39	26	22	2	0	2	4	23	0	33	2	0	3	1	.750	0	0-0 5	4.54	4.95

Reggie Sanders

Bats: R **Throws:** R **Pos:** RF-73; DH-12; PH-4; PR-1 **Ht:** 6'1" **Wt:** 205 **Born:** 12/1/1967 **Age:** 39

Year	Team	Lg	G	AB	H	2B	3B	HR	(Hm	Rd)	TB	R	RBI	RC	TBB	IBB	SO	HBP	SH	SF	SB	CS	SB%	GDP	Avg	OBP	Slg
1991	Cin	NL	9	40	8	0	0	1	(0	1)	11	6	3	1	0	0	9	0	0	0	1	1	.50	1	.200	.200	.275
1992	Cin	NL	116	385	104	26	6	12	(6	6)	178	62	36	64	48	2	98	4	0	1	16	7	.70	6	.270	.356	.462
1993	Cin	NL	138	496	136	16	4	20	(8	12)	220	90	83	76	51	7	118	5	3	8	27	10	.73	10	.274	.343	.444
1994	Cin	NL	107	400	105	20	8	17	(10	7)	192	66	62	65	41	1	**114**	2	1	3	21	9	.70	2	.263	.332	.480
1995	Cin	NL	133	484	148	36	6	28	(9	19)	280	91	99	109	69	4	122	8	0	6	36	12	.75	9	.306	.397	.579
1996	Cin	NL	81	287	72	17	1	14	(7	7)	133	49	33	47	44	4	86	2	0	1	24	8	.75	6	.251	.353	.463
1997	Cin	NL	86	312	79	19	2	19	(11	8)	159	52	56	53	42	3	93	3	1	0	13	7	.65	9	.253	.347	.510
1998	Cin	NL	135	481	129	18	6	14	(7	7)	201	83	59	69	51	2	137	7	4	2	20	9	.69	10	.268	.346	.418
1999	SD	NL	133	478	136	24	7	26	(11	15)	252	92	72	94	65	1	108	6	0	1	36	13	.73	10	.285	.376	.527
2000	Atl	NL	103	340	79	23	1	11	(4	7)	137	43	37	42	32	2	78	2	3	0	21	4	.84	9	.232	.302	.403
2001	Ari	NL	126	441	116	21	3	33	(19	14)	242	84	90	80	46	7	126	5	1	3	14	10	.58	2	.263	.337	.549
2002	SF	NL	140	505	126	23	6	23	(12	11)	230	75	85	65	47	3	121	12	0	7	18	6	.75	14	.250	.324	.455
2003	Pit	NL	130	453	129	27	4	31	(17	14)	257	74	87	78	38	4	110	5	0	2	15	5	.75	10	.285	.345	.567
2004	StL	NL	135	446	116	27	3	22	(8	14)	215	64	67	65	33	5	118	4	1	3	21	5	.81	5	.260	.315	.482

Year	Team	Lg	G	AB	H	2B	3B	HR	(Hm Rd)	TB	R	RBI	RC	TBB	IBB	SO	HBP	SH	SF	SB	CS	SB%	GDP	Avg	OBP	Slg
									BATTING												**BASERUNNING**			**AVERAGES**		
2005	Stl	NL	93	295	80	14	2	21	(14 7)	161	49	54	49	28	1	75	4	0	2	14	1	.93	8	.271	.340	.546
2006	KC	AL	88	325	80	23	1	11	(7 4)	138	45	49	40	28	3	86	1	0	4	7	7	.50	10	.246	.304	.425
16 ML YEARS			1753	6168	1643	334	60	303	(150 153)	3006	1025	972	997	663	49	1599	70	14	43	304	114	.73	119	.266	.342	.487

Danny Sandoval

Bats: B **Throws:** R **Pos:** PH-19; 2B-8; SS-6　　　　**Ht:** 5'11" **Wt:** 200 **Born:** 4/7/1979 **Age:** 28

Year	Team	Lg	G	AB	H	2B	3B	HR	(Hm Rd)	TB	R	RBI	RC	TBB	IBB	SO	HBP	SH	SF	SB	CS	SB%	GDP	Avg	OBP	Slg
									BATTING												**BASERUNNING**			**AVERAGES**		
1998	Hickory	A	126	430	99	12	2	0	(- -)	115	43	30	31	29	0	88	5	14	2	13	15	.46	10	.230	.285	.267
1999	Burlgtn	A	76	255	58	5	1	3	(- -)	74	34	37	20	17	0	39	0	6	2	8	5	.62	7	.227	.274	.290
2000	Burlgtn	A	75	269	87	9	3	0	(- -)	102	34	34	39	18	1	22	2	8	1	37	18	.67	6	.323	.369	.379
2000	WinSa	A+	52	199	53	11	2	2	(- -)	74	29	17	25	18	1	21	1	7	0	11	7	.61	7	.266	.330	.372
2000	Charltt	AAA	2	8	1	0	0	0	(- -)	1	0	1	0	1	0	1	0	0	0	0	0	-	0	.125	.222	.125
2001	WinSa	A+	48	176	48	11	0	3	(- -)	68	25	14	24	11	1	31	3	6	2	11	2	.85	3	.273	.323	.386
2001	Brham	AA	58	203	57	7	1	0	(- -)	66	24	29	26	17	1	26	1	6	3	17	4	.81	5	.281	.335	.325
2002	Brham	AA	135	504	133	30	2	5	(- -)	182	86	45	62	45	1	56	5	10	3	39	24	.62	12	.264	.329	.361
2003	Brham	AA	130	478	137	30	2	3	(- -)	180	62	49	67	43	2	67	3	14	9	21	11	.66	9	.287	.343	.377
2004	Tulsa	AA	133	530	169	37	4	8	(- -)	238	73	66	88	37	3	64	2	10	1	22	10	.69	12	.319	.365	.449
2005	S-WB	AAA	104	390	129	20	0	7	(- -)	170	53	48	64	31	7	49	2	10	4	11	11	.50	16	.331	.379	.436
2006	Rdng	AA	8	31	9	1	0	0	(- -)	10	1	2	3	1	0	4	0	0	0	2	0	1.00	0	.290	.313	.323
2006	S-WB	AAA	91	345	88	17	1	2	(- -)	113	31	39	33	14	3	50	3	4	2	1	1	.50	8	.255	.288	.328
2005	Phi	NL	3	2	0	0	0	0	(0 0)	0	1	0	0	0	0	1	0	0	0	0	0	-	0	.000	.000	.000
2006	Phi	NL	28	38	8	1	0	0	(0 0)	9	1	4	4	4	0	3	0	0	1	0	0	-	2	.211	.279	.237
2 ML YEARS			31	40	8	1	0	0	(0 0)	9	2	4	4	4	0	4	0	0	1	0	0	-	2	.200	.267	.225

Ervin Santana

Pitches: R **Bats:** R **Pos:** SP-33　　　　**Ht:** 6'2" **Wt:** 160 **Born:** 12/12/1982 **Age:** 24

Year	Team	Lg	G	GS	CG	GF	IP	BFP	H	R	ER	HR	SH	SF	HB	TBB	IBB	SO	WP	Bk	W	L	Pct	ShO	Sv-Op Hld	ERC	ERA
			HOW MUCH HE PITCHED						**WHAT HE GAVE UP**												**THE RESULTS**						
2001	Angels	R	10	9	1	0	58.2	251	40	27	21	0	2	0	2	35	0	69	8	1	3	2	.600	0	0- - -	2.52	3.22
2001	Provo	R+	4	4	0	0	18.2	88	19	17	16	1	0	2	2	12	1	22	3	1	2	1	.667	0	0- - -	5.03	7.71
2002	CRpds	A	27	27	0	0	147.0	625	133	75	68	10	2	8	6	48	3	146	9	3	14	8	.636	0	0- - -	3.13	4.16
2003	RCuca	A+	20	20	1	0	124.2	508	98	44	35	9	0	0	7	36	0	130	14	0	10	2	.833	0	0- - -	2.56	2.53
2003	Ark	AA	6	6	0	0	29.2	124	23	15	13	4	1	1	3	12	0	23	1	0	1	1	.500	0	0- - -	3.52	3.94
2004	Ark	AA	8	8	0	0	43.2	190	41	19	16	3	3	0	4	18	0	48	5	0	2	1	.667	0	0- - -	3.91	3.30
2005	Ark	AA	7	7	0	0	39.0	166	34	12	10	2	0	0	2	15	0	32	1	0	5	1	.833	0	0- - -	3.15	2.31
2005	Salt Lk	AAA	3	3	0	0	19.1	79	19	11	9	2	0	1	2	2	0	17	0	0	1	0	1.000	0	0- - -	3.28	4.19
2005	LAA	AL	23	23	1	0	133.2	583	139	73	69	17	1	4	8	47	2	99	4	2	12	8	.600	1	0-0 0	4.51	4.65
2006	LAA	AL	33	33	0	0	204.0	846	181	106	97	21	4	10	11	70	2	141	10	2	16	8	.667	0	0-0 0	3.51	4.28
2 ML YEARS			56	56	1	0	337.2	1429	320	179	166	38	5	14	19	117	4	240	14	2	28	16	.636	1	0-0 0	3.90	4.42

Johan Santana

Pitches: L **Bats:** L **Pos:** SP-34　　　　**Ht:** 6'0" **Wt:** 210 **Born:** 3/13/1979 **Age:** 28

Year	Team	Lg	G	GS	CG	GF	IP	BFP	H	R	ER	HR	SH	SF	HB	TBB	IBB	SO	WP	Bk	W	L	Pct	ShO	Sv-Op Hld	ERC	ERA
			HOW MUCH HE PITCHED						**WHAT HE GAVE UP**												**THE RESULTS**						
2000	Min	AL	30	5	0	9	86.0	398	102	64	62	11	1	3	2	54	0	64	5	2	2	3	.400	0	0-0 0	6.59	6.49
2001	Min	AL	15	4	0	5	43.2	195	50	25	23	6	2	3	3	16	0	28	3	0	1	0	1.000	0	0-0 0	5.36	4.74
2002	Min	AL	27	14	0	2	108.1	452	84	41	36	7	3	3	1	49	0	137	15	2	8	6	.571	0	1-1 3	2.86	2.99
2003	Min	AL	45	18	0	7	158.1	644	127	56	54	17	2	4	3	47	1	169	6	2	12	3	.800	0	0-0 5	2.73	3.07
2004	Min	AL	34	34	1	0	228.0	881	156	70	66	24	3	3	9	54	0	265	7	0	20	6	.769	1	0-0 0	2.07	2.61
2005	Min	AL	33	33	3	0	231.2	910	180	77	74	22	6	2	1	45	1	238	8	0	16	7	.696	2	0-0 0	2.14	2.87
2006	Min	AL	34	34	1	0	233.2	923	186	79	72	24	6	4	4	47	0	245	4	1	19	6	.760	0	0-0 0	2.36	2.77
7 ML YEARS			218	142	5	23	1089.2	4403	885	412	387	111	23	22	23	312	2	1146	48	7	78	31	.716	3	1-1 8	2.75	3.20

Julio Santana

Pitches: R **Bats:** R **Pos:** RP-7　　　　**Ht:** 6'0" **Wt:** 210 **Born:** 1/20/1974 **Age:** 33

Year	Team	Lg	G	GS	CG	GF	IP	BFP	H	R	ER	HR	SH	SF	HB	TBB	IBB	SO	WP	Bk	W	L	Pct	ShO	Sv-Op Hld	ERC	ERA
			HOW MUCH HE PITCHED						**WHAT HE GAVE UP**												**THE RESULTS**						
2006	Rdng*	AA	2	0	0	0	2.0	9	1	1	0	0	0	0	0	0	0	3	0	0	0	0	-	0	0- - -	0.42	0.00
1997	Tex	AL	30	14	0	3	104.0	496	141	86	78	16	1	5	4	49	2	64	8	1	4	6	.400	0	0-1 1	7.06	6.75
1998	2 Tms	AL	35	19	1	5	145.2	630	151	77	71	18	2	5	5	62	3	61	3	0	5	6	.455	0	0-0 0	4.75	4.39
1999	TB	AL	22	5	0	7	55.1	261	66	49	45	10	1	1	7	32	0	34	0	0	1	4	.200	0	0-0 0	7.29	7.32
2000	Mon	NL	36	4	0	8	66.2	293	69	45	42	11	1	2	2	33	2	58	2	0	1	5	.167	0	0-2 1	5.31	5.67
2002	Det	AL	38	0	0	8	57.0	239	49	19	18	8	3	0	2	28	2	38	3	1	3	5	.375	0	0-1 7	4.13	2.84
2005	Mil	NL	41	0	0	12	42.0	177	34	21	21	6	1	3	0	19	4	49	5	0	3	5	.375	0	1-4 11	3.36	4.50
2006	Phi	NL	7	0	0	2	8.1	43	8	9	7	1	0	2	1	9	1	4	0	0	0	0	-	0	0-0 0	6.86	7.56
98	Tex	AL	3	0	0	0	5.1	27	7	5	5	0	0	0	0	4	1	1	0	0	0	0	-	0	0-0 0	5.97	8.44
98	TB	AL	32	19	1	5	140.1	603	144	72	66	18	2	5	5	58	2	60	3	0	5	6	.455	0	0-0 0	4.70	4.23
7 ML YEARS			209	42	1	46	479.0	2139	518	306	282	70	9	18	21	232	14	308	21	2	17	31	.354	0	1-8 20	5.42	5.30

Ramon Santiago

Bats: B **Throws:** R **Pos:** SS-27; 2B-12; PR-7; PH-4; 3B-1; DH-1   **Ht:** 5'11" **Wt:** 175 **Born:** 8/31/1979 **Age:** 27

Year	Team	Lg	G	AB	H	2B	3B	HR	(Hm	Rd)	TB	R	RBI	RC	TBB	IBB	SO	HBP	SH	SF	SB	CS	SB%	GDP	Avg	OBP	Slg
2006	Toledo*	AAA	25	83	21	6	0	2	(-	-)	33	13	12	11	9	0	18	1	7	0	2	1	.67	0	.253	.333	.398
2002	Det	AL	65	222	54	5	5	4	(3	1)	81	33	20	23	13	0	48	8	4	2	8	5	.62	2	.243	.306	.365
2003	Det	AL	141	444	100	18	1	2	(1	1)	126	41	29	38	33	0	66	10	18	2	10	4	.71	9	.225	.292	.284
2004	Sea	AL	19	39	7	1	0	0	(0	0)	8	8	2	1	3	0	3	1	2	0	0	0	-	1	.179	.256	.205
2005	Sea	AL	8	8	1	0	0	0	(0	0)	1	2	0	1	1	0	2	3	1	0	0	0	-	0	.125	.417	.125
2006	Det	AL	43	80	18	1	1	0	(0	0)	21	9	3	3	1	0	14	1	4	0	2	0	1.00	1	.225	.244	.263
	5 ML YEARS		276	793	180	25	7	6	(4	2)	237	93	54	66	51	0	133	23	29	4	20	9	.69	13	.227	.292	.299

Chad Santos

Bats: L **Throws:** L **Pos:** 1B-3   **Ht:** 5'11" **Wt:** 220 **Born:** 4/28/1981 **Age:** 26

Year	Team	Lg	G	AB	H	2B	3B	HR	(Hm	Rd)	TB	R	RBI	RC	TBB	IBB	SO	HBP	SH	SF	SB	CS	SB%	GDP	Avg	OBP	Slg
1999	Royals	R	48	177	48	9	0	4	(-	-)	69	20	35	22	12	0	54	1	1	1	1	0	1.00	4	.271	.319	.390
2000	Spkane	A-	73	267	67	18	0	14	(-	-)	127	40	47	45	36	3	103	2	3	0	1	0	1.00	1	.251	.344	.476
2000	CtnWV	A	59	187	39	9	2	4	(-	-)	64	16	18	20	27	3	62	0	2	1	0	1	.00	4	.209	.307	.342
2001	Burlgtn	A	121	444	112	32	0	16	(-	-)	192	58	83	67	52	4	101	6	1	3	0	1	.00	14	.252	.337	.432
2002	Wilmg	A+	110	379	91	21	0	9	(-	-)	139	46	54	49	46	3	122	6	6	2	0	0	-	9	.240	.330	.367
2003	Wichta	AA	111	396	107	21	3	11	(-	-)	167	48	49	58	35	2	116	3	1	3	3	0	1.00	14	.270	.332	.422
2004	Wichta	AA	130	471	123	27	3	21	(-	-)	219	59	68	74	46	5	119	4	0	3	3	1	.75	14	.261	.330	.465
2005	Omha	AAA	120	433	112	26	0	16	(-	-)	186	50	64	62	38	1	133	5	1	1	2	1	.67	17	.259	.325	.430
2006	SnJos	A+	14	55	13	3	1	2	(-	-)	24	5	11	6	2	0	18	1	0	1	0	0	-	1	.236	.271	.436
2006	Fresno	AAA	91	353	92	18	1	14	(-	-)	154	40	70	48	24	1	86	1	0	3	0	0	-	13	.261	.307	.436
2006	SF	NL	3	7	3	0	0	1	(1	0)	6	2	2	3	1	0	2	0	0	0	0	0	-	0	.429	.500	.857

Victor Santos

Pitches: R **Bats:** R **Pos:** SP-19; RP-6   **Ht:** 6'2" **Wt:** 205 **Born:** 10/2/1976 **Age:** 30

Year	Team	Lg	G	GS	CG	GF	IP	BFP	H	R	ER	HR	SH	SF	HB	TBB	IBB	SO	WP	Bk	W	L	Pct	ShO	Sv-Op	Hld	ERC	ERA
2006	Indy*	AAA	1	1	0	0	5.0	15	1	0	0	0	0	0	0	0	0	0	0	0	1	0	1.000	0	0- -	-	0.10	0.00
2001	Det	AL	33	7	0	6	76.1	335	62	33	28	9	1	3	3	49	4	52	0	0	2	2	.500	0	0-0	2	4.18	3.30
2002	Col	NL	24	2	0	6	26.0	140	41	30	30	3	3	1	0	22	3	25	2	0	0	4	.000	0	0-0	1	9.37	10.38
2003	Tex	AL	8	4	0	2	25.2	117	29	21	20	5	1	1	1	16	1	15	0	0	2	2	.000	0	0-0	0	6.82	7.01
2004	Mil	NL	31	28	0	2	154.0	684	169	95	85	18	6	7	7	57	5	115	2	1	11	12	.478	0	0-0	0	4.73	4.97
2005	Mil	NL	29	24	1	2	141.2	640	153	87	72	20	5	1	5	60	8	89	7	0	4	13	.235	0	0-0	0	4.89	4.57
2006	Pit	NL	25	19	0	3	115.1	522	150	80	73	16	5	4	4	42	3	81	5	0	5	9	.357	0	0-0	0	6.20	5.70
	6 ML YEARS		150	84	1	21	539.0	2438	604	346	308	71	21	17	20	246	24	377	16	1	22	42	.344	0	0-0	3	5.30	5.14

Dennis Sarfate

Pitches: R **Bats:** R **Pos:** RP-8   **Ht:** 6'4" **Wt:** 210 **Born:** 4/9/1981 **Age:** 26

Year	Team	Lg	G	GS	CG	GF	IP	BFP	H	R	ER	HR	SH	SF	HB	TBB	IBB	SO	WP	Bk	W	L	Pct	ShO	Sv-Op	Hld	ERC	ERA
2001	Ogden	R+	9	4	0	1	22.1	100	20	13	12	4	1	0	2	10	0	32	2	0	1	2	.333	0	1- -	-	4.45	4.84
2002	Brewrs	R	5	5	0	0	14.0	56	6	4	4	0	0	0	1	7	0	22	0	2	0	0	-	0	0- -	-	1.35	2.57
2002	Ogden	R+	1	0	0	0	1.0	6	2	1	1	0	0	0	0	1	0	2	0	0	0	0	-	0	0- -	-	12.01	9.00
2003	Beloit	A	26	26	0	0	139.2	581	114	50	44	11	4	5	3	66	0	140	5	2	12	2	.857	0	0- -	-	3.35	2.84
2004	Hntsvl	AA	28	25	0	2	129.0	566	128	71	58	12	10	8	9	78	0	113	6	2	7	12	.368	0	0- -	-	5.30	4.05
2005	Hntsvl	AA	24	24	1	0	130.0	567	120	65	56	13	5	4	10	59	1	110	11	1	9	9	.500	0	0- -	-	4.14	3.88
2005	Nashv	AAA	2	1	0	1	12.0	46	6	3	3	1	0	1	1	4	0	10	0	0	0	1	.000	0	0- -	-	1.61	2.25
2006	Nashv	AAA	34	21	0	7	125.0	565	125	63	51	7	7	3	6	78	0	117	10	0	10	7	.588	0	0- -	-	4.87	3.67
2006	Mil	NL	8	0	0	5	8.1	38	9	4	4	0	0	0	0	4	1	11	2	0	0	0	-	0	0-0	0	3.77	4.32

Scott Sauerbeck

Pitches: L **Bats:** R **Pos:** RP-46   **Ht:** 6'3" **Wt:** 200 **Born:** 11/9/1971 **Age:** 35

Year	Team	Lg	G	GS	CG	GF	IP	BFP	H	R	ER	HR	SH	SF	HB	TBB	IBB	SO	WP	Bk	W	L	Pct	ShO	Sv-Op	Hld	ERC	ERA
2006	Stcktn*	A+	1	0	0	0	1.0	3	2	0	0	0	0	0	0	0	0	0	0	0	0	0	-	0	0- -	-	12.84	0.00
2006	Scrmto*	AAA	1	0	0	0	2.0	8	2	0	0	0	0	0	0	1	0	2	0	0	0	0	-	0	0- -	-	4.15	0.00
1999	Pit	NL	65	0	0	16	67.2	287	53	19	15	6	4	0	4	38	5	55	3	0	4	1	.800	0	2-5	10	3.60	2.00
2000	Pit	NL	75	0	0	13	75.2	349	76	36	34	4	3	3	1	61	8	83	9	2	5	4	.556	0	1-4	13	5.31	4.04
2001	Pit	NL	70	0	0	14	62.2	281	61	41	39	4	2	0	2	40	6	79	3	0	2	2	.500	0	2-4	19	4.60	5.60
2002	Pit	NL	78	0	0	21	62.2	255	50	18	16	4	0	0	1	27	4	70	2	1	5	4	.556	0	0-0	28	2.91	2.30
2003	2 Tms		79	0	0	13	56.2	260	47	34	30	6	2	1	5	43	5	50	1	0	3	5	.375	0	0-5	18	4.73	4.76
2005	Cle	AL	58	0	0	10	35.2	157	35	18	16	4	1	1	4	16	2	35	2	0	1	0	1.000	0	0-2	14	4.65	4.04
2006	2 Tms	AL	46	0	0	11	25.1	121	22	17	14	3	2	0	7	18	1	17	0	0	0	1	.000	0	0-2	5	5.70	4.97
	03	Pit	NL	53	0	0	11	40.0	173	30	20	18	5	2	0	1	25	2	32	0	0	3	4	.429	0	0-4	16	3.75	4.05
	03	Bos		26	0	0	2	16.2	87	17	14	12	1	0	1	4	18	3	18	1	0	0	1	-	0	0-1	2	7.20	6.48
	06	Cle	AL	24	0	0	8	13.0	57	9	9	9	2	1	0	1	9	1	11	0	0	0	1	.000	0	0-2	2	4.05	6.23
	06	Oak		22	0	0	3	12.1	64	13	8	5	1	1	0	6	9	0	6	0	0	0	0	-	0	0-0	3	7.54	3.65
	7 ML YEARS		471	0	0	98	386.1	1710	344	183	164	31	14	5	24	243	31	389	20	3	20	17	.541	0	5-22	107	4.37	3.82

Joe Saunders

Pitches: L Bats: L Pos: SP-13   Ht: 6'3" Wt: 210 Born: 6/16/1981 Age: 26

Year	Team	Lg	G	GS	CG	GF	IP	BFP	H	R	ER	HR	SH	SF	HB	TBB	IBB	SO	WP	Bk	W	L	Pct	ShO	Sv-Op	Hld	ERC	ERA
							HOW MUCH HE PITCHED						**WHAT HE GAVE UP**											**THE RESULTS**				
2002	Provo	R	8	8	0	0	32.1	146	40	19	13	1	2	1	1	11	0	21	3	0	2	1	.667	0	0--	-	4.78	3.62
2002	CRpds	A	5	5	0	0	28.2	111	16	7	6	2	1	0	2	9	0	27	2	0	3	1	.750	0	0--	-	1.66	1.88
2004	RCuca	A+	19	19	0	0	105.2	446	106	49	40	13	2	3	5	23	0	76	5	1	9	7	.563	0	0--	-	3.68	3.41
2004	Ark	AA	8	8	0	0	39.0	182	51	26	25	5	5	2	5	14	0	25	2	0	4	3	.571	0	0--	-	6.52	5.77
2005	Ark	AA	18	18	2	0	105.2	456	107	52	41	9	0	2	3	32	0	80	2	0	7	4	.636	1	0--	-	3.71	3.49
2005	Salt Lk	AAA	9	9	1	0	55.0	251	65	38	28	3	3	4	1	21	0	29	1	0	3	3	.500	1	0--	-	4.67	4.58
2006	Salt Lk	AAA	21	20	1	1	135.0	545	117	44	40	12	2	1	3	38	0	97	2	0	10	4	.714	1	0--	-	2.98	2.67
2005	LAA	AL	2	2	0	0	9.1	41	10	8	8	3	0	0	0	4	0	4	1	0	0	0	-	0	0-0	0	6.27	7.71
2006	LAA	AL	13	13	0	0	70.2	302	71	42	37	6	1	2	1	29	1	51	2	1	7	3	.700	0	0-0	0	4.13	4.71
2 ML YEARS			15	15	0	0	80.0	343	81	50	45	9	1	2	1	33	1	55	3	1	7	3	.700	0	0-0	0	4.38	5.06

Curt Schilling

Pitches: R Bats: R Pos: SP-31   Ht: 6'5" Wt: 235 Born: 11/14/1966 Age: 40

Year	Team	Lg	G	GS	CG	GF	IP	BFP	H	R	ER	HR	SH	SF	HB	TBB	IBB	SO	WP	Bk	W	L	Pct	ShO	Sv-Op	Hld	ERC	ERA
							HOW MUCH HE PITCHED						**WHAT HE GAVE UP**											**THE RESULTS**				
1988	Bal	AL	4	4	0	0	14.2	76	22	16	16	3	0	3	1	10	1	4	2	0	0	3	.000	0	0-0	0	9.43	9.82
1989	Bal	AL	5	1	0	0	8.2	38	10	6	6	2	0	0	0	3	0	6	1	0	0	1	.000	0	0-0	0	5.74	6.23
1990	Bal	AL	35	0	0	16	46.0	191	38	13	13	1	2	4	0	19	0	32	0	0	1	2	.333	0	3-9	5	2.68	2.54
1991	Hou	NL	56	0	0	34	75.2	336	79	35	32	2	5	1	0	39	7	71	4	1	3	5	.375	0	8-11	5	4.08	3.81
1992	Phi	NL	42	26	10	10	226.1	895	165	67	59	11	7	8	1	59	4	147	4	0	14	11	.560	4	2-3	0	1.86	2.35
1993	Phi	NL	34	34	7	0	235.1	982	234	114	105	23	9	7	4	57	6	186	9	3	16	7	.696	2	0-0	0	3.44	4.02
1994	Phi	NL	13	13	1	0	82.1	360	87	42	41	10	6	1	3	28	3	58	3	1	2	8	.200	0	0-0	0	4.36	4.48
1995	Phi	NL	17	17	1	0	116.0	473	96	52	46	12	5	2	3	26	2	114	0	1	7	5	.583	0	0-0	0	2.55	3.57
1996	Phi	NL	26	26	8	0	183.1	732	149	69	65	16	6	4	3	50	5	182	5	0	9	10	.474	2	0-0	0	2.59	3.19
1997	Phi	NL	35	35	7	0	254.1	1009	208	96	84	25	8	8	6	58	3	319	1	1	17	11	.607	2	0-0	0	2.55	2.97
1998	Phi	NL	35	35	15	0	268.2	1089	236	101	97	23	14	7	6	61	3	300	12	0	15	14	.517	2	0-0	0	2.75	3.25
1999	Phi	NL	24	24	8	0	180.1	735	159	74	71	25	11	3	5	44	0	152	4	0	15	6	.714	1	0-0	0	3.20	3.54
2000	2 Tms	NL	29	29	8	0	210.1	862	204	90	89	27	11	4	1	45	4	168	4	0	11	12	.478	2	0-0	0	3.38	3.81
2001	Ari	NL	35	35	6	0	256.2	1021	237	86	85	37	8	5	1	39	0	293	4	0	22	6	.786	1	0-0	0	3.03	2.98
2002	Ari	NL	36	35	5	0	259.1	1017	218	95	93	29	4	3	3	33	1	316	6	0	23	7	.767	1	0-0	0	2.33	3.23
2003	Ari	NL	24	24	3	0	168.0	673	144	58	55	17	11	1	3	32	2	194	4	0	8	9	.471	2	0-0	0	2.59	2.95
2004	Bos	AL	32	32	3	0	226.2	910	206	84	84	23	3	6	5	35	0	203	3	0	21	6	.778	0	0-0	0	2.75	3.26
2005	Bos	AL	32	11	0	21	93.1	418	121	59	59	12	3	5	3	22	0	87	1	1	8	5	.500	0	9-11	0	5.45	5.69
2006	Bos	AL	31	31	0	0	204.0	834	220	90	90	28	5	2	3	28	1	183	1	0	15	7	.682	0	0-0	0	3.83	3.97
00	Phi	NL	16	16	4	0	112.2	474	110	49	49	17	5	1	1	32	4	96	4	0	6	6	.500	1	0-0	0	3.79	3.91
00	Ari	NL	13	13	4	0	97.2	388	94	41	40	10	6	3	0	13	0	72	0	0	5	6	.455	1	0-0	0	2.91	3.69
19 ML YEARS			545	412	82	81	3110.0	12651	2833	1250	1188	326	118	74	50	688	42	3015	72	8	207	138	.600	19	22-34	10	2.99	3.44

Jason Schmidt

Pitches: R Bats: R Pos: SP-32   Ht: 6'5" Wt: 210 Born: 1/29/1973 Age: 34

Year	Team	Lg	G	GS	CG	GF	IP	BFP	H	R	ER	HR	SH	SF	HB	TBB	IBB	SO	WP	Bk	W	L	Pct	ShO	Sv-Op	Hld	ERC	ERA
							HOW MUCH HE PITCHED						**WHAT HE GAVE UP**											**THE RESULTS**				
1995	Atl	NL	9	2	0	1	25.0	119	27	17	16	2	2	4	1	18	3	19	1	0	2	2	.500	0	0-1	0	5.56	5.76
1996	2 Tms	NL	19	17	1	0	96.1	445	108	67	61	10	4	9	2	53	0	74	8	1	5	6	.455	0	0-0	0	5.46	5.70
1997	Pit	NL	32	32	0	0	187.2	825	193	106	96	16	10	3	9	76	2	136	8	0	10	9	.526	0	0-0	0	4.31	4.60
1998	Pit	NL	33	33	0	0	214.1	916	228	106	97	24	10	3	4	71	3	158	15	1	11	14	.440	0	0-0	0	4.35	4.07
1999	Pit	NL	33	33	2	0	212.2	937	219	110	99	24	7	7	3	85	4	148	6	4	13	11	.542	0	0-0	0	4.30	4.19
2000	Pit	NL	11	11	0	0	63.1	295	71	43	38	6	1	2	1	41	2	51	1	0	2	5	.286	0	0-0	0	5.77	5.40
2001	2 Tms	NL	25	25	1	0	150.1	641	138	75	68	13	5	3	7	61	3	142	8	1	13	7	.650	0	0-0	0	3.72	4.07
2002	SF	NL	29	29	2	0	185.1	769	148	78	71	15	11	5	2	73	1	196	12	0	13	8	.619	2	0-0	0	2.87	3.45
2003	SF	NL	29	29	5	0	207.2	819	152	56	54	14	6	3	5	46	1	208	7	1	17	5	.773	3	0-0	0	1.93	2.34
2004	SF	NL	32	32	4	0	225.0	907	165	84	80	18	7	3	3	77	3	251	7	1	18	7	.720	3	0-0	0	2.37	3.20
2005	SF	NL	29	29	0	0	172.0	757	160	90	84	16	8	8	5	85	4	165	7	1	12	7	.632	0	0-0	0	4.04	4.40
2006	SF	NL	32	32	3	0	213.1	894	189	94	85	21	7	7	6	80	6	180	11	1	11	9	.550	1	0-0	0	3.43	3.59
96	Atl	NL	13	11	0	0	58.2	274	69	48	44	8	3	6	0	32	0	48	5	1	3	4	.429	0	0-0	0	5.92	6.75
96	Pit	NL	6	6	1	0	37.2	171	39	19	17	2	1	3	2	21	0	26	3	0	2	2	.500	0	0-0	0	4.75	4.06
01	Pit	NL	14	14	1	0	84.0	357	81	46	43	11	3	2	7	28	2	77	3	1	6	6	.500	0	0-0	0	4.17	4.61
01	SF	NL	11	11	0	0	66.1	284	57	29	25	2	2	1	0	33	1	65	5	0	7	1	.875	0	0-0	0	3.16	3.39
12 ML YEARS			313	304	20	1	1953.0	8324	1798	926	849	179	78	57	48	766	32	1728	91	11	127	90	.585	9	0-1	0	3.61	3.91

Brian Schneider

Bats: L Throws: R Pos: C-123; PH-5; 1B-1; PR-1   Ht: 6'1" Wt: 195 Born: 11/26/1976 Age: 30

Year	Team	Lg	G	AB	H	2B	3B	HR	(Hm	Rd)	TB	R	RBI	RC	TBB	IBB	SO	HBP	SH	SF	SB	CS	SB%	GDP	Avg	OBP	Slg
									BATTING													**BASERUNNING**				**AVERAGES**	
2006	Ptomc*	A+	2	9	2	1	0	0	(-	-)	3	1	1	0	0	0	2	0	0	0	0	0	-	0	.222	.222	.333
2000	Mon	NL	45	115	27	6	0	0	(0	0)	33	6	11	8	7	2	24	0	0	1	0	1	.00	1	.235	.276	.287
2001	Mon	NL	27	41	13	3	0	1	(1	0)	19	4	6	8	6	1	3	0	0	0	0	0	-	0	.317	.396	.463
2002	Mon	NL	73	207	57	19	0	6	(3	2)	95	21	29	29	21	8	41	0	2	2	1	2	.33	7	.275	.339	.459
2003	Mon	NL	108	335	77	26	1	9	(9	0)	132	34	46	36	37	8	75	2	1	2	0	2	.00	12	.230	.309	.394
2004	Mon	NL	135	436	112	20	3	12	(5	7)	174	40	49	52	42	10	63	3	5	2	0	1	.00	9	.257	.325	.399
2005	Was	NL	116	369	99	20	1	10	(5	5)	151	38	44	48	29	7	68	4	6	2	1	0	1.00	10	.268	.330	.409
2006	Was	NL	124	410	105	18	0	4	(3	1)	135	30	55	45	38	10	67	2	2	3	2	2	.50	14	.256	.320	.329
7 ML YEARS			628	1913	490	112	7	41	(26	15)	739	173	240	226	180	46	321	13	12	13	4	8	.33	53	.256	.322	.386

Scott Schoeneweis

Pitches: L **Bats:** L **Pos:** RP-71   **Ht:** 6'0" **Wt:** 190 **Born:** 10/2/1973 **Age:** 33

Year	Team	Lg	G	GS	CG	GF	IP	BFP	H	R	ER	HR	SH	SF	HB	TBB	IBB	SO	WP	Bk	W	L	Pct	ShO	Sv-Op	Hld	ERC	ERA
1999	LAA	AL	31	0	0	6	39.1	175	47	27	24	4	0	1	0	14	1	22	1	0	1	1	.500	0	0-0	3	4.99	5.49
2000	LAA	AL	27	27	1	0	170.0	742	183	112	103	21	2	5	6	67	2	78	4	3	7	10	.412	1	0-0	0	4.84	5.45
2001	LAA	AL	32	32	1	0	205.1	910	227	122	116	21	3	8	14	77	2	104	4	1	10	11	.476	0	0-0	0	4.87	5.08
2002	LAA	AL	54	15	0	4	118.0	510	119	68	64	17	1	5	5	49	4	65	1	1	9	8	.529	0	1-4	11	4.68	4.88
2003	2 Tms	AL	59	0	0	19	64.2	276	63	35	30	3	2	1	4	19	5	56	3	0	3	2	.600	0	0-2	4	3.25	4.18
2004	CWS	AL	20	19	0	0	112.2	500	129	74	70	17	3	2	3	49	0	69	3	0	6	9	.400	0	0-0	0	5.65	5.59
2005	Tor	AL	80	0	0	15	57.0	250	54	23	21	2	1	0	4	25	5	43	2	0	3	4	.429	0	1-4	21	3.56	3.32
2006	2 Tms	AL	71	0	0	16	51.2	221	48	28	28	4	1	0	2	24	6	29	3	0	4	2	.667	0	4-6	19	3.79	4.88
03	LAA	AL	39	0	0	12	38.2	163	37	19	17	2	1	1	3	10	3	29	1	0	1	1	.500	0	0-1	4	3.14	3.96
03	CWS	AL	20	0	0	7	26.0	113	26	16	13	1	1	0	1	9	2	27	2	0	2	1	.667	0	0-1	0	3.41	4.50
06	Tor	AL	55	0	0	8	37.1	161	39	27	27	3	1	0	1	16	5	18	2	0	2	2	.500	0	1-3	18	4.27	6.51
06	Cin	NL	16	0	0	8	14.1	60	9	1	1	1	0	0	1	8	1	11	1	0	2	0	1.000	0	3-3	1	2.64	0.63
	8 ML YEARS		374	93	2	60	818.2	3584	870	489	456	89	13	22	38	324	25	466	21	5	43	47	.478	1	6-16	58	4.65	5.01

Chris Schroder

Pitches: R **Bats:** R **Pos:** RP-21   **Ht:** 6'3" **Wt:** 210 **Born:** 8/20/1978 **Age:** 28

Year	Team	Lg	G	GS	CG	GF	IP	BFP	H	R	ER	HR	SH	SF	HB	TBB	IBB	SO	WP	Bk	W	L	Pct	ShO	Sv-Op	Hld	ERC	ERA
2001	Vrmnt	A-	11	0	0	7	12.0	48	8	2	2	1	0	0	0	5	0	18	0	0	0	0	-	0	2--	-	2.32	1.50
2001	Jupiter	A+	10	0	0	2	15.2	64	12	5	4	1	0	0	0	4	0	20	4	0	1	0	1.000	0	0--	-	2.04	2.30
2002	Clinton	A	22	0	0	20	27.1	113	15	7	5	1	1	0	2	14	1	42	1	0	1	3	.250	0	10--	-	1.93	1.65
2002	BrvdCt	A+	23	0	0	21	29.2	118	13	6	5	2	0	1	0	19	1	36	2	0	2	2	.500	0	6--	-	1.87	1.52
2003	Hrsbrg	AA	49	0	0	22	82.1	353	68	29	26	5	6	4	2	47	1	81	1	0	9	2	.818	0	4--	-	3.61	2.84
2004	Hrsbrg	AA	32	0	0	22	48.1	205	39	13	13	3	0	0	5	17	2	51	2	0	2	2	.500	0	11--	-	2.88	2.42
2004	Edmtn	AAA	17	1	0	5	26.2	120	34	13	13	3	0	0	1	15	0	32	2	0	2	1	.667	0	0--	-	7.07	4.39
2005	Hrsbrg	AA	16	0	0	5	23.0	100	20	13	12	4	3	1	1	11	3	28	1	0	2	3	.400	0	0--	-	4.09	4.70
2005	NewOr	AAA	19	0	0	8	23.0	106	21	21	20	6	2	0	4	15	1	29	1	1	2	0	1.000	0	4--	-	6.56	7.83
2005	Nats	R	1	0	0	0	1.0	5	2	1	1	0	0	0	0	0	0	3	0	0	0	0	-	0	0--	-	7.48	9.00
2005	Ptomc	A+	5	0	0	2	7.0	30	7	3	0	0	0	1	1	2	0	10	0	0	0	0	-	0	1--	-	3.51	0.00
2006	Hrsbrg	AA	9	0	0	3	14.1	66	18	9	8	2	0	0	0	6	2	13	3	0	2	0	1.000	0	1--	-	5.66	5.02
2006	NewOr	AAA	28	0	0	5	47.1	188	25	9	8	2	2	1	3	16	1	60	2	0	2	1	.667	0	1--	-	1.43	1.52
2006	Was	NL	21	0	0	3	28.1	127	23	21	20	7	1	3	5	15	3	39	0	0	0	2	.000	0	0-1	1	5.07	6.35

Skip Schumaker

Bats: L **Throws:** R **Pos:** LF-13; RF-9; PH-7; CF-5; PR-1   **Ht:** 5'10" **Wt:** 175 **Born:** 2/3/1980 **Age:** 27

Year	Team	Lg	G	AB	H	2B	3B	HR	(Hm	Rd)	TB	R	RBI	RC	TBB	IBB	SO	HBP	SH	SF	SB	CS	SB%	GDP	Avg	OBP	Slg
2001	NewJrs	A-	49	162	41	10	1	0	(-	-)	53	22	14	22	29	1	33	1	2	1	1	2	.33	4	.253	.368	.327
2002	Ptomc	A+	136	551	158	22	4	2	(-	-)	194	71	44	69	45	3	84	2	6	2	26	16	.62	10	.287	.342	.352
2003	Tenn	AA	91	342	86	20	3	2	(-	-)	118	43	22	41	37	2	54	4	2	2	6	6	.50	4	.251	.330	.345
2004	Tenn	AA	138	516	163	29	6	4	(-	-)	216	78	43	86	60	3	61	2	4	1	19	14	.58	7	.316	.389	.419
2005	Memp	AAA	115	443	127	24	3	7	(-	-)	178	66	34	62	29	1	54	2	8	5	13	3	.81	15	.287	.330	.402
2006	Memp	AAA	95	369	113	13	3	3	(-	-)	141	47	27	52	23	1	48	3	4	4	11	4	.73	12	.306	.348	.382
2005	StL	NL	27	24	6	1	0	0	(0	0)	7	9	1	2	2	0	2	0	0	0	1	0	1.00	0	.250	.308	.292
2006	StL	NL	28	54	10	1	0	1	(0	1)	14	3	2	2	5	1	6	0	1	0	2	1	.67	1	.185	.254	.259
	2 ML YEARS		55	78	16	2	0	1	(0	1)	21	12	3	4	7	1	8	0	1	0	3	1	.75	1	.205	.271	.269

Luke Scott

Bats: L **Throws:** R **Pos:** LF-50; RF-13; PH-7; CF-1; PR-1   **Ht:** 6'0" **Wt:** 210 **Born:** 6/25/1978 **Age:** 29

Year	Team	Lg	G	AB	H	2B	3B	HR	(Hm	Rd)	TB	R	RBI	RC	TBB	IBB	SO	HBP	SH	SF	SB	CS	SB%	GDP	Avg	OBP	Slg
2002	Clmbs	A	49	171	44	15	4	7	(-	-)	88	28	32	32	21	0	58	3	1	2	9	1	.90	3	.257	.345	.515
2002	Kinston	A+	48	163	39	7	1	8	(-	-)	72	22	30	24	16	0	47	5	2	0	2	1	.67	2	.239	.326	.442
2003	Kinston	A+	67	241	67	12	1	13	(-	-)	120	37	44	43	27	0	62	4	0	0	6	3	.67	0	.278	.360	.498
2003	Akron	AA	50	183	50	13	1	7	(-	-)	86	21	37	27	11	0	37	2	3	3	0	1	.00	1	.273	.317	.470
2004	Salem	A+	66	241	67	20	1	8	(-	-)	113	45	35	46	41	4	58	0	0	5	6	1	.86	5	.278	.376	.469
2004	RdRck	AA	63	208	62	17	0	19	(-	-)	136	45	62	53	33	1	43	6	1	5	0	2	.00	4	.298	.401	.654
2005	RdRck	AAA	103	398	114	25	4	31	(-	-)	240	69	87	85	43	1	96	6	0	2	2	2	.50	4	.286	.363	.603
2006	RdRck	AAA	87	318	95	15	1	20	(-	-)	172	63	63	71	52	6	66	5	1	5	6	1	.86	3	.299	.400	.541
2005	Hou	NL	34	80	15	4	2	0	(0	0)	23	6	4	6	9	1	23	0	0	1	1	1	.50	0	.188	.270	.288
2006	Hou	NL	65	214	72	19	6	10	(8	2)	133	31	37	48	30	4	43	4	0	1	2	1	.67	2	.336	.426	.621
	2 ML YEARS		99	294	87	23	8	10	(8	2)	156	37	41	54	39	5	66	4	0	1	3	2	.60	2	.296	.385	.531

Marco Scutaro

Bats: R **Throws:** R **Pos:** SS-69; 2B-37; 3B-12; PH-3; LF-2; PR-1   **Ht:** 5'10" **Wt:** 190 **Born:** 10/30/1975 **Age:** 31

Year	Team	Lg	G	AB	H	2B	3B	HR	(Hm	Rd)	TB	R	RBI	RC	TBB	IBB	SO	HBP	SH	SF	SB	CS	SB%	GDP	Avg	OBP	Slg
2002	NYM	NL	27	36	8	0	1	1	(0	1)	13	2	6	2	0	0	11	0	1	1	0	1	.00	1	.222	.216	.361
2003	NYM	NL	48	75	16	4	0	2	(0	2)	26	10	6	10	13	2	14	1	1	1	2	0	1.00	1	.213	.333	.347
2004	Oak	AL	137	455	124	32	1	7	(6	1)	179	50	43	48	16	1	58	0	5	1	0	0	-	9	.273	.297	.393
2005	Oak	AL	118	381	94	22	3	9	(5	4)	149	48	37	45	36	1	48	0	4	2	5	2	.71	6	.247	.310	.391
2006	Oak	AL	117	365	97	21	6	5	(1	4)	145	52	41	47	50	0	66	0	3	5	5	1	.83	16	.266	.350	.397
	5 ML YEARS		447	1312	339	79	11	24	(13	11)	512	162	133	152	115	4	197	1	14	10	12	4	.75	33	.258	.316	.390

Rudy Seanez

Pitches: R **Bats:** R **Pos:** RP-49   **Ht:** 5'11" **Wt:** 200 **Born:** 10/20/1968 **Age:** 38

Year	Team	Lg	G	GS	CG	GF	IP	BFP	H	R	ER	HR	SH	SF	HB	TBB	IBB	SO	WP	Bk	W	L	Pct	ShO	Sv-Op	Hld	ERC	ERA
1989	Cle	AL	5	0	0	2	5.0	20	1	2	2	0	0	2	0	4	1	7	1	1	0	0	-	0	0-0	0	0.94	3.60
1990	Cle	AL	24	0	0	12	27.1	127	22	17	17	2	0	1	1	25	1	24	5	0	2	1	.667	0	0-0	3	4.85	5.60
1991	Cle	AL	5	0	0	0	5.0	33	10	12	9	2	0	0	0	7	0	7	2	0	0	0	-	0	0-1	0	17.96	16.20
1993	SD	NL	3	0	0	3	3.1	20	8	6	5	1	1	0	0	2	0	1	0	0	0	0	-	0	0-0	0	16.31	13.50
1994	LAD	NL	17	0	0	6	23.2	104	24	7	7	2	4	2	1	9	1	18	3	0	1	1	.500	0	0-1	1	4.01	2.66
1995	LAD	NL	37	0	0	12	34.2	159	39	27	26	5	3	0	1	18	3	29	0	0	1	3	.250	0	3-4	6	5.57	6.75
1998	Atl	NL	34	0	0	8	36.0	148	25	13	11	2	1	2	1	16	0	50	2	0	4	1	.800	0	2-4	8	2.44	2.75
1999	Atl	NL	56	0	0	13	53.2	225	47	21	20	3	0	2	1	21	1	41	3	0	6	1	.857	0	3-8	18	3.12	3.35
2000	Atl	NL	23	0	0	8	21.0	89	15	11	10	3	1	0	1	9	1	20	0	0	2	4	.333	0	2-3	6	2.95	4.29
2001	2 Tms		38	0	0	8	36.0	150	23	12	11	4	0	1	1	19	0	41	4	0	0	2	.000	0	1-3	9	2.78	2.75
2002	Tex	AL	33	0	0	4	33.0	150	28	25	21	5	3	1	0	24	1	40	6	0	1	3	.250	0	0-4	10	4.77	5.73
2003	Bos	AL	9	0	0	4	8.2	44	11	7	6	2	0	1	0	6	1	9	3	0	0	1	.000	0	0-1	0	7.45	6.23
2004	2 Tms		39	0	0	15	46.0	193	39	17	17	3	0	3	0	19	3	46	4	0	3	2	.600	0	0-2	4	2.96	3.33
2005	SD	NL	57	0	0	9	60.1	248	49	19	18	4	2	1	2	22	4	84	4	0	7	1	.875	0	0-2	11	2.76	2.69
2006	2 Tms		49	0	0	22	53.0	249	58	32	29	8	0	1	1	32	4	54	7	0	3	3	.500	0	0-2	3	5.68	4.92
01	SD	NL	26	0	0	8	24.0	102	15	8	7	3	0	1	1	15	0	24	1	0	0	2	.000	0	1-3	5	3.21	2.63
01	Atl	NL	12	0	0	0	12.0	48	8	4	4	1	0	0	0	4	0	17	3	0	0	0	-	0	0-0	4	1.99	3.00
04	KC	AL	16	0	0	7	23.0	100	21	10	10	0	0	3	0	11	2	21	3	0	0	1	.000	0	0-1	1	3.01	3.91
04	Fla	NL	23	0	0	8	23.0	93	18	7	7	3	0	0	0	8	1	25	1	0	3	1	.750	0	0-1	3	2.87	2.74
06	Bos	AL	41	0	0	16	46.2	216	51	28	25	6	0	1	1	26	1	48	7	0	2	1	.667	0	0-1	3	5.44	4.82
06	SD	NL	8	0	0	6	6.1	33	7	4	4	2	0	0	0	6	3	6	0	0	1	2	.333	0	0-1	0	7.49	5.68
15 ML YEARS			429	0	0	126	446.2	1959	399	228	209	46	15	17	10	233	21	471	44	1	30	23	.566	0	11-35	79	3.95	4.21

Bobby Seay

Pitches: L **Bats:** L **Pos:** RP-14   **Ht:** 6'2" **Wt:** 235 **Born:** 6/20/1978 **Age:** 29

Year	Team	Lg	G	GS	CG	GF	IP	BFP	H	R	ER	HR	SH	SF	HB	TBB	IBB	SO	WP	Bk	W	L	Pct	ShO	Sv-Op	Hld	ERC	ERA
2006	Toledo*	AAA	24	1	0	1	24.2	101	25	15	13	3	2	2	1	6	2	14	0	1	1	2	.333	0	0- -	1	3.84	4.74
2001	TB	AL	12	0	0	4	13.0	58	13	11	9	3	2	0	1	5	1	12	1	0	1	1	.500	0	0-0	0	5.03	6.23
2003	TB	AL	12	0	0	2	9.0	39	7	3	3	0	0	2	0	6	0	5	0	0	0	0	-	0	0-1	0	3.17	3.00
2004	TB	AL	21	0	0	6	22.2	95	21	6	6	2	0	0	2	5	1	17	1	0	0	0	-	0	0-0	0	3.15	2.38
2005	Col	NL	17	0	0	5	11.2	58	18	11	11	3	1	0	0	8	1	11	0	1	0	0	-	0	0-1	1	10.28	8.49
2006	Det	AL	14	0	0	6	15.1	71	14	11	11	1	1	1	3	9	1	12	0	0	0	0	-	0	0-0	0	4.65	6.46
5 ML YEARS			76	0	0	23	71.2	321	73	42	40	9	4	3	6	33	4	57	2	1	1	1	.500	0	0-2	1	4.83	5.02

Aaron Sele

Pitches: R **Bats:** R **Pos:** SP-15; RP-13   **Ht:** 6'3" **Wt:** 220 **Born:** 6/25/1970 **Age:** 37

Year	Team	Lg	G	GS	CG	GF	IP	BFP	H	R	ER	HR	SH	SF	HB	TBB	IBB	SO	WP	Bk	W	L	Pct	ShO	Sv-Op	Hld	ERC	ERA
2006	LsVgs*	AAA	5	5	0	0	29.2	117	25	8	8	1	0	1	5	0	0	28	0	0	3	0	1.000	0	0- -	-	2.15	2.43
1993	Bos	AL	18	18	0	0	111.2	484	100	42	34	5	2	5	7	48	2	93	5	0	7	2	.778	0	0-0	0	3.40	2.74
1994	Bos	AL	22	22	2	0	143.1	615	140	68	61	13	4	5	9	60	2	105	4	0	8	7	.533	0	0-0	0	4.26	3.83
1995	Bos	AL	6	6	0	0	32.1	146	32	14	11	3	1	1	3	14	0	21	3	0	3	1	.750	0	0-0	0	4.35	3.06
1996	Bos	AL	29	29	1	0	157.1	722	192	110	93	14	6	7	8	67	2	137	2	0	7	11	.389	0	0-0	0	5.56	5.32
1997	Bos	AL	33	33	1	0	177.1	810	196	115	106	25	5	7	15	80	4	122	7	0	13	12	.520	0	0-0	0	5.47	5.38
1998	Tex	AL	33	33	3	0	212.2	954	239	116	100	14	5	7	13	84	6	167	4	0	19	11	.633	2	0-0	0	4.69	4.23
1999	Tex	AL	33	33	2	0	205.0	920	244	115	109	21	1	3	12	70	3	186	4	0	18	9	.667	2	0-0	0	5.17	4.79
2000	Sea	AL	34	34	2	0	211.2	908	221	110	106	17	5	8	5	74	7	137	5	0	17	10	.630	2	0-0	0	4.06	4.51
2001	Sea	AL	34	34	2	0	215.0	899	216	93	86	25	5	9	7	51	2	114	1	0	15	5	.750	1	0-0	0	3.70	3.60
2002	LAA	AL	26	26	1	0	160.0	706	190	92	87	21	5	10	7	49	2	82	5	0	8	9	.471	0	0-0	0	5.20	4.89
2003	LAA	AL	25	25	0	0	121.2	553	135	82	78	17	2	5	12	58	1	53	5	0	7	11	.389	0	0-0	0	5.77	5.77
2004	LAA	AL	28	24	0	1	132.0	593	163	84	74	16	3	8	5	51	2	51	4	2	9	4	.692	0	0-0	0	5.77	5.05
2005	Sea	AL	21	21	1	0	116.0	523	147	76	73	18	1	9	5	41	2	53	2	0	6	12	.333	0	0-0	0	6.11	5.66
2006	LAD	NL	28	15	0	4	103.1	451	120	57	52	11	4	1	2	30	2	57	3	0	8	6	.571	0	0-1	0	4.66	4.53
14 ML YEARS			370	352	15	5	2099.1	9284	2335	1174	1070	220	49	85	110	777	37	1378	54	2	145	110	.569	9	0-1	0	4.83	4.59

Jae Seo

Pitches: R **Bats:** R **Pos:** SP-26; RP-10   **Ht:** 6'0" **Wt:** 230 **Born:** 5/24/1977 **Age:** 30

Year	Team	Lg	G	GS	CG	GF	IP	BFP	H	R	ER	HR	SH	SF	HB	TBB	IBB	SO	WP	Bk	W	L	Pct	ShO	Sv-Op	Hld	ERC	ERA
2002	NYM	NL	1	0	0	1	1.0	3	0	0	0	0	0	0	0	0	0	1	0	0	0	0	-	0	0-0	0	0.00	0.00
2003	NYM	NL	32	31	0	0	188.1	806	193	94	80	18	8	4	6	46	11	110	2	0	9	12	.429	0	0-0	0	3.54	3.82
2004	NYM	NL	24	21	0	1	117.2	512	133	67	64	17	12	3	2	50	7	54	0	1	5	10	.333	0	0-0	0	5.39	4.90
2005	NYM	NL	14	14	1	0	90.1	363	84	26	26	9	9	3	1	16	0	59	2	0	8	2	.800	0	0-0	0	2.91	2.59
2006	2 Tms		36	26	0	5	157.0	707	197	101	93	31	6	8	4	56	4	88	5	1	3	12	.200	0	0-1	0	6.26	5.33
06	LAD	NL	19	10	0	5	67.0	296	75	45	43	14	3	3	1	25	1	49	1	1	2	4	.333	0	0-0	0	5.49	5.78
06	TB	AL	17	16	0	0	90.0	411	122	56	50	17	3	5	3	31	3	39	4	0	1	8	.111	0	0-1	0	6.85	5.00
5 ML YEARS			107	92	1	7	554.1	2391	607	288	263	75	35	18	13	168	22	312	9	2	25	36	.410	0	0-1	0	4.52	4.27

Richie Sexson

Bats: R Throws: R Pos: 1B-150; DH-8; PH-1   Ht: 6'8" Wt: 235 Born: 12/29/1974 Age: 32

Year	Team	Lg	G	AB	H	2B	3B	HR	(Hm	Rd)	TB	R	RBI	RC	TBB	IBB	SO	HBP	SH	SF	SB	CS	SB%	GDP	Avg	OBP	Slg
1997	Cle	AL	5	11	3	0	0	0	(0	0)	3	1	0	0	0	0	2	0	0	0	0	0	-	2	.273	.273	.273
1998	Cle	AL	49	174	54	14	1	11	(9	2)	103	28	35	33	6	0	42	3	0	0	1	1	.50	3	.310	.344	.592
1999	Cle	AL	134	479	122	17	7	31	(18	13)	246	72	116	70	34	0	117	4	0	8	3	3	.50	19	.255	.305	.514
2000	2 Tms		148	537	146	30	1	30	(15	15)	268	89	91	91	59	2	159	7	0	4	2	0	1.00	11	.272	.349	.499
2001	Mil	NL	158	598	162	24	3	45	(28	17)	327	94	125	103	60	5	178	6	0	3	2	4	.33	20	.271	.342	.547
2002	Mil	NL	157	570	159	37	2	29	(13	16)	287	86	102	98	70	7	136	8	0	4	0	0	-	17	.279	.363	.504
2003	Mil	NL	162	606	165	28	2	45	(23	22)	332	97	124	116	98	7	151	9	0	5	2	3	.40	18	.272	.379	.548
2004	Ari	NL	23	90	21	4	0	9	(6	3)	52	20	23	18	14	0	21	0	0	0	0	0	-	2	.233	.337	.578
2005	Sea	AL	156	558	147	36	1	39	(21	18)	302	99	121	117	89	4	167	6	0	3	1	1	.50	14	.263	.369	.541
2006	Sea	AL	158	591	156	40	0	34	(17	17)	298	75	107	92	64	5	154	4	0	4	1	1	.50	17	.264	.338	.504
00	Cle	AL	91	324	83	16	1	16	(8	8)	149	45	44	45	25	0	96	4	0	3	1	0	1.00	8	.256	.315	.460
00	Mil	NL	57	213	63	14	0	14	(7	7)	119	44	47	46	34	2	63	3	0	1	1	0	1.00	3	.296	.398	.559
10 ML YEARS			1150	4214	1135	230	17	273	(150	123)	2218	661	844	738	494	30	1127	47	0	31	12	13	.48	123	.269	.350	.526

Brian Shackelford

Pitches: L Bats: L Pos: RP-26   Ht: 6'1" Wt: 195 Born: 8/30/1976 Age: 30

			HOW MUCH HE PITCHED					WHAT HE GAVE UP										THE RESULTS						
Year	Team	Lg	G	GS	CG	GF	IP	BFP	H	R	ER	HR	SH	SF	HB	TBB	IBB	SO	WP	Bk	W	L	Pct	ShO	Sv-Op	Hld	ERC	ERA
2001	Wichta	AA	1	0	0	0	1.0	7	3	2	2	0	4	6	0	1	0	0	0	0	0	0	-	0	0- -	-	19.55	18.00
2002	Wichta	AA	22	0	0	7	25.2	126	23	12	10	1	2	0	3	26	2	15	6	1	3	1	.750	0	0- -	-	5.70	3.51
2003	Chatt	AA	13	1	0	0	20.0	102	26	18	14	3	14	9	5	14	2	19	2	1	3	2	.600	0	1- -	-	8.55	6.30
2003	Ptomc	A+	18	0	0	5	27.1	111	17	6	6	1	0	2	4	8	0	20	1	0	1	0	1.000	0	1- -	-	1.86	1.98
2003	Lsvlle	AAA	12	0	0	4	15.2	70	15	4	4	0	1	1	1	7	0	10	0	0	1	0	1.000	0	0- -	-	3.45	2.30
2004	Lsvlle	AAA	59	0	0	13	73.0	319	58	31	29	6	0	0	1	42	1	63	4	2	8	1	.889	0	0- -	-	3.46	3.58
2005	Lsvlle	AAA	31	0	0	8	32.2	143	35	19	19	1	3	0	2	10	0	21	1	0	1	6	.143	0	1- -	-	3.81	5.23
2006	Lsvlle	AAA	34	0	0	8	29.2	131	29	6	6	0	1	2	2	14	0	23	1	0	1	0	1.000	0	1- -	-	3.75	1.82
2005	Cin	NL	37	0	0	5	29.2	119	21	9	8	2	0	1	6	9	1	17	3	1	1	0	1.000	0	0-0	3	2.76	2.43
2006	Cin	NL	26	0	0	9	16.1	79	18	13	13	4	0	0	2	10	0	15	1	0	1	0	1.000	0	0-0	2	7.10	7.16
2 ML YEARS			63	0	0	14	46.0	198	39	22	21	6	0	1	8	19	1	32	4	1	2	0	1.000	0	0-0	5	4.19	4.11

Josh Sharpless

Pitches: R Bats: R Pos: RP-14   Ht: 6'5" Wt: 235 Born: 1/26/1981 Age: 26

			HOW MUCH HE PITCHED					WHAT HE GAVE UP										THE RESULTS						
Year	Team	Lg	G	GS	CG	GF	IP	BFP	H	R	ER	HR	SH	SF	HB	TBB	IBB	SO	WP	Bk	W	L	Pct	ShO	Sv-Op	Hld	ERC	ERA
2003	Wmspt	A-	22	0	0	9	31.1	130	19	9	9	2	1	0	2	17	0	45	0	0	1	1	.500	0	5- -	-	2.53	2.59
2004	Hickory	A+	44	0	0	21	74.1	323	42	28	25	4	0	3	0	55	2	109	8	0	6	2	.750	0	4- -	-	2.74	3.03
2005	Lynbrg	A+	17	0	0	9	27.0	99	7	1	0	0	0	0	0	11	0	46	0	0	3	0	1.000	0	5- -	-	0.64	0.00
2005	Altna	AA	7	0	0	2	9.1	39	6	3	3	0	0	1	0	3	0	13	1	0	1	0	1.000	0	0- -	-	1.40	2.89
2006	Altna	AA	14	0	0	11	21.0	80	8	2	2	0	1	0	0	9	0	30	0	0	2	0	1.000	0	8- -	-	0.95	0.86
2006	Indy	AAA	23	0	0	9	33.0	146	32	11	9	1	1	2	0	15	2	30	3	0	1	1	.500	0	1- -	-	3.43	2.45
2006	Pit	NL	14	0	0	3	12.0	53	7	2	2	0	1	1	0	11	1	7	2	0	0	0	-	0	0-0	2	2.86	1.50

Ryan Shealy

Bats: R Throws: R Pos: 1B-53; PH-3   Ht: 6'5" Wt: 250 Born: 8/29/1979 Age: 27

Year	Team	Lg	G	AB	H	2B	3B	HR	(Hm	Rd)	TB	R	RBI	RC	TBB	IBB	SO	HBP	SH	SF	SB	CS	SB%	GDP	Avg	OBP	Slg
2002	Casper	R+	69	231	85	21	1	19	(-	-)	165	55	70	79	50	7	52	18	0	9	0	0	-	7	.368	.497	.714
2003	Visalia	A+	93	341	102	31	1	14	(-	-)	177	70	73	71	42	0	72	14	0	7	0	0	-	5	.299	.391	.519
2004	Tulsa	AA	132	469	149	32	3	29	(-	-)	274	88	99	111	61	7	123	16	2	4	1	1	.50	10	.318	.411	.584
2005	ColSpr	AAA	108	411	135	30	2	26	(-	-)	247	85	88	95	41	2	81	7	2	7	4	0	1.00	4	.328	.393	.601
2006	ColSpr	AAA	58	222	63	16	1	15	(-	-)	126	37	55	44	20	1	34	4	0	2	0	0	-	9	.284	.351	.568
2005	Col	NL	36	91	30	7	0	2	(0	2)	43	14	16	14	13	0	22	0	0	0	1	0	1.00	6	.330	.413	.473
2006	2 Tms		56	202	56	12	1	7	(5	2)	91	31	37	32	15	1	54	2	0	0	1	1	.50	5	.277	.333	.450
06	Col	NL	5	9	2	2	0	0	(0	0)	4	2	1	0	0	0	4	0	0	0	0	0	-	0	.222	.222	.444
06	KC	AL	51	193	54	10	1	7	(5	2)	87	29	36	32	15	1	50	2	0	0	1	1	.50	5	.280	.338	.451
2 ML YEARS			92	293	86	19	1	9	(5	4)	134	45	53	46	28	1	76	2	0	0	2	1	.67	11	.294	.359	.457

Ben Sheets

Pitches: R Bats: R Pos: SP-17   Ht: 6'1" Wt: 220 Born: 7/18/1978 Age: 28

			HOW MUCH HE PITCHED					WHAT HE GAVE UP										THE RESULTS						
Year	Team	Lg	G	GS	CG	GF	IP	BFP	H	R	ER	HR	SH	SF	HB	TBB	IBB	SO	WP	Bk	W	L	Pct	ShO	Sv-Op	Hld	ERC	ERA
2006	Brewrs*	R	1	1	0	0	4.1	19	5	5	5	0	0	0	0	2	0	8	2	0	0	0	-	0	0- -	-	4.57	10.38
2006	Nashv*	AAA	3	3	0	0	15.0	58	9	4	4	1	1	0	0	5	0	15	3	0	2	1	.667	0	0- -	-	1.66	2.40
2006	Hntsvl*	AA	1	1	0	0	2.2	13	4	2	1	0	0	0	0	0	0	5	1	0	0	0	-	0	0- -	-	4.08	3.38
2001	Mil	NL	25	25	1	0	151.1	653	166	89	80	23	8	5	5	48	6	94	3	0	11	10	.524	1	0-0	0	4.78	4.76
2002	Mil	NL	34	34	1	0	216.2	934	237	105	100	21	10	0	10	70	10	170	9	0	11	16	.407	0	0-0	0	4.45	4.15
2003	Mil	NL	34	34	1	0	220.2	931	232	122	109	29	11	6	6	43	2	157	7	0	11	13	.458	0	0-0	0	3.83	4.45
2004	Mil	NL	34	34	1	0	237.0	937	201	85	71	25	6	4	4	32	1	264	8	1	12	14	.462	0	0-0	0	2.37	2.70
2005	Mil	NL	22	22	3	0	156.2	633	142	66	58	19	6	2	2	25	1	141	7	0	10	9	.526	0	0-0	0	2.81	3.33
2006	Mil	NL	17	17	0	0	106.0	430	105	47	45	9	6	5	2	11	1	116	3	0	6	7	.462	0	0-0	0	2.84	3.82
6 ML YEARS			166	166	11	0	1088.1	4518	1083	514	463	126	47	22	29	229	21	942	37	1	61	69	.469	1	0-0	0	3.49	3.83

Gary Sheffield

Bats: R **Throws:** R **Pos:** RF-21; 1B-9; DH-9; PH-1   **Ht:** 6'0" **Wt:** 215 **Born:** 11/18/1968 **Age:** 38

							BATTING													BASERUNNING				AVERAGES		
Year	Team	Lg	G	AB	H	2B	3B	HR	(Hm | Rd)	TB	R	RBI	RC	TBB	IBB	SO	HBP	SH	SF	SB	CS	SB%	GDP	Avg	OBP	Slg
2006	Trntn*	AA	1	3	1	0	0	0	(- | -)	1	0	1	0	0	0	1	0	0	0	0	0	-	0	.333	.250	.333
1988	Mil	AL	24	80	19	1	0	4	(1 | 3)	32	12	12	8	7	0	7	0	1	1	3	1	.75	5	.238	.295	.400
1989	Mil	AL	95	368	91	18	0	5	(2 | 3)	124	34	32	38	27	0	33	4	3	3	10	6	.63	4	.247	.303	.337
1990	Mil	AL	125	487	143	30	1	10	(3 | 7)	205	67	67	73	44	1	41	3	4	9	25	10	.71	11	.294	.350	.421
1991	Mil	AL	50	175	34	12	2	2	(2 | 0)	56	25	22	15	19	1	15	3	1	5	5	5	.50	3	.194	.277	.320
1992	SD	NL	146	557	184	34	3	33	(23 | 10)	323	87	100	113	48	5	40	6	0	7	5	6	.45	19	.330	.385	.580
1993	2 Tms	NL	140	494	145	20	5	20	(10 | 10)	235	67	73	84	47	6	64	9	0	7	17	5	.77	11	.294	.361	.476
1994	Fla	NL	87	322	89	16	1	27	(15 | 12)	188	61	78	68	51	11	50	6	0	5	12	6	.67	10	.276	.380	.584
1995	Fla	NL	63	213	69	8	0	16	(4 | 12)	125	46	46	60	55	8	45	4	0	2	19	4	.83	3	.324	.467	.587
1996	Fla	NL	161	519	163	33	1	42	(19 | 23)	324	118	120	144	142	19	66	10	0	6	16	9	.64	16	.314	.465	.624
1997	Fla	NL	135	444	111	22	1	21	(13 | 8)	198	86	71	92	121	11	79	15	0	2	11	7	.61	7	.250	.424	.446
1998	2 Tms	NL	130	437	132	27	2	22	(11 | 11)	229	73	85	102	95	12	46	8	0	9	22	7	.76	7	.302	.428	.524
1999	LAD	NL	152	549	165	20	0	34	(19 | 15)	287	103	101	118	101	4	64	4	0	9	11	5	.69	10	.301	.407	.523
2000	LAD	NL	141	501	163	24	3	43	(23 | 20)	322	105	109	131	101	7	71	4	0	6	4	6	.40	13	.325	.438	.643
2001	LAD	NL	143	515	160	28	2	36	(16 | 20)	300	98	100	120	94	13	67	4	0	5	10	4	.71	12	.311	.417	.583
2002	Atl	NL	135	492	151	26	0	25	(10 | 15)	252	82	84	102	72	2	53	11	0	4	12	2	.86	16	.307	.404	.512
2003	Atl	NL	155	576	190	37	2	39	(20 | 19)	348	126	132	134	86	6	55	8	0	8	18	4	.82	16	.330	.419	.604
2004	NYY	AL	154	573	166	30	1	36	(19 | 17)	306	117	121	123	92	7	83	11	0	8	5	6	.45	16	.290	.393	.534
2005	NYY	AL	154	584	170	27	0	34	(19 | 15)	299	104	123	130	78	7	76	8	0	5	10	2	.83	11	.291	.379	.512
2006	NYY	AL	39	151	45	5	0	6	(5 | 1)	68	22	25	21	13	2	16	1	0	1	5	1	.83	6	.298	.355	.450
93	SD	NL	68	258	76	12	2	10	(6 | 4)	122	34	36	40	18	0	30	3	0	3	5	1	.83	9	.295	.344	.473
93	Fla	NL	72	236	69	8	3	10	(4 | 6)	113	33	37	44	29	6	34	6	0	4	12	4	.75	2	.292	.378	.479
98	Fla	NL	40	136	37	11	1	6	(6 | 0)	68	21	28	27	26	1	16	2	0	2	4	2	.67	3	.272	.392	.500
98	LAD	NL	90	301	95	16	1	16	(5 | 11)	161	52	57	75	69	11	30	6	0	7	18	5	.78	4	.316	.444	.535
	19 ML YEARS		2229	8037	2390	418	24	455	(230 | 225)	4221	1433	1501	1676	1293	122	971	119	9	102	220	96	.70	196	.297	.398	.525

Chris Shelton

Bats: R **Throws:** R **Pos:** 1B-115; PH-6   **Ht:** 6'0" **Wt:** 215 **Born:** 6/26/1980 **Age:** 27

							BATTING													BASERUNNING				AVERAGES		
Year	Team	Lg	G	AB	H	2B	3B	HR	(Hm | Rd)	TB	R	RBI	RC	TBB	IBB	SO	HBP	SH	SF	SB	CS	SB%	GDP	Avg	OBP	Slg
2006	Toledo*	AAA	28	109	29	6	2	3	(- | -)	48	20	14	19	18	0	37	1	0	1	1	0	1.00	2	.266	.372	.440
2004	Det	AL	27	46	9	1	0	1	(0 | 1)	13	6	3	4	9	0	14	0	0	1	0	0	-	2	.196	.321	.283
2005	Det	AL	107	388	116	22	3	18	(10 | 8)	198	61	59	65	34	0	87	5	0	4	0	0	-	12	.299	.360	.510
2006	Det	AL	115	373	102	16	4	16	(5 | 11)	174	50	47	50	34	1	107	4	0	1	1	2	.33	10	.273	.340	.466
	3 ML YEARS		249	807	227	39	7	35	(16 | 19)	385	117	109	119	77	1	208	9	0	6	1	2	.33	24	.281	.348	.477

George Sherrill

Pitches: L **Bats:** L **Pos:** RP-72   **Ht:** 6'0" **Wt:** 225 **Born:** 4/19/1977 **Age:** 30

			HOW MUCH HE PITCHED						WHAT HE GAVE UP											THE RESULTS						
Year	Team	Lg	G	GS	CG	GF	IP	BFP	H	R	ER	HR	SH	SF	HB	TBB	IBB	SO	WP	Bk	W	L	Pct	ShO	Sv-Op	Hld	ERC	ERA
2004	Sea	AL	21	0	0	4	23.2	104	24	12	10	3	0	1	1	9	1	16	4	1	2	1	.667	0	0-0	3	4.31	3.80
2005	Sea	AL	29	0	0	2	19.0	77	13	12	11	3	1	1	1	7	2	24	0	0	4	3	.571	0	0-0	9	2.70	5.21
2006	Sea	AL	72	0	0	6	40.0	174	30	19	19	0	4	2	0	27	4	42	0	0	2	4	.333	0	1-1	17	2.86	4.28
	3 ML YEARS		122	0	0	12	82.2	355	67	43	40	6	5	4	2	43	7	82	4	1	8	8	.500	0	1-1	29	3.24	4.35

James Shields

Pitches: R **Bats:** R **Pos:** SP-21   **Ht:** 6'4" **Wt:** 215 **Born:** 12/20/1981 **Age:** 25

			HOW MUCH HE PITCHED						WHAT HE GAVE UP											THE RESULTS						
Year	Team	Lg	G	GS	CG	GF	IP	BFP	H	R	ER	HR	SH	SF	HB	TBB	IBB	SO	WP	Bk	W	L	Pct	ShO	Sv-Op	Hld	ERC	ERA
2001	HudVal	A-	5	5	0	0	27.1	113	27	8	7	1	1	0	1	5	0	25	1	1	2	1	.667	0	0- -	-	2.90	2.30
2001	CtnSC	A	10	10	2	0	71.1	284	63	24	21	7	3	2	2	10	0	60	2	1	4	5	.444	1	0- -	-	2.58	2.65
2003	Bkrsfld	A	26	24	0	1	143.2	632	161	85	71	19	3	2	12	38	0	119	6	4	10	10	.500	0	1- -	-	4.76	4.45
2004	Mont	AA	4	4	0	0	18.1	84	24	16	16	4	3	0	0	8	0	14	0	0	0	3	.000	0	0- -	-	7.12	7.85
2004	Bkrsfld	A	20	20	1	0	117.0	488	119	61	55	13	4	5	9	33	0	92	6	0	8	5	.615	1	0- -	-	4.22	4.23
2005	Mont	AA	17	16	0	1	109.1	434	95	36	34	6	5	2	6	31	0	104	7	0	7	5	.583	0	0- -	-	2.98	2.80
2005	Drham	AAA	1	1	0	0	6.0	29	9	4	4	0	0	0	0	3	0	6	1	0	1	0	1.000	0	0- -	-	6.72	6.00
2006	Drham	AAA	10	10	0	0	61.1	241	60	24	18	3	3	1	2	6	0	64	4	1	3	2	.600	0	0- -	-	2.70	2.64
2006	TB	AL	21	21	1	0	124.2	540	141	69	67	18	4	3	5	38	5	104	9	0	6	8	.429	0	0-0	0	4.92	4.84

Scot Shields

Pitches: R **Bats:** R **Pos:** RP-74   **Ht:** 6'1" **Wt:** 170 **Born:** 7/22/1975 **Age:** 31

			HOW MUCH HE PITCHED						WHAT HE GAVE UP											THE RESULTS						
Year	Team	Lg	G	GS	CG	GF	IP	BFP	H	R	ER	HR	SH	SF	HB	TBB	IBB	SO	WP	Bk	W	L	Pct	ShO	Sv-Op	Hld	ERC	ERA
2001	LAA	AL	8	0	0	6	11.0	48	8	1	0	0	0	0	1	7	0	7	2	0	0	0	-	0	0-0	0	3.10	0.00
2002	LAA	AL	29	1	0	13	49.0	188	31	13	12	4	1	0	1	21	1	30	3	0	5	3	.625	0	0-0	3	2.35	2.20
2003	LAA	AL	44	13	0	5	148.1	609	138	56	47	12	3	4	5	38	6	111	4	0	5	6	.455	0	1-1	3	3.12	2.85
2004	LAA	AL	60	0	0	12	105.1	454	97	42	39	6	2	2	3	40	5	109	4	0	8	2	.800	0	4-7	17	3.24	3.33
2005	LAA	AL	78	0	0	21	91.2	375	66	33	28	5	4	3	2	37	2	98	12	0	10	11	.476	0	7-13	33	2.37	2.75
2006	LAA	AL	74	0	0	13	87.2	351	70	30	28	8	3	1	1	24	4	84	8	0	7	7	.500	0	2-8	31	2.48	2.87
	6 ML YEARS		293	14	0	70	493.0	2025	410	175	154	35	13	10	13	167	18	439	33	0	35	29	.547	0	14-29	87	2.81	2.81

Jason Shiell

Pitches: R Bats: R Pos: SP-3; RP-1   Ht: 6'0" Wt: 180 Born: 10/19/1976 Age: 30

Year	Team	Lg	G	GS	CG	GF	IP	BFP	H	R	ER	HR	SH	SF	HB	TBB	IBB	SO	WP	Bk	W	L	Pct	ShO	Sv-Op	Hld	ERC	ERA
2006	Rchmd*	AAA	9	9	0	0	52.0	221	51	26	26	3	6	3	2	16	0	34	2	0	2	4	.333	0	0--	-	3.46	4.50
2002	SD	NL	3	0	0	0	1.1	13	7	4	4	0	0	0	0	3	0	1	0	0	0	0	-	0	0-0	0	48.76	27.00
2003	Bos	AL	17	0	0	6	23.1	110	23	13	12	4	0	0	2	17	2	23	2	0	2	0	1.000	0	1-2	0	6.06	4.63
2006	Atl	NL	4	3	0	0	15.2	80	23	15	15	5	2	1	1	9	1	14	0	0	0	2	.000	0	0-0	0	9.62	8.62
	3 ML YEARS		24	3	0	6	40.1	203	53	32	31	9	2	1	3	29	3	38	2	0	2	2	.500	0	1-2	0	8.54	6.92

Kelly Shoppach

Bats: R Throws: R Pos: C-40; PH-4   Ht: 6'0" Wt: 220 Born: 4/29/1980 Age: 27

Year	Team	Lg	G	AB	H	2B	3B	HR	(Hm	Rd)	TB	R	RBI	RC	TBB	IBB	SO	HBP	SH	SF	SB	CS	SB%	GDP	Avg	OBP	Slg
2002	Srsota	A+	116	414	112	35	1	10	(-	-)	179	54	66	69	59	2	112	6	0	1	2	1	.67	11	.271	.369	.432
2003	Portlnd	AA	92	340	96	30	2	12	(-	-)	166	45	60	60	35	2	83	5	0	5	0	0	-	10	.282	.353	.488
2004	Pwtckt	AAA	113	399	93	25	0	22	(-	-)	184	62	64	61	46	0	138	6	1	2	0	0	-	7	.233	.320	.461
2005	Pwtckt	AAA	102	371	94	16	0	26	(-	-)	188	60	75	68	46	2	116	12	0	3	0	0	-	9	.253	.352	.507
2006	Buffalo	AAA	21	78	22	8	0	4	(-	-)	42	11	9	14	6	0	25	3	0	0	0	1	.00	1	.282	.356	.538
2005	Bos	AL	9	15	0	0	0	0	(0	0)	0	1	0	0	0	0	7	1	0	0	0	0	-	0	.000	.063	.000
2006	Cle	AL	41	110	27	6	0	3	(2	1)	42	7	16	13	8	0	45	0	2	0	0	0	-	2	.245	.297	.382
	2 ML YEARS		50	125	27	6	0	3	(2	1)	42	8	16	13	8	0	52	1	2	0	0	0	-	2	.216	.269	.336

Brian Shouse

Pitches: L Bats: L Pos: RP-65   Ht: 5'11" Wt: 190 Born: 9/26/1968 Age: 38

Year	Team	Lg	G	GS	CG	GF	IP	BFP	H	R	ER	HR	SH	SF	HB	TBB	IBB	SO	WP	Bk	W	L	Pct	ShO	Sv-Op	Hld	ERC	ERA
2006	Frisco*	AA	2	0	0	0	2.0	9	2	0	0	0	1	0	0	1	1	1	0	0	0	0	-	0	0--	-	2.79	0.00
2006	Okla*	AAA	5	0	0	4	5.0	26	7	5	3	1	0	0	0	4	0	3	0	0	0	1	.000	0	0--	-	8.96	5.40
1993	Pit	NL	6	0	0	1	4.0	22	7	4	4	1	0	1	0	2	0	3	1	0	0	0	-	0	0-0	0	9.92	9.00
1998	Bos	AL	7	0	0	4	8.0	36	9	5	5	2	0	0	0	4	0	5	0	0	0	1	.000	0	0-0	1	6.42	5.63
2002	KC	AL	23	0	0	7	14.2	71	15	10	10	3	1	1	2	9	1	11	2	0	0	0	-	0	0-2	6	6.11	6.14
2003	Tex	AL	62	0	0	14	61.0	253	62	24	21	1	3	0	4	14	6	40	0	0	0	1	.000	0	1-1	19	3.10	3.10
2004	Tex	AL	53	0	0	14	44.1	184	36	12	11	3	2	1	1	18	3	34	0	0	2	0	1.000	0	0-0	12	2.87	2.23
2005	Tex	AL	64	0	0	12	53.1	233	55	37	31	7	2	3	3	18	4	35	2	0	3	2	.600	0	0-2	11	4.29	5.23
2006	2 Tms	AL	65	0	0	10	38.1	174	40	18	17	4	1	1	6	18	5	23	0	0	1	3	.250	0	2-5	15	5.06	3.99
	06 Tex	AL	6	0	0	2	4.1	20	6	2	2	1	0	0	0	1	1	3	0	0	0	0	-	0	0-1	1	6.09	4.15
	06 Mil	NL	59	0	0	8	34.0	154	34	16	15	3	1	1	6	17	4	20	0	0	1	3	.250	0	2-4	14	4.92	3.97
	7 ML YEARS		280	0	0	62	223.2	973	224	110	99	21	9	8	16	83	19	151	5	0	6	7	.462	0	3-8	51	4.07	3.98

Ruben Sierra

Bats: B Throws: R Pos: PH-8; DH-7   Ht: 6'1" Wt: 220 Born: 10/6/1965 Age: 41

Year	Team	Lg	G	AB	H	2B	3B	HR	(Hm	Rd)	TB	R	RBI	RC	TBB	IBB	SO	HBP	SH	SF	SB	CS	SB%	GDP	Avg	OBP	Slg
2006	FtMyrs*	A+	3	12	3	1	0	0	(-	-)	4	2	1	1	1	0	3	0	0	0	0	0	-	0	.250	.308	.333
2006	Roch*	AAA	2	6	2	0	0	0	(-	-)	2	1	2	1	2	0	2	0	0	0	0	0	-	1	.333	.500	.333
1986	Tex	AL	113	382	101	13	10	16	(8	8)	182	50	55	52	22	3	65	1	1	5	7	8	.47	8	.264	.302	.476
1987	Tex	AL	158	643	169	35	4	30	(15	15)	302	97	109	86	39	4	114	2	0	12	16	11	.59	18	.263	.302	.470
1988	Tex	AL	156	615	156	32	2	23	(15	8)	261	77	91	78	44	10	91	1	0	8	18	4	.82	15	.254	.301	.424
1989	Tex	AL	162	634	194	35	14	29	(21	8)	344	101	119	118	43	2	82	2	0	10	8	2	.80	7	.306	.347	.543
1990	Tex	AL	159	608	170	37	2	16	(10	6)	259	70	96	84	49	13	86	1	0	9	9	0	1.00	15	.280	.330	.426
1991	Tex	AL	161	661	203	44	5	25	(12	13)	332	110	116	114	56	7	91	0	0	9	16	4	.80	17	.307	.357	.502
1992	2 Tms	AL	151	601	167	34	7	17	(10	7)	266	83	87	86	45	12	68	0	0	10	14	4	.78	11	.278	.323	.443
1993	Oak	AL	158	630	147	23	5	22	(9	13)	246	77	101	70	52	16	97	0	0	10	25	5	.83	17	.233	.288	.390
1994	Oak	AL	110	426	114	21	1	23	(11	12)	206	71	92	58	23	4	64	0	0	11	8	5	.62	15	.268	.298	.484
1995	2 Tms	AL	126	479	126	32	0	19	(8	11)	215	73	86	69	46	4	76	0	0	8	5	4	.56	8	.263	.323	.449
1996	2 Tms	AL	142	518	128	26	2	12	(4	8)	194	61	72	62	60	12	83	0	0	9	4	4	.50	12	.247	.320	.375
1997	2 Tms	AL	39	138	32	5	3	3	(3	0)	52	10	12	14	9	2	34	0	0	1	0	0	-	1	.232	.277	.377
1998	CWS	AL	27	74	16	4	1	4	(0	4)	34	7	11	8	3	0	11	0	0	0	2	0	1.00	2	.216	.247	.459
2000	Tex	AL	20	60	14	0	0	1	(0	1)	17	5	7	5	4	0	9	0	0	0	1	0	1.00	1	.233	.281	.283
2001	Tex	AL	94	344	100	22	1	23	(13	10)	193	55	67	58	19	0	52	0	0	6	2	0	1.00	13	.291	.322	.561
2002	Sea	AL	122	419	113	23	0	13	(6	7)	175	47	60	47	31	5	66	0	0	2	4	0	1.00	17	.270	.319	.418
2003	2 Tms	AL	106	307	83	17	1	9	(7	2)	129	33	43	35	27	3	47	0	0	2	2	1	.67	9	.270	.327	.420
2004	NYY	AL	107	307	75	12	1	17	(8	9)	140	40	65	46	25	4	55	0	0	6	1	0	1.00	4	.244	.296	.456
2005	NYY	AL	61	170	39	12	0	4	(3	1)	63	14	29	19	9	1	41	0	0	2	0	0	-	2	.229	.265	.371
2006	Min	AL	14	28	5	1	0	0	(0	0)	6	3	4	2	0	0	7	0	0	0	0	0	-	0	.179	.273	.214
	92 Tex	AL	124	500	139	30	6	14	(8	6)	223	66	70	70	31	6	59	0	0	8	12	4	.75	9	.278	.315	.446
	92 Oak	AL	27	101	28	4	1	3	(2	1)	43	17	17	16	14	6	9	0	0	2	2	0	1.00	2	.277	.359	.426
	95 Oak	AL	70	264	70	17	0	12	(3	9)	123	40	42	40	24	2	42	0	0	3	4	4	.50	2	.265	.323	.466
	95 NYY	AL	56	215	56	15	0	7	(5	2)	92	33	44	29	22	2	34	0	0	5	1	0	1.00	6	.260	.322	.428
	96 NYY	AL	96	360	93	17	1	11	(4	7)	145	39	52	46	40	11	58	0	0	7	1	3	.25	10	.258	.327	.403
	96 Det	AL	46	158	35	9	1	1	(0	1)	49	22	20	16	20	1	25	0	0	2	3	1	.75	2	.222	.306	.310
	97 Cin	NL	25	90	22	5	1	2	(2	0)	35	6	7	10	6	1	21	0	0	0	0	0	-	0	.244	.292	.389
	97 Tor	AL	14	48	10	0	2	1	(1	0)	17	4	5	4	3	1	13	0	0	1	0	0	-	1	.208	.250	.354
	03 Tex	AL	43	133	35	9	0	3	(5	1)	53	14	12	15	14	1	27	0	0	0	1	1	.50	2	.263	.333	.398
	03 NYY	AL	63	174	48	8	1	6	(5	1)	76	19	31	20	13	2	20	0	0	2	1	0	1.00	9	.276	.323	.437
	20 ML YEARS		2186	8044	2152	428	59	306	(163	143)	3616	1084	1322	1111	610	102	1239	7	1	120	142	52	.73	193	.268	.315	.450

Brian Sikorski

Pitches: R Bats: R Pos: RP-30　　　　　　　　　　Ht: 6'1" Wt: 190 Born: 7/27/1974 Age: 32

Year	Team	Lg	G	GS	CG	GF	IP	BFP	H	R	ER	HR	SH	SF	HB	TBB	IBB	SO	WP	Bk	W	L	Pct	ShO	Sv-Op	Hld	ERC	ERA
1995	Auburn	A-	23	0	0	19	34.1	137	22	8	8	1	0	1	0	14	2	35	1	0	1	2	.333	0	12--	-	1.76	2.10
1995	QuadC	A	2	0	0	1	3.0	11	1	1	0	0	0	0	0	0	0	4	0	0	1	0	1.000	0	0--	-	0.23	0.00
1996	QuadC	A	26	25	1	0	166.2	704	140	79	58	12	4	7	10	70	2	150	7	9	11	8	.579	0	0--	-	3.31	3.13
1997	Kissim	A+	11	11	0	0	67.2	279	64	29	23	2	0	1	6	16	0	46	0	3	8	2	.800	0	0--	-	3.08	3.06
1997	Jacksn	AA	17	17	0	0	93.1	402	91	55	48	8	5	2	4	31	2	74	0	2	5	5	.500	0	0--	-	3.66	4.63
1998	Jacksn	AA	15	15	0	0	97.1	419	83	50	44	13	3	2	6	44	1	80	3	1	6	4	.600	0	0--	-	3.90	4.07
1998	NewOrl	AAA	15	14	1	0	84.0	371	86	57	54	9	2	4	6	32	1	64	2	1	5	8	.385	0	0--	-	4.41	5.79
1999	NewOr	AAA	28	27	2	0	158.1	699	169	92	87	25	8	1	9	58	1	122	6	2	7	10	.412	1	0--	-	4.94	4.95
2000	Okla	AAA	24	23	5	1	140.1	591	131	73	63	9	2	8	3	60	1	99	3	5	10	9	.526	2	1--	-	3.71	4.04
2001	Okla	AAA	14	14	1	0	87.1	354	89	37	35	8	2	4	2	23	0	73	0	1	6	4	.600	0	0--	-	3.85	3.61
2006	Portlnd	AAA	22	0	0	14	28.2	118	25	12	10	3	0	0	0	7	1	44	0	0	2	3	.400	0	7--	-	2.73	3.14
2000	Tex	AL	10	5	0	2	37.2	187	46	31	24	9	0	1	1	25	1	32	1	0	1	3	.250	0	0-0	-	7.48	5.73
2006	2 Tms		30	0	0	10	34.0	142	36	19	19	8	1	1	1	7	1	38	3	0	3	2	.600	0	0-1	2	4.66	5.03
06	SD	NL	13	0	0	4	14.1	60	16	9	9	4	0	0	0	3	1	14	2	0	1	1	.500	0	0-0	0	5.16	5.65
06	Cle	AL	17	0	0	6	19.2	82	20	10	10	4	1	1	1	4	0	24	1	0	2	1	.667	0	0-1	2	4.31	4.58
2 ML YEARS			40	5	0	12	71.2	329	82	50	43	17	1	2	2	32	2	70	4	0	4	5	.444	0	0-1	2	6.13	5.40

Carlos Silva

Pitches: R Bats: R Pos: SP-31; RP-5　　　　　　　Ht: 6'4" Wt: 245 Born: 4/23/1979 Age: 28

Year	Team	Lg	G	GS	CG	GF	IP	BFP	H	R	ER	HR	SH	SF	HB	TBB	IBB	SO	WP	Bk	W	L	Pct	ShO	Sv-Op	Hld	ERC	ERA
2002	Phi	NL	68	0	0	21	84.0	350	88	34	30	4	9	3	4	22	6	41	3	0	5	0	1.000	0	1-5	8	3.60	3.21
2003	Phi	NL	62	1	0	15	87.1	381	92	43	43	7	6	1	8	37	5	48	12	1	3	1	.750	0	1-3	4	4.71	4.43
2004	Min	AL	33	33	1	0	203.0	869	255	100	95	23	6	0	5	35	2	76	5	1	14	8	.636	1	0-0	-	4.89	4.21
2005	Min	AL	27	27	2	0	188.1	749	212	83	72	25	2	5	3	9	2	71	0	0	9	8	.529	0	0-0	-	3.78	3.44
2006	Min	AL	36	31	0	2	180.1	811	246	130	119	38	6	7	7	32	4	70	1	0	11	15	.423	0	0-0	-	6.23	5.94
5 ML YEARS			226	92	3	38	743.0	3160	893	390	359	97	29	16	27	135	19	306	21	2	42	32	.568	1	2-8	14	4.76	4.35

Randall Simon

Bats: L Throws: L Pos: PH-23　　　　　　　　　　Ht: 6'0" Wt: 240 Born: 5/25/1975 Age: 32

										BATTING													BASERUNNING				AVERAGES		
Year	Team	Lg	G	AB	H	2B	3B	HR	(Hm	Rd)	TB	R	RBI	RC	TBB	IBB	SO	HBP	SH	SF	SB	CS	SB%	GDP	Avg	OBP	Slg
2006	Okla*	AAA	19	63	20	5	0	1	(-	-)	28	3	7	11	7	0	7	1	0	1	0	0	-	3	.317	.389	.444
2006	Rngrs*	R	5	18	5	1	0	0	(-	-)	6	2	3	1	1	0	0	0	0	0	0	0	-	-	.278	.316	.333
2006	Tijuana*	Mex	63	233	81	13	0	18	(-	-)	148	46	69	60	29	4	18	4	0	4	1	0	1.00	10	.348	.422	.635
1997	Atl	NL	13	14	6	1	0	0	(0	0)	7	2	1	3	1	0	2	0	0	0	0	0	-	1	.429	.467	.500
1998	Atl	NL	7	16	3	0	0	0	(0	0)	3	2	4	0	0	0	1	0	0	0	0	0	-	-	.188	.176	.188
1999	Atl	NL	90	218	69	16	0	5	(2	3)	100	26	25	33	17	6	25	1	0	1	2	2	.50	10	.317	.367	.459
2001	Det	AL	81	256	78	14	2	6	(1	5)	114	28	37	36	15	2	28	0	1	2	0	1	.00	9	.305	.341	.445
2002	Det	NL	130	482	145	17	1	19	(13	6)	221	51	82	69	13	5	30	4	0	7	0	1	.00	13	.301	.320	.459
2003	2 Tms	NL	124	410	113	17	0	16	(4	12)	178	47	72	61	16	2	37	4	0	1	0	0	-	7	.276	.309	.434
2004	2 Tms		69	192	36	6	0	3	(0	3)	51	16	14	10	18	5	19	3	0	1	0	0	-	8	.188	.266	.266
2006	Phi	NL	23	21	5	0	0	0	(0	0)	5	0	2	2	2	0	6	0	0	0	0	0	-	-	.238	.304	.238
03	Pit	NL	91	307	84	14	0	10	(4	6)	128	34	51	40	12	1	30	2	0	0	0	0	-	6	.274	.305	.417
03	ChC	NL	33	103	29	3	0	6	(0	6)	50	13	21	21	4	1	7	2	0	1	0	0	-	1	.282	.318	.485
04	Pit	NL	61	175	34	6	0	3	(0	3)	49	14	14	10	15	5	17	2	0	1	0	0	-	8	.194	.264	.280
04	TB	AL	8	17	2	0	0	0	(0	0)	2	2	0	0	3	0	2	1	0	0	0	0	-	-	.118	.286	.118
8 ML YEARS			537	1609	455	71	3	49	(20	29)	679	172	237	214	82	20	148	12	1	13	2	4	.33	48	.283	.320	.422

Allan Simpson

Pitches: R Bats: R Pos: RP-2　　　　　　　　　　Ht: 6'4" Wt: 200 Born: 8/26/1977 Age: 29

Year	Team	Lg	G	GS	CG	GF	IP	BFP	H	R	ER	HR	SH	SF	HB	TBB	IBB	SO	WP	Bk	W	L	Pct	ShO	Sv-Op	Hld	ERC	ERA
2006	Nashv*	AAA	42	0	0	26	56.2	242	45	26	21	7	4	4	5	27	1	53	3	2	2	4	.333	0	10--	-	3.72	3.34
2004	Col	NL	32	0	0	9	39.0	183	44	26	22	4	3	4	4	20	0	46	3	0	2	1	.667	0	0-1	1	5.64	5.08
2005	2 Tms	NL	11	0	0	2	7.1	36	6	10	10	1	0	1	1	8	0	6	2	0	0	1	.000	0	0-1	0	6.69	12.27
2006	Mil	NL	2	0	0	1	2.2	14	1	2	1	0	1	0	0	4	0	5	1	0	0	0	-	0	0-0	0	3.49	3.38
05	Col	NL	2	0	0	0	0.2	8	3	5	5	0	0	1	0	3	0	0	1	0	0	0	-	0	0-0	0	50.38	67.50
05	Cin	NL	9	0	0	2	6.2	28	3	5	5	1	0	0	1	5	0	6	1	0	0	1	.000	0	0-1	0	3.41	6.75
3 ML YEARS			45	0	0	12	49.0	233	51	38	33	5	3	6	5	32	0	57	6	0	2	2	.500	0	0-2	1	5.68	6.06

Andy Sisco

Pitches: L Bats: L Pos: RP-65　　　　　　　　　　Ht: 6'10" Wt: 270 Born: 1/13/1983 Age: 24

Year	Team	Lg	G	GS	CG	GF	IP	BFP	H	R	ER	HR	SH	SF	HB	TBB	IBB	SO	WP	Bk	W	L	Pct	ShO	Sv-Op	Hld	ERC	ERA
2001	Cubs	R	10	7	0	0	34.1	148	36	28	20	1	1	6	6	10	0	31	2	1	1	0	1.000	0	0--	-	4.19	5.24
2002	Boise	A-	14	14	0	0	77.2	323	51	23	21	3	3	0	6	39	0	101	6	0	7	2	.778	0	0--	-	2.52	2.43
2003	Lansng	A	19	19	3	0	94.0	389	76	44	37	3	1	0	5	31	0	99	8	0	6	8	.429	0	0--	-	2.54	3.54
2004	Dytona	A+	26	25	0	0	126.0	561	118	64	59	11	8	6	7	65	1	134	9	1	4	10	.286	0	0--	-	4.24	4.21
2006	Omha	AAA	3	0	0	2	4.2	18	3	1	1	0	0	0	0	1	0	6	1	0	0	0	-	0	1--	-	2.16	1.93
2005	KC	AL	67	0	0	13	75.1	329	68	27	26	6	2	3	2	42	4	76	2	0	2	5	.286	0	0-5	14	4.04	3.11
2006	KC	AL	65	0	0	16	58.1	278	66	47	46	8	4	5	1	40	6	52	4	0	1	3	.250	0	1-5	5	6.14	7.10
2 ML YEARS			132	0	0	29	133.2	607	134	74	72	14	6	8	3	82	10	128	6	0	3	8	.273	0	1-10	19	4.93	4.85

Grady Sizemore

Bats: L Throws: L Pos: CF-160; PH-2; DH-1   Ht: 6'2" Wt: 200 Born: 8/2/1982 Age: 24

Year	Team	Lg	G	AB	H	2B	3B	HR	(Hm	Rd)	TB	R	RBI	RC	TBB	IBB	SO	HBP	SH	SF	SB	CS	SB%	GDP	Avg	OBP	Slg
2004	Cle	AL	43	138	34	6	2	4	(2	2)	56	15	24	21	14	0	34	5	0	2	2	0	1.00	0	.246	.333	.406
2005	Cle	AL	158	640	185	37	11	22	(10	12)	310	111	81	101	52	1	132	7	5	2	22	10	.69	17	.289	.348	.484
2006	Cle	AL	162	655	190	53	11	28	(14	14)	349	134	76	121	78	8	153	13	1	4	22	6	.79	2	.290	.375	.533
	3 ML YEARS		363	1433	409	96	24	54	(26	28)	715	260	181	243	144	9	319	25	6	8	46	16	.74	19	.285	.359	.499

Doug Slaten

Pitches: L Bats: L Pos: RP-9   Ht: 6'5" Wt: 200 Born: 2/4/1980 Age: 27

HOW MUCH HE PITCHED / WHAT HE GAVE UP / THE RESULTS

Year	Team	Lg	G	GS	CG	GF	IP	BFP	H	R	ER	HR	SH	SF	HB	TBB	IBB	SO	WP	Bk	W	L	Pct	ShO	Sv-Op	Hld	ERC	ERA
2000	DBcks	R	9	4	0	3	9.1	40	7	1	1	0	0	0	2	3	0	7	0	0	0	0	-	0	0- -	-	2.51	0.96
2001	Lancst	A+	28	27	1	0	157.2	723	207	105	84	16	5	5	4	45	3	110	6	5	9	8	.529	0	0- -	-	5.42	4.79
2002	Lancst	A+	8	8	0	0	35.0	183	59	43	35	4	1	3	3	12	0	23	5	3	1	6	.143	0	0- -	-	8.18	9.00
2002	Sbend	A	7	0	0	2	14.1	63	18	8	7	0	1	0	0	4	0	5	1	0	0	0	-	0	0- -	-	4.34	4.40
2003	Lancst	A+	32	19	0	3	119.1	555	146	94	80	13	3	1	10	47	0	78	4	3	6	7	.462	0	0- -	-	5.70	6.03
2004	ElPaso	AA	11	0	0	2	9.0	53	16	13	10	1	1	1	0	10	0	6	0	0	0	1	.000	0	0- -	-	12.15	10.00
2004	Sbend	A	36	0	0	16	44.0	191	44	13	11	2	0	0	2	13	1	40	3	0	5	2	.714	0	5- -	-	3.35	2.25
2005	Tenn	AA	58	0	0	6	61.1	270	61	45	29	2	5	3	3	26	0	72	3	2	2	2	.500	0	1- -	-	3.81	4.26
2006	Tenn	AA	40	0	0	24	43.0	168	31	12	9	1	2	2	1	15	0	59	3	0	2	3	.400	0	8- -	-	2.14	1.88
2006	Tucsn	AAA	18	0	0	6	20.0	77	10	2	1	0	2	2	0	7	0	21	0	0	2	1	.667	0	2- -	-	1.12	0.45
2006	Ari	NL	9	0	0	0	5.2	21	3	0	0	0	1	0	0	2	1	3	0	0	0	0	-	0	0-0	2	1.11	0.00

Terrmel Sledge

Bats: L Throws: L Pos: PH-19; LF-12; RF-10   Ht: 6'0" Wt: 185 Born: 3/18/1977 Age: 30

Year	Team	Lg	G	AB	H	2B	3B	HR	(Hm	Rd)	TB	R	RBI	RC	TBB	IBB	SO	HBP	SH	SF	SB	CS	SB%	GDP	Avg	OBP	Slg
2006	Team*	AAA	101	367	114	18	5	24	(-	-)	214	69	73	85	59	0	75	1	1	6	5	3	.63	9	.311	.402	.583
2004	Mon	NL	133	398	107	20	6	15	(6	9)	184	45	62	66	40	4	66	1	6	1	3	3	.50	2	.269	.336	.462
2005	Was	NL	20	37	9	0	1	1	(0	1)	14	7	8	4	7	1	8	0	0	2	2	1	.67	3	.243	.348	.378
2006	SD	NL	38	70	16	3	0	2	(0	2)	25	7	7	6	8	0	17	0	0	0	0	0	-	1	.229	.308	.357
	3 ML YEARS		191	505	132	23	7	18	(6	12)	223	59	77	76	55	5	91	1	6	3	5	4	.56	6	.261	.333	.442

Brian Slocum

Pitches: R Bats: R Pos: RP-6; SP-2   Ht: 6'4" Wt: 200 Born: 3/27/1981 Age: 26

HOW MUCH HE PITCHED / WHAT HE GAVE UP / THE RESULTS

Year	Team	Lg	G	GS	CG	GF	IP	BFP	H	R	ER	HR	SH	SF	HB	TBB	IBB	SO	WP	Bk	W	L	Pct	ShO	Sv-Op	Hld	ERC	ERA
2002	MhVlly	A	11	11	0	0	55.1	223	47	19	16	7	1	2	2	14	0	48	3	0	5	2	.714	0	0- -	-	2.38	2.60
2003	Kinston	A	22	21	0	1	107.0	469	112	61	53	7	0	2	5	41	0	66	1	0	6	7	.462	0	1- -	-	4.20	4.46
2004	Kinston	A	25	25	2	0	135.0	568	136	66	65	13	5	7	6	41	0	102	11	0	15	6	.714	2	0- -	-	3.95	4.33
2005	Akron	AA	21	18	1	2	102.1	436	98	52	50	9	7	3	6	36	0	95	2	0	7	5	.583	0	0- -	-	3.82	4.40
2006	Buffalo	AAA	27	15	0	4	94.0	394	78	42	35	5	2	2	9	37	2	91	6	0	6	3	.667	0	1- -	-	3.18	3.35
2006	Cle	AL	8	2	0	1	17.2	85	27	11	11	3	0	0	1	9	0	11	2	0	0	0	-	0	0-0	0	8.99	5.60

Aaron Small

Pitches: R Bats: R Pos: RP-8; SP-3   Ht: 6'5" Wt: 235 Born: 11/23/1971 Age: 35

HOW MUCH HE PITCHED / WHAT HE GAVE UP / THE RESULTS

Year	Team	Lg	G	GS	CG	GF	IP	BFP	H	R	ER	HR	SH	SF	HB	TBB	IBB	SO	WP	Bk	W	L	Pct	ShO	Sv-Op	Hld	ERC	ERA
2006	Clmbs*	AAA	11	8	0	1	41.2	197	64	29	26	4	0	1	1	12	0	17	0	0	2	4	.333	0	0- -	-	6.91	5.62
1994	Tor	AL	1	0	0	1	2.0	13	5	2	2	1	0	1	0	2	0	0	0	0	0	0	-	0	0-0	0	21.61	9.00
1995	Fla	NL	7	0	0	1	6.1	32	7	2	1	1	0	0	0	6	0	5	0	0	1	0	1.000	0	0-0	0	7.30	1.42
1996	Oak	AL	12	3	0	4	28.2	144	37	28	26	3	0	1	1	22	1	17	2	0	1	3	.250	0	0-0	0	7.42	8.16
1997	Oak	AL	71	0	0	22	96.2	425	109	50	46	6	5	6	3	40	6	57	4	0	9	5	.643	0	4-6	8	4.67	4.28
1998	2 Tms		47	0	0	13	67.2	304	83	48	42	8	5	1	4	22	4	33	4	0	4	2	.667	0	0-2	4	5.38	5.59
2002	Atl	NL	1	0	0	1	0.1	5	2	1	1	0	0	0	0	2	0	1	1	0	0	0	-	0	0-0	0	71.88	27.00
2004	Fla	NL	7	0	0	0	16.1	78	24	15	15	5	1	0	0	7	0	8	1	0	0	0	-	0	0-0	1	8.84	8.27
2005	NYY	AL	15	9	1	1	76.0	316	71	27	27	4	1	2	5	24	0	37	0	0	10	0	1.000	1	0-1	0	3.39	3.20
2006	NYY	AL	11	3	0	2	27.2	137	42	29	26	9	0	1	1	12	1	12	0	0	0	3	.000	0	0-0	0	9.32	8.46
98	Oak	AL	24	0	0	4	36.0	174	51	34	29	3	3	1	3	14	3	19	4	0	1	1	.500	0	0-0	3	6.49	7.25
98	Ari	NL	23	0	0	9	31.2	130	32	14	13	5	2	0	1	8	1	14	0	0	3	1	.750	0	0-2	1	4.14	3.69
	9 ML YEARS		172	15	1	45	321.2	1454	380	202	186	37	12	12	14	137	12	170	12	0	25	13	.658	1	4-9	13	5.50	5.20

Jason Smith

Bats: L Throws: R Pos: PH-24; 2B-18; 1B-6; 3B-3; SS-1; PR-1   Ht: 6'3" Wt: 200 Born: 7/24/1977 Age: 29

Year	Team	Lg	G	AB	H	2B	3B	HR	(Hm	Rd)	TB	R	RBI	RC	TBB	IBB	SO	HBP	SH	SF	SB	CS	SB%	GDP	Avg	OBP	Slg
2006	ColSpr*	AAA	41	141	41	9	5	4	(-	-)	72	26	23	26	15	0	41	0	1	2	3	1	.75	3	.291	.354	.511
2001	ChC	NL	2	1	0	0	0	0	(0	0)	0	0	0	0	0	0	1	0	0	0	0	0	-	0	.000	.000	.000
2002	TB	AL	26	65	13	1	2	1	(0	1)	21	9	6	5	2	0	24	0	2	0	3	0	1.00	0	.200	.224	.323
2003	TB	AL	1	4	1	0	0	0	(0	0)	1	0	0	0	0	0	0	0	0	0	0	0	-	0	.250	.250	.250
2004	Det	AL	61	155	37	7	4	5	(0	5)	67	20	19	13	8	0	37	1	5	0	1	2	.33	0	.239	.280	.432
2005	Det	AL	27	58	11	1	2	0	(0	0)	16	4	2	4	0	0	16	1	4	0	2	1	.67	0	.190	.203	.276
2006	Col	NL	49	99	26	1	0	5	(1	4)	42	9	13	15	7	1	29	2	0	0	3	0	1.00	1	.263	.324	.424
	6 ML YEARS		166	382	88	10	8	11	(1	10)	147	42	40	37	17	1	107	4	11	0	9	3	.75	1	.230	.270	.385

Matt Smith

Pitches: L **Bats:** L **Pos:** RP-26 **Ht:** 6'5" **Wt:** 225 **Born:** 6/15/1979 **Age:** 28

			HOW MUCH HE PITCHED						WHAT HE GAVE UP												THE RESULTS							
Year	Team	Lg	G	GS	CG	GF	IP	BFP	H	R	ER	HR	SH	SF	HB	TBB	IBB	SO	WP	Bk	W	L	Pct	ShO	Sv-Op	Hld	ERC	ERA
2000	StlsInd	A-	14	14	0	0	75.2	308	74	32	20	1	3	0	2	20	0	59	4	0	5	4	.556	0	0--	-	3.05	2.38
2001	Grnsbr	A	16	16	1	0	97.1	389	69	37	28	1	3	1	3	32	0	116	8	0	5	3	.625	0	0--	-	1.89	2.59
2001	Tampa	A+	11	11	0	0	68.2	276	54	21	17	2	1	1	1	22	0	71	4	4	6	2	.750	0	0--	-	2.30	2.23
2002	Nrwich	AA	17	17	0	0	89.1	419	112	63	54	8	3	3	9	37	0	70	11	0	3	8	.273	0	0--	-	5.91	5.44
2002	Tampa	A+	8	6	0	1	27.1	133	37	23	20	1	0	4	0	17	0	20	2	0	0	4	.000	0	0--	-	6.56	6.59
2003	Tampa	A+	6	6	0	0	32.1	131	20	11	8	0	0	4	1	12	0	25	1	0	2	3	.400	0	0--	-	1.56	2.23
2003	Trntn	AA	9	9	0	0	50.2	226	57	29	24	6	1	3	2	24	0	36	0	0	2	3	.400	0	0--	-	5.50	4.26
2004	Trntn	AA	14	11	0	0	61.2	271	67	34	34	5	2	2	1	31	1	56	3	0	4	4	.500	0	0--	-	5.01	4.96
2005	Clmbs	AAA	25	0	0	7	27.2	122	24	9	8	3	1	0	3	13	1	33	0	0	2	0	1.000	0	1--	-	3.98	2.60
2005	Trntn	AA	22	4	0	5	54.2	228	46	24	17	2	2	2	0	23	0	59	3	1	3	4	.429	0	2--	-	2.89	2.80
2006	Clmbs	AAA	24	0	0	5	26.0	111	27	9	6	3	1	0	1	8	1	22	1	0	0	1	.000	0	0--	-	4.15	2.08
2006	S-WB	AAA	9	0	0	6	9.0	40	5	2	2	1	2	0	1	6	0	6	0	0	0	0	-	0	4--	-	3.02	2.00
2006	Clrwtr	A+	2	0	0	1	2.0	6	0	0	0	0	0	0	0	0	0	6	0	0	0	0	-	0	0--	-	0.00	0.00
2006	2 Tms		26	0	0	9	20.2	77	7	2	2	0	0	0	0	12	1	21	0	0	0	1	.000	0	0-0	6	1.13	0.87
06	NYY	AL	12	0	0	6	12.0	46	4	0	0	0	0	0	0	8	1	9	0	0	0	0	-	0	0-0	0	1.23	0.00
06	Phi	NL	14	0	0	3	8.2	31	3	2	2	0	0	0	0	4	0	12	0	0	0	1	.000	0	0-0	6	0.98	2.08

Mike Smith

Pitches: R **Bats:** R **Pos:** SP-1 **Ht:** 5'11" **Wt:** 205 **Born:** 9/19/1977 **Age:** 29

			HOW MUCH HE PITCHED						WHAT HE GAVE UP												THE RESULTS							
Year	Team	Lg	G	GS	CG	GF	IP	BFP	H	R	ER	HR	SH	SF	HB	TBB	IBB	SO	WP	Bk	W	L	Pct	ShO	Sv-Op	Hld	ERC	ERA
2000	Queens	A-	14	12	0	0	51.0	205	41	18	13	1	1	2	2	17	0	55	9	1	2	2	.500	0	0--	-	2.48	2.29
2001	CtnWV	A	14	14	2	0	94.1	378	78	32	22	2	1	2	6	21	0	85	6	0	5	5	.500	1	0--	-	2.28	2.10
2001	Tenn	AA	14	14	1	0	93.0	393	80	32	25	7	4	1	8	26	2	77	6	0	6	2	.750	0	0--	-	2.93	2.42
2002	Syrcse	AAA	20	20	1	0	121.2	505	106	51	47	10	0	2	6	43	0	76	3	0	8	4	.667	1	0--	-	3.31	3.48
2003	Syrcse	AAA	26	21	2	0	131.1	583	140	80	73	13	5	5	11	58	1	89	16	0	8	9	.471	0	1--	-	5.00	5.00
2004	Syrcse	AAA	35	15	0	12	109.0	508	123	80	64	12	2	5	12	53	0	72	9	0	4	6	.400	0	0--	-	5.65	5.28
2005	Rdng	AA	28	28	1	0	170.2	756	162	97	85	18	10	5	23	82	0	113	14	1	5	14	.263	0	0--	-	4.72	4.48
2005	S-WB	AAA	1	1	0	0	3.2	20	5	4	4	1	0	0	1	3	0	2	0	0	0	0	-	0	0--	-	10.78	9.82
2006	Roch	AAA	28	24	2	1	150.2	657	152	76	65	12	2	6	9	57	1	110	6	0	11	5	.688	1	0--	-	4.11	3.88
2002	Tor	AL	14	6	0	3	35.1	174	43	28	26	3	3	1	7	20	0	16	2	0	0	3	.000	0	0-0	0	6.66	6.62
2006	Min	AL	1	1	0	0	3.0	18	5	4	4	1	0	0	1	3	0	1	0	0	0	0	-	0	0-0	0	14.84	12.00
	2 ML YEARS		15	7	0	3	38.1	192	48	32	30	4	3	1	8	23	0	17	2	0	0	3	.000	0	0-0	0	7.24	7.04

Travis Smith

Pitches: R **Bats:** R **Pos:** SP-1 **Ht:** 5'10" **Wt:** 170 **Born:** 11/7/1972 **Age:** 34

			HOW MUCH HE PITCHED						WHAT HE GAVE UP												THE RESULTS							
Year	Team	Lg	G	GS	CG	GF	IP	BFP	H	R	ER	HR	SH	SF	HB	TBB	IBB	SO	WP	Bk	W	L	Pct	ShO	Sv-Op	Hld	ERC	ERA
2006	Rchmd*	AAA	8	8	0	0	46.1	194	41	15	15	2	0	1	2	16	1	44	1	0	3	1	.750	0	0--	-	3.00	2.91
2006	Memp*	AAA	15	15	1	0	89.0	391	109	60	56	9	4	2	3	26	3	49	4	1	5	6	.455	0	0--	-	5.09	5.66
1998	Mil	NL	1	0	0	0	2.0	7	1	0	0	0	0	0	0	0	0	1	0	0	0	0	-	0	0-0	0	0.54	0.00
2002	StL	NL	12	10	0	0	54.0	244	69	44	43	10	7	0	3	20	0	32	2	0	4	2	.667	0	0-0	0	6.63	7.17
2004	Atl	NL	16	4	0	4	40.2	180	48	28	28	12	3	0	1	12	2	26	1	0	2	3	.400	0	0-0	1	6.12	6.20
2005	Fla	NL	12	0	0	4	10.2	52	17	8	8	1	0	1	0	5	1	9	0	0	0	0	-	0	0-0	0	7.89	6.75
2006	Atl	NL	1	1	0	0	4.1	19	5	4	2	0	1	1	0	1	0	1	1	0	0	1	.000	0	0-0	0	3.47	4.15
	5 ML YEARS		42	15	0	8	111.2	502	140	84	81	23	11	2	4	38	3	69	4	0	6	6	.500	0	0-0	1	6.29	6.53

John Smoltz

Pitches: R **Bats:** R **Pos:** SP-35 **Ht:** 6'3" **Wt:** 220 **Born:** 5/15/1967 **Age:** 40

			HOW MUCH HE PITCHED						WHAT HE GAVE UP												THE RESULTS							
Year	Team	Lg	G	GS	CG	GF	IP	BFP	H	R	ER	HR	SH	SF	HB	TBB	IBB	SO	WP	Bk	W	L	Pct	ShO	Sv-Op	Hld	ERC	ERA
1988	Atl	NL	12	12	0	0	64.0	297	74	40	39	10	2	0	2	33	4	37	2	1	2	7	.222	0	0-0	0	5.86	5.48
1989	Atl	NL	29	29	5	0	208.0	847	160	79	68	15	10	7	2	72	2	168	8	3	12	11	.522	0	0-0	0	2.50	2.94
1990	Atl	NL	34	34	6	0	231.1	966	206	109	99	20	9	8	1	**90**	3	170	**14**	3	14	11	.560	2	0-0	0	3.37	3.85
1991	Atl	NL	36	36	5	0	229.2	947	206	101	97	16	9	9	3	77	1	148	**20**	2	14	13	.519	2	0-0	0	3.15	3.80
1992	Atl	NL	35	35	9	0	246.2	1021	206	90	78	17	7	8	5	80	5	**215**	17	1	15	12	.556	3	0-0	0	2.73	2.85
1993	Atl	NL	35	35	3	0	243.2	1028	208	104	98	23	13	4	6	100	12	208	13	1	15	11	.577	0	0-0	0	3.29	3.62
1994	Atl	NL	21	21	1	0	134.2	568	120	69	62	15	7	6	4	48	4	113	7	0	6	10	.375	0	0-0	0	3.44	4.14
1995	Atl	NL	29	29	2	0	192.2	808	166	76	68	15	13	5	4	72	8	193	13	0	12	7	.632	1	0-0	0	3.08	3.18
1996	Atl	NL	35	35	6	0	**253.2**	995	199	93	83	19	12	4	2	55	3	**276**	10	1	**24**	8	**.750**	2	0-0	0	2.17	2.94
1997	Atl	NL	35	**35**	7	0	**256.0**	1043	**234**	97	86	21	10	3	1	63	9	241	10	1	15	12	.556	2	0-0	0	2.89	3.02
1998	Atl	NL	26	26	2	0	167.2	681	145	58	54	10	4	2	4	44	2	173	3	1	17	3	**.850**	2	0-0	0	2.67	2.90
1999	Atl	NL	29	29	1	0	186.1	746	168	70	66	14	10	5	4	40	2	156	2	0	11	8	.579	1	0-0	0	2.81	3.19
2001	Atl	NL	36	5	0	20	59.0	238	53	24	22	7	1	2	2	10	2	57	0	0	3	3	.500	0	10-11	5	2.85	3.36
2002	Atl	NL	75	0	0	68	80.1	319	59	30	29	4	2	1	0	24	1	85	1	1	3	2	.600	0	**55-59**	0	2.06	3.25
2003	Atl	NL	62	0	0	55	64.1	244	48	9	8	2	0	1	0	8	1	73	2	0	2	0	.000	0	45-49	0	1.50	1.12
2004	Atl	NL	73	0	0	61	81.2	323	75	25	25	8	4	0	0	13	2	85	6	0	0	1	.000	0	44-49	0	2.73	2.76
2005	Atl	NL	33	33	3	0	229.2	932	210	83	78	18	10	3	1	53	7	169	2	1	14	7	.667	1	0-0	0	2.83	3.06
2006	Atl	NL	35	**35**	3	0	232.0	960	221	93	90	23	**4**	**10**	9	55	4	211	5	0	**16**	9	.640	1	0-0	0	3.32	3.49
	18 ML YEARS		670	429	53	204	3161.1	12957	2758	1250	1150	257	127	78	50	937	72	2778	135	16	193	137	.585	16	154-168	5	2.91	3.27

Ian Snell

Pitches: R Bats: R Pos: SP-32   Ht: 5'11" Wt: 190 Born: 10/30/1981 Age: 25

			HOW MUCH HE PITCHED							WHAT HE GAVE UP											THE RESULTS							
Year	Team	Lg	G	GS	CG	GF	IP	BFP	H	R	ER	HR	SH	SF	HB	TBB	IBB	SO	WP	Bk	W	L	Pct	ShO	Sv-Op	Hld	ERC	ERA
2004	Pit	NL	3	1	0	1	12.0	56	14	10	10	2	0	0	0	9	0	9	0	0	0	1	.000	0	0-0	0	7.31	7.50
2005	Pit	NL	15	5	0	2	42.0	189	43	25	24	5	2	1	1	24	3	34	4	0	1	2	.333	0	0-0	1	5.03	5.14
2006	Pit	NL	32	32	0	0	186.0	813	198	104	98	29	16	6	2	74	4	169	8	0	14	11	.560	0	0-0	0	4.86	4.74
	3 ML YEARS		50	38	0	3	240.0	1058	255	139	132	36	18	7	3	107	7	212	12	0	15	14	.517	0	0-0	1	5.01	4.95

Chris Snelling

Bats: L Throws: L Pos: RF-33; PH-5; LF-1; CF-1   Ht: 5'10" Wt: 205 Born: 12/3/1981 Age: 25

						BATTING																	BASERUNNING				AVERAGES		
Year	Team	Lg	G	AB	H	2B	3B	HR	(Hm	Rd)	TB	R	RBI	RC	TBB	IBB	SO	HBP	SH	SF	SB	CS	SB%	GDP	Avg	OBP	Slg
2006	Tacom*	AAA	69	241	52	13	1	5	(-	-)	82	36	39	30	31	2	60	11	2	5	4	2	.67	7	.216	.326	.340
2002	Sea	AL	8	27	4	0	0	1	(0	1)	7	2	3	3	2	0	4	0	0	0	0	0	-	2	.148	.207	.259
2005	Sea	AL	15	29	8	2	0	1	(1	0)	13	4	1	3	5	0	2	0	1	0	0	2	.00	0	.276	.382	.448
2006	Sea	AL	36	96	24	6	1	3	(2	1)	41	14	8	11	13	0	38	4	5	1	2	1	.67	0	.250	.360	.427
	3 ML YEARS		59	152	36	8	1	5	(3	2)	61	20	12	17	20	0	44	4	6	1	2	3	.40	2	.237	.339	.401

J.T. Snow

Bats: L Throws: L Pos: 1B-26; PH-12; DH-1   Ht: 6'2" Wt: 210 Born: 2/26/1968 Age: 39

						BATTING																	BASERUNNING				AVERAGES		
Year	Team	Lg	G	AB	H	2B	3B	HR	(Hm	Rd)	TB	R	RBI	RC	TBB	IBB	SO	HBP	SH	SF	SB	CS	SB%	GDP	Avg	OBP	Slg
1992	NYY	AL	7	14	2	1	0	0	(0	0)	3	1	2	2	5	1	5	0	0	0	0	0	-	0	.143	.368	.214
1993	LAA	AL	129	419	101	18	2	16	(10	6)	171	60	57	57	55	4	88	2	7	6	3	0	1.00	10	.241	.328	.408
1994	LAA	AL	61	223	49	4	0	8	(7	1)	77	22	30	22	19	1	48	3	2	1	0	1	.00	2	.220	.289	.345
1995	LAA	AL	143	544	157	22	1	24	(14	10)	253	80	102	85	52	4	91	3	5	2	2	1	.67	16	.289	.353	.465
1996	LAA	AL	155	575	148	20	1	17	(8	9)	221	69	67	67	56	6	96	5	2	3	1	6	.14	19	.257	.327	.384
1997	SF	NL	157	531	149	36	1	28	(14	14)	271	81	104	105	96	13	124	1	2	7	6	4	.60	8	.281	.387	.510
1998	SF	NL	138	435	108	29	1	15	(9	6)	184	65	79	60	58	3	84	0	0	7	1	2	.33	12	.248	.332	.423
1999	SF	NL	161	570	156	25	2	24	(7	17)	257	93	98	93	86	7	121	5	1	6	0	4	.00	16	.274	.370	.451
2000	SF	NL	155	536	152	33	2	19	(10	9)	246	82	96	87	66	6	129	11	0	14	1	3	.25	20	.284	.365	.459
2001	SF	NL	101	285	70	12	1	8	(3	5)	108	43	34	44	55	10	81	4	0	4	0	0	-	2	.246	.371	.379
2002	SF	NL	143	422	104	26	2	6	(1	5)	152	47	53	54	59	5	90	7	0	6	0	0	-	11	.246	.344	.360
2003	SF	NL	103	330	90	18	3	8	(2	6)	138	48	51	59	55	0	55	8	1	2	1	2	.33	7	.273	.387	.418
2004	SF	NL	107	346	113	32	1	12	(5	7)	183	62	60	79	58	0	61	7	2	4	4	0	1.00	6	.327	.429	.529
2005	SF	NL	117	367	101	17	2	4	(1	3)	134	40	40	48	32	1	61	7	2	2	1	0	1.00	6	.275	.343	.365
2006	Bos	AL	38	44	9	0	0	0	(0	0)	9	5	4	5	8	0	8	1	0	0	0	0	-	1	.205	.340	.205
	15 ML YEARS		1715	5641	1509	293	19	189	(91	98)	2407	798	877	867	760	61	1142	64	24	64	20	23	.47	135	.268	.357	.427

Chris Snyder

Bats: R Throws: R Pos: C-60; PH-2   Ht: 6'3" Wt: 230 Born: 2/12/1981 Age: 26

						BATTING																	BASERUNNING				AVERAGES		
Year	Team	Lg	G	AB	H	2B	3B	HR	(Hm	Rd)	TB	R	RBI	RC	TBB	IBB	SO	HBP	SH	SF	SB	CS	SB%	GDP	Avg	OBP	Slg
2004	Ari	NL	29	96	23	6	0	5	(1	4)	44	10	15	11	13	1	25	0	0	1	0	0	-	1	.240	.327	.458
2005	Ari	NL	115	326	66	14	0	6	(2	4)	98	24	28	25	40	5	87	4	3	0	0	1	.00	6	.202	.297	.301
2006	Ari	NL	61	184	51	9	0	6	(4	2)	78	19	32	27	22	4	39	1	1	5	0	0	-	5	.277	.349	.424
	3 ML YEARS		205	606	140	29	0	17	(7	10)	220	53	75	63	75	10	151	5	4	6	0	1	.00	12	.231	.318	.363

Kyle Snyder

Pitches: R Bats: B Pos: SP-11; RP-6   Ht: 6'8" Wt: 215 Born: 9/9/1977 Age: 29

					HOW MUCH HE PITCHED							WHAT HE GAVE UP											THE RESULTS							
Year	Team	Lg	G	GS	CG	GF	IP	BFP	H	R	ER	HR	SH	SF	HB	TBB	IBB	SO	WP	Bk	W	L	Pct	ShO	Sv-Op	Hld	ERC	ERA
2006	Omha*	AAA	10	9	0	1	60.1	253	63	36	26	4	2	2	1	9	0	43	5	2	0	4	.000	0	1--	1	3.13	3.88
2006	Pwtckt*	AAA	3	3	0	0	20.1	82	24	8	8	1	0	0	1	2	0	7	0	0	1	1	.500	0	0--	-	3.95	3.54
2003	KC	AL	15	15	0	0	85.1	364	94	52	49	11	0	9	2	21	3	39	4	0	1	6	.143	0	0-0	0	4.29	5.17
2005	KC	AL	13	3	0	4	36.0	169	55	29	27	3	0	2	1	10	1	19	1	0	1	3	.250	0	0-0	0	6.70	6.75
2006	2 Tms		17	11	0	3	60.1	287	87	51	44	12	0	2	2	20	3	57	3	0	4	5	.444	0	0-0	1	7.21	6.56
	06 KC	AL	1	1	0	0	2.0	19	10	9	5	1	0	0	0	1	0	2	0	0	0	0	-	0	0-0	0	36.36	22.50
	06 Bos	AL	16	10	0	3	58.1	268	77	42	39	11	0	2	2	19	3	55	3	0	4	5	.444	0	0-0	1	6.38	6.02
	3 ML YEARS		45	29	0	7	181.2	820	236	132	120	26	0	13	5	51	7	115	8	0	6	14	.300	0	0-0	1	5.69	5.94

Alay Soler

Pitches: R Bats: R Pos: SP-8   Ht: 6'1" Wt: 240 Born: 10/9/1979 Age: 27

					HOW MUCH HE PITCHED							WHAT HE GAVE UP											THE RESULTS							
Year	Team	Lg	G	GS	CG	GF	IP	BFP	H	R	ER	HR	SH	SF	HB	TBB	IBB	SO	WP	Bk	W	L	Pct	ShO	Sv-Op	Hld	ERC	ERA
2006	Bklyn	A-	1	1	0	0	4.1	18	2	3	3	1	0	0	0	2	0	9	0	1	0	1	.000	0	0--	-	2.12	6.23
2006	Bnghtn	AA	3	3	0	0	19.2	77	16	6	6	0	0	2	0	3	0	22	0	0	1	0	1.000	0	0--	-	1.66	2.75
2006	StLuci	A+	6	6	0	0	30.0	110	13	2	2	0	0	0	0	9	0	33	1	0	2	0	1.000	0	0--	-	0.88	0.60
2006	Norfolk	AAA	2	2	0	0	10.0	46	13	7	7	0	1	0	0	4	0	12	1	1	1	1	.500	0	0--	-	5.01	6.30
2006	NYM	NL	8	8	1	0	45.0	208	50	33	30	7	2	2	1	21	1	23	3	0	2	3	.400	1	0-0	0	5.30	6.00

Alfonso Soriano

Bats: R **Throws:** R **Pos:** LF-158; PH-1 **Ht:** 6'1" **Wt:** 180 **Born:** 1/7/1976 **Age:** 31

									BATTING												BASERUNNING				AVERAGES		
Year	Team	Lg	G	AB	H	2B	3B	HR	(Hm	Rd)	TB	R	RBI	RC	TBB	IBB	SO	HBP	SH	SF	SB	CS	SB%	GDP	Avg	OBP	Slg
1999	NYY	AL	9	8	1	0	0	1	(1	0)	4	2	1	0	0	0	3	0	0	0	0	1	.00	0	.125	.125	.500
2000	NYY	AL	22	50	9	3	0	2	(0	2)	18	5	3	4	1	0	15	0	2	0	2	0	1.00	0	.180	.196	.360
2001	NYY	AL	158	574	154	34	3	18	(8	10)	248	77	73	77	29	0	125	3	3	5	43	14	.75	7	.268	.304	.432
2002	NYY	AL	156	696	209	51	2	39	(17	22)	381	128	102	121	23	1	157	14	1	7	41	13	.76	8	.300	.332	.547
2003	NYY	AL	156	682	198	36	5	38	(15	23)	358	114	91	110	38	7	130	12	0	2	35	8	.81	8	.290	.338	.525
2004	Tex	AL	145	608	170	32	4	28	(12	16)	294	77	91	90	33	4	121	10	0	7	18	5	.78	7	.280	.324	.484
2005	Tex	AL	156	637	171	43	2	36	(25	11)	326	102	104	93	33	3	125	7	0	5	30	2	.94	6	.268	.309	.512
2006	Was	NL	159	647	179	41	2	46	(24	22)	362	119	95	114	67	16	160	9	2	3	41	17	.71	3	.277	.351	.560
8 ML YEARS			961	3902	1091	240	18	208	(102	106)	1991	624	560	609	224	31	836	55	8	29	210	60	.78	39	.280	.325	.510

Rafael Soriano

Pitches: R **Bats:** R **Pos:** RP-53 **Ht:** 6'1" **Wt:** 220 **Born:** 12/19/1979 **Age:** 27

			HOW MUCH HE PITCHED						WHAT HE GAVE UP											THE RESULTS						
Year	Team	Lg	G	GS	CG	GF	IP	BFP	H	R	ER	HR	SH	SF	HB	TBB	IBB	SO	WP	Bk	W	L	Pct	ShO	Sv-Op	Hld	ERC	ERA
2002	Sea	AL	10	8	0	1	47.1	202	45	25	24	8	1	0	0	16	1	32	2	0	0	3	.000	0	1-1	0	3.93	4.56
2003	Sea	AL	40	0	0	12	53.0	201	30	9	9	2	0	1	3	12	1	68	0	0	3	0	1.000	0	1-2	5	1.32	1.53
2004	Sea	AL	6	0	0	3.1	23	9	6	5	0	0	0	0	3	0	3	0	0	3	.000	0	0-1	0	15.97	13.50		
2005	Sea	AL	7	0	0	4	7.1	30	6	2	2	0	0	1	1	1	0	9	0	0	0	0	-	0	0-0	1	2.00	2.45
2006	Sea	AL	53	0	0	14	60.0	241	44	15	15	6	1	1	2	21	0	65	2	0	1	2	.333	0	2-6	18	2.64	2.25
5 ML YEARS			116	8	0	31	171.0	697	134	57	55	16	2	3	6	53	2	177	4	0	4	8	.333	0	4-10	24	2.66	2.89

Jorge Sosa

Pitches: R **Bats:** R **Pos:** RP-32; SP-13 **Ht:** 6'2" **Wt:** 175 **Born:** 4/28/1977 **Age:** 30

			HOW MUCH HE PITCHED						WHAT HE GAVE UP											THE RESULTS						
Year	Team	Lg	G	GS	CG	GF	IP	BFP	H	R	ER	HR	SH	SF	HB	TBB	IBB	SO	WP	Bk	W	L	Pct	ShO	Sv-Op	Hld	ERC	ERA
2002	TB	AL	31	14	0	10	99.1	434	88	63	61	16	0	5	2	54	0	48	5	0	2	7	.222	0	0-0	1	4.51	5.53
2003	TB	AL	29	19	1	4	128.2	566	137	71	66	14	4	5	4	60	4	72	8	1	5	12	.294	1	0-0	0	4.93	4.62
2004	TB	AL	43	8	0	6	99.1	447	100	67	61	17	2	4	1	54	3	94	2	0	4	7	.364	0	1-1	6	5.17	5.53
2005	Atl	NL	44	20	0	5	134.0	577	122	42	38	12	5	2	0	64	8	85	3	0	13	3	.813	0	0-0	4	3.70	2.55
2006	2 Tms	NL	45	13	0	12	118.0	524	138	79	71	30	7	4	1	40	6	75	2	0	3	11	.214	0	4-7	0	5.88	5.42
06 Atl		NL	26	13	0	8	87.1	394	105	61	53	20	5	4	1	32	5	58	2	0	3	10	.231	0	3-6	0	6.00	5.46
06 StL		NL	19	0	0	4	30.2	130	33	18	18	10	2	0	0	8	1	17	0	0	0	1	.000	0	1-1	0	5.48	5.28
5 ML YEARS			192	74	1	37	579.1	2548	585	322	297	89	18	20	8	272	21	374	20	1	27	40	.403	1	5-8	11	4.80	4.61

Geovany Soto

Bats: R **Throws:** R **Pos:** C-7; PH-4 **Ht:** 6'1" **Wt:** 230 **Born:** 1/20/1983 **Age:** 24

									BATTING												BASERUNNING				AVERAGES		
Year	Team	Lg	G	AB	H	2B	3B	HR	(Hm	Rd)	TB	R	RBI	RC	TBB	IBB	SO	HBP	SH	SF	SB	CS	SB%	GDP	Avg	OBP	Slg
2001	Cubs	R	41	150	39	16	0	1	(-	-)	58	18	20	21	15	1	33	3	1	0	1	0	1.00	3	.260	.339	.387
2002	Cubs	R	44	156	42	10	2	3	(-	-)	65	24	24	22	13	1	35	3	1	2	0	2	.00	2	.269	.333	.417
2002	Boise	A-	1	5	2	0	0	0	(-	-)	2	1	0	0	0	0	1	0	0	0	0	0	-	0	.400	.400	.400
2003	Dytona	A+	89	297	72	12	2	2	(-	-)	94	26	38	32	31	0	58	2	4	6	0	0	-	10	.242	.313	.316
2004	WTenn	AA	104	332	90	16	0	9	(-	-)	133	47	48	50	40	1	71	5	1	3	1	2	.33	10	.271	.355	.401
2005	Iowa	AAA	91	292	74	14	0	4	(-	-)	100	30	39	39	48	0	77	0	3	2	0	1	.00	15	.253	.357	.342
2006	Iowa	AAA	108	342	93	21	0	6	(-	-)	132	34	38	49	41	2	74	3	3	2	0	1	.00	10	.272	.353	.386
2005	ChC	NL	1	1	0	0	0	0	(0	0)	0	0	0	0	0	0	0	0	0	0	0	0	-	0	.000	.000	.000
2006	ChC	NL	11	25	5	1	0	0	(0	0)	6	1	2	0	0	0	5	1	0	0	0	0	-	0	.200	.231	.240
2 ML YEARS			12	26	5	1	0	0	(0	0)	6	1	2	0	0	0	5	1	0	0	0	0	-	0	.192	.222	.231

Jeremy Sowers

Pitches: L **Bats:** L **Pos:** SP-14 **Ht:** 6'1" **Wt:** 180 **Born:** 5/17/1983 **Age:** 24

			HOW MUCH HE PITCHED						WHAT HE GAVE UP											THE RESULTS						
Year	Team	Lg	G	GS	CG	GF	IP	BFP	H	R	ER	HR	SH	SF	HB	TBB	IBB	SO	WP	Bk	W	L	Pct	ShO	Sv-Op	Hld	ERC	ERA
2005	Kinston	A+	13	13	0	0	71.1	292	60	25	22	5	0	1	0	19	0	75	4	0	8	3	.727	0	0- -	-	2.51	2.78
2005	Akron	AA	13	13	0	0	82.1	323	74	25	19	8	2	2	3	9	1	70	2	0	5	1	.833	0	0- -	-	2.59	2.08
2005	Buffalo	AAA	1	1	0	0	5.2	25	7	1	1	0	0	0	0	1	0	4	1	0	1	0	1.000	0	0- -	-	3.70	1.59
2006	Buffalo	AAA	15	15	2	0	97.1	383	78	20	15	1	4	1	1	29	1	54	2	0	9	1	.900	2	0- -	-	2.20	1.39
2006	Cle	AL	14	14	2	0	88.1	360	85	36	35	10	1	0	2	20	1	35	1	0	7	4	.636	2	0-0	0	3.41	3.57

Justin Speier

Pitches: R **Bats:** R **Pos:** RP-58 **Ht:** 6'4" **Wt:** 205 **Born:** 11/6/1973 **Age:** 33

			HOW MUCH HE PITCHED						WHAT HE GAVE UP											THE RESULTS						
Year	Team	Lg	G	GS	CG	GF	IP	BFP	H	R	ER	HR	SH	SF	HB	TBB	IBB	SO	WP	Bk	W	L	Pct	ShO	Sv-Op	Hld	ERC	ERA
1998	2 Tms	NL	19	0	0	10	20.2	99	27	20	20	7	2	1	0	13	1	17	3	0	0	3	.000	0	0-1	1	8.94	8.71
1999	Atl	NL	19	0	0	8	28.2	127	28	18	18	8	0	1	0	13	1	22	0	0	0	0	-	0	0-0	0	5.27	5.65
2000	Cle	AL	47	0	0	12	68.1	290	57	27	25	9	2	4	4	28	3	69	7	1	5	2	.714	0	0-1	6	3.56	3.29
2001	2 Tms	AL	54	0	0	10	76.2	324	71	40	39	13	2	7	8	20	3	62	6	1	6	3	.667	0	0-1	4	3.93	4.58
2002	Col	NL	63	0	0	7	62.1	259	51	31	30	9	0	1	3	19	4	47	1	2	5	1	.833	0	1-4	18	4.36	4.33
2003	Col	NL	72	0	0	31	73.1	319	73	37	33	11	1	4	7	23	6	66	0	0	3	1	.750	0	9-12	12	4.27	4.05
2004	Tor	AL	62	0	0	32	69.0	294	61	32	30	8	6	3	5	25	6	52	4	0	3	8	.273	0	7-11	7	3.52	3.91
2005	Tor	AL	65	0	0	36	66.2	264	48	20	19	10	4	0	3	15	2	56	1	1	3	2	.600	0	0-4	11	2.38	2.57
2006	Tor	AL	58	0	0	8	51.1	222	47	18	17	5	0	0	1	21	3	55	0	0	2	0	1.000	0	0-3	25	3.55	2.98

Year	Team	Lg	G	GS	CG	GF	IP	BFP	H	R	ER	HR	SH	SF	HB	TBB	IBB	SO	WP	Bk	W	L	Pct	ShO	Sv-Op	Hld	ERC	ERA
98	ChC	NL	1	0	0	0	1.1	7	2	2	2	0	0	0	0	1	0	2	1	0	0	0	-	0	0-0	0	7.52	13.50
98	Fla	NL	18	0	0	10	19.1	92	25	18	18	7	2	1	0	12	1	15	2	0	0	3	.000	0	0-1	1	9.02	8.38
01	Cle	AL	12	0	0	2	20.2	96	24	16	16	5	0	3	3	8	0	15	2	0	2	0	1.000	0	0-0	0	6.61	6.97
01	Col	NL	42	0	0	8	56.0	228	47	24	23	8	2	4	5	12	3	47	4	1	4	3	.571	0	0-1	4	3.04	3.70
	9 ML YEARS		459	0	0	154	517.0	2198	463	243	231	80	17	21	31	177	29	446	26	5	27	20	.574	0	17-37	84	3.76	4.02

Scott Spiezio

Bats: B Throws: R Pos: PH-43; 3B-38; LF-35; 1B-13; 2B-8; DH-5   Ht: 6'2" Wt: 220 Born: 9/21/1972 Age: 34

			BATTING															BASERUNNING				AVERAGES		
Year	Team	Lg	G	AB	H	2B	3B	HR	(Hm | Rd)	TB	R	RBI	RC	TBB	IBB	SO	HBP	SH	SF	SB	CS	SB%	GDP	Avg	OBP	Slg
1996	Oak	AL	9	29	9	2	0	2	(1 | 1)	17	6	8	6	4	1	4	0	2	0	0	1	.00	0	.310	.394	.586
1997	Oak	AL	147	538	131	28	4	14	(6 | 8)	209	58	65	61	44	2	75	1	3	4	9	3	.75	13	.243	.300	.388
1998	Oak	AL	114	406	105	19	1	9	(6 | 3)	153	54	50	50	44	3	56	2	7	2	1	3	.25	10	.259	.333	.377
1999	Oak	AL	89	247	60	24	0	8	(3 | 5)	108	31	33	35	29	3	36	2	1	3	0	0	-	5	.243	.324	.437
2000	LAA	AL	123	297	72	11	2	17	(10 | 7)	138	47	49	47	40	2	56	3	1	4	1	2	.33	5	.242	.334	.465
2001	LAA	AL	139	457	124	29	4	13	(8 | 5)	200	57	54	65	34	4	65	5	3	4	5	2	.71	6	.271	.326	.438
2002	LAA	AL	153	491	140	34	2	12	(7 | 5)	214	80	82	86	67	7	52	4	3	6	6	7	.46	12	.285	.371	.436
2003	LAA	AL	158	521	138	36	7	16	(7 | 9)	236	69	83	72	46	8	66	5	2	7	6	3	.67	12	.265	.326	.453
2004	Sea	AL	112	367	79	12	3	10	(5 | 5)	127	38	41	31	36	2	60	4	2	6	4	1	.80	7	.215	.288	.346
2005	Sea	AL	29	47	3	1	0	1	(0 | 1)	7	2	1	2	4	0	18	0	0	1	0	0	-	1	.064	.137	.149
2006	StL	NL	119	276	75	15	4	13	(4 | 9)	137	44	52	52	37	1	66	5	1	2	1	0	1.00	1	.272	.366	.496
	11 ML YEARS		1192	3676	936	211	27	115	(57 | 58)	1546	486	518	505	385	33	554	31	25	38	33	22	.60	72	.255	.327	.421

Ryan Spilborghs

Bats: R Throws: R Pos: PH-25; CF-24; RF-15; LF-10; DH-1   Ht: 6'1" Wt: 190 Born: 9/5/1979 Age: 27

			BATTING															BASERUNNING				AVERAGES		
Year	Team	Lg	G	AB	H	2B	3B	HR	(Hm | Rd)	TB	R	RBI	RC	TBB	IBB	SO	HBP	SH	SF	SB	CS	SB%	GDP	Avg	OBP	Slg
2002	Tri-Cit	A-	71	261	60	11	1	4	(- | -)	85	34	34	28	29	1	61	3	1	1	11	7	.61	5	.230	.313	.326
2003	Ashvlle	A	119	434	122	22	2	15	(- | -)	193	78	61	75	63	0	96	8	1	4	10	11	.48	4	.281	.379	.445
2004	Visalia	A+	125	444	115	26	3	8	(- | -)	171	59	57	66	64	0	98	6	2	4	8	6	.57	13	.259	.357	.385
2005	Tulsa	AA	71	255	87	23	3	6	(- | -)	134	52	54	59	42	2	49	2	0	2	10	3	.77	7	.341	.435	.525
2005	ColSpr	AAA	60	227	77	23	5	5	(- | -)	125	49	30	49	22	0	53	3	1	0	7	3	.70	5	.339	.405	.551
2006	ColSpr	AAA	68	269	91	20	1	5	(- | -)	128	50	34	53	30	0	49	1	1	5	8	2	.80	10	.338	.400	.476
2005	Col	NL	1	4	2	0	0	0	(0 | 0)	2	0	1	1	0	0	1	0	0	0	0	0	-	0	.500	.500	.500
2006	Col	NL	67	167	48	6	3	4	(3 | 1)	72	26	21	22	14	0	30	0	2	3	5	2	.71	7	.287	.337	.431
	2 ML YEARS		68	171	50	6	3	4	(3 | 1)	74	26	22	23	14	0	31	0	2	3	5	2	.71	7	.292	.340	.433

Russ Springer

Pitches: R Bats: R Pos: RP-72   Ht: 6'4" Wt: 215 Born: 11/7/1968 Age: 38

			HOW MUCH HE PITCHED						WHAT HE GAVE UP												THE RESULTS							
Year	Team	Lg	G	GS	CG	GF	IP	BFP	H	R	ER	HR	SH	SF	HB	TBB	IBB	SO	WP	Bk	W	L	Pct	ShO	Sv-Op	Hld	ERC	ERA
1992	NYY	AL	14	0	0	5	16.0	75	18	11	11	0	0	0	1	10	0	12	0	0	0	0	-	0	0-0	2	5.15	6.19
1993	LAA	AL	14	9	1	3	60.0	278	73	48	48	11	1	1	3	32	1	31	6	0	1	6	.143	0	0-0	0	6.87	7.20
1994	LAA	AL	18	5	0	6	45.2	198	53	28	28	9	1	1	0	14	0	28	2	0	2	2	.500	0	2-3	1	5.38	5.52
1995	2 Tms		33	6	0	6	78.1	350	82	48	46	16	2	2	7	35	4	70	2	0	1	2	.333	0	1-2	0	5.63	5.29
1996	Phi	NL	51	7	0	12	96.2	437	106	60	50	12	5	3	1	38	6	94	5	0	3	10	.231	0	0-3	6	4.57	4.66
1997	Hou	NL	54	0	0	13	55.1	241	48	28	26	4	1	2	4	27	2	74	4	0	3	3	.500	0	3-7	9	3.69	4.23
1998	2 Tms		48	0	0	14	52.2	232	51	26	24	4	2	1	1	30	4	56	5	0	5	4	.556	0	0-4	7	4.38	4.10
1999	Atl	NL	49	0	0	8	47.1	194	31	20	18	5	0	2	2	22	2	49	0	0	2	1	.667	0	1-1	8	2.63	3.42
2000	Ari	NL	52	0	0	10	62.0	282	63	36	35	11	2	3	2	34	6	59	3	0	2	4	.333	0	0-2	3	5.25	5.08
2001	Ari	NL	18	0	0	9	17.2	79	20	16	14	5	1	1	0	4	0	12	2	0	0	0	-	0	1-1	2	5.13	7.13
2003	StL	NL	17	0	0	4	17.1	77	19	16	16	8	0	0	1	6	0	11	1	0	1	1	.500	0	0-1	5	7.27	8.31
2004	Hou	NL	16	0	0	3	13.2	62	15	4	4	1	0	1	1	6	0	9	2	0	0	1	.000	0	0-0	5	4.84	2.63
2005	Hou	NL	62	0	0	11	59.0	246	49	34	31	9	1	0	3	21	3	54	2	0	4	4	.500	0	0-3	10	3.45	4.73
2006	Hou	NL	72	0	0	17	59.2	240	46	23	23	10	2	0	4	16	1	46	2	0	1	1	.500	0	0-0	9	3.03	3.47
95	LAA	AL	19	6	0	3	51.2	238	60	37	35	11	1	0	5	25	1	38	1	0	1	2	.333	0	1-2	0	6.69	6.10
95	Phi	NL	14	0	0	3	26.2	112	22	11	11	5	1	2	2	10	3	32	1	0	0	0	-	0	0-0	0	3.73	3.71
98	Ari	NL	26	0	0	13	32.2	140	29	16	15	4	0	0	1	14	1	37	3	0	4	3	.571	0	0-3	1	3.77	4.05
98	Atl	NL	22	0	0	1	20.0	92	22	10	9	0	2	1	0	16	3	19	2	0	1	1	.500	0	0-1	6	5.36	4.05
	14 ML YEARS		518	27	1	121	681.1	2991	674	398	374	105	18	17	30	295	29	605	36	0	25	39	.391	0	8-27	67	4.62	4.94

Chris Spurling

Pitches: R Bats: R Pos: RP-16   Ht: 6'5" Wt: 240 Born: 6/28/1977 Age: 30

			HOW MUCH HE PITCHED						WHAT HE GAVE UP												THE RESULTS							
Year	Team	Lg	G	GS	CG	GF	IP	BFP	H	R	ER	HR	SH	SF	HB	TBB	IBB	SO	WP	Bk	W	L	Pct	ShO	Sv-Op	Hld	ERC	ERA
2006	Toledo*	AAA	49	0	0	19	66.0	263	61	20	15	4	6	1	3	10	4	34	1	0		4	.200	0	5--	-	2.62	2.05
2003	Det	AL	66	0	0	18	77.0	326	78	42	40	9	3	5	3	22	1	38	2	1	1	3	.250	0	3-6	5	3.97	4.68
2005	Det	AL	56	0	0	8	70.2	284	58	30	27	8	3	5	2	22	6	26	4	0	3	4	.429	0	0-1	11	2.91	3.44
2006	2 Tms		16	0	0	3	21.1	95	25	12	12	5	0	0	0	8	3	7	0	0	0	0	-	0	0-1	0	5.73	5.06
06	Det	AL	9	0	0	3	11.1	49	13	4	4	2	0	0	0	4	2	4	0	0	0	0	-	0	0-0	0	5.10	3.18
06	Mil	NL	7	0	0	0	10.0	46	12	8	8	3	0	0	0	4	1	3	0	0	0	0	-	0	0-1	0	6.46	7.20
	3 ML YEARS		138	0	0	29	169.0	705	161	84	79	22	6	10	5	52	10	71	6	1	4	7	.364	0	3-8	16	3.72	4.21

Matt Stairs

Bats: L **Throws:** R **Pos:** DH-82; PH-27; 1B-12; LF-2; RF-1   **Ht:** 5'9" **Wt:** 215 **Born:** 2/27/1968 **Age:** 39

Year	Team	Lg	G	AB	H	2B	3B	HR	(Hm	Rd)	TB	R	RBI	RC	TBB	IBB	SO	HBP	SH	SF	SB	CS	SB%	GDP	Avg	OBP	Slg
1992	Mon	NL	13	30	5	2	0	0	(0	0)	7	2	5	3	7	0	7	0	0	1	0	0	-	0	.167	.316	.233
1993	Mon	NL	6	8	3	1	0	0	(0	0)	4	1	2	1	0	0	1	0	0	0	0	0	-	1	.375	.375	.500
1995	Bos	AL	39	88	23	7	1	1	(0	1)	35	8	17	9	4	0	14	1	1	1	0	1	.00	4	.261	.298	.398
1996	Oak	AL	61	137	38	5	1	10	(5	5)	75	21	23	27	19	2	23	1	0	1	1	1	.50	2	.277	.367	.547
1997	Oak	AL	133	352	105	19	0	27	(20	7)	205	62	73	77	50	1	60	3	1	4	3	2	.60	6	.298	.386	.582
1998	Oak	AL	149	523	154	33	1	26	(16	10)	267	88	106	96	59	4	93	6	1	4	8	3	.73	13	.294	.370	.511
1999	Oak	AL	146	531	137	26	3	38	(15	23)	283	94	102	101	89	6	124	2	0	1	2	7	.22	8	.258	.366	.533
2000	Oak	AL	143	476	108	26	0	21	(9	12)	197	74	81	69	78	4	122	1	1	6	2	2	.71	7	.227	.333	.414
2001	ChC	NL	128	340	85	21	0	17	(5	12)	157	48	61	57	52	7	76	7	1	3	2	3	.40	4	.250	.358	.462
2002	Mil	NL	107	270	66	15	0	16	(6	10)	129	41	41	38	36	4	50	8	0	1	2	0	1.00	7	.244	.349	.478
2003	Pit	NL	121	305	89	20	1	20	(13	7)	171	49	57	58	45	3	64	5	0	2	0	1	.00	7	.292	.389	.561
2004	KC	AL	126	439	117	21	3	18	(6	12)	198	48	66	65	49	2	92	5	0	3	1	0	1.00	15	.267	.345	.451
2005	KC	AL	127	396	109	26	1	13	(5	8)	176	55	66	70	60	4	69	5	0	5	1	2	.33	9	.275	.373	.444
2006	3 Tms		117	348	86	21	0	13	(6	7)	146	42	51	51	40	3	86	3	0	2	0	0	-	7	.247	.328	.420
06	KC	AL	77	226	59	14	0	8	(3	5)	97	31	32	35	31	2	52	2	0	2	0	0	-	5	.261	.352	.429
06	Tex	AL	26	81	17	4	0	3	(2	1)	30	6	11	10	6	1	22	1	0	0	0	0	-	1	.210	.273	.370
06	Det	AL	14	41	10	3	0	2	(1	1)	19	5	8	6	3	0	12	0	0	0	0	0	-	1	.244	.295	.463
14 ML YEARS			1416	4243	1125	243	11	220	(106	114)	2050	633	751	722	588	40	881	47	5	34	25	22	.53	90	.265	.358	.483

Jason Standridge

Pitches: R **Bats:** R **Pos:** RP-21   **Ht:** 6'4" **Wt:** 230 **Born:** 11/9/1978 **Age:** 28

Year	Team	Lg	G	GS	CG	GF	IP	BFP	H	R	ER	HR	SH	SF	HB	TBB	IBB	SO	WP	Bk	W	L	Pct	ShO	Sv-Op	Hld	ERC	ERA
2006	Lsvlle*	AAA	37	0	0	9	46.0	194	40	16	15	2	3	2	2	15	1	43	1	0	2	2	.500	0	0- -	-	2.80	2.93
2001	TB	AL	9	1	0	6	19.1	87	19	10	10	5	0	0	0	14	1	9	0	0	0	0	-	0	0-0	0	6.63	4.66
2002	TB	AL	1	0	0	0	3.0	18	7	3	3	1	0	0	0	4	0	1	0	0	0	0	-	0	0-0	0	22.36	9.00
2003	TB	AL	8	7	1	1	35.1	157	38	25	25	7	1	1	1	16	0	20	4	0	0	5	.000	0	0-0	0	5.60	6.37
2004	TB	AL	3	1	0	1	10.0	48	14	10	10	5	0	1	0	4	0	7	1	0	0	0	-	0	0-0	0	9.60	9.00
2005	2 Tms		34	0	0	0	33.1	156	45	17	17	3	2	0	1	17	8	19	2	0	2	2	.500	0	0-0	0	6.33	4.59
2006	Cin	NL	21	0	0	2	18.2	86	17	14	10	2	1	0	1	14	0	18	0	0	1	1	.500	0	0-0	1	5.23	4.82
05	Tex	AL	2	0	0	0	2.1	16	7	3	3	0	0	0	1	1	1	2	1	0	0	0	-	0	0-0	0	14.52	11.57
05	Cin	NL	32	0	0	0	31.0	140	38	14	14	3	2	0	0	16	7	17	1	0	2	2	.500	0	0-0	0	5.76	4.06
6 ML YEARS			76	9	1	16	119.2	552	140	79	75	23	4	2	3	69	9	74	7	0	3	8	.273	0	0-0	6	6.60	5.64

Mike Stanton

Pitches: L **Bats:** L **Pos:** RP-82   **Ht:** 6'1" **Wt:** 215 **Born:** 6/2/1967 **Age:** 40

Year	Team	Lg	G	GS	CG	GF	IP	BFP	H	R	ER	HR	SH	SF	HB	TBB	IBB	SO	WP	Bk	W	L	Pct	ShO	Sv-Op	Hld	ERC	ERA
1989	Atl	NL	20	0	0	10	24.0	94	17	4	4	0	4	0	0	8	1	27	1	0	0	1	.000	0	7-8	2	1.72	1.50
1990	Atl	NL	7	0	0	4	7.0	42	16	16	14	1	1	0	1	4	2	7	1	0	0	3	.000	0	2-3	0	13.58	18.00
1991	Atl	NL	74	0	0	20	78.0	314	62	27	25	6	6	0	1	21	6	54	0	0	5	5	.500	0	7-10	15	2.31	2.88
1992	Atl	NL	65	0	0	23	63.2	264	59	32	29	6	1	2	2	20	2	44	3	0	5	4	.556	0	8-11	15	3.42	4.10
1993	Atl	NL	63	0	0	41	52.0	236	51	35	27	4	5	2	0	29	7	43	1	0	4	6	.400	0	27-33	5	4.08	4.67
1994	Atl	NL	49	0	0	15	45.2	197	41	18	18	2	2	1	3	26	3	35	1	0	3	1	.750	0	3-4	10	4.01	3.55
1995	2 Tms		48	0	0	22	40.1	178	48	23	19	6	2	1	1	14	2	23	2	1	2	1	.667	0	1-3	8	5.41	4.24
1996	2 Tms		81	0	0	28	78.2	327	78	32	32	11	4	2	0	27	5	60	3	2	4	4	.500	0	1-6	22	4.08	3.66
1997	NYY	AL	64	0	0	15	66.2	283	50	19	19	3	2	0	3	34	2	70	3	2	6	1	.857	0	3-5	26	2.88	2.57
1998	NYY	AL	67	0	0	26	79.0	330	71	51	48	13	1	2	4	26	1	69	0	0	4	1	.800	0	6-10	18	3.88	5.47
1999	NYY	AL	73	1	0	10	62.1	271	71	30	30	5	4	2	1	18	4	59	2	0	2	2	.500	0	0-5	21	4.23	4.33
2000	NYY	AL	69	0	0	20	68.0	291	68	32	31	5	2	4	2	24	2	75	1	0	2	3	.400	0	0-4	15	3.78	4.10
2001	NYY	AL	76	0	0	16	80.1	342	80	25	23	4	2	3	4	29	9	78	3	1	9	4	.692	0	0-1	23	3.61	2.58
2002	NYY	AL	79	0	0	25	78.0	323	73	29	26	4	4	7	0	28	3	44	4	0	7	1	.875	0	6-9	17	3.23	3.00
2003	NYM	NL	50	0	0	24	45.1	194	37	25	23	6	1	3	2	19	4	34	2	1	2	7	.222	0	5-7	10	3.33	4.57
2004	NYM	NL	83	0	0	19	77.0	337	70	32	27	6	3	3	3	33	6	58	1	0	2	6	.250	0	0-6	25	3.41	3.16
2005	3 Tms		59	0	0	12	42.2	185	49	24	22	3	3	1	0	15	4	27	1	1	3	3	.500	0	0-1	9	4.42	4.64
2006	2 Tms	NL	82	0	0	22	67.2	290	70	30	30	2	2	4	2	27	11	48	5	1	7	7	.500	0	8-14	15	3.67	3.99
95	Atl	NL	26	0	0	10	19.1	94	31	14	12	3	2	1	1	6	2	13	1	1	1	1	.500	0	1-2	4	7.86	5.59
95	Bos	AL	22	0	0	12	21.0	84	17	9	7	3	0	0	0	8	0	10	1	0	1	0	1.000	0	0-1	4	3.37	3.00
96	Bos	AL	59	0	0	19	56.1	239	58	24	24	9	3	2	0	23	4	46	3	2	4	3	.571	0	1-5	15	4.71	3.83
96	Tex	AL	22	0	0	9	22.1	88	20	8	8	2	1	0	0	4	1	14	0	0	0	1	.000	0	0-1	7	2.62	3.22
05	NYY	AL	28	0	0	6	14.0	64	17	11	11	1	0	1	0	6	0	12	1	0	1	2	.333	0	0-0	4	5.17	7.07
05	Was	NL	30	0	0	6	27.2	118	31	13	11	2	3	0	0	9	4	14	0	1	2	1	.667	0	0-1	5	4.11	3.58
05	Bos	AL	1	0	0	0	1.0	3	1	0	0	0	0	0	0	0	0	1	0	0	0	0	-	0	0-0	0	2.79	0.00
06	Was	NL	56	0	0	7	44.1	196	47	22	22	1	2	3	1	21	11	30	2	1	3	5	.375	0	0-3	10	3.81	4.47
06	SF	NL	26	0	0	15	23.1	94	23	8	8	1	0	1	1	6	0	18	3	0	4	2	.667	0	8-11	5	3.39	3.09
18 ML YEARS			1109	1	0	352	1056.1	4499	1011	484	447	87	52	35	28	402	74	855	34	9	67	60	.528	0	84-140	256	3.65	3.81

Tim Stauffer

Pitches: R **Bats:** R **Pos:** SP-1   **Ht:** 6'1" **Wt:** 205 **Born:** 6/2/1982 **Age:** 25

Year	Team	Lg	G	GS	CG	GF	IP	BFP	H	R	ER	HR	SH	SF	HB	TBB	IBB	SO	WP	Bk	W	L	Pct	ShO	Sv-Op	Hld	ERC	ERA
2004	Lk Els	A+	6	6	0	0	35.1	139	28	10	7	0	1	2	1	9	0	30	0	0	2	0	1.000	0	0- -	-	2.01	1.78
2004	Mobile	AA	8	8	1	0	51.1	223	56	17	15	3	0	0	0	13	1	33	2	0	3	2	.600	0	0- -	-	3.60	2.63
2004	Portlnd	AAA	14	14	0	0	81.1	353	83	46	32	15	4	3	3	26	1	50	1	1	6	3	.667	0	0- -	-	4.53	3.54
2005	Portlnd	AAA	13	13	1	0	75.1	333	90	48	43	5	3	3	5	17	0	64	3	0	3	5	.375	1	0- -	-	4.47	5.14
2006	Portlnd	AAA	28	26	0	0	153.0	703	199	108	94	20	7	13	9	52	1	89	4	0	7	12	.368	0	0- -	-	6.07	5.53

Year	Team	Lg	G	GS	CG	GF	IP	BFP	H	R	ER	HR	SH	SF	HB	TBB	IBB	SO	WP	Bk	W	L	Pct	ShO	Sv-Op	Hld	ERC	ERA
2005	SD	NL	15	14	0	0	81.0	355	92	50	48	10	2	0	2	29	0	49	0	0	3	6	.333	0	0-0	0	5.00	5.33
2006	SD	NL	1	1	0	0	6.0	21	3	2	1	0	0	0	0	1	0	2	0	0	1	0	1.000	0	0-0	0	0.84	1.50
	2 ML YEARS		16	15	0	0	87.0	376	95	52	49	10	2	0	2	30	0	51	0	0	4	6	.400	0	0-0	0	4.63	5.07

Steve Stemle

Pitches: R Bats: R Pos: RP-5 **Ht: 6'4" Wt: 200 Born: 5/20/1977 Age: 30**

			HOW MUCH HE PITCHED						WHAT HE GAVE UP												THE RESULTS						
Year	Team	Lg	G	GS	CG	GF	IP	BFP	H	R	ER	HR	SH	SF	HB	TBB	IBB	SO	WP	Bk	W	L	Pct	ShO	Sv-Op	Hld	ERC	ERA
1998	NewJrs	A-	9	9	0	0	44.1	184	37	17	9	1	0	0	1	14	0	47	4	1	3	3	.500	0	0--	-	2.43	1.83
1999	Peoria	A	28	28	0	0	148.0	688	177	104	90	11	3	5	6	67	0	113	12	0	7	10	.412	0	0--	-	5.31	5.47
2000	Ptomc	A+	26	26	1	0	150.0	678	169	89	80	15	2	4	12	59	1	84	16	0	9	10	.474	0	0--	-	5.06	4.80
2001	NwHav	AA	26	25	0	0	134.0	604	159	76	71	12	4	3	10	43	2	75	4	0	7	10	.412	0	0--	-	4.99	4.77
2002	NwHav	AA	8	7	0	0	43.1	190	45	24	21	3	2	2	3	15	1	26	0	0	5	2	.714	0	0--	-	4.06	4.36
2002	Memp	AAA	20	11	0	1	93.2	401	97	41	38	8	3	1	4	23	1	55	5	1	7	4	.636	0	0--	-	3.67	3.65
2003	Memp	AAA	26	26	1	0	156.0	659	155	71	60	12	2	1	5	36	4	89	3	0	6	11	.353	0	0--	-	3.27	3.46
2004	PlmBh	A+	3	1	0	0	6.0	23	5	1	1	0	0	0	3	0	2	2	0	0	2	0	1.000	0	0--	-	2.65	1.50
2004	Memp	AAA	54	0	0	11	76.1	326	85	28	28	7	1	0	0	12	0	42	1	0	6	3	.667	0	3--	-	3.61	3.30
2005	Omha	AAA	14	0	0	5	20.0	76	13	3	1	0	1	2	0	3	0	12	0	0	1	1	.500	0	3--	-	1.15	0.45
2005	KC	AL	7	0	0	1	10.2	43	10	6	6	0	0	0	0	4	0	9	0	0	0	0	-	0	0-0	1	3.12	5.06
2006	KC	AL	5	0	0	1	6.0	36	15	10	10	1	0	0	0	3	0	0	0	0	0	1	.000	0	0-1	0	15.10	15.00
	2 ML YEARS		12	0	0	2	16.2	79	25	16	16	1	0	0	0	7	0	9	0	0	0	1	.000	0	0-1	1	6.94	8.64

Adam Stern

Bats: L Throws: R Pos: CF-8; LF-2; PR-2 **Ht: 5'11" Wt: 180 Born: 2/12/1980 Age: 27**

			BATTING																			BASERUNNING				AVERAGES		
Year	Team	Lg	G	AB	H	2B	3B	HR	(Hm	Rd)	TB	R	RBI	RC	TBB	IBB	SO	HBP	SH	SF	SB	CS	SB%	GDP	Avg	OBP	Slg
2001	Jmstwn	A-	21	75	23	4	2	0	(-	-)	31	20	11	14	15	0	11	0	0	2	9	4	.69	0	.307	.413	.413
2002	MrtlBh	A+	119	462	117	22	10	3	(-	-)	168	65	47	56	27	2	89	3	10	1	40	8	.83	3	.253	.298	.364
2003	Braves	R	7	29	10	1	0	1	(-	-)	14	6	6	6	6	0	3	0	1	0	2	2	.50	1	.345	.457	.483
2003	MrtlBh	A+	28	103	20	2	0	0	(-	-)	22	11	6	7	13	0	21	0	4	1	7	3	.70	1	.194	.282	.214
2004	Grnville	AA	102	394	127	26	6	8	(-	-)	189	64	47	73	35	2	58	2	1	3	27	10	.73	2	.322	.378	.480
2005	Pwtckt	AAA	20	81	26	8	0	2	(-	-)	40	16	14	15	8	1	10	1	1	1	3	1	.75	2	.321	.385	.494
2006	Pwtckt	AAA	93	392	101	21	3	8	(-	-)	152	59	34	48	23	1	78	1	4	1	23	7	.77	5	.258	.300	.388
2005	Bos	AL	36	15	2	0	0	1	(0	1)	5	4	2	1	0	0	4	1	0	0	1	1	.50	0	.133	.188	.333
2006	Bos	AL	10	20	3	1	0	0	(0	0)	4	3	4	2	0	0	4	1	0	0	1	0	1.00	0	.150	.190	.200
	2 ML YEARS		46	35	5	1	0	1	(0	1)	9	7	6	3	0	0	8	2	0	0	2	1	.67	0	.143	.189	.257

Chris Stewart

Bats: R Throws: R Pos: C-5; PH-2; DH-1 **Ht: 6'4" Wt: 205 Born: 2/19/1982 Age: 25**

			BATTING																			BASERUNNING				AVERAGES		
Year	Team	Lg	G	AB	H	2B	3B	HR	(Hm	Rd)	TB	R	RBI	RC	TBB	IBB	SO	HBP	SH	SF	SB	CS	SB%	GDP	Avg	OBP	Slg
2002	Bristol	R+	42	158	44	9	0	1	(-	-)	56	25	12	19	12	0	17	2	0	0	2	3	.40	0	.278	.337	.354
2003	WinSa	A+	76	217	45	8	2	2	(-	-)	63	18	27	20	27	1	29	0	7	1	1	0	1.00	6	.207	.294	.290
2004	Brham	AA	83	260	60	11	2	1	(-	-)	78	26	17	24	22	0	59	4	13	2	2	4	.33	3	.231	.299	.300
2004	Charltt	AAA	5	14	1	1	0	0	(-	-)	2	1	1	0	1	0	3	1	0	0	0	0	-	0	.071	.188	.143
2005	Brham	AA	95	311	89	21	0	11	(-	-)	143	39	51	49	24	2	37	3	10	2	3	3	.50	7	.286	.341	.460
2006	Charltt	AAA	89	272	72	17	3	4	(-	-)	107	40	28	35	15	0	35	5	8	1	3	0	1.00	7	.265	.314	.393
2006	CWS	AL	6	8	0	0	0	0	(0	0)	0	0	0	0	0	0	2	0	0	0	0	0	-	0	.000	.000	.000

Shannon Stewart

Bats: R Throws: R Pos: LF-34; DH-10 **Ht: 5'11" Wt: 210 Born: 2/25/1974 Age: 33**

			BATTING																			BASERUNNING				AVERAGES		
Year	Team	Lg	G	AB	H	2B	3B	HR	(Hm	Rd)	TB	R	RBI	RC	TBB	IBB	SO	HBP	SH	SF	SB	CS	SB%	GDP	Avg	OBP	Slg
2006	Roch*	AAA	5	18	5	1	0	0	(-	-)	6	2	1	2	2	1	4	0	0	1	2	0	1.00	0	.278	.333	.333
1995	Tor	AL	12	38	8	0	0	0	(0	0)	8	2	1	3	5	0	5	1	0	0	2	0	1.00	0	.211	.318	.211
1996	Tor	AL	7	17	3	1	0	0	(0	0)	4	2	2	1	1	0	4	0	0	0	1	0	1.00	1	.176	.222	.235
1997	Tor	AL	44	168	48	13	7	0	(0	0)	75	25	22	29	19	1	24	4	0	2	10	3	.77	3	.286	.368	.446
1998	Tor	AL	144	516	144	29	3	12	(6	6)	215	90	55	88	67	1	77	15	6	1	51	18	.74	5	.279	.377	.417
1999	Tor	AL	145	608	185	28	2	11	(4	7)	250	102	67	95	59	0	83	8	3	4	37	14	.73	12	.304	.371	.411
2000	Tor	AL	136	583	186	43	5	21	(12	9)	302	107	69	106	37	1	79	6	1	4	20	5	.80	12	.319	.363	.518
2001	Tor	AL	155	640	202	44	7	12	(6	6)	296	103	60	109	46	1	72	11	0	1	27	10	.73	9	.316	.371	.463
2002	Tor	AL	141	577	175	38	6	10	(4	6)	255	103	45	92	54	2	60	9	0	1	14	2	.88	17	.303	.371	.442
2003	2 Tms	AL	136	573	176	44	7	13	(7	6)	263	90	73	93	52	3	66	6	2	11	4	6	.40	10	.307	.364	.459
2004	Min	AL	92	378	115	17	2	11	(5	6)	169	46	47	68	47	4	44	1	1	3	6	3	.67	5	.304	.380	.447
2005	Min	AL	132	551	151	27	3	10	(4	6)	214	69	56	68	34	2	73	8	1	5	7	5	.58	11	.274	.323	.388
2006	Min	AL	44	174	51	5	1	2	(0	2)	64	21	21	26	14	0	19	1	0	1	3	1	.75	2	.293	.347	.368
03	Tor	AL	71	303	89	22	2	7	(3	4)	136	47	35	51	27	2	30	2	0	8	1	2	.33	6	.294	.347	.449
03	Min	AL	65	270	87	22	0	6	(4	2)	127	43	38	42	25	1	36	4	2	3	3	4	.43	4	.322	.384	.470
	12 ML YEARS		1188	4823	1444	289	38	102	(48	54)	2115	760	518	778	435	15	606	70	14	33	182	67	.73	92	.299	.364	.439

Kelly Stinnett

Bats: R **Throws:** R **Pos:** C-41; PH-1 **Ht:** 5'11" **Wt:** 235 **Born:** 2/4/1970 **Age:** 37

Year	Team	Lg	G	AB	H	2B	3B	HR	(Hm	Rd)	TB	R	RBI	RC	TBB	IBB	SO	HBP	SH	SF	SB	CS	SB%	GDP	Avg	OBP	Slg
2006	Norfolk*	AAA	5	16	6	1	0	1	(-	-)	10	2	1	4	2	0	2	0	0	0	0	0	-	0	.375	.444	.625
1994	NYM	NL	47	150	38	6	2	2	(0	2)	54	20	14	18	11	1	28	5	0	1	2	0	1.00	3	.253	.323	.360
1995	NYM	NL	77	196	43	8	1	4	(1	3)	65	23	18	24	29	3	65	6	0	0	2	0	1.00	3	.219	.338	.332
1996	Mil	AL	14	26	2	0	0	0	(0	0)	2	1	0	0	2	0	11	1	0	0	0	0	-	0	.077	.172	.077
1997	Mil	AL	30	36	9	4	0	0	(0	0)	13	2	3	4	3	0	9	0	0	0	0	0	-	0	.250	.308	.361
1998	Ari	NL	92	274	71	14	1	11	(5	6)	120	35	34	41	35	3	74	6	1	2	0	1	.00	9	.259	.353	.438
1999	Ari	NL	88	284	66	13	0	14	(3	11)	121	36	38	37	24	2	83	5	2	2	2	1	.67	4	.232	.302	.426
2000	Ari	NL	76	240	52	7	0	8	(2	6)	83	22	33	23	19	4	56	6	0	0	0	1	.00	5	.217	.291	.346
2001	Cin	NL	63	187	48	11	0	9	(6	3)	86	27	25	27	17	3	61	5	1	1	2	2	.50	5	.257	.333	.460
2002	Cin	NL	34	93	21	5	0	3	(2	1)	35	10	13	13	15	1	25	0	0	0	2	0	1.00	1	.226	.333	.376
2003	2 Tms	NL	67	186	44	13	0	3	(2	1)	66	14	19	20	14	3	52	4	2	1	0	0	-	3	.237	.302	.355
2004	KC	AL	20	59	18	0	0	3	(0	3)	27	10	7	9	5	0	16	2	3	0	0	0	-	0	.305	.379	.458
2005	Ari	NL	59	129	32	4	0	6	(2	4)	54	15	12	9	12	3	32	1	1	0	0	0	-	4	.248	.317	.419
2006	2 Tms	NL	41	91	19	3	0	1	(1	0)	25	6	9	7	5	1	33	1	2	0	0	0	-	0	.209	.258	.275
03	Cin	NL	60	179	41	13	0	3	(2	1)	63	14	19	18	13	3	51	4	2	1	0	0	-	3	.229	.294	.352
03	Phi	NL	7	7	3	0	0	0	(0	0)	3	0	0	2	1	0	1	0	0	0	0	0	-	0	.429	.500	.429
06	NYY	AL	34	79	18	3	0	1	(1	0)	24	6	9	7	5	1	29	1	2	0	0	0	-	0	.228	.282	.304
06	NYM	NL	7	12	1	0	0	0	(0	0)	1	0	0	0	0	0	4	0	0	0	0	0	-	0	.083	.083	.083
13 ML YEARS			708	1951	463	88	4	64	(23	41)	751	221	225	232	191	24	545	42	12	7	10	5	.67	37	.237	.318	.385

Phil Stockman

Pitches: R **Bats:** R **Pos:** RP-4 **Ht:** 6'8" **Wt:** 250 **Born:** 1/25/1980 **Age:** 27

Year	Team	Lg	G	GS	CG	GF	IP	BFP	H	R	ER	HR	SH	SF	HB	TBB	IBB	SO	WP	Bk	W	L	Pct	ShO	Sv-Op	Hld	ERC	ERA
1998	DBcks	R	1	0	0	0	0.1	3	2	0	0	0	0	0	0	2	0	1	0	0	0	0	-	0	0- -	-	120.2	0.00
2000	DBcks	R	14	2	0	5	41.2	194	40	22	12	2	0	0	2	23	0	40	3	1	3	2	.600	0	1- -	-	4.04	2.59
2000	Msoula	R+	2	2	0	0	11.0	46	10	3	3	0	0	0	0	3	0	4	0	0	2	0	1.000	0	0- -	-	2.41	2.45
2001	Lancst	A+	8	0	0	1	17.2	70	11	11	10	2	1	4	1	9	0	18	1	0	0	0	-	0	0- -	-	2.92	5.09
2001	Yakima	A-	15	14	0	0	76.0	329	81	39	36	5	3	1	5	22	0	48	5	0	3	4	.429	0	0- -	-	4.02	4.26
2002	Lancst	A+	20	20	0	0	108.1	463	91	58	53	10	4	1	7	58	0	108	7	0	7	5	.583	0	0- -	-	3.99	4.40
2003	ElPaso	AA	26	26	0	0	147.2	648	137	75	65	9	8	6	9	64	0	146	2	0	11	7	.611	0	0- -	-	3.70	3.96
2003	Tucsn	AAA	2	1	0	0	9.0	37	8	1	1	0	1	0	1	4	0	5	0	1	1	1	.500	0	0- -	-	3.56	1.00
2004	Tucsn	AAA	12	12	0	0	56.1	263	60	39	36	2	7	8	0	36	0	35	1	1	3	2	.600	0	0- -	-	4.81	5.75
2004	ElPaso	AA	6	6	1	0	27.0	120	17	13	8	1	2	2	4	20	0	21	2	0	1	3	.250	0	0- -	-	3.41	2.67
2005	Tucsn	AAA	17	4	0	1	31.2	158	35	29	22	4	3	3	1	27	0	16	1	0	1	1	.500	0	0- -	-	6.75	6.25
2005	Tenn	AA	47	1	0	7	36.0	165	31	16	13	2	4	3	4	24	2	30	2	0	1	3	.250	0	1- -	-	4.27	3.25
2006	Rome	A	3	3	0	0	3.0	15	5	3	0	0	0	0	0	3	0	6	0	0	0	1	.000	0	0- -	-	11.06	0.00
2006	Missi	AA	3	0	0	0	7.1	25	1	0	0	0	0	0	0	2	0	12	0	0	0	0	-	0	0- -	-	0.25	0.00
2006	Rchmd	AAA	18	0	0	10	33.1	122	13	3	3	0	0	1	0	10	1	41	1	0	0	0	-	0	2- -	-	0.75	0.81
2006	Atl	NL	4	0	0	1	4.0	19	3	1	1	0	2	0	0	4	2	4	0	0	0	0	-	0	0-0	0	3.15	2.25

Brian Stokes

Pitches: R **Bats:** R **Pos:** SP-4; RP-1 **Ht:** 6'1" **Wt:** 205 **Born:** 9/7/1979 **Age:** 27

Year	Team	Lg	G	GS	CG	GF	IP	BFP	H	R	ER	HR	SH	SF	HB	TBB	IBB	SO	WP	Bk	W	L	Pct	ShO	Sv-Op	Hld	ERC	ERA
1999	Princtn	R+	33	0	0	27	37.0	163	33	20	16	2	2	1	1	21	0	39	8	1	2	3	.400	0	9- -	-	3.88	3.89
2000	CtnSC	A	46	0	0	16	74.0	293	45	24	20	1	2	1	4	34	2	66	10	0	6	5	.455	0	5- -	-	1.95	2.43
2001	Bkrsfld	A+	32	20	1	5	128.2	565	118	65	56	11	4	5	8	64	0	92	9	0	8	6	.571	0	1- -	-	4.12	3.92
2002	Bkrsfld	A+	28	28	1	0	165.2	704	156	79	60	13	4	6	8	57	1	152	10	0	10	7	.588	1	0- -	-	3.56	3.26
2003	Orlndo	AA	10	10	0	0	50.2	220	55	26	18	2	0	2	4	13	0	33	1	1	2	5	.286	0	0- -	-	3.85	3.20
2005	Visalia	A+	4	4	0	0	17.0	71	15	8	8	3	0	1	0	5	0	21	0	0	1	2	.333	0	0- -	-	3.45	4.24
2005	Mont	AA	16	16	1	0	93.1	379	82	36	36	8	3	1	2	28	2	70	4	0	4	6	.400	0	0- -	-	3.05	3.47
2006	Drham	AAA	29	23	0	1	133.2	579	134	75	61	8	3	4	8	49	0	103	7	0	7	7	.500	0	0- -	-	3.91	4.11
2006	TB	AL	5	4	0	0	24.0	110	31	13	13	2	0	3	1	9	0	15	0	0	1	0	1.000	0	0-0	0	5.75	4.88

Huston Street

Pitches: R **Bats:** R **Pos:** RP-69 **Ht:** 6'0" **Wt:** 190 **Born:** 8/2/1983 **Age:** 23

Year	Team	Lg	G	GS	CG	GF	IP	BFP	H	R	ER	HR	SH	SF	HB	TBB	IBB	SO	WP	Bk	W	L	Pct	ShO	Sv-Op	Hld	ERC	ERA
2004	Kane	A	9	0	0	7	10.2	46	9	2	2	0	0	0	0	5	1	14	1	0	0	1	.000	0	4- -	-	2.60	1.69
2004	Mdland	AA	10	0	0	8	13.1	53	10	2	2	0	0	0	1	3	0	14	1	0	1	0	1.000	0	3- -	-	1.83	1.35
2004	Scrmto	AAA	2	0	0	1	2.0	8	2	0	0	0	0	0	0	2	0	1	0	0	0	0	-	0	1- -	-	1.95	0.00
2005	Oak	AL	67	0	0	47	78.1	306	53	17	15	3	3	2	2	26	4	72	1	0	5	1	.833	0	23-27	0	1.87	1.72
2006	Oak	AL	69	0	0	55	70.2	290	64	28	26	4	3	2	2	13	3	67	4	0	4	4	.500	0	37-48	1	2.49	3.31
2 ML YEARS			136	0	0	102	149.0	596	117	45	41	7	6	4	4	39	7	139	5	0	9	5	.643	0	60-75	1	2.16	2.48

Eric Stults

Pitches: L **Bats:** L **Pos:** RP-4; SP-2 **Ht:** 6'0" **Wt:** 215 **Born:** 12/9/1979 **Age:** 27

Year	Team	Lg	G	GS	CG	GF	IP	BFP	H	R	ER	HR	SH	SF	HB	TBB	IBB	SO	WP	Bk	W	L	Pct	ShO	Sv-Op	Hld	ERC	ERA
2002	Gr Falls	R+	5	0	0	1	8.0	34	6	4	2	0	0	0	0	3	0	9	0	0	1	0	1.000	0	1- -	-	1.94	2.25
2002	VeroB	A+	13	6	0	1	42.0	185	39	19	14	3	2	2	1	20	0	40	2	0	3	1	.750	0	0- -	-	3.79	3.00
2002	Jaxnvl	AA	1	0	0	0	1.0	3	0	0	0	0	0	0	0	0	0	0	0	0	0	0	-	0	0- -	-	0.00	0.00
2003	Jaxnvl	AA	9	7	0	1	38.0	169	46	23	21	5	2	3	0	13	0	14	0	0	3	4	.429	0	1- -	-	5.30	4.97

		HOW MUCH HE PITCHED						WHAT HE GAVE UP													THE RESULTS							
Year	Team	Lg	G	GS	CG	GF	IP	BFP	H	R	ER	HR	SH	SF	HB	TBB	IBB	SO	WP	Bk	W	L	Pct	ShO	Sv-Op	Hld	ERC	ERA
2003	VeroB	A+	1	1	0	0	3.0	13	6	2	2	0	0	0	0	1	0	1	0	0	0	1	.000	0	0--	-	11.17	6.00
2004	Clmbs	A	12	0	0	8	21.2	89	18	8	6	0	0	0	0	6	0	16	1	0	1	2	.333	0	3--	-	2.07	2.49
2004	VeroB	A+	7	0	0	0	10.0	46	11	4	3	0	0	0	1	4	0	6	0	0	2	1	.667	0	1--	-	4.16	2.70
2005	Jaxnvl	AA	12	12	0	0	68.0	291	73	33	25	6	2	1	0	14	0	58	2	0	4	3	.571	0	0--	-	3.56	3.31
2005	LsVgs	AAA	15	14	0	0	78.0	360	107	60	57	15	1	2	1	24	0	60	1	0	3	7	.300	0	0--	-	6.64	6.58
2006	LsVgs	AAA	26	26	1	0	153.1	658	153	85	72	10	5	9	5	68	5	128	7	0	10	11	.476	0	0--	-	4.15	4.23
2006	LAD	NL	6	2	0	2	17.2	73	17	12	11	4	2	0	0	7	0	5	0	0	1	0	1.000	0	0-0	0	4.91	5.60

Tanyon Sturtze

Pitches: R **Bats:** R **Pos:** RP-18   **Ht:** 6'5" **Wt:** 230 **Born:** 10/12/1970 **Age:** 36

		HOW MUCH HE PITCHED						WHAT HE GAVE UP													THE RESULTS							
Year	Team	Lg	G	GS	CG	GF	IP	BFP	H	R	ER	HR	SH	SF	HB	TBB	IBB	SO	WP	Bk	W	L	Pct	ShO	Sv-Op	Hld	ERC	ERA
1995	ChC	NL	2	0	0	0	2.0	9	2	2	2	1	0	0	0	1	0	0	0	0	0	0	-	0	0-0	0	7.30	9.00
1996	ChC	NL	6	0	0	3	11.0	51	16	11	11	3	0	0	0	5	0	7	0	0	1	0	1.000	0	0-0	0	8.87	9.00
1997	Tex	AL	9	5	0	1	32.2	155	45	30	30	6	0	4	0	18	0	18	1	1	1	1	.500	0	0-0	0	7.84	8.27
1999	CWS	AL	1	1	0	0	6.0	22	4	0	0	0	0	0	0	2	0	2	0	0	0	0	-	0	0-0	0	1.73	0.00
2000	2 Tms	AL	29	6	0	9	68.1	300	72	39	36	8	1	2	3	29	1	44	2	0	5	2	.714	0	0-0	0	4.80	4.74
2001	TB	AL	39	27	0	6	195.1	837	200	98	96	23	2	10	9	79	0	110	11	0	11	12	.478	0	1-3	3	4.65	4.42
2002	TB	AL	33	33	4	0	224.0	**1008**	271	141	129	33	7	6	9	**89**	2	137	7	2	4	**18**	.182	0	0-0	0	5.87	5.18
2003	Tor	AL	40	8	0	7	89.1	415	107	67	59	14	2	2	7	43	3	54	6	0	7	6	.538	0	0-0	1	6.30	5.94
2004	NYY	AL	28	3	0	7	77.1	337	75	49	47	9	2	1	6	33	2	56	2	1	6	2	.750	0	1-1	1	4.42	5.47
2005	NYY	AL	64	1	0	12	78.0	332	76	43	41	10	1	2	6	27	1	45	3	0	5	3	.625	0	1-6	16	4.26	4.73
2006	NYY	AL	18	0	0	2	10.2	56	17	10	9	3	0	1	1	6	0	6	0	0	0	0	-	0	0-0	3	10.37	7.59
00	CWS	AL	10	1	0	2	15.2	85	25	23	21	4	0	2	2	15	0	6	1	0	1	2	.333	0	0-0	0	12.84	12.06
00	TB	AL	19	5	0	7	52.2	215	47	16	15	4	1	0	1	14	1	38	1	0	4	0	1.000	0	0-0	0	2.89	2.56
11 ML YEARS			269	84	4	47	794.2	3522	885	490	460	110	15	28	41	332	9	479	32	4	40	44	.476	0	3-10	24	5.35	5.21

Cory Sullivan

Bats: L **Throws:** L **Pos:** CF-114; PH-19; PR-3   **Ht:** 6'0" **Wt:** 190 **Born:** 8/20/1979 **Age:** 27

			BATTING																		BASERUNNING				AVERAGES		
Year	Team	Lg	G	AB	H	2B	3B	HR	(Hm	Rd)	TB	R	RBI	RC	TBB	IBB	SO	HBP	SH	SF	SB	CS	SB%	GDP	Avg	OBP	Slg
2001	Ashvlle	A	67	258	71	12	1	5	(-	-)	100	36	22	35	25	0	56	2	0	0	13	9	.59	2	.275	.344	.388
2002	Salem	A+	138	560	161	42	6	12	(-	-)	251	90	67	91	36	3	70	12	7	7	26	5	.84	8	.288	.340	.448
2003	Tulsa	AA	135	557	167	34	8	5	(-	-)	232	81	61	81	39	3	83	4	5	5	17	13	.57	4	.300	.347	.417
2005	Col	NL	139	378	111	15	4	4	(1	3)	146	64	30	54	28	0	83	3	10	5	12	3	.80	6	.294	.343	.386
2006	Col	NL	126	386	103	26	10	2	(0	2)	155	47	30	47	32	3	100	1	19	5	10	6	.63	5	.267	.321	.402
2 ML YEARS			265	764	214	41	14	6	(1	5)	301	111	60	101	60	3	183	4	29	10	22	9	.71	11	.280	.332	.394

Jeff Suppan

Pitches: R **Bats:** R **Pos:** SP-32   **Ht:** 6'2" **Wt:** 220 **Born:** 1/2/1975 **Age:** 32

		HOW MUCH HE PITCHED						WHAT HE GAVE UP													THE RESULTS							
Year	Team	Lg	G	GS	CG	GF	IP	BFP	H	R	ER	HR	SH	SF	HB	TBB	IBB	SO	WP	Bk	W	L	Pct	ShO	Sv-Op	Hld	ERC	ERA
1995	Bos	AL	8	3	0	1	22.2	100	29	15	15	4	1	1	0	5	1	19	0	0	1	2	.333	0	0-0	1	5.43	5.96
1996	Bos	AL	8	4	0	2	22.2	107	29	19	19	3	1	4	1	13	0	13	3	0	1	1	.500	0	0-0	0	7.03	7.54
1997	Bos	AL	23	22	0	1	112.1	503	140	75	71	12	0	4	4	36	1	67	5	0	7	3	.700	0	0-0	0	5.39	5.69
1998	2 Tms		17	14	1	2	78.2	345	91	56	50	13	3	2	1	22	1	51	2	0	1	7	.125	0	0-0	0	4.95	5.72
1999	KC	AL	32	32	4	0	208.2	887	222	113	105	28	7	5	3	62	4	103	5	1	10	12	.455	1	0-0	0	4.33	4.53
2000	KC	AL	35	33	3	0	217.0	948	240	121	119	**36**	5	6	7	84	3	128	7	1	10	9	.526	1	0-0	0	5.31	4.94
2001	KC	AL	34	34	1	0	218.1	946	227	120	106	26	5	6	12	74	3	120	6	0	10	14	.417	0	0-0	0	4.40	4.37
2002	KC	AL	33	33	3	0	208.0	912	229	134	123	32	4	11	7	68	3	109	10	1	9	16	.360	1	0-0	0	4.84	5.32
2003	2 Tms		32	31	3	0	204.0	873	217	98	95	23	11	6	8	51	5	110	7	0	13	11	.542	2	0-0	0	4.03	4.19
2004	StL	NL	31	31	0	0	188.0	811	192	98	87	25	8	5	8	65	1	110	4	1	16	9	.640	0	0-0	0	4.38	4.16
2005	StL	NL	32	32	0	0	194.1	834	206	93	77	24	11	5	7	63	1	114	6	1	16	10	.615	0	0-0	0	4.46	3.57
2006	StL	NL	32	32	0	0	190.0	837	207	100	87	21	9	3	8	69	6	104	8	0	12	7	.632	0	0-0	0	4.62	4.12
98	Ari	NL	13	13	1	0	66.0	299	82	55	49	12	3	2	1	21	1	39	2	0	1	7	.125	0	0-0	0	5.73	6.68
98	KC	AL	4	1	0	2	12.2	46	9	1	1	1	0	0	0	1	0	12	0	0	0	0	-	0	0-0	0	1.51	0.71
03	Pit	NL	21	21	3	0	141.0	597	147	57	56	11	10	2	6	31	5	78	3	0	10	7	.588	2	0-0	0	3.55	3.57
03	Bos	AL	11	10	0	0	63.0	276	70	41	39	12	1	4	2	20	0	32	4	0	3	4	.429	0	0-0	0	5.15	5.57
12 ML YEARS			317	301	15	6	1864.2	8103	2029	1042	954	247	65	58	66	612	29	1048	63	5	106	101	.512	5	0-0	1	4.65	4.60

Ichiro Suzuki

Bats: L **Throws:** R **Pos:** RF-121; CF-39; DH-2; PH-1   **Ht:** 5'9" **Wt:** 170 **Born:** 10/22/1973 **Age:** 33

			BATTING																		BASERUNNING				AVERAGES		
Year	Team	Lg	G	AB	H	2B	3B	HR	(Hm	Rd)	TB	R	RBI	RC	TBB	IBB	SO	HBP	SH	SF	SB	CS	SB%	GDP	Avg	OBP	Slg
2001	Sea	AL	157	**692**	**242**	34	8	8	(5	3)	316	127	69	124	30	10	53	8	4	4	**56**	14	.80	3	**.350**	.381	.457
2002	Sea	AL	157	647	208	27	8	8	(4	4)	275	111	51	110	68	**27**	62	5	3	5	31	**15**	.67	8	.321	.388	.425
2003	Sea	AL	159	679	212	29	8	13	(8	5)	296	111	62	107	36	7	69	6	3	1	34	8	.81	5	.312	.352	.436
2004	Sea	AL	161	**704**	**262**	24	5	8	(4	4)	320	101	60	125	49	**19**	63	4	2	3	36	11	.77	6	**.372**	.414	.455
2005	Sea	AL	**162**	679	206	21	12	15	(8	7)	296	111	68	109	48	23	66	4	2	5	33	8	.80	5	.303	.350	.436
2006	Sea	AL	161	**695**	224	20	9	9	(6	3)	289	110	49	107	49	16	71	5	1	2	45	2	**.96**	2	.322	.370	.416
6 ML YEARS			957	4096	1354	155	50	61	(35	26)	1792	671	359	682	280	102	384	32	15	21	235	58	.80	27	.331	.376	.438

Brian Sweeney

Pitches: R **Bats:** R **Pos:** RP-37   **Ht:** 6'2" **Wt:** 200 **Born:** 6/13/1974 **Age:** 33

			HOW MUCH HE PITCHED					WHAT HE GAVE UP												THE RESULTS						
Year	Team	Lg	G	GS	CG	GF	IP	BFP	H	R	ER	HR	SH	SF	HB	TBB	IBB	SO	WP	Bk	W	L	Pct	ShO	Sv-Op Hld	ERC	ERA
2006	Portlnd*	AAA	7	5	0	0	30.2	126	33	17	16	3	1	0	0	7	0	22	1	0	2	1	.667	0	0- -	3.92	4.70
2003	Sea	AL	5	0	0	2	9.1	35	7	2	2	0	0	0	1	1	0	7	0	0	0	0	-	0	0-0 0	1.66	1.93
2004	SD	NL	7	2	0	1	14.1	63	20	9	9	1	0	0	0	2	0	10	1	0	1	0	1.000	0	0-0 0	5.12	5.65
2006	SD	NL	37	0	0	15	56.1	237	53	22	20	6	5	2	1	16	5	23	2	0	2	0	1.000	0	2-3 0	3.24	3.20
	3 ML YEARS		49	2	0	18	80.0	335	80	33	31	7	5	2	2	19	5	40	3	0	3	0	1.000	0	2-3 0	3.35	3.49

Mark Sweeney

Bats: L **Throws:** L **Pos:** 1B-53; PH-47; LF-21   **Ht:** 6'1" **Wt:** 215 **Born:** 10/26/1969 **Age:** 37

						BATTING														BASERUNNING				AVERAGES		
Year	Team	Lg	G	AB	H	2B	3B	HR	(Hm	Rd)	TB	R	RBI	RC	TBB	IBB	SO	HBP	SH	SF	SB	CS	SB%	GDP	Avg	OBP	Slg
1995	StL	NL	37	77	21	2	0	2	(0	2)	29	5	13	10	10	0	15	0	1	2	1	1	.50	3	.273	.348	.377
1996	StL	NL	98	170	45	9	0	3	(0	3)	63	32	22	27	33	2	29	1	5	0	3	0	1.00	4	.265	.387	.371
1997	2 Tms	NL	115	164	46	7	0	2	(2	0)	59	16	23	22	20	1	32	1	1	2	2	3	.40	3	.280	.358	.360
1998	SD	NL	122	192	45	8	3	2	(1	1)	65	17	15	21	26	0	37	1	0	3	1	2	.33	5	.234	.324	.339
1999	Cin	NL	37	31	11	3	0	2	(1	1)	20	6	7	7	4	1	9	0	0	0	0	0	-	2	.355	.429	.645
2000	Mil	NL	71	73	16	6	0	1	(0	1)	25	9	6	9	12	1	18	1	1	0	0	0	-	1	.219	.337	.342
2001	Mil	NL	48	89	23	3	1	3	(1	2)	37	9	11	14	12	0	23	0	2	0	2	1	.67	0	.258	.347	.416
2002	SD	NL	48	65	11	3	0	1	(0	1)	17	3	4	7	4	0	19	0	0	0	0	0	-	1	.169	.217	.262
2003	Col	NL	67	97	25	9	0	2	(1	1)	40	13	14	15	9	1	27	0	0	0	1	0	1.00	2	.258	.321	.412
2004	Col	NL	122	177	47	12	2	9	(6	3)	90	25	40	36	32	2	51	2	0	4	1	0	1.00	6	.266	.377	.508
2005	SD	NL	135	221	65	12	1	8	(3	5)	103	31	40	37	40	3	58	0	1	5	4	0	1.00	6	.294	.395	.466
2006	SF	NL	114	259	65	15	2	5	(0	5)	99	32	37	34	28	3	50	3	0	1	0	1	.00	6	.251	.330	.382
97	StL	NL	44	61	13	3	0	0	(0	0)	16	5	4	5	9	1	14	1	1	1	0	1	.00	2	.213	.319	.262
97	SD	NL	71	103	33	4	0	2	(2	0)	43	11	19	17	11	0	18	0	0	1	2	2	.50	1	.320	.383	.417
	12 ML YEARS		1014	1615	420	89	9	40	(15	25)	647	198	232	233	230	14	368	9	11	17	14	9	.61	35	.260	.352	.401

Mike Sweeney

Bats: R **Throws:** R **Pos:** DH-59; PH-1   **Ht:** 6'3" **Wt:** 220 **Born:** 7/22/1973 **Age:** 33

						BATTING														BASERUNNING				AVERAGES		
Year	Team	Lg	G	AB	H	2B	3B	HR	(Hm	Rd)	TB	R	RBI	RC	TBB	IBB	SO	HBP	SH	SF	SB	CS	SB%	GDP	Avg	OBP	Slg
2006	Burlgtn*	A	2	7	1	0	0	1	(-	-)	4	2	1	1	1	0	2	0	0	0	0	0	-	0	.143	.250	.571
2006	Wichta*	AA	4	13	5	1	0	2	(-	-)	12	3	5	4	2	0	2	0	0	0	0	0	-	0	.385	.467	.923
2006	Omha*	AAA	5	15	5	2	0	1	(-	-)	10	3	4	4	5	0	1	0	0	1	0	0	-	2	.333	.476	.667
1995	KC	AL	4	4	1	0	0	0	(0	0)	1	1	0	0	0	0	0	0	0	0	0	0	-	0	.250	.250	.250
1996	KC	AL	50	165	46	10	0	4	(1	3)	68	23	24	23	18	0	21	4	0	3	1	2	.33	7	.279	.358	.412
1997	KC	AL	84	240	58	8	0	7	(5	2)	87	30	31	25	17	0	33	6	1	2	3	2	.60	8	.242	.306	.363
1998	KC	AL	92	282	73	18	0	8	(6	2)	115	32	35	35	24	1	38	2	2	1	2	3	.40	7	.259	.320	.408
1999	KC	AL	150	575	185	44	2	22	(10	12)	299	101	102	109	54	0	48	10	0	4	6	1	.86	21	.322	.387	.520
2000	KC	AL	159	618	206	30	0	29	(17	12)	323	105	144	128	71	5	67	15	0	13	8	3	.73	15	.333	.407	.523
2001	KC	AL	147	559	170	46	0	29	(14	15)	303	97	99	109	64	13	64	2	1	6	10	3	.77	13	.304	.374	.542
2002	KC	AL	126	471	160	31	1	24	(14	10)	265	81	86	112	61	10	46	6	0	7	9	7	.56	9	.340	.417	.563
2003	KC	AL	108	392	115	18	1	16	(7	9)	183	62	83	83	64	5	56	2	0	5	3	2	.60	13	.293	.391	.467
2004	KC	AL	106	411	118	23	0	22	(8	14)	207	56	79	75	33	9	44	6	0	2	3	2	.60	7	.287	.347	.504
2005	KC	AL	122	470	141	39	0	21	(7	14)	243	63	83	80	33	7	61	4	1	6	3	0	1.00	16	.300	.347	.517
2006	KC	AL	60	217	56	15	0	8	(4	4)	95	23	33	33	28	5	48	4	0	3	2	0	1.00	5	.258	.349	.438
	12 ML YEARS		1208	4404	1329	282	4	190	(93	97)	2189	674	799	812	467	55	526	61	5	52	50	25	.67	121	.302	.373	.497

Ryan Sweeney

Bats: L **Throws:** L **Pos:** CF-7; LF-6; RF-6; PH-3; DH-1; PR-1   **Ht:** 6'4" **Wt:** 200 **Born:** 2/20/1985 **Age:** 22

						BATTING														BASERUNNING				AVERAGES		
Year	Team	Lg	G	AB	H	2B	3B	HR	(Hm	Rd)	TB	R	RBI	RC	TBB	IBB	SO	HBP	SH	SF	SB	CS	SB%	GDP	Avg	OBP	Slg
2003	Bristol	R+	19	67	21	3	0	2	(-	-)	30	11	5	12	7	0	10	1	1	0	3	0	1.00	1	.313	.387	.448
2003	Gr Falls	R+	10	34	12	2	0	0	(-	-)	14	0	4	4	2	0	3	0	0	0	2	2	.00	1	.353	.389	.412
2004	WinSa	A+	134	515	146	22	3	7	(-	-)	195	71	66	69	40	1	65	7	3	2	8	6	.57	3	.283	.342	.379
2005	Brham	AA	113	429	128	22	3	1	(-	-)	159	64	47	60	35	4	53	7	7	5	6	6	.50	5	.298	.357	.371
2006	Charltt	AAA	118	449	133	25	3	13	(-	-)	203	64	70	71	35	5	73	3	3	2	7	7	.50	9	.296	.350	.452
2006	CWS	AL	18	35	8	0	0	0	(0	0)	8	1	5	1	0	0	7	0	0	0	0	0	-	1	.229	.229	.229

Nick Swisher

Bats: B **Throws:** L **Pos:** 1B-90; LF-79; DH-2; CF-1; RF-1; PH-1; PR-1   **Ht:** 6'0" **Wt:** 215 **Born:** 11/25/1980 **Age:** 26

						BATTING														BASERUNNING				AVERAGES		
Year	Team	Lg	G	AB	H	2B	3B	HR	(Hm	Rd)	TB	R	RBI	RC	TBB	IBB	SO	HBP	SH	SF	SB	CS	SB%	GDP	Avg	OBP	Slg
2004	Oak	AL	20	60	15	4	0	2	(1	1)	25	11	8	8	8	0	11	2	0	1	0	0	-	2	.250	.352	.417
2005	Oak	AL	131	462	109	32	1	21	(11	10)	206	66	74	62	55	3	110	4	0	1	0	1	.00	9	.236	.322	.446
2006	Oak	AL	157	556	141	24	2	35	(17	18)	274	106	95	95	97	7	152	11	2	6	1	2	.33	13	.254	.372	.493
	3 ML YEARS		308	1078	265	60	3	58	(29	29)	505	183	177	165	160	10	273	17	2	8	1	3	.25	24	.246	.350	.468

Jon Switzer

Pitches: L **Bats:** L **Pos:** RP-40   **Ht:** 6'3" **Wt:** 190 **Born:** 8/13/1979 **Age:** 27

Year	Team	Lg	G	GS	CG	GF	IP	BFP	H	R	ER	HR	SH	SF	HB	TBB	IBB	SO	WP	Bk	W	L	Pct	ShO	Sv-Op	Hld	ERC	ERA
2006	Drham*	AAA	26	0	0	10	31.0	129	22	4	3	1	0	0	1	13	0	29	1	0	3	0	1.000	0	3--	-	2.26	0.87
2003	TB	AL	5	0	0	1	9.2	46	13	8	8	2	0	1	4	3	0	7	1	0	0	0	-	0	0-0	0	8.88	7.45
2005	TB	AL	2	0	0	0	4.0	25	5	4	3	0	0	0	0	7	0	5	0	0	0	0	-	0	0-0	0	9.71	6.75
2006	TB	AL	40	0	0	6	33.2	157	38	19	17	5	2	1	1	19	3	18	3	0	2	2	.500	0	0-3	5	5.78	4.54
	3 ML YEARS		47	0	0	7	47.1	228	56	31	28	7	2	2	5	29	3	30	4	0	2	2	.500	0	0-3	5	6.72	5.32

So Taguchi

Bats: R **Throws:** R **Pos:** LF-70; CF-59; PH-21; RF-7; 2B-1; DH-1; PR-1   **Ht:** 5'10" **Wt:** 165 **Born:** 7/2/1969 **Age:** 37

Year	Team	Lg	G	AB	H	2B	3B	HR	(Hm	Rd)	TB	R	RBI	RC	TBB	IBB	SO	HBP	SH	SF	SB	CS	SB%	GDP	Avg	OBP	Slg
2002	StL	NL	19	15	6	0	0	0	(0	0)	6	4	2	4	2	0	1	0	2	0	1	0	1.00	0	.400	.471	.400
2003	StL	NL	43	54	14	3	1	3	(1	2)	28	9	13	11	4	1	11	0	1	0	0	0	-	2	.259	.310	.519
2004	StL	NL	109	179	52	10	2	3	(1	2)	75	26	25	27	12	1	23	2	10	3	6	3	.67	6	.291	.337	.419
2005	StL	NL	143	396	114	21	2	8	(5	3)	163	45	53	59	20	2	62	2	2	4	11	2	.85	11	.288	.322	.412
2006	StL	NL	134	316	84	19	1	2	(0	2)	111	46	31	35	32	1	48	2	9	2	11	3	.79	9	.266	.335	.351
	5 ML YEARS		448	960	270	53	6	16	(7	9)	383	130	124	136	70	5	145	6	24	9	29	8	.78	28	.281	.331	.399

Brian Tallet

Pitches: L **Bats:** L **Pos:** RP-43; SP-1   **Ht:** 6'6" **Wt:** 215 **Born:** 9/21/1977 **Age:** 29

Year	Team	Lg	G	GS	CG	GF	IP	BFP	H	R	ER	HR	SH	SF	HB	TBB	IBB	SO	WP	Bk	W	L	Pct	ShO	Sv-Op	Hld	ERC	ERA
2006	Syrcse*	AAA	20	0	0	9	25.1	117	32	17	16	4	2	1	3	10	1	21	1	0	1	2	.333	0	3--	-	6.58	5.68
2002	Cle	AL	2	2	0	0	12.0	47	9	3	2	0	0	4	1	4	0	5	0	0	1	0	1.000	0	0-0	0	2.31	1.50
2003	Cle	AL	5	3	0	1	19.0	87	23	14	10	2	2	0	1	8	0	9	0	0	1	2	.000	0	0-0	0	5.65	4.74
2005	Cle	AL	2	0	0	0	4.2	24	6	4	4	2	0	0	1	3	0	2	0	0	0	0	-	0	0-0	0	10.55	7.71
2006	Tor	AL	44	1	0	8	54.1	229	45	24	23	5	1	5	3	31	4	37	2	1	3	0	1.000	0	0-0	5	3.97	3.81
	4 ML YEARS		53	6	0	9	90.0	387	83	45	39	9	3	5	6	46	4	53	2	1	4	2	.667	0	0-0	5	4.38	3.90

Taylor Tankersley

Pitches: L **Bats:** L **Pos:** RP-49   **Ht:** 6'1" **Wt:** 220 **Born:** 3/7/1983 **Age:** 24

Year	Team	Lg	G	GS	CG	GF	IP	BFP	H	R	ER	HR	SH	SF	HB	TBB	IBB	SO	WP	Bk	W	L	Pct	ShO	Sv-Op	Hld	ERC	ERA
2004	Jmstwn	A-	6	6	0	0	26.2	116	21	14	10	2	4	4	0	8	0	32	1	2	1	1	.500	0	0--	-	2.21	3.38
2005	Grnsbr	A	12	12	0	0	66.0	297	74	45	38	12	0	1	2	25	0	63	3	1	2	7	.222	0	0--	-	5.33	5.18
2005	Jupiter	A+	4	4	1	0	24.0	102	21	10	9	1	0	1	0	9	0	19	0	0	1	0	1.000	0	0--	-	2.85	3.38
2006	Carlina	AA	22	0	0	14	28.1	110	11	4	3	0	6	1	1	14	1	40	1	0	4	1	.800	0	6--	-	1.13	0.95
2006	Fla	NL	49	0	0	10	41.0	178	33	14	13	4	3	3	1	26	5	46	3	0	2	1	.667	0	3-7	22	3.80	2.85

Jack Taschner

Pitches: L **Bats:** L **Pos:** RP-24   **Ht:** 6'3" **Wt:** 210 **Born:** 4/21/1978 **Age:** 29

Year	Team	Lg	G	GS	CG	GF	IP	BFP	H	R	ER	HR	SH	SF	HB	TBB	IBB	SO	WP	Bk	W	L	Pct	ShO	Sv-Op	Hld	ERC	ERA
1999	SlmKzr	A-	7	6	0	0	28.2	118	26	12	8	1	0	0	0	10	0	36	0	0	3	2	.600	0	0--	-	2.99	2.51
2000	SnJos	A+	10	2	0	1	26.1	119	23	17	12	0	0	1	4	17	0	22	3	3	2	2	.500	0	1--	-	4.17	4.10
2001	SnJos	A+	14	14	0	0	65.2	292	62	33	30	7	1	3	5	29	0	72	8	2	4	4	.500	0	0--	-	4.19	4.11
2003	Nrwich	AA	34	12	0	10	75.2	347	78	53	48	7	0	2	5	45	0	46	6	0	0	6	.000	0	0--	-	5.24	5.71
2004	Nrwich	AA	14	10	0	1	58.0	237	47	17	16	5	2	1	0	16	0	55	3	0	3	1	.750	0	0--	-	2.48	2.48
2004	Fresno	AAA	18	9	0	4	53.1	263	71	59	55	14	1	2	3	32	1	44	3	0	4	7	.364	0	0--	-	8.45	9.28
2005	Fresno	AAA	44	0	0	26	49.1	202	30	9	9	3	1	1	1	24	0	62	3	0	3	0	1.000	0	10--	-	2.16	1.64
2006	Fresno	AAA	45	0	0	34	49.1	210	49	21	20	5	4	1	2	17	0	68	2	0	6	7	.462	0	14--	-	4.02	3.65
2005	SF	NL	24	0	0	7	22.2	95	15	5	4	0	0	1	0	13	0	19	0	0	2	0	1.000	0	0-1	3	2.25	1.59
2006	SF	NL	24	0	0	6	19.1	101	31	23	18	4	0	2	2	7	0	15	3	0	0	1	.000	0	0-1	3	8.55	8.38
	2 ML YEARS		48	0	0	13	42.0	196	46	28	22	4	0	3	2	20	0	34	3	0	2	1	.667	0	0-2	6	4.90	4.71

Jordan Tata

Pitches: R **Bats:** R **Pos:** RP-8   **Ht:** 6'6" **Wt:** 220 **Born:** 9/20/1981 **Age:** 25

Year	Team	Lg	G	GS	CG	GF	IP	BFP	H	R	ER	HR	SH	SF	HB	TBB	IBB	SO	WP	Bk	W	L	Pct	ShO	Sv-Op	Hld	ERC	ERA
2003	Oneont	A-	16	12	0	2	73.1	306	64	32	21	1	5	4	6	20	0	60	4	1	4	3	.571	0	1--	-	2.63	2.58
2004	W Mich	A	28	28	1	0	166.1	705	167	77	62	7	12	3	9	68	2	116	15	0	8	11	.421	0	0--	-	4.04	3.35
2005	Lkland	A+	25	25	2	0	155.0	628	138	55	48	12	2	1	8	41	1	134	11	1	13	2	.867	2	0--	-	3.08	2.79
2006	Toledo	AAA	21	21	1	0	122.0	530	117	58	52	11	5	4	7	49	2	86	10	0	10	6	.625	1	0--	-	3.96	3.84
2006	Det	AL	8	0	0	2	14.2	65	14	11	10	1	0	2	0	7	1	6	0	0	0	0	-	0	0-0	0	3.69	6.14

Fernando Tatis

Bats: R **Throws:** R **Pos:** PH-9; DH-7; 3B-5; 1B-4; LF-3; PR-3; 2B-1; RF-1   **Ht:** 5'10" **Wt:** 195 **Born:** 1/1/1975 **Age:** 32

Year	Team	Lg	G	AB	H	2B	3B	HR	(Hm	Rd)	TB	R	RBI	RC	TBB	IBB	SO	HBP	SH	SF	SB	CS	SB%	GDP	Avg	OBP	Slg
2006	Ottawa*	AAA	90	326	97	15	2	7			137	44	37	54	36	0	56	4	0	3	8	2	.80	3	.298	.372	.420
1997	Tex	AL	60	223	57	9	0	8	(6	2)	90	29	29	26	14	0	42	0	2	2	3	0	1.00	5	.256	.297	.404
1998	2 Tms		150	532	147	33	4	11	(6	5)	221	69	58	69	36	3	123	6	4	1	13	5	.72	16	.276	.329	.415

246

Year	Team	Lg	G	AB	H	2B	3B	HR	(Hm	Rd)	TB	R	RBI	RC	TBB	IBB	SO	HBP	SH	SF	SB	CS	SB%	GDP	Avg	OBP	Slg
1999	StL	NL	149	537	160	31	2	34	(16	18)	297	104	107	117	82	4	128	16	0	4	21	9	.70	11	.298	.404	.553
2000	StL	NL	96	324	82	21	1	18	(11	7)	159	59	64	58	57	1	94	10	1	2	2	3	.40	13	.253	.379	.491
2001	Mon	NL	41	145	37	9	0	2	(0	2)	52	20	11	18	16	0	43	4	0	3	0	0	-	5	.255	.339	.359
2002	Mon	NL	114	381	87	18	1	15	(5	10)	152	43	55	39	35	1	90	8	1	5	2	2	.50	15	.228	.303	.399
2003	Mon	NL	53	175	34	6	0	2	(1	1)	46	15	15	15	18	0	40	3	0	0	2	1	.67	7	.194	.281	.263
2006	Bal	AL	28	56	14	6	1	2	(1	1)	28	7	8	9	6	1	17	0	0	2	0	0	-	2	.250	.313	.500
98	Tex	AL	95	330	89	17	2	3	(1	2)	119	41	32	33	12	2	66	4	4	0	6	2	.75	10	.270	.303	.361
98	StL	AL	55	202	58	16	2	8	(5	3)	102	28	26	36	24	1	57	2	0	1	7	3	.70	6	.287	.367	.505
8 ML YEARS			691	2373	618	133	9	92	(46	46)	1045	346	347	351	264	10	577	47	8	19	43	20	.68	75	.260	.344	.440

Ty Taubenheim

Pitches: R Bats: R Pos: SP-7; RP-5 Ht: 6'5" Wt: 200 Born: 11/17/1982 Age: 24

Year	Team	Lg	G	GS	CG	GF	IP	BFP	H	R	ER	HR	SH	SF	HB	TBB	IBB	SO	WP	Bk	W	L	Pct	ShO	Sv-Op	Hld	ERC	ERA
2003	Helena	R+	14	0	0	2	50.1	196	47	13	12	3	4	0	2	3	0	44	2	1	6	1	.857	0	1--	-	2.41	2.15
2004	Beloit	A	47	0	0	36	92.1	378	81	41	37	10	1	0	3	17	0	106	2	0	5	3	.625	0	12--	-	2.72	3.61
2005	BrvdCt	A+	16	16	2	0	106.0	420	86	34	31	7	3	1	9	26	0	75	8	0	10	2	.833	1	0--	-	2.69	2.63
2005	Hntsvl	AA	11	11	0	0	64.0	281	64	36	31	7	8	4	1	24	1	44	3	0	2	6	.250	0	0--	-	3.98	4.36
2006	Syrcse	AAA	18	14	0	0	75.2	310	75	25	24	9	2	0	3	18	0	48	4	0	2	4	.333	0	0--	-	3.77	2.85
2006	Tor	AL	12	7	0	1	35.0	167	40	22	19	5	1	2	4	18	0	26	1	0	1	5	.167	0	0-0	-	6.05	4.89

Julian Tavarez

Pitches: R Bats: L Pos: RP-52; SP-6 Ht: 6'2" Wt: 195 Born: 5/22/1973 Age: 34

Year	Team	Lg	G	GS	CG	GF	IP	BFP	H	R	ER	HR	SH	SF	HB	TBB	IBB	SO	WP	Bk	W	L	Pct	ShO	Sv-Op	Hld	ERC	ERA
1993	Cle	AL	8	7	0	0	37.0	172	53	29	27	7	0	1	2	13	2	19	3	1	2	2	.500	0	0-0	0	7.48	6.57
1994	Cle	AL	1	1	0	0	1.2	14	6	8	4	1	0	1	0	1	1	0	0	0	0	1	.000	0	0-0	0	24.13	21.60
1995	Cle	AL	57	0	0	15	85.0	350	76	36	23	7	0	2	3	21	0	68	3	2	10	2	.833	0	0-4	19	2.93	2.44
1996	Cle	AL	51	4	0	13	80.2	353	101	49	48	9	5	4	1	22	5	46	1	0	4	7	.364	0	0-0	13	5.12	5.36
1997	SF	NL	89	0	0	13	88.1	378	91	43	38	6	3	8	4	34	5	38	4	0	6	4	.600	0	0-3	26	4.13	3.87
1998	SF	NL	60	0	0	12	85.1	374	96	41	36	5	8	5	8	36	11	52	1	1	5	3	.625	0	1-6	10	4.89	3.80
1999	SF	NL	47	0	0	12	54.2	258	65	38	36	7	3	2	8	25	3	33	4	1	2	0	1.000	0	0-2	5	6.10	5.93
2000	Col	NL	51	12	1	8	120.0	530	124	68	59	11	3	4	7	53	9	62	2	1	11	5	.688	0	1-1	6	4.49	4.43
2001	ChC	NL	34	28	0	1	161.1	712	172	98	81	13	8	4	11	69	4	107	2	1	10	9	.526	0	0-0	2	4.70	4.52
2002	Fla	NL	29	27	0	1	153.2	714	188	100	92	9	13	2	15	74	7	67	7	2	10	12	.455	0	0-1	0	5.75	5.39
2003	Pit	NL	64	0	0	29	83.2	350	75	37	34	1	9	1	5	27	8	39	3	0	3	3	.500	0	11-14	9	2.72	3.66
2004	StL	NL	77	0	0	27	64.1	268	57	21	17	1	3	1	6	19	0	48	2	1	7	4	.636	0	4-6	19	2.87	2.38
2005	StL	NL	74	0	0	16	65.2	278	68	28	25	6	3	3	8	19	4	47	1	0	2	3	.400	0	4-6	32	4.29	3.43
2006	Bos	AL	58	6	1	11	98.2	431	110	54	49	10	3	6	6	44	3	56	2	0	5	4	.556	0	1-3	5	5.32	4.47
14 ML YEARS			700	85	2	158	1180.0	5182	1282	650	569	93	58	39	84	457	62	682	35	10	77	59	.566	0	22-46	143	4.61	4.34

Willy Taveras

Bats: R Throws: R Pos: CF-138; PH-13; PR-5 Ht: 6'0" Wt: 160 Born: 12/25/1981 Age: 25

Year	Team	Lg	G	AB	H	2B	3B	HR	(Hm	Rd)	TB	R	RBI	RC	TBB	IBB	SO	HBP	SH	SF	SB	CS	SB%	GDP	Avg	OBP	Slg
2004	Hou	NL	10	1	0	0	0	0	(0	0)	0	2	0	0	0	0	1	0	1	0	1	0	1.00	0	.000	.000	.000
2005	Hou	NL	152	592	172	13	4	3	(2	1)	202	82	29	61	25	1	103	7	7	4	34	11	.76	4	.291	.325	.341
2006	Hou	NL	149	529	147	19	5	1	(0	1)	179	83	30	64	34	0	88	11	11	2	33	9	.79	6	.278	.333	.338
3 ML YEARS			311	1122	319	32	9	4	(2	2)	381	167	59	125	59	1	192	18	19	6	68	20	.77	10	.284	.329	.340

Mark Teahen

Bats: L Throws: R Pos: 3B-109; PH-2 Ht: 6'3" Wt: 220 Born: 9/6/1981 Age: 25

Year	Team	Lg	G	AB	H	2B	3B	HR	(Hm	Rd)	TB	R	RBI	RC	TBB	IBB	SO	HBP	SH	SF	SB	CS	SB%	GDP	Avg	OBP	Slg
2002	Vancvr	A-	13	57	23	5	1	0	(-	-)	30	10	6	13	5	0	9	0	0	1	4	1	.80	0	.404	.444	.526
2002	Mdest	A+	59	234	56	9	1	1	(-	-)	70	25	26	22	21	1	53	2	0	0	1	2	.33	4	.239	.307	.299
2003	Mdest	A+	121	453	128	27	4	3	(-	-)	172	68	71	72	66	1	113	6	0	5	4	0	1.00	19	.283	.377	.380
2004	Mdland	AA	53	197	66	15	4	6	(-	-)	107	31	36	44	29	3	44	1	0	2	0	0	-	12	.335	.419	.543
2004	Scrmto	AAA	26	69	19	8	0	0	(-	-)	27	9	10	10	11	0	22	1	0	0	0	1	.00	1	.275	.383	.391
2004	Omha	AAA	66	246	69	15	1	8	(-	-)	110	33	31	39	21	0	69	4	1	2	0	0	-	4	.280	.344	.447
2005	Omha	AAA	8	27	7	2	0	0	(-	-)	9	4	4	4	7	0	9	0	0	0	0	0	-	1	.259	.412	.333
2006	Omha	AAA	24	79	30	8	4	2	(-	-)	52	14	14	24	19	3	12	0	0	0	0	0	-	2	.380	.500	.658
2005	KC	AL	130	447	110	29	4	7	(3	4)	168	60	55	52	40	2	107	1	2	1	7	2	.78	13	.246	.309	.376
2006	KC	AL	109	393	114	21	7	18	(9	9)	203	70	69	79	40	2	85	2	2	2	10	0	1.00	5	.290	.357	.517
2 ML YEARS			239	840	224	50	11	25	(12	13)	371	130	124	131	80	4	192	3	4	3	17	2	.89	18	.267	.332	.442

Mark Teixeira

Bats: B Throws: R Pos: 1B-159; DH-3 Ht: 6'3" Wt: 220 Born: 4/11/1980 Age: 27

Year	Team	Lg	G	AB	H	2B	3B	HR	(Hm	Rd)	TB	R	RBI	RC	TBB	IBB	SO	HBP	SH	SF	SB	CS	SB%	GDP	Avg	OBP	Slg
2003	Tex	AL	146	529	137	29	5	26	(19	7)	254	66	84	78	44	5	120	14	0	2	1	2	.33	14	.259	.331	.480
2004	Tex	AL	145	545	153	34	2	38	(18	20)	305	101	112	120	68	12	117	10	0	2	4	1	.80	6	.281	.370	.560
2005	Tex	AL	162	644	194	41	3	43	(30	13)	370	112	144	148	72	5	124	11	0	3	4	0	1.00	18	.301	.379	.575
2006	Tex	AL	162	628	177	45	1	33	(12	21)	323	99	110	114	89	12	128	4	0	6	2	0	1.00	17	.282	.371	.514
4 ML YEARS			615	2346	661	149	11	140	(79	61)	1252	378	450	460	273	34	489	39	0	13	11	3	.79	55	.282	.364	.534

Miguel Tejada

Bats: R Throws: R Pos: SS-150; DH-12   Ht: 5'9" Wt: 215 Born: 5/25/1976 Age: 31

								BATTING												BASERUNNING				AVERAGES		
Year	Team	Lg	G	AB	H	2B	3B	HR	(Hm Rd)	TB	R	RBI	RC	TBB	IBB	SO	HBP	SH	SF	SB	CS	SB%	GDP	Avg	OBP	Slg
1997	Oak	AL	26	99	20	3	2	2	(1 1)	33	10	10	7	2	0	22	3	0	0	2	0	1.00	3	.202	.240	.333
1998	Oak	AL	105	365	85	20	1	11	(5 6)	140	53	45	40	28	0	86	7	4	3	5	6	.45	8	.233	.298	.384
1999	Oak	AL	159	593	149	33	4	21	(12 9)	253	93	84	82	57	3	94	10	9	5	8	7	.53	11	.251	.325	.427
2000	Oak	AL	160	607	167	32	1	30	(16 14)	291	105	115	99	66	6	102	4	2	2	6	0	1.00	15	.275	.349	.479
2001	Oak	AL	162	622	166	31	3	31	(17 14)	296	107	113	94	43	5	89	13	1	4	11	5	.69	14	.267	.326	.476
2002	Oak	AL	162	662	204	30	0	34	(17 17)	336	108	131	123	38	3	84	11	0	4	7	2	.78	21	.308	.354	.508
2003	Oak	AL	162	636	177	42	0	27	(15 12)	300	98	106	103	53	7	65	6	0	8	10	0	1.00	12	.278	.336	.472
2004	Bal	AL	162	653	203	40	2	34	(17 17)	349	107	150	124	48	6	73	10	0	14	4	1	.80	24	.311	.360	.534
2005	Bal	AL	162	654	199	50	5	26	(16 10)	337	89	98	102	40	9	83	7	0	3	5	1	.83	26	.304	.349	.515
2006	Bal	AL	162	648	214	37	0	24	(17 7)	323	99	100	99	46	10	79	9	0	6	6	2	.75	28	.330	.379	.498
10 ML YEARS			1422	5539	1584	318	18	240	(133 107)	2658	869	952	873	421	49	777	80	16	49	64	24	.73	162	.286	.342	.480

Robinson Tejeda

Pitches: R Bats: R Pos: SP-14   Ht: 6'3" Wt: 230 Born: 3/24/1982 Age: 25

			HOW MUCH HE PITCHED					WHAT HE GAVE UP												THE RESULTS							
Year	Team	Lg	G	GS	CG	GF	IP	BFP	H	R	ER	HR	SH	SF	HB	TBB	IBB	SO	WP	Bk	W	L	Pct	ShO	Sv-Op	Hld	ERC	ERA
1999	Phillies	R	12	9	0	2	46.1	213	47	27	22	5	3	1	2	27	0	39	1	1	1	3	.250	0	0- -	-	5.05	4.27
2000	Phillies	R	10	6	1	1	39.0	173	44	30	24	3	1	2	2	12	0	22	5	1	2	5	.286	1	0- -	-	4.42	5.54
2001	Lakwd	A	20	24	1	0	150.2	638	128	74	57	10	6	5	8	58	1	152	11	2	8	9	.471	1	0- -	-	3.14	3.40
2002	Clrwtr	A+	17	17	1	0	99.2	420	73	48	44	14	2	4	5	48	0	87	3	1	4	8	.333	0	0- -	-	3.38	3.97
2003	Lakwd	A	5	4	0	0	18.2	89	17	11	11	4	3	4	1	16	0	20	1	0	0	3	.000	0	0- -	-	6.49	5.30
2003	Clrwtr	A+	11	11	1	0	64.2	270	53	25	23	4	4	1	2	23	0	42	3	0	2	4	.333	0	0- -	-	2.78	3.20
2004	Rdng	AA	27	26	0	0	150.1	658	148	93	86	29	6	8	6	59	0	133	6	1	8	14	.364	0	0- -	-	4.72	5.15
2005	S-WB	AAA	5	5	0	0	28.1	119	21	8	7	0	0	3	0	13	0	28	0	0	2	0	1.000	0	0- -	-	2.23	2.22
2006	Rngrs	R	2	2	0	0	4.0	16	4	3	3	0	0	0	0	0	0	6	0	0	0	0	-	0	0- -	-	1.95	6.75
2006	Okla	AAA	15	15	0	0	80.0	336	61	30	28	7	0	1	3	42	0	79	4	0	6	2	.750	0	0- -	-	3.36	3.15
2005	Phi	NL	26	13	0	5	85.2	371	67	36	34	5	3	2	8	51	4	72	3	1	4	3	.571	0	0-0	1	3.64	3.57
2006	Tex	AL	14	14	0	0	73.2	329	83	40	35	10	1	5	3	32	1	40	1	1	5	5	.500	0	0-0	0	5.41	4.28
2 ML YEARS			40	27	0	5	159.1	700	150	76	69	15	4	7	11	83	5	112	4	2	9	8	.529	0	0-0	1	4.44	3.90

Luis Terrero

Bats: R Throws: R Pos: LF-16; CF-6; PR-6; RF-4; PH-4; DH-1   Ht: 6'3" Wt: 225 Born: 5/18/1980 Age: 27

								BATTING												BASERUNNING				AVERAGES		
Year	Team	Lg	G	AB	H	2B	3B	HR	(Hm Rd)	TB	R	RBI	RC	TBB	IBB	SO	HBP	SH	SF	SB	CS	SB%	GDP	Avg	OBP	Slg
2006	Ottawa*	AAA	84	302	96	21	2	16	(- -)	169	52	44	60	16	0	61	8	2	1	18	9	.67	4	.318	.367	.560
2003	Ari	NL	5	4	1	0	0	0	(0 0)	1	0	0	1	0	0	1	1	0	0	0	0	-	0	.250	.400	.250
2004	Ari	NL	62	229	56	14	0	4	(2 2)	82	21	14	25	20	2	78	5	1	0	10	2	.83	5	.245	.319	.358
2005	Ari	NL	88	161	37	6	1	4	(2 2)	57	23	20	17	14	0	40	6	2	1	3	2	.60	5	.230	.313	.354
2006	Bal	AL	27	40	8	1	0	1	(0 1)	12	4	6	3	1	0	7	1	0	0	0	3	.00	0	.200	.238	.300
4 ML YEARS			182	434	102	21	1	9	(4 5)	152	48	40	46	35	2	126	13	3	1	13	7	.65	10	.235	.311	.350

Marcus Thames

Bats: R Throws: R Pos: LF-54; DH-45; PH-8; RF-5; PR-1   Ht: 6'2" Wt: 220 Born: 3/6/1977 Age: 30

								BATTING												BASERUNNING				AVERAGES		
Year	Team	Lg	G	AB	H	2B	3B	HR	(Hm Rd)	TB	R	RBI	RC	TBB	IBB	SO	HBP	SH	SF	SB	CS	SB%	GDP	Avg	OBP	Slg
2002	NYY	AL	7	13	3	1	0	1	(1 0)	7	2	2	2	0	0	4	0	0	0	0	0	-	0	.231	.231	.538
2003	Tex	AL	30	73	15	2	0	1	(0 1)	20	12	4	5	8	0	18	2	0	1	0	1	.00	0	.205	.298	.274
2004	Det	AL	61	165	42	12	0	10	(5 5)	84	24	33	30	16	0	42	2	0	1	0	1	.00	3	.255	.326	.509
2005	Det	AL	38	107	21	2	0	7	(3 4)	44	11	16	10	9	1	38	1	0	1	0	0	-	1	.196	.263	.411
2006	Det	AL	110	348	89	20	2	26	(11 15)	191	61	60	60	37	0	92	4	0	1	1	1	.50	3	.256	.333	.549
5 ML YEARS			246	706	170	37	2	45	(20 25)	346	110	115	107	70	1	194	9	0	4	1	3	.25	6	.241	.316	.490

Ryan Theriot

Bats: R Throws: R Pos: 2B-39; PH-13; SS-2; 3B-1; PR-1   Ht: 5'11" Wt: 175 Born: 12/7/1979 Age: 27

								BATTING												BASERUNNING				AVERAGES		
Year	Team	Lg	G	AB	H	2B	3B	HR	(Hm Rd)	TB	R	RBI	RC	TBB	IBB	SO	HBP	SH	SF	SB	CS	SB%	GDP	Avg	OBP	Slg
2001	Dytona	A+	30	103	21	5	0	0	(- -)	26	20	9	10	21	0	17	1	3	1	2	4	.33	2	.204	.341	.252
2002	Lansng	A	130	489	123	19	4	1	(- -)	153	75	37	60	59	1	77	4	3	3	32	8	.80	3	.252	.335	.313
2003	Lansng	A	58	220	57	8	1	1	(- -)	70	29	17	30	31	1	34	1	5	0	21	5	.81	4	.259	.353	.318
2003	WTenn	AA	53	178	42	3	0	1	(- -)	48	20	9	19	29	1	21	3	4	1	9	8	.53	6	.236	.351	.270
2004	Dytona	A+	103	330	90	14	3	1	(- -)	113	47	34	45	48	0	43	3	6	3	13	11	.54	4	.273	.367	.342
2005	WTenn	AA	120	448	136	28	4	1	(- -)	175	52	53	69	45	2	38	1	4	5	24	10	.71	8	.304	.365	.391
2006	Iowa	AAA	73	280	85	11	5	0	(- -)	106	41	22	43	27	1	34	2	1	2	14	3	.82	5	.304	.367	.379
2005	ChC	NL	9	13	2	1	0	0	(0 0)	3	3	0	0	1	0	2	0	0	0	0	0	-	0	.154	.214	.231
2006	ChC	NL	53	134	44	11	3	3	(3 0)	70	34	16	31	17	0	18	2	6	0	13	2	.87	5	.328	.412	.522
2 ML YEARS			62	147	46	12	3	3	(3 0)	73	37	16	31	18	0	20	2	6	0	13	2	.87	5	.313	.395	.497

Frank Thomas

Bats: R **Throws:** R **Pos:** DH-135; PH-2 **Ht:** 6'5" **Wt:** 275 **Born:** 5/27/1968 **Age:** 39

Year	Team	Lg	G	AB	H	2B	3B	HR	(Hm	Rd)	TB	R	RBI	RC	TBB	IBB	SO	HBP	SH	SF	SB	CS	SB%	GDP	Avg	OBP	Slg
1990	CWS	AL	60	191	63	11	3	7	(2	5)	101	39	31	46	44	0	54	2	0	3	0	1	.00	5	.330	.454	.529
1991	CWS	AL	158	559	178	31	2	32	(24	8)	309	104	109	**134**	138	13	112	1	0	3	1	2	.33	20	.318	**.453**	.553
1992	CWS	AL	160	573	185	**46**	2	24	(10	14)	307	108	115	**132**	122	6	88	5	0	11	6	3	.67	19	.323	**.439**	.536
1993	CWS	AL	153	549	174	36	0	41	**(26**	15)	333	106	128	137	112	23	54	2	0	13	4	2	.67	10	.317	.426	.607
1994	CWS	AL	113	399	141	34	1	38	**(22**	16)	291	**106**	101	127	109	12	61	2	0	7	2	3	.40	15	.353	**.487**	.729
1995	CWS	AL	**145**	493	152	27	0	40	(15	**25)**	299	102	111	132	**136**	**29**	74	6	0	**12**	3	2	.60	14	.308	.454	.606
1996	CWS	AL	141	527	184	26	0	40	(16	24)	330	110	134	137	109	**26**	70	5	0	8	1	1	.50	25	.349	.459	.626
1997	CWS	AL	146	530	184	35	0	35	(16	19)	324	110	125	**139**	109	9	69	3	0	7	1	1	.50	15	**.347**	.456	.611
1998	CWS	AL	160	585	155	35	2	29	(15	14)	281	109	109	111	110	2	93	6	0	11	7	0	1.00	14	.265	.381	.480
1999	CWS	AL	135	486	148	36	0	15	(9	6)	229	74	77	95	87	13	66	9	0	8	3	3	.50	15	.305	.414	.471
2000	CWS	AL	159	582	191	44	0	43	**(30**	13)	364	115	143	**148**	112	18	94	5	0	8	1	3	.25	13	.328	.436	.625
2001	CWS	AL	20	68	15	3	0	4	(2	2)	30	8	10	10	10	2	12	0	0	1	0	0	-	0	.221	.316	.441
2002	CWS	AL	148	523	132	29	1	28	(24	4)	247	77	92	96	88	2	115	7	0	10	3	0	1.00	10	.252	.361	.472
2003	CWS	AL	153	546	146	35	0	42	**(29**	13)	307	87	105	115	100	4	115	12	0	4	0	0	-	11	.267	.390	.562
2004	CWS	AL	74	240	65	16	0	18	(14	4)	135	53	49	59	64	3	57	6	0	1	0	2	.00	2	.271	.434	.563
2005	CWS	AL	34	105	23	3	0	12	(9	3)	62	19	26	18	16	0	31	0	0	3	0	0	-	2	.219	.315	.590
2006	Oak	AL	137	466	126	11	0	39	(23	16)	254	77	114	99	81	3	81	6	0	6	0	0	-	13	.270	.381	.545
17 ML YEARS			2096	7422	2262	458	11	487	(286	201)	4203	1404	1579	1735	1547	165	1246	77	0	115	32	23	.58	203	.305	.424	.566

Jim Thome

Bats: L **Throws:** R **Pos:** DH-136; PH-4; 1B-3 **Ht:** 6'4" **Wt:** 245 **Born:** 8/27/1970 **Age:** 36

Year	Team	Lg	G	AB	H	2B	3B	HR	(Hm	Rd)	TB	R	RBI	RC	TBB	IBB	SO	HBP	SH	SF	SB	CS	SB%	GDP	Avg	OBP	Slg
1991	Cle	AL	27	98	25	4	2	1	(0	1)	36	7	9	9	5	1	16	1	0	0	1	1	.50	4	.255	.298	.367
1992	Cle	AL	40	117	24	3	1	2	(1	1)	35	8	12	9	10	2	34	2	0	2	2	0	1.00	3	.205	.275	.299
1993	Cle	AL	47	154	41	11	0	7	(5	2)	73	28	22	30	29	1	36	4	0	5	2	1	.67	3	.266	.385	.474
1994	Cle	AL	98	321	86	20	1	20	(10	10)	168	58	52	56	46	5	84	0	1	1	3	3	.50	11	.268	.359	.523
1995	Cle	AL	137	452	142	29	3	25	(13	12)	252	92	73	109	97	3	113	5	0	3	4	3	.57	8	.314	.438	.558
1996	Cle	AL	151	505	157	28	5	38	(18	20)	309	122	116	132	123	8	141	6	0	2	2	2	.50	13	.311	.450	.612
1997	Cle	AL	147	496	142	25	0	40	(17	23)	287	104	102	120	**120**	9	146	3	0	8	1	1	.50	9	.286	.423	.579
1998	Cle	AL	123	440	129	34	2	30	(18	12)	257	89	85	104	89	8	141	4	0	4	1	0	1.00	7	.293	.413	.584
1999	Cle	AL	146	494	137	27	2	33	(19	14)	267	101	108	116	**127**	13	**171**	4	0	4	0	0	-	6	.277	.426	.540
2000	Cle	AL	158	557	150	33	1	37	(21	16)	296	106	106	119	118	4	171	4	0	5	1	0	1.00	8	.269	.398	.531
2001	Cle	AL	156	526	153	26	1	49	**(30**	19)	328	101	124	130	111	14	**185**	4	0	3	0	1	.00	9	.291	.416	.624
2002	Cle	AL	147	480	146	19	2	52	**(30**	22)	325	101	118	139	**122**	18	139	5	0	6	1	2	.33	5	.304	.445	**.677**
2003	Phi	NL	159	578	154	30	3	**47**	(28	19)	331	111	131	125	111	11	**182**	4	0	5	0	3	.00	5	.266	.385	.573
2004	Phi	NL	143	508	139	28	1	42	(19	23)	295	97	105	97	104	26	144	2	0	4	0	2	.00	10	.274	.396	.581
2005	Phi	NL	59	193	40	7	0	7	(6	1)	68	26	30	25	45	4	59	2	0	2	0	0	-	5	.207	.360	.352
2006	CWS	AL	143	490	141	26	0	42	**(25**	17)	293	108	109	120	107	12	147	6	0	7	0	0	-	4	.288	.416	.598
16 ML YEARS			1881	6409	1806	350	24	472	(260	212)	3620	1259	1302	1440	1364	139	1909	56	1	61	18	19	.49	110	.282	.409	.565

Brad Thompson

Pitches: R **Bats:** R **Pos:** RP-42; SP-1 **Ht:** 6'1" **Wt:** 190 **Born:** 1/31/1982 **Age:** 25

Year	Team	Lg	G	GS	CG	GF	IP	BFP	H	R	ER	HR	SH	SF	HB	TBB	IBB	SO	WP	Bk	W	L	Pct	ShO	Sv-Op	Hld	ERC	ERA
2003	Peoria	A	30	4	0	7	65.0	275	70	23	21	2	2	0	6	10	2	43	4	2	5	3	.625	0	0--	-	3.38	2.91
2003	PlmBh	A+	2	1	0	0	6.0	21	3	0	0	4	1	0	0	0	0	4	0	0	1	1	.500	0	0--	-	0.54	0.00
2004	Tenn	AA	13	12	2	0	72.1	284	56	19	19	6	4	3	9	11	0	57	1	0	8	2	.800	2	0--	-	2.38	2.36
2004	Memp	AAA	3	3	0	0	14.2	67	20	10	9	3	0	0	0	3	0	10	0	0	1	0	1.000	0	0--	-	6.04	5.52
2005	Memp	AAA	9	0	0	4	13.2	60	12	5	5	1	2	0	1	7	5	11	0	1	2	1	.667	0	0--	-	3.29	3.29
2006	Memp	AAA	14	5	0	2	42.2	166	36	12	10	3	2	3	2	6	1	33	0	0	2	0	1.000	0	0--	-	2.32	2.11
2005	StL	NL	40	0	0	8	55.0	225	46	22	18	5	3	0	4	15	2	29	0	0	4	0	1.000	0	1-1	7	2.90	2.95
2006	StL	NL	43	1	0	16	56.2	245	58	23	21	4	3	0	5	20	3	32	1	0	2		.333	0	0-0	3	4.11	3.34
2 ML YEARS			83	1	0	24	111.2	470	104	45	39	9	6	0	9	35	5	61	1	0	5	2	.714	0	1-1	10	3.50	3.14

Kevin Thompson

Bats: R **Throws:** R **Pos:** RF-10; PR-6; LF-3; CF-2; DH-2; PH-1 **Ht:** 5'10" **Wt:** 185 **Born:** 9/18/1979 **Age:** 27

Year	Team	Lg	G	AB	H	2B	3B	HR	(Hm	Rd)	TB	R	RBI	RC	TBB	IBB	SO	HBP	SH	SF	SB	CS	SB%	GDP	Avg	OBP	Slg
2000	Yanks	R	20	75	20	7	1	2	(-	-)	35	13	9	12	10	0	14	1	0	1	2	3	.40	1	.267	.356	.467
2001	StIsInd	A-	68	260	68	11	4	6	(-	-)	105	46	33	41	36	0	48	5	1	2	11	5	.69	5	.262	.360	.404
2002	Grnsbr	A-	62	226	64	24	3	3	(-	-)	103	44	31	45	37	1	42	6	0	1	14	3	.82	4	.283	.396	.456
2002	Tampa	A+	25	87	16	5	0	0	(-	-)	21	10	7	9	13	0	15	2	2	2	11	1	.92	3	.184	.298	.241
2002	StIsInd	A-	36	139	42	5	2	4	(-	-)	63	25	14	24	11	1	24	0	1	1	6	3	.67	1	.302	.376	.453
2003	Tampa	A+	44	163	54	13	4	5	(-	-)	90	42	25	41	32	2	27	2	0	6	16	5	.76	3	.331	.433	.552
2003	Trntn	AA	86	328	74	16	2	5	(-	-)	109	48	20	42	37	1	57	4	3	2	47	8	.85	5	.226	.310	.332
2004	Trntn	AA	11	45	16	4	0	2	(-	-)	26	12	6	11	4	0	7	1	0	0	9	2	.82	0	.356	.420	.578
2004	Trntn	AA	69	270	76	17	0	9	(-	-)	120	43	17	46	30	1	40	4	2	0	29	10	.74	8	.281	.362	.444
2005	Trntn	AA	81	313	103	28	5	12	(-	-)	177	59	43	79	53	1	68	6	2	3	25	6	.81	5	.329	.432	.565
2005	Clmbs	AAA	58	209	52	17	0	2	(-	-)	75	28	28	29	23	0	45	6	4	4	18	5	.78	4	.249	.335	.359
2006	Clmbs	AAA	91	362	96	22	5	9	(-	-)	155	69	44	57	44	1	63	2	4	4	17	7	.71	3	.265	.345	.428
2006	NYY	AL	19	30	9	3	0	1	(1	0)	15	5	6	6	6	0	9	0	1	0	2	0	1.00	3	.300	.417	.500

Mike Thompson

Pitches: R **Bats:** R **Pos:** SP-16; RP-3   **Ht:** 6'4" **Wt:** 200 **Born:** 11/6/1980 **Age:** 26

Year	Team	Lg	G	GS	CG	GF	IP	BFP	H	R	ER	HR	SH	SF	HB	TBB	IBB	SO	WP	Bk	W	L	Pct	ShO	Sv-Op	Hld	ERC	ERA
1999	Padres	R	13	13	0	0	65.0	300	78	52	44	8	2	3	4	27	0	62	3	4	1	7	.125	0	0--	-	5.68	6.09
2000	Idaho	A	14	14	0	0	72.2	339	99	56	48	8	1	1	8	30	0	52	8	0	6	4	.600	0	0--	-	7.02	5.94
2000	FtWyn	R+	6	6	0	0	26.1	122	28	19	15	1	2	3	5	15	0	17	3	0	1	3	.250	0	0--	-	5.48	5.13
2001	FtWyn	A	1	1	0	0	6.0	28	8	4	4	0	0	0	0	2	0	1	0	0	0	1	.000	0	0--	-	4.83	6.00
2001	Lk Els	A+	19	12	0	1	74.0	318	82	46	44	7	5	2	3	25	0	39	5	2	5	4	.556	0	0--	-	4.67	5.35
2002	Mobile	AA	25	22	0	1	123.0	573	144	93	76	14	3	6	7	53	0	79	3	1	5	7	.417	0	0--	-	5.40	5.56
2002	Mobile	AA	1	1	0	0	5.0	19	5	2	2	1	0	0	0	0	0	0	0	0	1	0	1.000	0	0--	-	3.24	3.60
2003	Lk Els	A+	28	22	0	1	136.1	590	163	78	67	8	4	6	2	31	0	75	7	0	10	11	.476	0	0--	-	4.27	4.42
2004	Mobile	AA	35	18	0	4	121.1	498	128	50	46	13	14	3	8	31	2	69	2	0	10	2	.833	0	0--	-	4.30	3.41
2005	Mobile	AA	18	18	2	0	114.2	487	116	50	41	6	6	2	5	27	0	68	5	0	6	6	.500	1	0--	-	3.31	3.22
2005	Portlnd	AAA	9	9	0	0	60.0	240	58	22	21	6	2	0	0	13	0	25	1	0	4	2	.667	0	0--	-	3.29	3.15
2006	Portlnd	AAA	13	13	0	0	69.1	288	69	30	29	4	0	2	4	20	1	41	1	0	6	1	.857	0	0--	-	3.62	3.76
2006	SD	NL	19	16	0	2	92.0	405	103	56	51	13	5	2	7	30	4	35	1	0	4	5	.444	0	0-0	0	5.03	4.99

John Thomson

Pitches: R **Bats:** R **Pos:** SP-15; RP-3   **Ht:** 6'3" **Wt:** 220 **Born:** 10/1/1973 **Age:** 33

Year	Team	Lg	G	GS	CG	GF	IP	BFP	H	R	ER	HR	SH	SF	HB	TBB	IBB	SO	WP	Bk	W	L	Pct	ShO	Sv-Op	Hld	ERC	ERA
2006	Rome*	A	1	1	0	0	1.2	6	3	2	2	0	0	0	0	0	0	0	0	0	0	1	.000	0	0--	-	8.49	10.80
2006	Missi*	AA	1	1	0	0	1.0	6	2	1	1	0	0	0	0	1	0	1	0	0	0	0	-	0	0--	-	12.01	9.00
1997	Col	NL	27	27	2	0	166.1	721	193	94	87	15	10	3	5	51	0	106	2	0	7	9	.438	1	0-0	0	4.74	4.71
1998	Col	NL	26	26	2	0	161.0	680	174	86	86	21	8	5	0	49	0	106	4	2	8	11	.421	0	0-0	0	4.45	4.81
1999	Col	NL	14	13	1	1	62.2	305	85	62	56	11	4	2	1	36	1	34	2	0	1	10	.091	0	0-0	0	7.60	8.04
2001	Col	NL	14	14	1	0	93.2	386	84	46	42	15	3	3	4	25	3	68	1	0	4	5	.444	1	0-0	0	3.52	4.04
2002	2 Tms	NL	30	30	0	0	181.2	800	201	116	95	28	13	10	2	44	9	107	2	0	9	14	.391	0	0-0	0	4.24	4.71
2003	Tex	AL	35	35	3	0	217.0	910	234	125	117	27	7	4	4	49	2	136	5	0	13	14	.481	1	0-0	0	4.10	4.85
2004	Atl	NL	33	33	0	0	198.1	834	210	93	82	20	11	4	6	52	5	133	3	0	14	8	.636	0	0-0	0	4.01	3.72
2005	Atl	NL	17	17	1	0	98.2	427	111	52	49	6	2	4	2	28	2	61	3	0	4	6	.400	0	0-0	0	4.09	4.47
2006	Atl	NL	18	15	0	1	80.1	361	93	55	43	11	5	7	2	32	4	46	1	0	2	7	.222	0	0-0	1	5.26	4.82
02	Col	NL	21	21	0	0	127.1	550	136	77	69	21	7	7	2	27	6	76	2	0	7	8	.467	0	0-0	0	4.02	4.88
02	NYM	NL	9	9	0	0	54.1	250	65	39	26	7	6	3	0	17	3	31	0	0	2	6	.250	0	0-0	0	4.74	4.31
9 ML YEARS			214	210	10	2	1259.2	5424	1385	729	657	154	58	45	26	366	26	797	23	2	62	84	.425	3	0-0	1	4.42	4.69

Scott Thorman

Bats: L **Throws:** R **Pos:** LF-21; PH-19; 1B-18   **Ht:** 6'3" **Wt:** 235 **Born:** 1/6/1982 **Age:** 25

Year	Team	Lg	G	AB	H	2B	3B	HR	(Hm	Rd)	TB	R	RBI	RC	TBB	IBB	SO	HBP	SH	SF	SB	CS	SB%	GDP	Avg	OBP	Slg
2000	Braves	R	29	97	22	7	1	1	(-	-)	34	15	19	12	12	0	23	4	0	2	0	1	.00	1	.227	.330	.351
2002	Macon	A	127	470	138	38	3	16	(-	-)	230	57	82	86	51	5	83	7	0	6	2	2	.50	16	.294	.367	.489
2003	MrtlBh	A	124	445	108	26	2	12	(-	-)	174	44	56	57	42	6	79	4	0	4	0	0	-	13	.243	.311	.391
2004	MrtlBh	A	43	154	46	11	1	4	(-	-)	71	20	29	27	12	2	19	5	0	5	1	0	1.00	4	.299	.358	.461
2004	Grnville	AA	94	345	87	14	3	11	(-	-)	140	31	51	48	39	1	73	0	0	3	5	3	.63	3	.252	.326	.406
2005	Missi	AA	90	348	106	21	2	15	(-	-)	176	49	65	63	28	5	76	4	0	3	2	2	.50	3	.305	.360	.506
2005	Rchmd	AAA	52	210	58	10	3	6	(-	-)	92	23	27	29	9	0	42	3	0	2	0	0	-	3	.276	.313	.438
2006	Rchmd	AAA	81	309	92	16	2	15	(-	-)	157	38	48	57	31	6	48	1	0	3	4	2	.67	6	.298	.360	.508
2006	Atl	NL	55	128	30	11	0	5	(3	2)	56	13	14	14	5	0	21	0	0	0	1	0	1.00	0	.234	.263	.438

Matt Thornton

Pitches: L **Bats:** L **Pos:** RP-63   **Ht:** 6'6" **Wt:** 235 **Born:** 9/15/1976 **Age:** 30

Year	Team	Lg	G	GS	CG	GF	IP	BFP	H	R	ER	HR	SH	SF	HB	TBB	IBB	SO	WP	Bk	W	L	Pct	ShO	Sv-Op	Hld	ERC	ERA
2004	Sea	AL	19	1	0	8	32.2	148	30	15	15	2	2	1	0	25	1	30	2	0	1	2	.333	0	0-0	0	4.75	4.13
2005	Sea	AL	55	0	0	15	57.0	262	54	33	33	13	1	1	0	42	2	57	7	0	0	4	.000	0	0-1	5	6.06	5.21
2006	CWS	AL	63	0	0	20	54.0	227	46	20	20	5	1	3	1	21	4	49	1	0	5	3	.625	0	2-5	18	3.12	3.33
3 ML YEARS			137	1	0	43	143.2	637	130	68	68	20	4	5	1	88	7	136	10	0	6	9	.400	0	2-6	23	4.61	4.26

Joe Thurston

Bats: L **Throws:** R **Pos:** PH-10; 2B-4; PR-4; LF-2; RF-1   **Ht:** 5'11" **Wt:** 190 **Born:** 9/29/1979 **Age:** 27

Year	Team	Lg	G	AB	H	2B	3B	HR	(Hm	Rd)	TB	R	RBI	RC	TBB	IBB	SO	HBP	SH	SF	SB	CS	SB%	GDP	Avg	OBP	Slg
2006	S-WB*	AAA	127	479	135	29	9	9	(-	-)	209	74	55	76	43	2	65	7	14	1	20	10	.67	3	.282	.349	.436
2002	LAD	NL	8	13	6	1	0	0	(0	0)	7	1	1	3	0	0	1	0	1	0	0	0	-	0	.462	.429	.538
2003	LAD	NL	12	10	2	0	0	0	(0	0)	2	2	0	0	1	0	1	0	0	0	0	0	-	0	.200	.273	.200
2004	LAD	NL	17	17	3	1	1	0	(0	0)	6	1	1	1	0	0	5	0	0	1	0	0	-	0	.176	.167	.353
2006	Phi	NL	18	18	4	1	0	0	(0	0)	5	3	0	1	1	0	2	1	0	0	0	0	-	0	.222	.300	.278
4 ML YEARS			55	58	15	3	1	0	(0	0)	20	7	2	5	2	0	9	1	1	2	0	0	-	0	.259	.286	.345

Terry Tiffee

Bats: B Throws: R Pos: PH-9; 3B-6; DH-5; 1B-3   Ht: 6'3" Wt: 215 Born: 4/21/1979 Age: 28

Year	Team	Lg	G	AB	H	2B	3B	HR	(Hm	Rd)	TB	R	RBI	RC	TBB	IBB	SO	HBP	SH	SF	SB	CS	SB%	GDP	Avg	OBP	Slg
2006	Roch*	AAA	79	308	84	20	0	4	(-	-)	116	37	38	38	20	1	50	0	0	3	1	0	1.00	7	.273	.314	.377
2004	Min	AL	17	44	12	4	0	2	(1	1)	22	7	8	5	3	0	3	1	0	0	0	0	-	2	.273	.333	.500
2005	Min	AL	54	150	31	8	1	1	(1	0)	44	9	15	8	8	1	15	0	0	1	1	0	1.00	10	.207	.245	.293
2006	Min	AL	20	45	11	1	0	2	(1	1)	18	4	6	5	4	1	8	0	0	0	0	1	.00	2	.244	.306	.400
	3 ML YEARS		91	239	54	13	1	5	(3	2)	84	20	29	18	15	2	26	1	0	1	1	1	.50	14	.226	.273	.351

Mike Timlin

Pitches: R Bats: R Pos: RP-68   Ht: 6'4" Wt: 210 Born: 3/10/1966 Age: 41

Year	Team	Lg	G	GS	CG	GF	IP	BFP	H	R	ER	HR	SH	SF	HB	TBB	IBB	SO	WP	Bk	W	L	Pct	ShO	Sv-Op	Hld	ERC	ERA
1991	Tor	AL	63	3	0	17	108.1	463	94	43	38	6	6	2	1	50	11	85	5	0	11	6	.647	0	3-8	9	3.14	3.16
1992	Tor	AL	26	0	0	14	43.2	190	45	23	20	0	2	1	1	20	5	35	0	0	0	2	.000	0	1-1	1	3.68	4.12
1993	Tor	AL	54	0	0	27	55.2	254	63	32	29	7	1	3	1	27	3	49	1	0	4	2	.667	0	1-4	5	5.32	4.69
1994	Tor	AL	34	0	0	16	40.0	179	41	25	23	5	0	0	2	20	0	38	3	0	1	0	.000	0	2-4	5	5.01	5.18
1995	Tor	AL	31	0	0	19	42.0	179	38	13	10	1	3	0	2	17	5	36	3	1	4	3	.571	0	5-9	4	3.04	2.14
1996	Tor	AL	59	0	0	56	56.2	230	47	25	23	4	2	3	2	18	4	52	3	0	1	6	.143	0	31-38	2	2.74	3.65
1997	2 Tms	AL	64	0	0	31	72.2	297	69	30	26	8	6	1	1	20	5	45	1	1	6	4	.600	0	10-18	9	3.40	3.22
1998	Sea	AL	70	0	0	40	79.1	321	78	26	26	5	4	2	3	16	2	60	0	0	3	3	.500	0	19-24	6	3.17	2.95
1999	Bal	AL	62	0	0	52	63.0	261	51	30	25	9	1	1	5	23	3	50	1	0	3	9	.250	0	27-36	0	3.46	3.57
2000	2 Tms	AL	62	0	0	40	64.2	295	67	33	30	8	7	2	4	35	6	52	0	0	5	5	.556	0	12-18	6	5.08	4.18
2001	StL	NL	67	0	0	19	72.2	302	78	35	33	6	1	2	3	19	4	47	3	1	4	5	.444	0	3-7	12	3.95	4.09
2002	2 Tms	NL	72	1	0	17	96.2	376	75	35	32	15	2	1	5	14	2	50	3	0	4	6	.400	0	0-4	20	2.46	2.98
2003	Bos	AL	72	0	0	13	83.2	340	77	37	33	11	4	1	4	9	3	65	0	0	6	4	.600	0	2-6	17	2.81	3.55
2004	Bos	AL	76	0	0	12	76.1	320	75	35	35	8	3	1	5	19	3	56	1	0	5	4	.556	0	1-4	20	3.64	4.13
2005	Bos	AL	81	0	0	27	80.1	342	86	23	20	2	3	6	2	20	5	59	0	0	7	3	.700	0	13-20	24	3.35	2.24
2006	Bos	AL	68	0	0	22	64.0	279	78	33	31	7	4	1	2	16	4	30	3	0	6	6	.500	0	9-17	21	4.86	4.36
	97 Tor	AL	38	0	0	26	47.0	190	41	17	15	6	4	1	1	15	4	36	1	1	3	2	.600	0	9-13	2	3.30	2.87
	97 Sea	AL	26	0	0	5	25.2	107	28	13	11	2	2	0	0	5	1	9	0	0	3	2	.600	0	1-5	7	3.59	3.86
	00 Bal	AL	37	0	0	31	35.0	157	37	22	19	6	5	1	2	15	3	26	0	0	2	3	.400	0	11-15	1	5.08	4.89
	00 StL	NL	25	0	0	9	29.2	138	30	11	11	2	2	1	2	20	3	26	0	0	3	1	.750	0	1-3	5	5.05	3.34
	02 StL	NL	42	1	0	10	61.0	236	48	19	17	9	2	0	4	7	2	35	1	0	3	1	.250	0	0-2	12	2.41	2.51
	02 Phi	NL	30	0	0	7	35.2	140	27	16	15	6	0	1	1	7	0	15	2	0	1	3	.500	0	0-2	8	2.55	3.79
	16 ML YEARS		961	4	0	422	1099.2	4633	1062	478	434	102	49	27	43	343	65	809	30	3	69	68	.504	0	139-218	165	3.57	3.55

Brett Tomko

Pitches: R Bats: R Pos: RP-29; SP-15   Ht: 6'2" Wt: 225 Born: 4/7/1973 Age: 34

Year	Team	Lg	G	GS	CG	GF	IP	BFP	H	R	ER	HR	SH	SF	HB	TBB	IBB	SO	WP	Bk	W	L	Pct	ShO	Sv-Op	Hld	ERC	ERA
2006	LsVgs*	AAA	2	0	0	0	2.0	9	3	0	0	0	0	0	0	1	0	3	0	0	0	0	-	0	0- -	-	7.26	0.00
1997	Cin	NL	22	19	0	1	126.0	519	106	50	48	14	5	9	4	47	4	95	5	0	11	7	.611	0	0-0	0	3.31	3.43
1998	Cin	NL	34	34	1	0	210.2	887	198	111	104	22	12	2	7	64	3	162	9	1	13	12	.520	0	0-0	0	3.50	4.44
1999	Cin	NL	33	26	1	1	172.0	744	175	103	94	31	9	5	4	60	10	132	8	0	5	7	.417	0	0-0	1	4.51	4.92
2000	Sea	AL	32	8	0	10	92.1	401	92	53	48	12	5	5	3	40	4	59	1	1	7	5	.583	0	1-2	3	4.49	4.68
2001	Sea	AL	11	4	0	1	34.2	164	42	24	20	9	1	2	0	15	2	22	1	0	3	1	.750	0	0-1	0	6.31	5.19
2002	SD	NL	32	32	3	0	204.1	871	212	107	102	31	6	8	2	60	9	126	3	0	10	10	.500	0	0-0	0	4.18	4.49
2003	StL	NL	33	32	2	0	202.2	903	252	126	119	31	12	3	5	57	2	114	6	0	13	9	.591	0	0-0	0	5.63	5.28
2004	SF	NL	32	31	2	0	194.0	825	196	98	87	19	7	1	0	64	3	108	10	0	11	7	.611	1	0-0	0	3.82	4.04
2005	SF	NL	33	30	3	1	190.2	823	205	99	95	20	6	5	7	57	11	114	5	0	8	15	.348	0	1-1	1	4.18	4.48
2006	LAD	NL	44	15	0	2	112.1	491	123	67	59	17	7	7	2	29	0	76	3	1	8	7	.533	0	0-3	5	4.37	4.73
	10 ML YEARS		306	231	12	17	1539.2	6628	1601	838	776	210	70	47	34	493	48	1008	51	3	89	80	.527	1	2-7	10	4.26	4.54

Yorvit Torrealba

Bats: R Throws: R Pos: C-63; PH-3   Ht: 5'11" Wt: 200 Born: 7/19/1978 Age: 28

Year	Team	Lg	G	AB	H	2B	3B	HR	(Hm	Rd)	TB	R	RBI	RC	TBB	IBB	SO	HBP	SH	SF	SB	CS	SB%	GDP	Avg	OBP	Slg
2006	ColSpr*	AAA	10	36	6	2	0	0	(-	-)	8	0	2	1	4	0	9	0	0	0	0	0	-	3	.167	.250	.222
2001	SF	NL	3	4	2	0	1	0	(0	0)	4	0	2	2	0	0	0	0	0	0	0	0	-	0	.500	.500	1.000
2002	SF	NL	53	136	38	10	0	2	(0	2)	54	17	14	16	14	2	20	2	3	0	0	0	-	11	.279	.355	.397
2003	SF	NL	66	200	52	10	2	4	(3	1)	78	22	29	25	14	1	39	2	3	2	1	0	1.00	3	.260	.312	.390
2004	SF	NL	64	172	39	7	3	6	(3	3)	70	19	23	23	17	3	31	2	4	1	2	0	1.00	7	.227	.302	.407
2005	2 Tms	NL	76	201	47	12	0	3	(2	1)	68	32	15	14	16	1	50	2	5	0	1	0	1.00	8	.234	.297	.338
2006	Col	NL	65	223	55	16	3	7	(3	4)	98	23	43	30	11	1	49	4	2	1	4	3	.57	7	.247	.293	.439
	05 SF	NL	34	93	21	8	0	1	(1	0)	32	18	7	7	9	1	25	1	2	0	1	0	1.00	3	.226	.301	.344
	05 Sea	AL	42	108	26	4	0	2	(1	1)	36	14	8	7	7	0	25	1	3	0	0	0	-	5	.241	.293	.333
	6 ML YEARS		327	936	233	55	9	22	(11	11)	372	113	126	105	72	8	189	12	17	4	8	3	.73	36	.249	.310	.397

Salomon Torres

Pitches: R Bats: R Pos: RP-94   Ht: 5'11" Wt: 210 Born: 3/11/1972 Age: 35

Year	Team	Lg	G	GS	CG	GF	IP	BFP	H	R	ER	HR	SH	SF	HB	TBB	IBB	SO	WP	Bk	W	L	Pct	ShO	Sv-Op	Hld	ERC	ERA
1993	SF	NL	8	8	0	0	44.2	196	37	21	20	5	7	1	2	27	3	23	3	1	3	5	.375	0	0-0	0	3.95	4.03
1994	SF	NL	16	14	1	2	84.1	378	95	55	51	10	4	8	7	34	2	42	4	1	2	8	.200	0	0-0	0	5.29	5.44
1995	2 Tms		20	14	1	4	80.0	384	100	61	56	16	1	0	2	49	3	47	1	2	3	9	.250	0	0-0	0	7.30	6.30
1996	Sea	AL	10	7	1	1	49.0	212	44	27	25	5	3	1	3	23	2	36	1	0	3	3	.500	1	0-0	0	3.98	4.59

251

Year	Team	Lg	G	GS	CG	GF	IP	BFP	H	R	ER	HR	SH	SF	HB	TBB	IBB	SO	WP	Bk	W	L	Pct	ShO	Sv-Op	Hld	ERC	ERA
1997	2 Tms		14	0	0	4	25.2	127	32	29	28	2	3	1	3	15	0	11	3	0	0	0	-	0	0-0	0	6.44	9.82
2002	Pit	NL	5	5	0	0	30.0	127	28	10	9	2	2	0	3	13	1	12	0	0	2	1	.667	0	0-0	0	4.07	2.70
2003	Pit	NL	41	16	0	7	121.0	518	128	65	64	19	4	1	7	42	5	84	3	0	7	5	.583	0	2-3	6	4.88	4.76
2004	Pit	NL	84	0	0	20	92.0	380	87	33	27	6	9	3	6	22	6	62	5	0	7	7	.500	0	0-4	30	3.12	2.64
2005	Pit	NL	78	0	0	32	94.2	388	76	34	29	7	3	2	5	36	7	55	5	0	5	5	.500	0	3-3	8	2.91	2.76
2006	SF	NL	94	0	0	24	93.1	411	98	42	34	6	7	2	6	38	9	72	3	0	3	6	.333	0	12-15	20	4.23	3.28
95	SF		4	1	0	2	8.0	40	13	8	8	4	0	0	0	7	0	2	0	0	0	1	.000	0	0-0	0	15.31	9.00
95	Sea	AL	16	13	1	2	72.0	344	87	53	48	12	1	0	2	42	3	45	1	2	3	8	.273	0	0-0	0	6.55	6.00
97	Sea	AL	2	0	0	1	3.1	21	7	10	10	0	0	0	1	3	0	0	0	0	0	0	-	0	0-0	0	13.67	27.00
97	Mon	NL	12	0	0	3	22.1	106	25	19	18	2	3	1	2	12	0	11	3	0	0	0	-	0	0-0	0	5.47	7.25
10 ML YEARS			370	64	3	94	714.2	3121	725	377	343	78	43	19	43	299	38	444	28	4	35	49	.417	1	17-25	64	4.48	4.32

Josh Towers

Pitches: R **Bats:** R **Pos:** SP-12; RP-3   **Ht:** 6'1" **Wt:** 180 **Born:** 2/26/1977 **Age:** 30

Year	Team	Lg	G	GS	CG	GF	IP	BFP	H	R	ER	HR	SH	SF	HB	TBB	IBB	SO	WP	Bk	W	L	Pct	ShO	Sv-Op	Hld	ERC	ERA
2006	Syrcse*	AAA	15	15	0	0	101.1	426	121	53	45	12	1	4	6	11	1	76	2	0	5	5	.500	0	0--	-	4.43	4.00
2001	Bal	AL	24	20	1	2	140.1	586	165	74	70	21	3	4	6	16	0	58	1	0	8	10	.444	1	0-0	0	4.51	4.49
2002	Bal	AL	5	3	0	1	27.1	124	42	24	24	11	1	2	0	5	0	13	1	0	0	3	.000	0	0-0	0	9.00	7.90
2003	Tor	AL	14	8	1	2	64.1	265	67	34	32	15	0	2	4	7	1	42	1	0	8	1	.889	0	1-1	0	4.26	4.48
2004	Tor	AL	21	21	0	0	116.1	518	148	70	66	16	2	4	9	26	4	51	0	1	9	9	.500	0	0-0	0	5.50	5.11
2005	Tor	AL	33	33	2	0	208.2	876	237	101	86	24	3	7	6	29	2	112	1	1	13	12	.520	1	0-0	0	4.02	3.71
2006	Tor	AL	15	12	0	1	62.0	295	93	62	58	17	1	3	3	17	3	35	1	1	2	10	.167	0	0-0	0	8.05	8.42
6 ML YEARS			112	97	4	6	619.0	2664	752	365	336	104	10	22	28	100	10	311	5	3	40	45	.471	2	1-1	0	5.01	4.89

Billy Traber

Pitches: L **Bats:** L **Pos:** SP-8; RP-7   **Ht:** 6'5" **Wt:** 200 **Born:** 9/18/1979 **Age:** 27

Year	Team	Lg	G	GS	CG	GF	IP	BFP	H	R	ER	HR	SH	SF	HB	TBB	IBB	SO	WP	Bk	W	L	Pct	ShO	Sv-Op	Hld	ERC	ERA
2001	StLuci	A+	18	18	0	0	101.2	415	85	36	30	2	3	2	5	23	0	79	4	1	6	5	.545	0	0--	-	2.22	2.66
2001	Bnghtn	AA	8	8	0	0	42.2	188	50	25	21	4	1	3	2	13	1	45	4	1	4	3	.571	0	0--	-	4.80	4.43
2001	Norfolk	AAA	1	1	0	0	7.0	26	5	3	1	0	0	0	0	0	0	1	1	0	1	0	1.000	0	0--	-	1.04	1.29
2002	Akron	AA	18	17	2	0	107.2	436	99	38	33	8	1	0	7	20	0	82	2	0	13	2	.867	2	0--	-	2.95	2.76
2002	Buffalo	AAA	9	9	0	0	54.2	229	58	22	20	3	1	4	2	12	0	33	1	1	4	3	.571	0	0--	-	3.58	3.29
2005	Kinston	A+	4	4	0	0	21.2	86	19	12	12	2	1	1	0	6	0	13	1	1	2	2	.500	0	0--	-	3.00	4.98
2005	Akron	AA	5	5	0	0	34.0	133	25	11	10	2	0	0	1	5	0	27	0	0	3	2	.600	0	0--	-	1.67	2.65
2005	Buffalo	AAA	19	12	0	0	76.2	355	96	59	49	7	2	3	2	30	1	55	5	0	3	7	.300	0	0--	-	5.44	5.75
2006	NewOr	AAA	21	21	1	0	124.1	541	143	62	56	8	6	4	11	26	2	102	4	1	7	7	.500	0	0--	-	4.23	4.05
2003	Cle	AL	33	18	1	0	111.2	503	132	67	65	15	4	3	5	40	4	88	6	0	6	9	.400	1	0-0	1	5.31	5.24
2006	Was	NL	15	8	0	0	43.1	202	53	33	31	5	3	1	8	14	2	25	0	0	4	3	.571	0	0-0	2	5.81	6.44
2 ML YEARS			48	26	1	0	155.0	705	185	100	96	20	7	4	13	54	6	113	6	0	10	12	.455	1	0-0	3	5.45	5.57

Sean Tracey

Pitches: R **Bats:** L **Pos:** RP-7   **Ht:** 6'3" **Wt:** 210 **Born:** 11/14/1980 **Age:** 26

Year	Team	Lg	G	GS	CG	GF	IP	BFP	H	R	ER	HR	SH	SF	HB	TBB	IBB	SO	WP	Bk	W	L	Pct	ShO	Sv-Op	Hld	ERC	ERA
2002	Bristol	R+	13	12	0	0	65.2	261	57	27	22	4	1	0	4	19	0	50	1	0	5	2	.714	0	0--	-	3.07	3.02
2003	Knapol	A	14	9	0	0	41.2	231	51	54	44	4	5	2	11	46	0	28	16	1	2	7	.222	0	0--	-	9.40	9.50
2003	Gr Falls	R+	16	12	1	1	92.2	394	90	45	38	5	5	5	14	22	0	74	5	0	8	5	.615	0	0--	-	3.57	3.69
2004	WinSa	A+	27	27	0	0	148.1	616	108	60	45	5	11	5	23	69	0	130	12	1	9	8	.529	0	0--	-	3.07	2.73
2005	Brham	AA	28	28	2	0	163.2	695	154	80	74	13	3	5	14	76	1	106	12	0	14	6	.700	0	0--	-	4.34	4.07
2006	Charltt	AAA	29	20	1	3	129.2	572	111	67	62	17	6	5	19	76	1	102	20	2	8	9	.471	1	0--	-	4.89	4.30
2006	CWS	AL	7	0	0	5	8.0	34	4	3	3	2	0	0	1	5	0	3	4	0	0	0	-	0	0-0	0	3.65	3.38

Steve Trachsel

Pitches: R **Bats:** R **Pos:** SP-30   **Ht:** 6'4" **Wt:** 205 **Born:** 10/31/1970 **Age:** 36

Year	Team	Lg	G	GS	CG	GF	IP	BFP	H	R	ER	HR	SH	SF	HB	TBB	IBB	SO	WP	Bk	W	L	Pct	ShO	Sv-Op	Hld	ERC	ERA
1993	ChC	NL	3	3	0	0	19.2	78	16	10	10	4	1	1	0	3	0	14	1	0	0	2	.000	0	0-0	0	2.71	4.58
1994	ChC	NL	22	22	1	0	146.0	612	133	57	52	19	3	3	3	54	4	108	6	0	9	7	.563	0	0-0	0	3.74	3.21
1995	ChC	NL	30	29	2	0	160.2	722	174	104	92	25	12	5	0	76	8	117	2	1	7	13	.350	0	0-0	0	5.13	5.15
1996	ChC	NL	31	31	3	0	205.0	845	181	82	69	30	3	3	8	62	3	132	5	2	13	9	.591	2	0-0	0	3.52	3.03
1997	ChC	NL	34	34	4	0	201.1	878	225	110	101	32	8	11	5	69	6	160	4	1	8	12	.400	0	0-0	0	5.04	4.51
1998	ChC	NL	33	33	1	0	208.0	894	204	107	103	27	9	7	8	84	5	149	3	2	15	8	.652	0	0-0	0	4.35	4.46
1999	ChC	NL	34	34	4	0	205.2	894	226	133	127	32	6	**14**	3	64	4	149	8	3	8	18	.308	1	0-0	0	4.69	5.56
2000	2 Tms	NL	34	34	3	0	200.2	882	232	116	107	26	6	6	6	74	2	110	4	0	8	15	.348	1	0-0	0	5.25	4.80
2001	NYM	NL	28	28	1	0	173.2	726	168	90	86	28	8	7	3	47	7	144	4	0	11	13	.458	1	0-0	0	3.80	4.46
2002	NYM	NL	30	30	1	0	173.2	741	170	80	65	16	6	6	6	69	4	105	4	0	11	11	.500	0	0-0	0	3.88	3.37
2003	NYM	NL	33	33	2	0	204.2	857	204	90	86	26	8	8	3	65	9	111	5	2	16	10	.615	2	0-0	0	3.97	3.78
2004	NYM	NL	33	33	0	0	202.2	881	203	104	90	25	11	8	6	83	9	117	4	2	12	13	.480	0	0-0	0	4.31	4.00
2005	NYM	NL	6	6	0	0	37.0	157	37	20	17	6	2	2	1	12	0	24	1	0	1	4	.200	0	0-0	0	4.34	4.14
2006	NYM	NL	30	30	1	0	164.2	736	185	94	91	23	4	7	4	78	1	79	4	0	15	8	.652	0	0-0	0	5.55	4.97
00	TB	AL	23	23	3	0	137.2	606	160	76	70	16	2	5	6	49	1	78	3	0	6	10	.375	1	0-0	0	5.19	5.24
00	Tor	AL	11	11	0	0	63.0	276	72	40	37	10	4	1	0	25	1	32	1	0	2	5	.286	0	0-0	0	5.38	5.29
14 ML YEARS			381	380	19	0	2303.1	9903	2358	1197	1096	319	90	85	49	840	62	1519	55	13	134	143	.484	7	0-0	0	4.41	4.28

Chad Tracy

Bats: L **Throws:** R **Pos:** 3B-147; 1B-6; PH-6; DH-2 **Ht:** 6'2" **Wt:** 200 **Born:** 5/22/1980 **Age:** 27

Year	Team	Lg	G	AB	H	2B	3B	HR	(Hm	Rd)	TB	R	RBI	RC	TBB	IBB	SO	HBP	SH	SF	SB	CS	SB%	GDP	Avg	OBP	Slg
2004	Ari	NL	143	481	137	29	3	8	(6	2)	196	45	53	63	45	3	60	0	1	5	2	3	.40	11	.285	.343	.407
2005	Ari	NL	145	503	155	34	4	27	(9	18)	278	73	72	82	35	4	78	8	1	6	3	1	.75	10	.308	.359	.553
2006	Ari	NL	154	597	168	41	0	20	(14	6)	269	91	80	85	54	5	129	5	1	5	5	1	.83	11	.281	.343	.451
3 ML YEARS			442	1581	460	104	7	55	(29	26)	743	209	205	230	134	12	267	13	3	16	10	5	.67	32	.291	.348	.470

Matt Treanor

Bats: R **Throws:** R **Pos:** C-61; PH-9; PR-1 **Ht:** 6'0" **Wt:** 205 **Born:** 3/3/1976 **Age:** 31

Year	Team	Lg	G	AB	H	2B	3B	HR	(Hm	Rd)	TB	R	RBI	RC	TBB	IBB	SO	HBP	SH	SF	SB	CS	SB%	GDP	Avg	OBP	Slg
2004	Fla	NL	29	55	13	2	0	0	(0	0)	15	7	1	4	4	0	13	2	0	0	0	0	-	3	.236	.311	.273
2005	Fla	NL	58	134	27	8	0	0	(0	0)	35	10	13	13	16	1	28	3	1	0	0	0	-	5	.201	.301	.261
2006	Fla	NL	67	157	36	6	1	2	(0	2)	50	12	14	16	19	4	34	5	2	2	0	1	.00	4	.229	.328	.318
3 ML YEARS			154	346	76	16	1	2	(0	2)	100	29	28	33	39	5	75	10	3	2	0	1	.00	12	.220	.315	.289

Chin-hui Tsao

Pitches: R **Bats:** R **Pos:** P **Ht:** 6'2" **Wt:** 190 **Born:** 6/2/1981 **Age:** 26

Year	Team	Lg	G	GS	CG	GF	IP	BFP	H	R	ER	HR	SH	SF	HB	TBB	IBB	SO	WP	Bk	W	L	Pct	ShO	Sv-Op	Hld	ERC	ERA
2003	Col	NL	9	8	0	1	43.1	196	48	30	29	11	3	0	4	20	1	29	0	0	3	3	.500	0	0-0	0	6.56	6.02
2004	Col	NL	10	0	0	5	9.1	37	7	4	4	2	1	0	0	1	0	11	0	0	0	0	-	0	1-2	1	2.21	3.86
2005	Col	NL	10	0	0	9	11.0	56	16	8	8	3	1	1	1	5	1	4	1	0	1	0	1.000	0	3-4	0	8.44	6.55
3 ML YEARS			29	8	0	15	63.2	289	71	42	41	16	5	1	5	26	2	44	1	0	4	3	.571	0	4-6	1	6.16	5.80

Michael Tucker

Bats: L **Throws:** R **Pos:** PH-17; LF-16; RF-2; 1B-1 **Ht:** 6'2" **Wt:** 210 **Born:** 6/25/1971 **Age:** 36

Year	Team	Lg	G	AB	H	2B	3B	HR	(Hm	Rd)	TB	R	RBI	RC	TBB	IBB	SO	HBP	SH	SF	SB	CS	SB%	GDP	Avg	OBP	Slg
2006	Norfolk*	AAA	83	275	73	18	2	6	(-	-)	113	44	33	48	49	0	45	5	0	4	10	3	.77	5	.265	.381	.411
1995	KC	AL	62	177	46	10	4	4	(1	3)	68	23	17	22	18	2	51	1	2	0	2	3	.40	3	.260	.332	.384
1996	KC	AL	108	339	88	18	4	12	(2	10)	150	55	53	53	40	1	69	7	3	4	10	4	.71	7	.260	.346	.442
1997	Atl	NL	138	499	141	25	7	14	(5	9)	222	80	56	76	44	0	116	6	4	1	12	7	.63	7	.283	.347	.445
1998	Atl	NL	130	414	101	27	3	13	(10	3)	173	54	46	58	49	10	112	3	1	2	8	3	.73	4	.244	.327	.418
1999	Cin	NL	133	296	75	8	5	11	(5	6)	126	55	44	44	37	3	81	3	0	4	11	4	.73	5	.253	.338	.426
2000	Cin	NL	148	270	72	13	4	15	(7	8)	138	55	36	53	44	1	64	7	0	2	13	6	.68	6	.267	.381	.511
2001	2 Tms	NL	149	436	110	19	8	12	(4	8)	181	62	61	59	46	4	102	2	10	6	16	8	.67	8	.252	.322	.415
2002	KC	AL	144	475	118	27	6	12	(10	2)	193	65	56	64	56	1	105	3	7	2	23	9	.72	5	.248	.330	.406
2003	KC	AL	104	389	102	20	5	13	(8	5)	171	61	55	60	39	3	88	2	6	2	8	10	.44	8	.262	.331	.440
2004	SF	NL	140	464	119	21	6	13	(4	9)	191	77	62	68	70	3	106	2	6	5	5	2	.71	5	.256	.353	.412
2005	2 Tms	NL	126	268	64	16	1	5	(1	4)	97	35	36	36	31	3	52	2	2	4	4	0	1.00	7	.239	.318	.362
2006	NYM	NL	35	56	11	4	0	1	(0	1)	18	3	6	8	16	0	14	1	0	1	2	0	1.00	2	.196	.378	.321
01	Cin	NL	86	231	56	10	1	7	(1	6)	89	31	30	28	23	1	55	1	5	5	12	5	.71	4	.242	.308	.385
01	ChC	NL	63	205	54	9	7	5	(3	2)	92	31	31	31	23	3	47	1	5	1	4	3	.57	4	.263	.339	.449
05	SF	NL	104	250	60	16	1	5	(1	4)	93	32	33	33	28	3	48	2	2	4	4	0	1.00	6	.240	.317	.372
05	Phi	NL	22	18	4	0	0	0	(0	0)	4	3	3	3	3	0	4	0	0	0	0	0	-	1	.222	.333	.222
12 ML YEARS			1417	4083	1047	208	49	125	(57	68)	1728	625	528	601	490	31	960	39	41	33	114	56	.67	67	.256	.339	.423

Troy Tulowitzki

Bats: R **Throws:** R **Pos:** SS-25; PH-1 **Ht:** 6'3" **Wt:** 205 **Born:** 10/10/1984 **Age:** 22

Year	Team	Lg	G	AB	H	2B	3B	HR	(Hm	Rd)	TB	R	RBI	RC	TBB	IBB	SO	HBP	SH	SF	SB	CS	SB%	GDP	Avg	OBP	Slg
2005	Mdest	A+	22	94	25	6	0	4	(-	-)	43	17	14	15	9	0	18	2	0	0	1	0	1.00	2	.266	.343	.457
2006	Tulsa	AA	104	423	123	34	2	13	(-	-)	200	75	61	76	46	3	71	10	1	5	6	5	.55	8	.291	.370	.473
2006	Col	NL	25	96	23	2	0	1	(0	1)	28	15	6	10	10	3	25	1	1	0	3	0	1.00	1	.240	.318	.292

Derrick Turnbow

Pitches: R **Bats:** R **Pos:** RP-64 **Ht:** 6'3" **Wt:** 210 **Born:** 1/25/1978 **Age:** 29

Year	Team	Lg	G	GS	CG	GF	IP	BFP	H	R	ER	HR	SH	SF	HB	TBB	IBB	SO	WP	Bk	W	L	Pct	ShO	Sv-Op	Hld	ERC	ERA
2000	LAA	AL	24	1	0	16	38.0	181	36	21	20	7	0	0	2	36	0	25	3	1	0	0	-	0	0-0	0	7.05	4.74
2003	LAA	AL	11	0	0	7	15.1	53	7	1	1	0	0	0	0	3	0	15	0	0	2	0	1.000	0	0-0	0	0.79	0.59
2004	LAA	AL	4	0	0	4	6.1	26	2	0	0	0	0	0	0	7	0	3	0	0	0	0	-	0	0-0	0	2.47	0.00
2005	Mil	NL	69	0	0	62	67.1	271	49	15	13	5	0	1	1	24	2	64	9	0	7	1	.875	0	39-43	2	2.35	1.74
2006	Mil	NL	64	0	0	49	56.1	266	56	51	43	8	2	1	4	39	2	69	6	1	4	9	.308	0	24-32	4	5.69	6.87
5 ML YEARS			172	1	0	138	183.1	797	150	88	77	20	2	1	7	109	4	176	18	2	13	10	.565	0	63-75	6	4.01	3.78

Jason Tyner

Bats: L Throws: L Pos: LF-33; CF-18; DH-12; RF-1; PH-1; PR-1   Ht: 6'1" Wt: 175 Born: 4/23/1977 Age: 30

Year Team	Lg	G	AB	H	2B	3B	HR	(Hm Rd)	TB	R	RBI	RC	TBB	IBB	SO	HBP	SH	SF	SB	CS	SB%	GDP	Avg	OBP	Slg
2006 Roch*	AAA	80	316	104	14	5	0	(- -)	128	52	22	51	25	2	39	3	4	4	8	2	.80	2	.329	.379	.405
2000 2 Tms		50	124	28	4	0	0	(0 0)	32	9	13	9	5	0	16	2	8	3	7	2	.78	2	.226	.261	.258
2001 TB	AL	105	396	111	8	5	0	(0 0)	129	51	21	43	15	0	42	3	5	1	31	6	.84	6	.280	.311	.326
2002 TB	AL	44	168	36	2	1	0	(0 0)	40	17	9	8	7	0	19	1	3	1	7	1	.88	1	.214	.249	.238
2003 TB	AL	46	90	25	7	0	0	(0 0)	32	12	6	12	10	0	12	0	2	0	2	1	.67	1	.278	.350	.356
2005 Min	AL	18	56	18	1	1	0	(0 0)	21	8	5	8	4	0	4	0	0	0	2	0	1.00	1	.321	.367	.375
2006 Min	AL	62	218	68	5	2	0	(0 0)	77	29	18	30	11	2	18	1	0	2	4	2	.67	5	.312	.345	.353
00 NYM	NL	13	41	8	2	0	0	(0 0)	10	3	5	2	1	0	4	1	3	2	1	1	.50	1	.195	.222	.244
00 TB	AL	37	83	20	2	0	0	(0 0)	22	6	8	7	4	0	12	1	5	1	6	1	.86	1	.241	.281	.265
6 ML YEARS		325	1052	286	27	9	0	(0 0)	331	126	72	110	52	2	111	7	18	7	53	12	.82	17	.272	.309	.315

Dan Uggla

Bats: R Throws: R Pos: 2B-151; PH-3; DH-1   Ht: 5'11" Wt: 200 Born: 3/11/1980 Age: 27

Year Team	Lg	G	AB	H	2B	3B	HR	(Hm Rd)	TB	R	RBI	RC	TBB	IBB	SO	HBP	SH	SF	SB	CS	SB%	GDP	Avg	OBP	Slg
2001 Yakima	A-	72	278	77	21	0	5	(- -)	113	39	40	40	20	0	52	9	1	4	8	4	.67	9	.277	.341	.406
2002 Lancst	A	54	184	42	7	2	3	(- -)	62	21	16	20	21	0	51	2	2	2	3	2	.60	2	.228	.311	.337
2002 Sbend	A	53	171	34	5	1	2	(- -)	47	16	10	14	23	0	34	0	3	2	0	2	.00	2	.199	.291	.275
2003 Lancst	A+	134	534	155	31	7	23	(- -)	269	104	90	98	46	0	105	11	11	6	24	9	.73	7	.290	.355	.504
2004 ElPaso	AA	83	294	76	12	2	4	(- -)	104	29	30	31	15	0	55	4	2	2	10	7	.59	6	.259	.302	.354
2004 Lancst	A+	37	140	47	13	3	6	(- -)	84	29	38	33	17	1	21	4	1	0	2	4	.33	0	.336	.422	.600
2005 Tenn	AA	135	498	148	33	3	21	(- -)	250	88	87	96	52	5	103	14	3	2	15	8	.65	10	.297	.378	.502
2006 Fla	NL	154	611	172	26	7	27	(10 17)	293	105	90	97	48	1	123	9	7	8	6	6	.50	5	.282	.339	.480

B.J. Upton

Bats: R Throws: R Pos: 3B-50; PR-1   Ht: 6'3" Wt: 180 Born: 8/21/1984 Age: 22

Year Team	Lg	G	AB	H	2B	3B	HR	(Hm Rd)	TB	R	RBI	RC	TBB	IBB	SO	HBP	SH	SF	SB	CS	SB%	GDP	Avg	OBP	Slg
2003 CtnSC	A	101	384	116	22	6	7	(- -)	171	70	46	69	57	0	80	5	1	6	38	17	.69	8	.302	.394	.445
2003 Orlndo	AA	29	105	29	8	0	1	(- -)	40	14	16	15	16	0	25	2	2	2	2	4	.33	1	.276	.376	.381
2004 Mont	AA	29	104	34	7	1	2	(- -)	49	21	15	20	14	1	28	0	2	0	3	0	1.00	1	.327	.407	.471
2004 Drham	AAA	69	264	82	17	1	12	(- -)	137	65	36	54	42	0	72	3	4	0	17	5	.77	9	.311	.411	.519
2005 Drham	AAA	139	545	165	36	6	18	(- -)	267	98	74	111	78	1	127	4	1	3	44	13	.77	15	.303	.392	.490
2006 Drham	AAA	106	398	107	18	4	8	(- -)	157	72	41	67	65	0	89	4	0	3	46	17	.73	8	.269	.374	.394
2004 TB	AL	45	159	41	8	2	4	(2 2)	65	19	12	22	15	0	46	1	1	1	4	1	.80	1	.258	.324	.409
2006 TB	AL	50	175	43	5	0	1	(1 0)	51	20	10	17	13	0	40	1	0	0	11	3	.79	1	.246	.302	.291
2 ML YEARS		95	334	84	13	2	5	(3 2)	116	39	22	39	28	0	86	2	1	1	15	4	.79	2	.251	.312	.347

Juan Uribe

Bats: R Throws: R Pos: SS-132; PH-1; PR-1   Ht: 6'0" Wt: 220 Born: 3/22/1979 Age: 28

Year Team	Lg	G	AB	H	2B	3B	HR	(Hm Rd)	TB	R	RBI	RC	TBB	IBB	SO	HBP	SH	SF	SB	CS	SB%	GDP	Avg	OBP	Slg
2001 Col	NL	72	273	82	15	11	8	(3 5)	143	32	53	44	8	1	55	2	0	0	3	0	1.00	6	.300	.325	.524
2002 Col	NL	155	566	136	25	7	6	(4 2)	193	69	49	53	34	1	120	5	7	6	2	2	.82	17	.240	.286	.341
2003 Col	NL	87	316	80	19	3	10	(6 4)	135	45	33	45	17	0	60	3	6	1	7	2	.78	3	.253	.297	.427
2004 CWS	AL	134	502	142	31	6	23	(16 7)	254	82	74	81	32	1	96	3	11	5	9	11	.45	10	.283	.327	.506
2005 CWS	AL	146	481	121	23	3	16	(10 6)	198	58	71	59	34	0	77	4	11	10	4	6	.40	7	.252	.301	.412
2006 CWS	AL	132	463	109	28	2	21	(13 8)	204	53	71	52	13	1	82	3	9	7	1	1	.50	10	.235	.257	.441
6 ML YEARS		726	2601	670	141	32	84	(52 32)	1127	339	351	334	138	4	490	20	44	29	33	22	.60	53	.258	.297	.433

Chase Utley

Bats: L Throws: R Pos: 2B-156; 1B-2; DH-1; PH-1   Ht: 6'1" Wt: 185 Born: 12/17/1978 Age: 28

Year Team	Lg	G	AB	H	2B	3B	HR	(Hm Rd)	TB	R	RBI	RC	TBB	IBB	SO	HBP	SH	SF	SB	CS	SB%	GDP	Avg	OBP	Slg
2003 Phi	NL	43	134	32	10	1	2	(1 1)	50	13	21	19	11	0	22	6	0	1	2	0	1.00	3	.239	.322	.373
2004 Phi	NL	94	267	71	11	2	13	(8 5)	125	36	57	37	15	1	40	2	1	2	4	1	.80	5	.266	.308	.468
2005 Phi	NL	147	543	158	39	6	28	(12 16)	293	93	105	102	69	5	109	9	0	7	16	3	.84	10	.291	.376	.540
2006 Phi	NL	160	658	203	40	4	32	(16 16)	347	131	102	122	63	1	132	14	0	4	15	4	.79	9	.309	.379	.527
4 ML YEARS		444	1602	464	100	13	75	(37 38)	815	273	285	280	158	7	303	31	1	14	37	8	.82	27	.290	.362	.509

Javier Valentin

Bats: B Throws: R Pos: PH-55; C-46; 1B-2; DH-1   Ht: 5'10" Wt: 210 Born: 9/19/1975 Age: 31

Year Team	Lg	G	AB	H	2B	3B	HR	(Hm Rd)	TB	R	RBI	RC	TBB	IBB	SO	HBP	SH	SF	SB	CS	SB%	GDP	Avg	OBP	Slg
1997 Min	AL	4	7	2	0	0	0	(0 0)	2	1	0	1	0	0	3	0	0	0	0	0	-		.286	.286	.286
1998 Min	AL	55	162	32	7	1	3	(1 2)	50	11	18	10	11	1	30	0	3	1	0	0	-	7	.198	.247	.309
1999 Min	AL	78	218	54	12	1	5	(2 3)	83	22	28	27	22	0	39	1	1	5	0	0	-	2	.248	.313	.381
2002 Min	AL	4	4	2	0	0	0	(0 0)	2	0	0	0	0	0	0	0	0	0	0	0	-		.500	.500	.500
2003 TB	AL	49	135	30	7	1	3	(2 1)	48	13	15	11	5	0	31	1	0	1	0	0	-	7	.222	.254	.356
2004 Cin	NL	82	202	47	10	1	6	(2 4)	77	18	20	20	17	3	36	1	0	2	0	0	-	4	.233	.293	.381

Year	Team	Lg	G	AB	H	2B	3B	HR	(Hm	Rd)	TB	R	RBI	RC	TBB	IBB	SO	HBP	SH	SF	SB	CS	SB%	GDP	Avg	OBP	Slg
2005	Cin	NL	76	221	62	11	0	14	(7	7)	115	36	50	41	30	3	37	0	0	3	0	0	-	5	.281	.362	.520
2006	Cin	NL	92	186	50	6	1	8	(6	2)	82	24	27	17	13	3	29	0	0	2	0	0	-	5	.269	.313	.441
8 ML YEARS			440	1135	279	53	5	39	(20	19)	459	125	158	127	98	10	205	3	4	14	0	0	-	30	.246	.304	.404

Jose Valentin

Bats: L **Throws:** R **Pos:** 2B-94; PH-40; LF-6; RF-2; 1B-1; 3B-1   **Ht:** 5'10" **Wt:** 190 **Born:** 10/12/1969 **Age:** 37

									BATTING												BASERUNNING				AVERAGES		
Year	Team	Lg	G	AB	H	2B	3B	HR	(Hm	Rd)	TB	R	RBI	RC	TBB	IBB	SO	HBP	SH	SF	SB	CS	SB%	GDP	Avg	OBP	Slg
1992	Mil	AL	4	3	0	0	0	0	(0	0)	0	1	1	0	0	0	0	0	0	1	0	0	-	0	.000	.000	.000
1993	Mil	AL	19	53	13	1	2	1	(1	0)	21	10	7	8	7	1	16	1	2	0	1	0	1.00	1	.245	.344	.396
1994	Mil	AL	97	285	68	19	0	11	(8	3)	120	47	46	43	38	1	75	2	4	2	12	3	.80	1	.239	.330	.421
1995	Mil	AL	112	338	74	23	3	11	(3	8)	136	62	49	42	37	0	83	0	7	4	16	8	.67	0	.219	.293	.402
1996	Mil	AL	154	552	143	33	7	24	(10	14)	262	90	95	91	66	9	145	0	6	4	17	4	.81	4	.259	.336	.475
1997	Mil	AL	136	494	125	23	1	17	(4	13)	201	58	58	64	39	4	109	4	4	5	19	8	.70	5	.253	.310	.407
1998	Mil	NL	151	428	96	24	0	16	(7	9)	168	65	49	57	63	8	105	1	2	3	10	7	.59	2	.224	.323	.393
1999	Mil	NL	89	256	58	9	1	12	(3	7)	107	45	38	40	48	7	52	2	2	5	3	2	.60	3	.227	.347	.418
2000	CWS	AL	144	568	155	37	6	25	(16	9)	279	107	92	97	59	1	106	4	13	4	19	2	.90	11	.273	.343	.491
2001	CWS	AL	124	438	113	22	2	28	(14	14)	223	74	68	74	50	2	114	3	8	3	9	6	.60	7	.258	.336	.509
2002	CWS	AL	135	474	118	26	4	25	(15	10)	227	70	75	75	43	2	99	2	3	5	3	3	.50	9	.249	.311	.479
2003	CWS	AL	144	503	119	26	2	28	(14	14)	233	79	74	72	54	4	114	3	7	2	8	3	.73	6	.237	.313	.463
2004	CWS	AL	125	450	97	20	3	30	(16	14)	213	73	70	64	43	4	139	3	6	2	8	6	.57	5	.216	.287	.473
2005	LAD	NL	56	147	25	4	2	2	(0	2)	39	17	14	15	31	2	38	4	0	2	3	1	.75	2	.170	.326	.265
2006	NYM	NL	137	384	104	24	3	18	(11	7)	188	56	62	57	37	5	71	0	5	6	6	2	.75	5	.271	.330	.490
15 ML YEARS			1627	5373	1308	291	40	246	(122	124)	2417	854	798	799	615	50	1266	29	69	48	134	55	.71	61	.243	.322	.450

Jose Valverde

Pitches: R **Bats:** R **Pos:** RP-44   **Ht:** 6'4" **Wt:** 255 **Born:** 7/24/1979 **Age:** 27

			HOW MUCH HE PITCHED						WHAT HE GAVE UP											THE RESULTS						
Year	Team	Lg	G	GS	CG	GF	IP	BFP	H	R	ER	HR	SH	SF	HB	TBB	IBB	SO	WP	Bk	W	L	Pct	ShO	Sv-Op Hld	ERC	ERA
2006	Tucsn*	AAA	15	0	0	9	17.2	75	13	9	6	1	0	0	0	10	0	18	1	0	1	0	1.000	0	3- - -	2.96	3.06
2003	Ari	NL	54	0	0	33	50.1	204	24	16	12	4	0	1	2	26	2	71	2	0	2	1	.667	0	10-11 8	1.77	2.15
2004	Ari	NL	29	0	0	20	29.2	131	23	17	14	7	3	2	1	17	4	38	4	0	1	2	.333	0	8-10 5	4.25	4.25
2005	Ari	NL	61	0	0	34	66.1	268	51	19	18	5	3	1	2	20	1	75	3	0	3	4	.429	0	15-17 7	2.43	2.44
2006	Ari	NL	44	0	0	35	49.1	223	50	32	32	6	1	3	2	22	3	69	2	0	2	3	.400	0	18-22 1	4.42	5.84
4 ML YEARS			188	0	0	122	195.2	826	148	84	76	22	7	7	7	85	10	253	11	0	8	10	.444	0	51-60 21	2.98	3.50

John Van Benschoten

Pitches: R **Bats:** R **Pos:** P   **Ht:** 6'4" **Wt:** 215 **Born:** 4/14/1980 **Age:** 27

			HOW MUCH HE PITCHED						WHAT HE GAVE UP											THE RESULTS						
Year	Team	Lg	G	GS	CG	GF	IP	BFP	H	R	ER	HR	SH	SF	HB	TBB	IBB	SO	WP	Bk	W	L	Pct	ShO	Sv-Op Hld	ERC	ERA
2001	Wmspt	A-	9	9	0	0	25.2	104	23	11	10	0	0	0	1	10	0	19	5	0	0	2	.000	0	0- - -	3.09	3.51
2002	Hickory	A	27	27	0	0	148.0	620	119	57	46	6	4	2	7	62	1	145	7	0	11	4	.733	0	0- - -	2.86	2.80
2003	Lynbrg	A+	9	9	0	0	48.2	192	33	14	12	1	1	0	1	18	0	49	1	0	6	0	1.000	0	0- - -	1.94	2.22
2003	Altna	AA	17	17	1	0	90.1	399	95	46	37	5	4	1	6	34	1	78	2	2	7	6	.538	0	0- - -	4.16	3.69
2004	Nashv	AAA	23	23	0	0	131.2	574	135	75	69	16	2	3	9	49	1	101	4	1	4	11	.267	0	0- - -	4.54	4.72
2006	Pirates	R	1	1	-	0	6.0	21	1	3	3	1	-	-	0	2	-	4	1	0	0	1	.000	-	0- - -	0.75	4.50
2006	Altna	AA	1	1	0	0	5.0	21	3	2	2	0	0	1	0	3	0	3	1	0	1	0	1.000	0	0- - -	2.03	3.60
2006	Indy	AAA	3	3	0	0	11.2	51	10	7	7	2	0	1	0	7	0	13	0	0	1	1	.500	0	0- - -	4.58	5.40
2004	Pit	NL	6	5	0	0	28.2	135	33	27	22	3	2	2	2	19	0	18	1	0	1	3	.250	0	0-0 0	6.47	6.91

Jermaine Van Buren

Pitches: R **Bats:** R **Pos:** RP-10   **Ht:** 6'1" **Wt:** 220 **Born:** 7/2/1980 **Age:** 26

			HOW MUCH HE PITCHED						WHAT HE GAVE UP											THE RESULTS						
Year	Team	Lg	G	GS	CG	GF	IP	BFP	H	R	ER	HR	SH	SF	HB	TBB	IBB	SO	WP	Bk	W	L	Pct	ShO	Sv-Op Hld	ERC	ERA
1998	Rckies	R	12	11	1	0	65.0	259	42	20	16	2	0	0	3	22	0	92	3	2	7	2	.778	1	0- - -	1.80	2.22
1998	Portlnd	A-	2	2	0	0	10.0	44	7	4	4	0	0	2	1	7	0	9	1	1	0	0	-	0	0- - -	3.21	3.60
1999	Ashvlle	A	28	28	0	0	143.0	642	143	87	78	16	1	13	19	70	0	133	19	2	7	10	.412	0	0- - -	5.10	4.91
2000	Portlnd	A-	13	13	0	0	69.0	291	54	27	20	1	4	2	3	30	0	41	3	2	4	5	.444	0	0- - -	2.61	2.61
2001	Casper	R+	6	3	1	0	23.2	106	25	15	14	2	1	1	0	10	0	25	1	0	3	0	1.000	0	0- - -	4.26	5.32
2001	Tri-Cit	A-	1	1	0	0	5.0	25	7	4	4	0	0	0	0	3	0	2	0	0	1	0	1.000	0	0- - -	6.28	7.20
2002	Ashvlle	A	30	17	0	4	107.0	480	115	71	59	13	4	10	14	44	1	88	6	5	6	9	.400	0	0- - -	5.26	4.96
2004	Lansng	A	3	0	0	1	5.0	26	6	1	1	0	0	0	1	5	0	7	2	0	0	1	.000	0	0- - -	7.80	1.80
2004	WTenn	AA	51	0	0	46	53.0	206	23	11	11	2	0	0	1	24	0	64	4	0	3	2	.600	0	21- - -	1.32	1.87
2004	Iowa	AAA	3	0	0	2	4.1	16	3	1	1	1	0	0	0	0	0	5	0	0	0	0	-	0	1- - -	1.70	2.08
2005	Iowa	AAA	52	0	0	42	54.2	219	33	13	12	5	5	1	3	22	2	65	1	0	2	3	.400	0	25- - -	2.14	1.98
2006	Pwtckt	AAA	33	0	0	26	45.1	185	37	16	15	2	3	2	2	18	0	46	2	0	4	0	1.000	0	16- - -	2.95	2.98
2005	ChC	NL	6	0	0	1	6.0	27	2	2	2	0	1	0	0	9	2	3	0	0	0	2	.000	0	0-0 0	3.20	3.00
2006	Bos	AL	10	0	0	1	13.0	65	14	17	17	1	1	1	0	15	1	8	0	0	1	0	1.000	0	0-0 2	7.45	11.77
2 ML YEARS			16	0	0	1	19.0	92	16	19	19	1	2	1	0	24	3	11	0	0	1	2	.333	0	0-0 2	6.05	9.00

Claudio Vargas

Pitches: R Bats: R Pos: SP-30; RP-1 Ht: 6'3" Wt: 230 Born: 6/19/1978 Age: 29

				HOW MUCH HE PITCHED					WHAT HE GAVE UP									THE RESULTS						
Year	Team	Lg	G	GS	CG	GF	IP	BFP	H	R	ER	HR	SH	SF	HB	TBB	IBB	SO	WP	Bk	W	L	Pct	ShO	Sv-Op	Hld	ERC	ERA
2003	Mon	NL	23	20	0	0	114.0	492	111	59	55	16	5	4	7	41	5	62	2	0	6	8	.429	0	0-0	0	4.21	4.34
2004	Mon	NL	45	14	0	6	118.1	530	120	75	69	26	4	4	7	64	7	89	8	0	5	5	.500	0	0-0	3	5.84	5.25
2005	2 Tms	NL	25	23	0	0	132.1	586	146	81	77	25	6	1	7	47	5	95	6	0	9	9	.500	0	0-0	0	5.28	5.24
2006	Ari	NL	31	30	0	1	167.2	747	185	101	90	27	8	3	8	52	2	123	9	1	12	10	.545	0	0-0	0	4.81	4.83
	05 Was	NL	4	4	0	0	12.2	66	22	15	13	4	0	0	0	7	2	5	0	0	0	3	.000	0	0-0	0	11.04	9.24
	05 Ari	NL	21	19	0	0	119.2	520	124	66	64	21	6	1	7	40	3	90	6	0	9	6	.600	0	0-0	0	4.74	4.81
	4 ML YEARS		124	87	0	7	532.1	2355	562	316	291	94	23	12	29	204	19	369	25	1	32	32	.500	0	0-0	3	5.02	4.92

Jason Vargas

Pitches: L Bats: L Pos: RP-7; SP-5 Ht: 6'0" Wt: 215 Born: 2/2/1983 Age: 24

				HOW MUCH HE PITCHED					WHAT HE GAVE UP									THE RESULTS						
Year	Team	Lg	G	GS	CG	GF	IP	BFP	H	R	ER	HR	SH	SF	HB	TBB	IBB	SO	WP	Bk	W	L	Pct	ShO	Sv-Op	Hld	ERC	ERA
2004	Jmstwn	A-	8	8	0	0	41.1	168	35	17	9	2	0	0	3	13	0	41	3	0	3	1	.750	0	0- -	-	2.94	1.96
2004	Grnsbr	A	3	3	0	0	19.0	68	9	5	5	1	2	0	0	2	0	17	0	0	2	1	.667	0	0- -	-	0.78	2.37
2005	Grnsbr	A	5	5	0	0	33.2	127	16	4	3	1	1	0	2	10	0	33	1	0	4	1	.800	0	0- -	-	1.20	0.80
2005	Jupiter	A+	9	9	0	0	55.1	227	47	24	21	6	0	0	0	14	0	60	0	0	2	3	.400	0	0- -	-	2.72	3.42
2005	Carlina	AA	3	3	0	0	19.0	77	13	6	6	3	2	0	0	7	0	25	0	0	1	0	1.000	0	0- -	-	2.61	2.84
2006	Albq	AAA	13	13	0	0	69.0	321	98	60	57	11	4	2	5	28	3	51	0	1	3	6	.333	0	0- -	-	7.59	7.43
2005	Fla	NL	17	13	1	0	73.2	325	71	34	33	4	4	1	4	31	4	59	0	0	5	5	.500	0	0-0	0	3.68	4.03
2006	Fla	NL	12	5	0	3	43.0	213	50	39	35	9	4	4	4	30	3	25	2	0	1	2	.333	0	0-0	0	7.30	7.33
	2 ML YEARS		29	18	1	3	116.2	538	121	73	68	13	8	5	8	61	7	84	2	0	6	7	.462	0	0-0	0	4.93	5.25

Jason Varitek

Bats: B Throws: R Pos: C-99; PH-7 Ht: 6'2" Wt: 230 Born: 4/11/1972 Age: 35

								BATTING													BASERUNNING				AVERAGES		
Year	Team	Lg	G	AB	H	2B	3B	HR	(Hm	Rd)	TB	R	RBI	RC	TBB	IBB	SO	HBP	SH	SF	SB	CS	SB%	GDP	Avg	OBP	Slg
2006	Pwtckt*	AAA	2	7	3	0	0	1	(-	-)	6	2	1	2	0	0	3	0	0	0	0	0	-	0	.429	.429	.857
1997	Bos	AL	1	1	1	0	0	0	(0	0)	1	0	0	1	0	0	0	0	0	0	0	0	-	0	1.000	1.000	1.000
1998	Bos	AL	86	221	56	13	0	7	(1	6)	90	31	33	26	17	1	45	2	4	3	2	2	.50	8	.253	.309	.407
1999	Bos	AL	144	483	130	39	2	20	(12	8)	233	70	76	75	46	2	85	2	5	8	1	2	.33	13	.269	.330	.482
2000	Bos	AL	139	448	111	31	1	10	(2	8)	174	55	65	59	60	3	84	6	1	4	1	1	.50	16	.248	.342	.388
2001	Bos	AL	51	174	51	11	1	7	(2	5)	85	19	25	30	21	3	35	1	1	1	0	0	-	6	.293	.371	.489
2002	Bos	AL	132	467	124	27	1	10	(6	4)	183	58	61	52	41	3	95	7	1	3	4	3	.57	13	.266	.332	.392
2003	Bos	AL	142	451	123	31	1	25	(13	12)	231	63	85	79	51	8	106	7	5	7	3	2	.60	10	.273	.351	.512
2004	Bos	AL	137	463	137	30	1	18	(8	10)	223	67	73	79	62	9	126	10	0	1	10	3	.77	11	.296	.390	.482
2005	Bos	AL	133	470	132	30	1	22	(7	15)	230	70	70	78	62	3	117	3	1	3	2	0	1.00	10	.281	.366	.489
2006	Bos	AL	103	365	87	19	2	12	(2	10)	146	46	55	45	46	7	87	2	1	2	1	2	.33	10	.238	.325	.400
	10 ML YEARS		1068	3543	952	231	10	131	(53	78)	1596	479	543	524	406	39	780	40	19	32	24	15	.62	97	.269	.348	.450

Javier Vazquez

Pitches: R Bats: R Pos: SP-32; RP-1 Ht: 6'2" Wt: 215 Born: 7/25/1976 Age: 30

				HOW MUCH HE PITCHED					WHAT HE GAVE UP									THE RESULTS						
Year	Team	Lg	G	GS	CG	GF	IP	BFP	H	R	ER	HR	SH	SF	HB	TBB	IBB	SO	WP	Bk	W	L	Pct	ShO	Sv-Op	Hld	ERC	ERA
1998	Mon	NL	33	32	0	1	172.1	764	196	121	116	31	9	4	11	68	2	139	2	0	5	15	.250	0	0-0	0	5.79	6.06
1999	Mon	NL	26	26	3	0	154.2	667	154	98	86	20	3	3	4	52	4	113	2	0	9	8	.529	1	0-0	0	4.02	5.00
2000	Mon	NL	33	33	2	0	217.2	945	247	104	98	24	11	3	5	61	10	196	3	0	11	9	.550	1	0-0	0	4.45	4.05
2001	Mon	NL	32	32	5	0	223.2	898	197	92	85	24	9	2	3	44	4	208	3	1	16	11	.593	3	0-0	0	2.75	3.42
2002	Mon	NL	34	34	4	0	230.1	971	243	111	100	28	15	7	4	49	6	179	3	0	10	13	.435	0	0-0	0	3.80	3.91
2003	Mon	NL	34	34	4	0	230.2	938	198	93	83	28	6	6	4	57	5	241	11	1	13	12	.520	1	0-0	0	2.90	3.24
2004	NYY	AL	32	32	0	0	198.0	849	195	114	108	33	4	8	11	60	3	150	12	2	14	10	.583	0	0-0	0	4.23	4.91
2005	Ari	NL	33	33	3	0	215.2	904	223	112	106	35	13	3	5	46	4	192	7	0	11	15	.423	1	0-0	0	4.00	4.42
2006	CWS	AL	33	32	1	0	202.2	872	206	116	109	23	2	4	15	56	2	184	7	0	11	12	.478	0	0-0	0	4.02	4.84
	9 ML YEARS		290	288	20	1	1845.2	7808	1859	961	891	246	72	40	62	493	40	1602	50	4	100	105	.488	7	0-0	0	3.91	4.34

Ramon Vazquez

Bats: L Throws: R Pos: 3B-14; 2B-7; SS-7; PH-7; PR-4 Ht: 5'11" Wt: 170 Born: 8/21/1976 Age: 30

								BATTING													BASERUNNING				AVERAGES		
Year	Team	Lg	G	AB	H	2B	3B	HR	(Hm	Rd)	TB	R	RBI	RC	TBB	IBB	SO	HBP	SH	SF	SB	CS	SB%	GDP	Avg	OBP	Slg
2006	Buffalo*	AAA	28	99	24	2	1	2	(-	-)	34	19	11	15	22	1	27	0	1	1	2	1	.67	2	.242	.377	.343
2001	Sea	AL	17	35	8	0	0	0	(0	0)	8	5	4	2	0	0	3	0	1	1	0	0	-	0	.229	.222	.229
2002	SD	NL	128	423	116	21	5	2	(0	2)	153	50	32	55	45	3	79	1	3	2	7	2	.78	6	.274	.344	.362
2003	SD	NL	116	422	110	17	4	3	(1	2)	144	56	30	49	52	2	88	2	5	3	10	3	.77	4	.261	.342	.341
2004	SD	NL	52	115	27	3	2	1	(1	0)	37	12	13	9	11	2	24	0	4	2	1	1	.50	2	.235	.297	.322
2005	2 Tms	AL	39	85	18	5	0	0	(0	0)	23	7	5	5	9	0	17	0	2	0	0	0	-	0	.212	.256	.271
2006	Cle	AL	34	67	14	2	0	1	(1	0)	19	11	8	7	6	0	18	0	2	2	0	0	-	3	.209	.267	.284
	05 Bos	AL	27	61	12	2	0	0	(0	0)	14	6	4	3	3	0	14	0	2	0	0	0	-	0	.197	.234	.230
	05 Cle	AL	12	24	6	3	0	0	(0	0)	9	1	1	2	2	0	3	0	0	0	0	0	-	0	.250	.308	.375
	6 ML YEARS		386	1147	293	48	11	7	(3	4)	384	141	92	127	119	7	229	3	17	10	18	6	.75	15	.255	.324	.335

Mike Venafro

Pitches: L Bats: L Pos: RP-7   Ht: 5'10" Wt: 180 Born: 8/2/1973 Age: 33

Year	Team	Lg	G	GS	CG	GF	IP	BFP	H	R	ER	HR	SH	SF	HB	TBB	IBB	SO	WP	Bk	W	L	Pct	ShO	Sv-Op	Hld	ERC	ERA
2006	Lsvlle*	AAA	36	0	0	8	22.0	92	19	6	6	0	0	0	1	8	3	18	1	0	0	0	-	0	2- -	-	2.50	2.45
2006	ColSpr*	AAA	20	0	0	5	16.1	63	10	4	4	1	0	0	1	5	0	10	2	0	3	1	.750	0	0- -	-	1.82	2.20
1999	Tex	AL	65	0	0	11	68.1	283	63	29	25	4	5	2	3	22	0	37	0	0	3	2	.600	0	0-1	19	3.30	3.29
2000	Tex	AL	77	0	0	21	56.1	248	64	27	24	2	2	4	4	21	4	32	1	0	3	1	.750	0	1-2	17	4.49	3.83
2001	Tex	AL	70	0	0	20	60.0	266	54	35	32	2	2	4	7	28	4	29	3	0	5	5	.500	0	4-8	21	3.58	4.80
2002	Oak	AL	47	0	0	8	37.0	168	45	22	19	5	4	2	2	14	2	16	1	0	2	2	.500	0	0-0	15	5.65	4.62
2003	TB	AL	24	0	0	6	19.0	85	24	10	10	1	0	1	3	3	0	9	1	0	1	0	1.000	0	0-0	4	4.89	4.74
2004	LAD	NL	17	0	0	2	9.0	42	11	5	4	1	1	0	2	3	1	6	0	0	0	0	-	0	0-0	2	5.90	4.00
2006	Col	NL	7	0	0	0	3.2	15	3	1	1	0	0	0	0	3	0	2	0	0	1	0	1.000	0	0-0	0	4.38	2.45
	7 ML YEARS		307	0	0	68	253.1	1107	264	129	115	15	14	13	21	94	11	131	6	0	15	10	.600	0	5-11	78	4.18	4.09

Mike Vento

Bats: R Throws: R Pos: RF-8; PH-1; PR-1   Ht: 6'0" Wt: 195 Born: 5/25/1978 Age: 29

							BATTING														BASERUNNING				AVERAGES		
Year	Team	Lg	G	AB	H	2B	3B	HR	(Hm	Rd)	TB	R	RBI	RC	TBB	IBB	SO	HBP	SH	SF	SB	CS	SB%	GDP	Avg	OBP	Slg
1998	Oneont	A-	43	148	45	9	3	1	(-	-)	63	25	23	25	14	0	28	5	0	2	8	3	.73	1	.304	.379	.426
1999	Tampa	A+	70	255	66	10	1	7	(-	-)	99	37	28	31	17	1	69	3	0	2	2	3	.40	1	.259	.310	.388
1999	Grnsbr	A	40	148	37	11	1	3	(-	-)	59	20	16	20	14	1	46	2	0	1	3	1	.75	1	.250	.321	.399
2000	Tampa	A+	10	30	5	0	0	1	(-	-)	8	1	4	2	4	0	12	1	1	1	1	0	1.00	0	.167	.278	.267
2000	Grnsbr	A	84	318	83	15	2	6	(-	-)	120	49	52	49	47	0	66	11	2	3	13	8	.62	11	.261	.372	.377
2001	Tampa	A+	130	457	137	26	10	20	(-	-)	237	71	87	87	45	1	88	9	0	3	13	10	.57	9	.300	.372	.519
2002	Nrwich	AA	64	227	54	16	2	4	(-	-)	86	29	26	28	25	1	49	1	2	2	3	3	.50	6	.238	.314	.379
2003	Trntn	AA	81	314	95	19	3	9	(-	-)	147	46	56	52	22	1	52	5	0	4	4	4	.50	6	.303	.354	.468
2003	Clmbs	AAA	51	184	56	14	1	5	(-	-)	87	28	31	31	14	0	36	3	0	0	1	2	.33	6	.304	.363	.473
2004	Clmbs	AAA	122	451	124	28	1	15	(-	-)	199	64	72	68	34	3	77	9	0	7	2	3	.40	8	.275	.333	.441
2005	Clmbs	AAA	130	501	146	37	2	12	(-	-)	223	62	84	84	49	1	96	13	1	7	1	4	.20	13	.291	.365	.445
2006	NewOr	AAA	62	217	74	14	0	7	(-	-)	109	34	33	42	20	2	35	1	0	2	3	4	.43	5	.341	.396	.502
2006	Nats	R	6	20	5	0	0	1	(-	-)	8	3	4	3	4	0	1	0	0	0	0	0	-	0	.250	.375	.400
2005	NYY	AL	2	2	0	0	0	0	(0	0)	0	0	0	0	0	0	1	0	0	0	0	0	-	0	.000	.000	.000
2006	Was	NL	9	18	5	1	0	0	(0	0)	6	3	1	3	4	1	5	0	0	0	0	0	-	0	.278	.409	.333
	2 ML YEARS		11	20	5	1	0	0	(0	0)	6	3	1	3	4	1	6	0	0	0	0	0	-	0	.250	.375	.300

Jose Veras

Pitches: R Bats: R Pos: RP-12   Ht: 6'5" Wt: 230 Born: 10/20/1980 Age: 26

Year	Team	Lg	G	GS	CG	GF	IP	BFP	H	R	ER	HR	SH	SF	HB	TBB	IBB	SO	WP	Bk	W	L	Pct	ShO	Sv-Op	Hld	ERC	ERA
1998	DRays	R	5	4	0	0	16.0	79	19	14	12	1	0	0	1	12	0	19	1	0	1	1	.500	0	0- -	-	6.49	6.75
1999	Princtn	R	14	14	0	0	60.2	299	74	57	48	5	1	4	7	50	1	48	10	1	3	5	.375	0	0- -	-	7.64	7.12
2000	CtnSC	A	20	20	1	0	106.2	493	125	74	57	7	2	1	11	41	0	102	11	1	8	8	.500	0	0- -	-	5.07	4.81
2001	Bkrsfld	A+	27	27	0	0	153.0	658	163	104	77	13	5	4	20	55	0	138	14	2	9	8	.529	0	0- -	-	4.72	4.53
2002	HudVal	A	2	2	0	0	7.0	28	2	0	0	0	0	0	0	5	0	7	0	0	0	0	-	0	0- -	-	1.21	0.00
2002	Bkrsfld	A+	11	11	0	0	59.0	283	77	44	35	10	1	5	3	30	0	57	2	2	3	4	.429	0	0- -	-	7.08	5.34
2003	Orlndo	AA	27	22	1	1	131.0	551	108	59	50	11	3	3	6	53	0	118	8	1	6	9	.400	1	0- -	-	3.20	3.44
2003	Drham	AAA	3	0	0	0	5.1	27	9	5	5	2	0	0	1	1	0	3	1	0	0	0	-	0	0- -	-	10.48	8.44
2004	Drham	AAA	30	10	0	4	84.1	392	101	55	49	9	5	4	7	33	3	63	5	1	6	5	.545	0	0- -	-	5.41	5.23
2004	Mont	A	3	3	0	0	10.0	43	10	7	7	2	0	1	0	7	0	6	1	0	1	0	1.000	0	0- -	-	6.55	6.30
2005	Okla	AAA	57	0	0	47	61.2	284	63	27	26	4	2	2	2	33	3	72	5	2	3	5	.375	0	24- -	-	4.38	3.79
2006	Clmbs	AAA	50	0	0	35	59.2	220	49	17	16	3	4	2	1	19	2	68	1	0	5	3	.625	0	21- -	-	2.85	2.41
2006	NYY	AL	12	0	0	4	11.0	43	8	5	5	2	0	0	5	0	6	1	1	0	0	-	0	1-1	1	3.55	4.09

Justin Verlander

Pitches: R Bats: R Pos: SP-30   Ht: 6'5" Wt: 200 Born: 2/20/1983 Age: 24

Year	Team	Lg	G	GS	CG	GF	IP	BFP	H	R	ER	HR	SH	SF	HB	TBB	IBB	SO	WP	Bk	W	L	Pct	ShO	Sv-Op	Hld	ERC	ERA
2005	Lkland	A+	13	13	2	0	86.0	347	70	19	16	3	4	2	7	19	0	104	8	1	9	2	.818	0	0- -	-	2.34	1.67
2005	Erie	AA	7	7	0	0	32.2	116	11	1	1	1	1	0	1	7	0	32	0	1	2	0	1.000	0	0- -	-	0.65	0.28
2005	Det	AL	2	2	0	0	11.1	54	15	9	9	1	0	0	1	5	0	7	1	0	0	2	.000	0	0-0	0	6.41	7.15
2006	Det	AL	30	30	1	0	186.0	776	187	78	75	21	2	4	6	60	1	124	5	1	17	9	.654	1	0-0	0	4.12	3.63
	2 ML YEARS		32	32	1	0	197.1	830	202	87	84	22	2	4	7	65	1	131	6	1	17	11	.607	1	0-0	0	4.24	3.83

Shane Victorino

Bats: B Throws: R Pos: CF-67; LF-44; PH-41; RF-21; PR-8   Ht: 5'9" Wt: 180 Born: 11/30/1980 Age: 26

							BATTING														BASERUNNING				AVERAGES		
Year	Team	Lg	G	AB	H	2B	3B	HR	(Hm	Rd)	TB	R	RBI	RC	TBB	IBB	SO	HBP	SH	SF	SB	CS	SB%	GDP	Avg	OBP	Slg
2003	SD	NL	36	73	11	1	0	0	(0	0)	13	8	4	1	7	0	17	1	1	1	7	2	.78	5	.151	.232	.178
2005	Phi	NL	21	17	5	0	0	2	(1	1)	11	5	8	4	0	0	3	0	0	2	0	0	-	0	.294	.263	.647
2006	Phi	NL	153	415	119	19	8	6	(3	3)	172	70	46	58	24	0	54	14	8	1	4	3	.57	5	.287	.346	.414
	3 ML YEARS		210	505	135	21	8	8	(4	4)	196	83	58	63	31	0	74	15	9	4	11	5	.69	10	.267	.326	.388

Jose Vidro

Bats: B Throws: R Pos: 2B-107; PH-10; 1B-8; DH-2   Ht: 5'11" Wt: 195 Born: 8/27/1974 Age: 32

							BATTING													BASERUNNING				AVERAGES		
Year	Team	Lg	G	AB	H	2B	3B	HR	(Hm | Rd)	TB	R	RBI	RC	TBB	IBB	SO	HBP	SH	SF	SB	CS	SB%	GDP	Avg	OBP	Slg
2006	Ptomc*	A+	1	3	1	1	0	0	(- | -)	2	0	0	0	0	0	0	0	0	0	0	0	-	0	.333	.333	.667
2006	Hrsbrg*	AA	3	8	2	0	0	0	(- | -)	2	0	1	1	2	0	0	0	0	0	0	0	-	1	.250	.400	.250
1997	Mon	NL	67	169	42	12	1	2	(0 | 2)	62	19	17	19	11	0	20	2	0	3	1	0	1.00	1	.249	.297	.367
1998	Mon	NL	83	205	45	12	0	0	(0 | 0)	57	24	18	19	27	0	33	4	6	3	2	2	.50	5	.220	.318	.278
1999	Mon	NL	140	494	150	45	2	12	(5 | 7)	235	67	59	76	29	2	51	4	2	2	0	4	.00	12	.304	.346	.476
2000	Mon	NL	153	606	200	51	2	24	(11 | 13)	327	101	97	115	49	4	69	2	0	6	5	4	.56	17	.330	.379	.540
2001	Mon	NL	124	486	155	34	1	15	(6 | 9)	236	82	59	81	31	2	49	10	2	2	4	1	.80	18	.319	.371	.486
2002	Mon	NL	152	604	190	43	3	19	(11 | 8)	296	103	96	112	60	1	70	3	11	3	2	1	.67	12	.315	.378	.490
2003	Mon	NL	144	509	158	36	0	15	(7 | 8)	239	77	65	89	69	6	50	7	2	5	3	2	.60	16	.310	.397	.470
2004	Mon	NL	110	412	121	24	0	14	(6 | 8)	187	51	60	59	49	7	43	0	4	2	3	1	.75	14	.294	.367	.454
2005	Was	NL	87	309	85	21	2	7	(2 | 5)	131	38	32	41	31	3	30	1	2	4	0	0	-	8	.275	.339	.424
2006	Was	NL	126	463	134	26	1	7	(3 | 4)	183	52	47	60	41	3	48	3	0	4	1	0	1.00	16	.289	.348	.395
	10 ML YEARS		1186	4257	1280	304	12	115	(51 | 64)	1953	614	550	671	397	28	463	36	29	34	21	15	.58	119	.301	.363	.459

Carlos Villanueva

Pitches: R Bats: B Pos: SP-6; RP-4   Ht: 6'2" Wt: 190 Born: 11/28/1983 Age: 23

			HOW MUCH HE PITCHED						WHAT HE GAVE UP											THE RESULTS						
Year	Team	Lg	G	GS	CG	GF	IP	BFP	H	R	ER	HR	SH	SF	HB	TBB	IBB	SO	WP	Bk	W	L	Pct	ShO	Sv-Op	Hld	ERC	ERA
2002	Giants	R	19	0	0	9	30.1	113	24	3	2	1	0	0	1	2	0	23	0	0	4	0	1.000	0	3- -	-	1.64	0.59
2003	Giants	R	12	10	0	0	59.0	247	64	31	26	1	0	1	2	13	0	67	5	0	3	6	.333	0	0- -	-	3.46	3.97
2004	Beloit	A	25	21	1	2	114.2	482	102	67	48	20	4	6	9	30	1	113	5	2	8	8	.500	1	1- -	-	3.67	3.77
2005	BrvdCt	A+	21	21	0	0	112.1	447	78	31	29	11	0	2	3	32	0	124	8	4	8	1	.889	0	0- -	-	2.15	2.32
2005	Hntsvl	AA	4	4	0	0	20.2	94	21	18	17	3	1	1	1	9	0	14	1	0	1	3	.250	0	0- -	-	4.67	7.40
2006	Hntsvl	AA	11	10	1	0	62.1	259	60	31	26	6	1	0	1	14	0	59	6	0	4	5	.444	1	0- -	-	3.21	3.75
2006	Nashv	AAA	11	9	1	0	66.1	263	42	20	20	6	3	1	2	26	0	61	2	0	7	1	.875	0	0- -	-	2.23	2.71
2006	Mil	NL	10	6	0	2	53.2	215	43	22	22	8	1	0	4	11	1	39	0	0	2	2	.500	0	0-0	0	2.85	3.69

Oscar Villarreal

Pitches: R Bats: L Pos: RP-54; SP-4   Ht: 6'0" Wt: 215 Born: 11/22/1981 Age: 25

			HOW MUCH HE PITCHED						WHAT HE GAVE UP											THE RESULTS						
Year	Team	Lg	G	GS	CG	GF	IP	BFP	H	R	ER	HR	SH	SF	HB	TBB	IBB	SO	WP	Bk	W	L	Pct	ShO	Sv-Op	Hld	ERC	ERA
2003	Ari	NL	86	1	0	14	98.0	422	80	40	28	6	9	3	3	46	10	80	3	2	10	7	.588	0	0-4	10	2.97	2.57
2004	Ari	NL	17	0	0	4	18.0	84	25	14	14	3	3	0	1	7	1	17	5	0	0	2	.000	0	0-0	2	7.13	7.00
2005	Ari	NL	11	0	0	3	13.2	57	11	8	8	2	2	1	1	6	2	5	0	0	2	0	1.000	0	0-2	2	3.59	5.27
2006	Atl	NL	58	4	0	11	92.1	397	93	41	37	13	5	4	5	27	3	55	4	0	9	1	.900	0	0-4	2	4.10	3.61
	4 ML YEARS		172	5	0	29	222.0	960	209	103	87	24	19	8	10	86	16	157	12	2	21	10	.677	0	0-10	16	3.78	3.53

Ron Villone

Pitches: L Bats: L Pos: RP-70   Ht: 6'3" Wt: 245 Born: 1/16/1970 Age: 37

			HOW MUCH HE PITCHED						WHAT HE GAVE UP											THE RESULTS						
Year	Team	Lg	G	GS	CG	GF	IP	BFP	H	R	ER	HR	SH	SF	HB	TBB	IBB	SO	WP	Bk	W	L	Pct	ShO	Sv-Op	Hld	ERC	ERA
1995	2 Tms		38	0	0	15	45.0	212	44	31	29	11	3	1	1	34	0	63	3	0	2	3	.400	0	1-5	6	6.57	5.80
1996	2 Tms		44	0	0	19	43.0	182	31	15	15	6	0	2	5	25	0	38	2	0	1	1	.500	0	2-3	9	4.08	3.14
1997	Mil	AL	50	0	0	15	52.2	238	54	23	20	4	2	0	1	36	2	40	3	0	1	0	1.000	0	0-2	8	5.30	3.42
1998	Cle	AL	25	0	0	6	27.0	129	30	18	18	3	2	2	2	22	0	15	0	0	0	0	-	0	0-0	1	7.01	6.00
1999	Cin	NL	29	22	0	2	142.2	610	114	70	67	8	9	3	5	73	2	97	6	0	9	7	.563	0	2-2	0	3.20	4.23
2000	Cin	NL	35	23	2	5	141.0	643	154	95	85	22	10	8	9	78	3	77	7	0	10	10	.500	0	0-1	1	5.97	5.43
2001	2 Tms	NL	53	12	0	12	114.2	523	133	81	75	18	1	1	5	53	5	113	4	1	6	10	.375	0	0-0	6	5.81	5.89
2002	Pit	NL	45	7	0	6	93.0	399	95	63	60	8	5	3	5	34	3	55	1	0	4	6	.400	0	0-1	0	4.18	5.81
2003	Hou	NL	19	19	0	0	106.2	449	91	51	49	16	3	3	5	48	1	91	1	0	6	6	.500	0	0-0	0	4.04	4.13
2004	Sea	AL	56	10	0	14	117.0	523	102	64	53	12	4	4	12	64	3	86	6	0	8	6	.571	0	0-1	7	4.26	4.08
2005	2 Tms	NL	79	0	0	24	64.0	287	57	34	29	4	3	5	7	35	2	70	3	1	5	5	.500	0	1-9	21	4.09	4.08
2006	NYY	AL	70	0	0	19	80.1	365	75	48	45	9	6	4	4	51	9	72	5	0	3	3	.500	0	0-1	6	4.69	5.04
95	Sea	AL	19	0	0	7	19.1	101	20	19	17	6	3	0	1	23	0	26	1	0	0	2	.000	0	0-3	3	9.67	7.91
95	SD	NL	19	0	0	8	25.2	111	24	12	12	5	0	1	0	11	0	37	2	0	2	1	.667	0	1-2	3	4.44	4.21
96	SD	NL	21	0	0	9	18.1	78	17	6	6	2	0	0	1	7	0	19	0	0	1	1	.500	0	0-1	4	3.90	2.95
96	Mil	AL	23	0	0	10	24.2	104	14	9	9	4	0	2	4	18	0	19	2	0	0	0	-	0	2-2	5	4.21	3.28
01	Col	NL	22	6	0	6	46.2	222	56	35	33	6	1	1	1	29	4	48	2	0	1	3	.250	0	0-0	2	6.30	6.36
01	Hou	NL	31	6	0	6	68.0	301	77	46	42	12	0	0	4	24	1	65	2	1	5	7	.417	0	0-0	4	5.46	5.56
05	Sea	AL	52	0	0	14	40.1	178	33	14	11	2	1	3	5	23	1	41	2	1	2	3	.400	0	1-6	17	3.79	2.45
05	Fla	NL	27	0	0	10	23.2	109	24	20	18	2	2	2	2	12	1	29	1	0	3	2	.600	0	0-3	4	4.61	6.85
	12 ML YEARS		543	93	2	137	1027.0	4560	980	593	545	121	48	36	61	553	30	817	41	2	55	57	.491	0	6-24	65	4.70	4.78

Jose Vizcaino

Bats: B Throws: R Pos: PH-29; SS-26; 2B-18; 1B-11; PR-7; 3B-2   Ht: 6'1" Wt: 190 Born: 3/26/1968 Age: 39

							BATTING													BASERUNNING				AVERAGES		
Year	Team	Lg	G	AB	H	2B	3B	HR	(Hm	Rd)	TB	R	RBI	RC	TBB	IBB	SO	HBP	SH	SF	SB	CS	SB%	GDP	Avg	OBP	Slg
1989	LAD	NL	7	10	2	0	0	0	(0	0)	2	2	0	0	0	0	1	0	1	0	0	0	-	0	.200	.200	.200
1990	LAD	NL	37	51	14	1	1	0	(0	0)	17	3	2	5	4	1	8	0	4	0	1	1	.50	1	.275	.327	.333
1991	ChC	NL	93	145	38	5	0	0	(0	0)	43	7	10	12	5	0	18	0	2	2	2	1	.67	1	.262	.283	.297
1992	ChC	NL	86	285	64	10	4	1	(0	1)	85	25	17	21	14	2	35	0	5	1	3	0	1.00	4	.225	.260	.298
1993	ChC	NL	151	551	158	19	4	4	(1	3)	197	74	54	68	46	2	71	3	8	9	12	9	.57	9	.287	.340	.358
1994	NYM	NL	103	410	105	13	3	3	(1	2)	133	47	33	39	33	3	62	2	5	6	1	11	.08	5	.256	.310	.324
1995	NYM	NL	135	509	146	21	5	3	(2	1)	186	66	56	60	35	4	76	1	13	3	8	3	.73	14	.287	.332	.365

258

BATTING

Year	Team	Lg	G	AB	H	2B	3B	HR	(Hm	Rd)	TB	R	RBI	RC	TBB	IBB	SO	HBP	SH	SF	SB	CS	SB%	GDP	Avg	OBP	Slg
1996	2 Tms		144	542	161	17	8	1	(1	0)	197	70	45	68	35	0	82	3	10	3	15	7	.68	8	.297	.341	.363
1997	SF	NL	151	568	151	19	7	5	(1	4)	199	77	50	62	48	1	87	0	13	1	8	8	.50	13	.266	.323	.350
1998	LAD	NL	67	237	62	9	0	3	(0	3)	80	30	29	25	17	0	35	1	10	2	7	3	.70	4	.262	.311	.338
1999	LAD	NL	94	266	67	9	0	1	(1	0)	79	27	29	23	20	0	23	1	9	2	2	1	.67	9	.252	.304	.297
2000	2 Tms		113	267	67	10	2	0	(0	0)	81	32	14	23	22	3	43	1	5	2	6	7	.46	6	.251	.308	.303
2001	Hou	NL	107	256	71	8	3	1	(1	0)	88	38	14	28	15	0	33	2	9	0	3	2	.60	6	.277	.322	.344
2002	Hou	NL	125	406	123	19	2	5	(4	1)	161	53	37	53	24	2	40	1	5	2	3	5	.38	5	.303	.342	.397
2003	Hou	NL	91	189	47	7	3	3	(2	1)	69	14	26	24	8	3	22	1	4	1	0	1	.00	5	.249	.281	.365
2004	Hou	NL	138	358	98	21	3	3	(1	2)	134	34	33	40	20	5	39	0	5	2	1	1	.50	8	.274	.311	.374
2005	Hou	NL	98	187	46	10	2	1	(1	0)	63	15	23	22	15	4	40	0	1	2	2	0	1.00	2	.246	.299	.337
2006	2 Tms		80	142	33	6	0	2	(0	2)	45	19	8	16	17	3	14	0	2	0	0	2	.00	5	.232	.314	.317
96	NYM	NL	96	363	110	12	6	1	(1	0)	137	47	32	49	28	0	58	3	6	2	9	5	.64	6	.303	.356	.377
96	Cle	AL	48	179	51	5	2	0	(0	0)	60	23	13	19	7	0	24	0	4	1	6	2	.75	2	.285	.310	.335
00	LAD	NL	40	93	19	2	1	0	(0	0)	23	9	4	6	10	3	15	1	2	0	1	0	1.00	3	.204	.288	.247
00	NYY	AL	73	174	48	8	1	0	(0	0)	58	23	10	17	12	0	28	0	3	2	5	7	.42	3	.276	.319	.333
06	SF	NL	64	119	25	3	0	1	(0	1)	31	16	5	10	16	3	10	0	1	0	0	2	.00	3	.210	.304	.261
06	StL	NL	16	23	8	3	0	1	(0	1)	14	3	3	6	1	0	4	0	1	0	0	0	-	2	.348	.375	.609
18 ML YEARS			1820	5379	1453	204	47	36	(16	20)	1859	633	480	589	378	33	729	16	107	38	74	62	.54	105	.270	.318	.346

Luis Vizcaino

Pitches: R Bats: R Pos: RP-70   Ht: 5'11" Wt: 185 Born: 8/6/1974 Age: 32

	HOW MUCH HE PITCHED						WHAT HE GAVE UP												THE RESULTS							
Year	Team	Lg	G	GS	CG	GF	IP	BFP	H	R	ER	HR	SH	SF	HB	TBB	IBB	SO	WP	Bk	W	L	Pct	ShO	Sv-Op	Hld	ERC	ERA
1999	Oak	AL	1	0	0	1	3.1	16	3	2	2	1	0	0	0	3	0	2	1	0	0	0	-	0	0-0	0	7.01	5.40
2000	Oak	AL	12	0	0	1	19.1	96	25	17	16	2	0	1	2	11	0	18	1	0	0	1	.000	0	0-0	0	6.83	7.45
2001	Oak	AL	36	0	0	15	36.2	156	38	19	19	8	0	1	0	12	1	31	3	0	2	1	.667	0	1-1	3	4.80	4.66
2002	Mil	NL	76	0	0	30	81.1	326	55	27	27	6	3	3	3	30	4	79	3	2	5	3	.625	0	5-6	19	2.20	2.99
2003	Mil	NL	75	0	0	21	62.0	272	64	45	44	16	2	1	1	25	3	61	3	0	4	3	.571	0	0-6	9	5.37	6.39
2004	Mil	NL	73	0	0	21	72.0	298	61	35	30	12	1	5	1	24	3	63	9	0	4	4	.500	0	1-5	21	3.40	3.75
2005	CWS	AL	65	0	0	20	70.0	305	74	30	29	8	4	1	2	29	6	43	3	0	6	5	.545	0	0-3	9	4.58	3.73
2006	Ari	NL	70	0	0	15	65.1	272	51	26	26	8	2	0	4	29	6	72	1	0	4	6	.400	0	0-2	25	3.34	3.58
8 ML YEARS			408	0	0	124	410.0	1741	371	201	193	61	12	12	13	163	23	369	24	2	25	23	.521	0	7-23	86	3.92	4.24

Omar Vizquel

Bats: B Throws: R Pos: SS-152; PH-2; PR-2   Ht: 5'9" Wt: 175 Born: 4/24/1967 Age: 40

BATTING

Year	Team	Lg	G	AB	H	2B	3B	HR	(Hm	Rd)	TB	R	RBI	RC	TBB	IBB	SO	HBP	SH	SF	SB	CS	SB%	GDP	Avg	OBP	Slg
1989	Sea	AL	143	387	85	7	3	1	(1	0)	101	45	20	25	28	0	40	1	13	2	1	4	.20	6	.220	.273	.261
1990	Sea	AL	81	255	63	3	2	2	(0	2)	76	19	18	22	18	0	22	0	10	2	4	1	.80	7	.247	.295	.298
1991	Sea	AL	142	426	98	16	4	1	(1	0)	125	42	41	39	45	0	37	0	8	3	7	2	.78	8	.230	.302	.293
1992	Sea	AL	136	483	142	20	4	0	(0	0)	170	49	21	54	32	0	38	2	9	1	15	5	.54	14	.294	.340	.352
1993	Sea	AL	158	560	143	14	2	2	(1	1)	167	68	31	53	50	2	71	4	13	3	12	14	.46	7	.255	.319	.298
1994	Cle	AL	69	286	78	10	1	1	(0	1)	93	39	33	32	23	0	23	0	11	2	13	4	.76	4	.273	.325	.325
1995	Cle	AL	136	542	144	28	0	6	(3	3)	190	87	56	70	59	0	59	1	10	10	29	11	.73	4	.266	.333	.351
1996	Cle	AL	151	542	161	36	1	9	(2	7)	226	98	64	87	56	0	42	4	12	9	35	9	.80	10	.297	.362	.417
1997	Cle	AL	153	565	158	23	6	5	(3	2)	208	89	49	75	57	1	58	2	16	1	43	12	.78	16	.280	.347	.368
1998	Cle	AL	151	576	166	30	6	2	(0	2)	214	86	50	82	62	1	64	4	12	6	37	12	.76	10	.288	.358	.372
1999	Cle	AL	144	574	191	36	4	5	(0	3)	250	112	66	106	65	0	50	1	17	7	42	9	.82	8	.333	.397	.436
2000	Cle	AL	156	613	176	27	3	7	(1	6)	230	101	66	92	87	0	72	5	7	5	22	10	.69	13	.287	.377	.375
2001	Cle	AL	155	611	156	26	8	2	(2	0)	204	84	50	66	61	0	72	2	15	4	13	9	.59	14	.255	.323	.334
2002	Cle	AL	151	582	160	31	5	14	(9	5)	243	85	72	91	56	3	64	8	7	10	18	10	.64	7	.275	.341	.418
2003	Cle	AL	64	250	61	13	2	2	(2	0)	84	43	19	25	29	0	20	0	5	1	8	3	.73	11	.244	.321	.336
2004	Cle	AL	148	567	165	28	3	7	(2	5)	220	82	59	86	57	0	62	1	20	6	19	6	.76	12	.291	.353	.388
2005	SF	NL	152	568	154	28	4	3	(0	3)	199	66	45	76	56	0	58	5	20	2	24	10	.71	10	.271	.341	.350
2006	SF	NL	153	579	171	22	10	4	(2	2)	225	88	58	90	56	3	51	6	13	5	24	7	.77	13	.295	.361	.389
18 ML YEARS			2443	8966	2472	398	68	73	(32	41)	3225	1283	818	1171	897	10	903	46	218	80	366	146	.71	174	.276	.342	.360

Ryan Vogelsong

Pitches: R Bats: R Pos: RP-20   Ht: 6'3" Wt: 215 Born: 7/22/1977 Age: 29

	HOW MUCH HE PITCHED						WHAT HE GAVE UP												THE RESULTS							
Year	Team	Lg	G	GS	CG	GF	IP	BFP	H	R	ER	HR	SH	SF	HB	TBB	IBB	SO	WP	Bk	W	L	Pct	ShO	Sv-Op	Hld	ERC	ERA
2006	Indy*	AAA	11	10	1	0	67.2	269	54	23	20	5	3	1	4	12	3	43	1	0	4	5	.444	0	0- -	-	2.20	2.66
2000	SF	NL	4	0	0	3	6.0	24	4	0	0	0	0	0	0	2	0	6	0	0	0	0	-	0	0-0	0	1.57	0.00
2001	2 Tms	NL	15	2	0	8	34.2	164	39	31	26	6	0	1	2	20	1	24	2	0	0	5	.000	0	0-0	0	6.20	6.75
2003	Pit	NL	6	5	0	0	22.0	108	30	19	16	1	3	1	2	9	3	15	1	0	2	2	.500	0	0-0	0	5.72	6.55
2004	Pit	NL	31	26	0	4	133.0	610	148	97	96	22	8	6	10	67	7	92	3	0	6	13	.316	0	0-0	0	5.89	6.50
2005	Pit	NL	44	0	0	19	81.1	369	82	43	40	5	1	4	8	40	1	52	7	0	2	2	.500	0	0-1	4	4.51	4.43
2006	Pit	NL	20	0	0	7	38.0	178	44	27	27	2	5	4	7	16	2	27	4	1	0	0	-	0	0-0	0	5.31	6.39
01	SF	NL	13	0	0	8	28.2	130	29	21	18	5	0	1	2	14	0	17	2	0	0	3	.000	0	0-0	0	5.26	5.65
01	Pit	NL	2	2	0	0	6.0	34	10	10	8	1	0	0	0	6	1	7	0	0	0	2	.000	0	0-0	0	11.03	12.00
6 ML YEARS			120	33	0	41	315.0	1453	347	217	205	36	17	16	29	154	14	216	17	1	10	22	.313	0	0-1	1	5.38	5.86

Edison Volquez

Pitches: R Bats: R Pos: SP-8   Ht: 6'0" Wt: 200 Born: 7/3/1983 Age: 23

Year	Team	Lg	G	GS	CG	GF	IP	BFP	H	R	ER	HR	SH	SF	HB	TBB	IBB	SO	WP	Bk	W	L	Pct	ShO	Sv-Op	Hld	ERC	ERA
2003	Rngrs	R	10	4	0	1	27.0	116	24	14	12	1	0	0	2	11	0	28	4	0	2	1	.667	0	1--	-	3.32	4.00
2004	Stcktn	A+	8	8	0	0	39.2	164	31	16	13	6	3	3	2	14	0	34	2	0	4	1	.800	0	0--	-	3.23	2.95
2004	Clinton	A	21	15	0	3	87.2	372	82	49	41	8	2	3	3	27	1	74	4	0	4	4	.500	0	3--	-	3.38	4.21
2005	Bkrsfld	A+	11	11	1	1	66.2	276	64	34	31	9	0	0	7	12	0	77	3	0	5	4	.556	0	0--	-	3.67	4.19
2005	Frisco	AA	10	10	1	0	58.2	251	58	29	27	6	1	1	1	17	0	49	1	0	1	5	.167	1	0--	-	3.60	4.14
2005	Rngrs	R	1	1	0	0	2.0	8	2	0	0	0	0	0	0	0	0	2	1	0	0	0	-	0	0--	-	1.95	0.00
2006	Okla	AAA	21	21	0	0	120.2	509	86	51	43	9	5	4	4	72	0	130	3	2	6	6	.500	0	0--	-	3.25	3.21
2005	Tex	AL	6	3	0	0	12.2	75	25	22	20	3	0	1	2	10	0	11	0	0	0	4	.000	0	0-0	0	14.15	14.21
2006	Tex	AL	8	8	0	0	33.1	164	52	28	27	7	0	1	1	17	0	15	0	0	1	6	.143	0	0-0	0	9.27	7.29
	2 ML YEARS		14	11	0	0	46.0	239	77	50	47	10	0	2	3	27	0	26	0	0	1	10	.091	0	0-0	0	10.58	9.20

Doug Waechter

Pitches: R Bats: R Pos: SP-10; RP-1   Ht: 6'4" Wt: 210 Born: 1/28/1981 Age: 26

Year	Team	Lg	G	GS	CG	GF	IP	BFP	H	R	ER	HR	SH	SF	HB	TBB	IBB	SO	WP	Bk	W	L	Pct	ShO	Sv-Op	Hld	ERC	ERA
2006	Drham*	AAA	17	15	1	0	79.0	387	129	82	73	7	6	5	0	24	1	45	6	0	1	12	.077	0	0--	-	7.28	8.32
2003	TB	AL	6	5	1	0	35.1	145	29	13	13	4	0	0	1	15	0	29	0	0	3	2	.600	1	0-0	0	3.48	3.31
2004	TB	AL	14	14	0	0	70.1	309	68	54	47	20	0	2	4	33	1	36	1	1	5	7	.417	0	0-0	0	5.74	6.01
2005	TB	AL	29	25	0	3	157.0	692	191	109	98	29	4	4	3	38	5	87	4	2	5	12	.294	0	0-0	0	5.29	5.62
2006	TB	AL	11	10	0	0	53.0	249	67	40	39	6	3	6	5	19	1	25	0	0	1	4	.200	0	0-0	0	5.79	6.62
	4 ML YEARS		60	54	1	3	315.2	1395	355	216	197	59	7	12	13	105	7	177	5	3	14	25	.359	1	0-0	0	5.27	5.62

Billy Wagner

Pitches: L Bats: L Pos: RP-70   Ht: 5'11" Wt: 205 Born: 7/25/1971 Age: 35

Year	Team	Lg	G	GS	CG	GF	IP	BFP	H	R	ER	HR	SH	SF	HB	TBB	IBB	SO	WP	Bk	W	L	Pct	ShO	Sv-Op	Hld	ERC	ERA
1995	Hou	NL	1	0	0	0	0.1	1	0	0	0	0	0	0	0	0	0	0	0	0	0	0	-	0	0-0	0	0.00	0.00
1996	Hou	NL	37	0	0	20	51.2	212	28	16	14	6	7	2	3	30	2	67	1	0	2	2	.500	0	9-13	1	2.61	2.44
1997	Hou	NL	62	0	0	49	66.1	277	49	23	21	5	3	1	3	30	1	106	3	0	7	8	.467	0	23-29	1	2.85	2.85
1998	Hou	NL	58	0	0	50	60.0	247	46	19	18	6	4	0	0	25	1	97	2	0	4	3	.571	0	30-35	1	2.87	2.70
1999	Hou	NL	66	0	0	55	74.2	286	35	14	13	5	2	1	1	23	1	124	2	0	4	1	.800	0	39-42	1	1.20	1.57
2000	Hou	NL	28	0	0	19	27.2	129	28	19	19	6	0	0	1	18	0	28	7	0	2	4	.333	0	6-15	0	6.15	6.18
2001	Hou	NL	64	0	0	58	62.2	251	44	19	19	5	3	1	5	20	0	79	3	0	2	5	.286	0	39-41	0	2.42	2.73
2002	Hou	NL	70	0	0	61	75.0	289	51	21	21	7	2	3	2	22	5	88	6	0	4	2	.667	0	35-41	0	2.08	2.52
2003	Hou	NL	78	0	0	67	86.0	335	52	18	17	8	1	0	3	23	5	105	4	0	1	4	.200	0	44-47	0	1.63	1.78
2004	Phi	NL	45	0	0	38	48.1	182	31	16	13	5	3	0	2	6	1	59	1	0	4	0	1.000	0	21-25	1	1.52	2.42
2005	Phi	NL	75	0	0	70	77.2	297	45	17	13	6	0	2	3	20	2	87	3	1	4	3	.571	0	38-41	0	1.53	1.51
2006	NYM	NL	70	0	0	59	72.1	297	59	22	18	7	2	0	4	21	1	94	2	0	3	2	.600	0	40-45	0	2.83	2.24
	12 ML YEARS		654	0	0	546	702.2	2803	468	204	186	66	27	10	27	238	19	934	34	1	37	34	.521	0	324-374	7	2.19	2.38

Ryan Wagner

Pitches: R Bats: R Pos: RP-26   Ht: 6'4" Wt: 225 Born: 7/15/1982 Age: 24

Year	Team	Lg	G	GS	CG	GF	IP	BFP	H	R	ER	HR	SH	SF	HB	TBB	IBB	SO	WP	Bk	W	L	Pct	ShO	Sv-Op	Hld	ERC	ERA
2006	Lsvlle*	AAA	35	0	0	11	38.1	182	55	29	27	3	2	5	1	14	1	28	5	0	1	3	.250	0	1--	-	6.36	6.34
2006	NewOr*	AAA	6	0	0	2	9.0	35	8	4	4	0	0	1	0	2	0	5	0	0	0	0	-	0	0--	-	2.31	4.00
2003	Cin	NL	17	0	0	3	21.2	88	13	4	4	2	0	1	0	12	1	25	4	0	2	0	1.000	0	0-1	6	2.46	1.66
2004	Cin	NL	49	0	0	5	51.2	242	59	31	27	7	2	3	2	27	2	37	6	0	3	2	.600	0	0-3	8	5.66	4.70
2005	Cin	NL	42	0	0	8	45.2	210	56	33	31	4	1	3	4	17	1	39	2	0	3	2	.600	0	0-1	12	5.48	6.11
2006	Was	NL	26	0	0	5	30.2	141	36	21	16	3	1	0	2	15	3	20	3	1	3	3	.500	0	0-2	3	5.55	4.70
	4 ML YEARS		134	0	0	21	149.2	681	164	89	78	16	4	7	8	71	7	121	15	1	11	7	.611	0	0-7	29	5.07	4.69

Adam Wainwright

Pitches: R Bats: R Pos: RP-61   Ht: 6'7" Wt: 205 Born: 8/30/1981 Age: 25

Year	Team	Lg	G	GS	CG	GF	IP	BFP	H	R	ER	HR	SH	SF	HB	TBB	IBB	SO	WP	Bk	W	L	Pct	ShO	Sv-Op	Hld	ERC	ERA
2000	Braves	R	7	5	0	1	32.0	121	15	5	4	1	0	0	0	10	0	42	1	1	4	0	1.000	0	0--	-	1.08	1.13
2000	Danvle	R+	6	6	0	0	29.1	118	28	13	12	3	1	0	1	2	0	39	1	0	2	2	.500	0	0--	-	2.69	3.68
2001	Macon	A	28	28	1	0	164.2	686	144	89	69	9	7	2	8	48	1	184	9	2	10	10	.500	0	0--	-	2.84	3.77
2002	MrtlBh	A+	28	28	1	0	163.1	705	149	67	60	7	1	2	10	66	0	167	11	3	9	6	.600	0	0--	-	3.42	3.31
2003	Grnville	AA	27	27	1	0	149.2	619	133	59	56	9	2	3	7	37	0	128	4	2	10	8	.556	0	0--	-	2.80	3.37
2004	Memp	AAA	12	12	0	0	63.2	287	68	47	38	12	7	1	3	28	0	64	2	1	4	4	.500	0	0--	-	5.42	5.37
2005	Memp	AAA	29	29	0	0	182.0	801	204	98	89	18	7	6	5	51	6	147	11	1	10	10	.500	0	0--	-	4.25	4.40
2005	StL	NL	2	0	0	1	2.0	9	2	3	3	1	0	0	0	1	0	0	0	0	0	0	-	0	0-0	0	7.30	13.50
2006	StL	NL	61	0	0	10	75.0	309	64	26	26	6	4	1	4	22	2	72	3	0	2	1	.667	0	3-5	17	2.92	3.12
	2 ML YEARS		63	0	0	11	77.0	318	66	29	29	7	4	1	4	23	2	72	3	0	2	1	.667	0	3-5	17	3.02	3.39

Tim Wakefield

Pitches: R Bats: R Pos: SP-23   Ht: 6'2" Wt: 210 Born: 8/2/1966 Age: 40

			HOW MUCH HE PITCHED						WHAT HE GAVE UP												THE RESULTS							
Year	Team	Lg	G	GS	CG	GF	IP	BFP	H	R	ER	HR	SH	SF	HB	TBB	IBB	SO	WP	Bk	W	L	Pct	ShO	Sv-Op	Hld	ERC	ERA
1992	Pit	NL	13	13	4	0	92.0	373	76	26	22	3	6	4	1	35	1	51	3	1	8	1	.889	1	0-0	0	2.72	2.15
1993	Pit	NL	24	20	3	1	128.1	595	145	83	80	14	7	5	9	75	2	59	6	0	6	11	.353	2	0-0	0	5.97	5.61
1995	Bos	AL	27	27	6	0	195.1	804	163	76	64	22	3	7	9	68	0	119	11	0	16	8	.667	1	0-0	0	3.28	2.95
1996	Bos	AL	32	32	6	0	211.2	963	238	151	121	38	1	9	12	90	0	140	4	1	14	13	.519	0	0-0	0	5.68	5.14
1997	Bos	AL	35	29	4	2	201.1	866	193	109	95	24	3	7	16	87	5	151	6	0	12	15	.444	2	0-0	1	4.47	4.25
1998	Bos	AL	36	33	2	1	216.0	939	211	123	110	30	1	8	14	79	1	146	6	1	17	8	.680	0	0-0	0	4.30	4.58
1999	Bos	AL	49	17	0	28	140.0	635	146	93	79	19	1	8	5	72	2	104	1	0	6	11	.353	0	15-18	5	5.12	5.08
2000	Bos	AL	51	17	0	13	159.1	706	170	107	97	31	4	8	4	65	3	102	4	0	6	10	.375	0	0-1	3	5.23	5.48
2001	Bos	AL	45	17	0	5	168.2	732	156	84	73	13	3	9	18	73	5	148	5	1	9	12	.429	0	3-5	3	4.02	3.90
2002	Bos	AL	45	15	0	10	163.1	657	121	57	51	15	1	4	9	51	2	134	5	2	11	5	.688	0	3-5	5	2.54	2.81
2003	Bos	AL	35	33	0	2	202.1	872	193	106	92	23	2	4	12	71	0	169	8	0	11	7	.611	0	1-1	0	3.92	4.09
2004	Bos	AL	32	30	0	0	188.1	831	197	121	102	29	2	4	16	63	3	116	9	0	12	10	.545	0	0-0	1	4.73	4.87
2005	Bos	AL	33	33	3	0	225.1	943	210	113	104	35	1	6	11	68	4	151	8	0	16	12	.571	0	0-1	0	3.87	4.15
2006	Bos	AL	23	23	1	0	140.0	610	135	80	72	19	1	3	10	51	0	90	6	0	7	11	.389	0	0-0	0	4.22	4.63
14 ML YEARS			480	339	29	62	2432.0	10526	2354	1329	1162	315	36	86	146	948	28	1680	82	6	151	134	.530	6	22-30	13	4.28	4.30

Jamie Walker

Pitches: L Bats: L Pos: RP-56   Ht: 6'2" Wt: 185 Born: 7/1/1971 Age: 35

			HOW MUCH HE PITCHED						WHAT HE GAVE UP												THE RESULTS							
Year	Team	Lg	G	GS	CG	GF	IP	BFP	H	R	ER	HR	SH	SF	HB	TBB	IBB	SO	WP	Bk	W	L	Pct	ShO	Sv-Op	Hld	ERC	ERA
1997	KC	AL	50	0	0	15	43.0	197	46	28	26	6	2	2	3	20	3	24	2	0	3	3	.500	0	0-1	3	5.10	5.44
1998	KC	AL	6	2	0	2	17.1	86	30	20	19	5	1	1	2	3	0	15	0	0	0	1	.000	0	0-0	1	9.69	9.87
2002	Det	AL	57	0	0	16	43.2	175	32	19	18	9	0	1	4	9	1	40	1	1	1	1	.500	0	1-4	5	2.86	3.71
2003	Det	AL	78	0	0	19	65.0	273	61	30	24	9	5	2	2	17	1	45	1	0	4	3	.571	0	3-7	12	3.51	3.32
2004	Det	AL	70	0	0	18	64.2	277	69	28	23	8	1	1	1	12	3	53	4	0	3	4	.429	0	1-7	18	3.65	3.20
2005	Det	AL	66	0	0	11	48.2	208	49	22	20	5	1	2	2	13	3	30	0	0	4	3	.571	0	0-2	14	3.63	3.70
2006	Det	AL	56	0	0	14	48.0	196	47	15	15	8	1	0	0	8	3	37	1	0	0	1	.000	0	0-0	11	3.38	2.81
7 ML YEARS			383	2	0	95	330.1	1412	334	162	145	50	11	8	14	82	14	244	9	1	15	16	.484	0	5-21	64	3.93	3.95

Pete Walker

Pitches: R Bats: R Pos: RP-23   Ht: 6'2" Wt: 195 Born: 4/8/1969 Age: 38

			HOW MUCH HE PITCHED						WHAT HE GAVE UP												THE RESULTS							
Year	Team	Lg	G	GS	CG	GF	IP	BFP	H	R	ER	HR	SH	SF	HB	TBB	IBB	SO	WP	Bk	W	L	Pct	ShO	Sv-Op	Hld	ERC	ERA
1995	NYM	NL	13	0	0	10	17.2	79	24	9	9	3	0	1	0	5	0	5	0	0	1	0	1.000	0	0-0	1	6.35	4.58
1996	SD	NL	1	0	0	0	0.2	5	0	0	0	0	0	0	0	3	0	1	0	0	0	0	-	0	0-0	0	13.05	0.00
2000	Col	NL	3	0	0	1	4.2	27	10	9	9	1	0	0	0	4	0	2	0	0	0	0	-	0	0-0	0	15.29	17.36
2001	NYM	NL	2	0	0	1	6.2	25	6	2	2	0	0	0	0	0	0	4	0	0	0	0	-	0	0-0	0	1.63	2.70
2002	2 Tms		38	20	0	4	140.1	599	145	73	68	18	4	6	3	51	5	80	2	1	10	5	.667	0	1-1	3	4.41	4.36
2003	Tor	AL	23	7	0	2	55.1	242	59	31	30	11	2	1	2	24	2	29	2	0	2	2	.500	0	0-0	2	5.51	4.88
2005	Tor	AL	41	4	0	8	84.0	358	81	33	33	10	0	4	2	33	0	43	2	0	6	6	.500	0	2-5	4	4.11	3.54
2006	Tor	AL	23	0	0	9	30.0	138	37	24	18	5	0	0	0	13	2	27	0	1	1	1	.500	0	1-1	3	5.93	5.40
02	NYM	NL	1	0	0	0	1.0	5	2	1	1	0	0	0	0	0	0	0	0	0	0	0	-	0	0-0	0	7.48	9.00
02	Tor	NL	37	20	0	4	139.1	594	143	72	67	18	4	6	3	51	5	80	2	1	10	5	.667	0	1-1	3	4.39	4.33
8 ML YEARS			144	31	0	35	339.1	1473	362	181	169	48	6	12	7	133	9	191	6	2	20	14	.588	0	4-7	13	4.82	4.48

Todd Walker

Bats: L Throws: R Pos: 2B-60; 1B-40; 3B-23; PH-17; DH-5   Ht: 6'0" Wt: 185 Born: 5/25/1973 Age: 34

			BATTING																			BASERUNNING				AVERAGES		
Year	Team	Lg	G	AB	H	2B	3B	HR	(Hm	Rd)	TB	R	RBI	RC	TBB	IBB	SO	HBP	SH	SF		SB	CS	SB%	GDP		Avg	OBP	Slg
1996	Min	AL	25	82	21	6	0	0	(0	0)	27	8	6	7	4	0	13	0	0	3		3	0	1.00	4		.256	.281	.329
1997	Min	AL	52	156	37	7	1	3	(1	2)	55	15	16	16	11	1	30	1	1	2		7	0	1.00	5		.237	.288	.353
1998	Min	AL	143	528	167	41	3	12	(7	5)	250	85	62	90	47	9	65	2	0	4		19	7	.73	13		.316	.372	.473
1999	Min	AL	143	531	148	37	4	6	(4	2)	211	62	46	70	52	5	83	1	0	2		18	10	.64	15		.279	.343	.397
2000	2 Tms		80	248	72	11	4	9	(5	4)	118	42	44	43	27	0	29	1	1	6		7	1	.88	5		.290	.355	.476
2001	2 Tms	NL	151	551	163	35	2	17	(13	4)	253	93	75	84	51	1	82	1	4	3		1	8	.11	14		.296	.355	.459
2002	Cin	NL	155	612	183	42	3	11	(7	4)	264	79	64	90	50	7	81	3	7	3		8	5	.62	9		.299	.353	.431
2003	Bos	AL	144	587	166	38	4	13	(6	7)	251	92	85	84	48	0	54	1	1	10		1	1	.50	17		.283	.333	.428
2004	ChC	NL	129	372	102	19	4	15	(6	9)	174	60	50	61	43	8	52	4	1	4		3	0	.00	2		.274	.352	.468
2005	ChC	NL	110	397	121	25	3	12	(5	7)	188	50	40	56	31	1	40	1	2	2		1	1	.50	8		.305	.355	.474
2006	2 Tms	NL	138	442	123	22	2	9	(4	5)	176	56	53	60	55	2	38	1	1	5		2	1	.67	8		.278	.356	.398
00	Min	AL	23	77	18	1	0	2	(0	2)	25	14	8	7	7	0	10	0	0	3		3	0	1.00	3		.234	.287	.325
00	Col	NL	57	171	54	10	4	7	(5	2)	93	28	36	36	20	0	19	1	1	3		4	1	.80	2		.316	.385	.544
01	Col	NL	85	290	86	18	2	12	(10	2)	144	52	43	47	25	1	40	0	3	3		1	3	.25	8		.297	.349	.497
01	Cin	NL	66	261	77	17	0	5	(3	2)	109	41	32	37	26	0	42	1	1	0		0	5	.00	6		.295	.361	.418
06	ChC	NL	94	318	88	16	1	6	(3	3)	124	38	40	40	38	1	27	1	1	4		0	1	.00	7		.277	.352	.390
06	SD	NL	44	124	35	6	1	3	(1	2)	52	18	13	20	17	1	11	0	0	1		2	0	1.00	1		.282	.366	.419
11 ML YEARS			1270	4506	1303	283	30	107	(58	49)	1967	642	541	661	419	34	567	16	18	44		66	37	.64	100		.289	.349	.437

Tyler Walker

Pitches: R Bats: R Pos: RP-26   Ht: 6'3" Wt: 260 Born: 5/15/1976 Age: 31

Year	Team	Lg	G	GS	CG	GF	IP	BFP	H	R	ER	HR	SH	SF	HB	TBB	IBB	SO	WP	Bk	W	L	Pct	ShO	Sv-Op	Hld	ERC	ERA
2002	NYM	NL	5	1	0	3	10.2	49	11	7	7	3	0	0	0	5	1	7	0	0	1	0	1.000	0	0-0	0	5.46	5.91
2004	SF	NL	52	0	0	13	63.2	275	69	31	30	8	3	7	1	24	1	48	1	0	5	1	.833	0	1-1	5	4.76	4.24
2005	SF	NL	67	0	0	39	61.2	279	68	31	29	9	5	1	3	27	6	54	4	0	6	4	.600	0	23-28	2	5.15	4.23
2006	2 Tms		26	0	0	17	25.1	111	27	20	20	1	1	0	0	12	0	19	1	0	1	4	.200	0	10-14	1	4.35	7.11
06	SF	NL	6	0	0	1	5.1	28	9	9	9	1	0	0	0	5	0	3	1	0	0	1	.000	0	0-2	1	12.35	15.19
06	TB	AL	20	0	0	16	20.0	83	18	11	11	0	1	0	0	7	0	16	0	0	1	3	.250	0	10-12	0	2.70	4.95
	4 ML YEARS		150	1	0	72	161.1	714	175	89	86	21	9	8	4	68	8	128	6	0	13	9	.591	0	34-43	8	4.89	4.80

Les Walrond

Pitches: L Bats: L Pos: RP-8; SP-2   Ht: 6'3" Wt: 205 Born: 11/7/1976 Age: 30

Year	Team	Lg	G	GS	CG	GF	IP	BFP	H	R	ER	HR	SH	SF	HB	TBB	IBB	SO	WP	Bk	W	L	Pct	ShO	Sv-Op	Hld	ERC	ERA
1998	NewJrs	A-	13	10	0	0	51.2	228	52	31	23	1	1	2	0	24	0	52	3	0	2	4	.333	0	0- -	-	3.73	4.01
1999	Peoria	A	21	20	0	0	109.0	489	115	77	69	12	2	5	3	59	0	78	6	0	7	10	.412	0	0- -	-	5.19	5.70
2000	Ptomc	A+	27	27	0	0	151.0	632	134	66	56	9	1	3	7	54	0	153	12	1	10	5	.667	0	0- -	-	3.23	3.34
2001	NwHav	AA	16	16	1	0	81.1	354	68	41	35	5	3	3	2	46	0	67	6	0	2	8	.200	0	0- -	-	3.61	3.87
2002	NwHav	AA	4	4	0	0	22.1	96	19	8	6	2	0	0	0	10	0	31	3	0	2	1	.667	0	0- -	-	3.30	2.42
2002	Memp	AAA	28	18	0	2	123.0	538	127	75	68	20	3	1	1	63	2	111	8	0	8	7	.533	0	0- -	-	5.30	4.98
2003	Memp	AAA	10	1	0	2	17.1	71	12	2	2	0	0	1	0	7	1	14	0	0	0	0	-	0	0- -	-	1.77	1.04
2003	Tenn	AA	4	0	0	0	6.2	28	4	2	2	1	0	0	0	4	0	7	0	0	0	0	-	0	0- -	-	2.97	2.70
2003	Omha	AAA	18	0	0	5	25.2	109	19	9	7	1	1	1	1	9	0	20	4	1	3	1	.750	0	2- -	-	2.17	2.45
2003	Wichta	AAA	2	2	0	0	11.0	43	7	4	4	2	0	0	0	2	0	9	2	0	2	0	1.000	0	0- -	-	1.81	3.27
2004	Wichta	AA	8	6	0	0	39.0	165	30	19	19	2	3	1	3	17	0	34	3	0	3	3	.500	0	0- -	-	2.91	4.38
2004	Omha	AAA	19	19	1	0	123.2	515	114	46	42	12	6	4	3	41	0	107	7	2	11	5	.688	1	0- -	-	3.49	3.06
2005	Albq	AAA	15	15	2	0	86.2	373	97	50	44	13	2	0	1	37	0	61	2	3	4	5	.444	2	0- -	-	5.51	4.57
2006	Iowa	AAA	31	20	0	2	133.1	580	134	72	59	11	6	3	7	59	6	104	8	0	10	5	.667	0	0- -	-	4.33	3.98
2003	KC	AL	7	0	0	2	8.0	41	11	9	9	2	0	0	0	7	1	6	1	0	0	2	.000	0	0-0	1	9.58	10.13
2006	ChC	NL	10	2	0	0	17.1	84	19	13	12	2	1	1	0	12	1	21	0	0	0	1	.000	0	0-0	0	5.62	6.23
	2 ML YEARS		17	2	0	2	25.1	125	30	22	21	4	1	1	0	19	2	27	1	0	0	3	.000	0	0-0	1	6.79	7.46

Chien-Ming Wang

Pitches: R Bats: R Pos: SP-33; RP-1   Ht: 6'3" Wt: 220 Born: 3/31/1980 Age: 27

Year	Team	Lg	G	GS	CG	GF	IP	BFP	H	R	ER	HR	SH	SF	HB	TBB	IBB	SO	WP	Bk	W	L	Pct	ShO	Sv-Op	Hld	ERC	ERA
2000	StIsInd	A-	14	14	2	0	87.0	359	77	34	24	2	3	1	2	21	1	75	7	1	4	4	.500	1	0- -	-	2.41	2.48
2002	StIsInd	A-	13	13	0	0	78.1	312	63	23	15	2	3	3	0	14	0	64	1	2	6	1	.857	0	0- -	-	1.80	1.72
2003	Trntn	AA	21	21	2	0	122.0	541	143	71	63	7	0	0	2	32	2	84	3	1	7	6	.538	1	0- -	-	4.14	4.65
2003	Yanks	R	1	1	0	0	3.0	11	2	0	0	0	0	0	0	0	0	2	0	0	0	0	-	0	0- -	-	0.91	0.00
2004	Trntn	AA	18	18	0	0	109.0	465	112	53	49	6	6	5	3	26	0	90	2	0	6	5	.545	0	0- -	-	3.35	4.05
2004	Clmbs	AAA	6	5	2	1	40.1	160	31	9	9	3	1	0	1	8	0	35	0	0	5	1	.833	1	0- -	-	2.06	2.01
2005	Clmbs	AAA	6	6	0	0	34.0	148	40	16	16	4	1	2	0	6	0	21	1	0	2	1	.667	0	0- -	-	4.20	4.24
2005	NYY	AL	18	17	0	0	116.1	486	113	58	52	9	3	4	6	32	3	47	3	0	8	5	.615	0	0-0	0	3.47	4.02
2006	NYY	AL	34	33	2	1	218.0	900	233	92	88	12	3	2	2	52	4	76	6	1	19	6	.760	1	1-1	0	3.62	3.63
	2 ML YEARS		52	50	2	1	334.1	1386	346	150	140	21	6	6	8	84	7	123	9	1	27	11	.711	1	1-1	0	3.57	3.77

Daryle Ward

Bats: L Throws: L Pos: PH-75; 1B-10; RF-10; LF-4; DH-3   Ht: 6'2" Wt: 240 Born: 6/27/1975 Age: 32

Year	Team	Lg	G	AB	H	2B	3B	HR	(Hm	Rd)	TB	R	RBI	RC	TBB	IBB	SO	HBP	SH	SF	SB	CS	SB%	GDP	Avg	OBP	Slg
1998	Hou	NL	4	3	1	0	0	0	(0	0)	1	1	0	1	1	0	2	0	0	0	0	0	-	0	.333	.500	.333
1999	Hou	NL	64	150	41	6	0	8	(2	6)	71	11	30	21	9	0	31	0	0	2	0	0	-	3	.273	.311	.473
2000	Hou	NL	119	264	68	10	2	20	(13	7)	142	36	47	40	15	2	60	0	0	2	0	0	-	6	.258	.295	.538
2001	Hou	NL	95	213	56	15	0	9	(5	4)	98	21	39	31	19	4	48	1	0	2	0	0	-	3	.263	.323	.460
2002	Hou	NL	136	453	125	31	0	12	(9	3)	192	41	72	61	33	5	82	1	0	4	1	3	.25	9	.276	.324	.424
2003	LAD	NL	52	109	20	1	0	0	(0	0)	21	6	9	1	3	0	19	1	0	1	0	0	-	4	.183	.211	.193
2004	Pit	NL	79	293	73	17	2	15	(8	7)	139	39	57	40	22	3	45	3	0	3	0	0	-	8	.249	.305	.474
2005	Pit	NL	133	407	106	21	1	12	(7	5)	165	46	63	49	37	10	60	1	0	8	0	2	.00	18	.260	.318	.405
2006	2 Tms		98	130	40	10	0	7	(3	4)	71	17	26	26	15	1	27	2	0	3	0	1	.00	5	.308	.380	.546
06	Was	NL	78	104	32	9	0	6	(3	3)	59	15	19	19	14	1	21	2	0	3	0	1	.00	5	.308	.390	.567
06	Atl	NL	20	26	8	1	0	1	(0	1)	12	2	7	7	1	0	6	0	0	0	0	0	-	0	.308	.333	.462
	9 ML YEARS		780	2022	530	111	5	83	(47	36)	900	218	343	270	154	25	375	9	0	25	1	6	.14	56	.262	.314	.445

John Wasdin

Pitches: R Bats: R Pos: SP-5; RP-4   Ht: 6'2" Wt: 190 Born: 8/5/1972 Age: 34

Year	Team	Lg	G	GS	CG	GF	IP	BFP	H	R	ER	HR	SH	SF	HB	TBB	IBB	SO	WP	Bk	W	L	Pct	ShO	Sv-Op	Hld	ERC	ERA
2006	Okla*	AAA	13	9	1	0	63.0	254	52	23	14	2	2	2	2	17	1	62	1	0	3	3	.500	1	0- -	-	2.36	2.00
1995	Oak	AL	5	2	0	3	17.1	69	14	9	9	4	0	0	1	3	0	6	0	0	1	1	.500	0	0-0	0	3.19	4.67
1996	Oak	AL	25	21	1	2	131.1	575	145	96	87	24	3	6	4	50	5	75	2	2	8	7	.533	0	0-1	0	5.32	5.96
1997	Bos	AL	53	7	0	10	124.2	515	121	68	61	18	4	7	3	38	4	84	4	0	4	6	.400	0	0-2	0	3.82	4.40
1998	Bos	AL	47	8	0	13	96.0	424	111	57	56	14	3	6	2	27	8	59	1	0	6	6	.600	0	0-1	0	4.70	5.25
1999	Bos	AL	45	0	0	17	74.1	302	66	38	34	14	2	2	0	18	0	57	2	0	8	3	.727	0	2-5	0	3.41	4.12
2000	2 Tms		39	4	1	12	80.1	352	90	48	48	14	1	7	5	24	3	71	3	0	1	6	.143	0	1-2	0	5.09	5.38
2001	2 Tms		44	0	0	7	74.0	330	86	44	42	11	0	5	6	24	6	64	3	0	3	2	.600	0	0-5	0	5.27	5.11

Year	Team	Lg	G	GS	CG	GF	IP	BFP	H	R	ER	HR	SH	SF	HB	TBB	IBB	SO	WP	Bk	W	L	Pct	ShO	Sv-Op	Hld	ERC	ERA
2003	Tor	AL	3	2	0	0	5.0	35	16	13	13	2	0	1	0	4	0	5	0	0	0	1	.000	0	0-0	0	25.15	23.40
2004	Tex	AL	15	10	0	0	65.0	301	83	52	49	18	1	2	3	23	2	36	0	0	2	4	.333	0	0-0	0	6.97	6.78
2005	Tex	AL	31	6	0	7	75.2	319	77	37	36	9	1	2	1	20	2	44	2	0	3	2	.600	0	4-6	4	3.77	4.28
2006	Bos	AL	9	5	0	3	30.0	141	33	19	17	6	0	0	4	13	0	16	0	0	2	2	.500	0	0-0	0	5.93	5.10
00	Bos	AL	25	1	0	10	44.2	198	48	25	25	8	0	5	2	15	2	36	1	0	1	3	.250	0	1-2	0	4.83	5.04
00	Col	NL	14	3	1	2	35.2	154	42	23	23	6	1	2	3	9	1	35	2	0	0	3	.000	0	0-0	0	5.43	5.80
01	Col	NL	18	0	0	2	24.1	110	32	19	19	7	0	1	1	8	2	17	1	0	2	1	.667	0	0-3	0	7.27	7.03
01	Bal	AL	26	0	0	5	49.2	220	54	25	23	4	0	4	5	16	4	47	2	0	1	1	.500	0	0-2	0	4.36	4.17
11 ML YEARS			316	65	2	74	773.2	3382	842	481	452	134	15	38	29	244	30	517	17	2	38	38	.500	0	7-22	4	4.82	5.26

Jarrod Washburn

Pitches: L Bats: L Pos: SP-31   Ht: 6'1" Wt: 190 Born: 8/13/1974 Age: 32

Year	Team	Lg	G	GS	CG	GF	IP	BFP	H	R	ER	HR	SH	SF	HB	TBB	IBB	SO	WP	Bk	W	L	Pct	ShO	Sv-Op	Hld	ERC	ERA
1998	LAA	AL	15	11	0	0	74.0	317	70	40	38	11	2	3	3	27	1	48	0	0	6	3	.667	0	0-0	1	4.09	4.62
1999	LAA	AL	16	10	0	3	61.2	264	61	36	36	6	1	2	1	26	0	39	2	0	4	5	.444	0	0-0	1	4.20	5.25
2000	LAA	AL	14	14	0	0	84.1	340	64	38	35	16	1	3	1	37	0	49	1	0	7	2	.778	0	0-0	0	3.66	3.74
2001	LAA	AL	30	30	1	0	193.1	813	196	89	81	25	4	4	7	54	4	126	3	0	11	10	.524	0	0-0	0	4.03	3.77
2002	LAA	AL	32	32	1	0	206.0	852	183	75	72	19	4	7	3	59	1	139	5	1	18	6	.750	0	0-0	0	3.02	3.15
2003	LAA	AL	32	32	2	0	207.1	876	205	106	102	34	5	6	11	54	4	118	4	1	10	15	.400	0	0-0	0	4.07	4.43
2004	LAA	AL	25	25	1	0	149.1	640	159	81	77	20	2	4	4	40	1	86	5	0	11	8	.579	1	0-0	0	4.23	4.64
2005	LAA	AL	29	29	1	0	177.1	740	184	66	63	19	4	6	8	51	0	94	2	0	8	8	.500	1	0-0	0	4.19	3.20
2006	Sea	AL	31	31	0	0	187.0	809	198	103	97	25	3	6	7	55	2	103	3	0	8	14	.364	0	0-0	0	4.33	4.67
9 ML YEARS			224	214	6	3	1340.1	5651	1320	634	601	175	26	41	45	403	13	802	25	2	83	71	.539	2	0-0	2	3.95	4.04

Brandon Watson

Bats: L Throws: R Pos: CF-8; PH-1; PR-1   Ht: 6'1" Wt: 170 Born: 9/30/1981 Age: 25

Year	Team	Lg	G	AB	H	2B	3B	HR	(Hm	Rd)	TB	R	RBI	RC	TBB	IBB	SO	HBP	SH	SF	SB	CS	SB%	GDP	Avg	OBP	Slg
1999	Expos	R	33	119	36	2	0	0	(-	-)	38	15	12	12	1	1	11	1	2	2	4	2	.67	0	.303	.309	.319
2000	Vrmnt	A-	69	278	81	9	1	0	(-	-)	92	53	30	37	25	0	38	3	4	2	26	9	.74	4	.291	.354	.331
2001	Clinton	A	117	489	160	16	9	2	(-	-)	200	74	38	73	29	0	65	1	3	3	33	20	.62	6	.327	.364	.409
2002	BrvdCt	A+	111	424	113	16	2	0	(-	-)	133	57	24	43	27	0	53	3	11	2	22	13	.63	5	.267	.314	.314
2002	Hrsbrg	AA	2	6	2	0	0	0	(-	-)	2	2	0	1	1	0	0	0	0	0	0	0	-	0	.333	.429	.333
2003	Hrsbrg	AA	139	565	180	17	6	1	(-	-)	212	86	39	78	38	2	60	3	11	4	18	17	.51	7	.319	.362	.375
2004	Edmtn	AAA	139	526	154	17	3	2	(-	-)	183	74	41	64	31	2	68	1	6	2	22	10	.69	3	.293	.332	.348
2005	Hrsbrg	AA	34	146	36	1	0	0	(-	-)	37	13	6	10	7	0	21	2	1	0	7	5	.58	2	.247	.290	.253
2005	NewOr	AAA	88	372	132	15	3	1	(-	-)	156	69	25	65	28	0	33	1	5	2	31	13	.70	5	.355	.400	.419
2006	NewOr	AAA	21	82	25	3	1	0	(-	-)	30	11	13	10	3	0	10	0	1	1	2	1	.67	2	.305	.326	.366
2006	Nats	R	2	6	2	0	0	0	(-	-)	2	1	0	1	1	0	1	0	0	0	0	0	-	0	.333	.429	.333
2006	Lsvlle	AAA	42	137	37	3	0	0	(-	-)	40	16	8	14	11	1	12	0	4	0	6	2	.75	1	.270	.324	.292
2005	Was	NL	25	40	7	1	1	1	(0	1)	13	8	5	3	4	0	8	0	4	0	0	2	.00	0	.175	.250	.325
2006	2 Tms	NL	10	28	5	0	0	0	(0	0)	5	0	0	1	1	0	3	0	0	0	1	2	.33	0	.179	.207	.179
06	Was	NL	9	28	5	0	0	0	(0	0)	5	0	0	1	1	0	3	0	0	0	0	2	.00	0	.179	.207	.179
06	Cin	NL	1	0	0	0	0	0	(0	0)	0	0	0	0	0	0	0	0	0	0	1	0	1.00	0	-	-	-
2 ML YEARS			35	68	12	1	1	1	(0	1)	18	8	5	4	5	0	11	0	4	0	1	4	.20	0	.176	.233	.265

David Weathers

Pitches: R Bats: R Pos: RP-67   Ht: 6'3" Wt: 230 Born: 9/25/1969 Age: 37

Year	Team	Lg	G	GS	CG	GF	IP	BFP	H	R	ER	HR	SH	SF	HB	TBB	IBB	SO	WP	Bk	W	L	Pct	ShO	Sv-Op	Hld	ERC	ERA
1991	Tor	AL	15	0	0	4	14.2	79	15	9	8	1	2	1	2	17	3	13	0	0	1	0	1.000	0	0-0	1	6.88	4.91
1992	Tor	AL	2	0	0	0	3.1	15	5	3	3	1	0	0	0	2	0	3	0	0	0	0	-	0	0-0	0	10.97	8.10
1993	Fla	NL	14	6	0	2	45.2	202	57	26	26	3	2	0	1	13	1	34	6	0	2	3	.400	0	0-0	0	4.86	5.12
1994	Fla	NL	24	24	0	0	135.0	621	166	87	79	13	12	4	4	59	9	72	7	1	8	12	.400	0	0-0	0	5.52	5.27
1995	Fla	NL	28	15	0	0	90.1	416	104	68	60	8	7	3	5	52	3	60	3	0	4	5	.444	0	0-0	1	5.79	5.98
1996	2 Tms		42	12	0	9	88.2	409	108	60	54	8	5	2	6	42	5	53	3	0	2	4	.333	0	0-0	3	5.80	5.48
1997	2 Tms	AL	19	1	0	5	25.2	126	38	24	24	3	2	1	1	15	0	18	3	0	1	3	.250	0	0-1	0	8.27	8.42
1998	2 Tms	NL	44	9	0	9	110.0	492	130	69	60	6	6	2	3	41	3	94	7	2	6	5	.545	0	0-1	3	4.73	4.91
1999	Mil	NL	63	0	0	14	93.0	414	102	49	48	14	4	4	2	38	3	74	1	1	7	4	.636	0	2-6	9	5.04	4.65
2000	Mil	NL	69	0	0	23	76.1	320	73	29	26	7	4	1	2	32	8	50	0	0	3	5	.375	0	1-7	14	3.90	3.07
2001	2 Tms	NL	80	0	0	25	86.0	351	65	24	23	6	10	3	3	34	8	66	0	0	4	5	.444	0	4-10	16	2.59	2.41
2002	NYM	NL	71	0	0	12	77.1	331	69	30	25	6	5	0	6	36	7	61	2	0	6	3	.667	0	0-5	18	3.60	2.91
2003	NYM	NL	77	0	0	20	87.2	384	87	33	30	6	8	0	6	40	6	75	1	0	1	6	.143	0	7-9	26	4.21	3.08
2004	3 Tms	NL	66	2	0	20	87.2	387	85	44	38	12	5	2	5	35	2	61	1	1	7	7	.500	0	0-4	12	5.01	4.15
2005	Cin	NL	73	0	0	41	77.2	331	71	36	34	7	4	2	2	29	2	61	4	0	7	4	.636	0	15-19	8	3.46	3.94
2006	Cin	NL	67	0	0	32	73.2	314	61	31	29	12	5	3	2	34	4	50	0	0	4	4	.500	0	12-19	9	3.79	3.54
96	NYY	AL	31	8	0	8	71.1	329	85	41	36	7	5	1	4	28	4	40	2	0	2	2	.500	0	0-0	3	5.35	4.54
96	NYY	AL	11	4	0	1	17.1	90	23	19	18	1	0	1	2	14	1	13	1	0	0	2	.000	0	0-0	0	7.66	9.35
97	NYY	AL	10	0	0	3	9.0	47	15	10	10	1	0	0	0	7	0	4	2	0	0	1	.000	0	0-1	0	10.26	10.00
97	Cle	AL	9	1	0	2	16.2	79	23	14	14	2	2	1	1	8	0	14	1	0	1	2	.333	0	0-0	0	7.23	7.56
98	Cin	NL	16	9	0	0	62.1	294	86	47	43	3	4	1	1	27	2	51	5	1	2	4	.333	0	0-0	0	6.04	6.21
98	Mil	NL	28	0	0	9	47.2	198	44	22	17	3	2	1	2	14	1	43	2	1	4	1	.800	0	0-1	3	3.15	3.21
01	Mil	NL	52	0	0	21	57.2	233	37	14	13	3	8	1	2	25	7	46	0	0	3	4	.429	0	4-7	10	2.01	2.03
01	ChC	NL	28	0	0	4	28.1	118	28	10	10	3	2	2	1	9	1	20	0	0	1	1	.500	0	0-3	6	3.90	3.18
04	NYM	NL	32	0	0	10	33.2	156	41	19	16	5	2	2	2	15	0	25	1	1	5	3	.625	0	0-1	6	6.15	4.28

	HOW MUCH HE PITCHED						WHAT HE GAVE UP											THE RESULTS					
Year	Team	Lg	G	GS	CG	GF	IP	BFP	H	R	ER	HR	SH	SF	HB	TBB	IBB	SO	WP	Bk	W	L	Pct	ShO	Sv-Op	Hld	ERC	ERA
04	Hou	NL	26	0	0	9	32.0	137	31	20	17	5	2	0	3	13	1	26	0	0	1	4	.200	0	0-3	5	4.77	4.78
04	Fla	NL	8	2	0	1	16.2	64	13	5	5	2	1	0	0	7	1	10	0	0	1	0	1.000	0	0-0	1	3.28	2.70
16 ML YEARS			754	69	0	216	1167.1	5165	1236	622	567	113	82	32	47	519	64	845	38	5	63	70	.474	0	41-81	120	4.65	4.37

Jeff Weaver

Pitches: R Bats: R Pos: SP-31   **Ht: 6'5" Wt: 200 Born: 8/22/1976 Age: 30**

	HOW MUCH HE PITCHED						WHAT HE GAVE UP											THE RESULTS					
Year	Team	Lg	G	GS	CG	GF	IP	BFP	H	R	ER	HR	SH	SF	HB	TBB	IBB	SO	WP	Bk	W	L	Pct	ShO	Sv-Op	Hld	ERC	ERA
1999	Det	AL	30	29	0	1	163.2	717	176	104	101	27	5	5	17	56	2	114	0	0	9	12	.429	0	0-0	0	5.21	5.55
2000	Det	AL	31	30	2	0	200.0	849	205	102	96	26	3	9	15	52	2	136	3	2	11	15	.423	0	0-0	0	4.18	4.32
2001	Det	AL	33	33	5	0	229.1	985	235	116	104	19	12	7	14	68	4	152	3	0	13	16	.448	0	0-0	0	3.89	4.08
2002	2 Tms	AL	32	25	3	3	199.2	840	193	88	78	16	6	3	11	48	4	132	6	0	11	11	.500	3	2-2	0	3.30	3.52
2003	NYY	AL	32	24	0	3	159.1	735	211	113	106	16	9	9	11	47	2	93	2	0	7	9	.438	0	0-0	1	5.77	5.99
2004	LAD	NL	34	34	0	0	220.0	935	219	103	98	19	5	7	14	67	9	153	9	0	13	13	.500	0	0-0	0	3.79	4.01
2005	LAD	NL	34	34	3	0	224.0	930	220	111	105	35	8	3	18	43	1	157	2	0	14	11	.560	2	0-0	0	3.87	4.22
2006	2 Tms		31	31	0	0	172.0	770	213	117	110	34	7	4	10	47	1	107	5	0	8	14	.364	0	0-0	0	5.90	5.76
02	Det	AL	17	17	3	0	121.2	509	112	50	43	4	5	2	8	33	1	75	4	0	6	8	.429	3	0-0	0	2.94	3.18
02	NYY	AL	15	8	0	3	78.0	331	81	38	35	12	1	1	3	15	3	57	2	0	5	3	.625	0	2-2	0	3.86	4.04
06	LAA	AL	16	16	0	0	88.2	397	114	68	62	18	2	1	4	21	0	62	4	0	3	10	.231	0	0-0	0	6.03	6.29
06	StL	NL	15	15	0	0	83.1	373	99	49	48	16	5	3	6	26	1	45	1	0	5	4	.556	0	0-0	0	5.78	5.18
8 ML YEARS			257	240	13	7	1568.0	6761	1672	854	798	192	55	47	110	428	25	1044	30	2	86	101	.460	5	2-2	1	4.36	4.58

Jered Weaver

Pitches: R Bats: R Pos: SP-19   **Ht: 6'7" Wt: 205 Born: 10/4/1982 Age: 24**

	HOW MUCH HE PITCHED						WHAT HE GAVE UP											THE RESULTS					
Year	Team	Lg	G	GS	CG	GF	IP	BFP	H	R	ER	HR	SH	SF	HB	TBB	IBB	SO	WP	Bk	W	L	Pct	ShO	Sv-Op	Hld	ERC	ERA
2005	RCuca	A+	7	7	0	0	33.0	131	25	18	14	3	0	1	1	7	0	49	1	0	4	1	.800	0	0- -	-	2.17	3.82
2005	Ark	AA	8	8	0	0	43.0	192	43	22	19	5	0	1	0	19	0	46	1	0	3	3	.500	0	0- -	-	4.23	3.98
2006	Salt Lk	AAA	12	11	2	0	77.0	295	63	19	18	7	0	1	2	10	0	93	0	0	6	1	.857	2	0- -	-	2.24	2.10
2006	LAA	AL	19	19	0	0	123.0	490	94	36	35	15	2	2	3	33	1	105	2	0	11	2	.846	0	0-0	0	2.57	2.56

Brandon Webb

Pitches: R Bats: R Pos: SP-33   **Ht: 6'2" Wt: 230 Born: 5/9/1979 Age: 28**

	HOW MUCH HE PITCHED						WHAT HE GAVE UP											THE RESULTS					
Year	Team	Lg	G	GS	CG	GF	IP	BFP	H	R	ER	HR	SH	SF	HB	TBB	IBB	SO	WP	Bk	W	L	Pct	ShO	Sv-Op	Hld	ERC	ERA
2003	Ari	NL	29	28	1	1	180.2	750	140	65	57	12	9	1	13	68	4	172	9	1	10	9	.526	1	0-0	0	2.80	2.84
2004	Ari	NL	35	35	1	0	208.0	933	194	111	83	17	14	6	11	119	11	164	17	1	7	16	.304	0	0-0	0	4.32	3.59
2005	Ari	NL	33	33	1	0	229.0	943	229	98	90	21	10	7	2	59	4	172	14	1	14	12	.538	0	0-0	0	3.54	3.54
2006	Ari	NL	33	33	5	0	235.0	950	216	91	81	15	10	6	6	50	4	178	5	2	16	8	.667	3	0-0	0	2.81	3.10
4 ML YEARS			130	129	8	1	852.2	3576	779	365	311	65	43	20	32	296	23	686	45	5	47	45	.511	4	0-0	0	3.36	3.28

Rickie Weeks

Bats: R Throws: R Pos: 2B-92; PH-2; DH-1   **Ht: 6'0" Wt: 205 Born: 9/13/1982 Age: 24**

	BATTING																	BASERUNNING				AVERAGES		
Year	Team	Lg	G	AB	H	2B	3B	HR	(Hm | Rd)	TB	R	RBI	RC	TBB	IBB	SO	HBP	SH	SF	SB	CS	SB%	GDP	Avg	OBP	Slg
2003	Mil	NL	7	12	2	1	0	0	(0 | 0)	3	1	0	0	1	0	6	1	0	0	0	0	-	0	.167	.286	.250
2005	Mil	NL	96	360	86	13	2	13	(8 | 5)	142	56	42	49	40	2	96	11	2	1	15	2	.88	11	.239	.333	.394
2006	Mil	NL	95	359	100	15	3	8	(6 | 2)	145	73	34	53	30	1	92	19	2	3	19	5	.79	6	.279	.363	.404
3 ML YEARS			198	731	188	29	5	21	(14 | 7)	290	130	76	102	71	3	194	31	4	4	34	7	.83	17	.257	.346	.397

Todd Wellemeyer

Pitches: R Bats: R Pos: RP-46   **Ht: 6'3" Wt: 205 Born: 8/30/1978 Age: 28**

	HOW MUCH HE PITCHED						WHAT HE GAVE UP											THE RESULTS					
Year	Team	Lg	G	GS	CG	GF	IP	BFP	H	R	ER	HR	SH	SF	HB	TBB	IBB	SO	WP	Bk	W	L	Pct	ShO	Sv-Op	Hld	ERC	ERA
2003	ChC	NL	15	0	0	8	27.2	122	25	22	20	5	1	0	0	19	1	30	0	0	1	1	.500	0	1-1	1	5.33	6.51
2004	ChC	NL	20	0	0	7	24.1	119	27	16	16	1	3	2	0	20	2	30	0	1	2	1	.667	0	0-0	0	5.67	5.92
2005	ChC	NL	22	0	0	6	32.1	146	32	23	22	7	2	1	0	22	1	32	3	0	2	1	.667	0	1-1	3	6.09	6.12
2006	2 Tms		46	0	0	10	78.1	345	68	38	36	6	3	6	4	50	3	54	9	0	1	4	.200	0	1-1	3	4.28	4.14
06	Fla	NL	18	0	0	6	21.1	97	20	13	13	1	1	3	2	13	1	17	2	0	0	2	.000	0	0-0	0	4.41	5.48
06	KC	AL	28	0	0	4	57.0	248	48	25	23	5	2	3	2	37	2	37	7	0	1	2	.333	0	1-1	3	4.23	3.63
4 ML YEARS			103	0	0	31	162.2	732	152	99	94	19	9	9	4	111	7	146	12	1	6	7	.462	0	3-3	7	5.02	5.20

David Wells

Pitches: L Bats: L Pos: SP-13   **Ht: 6'3" Wt: 250 Born: 5/20/1963 Age: 44**

	HOW MUCH HE PITCHED						WHAT HE GAVE UP											THE RESULTS					
Year	Team	Lg	G	GS	CG	GF	IP	BFP	H	R	ER	HR	SH	SF	HB	TBB	IBB	SO	WP	Bk	W	L	Pct	ShO	Sv-Op	Hld	ERC	ERA
2006	Pwtckt*	AAA	2	2	0	0	10.0	44	10	9	9	2	0	1	1	4	0	4	0	0	1	1	.500	0	0- -	-	5.23	8.10
1987	Tor	AL	18	2	0	6	29.1	132	37	14	13	0	1	0	0	12	0	32	4	0	4	3	.571	0	1-2	2	4.91	3.99
1988	Tor	AL	41	0	0	15	64.1	279	65	36	33	12	2	2	2	31	9	56	6	2	3	5	.375	0	4-6	8	5.11	4.62
1989	Tor	AL	54	0	0	19	86.1	352	66	25	23	5	3	2	0	28	7	78	6	3	7	4	.636	0	2-9	8	2.16	2.40
1990	Tor	AL	43	25	0	8	189.0	759	165	72	66	14	9	2	2	45	3	115	7	1	11	6	.647	0	3-3	3	2.67	3.14
1991	Tor	AL	40	28	2	3	198.1	811	188	88	82	24	6	6	2	49	1	106	10	3	15	10	.600	0	1-2	3	3.41	3.72
1992	Tor	AL	41	14	0	14	120.0	529	138	84	72	16	3	4	8	36	6	62	3	1	7	9	.438	0	2-4	3	4.98	5.40

	HOW MUCH HE PITCHED						WHAT HE GAVE UP													THE RESULTS							
Year	Team	Lg	G	GS	CG	GF	IP	BFP	H	R	ER	HR	SH	SF	HB	TBB	IBB	SO	WP	Bk	W	L	Pct	ShO	Sv-Op	Hld	ERC	ERA
1993	Det	AL	32	30	0	0	187.0	776	183	93	87	26	3	3	7	42	6	139	13	0	11	9	.550	1	0-0	1	3.64	4.19
1994	Det	AL	16	16	5	0	111.1	464	113	54	49	13	3	1	2	24	6	71	5	0	5	7	.417	1	0-0	0	3.54	3.96
1995	2 Tms		29	29	6	0	203.0	839	194	88	73	23	7	3	2	53	9	133	7	2	16	8	.667	0	0-0	0	3.37	3.24
1996	Bal	AL	34	34	3	0	224.1	946	247	132	128	32	8	14	7	51	7	130	4	2	11	14	.440	0	0-0	0	4.39	5.14
1997	NYY	AL	32	32	5	0	218.0	922	239	109	102	24	7	3	6	45	0	156	8	0	16	10	.615	2	0-0	0	4.04	4.21
1998	NYY	AL	30	30	8	0	214.1	851	195	86	83	29	2	2	1	29	0	163	2	0	18	4	.818	5	0-0	0	2.83	3.49
1999	Tor	AL	34	34	7	0	231.2	987	246	132	124	32	6	6	6	62	2	169	1	0	17	10	.630	1	0-0	0	4.26	4.82
2000	Tor	AL	35	35	9	0	229.2	972	266	115	105	23	6	7	8	31	0	166	9	1	20	8	.714	1	0-0	0	4.05	4.11
2001	CWS	AL	16	16	1	0	100.2	432	120	55	50	12	2	2	3	21	1	59	2	0	5	7	.417	0	0-0	1	4.69	4.47
2002	NYY	AL	31	31	2	0	206.1	873	210	100	86	21	6	5	5	45	2	137	4	0	19	7	.731	1	0-0	0	3.50	3.75
2003	NYY	AL	31	30	4	0	213.0	887	242	101	98	24	6	7	8	20	0	101	3	0	15	7	.682	0	0-0	0	3.87	4.14
2004	SD	NL	31	31	0	0	195.2	804	203	85	81	23	14	4	2	20	1	101	2	1	12	8	.600	0	0-0	0	3.23	3.73
2005	SD	NL	30	30	2	0	184.0	780	220	95	91	21	1	6	9	21	0	107	4	1	15	7	.682	0	0-0	0	4.36	4.45
2006	2 Tms		13	13	0	0	75.1	324	97	41	37	11	2	1	0	12	0	38	0	0	3	5	.375	0	0-0	0	5.14	4.42
95	Det	AL	18	18	3	0	130.1	539	120	54	44	17	3	2	2	37	5	83	6	1	10	3	.769	0	0-0	0	3.40	3.04
95	Cin	NL	11	11	3	0	72.2	300	74	34	29	6	4	1	0	16	4	50	1	1	6	5	.545	0	0-0	0	3.31	3.59
06	Bos	AL	8	8	0	0	47.0	206	64	30	26	10	1	1	0	8	0	24	0	0	2	3	.400	0	0-0	0	6.16	4.98
06	SD	NL	5	5	0	0	28.1	118	33	11	11	1	1	0	0	4	0	14	0	0	1	2	.333	0	0-0	0	3.58	3.49
20 ML YEARS			631	460	54	65	3281.2	13719	3434	1605	1483	385	97	80	80	677	60	2119	100	17	230	148	.608	12	13-26	28	3.77	4.07

Kip Wells

Pitches: R Bats: R Pos: SP-9   Ht: 6'3" Wt: 205 Born: 4/21/1977 Age: 30

	HOW MUCH HE PITCHED						WHAT HE GAVE UP													THE RESULTS							
Year	Team	Lg	G	GS	CG	GF	IP	BFP	H	R	ER	HR	SH	SF	HB	TBB	IBB	SO	WP	Bk	W	L	Pct	ShO	Sv-Op	Hld	ERC	ERA
2006	Lynbrg*	A+	1	1	0	0	6.0	23	3	0	0	0	0	0	2	2	0	5	0	0	1	0	1.000	0	0- -	-	1.99	0.00
2006	Altna*	AA	1	1	0	0	7.1	27	6	3	3	1	0	0	0	1	0	4	1	0	1	0	1.000	0	0- -	-	2.53	3.68
1999	CWS	AL	7	7	0	0	35.2	153	33	17	16	2	0	2	3	15	0	29	1	2	4	1	.800	0	0-0	0	3.80	4.04
2000	CWS	AL	20	20	0	0	98.2	468	126	76	66	15	1	3	2	58	4	71	7	0	6	9	.400	0	0-0	0	7.01	6.02
2001	CWS	AL	40	20	0	3	133.1	603	145	80	71	14	8	6	12	61	5	99	14	0	10	11	.476	0	0-2	6	5.16	4.79
2002	Pit	NL	33	33	1	0	198.1	845	197	92	79	21	7	5	7	71	11	134	7	0	12	14	.462	1	0-0	0	4.00	3.58
2003	Pit	NL	31	31	1	0	197.1	835	171	77	72	24	15	2	7	76	7	147	7	0	10	9	.526	0	0-0	0	3.49	3.28
2004	Pit	NL	24	24	0	0	138.1	621	145	71	70	14	5	6	6	66	4	116	3	0	5	7	.417	0	0-0	0	4.77	4.55
2005	Pit	NL	33	33	1	0	182.0	828	186	116	103	23	9	10	12	99	8	132	8	0	8	18	.308	1	0-0	0	5.14	5.09
2006	2 Tms		9	9	0	0	44.1	208	61	33	32	3	1	1	4	21	1	20	5	0	2	5	.286	0	0-0	0	6.90	6.50
06	Pit	NL	7	7	0	0	36.1	168	46	27	27	3	1	1	4	18	1	16	5	0	1	5	.167	0	0-0	0	6.51	6.69
06	Tex	AL	2	2	0	0	8.0	40	15	6	5	0	0	0	0	3	0	4	0	0	1	0	1.000	0	0-0	0	8.77	5.63
8 ML YEARS			197	177	3	3	1028.0	4561	1064	562	509	116	46	35	53	467	40	748	52	2	57	74	.435	2	0-2	6	4.73	4.46

Vernon Wells

Bats: R Throws: R Pos: CF-150; DH-4   Ht: 6'1" Wt: 225 Born: 12/8/1978 Age: 28

	BATTING																		BASERUNNING				AVERAGES		
Year	Team	Lg	G	AB	H	2B	3B	HR	(Hm | Rd)	TB	R	RBI	RC	TBB	IBB	SO	HBP	SH	SF	SB	CS	SB%	GDP	Avg	OBP	Slg
1999	Tor	AL	24	88	23	5	0	1	(1 | 0)	31	8	8	7	4	0	18	0	0	0	1	1	.50	6	.261	.293	.352
2000	Tor	AL	3	2	0	0	0	0	(0 | 0)	0	0	0	0	0	0	0	0	0	0	0	0	-	0	.000	.000	.000
2001	Tor	AL	30	96	30	8	0	1	(1 | 0)	41	14	6	16	5	0	15	1	0	1	5	0	1.00	6	.313	.350	.427
2002	Tor	AL	159	608	167	34	4	23	(10 | 13)	278	87	100	88	27	0	85	3	2	8	9	4	.69	15	.275	.305	.457
2003	Tor	AL	161	678	215	49	5	33	(13 | 20)	373	118	117	124	42	2	80	7	0	8	4	1	.80	21	.317	.359	.550
2004	Tor	AL	134	536	146	34	2	23	(14 | 9)	253	82	67	72	51	2	83	2	0	1	9	2	.82	17	.272	.337	.472
2005	Tor	AL	156	620	167	30	3	28	(14 | 14)	287	78	97	96	47	3	86	3	0	8	8	3	.73	13	.269	.320	.463
2006	Tor	AL	154	611	185	40	5	32	(24 | 8)	331	91	106	107	54	0	90	3	0	9	17	4	.81	13	.303	.357	.542
8 ML YEARS			821	3239	933	200	19	141	(77 | 64)	1594	478	501	510	230	7	457	19	2	35	53	15	.78	85	.288	.336	.492

Jayson Werth

Bats: R Throws: R Pos: OF   Ht: 6'5" Wt: 210 Born: 5/20/1979 Age: 28

	BATTING																		BASERUNNING				AVERAGES		
Year	Team	Lg	G	AB	H	2B	3B	HR	(Hm | Rd)	TB	R	RBI	RC	TBB	IBB	SO	HBP	SH	SF	SB	CS	SB%	GDP	Avg	OBP	Slg
2002	Tor	AL	15	46	12	2	1	0	(0 | 0)	16	4	6	5	6	0	11	0	0	1	1	0	1.00	4	.261	.340	.348
2003	Tor	AL	26	48	10	4	0	2	(0 | 2)	20	7	10	6	3	0	22	0	0	0	1	0	1.00	0	.208	.255	.417
2004	LAD	NL	89	290	76	11	3	16	(11 | 5)	141	56	47	47	30	0	85	4	1	4	4	1	.80	1	.262	.338	.486
2005	LAD	NL	102	337	79	22	2	7	(1 | 6)	126	46	43	44	48	2	114	6	1	3	11	2	.85	10	.234	.338	.374
4 ML YEARS			232	721	177	39	6	25	(12 | 13)	303	113	106	102	87	2	232	10	2	5	17	3	.85	15	.245	.333	.420

Jake Westbrook

Pitches: R Bats: R Pos: SP-32   Ht: 6'3" Wt: 200 Born: 9/29/1977 Age: 29

	HOW MUCH HE PITCHED						WHAT HE GAVE UP													THE RESULTS							
Year	Team	Lg	G	GS	CG	GF	IP	BFP	H	R	ER	HR	SH	SF	HB	TBB	IBB	SO	WP	Bk	W	L	Pct	ShO	Sv-Op	Hld	ERC	ERA
2000	NYY	AL	3	2	0	1	6.2	38	15	10	10	1	0	2	0	4	1	1	0	0	0	2	.000	0	0-0	0	13.53	13.50
2001	Cle	AL	23	6	0	3	64.2	290	79	43	42	6	1	5	4	22	4	48	4	0	4	4	.500	0	0-0	5	5.25	5.85
2002	Cle	AL	11	4	0	1	41.2	185	50	30	27	6	2	1	1	12	1	20	1	0	1	3	.250	0	0-0	2	5.12	5.83
2003	Cle	AL	34	22	1	4	133.0	580	142	70	64	9	4	3	12	56	1	58	3	0	7	10	.412	0	0-0	1	4.78	4.33
2004	Cle	AL	33	30	5	2	215.2	895	208	95	81	19	6	6	5	61	3	116	4	1	14	9	.609	1	0-0	0	3.45	3.38
2005	Cle	AL	34	34	2	0	210.2	895	218	121	105	19	5	4	7	56	3	119	3	0	15	15	.500	0	0-0	0	3.78	4.49
2006	Cle	AL	32	32	3	0	211.1	904	247	106	98	15	5	4	4	55	4	109	5	0	15	10	.600	2	0-0	0	4.39	4.17
7 ML YEARS			170	130	11	11	883.2	3787	959	475	427	75	23	25	33	266	17	471	20	1	56	53	.514	3	0-2	7	4.22	4.35

Dan Wheeler

Pitches: R Bats: R Pos: RP-75   Ht: 6'3" Wt: 220 Born: 12/10/1977 Age: 29

Year	Team	Lg	G	GS	CG	GF	IP	BFP	H	R	ER	HR	SH	SF	HB	TBB	IBB	SO	WP	Bk	W	L	Pct	ShO	Sv-Op	Hld	ERC	ERA
1999	TB	AL	6	6	0	0	30.2	136	35	20	20	7	1	0	0	13	1	32	1	0	0	4	.000	0	0-0	0	5.96	5.87
2000	TB	AL	11	2	0	6	23.0	111	29	14	14	2	1	1	2	11	2	17	2	0	1	1	.500	0	0-1	1	5.87	5.48
2001	TB	AL	13	0	0	3	17.2	87	30	17	17	3	0	2	0	5	0	12	1	1	1	0	1.000	0	0-0	0	8.38	8.66
2003	NYM	NL	35	0	0	10	51.0	215	49	23	21	6	0	3	1	17	4	35	1	0	1	3	.250	0	2-3	0	3.69	3.71
2004	2 Tms	NL	46	1	0	11	65.0	287	76	33	31	10	2	1	1	20	2	55	4	1	3	1	.750	0	0-0	5	5.05	4.29
2005	Hou	NL	71	0	0	20	73.1	288	53	18	18	7	5	1	3	19	3	69	0	0	2	3	.400	0	3-5	17	2.22	2.21
2006	Hou	NL	75	0	0	25	71.1	295	58	22	20	5	3	3	2	24	8	68	0	0	3	5	.375	0	9-12	24	2.57	2.52
04	NYM	NL	32	1	0	7	50.2	232	65	29	27	9	2	1	0	17	2	46	4	1	3	1	.750	0	0-0	3	5.91	4.80
04	Hou	NL	14	0	0	4	14.1	55	11	4	4	1	0	0	1	3	0	9	0	0	0	0	-	0	0-0	2	2.35	2.51
	7 ML YEARS		257	9	0	75	332.0	1419	330	147	141	40	12	11	9	109	20	288	9	2	11	17	.393	0	14-21	47	3.90	3.82

Rick White

Pitches: R Bats: R Pos: RP-64   Ht: 6'4" Wt: 240 Born: 12/23/1968 Age: 38

Year	Team	Lg	G	GS	CG	GF	IP	BFP	H	R	ER	HR	SH	SF	HB	TBB	IBB	SO	WP	Bk	W	L	Pct	ShO	Sv-Op	Hld	ERC	ERA
1994	Pit	NL	43	5	0	23	75.1	317	79	35	32	9	7	5	6	17	3	38	2	2	4	5	.444	0	6-9	3	4.11	3.82
1995	Pit	NL	15	9	0	2	55.0	247	66	33	29	3	3	3	2	18	0	29	2	0	2	3	.400	0	0-0	0	4.70	4.75
1998	TB	AL	38	3	0	12	68.2	289	66	32	29	8	0	3	2	23	2	39	3	0	2	6	.250	0	0-0	2	3.82	3.80
1999	TB	AL	63	1	0	11	108.0	480	132	56	49	8	2	5	1	38	5	81	3	0	5	3	.625	0	0-2	4	4.96	4.08
2000	2 Tms	NL	66	0	0	14	99.2	420	83	44	39	9	1	3	7	38	5	67	3	0	5	9	.357	0	3-7	4	3.21	3.52
2001	NYM	NL	55	0	0	15	69.2	299	71	38	30	7	2	2	2	17	4	51	1	0	4	5	.444	0	2-4	10	3.52	3.88
2002	2 Tms	NL	61	0	0	10	62.2	264	62	33	30	4	3	4	1	21	5	41	3	0	5	7	.417	0	0-1	16	3.49	4.31
2003	2 Tms	NL	49	0	0	15	67.0	293	74	48	43	13	2	2	4	21	2	54	2	0	1	2	.333	0	1-1	4	5.22	5.23
2004	Cle	AL	59	0	0	20	78.1	340	88	52	46	15	6	3	2	29	7	44	2	0	5	5	.500	0	1-3	2	5.41	5.29
2005	Pit	NL	71	0	0	23	75.0	338	90	39	31	3	9	4	4	29	10	40	4	0	4	7	.364	0	2-3	12	4.71	3.72
2006	2 Tms	NL	64	0	0	20	64.2	276	72	44	37	8	5	2	3	20	1	40	4	2	4	1	.800	0	1-2	7	4.82	5.15
00	TB	AL	44	0	0	8	71.1	293	57	30	27	7	1	2	5	26	3	47	3	0	3	6	.333	0	2-5	2	3.09	3.41
00	NYM	NL	22	0	0	6	28.1	127	26	14	12	2	0	1	2	12	2	20	0	0	2	3	.400	0	1-2	2	3.51	3.81
02	Col	NL	41	0	0	8	40.2	182	49	30	28	4	1	4	1	18	4	27	3	0	2	6	.250	0	0-1	9	5.47	6.20
02	StL	NL	20	0	0	2	22.0	82	13	3	2	0	2	0	0	3	1	14	0	0	3	1	.750	0	0-0	7	0.94	0.82
03	CWS	AL	34	0	0	12	47.2	207	56	39	35	11	1	2	1	13	2	37	0	0	1	2	.333	0	1-1	3	5.58	6.61
03	Hou	NL	15	0	0	3	19.1	86	18	9	8	2	1	0	3	8	0	17	2	0	0	0	-	0	0-0	1	4.33	3.72
06	Cin	NL	26	0	0	10	27.1	118	34	23	19	5	3	2	1	5	1	17	2	2	1	0	1.000	0	1-2	2	5.35	6.26
06	Phi	NL	38	0	0	10	37.1	158	38	21	18	3	2	0	2	15	0	23	2	0	3	1	.750	0	0-0	5	4.42	4.34
	11 ML YEARS		584	18	0	165	824.0	3563	883	454	395	87	40	36	34	271	44	524	29	4	41	53	.436	0	16-32	64	4.34	4.31

Rondell White

Bats: R Throws: R Pos: DH-53; LF-38; PH-9   Ht: 6'1" Wt: 225 Born: 2/23/1972 Age: 35

Year	Team	Lg	G	AB	H	2B	3B	HR	(Hm	Rd)	TB	R	RBI	RC	TBB	IBB	SO	HBP	SH	SF	SB	CS	SB%	GDP	Avg	OBP	Slg
2006	Roch*	AAA	13	51	12	0	0	1	(-	-)	15	8	5	3	1	0	6	0	0	1	0	0	-	3	.235	.245	.294
1993	Mon	NL	23	73	19	3	1	2	(1	1)	30	9	15	9	7	0	16	0	2	1	1	2	.33	2	.260	.321	.411
1994	Mon	NL	40	97	27	10	1	2	(1	1)	45	16	13	16	9	0	18	3	0	0	1	1	.50	1	.278	.358	.464
1995	Mon	NL	130	474	140	33	4	13	(6	7)	220	87	57	79	41	1	87	6	0	4	25	5	.83	11	.295	.356	.464
1996	Mon	NL	88	334	98	19	4	6	(2	4)	143	35	41	46	22	0	53	2	0	1	14	6	.70	11	.293	.340	.428
1997	Mon	NL	151	592	160	29	5	28	(9	19)	283	84	82	84	31	3	111	10	1	4	16	8	.67	18	.270	.316	.478
1998	Mon	NL	97	357	107	21	2	17	(9	8)	183	54	58	65	30	2	57	7	0	3	16	7	.70	7	.300	.363	.513
1999	Mon	NL	138	539	168	26	6	22	(10	12)	272	83	64	91	32	2	85	11	0	6	10	6	.63	17	.312	.359	.505
2000	2 Tms	NL	94	357	110	26	0	13	(3	10)	176	59	61	64	33	0	79	4	0	2	5	3	.63	4	.311	.374	.493
2001	ChC	NL	95	323	99	19	1	17	(7	10)	171	43	50	57	26	4	56	7	1	0	1	0	1.00	14	.307	.371	.529
2002	NYY	AL	126	455	109	21	0	14	(5	9)	172	59	62	43	25	1	86	8	1	5	1	2	.33	11	.240	.288	.378
2003	2 Tms	NL	137	488	141	23	4	22	(5	17)	238	62	87	72	31	2	79	10	0	5	1	4	.20	13	.289	.341	.488
2004	Det	AL	121	448	121	21	2	19	(5	14)	203	76	67	69	39	4	77	8	0	3	1	2	.33	13	.270	.337	.453
2005	Det	AL	97	374	117	24	3	12	(7	5)	183	49	53	61	17	0	48	5	0	4	1	0	1.00	8	.313	.348	.489
2006	Min	AL	99	337	83	17	1	7	(4	3)	123	32	38	27	11	2	54	4	0	3	1	1	.50	11	.246	.276	.365
00	Mon	NL	75	290	89	24	0	11	(3	8)	146	52	54	53	28	0	67	2	0	2	5	1	.83	4	.307	.370	.503
00	ChC	NL	19	67	22	2	0	2	(0	2)	30	7	7	11	5	0	12	2	0	0	0	2	.00	0	.328	.392	.448
03	SD	NL	115	413	115	17	3	18	(4	14)	192	49	66	54	25	2	71	8	0	3	1	4	.20	11	.278	.330	.465
03	KC	AL	22	75	26	6	1	4	(1	3)	46	13	21	18	6	0	8	2	0	2	0	0	-	2	.347	.400	.613
	14 ML YEARS		1436	5248	1500	292	34	194	(74	120)	2442	748	748	783	354	21	906	85	5	41	94	47	.67	141	.286	.339	.465

Bob Wickman

Pitches: R Bats: R Pos: RP-57   Ht: 6'1" Wt: 240 Born: 2/6/1969 Age: 38

Year	Team	Lg	G	GS	CG	GF	IP	BFP	H	R	ER	HR	SH	SF	HB	TBB	IBB	SO	WP	Bk	W	L	Pct	ShO	Sv-Op	Hld	ERC	ERA
1992	NYY	AL	8	8	0	0	50.1	213	51	25	23	2	1	3	2	20	0	21	3	0	6	1	.857	0	0-0	0	3.99	4.11
1993	NYY	AL	41	19	1	9	140.0	629	156	82	72	13	4	1	5	69	7	70	2	0	14	4	.778	1	4-8	2	5.16	4.63
1994	NYY	AL	53	0	0	19	70.0	286	54	26	24	3	0	5	1	27	3	56	2	0	5	4	.556	0	6-10	11	2.45	3.09
1995	NYY	AL	63	1	0	14	80.0	347	77	38	36	6	4	1	5	33	3	51	2	0	2	4	.333	0	1-10	21	3.92	4.05
1996	2 Tms	AL	70	0	0	18	95.2	429	106	50	47	10	2	4	5	44	3	75	4	0	7	1	.875	0	0-4	10	5.17	4.42
1997	Mil	AL	74	0	0	20	95.2	405	89	32	29	6	3	6	3	41	7	78	8	0	7	6	.538	0	1-5	28	3.76	2.73
1998	Mil	NL	72	0	0	51	82.1	357	79	38	34	5	10	3	4	39	2	71	1	0	6	9	.400	0	25-32	0	4.05	3.72
1999	Mil	NL	71	0	0	63	74.1	331	75	31	28	6	3	2	2	38	6	60	2	0	3	8	.273	0	37-45	0	4.38	3.39
2000	2 Tms	AL	69	0	0	60	72.2	309	64	30	25	1	3	1	1	32	5	55	2	0	3	5	.375	0	30-37	0	2.92	3.10
2001	Cle	AL	70	0	0	56	67.2	270	61	18	18	4	0	0	2	14	2	66	2	0	5	0	1.000	0	32-35	4	2.69	2.39
2002	Cle	AL	36	0	0	30	34.1	159	42	22	17	3	0	0	1	10	0	36	0	0	1	3	.250	0	20-22	0	4.72	4.46

HOW MUCH HE PITCHED							WHAT HE GAVE UP												THE RESULTS							
Year	Team	Lg	G	GS	CG	GF	IP	BFP	H	R	ER	HR	SH	SF	HB	TBB	IBB	SO	WP	Bk	W	L	Pct	ShO	Sv-Op	Hld	ERC	ERA
2004	Cle	AL	30	0	0	21	29.2	129	33	14	14	4	0	0	2	10	0	26	0	0	0	2	.000	0	13-14	4	5.09	4.25
2005	Cle	AL	64	0	0	55	62.0	257	57	17	17	9	2	2	1	21	3	41	0	1	0	4	.000	0	**45-50**	4	3.74	2.47
2006	2 Tms		57	0	0	55	54.0	233	53	22	16	2	5	3	1	13	0	42	1	0	1	6	.143	0	33-37	0	2.89	2.67
96	NYY	AL	58	0	0	14	79.0	358	94	41	41	7	1	4	5	34	1	61	3	0	4	1	.800	0	0-3	6	5.51	4.67
96	Mil	AL	12	0	0	4	16.2	71	12	9	6	3	1	0	0	10	2	14	1	0	3	0	1.000	0	0-1	4	3.66	3.24
00	Mil	NL	43	0	0	36	46.0	194	37	18	15	1	0	1	1	20	2	44	2	0	2	2	.500	0	16-20	7	2.62	2.93
00	Cle	AL	26	0	0	24	26.2	115	27	12	10	0	3	0	0	12	3	11	0	0	1	3	.250	0	14-17	0	3.47	3.38
06	Cle	AL	29	0	0	29	28.0	126	29	15	13	1	4	3	1	11	0	17	1	0	1	4	.200	0	15-18	0	3.79	4.18
06	Atl	NL	28	0	0	26	26.0	107	24	7	3	1	1	0	0	2	0	25	0	0	0	2	.000	0	18-19	0	1.99	1.04
14 ML YEARS			778	28	1	471	1008.2	4354	997	445	400	76	40	27	35	411	41	748	29	1	60	57	.513	1	247-309	89	3.95	3.57

Chris Widger

Bats: R **Throws:** R **Pos:** C-28; PH-8; DH-4   **Ht:** 6'2" **Wt:** 220 **Born:** 5/21/1971 **Age:** 36

BATTING																					BASERUNNING				AVERAGES		
Year	Team	Lg	G	AB	H	2B	3B	HR	(Hm	Rd)	TB	R	RBI	RC	TBB	IBB	SO	HBP	SH	SF	SB	CS	SB%	GDP	Avg	OBP	Slg
1995	Sea	AL	23	45	9	0	0	1	(1	0)	12	2	2	3	3	0	11	0	0	1	0	0	-	0	.200	.245	.267
1996	Sea	AL	8	11	2	0	0	0	(0	0)	2	1	0	0	0	0	5	1	0	0	0	0	-	0	.182	.250	.182
1997	Mon	NL	91	278	65	20	3	7	(4	3)	112	30	37	32	22	1	59	1	2	2	2	0	1.00	7	.234	.290	.403
1998	Mon	NL	125	417	97	18	1	15	(6	9)	162	36	53	46	29	2	85	0	0	2	6	1	.86	5	.233	.281	.388
1999	Mon	NL	124	383	101	24	1	14	(11	3)	169	42	56	53	28	0	86	7	0	1	1	4	.20	5	.264	.325	.441
2000	2 Tms		96	292	68	17	2	13	(6	7)	128	32	35	39	30	3	63	1	0	1	1	2	.33	5	.233	.306	.438
2002	NYY	AL	21	64	19	5	0	0	(0	0)	24	4	5	8	2	0	9	2	0	0	0	0	-	0	.297	.338	.375
2003	StL	NL	44	102	24	9	0	0	(0	0)	33	9	14	10	6	1	20	1	1	2	0	0	-	0	.235	.279	.324
2005	CWS	AL	45	141	34	8	0	4	(2	2)	54	18	11	12	10	0	22	1	2	0	0	2	.00	5	.241	.296	.383
2006	2 Tms	AL	36	93	16	3	0	1	(0	1)	22	6	9	5	11	0	24	0	1	2	0	0	-	2	.172	.255	.237
00	Mon	NL	86	281	67	17	2	12	(6	6)	124	31	34	38	29	3	61	1	0	1	1	2	.33	5	.238	.311	.441
00	Sea	AL	10	11	1	0	0	1	(0	1)	4	1	1	1	1	0	2	0	0	0	0	0	-	0	.091	.167	.364
06	CWS	AL	27	76	14	3	0	1	(0	1)	20	6	7	4	9	0	20	0	0	2	0	0	-	1	.184	.264	.263
06	Bal	AL	9	17	2	0	0	0	(0	0)	2	0	2	1	2	0	4	0	1	0	0	0	-	1	.118	.211	.118
10 ML YEARS			613	1826	435	104	7	55	(30	25)	718	180	222	208	141	7	384	14	6	11	10	9	.53	34	.238	.296	.393

Ty Wigginton

Bats: R **Throws:** R **Pos:** 1B-45; 2B-43; 3B-34; RF-7; LF-5; PH-3; DH-1   **Ht:** 6'0" **Wt:** 225 **Born:** 10/11/1977 **Age:** 29

BATTING																					BASERUNNING				AVERAGES		
Year	Team	Lg	G	AB	H	2B	3B	HR	(Hm	Rd)	TB	R	RBI	RC	TBB	IBB	SO	HBP	SH	SF	SB	CS	SB%	GDP	Avg	OBP	Slg
2006	Drham*	AAA	2	8	3	2	0	1	(-	-)	8	2	2	2	0	0	2	0	0	0	0	0	-	0	.375	.375	1.000
2002	NYM	NL	46	116	35	8	0	6	(4	2)	61	18	18	15	8	0	19	2	0	1	2	1	.67	4	.302	.354	.526
2003	NYM	NL	156	573	146	36	6	11	(4	7)	227	73	71	76	46	2	124	9	1	4	12	2	.86	15	.255	.318	.396
2004	2 Tms	NL	144	494	129	30	2	17	(6	11)	214	63	66	59	45	6	82	2	1	3	7	1	.88	15	.261	.324	.433
2005	Pit	NL	57	155	40	9	1	7	(1	6)	72	20	25	22	14	0	30	1	1	0	0	1	.00	3	.258	.324	.465
2006	TB	AL	122	444	122	25	1	24	(18	6)	221	55	79	69	32	3	97	6	1	3	4	3	.57	11	.275	.330	.498
04	NYM	NL	86	312	89	23	2	12	(5	7)	152	46	42	38	23	4	48	1	1	2	6	1	.86	11	.285	.334	.487
04	Pit	NL	58	182	40	7	0	5	(1	4)	62	17	24	21	22	2	34	1	0	1	1	0	1.00	4	.220	.306	.341
5 ML YEARS			525	1782	472	108	10	65	(33	32)	795	229	259	241	145	11	352	20	4	11	25	8	.76	48	.265	.325	.446

Brad Wilkerson

Bats: L **Throws:** L **Pos:** LF-80; DH-12; RF-3; CF-1; PH-1   **Ht:** 6'0" **Wt:** 205 **Born:** 6/1/1977 **Age:** 30

BATTING																					BASERUNNING				AVERAGES		
Year	Team	Lg	G	AB	H	2B	3B	HR	(Hm	Rd)	TB	R	RBI	RC	TBB	IBB	SO	HBP	SH	SF	SB	CS	SB%	GDP	Avg	OBP	Slg
2001	Mon	NL	47	117	24	7	2	1	(1	0)	38	11	5	12	17	1	41	0	1	1	2	1	.67	2	.205	.304	.325
2002	Mon	NL	153	507	135	27	8	20	(12	8)	238	92	59	83	81	7	161	5	6	4	7	8	.47	5	.266	.370	.469
2003	Mon	NL	146	504	135	34	4	19	(9	10)	234	78	77	90	89	0	155	4	2	3	13	10	.57	5	.268	.380	.464
2004	Mon	NL	160	572	146	39	2	32	(15	17)	285	112	67	95	106	8	152	4	3	3	13	6	.68	6	.255	.374	.498
2005	Was	NL	148	565	140	42	7	11	(6	5)	229	76	57	83	84	9	147	7	3	2	8	10	.44	5	.248	.351	.405
2006	Tex	AL	95	320	71	15	2	15	(5	10)	135	56	44	39	37	1	116	3	2	3	3	2	.60	6	.222	.306	.422
6 ML YEARS			749	2585	651	164	25	98	(48	50)	1159	425	309	402	414	26	772	23	17	16	46	37	.55	30	.252	.358	.448

Bernie Williams

Bats: B **Throws:** R **Pos:** RF-58; DH-30; CF-28; PH-23; LF-5; PR-2   **Ht:** 6'2" **Wt:** 205 **Born:** 9/13/1968 **Age:** 38

BATTING																					BASERUNNING				AVERAGES		
Year	Team	Lg	G	AB	H	2B	3B	HR	(Hm	Rd)	TB	R	RBI	RC	TBB	IBB	SO	HBP	SH	SF	SB	CS	SB%	GDP	Avg	OBP	Slg
1991	NYY	AL	85	320	76	19	4	3	(1	2)	112	43	34	41	48	0	57	1	2	3	10	5	.67	4	.238	.336	.350
1992	NYY	AL	62	261	73	14	2	5	(3	2)	106	39	26	37	29	1	36	1	2	0	7	6	.54	5	.280	.354	.406
1993	NYY	AL	139	567	152	31	4	12	(5	7)	227	67	68	71	53	4	106	4	1	3	9	9	.50	17	.268	.333	.400
1994	NYY	AL	108	408	118	29	1	12	(4	8)	185	80	57	70	61	2	54	3	1	2	16	9	.64	11	.289	.384	.453
1995	NYY	AL	144	563	173	29	9	18	(7	11)	274	93	82	105	75	1	98	5	2	3	8	6	.57	12	.307	.392	.487
1996	NYY	AL	143	551	168	26	7	29	(12	17)	295	108	102	113	82	8	72	0	1	7	17	4	.81	15	.305	.391	.535
1997	NYY	AL	129	509	167	35	6	21	(13	8)	277	107	100	109	73	7	80	1	0	8	15	8	.65	10	.328	.408	.544
1998	NYY	AL	128	499	169	30	5	26	(14	12)	287	101	97	110	74	9	81	1	0	4	15	9	.63	19	.339	.422	.575
1999	NYY	AL	158	591	202	28	6	25	(11	14)	317	116	115	131	100	**17**	95	1	0	5	9	10	.47	11	.342	.435	.536
2000	NYY	AL	141	537	165	37	6	30	(15	15)	304	108	121	112	71	11	84	5	0	3	13	5	.72	15	.307	.391	.566
2001	NYY	AL	146	540	166	38	0	26	(14	12)	282	102	94	108	78	11	67	6	0	9	11	5	.69	15	.307	.395	.522
2002	NYY	AL	154	612	204	37	2	19	(13	6)	302	102	102	124	83	7	97	3	0	1	8	4	.67	19	.333	.415	.493
2003	NYY	AL	119	445	117	19	1	15	(5	10)	183	77	64	66	71	8	61	3	0	2	5	0	1.00	21	.263	.367	.411
2004	NYY	AL	148	561	147	29	1	22	(13	9)	244	105	70	82	85	5	96	2	1	2	1	5	.17	19	.262	.360	.435

(Batting — continued)

Year	Team	Lg	G	AB	H	2B	3B	HR	(Hm	Rd)	TB	R	RBI	RC	TBB	IBB	SO	HBP	SH	SF	SB	CS	SB%	GDP	Avg	OBP	Slg
2005	NYY	AL	141	485	121	19	1	12	(7	5)	178	53	64	62	53	1	75	1	1	6	1	2	.33	16	.249	.321	.367
2006	NYY	AL	131	420	118	29	0	12	(6	6)	183	65	61	52	33	5	53	2	1	6	2	0	1.00	14	.281	.332	.436
16 ML YEARS			2076	7869	2336	449	55	287	(143	144)	3756	1366	1257	1393	1069	97	1212	39	12	64	147	87	.63	223	.297	.381	.477

Dave Williams

Pitches: L Bats: L Pos: SP-13; RP-1   Ht: 6'3" Wt: 230 Born: 3/12/1979 Age: 28

			HOW MUCH HE PITCHED						WHAT HE GAVE UP												THE RESULTS							
Year	Team	Lg	G	GS	CG	GF	IP	BFP	H	R	ER	HR	SH	SF	HB	TBB	IBB	SO	WP	Bk	W	L	Pct	ShO	Sv-Op	Hld	ERC	ERA
2006	Mets*	R	2	2	0	0	8.0	26	2	0	0	0	1	0	0	0	0	10	0	0	1	0	1.000	0	0- -	-	0.14	0.00
2006	Norfolk*	AAA	7	6	0	0	36.2	152	33	20	15	3	0	0	2	10	0	17	0	0	2	2	.500	0	0- -	-	3.14	3.68
2001	Pit	NL	22	18	0	1	114.0	472	100	53	47	15	3	8	7	45	4	57	0	0	3	7	.300	0	0-0	1	3.89	3.71
2002	Pit	NL	9	9	0	0	43.1	195	38	26	24	9	2	1	4	24	2	33	2	2	2	5	.286	0	0-0	0	4.99	4.98
2004	Pit	NL	10	6	0	0	38.2	162	31	21	19	4	1	1	3	13	2	33	0	0	2	3	.400	0	0-0	0	2.97	4.42
2005	Pit	NL	25	25	1	0	138.2	600	137	74	68	20	7	2	8	58	5	88	3	0	10	11	.476	1	0-0	0	4.62	4.41
2006	2 Tms	NL	14	13	0	1	69.0	320	93	52	50	14	6	3	6	20	1	32	2	1	5	4	.556	0	0-0	0	6.82	6.52
06	Cin	NL	8	8	0	0	40.0	194	54	34	32	9	3	3	4	16	0	16	1	1	2	3	.400	0	0-0	0	7.46	7.20
06	NYM	NL	6	5	0	1	29.0	126	39	18	18	5	3	0	2	4	1	16	1	0	3	1	.750	0	0-0	0	5.93	5.59
5 ML YEARS			80	71	1	2	403.2	1749	399	226	208	62	19	15	28	160	14	243	7	3	22	30	.423	1	0-0	1	4.64	4.64

Jerome Williams

Pitches: R Bats: R Pos: RP-3; SP-2   Ht: 6'3" Wt: 240 Born: 12/4/1981 Age: 25

			HOW MUCH HE PITCHED						WHAT HE GAVE UP												THE RESULTS							
Year	Team	Lg	G	GS	CG	GF	IP	BFP	H	R	ER	HR	SH	SF	HB	TBB	IBB	SO	WP	Bk	W	L	Pct	ShO	Sv-Op	Hld	ERC	ERA
2006	Iowa*	AAA	29	16	1	2	111.2	500	145	66	59	17	9	6	3	35	1	52	3	0	5	7	.417	1	0- -	-	6.05	4.76
2003	SF	NL	21	21	2	0	131.0	545	116	54	48	10	6	3	7	49	3	88	2	1	7	5	.583	1	0-0	0	3.42	3.30
2004	SF	NL	22	22	0	0	129.1	559	123	69	61	14	4	9	17	44	1	80	2	1	10	7	.588	0	0-0	0	4.14	4.24
2005	2 Tms	NL	22	20	0	0	122.2	532	119	62	58	14	11	8	10	49	1	70	2	0	6	10	.375	0	0-0	1	4.34	4.26
2006	ChC	NL	5	2	0	1	12.1	61	15	12	10	2	0	3	1	11	1	5	0	0	0	2	.000	0	0-0	0	8.42	7.30
05	SF	NL	4	3	0	0	16.2	73	21	12	12	2	1	0	1	4	1	11	0	0	0	2	.000	0	0-0	0	5.32	6.48
05	ChC	NL	18	17	0	0	106.0	459	98	50	46	12	10	8	9	45	0	59	2	0	6	8	.429	0	0-0	1	4.19	3.91
4 ML YEARS			70	65	2	1	395.1	1697	373	197	177	40	21	23	35	153	6	243	6	2	23	24	.489	1	0-0	1	4.08	4.03

Todd Williams

Pitches: R Bats: R Pos: RP-62   Ht: 6'3" Wt: 220 Born: 2/13/1971 Age: 36

			HOW MUCH HE PITCHED						WHAT HE GAVE UP												THE RESULTS							
Year	Team	Lg	G	GS	CG	GF	IP	BFP	H	R	ER	HR	SH	SF	HB	TBB	IBB	SO	WP	Bk	W	L	Pct	ShO	Sv-Op	Hld	ERC	ERA
2006	Bowie*	AA	4	1	0	0	4.0	17	4	2	2	0	0	0	0	1	0	5	0	0	0	0	-	0	0- -	-	2.77	4.50
1995	LAD	NL	16	0	0	5	19.1	83	19	11	11	3	3	1	0	7	2	8	0	0	2	2	.500	0	0-1	0	4.01	5.12
1998	Cin	NL	6	0	0	2	9.1	50	15	8	8	1	0	0	0	6	0	4	0	0	0	1	.000	0	0-0	0	8.58	7.71
1999	Sea	AL	13	0	0	7	9.2	47	11	5	5	1	1	0	1	7	0	7	0	0	0	0	-	0	0-0	0	6.67	4.66
2001	NYY	AL	15	0	0	6	15.1	82	22	9	8	1	0	3	2	9	2	13	0	0	1	0	1.000	0	0-0	1	7.01	4.70
2004	Bal	AL	29	0	0	7	31.1	126	26	10	10	2	0	0	5	9	0	13	1	0	2	0	1.000	0	0-0	3	3.25	2.87
2005	Bal	AL	72	0	0	12	76.1	321	72	34	28	5	2	4	3	26	4	38	4	1	5	5	.500	0	1-3	18	3.40	3.30
2006	Bal	AL	62	0	0	5	57.0	260	76	36	30	8	3	1	2	19	3	24	6	0	2	4	.333	0	1-5	13	6.19	4.74
7 ML YEARS			213	0	0	44	218.1	969	241	113	100	21	9	9	13	83	11	107	11	1	12	12	.500	0	2-9	35	4.72	4.12

Woody Williams

Pitches: R Bats: R Pos: SP-24; RP-1   Ht: 6'0" Wt: 200 Born: 8/19/1966 Age: 40

			HOW MUCH HE PITCHED						WHAT HE GAVE UP												THE RESULTS							
Year	Team	Lg	G	GS	CG	GF	IP	BFP	H	R	ER	HR	SH	SF	HB	TBB	IBB	SO	WP	Bk	W	L	Pct	ShO	Sv-Op	Hld	ERC	ERA
2006	Lk Els*	A+	1	1	0	0	3.0	11	0	0	0	0	0	0	1	1	0	5	0	0	0	0	-	0	0- -	-	0.46	0.00
2006	Portlnd*	AAA	1	1	0	0	2.2	18	8	6	6	1	0	0	0	2	0	2	1	0	0	1	.000	0	0- -	-	22.87	20.25
1993	Tor	AL	30	0	0	9	37.0	172	40	18	18	2	2	1	1	22	3	24	2	1	3	1	.750	0	0-2	4	4.85	4.38
1994	Tor	AL	38	0	0	14	59.1	253	44	24	24	5	1	2	2	33	1	56	4	0	1	3	.250	0	0-0	5	3.25	3.64
1995	Tor	AL	23	3	0	10	53.2	232	44	23	22	6	2	0	2	28	1	41	0	0	1	2	.333	0	0-1	1	3.72	3.69
1996	Tor	AL	12	10	1	0	59.0	255	64	33	31	8	2	1	1	21	1	43	2	0	4	5	.444	0	0-0	0	4.73	4.73
1997	Tor	AL	31	31	0	0	194.2	833	201	98	94	31	6	8	5	66	3	124	7	0	9	14	.391	0	0-0	0	4.55	4.35
1998	Tor	AL	32	32	1	0	209.2	894	196	112	104	36	5	6	2	81	3	151	2	1	10	9	.526	1	0-0	0	4.15	4.46
1999	SD	NL	33	33	0	0	208.1	887	213	106	102	33	9	9	2	73	5	137	9	0	12	12	.500	0	0-0	0	4.46	4.41
2000	SD	NL	23	23	4	0	168.0	700	152	74	70	23	4	3	3	54	2	111	4	0	10	8	.556	0	0-0	0	3.55	3.75
2001	2 Tms	NL	34	34	3	0	220.0	922	224	110	99	35	13	8	8	56	5	154	5	0	15	9	.625	1	0-0	0	4.15	4.05
2002	StL	NL	17	17	1	0	103.1	412	84	30	29	10	3	1	4	25	2	76	2	0	9	4	.692	0	0-0	0	2.63	2.53
2003	StL	NL	34	33	0	1	220.2	944	220	101	95	20	11	6	11	55	2	153	3	0	18	9	.667	0	0-1	0	3.52	3.87
2004	StL	NL	31	31	0	0	189.2	817	193	93	88	20	9	5	9	58	3	131	12	1	11	8	.579	0	0-0	0	3.97	4.18
2005	SD	NL	28	28	0	0	159.2	697	174	92	86	24	6	5	3	51	1	106	1	0	9	12	.429	0	0-0	0	4.65	4.85
2006	StL	NL	25	24	0	0	145.1	624	152	68	59	21	7	5	7	35	3	72	4	1	12	5	.706	0	0-0	0	4.12	3.65
01	SD	NL	23	23	0	0	145.0	632	170	88	80	28	8	8	5	37	4	102	4	0	8	8	.500	0	0-0	0	5.26	4.97
01	StL	NL	11	11	3	0	75.0	290	54	22	19	7	5	0	3	19	1	52	1	0	7	1	.875	1	0-0	0	2.24	2.28
14 ML YEARS			391	299	10	34	2028.1	8642	2001	982	921	274	80	60	60	658	35	1379	57	4	124	101	.551	2	0-4	10	4.03	4.09

Scott Williamson

Pitches: R **Bats:** R **Pos:** RP-42   **Ht:** 6'0" **Wt:** 185 **Born:** 2/17/1976 **Age:** 31

Year	Team	Lg	G	GS	CG	GF	IP	BFP	H	R	ER	HR	SH	SF	HB	TBB	IBB	SO	WP	Bk	W	L	Pct	ShO	Sv-Op	Hld	ERC	ERA
2006	Peoria*	A	1	0	0	0	1.0	4	1	1	1	0	1	0	1	0	0	1	1	0	0	0	-	0	0--	-	1.95	9.00
2006	Iowa*	AAA	4	0	0	1	5.0	22	4	1	1	0	1	0	1	2	0	5	1	0	0	0	-	0	1--	-	2.96	1.80
1999	Cin	NL	62	0	0	40	93.1	366	54	29	25	8	5	2	1	43	6	107	13	0	12	7	.632	0	19-26	5	2.05	2.41
2000	Cin	NL	48	10	0	13	112.0	495	92	45	41	7	4	2	3	75	7	136	21	1	5	8	.385	0	6-8	6	3.85	3.29
2001	Cin	NL	2	0	0	0	0.2	6	1	0	0	0	0	0	0	2	0	0	1	0	0	0	-	0	0-0	1	24.61	0.00
2002	Cin	NL	63	0	0	23	74.0	299	46	27	24	5	5	2	2	36	5	84	8	1	3	4	.429	0	8-12	8	2.24	2.92
2003	2 Tms		66	0	0	40	62.2	276	54	30	29	7	2	1	1	34	6	74	11	0	5	4	.556	0	21-28	5	3.78	4.16
2004	Bos	AL	28	0	0	5	28.2	120	11	6	4	0	0	3	3	18	1	28	4	0	0	1	.000	0	1-2	3	1.47	1.26
2005	ChC	NL	17	0	0	4	14.1	65	15	9	9	3	2	0	2	6	0	23	4	1	0	0	-	0	0-0	3	5.79	5.65
2006	2 Tms		42	0	0	10	39.1	176	41	26	25	4	0	2	1	22	1	42	8	1	2	4	.333	0	0-0	3	5.09	5.72
03	Cin	NL	42	0	0	34	42.1	187	34	15	15	6	2	0	1	25	4	53	7	0	5	3	.625	0	21-26	0	3.87	3.19
03	Bos	AL	24	0	0	6	20.1	89	20	15	14	1	0	1	0	9	2	21	4	0	0	1	.000	0	0-2	5	3.58	6.20
06	ChC	NL	31	0	0	5	28.1	127	27	17	16	2	0	1	1	16	1	32	7	1	2	3	.400	0	0-0	3	4.28	5.08
06	SD	NL	11	0	0	5	11.0	49	14	9	9	2	0	1	0	6	0	10	1	0	0	1	.000	0	0-0	0	7.42	7.36
	8 ML YEARS		328	10	0	135	425.0	1803	314	172	157	34	18	12	14	236	26	494	70	4	27	28	.491	0	55-76	34	3.14	3.32

Josh Willingham

Bats: R **Throws:** R **Pos:** LF-132; PH-5; DH-3; C-2; 1B-2; PR-1   **Ht:** 6'1" **Wt:** 200 **Born:** 2/17/1979 **Age:** 28

Year	Team	Lg	G	AB	H	2B	3B	HR	(Hm	Rd)	TB	R	RBI	RC	TBB	IBB	SO	HBP	SH	SF	SB	CS	SB%	GDP	Avg	OBP	Slg
2006	Carlina*	AA	2	8	2	0	0	0	(-	-)	2	0	0	0	0	0	3	0	0	0	0	0	-	0	.250	.250	.250
2004	Fla	NL	12	25	5	0	0	1	(0	1)	8	2	1	1	4	0	8	0	0	0	0	0	-	1	.200	.310	.320
2005	Fla	NL	16	23	7	1	0	0	(0	0)	8	3	4	3	2	0	5	2	1	0	0	0	-	1	.304	.407	.348
2006	Fla	NL	142	502	139	28	2	26	(11	15)	249	62	74	74	54	2	109	11	0	6	2	0	1.00	13	.277	.356	.496
	3 ML YEARS		170	550	151	29	2	27	(11	16)	265	67	79	78	60	2	122	13	1	6	2	0	1.00	15	.275	.356	.482

Dontrelle Willis

Pitches: L **Bats:** L **Pos:** SP-34   **Ht:** 6'4" **Wt:** 240 **Born:** 1/12/1982 **Age:** 25

Year	Team	Lg	G	GS	CG	GF	IP	BFP	H	R	ER	HR	SH	SF	HB	TBB	IBB	SO	WP	Bk	W	L	Pct	ShO	Sv-Op	Hld	ERC	ERA
2003	Fla	NL	27	27	2	0	160.2	668	148	61	59	13	3	1	3	58	0	142	7	1	14	6	.700	2	0-0	0	3.49	3.30
2004	Fla	NL	32	32	0	0	197.0	848	210	99	88	20	8	2	8	61	8	139	2	0	10	11	.476	0	0-0	0	4.21	4.02
2005	Fla	NL	34	34	7	0	236.1	960	213	79	69	11	14	5	8	55	3	170	2	1	**22**	10	.688	**5**	0-0	0	2.71	2.63
2006	Fla	NL	34	34	4	0	223.1	975	234	106	96	21	11	6	**19**	83	6	160	6	1	12	12	.500	1	0-0	0	4.53	3.87
	4 ML YEARS		127	127	15	0	817.1	3451	805	345	312	65	36	14	38	257	17	611	17	3	58	39	.598	8	0-0	0	3.70	3.44

Reggie Willits

Bats: B **Throws:** R **Pos:** CF-19; PR-6; PH-4; RF-1; DH-1   **Ht:** 5'11" **Wt:** 185 **Born:** 5/30/1981 **Age:** 26

Year	Team	Lg	G	AB	H	2B	3B	HR	(Hm	Rd)	TB	R	RBI	RC	TBB	IBB	SO	HBP	SH	SF	SB	CS	SB%	GDP	Avg	OBP	Slg
2003	Provo	R	59	230	69	14	4	4	(-	-)	103	53	27	46	37	0	52	6	3	0	14	4	.78	2	.300	.410	.448
2004	RCuca	A+	135	526	150	17	5	5	(-	-)	192	99	52	84	73	2	112	8	8	10	44	15	.75	9	.285	.374	.365
2005	Ark	AA	123	487	148	23	6	2	(-	-)	189	75	46	80	54	0	78	8	4	8	40	14	.74	5	.304	.377	.388
2006	Salt Lk	AAA	97	352	115	18	4	3	(-	-)	150	85	39	75	77	2	50	2	4	2	31	15	.67	5	.327	.448	.426
2006	LAA	AL	28	45	12	1	0	0	(0	0)	13	12	2	6	11	0	10	0	2	0	4	3	.57	0	.267	.411	.289

Brian Wilson

Pitches: R **Bats:** R **Pos:** RP-31   **Ht:** 6'1" **Wt:** 205 **Born:** 3/16/1982 **Age:** 25

Year	Team	Lg	G	GS	CG	GF	IP	BFP	H	R	ER	HR	SH	SF	HB	TBB	IBB	SO	WP	Bk	W	L	Pct	ShO	Sv-Op	Hld	ERC	ERA
2004	Hgrstn	A	23	3	0	12	57.1	259	63	37	34	7	0	0	3	22	1	41	1	0	2	5	.286	0	3--	-	4.82	5.34
2005	Augsta	A	26	0	0	24	33.0	129	23	7	3	0	1	0	3	7	0	30	0	0	5	1	.833	0	13--	-	1.64	0.82
2005	Nrwich	AA	15	0	0	15	15.2	58	6	1	1	0	0	0	1	5	0	22	0	0	0	0	-	0	8--	-	0.90	0.57
2005	Fresno	AAA	9	0	0	2	11.1	52	8	7	5	0	1	1	0	8	0	13	1	0	1	1	.500	0	0--	-	2.72	3.97
2006	SnJos	A+	1	0	0	0	1.0	5	1	1	1	0	0	0	0	1	0	1	0	0	0	0	-	0	0--	-	5.48	9.00
2006	Fresno	AAA	24	0	0	14	28.0	115	20	9	9	2	0	1	4	14	0	30	0	0	1	3	.250	0	7--	-	2.93	2.89
2006	SF	NL	31	0	0	9	30.0	141	32	19	18	1	1	4	1	21	2	23	0	0	2	3	.400	0	1-2	4	5.11	5.40

C.J. Wilson

Pitches: L **Bats:** L **Pos:** RP-44   **Ht:** 6'1" **Wt:** 215 **Born:** 11/18/1980 **Age:** 26

Year	Team	Lg	G	GS	CG	GF	IP	BFP	H	R	ER	HR	SH	SF	HB	TBB	IBB	SO	WP	Bk	W	L	Pct	ShO	Sv-Op	Hld	ERC	ERA
2001	Pulaski	R+	8	8	0	0	37.2	149	24	6	4	2	0	0	4	9	0	49	0	0	1	0	1.000	0	0--	-	1.75	0.96
2001	Savann	A	5	5	2	0	34.0	141	30	13	12	2	2	1	1	9	0	26	3	2	1	2	.333	0	0--	-	2.74	3.18
2002	Charltt	A+	26	15	0	2	106.0	445	86	48	36	4	2	0	6	41	1	76	7	0	10	2	.833	0	1--	-	2.78	3.06
2002	Tulsa	AA	5	5	0	0	30.0	125	23	6	6	0	1	0	1	12	0	17	1	0	1	0	1.000	0	0--	-	2.29	1.80
2003	Frisco	AA	22	21	0	0	123.0	542	135	79	69	11	1	1	8	38	3	89	6	0	6	9	.400	0	0--	-	4.37	5.05
2005	Bkrsfld	A+	4	4	0	0	13.2	55	10	5	5	2	0	0	0	4	0	14	0	0	0	0	-	0	0--	-	2.51	3.29
2005	Frisco	AA	12	12	0	0	44.2	199	51	32	22	7	1	2	3	14	0	43	0	0	0	4	.000	0	0--	-	5.20	4.43
2006	Frisco	AA	4	0	0	0	3.1	15	3	1	1	0	0	0	0	2	0	6	1	0	0	0	-	0	0--	-	3.46	2.70
2006	Okla	AAA	9	0	0	4	11.0	48	10	3	3	0	0	0	0	5	0	17	1	0	1	0	1.000	0	2--	-	3.01	2.45

Year	Team	Lg	G	GS	CG	GF	IP	BFP	H	R	ER	HR	SH	SF	HB	TBB	IBB	SO	WP	Bk	W	L	Pct	ShO	Sv-Op	Hld	ERC	ERA
2005	Tex	AL	24	6	0	5	48.0	220	63	39	37	5	1	2	2	18	1	30	4	1	1	7	.125	0	1-1	4	6.03	6.94
2006	Tex	AL	44	0	0	12	44.1	191	39	23	20	7	1	0	5	18	1	43	0	0	2	4	.333	0	1-2	7	4.25	4.06
2 ML YEARS			68	6	0	17	92.1	411	102	62	57	12	2	2	7	36	2	73	4	1	3	11	.214	0	2-3	11	5.16	5.56

Craig Wilson

Bats: R **Throws:** R **Pos:** 1B-78; RF-32; PH-27; PR-3; DH-1   **Ht:** 6'2" **Wt:** 220 **Born:** 11/30/1976 **Age:** 30

Year	Team	Lg	G	AB	H	2B	3B	HR	(Hm	Rd)	TB	R	RBI	RC	TBB	IBB	SO	HBP	SH	SF	SB	CS	SB%	GDP	Avg	OBP	Slg
2001	Pit	NL	88	158	49	3	1	13	(8	5)	93	27	32	34	15	1	53	7	1	2	3	1	.75	4	.310	.390	.589
2002	Pit	NL	131	368	97	16	1	16	(3	13)	163	48	57	55	32	0	116	21	1	2	2	3	.40	10	.264	.355	.443
2003	Pit	NL	116	309	81	15	4	18	(9	9)	158	49	48	49	35	4	89	13	0	1	3	1	.75	6	.262	.360	.511
2004	Pit	NL	155	561	148	35	5	29	(16	13)	280	97	82	84	50	3	169	30	0	3	2	2	.50	10	.264	.354	.499
2005	Pit	NL	59	197	52	14	1	5	(3	2)	83	23	22	28	30	2	69	10	0	1	3	0	1.00	6	.264	.387	.421
2006	2 Tms		125	359	90	15	2	17	(10	7)	160	53	49	48	28	2	122	6	0	2	1	0	1.00	10	.251	.314	.446
06	Pit	NL	85	255	68	11	2	13	(8	5)	122	38	41	43	24	2	88	5	0	2	1	0	1.00	6	.267	.339	.478
06	NYY	AL	40	104	22	4	0	4	(2	2)	38	15	8	5	4	0	34	1	0	0	0	0	-	4	.212	.248	.365
6 ML YEARS			674	1952	517	98	14	98	(49	49)	937	297	290	298	190	12	618	87	2	11	14	7	.67	46	.265	.354	.480

Jack Wilson

Bats: R **Throws:** R **Pos:** SS-131; PH-11; PR-1   **Ht:** 6'0" **Wt:** 185 **Born:** 12/29/1977 **Age:** 29

Year	Team	Lg	G	AB	H	2B	3B	HR	(Hm	Rd)	TB	R	RBI	RC	TBB	IBB	SO	HBP	SH	SF	SB	CS	SB%	GDP	Avg	OBP	Slg
2001	Pit	NL	108	390	87	17	1	3	(0	3)	115	44	25	27	16	2	70	1	17	1	1	3	.25	4	.223	.255	.295
2002	Pit	NL	147	527	133	22	4	4	(2	2)	175	77	47	60	37	2	74	4	17	1	5	2	.71	7	.252	.306	.332
2003	Pit	NL	150	558	143	21	3	9	(2	7)	197	58	62	62	36	3	74	4	11	6	5	5	.50	11	.256	.303	.353
2004	Pit	NL	157	652	201	41	12	11	(7	4)	299	82	59	84	26	0	71	3	7	5	8	4	.67	15	.308	.335	.459
2005	Pit	NL	158	587	151	24	7	8	(3	5)	213	60	52	60	31	6	58	6	11	4	7	3	.70	11	.257	.299	.363
2006	Pit	NL	142	543	148	27	1	8	(5	3)	201	70	35	58	33	0	65	4	9	5	4	3	.57	15	.273	.316	.370
6 ML YEARS			862	3257	863	152	28	43	(19	24)	1200	391	280	351	179	13	412	22	72	22	30	20	.60	63	.265	.306	.368

Kris Wilson

Pitches: R **Bats:** R **Pos:** RP-4; SP-1   **Ht:** 6'4" **Wt:** 220 **Born:** 8/6/1976 **Age:** 30

Year	Team	Lg	G	GS	CG	GF	IP	BFP	H	R	ER	HR	SH	SF	HB	TBB	IBB	SO	WP	Bk	W	L	Pct	ShO	Sv-Op	Hld	ERC	ERA
2006	Trntn*	AA	2	2	0	0	8.2	40	13	10	9	4	0	0	0	2	1	2	0	0	0	2	.000	0	0--	-	9.12	9.35
2006	Clmbs*	AAA	21	21	2	0	132.1	539	120	54	50	7	1	5	10	24	1	103	5	0	9	6	.600	1	0--	-	2.74	3.40
2000	KC	AL	20	0	0	5	34.1	145	38	16	16	3	1	1	0	11	3	17	0	0	0	1	.000	0	0-1	0	4.25	4.19
2001	KC	AL	29	15	0	6	109.1	487	132	78	63	26	1	3	7	32	0	67	1	0	6	5	.545	0	1-1	0	6.17	5.19
2002	KC	AL	12	0	0	4	18.2	91	29	18	17	7	0	2	2	5	0	10	0	0	2	0	1.000	0	0-2	0	9.63	8.20
2003	KC	AL	29	4	0	7	72.2	328	92	49	43	13	0	4	6	16	3	42	0	1	6	3	.667	0	0-1	1	5.69	5.33
2006	NYY	AL	5	1	0	1	8.1	42	14	8	8	4	0	0	0	4	0	6	0	0	0	0	-	0	0-0	0	12.24	8.64
5 ML YEARS			95	20	0	23	243.1	1093	305	169	147	53	2	10	15	68	6	142	1	1	14	9	.609	0	1-5	1	6.18	5.44

Paul Wilson

Pitches: R **Bats:** R **Pos:** P   **Ht:** 6'5" **Wt:** 210 **Born:** 3/28/1973 **Age:** 34

Year	Team	Lg	G	GS	CG	GF	IP	BFP	H	R	ER	HR	SH	SF	HB	TBB	IBB	SO	WP	Bk	W	L	Pct	ShO	Sv-Op	Hld	ERC	ERA
2006	Dayton*	A	1	1	-	0	7.0	31	10	6	4	1	-	-	0	0	-	4	0	0	0	1	.000	-	0--	-	5.09	5.14
2006	Srsota*	A+	1	1	-	0	6.0	28	9	2	2	0	-	-	1	1	-	1	0	0	1	0	1.000	-	0--	-	6.02	3.00
2006	Lsvlle*	AAA	2	2	0	0	11.0	53	15	11	6	4	0	0	2	1	0	3	0	0	0	2	.000	0	0--	-	7.28	4.91
1996	NYM	NL	26	26	1	0	149.0	677	157	102	89	15	7	3	10	71	11	109	3	3	5	12	.294	0	0-0	1	4.77	5.38
2000	TB	AL	11	7	0	0	51.0	206	38	20	19	1	2	2	4	16	2	40	1	0	1	4	.200	0	0-0	1	2.17	3.35
2001	TB	AL	37	24	0	6	151.1	674	165	94	82	21	3	12	13	52	2	119	7	0	8	9	.471	0	0-1	0	4.94	4.88
2002	TB	AL	30	30	1	0	193.2	851	219	113	104	29	2	6	13	67	2	111	4	1	6	12	.333	0	0-0	0	5.30	4.83
2003	Cin	NL	28	28	0	0	166.2	730	190	97	86	24	7	0	7	50	5	93	1	0	8	10	.444	0	0-0	0	4.92	4.64
2004	Cin	NL	29	29	1	0	183.2	798	192	93	89	26	10	8	8	63	5	117	7	0	11	6	.647	0	0-0	0	4.53	4.36
2005	Cin	NL	9	9	0	0	46.1	224	68	41	40	10	2	3	4	17	1	30	2	0	1	5	.167	0	0-0	0	8.05	7.77
7 ML YEARS			170	153	3	6	941.2	4160	1029	560	509	126	33	34	59	336	28	619	25	4	40	58	.408	0	0-1	1	4.88	4.86

Preston Wilson

Bats: R **Throws:** R **Pos:** LF-102; RF-24; CF-7; PH-7   **Ht:** 6'2" **Wt:** 215 **Born:** 7/19/1974 **Age:** 32

Year	Team	Lg	G	AB	H	2B	3B	HR	(Hm	Rd)	TB	R	RBI	RC	TBB	IBB	SO	HBP	SH	SF	SB	CS	SB%	GDP	Avg	OBP	Slg
1998	2 Tms	NL	22	51	8	2	0	1	(1	0)	13	7	3	3	6	0	21	1	2	0	1	1	.50	0	.157	.259	.255
1999	Fla	NL	149	482	135	21	4	26	(8	18)	242	67	71	81	46	3	156	9	0	6	11	4	.73	15	.280	.350	.502
2000	Fla	NL	161	605	160	35	3	31	(12	19)	294	94	121	97	55	1	187	8	0	6	36	14	.72	11	.264	.331	.486
2001	Fla	NL	123	468	128	30	2	23	(9	14)	231	70	71	73	36	2	107	6	0	3	20	8	.71	14	.274	.331	.494
2002	Fla	NL	141	510	124	22	2	23	(8	15)	219	80	65	58	58	3	140	9	2	3	20	11	.65	17	.243	.329	.429
2003	Col	NL	155	600	169	43	1	36	(21	15)	322	94	141	111	54	1	139	4	0	3	14	7	.67	23	.282	.343	.537
2004	Col	NL	58	202	50	11	0	6	(3	3)	79	24	29	19	17	2	49	3	0	0	2	1	.67	9	.248	.315	.391
2005	2 Tms	NL	139	520	135	29	2	25	(13	12)	243	73	90	72	45	0	148	7	1	3	6	6	.50	18	.260	.325	.467
2006	2 Tms	NL	135	501	132	25	2	17	(12	5)	212	66	59	57	29	3	121	4	0	3	12	2	.86	20	.263	.307	.423
98	NYM	NL	8	20	6	2	0	0	(0	0)	8	3	2	3	2	0	8	0	0	0	1	1	.50	0	.300	.364	.400
98	Fla	NL	14	31	2	0	0	1	(1	0)	5	4	1	0	4	0	13	1	2	0	0	0	-	0	.065	.194	.161
05	Col	NL	71	267	69	15	1	15	(10	5)	131	39	47	33	25	0	77	1	1	2	3	2	.60	8	.258	.322	.491

Year	Team	Lg	G	AB	H	2B	3B	HR	(Hm	Rd)	TB	R	RBI	RC	TBB	IBB	SO	HBP	SH	SF	SB	CS	SB%	GDP	Avg	OBP	Slg
																					BASERUNNING				AVERAGES		
05	Was	NL	68	253	66	14	1	10	(3	7)	112	34	43	39	20	0	71	6	0	1	3	4	.43	10	.261	.329	.443
06	Hou	NL	102	390	105	22	2	9	(7	2)	158	40	55	44	22	2	94	2	0	3	6	2	.75	18	.269	.309	.405
06	StL	NL	33	111	27	3	0	8	(5	3)	54	18	17	16	7	1	27	2	0	0	6	0	1.00	2	.243	.300	.486
9 ML YEARS			1083	3939	1041	218	16	188	(87	101)	1855	567	663	574	346	15	1068	51	5	27	122	54	.69	127	.264	.330	.471

Vance Wilson

Bats: R **Throws:** R **Pos:** C-55; PH-5   **Ht:** 5'11" **Wt:** 215 **Born:** 3/17/1973 **Age:** 34

Year	Team	Lg	G	AB	H	2B	3B	HR	(Hm	Rd)	TB	R	RBI	RC	TBB	IBB	SO	HBP	SH	SF	SB	CS	SB%	GDP	Avg	OBP	Slg
1999	NYM	NL	1	0	0	0	0	0	(0	0)	0	0	0	0	0	0	0	0	0	0	0	0	-	0	-	-	-
2000	NYM	NL	4	4	0	0	0	0	(0	0)	0	0	0	0	0	0	2	0	0	0	0	0	-	0	.000	.000	.000
2001	NYM	NL	32	57	17	3	0	0	(0	0)	20	3	6	6	2	0	16	2	0	1	0	1	.00	1	.298	.339	.351
2002	NYM	NL	74	163	40	7	0	5	(3	2)	62	19	26	21	5	0	32	8	2	0	0	1	.00	4	.245	.301	.380
2003	NYM	NL	96	268	65	9	1	8	(3	5)	100	28	39	31	15	1	56	5	2	2	1	2	.33	6	.243	.293	.373
2004	NYM	NL	79	157	43	10	1	4	(1	3)	67	18	21	23	11	2	24	5	1	3	1	0	1.00	5	.274	.335	.427
2005	Det	AL	61	152	30	4	0	3	(1	2)	43	18	19	13	11	0	26	6	2	2	0	0	-	6	.197	.275	.283
2006	Det	AL	56	152	43	9	0	5	(3	2)	67	18	18	17	2	0	33	3	10	1	0	4	.00	1	.283	.304	.441
8 ML YEARS			403	953	238	42	2	25	(11	14)	359	104	129	111	46	3	189	29	17	9	2	8	.20	23	.250	.302	.377

Jason Windsor

Pitches: R **Bats:** R **Pos:** SP-3; RP-1   **Ht:** 6'2" **Wt:** 235 **Born:** 7/16/1982 **Age:** 24

	HOW MUCH HE PITCHED						WHAT HE GAVE UP											THE RESULTS						
Year	Team	Lg	G	GS	CG	GF	IP	BFP	H	R	ER	HR	SH	SF	HB	TBB	IBB	SO	WP	Bk	W	L	Pct	ShO	Sv-Op	Hld	ERC	ERA
2004	Vancvr	A-	4	0	0	3	5.0	19	4	0	0	0	0	0	0	0	0	5	0	0	0	0	-	0	1- -	-	1.27	0.00
2004	Kane	A	9	0	0	3	13.0	55	11	4	4	0	0	0	0	5	1	13	1	0	1	0	1.000	0	3- -	-	2.37	2.77
2005	Stcktn	A	10	10	0	0	55.1	226	52	28	22	5	0	2	2	8	0	64	1	0	2	2	.500	0	0- -	-	2.83	3.58
2005	Mdland	AA	11	11	0	0	56.2	260	69	40	36	5	0	5	3	23	1	39	0	0	3	6	.333	0	0- -	-	5.43	5.72
2006	Mdland	AA	6	6	0	0	33.1	130	27	12	11	2	0	1	0	10	0	35	1	0	4	1	.800	0	0- -	-	2.56	2.97
2006	Scrmto	AAA	20	20	1	0	118.0	510	128	53	50	7	3	3	2	32	0	123	2	0	13	1	.929	0	0- -	-	3.78	3.81
2006	Oak	AL	4	3	0	1	13.2	65	21	12	10	2	2	2	0	5	0	6	0	0	0	1	.000	0	0-0	0	7.64	6.59

Joe Winkelsas

Pitches: R **Bats:** R **Pos:** RP-7   **Ht:** 6'3" **Wt:** 188 **Born:** 9/14/1973 **Age:** 33

	HOW MUCH HE PITCHED						WHAT HE GAVE UP											THE RESULTS						
Year	Team	Lg	G	GS	CG	GF	IP	BFP	H	R	ER	HR	SH	SF	HB	TBB	IBB	SO	WP	Bk	W	L	Pct	ShO	Sv-Op	Hld	ERC	ERA
1996	Danvle	R+	8	0	0	6	11.1	54	11	10	9	0	0	4	4	4	0	9	2	0	1	1	.500	0	2- -	-	4.12	7.15
1997	Macon	A	38	0	0	15	62.2	242	44	17	14	1	3	0	4	13	0	45	4	2	3	2	.600	0	5- -	-	1.66	2.01
1997	Drham	A+	13	0	0	8	19.0	93	24	18	15	0	5	2	4	11	1	17	1	0	1	4	.200	0	1- -	-	6.32	7.11
1998	Danvle	A+	50	0	0	36	69.0	298	66	26	17	3	7	0	3	24	8	53	0	0	6	9	.400	0	22- -	-	3.17	2.22
1998	Grnville	AA	4	0	0	0	4.1	20	3	2	2	0	0	0	0	4	0	3	0	0	0	0	-	0	0- -	-	3.50	4.15
1999	Grnville	AA	55	0	0	40	62.1	280	71	32	26	5	2	0	2	30	6	38	3	1	4	4	.500	0	12- -	-	5.07	3.75
2000	Rchmd	AAA	4	0	0	1	5.0	33	12	9	8	1	2	0	1	5	2	1	0	0	0	1	.000	0	0- -	-	17.20	14.40
2001	MrtlBh	A+	4	0	0	4	6.0	20	2	0	0	0	0	0	0	1	0	5	0	0	1	0	1.000	0	3- -	-	0.47	0.00
2001	Grnville	AA	20	0	0	11	33.0	133	24	12	12	0	2	0	0	14	2	14	3	2	4	2	.667	0	3- -	-	2.05	3.27
2002	Grnville	AA	2	0	0	2	2.0	9	1	0	0	0	0	0	1	1	0	0	0	0	0	0	-	0	2- -	-	2.80	0.00
2002	Rchmd	AAA	16	0	0	6	25.2	107	25	6	6	0	4	0	0	9	3	13	1	0	1	2	.333	0	2- -	-	2.93	2.10
2003	Grnville	AA	23	0	0	8	27.2	115	26	11	9	2	0	3	3	8	0	14	0	0	1	1	.500	0	4- -	-	3.64	2.93
2004	WinSa	A+	1	0	0	0	1.1	8	4	1	1	0	0	0	1	0	0	1	0	0	0	0	-	0	0- -	-	20.65	6.75
2004	Charltt	AAA	5	0	0	1	10.0	48	15	7	7	1	0	0	0	3	0	5	1	0	0	0	-	0	0- -	-	6.49	6.30
2005	Charltt	AAA	4	0	0	1	8.1	38	11	6	6	2	0	1	0	4	1	3	0	0	0	0	-	0	0- -	-	7.48	6.48
2006	Hntsvl	AA	13	0	0	10	15.2	66	15	3	3	1	1	0	1	2	0	15	0	0	1	1	.500	0	4- -	-	2.71	1.72
2006	Nashv	AAA	6	0	0	6	10.2	47	11	6	6	0	2	0	2	2	0	7	0	0	1	3	.250	0	1- -	-	3.35	5.06
1999	Atl	NL	1	0	0	0	0.1		4	2	2	0	1	0	0	1	1	0			0	0	-	0	0-0	0	-	54.00
2006	Mil	NL	7	0	0	1	7.0	35	9	7	6	1	0	0	0	6	0	4	0	0	0	1	.000	0	0-0	0	8.18	7.71
2 ML YEARS			8	0	0	1	7.1	35	13	9	8	1	1	0	0	7	1	4	0	0	0	1	.000	0	0-0	0	13.69	9.82

Randy Winn

Bats: B **Throws:** R **Pos:** RF-89; CF-59; LF-20; PH-8; PR-2   **Ht:** 6'2" **Wt:** 195 **Born:** 6/9/1974 **Age:** 33

Year	Team	Lg	G	AB	H	2B	3B	HR	(Hm	Rd)	TB	R	RBI	RC	TBB	IBB	SO	HBP	SH	SF	SB	CS	SB%	GDP	Avg	OBP	Slg
1998	TB	AL	109	338	94	9	9	1	(0	1)	124	51	17	44	29	0	69	1	11	0	26	12	.68	2	.278	.337	.367
1999	TB	AL	79	303	81	16	4	2	(2	0)	111	44	24	32	17	0	63	1	1	2	9	9	.50	3	.267	.307	.366
2000	TB	AL	51	159	40	5	0	1	(1	0)	48	28	16	18	26	0	25	2	2	1	6	7	.46	2	.252	.362	.302
2001	TB	AL	128	429	117	25	6	6	(3	3)	172	54	50	56	38	0	81	6	5	2	12	10	.55	10	.273	.339	.401
2002	TB	AL	152	607	181	39	9	14	(9	5)	280	87	75	104	35	3	109	6	1	5	27	8	.77	9	.298	.360	.461
2003	Sea	AL	157	600	177	37	4	11	(6	5)	255	103	75	96	41	0	108	8	6	5	23	5	.82	9	.295	.346	.425
2004	Sea	AL	157	626	179	34	6	14	(6	8)	267	84	81	91	53	1	98	8	9	7	21	7	.75	16	.286	.346	.427
2005	2 Tms		160	617	189	47	6	20	(9	11)	308	85	63	95	48	4	91	5	10	3	19	11	.63	11	.306	.360	.499
2006	SF	NL	149	573	150	34	5	11	(6	5)	227	82	56	69	48	3	63	7	3	4	10	8	.56	7	.262	.324	.396
05	Sea	AL	102	386	106	25	1	6	(2	4)	151	46	37	52	37	3	53	4	6	3	12	6	.67	7	.275	.342	.391
05	SF	NL	58	231	83	22	5	14	(7	7)	157	39	26	43	11	1	38	1	4	0	7	5	.58	4	.359	.391	.680
9 ML YEARS			1142	4252	1208	246	49	80	(41	39)	1792	618	457	605	355	11	707	44	48	29	153	77	.67	69	.284	.343	.421

Dewayne Wise

Bats: L **Throws:** L **Pos:** PH-11; LF-9; CF-5; RF-4; PR-3 **Ht:** 6'1" **Wt:** 180 **Born:** 2/24/1978 **Age:** 29

Year Team	Lg	G	AB	H	2B	3B	HR	(Hm Rd)	TB	R	RBI	RC	TBB	IBB	SO	HBP	SH	SF	SB	CS	SB%	GDP	Avg	OBP	Slg
2006 Chatt*	AA	13	50	21	7	0	3	(- -)	37	11	7	15	3	0	9	1	0	1	1	0	1.00	0	.420	.455	.740
2006 Lsvlle*	AAA	44	154	41	10	4	4	(- -)	71	27	21	25	13	2	29	4	7	2	6	2	.75	1	.266	.335	.461
2000 Tor	AL	28	22	3	0	0	0	(0 0)	3	3	0	0	1	0	5	1	0	0	1	0	1.00	0	.136	.208	.136
2002 Tor	AL	42	112	20	1	1	3	(2 1)	35	14	13	8	4	0	15	0	0	0	5	0	1.00	0	.179	.207	.313
2004 Atl	NL	77	162	37	9	4	6	(3 3)	72	24	17	20	9	1	28	1	2	1	6	1	.86	1	.228	.272	.444
2006 Cin	NL	31	38	7	2	0	0	(0 0)	9	3	1	0	0	0	6	0	2	0	0	0	-	2	.184	.184	.237
4 ML YEARS		178	334	67	15	5	9	(5 4)	119	44	31	28	14	1	54	2	4	1	12	1	.92	3	.201	.236	.356

Matt Wise

Pitches: R **Bats:** R **Pos:** RP-40 **Ht:** 6'4" **Wt:** 200 **Born:** 11/18/1975 **Age:** 31

Year Team	Lg	G	GS	CG	GF	IP	BFP	H	R	ER	HR	SH	SF	HB	TBB	IBB	SO	WP	Bk	W	L	Pct	ShO	Sv-Op	Hld	ERC	ERA
2000 LAA	AL	8	6	0	0	37.1	163	40	23	23	7	0	2	1	13	1	20	1	0	3	3	.500	0	0-0	0	4.96	5.54
2001 LAA	AL	11	9	0	2	49.1	211	47	27	24	11	2	1	2	18	1	50	0	1	1	4	.200	0	0-0	0	4.65	4.38
2002 LAA	AL	7	0	0	6	8.1	33	7	3	3	0	1	0	1	1	0	6	0	0	0	0	-	0	0-0	0	2.07	3.24
2004 Mil	NL	30	3	0	5	52.2	222	51	27	26	3	1	2	2	15	1	30	2	0	1	2	.333	0	0-0	3	3.27	4.44
2005 Mil	NL	49	0	0	11	64.1	262	37	25	24	6	1	2	3	25	5	62	1	1	4	4	.500	0	1-3	14	1.83	3.36
2006 Mil	NL	40	0	0	9	44.1	188	45	24	19	6	3	1	2	14	2	27	0	1	5	6	.455	0	0-4	14	4.23	3.86
6 ML YEARS		145	18	0	33	256.1	1079	227	129	119	33	8	8	11	86	10	195	4	2	14	19	.424	0	1-7	27	3.48	4.18

Jay Witasick

Pitches: R **Bats:** R **Pos:** RP-20 **Ht:** 6'4" **Wt:** 240 **Born:** 8/28/1972 **Age:** 34

Year Team	Lg	G	GS	CG	GF	IP	BFP	H	R	ER	HR	SH	SF	HB	TBB	IBB	SO	WP	Bk	W	L	Pct	ShO	Sv-Op	Hld	ERC	ERA
2006 Stcktn*	A+	3	3	0	0	5.0	20	4	2	2	0	0	0	1	1	0	6	0	0	0	0	-	0	0--	-	2.46	3.60
2006 Scrmto*	AAA	12	0	0	2	14.0	57	10	7	6	2	1	0	1	4	0	6	1	0	1	0	1.000	0	0--	-	2.63	3.86
1996 Oak	AL	12	0	0	6	13.0	55	12	9	9	5	0	1	0	5	0	12	2	0	1	1	.500	0	0-1	0	5.52	6.23
1997 Oak	AL	8	0	0	1	11.0	53	14	7	7	2	1	0	0	6	0	8	0	0	0	0	-	0	0-0	1	6.81	5.73
1998 Oak	AL	7	3	0	1	27.0	131	36	24	19	9	0	0	0	15	1	29	2	0	1	3	.250	0	0-0	0	8.53	6.33
1999 KC	AL	32	28	1	2	158.1	732	191	108	98	23	4	8	8	83	1	102	4	2	9	12	.429	1	0-0	0	6.45	5.57
2000 2 Tms		33	25	2	2	150.0	697	178	107	97	24	8	4	7	73	5	121	5	1	6	10	.375	0	0-0	0	6.09	5.82
2001 2 Tms		63	0	0	17	79.0	352	78	41	29	8	3	2	6	33	4	106	4	0	8	2	.800	0	1-4	10	4.22	3.30
2002 SF	NL	44	0	0	9	68.1	276	58	19	18	3	2	1	4	21	3	54	3	0	1	0	1.000	0	0-0	4	2.78	2.37
2003 SD	NL	46	0	0	14	45.2	202	42	24	23	6	3	1	1	25	4	42	5	0	3	7	.300	0	2-7	12	4.34	4.53
2004 SD	NL	44	0	0	20	61.2	266	57	28	22	8	3	2	1	26	2	57	4	0	1	0	1.000	0	1-3	2	3.92	3.21
2005 2 Tms		60	0	0	11	63.1	277	53	26	20	4	4	0	6	29	5	73	5	0	1	5	.167	0	1-4	17	3.31	2.84
2006 Oak	AL	20	0	0	8	22.2	111	25	17	17	3	0	0	1	21	2	23	1	0	1	0	1.000	0	0-0	2	7.25	6.75
00 KC	AL	22	14	2	2	89.1	410	109	65	59	15	3	3	4	38	0	67	3	0	3	8	.273	0	0-0	0	6.19	5.94
00 SD	NL	11	11	0	0	60.2	287	69	42	38	9	5	1	3	35	5	54	2	1	3	2	.600	0	0-0	0	5.94	5.64
01 SD	NL	31	0	0	9	38.2	164	31	14	8	3	3	0	4	15	3	53	3	0	5	2	.714	0	1-3	5	3.05	1.86
01 NYY	AL	32	0	0	8	40.1	188	47	27	21	5	0	2	2	18	1	53	1	0	3	0	1.000	0	0-1	5	5.43	4.69
05 Col	NL	32	0	0	7	35.2	148	27	11	10	2	4	0	3	12	3	40	2	0	0	4	.000	0	0-1	11	2.43	2.52
05 Oak	AL	28	0	0	4	27.2	129	26	15	10	2	0	0	3	17	2	33	3	0	1	1	.500	0	1-3	6	4.54	3.25
11 ML YEARS		369	56	3	91	700.0	3152	744	410	359	95	28	19	34	337	27	627	35	3	31	41	.431	1	5-19	48	5.15	4.62

Kevin Witt

Bats: L **Throws:** R **Pos:** DH-10; 1B-5; PH-4 **Ht:** 6'4" **Wt:** 220 **Born:** 1/5/1976 **Age:** 31

Year Team	Lg	G	AB	H	2B	3B	HR	(Hm Rd)	TB	R	RBI	RC	TBB	IBB	SO	HBP	SH	SF	SB	CS	SB%	GDP	Avg	OBP	Slg
2006 Drham*	AAA	128	485	141	29	1	36	(- -)	280	82	99	99	50	8	132	4	0	3	0	0	-	14	.291	.360	.577
1998 Tor	AL	5	7	1	0	0	0	(0 0)	1	0	0	0	0	0	3	0	0	0	0	0	-	0	.143	.143	.143
1999 Tor	AL	15	34	7	1	0	1	(1 0)	11	3	5	3	2	0	9	0	1	0	0	0	-	0	.206	.250	.324
2001 SD	NL	14	27	5	0	0	2	(1 1)	11	5	5	3	2	0	7	0	0	1	0	0	-	0	.185	.233	.407
2003 Det	AL	93	270	71	9	0	10	(4 6)	110	25	26	24	15	0	68	1	0	3	1	1	.50	5	.263	.301	.407
2006 TB	AL	19	61	9	2	0	2	(1 1)	17	5	5	1	0	0	21	0	0	0	0	0	-	1	.148	.148	.279
5 ML YEARS		146	399	93	12	0	15	(7 8)	150	38	41	31	19	0	108	1	1	4	1	1	.50	6	.233	.267	.376

Randy Wolf

Pitches: L **Bats:** L **Pos:** SP-12 **Ht:** 6'0" **Wt:** 205 **Born:** 8/22/1976 **Age:** 30

Year Team	Lg	G	GS	CG	GF	IP	BFP	H	R	ER	HR	SH	SF	HB	TBB	IBB	SO	WP	Bk	W	L	Pct	ShO	Sv-Op	Hld	ERC	ERA
2006 Lakwd*	A	2	2	0	0	8.0	29	2	1	1	0	1	1	0	3	0	7	0	0	0	0	-	0	0--	-	0.57	1.13
2006 Clrwtr*	A+	2	2	0	0	5.2	25	6	1	0	0	0	1	0	4	0	4	1	0	0	0	-	0	0--	-	5.12	0.00
2006 Rdng*	AA	3	3	0	0	12.0	58	15	10	9	2	0	1	0	7	0	11	3	0	1	1	.500	0	0--	-	5.32	6.75
1999 Phi	NL	22	21	0	0	121.2	552	126	78	75	20	5	1	5	67	0	116	4	0	6	9	.400	0	0-0	0	5.54	5.55
2000 Phi	NL	32	32	1	0	206.1	889	210	107	100	25	10	8	8	83	2	160	1	0	11	9	.550	0	0-0	0	4.54	4.36
2001 Phi	NL	28	25	4	1	163.0	684	150	74	67	15	11	7	10	51	4	152	1	0	10	11	.476	2	0-0	0	3.46	3.70
2002 Phi	NL	31	31	3	0	210.2	855	172	77	75	23	7	6	7	63	5	172	4	0	11	9	.550	2	0-0	0	2.88	3.20
2003 Phi	NL	33	33	2	0	200.0	850	176	101	94	27	8	4	6	78	4	177	6	0	16	10	.615	2	0-0	0	3.67	4.23
2004 Phi	NL	23	23	1	0	136.2	585	145	73	65	20	6	3	5	36	4	89	2	0	5	8	.385	0	0-0	0	4.29	4.28
2005 Phi	NL	13	13	0	0	80.0	346	87	40	39	14	4	1	6	26	2	61	1	0	4	6	.400	0	0-0	0	5.17	4.39
2006 Phi	NL	12	12	0	0	56.2	261	63	37	35	13	2	3	2	33	2	44	2	0	4	0	1.000	0	0-0	0	6.63	5.56
8 ML YEARS		194	190	11	1	1175.0	5022	1129	587	550	157	53	33	49	437	23	971	21	0	69	60	.535	7	0-0	0	4.13	4.21

Tony Womack

Bats: L Throws: R Pos: 2B-21; PH-9   Ht: 5'9" Wt: 175 Born: 9/25/1969 Age: 37

										BATTING											BASERUNNING				AVERAGES		
Year	Team	Lg	G	AB	H	2B	3B	HR	(Hm	Rd)	TB	R	RBI	RC	TBB	IBB	SO	HBP	SH	SF	SB	CS	SB%	GDP	Avg	OBP	Slg
2006	Iowa*	AAA	5	15	7	1	0	0	(-	-)	8	2	1	4	3	0	3	0	2	0	3	1	.75	0	.467	.556	.533
1993	Pit	NL	15	24	2	0	0	0	(0	0)	2	5	0	0	3	0	3	0	1	0	2	0	1.00	0	.083	.185	.083
1994	Pit	NL	5	12	4	0	0	0	(0	0)	4	4	1	2	2	0	3	0	0	0	0	0	-	0	.333	.429	.333
1996	Pit	NL	17	30	10	3	1	0	(0	0)	15	11	7	8	6	0	1	1	3	0	2	0	1.00	0	.333	.459	.500
1997	Pit	NL	155	641	178	26	9	6	(5	1)	240	85	50	87	43	2	109	3	2	0	60	7	.90	6	.278	.326	.374
1998	Pit	NL	159	655	185	26	7	3	(2	1)	234	85	45	84	38	1	94	0	6	5	58	8	.88	4	.282	.319	.357
1999	Ari	NL	144	614	170	25	10	4	(1	3)	227	111	41	88	52	0	68	2	9	7	72	13	.85	4	.277	.332	.370
2000	Ari	NL	146	617	167	21	14	7	(4	3)	237	95	57	78	30	0	74	5	2	5	45	11	.80	6	.271	.307	.384
2001	Ari	NL	125	481	128	19	5	3	(2	1)	166	66	30	54	23	2	54	6	7	1	28	7	.80	4	.266	.307	.345
2002	Ari	NL	153	590	160	23	5	4	(4	1)	208	90	57	76	46	2	80	4	6	6	29	12	.71	9	.271	.325	.353
2003	3 Tms	NL	103	349	79	14	4	2	(2	0)	107	43	22	23	9	0	47	3	2	1	13	5	.72	7	.226	.251	.307
2004	StL	NL	145	553	170	22	3	5	(3	2)	213	91	38	77	36	1	60	3	8	6	26	5	.84	6	.307	.349	.385
2005	NYY	AL	108	329	82	8	1	0	(0	0)	92	46	15	27	12	0	49	1	7	2	27	5	.84	7	.249	.276	.280
2006	2 Tms	NL	28	68	18	3	0	1	(0	1)	24	7	5	8	8	1	7	0	4	0	1	1	.50	0	.265	.342	.353
03	Ari	NL	61	219	52	10	3	2	(2	0)	74	30	15	16	8	0	27	2	1	1	8	3	.73	6	.237	.270	.338
03	Col	NL	21	79	15	2	0	0	(0	0)	17	9	5	3	0	0	9	1	1	0	3	1	.75	1	.190	.200	.215
03	ChC	NL	21	51	12	2	1	0	(0	0)	16	4	2	4	1	0	11	0	0	0	2	1	.67	0	.235	.250	.314
06	Cin	NL	9	18	4	2	0	0	(0	0)	6	1	3	4	4	1	3	0	1	0	0	0	-	0	.222	.364	.333
06	ChC	NL	19	50	14	1	0	1	(0	1)	18	6	2	4	4	0	4	0	3	0	1	1	.50	0	.280	.333	.360
13 ML YEARS			1303	4963	1353	190	59	36	(23	13)	1769	739	368	612	308	9	649	28	57	33	363	74	.83	53	.273	.317	.356

Jason Wood

Bats: R Throws: R Pos: PH-7; 1B-5; 2B-1   Ht: 6'1" Wt: 200 Born: 12/16/1969 Age: 37

										BATTING											BASERUNNING				AVERAGES		
Year	Team	Lg	G	AB	H	2B	3B	HR	(Hm	Rd)	TB	R	RBI	RC	TBB	IBB	SO	HBP	SH	SF	SB	CS	SB%	GDP	Avg	OBP	Slg
2006	Albq*	AAA	123	441	127	23	3	11	(-	-)	189	64	77	68	42	1	92	2	1	8	1	1	.50	22	.288	.347	.429
1998	2 Tms	AL	13	24	8	2	0	1	(0	1)	13	6	1	4	3	0	5	0	0	0	0	1	.00	0	.333	.407	.542
1999	Det	AL	27	44	7	1	0	1	(1	0)	11	5	8	1	2	0	13	0	1	0	0	0	-	0	.159	.196	.250
2006	Fla	NL	12	13	6	2	0	0	(0	0)	8	3	1	4	1	0	2	0	0	0	1	0	1.00	0	.462	.500	.615
98	Oak	AL	3	1	0	0	0	0	(0	0)	0	1	0	0	0	0	1	0	0	0	0	0	-	0	.000	.000	.000
98	Det	AL	10	23	8	2	0	1	(0	1)	13	5	1	4	3	0	4	0	0	0	0	1	.00	0	.348	.423	.565
3 ML YEARS			52	81	21	5	0	2	(1	1)	32	14	10	9	6	0	20	0	1	0	1	1	.50	0	.259	.310	.395

Kerry Wood

Pitches: R Bats: R Pos: SP-4   Ht: 6'5" Wt: 225 Born: 6/16/1977 Age: 30

			HOW MUCH HE PITCHED						WHAT HE GAVE UP											THE RESULTS					
Year	Team	Lg	G	GS	CG	GF	IP	BFP	H	R	ER	HR	SH	SF	HB	TBB	IBB	SO	WP	Bk	W	L	Pct	ShO	Sv-Op Hld	ERC	ERA
2006	Peoria*	A	1	1	0	0	5.0	22	1	0	0	0	0	0	1	1	0	12	0	0	0	0	-	0	0- - -	0.41	0.00
2006	Iowa*	AAA	1	1	0	0	5.0	22	5	1	1	0	0	0	1	2	0	3	0	0	0	1	.000	0	0- - -	3.28	1.80
1998	ChC	NL	26	26	1	0	166.2	699	117	69	63	14	2	4	11	85	1	233	6	3	13	6	.684	1	0-0 -	3.03	3.40
2000	ChC	NL	23	23	1	0	137.0	603	112	77	73	17	7	5	9	87	0	132	5	1	8	7	.533	0	0-0 -	4.43	4.80
2001	ChC	NL	28	28	1	0	174.1	740	127	70	65	16	4	5	10	92	3	217	9	0	12	6	.667	1	0-0 -	3.22	3.36
2002	ChC	NL	33	33	4	0	213.2	895	169	92	87	22	13	5	16	97	5	217	8	1	12	11	.522	1	0-0 -	3.46	3.66
2003	ChC	NL	32	32	4	0	211.0	887	152	77	75	24	11	6	21	100	2	266	10	0	14	11	.560	2	0-0 -	3.31	3.20
2004	ChC	NL	22	22	0	0	140.1	595	127	62	58	16	6	6	11	51	0	144	7	0	8	9	.471	0	0-0 -	3.83	3.72
2005	ChC	NL	21	10	0	4	66.0	273	52	32	31	14	2	1	2	26	0	77	0	0	3	4	.429	0	0-0 -	3.75	4.23
2006	ChC	NL	4	4	0	0	19.2	86	19	13	9	5	0	2	1	8	0	13	1	0	1	2	.333	0	0-0 -	5.17	4.12
8 ML YEARS			189	178	11	4	1128.2	4778	875	492	461	128	45	34	81	546	11	1299	46	5	71	56	.559	5	0-0 4	3.54	3.68

Mike Wood

Pitches: R Bats: R Pos: RP-16; SP-7   Ht: 6'3" Wt: 220 Born: 4/26/1980 Age: 27

			HOW MUCH HE PITCHED						WHAT HE GAVE UP											THE RESULTS					
Year	Team	Lg	G	GS	CG	GF	IP	BFP	H	R	ER	HR	SH	SF	HB	TBB	IBB	SO	WP	Bk	W	L	Pct	ShO	Sv-Op Hld	ERC	ERA
2006	Wichta*	AA	2	2	0	0	4.0	17	5	4	3	0	0	0	0	0	0	3	1	0	0	0	-	0	0- - -	3.14	6.75
2006	Omha*	AAA	4	4	0	0	15.2	68	22	12	11	3	1	1	0	3	0	5	1	0	0	2	.000	0	0- - -	6.53	6.32
2003	Oak	AL	7	1	0	2	13.2	72	24	17	16	1	1	0	2	7	2	15	2	0	2	1	.667	0	0-0 -	9.45	10.54
2004	KC	AL	17	17	0	0	100.0	432	112	67	66	16	5	2	6	28	3	54	6	1	3	8	.273	0	0-0 -	4.96	5.94
2005	KC	AL	47	10	0	10	115.0	520	129	66	57	18	5	5	8	52	5	60	7	0	5	8	.385	0	2-2 7	5.67	4.46
2006	KC	AL	23	7	0	2	64.2	307	86	51	41	10	1	2	7	23	3	29	3	0	3	3	.500	0	0-0 1	6.57	5.71
4 ML YEARS			94	35	0	14	293.1	1331	351	201	180	45	12	9	23	110	13	158	18	1	13	20	.394	0	2-2 8	5.79	5.52

Jake Woods

Pitches: L Bats: L Pos: RP-29; SP-8   Ht: 6'1" Wt: 190 Born: 9/3/1981 Age: 25

			HOW MUCH HE PITCHED						WHAT HE GAVE UP											THE RESULTS					
Year	Team	Lg	G	GS	CG	GF	IP	BFP	H	R	ER	HR	SH	SF	HB	TBB	IBB	SO	WP	Bk	W	L	Pct	ShO	Sv-Op Hld	ERC	ERA
2001	Provo	R+	15	14	1	1	64.2	294	70	41	38	6	2	3	2	29	0	84	2	2	4	3	.571	1	0- - -	4.71	5.29
2002	CRpds	A	27	27	1	0	153.1	642	128	66	52	12	4	3	11	54	0	121	5	0	10	5	.667	0	0- - -	3.12	3.05
2003	RCuca	A+	28	28	2	0	171.1	746	178	90	76	9	3	1	8	54	0	109	2	2	12	7	.632	1	0- - -	3.76	3.99
2004	Ark	AA	14	14	1	0	90.0	374	86	29	27	5	7	4	4	19	0	60	5	0	9	2	.818	0	0- - -	2.97	2.70
2004	Salt Lk	AAA	15	14	1	1	83.0	398	107	67	56	13	2	3	4	42	0	60	2	1	6	4	.600	0	0- - -	6.82	6.07
2005	Salt Lk	AAA	15	5	0	2	36.2	177	50	27	24	7	0	1	2	17	2	36	1	0	3	1	.750	0	0- - -	7.33	5.89
2005	LAA	AL	28	0	0	10	27.2	122	30	18	14	7	1	0	2	8	0	20	2	0	1	1	.500	0	0-0 2	5.44	4.55
2006	Sea	AL	37	8	0	10	105.0	473	115	51	49	12	2	2	2	53	5	66	4	0	7	4	.636	0	1-1 2	5.16	4.20
2 ML YEARS			65	8	0	20	132.2	595	145	69	63	19	3	2	4	61	5	86	6	0	8	5	.615	0	1-1 4	5.23	4.27

Chris Woodward

Bats: R Throws: R Pos: 2B-39; PH-15; SS-13; 3B-11; LF-7; RF-2; 1B-1   Ht: 6'0" Wt: 190 Born: 6/27/1976 Age: 31

								BATTING														BASERUNNING				AVERAGES		
Year	Team	Lg	G	AB	H	2B	3B	HR	(Hm	Rd)	TB	R	RBI	RC	TBB	IBB	SO	HBP	SH	SF		SB	CS	SB%	GDP	Avg	OBP	Slg
1999	Tor	AL	14	26	6	1	0	0	(0	0)	7	1	2	2	2	0	6	0	0	1		0	0	-	1	.231	.276	.269
2000	Tor	AL	37	104	19	7	0	3	(1	2)	35	16	14	9	10	3	28	0	1	0		1	0	1.00	1	.183	.254	.337
2001	Tor	AL	37	63	12	3	2	2	(2	0)	25	9	5	4	1	0	14	0	2	0		0	1	.00	1	.190	.203	.397
2002	Tor	AL	90	312	86	13	4	13	(9	4)	146	48	45	45	26	0	72	3	1	8		3	0	1.00	8	.276	.330	.468
2003	Tor	AL	104	349	91	22	2	7	(4	3)	138	49	45	42	28	0	72	3	0	6		1	2	.33	6	.261	.316	.395
2004	Tor	AL	69	213	50	13	4	1	(0	1)	74	21	24	24	14	0	46	1	2	2		1	2	.33	3	.235	.283	.347
2005	NYM	NL	81	173	49	10	0	3	(2	1)	68	16	18	20	13	0	46	2	2	2		0	0	-	2	.283	.337	.393
2006	NYM	NL	83	222	48	10	1	3	(2	1)	69	25	25	18	23	2	55	1	4	3		1	1	.50	2	.216	.289	.311
	8 ML YEARS		515	1462	361	79	13	32	(20	12)	562	185	178	164	117	5	339	10	12	22		7	6	.54	24	.247	.303	.384

Tim Worrell

Pitches: R Bats: R Pos: RP-23   Ht: 6'4" Wt: 240 Born: 7/5/1967 Age: 39

			HOW MUCH HE PITCHED						WHAT HE GAVE UP											THE RESULTS							
Year	Team	Lg	G	GS	CG	GF	IP	BFP	H	R	ER	HR	SH	SF	HB	TBB	IBB	SO	WP	Bk	W	L	Pct	ShO	Sv-Op	Hld	ERC	ERA
1993	SD	NL	21	16	0	1	100.2	443	104	63	55	11	8	5	0	43	5	52	3	0	2	7	.222	0	0-0	1	4.31	4.92
1994	SD	NL	3	3	0	0	14.2	59	9	7	6	0	1	0	0	5	0	14	0	0	0	1	.000	0	0-0	0	1.40	3.68
1995	SD	NL	9	0	0	4	13.1	63	16	7	7	2	1	0	1	6	0	13	1	0	1	0	1.000	0	0-0	0	6.01	4.73
1996	SD	NL	50	11	0	8	121.0	510	109	45	41	9	3	1	6	39	1	99	0	0	9	7	.563	0	1-2	10	3.22	3.05
1997	SD	NL	60	10	0	14	106.1	483	116	67	61	14	6	6	7	50	2	81	2	1	4	8	.333	0	3-7	16	5.34	5.16
1998	3 Tms	AL	43	9	0	5	103.0	440	106	62	60	16	2	3	1	29	3	82	2	0	2	7	.222	0	0-3	6	4.10	5.24
1999	Oak	AL	53	0	0	17	69.0	309	69	38	32	6	1	1	3	34	1	62	1	0	2	2	.500	0	0-5	5	4.42	4.15
2000	2 Tms	NL	59	0	0	29	69.1	307	72	26	23	10	4	1	1	29	11	57	1	0	5	6	.455	0	3-6	12	4.42	2.99
2001	SF	NL	73	0	0	12	78.1	339	71	33	30	4	3	4	3	33	4	63	2	0	2	5	.286	0	0-3	13	3.32	3.45
2002	SF	NL	80	0	0	23	72.0	296	55	21	18	3	3	4	0	30	2	55	0	0	8	2	.800	0	0-1	23	2.47	2.25
2003	SF	NL	76	0	0	64	78.1	335	74	35	25	5	3	3	0	28	6	65	5	0	4	4	.500	0	38-45	1	3.19	2.87
2004	Phi	NL	77	0	0	36	78.1	327	75	36	32	10	4	5	2	21	4	64	0	0	5	6	.455	0	19-27	20	3.53	3.68
2005	2 Tms	NL	51	0	0	17	48.2	220	59	30	22	8	4	5	2	12	2	39	0	1	1	2	.333	0	1-4	12	5.10	4.07
2006	SF	NL	23	0	0	12	20.1	99	28	18	17	9	0	0	1	7	0	12	0	0	3	2	.600	0	6-8	1	8.73	7.52
98	Det	AL	15	9	0	0	61.2	265	66	42	41	11	0	1	1	19	2	47	0	0	2	6	.250	0	0-1	0	4.68	5.98
98	Cle	AL	3	0	0	1	5.1	24	6	3	3	0	0	2	0	2	0	2	0	0	0	0	-	0	0-0	0	3.84	5.06
98	Oak	AL	25	0	0	4	36.0	151	34	17	16	5	2	0	0	8	1	33	2	0	0	1	.000	0	0-2	6	3.20	4.00
00	Bal	AL	5	0	0	2	7.1	39	12	6	6	3	0	0	0	5	3	5	0	0	2	2	.500	0	0-0	0	11.13	7.36
00	ChC	NL	54	0	0	27	62.0	268	60	20	17	7	4	1	1	24	8	52	1	0	3	4	.429	0	3-6	12	3.75	2.47
05	Phi	NL	19	0	0	9	17.0	83	29	17	14	4	1	1	1	3	0	17	0	1	0	1	.000	0	1-3	3	8.79	7.41
05	Ari	NL	32	0	0	8	31.2	137	30	13	8	4	3	4	1	9	2	22	0	0	1	1	.500	0	0-1	9	3.40	2.27
	14 ML YEARS		678	49	0	242	973.2	4230	963	488	429	107	42	39	27	366	41	758	17	2	48	59	.449	0	71-111	120	3.99	3.97

David Wright

Bats: R Throws: R Pos: 3B-153; DH-1   Ht: 6'0" Wt: 200 Born: 12/20/1982 Age: 24

								BATTING														BASERUNNING				AVERAGES		
Year	Team	Lg	G	AB	H	2B	3B	HR	(Hm	Rd)	TB	R	RBI	RC	TBB	IBB	SO	HBP	SH	SF		SB	CS	SB%	GDP	Avg	OBP	Slg
2004	NYM	NL	69	263	77	17	1	14	(8	6)	138	41	40	42	14	0	40	3	0	3		6	0	1.00	7	.293	.332	.525
2005	NYM	NL	160	575	176	42	1	27	(12	15)	301	99	102	105	72	2	113	7	0	3		17	7	.71	16	.306	.388	.523
2006	NYM	NL	154	582	181	40	5	26	(13	13)	309	96	116	119	66	13	113	5	0	8		20	5	.80	15	.311	.381	.531
	3 ML YEARS		383	1420	434	99	7	67	(33	34)	748	236	258	266	152	15	266	15	0	14		43	12	.78	38	.306	.375	.527

Jamey Wright

Pitches: R Bats: R Pos: SP-21; RP-13   Ht: 6'6" Wt: 235 Born: 12/24/1974 Age: 32

			HOW MUCH HE PITCHED						WHAT HE GAVE UP											THE RESULTS							
Year	Team	Lg	G	GS	CG	GF	IP	BFP	H	R	ER	HR	SH	SF	HB	TBB	IBB	SO	WP	Bk	W	L	Pct	ShO	Sv-Op	Hld	ERC	ERA
1996	Col	NL	16	15	0	0	91.1	406	105	60	50	8	4	2	7	41	1	45	1	2	4	4	.500	0	0-0	1	5.50	4.93
1997	Col	NL	26	26	1	0	149.2	698	198	113	104	19	8	3	11	71	3	59	6	2	8	12	.400	0	0-0	0	6.96	6.25
1998	Col	NL	34	34	1	0	206.1	919	235	143	130	24	8	6	11	95	3	86	6	3	9	14	.391	0	0-0	0	5.57	5.67
1999	Col	NL	16	16	0	0	94.1	423	110	52	51	10	3	4	4	54	3	49	3	0	4	3	.571	0	0-0	0	6.19	4.87
2000	Mil	NL	26	25	0	1	164.2	718	157	81	75	12	4	6	18	88	5	96	9	2	7	9	.438	0	0-0	0	4.67	4.10
2001	Mil	NL	33	33	1	0	194.2	868	201	115	106	26	7	5	20	98	10	129	6	1	11	12	.478	1	0-0	0	5.36	4.90
2002	2 Tms	NL	23	22	1	0	129.1	585	130	80	76	17	9	6	11	75	9	77	9	0	7	13	.350	1	0-0	0	5.35	5.29
2003	KC	AL	4	4	2	0	25.1	106	23	14	12	1	0	0	1	11	0	19	0	0	1	2	.333	1	0-0	0	3.53	4.26
2004	Col	NL	14	14	0	0	78.2	361	82	39	36	8	1	1	6	45	3	41	3	0	2	3	.400	0	0-0	0	5.26	4.12
2005	Col	NL	34	27	0	0	171.1	782	201	119	104	22	4	3	15	81	4	101	4	2	8	16	.333	0	0-0	1	6.02	5.46
2006	SF	NL	34	21	0	2	156.0	676	167	95	90	16	5	4	10	64	4	79	6	0	6	10	.375	0	0-0	0	4.89	5.19
02	Mil	NL	19	19	1	0	114.1	515	115	72	68	15	9	6	11	63	8	69	8	0	5	13	.278	1	0-0	0	5.28	5.35
02	StL	NL	4	3	0	0	15.0	70	15	8	8	2	0	0	0	12	1	8	1	0	2	0	1.000	0	0-0	0	5.87	4.80
	11 ML YEARS		260	237	6	4	1461.2	6542	1609	911	834	163	53	40	114	723	45	781	51	12	67	98	.406	3	0-0	2	5.52	5.14

Jaret Wright

Pitches: R Bats: R Pos: SP-27; RP-3   Ht: 6'2" Wt: 230 Born: 12/29/1975 Age: 31

			HOW MUCH HE PITCHED						WHAT HE GAVE UP											THE RESULTS							
Year	Team	Lg	G	GS	CG	GF	IP	BFP	H	R	ER	HR	SH	SF	HB	TBB	IBB	SO	WP	Bk	W	L	Pct	ShO	Sv-Op	Hld	ERC	ERA
1997	Cle	AL	16	16	0	0	90.1	388	81	45	44	9	3	4	5	35	0	63	1	0	8	3	.727	0	0-0	0	3.63	4.38
1998	Cle	AL	32	32	1	0	192.2	855	207	109	101	22	4	6	11	87	4	140	6	0	12	10	.545	1	0-0	0	5.07	4.72
1999	Cle	AL	26	26	0	0	133.2	609	144	99	90	18	3	3	7	77	1	91	4	0	8	10	.444	0	0-0	0	5.77	6.06
2000	Cle	AL	9	9	1	0	51.2	217	44	27	27	6	0	1	0	28	0	36	2	0	3	4	.429	1	0-0	0	4.13	4.70
2001	Cle	AL	7	7	0	0	29.0	140	36	23	21	2	2	1	0	22	0	18	1	1	2	2	.500	0	0-0	0	6.82	6.52

274

Year	Team	Lg	G	GS	CG	GF	IP	BFP	H	R	ER	HR	SH	SF	HB	TBB	IBB	SO	WP	Bk	W	L	Pct	ShO	Sv-Op	Hld	ERC	ERA
							HOW MUCH HE PITCHED						**WHAT HE GAVE UP**											**THE RESULTS**					
2002	Cle	AL	8	6	0	1	18.1	116	40	34	32	3	0	3	2	19	0	12	1	0	2	3	.400	0	0-0	0	15.90	15.71
2003	2 Tms	NL	50	0	0	17	56.1	269	76	46	46	9	2	4	3	31	2	50	12	0	2	5	.286	0	2-5	4	7.59	7.35
2004	Atl	NL	32	32	0	0	186.1	781	168	79	68	11	8	6	3	70	5	159	3	0	15	8	.652	0	0-0	0	3.20	3.28
2005	NYY	AL	13	13	0	0	63.2	302	81	51	43	8	0	5	6	32	1	34	4	0	5	5	.500	0	0-0	0	6.72	6.08
2006	NYY	AL	30	27	0	0	140.1	625	157	76	70	10	3	3	7	57	0	84	6	0	11	7	.611	0	0-0	1	4.78	4.49
03	SD	NL	39	0	0	14	47.1	233	69	44	44	9	1	4	2	28	2	41	10	0	1	5	.167	0	2-4	1	8.71	8.37
03	Atl	NL	11	0	0	3	9.0	36	7	2	2	0	1	0	1	3	0	9	2	0	1	0	1.000	0	0-1	3	2.51	2.00
10 ML YEARS			223	168	2	18	962.1	4302	1034	589	542	98	25	36	45	458	13	687	40	1	68	57	.544	2	2-5	5	5.02	5.07

Mike Wuertz

Pitches: R Bats: R Pos: RP-41 Ht: 6'3" Wt: 205 Born: 12/15/1978 Age: 28

Year	Team	Lg	G	GS	CG	GF	IP	BFP	H	R	ER	HR	SH	SF	HB	TBB	IBB	SO	WP	Bk	W	L	Pct	ShO	Sv-Op	Hld	ERC	ERA
							HOW MUCH HE PITCHED						**WHAT HE GAVE UP**											**THE RESULTS**					
2006	Iowa*	AAA	30	0	0	24	41.2	168	30	10	8	2	1	0	1	9	1	67	3	0	6	0	1.000	0	10- -		1.68	1.73
2004	ChC	NL	31	0	0	11	29.0	124	22	14	14	4	4	2	0	17	1	30	2	1	1	0	1.000	0	1-1	1	3.67	4.34
2005	ChC	NL	75	0	0	12	75.2	319	60	36	32	6	3	2	0	40	7	89	7	0	6	2	.750	0	0-3	18	3.17	3.81
2006	ChC	NL	41	0	0	4	40.2	175	35	14	12	5	3	0	1	16	2	42	1	0	3	1	.750	0	0-1	6	3.37	2.66
3 ML YEARS			147	0	0	27	145.1	618	117	64	58	15	10	4	1	73	10	161	10	1	10	3	.769	0	1-5	25	3.33	3.59

Esteban Yan

Pitches: R Bats: R Pos: RP-27 Ht: 6'4" Wt: 255 Born: 6/22/1975 Age: 32

Year	Team	Lg	G	GS	CG	GF	IP	BFP	H	R	ER	HR	SH	SF	HB	TBB	IBB	SO	WP	Bk	W	L	Pct	ShO	Sv-Op	Hld	ERC	ERA
							HOW MUCH HE PITCHED						**WHAT HE GAVE UP**											**THE RESULTS**					
2006	Omha*	AAA	11	0	0	4	19.2	93	24	16	16	3	2	0	1	9	1	16	4	0	0	1	.000	0	0- -		5.99	7.32
1996	Bal	AL	4	0	0	2	9.1	42	13	7	6	3	0	0	1	3	1	7	0	0	0	0	-	0	0-0		7.88	5.79
1997	Bal	AL	3	2	0	0	9.2	58	20	18	17	3	0	1	2	7	0	4	1	0	0	1	1.000	0	0-0		15.60	15.83
1998	TB	AL	64	0	0	18	88.2	381	78	41	38	11	1	3	5	41	2	77	6	0	5	4	.556	0	1-5	8	4.02	3.86
1999	TB	AL	50	1	0	15	61.0	286	77	41	40	8	6	3	9	32	4	46	2	0	3	4	.429	0	0-3	7	7.13	5.90
2000	TB	AL	43	20	0	8	137.2	618	158	98	95	26	4	6	11	42	0	111	7	1	7	8	.467	0	0-2	3	5.46	6.21
2001	TB	AL	54	0	0	51	62.1	264	64	34	27	7	3	1	5	11	1	64	5	0	4	6	.400	0	22-31	0	3.68	3.90
2002	TB	AL	55	0	0	47	69.0	305	70	35	33	10	2	1	3	29	1	53	5	1	7	8	.467	0	19-27	0	4.67	4.30
2003	2 Tms		54	0	0	23	66.2	309	84	48	47	13	2	4	7	23	5	53	9	0	2	1	.667	0	1-1	4	6.39	6.35
2004	Det	AL	69	0	0	27	87.0	379	92	43	37	8	4	3	4	32	5	69	7	0	3	6	.333	0	7-17	11	4.32	3.83
2005	LAA	AL	49	0	0	21	66.2	293	66	36	34	8	3	4	0	30	4	45	5	0	1	1	.500	0	0-0	1	4.21	4.59
2006	2 Tms		27	0	0	12	37.1	161	32	25	23	8	2	3	1	20	4	24	5	0	1	0	1.000	0	1-1	6	4.58	5.54
03	Tex	AL	15	0	0	6	23.1	110	31	19	18	5	0	0	2	7	1	25	5	0	0	1	.000	0	0-0	1	6.64	6.94
03	StL	NL	39	0	0	17	43.1	199	53	29	29	8	2	4	5	16	4	28	4	0	2	0	1.000	0	1-1	3	6.26	6.02
06	LAA	AL	13	0	0	8	22.1	98	19	18	17	4	1	1	1	13	2	16	4	0	0	0	-	0	0-0		4.56	6.85
06	Cin	NL	14	0	0	4	15.0	63	13	7	6	4	1	2	0	7	2	8	1	0	1	0	1.000	0	1-1		4.60	3.60
11 ML YEARS			472	23	0	224	695.1	3096	754	426	397	105	27	29	47	270	27	553	52	2	33	39	.458	0	51-87	34	5.09	5.14

Tyler Yates

Pitches: R Bats: R Pos: RP-56 Ht: 6'4" Wt: 240 Born: 8/7/1977 Age: 29

Year	Team	Lg	G	GS	CG	GF	IP	BFP	H	R	ER	HR	SH	SF	HB	TBB	IBB	SO	WP	Bk	W	L	Pct	ShO	Sv-Op	Hld	ERC	ERA
							HOW MUCH HE PITCHED						**WHAT HE GAVE UP**											**THE RESULTS**					
1998	As	R	15	0	0	8	23.0	107	28	12	10	0	0	0	0	14	0	20	1	2	0	0		0	2- -		5.68	3.91
1998	SoOre	A-	2	0	0	1	2.1	9	2	0	0	0	0	0	0	0	0	1	0	0	0	0		0	1- -		1.44	0.00
1999	Visalia	A+	47	1	0	19	82.1	382	98	64	50	12	3	2	4	35	3	74	12	0	2	5	.286	0	4- -		5.67	5.47
2000	Mdest	A+	30	0	0	5	56.2	237	50	23	18	2	1	1	1	23	4	61	8	0	4	2	.667	0	1- -		3.01	2.86
2000	Mdland	AA	22	0	0	8	26.1	121	28	20	18	2	2	2	0	15	3	24	2	0	1	1	.500	0	0- -		4.65	6.15
2001	Mdland	AA	56	0	0	35	62.2	282	66	39	30	4	1	0	1	27	8	61	7	0	4	6	.400	0	17- -		3.97	4.31
2001	Scrmto	AAA	4	0	0	2	5.1	20	3	0	0	0	0	0	1	1	0	3	0	0	1	0	1.000	0	1- -		1.41	0.00
2002	Norfolk	AAA	24	0	0	20	34.0	142	29	10	5	1	1	0	0	13	1	34	0	0	2	2	.500	0	6- -		2.69	1.32
2003	StLuci	A+	14	11	0	0	48.0	205	41	28	23	5	0	2	2	24	0	49	2	0	1	2	.333	0	0- -		3.89	4.31
2003	Bnghtn	AA	8	8	0	0	39.1	167	33	21	19	4	3	4	1	17	0	36	2	2	1	2	.333	0	0- -		3.40	4.35
2003	Norfolk	AAA	4	4	0	0	20.0	86	22	9	9	1	0	0	0	9	0	15	1	0	1	2	.333	0	0- -		4.90	4.05
2004	Norfolk	AAA	30	1	0	12	39.2	172	28	18	14	2	0	0	3	22	0	43	3	0	6	2	.750	0	4- -		2.95	3.18
2006	Rchmd	AAA	7	0	0	0	8.1	32	6	2	2	0	1	0	0	3	0	10	0	0	0	0	-	0	0- -		1.99	2.16
2004	NYM	NL	21	7	0	2	46.2	228	61	36	33	6	2	2	3	25	3	35	1	1	2	4	.333	0	0-0	2	6.73	6.36
2006	Atl	NL	56	0	0	11	50.0	217	42	23	22	6	2	0	0	31	8	46	1	0	2	5	.286	0	1-6	12	3.95	3.96
2 ML YEARS			77	7	0	13	96.2	445	103	59	55	12	4	2	3	56	11	81	2	1	4	9	.308	0	1-6	14	5.24	5.12

Kevin Youkilis

Bats: R Throws: R Pos: 1B-127; LF-18; 3B-16; PH-1 Ht: 6'1" Wt: 220 Born: 3/15/1979 Age: 28

Year	Team	Lg	G	AB	H	2B	3B	HR	(Hm	Rd)	TB	R	RBI	RC	TBB	IBB	SO	HBP	SH	SF	SB	CS	SB%	GDP	Avg	OBP	Slg
			BATTING																		**BASERUNNING**				**AVERAGES**		
2004	Bos	AL	72	208	54	11	0	7	(2	5)	86	38	35	36	33	0	45	4	0	3	0	1	.00	1	.260	.367	.413
2005	Bos	AL	44	79	22	7	0	1	(0	1)	32	11	9	13	14	0	19	2	0	0	0	1	.00	0	.278	.400	.405
2006	Bos	AL	147	569	159	42	2	13	(6	7)	244	100	72	104	91	0	120	9	0	11	5	2	.71	12	.279	.381	.429
3 ML YEARS			263	856	235	60	2	21	(8	13)	362	149	116	153	138	0	184	15	0	14	5	4	.56	13	.275	.379	.423

Shane Youman

Pitches: L **Bats:** L **Pos:** SP-3; RP-2   **Ht:** 6'4" **Wt:** 220 **Born:** 10/11/1979 **Age:** 27

			HOW MUCH HE PITCHED						WHAT HE GAVE UP										THE RESULTS						
Year	Team	Lg	G	GS	CG	GF	IP	BFP	H	R	ER	HR	SH	SF	HB	TBB	IBB	SO	WP	Bk	W	L	Pct	ShO	Sv-Op	Hld	ERC	ERA
2002	Wmspt	A-	20	0	0	12	37.1	143	25	7	6	1	1	0	2	8	0	48	1	0	4	0	1.000	0	5- -	-	1.59	1.45
2003	Hickory	A+	40	1	0	28	50.1	236	51	31	26	2	4	1	2	35	2	58	5	0	6	3	.667	0	12- -	-	4.87	4.65
2004	Lynbrg	A+	47	0	0	11	74.0	325	67	28	26	5	1	1	1	35	5	62	2	0	4	2	.667	0	2- -	-	3.46	3.16
2005	Altna	AA	44	5	0	15	101.0	457	102	54	44	10	10	0	2	48	4	77	5	0	8	6	.571	0	2- -	-	4.30	3.92
2006	Altna	AA	23	11	0	3	95.1	375	70	27	16	4	3	2	1	20	1	64	1	0	7	2	.778	0	1- -	-	1.71	1.51
2006	Indy	AAA	8	7	0	0	42.1	175	42	20	19	2	2	1	0	10	0	19	2	0	4	0	1.000	0	0- -	-	3.07	4.04
2006	Pit	NL	5	3	0	0	21.2	88	15	7	7	1	2	1	0	10	0	5	0	0	0	2	.000	0	0-0	0	2.37	2.91

Chris Young

Pitches: R **Bats:** R **Pos:** SP-31   **Ht:** 6'10" **Wt:** 260 **Born:** 5/25/1979 **Age:** 28

			HOW MUCH HE PITCHED						WHAT HE GAVE UP										THE RESULTS						
Year	Team	Lg	G	GS	CG	GF	IP	BFP	H	R	ER	HR	SH	SF	HB	TBB	IBB	SO	WP	Bk	W	L	Pct	ShO	Sv-Op	Hld	ERC	ERA
2004	Tex	AL	7	7	0	0	36.1	158	36	21	19	7	1	0	2	10	0	27	1	0	3	2	.600	0	0-0	0	4.26	4.71
2005	Tex	AL	31	31	0	0	164.2	700	162	84	78	19	2	4	7	45	2	137	3	0	12	7	.632	0	0-0	0	3.71	4.26
2006	SD	NL	31	31	0	0	179.1	735	134	72	69	28	8	3	6	69	4	164	6	1	11	5	.688	0	0-0	0	3.12	3.46
	3 ML YEARS		69	69	0	0	380.1	1593	332	177	166	54	11	7	15	124	6	328	10	1	26	14	.650	0	0-0	0	3.48	3.93

Chris Young

Bats: R **Throws:** R **Pos:** CF-24; PR-6; PH-2   **Ht:** 6'2" **Wt:** 180 **Born:** 9/5/1983 **Age:** 23

			BATTING																	BASERUNNING				AVERAGES		
Year	Team	Lg	G	AB	H	2B	3B	HR	(Hm	Rd)	TB	R	RBI	RC	TBB	IBB	SO	HBP	SH	SF	SB	CS	SB%	GDP	Avg	OBP	Slg
2002	WhSox	R	55	184	40	13	1	5	(-	-)	70	26	17	21	19	0	54	5	2	0	7	8	.47	1	.217	.308	.380
2003	Bristol	R+	64	238	69	18	3	7	(-	-)	114	47	28	43	23	0	40	4	3	4	21	7	.75	0	.290	.357	.479
2003	Gr Falls	R+	10	34	6	3	0	0	(-	-)	9	5	0	1	1	0	10	0	0	0	0	0	-	0	.176	.200	.265
2004	Knapol	A	135	465	122	31	5	24	(-	-)	235	83	56	91	66	1	145	11	6	3	31	9	.78	2	.262	.365	.505
2005	Brham	AA	126	466	129	41	3	26	(-	-)	254	100	77	101	70	1	129	7	7	3	32	6	.84	4	.277	.377	.545
2006	Tucsn	AAA	100	402	111	32	4	21	(-	-)	214	78	77	81	52	2	71	6	1	5	17	5	.77	6	.276	.363	.532
2006	Ari	NL	30	70	17	4	0	2	(1	1)	27	10	10	11	6	0	12	1	0	1	2	1	.67	0	.243	.308	.386

Delmon Young

Bats: R **Throws:** R **Pos:** RF-30; CF-1   **Ht:** 6'3" **Wt:** 205 **Born:** 9/14/1985 **Age:** 21

			BATTING																	BASERUNNING				AVERAGES		
Year	Team	Lg	G	AB	H	2B	3B	HR	(Hm	Rd)	TB	R	RBI	RC	TBB	IBB	SO	HBP	SH	SF	SB	CS	SB%	GDP	Avg	OBP	Slg
2004	CtnSC	A	131	513	165	26	5	25	(-	-)	276	95	116	108	53	6	120	6	0	6	21	6	.78	11	.322	.388	.538
2005	Mont	AA	84	330	111	13	4	20	(-	-)	192	59	71	74	25	5	66	7	0	8	25	8	.76	10	.336	.386	.582
2005	Drham	AAA	52	228	65	13	3	6	(-	-)	102	33	28	30	4	0	33	2	0	0	7	4	.64	6	.285	.303	.447
2006	Drham	AAA	86	342	108	22	4	8	(-	-)	162	50	59	59	15	1	65	3	0	10	22	4	.85	12	.316	.341	.474
2006	TB	AL	30	126	40	9	1	3	(1	2)	60	16	10	15	1	0	24	3	0	1	2	2	.50	0	.317	.336	.476

Delwyn Young

Bats: B **Throws:** R **Pos:** PH-4; PR-2; LF-1; RF-1   **Ht:** 5'8" **Wt:** 210 **Born:** 6/30/1982 **Age:** 25

			BATTING																	BASERUNNING				AVERAGES		
Year	Team	Lg	G	AB	H	2B	3B	HR	(Hm	Rd)	TB	R	RBI	RC	TBB	IBB	SO	HBP	SH	SF	SB	CS	SB%	GDP	Avg	OBP	Slg
2002	Gr Falls	R	59	240	72	18	1	10	(-	-)	122	42	41	46	27	2	60	4	0	0	4	2	.67	2	.300	.380	.508
2003	SoGA	A	119	443	143	38	7	15	(-	-)	240	67	73	90	36	1	87	8	2	4	5	2	.71	2	.323	.381	.542
2004	VeroB	A+	129	470	132	36	3	22	(-	-)	240	76	85	89	57	8	134	7	2	4	11	4	.73	13	.281	.364	.511
2005	Jaxnvl	AA	95	371	110	25	1	16	(-	-)	185	52	62	63	27	4	86	3	1	4	1	3	.25	9	.296	.346	.499
2005	LsVgs	AAA	36	160	52	12	0	4	(-	-)	76	23	14	27	8	0	35	1	1	0	0	0	-	3	.325	.361	.475
2006	LsVgs	AAA	140	532	145	42	1	18	(-	-)	243	76	98	80	42	5	104	3	1	5	3	4	.43	11	.273	.326	.457
2006	LAD	NL	8	5	0	0	0	0	(0	0)	0	0	0	0	0	0	1	0	0	0	0	0	-	0	.000	.000	.000

Dmitri Young

Bats: B **Throws:** R **Pos:** DH-44; PH-5; 1B-3   **Ht:** 6'2" **Wt:** 220 **Born:** 10/11/1973 **Age:** 33

			BATTING																	BASERUNNING				AVERAGES		
Year	Team	Lg	G	AB	H	2B	3B	HR	(Hm	Rd)	TB	R	RBI	RC	TBB	IBB	SO	HBP	SH	SF	SB	CS	SB%	GDP	Avg	OBP	Slg
2006	Lkland*	A+	2	5	2	1	0	0	(-	-)	3	1	0	1	1	0	1	0	0	0	0	0	-	0	.400	.500	.600
2006	Erie*	AA	6	20	3	1	0	0	(-	-)	4	2	1	1	4	0	6	0	0	0	0	0	-	0	.150	.292	.200
2006	Toledo*	AAA	8	31	14	3	0	1	(-	-)	20	4	6	9	4	0	4	0	0	0	0	0	-	0	.452	.514	.645
1996	StL	NL	16	29	7	0	0	0	(0	0)	7	3	2	2	4	0	5	1	0	0	0	1	1.00	1	.241	.353	.241
1997	StL	NL	110	333	86	14	3	5	(2	3)	121	38	34	40	38	3	63	2	1	3	6	5	.55	8	.258	.335	.363
1998	Cin	NL	144	536	166	48	1	14	(3	11)	258	81	83	88	47	4	94	2	0	5	2	4	.33	16	.310	.364	.481
1999	Cin	NL	127	373	112	30	2	14	(9	5)	188	63	56	63	30	1	71	2	0	4	3	1	.75	11	.300	.352	.504
2000	Cin	NL	152	548	166	37	6	18	(6	12)	269	68	88	86	36	6	80	3	1	5	0	3	.00	16	.303	.346	.491
2001	Cin	NL	142	540	163	28	3	21	(8	13)	260	68	69	83	37	10	77	5	1	3	8	5	.62	22	.302	.350	.481
2002	Det	AL	54	201	57	14	0	7	(5	2)	92	25	27	27	12	5	39	2	0	1	2	0	1.00	12	.284	.329	.458
2003	Det	AL	155	562	167	34	7	29	(10	19)	302	78	85	101	58	16	130	11	0	4	1	1	.67	16	.297	.372	.537
2004	Det	AL	104	389	106	23	2	18	(8	10)	187	72	60	57	33	4	71	6	0	4	0	1	.00	8	.272	.336	.481
2005	Det	AL	126	469	127	25	3	21	(10	11)	221	61	72	60	29	7	100	9	0	1	1	0	1.00	16	.271	.325	.471
2006	Det	AL	48	172	43	4	1	7	(2	5)	70	19	23	20	11	0	39	0	0	1	1	1	.50	3	.250	.293	.407
	11 ML YEARS		1178	4152	1200	257	28	154	(63	91)	1975	576	599	627	335	56	769	43	3	31	25	22	.53	129	.289	.346	.476

Eric Young

Bats: R **Throws:** R **Pos:** LF-37; PH-21; PR-6; 2B-2; CF-2; RF-1   **Ht:** 5'9" **Wt:** 185 **Born:** 5/11/1967 **Age:** 40

										BATTING										BASERUNNING				AVERAGES		
Year	Team	Lg	G	AB	H	2B	3B	HR	(Hm | Rd)	TB	R	RBI	RC	TBB	IBB	SO	HBP	SH	SF	SB	CS	SB%	GDP	Avg	OBP	Slg
2006	Okla*	AAA	9	27	6	2	3	0	(- | -)	14	3	1	4	4	0	4	2	0	0	0	2	.00	0	.222	.364	.519
1992	LAD	NL	49	132	34	1	0	1	(0 | 1)	38	9	11	12	8	0	9	0	4	0	6	1	.86	3	.258	.300	.288
1993	Col	NL	144	490	132	16	8	3	(3 | 0)	173	82	42	66	63	3	41	4	4	4	42	19	.69	9	.269	.355	.353
1994	Col	NL	90	228	62	13	1	7	(6 | 1)	98	37	30	40	38	1	17	2	5	2	18	7	.72	3	.272	.378	.430
1995	Col	NL	120	366	116	21	9	6	(5 | 1)	173	68	36	73	49	3	29	5	3	1	35	12	.74	4	.317	.404	.473
1996	Col	NL	141	568	184	23	4	8	(7 | 1)	239	113	74	99	47	1	31	21	2	5	53	19	.74	9	.324	.393	.421
1997	2 Tms	NL	155	622	174	33	8	8	(2 | 6)	247	106	61	93	71	1	54	9	10	6	45	14	.76	18	.280	.359	.397
1998	LAD	NL	117	452	129	24	1	8	(7 | 1)	179	78	43	70	45	0	32	5	9	2	42	13	.76	4	.285	.355	.396
1999	LAD	NL	119	456	128	24	2	2	(2 | 0)	162	73	41	65	63	0	26	5	6	4	51	22	.70	12	.281	.371	.355
2000	ChC	NL	153	607	180	40	2	6	(5 | 1)	242	98	47	99	63	1	39	8	7	5	54	7	.89	12	.297	.367	.399
2001	ChC	NL	149	603	168	43	4	6	(4 | 2)	237	98	42	78	42	1	45	9	15	3	31	14	.69	15	.279	.333	.393
2002	Mil	NL	138	496	139	29	3	3	(2 | 1)	183	57	28	53	39	0	38	6	8	4	31	11	.74	14	.280	.338	.369
2003	2 Tms	NL	135	475	119	20	1	15	(7 | 8)	186	80	34	54	57	2	44	5	2	2	28	12	.70	12	.251	.336	.392
2004	Tex	AL	104	344	99	25	2	1	(1 | 0)	131	55	27	54	43	0	28	8	4	3	14	9	.61	9	.288	.377	.381
2005	SD	NL	56	142	39	9	0	2	(0 | 2)	54	22	12	17	18	0	12	0	3	0	7	6	.54	4	.275	.356	.380
2006	Tex	AL	60	138	28	6	1	3	(2 | 1)	45	20	15	10	14	1	17	2	2	3	8	2	.80	7	.203	.280	.326
97	Col	NL	118	468	132	29	6	6	(2 | 4)	191	78	45	71	57	0	37	5	8	5	32	12	.73	16	.282	.363	.408
97	LAD	NL	37	154	42	4	2	2	(0 | 2)	56	28	16	22	14	1	17	4	2	1	13	2	.87	2	.273	.347	.364
03	Mil	NL	109	404	105	18	1	15	(7 | 8)	170	71	31	51	48	2	34	4	2	1	25	7	.78	9	.260	.344	.421
03	SF	NL	26	71	14	2	0	0	(0 | 0)	16	9	3	3	9	0	10	1	0	1	3	5	.38	3	.197	.293	.225
06	SD	NL	56	128	26	5	0	3	(2 | 1)	40	19	13	8	13	1	16	2	1	3	8	2	.80	6	.203	.281	.313
06	Tex	AL	4	10	2	1	1	0	(0 | 0)	5	1	2	2	1	0	1	0	1	0	0	0	-	1	.200	.273	.500
15 ML YEARS			1730	6119	1731	327	46	79	(53 | 26)	2387	996	543	883	660	14	462	89	84	44	465	168	.73	135	.283	.359	.390

Michael Young

Bats: R **Throws:** R **Pos:** SS-155; DH-7   **Ht:** 6'1" **Wt:** 200 **Born:** 10/19/1976 **Age:** 30

										BATTING										BASERUNNING				AVERAGES		
Year	Team	Lg	G	AB	H	2B	3B	HR	(Hm | Rd)	TB	R	RBI	RC	TBB	IBB	SO	HBP	SH	SF	SB	CS	SB%	GDP	Avg	OBP	Slg
2000	Tex	AL	2	2	0	0	0	0	(0 | 0)	0	0	0	0	0	0	1	0	0	0	0	0	-	0	.000	.000	.000
2001	Tex	AL	106	386	96	18	4	11	(7 | 4)	155	57	49	45	26	0	91	3	9	5	3	1	.75	9	.249	.298	.402
2002	Tex	AL	156	573	150	26	8	9	(3 | 6)	219	77	62	64	41	1	112	0	13	6	6	7	.46	14	.262	.308	.382
2003	Tex	AL	160	666	204	33	9	14	(9 | 5)	297	106	72	106	36	1	103	1	3	7	13	2	.87	14	.306	.339	.446
2004	Tex	AL	160	690	216	33	9	22	(9 | 13)	333	114	99	124	44	1	89	1	0	4	12	3	.80	11	.313	.353	.483
2005	Tex	AL	159	668	221	40	5	24	(12 | 12)	343	114	91	131	58	0	91	3	0	3	5	2	.71	20	.331	.385	.513
2006	Tex	AL	162	691	217	52	3	14	(8 | 6)	317	93	103	120	48	0	96	1	0	8	7	3	.70	27	.314	.356	.459
7 ML YEARS			905	3676	1104	202	38	94	(48 | 46)	1664	561	476	590	253	3	583	9	25	33	46	18	.72	95	.300	.344	.453

Carlos Zambrano

Pitches: R **Bats:** B **Pos:** SP-33   **Ht:** 6'5" **Wt:** 255 **Born:** 6/1/1981 **Age:** 26

			HOW MUCH HE PITCHED						WHAT HE GAVE UP											THE RESULTS						
Year	Team	Lg	G	GS	CG	GF	IP	BFP	H	R	ER	HR	SH	SF	HB	TBB	IBB	SO	WP	Bk	W	L	Pct	ShO	Sv-Op	Hld	ERC	ERA
2001	ChC	NL	6	1	0	1	7.2	42	11	13	13	2	1	1	1	8	0	4	1	0	1	2	.333	0	0-1	0	11.86	15.26
2002	ChC	NL	32	16	0	3	108.1	477	94	53	44	9	9	1	4	63	0	93	6	0	4	8	.333	0	0-0	0	4.02	3.66
2003	ChC	NL	32	32	3	0	214.0	907	188	88	74	9	11	6	10	94	12	168	6	1	13	11	.542	1	0-0	0	3.28	3.11
2004	ChC	NL	31	31	1	0	209.2	887	174	73	64	14	10	3	20	81	4	188	6	2	16	8	.667	1	0-0	0	3.20	2.75
2005	ChC	NL	33	33	2	0	223.1	909	170	88	81	21	9	5	8	86	3	202	7	0	14	6	.700	0	0-0	0	2.86	3.26
2006	ChC	NL	33	33	0	0	214.0	917	162	91	81	20	11	4	9	115	4	210	9	1	16	7	.696	0	0-0	0	3.34	3.41
6 ML YEARS			167	146	6	4	977.0	4139	799	406	357	75	51	20	52	447	25	865	35	4	64	42	.604	2	0-1	0	3.31	3.29

Victor Zambrano

Pitches: R **Bats:** B **Pos:** SP-5   **Ht:** 6'0" **Wt:** 205 **Born:** 8/6/1975 **Age:** 31

			HOW MUCH HE PITCHED						WHAT HE GAVE UP											THE RESULTS						
Year	Team	Lg	G	GS	CG	GF	IP	BFP	H	R	ER	HR	SH	SF	HB	TBB	IBB	SO	WP	Bk	W	L	Pct	ShO	Sv-Op	Hld	ERC	ERA
2001	TB	AL	36	0	0	19	51.1	212	38	21	18	6	2	0	3	18	0	58	4	0	6	2	.750	0	2-6	5	2.80	3.16
2002	TB	AL	42	11	0	11	114.0	519	120	77	70	15	7	8	4	68	5	73	10	0	8	8	.500	0	1-3	6	5.52	5.53
2003	TB	AL	34	28	1	2	188.1	836	165	97	88	21	3	10	20	106	2	132	15	3	12	10	.545	0	0-0	2	4.51	4.21
2004	2 Tms		26	25	0	2	142.0	650	119	77	69	13	1	10	16	102	2	123	6	0	11	7	.611	0	0-0	1	4.75	4.37
2005	NYM	NL	31	27	0	2	166.1	748	170	85	77	12	6	6	15	77	2	112	8	2	7	12	.368	0	0-0	0	4.55	4.17
2006	NYM	NL	5	5	0	0	21.1	97	25	16	16	5	0	0	0	11	0	15	1	0	1	2	.333	0	0-0	0	6.69	6.75
04	TB	AL	23	22	0	2	128.0	588	107	68	63	13	0	10	16	96	2	109	5	0	9	7	.563	0	0-0	1	5.01	4.43
04	NYM	NL	3	3	0	0	14.0	62	12	9	6	0	1	0	0	6	0	14	1	0	2	0	1.000	0	0-0	0	2.57	3.86
6 ML YEARS			174	96	1	34	683.1	3062	637	373	338	72	19	34	58	382	11	513	44	5	45	41	.523	0	3-9	14	4.66	4.45

Gregg Zaun

Bats: B **Throws:** R **Pos:** C-72; DH-19; PH-18   **Ht:** 5'10" **Wt:** 190 **Born:** 4/14/1971 **Age:** 36

										BATTING										BASERUNNING				AVERAGES		
Year	Team	Lg	G	AB	H	2B	3B	HR	(Hm	Rd)	TB	R	RBI	RC	TBB	IBB	SO	HBP	SH	SF	SB	CS	SB%	GDP	Avg	OBP	Slg
2006	Dnedin*	A+	1	4	0	0	0	0	(-	-)	0	0	0	0	0	0	1	0	0	0	0	0	-	0	.000	.000	.000
1995	Bal	AL	40	104	27	5	0	3	(1	2)	41	18	14	15	16	0	14	0	2	0	1	1	.50	2	.260	.358	.394
1996	2 Tms		60	139	34	9	1	2	(1	1)	51	20	15	16	14	3	20	2	1	2	1	0	1.00	5	.245	.318	.367
1997	Fla	NL	58	143	43	10	2	2	(0	2)	63	21	20	27	26	4	18	2	1	0	1	0	1.00	8	.301	.415	.441
1998	Fla	NL	106	298	56	12	2	5	(2	3)	87	19	29	23	35	2	52	1	2	5	5	2	.71	7	.188	.274	.292
1999	Tex	AL	43	93	23	2	1	1	(0	1)	30	12	12	10	10	0	7	0	1	2	1	0	1.00	4	.247	.314	.323
2000	KC	AL	83	234	64	11	0	7	(2	5)	96	36	33	40	43	3	34	3	0	2	3	1	.70	4	.274	.390	.410

Year	Team	Lg	G	AB	H	2B	3B	HR	(Hm	Rd)	TB	R	RBI	RC	TBB	IBB	SO	HBP	SH	SF	SB	CS	SB%	GDP	Avg	OBP	Slg
2001	KC	AL	39	125	40	9	0	6	(1	5)	67	15	18	24	12	0	16	0	0	1	1	2	.33	2	.320	.377	.536
2002	Hou	NL	76	185	41	7	1	3	(3	0)	59	18	24	17	12	1	36	2	2	1	1	0	1.00	4	.222	.275	.319
2003	2 Tms	NL	74	166	38	8	0	4	(1	3)	58	15	21	20	19	0	21	1	1	2	1	1	.50	5	.229	.309	.349
2004	Tor	AL	107	338	91	24	0	6	(2	4)	133	46	36	50	47	3	61	6	0	1	0	2	.00	7	.269	.367	.393
2005	Tor	AL	133	434	109	18	1	11	(7	4)	162	61	61	65	73	2	70	0	0	5	2	3	.40	11	.251	.355	.373
2006	Tor	AL	99	290	79	19	0	12	(7	5)	134	39	40	41	41	3	42	3	0	5	0	2	.00	10	.272	.363	.462
96	Bal	AL	50	108	25	8	1	1	(1	0)	38	16	13	12	11	2	15	2	0	2	0	0	-	3	.231	.309	.352
96	Fla	NL	10	31	9	1	0	1	(0	1)	13	4	2	4	3	1	5	0	1	0	1	0	1.00	2	.290	.353	.419
03	Hou	NL	59	120	26	7	0	1	(1	0)	36	9	13	12	14	0	14	1	1	2	1	0	1.00	5	.217	.299	.300
03	Col	NL	15	46	12	1	0	3	(0	3)	22	6	8	8	5	0	7	0	0	0	0	1	.00	0	.261	.333	.478
12 ML YEARS			918	2549	645	134	8	62	(27	35)	981	320	323	348	348	21	391	20	10	23	21	16	.57	62	.253	.345	.385

Ryan Zimmerman

Bats: R **Throws:** R **Pos:** 3B-157   **Ht:** 6'3" **Wt:** 210 **Born:** 9/28/1984 **Age:** 22

Year	Team	Lg	G	AB	H	2B	3B	HR	(Hm	Rd)	TB	R	RBI	RC	TBB	IBB	SO	HBP	SH	SF	SB	CS	SB%	GDP	Avg	OBP	Slg
2005	Savann	A	4	17	8	2	1	2	(-	-)	18	5	6	6	0	0	3	0	0	0	0	1	.00	0	.471	.471	1.059
2005	Hrsbrg	AA	63	233	76	20	0	9	(-	-)	123	40	32	43	15	3	34	2	1	1	5	5	.17	3	.326	.371	.528
2005	Was	NL	20	58	23	10	0	0	(0	0)	33	6	6	9	3	0	12	0	0	1	0	0	-	1	.397	.419	.569
2006	Was	NL	157	614	176	47	3	20	(10	10)	289	84	110	101	61	7	120	2	1	4	11	8	.58	15	.287	.351	.471
2 ML YEARS			177	672	199	57	3	20	(10	10)	322	90	116	110	64	7	132	2	1	5	11	8	.58	16	.296	.357	.479

Barry Zito

Pitches: L **Bats:** L **Pos:** SP-34   **Ht:** 6'4" **Wt:** 210 **Born:** 5/13/1978 **Age:** 29

			HOW MUCH HE PITCHED						WHAT HE GAVE UP											THE RESULTS						
Year	Team	Lg	G	GS	CG	GF	IP	BFP	H	R	ER	HR	SH	SF	HB	TBB	IBB	SO	WP	Bk	W	L	Pct	ShO	Sv-Op Hld	ERC	ERA
2000	Oak	AL	14	14	1	0	92.2	376	64	30	28	6	1	0	2	45	2	78	2	0	7	4	.636	1	0-0 0	2.63	2.72
2001	Oak	AL	35	35	3	0	214.1	902	184	92	83	18	5	4	13	80	0	205	6	1	17	8	.680	2	0-0 0	3.33	3.49
2002	Oak	AL	35	35	1	0	229.1	939	182	79	70	24	9	7	9	78	2	182	2	1	23	5	.821	0	0-0 0	2.92	2.75
2003	Oak	AL	35	35	4	0	231.2	957	186	98	85	19	7	7	6	88	3	146	4	0	14	12	.538	1	0-0 0	2.91	3.30
2004	Oak	AL	34	34	0	0	213.0	926	216	116	106	28	7	9	9	81	2	163	4	1	11	11	.500	0	0-0 0	4.45	4.48
2005	Oak	AL	35	35	0	0	228.1	953	185	106	98	26	8	7	13	89	0	171	4	0	14	13	.519	0	0-0 0	3.32	3.86
2006	Oak	AL	34	34	0	0	221.0	945	211	99	94	27	7	6	13	99	5	151	4	2	16	10	.615	0	0-0 0	4.47	3.83
7 ML YEARS			222	222	9	0	1430.1	5998	1228	620	564	148	44	40	65	560	14	1096	26	5	102	63	.618	4	0-0 0	3.47	3.55

Ben Zobrist

Bats: B **Throws:** R **Pos:** SS-52; PH-2   **Ht:** 6'3" **Wt:** 200 **Born:** 5/26/1981 **Age:** 26

Year	Team	Lg	G	AB	H	2B	3B	HR	(Hm	Rd)	TB	R	RBI	RC	TBB	IBB	SO	HBP	SH	SF	SB	CS	SB%	GDP	Avg	OBP	Slg
2004	Tri-Cit	A-	68	259	87	14	3	4	(-	-)	119	50	45	56	43	0	31	4	4	2	15	4	.79	5	.336	.435	.459
2005	Lxngtn	A	68	247	75	17	2	2	(-	-)	102	45	32	49	47	2	35	5	4	7	16	5	.76	2	.304	.415	.413
2005	Salem	A+	42	141	47	12	1	3	(-	-)	70	25	13	35	37	1	17	1	1	0	2	1	.67	3	.333	.475	.496
2006	CpChr	AA	83	315	103	25	6	3	(-	-)	149	57	30	67	55	1	46	5	5	1	9	5	.64	7	.327	.434	.473
2006	Drham	AAA	18	69	21	3	1	0	(-	-)	26	12	6	11	10	0	9	1	2	0	4	1	.80	0	.304	.400	.377
2006	TB	AL	52	183	41	6	2	2	(2	0)	57	10	18	13	10	1	26	0	2	3	2	3	.40	2	.224	.260	.311

Joel Zumaya

Pitches: R **Bats:** R **Pos:** RP-62   **Ht:** 6'3" **Wt:** 210 **Born:** 11/9/1984 **Age:** 22

			HOW MUCH HE PITCHED						WHAT HE GAVE UP											THE RESULTS						
Year	Team	Lg	G	GS	CG	GF	IP	BFP	H	R	ER	HR	SH	SF	HB	TBB	IBB	SO	WP	Bk	W	L	Pct	ShO	Sv-Op Hld	ERC	ERA
2002	Tigers	A-	9	8	0	0	37.1	143	21	9	8	2	0	2	1	11	0	46	3	0	2	1	.667	0	0- - -	1.46	1.93
2003	W Mich	A	19	19	0	0	90.1	376	69	35	28	3	3	2	3	38	0	126	4	0	7	5	.583	0	0- - -	2.57	2.79
2004	Lkland	A+	20	20	1	0	115.2	479	90	60	56	10	7	4	9	58	0	108	7	1	7	7	.500	1	0- - -	3.58	4.36
2004	Erie	AA	4	4	0	0	20.0	90	19	20	14	6	1	1	2	10	0	29	0	0	2	2	.500	0	0- - -	6.04	6.30
2005	Erie	AA	18	18	0	0	107.1	438	71	40	33	8	1	4	2	52	0	143	4	4	8	3	.727	0	0- - -	2.53	2.77
2005	Toledo	AAA	8	8	1	0	44.0	186	30	13	13	2	1	1	5	24	1	56	2	0	1	2	.333	0	0- - -	2.95	2.66
2006	Det	AL	62	0	0	12	83.1	350	56	20	18	6	2	4	2	42	2	97	4	0	6	3	.667	0	1-6 30	2.55	1.94

2006 Fielding Statistics

This section contains all of the traditional fielding statistics for the 2006 season. However, these fielding stats are not official. You will most likely find some differences when the official Major League Baseball numbers arrive later this year. However, we feel that publishing an unofficial statistical fielding record in November is better than waiting for the official totals; we hope you will agree. Even though our statistics are unofficial, it does not mean that they are less accurate.

You will notice that each position is broken down into "The Regulars" and "The Rest" so you can get a truer sense of how the starters compare to each other, without having to sort through the September call-ups. Of course, if you are really interested in knowing how many putouts Delmon Young had, then we have that too.

The last column for the non-catchers is range factor labeled "Rng". Range Factor is the number of successful chances (Putouts plus Assists) times nine, divided by the number of Defensive Innings played.

Be sure to check out our "Catchers Special" section for our catcher ERA and stolen base numbers. Catching in the big leagues is demanding both physically and mentally, which helps us understand why certain catchers are still being employed despite hovering around the Mendoza Line offensively.

A couple of clarifications should be made. One, **PCS** is the number of Total Caught Stealing attributed to the pitcher, not the catcher in question. So, **CS%** is the percentage of runners caught stealing not including PCS. Two, if you are looking for pitcher's fielding statistics, you will find them in the "Pitchers Hitting, Fielding, & Holding Runners" section. And finally, if you are interested in seeing fielding leader boards you can find them for position players in the Leader Board section, and in The Fielding Bible Awards section.

First Basemen - Regulars

Player	Tm	G	GS	Inn	PO	A	E	DP	Pct.	Rng
Casey,Sean	TOT	106	102	874.1	937	34	2	84	.998	-
Lee,Travis	TB	112	96	864.2	852	58	2	97	.998	-
Teixeira,Mark	Tex	159	159	1399.0	1481	88	4	157	.997	-
Helton,Todd	Col	145	145	1272.1	1365	86	4	156	.997	-
Sexson,Richie	Sea	150	149	1310.1	1233	110	4	114	.997	-
Garciaparra,N	LAD	118	117	1017.0	1058	61	4	113	.996	-
Hatteberg,Scott	Cin	131	122	1088.2	997	69	4	85	.996	-
Mientkiewicz,D	KC	90	82	724.2	748	42	3	83	.996	-
Pujols,Albert	StL	143	142	1244.1	1345	110	6	145	.996	-
LaRoche,Adam	Atl	142	130	1153.1	1116	96	5	109	.996	-
Youkilis,Kevin	Bos	127	117	1030.0	1033	70	5	110	.995	-
Millar,Kevin	Bal	98	97	792.1	764	62	4	74	.995	-
Konerko,Paul	CWS	140	139	1181.2	1168	67	6	112	.995	-
Gonzalez,Adrian	SD	155	149	1341.0	1240	115	7	117	.995	-
Johnson,Dan	Oak	85	77	714.2	686	63	4	96	.995	-
Morneau,Justin	Min	153	152	1346.1	1295	111	8	112	.994	-
Shelton,Chris	Det	115	100	913.0	994	55	6	93	.994	-
Berkman,Lance	Hou	112	105	923.0	962	69	6	96	.994	-
Overbay,Lyle	Tor	145	139	1233.0	1355	94	9	124	.994	-
Delgado,Carlos	NYM	141	141	1246.1	1199	70	8	94	.994	-
Swisher,Nick	Oak	90	80	700.0	665	42	5	55	.993	-
Jacobs,Mike	Fla	124	120	972.0	930	57	7	100	.993	-
Fielder,Prince	Mil	152	150	1319.1	1258	87	11	112	.992	-
Howard,Ryan	Phi	159	157	1412.0	1369	91	14	139	.991	-
Jackson,Conor	Ari	129	127	1078.2	1107	81	12	110	.990	-
Johnson,Nick	Was	147	143	1252.1	1159	93	15	91	.988	-
Broussard,Ben	TOT	90	69	641.2	651	59	9	69	.987	-

First Basemen - The Rest

Player	Tm	G	GS	Inn	PO	A	E	DP	Pct.	Rng
Alfonzo,Edgardo	LAA	2	0	3.0	0	1	0	0	1.000	-
Amezaga,Alfredo	Fla	2	0	2.0	4	0	0	0	1.000	-
Anderson,Marlon	Was	2	0	5.0	2	0	0	0	1.000	-
Atkins,Garrett	Col	3	0	5.0	5	0	0	1	1.000	-
Aurilia,Rich	Cin	47	37	329.2	301	26	2	34	.994	-
Ausmus,Brad	Hou	1	0	0.2	0	0	0	0	-	-
Baker,Jeff	Col	1	0	3.0	4	0	0	0	1.000	-
Barajas,Rod	Tex	5	1	12.0	14	1	0	0	1.000	-
Barker,Kevin	Tor	2	1	12.0	13	0	0	0	1.000	-
Bellhorn,Mark	SD	18	11	97.1	90	6	2	9	.980	-
Bennett,Gary	StL	1	0	1.0	0	0	0	0	-	-
Blake,Casey	Cle	9	7	62.0	62	1	1	6	.984	-
Blanco,Henry	ChC	6	6	47.0	34	3	0	3	1.000	-
Bloomquist,Wil	Sea	4	0	5.2	6	0	0	0	1.000	-
Blum,Geoff	SD	2	0	2.1	4	0	0	2	1.000	-
Borchard,Joe	Fla	1	0	2.0	2	0	0	1	1.000	-
Bowen,Rob	SD	1	0	1.0	1	0	0	0	1.000	-
Branyan,Russell	TB	2	1	9.0	8	0	0	1	1.000	-
Broussard,Ben	Cle	80	60	569.2	577	51	7	57	.989	-
Broussard,Ben	Sea	10	9	72.0	74	8	2	12	.976	-
Cairo,Miguel	NYY	16	6	71.2	60	5	0	5	1.000	-
Casey,Sean	Pit	55	55	461.1	470	20	0	44	1.000	-
Casey,Sean	Det	51	47	413.0	467	14	2	40	.996	-
Castilla,Vinny	Col	7	1	21.0	19	0	0	3	1.000	-
Cirillo,Jeff	Mil	14	11	98.1	110	5	0	3	1.000	-
Clark,Tony	Ari	53	23	256.1	274	21	2	26	.993	-
Conine,Jeff	Bal	73	47	446.2	422	30	2	47	.996	-
Coste,Chris	Phi	2	0	4.1	3	0	0	1	1.000	-
Cuddyer,Michael	Min	6	6	52.0	48	3	0	4	1.000	-
Damon,Johnny	NYY	1	0	2.0	3	0	0	0	1.000	-
DeRosa,Mark	Tex	1	1	9.0	4	1	0	1	1.000	-
Dobbs,Greg	Sea	3	0	8.1	10	0	0	3	1.000	-
Doumit,Ryan	Pit	28	27	208.1	212	12	3	22	.987	-
Duncan,Chris	StL	11	7	61.1	54	3	0	6	1.000	-
Dunn,Adam	Cin	2	2	17.0	15	1	1	2	.941	-
Easley,Damion	Ari	3	0	6.1	6	1	0	0	1.000	-
Edmonds,Jim	StL	6	4	40.2	43	2	0	5	1.000	-
Ellis,Mark	Oak	1	0	3.0	1	0	0	0	1.000	-
Encarnacion,Ed	Cin	2	1	9.0	9	0	0	1	1.000	-
Erstad,Darin	LAA	13	0	28.0	31	1	0	1	1.000	-
Fick,Robert	Was	13	6	59.0	57	5	0	4	1.000	-

Player	Tm	G	GS	Inn	PO	A	E	DP	Pct.	Rng
Franco,Julio	NYM	27	20	194.0	197	5	1	22	.995	-
Gall,John	StL	1	0	0.2	0	0	0	0	-	-
Garko,Ryan	Cle	45	45	396.0	398	30	6	50	.986	-
German,Esteban	KC	1	1	9.0	8	1	0	2	1.000	-
Giambi,Jason	NYY	68	64	480.0	457	11	7	43	.985	-
Gload,Ross	CWS	49	20	247.1	266	13	4	24	.986	-
Gomez,Chris	Bal	27	14	138.0	116	7	0	14	1.000	-
Gonzalez,Alex S	Phi	3	3	23.0	17	4	0	2	1.000	-
Gonzalez,Luis A	Col	7	3	32.0	40	1	0	5	1.000	-
Graffanino,Tony	KC	16	13	99.0	96	6	2	14	.981	-
Green,Nick	NYY	1	0	1.0	1	1	0	0	1.000	-
Green,Shawn	Ari	12	10	96.0	105	6	0	12	1.000	-
Green,Shawn	NYM	1	0	2.0	2	0	0	0	1.000	-
Greene,Todd	SF	5	0	12.0	10	3	0	1	1.000	-
Guiel,Aaron	NYY	15	9	68.0	69	1	0	2	1.000	-
Guillen,Carlos	Det	8	4	39.0	30	4	0	4	1.000	-
Guzman,Joel	LAD	1	0	1.0	1	0	0	0	1.000	-
Hafner,Travis	Cle	4	4	33.1	18	4	0	2	1.000	-
Hairston,Jerry	ChC	1	0	6.1	4	0	0	1	1.000	-
Hammock,Robby	Ari	1	0	1.0	2	0	0	0	1.000	-
Hannahan,Jack	Det	1	1	8.0	6	0	0	0	1.000	-
Hart,Corey	Mil	2	1	8.0	8	0	1	1	.889	-
Helms,Wes	Fla	88	42	432.1	375	25	0	48	1.000	-
Hernandez,Jose	Pit	18	10	99.1	96	11	1	15	.991	-
Hernandez,Jose	Phi	1	0	3.0	2	0	0	0	1.000	-
Hernandez,Ram	Bal	2	0	5.0	5	0	0	0	1.000	-
Hillenbrand,Shea	Tor	19	17	144.1	136	12	2	14	.987	-
Hillenbrand,Shea	SF	58	51	453.0	422	35	1	29	.998	-
Hinske,Eric	Tor	4	1	14.0	15	0	0	1	1.000	-
Hinske,Eric	Bos	12	11	86.0	91	6	1	9	.990	-
House,J.R.	Hou	2	1	8.0	8	0	0	0	1.000	-
Huff,Aubrey	Hou	3	0	8.0	6	3	0	1	1.000	-
Ishikawa,Travis	SF	10	6	55.0	50	8	0	6	1.000	-
Jordan,Brian	Atl	25	18	142.2	137	9	2	13	.986	-
Kendrick,Howie	LAA	44	42	351.1	329	29	2	42	.994	-
Kent,Jeff	LAD	9	5	46.1	52	0	0	6	1.000	-
Keppinger,Jeff	KC	4	3	30.0	37	1	0	1	1.000	-
Kotchman,Casey	LAA	26	22	197.0	180	15	0	12	1.000	-
Kotsay,Mark	Oak	4	4	24.0	28	0	2	6	.933	-
Lamb,Mike	Hou	68	54	503.0	473	41	5	48	.990	-
Lane,Jason	Hou	1	0	1.0	3	0	0	0	1.000	-
LeCroy,Matthew	Was	6	2	22.0	19	1	1	2	.952	-
Lee,Derrek	ChC	47	44	393.2	369	26	5	34	.988	-
Loney,James	LAD	39	20	228.2	212	15	1	17	.996	-
Loretta,Mark	Bos	11	9	75.0	74	9	0	8	1.000	-
Luna,Hector	StL	6	1	19.2	25	1	0	3	1.000	-
Mabry,John	ChC	51	38	352.1	312	29	2	21	.994	-
Marrero,Eli	Col	7	7	61.0	58	8	0	8	1.000	-
Marrero,Eli	NYM	1	0	1.0	1	0	0	0	1.000	-
Martinez,Ramon	LAD	1	0	3.0	5	0	0	2	1.000	-
Martinez,Victor	Cle	22	19	166.1	149	5	0	15	1.000	-
McPherson,D	LAA	6	3	30.2	32	0	0	5	1.000	-
Melhuse,Adam	Oak	2	1	10.0	9	0	0	1	1.000	-
Molina,Jose	LAA	3	0	5.0	4	0	0	2	1.000	-
Molina,Yadier	StL	4	0	5.0	5	0	1	1	.833	-
Moore,Scott	ChC	6	6	46.0	43	2	1	1	.978	-
Morales,Kendry	LAA	56	49	453.2	422	37	5	40	.989	-
Morse,Mike	Sea	2	1	10.0	11	0	0	2	1.000	-
Munson,Eric	Hou	4	2	25.0	29	1	0	4	1.000	-
Nady,Xavier	NYM	1	0	4.0	3	0	0	1	1.000	-
Nady,Xavier	Pit	34	25	236.1	247	32	2	29	.993	-
Nelson,John	StL	1	0	1.0	1	0	0	0	1.000	-
Nevin,Phil	Tex	1	1	8.1	8	0	0	2	1.000	-
Nevin,Phil	ChC	38	33	282.0	250	17	0	26	1.000	-
Nevin,Phil	Min	5	4	32.2	29	1	0	6	1.000	-
Newhan,David	Bal	1	0	3.0	3	1	0	1	1.000	-
Niekro,Lance	SF	58	48	431.1	418	36	5	38	.989	-
Norton,Greg	TB	25	22	172.0	154	9	1	12	.994	-
Olivo,Miguel	Fla	5	0	9.0	4	1	0	1	1.000	-
Ortiz,David	Bos	10	10	68.0	62	6	2	8	.971	-
Pena,Carlos	Bos	17	8	80.0	81	5	1	15	.989	-
Perez,Eduardo	Cle	29	27	196.0	209	14	2	23	.991	-
Perez,Eduardo	Sea	5	1	15.1	10	2	0	2	1.000	-
Perez,Tomas	TB	1	1	8.0	8	0	0	0	1.000	-

Player	Tm	G	GS	Inn	PO	A	E	DP	Pct.	Rng
Petagine,Rob	Sea	9	2	25.0	23	4	0	3	1.000	-
Phillips,Andy	NYY	94	49	533.0	536	27	7	56	.988	-
Phillips,Jason	Tor	6	4	25.0	23	0	1	1	.958	-
Phillips,Paul	KC	5	3	34.1	34	0	0	4	1.000	-
Posada,Jorge	NYY	1	0	3.0	2	0	0	2	1.000	-
Quinlan,Robb	LAA	54	46	384.0	351	24	3	40	.992	-
Randa,Joe	Pit	15	5	69.1	69	4	1	5	.986	-
Rodriguez,Ivan	Det	7	7	55.0	56	6	1	6	.984	-
Rodriguez,Luis	Min	1	0	1.0	1	0	0	0	1.000	-
Saenz,Olmedo	LAD	30	20	164.1	173	7	2	27	.989	-
Santos,Chad	SF	3	2	19.2	17	1	1	1	.947	-
Schneider,Brian	Was	1	0	3.0	1	0	0	0	1.000	-
Shealy,Ryan	Col	2	1	10.0	13	0	0	1	1.000	-
Shealy,Ryan	KC	51	51	453.0	417	26	3	58	.993	-
Sheffield,Gary	NYY	9	9	57.0	56	3	1	4	.983	-
Smith,Jason	Col	6	5	43.0	34	3	0	1	1.000	-
Snow,J.T.	Bos	26	7	102.1	84	9	1	9	.989	-
Spiezio,Scott	StL	13	7	55.0	57	3	0	3	1.000	-
Stairs,Matt	KC	11	9	76.1	67	1	0	7	1.000	-
Stairs,Matt	Tex	1	0	3.0	2	0	0	1	1.000	-
Sweeney,Mark	SF	53	47	395.1	362	36	2	35	.995	-
Tatis,Fernando	Bal	4	4	34.0	40	2	0	3	1.000	-
Thome,Jim	CWS	3	3	20.0	21	0	0	1	1.000	-
Thorman,Scott	Atl	18	11	118.1	111	9	1	13	.992	-
Tiffee,Terry	Min	3	0	7.1	8	0	1	0	.889	-
Tracy,Chad	Ari	6	2	21.1	23	1	1	2	.960	-
Tucker,Michael	NYM	1	1	9.0	8	0	0	1	1.000	-
Utley,Chase	Phi	2	2	18.0	15	0	0	1	1.000	-
Valentin,Javier	Cin	2	0	1.1	2	0	0	0	1.000	-
Valentin,Jose	NYM	1	0	3.0	3	0	0	0	1.000	-
Vidro,Jose	Was	8	8	61.0	54	3	0	7	1.000	-
Vizcaino,Jose	SF	10	7	63.1	77	1	2	7	.975	-
Vizcaino,Jose	StL	1	0	1.0	1	0	0	0	1.000	-
Walker,Todd	ChC	37	35	311.2	272	19	3	17	.990	-
Walker,Todd	SD	3	2	22.0	26	1	0	1	1.000	-
Ward,Daryle	Was	6	3	34.0	29	1	1	2	.968	-
Ward,Daryle	Atl	4	3	27.0	26	2	0	2	1.000	-
Wigginton,Ty	TB	45	37	329.2	300	28	1	26	.997	-
Willingham,Josh	Fla	2	0	3.0	5	0	0	1	1.000	-
Wilson,Craig	Pit	43	40	360.1	344	19	1	42	.997	-
Wilson,Craig	NYY	35	25	228.0	226	8	2	22	.992	-
Witt,Kevin	TB	5	5	37.0	28	1	2	1	.935	-
Wood,Jason	Fla	5	0	13.0	16	1	0	2	1.000	-
Woodward,Chris	NYM	1	0	2.0	2	0	0	0	1.000	-
Young,Dmitri	Det	3	3	20.0	19	5	3	3	.889	-

Second Basemen - Regulars

Player	Tm	G	GS	Inn	PO	A	E	DP	Pct.	Rng
Carroll,Jamey	Col	109	102	894.2	187	396	3	99	.995	5.86
Kinsler,Ian	Tex	119	117	1032.0	247	393	18	94	.973	5.58
Valentin,Jose	NYM	94	87	782.1	194	286	6	52	.988	5.52
Miles,Aaron	StL	88	71	649.2	165	232	10	58	.975	5.50
Hudson,Orlando	Ari	157	151	1349.0	311	510	13	115	.984	5.48
Kent,Jeff	LAD	108	107	887.2	217	313	8	73	.985	5.37
Ellis,Mark	Oak	123	121	1070.0	273	357	2	91	.997	5.30
Polanco,Placido	Det	108	107	943.0	224	325	6	81	.989	5.24
Utley,Chase	Phi	156	155	1367.1	357	425	18	114	.978	5.15
Grudzielanek,M	KC	132	130	1111.0	261	372	4	107	.994	5.13
Hill,Aaron	Tor	112	106	914.1	174	345	7	92	.987	5.11
Uggla,Dan	Fla	151	150	1304.1	313	423	15	111	.980	5.08
Castillo,Jose	Pit	145	141	1235.0	343	351	18	107	.975	5.06
Cano,Robinson	NYY	118	115	1009.0	230	333	9	73	.984	5.02
Weeks,Rickie	Mil	92	90	794.0	177	261	22	66	.952	4.96
Belliard,Ronnie	TOT	145	141	1216.1	267	403	11	96	.984	4.96
Phillips,Brand	Cin	142	136	1216.1	331	334	16	83	.977	4.92
Giles,Marcus	Atl	134	132	1149.2	259	368	11	81	.983	4.91
Loretta,Mark	Bos	138	133	1172.0	246	389	4	99	.994	4.88
Durham,Ray	SF	133	132	1138.2	271	341	11	81	.982	4.84
Barfield,Josh	SD	147	138	1259.0	294	381	9	85	.987	4.83
Iguchi,Tadahito	CWS	136	136	1209.1	270	371	8	75	.988	4.77
Lopez,Jose	Sea	150	148	1322.0	282	416	16	95	.978	4.75
Vidro,Jose	Was	107	105	901.2	224	250	5	53	.990	4.73
Castillo,Luis	Min	142	142	1239.1	268	378	6	78	.991	4.69

Player	Tm	G	GS	Inn	PO	A	E	DP	Pct.	Rng
Biggio,Craig	Hou	129	127	1062.0	218	334	6	80	.989	4.68
Cantu,Jorge	TB	103	103	898.2	210	252	13	65	.973	4.63
Roberts,Brian	Bal	137	135	1167.2	214	375	9	98	.985	4.54
Kennedy,Adam	LAA	133	127	1140.2	205	360	9	76	.984	4.46

Second Basemen - The Rest

Player	Tm	G	GS	Inn	PO	A	E	DP	Pct.	Rng
Adams,Russ	Tor	50	35	324.2	58	99	2	18	.987	4.35
Alfonzo,Edgardo	Tor	12	12	99.0	14	31	0	4	1.000	4.09
Amezaga,Alfredo	Fla	23	12	127.0	33	41	2	15	.974	5.24
Anderson,Marlon	Was	32	26	231.1	51	71	5	13	.961	4.75
Anderson,Marlon	LAD	1	0	2.0	0	1	0	0	1.000	4.50
Aurilia,Rich	Cin	10	4	41.0	13	14	0	2	1.000	5.93
Ausmus,Brad	Hou	2	0	3.0	0	1	0	0	1.000	3.00
Aybar,Erick	LAA	3	0	6.0	1	3	0	0	1.000	6.00
Aybar,Willy	LAD	15	10	98.1	25	42	1	11	.985	6.13
Barmes,Clint	Col	4	0	14.0	2	9	0	1	1.000	7.07
Barnwell,Chris	Mil	3	2	19.2	3	4	1	1	.875	3.20
Bautista,Jose	Pit	3	2	21.2	9	9	0	3	1.000	7.48
Bellhorn,Mark	SD	11	10	84.1	22	33	0	5	1.000	5.87
Belliard,Ronnie	Cle	91	88	768.1	169	252	8	53	.981	4.93
Belliard,Ronnie	StL	54	53	448.0	98	151	3	43	.988	5.00
Beltre,Adrian	Sea	1	0	1.0	0	0	0	0	-	.00
Betemit,Wilson	Atl	10	9	69.0	26	20	0	7	1.000	6.00
Blanco,Andres	KC	7	2	27.0	5	8	0	3	1.000	4.33
Bloomquist,Wil	Sea	15	14	123.2	20	31	2	6	.962	3.71
Blum,Geoff	SD	1	1	9.0	3	6	0	1	1.000	9.00
Boone,Aaron	Cle	1	0	2.1	1	1	0	0	1.000	7.71
Bruntlett,Eric	Hou	23	3	48.0	13	17	2	5	.938	5.63
Burke,Chris	Hou	69	32	345.2	68	117	5	26	.974	4.82
Bynum,Freddie	ChC	31	14	117.2	34	32	5	7	.930	5.05
Cairo,Miguel	NYY	45	36	323.2	79	116	2	28	.990	5.42
Callaspo,Alberto	Ari	3	3	26.0	7	11	1	2	.947	6.23
Cannizaro,Andy	NYY	2	0	6.0	0	0	0	0	-	.00
Casilla,Alexi	Min	4	1	13.0	5	8	0	4	1.000	9.00
Castro,Bernie	Was	29	24	228.0	65	58	2	13	.984	4.86
Castro,Juan	Cin	1	1	5.0	0	2	0	0	1.000	3.60
Cedeno,Ronny	ChC	15	14	126.2	35	37	2	7	.973	5.12
Cintron,Alex	CWS	26	23	203.2	43	59	1	9	.990	4.51
Cirillo,Jeff	Mil	12	10	91.2	20	30	0	9	1.000	4.91
Cora,Alex	Bos	18	10	95.1	18	24	1	6	.977	3.97
Counsell,Craig	Ari	2	2	16.0	5	7	0	0	1.000	6.75
de la Rosa,Tomas	SF	2	0	5.0	0	2	0	1	1.000	3.60
DeRosa,Mark	Tex	26	26	222.2	50	86	1	16	.993	5.50
Easley,Damion	Ari	9	5	46.2	16	16	0	7	1.000	6.17
Fahey,Brandon	Bal	13	12	106.0	29	34	0	11	1.000	5.35
Figgins,Chone	LAA	9	7	62.0	9	19	1	6	.966	4.06
Figueroa,Luis	Tor	5	1	15.0	4	5	1	2	.900	5.40
Frandsen,Kevin	SF	28	19	177.0	35	51	2	6	.977	4.37
Freel,Ryan	Cin	13	11	91.0	23	25	1	2	.980	4.75
German,Esteban	KC	26	16	164.0	36	41	1	12	.987	4.23
Gomez,Chris	Bal	13	13	118.1	37	33	1	10	.986	5.32
Gonzalez,Luis A	Col	32	25	217.0	51	69	2	7	.984	4.98
Graffanino,Tony	KC	10	9	78.1	19	24	0	7	1.000	4.94
Graffanino,Tony	Mil	57	56	486.1	111	119	3	20	.987	4.26
Green,Andy	Ari	6	1	22.0	2	8	0	2	1.000	4.09
Green,Nick	TB	4	4	32.0	7	8	0	2	1.000	4.22
Green,Nick	NYY	19	11	103.0	37	29	1	6	.985	5.77
Hairston,Jerry	ChC	24	18	152.2	30	33	0	7	1.000	3.71
Hairston,Jerry	Tex	1	1	9.0	2	2	1	1	.800	4.00
Hall,Bill	Mil	4	4	34.0	6	9	0	1	1.000	3.97
Harris,Brendan	Was	4	2	22.0	5	4	0	0	1.000	3.68
Harris,Brendan	Cin	3	1	12.0	4	3	0	2	1.000	5.25
Harris,Willie	Bos	1	0	2.0	0	0	0	0	-	.00
Hernandez,An	NYM	13	12	111.0	26	27	0	3	1.000	4.30
Hernandez,Jose	Pit	3	1	13.0	1	6	0	1	1.000	4.85
Hooper,Kevin	Det	3	0	6.0	0	3	0	1	1.000	4.50
Infante,Omar	Det	37	34	307.1	65	108	4	30	.977	5.07
Inglett,Joe	Cle	53	47	417.1	112	142	4	43	.984	5.48
Izturis,Cesar	LAD	1	1	9.0	4	8	0	2	1.000	12.00
Izturis,Maicer	LAA	4	3	24.0	4	7	0	2	1.000	4.13
Jackson,Damian	Was	11	5	53.1	9	18	0	3	1.000	4.56
Jimenez,D'Ang	Tex	16	14	130.2	35	33	4	12	.944	4.68

Player	Tm	G	GS	Inn	PO	A	E	DP	Pct.	Rng
Jimenez,D'Ang	Oak	2	1	11.0	2	1	0	0	1.000	2.45
Kendrick,Howie	LAA	28	25	220.0	48	67	0	24	1.000	4.70
Keppinger,Jeff	KC	1	1	8.0	3	3	0	2	1.000	6.75
Lamb,Mike	Hou	2	0	7.0	2	1	0	1	1.000	3.86
Lugo,Julio	LAD	29	14	159.1	37	63	2	11	.980	5.65
Luna,Hector	StL	41	35	300.1	69	94	4	22	.976	4.88
Luna,Hector	Cle	20	20	169.1	39	50	5	14	.947	4.73
Martinez,Ramon	LAD	39	27	259.1	55	79	0	13	1.000	4.65
Matsui,Kaz	NYM	31	30	276.0	72	85	1	22	.994	5.12
Matsui,Kaz	Col	21	21	187.0	48	73	2	26	.984	5.82
McDonald,John	Tor	10	5	43.2	11	15	0	3	1.000	5.36
McEwing,Joe	Hou	2	0	3.0	1	2	0	0	1.000	9.00
Merloni,Lou	Cle	3	3	23.0	3	3	0	0	1.000	2.35
Meyer,Drew	Tex	3	3	28.0	8	6	0	1	1.000	4.50
Mora,Melvin	Bal	1	0	3.0	0	2	0	0	1.000	6.00
Nunez,Abraham	Phi	6	5	49.2	7	13	0	2	1.000	3.62
Olmedo,Ray	Cin	5	4	40.1	5	13	2	2	.900	4.02
Orr,Pete	Atl	32	16	161.2	31	63	0	12	1.000	5.23
Ozuna,Pablo	CWS	6	3	36.0	5	12	1	1	.944	4.25
Pedroia,Dustin	Bos	27	19	172.0	45	73	3	17	.975	6.17
Perez,Antonio	Oak	2	1	9.0	1	1	0	1	1.000	2.00
Perez,Neifi	ChC	53	33	327.0	72	107	5	23	.973	4.93
Perez,Neifi	Det	14	14	119.0	34	42	0	12	1.000	5.75
Perez,Tomas	TB	22	18	161.1	27	58	1	12	.988	4.74
Phillips,Andy	NYY	1	0	2.0	0	1	0	0	1.000	4.50
Prado,Martin	Atl	11	5	61.0	15	26	1	4	.976	6.05
Punto,Nick	Min	17	13	114.2	21	50	2	9	.973	5.57
Quintanilla,Om	Col	3	2	19.0	8	4	0	2	1.000	5.68
Roberts,Ryan	Tor	7	3	31.2	8	11	0	3	1.000	5.40
Robles,Oscar	LAD	13	3	44.2	9	10	0	4	1.000	3.83
Rodriguez,Ivan	Det	1	0	2.0	1	0	0	0	1.000	4.50
Rodriguez,Luis	Min	14	6	72.1	11	26	1	6	.974	4.60
Rogers,Eddie	Bal	4	2	22.0	3	5	0	2	1.000	3.27
Rouse,Mike	Oak	7	6	60.0	9	16	0	4	1.000	3.75
Sanchez,Angel	KC	4	4	38.0	13	22	0	3	1.000	8.29
Sanchez,Freddy	Pit	23	18	165.1	39	39	0	15	1.000	4.25
Sandoval,Danny	Phi	8	2	33.0	7	7	0	1	1.000	3.82
Santiago,Ramon	Det	12	7	70.2	14	19	0	4	1.000	4.20
Scutaro,Marco	Oak	37	33	301.2	73	93	1	32	.994	4.95
Smith,Jason	Col	18	12	115.2	32	46	2	12	.975	6.07
Spiezio,Scott	StL	8	2	26.2	7	13	0	4	1.000	6.75
Taguchi,So	StL	1	0	2.0	1	1	0	0	1.000	9.00
Tatis,Fernando	Bal	1	0	2.0	0	0	0	0	-	.00
Theriot,Ryan	ChC	39	30	281.2	62	59	2	11	.984	3.87
Thurston,Joe	Phi	4	0	10.1	6	2	0	1	1.000	6.97
Vazquez,Ramon	Cle	7	4	43.0	8	20	0	5	1.000	5.86
Vizcaino,Jose	SF	16	10	109.0	30	41	0	7	1.000	5.86
Vizcaino,Jose	StL	2	0	3.0	0	1	0	0	1.000	3.00
Walker,Todd	ChC	46	41	329.1	76	93	4	24	.977	4.62
Walker,Todd	SD	14	13	108.1	21	32	1	8	.981	4.40
Wigginton,Ty	TB	43	37	328.1	66	115	0	30	1.000	4.96
Womack,Tony	Cin	5	5	40.0	11	17	0	2	1.000	6.30
Womack,Tony	ChC	16	12	104.0	27	39	0	9	1.000	5.71
Wood,Jason	Fla	1	0	2.0	0	0	0	0	-	.00
Woodward,Chris	NYM	39	33	292.0	72	93	4	20	.976	5.09
Young,Eric	SD	1	0	3.0	0	0	0	0	-	.00
Young,Eric	Tex	1	1	9.0	2	6	0	2	1.000	8.00

Third Basemen - Regulars

Player	Tm	G	GS	Inn	PO	A	E	DP	Pct.	Rng
Inge,Brandon	Det	159	156	1392.0	135	397	22	34	.960	3.44
Sanchez,Freddy	Pit	99	92	821.2	59	243	6	24	.981	3.31
Crede,Joe	CWS	149	146	1260.0	114	339	10	34	.978	3.24
Lowell,Mike	Bos	153	148	1298.2	143	313	6	39	.987	3.16
Teahen,Mark	KC	109	104	923.2	80	235	14	31	.957	3.07
Koskie,Corey	Mil	70	69	603.1	54	150	7	11	.967	3.04
Rolen,Scott	StL	142	141	1215.2	93	318	15	32	.965	3.04
Beltre,Adrian	Sea	155	155	1358.0	136	323	15	31	.968	3.04
Chavez,Eric	Oak	134	133	1165.2	105	281	5	42	.987	2.98
Feliz,Pedro	SF	159	154	1372.1	117	330	21	29	.955	2.93
Ensberg,Morgan	Hou	117	106	975.0	81	230	12	24	.963	2.87
Glaus,Troy	Tor	145	135	1175.0	95	271	14	37	.963	2.80
Bell,David	TOT	143	138	1216.0	82	296	19	26	.952	2.80

Player	Tm	G	GS	Inn	PO	A	E	DP	Pct.	Rng
Huff,Aubrey	TOT	90	85	699.2	61	156	5	17	.977	2.79
Zimmerman,Ryan	Was	157	157	1368.1	152	260	15	30	.965	2.71
Mora,Melvin	Bal	154	154	1323.0	100	296	17	18	.959	2.69
Punto,Nick	Min	89	88	766.0	53	176	9	17	.962	2.69
Jones,Chipper	Atl	105	104	888.1	87	177	18	21	.936	2.67
Nunez,Abraham	Phi	74	69	632.0	36	151	8	10	.959	2.66
Blalock,Hank	Tex	122	120	1062.2	72	237	12	20	.963	2.62
Encarnacion,Ed	Cin	111	109	931.1	74	196	25	16	.915	2.61
Wright,David	NYM	153	153	1365.1	107	288	19	30	.954	2.60
Boone,Aaron	Cle	101	97	842.2	56	186	16	15	.938	2.59
Cabrera,Miguel	Fla	157	157	1334.0	114	266	17	31	.957	2.56
Tracy,Chad	Ari	147	143	1278.0	101	260	25	27	.935	2.54
Atkins,Garrett	Col	157	157	1381.1	98	286	19	35	.953	2.50
Rodriguez,Alex	NYY	151	148	1287.2	96	261	24	24	.937	2.50
Izturis,Maicer	LAA	87	78	707.1	45	145	13	12	.936	2.42
Ramirez,Aramis	ChC	156	155	1353.0	110	252	13	17	.965	2.41
Betemit,Wilson	TOT	79	65	602.0	32	123	7	18	.957	2.32

Third Basemen - The Rest

Player	Tm	G	GS	Inn	PO	A	E	DP	Pct.	Rng
Alexander,Manny	SD	13	0	33.1	2	7	1	1	.900	2.43
Alfonzo,Edgardo	LAA	15	10	100.2	5	20	0	1	1.000	2.24
Amezaga,Alfredo	Fla	4	0	5.0	1	0	0	0	1.000	1.80
Arias,Joaquin	Tex	1	1	8.0	1	4	0	0	1.000	5.63
Aurilia,Rich	Cin	52	39	356.0	24	78	5	7	.953	2.58
Aybar,Willy	LAD	29	25	214.1	9	50	5	2	.922	2.48
Aybar,Willy	Atl	32	27	241.1	14	40	3	3	.947	2.01
Barnwell,Chris	Mil	3	1	13.2	2	3	0	0	1.000	3.29
Batista,Tony	Min	50	50	434.0	27	97	6	6	.954	2.57
Bautista,Jose	Pit	33	31	267.1	22	56	6	5	.929	2.63
Bell,David	Phi	90	88	781.1	55	186	14	22	.945	2.78
Bell,David	Mil	53	50	434.2	27	110	5	4	.965	2.84
Bellhorn,Mark	SD	50	34	323.2	28	66	4	8	.959	2.61
Belliard,Ronnie	Cle	1	1	9.1	1	1	0	0	1.000	1.93
Betemit,Wilson	Atl	30	20	203.2	8	40	3	9	.941	2.12
Betemit,Wilson	LAD	49	45	398.1	24	83	4	9	.964	2.42
Bloomquist,Wil	Sea	12	6	70.0	5	15	0	4	1.000	2.57
Blum,Geoff	SD	34	17	200.1	18	36	0	1	1.000	2.43
Branyan,Russell	TB	5	3	33.1	1	6	3	0	.700	1.89
Branyan,Russell	SD	26	24	181.2	14	28	3	3	.933	2.08
Bruntlett,Eric	Hou	2	1	10.0	1	2	0	0	1.000	2.70
Burroughs,Sean	TB	7	6	57.0	6	20	1	4	.963	4.11
Cairo,Miguel	NYY	8	4	41.0	3	8	0	0	1.000	2.41
Callaspo,Alberto	Ari	2	0	5.0	1	1	0	0	1.000	3.60
Cannizaro,Andy	NYY	2	1	9.0	0	0	0	0	-	.00
Carroll,Jamey	Col	8	1	28.0	3	8	1	2	.917	3.54
Castilla,Vinny	SD	69	65	575.0	54	111	5	8	.971	2.58
Castilla,Vinny	Col	1	1	9.0	1	3	0	0	1.000	4.00
Castro,Juan	Cin	19	5	64.0	4	16	0	2	1.000	2.81
Cintron,Alex	CWS	11	6	63.0	8	20	3	0	.903	4.00
Cirillo,Jeff	Mil	42	30	274.0	27	64	2	8	.978	2.99
Clark,Howie	Bal	1	0	2.0	0	0	0	0	-	.00
Conine,Jeff	Bal	1	0	3.0	0	0	0	0	-	.00
Cora,Alex	Bos	11	4	50.2	3	7	0	2	1.000	1.78
Counsell,Craig	Ari	7	2	23.0	2	6	0	0	1.000	3.13
de la Rosa,Tomas	SF	2	0	2.0	0	0	0	0	-	.00
DeRosa,Mark	Tex	40	39	342.2	19	82	3	6	.971	2.65
Dobbs,Greg	Sea	2	0	2.0	1	0	0	0	1.000	4.50
Dorta,Melvin	Was	3	1	17.0	0	3	0	0	1.000	1.59
Easley,Damion	Ari	20	14	121.2	10	18	3	2	.903	2.07
Edwards,Mike	Pit	3	2	19.0	2	3	0	0	1.000	2.37
Fahey,Brandon	Bal	1	0	5.2	1	1	0	0	1.000	3.18
Fields,Josh	CWS	6	4	36.0	5	12	0	0	1.000	4.25
Figgins,Chone	LAA	34	32	280.1	22	50	10	4	.878	2.31
Franco,Julio	NYM	3	2	20.0	0	6	0	0	1.000	2.70
Freel,Ryan	Cin	13	9	88.1	7	25	0	2	1.000	3.26
German,Esteban	KC	24	20	181.0	9	43	4	5	.929	2.59
Gomez,Chris	Bal	5	4	37.1	3	10	2	1	.867	3.13
Gonzalez,Alex S	Phi	2	1	8.2	1	0	1	0	.500	1.04
Gonzalez,Luis A	Col	3	1	11.0	0	1	0	0	1.000	2.45
Graffanino,Tony	KC	27	26	215.1	15	63	2	2	.975	3.26
Green,Andy	Ari	7	3	32.0	1	8	0	0	1.000	2.53
Green,Nick	NYY	17	8	80.0	7	18	2	4	.926	2.81

282

Player	Tm	G	GS	Inn	PO	A	E	DP	Pct.	Rng
Guzman,Joel	LAD	6	5	43.2	0	7	0	1	1.000	1.44
Hairston,Jerry	Tex	1	1	8.0	1	1	0	0	1.000	2.25
Hall,Bill	Mil	11	10	86.0	5	15	2	2	.909	2.09
Hall,Toby	TB	1	0	1.0	0	0	0	0	-	.00
Harris,Brendan	Was	3	2	20.0	1	5	0	0	1.000	2.70
Hattig,John	Tor	10	7	63.0	4	14	0	1	1.000	2.57
Helms,Wes	Fla	24	5	94.1	7	23	2	0	.938	2.86
Hernandez,Jose	Pit	4	1	15.0	0	7	0	0	1.000	4.20
Hernandez,Jose	Phi	7	4	38.1	2	11	0	3	1.000	3.05
Hillenbrand,Shea	Tor	17	15	122.1	6	18	5	2	.828	1.77
Hillenbrand,Shea	SF	8	7	53.1	4	8	1	0	.923	2.03
Hinske,Eric	Tor	5	0	64.0	3	14	0	1	1.000	2.39
Hooper,Kevin	Det	2	0	2.0	0	2	0	0	1.000	9.00
Huff,Aubrey	TB	60	60	479.2	38	109	3	14	.980	2.76
Huff,Aubrey	Hou	30	25	220.0	23	47	2	3	.972	2.86
Infante,Omar	Det	7	6	51.0	3	8	0	0	1.000	1.94
Izturis,Cesar	LAD	28	28	252.0	12	73	4	3	.955	3.04
Jackson,Damian	Was	6	1	21.0	1	5	4	1	.600	2.57
Jimenez,D'Ang	Tex	2	1	10.0	0	1	0	0	1.000	.90
Jimenez,D'Ang	Oak	3	0	9.0	1	1	1	0	.667	2.00
Kendrick,Howie	LAA	1	1	6.0	0	0	0	0	-	.00
Keppinger,Jeff	KC	12	12	106.1	7	30	2	2	.949	3.13
Kouzmanoff,Kevin	Cle	2	2	16.0	2	4	1	0	.857	3.38
Lamb,Mike	Hou	36	30	263.2	24	70	6	8	.940	3.21
Lugo,Julio	LAD	16	13	115.0	10	29	1	4	.975	3.05
Luna,Hector	StL	2	1	9.0	1	4	0	0	1.000	5.00
Luna,Hector	Cle	2	2	17.0	0	0	0	0	-	.00
Mabry,John	ChC	2	0	2.0	0	1	0	0	1.000	4.50
Mackowiak,Rob	CWS	6	2	25.0	0	4	0	0	1.000	1.44
Marrero,Eli	NYM	1	0	2.0	0	1	0	0	1.000	4.50
Marte,Andy	Cle	50	49	428.0	32	118	6	14	.962	3.15
Martinez,Ramon	LAD	20	5	86.2	8	20	2	4	.933	2.91
Mateo,Henry	Was	2	1	10.0	0	1	0	0	1.000	.90
McDonald,John	Tor	2	0	4.0	0	0	0	0	-	.00
McPherson,D	LAA	31	25	228.1	13	49	3	4	.954	2.44
Melhuse,Adam	Oak	3	1	12.0	0	2	0	0	1.000	1.50
Merloni,Lou	Cle	3	1	17.1	1	3	0	2	1.000	2.08
Miles,Aaron	StL	1	0	2.1	0	0	0	0	-	.00
Moore,Scott	ChC	5	3	32.0	3	4	0	0	1.000	1.97
Morse,Mike	Sea	5	1	16.2	0	3	0	1	1.000	1.62
Mueller,Bill	LAD	30	30	256.0	15	60	8	7	.904	2.64
Olmedo,Ray	Cin	3	0	6.0	0	0	0	0	-	.00
Orr,Pete	Atl	10	7	64.0	5	15	0	1	1.000	2.81
Ozuna,Pablo	CWS	17	4	65.0	5	11	0	0	1.000	2.22
Pena,Brayan	Atl	1	0	3.0	0	1	0	0	1.000	3.00
Pena,Tony F	Atl	1	0	3.0	0	0	0	0	-	.00
Perez,Antonio	Oak	27	20	187.0	20	47	4	4	.944	3.22
Perez,Neifi	ChC	10	4	51.0	3	9	0	0	1.000	2.12
Perez,Neifi	Det	1	0	1.0	0	0	0	0	-	.00
Perez,Tomas	TB	40	13	162.1	15	37	2	4	.963	2.88
Phillips,Andy	NYY	10	1	26.0	1	6	0	1	1.000	2.42
Prado,Martin	Atl	8	4	38.0	2	4	1	0	.857	1.42
Quinlan,Robb	LAA	18	16	130.0	11	24	1	1	.972	2.42
Randa,Joe	Pit	42	36	312.0	31	70	4	7	.962	2.91
Robles,Oscar	LAD	6	2	16.1	0	6	1	0	.857	3.31
Rodriguez,Luis	Min	29	18	188.1	18	41	0	8	1.000	2.82
Rogers,Eddie	Bal	4	1	18.0	1	1	1	0	.667	1.00
Rottino,Vinny	Mil	3	2	14.0	2	3	0	0	1.000	3.21
Saenz,Olmedo	LAD	16	9	78.0	6	24	2	0	.938	3.46
Santiago,Ramon	Det	1	0	2.0	0	2	0	0	1.000	9.00
Scutaro,Marco	Oak	12	8	78.0	4	21	3	1	.893	2.88
Smith,Jason	Col	3	2	18.0	2	4	0	0	1.000	3.00
Spiezio,Scott	StL	38	19	202.2	10	45	4	4	.932	2.44
Tatis,Fernando	Bal	5	3	30.0	1	8	0	0	1.000	2.70
Theriot,Ryan	ChC	1	0	1.0	0	0	0	0	-	.00
Tiffee,Terry	Min	6	6	51.0	3	13	1	2	.941	2.82
Upton,B.J.	TB	50	48	412.2	38	88	13	6	.906	2.75
Valentin,Jose	NYM	1	1	8.0	1	1	0	0	1.000	2.25
Vazquez,Ramon	Cle	14	10	93.0	4	20	1	1	.960	2.32
Vizcaino,Jose	SF	2	0	2.0	0	1	0	0	1.000	4.50
Walker,Todd	SD	23	22	149.2	12	31	5	2	.896	2.59
Wigginton,Ty	TB	34	32	274.1	16	63	5	6	.940	2.59
Woodward,Chris	NYM	11	6	66.0	4	17	0	2	1.000	2.86
Youkilis,Kevin	Bos	16	10	92.0	11	27	3	1	.927	3.72

Shortstops - Regulars

Player	Tm	G	GS	Inn	PO	A	E	DP	Pct.	Rng
Counsell,Craig	Ari	88	83	736.2	127	296	9	75	.979	5.17
Furcal,Rafael	LAD	156	156	1371.0	269	492	27	117	.966	5.00
Wilson,Jack	Pit	131	129	1130.0	198	425	18	87	.972	4.96
Peralta,Jhonny	Cle	147	145	1275.1	235	459	16	94	.977	4.90
Young,Michael	Tex	155	155	1356.1	241	493	14	113	.981	4.87
Everett,Adam	Hou	149	146	1292.1	202	479	7	103	.990	4.74
Barmes,Clint	Col	125	122	1072.2	192	372	18	89	.969	4.73
Eckstein,David	StL	120	119	1029.0	178	363	6	87	.989	4.73
Uribe,Juan	CWS	132	127	1130.0	217	373	14	83	.977	4.70
McDonald,John	Tor	90	76	661.2	106	232	14	57	.960	4.60
Lugo,Julio	TOT	81	74	647.2	117	212	16	41	.954	4.57
Tejada,Miguel	Bal	150	150	1293.2	239	417	19	108	.972	4.56
Ramirez,Hanley	Fla	154	153	1323.1	258	410	26	110	.963	4.54
Crosby,Bobby	Oak	95	95	828.0	145	268	12	59	.972	4.49
Berroa,Angel	KC	131	129	1117.1	188	367	18	93	.969	4.47
Betancourt,Yun	Sea	157	156	1374.1	251	430	20	95	.971	4.46
Guillen,Carlos	Det	145	144	1235.0	178	427	28	88	.956	4.41
Bartlett,Jason	Min	99	99	879.2	131	298	13	45	.971	4.39
Clayton,Royce	TOT	129	121	1055.0	171	340	18	54	.966	4.36
Gonzalez,Alex	Bos	111	110	966.1	163	305	7	68	.985	4.36
Rollins,Jimmy	Phi	157	156	1378.0	213	446	11	95	.984	4.30
Cabrera,Orlando	LAA	152	152	1321.1	253	377	16	99	.975	4.29
Vizquel,Omar	SF	152	148	1281.1	205	389	4	86	.993	4.17
Renteria,Edgar	Atl	146	146	1265.1	185	399	13	75	.978	4.15
Jeter,Derek	NYY	150	149	1292.1	214	381	15	81	.975	4.14
Hall,Bill	Mil	127	126	1090.1	173	321	17	56	.967	4.08
Greene,Khalil	SD	113	111	997.2	139	309	9	62	.980	4.04
Cedeno,Ronny	ChC	134	130	1129.2	148	356	23	64	.956	4.02
Lopez,Felipe	TOT	155	152	1337.0	187	389	28	79	.954	3.88
Reyes,Jose	NYM	149	148	1320.1	176	390	17	71	.971	3.86

Shortstops - The Rest

Player	Tm	G	GS	Inn	PO	A	E	DP	Pct.	Rng
Adams,Russ	Tor	36	31	271.0	41	87	10	18	.928	4.25
Alexander,Manny	SD	9	9	75.0	12	27	1	8	.975	4.68
Amezaga,Alfredo	Fla	11	4	54.1	5	21	0	5	1.000	4.31
Andino,Robert	Fla	9	5	55.2	7	20	1	2	.964	4.37
Arias,Joaquin	Tex	5	2	20.0	6	9	0	2	1.000	6.75
Aurilia,Rich	Cin	26	25	198.2	37	68	1	17	.991	4.76
Aybar,Erick	LAA	19	6	75.1	13	22	4	6	.897	4.18
Barnwell,Chris	Mil	8	2	29.1	13	11	1	3	.960	7.36
Betemit,Wilson	Atl	18	10	92.0	20	33	5	10	.914	5.18
Blanco,Andres	KC	25	22	200.0	30	77	5	25	.955	4.82
Bloomquist,Wil	Sea	17	6	65.1	9	23	0	3	1.000	4.41
Blum,Geoff	SD	49	42	391.0	72	129	6	28	.971	4.63
Bruntlett,Eric	Hou	21	13	144.2	20	57	4	9	.951	4.79
Burke,Chris	Hou	8	3	31.2	2	8	1	1	.909	2.84
Cairo,Miguel	NYY	14	10	99.1	18	28	1	8	.979	4.17
Callaspo,Alberto	Ari	4	3	34.0	4	9	1	2	.929	3.44
Cannizaro,Andy	NYY	10	0	17.0	5	5	1	0	.909	5.29
Carroll,Jamey	Col	10	7	62.0	9	24	1	6	.971	4.79
Casilla,Alexi	Min	2	0	2.0	1	2	0	2	1.000	13.50
Castro,Juan	Min	50	48	408.0	66	148	7	27	.968	4.72
Castro,Juan	Cin	27	13	140.2	23	42	1	11	.985	4.16
Cintron,Alex	CWS	41	35	319.0	50	94	4	19	.973	4.06
Cirillo,Jeff	Mil	3	2	19.0	4	3	0	2	1.000	3.32
Clayton,Royce	Was	86	83	720.1	110	240	11	39	.970	4.37
Clayton,Royce	Cin	43	38	334.2	61	100	7	15	.958	4.33
Cora,Alex	Bos	63	47	434.0	66	166	6	46	.975	4.81
de la Rosa,Tomas	SF	8	2	33.0	7	7	1	0	.933	3.82
DeRosa,Mark	Tex	7	4	42.0	9	19	0	5	1.000	6.00
Dorta,Melvin	Was	3	1	16.0	1	9	1	0	.909	5.63
Drew,Stephen	Ari	56	52	480.1	73	150	5	34	.978	4.18
Easley,Damion	Ari	27	24	204.2	23	58	2	9	.976	3.56
Fahey,Brandon	Bal	17	10	97.1	11	32	3	11	.935	3.98
Feliz,Pedro	SF	2	1	10.0	4	0	0	0	1.000	3.60
Figgins,Chone	LAA	2	0	3.0	0	1	0	0	1.000	3.00
Figueroa,Luis	Tor	2	1	12.0	2	2	0	0	1.000	3.00
Frandsen,Kevin	SF	3	2	17.0	3	5	1	2	.889	4.24
German,Esteban	KC	1	0	2.0	0	0	0	0	-	.00
Glaus,Troy	Tor	8	8	55.1	5	18	0	2	1.000	3.74

Player	Tm	G	GS	Inn	PO	A	E	DP	Pct.	Rng
Gomez,Chris	Bal	6	2	27.0	5	7	0	2	1.000	4.00
Gonzalez,Alex S	Phi	3	2	21.0	2	4	0	0	1.000	2.57
Graffanino,Tony	KC	9	9	75.0	10	15	1	3	.962	3.00
Graffanino,Tony	Mil	4	3	29.1	4	13	0	3	1.000	5.22
Green,Andy	Ari	2	0	4.0	0	1	1	0	.500	2.25
Green,Nick	TB	10	7	67.0	10	21	0	6	1.000	4.16
Green,Nick	NYY	10	3	35.0	10	11	2	4	.913	5.40
Grudzielanek,M	KC	4	1	11.2	0	1	0	0	1.000	.77
Hairston,Jerry	Tex	3	1	12.0	4	6	0	3	1.000	7.50
Hardy,J.J.	Mil	32	29	257.2	51	90	2	24	.986	4.92
Harris,Brendan	Was	5	3	26.1	5	7	1	1	.923	4.10
Hernandez,An	NYM	10	3	44.0	3	7	0	0	1.000	2.05
Hernandez,Jose	Pit	9	6	65.0	12	25	0	6	1.000	5.12
Hernandez,Jose	Phi	2	0	7.0	1	4	0	1	1.000	6.43
Hill,Aaron	Tor	63	46	428.1	60	129	12	19	.940	3.97
Infante,Omar	Det	10	3	40.0	7	16	1	5	.958	5.18
Inglett,Joe	Cle	1	1	9.0	3	1	0	0	1.000	4.00
Izturis,Cesar	LAD	2	1	12.0	1	5	0	2	1.000	4.50
Izturis,Cesar	ChC	21	17	160.2	33	44	2	8	.975	4.31
Izturis,Maicer	LAA	10	4	53.0	9	13	1	7	.957	3.74
Jackson,Damian	Was	16	4	57.1	8	12	4	0	.833	3.14
Jimenez,D'Ang	Oak	3	3	26.0	3	7	0	0	1.000	3.46
Lopez,Felipe	Cin	84	82	735.2	98	227	14	45	.959	3.98
Lopez,Felipe	Was	71	70	601.1	89	162	14	34	.947	3.76
Lugo,Julio	TB	73	72	620.1	114	201	14	41	.957	4.57
Lugo,Julio	LAD	8	2	27.1	3	11	2	0	.875	4.61
Luna,Hector	StL	14	6	68.0	9	17	0	4	1.000	3.44
Luna,Hector	Cle	10	10	87.0	15	34	0	10	1.000	5.07
Martinez,Ramon	LAD	12	3	50.0	6	17	0	5	1.000	4.14
Mateo,Henry	Was	3	1	15.0	4	3	1	1	.875	4.20
Matsui,Kaz	Col	3	3	26.0	4	1	0	1	1.000	1.73
Merloni,Lou	Cle	3	1	9.0	1	4	0	1	1.000	4.00
Meyer,Drew	Tex	1	0	1.0	0	0	1	0	.000	.00
Miles,Aaron	StL	39	33	298.0	55	108	7	26	.959	4.92
Morse,Mike	Sea	1	0	1.0	0	0	0	0	-	.00
Navarro,Oswaldo	Sea	2	0	6.0	0	3	1	2	.750	4.50
Nelson,John	StL	1	0	2.0	1	1	0	0	1.000	9.00
Nunez,Abraham	Phi	3	2	21.0	0	4	0	1	1.000	1.71
Olmedo,Ray	Cin	4	2	21.0	4	6	1	3	.909	4.29
Ordaz,Luis	TB	1	0	5.0	1	1	0	0	1.000	3.60
Pedroia,Dustin	Bos	6	5	41.0	7	13	1	4	.952	4.39
Pena,Tony F	Atl	22	6	84.0	14	28	1	7	.977	4.50
Perez,Antonio	Oak	4	3	25.0	6	8	0	3	1.000	5.04
Perez,Neifi	ChC	21	13	131.2	24	36	2	7	.968	4.10
Perez,Neifi	Det	7	4	40.0	9	17	1	7	.963	5.85
Perez,Tomas	TB	36	33	287.1	47	96	5	24	.966	4.48
Phillips,Brand	Cin	3	2	15.0	1	3	1	0	.800	2.40
Punto,Nick	Min	26	15	146.2	14	50	2	7	.970	3.93
Quintanilla,Om	Col	8	7	62.2	10	26	0	7	1.000	5.17
Rodriguez,Luis	Min	2	0	3.0	0	1	1	0	.500	3.00
Rogers,Eddie	Bal	1	0	1.0	0	0	0	0	-	.00
Sanchez,Angel	KC	4	1	20.1	2	9	0	2	1.000	4.87
Sanchez,Freddy	Pit	28	27	240.0	47	88	4	24	.971	5.06
Sandoval,Danny	Phi	6	2	33.1	5	9	1	4	.933	3.78
Santiago,Ramon	Det	27	11	133.0	17	48	0	6	1.000	4.40
Scutaro,Marco	Oak	69	61	572.2	87	168	9	38	.966	4.01
Smith,Jason	Col	1	0	3.2	0	1	0	0	1.000	2.45
Theriot,Ryan	ChC	2	2	17.0	3	3	1	1	.857	3.18
Tulowitzki,Troy	Col	25	23	220.1	47	69	2	25	.983	4.74
Vazquez,Ramon	Cle	7	5	43.0	8	15	3	3	.885	4.81
Vizcaino,Jose	SF	19	8	88.1	15	34	2	3	.961	4.99
Vizcaino,Jose	StL	7	3	32.2	9	10	2	3	.905	5.23
Woodward,Chris	NYM	13	11	97.0	13	34	1	10	.979	4.36
Zobrist,Ben	TB	52	50	440.2	86	147	9	31	.963	4.76

Left Fielders - Regulars

Player	Tm	G	GS	Inn	PO	A	E	DP	Pct.	Rng
Swisher,Nick	Oak	79	71	654.2	170	5	3	3	.983	2.41
Soriano,Alfonso	Was	158	158	1373.2	326	22	11	9	.969	2.28
Crawford,Carl	TB	148	144	1252.1	302	9	3	0	.990	2.24
Roberts,Dave	SD	116	108	970.0	239	0	0	0	1.000	2.22
Anderson,Garret	LAA	94	94	812.2	192	1	0	0	1.000	2.14
Bay,Jason	Pit	157	157	1373.0	316	10	3	1	.991	2.14

Player	Tm	G	GS	Inn	PO	A	E	DP	Pct.	Rng
Brown,Emil	KC	87	84	719.1	163	7	1	2	.994	2.13
Murton,Matt	ChC	133	122	1049.0	240	3	3	2	.988	2.08
Cabrera,Melky	NYY	116	112	998.2	217	12	1	1	.996	2.06
Podsednik,Scott	CWS	135	121	1086.2	245	4	8	0	.969	2.06
Langerhans,Ryan	Atl	104	78	706.0	156	2	1	0	.994	2.01
Ibanez,Raul	Sea	158	158	1396.2	301	11	2	0	.994	2.01
Bonds,Barry	SF	116	115	875.0	188	6	3	0	.985	2.00
Wilkerson,Brad	Tex	80	76	664.1	139	7	1	3	.993	1.98
Michaels,Jason	Cle	117	115	1009.1	214	6	2	2	.991	1.96
Dunn,Adam	Cin	156	156	1321.0	279	7	12	1	.960	1.95
Burrell,Pat	Phi	126	126	987.2	204	8	3	1	.986	1.93
Johnson,Reed	Tor	100	64	635.1	129	7	1	0	.993	1.93
Holliday,Matt	Col	153	153	1334.1	277	8	6	1	.979	1.92
Ethier,Andre	LAD	109	99	895.2	172	9	6	1	.968	1.82
Willingham,Josh	Fla	132	129	1069.2	206	5	7	0	.968	1.78
Gonzalez,Luis	Ari	150	149	1315.0	256	3	1	1	.996	1.77
Floyd,Cliff	NYM	92	91	768.1	148	3	2	0	.987	1.77
Catalanotto,Fr	Tor	101	94	760.0	140	9	0	3	1.000	1.76
Monroe,Craig	Det	113	105	927.1	168	12	3	2	.984	1.75
Lee,Carlos	TOT	149	148	1259.1	227	5	6	0	.975	1.66
Wilson,Preston	TOT	102	100	873.0	156	2	0	0	1.000	1.63
Ramirez,Manny	Bos	123	123	1031.1	175	7	2	0	.989	1.59

Left Fielders - The Rest

Player	Tm	G	GS	Inn	PO	A	E	DP	Pct.	Rng
Abercrombie,Reggie	Fla	3	0	5.0	0	0	0	0	-	.00
Aguila,Chris	Fla	15	3	43.1	5	1	0	0	1.000	1.25
Alou,Moises	SF	11	10	79.0	19	0	0	0	1.000	2.16
Amezaga,Alfredo	Fla	14	1	28.1	11	0	0	0	1.000	3.49
Anderson,Drew	Mil	1	1	7.1	0	0	0	0	-	.00
Anderson,Marlon	LAD	15	14	115.2	19	0	1	0	.950	1.48
Baker,Jeff	Col	2	1	10.0	1	0	0	0	1.000	.90
Bautista,Jose	Pit	6	5	50.0	9	0	0	0	1.000	1.62
Berkman,Lance	Hou	5	2	25.2	5	0	0	0	1.000	1.75
Bigbie,Larry	StL	11	4	44.1	8	0	0	0	1.000	1.62
Bloomquist,Wil	Sea	3	0	10.0	2	0	0	0	1.000	1.80
Bocachica,Hiram	Oak	1	0	1.0	1	0	0	0	1.000	9.00
Bohn,T.J.	Sea	1	0	3.0	0	0	1	0	.000	.00
Borchard,Joe	Fla	15	9	77.0	17	1	0	0	1.000	2.10
Botts,Jason	Tex	1	0	1.0	1	0	0	0	1.000	9.00
Bourn,Michael	Phi	1	0	2.0	0	0	0	0	-	.00
Branyan,Russell	TB	1	1	7.0	3	0	0	0	1.000	3.86
Brown,Adrian	Tex	3	1	13.0	0	0	0	0	-	.00
Bruntlett,Eric	Hou	6	0	18.1	3	0	0	0	1.000	1.47
Burke,Chris	Hou	19	13	119.0	14	0	0	0	1.000	1.06
Bynum,Freddie	ChC	13	7	80.2	19	0	2	0	.905	2.12
Byrd,Marlon	Was	3	0	6.2	2	0	0	0	1.000	2.70
Byrnes,Eric	Ari	12	3	43.1	10	0	0	0	1.000	2.08
Cairo,Miguel	NYY	1	1	11.0	3	0	0	0	1.000	2.45
Castro,Bernie	Was	2	0	4.0	0	0	0	0	-	.00
Cepicky,Matt	Fla	1	0	1.0	0	0	0	0	-	.00
Chavez,Endy	NYM	43	22	239.2	55	4	0	0	1.000	2.22
Choo,Shin-Soo	Cle	9	9	77.2	14	0	1	0	.933	1.62
Church,Ryan	Was	2	0	4.0	2	1	0	0	1.000	6.75
Clark,Brady	Mil	3	0	7.0	3	0	0	0	1.000	3.86
Clark,Doug	Oak	1	0	0.1	0	0	0	0	-	.00
Clevlen,Brent	Det	8	0	17.0	6	0	0	0	1.000	3.18
Conine,Jeff	Bal	56	53	429.1	84	5	1	1	.989	1.87
Conine,Jeff	Phi	12	0	26.0	4	0	1	0	.800	1.38
Costa,Shane	KC	5	5	42.0	10	0	0	0	1.000	2.14
Crosby,Bubba	NYY	10	3	45.0	11	1	0	0	1.000	2.40
Cruz,Jose	LAD	40	32	279.2	60	0	0	0	1.000	1.93
Cruz,Nelson	Tex	1	0	3.0	0	0	0	0	-	.00
Cuddyer,Michael	Min	1	0	2.0	0	0	0	0	-	.00
Cust,Jack	SD	1	0	2.0	0	0	0	0	-	.00
DaVanon,Jeff	Ari	8	2	28.0	7	0	1	0	.875	2.25
DeJesus,David	KC	73	60	544.2	138	5	2	0	.986	2.36
Dellucci,David	Phi	45	31	279.2	59	1	0	0	1.000	1.93
Denorfia,Chris	Cin	11	1	27.0	4	0	0	0	1.000	1.33
DeRosa,Mark	Tex	5	4	37.0	7	1	0	0	1.000	1.95
Diaz,Matt	Atl	95	62	587.1	163	5	4	1	.977	2.57
Diaz,Victor	NYM	4	2	20.0	4	0	1	0	.800	1.80
Duncan,Chris	StL	49	40	327.1	66	2	3	0	.958	1.87

Player	Tm	G	GS	Inn	PO	A	E	DP	Pct.	Rng
Ellison,Jason	SF	44	5	112.2	26	1	2	0	.931	2.16
Encarnacion,Ju	StL	1	1	6.0	0	0	0	0	-	.00
Everett,Carl	Sea	1	1	9.0	1	0	0	0	1.000	1.00
Fahey,Brandon	Bal	53	43	372.0	101	2	5	1	.954	2.49
Feliz,Pedro	SF	3	0	3.0	1	0	0	0	1.000	3.00
Fields,Josh	CWS	1	0	1.0	0	0	0	0	-	.00
Figgins,Chone	LAA	16	9	90.2	16	1	0	0	1.000	1.69
Fiorentino,Jeff	Bal	15	11	104.0	28	3	0	1	1.000	2.68
Ford,Lew	Min	64	30	321.1	72	1	0	0	1.000	2.04
Freel,Ryan	Cin	13	3	41.2	10	1	0	0	1.000	2.38
Freeman,Choo	Col	5	1	18.0	6	0	0	0	1.000	3.00
Gall,John	StL	2	1	8.2	2	0	0	0	1.000	2.08
German,Esteban	KC	14	9	78.1	17	1	1	1	.947	2.07
Gload,Ross	CWS	4	1	12.0	2	0	0	0	1.000	1.50
Gomez,Alexis	Det	32	5	103.0	25	1	0	0	1.000	2.27
Gonzalez,Alex S	Phi	1	0	1.0	0	0	0	0	-	.00
Gonzalez,Luis A	Col	1	1	6.2	4	0	0	0	1.000	5.40
Green,Andy	Ari	7	4	38.0	10	0	0	0	1.000	2.37
Gross,Gabe	Mil	20	15	124.0	36	4	1	0	.976	2.90
Guiel,Aaron	KC	3	2	17.0	3	0	0	0	1.000	1.59
Guiel,Aaron	NYY	4	1	18.0	3	0	0	0	1.000	1.50
Gutierrez,Franklin	Cle	10	10	83.0	21	0	1	0	.955	2.28
Guzman,Freddy	Tex	1	1	8.0	1	0	0	0	1.000	1.13
Guzman,Joel	LAD	1	0	1.0	0	0	0	0	-	.00
Hairston,Jerry	ChC	3	1	12.0	3	0	0	0	1.000	2.25
Hairston,Jerry	Tex	35	13	141.1	31	5	0	1	1.000	2.29
Hairston,Scott	Ari	5	3	24.1	8	0	0	0	1.000	2.96
Harris,Willie	Bos	11	2	33.0	10	1	0	0	1.000	3.00
Hart,Corey	Mil	26	17	164.1	37	1	1	0	.974	2.08
Helms,Wes	Fla	1	0	2.0	1	0	0	0	1.000	4.50
Hernandez,Jose	Pit	3	0	4.0	1	0	0	0	1.000	2.25
Hinske,Eric	Tor	1	0	1.0	0	0	0	0	-	.00
Hinske,Eric	Bos	5	3	23.0	5	0	0	0	1.000	1.96
Hollandsworth,T	Cle	30	24	212.1	56	4	0	0	1.000	2.54
Hollandsworth,T	Cin	1	1	8.0	1	1	0	0	1.000	2.25
Hollins,Damon	TB	18	10	102.0	27	1	2	1	.933	2.47
Hopper,Norris	Cin	1	0	3.0	1	0	0	0	1.000	3.00
Inglett,Joe	Cle	6	4	41.0	8	0	0	0	1.000	1.76
Jackson,Damian	Was	2	0	7.0	0	0	0	0	-	.00
Johnson,Ben	SD	22	18	167.1	48	1	0	0	1.000	2.64
Jordan,Brian	Atl	3	2	14.0	3	0	0	0	1.000	1.93
Kapler,Gabe	Bos	21	4	63.0	18	2	0	0	1.000	2.86
Kemp,Matt	LAD	11	8	72.1	18	1	1	1	.950	2.36
Keppinger,Jeff	KC	1	0	1.0	0	0	0	0	-	.00
Kielty,Bobby	Oak	44	40	335.2	80	0	1	0	.988	2.14
Kubel,Jason	Min	30	24	204.0	33	1	2	0	.944	1.50
Lane,Jason	Hou	6	1	23.0	6	0	0	0	1.000	2.35
Lawton,Matt	Sea	1	1	9.0	0	0	0	0	-	.00
Ledee,Ricky	LAD	7	5	37.2	3	0	0	0	1.000	.72
Ledee,Ricky	NYM	2	1	9.1	0	0	0	0	-	.00
Lee,Carlos	Mil	98	97	835.1	145	4	4	0	.974	1.61
Lee,Carlos	Tex	51	51	424.0	82	1	2	0	.976	1.76
Lewis,Fred	SF	6	1	18.0	7	0	1	0	.875	3.50
Lind,Adam	Tor	2	2	17.0	4	0	0	0	1.000	2.12
Linden,Todd	SF	40	7	128.0	31	1	0	0	1.000	2.25
Lombard,George	Was	3	2	24.0	8	0	0	0	1.000	3.00
Long,Terrence	NYY	2	2	17.0	2	1	0	0	1.000	1.59
Lugo,Julio	LAD	1	1	7.0	0	0	0	0	-	.00
Luna,Hector	StL	17	12	111.1	24	0	1	0	.960	1.94
Mabry,John	ChC	5	2	17.0	8	0	0	0	1.000	4.24
Mackowiak,Rob	CWS	28	2	65.1	11	1	0	0	1.000	1.65
Maier,Mitch	KC	2	0	8.0	0	0	0	0	-	.00
Markakis,Nick	Bal	26	24	197.1	59	1	1	0	.984	2.74
Marrero,Eli	Col	3	2	21.0	6	1	1	0	.875	3.00
Marrero,Eli	NYM	3	3	27.0	3	0	0	0	1.000	1.00
Matos,Luis	Bal	31	10	123.1	21	0	0	0	1.000	1.53
Matos,Luis	Was	1	0	3.0	2	0	0	0	1.000	6.00
Matsui,Hideki	NYY	36	36	289.0	82	1	1	1	.988	2.58
McCracken,Q	Cin	7	0	14.0	3	0	0	0	1.000	1.93
McLouth,Nate	Pit	3	0	8.0	2	0	0	0	1.000	2.25
Mench,Kevin	Tex	17	15	130.2	16	1	1	0	.944	1.17
Mench,Kevin	Mil	38	31	277.0	64	1	1	0	.985	2.11
Milledge,Lastings	NYM	26	21	194.0	42	3	1	0	.978	2.09
Mohr,Dustan	Bos	7	0	13.0	3	0	0	0	1.000	2.08
Morse,Mike	Sea	2	1	10.0	1	0	0	0	1.000	.90
Mottola,Chad	Tor	3	2	15.0	2	0	0	0	1.000	1.20
Murphy,David	Bos	6	1	20.0	1	0	0	0	1.000	.45
Murphy,Tommy	LAA	2	0	2.0	1	0	0	0	1.000	4.50
Nevin,Phil	ChC	8	8	64.0	7	0	0	0	1.000	.98
Newhan,David	Bal	17	15	120.0	25	0	2	0	.926	1.88
Norton,Greg	TB	3	2	17.0	2	1	0	0	1.000	1.59
Ozuna,Pablo	CWS	39	38	272.0	45	3	0	0	1.000	1.59
Pagan,Angel	ChC	39	22	211.1	44	2	1	0	.979	1.96
Palmeiro,Orl	Hou	12	4	42.2	8	0	0	0	1.000	1.69
Paul,Josh	TB	1	0	1.0	0	0	0	0	-	.00
Payton,Jay	Oak	62	51	454.0	118	3	2	0	.984	2.40
Pena,Carlos	Bos	1	1	7.0	0	0	0	0	-	.00
Pena,Wily Mo	Bos	18	11	113.0	24	3	1	0	.964	2.15
Perez,Timo	StL	3	1	13.2	3	0	0	0	1.000	1.98
Perez,Tomas	TB	1	0	2.0	0	0	0	0	-	.00
Piedra,Jorge	Col	2	1	7.0	2	0	0	0	1.000	2.57
Pride,Curtis	LAA	8	4	36.0	8	0	0	0	1.000	2.00
Punto,Nick	Min	1	0	4.0	1	0	0	0	1.000	2.25
Quentin,Carlos	Ari	2	1	11.0	1	0	0	0	1.000	.82
Quinlan,Robb	LAA	11	0	26.0	11	0	0	0	1.000	3.81
Rabe,Josh	Min	10	5	55.0	22	0	2	0	.917	3.60
Reed,Eric	Fla	1	0	2.0	0	0	0	0	-	.00
Reese,Kevin	NYY	2	1	9.0	1	0	1	0	.500	1.00
Repko,Jason	LAD	13	3	48.2	12	0	1	0	.923	2.22
Restovich,Mike	ChC	1	0	5.0	0	0	0	0	-	.00
Rivera,Juan	LAA	56	54	478.1	126	7	3	1	.978	2.50
Roberson,Chris	Phi	30	0	49.0	6	0	0	0	1.000	1.10
Robinson,Kerry	KC	1	0	2.0	1	0	0	0	1.000	4.50
Rodriguez,John	StL	41	28	227.2	47	1	0	0	1.000	1.90
Rogers,Eddie	Bal	3	1	13.0	3	0	1	0	.750	2.08
Ross,Cody	LAD	1	0	0.2	0	0	0	0	-	.00
Ross,Cody	Cin	1	1	9.0	1	0	0	0	1.000	1.00
Ross,Cody	Fla	39	20	205.0	40	0	0	0	1.000	1.76
Rottino,Vinny	Mil	2	1	10.2	3	0	0	0	1.000	2.53
Salmon,Tim	LAA	1	1	7.0	2	0	0	0	1.000	2.57
Schumaker,Skip	StL	13	5	63.0	13	0	0	0	1.000	1.86
Scott,Luke	Hou	50	48	417.0	81	1	0	1	1.000	1.77
Scutaro,Marco	Oak	2	0	6.0	1	0	0	0	1.000	1.50
Sledge,Terrmel	SD	12	10	82.0	23	0	1	0	.958	2.52
Snelling,Chris	Sea	1	1	9.0	2	0	0	0	1.000	2.00
Spiezio,Scott	StL	35	28	216.0	34	1	1	0	.972	1.46
Spilborghs,Ryan	Col	10	3	50.1	14	1	0	1	1.000	2.68
Stairs,Matt	KC	2	2	14.0	4	0	0	0	1.000	2.57
Stern,Adam	Bos	2	0	4.0	2	0	0	0	1.000	4.50
Stewart,Shannon	Min	34	34	286.0	58	3	1	1	.984	1.92
Sweeney,Mark	SF	21	13	113.1	24	0	1	0	.960	1.91
Sweeney,Ryan	CWS	6	0	12.0	2	0	0	0	1.000	1.50
Taguchi,So	StL	70	35	361.2	87	1	1	0	.989	2.19
Tatis,Fernando	Bal	3	3	22.0	3	1	0	0	1.000	1.64
Terrero,Luis	Bal	16	2	38.0	12	2	0	0	1.000	3.32
Thames,Marcus	Det	54	52	400.2	70	1	2	0	.973	1.59
Thompson,Kevin	NYY	3	1	15.0	6	0	0	0	1.000	3.60
Thorman,Scott	Atl	21	20	131.0	19	1	0	0	1.000	1.37
Thurston,Joe	Phi	2	2	14.0	4	1	0	0	1.000	3.21
Tucker,Michael	NYM	16	12	115.0	22	2	0	0	1.000	1.88
Tyner,Jason	Min	33	32	281.0	86	4	1	1	.989	2.88
Valentin,Jose	NYM	6	5	47.1	12	1	0	0	1.000	2.47
Victorino,Shane	Phi	44	3	101.0	22	2	0	0	1.000	2.14
Ward,Daryle	Was	2	2	14.0	5	0	0	0	1.000	3.21
Ward,Daryle	Atl	2	0	3.0	1	0	0	0	1.000	3.00
White,Rondell	Min	38	37	286.0	57	0	0	0	1.000	1.79
Wigginton,Ty	TB	5	5	39.0	9	0	2	0	.818	2.08
Williams,Bernie	NYY	5	5	41.0	12	0	0	0	1.000	2.63
Wilson,Preston	Hou	94	94	823.0	147	2	0	0	1.000	1.63
Wilson,Preston	StL	8	5	50.0	9	0	0	0	1.000	1.62
Winn,Randy	SF	20	10	100.2	27	0	0	0	1.000	2.41
Wise,Dewayne	Cin	9	0	22.0	4	0	0	0	1.000	1.64
Woodward,Chris	NYM	7	5	40.2	10	0	0	0	1.000	2.21
Youkilis,Kevin	Bos	18	17	134.0	36	3	0	0	1.000	2.62
Young,Delwyn	LAD	1	0	2.0	0	0	0	0	-	.00
Young,Eric	SD	36	26	242.1	48	0	1	0	.980	1.78
Young,Eric	Tex	1	1	9.0	4	0	0	0	1.000	4.00

Center Fielders - Regulars

Player	Tm	G	GS	Inn	PO	A	E	DP	Pct.	Rng
Gathright,Joey	TOT	130	112	1016.2	341	6	3	4	.991	3.07
Patterson,Corey	Bal	134	122	1078.2	345	7	4	4	.989	2.94
Anderson,Brian	CWS	134	106	966.0	305	3	2	1	.994	2.87
Beltran,Carlos	NYM	136	136	1184.0	357	13	2	6	.995	2.81
Baldelli,Rocco	TB	91	85	749.1	228	6	5	3	.979	2.81
Taveras,Willy	Hou	138	120	1116.2	335	9	5	2	.986	2.77
Sizemore,Grady	Cle	160	159	1379.1	409	7	3	1	.993	2.71
Figgins,Chone	LAA	96	93	829.0	242	7	5	3	.980	2.70
Finley,Steve	SF	130	103	973.1	287	5	1	1	.997	2.70
Cameron,Mike	SD	141	139	1244.0	367	4	6	4	.984	2.70
Granderson,C	Det	157	143	1312.0	385	3	1	0	.997	2.66
Jones,Andruw	Atl	153	152	1317.1	377	4	2	1	.995	2.60
Edmonds,Jim	StL	99	92	792.1	223	4	3	0	.987	2.58
Rowand,Aaron	Phi	107	102	900.2	251	6	5	2	.981	2.57
Hunter,Torii	Min	143	143	1232.1	343	8	4	4	.989	2.56
Damon,Johnny	NYY	131	129	1086.2	306	3	3	1	.990	2.56
Clark,Brady	Mil	114	105	910.2	250	2	4	0	.984	2.49
Crisp,Coco	Bos	103	100	900.2	246	3	1	3	.996	2.49
Matthews Jr.,G	Tex	142	141	1227.0	331	8	7	2	.980	2.49
Kotsay,Mark	Oak	127	116	1047.0	281	6	2	2	.993	2.47
Sullivan,Cory	Col	114	92	841.0	225	4	1	0	.996	2.45
Griffey Jr.,Ken	Cin	100	100	870.1	229	6	5	0	.979	2.43
Pierre,Juan	ChC	162	162	1426.0	379	5	0	0	1.000	2.42
Byrnes,Eric	Ari	123	117	1051.0	270	5	1	1	.996	2.35
Wells,Vernon	Tor	150	147	1290.1	332	4	4	3	.988	2.34
Lofton,Kenny	LAD	120	114	961.0	241	4	3	0	.988	2.29
Duffy,Chris	Pit	77	75	671.2	166	4	3	2	.983	2.28

Center Fielders - The Rest

Player	Tm	G	GS	Inn	PO	A	E	DP	Pct.	Rng
Abercrombie,Reggie	Fla	87	66	591.1	172	3	5	0	.972	2.66
Abreu,Bobby	Phi	1	0	2.0	0	0	0	0	-	.00
Abreu,Bobby	NYY	1	0	4.0	1	0	0	0	1.000	2.25
Aguila,Chris	Fla	1	0	3.0	1	0	0	0	1.000	3.00
Amezaga,Alfredo	Fla	75	64	529.0	155	2	4	0	.975	2.67
Anderson,Marlon	Was	7	5	41.0	16	1	1	1	.944	3.73
Bautista,Jose	Pit	57	46	418.1	114	5	2	1	.983	2.56
Bloomquist,Wil	Sea	48	35	320.1	89	2	0	0	1.000	2.56
Bocachica,Hiram	Oak	4	2	22.0	2	0	0	0	1.000	.82
Borchard,Joe	Sea	3	2	16.0	4	1	0	0	1.000	2.81
Brown,Adrian	Tex	10	6	60.0	24	1	1	0	.962	3.75
Bruntlett,Eric	Hou	8	4	39.0	11	0	0	0	1.000	2.54
Burke,Chris	Hou	38	36	284.1	72	2	1	0	.987	2.34
Bynum,Freddie	ChC	2	0	6.0	2	0	0	0	1.000	3.00
Byrd,Marlon	Was	57	44	393.1	125	1	1	0	.992	2.88
Cabrera,Melky	NYY	4	1	23.0	8	0	0	0	1.000	3.13
Chavez,Endy	NYM	39	25	264.1	83	2	0	2	1.000	2.89
Choo,Shin-Soo	Sea	4	4	36.0	16	1	1	0	.944	4.25
Church,Ryan	Was	51	42	369.2	122	1	2	1	.984	2.99
Clevlen,Brent	Det	13	9	70.0	19	2	0	1	1.000	2.70
Coats,Buck	ChC	3	0	4.0	1	0	0	0	1.000	2.25
Costa,Shane	KC	21	18	159.0	49	0	1	0	.980	2.77
Crawford,Carl	TB	2	1	9.0	2	1	0	0	1.000	3.00
Crosby,Bubba	NYY	24	9	117.0	34	0	0	0	1.000	2.62
Cruz,Jose	LAD	15	8	92.2	32	0	0	0	1.000	3.11
Cruz,Nelson	Tex	2	0	3.0	0	0	0	0	-	.00
DaVanon,Jeff	Ari	36	30	259.1	62	0	1	0	.984	2.15
DeJesus,David	KC	61	53	479.2	149	7	1	1	.994	2.93
Denorfia,Chris	Cin	12	10	85.1	20	0	0	0	1.000	2.11
Ellison,Jason	SF	4	1	14.1	3	0	0	0	1.000	1.88
Encarnacion,Ju	StL	32	27	230.2	46	0	2	0	.958	1.79
Erstad,Darin	LAA	27	25	219.2	71	1	0	0	1.000	2.95
Escobar,Alex	Was	23	19	174.2	61	1	1	0	.984	3.19
Fiorentino,Jeff	Bal	1	0	1.0	0	0	0	0	-	.00
Ford,Lew	Min	13	2	41.0	7	0	1	0	.875	1.54
Francoeur,Jeff	Atl	2	0	3.0	1	0	0	0	1.000	3.00
Freel,Ryan	Cin	54	44	400.0	127	4	0	0	1.000	2.95
Freeman,Choo	Col	44	35	321.0	101	0	1	0	.990	2.83
Gathright,Joey	TB	54	50	438.0	155	2	1	2	.994	3.23
Gathright,Joey	KC	76	62	578.2	186	4	2	0	.990	2.96
German,Esteban	KC	11	8	71.1	19	0	0	0	.905	2.40

Player	Tm	G	GS	Inn	PO	A	E	DP	Pct.	Rng
Gross,Gabe	Mil	33	29	253.2	72	2	1	1	.987	2.63
Guiel,Aaron	KC	2	2	17.0	6	0	0	0	1.000	3.18
Guiel,Aaron	NYY	3	0	7.0	3	0	0	0	1.000	3.86
Gutierrez,Franklin	Cle	7	2	27.0	14	0	0	0	1.000	4.67
Guzman,Freddy	Tex	2	1	11.0	4	0	0	0	1.000	3.27
Gwynn,Tony	Mil	19	14	129.2	42	1	0	0	1.000	2.98
Hairston,Jerry	Tex	12	5	51.0	16	3	0	1	1.000	3.35
Hall,Bill	Mil	7	3	32.0	11	1	0	0	1.000	3.38
Harris,Willie	Bos	24	7	91.2	27	0	0	0	1.000	2.65
Hart,Corey	Mil	6	2	23.0	3	0	0	0	1.000	1.17
Hermida,Jeremy	Fla	9	6	53.0	20	0	0	0	1.000	3.40
Hollandsworth,T	Cle	2	0	6.0	0	0	0	0	-	.00
Hollins,Damon	TB	33	25	216.0	55	0	0	0	1.000	2.29
Hopper,Norris	Cin	2	1	14.0	1	1	0	0	1.000	1.29
Infante,Omar	Det	4	3	19.0	1	0	0	0	1.000	.47
Inglett,Joe	Cle	3	1	11.0	6	0	0	0	1.000	4.91
Jackson,Damian	Was	22	15	141.2	44	0	2	0	.957	2.80
Jimerson,Char	Hou	1	0	1.0	0	0	0	0	-	.00
Johnson,Ben	SD	17	10	110.2	40	0	0	0	1.000	3.25
Johnson,Reed	Tor	16	11	106.0	20	0	0	0	1.000	1.87
Jones,Adam	Sea	26	23	193.0	67	5	3	1	.960	3.36
Jordan,Brian	Atl	2	0	5.0	3	0	0	0	1.000	5.40
Kapler,Gabe	Bos	14	11	95.0	17	0	0	0	1.000	1.61
Kearns,Austin	Was	5	4	29.0	8	1	0	0	1.000	2.79
Kemp,Matt	LAD	29	19	189.2	37	0	3	0	.925	1.76
Lane,Jason	Hou	5	1	17.0	5	0	0	0	1.000	2.65
Langerhans,Ryan	Atl	24	10	116.0	40	0	0	0	1.000	3.10
Lawton,Matt	Sea	5	5	35.0	10	0	0	0	1.000	2.57
Lewis,Fred	SF	1	0	1.0	1	0	0	0	1.000	9.00
Logan,Nook	Was	26	25	220.0	59	0	1	0	.983	2.41
Long,Terrence	NYY	2	0	3.0	2	0	0	0	1.000	6.00
Mackowiak,Rob	CWS	63	51	436.0	119	0	4	0	.967	2.46
Markakis,Nick	Bal	9	8	62.0	15	0	0	0	1.000	2.18
Marrero,Eli	NYM	2	1	13.0	3	0	1	0	.750	2.08
Mateo,Henry	Was	1	0	1.0	0	0	0	0	-	.00
Matos,Luis	Bal	9	9	73.0	18	0	0	0	1.000	2.22
Matos,Luis	Was	3	1	9.1	2	1	0	0	1.000	2.89
McCracken,Q	Cin	6	4	40.0	15	0	1	0	.938	3.38
McLouth,Nate	Pit	42	41	345.0	84	1	1	1	.988	2.22
Mohr,Dustan	Bos	13	10	77.0	25	0	0	0	1.000	2.92
Monroe,Craig	Det	8	7	47.0	13	0	1	0	.929	2.49
Murphy,David	Bos	8	4	36.0	9	0	0	0	1.000	2.25
Murphy,Tommy	LAA	29	14	145.2	50	2	0	2	1.000	3.21
Newhan,David	Bal	19	18	161.1	34	0	0	0	1.000	1.90
Nix,Laynce	Tex	9	9	78.1	21	2	0	2	1.000	2.64
Nix,Laynce	Mil	9	9	76.2	20	0	0	0	1.000	2.35
Owens,Jerry	CWS	4	2	12.0	5	0	0	0	1.000	3.75
Pagan,Angel	ChC	2	0	3.0	1	0	0	0	1.000	3.00
Payton,Jay	Oak	46	44	380.2	105	1	3	0	.972	2.51
Pena,Wily Mo	Bos	27	25	194.0	59	0	0	0	1.000	2.74
Piedra,Jorge	Col	1	1	7.0	2	0	0	0	1.000	2.57
Punto,Nick	Min	2	1	16.0	5	0	0	0	1.000	2.81
Reed,Eric	Fla	31	8	112.0	33	1	0	1	1.000	2.73
Reed,Jeremy	Sea	64	55	507.1	129	3	1	0	.992	2.34
Repko,Jason	LAD	40	21	217.0	52	4	1	2	.982	2.32
Rios,Alex	Tor	6	4	32.0	6	1	0	0	1.000	1.97
Rivera,Juan	LAA	20	19	143.1	34	3	2	0	.949	2.32
Roberts,Dave	SD	13	13	104.0	34	1	0	0	1.000	2.83
Robinson,Kerry	KC	15	14	120.2	37	1	0	0	1.000	2.83
Ross,Cody	Fla	21	18	145.0	40	1	1	0	.976	2.54
Salazar,Jeffrey	Col	14	13	111.1	25	0	0	0	1.000	2.02
Schumaker,Skip	StL	5	3	25.0	10	0	0	0	1.000	3.60
Scott,Luke	Hou	1	0	1.0	0	0	0	0	-	.00
Snelling,Chris	Sea	1	0	1.0	0	0	0	0	-	.00
Spilborghs,Ryan	Col	24	21	167.0	43	2	0	1	1.000	2.43
Stern,Adam	Bos	8	5	47.0	16	1	0	0	1.000	3.26
Suzuki,Ichiro	Sea	39	38	338.0	114	1	1	0	.991	3.06
Sweeney,Ryan	CWS	7	3	35.0	8	0	0	0	1.000	2.06
Swisher,Nick	Oak	1	1	2.0	3	0	0	0	1.000	13.50
Taguchi,So	StL	59	35	353.1	90	2	5	0	.948	2.34
Terrero,Luis	Bal	6	5	43.0	16	1	1	1	.944	3.56
Thompson,Kevin	NYY	2	0	3.0	1	0	0	0	1.000	3.00
Tyner,Jason	Min	18	16	150.0	43	0	0	0	1.000	2.58
Victorino,Shane	Phi	67	60	557.2	161	6	0	2	1.000	2.70

Player	Tm	G	GS	Inn	PO	A	E	DP	Pct.	Rng
Watson,Brandon	Was	8	7	56.2	17	0	0	0	1.000	2.70
Wilkerson,Brad	Tex	1	0	1.0	0	0	0	0	-	.00
Williams,Bernie	NYY	28	23	200.0	44	0	0	0	1.000	1.98
Willits,Reggie	LAA	19	11	115.0	36	1	1	0	.974	2.90
Wilson,Preston	Hou	2	1	9.2	2	0	0	0	1.000	1.86
Wilson,Preston	StL	5	4	28.1	8	0	1	0	.889	2.54
Winn,Randy	SF	59	57	441.0	137	2	0	0	1.000	2.84
Wise,Dewayne	Cin	5	3	36.0	14	1	1	0	.938	3.75
Young,Chris	Ari	24	15	149.1	50	1	0	0	1.000	3.07
Young,Delmon	TB	1	1	8.0	4	0	0	0	1.000	4.50
Young,Eric	SD	2	0	5.0	2	0	0	0	1.000	3.60

Right Fielders - Regulars

Player	Tm	G	GS	Inn	PO	A	E	DP	Pct.	Rng
Winn,Randy	SF	89	69	652.2	184	6	3	1	.984	2.62
Sanders,Reggie	KC	73	70	601.0	170	4	2	0	.989	2.61
Kearns,Austin	TOT	144	139	1228.2	346	7	7	2	.981	2.59
Markakis,Nick	Bal	127	100	917.1	240	7	1	0	.996	2.42
Blake,Casey	Cle	93	93	814.1	210	6	3	0	.986	2.39
Drew,J.D.	LAD	135	131	1118.0	284	3	5	0	.983	2.31
Dye,Jermaine	CWS	146	145	1245.0	305	4	6	2	.981	2.23
Hawpe,Brad	Col	145	134	1197.2	280	16	4	3	.987	2.22
Nixon,Trot	Bos	110	100	891.1	212	6	1	2	.995	2.20
Suzuki,Ichiro	Sea	121	120	1061.2	250	8	2	3	.992	2.19
Bradley,Milton	Oak	94	94	802.2	191	4	4	0	.980	2.19
Alou,Moises	SF	81	80	646.2	154	1	4	0	.975	2.16
Guerrero,Vladimir	LAA	126	126	1090.0	251	7	11	2	.959	2.13
Rios,Alex	Tor	124	104	953.0	218	7	1	2	.996	2.12
Abreu,Bobby	TOT	154	149	1293.0	291	11	3	0	.990	2.10
Jones,Jacque	ChC	143	139	1205.0	275	5	7	2	.976	2.09
Francoeur,Jeff	Atl	162	162	1421.2	317	12	9	4	.973	2.08
Hermida,Jeremy	Fla	85	78	683.2	157	1	8	0	.952	2.08
Jenkins,Geoff	Mil	133	126	1101.0	247	6	6	2	.977	2.07
Lane,Jason	Hou	89	73	679.1	155	1	0	0	1.000	2.07
Encarnacion,Ju	StL	125	111	983.1	219	4	4	0	.982	2.04
Nady,Xavier	TOT	99	97	854.2	187	6	4	0	.980	2.03
Giles,Brian	SD	158	158	1398.2	299	7	7	2	.978	1.97
Ordonez,Magglio	Det	148	147	1268.0	258	9	7	1	.974	1.90
Cuddyer,Michael	Min	142	137	1227.1	244	11	5	2	.981	1.87
Green,Shawn	TOT	131	128	1121.1	220	1	5	1	.978	1.77
Burnitz,Jeromy	Pit	84	79	643.0	120	1	4	0	.984	1.69

Right Fielders - The Rest

Player	Tm	G	GS	Inn	PO	A	E	DP	Pct.	Rng
Abercrombie,Reggie	Fla	13	1	24.1	4	0	0	0	1.000	1.48
Abreu,Bobby	Phi	97	95	846.0	178	5	1	0	.995	1.95
Abreu,Bobby	NYY	57	54	447.0	113	6	2	0	.983	2.40
Aguila,Chris	Fla	24	15	135.1	33	1	0	0	1.000	2.26
Amezaga,Alfredo	Fla	2	1	9.0	0	0	0	0	-	.00
Anderson,Drew	Mil	1	0	2.0	1	0	0	0	1.000	4.50
Anderson,Marlon	Was	10	8	69.0	14	1	2	1	.882	1.96
Anderson,Marlon	LAD	1	1	7.0	2	0	0	0	1.000	2.57
Baker,Jeff	Col	10	9	77.1	10	1	0	0	1.000	1.28
Barker,Kevin	Tor	1	1	8.0	1	0	1	0	.500	1.13
Bautista,Jose	Pit	25	17	172.2	31	1	0	0	1.000	1.67
Bellhorn,Mark	SD	1	0	3.0	0	0	0	0	-	.00
Berkman,Lance	Hou	42	37	305.2	56	3	3	2	.952	1.74
Bigbie,Larry	StL	1	0	2.0	1	0	0	0	1.000	4.50
Bloomquist,Wil	Sea	12	5	52.0	13	0	0	0	1.000	2.25
Blum,Geoff	SD	1	0	4.0	1	0	0	0	1.000	2.25
Bocachica,Hiram	Oak	3	0	14.0	2	0	0	0	1.000	1.29
Bohn,T.J.	Sea	17	2	44.0	7	0	0	0	1.000	1.43
Borchard,Joe	Fla	55	37	332.1	84	6	2	1	.978	2.44
Bourn,Michael	Phi	14	0	34.1	8	0	0	0	1.000	2.10
Branyan,Russell	TB	54	44	357.1	86	5	3	0	.968	2.29
Brown,Adrian	Tex	11	1	20.2	7	2	0	1	1.000	3.92
Brown,Emil	KC	54	46	414.0	110	3	2	0	.983	2.46
Bruntlett,Eric	Hou	5	1	13.2	4	0	1	0	.833	3.29
Burke,Chris	Hou	7	3	31.2	10	0	0	0	1.000	2.84
Bynum,Freddie	ChC	8	1	26.0	6	0	0	0	1.000	2.08
Byrd,Marlon	Was	18	7	83.0	23	0	1	0	.958	2.49
Byrnes,Eric	Ari	10	10	86.0	17	0	0	0	1.000	1.78
Cabrera,Melky	NYY	8	8	69.2	20	0	1	0	.952	2.58
Catalanotto,Fr	Tor	1	1	8.0	3	0	1	0	.750	3.38
Cepicky,Matt	Fla	5	4	32.0	8	0	0	0	1.000	2.25
Chavez,Endy	NYM	45	32	310.2	71	3	0	1	1.000	2.14
Choo,Shin-Soo	Cle	30	29	256.2	67	2	1	1	.986	2.42
Church,Ryan	Was	14	10	97.0	20	0	0	0	1.000	1.86
Clark,Brady	Mil	7	1	18.1	4	0	0	0	1.000	1.96
Clevlen,Brent	Det	13	0	23.0	4	1	0	0	1.000	1.96
Coats,Buck	ChC	1	1	8.1	2	0	0	0	1.000	2.16
Conine,Jeff	Bal	1	0	2.0	1	0	0	0	1.000	4.50
Conine,Jeff	Phi	25	21	171.1	32	0	0	0	1.000	1.68
Costa,Shane	KC	39	34	307.0	83	0	5	0	.943	2.43
Crosby,Bubba	NYY	31	7	91.1	19	0	0	0	1.000	1.87
Cruz,Jose	LAD	24	14	144.1	37	0	0	0	1.000	2.31
Cruz,Nelson	Tex	38	35	307.1	69	4	0	1	1.000	2.14
DaVanon,Jeff	Ari	16	12	120.1	23	0	0	0	1.000	1.72
Davis,Rajai	Pit	1	0	3.0	0	0	0	0	-	.00
Dellucci,David	Phi	31	26	188.0	36	0	1	0	.973	1.72
Denorfia,Chris	Cin	15	14	118.1	34	2	0	1	1.000	2.74
DeRosa,Mark	Tex	60	59	512.0	125	4	1	1	.992	2.27
Diaz,Matt	Atl	6	6	13.0	3	0	0	0	1.000	2.08
Dobbs,Greg	Sea	3	0	4.0	1	0	0	0	1.000	2.25
Duncan,Chris	StL	24	19	151.1	41	0	3	0	.932	2.44
Easley,Damion	Ari	1	1	7.0	0	0	0	0	-	.00
Ellison,Jason	SF	17	7	72.2	17	1	0	0	1.000	2.23
Escobar,Alex	Was	1	0	2.0	1	0	0	0	1.000	4.50
Everett,Carl	Sea	1	1	9.0	2	0	0	0	1.000	2.00
Fahey,Brandon	Bal	1	1	5.0	0	0	0	0	-	.00
Fick,Robert	Was	6	3	32.0	4	0	0	0	1.000	1.13
Figgins,Chone	LAA	6	4	37.2	7	0	0	0	1.000	1.67
Fiorentino,Jeff	Bal	1	0	2.0	0	0	0	0	-	.00
Ford,Lew	Min	22	20	169.0	53	3	1	2	.982	2.98
Freel,Ryan	Cin	42	41	360.2	101	7	5	1	.956	2.70
Freeman,Choo	Col	2	0	2.0	0	0	0	0	-	.00
Gibbons,Jay	Bal	44	44	348.2	97	1	2	0	.980	2.53
Gload,Ross	CWS	15	7	73.0	14	0	0	0	1.000	1.73
Gomes,Jonny	TB	8	6	60.0	19	0	0	0	1.000	2.85
Gomez,Alexis	Det	21	10	113.0	19	1	0	0	1.000	1.59
Gonzalez,Luis A	Col	6	5	37.0	6	0	0	0	1.000	1.46
Green,Nick	TB	1	1	6.0	1	0	0	0	1.000	1.50
Green,Shawn	Ari	100	98	857.1	164	1	2	1	.988	1.73
Green,Shawn	NYM	31	30	264.0	56	0	3	0	.949	1.91
Gross,Gabe	Mil	8	3	38.1	13	0	0	0	1.000	3.05
Guiel,Aaron	KC	9	9	77.2	21	1	0	0	1.000	2.55
Guiel,Aaron	NYY	11	11	109.0	26	1	0	0	1.000	2.23
Guillen,Jose	Was	68	64	537.2	163	3	2	0	.988	2.78
Gutierrez,Franklin	Cle	28	24	212.0	50	1	2	0	.962	2.17
Guzman,Freddy	Tex	1	0	1.0	0	0	0	0	-	.00
Hairston,Jerry	ChC	5	2	21.1	6	0	0	0	1.000	2.53
Hairston,Jerry	Tex	7	3	31.2	6	0	0	0	1.000	1.71
Harris,Willie	Bos	1	1	9.0	1	0	0	0	1.000	1.00
Hart,Corey	Mil	37	32	266.0	63	2	0	0	1.000	2.20
Hernandez,Jose	Pit	7	2	24.0	9	0	0	0	1.000	3.38
Hernandez,Jose	Phi	2	1	9.0	2	0	0	0	1.000	2.00
Hinske,Eric	Tor	30	28	214.0	41	2	0	1	1.000	1.81
Hinske,Eric	Bos	10	7	61.0	10	1	0	0	1.000	1.62
Hollandsworth,T	Cle	15	10	93.0	20	0	2	0	.909	1.94
Hollandsworth,T	Cin	19	12	118.1	22	0	0	0	1.000	1.67
Hollins,Damon	TB	78	46	463.2	134	4	2	0	.986	2.68
Hopper,Norris	Cin	13	8	70.0	25	1	0	1	1.000	3.34
Huff,Aubrey	Hou	37	34	270.2	40	1	2	0	.953	1.36
Hyzdu,Adam	Tex	1	1	9.0	3	0	0	0	1.000	3.00
Jackson,Damian	Was	2	0	2.1	0	0	0	0	-	.00
Jimerson,Char	Hou	9	0	14.0	6	0	0	0	1.000	3.86
Johnson,Ben	SD	4	0	11.0	0	0	0	0	-	.00
Johnson,Reed	Tor	30	28	242.1	64	3	0	1	1.000	2.49
Jordan,Brian	Atl	1	0	1.2	0	0	0	0	-	.00
Kapler,Gabe	Bos	37	17	177.2	48	2	0	1	1.000	2.53
Kearns,Austin	Cin	85	84	746.1	207	5	2	1	.991	2.56
Kearns,Austin	Was	59	55	482.1	139	2	5	1	.966	2.63
Kemp,Matt	LAD	10	6	71.2	8	1	1	0	.900	1.13
Kielty,Bobby	Oak	31	27	255.0	56	3	0	0	1.000	2.08
Kubel,Jason	Min	7	5	40.0	7	0	0	0	1.000	1.58
Laird,Gerald	Tex	1	0	2.0	0	0	0	0	-	.00

Player	Tm	G	GS	Inn	PO	A	E	DP	Pct.	Rng
Langerhans,Ryan	Atl	2	0	5.0	0	0	0	0	-	.00
Lawton,Matt	Sea	2	0	5.0	1	0	0	0	1.000	1.80
Ledee,Ricky	LAD	2	1	10.1	1	0	0	0	1.000	.87
Ledee,Ricky	NYM	3	2	18.1	5	0	0	0	1.000	2.45
Linden,Todd	SF	12	4	45.2	9	0	0	0	1.000	1.77
Lombard,George	Was	5	1	16.0	5	1	1	0	.857	3.38
Loney,James	LAD	2	0	6.0	0	0	0	0	-	.00
Long,Terrence	NYY	7	6	54.1	18	0	1	0	.947	2.98
Lugo,Julio	LAD	2	2	13.0	1	0	0	0	1.000	.69
Luna,Hector	StL	1	0	1.0	0	0	0	0	-	.00
Luna,Hector	Cle	1	1	8.0	0	0	0	0	-	.00
Mabry,John	ChC	7	2	25.2	4	0	0	0	1.000	1.40
Mackowiak,Rob	CWS	21	7	100.0	19	1	0	0	1.000	1.80
Maier,Mitch	KC	2	2	21.1	4	0	1	0	.800	1.69
Marrero,Eli	Col	3	3	23.0	7	0	0	0	1.000	2.74
Marrero,Eli	NYM	2	1	10.0	4	0	0	0	1.000	3.60
Martinez,Ramon	LAD	1	1	6.0	1	0	0	0	1.000	1.50
Matos,Luis	Bal	13	11	94.0	28	0	0	0	1.000	2.68
Matthews Jr.,G	Tex	3	3	26.0	9	0	0	0	1.000	3.12
McAnulty,Paul	SD	1	0	2.0	0	0	0	0	-	.00
McCracken,Q	Cin	2	1	10.0	3	0	0	0	1.000	2.70
McLouth,Nate	Pit	39	14	164.1	23	0	1	0	.958	1.26
Mench,Kevin	Tex	57	57	488.2	112	2	0	1	1.000	2.10
Meyer,Drew	Tex	1	0	4.0	0	0	0	0	-	.00
Michaels,Jason	Cle	1	1	9.0	2	0	0	0	1.000	2.00
Milledge,Lastings	NYM	24	24	205.1	38	1	1	0	.975	1.71
Mohr,Dustan	Bos	5	1	11.0	2	0	0	0	1.000	1.64
Morse,Mike	Sea	7	4	36.0	8	1	0	0	1.000	2.25
Mottola,Chad	Tor	2	0	3.0	1	0	0	0	1.000	3.00
Murphy,David	Bos	2	1	9.1	2	0	0	0	1.000	1.93
Murphy,Tommy	LAA	12	2	39.0	13	0	0	0	1.000	3.00
Nady,Xavier	NYM	71	70	620.2	137	5	4	0	.973	2.06
Nady,Xavier	Pit	28	27	234.0	50	1	0	0	1.000	1.96
Nevin,Phil	ChC	2	2	13.0	2	0	0	0	1.000	1.38
Newhan,David	Bal	3	2	16.0	6	0	0	0	1.000	3.38
Norton,Greg	TB	28	26	207.1	40	0	2	0	.952	1.74
Olmedo,Ray	Cin	1	0	1.0	0	0	0	0	-	.00
Ortmeier,Dan	SF	3	1	12.0	4	0	0	0	1.000	3.00
Owens,Jerry	CWS	1	0	1.0	1	0	0	0	1.000	9.00
Ozuna,Pablo	CWS	1	0	2.0	0	0	0	0	-	.00
Pagan,Angel	ChC	21	15	134.2	41	0	0	0	1.000	2.74
Palmeiro,Orl	Hou	11	2	45.0	7	0	0	0	1.000	1.40
Payton,Jay	Oak	45	41	377.0	89	1	2	0	.978	2.15
Pena,Wily Mo	Bos	39	35	282.0	63	2	2	0	.970	2.07
Perez,Eduardo	Cle	5	4	30.1	4	2	0	0	1.000	1.78
Perez,Timo	StL	4	2	21.1	3	0	0	0	1.000	1.27
Perez,Tomas	TB	4	3	28.0	11	0	0	0	1.000	3.54
Piedra,Jorge	Col	2	1	10.0	3	0	0	0	1.000	2.70
Pride,Curtis	LAA	3	1	12.0	4	0	0	0	1.000	3.00
Quentin,Carlos	Ari	44	41	389.0	96	3	2	0	.980	2.29
Quinlan,Robb	LAA	5	0	11.0	2	0	0	0	1.000	1.64
Rabe,Josh	Min	1	0	1.0	0	0	0	0	-	.00
Reese,Kevin	NYY	2	1	11.0	1	0	0	0	1.000	.82
Repko,Jason	LAD	14	4	64.0	18	0	0	0	1.000	2.53
Restovich,Mike	ChC	2	0	5.0	1	0	0	0	1.000	1.80
Rivera,Juan	LAA	33	26	242.0	50	3	1	0	.981	1.97
Roberson,Chris	Phi	21	2	54.2	13	0	0	0	1.000	2.14
Robinson,Kerry	KC	1	1	5.1	2	0	0	0	1.000	3.38
Rodriguez,John	StL	15	8	74.1	21	0	1	0	.955	2.54
Rogers,Eddie	Bal	1	0	1.0	0	0	0	0	-	.00
Ross,Cody	LAD	2	2	18.0	4	0	0	0	1.000	2.00
Ross,Cody	Fla	32	26	216.2	45	2	1	0	.979	1.95
Salazar,Jeffrey	Col	1	0	1.0	0	0	0	0	-	.00
Salmon,Tim	LAA	3	3	19.0	1	0	0	0	1.000	.47
Schumaker,Skip	StL	9	2	26.0	4	0	0	0	1.000	1.38
Scott,Luke	Hou	13	8	78.1	15	1	0	0	1.000	1.84
Sheffield,Gary	NYY	21	20	165.0	39	1	1	0	.976	2.18
Sledge,Terrmel	SD	10	4	43.0	9	1	0	0	1.000	2.09
Snelling,Chris	Sea	33	30	235.0	43	2	1	0	.978	1.72
Spilborghs,Ryan	Col	15	10	99.1	18	1	1	0	.950	1.72
Stairs,Matt	Tex	1	1	8.0	1	0	0	0	1.000	1.13
Sweeney,Ryan	CWS	6	3	28.0	13	0	0	0	1.000	4.18
Swisher,Nick	Oak	1	0	3.0	1	0	0	0	1.000	3.00
Taguchi,So	StL	7	1	19.2	5	0	0	0	1.000	2.29
Tatis,Fernando	Bal	1	1	8.0	4	0	0	0	1.000	4.50
Terrero,Luis	Bal	4	3	25.0	5	0	0	0	1.000	1.80
Thames,Marcus	Det	5	5	44.0	14	0	0	0	1.000	2.86
Thompson,Kevin	NYY	10	6	64.0	15	0	0	0	1.000	2.11
Thurston,Joe	Phi	1	0	1.0	1	0	0	0	1.000	9.00
Tucker,Michael	NYM	2	1	10.0	4	0	0	0	1.000	3.60
Tyner,Jason	Min	1	0	2.0	0	0	0	0	-	.00
Valentin,Jose	NYM	2	1	9.1	1	1	0	0	1.000	1.93
Vento,Mike	Was	8	5	49.0	13	0	0	0	1.000	2.39
Victorino,Shane	Phi	21	17	156.0	38	3	0	1	1.000	2.37
Ward,Daryle	Was	10	9	66.0	13	0	0	0	1.000	1.77
Wigginton,Ty	TB	7	5	45.2	10	0	0	0	1.000	2.36
Wilkerson,Brad	Tex	3	2	21.0	4	0	0	0	1.000	1.71
Williams,Bernie	NYY	58	49	425.1	98	1	1	0	.990	2.09
Willits,Reggie	LAA	1	0	2.0	0	0	0	0	-	.00
Wilson,Craig	Pit	30	23	194.0	37	2	0	0	1.000	1.81
Wilson,Craig	NYY	2	0	7.0	2	0	0	0	1.000	2.57
Wilson,Preston	Hou	5	4	30.1	6	0	0	0	1.000	1.78
Wilson,Preston	StL	19	18	150.2	31	0	1	0	.969	1.85
Wise,Dewayne	Cin	4	2	21.0	0	0	0	0	-	.00
Woodward,Chris	NYM	2	1	13.0	2	0	0	0	1.000	1.38
Young,Delmon	TB	30	29	252.1	50	4	1	0	.982	1.93
Young,Delwyn	LAD	1	0	2.0	0	0	0	0	-	.00
Young,Eric	SD	2	0	2.0	0	0	0	0	-	.00

Catchers - Regulars

Player	Tm	G	GS	Inn	PO	A	E	DP	PB	Pct.
Ausmus,Brad	Hou	138	124	1124.2	933	60	2	8	1	.998
Rodriguez,Ivan	Det	123	121	1054.1	747	53	2	7	4	.998
Miller,Damian	Mil	98	98	840.0	649	43	2	2	3	.997
Molina,Bengie	Tor	99	98	842.0	615	47	2	6	11	.997
Pierzynski,A.J.	CWS	132	126	1125.0	800	57	3	4	10	.997
Estrada,Johnny	Ari	108	103	924.2	686	47	3	10	4	.996
Mauer,Joe	Min	120	119	1059.1	868	42	4	6	5	.996
Molina,Yadier	StL	127	118	1037.1	736	77	4	6	7	.995
Kendall,Jason	Oak	141	141	1254.0	924	53	5	9	7	.995
Varitek,Jason	Bos	99	94	822.1	648	27	4	3	1	.994
Barrett,Michael	ChC	102	96	852.0	729	40	5	7	10	.994
Schneider,Brian	Was	123	111	990.1	695	52	5	8	5	.993
Martin,Russell	LAD	117	114	1015.0	789	61	6	8	5	.993
Johjima,Kenji	Sea	144	131	1172.2	881	59	7	9	10	.993
Alfonzo,Eliezer	SF	84	80	700.1	568	30	5	3	1	.992
Olivo,Miguel	Fla	109	109	971.1	733	64	7	11	10	.991
Buck,John	KC	112	107	930.1	616	36	6	6	5	.991
Hall,Toby	TOT	82	69	628.0	396	28	4	3	3	.991
Martinez,Victor	Cle	133	127	1110.0	755	44	8	5	4	.990
Posada,Jorge	NYY	124	121	1050.1	789	66	9	7	13	.990
McCann,Brian	Atl	124	118	1016.1	779	38	9	4	5	.989
Paulino,Ronny	Pit	124	117	1047.0	804	67	11	3	9	.988
Lo Duca,Paul	NYM	118	117	1027.0	802	59	11	4	9	.987
Napoli,Mike	LAA	77	72	716.1	576	47	8	2	2	.987
Piazza,Mike	SD	99	99	718.0	554	33	8	3	7	.987
Molina,Jose	LAA	76	71	603.1	504	48	8	4	5	.986
Hernandez,Ram	Bal	135	126	1094.1	793	69	13	5	13	.985
Navarro,Dioner	TOT	78	75	653.2	479	37	8	3	6	.985
Ross,Dave	Cin	75	73	620.2	480	33	8	5	5	.985
Barajas,Rod	Tex	94	94	825.0	591	35	10	1	5	.984

Catchers - The Rest

Player	Tm	G	GS	Inn	PO	A	E	DP	PB	Pct.
Alomar Jr.,Sandy	LAD	18	11	115.1	80	2	1	1	1	.988
Alomar Jr.,Sandy	CWS	17	14	126.0	96	4	1	1	0	.990
Ardoin,Danny	Col	35	33	288.1	205	14	3	1	1	.986
Ardoin,Danny	Bal	4	3	35.0	35	1	0	0	0	1.000
Bako,Paul	KC	53	44	392.0	258	19	2	1	4	.993
Bard,Josh	Bos	7	6	53.0	35	4	0	2	10	1.000
Bard,Josh	SD	71	50	494.2	385	31	3	6	0	.993
Bennett,Gary	StL	56	43	385.1	243	14	3	1	1	.988
Blanco,Henry	ChC	69	59	526.0	468	33	1	9	2	.994
Bowen,Rob	SD	65	8	202.0	145	13	1	1	3	.994
Brown,Jeremy	Oak	1	0	1.0	2	0	0	0	0	1.000
Castro,Ramon	NYM	37	32	307.1	267	16	1	3	1	.996

Player	Tm	G	GS	Inn	PO	A	E	DP	PB	Pct.
Chavez,Raul	Bal	15	8	75.0	60	5	1	1	0	.985
Closser,JD	Col	29	27	239.2	173	13	2	3	1	.989
Colina,Alvin	Col	1	1	9.0	8	0	0	0	0	1.000
Coste,Chris	Phi	54	46	434.1	328	12	4	0	4	.988
Cota,Humberto	Pit	33	29	242.1	179	16	0	1	5	1.000
Diaz,Einar	LAD	1	0	1.0	0	0	0	0	0	-
DiFelice,Mike	NYM	15	9	84.0	71	3	2	0	0	.974
Doumit,Ryan	Pit	11	10	91.2	66	12	1	0	2	.987
Fasano,Sal	Phi	50	42	365.2	267	24	3	2	2	.990
Fasano,Sal	NYY	27	16	152.2	104	9	1	0	2	.991
Fick,Robert	Was	26	18	164.0	104	7	1	2	4	.991
Gonzalez,Wiki	Was	12	11	90.0	62	8	2	0	2	.972
Greene,Todd	SF	42	37	326.0	196	13	1	1	1	.995
Hall,Toby	TB	61	55	494.0	312	20	3	2	3	.991
Hall,Toby	LAD	21	14	134.0	84	8	1	1	0	.989
Harper,Brandon	Was	14	13	104.0	77	1	1	0	0	.987
Heintz,Chris	Min	2	0	2.0	0	0	0	0	0	-
Hoover,Paul	Fla	3	1	8.1	7	0	1	0	1	.875
House,J.R.	Hou	3	1	12.0	10	1	0	0	1	1.000
Huckaby,Ken	Bos	8	1	20.0	11	0	0	0	0	1.000
Iannetta,Christopher	Col	21	20	191.2	139	8	0	3	2	1.000
Knoedler,Justin	SF	5	0	12.0	11	0	0	0	1	1.000
Laird,Gerald	Tex	71	65	578.1	392	30	6	5	5	.986
Laker,Tim	Cle	4	4	33.0	24	1	0	1	0	1.000
LaRue,Jason	Cin	63	57	512.1	376	36	2	9	3	.995
LeCroy,Matthew	Was	13	9	88.0	60	1	2	0	0	.968
Lieberthal,Mike	Phi	60	56	484.0	429	32	4	2	4	.991
Lopez,Javy	Bal	21	19	171.2	123	10	0	1	1	1.000
Lopez,Javy	Bos	17	15	137.0	98	5	1	1	2	.990
Maldonado,Carlos	Pit	8	6	54.0	27	3	1	0	0	.968
Marrero,Eli	Col	5	1	14.0	11	1	0	1	0	1.000
Marrero,Eli	NYM	2	0	3.0	1	0	0	0	0	1.000
Matheny,Mike	SF	46	44	391.1	252	17	1	2	2	.996
Mathis,Jeff	LAA	20	14	133.0	92	6	3	1	1	.970
Melhuse,Adam	Oak	24	21	196.2	131	12	0	3	3	1.000
Miller,Corky	Bos	1	1	9.0	6	0	0	0	0	1.000
Mirabelli,Doug	SD	9	5	49.0	37	2	0	0	1	1.000
Mirabelli,Doug	Bos	57	45	400.0	298	18	2	3	11	.994
Moeller,Chad	Mil	29	25	231.0	193	14	1	0	0	.995
Montero,Miguel	Ari	5	4	40.0	36	4	0	0	1	1.000
Munson,Eric	Hou	37	30	275.1	198	9	1	1	4	.995
Navarro,Dioner	LAD	24	23	195.0	149	3	1	1	1	.993
Navarro,Dioner	TB	54	52	458.2	330	34	7	2	5	.981
Nevin,Phil	ChC	1	0	1.0	1	0	0	0	0	1.000
Nieves,Wil	NYY	6	1	19.0	15	1	0	0	1	1.000
Ojeda,Miguel	Col	24	19	174.2	126	9	1	0	0	.993
Ojeda,Miguel	Tex	5	3	28.0	21	2	0	0	1	1.000
Paul,Josh	TB	52	47	400.1	303	22	0	4	0	1.000
Pena,Brayan	Atl	15	5	71.0	30	2	0	0	0	1.000
Phillips,Jason	Tor	9	5	45.0	41	1	0	0	0	1.000
Phillips,Paul	KC	13	11	104.0	75	8	1	2	1	.988
Pratt,Todd	Atl	54	39	354.0	279	11	4	2	3	.986
Quintero,Humb	Hou	10	7	56.2	42	6	0	3	1	1.000
Quiroz,Guill	Sea	1	1	8.0	5	0	0	0	0	1.000
Redmond,Mike	Min	43	43	378.0	317	21	0	2	0	1.000
Reyes,Jose A	ChC	2	0	5.0	7	0	0	0	0	1.000
Riggans,Shawn	TB	8	8	67.1	56	4	0	1	0	1.000
Rivera,Mike	Mil	44	39	352.2	299	31	4	2	0	.988
Rivera,Rene	Sea	35	30	266.0	223	11	3	3	6	.987
Rose,Mike	StL	4	0	7.0	10	0	0	0	0	1.000
Rottino,Vinny	Mil	1	0	2.0	3	0	0	0	0	1.000
Ruiz,Carlos	Phi	24	18	176.1	148	10	3	1	1	.981
Shoppach,Kelly	Cle	40	31	280.1	208	20	2	5	3	.991
Snyder,Chris	Ari	60	55	495.0	394	35	2	6	6	.995
Soto,Geovany	ChC	7	7	55.0	66	4	1	0	0	.986
Stewart,Chris	CWS	5	1	15.0	17	2	0	0	0	1.000
Stinnett,Kelly	NYY	34	24	221.2	169	10	2	3	1	.989
Stinnett,Kelly	NYM	7	4	40.0	35	5	1	1	0	.976
Torrealba,Yorv	Col	63	61	530.0	336	35	5	7	4	.987
Treanor,Matt	Fla	61	50	439.2	375	25	3	1	2	.993
Valentin,Javier	Cin	46	32	312.2	247	17	7	1	2	.974
Widger,Chris	CWS	22	21	183.0	102	5	3	0	3	.973
Widger,Chris	Bal	6	5	43.0	32	3	0	1	0	1.000
Willingham,Josh	Fla	2	2	14.0	11	1	0	0	1	1.000

Player	Tm	G	GS	Inn	PO	A	E	DP	PB	Pct.
Wilson,Vance	Det	55	41	393.2	285	27	1	2	2	.997
Zaun,Gregg	Tor	72	59	541.1	438	31	3	2	4	.994

Catchers Special - Regulars

Player	Tm	G	GS	Inn	SBA	CS	PCS	CS%	ER	CERA
Piazza,Mike	SD	99	99	718.0	110	13		.12	281	3.52
Napoli,Mike	LAA	94	77	716.1	55	17	1	.30	299	3.76
Ausmus,Brad	Hou	138	124	1124.2	77	17	5	.17	477	3.82
Rodriguez,Ivan	Det	123	121	1054.1	51	26	5	.46	449	3.83
Mauer,Joe	Min	120	119	1059.1	58	22	5	.32	461	3.92
Martin,Russell	LAD	117	114	1015.0	103	32	7	.26	443	3.93
Molina,Jose	LAA	76	71	603.1	47	20	1	.41	267	3.98
Kendall,Jason	Oak	141	141	1254.0	102	31	8	.24	570	4.09
Paulino,Ronny	Pit	124	117	1047.0	105	38	14	.26	488	4.19
Ross,Dave	Cin	75	73	620.2	31	14	2	.41	294	4.26
Lo Duca,Paul	NYM	118	117	1027.0	111	27	5	.21	495	4.32
Posada,Jorge	NYY	134	121	1050.1	102	38	4	.35	510	4.37
Molina,Bengie	Tor	99	98	842.0	83	15	2	.16	412	4.40
McCann,Brian	Atl	124	118	1016.1	91	21	1	.22	498	4.41
Olivo,Miguel	Fla	124	109	971.1	78	30	5	.34	476	4.41
Estrada,Johnny	Ari	108	103	924.2	93	27	6	.24	457	4.45
Pierzynski,A.J.	CWS	132	126	1125.0	115	25	4	.19	559	4.47
Alfonzo,Eliezer	SF	84	80	700.1	70	18	5	.20	350	4.50
Martinez,Victor	Cle	133	127	1110.0	122	22	5	.15	556	4.51
Molina,Yadier	StL	127	118	1037.1	66	29	3	.41	522	4.53
Miller,Damian	Mil	98	98	840.0	53	17	4	.27	427	4.58
Barrett,Michael	ChC	102	96	852.0	110	21	5	.15	435	4.60
Barajas,Rod	Tex	94	94	825.0	57	19	4	.28	434	4.73
Johjima,Kenji	Sea	144	131	1172.2	86	29	7	.28	627	4.81
Varitek,Jason	Bos	99	94	822.1	59	13	3	.18	442	4.84
Navarro,Dioner	TOT	78	75	653.2	68	20	2	.27	355	4.89
Hall,Toby	TOT	82	69	628.0	58	16	4	.22	357	5.12
Hernandez,Ram	Bal	135	126	1094.1	97	42	7	.39	637	5.24
Schneider,Brian	Was	123	111	990.1	83	25	3	.28	581	5.28
Buck,John	KC	112	107	930.1	50	17	4	.28	590	5.71

Catchers Special - The Rest

Player	Tm	G	GS	Inn	SBA	CS	PCS	CS%	ER	CERA
Alomar Jr.,Sandy	LAD	18	11	115.1	15	1	0	.07	78	6.09
Alomar Jr.,Sandy	CWS	17	14	126.0	12	4	2	.20	67	4.79
Ardoin,Danny	Col	35	33	288.1	27	7	0	.26	124	3.87
Ardoin,Danny	Bal	5	4	35.0	1	0	0	.00	23	5.91
Bako,Paul	KC	53	44	392.0	29	9	1	.29	250	5.74
Bard,Josh	Bos	7	6	53.0	13	1	0	.08	31	5.26
Bard,Josh	SD	71	50	494.2	51	10	1	.18	235	4.28
Bennett,Gary	StL	56	43	385.1	29	3	0	.10	196	4.58
Blanco,Henry	ChC	69	59	526.0	42	18	3	.38	289	4.94
Bowen,Rob	SD	65	8	202.0	9	1	0	.11	76	3.39
Brown,Jeremy	Oak	1	0	1.0	0	0	0	-	1	9.00
Castro,Ramon	NYM	37	32	307.1	26	9	0	.35	144	4.22
Chavez,Raul	Bal	15	8	75.0	5	3	1	.50	62	7.44
Closser,JD	Col	29	27	239.2	25	8	2	.26	108	4.06
Colina,Alvin	Col	1	1	9.0	0	0	0	-	8	8.00
Coste,Chris	Phi	54	46	434.1	31	6	0	.19	215	4.46
Cota,Humberto	Pit	33	29	242.1	27	9	4	.22	164	6.09
Diaz,Einar	LAD	1	0	1.0	0	0	0	-	0	0.00
DiFelice,Mike	NYM	15	9	84.0	8	1	0	.13	23	2.46
Doumit,Ryan	Pit	11	10	91.2	15	4	2	.15	62	6.09
Fasano,Sal	Phi	50	42	365.2	37	8	1	.19	197	4.85
Fasano,Sal	NYY	27	16	152.2	9	3	0	.33	82	4.83
Fick,Robert	Was	26	18	164.0	18	1	0	.06	83	4.55
Gonzalez,Wiki	Was	12	11	90.0	9	3	0	.33	33	3.30
Greene,Todd	SF	42	37	326.0	31	11	4	.26	195	5.38
Hall,Toby	TB	61	55	494.0	44	11	3	.20	276	5.03
Hall,Toby	LAD	21	14	134.0	14	5	1	.31	81	5.44
Harper,Brandon	Was	14	13	104.0	9	0	0	.00	66	5.71
Heintz,Chris	Min	2	0	2.0	0	0	0	-	1	4.50
Hoover,Paul	Fla	3	1	8.1	1	0	0	.00	3	3.24
House,J.R.	Hou	3	1	12.0	0	0	0	-	4	4.50
Huckaby,Ken	Bos	8	1	20.0	0	0	0	-	8	3.60
Iannetta,Christopher	Col	21	20	191.2	21	3	0	.14	130	6.10
Knoedler,Justin	SF	5	0	12.0	2	0	0	.00	8	6.00

Player	Tm	G	GS	Inn	SBA	CS	PCS	CS%	ER	CERA
Laird,Gerald	Tex	71	65	578.1	46	21	2	.43	282	4.39
Laker,Tim	Cle	4	4	33.0	10	1	1	.00	17	4.64
LaRue,Jason	Cin	63	57	512.1	36	13	2	.32	252	4.43
LeCroy,Matthew	Was	13	9	88.0	21	1	1	.00	40	4.09
Lieberthal,Mike	Phi	60	56	484.0	47	18	4	.33	255	4.74
Lopez,Javy	Bal	21	19	171.2	22	4	2	.10	97	5.09
Lopez,Javy	Bos	17	15	137.0	17	2	1	.06	85	5.58
Maldonado,Carlos	Pit	8	6	54.0	7	1	0	.14	11	1.83
Marrero,Eli	Col	5	1	14.0	2	0	0	.00	8	5.14
Marrero,Eli	NYM	2	0	3.0	0	0	0	-	0	0.00
Matheny,Mike	SF	46	44	391.1	35	11	3	.25	184	4.23
Mathis,Jeff	LAA	20	14	133.0	15	3	0	.20	86	5.82
Melhuse,Adam	Oak	24	21	196.2	27	10	2	.32	109	4.99
Miller,Corky	Bos	1	1	9.0	0	0	0	-	5	5.00
Mirabelli,Doug	SD	9	5	49.0	6	2	1	.20	39	7.16
Mirabelli,Doug	Bos	57	45	400.0	42	7	1	.15	202	4.55
Moeller,Chad	Mil	29	25	231.0	28	6	3	.12	139	5.42
Montero,Miguel	Ari	5	4	40.0	4	1	0	.25	21	4.73
Munson,Eric	Hou	37	30	275.1	23	8	4	.21	150	4.90
Navarro,Dioner	LAD	24	23	195.0	16	0	0	.00	84	3.88
Navarro,Dioner	TB	54	52	458.2	52	20	2	.36	271	5.32
Nevin,Phil	ChC	1	0	1.0	0	0	0	-	0	0.00
Nieves,Wil	NYY	6	1	19.0	3	1	0	.33	10	4.74
Ojeda,Miguel	Col	24	19	174.2	14	3	2	.08	94	4.84
Ojeda,Miguel	Tex	5	3	28.0	4	0	0	.00	17	5.46
Paul,Josh	TB	52	47	400.1	55	12	3	.17	205	4.61
Pena,Brayan	Atl	15	5	71.0	3	0	0	.00	34	4.31
Phillips,Jason	Tor	9	5	45.0	7	0	0	.00	21	4.20
Phillips,Paul	KC	13	11	104.0	9	4	0	.44	59	5.11
Pratt,Todd	Atl	54	39	354.0	37	9	2	.20	204	5.19
Quintero,Humb	Hou	10	7	56.2	5	3	0	.60	35	5.56
Quiroz,Guill	Sea	1	1	8.0	0	0	0	-	5	5.63
Redmond,Mike	Min	43	43	378.0	27	9	1	.31	170	4.05
Reyes,Jose A	ChC	2	0	5.0	0	0	0	-	2	3.60
Riggans,Shawn	TB	8	8	67.1	3	3	0	1.00	32	4.28
Rivera,Mike	Mil	44	39	352.2	47	8	0	.17	197	5.03
Rivera,Rene	Sea	35	30	266.0	24	9	4	.25	107	3.62
Rose,Mike	StL	4	0	7.0	0	0	0	-	3	3.86
Rottino,Vinny	Mil	1	0	2.0	0	0	0	-	2	9.00
Ruiz,Carlos	Phi	24	18	176.1	14	3	1	.15	81	4.13
Shoppach,Kelly	Cle	40	31	280.1	30	11	1	.34	128	4.11
Snyder,Chris	Ari	60	55	495.0	38	17	4	.38	250	4.55
Soto,Geovany	ChC	7	7	55.0	5	0	0	.00	32	5.24
Stewart,Chris	CWS	5	1	15.0	3	2	0	.67	8	4.80
Stinnett,Kelly	NYY	34	24	221.2	25	5	1	.17	108	4.38
Stinnett,Kelly	NYM	7	4	40.0	6	3	0	.50	13	2.93
Torrealba,Yorv	Col	63	61	530.0	52	21	5	.34	277	4.70
Treanor,Matt	Fla	61	50	439.2	34	16	3	.42	205	4.20
Valentin,Javier	Cin	46	32	312.2	18	8	1	.41	182	5.24
Widger,Chris	CWS	22	21	183.0	20	3	0	.15	109	5.36
Widger,Chris	Bal	6	5	43.0	5	1	0	.20	25	5.23
Willingham,Josh	Fla	2	2	14.0	2	0	0	.00	12	7.71
Wilson,Vance	Det	55	41	393.2	33	9	1	.25	171	3.91
Zaun,Gregg	Tor	72	59	541.1	72	17	5	.18	261	4.34

Baserunning

Bill James

Who is the best baserunner in the major leagues? Who is the worst? Who is on the list? Who isn't as good as the public thinks? Who is better than the announcers say?

Last year we began an effort to better document baserunning. We have added some things to the record this year, and I have actual answers to the questions above. . .I'm not just teasing you with the possibility that I could come up with answers if I wanted to.

Our baserunning analysis looks at six factors to evaluate baserunning. These are not *everything* that could be studied, but it's a pretty good start. The factors we look at, and document in the chart that follows, are:

1) **Runners going from first to third on a single**. Mike Cameron was on first base when a single was hit into the outfield 16 times last year and made it to third 11 times, the best percentage for any player with 15 or more opportunities. Frank Thomas was on first base when a single was hit 23 times, and was 0-for-23.

2) **Scoring from second on a single**. Grady Sizemore last year scored from second on a single 25 times in 29 opportunities, the highest percentage of any player with 20 chances (although Ryan Langerhans was 13 for 13, and Corey Patterson and Ricky Weeks were both 18 for 19). Jorge Posada was 6 for 21, Josh Bard 1 for 12, Bengie Molina 0 for 7.

3) **Scoring from first on a double**. J.D. Drew scored from first on a double last year (2006) 8 times in 8 chances; Bengie Molina was 0 for 8.

4) **Bases Taken**. We've added a new category this year, Bases Taken, which could be generally defined as "the offensive side of events which are usually documented only as defensive failures." A player is credited with a Base Taken whenever he moves up a base on

a) a Wild Pitch,
b) a Passed Ball,
c) a Balk,
d) a Sacrifice Fly, or
e) Defensive Indifference.

Taken as a group, these events—Bases Taken—are significantly more common than Stolen Bases—and who benefits from them, if you look, bears an obvious relationship to speed. Ichiro led the majors in Bases Taken with 33, although Orlando Cabrera was better per time on base. The least likely players to take a base off the defense were Garrett Atkins, Jason Giambi and Adam Dunn.

5) **Baserunning outs**. We actually have three categories of outs. "Out Adv." is runners thrown out attempting to go first to third on a single, attempting to score from second on a single or attempting to score from first on a double. "Doubled Off" is runners doubled off base on a ball hit in the air, and "BR Outs" is runners thrown out attempting to advance on a Wild Pitch, a Passed Ball or a Sac Fly. There are so few of these, the Baserunning Outs, that we didn't print the data separately. And, also, there are other baserunning outs that we may worry about in some future year.

6) **Runs Scored as a Percentage of Times on Base**. You can't rely too heavily on runs scored as a percentage of times on base (excluding home runs), because the ratio is heavily colored by offensive context. But you can't ignore it, either, because the purpose of good baserunning is to score runs. We tried to give the category an appropriate weight.

As to how we combine these six factors into a rating. . .let's do Carlos Beltran. I am on record as saying that Carlos Beltran is probably the best baserunner in the majors, but let's look at the data. Beltran was on first when a single was hit 20 times in 2006, and made it to third base 9 times. The major league average was 28%, so Beltran was 3.4 bases better than an average runner.

Beltran was on second when a single was hit 22 times, and he scored 13 times, or 59%. The major league average was 60%, so Beltran was a tick below average there. Adding this to the first-to-third data, CB is now +3.2.

Beltran was on first when a double was doubled 6 times, and he scored 3 of the 6. The major league average was 42%, so Beltran is +.48. Adding this to the earlier data, this brings him up to +3.7.

Beltran was on base 226 times last year, not counting home runs, and took 23 bases from the defense. The major league average was .073 bases taken per time on base, so Beltran is +6.6 there. This brings him up to 10.3 bases better than an average baserunner.

Beltran was not thrown out advancing on the bases, and was doubled off only once—a total of one baserunning out. The major league average is essentially one baserunning out per 100 times on base, so Beltran is +1.1 in this category.

This category, however, receives triple points. Making an out on the bases is far more important, on a one-to-one basis, than picking up an extra base. For a runner in scoring position to try to take an extra base is not a breakeven gamble, or anything like a breakeven gamble. It's not even like a stolen base attempt, which breaks even about 65 to 67%; it's higher than that. We give triple weight, in evaluating baserunning, to this category, so that one baserunning out negates three bases gained.

Beltran gets 3.3 points for not making outs on the bases, which brings him up to +13.5. Beltran, on base 226 times, scored 86 runs, not counting his home runs. The major league average is .28 (.280910) runs scored per time on base. Beltran exceeded expectations by 21 runs.

That's heavily context-driven, of course. A player who bats in front of Carlos Delgado is going to do better than a player who bats in front of John McDonald. A player who hits doubles and triples is going to do better than a player who draws walks and hits singles. A player who bats leadoff is going to score more runs than a player who bats third or fourth, even with equally good hitters coming up behind him.

Still, you can't ignore stats just because they're context-driven, or you'll wind up ignoring everything. Scoring runs is the name of the game. We give Beltran credit for scoring more runs than expected, but one point for each three runs scored. +21 becomes +7. Adding to the +13.5 that Beltran had before, his score is, or rounds off to, +21.

He was not the best baserunner in the major leagues last year. He was ninth on the list, the top ten being:

1.	Chone Figgins	+28
2.	Chase Utley	+27
3.	Mark Ellis	+23
4.	Orlando Cabrera	+23
5.	David DeJesus	+23
6.	Jose Reyes	+22
7.	Mark Teahen	+22
8.	Willy Taveras	+21
9.	Carlos Beltran	+21
10.	Hanley Ramirez	+21

After that we have Johnny Damon, Grady Sizemore, Juan Pierre, Corey Patterson, Scott Podsednik, Marcus Giles, Jason Michaels, Mark Grudzielanek, Felipe Lopez, Carlos Guillen, Melky Cabrera, Brandon Fahey, Steve Finley and Shane Victorino.

The worst baserunner of 2006 was (drum roll, please. . .pratfall. . .band plays "Baby Elephant Walk"). . .Josh Willingham. Overcoming Frank Thomas' huge advantage in natural slowness augmented by age and Adrian Gonzalez' uncanny propensity for being doubled off, Willingham was 2-for-15 going first-to-third on a single, 1-for-11 scoring from second on a single, 2-for-5 scoring on a double (which is average, actually), was thrown out three times advancing while taking only six bases from the defense, and scored only 61 runs despite hitting 25 homers and being on base over 200 times on other events. The bottom ten are:

1.	Willingham	-30
2.	Yo Adrian Gonzalez	-25
3.	Mike Piazza	-25
4.	Frank Thomas	-23
5.	Jason Giambi	-23
6.	Ryan Howard	-21

7.	Pat Burrell	-21
8.	Travis Hafner	-21
9.	Victor Martinez	-20
10.	Juan Rivera	-20

Followed by Joe Crede, Kenji Johjima, Richie Sexson, Javy Lopez, Jorge Posada, Willy Aybar, Jermaine Dye, Bengie Molina, Mike Jacobs, Jacque Jones, Kevin Millar, Mike Lowell, Brian McCann, Paul Konerko and Khalil Greene.

The 25 best baserunners include, by my count, 9 center fielders, 5 shortstops, no catchers, no DHs, no first basemen. The 25 worst baserunners include 7 catchers, 7 first basemen, 2 DHs, one shortstop, no center fielders.

All of that is more or less as you would expect it to be. Maybe it's an upset that Frank Thomas isn't last, but he's close. You would expect Giambi, Hafner, Piazza and Bengie Molina to be prominently featured on a worst-baserunners list, and Figgins, Reyes, Taveras and Beltran to be on a best-baserunners list. You would expect the best baserunners to be mostly center fielders and shortstops; you would expect the worst baserunners to be mostly catchers and first basemen and DHs.

We turn our attention, then, to the issue of who *didn't* grade out the way you would expect him to. The biggest surprise, to me, is Ichiro Suzuki. Suzuki led the majors in Bases Taken, 33, as noted above, and he picks up some points for scoring runs in 34% of his times on base. Apart from that, his baserunning numbers range from ordinary to ugly. In 2005, Ichiro's stats on going first-to-third on a single, scoring from second on a single and scoring from first on a double were all exceptionally good. In 2006 they were all below average. In 2005 Ichiro was thrown out advancing once. In 2006 he was out advancing 3 times, and doubled off base 5 times. His total of 8 baserunning outs was the highest in the major leagues, one more than Adrian Gonzalez. Maybe it was just a fluke year—and maybe, at 32, he isn't what he used to be.

The American League MVP contest for 2006 appears to be Derek Jeter against David Ortiz. This book will be in the stores before the winner is announced, but I am assuming that it will be Derek Jeter.

Derek Jeter has a halo effect that would crush concrete. His teams win a lot of games, and he's likeable and polite and the media loves him, so any area of performance that is poorly documented or poorly understood—defense, baserunning, clutch hitting, leadership—the media will use as a rag to polish Derek Jeter's trophies. He gets lots of credit for being a great baserunner. The highlight of the Red Sox season, for me, was a moment when the network announcers were going on at some length about what a perfect baserunner Derek Jeter is, how he never gets thrown out on the bases and is always alert to picking up an extra base. Toward the end of this paean, Kevin Youkilis gunned the ball to second base on a 5-3 groundout, and nailed Jeter off second. Kevin, I could have kissed ya'.

But this is not partisan debate; this is ice-cold sabermetrics. Jeter scored 118 runs in his presumptive MVP season, and scored runs in 34% of his on-base opportunities. We credit him with scoring 17 runs more than expected given his times on base, and give him +5.6 points for that. Setting aside this frankly suspect advantage, Jeter's baserunning numbers are generally poor—as in, worse than the league average, and worse than David Ortiz. Jeter was 9-for-36 going from first to third on a single, 10-for-23 scoring from second on a single, and 2-for-7 scoring from second on a double. All of these numbers are below average. His basepath outs were above average.

At the same time, David Ortiz' baserunning numbers are surprisingly good. Ortiz was 8-for-17 scoring from second on a single—which incidentally is harder to do in Fenway than it is in Yankee Stadium—and he was 2-for-5 scoring from first on a double. He was not doubled off base, and he was not thrown out advancing. He was able to advance fairly often without being thrown out.

Having watched almost every Red Sox game for several years, I can say without hesitation that David Ortiz is a much better baserunner than most people think he is. He is slow, but he is alert, he reads the ball well off the bat, he hustles, and he knows what he can do. Do I really believe that he is a better baserunner than Derek Jeter? No, of course not; that's not what our chart shows, and it's not what I believe. What I believe is that the difference between them as baserunners is a fourth of what the media generally assumes it is.

Another surprise is Khalil Greene. . .he actually doesn't have ANY good baserunning numbers. Joey Gathright, one of the fastest players in baseball, we have rated as a below-average baserunner. I did not expect the high ranking to Chase Utley, although people tell me he does everything well. The high rating for Albert Pujols is not a surprise to me, although it will be to some people.

Note: Chart includes all players who have been on base 50 or more times during the 2006 season.

2006 Baserunning

Player	On Base	Scored	First to Third Moved	First to Third Chances	Second to Home Moved	Second to Home Chances	First to Home Moved	First to Home Chances	Bases Taken	Out Adv.	Doubled Off	BR Outs	Rating
Abercrombie, Reggie	103	32%	2	8	15	19	3	5	7	0	0	0	+8
Abreu, Bobby	284	29%	5	15	13	18	3	6	22	0	1	1	+11
Adams, Russ	87	32%	3	15	3	9	0	0	8	1	0	1	-1
Alfonzo, Eliezer	93	16%	1	9	1	4	1	1	5	0	0	0	-5
Alou, Moises	124	24%	0	9	3	9	0	3	7	0	0	0	-6
Amezaga, Alfredo	140	27%	4	8	11	12	3	4	12	0	1	1	+10
Anderson, Brian	123	30%	1	8	11	15	0	0	9	0	2	2	0
Anderson, Garret	186	24%	6	27	10	15	1	3	7	0	0	0	-4
Anderson, Marlon	104	29%	7	11	2	2	1	2	12	0	1	1	+10
Atkins, Garrett	274	32%	7	28	21	29	2	8	7	0	1	1	-3
Aurilia, Rich	156	24%	5	12	11	14	0	5	10	0	0	0	+3
Ausmus, Brad	174	20%	4	18	8	15	3	4	11	2	1	3	-11
Aybar, Willy	105	26%	3	17	3	12	1	2	4	2	1	3	-16
Baldelli, Rocco	129	33%	4	10	8	12	0	1	15	0	3	3	+4
Barajas, Rod	108	35%	3	17	5	11	3	5	6	0	0	0	+1
Bard, Josh	114	18%	4	10	1	12	0	1	7	0	0	0	-7
Barfield, Josh	210	28%	8	17	16	21	4	5	16	0	1	1	+12
Barmes, Clint	159	30%	1	8	10	12	5	6	12	0	1	1	+8
Barrett, Michael	153	24%	6	18	5	10	1	3	6	1	1	2	-9
Bartlett, Jason	145	28%	6	19	9	17	0	1	15	0	3	3	-1
Batista, Tony	61	31%	0	6	6	11	0	0	8	0	0	0	+4
Bautista, Jose	151	27%	6	21	9	14	1	2	11	0	1	1	+2
Bay, Jason	263	25%	6	22	9	20	3	7	18	0	1	1	-2
Bell, David	204	24%	2	24	11	15	5	8	12	0	1	1	-3
Bellhorn, Mark	83	21%	6	12	1	3	1	2	8	0	1	1	+2
Belliard, Ronnie	193	25%	11	23	8	19	2	3	18	1	1	2	+4
Beltran, Carlos	226	38%	9	20	13	22	3	6	23	0	1	1	+21
Beltre, Adrian	225	28%	7	22	18	25	2	5	18	2	0	2	+6
Bennett, Gary	52	17%	2	5	3	5	1	1	0	0	0	0	-3
Berkman, Lance	241	20%	8	19	9	13	1	8	12	0	0	0	-3
Berroa, Angel	142	25%	9	19	3	6	3	4	11	0	0	0	+8
Betancourt, Yuniesky	203	29%	11	31	13	18	3	4	17	1	4	6	-3
Betemit, Wilson	132	23%	1	11	5	8	2	3	5	0	1	1	-7
Biggio, Craig	183	31%	7	27	11	20	5	6	18	0	3	3	+4
Blake, Casey	166	26%	4	24	14	17	4	5	7	1	1	2	-4
Blalock, Hank	214	28%	2	23	8	19	3	5	13	0	2	2	-9
Blanco, Henry	83	20%	0	12	1	6	1	1	4	0	0	0	-7
Bloomquist, Willie	114	30%	4	13	9	12	0	1	7	0	0	0	+5
Blum, Geoff	95	24%	2	13	8	8	3	5	6	0	0	0	+3
Bonds, Barry	205	23%	5	20	7	16	1	5	11	0	1	1	-8
Boone, Aaron	127	33%	4	14	7	9	1	8	9	1	1	2	-1
Borchard, Joe	86	26%	1	5	6	11	0	4	3	0	0	0	-4
Bowen, Rob	58	32%	0	3	2	3	0	1	4	0	0	0	+1
Bradley, Milton	152	25%	2	15	9	12	2	2	13	1	1	2	0
Branyan, Russell	80	23%	1	6	4	7	2	2	5	0	0	0	+1
Broussard, Ben	151	26%	7	21	11	15	1	2	14	1	3	4	-2
Brown, Emil	226	26%	7	23	11	21	2	4	10	1	1	2	-7
Bruntlett, Eric	55	20%	1	2	3	6	0	0	3	0	1	1	-4
Buck, John	128	20%	3	16	7	15	0	0	10	1	0	1	-5
Burke, Chris	144	34%	4	15	10	15	1	2	15	0	1	2	+7
Burnitz, Jeromy	93	20%	1	14	5	11	0	3	9	0	0	0	-3
Burrell, Pat	203	25%	5	20	10	22	0	4	8	1	2	4	-20
Byrd, Marlon	82	28%	3	14	7	8	1	3	6	0	0	0	+3
Byrnes, Eric	195	28%	6	22	12	18	4	5	15	0	0	0	+10
Cabrera, Melky	209	32%	8	21	12	17	3	5	22	1	1	2	+15
Cabrera, Miguel	284	30%	6	32	22	33	6	15	19	1	1	2	+2
Cabrera, Orlando	240	35%	9	30	29	37	3	6	29	1	2	3	+24
Cairo, Miguel	81	34%	4	8	3	5	0	1	7	0	0	0	+7
Cameron, Mike	226	29%	11	16	15	22	1	3	19	0	2	2	+12

2006 Baserunning

Player	On Base	Scored	First to Third		Second to Home		First to Home		Bases Taken	Out Adv.	Doubled Off	BR Outs	Rating
			Moved	Chances	Moved	Chances	Moved	Chances					
Cano, Robinson	196	23%	6	21	8	19	3	6	10	1	1	2	-10
Cantu, Jorge	129	20%	2	12	8	11	4	8	11	0	0	0	+3
Carroll, Jamey	213	37%	9	20	18	25	2	5	17	0	3	3	+11
Casey, Sean	151	25%	5	19	8	14	1	4	8	0	0	0	-1
Castilla, Vinny	81	25%	5	13	1	4	2	5	10	0	0	0	+6
Castillo, Jose	183	21%	8	20	12	16	1	3	12	0	0	0	+5
Castillo, Luis	252	32%	13	33	17	21	3	6	15	0	2	2	+10
Castro, Juan	81	18%	1	10	3	6	1	2	5	1	0	1	-6
Catalanotto, Frank	193	25%	2	20	8	15	2	5	9	2	0	2	-12
Cedeno, Ronny	169	26%	8	19	12	17	2	3	7	1	1	2	-2
Chavez, Endy	151	29%	1	4	6	10	1	1	6	0	0	0	+0
Chavez, Eric	190	27%	7	23	10	16	3	6	7	2	0	2	-6
Choo, Shin-Soo	72	27%	2	4	5	8	0	0	4	0	1	1	-1
Church, Ryan	81	14%	1	8	4	8	0	0	7	1	0	1	-5
Cintron, Alex	104	28%	8	14	3	8	0	0	11	1	0	1	+6
Cirillo, Jeff	118	25%	4	9	6	9	3	6	14	0	1	1	+7
Clark, Brady	181	25%	1	21	11	17	4	8	15	1	0	2	-4
Clayton, Royce	168	27%	4	14	12	17	2	5	16	1	1	2	+4
Conine, Jeff	198	22%	10	24	12	21	0	3	14	1	2	3	-6
Cora, Alex	102	29%	2	5	9	11	2	3	7	0	0	0	+7
Costa, Shane	78	25%	1	7	3	5	1	1	9	0	0	0	+5
Coste, Chris	79	22%	0	6	1	4	0	1	6	0	0	0	-2
Counsell, Craig	150	34%	6	18	8	11	1	4	12	1	0	1	+7
Crawford, Carl	240	29%	3	19	16	18	4	7	24	2	2	4	+7
Crede, Joe	177	25%	4	21	9	16	2	3	10	3	3	6	-19
Crisp, Coco	150	33%	6	16	9	13	4	5	13	0	1	1	+11
Crosby, Bobby	128	25%	4	13	5	8	2	3	8	1	2	3	-6
Cruz, Jose	97	29%	4	8	4	6	0	3	5	1	0	1	-1
Cuddyer, Mike	234	33%	8	19	15	25	3	9	18	1	0	1	+11
Damon, Johnny	236	38%	9	23	21	28	4	8	23	0	3	3	+19
DaVanon, Jeff	100	33%	6	10	6	8	2	6	6	0	1	1	+4
DeJesus, David	206	35%	12	25	19	21	6	11	20	1	1	2	+24
Delgado, Carlos	195	26%	4	24	8	14	2	6	17	0	3	3	-5
Dellucci, David	105	26%	3	10	4	9	3	4	5	0	0	0	+0
DeRosa, Mark	222	29%	5	22	13	16	2	7	21	1	2	3	+5
Diaz, Matt	131	22%	3	12	6	11	1	2	8	1	1	2	-7
Doumit, Ryan	58	15%	0	2	3	5	1	1	6	0	0	0	+1
Drew, J.D.	236	27%	9	29	11	22	8	8	19	0	1	1	+8
Drew, Stephen	85	25%	1	8	6	6	2	4	8	0	0	0	+5
Duffy, Chris	122	36%	5	13	13	21	0	2	12	0	2	2	+5
Duncan, Chris	98	38%	0	10	10	11	1	2	6	0	0	0	+6
Dunn, Adam	218	27%	3	24	11	19	2	6	7	0	1	1	-11
Durham, Ray	187	28%	4	14	15	22	3	6	14	2	1	3	-1
Dye, Jermaine	210	27%	5	20	10	21	1	4	13	3	2	5	-15
Easley, Damion	72	20%	2	9	1	4	0	1	9	1	0	1	-1
Eckstein, David	209	31%	10	38	19	27	0	1	13	0	1	1	+5
Edmonds, Jim	135	23%	4	10	5	9	4	6	8	1	2	4	-9
Ellis, Mark	159	33%	11	20	8	16	3	4	23	0	0	0	+24
Encarnacion, Edwin	171	26%	5	15	11	14	1	5	11	0	1	1	+2
Encarnacion, Juan	197	27%	4	18	11	20	2	6	14	0	3	3	-6
Ensberg, Morgan	182	24%	5	28	8	11	0	1	11	0	0	0	-1
Estrada, Johnny	145	22%	3	13	5	15	2	4	7	1	1	2	-12
Ethier, Andre	161	24%	1	15	12	18	5	5	6	0	1	1	-5
Everett, Adam	186	24%	2	7	12	21	2	4	12	0	0	0	+2
Everett, Carl	98	26%	2	15	7	8	0	1	10	0	1	1	+2
Fahey, Brandon	116	29%	6	19	7	8	4	5	14	0	0	0	+14
Fasano, Sal	55	12%	0	1	0	4	0	1	1	0	1	1	-10
Feliz, Pedro	186	28%	2	16	10	23	0	5	8	1	0	1	-11
Fielder, Prince	206	26%	3	20	5	12	1	5	19	2	1	3	-6
Figgins, Chone	241	34%	14	28	12	20	10	12	25	0	1	1	+28
Finley, Steve	170	35%	7	20	12	18	3	5	14	0	0	0	+14

297

2006 Baserunning

Player	On Base	Scored	First to Third Moved	First to Third Chances	Second to Home Moved	Second to Home Chances	First to Home Moved	First to Home Chances	Bases Taken	Out Adv.	Doubled Off	BR Outs	Rating
Floyd, Cliff	119	28%	4	10	8	12	1	3	8	0	0	0	+5
Ford, Lew	91	39%	6	15	9	12	1	4	4	0	1	1	+3
Franco, Julio	61	19%	1	6	3	3	1	2	1	0	0	0	-3
Francoeur, Jeff	207	26%	11	20	7	10	5	11	23	1	0	2	+13
Freel, Ryan	199	29%	6	15	9	17	7	9	16	0	0	0	+12
Freeman, Choo	74	29%	2	3	5	9	1	1	7	0	0	0	+6
Furcal, Rafael	275	35%	12	33	14	23	4	10	22	0	3	3	+11
Garciaparra, Nomar	184	33%	3	11	10	22	2	6	16	2	0	2	+2
Garko, Ryan	74	28%	0	10	2	8	0	2	3	0	0	0	-7
Gathright, Joey	172	33%	3	12	10	19	1	3	12	2	1	3	-3
German, Esteban	159	25%	6	19	7	12	3	9	13	2	0	2	-1
Giambi, Jason	211	26%	4	23	10	22	0	7	6	1	2	3	-22
Gibbons, Jay	122	17%	0	8	3	11	0	4	9	0	0	0	-8
Giles, Brian	270	27%	9	36	15	21	8	15	11	1	2	3	-8
Giles, Marcus	218	34%	9	26	14	20	5	10	25	1	2	3	+16
Glaus, Troy	203	33%	8	29	6	14	6	8	9	0	2	2	-2
Gload, Ross	71	26%	0	5	8	10	0	4	7	2	2	4	-9
Gomes, Jonny	134	24%	3	14	5	9	2	4	15	1	0	1	+4
Gomez, Chris	62	19%	1	8	3	4	0	0	2	0	0	0	-3
Gonzalez, Adrian	216	27%	2	16	6	18	2	10	16	0	6	7	-24
Gonzalez, Alex	130	30%	6	18	11	19	0	4	11	0	1	1	+2
Gonzalez, Luis	235	33%	4	26	21	27	6	6	13	0	0	0	+12
Graffanino, Tony	192	31%	9	19	12	15	6	8	18	0	3	3	+12
Granderson, Curtis	219	32%	5	26	15	24	7	12	18	0	0	0	+12
Green, Shawn	207	28%	4	27	9	18	4	9	14	1	0	1	-3
Greene, Khalil	152	26%	2	11	10	19	2	7	9	2	2	4	-14
Greene, Todd	61	22%	1	3	2	7	0	1	1	0	0	0	-5
Griffey Jr., Ken	130	26%	2	16	6	10	3	7	11	0	2	2	-4
Gross, Gabe	93	35%	2	5	11	13	1	1	11	0	0	0	+14
Grudzielanek, Mark	207	37%	5	21	16	23	6	11	18	1	0	1	+15
Guerrero, Vladimir	235	25%	6	21	10	17	2	6	17	1	1	2	-2
Guiel, Aaron	51	35%	3	7	5	7	0	0	2	0	0	0	+3
Guillen, Carlos	249	32%	13	27	11	16	2	6	22	1	1	2	+15
Guillen, Jose	70	27%	3	7	4	6	1	1	2	0	0	0	+1
Hafner, Travis	212	27%	4	26	11	20	5	10	8	2	3	5	-20
Hairston, Jerry	76	32%	3	6	3	5	1	3	9	0	1	1	+5
Hall, Bill	198	33%	5	15	15	20	1	2	21	1	1	2	+14
Hall, Toby	84	10%	1	8	1	5	0	1	5	2	0	2	-13
Hart, Corey	88	26%	0	5	3	6	1	2	6	0	1	1	-3
Hatteberg, Scott	207	23%	8	23	10	20	2	5	14	0	0	0	+1
Hawpe, Brad	217	20%	8	20	8	12	3	7	11	0	0	0	0
Helms, Wes	106	17%	2	5	4	6	0	1	3	0	0	0	-4
Helton, Todd	264	29%	10	34	21	29	4	12	22	1	0	1	+12
Hermida, Jeremy	122	26%	4	11	6	9	2	4	6	0	0	0	+2
Hernandez, Jose	59	15%	1	8	2	3	0	2	3	0	0	0	-4
Hernandez, Ramon	197	21%	7	19	7	17	2	7	17	0	0	0	+2
Hill, Aaron	230	27%	10	25	11	16	3	3	20	0	1	1	+13
Hillenbrand, Shea	177	29%	10	21	11	17	1	4	16	1	2	3	+4
Hinske, Eric	107	28%	5	13	5	8	1	1	6	1	1	2	-2
Hollandsworth, Todd	65	30%	1	6	5	5	0	1	4	0	0	0	+3
Holliday, Matt	252	33%	7	21	12	20	3	11	13	1	0	1	+3
Hollins, Damon	98	22%	2	11	4	9	0	4	6	1	0	1	-7
Howard, Ryan	254	18%	4	24	9	16	8	14	12	2	2	4	-21
Hudson, Orlando	243	29%	12	23	12	19	3	5	19	0	2	2	+11
Huff, Aubrey	168	21%	8	20	5	7	2	5	13	0	1	1	+2
Hunter, Torii	205	26%	10	15	10	13	2	4	18	2	1	3	+8
Ibanez, Raul	235	29%	8	22	10	21	4	8	22	1	1	2	+7
Iguchi, Tadahito	222	35%	11	30	18	23	0	5	19	3	2	5	+5
Infante, Omar	92	33%	3	9	5	8	2	2	7	0	1	1	+4
Inge, Brandon	188	29%	5	15	13	18	6	8	11	2	2	4	-2
Inglett, Joe	84	28%	1	5	2	5	1	2	10	0	0	0	+5

2006 Baserunning

Player	On Base	Scored	First to Third		Second to Home		First to Home		Bases Taken	Out Adv.	Doubled Off	BR Outs	Rating
			Moved	Chances	Moved	Chances	Moved	Chances					
Izturis, Cesar	72	18%	3	8	2	3	0	2	2	0	0	0	-3
Izturis, Maicer	168	35%	11	24	12	17	4	7	13	0	2	2	+11
Jackson, Conor	217	27%	7	24	5	10	1	3	21	1	5	6	-8
Jacobs, Mike	153	22%	1	21	5	16	3	7	7	1	0	1	-15
Jenkins, Geoff	188	23%	6	20	9	15	2	7	15	0	1	1	+1
Jeter, Derek	310	33%	9	36	10	23	2	7	26	1	2	3	+3
Johjima, Kenji	189	22%	4	27	10	19	2	5	10	3	1	4	-19
Johnson, Ben	60	25%	0	3	4	8	0	1	3	0	1	1	-5
Johnson, Dan	109	19%	1	12	2	5	0	1	4	0	1	1	-11
Johnson, Nick	260	29%	10	25	11	23	5	12	22	2	0	2	+6
Johnson, Reed	214	34%	5	22	13	22	4	10	19	1	1	2	+7
Jones, Andruw	226	29%	5	18	10	14	5	6	14	0	0	0	+9
Jones, Chipper	186	32%	4	18	15	20	3	5	6	0	2	3	-5
Jones, Jacque	187	24%	5	17	8	18	1	4	14	2	3	5	-14
Kapler, Gabe	72	26%	0	5	4	6	2	3	6	0	1	1	-1
Kearns, Austin	225	27%	9	20	11	18	5	8	23	0	4	4	+6
Kemp, Matt	53	43%	2	5	4	6	1	1	6	0	1	1	+5
Kendall, Jason	251	29%	6	30	8	19	4	9	23	1	2	3	-1
Kendrick, Howie	101	20%	5	11	4	8	1	2	8	1	0	1	-1
Kennedy, Adam	179	25%	4	17	13	16	1	1	18	0	1	1	+9
Kent, Jeff	186	25%	4	15	7	14	3	9	9	2	1	3	-12
Kielty, Bobby	103	26%	2	11	5	6	2	3	6	0	0	0	+2
Kinsler, Ian	165	30%	2	8	3	9	4	9	17	2	1	3	+0
Konerko, Paul	228	27%	1	26	9	29	1	6	16	0	1	1	-14
Koskie, Corey	97	17%	1	7	4	7	1	1	10	1	0	1	-1
Kotsay, Mark	195	25%	6	24	12	24	2	5	15	4	0	4	-10
Kubel, Jason	60	25%	2	7	2	4	2	4	1	0	2	2	-8
Laird, Gerald	98	39%	3	12	7	10	2	6	11	0	0	0	+11
Lamb, Mike	149	38%	5	19	9	14	2	6	12	0	0	0	+11
Lane, Jason	99	29%	5	11	6	8	5	7	7	0	1	1	+5
Langerhans, Ryan	135	28%	1	13	13	13	2	4	5	0	0	0	+2
LaRoche, Adam	175	32%	3	24	12	19	1	5	14	0	0	0	+5
LaRue, Jason	74	18%	1	7	3	6	0	2	3	0	0	0	-5
Lee, Carlos	237	27%	9	24	13	27	2	11	19	1	1	2	-1
Lee, Derrek	69	31%	1	10	3	6	0	0	6	0	0	0	+1
Lee, Travis	116	20%	2	8	4	11	0	2	10	0	1	1	-5
Lieberthal, Mike	72	18%	1	9	1	8	0	1	7	1	1	2	-10
Lo Duca, Paul	203	36%	5	27	9	19	0	4	15	1	2	3	-3
Lofton, Kenny	214	35%	4	23	15	23	4	7	20	2	3	5	+1
Lopez, Felipe	262	33%	2	26	14	18	3	4	26	0	1	1	+15
Lopez, Javy	116	24%	1	11	6	14	0	3	4	2	0	3	-17
Lopez, Jose	227	29%	7	20	11	18	5	7	17	1	2	3	+3
Loretta, Mark	256	27%	10	26	9	18	1	9	30	2	1	3	+7
Lowell, Mike	227	25%	5	21	7	20	1	7	17	2	2	4	-14
Lugo, Julio	168	33%	7	22	12	17	0	4	18	0	2	2	+9
Luna, Hector	135	25%	3	8	9	13	1	3	8	0	3	3	-6
Mabry, John	65	16%	0	6	1	5	0	1	2	0	0	0	-7
Mackowiak, Rob	113	23%	7	14	3	8	0	0	9	1	1	2	-3
Markakis, Nick	197	28%	7	26	9	18	3	5	20	0	0	0	+11
Martin, Russell	183	30%	5	12	9	20	1	2	14	1	1	2	+0
Martinez, Ramon	75	24%	1	10	2	3	1	2	5	1	0	1	-4
Martinez, Victor	261	25%	3	34	9	20	1	9	15	1	2	3	-20
Matheny, Mike	51	13%	1	2	0	2	1	2	3	0	0	0	-2
Matos, Luis	54	25%	2	6	5	7	0	1	4	0	1	1	-1
Matsui, Hideki	76	31%	1	8	5	9	0	2	7	0	0	0	+2
Matsui, Kaz	87	33%	2	10	6	8	1	2	5	0	0	0	+3
Matthews Jr., Gary	257	32%	5	28	20	30	3	10	20	1	0	1	+7
Mauer, Joe	267	27%	8	32	18	27	2	6	23	0	0	0	+11
McCann, Brian	176	21%	3	17	5	16	0	2	11	1	1	2	-14
McDonald, John	81	39%	4	11	7	9	2	5	13	1	0	1	+12
McLouth, Nate	91	47%	5	9	7	11	1	4	10	0	1	1	+11

2006 Baserunning

Player	On Base	Scored	First to Third Moved	First to Third Chances	Second to Home Moved	Second to Home Chances	First to Home Moved	First to Home Chances	Bases Taken	Out Adv.	Doubled Off	BR Outs	Rating
Mench, Kevin	164	19%	5	16	2	5	2	2	11	0	2	2	-6
Michaels, Jason	188	36%	8	17	12	17	7	11	14	0	1	1	+15
Mientkiewicz, Doug	135	24%	1	11	4	16	3	5	9	1	0	1	-8
Miles, Aaron	167	27%	3	10	7	20	1	5	11	0	2	2	-8
Millar, Kevin	187	26%	1	24	8	18	0	6	15	1	1	3	-14
Milledge, Lastings	58	17%	1	4	1	3	0	1	3	0	0	0	-3
Miller, Damian	120	23%	5	10	7	15	0	2	12	2	0	2	-2
Mirabelli, Doug	53	13%	1	7	0	3	0	1	2	1	0	1	-9
Molina, Bengie	144	17%	1	15	0	7	0	8	10	0	1	1	-15
Molina, Jose	65	21%	1	8	5	9	1	2	4	0	1	1	-5
Molina, Yadier	131	17%	0	6	5	15	1	1	6	1	0	1	-12
Monroe, Craig	168	36%	6	23	14	18	2	3	10	2	1	3	+2
Mora, Melvin	250	32%	14	41	19	31	6	12	10	2	1	3	-3
Morales, Kendry	61	26%	1	7	3	7	1	3	6	2	0	2	-5
Morneau, Justin	228	27%	4	29	11	19	2	6	15	0	1	1	-3
Murton, Matt	205	27%	11	27	10	15	3	7	13	0	0	0	+8
Nady, Xavier	173	23%	3	15	10	20	0	2	7	0	0	0	-7
Napoli, Mike	109	28%	2	8	6	9	3	6	6	1	0	1	-1
Navarro, Dioner	97	22%	3	10	1	6	1	1	5	0	0	0	-3
Nevin, Phil	148	21%	1	16	10	15	0	0	8	0	0	0	-4
Niekro, Lance	66	33%	2	6	4	4	1	1	5	0	0	0	+6
Nixon, Trot	176	28%	5	19	9	19	2	6	12	0	1	1	-1
Norton, Greg	114	26%	2	12	9	11	1	3	10	1	1	2	-1
Nunez, Abraham	131	30%	2	10	10	13	0	2	10	0	1	1	+3
Olivo, Miguel	137	26%	1	8	10	14	0	2	15	0	0	0	+8
Ordonez, Magglio	224	25%	6	21	14	21	2	6	16	1	2	3	-3
Orr, Pete	57	36%	1	5	3	4	3	3	5	0	0	0	+6
Ortiz, David	246	24%	4	26	8	17	2	5	19	0	0	0	+0
Overbay, Lyle	224	26%	8	33	12	19	2	8	12	2	1	3	-10
Ozuna, Pablo	96	23%	4	12	8	9	2	4	5	0	0	0	+3
Pagan, Angel	68	33%	4	10	3	7	1	1	6	0	1	1	+2
Patterson, Corey	169	34%	8	18	18	19	1	2	16	1	1	2	+16
Paul, Josh	65	21%	2	7	3	4	0	0	1	0	2	2	-9
Paulino, Ronny	182	17%	1	16	7	11	2	11	7	0	0	0	-13
Payton, Jay	218	31%	5	19	10	17	3	7	18	1	0	1	+7
Pena, Wily Mo	102	24%	3	10	5	9	2	2	8	0	0	0	+3
Peralta, Jhonny	209	33%	2	20	10	25	3	11	15	1	0	1	-3
Perez, Eduardo	66	19%	1	9	5	8	0	0	2	0	0	0	-4
Perez, Neifi	97	29%	1	9	9	12	3	5	8	0	1	1	+3
Perez, Tomas	71	40%	5	9	4	9	1	3	10	1	0	1	+8
Phillips, Andy	90	25%	1	5	6	9	0	3	7	0	1	1	-2
Phillips, Brandon	201	23%	5	12	7	11	0	0	18	1	3	4	-3
Piazza, Mike	144	11%	0	12	1	2	0	4	4	1	1	3	-24
Pierre, Juan	270	31%	14	28	13	20	1	2	28	1	2	3	+17
Pierzynski, A.J.	180	27%	3	20	8	20	2	4	15	1	0	1	-3
Podsednik, Scott	209	39%	6	21	11	22	4	7	21	0	1	1	+16
Polanco, Placido	176	30%	9	33	8	14	2	5	14	1	0	1	+4
Posada, Jorge	196	21%	2	28	6	21	0	2	10	0	0	0	-16
Pujols, Albert	241	29%	10	17	8	10	4	8	18	1	0	1	+13
Punto, Nick	203	35%	10	30	11	17	4	6	16	0	3	3	+7
Quentin, Carlos	64	21%	3	5	2	4	0	1	3	0	1	1	-3
Quinlan, Robb	93	20%	3	6	6	6	0	1	3	0	0	0	0
Ramirez, Aramis	216	25%	6	22	11	23	2	4	17	1	0	1	+0
Ramirez, Hanley	248	41%	8	23	16	26	2	4	25	0	2	2	+21
Ramirez, Manny	223	19%	6	27	9	14	2	4	14	2	1	3	-11
Randa, Joe	75	25%	2	13	2	6	1	2	9	0	1	1	-1
Redmond, Mike	76	26%	1	8	2	7	1	3	8	1	0	1	-2
Reed, Jeremy	61	34%	3	4	6	8	0	0	5	0	0	0	+7
Renteria, Edgar	250	34%	10	24	16	20	2	7	23	1	4	5	+9
Repko, Jason	65	27%	3	6	5	6	0	0	8	0	0	0	+8
Reyes, Jose	255	40%	8	19	17	27	6	9	23	1	1	2	+22

300

2006 Baserunning

Player	On Base	Scored	First to Third Moved	First to Third Chances	Second to Home Moved	Second to Home Chances	First to Home Moved	First to Home Chances	Bases Taken	Out Adv.	Doubled Off	BR Outs	Rating
Rios, Alex	175	29%	6	16	12	14	1	2	10	0	1	1	+5
Rivera, Juan	178	23%	6	25	12	20	0	2	8	1	4	5	-19
Roberts, Brian	221	33%	6	13	22	30	0	0	21	0	3	3	+13
Roberts, Dave	219	35%	2	18	21	30	5	9	11	2	2	4	-4
Rodriguez, Alex	250	31%	5	23	17	22	4	5	14	1	1	2	+4
Rodriguez, Ivan	196	31%	5	18	16	22	6	6	14	0	0	0	+14
Rodriguez, John	83	34%	1	8	5	6	0	0	4	0	0	0	+2
Rolen, Scott	220	32%	6	23	17	26	2	5	19	1	0	1	+11
Rollins, Jimmy	248	41%	8	36	22	36	4	7	22	2	2	4	+9
Ross, Cody	82	24%	5	8	6	10	1	2	9	0	0	0	+8
Ross, Dave	87	18%	1	5	4	7	1	1	3	1	1	2	-10
Rowand, Aaron	153	30%	10	16	4	5	2	4	14	0	1	1	+13
Saenz, Olmedo	69	27%	0	6	1	3	0	2	1	0	0	0	-5
Salmon, Tim	88	23%	5	11	1	3	2	2	6	0	2	2	-3
Sanchez, Freddy	257	30%	9	37	24	33	2	6	25	1	1	2	+12
Sanders, Reggie	113	30%	4	14	7	10	1	4	9	2	0	2	-1
Schneider, Brian	158	16%	3	12	7	15	1	4	12	0	0	0	-4
Scott, Luke	99	21%	1	5	5	10	0	0	5	0	0	0	-3
Scutaro, Marco	159	29%	6	18	7	15	1	7	13	0	3	3	-5
Sexson, Richie	208	19%	3	23	9	21	2	4	12	3	0	3	-19
Shealy, Ryan	73	32%	1	8	5	10	0	1	6	0	0	0	+1
Sheffield, Gary	61	26%	3	6	2	4	0	1	4	0	1	1	-2
Shelton, Chris	131	25%	7	17	4	8	1	3	10	0	1	1	+2
Sizemore, Grady	271	39%	12	37	25	29	2	4	29	0	6	6	+19
Snyder, Chris	74	17%	0	5	3	6	0	2	1	0	2	2	-14
Soriano, Alfonso	233	31%	7	23	20	32	2	4	17	1	1	2	+5
Spiezio, Scott	111	27%	5	10	5	8	0	2	8	0	1	1	+2
Spilborghs, Ryan	61	36%	0	7	4	6	0	1	1	0	2	2	-8
Stairs, Matt	129	22%	3	6	8	10	3	5	5	1	0	2	-5
Stewart, Shannon	73	26%	1	10	2	4	1	2	8	0	1	1	-1
Sullivan, Cory	150	30%	2	13	8	11	0	1	10	2	0	2	-2
Suzuki, Ichiro	296	34%	10	36	13	22	4	14	33	3	5	8	+0
Sweeney, Mark	104	25%	2	11	2	5	1	6	4	0	0	0	-5
Sweeney, Mike	86	17%	1	6	2	7	0	0	7	0	0	0	-3
Swisher, Nick	229	31%	8	25	9	14	3	11	22	2	1	3	+5
Taguchi, So	141	31%	1	14	10	12	5	6	11	1	2	3	0
Taveras, Willy	228	35%	12	22	24	30	6	6	19	0	3	3	+21
Teahen, Mark	157	33%	9	22	11	16	2	3	21	0	0	0	+22
Teixeira, Mark	257	25%	5	19	22	34	2	5	17	3	1	4	-7
Tejada, Miguel	281	26%	9	33	13	26	4	12	21	0	1	1	+1
Thames, Marcus	116	30%	1	17	5	10	1	3	5	0	1	1	-7
Theriot, Ryan	66	46%	3	3	6	8	1	4	6	0	1	1	+7
Thomas, Frank	185	20%	0	23	3	15	2	9	10	0	2	2	-23
Thome, Jim	227	29%	7	28	19	30	1	9	11	1	1	2	-7
Torrealba, Yorvit	77	20%	2	6	4	7	0	0	9	0	2	2	-2
Tracy, Chad	225	31%	4	24	15	26	9	11	21	2	2	4	+3
Treanor, Matt	67	14%	1	3	1	4	0	0	4	0	0	0	-3
Tyner, Jason	95	30%	6	15	5	14	1	4	17	0	1	1	+8
Uggla, Dan	218	35%	10	25	11	15	5	8	15	1	1	2	+12
Upton, B.J.	62	30%	0	3	8	9	0	0	6	0	1	1	+3
Uribe, Juan	122	26%	0	8	6	10	0	3	10	0	1	1	-3
Utley, Chase	262	37%	12	28	20	29	9	11	19	0	0	0	+27
Valentin, Javier	59	27%	4	7	5	6	0	2	2	0	0	0	+2
Valentin, Jose	133	28%	6	12	6	8	0	3	10	1	1	2	+1
Varitek, Jason	136	25%	1	13	6	13	2	6	12	0	0	0	0
Victorino, Shane	178	35%	7	19	7	10	4	6	16	0	1	1	+14
Vidro, Jose	187	24%	7	22	4	12	1	6	14	0	0	2	-6
Vizcaino, Jose	63	26%	4	7	2	4	0	2	4	0	1	1	-1
Vizquel, Omar	240	35%	8	24	12	22	3	6	17	1	0	1	+10
Walker, Todd	184	25%	5	22	6	11	5	7	10	0	1	1	-2
Ward, Daryle	52	19%	0	2	1	3	1	2	3	0	0	0	-2

301

2006 Baserunning

Player	On Base	Scored	First to Third Moved	First to Third Chances	Second to Home Moved	Second to Home Chances	First to Home Moved	First to Home Chances	Bases Taken	Out Adv.	Doubled Off	BR Outs	Rating
Weeks, Rickie	165	39%	9	26	18	19	3	6	16	3	2	5	+9
Wells, Vernon	237	24%	3	12	14	19	3	5	10	0	0	1	-3
White, Rondell	112	22%	6	12	5	10	1	2	8	0	2	2	-3
Wigginton, Ty	151	20%	4	13	7	10	2	6	4	0	2	2	-11
Wilkerson, Brad	104	39%	4	12	5	9	1	6	11	1	0	2	+3
Williams, Bernie	157	33%	3	14	9	14	1	7	10	1	3	4	-8
Willingham, Josh	204	17%	2	15	1	11	2	5	6	3	1	4	-30
Wilson, Craig	121	29%	2	9	3	8	3	6	9	0	0	0	+3
Wilson, Jack	199	31%	4	20	13	19	6	11	17	1	2	3	+3
Wilson, Preston	175	23%	6	17	12	16	1	3	13	0	3	3	-3
Wilson, Vance	51	25%	2	5	2	3	0	2	2	0	0	0	-1
Winn, Randy	219	31%	11	38	18	24	0	4	9	0	3	3	-4
Woodward, Chris	74	29%	4	8	5	7	1	1	2	0	3	3	-7
Wright, David	247	28%	12	23	10	15	5	11	15	0	1	1	+8
Youkilis, Kevin	265	32%	9	36	24	33	0	8	24	1	1	2	+11
Young, Dmitri	54	22%	2	5	3	4	0	1	3	1	0	1	-3
Young, Eric	53	32%	0	4	4	6	0	0	2	0	0	0	0
Young, Michael	286	27%	5	21	17	30	6	11	15	2	1	3	-7
Zaun, Gregg	115	23%	8	21	3	10	1	3	9	1	0	1	-2
Zimmerman, Ryan	244	26%	10	24	10	12	2	6	19	1	1	2	+7
Zobrist, Ben	59	13%	3	7	1	4	0	0	2	0	0	0	-4

Pitchers Hitting, Fielding & Holding Runners, and Hitters Pitching

Have you ever wondered how a pitcher performed at the plate? What about how position players do in the rare occasions when they are called on to pitch? All of this information can be found in the forthcoming pages. Pitchers have their 2006 and career hitting statistics present, as well as their 2006 fielding statistics and data on how well they held runners in 2006. All active position players who have pitched have their career pitching statistics listed, as well as any 2006 pitching statistics that they may have accrued.

Pitchers Hitting, Fielding and Holding Runners

Pitcher	T	2006 Hitting						Career Hitting										2006 Fielding and Holding Runners											
		Avg	AB	H	HR	RBI	SH	Avg	AB	H	2B	3B	HR	RBI	BB	SO	SH	G	Inn	PO	A	E	DP	Pct	SBA	CS	PCS	PPO	CS%
Aardsma,David, ChC	R	.000	2	0	0	0	1	.000	2	0	0	0	0	0	0	0	1	45	53.0	1	5	0	1	1.000	5	0	0	0	.00
Abreu,Winston, Bal	R	-	0	0	0	0	0	-	0	0	0	0	0	0	0	0	0	7	8.0	1	0	0	0	1.000	0	0	0	0	-
Accardo,Jeremy, SF-Tor	R	.000	5	0	0	0	0	.143	7	1	0	0	0	0	0	1	0	65	69.0	2	12	0	0	1.000	7	1	0	0	.14
Adams,Mike, Mil	R	-	0	0	0	0	0	-	0	0	0	0	0	0	0	0	0	2	2.1	0	0	0		-	1	0	0	0	.00
Adkins,Jon, SD	R	.000	1	0	0	0	0	.000	1	0	0	0	0	0	0	1	0	55	54.1	1	12	1	2	.929	3	1	0	0	.33
Affeldt,Jeremy, KC-Col	L	.000	3	0	0	0	0	.222	9	2	0	0	0	2	1	2	0	54	97.1	1	13	1		.933	8	0	0	0	.00
Albers,Matt, Hou	R	.000	4	0	0	0	0	.000	4	0	0	0	0	0	0	3	0	4	15.0	4	4	0	1	1.000	1	0	0	0	.00
Alfonseca,Ant, Tex	R	-	0	0	0	0	0	.154	13	2	0	0	0	2	0	8	1	19	16.0	1	3	0		1.000	1	1	0	0	1.00
Alvarez,Abe, Bos	L	.000	1	0	0	0	0	.000	1	0	0	0	0	0	0	1	0	1	3.0	0	0	0	0	-	0	0	0	0	-
Andrade,Steve, KC	R	-	0	0	0	0	0	-	0	0	0	0	0	0	0	0	0	4	4.2	0	1	0		1.000	1	0	0	0	.00
Aquino,Greg, Ari	R	.000	1	0	0	0	0	.000	2	0	0	0	0	0	0	0	0	42	48.1	5	6	0	2	1.000	4	1	0	0	.25
Armas Jr.,Tony, Was	R	.060	50	3	0	1	5	.096	239	23	1	1	0	8	4	87	25	30	154.0	7	20	0	0	1.000	13	2	0	0	.15
Arroyo,Bronson, Cin	R	.111	81	9	2	6	10	.096	136	13	5	0	2	7	4	64	13	35	240.2	29	33	0	4	1.000	10	5	0	0	.50
Asencio,Miguel, Col	R	.000	3	0	0	0	0	.000	5	0	0	0	0	0	0	3	0	3	7.2	2	0	0	0	1.000	1	0	0	0	.00
Astacio,Ezeq, Hou	R	-	0	0	0	0	0	.143	21	3	0	0	0	0	0	12	0	6	5.2	1	1	0	0	1.000	1	0	0	0	.00
Astacio,Pedro, Was	R	.200	25	5	0	0	7	.133	676	90	7	1	0	28	5	256	89	17	90.1	6	16	0	1	1.000	5	1	0	0	.20
Backe,Brandon, Hou	R	.143	14	2	0	0	0	.227	75	17	2	2	1	12	5	26	8	8	43.0	5	4	0	1	1.000	1	1	0	1	1.00
Baek,Cha Seung, Sea	R	-	0	0	0	0	0	-	0	0	0	0	0	0	0	0	0	6	34.1	5	4	1	0	.900	2	1	0	0	.50
Baez,Danys, LAD-Atl	R	-	0	0	0	0	0	.000	3	0	0	0	0	0	0	0	0	57	59.2	7	9	1		.941	7	2	0	0	.29
Bajenaru,Jeff, Ari	R	-	0	0	0	0	0	-	0	0	0	0	0	0	0	0	0	1	1.0	0	1	0	0	1.000	0	0	0	0	-
Baker,Scott, Min	R	.000	3	0	0	0	0	.000	3	0	0	0	0	0	0	3	0	16	83.1	5	6	0	0	1.000	8	3	0	0	.38
Bannister,Brian, NYM	R	.333	12	4	0	2	1	.333	12	4	3	0	0	2	0	3	1	8	38.0	1	4	0	0	1.000	8	1	0	0	.13
Barry,Kevin, Atl	R	.000	2	0	0	0	0	.000	2	0	0	0	0	0	0	1	0	19	25.2	3	7	0	0	1.000	5	0	0	0	.00
Barzilla,Phil, Hou	L	-	0	0	0	0	0	-	0	0	0	0	0	0	0	0	0	1	0.1	0	0	0	0	-	0	0	0	0	-
Batista,Miguel, Ari	R	.100	60	6	0	4	9	.095	284	27	5	0	2	9	11	160	23	34	206.1	12	34	4	2	.920	22	7	2	0	.32
Bauer,Rick, Tex	R	-	0	0	0	0	0	-	0	0	0	0	0	0	0	0	0	58	71.0	4	5	1	2	.900	6	2	0	0	.33
Bautista,Denny, KC-Col	R	.000	1	0	0	0	0	.000	1	0	0	0	0	0	0	0	0	12	41.2	7	6	0	0	1.000	4	2	1	0	.50
Bayliss,Jonah, Pit	R	-	0	0	0	0	0	-	0	0	0	0	0	0	0	0	0	11	14.2	0	1	0	0	1.000	2	0	0	0	.00
Beam,T.J., NYY	R	.000	1	0	0	0	0	.000	1	0	0	0	0	0	0	1	0	20	18.0	1	1	0	0	1.000	1	0	0	0	.00
Bean,Colter, NYY	R	-	0	0	0	0	0	-	0	0	0	0	0	0	0	0	0	2	2.0	0	0	0	0	-	1	0	0	0	.00
Beckett,Josh, Bos	R	.429	7	3	1	3	0	.149	194	29	8	0	2	14	10	73	25	33	204.2	14	24	0	3	1.000	16	1	0	0	.06
Bedard,Erik, Bal	L	.000	2	0	0	0	0	.000	6	0	0	0	0	0	1	3	0	33	196.1	7	26	1	0	.971	6	2	0	0	.33
Beimel,Joe, LAD	L	.000	1	0	0	0	0	.238	42	10	1	0	0	1	2	16	6	62	70.0	4	25	1	1	.967	7	4	3	3	.57
Belisle,Matt, Cin	R	.000	5	0	0	0	2	.077	13	1	0	0	0	0	0	6	3	30	40.0	1	5	0	0	1.000	1	0	0	0	.00
Bell,Heath, NYM	R	.000	1	0	0	0	0	.000	5	0	0	0	0	0	0	2	0	22	37.0	0	7	0	1	1.000	4	2	0	0	.50
Benitez,Armando, SF	R	-	0	0	0	0	0	.000	8	0	0	0	0	2	0	4	0	41	38.1	1	2	0	0	1.000	6	0	0	0	.00
Benoit,Joaquin, Tex	R	-	0	0	0	0	0	.000	9	0	0	0	0	0	0	4	0	56	79.2	4	4	0	0	1.000	1	0	0	0	.00
Benson,Kris, Bal	R	.111	9	1	1	2	0	.130	316	41	7	0	1	22	15	126	46	30	183.0	15	25	2	2	.952	18	6	0	0	.33
Bergmann,Jason, Was	R	.000	8	0	0	0	2	.091	11	1	0	0	0	0	2	2	0	29	64.2	5	4	0	0	1.000	2	1	0	0	.50
Bernero,Adam, Phi-KC	R	-	0	0	0	0	0	.063	16	1	0	0	0	0	0	9	3	4	15.0	0	1	0	0	1.000	1	0	0	0	.00
Betancourt,Raf, Cle	R	-	0	0	0	0	0	-	0	0	0	0	0	0	0	0	0	50	56.2	2	1	0	0	1.000	10	2	0	0	.20
Billingsley,Chad, LAD	R	.083	24	2	0	2	1	.083	24	2	0	0	0	2	2	15	1	18	90.0	2	7	0	1	1.000	10	5	0	1	.50
Birkins,Kurt, Bal	L	-	0	0	0	0	0	-	0	0	0	0	0	0	0	0	0	35	31.0	0	7	0	1	1.000	1	1	1	0	1.00
Blanton,Joe, Oak	R	.000	2	0	0	0	1	.200	5	1	0	0	0	0	0	1	2	32	194.1	13	14	4	0	.871	18	5	1	0	.28
Bonderman,Jer, Det	R	.000	4	0	0	0	0	.000	19	0	0	0	0	0	0	12	0	34	214.0	13	16	1	0	.967	16	2	1	0	.13
Bonser,Boof, Min	R	.000	3	0	0	0	1	.000	3	0	0	0	0	0	0	0	0	18	100.1	4	9	0	0	1.000	7	3	0	2	.43
Booker,Chris, KC-Was	R	-	0	0	0	0	0	-	0	0	0	0	0	0	0	0	0	11	8.1	0	0	0	0	-	1	0	0	0	.00
Bootcheck,Chris, LAA	R	-	0	0	0	0	0	-	0	0	0	0	0	0	0	0	0	7	10.1	0	2	0	0	1.000	0	0	0	0	-
Borkowski,Dave, Hou	R	.000	5	0	0	0	0	.000	5	0	0	0	0	0	0	1	0	40	71.0	8	7	0	0	1.000	1	0	0	0	.00
Borowski,Joe, Fla	R	-	0	0	0	0	0	.222	9	2	0	0	0	0	0	7	1	72	69.2	1	3	1	0	.800	5	1	0	0	.20
Bowie,Micah, Was	L	.000	1	0	0	0	0	.200	15	3	0	0	0	3	1	3	0	15	19.2	1	4	0	0	1.000	0	0	0	0	-
Boyer,Blaine, Atl	R	-	0	0	0	0	0	-	0	0	0	0	0	0	0	0	0	2	0.2	0	0	0	0	-	0	0	0	0	-
Bradford,Chad, NYM	R	-	0	0	0	0	0	-	0	0	0	0	0	0	0	0	0	70	62.0	3	10	0	0	1.000	3	0	0	0	.00
Braun,Ryan, KC	R	-	0	0	0	0	0	-	0	0	0	0	0	0	0	0	0	9	10.2	0	0	1	0	.000	1	1	0	0	1.00
Bray,Bill, Was-Cin	L	.000	1	0	0	0	0	.000	1	0	0	0	0	0	0	1	0	48	50.2	1	6	1	0	.875	2	1	0	0	.50
Brazelton,Dewon, SD	R	.250	4	1	0	1	0	.167	6	1	1	0	0	1	0	2	0	9	18.0	0	2	1	0	.667	3	0	0	0	.00
Brazoban,Yhency, LAD	R	-	0	0	0	0	0	.000	3	0	0	0	0	0	0	2	0	5	5.0	1	0	0	0	1.000	1	0	0	0	.00
Breslow,Craig, Bos	L	-	0	0	0	0	0	.000	1	0	0	0	0	0	0	0	0	13	12.0	0	1	0	0	1.000	2	0	0	0	.00
Brito,Eude, Phi	L	.000	6	0	0	0	0	.077	13	1	0	0	0	0	1	6	0	5	18.1	2	2	0	0	1.000	1	0	0	0	.00
Britton,Chris, Bal	R	-	0	0	0	0	0	-	0	0	0	0	0	0	0	0	0	52	53.2	0	4	0	0	1.000	7	1	0	0	.14
Brocail,Doug, SD	R	-	0	0	0	0	0	-	0	0	0	0	0	0	0	0	0	25	28.1	9	4	0	1	1.000	1	0	0	0	.00
Brower,Jim, Bal-SD	R	-	0	0	0	0	0	.203	59	12	1	0	0	4	1	20	4	18	20.0	1	1	0	0	1.000	2	1	0	0	.50
Brown,Andrew, Cle	R	-	0	0	0	0	0	-	0	0	0	0	0	0	0	0	0	9	10.0	0	2	0	0	1.000	0	0	0	0	-
Broxton,Jon, LAD	R	.000	2	0	0	0	1	.000	2	0	0	0	0	0	1	2	1	68	76.1	0	5	0	0	1.000	7	2	0	0	.29
Bruney,Brian, NYY	R	-	0	0	0	0	0	.000	1	0	0	0	0	0	0	0	0	19	20.2	1	2	0	1	1.000	2	1	0	0	.00
Buchholz,Taylor, Hou	R	.033	30	1	0	0	4	.033	30	1	0	0	0	0	1	11	4	22	113.0	15	8	0	0	1.000	12	1	0	0	.08
Buehrle,Mark, CWS	L	.000	4	0	0	0	1	.080	25	2	0	0	0	1	1	13	3	32	204.0	9	35	1	3	.978	11	7	4	6	.64
Bulger,Jason, LAA	R	-	0	0	0	0	0	-	0	0	0	0	0	0	0	0	0	2	1.2	0	0	0	0	-	0	0	0	0	-

Pitchers Hitting, Fielding and Holding Runners

Pitcher	T	2006 Hitting						Career Hitting										2006 Fielding and Holding Runners											
		Avg	AB	H	HR	RBI	SH	Avg	AB	H	2B	3B	HR	RBI	BB	SO	SH	G	Inn	PO	A	E	DP	Pct	SBA	CS	PCS	PPO	CS%
Burgos,Ambiorix, KC	R	-	0	0	0	0	0	-	0	0	0	0	0	0	0	0	0	68	73.1	0	8	0	1	1.000	5	0	0	0	.00
Burnett,A.J., Tor	R	.000	3	0	0	0	0	.133	256	34	6	3	3	9	12	124	33	21	135.2	6	16	1	2	.957	22	4	0	1	.18
Burns,Mike, Cin-Bos	R	-	0	0	0	0	0	-	0	0	0	0	0	0	0	0	0	18	21.0	2	2	0	1	1.000	1	1	0	0	1.00
Burres,Brian, Bal	L	-	0	0	0	0	0	-	0	0	0	0	0	0	0	0	0	11	8.0	1	0	0	0	1.000	2	0	0	0	.00
Bush,David, Mil	R	.177	62	11	0	9	9	.172	64	11	3	0	0	9	0	25	9	34	210.0	16	29	1	2	.978	26	8	1	0	.31
Byrd,Paul, Cle	R	.250	4	1	0	0	2	.161	149	24	0	0	0	10	12	37	27	31	179.0	10	16	5	4	.839	23	5	0	1	.22
Byrdak,Tim, Bal	L	-	0	0	0	0	0	-	0	0	0	0	0	0	0	0	0	16	7.0	0	1	1	0	.500	0	0	0	0	-
Cabrera,Daniel, Bal	R	.000	1	0	0	0	1	.000	6	0	0	0	0	0	0	6	1	26	148.0	4	13	0	2	1.000	16	5	0	0	.31
Cabrera,Fern, Cle	R	-	0	0	0	0	0	-	0	0	0	0	0	0	0	0	0	51	60.2	2	7	0	0	1.000	17	6	2	0	.35
Cain,Matt, SF	R	.140	57	8	0	1	8	.125	72	9	3	0	0	1	1	34	9	32	190.2	17	15	3	0	.914	18	3	0	0	.17
Calero,Kiko, Oak	R	-	0	0	0	0	0	.167	6	1	0	0	0	0	1	2	0	70	58.0	1	5	1	0	.857	9	3	3	0	.33
Camp,Shawn, TB	R	-	0	0	0	0	0	-	0	0	0	0	0	0	0	0	0	75	75.0	6	13	1	2	.950	8	2	0	0	.25
Campbell,Brett, Was	R	-	0	0	0	0	0	-	0	0	0	0	0	0	0	0	0	4	4.1	0	0	0	0	-	2	1	0	0	.50
Campillo,Jorge, Sea	R	-	0	0	0	0	0	-	0	0	0	0	0	0	0	0	0	1	2.1	1	0	0	0	1.000	0	0	0	0	-
Capellan,Jose, Mil	R	.000	2	0	0	0	0	.000	4	0	0	0	0	0	0	3	0	61	71.2	0	7	0	0	1.000	13	3	0	0	.23
Capps,Matt, Pit	R	.000	2	0	0	0	0	.000	2	0	0	0	0	0	1	1	0	85	80.2	4	10	2	0	.875	6	3	0	0	.50
Capuano,Chris, Mil	L	.118	68	8	0	3	5	.147	177	26	6	0	0	14	5	83	10	34	221.1	14	31	2	1	.957	4	3	2	4	.75
Carmona,Fausto, Cle	R	-	0	0	0	0	0	-	0	0	0	0	0	0	0	0	0	38	74.2	9	15	0	1	1.000	12	2	1	0	.17
Carpenter,Chris, StL	R	.127	71	9	0	2	9	.095	221	21	2	0	0	5	7	76	25	32	221.2	11	25	0	3	1.000	10	7	0	0	.70
Carrara,Giov, LAD	R	-	0	0	0	0	0	.097	31	3	0	0	0	0	1	11	4	25	27.2	2	2	0	0	1.000	4	0	0	0	.00
Carrasco,Hector, LAA	R	-	0	0	0	0	0	.038	26	1	0	0	0	0	0	19	2	56	100.1	6	19	2	2	.926	2	0	0	0	.00
Carter,Lance, LAD	R	-	0	0	0	0	0	-	0	0	0	0	0	0	0	0	0	10	11.2	0	4	0	0	1.000	0	0	0	0	-
Casilla,Santiago, Oak	R	-	0	0	0	0	0	-	0	0	0	0	0	0	0	0	0	2	2.1	0	1	1	0	.500	1	0	0	0	.00
Cassidy,Scott, SD	R	.000	1	0	0	0	0	.000	2	0	0	0	0	0	1	2	0	42	42.2	1	7	0	0	1.000	5	4	1	0	.80
Castro,Fabio, Tex-Phi	L	.000	2	0	0	0	0	.000	2	0	0	0	0	0	0	1	0	20	31.2	0	6	1	1	.857	1	0	0	0	.00
Chacin,Gustavo, Tor	L	-	0	0	0	0	0	.000	7	0	0	0	0	0	0	2	1	17	87.1	4	8	0	0	1.000	5	0	0	0	.00
Chacon,Shawn, NYY-Pit	R	.067	15	1	0	1	2	.147	163	24	4	0	1	10	3	66	16	26	109.0	3	17	1	2	.952	11	2	0	0	.18
Chen,Bruce, Bal	L	1.000	1	1	0	0	0	.130	115	15	1	0	0	3	2	53	17	40	98.2	6	12	0	1	1.000	15	6	3	0	.40
Chick,Travis, Sea	R	-	0	0	0	0	0	-	0	0	0	0	0	0	0	0	0	3	5.0	0	0	0	0	-	0	0	0	0	-
Childers,Jason, TB	R	-	0	0	0	0	0	-	0	0	0	0	0	0	0	0	0	5	7.2	1	1	1	0	.667	1	0	0	0	.00
Choate,Randy, Ari	L	-	0	0	0	0	0	.000	5	0	0	0	0	0	0	3	0	30	16.0	0	5	0	1	1.000	0	0	0	0	-
Chulk,Vinnie, Tor-SF	R	.000	1	0	0	0	0	.000	1	0	0	0	0	0	0	0	0	48	46.1	3	5	0	0	1.000	1	0	0	0	.00
Claussen,Bran, Cin	L	.095	21	2	0	1	3	.101	99	10	0	0	0	2	4	40	11	14	77.0	7	14	0	1	1.000	10	3	2	0	.30
Clemens,Roger, Hou	R	.074	27	2	0	0	7	.169	177	30	6	0	0	12	13	61	18	19	113.1	4	15	1	3	.950	16	2	0	0	.13
Clement,Matt, Bos	R	.333	3	1	0	0	0	.095	348	33	5	1	0	12	14	174	43	12	65.1	6	4	0	0	1.000	2	1	0	0	.50
Coffey,Todd, Cin	R	-	0	0	0	0	0	.000	3	0	0	0	0	0	0	3	0	81	78.0	2	7	0	0	1.000	2	2	0	0	1.00
Colome,Jesus, TB	R	-	0	0	0	0	0	.000	1	0	0	0	0	0	0	1	1	1	0.1	0	0	0	0	-	0	0	0	0	-
Colon,Bartolo, LAA	R	.000	1	0	0	0	1	.125	80	10	0	0	0	5	0	47	5	10	56.1	4	7	1	0	.917	4	3	0	0	.75
Colon,Roman, Det	R	-	0	0	0	0	0	.000	7	0	0	0	0	0	0	5	1	20	38.2	2	4	0	0	1.000	2	2	0	0	1.00
Condrey,Clay, Phi	R	.000	2	0	0	0	0	.111	18	2	0	0	0	0	0	10	0	21	28.2	2	4	0	0	1.000	2	1	1	0	.50
Contreras,Jose, CWS	R	.000	4	0	0	0	0	.000	18	0	0	0	0	0	3	11	0	30	196.0	8	21	2	1	.935	27	6	0	0	.22
Cook,Aaron, Col	R	.052	58	3	0	0	13	.111	162	18	0	1	0	5	8	53	22	32	212.2	22	45	2	4	.971	12	5	1	1	.42
Corcoran,Roy, Was	R	.000	1	0	0	0	0	.000	2	0	0	0	0	0	1	2	0	6	5.2	0	1	0	0	1.000	1	0	0	0	.00
Corcoran,Tim, TB	R	.000	4	0	0	0	1	.000	4	0	0	0	0	0	0	3	1	21	90.1	7	10	0	1	1.000	16	6	0	0	.38
Cordero,Chad, Was	R	.000	2	0	0	0	0	.000	4	0	0	0	0	0	0	3	2	68	73.1	2	10	1	0	.923	4	1	0	0	.25
Cordero,Franc, Tex-Mil	R	-	0	0	0	0	0	.000	1	0	0	0	0	0	0	1	0	77	75.1	5	6	1	1	1.000	6	2	0	0	.33
Corey,Bryan, Tex-Bos	R	-	0	0	0	0	0	-	0	0	0	0	0	0	0	0	0	32	39.0	1	6	1	0	.875	1	0	0	0	.00
Cormier,Lance, Atl	R	.083	12	1	0	0	2	.192	26	5	1	0	0	2	1	7	4	29	73.2	3	8	0	0	1.000	8	3	0	0	.38
Cormier,Rheal, Phi-Cin	L	-	0	0	0	0	0	.188	192	36	4	1	0	12	5	45	30	64	48.0	7	13	0	2	1.000	1	0	0	0	.00
Corpas,Manuel, Col	R	-	0	0	0	0	0	-	0	0	0	0	0	0	0	0	0	35	32.1	1	0	0	0	1.000	4	1	0	0	.25
Correia,Kevin, SF	R	.083	12	1	0	0	0	.119	42	5	1	0	0	2	4	19	2	48	69.2	3	3	0	0	1.000	6	3	1	0	.50
Cortes,David, Col	R	-	0	0	0	0	0	.000	2	0	0	0	0	0	0	0	0	30	29.1	1	5	0	0	1.000	0	0	0	0	-
Cotts,Neal, CWS	L	-	0	0	0	0	0	1.000	1	1	1	0	0	0	0	0	0	70	54.0	4	9	0	1	1.000	2	0	0	0	.00
Crain,Jesse, Min	R	-	0	0	0	0	0	-	0	0	0	0	0	0	0	0	0	68	76.2	8	8	1	0	.941	5	1	0	0	.20
Cruceta,Franc, Sea	R	-	0	0	0	0	0	-	0	0	0	0	0	0	0	0	0	4	6.2	1	1	0	0	1.000	0	0	0	0	-
Cruz,Juan, Ari	R	.000	21	0	0	0	2	.118	68	8	1	1	0	2	4	26	7	31	94.2	8	10	2	1	.900	10	3	0	0	.30
Daigle,Casey, Ari	R	.000	1	0	0	0	0	.111	18	2	2	0	0	0	0	8	1	10	12.1	0	1	0	0	1.000	0	0	0	0	-
Davies,Kyle, Atl	R	.043	23	1	1	1	1	.105	38	4	0	0	1	5	2	11	11	14	63.1	3	5	0	0	1.000	5	1	0	1	.20
Davis,Doug, Mil	L	.046	65	3	0	2	11	.071	226	16	3	1	0	5	3	111	21	34	203.1	6	25	1	3	.969	19	4	2	0	.21
Davis,Jason, Cle	R	-	0	0	0	0	0	.111	9	1	0	0	1	1	0	5	2	39	55.1	4	6	1	0	.909	5	1	0	0	.20
Day,Zach, Col-Was	R	.000	12	0	0	0	2	.057	105	6	0	0	1	3	2	51	9	8	40.0	1	4	0	1	1.000	10	1	0	0	.10
de la Rosa,Jor, Mil-KC	L	.000	5	0	0	0	0	.000	11	0	0	0	0	0	0	10	1	28	79.0	3	6	1	0	.900	11	1	1	0	.09
DeJean,Mike, Col	R	-	0	0	0	0	0	.059	17	1	1	0	0	0	0	10	1	2	1.2	0	0	0	0	-	0	0	0	0	-
Delcarmen,Manny, Bos	R	-	0	0	0	0	0	-	0	0	0	0	0	0	0	0	0	50	53.1	4	5	0	0	1.000	5	0	0	0	.00
Demaria,Chris, Mil	R	-	0	0	0	0	0	-	0	0	0	0	0	0	0	0	0	10	13.2	1	1	1	0	.667	0	0	0	0	-
Dempster,Ryan, ChC	R	.000	2	0	0	0	0	.077	313	24	5	1	0	7	6	135	32	74	75.0	3	8	1	0	.917	5	0	0	0	.00
Dessens,Elmer, KC-LAD	R	.000	1	0	0	0	0	.167	234	39	4	1	0	16	20	63	37	62	77.0	3	13	0	0	1.000	5	2	0	0	.40
Devine,Joey, Atl	R	-	0	0	0	0	0	.000	1	0	0	0	0	0	0	1	0	10	6.1	0	0	0	0	-	0	0	0	0	-
Diaz,Joselo, KC	R	-	0	0	0	0	0	-	0	0	0	0	0	0	0	0	0	4	6.2	1	0	0	1	1.000	0	0	0	0	-
Dickey,R.A., Tex	R	-	0	0	0	0	0	1.000	1	1	0	0	0	0	0	0	0	1	3.1	0	0	0	0	-	0	0	0	0	-

Pitchers Hitting, Fielding and Holding Runners

Pitcher	T	2006 Hitting						Career Hitting										2006 Fielding and Holding Runners											
		Avg	AB	H	HR	RBI	SH	Avg	AB	H	2B	3B	HR	RBI	BB	SO	SH	G	Inn	PO	A	E	DP	Pct	SBA	CS	PCS	PPO	CS%
DiNardo,Lenny, Bos	L	.000	1	0	0	0	0	.000	1	0	0	0	0	0	0	1	0	13	39.0	0	6	2	1	.750	1	1	0	0	1.00
Dohmann,Scott, Col-KC	R	.000	1	0	0	0	0	.000	3	0	0	0	0	0	0	2	1	48	48.1	1	2	0	0	1.000	5	1	0	0	.20
Donnelly,Brend, LAA	R	-	0	0	0	0	0	.000	1	0	0	0	0	0	0	0	0	62	64.0	3	3	1	0	.857	1	0	0	0	.00
Dotel,Octavio, NYY	R	-	0	0	0	0	0	.068	74	5	0	0	0	1	5	42	9	14	10.0	0	2	0	0	1.000	1	0	0	0	.00
Downs,Scott, Tor	L	-	0	0	0	0	0	.068	44	3	0	0	0	1	3	17	10	59	77.0	6	15	0	1	1.000	2	1	0	0	.50
Drese,Ryan, Was	R	.000	3	0	0	0	0	.120	25	3	1	0	0	1	14	6	2	8.2	0	1	0	0	1.000	3	2	1	0	.67
DuBose,Eric, Bal	L	-	0	0	0	0	0	.000	2	0	0	0	0	0	0	2	0	2	4.2	0	1	0	1	1.000	0	0	0	0	-
Duchscherer,J, Oak	R	-	0	0	0	0	0	-	0	0	0	0	0	0	0	0	0	53	55.2	4	12	0	0	1.000	6	1	0	2	.17
Duckworth,Br, KC	R	.333	3	1	0	0	0	.214	112	24	4	0	8	10	22	10	10	45.2	5	3	0	0	1.000	1	1	0	1	1.00
Duke,Zach, Pit	L	.191	68	13	0	7	9	.177	96	17	3	0	8	3	42	9	34	215.1	8	52	1	3	.984	25	12	7	0	.48
Dunn,Scott, TB	R	-	0	0	0	0	0	-	0	0	0	0	0	0	0	0	0	7	7.2	0	0	0	0	-	0	0	0	0	-
Durbin,Chad, Det	R	-	0	0	0	0	0	.000	2	0	0	0	0	0	0	0	1	3	6.0	0	0	0	0	-	0	0	0	0	-
Eaton,Adam, Tex	R	-	0	0	0	0	0	.191	251	48	13	1	2	19	24	85	17	13	65.0	4	5	0	1	1.000	7	5	0	0	.71
Eischen,Joey, Was	L	.000	2	0	0	0	1	.179	28	5	1	0	0	1	1	12	1	22	14.2	1	1	0	0	1.000	3	0	0	0	.00
Elarton,Scott, KC	R	.333	3	1	0	0	1	.140	164	23	3	0	0	3	5	52	28	20	114.2	3	13	0	0	1.000	7	3	0	2	.43
Embree,Alan, SD	L	.000	1	0	0	0	0	.000	3	0	0	0	0	0	1	2	0	73	52.1	3	3	1	0	.857	13	1	0	0	.08
Erickson,Scott, NYY	R	-	0	0	0	0	0	.114	35	4	1	0	0	1	4	15	5	9	11.1	0	2	0	0	1.000	2	0	0	0	.00
Escobar,Kelvim, LAA	R	.000	4	0	0	0	0	.048	21	1	0	0	0	1	0	11	1	30	189.1	7	18	0	2	1.000	24	10	0	0	.42
Estes,Shawn, SD	L	.000	1	0	0	0	0	.157	489	77	14	2	4	28	15	163	73	1	6.0	0	0	0	0	-	0	0	0	0	-
Etherton,Seth, KC	R	-	0	0	0	0	0	.111	9	1	0	0	0	0	1	2	3	2	7.2	0	0	0	0	-	0	0	0	0	-
Eveland,Dana, Mil	L	.000	7	0	0	0	1	.000	8	0	0	0	0	0	0	4	2	9	27.2	0	2	0	0	1.000	7	2	1	0	.29
Eyre,Scott, ChC	L	.000	1	0	0	0	0	.167	12	2	0	0	0	0	1	6	0	74	61.1	1	8	0	0	1.000	5	1	0	0	.20
Eyre,Willie, Min	R	.000	1	0	0	0	0	.000	1	0	0	0	0	0	0	1	0	42	59.1	3	5	0	0	1.000	2	1	0	0	.50
Falkenborg,Br, StL	R	.000	1	0	0	0	0	.000	3	0	0	0	0	0	1	3	0	5	6.1	0	1	0	0	1.000	1	1	0	0	1.00
Farnsworth,Kyle, NYY	R	-	0	0	0	0	0	.074	54	4	1	0	0	3	2	18	8	72	66.0	3	7	0	0	1.000	8	2	0	0	.25
Fassero,Jeff, SF	L	.250	4	1	0	0	1	.083	276	23	2	1	0	6	18	151	45	10	15.0	2	3	0	0	1.000	1	1	1	0	1.00
Feierabend,Ryan, Sea	L	-	0	0	0	0	0	-	0	0	0	0	0	0	0	0	0	4	17.0	3	2	0	0	1.000	1	1	1	0	1.00
Feldman,Scott, Tex	R	-	0	0	0	0	0	-	0	0	0	0	0	0	0	0	0	36	41.1	1	11	3	1	.800	3	1	0	0	.33
Feliciano,Pedro, NYM	L	.000	0	0	0	0	0	.000	6	0	0	0	0	0	1	2	1	64	60.1	3	7	2	0	.833	1	1	0	1	1.00
Fernandez,Jared, Mil	R	-	0	0	0	0	0	.095	21	2	0	0	0	1	1	10	3	4	6.1	0	2	0	0	1.000	0	0	0	0	-
Field,Nate, Col	R	-	0	0	0	0	0	-	0	0	0	0	0	0	0	0	0	14	9.0	0	0	0	0	-	0	0	0	0	-
Flores,Randy, StL	L	-	0	0	0	0	0	.000	7	0	0	0	0	0	0	4	0	65	41.2	1	8	0	1	1.000	3	2	1	0	.67
Flores,Ron, Oak	L	.000	1	0	0	0	0	.000	1	0	0	0	0	0	0	0	0	25	29.2	1	2	0	0	1.000	1	0	0	0	.00
Floyd,Gavin, Phi	R	.043	23	1	0	0	0	.048	42	2	0	0	0	0	0	22	0	11	54.1	4	6	1	0	.909	13	2	1	0	.15
Fogg,Josh, Col	R	.098	51	5	0	2	15	.116	251	29	3	0	0	10	10	84	41	31	172.0	11	29	3	1	.930	14	6	2	0	.43
Fortunato,Bart, NYM	R	-	0	0	0	0	0	-	0	0	0	0	0	0	0	0	0	2	3.0	1	0	0	0	1.000	0	0	0	0	-
Fossum,Casey, TB	L	.000	2	0	0	0	0	.087	46	4	0	0	0	0	1	16	4	25	130.0	6	21	1	0	.964	15	3	2	0	.20
Foulke,Keith, Bos	R	-	0	0	0	0	0	.125	16	2	0	0	0	0	0	5	2	44	49.2	1	5	1	0	.857	1	0	0	0	.00
Francis,Jeff, Col	L	.115	61	7	0	6	9	.101	129	13	2	0	0	10	15	51	19	32	199.0	4	38	0	2	1.000	28	7	4	1	.25
Francisco,Frank, Tex	R	-	0	0	0	0	0	-	0	0	0	0	0	0	0	0	0	8	7.1	2	0	0	0	1.000	1	1	0	0	1.00
Franklin,Ryan, Phi-Cin	R	.000	4	0	0	0	0	.067	15	1	0	0	0	0	2	7	2	66	77.1	4	10	1	0	.933	7	3	0	1	.43
Franklin,Wayne, Atl	L	-	0	0	0	0	0	.157	70	11	1	0	0	5	3	22	12	11	7.2	1	0	0	0	1.000	2	0	0	0	.00
Frasor,Jason, Tor	R	-	0	0	0	0	0	-	0	0	0	0	0	0	0	0	0	51	50.0	4	8	1	0	.923	5	1	0	0	.20
Fruto,Emiliano, Sea	R	-	0	0	0	0	0	-	0	0	0	0	0	0	0	0	0	23	36.0	2	5	0	1	1.000	3	0	0	1	.00
Fuentes,Brian, Col	L	-	0	0	0	0	0	.000	1	0	0	0	0	0	0	0	0	66	65.1	1	6	1	0	.875	4	1	0	0	.25
Fulchino,Jeff, Fla	R	-	0	0	0	0	0	-	0	0	0	0	0	0	0	0	0	1	0.1	1	0	0	0	1.000	0	0	0	0	-
Fultz,Aaron, Phi	L	.000	4	0	0	0	0	.263	19	5	0	0	0	0	0	3	1	66	71.1	2	14	2	1	.889	7	2	0	0	.29
Gabbard,Kason, Bos	L	-	0	0	0	0	0	-	0	0	0	0	0	0	0	0	0	7	25.2	3	1	0	0	1.000	2	1	0	0	.50
Gagne,Eric, LAD	R	-	0	0	0	0	0	.140	86	12	2	1	1	3	1	25	12	2	2.0	0	0	0	0	-	0	0	0	0	-
Gallo,Mike, Hou	L	.000	1	0	0	0	0	.000	4	0	0	0	0	0	0	1	0	23	16.1	0	2	0	0	1.000	1	0	0	0	.00
Garcia,Freddy, CWS	R	.200	5	1	0	0	1	.195	41	8	1	0	0	2	0	12	11	33	216.1	12	18	2	2	.938	42	2	0	0	.05
Garcia,Jose, Fla	R	.500	2	1	0	0	0	.500	2	1	0	0	0	0	0	0	0	5	11.0	0	1	0	0	1.000	0	0	0	0	.00
Garland,Jon, CWS	R	.200	5	1	1	2	2	.176	17	3	0	0	1	3	1	5	5	33	211.1	12	34	3	10	.939	13	7	0	0	.54
Garza,Matt, Min	R	-	0	0	0	0	0	-	0	0	0	0	0	0	0	0	0	10	50.0	5	1	0	0	1.000	2	0	0	0	.00
Gaudin,Chad, Oak	R	-	0	0	0	0	0	.000	1	0	0	0	0	0	0	1	0	55	64.0	4	3	1	0	.875	6	0	0	0	.00
Geary,Geoff, Phi	R	.200	5	1	0	1	0	.167	12	2	1	0	0	1	1	7	0	81	91.1	7	14	1	4	.955	6	2	0	0	.33
German,Franklyn, Fla	R	-	0	0	0	0	0	.000	1	0	0	0	0	0	0	1	0	12	12.0	1	2	0	0	1.000	0	0	0	0	-
Germano,Justin, Cin	R	.000	2	0	0	0	1	.000	9	0	0	0	0	0	0	5	2	2	6.2	1	0	0	0	1.000	0	0	0	0	-
Glavine,Tom, NYM	L	.170	53	9	0	2	10	.186	1248	232	24	2	1	85	92	319	201	32	198.0	11	43	4	3	.931	15	9	2	0	.60
Gobble,Jimmy, KC	L	.000	0	0	0	0	1	.000	2	0	0	0	0	0	0	1	1	60	84.0	4	10	0	1	1.000	6	2	1	0	.33
Gonzalez,Edgar, Ari	R	.077	13	1	0	0	0	.133	30	4	0	0	0	0	6	2	0	11	42.2	0	4	0	0	1.000	4	1	0	0	.25
Gonzalez,Enrique, Ari	R	.281	32	9	0	3	3	.281	32	9	1	0	0	3	0	8	3	22	106.1	8	13	1	1	.955	8	6	0	0	.75
Gonzalez,G., NYM-Mil	R	.000	8	0	0	0	2	.116	86	10	1	0	0	3	4	28	18	24	56.0	1	4	1	0	.833	5	2	0	0	.40
Gonzalez,Mike, Pit	L	.000	1	0	0	0	0	.500	2	1	1	0	0	2	0	0	0	54	54.0	2	6	0	0	1.000	3	0	0	0	.00
Gordon,Tom, Phi	R	-	0	0	0	0	0	.000	2	0	0	0	0	0	0	0	0	59	59.1	5	8	0	0	1.000	6	0	0	0	.00
Gorzelanny,Tom, Pit	L	.000	19	0	0	1	1	.000	20	0	0	0	0	1	1	12	2	11	61.2	3	18	3	0	.875	6	2	2	0	.33
Gosling,Mike, Cin	L	-	0	0	0	0	0	.000	12	0	0	0	0	0	1	8	2	1	1.1	0	0	0	0	-	0	0	0	0	-
Grabow,John, Pit	L	.000	1	0	0	0	0	.000	1	0	0	0	0	0	0	1	0	72	69.2	4	13	0	0	1.000	3	1	0	0	.33
Graves,Danny, Cle	R	-	0	0	0	0	0	.105	76	8	0	0	2	3	1	25	5	13	14.0	1	3	1	0	.800	1	0	0	0	.00
Green,Sean, Sea	R	-	0	0	0	0	0	-	0	0	0	0	0	0	0	0	0	24	32.0	1	3	0	0	1.000	1	0	0	0	.00

Pitchers Hitting, Fielding and Holding Runners

Pitcher	T	2006 Hitting						Career Hitting										2006 Fielding and Holding Runners											
		Avg	AB	H	HR	RBI	SH	Avg	AB	H	2B	3B	HR	RBI	BB	SO	SH	G	Inn	PO	A	E	DP	Pct	SBA	CS	PCS	PPO	CS%
Gregg,Kevin, LAA	R	.000	3	0	0	0	0	.000	3	0	0	0	0	0	0	2	0	32	78.1	2	4	2	0	.750	5	0	0	1	.00
Greinke,Zack, KC	R	-	0	0	0	0	0	.250	4	1	0	0	1	1	0	1	0	3	6.1	0	1	0	0	1.000	0	0	0	0	-
Grilli,Jason, Det	R	-	0	0	0	0	0	-	0	0	0	0	0	0	0	0	0	51	62.0	2	6	0	0	1.000	3	1	0	0	.33
Grimsley,Jason, Ari	R	.000	4	0	0	0	0	.093	43	4	0	0	0	2	5	13	5	19	27.2	0	3	1	1	.750	0	0	0	0	-
Gryboski,Kevin, Was	R	-	0	0	0	0	0	.000	1	0	0	0	0	0	0	1	0	6	5.2	0	1	0	0	1.000	0	0	0	0	-
Guardado,Eddie, Sea-Cin	L	-	0	0	0	0	0	.000	1	0	0	0	0	0	0	1	0	43	37.0	1	3	0	0	1.000	1	1	0	0	1.00
Guerrier,Matt, Min	R	-	0	0	0	0	0	.000	2	0	0	0	0	0	0	1	0	39	69.2	7	11	1	0	.947	4	3	1	0	.75
Guthrie,Jeremy, Cle	R	-	0	0	0	0	0	-	0	0	0	0	0	0	0	0	0	9	19.1	0	5	0	1	1.000	3	1	0	0	.33
Guzman,Angel, ChC	R	.167	12	2	0	2	4	.167	12	2	1	0	0	2	0	4	4	15	56.0	3	5	0	0	1.000	8	3	0	0	.38
Haeger,Charlie, CWS	R	-	0	0	0	0	0	-	0	0	0	0	0	0	0	0	0	7	18.1	1	5	0	0	1.000	3	1	0	0	.33
Halama,John, Bal	L	-	0	0	0	0	0	.115	26	3	1	0	0	0	3	12	3	17	29.1	0	9	1	0	.900	3	2	2	0	.67
Halladay,Roy, Tor	R	.000	3	0	0	0	0	.034	29	1	0	0	0	0	0	12	2	32	220.0	25	31	1	2	.982	25	5	0	0	.20
Halsey,Brad, Oak	L	-	0	0	0	0	0	.080	50	4	0	0	0	2	6	19	6	52	94.1	4	15	1	2	.950	13	3	3	0	.23
Hamels,Cole, Phi	L	.114	44	5	0	3	2	.114	44	5	0	0	0	3	6	24	2	23	132.1	4	20	0	0	1.000	11	2	0	0	.18
Hammel,Jason, TB	R	-	0	0	0	0	0	-	0	0	0	0	0	0	0	0	0	9	44.0	2	7	0	1	1.000	3	2	0	1	.67
Hammond,Chris, Cin	L	-	0	0	0	0	0	.202	238	48	7	1	4	14	28	96	19	29	28.2	0	5	0	0	1.000	0	0	0	0	-
Hampson,Justin, Col	L	.000	3	0	0	0	1	.000	3	0	0	0	0	0	1	1	1	5	12.0	0	0	0	0	-	1	0	0	0	.00
Hamulack,Tim, LAD	L	.000	1	0	0	0	0	.000	1	0	0	0	0	0	0	0	0	33	34.0	1	5	1	0	.857	0	0	0	0	-
Hancock,Josh, StL	R	.000	6	0	0	0	1	.087	23	2	0	0	0	1	4	18	2	62	77.0	3	8	1	0	.917	4	0	0	0	.00
Hansack,Devern, Bos	R	-	0	0	0	0	0	-	0	0	0	0	0	0	0	0	0	2	10.0	2	0	0	0	1.000	0	0	0	0	-
Hansen,Craig, Bos	R	-	0	0	0	0	0	-	0	0	0	0	0	0	0	0	0	38	38.0	4	2	1	0	.857	4	0	0	0	.00
Harang,Aaron, Cin	R	.108	74	8	0	2	5	.066	226	15	1	0	0	5	1	122	13	36	234.1	13	31	2	0	.957	24	8	1	0	.33
Harden,Rich, Oak	R	-	0	0	0	0	0	.000	5	0	0	0	0	0	0	3	0	9	46.2	6	7	0	0	1.000	5	3	0	0	.60
Haren,Danny, Oak	R	.000	7	0	0	0	0	.082	49	4	3	0	0	3	1	18	3	34	223.0	19	24	1	1	.977	14	4	0	1	.29
Harper,Travis, TB	R	-	0	0	0	0	0	.000	1	0	0	0	0	0	0	1	0	30	42.0	5	2	0	1	1.000	2	1	0	0	.50
Harris,Jeff, Sea	R	-	0	0	0	0	0	-	0	0	0	0	0	0	0	0	0	3	3.1	0	0	0	0	-	0	0	0	0	-
Harville,Chad, TB	R	-	0	0	0	0	0	.000	2	0	0	0	0	0	0	2	0	32	41.0	7	9	0	1	1.000	8	1	0	0	.13
Hawkins,LaTroy, Bal	R	-	0	0	0	0	0	.000	5	0	0	0	0	0	0	4	1	60	60.1	4	7	1	1	.917	9	2	0	0	.22
Heilman,Aaron, NYM	R	-	0	0	0	0	0	.023	43	1	0	0	0	1	2	23	5	74	87.0	2	16	1	0	.947	9	0	0	0	.00
Helling,Rick, Mil	R	.000	3	0	0	0	0	.061	115	7	1	0	0	1	8	48	10	20	35.0	1	1	0	0	1.000	2	0	0	0	.00
Hendrickson,Ben, Mil	R	.000	3	0	0	0	0	.105	19	2	0	0	0	1	1	12	1	4	12.0	0	0	0	0	-	5	0	0	0	.00
Hendrickson,Ma, TB-LAD	L	.000	19	0	0	0	2	.086	35	3	0	0	1	1	3	22	2	31	164.2	4	23	3	1	.897	12	3	2	0	.25
Henn,Sean, NYY	L	-	0	0	0	0	0	-	0	0	0	0	0	0	0	0	0	4	9.1	0	2	0	0	1.000	0	0	0	0	-
Hennessey,Brad, SF	R	.222	27	6	0	0	3	.228	79	18	2	0	2	7	1	25	5	34	99.1	5	12	1	1	.944	14	3	1	1	.21
Hensley,Clay, SD	R	.083	48	4	0	2	5	.093	54	5	2	0	0	2	3	31	5	37	187.0	16	26	2	0	.955	16	4	0	1	.25
Herges,Matt, Fla	R	-	0	0	0	0	0	.222	27	6	0	0	0	1	1	14	2	66	71.0	1	8	1	0	.900	2	2	0	0	1.00
Hermanson,Dustin, CWS	R	-	0	0	0	0	0	.093	322	30	5	0	2	10	20	161	40	6	6.2	0	1	0	0	1.000	0	0	0	0	-
Hernandez,Fel, Sea	R	.000	4	0	0	0	1	.000	4	0	0	0	0	0	0	3	1	31	191.0	16	25	0	0	1.000	19	5	1	0	.26
Hernandez,Liv, Was-Ari	R	.206	68	14	1	6	13	.234	714	167	33	2	8	68	6	100	82	34	216.0	16	32	4	4	.923	18	4	1	1	.22
Hernandez,Orl, Ari-NYM	R	.174	46	8	0	2	7	.147	68	10	1	1	0	2	1	23	9	29	162.1	18	17	0	3	1.000	27	7	0	0	.26
Hernandez,Rob, Pit-NYM	R	-	0	0	0	0	0	.500	2	1	0	0	0	0	0	1	0	68	63.2	1	5	2	0	.750	8	2	0	0	.25
Hernandez,Run, KC	R	-	0	0	0	0	0	.000	5	0	0	0	0	0	0	1	0	21	109.2	3	12	1	2	.938	4	2	0	0	.50
Hill,Rich, ChC	L	.100	30	3	0	0	3	.139	36	5	1	0	0	0	1	13	3	17	99.1	2	7	1	0	.900	13	3	1	0	.23
Hill,Shawn, Was	R	.167	6	1	0	0	2	.125	8	1	0	0	0	0	6	3	5	6	36.2	4	9	0	2	1.000	3	1	0	0	.33
Hirsh,Jason, Hou	R	.000	15	0	0	0	2	.000	15	0	0	0	0	0	9	2	2	9	44.2	2	3	1	0	.833	3	1	0	0	.33
Hoey,James, Bal	R	-	0	0	0	0	0	-	0	0	0	0	0	0	0	0	0	12	9.2	3	2	0	0	1.000	1	0	0	0	.00
Hoffman,Trevor, SD	R	-	0	0	0	0	0	.121	33	4	2	0	0	5	0	10	2	65	63.0	6	5	0	2	1.000	2	0	0	0	.00
Holtz,Mike, Bos	L	-	0	0	0	0	0	.000	3	0	0	0	0	0	0	2	0	3	1.2	1	0	0	0	1.000	0	0	0	0	-
Howell,J.P., TB	L	-	0	0	0	0	0	.000	3	0	0	0	0	0	0	1	0	8	42.1	4	7	0	3	1.000	4	1	0	0	.25
Howry,Bob, ChC	R	1.000	1	1	0	0	0	.500	2	1	0	0	0	0	0	0	0	84	76.2	5	3	0	1	1.000	9	5	0	0	.56
Huber,Jonathan, Sea	R	-	0	0	0	0	0	-	0	0	0	0	0	0	0	0	0	16	16.2	3	2	0	0	1.000	1	1	0	0	1.00
Hudson,Luke, KC	R	-	0	0	0	0	0	.244	41	10	2	0	0	5	3	12	3	26	102.0	12	12	1	2	.960	3	2	0	0	.67
Hudson,Tim, Atl	R	.095	63	6	0	3	14	.117	154	18	4	1	0	10	7	53	18	35	218.1	17	30	2	1	1.000	27	4	1	1	.15
Hughes,Travis, Was	R	1.000	1	1	0	0	0	1.000	1	1	0	0	0	0	0	0	0	8	11.1	2	1	0	0	1.000	0	0	0	0	-
Humber,Philip, NYM	R	-	0	0	0	0	0	-	0	0	0	0	0	0	0	0	0	2	2.0	0	0	0	0	-	1	0	0	0	.00
Isringhausen,Jason, StL	R	-	0	0	0	0	0	.206	102	21	4	1	2	16	5	35	8	59	58.1	5	10	1	0	.938	6	1	0	0	.17
Jackson,Edwin, TB	R	-	0	0	0	0	0	.150	20	3	0	0	0	2	2	5	3	23	36.1	3	3	0	1	1.000	3	0	0	0	.00
Jackson,Zach, Mil	L	.111	9	1	0	0	4	.111	9	1	0	0	0	0	0	2	4	8	38.1	1	2	1	0	.750	4	0	0	0	.00
James,Chuck, Atl	L	.029	35	1	0	0	4	.056	36	2	0	0	0	1	1	14	4	25	119.0	3	13	0	1	1.000	17	3	1	0	.18
Janssen,Casey, Tor	R	.000	1	0	0	0	0	.000	1	0	0	0	0	0	0	0	0	19	94.0	8	14	0	1	1.000	5	3	0	2	.60
Jarvis,Kevin, Ari-Bos	R	-	0	0	0	0	0	.160	188	30	6	0	1	14	13	62	23	9	28.0	1	5	0	0	1.000	2	0	0	1	.00
Jenks,Bobby, CWS	R	-	0	0	0	0	0	-	0	0	0	0	0	0	0	0	0	67	69.2	5	6	1	1	.917	13	2	0	0	.15
Jennings,Jason, Col	R	.129	62	8	0	2	10	.219	302	66	14	0	2	25	16	72	27	32	212.0	14	25	1	3	.975	23	7	0	0	.30
Jimenez,Cesar, Sea	L	-	0	0	0	0	0	-	0	0	0	0	0	0	0	0	0	4	7.1	0	0	0	0	-	0	0	0	0	-
Jimenez,Ubaldo, Col	R	.333	3	1	0	0	0	.333	3	1	0	0	0	0	0	1	0	2	7.2	0	2	0	0	1.000	3	1	0	0	.33
Johnson,J., Cle-Bos-Cin	R	.000	1	0	0	0	0	.120	25	3	0	0	1	1	2	16	3	24	115.0	7	9	1	0	.941	19	0	0	0	.00
Johnson,Jim, Bal	R	-	0	0	0	0	0	-	0	0	0	0	0	0	0	0	0	1	3.0	0	0	0	0	-	1	0	0	0	.00
Johnson,Josh, Fla	R	.095	42	4	0	3	6	.109	46	5	2	0	0	3	1	25	6	31	157.0	5	26	0	2	1.000	17	8	2	0	.47
Johnson,Randy, NYY	L	.167	6	1	0	0	0	.127	534	68	13	0	1	35	13	247	35	33	205.0	2	26	1	0	.966	31	10	1	0	.32
Johnson,Tyler, StL	L	.000	1	0	0	0	0	.000	1	0	0	0	0	0	0	1	0	56	36.1	4	2	1	0	.857	3	0	0	0	.00

Pitchers Hitting, Fielding and Holding Runners

Pitcher	T	2006 Hitting						Career Hitting										2006 Fielding and Holding Runners											
		Avg	AB	H	HR	RBI	SH	Avg	AB	H	2B	3B	HR	RBI	BB	SO	SH	G	Inn	PO	A	E	DP	Pct	SBA	CS	PCS	PPO	CS%
Jones,Greg, LAA	R	-	0	0	0	0	0											5	6.0					-	1	0	0	0	.00
Jones,Todd, Det	R	-	0	0	0	0	0	.211	19	4	1	0	0	0	1	6	0	62	64.0	2	10	0	1	1.000	0	0	0	0	-
Julio,Jorge, NYM-Ari	R	.000	1	0	0	0	0	.000	1	0	0	0	0	0	0	1	0	62	66.0	1	1	0	0	1.000	7	2	0	0	.29
Karsay,Steve, Oak	R	-	0	0	0	0	0	.000	4	0	0	0	0	0	0	2	0	9	9.1	1	0	0	0	1.000	0	0	0	0	-
Karstens,Jeff, NYY	R	-	0	0	0	0	0	-										8	42.2	4	6	1	1	.909	2	0	0	0	.00
Kazmir,Scott, TB	L	.000	3	0	0	0	0	.000	4	0	0	0	0	0	0	2	0	24	144.2	5	11	1	1	.941	18	3	2	3	.17
Keisler,Randy, Oak	L	-	0	0	0	0	0	.211	19	4	2	0	1	2	0	5	0	11	10.0	0	0	0	0	-	1	1	0	0	1.00
Kennedy,Joe, Oak	L	-	0	0	0	0	0	.170	88	15	1	1	0	6	3	25	9	39	35.0	1	3	0	0	1.000	0	0	0	0	-
Kensing,Logan, Fla	R	.000	1	0	0	0	0	.000	3	0	0	0	0	0	0	2	1	37	37.2	3	0	0	0	1.000	4	1	0	0	.25
Keppel,Bobby, KC	R	.000	2	0	0	0	0	.000	2	0	0	0	0	0	0	1	0	8	34.1	2	7	0	2	1.000	2	1	0	1	.50
Kim,Byung-Hyun, Col	R	.160	50	8	0	4	6	.142	120	17	2	0	0	9	4	27	12	27	155.0	7	19	1	2	.963	31	7	1	1	.23
Kim,Sun-Woo, Col-Cin	R	.500	2	1	0	0	0	.183	60	11	3	0	0	8	0	17	10	8	13.2	1	2	0	0	1.000	0	0	0	0	-
King,Ray, Col	L	.000	1	0	0	0	0	.000	6	0	0	0	0	0	0	0	3	67	44.2	4	3	0	0	1.000	3	1	0	0	.33
Kinney,Josh, StL	R	-	0	0	0	0	0	-										21	25.0	4	2	1	0	.857	1	0	0	0	.00
Kline,Steve, SF	L	-	0	0	0	0	0	.154	13	2	1	0	0	2	0	5	4	72	51.2	5	10	1	0	.938	1	1	1	0	1.00
Kolb,Dan, Mil	R	-	0	0	0	0	0	.000	1	0	0	0	0	0	0	1	0	53	48.1	0	4	1	0	.800	2	0	0	0	.00
Komine,Shane, Oak	R	-	0	0	0	0	0	-										2	9.0	0	0	0	0	-	0	0	0	0	-
Koplove,Mike, Ari	R	.000	1	0	0	0	0	.000	5	0	0	0	0	0	0	0	2	2	3.0	0	2	0	0	1.000	2	0	0	0	.00
Koronka,John, Tex	L	.000	6	0	0	0	0	.000	10	0	0	0	0	0	1	5	0	23	125.0	4	11	0	1	1.000	12	3	2	0	.25
Kuo,Hong-Chih, LAD	L	.125	8	1	0	0	3	.125	8	1	1	0	0	0	0	6	3	28	59.2	2	6	0	0	1.000	9	4	2	0	.44
Lackey,John, LAA	R	.000	3	0	0	0	0	.000	14	0	0	0	0	0	0	4	0	33	217.2	10	26	0	1	1.000	16	4	0	0	.25
Lara,Juan, Cle	L	-	0	0	0	0	0	-										9	5.0	0	0	0	0	-	2	0	0	0	.00
League,Brandon, Tor	R	-	0	0	0	0	0	-										33	42.2	3	13	2	0	.889	2	1	0	0	.50
Ledezma,Wil, Det	L	-	0	0	0	0	0	-										24	60.1	3	6	1	0	.900	3	1	0	0	.33
Lee,Cliff, Cle	L	.167	6	1	0	0	0	.118	17	2	0	0	0	0	0	5	0	33	200.2	3	17	1	0	.952	10	3	1	0	.30
Lehr,Justin, Mil	R	-	0	0	0	0	0	.000	3	0	0	0	0	0	0	2	0	16	15.2	1	3	0	1	1.000	4	0	0	0	.00
Lerew,Anthony, Atl	R	-	0	0	0	0	0	-										1	2.0	0	0	0	0	-	0	0	0	0	-
Lester,Jon, Bos	L	.000	4	0	0	0	0	.000	4	0	0	0	0	0	0	3	0	15	81.1	0	11	0	0	1.000	15	6	5	1	.40
Lewis,Colby, Det	R	-	0	0	0	0	0	.000	1	0	0	0	0	0	0	1	0	2	3.0	0	0	0	0	-	0	0	0	0	-
Lidge,Brad, Hou	R	-	0	0	0	0	0	.286	7	2	1	0	0	2	0	4	0	78	75.0	5	2	0	0	.846	7	0	0	0	.00
Lidle,Cory, Phi-NYY	R	.088	34	3	0	0	4	.129	170	22	4	1	1	8	9	87	21	31	170.2	12	34	1	4	.979	16	8	0	0	.50
Lieber,Jon, Phi	R	.094	53	5	0	0	6	.142	590	84	17	0	0	24	26	222	53	27	168.0	15	19	3	0	.919	11	3	0	0	.27
Lilly,Ted, Tor	L	.000	3	0	0	0	0	.043	23	1	0	0	0	0	0	10	4	32	181.2	7	24	1	0	.969	17	3	2	0	.18
Lima,Jose, NYM	R	.000	5	0	0	0	1	.130	292	38	4	0	0	10	7	101	44	4	17.1	1	4	1	1	.833	1	0	0	0	.00
Linebrink,Scott, SD	R	1.000	1	1	0	0	0	.235	17	4	1	0	0	0	0	9	2	73	75.2	6	7	0	1	1.000	9	1	0	0	.11
Liriano,Francisco, Min	L	.200	5	1	0	1	1	.200	5	1	0	0	0	1	1	3	1	28	121.0	3	6	1	0	.900	9	0	0	0	.00
Littleton,Wes, Tex	R	-	0	0	0	0	0	-										33	36.1	1	7	0	1	1.000	2	1	0	0	.50
Livingston,Bobby, Sea	L	-	0	0	0	0	0	-										3	5.0	1	1	0	0	1.000	0	0	0	0	-
Loaiza,Esteban, Oak	R	.000	5	0	0	0	1	.167	258	43	4	1	0	15	3	66	31	26	154.2	5	15	1	0	.952	13	3	0	0	.23
Loe,Kameron, Tex	R	-	0	0	0	0	0	-										15	78.1	3	11	2	0	.875	5	0	0	0	.00
Loewen,Adam, Bal	L	.000	2	0	0	0	0	.000	2	0	0	0	0	0	0	0	0	22	112.1	2	13	0	0	1.000	18	7	3	0	.39
Logan,Boone, CWS	L	-	0	0	0	0	0	-										21	17.1	1	3	1	0	.800	0	0	0	0	-
Lohse,Kyle, Min-Cin	R	.174	23	4	0	3	1	.186	43	8	2	0	0	4	0	18	5	34	126.2	12	25	0	1	1.000	5	3	1	1	.60
Looper,Braden, StL	R	.500	2	1	0	0	0	.200	10	2	1	0	0	0	0	5	1	69	73.1	6	10	0	2	1.000	4	1	0	0	.25
Lopez,Javier, Bos	L	-	0	0	0	0	0	.143	7	1	0	0	0	1	0	3	1	27	16.2	1	2	0	0	1.000	2	0	0	0	.00
Lopez,Rodrigo, Bal	R	.000	2	0	0	0	1	.050	20	1	0	0	0	0	0	12	1	36	189.0	12	18	1	0	.968	19	10	1	0	.53
Lowe,Derek, LAD	R	.094	64	6	0	3	10	.121	149	18	5	0	0	8	8	44	22	35	218.0	19	48	3	4	.957	30	4	1	0	.13
Lowe,Mark, Sea	R	-	0	0	0	0	0	-										15	18.2	0	1	1	0	.500	0	0	0	0	-
Lowry,Noah, SF	L	.152	46	7	1	2	8	.214	140	30	8	0	1	9	6	33	23	27	159.1	10	20	2	1	.938	10	4	0	0	.40
Lugo,Ruddy, TB	R	-	0	0	0	0	0	-										64	85.0	9	9	0	0	1.000	5	3	0	0	.60
Lyon,Brandon, Ari	R	-	0	0	0	0	0	-										68	69.1	1	8	0	1	1.000	2	0	0	0	.00
Mabeus,Chris, Mil	R	-	0	0	0	0	0	-										1	1.2	0	0	0	0	-	0	0	0	0	-
MacDougal,M., KC-CWS	R	-	0	0	0	0	0	-										29	29.0	0	3	0	0	1.000	2	0	0	0	.00
Maddux,Greg, ChC-LAD	R	.132	68	9	0	7	6	.174	1474	257	33	2	5	81	32	385	165	34	210.0	14	52	0	9	1.000	31	6	1	0	.19
Madson,Ryan, Phi	R	.182	33	6	0	2	4	.143	42	6	1	0	0	2	2	15	0	50	134.1	9	20	0	1	1.000	20	6	0	1	.30
Mahay,Ron, Tex	L	-	0	0	0	0	0	.286	7	2	1	0	0	0	0	2	0	62	57.0	0	2	1	0	.667	4	2	1	0	.50
Maholm,Paul, Pit	L	.109	55	6	0	2	1	.114	70	8	0	0	0	2	4	37	2	30	176.0	10	41	2	2	.962	24	11	8	1	.46
Maine,John, NYM	R	.036	28	1	0	0	3	.036	28	1	1	0	0	0	0	16	3	16	90.0	3	11	0	1	1.000	9	3	0	0	.33
Majewski,Gary, Was-Cin	R	.000	3	0	0	0	1	.000	11	0	0	0	0	0	0	6	2	65	70.1	5	9	1	1	.933	5	3	0	0	.60
Manon,Julio, Bal	R	-	0	0	0	0	0	.000	1	0	0	0	0	0	0	1	0	22	20.0	3	0	0	0	1.000	2	1	0	0	.50
Marcum,Shaun, Tor	R	-	0	0	0	0	0	-										21	78.1	2	10	0	0	1.000	3	1	0	0	.50
Marmol,Carlos, ChC	R	.261	23	6	1	1	1	.261	23	6	1	0	1	1	0	7	1	19	77.0	3	7	3	0	.769	16	5	1	1	.31
Maroth,Mike, Det	L	-	0	0	0	0	0	.250	16	4	0	0	0	0	2	10	3	13	53.2	1	13	0	1	1.000	2	1	0	0	.50
Marquis,Jason, StL	R	.179	78	14	0	5	4	.223	310	69	19	2	2	26	7	68	15	33	194.1	13	30	1	3	.977	15	5	0	0	.33
Marshall,Sean, ChC	L	.125	40	5	1	2	3	.125	40	5	0	0	1	2	0	19	3	24	125.2	3	21	1	0	.960	17	5	2	0	.29
Marte,Damaso, Pit	L	.000	2	0	0	0	0	.000	6	0	0	0	0	0	0	1	0	75	58.1	1	10	1	0	.917	6	2	1	2	.33
Martin,Tom, Col	L	.000	4	0	0	0	0	.000	11	0	0	0	0	0	0	4	0	68	60.1	2	10	2	1	.857	4	2	1	0	.50
Martinez,Carlos, Fla	R	-	0	0	0	0	0	-										12	10.1	1	0	0	0	1.000	3	2	0	0	.67
Martinez,Pedro, NYM	R	.105	38	4	0	1	9	.094	372	35	4	2	0	13	14	163	53	23	132.2	7	13	5	0	.800	14	1	0	0	.07
Masset,Nick, Tex	R	-	0	0	0	0	0	-										8	8.2	0	3	0	0	1.000	0	0	0	0	-

Pitchers Hitting, Fielding and Holding Runners

Pitcher	T	Avg	AB	H	HR	RBI	SH	Avg	AB	H	2B	3B	HR	RBI	BB	SO	SH	G	Inn	PO	A	E	DP	Pct	SBA	CS	PCS	PPO	CS%
		2006 Hitting						**Career Hitting**										**2006 Fielding and Holding Runners**											
Mastny,Tom, Cle	R	-	0	0	0	0	0	-	0	0	0	0	0	0	0	0	0	15	16.1	1	1	0	0	1.000	0	0	0	0	-
Mateo,Juan, ChC	R	.000	12	0	0	0	2	.000	12	0	0	0	0	0	0	9	2	11	45.2	0	5	0	1	1.000	2	1	0	0	.50
Mateo,Julio, Sea	R	-	0	0	0	0	0	-	0	0	0	0	0	0	0	0	0	48	53.2	1	4	1	1	.833	5	1	0	0	.20
Mathieson,Scott, Phi	R	.143	7	1	0	0	2	.143	7	1	0	0	0	0	0	4	2	9	37.1	0	7	1	0	.875	1	0	0	0	.00
Mays,Joe, KC-Cin	R	.222	9	2	0	3	1	.250	24	6	2	0	0	3	3	9	4	13	50.2	3	5	0	0	1.000	1	0	0	0	.00
McBride,Macay, Atl	L	-	0	0	0	0	0	-	0	0	0	0	0	0	0	0	0	71	56.2	6	8	0	1	1.000	0	0	0	0	-
McCarthy,Bran, CWS	R	.000	1	0	0	0	0	.000	3	0	0	0	0	0	0	2	0	53	84.2	4	11	0	2	1.000	11	3	0	0	.27
McClung,Seth, TB	R	.000	1	0	0	0	1	.000	1	0	0	0	0	0	0	0	1	39	103.0	8	4	3	0	.800	20	5	1	0	.25
McGowan,Dustin, Tor	R	-	0	0	0	0	0	-	0	0	0	0	0	0	0	0	0	16	27.1	4	0	0	0	1.000	4	1	0	0	.25
McLeary,Marty, Pit	R	.000	5	0	0	0	0	.000	5	0	0	0	0	0	0	3	0	5	17.2	1	1	1	0	.667	4	0	0	0	.00
Meadows,Brian, TB	R	-	0	0	0	0	0	.117	180	21	3	0	0	8	8	76	19	53	69.2	2	3	0	0	1.000	6	1	0	0	.17
Meche,Gil, Sea	R	.000	4	0	0	0	0	.154	13	2	0	0	0	1	0	5	0	32	186.2	13	18	1	1	.969	12	7	1	1	.58
Medders,Brandon, Ari	R	.000	2	0	0	0	0	.000	3	0	0	0	0	0	0	0	0	60	71.2	8	8	1	0	.941	5	1	0	0	.20
Mercker,Kent, Cin	L	-	0	0	0	0	0	.113	248	28	5	2	1	18	11	115	22	37	28.1	1	2	0	1	1.000	1	0	0	0	.00
Meredith,Cla, SD	R	-	0	0	0	0	1	-	0	0	0	0	0	0	0	0	1	45	50.2	5	9	1	1	.933	5	1	0	0	.20
Mesa,Jose, Col	R	.000	1	0	0	0	0	.000	2	0	0	0	0	0	1	1	1	79	72.1	2	11	1	2	.929	3	3	0	0	1.00
Messenger,Randy, Fla	R	.000	2	0	0	0	0	.200	5	1	0	0	0	0	1	2	0	59	60.1	1	7	1	1	.889	7	1	0	0	.14
Miceli,Dan, TB	R	-	0	0	0	0	0	.091	22	2	0	0	0	0	0	10	0	33	32.0	2	2	1	0	.800	3	1	0	0	.33
Michalak,Chris, Cin	L	.250	8	2	0	0	2	.273	11	3	1	1	0	0	1	6	4	8	35.0	2	9	1	1	.917	4	2	2	0	.50
Miller,Andrew, Det	L	-	0	0	0	0	0	-	0	0	0	0	0	0	0	0	0	8	10.1	1	0	0	0	1.000	0	0	0	0	-
Miller,Matt, Cle	R	-	0	0	0	0	0	-	0	0	0	0	0	0	0	0	0	14	15.2	0	1	0	0	1.000	0	0	0	0	-
Miller,Trever, Hou	L	-	0	0	0	0	0	.167	6	1	1	0	0	0	0	1	2	70	50.2	3	4	0	1	1.000	3	1	0	0	.33
Miller,Wade, ChC	R	.143	7	1	0	0	0	.171	269	46	9	0	0	17	4	86	30	5	21.2	1	5	0	0	1.000	2	0	0	0	.00
Millwood,Kevin, Tex	R	.000	5	0	0	0	1	.122	433	53	14	0	2	24	19	196	51	34	215.0	13	29	0	4	1.000	13	3	0	0	.23
Milton,Eric, Cin	L	.224	49	11	0	3	6	.184	190	35	5	1	2	14	10	85	16	26	152.2	5	19	0	1	1.000	5	2	0	0	.40
Miner,Zach, Det	R	.167	6	1	0	0	0	.167	6	1	1	0	0	0	0	3	0	27	93.0	8	13	1	1	.954	13	5	1	0	.38
Misch,Patrick, SF	L	-	0	0	0	0	0	-	0	0	0	0	0	0	0	0	0	1	1.0	1	0	0	0	1.000	0	0	0	0	-
Mitre,Sergio, Fla	R	.167	12	2	0	1	2	.200	40	8	3	0	0	2	1	14	6	15	41.0	2	7	2	1	.818	7	2	1	0	.29
Moehler,Brian, Fla	R	.065	31	2	0	2	7	.050	101	5	1	0	0	5	4	42	13	29	122.0	8	18	1	1	.963	11	6	1	1	.55
Montero,Agustin, CWS	R	-	0	0	0	0	0	-	0	0	0	0	0	0	0	0	0	11	14.0	0	1	0	0	1.000	0	0	0	0	-
Morillo,Juan, Col	R	.000	1	0	0	0	0	.000	1	0	0	0	0	0	0	0	0	1	4.0	0	0	0	0	-	0	0	0	0	-
Morris,Matt, SF	R	.200	60	12	0	6	14	.161	479	77	15	0	1	34	26	195	70	33	207.2	20	28	3	4	.941	16	3	2	1	.19
Moseley,Dustin, LAA	R	-	0	0	0	0	0	-	0	0	0	0	0	0	0	0	0	3	11.0	0	1	0	0	1.000	2	0	0	0	.00
Mota,Guillermo, Cle-NYM	R	-	0	0	0	0	0	.212	33	7	1	0	2	6	0	17	0	52	55.2	4	0	0	0	1.000	10	1	0	0	.10
Moyer,Jamie, Sea-Phi	L	.095	21	2	0	1	3	.149	195	29	2	0	0	7	16	63	26	33	211.1	12	36	2	5	.960	19	8	5	0	.42
Moylan,Peter, Atl	R	-	0	0	0	0	0	-	0	0	0	0	0	0	0	0	0	15	15.0	0	1	0	0	1.000	2	0	0	0	.00
Mujica,Edward, Cle	R	-	0	0	0	0	0	-	0	0	0	0	0	0	0	0	0	10	18.1	1	0	0	0	1.000	1	1	1	0	1.00
Mulder,Mark, StL	L	.280	25	7	1	5	6	.156	109	17	2	0	1	9	9	44	8	17	93.1	1	28	0	2	1.000	6	1	0	0	.17
Mulholland,T, Ari	L	-	0	0	0	0	0	.111	619	69	13	1	2	23	13	281	53	5	3.0	0	1	0	0	1.000	0	0	0	0	-
Munter,Scott, SF	R	1.000	1	1	0	1	0	1.000	1	1	1	0	0	1	0	0	1	27	22.2	3	2	0	1	1.000	3	1	0	0	.33
Mussina,Mike, NYY	R	.000	4	0	0	0	0	.178	45	8	1	0	0	5	0	9	1	32	197.1	3	22	0	0	1.000	19	4	0	0	.21
Myers,Brett, Phi	R	.032	63	2	0	1	7	.129	264	34	7	0	0	9	12	87	34	31	198.0	13	25	0	1	1.000	18	5	2	0	.28
Myers,Mike, NYY	L	-	0	0	0	0	0	.000	1	0	0	0	0	0	0	1	0	62	30.2	0	7	0	0	1.000	6	2	1	0	.33
Nageotte,Clint, Sea	R	-	0	0	0	0	0	.000	2	0	0	0	0	0	0	2	0	1	1.0	1	0	0	0	1.000	1	0	0	0	.00
Narveson,Chris, StL	L	.000	1	0	0	0	0	.000	1	0	0	0	0	0	0	1	0	5	9.1	1	0	0	0	1.000	2	1	0	0	.50
Nathan,Joe, Min	R	.000	1	0	0	0	0	.159	63	10	3	0	2	4	3	17	10	64	68.1	3	5	2	0	.800	2	0	0	0	.00
Nelson,Jeff, CWS	R	-	0	0	0	0	0	.000	2	0	0	0	0	0	0	0	1	6	2.2	0	0	0	0	-	1	1	0	0	1.00
Nelson,Joe, KC	R	-	0	0	0	0	0	-	0	0	0	0	0	0	0	0	0	43	44.2	3	5	0	1	1.000	3	1	0	0	.33
Neshek,Pat, Min	R	-	0	0	0	0	0	-	0	0	0	0	0	0	0	0	0	32	37.0	2	1	0	0	1.000	5	2	0	0	.40
Nieve,Fernando, Hou	R	.125	16	2	0	1	5	.125	16	2	0	0	0	1	2	8	5	40	96.1	10	7	0	2	1.000	5	1	0	0	.20
Nippert,Dustin, Ari	R	.000	2	0	0	0	0	.167	6	1	0	0	0	1	5	0	2	10.0	2	1	0	0	1.000	1	0	0	0	.00
Nolasco,Ricky, Fla	R	.171	41	7	1	5	6	.171	41	7	0	0	1	5	2	19	6	35	140.0	8	13	4	2	.840	12	6	0	0	.50
Novoa,Roberto, ChC	R	.200	5	1	0	1	0	.167	6	1	1	0	0	1	0	2	0	66	76.0	1	3	1	0	.800	10	0	0	0	.00
Nunez,Leo, KC	R	-	0	0	0	0	0	-	0	0	0	0	0	0	0	0	0	7	13.1	1	2	0	1	1.000	0	0	0	0	-
O'Connor,Mike, Was	L	.065	31	2	0	1	1	.065	31	2	0	0	0	1	1	18	1	21	105.0	3	10	1	0	.929	18	1	0	0	.06
O'Flaherty,Eric, Sea	L	-	0	0	0	0	0	-	0	0	0	0	0	0	0	0	0	15	11.0	1	1	0	0	1.000	0	0	0	0	-
Ohka,Tomo, Mil	R	.161	31	5	0	6	3	.139	238	33	2	0	0	15	10	94	24	18	97.0	8	12	5	1	.800	6	2	0	1	.33
Ohman,Will, ChC	L	1.000	1	1	0	0	0	1.000	1	1	0	0	0	0	0	0	0	78	65.1	2	3	0	0	1.000	4	0	0	0	.00
Oliver,Darren, NYM	L	.133	15	2	0	2	0	.221	217	48	11	0	1	20	8	74	15	45	81.0	4	10	0	0	1.000	4	1	0	0	.25
Olsen,Scott, Fla	L	.190	58	11	0	8	6	.180	61	11	2	0	0	8	0	19	7	31	180.2	4	24	1	1	.966	16	8	3	0	.50
O'Malley,Ryan, ChC	L	.000	4	0	0	0	0	.000	4	0	0	0	0	0	0	3	0	2	12.2	0	2	0	0	1.000	1	1	1	0	1.00
Ortiz,Ramon, Was	R	.107	56	6	1	3	7	.076	132	10	0	0	1	3	4	56	14	33	190.2	12	21	3	0	.917	10	4	0	1	.40
Ortiz,Russ, Ari-Bal	R	.333	6	2	0	2	1	.208	462	96	22	0	6	44	34	122	56	26	63.0	5	8	0	1	1.000	9	5	2	1	.56
Orvella,Chad, TB	R	-	0	0	0	0	0	-	0	0	0	0	0	0	0	0	0	22	24.1	0	0	0	0	-	5	1	0	0	.20
Osoria,Franq, LAD	R	.000	2	0	0	0	0	.000	5	0	0	0	0	0	0	4	0	12	17.2	1	5	0	0	1.000	0	0	0	0	-
Oswalt,Roy, Hou	R	.152	66	10	1	8	20	.158	373	59	6	1	23	16	103	57	33	220.2	15	28	1	4	.977	11	6	1	0	.55
Otsuka,Akinori, Tex	R	-	0	0	0	0	0	.000	2	0	0	0	0	0	1	1	0	63	59.2	3	10	1	2	.929	4	2	0	0	.50
Owens,Henry, NYM	R	-	0	0	0	0	0	-	0	0	0	0	0	0	0	0	0	3	4.0	1	0	0	0	-	1	0	0	0	.00
Padilla,Vicente, Tex	R	.000	1	0	0	0	1	.092	206	19	3	1	0	13	14	109	20	33	200.0	12	22	1	1	.971	11	3	1	1	.27
Papelbon,Jonat, Bos	R	-	0	0	0	0	0	-	0	0	0	0	0	0	0	0	0	59	68.1	4	3	1	0	.875	5	1	0	0	.20

309

Pitchers Hitting, Fielding and Holding Runners

Pitcher	T	2006 Hitting						Career Hitting										2006 Fielding and Holding Runners											
		Avg	AB	H	HR	RBI	SH	Avg	AB	H	2B	3B	HR	RBI	BB	SO	SH	G	Inn	PO	A	E	DP	Pct	SBA	CS	PCS	PPO	CS%
Park,Chan Ho, SD	R	.268	41	11	0	5	7	.183	405	74	15	1	2	30	17	144	50	24	136.2	7	18	2	1	.926	9	0	0	0	.00
Paronto,Chad, Atl	R	.000	1	0	0	0	0	.000	1	0	0	0	0	0	0	0	1	65	56.2	2	8	0	0	1.000	6	4	1	0	.67
Patterson,John, Was	R	.250	8	2	0	0	2	.115	122	14	3	0	0	2	2	49	17	8	40.2	1	4	0	0	1.000	8	0	0	0	.00
Pauley,David, Bos	R	-	0	0	0	0	0	-	0	0	0	0	0	0	0	0	0	3	16.0	2	2	0	1	1.000	0	0	0	0	-
Peavy,Jake, SD	R	.167	60	10	2	9	8	.158	260	41	8	0	2	17	12	86	28	32	202.1	22	20	2	1	.955	31	6	0	0	.19
Pelfrey,Mike, NYM	R	.000	9	0	0	0	0	.000	9	0	0	0	0	0	0	4	0	4	21.1	1	3	0	0	1.000	3	1	0	0	.33
Pena,Tony, Ari	R	.000	2	0	0	0	0	.000	2	0	0	0	0	0	0	0	0	25	30.2	2	6	0	0	1.000	1	1	0	1	1.00
Penn,Hayden, Bal	R	-	0	0	0	0	0	.000	1	0	0	0	0	0	1	0	1	6	19.2	1	1	1	0	.667	2	0	0	0	.00
Penny,Brad, LAD	R	.185	65	12	0	5	5	.141	389	55	10	2	2	21	2	125	25	34	189.0	7	22	1	6	.967	28	8	1	1	.29
Peralta,Joel, KC	R	-	0	0	0	0	0	-	0	0	0	0	0	0	0	0	0	64	73.2	6	4	0	2	1.000	5	1	0	0	.20
Perez,Beltran, Was	R	.500	6	3	0	0	0	.500	6	3	0	0	0	0	1	2	0	8	21.0	2	4	0	0	1.000	6	2	0	0	.33
Perez,Juan, Pit	L	-	0	0	0	0	0	-	0	0	0	0	0	0	0	0	0	7	3.1	0	0	0	0	-	0	0	0	0	-
Perez,Odalis, LAD-KC	L	.067	15	1	0	0	1	.128	282	36	8	0	1	10	6	71	41	32	126.1	3	24	1	1	.964	12	3	1	0	.25
Perez,Oliver, Pit-NYM	L	.105	38	4	0	3	1	.162	198	32	0	0	0	10	8	67	24	22	112.2	1	13	2	0	.875	6	1	1	0	.17
Perez,Rafael, Cle	L	-	0	0	0	0	0	-	0	0	0	0	0	0	0	0	0	18	12.1	0	2	1	0	.667	3	0	0	0	.00
Perkins,Glen, Min	L	-	0	0	0	0	0	-	0	0	0	0	0	0	0	0	0	4	5.2	0	1	0	0	1.000	0	0	0	0	-
Petit,Yusmeiro, Fla	R	.200	5	1	0	0	0	.200	5	1	0	0	0	0	1	0	2	15	26.1	2	0	0	0	1.000	2	2	0	0	1.00
Pettitte,Andy, Hou	L	.194	62	12	1	5	10	.137	175	24	5	0	1	12	6	54	31	36	214.1	2	31	2	2	.943	13	3	3	1	.23
Pineiro,Joel, Sea	R	.000	4	0	0	0	2	.083	24	2	1	0	0	2	0	10	4	40	165.2	24	12	0	6	1.000	11	3	0	0	.27
Pinto,Renyel, Fla	L	.000	1	0	0	0	0	.000	1	0	0	0	0	0	0	0	0	27	29.2	2	2	0	0	1.000	0	0	0	0	-
Politte,Cliff, CWS	R	-	0	0	0	0	0	.121	33	4	1	0	0	3	3	14	1	33	30.0	0	3	0	0	1.000	3	0	0	0	.00
Ponson,Sidney, StL-NYY	R	.231	13	3	0	1	5	.143	63	9	3	0	0	1	3	20	11	19	85.0	5	9	1	1	.933	8	3	1	1	.38
Prior,Mark, ChC	R	.077	13	1	0	0	1	.201	204	41	10	0	1	13	8	81	22	9	43.2	3	5	2	1	.800	7	2	0	0	.29
Proctor,Scott, NYY	R	-	0	0	0	0	0	-	0	0	0	0	0	0	0	0	0	83	102.1	4	9	0	1	1.000	9	2	0	0	.22
Putz,J.J., Sea	R	-	0	0	0	0	0	-	0	0	0	0	0	0	0	0	0	72	78.1	2	7	1	0	.900	7	0	0	0	.00
Qualls,Chad, Hou	R	.000	0	0	0	0	0	.000	2	0	0	0	0	0	0	2	0	81	88.2	8	11	0	1	1.000	7	4	1	0	.57
Radke,Brad, Min	R	.000	1	0	0	0	1	.103	29	3	0	0	0	0	0	9	5	28	162.1	20	21	0	1	1.000	11	5	0	0	.45
Ramirez,Eliz, Cin	R	.192	26	5	0	3	2	.147	34	5	1	0	0	3	2	12	2	21	104.0	7	12	0	1	1.000	5	3	0	0	.60
Ramirez,Horacio, Atl	L	.125	24	3	0	0	3	.151	179	27	3	1	0	5	2	36	13	14	76.1	10	20	1	3	.968	6	1	0	0	.17
Ramirez,Ramon, Col	R	.500	4	2	0	0	1	.500	4	2	0	0	0	0	0	2	1	61	67.2	5	4	1	0	.900	2	0	0	0	.00
Ramirez,Santiago, Was	R	-	0	0	0	0	0	-	0	0	0	0	0	0	0	0	0	4	3.1	0	0	0	0	-	0	0	0	0	-
Rasner,Darrell, NYY	R	-	0	0	0	0	0	-	0	0	0	0	0	0	0	0	0	6	20.1	0	4	0	0	1.000	0	0	0	0	-
Rauch,Jon, Was	R	.000	4	0	0	0	0	.118	17	2	0	0	1	3	0	12	1	85	91.1	1	6	0	1	1.000	12	4	0	0	.33
Ray,Chris, Bal	R	-	0	0	0	0	0	-	0	0	0	0	0	0	0	0	0	61	66.0	3	6	1	0	.900	2	2	0	0	1.00
Ray,Ken, Atl	R	.000	1	0	0	0	0	.000	1	0	0	0	0	0	0	0	0	69	67.2	5	6	0	0	1.000	9	4	0	0	.44
Reames,Britt, Pit	R	-	0	0	0	0	0	.128	39	5	0	0	1	3	4	11	6	6	7.1	1	1	0	0	1.000	1	0	0	0	.00
Redman,Mark, KC	L	.000	1	0	0	0	1	.062	130	8	0	0	0	3	5	60	10	29	167.0	8	25	3	4	.917	11	6	1	0	.55
Reitsma,Chris, Atl	R	-	0	0	0	0	0	.103	87	9	1	0	0	5	3	42	14	27	28.0	3	3	0	0	1.000	1	0	0	0	.00
Remlinger,Mike, Atl	L	-	0	0	0	0	0	.073	110	8	3	0	0	8	8	37	19	36	22.1	1	5	1	2	.857	0	0	0	0	-
Resop,Chris, Fla	R	-	0	0	0	0	0	.000	1	0	0	0	0	0	0	0	0	22	21.1	1	0	0	0	1.000	4	1	0	0	.25
Reyes,Anthony, StL	R	.120	25	3	0	0	2	.103	29	3	0	0	0	0	0	11	2	17	85.1	2	5	0	0	1.000	7	2	0	0	.29
Reyes,Dennys, Min	L	-	0	0	0	0	0	.074	54	4	1	0	0	0	2	25	2	66	50.2	6	11	0	1	1.000	4	4	4	0	1.00
Rheinecker,John, Tex	L	-	0	0	0	0	0	-	0	0	0	0	0	0	0	0	0	21	70.2	2	20	0	1	1.000	7	5	1	0	.71
Rhodes,Arthur, Phi	L	-	0	0	0	0	0	.250	4	1	0	0	0	0	0	3	0	55	45.2	0	7	0	0	1.000	2	0	0	0	.00
Rincon,Juan, Min	R	-	0	0	0	0	0	.500	2	1	0	0	0	0	0	1	0	75	74.1	7	6	0	0	1.000	3	0	0	0	.00
Rincon,Ricardo, StL	L	-	0	0	0	0	0	.000	4	0	0	0	0	0	0	1	1	5	3.1	0	0	0	0	-	0	0	0	0	-
Ring,Royce, NYM	L	-	0	0	0	0	0	-	0	0	0	0	0	0	0	0	0	11	12.2	0	4	0	0	1.000	0	0	0	0	-
Riske,David, Bos-CWS	R	-	0	0	0	0	0	-	0	0	0	0	0	0	0	0	0	41	44.0	1	3	1	0	.800	4	1	0	0	.25
Rivera,Mariano, NYY	R	.000	1	0	0	0	0	.000	1	0	0	0	0	0	0	0	1	63	75.0	7	18	0	1	1.000	6	3	0	0	.50
Rivera,Saul, Was	R	.000	4	0	0	0	0	.000	4	0	0	0	0	0	0	2	0	54	60.1	2	8	1	0	.909	4	0	0	0	.00
Rleal,Sendy, Bal	R	-	0	0	0	0	0	-	0	0	0	0	0	0	0	0	0	42	46.2	6	1	1	0	.875	0	0	0	0	-
Robertson,Nate, Det	L	.167	6	1	0	1	0	.071	14	1	0	0	0	1	0	6	1	32	208.2	10	21	3	0	.912	14	5	1	0	.36
Rodney,Fernando, Det	R	.000	1	0	0	0	0	.000	1	0	0	0	0	0	0	0	0	63	71.2	5	9	1	0	.933	9	4	1	0	.44
Rodriguez,Eddy, Bal	R	-	0	0	0	0	0	.000	1	0	0	0	0	0	0	1	0	9	15.0	0	1	1	1	.500	1	0	0	0	.00
Rodriguez,Felix, Was	R	.000	1	0	0	0	0	.235	17	4	1	0	1	3	0	5	2	31	29.1	1	4	0	0	1.000	3	1	0	0	.33
Rodriguez,Fran, LAA	R	-	0	0	0	0	0	-	0	0	0	0	0	0	0	0	0	69	73.0	5	5	0	0	1.000	3	1	0	1	.33
Rodriguez,Wandy, Hou	L	.081	37	3	0	1	5	.117	77	9	0	0	0	2	3	26	6	30	135.2	6	15	1	1	.955	12	6	4	0	.50
Rogers,Brian, Pit	R	-	0	0	0	0	0	-	0	0	0	0	0	0	0	0	0	10	8.2	0	1	0	0	1.000	0	0	0	0	-
Rogers,Kenny, Det	L	.143	7	1	0	0	0	.143	63	9	1	1	0	4	4	23	4	34	204.0	14	38	5	2	.912	7	6	1	1	.86
Romero,Davis, Tor	L	-	0	0	0	0	0	-	0	0	0	0	0	0	0	0	0	7	16.1	3	0	0	0	1.000	5	0	0	0	.00
Romero,J.C., LAA	L	-	0	0	0	0	0	.333	3	1	1	0	0	0	0	1	0	65	48.1	7	3	0	0	1.000	3	1	1	0	.33
Roney,Matt, Oak	R	-	0	0	0	0	0	.500	2	1	0	0	0	0	0	1	0	3	4.0	0	0	0	0	-	0	0	0	0	-
Rosario,Francisco, Tor	R	.000	1	0	0	0	0	.000	1	0	0	0	0	0	0	0	0	17	23.0	0	3	0	0	1.000	8	0	0	0	.00
Rupe,Josh, Tex	R	-	0	0	0	0	0	-	0	0	0	0	0	0	0	0	0	16	29.0	2	5	0	0	1.000	1	0	0	0	.00
Rusch,Glendon, ChC	L	.200	15	3	0	0	3	.154	305	47	4	0	3	19	9	99	38	25	66.1	3	10	0	0	1.000	6	3	1	0	.50
Ryan,B.J., Tor	L	-	0	0	0	0	0	-	0	0	0	0	0	0	0	0	0	65	72.1	1	12	0	2	1.000	10	3	2	0	.30
Ryu,Jae Kuk, ChC	R	.000	1	0	0	0	0	.000	1	0	0	0	0	0	0	1	0	10	15.0	2	1	0	0	1.000	0	0	0	0	-
Saarloos,Kirk, Oak	R	-	0	0	0	0	0	.056	36	2	1	0	0	3	1	11	8	35	121.1	9	27	0	1	1.000	12	5	0	0	.42
Sabathia,C.C., Cle	L	.222	9	2	0	2	0	.265	34	9	1	0	1	6	1	10	1	28	192.2	7	15	3	1	.880	19	5	0	0	.26
Sadler,Billy, SF	R	-	0	0	0	0	0	-	0	0	0	0	0	0	0	0	0	5	4.0	0	0	0	0	-	0	0	0	0	-

Pitchers Hitting, Fielding and Holding Runners

Pitcher	T	2006 Hitting Avg	AB	H	HR	RBI	SH	Career Hitting Avg	AB	H	2B	3B	HR	RBI	BB	SO	SH	2006 Fielding and Holding Runners G	Inn	PO	A	E	DP	Pct	SBA	CS	PCS	PPO	CS%
Saito,Takashi, LAD	R	-	0	0	0	0	0	-	0	0	0	0	0	0	0	0	0	72	78.1	2	7	0	2	1.000	5	0	0	0	.00
Salas,Juan, TB	R	-	0	0	0	0	0	-	0	0	0	0	0	0	0	0	0	8	10.0	2	3	0	0	1.000	0	0	0	0	.00
Sampson,Chris, Hou	R	.000	5	0	0	0	2	.000	5	0	0	0	0	0	0	2	2	12	34.0	4	11	0	0	1.000	0	0	0	0	-
Sanches,Brian, Phi	R	-	0	0	0	0	0	-	0	0	0	0	0	0	0	0	0	18	21.1	1	0	0	0	1.000	1	1	0	0	1.00
Sanchez,Anibal, Fla	R	.114	35	4	0	2	3	.114	35	4	0	0	0	2	0	14	3	18	114.1	15	12	1	2	.964	7	1	0	0	.14
Sanchez,Duaner, NYM	R	.000	1	0	0	0	0	.111	9	1	1	0	0	2	0	2	1	49	55.1	4	5	1	0	.900	3	0	0	1	.00
Sanchez,Jonathan, SF	L	.000	7	0	0	0	0	.000	7	0	0	0	0	0	1	4	0	27	40.0	0	2	0	0	1.000	9	0	0	0	.00
Santana,Ervin, LAA	R	.250	4	1	0	0	0	.250	4	1	0	0	0	0	0	3	0	33	204.0	13	12	2	3	.926	14	9	0	0	.64
Santana,Johan, Min	L	.000	2	0	0	0	0	.250	24	6	0	0	0	2	0	4	0	34	233.2	12	31	1	2	.977	9	5	0	0	.56
Santana,Julio, Phi	R	.000	1	0	0	0	1	.100	20	2	0	0	0	1	0	11	1	7	8.1	0	1	0	0	1.000	0	0	0	0	-
Santos,Victor, Pit	R	.158	38	6	0	1	6	.099	121	12	2	0	0	2	2	47	16	25	115.1	5	8	1	1	.929	12	4	0	2	.33
Sarfate,Dennis, Mil	R	-	0	0	0	0	0	-	0	0	0	0	0	0	0	0	0	8	8.1	0	0	0	0	-	1	0	0	0	.00
Sauerbeck,Scott, Cle-Oak	L	-	0	0	0	0	0	.000	7	0	0	0	0	0	0	4	1	46	25.1	2	5	0	0	1.000	1	0	0	0	.00
Saunders,Joe, LAA	L	-	0	0	0	0	0	-	0	0	0	0	0	0	0	0	0	13	70.2	1	10	0	3	1.000	4	3	1	0	.75
Schilling,Curt, Bos	R	.500	2	1	0	0	0	.150	771	116	13	1	0	29	25	269	102	31	204.0	14	26	3	1	.930	11	5	0	3	.45
Schmidt,Jason, SF	R	.136	66	9	1	1	6	.104	584	61	9	0	6	20	22	278	88	32	213.1	10	19	0	1	1.000	20	8	0	2	.40
Schoeneweis,S, Tor-Cin	L	-	0	0	0	0	0	.286	7	2	1	0	0	1	2	2	0	71	51.2	6	7	0	2	1.000	6	1	0	0	.17
Schroder,Chris, Was	R	.000	2	0	0	0	0	.000	2	0	0	0	0	0	0	1	0	21	28.1	1	2	0	1	1.000	2	0	0	0	.00
Seanez,Rudy, Bos-SD	R	-	0	0	0	0	0	.000	4	0	0	0	0	0	1	4	0	49	53.0	4	4	0	0	1.000	7	0	0	0	.00
Seay,Bobby, Det	L	-	0	0	0	0	0	-	0	0	0	0	0	0	0	0	0	14	15.1	0	1	0	0	1.000	0	0	0	0	-
Sele,Aaron, LAD	R	.192	26	5	0	0	6	.167	54	9	2	0	0	1	2	12	11	28	103.1	3	10	0	0	1.000	8	2	0	0	.25
Seo,Jae, LAD-TB	R	.105	19	2	0	0	2	.115	131	15	3	0	0	5	9	45	11	36	157.0	4	20	0	2	1.000	12	7	0	1	.58
Shackelford,Br, Cin	L	-	0	0	0	0	0	.000	1	0	0	0	0	0	0	1	0	26	16.1	2	3	0	0	1.000	0	0	0	0	-
Sharpless,Josh, Pit	R	-	0	0	0	0	0	-	0	0	0	0	0	0	0	0	0	14	12.0	2	1	0	0	1.000	6	1	0	0	.17
Sheets,Ben, Mil	R	.030	33	1	0	0	3	.078	321	25	1	0	0	7	16	155	30	17	106.0	5	8	0	0	1.000	12	2	0	2	.17
Sherrill,George, Sea	L	-	0	0	0	0	0	-	0	0	0	0	0	0	0	0	0	72	40.0	0	7	0	0	1.000	6	2	2	0	.33
Shields,James, TB	R	.375	8	3	0	0	0	.375	8	3	0	0	0	0	0	3	0	21	124.2	14	15	0	1	1.000	11	4	2	2	.36
Shields,Scot, LAA	R	.000	1	0	0	0	0	.000	3	0	0	0	0	0	0	2	0	74	87.2	10	13	1	2	.958	10	0	0	0	.00
Shiell,Jason, Atl	R	.000	4	0	0	0	1	.000	4	0	0	0	0	0	1	3	1	4	15.2	3	1	3	0	.857	1	0	0	0	.00
Shouse,Brian, Tex-Mil	L	-	0	0	0	0	0	-	0	0	0	0	0	0	0	0	0	65	38.1	3	10	1	0	.929	4	2	0	0	.50
Sikorski,Brian, SD-Cle	R	-	0	0	0	0	0	-	0	0	0	0	0	0	0	0	0	30	34.0	0	3	0	0	1.000	5	2	0	2	.40
Silva,Carlos, Min	R	.333	3	1	0	0	0	.158	19	3	1	0	0	1	1	6	1	36	180.1	13	20	0	3	1.000	12	2	0	0	.17
Simpson,Allan, Mil	R	-	0	0	0	0	0	.000	1	0	0	0	0	0	0	0	0	2	2.2	0	0	0	0	-	0	0	0	0	-
Sisco,Andy, KC	L	-	0	0	0	0	0	.000	1	0	0	0	0	0	0	1	0	65	58.1	3	5	1	1	.889	6	1	0	0	.17
Slaten,Doug, Ari	L	-	0	0	0	0	0	-	0	0	0	0	0	0	0	0	0	9	5.2	0	2	0	0	1.000	0	0	0	0	-
Slocum,Brian, Cle	R	-	0	0	0	0	0	-	0	0	0	0	0	0	0	0	0	8	17.2	0	2	0	0	.000	2	1	0	0	.50
Small,Aaron, NYY	R	.000	1	0	0	0	1	.000	4	0	0	0	0	0	0	3	1	11	27.2	0	4	0	0	1.000	1	0	0	0	.00
Smith,Matt, NYY-Phi	L	-	0	0	0	0	0	-	0	0	0	0	0	0	0	0	0	26	20.2	2	3	0	1	1.000	2	1	1	0	.50
Smith,Mike, Min	R	-	0	0	0	0	0	-	0	0	0	0	0	0	0	0	0	1	3.0	0	0	0	0	-	0	0	0	0	-
Smith,Travis, Atl	R	.000	1	0	0	0	0	.143	28	4	0	0	0	2	0	8	2	1	4.1	0	0	0	0	-	0	0	0	0	-
Smoltz,John, Atl	R	.125	64	8	0	4	18	.166	871	145	25	2	5	58	77	337	122	35	232.0	20	33	2	1	.964	14	4	0	0	.29
Snell,Ian, Pit	R	.056	54	3	0	2	9	.047	64	3	1	0	0	2	2	33	10	32	186.0	9	24	0	1	1.000	21	5	0	0	.24
Snyder,Kyle, KC-Bos	R	-	0	0	0	0	0	.000	2	0	0	0	0	0	0	1	0	17	60.1	2	6	0	2	1.000	8	2	0	0	.25
Soler,Alay, NYM	R	.091	11	1	0	0	4	.091	11	1	0	0	0	0	0	6	4	8	45.0	3	6	1	0	.900	5	0	0	0	.00
Soriano,Rafael, Sea	R	-	0	0	0	0	0	.000	4	0	0	0	0	0	0	1	0	53	60.0	2	3	0	0	1.000	9	2	0	0	.22
Sosa,Jorge, Atl-StL	R	.125	24	3	3	3	6	.109	55	6	0	0	3	3	3	26	9	45	118.0	1	10	0	0	1.000	4	2	1	0	.50
Sowers,Jeremy, Cle	L	-	0	0	0	0	0	-	0	0	0	0	0	0	0	0	0	14	88.1	4	7	1	1	.917	3	1	0	0	.33
Speier,Justin, Tor	R	-	0	0	0	0	0	.176	17	3	0	0	0	0	0	8	0	58	51.1	4	5	0	1	1.000	10	1	1	0	.10
Springer,Russ, Hou	R	-	0	0	0	0	0	.077	26	2	0	0	0	0	0	16	4	72	59.2	3	6	1	0	.900	8	1	0	0	.13
Spurling,Chris, Det-Mil	R	-	0	0	0	0	0	-	0	0	0	0	0	0	0	0	0	16	21.1	0	2	0	0	1.000	1	1	0	0	1.00
Standridge,Jas, Cin	R	-	0	0	0	0	0	-	0	0	0	0	0	0	1	0	0	21	18.2	0	1	0	0	1.000	1	0	0	0	.00
Stanton,Mike, Was-SF	L	.000	2	0	0	0	0	.364	22	8	1	0	0	3	1	3	1	82	67.2	0	7	1	1	.875	8	4	3	1	.50
Stauffer,Tim, SD	R	.500	2	1	0	0	0	.154	26	4	1	0	0	1	0	11	3	1	6.0	0	0	0	0	-	1	1	0	0	1.00
Stemle,Steve, KC	R	-	0	0	0	0	0	-	0	0	0	0	0	0	0	0	0	5	6.0	0	2	0	1	1.000	1	0	0	0	.00
Stockman,Phil, Atl	R	-	0	0	0	0	0	-	0	0	0	0	0	0	0	0	0	4	4.0	0	0	0	0	-	2	0	0	0	.00
Stokes,Brian, TB	R	-	0	0	0	0	0	-	0	0	0	0	0	0	0	0	0	5	24.0	1	2	0	0	1.000	3	2	0	0	.67
Street,Huston, Oak	R	-	0	0	0	0	0	-	0	0	0	0	0	0	0	0	0	69	70.2	3	8	2	0	.846	6	1	1	0	.17
Stults,Eric, LAD	L	.600	5	3	0	0	1	.600	5	3	0	0	0	0	0	1	1	6	17.2	1	2	1	1	.750	0	0	0	0	-
Sturtze,Tanyon, NYY	R	-	0	0	0	0	0	.063	16	1	0	0	0	0	0	5	2	18	10.2	1	0	1	0	.500	1	0	0	0	.00
Suppan,Jeff, StL	R	.218	55	12	0	6	9	.196	250	49	4	0	1	15	12	53	36	32	190.0	8	25	0	2	1.000	15	3	0	1	.20
Sweeney,Brian, SD	R	.000	1	0	0	0	0	.000	5	0	0	0	0	0	0	3	0	37	56.1	3	13	0	2	1.000	3	0	0	0	.00
Switzer,Jon, TB	L	-	0	0	0	0	0	-	0	0	0	0	0	0	0	0	0	40	33.2	1	2	0	0	1.000	2	1	0	0	.50
Tallet,Brian, Tor	L	-	0	0	0	0	0	.000	2	0	0	0	0	0	0	1	0	44	54.1	2	8	1	0	.909	8	4	2	1	.50
Tankersley,Taylor, Fla	L	.000	2	0	0	0	0	.000	2	0	0	0	0	0	0	2	0	49	41.0	2	6	0	0	1.000	10	0	0	3	.00
Taschner,Jack, SF	L	-	0	0	0	0	0	-	0	0	0	0	0	0	0	0	0	24	19.1	1	5	1	0	.857	3	1	0	0	.33
Tata,Jordan, Det	R	-	0	0	0	0	0	-	0	0	0	0	0	0	0	0	0	8	14.2	1	1	0	0	1.000	0	0	0	0	-
Taubenheim,Ty, Tor	R	.333	3	1	0	0	0	.333	3	1	0	0	0	0	0	2	0	12	35.0	2	5	0	0	1.000	1	0	0	0	.00
Tavarez,Julian, Bos	R	-	0	0	0	0	0	.111	135	15	0	0	0	8	6	57	21	58	98.2	7	16	2	2	.920	2	0	0	0	.00
Tejeda,Robinson, Tex	R	.000	2	0	0	0	1	.091	22	2	0	1	0	0	0	10	6	14	73.2	3	7	1	0	.909	7	3	0	0	.43
Thompson,Brad, StL	R	.500	2	1	0	0	0	.250	8	2	0	0	0	0	0	3	1	43	56.2	5	9	0	0	1.000	2	1	0	0	.50

311

Pitchers Hitting, Fielding and Holding Runners

Pitcher	T	Avg	AB	H	HR	RBI	SH	Avg	AB	H	2B	3B	HR	RBI	BB	SO	SH	G	Inn	PO	A	E	DP	Pct	SBA	CS	PCS	PPO	CS%
		2006 Hitting						**Career Hitting**										**2006 Fielding and Holding Runners**											
Thompson,Mike, SD	R	.160	25	4	0	0	3	.160	25	4	0	0	0	0	1	12	3	19	92.0	8	16	1	1	.960	6	0	0	0	.00
Thomson,John, Atl	R	.267	30	8	0	4	2	.198	318	63	6	1	0	22	12	133	48	18	80.1	7	16	0	0	1.000	15	4	0	0	.27
Thornton,Matt, CWS	L	-	0	0	0	0	0	-	0	0	0	0	0	0	0	0	0	63	54.0	2	8	1	0	.909	4	0	0	0	.00
Timlin,Mike, Bos	R	-	0	0	0	0	0	.000	7	0	0	0	0	0	0	4	0	68	64.0	6	7	0	1	1.000	5	1	0	0	.20
Tomko,Brett, LAD	R	.120	25	3	0	0	5	.169	419	71	9	0	28	18	157	66	44	112.1	3	15	0	1	1.000	5	1	0	0	.20
Torres,Salomon, Pit	R	.200	5	1	0	0	0	.147	102	15	1	1	0	1	2	46	12	94	93.1	9	13	0	2	1.000	8	3	1	0	.38
Towers,Josh, Tor	R	.200	5	1	0	0	0	.067	15	1	0	0	0	0	0	3	2	15	62.0	7	6	1	0	.929	14	2	0	0	.14
Traber,Billy, Was	L	.077	13	1	0	1	2	.059	17	1	0	0	0	1	1	10	2	15	43.1	1	5	0	0	1.000	5	2	1	0	.40
Tracey,Sean, CWS	R	-	0	0	0	0	0	-	0	0	0	0	0	0	0	0	0	7	8.0	1	1	0	0	1.000	0	0	0	0	-
Trachsel,Steve, NYM	R	.140	50	7	1	2	4	.164	639	105	17	1	3	40	26	196	87	30	164.2	7	28	1	1	.972	19	7	0	1	.37
Turnbow,Derrick, Mil	R	.000	1	0	0	0	0	.000	2	0	0	0	0	0	0	1	0	64	56.1	4	3	2	0	.778	4	1	0	0	.25
Valverde,Jose, Ari	R	-	0	0	0	0	0	1.000	1	1	0	0	0	0	0	0	0	44	49.1	1	1	0	0	1.000	1	0	0	0	.00
Van Buren,Jermaine, Bos	R	-	0	0	0	0	0	-	0	0	0	0	0	0	0	0	0	10	13.0	0	1	0	0	1.000	5	0	0	0	.00
Vargas,Claudio, Ari	R	.098	51	5	0	4	9	.072	139	10	3	0	0	7	3	41	27	31	167.2	10	21	2	2	.939	17	5	3	0	.29
Vargas,Jason, Fla	L	.313	16	5	0	1	0	.310	42	13	3	0	0	3	2	9	0	12	43.0	1	7	0	1	1.000	6	0	0	0	.00
Vazquez,Javier, CWS	R	1.000	1	1	0	0	1	.215	427	92	10	2	1	24	17	68	73	33	202.2	7	29	0	2	1.000	14	4	2	0	.29
Venafro,Mike, Col	L	-	0	0	0	0	0	-	0	0	0	0	0	0	0	0	0	7	3.2	0	0	0	0	-	0	0	0	0	-
Veras,Jose, NYY	R	-	0	0	0	0	0	-	0	0	0	0	0	0	0	0	0	12	11.0	0	1	0	0	1.000	3	1	0	0	.33
Verlander,Just, Det	R	.000	1	0	0	0	1	.000	1	0	0	0	0	0	0	0	1	30	186.0	11	24	3	4	.921	6	5	1	7	.83
Villanueva,Carlos, Mil	R	.067	15	1	0	1	2	.067	15	1	0	0	0	1	0	9	2	10	53.2	2	9	0	1	1.000	2	0	0	0	.00
Villarreal,Osc, Atl	R	.000	7	0	0	0	2	.000	10	0	0	0	0	0	0	5	2	58	92.1	8	15	0	0	1.000	5	1	0	1	.20
Villone,Ron, NYY	L	-	0	0	0	0	0	.130	169	22	3	1	1	7	1	50	12	70	80.1	2	19	1	1	.955	4	3	2	1	.75
Vizcaino,Luis, Ari	R	-	0	0	0	0	0	.000	2	0	0	0	0	0	0	0	0	70	65.1	2	9	0	1	1.000	4	2	0	0	.50
Vogelsong,Ryan, Pit	R	.333	3	1	0	0	0	.186	59	11	4	0	0	3	4	24	12	20	38.0	2	12	0	1	1.000	7	1	0	0	.14
Volquez,Edison, Tex	R	-	0	0	0	0	0	-	0	0	0	0	0	0	0	0	0	8	33.1	4	2	0	1	1.000	5	1	0	0	.20
Waechter,Doug, TB	R	-	0	0	0	0	0	.000	5	0	0	0	0	0	0	0	0	11	53.0	0	4	1	0	.800	3	2	0	0	.67
Wagner,Billy, NYM	L	-	0	0	0	0	0	.100	20	2	0	0	0	1	1	12	0	70	72.1	1	11	0	0	1.000	9	4	1	0	.44
Wagner,Ryan, Was	R	.333	3	1	0	0	0	.250	4	1	0	0	0	0	0	2	1	26	30.2	2	7	0	0	1.000	3	0	0	0	.00
Wainwright,Adam, StL	R	.500	6	3	1	1	0	.500	6	3	1	0	1	1	0	0	0	61	75.0	3	7	1	0	.909	5	0	0	0	.00
Wakefield,Tim, Bos	R	.000	4	0	0	0	0	.125	96	12	2	0	1	4	2	35	13	23	140.0	13	12	0	1	1.000	28	4	0	2	.14
Walker,Jamie, Det	L	-	0	0	0	0	0	-	0	0	0	0	0	0	0	0	0	56	48.0	0	2	0	0	1.000	3	1	0	0	.33
Walker,Pete, Tor	R	-	0	0	0	0	0	.000	1	0	0	0	0	0	0	1	0	23	30.0	3	7	1	0	.909	3	0	0	0	.00
Walker,Tyler, SF-TB	R	-	0	0	0	0	0	.000	10	0	0	0	0	0	1	6	0	26	25.1	0	0	0	0	-	5	1	0	0	.20
Walrond,Les, ChC	L	.000	2	0	0	0	1	.000	2	0	0	0	0	0	0	1	1	10	17.1	1	4	0	0	1.000	1	0	0	0	.00
Wang,Chien-Ming, NYY	R	.000	4	0	0	0	0	.000	5	0	0	0	0	0	0	0	3	34	218.0	15	42	1	4	.983	20	11	1	0	.55
Wasdin,John, Tex	R	-	0	0	0	0	0	.200	15	3	1	0	0	1	1	5	1	9	30.0	1	1	0	0	1.000	3	1	0	0	.33
Washburn,Jarrod, Sea	L	.000	2	0	0	0	1	.267	30	8	0	0	0	3	4	8	7	31	187.0	7	24	0	0	1.000	10	5	2	0	.50
Weathers,David, Cin	R	.000	1	0	0	0	0	.101	139	14	0	2	4	7	85	16	67	73.2	2	3	1	0	.833	4	1	0	0	.25
Weaver,Jeff, LAA-StL	R	.133	30	4	0	3	6	.206	189	39	6	1	0	13	6	64	21	31	172.0	13	17	3	0	.909	17	8	0	2	.47
Weaver,Jered, LAA	R	-	0	0	0	0	0	-	0	0	0	0	0	0	0	0	0	19	123.0	7	8	2	0	.882	14	3	0	0	.21
Webb,Brandon, Ari	R	.151	73	11	0	9	10	.112	249	28	3	0	0	15	8	120	34	33	235.0	17	46	3	3	.955	33	9	2	0	.27
Wellemeyer,Todd, Fla-KC	R	.000	2	0	0	0	0	.143	7	1	0	0	0	1	3	1	0	46	78.1	3	12	0	2	1.000	7	1	1	0	.14
Wells,David, Bos-SD	L	.200	5	1	0	0	3	.120	125	15	1	0	4	3	41	14	13	75.1	2	6	0	0	1.000	7	0	0	1	.00
Wells,Kip, Pit-Tex	R	.091	11	1	0	0	1	.176	250	44	9	1	3	12	4	112	25	9	44.1	1	3	0	0	1.000	6	4	0	0	.67
Westbrook,Jake, Cle	R	.500	4	2	0	1	1	.200	10	2	1	0	0	1	1	6	3	32	211.1	33	40	1	1	.986	19	3	2	1	.16
Wheeler,Dan, Hou	R	-	0	0	0	0	0	.143	7	1	0	0	0	0	0	1	1	75	71.1	5	4	0	0	1.000	4	1	0	0	.25
White,Rick, Cin-Phi	R	-	0	0	0	0	0	.095	42	4	1	0	0	1	0	12	2	64	64.2	1	16	0	2	1.000	5	2	0	0	.40
Wickman,Bob, Cle-Atl	R	-	0	0	0	0	0	.000	2	0	0	0	0	0	0	0	0	57	54.0	3	6	2	1	.818	4	0	0	0	.00
Williams,Dave, Cin-NYM	L	.143	21	3	0	0	1	.123	122	15	3	0	1	9	4	64	9	14	69.0	1	18	0	1	1.000	6	4	2	0	.67
Williams,Jerome, ChC	R	.000	4	0	0	0	0	.110	109	12	0	0	1	1	50	18	5	12.1	0	1	1	0	.500	2	0	0	0	.00
Williams,Todd, Bal	R	-	0	0	0	0	0	-	0	0	0	0	0	0	0	0	0	62	57.0	6	13	1	2	.950	3	1	0	0	.33
Williams,Woody, SD	R	.204	54	11	0	4	6	.206	481	99	25	1	3	41	17	158	40	25	145.1	12	16	1	1	.966	10	0	0	0	.00
Williamson,Sc, ChC-SD	R	-	0	0	0	0	0	.043	23	1	0	0	0	3	14	7	42	39.1	5	8	0	1	1.000	17	3	2	0	.18
Willis,Dontrelle, Fla	L	.172	64	11	3	10	6	.222	288	64	8	2	6	28	16	51	18	34	223.1	11	44	5	4	.917	11	5	1	1	.45
Wilson,Brian, SF	R	.000	2	0	0	0	0	.000	2	0	0	0	0	0	0	0	1	31	30.0	1	3	0	0	1.000	4	2	0	0	.50
Wilson,C.J., Tex	R	-	0	0	0	0	0	-	0	0	0	0	0	0	0	0	0	44	44.1	0	7	0	0	1.000	8	3	1	0	.38
Wilson,Kris, NYY	R	-	0	0	0	0	0	.333	3	1	0	0	0	0	1	0	0	5	8.1	1	1	0	0	1.000	0	0	0	0	-
Windsor,Jason, Oak	R	-	0	0	0	0	0	-	0	0	0	0	0	0	0	0	0	4	13.2	0	1	1	0	.500	2	0	0	0	.00
Winkelsas,Joe, Mil	R	-	0	0	0	0	0	-	0	0	0	0	0	0	0	0	0	7	7.0	0	2	0	0	1.000	0	0	0	0	-
Wise,Matt, Mil	R	.000	1	0	0	0	0	.167	6	1	0	0	0	1	2	1	0	40	44.1	2	6	1	0	.889	2	1	0	0	.50
Witasick,Jay, Oak	R	-	0	0	0	0	0	.071	42	3	0	0	0	3	1	22	2	20	22.2	2	1	0	1	1.000	1	0	0	0	.00
Wolf,Randy, Phi	L	.190	21	4	0	4	0	.193	353	68	19	0	4	34	21	112	49	12	56.2	6	6	0	0	1.000	5	2	0	0	.40
Wood,Kerry, ChC	R	.500	6	3	0	2	0	.172	344	59	6	0	7	32	11	112	46	4	19.2	1	1	1	0	.667	3	1	0	0	.33
Wood,Mike, KC	R	.000	3	0	0	0	0	.000	5	0	0	0	0	0	0	2	0	23	64.2	4	12	1	0	.941	8	0	0	1	1.00
Woods,Jake, Sea	L	-	0	0	0	0	0	-	0	0	0	0	0	0	0	0	0	37	105.0	6	9	0	0	1.000	6	2	0	0	.33
Worrell,Tim, SF	R	.000	1	0	0	0	0	.099	81	8	1	0	4	4	43	10	23	20.1	3	1	1	0	.800	5	0	0	0	.00
Wright,Jamey, SF	R	.255	47	12	0	1	5	.147	435	64	15	1	1	17	12	174	50	34	156.0	10	28	2	1	.950	21	8	5	2	.38
Wright,Jaret, NYY	R	.000	3	0	0	1	0	.141	78	11	2	0	1	6	3	42	9	30	140.1	5	18	1	1	.958	7	4	0	0	.57
Wuertz,Mike, ChC	R	-	0	0	0	0	1	.000	1	0	0	0	0	0	0	3	1	41	40.2	2	3	1	0	.833	4	2	0	0	.50
Yan,Esteban, LAA-Cin	R	-	0	0	0	0	0	1.000	2	2	0	0	1	1	0	0	1	27	37.1	3	0	0	0	1.000	4	2	0	0	.50

Pitchers Hitting, Fielding and Holding Runners

Pitcher	T	2006 Hitting						Career Hitting										2006 Fielding and Holding Runners										
		Avg	AB	H	HR	RBI	SH	Avg	AB	H	2B	3B	HR	RBI	BB	SO	SH	G	Inn	PO	A	E	DP	Pct	SBA	CS	PCS	PPO	CS%
Yates,Tyler, Atl	R	-	0	0	0	0	0	.091	11	1	0	0	0	0	0	5	1	56	50.0	1	7	0	0	1.000	2	0	0	0	.00
Youman,Shane, Pit	L	.429	7	3	0	1	0	.429	7	3	0	0	0	1	0	3	0	5	21.2	2	4	0	0	1.000	0	0	0	0	-
Young,Chris, SD	R	.130	54	7	0	4	8	.119	59	7	2	1	0	4	0	29	8	31	179.1	8	12	0	2	1.000	45	4	0	1	.09
Zambrano,Carlos, ChC	R	.151	73	11	6	11	5	.212	330	70	13	2	10	28	5	122	23	33	214.0	12	33	4	4	.918	5	3	0	1	.60
Zambrano,Victor, NYM	R	.000	5	0	0	0	0	.123	73	9	1	1	0	3	0	28	8	5	21.1	1	1	0	0	1.000	3	1	0	0	.33
Zito,Barry, Oak	L	.000	3	0	0	0	1	.034	29	1	0	0	0	0	0	15	3	34	221.0	7	18	1	3	.962	20	12	2	0	.60
Zumaya,Joel, Det	R	-	0	0	0	0	0	-	0	0	0	0	0	0	0	0	0	62	83.1	2	4	1	1	.857	5	1	0	0	.20

Hitters Pitching

Player	2006 Pitching											Career Pitching										
	G	W	L	Sv	IP	H	R	ER	BB	SO	ERA	G	W	L	Sv	IP	H	R	ER	BB	SO	ERA
Burroughs,Sean, TB	0	0	0	0	0.0	0	0	0	0	0	-	1	0	0	0	1.0	4	3	3	0	0	27.00
Finley,Steve, SF	0	0	0	0	0.0	0	0	0	0	0	-	1	0	0	0	1.0	0	0	0	1	0	0.00
Gonzalez,Wiki, Was	0	0	0	0	0.0	0	0	0	0	0	-	1	0	0	0	1.0	0	0	0	1	0	0.00
Jimenez,D'Ang, Tex-Oak	0	0	0	0	0.0	0	0	0	0	0	-	1	0	0	0	1.1	0	0	0	0	0	0.00
Laker,Tim, Cle	0	0	0	0	0.0	0	0	0	0	0	-	2	0	0	0	2.0	2	0	0	2	1	0.00
Loretta,Mark, Bos	0	0	0	0	0.0	0	0	0	0	0	-	1	0	0	0	1.0	1	0	0	1	2	0.00
Mabry,John, ChC	0	0	0	0	0.0	0	0	0	0	0	-	2	0	0	0	1.0	6	7	7	4	0	63.00
Nunez,Abraham , Phi	0	0	0	0	0.0	0	0	0	0	0	-	1	0	0	0	0.1	0	0	0	0	0	0.00
Perez,Tomas, TB	0	0	0	0	0.0	0	0	0	0	0	-	1	0	0	0	0.1	0	0	0	0	0	0.00

Manufactured Runs

Bill James

Part I

The term "Manufactured Run", with the modern understanding of the term, emerged in the mid-1970s, at the time of a stolen base revival. They have these computer searches you can do now, searching old newspapers for combinations of words. Searches for combinations using "manufactured" and "run" and "baseball" get occasional random hits before 1975, mostly when a manufacturer of something buys a baseball team, but sometimes the term "manufactured runs" will turn up. Most of the time, however, these are uses like "the New York Yankees manufactured 8 runs on 11 hits Friday night", or "Chicago manufactured four runs in the seventh on two doubles and a two homers."

In the mid-1970s the term started to pop up in newspapers in the modern usage. As we use the term now, a manufactured run is a run put together out of small parts. The term is fairly ubiquitous; almost every broadcast, I would guess, contains some reference to manufactured runs or efforts to manufacture a run or to the importance of manufacturing runs. Every manager talks about it.

About three years ago, it occurred to me to ask, "What exactly *is* a manufactured run?" How do you define a manufactured run? How do you determine whether a given run is or is not manufactured? This led to a give and take between myself—Bill James—and Steve Moyer, who runs Baseball Info Solutions, the company which actually produces all of the information in this book. Eventually, last summer, we decided to stop arguing about it, and move forward with the data.

The general definition of a manufactured run is that *a run is considered a manufactured run if it is at least one-half created by the offense doing something other than playing station-to-station baseball.* We developed two types of Manufactured Runs, a sort of loose definition and a strict definition.

Manufactured Runs (Type 1) are runs created by deliberate acts such as bunting and stealing bases.

Manufactured Runs (Type 2) are runs created by things such as infield hits, taking advantage of the defense, moving up two bases on singles, advancing on outs, and advancing on throws.

As a general rule, if two singles are added together to make a run, that's a manufactured run. If you produce a run from a walk and a single, that's a manufactured run. If it's three hits, or if there is a walk and two hits, or if there is an extra-base hit involved, it generally is not a manufactured run.

We will need a more specific definition than that, and I will get to that in a moment, but first, why the two definitions?   OK, I admit it; we're trying to keep everybody happy.   Suppose that a team had a walk, a single (runner going to third) and a fly ball, leading to a run, and suppose further that there was then an official determination that this was a Manufactured Run.   You know what people are going to say.   People are going to say, at that point, "well, that's not *really* a manufactured run.   That's not what *I* mean when *I* say that a run was manufactured."

People are going to say that, because people like to say crap like that.   But at the same time, the fact is that when that sequence of events occurs, people absolutely are going to describe that as manufacturing a run, beyond any question.   The announcers are going to say that that team manufactured a run, the sportswriters are going to write that that run was manufactured, and nobody is going to have any problem with that—until you say officially that that was a manufactured run, at which moment the same people are going to step forward to debate learnedly the issue of what is and what is not a manufactured run.

So we used both definitions—the loose definition (MR-2) to match the way that the term is actually used every day at the ballpark, and the much stricter definition (MR-1) to accommodate the puritan impulse that causes people to insist that what goes into the record books must meet rigorous standards.   This is the more specific, point-by-point definition that I promised you earlier.   There are twelve rules:

1. Any run which scores without a hit is ALWAYS considered to be a manufactured run.

2. A run which scores on which the only hit(s) is (are) infield hit(s) is always considered to be a manufactured run.

3. A run which scores as a direct result of an extra base hit is NEVER considered a manufactured run (that is, if the RBI is credited to an extra base hit), with the exception of plays described in Rule 8.

4. Otherwise, a run is considered to be a manufactured run if TWO of the four bases do NOT result from the runner being forced along by a walk, a hit batsman, or a safe hit reaching the outfield.

5. Manufactured Runs are of two types, Type One (MR-1) and Type Two (MR-2).

6. Type One (MR-1) are those manufactured runs which involve at least one base resulting from one of four deliberate acts intended to manufacture a run, those acts being:

   a. A sacrifice bunt,
   b. A stolen base,
   c. A hit and run play,
   d. A bunt hit.

A sacrifice bunt, for purposes of this definition, includes any attempt at a sacrifice bunt which results in a positive outcome for the offense. In other words, if a team bunts in a sacrifice situation but the play results in a single or some other positive outcome, that counts as a sacrifice bunt for the purpose of determining whether a manufactured run is Type One or Type Two.

Also, a run is a Type One manufactured run if

      a. It is a manufactured run, and

      b. It is scored by a pinch runner.

7. Those manufactured runs which do not qualify as Type One are classified as Type Two.

8. The exception to rule (3) is that a run shall be considered a manufactured run if

      a. The run scores on a double or a triple, and

      b. There are TWO bases in the sequence resulting from the four acts outlined in rule 6.

In other words, if a batter reaches on a bunt hit and steals second, then scores on a double or a triple, that IS considered a manufactured run (MR-1), even though the run comes across the plate on an extra base hit.

9. A forceout or fielder's choice which does not improve the position of the baserunners should not be counted as contributing toward a manufactured run. Advancing on a forceout or a fielder's choice DOES count toward a manufactured run, if the play is one which improves the position of the baserunners.

10. A base "gained" on a double play does not count as contributing to a Manufactured Run. A run scored on a double play CAN be a manufactured run, if two OTHER bases are not attributable to forced advancement.

11. An "infield hit" is any safe hit fielded or retrieved by an infielder, with the exception of a ball hit in the air into the outfield, but subsequently retrieved by an infielder.

12. If a situation arises in which the scorer is simply unable to determine, consistent with these rules, whether a run is or is not a Manufactured Run, then the scorer will have to make a determination. He should be guided in this decision by whether he believes that a sportswriter or broadcaster, in that situation, would be likely to describe the sequence as manufacturing a run.

I'm sorry that's so complicated, but there's just no easy way to do it. The following scenarios may be used to sort out manufactured runs:

Single, single (runner goes to third), sacrifice fly.
      Manufactured run, Type 2.

Single, single (runner goes to third), ground out.
      Manufactured run, Type 2.

Single, single (runner goes to third), single.

NOT a manufactured run unless one of the hits is an infield hit. If one of the hits is an infield hit, MR-2.

Single, stolen base, single, run scores.

Manufactured run, Type 1.

Single, stolen base, walk, ground out, sac fly.

MR-1.

Single, stolen base, walk, ground out (runners move up), infield hit (run scores and other runner moves up), sacrifice fly, walk, home run.

Five runs score. The first two runs, which scored BEFORE the home run, are MR-1. The other three runs are not manufactured runs.

Double, ground out, ground out.

MR-2.

Single, stolen base, ground out, ground out.

MR-1.

Double, ground out, single.

Run is not manufactured.

Double, infield hit (runner holds), single (runners move up two), sacrifice bunt scores run.

Two runs score. The first run is NOT considered a manufactured run. The second run is MR-1.

Double, infield hit (runner advances), single (runners move up two), sacrifice bunt scores run.

Same thing. Only one base of the first run is not accounted for by a hit to the outfield. . .therefore it is not a manufactured run. The second run, which results from an infield hit, a single and a sac bunt, is an MR-1.

Double, stolen base, single.

No manufactured run.

Single, stolen base, single (runs scores).

MR-1.

Bunt hit, sacrifice bunt, double.

MR-1 (Under Rule 8).

Single, SB + E-2, IBB, GIDP.

MR-1.   The double play does not contribute toward the run being scored as manufactured, but two of the four bases are due to the baserunners' initiative in stealing the base, leading to the error.   The subsequent double play does not negate these.

Part II

After I wrote these rules, or wrote some of these rules, I went into Retrosheet, and downloaded the play-by-play for three teams from 1959—the Cubs, the Dodgers and the White Sox.   The White Sox, who were called the Go-Go Sox, were famous for manufacturing runs (although the term was not in general use at that time.)

Anyway, my goal was to study the play-by-play for these teams, and see if I could gain a better understanding of the role of Manufactured Runs in an offense, and of the difficulties involved in deciding what was and what was not a manufactured run.   Situations do arise in which it is all but impossible to determine whether something was or was not a Manufactured Run.   Here's one; this happened May 20, 1959, Philadelphia at Chicago.

Moe Drabowsky reaches on a leadoff double.

Tony Taylor bunts back to the mound.   The pitcher, Don Cardwell, throws to third, but throws high and late, all safe on Fielder's Choice.

Alvin Dark grounds to second, 4-6 forceout, run scores.

Ernie Banks doubles, Dark to third.

Walt Moryn grounds to second, Dark tries to score and is out at home (4-2).   Banks goes to third, Moryn to first.

Passed Ball. . .Banks scores, Moryn to second.

Dale Long singles, Moryn scores.

Bobby Thomson grounds to short, ending the inning.

Three runs in the inning.   OK, take the rules I laid out before, and tell me which of those runs are Manufactured and which aren't.   It can be done, and I THINK I know the answer, but. . .it ain't easy.

The Cubs in 1959 had 156 Manufactured Runs, of which 34 were Type 1 and 122 were Type 2.   As to the role this played in the success of the team . . .first of all, they didn't manufacture a huge number of runs. As we will see in a moment, most of the major league teams in 2006 manufactured significantly more runs, both MR-1 and MR-2, than did the 1959 Cubs. But what I really wish is that I had some way to estimate how many runs the Cubs cost themselves that year with ill-fated efforts to manufacture a run. The number had to be at least 75, and it may have been 150; they were constantly shooting themselves in the foot with busted hit-and-run plays, failed bunts, and unsuccessful attempts to move up a base on a fly to the outfield. It's almost comical, at a distance of 47 years. . .you get the feeling that these people believed strongly in manufacturing runs, only they were just really lousy at it.

The '59 White Sox are all different—they were really, really good at manufacturing runs. I didn't make it all the way through the season, scoring MR by hand, but my estimate is that the '59 White Sox probably had about 230 Manufactured Runs, including about 90 MR-1. Luis Aparicio scored 98 runs in 1959. I'm confident that more than half of those—more than 50 of them—were Manufactured Runs. The '59 Dodgers were also good at manufacturing runs, at least compared to the '59 Cubs. How they would compare to modern teams. . .I don't have enough data to say.

The other thing I learned from doing this study was that Tony Taylor was a wild man on the basepaths. I never knew this. . .I am old enough to remember Tony Taylor as a player, but I was a kid, and I didn't really understand anything except what the announcers told me. But he was amazing. . .he was like Alfredo Griffin. In one game (June 12 vs. Milwaukee) Taylor scored from second base on a tap to the catcher (2-3), and then later in the game was thrown out at home trying to score from first on a single to left field. On July 16 he scored from first on an infield single, drawing a throw from the first baseman by going first to third, then scoring when the throw went wild.

He was also thrown out many times doing stuff like this. But having said that, Taylor at least was actually good at this one-run stuff. . .really good. Maybe the cost was a little high, but the benefits are obvious. Taylor scored 32 Manufactured Runs. . .32 of his 96 runs scored, as opposed to 14 of 97 for Ernie Banks. Of course, 45 of Banks' runs were home runs, but setting those aside, Taylor's percentage is still higher, although not as high as Alvin Dark (22 of 60.) Pitcher Bob Anderson scored 6 runs, 5 of them Manufactured Runs, because whenever he got on base Taylor would find some way to move him along. The problem was that Taylor was playing on a team with a seemingly endless list of aging, ineffective sluggers. . .Irv Noren, Walt Moryn, Dale Long, Cal Neeman, Randy Jackson, etc. One of the aging sluggers, Bobby Thomson, was actually surprisingly effective at the one-run game as well.

Ahh, living in the Baseball Past. Retrosheet is great, isn't it?

Part III

We come now to the purpose of the present effort, which is to begin collecting and publishing information about the runs manufactured by current teams. Which modern teams are good at manufacturing runs? Which are not so good?

The best team in baseball in 2006 at manufacturing runs, by far, was the Minnesota Twins. The Twins had 224 Manufactured Runs. No other major league team was over 200.

The Cubs worked harder at it. The Cubs had 99 MR-1, or "intentionally Manufactured Runs", if you will. The Cubs had 170 stolen base attempts, which is a lot, and were third in the majors in Sacrifice Bunts. Unfortunately, despite a .268 team batting average, 17th in the majors, they were 28th among the 30 teams in runs scored, so it is hard to describe their efforts to manufacture runs as an unqualified success. But you have to give them an A for effort.

The Rockies, who find that they can bunt very successfully in the thin air up there, also had 81 Type 1 Manufactured Runs, which, again, is probably not an unqualified success from 111 Sacrifice Bunts and 135 Stolen Base Attempts.

For whatever it is worth, the Philadelphia Phillies, who were last in the majors in MR-1, with 33, were first in the National League in Runs Scored, with 865. The Yankees, who led the majors in runs scored, were middle-of-the-pack in Manufactured Runs.

There is probably some predictable relationship between one-run strategies and MR-1. There is probably some predictable relationship between batting average, home runs, on-base percentage, strikeouts and Manufactured Runs. There is probably some predictable relationship between Manufactured Runs and Winning Percentage, or Manufactured Runs and post-season success.

All of that will be interesting to study in upcoming years, but we're getting way ahead of ourselves. First we create the data, mostly through the hard work of Damon Lichtenwalner. Later on, we can pick it apart and figure out what it means.

Team	MR	MR1	MR2
Minnesota Twins	224	84	140
Los Angeles Angels	190	80	110
Kansas City Royals	186	57	129
Baltimore Orioles	184	74	110
Seattle Mariners	176	46	130
Tampa Bay Devil Rays	166	63	103
New York Yankees	163	59	104
Chicago White Sox	160	49	111
Boston Red Sox	147	39	108
Oakland Athletics	142	37	105
Texas Rangers	142	36	106
Cleveland Indians	139	43	96
Toronto Blue Jays	139	42	97
Detroit Tigers	124	41	83

Team	MR	MR1	MR2
Colorado Rockies	198	81	117
Washington Nationals	185	85	100
Chicago Cubs	175	99	76
Florida Marlins	175	69	106
Los Angeles Dodgers	172	72	100
Arizona Diamondbacks	169	56	113
Pittsburgh Pirates	167	58	109
St Louis Cardinals	164	43	121
Houston Astros	161	67	94
New York Mets	158	61	97
Milwaukee Brewers	151	44	107
Philadelphia Phillies	148	33	115
San Francisco Giants	144	53	91
Atlanta Braves	143	50	93
San Diego Padres	141	68	73
Cincinnati Reds	135	57	78

322

The Manager's Record

Bill James

Some ten years ago—or maybe it was 40, I'm not sure—it occurred to me that nobody could describe how one manager was functionally different from another. Personalities and clubhouse management. . .those things we understand a little bit. There are high-pressure managers who set high expectations and become very annoyed when players fail, and there are "long season" managers who roll with the punches and figure that the player who is forgiven today's trespasses may have a better chance to come through tommorrow. There are smiling managers and there are frowning managers. There are emotionally involved managers, and there are arms-length managers. There are successful managers of all types, and there are dismal failures of all types.

I am not talking about that; I am talking about in the game. What does one manager do, in practice, that makes him different from another manager? For several years we have been trying to identify very specific questions, with very specific answers, that can be used to describe managerial tendencies. It's a long process. Whereas fielding stats now are about where batting stats were in 1940, managerial stats are closer to where batting stats were in 1878. We have a long ditch in front of us, decades of asking very specific questions about managers, finding the answers, turning the answers into data, compiling years worth of data, and then studying the data to find out that we haven't actually learned anything and we need to start over.

The standards keep changing on us, for one thing. What was a quick hook ten years ago is a slow hook now; what was a high number of relievers to use in a season ten years ago is a pittance now. The fact that the standards keep changing is interesting to know in itself, but not *that* interesting, and it interferes with the development of markers by which to make sense of this stuff. The numbers ".258" and ".285" don't look all that much different, intuitively; it takes time and experience to learn to see differences that, once you're in, may seem highly significant. What is normal in the National League is abnormal in the American League, and managers keep drifting from one league to the other, which screws up their ratios.

It's like pulling teeth, but we keep pulling. OK, these are the specific questions we ask in compiling a manager's record:

1) *How many different lineups did he use?* This is charted under the heading "LUp". Joe Maddon of Tampa Bay used 145 different starting lineups last year; Charlie Manuel of Philadelphia used only 81.

This clearly is an identifiable manager tendency. Bobby Cox and Tony LaRussa have both been major league managers for decades, both highly successful. Since 1994 Cox has averaged 91 different lineups per season; LaRussa, 131. Last year Cox used 85 different lineups, LaRussa, 131. Our data for the National League teams don't consider the pitcher to be a part of the lineup.

2) *What percentage of the players in his starting lineup, over the course of the season, had the platoon advantage at the start of the game?* We enter this data under the heading "PL%".

This data would probably have been more interesting in earlier decades than it is now, when some managers platooned more. In the mid-1980s, Bobby Cox had a team that platooned at five positions. Whitey Herzog, I think, had teams that had an 85% platoon advantage in the starting lineup. You can't imagine anybody doing that now, when 12-man bullpens have shrunk the typical bench to a backup catcher and Damian Jackson.

Platoon percentages range from about 50% to about 65%. Bob Melvin and Joe Torre are probably the managers who platoon most in modern baseball; Ned Yost, Tony LaRussa and Clint Hurdle are among those who platoon least. Having switch-hitters in the lineup affects the percentage, as the switch hitter always has the platoon advantage.

3) *How many pinch hitters did the manager use?* We call this "PH", because we figure that pinch hitters effect the acidity of the game.

Pinch hitting totals are hugely different between the leagues, and also vary widely from season to season by the same manager, based on the makeup of the team. You have Nook Logan in your lineup, you just kind of have to pinch hit. There is also some managerial tendency. The American League manager who uses a pinch hitter most often is probably Ozzie Guillen—135 times last year, 132 per season career average. Buck Showalter has used 96 pinch hitters over the last two years combined. In the National League Bobby Cox is a big pinch-hitter guy, while Felipe Alou is on the other end.

4) *How many pinch runners did the manager use?* (PR). Dusty Baker used only 9 pinch runners last year and has a career average of 23 per 162 games over the course of a long career, while Bruce Bochy used 64 last year and has averaged 42 per season. Bobby Cox has a career average of 49; Jim Leyland, 20. The norm is 30 to 35.

5) *How many defensive substitutes did the manager put into the game?* (DS). Eric Wedge used only 13 defensive substitutes last year and has a career average of 19 per season. Phil Garner used 47 last year and has a career average of 40. Joe Girardi used 66 last year, but as it was his first year managing, we don't know whether that represents his philosophy or just the team he was stuck with.

Using defensive substitutes may indicate a belief in the importance of defense—or it may indicate the opposite, that a manager is trying to get as much as he can out of some bangers and is covering for them when the game is on the line. Buddy Bell uses very few defensive substitutes, but in my opinion this isn't because he doesn't emphasize defense. It is because he emphasizes defense so much that he usually has his best fielders in the lineup when the game begins.

In the manager's box there is a line there, and then we go into the pitcher usage section, in which we ask:

6 and 7) *How many Quick Hooks (Quick) and Slow Hooks (Slow) did the manager have?* The definitions of these are given in the Glossary at the end of the book. The quickest hook in the majors last year was Ron Gardenhire; the slowest, Ozzie Guillen.

Ozzie had a Slow Hook last year because he has a strong starting rotation and, at least last year, a not-very-good bullpen. Gardenhire is just a Quick Hook; always has been, and he has the bullpen to make it work. Grady Little is a Quick Hook; his old bench coach, Jerry Narron, is a Slow Hook. Ned Yost is a Slow Hook.

We have defined these things in such a way now that they balance, and the ratio between Quick Hooks and Slow Hooks pretty quickly becomes a true indicator of the manager's tendency. In earlier years we tried to use static definitions, but the changes in the game kept undercutting us. One ballpark effect here. . .a manager working in a big hitter's park has to be a Slow Hook or his starting rotation will degenerate.

8) *How many Long Outings from his starting pitcher did this manager have?* (LO). A long outing is defined as "more than 120 pitches", which by the way is becoming an obsolete definition, since nobody throws more than 120 pitches anymore. We'll work on revising it, but my theory is that so many managers have been criticized for allowing their starting pitchers to run high pitch counts that nobody does anymore, and this whole area may be no longer of much interest.

I was doing some research early in the summer about the 1959 season, by the way, using Retrosheet. One of the many things that astonished me about that season, looking carefully at games played, is how many games there were in which starting pitchers were yanked after giving up two or three runs in the first or second inning. At that time the composition of the staff was very different. You'd have three or four guys on a staff who were spot starters/long relievers. If one of the spot starters was having a good day he might face 40 hitters and pitch a complete game—but if he got off to a rocky start, he might come out after six or seven hitters. Very, very different from modern baseball, not only on the "long start" end but also on the "short start" end.

9) *How many times did this manager use a reliever on consecutive days?* (RCD—"Relievers, Consecutive Days") This is a new entry to the record in this book, and I'm pretty excited about it. . .it certainly *appears* to be a valid variable, something that separates one manager from another. Dusty Baker used relievers on consecutive days 165 times last year, Phil Garner 157 times—as opposed to 48 for Eric Wedge, 52 for Jim Leyland. We'll have to get more data to know for sure what we have, but Jim Tracy has a career average of 135, data going back to 2002, and Ned Yost an average of 75. It certainly appears that there is a distinction among managers in terms of their willingness to use their relievers on back-to-back days.

One of the frustrations of doing this—trying to understand how one manager manages differently than his colleagues—is that managers are highly sensitive to meeting expectations, and thus reluctant to be seen as deviating from the consensus wisdom. Groupthink among managers is tremendously powerful—for good reasons. You can make an excellent living as a major league manager if you can just convince people that you know how these things are done. You can very easily get fired if people decide that you don't know how things are done. It's a high-risk, low-reward strategy—arguing with what everybody knows to be true. It is exceedingly rare to find a manager who is willing to step outside the box, state what he believes and battle to defend it, like Casey Stengel advocating platooning or Earl Weaver disparaging the bunt. That really only happens when a manager has been successful and reaches a point at which he no longer feels the pressure to conform.

So what will happen is, we'll spot some difference of opinion like this— one manager willing to use his relievers back-to-back, another manager not willing—and we'll point out that difference. And the difference will then immediately disappear, because as soon as it is pointed out that there is no consensus on this issue, a consensus will develop. There is a name for that syndrome, where the observation of a thing changes the thing itself. . .what is that called?

Anyway, this is frustrating to me, because what I am fundamentally interested in is the battle of ideas within the game—how changes in the way people think about the game change the game itself. History is essentially a battleground of ideas. I am always trying to figure out how people think, how managers think, and how that difference in philosophy shapes the game. But you can't ever figure it out because managers are more committed to keeping their jobs than they are to defending their ideas, so the differences in philosophy evaporate as soon as they are exposed. I'm ranting, aren't I?

10) *How willing is this manager to use his closer for more than one inning?* (LS, or "Long Saves".) This is another new addition to this year's book. John Gibbons in 2006 had 16 Long Saves; Bob Melvin had none. But Melvin had

11 in 2005, so this isn't necessarily a difference in philosophy; it may be just that he felt it was bad enough having to put Jorge Julio or Jose Valverde out there for one critical inning, God forbid he should try two.

11) *How many relievers did this manager use, over the course of the season?* The answer for all 30 major league managers last year was "too damned many", but just in case that doesn't work for you, we also included a specific count. Dusty Baker won the office pool with 542, which was in fact a new major league record, breaking the previous record of 521, by Felipe Alou in 2004. Whoo, boy.

There is another line across the chart then, and we move into "Tactics". In this area we ask five questions:

12) *How many stolen base attempts did the manager order or allow to occur on his watch?* (SBA). These numbers are higher in the National League than in the American, but Mike Scioscia, the Little Ball King, ordered (or allowed) 205 stolen base attempts in 2006—down 13 from the previous year, but still 24 more than any other major league manager. Four American League and seven National League managers had 150+ stolen base attempts last year; six American Leaguers and four National Leaguers had less than 100.

While the speed on the team certainly shapes the number of stolen base opportunities, this, obviously, is a philosophical split among managers, the value of the running game. Mike Scioscia has a career average of 183 stolen base attempts per season; Ken Macha, an average of 66.

13) *How many Sacrifice Bunt Attempts did the manager use?* (SacA). This is a league variable, with the pitchers hitting in the NL creating must-sacrifice situations, but American League totals last year ranged from 20 to 70, National League totals from 77 to 155. Bruce Bochy, who had the 77 in the National League, was actually *above* his career norm, which is 70, while Clint Hurdle, who had the 155, was apparently experimenting with a new lifestyle, having never before bunted like a madman (or had Clint Barmes and Cory Sullivan in the lineup). We're guessing that he won't bunt nearly as much with Tulowitski, or turn nearly so many of those annoying double plays.

14) *How many times did this manager have a Runner Moving when the pitch was thrown?* (RM, for Runners Moving). This is another new category this year. Runners Moving means Hit and Run attempts, rather than straight steals. Mike Scioscia also had 163 of these puppies, some of which were double-counted as stolen base attempts, while Ken Macha and Buck Showalter didn't have 163 between them. Bob Melvin had only 60 runners moving in Arizona, which again was very different from his total the previous year, but then his team was very different from the previous year.

15) *How many intentional walks did this manager use?* (IBB) Frank Robinson's Nationals issued 93 intentional walks in 2006, which was a career

high even for Frank, who has always made liberal use of the tactic. Buck Showalter issued only 18 intentional walks, which was *not* a career low for Buck, who has never much liked the IBB.

Some of you probably know that I don't much like the IBB, either, but I am trying to move the discussion of managers away from judgmental comments and establish a factual basis to compare one manager to another. The discussion of managers in the public press and on the radio revolves almost 100% around "this guy is great" or "this guy is an idiot." That's the only discussion you can have if you can't say specifically how it is that one manager is different from another. This is different from the discussion of anything else in the baseball world. You can debate the MVP award by stating specifically how David Ortiz is different from Derek Jeter. You can debate the Hall of Fame with a firm understanding of how Lee Smith is different from Bruce Sutter or Dennis Eckersley. My challenge has been to try to allow people to debate managers with a true understanding of how one manager is different from the other guy.

16) *How many pitchouts did the manager order?* (PO). Grady Little ordered 63 pitchouts last year and has a career average of 46 per season. His old bench coach, Jerry Narron, ordered only 11 last year and has a career average of 9 per season.

We wrap it up with the wins and losses, and that's our managerial record. We hope you get something out of it.

Felipe Alou

Year	Team	Lg	G	LUp	PL%	PH	PR	DS	Quick	Slow	LO	RCD	LS	Rel	SBA	SacA	RM	IBB	PO	W	L	Pct
1994	Expos	NL	114	72	.48	143	33	7	51	18	0			259	173	72		24	20	74	40	.649
1995	Expos	NL	144	116	.49	200	36	10	48	28	7			396	169	74		20	22	66	78	.458
1996	Expos	NL	162	113	.49	240	31	30	60	27	13			433	142	97		25	25	88	74	.543
1997	Expos	NL	162	138	.58	205	22	40	52	41	15			390	121	91		33	30	78	84	.481
1998	Expos	NL	162	133	.50	235	27	37	56	26	2			443	137	111		30	18	65	97	.401
1999	Expos	NL	162	143	.49	247	33	55	45	36	5			432	121	84		28	26	68	94	.420
2000	Expos	NL	162	120	.61	211	24	32	51	36	5			452	106	103		29	18	67	95	.414
2001	Expos	NL	53	40	.58	84	4	5	18	12	1			171	39	28		10	7	21	32	.396
2003	Giants	NL	161	127	.56	202	32	42	46	27	8	113	5	461	90	93	33	34	9	100	61	.621
2004	Giants	NL	162	138	.67	264	63	60	25	49	13	154	8	521	66	104	99	35	2	91	71	.562
2005	Giants	NL	162	139	.62	242	33	49	29	46	7	145	6	511	106	109	120	42	12	75	87	.463
2006	Giants	NL	162	123	.64	215	57	56	22	50	9	98	5	438	83	99	82	37	14	76	85	.472
	162-Game Average			129	.56	228	36	39	46	36	8	128	6	450	124	98	84	32	19	80	82	.494

Dusty Baker

Year	Team	Lg	G	LUp	PL%	PH	PR	DS	Quick	Slow	LO	RCD	LS	Rel	SBA	SacA	RM	IBB	PO	W	L	Pct
1994	Giants	NL	115	76	.53	177	16	9	29	25	2			288	154	88		24	78	55	60	.478
1995	Giants	NL	144	96	.41	230	36	13	32	50	8			381	184	101		33	77	67	77	.465
1996	Giants	NL	162	121	.51	250	17	15	24	58	15			425	166	103		45	96	68	94	.420
1997	Giants	NL	162	114	.71	212	17	22	46	25	17			481	170	85		37	93	90	72	.556
1998	Giants	NL	163	130	.62	224	20	12	43	38	8			433	153	111		51	41	89	74	.546
1999	Giants	NL	162	120	.62	233	16	16	30	51	27			450	165	113		28	40	86	76	.531
2000	Giants	NL	162	82	.56	233	26	22	38	50	25			384	118	86		16	37	97	65	.599
2001	Giants	NL	162	122	.48	261	22	19	40	48	10			439	99	95		32	45	90	72	.556
2002	Giants	NL	162	118	.43	226	34	37	29	56	21	106	8	417	95	88	25	44	40	95	66	.590
2003	Cubs	NL	162	114	.49	272	25	43	24	58	26	111	3	420	104	93	31	36	24	88	74	.543
2004	Cubs	NL	162	113	.44	293	27	19	37	38	13	129	8	460	94	106	54	33	56	89	73	.549
2005	Cubs	NL	162	121	.59	240	21	29	40	46	10	103	2	457	104	88	107	48	70	79	83	.488
2006	Cubs	NL	162	133	.56	271	9	26	45	39	7	165	2	542	170	107	134	44	46	66	96	.407
	162-Game Average			117	.54	248	23	22	36	46	15	123	5	443	141	100	70	37	59	84	78	.519

Buddy Bell

Year	Team	Lg	G	LUp	PL%	PH	PR	DS	Quick	Slow	LO	RCD	LS	Rel	SBA	SacA	RM	IBB	PO	W	L	Pct
1996	Tigers	AL	162	128	.50	123	29	17	17	27	26			426	137	63		40	13	53	109	.327
1997	Tigers	AL	162	116	.61	163	19	22	24	7	12			417	233	44		24	32	79	83	.488
1998	Tigers	AL	137	88	.58	102	25	7	15	15	10			362	143	24		29	38	52	85	.380
2000	Rockies	NL	162	106	.64	285	21	8	12	18	10			480	192	100		53	40	82	80	.506
2001	Rockies	NL	162	116	.61	314	27	14	18	30	8			476	186	108		43	43	73	89	.451
2002	Rockies	NL	22	15	.55	48	1	5	5	11	2	21	0	69	17	9	5	11	5	6	16	.273
2005	Royals	AL	112	93	.61	97	18	8	32	23	0	54	4	310	48	38	80	17	25	43	69	.384
2006	Royals	AL	152	132	.57	87	27	25	39	37	5	86	6	439	95	63	81	40	13	58	94	.382
	162-Game Average			120	.59	184	25	16	25	25	11	89	6	451	159	68	94	39	32	67	95	.414

Bruce Bochy

Year	Team	Lg	G	LUp	PL%	PH	PR	DS	Quick	Slow	LO	RCD	LS	Rel	SBA	SacA	RM	IBB	PO	W	L	Pct
1995	Padres	NL	144	96	.59	262	30	23	44	41	17			337	170	68		26	38	70	74	.486
1996	Padres	NL	162	114	.52	289	29	15	51	33	10			411	164	73		42	65	91	71	.562
1997	Padres	NL	162	111	.60	291	26	9	45	45	3			426	200	84		24	58	76	86	.469
1998	Padres	NL	162	110	.65	280	62	44	44	45	9			369	116	84		30	27	98	64	.605
1999	Padres	NL	162	137	.60	298	51	21	44	36	4			403	241	60		39	29	74	88	.457
2000	Padres	NL	162	134	.52	285	44	14	41	47	14			443	184	52		40	27	76	86	.469
2001	Padres	NL	162	116	.60	255	54	27	32	47	6			422	173	43		40	23	79	83	.488
2002	Padres	NL	162	123	.66	273	46	56	40	40	2	106	4	459	115	63	59	61	12	66	96	.407
2003	Padres	NL	162	134	.58	339	20	29	34	43	3	100	3	473	115	63	41	52	6	64	98	.395
2004	Padres	NL	162	96	.54	284	38	47	46	32	1	76	3	437	77	75	90	39	14	87	75	.537
2005	Padres	NL	162	128	.58	285	31	49	46	36	2	87	1	456	143	89	111	45	16	82	80	.506
2006	Padres	NL	162	111	.60	264	64	48	43	42	5	111	2	475	154	77	106	63	21	88	74	.543
	162-Game Average			119	.59	286	42	32	43	41	6	96	3	430	156	70	81	42	28	80	82	.494

Bobby Cox

Year	Team	Lg	G	LUp	PL%	PH	PR	DS	Quick	Slow	LO	RCD	LS	Rel	SBA	SacA	RM	IBB	PO	W	L	Pct
1994	Braves	NL	114	64	.60	163	30	25	22	31	5			244	79	83		39	44	68	46	.596
1995	Braves	NL	144	59	.56	224	48	40	41	34	13			339	116	77		38	41	90	54	.625
1996	Braves	NL	162	89	.62	254	32	27	48	43	19			408	126	90		48	34	96	66	.593
1997	Braves	NL	162	87	.64	276	58	29	40	37	23			374	166	112		46	13	101	62	.620
1998	Braves	NL	162	80	.64	245	28	25	44	33	14			354	141	97		26	40	106	56	.654
1999	Braves	NL	162	76	.58	272	51	34	44	39	13			394	214	89		37	54	103	59	.636
2000	Braves	NL	162	103	.59	252	72	11	52	41	6			376	204	109		34	59	95	67	.586
2001	Braves	NL	162	113	.57	278	50	23	49	40	4			412	131	84		55	90	88	74	.543
2002	Braves	NL	161	105	.48	289	38	44	58	30	5	113	9	469	115	84	37	63	46	101	59	.631
2003	Braves	NL	162	69	.52	262	49	45	40	45	5	113	10	489	90	85	23	69	49	101	61	.623
2004	Braves	NL	162	105	.70	263	80	28	49	33	4	128	16	483	118	104	75	50	22	96	66	.593
2005	Braves	NL	162	110	.69	247	54	35	46	27	1	125	7	484	124	104	93	52	11	90	72	.556
2006	Braves	NL	162	85	.58	299	24	35	44	38	8	144	3	522	87	99	56	69	24	79	83	.488
	162-Game Average			91	.60	264	49	32	46	37	10	125	9	425	136	97	57	50	42	96	66	.593

Billy Doran

Year	Team	Lg	G	LUp	PL%	PH	PR	DS	Quick	Slow	LO	RCD	LS	Rel	SBA	SacA	RM	IBB	PO	W	L	Pct
2006	Royals	AL	10	10	.50	5	2	0	4	0	0	4	0	34	4	7	4	5	0	4	6	.400
	162-Game Average			162	.50	81	32	0	65	0	0	65	0	551	65	113	65	81	0	65	97	.401

Terry Francona

Year	Team	Lg	G	LUp	PL%	PH	PR	DS	Quick	Slow	LO	RCD	LS	Rel	SBA	SacA	RM	IBB	PO	W	L	Pct
1997	Phillies	NL	162	98	.66	288	19	28	28	54	22			409	148	91		31	30	68	94	.420
1998	Phillies	NL	162	84	.53	256	20	19	34	57	20			385	142	85		23	16	75	87	.463
1999	Phillies	NL	162	85	.51	239	13	31	29	41	16			441	160	81		17	27	77	85	.475
2000	Phillies	NL	162	108	.53	278	17	14	38	43	25			414	132	89		17	16	65	97	.401
2004	Red Sox	AL	162	141	.65	139	87	60	39	48	2	105	8	437	98	18	84	28	27	98	64	.605
2005	Red Sox	AL	162	104	.67	110	46	37	25	55	3	99	3	442	57	21	79	28	11	95	67	.586
2006	Red Sox	AL	162	116	.59	93	54	49	36	42	2	94	9	454	74	33	95	25	16	86	76	.531
	162-Game Average			105	.59	200	37	34	33	49	13	99	7	426	116	60	86	24	20	81	81	.500

Ron Gardenhire

Year	Team	Lg	G	LUp	PL%	PH	PR	DS	Quick	Slow	LO	RCD	LS	Rel	SBA	SacA	RM	IBB	PO	W	L	Pct
2002	Twins	AL	161	111	.69	157	42	42	51	22	4	84	1	435	141	45	30	24	11	94	67	.584
2003	Twins	AL	162	126	.63	144	50	26	49	33	2	85	2	399	138	59	37	35	14	90	72	.556
2004	Twins	AL	163	131	.59	148	55	29	54	21	1	106	4	435	142	66	105	27	19	92	70	.568
2005	Twins	AL	162	135	.58	104	45	26	50	21	0	87	1	396	146	59	138	38	16	83	79	.512
2006	Twins	AL	162	97	.62	93	36	21	60	30	0	82	5	421	143	48	127	25	11	96	66	.593
	162-Game Average			120	.62	129	46	29	53	25	1	89	3	418	146	55	88	30	14	91	71	.562

Phil Garner

Year	Team	Lg	G	LUp	PL%	PH	PR	DS	Quick	Slow	LO	RCD	LS	Rel	SBA	SacA	RM	IBB	PO	W	L	Pct
1994	Brewers	AL	115	94	.53	53	33	24	31	35	0			252	96	46		16	23	53	62	.461
1995	Brewers	AL	144	120	.58	83	67	52	42	42	10			321	145	64		23	52	65	79	.451
1996	Brewers	AL	162	114	.58	115	48	46	50	36	13			385	149	72		20	82	80	82	.494
1997	Brewers	AL	161	128	.59	190	42	36	51	34	6			367	158	65		21	55	78	83	.484
1998	Brewers	NL	162	125	.59	265	54	46	52	43	6			416	140	85		21	59	74	88	.457
1999	Brewers	NL	112	69	.57	182	15	5	28	26	4			294	75	85		19	57	52	60	.464
2000	Tigers	AL	162	128	.53	126	30	25	35	38	8			429	121	58		13	26	79	83	.488
2001	Tigers	AL	162	116	.64	93	40	14	25	51	9			391	194	58		29	36	66	96	.407
2002	Tigers	AL	6	3	.63	1	1	0	1	3	2	2	0	15	4	0	3	2	0	0	6	.000
2004	Astros	NL	74	31	.54	163	28	35	27	14	3	71	4	241	78	40	36	24	7	48	26	.649
2005	Astros	NL	163	101	.48	251	40	63	55	34	5	118	3	434	159	99	148	29	10	89	73	.549
2006	Astros	NL	162	111	.47	287	17	47	55	36	4	157	2	497	115	123	114	65	26	82	80	.506
	162-Game Average			117	.56	185	42	40	46	40	7	140	4	413	147	81	121	29	44	78	84	.481

John Gibbons

Year	Team	Lg	G	LUp	PL%	PH	PR	DS	Quick	Slow	LO	RCD	LS	Rel	SBA	SacA	RM	IBB	PO	W	L	Pct
				LINEUPS		SUBSTITUTIONS			PITCHER USAGE						TACTICS					RESULTS		
2004	Blue Jays	AL	51	36	.68	55	3	2	15	8	2	22	1	130	34	2	39	11	21	20	30	.400
2005	Blue Jays	AL	162	124	.66	148	11	37	55	18	1	77	12	432	107	28	128	29	45	80	82	.494
2006	Blue Jays	AL	162	120	.53	112	32	40	58	32	2	94	16	482	98	20	126	56	40	87	75	.537
162-Game Average				121	.61	136	20	34	55	25	2	84	13	452	104	22	127	42	46	81	81	.500

Joe Girardi

Year	Team	Lg	G	LUp	PL%	PH	PR	DS	Quick	Slow	LO	RCD	LS	Rel	SBA	SacA	RM	IBB	PO	W	L	Pct
				LINEUPS		SUBSTITUTIONS			PITCHER USAGE						TACTICS					RESULTS		
2006	Marlins	NL	162	117	.50	250	44	66	46	39	4	76	3	438	168	97	105	58	42	78	84	.481
162-Game Average				117	.50	250	44	66	46	39	4	76	3	438	168	97	105	58	42	78	84	.481

Ozzie Guillen

Year	Team	Lg	G	LUp	PL%	PH	PR	DS	Quick	Slow	LO	RCD	LS	Rel	SBA	SacA	RM	IBB	PO	W	L	Pct
				LINEUPS		SUBSTITUTIONS			PITCHER USAGE						TACTICS					RESULTS		
2004	White Sox	AL	162	134	.55	160	46	15	27	65	5	86	8	399	129	79	77	36	17	83	79	.512
2005	White Sox	AL	162	112	.51	100	32	21	31	56	3	114	5	412	204	68	148	42	15	99	63	.611
2006	White Sox	AL	162	87	.60	135	42	38	27	67	4	83	7	398	141	61	83	59	27	90	72	.556
162-Game Average				111	.55	132	40	25	28	63	4	94	7	403	158	69	103	46	20	91	71	.562

Mike Hargrove

Year	Team	Lg	G	LUp	PL%	PH	PR	DS	Quick	Slow	LO	RCD	LS	Rel	SBA	SacA	RM	IBB	PO	W	L	Pct
				LINEUPS		SUBSTITUTIONS			PITCHER USAGE						TACTICS					RESULTS		
1994	Indians	AL	113	53	.67	79	18	31	23	31	3			222	179	43		22	40	66	47	.584
1995	Indians	AL	144	64	.66	101	34	21	36	23	12			335	185	40		12	22	100	44	.694
1996	Indians	AL	161	96	.56	115	20	25	39	31	14			382	210	58		31	41	99	62	.615
1997	Indians	AL	162	109	.58	86	17	14	34	46	14			429	177	60		30	37	86	75	.534
1998	Indians	AL	162	108	.62	88	21	32	29	39	19			423	203	53		39	47	89	73	.549
1999	Indians	AL	162	123	.66	99	25	22	41	44	15			466	197	82		36	28	97	65	.599
2000	Orioles	AL	162	107	.54	77	42	19	25	55	24			396	191	36		21	31	74	88	.457
2001	Orioles	AL	162	139	.53	82	27	20	39	42	3			392	186	57		17	71	63	98	.391
2002	Orioles	AL	162	125	.52	129	24	22	32	44	7	74	6	407	158	54	13	34	39	67	95	.414
2003	Orioles	AL	163	120	.52	78	37	22	29	52	11	89	5	425	125	67	45	43	16	71	91	.438
2005	Mariners	AL	162	97	.52	125	24	18	30	45	1	73	1	433	149	61	120	32	36	69	93	.426
2006	Mariners	AL	162	84	.51	121	21	20	24	47	3	81	14	429	143	39	119	50	17	78	84	.481
162-Game Average				106	.57	102	27	23	33	43	11	79	7	410	182	56	74	32	37	83	79	.512

Clint Hurdle

Year	Team	Lg	G	LUp	PL%	PH	PR	DS	Quick	Slow	LO	RCD	LS	Rel	SBA	SacA	RM	IBB	PO	W	L	Pct
				LINEUPS		SUBSTITUTIONS			PITCHER USAGE						TACTICS					RESULTS		
2002	Rockies	NL	140	100	.52	283	30	41	30	44	3	104	3	437	139	44	41	38	13	67	73	.479
2003	Rockies	NL	162	108	.47	317	17	32	35	40	0	87	4	500	100	82	26	51	16	74	88	.457
2004	Rockies	NL	162	131	.57	330	24	36	33	60	3	74	1	473	77	126	52	84	11	68	94	.420
2005	Rockies	NL	162	135	.60	273	21	40	42	60	1	89	2	459	97	114	119	54	22	67	95	.414
2006	Rockies	NL	162	111	.49	259	17	22	33	52	2	107	2	499	135	155	109	81	28	76	86	.469
162-Game Average				120	.53	301	22	35	36	53	2	95	2	487	113	107	71	63	19	72	90	.444

Tony LaRussa

Year	Team	Lg	G	LUp	PL%	PH	PR	DS	Quick	Slow	LO	RCD	LS	Rel	SBA	SacA	RM	IBB	PO	W	L	Pct
				LINEUPS		SUBSTITUTIONS			PITCHER USAGE						TACTICS					RESULTS		
1994	Athletics	AL	114	97	.62	89	28	14	43	21	5			308	130	31		23	32	51	63	.447
1995	Athletics	AL	144	120	.54	113	38	24	33	38	19			358	158	42		17	42	67	77	.465
1996	Cardinals	NL	162	120	.52	246	25	13	32	48	24			413	207	117		38	41	88	74	.543
1997	Cardinals	NL	162	146	.54	307	17	18	34	42	16			399	224	77		26	79	73	89	.451
1998	Cardinals	NL	162	146	.52	259	7	18	62	31	13			429	174	85		32	34	83	79	.512
1999	Cardinals	NL	161	138	.47	264	32	28	50	41	13			454	182	103		31	30	75	86	.466
2000	Cardinals	NL	162	137	.53	240	35	25	40	31	11			386	138	107		21	34	95	67	.586
2001	Cardinals	NL	162	117	.47	256	26	13	46	36	7			485	126	102		31	25	93	69	.574
2002	Cardinals	NL	162	117	.52	352	35	41	55	33	6	110	6	472	128	105	57	39	13	97	65	.599
2003	Cardinals	NL	162	126	.50	352	28	51	38	49	10	113	9	460	114	108	56	36	9	85	77	.525
2004	Cardinals	NL	162	119	.53	321	33	75	30	43	6	120	16	469	158	87	128	24	7	105	57	.648
2005	Cardinals	NL	162	138	.55	270	25	48	40	38	1	88	4	459	119	92	153	27	9	100	62	.617
2006	Cardinals	NL	162	131	.56	272	11	52	49	34	2	95	6	469	91	85	117	35	13	83	78	.516
162-Game Average				131	.53	266	27	33	44	39	11	105	8	440	155	91	102	30	29	87	75	.537

Jim Leyland

Year	Team	Lg	G	LINEUPS		SUBSTITUTIONS			PITCHER USAGE						TACTICS					RESULTS		
				LUp	PL%	PH	PR	DS	Quick	Slow	LO	RCD	LS	Rel	SBA	SacA	RM	IBB	PO	W	L	Pct
1995	Pirates	NL	144	124	.56	282	8	4	13	12	11			391	139	69		36	51	58	86	.403
1996	Pirates	NL	162	117	.53	299	18	14	27	8	11			422	175	101		31	46	73	89	.451
1997	Marlins	NL	162	105	.59	258	36	31	21	12	18			404	173	91		31	38	92	70	.568
1998	Marlins	NL	162	96	.59	277	13	15	18	24	31			420	172	91		45	31	54	108	.333
1999	Rockies	NL	162	124	.56	294	11	12	11	29	21			421	113	88		29	11	72	90	.444
2006	Tigers	AL	162	120	.53	81	34	37	52	31	2	52	3	390	100	57	124	35	9	95	67	.586
	162-Game Average			116	.56	253	20	19	24	20	16	52	3	416	148	84	124	35	32	75	87	.463

Grady Little

Year	Team	Lg	G	LINEUPS		SUBSTITUTIONS			PITCHER USAGE						TACTICS					RESULTS		
				LUp	PL%	PH	PR	DS	Quick	Slow	LO	RCD	LS	Rel	SBA	SacA	RM	IBB	PO	W	L	Pct
2002	Red Sox	AL	162	120	.59	138	54	23	59	27	2	53	11	338	108	32	25	29	46	93	69	.574
2003	Red Sox	AL	162	118	.64	130	80	32	43	36	4	78	4	437	123	32	42	41	28	95	67	.586
2006	Dodgers	NL	162	118	.67	291	34	37	56	26	1	106	9	454	177	82	137	40	63	88	74	.543
	162-Game Average			119	.63	186	56	31	53	30	2	79	9	410	136	49	68	37	46	92	70	.568

Ken Macha

Year	Team	Lg	G	LINEUPS		SUBSTITUTIONS			PITCHER USAGE						TACTICS					RESULTS		
				LUp	PL%	PH	PR	DS	Quick	Slow	LO	RCD	LS	Rel	SBA	SacA	RM	IBB	PO	W	L	Pct
2003	Athletics	AL	162	111	.57	140	29	23	44	38	4	72	12	364	62	31	28	42	9	96	66	.593
2004	Athletics	AL	163	119	.60	139	16	14	34	47	9	94	5	414	69	30	57	49	2	91	71	.562
2005	Athletics	AL	162	127	.62	83	17	11	43	36	4	79	13	410	53	29	53	42	13	88	74	.543
2006	Athletics	AL	162	121	.58	62	33	23	39	47	6	104	8	444	81	29	68	47	22	93	69	.574
	162-Game Average			120	.59	106	24	18	40	42	6	87	10	408	66	30	52	45	12	92	70	.568

Joe Maddon

Year	Team	Lg	G	LINEUPS		SUBSTITUTIONS			PITCHER USAGE						TACTICS					RESULTS		
				LUp	PL%	PH	PR	DS	Quick	Slow	LO	RCD	LS	Rel	SBA	SacA	RM	IBB	PO	W	L	Pct
2006	Devil Rays	AL	162	145	.57	81	26	51	40	37	1	79	10	444	186	51	126	39	48	61	101	.377
	162-Game Average			145	.57	81	26	51	40	37	1	79	10	444	186	51	126	39	48	61	101	.377

Charlie Manuel

Year	Team	Lg	G	LINEUPS		SUBSTITUTIONS			PITCHER USAGE						TACTICS					RESULTS		
				LUp	PL%	PH	PR	DS	Quick	Slow	LO	RCD	LS	Rel	SBA	SacA	RM	IBB	PO	W	L	Pct
2000	Indians	AL	162	102	.64	73	40	26	21	12	20			462	147	59		38	30	90	72	.556
2001	Indians	AL	162	114	.61	105	30	49	28	17	10			484	120	67		34	43	91	71	.562
2002	Indians	AL	87	68	.61	60	10	19	13	17	4	47	0	225	57	19	12	21	3	39	48	.448
2005	Phillies	NL	162	80	.64	265	36	19	42	28	3	119	6	442	143	86	76	51	11	88	74	.543
2006	Phillies	NL	162	81	.65	301	42	49	28	43	2	126	2	500	117	79	69	63	16	85	77	.525
	162-Game Average			98	.63	177	35	36	29	26	9	115	3	466	129	68	62	46	23	87	75	.537

Bob Melvin

Year	Team	Lg	G	LINEUPS		SUBSTITUTIONS			PITCHER USAGE						TACTICS					RESULTS		
				LUp	PL%	PH	PR	DS	Quick	Slow	LO	RCD	LS	Rel	SBA	SacA	RM	IBB	PO	W	L	Pct
2003	Mariners	AL	162	111	.62	81	62	33	27	46	7	56	6	366	145	44	37	24	5	93	69	.574
2004	Mariners	AL	162	151	.59	127	86	26	21	62	12	82	5	414	152	56	111	32	24	63	99	.389
2005	Diamondbacks	NL	162	120	.68	310	26	38	26	56	3	123	11	458	93	93	101	43	30	77	85	.475
2006	Diamondbacks	NL	162	114	.72	278	11	35	37	42	3	86	0	461	106	81	60	44	30	76	86	.469
	162-Game Average			124	.65	199	46	33	28	52	6	87	6	425	124	69	77	36	22	77	85	.475

Jerry Narron

Year	Team	Lg	G	LINEUPS		SUBSTITUTIONS			PITCHER USAGE						TACTICS					RESULTS		
				LUp	PL%	PH	PR	DS	Quick	Slow	LO	RCD	LS	Rel	SBA	SacA	RM	IBB	PO	W	L	Pct
2001	Rangers	AL	134	94	.66	92	14	19	9	18	6			340	106	29		16	5	62	72	.463
2002	Rangers	AL	162	128	.52	159	63	38	30	50	9	121	5	487	96	58	48	32	6	72	90	.444
2005	Reds	NL	93	73	.61	156	9	14	13	22	1	71	5	287	50	45	53	25	7	46	46	.500
2006	Reds	NL	162	140	.56	273	23	46	33	47	4	121	2	476	157	86	89	55	11	80	82	.494
	162-Game Average			128	.58	200	32	34	25	40	6	122	5	468	120	64	74	38	9	77	85	.475

Sam Perlozzo

Year	Team	Lg	G	LINEUPS		SUBSTITUTIONS			PITCHER USAGE						TACTICS					RESULTS		
				LUp	PL%	PH	PR	DS	Quick	Slow	LO	RCD	LS	Rel	SBA	SacA	RM	IBB	PO	W	L	Pct
2005	Orioles	AL	55	47	.61	28	23	26	15	11	0	46	2	180	41	24	25	3	8	23	32	.418
2006	Orioles	AL	162	124	.56	72	46	49	28	46	2	102	10	472	153	56	76	26	30	70	92	.432
	162-Game Average			128	.57	75	52	56	32	43	1	110	9	487	145	60	75	22	28	69	93	.426

Willie Randolph

Year	Team	Lg	G	LINEUPS		SUBSTITUTIONS			PITCHER USAGE						TACTICS					RESULTS		
				LUp	PL%	PH	PR	DS	Quick	Slow	LO	RCD	LS	Rel	SBA	SacA	RM	IBB	PO	W	L	Pct
2005	Mets	NL	162	105	.64	222	10	51	47	34	4	74	5	392	193	89	118	43	18	83	79	.512
2006	Mets	NL	162	101	.66	247	9	24	40	40	1	119	4	474	181	100	103	39	16	97	65	.599
	162-Game Average			103	.65	235	10	38	44	37	3	97	5	433	187	95	111	41	17	90	72	.556

Frank Robinson

Year	Team	Lg	G	LINEUPS		SUBSTITUTIONS			PITCHER USAGE						TACTICS					RESULTS		
				LUp	PL%	PH	PR	DS	Quick	Slow	LO	RCD	LS	Rel	SBA	SacA	RM	IBB	PO	W	L	Pct
2002	Expos	NL	162	121	.60	266	51	40	48	40	9	109	11	437	182	120	34	80	23	83	79	.512
2003	Expos	NL	162	134	.63	248	55	31	50	44	23	98	4	437	139	85	50	51	8	83	79	.512
2004	Expos	NL	162	131	.67	279	19	27	48	36	13	109	4	462	147	120	91	78	1	67	95	.414
2005	Nationals	NL	162	121	.60	266	48	35	45	47	16	140	3	470	90	115	109	77	4	81	81	.500
2006	Nationals	NL	162	110	.59	314	37	25	46	32	4	137	3	517	185	93	144	93	14	71	91	.438
	162-Game Average			123	.62	275	42	32	47	40	13	119	5	465	149	107	86	76	10	77	85	.475

Mike Scioscia

Year	Team	Lg	G	LINEUPS		SUBSTITUTIONS			PITCHER USAGE						TACTICS					RESULTS		
				LUp	PL%	PH	PR	DS	Quick	Slow	LO	RCD	LS	Rel	SBA	SacA	RM	IBB	PO	W	L	Pct
2000	Angels	AL	162	75	.62	110	41	4	56	42	6			441	145	63		32	40	82	80	.506
2001	Angels	AL	162	130	.62	118	30	8	29	41	5			384	168	66		33	50	75	87	.463
2002	Angels	AL	162	102	.64	170	60	24	34	32	5	88	8	400	168	61	41	24	29	99	63	.611
2003	Angels	AL	162	130	.64	134	54	40	50	48	1	60	4	375	190	64	79	38	25	77	85	.475
2004	Angels	AL	162	126	.57	115	43	46	35	40	3	61	11	343	189	69	196	27	32	92	70	.568
2005	Angels	AL	162	124	.65	92	37	37	47	37	1	88	9	379	218	58	160	24	43	95	67	.586
2006	Angels	AL	162	114	.63	103	45	38	38	48	2	99	9	380	205	37	163	27	22	89	73	.549
	162-Game Average			114	.62	120	44	28	41	41	3	79	8	386	183	60	128	29	34	87	75	.537

Buck Showalter

Year	Team	Lg	G	LINEUPS		SUBSTITUTIONS			PITCHER USAGE						TACTICS					RESULTS		
				LUp	PL%	PH	PR	DS	Quick	Slow	LO	RCD	LS	Rel	SBA	SacA	RM	IBB	PO	W	L	Pct
1994	Yankees	AL	113	79	.59	95	31	3	24	30	0			241	95	34		18	22	70	43	.619
1995	Yankees	AL	145	107	.68	124	30	20	29	42	37			302	80	27		15	29	79	65	.549
1998	Diamondbacks	NL	162	124	.62	252	17	15	34	40	7			368	111	68		18	13	65	97	.401
1999	Diamondbacks	NL	162	97	.63	220	20	17	37	48	25			382	176	75		34	15	100	62	.617
2000	Diamondbacks	NL	162	99	.60	250	32	11	46	26	18			390	141	89		36	10	85	77	.525
2003	Rangers	AL	162	133	.61	88	51	41	35	33	4	93	7	494	90	35	80	45	12	71	91	.438
2004	Rangers	AL	162	120	.64	98	18	24	47	30	3	82	10	468	105	29	70	29	5	89	73	.549
2005	Rangers	AL	162	98	.59	57	22	11	42	39	2	79	8	454	82	11	103	31	5	79	83	.488
2006	Rangers	AL	162	95	.57	39	34	22	41	25	0	85	4	489	77	30	68	18	8	80	82	.494
	162-Game Average			111	.62	142	30	19	39	36	11	85	7	418	111	46	80	28	14	84	78	.519

Joe Torre

Year	Team	Lg	G	LINEUPS		SUBSTITUTIONS			PITCHER USAGE						TACTICS					RESULTS		
				LUp	PL%	PH	PR	DS	Quick	Slow	LO	RCD	LS	Rel	SBA	SacA	RM	IBB	PO	W	L	Pct
1994	Cardinals	NL	115	79	.68	192	9	0	36	29	6			330	122	57		13	33	53	61	.465
1995	Cardinals	NL	47	36	.51	99	6	4	17	11	1			146	42	26		11	14	20	27	.426
1996	Yankees	AL	162	131	.57	92	62	55	59	23	22			411	142	53		27	19	92	70	.568
1997	Yankees	AL	162	118	.61	75	70	23	35	41	19			368	157	54		29	14	96	66	.593
1998	Yankees	AL	162	96	.62	94	36	28	43	38	27			334	216	44		18	9	114	48	.704
1999	Yankees	AL	162	76	.63	103	57	10	29	51	26			276	129	31		15	12	98	64	.605
2000	Yankees	AL	161	112	.63	86	49	27	43	53	27			382	147	22		16	8	87	74	.540
2001	Yankees	AL	161	94	.56	76	33	14	37	45	10			362	214	41		22	21	95	65	.594
2002	Yankees	AL	161	108	.62	92	60	31	37	48	10	86	13	334	138	34	38	44	17	103	58	.640
2003	Yankees	AL	163	104	.65	118	48	18	26	51	13	75	10	367	131	39	69	36	33	101	61	.623
2004	Yankees	AL	163	116	.65	99	42	47	47	35	3	129	10	436	117	48	126	32	33	101	61	.623

Year	Team	Lg	G	LINEUPS		SUBSTITUTIONS			PITCHER USAGE						TACTICS					RESULTS		
				LUp	PL%	PH	PR	DS	Quick	Slow	LO	RCD	LS	Rel	SBA	SacA	RM	IBB	PO	W	L	Pct
2005	Yankees	AL	162	117	.64	94	65	47	44	45	8	92	7	418	111	40	123	25	50	95	67	.586
2006	Yankees	AL	162	120	.66	108	50	59	50	28	1	109	7	489	174	48	115	41	50	97	65	.599
	162-Game Average			109	.62	111	49	30	42	42	14	98	9	389	154	45	94	27	26	96	66	.593

Jim Tracy

Year	Team	Lg	G	LINEUPS		SUBSTITUTIONS			PITCHER USAGE						TACTICS					RESULTS		
				LUp	PL%	PH	PR	DS	Quick	Slow	LO	RCD	LS	Rel	SBA	SacA	RM	IBB	PO	W	L	Pct
2001	Dodgers	NL	162	111	.50	264	34	20	46	42	8			409	131	81		25	10	86	76	.531
2002	Dodgers	NL	162	102	.52	331	44	37	48	35	3	118	9	423	133	80	35	45	18	92	70	.568
2003	Dodgers	NL	162	103	.64	269	22	64	52	29	6	148	11	438	116	97	32	35	10	85	77	.525
2004	Dodgers	NL	162	94	.70	336	34	19	48	31	4	128	16	459	143	79	90	47	7	93	69	.574
2005	Dodgers	NL	162	129	.64	303	31	37	44	40	6	126	2	459	93	76	97	34	17	71	91	.438
2006	Pirates	NL	162	121	.43	264	22	22	37	43	2	156	3	505	91	80	74	62	12	67	95	.414
	162-Game Average			110	.57	295	31	33	46	37	5	135	8	449	118	82	66	41	12	82	80	.506

Eric Wedge

Year	Team	Lg	G	LINEUPS		SUBSTITUTIONS			PITCHER USAGE						TACTICS					RESULTS		
				LUp	PL%	PH	PR	DS	Quick	Slow	LO	RCD	LS	Rel	SBA	SacA	RM	IBB	PO	W	L	Pct
2003	Indians	AL	162	145	.67	117	43	27	47	34	1	89	5	428	147	67	54	37	12	68	94	.420
2004	Indians	AL	162	114	.72	110	41	20	42	38	2	121	0	479	149	56	96	47	25	80	82	.494
2005	Indians	AL	162	111	.66	88	18	16	45	45	0	90	3	409	98	53	79	20	9	93	69	.574
2006	Indians	AL	162	111	.59	98	13	13	31	50	2	48	1	377	78	40	81	35	15	78	84	.481
	162-Game Average			120	.66	103	29	19	41	42	1	87	2	423	118	54	78	35	15	80	82	.494

Ned Yost

Year	Team	Lg	G	LINEUPS		SUBSTITUTIONS			PITCHER USAGE						TACTICS					RESULTS		
				LUp	PL%	PH	PR	DS	Quick	Slow	LO	RCD	LS	Rel	SBA	SacA	RM	IBB	PO	W	L	Pct
2003	Brewers	NL	162	97	.44	304	22	39	23	59	5	90	6	460	138	85	40	43	23	68	94	.420
2004	Brewers	NL	162	131	.60	317	28	20	39	40	9	63	2	423	178	79	78	27	7	67	94	.416
2005	Brewers	NL	162	99	.46	259	18	35	26	41	4	71	2	395	113	89	97	52	50	81	81	.500
2006	Brewers	NL	162	106	.48	238	12	14	33	44	3	77	4	427	108	80	77	34	16	75	87	.463
	162-Game Average			108	.50	280	20	27	30	46	5	75	4	427	134	83	73	39	24	73	89	.451

2006 American League Managers

Manager	G	LINEUPS		SUBSTITUTIONS			PITCHER USAGE						TACTICS					RESULTS		
		LUp	PL%	PH	PR	DS	Quick	Slow	LO	RCD	LS	Rel	SBA	SacA	RM	IBB	PO	W	L	Pct
Buddy Bell, KC	152	132	.57	87	27	25	39	37	5	86	6	439	95	63	81	40	13	58	94	.382
Billy Doran, KC	10	10	.50	5	2	0	4	0	0	4	0	34	4	7	4	5	0	4	6	.400
Terry Francona, Bos	162	116	.59	93	54	49	36	42	2	94	9	454	74	33	95	25	16	86	76	.531
Ron Gardenhire, Min	162	97	.62	93	36	21	60	30	0	82	5	421	143	48	127	25	11	96	66	.593
John Gibbons, Tor	162	120	.53	112	32	40	58	32	2	94	16	482	98	20	126	56	40	87	75	.537
Ozzie Guillen, CWS	162	87	.60	135	42	38	27	67	4	83	7	398	141	61	83	59	27	90	72	.556
Mike Hargrove, Sea	162	84	.51	121	21	20	24	47	3	81	14	429	100	39	119	50	17	78	84	.481
Jim Leyland, Det	162	120	.53	81	34	37	52	31	2	52	3	390	100	57	124	35	9	95	67	.586
Ken Macha, Oak	162	121	.58	62	33	23	39	47	6	104	8	444	81	29	68	47	22	93	69	.574
Joe Maddon, TB	162	145	.57	81	26	51	40	37	1	79	10	444	186	51	126	39	48	61	101	.377
Sam Perlozzo, Bal	162	124	.56	72	46	49	28	46	2	102	10	472	153	56	76	26	30	70	92	.432
Mike Scioscia, LAA	162	114	.63	103	45	38	38	48	2	99	9	380	205	37	163	27	22	89	73	.549
Buck Showalter, Tex	162	95	.57	39	34	22	41	25	0	85	4	489	77	30	68	18	8	80	82	.494
Joe Torre, NYY	162	120	.66	108	50	59	50	28	1	109	7	489	174	48	115	41	50	97	65	.599
Eric Wedge, Cle	162	111	.59	98	13	13	31	50	2	48	1	377	78	40	81	35	15	78	84	.481

2006 National League Managers

Manager	G	LINEUPS		SUBSTITUTIONS			PITCHER USAGE						TACTICS					RESULTS		
		LUp	PL%	PH	PR	DS	Quick	Slow	LO	RCD	LS	Rel	SBA	SacA	RM	IBB	PO	W	L	Pct
Felipe Alou, SF	162	123	.64	215	57	56	22	50	9	98	5	438	83	99	82	37	14	76	85	.472
Dusty Baker, ChC	162	133	.56	271	9	26	45	39	7	165	2	542	154	107	134	44	46	66	96	.407
Bruce Bochy, SD	162	111	.60	264	64	48	43	42	5	111	2	475	170	77	106	63	21	88	74	.543
Bobby Cox, Atl	162	85	.58	299	24	35	44	38	8	144	3	522	87	99	56	69	24	79	83	.488
Phil Garner, Hou	162	111	.47	287	17	47	55	36	4	157	2	497	115	123	114	65	26	82	80	.506
Joe Girardi, Fla	162	117	.50	250	44	66	46	39	4	76	3	438	168	97	105	58	42	78	84	.481
Clint Hurdle, Col	162	111	.49	259	17	22	33	52	2	107	2	499	135	155	109	81	28	76	86	.469
Tony LaRussa, StL	162	131	.56	272	11	52	49	34	2	95	6	469	91	85	117	35	13	83	78	.516
Grady Little, LAD	162	118	.67	291	34	37	56	26	1	106	9	454	177	82	137	40	63	88	74	.543
Charlie Manuel, Phi	162	81	.65	301	42	49	28	43	2	126	2	500	117	79	69	63	16	85	77	.525
Bob Melvin, Ari	162	114	.72	278	11	35	37	42	3	86	0	469	106	81	60	44	30	76	86	.469
Jerry Narron, Cin	162	140	.56	273	23	46	33	47	4	121	2	476	157	86	89	55	11	80	82	.494
Willie Randolph, NYM	162	101	.66	247	9	24	40	40	1	119	4	474	181	100	103	39	16	97	65	.599
Frank Robinson, Was	162	110	.59	314	37	25	46	32	4	137	3	517	185	93	144	93	14	71	91	.438
Jim Tracy, Pit	162	121	.43	264	22	22	37	43	2	156	3	505	91	80	74	62	12	67	95	.414
Ned Yost, Mil	162	106	.48	238	12	14	33	44	3	77	4	427	108	80	77	34	16	75	87	.463

2006 Park Indices

Park Indices are calculated in a way that neutralizes the effect of a team's makeup and isolates the effects of the park. This isolation is figured by comparing what both the team and its opponents accomplished at home, and comparing that to what the same team and its opponents accomplished on the road.

To calculate the Park Index for Home Runs in a given ballpark, we take the total Home Runs of both the home team and its opponents at the ballpark and compare it to the total Home Runs of the home team and its opponents in other games. We then divide each of those totals by the At Bats in the equivalent situations, so that if there are more at bats in either situation the index is not skewed. The result is then multiplied by 100 to yield the familiar form.

The park indices for Doubles, Triples, Walks, Strikeouts and Home Runs by Lefties and Righties are determined like Home Runs above—relative to At Bats. Indices of At Bats, Runs, Hits, Errors and Infield Fielding Errors (E-Infield) are calculated relative to Games. The three Batting Average Indices are calculated as is, since these are already relative to At Bats.

A park with an index of exactly 100 is neutral and can be said to have had no effect on that particular stat. An index above 100 means the ballpark favors that statistic. For example, if a park has a Home Run Index of 120, it was 20% easier to hit Home Runs in that park then the rest of the parks in that team's league.

There is one major change this season, and that is that we are no longer ignoring interleague games in the data. In the past we did not include interleague games due to the designated hitter rule only being used in AL parks as well as because the schedules are very unbalanced. However, we felt that having the complete data was more important than trying to remove some statistical "noise," so now if you are interested in a team's aggregate home/road splits you will be able to find them here as well.

In addition to the 2006 Park Indices, we have included 2004-2006 park data as well. You will notice that only 2005-2006 data is included in the case of RFK Stadium, and that only 2006 data is included for Busch Stadium (2003-2005 data from the old Busch stadium is shown as a comparison). Also, the dimensions changed in Citizens Bank Park and PETCO Park in Philadelphia and San Diego, respectively, so we have decided to show only the 2006 data from those parks while including the 2004-2005 numbers so you can see if the new dimensions had a major impact.

Finally, you may notice that for the first time we are including ballpark index leader boards in this section. These tables show how different ballparks compare to each other in several categories in an easy-to-read format. Take a look, and you may be able to see why a ballpark such as Camden Yards may be a home run hitter's park but not a hitter's park overall.

Arizona Diamondbacks - Chase Field

	2006 Season							2004-2006						
	Home Games			Away Games				Home Games			Away Games			
	D'Backs	Opp	Total	D'Backs	Opp	Total	Index	D'Backs	Opp	Total	D'Backs	Opp	Total	Index
G	81	81	162	81	81	162		243	243	486	243	243	486	
Avg	.283	.273	.278	.251	.260	.255	109	.269	.273	.271	.248	.267	.258	105
AB	2779	2894	5673	2866	2740	5606	101	8243	8671	16914	8496	8195	16691	101
R	403	429	832	370	359	729	114	1075	1347	2422	1009	1196	2205	110
H	786	791	1577	720	712	1432	110	2216	2371	4587	2110	2191	4301	107
2B	182	161	343	149	164	313	108	469	510	979	448	445	893	108
3B	27	27	54	11	22	33	162	67	73	140	36	57	93	149
HR	86	102	188	74	66	140	133	261	311	572	225	247	472	120
BB	250	291	541	254	245	499	107	767	918	1685	784	824	1608	103
SO	440	572	1012	525	543	1068	94	1427	1703	3130	1654	1603	3257	95
E	52	58	110	52	50	102	108	159	138	297	178	134	312	95
E-Infield	30	28	58	19	23	42	138	77	59	136	64	56	120	113
LHB-Avg	.278	.289	.278	.250	.321	.255	109	.260	.264	.262	.254	.264	.258	101
LHB-HR	25	0	25	17	1	18	154	76	63	139	56	49	105	132
RHB-Avg	.285	.273	.278	.252	.259	.256	109	.272	.276	.274	.246	.268	.257	107
RHB-HR	61	102	163	57	65	122	129	185	248	433	169	198	367	116

Atlanta Braves - Turner Field

	2006 Season							2004-2006						
	Home Games			Away Games				Home Games			Away Games			
	Braves	Opp	Total	Braves	Opp	Total	Index	Braves	Opp	Total	Braves	Opp	Total	Index
G	81	81	162	81	81	162		243	243	486	243	243	486	
Avg	.280	.271	.276	.261	.275	.268	103	.276	.265	.271	.261	.272	.266	102
AB	2732	2852	5584	2851	2748	5599	100	8145	8528	16673	8494	8174	16668	100
R	414	390	804	435	415	850	95	1233	1055	2288	1188	1092	2280	100
H	766	773	1539	744	756	1500	103	2252	2264	4516	2214	2227	4441	102
2B	157	150	307	155	154	309	100	471	417	888	453	422	875	101
3B	13	13	26	13	23	36	72	54	29	83	46	46	92	90
HR	100	95	195	122	88	210	93	281	244	525	303	238	541	97
BB	258	264	522	268	308	576	91	839	772	1611	808	843	1651	98
SO	560	577	1137	609	472	1081	105	1670	1603	3273	1741	1400	3141	104
E	43	62	105	56	39	95	111	146	158	304	155	141	296	103
E-Infield	17	27	44	25	19	44	100	72	65	137	69	62	131	105
LHB-Avg	.258	.273	.265	.259	.239	.251	106	.269	.269	.269	.273	.269	.272	99
LHB-HR	24	19	43	34	13	47	91	66	55	121	90	49	139	89
RHB-Avg	.288	.270	.279	.262	.283	.273	102	.279	.265	.271	.256	.273	.265	103
RHB-HR	76	76	152	88	75	163	94	215	189	404	213	189	402	100

Baltimore Orioles - Oriole Park at Camden Yards

	2006 Season							2004-2006						
	Home Games			Away Games				Home Games			Away Games			
	Orioles	Opp	Total	Orioles	Opp	Total	Index	Orioles	Opp	Total	Orioles	Opp	Total	Index
G	81	81	162	81	81	162		243	243	486	243	243	486	
Avg	.290	.277	.284	.265	.291	.277	102	.278	.268	.273	.274	.273	.274	100
AB	2776	2830	5606	2834	2730	5564	101	8259	8573	16832	8638	8160	16798	100
R	416	411	827	352	488	840	98	1156	1253	2409	1183	1276	2459	98
H	806	785	1591	750	794	1544	103	2296	2295	4591	2366	2230	4596	100
2B	137	131	268	151	155	306	87	426	385	811	477	414	891	91
3B	9	9	18	11	19	30	60	29	28	57	36	50	86	66
HR	100	106	206	64	110	174	118	275	279	554	247	276	523	106
BB	228	291	519	246	322	568	91	737	937	1674	712	943	1655	101
SO	400	509	909	478	507	985	92	1231	1582	2813	1498	1576	3074	91
E	45	57	102	57	48	105	97	162	163	325	157	167	324	100
E-Infield	18	24	42	21	20	41	102	62	68	130	62	69	131	99
LHB-Avg	.281	.285	.284	.238	.276	.258	110	.267	.260	.263	.251	.259	.255	103
LHB-HR	23	33	56	22	34	56	95	78	90	168	74	98	172	96
RHB-Avg	.293	.273	.284	.275	.298	.286	99	.282	.272	.277	.283	.282	.282	98
RHB-HR	77	73	150	42	76	118	129	197	189	386	173	178	351	110

Boston Red Sox - Fenway Park

	2006 Season							2004-2006						
	Home Games			Away Games				Home Games			Away Games			
	Red Sox	Opp	Total	Red Sox	Opp	Total	Index	Red Sox	Opp	Total	Red Sox	Opp	Total	Index
G	81	81	162	81	81	162		242	242	484	243	243	486	
Avg	.285	.274	.279	.253	.283	.268	104	.290	.266	.278	.265	.274	.269	103
AB	2754	2874	5628	2865	2763	5628	100	8275	8582	16857	8657	8242	16899	100
R	425	410	835	395	415	810	103	1411	1180	2591	1257	1209	2466	106
H	784	787	1571	726	783	1509	104	2400	2283	4683	2293	2257	4550	103
2B	186	204	390	141	144	285	137	591	579	1170	444	436	880	133
3B	8	14	22	8	14	22	100	26	46	72	36	54	90	80
HR	83	74	157	109	107	216	73	285	229	514	327	274	601	86
BB	322	249	571	350	260	610	94	973	697	1670	1002	693	1695	99
SO	493	555	1048	563	515	1078	97	1573	1633	3206	1709	1520	3229	100
E	23	57	80	43	38	81	99	144	166	310	148	136	284	110
E-Infield	15	24	39	16	17	33	118	73	73	146	50	56	106	138
LHB-Avg	.277	.285	.280	.249	.337	.275	102	.293	.267	.283	.259	.320	.279	102
LHB-HR	22	15	37	32	11	43	86	80	35	115	93	47	140	86
RHB-Avg	.288	.271	.279	.255	.275	.266	105	.289	.266	.276	.267	.265	.266	104
RHB-HR	61	59	120	77	96	173	69	205	194	399	234	227	461	86

Chicago Cubs - Wrigley Field

	2006 Season							2004-2006						
	Home Games			Away Games				Home Games			Away Games			
	Cubs	Opp	Total	Cubs	Opp	Total	Index	Cubs	Opp	Total	Cubs	Opp	Total	Index
G	81	81	162	81	81	162		244	244	488	242	242	484	
Avg	.279	.244	.262	.256	.265	.261	100	.275	.246	.260	.262	.255	.259	101
AB	2755	2801	5556	2832	2683	5515	101	8294	8466	16760	8505	7970	16475	101
R	374	429	803	342	405	747	107	1154	1140	2294	1054	1073	2127	107
H	770	684	1454	726	712	1438	101	2280	2085	4365	2230	2031	4261	102
2B	150	134	284	121	142	263	107	457	406	863	445	373	818	104
3B	24	21	45	22	11	33	135	51	45	96	47	37	84	112
HR	81	125	206	85	85	170	120	317	317	634	278	248	526	118
BB	196	316	512	199	371	570	89	650	870	1520	653	938	1591	94
SO	448	694	1142	480	556	1036	109	1397	2031	3428	1531	1821	3352	101
E	60	62	122	46	67	113	108	160	173	333	133	177	310	107
E-Infield	28	25	53	15	32	47	113	72	65	137	51	82	133	102
LHB-Avg	.257	.251	.254	.248	.264	.257	99	.265	.264	.265	.253	.255	.254	104
LHB-HR	25	43	68	21	33	54	117	86	79	165	68	51	119	123
RHB-Avg	.290	.241	.265	.259	.266	.262	101	.279	.241	.259	.265	.255	.260	100
RHB-HR	56	82	138	64	52	116	122	231	238	469	210	197	407	117

Chicago White Sox - U.S. Cellular Field

	2006 Season							2004-2006						
	Home Games			Away Games				Home Games			Away Games			
	White Sox	Opp	Total	White Sox	Opp	Total	Index	White Sox	Opp	Total	White Sox	Opp	Total	Index
G	81	81	162	81	81	162		243	243	486	243	243	486	
Avg	.281	.268	.274	.280	.274	.277	99	.271	.268	.269	.269	.260	.265	102
AB	2783	2933	5716	2874	2731	5605	102	8182	8635	16817	8538	8140	16678	101
R	461	392	853	407	402	809	105	1294	1172	2466	1180	1098	2278	108
H	781	786	1567	805	748	1553	101	2219	2312	4531	2298	2119	4417	103
2B	136	144	280	155	152	307	89	396	416	812	432	434	866	93
3B	6	14	20	14	17	31	63	26	35	61	36	43	79	77
HR	136	111	247	100	89	189	128	396	336	732	282	255	537	135
BB	258	236	494	244	197	441	110	751	725	1476	685	694	1379	106
SO	505	525	1030	551	487	1038	97	1496	1587	3083	1592	1478	3070	100
E	40	57	97	50	48	98	99	125	155	280	159	155	314	89
E-Infield	13	28	41	19	19	38	108	45	70	115	69	66	135	85
LHB-Avg	.240	.287	.261	.279	.294	.284	92	.255	.274	.265	.273	.266	.270	98
LHB-HR	31	41	72	33	14	47	158	105	107	212	92	56	148	142
RHB-Avg	.299	.262	.279	.281	.269	.274	102	.278	.265	.271	.268	.258	.263	103
RHB-HR	105	70	175	67	75	142	118	291	229	520	190	199	389	132

Cincinnati Reds - Great American Ballpark

	2006 Season							2004-2006						
	Home Games			Away Games				Home Games			Away Games			
	Reds	Opp	Total	Reds	Opp	Total	Index	Reds	Opp	Total	Reds	Opp	Total	Index
G	81	81	162	81	81	162		244	244	488	243	243	486	
Avg	.271	.273	.272	.244	.282	.263	103	.260	.277	.269	.252	.288	.270	100
AB	2692	2878	5570	2823	2793	5616	99	8094	8739	16833	8504	8337	16841	100
R	401	429	830	348	372	720	115	1186	1314	2500	1133	1283	2416	103
H	730	787	1517	689	789	1478	103	2108	2423	4531	2144	2405	4549	99
2B	129	171	300	162	161	323	94	431	557	988	482	514	996	99
3B	2	8	10	10	15	25	40	18	32	50	37	62	99	51
HR	124	117	241	93	96	189	129	342	365	707	291	303	594	119
BB	326	230	556	288	234	522	107	909	739	1648	915	789	1704	97
SO	579	565	1144	613	488	1101	105	1814	1607	3421	2016	1393	3409	100
E	64	39	103	64	46	110	94	160	123	283	185	135	320	88
E-Infield	28	16	44	16	15	31	142	62	55	117	61	46	107	109
LHB-Avg	.280	.277	.278	.262	.295	.280	99	.253	.276	.265	.259	.290	.274	97
LHB-HR	43	45	88	26	38	64	126	97	117	214	87	90	177	117
RHB-Avg	.268	.272	.270	.238	.277	.257	105	.263	.278	.271	.249	.288	.269	101
RHB-HR	81	72	153	67	58	125	128	245	248	493	204	213	417	120

Cleveland Indians - Jacobs Field

	2006 Season							2004-2006						
	Home Games			Away Games				Home Games			Away Games			
	Indians	Opp	Total	Indians	Opp	Total	Index	Indians	Opp	Total	Indians	Opp	Total	Index
G	81	81	162	81	81	162		243	243	486	243	243	486	
Avg	.280	.273	.276	.281	.291	.286	97	.272	.261	.267	.279	.272	.276	97
AB	2716	2831	5547	2903	2787	5690	97	8130	8507	16637	8774	8354	17128	97
R	435	368	803	435	414	849	95	1214	1097	2311	1304	1184	2488	93
H	760	772	1532	816	811	1627	94	2212	2224	4436	2451	2275	4726	94
2B	179	140	319	172	153	325	101	535	453	988	498	447	945	108
3B	12	10	22	15	13	28	81	32	27	59	54	39	93	65
HR	94	74	168	102	92	194	89	255	246	501	332	278	610	85
BB	287	221	508	269	208	477	109	884	711	1595	781	710	1491	110
SO	584	495	1079	620	453	1073	103	1595	1615	3210	1711	1498	3209	103
E	59	46	105	59	40	99	106	166	180	346	164	135	299	116
E-Infield	28	19	47	30	19	49	96	81	65	146	84	55	139	105
LHB-Avg	.269	.260	.264	.274	.255	.265	100	.257	.261	.259	.274	.254	.264	98
LHB-HR	33	33	66	40	27	67	107	86	84	170	111	86	197	89
RHB-Avg	.284	.280	.282	.285	.310	.297	95	.279	.262	.270	.282	.281	.282	96
RHB-HR	61	41	102	62	65	127	80	169	162	331	221	192	413	82

Colorado Rockies - Coors Field

	2006 Season							2004-2006						
	Home Games			Away Games				Home Games			Away Games			
	Rockies	Opp	Total	Rockies	Opp	Total	Index	Rockies	Opp	Total	Rockies	Opp	Total	Index
G	81	81	162	81	81	162		243	243	486	243	243	486	
Avg	.294	.282	.288	.247	.271	.259	111	.299	.295	.297	.242	.274	.257	115
AB	2752	2901	5653	2810	2699	5509	103	8368	8766	17134	8313	8038	16351	105
R	456	413	869	357	399	756	115	1403	1392	2795	983	1205	2188	128
H	809	818	1627	695	731	1426	114	2502	2584	5086	2010	2199	4209	121
2B	162	167	329	163	164	327	98	508	539	1047	428	485	913	109
3B	33	27	60	21	28	49	119	75	72	147	47	58	105	134
HR	75	93	168	82	62	144	114	272	287	559	237	241	478	112
BB	295	280	575	266	273	539	104	880	947	1827	758	907	1665	105
SO	490	491	981	618	461	1079	89	1511	1484	2995	1881	1396	3277	87
E	44	65	109	47	56	103	106	149	204	353	149	149	298	118
E-Infield	25	15	40	19	25	44	91	54	66	120	50	64	114	105
LHB-Avg	.317	.283	.297	.240	.237	.238	125	.316	.301	.308	.225	.264	.248	124
LHB-HR	18	22	40	13	21	34	114	74	78	152	46	86	132	116
RHB-Avg	.288	.282	.285	.249	.285	.265	108	.294	.292	.293	.247	.278	.261	112
RHB-HR	57	71	128	69	41	110	113	198	209	407	191	155	346	110

Detroit Tigers - Comerica Park

	2006 Season							2004-2006						
	Home Games			Away Games				Home Games			Away Games			
	Tigers	Opp	Total	Tigers	Opp	Total	Index	Tigers	Opp	Total	Tigers	Opp	Total	Index
G	81	81	162	81	81	162		243	243	486	243	243	486	
Avg	.273	.259	.265	.276	.254	.266	100	.274	.267	.271	.271	.268	.270	100
AB	2759	2877	5636	2883	2658	5541	102	8262	8620	16882	8605	8060	16665	101
R	392	349	741	430	326	756	98	1138	1144	2282	1234	1162	2396	95
H	752	744	1496	796	676	1472	102	2265	2305	4570	2335	2161	4496	102
2B	132	135	267	162	128	290	91	376	405	781	485	407	892	86
3B	22	20	42	18	18	36	115	89	63	152	50	47	97	155
HR	81	81	162	122	79	201	79	257	262	519	315	281	596	86
BB	213	251	464	217	238	455	100	661	752	1413	671	728	1399	100
SO	520	504	1024	613	499	1112	91	1529	1488	3017	1786	1417	3203	93
E	50	62	112	56	50	106	106	171	151	322	189	148	337	96
E-Infield	27	29	56	21	26	47	119	70	74	144	68	58	126	114
LHB-Avg	.275	.249	.258	.265	.268	.267	97	.279	.269	.273	.272	.274	.273	100
LHB-HR	16	36	52	33	41	74	72	72	103	175	85	130	215	82
RHB-Avg	.272	.266	.269	.281	.245	.265	101	.272	.266	.269	.271	.264	.268	101
RHB-HR	65	45	110	89	38	127	84	185	159	344	230	151	381	88

Florida Marlins - Dolphins Stadium

	2006 Season							2004-2006						
	Home Games			Away Games				Home Games			Away Games			
	Marlins	Opp	Total	Marlins	Opp	Total	Index	Marlins	Opp	Total	Marlins	Opp	Total	Index
G	81	81	162	81	81	162		242	242	484	244	244	488	
Avg	.258	.262	.260	.270	.272	.271	96	.263	.255	.259	.270	.271	.271	96
AB	2647	2807	5454	2855	2683	5538	98	7938	8338	16276	8552	8092	16644	99
R	353	371	724	405	401	806	90	1031	1037	2068	1162	1167	2329	90
H	683	735	1418	771	730	1501	94	2088	2125	4213	2312	2194	4506	94
2B	146	138	284	163	130	293	98	412	419	831	478	435	913	93
3B	25	27	52	17	20	37	143	62	65	127	44	64	108	120
HR	84	79	163	98	87	185	89	212	214	426	246	234	480	91
BB	268	320	588	229	302	531	112	796	873	1669	712	825	1537	111
SO	611	596	1207	638	492	1130	108	1558	1823	3381	1577	1506	3083	112
E	62	60	122	64	60	124	98	134	174	308	181	172	353	88
E-Infield	14	18	32	25	24	49	65	39	64	103	76	64	140	74
LHB-Avg	.258	.264	.261	.256	.248	.251	104	.271	.265	.268	.260	.262	.261	102
LHB-HR	25	24	49	24	36	60	89	53	62	115	61	82	143	85
RHB-Avg	.258	.261	.259	.275	.287	.280	93	.261	.250	.256	.273	.275	.274	93
RHB-HR	59	55	114	74	51	125	90	159	152	311	185	152	337	93

Houston Astros - Minute Maid Park

	2006 Season							2004-2006						
	Home Games			Away Games				Home Games			Away Games			
	Astros	Opp	Total	Astros	Opp	Total	Index	Astros	Opp	Total	Astros	Opp	Total	Index
G	81	81	162	81	81	162		243	243	486	244	244	488	
Avg	.254	.255	.255	.256	.256	.256	99	.267	.246	.256	.252	.261	.256	100
AB	2667	2864	5531	2854	2708	5562	99	7990	8376	16366	8461	8125	16586	99
R	372	367	739	363	352	715	103	1137	985	2122	1094	1041	2135	100
H	677	731	1408	730	694	1424	99	2135	2060	4195	2130	2117	4247	99
2B	143	156	299	132	165	297	101	405	405	810	445	458	903	91
3B	16	15	31	11	13	24	130	56	45	101	39	45	84	122
HR	98	94	192	76	88	164	118	287	263	550	235	248	483	115
BB	294	229	523	291	251	542	97	846	663	1509	810	782	1592	96
SO	516	604	1120	560	556	1116	101	1467	1894	3361	1645	1712	3357	101
E	41	36	77	39	56	95	81	147	139	286	123	151	274	105
E-Infield	25	14	39	17	20	37	105	72	56	128	49	74	123	104
LHB-Avg	.260	.289	.277	.252	.279	.267	104	.265	.266	.265	.245	.268	.256	104
LHB-HR	26	26	52	13	28	41	124	75	62	137	39	61	100	138
RHB-Avg	.252	.241	.247	.257	.247	.252	98	.268	.240	.254	.254	.258	.256	99
RHB-HR	72	68	140	63	60	123	115	212	201	413	196	187	383	110

Kansas City Royals - Ewing M. Kauffman Stadium

| | 2006 Season | | | | | | | 2004-2006 | | | | | | |
| | Home Games | | | Away Games | | | | Home Games | | | Away Games | | | |
	Royals	Opp	Total	Royals	Opp	Total	Index	Royals	Opp	Total	Royals	Opp	Total	Index
G	81	81	162	81	81	162		242	242	484	243	243	486	
Avg	.289	.294	.291	.254	.291	.272	107	.273	.288	.280	.256	.295	.275	102
AB	2769	2889	5658	2820	2747	5567	102	8124	8648	16772	8472	8235	16707	101
R	424	499	923	333	472	805	115	1119	1375	2494	1050	1425	2475	101
H	800	848	1648	715	800	1515	109	2214	2489	4703	2168	2428	4596	103
2B	177	191	368	158	150	308	118	448	560	1008	432	485	917	109
3B	19	16	35	18	11	29	119	52	55	107	48	47	95	112
HR	65	102	167	59	111	170	97	172	272	444	227	326	553	80
BB	252	336	588	222	301	523	111	705	861	1566	648	865	1513	103
SO	513	443	956	527	461	988	95	1425	1384	2809	1672	1324	2996	93
E	55	63	118	43	51	94	126	165	162	327	188	166	354	93
E-Infield	26	19	45	19	19	38	118	69	67	136	76	67	143	95
LHB-Avg	.277	.297	.288	.250	.279	.266	108	.263	.294	.280	.247	.285	.268	105
LHB-HR	18	28	46	21	39	60	69	50	94	144	68	125	193	76
RHB-Avg	.294	.292	.293	.255	.297	.275	107	.277	.285	.280	.259	.301	.279	101
RHB-HR	47	74	121	38	72	110	113	122	178	300	159	201	360	82

Los Angeles Angels - Angel Stadium of Anaheim

| | 2006 Season | | | | | | | 2004-2006 | | | | | | |
| | Home Games | | | Away Games | | | | Home Games | | | Away Games | | | |
	Angels	Opp	Total	Angels	Opp	Total	Index	Angels	Opp	Total	Angels	Opp	Total	Index
G	81	81	162	81	81	162		243	243	486	243	243	486	
Avg	.279	.257	.268	.270	.252	.261	102	.276	.256	.266	.275	.258	.267	100
AB	2745	2832	5577	2864	2709	5573	100	8240	8601	16841	8668	8150	16818	100
R	366	346	712	400	386	786	91	1118	1040	2158	1245	1069	2314	93
H	766	727	1493	773	683	1456	103	2277	2203	4480	2385	2102	4487	100
2B	148	147	295	161	153	314	94	398	441	839	461	442	903	93
3B	13	10	23	16	13	29	79	42	33	75	54	44	98	76
HR	69	72	141	90	86	176	80	217	240	457	251	246	497	92
BB	248	220	468	238	251	489	96	684	688	1372	699	728	1427	96
SO	450	596	1046	464	568	1032	101	1320	1766	3086	1384	1688	3072	100
E	61	45	106	63	40	103	103	157	149	306	144	171	315	97
E-Infield	26	15	41	34	14	48	85	61	53	114	63	69	132	86
LHB-Avg	.267	.261	.265	.265	.301	.272	97	.264	.275	.267	.279	.275	.278	96
LHB-HR	21	5	26	29	4	33	73	65	28	93	81	30	111	87
RHB-Avg	.284	.256	.268	.272	.248	.259	104	.281	.254	.266	.273	.256	.264	101
RHB-HR	48	67	115	61	82	143	82	152	212	364	170	216	386	93

Los Angeles Dodgers - Dodger Stadium

| | 2006 Season | | | | | | | 2004-2006 | | | | | | |
| | Home Games | | | Away Games | | | | Home Games | | | Away Games | | | |
	Dodgers	Opp	Total	Dodgers	Opp	Total	Index	Dodgers	Opp	Total	Dodgers	Opp	Total	Index
G	81	81	162	81	81	162		243	243	486	243	243	486	
Avg	.293	.265	.278	.260	.274	.267	104	.267	.254	.261	.260	.271	.265	98
AB	2733	2857	5590	2895	2798	5693	98	8029	8397	16426	8573	8160	16733	98
R	438	365	803	382	386	768	105	1144	1032	2176	1122	1158	2280	95
H	800	756	1556	752	768	1520	102	2145	2136	4281	2230	2208	4438	96
2B	159	159	318	148	164	312	104	399	411	810	418	458	876	94
3B	21	9	30	37	21	58	53	39	28	67	70	61	131	52
HR	88	78	166	65	74	139	122	268	260	528	237	252	489	110
BB	328	259	587	273	233	506	118	874	714	1588	805	770	1575	103
SO	443	582	1025	516	486	1002	104	1485	1694	3179	1660	1444	3104	104
E	63	54	117	52	48	100	117	148	161	309	146	153	299	103
E-Infield	28	26	54	20	19	39	138	57	62	119	56	63	119	100
LHB-Avg	.316	.286	.302	.256	.285	.271	111	.272	.258	.265	.265	.274	.269	98
LHB-HR	20	14	34	17	23	40	99	66	57	123	61	70	131	100
RHB-Avg	.286	.259	.272	.261	.271	.266	103	.266	.253	.259	.259	.269	.264	98
RHB-HR	68	64	132	48	51	99	131	202	203	405	176	182	358	114

Milwaukee Brewers - Miller Park

| | 2006 Season | | | | | | | 2004-2006 | | | | | | |
| | Home Games | | | Away Games | | | | Home Games | | | Away Games | | | |
	Brewers	Opp	Total	Brewers	Opp	Total	Index	Brewers	Opp	Total	Brewers	Opp	Total	Index
G	81	81	162	81	81	162		243	243	486	242	242	484	
Avg	.260	.251	.255	.256	.279	.267	95	.256	.246	.250	.254	.271	.262	95
AB	2639	2804	5443	2794	2690	5484	99	7980	8414	16394	8384	8154	16538	99
R	385	398	783	345	435	780	100	1099	1109	2208	991	1178	2169	101
H	685	703	1388	715	751	1466	95	2040	2066	4106	2131	2210	4341	94
2B	155	170	325	146	185	331	99	468	485	953	455	495	950	101
3B	14	16	30	6	16	22	137	46	43	89	25	50	75	120
HR	96	83	179	84	94	178	101	253	254	507	237	256	493	104
BB	273	258	531	229	256	485	110	847	786	1633	726	773	1499	110
SO	598	633	1231	635	512	1147	108	1834	1857	3691	1873	1559	3432	108
E	63	60	123	54	43	97	127	177	171	348	176	134	310	112
E-Infield	22	25	47	24	19	43	109	76	77	153	81	61	142	107
LHB-Avg	.270	.255	.261	.242	.290	.271	96	.257	.244	.249	.249	.282	.267	93
LHB-HR	23	23	46	21	42	63	74	68	71	139	56	91	147	96
RHB-Avg	.256	.248	.252	.260	.272	.266	95	.255	.246	.251	.256	.266	.260	96
RHB-HR	73	60	133	63	52	115	116	185	183	368	181	165	346	107

Minnesota Twins - Hubert H. Humphrey Metrodome Surface: AstroTurf

| | 2006 Season | | | | | | | 2004-2006 | | | | | | |
| | Home Games | | | Away Games | | | | Home Games | | | Away Games | | | |
	Twins	Opp	Total	Twins	Opp	Total	Index	Twins	Opp	Total	Twins	Opp	Total	Index
G	81	81	162	81	81	162		243	243	486	243	243	486	
Avg	.298	.251	.274	.276	.283	.279	98	.277	.257	.267	.265	.273	.269	99
AB	2743	2833	5576	2859	2753	5612	99	8218	8592	16810	8571	8286	16857	100
R	421	307	728	380	376	756	96	1176	998	2174	1093	1062	2155	101
H	818	712	1530	790	778	1568	98	2275	2205	4480	2268	2266	4534	99
2B	132	138	270	143	142	285	95	419	383	802	435	401	836	96
3B	23	12	35	11	11	22	160	51	31	82	39	43	82	100
HR	69	79	148	74	103	177	84	225	243	468	243	275	518	91
BB	223	151	374	267	205	472	80	725	499	1224	763	636	1399	88
SO	426	617	1043	446	547	993	106	1409	1744	3153	1423	1508	2931	108
E	42	51	93	42	56	98	95	140	157	297	148	167	315	94
E-Infield	15	16	31	16	24	40	78	63	49	112	53	65	118	95
LHB-Avg	.314	.192	.259	.274	.227	.253	102	.278	.225	.252	.260	.236	.249	102
LHB-HR	24	15	39	22	21	43	92	73	63	136	69	65	134	97
RHB-Avg	.290	.273	.281	.277	.303	.291	97	.276	.269	.273	.266	.288	.277	98
RHB-HR	45	64	109	52	82	134	82	152	180	332	174	210	384	88

New York Mets - Shea Stadium

| | 2006 Season | | | | | | | 2004-2006 | | | | | | |
| | Home Games | | | Away Games | | | | Home Games | | | Away Games | | | |
	Mets	Opp	Total	Mets	Opp	Total	Index	Mets	Opp	Total	Mets	Opp	Total	Index
G	81	81	162	81	81	162		243	243	486	243	243	486	
Avg	.256	.245	.250	.272	.262	.267	94	.257	.253	.255	.257	.260	.259	99
AB	2708	2833	5541	2850	2698	5548	100	8135	8494	16629	8460	8064	16524	101
R	395	347	742	439	384	823	90	1100	1015	2115	1140	1095	2235	95
H	693	694	1387	776	708	1484	93	2089	2148	4237	2177	2096	4273	99
2B	157	142	299	166	132	298	100	430	425	855	461	414	875	97
3B	19	8	27	22	10	32	84	41	22	63	52	41	93	67
HR	96	82	178	104	98	202	88	264	212	476	296	259	555	85
BB	278	264	542	269	263	532	102	784	795	1579	761	815	1576	100
SO	516	604	1120	555	557	1112	101	1575	1643	3218	1730	1507	3237	99
E	53	48	101	51	63	114	89	189	163	352	158	152	310	114
E-Infield	21	18	39	15	23	38	103	84	63	147	58	54	112	131
LHB-Avg	.250	.243	.246	.259	.267	.263	94	.255	.247	.251	.255	.261	.259	97
LHB-HR	22	27	49	22	33	55	87	55	61	116	60	80	140	81
RHB-Avg	.258	.246	.252	.277	.260	.269	94	.257	.255	.256	.258	.259	.259	99
RHB-HR	74	55	129	82	65	147	89	209	151	360	236	179	415	87

New York Yankees - Yankee Stadium

| | 2006 Season | | | | | | | 2004-2006 | | | | | | |
| | Home Games | | | Away Games | | | | Home Games | | | Away Games | | | |
	Yankees	Opp	Total	Yankees	Opp	Total	Index	Yankees	Opp	Total	Yankees	Opp	Total	Index
G	81	81	162	81	81	162		243	243	486	243	243	486	
Avg	.284	.253	.268	.285	.271	.278	96	.281	.262	.272	.272	.273	.272	100
AB	2710	2810	5520	2941	2780	5721	96	8164	8565	16729	8638	8232	16870	99
R	450	354	804	480	413	893	90	1373	1107	2480	1340	1257	2597	95
H	770	710	1480	838	753	1591	93	2297	2246	4543	2346	2244	4590	99
2B	155	147	302	172	147	319	98	406	431	837	461	462	923	91
3B	8	6	14	13	16	29	50	24	32	56	33	49	82	69
HR	111	85	196	99	85	184	110	363	254	617	318	262	580	107
BB	314	239	553	335	257	592	97	949	662	1611	1007	742	1749	93
SO	478	505	983	575	514	1089	94	1442	1605	3047	1582	1457	3039	101
E	55	49	104	49	51	100	104	153	173	326	145	164	309	106
E-Infield	23	24	47	19	22	41	115	68	83	151	54	76	130	116
LHB-Avg	.289	.238	.266	.272	.254	.264	101	.288	.257	.276	.270	.279	.274	101
LHB-HR	28	19	47	21	23	44	124	115	49	164	73	60	133	118
RHB-Avg	.282	.257	.269	.290	.276	.283	95	.278	.263	.270	.272	.271	.272	99
RHB-HR	83	66	149	78	62	140	106	248	205	453	245	202	447	104

Oakland Athletics - McAfee Coliseum

| | 2006 Season | | | | | | | 2004-2006 | | | | | | |
| | Home Games | | | Away Games | | | | Home Games | | | Away Games | | | |
	Athletics	Opp	Total	Athletics	Opp	Total	Index	Athletics	Opp	Total	Athletics	Opp	Total	Index
G	81	81	162	81	81	162		243	243	486	243	243	486	
Avg	.259	.268	.264	.261	.275	.268	98	.266	.254	.260	.262	.263	.262	99
AB	2675	2857	5532	2825	2757	5582	99	8211	8506	16717	8644	8158	16802	99
R	372	346	718	399	381	780	92	1168	1058	2226	1168	1069	2237	100
H	692	767	1459	737	758	1495	98	2187	2164	4351	2263	2142	4405	99
2B	128	159	287	138	130	268	108	451	447	898	461	390	851	106
3B	11	16	27	11	18	29	94	28	33	61	29	46	75	82
HR	84	71	155	91	91	182	86	255	230	485	264	250	514	95
BB	303	255	558	347	274	621	91	881	785	1666	914	792	1706	98
SO	455	484	939	521	519	1040	91	1305	1546	2851	1551	1566	3117	92
E	35	40	75	49	46	95	79	121	148	269	142	145	287	94
E-Infield	12	19	31	18	25	43	72	53	60	113	59	75	134	84
LHB-Avg	.263	.273	.269	.266	.261	.263	102	.284	.268	.275	.258	.257	.258	107
LHB-HR	20	24	44	30	22	52	89	78	94	172	69	91	160	105
RHB-Avg	.258	.267	.262	.259	.280	.269	97	.259	.247	.254	.263	.265	.264	96
RHB-HR	64	47	111	61	69	130	85	177	136	313	195	159	354	90

Philadelphia Phillies - Citizens Bank Park

| | 2006 Season | | | | | | | 2004-2005 | | | | | | |
| | Home Games | | | Away Games | | | | Home Games | | | Away Games | | | |
	Phillies	Opp	Total	Phillies	Opp	Total	Index	Phillies	Opp	Total	Phillies	Opp	Total	Index
G	81	81	162	81	81	162		162	162	324	162	162	324	
Avg	.274	.275	.275	.260	.275	.267	103	.273	.262	.268	.263	.255	.259	103
AB	2750	2877	5627	2937	2800	5737	98	5475	5726	11201	5710	5354	11064	101
R	444	420	864	421	392	813	106	851	791	1642	796	716	1512	109
H	754	791	1545	764	770	1534	101	1496	1502	2998	1503	1365	2868	105
2B	151	168	319	143	167	310	105	288	316	604	297	321	618	97
3B	15	17	32	26	23	49	67	34	37	71	24	27	51	138
HR	112	121	233	104	90	194	122	207	222	429	175	181	356	119
BB	301	255	556	325	257	582	97	654	463	1117	630	526	1156	95
SO	560	614	1174	643	524	1167	103	1011	1163	2174	1205	1066	2271	95
E	53	57	110	51	51	102	108	81	99	180	90	99	189	95
E-Infield	22	26	48	21	25	46	104	33	45	78	32	41	73	107
LHB-Avg	.279	.242	.260	.235	.262	.249	105	.284	.241	.261	.256	.246	.251	104
LHB-HR	33	33	66	31	21	52	142	56	58	114	39	54	93	117
RHB-Avg	.272	.287	.280	.270	.281	.275	102	.270	.270	.270	.266	.258	.262	103
RHB-HR	79	88	167	73	69	142	116	151	164	315	136	127	263	120

Pittsburgh Pirates - PNC Park

	2006 Season							2004-2006						
	Home Games			Away Games			Index	Home Games			Away Games			Index
	Pirates	Opp	Total	Pirates	Opp	Total		Pirates	Opp	Total	Pirates	Opp	Total	
G	81	81	162	81	81	162		242	242	484	243	243	486	
Avg	.283	.275	.279	.243	.287	.264	105	.270	.269	.270	.252	.274	.263	103
AB	2801	2891	5692	2757	2616	5373	106	8211	8485	16696	8403	7913	16316	103
R	380	367	747	311	430	741	101	1054	1104	2158	997	1206	2203	98
H	793	794	1587	669	751	1420	112	2220	2280	4500	2115	2172	4287	105
2B	161	166	327	125	134	259	119	453	489	942	392	428	820	112
3B	10	14	24	7	17	24	94	55	38	93	39	54	93	98
HR	70	64	134	71	92	163	78	207	202	409	215	265	480	83
BB	239	295	534	220	325	545	92	683	862	1545	662	946	1608	94
SO	568	543	1111	632	517	1149	91	1588	1593	3181	1770	1504	3274	95
E	41	51	92	63	56	119	77	154	153	307	170	158	328	94
E-Infield	21	23	44	30	23	53	83	67	69	136	70	69	139	98
LHB-Avg	.317	.266	.282	.264	.290	.281	101	.273	.252	.260	.260	.274	.269	97
LHB-HR	21	26	47	26	41	67	65	51	87	138	60	109	169	78
RHB-Avg	.272	.284	.277	.235	.284	.254	109	.269	.281	.275	.249	.275	.260	106
RHB-HR	49	38	87	45	51	96	87	156	115	271	155	156	311	86

San Diego Padres - PETCO Park

	2006 Season							2004-2005						
	Home Games			Away Games			Index	Home Games			Away Games			Index
	Padres	Opp	Total	Padres	Opp	Total		Padres	Opp	Total	Padres	Opp	Total	
G	81	81	162	81	81	162		162	162	324	162	162	324	
Avg	.245	.244	.244	.279	.255	.268	91	.256	.250	.253	.274	.272	.273	93
AB	2698	2844	5542	2878	2713	5591	99	5310	5631	10941	5765	5531	11296	97
R	315	337	652	416	342	758	86	637	660	1297	815	771	1586	82
H	661	693	1354	804	692	1496	91	1358	1409	2767	1579	1503	3082	90
2B	118	126	244	180	138	318	77	251	305	556	322	321	643	89
3B	22	16	38	16	19	35	110	44	43	87	27	35	62	145
HR	75	92	167	86	84	170	99	111	139	250	158	191	349	74
BB	282	237	519	282	231	513	102	588	452	1040	578	473	1051	102
SO	548	596	1144	556	501	1057	109	936	1165	2101	951	1047	1998	109
E	40	46	86	52	50	102	84	100	87	187	117	119	236	79
E-Infield	14	14	28	20	20	40	70	40	28	68	50	54	104	65
LHB-Avg	.246	.289	.255	.285	.232	.274	93	.251	.266	.256	.279	.275	.278	92
LHB-HR	26	3	29	16	2	18	151	29	19	48	48	35	83	62
RHB-Avg	.245	.241	.242	.278	.257	.266	91	.258	.248	.252	.272	.271	.272	93
RHB-HR	49	89	138	70	82	152	93	82	120	202	110	156	266	77

San Francisco Giants - Pacific Bell Park

	2006 Season							2004-2006						
	Home Games			Away Games			Index	Home Games			Away Games			Index
	Giants	Opp	Total	Giants	Opp	Total		Giants	Opp	Total	Giants	Opp	Total	
G	81	81	162	80	80	160		244	244	488	241	241	482	
Avg	.264	.253	.258	.254	.270	.262	99	.270	.262	.265	.258	.264	.261	102
AB	2674	2784	5458	2798	2665	5463	99	8037	8474	16511	8443	8102	16545	99
R	382	388	770	364	402	766	99	1134	1167	2301	1111	1138	2249	101
H	706	703	1409	712	719	1431	97	2166	2217	4383	2179	2142	4321	100
2B	162	143	305	135	144	279	109	473	441	914	437	444	881	104
3B	30	21	51	22	26	48	106	68	69	137	43	65	108	127
HR	61	68	129	102	85	187	69	213	214	427	261	251	512	84
BB	259	281	540	235	303	538	100	831	828	1659	799	896	1695	98
SO	410	522	932	481	470	951	98	1215	1565	2780	1451	1419	2870	97
E	48	51	99	43	42	85	115	145	154	299	137	131	268	110
E-Infield	24	18	42	15	27	42	99	67	55	122	58	62	120	100
LHB-Avg	.266	.266	.266	.260	.297	.276	96	.276	.264	.269	.270	.275	.272	99
LHB-HR	17	18	35	21	17	38	92	65	60	125	67	76	143	84
RHB-Avg	.263	.248	.256	.252	.263	.258	99	.268	.260	.264	.254	.260	.257	103
RHB-HR	44	50	94	81	68	149	63	148	154	302	194	175	369	83

Seattle Mariners - Safeco Field

	2006 Season							2004-2006						
	Home Games			Away Games				Home Games			Away Games			
	Mariners	Opp	Total	Mariners	Opp	Total	Index	Mariners	Opp	Total	Mariners	Opp	Total	Index
G	81	81	162	81	81	162		244	244	488	242	242	484	
Avg	.265	.255	.260	.277	.280	.279	93	.260	.256	.258	.271	.279	.275	94
AB	2706	2819	5525	2964	2792	5756	96	8197	8598	16795	8702	8192	16894	99
R	353	372	725	403	420	823	88	1020	1121	2141	1133	1245	2378	89
H	718	718	1436	822	782	1604	90	2130	2197	4327	2362	2284	4646	92
2B	123	160	283	143	167	310	95	394	467	861	437	444	881	98
3B	21	10	31	21	13	34	95	42	23	65	54	42	96	68
HR	81	86	167	91	97	188	93	215	272	487	223	302	525	93
BB	195	304	499	209	256	465	112	686	855	1541	676	776	1452	107
SO	481	571	1052	493	496	989	111	1555	1622	3177	1463	1373	2836	113
E	39	55	94	49	79	128	73	138	160	298	139	191	330	90
E-Infield	16	18	34	25	33	58	59	53	54	107	68	83	151	70
LHB-Avg	.245	.260	.254	.273	.296	.287	89	.259	.252	.255	.279	.277	.278	92
LHB-HR	13	38	51	17	43	60	80	61	102	163	49	112	161	93
RHB-Avg	.272	.251	.263	.279	.271	.275	96	.260	.258	.259	.269	.280	.274	95
RHB-HR	68	48	116	74	54	128	99	154	170	324	174	190	364	93

St Louis Cardinals - Busch Stadium

	2006 Season							2003-2005						
	Home Games			Away Games				Home Games			Away Games			
	Cardinals	Opp	Total	Cardinals	Opp	Total	Index	Cardinals	Opp	Total	Cardinals	Opp	Total	Index
G	80	80	160	81	81	162		243	243	486	243	243	486	
Avg	.273	.253	.263	.265	.284	.274	96	.282	.254	.268	.270	.266	.268	100
AB	2708	2793	5501	2814	2703	5517	101	8167	8454	16621	8598	8162	16760	99
R	399	348	747	382	414	796	95	1256	1010	2266	1280	1079	2359	96
H	738	708	1446	746	767	1513	97	2300	2147	4447	2318	2174	4492	99
2B	140	141	281	152	169	321	88	499	433	932	449	454	903	104
3B	14	12	26	13	22	35	75	36	31	67	46	39	85	79
HR	85	91	176	99	102	201	88	270	252	522	310	280	590	89
BB	273	251	524	258	253	511	103	831	678	1509	831	713	1544	99
SO	439	495	934	483	475	958	98	1382	1581	2963	1602	1403	3005	99
E	56	50	106	42	55	97	111	136	176	312	139	188	327	95
E-Infield	26	20	46	18	27	45	104	59	65	124	65	69	134	93
LHB-Avg	.241	.266	.248	.288	.326	.301	83	.290	.259	.278	.268	.273	.270	103
LHB-HR	23	14	37	18	17	35	108	73	33	106	69	42	111	94
RHB-Avg	.286	.252	.267	.256	.277	.267	100	.279	.253	.265	.270	.265	.268	99
RHB-HR	62	77	139	81	85	166	84	197	219	416	241	238	479	88

Tampa Bay Devil Rays - Tropicana Field Surface: NexTurf

	2006 Season							2004-2006						
	Home Games			Away Games				Home Games			Away Games			
	Devil Rays	Opp	Total	Devil Rays	Opp	Total	Index	Devil Rays	Opp	Total	Devil Rays	Opp	Total	Index
G	81	81	162	81	81	162		242	242	484	243	243	486	
Avg	.259	.275	.268	.250	.297	.273	98	.264	.266	.265	.260	.289	.274	97
AB	2659	2856	5515	2815	2741	5556	99	8046	8545	16591	8463	8156	16619	100
R	373	415	788	316	441	757	104	1122	1239	2361	1031	1395	2426	98
H	690	786	1476	705	814	1519	97	2127	2275	4402	2203	2354	4557	97
2B	129	161	290	138	173	311	94	401	459	860	433	514	947	91
3B	22	15	37	11	12	23	162	73	46	119	46	49	95	125
HR	100	99	199	90	81	171	117	245	287	532	247	279	526	101
BB	241	306	547	200	300	500	110	708	877	1585	614	924	1538	103
SO	538	520	1058	568	459	1027	104	1466	1527	2993	1574	1324	2898	103
E	55	53	108	61	30	91	119	175	148	323	184	119	303	107
E-Infield	26	20	46	25	11	36	128	73	57	130	68	39	107	122
LHB-Avg	.252	.236	.242	.266	.283	.274	88	.270	.259	.264	.267	.284	.276	95
LHB-HR	30	27	57	26	25	51	114	74	79	153	68	84	152	105
RHB-Avg	.262	.294	.277	.244	.303	.273	102	.262	.270	.266	.258	.291	.273	97
RHB-HR	70	72	142	64	56	120	119	171	208	379	179	195	374	100

Texas Rangers - The Ballpark in Arlington

	2006 Season							2004-2006						
	Home Games			Away Games				Home Games			Away Games			
	Rangers	Opp	Total	Rangers	Opp	Total	Index	Rangers	Opp	Total	Rangers	Opp	Total	Index
G	81	81	162	81	81	162		243	243	486	243	243	486	
Avg	.283	.273	.278	.272	.284	.278	100	.282	.274	.278	.259	.280	.269	103
AB	2802	2895	5697	2857	2706	5563	102	8368	8720	17088	8622	8196	16818	102
R	428	413	841	407	371	778	108	1388	1254	2642	1172	1182	2354	112
H	794	790	1584	777	768	1545	103	2361	2389	4750	2230	2294	4524	105
2B	191	149	340	166	134	300	111	509	469	978	482	423	905	106
3B	10	11	21	13	14	27	76	49	47	96	37	33	70	135
HR	93	85	178	90	77	167	104	362	262	624	308	241	549	112
BB	252	259	511	253	237	490	102	767	770	1537	733	795	1528	99
SO	537	487	1024	524	485	1009	99	1560	1452	3012	1712	1431	3143	94
E	51	49	100	47	49	96	104	165	138	303	158	140	298	102
E-Infield	29	28	57	14	27	41	139	77	78	155	69	71	140	111
LHB-Avg	.300	.277	.289	.258	.305	.277	104	.286	.274	.280	.261	.290	.274	102
LHB-HR	37	22	59	23	16	39	141	96	55	151	77	76	153	105
RHB-Avg	.278	.272	.275	.277	.279	.278	99	.281	.274	.277	.258	.277	.267	104
RHB-HR	56	63	119	67	61	128	92	266	207	473	231	165	396	115

Toronto Blue Jays - Rogers Centre Surface: AstroTurf

	2006 Season							2004-2006						
	Home Games			Away Games				Home Games			Away Games			
	Blue Jays	Opp	Total	Blue Jays	Opp	Total	Index	Blue Jays	Opp	Total	Blue Jays	Opp	Total	Index
G	81	81	162	81	81	162		243	243	486	242	242	484	
Avg	.295	.252	.274	.274	.271	.272	100	.278	.265	.272	.262	.267	.264	103
AB	2781	2856	5637	2815	2676	5491	103	8248	8587	16835	8460	8041	16501	102
R	449	358	807	360	396	756	107	1242	1141	2383	1061	1141	2202	108
H	821	721	1542	770	726	1496	103	2295	2277	4572	2214	2150	4364	104
2B	187	135	322	161	156	317	99	501	420	921	444	427	871	104
3B	17	15	32	10	6	16	195	61	36	97	39	33	72	132
HR	121	94	215	78	91	169	124	277	290	567	203	261	464	120
BB	246	251	497	268	253	521	93	759	764	1523	754	792	1546	97
SO	435	577	1012	471	499	970	102	1406	1607	3013	1538	1383	2921	101
E	40	40	80	59	35	94	85	147	154	301	138	138	276	109
E-Infield	14	12	26	24	16	40	65	59	59	118	60	62	122	96
LHB-Avg	.321	.234	.267	.277	.259	.268	100	.280	.249	.264	.273	.256	.265	99
LHB-HR	26	38	64	27	30	57	110	78	84	162	69	71	140	116
RHB-Avg	.287	.263	.276	.272	.277	.275	101	.278	.272	.275	.257	.272	.264	104
RHB-HR	95	56	151	51	61	112	131	199	206	405	134	190	324	121

Washington Nationals - RFK Stadium

	2006 Season							2005-2006						
	Home Games			Away Games				Home Games			Away Games			
	Nationals	Opp	Total	Nationals	Opp	Total	Index	Nationals	Opp	Total	Nationals	Opp	Total	Index
G	81	81	162	81	81	162		162	162	324	162	162	324	
Avg	.262	.263	.262	.261	.286	.274	96	.249	.255	.252	.264	.282	.273	92
AB	2684	2872	5556	2811	2730	5541	100	5256	5672	10928	5665	5480	11145	98
R	373	412	785	373	460	833	94	662	732	1394	723	813	1536	91
H	702	754	1456	735	781	1516	96	1309	1445	2754	1495	1546	3041	91
2B	143	147	290	179	158	337	86	288	282	570	345	302	647	90
3B	16	21	37	6	21	27	137	36	28	64	18	35	53	123
HR	74	91	165	90	102	192	86	120	157	277	161	176	337	84
BB	290	256	546	304	328	632	86	540	511	1051	545	612	1157	93
SO	531	507	1038	625	453	1078	96	1053	1053	2106	1193	904	2097	102
E	53	58	111	78	43	121	92	103	100	203	120	85	205	99
E-Infield	20	15	35	23	20	43	81	46	38	84	41	39	80	105
LHB-Avg	.264	.258	.261	.286	.265	.279	94	.256	.276	.263	.278	.266	.274	96
LHB-HR	20	9	29	24	17	41	70	29	13	42	42	17	59	73
RHB-Avg	.261	.264	.262	.251	.290	.272	96	.247	.251	.249	.258	.284	.272	92
RHB-HR	54	82	136	66	85	151	90	91	144	235	119	159	278	86

2006 American League Ballpark Index Rankings - Runs

Home Park	TOTALS											LHB		RHB	
	Avg	AB	R	H	2B	3B	HR	BB	SO	E	E-Inf	Avg	HR	Avg	HR
Royals (Ewing M. Kauffman Stadium)	107	102	115	109	118	119	97	111	95	126	118	108	69	107	113
Rangers (The Ballpark in Arlington)	100	102	108	103	111	76	104	102	99	104	139	104	141	99	92
Blue Jays (Rogers Centre)	100	103	107	103	99	195	124	93	102	85	65	100	110	101	131
White Sox (U.S. Cellular Field)	99	102	105	101	89	63	128	110	97	99	108	92	158	102	118
Devil Rays (Tropicana Field)	98	99	104	97	94	162	117	110	104	119	128	88	114	102	119
Red Sox (Fenway Park)	104	100	103	104	137	100	73	94	97	99	118	102	86	105	69
Orioles (Oriole Park at Camden Yards)	102	101	98	103	87	60	118	91	92	97	102	110	95	99	129
Tigers (Comerica Park)	100	102	98	102	91	115	79	100	91	106	119	97	72	101	84
Twins (Hubert H. Humphrey Metrodome)	98	99	96	98	95	160	84	80	106	95	78	102	92	97	82
Indians (Jacobs Field)	97	97	95	94	101	81	89	109	103	106	96	100	107	95	80
Athletics (McAfee Coliseum)	98	99	92	98	108	94	86	91	91	79	72	102	89	97	85
Angels (Angel Stadium of Anaheim)	102	100	91	103	94	79	80	96	101	103	85	97	73	104	82
Yankees (Yankee Stadium)	96	96	90	97	98	50	110	97	94	104	115	101	124	95	106
Mariners (Safeco Field)	93	96	88	90	95	95	93	112	111	73	59	89	80	96	99

2006 National League Ballpark Index Rankings - Runs

Home Park	TOTALS											LHB		RHB	
	Avg	AB	R	H	2B	3B	HR	BB	SO	E	E-Inf	Avg	HR	Avg	HR
Reds (Great American Ballpark)	103	99	115	103	94	40	129	107	105	94	142	99	126	105	128
Rockies (Coors Field)	111	103	115	114	98	119	114	104	89	106	91	125	114	108	113
Diamondbacks (Chase Field)	109	101	114	110	108	162	133	107	94	108	138	109	154	109	129
Cubs (Wrigley Field)	100	101	107	101	107	135	120	89	109	108	113	99	117	101	122
Phillies (Citizens Bank Park)	103	98	106	101	105	67	122	97	103	108	104	105	142	102	116
Dodgers (Dodger Stadium)	104	98	105	102	104	53	122	118	104	117	138	111	99	103	131
Astros (Minute Maid Park)	99	99	103	99	101	130	118	97	101	81	105	104	124	98	115
Pirates (PNC Park)	105	106	101	112	119	94	78	92	91	77	83	101	65	109	87
Brewers (Miller Park)	95	99	100	95	99	137	101	110	108	127	109	96	74	95	116
Giants (Pacific Bell Park)	99	99	99	97	109	106	69	100	98	115	99	96	92	99	63
Cardinals (Busch Stadium)	96	101	95	97	88	75	88	103	98	111	104	83	108	100	84
Braves (Turner Field)	103	100	95	103	100	72	93	91	105	111	100	106	91	102	94
Nationals (RFK Stadium)	96	100	94	96	86	137	86	86	96	92	81	94	70	96	90
Mets (Shea Stadium)	94	100	90	93	100	84	88	102	101	89	103	94	87	94	89
Marlins (Dolphins Stadium)	96	98	90	94	98	143	89	112	108	98	65	104	89	93	90
Padres (PETCO Park)	91	99	86	91	77	110	99	102	109	84	70	93	151	91	93

2006 AL Home Runs

Home Park	Index
White Sox	128
Blue Jays	124
Orioles	118
Devil Rays	117
Yankees	110
Rangers	104
Royals	97
Mariners	93
Indians	89
Athletics	86
Twins	84
Angels	80
Tigers	79
Red Sox	73

2006 AL LHB Home Runs

Home Park	Index
White Sox	158
Rangers	141
Yankees	124
Devil Rays	114
Blue Jays	110
Indians	107
Orioles	95
Twins	92
Athletics	89
Red Sox	86
Mariners	80
Angels	73
Tigers	72
Royals	69

2006 AL RHB Home Runs

Home Park	Index
Blue Jays	131
Orioles	129
Devil Rays	119
White Sox	118
Royals	113
Yankees	106
Mariners	99
Rangers	92
Athletics	85
Tigers	84
Angels	82
Twins	82
Indians	80
Red Sox	69

2006 NL Home Runs

Home Park	Index
Diamondbacks	133
Reds	129
Phillies	122
Dodgers	122
Cubs	120
Astros	118
Rockies	114
Brewers	101
Padres	99
Braves	93
Marlins	89
Mets	88
Cardinals	88
Nationals	86
Pirates	78
Giants	69

2006 NL LHB Home Runs

Home Park	Index
Diamondbacks	154
Padres	151
Phillies	142
Reds	126
Astros	124
Cubs	117
Rockies	114
Cardinals	108
Dodgers	99
Giants	92
Braves	91
Marlins	89
Mets	87
Brewers	74
Nationals	70
Pirates	65

2006 NL RHB Home Runs

Home Park	Index
Dodgers	131
Diamondbacks	129
Reds	128
Cubs	122
Brewers	116
Phillies	116
Astros	115
Rockies	113
Braves	94
Padres	93
Marlins	90
Nationals	90
Mets	89
Pirates	87
Cardinals	84
Giants	63

2006 AL Avg	
Home Park	Index
Royals	107
Red Sox	104
Angels	102
Orioles	102
Blue Jays	100
Rangers	100
Tigers	100
White Sox	99
Athletics	98
Twins	98
Devil Rays	98
Indians	97
Yankees	96
Mariners	93

2006 AL LHB Avg	
Home Park	Index
Orioles	110
Royals	108
Rangers	104
Twins	102
Athletics	102
Red Sox	102
Yankees	101
Blue Jays	100
Indians	100
Angels	97
Tigers	97
White Sox	92
Mariners	89
Devil Rays	88

2006 AL RHB Avg	
Home Park	Index
Royals	107
Red Sox	105
Angels	104
White Sox	102
Devil Rays	102
Tigers	101
Blue Jays	101
Orioles	99
Rangers	99
Athletics	97
Twins	97
Mariners	96
Indians	95
Yankees	95

2006 NL Avg	
Home Park	Index
Rockies	111
Diamondbacks	109
Pirates	105
Dodgers	104
Reds	103
Braves	103
Phillies	103
Cubs	100
Astros	99
Giants	99
Marlins	96
Cardinals	96
Nationals	96
Brewers	95
Mets	94
Padres	91

2006 NL LHB Avg	
Home Park	Index
Rockies	125
Dodgers	111
Diamondbacks	109
Braves	106
Phillies	105
Marlins	104
Astros	104
Pirates	101
Reds	99
Cubs	99
Brewers	96
Giants	96
Nationals	94
Mets	94
Padres	93
Cardinals	83

2006 NL RHB Avg	
Home Park	Index
Pirates	109
Diamondbacks	109
Rockies	108
Reds	105
Dodgers	103
Braves	102
Phillies	102
Cubs	101
Cardinals	100
Giants	99
Astros	98
Nationals	96
Brewers	95
Mets	94
Marlins	93
Padres	91

2006 AL Doubles	
Home Park	Index
Red Sox	137
Royals	118
Rangers	111
Athletics	108
Indians	101
Blue Jays	99
Yankees	98
Twins	95
Mariners	95
Devil Rays	94
Angels	94
Tigers	91
White Sox	89
Orioles	87

2006 AL Triples	
Home Park	Index
Blue Jays	195
Devil Rays	162
Twins	160
Royals	119
Tigers	115
Red Sox	100
Mariners	95
Athletics	94
Indians	81
Angels	79
Rangers	76
White Sox	63
Orioles	60
Yankees	50

2006 AL Errors	
Home Park	Index
Royals	126
Devil Rays	119
Indians	106
Tigers	106
Rangers	104
Yankees	104
Angels	103
White Sox	99
Red Sox	99
Orioles	97
Twins	95
Blue Jays	85
Athletics	79
Mariners	73

2006 NL Doubles	
Home Park	Index
Pirates	119
Giants	109
Diamondbacks	108
Cubs	107
Phillies	105
Dodgers	104
Astros	101
Mets	100
Braves	100
Brewers	99
Marlins	98
Rockies	98
Reds	94
Cardinals	88
Nationals	86
Padres	77

2006 NL Triples	
Home Park	Index
Diamondbacks	162
Marlins	143
Brewers	137
Nationals	137
Cubs	135
Astros	130
Rockies	119
Padres	110
Giants	106
Pirates	94
Mets	84
Cardinals	75
Braves	72
Phillies	67
Dodgers	53
Reds	40

2006 NL Errors	
Home Park	Index
Brewers	127
Dodgers	117
Giants	115
Cardinals	111
Braves	111
Cubs	108
Phillies	108
Diamondbacks	108
Rockies	106
Marlins	98
Reds	94
Nationals	92
Mets	89
Padres	84
Astros	81
Pirates	77

2004-2006 American League Ballpark Index Rankings - Runs

Home Park	TOTALS											LHB		RHB	
	Avg	AB	R	H	2B	3B	HR	BB	SO	E	E-Inf	Avg	HR	Avg	HR
Rangers (The Ballpark in Arlington)	103	102	112	105	106	135	112	99	94	102	111	102	105	104	115
White Sox (U.S. Cellular Field)	102	101	108	103	93	77	135	106	100	89	85	98	142	103	132
Blue Jays (Rogers Centre)	103	102	108	104	104	132	120	97	101	109	96	99	116	104	121
Red Sox (Fenway Park)	103	100	106	103	133	80	86	99	100	110	138	102	86	104	86
Royals (Ewing M. Kauffman Stadium)	102	101	101	103	109	112	80	103	93	93	95	105	76	101	82
Twins (Hubert H. Humphrey Metrodome)	99	100	101	99	96	100	91	88	108	94	95	102	97	98	88
Athletics (McAfee Coliseum)	99	99	100	99	106	82	95	98	92	94	84	107	105	96	90
Orioles (Oriole Park at Camden Yards)	100	100	98	100	91	66	106	101	91	100	99	103	96	98	110
Devil Rays (Tropicana Field)	97	100	98	97	91	125	101	103	103	107	122	95	105	97	100
Yankees (Yankee Stadium)	100	99	95	99	91	69	107	93	101	106	116	101	118	99	104
Tigers (Comerica Park)	100	101	95	102	86	155	86	100	93	96	114	100	82	101	88
Angels (Angel Stadium of Anaheim)	100	100	93	100	93	76	92	96	100	97	86	96	87	101	93
Indians (Jacobs Field)	97	97	93	94	108	65	85	110	103	116	105	98	89	96	82
Mariners (Safeco Field)	94	99	89	92	98	68	93	107	113	90	70	92	93	95	93

2004-2006 National League Ballpark Index Rankings - Runs

Home Park	TOTALS											LHB		RHB	
	Avg	AB	R	H	2B	3B	HR	BB	SO	E	E-Inf	Avg	HR	Avg	HR
Rockies (Coors Field)	115	105	128	121	109	134	112	105	87	118	105	124	116	112	110
Diamondbacks (Chase Field)	105	101	110	107	108	149	120	103	95	95	113	101	132	107	116
Phillies (Citizens Bank Park)	103	100	108	103	99	103	120	96	97	100	106	104	125	103	118
Cubs (Wrigley Field)	101	101	107	102	104	112	118	94	101	107	102	104	123	100	117
Reds (Great American Ballpark)	100	100	103	99	99	51	119	97	100	88	109	97	117	101	120
Brewers (Miller Park)	95	99	101	94	101	120	104	110	108	112	107	93	96	96	107
Giants (Pacific Bell Park)	102	99	101	100	104	127	84	98	97	110	100	99	84	103	83
Braves (Turner Field)	102	100	100	102	101	90	97	98	104	103	105	99	89	103	100
Astros (Minute Maid Park)	100	99	100	99	91	122	115	96	101	105	104	104	138	99	110
Pirates (PNC Park)	103	103	98	105	112	98	83	94	95	94	98	97	78	106	86
Dodgers (Dodger Stadium)	98	98	95	96	94	52	110	103	104	103	100	98	100	98	114
Cardinals (Busch Stadium) *	96	101	96	97	88	75	88	103	98	111	104	83	108	100	84
Mets (Shea Stadium)	99	101	95	99	97	67	85	100	99	114	131	97	81	99	87
Nationals (RFK Stadium)	92	98	91	91	90	123	84	93	102	99	105	96	73	92	86
Marlins (Dolphins Stadium)	96	99	90	94	93	120	91	111	112	88	74	102	85	93	93
Padres (PETCO Park)	92	98	83	90	85	132	82	102	109	81	67	92	79	92	83

2004-2006 AL Home Runs

Home Park	Index
White Sox	135
Blue Jays	120
Rangers	112
Yankees	107
Orioles	106
Devil Rays	101
Athletics	95
Mariners	93
Angels	92
Twins	91
Tigers	86
Red Sox	86
Indians	85
Royals	80

2004-2006 AL LHB Home Runs

Home Park	Index
White Sox	142
Yankees	118
Blue Jays	116
Athletics	105
Devil Rays	105
Rangers	105
Twins	97
Orioles	96
Mariners	93
Indians	89
Angels	87
Red Sox	86
Tigers	82
Royals	76

2004-2006 AL RHB Home Runs

Home Park	Index
White Sox	132
Blue Jays	121
Rangers	115
Orioles	110
Yankees	104
Devil Rays	100
Angels	93
Mariners	93
Athletics	90
Twins	88
Tigers	88
Red Sox	86
Indians	82
Royals	82

2004-2006 NL Home Runs

Home Park	Index
Phillies	120
Diamondbacks	120
Reds	119
Cubs	118
Astros	115
Rockies	112
Dodgers	110
Brewers	104
Braves	97
Marlins	91
Cardinals *	88
Mets	85
Nationals	84
Giants	84
Pirates	83
Padres	82

2004-2006 NL LHB Home Runs

Home Park	Index
Astros	138
Diamondbacks	132
Phillies	125
Cubs	123
Reds	117
Rockies	116
Cardinals *	108
Dodgers	100
Brewers	96
Braves	89
Marlins	85
Giants	84
Mets	81
Padres	79
Pirates	78
Nationals	73

2004-2006 NL RHB Home Runs

Home Park	Index
Reds	120
Phillies	118
Cubs	117
Diamondbacks	116
Dodgers	114
Rockies	110
Astros	110
Brewers	107
Braves	100
Marlins	93
Mets	87
Pirates	86
Nationals	86
Cardinals *	84
Giants	83
Padres	83

* Data for 2006 only

2004-2006 AL Avg	
Home Park	Index
Rangers	103
Red Sox	103
Blue Jays	103
Royals	102
White Sox	102
Tigers	100
Yankees	100
Angels	100
Orioles	100
Athletics	99
Twins	99
Devil Rays	97
Indians	97
Mariners	94

2004-2006 AL LHB Avg	
Home Park	Index
Athletics	107
Royals	105
Orioles	103
Rangers	102
Red Sox	102
Twins	102
Yankees	101
Tigers	100
Blue Jays	99
White Sox	98
Indians	98
Angels	96
Devil Rays	95
Mariners	92

2004-2006 AL RHB Avg	
Home Park	Index
Blue Jays	104
Rangers	104
Red Sox	104
White Sox	103
Angels	101
Royals	101
Tigers	101
Yankees	99
Twins	98
Orioles	98
Devil Rays	97
Athletics	96
Indians	96
Mariners	95

2004-2006 NL Avg	
Home Park	Index
Rockies	115
Diamondbacks	105
Phillies	103
Pirates	103
Braves	102
Giants	102
Cubs	101
Astros	100
Reds	100
Mets	99
Dodgers	98
Cardinals *	96
Marlins	96
Brewers	95
Nationals	92
Padres	92

2004-2006 NL LHB Avg	
Home Park	Index
Rockies	124
Phillies	104
Cubs	104
Astros	104
Marlins	102
Diamondbacks	101
Braves	99
Giants	99
Dodgers	98
Mets	97
Reds	97
Pirates	97
Nationals	96
Brewers	93
Padres	92
Cardinals *	83

2004-2006 NL RHB Avg	
Home Park	Index
Rockies	112
Diamondbacks	107
Pirates	106
Giants	103
Phillies	103
Braves	103
Reds	101
Cardinals *	100
Cubs	100
Mets	99
Astros	99
Dodgers	98
Brewers	96
Marlins	93
Padres	92
Nationals	92

2004-2006 AL Doubles	
Home Park	Index
Red Sox	133
Royals	109
Indians	108
Rangers	106
Athletics	106
Blue Jays	104
Mariners	98
Twins	96
White Sox	93
Angels	93
Yankees	91
Devil Rays	91
Orioles	91
Tigers	86

2004-2006 AL Triples	
Home Park	Index
Tigers	155
Rangers	135
Blue Jays	132
Devil Rays	125
Royals	112
Twins	100
Athletics	82
Red Sox	80
White Sox	77
Angels	76
Yankees	69
Mariners	68
Orioles	66
Indians	65

2004-2006 AL Errors	
Home Park	Index
Indians	116
Red Sox	110
Blue Jays	109
Devil Rays	107
Yankees	106
Rangers	102
Orioles	100
Angels	97
Tigers	96
Twins	94
Athletics	94
Royals	93
Mariners	90
White Sox	89

2004-2006 NL Doubles	
Home Park	Index
Pirates	112
Rockies	109
Diamondbacks	108
Giants	104
Cubs	104
Braves	101
Brewers	101
Phillies	99
Reds	99
Mets	97
Dodgers	94
Marlins	93
Astros	91
Nationals	90
Cardinals *	88
Padres	85

2004-2006 NL Triples	
Home Park	Index
Diamondbacks	149
Rockies	134
Padres	132
Giants	127
Nationals	123
Astros	122
Marlins	120
Brewers	120
Cubs	112
Phillies	103
Pirates	98
Braves	90
Cardinals *	75
Mets	67
Dodgers	52
Reds	51

2004-2006 NL Errors	
Home Park	Index
Rockies	118
Mets	114
Brewers	112
Cardinals *	111
Giants	110
Cubs	107
Astros	105
Dodgers	103
Braves	103
Phillies	100
Nationals	99
Diamondbacks	95
Pirates	94
Reds	88
Marlins	88
Padres	81

* Data for 2006 only

2006 Lefty/Righty Statistics

Lefty/righty splits for all batters and pitchers who appeared during the 2006 season are in this section. The batting side of each hitter is shown below his name; for pitchers the hand that he throws with is indicated. Go ahead and check out which players most benefited from having the platoon advantage, which ones had a "reverse platoon split," and which ones did equally well against left- and right-handed opponents.

Batters vs. Left-Handed and Right-Handed Pitchers

Batter	vs	Avg	AB	H	2B	3B	HR	RBI	BB	SO	OBP	Slg
Abad,Andy	L	-	0	0	0	0	0	0	0	0	-	-
Bats Left	R	.000	3	0	0	0	0	0	2	0	.400	.000
Abercrombie,Reggie	L	.220	82	18	5	0	1	5	6	26	.281	.317
Bats Right	R	.208	173	36	7	2	4	19	12	52	.266	.341
Abreu,Bobby	L	.293	167	49	11	2	3	26	31	47	.403	.437
Bats Left	R	.299	381	114	30	0	12	81	93	91	.433	.472
Adams,Russ	L	.135	37	5	0	0	1	4	3	7	.200	.216
Bats Left	R	.234	214	50	14	1	2	24	19	34	.295	.336
Aguila,Chris	L	.195	41	8	2	0	0	1	4	11	.267	.244
Bats Right	R	.259	54	14	6	1	0	6	5	15	.322	.407
Alexander,Manny	L	.182	22	4	1	1	0	4	2	2	.240	.318
Bats Right	R	.167	12	2	0	0	0	0	0	3	.167	.167
Alfonzo,Edgardo	L	.118	34	4	2	0	0	1	2	1	.167	.176
Bats Right	R	.132	53	7	0	0	0	4	5	3	.220	.132
Alfonzo,Eliezer	L	.246	61	15	2	0	1	4	0	11	.246	.328
Bats Right	R	.271	225	61	15	2	11	35	9	63	.316	.502
Alomar Jr.,Sandy	L	.327	52	17	5	0	1	10	1	5	.327	.481
Bats Right	R	.232	56	13	3	0	0	7	2	9	.259	.286
Alou,Moises	L	.349	83	29	10	0	6	19	8	8	.407	.687
Bats Right	R	.286	262	75	15	1	16	55	20	23	.334	.534
Amezaga,Alfredo	L	.091	55	5	1	0	0	3	8	11	.227	.109
Bats Both	R	.294	279	82	8	3	3	16	25	35	.354	.376
Anderson,Brian	L	.226	159	36	10	1	2	9	16	35	.298	.340
Bats Right	R	.223	206	46	13	0	6	24	14	55	.284	.374
Anderson,Drew	L	.000	1	0	0	0	0	0	0	1	.000	.000
Bats Left	R	.125	8	1	0	0	0	0	1	3	.222	.125
Anderson,Garret	L	.248	165	41	11	1	3	26	8	35	.280	.382
Bats Left	R	.294	378	111	17	1	14	59	30	60	.341	.455
Anderson,Marlon	L	.254	63	16	1	0	2	5	3	16	.284	.365
Bats Left	R	.310	216	67	15	4	10	33	22	33	.373	.556
Andino,Robert	L	.111	9	1	0	0	0	0	1	3	.200	.111
Bats Right	R	.200	15	3	1	0	0	2	0	3	.176	.267
Ardoin,Danny	L	.250	12	3	0	1	0	1	1	5	.357	.417
Bats Right	R	.173	110	19	5	0	0	2	8	28	.242	.218
Arias,Joaquin	L	.333	6	2	1	0	0	0	1	0	.429	.500
Bats Right	R	.800	5	4	0	0	0	1	0	0	.800	.800
Atkins,Garrett	L	.341	91	31	10	0	6	24	24	12	.475	.648
Bats Right	R	.327	511	167	38	1	23	96	55	64	.395	.540
Aurilia,Rich	L	.347	147	51	14	1	11	28	16	18	.406	.680
Bats Right	R	.276	293	81	11	0	12	42	18	33	.318	.437
Ausmus,Brad	L	.266	94	25	3	0	1	10	9	17	.333	.330
Bats Right	R	.220	345	76	13	1	1	29	36	54	.302	.272
Aybar,Erick	L	.250	8	2	0	0	0	1	0	2	.250	.250
Bats Both	R	.250	32	8	1	1	0	1	0	6	.250	.344
Aybar,Willy	L	.328	64	21	3	0	1	8	7	8	.403	.422
Bats Both	R	.263	179	47	15	0	3	22	21	28	.350	.397
Baker,Jeff	L	.438	16	7	2	0	3	9	1	1	.471	1.125
Bats Right	R	.341	41	14	5	2	2	12	0	13	.341	.707
Bako,Paul	L	.200	10	2	0	0	0	0	0	4	.200	.200
Bats Left	R	.210	143	30	3	0	0	10	11	42	.265	.231
Baldelli,Rocco	L	.297	74	22	7	2	1	11	5	15	.342	.486
Bats Right	R	.303	290	88	17	4	15	46	9	55	.338	.545
Barajas,Rod	L	.156	64	10	4	0	3	9	5	9	.217	.359
Bats Right	R	.279	280	78	16	0	8	32	12	42	.316	.421
Bard,Josh	L	.333	66	22	4	0	3	10	5	13	.384	.530
Bats Both	R	.333	183	61	16	0	6	30	25	29	.411	.519
Barfield,Josh	L	.331	121	40	10	0	7	20	10	15	.378	.587
Bats Right	R	.266	418	111	22	3	6	38	20	66	.299	.376
Barker,Kevin	L	.000	1	0	0	0	0	0	1	1	.500	.000
Bats Left	R	.250	16	4	1	0	1	1	0	9	.250	.500
Barmes,Clint	L	.267	86	23	7	0	2	14	6	9	.327	.419
Bats Right	R	.209	392	82	19	4	5	42	16	63	.249	.316
Barnwell,Chris	L	.100	10	1	0	0	0	0	0	1	.100	.100
Bats Right	R	.050	20	1	0	0	0	1	1	5	.095	.050
Barrett,Michael	L	.313	83	26	7	2	6	16	11	7	.396	.663
Bats Right	R	.305	292	89	18	1	10	37	22	34	.359	.476
Bartlett,Jason	L	.314	102	32	5	0	0	9	6	12	.368	.363
Bats Right	R	.307	231	71	13	2	2	23	16	34	.366	.407
Batista,Tony	L	.212	52	11	5	0	1	5	3	8	.268	.365
Bats Right	R	.246	126	31	7	0	4	16	12	19	.317	.397
Bautista,Jose	L	.283	113	32	4	2	7	15	16	29	.404	.540
Bats Right	R	.216	287	62	16	1	9	36	30	81	.306	.373
Bay,Jason	L	.304	138	42	8	2	9	30	31	39	.427	.587
Bats Right	R	.280	432	121	21	1	26	79	71	117	.386	.514
Bell,David	L	.281	121	34	7	2	1	18	9	17	.331	.397
Bats Right	R	.266	383	102	20	2	9	45	41	51	.340	.399

Batter	vs	Avg	AB	H	2B	3B	HR	RBI	BB	SO	OBP	Slg
Bellhorn,Mark	L	.224	76	17	4	0	3	10	7	25	.289	.395
Bats Both	R	.175	177	31	7	2	5	17	25	65	.283	.322
Belliard,Ronnie	L	.220	168	37	11	0	2	15	12	24	.271	.321
Bats Right	R	.295	376	111	19	1	11	52	24	57	.345	.439
Beltran,Carlos	L	.247	166	41	15	0	8	39	27	25	.352	.482
Bats Both	R	.288	344	99	23	1	33	77	68	74	.405	.648
Beltre,Adrian	L	.280	132	37	12	0	4	19	13	23	.351	.462
Bats Right	R	.264	488	129	27	4	21	70	34	95	.321	.465
Bennett,Gary	L	.400	35	14	1	0	2	6	4	4	.462	.600
Bats Right	R	.172	122	21	4	0	2	16	7	26	.217	.254
Berkman,Lance	L	.266	154	41	8	0	5	27	27	24	.374	.416
Bats Both	R	.335	382	128	21	0	40	109	71	82	.438	.704
Berroa,Angel	L	.217	129	28	5	0	4	17	1	25	.223	.349
Bats Right	R	.241	345	83	13	1	5	37	13	63	.272	.328
Betancourt,Yuniesky	L	.240	129	31	7	1	2	8	6	11	.279	.357
Bats Right	R	.303	429	130	21	5	6	39	11	43	.320	.417
Betemit,Wilson	L	.189	74	14	1	0	3	13	6	28	.250	.324
Bats Both	R	.281	299	84	22	0	15	40	30	74	.344	.505
Bigbie,Larry	L	.333	3	1	0	0	0	0	0	2	.333	.333
Bats Left	R	.227	22	5	1	0	0	1	3	7	.320	.273
Biggio,Craig	L	.297	111	33	8	0	6	12	12	16	.373	.532
Bats Right	R	.233	437	102	25	0	15	50	28	68	.288	.394
Blake,Casey	L	.272	114	31	3	0	10	24	17	23	.366	.561
Bats Right	R	.286	287	82	17	1	9	44	28	70	.352	.446
Blalock,Hank	L	.216	162	35	7	0	3	23	15	27	.281	.315
Bats Left	R	.284	429	122	19	3	13	66	36	71	.342	.434
Blanco,Andres	L	.500	18	9	2	1	0	5	0	4	.500	.722
Bats Both	R	.174	69	12	2	0	0	4	5	10	.240	.203
Blanco,Henry	L	.325	80	26	6	0	3	11	4	8	.357	.513
Bats Right	R	.236	161	38	9	2	3	26	10	30	.277	.373
Bloomquist,Willie	L	.253	99	25	2	1	1	5	6	8	.308	.323
Bats Right	R	.243	152	37	4	1	0	10	18	32	.328	.283
Blum,Geoff	L	.167	36	6	2	0	0	0	2	10	.211	.222
Bats Both	R	.267	240	64	15	1	4	34	15	41	.305	.388
Bocachica,Hiram	L	.500	2	1	0	0	0	0	2	1	.750	.500
Bats Right	R	.182	11	2	0	0	0	0	1	3	.250	.182
Bohn,T.J.	L	.100	10	1	0	0	0	0	1	5	.182	.100
Bats Right	R	.250	4	1	0	0	1	2	1	3	.400	1.000
Bonds,Barry	L	.255	106	27	4	0	8	22	33	18	.451	.519
Bats Left	R	.276	261	72	19	0	18	55	82	33	.456	.556
Boone,Aaron	L	.280	107	30	6	0	3	13	13	19	.369	.421
Bats Right	R	.239	247	59	13	1	4	33	14	43	.289	.348
Borchard,Joe	L	.148	61	9	2	0	1	3	4	14	.212	.230
Bats Both	R	.258	178	46	5	1	9	25	24	55	.353	.449
Botts,Jason	L	.100	10	1	0	0	0	1	1	4	.167	.100
Bats Both	R	.250	40	10	4	0	1	5	7	14	.354	.425
Bourn,Michael	L	.000	1	0	0	0	0	0	0	0	.000	.000
Bats Left	R	.143	7	1	0	0	0	0	1	3	.250	.143
Bowen,Rob	L	.167	18	3	0	0	0	1	5	7	.333	.167
Bats Both	R	.263	76	20	5	0	3	12	8	19	.341	.447
Bradley,Milton	L	.293	92	27	2	0	6	19	12	15	.375	.511
Bats Both	R	.270	259	70	12	2	8	33	39	50	.369	.425
Branyan,Russell	L	.220	41	9	1	0	4	6	3	21	.304	.537
Bats Left	R	.230	200	46	10	0	14	30	31	68	.332	.490
Broussard,Ben	L	.177	62	11	2	0	3	8	6	21	.261	.355
Bats Left	R	.308	370	114	19	0	18	55	20	82	.343	.505
Brown,Adrian	L	.133	15	2	0	0	0	1	0	6	.125	.133
Bats Both	R	.238	21	5	1	0	0	1	2	3	.304	.286
Brown,Emil	L	.236	157	37	10	1	8	27	18	32	.316	.465
Bats Right	R	.308	370	114	31	1	7	54	41	63	.375	.454
Brown,Jeremy	L	.500	2	1	1	0	0	0	0	0	.500	1.000
Bats Right	R	.250	8	2	1	0	0	0	1	1	.333	.375
Bruntlett,Eric	L	.350	40	14	3	0	0	5	5	7	.413	.425
Bats Right	R	.241	79	19	5	0	0	5	8	14	.318	.304
Buck,John	L	.246	114	28	4	1	6	14	13	26	.331	.456
Bats Right	R	.245	257	63	17	0	5	36	13	58	.295	.370
Burke,Chris	L	.327	101	33	6	0	2	8	7	24	.393	.446
Bats Right	R	.257	265	68	17	1	7	32	20	53	.330	.408
Burnitz,Jeromy	L	.224	58	13	2	0	1	6	3	19	.274	.310
Bats Left	R	.231	255	59	10	0	15	43	19	55	.293	.447
Burrell,Pat	L	.290	138	40	6	0	11	25	37	38	.440	.572
Bats Right	R	.244	324	79	18	1	18	70	61	93	.365	.472
Burroughs,Sean	L	.000	2	0	0	0	0	0	1	1	.333	.000
Bats Left	R	.211	19	4	1	0	0	1	3	6	.318	.263
Bynum,Freddie	L	.130	23	3	1	0	0	0	1	12	.200	.174
Bats Left	R	.283	113	32	4	5	4	12	8	32	.331	.513

Batters vs. Left-Handed and Right-Handed Pitchers

Batter	vs	Avg	AB	H	2B	3B	HR	RBI	BB	SO	OBP	Slg
Byrd,Marlon	L	.188	69	13	1	1	2	4	11	21	.309	.319
Bats Right	R	.242	128	31	7	0	3	14	11	26	.322	.367
Byrnes,Eric	L	.323	161	52	16	1	8	22	14	24	.377	.584
Bats Right	R	.244	401	98	21	2	18	57	20	64	.287	.441
Cabrera,Melky	L	.286	126	36	7	0	1	8	15	13	.359	.365
Bats Both	R	.278	334	93	19	2	6	42	41	46	.361	.401
Cabrera,Miguel	L	.321	134	43	14	0	6	28	26	30	.436	.560
Bats Right	R	.344	442	152	36	2	20	86	60	78	.429	.570
Cabrera,Orlando	L	.243	169	41	11	0	1	14	17	13	.316	.325
Bats Right	R	.297	438	130	34	1	8	58	34	45	.342	.434
Cairo,Miguel	L	.279	68	19	5	1	0	10	5	8	.333	.382
Bats Right	R	.221	154	34	7	2	0	20	8	23	.256	.292
Callaspo,Alberto	L	.278	18	5	0	0	0	1	1	2	.316	.278
Bats Both	R	.208	24	5	1	1	0	3	4	4	.286	.333
Cameron,Mike	L	.252	123	31	6	3	4	19	23	30	.362	.447
Bats Right	R	.273	429	117	28	6	18	64	48	112	.353	.492
Cannizaro,Andy	L	1.000	2	2	0	0	1	1	0	0	1.000	2.500
Bats Right	R	.000	6	0	0	0	0	0	1	1	.143	.000
Cano,Robinson	L	.287	129	37	9	1	0	11	6	15	.328	.372
Bats Left	R	.363	353	128	32	0	15	67	12	39	.378	.581
Cantu,Jorge	L	.233	116	27	5	1	6	21	4	13	.256	.448
Bats Right	R	.256	297	76	13	1	8	41	22	78	.309	.387
Carroll,Jamey	L	.359	103	37	4	1	1	7	16	8	.438	.447
Bats Right	R	.283	360	102	19	4	4	29	40	58	.359	.392
Casey,Sean	L	.287	108	31	6	0	4	23	4	18	.328	.454
Bats Left	R	.266	289	77	16	0	4	36	29	25	.340	.363
Casilla,Alexi	L	.000	1	0	0	0	0	0	0	0	.000	.000
Bats Both	R	.333	3	1	0	0	0	0	2	1	.600	.333
Castilla,Vinny	L	.203	74	15	2	0	1	6	3	12	.238	.270
Bats Right	R	.239	201	48	8	0	4	21	6	37	.265	.338
Castillo,Jose	L	.259	143	37	7	0	6	20	13	27	.321	.434
Bats Right	R	.251	375	94	18	0	8	45	19	71	.291	.363
Castillo,Luis	L	.256	195	50	10	2	2	12	19	12	.326	.359
Bats Both	R	.316	389	123	12	4	1	37	37	46	.374	.375
Castro,Bernie	L	.182	44	8	0	2	0	1	2	11	.217	.273
Bats Both	R	.258	66	17	1	1	0	9	7	7	.329	.303
Castro,Juan	L	.268	71	19	2	0	2	11	6	10	.321	.380
Bats Right	R	.244	180	44	8	3	1	17	5	26	.265	.339
Castro,Ramon	L	.269	26	7	1	0	1	4	4	7	.367	.423
Bats Right	R	.230	100	23	6	0	3	8	11	33	.310	.380
Catalanotto,Frank	L	.237	38	9	1	0	1	6	7	6	.348	.342
Bats Left	R	.306	399	122	35	2	6	50	45	31	.379	.449
Cedeno,Ronny	L	.230	152	35	3	1	2	13	4	28	.250	.303
Bats Right	R	.251	382	96	15	6	4	28	13	81	.279	.353
Cepicky,Matt	L	.500	2	1	0	0	0	0	0	1	.500	.500
Bats Left	R	.063	16	1	0	0	0	0	1	3	.118	.063
Chavez,Endy	L	.333	78	26	2	0	0	5	3	7	.358	.359
Bats Left	R	.298	275	82	20	5	4	37	21	37	.346	.451
Chavez,Eric	L	.197	127	25	3	0	5	16	20	29	.311	.339
Bats Left	R	.257	358	92	21	2	17	56	64	71	.364	.469
Chavez,Raul	L	.000	3	0	0	0	0	0	0	0	.000	.000
Bats Right	R	.200	25	5	0	0	0	0	1	4	.231	.200
Choo,Shin-Soo	L	.278	18	5	0	0	0	1	1	7	.350	.278
Bats Left	R	.281	139	39	12	3	3	21	17	43	.361	.475
Church,Ryan	L	.265	49	13	5	0	1	9	5	17	.321	.429
Bats Left	R	.279	147	41	12	1	9	26	21	43	.380	.558
Cintron,Alex	L	.274	62	17	1	0	0	5	3	5	.308	.290
Bats Both	R	.288	226	65	9	3	5	36	7	30	.311	.420
Cirillo,Jeff	L	.413	75	31	6	0	0	11	6	12	.451	.493
Bats Right	R	.282	188	53	10	0	3	15	15	21	.337	.383
Clark,Brady	L	.273	128	35	5	1	2	11	12	17	.338	.375
Bats Right	R	.258	287	74	9	1	2	18	31	43	.352	.317
Clark,Doug	L	-	0	0	0	0	0	0	0	0	-	-
Bats Left	R	.167	6	1	0	0	0	0	0	3	.167	.167
Clark,Howie	L	.500	2	1	0	0	0	0	0	1	.500	.500
Bats Left	R	.000	5	0	0	0	0	0	2	1	.286	.000
Clark,Tony	L	.125	24	3	0	0	2	5	5	10	.276	.125
Bats Both	R	.213	108	23	4	0	6	14	8	30	.280	.417
Clayton,Royce	L	.303	132	40	5	1	1	16	12	23	.365	.379
Bats Right	R	.239	322	77	25	0	1	24	18	62	.282	.326
Clevlen,Brent	L	.333	24	8	1	2	1	4	1	8	.360	.667
Bats Right	R	.200	15	3	0	0	2	2	1	7	.250	.600
Closser,JD	L	.083	12	1	0	0	0	1	2	6	.267	.083
Bats Both	R	.212	85	18	3	1	2	10	10	17	.292	.341
Coats,Buck	L	.000	3	0	0	0	0	0	0	2	.000	.000
Bats Left	R	.200	15	3	1	0	1	1	0	4	.200	.467

Batter	vs	Avg	AB	H	2B	3B	HR	RBI	BB	SO	OBP	Slg
Colina,Alvin	L	.250	4	1	0	0	0	1	0	1	.250	.250
Bats Right	R	.000	1	0	0	0	0	0	0	0	.000	.000
Conine,Jeff	L	.260	150	39	7	1	4	20	18	23	.337	.400
Bats Right	R	.271	339	92	19	3	6	46	22	42	.320	.398
Cora,Alex	L	.333	39	13	3	0	0	4	1	9	.366	.410
Bats Left	R	.219	196	43	4	2	1	14	18	20	.301	.276
Costa,Shane	L	.244	41	10	4	0	1	5	1	6	.256	.415
Bats Left	R	.281	196	55	16	1	2	18	5	23	.314	.403
Coste,Chris	L	.288	59	17	4	0	3	15	4	16	.333	.508
Bats Right	R	.345	139	48	10	0	4	17	6	15	.393	.504
Cota,Humberto	L	.125	24	3	0	0	0	2	4	2	.241	.125
Bats Right	R	.211	76	16	1	0	0	3	4	24	.250	.224
Counsell,Craig	L	.256	86	22	1	0	0	8	11	18	.347	.267
Bats Left	R	.255	286	73	13	4	4	22	20	29	.321	.371
Crawford,Carl	L	.288	163	47	6	3	4	26	10	31	.341	.436
Bats Left	R	.311	437	136	14	13	14	51	27	54	.351	.499
Crede,Joe	L	.273	183	50	13	0	10	34	17	16	.340	.508
Bats Right	R	.288	361	104	18	0	20	60	11	42	.313	.504
Crisp,Coco	L	.277	112	31	10	1	1	9	7	28	.325	.411
Bats Both	R	.259	301	78	12	1	7	27	24	39	.314	.375
Crosby,Bobby	L	.185	81	15	6	0	0	5	10	21	.272	.259
Bats Right	R	.242	277	67	6	0	9	35	26	55	.306	.361
Crosby,Bubba	L	.300	10	3	0	0	0	1	1	2	.364	.300
Bats Left	R	.195	77	15	3	1	1	5	3	19	.244	.299
Cruz,Jose	L	.313	67	21	8	0	2	6	13	12	.420	.522
Bats Both	R	.199	156	31	8	1	3	11	30	42	.324	.321
Cruz,Nelson	L	.217	46	10	1	0	3	11	2	7	.245	.435
Bats Right	R	.226	84	19	2	0	3	11	5	25	.270	.357
Cuddyer,Michael	L	.297	195	58	17	1	8	36	24	47	.376	.518
Bats Right	R	.276	362	100	24	4	16	73	38	83	.355	.497
Cust,Jack	L	-	0	0	0	0	0	0	0	0	-	-
Bats Left	R	.333	3	1	0	0	0	0	0	1	.333	.333
Damon,Johnny	L	.297	165	49	6	2	6	27	25	22	.395	.467
Bats Left	R	.280	428	120	29	3	18	53	42	63	.344	.488
DaVanon,Jeff	L	.205	39	8	1	0	0	3	7	12	.319	.231
Bats Both	R	.308	182	56	11	4	5	32	24	30	.383	.495
Davis,Rajai	L	.000	2	0	0	0	0	0	0	0	.000	.000
Bats Both	R	.167	12	2	1	0	0	0	2	3	.286	.250
de la Rosa,Tomas	L	.250	4	1	0	0	0	1	0	0	.400	.250
Bats Right	R	.333	12	4	0	0	0	1	0	3	.333	.333
DeCaster,Yurendell	L	-	0	0	0	0	0	0	0	0	-	-
Bats Right	R	.000	2	0	0	0	0	0	0	0	.000	.000
DeJesus,David	L	.307	140	43	16	3	3	14	16	16	.384	.529
Bats Left	R	.291	351	102	20	4	5	42	27	54	.355	.413
Delgado,Carlos	L	.226	159	36	9	2	7	33	16	44	.311	.440
Bats Left	R	.282	365	103	21	0	31	81	58	76	.382	.595
Dellucci,David	L	.200	20	4	1	0	2	4	3	5	.292	.550
Bats Left	R	.299	244	73	13	5	11	35	25	57	.375	.529
Denorfia,Chris	L	.317	41	13	3	0	0	5	4	8	.378	.390
Bats Right	R	.262	65	17	3	0	1	2	7	15	.342	.354
DeRosa,Mark	L	.342	146	50	15	0	7	27	13	27	.394	.589
Bats Right	R	.278	374	104	25	2	6	47	31	75	.342	.404
Diaz,Einar	L	.000	1	0	0	0	0	0	0	0	.000	.000
Bats Right	R	1.000	2	2	0	0	0	0	0	0	1.000	1.000
Diaz,Matt	L	.295	146	43	5	3	5	16	4	23	.327	.473
Bats Right	R	.358	151	54	10	1	2	16	7	26	.400	.477
Diaz,Victor	L	.143	7	1	0	0	0	0	0	3	.143	.143
Bats Right	R	.250	4	1	1	0	0	2	0	2	.250	.500
DiFelice,Mike	L	.143	7	1	1	0	0	0	1	4	.250	.286
Bats Right	R	.056	18	1	0	0	0	1	4	6	.227	.056
Dobbs,Greg	L	.000	1	0	0	0	0	0	0	1	.000	.000
Bats Left	R	.385	26	10	3	1	0	3	0	3	.407	.577
Dorta,Melvin	L	.333	6	2	1	0	0	0	1	1	.429	.500
Bats Right	R	.154	13	2	0	0	0	0	0	1	.154	.154
Doumit,Ryan	L	.208	24	5	1	0	0	0	3	6	.406	.250
Bats Both	R	.208	125	26	8	0	6	17	12	36	.303	.416
Drew,J.D.	L	.244	119	29	5	1	3	25	18	30	.338	.378
Bats Left	R	.296	375	111	29	5	17	75	71	76	.410	.536
Drew,Stephen	L	.350	40	14	3	2	1	3	3	17	.395	.600
Bats Left	R	.308	169	52	10	5	4	20	11	33	.348	.497
Duffy,Chris	L	.229	83	19	2	0	2	6	5	21	.286	.325
Bats Left	R	.264	231	61	12	3	0	12	14	50	.328	.342
Duncan,Chris	L	.170	47	8	1	0	2	3	3	14	.220	.319
Bats Left	R	.318	233	74	10	3	20	40	27	55	.390	.644
Dunn,Adam	L	.270	185	50	10	0	11	26	34	64	.393	.503
Bats Left	R	.215	376	81	14	0	29	66	78	130	.352	.484

Batters vs. Left-Handed and Right-Handed Pitchers

Batter	vs	Avg	AB	H	2B	3B	HR	RBI	BB	SO	OBP	Slg
Durham,Ray	L	.341	123	42	9	1	9	21	15	11	.413	.650
Bats Both	R	.277	375	104	21	6	17	72	36	50	.342	.501
Dye,Jermaine	L	.337	172	58	8	0	15	35	29	35	.429	.645
Bats Right	R	.305	367	112	19	3	29	85	30	83	.362	.610
Easley,Damion	L	.245	106	26	5	1	4	13	13	17	.339	.425
Bats Right	R	.217	83	18	1	0	5	15	8	13	.301	.410
Eckstein,David	L	.280	161	45	5	1	0	12	12	12	.352	.323
Bats Right	R	.298	339	101	13	0	2	11	19	29	.349	.354
Edmonds,Jim	L	.156	96	15	3	0	3	12	6	32	.198	.281
Bats Left	R	.295	254	75	15	0	16	58	47	69	.404	.543
Edwards,Mike	L	.000	2	0	0	0	0	0	1	0	.333	.000
Bats Right	R	.214	14	3	0	0	0	0	0	5	.214	.214
Ellis,Mark	L	.278	90	25	5	0	2	11	18	12	.402	.400
Bats Right	R	.242	351	85	20	1	9	41	22	64	.294	.382
Ellison,Jason	L	.269	26	7	0	1	1	3	2	2	.333	.462
Bats Right	R	.200	55	11	5	0	1	1	3	12	.241	.345
Encarnacion,Edwin	L	.248	113	28	9	0	5	24	18	23	.368	.460
Bats Right	R	.287	293	84	24	1	10	48	23	55	.355	.478
Encarnacion,Juan	L	.316	177	56	8	1	7	28	8	22	.346	.492
Bats Right	R	.261	380	99	17	4	12	51	22	64	.303	.421
Ensberg,Morgan	L	.245	94	23	2	0	9	19	38	23	.463	.553
Bats Right	R	.232	293	68	15	1	14	39	63	73	.370	.433
Erstad,Darin	L	.192	26	5	2	1	0	1	3	6	.300	.346
Bats Left	R	.232	69	16	6	0	0	4	3	12	.270	.319
Escobar,Alex	L	.400	30	12	1	1	3	10	3	8	.417	.800
Bats Right	R	.333	57	19	2	1	1	8	5	10	.381	.456
Estrada,Johnny	L	.296	98	29	2	0	3	17	4	9	.317	.408
Bats Both	R	.304	316	96	24	0	8	54	9	31	.331	.456
Ethier,Andre	L	.351	77	27	2	2	1	11	3	13	.378	.468
Bats Left	R	.298	319	95	18	5	10	44	31	64	.362	.480
Everett,Adam	L	.250	100	25	6	3	1	15	13	6	.333	.400
Bats Right	R	.237	414	98	22	3	5	44	21	65	.278	.341
Everett,Carl	L	.186	70	13	1	0	2	5	5	18	.269	.286
Bats Both	R	.239	238	57	7	0	9	28	24	39	.306	.382
Fahey,Brandon	L	.190	42	8	1	0	0	2	4	13	.277	.214
Bats Left	R	.244	209	51	7	2	2	21	19	35	.313	.325
Fasano,Sal	L	.241	54	13	4	0	1	5	4	17	.317	.370
Bats Right	R	.207	135	28	8	0	4	10	3	44	.246	.356
Feliz,Pedro	L	.212	132	28	7	2	3	19	10	23	.269	.364
Bats Right	R	.253	471	119	28	3	19	79	23	89	.285	.446
Fick,Robert	L	.273	44	12	1	0	0	1	2	9	.319	.295
Bats Left	R	.262	84	22	3	0	2	8	8	15	.326	.369
Fielder,Prince	L	.247	166	41	9	0	11	31	11	49	.319	.500
Bats Left	R	.280	403	113	26	1	17	50	48	76	.359	.476
Fields,Josh	L	.167	6	1	0	0	1	2	1	3	.286	.667
Bats Right	R	.143	14	2	2	0	0	0	4	5	.333	.286
Figgins,Chone	L	.233	172	40	8	1	3	12	19	38	.307	.343
Bats Both	R	.280	432	121	15	7	6	50	46	62	.348	.389
Figueroa,Luis	L	.000	2	0	0	0	0	0	0	1	.000	.000
Bats Both	R	.143	7	1	1	0	0	0	0	1	.143	.286
Finley,Steve	L	.255	98	25	4	4	0	9	6	14	.308	.378
Bats Left	R	.244	328	80	17	8	6	31	40	41	.323	.399
Fiorentino,Jeff	L	.182	11	2	0	0	0	2	0	1	.182	.182
Bats Left	R	.286	28	8	2	0	0	5	7	2	.432	.357
Floyd,Cliff	L	.179	84	15	6	0	3	16	7	13	.274	.357
Bats Left	R	.266	248	66	13	1	8	28	22	45	.342	.423
Ford,Lew	L	.206	102	21	3	0	4	8	4	16	.250	.353
Bats Right	R	.242	132	32	3	1	0	10	12	27	.315	.280
Franco,Julio	L	.227	66	15	3	0	0	8	5	25	.282	.273
Bats Right	R	.303	99	30	7	0	2	18	8	24	.361	.434
Francoeur,Jeff	L	.292	168	49	9	1	9	25	10	29	.335	.518
Bats Right	R	.248	483	120	15	5	20	78	13	103	.278	.424
Frandsen,Kevin	L	.200	10	2	0	0	1	3	0	1	.200	.500
Bats Right	R	.217	83	18	4	0	1	4	3	13	.293	.301
Freel,Ryan	L	.303	109	33	7	1	1	5	23	16	.424	.413
Bats Right	R	.261	345	90	23	1	7	22	34	82	.343	.394
Freeman,Choo	L	.276	76	21	2	2	1	6	8	12	.353	.395
Bats Right	R	.206	97	20	4	1	1	12	6	30	.252	.299
Furcal,Rafael	L	.324	142	46	10	3	5	19	15	13	.386	.542
Bats Both	R	.293	512	150	22	6	10	44	58	85	.365	.418
Gall,John	L	.333	6	2	0	0	0	1	0	2	.333	.333
Bats Right	R	.167	6	1	0	0	0	0	0	3	.167	.167
Garciaparra,Nomar	L	.341	85	29	7	0	5	16	11	8	.420	.600
Bats Right	R	.294	384	113	24	2	15	77	31	22	.355	.484
Garko,Ryan	L	.333	39	13	2	0	2	9	5	4	.400	.538
Bats Right	R	.281	146	41	10	0	5	36	9	33	.348	.452

Batter	vs	Avg	AB	H	2B	3B	HR	RBI	BB	SO	OBP	Slg
Gathright,Joey	L	.232	82	19	1	1	0	8	9	16	.344	.268
Bats Left	R	.239	301	72	11	2	1	33	33	59	.315	.299
German,Esteban	L	.347	118	41	7	3	1	15	17	20	.430	.483
Bats Right	R	.311	161	50	11	2	2	19	23	29	.416	.441
Giambi,Jason	L	.213	127	27	6	0	9	32	21	36	.356	.472
Bats Left	R	.270	319	86	19	0	28	81	89	70	.434	.592
Gibbons,Jay	L	.258	62	16	3	0	2	7	2	12	.277	.403
Bats Left	R	.281	281	79	20	0	11	39	30	36	.355	.470
Giles,Brian	L	.217	175	38	8	1	2	13	23	14	.315	.309
Bats Left	R	.282	429	121	29	0	12	70	81	46	.397	.434
Giles,Marcus	L	.229	144	33	6	1	3	13	12	26	.296	.347
Bats Right	R	.273	406	111	26	1	8	47	50	79	.357	.401
Gimenez,Hector	L	.000	1	0	0	0	0	0	0	0	.000	.000
Bats Both	R	.000	1	0	0	0	0	0	0	1	.000	.000
Glaus,Troy	L	.292	137	40	11	0	12	31	29	29	.413	.635
Bats Right	R	.238	403	96	16	0	26	73	57	105	.334	.471
Gload,Ross	L	.308	39	12	1	1	1	5	2	5	.341	.462
Bats Left	R	.333	117	39	7	1	2	13	4	10	.358	.462
Gomes,Jonny	L	.297	101	30	9	1	7	22	24	24	.438	.614
Bats Right	R	.187	284	53	12	0	13	37	37	92	.282	.366
Gomez,Alexis	L	.188	16	3	1	0	0	1	0	3	.188	.250
Bats Left	R	.287	87	25	4	2	1	5	6	18	.340	.414
Gomez,Chris	L	.333	48	16	2	0	1	3	5	3	.396	.438
Bats Right	R	.345	84	29	5	0	1	14	2	8	.382	.440
Gonzalez,Adrian	L	.312	141	44	10	0	5	20	5	33	.345	.489
Bats Left	R	.301	429	129	28	1	19	62	47	80	.367	.503
Gonzalez,Alex	L	.278	126	35	8	0	3	18	10	26	.333	.413
Bats Right	R	.244	262	64	16	2	6	32	12	41	.282	.389
Gonzalez,Alex S	L	.130	23	3	0	0	0	1	2	7	.200	.130
Bats Right	R	.077	13	1	0	0	0	0	0	3	.077	.077
Gonzalez,Luis	L	.259	174	45	15	1	3	16	16	19	.332	.408
Bats Left	R	.277	412	114	37	1	12	57	53	39	.360	.459
Gonzalez,Luis A	L	.219	32	7	3	0	1	4	1	9	.235	.406
Bats Right	R	.248	117	29	6	1	1	10	3	18	.279	.342
Gonzalez,Wiki	L	.222	9	2	0	0	0	1	1	2	.300	.222
Bats Right	R	.231	26	6	0	0	0	1	1	3	.250	.231
Graffanino,Tony	L	.275	142	39	10	0	4	17	12	20	.331	.430
Bats Right	R	.274	314	86	23	3	3	42	33	48	.351	.395
Granderson,Curtis	L	.218	147	32	8	3	4	16	10	49	.277	.395
Bats Left	R	.274	449	123	23	6	15	52	56	125	.353	.452
Green,Andy	L	.171	35	6	1	0	1	3	7	6	.310	.286
Bats Right	R	.196	51	10	3	0	0	3	6	14	.281	.255
Green,Nick	L	.150	40	6	1	0	0	0	3	11	.227	.175
Bats Right	R	.203	74	15	4	0	2	4	8	29	.280	.338
Green,Shawn	L	.267	165	44	11	1	6	23	15	33	.344	.455
Bats Left	R	.282	365	103	20	2	9	43	30	49	.343	.422
Greene,Khalil	L	.271	96	26	8	0	3	11	14	15	.372	.448
Bats Right	R	.237	316	75	18	2	12	44	25	72	.303	.421
Greene,Todd	L	.250	36	9	3	1	1	6	2	8	.289	.472
Bats Right	R	.301	123	37	9	1	1	11	8	37	.348	.415
Griffey Jr.,Ken	L	.204	147	30	4	0	9	29	9	27	.256	.415
Bats Left	R	.278	281	78	15	0	18	43	30	51	.346	.523
Gross,Gabe	L	.095	21	2	2	0	0	0	3	10	.208	.190
Bats Left	R	.294	187	55	13	0	9	38	33	50	.400	.508
Grudzielanek,Mark	L	.277	148	41	6	1	2	15	9	25	.316	.372
Bats Right	R	.305	400	122	26	3	5	37	19	44	.336	.423
Guerrero,Vladimir	L	.401	147	59	12	0	10	31	24	16	.483	.687
Bats Right	R	.307	460	141	22	1	23	85	26	52	.347	.509
Guiel,Aaron	L	.174	23	4	1	0	1	3	1	7	.208	.348
Bats Left	R	.257	109	28	5	0	6	15	13	24	.362	.468
Guillen,Carlos	L	.291	148	43	10	1	5	13	13	22	.354	.473
Bats Both	R	.332	395	131	31	4	14	72	58	65	.417	.537
Guillen,Jose	L	.200	60	12	4	0	3	10	5	10	.269	.417
Bats Right	R	.221	181	40	11	1	6	30	10	38	.279	.392
Gutierrez,Franklin	L	.262	42	11	2	0	1	4	1	5	.279	.381
Bats Right	R	.277	94	26	7	0	0	4	2	23	.292	.351
Guzman,Freddy	L	.500	4	2	0	0	0	0	1	0	.600	.500
Bats Both	R	.000	3	0	0	0	0	0	0	1	.250	.000
Guzman,Joel	L	.143	7	1	0	0	0	1	1	0	.250	.143
Bats Right	R	.250	12	3	0	0	0	2	2	2	.400	.250
Gwynn,Tony	L	.167	6	1	0	0	0	0	0	3	.167	.167
Bats Left	R	.268	71	19	2	1	0	4	2	12	.284	.324
Hafner,Travis	L	.321	184	59	12	1	16	46	38	47	.442	.658
Bats Left	R	.300	270	81	19	0	26	71	62	64	.436	.659
Hairston,Jerry	L	.153	72	11	1	0	0	4	7	16	.228	.167
Bats Right	R	.245	98	24	5	1	0	6	6	18	.302	.316

Batters vs. Left-Handed and Right-Handed Pitchers

Batter	vs	Avg	AB	H	2B	3B	HR	RBI	BB	SO	OBP	Slg
Hairston,Scott	L	.375	8	3	2	0	0	2	1	1	.444	.625
Bats Right	R	.429	7	3	0	0	0	0	0	4	.429	.429
Hall,Bill	L	.300	120	36	6	0	12	25	26	39	.422	.650
Bats Right	R	.261	417	109	33	4	23	60	37	123	.321	.525
Hall,Toby	L	.292	72	21	6	0	3	12	4	6	.333	.500
Bats Right	R	.248	206	51	11	0	5	19	6	16	.269	.374
Hammock,Robby	L	.000	0	0	0	0	0	0	0	0	-	
Bats Right	R	.500	2	1	1	0	0	0	0	0	.500	1.000
Hannahan,Jack	L	.000	1	0	0	0	0	0	0	0	.000	.000
Bats Left	R	.000	8	0	0	0	0	0	1	1	.111	.000
Hardy,J.J.	L	.294	34	10	1	0	3	6	4	6	.368	.588
Bats Right	R	.223	94	21	4	0	2	8	6	17	.267	.330
Harper,Brandon	L	.258	31	8	2	0	2	6	3	4	.333	.516
Bats Right	R	.400	10	4	1	0	0	0	1	0	.455	.500
Harris,Brendan	L	.313	16	5	1	0	1	2	3	3	.421	.563
Bats Right	R	.192	26	5	1	0	0	1	1	4	.250	.231
Harris,Willie	L	.250	8	2	1	0	0	0	0	0	.250	.375
Bats Left	R	.135	37	5	1	0	0	1	4	11	.250	.162
Hart,Corey	L	.304	79	24	3	0	3	15	7	16	.352	.456
Bats Right	R	.272	158	43	10	2	6	18	10	42	.315	.475
Hatteberg,Scott	L	.231	78	18	6	0	1	9	10	13	.333	.346
Bats Left	R	.302	378	114	22	0	12	42	64	28	.401	.455
Hattig,John	L	.000	3	0	0	0	0	0	1	1	.250	.000
Bats Both	R	.381	21	8	1	0	0	3	4	7	.480	.429
Hawpe,Brad	L	.232	69	16	3	1	3	10	7	25	.303	.435
Bats Left	R	.302	430	130	30	5	19	74	67	98	.395	.528
Heintz,Chris	L	-	0	0	0	0	0	0	0	0	-	
Bats Right	R	.000	0	0	0	0	0	0	0	0	.000	.000
Helms,Wes	L	.336	107	36	9	0	3	22	13	29	.414	.505
Bats Right	R	.323	133	43	10	5	7	25	8	26	.368	.632
Helton,Todd	L	.326	132	43	8	0	2	24	14	19	.392	.432
Bats Left	R	.295	414	122	32	5	13	57	75	45	.407	.490
Hermida,Jeremy	L	.219	73	16	2	0	1	2	7	18	.321	.288
Bats Left	R	.261	234	61	17	1	4	26	26	52	.336	.393
Hernandez,Anderson	L	.211	19	4	0	0	1	1	1	2	.250	.368
Bats Both	R	.128	47	6	1	1	0	2	0	10	.128	.191
Hernandez,Jose	L	.290	62	18	2	0	2	12	5	17	.343	.419
Bats Right	R	.244	90	22	2	1	1	7	7	23	.299	.322
Hernandez,Ramon	L	.291	127	37	7	0	10	30	19	16	.393	.583
Bats Right	R	.270	374	101	22	2	13	61	24	63	.324	.444
Hill,Aaron	L	.298	161	48	6	0	3	10	16	20	.362	.391
Bats Right	R	.288	385	111	22	3	3	40	26	46	.344	.384
Hillenbrand,Shea	L	.338	139	47	9	0	4	18	9	18	.373	.489
Bats Right	R	.256	391	100	18	1	17	50	12	62	.291	.437
Hinske,Eric	L	.167	48	8	3	0	1	4	8	16	.286	.292
Bats Left	R	.293	229	67	14	2	12	30	27	63	.367	.528
Hollandsworth,Todd	L	.174	23	4	1	0	0	4	1	10	.200	.217
Bats Left	R	.254	201	51	17	1	7	31	9	42	.284	.453
Holliday,Matt	L	.327	107	35	11	2	4	17	13	18	.405	.579
Bats Right	R	.325	495	161	34	3	30	97	34	91	.383	.588
Hollins,Damon	L	.240	129	31	8	0	9	18	8	32	.283	.512
Bats Right	R	.221	204	45	12	0	6	15	11	32	.260	.368
Hooper,Kevin	L	-	0	0	0	0	0	0	0	0	-	
Bats Right	R	.000	3	0	0	0	0	0	1	1	.250	.000
Hoover,Paul	L	.400	5	2	0	0	0	1	0	0	.400	.400
Bats Right	R	-	0	0	0	0	0	0	0	0	-	
Hopper,Norris	L	.571	21	12	1	0	1	3	3	1	.600	.762
Bats Right	R	.111	18	2	0	0	0	2	3	3	.238	.111
House,J.R.	L	.000	7	0	0	0	0	0	0	1	.000	.000
Bats Right	R	.000	2	0	0	0	0	0	0	0	.000	.000
Howard,Ryan	L	.279	197	55	5	1	16	45	22	76	.364	.558
Bats Left	R	.331	384	127	20	0	42	104	86	105	.453	.711
Huber,Justin	L	.125	8	1	0	0	0	0	1	3	.222	.125
Bats Right	R	.500	2	1	1	0	0	1	0	1	.500	1.000
Huckaby,Ken	L	.000	1	0	0	0	0	0	0	0	.000	.000
Bats Right	R	.250	4	1	0	0	0	0	0	0	.250	.250
Hudson,Orlando	L	.338	142	48	10	3	3	19	16	10	.398	.514
Bats Both	R	.270	437	118	24	6	12	48	45	68	.340	.435
Huff,Aubrey	L	.233	120	28	6	0	4	16	11	15	.303	.383
Bats Left	R	.278	334	93	19	2	17	50	39	49	.358	.500
Hunter,Torii	L	.319	160	51	9	1	8	29	18	31	.381	.538
Bats Right	R	.262	397	104	12	1	23	69	27	77	.316	.471
Hyzdu,Adam	L	.000	2	0	0	0	0	0	0	1	.000	.000
Bats Right	R	.500	2	1	0	0	0	0	0	0	.500	.500
Iannetta,Christopher	L	.231	13	3	1	0	1	3	6	2	.474	.538
Bats Right	R	.266	64	17	3	0	1	7	7	15	.342	.359
Ibanez,Raul	L	.243	185	45	10	0	4	36	16	43	.301	.362
Bats Left	R	.308	441	136	23	5	29	87	49	72	.375	.580
Iguchi,Tadahito	L	.252	206	52	11	0	6	19	26	42	.335	.393
Bats Right	R	.298	349	104	13	0	12	48	33	68	.363	.438
Infante,Omar	L	.286	70	20	3	0	2	5	3	14	.333	.414
Bats Right	R	.273	154	42	8	4	2	20	11	31	.321	.416
Inge,Brandon	L	.243	140	34	7	1	6	25	11	38	.301	.436
Bats Right	R	.256	402	103	22	1	21	58	32	90	.318	.473
Inglett,Joe	L	.217	23	5	1	0	0	0	2	5	.280	.261
Bats Left	R	.292	178	52	7	3	2	21	12	34	.339	.399
Ishikawa,Travis	L	.400	5	2	1	0	0	2	1	0	.500	.600
Bats Left	R	.263	19	5	2	1	0	2	0	6	.263	.474
Izturis,Cesar	L	.206	34	7	1	0	0	4	2	5	.270	.235
Bats Right	R	.253	158	40	8	1	1	14	10	9	.300	.335
Izturis,Maicer	L	.247	85	21	7	0	0	12	11	5	.333	.329
Bats Both	R	.307	267	82	14	3	5	32	27	30	.376	.438
Jackson,Conor	L	.296	162	48	7	0	5	20	21	27	.378	.432
Bats Right	R	.288	323	93	19	1	10	59	33	46	.362	.446
Jackson,Damian	L	.233	43	10	2	0	2	4	9	13	.365	.419
Bats Right	R	.178	73	13	4	1	2	6	3	26	.250	.342
Jacobs,Mike	L	.182	88	16	4	0	2	11	5	26	.234	.295
Bats Left	R	.281	381	107	33	1	18	66	40	79	.345	.514
Jenkins,Geoff	L	.133	98	13	2	0	2	7	12	43	.265	.214
Bats Left	R	.306	386	118	24	1	15	63	44	86	.381	.490
Jeter,Derek	L	.390	159	62	12	1	4	22	18	25	.458	.553
Bats Right	R	.328	464	152	27	2	10	75	51	77	.403	.459
Jimenez,D'Angelo	L	.188	16	3	1	0	0	4	3	1	.316	.250
Bats Both	R	.182	55	10	2	0	1	4	13	12	.338	.273
Jimerson,Charlton	L	.667	3	2	0	0	1	1	0	1	.667	1.667
Bats Right	R	.000	3	0	0	0	0	0	0	2	.000	.000
Johjima,Kenji	L	.263	114	30	7	0	0	9	5	10	.315	.325
Bats Right	R	.298	392	117	18	1	18	67	15	36	.337	.487
Johnson,Ben	L	.275	51	14	2	1	2	5	8	13	.383	.471
Bats Right	R	.232	69	16	3	1	2	7	6	23	.293	.391
Johnson,Dan	L	.217	46	10	3	0	0	4	3	15	.260	.283
Bats Left	R	.238	240	57	10	1	9	33	37	30	.335	.400
Johnson,Nick	L	.303	142	43	13	0	5	24	31	30	.438	.500
Bats Left	R	.285	358	102	33	0	18	53	79	69	.424	.528
Johnson,Reed	L	.323	164	53	9	1	3	13	15	23	.422	.445
Bats Right	R	.316	297	94	25	1	9	36	18	58	.370	.498
Jones,Adam	L	.235	17	4	0	0	0	0	1	6	.278	.235
Bats Right	R	.211	57	12	4	0	1	8	1	16	.224	.333
Jones,Andruw	L	.260	127	33	6	0	10	21	23	29	.390	.543
Bats Right	R	.263	438	115	23	0	31	108	59	98	.355	.527
Jones,Chipper	L	.293	92	27	4	2	6	22	3	17	.309	.576
Bats Both	R	.332	319	106	24	1	20	64	58	56	.434	.602
Jones,Jacque	L	.234	137	32	7	0	6	22	2	33	.261	.416
Bats Left	R	.303	396	120	24	1	21	59	33	83	.358	.528
Jordan,Brian	L	.180	50	9	0	0	0	5	5	9	.246	.180
Bats Right	R	.293	41	12	2	0	3	5	2	14	.341	.561
Kapler,Gabe	L	.265	68	18	5	0	1	1	8	7	.367	.382
Bats Right	R	.242	62	15	2	0	1	1	6	8	.309	.323
Kearns,Austin	L	.336	152	51	14	0	9	33	27	33	.434	.605
Bats Right	R	.236	385	91	19	2	15	53	49	102	.334	.413
Kemp,Matt	L	.229	48	11	3	1	0	2	1	18	.245	.333
Bats Right	R	.264	106	28	4	0	7	21	8	35	.308	.500
Kendall,Jason	L	.331	124	41	10	0	0	17	18	8	.421	.411
Bats Right	R	.285	428	122	13	0	1	33	35	46	.350	.322
Kendrick,Howie	L	.264	91	24	8	1	1	10	3	11	.299	.407
Bats Right	R	.295	176	52	13	0	3	20	6	33	.323	.420
Kennedy,Adam	L	.193	83	16	3	2	0	6	5	18	.256	.277
Bats Left	R	.291	368	107	23	4	4	49	34	54	.351	.408
Kent,Jeff	L	.347	98	34	6	0	6	16	17	16	.444	.592
Bats Right	R	.275	309	85	21	3	8	52	38	53	.365	.440
Keppinger,Jeff	L	.222	27	6	2	0	1	2	3	4	.300	.407
Bats Right	R	.303	33	10	0	0	1	6	2	2	.343	.394
Kielty,Bobby	L	.325	117	38	12	0	7	20	6	16	.358	.607
Bats Both	R	.229	153	35	8	1	1	16	16	33	.308	.314
Kinsler,Ian	L	.271	118	32	8	0	5	18	9	11	.315	.466
Bats Right	R	.292	305	89	19	1	9	37	31	53	.359	.449
Klesko,Ryan	L	1.000	1	1	1	0	0	1	0	0	1.000	2.000
Bats Left	R	.667	3	2	1	0	0	1	2	0	.800	.667
Knoedler,Justin	L	.000	1	0	0	0	0	0	0	0	.000	.000
Bats Right	R	.167	6	1	0	0	0	0	0	1	.167	.167
Knott,Jon	L	.000	3	0	0	0	0	0	0	1	.000	.000
Bats Right	R	-	0	0	0	0	0	0	0	0	-	

Batters vs. Left-Handed and Right-Handed Pitchers

Batter	vs	Avg	AB	H	2B	3B	HR	RBI	BB	SO	OBP	Slg
Konerko,Paul	L	.318	195	62	11	0	14	38	22	36	.394	.590
Bats Right	R	.310	371	115	19	0	21	75	38	68	.374	.531
Koskie,Corey	L	.263	57	15	5	0	1	5	2	14	.288	.404
Bats Left	R	.260	200	52	18	0	11	28	27	44	.357	.515
Kotchman,Casey	L	.214	14	3	0	0	0	2	1	1	.267	.214
Bats Left	R	.138	65	9	2	0	1	4	6	12	.211	.215
Kotsay,Mark	L	.265	117	31	6	1	3	14	5	17	.293	.410
Bats Left	R	.278	385	107	23	2	4	45	39	38	.343	.379
Kouzmanoff,Kevin	L	.167	12	2	0	0	0	0	0	5	.167	.167
Bats Right	R	.227	44	10	2	0	3	11	5	7	.306	.477
Kubel,Jason	L	.243	37	9	0	0	2	7	2	9	.282	.405
Bats Left	R	.240	183	44	8	0	6	19	10	36	.278	.383
Laird,Gerald	L	.400	85	34	8	0	3	9	2	13	.414	.600
Bats Right	R	.241	158	38	12	1	4	13	10	41	.291	.405
Laker,Tim	L	.400	5	2	1	0	0	2	0	3	.400	.600
Bats Right	R	.250	8	2	0	0	0	0	0	1	.250	.250
Lamb,Mike	L	.211	57	12	3	1	1	7	3	14	.250	.351
Bats Left	R	.324	324	105	19	2	11	38	32	41	.380	.497
Lane,Jason	L	.198	96	19	4	0	6	20	22	25	.344	.427
Bats Right	R	.203	192	39	6	0	9	25	27	50	.303	.375
Langerhans,Ryan	L	.308	39	12	1	0	0	6	6	11	.400	.333
Bats Left	R	.232	276	64	15	3	7	22	44	80	.343	.384
LaRoche,Adam	L	.241	112	27	6	0	7	20	11	36	.315	.482
Bats Left	R	.297	380	113	32	1	25	70	44	92	.366	.584
LaRue,Jason	L	.235	51	12	2	0	2	3	5	14	.328	.392
Bats Right	R	.179	140	25	3	0	6	18	22	37	.314	.329
Lawton,Matt	L	1.000	1	1	0	0	0	1	0	0	1.000	1.000
Bats Left	R	.231	26	6	0	0	0	0	2	2	.286	.231
LeCroy,Matthew	L	.229	35	8	1	0	1	5	8	10	.386	.343
Bats Right	R	.250	32	8	2	0	1	4	3	7	.306	.406
Ledee,Ricky	L	.111	9	1	0	0	0	1	0	3	.111	.111
Bats Left	R	.197	76	15	6	0	2	8	6	13	.256	.355
Lee,Carlos	L	.313	147	46	6	1	6	20	11	14	.354	.490
Bats Right	R	.296	477	141	31	0	31	96	47	51	.356	.556
Lee,Derrek	L	.292	48	14	4	0	0	3	7	8	.382	.375
Bats Right	R	.283	127	36	5	0	8	27	18	33	.362	.512
Lee,Travis	L	.226	93	21	2	0	7	13	6	21	.273	.473
Bats Left	R	.224	250	56	9	2	4	18	36	52	.325	.324
Leone,Justin	L	-	0	0	0	0	0	0	0	0	-	-
Bats Right	R	.000	1	0	0	0	0	0	0	0	.000	.000
Lewis,Fred	L	.500	2	1	1	0	0	1	0	0	.500	1.000
Bats Left	R	.444	9	4	0	0	0	1	0	3	.444	.444
Lieberthal,Mike	L	.286	42	12	1	0	2	8	2	3	.311	.452
Bats Right	R	.269	167	45	13	0	7	28	6	16	.317	.473
Lind,Adam	L	.444	9	4	1	0	0	2	2	0	.545	.556
Bats Left	R	.353	51	18	7	0	2	6	3	12	.389	.608
Linden,Todd	L	.208	24	5	0	0	1	2	3	7	.321	.333
Bats Both	R	.302	53	16	4	2	1	3	6	13	.373	.509
Lo Duca,Paul	L	.336	152	51	13	0	2	16	9	10	.373	.461
Bats Right	R	.311	360	112	26	1	3	33	15	28	.347	.414
Lofton,Kenny	L	.214	84	18	2	0	1	6	7	13	.275	.274
Bats Left	R	.319	385	123	13	12	2	35	38	29	.379	.431
Logan,Nook	L	.350	20	7	2	1	1	3	2	3	.409	.700
Bats Both	R	.286	70	20	1	0	0	5	4	17	.316	.300
Lombard,George	L	.000	9	0	0	0	0	0	1	5	.100	.000
Bats Right	R	.250	12	3	0	0	1	1	4	5	.438	.500
Loney,James	L	.350	20	7	1	1	0	4	0	2	.350	.500
Bats Left	R	.268	82	22	5	4	4	14	8	8	.341	.573
Long,Terrence	L	.143	7	1	1	0	0	0	1	5	.250	.286
Bats Left	R	.172	29	5	0	0	0	2	3	3	.250	.172
Lopez,Felipe	L	.246	175	43	8	0	2	20	18	49	.315	.326
Bats Both	R	.285	442	126	19	3	9	32	63	77	.375	.403
Lopez,Javy	L	.270	89	24	4	1	2	11	3	26	.293	.404
Bats Right	R	.245	253	62	16	0	6	24	17	50	.298	.379
Lopez,Jose	L	.331	151	50	7	1	4	23	8	15	.370	.470
Bats Right	R	.265	452	120	21	7	6	56	18	65	.301	.383
Loretta,Mark	L	.274	186	51	10	0	4	14	22	17	.355	.392
Bats Right	R	.290	449	130	23	0	1	45	27	46	.341	.347
Lowell,Mike	L	.241	166	40	11	0	4	18	17	22	.316	.380
Bats Right	R	.302	407	123	36	1	16	62	30	39	.349	.514
Lugo,Julio	L	.263	118	31	6	0	4	11	9	11	.318	.398
Bats Right	R	.284	317	90	18	2	8	26	30	65	.349	.429
Luna,Hector	L	.315	162	51	10	0	2	16	11	23	.358	.414
Bats Right	R	.261	188	49	11	2	4	22	16	37	.320	.404
Mabry,John	L	.316	19	6	1	0	1	7	3	7	.409	.526
Bats Left	R	.194	191	37	7	1	4	18	20	50	.270	.304
Mackowiak,Rob	L	.222	54	12	0	0	0	6	3	13	.288	.222
Bats Left	R	.308	201	62	12	1	5	17	25	46	.384	.453
Maier,Mitch	L	.000	5	0	0	0	0	0	1	2	.167	.000
Bats Left	R	.250	8	2	0	0	0	0	1	2	.333	.250
Maldonado,Carlos	L	-	0	0	0	0	0	0	0	0	-	-
Bats Right	R	.105	19	2	0	0	0	0	1	10	.150	.105
Markakis,Nick	L	.286	119	34	8	0	1	12	8	22	.333	.378
Bats Left	R	.293	372	109	17	2	15	50	35	50	.356	.470
Marrero,Eli	L	.138	29	4	0	0	1	2	8	9	.342	.241
Bats Right	R	.234	64	15	4	0	5	13	7	22	.315	.531
Marte,Andy	L	.227	44	10	5	0	2	6	4	7	.292	.477
Bats Right	R	.225	120	27	10	1	3	17	9	31	.285	.400
Martin,Russell	L	.366	71	26	5	0	2	16	11	6	.451	.521
Bats Right	R	.265	344	91	21	4	8	49	34	51	.335	.419
Martinez,Ramon	L	.289	38	11	2	0	0	5	4	8	.357	.342
Bats Right	R	.275	138	38	5	1	2	19	11	12	.333	.370
Martinez,Victor	L	.290	214	62	12	0	6	28	28	28	.373	.430
Bats Left	R	.332	358	119	25	0	10	65	43	50	.402	.486
Mateo,Henry	L	.214	14	3	1	0	1	3	2	0	.313	.500
Bats Both	R	.083	12	1	0	0	0	0	0	3	.083	.167
Matheny,Mike	L	.364	44	16	3	0	1	8	3	3	.404	.500
Bats Right	R	.181	116	21	5	0	2	10	6	27	.228	.276
Mathis,Jeff	L	.133	15	2	0	0	0	0	2	3	.235	.133
Bats Right	R	.150	40	6	2	0	2	6	5	11	.239	.350
Matos,Luis	L	.219	64	14	3	1	1	2	3	13	.254	.344
Bats Left	R	.194	72	14	6	0	1	3	7	10	.284	.319
Matsui,Hideki	L	.226	53	12	2	0	1	4	6	10	.305	.321
Bats Left	R	.336	119	40	7	0	7	25	21	13	.430	.571
Matsui,Kaz	L	.119	42	5	1	0	0	3	1	6	.143	.143
Bats Both	R	.299	201	60	11	3	3	23	10	35	.329	.428
Matthews Jr.,Gary	L	.314	137	43	13	1	7	19	15	25	.374	.577
Bats Both	R	.313	483	151	31	5	12	60	43	74	.370	.472
Mauer,Joe	L	.331	181	60	11	0	2	28	22	23	.401	.425
Bats Left	R	.356	340	121	25	4	11	56	57	31	.444	.550
McAnulty,Paul	L	.000	1	0	0	0	0	0	0	0	.000	.000
Bats Right	R	.250	12	3	1	0	1	3	2	4	.357	.583
McCann,Brian	L	.266	94	25	9	0	3	15	11	19	.352	.457
Bats Left	R	.351	348	122	25	0	21	78	30	35	.398	.603
McCracken,Quinton	L	.143	7	1	0	0	0	0	0	3	.143	.143
Bats Both	R	.217	46	10	1	1	1	2	4	6	.280	.348
McDonald,John	L	.230	87	20	4	0	1	12	9	11	.303	.310
Bats Right	R	.220	173	38	3	3	2	11	7	30	.254	.306
McEwing,Joe	L	.000	1	0	0	0	0	0	0	0	.000	.000
Bats Right	R	.000	5	0	0	0	0	0	0	2	.000	.000
McLouth,Nate	L	.260	50	13	2	1	3	6	1	8	.315	.520
Bats Left	R	.227	220	50	14	1	4	10	17	51	.288	.355
McPherson,Dallas	L	.231	13	3	0	0	2	2	1	6	.286	.692
Bats Left	R	.265	102	27	4	0	5	11	5	34	.299	.451
Melhuse,Adam	L	.222	18	4	0	0	1	3	1	4	.250	.389
Bats Both	R	.218	110	24	8	0	3	15	8	30	.277	.373
Mench,Kevin	L	.303	119	36	8	1	5	20	11	5	.364	.513
Bats Right	R	.257	327	84	16	1	8	48	16	54	.294	.385
Merloni,Lou	L	.222	9	2	0	0	0	1	1	2	.300	.222
Bats Right	R	.200	10	2	1	0	0	1	1	3	.273	.300
Meyer,Drew	L	.333	3	1	0	0	0	0	0	0	.333	.333
Bats Left	R	.182	11	2	0	0	0	0	0	8	.182	.182
Michaels,Jason	L	.291	189	55	15	0	5	27	17	30	.349	.450
Bats Right	R	.252	305	77	17	1	4	28	26	71	.312	.354
Mientkiewicz,Doug	L	.274	62	17	6	0	1	10	7	12	.375	.419
Bats Left	R	.286	252	72	18	2	3	33	28	38	.355	.409
Miles,Aaron	L	.291	86	25	6	0	0	7	12	17	.378	.360
Bats Both	R	.256	340	87	14	5	2	23	26	25	.310	.344
Millar,Kevin	L	.244	119	29	8	0	3	12	16	18	.336	.387
Bats Right	R	.283	311	88	18	0	12	52	43	56	.388	.457
Milledge,Lastings	L	.241	54	13	2	1	0	3	6	11	.349	.315
Bats Right	R	.241	112	27	5	1	4	19	6	28	.289	.411
Miller,Corky	L	.000	2	0	0	0	0	0	0	1	.000	.000
Bats Right	R	.000	2	0	0	0	0	0	0	0	.000	.000
Miller,Damian	L	.280	82	23	15	0	1	10	12	22	.365	.500
Bats Right	R	.241	249	60	13	0	5	28	21	64	.307	.353
Mirabelli,Doug	L	.200	55	11	4	0	1	2	7	19	.302	.327
Bats Right	R	.188	128	24	3	0	5	23	8	40	.252	.328
Moeller,Chad	L	.211	19	4	0	0	1	2	2	4	.286	.368
Bats Right	R	.177	79	14	3	0	1	3	2	22	.217	.253
Mohr,Dustan	L	.250	28	7	1	0	2	3	3	13	.323	.500
Bats Right	R	.000	12	0	0	0	0	0	0	7	.000	.000

Batters vs. Left-Handed and Right-Handed Pitchers

Batter	vs	Avg	AB	H	2B	3B	HR	RBI	BB	SO	OBP	Slg
Molina,Bengie	L	.358	148	53	6	1	10	28	5	12	.383	.615
Bats Right	R	.246	285	70	14	0	9	29	14	35	.286	.389
Molina,Jose	L	.218	87	19	6	0	2	7	5	15	.261	.356
Bats Right	R	.254	138	35	11	0	2	15	4	34	.281	.377
Molina,Yadier	L	.213	127	27	9	0	1	10	11	11	.296	.307
Bats Right	R	.217	290	63	17	0	5	39	15	30	.264	.328
Monroe,Craig	L	.271	140	38	13	0	2	21	12	33	.327	.407
Bats Right	R	.249	401	100	22	2	26	71	25	93	.292	.509
Montero,Miguel	L	.333	3	1	0	0	0	2	0	0	.333	.333
Bats Left	R	.231	13	3	1	0	0	1	1	3	.286	.308
Moore,Scott	L	.000	4	0	0	0	0	0	0	2	.200	.000
Bats Left	R	.294	34	10	2	0	2	5	2	8	.333	.529
Mora,Melvin	L	.253	166	42	6	0	7	23	19	26	.339	.416
Bats Right	R	.282	458	129	19	0	9	60	35	73	.343	.382
Morales,Kendry	L	.229	48	11	4	0	1	7	0	6	.229	.375
Bats Both	R	.235	149	35	6	1	4	15	17	22	.311	.369
Morneau,Justin	L	.315	213	67	13	0	13	47	12	32	.345	.559
Bats Left	R	.325	379	123	24	1	21	83	41	61	.391	.559
Morse,Mike	L	.438	32	14	4	0	0	9	2	4	.457	.563
Bats Right	R	.182	11	2	1	0	0	2	1	3	.231	.273
Mottola,Chad	L	.182	11	2	1	0	0	0	0	1	.182	.273
Bats Right	R	.400	5	2	1	0	0	0	0	2	.400	.600
Mueller,Bill	L	.280	25	7	1	0	0	2	2	1	.333	.320
Bats Both	R	.244	82	20	6	0	3	13	15	8	.364	.427
Munson,Eric	L	.318	22	7	3	0	1	7	1	5	.375	.591
Bats Left	R	.176	119	21	3	0	4	12	10	27	.250	.303
Murphy,David	L	.000	1	0	0	0	0	0	0	0	.000	.000
Bats Left	R	.238	21	5	1	0	1	2	4	4	.360	.429
Murphy,Tommy	L	.318	22	7	2	0	1	2	0	5	.318	.545
Bats Both	R	.188	48	9	2	1	0	4	5	16	.259	.271
Murton,Matt	L	.301	136	41	7	0	6	19	18	11	.385	.485
Bats Right	R	.295	319	94	15	3	7	43	27	51	.356	.426
Nady,Xavier	L	.336	107	36	5	0	6	20	13	16	.418	.551
Bats Right	R	.263	361	95	23	1	11	43	17	69	.312	.424
Napoli,Mike	L	.185	65	12	0	0	5	9	15	24	.346	.415
Bats Right	R	.241	203	49	13	0	11	33	36	66	.365	.468
Navarro,Dioner	L	.286	56	16	2	0	1	7	11	10	.403	.375
Bats Both	R	.245	212	52	7	0	5	21	20	41	.312	.349
Navarro,Oswaldo	L	-	0	0	0	0	0	0	0	0	-	-
Bats Both	R	.667	3	2	0	0	0	0	0	1	.667	.667
Nelson,John	L	-	0	0	0	0	0	0	0	0	-	-
Bats Right	R	.000	0	0	0	0	0	0	0	0	.000	.000
Nevin,Phil	L	.226	133	30	4	0	7	17	19	28	.325	.414
Bats Right	R	.246	264	65	9	0	15	51	29	78	.322	.451
Newhan,David	L	.182	22	4	0	0	1	3	1	6	.250	.318
Bats Left	R	.266	109	29	4	0	3	15	6	16	.303	.385
Niekro,Lance	L	.246	61	15	6	1	1	8	2	11	.270	.426
Bats Right	R	.246	138	34	3	1	4	23	9	21	.293	.370
Nieves,Wil	L	.000	2	0	0	0	0	0	0	1	.000	.000
Bats Right	R	.000	4	0	0	0	0	0	0	0	.000	.000
Nix,Laynce	L	.125	8	1	0	0	0	3	0	5	.125	.125
Bats Left	R	.169	59	10	2	0	1	7	0	23	.194	.254
Nixon,Trot	L	.204	93	19	4	0	2	10	16	20	.336	.312
Bats Left	R	.288	288	83	20	0	6	42	44	36	.385	.420
Norton,Greg	L	.283	60	17	1	0	3	10	12	16	.411	.450
Bats Both	R	.299	234	70	14	0	14	35	23	53	.364	.538
Nunez,Abraham	L	.171	82	14	0	0	1	7	11	17	.274	.207
Bats Both	R	.225	240	54	10	2	1	25	30	41	.314	.296
Ojeda,Miguel	L	.308	13	4	1	0	0	2	2	2	.400	.385
Bats Right	R	.230	74	17	4	0	2	13	6	17	.288	.365
Olivo,Miguel	L	.273	128	35	6	1	5	14	2	32	.285	.453
Bats Right	R	.258	302	78	16	2	11	44	7	71	.288	.434
Olmedo,Ray	L	.333	6	2	1	0	0	0	1	1	.429	.500
Bats Both	R	.184	38	7	1	0	1	4	3	3	.244	.289
Ordaz,Luis	L	-	0	0	0	0	0	0	0	0	-	-
Bats Right	R	.000	2	0	0	0	0	0	0	0	.000	.000
Ordonez,Magglio	L	.294	163	48	10	1	9	32	9	20	.333	.534
Bats Right	R	.300	430	129	22	0	15	72	36	67	.356	.456
Orr,Pete	L	.182	22	4	0	0	0	0	2	6	.250	.182
Bats Left	R	.265	132	35	3	4	1	8	3	24	.281	.371
Ortiz,David	L	.278	205	57	13	1	18	44	30	48	.373	.615
Bats Left	R	.292	353	103	16	1	36	93	89	69	.434	.649
Ortmeier,Dan	L	.000	2	0	0	0	0	0	0	1	.000	.000
Bats Both	R	.300	10	3	1	0	0	2	0	3	.300	.400
Overbay,Lyle	L	.284	162	46	8	0	3	18	4	31	.305	.389
Bats Left	R	.322	419	135	38	1	19	74	51	65	.395	.554
Owens,Jerry	L	.000	1	0	0	0	0	0	0	1	.000	.000
Bats Left	R	.375	8	3	1	0	0	0	0	1	.375	.500
Ozuna,Pablo	L	.322	143	46	11	2	2	15	6	11	.358	.469
Bats Right	R	.348	46	16	1	0	0	2	1	5	.388	.370
Pagan,Angel	L	.196	56	11	1	1	1	8	8	7	.292	.304
Bats Both	R	.272	114	31	5	1	4	10	7	21	.314	.439
Palmeiro,Orlando	L	.000	3	0	0	0	0	0	0	0	.000	.000
Bats Left	R	.259	116	30	6	1	0	17	6	16	.301	.328
Patterson,Corey	L	.207	121	25	1	2	3	14	4	29	.238	.322
Bats Left	R	.301	342	103	18	3	13	39	17	65	.341	.485
Paul,Josh	L	.333	39	13	1	0	0	2	6	11	.426	.359
Bats Right	R	.234	107	25	8	0	1	6	8	28	.287	.336
Paulino,Ronny	L	.339	115	39	6	0	2	15	11	15	.402	.443
Bats Right	R	.300	327	98	13	0	4	40	23	64	.346	.376
Payton,Jay	L	.296	142	42	6	1	6	22	9	11	.338	.479
Bats Right	R	.296	415	123	26	2	4	37	13	41	.320	.398
Pedroia,Dustin	L	.162	37	6	3	0	0	3	4	1	.262	.243
Bats Right	R	.212	52	11	1	0	2	4	3	6	.255	.346
Pena,Brayan	L	.200	15	3	1	0	0	1	2	1	.294	.267
Bats Both	R	.308	26	8	1	0	1	4	0	4	.308	.462
Pena,Carlos	L	.273	11	3	0	0	0	0	5	0	.273	.273
Bats Left	R	.273	22	6	2	0	1	3	4	5	.385	.500
Pena,Tony F	L	.278	18	5	2	0	0	1	1	6	.316	.389
Bats Right	R	.192	26	5	0	0	1	2	1	4	.222	.308
Pena,Wily Mo	L	.260	104	27	4	0	1	11	11	42	.333	.327
Bats Right	R	.326	172	56	11	2	10	31	9	48	.359	.587
Peralta,Jhonny	L	.267	176	47	9	0	5	17	13	57	.321	.403
Bats Right	R	.252	393	99	19	3	8	51	43	95	.323	.377
Perez,Antonio	L	.129	31	4	2	0	1	4	5	14	.250	.290
Bats Right	R	.090	67	6	3	1	0	4	5	30	.153	.164
Perez,Eduardo	L	.275	153	42	8	0	9	28	13	26	.331	.503
Bats Right	R	.152	33	5	2	0	0	5	5	7	.293	.212
Perez,Neifi	L	.265	98	26	0	2	8	14	2	14	.275	.408
Bats Both	R	.232	203	47	6	1	0	21	6	11	.252	.271
Perez,Timo	L	.400	5	2	0	0	1	1	0	2	.500	1.000
Bats Left	R	.154	26	4	1	0	0	2	3	2	.241	.192
Perez,Tomas	L	.178	73	13	4	0	1	6	4	19	.218	.274
Bats Both	R	.226	168	38	8	0	1	10	1	25	.227	.292
Petagine,Roberto	L	.000	2	0	0	0	0	0	0	3	.333	.000
Bats Left	R	.200	25	5	2	0	1	2	4	8	.310	.400
Phillips,Andy	L	.195	82	16	1	0	1	4	4	18	.233	.244
Bats Right	R	.262	164	43	10	3	6	25	11	38	.305	.470
Phillips,Brandon	L	.299	137	41	5	0	4	16	12	21	.351	.423
Bats Right	R	.268	399	107	23	1	13	59	23	67	.315	.429
Phillips,Jason	L	.290	31	9	4	0	0	4	1	3	.303	.419
Bats Right	R	.176	17	3	2	0	0	2	0	2	.222	.294
Phillips,Paul	L	.304	23	7	1	0	1	3	1	2	.333	.478
Bats Right	R	.262	42	11	2	0	0	2	0	6	.256	.310
Piazza,Mike	L	.359	103	37	6	0	8	20	11	12	.421	.650
Bats Right	R	.257	296	76	13	1	14	48	23	54	.314	.449
Piedra,Jorge	L	.000	6	0	0	0	0	0	0	3	.000	.000
Bats Left	R	.189	53	10	2	0	3	10	3	19	.246	.396
Pierre,Juan	L	.293	246	72	12	2	0	17	11	15	.341	.358
Bats Left	R	.291	453	132	20	11	3	23	21	23	.324	.404
Pierzynski,A.J.	L	.270	141	38	4	0	1	14	4	22	.304	.319
Bats Left	R	.304	368	112	20	0	15	50	18	50	.344	.481
Podsednik,Scott	L	.216	139	30	4	1	1	8	12	30	.281	.281
Bats Left	R	.278	385	107	23	5	2	37	42	66	.348	.379
Polanco,Placido	L	.272	136	37	8	1	2	20	8	12	.313	.390
Bats Right	R	.305	325	99	10	0	2	32	9	15	.335	.354
Posada,Jorge	L	.263	137	36	5	1	3	15	15	32	.348	.380
Bats Both	R	.284	328	93	22	1	20	78	49	65	.385	.540
Prado,Martin	L	.310	29	9	1	0	1	7	4	5	.394	.448
Bats Right	R	.154	13	2	0	1	0	2	1	2	.214	.308
Pratt,Todd	L	.176	68	12	5	0	4	12	8	25	.260	.426
Bats Right	R	.239	67	16	1	0	0	7	4	18	.284	.254
Pride,Curtis	L	.000	2	0	0	0	0	0	0	1	.000	.000
Bats Left	R	.240	25	6	2	0	1	2	6	7	.387	.440
Pujols,Albert	L	.336	137	46	9	0	10	26	24	10	.435	.620
Bats Right	R	.329	398	131	24	1	39	111	68	40	.429	.688
Punto,Nick	L	.331	163	54	6	3	0	12	16	15	.392	.405
Bats Both	R	.267	296	79	15	4	1	33	31	53	.330	.355
Quentin,Carlos	L	.171	41	7	2	1	2	10	4	8	.277	.415
Bats Right	R	.280	125	35	11	2	7	22	11	26	.364	.568
Quinlan,Robb	L	.326	138	45	8	0	7	19	6	17	.356	.536
Bats Right	R	.313	96	30	3	1	2	13	1	11	.327	.427

Batters vs. Left-Handed and Right-Handed Pitchers

Batter	vs	Avg	AB	H	2B	3B	HR	RBI	BB	SO	OBP	Slg
Quintanilla,Omar	L	.250	4	1	0	0	0	0	0	1	.250	.250
Bats Left	R	.167	30	5	1	1	0	3	3	8	.242	.267
Quintero,Humberto	L	.571	7	4	1	0	0	2	1	0	.625	.714
Bats Right	R	.214	14	3	1	0	0	0	0	3	.214	.286
Quiroz,Guillermo	L	-	0	0	0	0	0	0	0	0	-	-
Bats Right	R	.000	2	0	0	0	0	0	0	2	.000	.000
Rabe,Josh	L	.375	24	9	1	0	2	5	2	2	.423	.667
Bats Right	R	.200	25	5	0	0	1	2	0	9	.200	.320
Rabelo,Mike	L	.000	1	0	0	0	0	0	0	1	.000	.000
Bats Both	R	-	0	0	0	0	0	0	0	0	-	
Ramirez,Aramis	L	.261	142	37	8	1	9	32	17	21	.345	.521
Bats Right	R	.301	452	136	30	3	29	87	33	42	.354	.573
Ramirez,Hanley	L	.307	153	47	15	5	6	19	19	28	.385	.588
Bats Right	R	.288	480	138	31	6	11	40	37	100	.342	.446
Ramirez,Manny	L	.326	132	43	9	0	10	35	39	27	.477	.621
Bats Right	R	.319	317	101	18	1	25	67	61	75	.422	.618
Randa,Joe	L	.275	69	19	3	0	1	11	4	7	.307	.362
Bats Right	R	.263	137	36	10	0	3	17	12	19	.320	.401
Redmond,Mike	L	.443	70	31	7	0	0	9	3	1	.467	.543
Bats Right	R	.275	109	30	6	0	0	14	1	17	.298	.330
Reed,Eric	L	.000	1	0	0	0	0	0	0	1	.500	.000
Bats Left	R	.100	40	4	0	0	0	0	2	9	.163	.100
Reed,Jeremy	L	.000	23	0	0	0	0	0	1	6	.042	.000
Bats Left	R	.243	189	46	6	5	6	17	10	25	.286	.423
Reese,Kevin	L	-	0	0	0	0	0	0	0	0	1.000	
Bats Left	R	.417	12	5	0	0	0	1	1	1	.462	.417
Renteria,Edgar	L	.333	132	44	14	0	4	15	20	20	.418	.530
Bats Right	R	.281	466	131	26	2	10	55	42	69	.344	.410
Repko,Jason	L	.239	46	11	1	1	3	8	8	7	.375	.500
Bats Right	R	.262	84	22	4	0	0	8	7	17	.326	.310
Restovich,Mike	L	.222	9	2	1	0	0	1	0	3	.222	.333
Bats Right	R	.000	3	0	0	0	0	0	0	2	.250	.000
Reyes,Jose	L	.330	182	60	9	3	6	25	14	20	.378	.511
Bats Both	R	.288	465	134	21	14	13	56	39	61	.345	.477
Reyes,Jose A	L	.000	2	0	0	0	0	0	0	1	.000	.000
Bats Both	R	.333	3	1	0	0	0	2	0	2	.333	.333
Riggans,Shawn	L	.000	10	0	0	0	0	0	1	3	.091	.000
Bats Right	R	.263	19	5	1	0	0	1	3	4	.364	.316
Rios,Alex	L	.295	122	36	9	1	6	29	10	23	.341	.533
Bats Right	R	.305	328	100	24	5	11	53	25	66	.353	.509
Rivera,Juan	L	.351	134	47	11	0	7	27	7	14	.380	.590
Bats Right	R	.293	314	92	16	0	16	58	26	45	.355	.497
Rivera,Mike	L	.226	31	7	1	0	0	5	2	4	.273	.258
Bats Right	R	.279	111	31	8	0	6	19	8	17	.339	.514
Rivera,Rene	L	.087	23	2	0	0	1	2	1	9	.125	.217
Bats Right	R	.171	76	13	4	0	1	2	2	20	.203	.263
Roberson,Chris	L	.111	18	2	0	0	0	1	0	6	.158	.111
Bats Both	R	.261	23	6	0	1	0	0	0	3	.261	.348
Roberts,Brian	L	.235	170	40	10	1	1	11	25	32	.332	.324
Bats Both	R	.308	393	121	24	2	9	44	30	34	.354	.448
Roberts,Dave	L	.292	65	19	2	3	0	11	2	10	.310	.415
Bats Left	R	.293	434	127	16	10	2	33	49	51	.367	.389
Roberts,Ryan	L	-	0	0	0	0	0	0	0	0	-	-
Bats Right	R	.077	13	1	0	0	1	1	1	4	.143	.308
Robinson,Kerry	L	.182	11	2	0	0	0	0	0	1	.182	.182
Bats Left	R	.283	53	15	2	1	0	5	1	6	.296	.358
Robles,Oscar	L	.000	4	0	0	0	0	0	1	2	.200	.000
Bats Left	R	.172	29	5	0	1	0	0	4	3	.273	.241
Rodriguez,Alex	L	.294	136	40	6	1	10	30	33	29	.434	.574
Bats Right	R	.289	436	126	20	0	25	91	57	110	.377	.507
Rodriguez,Ivan	L	.340	156	53	11	0	5	22	12	28	.385	.506
Bats Right	R	.284	391	111	17	4	8	47	14	58	.310	.409
Rodriguez,John	L	.308	13	4	1	1	1	2	3	6	.471	.769
Bats Left	R	.300	170	51	11	2	1	17	18	39	.366	.406
Rodriguez,Luis	L	.250	24	6	0	0	0	1	3	3	.333	.250
Bats Both	R	.231	91	21	4	0	2	5	11	13	.311	.341
Rogers,Eddie	L	.154	13	2	0	0	0	1	0	1	.143	.154
Bats Right	R	.250	12	3	0	0	0	1	0	2	.250	.250
Rolen,Scott	L	.259	143	37	12	1	5	17	18	18	.335	.462
Bats Right	R	.310	378	117	36	0	17	78	38	51	.381	.540
Rollins,Jimmy	L	.277	177	49	9	2	9	17	11	18	.335	.503
Bats Both	R	.277	512	142	36	7	16	66	42	62	.333	.469
Rose,Mike	L	.000	2	0	0	0	0	0	0	0	.000	.000
Bats Both	R	.286	7	2	0	0	0	0	0	0	.286	.286
Ross,Cody	L	.245	102	25	6	1	9	28	8	25	.300	.588
Bats Right	R	.216	167	36	6	1	4	18	14	40	.289	.335
Ross,Dave	L	.316	76	24	4	1	11	19	12	22	.404	.829
Bats Right	R	.228	171	39	11	0	10	33	25	53	.330	.468
Rottino,Vinny	L	.143	7	1	1	0	0	1	1	0	.250	.286
Bats Right	R	.286	7	2	0	0	0	0	0	2	.286	.286
Rouse,Mike	L	.200	5	1	0	0	0	0	1	1	.333	.200
Bats Left	R	.316	19	6	3	0	0	2	0	3	.350	.474
Rowand,Aaron	L	.222	99	22	7	0	5	16	9	18	.304	.444
Bats Right	R	.275	306	84	17	3	7	31	9	58	.326	.418
Ruiz,Carlos	L	.263	19	5	0	1	1	1	3	2	.364	.526
Bats Right	R	.260	50	13	1	0	2	9	2	6	.296	.400
Saenz,Olmedo	L	.397	58	23	5	0	5	22	8	16	.457	.741
Bats Right	R	.248	121	30	10	0	6	26	6	31	.313	.479
Salazar,Jeffrey	L	.000	2	0	0	0	0	0	0	1	.000	.000
Bats Left	R	.294	51	15	4	0	1	8	11	15	.422	.431
Salmon,Tim	L	.298	104	31	5	1	7	15	15	19	.392	.567
Bats Right	R	.234	107	25	3	1	2	12	14	25	.331	.336
Sanchez,Angel	L	.250	12	3	0	0	0	0	0	3	.250	.250
Bats Right	R	.200	15	3	0	0	0	1	0	5	.188	.200
Sanchez,Freddy	L	.442	129	57	10	1	2	20	7	14	.460	.581
Bats Right	R	.316	453	143	43	1	4	65	24	38	.355	.442
Sanders,Reggie	L	.268	97	26	8	0	3	16	19	23	.385	.443
Bats Right	R	.237	228	54	15	1	8	33	9	63	.266	.417
Sandoval,Danny	L	.286	14	4	0	0	0	0	2	1	.375	.286
Bats Both	R	.167	24	4	1	0	0	4	2	2	.222	.208
Santiago,Ramon	L	.208	24	5	1	0	0	1	0	5	.208	.250
Bats Both	R	.232	56	13	0	1	0	2	1	9	.259	.268
Santos,Chad	L	.667	3	2	0	0	0	0	0	0	.667	.667
Bats Left	R	.250	4	1	0	0	1	2	1	2	.400	1.000
Schneider,Brian	L	.271	107	29	5	0	0	16	5	22	.304	.318
Bats Left	R	.251	303	76	13	0	4	39	33	45	.325	.333
Schumaker,Skip	L	.000	9	0	0	0	0	0	0	2	.000	.000
Bats Left	R	.222	45	10	1	0	1	2	5	4	.300	.311
Scott,Luke	L	.240	50	12	2	1	1	6	11	17	.397	.380
Bats Left	R	.366	164	60	17	5	9	31	19	26	.435	.695
Scutaro,Marco	L	.218	78	17	4	0	2	10	15	19	.340	.346
Bats Right	R	.279	287	80	17	6	3	31	35	47	.353	.411
Sexson,Richie	L	.204	137	28	11	0	7	20	25	40	.325	.438
Bats Right	R	.282	454	128	29	0	27	87	39	114	.342	.524
Shealy,Ryan	L	.185	54	10	5	0	1	6	7	17	.279	.333
Bats Right	R	.311	148	46	7	1	6	31	8	37	.354	.493
Sheffield,Gary	L	.344	32	11	0	0	2	8	4	1	.417	.531
Bats Right	R	.286	119	34	5	0	4	17	9	15	.338	.429
Shelton,Chris	L	.276	98	27	4	1	3	10	14	25	.377	.429
Bats Right	R	.273	275	75	12	3	13	37	20	82	.326	.480
Shoppach,Kelly	L	.314	35	11	5	0	2	7	3	10	.368	.629
Bats Right	R	.213	75	16	1	0	1	9	5	35	.263	.267
Sierra,Ruben	L	.250	8	2	0	0	0	2	0	1	.250	.250
Bats Both	R	.150	20	3	1	0	0	2	4	6	.280	.200
Simon,Randall	L	-	0	0	0	0	0	0	0	0	-	-
Bats Left	R	.238	21	5	0	0	0	2	2	6	.304	.238
Sizemore,Grady	L	.214	220	47	13	2	10	25	19	54	.290	.427
Bats Left	R	.329	435	143	40	9	18	51	59	99	.416	.586
Sledge,Terrmel	L	.400	5	2	0	0	0	1	0	1	.400	.400
Bats Left	R	.215	65	14	3	0	2	6	8	16	.301	.354
Smith,Jason	L	.400	5	2	0	0	2	3	2	0	.571	1.600
Bats Left	R	.255	94	24	1	0	3	10	5	29	.307	.362
Snelling,Chris	L	.091	11	1	0	0	0	0	1	2	.231	.182
Bats Left	R	.271	85	23	5	1	3	8	12	36	.376	.459
Snow,J.T.	L	.333	6	2	0	0	0	1	2	2	.500	.333
Bats Left	R	.184	87	16	3	0	0	8	6	31	.311	.184
Snyder,Chris	L	.246	65	16	3	0	2	15	10	11	.333	.385
Bats Right	R	.294	119	35	6	0	4	17	12	28	.358	.445
Soriano,Alfonso	L	.293	167	49	10	1	12	23	29	43	.401	.581
Bats Right	R	.280	480	130	31	1	34	72	38	117	.333	.552
Soto,Geovany	L	.133	15	2	0	0	0	1	0	3	.133	.133
Bats Right	R	.300	10	3	1	0	0	1	0	3	.364	.400
Spiezio,Scott	L	.318	85	27	2	1	0	10	8	14	.372	.365
Bats Both	R	.251	191	48	13	3	13	42	29	52	.363	.555
Spilborghs,Ryan	L	.323	62	20	3	0	1	6	5	9	.362	.419
Bats Right	R	.267	105	28	3	3	3	15	9	21	.322	.438
Stairs,Matt	L	.217	46	10	2	0	1	6	4	13	.265	.326
Bats Left	R	.252	302	76	19	0	12	45	38	73	.337	.434
Stern,Adam	L	.000	1	0	0	0	0	0	0	0	.000	.000
Bats Left	R	.158	19	3	1	0	0	4	0	4	.200	.211
Stewart,Chris	L	.000	2	0	0	0	0	0	0	0	.000	.000
Bats Right	R	.000	6	0	0	0	0	0	0	1	.000	.000

Batters vs. Left-Handed and Right-Handed Pitchers

Batter	vs	Avg	AB	H	2B	3B	HR	RBI	BB	SO	OBP	Slg
Stewart,Shannon	L	.288	52	15	2	0	0	4	7	7	.373	.327
Bats Right	R	.295	122	36	3	1	2	17	7	12	.336	.385
Stinnett,Kelly	L	.200	30	6	3	0	1	6	4	12	.294	.400
Bats Right	R	.213	61	13	0	0	0	3	1	21	.238	.213
Sullivan,Cory	L	.280	25	7	1	1	1	4	2	9	.310	.520
Bats Left	R	.266	361	96	25	9	1	26	30	91	.322	.393
Suzuki,Ichiro	L	.352	176	62	5	3	2	8	11	15	.397	.449
Bats Left	R	.312	519	162	15	6	7	41	38	56	.361	.405
Sweeney,Mark	L	.135	37	5	0	0	0	2	4	12	.238	.135
Bats Left	R	.270	222	60	15	2	5	35	24	38	.345	.423
Sweeney,Mike	L	.266	64	17	3	0	2	7	10	12	.365	.406
Bats Right	R	.255	153	39	12	0	6	26	18	36	.343	.451
Sweeney,Ryan	L	.286	7	2	0	0	0	0	0	3	.286	.286
Bats Left	R	.214	28	6	0	0	0	5	0	4	.214	.214
Swisher,Nick	L	.291	141	41	6	0	8	26	25	29	.406	.504
Bats Both	R	.241	415	100	18	2	27	69	72	123	.360	.489
Taguchi,So	L	.280	157	44	12	1	1	21	14	20	.337	.389
Bats Right	R	.252	159	40	7	0	1	10	18	28	.333	.314
Tatis,Fernando	L	.286	28	8	2	1	2	7	3	4	.333	.643
Bats Right	R	.214	28	6	4	0	0	1	3	13	.290	.357
Taveras,Willy	L	.254	118	30	5	1	0	6	9	18	.318	.314
Bats Left	R	.285	411	117	14	4	1	24	25	70	.338	.345
Teahen,Mark	L	.274	106	29	10	3	2	15	8	26	.333	.481
Bats Left	R	.296	287	85	11	4	16	54	32	59	.366	.530
Teixeira,Mark	L	.302	169	51	14	0	12	32	20	42	.379	.598
Bats Both	R	.275	459	126	31	1	21	78	69	86	.369	.484
Tejada,Miguel	L	.335	161	54	9	0	6	23	12	19	.375	.503
Bats Right	R	.329	487	160	28	0	18	77	34	60	.381	.497
Terrero,Luis	L	.182	33	6	1	0	1	2	0	6	.206	.303
Bats Right	R	.286	7	2	0	0	0	4	1	1	.375	.286
Thames,Marcus	L	.238	130	31	8	2	8	19	17	31	.331	.515
Bats Right	R	.266	218	58	12	0	18	41	20	61	.335	.569
Theriot,Ryan	L	.346	52	18	4	1	1	6	11	3	.460	.519
Bats Right	R	.317	82	26	7	2	2	10	6	15	.378	.524
Thomas,Frank	L	.245	106	26	4	0	9	18	31	23	.429	.538
Bats Right	R	.278	360	100	7	0	30	96	50	58	.365	.547
Thome,Jim	L	.236	191	45	6	0	6	24	31	66	.354	.361
Bats Left	R	.321	299	96	20	0	36	85	76	81	.454	.749
Thompson,Kevin	L	.182	11	2	0	0	0	0	4	6	.400	.182
Bats Right	R	.368	19	7	3	0	1	6	2	3	.429	.684
Thorman,Scott	L	.189	37	7	4	0	1	3	2	11	.231	.378
Bats Left	R	.253	91	23	7	0	4	11	3	10	.277	.462
Thurston,Joe	L	-	0	0	0	0	0	0	0	0	-	-
Bats Left	R	.222	18	4	1	0	0	0	1	2	.300	.278
Tiffee,Terry	L	.200	15	3	0	0	1	1	1	2	.250	.400
Bats Both	R	.267	30	8	1	0	1	5	3	6	.333	.400
Torrealba,Yorvit	L	.246	57	14	5	1	2	15	2	8	.283	.474
Bats Right	R	.247	166	41	11	2	5	28	9	41	.296	.428
Tracy,Chad	L	.231	182	42	9	0	4	23	13	48	.281	.346
Bats Left	R	.304	415	126	32	0	16	57	41	81	.370	.496
Treanor,Matt	L	.268	41	11	2	1	0	3	4	8	.348	.366
Bats Right	R	.216	116	25	4	0	2	11	15	26	.321	.302
Tucker,Michael	L	.294	17	5	2	0	0	2	3	3	.429	.412
Bats Left	R	.154	39	6	2	0	1	4	13	11	.358	.282
Tulowitzki,Troy	L	.150	20	3	1	0	0	0	2	5	.227	.200
Bats Right	R	.263	76	20	1	0	1	6	8	20	.311	.316
Tyner,Jason	L	.269	52	14	0	0	0	5	1	9	.283	.269
Bats Left	R	.325	166	54	5	2	0	13	10	9	.363	.380
Uggla,Dan	L	.307	153	47	11	0	4	13	12	25	.363	.458
Bats Right	R	.273	458	125	15	7	23	77	36	98	.331	.487
Upton,B.J.	L	.298	47	14	1	0	1	5	2	10	.327	.383
Bats Right	R	.227	128	29	4	0	0	5	11	30	.293	.258
Uribe,Juan	L	.224	192	43	12	1	4	27	5	41	.241	.359
Bats Right	R	.244	271	66	16	1	17	44	8	41	.268	.498
Utley,Chase	L	.301	216	65	14	3	5	24	25	63	.394	.463
Bats Left	R	.312	442	138	26	1	27	78	38	69	.371	.559
Valentin,Javier	L	.111	18	2	0	0	0	2	4	6	.273	.111
Bats Both	R	.286	168	48	6	1	8	25	9	23	.318	.476
Valentin,Jose	L	.219	96	21	6	0	2	11	12	18	.300	.344
Bats Both	R	.288	288	83	18	3	16	51	25	54	.341	.538
Varitek,Jason	L	.229	131	30	7	1	4	15	13	35	.299	.389
Bats Both	R	.244	234	57	12	1	8	40	33	52	.339	.406
Vazquez,Ramon	L	.286	7	2	1	0	0	0	0	3	.286	.429
Bats Left	R	.200	60	12	1	0	1	8	6	15	.265	.267
Vento,Mike	L	.250	8	2	1	0	0	0	2	1	.400	.375
Bats Right	R	.300	10	3	0	0	0	1	2	4	.417	.300
Victorino,Shane	L	.273	132	36	9	1	3	16	5	16	.340	.424
Bats Both	R	.293	283	83	10	7	3	30	19	38	.349	.410
Vidro,Jose	L	.323	133	43	7	0	3	13	10	15	.372	.444
Bats Both	R	.276	330	91	19	1	4	34	31	33	.339	.376
Vizcaino,Jose	L	.214	42	9	1	0	1	3	8	6	.340	.310
Bats Both	R	.240	100	24	5	0	1	5	9	8	.303	.320
Vizquel,Omar	L	.340	141	48	7	0	0	7	19	10	.423	.390
Bats Both	R	.281	438	123	15	10	4	51	37	41	.340	.388
Walker,Todd	L	.204	108	22	3	0	3	16	19	10	.320	.315
Bats Left	R	.302	334	101	19	2	6	37	36	28	.368	.425
Ward,Daryle	L	.059	17	1	0	0	0	0	2	10	.158	.059
Bats Left	R	.345	113	39	10	0	7	26	13	17	.412	.619
Watson,Brandon	L	.000	4	0	0	0	0	0	0	1	.000	.000
Bats Left	R	.208	24	5	0	0	0	0	1	2	.240	.208
Weeks,Rickie	L	.271	70	19	5	0	3	9	9	21	.369	.471
Bats Right	R	.280	289	81	10	3	5	25	21	71	.361	.388
Wells,Vernon	L	.333	156	52	9	0	6	24	15	22	.392	.506
Bats Right	R	.292	455	133	31	5	26	82	39	68	.346	.554
White,Rondell	L	.271	107	29	6	0	2	12	4	12	.301	.383
Bats Right	R	.235	230	54	11	1	5	26	7	42	.264	.357
Widger,Chris	L	.154	52	8	2	0	0	1	6	13	.237	.192
Bats Right	R	.195	41	8	1	0	1	8	5	11	.277	.293
Wigginton,Ty	L	.316	117	37	8	0	5	21	13	29	.385	.513
Bats Right	R	.260	327	85	17	1	19	58	19	68	.310	.492
Wilkerson,Brad	L	.190	63	12	2	0	2	8	7	25	.278	.317
Bats Left	R	.230	257	59	13	2	13	36	30	91	.313	.447
Williams,Bernie	L	.323	133	43	9	0	7	26	14	11	.387	.549
Bats Both	R	.261	287	75	20	0	5	35	19	42	.305	.383
Willingham,Josh	L	.299	134	40	8	1	11	26	23	25	.411	.619
Bats Right	R	.269	368	99	20	1	15	48	31	84	.334	.451
Willits,Reggie	L	.083	12	1	0	0	0	0	4	1	.313	.083
Bats Both	R	.333	33	11	1	0	0	2	7	9	.450	.364
Wilson,Craig	L	.278	133	37	6	1	7	24	12	38	.347	.496
Bats Right	R	.235	226	53	9	1	10	25	16	84	.294	.416
Wilson,Jack	L	.301	153	46	4	0	3	8	11	13	.348	.386
Bats Right	R	.262	390	102	23	1	5	27	22	52	.304	.364
Wilson,Preston	L	.292	113	33	3	1	6	22	12	27	.362	.496
Bats Right	R	.255	388	99	22	1	11	50	17	94	.290	.402
Wilson,Vance	L	.326	43	14	4	0	1	6	2	13	.356	.488
Bats Right	R	.266	109	29	5	0	4	12	0	20	.283	.422
Winn,Randy	L	.219	155	34	12	0	4	16	10	14	.280	.374
Bats Both	R	.278	418	116	22	5	7	40	38	49	.341	.404
Wise,Dewayne	L	.000	0	0	0	0	0	0	0	0	.000	.000
Bats Left	R	.206	34	7	2	0	0	1	0	5	.206	.265
Witt,Kevin	L	.167	6	1	0	0	0	0	0	1	.167	.167
Bats Left	R	.145	55	8	2	0	2	5	0	20	.145	.291
Womack,Tony	L	.250	16	4	0	0	0	0	1	4	.294	.250
Bats Left	R	.269	52	14	3	0	1	5	7	3	.356	.385
Wood,Jason	L	.500	4	2	0	0	0	1	0	2	.500	.500
Bats Right	R	.444	9	4	2	0	0	1	0	1	.500	.667
Woodward,Chris	L	.226	93	21	4	0	2	12	11	23	.302	.333
Bats Right	R	.209	129	27	6	1	1	13	12	32	.280	.295
Wright,David	L	.285	165	47	13	1	6	28	27	29	.385	.485
Bats Right	R	.321	417	134	27	4	20	88	39	84	.380	.549
Youkilis,Kevin	L	.270	163	44	10	1	3	19	33	33	.392	.399
Bats Right	R	.283	406	115	32	1	10	53	58	88	.376	.441
Young,Chris	L	.360	25	9	3	0	1	6	1	2	.385	.600
Bats Right	R	.178	45	8	1	0	1	4	5	10	.269	.267
Young,Delmon	L	.379	29	11	4	0	1	2	0	4	.379	.621
Bats Right	R	.299	97	29	5	1	2	8	1	20	.324	.433
Young,Delwyn	L	-	0	0	0	0	0	0	0	0	-	-
Bats Both	R	.000	5	0	0	0	0	0	0	0	.000	.000
Young,Dmitri	L	.136	22	3	1	0	0	1	2	7	.208	.182
Bats Both	R	.267	150	40	3	1	7	22	9	32	.306	.440
Young,Eric	L	.268	71	19	4	1	3	12	5	8	.329	.479
Bats Right	R	.134	67	9	2	0	0	3	9	9	.231	.164
Young,Michael	L	.295	166	49	16	0	4	17	15	24	.352	.464
Bats Right	R	.320	525	168	36	3	10	86	33	72	.357	.457
Zaun,Gregg	L	.373	51	19	7	0	2	6	10	2	.492	.627
Bats Both	R	.251	239	60	12	0	10	34	31	40	.333	.427
Zimmerman,Ryan	L	.280	150	42	13	0	4	25	21	25	.364	.447
Bats Right	R	.289	464	134	34	3	16	85	40	95	.346	.478
Zobrist,Ben	L	.212	52	11	3	1	0	4	1	5	.226	.308
Bats Both	R	.229	131	30	3	1	2	14	9	21	.273	.313
AL	L	.271	—	—	—	—	—	—	—	—	.340	.432
	R	.276	—	—	—	—	—	—	—	—	.339	.439

Pitchers vs. Left-Handed and Right-Handed Batters

Batter	vs	Avg	AB	H	2B	3B	HR	RBI	BB	SO	OBP	Slg
NL	L	.265	—	—	—	—	—	—	—	—	.339	.426
	R	.264	—	—	—	—	—	—	—	—	.332	.428

Pitchers vs. Left-Handed and Right-Handed Batters

Pitcher	vs	Avg	AB	H	2B	3B	HR	RBI	BB	SO	OBP	Slg
Aardsma,David	L	.190	63	12	2	0	2	6	10	15	.297	.317
Throws Right	R	.225	129	29	3	0	7	19	18	34	.320	.411
Abreu,Winston	L	.286	14	4	2	0	1	4	5	1	.474	.643
Throws Right	R	.300	20	6	4	0	0	2	1	5	.348	.500
Accardo,Jeremy	L	.241	108	26	4	0	3	12	13	25	.322	.361
Throws Right	R	.307	163	50	11	1	4	34	7	29	.331	.460
Adams,Mike	L	.000	5	0	0	0	0	0	1	1	.167	.000
Throws Right	R	.667	6	4	1	0	1	6	1	0	.714	1.333
Adkins,Jon	L	.287	87	25	3	1	1	14	12	10	.370	.379
Throws Right	R	.259	116	30	11	0	2	11	8	20	.315	.405
Affeldt,Jeremy	L	.212	113	24	5	1	5	19	18	17	.321	.407
Throws Left	R	.289	270	78	13	0	8	50	37	31	.374	.426
Albers,Matt	L	.333	27	9	3	0	0	4	7	6	.471	.444
Throws Right	R	.267	30	8	1	0	1	5	0	5	.267	.400
Alfonseca,Antonio	L	.452	31	14	1	0	3	8	3	0	.486	.774
Throws Right	R	.257	35	9	3	0	0	3	4	5	.333	.343
Alvarez,Abe	L	1.000	4	4	0	0	2	4	1	0	1.000	2.500
Throws Left	R	.111	9	1	1	0	0	0	1	2	.200	.222
Andrade,Steve	L	.286	7	2	0	0	0	2	2	3	.444	.286
Throws Right	R	.273	11	3	0	0	0	0	2	2	.385	.273
Aquino,Greg	L	.280	93	26	5	0	2	13	11	20	.362	.398
Throws Right	R	.286	98	28	6	0	6	17	13	31	.386	.531
Armas Jr.,Tony	L	.274	274	75	12	1	8	37	35	40	.360	.412
Throws Right	R	.284	324	92	22	2	11	49	29	57	.357	.466
Arroyo,Bronson	L	.283	449	127	25	3	22	57	37	61	.341	.499
Throws Right	R	.205	463	95	16	0	9	36	27	123	.252	.298
Asencio,Miguel	L	.133	15	2	1	0	0	3	2	3	.235	.200
Throws Right	R	.412	17	7	3	0	1	5	2	4	.500	.765
Astacio,Ezequiel	L	.182	11	2	1	0	0	0	2	2	.308	.273
Throws Right	R	.385	13	5	0	0	2	4	4	4	.529	.846
Astacio,Pedro	L	.270	174	47	9	4	7	30	18	23	.332	.489
Throws Right	R	.330	188	62	15	0	7	27	13	19	.374	.521
Backe,Brandon	L	.317	82	26	8	0	1	7	12	7	.400	.451
Throws Right	R	.205	83	17	4	0	3	11	6	12	.280	.361
Baek,Cha Seung	L	.211	57	12	3	0	3	8	9	6	.318	.421
Throws Right	R	.206	68	14	1	0	3	5	4	17	.270	.353
Baez,Danys	L	.295	105	31	10	0	2	15	10	15	.358	.448
Throws Right	R	.244	119	29	7	0	1	22	7	24	.308	.328
Bajenaru,Jeff	L	.667	3	2	0	0	1	1	0	0	.667	1.667
Throws Right	R	.500	4	2	0	0	2	3	0	0	.500	2.000
Baker,Scott	L	.349	175	61	14	2	9	31	12	25	.382	.606
Throws Right	R	.299	177	53	10	1	8	28	4	37	.326	.503
Bannister,Brian	L	.286	77	22	3	1	2	12	11	10	.359	.429
Throws Right	R	.185	65	12	3	1	2	6	11	9	.321	.354
Barry,Kevin	L	.194	36	7	3	0	0	3	8	9	.333	.278
Throws Right	R	.288	59	17	5	2	2	13	6	10	.358	.542
Barzilla,Phil	L	-	0	0	0	0	0	0	0	0	-	-
Throws Left	R	.500	2	1	0	0	0	0	0	0	.500	.500
Batista,Miguel	L	.321	383	123	24	6	10	50	55	61	.405	.493
Throws Right	R	.257	420	108	19	1	8	51	29	49	.312	.364
Bauer,Rick	L	.231	104	24	8	1	1	14	11	16	.311	.356
Throws Right	R	.299	164	49	5	1	3	24	14	19	.355	.396
Bautista,Denny	L	.272	81	22	6	1	1	11	7	13	.333	.407
Throws Right	R	.294	85	25	6	0	4	19	14	14	.408	.506
Bayliss,Jonah	L	.176	17	3	0	0	0	3	4	3	.333	.176
Throws Right	R	.270	37	10	2	0	1	6	7	12	.391	.405
Beam,T.J.	L	.357	28	10	7	0	2	6	5	5	.471	.821
Throws Right	R	.327	49	16	5	1	3	9	1	7	.353	.653
Bean,Colter	L	.333	3	1	0	0	0	2	2	0	.500	.333
Throws Right	R	.333	3	1	1	0	0	0	0	1	.500	.667
Beckett,Josh	L	.251	390	98	21	2	20	60	46	76	.330	.469
Throws Right	R	.238	390	93	23	2	16	49	28	82	.304	.431
Bedard,Erik	L	.204	152	31	5	0	1	9	22	36	.309	.257
Throws Left	R	.271	608	165	26	3	15	75	47	135	.326	.398
Beimel,Joe	L	.232	95	22	5	0	2	8	5	16	.267	.347
Throws Left	R	.279	172	48	14	0	5	21	16	14	.337	.448
Belisle,Matt	L	.245	49	12	1	0	2	7	3	9	.315	.388
Throws Right	R	.292	106	31	7	0	3	12	16	17	.384	.443
Bell,Heath	L	.308	65	20	4	0	0	10	8	18	.384	.369
Throws Right	R	.348	89	31	3	0	6	16	3	17	.370	.584
Benitez,Armando	L	.270	63	17	2	1	2	5	16	14	.413	.429
Throws Right	R	.265	83	22	2	0	4	12	5	17	.300	.434
Benoit,Joaquin	L	.191	115	22	3	0	3	9	19	34	.306	.296
Throws Right	R	.245	188	46	8	0	2	35	19	51	.319	.319
Benson,Kris	L	.303	350	106	20	0	21	56	36	42	.370	.540
Throws Right	R	.270	344	93	17	1	12	43	22	46	.313	.430

Pitcher	vs	Avg	AB	H	2B	3B	HR	RBI	BB	SO	OBP	Slg
Bergmann,Jason	L	.257	109	28	5	4	5	19	19	21	.362	.514
Throws Right	R	.351	151	53	13	2	7	29	8	33	.401	.603
Bernero,Adam	L	.243	37	9	1	0	3	7	2	11	.282	.514
Throws Right	R	.448	29	13	6	0	0	3	0	1	.448	.655
Betancourt,Rafael	L	.221	86	19	6	0	1	12	8	17	.281	.326
Throws Right	R	.254	130	33	5	0	6	16	3	31	.271	.431
Billingsley,Chad	L	.328	174	57	6	1	2	20	35	25	.443	.408
Throws Right	R	.213	164	35	9	0	5	14	23	34	.317	.360
Birkins,Kurt	L	.212	52	11	3	0	1	5	5	14	.300	.327
Throws Left	R	.230	61	14	1	0	3	7	11	13	.351	.393
Blanton,Joe	L	.314	357	112	17	4	7	41	27	44	.361	.443
Throws Right	R	.304	424	129	33	0	10	55	31	63	.353	.453
Bonderman,Jeremy	L	.284	405	115	27	8	11	52	42	88	.350	.472
Throws Right	R	.235	422	99	20	2	7	43	22	114	.275	.341
Bonser,Boof	L	.251	183	46	8	1	9	16	14	46	.305	.454
Throws Right	R	.280	207	58	12	0	9	29	10	38	.314	.469
Booker,Chris	L	.200	10	2	1	0	0	0	3	3	.385	.300
Throws Right	R	.333	24	8	1	0	4	7	1	4	.360	.875
Bootcheck,Chris	L	.250	20	5	0	0	1	3	3	4	.348	.400
Throws Right	R	.458	24	11	4	0	2	10	6	3	.567	.875
Borkowski,Dave	L	.259	108	28	10	1	3	9	13	20	.336	.454
Throws Right	R	.256	164	42	10	2	5	31	10	32	.297	.433
Borowski,Joe	L	.167	120	20	2	1	3	10	28	35	.324	.275
Throws Right	R	.291	148	43	11	1	4	18	5	29	.323	.459
Bowie,Micah	L	.273	22	6	1	0	0	1	1	2	.304	.318
Throws Left	R	.111	45	5	2	0	1	1	6	9	.216	.222
Boyer,Blaine	L	.750	4	3	0	0	0	0	1	0	.800	.750
Throws Right	R	.500	2	1	0	0	0	2	0	0	.500	.500
Bradford,Chad	L	.262	61	16	5	0	0	4	6	13	.328	.344
Throws Right	R	.251	171	43	9	0	1	24	7	32	.276	.322
Braun,Ryan	L	.357	14	5	1	0	1	2	1	1	.400	.643
Throws Right	R	.296	27	8	2	1	1	5	2	5	.333	.556
Bray,Bill	L	.329	79	26	4	0	1	10	6	15	.376	.418
Throws Left	R	.254	122	31	9	0	4	22	12	24	.324	.426
Brazelton,Dewon	L	.361	36	13	0	0	3	9	5	4	.419	.611
Throws Right	R	.349	43	15	4	1	3	13	4	5	.404	.698
Brazoban,Yhency	L	.333	9	3	1	0	0	0	2	2	.455	.444
Throws Right	R	.364	11	4	1	0	0	5	0	2	.333	.455
Breslow,Craig	L	.316	19	6	3	0	0	2	1	6	.350	.474
Throws Left	R	.222	27	6	2	0	0	4	5	6	.343	.296
Brito,Eude	L	.238	21	5	2	0	0	5	1	7	.261	.333
Throws Left	R	.320	50	16	6	0	2	11	11	2	.452	.560
Britton,Chris	L	.301	73	22	4	1	0	8	9	15	.378	.384
Throws Right	R	.186	129	24	3	2	4	16	8	26	.232	.333
Brocail,Doug	L	.280	50	14	1	0	0	6	6	5	.357	.300
Throws Right	R	.228	57	13	6	0	1	7	2	14	.250	.386
Brower,Jim	L	.342	38	13	5	1	1	14	5	7	.432	.605
Throws Right	R	.396	48	19	5	0	1	10	9	7	.516	.563
Brown,Andrew	L	.286	14	4	1	0	0	1	4	5	.444	.357
Throws Right	R	.095	21	2	0	0	0	1	4	2	.269	.095
Broxton,Jonathan	L	.244	119	29	6	2	4	14	23	43	.366	.429
Throws Right	R	.196	163	32	6	0	3	14	10	54	.246	.288
Bruney,Brian	L	.115	26	3	0	0	0	1	8	9	.343	.115
Throws Right	R	.229	48	11	3	0	1	6	7	16	.327	.354
Buchholz,Taylor	L	.249	205	51	14	1	11	38	15	34	.296	.488
Throws Right	R	.248	226	56	13	1	10	32	19	43	.310	.447
Buehrle,Mark	L	.238	160	38	4	0	8	24	6	23	.282	.413
Throws Left	R	.322	649	209	44	2	28	95	42	75	.362	.525
Bulger,Jason	L	.333	3	1	0	0	0	0	2	0	.600	.333
Throws Right	R	.000	3	0	0	0	0	1	1	1	.250	.000
Burgos,Ambiorix	L	.345	119	41	5	2	10	30	18	33	.436	.672
Throws Right	R	.249	169	42	6	1	6	27	19	39	.333	.402
Burnett,A.J.	L	.263	281	74	18	0	4	22	27	63	.337	.370
Throws Right	R	.264	242	64	18	0	10	38	12	55	.307	.463
Burns,Mike	L	.303	33	10	3	0	1	5	1	7	.324	.485
Throws Right	R	.484	62	30	7	1	1	15	3	9	.507	.677
Burres,Brian	L	.071	14	1	0	0	0	0	0	3	.071	.071
Throws Left	R	.313	16	5	0	0	1	3	1	3	.353	.500
Bush,David	L	.258	395	102	34	1	11	50	25	96	.304	.433
Throws Right	R	.246	403	99	17	2	15	57	13	70	.294	.409
Byrd,Paul	L	.369	347	128	20	5	12	57	27	23	.413	.559
Throws Right	R	.256	407	104	18	2	14	57	11	65	.282	.413
Byrdak,Tim	L	.381	21	8	4	0	0	5	2	0	.435	.571
Throws Left	R	.545	11	6	2	0	2	6	6	2	.706	1.273
Cabrera,Daniel	L	.231	273	63	13	1	5	30	49	78	.349	.341
Throws Right	R	.251	267	67	14	1	6	38	55	79	.379	.378

Pitchers vs. Left-Handed and Right-Handed Batters

Pitcher	vs	Avg	AB	H	2B	3B	HR	RBI	BB	SO	OBP	Slg
Cabrera,Fernando	L	.235	81	19	3	0	4	13	19	21	.376	.420
Throws Right	R	.248	137	34	7	1	8	24	13	50	.312	.489
Cain,Matt	L	.217	373	81	20	5	10	44	54	93	.318	.378
Throws Right	R	.227	335	76	18	2	8	36	33	86	.300	.364
Calero,Kiko	L	.278	72	20	2	0	2	5	14	25	.395	.389
Throws Right	R	.208	144	30	2	3	2	20	10	42	.258	.306
Camp,Shawn	L	.370	100	37	13	1	2	15	9	10	.432	.580
Throws Right	R	.284	197	56	5	0	7	32	10	43	.330	.416
Campbell,Brett	L	.300	10	3	0	0	1	3	1	2	.364	.600
Throws Right	R	.167	6	1	0	1	0	2	1	2	.375	.500
Campillo,Jorge	L	.250	4	1	0	0	0	1	0	0	.250	.250
Throws Right	R	.429	7	3	3	0	0	2	0	1	.429	.857
Capellan,Jose	L	.248	101	25	6	1	5	12	16	15	.353	.475
Throws Right	R	.242	165	40	11	2	6	26	15	43	.311	.442
Capps,Matt	L	.250	100	25	5	1	4	12	4	26	.279	.440
Throws Right	R	.275	204	56	12	0	8	38	8	30	.309	.451
Capuano,Chris	L	.273	154	42	7	0	3	20	2	32	.289	.377
Throws Left	R	.264	709	187	59	2	26	87	45	142	.311	.463
Carmona,Fausto	L	.299	134	40	7	1	4	18	18	18	.377	.455
Throws Right	R	.298	161	48	8	0	5	21	13	40	.372	.441
Carpenter,Chris	L	.266	365	97	19	3	10	36	23	83	.314	.416
Throws Right	R	.210	462	97	19	0	11	41	20	101	.252	.323
Carrara,Giovanni	L	.157	51	8	3	1	1	4	5	13	.232	.314
Throws Right	R	.333	57	19	3	1	4	14	2	12	.367	.632
Carrasco,Hector	L	.249	173	43	9	1	4	19	13	31	.309	.382
Throws Right	R	.240	208	50	9	1	6	22	14	41	.295	.380
Carter,Lance	L	.429	21	9	3	0	0	3	2	1	.458	.571
Throws Right	R	.286	28	8	2	0	1	6	6	4	.400	.464
Casilla,Santiago	L	.400	5	2	1	0	0	1	1	1	.500	.600
Throws Right	R	.000	3	0	0	0	0	0	1	1	.250	.000
Cassidy,Scott	L	.237	59	14	2	1	2	11	4	16	.286	.407
Throws Right	R	.255	98	25	7	1	6	17	15	33	.357	.531
Castro,Fabio	L	.071	28	2	0	0	0	3	4	4	.182	.071
Throws Left	R	.205	78	16	5	0	1	7	9	14	.300	.308
Chacin,Gustavo	L	.268	71	19	4	0	7	10	7	12	.350	.620
Throws Left	R	.266	267	71	21	2	12	38	31	35	.351	.494
Chacon,Shawn	L	.307	199	61	17	2	11	41	35	33	.413	.578
Throws Right	R	.273	231	63	15	1	12	33	28	29	.361	.502
Chen,Bruce	L	.328	125	41	5	1	10	26	9	21	.368	.624
Throws Left	R	.337	285	96	15	0	18	44	26	49	.389	.579
Chick,Travis	L	.500	10	5	1	0	0	1	4	1	.643	.600
Throws Right	R	.182	11	2	1	0	0	3	6	1	.471	.273
Childers,Jason	L	.357	14	5	0	0	1	2	1	2	.400	.571
Throws Right	R	.333	21	7	0	0	0	5	3	3	.400	.333
Choate,Randy	L	.294	34	10	3	1	0	3	3	9	.368	.441
Throws Left	R	.314	35	11	2	0	0	3	0	3	.351	.371
Chulk,Vinnie	L	.206	63	13	3	0	1	7	6	14	.271	.302
Throws Right	R	.282	117	33	5	0	5	27	14	29	.370	.453
Claussen,Brandon	L	.164	55	9	4	0	1	6	3	15	.242	.291
Throws Left	R	.331	254	84	18	0	13	42	25	42	.396	.555
Clemens,Roger	L	.254	185	47	11	2	2	13	17	44	.324	.368
Throws Right	R	.185	227	42	8	0	5	18	12	58	.231	.286
Clement,Matt	L	.307	140	43	7	0	5	26	21	12	.401	.464
Throws Right	R	.272	125	34	8	0	3	19	17	31	.381	.408
Coffey,Todd	L	.344	96	33	6	1	3	10	11	15	.411	.521
Throws Right	R	.243	214	52	10	3	4	24	16	45	.300	.374
Colome,Jesus	L	-	0	0	0	0	0	0	1	0	1.000	-
Throws Right	R	.000	1	0	0	0	0	0	0	0	.000	.000
Colon,Bartolo	L	.354	113	40	8	0	6	18	7	19	.398	.584
Throws Right	R	.261	119	31	8	0	5	16	4	12	.290	.454
Colon,Roman	L	.271	59	16	3	2	1	3	6	7	.338	.441
Throws Right	R	.323	93	30	6	0	5	15	8	18	.375	.548
Condrey,Clay	L	.383	47	18	4	0	2	7	3	9	.412	.596
Throws Right	R	.270	63	17	4	0	1	4	6	7	.333	.381
Contreras,Jose	L	.267	326	87	13	3	8	35	38	63	.339	.399
Throws Right	R	.248	432	107	21	4	12	55	17	71	.290	.398
Cook,Aaron	L	.314	449	141	31	7	13	51	36	43	.370	.501
Throws Right	R	.258	391	101	12	2	4	42	19	49	.294	.330
Corcoran,Roy	L	.625	16	10	0	1	1	6	2	2	.667	.938
Throws Right	R	.154	13	2	0	0	0	4	2	4	.250	.154
Corcoran,Tim	L	.281	167	47	12	0	6	28	27	27	.384	.461
Throws Right	R	.262	172	45	13	2	4	17	21	32	.345	.430
Cordero,Chad	L	.219	128	28	8	1	4	10	14	35	.297	.391
Throws Right	R	.212	146	31	4	1	9	18	8	34	.263	.438
Cordero,Francisco	L	.286	119	34	6	2	4	19	23	30	.408	.471
Throws Right	R	.219	160	35	6	0	3	20	9	54	.256	.313

Pitcher	vs	Avg	AB	H	2B	3B	HR	RBI	BB	SO	OBP	Slg
Corey,Bryan	L	.225	71	16	4	1	1	7	5	18	.282	.352
Throws Right	R	.257	74	19	7	0	0	11	10	10	.345	.351
Cormier,Lance	L	.271	133	36	3	1	4	15	25	21	.389	.398
Throws Right	R	.351	154	54	15	2	4	18	14	22	.400	.552
Cormier,Rheal	L	.286	84	24	5	1	4	15	6	9	.341	.512
Throws Left	R	.250	96	24	6	0	1	15	11	10	.339	.344
Corpas,Manuel	L	.281	64	18	4	1	1	4	2	10	.303	.422
Throws Right	R	.290	62	18	5	0	2	8	6	17	.371	.468
Correia,Kevin	L	.275	109	30	6	1	2	20	12	19	.339	.404
Throws Right	R	.218	156	34	14	0	3	15	10	38	.276	.365
Cortes,David	L	.279	43	12	1	0	1	7	4	4	.333	.372
Throws Right	R	.329	70	23	3	0	2	9	2	10	.351	.457
Cotts,Neal	L	.263	99	26	4	2	5	23	5	29	.318	.495
Throws Left	R	.314	121	38	9	1	7	18	19	14	.404	.579
Crain,Jesse	L	.259	116	30	2	0	3	10	8	21	.304	.353
Throws Right	R	.263	186	49	11	2	3	30	10	39	.307	.392
Cruceta,Francisco	L	.200	10	2	1	0	0	2	3	2	.357	.300
Throws Right	R	.471	17	8	2	0	2	7	3	0	.550	.941
Cruz,Juan	L	.263	167	44	11	0	5	24	23	33	.359	.419
Throws Right	R	.199	181	36	9	2	2	18	24	55	.319	.304
Daigle,Casey	L	.375	24	9	1	0	1	4	1	3	.385	.542
Throws Right	R	.238	21	5	0	0	0	1	5	4	.385	.238
Davies,Kyle	L	.333	144	48	7	2	9	33	21	28	.417	.597
Throws Right	R	.331	127	42	12	0	5	19	12	23	.397	.543
Davis,Doug	L	.314	191	60	14	1	4	32	16	44	.365	.461
Throws Left	R	.251	582	146	28	3	15	77	86	115	.349	.387
Davis,Jason	L	.316	79	25	6	1	0	13	7	8	.364	.418
Throws Right	R	.294	143	42	8	1	1	24	7	29	.335	.385
Day,Zach	L	.348	69	24	2	0	2	11	11	5	.444	.464
Throws Right	R	.284	95	27	3	1	3	14	10	14	.361	.432
de la Rosa,Jorge	L	.262	61	16	2	0	4	14	13	9	.395	.492
Throws Left	R	.266	244	65	12	0	10	23	41	58	.370	.439
DeJean,Mike	L	.000	2	0	0	0	0	0	1	0	.333	.000
Throws Right	R	.250	4	1	0	0	0	0	1	0	.400	.250
Delcarmen,Manny	L	.319	94	30	6	3	1	23	12	15	.398	.479
Throws Right	R	.302	126	38	3	2	1	17	5	30	.333	.381
Demaria,Chris	L	.263	19	5	2	0	3	6	5	5	.417	.842
Throws Right	R	.161	31	5	1	0	1	4	4	6	.297	.290
Dempster,Ryan	L	.307	127	39	7	2	2	17	19	33	.392	.441
Throws Right	R	.228	167	38	5	0	3	23	17	34	.307	.311
Dessens,Elmer	L	.264	121	32	5	1	1	18	12	19	.328	.347
Throws Right	R	.293	184	54	5	1	7	28	10	33	.333	.446
Devine,Joey	L	.333	12	4	0	0	0	4	5	6	.529	.333
Throws Right	R	.286	14	4	1	0	1	5	4	4	.474	.571
Diaz,Joselo	L	.333	12	4	0	0	1	6	4	1	.500	.583
Throws Right	R	.353	17	6	1	0	1	3	4	2	.500	.588
Dickey,R.A.	L	.000	3	0	0	0	0	0	1	1	.250	.000
Throws Right	R	.571	14	8	0	0	6	7	0	0	.571	1.857
DiNardo,Lenny	L	.383	47	18	3	1	1	8	1	5	.400	.553
Throws Left	R	.355	121	43	11	0	5	20	19	12	.443	.570
Dohmann,Scott	L	.357	56	20	1	0	7	15	18	13	.514	.750
Throws Right	R	.293	133	39	9	2	2	20	15	31	.382	.436
Donnelly,Brendan	L	.290	100	29	0	2	4	12	19	21	.415	.450
Throws Right	R	.204	142	29	5	0	4	17	9	32	.255	.324
Dotel,Octavio	L	.333	18	6	1	0	0	5	3	1	.429	.389
Throws Right	R	.414	29	12	3	1	2	8	8	6	.526	.793
Downs,Scott	L	.232	95	22	8	0	2	11	8	23	.298	.379
Throws Left	R	.258	198	51	13	0	7	23	22	38	.333	.429
Drese,Ryan	L	.250	8	2	0	0	0	2	0	3	.250	.250
Throws Right	R	.304	23	7	3	0	0	5	8	2	.484	.435
DuBose,Eric	L	.400	5	2	0	0	1	3	1	1	.500	1.000
Throws Left	R	.533	15	8	1	0	1	3	2	1	.588	.800
Duchscherer,Justin	L	.248	101	25	4	0	1	4	5	27	.283	.317
Throws Right	R	.241	112	27	2	0	3	10	4	24	.274	.339
Duckworth,Brandon	L	.232	69	16	2	0	0	10	12	14	.341	.261
Throws Right	R	.390	118	46	14	0	3	20	12	13	.451	.585
Duke,Zach	L	.264	144	38	6	0	2	13	12	30	.338	.347
Throws Left	R	.310	699	217	54	3	15	87	56	87	.362	.461
Dunn,Scott	L	.438	16	7	2	0	0	0	2	3	.550	.563
Throws Right	R	.435	23	10	4	0	2	10	2	1	.480	.870
Durbin,Chad	L	.286	7	2	0	0	0	0	0	1	.286	.286
Throws Right	R	.235	17	4	1	0	1	2	0	2	.235	.471
Eaton,Adam	L	.320	125	40	8	1	8	19	13	19	.393	.592
Throws Right	R	.279	136	38	5	0	3	18	11	24	.340	.382
Eischen,Joey	L	.087	23	2	1	0	1	5	6	9	.267	.261
Throws Left	R	.421	38	16	2	0	1	15	13	9	.566	.553

Pitchers vs. Left-Handed and Right-Handed Batters

Pitcher	vs	Avg	AB	H	2B	3B	HR	RBI	BB	SO	OBP	Slg
Elarton,Scott	L	.253	194	49	10	0	12	24	32	17	.360	.490
Throws Right	R	.278	245	68	17	1	14	37	20	32	.343	.527
Embree,Alan	L	.240	104	25	5	1	1	11	8	25	.295	.337
Throws Left	R	.258	97	25	4	1	3	18	7	28	.299	.412
Erickson,Scott	L	.333	21	7	0	0	0	5	4	1	.440	.333
Throws Right	R	.240	25	6	2	0	2	5	3	1	.387	.560
Escobar,Kelvim	L	.258	345	89	13	2	15	50	30	60	.320	.438
Throws Right	R	.270	381	103	25	0	2	28	20	87	.309	.352
Estes,Shawn	L	.000	1	0	0	0	0	0	1	0	.667	.000
Throws Left	R	.227	22	5	0	0	0	2	2	4	.292	.227
Etherton,Seth	L	.231	13	3	1	0	0	2	4	4	.389	.308
Throws Right	R	.368	19	7	1	0	3	7	2	0	.409	.895
Eveland,Dana	L	.419	43	18	5	0	2	14	5	14	.490	.674
Throws Left	R	.280	75	21	3	0	2	10	11	18	.396	.400
Eyre,Scott	L	.281	89	25	3	0	6	16	12	32	.359	.517
Throws Left	R	.255	141	36	6	1	5	16	18	41	.335	.418
Eyre,Willie	L	.379	103	39	9	1	5	19	14	6	.458	.631
Throws Right	R	.257	140	36	10	0	3	14	8	20	.312	.393
Falkenborg,Brian	L	.250	8	2	0	0	0	2	0	3	.250	.250
Throws Right	R	.200	15	3	1	0	0	0	0	2	.250	.267
Farnsworth,Kyle	L	.215	107	23	6	0	3	11	6	42	.263	.355
Throws Right	R	.264	148	39	4	0	5	25	22	33	.355	.392
Fassero,Jeff	L	.333	21	7	2	0	1	4	4	3	.440	.571
Throws Left	R	.381	42	16	1	1	3	9	4	4	.426	.667
Feierabend,Ryan	L	.231	13	3	1	0	0	1	0	1	.231	.308
Throws Left	R	.231	52	12	2	0	3	6	7	10	.322	.442
Feldman,Scott	L	.280	50	14	2	0	2	7	3	13	.357	.440
Throws Right	R	.259	108	28	3	0	2	14	7	17	.308	.343
Feliciano,Pedro	L	.231	117	27	4	0	2	11	5	44	.272	.316
Throws Left	R	.266	109	29	3	0	2	10	15	10	.354	.349
Fernandez,Jared	L	.375	16	6	1	1	2	5	1	1	.412	.938
Throws Right	R	.357	14	5	2	0	0	4	0	0	.357	.500
Field,Nate	L	.417	12	5	2	0	2	4	4	2	.563	1.083
Throws Right	R	.174	23	4	1	1	0	11	1	12	.208	.304
Flores,Randy	L	.258	93	24	3	0	2	15	10	23	.337	.355
Throws Left	R	.329	76	25	5	2	3	15	12	17	.416	.566
Flores,Ron	L	.323	31	10	1	0	1	7	2	11	.364	.452
Throws Left	R	.228	79	18	7	1	2	11	8	9	.292	.418
Floyd,Gavin	L	.306	98	30	10	1	6	19	20	11	.417	.612
Throws Right	R	.323	124	40	9	0	8	21	12	23	.387	.589
Fogg,Josh	L	.309	330	102	24	5	11	49	43	37	.389	.512
Throws Right	R	.291	357	104	24	5	13	49	17	56	.329	.496
Fortunato,Bartolome	L	.667	6	4	1	0	1	2	2	0	.750	1.333
Throws Right	R	.333	9	3	1	0	1	4	0	0	.400	.778
Fossum,Casey	L	.271	85	23	5	0	3	14	17	17	.410	.435
Throws Left	R	.263	429	113	22	2	15	62	46	71	.345	.429
Foulke,Keith	L	.301	103	31	9	0	6	15	3	18	.324	.563
Throws Right	R	.236	89	21	6	0	3	11	4	18	.268	.404
Francis,Jeff	L	.245	147	36	7	2	2	14	9	24	.319	.361
Throws Left	R	.252	600	151	39	5	16	71	60	93	.322	.413
Francisco,Frank	L	.000	12	0	0	0	0	0	1	2	.077	.000
Throws Right	R	.444	18	8	1	0	2	2	1	4	.474	.833
Franklin,Ryan	L	.265	98	26	8	2	2	6	19	13	.390	.449
Throws Right	R	.294	204	60	14	1	11	35	14	30	.345	.534
Franklin,Wayne	L	.308	13	4	1	0	1	2	2	2	.375	.615
Throws Left	R	.286	14	4	1	0	1	2	4	1	.421	.571
Frasor,Jason	L	.211	71	15	3	0	3	10	7	21	.282	.380
Throws Right	R	.262	122	32	3	0	5	22	10	30	.321	.410
Fruto,Emiliano	L	.267	45	12	2	0	0	5	10	9	.393	.311
Throws Right	R	.237	93	22	4	0	4	18	14	25	.349	.409
Fuentes,Brian	L	.183	60	11	0	0	4	9	4	28	.246	.383
Throws Left	R	.218	179	39	13	1	4	15	22	45	.319	.369
Fulchino,Jeff	L	-	0	0	0	0	0	0	0	0	-	-
Throws Right	R	.000	1	0	0	0	0	0	1	0	.500	.000
Fultz,Aaron	L	.268	97	26	5	1	0	24	7	29	.315	.340
Throws Left	R	.298	181	54	15	3	7	34	21	33	.369	.530
Gabbard,Kason	L	.250	20	5	0	0	0	3	6	8	.423	.250
Throws Left	R	.257	74	19	5	0	0	3	10	7	.345	.324
Gagne,Eric	L	.000	3	0	0	0	0	0	0	2	.000	.000
Throws Right	R	.000	3	0	0	0	0	0	1	1	.400	.000
Gallo,Mike	L	.360	25	9	1	0	0	3	1	3	.370	.400
Throws Left	R	.422	45	19	3	0	3	7	6	4	.509	.689
Garcia,Freddy	L	.262	397	104	18	3	9	41	27	62	.309	.390
Throws Right	R	.271	458	124	28	2	23	63	21	73	.308	.491
Garcia,Jose	L	.267	30	8	2	0	1	4	3	4	.333	.433
Throws Right	R	.154	13	2	1	0	0	1	2	4	.267	.231

Pitcher	vs	Avg	AB	H	2B	3B	HR	RBI	BB	SO	OBP	Slg
Garland,Jon	L	.290	359	104	17	4	10	39	19	50	.328	.443
Throws Right	R	.297	481	143	34	1	16	61	22	62	.329	.472
Garza,Matt	L	.245	102	25	7	0	1	14	13	21	.325	.343
Throws Right	R	.356	104	37	7	2	5	18	10	17	.409	.606
Gaudin,Chad	L	.261	92	24	4	3	2	7	19	7	.387	.435
Throws Right	R	.196	138	27	6	0	1	13	23	29	.309	.261
Geary,Geoff	L	.348	138	48	8	1	5	17	10	23	.396	.529
Throws Right	R	.249	221	55	5	1	1	16	10	37	.295	.294
German,Franklyn	L	.235	17	4	1	0	1	2	10	1	.519	.471
Throws Right	R	.125	24	3	1	0	0	3	4	5	.276	.167
Germano,Justin	L	.000	6	0	0	0	0	0	2	2	.250	.000
Throws Right	R	.381	21	8	1	0	1	4	1	6	.435	.571
Glavine,Tom	L	.202	168	34	9	0	3	12	13	40	.276	.310
Throws Left	R	.286	588	168	35	3	19	68	49	91	.339	.452
Gobble,Jimmy	L	.255	102	26	6	1	6	23	3	36	.276	.510
Throws Left	R	.294	235	69	19	0	6	29	26	44	.366	.451
Gonzalez,Edgar	L	.259	85	22	5	0	5	10	7	12	.312	.494
Throws Right	R	.288	80	23	9	1	2	10	2	16	.329	.500
Gonzalez,Enrique	L	.288	184	53	7	1	4	37	18	22	.350	.402
Throws Right	R	.265	230	61	10	2	10	32	16	44	.321	.457
Gonzalez,Geremi	L	.437	87	38	9	2	5	22	6	11	.468	.759
Throws Right	R	.237	139	33	9	0	5	21	17	33	.325	.410
Gonzalez,Mike	L	.163	43	7	1	0	1	4	5	16	.265	.256
Throws Left	R	.227	154	35	5	0	0	10	26	48	.341	.260
Gordon,Tom	L	.185	108	20	2	1	3	11	11	42	.258	.306
Throws Right	R	.277	119	33	6	0	6	18	11	26	.344	.479
Gorzelanny,Tom	L	.234	47	11	5	0	1	7	4	8	.321	.404
Throws Left	R	.224	174	39	8	0	2	18	27	32	.329	.305
Gosling,Mike	L	.000	1	0	0	0	0	0	1	1	.667	.000
Throws Left	R	.250	4	1	0	0	1	1	0	0	.250	1.000
Grabow,John	L	.275	91	25	5	0	2	10	6	30	.337	.396
Throws Left	R	.251	171	43	10	2	5	20	24	36	.340	.421
Graves,Danny	L	.348	23	8	1	1	0	0	3	1	.423	.478
Throws Right	R	.278	36	10	1	0	3	13	2	2	.308	.556
Green,Sean	L	.190	42	8	3	0	1	4	9	10	.346	.333
Throws Right	R	.325	80	26	5	0	1	10	4	5	.360	.425
Gregg,Kevin	L	.298	131	39	5	2	5	20	13	34	.359	.481
Throws Right	R	.268	183	49	7	0	5	22	8	37	.303	.388
Greinke,Zack	L	.400	10	4	0	0	0	1	2	2	.500	.400
Throws Right	R	.200	15	3	0	0	1	2	1	3	.250	.400
Grilli,Jason	L	.292	65	19	6	3	0	9	10	11	.382	.477
Throws Right	R	.249	169	42	6	0	6	25	15	20	.323	.391
Grimsley,Jason	L	.271	48	13	1	0	0	7	5	3	.340	.292
Throws Right	R	.288	59	17	4	0	4	13	3	7	.323	.559
Gryboski,Kevin	L	.500	16	8	1	0	2	6	1	1	.529	.938
Throws Right	R	.400	15	6	0	0	1	5	1	3	.471	.600
Guardado,Eddie	L	.234	47	11	3	0	1	4	1	12	.265	.362
Throws Left	R	.327	101	33	5	0	9	19	12	27	.395	.644
Guerrier,Matt	L	.333	108	36	7	1	3	14	12	16	.400	.500
Throws Right	R	.256	164	42	2	0	6	16	9	21	.288	.378
Guthrie,Jeremy	L	.394	33	13	5	0	0	6	11	5	.545	.545
Throws Right	R	.256	43	11	3	0	2	9	4	9	.347	.465
Guzman,Angel	L	.305	82	25	5	1	5	12	19	20	.453	.573
Throws Right	R	.309	139	43	8	1	4	26	18	40	.391	.468
Haeger,Charlie	L	.118	17	2	1	0	0	4	5	6	.318	.176
Throws Right	R	.204	49	10	0	1	0	7	8	13	.316	.245
Halama,John	L	.318	44	14	2	1	0	4	5	4	.388	.409
Throws Left	R	.329	73	24	3	0	6	20	8	8	.390	.616
Halladay,Roy	L	.259	394	102	21	2	9	38	13	56	.288	.391
Throws Right	R	.244	435	106	14	3	10	40	21	76	.279	.359
Halsey,Brad	L	.317	104	33	7	1	4	15	14	16	.405	.519
Throws Left	R	.277	271	75	11	0	7	37	32	37	.358	.395
Hamels,Cole	L	.207	92	19	6	0	4	10	9	28	.277	.402
Throws Left	R	.244	401	98	20	5	15	53	39	117	.310	.431
Hammel,Jason	L	.372	86	32	6	1	5	22	12	16	.444	.640
Throws Right	R	.299	97	29	9	1	2	14	9	16	.358	.474
Hammond,Chris	L	.286	49	14	1	0	3	9	0	10	.286	.490
Throws Left	R	.314	70	22	5	0	2	8	5	13	.360	.471
Hampson,Justin	L	.364	11	4	2	0	0	4	1	4	.462	.545
Throws Left	R	.349	43	15	3	2	3	9	4	5	.404	.721
Hamulack,Tim	L	.295	44	13	4	0	4	14	8	16	.426	.659
Throws Left	R	.250	92	23	4	0	3	14	14	18	.349	.391
Hancock,Josh	L	.239	117	28	10	1	4	20	8	15	.286	.444
Throws Right	R	.241	174	42	11	1	5	25	15	35	.301	.402
Hansack,Devern	L	.235	17	4	1	0	1	1	0	3	.235	.471
Throws Right	R	.111	18	2	0	0	1	1	1	5	.158	.278

Pitchers vs. Left-Handed and Right-Handed Batters

Pitcher	vs	Avg	AB	H	2B	3B	HR	RBI	BB	SO	OBP	Slg
Hansen,Craig	L	.344	64	22	5	0	3	12	3	10	.371	.563
Throws Right	R	.276	87	24	5	0	2	12	12	20	.379	.402
Harang,Aaron	L	.267	374	100	25	5	10	39	27	107	.318	.441
Throws Right	R	.270	526	142	29	0	18	59	29	109	.313	.428
Harden,Rich	L	.176	91	16	2	0	3	9	15	25	.287	.297
Throws Right	R	.211	71	15	3	0	2	8	11	24	.325	.338
Haren,Danny	L	.246	407	100	21	3	14	45	28	82	.296	.415
Throws Right	R	.268	462	124	22	3	17	54	17	94	.305	.439
Harper,Travis	L	.400	60	24	6	0	3	10	4	12	.438	.650
Throws Right	R	.322	118	38	9	1	3	20	9	20	.377	.492
Harris,Jeff	L	.000	4	0	0	0	0	0	0	0	.000	.000
Throws Right	R	.375	8	3	1	0	0	0	0	1	.375	.500
Harville,Chad	L	.284	67	19	3	0	3	9	9	12	.368	.463
Throws Right	R	.272	92	25	2	0	2	23	13	18	.358	.359
Hawkins,LaTroy	L	.323	99	32	8	2	2	12	10	12	.385	.505
Throws Right	R	.285	144	41	5	1	2	15	5	15	.305	.375
Heilman,Aaron	L	.231	147	34	4	2	2	14	22	35	.337	.327
Throws Right	R	.231	169	39	9	0	3	26	6	38	.260	.337
Helling,Rick	L	.250	48	12	8	0	2	8	10	11	.373	.542
Throws Right	R	.171	76	13	3	0	4	10	5	21	.220	.368
Hendrickson,Ben	L	.571	21	12	4	0	0	8	6	2	.643	.762
Throws Right	R	.265	34	9	2	0	0	8	3	6	.324	.324
Hendrickson,Mark	L	.287	129	37	6	0	2	14	16	25	.370	.380
Throws Left	R	.264	515	136	25	0	15	62	46	74	.326	.400
Henn,Sean	L	.357	14	5	0	0	1	1	0	1	.357	.571
Throws Left	R	.261	23	6	2	0	1	2	5	6	.400	.478
Hennessey,Brad	L	.230	148	34	9	2	5	20	23	16	.335	.419
Throws Right	R	.265	219	58	12	0	7	30	19	26	.347	.416
Hensley,Clay	L	.263	327	86	20	2	4	29	36	59	.337	.373
Throws Right	R	.239	368	88	17	1	11	48	40	63	.316	.380
Herges,Matt	L	.300	140	42	12	0	2	19	11	19	.359	.429
Throws Right	R	.340	153	52	8	1	3	35	17	17	.407	.464
Hermanson,Dustin	L	.167	12	2	1	0	1	1	0	2	.167	.500
Throws Right	R	.308	13	4	2	0	1	4	1	3	.400	.692
Hernandez,Felix	L	.281	388	109	21	1	18	65	34	91	.340	.479
Throws Right	R	.241	357	86	15	1	5	31	26	85	.300	.331
Hernandez,Livan	L	.302	427	129	17	4	15	55	46	58	.370	.466
Throws Right	R	.275	426	117	22	4	14	66	32	70	.325	.444
Hernandez,Orlando	L	.298	329	98	25	4	15	55	36	55	.373	.535
Throws Right	R	.200	285	57	15	2	7	26	25	109	.278	.340
Hernandez,Roberto	L	.293	99	29	7	0	3	12	20	19	.408	.455
Throws Right	R	.218	147	32	3	2	2	18	12	29	.281	.306
Hernandez,Runelvys	L	.325	191	62	12	0	12	42	26	20	.397	.576
Throws Right	R	.329	252	83	10	0	10	38	22	30	.391	.488
Hill,Rich	L	.262	61	16	3	1	2	3	9	17	.357	.443
Throws Left	R	.220	304	67	18	0	14	42	30	73	.292	.418
Hill,Shawn	L	.324	74	24	7	1	2	12	7	7	.386	.527
Throws Right	R	.268	71	19	2	1	0	4	5	9	.333	.324
Hirsh,Jason	L	.211	71	15	3	0	4	7	16	16	.360	.423
Throws Right	R	.303	109	33	5	0	7	17	6	13	.350	.541
Hoey,James	L	.375	16	6	3	1	1	8	3	1	.500	.875
Throws Right	R	.348	23	8	1	0	0	5	2	5	.385	.391
Hoffman,Trevor	L	.194	103	20	5	0	2	6	10	24	.272	.301
Throws Right	R	.214	131	28	3	0	4	9	3	26	.231	.328
Holtz,Mike	L	.333	3	1	0	0	0	1	1	0	.600	.333
Throws Left	R	.500	4	2	1	1	0	2	3	2	.714	1.250
Howell,J.P.	L	.400	40	16	3	0	1	3	2	6	.429	.550
Throws Left	R	.281	128	36	4	1	3	16	12	27	.352	.398
Howry,Bob	L	.247	89	22	3	0	3	6	8	23	.309	.382
Throws Right	R	.244	197	48	7	1	5	30	9	48	.283	.365
Huber,Jonathan	L	.067	15	1	0	0	0	0	1	4	.125	.067
Throws Right	R	.209	43	9	1	1	0	5	5	7	.292	.279
Hudson,Luke	L	.258	190	49	12	2	2	22	19	29	.330	.374
Throws Right	R	.293	205	60	9	2	5	26	19	35	.355	.429
Hudson,Tim	L	.281	434	122	23	9	17	74	44	58	.353	.493
Throws Right	R	.265	426	113	23	0	8	43	35	83	.325	.376
Hughes,Travis	L	.182	22	4	1	0	1	4	5	1	.345	.364
Throws Right	R	.450	20	9	2	0	1	5	1	3	.522	.700
Humber,Philip	L	.000	4	0	0	0	0	0	1	2	.200	.000
Throws Right	R	.000	2	0	0	0	0	0	0	0	.000	.000
Isringhausen,Jason	L	.270	89	24	4	0	4	13	19	22	.404	.449
Throws Right	R	.187	123	23	3	0	6	19	19	30	.299	.358
Jackson,Edwin	L	.233	60	14	5	1	0	12	14	13	.382	.350
Throws Right	R	.333	84	28	5	1	2	16	11	14	.406	.488
Jackson,Zach	L	.333	39	13	2	0	2	6	3	1	.409	.538
Throws Left	R	.294	119	35	8	1	4	17	11	21	.361	.479

Pitcher	vs	Avg	AB	H	2B	3B	HR	RBI	BB	SO	OBP	Slg
James,Chuck	L	.281	96	27	6	1	3	7	12	20	.364	.458
Throws Left	R	.218	339	74	15	1	17	43	35	71	.296	.419
Janssen,Casey	L	.292	168	49	10	1	5	20	14	16	.351	.452
Throws Right	R	.261	207	54	10	1	7	29	7	28	.300	.420
Jarvis,Kevin	L	.327	52	17	7	0	1	11	6	6	.410	.519
Throws Right	R	.348	66	23	7	2	2	16	5	7	.384	.606
Jenks,Bobby	L	.227	97	22	4	0	0	9	14	26	.319	.268
Throws Right	R	.268	164	44	10	0	5	23	17	54	.344	.421
Jennings,Jason	L	.254	378	96	18	7	6	32	62	66	.356	.386
Throws Right	R	.261	422	110	18	1	11	53	23	76	.302	.386
Jimenez,Cesar	L	.167	6	1	0	0	1	3	2	1	.375	.667
Throws Left	R	.429	28	12	4	0	3	10	2	2	.467	.893
Jimenez,Ubaldo	L	.182	11	2	0	0	0	0	1	1	.250	.182
Throws Right	R	.188	16	3	0	0	1	2	2	2	.278	.375
Johnson,Jason	L	.380	221	84	19	3	7	37	15	23	.416	.588
Throws Right	R	.297	256	76	12	0	7	37	20	31	.351	.426
Johnson,Jim	L	.375	8	3	0	0	0	2	1	0	.500	.375
Throws Right	R	.750	8	6	3	0	1	6	2	0	.727	1.500
Johnson,Josh	L	.246	276	68	8	2	7	30	35	59	.338	.366
Throws Right	R	.227	300	68	16	3	7	32	33	74	.305	.370
Johnson,Randy	L	.191	110	21	3	2	1	8	6	32	.254	.282
Throws Left	R	.259	667	173	36	1	27	106	54	140	.318	.438
Johnson,Tyler	L	.221	77	17	2	2	3	19	11	24	.330	.416
Throws Left	R	.276	58	16	2	0	2	11	12	13	.417	.414
Jones,Greg	L	.000	5	0	0	0	0	2	2	0	.222	.000
Throws Right	R	.444	18	8	1	1	1	3	0	1	.421	.778
Jones,Todd	L	.264	106	28	1	1	1	14	7	14	.313	.321
Throws Right	R	.284	148	42	6	3	3	16	4	14	.312	.426
Julio,Jorge	L	.185	124	23	5	0	6	12	17	38	.284	.371
Throws Right	R	.234	124	29	7	2	4	18	18	50	.336	.419
Karsay,Steve	L	.444	18	8	1	0	2	6	1	2	.450	.833
Throws Right	R	.263	19	5	0	1	2	2	2	3	.364	.684
Karstens,Jeff	L	.253	79	20	3	0	1	4	6	10	.306	.329
Throws Right	R	.233	86	20	6	1	5	14	5	6	.277	.500
Kazmir,Scott	L	.227	97	22	1	2	2	12	8	24	.283	.340
Throws Left	R	.242	454	110	28	3	13	42	44	139	.310	.403
Keisler,Randy	L	.353	17	6	2	0	0	4	1	3	.389	.471
Throws Left	R	.348	23	8	3	0	3	4	1	2	.375	.870
Kennedy,Joe	L	.326	43	14	2	2	0	3	3	12	.370	.465
Throws Left	R	.220	91	20	2	0	1	5	10	17	.304	.275
Kensing,Logan	L	.218	55	12	4	0	4	9	11	15	.358	.509
Throws Right	R	.222	81	18	3	1	2	9	8	30	.308	.358
Keppel,Bobby	L	.394	66	26	5	0	5	16	6	5	.432	.697
Throws Right	R	.264	72	19	3	0	1	3	9	15	.354	.347
Kim,Byung-Hyun	L	.325	305	99	21	2	13	49	43	51	.414	.534
Throws Right	R	.265	302	80	19	2	5	41	18	78	.310	.391
Kim,Sun-Woo	L	.471	34	16	2	0	3	9	2	4	.487	.794
Throws Right	R	.296	27	8	3	0	2	9	6	4	.412	.630
King,Ray	L	.299	77	23	5	2	3	13	7	14	.360	.532
Throws Left	R	.351	94	33	3	0	3	21	13	9	.427	.479
Kinney,Josh	L	.162	37	6	1	0	2	3	6	10	.279	.351
Throws Right	R	.208	53	11	2	0	1	2	2	12	.250	.302
Kline,Steve	L	.269	93	25	4	2	0	15	10	22	.346	.355
Throws Left	R	.280	100	28	6	0	3	17	16	11	.376	.430
Kolb,Dan	L	.323	65	21	4	0	1	13	7	7	.387	.431
Throws Right	R	.260	123	32	4	2	3	20	13	19	.328	.398
Komine,Shane	L	.250	12	3	0	0	0	0	6	1	.500	.250
Throws Right	R	.280	25	7	1	0	3	5	2	0	.333	.680
Koplove,Mike	L	.250	4	1	1	0	0	0	2	1	.500	.500
Throws Right	R	.500	8	4	1	0	0	1	0	0	.500	.625
Koronka,John	L	.274	124	34	5	0	7	25	7	12	.319	.484
Throws Left	R	.300	370	111	24	3	10	52	40	49	.368	.462
Kuo,Hong-Chih	L	.236	55	13	4	0	0	4	9	21	.344	.309
Throws Left	R	.247	166	41	10	1	3	20	24	50	.344	.373
Lackey,John	L	.263	391	103	22	1	5	39	47	78	.348	.363
Throws Right	R	.230	434	100	26	1	9	55	25	112	.277	.357
Lara,Juan	L	.091	11	1	0	0	0	0	1	1	.167	.091
Throws Left	R	.429	7	3	0	0	0	2	0	1	.429	.429
League,Brandon	L	.276	58	16	2	0	1	8	3	9	.323	.362
Throws Right	R	.178	101	18	0	0	2	7	6	20	.239	.238
Ledezma,Wil	L	.241	79	19	3	1	0	12	4	14	.286	.304
Throws Left	R	.261	157	41	8	1	5	16	19	25	.343	.420
Lee,Cliff	L	.261	176	46	11	0	6	21	7	25	.302	.426
Throws Left	R	.282	631	178	36	1	23	80	51	104	.338	.452
Lehr,Justin	L	.313	32	10	1	0	1	6	1	7	.324	.438
Throws Right	R	.424	33	14	4	2	1	15	6	5	.525	.758

Pitchers vs. Left-Handed and Right-Handed Batters

Pitcher	vs	Avg	AB	H	2B	3B	HR	RBI	BB	SO	OBP	Slg
Lerew,Anthony	L	.200	5	1	1	0	0	0	1	0	.333	.400
Throws Right	R	.667	6	4	0	0	0	5	2	1	.778	.667
Lester,Jon	L	.397	58	23	6	1	3	11	4	8	.431	.690
Throws Left	R	.271	251	68	14	0	4	30	39	52	.370	.375
Lewis,Colby	L	.429	7	3	1	0	0	0	0	2	.429	.571
Throws Right	R	.500	10	5	1	0	1	4	1	3	.545	.900
Lidge,Brad	L	.286	126	36	7	2	4	18	22	42	.400	.468
Throws Right	R	.201	164	33	5	1	6	24	14	62	.277	.354
Lidle,Cory	L	.290	307	89	26	2	15	42	30	50	.360	.534
Throws Right	R	.256	360	92	16	1	15	48	28	80	.319	.431
Lieber,Jon	L	.304	339	103	17	2	16	47	15	40	.334	.507
Throws Right	R	.278	335	93	17	2	11	40	9	60	.304	.439
Lilly,Ted	L	.202	124	25	4	0	1	6	13	22	.281	.258
Throws Left	R	.265	582	154	33	2	27	72	68	138	.344	.467
Lima,Jose	L	.412	34	14	4	0	2	12	6	4	.488	.706
Throws Right	R	.262	42	11	0	1	1	7	4	8	.354	.381
Linebrink,Scott	L	.204	162	33	4	1	4	11	13	38	.263	.315
Throws Right	R	.294	126	37	5	1	5	17	9	30	.341	.468
Liriano,Francisco	L	.202	84	17	1	0	1	4	7	26	.264	.250
Throws Left	R	.206	350	72	16	0	8	27	25	118	.259	.320
Littleton,Wes	L	.256	39	10	1	1	1	5	6	4	.375	.410
Throws Right	R	.157	83	13	0	0	1	3	7	13	.222	.193
Livingston,Bobby	L	.364	11	4	0	0	0	3	1	2	.500	.364
Throws Left	R	.385	13	5	1	0	2	7	5	1	.556	.923
Loaiza,Esteban	L	.319	270	86	20	4	9	36	22	45	.369	.522
Throws Right	R	.265	351	93	17	0	8	47	18	52	.303	.382
Loe,Kameron	L	.313	166	52	11	3	4	21	10	12	.354	.488
Throws Right	R	.321	165	53	9	0	6	28	12	22	.363	.485
Loewen,Adam	L	.277	94	26	4	0	1	13	18	26	.393	.351
Throws Left	R	.254	335	85	16	1	7	47	44	72	.350	.370
Logan,Boone	L	.357	28	10	0	0	1	9	6	6	.486	.464
Throws Left	R	.244	45	11	5	0	1	12	9	9	.386	.422
Lohse,Kyle	L	.288	215	62	13	0	4	26	20	40	.353	.405
Throws Right	R	.304	289	88	16	0	11	53	24	57	.362	.474
Looper,Braden	L	.284	95	27	8	0	1	12	14	16	.369	.400
Throws Right	R	.274	179	49	9	0	2	18	6	25	.300	.358
Lopez,Javier	L	.250	32	8	1	0	0	6	6	7	.385	.281
Throws Left	R	.208	24	5	2	0	1	10	4	4	.333	.417
Lopez,Rodrigo	L	.308	389	120	20	1	15	49	32	65	.363	.481
Throws Right	R	.296	385	114	29	3	17	64	27	71	.342	.519
Lowe,Derek	L	.270	404	109	17	2	10	47	41	48	.341	.396
Throws Right	R	.255	440	112	20	0	4	35	14	75	.280	.327
Lowe,Mark	L	.167	24	4	0	0	1	2	3	9	.310	.292
Throws Right	R	.205	39	8	3	0	0	4	6	11	.311	.282
Lowry,Noah	L	.312	125	39	11	3	4	15	16	18	.407	.544
Throws Left	R	.262	484	127	23	3	17	60	40	66	.317	.428
Lugo,Ruddy	L	.213	150	32	6	1	0	18	13	27	.282	.267
Throws Right	R	.264	163	43	9	2	4	23	24	21	.359	.417
Lyon,Brandon	L	.244	123	30	8	0	4	17	13	26	.314	.407
Throws Right	R	.270	141	38	16	2	3	21	9	20	.307	.475
Mabeus,Chris	L	.000	1	0	0	0	0	0	1	1	.500	.000
Throws Right	R	.500	8	4	2	0	1	4	2	1	.600	1.125
MacDougal,Mike	L	.281	32	9	3	0	1	3	1	4	.303	.469
Throws Right	R	.171	70	12	0	0	0	4	5	17	.237	.171
Maddux,Greg	L	.254	366	93	21	2	11	44	21	52	.293	.413
Throws Right	R	.284	443	126	32	3	9	55	16	65	.307	.431
Madson,Ryan	L	.307	267	82	20	3	11	37	28	48	.381	.528
Throws Right	R	.335	281	94	19	1	9	39	22	51	.391	.505
Mahay,Ron	L	.240	96	23	7	1	4	20	14	27	.336	.458
Throws Left	R	.258	120	31	3	1	3	13	14	29	.333	.375
Maholm,Paul	L	.224	156	35	8	0	1	9	20	44	.333	.295
Throws Left	R	.316	528	167	32	3	18	79	61	73	.391	.491
Maine,John	L	.231	169	39	7	0	6	11	23	34	.323	.379
Throws Right	R	.191	157	30	9	0	9	23	10	37	.247	.420
Majewski,Gary	L	.287	108	31	6	0	2	21	9	22	.342	.398
Throws Right	R	.281	171	48	14	3	3	18	20	21	.364	.450
Manon,Julio	L	.364	33	12	3	0	2	7	7	9	.475	.636
Throws Right	R	.216	51	11	1	1	3	8	9	13	.355	.451
Marcum,Shaun	L	.303	152	46	10	2	7	19	22	23	.390	.533
Throws Right	R	.256	160	41	10	0	7	24	16	42	.335	.450
Marmol,Carlos	L	.229	105	24	5	3	8	23	21	17	.362	.562
Throws Right	R	.263	179	47	13	0	6	24	38	42	.400	.436
Maroth,Mike	L	.260	50	13	0	0	3	6	6	5	.339	.440
Throws Left	R	.305	167	51	12	2	8	17	10	19	.348	.545
Marquis,Jason	L	.288	365	105	22	5	15	57	40	46	.363	.499
Throws Right	R	.291	399	116	21	5	20	70	35	50	.364	.519

Pitcher	vs	Avg	AB	H	2B	3B	HR	RBI	BB	SO	OBP	Slg
Marshall,Sean	L	.247	81	20	0	1	6	17	10	16	.351	.494
Throws Left	R	.275	408	112	21	1	14	57	49	61	.357	.434
Marte,Damaso	L	.225	89	20	2	0	2	12	8	33	.300	.315
Throws Left	R	.258	120	31	6	1	3	18	23	30	.381	.400
Martin,Tom	L	.276	98	27	7	2	3	20	10	24	.360	.480
Throws Left	R	.255	137	35	9	2	1	19	15	22	.331	.372
Martinez,Carlos	L	.250	12	3	0	0	0	1	4	3	.412	.250
Throws Right	R	.250	24	6	1	0	0	2	2	8	.296	.292
Martinez,Pedro	L	.231	234	54	7	0	6	26	25	59	.308	.338
Throws Right	R	.211	256	54	14	1	13	39	14	78	.270	.426
Masset,Nick	L	.250	16	4	1	1	0	2	1	2	.350	.438
Throws Right	R	.357	14	5	1	0	0	2	1	2	.375	.429
Mastny,Tom	L	.273	22	6	0	0	1	6	5	4	.393	.409
Throws Right	R	.282	39	11	2	0	0	4	3	10	.341	.333
Mateo,Juan	L	.277	65	18	8	0	1	11	10	16	.377	.446
Throws Right	R	.295	112	33	3	2	5	18	13	19	.375	.491
Mateo,Julio	L	.394	71	28	4	1	2	14	12	14	.482	.563
Throws Right	R	.246	138	34	7	1	4	24	10	17	.299	.399
Mathieson,Scott	L	.279	68	19	4	1	4	16	7	17	.342	.544
Throws Right	R	.337	86	29	10	0	4	18	9	11	.406	.593
Mays,Joe	L	.298	94	28	8	1	3	22	16	11	.400	.500
Throws Right	R	.397	126	50	13	0	8	31	10	14	.435	.690
McBride,Macay	L	.187	107	20	4	1	2	10	10	30	.263	.299
Throws Left	R	.308	107	33	6	2	0	13	22	16	.426	.402
McCarthy,Brandon	L	.197	117	23	2	0	6	18	16	29	.291	.368
Throws Right	R	.270	200	54	5	3	11	31	17	40	.327	.490
McClung,Seth	L	.299	197	59	11	0	5	27	37	28	.406	.431
Throws Right	R	.289	211	61	10	0	9	41	31	31	.378	.464
McGowan,Dustin	L	.327	55	18	5	0	2	12	15	9	.472	.527
Throws Right	R	.283	60	17	3	0	0	12	10	13	.394	.333
McLeary,Marty	L	.167	30	5	0	0	1	1	3	2	.242	.267
Throws Right	R	.333	36	12	1	0	0	3	3	6	.375	.361
Meadows,Brian	L	.254	130	33	7	2	6	22	10	22	.301	.477
Throws Right	R	.361	158	57	10	0	8	34	5	13	.373	.576
Meche,Gil	L	.240	338	81	21	1	10	37	44	79	.334	.396
Throws Right	R	.271	376	102	21	3	14	49	40	77	.346	.455
Medders,Brandon	L	.348	138	48	12	1	2	23	14	10	.412	.493
Throws Right	R	.196	143	28	5	0	3	18	14	37	.269	.294
Mercker,Kent	L	.260	50	13	4	0	5	9	5	9	.327	.640
Throws Left	R	.259	58	15	3	0	1	9	6	8	.323	.362
Meredith,Cla	L	.281	64	18	1	1	1	6	4	8	.333	.375
Throws Right	R	.107	112	12	1	0	2	9	2	29	.130	.170
Mesa,Jose	L	.270	126	34	2	1	6	17	17	13	.378	.444
Throws Right	R	.271	144	39	10	0	3	24	19	26	.352	.403
Messenger,Randy	L	.333	108	36	11	0	7	30	8	22	.385	.630
Throws Right	R	.267	135	36	8	0	1	13	16	23	.340	.348
Miceli,Dan	L	.130	54	7	2	0	2	9	13	12	.290	.278
Throws Right	R	.295	61	18	4	0	2	10	7	6	.371	.459
Michalak,Chris	L	.276	29	8	0	0	1	2	2	3	.344	.379
Throws Left	R	.312	109	34	9	0	5	15	14	7	.400	.532
Miller,Andrew	L	.333	9	3	0	1	0	3	7	1	.625	.556
Throws Left	R	.167	30	5	2	0	0	1	3	5	.286	.233
Miller,Matt	L	.250	20	5	0	0	2	4	4	2	.360	.550
Throws Right	R	.188	32	6	2	0	0	5	5	10	.325	.250
Miller,Trever	L	.221	86	19	2	0	4	9	7	32	.277	.384
Throws Left	R	.228	101	23	7	0	3	9	6	24	.295	.386
Miller,Wade	L	.273	44	12	2	0	4	11	14	12	.458	.591
Throws Right	R	.184	38	7	0	0	0	0	4	8	.262	.184
Millwood,Kevin	L	.285	417	119	20	1	13	52	38	89	.347	.432
Throws Right	R	.258	422	109	22	5	10	49	15	68	.286	.405
Milton,Eric	L	.225	151	34	2	1	7	19	5	32	.253	.391
Throws Left	R	.284	455	129	33	1	22	66	37	58	.341	.505
Miner,Zach	L	.316	152	48	10	2	5	23	19	24	.392	.507
Throws Right	R	.248	210	52	8	0	6	27	13	35	.289	.371
Misch,Patrick	L	.000	2	0	0	0	0	0	0	1	.000	.000
Throws Left	R	.667	3	2	0	0	0	0	0	0	.667	.667
Mitre,Sergio	L	.344	61	21	0	1	4	8	14	11	.474	.574
Throws Right	R	.232	99	23	2	0	3	14	6	20	.306	.343
Moehler,Brian	L	.351	268	94	17	4	9	47	21	23	.401	.545
Throws Right	R	.297	236	70	16	3	10	40	17	35	.350	.517
Montero,Agustin	L	.368	19	7	0	0	2	9	1	3	.364	.684
Throws Right	R	.229	35	8	1	0	1	5	1	4	.243	.343
Morillo,Juan	L	.625	8	5	1	0	3	6	1	1	.667	1.875
Throws Right	R	.273	11	3	1	0	0	1	2	3	.429	.364
Morris,Matt	L	.277	394	109	25	7	9	56	28	63	.332	.444
Throws Right	R	.261	418	109	29	2	13	56	35	54	.328	.433

Pitchers vs. Left-Handed and Right-Handed Batters

Pitcher	vs	Avg	AB	H	2B	3B	HR	RBI	BB	SO	OBP	Slg
Moseley,Dustin	L	.500	26	13	3	0	1	4	1	3	.519	.731
Throws Right	R	.375	24	9	0	0	2	7	1	0	.385	.625
Mota,Guillermo	L	.252	103	26	5	2	6	22	14	21	.336	.515
Throws Right	R	.261	111	29	4	0	5	13	10	25	.320	.432
Moyer,Jamie	L	.251	191	48	9	3	3	19	8	28	.289	.377
Throws Left	R	.285	632	180	43	4	30	81	43	80	.329	.508
Moylan,Peter	L	.192	26	5	0	0	1	5	3	3	.276	.308
Throws Right	R	.361	36	13	4	0	0	4	2	11	.395	.472
Mujica,Edward	L	.324	34	11	3	0	0	4	0	4	.324	.412
Throws Right	R	.341	41	14	2	0	1	9	0	8	.341	.463
Mulder,Mark	L	.241	83	20	4	0	2	8	5	19	.312	.361
Throws Left	R	.351	296	104	25	1	17	65	30	31	.413	.615
Mulholland,Terry	L	.250	8	2	2	0	0	2	0	1	.250	.500
Throws Left	R	.833	6	5	1	0	1	2	1	0	.857	1.500
Munter,Scott	L	.405	37	15	4	0	1	13	9	5	.511	.595
Throws Right	R	.333	45	15	3	0	0	13	9	2	.464	.400
Mussina,Mike	L	.223	359	80	11	1	13	47	19	90	.266	.368
Throws Right	R	.258	403	104	22	0	9	35	16	82	.291	.380
Myers,Brett	L	.259	343	89	19	3	8	26	43	86	.342	.402
Throws Right	R	.254	413	105	16	2	21	59	20	103	.291	.455
Myers,Mike	L	.254	71	18	3	2	2	14	4	18	.293	.437
Throws Left	R	.229	48	11	0	0	1	8	6	4	.351	.292
Nageotte,Clint	L	.500	2	1	0	0	0	0	1	0	.667	.500
Throws Right	R	.333	3	1	0	0	1	3	1	1	.500	1.333
Narveson,Chris	L	.000	6	0	0	0	0	0	2	3	.333	.000
Throws Left	R	.214	28	6	3	0	1	4	3	9	.290	.429
Nathan,Joe	L	.193	109	21	5	0	0	6	8	41	.244	.239
Throws Right	R	.130	131	17	2	2	3	7	8	54	.186	.244
Nelson,Jeff	L	.000	3	0	0	0	0	0	2	1	.400	.000
Throws Right	R	.429	7	3	1	0	1	2	3	1	.600	1.000
Nelson,Joe	L	.180	61	11	1	0	1	5	10	20	.296	.246
Throws Right	R	.252	103	26	13	1	4	16	14	24	.345	.515
Neshek,Pat	L	.244	45	11	0	0	4	6	4	16	.300	.511
Throws Right	R	.140	86	12	1	0	2	5	2	37	.159	.221
Nieve,Fernando	L	.262	164	43	7	0	8	19	29	27	.373	.451
Throws Right	R	.224	196	44	13	1	10	30	12	43	.272	.454
Nippert,Dustin	L	.333	27	9	1	0	4	9	4	7	.419	.815
Throws Right	R	.375	16	6	1	0	1	4	3	2	.474	.625
Nolasco,Ricky	L	.338	260	88	12	3	12	49	24	35	.390	.546
Throws Right	R	.240	288	69	13	2	8	27	17	64	.302	.382
Novoa,Roberto	L	.279	86	24	5	0	3	12	16	16	.404	.442
Throws Right	R	.255	208	53	10	1	12	36	16	37	.317	.486
Nunez,Leo	L	.211	19	4	0	0	0	2	4	1	.333	.211
Throws Right	R	.355	31	11	2	0	2	5	1	6	.412	.613
O'Connor,Mike	L	.250	76	19	4	2	2	10	8	17	.348	.434
Throws Left	R	.243	317	77	13	3	13	39	37	42	.325	.426
O'Flaherty,Eric	L	.238	21	5	2	0	0	1	0	3	.238	.333
Throws Left	R	.448	29	13	1	0	2	9	6	3	.543	.690
Ohka,Tomo	L	.265	170	45	9	0	7	26	19	25	.337	.441
Throws Right	R	.266	199	53	12	0	5	22	16	25	.332	.402
Ohman,Will	L	.157	102	16	4	0	2	5	13	42	.275	.255
Throws Left	R	.245	143	35	7	1	4	28	21	32	.343	.392
Oliver,Darren	L	.208	106	22	7	0	5	14	5	25	.252	.415
Throws Left	R	.244	197	48	8	1	8	26	16	35	.301	.416
Olsen,Scott	L	.178	157	28	7	1	4	12	11	47	.254	.312
Throws Left	R	.257	513	132	21	8	19	66	64	119	.341	.441
O'Malley,Ryan	L	.000	12	0	0	0	0	1	1	2	.143	.000
Throws Left	R	.286	35	10	0	1	0	2	6	2	.390	.343
Ortiz,Ramon	L	.316	376	119	27	1	16	61	39	41	.389	.521
Throws Right	R	.278	399	111	19	3	15	54	25	63	.336	.454
Ortiz,Russ	L	.378	111	42	11	0	8	30	23	17	.485	.694
Throws Right	R	.299	147	44	12	3	10	32	17	27	.380	.626
Orvella,Chad	L	.275	40	11	2	0	2	9	12	8	.442	.475
Throws Right	R	.391	64	25	6	1	4	21	8	9	.474	.703
Osoria,Franquelis	L	.500	26	13	2	0	3	7	2	3	.536	.923
Throws Right	R	.286	49	14	1	0	1	4	7	10	.386	.367
Oswalt,Roy	L	.264	368	97	23	2	6	32	19	75	.301	.386
Throws Right	R	.263	468	123	32	2	12	38	19	91	.297	.417
Otsuka,Akinori	L	.287	115	33	3	1	3	17	4	23	.308	.409
Throws Right	R	.190	105	20	1	1	0	1	7	24	.241	.219
Owens,Henry	L	.167	6	1	0	0	0	2	1	2	.250	.167
Throws Right	R	.375	8	3	0	0	0	2	3	0	.545	.375
Padilla,Vicente	L	.305	387	118	26	3	13	54	53	72	.401	.488
Throws Right	R	.228	386	88	21	1	8	41	17	84	.268	.350
Papelbon,Jonathan	L	.203	123	25	7	0	2	7	8	37	.248	.309
Throws Right	R	.128	117	15	3	1	1	4	5	38	.171	.197
Park,Chan Ho	L	.266	290	77	21	2	12	42	30	49	.341	.476
Throws Right	R	.278	248	69	10	2	8	30	14	47	.328	.431
Paronto,Chad	L	.288	73	21	2	1	1	8	6	11	.342	.384
Throws Right	R	.234	137	32	6	0	4	21	13	30	.312	.365
Patterson,John	L	.299	67	20	5	2	2	11	5	22	.355	.522
Throws Right	R	.188	85	16	4	0	2	9	4	20	.228	.306
Pauley,David	L	.450	40	18	5	0	1	4	4	4	.500	.650
Throws Right	R	.382	34	13	1	1	0	7	2	6	.447	.471
Peavy,Jake	L	.242	372	90	24	4	16	44	37	97	.317	.457
Throws Right	R	.243	400	97	24	3	7	43	25	118	.290	.370
Pelfrey,Mike	L	.278	36	10	2	0	0	5	7	6	.409	.333
Throws Right	R	.326	46	15	4	0	1	7	5	7	.407	.478
Pena,Tony	L	.382	68	26	7	1	4	14	5	12	.419	.691
Throws Right	R	.179	56	10	1	2	2	7	3	9	.220	.375
Penn,Hayden	L	.327	52	17	3	0	3	10	7	6	.407	.558
Throws Right	R	.467	45	21	4	1	5	19	6	2	.547	.933
Penny,Brad	L	.275	378	104	23	0	11	45	30	70	.331	.423
Throws Right	R	.283	361	102	30	1	8	44	24	78	.338	.438
Peralta,Joel	L	.338	80	27	6	2	4	23	9	13	.400	.613
Throws Right	R	.234	201	47	14	1	6	27	8	44	.268	.403
Perez,Beltran	L	.270	37	10	1	0	2	5	9	4	.413	.459
Throws Right	R	.171	35	6	1	0	1	5	4	5	.256	.286
Perez,Juan	L	.286	7	2	0	0	0	3	0	2	.375	.286
Throws Left	R	.500	6	3	0	1	1	3	1	1	.556	1.333
Perez,Odalis	L	.339	115	39	9	3	4	19	8	21	.392	.574
Throws Left	R	.315	413	130	30	3	14	68	23	60	.347	.504
Perez,Oliver	L	.260	77	20	1	0	3	16	12	28	.355	.390
Throws Left	R	.300	363	109	18	1	17	66	56	74	.394	.496
Perez,Rafael	L	.130	23	3	0	0	0	1	3	7	.231	.130
Throws Left	R	.269	26	7	0	0	2	5	3	8	.345	.500
Perkins,Glen	L	.250	8	2	0	0	0	0	0	5	.250	.250
Throws Left	R	.083	12	1	1	0	0	0	0	1	.083	.167
Petit,Yusmeiro	L	.381	63	24	2	4	2	13	7	10	.443	.635
Throws Right	R	.400	55	22	5	0	5	12	2	10	.414	.764
Pettitte,Andy	L	.259	158	41	12	1	5	19	14	33	.318	.443
Throws Left	R	.290	680	197	41	3	22	83	56	145	.344	.456
Pineiro,Joel	L	.287	307	88	27	2	10	50	39	38	.364	.485
Throws Right	R	.332	365	121	22	1	13	60	25	49	.388	.504
Pinto,Renyel	L	.150	40	6	1	0	1	4	11	17	.346	.250
Throws Left	R	.215	65	14	3	0	2	9	16	19	.366	.354
Politte,Cliff	L	.385	39	15	4	0	4	9	9	2	.500	.795
Throws Right	R	.340	94	32	9	0	5	20	6	13	.379	.596
Ponson,Sidney	L	.302	149	45	9	0	6	23	22	21	.395	.483
Throws Right	R	.330	191	63	18	0	4	25	14	27	.385	.487
Prior,Mark	L	.321	78	25	4	0	6	21	12	16	.419	.603
Throws Right	R	.226	93	21	4	0	3	15	16	22	.371	.366
Proctor,Scott	L	.204	147	30	5	1	5	18	13	37	.269	.354
Throws Right	R	.250	236	59	12	0	7	36	20	52	.307	.390
Putz,J.J.	L	.211	133	28	6	1	3	13	7	45	.254	.338
Throws Right	R	.204	152	31	2	0	1	12	6	59	.238	.237
Qualls,Chad	L	.227	132	30	6	0	4	16	10	25	.283	.364
Throws Right	R	.253	182	46	6	1	6	33	18	31	.333	.396
Radke,Brad	L	.303	297	90	20	3	10	45	13	37	.325	.492
Throws Right	R	.311	344	107	16	0	14	37	19	46	.346	.480
Ramirez,Elizardo	L	.290	200	58	14	1	8	36	18	30	.353	.490
Throws Right	R	.295	220	65	18	2	6	28	11	39	.343	.477
Ramirez,Horacio	L	.282	71	20	2	0	2	10	2	13	.307	.394
Throws Left	R	.289	225	65	11	0	4	24	29	24	.375	.391
Ramirez,Ramon	L	.274	113	31	8	2	3	12	12	18	.341	.460
Throws Right	R	.194	139	27	9	0	2	18	15	43	.274	.302
Ramirez,Santiago	L	.500	6	3	0	0	1	1	0	0	.500	1.000
Throws Right	R	.300	10	3	1	0	0	5	2	1	.417	.400
Rasner,Darrell	L	.189	37	7	2	1	0	0	1	5	.211	.297
Throws Right	R	.282	39	11	1	1	2	13	4	6	.364	.513
Rauch,Jon	L	.254	134	34	7	1	5	20	20	32	.344	.433
Throws Right	R	.216	204	44	6	0	8	19	16	54	.275	.363
Ray,Chris	L	.184	114	21	2	1	8	20	18	27	.296	.430
Throws Right	R	.202	119	24	3	0	2	9	9	24	.254	.277
Ray,Ken	L	.282	124	35	5	0	4	20	26	25	.404	.419
Throws Right	R	.237	131	31	7	0	5	21	12	25	.299	.405
Reames,Britt	L	.444	9	4	0	0	1	3	3	1	.538	.778
Throws Right	R	.318	22	7	2	0	1	6	2	5	.375	.545
Redman,Mark	L	.229	131	30	6	1	2	14	6	18	.261	.336
Throws Left	R	.326	528	172	36	4	17	83	57	58	.398	.506
Reitsma,Chris	L	.422	64	27	6	2	4	18	4	4	.457	.766
Throws Right	R	.302	63	19	4	0	3	11	4	9	.362	.508

Pitchers vs. Left-Handed and Right-Handed Batters

Pitcher	vs	Avg	AB	H	2B	3B	HR	RBI	BB	SO	OBP	Slg
Remlinger,Mike	L	.289	45	13	0	1	1	7	2	7	.347	.400
Throws Left	R	.298	47	14	3	0	1	6	7	12	.389	.426
Resop,Chris	L	.279	43	12	3	1	1	3	10	7	.426	.465
Throws Right	R	.341	41	14	5	0	0	4	6	3	.426	.463
Reyes,Anthony	L	.278	144	40	6	2	7	16	14	25	.340	.493
Throws Right	R	.249	177	44	11	4	10	27	20	47	.345	.525
Reyes,Dennys	L	.148	88	13	2	0	1	4	8	28	.219	.205
Throws Left	R	.244	90	22	3	0	2	5	7	21	.299	.344
Rheinecker,John	L	.197	66	13	1	0	0	2	7	9	.284	.212
Throws Left	R	.392	232	91	19	0	6	38	12	19	.425	.552
Rhodes,Arthur	L	.286	63	18	5	1	2	13	6	17	.357	.492
Throws Left	R	.248	117	29	9	0	0	9	24	31	.380	.325
Rincon,Juan	L	.222	117	26	2	0	0	5	9	27	.283	.239
Throws Right	R	.303	165	50	11	0	2	23	15	38	.366	.406
Rincon,Ricardo	L	.111	9	1	0	0	1	2	1	5	.200	.444
Throws Left	R	.714	7	5	2	0	0	2	3	1	.818	1.000
Ring,Royce	L	.150	20	3	1	0	0	0	2	7	.227	.200
Throws Left	R	.160	25	4	1	0	2	4	1	1	.192	.440
Riske,David	L	.280	50	14	2	0	1	7	12	8	.438	.380
Throws Right	R	.224	116	26	8	0	5	21	5	20	.258	.422
Rivera,Mariano	L	.192	130	25	2	0	1	9	4	22	.222	.231
Throws Right	R	.250	144	36	5	1	2	12	7	33	.299	.340
Rivera,Saul	L	.194	98	19	4	0	2	11	20	26	.333	.296
Throws Right	R	.290	138	40	4	1	2	21	12	15	.359	.377
Rleal,Sendy	L	.242	91	22	3	1	3	13	11	6	.317	.396
Throws Right	R	.310	84	26	5	0	7	21	12	13	.392	.619
Robertson,Nate	L	.181	193	35	9	1	2	9	5	44	.221	.269
Throws Left	R	.284	602	171	29	2	27	76	62	93	.351	.473
Rodney,Fernando	L	.202	109	22	2	0	4	11	16	25	.320	.330
Throws Right	R	.192	151	29	7	0	2	22	18	40	.299	.278
Rodriguez,Eddy	L	.318	22	7	2	0	1	4	3	2	.385	.545
Throws Right	R	.263	38	10	1	0	4	12	7	9	.370	.605
Rodriguez,Felix	L	.314	51	16	4	2	2	11	11	6	.422	.588
Throws Right	R	.254	63	16	4	0	3	12	5	9	.342	.460
Rodriguez,Francisco	L	.215	130	28	9	0	5	11	13	42	.287	.400
Throws Right	R	.179	134	24	9	0	1	10	15	56	.267	.269
Rodriguez,Wandy	L	.262	122	32	2	1	2	12	19	21	.366	.344
Throws Left	R	.298	409	122	35	4	15	70	44	77	.370	.513
Rogers,Brian	L	.444	9	4	0	0	2	4	0	0	.444	1.111
Throws Right	R	.280	25	7	0	2	0	0	2	7	.357	.440
Rogers,Kenny	L	.200	165	33	13	0	4	20	20	43	.296	.352
Throws Left	R	.268	605	162	28	2	19	66	42	56	.319	.415
Romero,Davis	L	.318	22	7	1	0	0	0	1	4	.348	.364
Throws Left	R	.286	42	12	4	0	1	5	5	6	.375	.452
Romero,J.C.	L	.202	89	18	6	0	1	15	13	13	.298	.303
Throws Left	R	.382	102	39	12	1	2	21	15	18	.455	.578
Roney,Matt	L	.250	4	1	0	0	0	0	1	0	.400	.250
Throws Right	R	.364	11	4	2	0	0	2	0	0	.333	.545
Rosario,Francisco	L	.310	29	9	0	0	2	5	8	8	.459	.517
Throws Right	R	.242	62	15	2	1	2	9	8	13	.338	.403
Rupe,Josh	L	.225	40	9	1	0	1	7	4	6	.311	.325
Throws Right	R	.320	75	24	3	0	1	8	5	8	.363	.400
Rusch,Glendon	L	.352	71	25	6	1	6	17	5	14	.395	.718
Throws Left	R	.308	198	61	11	0	15	35	28	45	.395	.591
Ryan,B.J.	L	.120	50	6	0	0	0	2	3	19	.167	.120
Throws Left	R	.182	198	36	2	0	3	9	17	67	.247	.237
Ryu,Jae Kuk	L	.360	25	9	2	1	3	5	5	6	.484	.880
Throws Right	R	.341	41	14	2	0	4	10	1	11	.372	.683
Saarloos,Kirk	L	.319	232	74	11	0	7	32	28	28	.396	.457
Throws Right	R	.298	252	75	17	3	12	40	25	24	.356	.532
Sabathia,C.C.	L	.271	107	29	4	1	3	13	8	35	.328	.411
Throws Left	R	.242	631	153	27	1	14	62	36	137	.288	.355
Sadler,Billy	L	.250	8	2	0	0	1	1	1	3	.333	.625
Throws Right	R	.333	9	3	2	0	1	4	1	3	.455	.889
Saito,Takashi	L	.227	132	30	9	1	1	13	10	43	.283	.333
Throws Right	R	.129	139	18	3	0	2	12	13	64	.206	.194
Salas,Juan	L	.200	25	5	1	1	0	2	2	6	.259	.320
Throws Right	R	.421	19	8	4	0	1	5	1	2	.429	.789
Sampson,Chris	L	.154	52	8	0	0	0	1	2	5	.200	.154
Throws Right	R	.243	70	17	2	0	3	8	3	10	.270	.400
Sanches,Brian	L	.282	39	11	4	0	3	4	6	11	.378	.615
Throws Right	R	.261	46	12	3	1	2	10	7	11	.358	.500
Sanchez,Anibal	L	.229	227	52	9	2	5	14	26	36	.310	.352
Throws Right	R	.202	188	38	7	1	4	20	20	36	.289	.314
Sanchez,Duaner	L	.276	87	24	7	0	2	16	13	18	.362	.425
Throws Right	R	.179	106	19	2	0	1	5	11	26	.275	.226

Pitcher	vs	Avg	AB	H	2B	3B	HR	RBI	BB	SO	OBP	Slg
Sanchez,Jonathan	L	.256	39	10	3	0	0	6	3	6	.333	.333
Throws Left	R	.248	117	29	7	1	2	23	20	27	.364	.376
Santana,Ervin	L	.254	350	89	17	3	12	46	46	54	.339	.423
Throws Right	R	.229	401	92	24	3	9	49	24	87	.286	.372
Santana,Johan	L	.254	169	43	8	2	6	18	12	37	.306	.432
Throws Left	R	.206	693	143	34	3	18	54	35	208	.247	.342
Santana,Julio	L	.143	14	2	0	0	0	1	7	1	.429	.143
Throws Right	R	.353	17	6	3	0	1	9	2	3	.409	.706
Santos,Victor	L	.264	193	51	9	2	7	26	19	41	.327	.440
Throws Right	R	.361	274	99	17	5	9	50	23	40	.416	.558
Sarfate,Dennis	L	.267	15	4	2	0	0	2	1	4	.313	.400
Throws Right	R	.263	19	5	2	0	0	2	3	7	.364	.368
Sauerbeck,Scott	L	.234	47	11	3	0	3	10	11	12	.419	.489
Throws Left	R	.234	47	11	2	1	0	5	7	5	.368	.319
Saunders,Joe	L	.220	50	11	2	0	0	4	3	11	.278	.260
Throws Left	R	.274	219	60	11	0	6	28	26	40	.348	.406
Schilling,Curt	L	.277	382	106	28	3	13	49	14	87	.304	.469
Throws Right	R	.275	414	114	23	2	15	38	14	96	.302	.449
Schmidt,Jason	L	.262	390	102	16	3	6	37	50	95	.345	.364
Throws Right	R	.215	404	87	19	4	15	48	30	85	.275	.394
Schoeneweis,Scott	L	.236	89	21	5	0	0	13	11	15	.333	.292
Throws Left	R	.257	105	27	4	1	4	13	13	14	.339	.429
Schroder,Chris	L	.255	47	12	3	0	4	16	12	16	.393	.574
Throws Right	R	.196	56	11	2	0	3	8	3	23	.292	.393
Seanez,Rudy	L	.266	94	25	3	2	3	18	17	23	.378	.436
Throws Right	R	.273	121	33	5	0	5	20	15	31	.355	.438
Seay,Bobby	L	.227	22	5	3	0	0	1	4	5	.414	.364
Throws Left	R	.257	35	9	0	0	1	6	5	7	.341	.343
Sele,Aaron	L	.280	186	52	11	4	7	25	18	28	.346	.495
Throws Right	R	.298	228	68	17	1	4	27	12	29	.335	.434
Seo,Jae	L	.310	297	92	24	3	13	44	28	37	.367	.542
Throws Right	R	.313	336	105	20	1	18	50	28	51	.367	.539
Shackelford,Brian	L	.175	40	7	1	1	0	4	3	10	.267	.250
Throws Left	R	.407	27	11	1	0	4	11	7	5	.529	.889
Sharpless,Josh	L	.000	8	0	0	0	0	1	5	1	.385	.000
Throws Right	R	.219	32	7	1	0	0	3	6	6	.333	.250
Sheets,Ben	L	.248	165	41	11	3	6	17	5	58	.270	.461
Throws Right	R	.266	241	64	22	0	3	25	6	58	.284	.394
Sherrill,George	L	.143	77	11	3	0	0	6	9	29	.230	.182
Throws Left	R	.297	64	19	4	0	0	9	18	13	.446	.359
Shields,James	L	.266	241	64	13	0	10	34	19	43	.323	.444
Throws Right	R	.309	249	77	20	0	8	31	19	61	.363	.486
Shields,Scot	L	.207	150	31	6	0	4	12	14	45	.274	.327
Throws Right	R	.227	172	39	9	0	4	21	10	39	.272	.349
Shiell,Jason	L	.423	26	11	4	0	3	8	2	4	.464	.923
Throws Right	R	.293	41	12	3	0	2	7	7	10	.400	.512
Shouse,Brian	L	.238	80	19	6	0	1	13	6	19	.319	.350
Throws Left	R	.309	68	21	3	1	3	14	12	4	.427	.515
Sikorski,Brian	L	.346	52	18	3	0	5	13	4	15	.404	.692
Throws Right	R	.225	80	18	5	0	3	7	3	23	.250	.400
Silva,Carlos	L	.329	362	119	23	2	22	60	19	39	.363	.586
Throws Right	R	.320	397	127	21	0	16	54	13	31	.345	.494
Simpson,Allan	L	.167	6	1	0	0	0	0	1	3	.286	.167
Throws Right	R	.000	3	0	0	0	0	1	3	2	.429	.000
Sisco,Andy	L	.318	88	28	6	0	3	24	17	20	.430	.489
Throws Left	R	.271	140	38	4	0	5	32	23	32	.365	.407
Slaten,Doug	L	.111	9	1	0	0	0	0	0	3	.111	.111
Throws Left	R	.222	9	2	0	0	0	0	2	0	.364	.222
Slocum,Brian	L	.367	30	11	2	0	0	2	4	4	.457	.433
Throws Right	R	.356	45	16	3	1	3	8	5	7	.420	.667
Small,Aaron	L	.358	53	19	4	1	3	9	7	6	.433	.642
Throws Right	R	.329	70	23	3	1	6	17	5	6	.377	.657
Smith,Matt	L	.167	18	3	0	0	0	2	8	6	.423	.167
Throws Left	R	.085	47	4	0	0	0	0	4	15	.157	.085
Smith,Mike	L	.375	8	3	1	0	0	1	1	1	.500	.500
Throws Right	R	.333	6	2	0	1	1	3	2	0	.500	1.167
Smith,Travis	L	.364	11	4	1	0	0	3	1	1	.385	.455
Throws Right	R	.200	5	1	1	0	0	0	0	0	.200	.400
Smoltz,John	L	.278	414	115	27	1	12	49	41	83	.348	.435
Throws Right	R	.226	468	106	22	3	11	37	14	128	.251	.357
Snell,Ian	L	.305	344	105	18	2	18	49	47	76	.386	.526
Throws Right	R	.251	371	93	25	1	11	49	27	93	.303	.412
Snyder,Kyle	L	.349	126	44	10	0	6	27	9	22	.399	.571
Throws Right	R	.314	137	43	10	0	6	18	11	35	.362	.518
Soler,Alay	L	.252	107	27	7	2	2	13	13	12	.333	.411
Throws Right	R	.307	75	23	5	0	5	17	8	11	.373	.573

Pitchers vs. Left-Handed and Right-Handed Batters

Pitcher	vs	Avg	AB	H	2B	3B	HR	RBI	BB	SO	OBP	Slg
Soriano,Rafael	L	.244	82	20	1	1	3	7	9	21	.315	.390
Throws Right	R	.179	134	24	5	1	3	16	12	44	.257	.299
Sosa,Jorge	L	.323	192	62	9	1	13	27	23	30	.395	.583
Throws Right	R	.271	280	76	18	0	17	48	17	45	.311	.518
Sowers,Jeremy	L	.225	71	16	1	0	4	9	3	12	.257	.408
Throws Left	R	.259	266	69	12	2	6	25	17	23	.309	.387
Speier,Justin	L	.183	71	13	1	1	3	12	6	23	.256	.352
Throws Right	R	.264	129	34	11	1	2	18	15	32	.340	.411
Springer,Russ	L	.253	79	20	3	2	5	16	6	13	.314	.532
Throws Right	R	.187	139	26	3	0	5	15	10	33	.257	.317
Spurling,Chris	L	.263	38	10	2	0	2	6	6	2	.364	.474
Throws Right	R	.306	49	15	3	0	3	11	2	5	.333	.551
Standridge,Jason	L	.200	25	5	0	0	1	3	5	8	.355	.320
Throws Right	R	.267	45	12	2	0	1	4	9	10	.389	.378
Stanton,Mike	L	.271	85	23	5	0	1	16	7	21	.330	.365
Throws Left	R	.276	170	47	13	0	1	20	20	27	.351	.371
Stauffer,Tim	L	.091	11	1	0	0	0	0	1	0	.167	.091
Throws Right	R	.222	9	2	0	0	0	2	0	2	.222	.222
Stemle,Steve	L	.429	14	6	1	1	0	5	2	0	.500	.643
Throws Right	R	.474	19	9	4	0	1	6	1	0	.500	.842
Stockman,Phil	L	.500	2	1	1	0	0	0	2	0	.750	1.000
Throws Right	R	.182	11	2	1	0	0	1	2	4	.308	.273
Stokes,Brian	L	.302	53	16	6	0	1	8	5	9	.350	.472
Throws Right	R	.341	44	15	2	0	1	7	4	6	.400	.455
Street,Huston	L	.274	117	32	8	1	3	22	8	31	.325	.436
Throws Right	R	.211	152	32	7	0	1	12	5	36	.236	.276
Stults,Eric	L	.412	17	7	3	0	1	2	4	1	.524	.765
Throws Left	R	.213	47	10	2	1	3	9	3	4	.260	.489
Sturtze,Tanyon	L	.333	12	4	0	0	1	3	3	0	.467	.583
Throws Right	R	.361	36	13	4	0	2	8	3	6	.415	.639
Suppan,Jeff	L	.301	339	102	23	1	10	39	33	54	.369	.463
Throws Right	R	.257	408	105	26	4	11	49	36	50	.321	.422
Sweeney,Brian	L	.263	99	26	1	1	3	11	7	8	.315	.384
Throws Right	R	.237	114	27	5	0	3	16	9	15	.290	.360
Switzer,Jon	L	.220	50	11	0	0	2	6	7	11	.310	.340
Throws Left	R	.321	84	27	6	0	3	10	12	7	.412	.500
Tallet,Brian	L	.217	60	13	3	0	2	5	8	12	.314	.367
Throws Left	R	.248	129	32	9	0	3	20	23	25	.361	.388
Tankersley,Taylor	L	.232	56	13	0	0	3	9	7	16	.313	.393
Throws Left	R	.225	89	20	2	1	1	16	19	30	.360	.303
Taschner,Jack	L	.275	40	11	0	0	0	6	3	8	.318	.275
Throws Left	R	.400	50	20	6	0	4	17	4	7	.456	.760
Tata,Jordan	L	.259	27	7	1	0	0	3	3	3	.323	.296
Throws Right	R	.241	29	7	0	0	1	5	4	3	.324	.345
Taubenheim,Ty	L	.262	61	16	3	2	2	12	13	11	.382	.475
Throws Right	R	.296	81	24	6	0	3	9	5	15	.367	.481
Tavarez,Julian	L	.248	161	40	14	1	5	33	24	28	.344	.441
Throws Right	R	.327	214	70	11	1	5	26	20	28	.397	.458
Tejeda,Robinson	L	.331	136	45	8	0	6	17	15	17	.401	.522
Throws Right	R	.250	152	38	5	0	4	16	17	23	.324	.362
Thompson,Brad	L	.281	89	25	7	1	1	11	6	12	.333	.416
Throws Right	R	.258	128	33	6	0	3	16	14	20	.349	.375
Thompson,Mike	L	.283	184	52	6	0	6	24	14	16	.340	.413
Throws Right	R	.288	177	51	13	0	7	26	16	19	.360	.480
Thomson,John	L	.276	152	42	8	1	5	23	19	22	.354	.441
Throws Right	R	.313	163	51	7	0	6	27	13	24	.359	.466
Thornton,Matt	L	.211	76	16	5	0	1	13	5	23	.253	.316
Throws Left	R	.240	125	30	2	1	4	11	16	26	.329	.368
Timlin,Mike	L	.306	124	38	5	0	2	17	7	15	.341	.395
Throws Right	R	.303	132	40	11	0	5	23	9	15	.357	.500
Tomko,Brett	L	.300	190	57	12	4	7	23	18	32	.362	.516
Throws Right	R	.258	256	66	12	2	10	40	11	44	.284	.438
Torres,Salomon	L	.281	139	39	6	0	2	14	15	26	.363	.367
Throws Right	R	.269	219	59	10	0	4	25	23	46	.344	.370
Towers,Josh	L	.325	114	37	5	1	9	27	7	16	.366	.623
Throws Right	R	.357	157	56	9	0	8	28	10	19	.398	.567
Traber,Billy	L	.256	43	11	3	0	0	8	5	10	.373	.326
Throws Left	R	.316	133	42	11	1	5	23	9	15	.378	.526
Tracey,Sean	L	.091	11	1	0	0	1	2	2	1	.286	.364
Throws Right	R	.176	17	3	0	0	1	3	3	2	.300	.353
Trachsel,Steve	L	.267	300	80	9	3	8	33	35	31	.340	.397
Throws Right	R	.306	343	105	30	0	15	51	43	48	.386	.525
Turnbow,Derrick	L	.245	106	26	6	1	3	18	16	32	.341	.406
Throws Right	R	.263	114	30	6	2	5	18	23	37	.404	.482
Valverde,Jose	L	.323	96	31	6	0	5	19	15	25	.407	.542
Throws Right	R	.192	99	19	3	1	1	13	7	44	.257	.273

Pitcher	vs	Avg	AB	H	2B	3B	HR	RBI	BB	SO	OBP	Slg
Van Buren,Jermaine	L	.350	20	7	3	0	1	6	9	3	.552	.650
Throws Right	R	.250	28	7	0	1	0	4	6	5	.371	.321
Vargas,Claudio	L	.275	327	90	19	4	14	46	25	46	.328	.486
Throws Right	R	.272	349	95	23	2	13	44	27	77	.335	.461
Vargas,Jason	L	.244	45	11	3	0	2	7	4	7	.340	.444
Throws Left	R	.310	126	39	10	2	7	31	26	18	.423	.587
Vazquez,Javier	L	.256	359	92	20	2	13	42	31	76	.321	.432
Throws Right	R	.261	436	114	22	2	10	56	25	108	.316	.390
Venafro,Mike	L	.200	5	1	0	0	0	1	2	2	.429	.200
Throws Left	R	.286	7	2	1	0	0	2	1	0	.375	.429
Veras,Jose	L	.188	16	3	0	0	1	4	2	4	.278	.375
Throws Right	R	.227	22	5	1	0	1	3	3	2	.320	.409
Verlander,Justin	L	.279	340	95	15	4	13	41	33	58	.343	.462
Throws Right	R	.253	363	92	18	0	8	30	27	66	.313	.369
Villanueva,Carlos	L	.226	106	24	6	2	4	9	6	24	.268	.434
Throws Right	R	.204	93	19	5	1	4	13	5	15	.275	.409
Villarreal,Oscar	L	.264	163	43	8	2	8	21	16	25	.328	.485
Throws Right	R	.259	193	50	10	0	5	26	11	30	.311	.389
Villone,Ron	L	.185	108	20	5	0	4	15	13	38	.290	.343
Throws Left	R	.286	192	55	13	0	5	27	38	34	.400	.432
Vizcaino,Luis	L	.163	104	17	3	2	2	10	15	29	.281	.288
Throws Right	R	.256	133	34	8	2	6	17	14	43	.336	.481
Vogelsong,Ryan	L	.239	46	11	2	0	2	10	9	10	.379	.413
Throws Right	R	.330	100	33	5	1	0	16	7	17	.391	.400
Volquez,Edison	L	.361	61	22	1	0	2	10	4	7	.394	.475
Throws Right	R	.357	84	30	4	0	5	16	13	8	.449	.583
Waechter,Doug	L	.284	95	27	5	0	3	15	5	9	.327	.432
Throws Right	R	.331	121	40	9	1	3	18	14	16	.401	.496
Wagner,Billy	L	.161	56	9	0	0	1	4	2	19	.190	.214
Throws Left	R	.234	214	50	5	0	6	17	19	75	.308	.341
Wagner,Ryan	L	.197	61	12	2	0	1	10	9	7	.300	.279
Throws Right	R	.387	62	24	3	0	2	9	6	13	.457	.532
Wainwright,Adam	L	.301	113	34	6	0	5	16	14	38	.380	.487
Throws Right	R	.182	165	30	9	0	1	9	8	34	.233	.255
Wakefield,Tim	L	.229	245	56	11	1	5	21	23	39	.295	.343
Throws Right	R	.263	300	79	20	0	14	48	28	51	.343	.470
Walker,Jamie	L	.238	80	19	9	0	3	8	3	23	.265	.463
Throws Left	R	.262	107	28	2	1	5	13	5	14	.295	.439
Walker,Pete	L	.318	44	14	2	1	3	9	8	12	.423	.614
Throws Right	R	.284	81	23	4	0	2	12	5	15	.326	.407
Walker,Tyler	L	.333	45	15	3	0	1	8	6	8	.412	.467
Throws Right	R	.226	53	12	2	0	0	6	6	11	.305	.264
Walrond,Les	L	.136	22	3	0	0	2	3	2	10	.200	.409
Throws Left	R	.333	48	16	4	0	0	8	10	11	.448	.417
Wang,Chien-Ming	L	.275	375	103	24	1	5	35	25	27	.321	.384
Throws Right	R	.279	466	130	20	0	7	48	27	49	.319	.367
Wasdin,John	L	.328	58	19	4	0	5	9	8	7	.435	.655
Throws Right	R	.212	66	14	3	0	1	8	5	9	.278	.303
Washburn,Jarrod	L	.317	139	44	9	0	6	18	11	25	.364	.511
Throws Left	R	.257	599	154	41	2	19	75	44	78	.313	.427
Weathers,David	L	.219	105	23	2	0	4	9	21	16	.352	.352
Throws Right	R	.230	165	38	10	0	8	24	13	34	.287	.436
Weaver,Jeff	L	.342	351	120	24	2	22	58	29	47	.398	.610
Throws Right	R	.265	351	93	18	3	12	48	18	60	.309	.436
Weaver,Jered	L	.250	208	52	10	1	13	26	15	49	.299	.495
Throws Right	R	.174	242	42	9	1	2	8	18	56	.239	.244
Webb,Brandon	L	.261	440	115	20	4	9	44	39	74	.321	.386
Throws Right	R	.231	438	101	24	2	6	35	11	104	.256	.336
Wellemeyer,Todd	L	.208	120	25	6	1	3	13	18	22	.312	.350
Throws Right	R	.265	162	43	11	1	3	24	32	32	.387	.401
Wells,David	L	.303	66	20	6	0	2	7	3	8	.333	.485
Throws Left	R	.317	243	77	10	1	9	31	9	30	.340	.477
Wells,Kip	L	.353	85	30	3	3	0	11	15	8	.455	.459
Throws Right	R	.323	96	31	9	0	3	15	6	12	.377	.510
Westbrook,Jake	L	.290	369	107	13	1	7	32	35	40	.355	.388
Throws Right	R	.300	466	140	27	1	8	58	20	69	.329	.414
Wheeler,Dan	L	.273	110	30	11	0	3	18	14	20	.357	.455
Throws Right	R	.183	153	28	9	1	2	11	10	48	.235	.294
White,Rick	L	.299	77	23	5	1	4	17	10	13	.393	.545
Throws Right	R	.290	169	49	6	0	4	22	10	27	.330	.396
Wickman,Bob	L	.267	101	27	6	0	1	17	9	23	.324	.356
Throws Right	R	.236	110	26	5	0	1	5	4	19	.265	.309
Williams,Dave	L	.283	46	13	2	0	2	5	4	11	.353	.457
Throws Left	R	.335	239	80	14	1	12	41	16	21	.384	.552
Williams,Jerome	L	.214	14	3	0	0	1	3	4	2	.368	.429
Throws Right	R	.375	32	12	3	1	1	7	7	3	.476	.625

Pitcher	vs	Avg	AB	H	2B	3B	HR	RBI	BB	SO	OBP	Slg
Williams,Todd	L	.342	79	27	4	1	2	16	8	6	.402	.494
Throws Right	R	.314	156	49	6	1	6	30	11	18	.365	.481
Williams,Woody	L	.245	274	67	12	2	10	23	21	38	.295	.412
Throws Right	R	.287	296	85	14	2	11	36	14	34	.332	.459
Williamson,Scott	L	.200	50	10	4	1	0	2	11	16	.339	.320
Throws Right	R	.307	101	31	6	0	4	18	11	26	.377	.485
Willis,Dontrelle	L	.244	127	31	3	0	3	18	13	42	.317	.339
Throws Left	R	.279	728	203	31	4	18	74	70	118	.355	.407
Wilson,Brian	L	.348	46	16	4	1	0	4	13	9	.475	.478
Throws Right	R	.235	68	16	0	1	1	8	8	14	.316	.309
Wilson,C.J.	L	.155	71	11	0	0	4	10	4	19	.241	.324
Throws Left	R	.292	96	28	6	0	3	19	14	24	.387	.448
Wilson,Kris	L	.200	15	3	0	0	2	6	1	5	.250	.600
Throws Right	R	.478	23	11	2	0	2	4	3	1	.538	.826
Windsor,Jason	L	.381	21	8	0	1	1	3	4	3	.462	.619
Throws Right	R	.371	35	13	2	0	1	8	1	3	.378	.514
Winkelsas,Joe	L	.300	10	3	1	0	0	5	1	2	.364	.400
Throws Right	R	.316	19	6	0	0	1	9	5	2	.458	.474
Wise,Matt	L	.206	68	14	1	0	3	10	4	11	.247	.353
Throws Right	R	.310	100	31	8	0	3	10	10	16	.384	.480
Witasick,Jay	L	.138	29	4	2	0	0	1	12	7	.405	.207
Throws Right	R	.350	60	21	3	0	3	13	9	16	.435	.550
Wolf,Randy	L	.079	38	3	0	0	1	5	4	12	.163	.158
Throws Left	R	.328	183	60	12	2	12	27	29	32	.421	.612
Wood,Kerry	L	.206	34	7	0	0	1	2	1	7	.229	.294
Throws Right	R	.293	41	12	3	1	4	10	7	6	.392	.707
Wood,Mike	L	.320	122	39	7	0	3	21	11	13	.382	.451
Throws Right	R	.309	152	47	9	1	7	27	12	16	.376	.520
Woods,Jake	L	.291	117	34	5	2	3	12	9	19	.339	.444
Throws Left	R	.273	297	81	23	1	9	48	44	47	.369	.448
Worrell,Tim	L	.256	43	11	3	0	3	8	4	8	.333	.535
Throws Right	R	.354	48	17	1	0	6	14	3	4	.392	.750
Wright,Jamey	L	.261	276	72	11	3	7	37	29	48	.335	.399
Throws Right	R	.300	317	95	12	4	9	49	35	31	.380	.448
Wright,Jaret	L	.314	261	82	18	3	7	29	33	41	.390	.487
Throws Right	R	.255	294	75	19	0	3	28	24	43	.324	.350
Wuertz,Mike	L	.184	49	9	2	1	1	5	4	14	.259	.327
Throws Right	R	.245	106	26	2	1	4	22	12	28	.322	.396
Yan,Esteban	L	.294	51	15	2	0	4	16	10	10	.403	.569
Throws Right	R	.202	84	17	5	0	4	15	10	14	.289	.405
Yates,Tyler	L	.217	69	15	4	1	2	11	17	23	.372	.391
Throws Right	R	.235	115	27	5	2	4	14	14	23	.318	.417
Youman,Shane	L	.235	17	4	0	0	0	2	3	0	.350	.235
Throws Left	R	.190	58	11	3	0	1	3	7	5	.273	.293
Young,Chris	L	.175	303	53	8	2	11	24	35	81	.267	.323
Throws Right	R	.234	346	81	12	3	17	38	34	83	.305	.434
Zambrano,Carlos	L	.249	370	92	23	4	10	36	75	79	.379	.414
Throws Right	R	.172	408	70	18	1	10	48	40	131	.254	.294
Zambrano,Victor	L	.344	32	11	3	0	2	8	7	3	.462	.625
Throws Right	R	.259	54	14	0	0	3	8	4	12	.310	.426
Zito,Barry	L	.260	150	39	3	0	6	19	24	33	.369	.400
Throws Left	R	.257	670	172	39	3	21	74	75	118	.339	.418
Zumaya,Joel	L	.183	109	20	1	1	2	15	21	38	.311	.266
Throws Right	R	.188	191	36	2	1	4	17	21	59	.273	.272
AL	L	.273	—	—	—	—	—	—	—	—	.344	.436
	R	.272	—	—	—	—	—	—	—	—	.332	.430
NL	L	.271	—	—	—	—	—	—	—	—	.348	.442
	R	.264	—	—	—	—	—	—	—	—	.329	.425

2006 Leader Boards

We've added two new charts to the most complete baseball leader boards in print. The new leader boards are "Highest First Swing %" and "Lowest First Swing %." These will enable you to see who likes to take a cut at the first pitch and who would rather take a more patient approach.

Many of our leader boards are derived from the complex pitch data we collect. Our pitch charting data is the most complete and thorough in baseball, and the information found in these leader boards cannot be found anywhere else. We have everything from the pitchers who blow away hitters with the fastest fastballs, to the hitters who hammer curveballs.

And speaking of hammering pitches, we have a leader board of the longest Home Runs hit this year. Check it out and see who is stretching the limits of the tape measure. Two years ago in 2005, Wily Mo Pena incredibly hit the two longest home runs of the season, with the longest one being 492 feet; you will soon see if anyone was able to top that in 2006.

Here are some definitions to help clarify some of the leader boards:

BPS stands for "Batting Average plus Slugging Percentage." We feel that BPS makes more sense than OPS for some leader boards because we wanted to know who was having success putting those balls in play, not just drawing walks.

OutZ is "Pitches Outside the Strike Zone."

Holds Adjusted Saves Percentage is calculated by dividing Holds plus Saves by Holds plus Saves Opportunities.

2006 American League Batting Leaders

Batting Average (minimum 502 PA)		On Base Percentage (minimum 502 PA)		Slugging Average (minimum 502 PA)		Home Runs	
Mauer,Joe, Min	.347	Ramirez,Manny, Bos	.439	Hafner,Travis, Cle	.659	Ortiz,David, Bos	54
Jeter,Derek, NYY	.343	Hafner,Travis, Cle	.439	Ortiz,David, Bos	.636	Dye,Jermaine, CWS	44
Cano,Robinson, NYY	.342	Mauer,Joe, Min	.429	Dye,Jermaine, CWS	.622	Hafner,Travis, Cle	42
Tejada,Miguel, Bal	.330	Jeter,Derek, NYY	.417	Ramirez,Manny, Bos	.619	Thome,Jim, CWS	42
Guerrero,Vladimir, LAA	.329	Thome,Jim, CWS	.416	Thome,Jim, CWS	.598	Thomas,Frank, Oak	39
Suzuki,Ichiro, Sea	.322	Giambi,Jason, NYY	.413	Morneau,Justin, Min	.559	Glaus,Troy, Tor	38
Morneau,Justin, Min	.321	Ortiz,David, Bos	.413	Giambi,Jason, NYY	.558	Giambi,Jason, NYY	37
Ramirez,Manny, Bos	.321	Guillen,Carlos, Det	.400	Guerrero,Vladimir, LAA	.552	4 tied with	35
Guillen,Carlos, Det	.320	Rodriguez,Alex, NYY	.392	Konerko,Paul, CWS	.551		
Johnson,Reed, Tor	.319	Martinez,Victor, Cle	.391	Thomas,Frank, Oak	.545		

Games		Plate Appearances		At Bats		Hits	
Sizemore,Grady, Cle	162	Suzuki,Ichiro, Sea	752	Suzuki,Ichiro, Sea	695	Suzuki,Ichiro, Sea	224
Teixeira,Mark, Tex	162	Sizemore,Grady, Cle	751	Young,Michael, Tex	691	Young,Michael, Tex	217
Tejada,Miguel, Bal	162	Young,Michael, Tex	748	Sizemore,Grady, Cle	655	Jeter,Derek, NYY	214
Young,Michael, Tex	162	Teixeira,Mark, Tex	727	Tejada,Miguel, Bal	648	Tejada,Miguel, Bal	214
Suzuki,Ichiro, Sea	161	Jeter,Derek, NYY	715	Loretta,Mark, Bos	635	Guerrero,Vladimir, LAA	200
Granderson,C, Det	159	Tejada,Miguel, Bal	709	Teixeira,Mark, Tex	628	Matthews Jr.,G, Tex	194
Ibanez,Raul, Sea	159	Mora,Melvin, Bal	705	Ibanez,Raul, Sea	626	Morneau,Justin, Min	190
Inge,Brandon, Det	159	Loretta,Mark, Bos	703	Mora,Melvin, Bal	624	Sizemore,Grady, Cle	190
Sexson,Richie, Sea	158	Ibanez,Raul, Sea	699	Jeter,Derek, NYY	623	Wells,Vernon, Tor	185
4 tied with	157	Matthews Jr.,G, Tex	690	2 tied with	620	Crawford,Carl, TB	183

Singles		Doubles		Triples		Total Bases	
Suzuki,Ichiro, Sea	186	Sizemore,Grady, Cle	53	Crawford,Carl, TB	16	Ortiz,David, Bos	355
Jeter,Derek, NYY	158	Young,Michael, Tex	52	Sizemore,Grady, Cle	11	Sizemore,Grady, Cle	349
Tejada,Miguel, Bal	153	Lowell,Mike, Bos	47	Granderson,C, Det	9	Dye,Jermaine, CWS	335
Young,Michael, Tex	148	Overbay,Lyle, Tor	46	Suzuki,Ichiro, Sea	9	Guerrero,Vladimir, LAA	335
Loretta,Mark, Bos	143	Cabrera,Orlando, LAA	45	Figgins,Chone, LAA	8	Morneau,Justin, Min	331
Castillo,Luis, Min	142	Teixeira,Mark, Tex	45	Lopez,Jose, Sea	8	Wells,Vernon, Tor	331
Kendall,Jason, Oak	139	Matthews Jr.,G, Tex	44	DeJesus,David, KC	7	Ibanez,Raul, Sea	323
Guerrero,Vladimir, LAA	132	Youkilis,Kevin, Bos	42	Punto,Nick, Min	7	Teixeira,Mark, Tex	323
Mora,Melvin, Bal	130	4 tied with	41	Teahen,Mark, KC	7	Tejada,Miguel, Bal	323
Crawford,Carl, TB	129			8 tied with	6	Young,Michael, Tex	317

Runs Scored		RBI		Walks		Strikeouts	
Sizemore,Grady, Cle	134	Ortiz,David, Bos	137	Ortiz,David, Bos	119	Granderson,C, Det	174
Jeter,Derek, NYY	118	Morneau,Justin, Min	130	Giambi,Jason, NYY	110	Sexson,Richie, Sea	154
Damon,Johnny, NYY	115	Ibanez,Raul, Sea	123	Thome,Jim, CWS	107	Sizemore,Grady, Cle	153
Ortiz,David, Bos	115	Rodriguez,Alex, NYY	121	Hafner,Travis, Cle	100	Peralta,Jhonny, Cle	152
Rodriguez,Alex, NYY	113	Dye,Jermaine, CWS	120	Ramirez,Manny, Bos	100	Swisher,Nick, Oak	152
Suzuki,Ichiro, Sea	110	Hafner,Travis, Cle	117	Swisher,Nick, Oak	97	Thome,Jim, CWS	147
Thome,Jim, CWS	108	Guerrero,Vladimir, LAA	116	Youkilis,Kevin, Bos	91	Rodriguez,Alex, NYY	139
Swisher,Nick, Oak	106	Thomas,Frank, Oak	114	Rodriguez,Alex, NYY	90	Glaus,Troy, Tor	134
Glaus,Troy, Tor	105	Giambi,Jason, NYY	113	Teixeira,Mark, Tex	89	Cuddyer,Michael, Min	130
2 tied with	103	Konerko,Paul, CWS	113	Glaus,Troy, Tor	86	2 tied with	128

2006 American League Batting Leaders

Intentional Walks		BA Bases Loaded (minimum 10 PA)		Sacrifice Hits		Sacrifice Flies	
Guerrero,Vladimir, LAA	25	Rivera,Juan, LAA	.667	Lopez,Jose, Sea	12	Cabrera,Orlando, LAA	11
Ortiz,David, Bos	23	Young,Michael, Tex	.615	Punto,Nick, Min	10	Morneau,Justin, Min	11
Mauer,Joe, Min	21	Crawford,Carl, TB	.600	Wilson,Vance, Det	10	Youkilis,Kevin, Bos	11
Hafner,Travis, Cle	16	Hafner,Travis, Cle	.571	Berroa,Angel, KC	9	Brown,Emil, KC	10
Ramirez,Manny, Bos	16	Pierzynski,A.J., CWS	.571	Castillo,Luis, Min	9	Rios,Alex, Tor	10
Suzuki,Ichiro, Sea	16	DeRosa,Mark, Tex	.563	Crawford,Carl, TB	9	Gomes,Jonny, TB	9
Ibanez,Raul, Sea	15	Figgins,Chone, LAA	.556	Fahey,Brandon, Bal	9	Konerko,Paul, CWS	9
Giambi,Jason, NYY	12	Blake,Casey, Cle	.545	Gathright,Joey, TB-KC	9	Wells,Vernon, Tor	9
Teixeira,Mark, Tex	12	Lopez,Jose, Sea	.545	Uribe,Juan, CWS	9	3 tied with	8
Thome,Jim, CWS	12	Millar,Kevin, Bal	.545	4 tied with	8		

BA Close & Late (minimum 50 PA)		Batting Average w/ RISP (minimum 100 PA)		SLG vs. LHP (minimum 125 PA)		SLG vs. RHP (minimum 377 PA)	
Bloomquist,Wil, Sea	.431	Young,Michael, Tex	.412	Guerrero,Vladimir, LAA	.687	Thome,Jim, CWS	.749
Hafner,Travis, Cle	.411	Polanco,Placido, Det	.396	Hafner,Travis, Cle	.658	Ortiz,David, Bos	.649
Matthews Jr.,G, Tex	.398	Jeter,Derek, NYY	.381	Dye,Jermaine, CWS	.645	Ramirez,Manny, Bos	.618
Catalanotto,Fr, Tor	.394	Konerko,Paul, CWS	.366	Glaus,Troy, Tor	.635	Dye,Jermaine, CWS	.610
Damon,Johnny, NYY	.361	Rios,Alex, Tor	.366	Ramirez,Manny, Bos	.621	Giambi,Jason, NYY	.592
Young,Michael, Tex	.356	Mauer,Joe, Min	.360	Molina,Bengie, Tor	.615	Sizemore,Grady, Cle	.586
Castillo,Luis, Min	.351	Dye,Jermaine, CWS	.351	Ortiz,David, Bos	.615	Ibanez,Raul, Sea	.580
Cuddyer,Michael, Min	.346	Teahen,Mark, KC	.350	Gomes,Jonny, TB	.614	Morneau,Justin, Min	.559
Kendall,Jason, Oak	.346	Rivera,Juan, LAA	.349	Teixeira,Mark, Tex	.598	Wells,Vernon, Tor	.554
Rios,Alex, Tor	.344	Crawford,Carl, TB	.348	Konerko,Paul, CWS	.590	Overbay,Lyle, Tor	.554

Leadoff Hitters OBP (minimum 150 PA)		Cleanup Hitters SLG (minimum 150 PA)		BA vs. LHP (minimum 125 PA)		BA vs. RHP (minimum 377 PA)	
Johnson,Reed, Tor	.391	Hafner,Travis, Cle	.662	Guerrero,Vladimir, LAA	.401	Mauer,Joe, Min	.356
Youkilis,Kevin, Bos	.385	Ramirez,Manny, Bos	.621	Jeter,Derek, NYY	.390	Martinez,Victor, Cle	.332
Sizemore,Grady, Cle	.374	Guerrero,Vladimir, LAA	.620	Molina,Bengie, Tor	.358	Guillen,Carlos, Det	.332
Kendall,Jason, Oak	.373	Teixeira,Mark, Tex	.570	Suzuki,Ichiro, Sea	.352	Sizemore,Grady, Cle	.329
Lugo,Julio, TB	.373	Ibanez,Raul, Sea	.554	Rivera,Juan, LAA	.351	Tejada,Miguel, Bal	.329
Matthews Jr.,G, Tex	.372	Konerko,Paul, CWS	.547	German,Esteban, KC	.347	Jeter,Derek, NYY	.328
Suzuki,Ichiro, Sea	.370	Thomas,Frank, Oak	.546	DeRosa,Mark, Tex	.342	Morneau,Justin, Min	.325
Ozuna,Pablo, CWS	.370	Wigginton,Ty, TB	.542	Rodriguez,Ivan, Det	.340	Overbay,Lyle, Tor	.322
Baldelli,Rocco, TB	.368	Glaus,Troy, Tor	.521	Dye,Jermaine, CWS	.337	Thome,Jim, CWS	.321
DeJesus,David, KC	.366	Tejada,Miguel, Bal	.503	Tejada,Miguel, Bal	.335	Young,Michael, Tex	.320

Home BA (minimum 251 PA)		Away BA (minimum 251 PA)		OBP vs. LHP (minimum 125 PA)		OBP vs. RHP (minimum 377 PA)	
Tejada,Miguel, Bal	.357	Cano,Robinson, NYY	.364	Guerrero,Vladimir, LAA	.483	Thome,Jim, CWS	.454
Ramirez,Manny, Bos	.355	Mauer,Joe, Min	.359	Ramirez,Manny, Bos	.477	Mauer,Joe, Min	.444
Jeter,Derek, NYY	.354	Jeter,Derek, NYY	.334	Jeter,Derek, NYY	.458	Giambi,Jason, NYY	.434
Guillen,Carlos, Det	.344	Kendall,Jason, Oak	.330	Hafner,Travis, Cle	.442	Ortiz,David, Bos	.434
Johnson,Reed, Tor	.342	Dye,Jermaine, CWS	.324	Gomes,Jonny, TB	.438	Ramirez,Manny, Bos	.422
Guerrero,Vladimir, LAA	.342	Konerko,Paul, CWS	.319	Rodriguez,Alex, NYY	.434	Guillen,Carlos, Det	.417
Suzuki,Ichiro, Sea	.339	Guerrero,Vladimir, LAA	.319	German,Esteban, KC	.430	Sizemore,Grady, Cle	.416
Catalanotto,Fr, Tor	.339	Damon,Johnny, NYY	.313	Dye,Jermaine, CWS	.429	Jeter,Derek, NYY	.403
Young,Michael, Tex	.338	Martinez,Victor, Cle	.313	Thomas,Frank, Oak	.429	Martinez,Victor, Cle	.402
Mauer,Joe, Min	.335	Rivera,Juan, LAA	.312	Johnson,Reed, Tor	.422	Overbay,Lyle, Tor	.395

2006 American League Batting Leaders

Stolen Bases			Caught Stealing			Highest SB Success Pct			Lowest SB Success Pct		
						(minimum 20 SBA)			(minimum 20 SBA)		
Crawford,Carl, TB		58	Podsednik,Scott, CWS		19	Suzuki,Ichiro, Sea		95.7	Kennedy,Adam, LAA		61.5
Figgins,Chone, LAA		52	Figgins,Chone, LAA		16	Cabrera,Orlando, LAA		90.0	Podsednik,Scott, CWS		67.8
Patterson,Corey, Bal		45	Castillo,Luis, Min		11	Jeter,Derek, NYY		87.2	Guillen,Carlos, Det		69.0
Suzuki,Ichiro, Sea		45	Damon,Johnny, NYY		10	Crawford,Carl, TB		86.6	Castillo,Luis, Min		69.4
Podsednik,Scott, CWS		40	Kennedy,Adam, LAA		10	Crisp,Coco, Bos		84.6	Izturis,Maicer, LAA		70.0
Roberts,Brian, Bal		36	Crawford,Carl, TB		9	Roberts,Brian, Bal		83.7	Gathright,Joey, TB-KC		71.0
Jeter,Derek, NYY		34	Gathright,Joey, TB-KC		9	Patterson,Corey, Bal		83.3	Damon,Johnny, NYY		71.4
Cabrera,Orlando, LAA		27	Guillen,Carlos, Det		9	Lugo,Julio, TB		81.8	Rios,Alex, Tor		71.4
Castillo,Luis, Min		25	Patterson,Corey, Bal		9	Wells,Vernon, Tor		81.0	Guerrero,Vladimir, LAA		75.0
Damon,Johnny, NYY		25	Betancourt,Yun, Sea		8	Sizemore,Grady, Cle		78.6	Figgins,Chone, LAA		76.5

Steals of Third			Grounded Into DP			Grounded Into DP Pct			Hit By Pitch		
						(minimum 50 GIDP Ops)					
Jeter,Derek, NYY		12	Tejada,Miguel, Bal		28	Patterson,Corey, Bal		0.00	Johnson,Reed, Tor		21
Roberts,Brian, Bal		12	Martinez,Victor, Cle		27	Thames,Marcus, Det		0.00	Giambi,Jason, NYY		16
Figgins,Chone, LAA		11	Young,Michael, Tex		27	Suzuki,Ichiro, Sea		2.00	Mora,Melvin, Bal		14
Cabrera,Orlando, LAA		9	Glaus,Troy, Tor		25	Sizemore,Grady, Cle		2.02	Johjima,Kenji, Sea		13
Podsednik,Scott, CWS		9	Konerko,Paul, CWS		25	Thome,Jim, CWS		2.74	Sizemore,Grady, Cle		13
Lugo,Julio, TB		8	Mauer,Joe, Min		24	Baldelli,Rocco, TB		3.45	DeJesus,David, KC		12
Suzuki,Ichiro, Sea		8	Lowell,Mike, Bos		22	Napoli,Mike, LAA		3.45	Jeter,Derek, NYY		12
Crawford,Carl, TB		6	Rodriguez,Alex, NYY		22	Damon,Johnny, NYY		3.77	Kendall,Jason, Oak		12
Wells,Vernon, Tor		6	Berroa,Angel, KC		21	Fahey,Brandon, Bal		3.85	Loretta,Mark, Bos		12
6 tied with		4	6 tied with		19	Gathright,Joey, TB-KC		3.90	Millar,Kevin, Bal		12

Pitches Seen			At Bats Per Home Run			Highest GB/FB Ratio			Lowest GB/FB Ratio		
			(minimum 502 PA)			(minimum 502 PA)			(minimum 502 PA)		
Sizemore,Grady, Cle		3019	Ortiz,David, Bos		10.3	Jeter,Derek, NYY		4.07	Thomas,Frank, Oak		0.47
Youkilis,Kevin, Bos		3009	Hafner,Travis, Cle		10.8	Castillo,Luis, Min		3.67	Giambi,Jason, NYY		0.66
Teixeira,Mark, Tex		2887	Thome,Jim, CWS		11.7	Grudzielanek,M, KC		2.65	Crede,Joe, CWS		0.71
Suzuki,Ichiro, Sea		2821	Thomas,Frank, Oak		11.9	Mauer,Joe, Min		2.53	Glaus,Troy, Tor		0.76
Ibanez,Raul, Sea		2805	Giambi,Jason, NYY		12.1	Kendall,Jason, Oak		2.52	Swisher,Nick, Oak		0.79
Young,Michael, Tex		2805	Dye,Jermaine, CWS		12.3	Tejada,Miguel, Bal		2.50	Youkilis,Kevin, Bos		0.80
Mora,Melvin, Bal		2796	Ramirez,Manny, Bos		12.8	Suzuki,Ichiro, Sea		2.23	Sizemore,Grady, Cle		0.86
Ortiz,David, Bos		2793	Glaus,Troy, Tor		14.2	Cano,Robinson, NYY		2.20	Konerko,Paul, CWS		0.88
Granderson,C, Det		2780	Swisher,Nick, Oak		15.9	DeRosa,Mark, Tex		2.19	Ortiz,David, Bos		0.90
Swisher,Nick, Oak		2761	Konerko,Paul, CWS		16.2	Berroa,Angel, KC		2.16	Thome,Jim, CWS		0.91

Pitches Per Plate App			Pct Pitches Taken			Best BPS on OutZ			Worst BPS on OutZ		
(minimum 502 PA)			(minimum 1500 Pitches)			(minimum 502 PA)			(minimum 502 PA)		
Youkilis,Kevin, Bos		4.43	Giambi,Jason, NYY		64.0	Markakis,Nick, Bal		.640	Peralta,Jhonny, Cle		.168
Giambi,Jason, NYY		4.38	Youkilis,Kevin, Bos		63.8	Martinez,Victor, Cle		.636	Iguchi,Tadahito, CWS		.228
Thomas,Frank, Oak		4.36	Castillo,Luis, Min		63.4	Guillen,Carlos, Det		.634	Swisher,Nick, Oak		.231
Thome,Jim, CWS		4.31	Mauer,Joe, Min		63.3	Pierzynski,A.J., CWS		.610	Monroe,Craig, Det		.246
Hafner,Travis, Cle		4.21	Podsednik,Scott, CWS		62.5	Rodriguez,Ivan, Det		.608	Granderson,C, Det		.252
Glaus,Troy, Tor		4.21	Thome,Jim, CWS		62.4	Loretta,Mark, Bos		.593	Inge,Brandon, Det		.260
Ramirez,Manny, Bos		4.16	Izturis,Maicer, LAA		62.3	Teixeira,Mark, Tex		.589	Mora,Melvin, Bal		.278
Inge,Brandon, Det		4.13	Hafner,Travis, Cle		61.6	Wells,Vernon, Tor		.578	DeJesus,David, KC		.282
Peralta,Jhonny, Cle		4.12	Nixon,Trot, Bos		61.3	Johnson,Reed, Tor		.578	Ordonez,Magglio, Det		.296
Dye,Jermaine, CWS		4.11	Kendall,Jason, Oak		61.3	Morneau,Justin, Min		.576	Sexson,Richie, Sea		.299

2006 American League Batting Leaders

Best BPS vs Fastballs
(minimum 251 PA)

Ramirez,Manny, Bos	1.102
Ortiz,David, Bos	1.093
Dye,Jermaine, CWS	1.018
Rios,Alex, Tor	1.016
Posada,Jorge, NYY	1.008
Rivera,Juan, LAA	1.004
Hafner,Travis, Cle	.992
Sizemore,Grady, Cle	.948
Konerko,Paul, CWS	.929
Mauer,Joe, Min	.929

Best BPS vs Curveballs
(minimum 50 PA)

Guerrero,Vladimir, LAA	1.219
Morneau,Justin, Min	1.204
Thome,Jim, CWS	.959
Wells,Vernon, Tor	.944
Crawford,Carl, TB	.923
Hafner,Travis, Cle	.805
Tejada,Miguel, Bal	.759
Crede,Joe, CWS	.755
Matthews Jr.,G, Tex	.755
2 tied with	.702

Best BPS vs Changeups
(minimum 50 PA)

Thome,Jim, CWS	1.424
Cuddyer,Michael, Min	1.139
Young,Michael, Tex	1.056
Inge,Brandon, Det	1.054
Ramirez,Manny, Bos	1.034
Overbay,Lyle, Tor	1.030
Jeter,Derek, NYY	1.020
Markakis,Nick, Bal	1.000
Cano,Robinson, NYY	.985
Morneau,Justin, Min	.980

Best BPS vs Sliders
(minimum 32 PA)

Giambi,Jason, NYY	1.016
Hafner,Travis, Cle	.986
Crawford,Carl, TB	.931
Damon,Johnny, NYY	.920
Pena,Wily Mo, Bos	.893
Graffanino,Tony, KC	.834
Ibanez,Raul, Sea	.834
Hill,Aaron, Tor	.833
Ortiz,David, Bos	.831
Thames,Marcus, Det	.831

OPS
(minimum 502 PA)

Hafner,Travis, Cle	1.098
Ramirez,Manny, Bos	1.058
Ortiz,David, Bos	1.049
Thome,Jim, CWS	1.014
Dye,Jermaine, CWS	1.007
Giambi,Jason, NYY	.971
Mauer,Joe, Min	.936
Guerrero,Vladimir, LAA	.934
Morneau,Justin, Min	.934
Konerko,Paul, CWS	.932

OPS First Half
(minimum 251 PA)

Hafner,Travis, Cle	1.111
Thome,Jim, CWS	1.065
Ramirez,Manny, Bos	1.049
Dye,Jermaine, CWS	1.043
Giambi,Jason, NYY	1.026
Ortiz,David, Bos	.997
Mauer,Joe, Min	.981
Wells,Vernon, Tor	.971
Rios,Alex, Tor	.968
Konerko,Paul, CWS	.943

OPS Second Half
(minimum 251 PA)

Ortiz,David, Bos	1.121
Guerrero,Vladimir, LAA	1.046
Sexson,Richie, Sea	1.012
Teixeira,Mark, Tex	.998
Guillen,Carlos, Det	.976
Dye,Jermaine, CWS	.966
Thomas,Frank, Oak	.956
Thome,Jim, CWS	.942
Sizemore,Grady, Cle	.941
Rodriguez,Alex, NYY	.939

OPS by Catchers
(minimum 251 PA)

Mauer,Joe, Min	.901
Posada,Jorge, NYY	.893
Hernandez,Ram, Bal	.853
Martinez,Victor, Cle	.844
Zaun,Gregg, Tor	.829
Napoli,Mike, LAA	.822
Laird,Gerald, Tex	.807
Johjima,Kenji, Sea	.790
Molina,Bengie, Tor	.783
Pierzynski,A.J., CWS	.782

OPS by First Basemen
(minimum 251 PA)

Giambi,Jason, NYY	1.051
Morneau,Justin, Min	.950
Konerko,Paul, CWS	.930
Broussard,Ben, Cle-Sea	.912
Overbay,Lyle, Tor	.898
Teixeira,Mark, Tex	.885
Millar,Kevin, Bal	.839
Sexson,Richie, Sea	.831
Shelton,Chris, Det	.809
Youkilis,Kevin, Bos	.779

OPS by Second Basemen
(minimum 251 PA)

Cano,Robinson, NYY	.877
Kinsler,Ian, Tex	.802
Iguchi,Tadahito, CWS	.771
Roberts,Brian, Bal	.758
Belliard,Ronnie, Cle	.754
Grudzielanek,M, KC	.751
Loretta,Mark, Bos	.735
Castillo,Luis, Min	.728
Lopez,Jose, Sea	.724
Kennedy,Adam, LAA	.723

OPS by Third Basemen
(minimum 251 PA)

Rodriguez,Alex, NYY	.931
Teahen,Mark, KC	.874
Glaus,Troy, Tor	.865
Crede,Joe, CWS	.831
Lowell,Mike, Bos	.808
Chavez,Eric, Oak	.799
Beltre,Adrian, Sea	.795
Blalock,Hank, Tex	.777
Inge,Brandon, Det	.776
Izturis,Maicer, LAA	.775

OPS by Shortstops
(minimum 251 PA)

Guillen,Carlos, Det	.946
Jeter,Derek, NYY	.918
Tejada,Miguel, Bal	.875
Lugo,Julio, TB	.871
Scutaro,Marco, Oak	.857
Young,Michael, Tex	.784
Bartlett,Jason, Min	.760
Cabrera,Orlando, LAA	.739
Betancourt,Yun, Sea	.713
Peralta,Jhonny, Cle	.711

OPS by Left Fielders
(minimum 251 PA)

Ramirez,Manny, Bos	1.047
Swisher,Nick, Oak	.980
Ibanez,Raul, Sea	.873
Johnson,Reed, Tor	.856
Catalanotto,Fr, Tor	.841
Crawford,Carl, TB	.837
DeJesus,David, KC	.800
Brown,Emil, KC	.783
Wilkerson,Brad, Tex	.777
Monroe,Craig, Det	.774

OPS by Center Fielders
(minimum 251 PA)

Sizemore,Grady, Cle	.909
Wells,Vernon, Tor	.906
Matthews Jr.,G, Tex	.875
Baldelli,Rocco, TB	.869
Damon,Johnny, NYY	.828
DeJesus,David, KC	.822
Hunter,Torii, Min	.816
Granderson,C, Det	.776
Patterson,Corey, Bal	.761
Kotsay,Mark, Oak	.718

OPS by Right Fielders
(minimum 251 PA)

Dye,Jermaine, CWS	1.008
Guerrero,Vladimir, LAA	.921
Markakis,Nick, Bal	.875
Rios,Alex, Tor	.850
Cuddyer,Michael, Min	.823
Bradley,Milton, Oak	.821
Ordonez,Magglio, Det	.816
Suzuki,Ichiro, Sea	.791
Blake,Casey, Cle	.786
Nixon,Trot, Bos	.781

OPS by Designated Hitters
(minimum 251 PA)

Hafner,Travis, Cle	1.084
Ortiz,David, Bos	1.025
Thome,Jim, CWS	.997
Thames,Marcus, Det	.945
Thomas,Frank, Oak	.924
Giambi,Jason, NYY	.904
Hillenbrand,Shea, Tor	.876
Anderson,Garret, LAA	.825
Sweeney,Mike, KC	.791
Salmon,Tim, LAA	.778

2006 American League Batting Leaders

OPS Batting Left vs. LHP		OPS Batting Left vs. RHP		OPS Batting Right vs. LHP		OPS Batting Right vs. RHP	
(minimum 125 PA)		(minimum 377 PA)		(minimum 125 PA)		(minimum 377 PA)	
Hafner,Travis, Cle	1.100	Thome,Jim, CWS	1.203	Guerrero,Vladimir, LAA	1.170	Ramirez,Manny, Bos	1.040
Ortiz,David, Bos	.988	Ortiz,David, Bos	1.083	Ramirez,Manny, Bos	1.098	Dye,Jermaine, CWS	.972
DeJesus,David, KC	.913	Giambi,Jason, NYY	1.026	Dye,Jermaine, CWS	1.074	Thomas,Frank, Oak	.912
Morneau,Justin, Min	.904	Sizemore,Grady, Cle	1.002	Gomes,Jonny, TB	1.052	Konerko,Paul, CWS	.905
Damon,Johnny, NYY	.862	Mauer,Joe, Min	.994	Glaus,Troy, Tor	1.048	Wells,Vernon, Tor	.900
Suzuki,Ichiro, Sea	.846	Ibanez,Raul, Sea	.955	Jeter,Derek, NYY	1.011	Rodriguez,Alex, NYY	.884
Giambi,Jason, NYY	.828	Guillen,Carlos, Det	.954	Rodriguez,Alex, NYY	1.008	Tejada,Miguel, Bal	.878
Mauer,Joe, Min	.826	Morneau,Justin, Min	.950	Molina,Bengie, Tor	.998	Sexson,Richie, Sea	.866
Crawford,Carl, TB	.777	Overbay,Lyle, Tor	.949	Konerko,Paul, CWS	.984	Lowell,Mike, Bos	.863
Sizemore,Grady, Cle	.717	Posada,Jorge, NYY	.925	DeRosa,Mark, Tex	.983	Jeter,Derek, NYY	.862

OPS vs. LHP		OPS vs. RHP		RC Per 27 Outs vs. LHP		RC Per 27 Outs vs. RHP	
(minimum 125 PA)		(minimum 377 PA)		(minimum 125 PA)		(minimum 377 PA)	
Guerrero,Vladimir, LAA	1.170	Thome,Jim, CWS	1.203	Ramirez,Manny, Bos	12.6	Thome,Jim, CWS	11.4
Hafner,Travis, Cle	1.100	Ortiz,David, Bos	1.083	Guerrero,Vladimir, LAA	12.0	Giambi,Jason, NYY	9.4
Ramirez,Manny, Bos	1.098	Ramirez,Manny, Bos	1.040	Jeter,Derek, NYY	9.9	Ortiz,David, Bos	9.4
Dye,Jermaine, CWS	1.074	Giambi,Jason, NYY	1.026	Dye,Jermaine, CWS	9.6	Sizemore,Grady, Cle	8.3
Gomes,Jonny, TB	1.052	Sizemore,Grady, Cle	1.002	Gomes,Jonny, TB	8.9	Morneau,Justin, Min	8.2
Glaus,Troy, Tor	1.048	Mauer,Joe, Min	.994	Hafner,Travis, Cle	8.8	Guillen,Carlos, Det	8.0
Jeter,Derek, NYY	1.011	Dye,Jermaine, CWS	.972	Molina,Bengie, Tor	8.6	Ramirez,Manny, Bos	7.8
Rodriguez,Alex, NYY	1.008	Ibanez,Raul, Sea	.955	Hernandez,Ram, Bal	8.3	Mauer,Joe, Min	7.8
Molina,Bengie, Tor	.998	Guillen,Carlos, Det	.954	Glaus,Troy, Tor	8.3	Posada,Jorge, NYY	7.7
Ortiz,David, Bos	.988	Morneau,Justin, Min	.950	German,Esteban, KC	8.1	Ibanez,Raul, Sea	7.6

Highest RBI %		Lowest RBI %		Highest Strikeout per PA		Lowest Strikeout per PA	
(minimum 502 PA)		(minimum 502 PA)		(minimum 502 PA)		(minimum 502 PA)	
Hafner,Travis, Cle	12.26	Suzuki,Ichiro, Sea	4.43	Granderson,C, Det	.256	Johjima,Kenji, Sea	.085
Thomas,Frank, Oak	11.78	Castillo,Luis, Min	4.79	Peralta,Jhonny, Cle	.241	Cabrera,Orlando, LAA	.086
Ortiz,David, Bos	11.68	Kendall,Jason, Oak	5.01	Thome,Jim, CWS	.241	Kendall,Jason, Oak	.086
Dye,Jermaine, CWS	11.39	Loretta,Mark, Bos	5.08	Sexson,Richie, Sea	.232	Payton,Jay, Oak	.088
Morneau,Justin, Min	11.20	Hill,Aaron, Tor	5.09	Swisher,Nick, Oak	.226	Castillo,Luis, Min	.089
Giambi,Jason, NYY	11.00	Betancourt,Yun, Sea	5.14	Monroe,Craig, Det	.215	Mauer,Joe, Min	.089
Thome,Jim, CWS	10.92	Podsednik,Scott, CWS	5.21	Inge,Brandon, Det	.213	Loretta,Mark, Bos	.090
Ibanez,Raul, Sea	10.61	Punto,Nick, Min	5.26	Glaus,Troy, Tor	.211	Betancourt,Yun, Sea	.092
Ramirez,Manny, Bos	10.55	Grudzielanek,M, KC	5.57	Rodriguez,Alex, NYY	.206	Suzuki,Ichiro, Sea	.094
Guerrero,Vladimir, LAA	10.53	Roberts,Brian, Bal	5.59	Cuddyer,Michael, Min	.205	Lowell,Mike, Bos	.097

Home Runs At Home		Home Runs Away		Longest Avg Home Run		Shortest Avg Home Run	
				(min 10 over the wall)		(min 10 over the wall)	
Glaus,Troy, Tor	25	Ortiz,David, Bos	32	Pena,Wily Mo, Bos	411	Ellis,Mark, Oak	370
Thome,Jim, CWS	25	Dye,Jermaine, CWS	23	Rodriguez,Alex, NYY	410	Barajas,Rod, Tex	375
Wells,Vernon, Tor	24	Hafner,Travis, Cle	21	Sexson,Richie, Sea	407	Millar,Kevin, Bal	376
Thomas,Frank, Oak	23	Teixeira,Mark, Tex	21	Hafner,Travis, Cle	406	Lugo,Julio, TB	376
Ortiz,David, Bos	22	Guerrero,Vladimir, LAA	19	Hinske,Eric, Tor-Bos	405	Lopez,Jose, Sea	376
Dye,Jermaine, CWS	21	Ramirez,Manny, Bos	19	Thome,Jim, CWS	401	Tejada,Miguel, Bal	377
Hafner,Travis, Cle	21	Swisher,Nick, Oak	18	Broussard,Ben, Cle-Sea	401	DeRosa,Mark, Tex	377
Konerko,Paul, CWS	21	4 tied with	17	Ortiz,David, Bos	401	Conine,Jeff, Bal	377
Giambi,Jason, NYY	20			Giambi,Jason, NYY	400	Payton,Jay, Oak	377
Rodriguez,Alex, NYY	20			Nevin,Phil, Tex-Min	400	Zaun,Gregg, Tor	377

2006 American League Batting Leaders

Under Age 26: AB Per HR

(minimum 502 PA)

Swisher,Nick, Oak	15.9
Morneau,Justin, Min	17.4
Sizemore,Grady, Cle	23.4
Markakis,Nick, Bal	30.7
Granderson,C, Det	31.4
Cano,Robinson, NYY	32.1
Crawford,Carl, TB	33.3
Blalock,Hank, Tex	36.9
Mauer,Joe, Min	40.1
Peralta,Jhonny, Cle	43.8

Under Age 26: OPS

(minimum 502 PA)

Mauer,Joe, Min	.936
Morneau,Justin, Min	.934
Sizemore,Grady, Cle	.907
Cano,Robinson, NYY	.890
Swisher,Nick, Oak	.864
Crawford,Carl, TB	.830
Markakis,Nick, Bal	.799
Granderson,C, Det	.773
Cabrera,Melky, NYY	.752
Hill,Aaron, Tor	.735

Under Age 26: RC/27 Outs

(minimum 502 PA)

Morneau,Justin, Min	7.4
Mauer,Joe, Min	7.3
Crawford,Carl, TB	6.7
Sizemore,Grady, Cle	6.7
Swisher,Nick, Oak	5.8
Cano,Robinson, NYY	5.7
Cabrera,Melky, NYY	5.1
Blalock,Hank, Tex	5.1
Granderson,C, Det	5.1
Markakis,Nick, Bal	4.8

Longest Home Run

Rodriguez,Alex, NYY, 6/15	480
Pena,Wily Mo, Bos, 7/31	475
Napoli,Mike, LAA, 6/23	470
Hafner,Travis, Cle, 6/19	461
Ibanez,Raul, Sea, 5/27	460
Belliard,Ronnie, Cle, 7/2	457
Dye,Jermaine, CWS, 7/8	456
Giambi,Jason, NYY, 4/16	451
Pena,Wily Mo, Bos, 8/8	451
3 tied with	450

Swing and Miss %

(minimum 1500 Pitches Seen)

Sexson,Richie, Sea	22.5
Wilkerson,Brad, Tex	22.0
Swisher,Nick, Oak	20.7
Gomes,Jonny, TB	20.4
Thome,Jim, CWS	20.0
Granderson,C, Det	19.8
Hafner,Travis, Cle	19.6
Thames,Marcus, Det	19.4
Rodriguez,Alex, NYY	18.6
Peralta,Jhonny, Cle	17.5

Highest First Swing %

(minimum 502 PA)

Guerrero,Vladimir, LAA	50.2
Pierzynski,A.J., CWS	42.5
Payton,Jay, Oak	39.0
Cano,Robinson, NYY	38.9
Monroe,Craig, Det	38.9
Ordonez,Magglio, Det	38.6
Hunter,Torii, Min	38.2
Wells,Vernon, Tor	37.8
Brown,Emil, KC	36.8
Berroa,Angel, KC	36.3

Lowest First Swing %

(minimum 502 PA)

Kendall,Jason, Oak	9.2
Johnson,Reed, Tor	10.2
Damon,Johnny, NYY	11.1
Castillo,Luis, Min	11.3
Youkilis,Kevin, Bos	11.5
Mauer,Joe, Min	12.5
Podsednik,Scott, CWS	13.3
Suzuki,Ichiro, Sea	14.5
Mora,Melvin, Bal	16.7
Thomas,Frank, Oak	17.1

Home RC Per 27 Outs

(minimum 251 PA)

Hafner,Travis, Cle	10.8
Giambi,Jason, NYY	10.5
Ramirez,Manny, Bos	10.1
Thome,Jim, CWS	9.6
Ortiz,David, Bos	9.0
Jeter,Derek, NYY	8.6
Posada,Jorge, NYY	8.2
Hernandez,Ram, Bal	8.1
Morneau,Justin, Min	8.0
Guerrero,Vladimir, LAA	7.9

Road RC Per 27 Outs

(minimum 251 PA)

Thomas,Frank, Oak	9.0
Mauer,Joe, Min	8.3
Hafner,Travis, Cle	8.3
Ramirez,Manny, Bos	8.2
Teixeira,Mark, Tex	8.2
Thome,Jim, CWS	8.1
Dye,Jermaine, CWS	7.7
Ortiz,David, Bos	7.6
Jeter,Derek, NYY	7.5
Damon,Johnny, NYY	7.2

2006 National League Batting Leaders

Batting Average (minimum 502 PA)		On Base Percentage (minimum 502 PA)		Slugging Average (minimum 502 PA)		Home Runs	
Sanchez,Freddy, Pit	.344	Pujols,Albert, StL	.431	Pujols,Albert, StL	.671	Howard,Ryan, Phi	58
Cabrera,Miguel, Fla	.339	Cabrera,Miguel, Fla	.430	Howard,Ryan, Phi	.659	Pujols,Albert, StL	49
Pujols,Albert, StL	.331	Johnson,Nick, Was	.428	Berkman,Lance, Hou	.621	Soriano,Alfonso, Was	46
Atkins,Garrett, Col	.329	Howard,Ryan, Phi	.425	Beltran,Carlos, NYM	.594	Berkman,Lance, Hou	45
Holliday,Matt, Col	.326	Berkman,Lance, Hou	.420	Holliday,Matt, Col	.586	Beltran,Carlos, NYM	41
Lo Duca,Paul, NYM	.318	Atkins,Garrett, Col	.409	Cabrera,Miguel, Fla	.568	Jones,Andruw, Atl	41
Berkman,Lance, Hou	.315	Helton,Todd, Col	.404	LaRoche,Adam, Atl	.561	Dunn,Adam, Cin	40
Howard,Ryan, Phi	.313	Bay,Jason, Pit	.396	Ramirez,Aramis, ChC	.561	Delgado,Carlos, NYM	38
Wright,David, NYM	.311	Drew,J.D., LAD	.393	Soriano,Alfonso, Was	.560	Ramirez,Aramis, ChC	38
Utley,Chase, Phi	.309	Hatteberg,Scott, Cin	.389	Atkins,Garrett, Col	.556	2 tied with	35

Games		Plate Appearances		At Bats		Hits	
Francoeur,Jeff, Atl	162	Rollins,Jimmy, Phi	758	Pierre,Juan, ChC	699	Pierre,Juan, ChC	204
Pierre,Juan, ChC	162	Pierre,Juan, ChC	750	Rollins,Jimmy, Phi	689	Utley,Chase, Phi	203
Dunn,Adam, Cin	160	Utley,Chase, Phi	739	Utley,Chase, Phi	658	Sanchez,Freddy, Pit	200
Feliz,Pedro, SF	160	Furcal,Rafael, LAD	736	Furcal,Rafael, LAD	654	Atkins,Garrett, Col	198
Utley,Chase, Phi	160	Soriano,Alfonso, Was	728	Francoeur,Jeff, Atl	651	Furcal,Rafael, LAD	196
Bay,Jason, Pit	159	Giles,Brian, SD	717	Reyes,Jose, NYM	647	Holliday,Matt, Col	196
Furcal,Rafael, LAD	159	Lopez,Felipe, Cin-Was	714	Soriano,Alfonso, Was	647	Cabrera,Miguel, Fla	195
Howard,Ryan, Phi	159	Howard,Ryan, Phi	704	Ramirez,Hanley, Fla	633	Reyes,Jose, NYM	194
Soriano,Alfonso, Was	159	Reyes,Jose, NYM	703	Lopez,Felipe, Cin-Was	617	Rollins,Jimmy, Phi	191
4 tied with	158	Ramirez,Hanley, Fla	700	Zimmerman,Ryan, Was	614	Ramirez,Hanley, Fla	185

Singles		Doubles		Triples		Total Bases	
Pierre,Juan, ChC	156	Sanchez,Freddy, Pit	53	Reyes,Jose, NYM	17	Howard,Ryan, Phi	383
Furcal,Rafael, LAD	140	Gonzalez,Luis, Ari	52	Pierre,Juan, ChC	13	Soriano,Alfonso, Was	362
Sanchez,Freddy, Pit	139	Cabrera,Miguel, Fla	50	Roberts,Dave, SD	13	Pujols,Albert, StL	359
Vizquel,Omar, SF	135	Atkins,Garrett, Col	48	Finley,Steve, SF	12	Holliday,Matt, Col	353
Lopez,Felipe, Cin-Was	128	Rolen,Scott, StL	48	Lofton,Kenny, LAD	12	Utley,Chase, Phi	347
Reyes,Jose, NYM	128	Zimmerman,Ryan, Was	47	Ramirez,Hanley, Fla	11	Atkins,Garrett, Col	335
Utley,Chase, Phi	127	Johnson,Nick, Was	46	Sullivan,Cory, Col	10	Berkman,Lance, Hou	333
Eckstein,David, StL	125	Ramirez,Hanley, Fla	46	Vizquel,Omar, SF	10	Ramirez,Aramis, ChC	333
Taveras,Willy, Hou	122	Holliday,Matt, Col	45	4 tied with	9	Rollins,Jimmy, Phi	329
Atkins,Garrett, Col	120	Rollins,Jimmy, Phi	45			Cabrera,Miguel, Fla	327

Runs Scored		RBI		Walks		Strikeouts	
Utley,Chase, Phi	131	Howard,Ryan, Phi	149	Bonds,Barry, SF	115	Dunn,Adam, Cin	194
Beltran,Carlos, NYM	127	Pujols,Albert, StL	137	Dunn,Adam, Cin	112	Howard,Ryan, Phi	181
Rollins,Jimmy, Phi	127	Berkman,Lance, Hou	136	Johnson,Nick, Was	110	Hall,Bill, Mil	162
Reyes,Jose, NYM	122	Jones,Andruw, Atl	129	Howard,Ryan, Phi	108	Soriano,Alfonso, Was	160
Holliday,Matt, Col	119	Atkins,Garrett, Col	120	Giles,Brian, SD	104	Bay,Jason, Pit	156
Pujols,Albert, StL	119	Ramirez,Aramis, ChC	119	Bay,Jason, Pit	102	Cameron,Mike, SD	142
Ramirez,Hanley, Fla	119	Beltran,Carlos, NYM	116	Ensberg,Morgan, Hou	101	Kearns,Austin, Cin-Was	135
Soriano,Alfonso, Was	119	Wright,David, NYM	116	Berkman,Lance, Hou	98	Francoeur,Jeff, Atl	132
Atkins,Garrett, Col	117	3 tied with	114	Burrell,Pat, Phi	98	Utley,Chase, Phi	132
Furcal,Rafael, LAD	113			Beltran,Carlos, NYM	95	Burrell,Pat, Phi	131

2006 National League Batting Leaders

Intentional Walks

Bonds,Barry, SF	38
Howard,Ryan, Phi	37
Pujols,Albert, StL	28
Cabrera,Miguel, Fla	27
Berkman,Lance, Hou	22
Soriano,Alfonso, Was	16
Helton,Todd, Col	15
Johnson,Nick, Was	15
Wright,David, NYM	13
Dunn,Adam, Cin	12

BA Bases Loaded
(minimum 10 PA)

Renteria,Edgar, Atl	.818
Pierre,Juan, ChC	.643
Chavez,Endy, NYM	.625
Atkins,Garrett, Col	.571
Helton,Todd, Col	.571
Valentin,Jose, NYM	.563
Garciaparra,N, LAD	.556
Counsell,Craig, Ari	.545
Sanchez,Freddy, Pit	.545
Taguchi,So, StL	.538

Sacrifice Hits

Oswalt,Roy, Hou	20
Barmes,Clint, Col	19
Sullivan,Cory, Col	19
Smoltz,John, Atl	18
Cedeno,Ronny, ChC	15
Fogg,Josh, Col	15
Hudson,Tim, Atl	14
Morris,Matt, SF	14
3 tied with	13

Sacrifice Flies

Delgado,Carlos, NYM	10
Bay,Jason, Pit	9
Jones,Andruw, Atl	9
Sanchez,Freddy, Pit	9
Berkman,Lance, Hou	8
Estrada,Johnny, Ari	8
Fielder,Prince, Mil	8
Rolen,Scott, StL	8
Uggla,Dan, Fla	8
Wright,David, NYM	8

BA Close & Late
(minimum 50 PA)

Anderson,Mar, Was-LAD	.400
Helms,Wes, Fla	.400
Jenkins,Geoff, Mil	.397
Lee,Carlos, Mil	.373
Durham,Ray, SF	.364
Bard,Josh, SD	.351
Jones,Andruw, Atl	.349
Wright,David, NYM	.348
Cabrera,Miguel, Fla	.342
Cirillo,Jeff, Mil	.339

Batting Average w/ RISP
(minimum 100 PA)

Bonds,Barry, SF	.423
Pujols,Albert, StL	.397
Sanchez,Freddy, Pit	.386
Berkman,Lance, Hou	.382
Cabrera,Miguel, Fla	.378
Garciaparra,N, LAD	.368
Wright,David, NYM	.365
Helton,Todd, Col	.347
Lee,Carlos, Mil	.347
McCann,Brian, Atl	.346

SLG vs. LHP
(minimum 125 PA)

Aurilia,Rich, Cin	.680
Durham,Ray, SF	.650
Hall,Bill, Mil	.650
Pujols,Albert, StL	.620
Willingham,Josh, Fla	.619
Kearns,Austin, Cin-Was	.605
Ramirez,Hanley, Fla	.588
Bay,Jason, Pit	.587
Barfield,Josh, SD	.587
Byrnes,Eric, Ari	.584

SLG vs. RHP
(minimum 377 PA)

Howard,Ryan, Phi	.711
Berkman,Lance, Hou	.704
Pujols,Albert, StL	.688
Beltran,Carlos, NYM	.648
McCann,Brian, Atl	.603
Jones,Chipper, Atl	.602
Delgado,Carlos, NYM	.595
Holliday,Matt, Col	.588
LaRoche,Adam, Atl	.584
Ramirez,Aramis, ChC	.573

Leadoff Hitters OBP
(minimum 150 PA)

Carroll,Jamey, Col	.372
Furcal,Rafael, LAD	.372
Soriano,Alfonso, Was	.368
Weeks,Rickie, Mil	.360
Bautista,Jose, Pit	.360
Freel,Ryan, Cin	.359
Roberts,Dave, SD	.359
Ramirez,Hanley, Fla	.358
Reyes,Jose, NYM	.354
Eckstein,David, StL	.351

Cleanup Hitters SLG
(minimum 150 PA)

Wright,David, NYM	.688
Howard,Ryan, Phi	.674
Holliday,Matt, Col	.578
Berkman,Lance, Hou	.573
Lee,Carlos, Mil	.573
Encarnacion,Ed, Cin	.569
Delgado,Carlos, NYM	.556
Bay,Jason, Pit	.549
Bonds,Barry, SF	.548
Edmonds,Jim, StL	.543

BA vs. LHP
(minimum 125 PA)

Sanchez,Freddy, Pit	.442
Aurilia,Rich, Cin	.347
Durham,Ray, SF	.341
Vizquel,Omar, SF	.340
Paulino,Ronny, Pit	.339
Hudson,Orlando, Ari	.338
Helms,Wes, Fla	.336
Pujols,Albert, StL	.336
Kearns,Austin, Cin-Was	.336
Lo Duca,Paul, NYM	.336

BA vs. RHP
(minimum 377 PA)

McCann,Brian, Atl	.351
Cabrera,Miguel, Fla	.344
Berkman,Lance, Hou	.335
Jones,Chipper, Atl	.332
Howard,Ryan, Phi	.331
Pujols,Albert, StL	.329
Atkins,Garrett, Col	.327
Holliday,Matt, Col	.325
Wright,David, NYM	.321
Lofton,Kenny, LAD	.319

Home BA
(minimum 251 PA)

Sanchez,Freddy, Pit	.388
Carroll,Jamey, Col	.375
Holliday,Matt, Col	.373
Cabrera,Miguel, Fla	.355
Atkins,Garrett, Col	.346
Pujols,Albert, StL	.345
Helton,Todd, Col	.338
Berkman,Lance, Hou	.335
Furcal,Rafael, LAD	.333
Utley,Chase, Phi	.329

Away BA
(minimum 251 PA)

Jones,Chipper, Atl	.355
Cabrera,Miguel, Fla	.323
Lofton,Kenny, LAD	.322
Barfield,Josh, SD	.319
Lo Duca,Paul, NYM	.318
Howard,Ryan, Phi	.318
Pujols,Albert, StL	.317
Beltran,Carlos, NYM	.317
Atkins,Garrett, Col	.313
Taveras,Willy, Hou	.313

OBP vs. LHP
(minimum 125 PA)

Ensberg,Morgan, Hou	.463
Sanchez,Freddy, Pit	.460
Bonds,Barry, SF	.451
Burrell,Pat, Phi	.440
Johnson,Nick, Was	.438
Cabrera,Miguel, Fla	.436
Pujols,Albert, StL	.435
Kearns,Austin, Cin-Was	.434
Bay,Jason, Pit	.427
Freel,Ryan, Cin	.424

OBP vs. RHP
(minimum 377 PA)

Howard,Ryan, Phi	.453
Berkman,Lance, Hou	.438
Jones,Chipper, Atl	.434
Pujols,Albert, StL	.429
Cabrera,Miguel, Fla	.429
Johnson,Nick, Was	.424
Drew,J.D., LAD	.410
Helton,Todd, Col	.407
Beltran,Carlos, NYM	.405
Hatteberg,Scott, Cin	.401

2006 National League Batting Leaders

<table>
<tr><td colspan="2">Stolen Bases</td></tr>
<tr><td>Reyes,Jose, NYM</td><td>64</td></tr>
<tr><td>Pierre,Juan, ChC</td><td>58</td></tr>
<tr><td>Ramirez,Hanley, Fla</td><td>51</td></tr>
<tr><td>Roberts,Dave, SD</td><td>49</td></tr>
<tr><td>Lopez,Felipe, Cin-Was</td><td>44</td></tr>
<tr><td>Soriano,Alfonso, Was</td><td>41</td></tr>
<tr><td>Freel,Ryan, Cin</td><td>37</td></tr>
<tr><td>Furcal,Rafael, LAD</td><td>37</td></tr>
<tr><td>Rollins,Jimmy, Phi</td><td>36</td></tr>
<tr><td>Taveras,Willy, Hou</td><td>33</td></tr>
</table>

Caught Stealing	
Pierre,Juan, ChC	20
Reyes,Jose, NYM	17
Soriano,Alfonso, Was	17
Ramirez,Hanley, Fla	15
Furcal,Rafael, LAD	13
Amezaga,Alfredo, Fla	12
Carroll,Jamey, Col	12
Lopez,Felipe, Cin-Was	12
Freel,Ryan, Cin	11
3 tied with	9

Highest SB Success Pct	
(minimum 20 SBA)	
Duffy,Chris, Pit	96.3
Phillips,Brand, Cin	92.6
Rollins,Jimmy, Phi	90.0
Byrnes,Eric, Ari	89.3
Roberts,Dave, SD	89.1
Lofton,Kenny, LAD	86.5
Beltran,Carlos, NYM	85.7
Abreu,Bobby, Phi	83.3
Barfield,Josh, SD	80.8
Wright,David, NYM	80.0

Lowest SB Success Pct	
(minimum 20 SBA)	
Carroll,Jamey, Col	45.5
Amezaga,Alfredo, Fla	62.5
Counsell,Craig, Ari	65.2
Clayton,Royce, Was-Cin	70.0
Soriano,Alfonso, Was	70.7
Cameron,Mike, SD	73.5
Renteria,Edgar, Atl	73.9
Furcal,Rafael, LAD	74.0
Pierre,Juan, ChC	74.4
Freel,Ryan, Cin	77.1

Steals of Third	
Soriano,Alfonso, Was	14
Pierre,Juan, ChC	12
Freel,Ryan, Cin	10
Phillips,Brand, Cin	8
Reyes,Jose, NYM	8
Lopez,Felipe, Cin-Was	7
Ramirez,Hanley, Fla	7
Beltran,Carlos, NYM	6
Chavez,Endy, NYM	6
Vizquel,Omar, SF	6

Grounded Into DP	
Atkins,Garrett, Col	24
Gonzalez,Adrian, SD	24
Castillo,Jose, Pit	22
Holliday,Matt, Col	22
Ausmus,Brad, Hou	21
Pujols,Albert, StL	20
Wilson,Preston, Hou-StL	20
Phillips,Brand, Cin	19
7 tied with	18

Grounded Into DP Pct	
(minimum 50 GIDP Ops)	
Dellucci,David, Phi	1.67
Spiezio,Scott, StL	1.82
Drew,Stephen, Ari	1.85
Barmes,Clint, Col	2.06
Soriano,Alfonso, Was	3.00
Drew,J.D., LAD	3.20
Abercrombie,Reggie, Fla	3.64
Ensberg,Morgan, Hou	3.75
Scott,Luke, Hou	3.92
Beltran,Carlos, NYM	4.14

Hit By Pitch	
Weeks,Rickie, Mil	19
Rowand,Aaron, Phi	18
Bautista,Jose, Pit	16
Eckstein,David, StL	15
Holliday,Matt, Col	15
Burke,Chris, Hou	14
Clark,Brady, Mil	14
Utley,Chase, Phi	14
Victorino,Shane, Phi	14
3 tied with	13

Pitches Seen	
Lopez,Felipe, Cin-Was	2951
Utley,Chase, Phi	2930
Dunn,Adam, Cin	2867
Howard,Ryan, Phi	2863
Soriano,Alfonso, Was	2839
Furcal,Rafael, LAD	2827
Ramirez,Hanley, Fla	2806
Rollins,Jimmy, Phi	2806
Bay,Jason, Pit	2770
Johnson,Nick, Was	2692

At Bats Per Home Run	
(minimum 502 PA)	
Howard,Ryan, Phi	10.0
Pujols,Albert, StL	10.9
Berkman,Lance, Hou	11.9
Beltran,Carlos, NYM	12.4
Jones,Andruw, Atl	13.8
Delgado,Carlos, NYM	13.8
Dunn,Adam, Cin	14.0
Soriano,Alfonso, Was	14.1
Hall,Bill, Mil	15.3
LaRoche,Adam, Atl	15.4

Highest GB/FB Ratio	
(minimum 502 PA)	
Pierre,Juan, ChC	2.87
Roberts,Dave, SD	2.73
Taveras,Willy, Hou	2.71
Murton,Matt, ChC	2.68
Jones,Jacque, ChC	2.49
Wilson,Preston, Hou-StL	2.37
Ausmus,Brad, Hou	2.32
Clayton,Royce, Was-Cin	2.21
Green,Shawn, Ari-NYM	2.17
Carroll,Jamey, Col	2.12

Lowest GB/FB Ratio	
(minimum 502 PA)	
Soriano,Alfonso, Was	0.63
Dunn,Adam, Cin	0.65
Burrell,Pat, Phi	0.72
Rolen,Scott, StL	0.80
Hall,Bill, Mil	0.83
Ramirez,Aramis, ChC	0.84
Barmes,Clint, Col	0.85
Beltran,Carlos, NYM	0.93
Byrnes,Eric, Ari	0.93
Cameron,Mike, SD	0.94

Pitches Per Plate App	
(minimum 502 PA)	
Burrell,Pat, Phi	4.32
Johnson,Nick, Was	4.29
Beltran,Carlos, NYM	4.20
Dunn,Adam, Cin	4.20
Carroll,Jamey, Col	4.16
Hall,Bill, Mil	4.16
Lopez,Felipe, Cin-Was	4.13
Kearns,Austin, Cin-Was	4.10
Freel,Ryan, Cin	4.09
Cameron,Mike, SD	4.09

Pct Pitches Taken	
(minimum 1500 Pitches)	
Hatteberg,Scott, Cin	66.0
Abreu,Bobby, Phi	65.9
Bonds,Barry, SF	65.5
Johnson,Nick, Was	65.0
Burrell,Pat, Phi	64.4
Giles,Brian, SD	63.2
Jackson,Conor, Ari	63.0
Beltran,Carlos, NYM	62.9
Lopez,Felipe, Cin-Was	62.5
Bautista,Jose, Pit	62.3

Best BPS on OutZ	
(minimum 502 PA)	
Cabrera,Miguel, Fla	.671
Pujols,Albert, StL	.618
Wright,David, NYM	.594
Furcal,Rafael, LAD	.575
Ramirez,Aramis, ChC	.566
Pierre,Juan, ChC	.561
Ramirez,Hanley, Fla	.554
Byrnes,Eric, Ari	.551
Zimmerman,Ryan, Was	.544
Rollins,Jimmy, Phi	.542

Worst BPS on OutZ	
(minimum 502 PA)	
Jenkins,Geoff, Mil	.170
Berkman,Lance, Hou	.189
Ausmus,Brad, Hou	.197
Jones,Andruw, Atl	.205
Dunn,Adam, Cin	.205
Castillo,Jose, Pit	.211
Wilson,Preston, Hou-StL	.223
Kearns,Austin, Cin-Was	.223
Cameron,Mike, SD	.237
Barmes,Clint, Col	.241

2006 National League Batting Leaders

Best BPS vs Fastballs
(minimum 251 PA)

Howard,Ryan, Phi	1.199
Pujols,Albert, StL	1.045
LaRoche,Adam, Atl	1.026
Berkman,Lance, Hou	1.024
Jones,Chipper, Atl	1.004
McCann,Brian, Atl	1.000
Atkins,Garrett, Col	.990
Jones,Andruw, Atl	.969
Utley,Chase, Phi	.968
Bonds,Barry, SF	.966

Best BPS vs Curveballs
(minimum 50 PA)

Berkman,Lance, Hou	1.141
Holliday,Matt, Col	.983
Ramirez,Hanley, Fla	.891
Hall,Bill, Mil	.869
Winn,Randy, SF	.834
Howard,Ryan, Phi	.831
Roberts,Dave, SD	.800
Cabrera,Miguel, Fla	.782
Willingham,Josh, Fla	.777
Hudson,Orlando, Ari	.755

Best BPS vs Changeups
(minimum 50 PA)

Garciaparra,N, LAD	1.180
Holliday,Matt, Col	1.121
Jones,Chipper, Atl	1.111
Pujols,Albert, StL	1.092
Soriano,Alfonso, Was	1.091
Beltran,Carlos, NYM	1.082
Rolen,Scott, StL	1.062
Ethier,Andre, LAD	1.042
Encarnacion,Ju, StL	.984
Hawpe,Brad, Col	.975

Best BPS vs Sliders
(minimum 32 PA)

Bard,Josh, SD	1.121
Estrada,Johnny, Ari	1.088
Anderson,Mar, Was-LAD	1.047
Holliday,Matt, Col	.962
Cabrera,Miguel, Fla	.931
Ethier,Andre, LAD	.915
Durham,Ray, SF	.889
Scott,Luke, Hou	.883
Ramirez,Aramis, ChC	.873
Delgado,Carlos, NYM	.845

OPS
(minimum 502 PA)

Pujols,Albert, StL	1.102
Howard,Ryan, Phi	1.084
Berkman,Lance, Hou	1.041
Cabrera,Miguel, Fla	.998
Beltran,Carlos, NYM	.982
Holliday,Matt, Col	.973
Atkins,Garrett, Col	.965
Johnson,Nick, Was	.948
Bay,Jason, Pit	.928
LaRoche,Adam, Atl	.915

OPS First Half
(minimum 251 PA)

Pujols,Albert, StL	1.138
Berkman,Lance, Hou	1.011
Garciaparra,N, LAD	1.004
Cabrera,Miguel, Fla	.998
Beltran,Carlos, NYM	.994
Rolen,Scott, StL	.975
Holliday,Matt, Col	.974
Bonds,Barry, SF	.971
Wright,David, NYM	.961
Johnson,Nick, Was	.959

OPS Second Half
(minimum 251 PA)

Howard,Ryan, Phi	1.260
Berkman,Lance, Hou	1.078
Pujols,Albert, StL	1.069
Atkins,Garrett, Col	1.062
LaRoche,Adam, Atl	1.042
Ramirez,Aramis, ChC	1.041
McCann,Brian, Atl	1.002
Cabrera,Miguel, Fla	.998
Durham,Ray, SF	.982
Delgado,Carlos, NYM	.980

OPS by Catchers
(minimum 251 PA)

McCann,Brian, Atl	.967
Ross,Dave, Cin	.913
Barrett,Michael, ChC	.898
Piazza,Mike, SD	.855
Martin,Russell, LAD	.805
Lo Duca,Paul, NYM	.776
Alfonzo,Eliezer, SF	.775
Estrada,Johnny, Ari	.775
Paulino,Ronny, Pit	.758
Olivo,Miguel, Fla	.721

OPS by First Basemen
(minimum 251 PA)

Pujols,Albert, StL	1.101
Howard,Ryan, Phi	1.080
Berkman,Lance, Hou	1.027
Johnson,Nick, Was	.951
LaRoche,Adam, Atl	.927
Delgado,Carlos, NYM	.914
Lamb,Mike, Hou	.895
Garciaparra,N, LAD	.880
Helton,Todd, Col	.880
Gonzalez,Adrian, SD	.863

OPS by Second Basemen
(minimum 251 PA)

Durham,Ray, SF	.904
Utley,Chase, Phi	.900
Valentin,Jose, NYM	.867
Kent,Jeff, LAD	.847
Uggla,Dan, Fla	.819
Carroll,Jamey, Col	.816
Hudson,Orlando, Ari	.812
Vidro,Jose, Was	.752
Weeks,Rickie, Mil	.751
Phillips,Brand, Cin	.738

OPS by Third Basemen
(minimum 251 PA)

Cabrera,Miguel, Fla	.998
Jones,Chipper, Atl	.998
Atkins,Garrett, Col	.963
Wright,David, NYM	.915
Ramirez,Aramis, ChC	.909
Sanchez,Freddy, Pit	.896
Rolen,Scott, StL	.887
Ensberg,Morgan, Hou	.851
Koskie,Corey, Mil	.846
Encarnacion,Ed, Cin	.835

OPS by Shortstops
(minimum 251 PA)

Hall,Bill, Mil	.857
Reyes,Jose, NYM	.842
Ramirez,Hanley, Fla	.830
Furcal,Rafael, LAD	.818
Rollins,Jimmy, Phi	.814
Renteria,Edgar, Atl	.799
Vizquel,Omar, SF	.752
Greene,Khalil, SD	.748
Lopez,Felipe, Cin-Was	.740
Eckstein,David, StL	.698

OPS by Left Fielders
(minimum 251 PA)

Bonds,Barry, SF	.995
Holliday,Matt, Col	.974
Bay,Jason, Pit	.930
Burrell,Pat, Phi	.926
Soriano,Alfonso, Was	.912
Lee,Carlos, Mil	.905
Ethier,Andre, LAD	.864
Willingham,Josh, Fla	.858
Dunn,Adam, Cin	.854
Diaz,Matt, Atl	.841

OPS by Center Fielders
(minimum 251 PA)

Beltran,Carlos, NYM	.988
Jones,Andruw, Atl	.895
Cameron,Mike, SD	.836
Byrnes,Eric, Ari	.823
Edmonds,Jim, StL	.797
Griffey Jr.,Ken, Cin	.787
Victorino,Shane, Phi	.785
Lofton,Kenny, LAD	.763
Rowand,Aaron, Phi	.738
Sullivan,Cory, Col	.732

OPS by Right Fielders
(minimum 251 PA)

Hawpe,Brad, Col	.900
Drew,J.D., LAD	.889
Alou,Moises, SF	.880
Abreu,Bobby, Phi	.862
Kearns,Austin, Cin-Was	.842
Jones,Jacque, ChC	.837
Encarnacion,Ju, StL	.800
Jenkins,Geoff, Mil	.796
Winn,Randy, SF	.790
Nady,Xavier, NYM-Pit	.786

OPS by Pitchers
(minimum 66 PA)

Zambrano,Carlos, ChC	.589
Willis,Dontrelle, Fla	.565
Hernandez,Liv, Was-Ari	.535
Suppan,Jeff, StL	.531
Pettitte,Andy, Hou	.513
Peavy,Jake, SD	.497
Morris,Matt, SF	.480
Glavine,Tom, NYM	.456
Duke,Zach, Pit	.438
Oswalt,Roy, Hou	.425

2006 National League Batting Leaders

OPS Batting Left vs. LHP
(minimum 125 PA)

Bonds,Barry, SF	.970
Johnson,Nick, Was	.938
Howard,Ryan, Phi	.922
Dunn,Adam, Cin	.896
Abreu,Bobby, Phi	.888
Utley,Chase, Phi	.857
Gonzalez,Adrian, SD	.834
Helton,Todd, Col	.824
Fielder,Prince, Mil	.819
Green,Shawn, Ari-NYM	.799

OPS Batting Left vs. RHP
(minimum 377 PA)

Howard,Ryan, Phi	1.164
Berkman,Lance, Hou	1.142
Beltran,Carlos, NYM	1.053
Jones,Chipper, Atl	1.036
McCann,Brian, Atl	1.001
Delgado,Carlos, NYM	.977
Johnson,Nick, Was	.952
LaRoche,Adam, Atl	.950
Drew,J.D., LAD	.946
Utley,Chase, Phi	.930

OPS Batting Right vs. LHP
(minimum 125 PA)

Aurilia,Rich, Cin	1.086
Hall,Bill, Mil	1.072
Durham,Ray, SF	1.063
Pujols,Albert, StL	1.055
Sanchez,Freddy, Pit	1.041
Kearns,Austin, Cin-Was	1.039
Willingham,Josh, Fla	1.030
Ensberg,Morgan, Hou	1.016
Bay,Jason, Pit	1.014
Burrell,Pat, Phi	1.012

OPS Batting Right vs. RHP
(minimum 377 PA)

Pujols,Albert, StL	1.117
Cabrera,Miguel, Fla	.999
Holliday,Matt, Col	.971
Atkins,Garrett, Col	.935
Wright,David, NYM	.929
Ramirez,Aramis, ChC	.927
Rolen,Scott, StL	.921
Bay,Jason, Pit	.900
Soriano,Alfonso, Was	.885
Jones,Andruw, Atl	.882

OPS vs. LHP
(minimum 125 PA)

Aurilia,Rich, Cin	1.086
Hall,Bill, Mil	1.072
Durham,Ray, SF	1.063
Pujols,Albert, StL	1.055
Sanchez,Freddy, Pit	1.041
Kearns,Austin, Cin-Was	1.039
Willingham,Josh, Fla	1.030
Ensberg,Morgan, Hou	1.016
Bay,Jason, Pit	1.014
Burrell,Pat, Phi	1.012

OPS vs. RHP
(minimum 377 PA)

Howard,Ryan, Phi	1.164
Berkman,Lance, Hou	1.142
Pujols,Albert, StL	1.117
Beltran,Carlos, NYM	1.053
Jones,Chipper, Atl	1.036
McCann,Brian, Atl	1.001
Cabrera,Miguel, Fla	.999
Delgado,Carlos, NYM	.977
Holliday,Matt, Col	.971
Johnson,Nick, Was	.952

RC Per 27 Outs vs. LHP
(minimum 125 PA)

Sanchez,Freddy, Pit	10.5
Pujols,Albert, StL	9.7
Aurilia,Rich, Cin	9.7
Bonds,Barry, SF	9.1
Burrell,Pat, Phi	9.0
Ensberg,Morgan, Hou	8.6
Kearns,Austin, Cin-Was	8.4
Hall,Bill, Mil	8.2
Willingham,Josh, Fla	8.0
Cabrera,Miguel, Fla	8.0

RC Per 27 Outs vs. RHP
(minimum 377 PA)

Berkman,Lance, Hou	11.5
Howard,Ryan, Phi	10.5
Pujols,Albert, StL	10.3
Jones,Chipper, Atl	9.4
McCann,Brian, Atl	9.2
Beltran,Carlos, NYM	8.8
Cabrera,Miguel, Fla	8.8
Wright,David, NYM	8.0
Helton,Todd, Col	7.9
Johnson,Nick, Was	7.7

Highest RBI %
(minimum 502 PA)

Pujols,Albert, StL	12.72
Berkman,Lance, Hou	12.50
Howard,Ryan, Phi	12.19
Beltran,Carlos, NYM	11.65
Delgado,Carlos, NYM	10.99
Jones,Andruw, Atl	10.90
Ramirez,Aramis, ChC	10.87
Cabrera,Miguel, Fla	10.29
Garciaparra,N, LAD	10.25
Wright,David, NYM	10.15

Lowest RBI %
(minimum 502 PA)

Eckstein,David, StL	2.86
Taveras,Willy, Hou	3.47
Freel,Ryan, Cin	3.60
Pierre,Juan, ChC	3.77
Wilson,Jack, Pit	3.85
Cedeno,Ronny, ChC	4.39
Ausmus,Brad, Hou	4.56
Carroll,Jamey, Col	4.66
Lopez,Felipe, Cin-Was	4.69
Clayton,Royce, Was-Cin	4.91

Highest Strikeout per PA
(minimum 502 PA)

Dunn,Adam, Cin	.284
Hall,Bill, Mil	.266
Howard,Ryan, Phi	.257
Jenkins,Geoff, Mil	.232
Burrell,Pat, Phi	.231
LaRoche,Adam, Atl	.230
Bay,Jason, Pit	.226
Wilson,Preston, Hou-StL	.225
Cameron,Mike, SD	.224
Soriano,Alfonso, Was	.220

Lowest Strikeout per PA
(minimum 502 PA)

Pierre,Juan, ChC	.051
Garciaparra,N, LAD	.057
Lo Duca,Paul, NYM	.069
Eckstein,David, StL	.074
Walker,Todd, ChC-SD	.075
Hatteberg,Scott, Cin	.076
Vizquel,Omar, SF	.077
Pujols,Albert, StL	.079
Lofton,Kenny, LAD	.080
Sanchez,Freddy, Pit	.082

Home Runs At Home

Howard,Ryan, Phi	29
Berkman,Lance, Hou	24
Pujols,Albert, StL	24
Soriano,Alfonso, Was	24
Dunn,Adam, Cin	22
Holliday,Matt, Col	22
Francoeur,Jeff, Atl	19
Jones,Andruw, Atl	19
Delgado,Carlos, NYM	18
Hall,Bill, Mil	18

Home Runs Away

Howard,Ryan, Phi	29
Beltran,Carlos, NYM	26
Pujols,Albert, StL	25
Ramirez,Aramis, ChC	24
Bay,Jason, Pit	22
Jones,Andruw, Atl	22
Soriano,Alfonso, Was	22
Berkman,Lance, Hou	21
LaRoche,Adam, Atl	21
Delgado,Carlos, NYM	20

Longest Avg Home Run
(min 10 over the wall)

Bonds,Barry, SF	407
Green,Shawn, Ari-NYM	407
Castillo,Jose, Pit	406
Saenz,Olmedo, LAD	405
Holliday,Matt, Col	405
Jones,Chipper, Atl	403
Anderson,Mar, Was-LAD	403
Piazza,Mike, SD	403
Dunn,Adam, Cin	403
Giles,Marcus, Atl	403

Shortest Avg Home Run
(min 10 over the wall)

Biggio,Craig, Hou	358
Winn,Randy, SF	365
Lane,Jason, Hou	372
Ensberg,Morgan, Hou	376
Bell,David, Phi-Mil	377
Giles,Brian, SD	379
Greene,Khalil, SD	379
Spiezio,Scott, StL	379
Burnitz,Jeromy, Pit	380
Hatteberg,Scott, Cin	380

2006 National League Batting Leaders

Under Age 26: AB Per HR	
(minimum 502 PA)	
Fielder,Prince, Mil	20.3
Cabrera,Miguel, Fla	22.2
Wright,David, NYM	22.4
Francoeur,Jeff, Atl	22.4
Jacobs,Mike, Fla	23.5
Gonzalez,Adrian, SD	23.8
Zimmerman,Ryan, Was	30.7
Phillips,Brand, Cin	31.5
Jackson,Conor, Ari	32.3
Reyes,Jose, NYM	34.1

Under Age 26: OPS	
(minimum 502 PA)	
Cabrera,Miguel, Fla	.998
Wright,David, NYM	.912
Gonzalez,Adrian, SD	.862
Reyes,Jose, NYM	.841
Ramirez,Hanley, Fla	.833
Fielder,Prince, Mil	.831
Zimmerman,Ryan, Was	.822
Jackson,Conor, Ari	.809
Murton,Matt, ChC	.809
Jacobs,Mike, Fla	.798

Under Age 26: RC/27 Outs	
(minimum 502 PA)	
Cabrera,Miguel, Fla	8.7
Wright,David, NYM	7.4
Reyes,Jose, NYM	6.8
Zimmerman,Ryan, Was	5.8
Ramirez,Hanley, Fla	5.7
Jackson,Conor, Ari	5.6
Murton,Matt, ChC	5.3
Gonzalez,Adrian, SD	5.1
Fielder,Prince, Mil	5.1
Jacobs,Mike, Fla	4.8

Longest Home Run		
Howard,Ryan, Phi, 4/23		496
Soriano,Alfonso, Was, 5/9		491
Holliday,Matt, Col, 9/3		481
Dunn,Adam, Cin, 4/6		480
Holliday,Matt, Col, 9/19		478
Fielder,Prince, Mil, 5/12		475
Weeks,Rickie, Mil, 4/29		475
Fielder,Prince, Mil, 5/29		471
Green,Sh, Ari-NYM, 4/11		470
Wright,David, NYM, 4/7		470

Swing and Miss %	
(minimum 1500 Pitches Seen)	
Howard,Ryan, Phi	24.2
Olivo,Miguel, Fla	20.9
Hawpe,Brad, Col	19.4
Jones,Jacque, ChC	19.2
Dunn,Adam, Cin	19.1
Jones,Andruw, Atl	18.8
Hall,Bill, Mil	18.4
Delgado,Carlos, NYM	18.3
Ensberg,Morgan, Hou	18.2
Kearns,Austin, Cin-Was	17.9

Highest First Swing %	
(minimum 502 PA)	
Francoeur,Jeff, Atl	49.9
Holliday,Matt, Col	44.5
Garciaparra,N, LAD	43.9
Barfield,Josh, SD	42.5
Berkman,Lance, Hou	40.0
Jacobs,Mike, Fla	38.6
Giles,Marcus, Atl	37.6
Castillo,Jose, Pit	37.4
Feliz,Pedro, SF	37.3
Hawpe,Brad, Col	37.0

Lowest First Swing %	
(minimum 502 PA)	
Carroll,Jamey, Col	8.8
Hatteberg,Scott, Cin	11.1
Beltran,Carlos, NYM	12.9
Eckstein,David, StL	13.7
Jackson,Conor, Ari	13.8
Johnson,Nick, Was	14.3
Pierre,Juan, ChC	15.1
Taveras,Willy, Hou	15.3
Wilson,Jack, Pit	15.3
Tracy,Chad, Ari	15.4

Home RC Per 27 Outs	
(minimum 251 PA)	
Pujols,Albert, StL	11.2
Berkman,Lance, Hou	10.6
Helton,Todd, Col	9.7
Holliday,Matt, Col	9.4
Howard,Ryan, Phi	9.3
Cabrera,Miguel, Fla	8.8
Sanchez,Freddy, Pit	8.4
Atkins,Garrett, Col	8.2
Furcal,Rafael, LAD	7.9
Wright,David, NYM	7.9

Road RC Per 27 Outs	
(minimum 251 PA)	
Beltran,Carlos, NYM	10.9
Jones,Chipper, Atl	10.0
Bonds,Barry, SF	9.6
Pujols,Albert, StL	9.2
Howard,Ryan, Phi	8.7
Berkman,Lance, Hou	8.6
Cabrera,Miguel, Fla	8.4
Atkins,Garrett, Col	7.7
LaRoche,Adam, Atl	7.7
Delgado,Carlos, NYM	7.7

2006 American League Pitching Leaders

Earned Run Average (minimum 162 IP)		Winning Percentage (minimum 15 Decisions)		Opponent Batting Average (minimum 162 IP)		Baserunners Per 9 IP (minimum 162 IP)	
Santana,Johan, Min	2.77	Liriano,Francisco, Min	.800	Santana,Johan, Min	.216	Santana,Johan, Min	9.13
Halladay,Roy, Tor	3.19	Halladay,Roy, Tor	.762	Santana,Ervin, LAA	.241	Halladay,Roy, Tor	10.10
Sabathia,C.C., Cle	3.22	Santana,Johan, Min	.760	Mussina,Mike, NYY	.241	Mussina,Mike, NYY	10.22
Mussina,Mike, NYY	3.51	Wang,Chien-Ming, NYY	.760	Beckett,Josh, Bos	.245	Sabathia,C.C., Cle	10.88
Lackey,John, LAA	3.56	Garland,Jon, CWS	.720	Lackey,John, LAA	.246	Schilling,Curt, Bos	11.07
Escobar,Kelvim, LAA	3.61	Mussina,Mike, NYY	.682	Sabathia,C.C., Cle	.247	Haren,Dan, Oak	11.26
Verlander,Just, Det	3.63	Schilling,Curt, Bos	.682	Johnson,Randy, NYY	.250	Santana,Ervin, LAA	11.56
Wang,Chien-Ming, NYY	3.63	Rogers,Kenny, Det	.680	Halladay,Roy, Tor	.251	Johnson,Randy, NYY	11.59
Bedard,Erik, Bal	3.76	Santana,Ervin, LAA	.667	Rogers,Kenny, Det	.253	Escobar,Kelvim, LAA	11.69
Zito,Barry, Oak	3.83	2 tied with	.654	Lilly,Ted, Tor	.254	Rogers,Kenny, Det	11.74

Games		Games Started		Complete Games		Shutouts	
Proctor,Scott, NYY	83	Bonderman,Jer, Det	34	Sabathia,C.C., Cle	6	Lackey,John, LAA	2
Camp,Shawn, TB	75	Haren,Dan, Oak	34	Halladay,Roy, Tor	4	Sabathia,C.C., Cle	2
Rincon,Juan, Min	75	Millwood,Kevin, Tex	34	Benson,Kris, Bal	3	Sowers,Jeremy, Cle	2
Shields,Scot, LAA	74	Santana,Johan, Min	34	Lackey,John, LAA	3	Westbrook,Jake, Cle	2
Farnsworth,Kyle, NYY	72	Zito,Barry, Oak	34	Westbrook,Jake, Cle	3	17 tied with	1
Putz,J.J., Sea	72	10 tied with	33	11 tied with	2		
Sherrill,George, Sea	72						
Calero,Kiko, Oak	70						
Cotts,Neal, CWS	70						
Villone,Ron, NYY	70						

Wins		Losses		No Decisions		Wild Pitches	
Santana,Johan, Min	19	Lopez,Rodrigo, Bal	18	Fossum,Casey, TB	13	Cabrera,Daniel, Bal	17
Wang,Chien-Ming, NYY	19	Silva,Carlos, Min	15	Meche,Gil, Sea	13	Contreras,Jose, CWS	16
Garland,Jon, CWS	18	Escobar,Kelvim, LAA	14	Bonderman,Jer, Det	12	Lackey,John, LAA	16
Garcia,Freddy, CWS	17	Hernandez,Fel, Sea	14	Byrd,Paul, Cle	12	Redman,Mark, KC	12
Johnson,Randy, NYY	17	Washburn,Jarrod, Sea	14	Halladay,Roy, Tor	11	Beckett,Josh, Bos	11
Rogers,Kenny, Det	17	Buehrle,Mark, CWS	13	Mussina,Mike, NYY	10	Burgos,Ambiorix, KC	11
Verlander,Just, Det	17	Haren,Dan, Oak	13	Wright,Jaret, NYY	10	Hernandez,Fel, Sea	11
6 tied with	16	Lilly,Ted, Tor	13	8 tied with	9	Haren,Dan, Oak	10
		Pineiro,Joel, Sea	13			Rodriguez,Fran, LAA	10
		Robertson,Nate, Det	13			Santana,Ervin, LAA	10

Strikeouts		Walks Allowed		Intentional Walks Allowed		Hit Batters	
Santana,Johan, Min	245	Cabrera,Daniel, Bal	104	Pineiro,Joel, Sea	13	Padilla,Vicente, Tex	17
Bonderman,Jer, Det	202	Zito,Barry, Oak	99	Jenks,Bobby, CWS	10	Vazquez,Javier, CWS	15
Lackey,John, LAA	190	Meche,Gil, Sea	84	McCarthy,Bran, CWS	9	Zito,Barry, Oak	13
Vazquez,Javier, CWS	184	Lilly,Ted, Tor	81	Villone,Ron, NYY	9	Fossum,Casey, TB	12
Schilling,Curt, Bos	183	Beckett,Josh, Bos	74	Mateo,Julio, Sea	8	Santana,Ervin, LAA	11
Haren,Dan, Oak	176	Lackey,John, LAA	72	Bonderman,Jer, Det	7	6 tied with	10
Hernandez,Fel, Sea	176	Padilla,Vicente, Tex	70	Halsey,Brad, Oak	7		
Johnson,Randy, NYY	172	Santana,Ervin, LAA	70	Politte,Cliff, CWS	7		
Mussina,Mike, NYY	172	Bedard,Erik, Bal	69	7 tied with	6		
Sabathia,C.C., Cle	172	McClung,Seth, TB	68				

2006 American League Pitching Leaders

Runs Allowed			Hits Allowed			Doubles Allowed			Home Runs Allowed	
Silva,Carlos, Min	130		Buehrle,Mark, CWS	247		Garland,Jon, CWS	51		Silva,Carlos, Min	38
Lopez,Rodrigo, Bal	129		Garland,Jon, CWS	247		Schilling,Curt, Bos	51		Beckett,Josh, Bos	36
Johnson,Randy, NYY	125		Westbrook,Jake, Cle	247		Blanton,Joe, Oak	50		Buehrle,Mark, CWS	36
Buehrle,Mark, CWS	124		Silva,Carlos, Min	246		Washburn,Jarrod, Sea	50		Benson,Kris, Bal	33
Pineiro,Joel, Sea	123		Blanton,Joe, Oak	241		Lopez,Rodrigo, Bal	49		Garcia,Freddy, CWS	32
Beckett,Josh, Bos	120		Lopez,Rodrigo, Bal	234		Pineiro,Joel, Sea	49		Lopez,Rodrigo, Bal	32
Byrd,Paul, Cle	120		Wang,Chien-Ming, NYY	233		Buehrle,Mark, CWS	48		Haren,Dan, Oak	31
Garcia,Freddy, CWS	116		Byrd,Paul, Cle	232		Lackey,John, LAA	48		Lee,Cliff, Cle	29
Vazquez,Javier, CWS	116		Garcia,Freddy, CWS	228		3 tied with	47		Robertson,Nate, Det	29
2 tied with	114		Millwood,Kevin, Tex	228					4 tied with	28

Run Support Per Nine IP (minimum 162 IP)			% Pitches In Strike Zone (minimum 162 IP)			Pitches Per Start (minimum 30 GS)			Pitches Per Batter (minimum 162 IP)	
Johnson,Randy, NYY	7.51		Byrd,Paul, Cle	57.5		Zito,Barry, Oak	107.8		Silva,Carlos, Min	3.32
Verlander,Just, Det	6.77		Silva,Carlos, Min	56.7		Lackey,John, LAA	106.4		Wang,Chien-Ming, NYY	3.39
Westbrook,Jake, Cle	6.73		Mussina,Mike, NYY	55.7		Schilling,Curt, Bos	104.7		Halladay,Roy, Tor	3.48
Byrd,Paul, Cle	6.59		Radke,Brad, Min	54.7		Garland,Jon, CWS	104.1		Robertson,Nate, Det	3.53
Mussina,Mike, NYY	6.52		Santana,Johan, Min	54.1		Meche,Gil, Sea	103.0		Buehrle,Mark, CWS	3.54
Lee,Cliff, Cle	6.50		Sabathia,C.C., Cle	53.8		Haren,Dan, Oak	102.6		Byrd,Paul, Cle	3.55
Vazquez,Javier, CWS	6.48		Bedard,Erik, Bal	53.7		Vazquez,Javier, CWS	102.5		Radke,Brad, Min	3.60
Rogers,Kenny, Det	6.40		Lee,Cliff, Cle	53.7		Westbrook,Jake, Cle	102.3		Lopez,Rodrigo, Bal	3.61
Garland,Jon, CWS	6.39		Johnson,Randy, NYY	53.3		Lee,Cliff, Cle	101.8		Garcia,Freddy, CWS	3.62
Padilla,Vicente, Tex	6.35		Schilling,Curt, Bos	53.3		Santana,Johan, Min	101.5		Westbrook,Jake, Cle	3.62

Quality Starts			Batters Faced			Innings Pitched			Most Pitches in a Game	
Santana,Johan, Min	24		Zito,Barry, Oak	945		Santana,Johan, Min	233.2		Schilling,Curt, Bos, 4/25	133
Lackey,John, LAA	23		Haren,Dan, Oak	930		Haren,Dan, Oak	223.0		Johnson,Randy, NYY, 7/19	129
Mussina,Mike, NYY	23		Santana,Johan, Min	923		Zito,Barry, Oak	221.0		Zito,Barry, Oak, 7/2	128
Millwood,Kevin, Tex	22		Lackey,John, LAA	922		Halladay,Roy, Tor	220.0		Vazquez,Jav, CWS, 9/10	127
Bedard,Erik, Bal	20		Garcia,Freddy, CWS	917		Wang,Chien-Ming, NYY	218.0		Meche,Gil, Sea, 7/9	126
Escobar,Kelvim, LAA	20		Millwood,Kevin, Tex	907		Lackey,John, LAA	217.2		Redman,Mark, KC, 9/16	126
Padilla,Vicente, Tex	20		Westbrook,Jake, Cle	904		Garcia,Freddy, CWS	216.1		Verlander,Just, Det, 9/2	126
Robertson,Nate, Det	20		Bonderman,Jer, Det	903		Millwood,Kevin, Tex	215.0		Zito,Barry, Oak, 5/27	126
Zito,Barry, Oak	20		Garland,Jon, CWS	900		Bonderman,Jer, Det	214.0		Meche,Gil, Sea, 9/27	125
6 tied with	19		Wang,Chien-Ming, NYY	900		2 tied with	211.1		Vazquez,Jav, CWS, 9/21	125

Stolen Bases Allowed			Caught Stealing Off			Stolen Base Pct Allowed (minimum 162 IP)			Pickoffs	
Garcia,Freddy, CWS	40		Zito,Barry, Oak	12		Rogers,Kenny, Det	14.3		Buehrle,Mark, CWS	10
Wakefield,Tim, Bos	24		Wang,Chien-Ming, NYY	11		Verlander,Just, Det	16.7		Verlander,Just, Det	8
Contreras,Jose, CWS	21		Escobar,Kelvim, LAA	10		Santana,Ervin, LAA	35.7		Lester,Jon, Bos	6
Johnson,Randy, NYY	21		Johnson,Randy, NYY	10		Buehrle,Mark, CWS	36.4		Kazmir,Scott, TB	5
Halladay,Roy, Tor	20		Lopez,Rodrigo, Bal	10		Zito,Barry, Oak	40.0		Moyer,Jamie, Sea	4
Johnson,Jason, Cle-Bos	19		Santana,Ervin, LAA	9		Meche,Gil, Sea	41.7		Reyes,Dennys, Min	4
Burnett,A.J., Tor	18		5 tied with	7		Santana,Johan, Min	44.4		Shields,James, TB	4
Byrd,Paul, Cle	18					Wang,Chien-Ming, NYY	45.0		8 tied with	3
Westbrook,Jake, Cle	16					Redman,Mark, KC	45.5			
4 tied with	15					Garland,Jon, CWS	46.2			

2006 American League Pitching Leaders

Strikeouts Per 9 IP
(minimum 162 IP)

Santana,Johan, Min	9.44
Bonderman,Jer, Det	8.50
Hernandez,Fel, Sea	8.29
Vazquez,Javier, CWS	8.17
Schilling,Curt, Bos	8.07
Sabathia,C.C., Cle	8.03
Lilly,Ted, Tor	7.93
Lackey,John, LAA	7.86
Mussina,Mike, NYY	7.84
Bedard,Erik, Bal	7.84

Opp On-Base Percentage
(minimum 162 IP)

Santana,Johan, Min	.258
Mussina,Mike, NYY	.279
Halladay,Roy, Tor	.283
Sabathia,C.C., Cle	.293
Haren,Dan, Oak	.301
Schilling,Curt, Bos	.303
Garcia,Freddy, CWS	.309
Johnson,Randy, NYY	.309
Santana,Ervin, LAA	.311
Lackey,John, LAA	.311

Opp Slugging Average
(minimum 162 IP)

Santana,Johan, Min	.360
Lackey,John, LAA	.360
Sabathia,C.C., Cle	.363
Bedard,Erik, Bal	.370
Halladay,Roy, Tor	.374
Mussina,Mike, NYY	.374
Wang,Chien-Ming, NYY	.375
Escobar,Kelvim, LAA	.393
Santana,Ervin, LAA	.395
Contreras,Jose, CWS	.398

Hits Per Nine Innings
(minimum 162 IP)

Santana,Johan, Min	7.16
Santana,Ervin, LAA	7.99
Mussina,Mike, NYY	8.39
Lackey,John, LAA	8.39
Beckett,Josh, Bos	8.40
Sabathia,C.C., Cle	8.50
Halladay,Roy, Tor	8.51
Johnson,Randy, NYY	8.52
Zito,Barry, Oak	8.59
Rogers,Kenny, Det	8.60

Home Runs Per Nine IP
(minimum 162 IP)

Wang,Chien-Ming, NYY	0.50
Lackey,John, LAA	0.58
Westbrook,Jake, Cle	0.64
Bedard,Erik, Bal	0.73
Bonderman,Jer, Det	0.76
Halladay,Roy, Tor	0.78
Blanton,Joe, Oak	0.79
Sabathia,C.C., Cle	0.79
Escobar,Kelvim, LAA	0.81
Contreras,Jose, CWS	0.92

Batting Average vs. LHB
(minimum 125 BF)

Robertson,Nate, Det	.181
Zumaya,Joel, Det	.183
Ray,Chris, Bal	.184
Villone,Ron, NYY	.185
Benoit,Joaquin, Tex	.191
Rivera,Mariano, NYY	.192
McCarthy,Bran, CWS	.197
Rogers,Kenny, Det	.200
Lilly,Ted, Tor	.202
Rodney,Fernando, Det	.202

Batting Average vs. RHB
(minimum 225 BF)

Weaver,Jered, LAA	.174
Liriano,Francisco, Min	.206
Santana,Johan, Min	.206
Hendrickson,Ma, TB	.223
Padilla,Vicente, Tex	.228
Santana,Ervin, LAA	.229
Lackey,John, LAA	.230
Bonderman,Jer, Det	.235
Beckett,Josh, Bos	.238
Carrasco,Hector, LAA	.240

Opp BA w/ RISP
(minimum 125 BF)

Santana,Johan, Min	.174
Kazmir,Scott, TB	.188
Wakefield,Tim, Bos	.193
Robertson,Nate, Det	.199
Halsey,Brad, Oak	.204
Cabrera,Daniel, Bal	.208
Villone,Ron, NYY	.210
Halladay,Roy, Tor	.213
Zito,Barry, Oak	.227
Proctor,Scott, NYY	.229

OBP vs. Leadoff Hitter
(minimum 150 BF)

Beckett,Josh, Bos	.231
Mussina,Mike, NYY	.235
Haren,Dan, Oak	.241
Contreras,Jose, CWS	.255
Lackey,John, LAA	.271
Wang,Chien-Ming, NYY	.273
Garcia,Freddy, CWS	.274
Santana,Ervin, LAA	.276
Halladay,Roy, Tor	.278
Hernandez,Fel, Sea	.281

Strikeouts / Walks Ratio
(minimum 162 IP)

Schilling,Curt, Bos	6.54
Santana,Johan, Min	5.21
Mussina,Mike, NYY	4.91
Haren,Dan, Oak	3.91
Sabathia,C.C., Cle	3.91
Halladay,Roy, Tor	3.88
Vazquez,Javier, CWS	3.29
Bonderman,Jer, Det	3.16
Millwood,Kevin, Tex	2.96
Escobar,Kelvim, LAA	2.94

Highest GB/FB Ratio
(minimum 162 IP)

Wang,Chien-Ming, NYY	4.10
Westbrook,Jake, Cle	3.43
Halladay,Roy, Tor	2.88
Hernandez,Fel, Sea	2.84
Pineiro,Joel, Sea	1.97
Bedard,Erik, Bal	1.88
Rogers,Kenny, Det	1.86
Bonderman,Jer, Det	1.78
Millwood,Kevin, Tex	1.56
Silva,Carlos, Min	1.54

Lowest GB/FB Ratio
(minimum 162 IP)

Lee,Cliff, Cle	0.79
Zito,Barry, Oak	0.97
Lilly,Ted, Tor	1.00
Santana,Ervin, LAA	1.01
Washburn,Jarrod, Sea	1.09
Johnson,Randy, NYY	1.12
Garcia,Freddy, CWS	1.13
Vazquez,Javier, CWS	1.15
Schilling,Curt, Bos	1.16
Benson,Kris, Bal	1.18

Sacrifice Flies Allowed

Benson,Kris, Bal	13
Radke,Brad, Min	10
Santana,Ervin, LAA	10
Blanton,Joe, Oak	9
McClung,Seth, TB	9
7 tied with	8

Sacrifice Hits Allowed

Benson,Kris, Bal	9
Lackey,John, LAA	8
Millwood,Kevin, Tex	8
Sabathia,C.C., Cle	8
Zito,Barry, Oak	7
9 tied with	6

GIDP Induced

Westbrook,Jake, Cle	35
Wang,Chien-Ming, NYY	33
Zito,Barry, Oak	31
Robertson,Nate, Det	30
Rogers,Kenny, Det	25
Tavarez,Julian, Bos	24
Garland,Jon, CWS	23
Halladay,Roy, Tor	23
Redman,Mark, KC	22
5 tied with	21

GIDP Per Nine IP
(minimum 162 IP)

Westbrook,Jake, Cle	1.49
Wang,Chien-Ming, NYY	1.36
Robertson,Nate, Det	1.29
Zito,Barry, Oak	1.26
Redman,Mark, KC	1.19
Pineiro,Joel, Sea	1.14
Rogers,Kenny, Det	1.10
Verlander,Just, Det	1.02
Garland,Jon, CWS	0.98
Blanton,Joe, Oak	0.97

2006 American League Pitching Leaders

Saves		Blown Saves		Save Pct (minimum 20 Save Ops)		Save Opportunities	
Rodriguez,Fran, LAA	47	Burgos,Ambiorix, KC	12	Nathan,Joe, Min	94.7	Rodriguez,Fran, LAA	51
Jenks,Bobby, CWS	41	Street,Huston, Oak	11	Rodriguez,Fran, LAA	92.2	Street,Huston, Oak	48
Ryan,B.J., Tor	38	Cordero,Franc, Tex	9	Rivera,Mariano, NYY	91.9	Jenks,Bobby, CWS	45
Jones,Todd, Det	37	Timlin,Mike, Bos	8	Jenks,Bobby, CWS	91.1	Jones,Todd, Det	43
Street,Huston, Oak	37	Proctor,Scott, NYY	7	Ryan,B.J., Tor	90.5	Putz,J.J., Sea	43
Nathan,Joe, Min	36	Putz,J.J., Sea	7	Otsuka,Akinori, Tex	88.9	Ryan,B.J., Tor	42
Putz,J.J., Sea	36	Jones,Todd, Det	6	Ray,Chris, Bal	86.8	Papelbon,Jonat, Bos	41
Papelbon,Jonat, Bos	35	Papelbon,Jonat, Bos	6	Jones,Todd, Det	86.0	Nathan,Joe, Min	38
Rivera,Mariano, NYY	34	Shields,Scot, LAA	6	Papelbon,Jonat, Bos	85.4	Ray,Chris, Bal	38
Ray,Chris, Bal	33	3 tied with	5	Putz,J.J., Sea	83.7	Rivera,Mariano, NYY	37

Easy Saves		Regular Saves		Tough Saves		Holds Adjusted Saves % (minimum 20 Save Ops)	
Jones,Todd, Det	26	Rodriguez,Fran, LAA	19	Putz,J.J., Sea	5	Nathan,Joe, Min	94.7
Jenks,Bobby, CWS	25	Rivera,Mariano, NYY	16	Jenks,Bobby, CWS	4	Rodriguez,Fran, LAA	92.2
Rodriguez,Fran, LAA	25	Ryan,B.J., Tor	16	Ryan,B.J., Tor	4	Rivera,Mariano, NYY	91.9
Nathan,Joe, Min	22	Street,Huston, Oak	16	Camp,Shawn, TB	3	Jenks,Bobby, CWS	91.1
Otsuka,Akinori, Tex	22	Papelbon,Jonat, Bos	15	Papelbon,Jonat, Bos	3	Otsuka,Akinori, Tex	90.7
Putz,J.J., Sea	20	Nathan,Joe, Min	13	Rodriguez,Fran, LAA	3	Ryan,B.J., Tor	90.7
Ray,Chris, Bal	18	Ray,Chris, Bal	13	Street,Huston, Oak	3	Ray,Chris, Bal	86.8
Ryan,B.J., Tor	18	Jenks,Bobby, CWS	12	Ray,Chris, Bal	2	Jones,Todd, Det	86.0
Street,Huston, Oak	18	Jones,Todd, Det	11	Walker,Tyler, TB	2	Papelbon,Jonat, Bos	85.7
2 tied with	17	Putz,J.J., Sea	11	13 tied with	1	Putz,J.J., Sea	85.4

Relief Wins		Relief Losses		Relief Games		Holds	
Mateo,Julio, Sea	9	Dessens,Elmer, KC	7	Proctor,Scott, NYY	83	Shields,Scot, LAA	31
Camp,Shawn, TB	7	Shields,Scot, LAA	7	Camp,Shawn, TB	75	Zumaya,Joel, Det	30
Carrasco,Hector, LAA	7	Carmona,Fausto, Cle	6	Rincon,Juan, Min	75	Proctor,Scott, NYY	26
Cordero,Franc, Tex	7	Farnsworth,Kyle, NYY	6	Shields,Scot, LAA	74	Rincon,Juan, Min	26
Nathan,Joe, Min	7	Jones,Todd, Det	6	Farnsworth,Kyle, NYY	72	Speier,Justin, Tor	25
Rodney,Fernando, Det	7	McCarthy,Bran, CWS	6	Putz,J.J., Sea	72	Calero,Kiko, Oak	23
Shields,Scot, LAA	7	Meadows,Brian, TB	6	Sherrill,George, Sea	72	Timlin,Mike, Bos	21
4 tied with	6	Timlin,Mike, Bos	6	Calero,Kiko, Oak	70	Farnsworth,Kyle, NYY	19
		4 tied with	5	Cotts,Neal, CWS	70	5 tied with	18
				Villone,Ron, NYY	70		

Relief Innings		Inherited Runners Scrd % (minimum 30 IR)		Relief Opp On Base Pct (minimum 50 IP)		Relief Opp Slugging Avg (minimum 50 IP)	
Proctor,Scott, NYY	102.1	Reyes,Dennys, Min	13.3	Papelbon,Jonat, Bos	.211	Ryan,B.J., Tor	.214
Shields,Scot, LAA	87.2	Jenks,Bobby, CWS	16.7	Nathan,Joe, Min	.212	Nathan,Joe, Min	.242
Carrasco,Hector, LAA	86.1	Putz,J.J., Sea	17.5	Ryan,B.J., Tor	.230	Papelbon,Jonat, Bos	.254
Lugo,Ruddy, TB	85.0	Gaudin,Chad, Oak	20.0	Putz,J.J., Sea	.245	Zumaya,Joel, Det	.270
Zumaya,Joel, Det	83.1	Schoeneweis,S, Tor	22.5	Reyes,Dennys, Min	.259	Reyes,Dennys, Min	.275
Villone,Ron, NYY	80.1	Benoit,Joaquin, Tex	22.7	Rivera,Mariano, NYY	.264	Putz,J.J., Sea	.284
Benoit,Joaquin, Tex	79.2	Myers,Mike, NYY	22.8	Shields,Scot, LAA	.273	Rivera,Mariano, NYY	.288
Putz,J.J., Sea	78.1	Street,Huston, Oak	23.3	Betancourt,Raf, Cle	.275	Rodney,Fernando, Det	.300
Crain,Jesse, Min	76.2	Villone,Ron, NYY	23.5	Street,Huston, Oak	.275	Benoit,Joaquin, Tex	.310
McCarthy,Bran, CWS	75.1	Mahay,Ron, Tex	23.7	Ray,Chris, Bal	.275	Otsuka,Akinori, Tex	.318

2006 American League Pitching Leaders

Relief Opp BA Vs LHB	
(minimum 50 AB)	
Downs,Scott, Tor	.177
Zumaya,Joel, Det	.183
Ray,Chris, Bal	.184
Villone,Ron, NYY	.185
Benoit,Joaquin, Tex	.191
Rivera,Mariano, NYY	.192
Nathan,Joe, Min	.193
Wellemeyer,Todd, KC	.198
Rodney,Fernando, Det	.202
Papelbon,Jonat, Bos	.203

Relief Opp BA Vs RHB	
(minimum 50 AB)	
Papelbon,Jonat, Bos	.128
Nathan,Joe, Min	.130
Rodriguez,Fran, LAA	.179
Soriano,Rafael, Sea	.179
Ryan,B.J., Tor	.182
Britton,Chris, Bal	.186
Zumaya,Joel, Det	.188
Otsuka,Akinori, Tex	.190
Rodney,Fernando, Det	.192
Gaudin,Chad, Oak	.196

Relief Opp Batting Average	
(minimum 50 IP)	
Nathan,Joe, Min	.158
Papelbon,Jonat, Bos	.167
Ryan,B.J., Tor	.169
Zumaya,Joel, Det	.187
Ray,Chris, Bal	.193
Rodney,Fernando, Det	.196
Reyes,Dennys, Min	.197
Rodriguez,Fran, LAA	.197
Downs,Scott, Tor	.197
Soriano,Rafael, Sea	.204

Relief Earned Run Average	
(minimum 50 IP)	
Reyes,Dennys, Min	0.89
Papelbon,Jonat, Bos	0.92
Ryan,B.J., Tor	1.37
Nathan,Joe, Min	1.58
Rodriguez,Fran, LAA	1.73
Rivera,Mariano, NYY	1.80
Zumaya,Joel, Det	1.94
Otsuka,Akinori, Tex	2.11
Soriano,Rafael, Sea	2.25
Putz,J.J., Sea	2.30

Rel OBP 1st Batter Faced	
(minimum 40 BF)	
Ryan,B.J., Tor	.125
Duchscherer,J, Oak	.132
Putz,J.J., Sea	.167
Britton,Chris, Bal	.192
Reyes,Dennys, Min	.197
Gaudin,Chad, Oak	.204
Calero,Kiko, Oak	.214
Grilli,Jason, Det	.216
Papelbon,Jonat, Bos	.220
Jones,Todd, Det	.226

Rel Opp BA w/ Runners On	
(minimum 50 IP)	
Papelbon,Jonat, Bos	.112
Downs,Scott, Tor	.134
Nathan,Joe, Min	.141
Ryan,B.J., Tor	.142
Reyes,Dennys, Min	.151
Gaudin,Chad, Oak	.170
Rivera,Mariano, NYY	.174
Duchscherer,J, Oak	.190
Rodriguez,Fran, LAA	.191
Soriano,Rafael, Sea	.192

Relief Opp BA w/ RISP	
(minimum 50 IP)	
Papelbon,Jonat, Bos	.082
Downs,Scott, Tor	.111
Ryan,B.J., Tor	.121
Reyes,Dennys, Min	.135
Nathan,Joe, Min	.145
Ray,Chris, Bal	.167
Carrasco,Hector, LAA	.169
Soriano,Rafael, Sea	.172
Duchscherer,J, Oak	.175
Zumaya,Joel, Det	.176

Fastest Avg Fastball-Relief	
(minimum 50 IP)	
Zumaya,Joel, Det	98.6
Farnsworth,Kyle, NYY	96.2
Thornton,Matt, CWS	96.0
Burgos,Ambiorix, KC	95.8
Jenks,Bobby, CWS	95.8
Putz,J.J., Sea	95.6
Davis,Jason, Cle	94.9
Rodriguez,Fran, LAA	94.8
Nathan,Joe, Min	94.8
Ray,Chris, Bal	94.8

Fastest Average Fastball	
(minimum 162 IP)	
Hernandez,Fel, Sea	95.2
Verlander,Just, Det	95.1
Beckett,Josh, Bos	94.7
Sabathia,C.C., Cle	93.7
Bonderman,Jer, Det	93.3
Escobar,Kelvim, LAA	93.1
Wang,Chien-Ming, NYY	93.1
Santana,Ervin, LAA	93.1
Santana,Johan, Min	93.1
Bedard,Erik, Bal	92.6

Slowest Average Fastball	
(minimum 162 IP)	
Redman,Mark, KC	84.1
Rogers,Kenny, Det	85.2
Buehrle,Mark, CWS	85.7
Zito,Barry, Oak	85.8
Byrd,Paul, Cle	86.1
Mussina,Mike, NYY	88.6
Lopez,Rodrigo, Bal	88.8
Washburn,Jarrod, Sea	88.8
Radke,Brad, Min	89.0
Lee,Cliff, Cle	89.0

Pitches 100+ Velocity	
Zumaya,Joel, Det	233
Farnsworth,Kyle, NYY	26
Verlander,Just, Det	19
Hernandez,Fel, Sea	7
Burgos,Ambiorix, KC	5
Thornton,Matt, CWS	5
Bautista,Denny, KC	3
Jenks,Bobby, CWS	3
3 tied with	2

Pitches 95+ Velocity	
Beckett,Josh, Bos	1072
Verlander,Just, Det	992
Hernandez,Fel, Sea	950
Zumaya,Joel, Det	884
Cabrera,Daniel, Bal	834
Burnett,A.J., Tor	677
Burgos,Ambiorix, KC	578
Putz,J.J., Sea	499
Farnsworth,Kyle, NYY	483
Thornton,Matt, CWS	473

Pitches Less Than 80 MPH	
Wakefield,Tim, Bos	1598
Zito,Barry, Oak	1200
Rogers,Kenny, Det	901
Moyer,Jamie, Sea	899
Redman,Mark, KC	832
Mussina,Mike, NYY	701
Buehrle,Mark, CWS	694
Fossum,Casey, TB	604
Byrd,Paul, Cle	594
Bedard,Erik, Bal	579

Lowest % Fastballs	
(minimum 162 IP)	
Buehrle,Mark, CWS	44.4
Garcia,Freddy, CWS	46.9
Rogers,Kenny, Det	49.5
Escobar,Kelvim, LAA	49.8
Meche,Gil, Sea	50.0
Halladay,Roy, Tor	50.0
Mussina,Mike, NYY	51.1
Zito,Barry, Oak	51.3
Byrd,Paul, Cle	51.8
Pineiro,Joel, Sea	53.4

Highest % Fastballs	
(minimum 162 IP)	
Wang,Chien-Ming, NYY	74.2
Silva,Carlos, Min	72.3
Padilla,Vicente, Tex	68.7
Garland,Jon, CWS	68.3
Beckett,Josh, Bos	68.2
Millwood,Kevin, Tex	68.0
Lee,Cliff, Cle	67.9
Westbrook,Jake, Cle	66.3
Verlander,Just, Det	65.7
Washburn,Jarrod, Sea	64.8

Highest % Curveballs	
(minimum 162 IP)	
Mussina,Mike, NYY	23.4
Halladay,Roy, Tor	23.4
Bedard,Erik, Bal	22.0
Lackey,John, LAA	21.3
Beckett,Josh, Bos	21.0
Hernandez,Fel, Sea	20.0
Zito,Barry, Oak	18.2
Meche,Gil, Sea	18.2
Blanton,Joe, Oak	17.1
Verlander,Just, Det	15.8

2006 American League Pitching Leaders

Highest % Changeups
(minimum 162 IP)

Rogers,Kenny, Det	29.0
Redman,Mark, KC	27.6
Santana,Johan, Min	25.5
Buehrle,Mark, CWS	20.1
Zito,Barry, Oak	18.7
Robertson,Nate, Det	17.0
Verlander,Just, Det	17.0
Vazquez,Javier, CWS	16.6
Byrd,Paul, Cle	15.3
Hernandez,Fel, Sea	14.8

Highest % Sliders
(minimum 162 IP)

Johnson,Randy, NYY	34.6
Bonderman,Jer, Det	33.0
Benson,Kris, Bal	24.6
Sabathia,C.C., Cle	23.1
Robertson,Nate, Det	22.5
Santana,Ervin, LAA	21.3
Byrd,Paul, Cle	21.1
Pineiro,Joel, Sea	19.8
Garcia,Freddy, CWS	19.3
Haren,Dan, Oak	18.9

Balks

Lilly,Ted, Tor	4
Burgos,Ambiorix, KC	3
12 tied with	2

Strikeout/Hit Ratio
(minimum 50 IP)

Nathan,Joe, Min	2.50
Ryan,B.J., Tor	2.05
Rodriguez,Fran, LAA	1.89
Papelbon,Jonat, Bos	1.88
Putz,J.J., Sea	1.76
Zumaya,Joel, Det	1.73
Liriano,Francisco, Min	1.62
Soriano,Rafael, Sea	1.48
Reyes,Dennys, Min	1.40
2 tied with	1.34

Opp BPS vs Fastballs
(minimum 251 BF)

Zumaya,Joel, Det	.514
Weaver,Jered, LAA	.576
Kazmir,Scott, TB	.610
Shields,Scot, LAA	.616
Lackey,John, LAA	.621
Santana,Ervin, LAA	.632
Padilla,Vicente, Tex	.645
Proctor,Scott, NYY	.648
Mussina,Mike, NYY	.648
Loewen,Adam, Bal	.661

Opp BPS vs Curveballs
(minimum 100 BF)

Burnett,A.J., Tor	.317
Meche,Gil, Sea	.423
Beckett,Josh, Bos	.426
Halladay,Roy, Tor	.455
Millwood,Kevin, Tex	.456
Bedard,Erik, Bal	.468
Hernandez,Fel, Sea	.487
Lilly,Ted, Tor	.520
Lackey,John, LAA	.548
Zito,Barry, Oak	.579

Opp BPS vs Changeups
(minimum 100 BF)

Santana,Johan, Min	.352
Rodney,Fernando, Det	.378
Saunders,Joe, LAA	.451
Carrasco,Hector, LAA	.480
Pineiro,Joel, Sea	.510
Westbrook,Jake, Cle	.529
Vazquez,Javier, CWS	.545
Mussina,Mike, NYY	.553
Verlander,Just, Det	.568
Sabathia,C.C., Cle	.582

Opp BPS vs Sliders
(minimum 64 BF)

Neshek,Pat, Min	.162
Fossum,Casey, TB	.261
Nathan,Joe, Min	.301
Cabrera,Fern, Cle	.304
Liriano,Francisco, Min	.356
Cabrera,Daniel, Bal	.361
Gobble,Jimmy, KC	.361
Gaudin,Chad, Oak	.382
Bonderman,Jer, Det	.397
Janssen,Casey, Tor	.397

Earned Runs

Lopez,Rodrigo, Bal	124
Silva,Carlos, Min	119
Pineiro,Joel, Sea	117
Beckett,Josh, Bos	114
Johnson,Randy, NYY	114
Buehrle,Mark, CWS	113
Garcia,Freddy, CWS	109
Vazquez,Javier, CWS	109
Millwood,Kevin, Tex	108
2 tied with	106

2006 National League Pitching Leaders

Earned Run Average		Winning Percentage		Opponent Batting Average		Baserunners Per 9 IP	
(minimum 162 IP)		(minimum 15 Decisions)		(minimum 162 IP)		(minimum 162 IP)	
Oswalt,Roy, Hou	2.98	James,Chuck, Atl	.733	Young,Chris, SD	.206	Carpenter,Chris, StL	10.03
Carpenter,Chris, StL	3.09	Williams,Woody, SD	.706	Zambrano,Carlos, ChC	.208	Webb,Brandon, Ari	10.42
Webb,Brandon, Ari	3.10	Zambrano,Carlos, ChC	.696	Cain,Matt, SF	.222	Young,Chris, SD	10.49
Arroyo,Bronson, Cin	3.29	Young,Chris, SD	.688	Carpenter,Chris, StL	.235	Oswalt,Roy, Hou	10.77
Zambrano,Carlos, ChC	3.41	Glavine,Tom, NYM	.682	Schmidt,Jason, SF	.238	Arroyo,Bronson, Cin	10.88
Young,Chris, SD	3.46	Lowe,Derek, LAD	.667	Olsen,Scott, Fla	.239	Maddux,Greg, ChC-LAD	10.97
Smoltz,John, Atl	3.49	Webb,Brandon, Ari	.667	Peavy,Jake, SD	.242	Bush,David, Mil	11.01
Schmidt,Jason, SF	3.59	Carpenter,Chris, StL	.652	Arroyo,Bronson, Cin	.243	Smoltz,John, Atl	11.06
Lowe,Derek, LAD	3.63	Oswalt,Roy, Hou	.652	Webb,Brandon, Ari	.246	Peavy,Jake, SD	11.34
Hensley,Clay, SD	3.71	Trachsel,Steve, NYM	.652	Francis,Jeff, Col	.250	Capuano,Chris, Mil	11.59

Games		Games Started		Complete Games		Shutouts	
Torres,Salomon, Pit	94	Arroyo,Bronson, Cin	35	Harang,Aaron, Cin	6	Carpenter,Chris, StL	3
Capps,Matt, Pit	85	Harang,Aaron, Cin	35	Carpenter,Chris, StL	5	Webb,Brandon, Ari	3
Rauch,Jon, Was	85	Hudson,Tim, Atl	35	Webb,Brandon, Ari	5	Bush,David, Mil	2
Howry,Bob, ChC	84	Pettitte,Andy, Hou	35	Willis,Dontrelle, Fla	4	Capuano,Chris, Mil	2
Stanton,Mike, Was-SF	82	Smoltz,John, Atl	35	7 tied with	3	Harang,Aaron, Cin	2
Coffey,Todd, Cin	81	7 tied with	34			Jennings,Jason, Col	2
Geary,Geoff, Phi	81					24 tied with	1
Qualls,Chad, Hou	81						
Mesa,Jose, Col	79						
2 tied with	78						

Wins		Losses		No Decisions		Wild Pitches	
Harang,Aaron, Cin	16	Marquis,Jason, StL	16	Young,Chris, SD	15	Batista,Miguel, Ari	14
Lowe,Derek, LAD	16	Ortiz,Ramon, Was	16	Batista,Miguel, Ari	14	Madson,Ryan, Phi	12
Penny,Brad, LAD	16	Cook,Aaron, Col	15	Suppan,Jeff, StL	13	Lidge,Brad, Hou	11
Smoltz,John, Atl	16	Duke,Zach, Pit	15	Davis,Doug, Mil	12	Schmidt,Jason, SF	11
Webb,Brandon, Ari	16	Morris,Matt, SF	15	Maholm,Paul, Pit	12	Jennings,Jason, Col	10
Zambrano,Carlos, ChC	16	Maddux,Greg, ChC-LAD	14	Myers,Brett, Phi	12	Cain,Matt, SF	9
5 tied with	15	Peavy,Jake, SD	14	Schmidt,Jason, SF	12	Julio,Jorge, NYM-Ari	9
		4 tied with	13	Capuano,Chris, Mil	11	Vargas,Claudio, Ari	9
				Fogg,Josh, Col	11	Zambrano,Carlos, ChC	9
				Lowe,Derek, LAD	11	7 tied with	8

Strikeouts		Walks Allowed		Intentional Walks Allowed		Hit Batters	
Harang,Aaron, Cin	216	Zambrano,Carlos, ChC	115	Francis,Jeff, Col	15	Willis,Dontrelle, Fla	19
Peavy,Jake, SD	215	Davis,Doug, Mil	102	Ortiz,Ramon, Was	14	Bush,David, Mil	18
Smoltz,John, Atl	211	Cain,Matt, SF	87	Fogg,Josh, Col	13	Ortiz,Ramon, Was	18
Zambrano,Carlos, ChC	210	Jennings,Jason, Col	85	Cook,Aaron, Col	11	Marquis,Jason, StL	16
Myers,Brett, Phi	189	Batista,Miguel, Ari	84	Peavy,Jake, SD	11	Morris,Matt, SF	14
Arroyo,Bronson, Cin	184	Willis,Dontrelle, Fla	83	Stanton,Mike, Was-SF	11	Armas Jr.,Tony, Was	13
Carpenter,Chris, StL	184	Maholm,Paul, Pit	81	Franklin,Ryan, Phi-Cin	10	Francis,Jeff, Col	13
Schmidt,Jason, SF	180	Schmidt,Jason, SF	80	Hudson,Tim, Atl	10	Hernandez,Orl, Ari-NYM	12
Cain,Matt, SF	179	Hudson,Tim, Atl	79	3 tied with	9	Maholm,Paul, Pit	12
2 tied with	178	2 tied with	78			Cruz,Juan, Ari	11

2006 National League Pitching Leaders

Runs Allowed		Hits Allowed		Doubles Allowed		Home Runs Allowed	
Marquis,Jason, StL	136	Duke,Zach, Pit	255	Capuano,Chris, Mil	66	Marquis,Jason, StL	35
Hudson,Tim, Atl	129	Hernandez,Liv, Was-Ari	246	Duke,Zach, Pit	60	Arroyo,Bronson, Cin	31
Ortiz,Ramon, Was	127	Cook,Aaron, Col	242	Oswalt,Roy, Hou	55	Ortiz,Ramon, Was	31
Hernandez,Liv, Was-Ari	125	Harang,Aaron, Cin	242	Harang,Aaron, Cin	54	Sosa,Jorge, Atl-StL	30
Morris,Matt, SF	123	Pettitte,Andy, Hou	238	Morris,Matt, SF	54	Capuano,Chris, Mil	29
Davis,Doug, Mil	118	Hudson,Tim, Atl	235	Maddux,Greg, ChC-LAD	53	Hernandez,Liv, Was-Ari	29
Batista,Miguel, Ari	116	Willis,Dontrelle, Fla	234	Penny,Brad, LAD	53	Milton,Eric, Cin	29
Duke,Zach, Pit	116	Batista,Miguel, Ari	231	Pettitte,Andy, Hou	53	Myers,Brett, Phi	29
Fogg,Josh, Col	115	Ortiz,Ramon, Was	230	Bush,David, Mil	51	Snell,Ian, Pit	29
Pettitte,Andy, Hou	114	Capuano,Chris, Mil	229	2 tied with	49	2 tied with	28

Run Support Per Nine IP		% Pitches In Strike Zone		Pitches Per Start		Pitches Per Batter	
(minimum 162 IP)		(minimum 162 IP)		(minimum 30 GS)		(minimum 162 IP)	
Trachsel,Steve, NYM	6.61	Oswalt,Roy, Hou	57.7	Arroyo,Bronson, Cin	110.1	Maddux,Greg, ChC-LAD	3.25
Fogg,Josh, Col	6.44	Maddux,Greg, ChC-LAD	56.5	Zambrano,Carlos, ChC	109.9	Cook,Aaron, Col	3.40
Davis,Doug, Mil	6.20	Bush,David, Mil	55.1	Schmidt,Jason, SF	108.2	Bush,David, Mil	3.49
Hudson,Tim, Atl	6.10	Lieber,Jon, Phi	54.5	Harang,Aaron, Cin	106.4	Lieber,Jon, Phi	3.49
Zambrano,Carlos, ChC	5.97	Penny,Brad, LAD	53.6	Willis,Dontrelle, Fla	106.3	Duke,Zach, Pit	3.50
Penny,Brad, LAD	5.95	Cook,Aaron, Col	53.3	Cain,Matt, SF	106.0	Webb,Brandon, Ari	3.51
Glavine,Tom, NYM	5.91	Capuano,Chris, Mil	53.2	Peavy,Jake, SD	104.8	Marquis,Jason, StL	3.54
Francis,Jeff, Col	5.83	Vargas,Claudio, Ari	53.0	Myers,Brett, Phi	103.7	Hudson,Tim, Atl	3.56
Batista,Miguel, Ari	5.76	Arroyo,Bronson, Cin	53.0	Jennings,Jason, Col	102.6	Batista,Miguel, Ari	3.59
Suppan,Jeff, StL	5.73	Morris,Matt, SF	52.9	Hernandez,Liv, Was-Ari	102.6	Lowe,Derek, LAD	3.59

Quality Starts		Batters Faced		Innings Pitched		Most Pitches in a Game	
Capuano,Chris, Mil	25	Harang,Aaron, Cin	993	Arroyo,Bronson, Cin	240.2	Hernandez,Liv, Was, 6/15	138
Oswalt,Roy, Hou	25	Arroyo,Bronson, Cin	992	Webb,Brandon, Ari	235.0	Harang,Aaron, Cin, 7/8	135
Smoltz,John, Atl	24	Willis,Dontrelle, Fla	975	Harang,Aaron, Cin	234.1	Schmidt,Jason, SF, 5/20	132
Arroyo,Bronson, Cin	23	Smoltz,John, Atl	960	Smoltz,John, Atl	232.0	Cain,Matt, SF, 6/19	131
Webb,Brandon, Ari	23	Hernandez,Liv, Was-Ari	959	Willis,Dontrelle, Fla	223.1	Hernandez,Liv, Was, 7/1	131
Glavine,Tom, NYM	22	Hudson,Tim, Atl	959	Carpenter,Chris, StL	221.2	Smoltz,John, Atl, 5/17	130
Myers,Brett, Phi	22	Webb,Brandon, Ari	950	Capuano,Chris, Mil	221.1	Francis,Jeff, Col, 7/24	129
Zambrano,Carlos, ChC	22	Capuano,Chris, Mil	936	Oswalt,Roy, Hou	220.2	Peavy,Jake, SD, 7/26	129
Peavy,Jake, SD	21	Duke,Zach, Pit	935	Hudson,Tim, Atl	218.1	3 tied with	128
5 tied with	20	Pettitte,Andy, Hou	929	Lowe,Derek, LAD	218.0		

Stolen Bases Allowed		Caught Stealing Off		Stolen Base Pct Allowed		Pickoffs	
Young,Chris, SD	41	Duke,Zach, Pit	12	Capuano,Chris, Mil	25.0	Maholm,Paul, Pit	9
Lowe,Derek, LAD	26	Maholm,Paul, Pit	11	Carpenter,Chris, StL	30.0	Duke,Zach, Pit	7
Maddux,Greg, ChC-LAD	25	Glavine,Tom, NYM	9	Glavine,Tom, NYM	40.0	Wright,Jamey, SF	7
Peavy,Jake, SD	25	Webb,Brandon, Ari	9	Zambrano,Carlos, ChC	40.0	Beimel,Joe, LAD	6
Kim,Byung-Hyun, Col	24	7 tied with	8	Oswalt,Roy, Hou	45.5	Capuano,Chris, Mil	6
Webb,Brandon, Ari	24			Arroyo,Bronson, Cin	50.0	Francis,Jeff, Col	5
Hudson,Tim, Atl	23			Olsen,Scott, Fla	50.0	Pettitte,Andy, Hou	4
Francis,Jeff, Col	21			Duke,Zach, Pit	52.0	Rodriguez,Wandy, Hou	4
Hernandez,Orl, Ari-NYM	20			Maholm,Paul, Pit	54.2	Stanton,Mike, Was-SF	4
Penny,Brad, LAD	20			Willis,Dontrelle, Fla	54.5	6 tied with	3

Note: Stolen Base Pct Allowed (minimum 162 IP)

2006 National League Pitching Leaders

Strikeouts Per 9 IP
(minimum 162 IP)

Peavy,Jake, SD	9.56
Hernandez,Orl, Ari-NYM	9.09
Zambrano,Carlos, ChC	8.83
Myers,Brett, Phi	8.59
Cain,Matt, SF	8.45
Harang,Aaron, Cin	8.30
Olsen,Scott, Fla	8.27
Young,Chris, SD	8.23
Smoltz,John, Atl	8.19
Snell,Ian, Pit	8.18

Opp On-Base Percentage
(minimum 162 IP)

Carpenter,Chris, StL	.279
Young,Chris, SD	.287
Webb,Brandon, Ari	.289
Arroyo,Bronson, Cin	.296
Smoltz,John, Atl	.298
Oswalt,Roy, Hou	.299
Bush,David, Mil	.299
Maddux,Greg, ChC-LAD	.301
Peavy,Jake, SD	.303
Capuano,Chris, Mil	.307

Opp Slugging Average
(minimum 162 IP)

Zambrano,Carlos, ChC	.351
Lowe,Derek, LAD	.360
Webb,Brandon, Ari	.361
Carpenter,Chris, StL	.364
Cain,Matt, SF	.371
Hensley,Clay, SD	.377
Schmidt,Jason, SF	.379
Young,Chris, SD	.382
Jennings,Jason, Col	.386
Smoltz,John, Atl	.393

Hits Per Nine Innings
(minimum 162 IP)

Young,Chris, SD	6.72
Zambrano,Carlos, ChC	6.81
Cain,Matt, SF	7.41
Carpenter,Chris, StL	7.88
Olsen,Scott, Fla	7.97
Schmidt,Jason, SF	7.97
Webb,Brandon, Ari	8.27
Arroyo,Bronson, Cin	8.30
Peavy,Jake, SD	8.32
Hensley,Clay, SD	8.37

Home Runs Per Nine IP
(minimum 162 IP)

Webb,Brandon, Ari	0.57
Lowe,Derek, LAD	0.58
Duke,Zach, Pit	0.71
Cook,Aaron, Col	0.72
Jennings,Jason, Col	0.72
Hensley,Clay, SD	0.72
Oswalt,Roy, Hou	0.73
Batista,Miguel, Ari	0.79
Francis,Jeff, Col	0.81
Davis,Doug, Mil	0.84

Batting Average vs. LHB
(minimum 125 BF)

Borowski,Joe, Fla	.167
Young,Chris, SD	.175
Olsen,Scott, Fla	.178
Julio,Jorge, NYM-Ari	.185
Glavine,Tom, NYM	.202
Linebrink,Scott, SD	.204
Cain,Matt, SF	.217
Weathers,David, Cin	.219
Cordero,Chad, Was	.220
Maholm,Paul, Pit	.224

Batting Average vs. RHB
(minimum 225 BF)

Zambrano,Carlos, ChC	.172
Clemens,Roger, Hou	.185
Hernandez,Orl, Ari-NYM	.200
Arroyo,Bronson, Cin	.205
Carpenter,Chris, StL	.210
Martinez,Pedro, NYM	.211
Schmidt,Jason, SF	.215
James,Chuck, Atl	.218
Hill,Rich, ChC	.220
Smoltz,John, Atl	.226

Opp BA w/ RISP
(minimum 125 BF)

Young,Chris, SD	.176
Billingsley,Chad, LAD	.191
Schmidt,Jason, SF	.197
Cruz,Juan, Ari	.216
Smoltz,John, Atl	.223
Martinez,Pedro, NYM	.223
Carpenter,Chris, StL	.224
Harang,Aaron, Cin	.228
Peavy,Jake, SD	.228
Oswalt,Roy, Hou	.229

OBP vs. Leadoff Hitter
(minimum 150 BF)

Lieber,Jon, Phi	.246
Capuano,Chris, Mil	.252
Carpenter,Chris, StL	.261
Arroyo,Bronson, Cin	.262
Cain,Matt, SF	.264
Francis,Jeff, Col	.268
Jennings,Jason, Col	.272
Myers,Brett, Phi	.275
Hernandez,Liv, Was-Ari	.276
Maddux,Greg, ChC-LAD	.281

Strikeouts / Walks Ratio
(minimum 162 IP)

Bush,David, Mil	4.37
Oswalt,Roy, Hou	4.37
Carpenter,Chris, StL	4.28
Lieber,Jon, Phi	4.17
Harang,Aaron, Cin	3.86
Smoltz,John, Atl	3.84
Capuano,Chris, Mil	3.70
Webb,Brandon, Ari	3.56
Peavy,Jake, SD	3.47
Maddux,Greg, ChC-LAD	3.16

Highest GB/FB Ratio
(minimum 162 IP)

Webb,Brandon, Ari	5.09
Lowe,Derek, LAD	4.82
Cook,Aaron, Col	3.24
Hudson,Tim, Atl	2.76
Maholm,Paul, Pit	2.43
Pettitte,Andy, Hou	2.33
Carpenter,Chris, StL	2.23
Maddux,Greg, ChC-LAD	2.21
Duke,Zach, Pit	2.18
Batista,Miguel, Ari	2.16

Lowest GB/FB Ratio
(minimum 162 IP)

Young,Chris, SD	0.50
Cain,Matt, SF	0.84
Hernandez,Orl, Ari-NYM	0.86
Hernandez,Liv, Was-Ari	0.96
Schmidt,Jason, SF	0.97
Peavy,Jake, SD	1.04
Arroyo,Bronson, Cin	1.06
Vargas,Claudio, Ari	1.07
Ortiz,Ramon, Was	1.14
Harang,Aaron, Cin	1.18

Sacrifice Flies Allowed

Perez,Oliver, Pit-NYM	10
Smoltz,John, Atl	10
Capuano,Chris, Mil	8
Davis,Doug, Mil	8
Hamels,Cole, Phi	8
Harang,Aaron, Cin	8
Hernandez,Liv, Was-Ari	8
8 tied with	7

Sacrifice Hits Allowed

Harang,Aaron, Cin	21
Davis,Doug, Mil	16
Hernandez,Liv, Was-Ari	16
Snell,Ian, Pit	16
Pettitte,Andy, Hou	14
Duke,Zach, Pit	13
5 tied with	12

GIDP Induced

Batista,Miguel, Ari	33
Willis,Dontrelle, Fla	32
Lowe,Derek, LAD	29
Webb,Brandon, Ari	29
Cook,Aaron, Col	28
Duke,Zach, Pit	27
Hensley,Clay, SD	27
Pettitte,Andy, Hou	26
3 tied with	24

GIDP Per Nine IP
(minimum 162 IP)

Batista,Miguel, Ari	1.44
Hensley,Clay, SD	1.30
Willis,Dontrelle, Fla	1.29
Lowe,Derek, LAD	1.20
Cook,Aaron, Col	1.18
Maholm,Paul, Pit	1.18
Suppan,Jeff, StL	1.14
Duke,Zach, Pit	1.13
Webb,Brandon, Ari	1.11
Pettitte,Andy, Hou	1.09

2006 National League Pitching Leaders

Saves

Hoffman,Trevor, SD	46
Wagner,Billy, NYM	40
Borowski,Joe, Fla	36
Gordon,Tom, Phi	34
Isringhausen,Jason, StL	33
Lidge,Brad, Hou	32
Fuentes,Brian, Col	30
Cordero,Chad, Was	29
4 tied with	24

Blown Saves

Isringhausen,Jason, StL	10
Capps,Matt, Pit	9
Dempster,Ryan, ChC	9
Linebrink,Scott, SD	9
Baez,Danys, LAD-Atl	8
Benitez,Armando, SF	8
Turnbow,Derrick, Mil	8
5 tied with	7

Save Pct
(minimum 20 Save Ops)

Gonzalez,Mike, Pit	100.0
Saito,Takashi, LAD	92.3
Hoffman,Trevor, SD	90.2
Wagner,Billy, NYM	88.9
Cordero,Chad, Was	87.9
Gordon,Tom, Phi	87.2
Lidge,Brad, Hou	84.2
Borowski,Joe, Fla	83.7
Fuentes,Brian, Col	83.3
Valverde,Jose, Ari	81.8

Save Opportunities

Hoffman,Trevor, SD	51
Wagner,Billy, NYM	45
Borowski,Joe, Fla	43
Isringhausen,Jason, StL	43
Gordon,Tom, Phi	39
Lidge,Brad, Hou	38
Fuentes,Brian, Col	36
Cordero,Chad, Was	33
Dempster,Ryan, ChC	33
Turnbow,Derrick, Mil	32

Easy Saves

Hoffman,Trevor, SD	28
Borowski,Joe, Fla	25
Fuentes,Brian, Col	24
Wagner,Billy, NYM	22
Gordon,Tom, Phi	21
Isringhausen,Jason, StL	21
Lidge,Brad, Hou	18
Gonzalez,Mike, Pit	17
Cordero,Chad, Was	16
Dempster,Ryan, ChC	15

Regular Saves

Hoffman,Trevor, SD	18
Wagner,Billy, NYM	18
Gordon,Tom, Phi	13
Lidge,Brad, Hou	12
Borowski,Joe, Fla	11
Cordero,Chad, Was	11
Isringhausen,Jason, StL	11
Saito,Takashi, LAD	10
3 tied with	9

Tough Saves

Cordero,Chad, Was	2
Cordero,Franc, Mil	2
Lidge,Brad, Hou	2
Reitsma,Chris, Atl	2
Remlinger,Mike, Atl	2
Stanton,Mike, Was-SF	2
Wheeler,Dan, Hou	2
18 tied with	1

Holds Adjusted Saves %
(minimum 20 Save Ops)

Gonzalez,Mike, Pit	100.0
Saito,Takashi, LAD	93.9
Hoffman,Trevor, SD	90.2
Wagner,Billy, NYM	88.9
Cordero,Chad, Was	87.9
Gordon,Tom, Phi	87.2
Lidge,Brad, Hou	86.4
Borowski,Joe, Fla	83.7
Fuentes,Brian, Col	83.3
Valverde,Jose, Ari	82.6

Relief Wins

Capps,Matt, Pit	9
Looper,Braden, StL	9
Villarreal,Osc, Atl	8
Cordero,Chad, Was	7
Feliciano,Pedro, NYM	7
Geary,Geoff, Phi	7
Linebrink,Scott, SD	7
Qualls,Chad, Hou	7
Stanton,Mike, Was-SF	7
4 tied with	6

Relief Losses

Dempster,Ryan, ChC	9
Turnbow,Derrick, Mil	9
Isringhausen,Jason, StL	8
Coffey,Todd, Cin	7
Franklin,Ryan, Phi-Cin	7
Marte,Damaso, Pit	7
Messenger,Randy, Fla	7
Stanton,Mike, Was-SF	7
4 tied with	6

Relief Games

Torres,Salomon, Pit	94
Capps,Matt, Pit	85
Rauch,Jon, Was	85
Howry,Bob, ChC	84
Stanton,Mike, Was-SF	82
Coffey,Todd, Cin	81
Geary,Geoff, Phi	81
Qualls,Chad, Hou	81
Mesa,Jose, Col	79
2 tied with	78

Holds

Linebrink,Scott, SD	36
Heilman,Aaron, NYM	27
Vizcaino,Luis, Ari	25
Wheeler,Dan, Hou	24
Lyon,Brandon, Ari	23
Qualls,Chad, Hou	23
Rhodes,Arthur, Phi	23
Tankersley,Taylor, Fla	22
Howry,Bob, ChC	21
Torres,Salomon, Pit	20

Relief Innings

Torres,Salomon, Pit	93.1
Geary,Geoff, Phi	91.1
Rauch,Jon, Was	91.1
Qualls,Chad, Hou	88.2
Heilman,Aaron, NYM	87.0
Oliver,Darren, NYM	81.0
Capps,Matt, Pit	80.2
Saito,Takashi, LAD	78.1
Coffey,Todd, Cin	78.0
Franklin,Ryan, Phi-Cin	77.1

Inherited Runners Scrd %
(minimum 30 IR)

Grabow,John, Pit	17.5
Miller,Trever, Hou	17.5
Bradford,Chad, NYM	18.9
Ohman,Will, ChC	19.5
Stanton,Mike, Was-SF	20.3
McBride,Macay, Atl	20.4
Eyre,Scott, ChC	21.4
Coffey,Todd, Cin	22.9
Rauch,Jon, Was	23.5
2 tied with	23.7

Relief Opp On Base Pct
(minimum 50 IP)

Meredith,Cla, SD	.207
Saito,Takashi, LAD	.243
Hoffman,Trevor, SD	.250
Springer,Russ, Hou	.277
Cordero,Chad, Was	.279
Oliver,Darren, NYM	.284
Wagner,Billy, NYM	.285
Miller,Trever, Hou	.286
Wheeler,Dan, Hou	.288
Bradford,Chad, NYM	.290

Relief Opp Slugging Avg
(minimum 50 IP)

Meredith,Cla, SD	.244
Gonzalez,Mike, Pit	.259
Saito,Takashi, LAD	.262
Wagner,Billy, NYM	.315
Sanchez,Duaner, NYM	.316
Hoffman,Trevor, SD	.316
Bradford,Chad, NYM	.328
Feliciano,Pedro, NYM	.332
Heilman,Aaron, NYM	.332
Ohman,Will, ChC	.335

2006 National League Pitching Leaders

Relief Opp BA Vs LHB	
(minimum 50 AB)	
Ohman,Will, ChC	.157
Vizcaino,Luis, Ari	.163
Borowski,Joe, Fla	.167
Gordon,Tom, Phi	.185
Julio,Jorge, NYM-Ari	.185
McBride,Macay, Atl	.187
Rivera,Saul, Was	.194
Hoffman,Trevor, SD	.194
Linebrink,Scott, SD	.204
Oliver,Darren, NYM	.208

Relief Opp BA Vs RHB	
(minimum 50 AB)	
Meredith,Cla, SD	.107
Saito,Takashi, LAD	.129
Sanchez,Duaner, NYM	.179
Wainwright,Adam, StL	.182
Wheeler,Dan, Hou	.183
Isringhausen,Jason, StL	.187
Springer,Russ, Hou	.187
Ramirez,Ramon, Col	.194
Medders,Brandon, Ari	.196
Broxton,Jon, LAD	.196

Relief Opp Batting Average	
(minimum 50 IP)	
Meredith,Cla, SD	.170
Saito,Takashi, LAD	.177
Hoffman,Trevor, SD	.205
Ohman,Will, ChC	.208
Fuentes,Brian, Col	.209
Julio,Jorge, NYM-Ari	.210
Springer,Russ, Hou	.211
Gonzalez,Mike, Pit	.213
Aardsma,David, ChC	.214
Vizcaino,Luis, Ari	.215

Relief Earned Run Average	
(minimum 50 IP)	
Meredith,Cla, SD	1.07
Saito,Takashi, LAD	2.07
Feliciano,Pedro, NYM	2.09
Hoffman,Trevor, SD	2.14
Gonzalez,Mike, Pit	2.17
Wagner,Billy, NYM	2.24
Wheeler,Dan, Hou	2.52
Broxton,Jon, LAD	2.59
Sanchez,Duaner, NYM	2.60
Bradford,Chad, NYM	2.90

Rel OBP 1st Batter Faced	
(minimum 40 BF)	
Meredith,Cla, SD	.178
Embree,Alan, SD	.219
Bradford,Chad, NYM	.229
Wagner,Billy, NYM	.229
Franklin,Ryan, Phi-Cin	.231
Ray,Ken, Atl	.232
Capps,Matt, Pit	.241
Beimel,Joe, LAD	.242
Fuentes,Brian, Col	.242
2 tied with	.250

Rel Opp BA w/ Runners On	
(minimum 50 IP)	
Meredith,Cla, SD	.114
Hoffman,Trevor, SD	.122
Wagner,Billy, NYM	.171
Broxton,Jon, LAD	.172
Fuentes,Brian, Col	.173
Miller,Trever, Hou	.176
Cordero,Chad, Was	.183
Vizcaino,Luis, Ari	.194
Julio,Jorge, NYM-Ari	.195
Springer,Russ, Hou	.198

Relief Opp BA w/ RISP	
(minimum 50 IP)	
Miller,Trever, Hou	.063
Broxton,Jon, LAD	.159
Meredith,Cla, SD	.159
Capellan,Jose, Mil	.171
Hoffman,Trevor, SD	.182
Cordero,Chad, Was	.185
Isringhausen,Jason, StL	.186
Gordon,Tom, Phi	.187
Wainwright,Adam, StL	.188
Fuentes,Brian, Col	.190

Fastest Avg Fastball-Relief	
(minimum 50 IP)	
Wagner,Billy, NYM	96.3
Lidge,Brad, Hou	95.7
Turnbow,Derrick, Mil	95.6
Julio,Jorge, NYM-Ari	95.3
Broxton,Jon, LAD	95.0
Yates,Tyler, Atl	94.6
Aardsma,David, ChC	94.3
Capellan,Jose, Mil	93.7
Novoa,Roberto, ChC	93.7
Hernandez,Rob, Pit-NYM	93.3

Fastest Average Fastball	
(minimum 162 IP)	
Penny,Brad, LAD	93.9
Cain,Matt, SF	93.4
Snell,Ian, Pit	92.8
Oswalt,Roy, Hou	92.7
Smoltz,John, Atl	92.7
Schmidt,Jason, SF	92.4
Batista,Miguel, Ari	92.2
Zambrano,Carlos, ChC	92.2
Peavy,Jake, SD	92.1
Vargas,Claudio, Ari	91.5

Slowest Average Fastball	
(minimum 162 IP)	
Maddux,Greg, ChC-LAD	83.4
Hernandez,Liv, Was-Ari	83.9
Glavine,Tom, NYM	85.3
Davis,Doug, Mil	85.6
Francis,Jeff, Col	86.0
Capuano,Chris, Mil	86.8
Fogg,Josh, Col	87.1
Jennings,Jason, Col	87.1
Trachsel,Steve, NYM	87.1
Duke,Zach, Pit	87.1

Pitches 100+ Velocity	
Wagner,Billy, NYM	5
Lidge,Brad, Hou	3
Novoa,Roberto, ChC	3
Turnbow,Derrick, Mil	3
Cordero,Franc, Mil	2
Julio,Jorge, NYM-Ari	2
Aardsma,David, ChC	1

Pitches 95+ Velocity	
Penny,Brad, LAD	817
Lidge,Brad, Hou	574
Wagner,Billy, NYM	541
Broxton,Jon, LAD	442
Julio,Jorge, NYM-Ari	437
Cain,Matt, SF	377
Turnbow,Derrick, Mil	375
Zambrano,Carlos, ChC	356
Aardsma,David, ChC	296
Novoa,Roberto, ChC	280

Pitches Less Than 80 MPH	
Arroyo,Bronson, Cin	1350
Hernandez,Liv, Was-Ari	1055
Hernandez,Orl, Ari-NYM	1013
Glavine,Tom, NYM	977
Morris,Matt, SF	867
Capuano,Chris, Mil	837
Lowry,Noah, SF	826
Francis,Jeff, Col	728
Maddux,Greg, ChC-LAD	679
Nolasco,Ricky, Fla	649

Lowest % Fastballs	
(minimum 162 IP)	
Davis,Doug, Mil	41.6
Arroyo,Bronson, Cin	42.6
Morris,Matt, SF	45.3
Smoltz,John, Atl	45.6
Carpenter,Chris, StL	47.3
Batista,Miguel, Ari	47.5
Hernandez,Orl, Ari-NYM	49.1
Ortiz,Ramon, Was	49.2
Myers,Brett, Phi	49.2
Glavine,Tom, NYM	49.3

Highest % Fastballs	
(minimum 162 IP)	
Cook,Aaron, Col	81.0
Webb,Brandon, Ari	76.2
Young,Chris, SD	73.1
Penny,Brad, LAD	72.6
Cain,Matt, SF	70.3
Oswalt,Roy, Hou	66.5
Schmidt,Jason, SF	65.5
Lowe,Derek, LAD	65.1
Zambrano,Carlos, ChC	64.9
Maddux,Greg, ChC-LAD	64.7

Highest % Curveballs	
(minimum 162 IP)	
Morris,Matt, SF	28.6
Carpenter,Chris, StL	21.7
Myers,Brett, Phi	20.7
Bush,David, Mil	20.6
Penny,Brad, LAD	19.0
Arroyo,Bronson, Cin	18.7
Hernandez,Orl, Ari-NYM	17.8
Trachsel,Steve, NYM	17.7
Duke,Zach, Pit	17.6
Maholm,Paul, Pit	17.4

2006 National League Pitching Leaders

Highest % Changeups
(minimum 162 IP)

Glavine,Tom, NYM	37.5
Maddux,Greg, ChC-LAD	26.7
Capuano,Chris, Mil	22.6
Fogg,Josh, Col	21.6
Francis,Jeff, Col	19.8
Schmidt,Jason, SF	18.9
Olsen,Scott, Fla	18.8
Jennings,Jason, Col	14.8
Duke,Zach, Pit	13.4
Vargas,Claudio, Ari	12.3

Highest % Sliders
(minimum 162 IP)

Lieber,Jon, Phi	35.4
Ortiz,Ramon, Was	33.6
Smoltz,John, Atl	31.8
Jennings,Jason, Col	28.6
Snell,Ian, Pit	26.0
Harang,Aaron, Cin	24.3
Hernandez,Liv, Was-Ari	24.1
Hernandez,Orl, Ari-NYM	23.8
Arroyo,Bronson, Cin	22.5
Hensley,Clay, SD	22.2

Balks

Hernandez,Orl, Ari-NYM	3
Morris,Matt, SF	3
Ortiz,Ramon, Was	3
Ramirez,Eliz, Cin	3
Cain,Matt, SF	2
Lowe,Derek, LAD	2
Meredith,Cla, SD	2
Rodriguez,Felix, Was	2
Webb,Brandon, Ari	2
White,Rick, Cin-Phi	2

Strikeout/Hit Ratio
(minimum 50 IP)

Saito,Takashi, LAD	2.23
Julio,Jorge, NYM-Ari	1.69
Wagner,Billy, NYM	1.59
Broxton,Jon, LAD	1.59
Gonzalez,Mike, Pit	1.52
Lidge,Brad, Hou	1.51
Fuentes,Brian, Col	1.46
Ohman,Will, ChC	1.45
Vizcaino,Luis, Ari	1.41
Miller,Trever, Hou	1.33

Opp BPS vs Fastballs
(minimum 251 BF)

Clemens,Roger, Hou	.518
Maine,John, NYM	.529
Martinez,Pedro, NYM	.543
Cruz,Juan, Ari	.558
Zambrano,Carlos, ChC	.565
Cain,Matt, SF	.601
Young,Chris, SD	.612
Webb,Brandon, Ari	.619
Sanchez,Anibal, Fla	.621
Lowe,Derek, LAD	.622

Opp BPS vs Curveballs
(minimum 100 BF)

Marshall,Sean, ChC	.330
Webb,Brandon, Ari	.373
Davis,Doug, Mil	.375
Bush,David, Mil	.436
Myers,Brett, Phi	.444
Cain,Matt, SF	.486
Morris,Matt, SF	.489
Carpenter,Chris, StL	.504
Oswalt,Roy, Hou	.510
2 tied with	.510

Opp BPS vs Changeups
(minimum 100 BF)

Reyes,Anthony, StL	.415
Hamels,Cole, Phi	.451
Duke,Zach, Pit	.527
Heilman,Aaron, NYM	.527
Wise,Matt, Mil	.543
Olsen,Scott, Fla	.546
Schmidt,Jason, SF	.564
James,Chuck, Atl	.578
Lowe,Derek, LAD	.594
Francis,Jeff, Col	.610

Opp BPS vs Sliders
(minimum 64 BF)

Olsen,Scott, Fla	.280
Feliciano,Pedro, NYM	.281
Cordero,Franc, Mil	.316
Oswalt,Roy, Hou	.320
Young,Chris, SD	.338
Julio,Jorge, NYM-Ari	.345
Lidge,Brad, Hou	.370
Eyre,Scott, ChC	.408
Saito,Takashi, LAD	.417
Rivera,Saul, Was	.427

Earned Runs

Marquis,Jason, StL	130
Hudson,Tim, Atl	118
Ortiz,Ramon, Was	118
Hernandez,Liv, Was-Ari	116
Morris,Matt, SF	115
Davis,Doug, Mil	111
Duke,Zach, Pit	107
Batista,Miguel, Ari	105
Fogg,Josh, Col	105
Bush,David, Mil	103

2006 American League Fielding Leaders

2B Pivot % (minimum 98 G)	
Hill,Aaron, Tor	0.761
Ellis,Mark, Oak	0.712
Lopez,Jose, Sea	0.711
Grudzielanek,M, KC	0.706
Loretta,Mark, Bos	0.704
Polanco,Placido, Det	0.692
Kennedy,Adam, LAA	0.661
Roberts,Brian, Bal	0.636
Kinsler,Ian, Tex	0.630
Iguchi,Tadahito, CWS	0.620

SS Pivot % (minimum 98 G)	
Peralta,Jhonny, Cle	0.679
Guillen,Carlos, Det	0.667
Uribe,Juan, CWS	0.654
Betancourt,Yun, Sea	0.634
Young,Michael, Tex	0.629
Cabrera,Orlando, LAA	0.625
Jeter,Derek, NYY	0.618
Berroa,Angel, KC	0.612
Tejada,Miguel, Bal	0.591
Gonzalez,Alex, Bos	0.550

Highest Pct CS by Catchers (minimum 50 SBA)	
Hernandez,Ram, Bal	38.9
Navarro,Dioner, TB	36.0
Posada,Jorge, NYY	34.7
Mauer,Joe, Min	32.1
Napoli,Mike, LAA	29.6
Barajas,Rod, Tex	28.3
Johjima,Kenji, Sea	27.8
Kendall,Jason, Oak	24.5
Pierzynski,A.J., CWS	18.9
Zaun,Gregg, Tor	17.9

Lowest Pct CS by Catchers (minimum 50 SBA)	
Martinez,Victor, Cle	14.5
Molina,Bengie, Tor	16.0
Paul,Josh, TB	17.3
Varitek,Jason, Bos	17.9
Zaun,Gregg, Tor	17.9
Pierzynski,A.J., CWS	18.9
Kendall,Jason, Oak	24.5
Johjima,Kenji, Sea	27.8
Barajas,Rod, Tex	28.3
Napoli,Mike, LAA	29.6

2B Double Play % (minimum 98 G)	
Hill,Aaron, Tor	0.640
Polanco,Placido, Det	0.615
Grudzielanek,M, KC	0.609
Ellis,Mark, Oak	0.588
Loretta,Mark, Bos	0.576
Kinsler,Ian, Tex	0.558
Lopez,Jose, Sea	0.555
Kennedy,Adam, LAA	0.554
Roberts,Brian, Bal	0.548
Iguchi,Tadahito, CWS	0.529

3B Double Play % (minimum 98 G)	
Chavez,Eric, Oak	0.534
Crede,Joe, CWS	0.492
Glaus,Troy, Tor	0.484
Lowell,Mike, Bos	0.451
Teahen,Mark, KC	0.439
Inge,Brandon, Det	0.397
Beltre,Adrian, Sea	0.366
Blalock,Hank, Tex	0.339
Boone,Aaron, Cle	0.333
Rodriguez,Alex, NYY	0.318

SS Double Play % (minimum 98 G)	
Berroa,Angel, KC	0.640
Betancourt,Yun, Sea	0.638
Guillen,Carlos, Det	0.634
Tejada,Miguel, Bal	0.616
Cabrera,Orlando, LAA	0.613
Peralta,Jhonny, Cle	0.603
Uribe,Juan, CWS	0.595
Gonzalez,Alex, Bos	0.594
Young,Michael, Tex	0.592
Jeter,Derek, NYY	0.568

Errors	
Guillen,Carlos, Det	28
Rodriguez,Alex, NYY	24
Inge,Brandon, Det	22
Betancourt,Yun, Sea	20
Hill,Aaron, Tor	19
Tejada,Miguel, Bal	19
Berroa,Angel, KC	18
Kinsler,Ian, Tex	18
Mora,Melvin, Bal	17
5 tied with	16

Fielding Errors	
Rodriguez,Alex, NYY	14
Guillen,Carlos, Det	13
Hernandez,Ram, Bal	12
Hill,Aaron, Tor	11
Adams,Russ, Tor	10
Barajas,Rod, Tex	10
Betancourt,Yun, Sea	10
Inge,Brandon, Det	10
Lugo,Julio, TB	9
8 tied with	8

Throwing Errors	
Berroa,Angel, KC	15
Guillen,Carlos, Det	15
Boone,Aaron, Cle	13
Figgins,Chone, LAA	12
Inge,Brandon, Det	12
Lopez,Jose, Sea	12
5 tied with	11

Range Factor for 2B (minimum 98 games)	
Kinsler,Ian, Tex	5.58
Ellis,Mark, Oak	5.30
Polanco,Placido, Det	5.24
Grudzielanek,M, KC	5.13
Hill,Aaron, Tor	5.11
Cano,Robinson, NYY	5.02
Loretta,Mark, Bos	4.88
Iguchi,Tadahito, CWS	4.77
Lopez,Jose, Sea	4.75
Castillo,Luis, Min	4.69

Range Factor for 3B (minimum 98 games)	
Inge,Brandon, Det	3.44
Crede,Joe, CWS	3.24
Lowell,Mike, Bos	3.16
Teahen,Mark, KC	3.07
Beltre,Adrian, Sea	3.04
Chavez,Eric, Oak	2.98
Glaus,Troy, Tor	2.80
Mora,Melvin, Bal	2.69
Blalock,Hank, Tex	2.62
Boone,Aaron, Cle	2.58

Range Factor for SS (minimum 98 games)	
Peralta,Jhonny, Cle	4.90
Young,Michael, Tex	4.87
Uribe,Juan, CWS	4.70
Tejada,Miguel, Bal	4.56
Berroa,Angel, KC	4.47
Betancourt,Yun, Sea	4.46
Guillen,Carlos, Det	4.41
Bartlett,Jason, Min	4.39
Gonzalez,Alex, Bos	4.36
Cabrera,Orlando, LAA	4.29

2006 National League Fielding Leaders

2B Pivot %
(minimum 98 G)

Carroll,Jamey, Col	0.809
Hudson,Orlando, Ari	0.782
Utley,Chase, Phi	0.717
Barfield,Josh, SD	0.709
Castillo,Jose, Pit	0.689
Uggla,Dan, Fla	0.687
Durham,Ray, SF	0.671
Giles,Marcus, Atl	0.671
Phillips,Brand, Cin	0.640
Kent,Jeff, LAD	0.630

SS Pivot %
(minimum 98 G)

Everett,Adam, Hou	0.702
Rollins,Jimmy, Phi	0.689
Ramirez,Hanley, Fla	0.648
Barmes,Clint, Col	0.645
Cedeno,Ronny, ChC	0.636
Furcal,Rafael, LAD	0.619
Wilson,Jack, Pit	0.600
Eckstein,David, StL	0.597
Clayton,Royce, Was-Cin	0.588
Reyes,Jose, NYM	0.577

Highest Pct CS by Catchers
(minimum 50 SBA)

Molina,Yadier, StL	41.3
Olivo,Miguel, Fla	34.2
Schneider,Brian, Was	27.5
Paulino,Ronny, Pit	26.4
Martin,Russell, LAD	26.0
Estrada,Johnny, Ari	24.1
McCann,Brian, Atl	22.2
Lo Duca,Paul, NYM	20.8
Alfonzo,Eliezer, SF	20.0
Bard,Josh, SD	18.0

Lowest Pct CS by Catchers
(minimum 50 SBA)

Piazza,Mike, SD	11.8
Barrett,Michael, ChC	15.2
Ausmus,Brad, Hou	16.7
Bard,Josh, SD	18.0
Alfonzo,Eliezer, SF	20.0
Lo Duca,Paul, NYM	20.8
McCann,Brian, Atl	22.2
Estrada,Johnny, Ari	24.1
Martin,Russell, LAD	26.0
Paulino,Ronny, Pit	26.4

2B Double Play %
(minimum 98 G)

Carroll,Jamey, Col	0.657
Utley,Chase, Phi	0.554
Hudson,Orlando, Ari	0.518
Uggla,Dan, Fla	0.517
Biggio,Craig, Hou	0.507
Giles,Marcus, Atl	0.497
Castillo,Jose, Pit	0.493
Barfield,Josh, SD	0.482
Durham,Ray, SF	0.469
Phillips,Brand, Cin	0.451

3B Double Play %
(minimum 98 G)

Jones,Chipper, Atl	0.467
Atkins,Garrett, Col	0.430
Sanchez,Freddy, Pit	0.412
Rolen,Scott, StL	0.408
Cabrera,Miguel, Fla	0.397
Zimmerman,Ryan, Was	0.387
Bell,David, Phi-Mil	0.359
Tracy,Chad, Ari	0.357
Ensberg,Morgan, Hou	0.353
Feliz,Pedro, SF	0.342

SS Double Play %
(minimum 98 G)

Rollins,Jimmy, Phi	0.676
Barmes,Clint, Col	0.662
Everett,Adam, Hou	0.654
Ramirez,Hanley, Fla	0.632
Wilson,Jack, Pit	0.618
Eckstein,David, StL	0.588
Furcal,Rafael, LAD	0.576
Cedeno,Ronny, ChC	0.573
Vizquel,Omar, SF	0.566
Renteria,Edgar, Atl	0.566

Errors

Lopez,Felipe, Cin-Was	28
Furcal,Rafael, LAD	27
Ramirez,Hanley, Fla	26
Tracy,Chad, Ari	26
Cedeno,Ronny, ChC	25
Encarnacion,Ed, Cin	25
Weeks,Rickie, Mil	22
Feliz,Pedro, SF	21
4 tied with	19

Fielding Errors

Encarnacion,Ed, Cin	16
Furcal,Rafael, LAD	15
Cedeno,Ronny, ChC	14
Lopez,Felipe, Cin-Was	14
Tracy,Chad, Ari	13
Weeks,Rickie, Mil	12
5 tied with	11

Throwing Errors

Feliz,Pedro, SF	16
Castillo,Jose, Pit	15
Ramirez,Hanley, Fla	15
Lopez,Felipe, Cin-Was	14
Atkins,Garrett, Col	13
Tracy,Chad, Ari	13
Clayton,Royce, Was-Cin	12
Furcal,Rafael, LAD	12
Miles,Aaron, StL	12
4 tied with	11

Range Factor for 2B
(minimum 98 games)

Carroll,Jamey, Col	5.86
Hudson,Orlando, Ari	5.48
Kent,Jeff, LAD	5.37
Utley,Chase, Phi	5.15
Uggla,Dan, Fla	5.08
Castillo,Jose, Pit	5.06
Phillips,Brand, Cin	4.92
Giles,Marcus, Atl	4.91
Durham,Ray, SF	4.84
Barfield,Josh, SD	4.83

Range Factor for 3B
(minimum 98 games)

Sanchez,Freddy, Pit	3.31
Rolen,Scott, StL	3.04
Feliz,Pedro, SF	2.93
Ensberg,Morgan, Hou	2.87
Bell,David, Phi-Mil	2.80
Zimmerman,Ryan, Was	2.71
Jones,Chipper, Atl	2.67
Encarnacion,Ed, Cin	2.61
Wright,David, NYM	2.60
Cabrera,Miguel, Fla	2.56

Range Factor for SS
(minimum 98 games)

Furcal,Rafael, LAD	5.00
Wilson,Jack, Pit	4.96
Everett,Adam, Hou	4.74
Barmes,Clint, Col	4.73
Eckstein,David, StL	4.73
Ramirez,Hanley, Fla	4.54
Clayton,Royce, Was-Cin	4.36
Rollins,Jimmy, Phi	4.30
Vizquel,Omar, SF	4.17
Renteria,Edgar, Atl	4.15

2006 Active Career Batting Leaders

Batting Average (minimum 1000 PA)		On Base Percentage (minimum 1000 PA)		Slugging Average (minimum 1000 PA)		Home Runs	
Helton,Todd	.333	Bonds,Barry	.443	Pujols,Albert	.629	Bonds,Barry	734
Pujols,Albert	.332	Helton,Todd	.430	Howard,Ryan	.624	Griffey Jr.,Ken	563
Suzuki,Ichiro	.331	Thomas,Frank	.424	Bonds,Barry	.608	Thomas,Frank	487
Guerrero,Vladimir	.325	Pujols,Albert	.419	Ramirez,Manny	.600	Thome,Jim	472
Mauer,Joe	.321	Berkman,Lance	.416	Helton,Todd	.593	Ramirez,Manny	470
Cano,Robinson	.319	Giambi,Jason	.413	Guerrero,Vladimir	.583	Rodriguez,Alex	464
Garciaparra,N	.318	Abreu,Bobby	.412	Hafner,Travis	.583	Sheffield,Gary	455
Jeter,Derek	.317	Ramirez,Manny	.411	Rodriguez,Alex	.573	Piazza,Mike	419
Ramirez,Manny	.314	Thome,Jim	.409	Berkman,Lance	.567	Delgado,Carlos	407
Sanchez,Freddy	.313	Giles,Brian	.408	Thomas,Frank	.566	Jones,Chipper	357

Games		At Bats		Hits		Total Bases	
Bonds,Barry	2860	Biggio,Craig	10359	Biggio,Craig	2930	Bonds,Barry	5784
Biggio,Craig	2709	Bonds,Barry	9507	Bonds,Barry	2841	Griffey Jr.,Ken	4622
Finley,Steve	2540	Finley,Steve	9303	Franco,Julio	2566	Biggio,Craig	4514
Franco,Julio	2472	Vizquel,Omar	8966	Finley,Steve	2531	Sheffield,Gary	4221
Vizquel,Omar	2443	Franco,Julio	8587	Vizquel,Omar	2472	Thomas,Frank	4203
Gonzalez,Luis	2316	Gonzalez,Luis	8352	Griffey Jr.,Ken	2412	Finley,Steve	4134
Griffey Jr.,Ken	2234	Griffey Jr.,Ken	8298	Sheffield,Gary	2390	Gonzalez,Luis	4043
Sheffield,Gary	2229	Sierra,Ruben	8044	Gonzalez,Luis	2373	Ramirez,Manny	3946
Sierra,Ruben	2186	Sheffield,Gary	8037	Rodriguez,Ivan	2354	Rodriguez,Alex	3875
Thomas,Frank	2096	Williams,Bernie	7869	Williams,Bernie	2336	Kent,Jeff	3815

Doubles		Triples		Runs Scored		RBI	
Biggio,Craig	637	Finley,Steve	124	Bonds,Barry	2152	Bonds,Barry	1930
Bonds,Barry	587	Lofton,Kenny	110	Biggio,Craig	1776	Griffey Jr.,Ken	1608
Gonzalez,Luis	547	Damon,Johnny	85	Griffey Jr.,Ken	1467	Thomas,Frank	1579
Kent,Jeff	501	Bonds,Barry	77	Lofton,Kenny	1442	Ramirez,Manny	1516
Rodriguez,Ivan	473	Durham,Ray	77	Finley,Steve	1434	Sheffield,Gary	1501
Thomas,Frank	458	Vizquel,Omar	68	Sheffield,Gary	1433	Kent,Jeff	1380
Griffey Jr.,Ken	449	Crawford,Carl	65	Thomas,Frank	1404	Rodriguez,Alex	1347
Williams,Bernie	449	Gonzalez,Luis	65	Williams,Bernie	1366	Gonzalez,Luis	1324
Finley,Steve	446	3 tied with	61	Rodriguez,Alex	1358	Sierra,Ruben	1322
Ramirez,Manny	438			Gonzalez,Luis	1312	Thome,Jim	1302

Walks		Intentional Walks		Hit By Pitch		Strikeouts	
Bonds,Barry	2426	Bonds,Barry	645	Biggio,Craig	282	Thome,Jim	1909
Thomas,Frank	1547	Griffey Jr.,Ken	216	Kendall,Jason	209	Biggio,Craig	1641
Thome,Jim	1364	Guerrero,Vladimir	194	Delgado,Carlos	149	Sanders,Reggie	1599
Sheffield,Gary	1293	Thomas,Frank	165	Giambi,Jason	127	Edmonds,Jim	1512
Biggio,Craig	1137	Delgado,Carlos	159	Easley,Damion	120	Griffey Jr.,Ken	1494
Giambi,Jason	1089	Ramirez,Manny	154	Sheffield,Gary	119	Bonds,Barry	1485
Griffey Jr.,Ken	1077	Helton,Todd	146	Jeter,Derek	115	Delgado,Carlos	1483
Jones,Chipper	1070	Piazza,Mike	146	Kent,Jeff	113	Ramirez,Manny	1451
Williams,Bernie	1069	Gonzalez,Luis	145	Gonzalez,Luis	107	Kent,Jeff	1409
Gonzalez,Luis	1058	Thome,Jim	139	Rodriguez,Alex	106	Rodriguez,Alex	1404

2006 Active Career Batting Leaders

Sacrifice Hits		Sacrifice Flies		Stolen Bases		Seasons Played	
Vizquel,Omar	218	Sierra,Ruben	120	Lofton,Kenny	599	Clemens,Roger	23
Glavine,Tom	201	Thomas,Frank	115	Bonds,Barry	509	Franco,Julio	22
Maddux,Greg	165	Sheffield,Gary	102	Young,Eric	465	Bonds,Barry	21
Smoltz,John	122	Conine,Jeff	96	Biggio,Craig	410	Maddux,Greg	21
Clayton,Royce	110	Kent,Jeff	95	Vizquel,Omar	366	Glavine,Tom	20
Vizcaino,Jose	107	Gonzalez,Luis	91	Womack,Tony	363	Moyer,Jamie	20
Schilling,Curt	102	Bonds,Barry	89	Pierre,Juan	325	Mulholland,T	20
Perez,Neifi	96	Griffey Jr.,Ken	85	Finley,Steve	320	Sierra,Ruben	20
Biggio,Craig	94	Vizquel,Omar	80	Castillo,Luis	306	Wells,David	20
Finley,Steve	91	2 tied with	78	Damon,Johnny	306	5 tied with	19

| At Bats Per Home Run | | Grounded Into DP | | Highest SB Success Pct | | Lowest SB Success Pct | |
(minimum 1000 AB)				(minimum 100 SBA)		(minimum 100 SBA)	
Bonds,Barry	13.0	Franco,Julio	310	Beltran,Carlos	87.6	Vizcaino,Jose	54.4
Thome,Jim	13.6	Rodriguez,Ivan	256	Womack,Tony	83.1	Perez,Neifi	55.9
Pujols,Albert	14.0	Castilla,Vinny	224	Crawford,Carl	82.8	Burnitz,Jeromy	56.1
Ramirez,Manny	14.0	Williams,Bernie	223	Reyes,Jose	80.8	Edmonds,Jim	57.8
Dunn,Adam	14.3	Piazza,Mike	220	Cabrera,Orlando	80.6	Gonzalez,Luis	59.3
Rodriguez,Alex	14.6	Clayton,Royce	208	Roberts,Dave	80.5	Anderson,Garret	61.9
Griffey Jr.,Ken	14.7	Thomas,Frank	203	Patterson,Corey	80.4	Kent,Jeff	62.4
Delgado,Carlos	14.9	Sheffield,Gary	196	Suzuki,Ichiro	80.2	Williams,Bernie	62.8
Hafner,Travis	15.0	Kent,Jeff	194	Rodriguez,Alex	80.1	Hollandsworth,T	63.6
Thomas,Frank	15.2	Sierra,Ruben	193	Jeter,Derek	80.1	Kotsay,Mark	63.8

| Strikeouts / Walks Ratio | | At Bats Per GIDP | | OPS | | Secondary Average | |
(minimum 1000 AB)		(minimum 1000 AB)		(minimum 1000 PA)		(minimum 1000 PA)	
Bonds,Barry	.612	Suzuki,Ichiro	151.7	Bonds,Barry	1.051	Bonds,Barry	.618
Giles,Brian	.687	Mackowiak,Rob	132.1	Pujols,Albert	1.048	Thome,Jim	.499
Young,Eric	.700	Maddux,Greg	122.8	Helton,Todd	1.023	Dunn,Adam	.487
Sheffield,Gary	.751	Reyes,Jose	122.5	Howard,Ryan	1.023	Thomas,Frank	.474
Helton,Todd	.794	Roberts,Dave	116.0	Ramirez,Manny	1.011	Howard,Ryan	.474
Pujols,Albert	.799	Branyan,Russell	113.7	Thomas,Frank	.990	Berkman,Lance	.463
Thomas,Frank	.805	Taveras,Willy	112.2	Hafner,Travis	.985	Ramirez,Manny	.451
Mauer,Joe	.874	Crawford,Carl	106.1	Berkman,Lance	.983	Pujols,Albert	.448
Kendall,Jason	.890	Damon,Johnny	102.6	Thome,Jim	.974	Abreu,Bobby	.446
Palmeiro,Orl	.892	Patterson,Corey	101.5	Guerrero,Vladimir	.973	Giambi,Jason	.446

| Highest Strikeout per PA | | Lowest Strikeout per PA | | At Bats Per RBI | |
(minimum 1000 PA)		(minimum 1000 PA)		(minimum 1000 AB)	
Branyan,Russell	.348	Pierre,Juan	.055	Ramirez,Manny	4.3
Pena,Wily Mo	.314	Young,Eric	.066	Pujols,Albert	4.6
Smoltz,John	.314	Polanco,Placido	.067	Hafner,Travis	4.7
Bellhorn,Mark	.290	Lo Duca,Paul	.069	Thomas,Frank	4.7
Wilson,Craig	.276	Eckstein,David	.075	Delgado,Carlos	4.7
Brown,Emil	.274	Kendall,Jason	.075	Ortiz,David	4.8
Hernandez,Jose	.273	Hall,Toby	.082	Berkman,Lance	4.9
Howard,Ryan	.269	Cabrera,Orlando	.084	Giambi,Jason	4.9
Dunn,Adam	.267	Sanchez,Freddy	.085	Thome,Jim	4.9
Pena,Carlos	.261	3 tied with	.086	Bonds,Barry	4.9

2006 Active Career Pitching Leaders

Earned Run Average		Winning Percentage		Opponent Batting Average		Baserunners Per 9 IP	
(minimum 750 IP)		(minimum 100 Decisions)		(minimum 750 IP)		(minimum 750 IP)	
Rivera,Mariano	2.29	Santana,Johan	.716	Hoffman,Trevor	.208	Hoffman,Trevor	9.48
Hoffman,Trevor	2.71	Martinez,Pedro	.691	Martinez,Pedro	.209	Rivera,Mariano	9.66
Martinez,Pedro	2.81	Oswalt,Roy	.676	Rivera,Mariano	.213	Martinez,Pedro	9.67
Oswalt,Roy	3.05	Hudson,Tim	.665	Wood,Kerry	.215	Santana,Johan	10.08
Maddux,Greg	3.07	Halladay,Roy	.664	Johnson,Randy	.217	Foulke,Keith	10.10
Clemens,Roger	3.10	Clemens,Roger	.662	Santana,Johan	.220	Schilling,Curt	10.33
Santana,Johan	3.20	Johnson,Randy	.656	Foulke,Keith	.223	Maddux,Greg	10.47
Johnson,Randy	3.22	Mulder,Mark	.644	Nelson,Jeff	.224	Smoltz,John	10.66
Smoltz,John	3.27	Pettitte,Andy	.641	Zambrano,Carlos	.224	Mussina,Mike	10.72
Webb,Brandon	3.28	Mussina,Mike	.641	Clemens,Roger	.228	Clemens,Roger	10.81

Games		Games Started		Complete Games		Shutouts	
Stanton,Mike	1109	Clemens,Roger	690	Clemens,Roger	118	Clemens,Roger	46
Mesa,Jose	966	Maddux,Greg	673	Maddux,Greg	108	Johnson,Randy	37
Timlin,Mike	961	Glavine,Tom	635	Johnson,Randy	98	Maddux,Greg	35
Hernandez,Rob	960	Johnson,Randy	546	Schilling,Curt	82	Glavine,Tom	24
Jones,Todd	874	Moyer,Jamie	518	Mussina,Mike	57	Mussina,Mike	23
Hoffman,Trevor	821	Mussina,Mike	475	Glavine,Tom	55	Schilling,Curt	19
Myers,Mike	811	Wells,David	460	Wells,David	54	Erickson,Scott	17
Gordon,Tom	809	Rogers,Kenny	433	Smoltz,John	53	Martinez,Pedro	17
Nelson,Jeff	798	Smoltz,John	429	Erickson,Scott	51	Smoltz,John	16
Guardado,Eddie	781	Schilling,Curt	412	2 tied with	46	3 tied with	12

Wins		Losses		Innings Pitched		Batters Faced	
Clemens,Roger	348	Maddux,Greg	203	Clemens,Roger	4817.2	Clemens,Roger	19820
Maddux,Greg	333	Glavine,Tom	191	Maddux,Greg	4616.1	Maddux,Greg	18787
Glavine,Tom	290	Clemens,Roger	178	Glavine,Tom	4149.2	Glavine,Tom	17468
Johnson,Randy	280	Moyer,Jamie	166	Johnson,Randy	3798.2	Johnson,Randy	15644
Mussina,Mike	239	Wells,David	148	Moyer,Jamie	3351.0	Moyer,Jamie	14235
Wells,David	230	Johnson,Randy	147	Wells,David	3281.2	Wells,David	13719
Moyer,Jamie	216	Trachsel,Steve	143	Mussina,Mike	3210.1	Rogers,Kenny	13223
Rogers,Kenny	207	Mulholland,T	142	Smoltz,John	3161.1	Mussina,Mike	13118
Schilling,Curt	207	Radke,Brad	139	Schilling,Curt	3110.0	Smoltz,John	12957
Martinez,Pedro	206	Rogers,Kenny	139	Rogers,Kenny	3066.0	Schilling,Curt	12651

Strikeouts		Walks Allowed		Hit Batters		Wild Pitches	
Clemens,Roger	4604	Clemens,Roger	1549	Johnson,Randy	178	Clemens,Roger	136
Johnson,Randy	4544	Johnson,Randy	1409	Clemens,Roger	154	Smoltz,John	135
Maddux,Greg	3169	Glavine,Tom	1399	Wakefield,Tim	146	Gordon,Tom	105
Schilling,Curt	3015	Rogers,Kenny	1079	Martinez,Pedro	129	Clement,Matt	101
Martinez,Pedro	2998	Wakefield,Tim	948	Park,Chan Ho	126	Johnson,Randy	101
Smoltz,John	2778	Moyer,Jamie	946	Maddux,Greg	125	Wells,David	100
Mussina,Mike	2572	Gordon,Tom	944	Rogers,Kenny	117	Grimsley,Jason	96
Glavine,Tom	2481	Maddux,Greg	944	Wright,Jamey	114	Schmidt,Jason	91
Wells,David	2119	Smoltz,John	937	Moyer,Jamie	112	Fassero,Jeff	86
Moyer,Jamie	1992	Erickson,Scott	865	Astacio,Pedro	111	2 tied with	82

2006 Active Career Pitching Leaders

Saves

Hoffman,Trevor	482
Rivera,Mariano	413
Hernandez,Rob	326
Wagner,Billy	324
Mesa,Jose	320
Benitez,Armando	280
Jones,Todd	263
Isringhausen,Jason	249
Wickman,Bob	247
Foulke,Keith	190

Save Pct
(minimum 50 Save Ops)

Gagne,Eric	96.4
Smoltz,John	91.7
Nathan,Joe	89.9
Hoffman,Trevor	89.6
Jenks,Bobby	88.7
Rivera,Mariano	88.2
Wagner,Billy	86.6
Cordero,Chad	85.8
Valverde,Jose	85.0
Isringhausen,Jason	84.7

Home Runs Allowed

Moyer,Jamie	414
Wells,David	385
Johnson,Randy	361
Clemens,Roger	354
Mussina,Mike	345
Radke,Brad	326
Schilling,Curt	326
Glavine,Tom	322
Trachsel,Steve	319
Maddux,Greg	318

Strikeouts Per 9 IP
(minimum 750 IP)

Johnson,Randy	10.77
Wood,Kerry	10.36
Martinez,Pedro	10.20
Hoffman,Trevor	9.81
Nelson,Jeff	9.51
Santana,Johan	9.47
Peavy,Jake	8.85
Rhodes,Arthur	8.84
Remlinger,Mike	8.74
Schilling,Curt	8.73

Opp On-Base Percentage
(minimum 750 IP)

Hoffman,Trevor	.264
Rivera,Mariano	.269
Martinez,Pedro	.270
Santana,Johan	.279
Foulke,Keith	.279
Schilling,Curt	.285
Maddux,Greg	.290
Smoltz,John	.292
Mussina,Mike	.293
Clemens,Roger	.294

Opp Slugging Average
(minimum 750 IP)

Rivera,Mariano	.290
Carrasco,Hector	.315
Martinez,Pedro	.327
Nelson,Jeff	.331
Hoffman,Trevor	.336
Clemens,Roger	.340
Zambrano,Carlos	.344
Johnson,Randy	.346
Isringhausen,Jason	.351
Maddux,Greg	.353

Hits Per Nine Innings
(minimum 750 IP)

Martinez,Pedro	6.85
Hoffman,Trevor	6.86
Wood,Kerry	6.98
Rivera,Mariano	7.05
Johnson,Randy	7.14
Nelson,Jeff	7.26
Santana,Johan	7.31
Zambrano,Carlos	7.36
Foulke,Keith	7.43
Clemens,Roger	7.63

Home Runs Per Nine IP
(minimum 750 IP)

Rivera,Mariano	0.46
Maddux,Greg	0.62
Nelson,Jeff	0.63
Clemens,Roger	0.66
Wickman,Bob	0.68
Webb,Brandon	0.69
Zambrano,Carlos	0.69
Carrasco,Hector	0.69
Glavine,Tom	0.70
Tavarez,Julian	0.71

Strikeouts / Walks Ratio
(minimum 750 IP)

Schilling,Curt	4.38
Martinez,Pedro	4.28
Sheets,Ben	4.11
Oswalt,Roy	3.86
Hoffman,Trevor	3.86
Foulke,Keith	3.84
Lieber,Jon	3.74
Santana,Johan	3.67
Mussina,Mike	3.58
Rivera,Mariano	3.46

Stolen Base Pct Allowed
(minimum 750 IP)

Carpenter,Chris	38.3
Maroth,Mike	40.0
Mulholland,T	41.2
Buehrle,Mark	41.4
Rogers,Kenny	41.7
Zambrano,Carlos	44.7
Meche,Gil	45.5
Santana,Johan	47.8
Oswalt,Roy	49.1
Redman,Mark	50.0

GIDP Induced

Glavine,Tom	392
Maddux,Greg	392
Clemens,Roger	321
Rogers,Kenny	317
Erickson,Scott	310
Moyer,Jamie	274
Mulholland,T	266
Pettitte,Andy	262
Wells,David	254
Mussina,Mike	251

GIDP Per Nine IP
(minimum 750 IP)

Tavarez,Julian	1.30
Estes,Shawn	1.29
Westbrook,Jake	1.29
Wright,Jamey	1.19
Erickson,Scott	1.18
Wickman,Bob	1.15
Schoeneweis,S	1.13
Mulder,Mark	1.12
Graves,Danny	1.09
Garland,Jon	1.07

Complete Game %
(minimum 100 GS)

Schilling,Curt	0.20
Johnson,Randy	0.18
Clemens,Roger	0.17
Maddux,Greg	0.16
Erickson,Scott	0.14
Mulholland,T	0.14
Hernandez,Liv	0.13
Halladay,Roy	0.13
Mulder,Mark	0.13
Smoltz,John	0.12

Quality Start Pct
(minimum 100 GS)

Oswalt,Roy	70.6
Martinez,Pedro	69.9
Johnson,Randy	68.3
Webb,Brandon	66.7
Schilling,Curt	66.5
Zambrano,Carlos	66.4
Maddux,Greg	66.1
Clemens,Roger	65.9
Glavine,Tom	64.3
Prior,Mark	64.2

Walks Per 9 IP
(minimum 750 IP)

Radke,Brad	1.63
Lieber,Jon	1.71
Maddux,Greg	1.84
Wells,David	1.86
Sheets,Ben	1.89
Oswalt,Roy	1.97
Schilling,Curt	1.99
Mussina,Mike	2.02
Buehrle,Mark	2.07
Foulke,Keith	2.16

Games Finished

Hoffman,Trevor	682
Hernandez,Rob	647
Mesa,Jose	612
Rivera,Mariano	600
Wagner,Billy	546
Jones,Todd	528
Benitez,Armando	501
Wickman,Bob	471
Timlin,Mike	422
Foulke,Keith	397

2006 American League Bill James Leaders

Top Game Scores

Pitcher	Date	Opp	IP	H	R	ER	BB	SO	GS
Lackey,John, LAA	7/7	Oak	9.0	1	0	0	0	10	95
Kazmir,Scott, TB	7/3	Bos	9.0	2	0	0	2	10	91
Bedard,Erik, Bal	6/21	Fla	8.0	2	0	0	0	12	90
Santana,Johan, Min	9/5	TB	8.0	2	0	0	1	12	89
Sabathia,C.C., Cle	7/7	Bal	9.0	3	0	0	0	7	88
Liriano,Francisco, Min	7/2	Mil	8.0	3	0	0	1	12	87
Marcum,Shaun, Tor	9/25	Bos	8.0	2	0	0	1	10	87
Cabrera,Daniel, Bal	9/28	NYY	9.0	1	1	0	2	5	86
Loaiza,Esteban, Oak	8/23	Tor	9.0	4	0	0	0	7	86
8 tied with									85

Worst Game Scores

Pitcher	Date	Opp	IP	H	R	ER	BB	SO	GS
Hudson,Luke, KC	8/13	Cle	0.1	8	11	10	3	1	-9
Pineiro,Joel, Sea	8/15	Oak	3.2	12	9	9	5	1	-3
Millwood,Kevin, Tex	5/9	Min	1.1	9	9	9	1	0	-1
Redman,Mark, KC	9/23	Det	0.1	7	9	9	2	0	-1
Lopez,Rodrigo, Bal	7/4	CWS	2.2	10	9	9	1	0	1
Buehrle,Mark, CWS	7/2	ChC	5.0	13	11	10	0	4	3
Affeldt,Jeremy, KC	5/27	NYY	5.1	11	10	10	2	0	4
Koronka,John, Tex	7/17	Tor	3.2	11	9	9	0	1	4
Penn,Hayden, Bal	9/3	Oak	0.2	8	8	8	0	0	4
2 tied with									5

Runs Created

Jeter,Derek, NYY	132
Ortiz,David, Bos	129
Sizemore,Grady, Cle	121
Young,Michael, Tex	120
Thome,Jim, CWS	119
Hafner,Travis, Cle	118
Morneau,Justin, Min	118
Dye,Jermaine, CWS	116
3 tied with	114

Runs Created Per 27 Outs

Hafner,Travis, Cle	9.6
Ramirez,Manny, Bos	9.3
Thome,Jim, CWS	8.8
Ortiz,David, Bos	8.3
Giambi,Jason, NYY	8.0
Jeter,Derek, NYY	8.0
Dye,Jermaine, CWS	7.8
Morneau,Justin, Min	7.4
Thomas,Frank, Oak	7.3
Mauer,Joe, Min	7.3

Offensive Winning %

Hafner,Travis, Cle	.795
Ramirez,Manny, Bos	.775
Thome,Jim, CWS	.754
Giambi,Jason, NYY	.737
Jeter,Derek, NYY	.735
Ortiz,David, Bos	.732
Dye,Jermaine, CWS	.709
Thomas,Frank, Oak	.699
Morneau,Justin, Min	.697
Mauer,Joe, Min	.694

Secondary Average
(minimum 502 PA)

Hafner,Travis, Cle	.570
Ortiz,David, Bos	.565
Giambi,Jason, NYY	.556
Thome,Jim, CWS	.529
Ramirez,Manny, Bos	.521
Thomas,Frank, Oak	.448
Dye,Jermaine, CWS	.429
Glaus,Troy, Tor	.426
Rodriguez,Alex, NYY	.416
Swisher,Nick, Oak	.415

Isolated Power
(minimum 502 PA)

Hafner,Travis, Cle	.350
Ortiz,David, Bos	.349
Thome,Jim, CWS	.310
Dye,Jermaine, CWS	.306
Giambi,Jason, NYY	.305
Ramirez,Manny, Bos	.298
Thomas,Frank, Oak	.275
Glaus,Troy, Tor	.261
Sizemore,Grady, Cle	.243
Sexson,Richie, Sea	.240

Power / Speed Number

Crawford,Carl, TB	27.5
Sizemore,Grady, Cle	24.6
Damon,Johnny, NYY	24.5
Wells,Vernon, Tor	22.2
Rodriguez,Alex, NYY	21.0
Guerrero,Vladimir, LAA	20.6
Jeter,Derek, NYY	19.8
Guillen,Carlos, Det	19.5
Hunter,Torii, Min	17.3
Roberts,Brian, Bal	15.7

Speed Scores (2005-2006)

Crawford,Carl, TB	8.36
Suzuki,Ichiro, Sea	8.28
Figgins,Chone, LAA	7.95
Damon,Johnny, NYY	7.78
Sizemore,Grady, Cle	7.72
Podsednik,Scott, CWS	7.48
Lugo,Julio, TB	7.17
Cabrera,Orlando, LAA	7.01
Crisp,Coco, Bos	6.86
DeJesus,David, KC	6.68

Cheap Wins

Blanton,Joe, Oak	7
Garcia,Freddy, CWS	5
Garland,Jon, CWS	5
Johnson,Randy, NYY	5
Robertson,Nate, Det	5
Verlander,Just, Det	5
Wang,Chien-Ming, NYY	5
Zito,Barry, Oak	5
6 tied with	4

Tough Losses

Escobar,Kelvim, LAA	6
Robertson,Nate, Det	6
Hernandez,Fel, Sea	5
Moyer,Jamie, Sea	5
Washburn,Jarrod, Sea	5
Benson,Kris, Bal	4
Johnson,Randy, NYY	4
Lilly,Ted, Tor	4
Zito,Barry, Oak	4
6 tied with	3

2006 National League Bill James Leaders

Top Game Scores

Pitcher	Date	Opp	IP	H	R	ER	BB	SO	GS
Hill,Rich, ChC	9/16	Cin	9.0	2	0	0	1	10	92
Willis,Dontrelle, Fla	9/10	Phi	9.0	3	0	0	1	12	92
Francis,Jeff, Col	7/24	StL	9.0	2	0	0	0	8	91
Peavy,Jake, SD	9/2	Cin	9.0	2	1	1	2	14	91
Carpenter,Chris, StL	7/14	LAD	9.0	2	0	0	0	7	90
Webb,Brandon, Ari	9/9	StL	9.0	1	0	0	0	5	90
Sanchez,Anibal, Fla	9/6	Ari	9.0	0	0	0	4	6	89
Astacio,Pedro, Was	8/15	Atl	9.0	2	0	0	0	5	88
Lowry,Noah, SF	8/21	Ari	9.0	2	0	0	1	6	88
5 tied with									87

Worst Game Scores

Pitcher	Date	Opp	IP	H	R	ER	BB	SO	GS
Marquis,Jason, StL	6/21	CWS	5.0	14	13	13	1	3	-11
Marquis,Jason, StL	7/18	Atl	5.0	14	12	12	2	4	-7
Davies,Kyle, Atl	9/23	Col	2.1	12	9	9	1	1	-3
Hirsh,Jason, Hou	8/22	Cin	2.2	9	10	10	5	2	-3
Lowry,Noah, SF	9/18	Col	1.1	9	9	9	2	0	-2
Hernandez,Orl, NYM	8/15	Phi	4.0	10	11	11	4	5	-1
Brazelton,Dewon, SD	4/8	Col	2.1	11	9	9	2	3	0
Madson,Ryan, Phi	4/20	Was	1.0	7	9	9	4	1	0
Williams,Dave, NYM	9/11	Fla	3.0	11	9	9	2	1	0
Mulder,Mark, StL	6/20	CWS	2.1	10	9	9	0	0	1

Runs Created

Pujols,Albert, StL	146
Berkman,Lance, Hou	138
Howard,Ryan, Phi	138
Cabrera,Miguel, Fla	132
Atkins,Garrett, Col	129
Utley,Chase, Phi	122
Beltran,Carlos, NYM	121
Reyes,Jose, NYM	121
Wright,David, NYM	119
Helton,Todd, Col	118

Runs Created Per 27 Outs

Pujols,Albert, StL	10.2
Berkman,Lance, Hou	9.5
Howard,Ryan, Phi	9.0
Cabrera,Miguel, Fla	8.7
Beltran,Carlos, NYM	8.4
Atkins,Garrett, Col	8.0
Helton,Todd, Col	7.9
Wright,David, NYM	7.4
Johnson,Nick, Was	7.4
Utley,Chase, Phi	6.9

Offensive Winning %

Pujols,Albert, StL	.825
Berkman,Lance, Hou	.789
Cabrera,Miguel, Fla	.784
Beltran,Carlos, NYM	.769
Howard,Ryan, Phi	.763
Wright,David, NYM	.724
Johnson,Nick, Was	.720
Atkins,Garrett, Col	.707
Helton,Todd, Col	.706
Reyes,Jose, NYM	.686

Secondary Average
(minimum 502 PA)

Beltran,Carlos, NYM	.541
Howard,Ryan, Phi	.532
Pujols,Albert, StL	.525
Berkman,Lance, Hou	.494
Johnson,Nick, Was	.470
Dunn,Adam, Cin	.469
Burrell,Pat, Phi	.457
Soriano,Alfonso, Was	.450
Bay,Jason, Pit	.444
Delgado,Carlos, NYM	.424

Isolated Power
(minimum 502 PA)

Howard,Ryan, Phi	.346
Pujols,Albert, StL	.340
Beltran,Carlos, NYM	.320
Berkman,Lance, Hou	.306
Hall,Bill, Mil	.283
Soriano,Alfonso, Was	.283
Delgado,Carlos, NYM	.282
LaRoche,Adam, Atl	.276
Ramirez,Aramis, ChC	.269
Jones,Andruw, Atl	.269

Power / Speed Number

Soriano,Alfonso, Was	43.4
Rollins,Jimmy, Phi	29.5
Reyes,Jose, NYM	29.3
Ramirez,Hanley, Fla	25.5
Byrnes,Eric, Ari	25.5
Beltran,Carlos, NYM	25.0
Cameron,Mike, SD	23.4
Wright,David, NYM	22.6
Furcal,Rafael, LAD	21.3
Utley,Chase, Phi	20.4

Speed Scores (2005-2006)

Reyes,Jose, NYM	8.88
Pierre,Juan, ChC	8.06
Lofton,Kenny, LAD	8.05
Rollins,Jimmy, Phi	8.01
Roberts,Dave, SD	7.95
Taveras,Willy, Hou	7.69
Furcal,Rafael, LAD	7.60
Freel,Ryan, Cin	7.30
Cameron,Mike, SD	7.08
Beltran,Carlos, NYM	7.01

Cheap Wins

Trachsel,Steve, NYM	8
Fogg,Josh, Col	6
Pettitte,Andy, Hou	6
Hernandez,Liv, Was-Ari	5
Batista,Miguel, Ari	4
Jennings,Jason, Col	4
Lieber,Jon, Phi	4
Lowe,Derek, LAD	4
Maddux,Greg, ChC-LAD	4
Williams,Woody, SD	4

Tough Losses

Capuano,Chris, Mil	5
Hensley,Clay, SD	5
Peavy,Jake, SD	5
12 tied with	4

Additional Bill James Leaders

AL Batters Win Shares		NL Batters Win Shares		AL Pitchers Win Shares		NL Pitchers Win Shares	
(2006)		(2006)		(2006)		(2006)	
Jeter,Derek, NYY	32	Pujols,Albert, StL	37	Santana,Johan, Min	24	Arroyo,Bronson, Cin	20
Mauer,Joe, Min	30	Beltran,Carlos, NYM	34	Halladay,Roy, Tor	20	Oswalt,Roy, Hou	20
Ortiz,David, Bos	27	Cabrera,Miguel, Fla	33	Nathan,Joe, Min	20	Webb,Brandon, Ari	20
Ramirez,Manny, Bos	27	Berkman,Lance, Hou	31	Papelbon,Jonat, Bos	19	Carpenter,Chris, StL	19
Morneau,Justin, Min	26	Wright,David, NYM	30	Ryan,B.J., Tor	19	Harang,Aaron, Cin	18
Young,Michael, Tex	26	Howard,Ryan, Phi	29	Putz,J.J., Sea	17	Saito,Takashi, LAD	18
Dye,Jermaine, CWS	25	Reyes,Jose, NYM	28	Rodriguez,Fran, LAA	17	Zambrano,Carlos, ChC	17
Guillen,Carlos, Det	25	Furcal,Rafael, LAD	27	Zito,Barry, Oak	17	Lowe,Derek, LAD	15
Ibanez,Raul, Sea	25	Utley,Chase, Phi	27	4 tied with	16	Schmidt,Jason, SF	15
Rodriguez,Alex, NYY	25	Soriano,Alfonso, Was	26			Smoltz,John, Atl	15

Batters Win Shares		Pitchers Win Shares		2006 AL Component ERA		2006 NL Component ERA	
(Career)		(Career)		(minimum 162 IP)		(minimum 162 IP)	
Bonds,Barry	686	Clemens,Roger	432	Santana,Johan, Min	2.36	Carpenter,Chris, StL	2.75
Biggio,Craig	422	Maddux,Greg	383	Halladay,Roy, Tor	2.87	Webb,Brandon, Ari	2.81
Sheffield,Gary	402	Johnson,Randy	305	Mussina,Mike, NYY	3.01	Young,Chris, SD	3.12
Thomas,Frank	383	Glavine,Tom	303	Sabathia,C.C., Cle	3.13	Oswalt,Roy, Hou	3.19
Griffey Jr.,Ken	367	Smoltz,John	272	Lackey,John, LAA	3.31	Smoltz,John, Atl	3.32
Rodriguez,Alex	340	Martinez,Pedro	249	Santana,Ervin, LAA	3.51	Zambrano,Carlos, ChC	3.34
Ramirez,Manny	334	Mussina,Mike	248	Bonderman,Jer, Det	3.58	Cain,Matt, SF	3.35
Piazza,Mike	320	Schilling,Curt	242	Wang,Chien-Ming, NYY	3.62	Arroyo,Bronson, Cin	3.37
Kent,Jeff	313	Wells,David	207	Escobar,Kelvim, LAA	3.67	Maddux,Greg, ChC-LAD	3.39
Williams,Bernie	311	Rogers,Kenny	199	Haren,Dan, Oak	3.72	Peavy,Jake, SD	3.42

Highest Avg Game Score		Lowest Avg Game Score		Lowest Offensive Win %	
(AL - minimum 30 GS)		(AL - minimum 30 GS)		(AL)	
Santana,Johan, Min	62.21	Silva,Carlos, Min	39.81	Berroa,Angel, KC	.143
Halladay,Roy, Tor	56.38	Byrd,Paul, Cle	43.77	Betancourt,Yun, Sea	.389
Mussina,Mike, NYY	55.09	Buehrle,Mark, CWS	45.00	Peralta,Jhonny, Cle	.389
Lackey,John, LAA	54.88	Blanton,Joe, Oak	45.10	Podsednik,Scott, CWS	.396
Schilling,Curt, Bos	53.97	Benson,Kris, Bal	46.90	Grudzielanek,M, KC	.424
Haren,Dan, Oak	52.82	Washburn,Jarrod, Sea	47.71	Hill,Aaron, Tor	.436
Bonderman,Jer, Det	52.71	Lee,Cliff, Cle	47.79	Kotsay,Mark, Oak	.438
Escobar,Kelvim, LAA	52.63	Garland,Jon, CWS	48.13	Michaels,Jason, Cle	.439
Bedard,Erik, Bal	52.52	Westbrook,Jake, Cle	48.31	Loretta,Mark, Bos	.442
Verlander,Just, Det	52.33	Meche,Gil, Sea	49.50	Punto,Nick, Min	.451

Highest Avg Game Score		Lowest Avg Game Score		Lowest Offensive Win %	
(NL - minimum 30 GS)		(NL - minimum 30 GS)		(NL)	
Carpenter,Chris, StL	59.06	Marquis,Jason, StL	42.79	Cedeno,Ronny, ChC	.207
Webb,Brandon, Ari	57.85	Ortiz,Ramon, Was	43.15	Ausmus,Brad, Hou	.216
Oswalt,Roy, Hou	57.19	Fogg,Josh, Col	43.19	Barmes,Clint, Col	.270
Zambrano,Carlos, ChC	57.06	Trachsel,Steve, NYM	44.70	Everett,Adam, Hou	.299
Smoltz,John, Atl	56.74	Armas Jr.,Tony, Was	45.83	Clayton,Royce, Was-Cin	.302
Arroyo,Bronson, Cin	56.34	Maholm,Paul, Pit	46.13	Castillo,Jose, Pit	.339
Young,Chris, SD	56.29	Batista,Miguel, Ari	46.42	Biggio,Craig, Hou	.368
Schmidt,Jason, SF	55.31	Hernandez,Liv, Was-Ari	46.71	Wilson,Jack, Pit	.373
Peavy,Jake, SD	55.06	Duke,Zach, Pit	46.79	Feliz,Pedro, SF	.404
Harang,Aaron, Cin	54.20	Vargas,Claudio, Ari	47.07	Wilson,Preston, Hou-StL	.411

Win Shares

Bill James initially devised Win Shares as a way of relating a player's individual statistics to the number of wins he contributed to his team. As a single number, Win Shares allow us to easily compare the accomplishments of each player.

The following pages contain the sum of a player's Win Shares prior to 1997, then individual season totals from 1997 through 2006. Career numbers are also included for each player.

We credit a team with three Win Shares for each win. If a team wins 100 games, the players on the team will be credited with 300 Win Shares—or 300 thirds-of-a-win. If a team wins 70 games, the players on the team will be credited with 210 Win Shares, and so on and so forth.

The quality of the team does not affect an individual player's Win Shares. A great player on a bad team will rate just as well as a great player on a good team. For example, Carlos Beltran had 34 Win Shares for the New York Mets who won the NL East, while Miguel Cabrera had 33 Win Shares for a Florida Marlins team that finished 19 games behind the Mets in the NL East standings.

Win Shares are also a great tool for evaluating award voting and Hall of Fame credentials. Take a look and see if this year's Most Valuable Player, Cy Young, and Rookie of the Year award winners match up with the Win Shares leaders. Based on Win Shares, the major award winners should be Albert Pujols (NL MVP), Derek Jeter (AL MVP), and Johan Santana (AL Cy Young). The NL Cy Young race should be quite interesting, as Brandon Webb, Bronson Arroyo, and Roy Oswalt all finished tied for the NL lead among pitchers with 20 Win Shares, and Chris Carpenter was right behind them with 19. Overall, a good benchmark for an MVP caliber season for a position player is 30 Win Shares; similarly 20 Win Shares would indicate a Cy Young caliber season.

Win Shares can also be used to assess the value of trades. Does your favorite team have a net gain or loss from their transactions? Win Shares also adjust for offensive environment, so it is a great tool to use for looking at the greatest individual seasons in baseball history as well as the greatest players of all time. For a complete description of how Win Shares are calculated as well as countless essays using Win Shares to analyze various facets of the game, please consult Bill James' book titled *Win Shares*.

WIN SHARES BY YEAR

Player	<97	97	98	99	00	01	02	03	04	05	06	Career
Aardsma,David									0		4	4
Abad,Andy							0					0
Abercrombie,Reggie											3	3
Abreu,Bobby	0	6	26	26	23	26	29	28	33	25	27	249
Abreu,Winston											0	0
Accardo,Jeremy										2	4	6
Adams,Mike									5	1	0	6
Adams,Russ									2	10	3	15
Adkins,Jon								0	3	0	3	6
Affeldt,Jeremy							5	12	4	1	3	25
Aguila,Chris								0	0	0		0
Albers,Matt											0	0
Alexander,Manny	4	6	3	4	3				1	0	1	22
Alfonseca,Ant		0	3	11	10	9	7	1	8	1	0	50
Alfonzo,Edgardo	14	28	22	29	36	15	26	17	15	9	0	211
Alfonzo,Eliezer											9	9
Alomar Jr.,Sandy	60	18	6	4	8	4	5	4	1	2	3	115
Alou,Moises	89	23	29		17	21	9	20	23	18	14	263
Alvarez,Abe									0	0	0	0
Amezaga,Alfredo								2	1	1	5	9
Anderson,Brian J	13	2	9	7	14	2	5	12	2	0		66
Anderson,Brian										0	5	5
Anderson,Drew											0	0
Anderson,Garret	17	16	18	16	15	17	23	25	14	16	14	191
Anderson,Marlon			2	8	2	16	10	12	3	4	8	65
Andino,Robert									0	0	0	0
Andrade,Steve											0	0
Aquino,Greg									6	0	3	9
Ardoin,Danny				0					0	3	2	5
Arias,Joaquin											1	1
Armas Jr.,Tony				0	5	12	7	4	2	2	4	36
Arroyo,Bronson					0	3	2	2	11	11	20	49
Asencio,Miguel							6	3			0	9
Astacio,Ezeq									0	0	0	0
Astacio,Pedro	36	10	6	19	11	7	5	0	0	5	1	100
Atkins,Garrett								0	2	13	23	38
Aurilia,Rich	7	5	13	18	20	33	15	13	7	16	15	162
Ausmus,Brad	29	13	14	17	16	10	10	12	7	15	7	150
Ayala,Luis								11	10	8		29
Aybar,Erick											1	1
Aybar,Willy										6	6	12
Backe,Brandon							0	1	5	7	3	16
Baek,Cha Seung								0			3	3
Baez,Danys					6	11	9	10	10	6		52
Bajenaru,Jeff									0	0	0	0
Baker,Jeff										1	3	4
Baker,Scott										4	0	4
Bako,Paul			5	5	5	3	3	5	2	1	2	31
Baldelli,Rocco								14	14		12	40
Balfour,Grant						0		2	3			5
Bannister,Brian											3	3
Barajas,Rod				1	0	1	3	5	9	11	7	37
Bard,Josh							1	7	2	2	10	22
Barfield,Josh											18	18
Barker,Kevin					0						0	0
Barmes,Clint								1	3	9	6	19
Barnwell,Chris											0	0
Barrett,Michael			1	11	1	2	12	7	14	18	13	79
Barry,Kevin											1	1
Bartlett,Jason									0	6	13	19
Barzilla,Phil											0	0
Batista,Miguel	0	0	6	6	0	11	9	14	11	8	10	75
Batista,Tony	9	2	10	21	18	12	14	11	12		4	113
Bauer,Rick						0	5	2	3	0	6	16
Bautista,Denny								0	1	1		2
Bautista,Jose									0	0	9	9
Bay,Jason								5	15	30	21	71
Bayliss,Jonah										0	1	1
Beam,T.J.											0	0
Bean,Colter										0	0	0
Beckett,Josh						3	5	11	9	12	11	51
Bedard,Erik							0		6	8	13	27
Beimel,Joe						4	3	2	0	1	7	17

WIN SHARES BY YEAR

Player	<97	97	98	99	00	01	02	03	04	05	06	Career
Belisle,Matt								0		4	3	7
Bell,David	3	2	10	16	8	14	18	5	20	9	13	118
Bell,Heath									2	0	1	3
Bellhorn,Mark		5	0		0	1	18	4	20	5	4	57
Belliard,Ronnie			0	0	17	13	1	11	18	18	11	89
Beltran,Carlos			2	18	5	27	20	28	29	21	34	184
Beltre,Adrian			4	15	22	12	16	15	33	13	17	147
Benitez,Armando	5	11	10	19	17	14	12	10	18	4	6	126
Bennett,Gary	0		1	2	3	1	4	6	2	5	2	26
Benoit,Joaquin							0	3	5	4	4	22
Benson,Kris			12	14		5		2	10	10	8	61
Bergmann,Jason										2	0	2
Berkman,Lance				1	10	32	29	25	30	20	31	178
Bernero,Adam					2	0	1	1	1	1	2	8
Berroa,Angel						1	1	16	12	12	4	46
Betancourt,Raf								4	5	7	5	21
Betancourt,Yun										3	13	16
Betemit,Wilson						0			1	7	9	17
Bigbie,Larry						2	0	9	10	5	0	26
Biggio,Craig	202	38	35	31	11	25	15	20	16	18	11	422
Billingsley,Chad											6	6
Birkins,Kurt											2	2
Blake,Casey				1	0	1	0	11	17	9	11	50
Blalock,Hank						1	17	24	14	13		69
Blanco,Andres									3	1	2	6
Blanco,Henry	0			6	9	6	4	2	5	5	6	43
Blanton,Joe									0	13	10	23
Bloomquist,Wil							3	3	2	4	5	17
Blum,Geoff				3	10	8	15	5	3	7	6	57
Bocachica,Hiram					0	3	1	0	1	0	0	5
Bohn,T.J.											0	0
Bonderman,Jer								2	8	9	13	32
Bonds,Barry	348	36	34	19	32	54	49	39	48	2	25	686
Bonser,Boof											6	6
Booker,Chris										0	1	1
Boone,Aaron		0	6	15	10	13	19	23		9	7	102
Bootcheck,Chris								0		1	0	1
Borchard,Joe							1	0	1	0	4	6
Borkowski,Dave			1	0	0			2		4		7
Borowski,Joe	2	2	0			0	8	14	0	3	9	38
Botts,Jason										0	1	1
Bourn,Michael											0	0
Bowen,Rob								0	1		2	3
Bowie,Micah			0			2	0				3	5
Boyer,Blaine										4	0	4
Bradford,Chad			3	0	2	3	9	9	5	2	7	40
Bradley,Milton					3	3	6	18	16	10	13	69
Branyan,Russell			0	1	5	10	8	6	5	9	6	50
Braun,Ryan											0	0
Bray,Bill											3	3
Brazelton,Dewon							1	0	5	0	0	6
Brazoban,Yhency									4	4	0	8
Breslow,Craig										1	1	2
Brito,Eude										1	0	1
Britton,Chris											4	4
Brocail,Doug	8	7	8	12	5				4	3	1	48
Broussard,Ben							0	9	16	10	11	46
Brower,Jim			2	1	8	5	7	8	1	0		32
Brown,Adrian		1	2	3	9	0	2	0	0		1	18
Brown,Andrew											1	1
Brown,Emil		1	0	0	1	2				18	13	35
Brown,Jeremy											0	0
Broxton,Jon										0	9	9
Bruney,Brian									2	0	3	5
Bruntlett,Eric								1	2	3	4	10
Buchholz,Taylor											1	1
Buck,John									4	10	8	22
Buehrle,Mark					4	18	17	13	17	22	9	100
Bulger,Jason										1	0	1
Burgos,Ambiorix										4	3	7
Burke,Chris									0	6	10	16
Burnett,A.J.				3	5	9	14	0	7	11	9	58
Burnitz,Jeromy	17	20	19	19	16	18	7	12	17	16	5	166

Player	<97	97	98	99	00	01	02	03	04	05	06	Career
Burns,Mike										1	0	1
Burrell,Pat					12	17	25	9	14	24	15	116
Burres,Brian											1	1
Burroughs,Sean							3	16	16	6	1	42
Bush,David									7	6	12	25
Bynum,Freddie										0	3	3
Byrd,Marlon							0	16	5	6	2	29
Byrd,Paul	5	1	7	10	0	6	19		7	13	6	74
Byrdak,Tim			0	0	0					1	0	1
Byrnes,Eric				0	1	2	16	17	9	13		58
Cabrera,Daniel								8	7	7		22
Cabrera,Fern								0	4	2		6
Cabrera,Melky										0	13	13
Cabrera,Miguel								12	19	27	33	91
Cabrera,Orlando		0	6	8	9	26	14	20	11	15	18	127
Cain,Matt										5	11	16
Cairo,Miguel	0	0	10	10	10	4	3	3	14	5	5	64
Calero,Kiko								3	6	5	7	21
Callaspo,Alberto											1	1
Cameron,Mike	0	17	6	19	19	29	18	21	15	11	25	180
Camp,Shawn									4	0	5	9
Campbell,Brett											0	0
Campillo,Jorge											0	0
Cannizaro,Andy											0	0
Cano,Robinson										12	17	29
Cantu,Jorge									4	18	5	27
Capellan,Jose									0	1	5	6
Capps,Matt										0	7	7
Capuano,Chris								1	4	13	14	32
Carmona,Fausto											1	1
Carpenter,Chris		2	11	9	5	13	3		12	20	19	94
Carrara,Giov	0	0			0	8	7	0	7	5	1	28
Carrasco,Hector	17	4	5	3	6	4		2		10	8	59
Carroll,Jamey							3	3	6	9	13	34
Carter,Lance				0			4	10	6	2	0	22
Casey,Sean		0	10	23	17	18	6	17	28	13	10	142
Casilla,Alexi											0	0
Casilla,Santiago									0	0	0	0
Cassidy,Scott							2			0	4	6
Castilla,Vinny	45	21	21	11	3	13	1	14	12	10	2	153
Castillo,Jose									9	9	7	25
Castillo,Luis	3	3	3	14	18	14	20	22	22	18	18	155
Castro,Bernie										3	1	4
Castro,Fabio											3	3
Castro,Juan	2	1	3	0	3	1	2	8	5	7	6	38
Castro,Ramon				1	3	0	4	2	1	7	2	20
Catalanotto,Fr		1	4	5	8	17	7	15	5	16	14	92
Cedeno,Ronny										2	5	7
Cepicky,Matt							1	0	0	0	0	1
Chacin,Gustavo									1	14	5	20
Chacon,Shawn						7	4	9	2	11	1	34
Chavez,Endy						0	3	10	10	1	13	37
Chavez,Eric			2	9	16	26	24	25	18	20	16	156
Chavez,Raul	0	0	0		0		0	1	3	2	0	6
Chen,Bruce			1	1	11	4	1	0	4	13	0	35
Chick,Travis											0	0
Childers,Jason											0	0
Choate,Randy					1	4	0	0	3	0	1	9
Choo,Shin-Soo										0	4	4
Chulk,Vinnie								0	4	5	2	11
Church,Ryan									1	8	9	18
Cintron,Alex						0	1	14	8	7	6	36
Cirillo,Jeff	32	24	26	22	19	14	9	3	1	6	8	164
Clark,Brady				0	4	1	7	12	22	8		54
Clark,Doug										0	0	0
Clark,Howie							0	3	1		0	4
Clark,Tony	10	24	15	19	6	16	1	4	7	18	0	120
Claussen,Bran								1	0	7	1	9
Clayton,Royce	53	13	12	15	8	10	8	7	11	11	7	155
Clemens,Roger	250	32	25	10	16	19	11	15	19	24	11	432
Clement,Matt			1	6	5	4	11	10	12	11	1	61
Clevlen,Brent											2	2
Closser,JD									2	2	2	6
Coats,Buck											0	0
Coffey,Todd										3	9	12
Colina,Alvin											0	0
Colome,Jesus					4	0	4	5	2	0		15
Colon,Bartolo		2	16	16	15	14	22	17	10	18	1	131
Colon,Roman									2	1	2	5
Condrey,Clay							2	0			2	4
Conine,Jeff	70	9	6	10	9	24	9	16	17	10	8	188
Contreras,Jose								7	6	17	13	43
Cook,Aaron							2	3	6	6	12	29
Cora,Alex			1	0	6	6	13	13	17	5	6	67
Corcoran,Roy									1	0	0	1
Corcoran,Tim										0	5	5
Cordero,Chad								2	12	15	12	41
Cordero,Franc				2	3	0	8	12	17	11	12	65
Corey,Bryan					0						3	3
Cormier,Lance									0	4	2	6
Cormier,Rheal	33	0		5	4	4	1	14	7	1	6	75
Corpas,Manuel											3	3
Correia,Kevin								3	0	2	6	11
Cortes,David		0						0		5	2	7
Costa,Shane										0	3	3
Coste,Chris											8	8
Cota,Humberto						0	0	0	2	6	1	9
Cotts,Neal								0	2	9	2	13
Counsell,Craig	0	8	13	2	5	14	15	5	10	22	9	103
Crain,Jesse									4	10	7	21
Crawford,Carl							6	13	20	22	21	82
Crede,Joe					0	1	6	13	8	15	19	62
Crisp,Coco							3	7	14	20	9	53
Crosby,Bobby								0	14	12	8	34
Crosby,Bubba								0	1	2	1	4
Cruceta,Franc										0	0	0
Cruz,Jose		11	12	11	15	16	13	17	14	11	4	124
Cruz,Juan						4	3	0	7	0	6	20
Cruz,Nelson										0	3	3
Cuddyer,Michael						0	3	1	10	7	22	43
Cust,Jack						0	0	4	0		0	4
Daigle,Casey									0		1	1
Damon,Johnny	15	11	17	18	26	17	22	18	26	25	21	216
DaVanon,Jeff			0			1	1	12	9	4	7	34
Davies,Kyle										4	0	4
Davis,Doug				0	5	8	3	7	16	12	8	59
Davis,Jason							2	5	2	2	4	15
Davis,Rajai											0	0
Day,Zach							3	8	6	0	1	18
de la Rosa,Jor									0	2	2	4
de la Rosa,Tomas							3	0			0	3
DeCaster,Yurendell											0	0
DeJean,Mike		7	9	0	4	8	8	6	2	5	1	50
DeJesus,David								0	9	16	14	39
Delcarmen,Manny										1	3	4
Delgado,Carlos	15	18	24	21	36	23	26	32	16	29	22	262
Dellucci,David		1	10	5	1	7	4	4	10	15	8	65
Demaria,Chris										0	0	0
Dempster,Ryan			0	6	17	7	4	0	2	14	6	56
Denorfia,Chris										0	2	2
DeRosa,Mark			0	0	1	6	7	5	2	4	14	39
Dessens,Elmer	1	1	1	10	10	15	7	5	4	5		59
Devine,Joey										0	0	0
Diaz,Einar	0	0	1	8	6	15	4	5	2	2	0	43
Diaz,Joselo											0	0
Diaz,Matt								0	0	2	7	9
Diaz,Victor									1	7	0	8
Dickey,R.A.						0			6		4	10
DiFelice,Mike	0	6	5	8	2	1	4	6	0	0	0	32
DiNardo,Lenny									1	1	0	2
Dobbs,Greg									1	2	1	4
Dohmann,Scott									3	1	1	5
Donnelly,Brend							6	12	5	6	5	34
Dorta,Melvin											0	0
Dotel,Octavio				3	7	12	17	12	14	2	0	67
Doumit,Ryan										6	2	8

Player	<97	97	98	99	00	01	02	03	04	05	06	Career
Downs,Scott				3				0	0	5	6	14
Drese,Ryan						3	2	0	15	2	0	22
Drew,J.D.			3	10	18	22	15	13	31	12	19	143
Drew,Stephen											6	6
DuBose,Eric							1	5	1	0	0	7
Duchscherer,J							0		1	9	11	10	31
Duckworth,Br						5	2	2	0	0	0	9
Duffy,Chris										5	6	11
Duke,Zach										10	10	20
Duncan,Chris										0	10	10
Dunn,Adam						10	20	13	29	25	18	115
Dunn,Scott									0	0	0	0
Durbin,Chad				0	0	8	0	0	1		1	10
Durham,Ray	25	13	25	20	19	21	20	16	19	14	20	212
Dye,Jermaine	5	2	2	16	21	18	13	2	12	17	25	133
Easley,Damion	21	18	23	13	14	15	5	0	8	9	5	131
Eaton,Adam					9	5	0	7	6	5	4	36
Eckstein,David						12	21	11	10	27	13	94
Edmonds,Jim	47	19	24	5	29	30	29	22	33	25	11	274
Edwards,Mike								0	3	0		3
Eischen,Joey	4	0				1	9	5	1	3	0	23
Elarton,Scott			5	10	11	0		0	5	7	4	42
Ellis,Mark							14	18		21	14	67
Ellison,Jason								0	1	6	0	7
Embree,Alan	1	6	3	6	3	2	7	5	4	0	5	42
Encarnacion,Ed									4	14		18
Encarnacion,Ju		1	4	8	14	5	14	15	12	18	15	106
Ensberg,Morgan					0		2	15	11	27	16	71
Erickson,Scott	75	16	15	12	0		2		0	0	0	120
Erstad,Darin	3	19	21	9	30	14	17	3	15	15	1	147
Escobar,Alex						1		1	3		4	9
Escobar,Kelvim		6	7	7	8	11	9	12	14	5	12	91
Estes,Shawn	4	16	3	6	10	7	4	0	9	5	0	64
Estrada,Johnny						5	0	0	18	9	13	45
Etherton,Seth				3			0		0	0	0	3
Ethier,Andre											11	11
Eveland,Dana										0	0	0
Everett,Adam						0	1	11	12	14	13	51
Everett,Carl	10	13	16	25	24	11	10	21	5	11	2	148
Eyre,Scott		2	2	0	0	2	4	5	4	9	5	33
Eyre,Willie											2	2
Fahey,Brandon											4	4
Falkenborg,Br			0					0	0	0		0
Farnsworth,Kyle				5	0	9	0	7	3	14	5	43
Fasano,Sal	4	1	7	3	2	2	0			3	3	25
Fassero,Jeff	65	17	14	1	8	10	2	0	4	5	0	126
Feierabend,Ryan											1	1
Feldman,Scott										1	3	4
Feliciano,Pedro							0	3	1		8	12
Feliz,Pedro					0	0	2	8	9	9	13	41
Fernandez,Jared						0	2	2	0		0	4
Fick,Robert			2	2	4	10	12	14	2	6	1	53
Field,Nate							0	2	3	0	1	6
Fielder,Prince										2	16	18
Fields,Josh											0	0
Figgins,Chone							0	8	20	22	17	67
Figueroa,Luis					0							0
Finley,Steve	128	19	15	24	21	15	24	18	16	6	10	296
Fiorentino,Jeff										0	1	1
Flores,Randy						1			2	3	1	7
Flores,Ron										1	3	4
Floyd,Cliff	17	5	18	9	19	26	22	15	13	24	9	177
Floyd,Gavin									2	0	0	2
Fogg,Josh						2	10	4	7	3	6	32
Ford,Lew								4	21	12	3	40
Fortunato,Bart									3			3
Fossum,Casey						2	6	3	0	5	4	20
Foulke,Keith		4	5	16	16	17	9	21	18	3	4	113
Francis,Jeff									2	6	13	21
Francisco,Frank									6		0	6
Franco,Julio	232	9		0		3	6	6	12	7	3	278
Francoeur,Jeff										12	15	27
Frandsen,Kevin											0	0

Player	<97	97	98	99	00	01	02	03	04	05	06	Career
Franklin,Ryan		1				5	6	13	6	6	4	41
Franklin,Wayne			1	0	2	4	1	0	0			8
Frasor,Jason									9	6	4	19
Freel,Ryan				0				3	19	11	11	44
Freeman,Choo									1	0	3	4
Fruto,Emiliano											1	1
Fuentes,Brian						1	2	10	2	14	12	41
Fulchino,Jeff											0	0
Fultz,Aaron					3	3	1	3	3	7	4	24
Furcal,Rafael					17	9	20	25	20	26	27	144
Gabbard,Kason											2	2
Gagne,Eric				3	2	4	20	25	19	3	1	77
Gall,John										1	0	1
Gallo,Mike								3	2	2	0	7
Garcia,Freddy				16	8	18	11	8	15	17	14	107
Garcia,Jose										0		0
Garciaparra,N	2	26	27	32	29	3	26	25	11	5	17	203
Garko,Ryan										0	6	6
Garland,Jon					1	8	8	10	11	20	15	73
Garza,Matt											1	1
Gathright,Joey									0	4	7	11
Gaudin,Chad								3	1	0	7	11
Geary,Geoff								0	1	3	10	14
German,Esteban							0	0	2	1	11	14
German,Franklyn							2	0	0	4	1	7
Germano,Justin									0		0	0
Gerut,Jody								14	10	3		27
Giambi,Jason	20	18	23	30	38	38	34	28	8	24	22	283
Gibbons,Jay						4	12	18	4	15	9	62
Giles,Brian	7	13	14	27	27	29	31	25	23	32	21	249
Giles,Marcus						9	5	28	17	23	17	99
Gimenez,Hector											0	0
Glaus,Troy			3	16	25	21	22	9	8	23	16	143
Glavine,Tom	141	21	23	14	21	16	19	7	14	14	13	303
Gload,Ross				0		0			7	0	4	11
Gobble,Jimmy								3	5	1	4	13
Gomes,Jonny								0	0	14	6	20
Gomez,Alexis							0		0	0	3	3
Gomez,Chris	27	7	15	6	1	8	11	2	8	4	5	94
Gonzalez,Adrian									1	1	16	18
Gonzalez,Alex			1	11	3	10	3	20	15	14	10	87
Gonzalez,Alex S	22	10	9	6	11	16	13	16	5	7	0	115
Gonzalez,Edgar								1	0	0	3	4
Gonzalez,Enrique											3	3
Gonzalez,Geremi		9	2					8	0	1	1	21
Gonzalez,Luis	91	12	12	26	27	37	27	24	10	19	12	297
Gonzalez,Luis A									7	9	1	17
Gonzalez,Mike								0	8	6	11	25
Gonzalez,Wiki			1	6	7	5	1			1	1	22
Gordon,Tom	82	15	17	2		8	3	11	15	10	10	173
Gorzelanny,Tom										0	3	3
Gosling,Mike									1	1	0	2
Grabow,John								0	1	2	5	8
Graffanino,Tony	1	6	4	7	6	3	7	9	7	13	12	75
Granderson,C									0	6	20	26
Graves,Danny	2	0	8	16	18	11	17	3	6	0	0	81
Green,Andy									1	1	0	2
Green,Nick									8	6	2	16
Green,Sean											2	2
Green,Shawn	18	14	21	24	22	34	29	20	15	17	11	225
Greene,Khalil								1	20	16	13	50
Greene,Todd	1	4	1	3	0	0	1	1	3	3	5	22
Gregg,Kevin								2	6	2	4	14
Greinke,Zack									9	3	1	13
Griffey Jr.,Ken	179	36	29	31	24	14	5	6	15	19	9	367
Grilli,Jason					0	1			0	1	4	6
Grimsley,Jason	11			6	5	8	7	4	4	0	1	46
Gross,Gabe									2	2	10	14
Grudzielanek,M	20	14	13	13	15	17	12	18	8	18	13	161
Gryboski,Kevin							4	3	5	1	0	13
Guardado,Eddie	11	3	5	4	8	12	14	15	8	10	3	93
Guerrero,Vladimir	0	10	29	28	29	23	28	18	27	27	24	243
Guerrier,Matt									0	5	5	10

WIN SHARES BY YEAR

Player	<97	97	98	99	00	01	02	03	04	05	06	Career
Guiel,Aaron							4	12	0	2	2	20
Guillen,Carlos			2	0	8	14	12	12	22	8	25	103
Guillen,Jose		7	11	3	6	2	2	20	20	15	3	89
Guthrie,Jeremy									1	0	0	1
Gutierrez,Franklin										0	1	1
Guzman,Angel										0	0	0
Guzman,Cristian					5	12	18	14	13	16	6	84
Guzman,Freddy									1		0	1
Guzman,Joel											0	0
Gwynn,Tony											1	1
Haeger,Charlie											2	2
Hafner,Travis							1	7	21	26	24	79
Hairston,Jerry			0	5	4	10	12	7	8	9	1	56
Hairston,Scott									3	0	0	3
Halama,John			0	13	6	4	6	4	6	0	1	40
Hall,Bill							1	4	7	17	20	49
Hall,Toby					0	6	7	10	8	11	3	45
Halladay,Roy			2	10	0	9	21	23	9	15	20	109
Halsey,Brad									0	6	5	11
Hamels,Cole											8	8
Hammel,Jason											0	0
Hammock,Robby								6	3	0		9
Hammond,Chris	35	2	0			13	7	6	4	0		67
Hampson,Justin											0	0
Hampton,Mike	22	11	15	26	19	11	5	11	10	6		136
Hamulack,Tim										0	0	0
Hancock,Josh							0	0	2	1	5	8
Hannahan,Jack											0	0
Hansack,Devern											1	1
Hansen,Craig										0	0	0
Harang,Aaron							4	2	5	11	18	40
Harden,Rich								4	14	12	4	34
Hardy,J.J.										11	3	14
Haren,Danny								1	2	13	14	30
Harper,Brandon											1	1
Harper,Travis					2	0	3	6	6	1	2	20
Harris,Brendan									0	1	0	1
Harris,Jeff										3	0	3
Harris,Willie						0	2	2	10	4	1	19
Hart,Corey									0	0	5	5
Harville,Chad			0		1		0	2	1	1		5
Hatteberg,Scott	0	6	11	4	5	5	16	14	17	8	15	101
Hattig,John											1	1
Hawkins,LaTroy	0	2	6	3	12	3	11	13	16	5	4	75
Hawpe,Brad									1	8	15	24
Heilman,Aaron	0							0	0	10	8	18
Heintz,Chris										1	0	1
Helling,Rick	5	6	15	12	15	7	8	6		5	2	81
Helms,Wes			1	0	5	1	12	4		5	10	38
Helton,Todd		2	17	19	29	26	27	34	30	25	21	230
Hendrickson,Ben								0		0		0
Hendrickson,Ma							4	4	7	4	8	27
Henn,Sean										0	0	0
Hennessey,Brad									1	6	6	13
Hensley,Clay										5	11	16
Herges,Matt				1	10	9	4	7	3	1	3	38
Hermanson,Dustin	0	10	13	12	9	8	0	4	9	14	0	79
Hermida,Jeremy										3	6	9
Hernandez,An										0	1	1
Hernandez,Fel										8	8	16
Hernandez,Jose	14	4	16	16	9	13	19	6	9	2	3	111
Hernandez,Liv	1	8	6	9	14	5	7	22	19	13	10	114
Hernandez,Orl			13	14	12	4	11		8	5	7	74
Hernandez,Ram				6	10	13	12	19	13	10	21	104
Hernandez,Rob	57	15	10	14	12	9	7	3	1	10	5	143
Hernandez,Run							5	6		4	1	16
Hill,Aaron										9	14	23
Hill,Rich										0	5	5
Hill,Shawn									0	1	1	1
Hillenbrand,Shea						5	17	11	13	15	8	69
Hinske,Eric							22	12	6	11	7	58
Hirsh,Jason											0	0
Hoey,James											0	0

WIN SHARES BY YEAR

Player	<97	97	98	99	00	01	02	03	04	05	06	Career
Hoffman,Trevor	47	11	20	14	13	9	8	1	11	10	14	158
Hollandsworth,T	21	7	6	7	8	4	12	5	6	4	4	84
Holliday,Matt									9	17	19	45
Hollins,Damon		0							0	7	3	10
Holtz,Mike							0			0	0	0
Hooper,Kevin										0	0	0
Hoover,Paul							0				0	0
Hopper,Norris										2		2
House,J.R.								0	0			0
Howard,Ryan									1	10	29	40
Howell,J.P.										1	2	3
Howry,Bob			7	10	9	5	3	0	4	11	9	58
Huber,Jonathan											3	3
Huber,Justin										0	0	0
Huckaby,Ken						0	2	0	0	1	0	3
Hudson,Luke								0	4	1	5	10
Hudson,Orlando							7	18	16	15	20	76
Hudson,Tim				12	15	17	23	23	16	14	7	127
Huff,Aubrey					3	5	12	21	20	14	9	84
Hughes,Travis									0	0	0	0
Humber,Philip											0	0
Hunter,Torii		0	0	5	8	19	20	15	13	11	17	108
Hyzdu,Adam					1	1	6	1	0	0	0	9
Iannetta,Christopher											1	1
Ibanez,Raul	0	0	1	4	1	9	12	15	12	17	25	96
Iguchi,Tadahito										18	19	37
Infante,Omar							3	3	12	7	5	30
Inge,Brandon						3	4	5	13	17	17	59
Inglett,Joe											6	6
Ishikawa,Travis											1	1
Isringhausen,Jason	14	0		4	10	14	13	7	15	12	8	97
Izturis,Cesar						4	4	11	25	6	3	53
Izturis,Maicer									1	6	13	20
Jackson,Conor										0	12	12
Jackson,Damian	1	1	2	11	15	11	6	2	0	8	1	58
Jackson,Edwin								2	0	0	1	3
Jackson,Zach											1	1
Jacobs,Mike										5	12	17
James,Chuck										1	8	9
Janssen,Casey											4	4
Jarvis,Kevin	0	1		0	4	7	1	0	0	0	0	13
Jenkins,Geoff			1	18	20	11	4	20	12	20	15	121
Jenks,Bobby										6	12	18
Jennings,Jason						3	14	9	9	5	14	54
Jeter,Derek	19	19	27	35	23	28	24	18	26	26	32	277
Jimenez,Cesar											0	0
Jimenez,D'Ang					1	8	13	17	23	1	1	64
Jimenez,Ubaldo											0	0
Jimerson,Char										0	0	0
Johjima,Kenji											20	20
Johnson,Ben										1	2	3
Johnson,Dan										9	5	14
Johnson,Jason		0	2	4	0	9	5	10	6	8	2	46
Johnson,Jim											0	0
Johnson,Josh										1	12	13
Johnson,Nick						0	11	14	6	20	25	76
Johnson,Randy	106	23	19	26	26	26	29	6	21	15	8	305
Johnson,Reed								11	9	10	16	46
Johnson,Tyler										0	1	1
Jones,Adam											1	1
Jones,Andruw	3	13	26	28	30	22	27	23	17	21	22	232
Jones,Chipper	46	23	29	32	27	29	31	26	18	18	22	301
Jones,Greg								1	0			1
Jones,Jacque				9	11	10	25	14	13	13	15	110
Jones,Todd	26	13	7	10	10	5	6	1	6	15	9	108
Jordan,Brian	58	1	21	22	14	19	18	7	2	4	0	166
Julio,Jorge						1	13	6	8	1	7	36
Kapler,Gabe			0	8	10	13	7	4	5	1	2	50
Karsay,Steve	6	3	0	9	11	11	11		1	0	0	52
Karstens,Jeff											3	3
Kazmir,Scott									1	10	13	24
Kearns,Austin							16	12	5	10	17	60
Keisler,Randy					0	0			0	0	1	1

411

WIN SHARES BY YEAR

Player	<97	97	98	99	00	01	02	03	04	05	06	Career
Kemp,Matt											3	3
Kendall,Jason	12	22	26	13	24	9	14	20	25	14	23	202
Kendrick,Howie											6	6
Kennedy,Adam				2	11	8	17	14	13	17	15	97
Kennedy,Joe						6	9	0	13	3	6	37
Kensing,Logan									0	0	2	2
Kent,Jeff	63	22	25	23	37	27	28	20	22	28	18	313
Keppel,Bobby											1	1
Keppinger,Jeff								2			1	3
Kielty,Bobby						1	15	12	4	10	8	50
Kim,Byung-Hyun				2	8	16	20	14	0	6	5	71
Kim,Sun-Woo						1	3	0	5	4	0	13
King,Ray				0	4	5	5	5	8	3	2	32
Kinney,Josh											2	2
Kinsler,Ian											12	12
Klesko,Ryan	47	16	13	18	23	29	30	13	18	15	1	223
Kline,Steve		1	6	7	9	12	6	5	7	3	5	61
Knoedler,Justin									0	0	0	0
Knott,Jon										0	0	0
Kolb,Dan				2	0	1	2	9	11	0	3	28
Komine,Shane											0	0
Konerko,Paul		0	1	14	15	17	17	4	20	24	21	133
Koplove,Mike						0	7	5	6	2	0	20
Koronka,John										0	4	4
Koskie,Corey			0	13	17	24	18	21	13	6	9	121
Kotchman,Casey									2	4	0	6
Kotsay,Mark		1	13	6	12	16	22	14	21	19	11	135
Kouzmanoff,Kevin											1	1
Kroon,Marc	0	0	0									0
Kubel,Jason									3		1	4
Kuo,Hong-Chih										0	3	3
Lackey,John							7	8	10	16	16	57
Laird,Gerald								1	3	1	5	10
Laker,Tim	4	0	1	0		1		4	2	0	0	12
Lamb,Mike				6	8	7	0	12	6	9		48
Lane,Jason						3	1	5	14	7		30
Langerhans,Ryan						0	0			12	8	20
Lara,Juan											0	0
LaRoche,Adam									7	11	16	34
LaRue,Jason				2	3	9	11	10	15	17	5	72
Lawrence,Brian						6	8	8	8	4		34
Lawton,Matt	11	14	21	8	20	20	9	10	15	13	1	142
League,Brandon									1	0	5	6
LeCroy,Matthew				2	3	4	12	4	8	2		35
Ledee,Ricky			2	9	10	4	4	7	5	7	0	48
Ledezma,Wil								2	3	0	4	9
Lee,Carlos				10	14	15	17	20	22	21	22	141
Lee,Cliff							1	3	6	13	10	33
Lee,Derrek			2	10	1	16	16	22	25	19	34	4	149
Lee,Travis			13	8	6	15	13	13	0	10	3	81
Lehr,Justin									2	2	0	4
Leone,Justin									3		0	3
Lerew,Anthony										0	0	0
Lester,Jon											5	5
Lewis,Colby							0	1	1		0	2
Lewis,Fred											1	1
Lidge,Brad							1	8	22	15	7	53
Lidle,Cory		6		0	4	13	13	5	7	7	7	62
Lieber,Jon	15	9	8	13	12	16	7		10	12	6	108
Lieberthal,Mike	4	15	8	20	14	3	15	16	9	11	6	121
Lilly,Ted				0	0	3	6	10	15	4	11	49
Lima,Jose	5	1	14	18	2	4	0	5	9	0	0	58
Lind,Adam											3	3
Linden,Todd								1	0	1	2	4
Linebrink,Scott					1	1	0	5	10	11	8	36
Liriano,Francisco										0	16	16
Littleton,Wes											6	6
Livingston,Bobby											0	0
Lo Duca,Paul			0	2	2	28	19	19	20	11	16	117
Loaiza,Esteban	7	11	6	8	12	8	4	23	7	12	7	105
Loe,Kameron									0	8	2	10
Loewen,Adam											4	4
Lofton,Kenny	114	21	21	16	17	13	19	18	7	15	12	273

WIN SHARES BY YEAR

Player	<97	97	98	99	00	01	02	03	04	05	06	Career
Logan,Boone											0	0
Logan,Nook									3	5	2	10
Lohse,Kyle				3	11	11	6	10	4			45
Lombard,George		0	0	0			4	0			0	4
Loney,James											3	3
Long,Terrence			0	18	17	12	11	5	9	0		72
Looper,Braden		0	5	5	7	11	12	13	6	8		67
Lopez,Felipe						5	6	3	9	21	16	60
Lopez,Javier								7	0	0	2	9
Lopez,Javy	34	19	25	11	16	13	10	30	19	12	5	194
Lopez,Jose									3	5	16	24
Lopez,Rodrigo				0		15	2	14	8	4		43
Loretta,Mark	3	12	16	14	12	9	10	24	32	15	17	164
Lowe,Derek		1	7	19	19	11	22	12	6	11	15	123
Lowe,Mark										3		3
Lowell,Mike			0	8	20	20	19	23	22	8	16	136
Lowry,Noah								1	6	15	7	29
Lugo,Julio				9	9	9	14	20	24	13		98
Lugo,Ruddy											7	7
Luna,Hector									4	5	9	18
Lyon,Brandon					4	0	5			0	6	15
Mabeus,Chris										0		0
Mabry,John	23	8	5	3	3	1	8	2	3	3	3	67
MacDougal,Mike						1	0	9	0	8	5	23
Mackowiak,Rob						4	12	6	14	12	6	54
Maddux,Greg	205	26	25	17	24	20	19	11	13	11	12	383
Madson,Ryan								0	9	6	4	19
Mahay,Ron	0	3	2	3	1	2	0	5	8	0	4	28
Maholm,Paul										4	7	11
Maier,Mitch											0	0
Maine,John									0	0	6	6
Majewski,Gary									1	8	4	13
Maldonado,Carlos											0	0
Manon,Julio								2			0	2
Marcum,Shaun										1	3	4
Markakis,Nick											12	12
Marmol,Carlos											1	1
Maroth,Mike							6	4	11	8	4	33
Marquis,Jason					1	8	3	1	14	12	2	41
Marrero,Eli		1	6	5	5	7	14	3	12	1	3	57
Marshall,Sean											2	2
Marte,Andy										0	4	4
Marte,Damaso			0		1	9	15	9	4	4		42
Martin,Russell											14	14
Martin,Tom	7	0	0	2	0	0	5	2	0	3		19
Martinez,Carlos										1		1
Martinez,Pedro	52	26	21	27	29	12	21	20	16	19	6	249
Martinez,Ramon		0	5	7	9	9	7	6	2	5		50
Martinez,Victor							1	3	20	22	18	64
Masset,Nick											1	1
Mastny,Tom											1	1
Mateo,Henry				0	0		2	0	0	0		2
Mateo,Juan											1	1
Mateo,Julio							1	7	3	7	4	22
Matheny,Mike	7	8	4	3	14	8	9	13	11	17	2	96
Mathieson,Scott											0	0
Mathis,Jeff										0	0	0
Matos,Luis					2	3	0	14	3	12	0	34
Matsui,Hideki								19	28	23	6	76
Matsui,Kaz									13	5	7	25
Matthews Jr.,G				1	1	10	10	9	11	11	21	74
Mauer,Joe									6	22	30	58
Mays,Joe		10	6	22	2	2			2	0		44
McAnulty,Paul										0	1	1
McBride,Macay										0	4	4
McCann,Brian										6	22	28
McCarthy,Bran										5	5	10
McClung,Seth								2		1	2	5
McCracken,Q	7	8	12	2	0	0	14	1	2	2	0	48
McDonald,John				0	0	0	5	2	1	4	3	15
McEwing,Joe			0	11	2	8	2	5	4	1	0	33
McGowan,Dustin										0	0	0
McLeary,Marty								0			2	2

412

Player	<97	97	98	99	00	01	02	03	04	05	06	Career
McLouth,Nate										1	2	3
McPherson,D									1	6	3	10
Meadows,Brian			4	4	7	0	3	3	5	3	4	33
Meche,Gil			6	6				8	5	5	8	38
Medders,Brandon										5	6	11
Melhuse,Adam				0	0			4	5	2	1	12
Mench,Kevin							10	4	13	12	9	48
Mercker,Kent	43	9	5	6	1		1	6	7	5	2	85
Meredith,Cla										0	9	9
Merloni,Lou			4	2	3	2	6	5	5	0		27
Mesa,Jose	50	11	5	5	3	14	13	0	12	5	6	124
Messenger,Randy										1	1	2
Meyer,Drew											0	0
Miceli,Dan	7	5	8	4	5	3	0	6	7	1	3	49
Michaels,Jason						0	3	5	10	12	9	39
Michalak,Chris						1					2	3
Mientkiewicz,D			0	3	0	18	17	20	6	4	8	76
Miles,Aaron								1	12	8	10	31
Millar,Kevin			0	12	10	20	14	16	17	11	13	113
Milledge,Lastings											4	4
Miller,Andrew											0	0
Miller,Corky						2	5	1	0	0	0	8
Miller,Damian		2	6	10	11	10	10	10	14	8	9	90
Miller,Matt								1	5	4	1	11
Miller,Trever	0		4	2	0			4	4	2	6	22
Miller,Wade				0	4	17	13	9	7	4	1	55
Millwood,Kevin		3	10	22	10	5	19	11	5	14	13	112
Milton,Eric			6	12	11	15	9	2	9	0	7	71
Miner,Zach											4	4
Mirabelli,Doug	1	0	1	3	6	7	4	2	7	4	2	37
Misch,Patrick											0	0
Mitre,Sergio								0	0	2	0	2
Moehler,Brian	0	9	17	10	10	1	2	0		5	0	54
Moeller,Chad				2	0	6	6	5	3	1		23
Mohr,Dustan						1	11	6	9	3	0	30
Molina,Bengie			0	3	13	7	10	16	11	15	11	86
Molina,Jose				0		1	2	2	6	7	5	23
Molina,Yadier									5	14	9	28
Monroe,Craig						1	0	10	11	13	13	48
Montero,Agustin										1		1
Montero,Miguel											0	0
Moore,Scott											1	1
Mora,Melvin				0	12	11	16	16	24	20	18	117
Morales,Kendry											2	2
Morillo,Juan											0	0
Morneau,Justin								1	9	7	26	43
Morris,Matt		16	10		6	17	14	10	7	9	8	97
Morse,Mike										5	2	7
Moseley,Dustin											0	0
Mota,Guillermo				5	1	2	2	14	12	3	3	42
Mottola,Chad	1			0	0				0		0	1
Moyer,Jamie	63	14	18	18	5	15	16	18	5	12	10	194
Moylan,Peter											1	1
Mueller,Bill	9	14	18	12	10	8	12	23	12	19	3	140
Mujica,Edward											1	1
Mulder,Mark					5	18	19	17	15	13	1	88
Mulholland,T	60	8	12	11	7	3	3	3	4	3	0	114
Munson,Eric					0	0	0	7	9	0	1	17
Munter,Scott										4	0	4
Murphy,David											0	0
Murphy,Tommy											2	2
Murton,Matt										4	13	17
Mussina,Mike	92	19	15	17	18	20	15	19	9	10	14	248
Myers,Brett							3	9	4	14	12	42
Myers,Mike	3	1	6	2	7	4	3	1	3	4	3	37
Nady,Xavier					0			7	1	8	12	28
Nageotte,Clint									0	0	0	0
Napoli,Mike											10	10
Narveson,Chris											0	0
Nathan,Joe				5	2		1	11	19	17	20	75
Navarro,Dioner									0	4	5	9
Navarro,Oswaldo											0	0
Nelson,Jeff	28	8	4	2	9	8	3	6	2	2	0	72

Player	<97	97	98	99	00	01	02	03	04	05	06	Career
Nelson,Joe				0					0		5	5
Nelson,John											0	0
Neshek,Pat											6	6
Nevin,Phil	7	6	2	19	22	31	12	9	21	7	7	143
Newhan,David			1	0	0				13	2	0	16
Niekro,Lance									0	6	3	9
Nieve,Fernando											6	6
Nieves,Wil							1			0	0	1
Nippert,Dustin										1	0	1
Nix,Laynce								4	7	4	0	15
Nixon,Trot	0		0	10	14	20	16	19	4	15	10	108
Nolasco,Ricky											5	5
Norton,Greg	0	1	4	11	3	3	3	4	0		9	38
Novoa,Roberto									1	3	4	8
Nunez,Abraham		1	1	4	1	6	5	4	2	12	4	40
Nunez,Leo										0	1	1
O'Connor,Mike											3	3
O'Flaherty,Eric											0	0
Ohka,Tomo				0	6	2	14	12	5	10	4	53
Ohman,Will				0	0					4	5	9
Ojeda,Miguel								4	6	1	1	12
Oliver,Darren	21	12	4	13	0	3	3	10	1		6	73
Olivo,Miguel							1	8	7	7	13	36
Olmedo,Ray								2	0	1	0	3
Olsen,Scott										1	10	11
O'Malley,Ryan											1	1
Ordaz,Luis							1				0	1
Ordonez,Magglio		3	13	20	22	25	25	23	8	10	19	168
Orr,Pete										3	2	5
Ortiz,David		2	9	0	8	7	11	15	24	30	27	133
Ortiz,Ramon				1	6	12	14	5	7	3	3	51
Ortiz,Russ			3	12	7	15	13	16	12	0	1	79
Ortmeier,Dan										0	0	0
Orvella,Chad										3	0	3
Osoria,Franq										1	0	1
Oswalt,Roy						15	20	10	18	21	20	104
Otsuka,Akinori									11	4	13	28
Overbay,Lyle						0	0	6	17	17	17	57
Owens,Henry										0		0
Owens,Jerry										0		0
Ozuna,Pablo						1		1	1	4	6	13
Padilla,Vicente				0	6	3	14	13	5	6	12	59
Pagan,Angel											3	3
Palmeiro,Orl	3	1	5	6	7	4	8	6	3	6	1	50
Papelbon,Jonat										4	19	23
Park,Chan Ho	7	13	13	6	18	16	5	0	4	5	4	91
Paronto,Chad						0	2	0			4	6
Patterson,Corey					0	3	8	13	17	4	13	58
Patterson,John							3	0	2	14	2	21
Paul,Josh				0	3	4	2	1	2	1	4	17
Pauley,David											0	0
Paulino,Ronny										0	14	14
Pavano,Carl				6	3	8	0	3	9	19	3	51
Payton,Jay			0	0	14	3	15	15	15	12	15	89
Peavy,Jake							3	7	15	16	12	53
Pedroia,Dustin											2	2
Pelfrey,Mike											0	0
Pena,Brayan										0	1	1
Pena,Carlos						3	11	9	11	7	0	41
Pena,Tony										1		1
Pena,Tony F											0	0
Pena,Wily Mo							0	1	14	6	8	29
Penn,Hayden										0	0	0
Penny,Brad					5	12	4	10	10	9	11	61
Peralta,Jhonny								4	0	25	15	44
Peralta,Joel										2	5	7
Perez,Antonio								3	0	10	1	14
Perez,Beltran											1	1
Perez,Eduardo	6	0	4	2	1		3	7	1	7	5	36
Perez,Juan											0	0
Perez,Neifi	0	9	12	14	15	11	6	8	7	12	4	98
Perez,Odalis			1	1		3	17	6	13	4	2	47
Perez,Oliver							4	1	16	2	0	23

WIN SHARES BY YEAR

Player	<97	97	98	99	00	01	02	03	04	05	06	Career
Perez,Rafael											1	1
Perez,Timo					2	4	14	5	6	1	0	32
Perez,Tomas	4	2	0		1	5	4	5	4	1	3	29
Perkins,Glen											1	1
Petagine,Rob	4	0	2							1	0	7
Petit,Yusmeiro											0	0
Pettitte,Andy	29	20	13	10	14	13	11	15	5	21	12	163
Phillips,Andy									0	0	1	1
Phillips,Brand							1	4	0	0	14	19
Phillips,Jason						0	1	13	5	7	0	26
Phillips,Paul									0	2	2	4
Piazza,Mike	113	39	33	21	28	21	19	11	12	12	11	320
Piedra,Jorge									2	3	0	5
Pierre,Juan				3	17	15	20	22	14	15		106
Pierzynski,A.J.			1	0	3	15	18	22	12	11	14	96
Pineiro,Joel				0	7	14	13	5	3	0		42
Pinto,Renyel											2	2
Podsednik,Scott						0	1	22	13	12	9	57
Polanco,Placido			2	3	11	14	16	18	17	22	14	117
Politte,Cliff			0	0	5	3	7	3	4	12	0	34
Ponson,Sidney			5	10	11	4	10	15	8	0	3	66
Posada,Jorge	0	6	15	10	29	23	22	28	21	19	24	197
Prado,Martin											2	2
Pratt,Todd	9	5	2	5	5	2	7	5	4	6	2	52
Pride,Curtis	11	2	2		0	1		0	0	0	1	17
Prior,Mark							8	22	7	12	0	49
Proctor,Scott									1	0	9	10
Pujols,Albert						29	32	41	37	34	37	210
Punto,Nick						0	0	1	4	6	12	23
Putz,J.J.								0	3	5	17	25
Qualls,Chad									4	7	9	20
Quentin,Carlos											5	5
Quinlan,Robb								0	8	2	8	18
Quintanilla,Om										1	0	1
Quintero,Humb								0	1	1	0	2
Quiroz,Guill									0	0	0	0
Rabe,Josh											1	1
Rabelo,Mike											0	0
Radke,Brad	21	16	14	17	15	17	6	12	18	11	10	157
Ramirez,Aramis			2	0	3	27	6	19	19	18	21	115
Ramirez,Eliz									1	0	3	4
Ramirez,Hanley										0	25	25
Ramirez,Horacio							9	5	8	3		25
Ramirez,Manny	59	21	25	35	27	25	29	28	25	33	27	334
Ramirez,Ramon											7	7
Ramirez,Santiago											0	0
Randa,Joe	10	16	9	17	18	11	10	14	13	15	2	135
Rasner,Darrell										0	1	1
Rauch,Jon							0		4	2	8	14
Ray,Chris										4	12	16
Ray,Ken		0									4	4
Reames,Britt				3	2	1	0			0	0	6
Redman,Mark			0	10	3	10	11	10	4	6		54
Redmond,Mike			4	12	5	6	13	1	6	7	6	60
Reed,Eric											0	0
Reed,Jeremy								3	9	1		13
Reese,Kevin										0	1	1
Reitsma,Chris						3	7	8	7	9	0	34
Remlinger,Mike	2	9	5	12	12	9	11	6	4	1	1	72
Renteria,Edgar	15	15	11	13	15	13	26	25	16	15	19	183
Repko,Jason										5	4	9
Resop,Chris										0	1	1
Restovich,Mike							0	2	1	1	0	4
Reyes,Anthony										1	3	4
Reyes,Dennys		2	2	5	2	1	4	0	4	1	9	30
Reyes,Jose								12	4	16	28	60
Reyes,Jose A											0	0
Rheinecker,John											2	2
Rhodes,Arthur	16	10	7	2	6	12	11	4	2	6	3	79
Riggans,Shawn											1	1
Rincon,Juan						0	0	7	12	10	8	37
Rincon,Ricardo		7	9	3	3	6	6	6	4	2	0	46
Ring,Royce										0	1	1

WIN SHARES BY YEAR

Player	<97	97	98	99	00	01	02	03	04	05	06	Career
Rios,Alex									7	9	18	34
Riske,David			0		3	2	10	7	5	4		31
Rivera,Juan						0	1	4	12	9	18	44
Rivera,Mariano	20	15	14	17	16	19	9	18	18	19	16	181
Rivera,Mike					0	1	0				4	5
Rivera,Rene									0	2	2	4
Rivera,Saul											5	5
Rleal,Sendy											2	2
Roberson,Chris											0	0
Roberts,Brian						3	2	13	16	28	13	75
Roberts,Dave			2		0	0	19	8	12	14	19	74
Roberts,Ryan											0	0
Robertson,Nate							0	1	8	7	14	30
Robinson,Kerry				0	0	4	4	3	2		0	13
Robles,Oscar										9	0	9
Rodney,Fernando							0	1		6	8	15
Rodriguez,Alex	36	22	30	23	37	37	35	32	29	34	25	340
Rodriguez,Eddy								2		0		2
Rodriguez,Felix	1	2	1	4	9	12	5	8	7	1	0	50
Rodriguez,Fran							1	9	17	14	17	58
Rodriguez,Ivan	88	26	27	28	19	18	11	23	22	10	24	296
Rodriguez,John										5	6	11
Rodriguez,Luis										6	1	7
Rodriguez,Wandy										2	2	4
Rogers,Brian											0	0
Rogers,Eddie						0				0	0	0
Rogers,Kenny	80	2	19	12	15	2	15	11	14	15	14	199
Rolen,Scott	2	29	30	15	18	29	26	25	35	5	21	235
Rollins,Jimmy					1	20	17	19	24	21	25	127
Romero,Davis											1	1
Romero,J.C.				1	0	1	14	3	8	5	0	32
Roney,Matt								2			0	2
Rosario,Francisco											0	0
Rose,Mike								0	0	0	0	0
Ross,Cody								1		0	6	7
Ross,Dave							1	4	2	3	13	23
Rottino,Vinny											0	0
Rouse,Mike											1	1
Rowand,Aaron						5	7	6	20	18	7	63
Ruiz,Carlos											2	2
Rupe,Josh										1	2	3
Rusch,Glendon		5	5	0	11	6	7	0	10	6	0	50
Ryan,B.J.			2	2	3	3	6	11	14	19		60
Ryu,Jae Kuk											0	0
Saarloos,Kirk							1	2	2	9	6	20
Sabathia,C.C.						12	13	13	11	12	15	76
Sadler,Billy											0	0
Saenz,Olmedo	0		7	8	1	5			4	11	7	43
Saito,Takashi											18	18
Salas,Juan											0	0
Salazar,Jeffrey											2	2
Salmon,Tim	88	29	22	14	23	11	21	17	3		4	232
Sampson,Chris											4	4
Sanches,Brian											0	0
Sanchez,Angel											0	0
Sanchez,Anibal											10	10
Sanchez,Duaner							0	0	6	7	6	19
Sanchez,Freddy							0	0	0	12	23	35
Sanchez,Jonathan											2	2
Sanders,Reggie	78	13	14	19	6	14	14	18	14	11	5	206
Sandoval,Danny										0	1	1
Santana,Ervin										6	12	18
Santana,Johan					2	2	10	16	26	23	24	103
Santana,Julio		0	8	0	1		5			3	0	17
Santiago,Ramon							4	5	0	0	1	10
Santos,Chad										1		1
Santos,Victor						5	0	0	5	3	1	14
Sarfate,Dennis											0	0
Sauerbeck,Scott				9	6	3	9	3		2	0	32
Saunders,Joe										0	4	4
Schilling,Curt	64	22	22	15	16	24	24	15	21	4	15	242
Schmidt,Jason	2	8	11	13	1	9	10	22	19	9	15	119
Schneider,Brian					1	2	7	13	17	16	9	65

414

Player	<97	97	98	99	00	01	02	03	04	05	06	Career
Schoeneweis,S				1	6	9	5	3	4	6	6	40
Schroder,Chris											0	0
Schumaker,Skip										0	0	0
Scott,Luke										0	11	11
Scutaro,Marco							0	2	11	11	11	35
Seanez,Rudy	3		5	7	2	3	1	0	4	7	2	34
Seay,Bobby						0		1	2	0	0	3
Sele,Aaron	31	7	14	13	12	14	5	2	5	2	5	110
Seo,Jae						0	9	3	9	4		25
Sexson,Richie		0	5	10	16	19	21	26	3	24	19	143
Shackelford,Br									3	0		3
Sharpless,Josh											2	2
Shealy,Ryan										2	6	8
Sheets,Ben					6	8	9	21	11	7		62
Sheffield,Gary	139	22	30	24	31	30	26	35	30	31	4	402
Shelton,Chris									0	13	8	21
Sherrill,George								1	2	3		6
Shields,James											6	6
Shields,Scot						2	6	12	11	13	11	55
Shiell,Jason						0	1			0		1
Shoppach,Kelly										0	3	3
Shouse,Brian	0		0				0	6	6	2	3	17
Sierra,Ruben	191	1	1		1	6	7	5	8	2	0	222
Sikorski,Brian				1							1	2
Silva,Carlos						7	5	14	14	2		42
Simon,Randall		1	0	4		7	13	11	0		0	36
Simpson,Allan								2	0	0		2
Sisco,Andy										5	0	5
Sizemore,Grady									5	24	24	53
Slaten,Doug											1	1
Sledge,Terrmel								13	1	1		15
Slocum,Brian										0	0	0
Small,Aaron	1	7	2			0			0	7	0	17
Smith,Jason						0	0	0	2	1	3	6
Smith,Matt											4	4
Smith,Mike					0						0	0
Smith,Travis			0			0		0	0	0		0
Smoltz,John	126	21	16	18		8	17	16	16	19	15	272
Snell,Ian									0	1	8	9
Snelling,Chris						0			1	2		3
Snow,J.T.	34	28	13	18	16	6	11	14	19	10	1	170
Snyder,Chris									2	4	7	13
Snyder,Kyle							4		0	1		5
Soler,Alay											0	0
Soriano,Alfonso				0	0	16	28	27	16	16	26	129
Soriano,Rafael						1	7	0	1	7		16
Sosa,Jorge						2	5	3	14	2		26
Soto,Geovany									0	0		0
Sowers,Jeremy											7	7
Speier,Justin			0	1	7	5	7	8	7	7	6	48
Spiezio,Scott	2	10	10	6	6	9	17	12	4	0	12	88
Spilborghs,Ryan										0	3	3
Springer,Russ	9	3	3	5	3	0		0	1	3	5	32
Spurling,Chris								4		5	1	10
Stairs,Matt	6	15	20	20	10	11	7	13	11	14	7	134
Standridge,Jas						1	0	0	0	2	1	4
Stanton,Mike	41	9	4	4	6	10	10	3	7	2	8	104
Stauffer,Tim										0	1	1
Stemle,Steve									0	0	0	0
Stern,Adam									0	0	0	0
Stewart,Chris											0	0
Stewart,Shannon	0	7	18	17	17	18	17	19	13	11	5	142
Stinnett,Kelly	8	1	10	6	5	5	4	4	2	1	2	48
Stockman,Phil											0	0
Stokes,Brian											1	1
Street,Huston										16	14	30
Stults,Eric											1	1
Sturtze,Tanyon	0	0			1	6	11	6	2	3	4	33
Sullivan,Cory										10	6	16
Suppan,Jeff	1	4	2	12	12	12	9	14	9	13	12	100
Suzuki,Ichiro					36	26	23	27	22	24		158
Sweeney,Brian								1	0		5	6
Sweeney,Mark	8	5	3	0	0	1	0	2	6	9	5	39

Player	<97	97	98	99	00	01	02	03	04	05	06	Career
Sweeney,Mike	4	5	8	16	26	18	18	15	14	16	5	145
Sweeney,Ryan											0	0
Swisher,Nick							1	12	20			33
Switzer,Jon						0			0	2		2
Taguchi,So					1	3	6	12	6			28
Tallet,Brian			2	0				0	4			6
Tankersley,Taylor									5			5
Taschner,Jack								3	0			3
Tata,Jordan									0			0
Tatis,Fernando		3	9	23	11	2	6	1			2	57
Taubenheim,Ty									1			1
Tavarez,Julian	14	6	5	1	10	6	2	10	9	6	5	74
Taveras,Willy								0	13	13		26
Teahen,Mark									9	18		27
Teixeira,Mark							13	24	33	21		91
Tejada,Miguel		1	7	20	23	25	32	25	28	26	23	210
Tejada,Robinson									5	4		9
Terrero,Luis						0	3	3	0			6
Thames,Marcus						0	0	6	1	11		18
Theriot,Ryan									0	6		6
Thomas,Frank	193	39	25	16	34	1	16	23	12	3	21	383
Thome,Jim	70	26	19	26	20	31	33	30	20	4	25	304
Thompson,Brad									5	5		10
Thompson,Kevin									1			1
Thompson,Mike									2			2
Thomson,John		10	9	0		7	7	11	13	4	2	63
Thorman,Scott									2			2
Thornton,Matt							2	1	7			10
Thurston,Joe				1	0	0			0			1
Tiffee,Terry							1	0	1			2
Timlin,Mike	34	9	12	9	6	5	8	8	7	14	6	118
Tomko,Brett		10	9	6	5	1	6	6	10	8	5	66
Torrealba,Yorv					1	4	7	4	4	6		26
Torres,Salomon	6	0			3	5	11	10	9			44
Towers,Josh				6	0	5	6	13	0			30
Traber,Billy							3		0			3
Tracey,Sean									1			1
Trachsel,Steve	30	9	13	6	11	8	10	13	10	1	6	117
Tracy,Chad							11	19	14			44
Treanor,Matt							1	2	5			8
Tsao,Chin-hui						1	1	0				2
Tucker,Michael	12	15	11	10	7	10	8	9	14	7	2	105
Tulowitzki,Troy									1			1
Turnbow,Derrick				2		2	1	17	2			24
Tyner,Jason				1	6	1	2		2	7		19
Uggla,Dan									23			23
Upton,B.J.						4		2				6
Uribe,Juan				7	10	9	18	17	11			72
Utley,Chase						5	8	25	27			65
Valentin,Javier	0	2	5			0	2	4	11	3		27
Valentin,Jose	42	13	15	8	24	15	16	18	14	2	15	182
Valverde,Jose						11	3	13	4			31
Van Benschoten,J							0					0
Van Buren,Jermaine								0	0			0
Vargas,Claudio						6	3	6	7			22
Vargas,Jason							4	1				5
Varitek,Jason	0	5	12	7	8	12	17	18	18	7		104
Vazquez,Javier		0	8	14	21	13	21	9	12	11		109
Vazquez,Ramon				0	14	10	1	1	1			27
Venafro,Mike		7	6	4	2	1	0		1			21
Vento,Mike							0	1				1
Veras,Jose								1				1
Verlander,Just							0	15				15
Victorino,Shane						0	1	11				12
Vidro,Jose		3	2	11	25	18	29	19	11	10	12	140
Villanueva,Carlos								4				4
Villarreal,Osc						11	0	1	7			19
Villone,Ron	7	4	1	8	5	3	2	5	6	5	3	49
Vizcaino,Jose	59	17	8	4	3	4	11	4	8	4	3	125
Vizcaino,Luis				0	0	2	8	1	6	6	7	30
Vizquel,Omar	84	14	18	22	16	12	21	5	18	20	20	250
Vogelsong,Ryan				1	0		0	0	3	0		4
Volquez,Edison								0	0			0

WIN SHARES BY YEAR

Player	<97	97	98	99	00	01	02	03	04	05	06	Career
Waechter,Doug								3	1	3	0	7
Wagner,Billy	8	11	11	20	1	13	16	19	10	18	14	141
Wagner,Ryan								3	2	1	1	7
Wainwright,Adam										0	9	9
Wakefield,Tim	39	12	11	8	5	11	15	12	8	15	7	143
Walker,Jamie		2	0				4	7	6	4	5	28
Walker,Pete	1			0	1	9	3			7	1	22
Walker,Todd	1	2	19	9	5	12	22	15	13	13	11	122
Walker,Tyler							0		4	7	3	14
Walrond,Les							0				0	0
Wang,Chien-Ming										7	16	23
Ward,Daryle			0	3	3	5	10	0	7	7	6	41
Wasdin,John	5	7	4	7	3	3		0	1	6	1	37
Washburn,Jarrod			4	3	7	15	18	10	8	14	7	86
Watson,Brandon										0	0	0
Weathers,David	8	0	4	6	7	10	7	8	5	8	10	73
Weaver,Jeff				7	12	13	14	2	11	13	3	75
Weaver,Jered											14	14
Webb,Brandon								17	11	17	20	65
Weeks,Rickie								0		9	10	19
Wellemeyer,Todd								0	1	0	4	5
Wells,David	87	12	18	13	18	5	15	14	10	11	4	207
Wells,Kip				3	2	6	13	16	6	3	0	49
Wells,Vernon				1	0	3	18	26	13	20	24	105
Werth,Jayson							1	1	11	9		22
Westbrook,Jake					0	2	1	6	15	8	13	45
Wheeler,Dan				1	1	0		3	3	10	12	30
White,Rick	9		5	7	9	5	5	1	3	5	2	51
White,Rondell	31	17	16	15	14	12	6	15	11	12	1	150
Wickman,Bob	32	11	11	11	12	14	4		3	10	8	116
Widger,Chris	0	5	10	8	4		2	2		2	0	33
Wigginton,Ty							3	15	10	4	13	45
Wilkerson,Brad						1	17	18	19	19	5	79
Williams,Bernie	99	24	27	33	26	24	30	13	16	11	8	311
Williams,Dave						7	1		2	6	1	17
Williams,Jerome								9	7	6	0	22
Williams,Todd	1		0	1		1			3	7	2	15
Williams,Woody	14	11	12	10	12	11	10	13	8	3	10	114
Williamson,Sc			17	11	0	10	7	4	0	1		50
Willingham,Josh									0	0	14	14
Willis,Dontrelle								14	9	22	13	58
Willits,Reggie											1	1
Wilson,Brian											1	1
Wilson,C.J.										0	3	3
Wilson,Craig						8	11	10	16	5	8	58
Wilson,Jack						5	12	11	22	14	12	76
Wilson,Kris				2	4	0	4				0	10
Wilson,Paul	1					4	6	7	5	7	0	30
Wilson,Preston			1	13	20	10	10	20	2	14	9	99
Wilson,Vance			0	0	1	5	7	5	3	5		26
Windsor,Jason											0	0
Winkelsas,Joe				0							0	0
Winn,Randy			5	4	2	10	23	21	17	22	13	117
Wise,Dewayne					0		1		3		0	4
Wise,Matt				2	2	1		3	7	4		19
Witasick,Jay	0	0	0	5	3	6	6	2	3	6	0	31
Witt,Kevin			0	0		2					0	3
Wolf,Randy				4	13	11	15	12	6	4	2	67
Womack,Tony	3	18	17	14	16	10	15	3	18	3	2	119
Wood,Jason			0	0							1	1
Wood,Kerry			14		7	13	12	18	9	4	2	79
Wood,Mike								0	2	5	1	8
Woods,Jake										1	6	7
Woodward,Chris				0	2	1	10	9	4	4	3	33
Worrell,Tim	14	3	3	4	7	5	9	13	10	4	0	72
Wright,David									9	26	30	65
Wright,Jamey	5	3	8	7	9	7	2	2	5	4	4	56
Wright,Jaret		6	11	3	3	0	0	1	14	1	7	46
Wuertz,Mike									2	6	4	12
Yan,Esteban	0	0	7	2	4	8	7	1	7	2	2	40
Yates,Tyler										0	3	3
Youkilis,Kevin									8	3	22	33
Youman,Shane											2	2

WIN SHARES BY YEAR

Player	<97	97	98	99	00	01	02	03	04	05	06	Career
Young,Chris									2	10	12	24
Young,Chris										2		2
Young,Delmon											2	2
Young,Delwyn											0	0
Young,Dmitri	0	5	16	10	14	13	5	19	8	9	2	101
Young,Eric	49	17	17	14	18	16	9	9	9	4	0	162
Young,Michael					0	7	11	21	25	29	26	119
Zambrano,Carlos						0	5	18	20	18	17	78
Zambrano,Victor						6	4	10	8	7	0	35
Zaun,Gregg	6	9	3	3	9	4	2	2	11	14	8	71
Zimmerman,Ryan										2	24	26
Zito,Barry					9	15	25	18	12	13	17	109
Zobrist,Ben											2	2
Zumaya,Joel											12	12

Projected Batting Records for 2007

Bill James

You're a baseball fan, right? You know who is having a good year, who is not having such a good year. So take a look at the players below. One of these lines represents the player's actual batting record in 2006; the other line is the batting record that we had projected for him in these pages a year ago. The real season is always the same, in every pair... that is, it's always either the top or the bottom; it's not the top sometimes and the bottom sometimes. Which one is the actual batting record?

Hitter	G	AB	R	H	D	T	HR	RBI	BB	SO	SB	Avg	Slg
Perez,Eduardo	80	186	22	47	10	0	9	33	18	33	0	.253	.452
Perez,Eduardo	79	186	27	46	9	0	10	31	24	39	1	.247	.457

Hitter	G	AB	R	H	D	T	HR	RBI	BB	SO	SB	Avg	Slg
Catalanotto,Frank	128	437	56	131	36	2	7	56	52	37	1	.300	.439
Catalanotto,Frank	128	442	64	130	30	3	9	54	37	58	2	.294	.437

Hitter	G	AB	R	H	D	T	HR	RBI	BB	SO	SB	Avg	Slg
Garciaparra,Nomar	122	469	82	142	31	2	20	93	42	30	3	.303	.505
Garciaparra,Nomar	115	462	75	142	32	3	18	74	32	46	4	.307	.506

Hitter	G	AB	R	H	D	T	HR	RBI	BB	SO	SB	Avg	Slg
Brown,Emil	147	527	77	151	41	2	15	81	59	95	6	.287	.457
Brown,Emil	148	536	72	152	30	3	16	80	44	99	10	.284	.440

Hitter	G	AB	R	H	D	T	HR	RBI	BB	SO	SB	Avg	Slg
Castillo,Luis	142	584	84	173	22	6	3	49	56	58	25	.296	.370
Castillo,Luis	147	560	91	170	17	4	4	38	73	59	20	.304	.370

Hitter	G	AB	R	H	D	T	HR	RBI	BB	SO	SB	Avg	Slg
Williams,Bernie	131	420	65	118	29	0	12	61	33	53	2	.281	.436
Williams,Bernie	118	414	64	113	21	1	14	61	56	68	2	.273	.430

Hitter	G	AB	R	H	D	T	HR	RBI	BB	SO	SB	Avg	Slg
Youkilis,Kevin	147	569	100	159	42	2	13	72	91	120	5	.279	.429
Youkilis,Kevin	149	500	86	139	38	1	14	68	95	91	4	.278	.442

Hitter	G	AB	R	H	D	T	HR	RBI	BB	SO	SB	Avg	Slg
Cintron,Alex	91	288	35	82	10	3	5	41	10	35	10	.285	.392
Cintron,Alex	105	298	36	85	19	3	5	33	16	26	1	.285	.419

Hitter	G	AB	R	H	D	T	HR	RBI	BB	SO	SB	Avg	Slg
Buck,John	114	371	37	91	21	1	11	50	26	84	0	.245	.396
Buck,John	118	389	46	98	22	1	13	56	23	87	2	.252	.414

Hitter	G	AB	R	H	D	T	HR	RBI	BB	SO	SB	Avg	Slg
Molina,Jose	78	225	18	54	17	0	4	22	9	49	1	.240	.369
Molina,Jose	81	196	20	49	8	0	4	24	11	41	2	.250	.352

Hitter	G	AB	R	H	D	T	HR	RBI	BB	SO	SB	Avg	Slg
Wilson,Jack	142	543	70	148	27	1	8	35	33	65	4	.273	.370
Wilson,Jack	158	614	71	167	29	5	9	57	34	68	6	.272	.379

Hitter	G	AB	R	H	D	T	HR	RBI	BB	SO	SB	Avg	Slg
Burrell,Pat	144	462	80	119	24	1	29	95	98	131	0	.258	.502
Burrell,Pat	149	527	72	137	30	1	28	97	87	152	0	.260	.480

Hitter	G	AB	R	H	D	T	HR	RBI	BB	SO	SB	Avg	Slg
Jones,Andruw	156	565	107	148	29	0	41	129	82	127	4	.262	.531
Jones,Andruw	159	602	102	162	32	3	42	113	69	126	7	.269	.542

Hitter	G	AB	R	H	D	T	HR	RBI	BB	SO	SB	Avg	Slg
Rolen,Scott	142	521	94	154	48	1	22	95	56	69	7	.296	.518
Rolen,Scott	146	503	90	144	35	2	26	98	70	93	6	.286	.519

Hitter	G	AB	R	H	D	T	HR	RBI	BB	SO	SB	Avg	Slg
Ordonez,Magglio	155	593	82	177	32	1	24	104	45	87	1	.298	.477
Ordonez,Magglio	145	520	80	157	34	1	23	93	50	62	4	.302	.504

Hitter	G	AB	R	H	D	T	HR	RBI	BB	SO	SB	Avg	Slg
Freel,Ryan	132	454	67	123	30	2	8	27	57	98	37	.271	.399
Freel,Ryan	128	469	74	126	24	3	5	31	56	69	37	.269	.365

Hitter	G	AB	R	H	D	T	HR	RBI	BB	SO	SB	Avg	Slg
Vidro,Jose	126	463	52	134	26	1	7	47	41	48	1	.289	.395
Vidro,Jose	127	471	59	139	27	1	11	55	49	51	1	.295	.427

Hitter	G	AB	R	H	D	T	HR	RBI	BB	SO	SB	Avg	Slg
Anderson,Garret	141	543	63	152	28	2	17	85	38	95	1	.280	.433
Anderson,Garret	139	524	63	151	34	1	19	86	25	79	2	.288	.466

Hitter	G	AB	R	H	D	T	HR	RBI	BB	SO	SB	Avg	Slg
Belliard,Ronnie	147	544	63	148	30	1	13	67	36	81	2	.272	.403
Belliard,Ronnie	150	581	81	160	41	2	14	71	54	86	3	.275	.425

Hitter	G	AB	R	H	D	T	HR	RBI	BB	SO	SB	Avg	Slg
Delgado,Carlos	144	524	89	139	30	2	38	114	74	120	0	.265	.548
Delgado,Carlos	150	551	94	155	38	1	36	118	93	136	0	.281	.550

Hitter	G	AB	R	H	D	T	HR	RBI	BB	SO	SB	Avg	Slg
Graffanino,Tony	129	456	68	125	33	3	7	59	45	68	5	.274	.406
Graffanino,Tony	118	405	67	112	18	2	7	42	37	55	7	.277	.383

Hitter	G	AB	R	H	D	T	HR	RBI	BB	SO	SB	Avg	Slg
Beltre,Adrian	156	620	88	166	39	4	25	89	47	118	11	.268	.465
Beltre,Adrian	149	532	70	146	30	2	25	85	41	90	4	.274	.479

Hitter	G	AB	R	H	D	T	HR	RBI	BB	SO	SB	Avg	Slg
Sexson,Richie	158	591	75	156	40	0	34	107	64	154	1	.264	.504
Sexson,Richie	145	549	89	143	30	1	37	112	77	158	1	.260	.521

Hitter	G	AB	R	H	D	T	HR	RBI	BB	SO	SB	Avg	Slg
Guerrero,Vladimir	156	607	92	200	34	1	33	116	50	68	15	.329	.552
Guerrero,Vladimir	150	567	104	187	35	3	36	114	64	63	15	.330	.593

Hitter	G	AB	R	H	D	T	HR	RBI	BB	SO	SB	Avg	Slg
Fielder,Prince	157	569	82	154	35	1	28	81	59	125	7	.271	.483
Fielder,Prince	152	539	72	146	30	0	33	101	58	138	9	.271	.510

Hitter	G	AB	R	H	D	T	HR	RBI	BB	SO	SB	Avg	Slg
Furcal,Rafael	159	654	113	196	32	9	15	63	73	98	37	.300	.445
Furcal,Rafael	155	627	109	179	32	6	13	58	64	82	37	.285	.418

Hitter	G	AB	R	H	D	T	HR	RBI	BB	SO	SB	Avg	Slg
Martinez,Victor	153	572	82	181	37	0	16	93	71	78	0	.316	.465
Martinez,Victor	141	526	75	160	37	0	20	89	61	67	0	.304	.489

Hitter	G	AB	R	H	D	T	HR	RBI	BB	SO	SB	Avg	Slg
Grudzielanek,Mark	134	548	85	163	32	4	7	52	28	69	3	.297	.409
Grudzielanek,Mark	134	511	64	145	26	2	7	48	27	78	6	.284	.384

Hitter	G	AB	R	H	D	T	HR	RBI	BB	SO	SB	Avg	Slg
Ramirez,Aramis	157	594	93	173	38	4	38	119	50	63	2	.291	.561
Ramirez,Aramis	147	562	81	163	34	1	33	104	43	78	1	.290	.530

Hitter	G	AB	R	H	D	T	HR	RBI	BB	SO	SB	Avg	Slg
Navarro,Dioner	81	268	28	68	9	0	6	28	31	51	2	.254	.354
Navarro,Dioner	119	361	40	95	18	0	7	35	38	39	2	.263	.371

As you no doubt have figured out, clever weasel that you are, the top lines above represent what these players actually did; the bottom lines represent what we had projected them to do.

Two points here. First, if you think that I've shown you here all of our really good projections from last year, you're wrong; actually, I've only shown you about 15 to 20% of them. (We always hi-light a much higher percentage of our bad projections than we do our good ones.) And second, we really don't know anything or very much about projecting performance for hitters that you don't know. It's just that, in any major league season, there are a large number of hitters who are going to do exactly what you would have projected them to do, had you taken the time to make projections.

This doesn't include just veteran players... it includes rookies and first-year regulars like Kevin Youkilis, Dioner Navarro, and Prince Fielder. The charts above include numerous players who historically have been up and down-Nomar Garciaparra, Aramis Ramirez, Adrian Beltre and Pat Burrell. It includes players coming back from devastating injuries (Magglio Ordonez and Scott Rolen); it includes an eleven-year veteran who had never played this much in a season before (Tony Graffanino).

When our projections are wrong, what we are most often wrong about is playing time. We make these projections, the ones printed here, in early October, just after the previous season ends, before trades and free agent signings and spring training and snapped tendons. With regard to Yuniesky Betancourt, we had projected what he would hit very accurately, but we had projected him to play 60 games, 209 at bats; he actually had 157 and 558. Darrin Erstad and Delmon Young, on the other hand, we had projected for much more playing time than they actually received... ditto for Russ Adams, Matt LeCroy, Jason LaRue, Hideki Matsui, Dallas McPherson, Dmitri Young, Cliff Floyd, Bill Mueller, Bobby Crosby, Dan Johnson, Mike Sweeney, Humberto Quintaro, and many others. Derrek Lee, Gary Sheffield, Ryan Klesko and Sean Burroughs. We had projected that Shannon Stewart should hit .293, and he did, but we had projected that he would do this in 133 games, rather than 44. There aren't as many players who get playing time that we don't project, like Yuniesky Betancourt, because if we suspect that a player might play regularly, we project that he will play regularly. We figure it is our job to put ourselves on record as to what a player is capable of doing. Prince Fielder and Delmon Young... a year ago we projected them both to play. Fielder did; Delmon didn't. That's OK. But if one of them did play and we hadn't printed a projection for him, we'd feel bad about that, because we would feel that we failed to give you our assessment of the player's abilities.

And sometimes, of course, we're just entirely wrong. These are the most interesting cases, the "stories" of the season, the players who do what no one-or at least no one in our office-would have expected them to do. Jermaine Dye:

Hitter	Season	G	AB	R	H	D	T	HR	RBI	BB	SO	SB	Avg	Slg
Dye,Jermaine	Actual	146	539	103	170	27	3	44	120	59	118	7	.315	.622
Dye,Jermaine	Projected	133	499	75	132	27	1	24	82	46	102	7	.265	.467

We had projected more or less the same season for Gary Matthews Jr. that we had for Luis Matos:

Hitter	Season	G	AB	R	H	D	T	HR	RBI	BB	SO	SB	Avg	Slg
Matthews Jr.,Gary	Actual	147	620	102	194	44	6	19	79	58	99	10	.313	.495
Matthews Jr.,Gary	Projected	133	458	68	116	25	2	14	51	50	94	9	.253	.408

Hitter	Season	G	AB	R	H	D	T	HR	RBI	BB	SO	SB	Avg	Slg
Matos,Luis	Actual	69	136	16	28	9	1	2	5	10	23	7	.206	.331
Matos,Luis	Projected	116	386	53	105	22	2	7	39	28	61	16	.272	.394

Whereas on the Milwaukee Brewers, we had apparently mixed up Bill Hall with Rickie Weeks:

Hitter	Season	G	AB	R	H	D	T	HR	RBI	BB	SO	SB	Avg	Slg
Hall,Bill	Actual	148	537	101	145	39	4	35	85	63	162	8	.270	.553
Hall,Bill	Projected	129	436	58	118	29	3	13	52	30	92	14	.271	.440

Hitter	Season	G	AB	R	H	D	T	HR	RBI	BB	SO	SB	Avg	Slg
Weeks,Rickie	Actual	95	359	73	100	15	3	8	34	30	92	19	.279	.404
Weeks,Rickie	Projected	155	574	98	153	28	8	26	86	67	144	27	.267	.479

An understandable confusion, I'm sure you'll agree. Here's a kind of Newgate Calendar of our worst offenses from last season:

Hitter	Season	G	AB	R	H	D	T	HR	RBI	BB	SO	SB	Avg	Slg
Wilkerson,Brad	Actual	95	320	56	71	15	2	15	44	37	116	3	.222	.422
Wilkerson,Brad	Projected	156	574	82	147	32	4	16	59	100	162	9	.256	.409

Hitter	Season	G	AB	R	H	D	T	HR	RBI	BB	SO	SB	Avg	Slg
Rios,Alexis	Actual	128	450	68	136	33	6	17	82	35	89	15	.302	.516
Rios,Alexis	Projected	116	374	55	109	21	5	6	43	25	69	11	.291	.422

Hitter	Season	G	AB	R	H	D	T	HR	RBI	BB	SO	SB	Avg	Slg
Cuddyer,Mike	Actual	150	557	102	158	41	5	24	109	62	130	6	.284	.504
Cuddyer,Mike	Projected	129	438	63	118	25	4	16	51	46	88	5	.269	.454

Hitter	Season	G	AB	R	H	D	T	HR	RBI	BB	SO	SB	Avg	Slg
Varitek,Jason	Actual	103	365	46	87	19	2	12	55	46	87	1	.238	.400
Varitek,Jason	Projected	140	492	66	131	32	1	20	75	61	124	3	.266	.457

Hitter	Season	G	AB	R	H	D	T	HR	RBI	BB	SO	SB	Avg	Slg
Johnson,Reed	Actual	134	461	86	147	34	2	12	49	33	81	8	.319	.479
Johnson,Reed	Projected	131	415	61	114	22	3	8	53	23	72	5	.275	.400

Hitter	Season	G	AB	R	H	D	T	HR	RBI	BB	SO	SB	Avg	Slg
Sanchez,Freddy	Actual	157	582	85	200	53	2	6	85	31	52	3	.344	.473
Sanchez,Freddy	Projected	137	492	69	148	32	2	6	46	36	44	5	.301	.411

Hitter	Season	G	AB	R	H	D	T	HR	RBI	BB	SO	SB	Avg	Slg
Byrnes,Eric	Actual	143	562	82	150	37	3	26	79	34	88	25	.267	.482
Byrnes,Eric	Projected	120	379	55	96	25	4	11	43	31	72	7	.253	.427

Hitter	Season	G	AB	R	H	D	T	HR	RBI	BB	SO	SB	Avg	Slg
Aurilia,Rich	Actual	122	440	61	132	25	1	23	70	34	51	3	.300	.518
Aurilia,Rich	Projected	119	371	49	99	20	1	11	48	31	63	1	.267	.415

Hitter	Season	G	AB	R	H	D	T	HR	RBI	BB	SO	SB	Avg	Slg
Cantu,Jorge	Actual	107	413	40	103	18	2	14	62	26	91	1	.249	.404
Cantu,Jorge	Projected	150	570	71	158	42	1	21	92	22	79	1	.277	.465

Hitter	Season	G	AB	R	H	D	T	HR	RBI	BB	SO	SB	Avg	Slg
Helton,Todd	Actual	145	546	94	165	40	5	15	81	91	64	3	.302	.476
Helton,Todd	Projected	155	569	112	189	48	2	30	108	111	85	3	.332	.582

Hitter	Season	G	AB	R	H	D	T	HR	RBI	BB	SO	SB	Avg	Slg
Holliday,Matt	Actual	155	602	119	196	45	5	34	114	47	110	10	.326	.586
Holliday,Matt	Projected	154	548	84	163	32	5	20	89	44	87	13	.297	.484

Hitter	Season	G	AB	R	H	D	T	HR	RBI	BB	SO	SB	Avg	Slg
Wigginton,Ty	Actual	122	444	55	122	25	1	24	79	32	97	4	.275	.498
Wigginton,Ty	Projected	74	176	24	47	11	1	6	25	18	31	3	.267	.443

Hitter	Season	G	AB	R	H	D	T	HR	RBI	BB	SO	SB	Avg	Slg
Teahen,Mark	Actual	109	393	70	114	21	7	18	69	40	85	10	.290	.517
Teahen,Mark	Projected	145	502	71	128	35	4	8	66	50	112	8	.255	.388

Hitter	Season	G	AB	R	H	D	T	HR	RBI	BB	SO	SB	Avg	Slg
Thomas,Frank	Actual	137	466	77	126	11	0	39	114	81	81	0	.270	.545
Thomas,Frank	Projected	90	283	45	71	16	0	18	52	52	66	0	.251	.498

Hitter	Season	G	AB	R	H	D	T	HR	RBI	BB	SO	SB	Avg	Slg
Cedeno,Ronny	Actual	151	534	51	131	18	7	6	41	17	109	8	.245	.339
Cedeno,Ronny	Projected	116	335	50	104	18	1	8	38	23	43	16	.310	.442

Hitter	Season	G	AB	R	H	D	T	HR	RBI	BB	SO	SB	Avg	Slg
Ross,Dave	Actual	90	247	37	63	15	1	21	52	37	75	0	.255	.579
Ross,Dave	Projected	65	151	17	37	8	1	6	20	11	36	0	.245	.430

Hitter	Season	G	AB	R	H	D	T	HR	RBI	BB	SO	SB	Avg	Slg
Carroll,Jamey	Actual	136	463	84	139	23	5	5	36	56	66	10	.300	.404
Carroll,Jamey	Projected	104	248	32	65	9	1	1	17	27	37	3	.262	.319

Hitter	Season	G	AB	R	H	D	T	HR	RBI	BB	SO	SB	Avg	Slg
Barmes,Clint	Actual	131	478	57	105	26	4	7	56	22	72	5	.220	.335
Barmes,Clint	Projected	147	577	85	163	35	2	15	70	26	62	9	.282	.428

Hitter	Season	G	AB	R	H	D	T	HR	RBI	BB	SO	SB	Avg	Slg
Morneau,Justin	Real	157	592	97	190	37	1	34	130	53	93	3	.321	.559
Morneau,Justin	Imaginary	135	474	66	125	25	3	25	83	44	86	0	.264	.487

Hitter	Season	G	AB	R	H	D	T	HR	RBI	BB	SO	SB	Avg	Slg
Atkins,Garrett	True	157	602	117	198	48	1	29	120	79	76	4	.329	.556
Atkins,Garrett	Fake	142	537	72	154	33	1	15	83	47	68	0	.287	.436

Hitter	Season	G	AB	R	H	D	T	HR	RBI	BB	SO	SB	Avg	Slg
Snelling,Chris	Reality	36	96	14	24	6	1	3	8	13	38	2	.250	.427
Snelling,Chris	Dream	116	394	61	125	26	2	10	56	45	66	2	.317	.470

Hitter	Season	G	AB	R	H	D	T	HR	RBI	BB	SO	SB	Avg	Slg
McCann,Brian	Honest	130	442	61	147	34	0	24	93	41	54	2	.333	.572
McCann,Brian	Simulated	89	311	41	85	19	1	10	44	38	45	3	.273	.437

Hitter	Season	G	AB	R	H	D	T	HR	RBI	BB	SO	SB	Avg	Slg
DeRosa,Mark	Him	136	520	78	154	40	2	13	74	44	102	4	.296	.456
DeRosa,Mark	Us	67	167	24	43	8	0	4	18	13	29	1	.257	.377

Hitter	Season	G	AB	R	H	D	T	HR	RBI	BB	SO	SB	Avg	Slg
Doumit,Ryan	Actual	61	149	15	31	9	0	6	17	15	42	0	.208	.389
Doumit,Ryan	Projected	127	388	59	111	24	1	16	65	24	78	3	.286	.477

Hitter	Season	G	AB	R	H	D	T	HR	RBI	BB	SO	SB	Avg	Slg
Lane,Jason	Actual	112	288	44	58	10	0	15	45	49	75	1	.201	.392
Lane,Jason	Projected	142	519	73	143	38	3	24	86	39	94	6	.276	.499

Hitter	Season	G	AB	R	H	D	T	HR	RBI	BB	SO	SB	Avg	Slg
Hermida,Jeremy	Actual	99	307	37	77	19	1	5	28	33	70	4	.251	.368
Hermida,Jeremy	Not	145	521	103	145	36	3	27	90	141	126	33	.278	.514

422

On the pages that follow are our projected batting records for all major league players in the year 2007. These will prove, in retrospect, to have been exactly as accurate as the projections for 2006 were. It is what it is; we are not soothsayers or mystics with crystal balls; we're just a bunch of hairy accountants with spreadsheets. Sometimes we're right, and sometimes we're wrong, and sometimes we're sorry we brought up the subject.

Addendum from Baseball Info Solutions:

The injury projections are courtesy of Sig Mejdal, now Senior Quantitative Analyst for the St. Louis Cardinals. Missing injury projections are not really missing at all, they're simply players who could not be projected due to insufficient data.

In the "Projected Career Totals" section, let it be known that we won't do a projection for players less than 25 years of age or for players who haven't played at least a few hundred games in the majors. We also won't do a projection for players whose careers are over or virtually over.

2007 Hitter Projections

Hitter	Team	Age	Inj	G	AB	H	2B	3B	HR	R	RBI	RC	BB	SO	SB	CS	SB%	Avg	OBP	Slg	OPS
Abreu,Bobby	NYY	33	high	160	588	170	43	2	21	104	99	118	123	141	26	9	.74	.289	.415	.476	.891
Adams,Russ	Tor	26	low	114	361	93	20	4	5	48	41	44	36	47	4	2	.67	.258	.327	.371	.703
Aguila,Chris	Fla	28	low	81	177	50	10	1	4	23	22	25	15	37	4	2	.67	.282	.339	.418	.757
Alfonzo,Eliezer	SF	28	med	110	367	97	19	2	13	39	49	47	16	84	2	1	.67	.264	.302	.433	.736
Alou,Moises	SF	40	high	134	503	143	28	1	23	67	83	85	53	56	3	2	.60	.284	.355	.481	.836
Amezaga,Alfredo	Fla	29	low	92	205	54	9	1	2	26	16	23	17	29	9	5	.64	.263	.326	.346	.672
Anderson,Brian	CWS	25	med	82	197	51	12	1	6	27	21	26	16	47	2	2	.50	.259	.324	.421	.745
Anderson,Garret	LAA	35	high	138	510	143	31	1	17	60	82	72	27	85	2	1	.67	.280	.317	.445	.762
Anderson,Marlon	LAD	33	med	107	230	60	12	1	6	29	26	29	18	39	4	2	.67	.261	.320	.400	.720
Atkins,Garrett	Col	27	med	157	605	188	45	1	22	97	104	114	67	71	2	1	.67	.311	.383	.498	.881
Aurilia,Rich	Cin	35	med	132	459	127	24	1	17	61	63	67	37	67	2	1	.67	.277	.333	.444	.778
Ausmus,Brad	Hou	38	high	123	360	85	14	1	3	34	33	34	37	57	2	2	.50	.236	.316	.306	.621
Aybar,Erick	LAA	23	low	124	466	122	24	4	6	69	44	48	20	51	44	22	.67	.262	.292	.369	.661
Aybar,Willy	Atl	24	med	79	268	74	18	1	6	32	35	38	28	37	2	2	.50	.276	.351	.418	.769
Baker,Jeff	Col	26	med	44	129	38	9	1	5	17	24	22	9	27	2	1	.67	.295	.341	.496	.837
Baldelli,Rocco	TB	25	low	123	461	141	29	5	16	74	68	77	23	81	13	5	.72	.306	.348	.495	.843
Barajas,Rod	Tex	31	med	122	439	108	27	0	16	55	61	52	23	72	0	0	.00	.246	.288	.417	.705
Bard,Josh	SD	29	med	92	251	71	17	0	7	28	36	38	25	37	1	0	1.00	.283	.348	.434	.782
Barfield,Josh	SD	24	med	150	536	155	30	2	13	72	63	77	36	86	22	7	.76	.289	.335	.425	.760
Barmes,Clint	Col	28	med	79	322	85	20	1	7	43	35	37	14	40	3	2	.60	.264	.305	.398	.703
Barrett,Michael	ChC	30	med	130	460	128	31	2	16	57	61	71	40	59	0	0	.00	.278	.341	.459	.800
Bartlett,Jason	Min	27	low	140	485	142	31	4	4	73	44	66	37	63	14	8	.64	.293	.350	.398	.748
Barton,Daric	Oak	21		75	207	54	13	2	3	30	28	29	33	33	1	1	.50	.261	.363	.386	.749
Bautista,Jose	Pit	26	med	95	262	66	16	1	10	35	35	37	29	62	2	2	.50	.252	.344	.435	.780
Bay,Jason	Pit	28	high	157	578	173	34	4	35	105	109	129	97	141	13	4	.76	.299	.405	.554	.959
Bell,David	Mil	34	high	143	497	126	27	1	11	56	60	60	48	70	2	1	.67	.254	.325	.378	.704
Bellhorn,Mark	SD	32	med	95	247	53	14	1	8	35	28	30	39	90	1	1	.50	.215	.326	.377	.703
Belliard,Ronnie	StL	32	high	153	586	158	38	1	14	76	70	78	50	89	3	2	.60	.270	.330	.410	.740
Beltran,Carlos	NYM	30	high	153	582	161	35	4	32	114	105	111	80	108	22	6	.79	.277	.368	.515	.883
Beltre,Adrian	Sea	28	high	154	582	158	34	2	26	78	89	89	46	104	8	4	.67	.271	.331	.471	.802
Bennett,Gary	StL	35	med	70	169	38	7	0	2	13	19	14	14	31	0	0	.00	.225	.288	.302	.590
Berkman,Lance	Hou	31	high	153	552	168	38	2	36	101	118	132	107	106	4	3	.57	.304	.423	.576	.999
Berroa,Angel	KC	29	med	116	377	97	17	2	8	45	40	41	15	69	5	2	.71	.257	.300	.377	.677
Betancourt,Yuniesky	Sea	25	low	157	557	155	29	7	8	63	51	66	20	49	12	9	.57	.278	.304	.399	.703
Betemit,Wilson	LAD	26	med	125	400	107	22	3	14	54	51	58	38	95	2	2	.50	.268	.331	.443	.774
Bigbie,Larry	StL	29	med	55	127	34	7	0	3	17	14	17	13	31	2	1	.67	.268	.336	.394	.729
Biggio,Craig	Hou	41	high	115	451	112	27	1	14	63	45	56	36	75	4	2	.67	.248	.325	.406	.730
Blake,Casey	Cle	33	high	138	499	127	28	1	20	70	65	69	49	117	6	4	.60	.255	.327	.435	.762
Blalock,Hank	Tex	26	med	155	599	164	35	2	23	85	95	91	56	111	1	1	.50	.274	.339	.454	.793
Blanco,Andres	KC	23	low	75	255	60	8	3	1	26	19	21	16	36	4	3	.57	.235	.283	.302	.585
Blanco,Henry	ChC	35	med	97	298	67	16	1	7	28	36	30	23	53	0	0	.00	.225	.283	.356	.638
Bloomquist,Willie	Sea	29	med	86	187	48	8	1	1	26	16	19	15	28	10	4	.71	.257	.319	.326	.645
Blum,Geoff	SD	34	med	123	361	86	20	1	7	38	40	38	29	64	1	1	.50	.238	.298	.357	.656
Bocachica,Hiram	Oak	31		124	343	91	17	1	6	52	45	52	35	70	16	7	.70	.265	.333	.452	.785
Bonds,Barry	SF	42	high	121	381	113	22	1	32	86	80	114	143	56	4	2	.67	.297	.495	.612	1.107
Boone,Aaron	Cle	34	med	94	269	67	14	1	8	35	36	33	21	50	5	2	.71	.249	.322	.398	.720
Borchard,Joe	Fla	28	med	58	163	40	7	0	8	21	19	22	16	45	1	0	1.00	.245	.317	.436	.752
Botts,Jason	Tex	26	low	51	123	33	8	1	5	19	19	20	15	34	2	1	.67	.268	.348	.472	.819
Bowen,Rob	SD	26	low	94	240	58	14	0	7	35	27	30	29	64	0	0	.00	.242	.323	.388	.711
Bradley,Milton	Oak	29	high	123	463	127	26	2	17	70	64	75	62	94	12	6	.67	.274	.364	.449	.813
Branyan,Russell	SD	31	high	114	364	84	18	1	23	50	59	56	51	144	2	1	.67	.231	.329	.475	.804
Broussard,Ben	Sea	30	high	118	372	98	21	2	16	49	55	54	30	86	2	1	.67	.263	.327	.460	.786
Brown,Emil	KC	32	high	128	433	123	28	2	13	59	64	67	41	75	5	2	.71	.284	.351	.448	.800
Bruntlett,Eric	Hou	29	low	97	196	47	8	1	3	26	18	21	22	35	6	3	.67	.240	.320	.337	.656
Buck,John	KC	26	med	121	418	104	24	1	13	47	60	50	27	90	0	0	.00	.249	.299	.404	.703
Burke,Chris	Hou	27	med	121	481	126	26	5	9	71	42	60	37	83	18	7	.72	.262	.324	.393	.717
Burnitz,Jeromy	Pit	38	high	130	423	101	20	1	21	58	66	57	44	99	3	2	.60	.239	.319	.440	.759
Burrell,Pat	Phi	30	high	139	480	124	27	1	27	71	92	87	86	138	0	0	.00	.258	.374	.488	.862
Byrd,Marlon	Was	29	med	74	187	49	11	1	4	26	20	23	16	36	3	2	.60	.262	.337	.396	.732
Byrnes,Eric	Ari	31	med	139	494	128	33	3	19	73	63	70	36	83	17	5	.77	.259	.316	.453	.769
Cabrera,Melky	NYY	22	low	130	460	131	24	2	10	69	60	67	46	57	12	4	.75	.285	.351	.411	.762
Cabrera,Miguel	Fla	24	med	160	609	200	48	3	32	113	125	142	80	119	7	4	.64	.328	.412	.575	.986
Cabrera,Orlando	LAA	32	high	155	604	162	41	2	10	78	69	77	47	58	20	6	.77	.268	.324	.392	.717
Cairo,Miguel	NYY	33	high	95	254	65	13	1	2	31	25	26	15	32	11	4	.73	.256	.308	.339	.646
Cameron,Mike	SD	34	med	136	523	131	31	4	21	80	76	79	68	146	20	8	.71	.250	.343	.446	.789
Cano,Robinson	NYY	24	med	149	557	181	44	3	17	80	83	99	23	60	4	2	.67	.325	.354	.506	.860
Cantu,Jorge	TB	25	med	128	476	126	31	1	17	55	75	63	23	84	1	0	1.00	.265	.303	.441	.744
Carroll,Jamey	Col	33	med	129	371	104	17	2	3	59	29	47	43	49	6	5	.55	.280	.360	.361	.721
Casey,Sean	Det	32	med	128	450	133	27	1	11	61	65	69	41	46	1	1	.50	.296	.363	.433	.797
Castillo,Jose	Pit	26	high	135	448	120	22	2	12	55	60	57	30	76	6	4	.60	.268	.317	.406	.723
Castillo,Luis	Min	31	med	147	568	169	18	4	3	87	44	77	67	61	24	12	.67	.298	.373	.359	.732
Castro,Bernie	Was	27	low	56	129	35	4	1	0	17	9	14	10	16	11	3	.79	.271	.324	.318	.642
Castro,Juan	Cin	35	high	120	341	83	17	1	5	30	34	32	16	55	1	1	.50	.243	.277	.343	.620
Castro,Ramon	NYM	31	med	84	230	55	13	0	8	27	29	30	28	60	0	0	.00	.239	.324	.400	.724
Catalanotto,Frank	Tor	33	high	135	465	139	34	3	9	65	57	75	46	50	2	1	.67	.299	.369	.443	.812
Cedeno,Ronny	ChC	24	low	99	284	77	12	3	4	32	25	32	12	49	6	4	.60	.271	.308	.377	.684
Chavez,Endy	NYM	29	low	89	220	60	11	2	2	29	19	26	15	24	8	3	.73	.273	.319	.368	.687
Chavez,Eric	Oak	29	high	150	573	151	34	2	28	90	95	96	79	116	4	2	.67	.264	.355	.476	.831
Choo,Shin-Soo	Cle	24	low	119	382	107	23	3	10	60	46	61	47	89	22	7	.76	.280	.360	.432	.792
Church,Ryan	Was	28	low	99	272	71	15	1	11	37	42	40	29	67	6	2	.75	.261	.337	.445	.781

424

2007 Hitter Projections

PLAYER				BATTING											BASERUNNING			AVERAGES			
Hitter	Team	Age	Inj	G	AB	H	2B	3B	HR	R	RBI	RC	BB	SO	SB	CS	SB%	Avg	OBP	Slg	OPS
Cintron,Alex	CWS	28	low	94	294	83	17	2	5	35	33	37	14	32	5	3	.62	.282	.317	.405	.722
Cirillo,Jeff	Mil	37	high	99	241	66	13	0	4	30	29	30	21	33	1	1	.50	.274	.340	.378	.717
Clark,Brady	Mil	34	med	139	420	114	20	1	7	53	40	53	42	55	5	4	.56	.271	.352	.374	.726
Clark,Tony	Ari	35	high	91	193	47	10	0	11	24	34	28	20	56	0	0	.00	.244	.321	.466	.787
Clayton,Royce	Cin	37	high	139	470	118	24	1	5	55	42	48	35	96	10	5	.67	.251	.307	.338	.645
Closser,JD	Col	27	low	71	181	48	12	1	5	22	23	26	20	32	3	1	.75	.265	.342	.425	.767
Conine,Jeff	Phi	41	high	124	272	72	15	1	5	28	35	34	24	40	2	1	.67	.265	.331	.382	.713
Cora,Alex	Bos	31	med	111	301	73	12	2	3	32	26	29	23	38	5	3	.62	.243	.313	.326	.639
Costa,Shane	KC	25	low	107	355	100	25	2	9	43	41	50	18	38	5	1	.83	.282	.324	.439	.763
Coste,Chris	Phi	34	med	68	203	55	12	0	6	22	28	27	12	32	1	0	1.00	.271	.321	.419	.740
Cota,Humberto	Pit	28	low	60	134	32	7	0	3	13	16	14	9	33	0	0	.00	.239	.292	.358	.650
Counsell,Craig	Ari	36	high	129	452	111	19	2	4	62	32	47	51	63	15	8	.65	.246	.330	.323	.653
Crawford,Carl	TB	25	low	156	633	190	26	14	15	100	76	101	34	88	55	13	.81	.300	.339	.457	.795
Crede,Joe	CWS	29	med	147	513	138	29	0	27	70	83	77	31	66	0	0	.00	.269	.318	.483	.802
Crisp,Coco	Bos	27	med	136	511	145	30	3	11	74	54	73	41	76	23	9	.72	.284	.337	.419	.756
Crosby,Bobby	Oak	27	high	120	431	110	25	2	15	63	55	61	46	84	9	3	.75	.255	.330	.427	.757
Cruz,Jose	LAD	33	high	87	248	60	14	1	10	35	31	37	39	61	4	2	.67	.242	.345	.427	.772
Cruz,Nelson	Tex	26	low	68	198	54	11	0	11	31	35	33	21	53	7	3	.70	.273	.342	.495	.837
Cuddyer,Michael	Min	28	med	151	568	158	38	4	23	93	88	95	63	119	6	3	.67	.278	.355	.481	.836
Damon,Johnny	NYY	33	med	154	627	179	35	4	17	115	75	98	68	82	22	8	.73	.285	.358	.435	.794
DaVanon,Jeff	Ari	33	med	115	304	82	15	2	7	49	37	45	46	54	13	6	.68	.270	.366	.401	.767
DeJesus,David	KC	27	low	134	524	156	35	5	10	85	61	82	50	71	7	5	.58	.298	.369	.441	.810
Delgado,Carlos	NYM	35	med	150	555	153	36	1	37	93	118	113	88	136	0	0	.00	.276	.387	.544	.931
Dellucci,David	Phi	33	med	128	354	90	16	3	17	60	52	56	48	93	4	2	.67	.254	.350	.460	.810
Denorfia,Chris	Cin	26	low	135	447	139	28	2	12	67	60	79	48	69	14	5	.74	.311	.379	.463	.842
DeRosa,Mark	Tex	32	high	122	444	121	28	1	10	63	54	59	36	86	3	2	.60	.273	.333	.408	.740
Diaz,Matt	Atl	29	low	110	348	110	25	3	10	46	49	59	17	58	7	4	.64	.316	.355	.491	.846
Doumit,Ryan	Pit	26	med	71	169	45	11	1	6	24	28	24	13	37	0	0	.00	.266	.361	.450	.811
Drew,J.D.	LAD	31	high	138	499	141	27	3	24	92	82	96	91	109	4	3	.57	.283	.398	.493	.891
Drew,Stephen	Ari	24	low	136	484	135	27	7	16	64	59	74	38	85	5	3	.62	.279	.331	.463	.794
Duffy,Chris	Pit	27	med	87	281	80	14	3	3	44	24	38	19	50	22	6	.79	.285	.343	.388	.731
Duncan,Chris	StL	26	low	153	554	151	27	3	33	90	90	99	66	135	1	1	.50	.273	.351	.511	.862
Dunn,Adam	Cin	27	high	161	579	140	32	1	43	108	99	114	123	194	7	3	.70	.242	.382	.523	.905
Durham,Ray	SF	35	low	146	549	155	33	4	19	91	72	89	60	77	9	5	.64	.282	.357	.461	.818
Dye,Jermaine	CWS	33	high	151	574	158	31	2	34	92	105	101	58	125	6	3	.67	.275	.348	.514	.862
Easley,Damion	Ari	37	high	88	184	43	9	1	6	23	22	22	18	32	2	1	.67	.234	.325	.391	.717
Eckstein,David	StL	32	med	148	589	166	24	2	4	85	42	68	45	49	10	6	.62	.282	.349	.350	.699
Edmonds,Jim	StL	37	high	142	488	130	32	1	30	85	90	95	86	149	5	3	.62	.266	.380	.520	.900
Ellis,Mark	Oak	30	med	125	410	112	22	2	10	64	47	57	41	59	3	2	.60	.273	.348	.410	.758
Ellison,Jason	SF	29	low	80	120	34	7	1	1	17	8	15	8	15	3	2	.60	.283	.333	.383	.717
Encarnacion,Edwin	Cin	24	low	148	557	154	44	1	23	81	91	92	55	108	9	4	.69	.276	.350	.483	.833
Encarnacion,Juan	StL	31	high	147	522	141	28	3	17	67	75	70	34	91	7	5	.58	.270	.322	.433	.755
Ensberg,Morgan	Hou	31	med	146	503	131	25	2	27	80	82	90	93	110	3	2	.60	.260	.380	.479	.859
Erstad,Darin	LAA	33	high	85	259	70	13	1	4	35	27	31	19	43	6	2	.75	.270	.327	.375	.702
Escobar,Alex	Was	28	low	53	130	37	7	1	6	20	22	22	13	28	2	1	.67	.285	.350	.492	.842
Estrada,Johnny	Ari	31	med	126	450	131	31	0	10	46	70	63	24	44	0	0	.00	.291	.334	.427	.761
Ethier,Andre	LAD	25	low	151	592	181	32	6	17	88	82	99	54	107	7	6	.54	.306	.367	.466	.833
Everett,Adam	Hou	30	low	145	505	127	26	3	8	62	51	54	31	79	11	5	.69	.251	.303	.362	.665
Everett,Carl	Sea	36	high	79	205	52	9	1	8	26	32	27	18	41	1	1	.50	.254	.335	.424	.759
Fahey,Brandon	Bal	26	low	61	180	49	7	1	1	24	16	21	18	26	5	3	.62	.272	.345	.339	.684
Fasano,Sal	NYY	35	med	52	125	28	6	0	5	12	14	13	6	33	0	0	.00	.224	.281	.392	.673
Feliz,Pedro	SF	32	low	144	491	122	27	2	19	60	75	60	27	92	1	1	.50	.248	.289	.428	.717
Fick,Robert	Was	33	high	54	163	41	8	0	4	18	21	19	17	28	1	1	.50	.252	.330	.374	.704
Fielder,Prince	Mil	23	med	157	528	148	33	1	30	78	87	96	58	113	7	3	.70	.280	.360	.517	.877
Fields,Josh	CWS	24		135	489	134	31	2	22	81	73	82	55	143	12	5	.71	.274	.347	.481	.828
Figgins,Chone	LAA	29	med	156	612	172	25	9	8	98	60	85	62	100	46	16	.74	.281	.348	.391	.739
Finley,Steve	SF	42	high	47	116	28	5	1	3	14	14	14	12	17	2	1	.67	.241	.319	.379	.708
Floyd,Cliff	NYM	34	high	124	416	111	26	1	19	62	67	67	47	83	8	3	.73	.267	.354	.471	.825
Ford,Lew	Min	30	med	103	286	79	17	1	6	44	31	39	26	42	9	4	.69	.276	.351	.406	.757
Franco,Julio	NYM	48	high	91	146	38	7	0	3	15	20	18	15	39	3	1	.75	.260	.333	.370	.703
Francoeur,Jeff	Atl	23	med	162	634	175	34	4	31	88	111	94	27	123	4	3	.57	.276	.314	.489	.803
Frandsen,Kevin	SF	25	low	59	148	40	11	1	2	20	14	17	5	15	3	2	.60	.270	.312	.399	.711
Freel,Ryan	Cin	31	high	139	508	136	29	3	7	78	33	68	61	88	38	14	.73	.268	.354	.378	.732
Freeman,Choo	Col	27	low	66	118	30	4	1	2	15	13	13	9	25	2	2	.50	.254	.307	.356	.663
Furcal,Rafael	LAD	29	med	158	631	181	32	6	13	108	59	95	66	91	32	12	.73	.287	.356	.418	.775
Garciaparra,Nomar	LAD	33	high	117	427	130	30	2	17	70	72	76	34	35	3	2	.60	.304	.364	.504	.868
Garko,Ryan	Cle	26	low	149	527	147	30	1	20	72	95	78	54	100	3	3	.50	.268	.341	.442	.783
Gathright,Joey	KC	26	low	88	206	54	7	2	1	34	18	24	21	37	17	6	.74	.262	.345	.330	.675
German,Esteban	KC	29	low	122	431	123	20	4	3	63	43	59	50	66	18	6	.75	.285	.362	.371	.734
Gerut,Jody	Pit	29		129	483	133	32	2	13	68	59	71	51	56	9	6	.60	.275	.347	.431	.778
Giambi,Jason	NYY	36	high	135	424	112	22	0	30	77	91	90	99	104	1	1	.50	.264	.419	.528	.947
Gibbons,Jay	Bal	30	high	117	394	105	25	1	17	48	58	59	32	56	0	0	.00	.266	.325	.464	.789
Giles,Brian	SD	36	high	160	601	170	38	4	21	96	94	111	113	71	9	4	.69	.283	.401	.464	.865
Giles,Marcus	Atl	29	high	148	569	160	39	2	15	95	66	88	65	105	12	5	.71	.281	.361	.436	.797
Glaus,Troy	Tor	30	high	146	540	137	30	1	37	95	100	106	88	139	4	3	.57	.254	.362	.519	.881
Gload,Ross	CWS	31	low	104	297	93	20	2	10	39	42	51	17	37	4	2	.67	.313	.352	.495	.847
Gomes,Jonny	TB	26	med	134	380	98	23	3	22	62	63	67	54	108	6	3	.67	.258	.359	.505	.864
Gomez,Alexis	Det	28	low	72	173	47	9	2	4	21	20	23	11	35	6	3	.67	.272	.315	.416	.731
Gomez,Chris	Bal	36	med	93	248	68	12	1	3	27	25	29	18	27	1	1	.50	.274	.328	.343	.695
Gonzalez,Adrian	SD	25	med	156	554	159	33	2	22	77	82	90	48	98	0	0	.00	.287	.345	.473	.818
Gonzalez,Alex	Bos	30	high	140	504	127	31	2	12	57	62	58	29	97	2	1	.67	.252	.301	.393	.693

2007 Hitter Projections

Hitter	Team	Age	Inj	G	AB	H	2B	3B	HR	R	RBI	RC	BB	SO	SB	CS	SB%	Avg	OBP	Slg	OPS
Gonzalez,Luis	Ari	39	high	144	475	131	32	1	18	74	70	80	66	61	1	1	.50	.276	.372	.461	.833
Gonzalez,Luis A	Col	28	low	72	186	53	10	1	4	23	21	25	10	27	1	1	.50	.285	.332	.414	.746
Gordon,Alex	KC	23		118	413	126	33	1	20	79	72	87	53	92	21	4	.84	.305	.384	.535	.919
Graffanino,Tony	Mil	35	med	76	279	76	16	1	4	43	31	35	26	43	4	2	.67	.272	.341	.380	.721
Granderson,Curtis	Det	26	med	159	588	164	32	11	21	94	75	97	63	156	11	6	.65	.279	.351	.478	.829
Green,Nick	NYY	28	low	85	199	46	11	1	4	25	18	20	16	52	2	1	.67	.231	.298	.357	.655
Green,Shawn	NYM	34	med	157	586	161	35	2	23	86	85	93	64	104	6	3	.67	.275	.353	.459	.812
Greene,Khalil	SD	27	med	140	506	132	34	2	17	65	71	70	43	96	6	3	.67	.261	.326	.437	.763
Greene,Todd	SF	36	high	66	185	47	10	0	7	18	25	22	8	44	0	0	.00	.254	.289	.422	.710
Griffey Jr.,Ken	Cin	37	high	105	406	107	20	0	26	62	72	70	48	82	1	1	.50	.264	.346	.505	.851
Gross,Gabe	Mil	27	med	91	203	53	14	1	5	30	26	30	28	47	3	1	.75	.261	.353	.414	.767
Grudzielanek,Mark	KC	37	high	140	539	154	29	2	7	71	49	67	29	77	4	2	.67	.286	.328	.386	.714
Guerrero,Vladimir	LAA	31	high	155	601	197	37	2	36	103	119	135	63	68	15	7	.68	.328	.397	.576	.973
Guiel,Aaron	NYY	34	high	86	252	63	14	0	11	40	38	36	28	55	1	1	.50	.250	.337	.437	.773
Guillen,Carlos	Det	31	high	142	537	161	33	4	15	91	75	91	62	88	13	8	.62	.300	.374	.460	.834
Guillen,Jose	Was	31	high	124	423	115	23	1	19	60	66	61	25	80	2	1	.67	.272	.329	.466	.795
Gutierrez,Franklin	Cle	24	low	49	105	27	8	0	2	18	10	13	10	23	3	2	.60	.257	.322	.390	.712
Guzman,Cristian	Was	29	high	139	399	103	18	5	5	51	34	43	21	58	9	5	.64	.258	.299	.366	.664
Gwynn,Tony	Mil	24	low	48	102	27	5	1	1	14	8	12	10	18	7	3	.70	.265	.330	.363	.693
Hafner,Travis	Cle	30	high	145	526	157	39	1	37	102	115	125	94	129	0	0	.00	.298	.413	.587	1.001
Hairston,Jerry	Tex	31	med	85	190	48	11	1	2	25	15	20	16	28	6	4	.60	.253	.330	.353	.683
Hairston,Scott	Ari	27	low	73	223	63	12	2	12	34	32	39	20	46	2	1	.67	.283	.342	.516	.857
Hall,Bill	Mil	27	med	150	526	141	36	3	24	82	71	83	48	131	11	7	.61	.268	.330	.485	.815
Hall,Toby	LAD	31	med	55	131	35	7	0	3	11	16	15	6	12	0	0	.00	.267	.314	.389	.704
Hardy,J.J.	Mil	24	med	115	417	105	24	0	13	53	55	54	45	57	1	1	.50	.252	.325	.403	.728
Harris,Willie	Bos	29	low	73	165	40	7	1	3	27	12	19	19	35	11	4	.73	.242	.324	.352	.676
Hart,Corey	Mil	25	low	112	350	99	25	3	13	54	55	57	29	77	19	8	.70	.283	.338	.483	.821
Hatteberg,Scott	Cin	37	high	114	400	106	21	0	9	49	47	54	55	41	1	1	.50	.265	.359	.385	.744
Hawpe,Brad	Col	28	low	152	586	170	37	5	26	80	101	111	83	132	5	4	.56	.290	.378	.503	.882
Helms,Wes	Fla	31	low	119	264	74	16	2	9	29	39	40	21	60	0	0	.00	.280	.345	.458	.803
Helton,Todd	Col	33	low	152	565	182	46	2	25	106	100	132	106	78	3	2	.60	.322	.433	.543	.977
Hermida,Jeremy	Fla	23	med	131	338	92	23	1	11	53	45	59	61	74	10	2	.83	.272	.388	.444	.832
Hernandez,Jose	Phi	37	med	70	124	31	5	0	4	14	15	15	11	38	0	0	.00	.250	.321	.387	.708
Hernandez,Ramon	Bal	31	high	132	485	131	27	1	19	59	79	71	40	71	1	0	1.00	.270	.335	.447	.782
Hill,Aaron	Tor	25	med	155	545	158	33	3	7	73	55	75	43	59	5	2	.71	.290	.351	.400	.751
Hillenbrand,Shea	SF	31	med	145	527	149	32	1	18	70	73	74	22	74	2	1	.67	.283	.326	.450	.776
Hinske,Eric	Bos	29	med	110	284	73	19	1	10	43	38	41	33	72	4	2	.67	.257	.341	.437	.777
Hollandsworth,Todd	Cin	34	high	66	162	42	11	1	5	20	21	22	13	38	1	1	.50	.259	.314	.432	.746
Holliday,Matt	Col	27	high	153	597	183	40	5	28	104	105	113	49	99	10	5	.67	.307	.368	.531	.899
Hollins,Damon	TB	33	med	97	175	44	11	0	7	21	21	23	12	30	2	1	.67	.251	.299	.434	.734
Howard,Ryan	Phi	27	high	160	586	191	33	1	56	106	148	167	100	168	0	0	.00	.326	.428	.672	1.101
Huber,Justin	KC	24	low	105	350	97	22	2	12	46	50	55	37	86	4	2	.67	.277	.346	.454	.801
Hudson,Orlando	Ari	29	low	152	562	157	33	6	13	78	66	81	52	83	7	5	.58	.279	.344	.429	.772
Huff,Aubrey	Hou	30	med	148	545	152	31	1	24	72	84	87	51	77	2	1	.67	.279	.346	.472	.818
Hunter,Torii	Min	31	high	142	545	146	30	2	26	83	88	82	43	107	13	7	.65	.268	.327	.473	.801
Iannetta,Christopher	Col	24	low	85	262	80	17	2	10	42	35	51	36	46	1	0	1.00	.305	.391	.500	.891
Ibanez,Raul	Sea	35	med	157	612	170	34	3	24	89	99	96	59	110	3	2	.60	.278	.343	.461	.804
Iguchi,Tadahito	CWS	32	high	130	485	138	22	1	15	79	63	72	50	91	9	5	.64	.285	.356	.427	.783
Infante,Omar	Det	25	low	115	370	94	19	4	7	45	38	43	24	64	9	4	.69	.254	.303	.384	.687
Inge,Brandon	Det	30	high	158	568	142	29	4	21	70	74	74	48	132	6	5	.55	.250	.314	.426	.740
Inglett,Joe	Cle	29	low	73	221	67	13	2	2	32	21	32	19	32	7	3	.70	.303	.361	.407	.768
Izturis,Cesar	ChC	27	med	143	489	128	24	4	2	54	40	50	30	46	8	5	.62	.262	.307	.339	.647
Izturis,Maicer	LAA	26	low	101	296	81	18	4	3	44	31	40	30	30	12	5	.71	.274	.345	.392	.736
Jackson,Conor	Ari	25	med	154	536	158	38	1	16	83	89	93	70	68	2	1	.67	.295	.382	.459	.841
Jackson,Damian	Was	33	med	90	197	45	10	1	4	29	17	21	22	50	6	3	.67	.228	.315	.350	.666
Jacobs,Mike	Fla	26	med	135	512	147	42	1	26	65	93	92	44	106	2	1	.67	.287	.345	.525	.870
Jenkins,Geoff	Mil	32	high	154	572	156	37	2	25	82	88	92	58	153	3	2	.60	.273	.351	.476	.827
Jeter,Derek	NYY	33	high	158	644	203	35	2	17	117	81	114	70	111	24	7	.77	.315	.393	.455	.848
Jimenez,D'Angelo	Oak	29	low	83	265	68	13	1	5	37	30	34	39	43	5	3	.62	.257	.354	.370	.724
Johjima,Kenji	Sea	31	med	135	488	143	25	1	18	59	75	72	20	40	3	1	.75	.293	.338	.459	.797
Johnson,Ben	SD	26	low	58	114	28	6	1	4	16	14	15	12	30	3	1	.75	.246	.317	.421	.739
Johnson,Dan	Oak	27	low	132	444	118	27	1	16	61	73	69	61	63	0	0	.00	.266	.354	.439	.794
Johnson,Kelly	Atl	25		71	221	61	14	2	7	36	32	37	33	43	5	2	.71	.276	.370	.452	.823
Johnson,Nick	Was	28	high	139	485	135	37	1	20	88	76	94	99	98	7	4	.64	.278	.411	.482	.893
Johnson,Reed	Tor	30	med	138	451	129	27	2	10	71	52	62	28	83	6	3	.67	.286	.349	.421	.771
Jones,Adam	Sea	21	low	57	145	39	7	1	5	22	19	20	10	33	6	2	.75	.269	.316	.434	.751
Jones,Andruw	Atl	30	high	159	594	157	32	2	40	102	115	108	74	131	5	3	.62	.264	.355	.527	.882
Jones,Chipper	Atl	35	med	133	484	142	30	1	27	84	90	101	83	87	6	3	.67	.293	.398	.527	.925
Jones,Jacque	ChC	32	high	149	534	145	29	1	23	73	75	78	38	118	9	5	.64	.272	.326	.459	.785
Kapler,Gabe	Bos	31	med	96	234	64	14	1	5	35	28	31	20	36	4	2	.67	.274	.336	.406	.742
Kearns,Austin	Was	27	high	139	506	135	33	2	24	83	87	87	72	130	6	3	.67	.267	.366	.482	.848
Kemp,Matt	LAD	22	low	154	576	179	39	6	20	111	98	108	49	123	23	6	.79	.311	.365	.503	.868
Kendall,Jason	Oak	33	high	145	564	166	27	1	3	75	50	71	54	49	9	6	.60	.291	.369	.358	.727
Kendrick,Howie	LAA	23	low	152	577	181	49	5	16	79	89	97	19	89	20	6	.77	.314	.339	.499	.838
Kennedy,Adam	LAA	31	med	147	505	142	28	3	7	64	54	65	39	82	17	9	.65	.281	.341	.390	.731
Kent,Jeff	LAD	39	high	144	538	154	35	2	23	83	93	94	61	95	3	2	.60	.286	.366	.487	.853
Keppinger,Jeff	KC	27	low	34	120	37	5	0	1	16	12	16	10	7	1	0	1.00	.308	.362	.375	.737
Kielty,Bobby	Oak	30	med	103	302	77	19	1	9	42	42	43	39	60	2	1	.67	.255	.346	.414	.760
Kinsler,Ian	Tex	25	low	155	539	145	33	1	20	84	74	79	47	78	15	6	.71	.269	.330	.445	.775
Klesko,Ryan	SD	36	high	135	414	111	25	1	17	59	68	70	68	75	4	3	.57	.268	.373	.457	.829
Konerko,Paul	CWS	31	high	158	589	168	30	0	35	91	109	108	66	105	1	0	1.00	.285	.364	.514	.878

2007 Hitter Projections

Hitter	Team	Age	Inj	G	AB	H	2B	3B	HR	R	RBI	RC	BB	SO	SB	CS	SB%	Avg	OBP	Slg	OPS
Koskie,Corey	Mil	34	high	116	411	107	28	1	16	58	58	64	54	101	5	3	.62	.260	.355	.450	.805
Kotchman,Casey	LAA	24	low	114	401	95	19	1	10	45	53	44	38	49	2	1	.67	.237	.305	.364	.669
Kotsay,Mark	Oak	31		146	589	167	34	3	12	75	66	83	53	67	7	5	.58	.284	.345	.413	.757
Kouzmanoff,Kevin	Cle	25	low	90	350	111	24	1	18	63	76	71	34	50	4	3	.57	.317	.378	.546	.923
Kubel,Jason	Min	25	med	75	230	61	11	1	9	31	34	32	17	43	3	1	.75	.265	.316	.439	.755
Laird,Gerald	Tex	27	low	83	264	72	16	2	8	41	32	38	20	54	5	2	.71	.273	.326	.439	.766
Lamb,Mike	Hou	31	low	124	338	94	18	2	11	51	46	50	31	56	1	1	.50	.278	.341	.441	.781
Lane,Jason	Hou	30	med	123	324	82	20	1	15	47	55	49	36	70	3	2	.60	.253	.331	.460	.791
Langerhans,Ryan	Atl	27	low	117	308	80	20	2	9	48	37	46	44	75	1	1	.50	.260	.356	.425	.781
LaRoche,Adam	Atl	27	med	151	513	144	39	1	29	80	89	95	55	113	0	0	.00	.281	.353	.530	.883
Laroche,Andy	LAD	23		128	457	131	26	0	18	74	77	78	63	77	9	5	.64	.287	.373	.462	.835
LaRue,Jason	Cin	33	med	106	338	80	19	1	13	39	46	43	34	97	1	1	.50	.237	.328	.414	.742
Lawton,Matt	Sea	35	med	82	138	35	7	0	4	21	17	19	19	20	4	2	.67	.254	.368	.391	.759
Lee,Carlos	Tex	31	high	161	623	180	39	1	33	100	112	111	56	79	14	6	.70	.289	.350	.514	.864
Lee,Derrek	ChC	31	high	151	572	166	36	2	32	95	93	113	79	127	15	8	.65	.290	.380	.528	.908
Lee,Travis	TB	32	low	84	200	49	10	1	6	24	25	26	24	39	3	1	.75	.245	.329	.395	.724
Lieberthal,Mike	Phi	35	high	114	329	90	21	0	11	39	47	47	24	37	0	0	.00	.274	.340	.438	.777
Lind,Adam	Tor	23	low	46	122	41	10	0	7	17	24	29	12	27	1	0	1.00	.336	.396	.590	.986
Linden,Todd	SF	27	low	80	190	49	10	1	6	28	22	26	21	49	3	1	.75	.258	.338	.416	.754
Lo Duca,Paul	NYM	35	med	136	516	148	31	1	8	62	60	67	32	41	3	2	.60	.287	.336	.397	.733
Lofton,Kenny	LAD	40	low	134	484	139	20	5	6	83	43	68	50	52	23	8	.74	.287	.356	.386	.743
Logan,Nook	Was	27	low	77	188	47	6	2	1	25	11	19	17	38	12	5	.71	.250	.312	.319	.631
Loney,James	LAD	23	low	137	498	152	36	4	11	72	70	82	42	60	9	5	.64	.305	.360	.460	.820
Lopez,Felipe	Was	27	high	149	575	156	30	4	15	90	67	84	66	124	27	11	.71	.271	.348	.416	.764
Lopez,Javy	Bos	36		121	381	103	20	1	14	44	54	53	25	78	0	0	.00	.270	.324	.438	.762
Lopez,Jose	Sea	23		151	567	158	36	5	11	75	77	73	24	70	5	3	.62	.279	.315	.418	.733
Loretta,Mark	Bos	35	high	148	590	171	31	1	7	75	59	78	52	59	4	2	.67	.290	.355	.381	.737
Lowell,Mike	Bos	33	high	146	502	137	36	0	18	66	77	76	48	62	2	1	.67	.273	.341	.452	.793
Lugo,Julio	LAD	31	high	149	564	156	30	3	11	85	55	77	53	96	26	11	.70	.277	.343	.399	.742
Luna,Hector	Cle	27	low	147	455	122	25	3	6	63	47	55	37	73	11	5	.69	.268	.326	.376	.702
Mabry,John	ChC	36	high	82	150	34	7	0	5	15	20	16	14	41	0	0	.00	.227	.297	.373	.670
Mackowiak,Rob	CWS	31	med	115	267	71	13	1	7	33	32	36	27	63	5	2	.71	.266	.342	.401	.743
Markakis,Nick	Bal	23	med	156	547	168	35	3	19	86	84	98	55	78	2	1	.67	.307	.373	.486	.859
Marte,Andy	Cle	23	low	137	459	115	34	2	18	59	69	67	52	100	1	1	.50	.251	.328	.451	.779
Martin,Russell	LAD	24	low	121	424	122	27	2	9	71	63	67	56	60	11	6	.65	.288	.375	.425	.799
Martinez,Ramon	LAD	34	low	72	181	49	9	1	2	20	21	22	15	24	0	0	.00	.271	.333	.365	.698
Martinez,Victor	Cle	28	high	147	557	171	39	0	18	79	93	101	68	77	0	0	.00	.307	.385	.474	.859
Matheny,Mike	SF	36	high	98	300	70	15	0	5	25	34	29	22	63	0	0	.00	.233	.292	.333	.626
Mathis,Jeff	LAA	24	low	49	118	29	8	1	3	16	13	14	8	24	1	1	.50	.246	.294	.407	.700
Matos,Luis	Was	28	high	63	134	35	8	1	3	18	13	17	10	23	6	2	.75	.261	.331	.403	.734
Matsui,Hideki	NYY	33	high	129	485	143	31	1	19	81	86	87	61	70	2	1	.67	.295	.376	.480	.856
Matsui,Kaz	Col	31	low	107	364	98	20	2	5	50	36	44	25	61	11	4	.73	.269	.320	.376	.696
Matthews Jr.,Gary	Tex	32	med	144	550	153	34	3	16	85	64	83	58	98	9	5	.64	.278	.349	.438	.787
Mauer,Joe	Min	24	low	130	487	161	33	3	12	77	73	98	69	50	8	3	.73	.331	.415	.485	.899
McCann,Brian	Atl	23	med	130	444	140	33	0	23	63	87	92	47	53	2	1	.67	.315	.383	.545	.928
McDonald,John	Tor	32	med	97	225	53	8	1	2	28	17	19	13	32	5	3	.62	.236	.283	.307	.590
McLouth,Nate	Pit	25	med	79	186	48	11	1	4	31	14	22	12	33	9	3	.75	.258	.320	.392	.713
McPherson,Dallas	LAA	26	med	81	250	61	13	2	15	36	42	36	18	90	3	2	.60	.244	.295	.492	.787
Melhuse,Adam	Oak	35	med	77	219	55	14	0	7	24	30	28	18	50	0	0	.00	.251	.308	.411	.719
Mench,Kevin	Mil	29	high	136	466	126	30	2	19	58	70	70	38	63	1	1	.50	.270	.332	.466	.798
Michaels,Jason	Cle	31	high	144	482	136	31	1	10	77	57	70	54	99	7	5	.58	.282	.357	.413	.770
Mientkiewicz,Doug	KC	33	med	100	292	77	20	1	6	35	35	41	38	45	2	1	.67	.264	.356	.401	.757
Miles,Aaron	StL	30	med	87	272	79	14	2	3	35	25	35	18	25	3	2	.60	.290	.339	.390	.729
Millar,Kevin	Bal	35		114	385	106	25	1	13	52	56	61	45	70	1	0	1.00	.275	.364	.447	.811
Milledge,Lastings	NYM	22	low	147	541	152	37	5	12	81	68	81	60	116	19	13	.59	.281	.356	.434	.790
Miller,Damian	Mil	37	high	105	364	90	23	0	8	38	42	43	36	95	0	0	.00	.247	.320	.376	.696
Mirabelli,Doug	Bos	36	med	56	150	32	8	0	5	15	20	16	15	49	0	0	.00	.213	.298	.367	.664
Moeller,Chad	Mil	32	low	56	131	30	6	0	3	13	14	13	11	29	0	0	.00	.229	.299	.344	.642
Mohr,Dustan	Bos	31	low	91	240	57	14	1	9	34	28	32	30	76	1	1	.50	.238	.327	.417	.744
Molina,Bengie	Tor	32	high	127	465	128	21	0	16	47	68	61	23	49	1	0	1.00	.275	.314	.424	.737
Molina,Jose	LAA	32	high	90	243	60	13	0	4	22	27	24	11	50	1	1	.50	.247	.282	.350	.632
Molina,Yadier	StL	24	high	118	360	88	19	0	6	30	46	36	24	32	1	1	.50	.244	.299	.347	.646
Monroe,Craig	Det	30	high	147	517	137	32	2	23	73	82	75	36	108	3	2	.60	.265	.316	.468	.783
Mora,Melvin	Bal	35	high	154	608	169	31	1	20	92	83	89	59	110	9	5	.64	.278	.353	.431	.784
Morales,Kendry	LAA	24	low	128	436	119	21	1	17	56	66	60	26	64	1	1	.50	.273	.314	.443	.757
Morneau,Justin	Min	26	med	157	593	174	35	2	34	91	118	111	55	94	2	1	.67	.293	.356	.531	.888
Munson,Eric	Hou	29	high	77	218	51	10	1	11	25	33	29	21	47	0	0	.00	.234	.307	.440	.747
Murphy,Tommy	LAA	27	low	56	116	30	6	1	3	15	13	14	7	25	4	3	.57	.259	.301	.405	.706
Murton,Matt	ChC	25	med	150	509	161	25	4	17	78	70	93	52	66	9	4	.69	.316	.383	.481	.864
Nady,Xavier	Pit	28	med	125	385	107	21	1	15	50	55	57	26	66	2	1	.67	.278	.333	.455	.788
Napoli,Mike	LAA	25	med	99	320	73	17	0	19	57	55	49	54	102	4	3	.57	.228	.345	.459	.804
Navarro,Dioner	TB	23	med	135	387	97	18	0	8	41	38	45	42	58	3	2	.60	.251	.326	.359	.685
Nevin,Phil	Min	36	high	103	304	77	14	0	14	40	52	44	33	80	1	0	1.00	.253	.330	.438	.768
Newhan,David	Bal	33	high	82	230	62	10	1	5	36	29	29	18	39	7	3	.70	.270	.328	.387	.715
Niekro,Lance	SF	28	low	82	202	53	11	1	7	25	29	26	10	30	0	0	.00	.262	.297	.431	.728
Nixon,Trot	Bos	33	high	128	449	125	28	2	16	71	69	75	64	74	1	1	.50	.278	.373	.457	.830
Norton,Greg	TB	34	med	103	318	79	15	0	14	41	44	44	38	80	1	1	.50	.248	.331	.428	.758
Nunez,Abraham	Phi	31	low	100	212	52	8	1	2	27	19	21	22	37	1	1	.50	.245	.319	.321	.640
Ojeda,Miguel	Tex	32	low	73	188	45	8	0	6	22	25	23	23	37	1	1	.50	.239	.325	.378	.703
Olivo,Miguel	Fla	28	med	126	408	103	22	3	14	52	55	48	18	93	6	4	.60	.252	.291	.424	.715
Ordonez,Magglio	Det	33	high	147	564	168	35	1	24	83	101	98	50	78	3	2	.60	.298	.359	.491	.850

2007 Hitter Projections

Hitter	Team	Age	Inj	G	AB	H	2B	3B	HR	R	RBI	RC	BB	SO	SB	CS	SB%	Avg	OBP	Slg	OPS
Ortiz,David	Bos	31	high	157	601	171	42	1	47	110	138	139	103	129	1	0	1.00	.285	.391	.592	.983
Overbay,Lyle	Tor	30	med	159	586	174	47	1	20	81	88	105	69	107	3	2	.60	.297	.373	.483	.856
Ozuna,Pablo	CWS	32	low	81	203	58	10	1	2	25	19	23	8	19	5	4	.56	.286	.322	.374	.697
Palmeiro,Orlando	Hou	38	low	83	108	28	5	0	1	12	11	11	10	14	1	1	.50	.259	.333	.333	.667
Patterson,Corey	Bal	27	high	147	575	150	27	5	20	81	63	75	31	133	39	11	.78	.261	.303	.430	.733
Paul,Josh	TB	32	med	77	188	46	9	0	2	21	17	18	16	42	1	1	.50	.245	.304	.324	.628
Paulino,Ronny	Pit	26	med	129	450	134	23	1	9	48	56	65	36	76	2	1	.67	.298	.351	.413	.764
Payton,Jay	Oak	34	high	100	295	82	14	1	8	39	35	38	17	33	3	2	.60	.278	.324	.414	.737
Pedroia,Dustin	Bos	23	low	157	619	176	47	3	10	79	72	91	67	43	3	3	.50	.284	.355	.418	.774
Pena,Carlos	Bos	29	low	68	152	39	8	1	8	23	24	25	22	42	1	1	.50	.257	.358	.480	.838
Pena,Tony F	Atl	26	low	40	114	30	5	1	1	14	9	12	5	23	4	2	.67	.263	.294	.351	.645
Pena,Wily Mo	Bos	25	med	121	415	115	20	1	23	57	68	67	31	127	2	1	.67	.277	.332	.496	.828
Pence,Hunter	Hou	24		39	109	30	6	1	6	19	19	19	11	22	4	1	.80	.275	.342	.514	.855
Peralta,Jhonny	Cle	25	low	138	523	146	32	3	15	80	69	79	52	124	0	0	.00	.279	.347	.438	.784
Perez,Antonio	Oak	27	low	66	125	31	6	1	3	17	14	15	12	34	2	1	.67	.248	.319	.384	.703
Perez,Eduardo	Sea	37	med	84	194	48	10	0	9	25	32	28	22	38	0	0	.00	.247	.330	.438	.768
Perez,Neifi	Det	34	low	106	297	76	14	1	3	32	27	29	11	27	2	1	.67	.256	.285	.340	.625
Phillips,Andy	NYY	30	low	76	154	40	8	1	7	23	21	22	11	32	1	1	.50	.260	.309	.461	.770
Phillips,Brandon	Cin	26	med	149	527	136	30	1	14	68	59	64	35	83	17	6	.74	.258	.308	.398	.706
Phillips,Jason	Tor	30	low	95	285	72	17	0	7	29	39	34	22	38	0	0	.00	.253	.315	.386	.701
Phillips,Paul	KC	30	low	45	100	24	5	0	2	11	10	10	5	11	0	0	.00	.240	.276	.350	.626
Piazza,Mike	SD	38	low	110	315	84	15	0	16	37	51	50	35	55	0	0	.00	.267	.344	.467	.810
Pie,Felix	ChC	22		51	171	49	11	2	6	25	17	27	13	37	6	4	.60	.287	.337	.480	.816
Pierre,Juan	ChC	29	low	158	633	189	25	8	2	89	42	81	38	37	49	20	.71	.299	.346	.373	.719
Pierzynski,A.J.	CWS	30	high	139	514	145	31	1	15	63	70	70	23	68	1	1	.50	.282	.325	.434	.759
Podsednik,Scott	CWS	31	high	130	511	138	27	4	5	78	41	64	50	88	40	17	.70	.270	.339	.368	.707
Polanco,Placido	Det	31	high	136	544	164	26	1	9	79	57	74	29	35	4	2	.67	.301	.346	.403	.749
Posada,Jorge	NYY	35	high	143	497	132	29	1	22	70	89	84	78	113	2	1	.67	.266	.373	.461	.834
Pujols,Albert	StL	27	low	155	591	197	46	2	50	136	141	169	94	59	7	3	.70	.333	.431	.672	1.102
Punto,Nick	Min	29	low	136	473	129	20	4	2	69	39	57	51	74	17	7	.71	.273	.344	.345	.688
Quentin,Carlos	Ari	24	low	158	631	170	48	5	25	104	100	105	72	98	9	3	.75	.269	.349	.480	.829
Quinlan,Robb	LAA	30	low	97	273	84	15	1	8	36	38	42	13	37	3	2	.60	.308	.341	.458	.799
Quintanilla,Omar	Col	25	low	62	177	46	10	1	2	22	13	20	12	27	2	1	.67	.260	.307	.362	.668
Quintero,Humberto	Hou	27	med	61	190	50	13	0	3	19	22	21	9	28	2	1	.67	.263	.296	.379	.675
Quiroz,Guillermo	Sea	25	low	43	105	26	6	0	4	11	18	13	8	25	0	0	.00	.248	.307	.419	.726
Ramirez,Aramis	ChC	29	high	151	577	169	36	1	35	87	111	108	47	70	1	1	.50	.293	.353	.541	.894
Ramirez,Hanley	Fla	23	low	158	594	169	41	9	14	104	59	94	53	102	46	16	.74	.285	.346	.455	.801
Ramirez,Manny	Bos	35	high	140	512	156	33	1	37	94	118	124	90	119	1	0	1.00	.305	.414	.590	1.004
Randa,Joe	Pit	37	low	80	225	61	14	1	5	27	29	30	18	32	0	0	.00	.271	.336	.409	.745
Redmond,Mike	Min	36	med	46	156	45	9	0	1	14	18	18	8	17	0	0	.00	.288	.343	.365	.709
Reed,Jeremy	Sea	26	low	118	402	110	24	4	8	59	42	54	35	52	9	7	.56	.274	.335	.413	.748
Renteria,Edgar	Atl	31	high	155	619	176	40	1	12	95	78	89	59	91	17	7	.71	.284	.349	.410	.759
Repko,Jason	LAD	26	low	90	197	48	8	1	5	30	19	22	17	41	10	4	.71	.244	.317	.371	.687
Reyes,Jose	NYM	24	low	147	605	175	29	14	13	107	65	94	39	69	58	15	.79	.289	.333	.448	.781
Riggans,Shawn	TB	26	low	51	152	43	9	0	4	16	20	21	11	33	1	0	1.00	.283	.331	.421	.752
Rios,Alex	Tor	26	low	151	519	155	34	7	14	80	75	85	38	95	16	7	.70	.299	.350	.472	.822
Rivera,Juan	LAA	28	low	134	456	137	30	0	20	63	76	79	34	53	1	1	.50	.300	.353	.498	.851
Rivera,Mike	Mil	30	low	62	186	47	9	0	8	21	29	23	11	34	1	1	.50	.253	.298	.430	.728
Roberts,Brian	Bal	29	med	151	602	172	39	3	10	94	59	90	66	79	32	11	.74	.286	.357	.410	.768
Roberts,Dave	SD	35	low	118	354	95	12	5	3	55	28	45	39	48	28	8	.78	.268	.346	.356	.702
Robles,Oscar	LAD	31	low	66	156	40	6	0	1	16	13	16	16	13	0	0	.00	.256	.329	.314	.644
Rodriguez,Alex	NYY	31	high	159	607	178	29	1	42	119	124	130	91	143	16	6	.73	.293	.395	.552	.947
Rodriguez,Ivan	Det	35	high	138	545	164	32	2	17	75	75	84	29	94	7	4	.64	.301	.339	.461	.799
Rodriguez,John	StL	29	low	92	225	60	12	2	8	31	33	34	24	54	1	0	1.00	.267	.343	.444	.787
Rodriguez,Luis	Min	27	low	66	126	33	7	0	1	15	11	14	13	14	0	0	.00	.262	.331	.341	.672
Rolen,Scott	StL	32	low	137	507	146	38	2	24	89	97	95	65	81	7	4	.64	.288	.378	.513	.890
Rollins,Jimmy	Phi	28	low	159	671	188	42	8	18	115	70	103	57	81	32	9	.78	.280	.339	.447	.786
Ross,Cody	Fla	26	low	66	138	34	8	1	6	20	20	19	12	32	1	1	.50	.246	.316	.449	.765
Ross,Dave	Cin	30	med	128	404	99	21	1	25	51	69	64	48	112	0	0	.00	.245	.330	.488	.817
Rowand,Aaron	Phi	29	med	143	531	145	33	2	16	78	65	71	29	101	12	6	.67	.273	.328	.433	.761
Ruiz,Carlos	Phi	28	low	89	258	74	16	2	9	35	39	42	25	35	2	2	.50	.287	.352	.469	.821
Saenz,Olmedo	LAD	36	high	61	142	37	9	0	7	19	25	21	12	35	0	0	.00	.261	.344	.472	.816
Sanchez,Freddy	Pit	29	med	155	562	179	44	2	6	77	67	88	36	49	4	2	.67	.319	.364	.436	.800
Sanders,Reggie	KC	39	high	114	374	93	20	1	18	53	57	52	34	102	10	5	.67	.249	.318	.452	.770
Santiago,Ramon	Det	27	low	53	105	23	4	1	1	13	9	9	8	16	3	1	.75	.219	.293	.305	.598
Schneider,Brian	Was	30	med	127	417	107	24	1	8	36	53	50	39	66	1	1	.50	.257	.323	.376	.700
Scott,Luke	Hou	29	low	143	485	138	30	5	26	72	82	93	60	101	6	3	.67	.285	.366	.528	.893
Scutaro,Marco	Oak	31	low	137	473	126	29	3	9	61	47	63	49	69	6	3	.67	.266	.335	.397	.733
Sexson,Richie	Sea	32	high	146	549	143	31	1	34	81	107	95	70	152	1	1	.50	.260	.349	.506	.856
Shealy,Ryan	KC	27	low	149	537	155	36	2	25	77	96	92	42	102	2	1	.67	.289	.341	.503	.844
Sheffield,Gary	NYY	38	low	123	470	137	22	0	26	82	88	90	69	61	8	4	.67	.291	.388	.504	.892
Shelton,Chris	Det	27	low	112	352	101	20	3	15	55	52	62	39	87	2	1	.67	.287	.363	.489	.852
Shoppach,Kelly	Cle	27	low	62	176	43	7	0	7	20	27	23	16	57	0	0	.00	.244	.307	.432	.739
Sizemore,Grady	Cle	24	low	162	647	190	45	10	27	127	87	122	70	131	21	9	.70	.294	.371	.519	.890
Sledge,Terrmel	SD	30	med	75	197	54	9	2	8	28	29	32	23	39	3	2	.60	.274	.350	.462	.812
Snelling,Chris	Sea	25	med	114	393	103	24	2	10	57	53	54	46	99	6	4	.60	.262	.342	.410	.752
Snyder,Chris	Ari	26	low	93	275	65	15	0	8	26	37	33	34	58	0	0	.00	.236	.323	.378	.701
Soriano,Alfonso	Was	31	high	158	644	177	41	2	38	105	95	108	46	146	31	12	.72	.275	.331	.522	.853
Spiezio,Scott	StL	34	high	85	197	47	11	1	6	25	28	24	21	41	1	1	.50	.239	.321	.396	.717
Spilborghs,Ryan	Col	27	low	60	227	73	16	2	5	35	28	41	22	40	7	3	.70	.322	.382	.476	.857
Stairs,Matt	Det	39	high	62	147	36	8	0	6	18	22	21	20	34	0	0	.00	.245	.351	.422	.773

428

2007 Hitter Projections

Hitter	Team	Age	Inj	G	AB	H	2B	3B	HR	R	RBI	RC	BB	SO	SB	CS	SB%	Avg	OBP	Slg	OPS
Stewart,Ian	Col	22		41	129	34	11	1	3	18	17	18	12	26	1	1	.50	.264	.326	.434	.760
Stewart,Shannon	Min	33	med	96	339	99	20	1	7	48	35	49	29	43	6	3	.67	.292	.357	.419	.775
Sullivan,Cory	Col	27	low	119	348	98	21	6	3	49	30	46	27	75	9	5	.64	.282	.335	.402	.737
Suzuki,Ichiro	Sea	33	med	157	661	210	23	5	10	102	54	102	47	67	33	9	.79	.318	.367	.413	.780
Sweeney,Mark	SF	37	med	121	175	45	10	1	5	21	27	25	24	41	0	0	.00	.257	.350	.411	.761
Sweeney,Mike	KC	33	high	118	455	131	30	0	20	64	82	79	51	70	4	2	.67	.288	.366	.486	.852
Swisher,Nick	Oak	26	med	153	562	140	34	2	32	100	97	96	88	135	1	1	.50	.249	.357	.488	.844
Taguchi,So	StL	37	med	122	282	75	15	1	3	35	31	32	21	39	7	3	.70	.266	.319	.358	.677
Taveras,Willy	Hou	25	low	153	541	158	17	4	2	85	30	65	32	83	34	11	.76	.292	.341	.349	.690
Teahen,Mark	KC	25	low	137	502	145	34	8	18	86	82	91	59	100	10	3	.77	.289	.366	.496	.862
Teixeira,Mark	Tex	27	med	160	624	179	43	3	39	106	124	127	81	126	2	1	.67	.287	.376	.553	.929
Tejada,Miguel	Bal	31	high	162	638	194	39	1	27	97	112	111	47	80	5	2	.71	.304	.360	.495	.856
Thames,Marcus	Det	30	med	112	379	97	21	2	23	59	60	62	41	89	1	1	.50	.256	.332	.504	.836
Theriot,Ryan	ChC	27	low	149	536	154	29	6	3	77	49	75	57	59	31	10	.76	.287	.357	.381	.737
Thomas,Frank	Oak	39	high	110	350	91	17	0	25	56	71	68	63	71	0	0	.00	.260	.380	.523	.903
Thome,Jim	CWS	36	high	144	510	134	25	1	38	94	103	108	110	162	0	0	.00	.263	.397	.539	.937
Thompson,Kevin	NYY	27	low	52	129	33	8	1	3	20	14	18	15	25	8	3	.73	.256	.333	.403	.736
Thorman,Scott	Atl	25	low	55	178	51	11	1	8	22	28	29	13	31	2	1	.67	.287	.335	.494	.829
Torrealba,Yorvit	Col	28	low	92	274	67	17	2	7	32	38	32	20	55	3	2	.60	.245	.303	.398	.701
Tracy,Chad	Ari	27	high	154	567	166	39	3	19	80	77	93	48	94	4	2	.67	.293	.352	.473	.825
Treanor,Matt	Fla	31	med	69	149	34	7	0	2	14	15	14	17	28	1	1	.50	.228	.320	.315	.635
Tulowitzki,Troy	Col	22	low	129	447	123	31	2	12	68	50	66	43	76	8	4	.67	.275	.340	.434	.774
Tyner,Jason	Min	30	low	63	167	49	6	1	0	23	12	20	12	17	4	2	.67	.293	.344	.341	.686
Uggla,Dan	Fla	27	low	157	614	175	32	5	28	104	95	102	52	115	8	5	.62	.285	.347	.490	.837
Upton,B.J.	TB	22	low	144	480	127	24	3	11	74	47	68	60	112	43	15	.74	.265	.348	.396	.743
Uribe,Juan	CWS	28	med	147	534	136	31	4	21	70	77	69	28	95	4	3	.57	.255	.296	.446	.741
Utley,Chase	Phi	28	med	152	568	168	38	3	27	100	99	106	58	102	12	4	.75	.296	.370	.516	.886
Valentin,Javier	Cin	31	low	93	221	58	11	1	9	27	34	31	19	35	0	0	.00	.262	.321	.443	.764
Valentin,Jose	NYM	37	high	120	370	87	19	2	17	54	52	50	40	85	5	3	.62	.235	.313	.435	.748
Varitek,Jason	Bos	35	high	129	468	121	29	1	17	60	69	69	56	118	2	1	.67	.259	.343	.434	.777
Victorino,Shane	Phi	26	low	147	538	143	21	8	12	81	55	67	36	75	11	6	.65	.266	.319	.401	.720
Vidro,Jose	Was	32	high	131	493	146	33	1	12	65	61	78	49	52	1	1	.50	.296	.363	.440	.803
Vizquel,Omar	SF	40	high	156	597	163	26	3	5	82	55	72	60	61	19	8	.70	.273	.343	.352	.695
Walker,Todd	SD	34	med	141	485	136	29	2	12	65	58	71	49	52	2	2	.50	.280	.349	.423	.772
Ward,Daryle	Atl	32	med	76	179	46	10	0	7	20	30	24	15	32	0	0	.00	.257	.318	.430	.748
Weeks,Rickie	Mil	24	med	148	542	147	30	6	16	96	63	82	57	128	23	7	.77	.271	.354	.437	.791
Wells,Vernon	Tor	28	med	156	618	178	40	3	30	91	100	108	50	89	12	4	.75	.288	.344	.508	.852
Werth,Jayson	LAD	28	high	102	337	84	20	2	12	51	51	49	42	99	13	4	.76	.249	.336	.427	.763
White,Rondell	Min	35	high	92	273	74	14	1	8	34	37	35	15	45	1	1	.50	.271	.323	.418	.741
Wigginton,Ty	TB	29	high	147	523	138	33	2	21	67	78	77	46	108	6	3	.67	.264	.328	.455	.783
Wilkerson,Brad	Tex	30	high	120	398	97	26	3	15	64	48	60	62	124	5	4	.56	.244	.351	.437	.788
Williams,Bernie	NYY	38	high	121	358	98	19	1	11	54	52	53	43	54	2	1	.67	.274	.355	.425	.779
Willingham,Josh	Fla	28	high	147	522	149	29	2	29	73	83	98	64	110	3	1	.75	.285	.370	.515	.885
Wilson,Craig	NYY	30	med	119	380	98	20	2	18	56	55	57	37	126	2	1	.67	.258	.344	.463	.807
Wilson,Jack	Pit	29	med	155	605	163	30	4	9	72	51	70	34	71	5	3	.62	.269	.313	.377	.689
Wilson,Preston	StL	32	high	128	441	115	24	1	19	58	71	62	36	116	9	5	.64	.261	.324	.449	.773
Wilson,Vance	Det	34	med	82	209	52	9	0	6	23	28	22	9	38	0	0	.00	.249	.293	.378	.671
Winn,Randy	SF	33	med	149	552	157	34	4	12	78	62	79	46	77	12	7	.63	.284	.346	.426	.772
Witt,Kevin	TB	31	low	46	107	29	6	0	6	15	19	17	8	29	0	0	.00	.271	.322	.495	.817
Wood,Brandon	LAA	22		63	229	61	23	11	0	12	12	28	0	55	0	0	.00	.266	.266	.463	.729
Woodward,Chris	NYM	31	med	90	223	55	13	1	4	26	26	25	19	54	1	1	.50	.247	.309	.368	.676
Wright,David	NYM	24	low	150	567	179	42	3	29	100	112	122	66	99	18	6	.75	.316	.392	.554	.946
Youkilis,Kevin	Bos	28	low	153	584	165	44	1	14	101	77	99	103	110	5	3	.62	.283	.395	.433	.828
Young,Chris	Ari	23	low	142	481	128	38	3	25	83	76	85	54	97	24	7	.77	.266	.341	.514	.855
Young,Delmon	TB	21	low	157	594	179	34	6	18	83	89	92	23	110	33	10	.77	.301	.330	.470	.799
Young,Dmitri	Det	33	med	95	307	84	17	1	13	41	43	46	24	65	1	1	.50	.274	.334	.463	.797
Young,Michael	Tex	30	high	161	674	209	41	4	17	101	91	110	48	97	7	4	.64	.310	.357	.458	.815
Zaun,Gregg	Tor	36	high	88	252	64	14	0	7	32	33	34	36	41	0	0	.00	.254	.352	.393	.745
Zimmerman,Ryan	Was	22	med	157	578	174	50	2	20	85	102	103	55	101	10	7	.59	.301	.363	.498	.861
Zobrist,Ben	TB	26	low	141	472	134	28	6	5	63	45	69	60	66	14	8	.64	.284	.365	.400	.765

Projected Career Totals for Active Players
Note: These projections assume that the player will be healthy.

PLAYER	BATTING												BASERUNNING			AVERAGES			
Hitter	G	AB	H	2B	3B	HR	R	RBI	RC	RC27	BB	SO	SB	CS	SB%	Avg	OBP	Slg	OPS
Abreu,Bobby	2536	9030	2626	637	52	331	1574	1489	1815	7.21	1780	2143	404	138	.75	.291	.406	.483	.889
Adams,Russ	1834	6104	1531	334	34	86	786	688	701	3.96	618	801	62	34	.65	.251	.320	.359	.679
Alou,Moises	2316	8317	2462	489	41	388	1261	1486	1539	6.79	483	1053	111	41	.73	.296	.363	.505	.868
Amezaga,Alfredo	996	2323	593	89	13	23	293	174	239	3.47	187	348	92	59	.61	.255	.317	.334	.651
Anderson,Garret	2275	8752	2562	533	34	297	1089	1404	1319	5.50	433	1281	76	46	.62	.293	.323	.463	.786
Anderson,Marlon	1372	3761	998	202	24	79	458	423	472	4.40	272	561	78	29	.73	.265	.316	.395	.711
Atkins,Garrett	2214	8399	2508	604	9	285	1255	1407	1470	6.47	915	1089	20	12	.62	.299	.370	.474	.844
Aurilia,Rich	1956	6882	1892	363	22	237	921	917	993	5.15	551	1050	29	21	.58	.275	.329	.437	.766
Ausmus,Brad	2060	6466	1618	275	32	80	736	628	705	3.74	652	1029	101	54	.65	.250	.324	.340	.664
Barajas,Rod	1312	4232	1007	256	1	149	505	576	474	3.82	224	746	1	1	.50	.238	.280	.405	.685
Bard,Josh	1514	4840	1318	309	1	133	500	670	689	5.08	473	749	5	2	.71	.272	.335	.419	.754
Barmes,Clint	1608	5823	1489	351	15	117	745	625	635	3.78	259	762	47	34	.58	.256	.295	.381	.676
Barrett,Michael	2085	7273	1936	472	35	225	840	906	1023	4.97	617	1004	11	15	.42	.266	.327	.434	.761
Bay,Jason	2104	7725	2174	457	36	427	1282	1363	1525	7.07	1252	2130	138	57	.71	.281	.385	.516	.901
Bell,David	1912	6418	1636	351	21	158	762	778	794	4.30	581	918	23	23	.50	.255	.320	.390	.710
Bellhorn,Mark	1040	2831	638	155	16	91	423	327	373	4.39	459	993	34	16	.68	.225	.337	.388	.724
Belliard,Ronnie	1993	7209	1925	464	26	156	948	834	955	4.67	665	1127	45	34	.57	.267	.330	.404	.734
Beltran,Carlos	2606	9874	2672	556	77	475	1794	1662	1742	6.21	1268	1894	385	89	.81	.271	.354	.487	.841
Beltre,Adrian	2798	10336	2758	581	35	432	1328	1532	1513	5.15	814	1883	131	66	.66	.267	.325	.455	.780
Bennett,Gary	700	1921	456	83	3	24	159	215	181	3.20	163	330	5	4	.56	.237	.301	.321	.623
Berkman,Lance	2382	8503	2506	574	25	514	1498	1709	1900	8.17	1635	1727	76	48	.61	.295	.411	.548	.960
Berroa,Angel	1797	6124	1558	269	35	119	729	620	640	3.61	241	1152	92	42	.69	.254	.296	.368	.664
Betemit,Wilson	1966	6273	1633	340	29	203	791	758	860	4.80	609	1585	26	18	.59	.260	.325	.421	.746
Bigbie,Larry	862	2285	603	110	5	54	301	251	229	4.55	229	576	38	15	.72	.264	.329	.387	.716
Biggio,Craig	3130	11821	3283	724	53	324	1970	1264	1803	5.41	1252	1892	423	127	.77	.278	.362	.430	.792
Blake,Casey	1214	4142	1052	238	8	163	584	534	566	4.71	394	967	45	36	.56	.254	.326	.433	.759
Blalock,Hank	2467	9392	2497	528	22	355	1285	1438	1368	5.15	897	1878	16	11	.59	.266	.331	.440	.771
Blanco,Henry	977	2835	632	157	12	70	276	328	290	3.41	246	522	4	10	.29	.223	.285	.361	.646
Bloomquist,Willie	855	1954	499	87	11	10	270	165	204	3.58	150	332	98	28	.78	.255	.313	.327	.639
Blum,Geoff	1479	4236	1033	228	14	95	471	479	475	3.83	346	739	22	20	.52	.244	.303	.372	.674
Bocachica,Hiram	1152	3283	823	158	8	130	460	385	437	4.51	323	713	105	58	.64	.251	.318	.422	.741
Bonds,Barry	3478	11539	3412	702	80	884	2566	2320	3187	10.01	3215	1798	527	148	.78	.296	.452	.600	1.052
Boone,Aaron	1375	4537	1175	248	18	147	608	642	602	4.60	348	823	124	38	.77	.259	.323	.419	.742
Borchard,Joe	1010	2649	615	99	2	119	332	302	319	4.06	249	734	9	11	.45	.232	.301	.406	.707
Bradley,Milton	1853	6693	1788	371	21	224	964	877	1014	5.29	876	1421	152	80	.66	.267	.355	.429	.785
Branyan,Russell	1355	3978	886	196	8	244	523	616	584	4.89	554	1647	18	10	.64	.223	.320	.460	.780
Broussard,Ben	1238	3632	949	205	19	151	472	539	521	5.03	300	831	21	12	.64	.261	.325	.453	.778
Brown,Emil	1028	3470	964	222	14	97	461	510	512	5.28	326	643	42	17	.71	.278	.342	.434	.776
Bruntlett,Eric	963	1886	453	83	8	31	254	177	202	3.60	198	346	52	26	.67	.240	.314	.342	.656
Buck,John	1834	6440	1551	363	11	199	681	877	729	3.87	423	1507	9	5	.64	.241	.293	.393	.686
Burke,Chris	1800	6273	1619	347	34	110	898	535	739	4.05	497	1129	180	86	.68	.258	.322	.377	.699
Burnitz,Jeromy	2071	6818	1708	348	30	368	1063	1147	1068	5.37	851	1642	81	63	.56	.251	.340	.472	.812
Burrell,Pat	2052	7177	1803	382	16	379	1006	1299	1214	5.87	1222	2139	5	1	.83	.251	.361	.467	.828
Byrd,Marlon	1259	3780	968	202	16	74	508	378	446	4.08	317	773	53	28	.65	.256	.323	.377	.699
Byrnes,Eric	1639	5458	1389	346	33	193	790	665	738	4.67	410	968	152	43	.78	.254	.315	.436	.751
Cabrera,Orlando	2278	8425	2227	547	34	148	1067	951	1054	4.37	621	817	240	70	.77	.264	.315	.390	.705
Cairo,Miguel	1399	3861	1017	189	29	35	484	372	428	3.85	230	461	146	46	.76	.263	.312	.355	.667
Cameron,Mike	2148	7550	1867	424	62	297	1159	1076	1119	5.03	963	2132	338	106	.76	.247	.338	.438	.776
Carroll,Jamey	1207	3457	946	156	21	22	541	251	419	4.47	395	517	50	41	.55	.274	.351	.350	.701
Casey,Sean	1876	6578	1953	402	12	176	916	962	1045	5.87	613	739	19	7	.73	.297	.363	.442	.804
Castillo,Jose	2142	7500	1934	364	21	195	869	959	886	4.10	507	1408	69	49	.58	.258	.305	.390	.695
Castillo,Luis	2297	8708	2528	264	67	44	1309	580	1142	4.66	1030	1118	424	191	.69	.290	.365	.351	.716
Castro,Juan	1326	3306	775	162	16	52	307	305	307	3.14	174	572	7	9	.44	.234	.271	.340	.612
Castro,Ramon	1127	3221	731	178	0	113	354	406	393	4.10	395	872	1	0	1.00	.227	.311	.387	.699
Catalanotto,Frank	1730	5590	1641	392	41	113	799	679	863	5.64	511	691	49	30	.62	.294	.360	.439	.799
Chavez,Endy	1179	3025	814	148	35	27	398	264	352	4.05	192	334	112	48	.70	.269	.311	.368	.679
Chavez,Eric	2489	9080	2373	523	26	435	1381	1484	1457	5.68	1187	1842	73	32	.70	.261	.346	.468	.814
Church,Ryan	1477	4686	1188	257	14	173	592	700	647	4.76	490	1177	68	35	.66	.254	.327	.425	.752
Cintron,Alex	1929	6519	1779	354	40	106	745	712	775	4.21	329	730	62	41	.60	.273	.308	.388	.697
Cirillo,Jeff	1776	5734	1693	358	19	119	840	763	891	5.68	590	748	64	39	.62	.295	.365	.427	.791
Clark,Brady	1354	3834	1043	181	8	67	488	380	486	4.45	381	495	69	47	.59	.272	.352	.376	.728
Clark,Tony	1541	4582	1204	244	10	254	638	822	756	5.80	514	1214	6	9	.40	.263	.338	.487	.824
Clayton,Royce	2541	8783	2247	429	59	124	1093	848	982	3.84	670	1699	257	114	.69	.256	.310	.360	.671
Conine,Jeff	2213	7388	2097	408	37	221	915	1122	1123	5.49	704	1235	55	32	.63	.284	.345	.439	.784
Cora,Alex	1608	4341	1043	169	37	51	453	375	423	3.31	319	572	56	29	.66	.240	.310	.331	.641
Counsell,Craig	1608	5231	1323	233	35	47	724	406	593	3.88	621	729	136	64	.68	.253	.338	.338	.676
Crede,Joe	1979	6903	1801	375	3	331	892	1069	957	4.87	407	982	4	8	.33	.261	.309	.460	.769
Crisp,Coco	2064	7769	2152	447	37	160	1082	798	1037	4.70	603	1186	253	124	.67	.277	.328	.406	.734
Crosby,Bobby	2073	7561	1843	443	19	239	1047	908	970	4.37	623	1605	101	48	.68	.244	.320	.402	.722
Cruz,Jose	1664	5474	1349	298	37	237	814	732	829	5.17	780	1343	121	46	.72	.246	.338	.444	.782
Cuddyer,Michael	1980	7054	1881	459	36	264	1078	1021	1085	5.42	780	1625	62	36	.63	.267	.344	.454	.798
Damon,Johnny	2621	10263	2922	548	101	242	1793	1180	1574	5.48	1034	1274	401	126	.76	.285	.350	.429	.779
DaVanon,Jeff	1174	3109	806	141	21	75	481	358	435	4.80	454	623	120	55	.69	.259	.352	.390	.742
DeJesus,David	1887	7128	2062	468	51	128	1112	798	1053	5.34	685	1042	77	62	.55	.289	.362	.423	.785
Delgado,Carlos	2507	8903	2461	590	20	583	1505	1862	1830	7.38	1422	2222	9	7	.56	.276	.385	.544	.929
Dellucci,David	1411	3593	922	165	40	146	570	512	544	5.24	450	936	50	30	.62	.257	.346	.447	.792
DeRosa,Mark	1205	3607	972	212	6	82	506	424	465	4.56	284	681	21	18	.54	.269	.329	.400	.729
Drew,J.D.	2088	7197	1986	373	51	342	1294	1138	1350	6.68	1267	1642	101	44	.70	.276	.388	.485	.872

430

Projected Career Totals for Active Players
Note: These projections assume that the player will be healthy.

PLAYER	BATTING												BASERUNNING			AVERAGES			
Hitter	G	AB	H	2B	3B	HR	R	RBI	RC	RC27	BB	SO	SB	CS	SB%	Avg	OBP	Slg	OPS
Dunn,Adam	2499	8951	2099	483	10	618	1584	1462	1646	6.21	1887	3109	104	45	.70	.234	.375	.498	.873
Durham,Ray	2551	9588	2657	559	92	270	1584	1129	1477	5.45	1039	1508	292	114	.72	.277	.351	.439	.790
Dye,Jermaine	2240	8149	2214	435	29	416	1231	1375	1331	5.79	764	1744	68	37	.65	.272	.338	.485	.823
Easley,Damion	1664	5264	1314	285	26	156	714	648	672	4.36	500	912	117	57	.67	.250	.328	.403	.730
Eckstein,David	1931	7323	2032	296	28	55	1041	530	842	4.08	559	638	158	77	.67	.277	.347	.348	.696
Edmonds,Jim	2439	8453	2347	538	24	492	1523	1507	1654	6.98	1328	2335	82	58	.59	.278	.376	.522	.898
Ellis,Mark	1637	5686	1501	300	28	127	851	616	741	4.58	571	903	37	21	.64	.264	.337	.394	.731
Ellison,Jason	936	1887	519	106	9	23	269	123	227	4.23	123	242	51	27	.65	.275	.322	.377	.699
Encarnacion,Juan	1985	7049	1880	363	57	231	902	988	941	4.66	448	1292	158	78	.67	.267	.316	.433	.749
Ensberg,Morgan	1713	5714	1454	272	19	288	852	896	953	5.77	977	1254	41	32	.56	.254	.367	.460	.827
Erstad,Darin	1691	6255	1767	329	32	127	950	729	874	5.00	492	965	190	60	.76	.282	.337	.406	.743
Estrada,Johnny	1511	5312	1486	352	0	106	515	778	688	4.68	296	597	0	0	.00	.280	.324	.406	.730
Everett,Adam	1674	5433	1332	266	28	84	650	543	553	3.46	332	905	120	50	.71	.245	.298	.351	.648
Everett,Carl	1598	5277	1420	278	27	220	765	862	804	5.34	482	1117	110	56	.66	.269	.339	.457	.797
Fasano,Sal	643	1615	355	71	0	69	180	194	167	3.44	96	453	2	3	.40	.220	.287	.392	.679
Feliz,Pedro	1342	4173	1035	223	24	159	507	627	507	4.19	223	800	14	11	.56	.248	.285	.427	.712
Fick,Robert	1247	3689	938	178	14	100	423	493	465	4.37	369	610	13	14	.48	.254	.325	.391	.716
Figgins,Chone	1786	6640	1840	266	85	77	1029	632	875	4.58	658	1118	443	172	.72	.277	.340	.378	.718
Finley,Steve	2726	9802	2651	468	127	317	1495	1224	1449	5.18	886	1372	327	123	.73	.270	.332	.441	.773
Floyd,Cliff	2022	6696	1826	430	25	299	1024	1076	1126	5.94	753	1353	178	57	.76	.273	.355	.478	.833
Ford,Lew	1058	2957	798	162	16	59	446	323	398	4.73	280	461	83	27	.75	.270	.348	.395	.743
Franco,Julio	2563	8733	2604	411	54	175	1292	1198	1352	5.64	918	1357	282	107	.72	.298	.365	.418	.782
Freel,Ryan	1326	4520	1192	241	26	59	679	279	588	4.44	553	833	306	116	.73	.264	.355	.368	.723
Furcal,Rafael	2532	9898	2759	482	82	187	1621	880	1399	4.98	1014	1504	449	165	.73	.279	.345	.401	.746
Garciaparra,Nomar	1902	7325	2268	498	61	301	1232	1226	1360	6.94	537	694	105	39	.73	.310	.361	.518	.878
Gathright,Joey	1405	3652	927	127	24	11	570	306	375	3.44	367	681	252	107	.70	.254	.332	.311	.642
Gerut,Jody	1282	4240	1124	276	16	113	565	508	587	4.83	439	541	62	43	.59	.265	.338	.418	.755
Giambi,Jason	2336	7891	2202	444	8	500	1401	1592	1683	7.67	1615	1719	20	13	.61	.279	.411	.527	.939
Gibbons,Jay	1366	4548	1195	274	10	199	565	674	661	5.12	365	659	2	6	.25	.263	.319	.459	.778
Giles,Brian	2308	8096	2320	504	60	352	1376	1352	1618	7.21	1534	1047	136	55	.71	.287	.401	.494	.895
Giles,Marcus	2158	8095	2231	551	25	207	1292	917	1209	5.30	911	1543	148	67	.69	.276	.354	.427	.781
Glaus,Troy	2389	8564	2100	457	11	539	1442	1506	1469	5.87	1373	2330	83	46	.64	.245	.352	.490	.842
Gload,Ross	1162	3266	988	209	11	103	409	457	522	5.91	193	433	30	17	.64	.303	.342	.468	.810
Gomes,Jonny	1786	5861	1452	324	26	319	889	918	947	5.52	831	1743	77	50	.61	.248	.347	.475	.823
Gomez,Chris	1498	4612	1203	234	18	63	515	487	529	4.00	415	739	36	33	.52	.261	.326	.360	.686
Gonzalez,Alex	2145	7554	1839	448	34	183	828	899	824	3.73	427	1550	38	25	.60	.243	.291	.384	.676
Gonzalez,Luis	2822	10014	2809	654	68	388	1547	1553	1733	6.18	1292	1341	125	86	.59	.281	.367	.476	.842
Gonzalez,Luis A	1617	5134	1432	285	14	119	609	575	661	4.62	273	788	22	20	.52	.279	.321	.409	.730
Graffanino,Tony	1418	4352	1162	231	27	76	670	458	560	4.51	417	727	75	36	.68	.267	.335	.385	.720
Granderson,Curtis	2182	8162	2179	451	97	284	1219	976	1247	5.36	901	2291	120	69	.63	.267	.340	.450	.791
Green,Nick	1022	2447	572	126	11	43	315	219	245	3.37	197	649	19	15	.56	.234	.303	.347	.650
Green,Shawn	2590	9318	2584	569	40	417	1439	1390	1570	6.00	999	1752	173	64	.73	.277	.352	.481	.833
Greene,Khalil	2154	7769	1916	514	23	244	934	982	982	4.34	669	1675	62	32	.66	.247	.313	.413	.726
Greene,Todd	954	2796	698	146	3	117	296	379	338	4.18	121	636	5	4	.56	.250	.284	.430	.714
Griffey Jr.,Ken	2796	10380	2932	549	36	681	1754	1944	2053	7.10	1320	1938	181	68	.73	.282	.365	.539	.904
Gross,Gabe	1187	2881	743	187	9	71	423	368	407	4.91	407	678	33	19	.63	.258	.351	.403	.754
Grudzielanek,Mark	2167	8275	2361	445	38	106	1097	739	1032	4.49	426	1159	141	57	.71	.285	.327	.387	.714
Guerrero,Vladimir	2884	10904	3468	636	48	633	1807	2055	2314	7.95	1111	1349	265	134	.66	.318	.385	.559	.944
Guiel,Aaron	784	2298	564	128	0	90	359	301	301	4.47	230	506	14	17	.45	.245	.328	.419	.746
Guillen,Carlos	2204	8040	2293	463	57	195	1273	1055	1230	5.49	890	1438	125	81	.61	.285	.357	.430	.786
Guillen,Jose	1939	6532	1751	348	26	255	863	974	891	4.82	361	1242	31	30	.51	.268	.321	.446	.768
Guzman,Cristian	1986	6582	1683	290	94	74	842	550	693	3.61	342	1002	157	87	.64	.256	.294	.361	.655
Hafner,Travis	1910	6810	1945	503	15	439	1223	1411	1488	7.95	1170	1785	7	4	.64	.286	.399	.557	.957
Hairston,Jerry	962	2803	719	154	17	34	373	234	321	3.89	243	372	121	59	.67	.257	.331	.360	.691
Hall,Bill	2326	8318	2114	563	39	333	1178	1067	1172	4.84	737	2303	138	93	.60	.254	.314	.451	.766
Hall,Toby	1231	3944	1028	212	1	80	338	474	429	3.81	177	358	2	8	.20	.261	.296	.376	.672
Harris,Willie	900	2019	481	72	9	23	313	131	206	3.39	216	417	118	43	.73	.238	.313	.317	.630
Hatteberg,Scott	1505	4845	1301	272	6	119	609	593	688	5.04	646	570	4	8	.33	.269	.359	.401	.759
Hawpe,Brad	1918	6891	1922	414	38	281	890	1130	1197	6.22	982	1653	42	34	.55	.279	.367	.472	.840
Helms,Wes	1382	3294	887	192	18	113	357	464	471	5.07	270	800	2	9	.18	.269	.332	.441	.773
Helton,Todd	2519	9110	2924	722	40	443	1708	1641	2142	8.95	1612	1289	49	34	.59	.321	.424	.555	.979
Hernandez,Jose	1657	4742	1197	198	33	172	637	618	611	4.43	395	1429	41	38	.52	.252	.312	.417	.729
Hernandez,Ramon	2030	7056	1843	376	10	258	837	1080	961	4.79	584	1065	12	1	.92	.261	.325	.427	.752
Hillenbrand,Shea	1594	5631	1592	334	17	179	737	776	776	4.98	229	772	23	13	.64	.283	.325	.443	.768
Hinske,Eric	1447	4306	1096	281	18	145	648	574	617	4.95	499	1063	72	31	.70	.255	.334	.429	.763
Hollandsworth,Todd	1402	3839	1034	235	25	116	529	482	542	4.94	313	856	80	47	.63	.269	.324	.434	.758
Holliday,Matt	2261	8547	2543	472	50	372	1389	1442	1515	6.49	702	1576	115	63	.65	.298	.360	.507	.867
Hollins,Damon	602	1432	350	82	1	54	169	173	172	4.10	90	257	18	9	.67	.244	.288	.416	.704
Howard,Ryan	2232	8291	2511	456	10	711	1356	1932	2077	9.34	1401	2603	0	1	.00	.303	.406	.618	1.024
Hudson,Orlando	1962	7088	1911	403	63	158	935	816	962	4.79	642	1145	77	47	.62	.270	.332	.411	.743
Huff,Aubrey	2000	7252	1999	397	16	309	920	1078	1123	5.53	648	1059	35	24	.59	.276	.338	.463	.801
Hunter,Torii	2093	7619	2000	413	33	327	1107	1184	1083	4.93	574	1555	180	91	.66	.263	.319	.454	.774
Ibanez,Raul	1742	5975	1666	328	34	227	865	950	934	5.60	558	1021	44	28	.61	.279	.340	.459	.799
Iguchi,Tadahito	1247	4627	1260	204	12	135	707	576	641	4.89	466	939	77	40	.66	.272	.342	.409	.751
Inge,Brandon	1661	5436	1320	268	40	176	635	668	660	4.12	456	1289	52	46	.53	.243	.306	.404	.710
Izturis,Cesar	2140	7471	1918	354	45	32	789	586	728	3.36	437	775	129	79	.61	.257	.299	.329	.628
Izturis,Maicer	1707	5721	1530	338	46	53	821	569	714	4.33	592	595	181	94	.66	.267	.338	.370	.709
Jackson,Damian	1128	2820	673	151	20	43	421	250	324	3.84	311	674	151	48	.76	.239	.320	.352	.672
Jenkins,Geoff	2002	7087	1918	455	26	316	1033	1093	1133	5.68	675	1881	41	18	.69	.271	.346	.476	.822

Projected Career Totals for Active Players

Note: These projections assume that the player will be healthy.

PLAYER	BATTING												BASERUNNING			AVERAGES			
Hitter	G	AB	H	2B	3B	HR	R	RBI	RC	RC27	BB	SO	SB	CS	SB%	Avg	OBP	Slg	OPS
Jeter,Derek	2942	11701	3604	597	60	298	2089	1428	1985	6.29	1221	2119	374	110	.77	.308	.383	.446	.828
Jimenez,D'Angelo	1334	4259	1088	208	23	76	568	457	543	4.39	593	747	68	43	.61	.255	.347	.369	.716
Johnson,Dan	1552	5172	1346	304	8	182	676	826	774	5.26	717	747	0	1	.00	.260	.346	.428	.773
Johnson,Nick	2069	7265	1947	530	6	276	1183	1091	1285	6.21	1421	1567	82	58	.59	.268	.398	.457	.855
Johnson,Reed	1478	4730	1330	270	22	102	728	551	626	4.74	283	898	54	32	.63	.281	.348	.412	.761
Jones,Andruw	3051	11125	2884	571	40	677	1798	2009	1876	5.87	1305	2516	166	75	.69	.259	.344	.500	.844
Jones,Chipper	2629	9545	2825	567	35	516	1698	1753	2008	7.70	1606	1609	155	57	.73	.296	.395	.520	.920
Jones,Jacque	1931	6755	1843	362	21	271	921	929	972	5.08	462	1488	115	63	.65	.273	.324	.453	.777
Kapler,Gabe	1368	3678	988	215	17	87	544	449	491	4.68	318	584	85	36	.70	.269	.329	.407	.736
Kearns,Austin	2232	8073	2076	524	21	360	1252	1335	1304	5.62	1157	2180	75	41	.65	.257	.357	.461	.818
Kendall,Jason	2459	9079	2670	456	33	83	1270	859	1235	4.93	867	795	203	101	.67	.294	.375	.379	.754
Kennedy,Adam	2060	6903	1903	369	48	95	865	721	864	4.41	501	1138	217	99	.69	.276	.333	.384	.717
Kent,Jeff	2673	9842	2808	641	51	433	1518	1745	1693	6.20	972	1825	105	63	.62	.285	.355	.493	.847
Kielty,Bobby	1192	3436	863	205	8	101	481	476	477	4.80	466	709	32	12	.73	.251	.345	.404	.749
Klesko,Ryan	2069	6532	1804	391	32	322	999	1143	1200	6.53	982	1252	97	47	.67	.276	.370	.494	.864
Konerko,Paul	2376	8555	2391	416	5	471	1261	1520	1481	6.25	913	1466	7	1	.88	.279	.353	.494	.847
Koskie,Corey	1646	5589	1479	364	16	203	807	797	870	5.44	742	1367	96	51	.65	.265	.358	.444	.802
Kotsay,Mark	2284	8519	2385	475	53	174	1092	942	1177	4.93	745	1026	122	74	.62	.280	.337	.409	.747
Lamb,Mike	1334	3756	1037	190	22	109	554	497	534	5.08	325	614	12	13	.48	.276	.334	.425	.759
Lane,Jason	1249	3312	808	196	13	151	454	520	468	4.83	351	765	27	16	.63	.244	.319	.448	.767
Langerhans,Ryan	1655	4756	1204	306	22	126	704	548	668	4.87	675	1214	15	13	.54	.253	.349	.406	.756
LaRoche,Adam	1992	6818	1827	509	6	351	996	1138	1149	5.98	722	1643	0	4	.00	.268	.337	.499	.836
LaRue,Jason	1351	4185	970	236	7	153	473	557	498	4.01	388	1245	17	14	.55	.232	.322	.401	.723
Lawton,Matt	1780	5808	1531	318	17	167	908	748	858	5.12	820	767	190	80	.70	.264	.365	.410	.776
Lee,Carlos	2323	8735	2468	520	13	433	1345	1504	1466	6.02	750	1224	170	66	.72	.283	.339	.494	.832
Lee,Derrek	2312	8169	2253	506	29	421	1276	1260	1479	6.41	1091	1980	162	81	.67	.276	.364	.499	.864
Lee,Travis	1396	4406	1122	226	18	135	554	570	605	4.76	534	838	67	24	.74	.255	.335	.406	.741
Lieberthal,Mike	1836	6283	1703	384	10	215	764	891	894	5.07	487	819	8	7	.53	.271	.335	.438	.773
Lo Duca,Paul	1610	5872	1675	345	9	110	725	703	780	4.80	391	469	29	26	.53	.285	.336	.403	.739
Lofton,Kenny	2427	9150	2702	418	123	139	1680	870	1457	5.72	1043	1134	659	175	.79	.295	.367	.413	.780
Logan,Nook	907	2168	555	74	22	10	285	130	226	3.53	189	411	118	50	.70	.256	.314	.324	.639
Lopez,Felipe	2463	9300	2413	482	44	236	1370	1035	1244	4.60	1066	2197	299	144	.67	.259	.336	.397	.733
Lopez,Javy	2128	7389	2064	374	22	332	899	1139	1133	5.51	491	1411	8	19	.30	.279	.330	.471	.801
Loretta,Mark	2133	7687	2247	402	23	100	1004	790	1056	5.01	709	806	61	41	.60	.292	.357	.390	.747
Lowell,Mike	2002	6983	1878	488	4	260	911	1070	1056	5.36	672	967	34	15	.69	.269	.334	.452	.786
Lugo,Julio	1938	7029	1907	358	37	133	1030	682	921	4.58	650	1304	264	112	.70	.271	.336	.390	.725
Luna,Hector	1822	5795	1526	329	23	72	771	596	677	4.06	485	982	129	68	.65	.263	.323	.365	.688
Mabry,John	1375	3525	928	189	6	100	393	461	457	4.55	293	748	7	12	.37	.263	.321	.405	.727
Mackowiak,Rob	1528	4216	1083	199	24	110	523	500	539	4.42	417	1064	78	35	.69	.257	.330	.394	.724
Martinez,Ramon	1167	2923	779	141	13	42	332	338	349	4.22	251	465	8	7	.53	.267	.325	.367	.692
Martinez,Victor	2155	8066	2361	524	1	248	1055	1290	1338	6.09	957	1192	1	3	.25	.293	.368	.450	.818
Matheny,Mike	1595	4678	1109	230	9	81	418	533	455	3.30	325	966	8	14	.36	.237	.292	.342	.634
Matos,Luis	632	1859	476	99	10	35	246	164	220	4.05	127	342	83	28	.75	.256	.314	.377	.691
Matsui,Hideki	1358	4937	1427	311	10	186	789	857	848	6.27	601	740	15	9	.62	.289	.365	.469	.834
Matsui,Kaz	1016	3293	869	174	18	43	435	316	382	4.05	231	578	84	30	.74	.264	.314	.367	.681
Matthews Jr.,Gary	1840	6303	1669	368	33	172	938	700	883	4.90	671	1238	112	56	.67	.265	.336	.416	.751
McDonald,John	858	1933	451	71	13	14	236	137	161	2.79	102	304	35	16	.69	.233	.278	.305	.583
Melhuse,Adam	786	2140	528	126	1	72	229	289	268	4.32	174	479	1	2	.33	.247	.303	.407	.711
Mench,Kevin	1678	5659	1506	353	19	225	700	824	823	5.14	455	827	15	11	.58	.266	.326	.454	.781
Michaels,Jason	1278	3739	1032	231	10	80	586	434	534	5.07	436	807	42	31	.58	.276	.352	.407	.759
Mientkiewicz,Doug	1275	3921	1048	260	10	81	487	475	554	4.98	516	586	19	18	.51	.267	.356	.401	.757
Miles,Aaron	1279	4167	1162	187	24	38	514	354	482	4.13	258	422	45	30	.60	.279	.323	.363	.685
Millar,Kevin	1547	4937	1388	325	15	173	679	743	801	5.86	561	887	8	7	.53	.281	.363	.458	.821
Miller,Damian	1356	4368	1118	280	4	110	478	533	558	4.46	426	1105	4	5	.44	.256	.325	.397	.722
Mirabelli,Doug	752	1915	434	105	2	73	209	264	234	4.11	211	563	3	0	1.00	.227	.312	.398	.710
Moeller,Chad	677	1814	409	88	6	40	182	184	180	3.32	149	424	2	4	.33	.225	.290	.347	.636
Mohr,Dustan	1108	2979	704	167	12	103	415	333	377	4.28	342	950	19	16	.54	.236	.319	.404	.723
Molina,Bengie	1703	5955	1606	258	3	182	577	849	733	4.38	285	620	4	7	.36	.270	.306	.406	.712
Molina,Jose	790	1992	479	98	2	35	187	212	189	3.23	97	438	12	7	.63	.240	.279	.344	.623
Monroe,Craig	1501	4963	1295	288	17	217	681	780	696	4.90	344	1039	35	23	.60	.261	.308	.457	.765
Mora,Melvin	1780	6346	1748	332	13	206	968	853	936	5.22	642	1199	109	60	.64	.275	.355	.429	.784
Morneau,Justin	2352	8666	2425	507	21	472	1260	1671	1507	6.26	831	1543	16	15	.52	.280	.343	.507	.850
Munson,Eric	1186	3659	804	152	6	171	374	526	428	3.89	354	831	9	2	.82	.220	.293	.405	.697
Nady,Xavier	1477	4551	1221	243	10	164	562	611	621	4.83	305	869	25	14	.64	.268	.327	.434	.761
Nevin,Phil	1471	4874	1302	240	6	239	672	857	782	5.68	522	1201	20	5	.80	.267	.340	.466	.806
Newhan,David	779	2138	561	88	12	48	326	263	262	4.26	169	385	59	22	.73	.262	.319	.382	.702
Nixon,Trot	1798	6008	1636	368	35	223	954	928	993	5.88	834	1109	35	18	.66	.272	.363	.457	.819
Norton,Greg	1080	2681	671	137	8	109	351	374	378	4.85	319	675	16	18	.47	.250	.331	.429	.760
Nunez,Abraham	1210	2878	699	102	21	24	343	250	286	3.38	287	514	39	18	.68	.243	.313	.318	.631
Ojeda,Miguel	827	2210	514	82	1	67	240	300	252	3.85	263	424	8	8	.50	.233	.316	.362	.678
Olivo,Miguel	1580	5102	1224	265	24	167	613	644	550	3.64	232	1315	73	47	.61	.240	.278	.399	.679
Ordonez,Magglio	2159	8104	2413	491	21	354	1212	1428	1418	6.42	709	1053	98	53	.65	.298	.356	.495	.851
Ortiz,David	2231	8088	2233	557	17	547	1365	1726	1686	7.48	1284	1823	9	2	.82	.276	.374	.552	.926
Overbay,Lyle	1793	6328	1826	495	4	199	844	916	1071	6.16	776	1251	26	15	.63	.289	.366	.462	.829
Ozuna,Pablo	516	1215	350	58	10	9	150	99	141	4.11	44	117	42	26	.62	.288	.325	.374	.700
Palmeiro,Orlando	1188	2340	644	115	14	13	306	231	287	4.33	259	236	38	28	.58	.275	.350	.353	.703
Patterson,Corey	2148	7686	1949	350	52	253	1044	817	935	4.15	410	1886	375	125	.75	.254	.296	.411	.708
Paul,Josh	719	1643	405	81	2	20	194	158	168	3.50	142	367	18	10	.64	.247	.306	.335	.640
Payton,Jay	1407	4569	1287	213	26	137	628	566	630	4.94	282	547	43	35	.55	.282	.327	.430	.756

432

Projected Career Totals for Active Players
Note: These projections assume that the player will be healthy.

PLAYER						BATTING							BASERUNNING			AVERAGES			
Hitter	G	AB	H	2B	3B	HR	R	RBI	RC	RC27	BB	SO	SB	CS	SB%	Avg	OBP	Slg	OPS
Pena,Carlos	1347	4256	1044	203	21	210	589	625	639	5.14	567	1258	30	21	.59	.245	.337	.451	.788
Perez,Antonio	1165	2747	671	139	13	57	360	289	318	3.94	267	727	48	22	.69	.244	.317	.367	.684
Perez,Eduardo	970	2271	559	111	3	101	298	369	314	4.73	248	488	19	13	.59	.246	.326	.431	.757
Perez,Neifi	1707	5930	1578	275	64	72	726	561	651	3.85	260	577	63	49	.56	.266	.295	.370	.666
Phillips,Brandon	2024	7116	1769	401	12	179	854	779	810	3.88	473	1209	163	74	.69	.249	.299	.384	.682
Phillips,Jason	1196	3676	903	206	0	85	360	475	413	3.87	294	504	0	4	.00	.246	.310	.371	.681
Piazza,Mike	2366	8296	2470	406	7	494	1188	1538	1621	7.21	931	1363	17	20	.46	.298	.369	.527	.896
Pierre,Juan	2215	8641	2562	321	100	27	1223	574	1088	4.47	534	533	605	247	.71	.296	.346	.366	.712
Pierzynski,A.J.	2036	7263	2023	433	20	191	864	967	947	4.68	321	977	12	16	.43	.279	.324	.423	.747
Podsednik,Scott	1074	3801	1032	191	33	39	586	297	492	4.44	371	647	325	114	.74	.272	.339	.370	.709
Polanco,Placido	2116	7810	2304	370	25	129	1108	798	1034	4.85	429	559	73	39	.65	.295	.340	.398	.739
Posada,Jorge	2103	7137	1873	417	8	311	1023	1242	1179	5.80	1134	1726	21	23	.48	.262	.369	.454	.823
Pujols,Albert	3060	11600	3752	867	23	867	2448	2559	3019	9.93	1814	1295	107	55	.66	.323	.419	.626	1.046
Punto,Nick	1174	3486	924	142	25	21	496	281	399	3.97	364	598	113	50	.69	.265	.332	.338	.670
Quinlan,Robb	1132	3355	1007	189	10	98	424	442	503	5.53	171	477	29	19	.60	.300	.336	.450	.786
Ramirez,Aramis	2622	9807	2750	582	19	531	1344	1758	1654	6.08	755	1391	20	17	.54	.280	.337	.506	.843
Ramirez,Manny	2766	9979	3041	641	17	691	1824	2228	2335	8.71	1637	2288	36	31	.54	.305	.405	.580	.985
Randa,Joe	1844	6327	1782	381	38	142	802	852	894	5.09	503	869	42	26	.62	.282	.337	.421	.758
Redmond,Mike	958	2902	832	157	2	17	263	316	342	4.29	171	337	1	2	.33	.287	.340	.360	.700
Reed,Jeremy	1940	6634	1757	405	42	117	921	671	842	4.41	619	871	119	89	.57	.265	.330	.391	.721
Renteria,Edgar	2859	10932	3073	634	30	190	1615	1281	1499	4.87	1002	1621	355	148	.71	.281	.341	.397	.738
Rios,Alex	2267	8047	2301	520	72	196	1155	1079	1188	5.28	603	1613	194	100	.66	.286	.336	.442	.778
Rivera,Juan	1865	6485	1875	413	2	258	837	1023	1032	5.79	483	852	17	23	.42	.289	.340	.473	.813
Roberts,Brian	2066	7937	2187	510	36	123	1192	750	1105	4.89	852	1112	343	130	.73	.276	.344	.395	.740
Roberts,Dave	1027	3240	869	111	54	30	515	260	430	4.57	359	421	282	74	.79	.268	.344	.364	.707
Rodriguez,Alex	3064	11709	3429	584	31	772	2234	2273	2432	7.54	1555	2669	335	102	.77	.293	.383	.546	.929
Rodriguez,Ivan	2800	10639	3168	635	50	356	1530	1483	1671	5.76	593	1661	140	72	.66	.298	.336	.467	.803
Rolen,Scott	2498	9078	2540	644	38	427	1548	1674	1653	6.51	1186	1738	136	63	.68	.280	.369	.500	.869
Rollins,Jimmy	2659	10769	2906	643	108	244	1701	1053	1488	4.83	885	1460	442	144	.75	.270	.327	.418	.745
Ross,Dave	1405	4504	1059	228	10	259	534	721	661	4.99	527	1299	0	0	.00	.235	.318	.463	.781
Rowand,Aaron	1935	6513	1740	390	24	195	932	785	844	4.54	361	1293	123	58	.68	.267	.325	.424	.749
Saenz,Olmedo	860	2067	548	133	5	93	283	346	316	5.39	175	458	3	4	.43	.265	.340	.469	.809
Sanchez,Freddy	1745	6200	1911	460	16	64	815	702	906	5.47	388	592	35	21	.62	.308	.352	.419	.770
Sanders,Reggie	2076	7125	1873	384	63	345	1150	1112	1149	5.56	747	1865	327	125	.72	.263	.338	.480	.817
Santiago,Ramon	1043	2547	561	92	13	28	304	199	208	2.68	180	401	56	30	.65	.220	.287	.300	.586
Schneider,Brian	1549	4901	1228	274	12	97	421	602	573	4.04	463	831	10	13	.43	.251	.318	.371	.689
Scutaro,Marco	1524	4958	1258	295	25	87	596	473	595	4.15	480	800	44	24	.65	.254	.317	.376	.693
Sexson,Richie	1962	7105	1856	393	20	441	1065	1378	1233	6.09	870	1975	16	16	.50	.261	.346	.508	.855
Sheffield,Gary	2784	10056	2952	510	24	554	1753	1860	2039	7.35	1585	1244	247	111	.69	.294	.393	.514	.908
Shelton,Chris	1794	6245	1754	361	32	257	927	886	1041	6.01	690	1557	17	12	.59	.281	.355	.472	.828
Snyder,Chris	1741	5814	1336	316	0	166	522	773	686	3.98	744	1261	0	1	.00	.230	.318	.370	.688
Soriano,Alfonso	2024	7904	2150	485	26	428	1239	1129	1255	5.55	502	1788	363	127	.74	.272	.324	.502	.826
Spiezio,Scott	1411	4130	1045	236	30	129	543	581	561	4.69	433	647	36	24	.60	.253	.326	.418	.745
Stairs,Matt	1604	4691	1234	267	11	237	687	817	787	5.88	647	985	25	22	.53	.263	.357	.476	.833
Stewart,Shannon	1698	6457	1907	381	42	133	980	684	986	5.54	573	820	204	81	.72	.295	.359	.429	.788
Sullivan,Cory	1677	5421	1493	317	55	44	738	442	670	4.36	424	1226	115	68	.63	.275	.327	.379	.706
Suzuki,Ichiro	1838	7478	2402	267	70	108	1171	628	1179	5.92	516	748	370	102	.78	.321	.369	.419	.788
Sweeney,Mark	1299	2084	538	116	11	53	253	303	296	4.95	295	481	15	9	.62	.258	.350	.401	.751
Sweeney,Mike	1863	6704	1969	429	4	286	977	1198	1186	6.47	719	894	65	34	.66	.294	.366	.487	.853
Swisher,Nick	2055	7394	1792	449	15	398	1234	1227	1198	5.56	1167	1870	5	4	.56	.242	.352	.469	.820
Taguchi,So	720	1546	424	83	7	22	201	188	193	4.42	113	231	42	14	.75	.274	.324	.380	.704
Teixeira,Mark	2454	9486	2609	631	28	558	1496	1802	1791	6.84	1205	2013	31	14	.69	.278	.367	.529	.895
Tejada,Miguel	2898	11262	3249	657	24	461	1667	1900	1810	5.84	837	1553	99	42	.70	.288	.344	.474	.818
Thames,Marcus	1228	4045	1010	219	10	235	612	632	628	5.36	433	986	9	10	.47	.250	.325	.483	.808
Thomas,Frank	2533	8760	2593	516	11	574	1601	1834	2030	8.53	1787	1530	32	23	.58	.296	.416	.554	.970
Thome,Jim	2518	8552	2342	449	25	619	1628	1708	1893	7.90	1821	2620	18	19	.49	.274	.402	.549	.952
Torrealba,Yorvit	1350	4209	1003	255	23	99	473	557	466	3.76	317	883	36	20	.64	.238	.297	.380	.678
Tracy,Chad	2238	8266	2347	566	25	268	1096	1073	1282	5.61	708	1457	39	23	.63	.284	.342	.456	.798
Tyner,Jason	660	1861	522	57	14	0	238	129	203	3.88	110	194	72	21	.77	.280	.323	.326	.649
Uribe,Juan	2309	8284	2061	469	58	293	1041	1130	1006	4.17	443	1577	67	47	.59	.249	.288	.426	.714
Utley,Chase	2172	8194	2298	522	32	357	1333	1362	1374	6.00	829	1656	132	56	.70	.280	.355	.483	.837
Valentin,Javier	773	1882	471	91	6	70	214	269	245	4.51	162	334	0	0	.00	.250	.307	.417	.724
Valentin,Jose	2110	6794	1632	360	45	308	1048	989	957	4.76	768	1607	149	64	.70	.240	.318	.442	.761
Varitek,Jason	1821	6156	1597	381	13	220	794	908	900	5.11	720	1482	35	21	.62	.259	.341	.433	.774
Victorino,Shane	1898	6334	1655	250	58	138	928	627	748	4.10	433	921	111	65	.63	.261	.317	.384	.702
Vidro,Jose	2223	7985	2324	536	16	196	1065	984	1236	5.66	774	891	28	21	.57	.291	.356	.436	.791
Vizquel,Omar	2983	10895	2976	479	77	88	1526	985	1347	4.33	1090	1107	417	170	.71	.273	.340	.355	.696
Walker,Todd	2004	6902	1958	420	38	163	951	816	1017	5.30	654	840	73	43	.63	.284	.345	.426	.771
Ward,Daryle	1082	2659	692	147	5	107	286	448	365	4.81	206	492	1	6	.14	.260	.313	.440	.753
Wells,Vernon	2444	9486	2659	587	36	418	1338	1463	1522	5.75	737	1427	135	56	.71	.280	.332	.482	.814
Werth,Jayson	1205	3744	935	218	15	134	561	563	528	4.81	465	1090	105	46	.70	.250	.336	.423	.759
White,Rondell	1654	5835	1657	321	36	212	820	828	866	5.43	387	1005	95	48	.66	.284	.337	.460	.797
Wigginton,Ty	1405	4586	1195	282	16	173	577	666	648	4.93	393	954	54	25	.68	.261	.324	.442	.766
Wilkerson,Brad	1561	5081	1239	325	37	188	813	597	762	5.08	807	1575	75	59	.56	.244	.351	.433	.785
Williams,Bernie	2474	9048	2647	509	56	322	1534	1418	1602	6.42	1211	1393	153	90	.63	.293	.376	.468	.844
Wilson,Craig	1456	4223	1077	216	22	200	612	604	622	5.12	413	1409	25	13	.66	.255	.347	.459	.806
Wilson,Jack	2174	8081	2122	382	47	110	937	676	883	3.83	452	1021	60	40	.60	.263	.304	.362	.667
Wilson,Preston	1712	5961	1546	328	20	270	820	981	866	5.02	510	1625	157	73	.68	.259	.324	.457	.781
Wilson,Vance	784	1945	481	84	2	52	209	259	202	3.57	91	374	2	8	.20	.247	.296	.373	.668

433

Projected Career Totals for Active Players
Note: These projections assume that the player will be healthy.

PLAYER	BATTING												BASERUNNING			AVERAGES			
Hitter	G	AB	H	2B	3B	HR	R	RBI	RC	RC27	BB	SO	SB	CS	SB%	Avg	OBP	Slg	OPS
Winn,Randy	1899	6806	1913	402	62	133	965	733	952	4.95	565	1091	204	105	.66	.281	.341	.417	.758
Woodward,Chris	1093	2847	691	157	19	57	341	334	319	3.83	235	690	11	8	.58	.243	.300	.371	.672
Youkilis,Kevin	1724	6209	1705	463	10	149	1046	814	1014	5.82	1105	1234	40	27	.60	.275	.386	.424	.811
Young,Dmitri	1561	5241	1490	316	32	197	714	747	827	5.70	419	1009	28	23	.55	.284	.343	.470	.812
Young,Michael	2422	9645	2856	542	61	233	1385	1229	1453	5.53	681	1536	89	44	.67	.296	.340	.437	.778
Zaun,Gregg	1436	4156	1038	218	8	104	512	519	545	4.52	575	669	23	17	.57	.250	.342	.381	.724

Pitcher Projections

Last year's Handbook contained a very thorough and entertaining introduction to our "new" pitcher projections explaining many of the mysteries behind them. If you have specific questions not answered here, I'd suggest referring back to your edition of the 2006 Bill James Handbook or picking up a copy if you don't already have one.

Our audience seemed to like these projections last year, so we decided to continue.

Things to keep in mind:

- Bill James doesn't have anything to do with these. He doesn't believe pitchers can be projected. The projections are the brainchild of John Dewan with lots of help from Pat Quinn and Damon Lichtenwalner and a little help from the rest of the Baseball Info Solutions staff.

- The projections are based on variables like past history (obviously), recent workload and role, age and minor league performance when applicable.

- Subjective adjustments are made when the computer needs help. For example, the computer has no way of knowing that Brandon McCarthy is set to move into the White Sox' starting rotation in 2007. The computer has no way of knowing the best guess in October, 2007 is that Kerry Wood is done as a starter. The vast majority of these subjective adjustments are only for role and playing time.

2007 Pitcher Projections

PLAYER				HOW MUCH			WHAT HE WILL GIVE UP					THE RESULTS					
Pitcher	Team	Age	Inj	G	GS	IP	H	HR	BB	SO	HB	W	L	Pct	Sv	BR/9	ERA
Aardsma,David	ChC	25	low	58	0	77	75	6	41	64	3	4	5	.444	0	13.9	4.32
Accardo,Jeremy	Tor	25	med	66	0	72	71	5	21	60	1	5	3	.625	0	11.6	3.50
Adkins,Jon	SD	29	med	57	0	56	64	9	21	37	2	2	4	.333	0	14.0	5.30
Affeldt,Jeremy	Col	28	high	65	4	90	97	9	43	61	2	5	5	.500	4	14.2	4.80
Aquino,Greg	Ari	29	high	33	0	42	40	6	19	41	3	2	3	.400	0	13.3	4.50
Armas Jr.,Tony	Was	29	high	32	32	167	164	22	78	119	11	8	11	.421	0	13.6	4.63
Arroyo,Bronson	Cin	30	high	34	34	227	226	25	67	151	13	12	13	.480	0	12.1	3.93
Astacio,Pedro	Was	37	high	24	24	132	144	20	44	94	6	6	9	.400	0	13.2	4.84
Ayala,Luis	Was	29	high	55	0	61	63	5	11	38	4	4	3	.571	0	11.5	3.69
Baek,Cha Seung	Sea	27	low	12	12	69	77	11	23	48	2	3	5	.375	0	13.3	4.83
Baez,Danys	Atl	29	med	42	0	43	40	4	17	33	3	3	2	.600	2	12.6	3.77
Baker,Scott	Min	25	med	15	15	76	82	9	19	58	3	4	4	.500	0	12.3	4.14
Bannister,Brian	NYM	26	med	18	18	97	98	9	33	77	4	6	5	.545	0	12.5	3.99
Batista,Miguel	Ari	36	med	34	32	206	216	20	84	124	6	11	12	.478	0	13.4	4.37
Bauer,Rick	Tex	30	med	58	0	68	77	8	27	38	3	3	5	.375	0	14.2	5.03
Bautista,Denny	Col	26	med	12	5	31	36	3	17	23	2	1	2	.333	0	16.0	5.52
Beckett,Josh	Bos	27	high	32	32	208	188	24	75	191	8	13	10	.565	0	11.7	3.68
Bedard,Erik	Bal	28	high	32	32	197	202	16	79	172	7	11	11	.500	0	13.2	4.11
Beimel,Joe	LAD	30	med	66	0	75	87	8	31	42	2	3	5	.375	0	14.4	5.16
Belisle,Matt	Cin	27	high	30	4	45	53	5	14	28	3	2	3	.400	0	14.0	5.00
Bell,Heath	NYM	29	med	19	0	36	35	3	11	37	1	2	2	.500	0	11.8	3.75
Benitez,Armando	SF	34	med	39	0	34	25	4	16	36	0	2	1	.667	6	10.9	3.18
Benoit,Joaquin	Tex	29	med	52	0	81	77	11	38	72	4	4	5	.444	0	13.2	4.44
Benson,Kris	Bal	32	high	26	26	166	174	22	56	100	6	8	10	.444	0	12.8	4.39
Bergmann,Jason	Was	25	med	31	12	98	92	12	40	94	6	5	6	.455	0	12.7	4.04
Betancourt,Rafael	Cle	32	med	52	0	62	57	6	16	62	0	5	2	.714	4	10.6	3.34
Billingsley,Chad	LAD	22	high	27	25	162	145	15	80	156	5	10	8	.556	0	12.8	3.89
Blanton,Joe	Oak	26	high	31	29	194	213	18	55	116	5	10	11	.476	0	12.7	4.18
Bonderman,Jeremy	Det	24	high	34	34	210	212	23	69	178	6	12	12	.500	0	12.3	3.94
Bonser,Boof	Min	25	low	25	25	147	147	22	53	141	3	8	9	.471	0	12.4	4.22
Borkowski,Dave	Hou	30	low	43	0	81	98	10	26	51	5	3	6	.333	0	14.3	5.22
Borowski,Joe	Fla	36	high	77	0	76	68	9	29	65	1	5	3	.625	38	11.6	3.67
Bowie,Micah	Was	32	low	32	0	43	39	2	22	42	2	3	2	.600	0	13.2	3.77
Bradford,Chad	NYM	32	med	67	0	64	62	4	17	44	4	4	3	.571	0	11.7	3.52
Bray,Bill	Cin	24	low	54	0	57	57	8	20	58	3	3	3	.500	0	12.6	4.26
Brocail,Doug	SD	40	med	37	0	41	43	2	15	33	2	2	2	.500	0	13.2	3.95
Broxton,Jonathan	LAD	23	med	73	0	82	66	5	34	102	2	6	3	.667	12	11.2	3.18
Bruney,Brian	NYY	25	high	49	0	58	49	6	42	66	4	3	3	.500	0	14.7	4.50
Buchholz,Taylor	Hou	25	low	14	11	63	65	11	22	43	2	3	4	.429	0	12.7	4.57
Buehrle,Mark	CWS	28	high	31	31	200	214	24	45	114	5	12	11	.522	0	11.9	3.96
Burgos,Ambiorix	KC	23	high	65	2	72	71	11	37	75	6	3	5	.375	4	14.2	5.00
Burnett,A.J.	Tor	30	high	28	28	191	170	15	77	172	8	13	9	.591	0	12.0	3.53
Burres,Brian	Bal	26		25	0	37	42	5	18	28	2	1	3	.250	0	15.1	5.59
Bush,David	Mil	27	high	32	31	216	229	27	43	152	17	11	13	.458	0	12.0	4.04
Byrd,Paul	Cle	36	high	29	29	177	200	25	38	95	6	10	10	.500	0	12.4	4.42
Cabrera,Daniel	Bal	26	high	27	27	168	156	14	102	150	7	9	10	.474	0	14.2	4.39
Cabrera,Fernando	Cle	25	med	55	0	66	54	7	28	77	1	5	3	.625	0	11.3	3.41
Cain,Matt	SF	22	high	33	33	212	173	23	98	201	7	13	10	.565	0	11.8	3.52
Calero,Kiko	Oak	32	med	64	0	52	42	5	19	56	1	4	2	.667	0	10.7	3.12
Camp,Shawn	TB	31	med	77	0	78	94	10	22	51	6	3	6	.333	0	14.1	5.08
Capellan,Jose	Mil	26	med	60	0	68	69	5	29	56	2	4	4	.500	0	13.2	4.10
Capps,Matt	Pit	23	med	83	0	76	79	10	9	60	3	5	4	.556	0	10.8	3.67
Capuano,Chris	Mil	28	high	32	32	214	216	31	66	171	11	11	13	.458	0	12.3	4.21
Carmona,Fausto	Cle	23	low	34	9	79	87	8	24	55	5	4	5	.444	0	13.2	4.44
Carpenter,Chris	StL	32	high	31	31	236	222	25	63	187	9	16	10	.615	0	11.2	3.55
Carrara,Giovanni	LAD	39	med	29	0	32	30	4	13	24	2	2	2	.500	0	12.7	3.94
Carrasco,Hector	LAA	37	med	55	1	102	91	9	38	81	5	6	5	.545	0	11.8	3.53
Cassidy,Scott	SD	31	med	36	0	35	31	4	14	35	1	2	2	.500	0	11.8	3.86
Chacin,Gustavo	Tor	26	high	25	25	158	168	21	58	98	7	8	10	.444	0	13.3	4.56
Chacon,Shawn	Pit	29	high	26	23	124	127	19	64	78	10	5	9	.357	0	14.6	5.23
Chen,Bruce	Bal	30	high	41	7	81	87	16	31	63	2	3	6	.333	0	13.3	5.11
Chulk,Vinnie	SF	28	med	58	0	51	48	7	22	41	2	3	3	.500	0	12.7	4.24
Claussen,Brandon	Cin	28	high	7	7	38	44	6	15	29	2	1	3	.250	0	14.4	5.45
Clemens,Roger	Hou	44	high	25	25	156	130	12	52	146	4	11	6	.647	0	10.7	3.12
Coffey,Todd	Cin	26	med	84	0	78	89	7	19	55	3	4	5	.444	3	12.8	4.27
Colon,Bartolo	LAA	34	high	28	28	198	196	27	63	147	4	11	11	.500	0	12.0	3.95
Condrey,Clay	Phi	31	low	25	0	32	42	4	10	16	1	1	2	.333	0	14.9	5.63
Contreras,Jose	CWS	35	high	29	29	186	175	23	67	143	9	11	10	.524	0	12.1	3.92
Cook,Aaron	Col	28	high	30	30	204	238	16	61	81	9	11	12	.478	0	13.6	4.54
Corcoran,Tim	TB	29	med	26	22	128	128	11	58	92	4	7	8	.467	0	13.4	4.15
Cordero,Chad	Was	25	high	68	0	73	60	6	25	68	2	5	3	.625	32	10.7	3.33
Cordero,Francisco	Mil	32	high	73	0	74	67	5	34	77	3	4	4	.500	43	12.6	3.65
Cormier,Lance	Atl	26	high	26	14	99	119	10	44	65	3	5	6	.455	0	15.1	5.45
Cormier,Rheal	Cin	40	med	61	0	45	44	5	15	29	2	3	2	.600	0	12.2	3.80
Correia,Kevin	SF	26	med	46	0	68	71	8	27	48	3	3	4	.429	0	13.4	4.50
Cotts,Neal	CWS	27	med	64	0	44	41	6	22	38	2	2	3	.400	0	13.3	4.50
Crain,Jesse	Min	25	med	69	0	78	73	6	24	52	3	5	4	.556	1	11.5	3.46
Cruz,Juan	Ari	28	med	32	12	83	73	7	40	81	7	5	4	.556	0	13.0	3.90
Davies,Kyle	Atl	23	high	15	15	63	66	8	31	51	1	3	4	.429	0	14.0	4.86
Davis,Doug	Mil	31	high	32	32	205	205	20	91	156	5	10	13	.435	0	13.2	4.21

436

2007 Pitcher Projections

	PLAYER			HOW MUCH			WHAT HE WILL GIVE UP					THE RESULTS					
Pitcher	Team	Age	Inj	G	GS	IP	H	HR	BB	SO	HB	W	L	Pct	Sv	BR/9	ERA
Davis,Jason	Cle	27	med	41	0	55	61	5	18	36	2	3	3	.500	0	13.3	4.42
de la Rosa,Jorge	KC	26	med	27	19	104	113	11	58	85	5	4	7	.364	0	15.2	5.28
Delcarmen,Manny	Bos	25	med	53	0	58	58	2	26	57	2	3	3	.500	0	13.3	3.88
Dempster,Ryan	ChC	30	high	72	0	76	77	7	39	63	3	4	5	.444	14	14.1	4.62
Dessens,Elmer	LAD	36	high	53	0	65	71	8	19	40	1	3	4	.429	0	12.6	4.43
Dohmann,Scott	KC	29	med	54	0	60	61	10	31	63	3	2	4	.333	0	14.2	5.25
Donnelly,Brendan	LAA	35	med	62	0	66	57	7	24	64	3	4	3	.571	0	11.5	3.41
Dotel,Octavio	NYY	33	high	35	0	41	33	5	18	50	2	3	2	.600	0	11.6	3.51
Downs,Scott	Tor	31	high	55	5	80	90	11	25	52	2	4	5	.444	0	13.2	4.73
Duchscherer,Justin	Oak	29	med	62	0	64	59	7	15	53	2	4	3	.571	2	10.7	3.38
Duke,Zach	Pit	24	high	32	32	225	247	15	63	132	6	12	13	.480	0	12.6	3.96
Eaton,Adam	Tex	29	high	24	24	124	129	16	43	95	6	6	7	.462	0	12.9	4.43
Elarton,Scott	KC	31	high	10	10	57	60	11	22	33	2	2	4	.333	0	13.3	5.21
Embree,Alan	SD	37	med	74	0	51	49	7	16	46	1	3	3	.500	0	11.6	3.88
Escobar,Kelvim	LAA	31	high	30	30	199	192	19	77	174	7	11	11	.500	0	12.5	3.89
Estes,Shawn	SD	34	high	11	11	50	53	6	25	32	2	2	3	.400	0	14.4	4.86
Eyre,Scott	ChC	35	med	65	0	51	48	5	24	47	1	3	3	.500	0	12.9	4.06
Eyre,Willie	Min	28	low	43	0	69	78	6	26	47	5	3	5	.375	0	14.2	4.83
Farnsworth,Kyle	NYY	31	high	67	0	62	55	7	28	68	2	4	3	.571	2	12.3	3.77
Feldman,Scott	Tex	24	med	30	0	36	35	3	12	25	2	2	2	.500	0	12.2	3.75
Feliciano,Pedro	NYM	30	low	61	0	59	59	6	23	48	3	3	3	.500	0	13.0	4.12
Flores,Randy	StL	31	high	62	0	39	41	4	16	30	2	2	2	.500	0	13.6	4.62
Flores,Ron	Oak	27	med	29	0	31	29	2	14	28	0	2	2	.500	0	12.5	3.77
Floyd,Gavin	Phi	24	med	17	14	105	119	12	49	74	9	5	7	.417	0	15.2	5.49
Fogg,Josh	Col	30	high	31	31	170	193	23	57	88	7	8	10	.444	0	13.6	4.92
Fossum,Casey	TB	29	high	19	19	97	105	14	40	75	8	4	7	.364	0	14.2	5.20
Foulke,Keith	Bos	34	high	43	0	51	45	6	12	46	3	4	2	.667	10	10.6	3.35
Francis,Jeff	Col	26	high	31	31	201	205	24	65	150	10	12	10	.545	0	12.5	4.12
Franklin,Ryan	Cin	34	med	61	0	75	81	12	24	39	3	3	5	.375	0	13.0	4.68
Frasor,Jason	Tor	29	med	51	0	50	47	5	23	47	2	3	3	.500	0	13.0	3.96
Fruto,Emiliano	Sea	23	low	24	0	44	39	4	25	48	3	2	3	.400	0	13.7	4.09
Fuentes,Brian	Col	31	high	65	0	66	56	7	29	75	7	4	3	.571	31	12.5	3.82
Fultz,Aaron	Phi	33	med	64	0	63	62	6	24	51	3	4	3	.571	0	12.7	4.00
Gabbard,Kason	Bos	25	low	12	6	43	45	4	23	33	2	2	3	.400	0	14.7	4.81
Gagne,Eric	LAD	31	high	35	0	41	30	4	13	50	2	3	1	.750	19	9.9	2.85
Garcia,Freddy	CWS	31	high	32	32	212	208	26	65	150	6	13	11	.542	0	11.8	3.86
Garland,Jon	CWS	27	high	32	32	217	228	29	68	116	6	12	12	.500	0	12.5	4.27
Gaudin,Chad	Oak	24	med	60	0	66	68	7	26	50	3	3	4	.429	0	13.2	4.23
Geary,Geoff	Phi	30	med	84	0	97	105	8	26	66	5	6	5	.545	0	12.6	4.08
Glavine,Tom	NYM	41	med	29	29	185	188	17	62	101	3	11	9	.550	0	12.3	3.89
Gobble,Jimmy	KC	25	med	64	3	72	82	11	26	46	2	3	5	.375	0	13.8	5.13
Gonzalez,Edgar	Ari	24	med	13	7	57	64	8	14	40	4	3	4	.429	0	12.9	4.74
Gonzalez,Enrique	Ari	24	low	27	20	120	129	10	39	86	4	7	7	.500	0	12.9	4.13
Gonzalez,Geremi	Mil	32	med	25	2	46	50	6	17	30	2	2	3	.400	0	13.5	4.89
Gonzalez,Mike	Pit	29	high	50	0	50	39	2	25	59	1	4	2	.667	40	11.7	3.24
Gordon,Tom	Phi	39	high	54	0	57	45	5	20	62	1	4	3	.571	36	10.4	3.00
Gorzelanny,Tom	Pit	24	med	27	27	147	135	8	57	122	6	9	7	.562	0	12.1	3.49
Grabow,John	Pit	28	med	75	0	72	74	8	32	68	2	3	5	.375	0	13.5	4.50
Green,Sean	Sea	28	low	29	0	40	39	1	21	28	3	2	2	.500	0	14.2	4.05
Gregg,Kevin	LAA	29	med	29	1	78	79	8	26	69	3	4	4	.500	0	12.5	3.92
Greinke,Zack	KC	23	high	21	13	96	106	13	25	68	6	5	6	.455	0	12.8	4.59
Grilli,Jason	Det	30	med	57	0	70	80	12	28	40	4	3	5	.375	0	14.4	5.53
Guerrier,Matt	Min	28	med	45	2	91	98	10	25	54	3	5	5	.500	0	12.5	4.15
Haeger,Charlie	CWS	23	low	31	4	82	81	5	47	59	6	4	5	.444	0	14.7	4.50
Halladay,Roy	Tor	30	high	30	30	205	197	17	47	142	6	14	8	.636	0	11.0	3.38
Halsey,Brad	Oak	26	high	48	5	77	86	8	25	44	4	4	5	.444	0	13.4	4.56
Hammel,Jason	TB	24	low	14	14	76	84	9	28	67	3	3	5	.375	0	13.6	4.74
Hampton,Mike	Atl	34	med	22	22	130	141	12	54	71	2	7	7	.500	0	13.6	4.50
Hamulack,Tim	LAD	30	med	29	0	31	28	3	17	31	1	2	2	.500	0	13.4	3.77
Hancock,Josh	StL	29	med	60	0	72	78	10	22	44	2	4	4	.500	0	12.8	4.50
Harang,Aaron	Cin	29	high	34	34	230	243	28	64	186	8	12	14	.462	0	12.3	4.15
Harden,Rich	Oak	25	high	26	26	162	135	12	69	152	3	11	7	.611	0	11.5	3.33
Haren,Dan	Oak	26	high	32	32	214	219	27	50	170	8	12	12	.500	0	11.6	3.87
Harper,Travis	TB	31	high	29	0	38	43	5	12	25	2	2	3	.400	0	13.5	4.97
Harville,Chad	TB	30	med	31	0	33	35	4	19	25	1	1	2	.333	0	15.0	5.18
Hawkins,LaTroy	Bal	34	med	52	0	53	55	5	16	38	0	3	3	.500	0	12.1	3.91
Heilman,Aaron	NYM	28	med	75	0	85	84	8	35	69	4	5	5	.500	0	13.0	4.13
Helling,Rick	Mil	36	med	21	1	36	39	6	13	25	2	2	2	.500	0	13.5	5.00
Hendrickson,Mark	LAD	33	high	32	21	142	165	17	43	74	3	7	9	.438	0	13.4	4.75
Hennessey,Brad	SF	27	high	34	14	100	106	10	39	51	5	5	6	.455	0	13.5	4.41
Hensley,Clay	SD	27	high	30	30	192	168	13	71	129	3	13	8	.619	0	11.3	3.28
Herges,Matt	Fla	37	low	65	0	69	81	7	26	46	3	3	4	.429	0	14.3	5.09
Hermanson,Dustin	CWS	34	high	31	0	38	38	5	13	24	1	2	2	.500	2	12.3	4.26
Hernandez,Felix	Sea	21	high	31	31	197	175	17	72	197	6	13	9	.591	0	11.6	3.47
Hernandez,Livan	Ari	32	high	34	34	233	246	25	78	151	8	12	14	.462	0	12.8	4.25
Hernandez,Orlando	NYM	37	high	27	27	163	158	22	58	136	11	9	9	.500	0	12.5	4.14
Hernandez,Roberto	NYM	42	med	65	0	63	62	7	28	49	2	4	3	.571	0	13.1	4.29
Hernandez,Runelvys	KC	29	high	26	26	147	170	20	63	79	6	6	11	.353	0	14.6	5.45
Hill,Rich	ChC	27	med	32	32	201	165	28	69	241	6	13	9	.591	0	10.8	3.40
Hirsh,Jason	Hou	25	low	17	17	89	80	9	33	75	6	5	5	.500	0	12.0	3.64
Hoffman,Trevor	SD	39	high	65	0	65	53	5	15	63	1	4	3	.571	45	9.6	2.77

2007 Pitcher Projections

Pitcher	Team	Age	Inj	G	GS	IP	H	HR	BB	SO	HB	W	L	Pct	Sv	BR/9	ERA
Howell,J.P.	TB	24	med	15	15	85	94	8	36	73	5	4	6	.400	0	14.3	4.87
Howry,Bob	ChC	33	med	81	0	77	69	8	24	63	3	5	3	.625	14	11.2	3.39
Huber,Jon	Sea	25	low	31	0	33	37	3	11	27	1	2	2	.500	0	13.4	4.36
Hudson,Luke	KC	30	high	29	29	172	176	18	69	114	11	9	11	.450	0	13.4	4.40
Hudson,Tim	Atl	31	high	34	34	223	220	19	71	147	10	15	10	.600	0	12.1	3.75
Isringhausen,Jason	StL	34	high	50	0	48	38	4	21	44	1	3	2	.600	30	11.2	3.19
Jackson,Edwin	TB	23	high	23	0	39	42	5	21	28	2	2	3	.400	0	15.0	5.08
James,Chuck	Atl	25	med	30	29	186	163	23	61	164	6	13	7	.650	0	11.1	3.53
Jarvis,Kevin	Bos	37	high	10	6	39	46	6	11	24	1	2	3	.400	0	13.4	5.08
Jenks,Bobby	CWS	26	med	61	0	68	60	4	31	80	3	4	3	.571	38	12.4	3.57
Jennings,Jason	Col	28	high	30	30	198	215	21	88	129	6	10	12	.455	0	14.0	4.77
Johnson,Jason	Cin	33	high	23	15	102	117	12	35	58	4	4	7	.364	0	13.8	4.85
Johnson,Josh	Fla	23	high	27	27	160	155	10	71	136	5	10	8	.556	0	13.0	3.88
Johnson,Randy	NYY	43	high	28	28	192	176	25	49	186	10	15	8	.652	0	11.0	3.98
Johnson,Tyler	StL	26	med	63	0	41	37	5	24	47	3	2	2	.500	0	14.0	4.61
Jones,Todd	Det	39	med	60	0	66	68	5	22	50	3	4	4	.500	28	12.7	3.95
Julio,Jorge	Ari	28	med	55	0	60	55	9	30	59	2	3	4	.429	4	13.0	4.35
Karstens,Jeff	NYY	24	low	15	12	85	93	11	25	64	2	5	5	.500	0	12.7	4.45
Kazmir,Scott	TB	23	high	27	27	164	148	13	73	171	6	10	8	.556	0	12.5	3.68
Kennedy,Joe	Oak	28	high	49	0	52	58	6	19	33	3	2	3	.400	0	13.8	4.85
Kim,Byung-Hyun	Col	28	high	29	29	172	176	18	69	147	13	10	9	.526	0	13.5	4.40
King,Ray	Col	33	med	67	0	47	46	4	20	31	2	3	2	.600	0	13.0	4.02
Kinney,Josh	StL	28	low	26	0	31	27	2	14	30	2	2	1	.667	0	12.5	3.48
Kline,Steve	SF	34	high	72	0	52	48	5	22	34	2	3	3	.500	0	12.5	3.81
Kolb,Dan	Mil	32	high	52	0	49	53	3	22	29	1	2	3	.400	0	14.0	4.41
Koronka,John	Tex	26	med	14	14	70	79	9	28	43	2	3	5	.375	0	14.0	5.01
Lackey,John	LAA	28	high	32	32	211	214	19	68	172	9	12	12	.500	0	12.4	3.88
League,Brandon	Tor	24	med	52	0	71	79	6	25	48	4	4	4	.500	0	13.7	4.56
Ledezma,Wil	Det	26	med	32	14	99	103	10	38	69	3	5	6	.455	0	13.1	4.27
Lee,Cliff	Cle	28	high	32	32	203	211	28	66	148	6	11	11	.500	0	12.5	4.30
Lester,Jon	Bos	23	med	14	14	78	77	7	40	72	3	4	5	.444	0	13.8	4.38
Lidge,Brad	Hou	30	high	77	0	78	60	7	33	110	5	5	3	.625	36	11.3	3.23
Lieber,Jon	Phi	37	high	29	29	192	210	26	32	125	5	12	10	.545	0	11.6	3.98
Lilly,Ted	Tor	31	high	31	31	182	176	28	76	153	6	10	11	.476	0	12.8	4.35
Linebrink,Scott	SD	30	med	71	0	76	66	7	26	67	2	5	3	.625	2	11.1	3.43
Liriano,Francisco	Min	23	high	22	22	145	121	12	45	179	2	11	5	.688	0	10.4	3.04
Littleton,Wes	Tex	24	low	49	0	58	59	7	19	43	3	3	3	.500	0	12.6	4.03
Loaiza,Esteban	Oak	35	high	30	30	197	219	22	54	137	6	10	12	.455	0	12.7	4.34
Loe,Kameron	Tex	25	high	15	15	77	93	9	26	47	1	3	5	.375	0	14.0	5.14
Lohse,Kyle	Cin	28	high	34	25	158	180	21	50	97	7	7	11	.389	0	13.5	4.84
Looper,Braden	StL	32	med	67	0	76	78	5	26	46	3	5	4	.556	0	12.7	3.91
Lopez,Rodrigo	Bal	31	high	38	24	187	208	27	58	124	5	9	12	.429	0	13.0	4.72
Lowe,Derek	LAD	34	high	34	32	222	229	19	62	135	8	14	11	.560	0	12.1	3.81
Lowry,Noah	SF	26	high	28	28	172	172	19	58	122	5	9	10	.474	0	12.3	3.98
Lugo,Ruddy	TB	27	low	67	0	92	86	4	44	67	4	5	5	.500	0	13.1	3.72
Lyon,Brandon	Ari	27	med	63	0	65	74	9	20	41	1	3	4	.429	0	13.2	4.71
MacDougal,Mike	CWS	30	med	60	0	57	56	4	26	48	4	3	3	.500	0	13.6	4.11
Maddux,Greg	LAD	41	med	34	34	216	222	24	36	135	6	14	10	.583	0	11.0	3.63
Madson,Ryan	Phi	26	high	65	8	118	130	15	38	92	8	6	7	.462	0	13.4	4.73
Mahay,Ron	Tex	36	med	65	0	58	58	8	27	53	1	3	4	.429	0	13.3	4.50
Maholm,Paul	Pit	25	high	28	28	170	182	14	73	119	10	8	11	.421	0	14.0	4.55
Maine,John	NYM	26	high	22	22	130	132	17	53	102	3	7	7	.500	0	13.0	4.36
Majewski,Gary	Cin	27	high	72	0	75	80	3	30	49	5	4	5	.444	0	13.8	4.20
Marcum,Shaun	Tor	25	med	26	23	120	128	21	36	105	5	6	8	.429	0	12.7	4.73
Maroth,Mike	Det	29	high	26	26	160	181	23	42	78	6	7	10	.412	0	12.9	4.61
Marquis,Jason	StL	28	high	32	32	177	188	26	68	101	9	9	11	.450	0	13.5	4.78
Marte,Damaso	Pit	32	med	72	0	61	52	6	29	65	3	4	3	.571	0	12.4	3.69
Martin,Tom	Col	37	high	69	0	64	68	8	29	46	4	3	4	.429	0	14.2	4.92
Martinez,Pedro	NYM	35	high	15	15	86	67	8	20	95	5	7	2	.778	0	9.6	2.83
Mateo,Julio	Sea	29	high	41	0	45	44	6	12	30	3	2	3	.400	0	11.8	4.00
McBride,Macay	Atl	24	med	75	0	63	65	5	34	59	1	3	4	.429	0	14.3	4.71
McCarthy,Brandon	CWS	23	med	30	30	200	191	38	64	180	4	11	11	.500	0	11.7	4.14
McClung,Seth	TB	26	high	50	1	54	58	8	31	42	3	2	4	.333	22	15.3	5.67
McGowan,Dustin	Tor	25	med	22	7	50	53	7	27	44	3	2	4	.333	0	14.9	5.40
Meadows,Brian	TB	31	med	55	0	75	88	10	20	37	1	3	5	.375	0	13.1	4.80
Meche,Gil	Sea	28	high	30	30	176	182	24	79	126	5	8	12	.400	0	13.6	4.76
Medders,Brandon	Ari	27	med	57	0	69	66	5	27	60	2	4	3	.571	0	12.4	3.65
Meredith,Cla	SD	24	med	65	0	78	73	7	17	62	2	5	3	.625	0	10.6	3.23
Mesa,Jose	Col	41	low	74	0	73	77	8	34	50	3	4	4	.500	0	14.1	4.68
Messenger,Randy	Fla	25	med	57	0	63	66	8	32	47	1	3	4	.429	0	14.1	4.86
Miceli,Dan	TB	36	high	43	0	45	43	6	20	40	1	2	3	.400	0	12.8	4.20
Michalak,Chris	Cin	36	low	15	12	70	84	13	22	30	4	2	5	.286	0	14.1	5.66
Miller,Matt	Cle	35	high	38	0	36	30	1	14	33	3	3	1	.750	0	11.8	3.35
Miller,Trever	Hou	34	med	77	0	55	52	6	24	49	5	3	3	.500	2	13.3	4.25
Miller,Wade	ChC	30	high	10	10	43	41	5	19	35	1	2	2	.500	0	12.8	3.98
Millwood,Kevin	Tex	32	high	34	34	228	227	23	65	177	6	14	11	.560	0	11.8	3.75
Milton,Eric	Cin	31	high	26	26	144	155	27	39	100	3	6	10	.375	0	12.3	4.69
Miner,Zach	Det	25	low	38	16	104	114	10	50	71	1	5	7	.417	0	14.3	4.85
Mitre,Sergio	Fla	26	med	21	11	72	78	9	28	53	4	4	4	.500	0	13.8	4.75
Moehler,Brian	Fla	35	med	33	17	120	155	15	33	61	4	5	8	.385	0	14.4	5.48
Morris,Matt	SF	32	high	32	32	210	215	24	56	139	9	12	12	.500	0	12.0	3.94

2007 Pitcher Projections

Pitcher	Team	Age	Inj	G	GS	IP	H	HR	BB	SO	HB	W	L	Pct	Sv	BR/9	ERA
Mota,Guillermo	NYM	33	high	51	0	55	49	6	22	46	1	4	2	.667	0	11.8	3.60
Moyer,Jamie	Phi	44	high	33	33	202	210	29	52	114	8	12	10	.545	0	12.0	4.10
Mulder,Mark	StL	29	high	11	11	54	56	6	18	33	2	3	3	.500	0	12.7	4.17
Mussina,Mike	NYY	38	high	29	29	172	170	20	36	146	4	12	7	.632	0	11.0	3.56
Myers,Brett	Phi	26	high	32	32	214	215	31	73	179	8	12	11	.522	0	12.4	4.29
Myers,Mike	NYY	38	low	65	0	34	32	3	15	25	3	2	2	.500	0	13.2	3.97
Nathan,Joe	Min	32	high	64	0	69	50	5	27	78	1	5	3	.625	36	10.2	2.74
Nelson,Joe	KC	32	low	56	0	59	49	8	30	68	4	3	3	.500	4	12.7	3.97
Neshek,Pat	Min	26	low	50	0	58	47	9	14	77	1	4	2	.667	0	9.6	3.10
Nieve,Fernando	Hou	24	low	45	5	77	73	12	31	69	3	4	5	.444	0	12.5	4.21
Nolasco,Ricky	Fla	24	med	33	24	140	148	18	43	121	10	8	8	.500	0	12.9	4.44
Novoa,Roberto	ChC	27	med	67	0	79	79	10	31	55	4	4	5	.444	0	13.0	4.44
Ohka,Tomo	Mil	31	high	25	25	134	146	16	38	74	4	7	8	.467	0	12.6	4.30
Ohman,Will	ChC	29	med	78	0	64	55	7	34	72	4	4	4	.500	0	13.1	3.94
Oliver,Darren	NYM	36	low	45	0	76	88	11	27	45	3	3	5	.375	0	14.0	5.21
Olsen,Scott	Fla	23	high	32	32	197	182	25	83	199	7	12	10	.545	0	12.4	3.97
Ortiz,Ramon	Was	34	high	33	33	189	211	31	65	114	11	8	13	.381	0	13.7	5.10
Ortiz,Russ	Bal	33	high	34	7	64	70	8	35	45	1	3	4	.429	0	14.0	4.76
Oswalt,Roy	Hou	29	high	32	31	224	218	18	48	183	8	15	10	.600	0	11.0	3.38
Otsuka,Akinori	Tex	35	med	55	0	53	46	3	18	50	1	4	2	.667	39	11.0	3.23
Padilla,Vicente	Tex	29	high	32	32	202	205	23	71	141	15	11	12	.478	0	13.0	4.23
Papelbon,Jonathan	Bos	26	high	27	27	184	151	17	48	181	8	14	6	.700	0	10.1	2.98
Park,Chan Ho	SD	34	high	16	13	84	88	11	38	65	7	4	6	.400	0	14.2	5.04
Paronto,Chad	Atl	31	low	72	0	64	68	5	26	46	4	4	3	.571	0	13.8	4.36
Patterson,John	Was	29	high	25	25	156	146	20	56	146	7	9	8	.529	0	12.1	3.87
Pavano,Carl	NYY	31	high	14	14	78	84	8	20	50	4	5	4	.556	0	12.5	4.15
Peavy,Jake	SD	26	high	33	33	219	193	24	70	219	8	14	10	.583	0	11.1	3.45
Penn,Hayden	Bal	22	med	16	16	86	96	13	39	74	1	3	6	.333	0	14.2	5.34
Penny,Brad	LAD	29	high	34	33	190	195	19	58	140	5	11	10	.524	0	12.2	3.93
Peralta,Joel	KC	31	med	67	0	76	77	9	22	64	4	4	4	.500	0	12.2	4.03
Perez,Odalis	KC	30	high	32	30	174	181	22	46	120	3	10	10	.500	0	11.9	3.93
Perez,Oliver	NYM	25	high	21	21	111	104	19	63	117	6	5	7	.417	0	14.0	5.03
Petit,Yusmeiro	Fla	22	low	16	4	43	44	7	10	38	1	3	2	.600	0	11.5	3.98
Pettitte,Andy	Hou	35	high	33	33	210	214	20	61	164	3	12	11	.522	0	11.9	3.77
Pineiro,Joel	Sea	28	high	45	18	144	156	18	48	92	5	7	9	.438	0	13.1	4.50
Pinto,Renyel	Fla	24	low	43	0	49	45	4	32	51	5	3	3	.500	0	15.1	4.59
Politte,Cliff	CWS	33	high	38	0	37	36	5	15	31	1	2	2	.500	0	12.6	4.14
Prior,Mark	ChC	26	high	20	20	128	114	16	45	145	6	8	6	.571	0	11.6	3.73
Proctor,Scott	NYY	30	med	80	0	95	93	15	34	85	3	6	5	.545	6	12.3	4.26
Putz,J.J.	Sea	30	high	70	0	81	73	8	23	80	3	5	4	.556	36	11.0	3.44
Qualls,Chad	Hou	28	med	83	0	87	93	8	26	56	6	4	5	.444	0	12.9	4.24
Ramirez,Elizardo	Cin	24	high	16	14	64	79	9	15	40	3	2	5	.286	0	13.6	5.20
Ramirez,Horacio	Atl	27	high	22	22	133	142	17	49	63	3	7	7	.500	0	13.1	4.53
Ramirez,Ramon	Col	25	low	60	0	71	72	10	28	61	1	4	4	.500	0	12.8	4.31
Rasner,Darrell	NYY	26	high	10	6	38	39	3	8	26	2	3	2	.600	0	11.6	3.79
Rauch,Jon	Was	28	high	85	0	90	83	13	32	73	2	5	5	.500	0	11.7	3.80
Ray,Chris	Bal	25	high	57	0	64	53	9	25	58	2	4	3	.571	27	11.2	3.52
Ray,Ken	Atl	32	low	61	0	62	67	8	36	41	2	3	4	.429	0	15.2	5.37
Redman,Mark	KC	33	high	30	30	176	192	19	58	102	5	9	11	.450	0	13.0	4.40
Reitsma,Chris	Atl	29	high	45	0	42	48	5	11	25	1	2	2	.500	0	12.9	4.50
Reyes,Anthony	StL	25	med	27	27	142	128	20	40	131	6	9	6	.600	0	11.0	3.61
Reyes,Dennys	Min	30	med	80	0	59	60	5	30	51	1	3	4	.429	0	13.9	4.42
Rhodes,Arthur	Phi	37	high	50	0	43	38	4	18	44	1	3	2	.600	0	11.9	3.56
Rincon,Juan	Min	28	med	75	0	71	64	3	27	69	2	5	3	.625	0	11.8	3.42
Riske,David	CWS	30	high	43	0	50	43	7	21	45	3	3	3	.500	0	12.1	3.78
Rivera,Mariano	NYY	37	high	54	0	66	53	3	14	57	3	5	2	.714	40	9.5	2.59
Rivera,Saul	Was	29	low	67	0	80	78	4	33	63	5	5	4	.556	0	13.0	3.83
Rleal,Sendy	Bal	27	low	25	0	30	31	5	11	21	0	1	2	.333	0	12.6	4.50
Robertson,Nate	Det	29	high	31	31	215	222	31	73	145	7	11	13	.458	0	12.6	4.40
Rodney,Fernando	Det	30	med	61	0	75	65	7	35	69	6	4	4	.500	2	12.7	3.84
Rodriguez,Francisco	LAA	25	high	77	0	82	55	7	34	110	1	6	3	.667	44	9.9	2.74
Rodriguez,Wandy	Hou	28	high	28	19	106	123	15	47	71	6	4	8	.333	0	14.9	5.60
Rogers,Kenny	Det	42	high	32	32	205	220	21	64	109	9	11	12	.478	0	12.9	4.26
Romero,J.C.	LAA	31	med	62	0	45	44	4	24	36	3	2	3	.400	0	14.2	4.40
Ryan,B.J.	Tor	31	high	59	0	67	51	4	30	83	2	4	3	.571	38	11.1	2.96
Saarloos,Kirk	Oak	28	high	31	16	116	132	13	44	52	6	5	8	.385	0	14.1	4.97
Sabathia,C.C.	Cle	26	high	30	30	211	199	20	72	170	7	14	9	.609	0	11.9	3.67
Sampson,Chris	Hou	29	low	17	10	68	71	8	9	36	2	4	3	.571	0	10.9	3.57
Sanchez,Anibal	Fla	23	med	25	24	168	160	16	65	146	7	11	8	.579	0	12.4	3.86
Sanchez,Duaner	NYM	27	high	68	0	71	67	7	30	52	4	4	4	.500	0	12.8	3.93
Santana,Ervin	LAA	24	high	32	32	199	191	21	68	148	11	11	11	.500	0	12.2	3.84
Santana,Johan	Min	28	high	32	32	233	186	23	62	245	5	19	7	.731	0	9.8	2.90
Santos,Victor	Pit	30	high	21	16	100	113	13	43	68	4	4	7	.364	0	14.4	5.22
Saunders,Joe	LAA	26	med	24	24	131	132	12	45	89	3	7	7	.500	0	12.4	3.92
Schilling,Curt	Bos	40	high	27	27	180	179	22	30	177	3	12	8	.600	0	10.6	3.50
Schmidt,Jason	SF	34	high	31	31	210	179	18	80	199	5	14	9	.609	0	11.3	3.34
Schoeneweis,Scott	Cin	33	high	66	0	53	56	5	21	31	2	2	3	.400	0	13.4	4.58
Schroder,Chris	Was	28	low	41	0	57	47	9	27	69	5	3	3	.500	0	12.5	3.95
Seanez,Rudy	SD	38	high	36	0	35	30	4	17	38	1	2	2	.500	0	12.3	3.86
Sele,Aaron	LAD	37	high	32	10	93	107	11	30	50	4	4	6	.400	0	13.6	4.84
Seo,Jae	TB	30	med	32	27	159	179	22	48	98	3	7	11	.389	0	13.0	4.70

439

2007 Pitcher Projections

PLAYER				HOW MUCH			WHAT HE WILL GIVE UP					THE RESULTS					
Pitcher	Team	Age	Inj	G	GS	IP	H	HR	BB	SO	HB	W	L	Pct	Sv	BR/9	ERA
Sheets,Ben	Mil	28	high	24	24	159	155	18	32	143	4	10	8	.556	0	10.8	3.45
Sherrill,George	Sea	30	med	71	0	34	29	2	14	38	1	2	1	.667	0	11.6	3.44
Shields,James	TB	25	low	23	23	145	155	15	39	135	6	8	8	.500	0	12.4	4.10
Shields,Scot	LAA	31	high	76	0	92	78	7	31	84	2	7	4	.636	4	10.9	3.13
Shouse,Brian	Mil	38	med	66	0	36	37	3	14	24	3	2	2	.500	0	13.5	4.25
Silva,Carlos	Min	28	high	35	32	192	235	27	33	77	6	9	13	.409	0	12.8	4.83
Sisco,Andy	KC	24	med	60	0	53	53	6	32	52	1	2	4	.333	0	14.6	4.92
Slaten,Doug	Ari	27	low	33	0	35	31	1	15	39	1	2	1	.667	0	12.1	3.34
Smith,Matt	Phi	28	low	36	0	40	36	4	19	39	1	3	2	.600	0	12.6	3.83
Smoltz,John	Atl	40	med	34	34	227	209	19	50	200	4	18	7	.720	0	10.4	3.17
Snell,Ian	Pit	25	high	31	31	194	198	26	67	167	3	10	12	.455	0	12.4	4.22
Snyder,Kyle	Bos	29	med	24	14	80	97	9	21	51	2	4	5	.444	0	13.5	4.84
Soriano,Rafael	Sea	27	med	42	0	43	35	4	13	46	2	3	2	.600	9	10.5	3.14
Sosa,Jorge	StL	30	high	49	6	105	108	17	47	68	1	5	7	.417	0	13.4	4.80
Sowers,Jeremy	Cle	24	low	25	25	158	160	12	41	93	3	11	7	.611	0	11.6	3.59
Speier,Justin	Tor	33	high	43	0	40	35	5	13	35	2	3	2	.600	0	11.2	3.60
Springer,Russ	Hou	38	high	72	0	61	56	10	23	51	3	3	4	.429	0	12.1	4.13
Stanton,Mike	SF	40	med	74	0	67	66	4	25	51	2	4	3	.571	0	12.5	3.76
Stokes,Brian	TB	27	med	10	8	48	53	4	19	35	2	2	3	.400	0	13.9	4.50
Street,Huston	Oak	23	high	64	0	68	58	3	17	64	2	4	3	.571	44	10.2	2.78
Stults,Eric	LAD	27	low	12	4	35	38	4	14	28	1	2	2	.500	0	13.6	4.63
Sturtze,Tanyon	NYY	36	high	26	0	42	45	5	17	26	2	2	2	.500	0	13.7	4.93
Suppan,Jeff	StL	32	high	33	33	206	220	26	68	114	8	11	12	.478	0	12.9	4.46
Sweeney,Brian	SD	33	low	27	0	44	48	5	11	27	1	2	3	.400	0	12.3	4.09
Switzer,Jon	TB	27	med	56	0	45	51	5	21	30	5	2	3	.400	0	15.4	5.60
Tallet,Brian	Tor	29	med	47	2	59	63	8	25	38	3	3	4	.429	0	13.9	4.88
Taschner,Jack	SF	29	med	36	0	32	33	4	14	30	1	1	2	.333	0	13.5	4.50
Tavarez,Julian	Bos	34	med	62	4	75	81	5	31	43	6	4	4	.500	0	14.2	4.56
Tejeda,Robinson	Tex	25	high	20	20	118	116	15	60	93	6	6	7	.462	0	13.9	4.65
Thompson,Brad	StL	25	high	37	0	56	54	5	15	36	3	4	2	.667	0	11.6	3.54
Thompson,Mike	SD	26	low	21	15	88	94	8	26	45	4	5	5	.500	0	12.7	4.09
Thomson,John	Atl	33	high	26	26	155	170	18	45	96	4	9	8	.529	0	12.7	4.30
Thornton,Matt	CWS	30	med	64	0	52	52	6	33	46	2	2	3	.400	2	15.1	5.02
Timlin,Mike	Bos	41	high	72	0	70	73	7	18	46	3	4	4	.500	5	12.1	3.86
Tomko,Brett	LAD	34	med	50	13	117	127	15	36	71	2	6	7	.462	0	12.7	4.46
Torres,Salomon	Pit	35	med	89	0	92	91	8	33	61	6	5	5	.500	4	12.7	3.91
Towers,Josh	Tor	30	high	16	12	70	87	12	11	39	3	3	5	.375	0	13.0	5.14
Traber,Billy	Was	27	low	26	13	76	89	7	22	56	6	3	5	.375	0	13.9	4.74
Trachsel,Steve	NYM	36	med	29	29	164	169	22	61	96	3	9	9	.500	0	12.8	4.34
Turnbow,Derrick	Mil	29	high	54	0	50	46	5	29	45	2	2	3	.400	0	13.9	4.32
Valverde,Jose	Ari	27	high	42	0	53	42	6	24	66	2	4	2	.667	32	11.5	3.40
Vargas,Claudio	Ari	29	high	31	30	180	190	32	67	130	9	8	12	.400	0	13.3	4.95
Vazquez,Javier	CWS	30	high	33	33	217	216	29	55	190	9	13	11	.542	0	11.6	3.86
Verlander,Justin	Det	24	high	31	31	194	184	20	62	137	7	12	10	.545	0	11.7	3.66
Villarreal,Oscar	Atl	25	high	50	8	105	106	12	37	70	5	6	5	.545	0	12.7	4.20
Villone,Ron	NYY	37	med	71	0	83	79	9	43	66	6	5	5	.500	0	13.9	4.45
Vizcaino,Luis	Ari	32	med	67	0	69	63	10	28	61	2	4	4	.500	0	12.1	3.91
Wagner,Billy	NYM	35	high	69	0	71	49	7	20	87	3	5	3	.625	38	9.1	2.66
Wagner,Ryan	Was	24	high	49	0	59	69	6	26	45	3	2	4	.333	0	14.9	5.34
Wainwright,Adam	StL	25	high	33	15	112	117	12	34	93	4	6	6	.500	0	12.5	4.02
Wakefield,Tim	Bos	40	high	28	24	152	146	21	55	108	10	8	8	.500	0	12.5	4.14
Walker,Jamie	Det	35	med	59	0	48	47	7	10	36	1	3	2	.600	0	10.9	3.75
Wang,Chien-Ming	NYY	27	high	32	32	214	232	15	52	98	5	14	10	.583	0	12.2	3.79
Washburn,Jarrod	Sea	32	high	29	29	179	183	23	53	103	6	9	11	.450	0	12.2	4.07
Weathers,David	Cin	37	med	64	0	75	71	8	32	56	3	4	4	.500	2	12.7	3.96
Weaver,Jeff	StL	30	high	32	32	188	203	24	51	123	13	10	11	.476	0	12.8	4.40
Weaver,Jered	LAA	24	low	25	25	166	141	19	41	163	3	12	7	.632	0	10.0	3.14
Webb,Brandon	Ari	28	high	30	30	219	206	17	70	172	7	14	10	.583	0	11.6	3.49
Wellemeyer,Todd	KC	28	high	41	3	101	98	9	64	87	3	5	7	.417	0	14.7	4.72
Wells,David	SD	44	high	21	21	131	147	16	21	75	4	7	7	.500	0	11.8	3.98
Wells,Kip	Tex	30	high	24	24	138	144	16	63	99	7	7	9	.438	0	14.0	4.70
Westbrook,Jake	Cle	29	high	31	31	222	241	18	65	117	7	13	12	.520	0	12.7	4.05
Wheeler,Dan	Hou	29	med	77	0	76	70	8	25	66	2	5	4	.556	4	11.5	3.55
White,Rick	Phi	38	high	69	0	70	77	8	24	45	3	4	4	.500	0	13.4	4.63
Wickman,Bob	Atl	38	high	64	0	62	61	5	21	50	2	4	3	.571	41	12.2	3.77
Williams,Dave	NYM	28	high	15	14	78	82	12	29	45	5	4	5	.444	0	13.4	4.85
Williams,Todd	Bal	36	med	62	0	54	64	5	.17	24	3	3	3	.500	0	14.0	4.67
Williams,Woody	SD	40	high	29	29	185	190	24	53	119	7	10	11	.476	0	12.2	4.04
Williamson,Scott	SD	31	high	32	0	32	25	3	18	37	2	2	2	.500	0	12.7	3.66
Willis,Dontrelle	Fla	25	high	34	34	229	227	18	73	169	12	15	10	.600	0	12.3	3.77
Wilson,C.J.	Tex	26	med	55	0	52	54	6	22	46	3	3	3	.500	0	13.7	4.50
Wilson,Paul	Cin	34	high	10	10	51	58	8	17	32	3	2	4	.333	0	13.8	5.12
Wise,Matt	Mil	31	med	38	0	43	39	5	14	32	2	3	2	.600	0	11.5	3.56
Witasick,Jay	Oak	34	high	31	0	37	36	4	18	34	2	2	2	.500	0	13.6	4.38
Wolf,Randy	Phi	30	high	25	25	142	141	20	54	114	6	8	8	.500	0	12.7	4.31
Wood,Kerry	ChC	30	high	35	4	52	43	7	24	57	4	3	3	.500	12	12.3	3.81
Wood,Mike	KC	27	high	20	3	52	61	7	18	28	3	2	4	.333	0	14.2	5.37
Woods,Jake	Sea	25	med	37	15	141	160	17	58	92	5	6	10	.375	0	14.2	5.11
Worrell,Tim	SF	39	med	33	0	32	32	4	12	25	1	2	2	.500	0	14.7	4.22
Wright,Jamey	SF	32	high	37	12	120	134	15	58	67	9	5	9	.357	0	15.1	5.40
Wright,Jaret	NYY	31	high	32	28	152	165	13	72	106	7	8	9	.471	0	14.4	4.80

440

2007 Pitcher Projections

PLAYER				HOW MUCH			WHAT HE WILL GIVE UP					THE RESULTS					
Pitcher	Team	Age	Inj	G	GS	IP	H	HR	BB	SO	HB	W	L	Pct	Sv	BR/9	ERA
Wuertz,Mike	ChC	28	med	65	0	66	53	6	27	78	1	5	3	.625	0	11.0	3.27
Yates,Tyler	Atl	29	low	71	0	62	62	6	37	54	2	3	4	.429	0	14.7	4.79
Youman,Shane	Pit	27		10	6	43	45	3	15	25	0	2	2	.500	0	12.6	3.98
Young,Chris	SD	28	high	31	31	186	174	26	64	155	7	11	10	.524	0	11.9	3.87
Zambrano,Carlos	ChC	26	high	32	32	212	173	17	98	191	11	14	10	.583	0	12.0	3.48
Zambrano,Victor	NYM	31	high	20	19	107	102	11	59	79	9	6	6	.500	0	14.3	4.63
Zito,Barry	Oak	29	high	32	32	218	195	24	87	161	11	13	11	.542	0	12.1	3.76
Zumaya,Joel	Det	22	low	59	0	88	63	6	47	108	3	6	3	.667	7	11.6	3.17

Career Assessments

This section is designed to give probabilities on players achieving important career milestones. The method (formerly under the name of "The Favorite Toy") was developed by Bill James and takes into account a player's age and performance level in predicting the probability that he will accumulate certain career stats. A detailed explanation of how the system works can be found in the glossary.

There was only one major milestone passed in 2006, and that was Trevor Hoffman breaking Lee Smith's all-time record for saves. This sets up a potentially huge year for milestones in 2007. Of course, the biggest one is Barry Bonds's controversial pursuit of Hank Aaron's 755 home runs. Assuming Bonds plays in 2007 and stays healthy, he should have an excellent chance of catching Aaron.

In addition to Bonds's run toward Aaron's record, there are several other milestones that could be reached in 2007. Frank Thomas, Manny Ramirez, Alex Rodriguez, and Jim Thome all have a good chance to reach 500 home runs. Provided he has good health Thomas should easily get there; Ramirez, Rodriguez, and Thome have more work to do than Thomas but should have a chance to reach the milestone with decent seasons. Craig Biggio should reach 3000 hits, and Ken Griffey Jr. has an outside chance of reaching 600 home runs (but will most likely have to wait until 2008).

It should be noted that the ages used in this section correspond to a player's 2006 age instead of the 2007 age used in the register.

Career Assessments

756 Home Runs
% chance to break record

Bonds,Barry	97%
Rodriguez,Alex	31%
Pujols,Albert	22%
Jones,Andruw	16%
Dunn,Adam	9%
Ortiz,David	7%
Ramirez,Manny	5%
Howard,Ryan	2%

4,257 Hits
% chance to break record

Cabrera,Miguel	< 1%

4,000 Hits
% chance to reach milestone

Jeter,Derek	6%
Cabrera,Miguel	5%
Rodriguez,Alex	5%
Crawford,Carl	3%
Pujols,Albert	2%
Tejada,Miguel	1%
Guerrero,Vladimir	1%
Pierre,Juan	< 1%

3,000 Hits
% chance to reach milestone

Biggio,Craig	99%
Jeter,Derek	71%
Rodriguez,Alex	63%
Guerrero,Vladimir	44%
Tejada,Miguel	38%
Damon,Johnny	37%
Renteria,Edgar	34%
Pujols,Albert	31%
Pierre,Juan	29%
Cabrera,Miguel	28%
Crawford,Carl	27%
Rollins,Jimmy	26%
Young,Michael	25%
Beltre,Adrian	23%
Bonds,Barry	22%
Rodriguez,Ivan	18%
Suzuki,Ichiro	18%
Furcal,Rafael	18%
Jones,Andruw	18%
Ramirez,Manny	16%
Anderson,Garret	16%
Reyes,Jose	15%
Helton,Todd	15%
Lee,Carlos	13%
Wells,Vernon	13%
Green,Shawn	12%
Teixeira,Mark	11%
Castillo,Luis	11%
Blalock,Hank	11%
Wright,David	10%
Sizemore,Grady	10%
Ramirez,Aramis	9%
Konerko,Paul	9%
Abreu,Bobby	9%
Griffey Jr.,Ken	9%
Kotsay,Mark	7%
Beltran,Carlos	6%
Soriano,Alfonso	5%
Holliday,Matt	2%
Roberts,Brian	2%
Ortiz,David	2%
Wilson,Jack	2%
Chavez,Eric	1%
Berkman,Lance	< 1%
Cabrera,Orlando	< 1%

700 Home Runs
% chance to reach milestone

Bonds,Barry	done
Rodriguez,Alex	50%
Pujols,Albert	31%
Jones,Andruw	27%
Ramirez,Manny	19%
Dunn,Adam	15%
Ortiz,David	13%
Griffey Jr.,Ken	12%
Howard,Ryan	6%
Guerrero,Vladimir	6%

2,298 RBI
% chance to break record

Rodriguez,Alex	27%
Pujols,Albert	16%
Jones,Andruw	12%
Ramirez,Manny	12%
Cabrera,Miguel	7%
Guerrero,Vladimir	5%
Ortiz,David	5%
Teixeira,Mark	3%

2,000 RBI
% chance to reach milestone

Bonds,Barry	76%
Rodriguez,Alex	62%
Ramirez,Manny	50%
Pujols,Albert	32%
Jones,Andruw	31%
Guerrero,Vladimir	23%
Ortiz,David	18%
Cabrera,Miguel	18%
Teixeira,Mark	13%
Delgado,Carlos	13%

600 Home Runs
% chance to reach milestone

Bonds,Barry	done
Griffey Jr.,Ken	96%
Rodriguez,Alex	90%
Ramirez,Manny	72%
Jones,Andruw	57%
Pujols,Albert	55%
Thome,Jim	36%
Dunn,Adam	32%
Ortiz,David	30%
Guerrero,Vladimir	27%

2,296 Runs Scored
% chance to break record

Rodriguez,Alex	25%
Pujols,Albert	14%
Bonds,Barry	14%
Jeter,Derek	8%
Rollins,Jimmy	5%
Cabrera,Miguel	3%
Damon,Johnny	3%

6,857 Total Bases
% chance to break record

Rodriguez,Alex	15%
Pujols,Albert	12%
Cabrera,Miguel	5%
Guerrero,Vladimir	4%
Jones,Andruw	1%

500 Home Runs
% chance to reach milestone

Bonds,Barry	done
Griffey Jr.,Ken	done
Thomas,Frank	99%
Ramirez,Manny	98%
Thome,Jim	97%
Rodriguez,Alex	97%
Delgado,Carlos	92%
Jones,Andruw	89%
Pujols,Albert	85%
Guerrero,Vladimir	75%

793 Doubles
% chance to break record

Cabrera,Miguel	15%
Helton,Todd	7%
Pujols,Albert	7%
Rollins,Jimmy	6%
Sizemore,Grady	4%
Tejada,Miguel	3%
Teixeira,Mark	2%
Beltre,Adrian	< 1%
Renteria,Edgar	< 1%
Wright,David	< 1%

1,000 Stolen Bases
% chance to reach milestone

Crawford,Carl	13%
Reyes,Jose	12%
Pierre,Juan	8%

300-Win Candidates

Bill James

When Randy Johnson celebrated his 30th birthday on September 10, 1993, he had a career record of 64 wins, 56 losses. Throughout almost all of the Unit's career it has been generally assumed that he found himself too late to be a 300-win candidate—a Hall of Famer, yes, but the kind of Hall of Famer who finishes 220-135, rather than the kind who finishes 302-170.

But Johnson is now 43, still winning games, and here he is, knocking on the door of 300 wins. This actually is not all that unusual; many or most of the pitchers who have won 300 games, historically, have been late starters and late bloomers. Through the age of 30 Wes Ferrell was 190-125, Early Wynn 101-102—yet Wynn won 300 games, and Ferrell did not. Through the age of 30 Juan Marichal was 170-77, Lefty Grove 115-57—yet Grove won 300 games. Through the age of 30 Robin Roberts was 189-142, Gaylord Perry 95-84—and yet. Through the age of 30 Hal Newhouser was 191-138, Phil Niekro was 54-40. Through the age of 30 Bob Feller was 192-112, Warren Spahn 108-72, both of them having missed several seasons during World War II. There is reason to believe that, if you want to win 300 games, the best policy is not to pitch too many innings before you turn 26.

Our current analysis (below) shows that it is likely that either Johnson or Tom Glavine will win 300 games, possibly both, and that it is likely that one other major league pitcher now active will as well, but that it's anybody's guess who the other one will be.

Name	2006 Age	R/L	W	L	EWL	Momentum	Chance
Tom Glavine	40	L	290	191	12.1	.695	.74
Randy Johnson	42	L	280	147	14.4	.771	.70
Mike Mussina	37	R	239	134	13.3	.688	.18
Johan Santana	27	L	78	31	17.1	.868	.16
Pedro Martinez	34	R	206	92	10.2	.798	.13
John Smoltz	39	R	193	137	13.4	.750	.10
Curt Schilling	39	R	207	138	12.8	.719	.09
Andy Pettitte	34	L	186	104	13.4	.748	.09
Livan Hernandez	31	R	123	117	11.6	.850	.08
Kenny Rogers	41	L	207	139	12.9	.707	.08
Roy Oswalt	28	R	98	47	14.2	.838	.08
Barry Zito	28	L	102	63	13.3	.832	.06
Jamie Moyer	43	L	216	166	10.2	.707	.06
Freddy Garcia	30	R	116	71	13.4	.793	.04
Tim Hudson	30	R	119	60	11.9	.796	.03
Chris Carpenter	31	R	100	68	14.0	.782	.03
Mark Buehrle	27	L	97	66	10.9	.813	.02
Javier Vazquez	29	R	100	105	11.4	.792	.02
Kevin Millwood	31	R	123	87	12.6	.742	.02
Jason Schmidt	33	R	127	90	11.8	.751	.01
Roy Halladay	29	R	95	48	12.8	.762	.01
Derek Lowe	33	R	100	82	12.7	.754	.01
(Less than 1%: David Wells, Brad Radke, Matt Morris.)							

Note: EWL = Established Win Level

Baseball Glossary

% Inherited Scored
The percentage of inherited baserunners a relief pitcher allows to score.

% Pitches Taken
The percentage of pitches that a batter does not swing at out of the total number of pitches thrown to him.

1st Batter Average
The Batting Average that a relief pitcher allows to the first batter he faces when he enters a game.

1st Batter OBP
The On-Base Percentage that a relief pitcher allows to the first batter he faces when he enters a game.

Active Career Batting Leaders
A list of batting leaders among active (appearing in the most recent season) players. An active player is eligible when he meets the minimum requirements for the following categories:

1,000 At Bats—Batting Average, On-Base Percentage, Slugging Average, At Bats Per HR, At Bats Per GDP, At Bats Per RBI, Strikeout to Walk Ratio
100 Stolen Base Attempts—Stolen Base Success Percentage

Active Career Pitching Leaders
A list of pitching leaders among active (appearing in the most recent season) players. An active player is eligible when he meets the minimum requirements for the following categories:

750 Innings Pitched—Earned Run Average, Opponent Batting Average, all "Per 9 Innings" categories, Strikeout to Walk Ratio
250 Games Started—Complete Game Frequency
100 Decisions—Win-Loss Percentage

AVG Allowed ScPos
The Batting Average allowed by a pitcher while pitching with runners in scoring position.

AVG Bases Loaded
The Batting Average of a hitter while batting with the bases loaded.

Batting Average
Hits divided by at bats.

Blown Save

When a relief pitcher enters a game in a Save Situation (see definition for Save Situation) and allows the other team to score the tying or go-ahead run.

Career Assessments

This method, once called the Favorite Toy, is a way to estimate the probability that a player will achieve a specific career goal. In this example, 3,000 hits will be used. The four components of the formula are Needed Hits, Years Remaining, Established Hit Level and Projected Remaining Hits.

Needed Hits. This is the number of Hits (or any statistic) that a player needs to reach a desired goal.

Years Remaining. This is the estimated number of years remaining in the player's career. It is determined using the player's age (on June 30th of the previous year; use 2003 when making the calculation after the 2003 season is complete). The formula is (42 - age) divided by two. This means a player who is 20 years old will have 11 remaining seasons, a player who is 25 years old will have 8.5 remaining seasons and a player who is 35 years old will have 3.5 remaining seasons. If the player is a catcher, then multiply his remaining seasons by .7. If a player is older than 39 (the Years Remaining calculation yields less than 1.5), consult the player's statistics for the most recent year. If the player either had 100 Hits or an Offensive Winning Percentage of .500 or greater, then the player will have 1.0 remaining seasons. If the player has both, he has 1.5 remaining seasons. If he has neither, he has .5 remaining seasons.

Established Hit Level. The Established Hit Level is a weighted average of the player's hits over the past three seasons. To calculate the Established Hit Level after the 2003 season is complete, add 2001 Hits, (2002 Hits multiplied by two) and (2003 Hits multiplied by three), then divide by six. If the Established Hit Level is less than 75% of the most recent performance (2003 Hits in this case), then the Established Hit Level is equal to .75 times the most recent performance.

Projected Remaining Hits. This is calculated by multiplying Years Remaining by the Established Hit Level.

The probability of achieving the specified goal is found by dividing Projected Remaining Hits by Need Hits, then subtracting .5. The maximum that any player has of achieving a goal is .97 raised to the power of (Need Hits / Established Hit Level). This prevents the possibility of a player reaching a goal from being higher than 100 percent, which is impossible.

Catcher's ERA

The ERA for a catcher is equal to the ERA of pitchers pitching while the catcher is playing behind the plate. It is calculated exactly like ERA for pitchers. Take the number of earned runs allowed while the catcher is playing, multiply it by 9 and then divide it by the total number of defensive innings that the catcher was behind the plate.

Cheap Win
A starting pitcher who wins the game with a game score under 50 gets credit for a cheap win. See Game Score.

Cleanup Slugging Average
The Slugging Average of a batter when he bats in the cleanup spot, or fourth, in the batting order.

Component ERA (ERC)
A statistic that estimates what a pitcher's ERA should have been, based on his pitching performance. The ERC formula is calculated as follows:

1. Subtract the pitcher's Home Runs Allowed from his Hits Allowed.
2. Multiply Step 1 by 1.255.
3. Multiply his Home Runs Allowed by four.
4. Add Steps 2 and 3 together.
5. Multiply Step 4 by .89.
6. Add his Walks and Hit Batsmen.
7. Multiply Step 6 by .475.
8. Add Steps 5 and 7 together.

This yields the pitcher's total base estimate (PTB), which is:

$$PTB = 0.89 \times (1.255 \times (H - HR) + 4 \times HR) + 0.475 \times (BB + HB)$$

For those pitchers for whom there is intentional walk data, use this formula instead:

$$PTB = 0.89 \times (1.255 \times (H - HR) + 4 \times HR) + 0.56 \times (BB + HB - IBB)$$

9. Add Hits and Walks and Hit Batsmen.
10. Multiply Step 9 by PTB.
11. Divide Step 10 by Batters Facing Pitcher. If BFP data is unavailable, approximate it by multiplying Innings Pitched by 2.9, then adding Step 9.
12. Multiply Step 11 by 9.
13. Divide Step 12 by Innings Pitched.
14. Subtract .56 from Step 13.

This is the pitcher's ERC, which is:

$$\frac{(H + BB + HB) \times PTB}{BFP \times IP} \times 9 - 0.56$$

If the result after Step 13 is less than 2.24, adjust the formula as follows:

$$\frac{(H + BB + HB) \times PTB}{BFP \times IP} \times 9 \times 0.75$$

Double Play %
Successful Double Plays divided by the number of Double Play opportunities. This statistic includes both the fielder who started the play and the pivot man.

Double Play Opportunity
A fielder is considered to have a double play opportunity when a ground ball is hit with a runner on first base and less than 2 outs and that fielder is involved in the play. This is used to calculate Double Play % and Pivot %.

Earned Run Average
The number of earned runs that a pitcher surrenders per nine innings that he pitches. It is calculated by multiplying the total earned runs allowed by nine and dividing by the total number of innings pitched.

Easy Save
This label is used to separate Saves by difficulty level (Easy or Tough). A Save is considered Easy if the relief pitcher enters the game, pitches one inning or less, and the first batter he faces does not at least represent the tying run.

Fielding Percentage
The percentage of plays a player makes in the field without making an error out of the total number of opportunities. It is calculated by adding (Putouts plus Assists) and dividing by (Putouts plus Assists plus Errors).

Games Finished
The relief pitcher who is in the game for each team when the game ends is credited with a Game Finished.

Game Score
To determine the starting pitcher's Game Score:
Start with 50.
Add 1 point for each out recorded by the starting pitcher.
Add 2 points for each inning the pitcher completes after the fourth inning.
Add 1 point for each strikeout.
Subtract 2 points for each hit allowed.
Subtract 4 points for each earned run allowed.
Subtract 2 points for an unearned run.
Subtract 1 point for each walk.

GDP
Grounded into Double Play

GDP Opportunity
This is a situation where the batter has a chance to ground into a double play. It occurs with at least a runner on first base and less than two outs.

Ground / Fly Ratio (Grd/Fly, GB/FB)

Calculated for both batters and pitchers. For batters, it is the number of groundballs hit divided by the number of flyballs hit. For pitchers, it is exactly the same but uses the number of groundballs and flyballs allowed. Every fair batted ball is included except for bunts and line drives.

Hold

A relief pitcher is given a Hold anytime he enters a game in a Save Situation (see definition for Save Situation), records one out or more, and exits the game without giving up the lead. If the pitcher finishes the game, then he will only earn credit for a Save. He cannot receive credit for both a Hold and a Save.

Holds Adjusted Saves Percentage

Holds plus Saves divided by Holds plus Saves Opportunities.

Inherited Runner

When a relief pitcher enters the game, any runner who is on base at the time is considered an Inherited Runner.

Isolated Power

Slugging Average minus Batting Average.

K/BB Ratio

Strikeouts divided by Walks.

Late & Close

A situation in a game that is very similar to a Save Situation. The following requirements are necessary for a Late & Close game:
1. The game is in the seventh inning or later AND
2. The batting team is either leading by one run or tied OR
3. The tying run is on base, at bat, or on deck.

Leadoff On-Base Percentage

The On-Base Percentage of a batter when he bats leadoff, or first, in the batting order.

Offensive Winning Percentage (OWP)

A player's Offensive Winning Percentage is the winning percentage of a hypothetical team which has an offense consisting of nine of that player, and pitching and defense which is average for the player's league. It is calculated by taking the square of RC/27 (see the definition for Runs Created per 27 Outs), dividing it by the sum of RC/27 and the square of the average runs scored per game in the league.

On-Base Percentage

(Hits plus Walks plus Hit by Pitcher) divided by (At Bats plus Walks plus Hit by Pitcher plus Sacrifice Flies).

$$\frac{H + BB + HBP}{AB + BB + HBP + SF}$$

Opponent Batting Average

Hits Allowed divided by (Batters Faced minus Walks minus Hit Batsmen minus Sacrifice Hits minus Sacrifice Flies minus Catcher's Interference).

$$\frac{H}{BFP - BB - HBP - SH - SF - CI}$$

PA*

Used in the denominator for the calculation of On-Base Percentage. It is calculated by subtracting (Sacrifice Hits plus Times Reached Base on Defensive Interference) from Plate Appearances (see definition for Plate Appearances).

Park Index

The Park Index of a given ballpark is the amount that the ballpark influences a given statistic. The following is a calculation of a park index using runs as the statistic:

1. Add Runs and Opponent Runs in home games.
2. Add At Bats and Opponent At Bats in home games. (If At Bats are unavailable, use home games.)
3. Divide Step 1 by Step 2.
4. Add Runs and Opponent Runs in road games.
5. Add At Bats and Opponent At Bats in road games. (If At Bats are unavailable, use road games.)
6. Divide Step 4 by Step 5.
7. Divide Step 3 by Step 6.
8. Multiply Step 7 by 100.

An index of 100 means the park is completely neutral and does not influence the particular statistic at all. A park index of 112 for runs indicates that teams score 12 percent more runs in this ballpark than a neutral park. A park index of 92 for runs means that teams tend to score 8 percent fewer runs in this ballpark than a neutral park.

PCS (Pitchers' Caught Stealing)

The number of runners officially scored as Caught Stealing where the pitcher initiated the play. The normal Caught Stealing is when a runner is out attempting to steal a base but the play was initiated by the catcher. PCS plays are often referred to as pickoffs, but differ when the runner breaks towards the next base as opposed to returning to the base he was currently on. Pickoffs occur when the pitcher throws to a base that a runner is leading from, and the runner is out attempting to return to that base. Pickoffs are not an official statistic.

Pitches per PA

The total number of pitches a hitter sees divided by his total Plate Appearances.

Pivot %

Successful Double Plays turned by pivot man divided by the number of Double Play opportunities with that pivot man involved.

Plate Appearances

At Bats plus Total Walks plus Hit By Pitcher plus Sacrifice Hits plus Sacrifice Flies plus Times Reached on Defensive Interference.

Power/Speed Number

A single number that reflects a combination of power and speed. To achieve a high Power/Speed Number, a player must score high in both power and speed. To calculate the Power/Speed Number, multiply Home Runs by Stolen Bases by two, and divide by the sum of Home Runs and Stolen Bases.

$$\frac{2 \times HR \times SB}{HR + SB}$$

PPO (Pitcher Pickoff)

The number of baserunners thrown out when a pitcher throws to a base with a leading baserunner, and the runner is tagged out attempting to return to the base. PPO is not an official statistic and does not count toward Caught Stealing totals.

Quality Start

A game where the starting pitcher pitches for at least six innings and allows no more than three earned runs.

Quality Start Percentage

Quality Starts divided by Games Started (see the definition for Quality Start).

Quick Hooks

Used in the Manager's Record. For Quick Hooks and Slow Hooks a score is calculated by adding the number of Pitches to 10 times the number of Runs Allowed for the starting pitcher. The bottom 25% of scores in the league are considered to be Quick Hooks.

Range Factor

The number of Successful Chances (Putouts plus Assists) times nine divided by the number of Defensive Innings Played. The average for a Regular Player at each position in 2006:
Second Base: 4.99
Third Base: 2.76
Shortstop: 4.44
Left Field: 2.01
Center Field: 2.61
Right Field: 2.15

Run Support Per 9 IP

The total number of runs scored by a pitcher's team while he is in the game multiplied by nine and divided by total Innings Pitched.

Runs Created

"Runs Created" is an estimate of the number of a team's runs which are created by each individual hitter. The Cincinnati Reds scored 820 runs last year, let us say. How many of those were created by Adam Dunn? How many by Ken Griffey Jr.? How many by Jason LaRue?

There are many different formulas for estimating runs created. . .did you want the one that involves swinging a dead cat in the cemetery under a full moon? Yeah, I don't blame you. . .worm-eaten persimmons are so hard to find in the modern world.

This is the one we use now; it is complicated enough. First, there is an "A" Factor in the formula, a "B" Factor, and a "C" factor. The "A" Factor, which represents the number of times the hitter is on base, is Hits, Plus Walks, Plus Hit Batsmen, Minus Caught Stealing, Minus Grounded Into Double Play. The "B" Factor, which represents the hitter's ability to advance other runners, is 1.125 times the player's Singles, plus 1.69 times his Doubles, plus 3.02 times his Triples, plus 3.73 times his Home Runs, plus .29 times his Walks and Hit Batsmen, not counting intentional walks, plus .492 times Sacrifice Hits, Sacrifice Flies and Stolen Bases, minus .04 times Strikeouts. The "C" Factor, which represents opportunities, is At Bats, Plus Walks, Plus Hit By Pitch, Plus Sacrifice Hits, Plus Sacrifice Flies.

Having made these initial calculations of the A, B and C factors, we then change the "A" factor to "A plus 2.4 times C".

We change the "B" factor to "B plus 3 times C".

We change the "C" factor to "9 times C".

Multiply A times B, divide by then new C ("9 times C"), and subtract .90 times by the original C.

This is our first, temporary estimate of the player's runs created. We what we have done here is to ask these questions:
  1. How many runs would a team probably score that consisted of eight "ordinary" type of hitters, plus this particular hitter?
  2. How many of those runs would be created by the eight ordinary type of hitters?
  3. What is the difference-and thus, how many runs did our player create?

To estimate this, we have placed our player in the context of eight hitters with a .300 on base percentage (2.4 divided by 8) and a .375 advancement percentage (3 divided by 8). For each trip through the batting order, the eight ordinary-type hitters would produce 9/10 of a run (2.4 times 3, divided by 8). The "9" in the denominator is eight ordinary hitters plus our man. The "-.9" being subtracted at the end is the runs created by the "ordinary" hitters. In essence, we have placed the hitter in a neutral solution, measured the neutral solution without our hitter, measured it with our hitter, and then estimated the contribution of this hitter as being the difference between the two.

We're not quite done. After that, we adjust the player's runs created estimate for his performance in two "run-sensitive" situations. Suppose that a player whose overall batting average is .250 has batted 100 times with runners in scoring position, and has gone 30-for-100. That's five hits better than expected, 30 hits where we would have expected 25. His team will score an extra five runs because he has done that, and so we increase the player's runs created estimate by five runs. If the player has hit poorly with runners in scoring position, we decrease it by the shortfall in the same way.

Suppose that a player has batted 250 times with runners on base, 250 times with the bases empty, and that he has hit 20 home runs overall. We would expect him to have hit 10 with men on base, 10 with the bases empty, right?

Suppose that he didn't. Suppose that he hit 12 with the bases empty, 8 with men on base. His team would score two runs less than expected because he did this, and we would thus penalize him two runs for the shortfall.
This is our second runs created estimate-the player's runs created, adjusted for his batting performance in run-sensitive situations.

Suppose, however, that we figure the runs created for all of the individuals on a team, and we add them up, and it doesn't match the runs actually scored by the team? What if the formulas say that the team should have scored 800 runs, but they actually scored 820?

Then obviously, the formulas missed. We're trying to measure the runs ACTUALLY created by each hitter as best we can, in the real world, not the theoretical impact of some combination of singles, doubles, triples and walks. If the actual number is different than the estimates, we have to adjust the estimates to fit the facts. In this case-820 runs scored with only 800 runs created-we would multiply each runs created estimate by 820/800, or 1.025. Then we round it off to an integer, and that's the player's estimated runs created.

Let go of that cat, Arthur. Heck, the moon isn't full for three weeks, anyway.

Runs Created per 27 Outs (RC/27)
This statistic estimates the number of runs per game that a team made up of nine of the same player would score. To calculate RC/27, multiply Runs Created by league outs per team game, divide the result by outs made by the player (the sum of at bats plus sacrifice hits plus sacrifice flies plus caught stealing plus grounded into double plays, minus hits). The formula written out is:

$$\frac{\frac{RC \times 3 \times LgIP}{2 \times LgG}}{AB - H + SH + SF + CS + GDP}$$

Save Percentage
A pitcher's Saves divided by the total number of Save Situations he faces (see definition for Save Situation).

Save Situation

A relief pitcher is in a Save Situation when he enters the game with his team in the lead, has the opportunity to finish the game, is not the winning pitcher of record at the time, and meets any one of the three following conditions:

  1. The pitcher's team is leading by no more than three runs and the pitcher has the chance to pitch for at least one inning,
OR
  2. The pitcher enters the game with the potential tying run on base, at bat, or on deck,
OR
  3. The pitcher pitches three or more effective innings regardless of the lead. The determination of a save in this situation is made by the official scorer.
It is not possible to have more than one save credited to a single team in a game.

SB Success Percentage

Stolen Bases divided by the number of Stolen Base attempts (Stolen Bases plus Caught Stealing).

$$\frac{SB}{SB + CS}$$

Secondary Average

A number meant to reflect everything else except for batting average. A player will have a high Secondary Average if he hits for power, takes walks and steals bases. It is calculated with the following formula:

$$\frac{TB - H + BB + SB}{AB}$$

Similarity Score

A number which reflects the similarity between two different statistical lines, either for a player or for a team. A score of 1,000 means that the statistical lines are identical.

Slow Hooks

Used in the Manager's Record. For Quick Hooks and Slow Hooks a score is calculated by adding the number of Pitches to 10 times the number of Runs Allowed. The top 25% of scores in the league are considered to be Slow Hooks.

Slugging Average

Total Bases divided by At Bats.

$$\frac{TB}{AB}$$

Speed Score

Speed Score is a number which evaluates how fast a player is. To calculate the Speed Score, start with the player's statistics over the last two seasons combined. A value will be found for each of the following six categories and will be combined for a final score at the end:

1. Stolen Base Percentage. The value of this category is:

$$\left(\frac{SB + 3}{SB + CS + 7} - 0.4 \right) \times 20$$

2. Frequency of Stolen Base Attempts. The value of this category is:

$$\frac{\sqrt{\dfrac{SB + CS}{Singles + BB + HBP}}}{0.07}$$

3. Percentage of Triples. This is calculated by taking the percentage of triples out of the number of balls put in play. To get the percentage, use this formula:

$$\frac{3B}{AB - HR - SO}$$

From this assign an integer from 0 to 10, based on the following chart:

Less than .001	0
.001 - .0023	1
.0023 - .0039	2
.0039 - .0058	3
.0058 - .0080	4
.0080 - .0105	5
.0105 - .013	6
.013 - .0158	7
.0158 - .0189	8
.0189 - .0223	9
.0223 or more	10

4. Runs Scored Percentage. This is calculated by taking the percentage of times the player scores a run out of the number of times the player is on base. To get the percentage, use this formula:

$$\frac{\left(\dfrac{R - HR}{H + HBP + BB - HR} - 0.1 \right)}{0.04}$$

5. Grounded Into Double Play Frequency. To get the frequency, use this formula:

$$\frac{0.055 - \left(\dfrac{GIDP}{AB - HR - SO}\right)}{0.005}$$

6. Range Factor. The value of this category depends on the players position:

Catcher—1
First Baseman—2
Designated Hitter—1.5
Second Baseman—1.25 x Range Factor
Third Baseman—1.51 x Range Factor
Shortstop—1.52 x Range Factor
Outfield—3 x Range Factor

For an explanation on Range Factor, consult the definition in this glossary. Remember to figure range factors over a two-year period.

If any category value is greater than 10, then reduce it to 10. If any value is less than zero, then increase the value to zero. All category values must fall within the zero to 10 range. The Speed Score is then calculated by discarding the lowest of the six values, and taking the average of the remaining five.

Total Bases
Hits plus Doubles plus (2 times Triples) plus (3 times Home Runs).

$$H + 2B + (2 \times 3B) + (3 \times HR)$$

Tough Loss
A starting pitcher who loses the game with a game score over 50 gets credit for a tough loss. See Game Score.

Tough Save
This label is used to separate Saves by difficulty level (Easy or Tough). A Save is considered Tough if the relief pitcher enters the game with the tying run on base.

Winning Percentage
Wins divided by (Wins plus Losses).

Baseball Info Solutions

Analyzing baseball statistics has taken the sport by storm ever since *Moneyball* brought statistical analysis into the public eye. However, in order to properly evaluate baseball statistics you need to have high quality, innovative data or you may draw the wrong conclusions. BIS has been supplying top notch, timely, and in-depth baseball data to its customers since 2002.

BIS collects a statistical snapshot of every important moment of every Major League Baseball game with the most advanced technology, resulting in a database that includes traditional data, pitch-by-pitch data, and defensive positioning data. The company also has the highest quality pitch charting data available anywhere, including pitch type, location, and velocity.

BIS provides comprehensive services to nearly half of the 30 Major League Baseball teams, as well as many sports agents, media, fantasy services, game companies, and private individuals.

John Dewan, the principal owner of BIS, has been on the cutting edge of baseball analysis for over 20 years. His experience goes all the way back to his days as Executive Director of Project Scoresheet, the Bill James led effort that pioneered the new wave of baseball statistics that are now common baseball terminology.

President Steve Moyer brings 15 years of baseball industry experience to BIS. His hands-on, can-do business demeanor helps set BIS apart from its competition.

The rest of the BIS team includes former professional and collegiate baseball players as well as programming and database management experts. Over the last four seasons, BIS has more than tripled its full-time staff.

BIS continues to grow within the industry while emphasizing personal attention to its customers. This focus on personal attention is evidenced by the fact that if you contact the office with an inquiry you are very likely to be able to speak to the company president directly.

To contact BIS:

Baseball Info Solutions
528 North New Street
Bethlehem, PA 18018-5752
610-814-0108
www.baseballinfosolutions.com

Notes

Notes

Notes

Notes

Notes

Notes

Notes

Notes

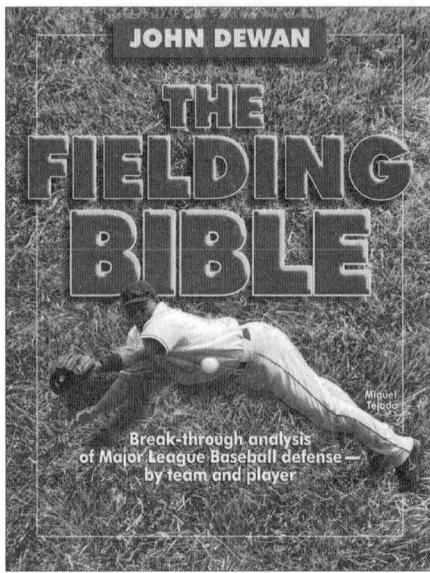

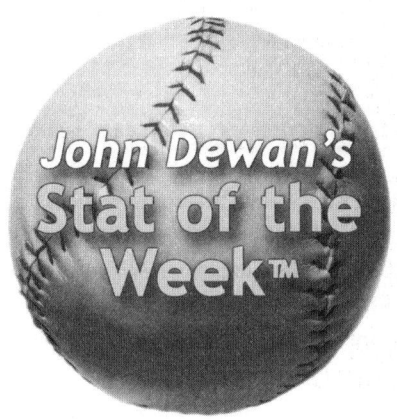

Career Registers for Your Favorite Team

We already know you love the comprehensive collection of stats in *The Bill James Handbook*, otherwise you wouldn't have bought it. But wouldn't it be nice to have the largest feature of the Handbook organized by team? For the first time ever, we are offering the Team Register, which compiles all the career statistics of each player on your favorite major league ball club, and it's FREE!

Just send an e-mail to info@actasports.com with "Handbook Free Gift" in the subject line, and include the following information:

Your First and Last Name
Mailing Address
E-Mail Address
Your Favorite MLB Team

As soon as we receive your e-mail, we will e-mail you a PDF version of a Team Register with all the players on your favorite team at the end of last season. So next year, you won't have to wonder how many wild pitches your Opening Day starter threw in 2006—you can check your personalized Team Register.

Limit one Team Register per customer.